8th Edition
Jobs
Almanac

ALL-IN-ONE CAREER GUIDE

Managing Editor:	Michelle Roy Kelly
Editor:	Heather L. Vinhateiro
Associate Editor:	Anne M. Grignon
Editorial Assistant:	Bethany L. Brown
Researchers:	Lesley Bolton Michael Paydos Jennifer M. Wood
Editorial Intern	Jennifer L. Carlson

Adams Media Corporation
HOLBROOK, MASSACHUSETTS

Published by Adams Media Corporation
260 Center Street, Holbrook MA 02343. U.S.A.

ISBN: 1-58062-443-X
ISSN: 1072-592X

Printed in Canada

A   B   C   D   E   F   G   H   I   J

"This publication is designed to provide accurate and authoritative information with regard to the subject matter covered. It is sold with the understanding that the publisher is not engaged in rendering legal, accounting, or other professional advice. If legal advice or other expert assistance is required, the services of a competent professional person should be sought."

—From a *Declaration of Principles* jointly adopted by a Committee of the American Bar Association and a Committee of Publishers and Associations

This book is available at quantity discounts for bulk purchases.
For information, call 800/872-5627 (in Massachusetts 781/767-8100) or
e-mail at jobbank@adamsonline.com.

Visit our exciting job and career site at http://www.careercity.com

Contents

The Nation's Job Market: An Overview

Where the Jobs Will Be

As the U.S. enters the new millennium, both the labor market and employment opportunities will reflect technological and sociological changes. The Internet will continue to be a major influence on the economy, and changes in the workplace, the labor force, jobseeking and consumer spending will result. Jobseekers must be aware of potential changes in employment opportunities, job growth, and top careers in order to plan for their futures.

The economy is expected to continue its exceptional growth, reaching $9.5 trillion by 2008. According to *Occupational Outlook Quarterly*, employment is expected to increase by 14 percent. Exports and imports are also expected to increase as international trade becomes a more intricate part of the U.S. economy. Consumer spending should increase and account for 68 percent of all economic activity.

Occupational Outlook Quarterly predicts that the service industries will account for 75 percent of job growth by 2008. This may be the only sector that experiences faster than average growth, as employment is expected to decrease in areas such as manufacturing and mining. According to *Occupational Outlook Quarterly*, manufacturing is expected to decrease to only 13 percent of total nonfarm wage and salary workers by the year 2008.

The way people look for jobs will change due to emerging technologies. According to *Newsweek*, Web-based jobseeking will continue to "revolutionize" the job search as employers and jobseekers post and review resumes over the Internet. Jobseekers can now search for jobs in any part of the world with a few clicks of the mouse. Gone are the days of shuffling through newspapers and cutting out classifieds. It is now possible to organize job searches based on skill level, job title, and personal preference.

Employers will also continue to benefit from Web-based recruiting. Instead of spending time weeding out hundreds of unacceptable paper resumes, companies can sort them electronically according to various qualifications. According to *Newsweek*, new job software will soon be able to match jobs and workers according to a number of specialized qualifications including salary, travel requirements, or tolerance for deadlines. Employers can also expect more out of potential employees during an interview. With increased access to information, jobseekers are expected to thoroughly research a company and be well-prepared in an interview.

The computer and health care industries are expected to be the fastest growing occupations over the next several years. Of the top 20 fastest growing occupations profiled in the *Occupational Outlook Quarterly*, eight are computer related and eight are in health care. The *Occupational Outlook Handbook* reports that special education teachers and social and recreation workers will also have a lot of opportunities for growth.

Projected job growth varies due to educational and training requirements. According to the *Occupational Outlook Handbook*, one-third of all employment growth expected for the 1998-2008 period will require at least a bachelor's degree. *Occupational Outlook Quarterly* reports that of the 20 fastest growing occupations through 2008, 12 will require at least an associate degree. However, those jobs not requiring any post secondary education will account for 57 percent of total job growth between 1998 and 2008.

Job opportunities do not always depend on the amount of job growth in an occupation or industry. Many job openings come from the need to replace workers who have retired or who enter other fields. This will be especially true over the next several years as the number of job openings resulting from replacement needs is expected to outnumber openings resulting from employment growth.

Innovations in communications technology are expected to have a profound effect on the workforce as well. According to *Time*, wireless communication will make virtually all information available at all times. This will decrease the need for physical presence while conducting business. Stocks for wireless companies have climbed considerably in recent months, and are expected to continue to do so. Mergers in the communications industry have created conglomerates that provide Internet access, wireless phone service, and long distance services.

The need for health care professionals is expected to increased significantly over the next several years. As the "baby boomers" increase in age and the elderly population continues to grow, the health care industry is expected to experience increased job growth. However, because hospitals and insurance companies are attempting to cut costs, it is the preventative and home health care fields that will be in high demand. Home health aides and medical assistants are the fastest growing occupations requiring short- or moderate-term on-the-job training.

The workplace is also expected to undergo significant changes over the next several years. Because employees are expected to work long hours, companies have already begun to cater to their personal needs. According to *Fortune*, companies are making an effort to incorporate many of the best aspects of home into the workplace. Some companies are providing gyms, dry-cleaning services, and even massage therapy for employees in return for 12-hour days and some weekends. Although the number of companies that currently provide these services are in the minority, it is a trend that is starting to spread and is expected to continue to do so as work pressures increase.

Technology will continue to be the key to finding jobs. As the computer industry and the Internet continue to expand, many of the "middleman" jobs may disappear. For example, people can tour homes over the Internet and book vacations through one of the many travel Websites which negates the need for personal realtors or travel agents. Consumers are cutting out the middleman in almost every industry as they choose to conduct their own research or business over the Internet instead.

Workforce Trends

The U.S. labor force will experience significant expansion through 2008. *Occupational Outlook Quarterly* reports that the labor force is projected to grow by 17 million workers from 1998-2008. At the same time, the internal make-up of the labor force will undergo other changes. As the "baby boomers" get older, the overall age distribution in the workforce will change. The "baby boom" generation will increase their participation in the labor force from 33 to 40 percent.

Ethnic and gender diversity will increase as white and non-Hispanic persons will constitute a smaller percentage of the workforce. African Americans, Asians, Hispanics and other minority groups are expected to experience increased employment growth by 2008. Both men and women should experience equal job growth, but the labor force participation rate will experience an overall decrease for men. According to *Occupational Outlook Quarterly*, women's share of the labor force is expected to reach 48 percent by 2008.

Although wage growth has remained fairly stagnant over the past several years, it will likely be affected by the growing economy. According to *Business Week*, the drop in consumer inflation following the Asian crisis temporarily slowed wage growth. Due to a shortage of qualified workers, however, employers will have to increase pay raises to attract and retain skilled employees. The recent trend in generous compensation packages is also likely to continue as companies attempt to offset salary increases with other perks.

Finally, the turnover rate for employees is expected to increase throughout future years. With the shortage of skilled workers, companies are constantly trying to attract employees from other business. As the power shifts in favor of the workers, loyalty to employers will soon be a thing of the past.

The Industry Outlook

Throughout the late 1990s the U.S. economy began to experience a transition from a goods-producing market to a services based one. Entering the 2000s, the shift continues, as service-producing industries are expected to account for nearly three-fourths of total job growth during the 1998-2008 period. Manufacturing industries should continue their slow decline as service-producing industries experience record-breaking growth.

The service industry is expected to create 11.8 million new jobs by the year 2008. According to the Bureau of Labor Statistics, business, health, and professional and miscellaneous services are expecting to take responsibility for three-fourths of the total job growth in the service industry. Computer data services is projected to be the fastest growing industry with job growth expected to increase by more than 100 percent by 2008.

The job growth experienced by construction and related industries in 1999 was partly due to consumer confidence and low interest rates. Industries responsible for providing materials to construction companies increased employment. The Bureau of Labor Statistics predicts that construction will increase by 9 percent during the 1998-2008 period.

The manufacturing industry continued to decline throughout much of 1999. Weaknesses in foreign economies reduced demand for U.S. exports and had an adverse affect on the manufacturing industry. According to the Bureau of Labor Statistics, manufacturing employment is expected to continue its decline through 2008. Advances in technologies, improved production methods, and weak foreign economies are considered to be the cause for this decline.

The finance, insurance, and real estate industries experienced moderate growth in 1999. According to the Bureau of Labor Statistics, demand for these services is expected to continue with employment increasing by 13 percent.

Government employment saw a resurgence in 1999 that is expected to continue through 2008. The rate of employment for this industry is expected to increase by 9 percent during this period. According to the Bureau of Labor Statistics, state and local government is expected to drive the employment growth, while federal government employment is expected to decline.

Working for the Federal Government

IMPORTANT NOTE: *Since application procedures for federal jobs may vary from city to city and may change as new legislation is passed, you should contact the Federal Employment Information Center (FEIC) nearest the location you would like to work to find out about specific paths to employment in that area. Check the government listings section of your phone directory for contact information.*

Uncle Sam wants you! The federal government is by far the nation's largest employer, with nearly 3,000,000 workers serving in a variety of professional positions across the country. For the most part, if a career exists in private business, someone somewhere has the same career working for the federal government. There are federal jobs in more than 200 career fields across the country and around the world. Traditionally, the federal government hires more than 300,000 new workers annually.

For example, if you are interested in finance, you can sign on with the nation's largest business. Science and technology, perhaps? Naturally, the government operates a number of renowned laboratories, medical facilities, and sophisticated computer systems, all of which need professionals to operate them. If you have an interest in protecting the public, becoming a federal law enforcement officer might be for you. Working for Uncle Sam certainly has its added advantages: As a federal employee, you have the opportunity to change jobs, offices, and agencies and still retain your benefits and service years.

Getting Started on Your Federal Job Search

Perhaps the most difficult part of finding a job in the federal government is ascertaining the application procedures. The process can be extremely frustrating, particularly when various efforts to "reinvent" government produce unfortunate and unexpected side effects like the closing of offices which once could readily distribute application information. Many of the nationwide locations of the **U.S. Office of Personnel Management (OPM)** -- long the best source for information on government jobs -- have either closed, or now offer little more than automated phone lines. Research for this section at various state employment offices, libraries, and colleges frequently turned up comments like, "Oh, we used to get that information sent to us on a regular basis...." But no more.

Fortunately, once you *do* figure out how to access the information -- and one of this section's primary goals is to assist you in that quest -- the OPM has done much to make the application process easier in recent years. For example, it has done away with **Standard Form 171 (SF-171)**, an application form which was once used in applying for most federal jobs. Jobseekers can now apply for most government jobs by sending a simple resume, or by using the **Optional Application For Federal Employment (OF-612)**. More information on these forms will be found later in this section.

The Federal Job Information Center (FJIC)

Your area FJIC is a good place to start. Representatives can usually provide you with numbers and addresses of OPM locations nationwide, and can offer other information and suggestions to assist you in your search. Check the government listings section (blue pages) of your phone directory for contact information.

The OPM is the government agency that is responsible for the hiring of all competitive service jobs. The agency is headquartered in Washington DC, but it also has five regional offices and a number of service centers located around the country. These offices are responsible for conducting OPM functions such as recruitment and job information. The main number for automated information in DC is 202/606-2700. To get a human voice, you can try 202/606-1800, although you may end up having to leave a voicemail message anyway.

Now a warning: Staffing is somewhat limited at these locations. The downtown location of the Boston office, for example, features a small sign reading "Federal Job Information Center," and a self-serve computer terminal that connects you to a database of government jobs, and allows you to order the information you need. The neighboring OPM office, however, has a sign posted that reads *"No Employment Information Available Here,"* so if you need a helpful human hand, you're out of luck.

The Federal Employment Information Highway

Recent efforts to streamline government *have* yielded one major benefit to jobseekers, in the form of the OPM's "Federal Employment Information Highway," composed of several systems that can be used to conduct a job search. These systems can be accessed by telephone, personal computer, or by visiting touch screen computer kiosks in various locations (usually the Federal Job Information Centers) nationwide. In addition to listing the latest job openings, these systems provide access to application materials and information on a wide range of federal employment-related topics and programs.

Some of the information available through these systems includes:

How to apply
Volunteer service
Postal employment
Overseas employment
Salary and benefits
Veteran's information

Aside from such general information, you can also tap into a vast database of jobs, updated regularly. You can access job openings by category (summer employment, entry-level professional, clerical and technical, trades and labor, and senior executive) and type (engineering, medical/health, administrative, computers, and mathematics). You can narrow your search by geographical area and by specific state.

Ultimately, you'll reach a listing of all available jobs that meet your specifications, including detailed descriptions and instructions on how to apply. This is particularly effective through the touch screen kiosks, which allow you the luxury of time that a long distance phone call does not. They also provide printouts of job listings and other information, all at no cost.

The Information Highway's three systems are as follows:

• **OPM's Career America Connection** at 912/757-3000, a telephone-based system that provides current worldwide federal job opportunities, salary and employee benefits information, special recruitment messages, and more. You can also record your request to have application packages, forms, and other employment-related literature mailed to you. This service is available 24 hours a day, seven days a week.

- **OPM's Federal Job Opportunities Bulletin Board (FJOB)** at 912/757-3100, a computer-based bulletin board system that also provides federal job information to jobseekers. You must have a personal computer with a modem to access this system. Many of the jobs listed have complete text announcements attached which can be downloaded or viewed online, or you may leave your name and address to have application packages mailed to you. This service is also available 24 hours a day, seven days a week. You can also find information on the Internet via Telnet at fjob.mail.opm.gov and File Transfer Protocol at ftp.fjob.mail.opm.gov. The OPM also has a Website, at http://www.opm.gov.

- **Federal Job Information "Touch Screen" Computer**, a computer-based system utilizing touch screen technology. A number of kiosks, located nationwide in OPM offices, federal office buildings, and other locations, allow you to access current worldwide federal job opportunities, online information, and more, with the touch of a finger. The computers are user-friendly, with colorful graphics and a cheerful voice (which can be turned off if desired). Printouts of information are generally available; job listings on these systems are updated daily.

The downside to the Federal Employment Information Highway is that if you need personal assistance with any of your questions, none of these automated systems can provide one. If you're unable to find and/or don't hear exactly what you're looking for among the choices listed, you may find yourself unsure whether that information doesn't exist -- or just can't be found.

Additional Online Resources

More jobseekers are jumping onto the Internet every day, and if you are online one of the best resources available to you is Fedworld, which like the OPM's Federal Job Opportunities Bulletin Board can also be reached with just a personal computer and a modem. Set up in November of 1992 by the National Technical Information Service, an agency of the United States Department of Commerce, Fedworld enables you to access over 130 computer bulletin board systems operated by the government. Its job files, updated Tuesday through Saturday, are obtained from FJOB, described above. You can reach them directly by using your computer to dial 912/757-3100.

Visit Fedworld's web address at http://www.fedworld.gov/ftp.htm; or use the Internet's File Transfer Protocol to connect to ftp.fedworld.gov/jobs. A wealth of job search information, including job listings by region, labor market data by state, and much more is available to jobseekers. You can also scan White House press releases, Environmental Protection Agency reports, and business updates in your spare time.

Other online resources include the **Federal Jobs Digest**, at http://www.jobsfed.com; and **Federal Jobs Central** (which charges a fee for its services), at http://www.fedjobs.com. Both sites offer listings for federal jobs in a variety of industries. Finally, the **Federal Register**, which publishes a variety of government documents, is available at http://www.access.gpo.gov. Information is updated on a daily basis.

Other Information Sources

Here is a brief summary of several of the most useful written sources of information on applying for federal jobs:

- **Federal Career Directory**: This comprehensive resource guide profiles approximately 176 federal agencies and departments, and includes information on typical entry-level jobs, personnel contacts, and student employment programs. Included are chapters on "How to Look for and Apply for a Government Job" and "Agency and Department Hiring by College Major." The directory is available at college placement offices and libraries throughout the country. One drawback: The most recent edition of this resource is from 1990, and some of the information is out of date.

- **X-118 Handbook**: By applying the qualification standards outlined in this handbook, personnel officers determine if an applicant will qualify for a particular position. If you are interested in learning more about the required qualifications for an occupation, you can find this handbook in OPM's library, as well as at some public and university libraries and agency personnel offices.

Federal Jobs in Washington DC

If you're looking for a job in Washington itself, the Washington Area Service Center (WASC), located in the OPM headquarters building, should be able to help you out. The address is 1900 E Street NW, or call 202/606-2525. (Again, you'll probably end up having to leave a voicemail message.)

Agencies in the Washington DC metropolitan area fill their vacancies in a variety of ways, sometimes independently from the OPM. For many federal jobs, you must apply directly for vacancies advertised by agencies. For others, you must take an entry-level test -- although most positions no longer require one. The first step is to find out which of the following procedures is the right one for your field.

Federal Clerical and Administrative Support Test

Many applicants refer to the Federal Clerical and Administrative Support test as the "Civil Service Exam." The test, which you can take at the FJIC, covers 64 different occupations at the GS-2 through GS-4 levels. "GS" stands for the General Schedule, a pay system that covers most white-collar jobs within the federal government. (More information on the GS is contained later in this section.) Applicants can obtain sample test materials and the testing schedule from the FJIC. The test is a good vehicle for recent high school graduates who are interested in beginning their federal careers.

Shared Case Examining

In Washington DC, many federal jobs are filled through "shared case examining" procedures. This means that agencies initially recruit and screen applications before sending them to the OPM for final evaluation. The OPM identifies the best qualified applicants and sends a list of these candidates back to the agency making the final selection. These jobs are typically in the financial, administrative, and social and physical sciences occupations (e.g., psychologists, economists, physicists, program analysts, etc.).

Delegated Examining

For occupations that are located primarily in one agency, the agency may be authorized to advertise, evaluate, and hire applicants independently from the OPM. The Federal Aviation Administration (FAA), for example, uses this authority for air traffic controller jobs. The FJIC has information about which agencies have this "delegated examining authority" for certain occupations. You should contact agencies directly to apply for these positions.

Direct Hire Authority

For occupations where there are critical shortages, such as nurses and engineers, the OPM has authorized agencies to use a "direct hire" approach to secure qualified applicants.

Best bets: computer, mathematics, engineering, and some health care occupations. Contact agency personnel offices directly if you are applying for a shortage occupation.

Other Avenues to Employment

Presidential Management Intern Programs: If you're in your last year of graduate school and have a strong interest in public management, you might want to consider the prestigious Presidential Management Intern (PMI) Program, which begins at the GS-9 level with career ladders to GS-12. You must apply for this two-year program during your final year of studies and be nominated by your school.

The program is open to students from a variety of disciplines, with an emphasis on leadership potential for public service and administration. Those with education or experience in financial management, health care policy or administration, criminal justice, and management information systems, among other backgrounds, are encouraged to apply.

If you would like more information, contact the dean of your graduate school, your career services department, or the OPM's Career America Connection.

Military Service and Veterans Programs: Your military service may count as general or specialized experience when applying for civilian positions. Also, as a veteran, you might receive preference over a non-veteran when looking for a federal job, as long as you are qualified for the available position. Qualified Vietnam vets, and other vets with a compensable disability of 30 percent or more, may be hired directly by agencies. The Veterans Programs Coordinator at individual federal agencies can provide program details and information on eligibility requirements.

Employment of People with Disabilities: The federal government actively promotes the employment of people with disabilities through selective placement procedures. This assistance includes individual job counseling, special testing for visually- and hearing-impaired applicants, and referral to agency coordinators for selective placement. Special accommodations such as interpreters, readers, and restructured work sites can also be provided for the disabled. Contact the Selective Placement Coordinator at the agency where you wish to work or your State Office of Vocational Rehabilitation for more information. You can also call 912/757-3000 for recorded information.

Student Employment Programs

The federal government also offers a variety of student employment programs to high school, undergraduate, and graduate students who are at least 16 years old and have U.S. citizenship. A government internship can be a great opportunity to gain experience. Contact your school's career placement center for more details.

Recently, the OPM consolidated its previous programs (e.g., Cooperative Education, Stay-in-School, Federal Junior Fellowship, and Summer Aid Programs) into the new **Student Educational Employment Program**. Most federal agencies use this program, although some do develop additional student, intern, or fellowship programs to meet their specific business needs.

The Student Educational Employment Program has two components -- student temporary employment and student career experience. It is available to all levels of students, from high school to professional degree students.

You are eligible if you are enrolled or accepted for enrollment as a degree-seeking student (diploma, certificate, etc.), and are taking at least half-time academic or vocational and technical course load in an accredited high school, technical or vocational school, two-

or four-year college or university, or graduate or professional school. You must also be a U.S. citizen or a national, although non-citizens may be eligible for employment under certain circumstances.

Summer Employment Programs

Summer job opportunities, beginning after May 12 and ending by September 30, are available nationwide, covering a wide variety of professions. Applicants must be at least 16 years old; most positions require U.S. citizenship. Those interested in a specific federal agency should contact that agency directly to obtain information on jobs, recruitment dates, and qualifications required. Check the government pages of your telephone directory for addresses and phone numbers of these agencies.

Information on summer jobs is also available through the "Federal Employment Information Highway" sources mentioned earlier. If you use the Federal Job Opportunities Bulletin Board, for example, when asked how you want to search for jobs, choose "series" and then enter "9999" for listings of specific positions.

Federal Pay Systems

The federal government has several different pay systems, the largest of which is called the **General Schedule (GS)**. It covers most white-collar jobs and consists of 15 numerical grade levels and their corresponding salaries. The higher the GS number, the higher the pay level. Under this system, specific jobs, such as engineers, accountants, and nurses, have special salary rates. However, not all jobs in the federal service fall under the GS pay system. The federal **Wage Grade (WG)** pay system covers blue-collar jobs in apprentice and journeyman trades and crafts occupations, e.g., electricians, mechanics, plumbers, carpenters, trades-helpers, etc. And finally, the **Senior Executive Schedule (ES)** covers high-level managerial and supervisory positions in the federal government.

The General Schedule

How do you know where you would fit into the GS pay system? Eligibility for federal jobs is determined by your education and/or work experience. With a high school degree or three months of general experience, you'll usually qualify for GS-2 grade level positions. To qualify for the GS-5 or GS-7 grade levels in professional and administrative jobs, you need a bachelor's degree or three years of increasingly responsible work experience after high school. If you have an undergraduate grade point average of 3.0 or higher, or membership in an academic honor society, you may qualify for the GS-7 grade level. Applicants with master's degrees are eligible for the GS-9 grade level, and those with doctoral degrees may be considered for the GS-11 level.

Career Ladders and Promotions

Grade levels for professional and administrative positions under the GS pay system increase first in two-grade intervals (i.e., GS-5, 7, 9, and 11) and then in 1-grade intervals (i.e., GS-12, 13, 14 and 15). Many federal jobs offer a "career ladder" of promotion potential. For example, an entry-level position's career ladder might go from GS-5 to GS-11. This means that an employee in that job could be promoted from GS-5 to 7 to 9 to 11, after performing successfully for at least one year at each level. Each grade increase typically means a salary increase of several thousand dollars. A summary of the current GS pay scales appears on the next page.

Starting Salaries Under the General Schedule
(As of January 2000)

| GS Level | Years of Government Service | | | | |
	1	2	3	4	5
1	$13,870	$14,332	$14,794	$15,252	$15,715
2	$15,594	$15,964	$16,481	$16,918	$17,107
3	$17,015	$17,582	$18,149	$18,716	$19,283
4	$19,100	$19,737	$20,374	$21,011	$21,648
5	$21,370	$22,082	$22,794	$23,506	$24,218
6	$23,820	$24,614	$25,408	$26,202	$26,996
7	$26,470	$27,352	$28,234	$29,116	$29,998
8	$29,315	$30,292	$31,269	$32,246	$33,223
9	$32,380	$33,459	$34,548	$35,617	$36,696
10	$35,658	$36,847	$38,036	$39,225	$40,414
11	$39,178	$40,484	$41,790	$43,096	$44,402
12	$46,955	$48,520	$50,085	$51,650	$53,215
13	$55,837	$57,698	$59,559	$61,420	$63,281
14	$65,983	$68,182	$70,381	$72,580	$74,779
15	$77,614	$80,201	$82,788	$85,375	$87,962

Benefits

The federal government offers such benefits as life insurance, retirement plans, a variety of health insurance plans, and paid leave. New employees earn 13 days of personal leave and 13 days of sick leave a year, and are also paid for 10 national holidays. Many federal agencies also offer a number of special benefits, including child care arrangements, credit unions, and recreational activities.

Work Schedules

Another benefit of a federal job is that federal employees are not always limited to a traditional work schedule. You may be able to work a part-time, flexible, or alternate work schedule. The flextime approach, for example, allows you flexibility in your work schedule while still working a 40-hour work week.

Age/Citizenship Requirements

The standard minimum age for starting a permanent job is 18. For some fields, such as law enforcement, there are higher age requirements for applicants. With few exceptions, federal employees must be U.S. citizens. However, some non-citizens may be selected for certain positions under special circumstances. Contact individual agencies to find out about such opportunities.

Equal Opportunity

The federal government is an Equal Opportunity Employer. Hiring and advancement are based on qualifications and performance regardless of such factors as race, color, religion, gender, age, national origin, political views, or disability.

Competitive Versus Excepted Services

The information in this section covers jobs in the federal competitive service, in which applicants compete for jobs based on a written exam and/or an evaluation of their education and work experience. However, in the case of such professions as lawyer and chaplain, and for jobs with some government agencies, including the Central Intelligence Agency and the General Accounting Office, hiring authorities are "excepted" from these procedures. Excepted agencies each have their own hiring methods, and should be contacted individually.

How to Apply

As mentioned earlier, Standard Form 171, once the required method of applying for most federal jobs, has gone the way of the dinosaur. It is still accepted for employment, but it is no longer insisted upon. In 1999 and for the foreseeable future, the **Optional Application For Federal Employment (OF-612)** is the preferred means of application for federal jobs. That said, the option does remain for you to simply submit a resume -- as long as it meets certain specifications.

What Your Federal Employment Application Should Include

Although the federal government no longer *requires* a standard application form for most jobs, some positions filled through automated procedures may require special forms or give specific instructions in the job announcement. In all cases, certain basic information is needed to evaluate your qualifications. If you decide to submit any format other than the OF-612, you must include:

- **Job Information** -- Announcement number, title, and grade of the job for which you're applying.

- **Personal Information** -- Full name, mailing address (with zip code), day and evening phone numbers (with area code), social security number, country of citizenship, veterans' preference, reinstatement eligibility, and highest federal civilian grade held.

- **Education** -- High school name and location, college or university name and location, major, and type of degree received (if no degree, show total credits earned and indicate whether semester or quarter hours).

- **Work Experience** -- Job title, duties and accomplishments, employer's name and address, supervisor's name and phone number, starting and ending dates (month and year), hours per week, and salary.

- **Other Qualifications** -- Job-related training courses, skills (for example, languages), certificates and licenses, honors, awards, and special accomplishments (for example, publications or memberships in professional or honor societies, leadership activities, public speaking, or performance awards).

Conclusion -- Outlook for the Future

As mentioned earlier, the federal government is the nation's largest single employer. And, about 87 percent of all federal employees work outside metropolitan Washington DC.

Little change is expected in the overall level of federal government employment through the next decade. Where the jobs are, on the other hand, is changing. Defense Department jobs -- which currently make up nearly half of all federal jobs -- are on the decline due to budget cuts. Hardest hit among Defense Department workers will be blue-collar workers, as three out of every four blue-collar workers in the federal government are employed by the Defense Department. As a group, though, virtually all other federal agencies should be adding more workers.

The reasons for rising and falling federal government employment are unique. Unlike any other employer in the nation, the government's payroll budget is determined by Congress and the President prior to each fiscal year, which runs from October 1 through September 30 of the following year. Whether operating at a surplus or a deficit, the federal government generally sticks to its payroll budget. As a result, federal employment is not affected by regular cycles in the economy, and employment levels tend to be relatively stable in the short run.

On the other hand, political changes can make staffing levels much more uncertain in the long run. Since each administration has different priorities, a change in administration can mean more hiring is done for some programs, and less for others. And in 1995, several government shutdowns resulted from an impasse between officials over the annual budget, putting many federal employees temporarily out of work. There's no guarantee that such work stoppages are a thing of the past, and not an indicator of the future.

The federal government has made numerous efforts in the past few years to streamline an undeniably unwieldy application process. Many of these efforts have been successful, and the sheer volume of information available today without leaving the comfort of one's home is impressive. Unfortunately, some automated advancements have combined with budget cuts to make finding the exact information you want a potentially frustrating venture. With any luck, some of the flaws in the current system will be corrected in the years to come.

The Job Search

This chapter is divided into four sections. The first section explains the fundamentals that every jobseeker should know, especially first-time jobseekers. The next three sections deal with special situations faced by specific types of jobseekers: those who are currently employed, those who have lost a job, and college students.

THE BASICS:
Things Everyone Needs to Know

Career Planning

The first step to finding your ideal job is to clearly define your objectives. This is better known as career planning (or life planning if you wish to emphasize the importance of combining the two). Career planning has become a field of study in and of itself.

If you are thinking of choosing or switching careers, we particularly emphasize two things. First, choose a career where you will enjoy most of the day-to-day tasks. This sounds obvious, but most of us have at some point found the idea of a glamour industry or prestigious job title attractive without thinking of the key consideration: Would we enjoy performing the *everyday* tasks the position entails?

The second key consideration is that you are not merely choosing a career, but also a lifestyle. Career counselors indicate that one of the most common problems people encounter in jobseeking is that they fail to consider how well-suited they are for a particular position or career. For example, some people, attracted to management consulting by good salaries, early responsibility, and high-level corporate exposure, do not adapt well to the long hours, heavy travel demands, and constant pressure to produce. Be sure to ask yourself how you might adapt to the day-to-day duties and working environment that a specific position entails. Then ask yourself how you might adapt to the demands of that career or industry as a whole.

Choosing Your Strategy

Assuming that you've established your career objectives, the next step of the job search is to develop a strategy. If you don't take the time to develop a plan, you may find yourself going in circles after several weeks of randomly searching for opportunities that always seem just beyond your reach.

The most common jobseeking techniques are:

- following up on help-wanted advertisements (in the newspaper or online)
- using employment services
- relying on personal contacts
- contacting employers directly (the Direct Contact method)

Each of these approaches can lead to better jobs. However, the Direct Contact method boasts twice the success rate of the others. So unless you have specific reasons to employ other strategies, Direct Contact should form the foundation of your job search.

If you choose to use other methods as well, try to expend at least half your energy on Direct Contact. Millions of other jobseekers have already proven that Direct Contact has been twice as effective in obtaining employment, so why not follow in their footsteps?

Setting Your Schedule

Okay, so now that you've targeted a strategy it's time to work out the details of your job search. The most important detail is setting up a schedule. Of course, since job searches aren't something most people do regularly, it may be hard to estimate how long each step will take. Nonetheless, it is important to have a plan so that you can monitor your progress.

When outlining your job search schedule, have a realistic time frame in mind. If you will be job-searching full-time, your search could take at least two months or more. If you can only devote part-time effort, it will probably take at least four months.

You probably know a few people who seem to spend their whole lives searching for a better job in their spare time. Don't be one of them. If you are presently working and don't feel like devoting a lot of energy to jobseeking right now, then wait. Focus on enjoying your present position, performing your best on the job, and storing up energy for when you are really ready to begin your job search.

Those of you who are currently unemployed should remember that *job-hunting is tough work, both physically and emotionally*. It is also intellectually demanding work that requires you to be at your best. So don't tire yourself out by working on your job campaign around the clock. At

> **The first step in beginning your job search is to clearly define your objectives.**

the same time, be sure to discipline yourself. The most logical way to manage your time while looking for a job is to keep your regular working hours.

If you are searching full-time and have decided to choose several different strategies, we recommend that you divide up each week, designating some time for each method. By trying several approaches at once, you can evaluate how promising each seems and alter your schedule accordingly. Keep in mind that the *majority of openings are filled without being advertised.* Remember also that positions advertised on the Internet are just as likely to already be filled as those found in the newspaper!

If you are searching part-time and decide to try several different contact methods, we recommend that you try them sequentially. You simply won't have enough time to put a meaningful amount of effort into more than one method at once. Estimate the length of your job search, and then allocate so many weeks or months for each contact method, beginning with Direct Contact. The purpose of setting this schedule is not to rush you to your goal but to help you periodically evaluate your progress.

The Direct Contact Method

Once you have scheduled your time, you are ready to begin your search in earnest. Beginning with the Direct Contact method, the first step is to develop a checklist for categorizing the types of firms for which you'd like to work. You might categorize firms by product line, size, customer type (such as industrial or consumer), growth prospects, or geographical location. Keep in mind, the shorter the list the easier it will be to locate a company that is right for you.

Next you will want to use this book to assemble your list of potential employers. Choose firms where *you* are most likely to be able to find a job. Try matching your skills with those that a specific job demands. Consider where your skills might be in demand, the degree of competition for employment, and the employment outlook at each company.

Separate your prospect list into three groups. The first 25 percent will be your primary target group, the next 25 percent will be your secondary group, and the remaining names will be your reserve group.

After you form your prospect list, begin working on your resume. Refer to the Resumes and Cover Letters section of this book for more information.

Once your resume is complete, begin researching your first batch of prospective employers. You will want to determine whether you would be happy working at the firms you are researching and to get a better idea of what their employment needs might be. You also need to obtain enough information to sound highly informed about the company during phone conversations and in mail correspondence. But don't go all out on your research yet! You probably won't be able to arrange interviews with some of these firms, so save your big research effort until you start to arrange interviews. Nevertheless, you should plan to spend several hours researching each firm. Do your research in batches to save time and energy. Start with this book, and find out what you can about each of the firms in your primary target group. For answers to specific questions, contact any pertinent professional associations that may be able to help you learn more about an employer. Read industry publications looking for articles on the firm. (Addresses of associations and names of important publications are listed after each section of employer listings in this book.) Then look up the company on the Internet or try additional resources at your local library. Keep organized, and maintain a folder on each firm.

> **The more you know about a company, the more likely you are to catch an interviewer's eye. (You'll also face fewer surprises once you get the job!)**

Information to look for includes: company size; president, CEO, or owners name; when the company was established; what each division does; and benefits that are important to you. An abundance of company information can be found electronically, through the World Wide Web or commercial online services. Researching companies online is a convenient means of obtaining information quickly and easily. If you have access to the Internet, you can search from your home at any time of day.

You may search a particular company's Website for current information that may be otherwise unavailable in print. In fact, many companies that maintain a site update their information daily. In addition, you may also search articles written about the company online. Most of the nation's largest newspapers, magazines, trade publications, and regional business periodicals have online versions of their publications. To find additional resources, use a search engine like Yahoo! or Alta Vista and type in the keyword "companies" or "employers."

If you discover something that really disturbs you about the firm (they are about to close their only local office), or if you discover that your chances of getting a job there are practically nil (they have just instituted a hiring freeze), then cross them off your prospect list. If possible, supplement your research efforts by contacting individuals who know the firm well. Ideally you should make an informal contact with someone at that particular firm, but often a direct competitor or a major customer will be able to supply you with just as much information. At the very least, try to obtain whatever printed information the company has available -- not just annual reports, but product brochures, company profiles, or catalogs. This information is often available on the company's Website.

Getting the Interview

Now it is time to make Direct Contact with the goal of arranging interviews. If you have read any books on job-searching, you may have noticed that most of these books tell you to avoid the personnel office like the plague. It is said that the personnel office never hires people; they screen candidates. Unfortunately, this is often the case. If you can identify the appropriate manager with the authority to hire you, you should try to contact that person directly.

The obvious means of initiating Direct Contact are:

- Mail (postal or electronic)
- Phone calls

Mail contact is a good choice if you have not been in the job market for a while. You can take your time to prepare a letter, say exactly what you want, and of course include your resume. Remember that employers receive many resumes every day. Don't be surprised if you do not get a response to your inquiry, *and don't spend weeks waiting for responses that may never come.* If you do send a letter, follow it up (or precede it) with a phone call. This will increase your impact, and because of the initial research you did, will underscore both your familiarity with and your interest in the firm. Bear in mind that your goal is to make your name a familiar one with prospective employers, so that when a position becomes available, your resume will be one of the first the hiring manager seeks out.

If you send a fax, always follow with a hard copy of your resume and cover letter in the mail. Often, through no fault of your own, a fax will come through illegibly and employers do not often have time to let candidates know.

Another alternative is to make a "cover call." Your cover call should be just like your cover letter: concise. Your first statement should interest the employer in you. Then try to subtly mention

DEVELOPING YOUR CONTACTS: NETWORKING

Some career counselors feel that the best route to a better job is through somebody you already know or through somebody to whom you can be introduced. These counselors recommend that you build your contact base beyond your current acquaintances by asking each one to introduce you, or refer you, to additional people in your field of interest.

The theory goes like this: You might start with 15 personal contacts, each of whom introduces you to three additional people, for a total of 45 additional contacts. Then each of these people introduces you to three additional people, which adds 135 additional contacts. Theoretically, you will soon know every person in the industry.

Of course, developing your personal contacts does not work quite as smoothly as the theory suggests because some people will not be able to introduce you to anyone. The further you stray from your initial contact base, the weaker your references may be. So, if you do try developing your own contacts, try to begin with as many people that you know personally as you can. Dig into your personal phone book and your holiday greeting card list and locate old classmates from school. Be particularly sure to approach people who perform your personal business such as your lawyer, accountant, banker, doctor, stockbroker, and insurance agent. These people develop a very broad contact base due to the nature of their professions.

your familiarity with the firm. Don't be overbearing; keep your introduction to three sentences or less. Be pleasant, self-confident, and relaxed. This will greatly increase the chances of the person at the other end of the line developing the conversation. But don't press. If you are asked to follow up with "something in the mail," this signals the conversation's natural end. Don't try to prolong the conversation once it has ended, and don't ask what they want to receive in the mail. Always send your resume and a highly personalized follow-up letter, reminding the addressee of the phone conversation. *Always* include a cover letter if you are asked to send a resume, and treat your resume and cover letter as a total package. Gear your letter toward the specific position you are applying for and prove why you would be a "good match" for the position.

> **Always include a cover letter if you are asked to send a resume.**

Unless you are in telephone sales, making smooth and relaxed cover calls will probably not come easily. Practice them on your own, and then with your friends or relatives.

> ## DON'T BOTHER WITH MASS MAILINGS OR BARRAGES OF PHONE CALLS
>
> Direct Contact does not mean burying every firm within a hundred miles with mail and phone calls. Mass mailings rarely work in the job hunt. This also applies to those letters that are personalized -- but dehumanized -- on an automatic typewriter or computer. Don't waste your time or money on such a project; you will fool no one but yourself.
>
> The worst part of sending out mass mailings, or making unplanned phone calls to companies you have not researched, is that you are likely to be remembered as someone with little genuine interest in the firm, who lacks sincerity -- somebody that nobody wants to hire.

If you obtain an interview as a result of a telephone conversation, be sure to send a thank-you note reiterating the points you made during the conversation. You will appear more professional and increase your impact. However, unless specifically requested, don't mail your resume once an interview has been arranged. Take it with you to the interview instead.

You should never show up to seek a professional position without an appointment. Even if you are somehow lucky enough to obtain an interview, you will appear so unprofessional that you will not be seriously considered.

Preparing for the Interview

As each interview is arranged, begin your in-depth research. You should arrive at an interview knowing the company upside-down and inside-out. You need to know the company's products, types of customers, subsidiaries, parent company, principal locations, rank in the industry, sales and profit trends, type of ownership, size, current plans, and much more. By this time you have probably narrowed your job search to one industry. Even if you haven't, you should still be familiar with common industry terms, the trends in the firm's industry, the firm's principal competitors and their relative performance, and the direction in which the industry leaders are headed.

Dig into every resource you can! Surf the Internet. Read the company literature, the trade press, the business press, and if the company is public, call your stockbroker (if you have one) and ask for additional information. If possible, speak to someone at the firm before the interview, or if not, speak to someone at a competing firm. The more time you spend, the better. Even if you feel extremely pressed for time, you should set aside several hours for pre-interview research.

If you have been out of the job market for some time, don't be surprised if you find yourself tense during your first few interviews. It will probably happen every time you re-enter the market, not just when you seek your first job after getting out of school.

> **You should arrive at an interview knowing the company upside-down and inside-out.**

HELP WANTED ADVERTISEMENTS

Only a small fraction of professional job openings are advertised. Yet the majority of jobseekers spend a lot of time studying the help wanted ads. As a result, the competition for advertised openings is often very severe.

A moderate-sized employer told us about their experience advertising in the help wanted section of a major Sunday newspaper:

It was a disaster. We had over 500 responses from this relatively small ad in just one week. We have only two phone lines in this office and one was totally knocked out. We'll never advertise for professional help again.

If you insist on following up on help wanted ads, then research a firm before you reply to an ad. Preliminary research might help to separate you from all of the other professionals responding to that ad, many of whom will have only a passing interest in the opportunity. It will also give you insight about a particular firm, to help you determine if it might be a good match. That said, your chances of obtaining a job through the want ads are still much smaller than they are with the Direct Contact method.

Tension is natural during an interview, but knowing you have done a thorough research job should put you more at ease. Make a list of questions that you think might be asked in each interview. Think out your answers carefully and practice them with a friend. Tape record your responses to the problem questions. (*See also in this chapter: Informational Interviews.*) If you feel particularly unsure of your interviewing skills, arrange your first interviews at firms you are not as interested in. (But remember it is common courtesy to seem enthusiastic about the possibility of working for any firm at which you interview.) Practice again on your own after these first few interviews. Go over the difficult questions that you were asked.

Take some time to really think about how you will convey your work history. Present "bad experiences" as "learning experiences." Instead of saying "I hated my position as a salesperson because I had to bother people on the phone," say "I realized that cold-calling was not my strong suit. Though I love working with people, I decided my talents would be best used in a more face-to-face atmosphere." Always find some sort of lesson from previous jobs, as they all have one.

Interview Attire

How important is the proper dress for a job interview? Buying a complete wardrobe, donning new shoes, and having your hair styled every morning are not enough to guarantee you a career position as an investment banker. But on the other hand, if you can't find a clean, conservative suit or won't take the time to wash your hair, then you are just wasting your time by interviewing at all.

Personal grooming is as important as finding appropriate clothes for a job interview. Careful grooming indicates both a sense of thoroughness and self-confidence. This is not the time to make a statement -- take out the extra earrings and avoid any garish hair colors not found in nature. Women should not wear excessive makeup, and both men and women should refrain from wearing any perfume or cologne (it only takes a small spritz to leave an allergic interviewer with a fit of sneezing and a bad impression of your meeting). Men should be freshly shaven, even if the interview is late in the day, and men with long hair should have it pulled back and neat.

Men applying for any professional position should wear a suit, preferably in a conservative color such as navy or charcoal gray. It is easy to get away with wearing the same dark suit to consecutive interviews at the same company; just be sure to wear a different shirt and tie for each interview.

Women should also wear a business suit. Professionalism still dictates a suit with a skirt, rather than slacks, as proper interview garb for women. This is usually true even at companies where pants are acceptable attire for female employees. As much as you may disagree with this guideline, the more prudent time to fight this standard is after you land the job.

The final selection of candidates for a job opening won't be determined by dress, of course. However, inappropriate dress can quickly eliminate a first-round candidate. So while you shouldn't spend a fortune on a new wardrobe, you should be sure that your clothes are adequate. The key is to dress at least as formally or slightly more formally and more conservatively than the position would suggest.

SKIRT VS. PANTS:
An Interview Dilemma

For those women who are still convinced that pants are acceptable interview attire, listen to the words of one career counselor from a prestigious New England college:

I had a student who told me that since she knew women in her industry often wore pants to work, she was going to wear pants to her interviews. Almost every recruiter commented that her pants were "too casual," and even referred to her as "the one with the pants." The funny thing was that one of the recruiters who commented on her pants had been wearing jeans!

What to Bring

Be complete. Everyone needs a watch, a pen, and a notepad. Finally, a briefcase or a leather-bound folder (containing extra, *unfolded*, copies of your resume) will help complete the look of professionalism.

Sometimes the interviewer will be running behind schedule. Don't be upset, be sympathetic. There is often pressure to interview a lot of candidates and to quickly fill a demanding position. So be sure to come to your interview with good reading material to keep yourself occupied and relaxed.

The Interview

The very beginning of the interview is the most important part because it determines the tone for the rest of it. Those first few moments are especially crucial. Do you smile when you meet? Do you establish enough eye contact, but not too much? Do you walk into the office with a self-assured and confident stride? Do you shake hands firmly? Do you make small talk easily without being garrulous? It is human nature to judge people by that first impression, so make sure it is a good one. But most of all, try to be yourself.

Often the interviewer will begin, after the small talk, by telling you about the company, the division, the department, or perhaps, the position. Because of your detailed research, the information about the company should be repetitive for you, and the interviewer would probably like nothing better than to avoid this regurgitation of the company biography. So if you can do so tactfully, indicate to the interviewer that you are very familiar with the firm. If he or she seems intent on providing you with background information, despite your hints, then acquiesce.

But be sure to remain attentive. If you can manage to generate a brief discussion of the company or the industry at this point, without being forceful, great. It will help to further build rapport, underscore your interest, and increase your impact.

Soon (if it didn't begin that way) the interviewer will begin the questions, many of which you will have already practiced. This period of the interview usually falls into one of two categories (or somewhere in between): either a structured interview, where the interviewer has a prescribed set of questions to ask; or an unstructured interview, where the interviewer will ask only leading questions to get you to talk about yourself, your experiences, and your goals. Try to sense as quickly as possible in which direction the interviewer wishes to proceed. This will make the interviewer feel more relaxed and in control of the situation.

Remember to keep attuned to the interviewer and make the length of your answers appropriate to the situation. If you are really unsure as to how detailed a response the interviewer is seeking, then ask.

> **The interviewer's job is to find a reason to turn you down; your job is to not provide that reason.**
>
> -John L. LaFevre, author, *How You Really Get Hired*
>
> Reprinted from the 1989/90 *CPC Annual*, with permission of the National Association of Colleges and Employers (formerly College Placement Council, Inc.), copyright holder.

As the interview progresses, the interviewer will probably mention some of the most important responsibilities of the position. If applicable, draw parallels between your experience and the demands of the position as detailed by the interviewer. Describe your past experience in the same manner that you do on your resume: emphasizing results and achievements and not merely describing activities. But don't exaggerate. Be on the level about your abilities.

The first interview is often the toughest, where many candidates are screened out. If you are interviewing for a very competitive position, you will have to make an impression that will last. Focus on a few of your greatest strengths that are relevant to the position. Develop these points carefully, state them again in different words, and then try to summarize them briefly at the end of the interview.

Often the interviewer will pause toward the end and ask if you have any questions. Particularly in a structured interview, this might be the one chance to really show your knowledge of and interest in the firm. Have a list prepared of specific questions that are of real interest to you. Let your questions subtly show your research and your knowledge of the firm's activities. It is wise to have an extensive list of questions, as several of them may be answered during the interview.

BE PREPARED:
Some Common Interview Questions

Tell me about yourself.

Why did you leave your last job?

What excites you in your current job?

What led you to apply for this position?

What are you looking for in a company?

Where would you like to be in five years?

How much overtime are you willing to work?

What would your previous/present employer tell me about you?

Tell me about a difficult situation that you
faced at your previous/present job.

What are your greatest strengths?

What are your weaknesses?

Describe a work situation where you took initiative
and went beyond your normal responsibilities.

Why should we hire you?

Do not turn your opportunity to ask questions into an interrogation. Avoid reading directly from your list of questions, and ask questions that you are fairly certain the interviewer can answer (remember how you feel when you cannot answer a question during an interview).

Even if you are unable to determine the salary range beforehand, do not ask about it during the first interview. You can always ask later. Above all, don't ask about fringe benefits until you have been offered a position. (Then be sure to get all the details.)

Try not to be negative about anything during the interview, particularly any past employer or any previous job. Be cheerful. Everyone likes to work with someone who seems to be happy. Even if you detest your current/former job or manager, do not make disparaging comments. The interviewer may construe this as a sign of a potential attitude problem and not consider you a strong candidate.

Don't let a tough question throw you off base. If you don't know the answer to a question, simply say so -- do not apologize. Just smile. Nobody can answer every question -- particularly some of the questions that are asked in job interviews.

Before your first interview, you may be able to determine how many rounds of interviews there usually are for positions at your level. (Of course it may differ quite a bit even within the different levels of one firm.) Usually you can count on attending at least two or three interviews, although some firms are known to give a minimum of six interviews for all professional positions. While you should be more relaxed as you return for subsequent interviews, the pressure will be on. The more prepared you are, the better.

Depending on what information you are able to obtain, you might want to vary your strategy quite a bit from interview to interview. For instance, if the first interview is a screening interview, then be sure a few of your strengths really stand out. On the other hand, if later interviews are primarily with people who are in a position to veto your hiring, but not to push it forward, then you should primarily focus on building rapport as opposed to reiterating and developing your key strengths.

If it looks as though your skills and background do not match the position the interviewer was hoping to fill, ask him or her if there is another division or subsidiary that perhaps could profit from your talents.

After the Interview

Write a follow-up letter immediately after the interview, while it is still fresh in the interviewer's mind (see the sample follow-up letter format found in the Resumes and Cover Letters chapter). Not only is this a thank-you, but it also gives you the chance to provide the interviewer with any details you may have forgotten (as long as they can be tactfully added in). If you haven't heard back from the interviewer within a week of sending your thank-you letter, call to stress your continued interest in the firm and the position. If you lost any points during the interview for any reason, this letter can help you regain footing. Be polite and make sure to stress your continued interest and competency to fill the position. Just don't forget to proofread it thoroughly. If you are unsure of the spelling of the interviewer's name, call the receptionist and ask.

THE BALANCING ACT:
Looking for a New Job While Currently Employed

For those of you who are still employed, job-searching will be particularly tiring because it must be done in addition to your normal work responsibilities. So don't overwork yourself to the point where you show up to interviews looking exhausted or start to slip behind at your current job. On the other hand, don't be tempted to quit your present job! The long hours are worth it. Searching for a job while you have one puts you in a position of strength.

Making Contact

If you must be at your office during the business day, then you have additional problems to deal with. How can you work interviews into the business day? And if you work in an open office, how can you even call to set up interviews? Obviously, you should keep up the effort and the appearances on your present job. So maximize your use of the lunch hour, early mornings, and late afternoons for calling. If you keep trying, you'll be surprised how often you will be able to reach the executive you are trying to contact during your out-of-office hours. You can catch people as early as 8 a.m. and as late as 6 p.m. on frequent occasions.

Scheduling Interviews

Your inability to interview at any time other than lunch just might work to your advantage. If you can, try to set up as many interviews as possible for your lunch hour. This will go a long way toward creating a relaxed atmosphere. But be sure the interviews don't stray too far from the agenda on hand.

> **Try calling as early as 8 a.m. and as late as 6 p.m. You'll be surprised how often you will be able to reach the executive you want during these times of the day.**

Lunchtime interviews are much easier to obtain if you have substantial career experience. People with less experience will often find no alternative to taking time off for interviews. If you have to take time off, you have to take time off. But try to do this as little as possible. Try to take the whole day off in order to avoid being blatantly obvious about your job search, and try to schedule two to three interviews for the same day. (It is very difficult to maintain an optimum level of energy at more than three interviews in one day.) Explain to the interviewer why you might have to juggle your interview schedule; he/she should honor the respect you're showing your current employer by minimizing your days off and will probably appreciate the fact that another prospective employer is interested in you.

References

What do you tell an interviewer who asks for references from your current employer? Just say that while you are happy to have your former employers contacted, you are trying to keep your job search confidential and would rather that your current employer not be contacted until you have been given a firm offer.

IF YOU'RE FIRED OR LAID OFF:
Picking Yourself Up and Dusting Yourself Off

If you've been fired or laid off, you are not the first and will not be the last to go through this traumatic experience. In today's changing economy, thousands of professionals lose their jobs every year. Even if you were terminated with just cause, do not lose heart. Remember, being fired is not a reflection on you as a person. It is usually a reflection of your company's staffing needs and its perception of your recent job performance and attitude. And if you were not performing up to par or enjoying your work, then you will probably be better off at another company anyway.

> **Be prepared for the question "Why were you fired?" during job interviews.**

A thorough job search could take months, so be sure to negotiate a reasonable severance package, if possible, and determine to what benefits, such as health insurance, you are still legally entitled. Also, register for unemployment compensation immediately. Don't be surprised to find other professionals collecting unemployment compensation -- it is for everyone who has lost their job.

Don't start your job search with a flurry of unplanned activity. Start by choosing a strategy and working out a plan. Now is not the time for major changes in your life. If possible, remain in the same career and in the same geographical location, at least until you have been working again for a while. On the other hand, if the only industry for which you are trained is leaving, or is severely depressed in your area, then you should give prompt consideration to moving or switching careers.

Avoid mentioning you were fired when arranging interviews, but be prepared for the question "Why were you fired?" during an interview. If you were laid off as a result of downsizing, briefly explain, being sure to reinforce that your job loss was not due to performance. If you were in fact fired, be honest, but try to detail the reason as favorably as possible and portray what you have learned from your mistakes. If you are confident one of your past managers will give you a good reference, tell the interviewer to contact that person. Do not to speak negatively of your past employer and try not to sound particularly worried about your status of being temporarily unemployed.

Finally, don't spend too much time reflecting on why you were let go or how you might have avoided it. Think positively, look to the future, and be sure to follow a careful plan during your job search.

THE COLLEGE STUDENT:
Conducting Your First Job Search

While you will be able to apply many of the basics covered earlier in this chapter to your job search, there are some situations unique to the college student's job search.

THE GPA QUESTION

You are interviewing for the job of your dreams. Everything is going well: You've established a good rapport, the interviewer seems impressed with your qualifications, and you're almost positive the job is yours. Then you're asked about your GPA, which is pitifully low. Do you tell the truth and watch your dream job fly out the window?

Never lie about your GPA (they may request your transcript, and no company will hire a liar). You can, however, explain if there is a reason you don't feel your grades reflect your abilities, and mention any other impressive statistics. For example, if you have a high GPA in your major, or in the last few semesters (as opposed to your cumulative college career), you can use that fact to your advantage.

Gaining Experience

Perhaps the biggest problem college students face is lack of experience. Many schools have internship programs designed to give students exposure to the field of their choice, as well as the opportunity to make valuable contacts. Check out your school's career services department to see what internships are available. If your school does not have a formal internship program, or if there are no available internships that appeal to you, try contacting local businesses and offering your services. Often, businesses will be more than willing to have an extra pair of hands (especially if those hands are unpaid!) for a day or two each week. Or try contacting school alumni to see if you can "shadow" them for a few days, and see what their daily duties are like.

Informational Interviews

Although many jobseekers do not do this, it can be extremely helpful to arrange an informational interview with a college alumnus or someone else who works in your desired industry. You interview them about their job, their company, and their industry with questions you have prepared in advance. This can be done over the phone but is usually done in person. This will provide you with a contact in the industry who may give you more valuable information -- or perhaps even a job opportunity -- in the future. Always follow up with a thank you letter that includes your contact information.

The goal is to try to begin building experience and establishing contacts
as early as possible in your college career.

What do you do if, for whatever reason, you weren't able to get experience directly related to your desired career? First, look at your previous jobs and see if there's anything you can highlight. Did you supervise or train other employees? Did you reorganize the accounting system, or boost productivity in some way? Accomplishments like these demonstrate leadership, responsibility, and innovation -- qualities that most companies look for in employees. And don't forget volunteer activities and school clubs, which can also showcase these traits.

On-Campus Recruiting

Companies will often send recruiters to interview on-site at various colleges. This gives students a chance to interview with companies that may not have interviewed them otherwise. This is particularly true if a company schedules "open" interviews, in which the only screening process is who is first in line at the sign-ups. Of course, since many more applicants gain interviews in this format, this also means that many more people are rejected. The on-campus interview is generally a screening interview, to see if it is worth the company's time to invite you in for a second interview. So do everything possible to make yourself stand out from the crowd.

The first step, of course, is to check out any and all information your school's career center has on the company. If the information seems out of date, check out the company on the Internet or call the company's headquarters and ask for any printed information.

Many companies will host an informational meeting for interviewees, often the evening before interviews are scheduled to take place. DO NOT MISS THIS MEETING. The recruiter will almost certainly ask if you attended. Make an effort to stay after the meeting and talk with the company's representatives. Not only does this give you an opportunity to find out more information about both the company and the position, it also makes you stand out in the recruiter's mind. If there's a particular company that you had your heart set on, but you weren't able to get an interview with them, attend the information session anyway. You may be able to persuade the recruiter to squeeze you into the schedule. (Or you may discover that the company really isn't the right fit for you after all.)

Try to check out the interview site beforehand. Some colleges may conduct "mock" interviews that take place in one of the standard interview rooms. Or you may be able to convince a career counselor (or even a custodian) to let you sneak a peek during off-hours. Either way, having an idea of the room's setup will help you to mentally prepare.

Arrive at least 15 minutes early to the interview. The recruiter may be ahead of schedule, and might meet you early. But don't be surprised if previous interviews have run over, resulting in your 30-minute slot being reduced to 20 minutes (or less). Don't complain or appear anxious; just use the time you do have as efficiently as possible to showcase the reasons *you* are the ideal candidate. Staying calm and composed in these situations will work to your advantage.

LAST WORDS

A parting word of advice. Again and again during your job search you will face rejection. You will be rejected when you apply for interviews. You will be rejected after interviews. For every job offer you finally receive, you probably will have been rejected many times. Don't let rejections slow you down. Keep reminding yourself that the sooner you go out, start your job search, and get those rejections flowing in, the closer you will be to obtaining the job you want.

RESUMES AND COVER LETTERS

When filling a position, an employer will often have 100-plus applicants, but time to interview only a handful of the most promising ones. As a result, he or she will reject most applicants after only briefly skimming their resumes.

Unless you have phoned and talked to the employer -- which you should do whenever you can -- you will be chosen or rejected for an interview entirely on the basis of your resume and cover letter. *Your cover letter must catch the employer's attention, and your resume must hold it.* (But remember -- a resume is no substitute for a job search campaign. *You* must seek a job. Your resume is only one tool, albeit a critical one.)

RESUME FORMAT:
Mechanics of a First Impression

The Basics

Employers dislike long resumes, so unless you have an unusually strong background with many years of experience and a diversity of outstanding achievements, keep your resume length to one page. If you must squeeze in more information than would otherwise fit, try using a smaller typeface or changing the margins. Watch also for "widows" at the end of paragraphs. You can often free up some space if you can shorten the information enough to get rid of those single words taking up an entire line. Another tactic is to decrease the font size and changing the spacing between lines.

Print your resume on standard 8 1/2" x 11" paper. Since recruiters often get resumes in batches of hundreds, a smaller-sized resume may be lost in the pile. Oversized resumes are likely to get crumpled at the edges, and won't fit easily in their files.

First impressions matter, so make sure the recruiter's first impression of your resume is a good one. Never hand-write your resume (or cover letter)! Print your resume on quality paper that has weight and texture, in a conservative color such as white, ivory, or pale gray. Good resume paper is easy to find at many stores that sell stationary or office products. Use *matching* paper and envelopes for both your resume and cover letter. One hiring manager at a major magazine throws out all resumes that arrive on paper that differs in color from the envelope!

Do not buy paper with images of clouds and rainbows in the background or anything that looks like casual stationary that you would send to your favorite aunt. Do not spray perfume or cologne on your resume. Do not include your picture with your resume unless you have a specific and appropriate reason to do so.

Another tip: Do a test print of your resume (and cover letter), to make sure the watermark is on the same side as the text so that you can read it. Also make sure it is right-side up. As trivial as this may sound, some recruiters check for this! One recruiter at a law firm in New Hampshire sheepishly admitted this is the first thing he checks. *"I open each envelope and check the watermarks on the resume and cover letter. Those candidates that have it wrong go into a different pile."*

Getting it on Paper

Modern photocomposition typesetting gives you the clearest, sharpest image, a wide variety of type styles, and effects such as italics, bold-facing, and book-like justified margins. It is also too expensive for many jobseekers. The quality of today's laser printers mean that a computer-generated resume can look just as impressive as one that has been professionally typeset.

A computer with a word processing or desktop publishing program is the most common way to generate your resume. This allows you the flexibility to make changes almost instantly and to store different drafts on disk. Word processing and desktop publishing programs also offer many different fonts to choose from, each taking up different amounts of space. (It is generally best to stay between 9-point and 12-point font size.) Many other options are also available, such as bold-facing or italicizing for emphasis and the ability to change and manipulate spacing. It is generally recommended to leave the right-hand margin unjustified as this keeps the spacing between the text even and therefore easier to read. It is not wrong to justify both margins of text, but if possible try it both ways before you decide if possible.

For a resume on paper, the end result will be largely determined by the quality of the printer you use. Laser printers will generally provide the best quality. Do not use a dot matrix printer.

Many companies now use scanning equipment to screen the resumes they receive, and certain paper, fonts, and other features are more compatible with this technology. White paper is preferable, as well as a standard font such as Courier or Helvetica. You should use at least a 10-point font, and avoid bolding, italics, underlining, borders, boxes, or graphics.

Household typewriters and office typewriters with nylon or other cloth ribbons are *not* good enough for typing your resume. If you don't have access to a quality word processing program, hire a professional with the resources to prepare your resume for you. Keep in mind that businesses such as Kinko's (open 24 hours) provide access to computers with quality printers.

Don't make your copies on an office photocopier. Only the personnel office may see the resume you mail. Everyone else may see only a copy of it, and copies of copies quickly become unreadable. Furthermore, sending photocopies of your resume or cover letter is completely unprofessional. Either print out each copy individually, or take your resume to a professional copy shop, which will generally offer professionally-maintained, extra-high-quality photocopiers and charge fairly reasonable prices. You want your resume to represent <u>you</u> with the look of polished quality.

Proof with Care

Whether you typed it or paid to have it produced professionally, mistakes on resumes are not only embarrassing, but will usually remove you from consideration (particularly if something obvious such as your name is misspelled). No matter how much you paid someone else to type, write, or typeset your resume, *you* lose if there is a mistake. So proofread it as carefully as possible. Get a friend to help you. Read your draft aloud as your friend checks the proof copy. Then have your friend read aloud while you check. Next, read it letter by letter to check spelling and punctuation.

If you are having it typed or typeset by a resume service or a printer, and you don't have time to proof it, pay for it and take it home. Proof it there and bring it back later to get it corrected and printed.

If you wrote your resume with a word processing program, use the built-in spell checker to double-check for spelling errors. Keep in mind that a spell checker will not find errors such as "to" for "two" or "wok" for "work." Many spell check programs do not recognize missing or misused punctuation, nor are they set to check the spelling of capitalized words. It's important that you still proofread your resume to check for grammatical mistakes and other problems, even <u>after</u> it has been spellchecked.

*If you find mistakes, do not make edits in pen or pencil
or use white-out to fix them on the final copy!*

Electronic Resumes

As companies rely increasingly on emerging technologies to find qualified candidates for job openings, you may opt to create an electronic resume in order to remain competitive in today's job market. Why is this important? Companies today sometimes request that resumes be submitted by e-mail, and many hiring managers regularly check online resume databases for candidates to fill unadvertised job openings. Other companies enlist the services of electronic employment database services, which charge jobseekers a nominal fee to have their resume posted to the database to be viewed by potential employers. Still other companies use their own automated applicant tracking systems, in which case your resume is fed through a scanner that sends the image to a computer which "reads" your resume, looking for keywords, and files it accordingly in its database.

Whether you're posting your resume online, e-mailing it directly to an employer, sending it to an electronic employment database, or sending it to a company you suspect uses an automated applicant tracking system, you must create some form of electronic resume to take advantage of the technology. Don't panic! An electronic resume is simply a modified version of your conventional resume. An electronic resume is one that is sparsely formatted, but filled with keywords and important facts.

In order to post your resume to the Internet -- either to an online resume database or through direct e-mail to an employer -- you will need to change the way your resume is formatted. Instead of a Word, WordPerfect, or other word processing document, save your resume as a plain text, DOS, or ASCII file. These three terms are basically interchangeable, and describe text at its simplest, most basic level, without the formatting such as boldface or italics that most jobseekers use to make their resumes look more interesting. If you use e-mail, you'll notice that all of your messages are written and received in this format. First, you should remove all formatting from your resume including boldface, italics, underlining, bullets, differing font sizes, and graphics. Then, convert and save your resume as a plain text file. Most word processing programs have a "save as" feature that allows you to save files in different formats. Here, you should choose "text only" or "plain text."

Another option is to create a resume in HTML (hypertext markup language), the text formatting language used to publish information on the World Wide Web. However, the real usefulness of HTML resumes is still being explored. Most of the major online databases do not accept HTML resumes, and the vast majority of companies only accept plain text resumes through their e-mail.

Finally, if you simply wish to send your resume to an electronic employment database or a company that uses an automated applicant tracking system, there is no need to convert your resume to a plain text file. The only change you need to make is to organize the information in your resume by keywords. Employers are likely to do keyword searches for information, such as degree held or knowledge of particular types of software. Therefore, using the right keywords or key phrases in your resume is critical to its ultimate success. Keywords are usually nouns or short phrases that the computer searches for which refer to experience, training, skills, and abilities. For example, let's say an employer searches an employment database for a sales representative with the following criteria:

BS/BA
exceeded quota
cold calls
high energy
willing to travel

Even if you have the right qualifications, neglecting to use these keywords would result in the computer passing over your resume. Although there is no way to know for sure which keywords employers are most likely to likely to search for, you can make educated guesses by checking the help-wanted ads or online job postings for your type of job. You should also arrange keywords in a keyword summary, a paragraph listing your qualifications that immediately follows your name and address (see sample letter in this chapter). In addition, choose a nondecorative font with clear, distinct characters, such as Helvetica or Times. It is more difficult for a scanner to accurately pick up the more unusual fonts. Boldface and all capital letters are best used only for major section headings, such as "Experience" and "Education." It is also best to avoid using italics or underlining, since this can cause the letters to bleed into one another.

For more specific information on creating and sending electronic resumes, see *The Adams Electronic Job Search Almanac.*

Types of Resumes

The most common resume formats are the functional resume, the chronological resume, and the combination resume. (Examples can be found at the end of this chapter.) A functional resume focuses on skills and de-emphasizes job titles, employers, etc. A functional resume is best if you have been out of the work force for a long time or are changing careers. It is also good if you want to highlight specific skills and strengths, especially if all of your work experience has been at one company. This format can also be a good choice if you are just out of school or have no experience in your desired field at all.

Choose a chronological format if you are currently working or were working recently, and if your most recent experiences relate to your desired field. Use reverse chronological order and include dates. To a recruiter your last job and your latest schooling are the most important, so put the last first and list the rest going back in time.

A combination resume is perhaps the most common. This resume simply combines elements of the functional and chronological resume formats. This is used by many jobseekers with a solid track record who find elements of both types useful.

Organization

Your name, phone number, e-mail address (if you have one), and a complete mailing address should be at the top of your resume. Try to make your name stand out by using a slightly larger font size or all capital letters. Be sure to spell out everything. Never abbreviate St. for Street or Rd. for Road. If you are a college student, you should also put your home address and phone number at the top. Change your message on your answering machine if necessary -- RUSH blaring in the background or your sorority sisters screaming may not come across well to all recruiters. If you think you may be moving within six months then include a second address and phone number of a trusted friend or relative who can reach you no matter where you are.

Remember that employers will keep your resume on file and
may contact you months later if a position opens that fits your qualifications.
All too often, candidates are unreachable because they have moved and had not previously provided
enough contact options on their resume.

Next, list your experience, then your education. If you are a recent graduate, list your education first, unless your experience is more important than your education. (For example, if you have just graduated from a teaching school, have some business experience, and are applying for a job in business, you would list your business experience first.)

Keep everything easy to find. Put the dates of your employment and education on the left of the page. Put the names of the companies you worked for and the schools you attended a few spaces to the right of the dates. Put the city and state, or the city and country, where you studied or worked to the right of the page.

The important thing is simply to break up the text in some logical way that makes your resume visually attractive and easy to scan, so experiment to see which layout works best for your resume. However you set it up, *stay consistent*. Inconsistencies in fonts, spacing, or tenses will make your resume look sloppy. Also, be sure to use tabs to keep your information vertically lined up, rather than the less precise space bar.

RESUME CONTENT:
Say it with Style

Sell Yourself

You are selling your skills and accomplishments in your resume, so it is important to inventory yourself and know yourself. If you have achieved something, say so. Put it in the best possible light. But avoid subjective statements, such as "I am a hard worker" or "I get along well with my coworkers." Just stick to the facts.

While you shouldn't hold back or be modest, don't exaggerate your achievements to the point of misrepresentation. <u>Be honest</u>. Many companies will immediately drop an applicant from consideration (or fire a current employee) upon discovering inaccurate or untrue information on a resume or other application material.

Write down the important (and pertinent) things you have done, but do it in as few words as possible. Your resume will be scanned, not read, and short, concise phrases are much more effective than long-winded sentences. Avoid the use of "I" when emphasizing your accomplishments. Instead, use brief phrases beginning with action verbs.

While some technical terms will be unavoidable, you should try to avoid excessive "technicalese." Keep in mind that the first person to see your resume may be a human resources person who won't necessarily know all the jargon -- and how can they be impressed by something they don't understand?

Keep it Brief

Also, try to hold your paragraphs to six lines or less. If you have more than six lines of information about one job or school, put it in two or more paragraphs. A short resume will be examined more carefully. Remember: Your resume usually has between eight and 45 seconds to catch an employer's eye. So make every second count.

Job Objective

A functional resume may require a job objective to give it focus. One or two sentences describing the job you are seeking can clarify in what capacity your skills will be best put to use. Be sure that your stated objective is in line with the position you're applying for.

Examples:

An entry-level editorial assistant position in the publishing industry.
A senior management position with a telecommunications firm.

Don't include a job objective on a chronological resume unless your previous work experiences are completely unrelated to the position for which you're applying. The presence of an overly specific job objective might eliminate you from consideration for other positions that a recruiter feels are a better match for your qualifications. But even if you don't put an objective on paper, having a career goal in mind can help give your resume a solid sense of direction.

Work Experience

Some jobseekers may choose to include both "Relevant Experience" and "Additional Experience" sections. This can be useful, as it allows the jobseeker to place more emphasis on certain experiences and to de-emphasize others.

Emphasize continued experience in a particular job area or continued interest in a particular industry. De-emphasize irrelevant positions. It is okay to include one opening line providing a general description of each company you've worked at. Delete positions that you held for less than four months (unless you are a very recent college grad or still in school). Stress your results and your achievements, elaborating on how you contributed in your previous jobs. Did you increase sales, reduce costs, improve a product, implement a new program? Were you promoted? Use specific numbers (i.e., quantities, percentages, dollar amounts) whenever possible.

Education

Keep it brief if you have more than two years of career experience. Elaborate more if you have less experience. If you are a recent college graduate, you may choose to include any high school activities that are directly relevant to your career. If you've been out of school for a while you don't need to list your education prior to college.

Mention degrees received and any honors or special awards. Note individual courses or projects you participated in that might be relevant for employers. For example, if you are an English major applying for a position as a business writer, be sure to mention any business or economics courses. Previous experience such as Editor-in-Chief of the school newspaper would be relevant as well.

If you are uploading your resume to an online job hunting site such as CareerCity, action verbs are still important, but the key words or key nouns that a computer would search for become more important. For example, if you're seeking an accounting position, key nouns that a computer would search for such as "Lotus 1-2-3" or "CPA" or "payroll" become very important.

Highlight Impressive Skills

Be sure to mention any computer skills you may have. You may wish to include a section entitled "Additional Skills" or "Computer Skills," in which you list any software programs you know. An additional skills section is also an ideal place to mention fluency in a foreign language.

> **Those things [marital status, church affiliations, etc.] have no place on a resume. Those are illegal questions, so why even put that information on your resume?**
>
> -Becky Hayes, Career Counselor
> Career Services, Rice University

USE ACTION VERBS

How you write your resume is just as important as *what* you write. In describing previous work experiences, the strongest resumes use short phrases beginning with action verbs. Below are a few you may want to use. (This list is not all-inclusive.)

achieved	developed	integrated	purchased
administered	devised	interpreted	reduced
advised	directed	interviewed	regulated
analyzed	discovered	invented	reorganized
arranged	distributed	launched	represented
assembled	eliminated	maintained	researched
assisted	established	managed	resolved
attained	evaluated	marketed	restored
budgeted	examined	mediated	restructured
built	executed	monitored	revised
calculated	expanded	negotiated	scheduled
collaborated	expedited	obtained	selected
collected	facilitated	operated	served
compiled	formulated	ordered	sold
completed	founded	organized	solved
computed	generated	participated	streamlined
conducted	headed	performed	studied
consolidated	identified	planned	supervised
constructed	implemented	prepared	supplied
consulted	improved	presented	supported
controlled	increased	processed	tested
coordinated	initiated	produced	trained
created	installed	proposed	updated
designed	instituted	provided	upgraded
determined	instructed	published	wrote

Personal Data

This section is optional, but if you choose to include it, keep it brief. A one-word mention of hobbies such as fishing, chess, baseball, cooking, etc., can give the person who will interview you a good way to open up the conversation. Team sports experience is looked at favorably. It doesn't hurt to include activities that are somewhat unusual (fencing, Akido, '70s music) or that somehow relate to the position or the company you're applying. For instance, it would be worth noting if you are a member of a professional organization in your industry of interest. Never include information about your age, alias, date of birth, health, physical characteristics, marital status, religious affiliation, or political/moral beliefs.

References

The most that is needed is the sentence "References available upon request" at the bottom of your resume. If you choose to leave it out, that's fine. This line is not really necessary. It is understood that references will most likely be asked for and provided by you later on in the interviewing process. Do not actually send references with your resume and cover letter unless specifically requested.

HIRING A RESUME WRITER:
Is it the Right Choice for You?

If you write reasonably well, it is to your advantage to write your own resume. Writing your resume forces you to review your experiences and figure out how to explain your accomplishments in clear, brief phrases. This will help you when you explain your work to interviewers. It is also easier to tailor your resume to each position you're applying for when you have put it together yourself.

If you write your resume, everything will be in your own words; it will sound like you. It will say what you want it to say. If you are a good writer, know yourself well, and have a good idea of which parts of your background employers are looking for, you should be able to write your own resume better than someone else. If you decide to write your resume yourself, have as many people as possible review and proofread it. Welcome objective opinions and other perspectives.

When to Get Help

If you have difficulty writing in "resume style" (which is quite unlike normal written language), if you are unsure which parts of your background to emphasize, or if you think your resume would make your case better if it did not follow one of the standard forms outlined either here or in a book on resumes, then you should consider having it professionally written.

Even some professional resume writers we know have had their resumes written with the help of fellow professionals. They sought the help of someone who can be objective about their background, as well as provide an experienced sounding board to help focus their thoughts.

If You Hire a Pro

The best way to choose a writer is by reputation: the recommendation of a friend, a personnel director, your school placement officer, or someone else knowledgeable in the field.

Important questions:
- "How long have you been writing resumes?"
- "If I'm not satisfied with what you write, will you go over it with me and change it?"
- "Do you charge by the hour or a flat rate?"

There is no sure relation between price and quality, except that you are unlikely to get a good writer for less than $50 for an uncomplicated resume and you shouldn't have to pay more than $300 unless your experience is very extensive or complicated. There will be additional charges for printing. Assume nothing no matter how much you pay. It is your career at stake if there are mistakes on your resume!

Few resume services will give you a firm price over the phone, simply because some resumes are too complicated and take too long to do for a predetermined price. Some services will quote you a price that applies to almost all of their customers. Once you decide to use a specific writer, you should insist on a firm price quote *before* engaging their services. Also, find out how expensive minor changes will be.

COVER LETTERS:
Quick, Clear, and Concise

Always mail a cover letter with your resume. In a cover letter you can show an interest in the company that you can't show in a resume. You can also point out one or two of your skills or accomplishments the company can put to good use.

Make it Personal

The more personal you can get, the better, so long as you keep it professional. If someone known to the person you are writing has recommended that you contact the company, get permission to include his/her name in the letter. If you can get the name of a person to send the letter to, address it directly to that person (after first calling the company to verify the spelling of the person's name, correct title, and mailing address). Be sure to put the person's name and title on both the letter and the envelope. This will ensure that your letter will get through to the proper person, even if a new person now occupies this position. It will not always be possible to get the name of a person. Always strive to get at least a title.

Be sure to mention something about why you have interest in the company -- *so many candidates apply for jobs with no apparent knowledge of what the company does!* This conveys the message that they just want any job.

Type cover letters in full. Don't try the cheap and easy ways, like using a computer mail merge program or photocopying the body of your letter and typing in the inside address and salutation. You will give the impression that you are mailing to a host of companies and have no particular interest in any one.

Print your cover letter on the same color and same high-quality paper as your resume.

Cover Letter Basic Format

Paragraph 1: State what the position is that you are seeking. It is not always necessary to state how you found out about the position -- often you will apply without knowing that a position is open.
Paragraph 2: Include what you know about the company and why you are interested in working there. Mention any prior contact with the company or someone known to the hiring person if relevant. Briefly state your qualifications and what you can offer. (Do not talk about what you cannot do).
Paragraph 3: Close with your phone number and where/when you can be reached. Make a request for an interview. State when you will follow-up by phone (or mail or e-mail if the ad requests no phone calls). Do not wait long -- generally five working days. If you say you're going to follow-up,

then actually do it! This phone call can get your resume noticed when it might otherwise sit in a stack of 225 other resumes.

Cover Letter Do's and Don'ts

- *Do* keep your cover letter brief and to the point.
- *Do* be sure it is error-free.
- *Do* accentuate what you can offer the company, not what you hope to gain from them.
- *Do* be sure your phone number and address is on your cover letter just in case it gets separated from your resume (this happens!).
- *Do* check the watermark by holding the paper up to a light -- be sure it is facing forward so it is readable -- on the same side as the text, and right-side up.
- *Do* sign your cover letter (or type your name if you are sending it electronically). Blue or black ink are both fine. Do not use red ink.
- *Don't* just repeat information verbatim from your resume.
- *Don't* overuse the personal pronoun "I."
- *Don't* send a generic cover letter -- show your personal knowledge of and interest in that particular company.

THANK YOU LETTERS:
Another Way to Stand Out

As mentioned earlier, *always* send a thank you letter after an interview (see the sample later in this section). So few candidates do this and it is yet another way for you to stand out. Be sure to mention something specific from the interview and restate your interest in the company and the position.

It is generally acceptable to handwrite your thank you letter on a generic thank you card (but *never* a postcard). Make sure handwritten notes are neat and legible. However, if you are in doubt, typing your letter is always the safe bet. If you met with several people it is fine to send them each an individual thank you letter. Call the company if you need to check on the correct spelling of their names.

Remember to:
- Keep it short.
- Proofread it carefully.
- Send it *promptly*.

FUNCTIONAL RESUME

LISA J. AMATO
237 Chimney Sweep Road
Newton MA 02459
617/555-1345
e-mail: lamato@baystate.net

Objective
A position as a graphic designer commensurate with my acquired skills and expertise.

Summary
Extensive experience in plate making, separations, color matching, background definition, printing, mechanicals, color corrections, and personnel supervision. A highly motivated manager and effective communicator. Proven ability to:

- **Create Commercial Graphics**
- **Produce Embossed Drawings**
- **Color Separate**
- **Control Quality**
- **Resolve Printing Problems**
- **Analyze Customer Satisfaction**

Qualifications
Printing:
Knowledgeable in black and white as well as color printing. Excellent judgment in determining acceptability of color reproduction through comparison with original. Proficient at producing four- or five-color corrections on all media, as well as restyling previously reproduced four-color artwork.

Customer Relations:
Routinely work closely with customers to ensure specifications are met. Capable of striking a balance between technical printing capabilities and need for customer satisfaction through entire production process.

Specialties:
Practiced at creating silk screen overlays for a multitude of processes including velo bind, GBC bind, and perfect bind. Creative design and timely preparation of posters, flyers, and personalized stationery.

Personnel Supervision:
Skillful at fostering atmosphere that encourages highly talented artists to balance high-level creativity with maximum production. Consistently beat production deadlines. Instruct new employees and students in both artistry and technical operations.

Experience
Graphic Arts Professor, Boston University, Boston MA (1996-1998).
Manager, Striking Graphics, Cambridge MA (1998-present).

Education
Massachusetts Conservatory of Art, Ph.D. 1996
University of Massachusetts, B.A. 1992

CHRONOLOGICAL RESUME

KATHRYN M. RYAN
6 Byron Avenue
Seattle, WA 98404
(206) 555-5449
e-mail:kmr@centco.com

EXPERIENCE

THE CENTER COMPANY   Seattle, WA
Systems Programmer   1996-present
- Develop and maintain customer accounting and order tracking database using a Visual Basic front end and SQL server.
- Plan and implement migration of company wide transition from mainframe based dumb terminals to a true client server environment using Windows NT Workstation and Server.
- Oversee general local and wide area network administration including the development of a variety of intranet modules to improve internal company communication and planning across divisions.

INFO TECH, INC.   Seattle, WA
Technical Manager   1994-1996
- Designed and managed the implementation of a network providing the legal community with a direct line to Supreme Court cases across the Internet using SQL Server and a variety of Internet tools.
- Developed a system to make the entire library catalog available online using PERL scripts and SQL.
- Used Visual Basic and Microsoft Access to create a registration system for university registrar.

EDUCATION

SALEM STATE UNIVERSITY   Salem, OR
    M.S. in Computer Science.   1993
    B.S. in Computer Science.   1991

COMPUTER SKILLS

- Programming Languages: Visual Basic, Java, C++, SQL, PERL
- Software: SQL Server, Internet Information Server, Oracle
- Operating Systems: Windows NT, UNIX, LINUX

CHRONOLOGICAL RESUME

KELLEY E. SHADRICK
70 Plymouth Avenue
East Providence RI 02914
401/555-5813 (h)
401/555-9211, x13 (w)

EDUCATION

Providence College, Providence RI
Bachelor of Arts in Elementary Education, 1996
- Graduated *magna cum laude*
- English minor
- Kappa Delta Pi member, inducted 1994

EXPERIENCE
September 1996-
Present

M.J. Newman Elementary School, Rumford RI
Kindergarten Teacher
- Instruct kindergartners in reading, spelling, language arts, and music.
- Participate in the selection of textbooks and learning aids.
- Organize and supervise class field trips and coordinate in-class presentations.

Summers
1993-1995

Boston YMCA, Youth Division, Boston MA
Child-care Counselor
- Oversaw summer program for low-income youth.
- Budgeted and coordinated special events and field trips, working with Program Director to initiate variations in the program.
- Served as Youth Advocate in cooperation with social worker to address the social needs and problems of participants.

Spring 1995

Gorham Elementary School, Cranston RI
Student Teacher
- Taught third-grade class in all elementary subjects.
- Designed and implemented a two-week unit on Native Americans.
- Assisted in revision of third-grade curriculum.

Fall 1994

Child Development Center, Providence RI
Daycare Worker
- Supervised preschool children on the playground and during athletic activities.
- Created a "Hot Corner," where children could quietly look at books or take a voluntary "time-out."

ADDITIONAL INTERESTS
Baseball, skiing, traveling, tennis, reading.

ELECTRONIC RESUME

CHRISTIN VUMBACO
9376 Foster Street
Cambridge, MA 02138
(617) 555-5643

KEYWORD SUMMARY

Senior financial manager with over ten years experience in Accounting and Systems Management, Budgeting, Forecasting, Cost Containment, Financial Reporting, and International Accounting. MBA in Management. Proficient in Lotus, Excel, Solomon, and Windows.

EXPERIENCE

COLWELL CORPORATION, Wellesley, MA
Director of Accounting and Budgets, 1994 to present
Direct staff of twenty in General Ledger, Accounts Payable, Accounts Receivable, and International Accounting.
Facilitate month-end closing process with parent company and auditors.
Implemented team-oriented cross-training program within accounting group, resulting in timely month-end closings and increased productivity of key accounting staff.
Developed and implemented a strategy for Sales and Use Tax Compliance in all fifty states.
Prepare monthly financial statements and analyses.

FRANKLIN AND DELANEY COMPANY, Melrose, MA
Senior Accountant, 1991-1994
Managed Accounts Payable, General Ledger, transaction processing, and financial reporting. Supervised staff of five.

Staff Accountant, 1989-1991
Managed Accounts Payable, including vouchering, cash disbursements, and bank reconciliation.
Wrote and issued policies.
Maintained supporting schedules used during year-end audits.
Trained new employees.

EDUCATION

MBA in Management, Northeastern University, Boston, MA, 1993
BS in Accounting, Boston College, Boston, MA, 1989

GENERAL MODEL
FOR A COVER LETTER

Your mailing address
Date

Contact's name
Contact's title
Company
Company's mailing address

Dear Mr./Ms. _____:

Immediately explain why your background makes you the best candidate for the position that you are applying for. Describe what prompted you to write (want ad, article you read about the company, networking contact, etc.). Keep the first paragraph short and hard-hitting.

Detail what you could contribute to this company. Show how your qualifications will benefit this firm. Describe your interest in the corporation. Subtly emphasizing your knowledge about this firm and your familiarity with the industry will set you apart from other candidates. Remember to keep this letter short; few recruiters will read a cover letter longer than half a page.

If possible, your closing paragraph should request specific action on the part of the reader. Include your phone number and the hours when you can be reached. Mention that if you do not hear from the reader by a specific date, you will follow up with a phone call. Lastly, thank the reader for their time, consideration, etc.

Sincerely,

(signature)

Your full name (typed)

Enclosure (use this if there are other materials, such as your resume,
            that are included in the same envelope)

SAMPLE COVER LETTER

70 Plymouth Avenue
East Providence RI 02914
January 13, 2001

Ms. Beverly Cross
Assistant Principal
Jonathon Daniels Elementary School
43 Mayflower Drive
Wallingford CT 06492

Dear Ms. Cross:

Janet Newell recently informed me of a possible opening for a third grade teacher at Jonathon Daniels Elementary School. With my experience instructing third-graders, both in schools and in summer programs, I feel I would be an ideal candidate for the position. Please accept this letter and the enclosed resume as my application.

Jonathon Daniels' educational philosophy that every child can learn and succeed interests me, since it mirrors my own. My current position at M.J. Newman Elementary has reinforced this philosophy, heightening my awareness of the different styles and paces of learning and increasing my sensitivity toward special needs children. Furthermore, as a direct result of my student teaching experience at Gorham Elementary School, I am comfortable, confident, and knowledgeable working with third-graders.

I look forward to discussing the position and my qualifications for it in more detail. I can be reached at 401/555-5813 evenings or 401/555-9211, x13 weekdays. If I do not hear from you before Tuesday of next week, I will call to see if we can schedule a time to meet. Thank you for your time and consideration.

Sincerely,

Kelley E. Shadrick

Kelley E. Shadrick

Enclosure

GENERAL MODEL FOR A
THANK YOU/FOLLOW-UP LETTER

Your mailing address
Date

Contact's name
Contact's title
Company
Company's mailing address

Dear Mr./Ms._____:

Remind the interviewer of the reason (i.e., a specific opening, an informational interview, etc.) you were interviewed, as well as the date. Thank him/her for the interview, and try to personalize your thanks by mentioning some specific aspect of the interview.

Confirm your interest in the organization (and in the opening, if you were interviewing for a particular position). Use specifics to re-emphasize that you have researched the firm in detail and have considered how you would fit into the company and the position. This is a good time to say anything you wish you had said in the initial meeting. Be sure to keep this letter brief; a half-page is plenty.

If appropriate, close with a suggestion for further action, such as a desire to have an additional interview, if possible. Mention your phone number and the hours that you can be reached. Alternatively, you may prefer to mention that you will follow up with a phone call in several days. Once again, thank the person for meeting with you, and state that you would be happy to provide any additional information about your qualifications.

Sincerely,

(signature)

Your full name (typed)

The Job Offer

In today's tough economy, one of the most nerve-racking steps on the trail to a new job is near the end of the path: deciding whether to accept an offer. On the one hand, if you've been in the job market for some time, your instinct may scream, "I'll take it, I'll take it," before the last syllables of the offer are out of the recruiter's mouth. On the other, you may also be worrying that the salary being offered won't even be enough to cover the cost of all those stamps you've used to send out resumes and cover letters over the past few months.

Faced with these conflicting emotions, it's easy to see how many job seekers can make unnecessary, costly mistakes during this final, vitally important stage. Far too many job seekers sell themselves short without even exploring their options. Others have wildly unrealistic expectations of what level of compensation they should expect. Still others get so wrapped up in money questions that they forget to consider any other issues, which is a big mistake.

Do You Want This Job?

If you're going to consider a job offer seriously, be confident that this is a job you really want. Are you willing to live and work in the area in question? Is the work schedule and way of life one you'd enjoy? If you're just graduating, is the job in the field you'd like to pursue?

Will It Help Your Career?

Whether or not a job will help your career progress is ultimately a much more important question than what your starting salary will be. In some organizations, you may be given a lot of responsibility right away but then find your progress blocked. Make sure you know if there are opportunities for advancement. Ask about performance reviews—how often are they conducted?

Do You Like the Environment?

Another important factor to consider is the kind of environment in which you'll be working. Is the company's atmosphere comfortable, challenging, and exciting? Consider specifics, including office or workstation setting, privacy, proximity to other staff, amount of space, noise level, and lighting. What is the level of interaction among coworkers? Some organizations strongly encourage teamwork and dialogue among staff, while others emphasize individual accomplishment. Which approach works better for you? Remember: if you don't like the work environment before you accept the job, you probably won't like it as an employee.

The Money Questions

The questions of salary and benefits strike fear into the hearts of job seekers young and old. But handling the inevitable money questions doesn't have to be difficult, and the more you think about them in advance, the easier they'll be to answer.

First, never try to negotiate salary or benefits until you've gotten an offer. At that point, don't worry about the recruiter withdrawing his or her handshake and showing you the door if you dare ask about flexibility in the company's offer. The worst case might be that the salary is set by company policy and the recruiter has no power to negotiate. Or else the recruiter may not be able to give you an immediate answer and will have to get back to you.

Negotiating a Salary

According to David G. Jensen, of Search Masters International, companies come in two types—those that won't negotiate salaries and those that will. He refers to these philosophies as "First offer, best offer" and "Negotiation is OK and expected." It's necessary to find out which type your company is before attempting to negotiate. You can determine this from

> ### Tell me about your salary expectations.
> I've become a little frustrated in the past year, because the downturn in our industry has caused limited promotional opportunities. Based on salary information published by our national association, the market price for someone with my experience and educational background is in the broad range of thirty to forty thousand dollars per year. Although I'm not certain how your salaries compare to the national norms, my feeling is that my value would certainly be in the upper half of this national range. I hope you'll share with me some of your salary ranges relative to the national norms.
>
> A well-prepared candidate can effectively turn this question around. Ask first for the company's salary range, then answer in general terms based on your qualifications in relation to the job requirements.

their response to an appropriately phrased question about more money or benefits. The idea is to first assure them of your interest, then give reasons for your proposed increase rather than just saying you need it or want it. For example, explain why their offer doesn't sufficiently cover your living expenses or moving expenses or the cost of maintaining a wardrobe if your position requires you to dress up. Their response to this will indicate whether they're willing to negotiate or not. David Jensen's Web page, at www.bio.com/hr/search/search_1.html, discusses these two approaches in greater detail, along with other aspects of job searching.

If you do negotiate, this doesn't mean you name a figure and the employer either matches it or doesn't. It means you're ready to listen to what the recruiter has to offer and give it consideration. To succeed in negotiation, both parties have to reach an agreement with which they're happy. If you succeed at winning yourself a bigger paycheck but antagonize your future boss in doing so, trouble lies ahead. If, on the other hand, you set realistic expectations and realize you may not get everything you want, you'll probably do just fine.

How Much Should You Expect?

Just how do you know how much you should expect? The answer is the same as in every other step of your job search: do your homework. Read the trade journals for your industry. Read the newspaper help-wanted ads. If possible, talk to current employees. The *Occupational Outlook Handbook,* available in libraries, lists salaries and other information about a variety of jobs.

Try to get objective comments. Alumni of your college or university in similar positions (or employed by the same organization) may be an excellent source of information. Doing this research will give you an idea of the salary level you can realistically expect.

Your Expectations

Setting realistic expectations is especially important for the entry-level job seeker or recent graduate. If you don't have a lot of professional experience, you don't leave the recruiter with much hard evidence on which to base a decision. Instead, you're asking him or her to take a leap of faith based on potential you've demonstrated in classes, internships, volunteering, or extracurricular activities. Without a track record of professional experience, your arsenal is missing a powerful weapon. This is why entry-level salaries are often determined by the marketplace, which leaves you with little leverage. Even so, that doesn't mean you can't give it a try.

On the other hand, if you have some experience under your belt and are looking for a mid-level or executive position, your negotiating power might be much greater. For a lucky (or unlucky) few at the top of the heap, salary and benefit negotiations can be as complex and painstakingly slow as watching the grass grow. If you're like most people, you're not in that group. Whatever your level of experience, your task is to try to figure out just how high the employer is likely to go.

Don't Mention It

If, after listening politely to the specifics of the offer, you're left hoping for a higher salary, greater health coverage, or something else, it's okay to (calmly) say so. Find out if the offer is firm. If it seems there may be some room to negotiate, make sure you have a figure in mind, because if the recruiter does have the freedom to barter, he or she will probably ask you to supply a figure.

When you're asked that question, rule number one is as follows: *Don't tip your hand by giving the interviewer a specific number for which you're willing to settle.* You don't want to take yourself out of the running by naming a figure that's absurdly optimistic, and you certainly don't want to risk naming a figure lower than what the employer is ready to offer. Instead of naming your price, say something like, "Based on my experience and skills and the demands of the position, I'd expect I'd earn an appropriate figure. Can you tell me what kind of range you have in mind?"

Of course, the recruiter may come back with "Well, how much were you interested in?"

> ### What do you reasonably expect to earn within five years?
>
> My expectation for the next five years is that my contributions will be recognized and appropriately rewarded. I realize that salary levels are based on a number of factors, including the company's profitability and the general business cycle that affects our industry, but I would expect to take on greater responsibility each year and to be appropriately compensated for my efforts and contributions.
>
> Again, turn this question around and ask what's typical for the career path. Then consider, based on your skills and performance, the areas you'll excel in. Leave it to the interviewer to determine the appropriate "time frames" for promotions. Don't speculate, or you'll risk sounding arrogant, unrealistic, or the opposite—too reserved or too tentative.

There's a limit to how far you can take this without antagonizing the other person, so if you can't get him or her to name a range, give in graciously and name your own. Be sure not to make the bottom number too low (because you may be stuck with it) or the range too large, and give yourself enough room at the top without being unrealistic. If you name a range of, say, $25,000–30,000, it may be that the company was considering a range of $22,000–28,000. Therefore, you should receive an offer in the mid-to-upper end of your range, depending on your experience and qualifications.

Get It in Writing

If you're somewhat content with the distribution of funds but haven't discussed health insurance and other benefits, like a 401(k) plan and vacation time, do so immediately. Then request that everything be outlined in writing, especially if you'll be leaving a job to take the new position. You have rights, and if something looks amiss, it's time to go back to the bargaining table—that is, if you're still interested. Regard with suspicion an employer who won't give you confirmation of the position in writing.

It's about Job Satisfaction

The point of your job search is not salary negotiation; it's finding a job you'll be happy with, that you'll grow with, and that will allow you to be yourself. If your starting salary isn't the one you dreamed about but the job presents the right opportunity, think about how much easier it'll be once you've had a chance to make yourself invaluable to the organization.

On the other hand, if the salary or benefits fall far short of your realistic expectations, despite all your efforts to negotiate, nothing says you have to take the job. Don't make the mistake of accepting a position with which you're fundamentally unhappy. Trust your instincts—if you're dissatisfied with the employer before your start date, don't bet the situation will get better.

Accounting and Management Consulting

You can expect to find the following types of companies in this chapter:
*Consulting and Research Firms • Industrial Accounting Firms
Management Services • Public Accounting Firms •Tax Preparation Companies*

Some helpful information: *The average salary for entry-level accountants is $25,000 - $30,000 per year, with experienced accountants and supervisors earning approximately $45,000 - $75,000.*

ABT ASSOCIATES INC.
55 Wheeler Street, Cambridge MA 02138. 617/492-7100. **Fax:** 617/492-5219. **Contact:** Human Resources. **World Wide Web address:** http://www.abtassoc.com. **Description:** One of the largest government and business consulting and research firms in the country. The company provides practical solutions to problems affecting a variety of clients including U.S. government agencies, corporations, foreign governments, and international organizations. Abt's practice spans five broad business lines: social and economic policy research and analysis; health care and environmental research; measurement services; business consulting and strategic planning; and international technical assistance and policy implementation. **Common positions include:** Administrative Assistant; Economist; Market Research Analyst; Researcher; Statistician. **Educational backgrounds include:** Economics; Health Care; Liberal Arts; Social Science. **Benefits:** 401(k); Dental Insurance; Disability Coverage; Employee Discounts; Life Insurance; Medical Insurance; Pension Plan; Profit Sharing; Public - Transit Available; Tuition Assistance. **Corporate headquarters location:** This Location. **Other U.S. locations:** Chicago IL; Bethesda MD. **International locations:** Egypt; Moscow; South Africa. **Number of employees at this location:** 450. **Number of employees worldwide:** 480.

AMERICAN INSTITUTE OF CERTIFIED PUBLIC ACCOUNTANTS (AICPA)
1455 Pennsylvania Avenue NW, 4th Floor, Washington DC 20004. 202/737-6600. **Contact:** Ms. Ela Work, Manager. **World Wide Web address:** http://www.aicpa.org. **Description:** A professional organization dedicated to serving the needs of the certified public accounting industry.

ARTHUR ANDERSEN
501 North 44th Street, Suite 300, Phoenix AZ 85008. 602/286-2000. **Fax:** 602/286-2195. **Contact:** Personnel. **World Wide Web address:** http://www.arthurandersen.com. **Description:** One of the largest certified public accounting firms in the world. Arthur Andersen's four key practice areas include Audit and Business Advisory, Tax and Business Advisory, Business Consulting, and Economic and Financial Consulting. NOTE: This firm does not accept unsolicited resumes. Please check the Website for available positions. **Corporate headquarters location:** Chicago IL. **Parent company:** Arthur Andersen Worldwide Organization is one of the leading providers of professional services in the world. With over 380 worldwide locations, the global practice of its member firms is conducted through two business units: Arthur Andersen and Andersen Consulting, which provides global management and technology

consulting. **Number of employees worldwide:** 91,000.
Other U.S. locations:
• 633 West Fifth Street, 25th Floor, Los Angeles CA 90071. 213/614-6500.
• 101 Second Street, Suite 1100, San Francisco CA 94105. 415/546-8200.

ARTHUR ANDERSEN
1010 Market Street, Suite 1000, St. Louis MO 63101. 314/621-6767. **Contact:** Human Resources. **World Wide Web address:** http://www.arthurandersen.com. **Description:** One of the largest certified public accounting firms in the world. Arthur Andersen's four key practice areas include Audit and Business Advisory, Tax and Business Advisory, Business Consulting, and Economic and Financial Consulting. NOTE: This firm does not accept unsolicited resumes. Please check the Website for available positions. **Corporate headquarters location:** Chicago IL. **Parent company:** Arthur Andersen Worldwide Organization ise of the leading providers of professional services in the world. With over 380 worldwide locations, the global practice of its member firms is conducted through two business units: Arthur Andersen and Andersen Consulting, which provides global management and technology consulting. **Number of employees at this location:** 200. **Number of employees worldwide:** 91,000.

ARTHUR ANDERSEN
1345 Avenue of the Americas, New York NY 10105. 212/708-4000. **Contact:** Recruiting Partner. **World Wide Web address:** http://www.arthurandersen.com. **Description:** One of the largest certified public accounting firms in the world. Arthur Andersen's four key practice areas include Audit and Business Advisory, Tax and Business Advisory, Business Consulting, and Economic and Financial Consulting. NOTE: This firm does not accept unsolicited resumes. Please check the Website for available positions. **Common positions include:** Accountant/Auditor; Actuary; Consultant; Economist; Financial Analyst; Systems Analyst. **Educational backgrounds include:** Accounting; Business Administration; Computer Science; Economics; Engineering; Finance; Liberal Arts; Mathematics. **Benefits:** 401(k); Dental Insurance; Disability Coverage; Life Insurance; Medical Insurance; Profit Sharing. **Corporate headquarters location:** Chicago IL. **Parent company:** Arthur Andersen Worldwide Organization is one of the leading providers of professional services in the world. With over 380 worldwide locations, the global practice of its member firms is conducted through two business units: Arthur Andersen and Andersen Consulting, which provides global management and technology consulting. **Operations at this facility include:** Business

Services; Management Consulting. **Number of employees worldwide:** 91,000.
Other U.S. locations:
- 225 Franklin Street, Boston MA 02110. 617/330-4000.
- 601 East Pratt Street, Baltimore MD 21202. 410/727-5800.

ARTHUR ANDERSEN
41 South High Street, Suite 2100, Huntington Center, Columbus OH 43215. 614/228-5651. **Fax:** 614/229-4225. **Contact:** Human Resources. **World Wide Web address:** http://www. arthurandersen.com. **Description:** One of the largest certified public accounting firms in the world. Arthur Andersen's four key practice areas include Audit and Business Advisory, Tax and Business Advisory, Business Consulting, and Economic and Financial Consulting. **NOTE:** This firm does not accept unsolicited resumes. Please check the Website for available positions. **Corporate headquarters location:** Chicago IL. **Parent company:** Arthur Andersen Worldwide Organization is one of the leading providers of professional services in the world. With over 380 worldwide locations, the global practice of its member firms is conducted through two business units: Arthur Andersen and Andersen Consulting, which provides global management and technology consulting.

ARTHUR ANDERSEN
100 Peabody Place, Suite 1100, Memphis TN 38103. 901/525-4451. **Contact:** Mark Mosley, Manager. **World Wide Web address:** http://www. arthurandersen.com. **Description:** One of the largest certified public accounting firms in the world. Arthur Andersen's four key practice areas include Audit and Business Advisory, Tax and Business Advisory, Business Consulting, and Economic and Financial Consulting. Founded in 1913. **NOTE:** This firm does not accept unsolicited resumes. Please check the Website for available positions. **Corporate headquarters location:** Chicago IL. **Parent company:** Arthur Andersen Worldwide Organization is one of the leading providers of professional services in the world. With over 380 worldwide locations, the global practice of its member firms is conducted through two business units: Arthur Andersen and Andersen Consulting, which provides global management and technology consulting. **Number of employees worldwide:** 91,000.

ARTHUR ANDERSEN
15 West South Temple Street, Suite 700, Salt Lake City UT 84101. 801/533-0820. **Contact:** Personnel. **World Wide Web address:** http://www. arthurandersen.com. **Description:** One of the largest certified public accounting firms in the world. Arthur Andersen's four key practice areas include Audit and Business Advisory, Tax and Business Advisory, Business Consulting, and Economic and Financial Consulting. **NOTE:** This firm does not accept unsolicited resumes. Please check the Website for available positions. **Corporate headquarters location:** Chicago IL. **Parent company:** Arthur Andersen Worldwide Organization is one of the leading providers of professional services in the world. With over 380 worldwide locations, the global practice of its member firms is conducted through two business units: Arthur Andersen and Andersen Consulting, which provides global management and technology consulting. **Number of employees worldwide:** 91,000.
Other U.S. locations:
- 801 Second Avenue, Suite 800, Seattle WA 98104. 206/623-8023.

ARTHUR ANDERSEN
One Biscayne Tower, Suite 2100, Miami FL 33131. 305/374-3700. **Contact:** Human Resources De. **World Wide Web address:** http://www. arthurandersen.com. **Description:** One of the largest certified public accounting firms in the world. Arthur Andersen's four key practice areas are Audit and Business Advisory, Tax and Business Advisory, Business Consulting, and Economic and Financial Consulting. **NOTE:** This firm does not accept unsolicited resumes. Please check the Website for available positions. **Corporate headquarters location:** Chicago IL. **Parent company:** Arthur Andersen Worldwide Organization is one of the leading providers of professional services in the world. With over 380 worldwide locations, the global practice of its member firms is conducted through two business units: Arthur Andersen and Andersen Consulting, which provides global management and technology consulting.
Other U.S. locations:
- 101 East Kennedy Boulevard, Suite 2200, Tampa FL 33602-5150. 813/222-4600.
- 3773 Howard Hughes Parkway, Suite 500S, Las Vegas NV 89109. 702/836-8600.
- 111 SW Columbia Street, Suite 1400, Portland OR 97201. 503/226-1331.

ARTHUR ANDERSEN
111 Monument Circle, Suite 4300, Bank One Center Tower, Indianapolis IN 46204. 317/634-3210. **Contact:** Dick Culp, Director of Human Resources. **World Wide Web address:** http://www. arthurandersen.com. **Description:** One of the largest certified public accounting firms in the world. Arthur Andersen's four key practice areas include Audit and Business Advisory, Tax and Business Advisory, Business Consulting, and Economic and Financial Consulting. **NOTE:** This firm does not accept unsolicited resumes. Please check the Website for available positions. **Corporate headquarters location:** Chicago IL. **International locations:** Worldwide. **Parent company:** Arthur Andersen Worldwide Organization is one of the leading providers of professional services in the world. With over 380 worldwide locations, the global practice of its member firms is conducted through two business units: Arthur Andersen and Andersen Consulting, which provides global management and technology consulting. **Number of employees worldwide:** 91,000.

ARTHUR ANDERSEN
2100 One PPG Place, Pittsburgh PA 15222. 412/232-0600. **Contact:** Gina Dialiso, Human Resources. **World Wide Web address:** http://www.arthurandersen.com. **Description:** One of the largest certified public accounting firms in the world. Arthur Andersen's four key practice areas include Audit and Business Advisory, Tax and Business Advisory, Business Consulting, and Economic and Financial Consulting. **NOTE:** This firm does not accept unsolicited resumes. Please check the Website for available positions. **Corporate headquarters location:** Chicago IL. **Parent company:** Arthur Andersen Worldwide Organization is one of the leading providers of professional services in the world. With over 380 worldwide locations, the global practice of its member firms is conducted through Arthur Andersen and Andersen Consulting, a global management and technology consulting firm.
Other U.S. locations:
- 1601 Market Street, Philadelphia PA 19103-2944. 215/241-7300.

ARTHUR ANDERSEN
6501 America's Parkway NE, Suite 400, Albuquerque NM 87110. 505/889-4700. **Contact:**

Human Resources. **World Wide Web address:** http://www.arthurandersen.com. **Description:** One of the largest certified public accounting firms in the world. Arthur Andersen's four key practice areas include Audit and Business Advisory, Tax and Business Advisory, Business Consulting, and Economic and Financial Consulting. **NOTE:** This firm does not accept unsolicited resumes. Please check the Website for available positions. **Corporate headquarters location:** Chicago IL. **Parent company:** Arthur Andersen Worldwide Organization is one of the leading providers of professional services in the world. With over 380 worldwide locations, the global practice of its member firms is conducted through two business units: Arthur Andersen and Andersen Consulting, which provides global management and technology consulting. **Number of employees worldwide:** 91,000.

ARTHUR ANDERSEN
Champion Plaza, 400 Atlantic Street, Stamford CT 06912. 203/353-3400. **Contact:** Human Resources. **World Wide Web address:** http://www. arthurandersen.com. **Description:** One of the largest certified public accounting firms in the world. Arthur Andersen's four key practice areas include Audit and Business Advisory, Tax and Business Advisory, Business Consulting, and Economic and Financial Consulting. **NOTE:** This firm does not accept unsolicited resumes. Please check the Website for available positions. **Corporate headquarters location:** Chicago IL. **Other U.S. locations:** Nationwide. **International locations:** Worldwide. **Parent company:** Arthur Andersen Worldwide Organization is one of the leading providers of professional services in the world. The global practice of its member firms is conducted through two business units: Arthur Andersen and Andersen Consulting, which provides global management and technology consulting. **Number of employees worldwide:** 91,000.

ARTHUR ANDERSEN
1225 17th Street, Suite 3100, Denver CO 80202. 303/295-1900. **Contact:** Human Resources. **World Wide Web address:** http://www. arthurandersen.com. **Description:** One of the largest certified public accounting firms in the world. Arthur Andersen's four key practice areas include Audit and Business Advisory, Tax and Business Advisory, Business Consulting, and Economic and Financial Consulting. **NOTE:** This firm does not accept unsolicited resumes. Please check the Website for available positions. **International locations:** Worldwide. **Parent company:** Arthur Andersen Worldwide Organization is one of the leading providers of professional services in the world. The global practice of its member firms is conducted through two business units: Arthur Andersen and Andersen Consulting, which provides global management and technology consulting.

ARTHUR ANDERSEN
171 Monroe Avenue NW, Suite 700, Grand Rapids MI 49503-2683. 616/451-2071. **Contact:** Recruiter. **World Wide Web address:** http://www. arthurandersen.com. **Description:** One of the largest certified public accounting firms in the world. Arthur Andersen's four key practice areas include Audit and Business Advisory, Tax and Business Advisory, Business Consulting, and Economic and Financial Consulting. **NOTE:** This firm does not accept unsolicited resumes. Please check the Website for available positions. **Corporate headquarters location:** Chicago IL. **Parent company:** Arthur Andersen Worldwide Organization is one of the leading providers of professional services in the world. With over 380

worldwide locations, the global practice of its member firms is conducted through two business units: Arthur Andersen and Andersen Consulting, which provides global management and technology consulting. **Number of employees worldwide:** 91,000.
Other U.S. locations:
• 2401 Plymouth Road, Suite A, Ann Arbor MI 48105. 734/761-6333.
• 500 Woodward Avenue, Suite 2700, Detroit MI 48226. 313/596-9000.

ARTHUR ANDERSEN
100 North Tryon Street, Suite 3800, Charlotte NC 28202-4000. 704/332-0092. **Contact:** Human Resources. **World Wide Web address:** http://www. arthurandersen.com. **Description:** One of the largest certified public accounting firms in the world. Arthur Andersen's four key practice areas include Audit and Business Advisory, Tax and Business Advisory, Business Consulting, and Economic and Financial Consulting. **NOTE:** This firm does not accept unsolicited resumes. Please check the Website for available positions. **Corporate headquarters location:** Chicago IL. **Other U.S. locations:** Nationwide. **International locations:** Worldwide. **Parent company:** Arthur Andersen Worldwide Organization is one of the leading providers of professional services in the world. With over 380 worldwide locations, the global practice of its member firms is conducted through two business units: Arthur Andersen and Andersen Consulting, which provides global management and technology consulting.

ARTHUR ANDERSEN
33 West Monroe Street, Chicago IL 60603. 312/580-0033. **Fax:** 312/507-6748. **Contact:** Human Resources. **E-mail address:** united.states@ arthurandersen.com. **World Wide Web address:** http://www.arthurandersen.com. **Description:** One of the largest certified public accounting firms in the world. Arthur Andersen's four key practice areas are Audit and Business Advisory, Tax and Business Advisory, Business Consulting, and Economic and Financial Consulting. **NOTE:** This firm does not accept unsolicited resumes. Please check the Website for available positions. **Corporate headquarters location:** This Location. **Parent company:** Arthur Andersen Worldwide Organization is one of the leading providers of professional services in the world. With over 380 worldwide locations, the global practice of its member firms is conducted through two business units: Arthur Andersen and Andersen Consulting, which provides global management and technology consulting.

ANDERSEN CONSULTING
1501 South Mopac Expressway, Austin TX 78746. 512/476-9949. **Contact:** Human Resources. **World Wide Web address:** http://www. andersenconsulting.com. **Description:** This location designs and installs business integration software for government use. Overall, Andersen Consulting provides services to help organizations effectively apply technology to their business advantage. By combining general business knowledge with information systems skills, the company develops solutions for clients in many industries manage technology. **Corporate headquarters location:** Chicago IL. **Parent company:** Arthur Andersen Worldwide Organization is one of the leading providers of professional services in the world. With over 380 worldwide locations, the global practice of its member firms is conducted through two business units: Arthur Andersen and Andersen Consulting, which provides global management and technology consulting.

AON CONSULTING
3565 Piedmont Road NE, Building 1, Suite 600, Atlanta GA 30305. 404/264-3141. **Fax:** 404/240-6099. **Contact:** Business Manager. **World Wide Web address:** http://www.aon.com. **Description:** An international human resources consulting and benefits brokerage firm providing integrated advisory and support services in retirement planning, health care management, organizational effectiveness, compensation, human resources-related communications, and information technologies. The company's organizational effectiveness services include advisory and support services in compensation, strategy development, organizational design, business process redesign, human resources development, management training and development, organizational communications, and information technology applications. Strategic health care services include advisory and support services in traditional group health and welfare programs, strategic health planning, strategic health care management, quality assurance, flexible benefits and compensation, financial management, data management, vendor oversight, and communications. Strategic retirement planning and educational services include consulting and support services in core actuarial applications, retirement health and welfare benefits, funding and investment strategy, record keeping and administration, employee sensing and communications, personalized retirement modeling, holistic lifestyle and family planning, and database information and proprietary studies. Information technologies services include human resources information systems development (information management strategies, systems, databases, software, and technology advisement) and human resources systems applications (human resources planning, record keeping, communication, and education). **Common positions include:** Account Manager; Administrative Assistant; Computer Programmer; Database Manager; Editor; Finance Director; Graphic Artist; Graphic Designer; Human Resources Manager; Insurance Agent/Broker; Paralegal; Project Manager; Sales Manager; Sales Representative; Software Engineer; Statistician; Underwriter/Assistant Underwriter. **Educational backgrounds include:** Business Administration; Communications; Computer Science; Finance; Health Care; Mathematics; Software Development; Software Tech. Support.
Other U.S. locations:
- 707 Wilshire Boulevard, Suite 5700, Los Angeles CA 90017. 213/630-2900.

AON CONSULTING
RADFORD DIVISION
2540 North First Street, Suite 400, San Jose CA 95131. 408/954-0900. **Contact:** Human Resources. **World Wide Web address:** http://www.aon.com. **Description:** An international human resources consulting and benefits brokerage firm providing integrated advisory and support services in retirement planning, health care management, organizational effectiveness, compensation, human resources-related communications, and information technologies. The company's organizational effectiveness services include advisory and support services in compensation, strategy development, organizational design, business process redesign, human resources development, management training and development, organizational communications, and information technology applications. Strategic health care services include advisory and support services in traditional group health and welfare programs, strategic health planning, strategic health care management, quality assurance, flexible benefits and compensation, financial and data management, vendor oversight,

and communications. Strategic retirement planning and educational services include consulting and support services in core actuarial applications, retirement health and welfare benefits, funding and investment strategy, recordkeeping and administration, employee sensing and communications, personalized retirement modeling, holistic lifestyle and family planning, and database information and proprietary studies. Information technologies services include human resources information systems development (information management strategies, systems, databases, software, and technology advisement) and human resources systems applications (human resources planning, recordkeeping, communication, and education).

ARONSON, FETRIDGE & WIEGLE
700 King Farm Boulevard, Suite 300, Rockville MD 20850. 301/231-6200. **Contact:** Lisa Cines, Partner. **World Wide Web address:** http://www.afwcpa.com. **Description:** A certified public accounting and consulting firm. **Number of employees at this location:** 100.

BBC RESEARCH & CONSULTING
3773 Cherry Creek North Drive, Suite 850, Denver CO 80209-3827. 303/321-2547. **Contact:** Jody Smith, Director. **World Wide Web address:** http://www.bbcresearch.com. **Description:** An economic research and management consulting firm. **Common positions include:** Computer Programmer; Economist; Financial Analyst; Management Analyst/Consultant; Marketing Specialist; Statistician. **Educational backgrounds include:** Business Administration; Economics; Finance. **Benefits:** Dental Insurance; Disability Coverage; Life Insurance; Medical Insurance; Pension Plan; Profit Sharing. **Corporate headquarters location:** This Location. **Listed on:** Privately held. **Number of employees at this location:** 30.

BDO SEIDMAN, LLP
233 North Michigan Avenue, Suite 2500, Chicago IL 60601. 312/856-9100. **Fax:** 312/856-1379. **Contact:** Nora McGee, Human Resources Manager. **World Wide Web address:** http://www.bdo.com. **Description:** A public accounting and consulting firm. **Common positions include:** Accountant/Auditor. **Educational backgrounds include:** Accounting. **Benefits:** 401(k); Dental Insurance; Disability Coverage; Life Insurance; Medical Insurance. **Special programs:** Internships. **Number of employees at this location:** 100.
Other U.S. locations:
- 40 Broad Street, Suite 500, Boston MA 02109. 617/422-0700.
- 330 East Kilborne Avenue, Suite 950, Milwaukee WI 53202. 414/272-5900.
- 130 East Randolph Drive, Suite 2800, Chicago IL 60601. 312/240-1236.

BAIN & COMPANY, INC.
2 Copley Place, Boston MA 02116. 617/572-2000. **Contact:** Human Resources. **World Wide Web address:** http://www.bain.com. **Description:** An international management consulting firm that helps major companies achieve higher levels of competitiveness and profitability. Founded in 1973. **Corporate headquarters location:** This Location. **Number of employees nationwide:** 1,000.
Other U.S. locations:
- One Embarcadero Center, Suite 3600, San Francisco CA 94111. 415/434-1022.

BAKER, NEWMAN & NOYES
100 Middle Street, Portland ME 04101. 207/879-2100. **Contact:** Human Resources. **E-mail address:**

mail@bnncpa.com. **World Wide Web address:** http://www.bnncpa.com. **Description:** A certified public accounting firm that provides a variety of services including audits and tax planning. **Number of employees at this location:** 120.

BANSLEY & KIENER
125 South Wacker Drive, Suite 1200, Chicago IL 60606-4496. 312/263-2700. **Contact:** Thomas Tyler, Partner. **Description:** A certified public accounting firm. **Common positions include:** Accountant/Auditor; Computer Programmer. **Educational backgrounds include:** Accounting; Computer Science. **Benefits:** 401(k); Dental Insurance; Life Insurance; Medical Insurance. **Corporate headquarters location:** This Location. **Operations at this facility include:** Service.

BENSON & NEFF
One Post Street, Suite 2150, San Francisco CA 94104-5225. 415/705-5615. **Contact:** Director of Personnel. **World Wide Web address:** http://www. bensonneff.com. **Description:** A certified public accounting firm offering accounting, auditing, tax, computer, and other consulting services. **Common positions include:** Accountant/Auditor. **Educational backgrounds include:** Accounting. **Benefits:** Disability Coverage; Life Insurance; Medical Insurance; Pension Plan. **Corporate headquarters location:** This Location. **Operations at this facility include:** Service.

BLUE & CO., LLC
P.O. Box 80069, Indianapolis IN 46280-0069. 317/848-8920. **Fax:** 317/573-2458. **Contact:** Pamela J. Fogle, Human Resources Officer. **World Wide Web address:** http://www.blueandco.com. **Description:** A public accounting and consulting firm with specialties in health care, manufacturing, construction, litigation support, and retirement planning. **Common positions include:** Accountant/Auditor; Consultant. **Educational backgrounds include:** Accounting. **Benefits:** 401(k); Disability Coverage; Life Insurance; Medical Insurance; Savings Plan; Tuition Assistance. **Special programs:** Internships. **Internship information:** Internships are offered January through April. Resumes should be sent to the above address. **Corporate headquarters location:** This Location. **Other U.S. locations:** KY. **Listed on:** Privately held. **Number of employees at this location:** 130. **Number of employees nationwide:** 200.

BOOZ-ALLEN & HAMILTON, INC.
8283 Greensboro Drive, McLean VA 22102. 703/902-5000. **Fax:** 703/902-3620. **Contact:** Recruiting Services Manager. **World Wide Web address:** http://www.bah.com. **Description:** A diversified, international, management consulting organization offering services in both the commercial and public sectors. The company's areas of expertise include strategy operations and technology. Specific services include corporate strategy and long-range planning; organization design; management changes; human resources management; financial management and control; acquisitions and divestiture; information systems and automation; manufacturing, inventory, and distribution control; marketing strategy and positioning; venture management; transportation and environmental systems; technology research; new products and process development; government programs; and regulatory compliance. **Common positions include:** Computer Scientist; Management Analyst/Consultant; Operations Research Analyst; Secretary; Software Engineer; Systems Analyst. **Educational backgrounds include:** Business Administration; Computer

Science; Engineering; Finance. **Benefits:** Dental Insurance; Disability Coverage; Life Insurance; Medical Insurance; Pension Plan; Savings Plan; Tuition Assistance. **Corporate headquarters location:** This Location. **International locations:** Worldwide. **Operations at this facility include:** Service.
Other U.S. locations:
• 101 Park Avenue, New York NY 10178. 212/551-6000.
• 901 Main Street, Suite 6500, Dallas TX 75202. 214/746-6500.
• 101 California Street, Suite 3300, San Francisco CA 94111. 415/391-1900.
• 229 Peachtree Street, Suite 1520, Atlanta GA 30303. 404/658-8000.

BOWMAN & COMPANY LLP
601 White Horse Road, Voorhees NJ 08043. 856/435-6200. **Contact:** Human Resources. **World Wide Web address:** http://www.bowmanllp.com. **Description:** A certified public accounting firm. Founded in 1939. **NOTE:** Entry-level positions are offered. **Common positions include:** Accountant/ Auditor. **Educational backgrounds include:** Accounting. **Benefits:** 401(k); Daycare Assistance; Disability Coverage; Life Insurance; Medical Insurance. **Special programs:** Internships; Co-ops. **Corporate headquarters location:** This Location. **Listed on:** Privately held. **Annual sales/revenues:** $5 - $10 million. **Number of employees at this location:** 90.

CERIDIAN EMPLOYER SERVICES
300 Embassy Row, Atlanta GA 30328. 678/441-2000. **Contact:** Personnel Department. **World Wide Web address:** http://www.ceridian.com. **Description:** Provides information management and data processing services that help customers accomplish functions related to the employment, compensation, and management of their workforce. **Corporate headquarters location:** Minneapolis MN. **Parent company:** Ceridian Corporation. **Listed on:** New York Stock Exchange.

CHESHIER AND FULLER, L.L.P.
14175 Proton Road, Dallas TX 75244-3604. 972/387-4300. **Toll-free phone:** 800/834-8586. **Fax:** 972/960-2810. **Contact:** Firm Administrator. **E-mail address:** cfllp@cheshier-fuller.com. **World Wide Web address:** http://www.cheshier-fuller.com. **Description:** Offers accounting, tax, audit, management advisory, business valuation, and litigation support services. Founded in 1956. **Common positions include:** Accountant; Administrative Assistant; Auditor; Secretary. **Educational backgrounds include:** Accounting; MBA; Microsoft Office; Microsoft Word; Spreadsheets. **Benefits:** 401(k); Cafeteria Plan; Casual Dress - Fridays; Disability Coverage; Life Insurance; Medical Insurance; Pension Plan; Profit Sharing; Sick Days (1 - 5); Vacation Days (6 - 10). **Special programs:** Training; Summer Jobs. **Office hours:** Monday - Friday, 8:30 a.m. - 5:30 p.m. **Corporate headquarters location:** This Location. **Listed on:** Privately held. **Annual sales/revenues:** Less than $5 million. **Number of employees at this location:** 35.

THE CHICAGO GROUP, INC.
744 North Wells Street, Chicago IL 60610. 312/751-0303. **Fax:** 312/751-0470. **Contact:** Human Resources. **Description:** A management consulting firm specializing in strategic marketing for utility, telecommunications, industrial, technology, and service businesses. **Common positions include:** Management Analyst/ Consultant; Technical Writer/Editor. **Educational backgrounds include:** Economics; Engineering;

Finance; Marketing. **Benefits:** Life Insurance; Medical Insurance; Profit Sharing. **Corporate headquarters location:** This Location. **Listed on:** Privately held. **Number of employees at this location:** 25.

CLIFTON GUNDERSON L.L.C.
P.O. Box 1835, Peoria IL 61656-1835. 309/671-4560. **Contact:** Human Resources. **World Wide Web address:** http://www.cliftoncpa.com. **Description:** A certified public accounting and consulting firm. **Common positions include:** Accountant/Auditor. **Educational backgrounds include:** Accounting. **Benefits:** Disability Coverage; Life Insurance; Medical Insurance; Pension Plan; Profit Sharing; Savings Plan. **Corporate headquarters location:** This Location. **Number of employees at this location:** 850.
Other U.S. locations:
- 9515 Deereco Road, Suite 500, Timonium MD 21093. 410/453-0900.
- P.O. Box 329, Sparta WI 54656. 608/269- 2424.
- 350 Interlocken Boulevard, Suite 350, Broomfield CO 80021. 303/466-8822.

COMPREHENSIVE BUSINESS SERVICES
P.O. Box 31147, Tucson AZ 85751. 520/881-7514. **Contact:** Human Resources Department. **World Wide Web address:** http://www. cbsaccounting.com. **Description:** Provides a wide range of accounting services to small business owners nationwide. Services include accounting and record keeping, payroll administration, budget and business planning, and consulting. **Other U.S. locations:** Nationwide. **Parent company:** Century Business Services.

CRAWFORD PIMENTEL & COMPANY
2150 Trade Zone Boulevard, Suite 200, San Jose CA 95131. 408/942-6888. **Fax:** 408/942-0194. **Contact:** Personnel. **E-mail address:** recruiting@ cpconet.com. **World Wide Web address:** http://www.1040tax.com. **Description:** A public accounting firm that also offers management advisory, technology consulting, and business consulting services. **Common positions include:** Accountant/Auditor. **Educational backgrounds include:** Accounting. **Benefits:** 401(k); Disability Coverage; Medical Insurance; Tuition Assistance. **Special programs:** Training. **Corporate headquarters location:** This Location. **Operations at this facility include:** Service. **Listed on:** Privately held. **Annual sales/revenues:** Less than $5 million. **Number of employees at this location:** 25.

DATABASE MARKETING GROUP INC.
2113 Wells Branch Parkway, Suite 4400, Austin TX 78728. 512/990-2000. **Contact:** Human Resources. **World Wide Web address:** http://www. leaddogs.com. **Description:** Provides management consulting for the marketing industry. Database Marketing Group also develops customized databases for client companies.

DELOITTE & TOUCHE
2901 North Central Avenue, Suite 1200, Phoenix AZ 85012. 602/234-5100. **Contact:** Personnel. **World Wide Web address:** http://www.us. deloitte.com. **Description:** An international firm of certified public accountants providing professional accounting, auditing, tax, and management consulting services to widely diversified clients. The company has a specialized program consisting of some 25 national industry groups and 50 functional groups that cross industry lines. Groups are involved in various disciplines including accounting, auditing, taxation management advisory

services, small and growing businesses, mergers and acquisitions, and computer applications.
Other U.S. locations:
- 50 Fremont Street, 31st Floor, San Francisco CA 94105. 415/247-4000.
- 1000 Wilshire Boulevard, Suite 1500, Los Angeles CA 90017. 213/688-0800.

DELOITTE & TOUCHE
P.O. Box 820, Wilton CT 06897-0820. 203/761-3000. **Fax:** 203/761-3062. **Contact:** Melissa Cox, Director of Human Resources. **World Wide Web address:** http://www.us.deloitte.com. **Description:** Deloitte & Touche is an international firm of certified public accountants providing professional accounting, auditing, management consulting, and tax services. The company has a specialized program consisting of some 25 national industry groups and 50 functional groups that cross industry lines. Group disciplines include accounting, auditing, taxation management advisory services, small and growing businesses, mergers and acquisitions, and computer applications. **Common positions include:** Accountant/Auditor; Actuary; Attorney; Computer Programmer; Financial Analyst; Management Analyst/Consultant; MIS Specialist; Systems Analyst. **Educational backgrounds include:** Accounting; Business Administration; Computer Science; Finance; Liberal Arts. **Benefits:** 401(k); Dental Insurance; Disability Coverage; Employee Discounts; Job Sharing; Life Insurance; Medical Insurance; Pension Plan; Tuition Assistance. **Special programs:** Internships. **Corporate headquarters location:** This Location. **Parent company:** Deloitte Touche Tohmatsu International is a global leader with nearly 90,000 employees in over 130 countries.
Other U.S. locations:
- 200 Berkeley Street, Boston MA 02116-5022. 617/261-8000.
- 1633 Broadway, New York NY 10019. 212/489-1600.

DELOITTE & TOUCHE
1750 Tysons Boulevard, McLean VA 22102. 703/251-1000. **Contact:** Human Resources. **World Wide Web address:** http://www.us.deloitte.com. **Description:** An international firm of certified public accountants, providing professional accounting, auditing, tax, and management consulting services to widely diversified clients. The company has a specialized program consisting of some 25 national industry groups and 50 functional groups that cross industry lines. Groups are involved in various disciplines including accounting, auditing, taxation management advisory services, small and growing businesses, mergers and acquisitions, and computer applications.

DELOITTE & TOUCHE
191 Peachtree Street, Suite 1500, Atlanta GA 30303. 404/220-1500. **Fax:** 404/220-1583. **Contact:** Human Resources. **World Wide Web address:** http://www.us.deloitte.com. **Description:** An international firm of certified public accountants providing professional accounting, auditing, tax, and management consulting services to widely diversified clients. Deloitte & Touche has a specialized program consisting of some 25 national industry groups and 50 functional groups that cross industry lines. Groups are involved in various disciplines including accounting, auditing, taxation management advisory services, small and growing businesses, mergers and acquisitions, and computer applications.

DELOITTE & TOUCHE
One City Center, St. Louis MO 63101. 314/342-4900. **Contact:** Human Resources. **World Wide**

Web address: http://www.us.deloitte.com.
Description: An international firm of certified
public accountants, providing professional
accounting, auditing, tax, and management
consulting services to widely diversified clients.
Deloitte & Touche has a specialized program
consisting of some 25 national industry groups and
50 functional groups that cross industry lines. The
groups are involved in various disciplines including
accounting, auditing, taxation management advisory
services, small and growing businesses, mergers and
acquisitions, and computer applications.

DELOITTE & TOUCHE
127 Public Square, Key Tower, Suite 2500,
Cleveland OH 44114-1303. 216/589-1300. **Fax:**
216/589-1369. **Contact:** Human Resources. **World
Wide Web address:** http://www.us.deloitte.com.
Description: An international firm of certified
public accountants providing professional
accounting, auditing, tax, and management
consulting services to widely diversified clients.
Deloitte & Touche offers a specialized program
consisting of 25 national industry groups and 50
functional groups that cross industry lines. Groups
are involved in various disciplines including
accounting, auditing, taxation, management
advisory services, small and growing businesses,
mergers and acquisitions, and computer
applications. **Common positions include:**
Accountant/Auditor. **Educational backgrounds
include:** Accounting. **Benefits:** Dental Insurance;
Life Insurance; Medical Insurance; Pension Plan;
Savings Plan. **Special programs:** Internships.
Corporate headquarters location: Wilton CT.
Other U.S. locations:
• 250 East Fifth Street, Suite 1900, Cincinnati
OH 45202. 513/241-2450.

DELOITTE & TOUCHE
2200 Ross Avenue, Suite 1600, Chase Tower,
Dallas TX 75201. 214/777-7000. **Contact:** Steve
Gass, Human Resources Director. **World Wide
Web address:** http://www.us.deloitte.com.
Description: Deloitte & Touche is an international
firm of certified public accountants, providing
professional accounting, auditing, tax, and
management consulting services to widely
diversified clients. Deloitte & Touche has a
specialized program consisting of some 25 national
industry groups and 50 functional (technical) groups
that cross industry lines. Groups are involved in
various disciplines including accounting, auditing,
taxation management advisory services, small and
growing businesses, mergers and acquisitions, and
computer applications. Deloitte & Touche has more
than 500 offices throughout the world. **Common
positions include:** Accountant/Auditor; Actuary.
Educational backgrounds include: Accounting.
Benefits: Dental Insurance; Disability Coverage;
Life Insurance; Medical Insurance; Savings Plan.
Special programs: Internships. **Corporate
headquarters location:** Wilton CT. **Operations at
this facility include:** Regional Headquarters.
Number of employees at this location: 450.
Other U.S. locations:
• 2500 City West Boulevard, Suite 700, Houston
TX 77042. 713/756-2420.
• 5550 Lyndon B. Johnson Freeway, Suite 700,
Dallas TX 75240. 972/776-6000.

DELOITTE & TOUCHE
50 South Main Street, Suite 1800, Salt Lake City
UT 84144. 801/328-4706. **Contact:** Mark Stevens,
Partner. **World Wide Web address:** http://www.
us.deloitte.com. **Description:** An international firm
of certified public accountants providing
professional accounting, auditing, tax, and
management consulting services to widely

diversified clients. The company has a specialized
program consisting of some 25 national industry
groups and 50 functional groups that cross industry
lines. Groups are involved in various disciplines
including accounting, auditing, taxation
management advisory services, small and growing
businesses, mergers and acquisitions, and computer
applications. **Common positions include:**
Accountant/Auditor. **Educational backgrounds
include:** Accounting. **Special programs:**
Internships. **Corporate headquarters location:**
Wilton CT. **Number of employees at this location:**
90.

DELOITTE & TOUCHE
700 Fifth Avenue, Suite 4500, Seattle WA 98104-
5044. 206/292-1800. **Contact:** Human Resources.
World Wide Web address: http://www.us.
deloitte.com. **Description:** An international firm of
certified public accountants providing professional
accounting, auditing, tax, and management
consulting services to widely diversified clients.
Deloitte & Touche has a specialized program
consisting of some 25 national industry groups and
50 functional groups that cross industry lines.
Groups are involved in various disciplines including
accounting, auditing, taxation management advisory
services, small and growing businesses, mergers and
acquisitions, and computer applications.

DELOITTE & TOUCHE
One Independent Drive, Suite 2801, Jacksonville FL
32202-5034. 904/356-0011. **Contact:** Human
Resources Director. **World Wide Web address:**
http://www.us.deloitte.com. **Description:** An
international firm of certified public accountants
providing professional accounting, auditing, tax,
and management consulting services. Deloitte &
Touche has a specialized program consisting of
some 25 national industry groups and 50 functional
groups that cross industry lines. Groups are
involved in various disciplines including
accounting, auditing, taxation management advisory
services, small and growing businesses, mergers and
acquisitions, and computer applications.
International locations: Worldwide.
Other U.S. locations:
• 201 East Kennedy Boulevard, Suite 1200,
Tampa FL 33602-5821. 813/273-8300.
• P.O. Box 2778, Raleigh NC 27602. 919/546-
8000.

DELOITTE & TOUCHE
424 Church Street, Suite 2400, Nashville TN 37219.
615/259-1800. **Contact:** Human Resources. **World
Wide Web address:** http://www.us.deloitte.com.
Description: An international firm of certified
public accountants providing professional
accounting, auditing, tax, and management
consulting services to widely diversified clients.
Deloitte & Touche has a specialized program
consisting of some 25 national industry groups and
50 functional groups that cross industry lines.
Groups are involved in various disciplines including
accounting, auditing, taxation, management
advisory services, small and growing businesses,
mergers and acquisitions, and computer
applications. **Corporate headquarters location:**
Wilton CT.

DELOITTE & TOUCHE
111 Monument Circle, Suite 2000, Indianapolis IN
46204. 317/464-8600. **Contact:** Human Resources.
World Wide Web address: http://www.us.
deloitte.com. **Description:** An international firm of
certified public accountants providing professional
accounting, auditing, tax, and management
consulting services to widely diversified clients.
Deloitte & Touche has a specialized program

consisting of some 25 national industry groups and 50 functional groups that cross industry lines. Groups are involved in various disciplines including accounting, auditing, taxation management advisory services, small and growing businesses, mergers and acquisitions, and computer applications.

DELOITTE & TOUCHE
3773 Howard Hughes Parkway, Suite 490 North, Las Vegas NV 89109. 702/893-3100. **Contact:** Human Resources. **World Wide Web address:** http://www.us.deloitte.com. **Description:** An international firm of certified public accountants providing professional accounting, auditing, tax, and management consulting services to widely diversified clients. Deloitte & Touche has a specialized program consisting of some 25 national industry groups and 50 functional groups that cross industry lines. Groups are involved in various disciplines including accounting, auditing, taxation, management advisory services, small and growing businesses, mergers and acquisitions, and computer applications. **Other U.S. locations:**
• 50 West Liberty Street, Suite 900, Reno NV 89501. 775/348-8808.

DELOITTE & TOUCHE
111 SW Fifth Avenue, Suite 3900, Portland OR 97204. 503/222-1341. **Contact:** Human Resources. **World Wide Web address:** http://www.us.deloitte.com. **Description:** An international firm of certified public accountants providing professional accounting, auditing, tax, and management consulting services to widely diversified clients. Deloitte & Touche has a specialized program consisting of some 25 national industry groups and 50 functional groups that cross industry lines. Groups are involved in various disciplines including accounting, auditing, taxation, management advisory services, small and growing businesses, mergers and acquisitions, and computer applications. **Number of employees at this location:** 200.

DELOITTE & TOUCHE
555 12th Street NW, Suite 500, Washington DC 20004. 202/879-5600. **Contact:** Human Resources. **World Wide Web address:** http://www.us.deloitte.com. **Description:** An international firm of certified public accountants, providing professional accounting, auditing, tax, and management consulting services to widely diversified clients. The company has a specialized program consisting of some 25 national industry groups and 50 functional groups that cross industry lines. Groups are involved in various disciplines including accounting, auditing, taxation management advisory services, small and growing businesses, mergers and acquisitions, and computer applications. **Other U.S. locations:**
• 2500 One PPG Place, Pittsburgh PA 15222. 412/338-7200.

DELOITTE & TOUCHE
1215 Laidley Tower, Charleston WV 25301. 304/342-5300. **Contact:** Managing Partner. **World Wide Web address:** http://www.us.deloitte.com. **Description:** An international firm of certified public accountants providing professional accounting, auditing, tax, and management consulting services to widely diversified clients. Deloitte & Touche has a specialized program consisting of some 25 national industry groups and 50 functional groups that cross industry lines. Groups are involved in various disciplines including accounting, auditing, taxation, management advisory services, small and growing businesses,

mergers and acquisitions, and computer applications. **Other U.S. locations:** Nationwide.

DELOITTE & TOUCHE
City Place One, 185 Asylum Street, Hartford CT 06103. 860/280-3000. **Contact:** Human Resources. **World Wide Web address:** http://www.us.deloitte.com. **Description:** An international firm of certified public accountants providing professional accounting, auditing, tax, and management consulting services to widely diversified clients. Deloitte & Touche has a specialized program consisting of some 25 national industry groups and 50 functional groups that cross industry lines. Groups are involved in various disciplines including accounting, auditing, taxation, management advisory services, small and growing businesses, mergers and acquisitions, and computer applications. **Corporate headquarters location:** Wilton CT. **Parent company:** Deloitte Touche Tohmatsu International is a global leader with nearly 90,000 employees in offices in over 130 countries.
Other U.S. locations:
• 2 Hilton Court, P.O. Box 319, Parsippany NJ 07054. 973/683-7000.

DELOITTE & TOUCHE LLP
555 17th Street, Suite 3600, Denver CO 80202-3942. 303/292-5400. **Contact:** Heather Cameron, Human Resources Director. **World Wide Web address:** http://www.us.deloitte.com. **Description:** An international firm of certified public accountants providing professional accounting, auditing, tax, and management consulting services to widely diversified clients. Deloitte & Touche LLP has a specialized program consisting of some 25 national industry groups and 50 functional groups that cross industry lines. Groups are involved in various disciplines including accounting, auditing, taxation management advisory services, small and growing businesses, mergers and acquisitions, and computer applications. **Common positions include:** Accountant/Auditor; Actuary; Financial Analyst; Management Analyst/Consultant; Systems Analyst. **Educational backgrounds include:** Accounting; Business Administration; Computer Science; Finance; Liberal Arts. **Benefits:** Daycare Assistance; Dental Insurance; Disability Coverage; Employee Discounts; Flextime Plan; Leave Time; Life Insurance; Medical Insurance. **Special programs:** Internships. **Other U.S. locations:** Nationwide.

DRAFFIN & TUCKER
P.O. Box 6, Albany GA 31702. 912/883-7878. **Contact:** Employment. **World Wide Web address:** http://www.draffin-tucker.com. **Description:** A certified public accounting firm.

EMA SERVICES, INC.
1970 Oakcrest Avenue, St. Paul MN 55113. 651/639-5600. **Toll-free phone:** 800/800-2110. **Fax:** 651/639-5635. **Contact:** Human Resources. **E-mail address:** hrinfo@ema-inc.com. **World Wide Web address:** http://www.ema-inc.com. **Description:** A specialized consulting firm that works with utilities and selected manufacturers to help clients develop and implement operational strategies for improving work practices, addressing organizational development, and leveraging technology. Services focus on helping clients improve productivity and long-term performance in competitive business environments. Founded in 1975. **NOTE:** Entry-level positions are offered. **Company slogan:** Linking people and technology for business results. **Common positions include:** Computer Programmer; Consultant; Database Manager; Design Engineer; Draftsperson;

Electrical/Electronics Engineer; Industrial Engineer; Management Analyst/Consultant; Manufacturing Engineer; Mechanical Engineer; MIS Specialist; Project Manager; Systems Analyst. **Educational backgrounds include:** Business Administration; Communications; Computer Science; Engineering; Software Development; Software Tech. Support. **Benefits:** 401(k); Dental Insurance; Disability Coverage; Flexible Schedule; Life Insurance; Medical Insurance; Profit Sharing; Telecommuting; Tuition Assistance. **Office hours:** Monday - Friday, 8:00 a.m. - 5:00 p.m. **Corporate headquarters location:** This Location. **Other U.S. locations:** Phoenix AZ; Tucson AZ; Los Angeles CA; Sacramento CA; San Francisco CA; Orlando FL; Boston MA; Philadelphia PA. **International locations:** Canada. **Listed on:** Privately held. **CEO:** Alan Manning. **Facilities Manager:** Peggy McCarthy. **Annual sales/revenues:** $21 - $50 million. **Number of employees at this location:** 80.

ECKERT, INGRUM, TINKLER, OLIPHANT, & FEATHERSTON, L.L.P.
P.O. Box 5821, San Angelo TX 76902-5821. 915/944-3571. **Fax:** 915/942-1093. **Contact:** Partner in Charge. **Description:** An accounting firm involved in bookkeeping, taxes, and auditing of various institutions including schools, governments, and banks. **NOTE:** Entry-level positions are offered. **Common positions include:** Accountant. **Educational backgrounds include:** Accounting. **Benefits:** Casual Dress - Daily; Medical Insurance; Sick Days (1 - 5); Vacation Days (6 - 10). **Office hours:** Monday - Friday, 8:00 a.m. - 12:00 p.m. and 1:00 p.m. - 5:00 p.m. **Corporate headquarters location:** This Location. **Annual sales/revenues:** Less than $5 million. **Number of employees at this location:** 15.

ELLIOT DAVIS & COMPANY LLP
P.O. Box 2227, Columbia SC 29202. 803/256-0002. **Contact:** Office Manager. **World Wide Web address:** http://www.edcocpa.com. **Description:** A corporate accounting firm.

ERNST & YOUNG
40 North Central Avenue, Suite 900, Phoenix AZ 85004. 602/452-8000. **Contact:** Personnel. **World Wide Web address:** http://www.ey.com. **Description:** A certified public accounting firm that also provides management consulting services. Services include data processing, financial modeling, financial feasibility studies, production planning and inventory management, management sciences, health care planning, human resources, cost accounting and budgeting systems. **Corporate headquarters location:** New York NY.
Other U.S. locations:
• 303 Almaden Boulevard, San Jose CA 95113. 408/947-5500.
• 555 California Street, Suite 1700, San Francisco CA 94104. 415/951-3000.

ERNST & YOUNG
1400 Pillsbury Center, 200 South Sixth Street, Minneapolis MN 55402. 612/343-1000. **Contact:** Recruiter. **World Wide Web address:** http://www. ey.com. **Description:** A certified public accounting firm that also provides management consulting services. Services include data processing, financial modeling, financial feasibility studies, production planning and inventory management, management sciences, health care planning, human resources, cost accounting, and budgeting systems. **Corporate headquarters location:** New York NY.

ERNST & YOUNG
1300 Chiquita Center, 250 East Fifth Street, Cincinnati OH 45202. 513/621-6454. **Contact:**

Personnel Department. **World Wide Web address:** http://www.ey.com. **Description:** A certified public accounting firm that also provides management consulting services. Services include data processing, financial modeling, financial feasibility studies, production planning and inventory management, management sciences, health care planning, human resources, cost accounting, and budgeting systems. **Corporate headquarters location:** New York NY.
Other U.S. locations:
• 10 West Broad Street, Suite 2300, Columbus OH 43215-3400. 614/222-3900.
• 1300 Huntington Building, 925 Euclid Avenue, Cleveland OH 44115-1405. 216/861- 5000.

ERNST & YOUNG
2121 San Jacinto, Suite 1500, Dallas TX 75201. 214/969-8000. **Fax:** 214/969-8587. **Contact:** Director of Human Resources. **World Wide Web address:** http://www.ey.com. **Description:** A certified public accounting firm that also provides management consulting services. Services include data processing, financial modeling, financial feasibility studies, production planning and inventory management, management sciences, health care planning, human resources, cost accounting, and budgeting systems. **Corporate headquarters location:** New York NY. **Other U.S. locations:** Nationwide. **Listed on:** Privately held.

ERNST & YOUNG
999 Third Avenue, Suite 3500, Seattle WA 98104. 206/621-1800. **Contact:** Human Resources. **World Wide Web address:** http://www.ey.com. **Description:** A certified public accounting firm that also provides management consulting services. Services include data processing, financial modeling, financial feasibility studies, production planning and inventory management, management sciences, health care planning, human resources, cost accounting, and budgeting systems. **Common positions include:** Accountant/Auditor; Actuary; Computer Programmer; Financial Analyst; Systems Analyst. **Educational backgrounds include:** Accounting; Business Administration; Computer Science; Economics; Finance. **Benefits:** Dental Insurance; Life Insurance; Medical Insurance; Pension Plan. **Corporate headquarters location:** New York NY.

ERNST & YOUNG
390 North Orange Avenue, Suite 1700, Orlando FL 32801. 407/872-6600. **Contact:** Human Resources Director. **World Wide Web address:** http://www. ey.com. **Description:** A certified public accounting firm that also provides management consulting services. Services include data processing, financial modeling, financial feasibility studies, production planning and inventory management, management sciences, health care planning, human resources, cost accounting, and budgeting systems. **Corporate headquarters location:** New York NY. **International locations:** Worldwide.
Other U.S. locations:
• 100 North Tampa Street, Suite 2200, Tampa FL 33602. 813/225-4800.

ERNST & YOUNG
701 Market Street, Gateway One, Suite 1400, St. Louis MO 63101-1860. 314/259-1000. **Contact:** Susan Chapman, Human Resources. **World Wide Web address:** http://www.ey.com. **Description:** A certified public accounting firm that also provides management consulting services. Services include data processing, financial modeling, financial feasibility studies, production planning and inventory management, management sciences, health care planning, human resources, cost

accounting, and budgeting systems. **Common positions include:** Accountant/Auditor; Auditor. **Educational backgrounds include:** Accounting; Business Administration. **Special programs:** Internships. **Corporate headquarters location:** New York NY.

ERNST & YOUNG
414 Union Street, Suite 2100, Nashville TN 37219-1779. 615/252-2000. **Contact:** Human Resources. **World Wide Web address:** http://www.ey.com. **Description:** A certified public accounting firm that also provides management consulting services. Services include data processing, financial modeling, financial feasibility studies, production planning and inventory management, management sciences, health care planning, human resources, cost accounting, and budgeting systems. **Corporate headquarters location:** New York NY.

ERNST & YOUNG
60 East South Temple, Suite 800, Salt Lake City UT 84111. 801/350-3300. **Contact:** Human Resources. **World Wide Web address:** http://www.ey.com. **Description:** A certified public accounting firm that also provides management consulting services. Services include data processing, financial modeling, financial feasibility studies, production planning and inventory management, management sciences, health care planning, human resources, cost accounting, and budgeting systems. **Corporate headquarters location:** New York NY.

ERNST & YOUNG LLP
600 Peachtree Street NE, Suite 2800, Atlanta GA 30308. 404/874-8300. **Contact:** Human Resources. **World Wide Web address:** http://www.ey.com. **Description:** A certified public accounting firm that also provides management consulting services. Services include data processing, financial modeling, financial feasibility studies, production planning and inventory management, management sciences, health care planning, human resources, cost accounting, and budgeting systems. **Common positions include:** Accountant/Auditor; Actuary; Administrator; Systems Analyst. **Educational backgrounds include:** Accounting; Business Administration; Computer Science; Economics; Finance; Mathematics. **Benefits:** Dental Insurance; Disability Coverage; Life Insurance; Medical Insurance; Pension Plan; Tuition Assistance. **Corporate headquarters location:** New York NY.

ERNST & YOUNG LLP
787 Seventh Avenue, 14th Floor, New York NY 10019. 212/773-3000. **Contact:** Human Resources. **World Wide Web address:** http://www.ey.com. **Description:** A certified public accounting firm that also provides management consulting services. Services include data processing, financial modeling, financial feasibility studies, production planning and inventory management, management sciences, health care planning, human resources, cost accounting, and budgeting systems. **Corporate headquarters location:** This Location.
Other U.S. locations:
- 2 Commerce Square, 2001 Market Street, Suite 4000, Philadelphia PA 19103. 215/448-5000.
- One North Charles Street, Baltimore MD 21201. 410/539-7940.
- 200 Clarendon Street, Boston MA 02116. 617/266-2000.
- Goodwin Square, 225 Asylum Street, Hartford CT 06103. 860/247-3100.

ERNST & YOUNG LLP
North City Center, Suite 2300, 110 Westberry Street, Fort Wayne IN 46802. 219/424-2233. **Contact:** Human Resources. **World Wide Web**

address: http://www.ey.com. **Description:** A certified public accounting firm that also provides management consulting services. Services include data processing, financial modeling, financial feasibility studies, production planning and inventory management, management sciences, health care planning, human resources, cost accounting, and budgeting systems. **Corporate headquarters location:** New York NY. **International locations:** Worldwide.
Other U.S. locations:
- One Indiana Square, Suite 3400, Indianapolis IN 46204. 317/681-7000.

ERNST & YOUNG LLP
One Oxford Centre, 28th Floor, Pittsburgh PA 15219. 412/644-7800. **Fax:** 412/644-0532. **Contact:** Michelle Ferris, Recruiting. **World Wide Web address:** http://www.ey.com. **Description:** A certified public accounting firm that also provides management consulting services. Services include data processing, financial modeling, financial feasibility studies, production planning and inventory management, management sciences, health care planning, human resources, cost accounting, and budgeting systems. **Corporate headquarters location:** New York NY.
Other U.S. locations:
- 125 Chubb Avenue, Lyndhurst NJ 07071. 201/872-2200.

ERNST & YOUNG LLP
P.O. Box 2938, San Antonio TX 78299. 210/228-9696. **Contact:** Human Resources. **World Wide Web address:** http://www.ey.com. **Description:** A certified public accounting firm that also provides management consulting services. Services include data processing, financial modeling, financial feasibility studies, production planning and inventory management, management sciences, health care planning, human resources, cost accounting, and budgeting systems. **Corporate headquarters location:** New York NY.
Other U.S. locations:
- 700 Lavaca Street, Suite 1400, Austin TX 78701. 512/478-9881.

ERNST & YOUNG LLP
101 North Tryon Street, Suite 1100, Charlotte NC 28246. 704/372-6300. **Contact:** Human Resources. **World Wide Web address:** http://www.ey.com. **Description:** A certified public accounting firm that also provides management consulting services. Services include data processing, financial modeling, financial feasibility studies, production planning and inventory management, management sciences, health care planning, human resources, cost accounting, and budgeting systems. **Corporate headquarters location:** New York NY. **Other U.S. locations:** Nationwide.

ERNST & YOUNG LLP
THE E&Y KENNETH LEVENTHAL REAL ESTATE GROUP DIVISION
1225 Connecticut Avenue NW, Washington DC 20036. 202/327-6000. **Contact:** Lulu Gonella, Human Resources Manager. **World Wide Web address:** http://www.ey.com. **Description:** A special practice unit of Ernst & Young LLP providing accounting and consulting services to the real estate and financial services industries. **NOTE:** Entry-level positions are offered. **Common positions include:** Accountant/Auditor. **Educational backgrounds include:** Accounting; Finance. **Benefits:** 401(k); Dental Insurance; Disability Coverage; Life Insurance; Medical Insurance; Pension Plan; Public Transit Available; Tuition Assistance. **Corporate headquarters location:** New York NY. **Other U.S. locations:**

Nationwide. **Number of employees at this location:** 70.

FAIR, ISAAC AND CO., INC.
8010 Corporate Drive, Suite G, White Marsh MD 21236. 410/931-7800. **Fax:** 410/931-7801. **Contact:** Human Resources. **World Wide Web address:** http://www.fairisaac.com. **Description:** Provides consulting services to financial institutions, service organizations, and government support institutions. Services include statistical analysis, database development and reporting, and actuarial management of customer portfolios through software decision support systems.

FIND/SVP, INC.
625 Sixth Avenue, 2nd Floor, New York NY 10011. 212/645-4500. **Fax:** 212/645-7681. **Contact:** Rowena Taylor, Human Resources Generalist. **World Wide Web address:** http://www.findsvp.com. **Description:** Provides business and management consulting, research, and advisory services. The company also offers seminars, conferences, and publications. Founded in 1969. **Corporate headquarters location:** This Location. **Listed on:** NASDAQ.

THE FORUM CORPORATION
One Exchange Place, 3rd Floor, Boston MA 02109. 617/523-7300. **Toll-free phone:** 800/367-8611. **Fax:** 617/973-2001. **Contact:** Aisling Mooney-Eddip, Recruiting Coordinator. **World Wide Web address:** http://www.forum.com. **Description:** An international training and consulting firm. Founded in 1971. **Common positions include:** Administrative Assistant; Computer Programmer; Consultant; Customer Service Rep.; Designer; Desktop Publishing Specialist; Editor; Sales Rep. **Educational backgrounds include:** Business Administration; Communications; Liberal Arts; Marketing. **Benefits:** 401(k); Dental Insurance; Disability Coverage; Life Insurance; Medical Insurance; Pension Plan; Profit Sharing; Savings Plan; Tuition Assistance. **Special programs:** Internships. **Office hours:** Monday - Friday, 9:00 a.m. - 5:30 p.m. **Corporate headquarters location:** This Location. **Other U.S. locations:** CA; DE; IL; NY; SC. **International locations:** Hong Kong; London. **Operations at this facility include:** Administration; Research and Development; Sales; Service. **Chairman and CEO:** John W. Humphrey. **Number of employees at this location:** 115. **Number of employees nationwide:** 260.

FRIEDMAN, EISENSTEIN, RAEMER & SCHWARTZ (FERS)
401 North Michigan Avenue, 26th Floor, Chicago IL 60611. 312/644-6000. **Contact:** Irwin Friedman, Managing Partner. **World Wide Web address:** http://www.fers.com. **Description:** An accounting firm.

THE FUTURES GROUP INTERNATIONAL
80 Glastonbury Boulevard, Glastonbury CT 06033. 860/633-3501. **Contact:** Human Resources. **World Wide Web address:** http://www.tfg.com. **Description:** A business and competitive intelligence consulting firm.

GARDINER, KAMYA & ASSOCIATES PC
1717 K Street NW, Suite 601, Washington DC 20036. 202/857-1777. **Fax:** 202/857-1778. **Contact:** Human Resources Manager. **E-mail address:** gardkamy@erols.com. **Description:** Provides auditing and accounting, management consulting, information systems services, and taxation services. **Company slogan:** Quality, Timeliness, Responsiveness, and Value. **Common positions include:** Accountant; Auditor; Bank Officer/Manager; Budget Analyst; Controller; Financial Analyst. **Educational backgrounds include:** Accounting; Finance. **Benefits:** 401(k); Casual Dress - Fridays; Dental Insurance; Disability Coverage; Financial Planning Assistance; Life Insurance; Medical Insurance; Tuition Assistance. **Corporate headquarters location:** This Location. **Other U.S. locations:** Nationwide. **Subsidiaries include:** GKA Staffing Resources, LLC. **CEO:** Chris Gardiner. **Sales Manager:** John Kamya. **Number of employees at this location:** 40.

GEMINUS CORPORATION
5281 Fountain Drive, Crown Point IN 46307. 219/791-2300. **Contact:** Human Resources. **World Wide Web address:** http://www.geminus.org. **Description:** Operates Head Start programs and performs accounting, marketing, and human resource functions for Southlake Center for Mental Health, an inpatient and outpatient mental health center, and Tri-City Mental Health, an outpatient mental health center. **Common positions include:** Claim Representative; Counselor; Medical Records Technician; Physician; Psychologist; Recreational Therapist; Registered Nurse; Social Worker; Teacher/Professor. **Benefits:** Dental Insurance; Disability Coverage; Employee Discounts; Life Insurance; Medical Insurance; Pension Plan; Tuition Assistance. **Special programs:** Internships. **Corporate headquarters location:** This Location. **Listed on:** Privately held. **Number of employees nationwide:** 1,200.

GENERAL ELECTRIC INFORMATION SERVICES
100 Edison Park Drive, Gaithersburg MD 20878. 301/340-4000. **Contact:** Human Resources. **World Wide Web address:** http://www.geis.com. **Description:** Provides business productivity solutions through management consulting. **Common positions include:** Computer Programmer; Electrical/Electronics Engineer; Financial Analyst; Instructor/Trainer; Management Trainee; Marketing Specialist; Services Sales Rep.; Systems Analyst; Teacher/Professor; Technical Writer/Editor. **Educational backgrounds include:** Business Administration; Computer Science; Engineering; Finance; Marketing. **Benefits:** Dental Insurance; Disability Coverage; Employee Discounts; Eye Care; Life Insurance; Medical Insurance; Pension Plan; Savings Plan; Tuition Assistance. **Special programs:** Internships. **Corporate headquarters location:** This Location. **Other U.S. locations:** Los Angeles CA; San Francisco CA; Atlanta GA; Chicago IL; Boston MA; Detroit MI; New York NY; Dallas TX; Houston TX. **Parent company:** General Electric Company (Fairfield CT) operates in the following areas: aircraft engines (jet engines, replacement parts, and repair services for commercial, military, executive, and commuter aircraft); appliances; broadcasting (NBC); industrial (lighting products, electrical distribution and control equipment, transportation systems products, electric motors and related products, a broad range of electrical and electronic industrial automation products, and a network of electrical supply houses); materials (plastics, ABS resins, silicones, superabrasives, and laminates); power systems (products for the generation, transmission, and distribution of electricity); technical products and systems (medical systems and equipment, as well as a full range of computer-based information and data interchange services for both internal use and external commercial and industrial customers); and capital services (consumer services, financing, and specialty insurance). **Listed on:** New York Stock Exchange. **Number of employees worldwide:** 230,000.

GILMORE, GANNAWAY, ANDREWS, SMITH & COMPANY
P.O. Drawer 1517, Roswell NM 88202-1517. 505/622-5200. **Physical address:** 2724 Wilshire Boulevard, Roswell NM 88201. **Contact:** Office Manager. **World Wide Web address:** http://www.ggas.com. **Description:** A certified public accounting firm.

GRANT THORNTON LLP
1600 Broadway, Suite 1800, Denver CO 80202. 303/861-5555. **Contact:** Managing Partner. **World Wide Web address:** http://www.grantthornton.com. **Description:** An international certified public accounting organization offering consulting and accounting services, as well as strategic and tactical planning assistance to a diverse clientele. **Common positions include:** Accountant/Auditor; Computer Programmer; Systems Analyst. **Educational backgrounds include:** Accounting; Computer Science. **Corporate headquarters location:** Chicago IL.
Other U.S. locations:
• 100 West Liberty, Suite 770, Reno NV 89501. 775/786-1520.

GRANT THORNTON LLP
2 Hopkins Plaza, Suite 700, Baltimore MD 21201. 410/685-4000. **Contact:** Recruiting Coordinator. **World Wide Web address:** http://www.grantthornton.com. **Description:** An international, certified public accounting organization offering a comprehensive scope of consulting and accounting services as well as strategic and tactical planning assistance to a diverse clientele. **Common positions include:** Accountant/Auditor; Computer Support Technician; Systems Analyst. **Other U.S. locations:** Nationwide.

GRANT THORNTON LLP
98 North Washington Street, Boston MA 02114. 617/723-7900. **Contact:** Human Resources. **World Wide Web address:** http://www.grantthornton.com. **Description:** An international certified public accounting organization offering consulting and accounting services as well as strategic and tactical planning assistance to a diversified client base. **Corporate headquarters location:** Chicago IL. **Other U.S. locations:** Nationwide.

GRANT THORNTON LLP
1717 Main Street, Suite 500, Dallas TX 75201. 214/855-7300. **Fax:** 214/561-2370. **Contact:** Human Resources. **World Wide Web address:** http://www.grantthornton.com. **Description:** An international certified public accounting organization offering consulting and accounting services as well as strategic and tactical planning assistance to a diverse clientele. **NOTE:** Entry-level positions are offered. **Common positions include:** Accountant/Auditor; Management Analyst/Consultant; Market Research Analyst; Software Engineer; Systems Analyst; Tax Specialist; Typist/Word Processor. **Educational backgrounds include:** Accounting; Business Administration; Computer Science; Engineering; M.I.S. **Benefits:** 401(k); Dental Insurance; Disability Coverage; Employee Discounts; Leave Time; Life Insurance; Medical Insurance; Public Transit Available; Telecommuting; Tuition Assistance. **Special programs:** Internships; Training. **Corporate headquarters location:** Chicago IL. **Other U.S. locations:** Nationwide. **Operations at this facility include:** Administration; Regional Headquarters; Sales; Service. **Listed on:** Privately held. **Annual sales/revenues:** More than $100 million. **Number of employees at this location:** 125. **Number of employees · nationwide:** 2,700. **Number of employees worldwide:** 23,000.

GRANT THORNTON LLP
P.O. Box 1097, Appleton WI 54912-1097. 920/830-3000. **Contact:** Human Resources. **World Wide Web address:** http://www.grantthornton.com. **Description:** An international, certified, public accounting firm offering a comprehensive scope of consulting and accounting services, as well as strategic and tactical planning assistance to a diverse clientele.
Other U.S. locations:
• P.O. Box 8100, Madison WI 53708-8100. 608/257-6761.
• 500 Pillsbury Center North, 200 South Sixth Street, Minneapolis MN 55402-1459. 612/332-0001.

GUNNIP & CO.
Little Falls Centre II, 2751 Centerville Road, Suite 300, Wilmington DE 19808. 302/225-5000. **Contact:** Human Resources. **World Wide Web address:** http://www.gunnip.com. **Description:** Provides accounting, auditing, tax, and management services to local, national, and international clients.

H&R BLOCK
2516 J. Dawson Road, Albany GA 31707. 912/883-5353. **Contact:** Human Resources. **World Wide Web address:** http://www.hrblock.com. **Description:** This location is a district office. Overall, H&R Block is primarily engaged in consumer tax preparation, operating more than 9,500 U.S. offices and preparing more than 10 million tax returns each year. The company also operates more than 800 offices in Canada. H&R Block has offices in over 750 Sears stores in both the United States and Canada. Many offices operate as franchises, and some operate on a seasonal basis. H&R Block is also engaged in a number of other tax-related activities including Group Tax Programs, Premium Tax Service, Tax Training Schools, and Real Estate Tax Awareness seminars. **Corporate headquarters location:** Kansas City MO.

H&R BLOCK
157 Pleasant Street, Malden MA 02148. 781/322-7453. **Contact:** Human Resources. **World Wide Web address:** http://www.hrblock.com. **Description:** Primarily engaged in consumer tax preparation, operating more than 9,500 offices nationwide, and preparing more than 10 million tax returns each year. The company also operates more than 800 offices in Canada. H&R Block has established offices in over 750 Sears stores in both the United States and Canada. Many offices operate as franchises, and some operate on a seasonal basis. H&R Block is also engaged in a number of other tax-related activities, including Group Tax Programs, Executive Tax Service, Tax Training Schools, and Real Estate Tax Awareness Seminars. **Corporate headquarters location:** Kansas City MO. **Listed on:** New York Stock Exchange.
Other U.S. locations:
• 275 Hancock Street, North Quincy MA 02171. 617/472-3535.
• 360 Merrimack Street, Lawrence MA 01843. 978/686-1371.

H&R BLOCK
3701 West NW Highway, Suite 210, Dallas TX 75220. 214/358-4560. **Contact:** Debbie Ruggeia, District Manager. **World Wide Web address:** http://www.hrblock.com. **Description:** Primarily engaged in consumer tax preparation, operating more than 9,500 United States offices and preparing more than 10 million tax returns each year. H&R Block has established offices in over 750 Sears stores in both the United States and Canada. The company is also engaged in a number of other tax-related activities including group tax programs,

executive tax service, tax training schools, and real estate tax awareness seminars. **Corporate headquarters location:** Kansas City MO. **Listed on:** New York Stock Exchange. **Number of employees nationwide:** 80,000.

H&R BLOCK
4400 Main Street, Kansas City MO 64111. 816/753-6900. **Contact:** Human Resources. **World Wide Web address:** http://www.hrblock.com. **Description:** Primarily engaged in consumer tax preparation. H&R Block has offices in over 750 Sears stores in both the United States and Canada. Many offices operate as franchises, and some operate on a seasonal basis. H&R Block is also engaged in a number of other tax-related activities including Group Tax Programs, Premium Tax Service, Tax Training Schools, and Real Estate Tax Awareness seminars. **Common positions include:** Accountant/Auditor; Advertising Clerk; Attorney; Buyer; Clerical Supervisor; Computer Programmer; Customer Service Representative; Editor; Human Resources Manager; Paralegal; Purchasing Agent/Manager; Quality Control Supervisor; Systems Analyst; Technical Writer/Editor. **Educational backgrounds include:** Accounting; Art/Design; Business Administration; Communications; Computer Science; Finance; Liberal Arts; Marketing. **Benefits:** 401(k); Dental Insurance; Disability Coverage; Employee Discounts; Life Insurance; Medical Insurance; Pension Plan; Profit Sharing; Savings Plan; Tuition Assistance. **Corporate headquarters location:** This Location. **Listed on:** New York Stock Exchange. **Number of employees at this location:** 300. **Number of employees nationwide:** 80,000.
Other U.S. locations:
- 121 South Eighth Street, Suite 1350, Minneapolis MN 55402. 612/339-0555.

HAY GROUP
100 Penn Square East, The Wanamaker Building, Philadelphia PA 19107. 215/861-2000. **Contact:** Human Resources. **World Wide Web address:** http://www.haygroup.com. **Description:** An international human resources and management consulting firm that provides a variety of services including total compensation planning, strategic management, business culture, employee surveys, and outplacement. **Common positions include:** Accountant/Auditor; Actuary; Computer Programmer; Customer Service Rep.; Human Resources Manager; Marketing Specialist; Systems Analyst. **Educational backgrounds include:** Business Administration; Computer Science; Economics; Human Resources. **Benefits:** Dental Insurance; Disability Coverage; Life Insurance; Medical Insurance; Pension Plan; Tuition Assistance. **Corporate headquarters location:** This Location.
Other U.S. locations:
- 5901 Peachtree Dunwoody Road, Building B, Suite 525, Atlanta GA 30328. 770/901-5600.

HEWITT ASSOCIATES
100 Half Day Road, Lincolnshire IL 60069. 847/295-5000. **Contact:** Human Resources. **World Wide Web address:** http://www.hewitt.com. **Description:** Hewitt Associates is an international firm of consultants and actuaries specializing in the design, financing, communication, and administration of employee benefit and compensation programs. **Corporate headquarters location:** This Location.
Other U.S. locations:
- 3350 Riverwood Parkway, Suite 80, Atlanta GA 30339. 770/956-7777.
- 45 South Seventh Street, Suite 2100, Minneapolis MN 55402. 612/339-7501.

HORNE CPA GROUP
P.O. Box 22964, Jackson MS 39225. 601/948-0940. **Contact:** Laura Weeks, Personnel Director. **World Wide Web address:** http://www.hcpag.com. **Description:** An accounting firm.

HOWARD JOHNSON AND COMPANY
1201 Third Avenue, Suite 2000, Seattle WA 98101. 206/625-1040. **Contact:** Human Resources. **World Wide Web address:** http://www.hjco.com. **Description:** An international benefits consulting company. Howard Johnson and Company works mainly with 401(k) plans and group benefits for corporations. **NOTE:** Please send resumes to Jean Revor, Human Resources, Howard Johnson and Company, 311 South Wacker Drive, Suite 6000, Chicago IL 60606. **Corporate headquarters location:** This Location.

INSOURCE MANAGEMENT GROUP (IMG)
1020 Holcombe Boulevard, Suite 1650, Houston TX 77030. 713/790-0800. **Fax:** 713/852-2151. **Contact:** Recruiting Group. **Description:** Offers management consulting services for the health care industry. Insource Management Group's services are organized into three main program areas: re-engineering; strategic information systems and project planning; and implementation. IMG also designs computer-based patient records systems for hospitals and medical centers. **Common positions include:** Accountant/Auditor; Clinical Lab Technician; Computer Programmer; Financial Analyst; Human Resources Manager; Licensed Practical Nurse; Medical Records Technician; Radiological Technologist; Registered Nurse; Systems Analyst. **Educational backgrounds include:** Accounting; Biology; Business Administration; Computer Science. **Benefits:** 401(k); Dental Insurance; Disability Coverage; Life Insurance; Medical Insurance. **Corporate headquarters location:** This Location. **Other U.S. locations:** Nationwide. **Number of employees at this location:** 65.

JACKSON HEWITT INC.
339 Jefferson Road, Parsippany NJ 07054. 973/496-1040. **Contact:** Human Resources. **World Wide Web address:** http://www.jacksonhewitt.com. **Description:** A full-service company specializing in computerized tax preparation and electronic filing. The foundation of Jackson Hewitt's tax service is Hewtax, a proprietary software program. The company offers a number of filing options including SuperFast Refund, through which customers receive a refund anticipation loan within one to two days of filing; Accelerated Check Refund, which allows Jackson Hewitt to set up a bank account for the IRS to deposit the taxpayer's refund; and a standard electronically filed return. Jackson Hewitt has locations in more than 210 Montgomery Ward stores, as well as other locations that are company-owned or franchised. The company also operates a travel agency, Campbell Travel. **Corporate headquarters location:** This Location. **Listed on:** NASDAQ. **Number of employees nationwide:** 200.

KPMG
One Arizona Center, 400 East Van Buren Street, Suite 1100, Phoenix AZ 85004. 602/253-2000. **Contact:** Tracy Oliver, Recruiting. **World Wide Web address:** http://www.kpmg.com. **Description:** KPMG delivers a wide range of value-added assurance, tax, and consulting services. **Corporate headquarters location:** Montvale NJ. **Parent company:** KPMG International has more than 85,000 employees worldwide, including 6,500 partners and 60,000 professional staff, serving clients in 155 countries. KPMG International is a leader among professional services firms engaged in

capturing, managing, assessing, and delivering information to create knowledge that will help its clients maximize shareholder value.
Other U.S. locations:
- 355 South Grand Avenue, Suite 2000, Los Angeles CA 90071.
- 3 Embarcadero Center, Suite 2100, San Francisco CA 94111. 415/951-0100.
- 650 Town Center Drive, Suite 1000, Costa Mesa CA 92626. 714/850-4300.
- P.O. Box 3939, Albuquerque NM 87190. 505/884-3939.

KPMG
3 Chestnut Ridge Road, Montvale NJ 07645. **Contact:** Personnel. **World Wide Web address:** http://www.kpmgcareers.com. **Description:** This location houses the company's administrative offices. Overall, KPMG delivers a wide range of value-added assurance, tax, and consulting services. **Corporate headquarters location:** This Location. **Other U.S. locations:** Nationwide. **Parent company:** KPMG International is a leader among professional services firms engaged in capturing, managing, assessing, and delivering information to create knowledge that will help its clients maximize shareholder value.
Other U.S. locations:
- 111 South Calvert Street, Baltimore MD 21202. 410/783-8304.
- 2001 M Street NW, Washington DC 20036. 202/467-3000.

KPMG
303 East Wacker Drive, Chicago IL 60601. 312/665-1000. **Contact:** Personnel. **World Wide Web address:** http://www.kpmg.com. **Description:** KPMG delivers a wide range of value-added assurance, tax, and consulting services. **Corporate headquarters location:** Montvale NJ. **Parent company:** KPMG International is a leader among professional services firms engaged in capturing, managing, assessing, and delivering information to create knowledge that will help its clients maximize shareholder value.

KPMG
99 High Street, Boston MA 02110-2371. 617/988-1000. **Contact:** Rachel Freeman, College Recruiter. **World Wide Web address:** http://www.kpmg.com. **Description:** KPMG delivers a wide range of value-added assurance, tax, and consulting services. **Common positions include:** Accountant/Auditor. **Educational backgrounds include:** Accounting; Business Administration; Finance. **Benefits:** Dental Insurance; Disability Coverage; Life Insurance; Medical Insurance; Pension Plan; Savings Plan. **Corporate headquarters location:** Montvale NJ. **Parent company:** KPMG International has more than 85,000 employees worldwide, including 6,500 partners and 60,000 professional staff, serving clients in 844 cities in 155 countries. KPMG International is a leader among professional services firms engaged in capturing, managing, assessing, and delivering information to create knowledge that will help its clients maximize shareholder value.
Other U.S. locations:
- 280 Park Avenue, New York NY 10017. 212/909-5000.

KPMG
90 South Seventh Street, 4200 Norwest Center, Minneapolis MN 55402. 612/305-5496. **Contact:** Nancy Joanis, Recruiting Coordinator. **World Wide Web address:** http://www.kpmg.com. **Description:** KPMG delivers a wide range of value-added assurance, tax, and consulting services. **Common positions include:** Accountant/Auditor; Management Analyst/Consultant; Tax Specialist.

Educational backgrounds include: Accounting; Finance; Health Care; Tax. **Benefits:** 401(k); Dental Insurance; Disability Coverage; Life Insurance; Medical Insurance; Pension Plan; Tuition Assistance. **Special programs:** Internships. **Corporate headquarters location:** Montvale NJ. **Parent company:** KPMG International has more than 85,000 employees worldwide including 6,500 partners and 60,000 professional staff members, serving clients in 844 cities in 155 countries. KPMG International is a leader among professional services firms engaged in capturing, managing, assessing, and delivering information to create knowledge that will help its clients maximize shareholder value.

KPMG
10 South Broadway, Suite 900, St. Louis MO 63102-1761. 314/444-1400. **Contact:** Anthony Casadonte, Human Resources Director. **World Wide Web address:** http://www.kpmg.com. **Description:** KPMG delivers a wide range of value-added assurance, tax, and consulting services. Founded in 1897. **Corporate headquarters location:** Montvale NJ. **Parent company:** KPMG International is a leader among professional services firms engaged in capturing, managing, assessing, and delivering information to create knowledge that will help its clients maximize shareholder value.

KPMG
200 Crescent Court, Suite 300, Dallas TX 75201. 214/754-2000. **Contact:** Personnel Department. **World Wide Web address:** http://www.kpmg.com. **Description:** Delivers a wide range of value-added assurance, tax, and consulting services. **Corporate headquarters location:** Montvale NJ. **Parent company:** KPMG International is a leader among professional services firms engaged in capturing, managing, assessing, and delivering information to create knowledge that will help its clients maximize shareholder value. KPMG International has more than 85,000 employees worldwide.
Other U.S. locations:
- 700 Louisiana Street, 31st Floor, Bank of America Center, Houston TX 77002. 713/319-2000.

KPMG
60 East South Temple, Suite 900, Salt Lake City UT 84111. 801/333-8000. **Contact:** Human Resources Director. **World Wide Web address:** http://www. kpmg.com. **Description:** KPMG delivers a wide range of value-added assurance, tax, and consulting services. **Corporate headquarters location:** Montvale NJ. **Parent company:** KPMG International has more than 85,000 employees worldwide including 6,500 partners and 60,000 professional staff, serving clients in 844 cities in 155 countries. KPMG International is a leader among professional services firms engaged in capturing, managing, assessing, and delivering information to create knowledge that will help its clients maximize shareholder value.

KPMG
One Biscayne Tower, 2 South Biscayne Boulevard, Suite 2800, Miami FL 33131-1802. 305/358-2300. **Contact:** Director of Human Resources. **World Wide Web address:** http://www.kpmg.com. **Description:** KPMG delivers a wide range of value-added assurance, tax, and consulting services. **Corporate headquarters location:** Montvale NJ. **International locations:** Worldwide. **Parent company:** KPMG International has more than 85,000 employees worldwide including 6,500 partners and 60,000 professional staff, serving clients in 844 cities in 155 countries. KPMG International is a leader among professional services firms engaged in capturing, managing, assessing,

and delivering information to create knowledge that will help its clients maximize shareholder value.
Other U.S. locations:
- 450 East Las Olas Boulevard, Suite 750, Fort Lauderdale FL 33301-3503. 954/524-6000.
- 301 North Elm Street, Suite 700, Greensboro NC 27401. 336/275-3394.
- P.O. Box 10529, Greenville SC 29603. 864/250-2600.

KPMG
1600 Market Street, 12th Floor, Philadelphia PA 19103. 215/299-3100. **Contact:** Human Resources. **World Wide Web address:** http://www.kpmg.com. **Description:** Delivers a wide range of value-added assurance, tax, and consulting services. **Corporate headquarters location:** Montvale NJ. **International locations:** Worldwide. **Parent company:** KPMG International is a leader among professional services firms engaged in capturing, managing, assessing, and delivering information to create knowledge that will help its clients maximize shareholder value.
Other U.S. locations:
- One Mellon Bank Center, 25th Floor, Pittsburgh PA 15219. 412/391-9710.

KPMG
1211 SW Fifth Avenue, Suite 2000, Portland OR 97204. 503/221-6500. **Contact:** Recruiting Coordinator. **World Wide Web address:** http://www.kpmg.com. **Description:** This location houses offices of the company's legal department as well as the top management staff. Overall, KPMG delivers a wide range of value-added assurance, tax, and consulting services. **Common positions include:** Accountant. **Educational backgrounds include:** Accounting; Business Administration; Finance. **Benefits:** 401(k); Life Insurance; Medical Insurance. **Corporate headquarters location:** Montvale NJ. **International locations:** Worldwide. **Parent company:** KPMG International is a leader among professional services firms engaged in capturing, managing, assessing, and delivering information to create knowledge that will help its clients maximize shareholder value.
Other U.S. locations:
- 3100 Two Union Square, 601 Union Street, Seattle WA 98101. 206/292-1500.

KPMG
88 Silva Lane, Middletown RI 02842. 401/849-2570. **Contact:** Human Resources. **World Wide Web address:** http://www.kpmg.com. **Description:** Delivers a wide range of value-added assurance, tax, and consulting services. **Corporate headquarters location:** Montvale NJ. **Other U.S. locations:** Nationwide. **Parent company:** KPMG International is a leader among professional services firms engaged in capturing, managing, assessing, and delivering information to create knowledge that will help its clients maximize shareholder value. KPMG International has more than 85,000 employees worldwide including 6,500 partners and 60,000 professional staff, serving clients in 844 cities in 155 countries.
Other U.S. locations:
- CityPlace II, 185 Asylum Street, Hartford CT 06103-4103. 860/522-3200.

A.T. KEARNEY, INC.
222 West Adams Street, Suite 2500, Chicago IL 60606. 312/648-0111. **Contact:** Human Resources. **World Wide Web address:** http://www.atkearney.com. **Description:** A general management consulting firm.
Other U.S. locations:
- One Memorial Drive, 14th Floor, Cambridge MA 02142-1301. 617/374-2600.

KEPNER-TREGOE, INC.
P.O. Box 704, Princeton NJ 08542. 609/921-2806. **Contact:** Human Resources Department. **World Wide Web address:** http://www.kepner-tregoe.com. **Description:** A worldwide management consulting firm. Product categories include strategy formulation, systems improvement, skill development, and specific issue resolution. Industry markets served are automotive, information technology, chemicals, financial services, and natural resources. **Common positions include:** Administrator; Consultant. **Benefits:** Dental Insurance; Disability Coverage; Life Insurance; Medical Insurance; Pension Plan; Savings Plan; Tuition Assistance. **Corporate headquarters location:** This Location.

LEMASTER & DANIELS
601 West Riverside Avenue, Suite 700, Spokane WA 99201. 509/624-4315. **Contact:** Human Resources. **World Wide Web address:** http://www.lemaster-daniels.com. **Description:** An accounting firm providing accounting, auditing, and tax services to clients.

ARTHUR D. LITTLE, INC.
25 Acorn Park, Cambridge MA 02140. 617/498-5290. **Fax:** 617/498-7227. **Contact:** Human Resources. **World Wide Web address:** http://www.arthurdlittle.com. **Description:** An employee-owned international management and technology consulting firm. The company offers services in three areas: management consulting; technology and product development; and environmental, health, and safety consulting. Services include cost reduction, total quality management consulting, market assessments, logistics management, telecommunications management, auditing, safety programs, software development, and toxicology. Clients operate in a variety of industries including aerospace, automobiles, telecommunications, electronics, and consumer products. **Common positions include:** Biological Scientist; Chemist; Economist; Engineer; Financial Analyst; Geologist/Geophysicist; Management Analyst/Consultant; Transportation/Traffic Specialist; Water Transportation Specialist. **Educational backgrounds include:** Biology; Chemistry; Economics; Engineering; Geology; Physics. **Benefits:** 401(k); Dental Insurance; Disability Coverage; Life Insurance; Medical Insurance; Pension Plan; Profit Sharing; Tuition Assistance. **Corporate headquarters location:** This Location. **Number of employees at this location:** 1,000.
Other U.S. locations:
- 1760 Market Street, 3rd Floor, Philadelphia PA 19103. 215/656-5400.
- Colonial Place One, 2111 Wilson Boulevard, Suite 1000, Arlington VA 22201. 703/526-8000.
- 505 Hamilton Avenue, Suite 201, Palo Alto CA 94301-2008. 650/752-2600.
- 3916 State Street, Suite 2A, Santa Barbara CA 93105. 805/563-7660.
- 1001 Fannin Street, Suite 2050, Houston TX 77002. 713/646-2200.

MMS (MEETING MANAGEMENT SERVICES)
1765 South Eighth Street, Suite T-6, Colorado Springs CO 80906. **Toll-free phone:** 800/544-2432. **Fax:** 719/473-8750. **Contact:** Executive Assistant. **World Wide Web address:** http://www.meetingexperts.com. **Description:** A management consulting firm offering media, travel, and meeting planning services. **Common positions include:** Travel Agent. **Benefits:** Dental Insurance; Employee Discounts; Life Insurance; Medical Insurance. **Special programs:** Internships. **Corporate headquarters location:** This Location.

Parent company: ICR. **Number of employees at this location:** 20. **Number of employees nationwide:** 2,000.

MACDONALD & PAGE
30 Long Creek Drive, South Portland ME 04106. 207/774-5701. **Contact:** Ralph Hendrix, Administrator. **World Wide Web address:** http://www.macpage.com. **Description:** Engaged in all types of accounting for both individual clients and corporations. **Number of employees at this location:** 50.

McGLADREY & PULLEN, LLP
801 Nicollet Avenue, Suite 1300, Minneapolis MN 55402. 612/332-4300. **Contact:** Kathy Pedersen, Human Resources Director. **World Wide Web address:** http://www.mcgladrey.com. **Description:** A certified public accounting firm providing audit, tax, management, data processing, and cost systems services. **Corporate headquarters location:** Davenport IA.
Other U.S. locations:
- P.O. Box 2470, Greensboro NC 27402. 336/273-4461.
- One Church Street, 8th Floor, New Haven CT 06510. 203/773-1909.
- 1699 East Woodfield Road, Suite 300, Schaumburg IL 60173. 847/517-7070.

MEADEN & MOORE, INC.
1100 Superior Avenue, Suite 1100, Cleveland OH 44114. 216/241-3272. **Contact:** Human Resources. **World Wide Web address:** http://www. meadenmoore.com. **Description:** Engaged in certified public accounting and business consulting.

WILLIAM M. MERCER, INC.
1166 Avenue of the Americas, New York NY 10036. 212/345-7000. **Contact:** National Recruiting Coordinator. **World Wide Web address:** http://www.wmmercer.com. **Description:** One of the world's largest actuarial and human resources management consulting firms. The company offers advice to organizations on all aspects of employee/management relationships. Services include retirement, health and welfare, performance and rewards, communication, investment, human resources administration, risk, finance and insurance, and health care provider consulting. **Corporate headquarters location:** This Location.
Other U.S. locations:
- 10 West Broad Street, Suite 1100, Columbus OH 43215-3475. 614/227-5500.
- 777 South Figueroa Street, Suite 2000, Los Angeles CA 90017. 213/346-2200.
- 1100 Town & Country Road, Suite 1500, Orange CA 92868. 714/648-3300.
- 301 Tresser Boulevard, Stamford CT 06901. 203/973-2000.
- 212 Carnegie Center, CN-5323, Princeton NJ 08543-5323. 609/520-2500.
- P.O. Box 27506, Richmond VA 23261. 804/344-3700.

MERCER MANAGEMENT CONSULTING
2300 N Street NW, Suite 800, Washington DC 20037. 202/778-7000. **Contact:** Recruiting. **World Wide Web address:** http://www.mercermc.com. **Description:** Provides strategy and management consulting services.

MERCER MANAGEMENT CONSULTING
3500 Chase Tower, 2200 Ross Avenue, Suite 3500, Dallas TX 75201. 214/758-1880. **Contact:** Human Resources. **World Wide Web address:** http://www. mercermc.com. **Description:** Provides strategy and management consulting services. **Corporate headquarters location:** New York NY.

MILLIMAN & ROBERTSON, INC.
1301 Fifth Avenue, Suite 3800, Seattle WA 98101. 206/624-7940. **Contact:** Personnel. **World Wide Web address:** http://www.milliman.com. **Description:** A nationwide actuarial service company. **Common positions include:** Actuary. **Educational backgrounds include:** Computer Science; Mathematics. **Benefits:** Life Insurance; Medical Insurance; Pension Plan; Profit Sharing; Savings Plan. **Corporate headquarters location:** This Location.

MOSS ADAMS LLP
1001 Fourth Avenue, Suite 2830, Seattle WA 98154. 206/223-1820. **Contact:** Human Resources. **World Wide Web address:** http://www. mossadams.com. **Description:** One of the nation's largest accounting and consulting firms.
Other U.S. locations:
- 1702 Broadway, Tacoma WA 98402. 253/572-4100.
- 222 SW Columbia, Portland OR 97201. 503/242-1447.

NATIONAL ASSOCIATION OF BLACK ACCOUNTANTS
7249-A Hanover Parkway, Greenbelt MD 20770. 301/474-6222. **Fax:** 301/474-3114. **Contact:** Charles Quinn, Program Coordinator. **Description:** A nonprofit membership organization for accounting and business professionals and students. The association has nationwide chapters. **Common positions include:** Accountant/Auditor; Administrative Manager; Budget Analyst; Chief Financial Officer; Controller; Financial Analyst. **Educational backgrounds include:** Accounting; Business Administration; Finance. **Benefits:** Dental Insurance; Disability Coverage; Life Insurance; Medical Insurance; Pension Plan; Tuition Assistance. **Special programs:** Internships. **Corporate headquarters location:** This Location. **Number of employees at this location:** 10.

NATIVE AMERICAN CONSULTANTS, INC.
725 Second Street NE, Washington DC 20002. 202/547-0576. **Contact:** Human Resources. **Description:** Provides consulting services to governmental agencies engaged in research for Native Americans. **Common positions include:** Civil Engineer; Computer Programmer; General Manager; Industrial Engineer; Mechanical Engineer; Systems Analyst; Technical Writer/Editor. **Educational backgrounds include:** Business Administration; Computer Science; Economics; Engineering; Liberal Arts. **Benefits:** Disability Coverage; Life Insurance; Medical Insurance; Pension Plan. **Corporate headquarters location:** This Location.

OLIVE, LLP
P.O. Box 44998, Indianapolis IN 46244. 317/383-4000. **Contact:** Kate Jackson, Human Resources Manager. **World Wide Web address:** http://www. olivellp.com. **Description:** A full-service certified public accounting and consulting firm. **Office hours:** Monday - Friday, 8:00 a.m. - 5:00 p.m. **Corporate headquarters location:** This Location. **CEO:** John Harris. **Information Systems Manager:** Bill Castetter.

O'SULLIVAN HICKS PATTON, LLP
316 South Baylen Street, Suite 200, Pensacola FL 32501. 850/435-7400. **Fax:** 850/435-2888. **Contact:** Kathy Anthony, Firm Administrator. **World Wide Web address:** http://www.ohp-cpas.com. **Description:** A full-service accounting and business consulting firm. **Common positions include:** Accountant/Auditor; Administrative Assistant. **Educational backgrounds include:**

Accounting; Microsoft Office; Microsoft Word. **Benefits:** 401(k); Casual Dress - Fridays; Daycare Assistance; Dental Insurance; Financial Planning Assistance; Medical Insurance; Pension Plan; Profit Sharing; Sick Days (6 - 10); Tuition Assistance; Vacation Days (10 - 20). **Special programs:** Co-ops. **Corporate headquarters location:** This Location. **Managing Partner:** Mort O'Sullivan.

PARADYME CORPORATION
One Harbison Way, Suite 114, Columbia SC 29212. 803/781-7810. **Contact:** Human Resources. **World Wide Web address:** http://www.paradyme.net. **Description:** Performs general accounting functions, as well as human resources, payroll, and workers' compensation for other companies.

PERFORMANCE DEVELOPMENT CORP.
109 Jefferson Avenue, Oak Ridge TN 37830. 865/482-9004. **Contact:** Sharon Kidwell, Personnel Administrator. **World Wide Web address:** http://www.pdcnet.com. **Description:** Develops entire management programs for clients.

PERSONNEL DECISIONS INTERNATIONAL (PDI)
700 Peavey Building, 730 Second Avenue South, Minneapolis MN 55402. 612/339-0927. **Fax:** 612/573-7800. **Contact:** Cathy Nelson, Human Resources Director. **Description:** A worldwide consulting firm of organizational psychologists and consultants who specialize in assessment-based development and who have created and implemented programs, services, and products that are tailored to client needs. PDI's services and products cover the selection and promotion of employees at all levels, the development of managers and executives, the fostering of a positive group dynamic for the organization as a whole, and outplacement and career transition. **Corporate headquarters location:** This Location.

PLANTE & MORAN, LLP
27400 Northwestern Highway, Southfield MI 48034. 248/352-2500. **Contact:** Personnel Director. **Description:** Provides accounting, tax, financial planning, and corporate finance services. **Common positions include:** Accountant/Auditor. **Educational backgrounds include:** Accounting. **Special programs:** Internships. **Corporate headquarters location:** This Location. **Number of employees at this location:** 500.

PRICEWATERHOUSECOOPERS
370 17th Street, Suite 3300, Denver CO 80202. 303/573-2800. **Contact:** Recruiting Department. **World Wide Web address:** http://www. pricewaterhousecoopers.com. **Description:** One of the largest certified public accounting firms in the world. **Corporate headquarters location:** New York NY.
Other U.S. locations:
- 2901 North Central Avenue, Suite 1000, Phoenix AZ 85012-2755. 602/280-1800.
- 350 South Grand Avenue, Los Angeles CA 90071. 213/356-6000.
- 333 Market Street, 21st Floor, San Francisco CA 94105. 415/957-3000.
- 400 South Hope Street, 22nd Floor, Los Angeles CA 90071-2889. 213/236-3000.
- 555 California Street, 36th Floor, San Francisco CA 94104. 415/393-8500.

PRICEWATERHOUSECOOPERS
1751 Pinnacle Drive, Suite 800, McLean VA 22102-3811. 703/918-3000. **Contact:** Human Resources. **World Wide Web address:** http://www. pricewaterhousecoopers.com. **Description:** One of the largest certified public accounting firms in the

world. **Corporate headquarters location:** New York NY.
Other U.S. locations:
- 1155 Peachtree Street, Suite 1100, Atlanta GA 30309. 404/870-1100.
- 50 Hurt Plaza, Suite 1700, Atlanta GA 30303. 404/658-1800.

PRICEWATERHOUSECOOPERS
203 North LaSalle Street, Chicago IL 60601. 312/701-5500. **Contact:** Human Resources. **World Wide Web address:** http://www. pricewaterhousecoopers.com. **Description:** One of the largest certified public accounting firms in the world. **Corporate headquarters location:** New York NY.
Other U.S. locations:
- 111 West Jackson Boulevard, 8th Floor, Chicago IL 60603. 312/419-1565.

PRICEWATERHOUSECOOPERS
1301 K Street NW, Suite 800 West, Washington DC 20005-3333. 202/414-1000. **Contact:** Human Resources. **World Wide Web address:** http://www. pricewaterhousecoopers.com. **Description:** One of the largest certified public accounting firms in the world. **Corporate headquarters location:** New York NY.
Other U.S. locations:
- 250 West Pratt Street, Suite 2100, Baltimore MD 21201-2304. 410/783-7600.

PRICEWATERHOUSECOOPERS
400 North Ashley Street, Suite 2800, Tampa FL 33602. 813/223-7577. **Contact:** Human Resources. **World Wide Web address:** http://www. pricewaterhousecoopers.com. **Description:** One of the world's largest certified public accounting firms. **Corporate headquarters location:** New York NY.
Other U.S. locations:
- First Union Financial Center, 200 South Biscayne Boulevard, Suite 1900, Miami FL 33131. 305/375-7400.

PRICEWATERHOUSECOOPERS
650 Third Avenue South, Suite 1300, Minneapolis MN 55402. 612/370-9300. **Fax:** 612/373-7170. **Contact:** Tracy Ellis, Recruiting Manager. **World Wide Web address:** http://www. pricewaterhousecoopers.com. **Description:** One of the largest certified public accounting firms in the world. **Special programs:** Internships. **Corporate headquarters location:** New York NY. **Number of employees at this location:** 450.

PRICEWATERHOUSECOOPERS
1301 Avenue of the Americas, New York NY 10019. 212/259-1000. **Contact:** Human Resources. **World Wide Web address:** http://www. pricewaterhousecoopers.com. **Description:** One of the largest certified public accounting firms in the world. **Corporate headquarters location:** This Location.
Other U.S. locations:
- 160 Federal Street, Boston MA 02110. 617/439-4390.
- 1177 Avenue of the Americas, New York NY 10036. 212/596-7000.
- 80 State Street, Albany NY 12207. 518/462-2030.
- One Lincoln Center, Syracuse NY 13202. 315/474-8541.

PRICEWATERHOUSECOOPERS
B.P. America Building, 200 Public Square, 27th Floor, Cleveland OH 44114-2301. 216/781-3700. **Contact:** Human Resources. **World Wide Web address:** http://www.pricewaterhousecoopers.com. **Description:** One of the largest certified public

accounting firms in the world. The firm provides public accounting, business advisory, management consulting, and taxation services. **Corporate headquarters location:** New York NY.
Other U.S. locations:
- 2200 Chemed Center, 255 East Fifth Street, Cincinnati OH 45202-4798. 513/621-1900.
- 100 East Broad Street, Suite 2100, Columbus OH 43215. 614/225-8700.

PRICEWATERHOUSECOOPERS
2400 Eleven Penn Center, 1835 Market Street, Philadelphia PA 19103. 215/963-8000. **Fax:** 215/963-8824. **Contact:** Linda York, Human Resources Supervisor. **World Wide Web address:** http://www.pricewaterhousecoopers.com. **Description:** One of the largest certified public accounting firms in the world. **Corporate headquarters location:** New York NY.
Other U.S. locations:
- 30 South 17th Street, Philadelphia PA 19103. 215/575-5000.
- 600 Grant Street, 52nd Floor, Pittsburgh PA 15219-2777. 412/355-6000.

PRICEWATERHOUSECOOPERS
2001 Ross Avenue, Suite 1800, Dallas TX 75201-2997. 214/999-1400. **Contact:** Kelly Shipley, Human Resources Coordinator. **World Wide Web address:** http://www.pricewaterhousecoopers.com. **Description:** One of the largest certified public accounting firms in the world. **Corporate headquarters location:** New York NY.
Other U.S. locations:
- 1201 Louisiana Street, Suite 2900, Houston TX 7002. 713/356-4000.
- 36 South State Street, Suite 1700, Salt Lake City UT 84111. 801/531-9666.
- 600 Congress Avenue, Suite 1800, Austin TX 78701-3236. 512/477-1300.

PRICEWATERHOUSECOOPERS
100 North Tryon Street, Suite 5400, Charlotte NC 28202. 704/375-8414. **Contact:** Human Resources. **World Wide Web address:** http://www.pricewaterhousecoopers.com. **Description:** One of the largest certified public accounting firms in the world. **Corporate headquarters location:** New York NY. **Other U.S. locations:** Nationwide.

PRICEWATERHOUSECOOPERS
3800 Howard Hughes Parkway, Suite 550, Las Vegas NV 89120. 702/691-5400. **Contact:** Human Resources. **World Wide Web address:** http://www.pricewaterhousecoopers.com. **Description:** One of the largest certified public accounting firms in the world. **Corporate headquarters location:** New York NY.
Other U.S. locations:
- 1850 North Central Avenue, Suite 700, Phoenix AZ 85004-4545. 602/379-5500.

PRICEWATERHOUSECOOPERS
100 Pearl Street, Hartford CT 06103. 860/240-2000. **Contact:** Human Resources. **World Wide Web address:** http://www.pricewaterhousecoopers.com. **Description:** One of the largest certified public accounting firms in the world. **Corporate headquarters location:** New York NY.
Other U.S. locations:
- One Canterbury Green, Stamford CT 06901. 203/326-8400.
- P.O. Box 5080, 2 Wall Street, Manchester NH 03108. 603/669-2200.

PRICEWATERHOUSECOOPERS
1001 Fourth Avenue, Suite 4200, Seattle WA 98154-1101. 206/622-1505. **Contact:** Human Resources. **World Wide Web address:** http://www.

pricewaterhousecoopers.com. **Description:** One of the largest certified public accounting firms in the world. **Corporate headquarters location:** New York NY.
Other U.S. locations:
- 999 Third Avenue, Suite 1800, Seattle WA 98104-4045. 206/622-8700.
- 121 SW Morrison Street, Suite 1800, Portland OR 97204. 503/224-9040.
- 1300 SW Fifth Avenue, Suite 3100, Portland OR 97201. 503/417-2400.

PRICEWATERHOUSECOOPERS NATIONAL ADMINISTRATIVE CENTER
3109 West Dr. Martin Luther King Jr. Boulevard, Tampa FL 33607. 813/348-7000. **Fax:** 813/348-7002. **Contact:** Director of Human Resources. **World Wide Web address:** http://www. pricewaterhousecoopers.com. **Description:** One of the world's largest certified public accounting firms.

RGL GALLAGHER
136 East South Temple, Suite 1770, Salt Lake City UT 84111. 801/355-0400. **Contact:** Personnel. **World Wide Web address:** http://www.rglslc.com. **Description:** A certified public accounting firm. **Parent company:** RGL International.

RSM McGLADREY, INC.
227 West First Street, Suite 700, Duluth MN 55802. 218/727-8253. **Fax:** 218/727-1438. **Contact:** Karen S. Andresen, Recruiter. **E-mail address:** karen-andresen@rsmi.com. **World Wide Web address:** http://www.rsmmcgladrey.com. **Description:** Provides accounting and auditing services, business planning, taxation, and consulting services. **Common positions include:** Accountant/Auditor; Bank Officer/Manager; Branch Manager; Chemist; Civil Engineer; Clerical Supervisor; Computer Programmer; Credit Manager; Customer Service Rep. Financial Analyst; General Manager; Health Services Manager; Hotel Manager; Human Resources Specialist; Management Analyst/ Consultant; Manufacturer's/Wholesaler's Sales Rep.; MIS Specialist; Operations/Production Manager; Paralegal; Property and Real Estate Manager; Purchasing Agent/Manager; Quality Control Supervisor; Systems Analyst; Telecommunications Manager. **Educational backgrounds include:** Accounting; Economics; Management/Planning; Personnel Relations. **Corporate headquarters location:** Minneapolis MN.
Other U.S. locations:
- 212 North Bradley Street, 2nd Floor, Davenport IA 52801. 319/324-0447.

GERALD T. REILLY & CO.
424 Adams Street, Milton MA 02186. 617/696-8900. **Contact:** Human Resources Department. **World Wide Web address:** http://www. gtreilly.com. **Description:** An accounting firm.

RIGHT MANAGEMENT CONSULTANTS
1818 Market Street, 33rd Floor, Philadelphia PA 19103. 215/988-1588. **Contact:** Human Resources. **World Wide Web address:** http://www.right.com. **Description:** Provides management consulting services.

ROBBINS-GIOIA, INC.
11 Canal Center Plaza, Suite 200, Alexandria VA 22314. 703/548-7006. **Fax:** 703/548-3724. **Contact:** Angela Thompson, Human Resources Manager. **Description:** A management consulting firm. The company's services include program/ project management, configuration management, cost-estimation, acquisition management, software development, systems design, technical support, life cycle management, and risk management. Robbins-

Gioia functions as a prime contractor, team member, or subcontractor in various industries including manufacturing, telecommunications, electronics, and state and local government. The company has experience managing large projects in logistics, mergers, personnel, finance, automated data processing, information resource management, systems integration, and new product development. **NOTE:** Entry-level positions are offered. **Common positions include:** Computer Programmer; Cost Estimator; Database Manager; MIS Specialist; Operations/Production Manager; Project Manager; Systems Analyst. **Educational backgrounds include:** Business Administration; Computer Science; Liberal Arts. **Benefits:** 401(k); Daycare Assistance; Dental Insurance; Disability Coverage; Financial Planning Assistance; Life Insurance; Medical Insurance; Tuition Assistance. **Corporate headquarters location:** This Location. **Other U.S. locations:** Nationwide.

RUBIN, BROWN, GORNSTEIN & CO. LLP
230 South Bemiston, St. Louis MO 63105. 314/727-8150. **Fax:** 314/727-9195. **Contact:** Laura E. Asher, Human Resources Director. **World Wide Web address:** http://www.rbgco.com. **Description:** A public accounting firm operating primarily in the St. Louis metropolitan area. Services and specialties include accounting, audit, and tax services; and computer, employee benefit plan, legal support management, personal financial, and acquisition consulting services. The company provides services to accounting firms, automotive dealerships, financial services firms including financial institutions and mortgage banks, government agencies, health care companies, hospitality firms, law firms, manufacturing companies, international business consultants, nonprofit organizations, real estate and construction firms, and retailers. **Common positions include:** Accountant/Auditor; Computer Programmer; Systems Analyst. **Educational backgrounds include:** Accounting; Computer Science. **Benefits:** 401(k); Dental Insurance; Disability Coverage; Employee Discounts; Life Insurance; Medical Insurance; Pension Plan; Profit Sharing; Savings Plan; Tuition Assistance. **Special programs:** Internships. **Corporate headquarters location:** This Location. **Number of employees at this location:** 200.

KURT SALMON ASSOCIATES, INC.
103 Carnegie Center, Suite 205, Princeton NJ 08540. 609/452-8700. **Contact:** Recruiting. **World Wide Web address:** http://www.kurtsalmon.com. **Description:** Provides management consulting to logistics and consumer products companies.

SCHATZ, FLETCHER & ASSOCIATES
P.O. Box 1071, Augusta ME 04332. 207/622-4766. **Physical address:** 227 Water Street, Augusta ME. **Contact:** Human Resources. **World Wide Web address:** http://www.sfacpa.com. **Description:** A general accounting firm.

SCHECHTER DOKKEN KANTER
100 Washington Avenue South, Suite 1600, Minneapolis MN 55401. 612/332-5500. **Contact:** Human Resources. **Description:** A regional accounting and management consulting firm performing audits, accounting, tax, employee benefits plan consulting, litigation support, and management consulting services. **Common positions include:** Accountant/Auditor. **Educational backgrounds include:** Accounting; Business Administration. **Benefits:** Disability Coverage; Medical Insurance; Profit Sharing; Savings Plan. **Corporate headquarters location:** This Location. **Operations at this facility include:** Service. **Number of employees at this location:** 50.

SYNYGY, INC.
One Belmont Avenue, 10th Floor, Bala-Cynwyd PA 19004. 610/664-7433. **Fax:** 610/664-7343. **Contact:** Stephanie Salamon, Technical Recruiter. **E-mail address:** salamon@synygy.com. **World Wide Web address:** http://www.synygy.com. **Description:** A management consulting and information technology company. Founded in 1991. **NOTE:** Entry-level positions are offered. **Company slogan:** Turning information into action. **Common positions include:** Computer Programmer; Consultant; Sales Rep. **Educational backgrounds include:** Business Administration; Computer Science; Engineering. **Benefits:** 401(k); Dental Insurance; Medical Insurance. **Special programs:** Summer Jobs. **Office hours:** Monday - Friday, 9:00 a.m. - 6:00 p.m. **Corporate headquarters location:** This Location. **Listed on:** Privately held. **CEO:** Mark Stiffler. **Annual sales/revenues:** $5 - $10 million. **Number of employees at this location:** 50.

TOWERS PERRIN
335 Madison Avenue, New York NY 10017. 212/309-3400. **Contact:** Recruiting Coordinator. **World Wide Web address:** http://www.towers.com. **Description:** A management consulting firm. **Corporate headquarters location:** This Location. **Other U.S. locations:**
- 100 Summit Lake Drive, Valhalla NY 10595. 914/745-4000.
- 8300 Norman Center Drive, Suite 600, Minneapolis MN 55437. 952/897-3300.

TRANSPECTIVE GROUP
8 Cedar Street, Suite 64, Woburn MA 01801. 781/932-9092. **Contact:** Human Resources. **World Wide Web address:** http://www.transpective.com. **Description:** Provides management consulting for a wide variety of industries.

U.S. COUNSELING SERVICES, INC.
GIBRALTAR CONSULTANTS
120 Bishop's Way, Brookfield WI 53008-0951. 262/784-5600. **Fax:** 262/784-0261. **Contact:** Michelle C. Bahringer, Human Resources Assistant. **World Wide Web address:** http://www.uscounselingservices.com. **Description:** Provides consulting services for the management of technical equipment for the health care industry. **Common positions include:** Account Manager; Account Rep.; Administrative Assistant; Auditor; Biomedical Engineer; Computer Programmer; Sales Executive; Sales Rep.; Systems Analyst; Typist/Word Processor. **Educational backgrounds include:** Business Administration; Computer Science; Engineering; Health Care. **Benefits:** Disability Coverage; Life Insurance; Medical Insurance; Profit Sharing; Tuition Assistance. **Corporate headquarters location:** This Location. **Other U.S. locations:** Nationwide. **Listed on:** Privately held. **Number of employees at this location:** 70.

WIPFLI ULLRICH BERTELSON
500 Third Street, Suite 303, P.O. Box 8010, Wausau WI 54402-8010. 715/845-3111. **Contact:** Human Resources. **World Wide Web address:** http://www.wipfli.com. **Description:** A certified public accounting firm specializing in human resources, management consulting, employee benefits, retirement and estate planning, information services, and business process improvement.

WOODEN & BENSON
100 West Pennsylvania Avenue, Suite 200, Towson MD 21204. 410/825-4860. **Contact:** Human Resources. **World Wide Web address:** http://www.woodenbenson.com. **Description:** Provides accounting, auditing, tax, and consulting services.

For more information on career opportunities in accounting and management consulting:

Associations

AMERICAN ACCOUNTING ASSOCIATION
5717 Bessie Drive, Sarasota FL 34233. 941/921-7747. World Wide Web address: http://www.aaa-edu.org. An academically-oriented accounting association that offers two quarterly journals, a semi-annual journal, a newsletter, and a wide variety of continuing education programs.

AMERICAN INSTITUTE OF CERTIFIED PUBLIC ACCOUNTANTS (AICPA)
1211 Avenue of the Americas, New York NY 10036. 212/596-6200. World Wide Web address: http://www.aicpa.org. A national professional organization for all CPAs.

AMERICAN MANAGEMENT ASSOCIATION INTERNATIONAL
1601 Broadway, 8th Floor, New York NY 10019. 212/586-8100. Fax: 212/903-8168. World Wide Web address: http://www.amanet.org. Provides a variety of publications, training videos, and courses, as well as an Information Resource Center, which provides management information, and a library service.

ASSOCIATION OF GOVERNMENT ACCOUNTANTS
2208 Mount Vernon Avenue, Alexandria VA 22301. 703/684-6931. World Wide Web address: http://www.agacgfm.org. Serves financial management professionals and offers continuing education workshops.

ASSOCIATION OF MANAGEMENT CONSULTING FIRMS
380 Lexington Avenue, Suite 1700, New York NY 10168. 212/551-7887. World Wide Web address: http://www.amcf.org.

THE INSTITUTE OF INTERNAL AUDITORS
249 Maitland Avenue, Altamonte Springs FL 32701. 407/830-7600. World Wide Web address: http://www.theiia.org. Publishes magazines and newsletters. The institute provides information on current issues, a network of more than 50,000 members in 100 countries, professional development and research services, and also offers continuing education seminars.

INSTITUTE OF MANAGEMENT ACCOUNTANTS
10 Paragon Drive, Montvale NJ 07645. 201/573-9000. World Wide Web address: http://www.imanet.org. Offers a Certified Management Accountant Program, periodicals, seminars, educational programs, a financial management network, and networking services.

INSTITUTE OF MANAGEMENT CONSULTANTS
1200 19th Street NW, Suite 300, Washington DC 20036. Toll-free phone: 800/221-2557. World Wide Web address: http://www.imcusa.org. Offers certification programs, professional development, and a directory of members.

NATIONAL ASSOCIATION OF TAX PRACTITIONERS
720 Association Drive, Appleton WI 54914-1483. 920/749-1040. World Wide Web address: http://www.natptax.com. Offers seminars, research, newsletters, preparer worksheets, state chapters, insurance, and other tax-related services.

NATIONAL SOCIETY OF ACCOUNTANTS
1010 North Fairfax Street, Alexandria VA 22314. 703/549-6400. World Wide Web address: http://www.nsacct.org. Offers professional development services, government representation, a variety of publications, practice aids, low-cost group insurance, annual seminars, and updates for members on new tax laws.

Career Fairs

CAREER FAIRS INTERNATIONAL
World Wide Web address: http://www.career-fairs.com. Organizes career fairs in the fields of accounting, banking, finance, and insurance.

Magazines

CPA JOURNAL
The New York State Society, 530 Fifth Avenue, 5th Floor, New York NY 10036. 212/719-8300. World Wide Web address: http://www.nysscpa.org. Published monthly.

CPA LETTER
American Institute of Certified Public Accountants, 1211 Avenue of the Americas, New York NY 10036. 212/596-6200. World Wide Web address: http://www.aicpa.org/pubs/cpaltr/index.htm

JOURNAL OF ACCOUNTANCY
American Institute of Certified Public Accountants, 1211 Avenue of the Americas, New York NY 10036. 212/596-6200. World Wide Web address: http://www.aicpa.org.

Online Services

ACCOUNTANTS FORUM
Go: Aicpa. A CompuServe forum sponsored by the American Institute of Certified Public Accountants.

ACCOUNTING & FINANCE JOBS
World Wide Web address: http://www.accountingjobs.com. Provides national and international job listings and offers links to related sites.

ACCOUNTING NET
World Wide Web address: http://www.accountingnet.com. Provides national and international job listings and offers links to related sites.

ACCOUNTING.COM
World Wide Web address: http://www.accounting.com. Offers job listings, discussion groups, and resume writing tips.

FINANCIAL, ACCOUNTING, AND INSURANCE JOBS PAGE
World Wide Web address: http://www.nationjob.com/financial. This Website provides a list of financial, accounting, and insurance job openings.

JOBS IN ACCOUNTING
World Wide Web address: http://www.cob.ohio-state.edu/dept/fin/jobs/account.htm#Link7. Provides information on the accounting profession, including salaries, trends, and resources.

Advertising, Marketing, and Public Relations

You can expect to find the following types of companies in this chapter:

Advertising Agencies • Direct Mail Marketers
Market Research Firms • Public Relations Firms

Some helpful information: *The average salary for an entry-level assistant position in an advertising/marketing agency is $25,000 - $30,000 annually, and these coveted positions are very difficult to attain. Senior agents and supervisors often earn $50,000 or more, while partners and executives frequently exceed $100,000 per year in this highly competitive field. Entry-level positions in public relations firms usually earn under $25,000 per year, with higher salaries in a corporate setting. Experienced representatives earn an average of $50,000 (higher figures are usually reserved for those with 10 or more years of experience).*

A&R PARTNERS
201 Baldwin Avenue, San Mateo CA 94401-3914. 650/762-2800. **Fax:** 650/762-2801. **Contact:** Zelda Rudin, Senior Partner. **E-mail address:** zrudin@arpartners.com. **World Wide Web address:** http://www.arpartners.com. **Description:** A public relations firm. **NOTE:** Entry-level positions are offered. **Common positions include:** Account Manager; Controller; Editorial Assistant; Human Resources Manager; Internet Services Manager; Market Research Analyst; Public Relations Specialist. **Educational backgrounds include:** Accounting; Communications; Computer Science; Marketing; Public Relations. **Benefits:** 401(k); Dental Insurance; Disability Coverage; Financial Planning Assistance; Flexible Benefits; Life Insurance; Medical Insurance; Pension Plan; Profit Sharing; Tuition Assistance. **Special programs:** Apprenticeships; Internships; Training. **Corporate headquarters location:** This Location. **President and Managing Partner:** Robert Angus.

AB DATA
8050 North Port Washington Road, Milwaukee WI 53211. 414/352-4404. **Fax:** 414/352-3994. **Contact:** Katrina Milinkovich, Corporate Human Resources Director. **E-mail address:** kmilinko@abdata.com. **World Wide Web address:** http://www.abdata.com. **Description:** A full-service, direct mail marketing company that primarily serves nonprofit and democratic political clients. **NOTE:** Entry-level positions are offered. **Common positions include:** Accountant; Administrative Assistant; Buyer; Computer Operator; Computer Programmer; Controller; Customer Service Rep.; Database Manager; Graphic Artist; Human Resources Manager; Marketing Manager; MIS Specialist; Production Manager; Sales Executive; Sales Rep.; Secretary; Systems Analyst; Technical Writer. **Educational backgrounds include:** Accounting; Art/Design; Communications; Computer Science; Finance; Marketing. **Benefits:** 401(k); Dental Insurance; Disability Coverage; Life Insurance; Medical Insurance. **Corporate headquarters location:** This Location. **Other U.S. locations:** Washington DC. **Annual sales/revenues:** $5 - $10 million. **Number of employees at this location:** 85. **Number of employees nationwide:** 100.

AMD INDUSTRIES, INC.
4620 West 19th Street, Cicero IL 60804. 708/863-8900. **Fax:** 708/863-2065. **Contact:** Human Resources Director. **World Wide Web address:** http://www.amdpop.com. **Description:** Produces and sells point-of-purchase (P.O.P.) displays. **Common positions include:** Accountant; Buyer; Computer Programmer; Cost Estimator; Customer Service Rep.; Designer; Draftsperson; General Manager; Purchasing Agent. **Educational backgrounds include:** Accounting; Art/Design; Engineering; Finance; Marketing. **Benefits:** Life Insurance; Medical Insurance; Savings Plan. **Corporate headquarters location:** This Location. **Other U.S. locations:** OH; WI. **Listed on:** Privately held. **Number of employees at this location:** 100.

ABRAMSON LABUS VAN DE VELDE
1140 Connecticut Avenue NW, Suite 200, Washington DC 20036. 202/822-8844. **Fax:** 202/822-0899. **Contact:** Human Resources. **World Wide Web address:** http://www.alvweb.com. **Description:** An agency specializing in radio and television advertising. **Common positions include:** Advertising Clerk; Commercial Artist; Marketing Specialist; Public Relations Specialist. **Educational backgrounds include:** Art/Design; Communications; Marketing. **Benefits:** 401(k); Dental Insurance; Disability Coverage; Life Insurance; Medical Insurance; Profit Sharing; Tuition Assistance. **Special programs:** Internships. **Corporate headquarters location:** This Location. **Listed on:** Privately held. **Annual sales/revenues:** $21 - $50 million.

ACCESS COMMUNICATIONS
101 Howard Street, 2nd Floor, San Francisco CA 94105-1629. 415/904-7070. **Fax:** 415/904-7055. **Contact:** Human Resources. **E-mail address:** info@accesspr.com. **World Wide Web address:** http://www.accesspr.com. **Description:** A public relations firm whose clients include software and other high-tech corporations. **Corporate headquarters location:** This Location.

THE ACKERLEY GROUP, INC.
1301 Fifth Avenue, Suite 4000, Seattle WA 98101. 206/624-2888. **Contact:** Personnel Department. **World Wide Web address:** http://www.ackerley.com. **Description:** Operates a group of media and entertainment companies including an outdoor advertising agency, 17 television stations, five radio stations, and a sports/entertainment division that operates the NBA's Seattle SuperSonics and the WNBA's Seattle Storm. **Corporate headquarters location:** This Location. **Subsidiaries include:** AK Media/Massachusetts; AK Media/Northwest; Full House Sports & Entertainment. **Listed on:** New York Stock Exchange. **Stock exchange symbol:** AK.

ACKERMAN McQUEEN, INC.
545 East John Carpenter Freeway, Suite 600, Irving TX 75062-3932. 972/444-9000. **Fax:** 972/869-4363. **Contact:** Personnel. **World Wide Web address:** http://www.am.com. **Description:** A full-service advertising agency. Founded in 1939. **NOTE:** Entry-level positions are offered. **Common positions include:** Administrative Assistant; Advertising Executive; Computer Support Technician; Desktop Publishing Specialist; Graphic Designer; Technical Writer. **Educational backgrounds include:** Advertising; Art; Business Administration; Communications; Journalism; Liberal Arts; Marketing; Microsoft Word; Public Relations; QuarkXPress; Spreadsheets. **Benefits:** 401(k); Casual Dress - Fridays; Dental Insurance; Life Insurance; Medical Insurance; Sick Days (1 - 5). **Special programs:** Internships. **Internship information:** Unpaid internships are offered each fall, spring, and summer semester for college credit. **Corporate headquarters location:** Oklahoma City OK. **Other U.S. locations:** Colorado Springs CO; Tulsa OK. **CEO:** Angus McQueen. **Annual sales/revenues:** More than $100 million.

ADSTREET INC.
1145-D Executive Circle, Cary NC 27511. 919/481-3004. **Contact:** Rich Styles, President. **World Wide Web address:** http://www.adstreet.com. **Description:** A full-service advertising and public relations agency offering creative advertising work, sports marketing, and media buying services. **Educational backgrounds include:** Art/Design; Marketing. **Corporate headquarters location:** This Location.

ADVO INC.
One Univac Lane, P.O. Box 755, Windsor CT 06095. 860/285-6100. **Contact:** Personnel. **World Wide Web address:** http://www.advo.com. **Description:** A direct mail advertising company. **Common positions include:** Accountant; Buyer; Computer Programmer; Customer Service Rep.; Financial Analyst; Human Resources Manager; Management Trainee; Purchasing Agent; Systems Analyst. **Educational backgrounds include:** Accounting; Computer Science; Finance; Marketing. **Benefits:** 401(k); Dental Insurance; Disability Coverage; Life Insurance; Medical Insurance. **Corporate headquarters location:** This Location. **Number of employees nationwide:** 5,500.

AEGIS COMMUNICATIONS GROUP
7880 Bent Branch Drive, Suite 150, Irving TX 75063. 972/830-1800. **Fax:** 972/830-1801. **Contact:** Personnel. **World Wide Web address:** http://www.aegiscomgroup.com. **Description:** A teleservices provider that offers integrated marketing services to large corporations. Services include customer acquisition, customer care, and marketing research. **Corporate headquarters location:** This Location. **Listed on:** NASDAQ.

AMMIRATI PURIS LINTAS
One Dag Hammarskjold Plaza, 37th Floor, New York NY 10017. 212/605-8645. **Fax:** 212/605-4708. **Contact:** Sarah Zieff, Human Resources Supervisor. **Description:** An advertising agency. **Corporate headquarters location:** This Location. **Parent company:** The Interpublic Group of Companies, Inc.

ASSOCIATED MERCHANDISING CORP.
500 Seventh Avenue, New York NY 10018. 212/819-6600. **Contact:** Roger Bush, Human Resources. **World Wide Web address:** http://www.theamc.com. **Description:** Performs retail product development and international apparel-sourcing services for retail clients. **Common positions include:** Accountant; Buyer; Commercial Artist; Computer Programmer; Customer Service Representative; Operations Manager; Product Manager; Quality Control Supervisor. **Educational backgrounds include:** Accounting; Art History; Business Administration; Computer Science; Marketing. **Benefits:** Dental Insurance; Disability Coverage; Employee Discounts; Life Insurance; Medical Insurance; Pension Plan; Savings Plan. **Corporate headquarters location:** This Location. **Other U.S. locations:** Miami FL; Minneapolis MN. **Operations at this facility include:** Administration; Research and Development; Service. **Number of employees nationwide:** 400.

FREDERICK ATKINS INC.
1515 Broadway, New York NY 10036. 212/840-7000. **Fax:** 212/536-7467. **Contact:** Margaret Gonzalez, Personnel Manager. **Description:** An international merchandising and marketing consulting firm that works with 25 department store chains specializing in trend analysis, fashion forecasting, and product development. **Common positions include:** Accountant; Buyer; Clerical Supervisor; Computer Programmer; Designer; Human Resources Manager; MIS Specialist; Product Manager; Quality Control Supervisor; Systems Analyst. **Educational backgrounds include:** Accounting; Art; Computer Science; Liberal Arts; Marketing. **Benefits:** 401(k); Dental Insurance; Disability Coverage; Employee Discounts; Life Insurance; Medical Insurance; Pension Plan; Public Transit Available; Tuition Assistance. **Corporate headquarters location:** This Location. **Other U.S. locations:** Los Angeles CA. **Operations at this facility include:** Administration; Sales. **Listed on:** Privately held. **Number of employees at this location:** 350. **Number of employees nationwide:** 370.

AVISO INC.
1336 C Park Street, Alameda CA 94501. 510/865-5100. **Fax:** 510/865-5165. **Contact:** Human Resources. **World Wide Web address:** http://www.avisoinc.com. **Description:** A marketing and communications firm that primarily serves the real estate and development industries. **Corporate headquarters location:** This Location.

N.W. AYER INC.
825 Eighth Avenue, New York NY 10019. 212/474-5000. **Contact:** Donna Milch, Personnel Director. **Description:** A national advertising agency. **Corporate headquarters location:** This Location. **Other U.S. locations:** Los Angeles CA; Detroit MI. **Number of employees nationwide:** 1,275.

BBDO WORLDWIDE INC.
1285 Avenue of the Americas, New York NY 10019. 212/459-5000. **Contact:** Human Resources. **World Wide Web address:** http://www.bbdo.com. **Description:** Operates a worldwide network of advertising agencies with related businesses in public relations, direct marketing, sales promotion, graphic design, graphic arts, and printing. **Corporate headquarters location:** This Location. **Other area locations:** 437 Madison Avenue, New York NY. **Other U.S. locations:** Los Angeles CA; San Francisco CA; Miami FL; Atlanta GA; Chicago IL; Southfield MI; Minneapolis MN; Houston TX. **International locations:** Worldwide.

BBK COMMUNICATIONS
2310 Washington Street, Newton MA 02162. 617/630-4477. **Contact:** Human Resources. **World Wide Web address:** http://www.bbkweb.com. **Description:** An integrated advertising and public relations agency serving the health policies,

technologies, managed care, and pharmaceutical fields. **NOTE:** Please indicate the department to which you are applying. **Common positions include:** Advertising Clerk; Designer; Editor; Public Relations Specialist; Technical Writer. **Educational backgrounds include:** Accounting; Art; Communications; Health Care; Liberal Arts; Marketing. **Corporate headquarters location:** This Location. **Listed on:** Privately held.

BRSG (BLACK ROGERS SULLIVAN GOODNIGHT)
1900 St. James Place, Suite 800, Houston TX 77056. 713/781-6666. **Fax:** 713/783-1592. **Contact:** Stacy Jacob, Senior Vice President/ Director of Corporate Resources. **Description:** A marketing communications firm. **Common positions include:** Accountant; Advertising Clerk; Graphic Artist; Marketing Manager; Payroll Clerk; Public Relations Specialist; Receptionist; Systems Analyst. **Educational backgrounds include:** Accounting; Advertising; Art/Design; Business Administration; Communications; Finance; Marketing. **Benefits:** Dental Insurance; Disability Coverage; Life Insurance; Medical Insurance; Savings Plan. **Special programs:** Internships. **Office hours:** Monday - Friday, 8:00 a.m. - 5:00 p.m. **Corporate headquarters location:** This Location. **Other U.S. locations:** Austin TX. **Operations at this facility include:** Research and Development. **CEO:** Scott Black. **Number of employees at this location:** 60. **Number of employees nationwide:** 85.

BALL ADVERTISING GROUP
424 South Lincoln, Casper WY 82601. 307/234-3472. **Contact:** Ken Ball, President. **World Wide Web address:** http://www.balladvertising.com. **Description:** An advertising agency that offers logo designs, ad campaigns, and media placements.

BATES SOUTHWEST
5847 San Felipe, Suite 400, Houston TX 77057. 713/266-7676. **Contact:** Sue Wiseman, Human Resources Manager. **Description:** An advertising agency. **Common positions include:** Accountant; Advertising Clerk; Copywriter; Human Resources Manager; Public Relations Specialist. **Benefits:** 401(k); Dental Insurance; Disability Coverage; Life Insurance; Medical Insurance; Pension Plan; Profit Sharing. **Special programs:** Internships. **Corporate headquarters location:** New York NY. **Other U.S. locations:** Nationwide. **Operations at this facility include:** Administration; Divisional Headquarters. **Number of employees at this location:** 100. **Number of employees nationwide:** 800.

BATES USA
498 Seventh Avenue, New York NY 10018. 212/297-7000. **Contact:** Personnel. **World Wide Web address:** http://www.bates.com. **Description:** An advertising and public relations agency. **Corporate headquarters location:** This Location. **Other U.S. locations:**
• 117 East Washington Street, Indianapolis IN 46204. 317/686-7800.

BERNSTEIN-REIN ADVERTISING, INC.
4600 Madison Avenue, Suite 1500, Kansas City MO 64112. 816/756-0640. **Contact:** Human Resources. **Description:** An advertising agency. **Corporate headquarters location:** This Location.

BERRY BROWN ADVERTISING
3100 McKinnon Street, Suite 1100, Dallas TX 75201-1046. 214/871-1001. **Fax:** 214/871-1137. **Contact:** Ms. Virdie Horton, Personnel Manager. **Description:** An advertising agency. **Common positions include:** Accountant; Administrative Manager; Clerical Supervisor; Commercial Artist; Computer Operator; Marketing Manager; Media Specialist; Payroll Clerk; Receptionist; Secretary; Typist. **Educational backgrounds include:** Accounting; Art/Design; Business Administration; Communications; Liberal Arts; Marketing. **Benefits:** Dental Insurance; Disability Coverage; Life Insurance; Medical Insurance; Pension Plan; Profit Sharing; Savings Plan; Tuition Assistance. **Special programs:** Internships. **Corporate headquarters location:** This Location.

THE BERRY COMPANY
P.O. Box 6000, Dayton OH 45401-6000. 937/296-2070. **Fax:** 937/296-4945. **Contact:** Kelley C. Bazelak, Employment Services Coordinator. **World Wide Web address:** http://www.lmberry.com. **Description:** Engaged in the sale and marketing of Yellow Pages advertising. **Common positions include:** Advertising Clerk; Computer Programmer; Customer Service Representative; Services Sales Representative. **Educational backgrounds include:** Business Administration; Communications; Marketing. **Benefits:** Dental Insurance; Disability Coverage; Life Insurance; Medical Insurance; Pension Plan; Savings Plan; Tuition Assistance. **Corporate headquarters location:** This Location. **Parent company:** BellSouth Corporation. **Number of employees at this location:** 750. **Number of employees nationwide:** 2,400.

BLACKWOOD MARTIN/CJRW
P.O. Box 1968, Fayetteville AR 72702. 501/442-9803. **Fax:** 501/442-3092. **Contact:** Jennifer Cross, Office Manager. **Description:** A full-service advertising and promotions agency. The company's primary focus is on print production including package design, FSIs, and coupons for the retail food business. Founded in 1978. **Common positions include:** Advertising Executive; Copywriter; Graphic Designer. **Educational backgrounds include:** Art/Design; Marketing. **Benefits:** 401(k); Dental Insurance; ESOP; Life Insurance; Medical Insurance. **Special programs:** Internships. **President:** Mark Blackwood. **Annual sales/revenues:** $11 - $20 million. **Number of employees at this location:** 45.

BLAIR TELEVISION
1290 Sixth Avenue, New York NY 10104. 212/603-5770. **Contact:** Personnel. **Description:** Provides the media industry with national sales, marketing, and research services. Blair Television represents 140 TV stations and provides services to advertising agency/buying accounts and spot TV advertisers. **Common positions include:** Researcher; Sales Executive. **Educational backgrounds include:** Communications; Liberal Arts; Marketing. **Benefits:** 401(k); Dental Insurance; Disability Coverage; Life Insurance; Medical Insurance. **Corporate headquarters location:** This Location. **Other U.S. locations:** Los Angeles CA; San Francisco CA; Denver CO; Miami FL; Tampa FL; Atlanta GA; Chicago IL; Boston MA; Detroit MI; St. Louis MO; Charlotte NC; Philadelphia PA; Austin TX; Dallas TX; Houston TX; Seattle WA. **Number of employees at this location:** 250. **Number of employees nationwide:** 500.

BLANC & OTUS
4 Embarcadero Center, 8th Floor, San Francisco CA 94111. 415/512-0500. **Contact:** Human Resources. **Description:** A public relations firm that primarily serves the high-tech industry. **Corporate headquarters location:** This Location.

BOZELL WORLDWIDE
40 West 23rd Street, New York NY 10010. 212/727-5000. **Contact:** Personnel Manager. **World Wide Web address:** http://www.bozell.com.

Description: A full-service advertising agency. that also offers public relations services such as corporate relations, marketing support, employee relations, financial relations, government affairs, and community relations. **Corporate headquarters location:** This Location.
Other U.S. locations:
- 625 North Michigan Avenue, Chicago IL 60611. 312/988-2000.

THE BRADFORD GROUP
9333 North Milwaukee Avenue, Niles IL 60714. 847/966-2770. **Contact:** Lisa Prazuch, Recruiter. **Description:** An international direct marketing company specializing in fine arts and collectibles. **NOTE:** Entry-level positions are offered. **Common positions include:** Customer Service Rep.; Designer; Market Research Analyst; Marketing Specialist. **Educational backgrounds include:** Art; Marketing. **Benefits:** 401(k); Dental Insurance; Disability Coverage; Employee Discounts; Life Insurance; Medical Insurance; Profit Sharing; Tuition Assistance. **Special programs:** Internships. **Corporate headquarters location:** This Location. **Number of employees nationwide:** 1,000.

BRAND FUSION
601 California Street, Suite 1501, San Francisco CA 94108. 415/433-8200. **Contact:** Personnel. **Description:** A public relations firm that serves the banking, law, and public service fields. **Corporate headquarters location:** This Location.

BURGESS ADVERTISING ASSOCIATES
1290 Congress Street, Portland ME 04102-2150. 207/775-5227. **Contact:** Human Resources. **Description:** Offers a complete range of advertising services from print to television. **Company slogan:** Advertising that works. **Benefits:** Dental Insurance; Disability Coverage; Life Insurance; Medical Insurance. **Corporate headquarters location:** This Location. **Number of employees at this location:** 15.

BURKE GIBSON INC.
702 Third Street SW, Auburn WA 98001. 253/735-4444. **Contact:** Human Resources. **World Wide Web address:** http://www.burkegibsoninc.com. **Description:** Designs and manufactures point-of-purchase advertising displays for retail and warehouse sales. **Corporate headquarters location:** This Location.

BURSON-MARSTELLER
230 Park Avenue South, New York NY 10003. 212/614-4000. **Contact:** Personnel. **World Wide Web address:** http://www.bm.com. **Description:** A public relations agency. **Common positions include:** Public Relations Specialist. **Educational backgrounds include:** Communications; Liberal Arts; Marketing. **Benefits:** 401(k); Dental Insurance; Disability Coverage; Life Insurance; Medical Insurance; Tuition Assistance. **Special programs:** Internships. **Corporate headquarters location:** This Location. **Other U.S. locations:** Los Angeles CA; Sacramento CA; San Diego CA; San Francisco CA; Washington DC; Miami FL; Chicago IL; Pittsburgh PA; Dallas TX. **Subsidiaries include:** Cohn & Wolfe, Public Relations. **Parent company:** Young & Rubicam, Inc. **Number of employees at this location:** 350. **Number of employees worldwide:** 2,000.

CAMPBELL-EWALD COMPANY
30400 Van Dyke, Warren MI 48093. 810/574-3400. **Contact:** Personnel. **Description:** An advertising agency. **Common positions include:** Account Representative; Art Director; Buyer; Copywriter; Marketing Specialist; Media Specialist; Technical Writer. **Educational backgrounds include:** Business Administration; Liberal Arts; Marketing. **Benefits:** Dental Insurance; Disability Coverage; Life Insurance; Medical Insurance; Savings Plan; Stock Option; Tuition Assistance. **Corporate headquarters location:** This Location. **Other U.S. locations:** Los Angeles CA; New York NY. **Parent company:** The Interpublic Group of Companies, Inc. **Operations at this facility include:** Administration; Service. **Number of employees at this location:** 800.

CARLSON COMPANIES, INC.
CARLSON MARKETING GROUP
P.O. Box 59159, Minneapolis MN 55459-8246. 612/540-5000. **Contact:** Mr. Vern Lovstad, Human Resources. **World Wide Web address:** http://www.carlson.com. **Description:** A diversified corporation doing business through a variety of subsidiaries. Business areas include hotels, restaurant operations, and retail and wholesale travel. Carlson Marketing Group (also at this location) provides a variety of marketing services for sporting events and airlines; incentive programs for employees of other companies; and strategic consulting services to help client companies create customer/brand loyalty. **Corporate headquarters location:** This Location. **Number of employees nationwide:** 50,000.

CARMICHAEL-LYNCH ADVERTISING
800 Hennepin Avenue, Minneapolis MN 55403. 612/334-6000. **Fax:** 612/334-6171. **Contact:** Julie Sprint, Personnel Director. **Description:** A full-service advertising agency that offers services including direct marketing, public relations, new media design, and market research. Founded in 1962. **NOTE:** Entry-level positions are offered. **Common positions include:** Account Manager; Account Rep.; Accountant; Administrative Assistant; Art Director; Graphic Designer; Market Research Analyst; Production Manager; Public Relations Specialist; Secretary. **Educational backgrounds include:** Accounting; Advertising; Art; Communications; Journalism; Marketing; Public Relations. **Benefits:** 401(k); Dental Insurance; Disability Coverage; Employee Discounts; Flexible Dependent Care; Life Insurance; Medical Insurance; Pension Plan; Profit Sharing; Savings Plan; Tuition Assistance. **Special programs:** Internships; Training. **Corporate headquarters location:** This Location. **Operations at this facility include:** Administration; Research and Development; Service. **Annual sales/revenues:** More than $100 million. **Number of employees at this location:** 200.

CATALINA MARKETING CORPORATION
11300 Ninth Street North, St. Petersburg FL 33716. 727/579-5000. **Contact:** Human Resources. **World Wide Web address:** http://www.catmktg.com. **Description:** Provides marketing services for consumer product manufacturers and supermarket retailers. The company's point-of-scan electronic marketing network delivers checkout coupons to consumers at supermarket checkouts based on their purchases. The company also provides Internet information on retail grocery promoters. **NOTE:** Entry-level positions are offered. **Common positions include:** Accountant; Clerical Supervisor; Computer Programmer; Customer Service Rep.; Electrical Engineer; Financial Analyst; Human Resources Manager; Market Research Analyst; Purchasing Agent; Systems Analyst. **Educational backgrounds include:** Accounting; Business Administration; Computer Science; Finance; Marketing. **Benefits:** 401(k); Dental Insurance; Disability Coverage; Life Insurance; Medical Insurance; Savings Plan. **Corporate headquarters location:** This Location. **Other U.S. locations:**

Nationwide. **Subsidiaries include:** Catalina Electronic Clearing Services; Health Resource Publishing Company. **Operations at this facility include:** Administration; Divisional Headquarters. **Listed on:** New York Stock Exchange. **Annual sales/revenues:** $51 - $100 million. **Number of employees at this location:** 170. **Number of employees worldwide:** 550.

CERRELL ASSOCIATES, INC.
320 North Larchmont Boulevard, 2nd Floor, Los Angeles CA 90004. 323/466-3445. **Contact:** Human Resources. **Description:** A public relations company specializing in local public affairs, issues management, and political campaigning. **Common positions include:** Account Manager; Secretary. **Benefits:** 401(k); Life Insurance; Medical Insurance; Profit Sharing. **Special programs:** Internships. **Corporate headquarters location:** This Location.

CITIGATE DEWE ROGERSON, INC.
1440 Broadway, 16th Floor, New York NY 10018. 212/688-6840. **Fax:** 212/838-3393. **Contact:** Jody Johnson, Director of Human Resources. **E-mail address:** jjohnson@dewerogerson.com. **World Wide Web address:** http://www.dewerogerson.com. **Description:** A public relations agency specializing in financial communications, market research, media relations, and shareholder intelligence. **NOTE:** Entry-level positions are offered. **Common positions include:** Account Rep.; Administrative Assistant; Fund Manager; Graphic Artist; Graphic Designer; Marketing Manager; Marketing Specialist; Multimedia Designer; Online Content Specialist; Public Relations Specialist. **Educational backgrounds include:** Communications; Finance; Marketing; Public Relations. **Benefits:** 401(k); Dental Insurance; Disability Coverage; Financial Planning Assistance; Life Insurance; Medical Insurance; Pension Plan; Tuition Assistance. **Special programs:** Internships. **Corporate headquarters location:** This Location. **International locations:** China; England; India; Japan. **Parent company:** Incepta Group plc. **Listed on:** Privately held. **Number of employees at this location:** 90. **Number of employees worldwide:** 300.

CLARION MARKETING & COMMUNICATIONS
Greenwich Office Park, Building 5, Greenwich CT 06831. 203/862-6000. **Contact:** Personnel. **World Wide Web address:** http://www.clarionmarketing.com. **Description:** Provides marketing services in the promotion, direct, interactive, brand communications, sports, and consulting areas. **Corporate headquarters location:** This Location.

CLARKE & COMPANY
535 Boylston Street, 8th Floor, Boston MA 02116. 617/536-3003. **Recorded jobline:** 617/867-2299. **Contact:** Personnel. **World Wide Web address:** http://www.clarkeco.com. **Description:** A public relations agency. **Common positions include:** Public Relations Specialist. **Educational backgrounds include:** Communications; Journalism; Liberal Arts; Public Relations. **Benefits:** 401(k); Dental Insurance; Disability Coverage; Medical Insurance; Tuition Assistance. **Special programs:** Internships. **Corporate headquarters location:** This Location. **Number of employees at this location:** 50.

COLLE & McVOY MARKETING
8500 Normandale Lake Boulevard, Suite 2400, Bloomington MN 55437. 952/897-7500. **Contact:** Elizabeth Laseski, Recruiting Manager. **World Wide Web address:** http://www.collemcvoy.com. **Description:** An advertising agency. Founded in 1935. **Company slogan:** Connect/compel. **Common positions include:** Accountant; Administrative Assistant; Advertising Clerk; Advertising Executive; Bank Officer; CFO; Computer Support Technician; Computer Technician; Content Developer; Controller; Database Manager; Desktop Publishing Specialist; Event Planner; Graphic Artist; Graphic Designer; Help-Desk Technician; Human Resources Manager; Internet Services Manager; Intranet Developer; Market Research Analyst; Marketing Specialist; Media Planner; MIS Manager; Multimedia Designer; Public Relations Specialist; Systems Analyst; Technical Writer; Video Production Coordinator; Web Advertising Specialist; Webmaster; Website Developer. **Educational backgrounds include:** Accounting; Art; ASP; Business Administration; Communications; Computer Science; Economics; HTML; Internet Development; Java; Liberal Arts; Marketing; MBA; Microsoft Office; Microsoft Word; Public Relations; Visual Basic. **Benefits:** 401(k); Casual Dress - Daily; Dental Insurance; Disability Coverage; Flexible Schedule; Medical Insurance; Profit Sharing; Relocation Assistance; Savings Plan; Sick Days (6 - 10); Telecommuting; Tuition Assistance; Vacation Days (10 - 20). **Office hours:** Monday - Friday, 8:00 a.m. - 5:00 p.m. **Subsidiaries include:** Sable Advertising Systems. **Parent company:** MDC Corporation. **CEO:** Jim Bergeson. **Annual sales/revenues:** $21 - $50 million. **Number of employees at this location:** 280. **Number of projected hires for 2000 - 2001 at this location:** 50.

COMMONWEALTH CREATIVE ASSOCIATES
345 Union Avenue, Framingham MA 01702. 508/620-6664. **Contact:** Personnel. **Description:** A full-service advertising agency. **Common positions include:** Art Director; Graphic Artist. **Educational backgrounds include:** Art/Design. **Benefits:** 401(k); Dental Insurance; Medical Insurance; Profit Sharing. **Corporate headquarters location:** This Location. **Operations at this facility include:** Administration; Sales. **Listed on:** Privately held. **Number of employees at this location:** 10.

CONNECT PUBLIC RELATIONS
80 East 100 North, Provo UT 84606. 801/373-7888. **Fax:** 801/373-8680. **Contact:** Personnel. **E-mail address:** info@connectpr.com. **World Wide Web address:** http://www.connectpr.com. **Description:** A public relations and marketing firm with clients in the computer networking field. Founded in 1990. **Common positions include:** Accountant; Administrative Assistant; Administrative Manager; Computer Engineer; Computer Support Technician; Computer Technician; Database Administrator; Database Manager; Event Planner; Human Resources Manager; Public Relations Specialist; Secretary. **Benefits:** 401(k); Casual Dress - Daily; Dental Insurance; Flexible Schedule; Life Insurance; Medical Insurance; Profit Sharing; Sick Days (1 - 5); Vacation Days (10 - 20). **Special programs:** Internships. **Corporate headquarters location:** This Location. **Other U.S. locations:** San Francisco CA. **Listed on:** Privately held. **Number of employees at this location:** 30.

CONTINENTAL PROMOTION GROUP
7405 East Monte Cristo Avenue, Scottsdale AZ 85260. 480/606-9300. **Toll-free phone:** 800/554-9838. **Fax:** 480/606-4314. **Contact:** Personnel. **World Wide Web address:** http://www.cpginc.com. **Description:** Provides promotional services including rebate offers, sweepstakes, and premium fulfillment. Founded in 1989. **Corporate headquarters location:** This Location. **International locations:** Canada; United Kingdom.

COOK MARKETING COMMUNICATIONS
225 Water Street, Suite 1600, Jacksonville FL 32202. 904/353-3911. **Contact:** Personnel. **World Wide Web address:** http://www.cookmc.com. **Description:** An advertising and public relations firm. **Common positions include:** Account Rep.; Advertising Clerk; Art Director; Commercial Artist; Copywriter; Marketing Specialist; Media Specialist; Public Relations Specialist. **Educational backgrounds include:** Advertising; Art/Design; Business Administration; Communications; Marketing; Public Relations. **Benefits:** 401(k); Dental Insurance; Disability Coverage; Life Insurance; Medical Insurance; Stock Option. **Special programs:** Internships. **Corporate headquarters location:** This Location. **Other U.S. locations:** Charlotte NC. **Listed on:** Privately held.

CRANFORD JOHNSON ROBINSON WOODS
Capitol Center, 303 West Capitol Avenue, Little Rock AR 72201. 501/376-6251. **Contact:** Fran Fields, Vice President of Human Resources. **E-mail address:** fran.fields@cjrw.com. **World Wide Web address:** http://www.cjrw.com. **Description:** A full-service advertising agency. **Common positions include:** Administrative Assistant; Art Director; Copywriter; Media Buyer; Public Relations Manager. **Number of employees at this location:** 90. **Number of employees nationwide:** 140.

CUNNINGHAM COMMUNICATION, INC.
1510 Page Mill Road, Palo Alto CA 94304. 650/858-3700. **Contact:** Human Resources. **World Wide Web address:** http://www.cunningham.com. **Description:** A public relations agency specializing in the high-tech field. **Common positions include:** Management Analyst; PR Specialist. **Educational backgrounds include:** Communications; English; Journalism; Marketing. **Benefits:** 401(k); Daycare Assistance; Dental Insurance; Disability Coverage; Employee Discounts; Life Insurance; Medical Insurance; Profit Sharing; Tuition Assistance. **Corporate headquarters location:** This Location. **Other U.S. locations:** Cambridge MA; Austin TX. **Operations at this facility include:** Administration; Service. **Listed on:** Privately held. **Number of employees at this location:** 55. **Number of employees nationwide:** 80.

CUSHMAN/AMBERG COMMUNICATIONS
180 North Michigan Avenue, Suite 1600, Chicago IL 60601. 312/263-2500. **Contact:** Thomas Amberg. **World Wide Web address:** http://www.cushmanpr.com. **Description:** A public relations agency. **Common positions include:** Public Relations Specialist. **Educational backgrounds include:** Communications; Public Relations. **Corporate headquarters location:** This Location.

CYRK, INC.
3 Pond Road, Gloucester MA 01930. 978/283-5800. **Fax:** 978/282-0639. **Contact:** Frank White, Employment Marketing Manager. **E-mail address:** employment@cyrk.com. **World Wide Web address:** http://www.cyrk.com. **Description:** Cyrk Designs, develops, manufactures, and distributes products for promotional programs. The company also provides integrated marketing services to national and international clients. **Common positions include:** Account Manager; Account Rep.; Accountant; Administrative Assistant; Budget Analyst; Credit Manager; Customer Service Rep.; Desktop Publishing Specialist; Financial Analyst; Graphic Artist; Graphic Designer; Marketing Manager; Marketing Specialist; Purchasing Agent; Secretary. **Educational backgrounds include:** Accounting; Art; Business Administration; Finance; Marketing. **Benefits:** 401(k); Casual Dress - Daily; Dental Insurance; Employee Discounts; Life

Insurance; Medical Insurance; Savings Plan. **Corporate headquarters location:** This Location. **Other U.S. locations:** Nationwide. **Annual sales/revenues:** More than $100 million.

DDB NEEDHAM WORLDWIDE, INC.
437 Madison Avenue, New York NY 10022. 212/415-2000. **Contact:** Wendy Raye, Personnel Manager. **World Wide Web address:** http://www.ddbn.com. **Description:** A full-service, international advertising agency. **Common positions include:** Advertising Executive; Media Specialist. **Educational backgrounds include:** Business Administration; Marketing. **Benefits:** 401(k); Dental Insurance; Disability Coverage; Life Insurance; Medical Insurance; Profit Sharing; Tuition Assistance. **Special programs:** Internships. **Corporate headquarters location:** This Location. **Other U.S. locations:** Los Angeles CA; Chicago IL. **Parent company:** Omnicom Group (also at this location, 212/415-3600) is a holding company that provides advertising, marketing, media buying, and interactive media services through its subsidiaries. **Number of employees at this location:** 400.

DAILEY & ASSOCIATES ADVERTISING
8687 Melrose Avenue, Suite G300, West Hollywood CA 90069. 310/360-3100. **Contact:** Jean Anne Hutchinson, Director of Personnel Administration. **World Wide Web address:** http://www.daileyads.com. **Description:** A full-service advertising agency.

DAVISELEN
865 South Figueroa Street, 12th Floor, Los Angeles CA 90017. 213/688-7000. **Fax:** 213/688-7288. **Contact:** Personnel. **World Wide Web address:** http://www.daviselen.com. **Description:** A full-service advertising agency. **NOTE:** Entry-level positions are offered. **Common positions include:** Administrative Assistant; Advertising Clerk; Buyer; Computer Operator; MIS Specialist. **Educational backgrounds include:** Advertising. **Special programs:** Internships. **Corporate headquarters location:** This Location. **Other U.S. locations:** Phoenix AZ; San Francisco CA; Portland OR.

DAWSON MARKETING GROUP
390 Main Street, Suite 200, Woburn MA 01801. 781/933-8855. **Fax:** 781/933-1155. **Contact:** Karen Heidenrich, Vice President of Personnel. **World Wide Web address:** http://www.dawsonmarketing.com. **Description:** An advertising and marketing consulting firm. The company offers services in market and strategic planning, creative support, advertising in all types of media, public relations, trade show and exhibit management, and special events planning. Founded in 1988. **NOTE:** Entry-level positions are offered. **Common positions include:** Account Manager; Account Rep.; Administrative Assistant; Advertising Executive; Event Planner; Graphic Artist; Graphic Designer; Marketing Specialist; Public Relations Specialist. **Educational backgrounds include:** Art/Design; Communications; Liberal Arts; Marketing; Public Relations. **Benefits:** Flexible Schedule; Job Sharing; Medical Insurance; Profit Sharing; Telecommuting. **Special programs:** Co-ops; Internships; Summer Jobs. **Corporate headquarters location:** This Location. **President:** James F. Dawson.

DECISION ANALYST, INC.
604 Avenue H East, Arlington TX 76011. 817/640-6166. **Fax:** 817/640-6567. **Contact:** Personnel. **World Wide Web address:** http://www.decisionanalyst.com. **Description:** A market research and consulting firm offering product testing, tracking research, and Internet surveys. **Corporate headquarters location:** This Location.

DIALAMERICA MARKETING INC.
2952 East Covenater Drive, Bloomington IN 47401. 812/332-2628. **Fax:** 812/333-7238. **Contact:** Jason Kaylor, Employment Coordinator. **World Wide Web address:** http://www.dialamerica.com/ bloomington. **Description:** A full-service marketing firm. **Common positions include:** Administrative Manager; Assistant Manager; Branch Manager; Clerical Supervisor; Management Trainee; Sales Representative. **Educational backgrounds include:** Business Administration; Communications; Education; Liberal Arts; Marketing; Microsoft Office; Microsoft Word; Public Relations; Spreadsheets. **Benefits:** 401(k); Dental Insurance; Life Insurance; Medical Insurance; Tuition Assistance. **Office hours:** Monday - Friday, 8:00 a.m. - 10:00 p.m. **Corporate headquarters location:** Mahwah NJ. **Other U.S. locations:** Nationwide. **Listed on:** Privately held. **Facilities Manager:** Mike Patton. **Sales Manager:** Becky Gerhardt. **Number of employees at this location:** 300. **Number of employees nationwide:** 12,000.

DIMAC DIRECT COMMUNICATIONS
One Corporate Woods Drive, Bridgeton MO 63044. 314/344-8000. **Fax:** 314/209-5637. **Contact:** Doreen Nersesian, Employee Relations. **World Wide Web address:** http://www.dimac.com. **Description:** Provides direct marketing programs including direct mail advertising and sales promotions. **Common positions include:** Advertising Executive; Computer Programmer; Copywriter; Graphic Artist; Systems Analyst. **Educational backgrounds include:** Communications; Computer Science; Marketing. **Benefits:** 401(k); Dental Insurance; Disability Coverage; Life Insurance; Medical Insurance; Tuition Assistance. **Special programs:** Internships. **Corporate headquarters location:** This Location. **Other U.S. locations:** Hayward CA; Los Angeles CA; Boston MA; Farmington NY; New York NY. **Parent company:** Dimac Corporation. **Operations at this facility include:** Service. **Number of employees at this location:** 700. **Number of employees nationwide:** 2,600.

DOE-ANDERSON ADVERTISING
620 West Main Street, Louisville KY 40202. 502/589-1700. **Fax:** 502/587-8349. **Contact:** Crystal L. Graham, Personnel Manager. **E-mail address:** cgraham@doeanderson.com. **World Wide Web address:** http://www.doeanderson.com. **Description:** A full-service advertising and public relations agency. Founded in 1915. **NOTE:** Entry-level positions are offered. **Common positions include:** Accountant; Advertising Executive; Computer Programmer; Graphic Artist; Graphic Designer; Personnel Manager; Production Manager; Public Relations Specialist; Webmaster. **Educational backgrounds include:** Art/Design; Communications; Computer Science; Marketing; Public Relations. **Benefits:** 401(k); Disability Coverage; Life Insurance; Medical Insurance; Profit Sharing. **Special programs:** Internships. **Corporate headquarters location:** This Location. **Annual sales/revenues:** $51 - $100 million. **Number of employees at this location:** 110.

R.H. DONNELLEY
One Manhattanville Road, Purchase NY 10577. 914/933-6800. **Contact:** Human Resources. **World Wide Web address:** http://www.rhdonnelley.com. **Description:** Engaged in selling advertising space in 500 Yellow Pages directories and also provides telemarketing services. **Common positions include:** Accountant; Claim Rep.; Commercial Artist; Computer Programmer; Credit Manager; Customer Service Rep.; Department Manager; Draftsperson; Financial Analyst; General Manager; Human Resources Manager; Marketing Specialist; Operations Manager; Purchasing Agent; Sales Rep.; Systems Analyst. **Educational backgrounds include:** Accounting; Art; Business Administration; Communications; Computer Science; Economics; Finance; Liberal Arts; Marketing; Sales. **Benefits:** Dental Insurance; Disability Coverage; Life Insurance; Medical Insurance; Pension Plan; Profit Sharing; Savings Plan; Tuition Assistance. **Corporate headquarters location:** This Location.

DOREMUS & COMPANY, INC.
200 Varick Street, 11th Floor, New York NY 10014. 212/366-3000. **Contact:** Human Resources. **World Wide Web address:** http://www.doremus.com. **Description:** An advertising agency specializing in corporate and financial advertising. Founded in 1903. **NOTE:** Entry-level positions are offered. **Common positions include:** Advertising Executive; Graphic Artist; Sales Executive. **Educational backgrounds include:** Accounting; Art/Design; Business Administration; Finance; Liberal Arts; Marketing. **Benefits:** 401(k); Dental Insurance; Disability Coverage; Life Insurance; Medical Insurance; Profit Sharing. **Special programs:** Internships. **Corporate headquarters location:** This Location. **Other U.S. locations:** San Francisco CA. **International locations:** London, England; Tokyo, Japan. **Parent company:** Omnicom Group. **Annual sales/revenues:** More than $100 million. **Number of employees at this location:** 100.

THE DOZIER COMPANY
P.O. Box 565125, Dallas TX 75356. 214/744-2800. **Fax:** 214/744-1240. **Contact:** Human Resources. **Description:** A full-service advertising and public relations agency. Founded in 1987. **Common positions include:** Administrative Assistant; Advertising Clerk; Advertising Executive; Editor; Editorial Assistant; Graphic Artist; Graphic Designer; Marketing Manager; Marketing Specialist; Media Planner; Public Relations Specialist; Typist; Web Advertising Specialist. **Educational backgrounds include:** Art/Design; Marketing; Microsoft Word; Public Relations; Publishing; QuarkXPress. **Benefits:** Life Insurance; Medical Insurance. **Special programs:** Internships. **Corporate headquarters location:** This Location. **Number of employees at this location:** 10.

EARLE PALMER BROWN
6400 Goldsboro Road, Suite 500, Bethesda MD 20817. 301/263-2200. **Fax:** 301/263-2357. **Contact:** Personnel. **World Wide Web address:** http://www.epb.com. **Description:** An agency offering advertising, public relations, marketing research, direct marketing, and sales promotion services. **Common positions include:** Account Manager; Account Rep.; Accountant; Advertising Clerk; Artist; Computer Programmer; Copywriter; Financial Analyst; Public Relations Specialist; Systems Analyst. **Educational backgrounds include:** Accounting; Art/Design; Communications; Marketing. **Benefits:** 401(k); Dental Insurance; Disability Coverage; EAP; Employee Discounts; Life Insurance; Medical Insurance; Tuition Assistance; Vision Insurance. **Special programs:** Internships. **Corporate headquarters location:** New York NY. **Operations at this facility include:** Administration. **Listed on:** Privately held. **Number of employees nationwide:** 750. **Other U.S. locations:**
- One South Broad Street, Philadelphia PA 19107. 215/399-2400.

EISNER & ASSOCIATES, INC.
509 South Exeter Street, Baltimore MD 21202. 410/685-3390. **Fax:** 410/843-4471. **Contact:** Sue Holland, Director of Personnel. **Description:** An

advertising and public relations agency. **Common positions include:** Advertising Clerk. **Educational backgrounds include:** Accounting; Art/Design; Business Administration; Communications; Liberal Arts; Marketing. **Benefits:** 401(k); Dental Insurance; Disability Coverage; Life Insurance; Medical Insurance. **Special programs:** Internships. **Corporate headquarters location:** This Location. **Operations at this facility include:** Administration. **Number of employees at this location:** 65.

ENTERTAINMENT PUBLICATIONS, INC.
2125 Butterfield Road, Troy MI 48084. 248/637-8400. **Contact:** Sue Rancilio, Corporate Recruiter. **World Wide Web address:** http://www.entertainment.com. **Description:** Develops and markets discount programs, promotions, and directories. Founded in 1962. **Common positions include:** Accountant; Administrative Manager; Advertising Clerk; Branch Manager; Clerical Supervisor; Computer Programmer; Customer Service Rep.; Editor; General Manager; Human Resources Manager; Library Technician; Management Trainee; Operations Manager; Purchasing Agent; Sales Manager; Services Analyst; Systems Analyst; Technical Writer/Editor. **Educational backgrounds include:** Accounting; Art; Business Administration; Communications; Computer Science; Economics; Finance; Liberal Arts; Marketing. **Benefits:** 401(k); Dental Insurance; Disability Coverage; Employee Discounts; Life Insurance; Medical Insurance; Tuition Assistance; Vision Insurance. **Corporate headquarters location:** This Location. **Parent company:** Cendant Corporation. **Operations at this facility include:** Administration; Sales; Service. **Number of employees at this location:** 300. **Number of employees nationwide:** 1,300.

EURO RSCG TATHAM
36 East Grand Street, Chicago IL 60611. 312/337-4400. **Contact:** Eileen Donahue, Personnel Manager. **Description:** An advertising agency. **Common positions include:** Advertising Executive; Art Director; Computer Programmer; Designer; Media Specialist. **Educational backgrounds include:** Art/Design; Business Administration; Communications. **Benefits:** 401(k); Dental Insurance; Disability Coverage; Employee Discounts; Life Insurance; Medical Insurance; Profit Sharing. **Corporate headquarters location:** This Location. **Operations at this facility include:** Administration; Research and Development; Sales. **Number of employees at this location:** 320.

EXPERIAN
949 West Bond Street, Lincoln NE 68521. 402/475-9541. **Fax:** 402/473-9761. **Recorded jobline:** 800/705-3961. **Contact:** Ruth Liedle, Personnel Representative. **E-mail address:** lincoln.resume@experian.com. **World Wide Web address:** http://www.experian.com. **Description:** A global information solutions company that supplies consumer and business credit, direct marketing, and real estate information services. **NOTE:** Part-time jobs and second and third shifts are offered. **Common positions include:** Account Manager; Account Rep.; Accountant; Administrative Assistant; AS400 Programmer Analyst; CFO; Clerical Supervisor; Computer Operator; Computer Programmer; Computer Support Technician; Computer Technician; Controller; Customer Service Rep.; Database Administrator; Database Manager; Finance Director; Help-Desk Technician; Human Resources Manager; Market Research Analyst; Marketing Manager; Network Administrator; Project Manager; Purchasing Agent; Sales Executive; Sales Manager; Sales Rep.; SQL Programmer; Systems Analyst; Technical Support

Manager; Vice President of Sales. **Educational backgrounds include:** Accounting; AS400 Certification; Business Administration; C/C++; Computer Science; Finance; HTML; Java; Marketing; Mathematics; MCSE; Microsoft Office; Microsoft Word; Novell; QuarkXPress; SAS Programming; Software Development; Software Tech. Support; Spreadsheets; SQL; Visual Basic. **Benefits:** 401(k); Casual Dress - Fridays; Dental Insurance; Employee Discounts; Flexible Schedule; Life Insurance; Medical Insurance; Pension Plan; Savings Plan; Tuition Assistance; Vacation Days. **Special programs:** Internships. **Office hours:** Monday - Friday, 8:00 a.m. - 5:00 p.m. **Corporate headquarters location:** Orange CA. **Other U.S. locations:** Nationwide. **International locations:** Worldwide. **Parent company:** The Great Universal Stores. **Operations at this facility include:** Sales. **Listed on:** New York Stock Exchange. **President:** Mac Rodgers. **Number of employees nationwide:** 7,500. **Number of employees worldwide:** 12,000.

THE FIELD COMPANIES
P.O. Box 78, Watertown MA 02472. 617/926-5550. **Physical address:** 385 Pleasant Street, Watertown MA. **Fax:** 617/924-9011. **Contact:** Mr. J. McDonald, Personnel Representative. **Description:** Provides direct mail services such as list procurement and post office delivery. **NOTE:** Entry-level positions are offered. **Common positions include:** Account Manager; Computer Operator; Customer Service Rep.; Human Resources Manager; Production Manager; Project Manager; Sales Rep.; Typist. **Benefits:** 401(k); Medical Insurance; Public Transit Available. **Corporate headquarters location:** This Location. **Listed on:** Privately held. **Number of employees at this location:** 70.

FITZGERALD MARKETING COMMUNICATIONS
5950 Hazeltine National Drive, Suite 460, Orlando FL 32811. 407/251-1020. **Fax:** 407/251-1042. **Contact:** Personnel Director. **Description:** A full-service advertising and public relations agency that specializes in business-to-business marketing communications for the high-tech industry. **Common positions include:** Account Manager; Account Rep.; Accountant; Administrative Assistant; Advertising Executive; Graphic Artist; Graphic Designer; Production Manager; Public Relations Specialist; Technical Writer. **Educational backgrounds include:** Art; Communications; Marketing; Public Relations. **Benefits:** 401(k); Dental Insurance; Medical Insurance; Profit Sharing. **Special programs:** Internships. **Corporate headquarters location:** This Location. **Operations at this facility include:** Administration; Sales. **President/Owner:** Bernie Fitzgerald.

FOOTE, CONE & BELDING
733 Front Street, San Francisco CA 94111. 415/820-8000. **Fax:** 415/820-8456. **Contact:** Eileen McCarthy, Personnel Manager. **E-mail address:** sf-resume@fcb.com. **World Wide Web address:** http://www.fcbsf.com. **Description:** One of the five largest marketing agencies in the world. Foote Cone & Belding develops integrated marketing campaigns for a broad range of clients. The firm offers additional services such as merchandising, product research, package design, e-business marketing, direct marketing, sports marketing, and events marketing. **NOTE:** Entry-level positions are offered. **Common positions include:** Accountant; Administrative Assistant; Advertising Clerk; Advertising Executive; AS400 Programmer Analyst; Attorney; Auditor; CFO; Computer Support Technician; Content Developer; Controller; Database Administrator; Database Manager; Event Planner; Finance Director; Financial Analyst;

General Manager; Graphic Designer; Help-Desk Technician; Human Resources Manager; Industrial Engineer; Internet Services Manager; Intranet Developer; Market Research Analyst; Media Planner; MIS Specialist; Multimedia Designer; Network Engineer; Software Engineer; Systems Analyst; Systems Manager; Video Production Coordinator; Web Advertising Specialist; Webmaster; Website Developer. **Educational backgrounds include:** Accounting; Art/Design; AS400 Certification; ASP; Business Administration; C/C++; CGI; Communications; Economics; Finance; HTML; Internet Development; Java; Liberal Arts; Marketing; Mathematics; MBA; Microsoft Office; Microsoft Word; QuarkXPress. **Benefits:** 401(k); Casual Dress - Daily; Dental Insurance; Disability Coverage; Employee Discounts; Financial Planning Assistance; Flexible Schedule; Life Insurance; Medical Insurance; Pension Plan; Profit Sharing; Public Transit Available; Relocation Assistance; Savings Plan; Telecommuting; Tuition Assistance. **Special programs:** Internships; Training. **Corporate headquarters location:** Chicago IL. **Other U.S. locations:** Nationwide. **Parent company:** True North Communications. **Chairman and CEO:** Geoff Thompson. **Number of employees at this location:** 400.

FRANCO PUBLIC RELATIONS GROUP
400 Renaissance Center, Suite 1050, Detroit MI 48243. 313/567-2300. **Contact:** Controller. **World Wide Web address:** http://www.franco.com. **Description:** A full-service public relations firm. **Common positions include:** Graphic Artist; Public Relations Specialist; Video Producer. **Educational backgrounds include:** Art; Communications; Marketing. **Benefits:** 401(k); Dental Insurance; Disability Coverage; Life Insurance; Medical Insurance; Profit Sharing. **Special programs:** Internships. **Corporate headquarters location:** This Location. **Subsidiaries include:** Brightlines Creative; The Comark Group Inc.

GCI GROUP
188 The Embarcadero, 5th Floor, San Francisco CA 94105. 415/974-6200. **Fax:** 415/974-6226. **Contact:** Personnel. **World Wide Web address:** http://www.gcigroup.com. **Description:** A high-tech public relations firm. **Corporate headquarters location:** New York NY.

GCI KAMER SINGER
74 New Montgomery Street, Suite 450, San Francisco CA 94105. 415/512-6800. **Fax:** 415/512-6875. **Contact:** Human Resources. **World Wide Web address:** http://www.kamersinger.com. **Description:** A public relations firm.

GE FINANCIAL ASSURANCE PARTNERSHIP MARKETING
200 North Martingale Road, Schaumburg IL 60173. 847/605-3000. **Contact:** Personnel. **Description:** One of the largest telemarketing and direct mail companies. The company offers retail, wholesale, enhancement, and employee assistance and benefit programs. The company also markets several auto, dental, and legal services plans. **Common positions include:** Accountant; Administrative Worker; Customer Service Rep.; Marketing Specialist; Travel Agent. **Benefits:** 401(k); Dental Insurance; Disability Coverage; Life Insurance; Medical Insurance; Tuition Assistance. **Corporate headquarters location:** This Location. **Parent company:** Montgomery Ward & Company, Inc.

GSD&M ADVERTISING
828 West Sixth Street, Austin TX 78703. 512/427-4736. **Contact:** Human Resources. **Description:** An

advertising agency. **Corporate headquarters location:** This Location. **Number of employees at this location:** 300.

GAGE MARKETING GROUP
10000 Highway 55, Minneapolis MN 55441. 612/595-3800. **Contact:** Human Resources. **World Wide Web address:** http://www.gage.com. **Description:** Provides a wide range of integrated marketing services through the following five divisions: Gage Print Services, Gage Marketing Communications, Gage In-Store Marketing, Gage Trade Support Services, and Gage Automotive. **Corporate headquarters location:** This Location. **Other area locations:** Howard Lake MN; Long Lake MN; Maple Plain MN; New Brighton MN; Roseville MN; Wayzata MN. **Other U.S. locations:** Newport Beach CA; Kankakee IL; Plymouth MI; El Paso TX. **International locations:** Mexico.

GARTNERGROUP, INC.
56 Top Gallant Road, Stamford CT 06904. 203/964-0096. **Fax:** 203/316-6436. **Contact:** Pat Moses, Vice President of Personnel. **World Wide Web address:** http://www.gartner.com. **Description:** A market research and consulting firm providing strategic decision support. **Common positions include:** Accountant/Auditor; Administrator; Computer Programmer; Financial Analyst; Human Resources Manager; Marketing Specialist; Systems Analyst; Technical Writer/Editor. **Educational backgrounds include:** Accounting; Business Administration; Computer Science; Liberal Arts. **Benefits:** Dental Insurance; Disability Coverage; Life Insurance; Medical Insurance; Savings Plan; Stock Option; Tuition Assistance. **Special programs:** Internships. **Corporate headquarters location:** This Location. **International locations:** Worldwide. **Operations at this facility include:** Research and Development; Sales.

THE GESSERT GROUP
5369 North 118th Court, Milwaukee WI 53225. 414/466-3400. **Contact:** Personnel Department. **World Wide Web address:** http://www.gessert. com. **Description:** A marketing and multimedia communications company specializing in the health care industry. The company's services also include print work and video production. **Corporate headquarters location:** This Location.

GOLDBERG MARCHESANO PARTNERS
1700 Wisconsin Avenue NW, Washington DC 20007. 202/337-0700. **Fax:** 202/298-3477. **Contact:** Ms. Pat Nordine, Office Manager. **Description:** A full-service advertising agency. **Common positions include:** Account Rep.; Accountant; Administrative Worker; Administrator; Buyer; Commercial Artist; Marketing Specialist; Media Specialist; Operations Manager; Typist. **Educational backgrounds include:** Accounting; Art; Business Administration; Communications; Finance; Liberal Arts; Marketing. **Benefits:** Dental Insurance; Medical Insurance; Pension Plan. **Special programs:** Internships. **Corporate headquarters location:** This Location. **Operations at this facility include:** Administration; Service. **Number of employees at this location:** 50.

GRAY RAMBUSCH, INC.
One Washington Mall, Suite 10, Boston MA 02108-2603. 617/367-0100. **Contact:** Human Resources. **Description:** An advertising firm.

GREY INC.
777 Third Avenue, New York NY 10017. 212/546-2000. **Contact:** Human Resources. **World Wide Web address:** http://www.grey.com. **Description:** A worldwide advertising agency that offers

marketing, consultation, direct response, research, product publicity, public relations, sales promotion, and cooperative advertising services. **Common positions include:** Account Representative; Art Director; Copywriter; Media Specialist; Researcher. **Educational backgrounds include:** Business Administration; Communications; Liberal Arts; Marketing. **Benefits:** Dental Insurance; Employee Discounts; Life Insurance; Medical Insurance; Profit Sharing; Stock Option; Tuition Assistance. **Special programs:** Internships. **Corporate headquarters location:** This Location. **Other U.S. locations:** Los Angeles CA; San Francisco CA. **Subsidiaries include:** GCI-APCO, specializing in public relations; Grey Direct, specializing in direct response marketing; J. Brown/LMC, specializing in cooperative advertising; FOVA, specializing in providing marketing to the Hispanic community; Grey Directory Marketing, specializing in Yellow Pages advertising. **Listed on:** NASDAQ.

HMG WORLDWIDE CORPORATION
475 10th Avenue, 12th Floor, New York NY 10018. 212/736-2300. **Contact:** Personnel. **Description:** Identifies the in-store marketing needs of its clients and integrates research, creative design, engineering, production, package design, and related services into point-of-purchase merchandising display systems. **Corporate headquarters location:** This Location. **Other U.S. locations:** IL; NJ. **Subsidiaries include:** Creative Displays, Inc.; Electronic Voting Systems, Inc.; HMG Europe B.V.; HMG Worldwide In-Store Marketing, Inc.; Intermark Corporation.

HARTE-HANKS, INC.
P.O. Box 269, San Antonio TX 78291-0269. 210/829-9000. **Contact:** Carolyn Oatman, Director of Human Resources. **World Wide Web address:** http://www.harte-hanks.com. **Description:** Provides direct marketing services for various companies and publishes a weekly shopping guide. **Corporate headquarters location:** This Location.

THE HIBBERT GROUP
400 Pennington Avenue, Trenton NJ 08618. 609/394-7500. **Fax:** 609/392-5946. **Contact:** Jennifer Robinson, Personnel Administrator. **Description:** Offers direct marketing services including literature fulfillment, data services, telemarketing, and direct mail. **Educational backgrounds include:** Computer Science; Marketing. **Benefits:** 401(k); Disability Coverage; Employee Discounts; Life Insurance; Medical Insurance; Tuition Assistance. **Corporate headquarters location:** This Location. **Other U.S. locations:** Denver CO. **Number of employees nationwide:** 600.

HILL AND KNOWLTON INC.
466 Lexington Avenue, 3rd Floor, New York NY 10017. 212/885-0300. **Contact:** Sharon James, Personnel Director. **World Wide Web address:** http://www.hillandknowlton.com. **Description:** One of the largest public relations/public affairs counseling firms in the world. **Corporate headquarters location:** This Location. **Other U.S. locations:** San Francisco CA; Washington DC. **International locations:** Worldwide.

HOLLAND MARK EDMUND INGALLS
312 Stuart Street, Boston MA 02116. 617/295-7000. **Fax:** 617/295-7514. **Contact:** Personnel. **World Wide Web address:** http://www.ingallsboston.com. **Description:** A full-service marketing agency.

THE HORN GROUP, INC.
612 Howard Street, Suite 100, San Francisco CA 94105. 415/905-4000. **Fax:** 415/905-4001.

Contact: Jennifer Logan, Director of Training. **World Wide Web address:** http://www.horngroup.com. **Description:** A public relations firm that focuses on the high-tech industry. **NOTE:** Entry-level positions are offered. **Company slogan:** Pride, passion, results. **Common positions include:** Account Manager; Account Rep.; Accountant; Administrative Assistant; Finance Director; Human Resources Manager; MIS Manager; Operations Manager; Public Relations Specialist. **Educational backgrounds include:** Business Administration; Communications; Marketing; Public Relations. **Benefits:** 401(k); Dental Insurance; Disability Coverage; Extensive Vacation; Life Insurance; Medical Insurance; Performance Bonus; Profit Sharing; Public Transit Available; Savings Plan; Tuition Assistance; Vision Insurance. **Special programs:** Internships; Summer Jobs. **Office hours:** Monday - Friday, 8:30 a.m. - 5:30 p.m. **Corporate headquarters location:** This Location. **Other U.S. locations:** Braintree MA. **Number of employees at this location:** 40. **Number of employees nationwide:** 50.

HUSK JENNINGS ADVERTISING
50 North Laura Street, Suite 2600, Jacksonville FL 32202. 904/354-2600. **Fax:** 904/354-7226. **Contact:** Manager. **World Wide Web address:** http://www.huskjennings.com. **Description:** An advertising, marketing, and public relations agency. **Common positions include:** Administrative Manager; Public Relations Specialist. **Educational backgrounds include:** Art/Design; Marketing. **Benefits:** 401(k); Dental Insurance; Life Insurance; Medical Insurance; Profit Sharing. **Corporate headquarters location:** This Location.

ICT GROUP, INC.
800 Town Center Drive, Langhorne PA 19047. 215/757-0200. **Fax:** 215/757-7877. **Contact:** Personnel. **World Wide Web address:** http://www.ictgroup.com. **Description:** A direct marketing agency engaged in telemarketing, customer service, and market research. **Common positions include:** Branch Manager; Computer Programmer; Operations Manager. **Benefits:** 401(k); Dental Insurance; Disability Coverage; Life Insurance; Medical Insurance; Profit Sharing. **Corporate headquarters location:** This Location. **Number of employees nationwide:** 2,140.

THE INTERPUBLIC GROUP OF COMPANIES
1271 Sixth Avenue, New York NY 10020. 212/399-8000. **Contact:** Doris Weil, Director of Corporate Human Resources. **World Wide Web address:** http://www.interpublic.com. **Description:** An advertising agency. The company plans, creates, and implements advertising campaigns in various media through either its own subsidiaries or contracts with local agencies. Other activities include publishing, market research, public relations, product development, and sales promotion. Interpublic's international business groups include McCann-Erickson WorldGroup and The Lowe Group. **Corporate headquarters location:** This Location.

IPSOS-ASI
130 North Brand Boulevard, Suite 300, Glendale CA 91203. 818/637-5600. **Contact:** Personnel Department. **Description:** Conducts market research for manufacturers and distributors. **Corporate headquarters location:** This Location. **Subsidiaries include:** Interconnect Phone Company designs, markets, and installs custom-designed phone communications systems.

JORDAN McGRATH CASE & PARTNERS
110 Fifth Avenue, New York NY 10011. 212/463-1000. **Fax:** 212/463-1096. **Contact:** Christine

Martin, Director of Human Resources. **E-mail address:** cmartin@jmcp.com. **World Wide Web address:** http://www.jmcp.com. **Description:** An advertising agency. Founded in 1980. **NOTE:** Entry-level positions are offered. **Common positions include:** Account Manager; Administrative Assistant; Advertising Executive; Designer; Graphic Artist; Graphic Designer; Market Research Analyst; Video Production Coordinator. **Educational backgrounds include:** Art/Design; Business Administration; Communications; Liberal Arts; Marketing. **Benefits:** 401(k); Dental Insurance; Disability Coverage; Life Insurance; Medical Insurance; Profit Sharing. **Special programs:** Apprenticeships; Internships; Training. **Corporate headquarters location:** This Location. **Operations at this facility include:** Service. **Number of employees at this location:** 330.

KETCHUM
6 PPG Place, Pittsburgh PA 15222. 412/456-3500. **Contact:** Human Resources. **World Wide Web address:** http://www.ketchum.com. **Description:** A public relations and advertising agency that specializes in directory advertising. **Corporate headquarters location:** This Location.
Other U.S. locations:
• 292 Madison Avenue, 11th Floor, New York NY 10017.

LCS DIRECT MARKETING SERVICES
120 Brighton Road, Clifton NJ 07012. 973/778-5588. **Fax:** 973/778-7485. **Contact:** Personnel. **World Wide Web address:** http://www.lcsi.com. **Description:** A direct marketing firm. **Common positions include:** Accountant; Clerical Supervisor; Computer Programmer; Customer Service Rep.; Management Trainee; Systems Analyst. **Educational backgrounds include:** Business Administration; Computer Science; Marketing. **Benefits:** 401(k); Dental Insurance; Disability Coverage; Life Insurance; Medical Insurance; Stock Option. **Corporate headquarters location:** This Location. **Other area locations:** Weehawken NJ. **Other U.S. locations:** Dover DE. **Subsidiaries include:** Catalog Resources Inc.; The SpeciaLISTS. **Operations at this facility include:** Administration; Sales; Service. **Listed on:** NASDAQ. **Number of employees at this location:** 500. **Number of employees nationwide:** 800.

E.B. LANE & ASSOCIATES, INC.
733 West McDowell Road, Phoenix AZ 85007. 602/258-5263. **Contact:** Sharon Thompson, Human Resources Manager. **Description:** A full-service advertising agency specializing in media buying, print media, public relations, radio producing, and television producing. **Corporate headquarters location:** This Location.

LEVLANE ADVERTISING/PR/INTERACTIVE
One Belmont Avenue, Suite 703, Bala-Cynwyd PA 19004. 610/667-7313. **Fax:** 610/667-3176. **Contact:** Shelley Carter, Assistant to the President. **E-mail address:** scarter@levlane.com. **World Wide Web address:** http://www.levlane.com. **Description:** An advertising agency and public relations firm. **NOTE:** Entry-level positions are offered. **Common positions include:** Advertising Executive; Computer Support Technician; Controller; Copywriter; Graphic Designer; Help-Desk Technician; Media Planner; Multimedia Designer; Network Administrator; Public Relations Specialist; Technical Writer; Video Production Coordinator; Web Advertising Specialist; Website Developer. **Educational backgrounds include:** Art/Design; Journalism; Liberal Arts; Marketing; MBA; Microsoft Office; Microsoft Word; Public Relations; QuarkXPress. **Benefits:** 401(k); Casual

Dress - Daily; Dental Insurance; Disability Coverage; Life Insurance; Medical Insurance; Profit Sharing. **Special programs:** Apprenticeships; Internships. **Corporate headquarters location:** This Location. **Other U.S. locations:** Tampa FL. **Annual sales/revenues:** $21 - $50 million. **Number of employees at this location:** 40. **Number of employees nationwide:** 55.

LIGGETT-STASHOWER, INC.
1228 Euclid Avenue, Cleveland OH 44115. 216/348-8500. **Toll-free phone:** 800/877-4573. **Fax:** 216/861-1284. **Contact:** Nancy Disbrow, Vice President/Secretary. **World Wide Web address:** http://www.liggett.com. **Description:** An advertising agency. **President/CEO:** Terrence McGovern.

THE LORD GROUP
20 Cooper Square, 5th Floor, New York NY 10003-7112. 212/780-5400. **Contact:** Human Resources Department. **Description:** An advertising agency specializing in large media campaigns. **Corporate headquarters location:** This Location. **Other U.S. locations:** Los Angeles CA.

LOWE GROB HEALTH & SCIENCE
One Brattle Square, Cambridge MA 02138. 617/876-9300. **Fax:** 617/661-4513. **Contact:** Personnel. **E-mail address:** info@lowegrob.com. **World Wide Web address:** http://www.lowegrob.com. **Description:** Provides advertising, consulting, market research, and public relations services to companies primarily in the biotech, health, medical, and scientific industries. **NOTE:** Entry-level positions are offered. **Common positions include:** Administrative Assistant; Advertising Executive; Graphic Artist; Market Research Analyst; MIS Specialist; Operations Manager; Production Manager; Public Relations Specialist. **Educational backgrounds include:** Art/Design; Business Administration; Health Care; Marketing; Microsoft Word; Public Relations; QuarkXPress. **Benefits:** 401(k); Casual Dress - Daily; Dental Insurance; Disability Coverage; Life Insurance; Medical Insurance; Pension Plan; Savings Plan. **Special programs:** Internships. **Corporate headquarters location:** New York NY. **Annual sales/revenues:** $11 - $20 million.

LYONS LAVEY NICKEL SWIFT INC.
220 East 42nd Street, 3rd Floor, New York NY 10017. 212/771-3000. **Fax:** 212/771-3510. **Contact:** Emilie Kovit, Personnel Manager. **E-mail address:** ekovit@llns.com. **World Wide Web address:** http://www.llns.com. **Description:** An advertising agency for pharmaceutical firms. Founded in 1972. **NOTE:** Entry-level positions are offered. **Common positions include:** Administrative Assistant; Advertising Clerk; Advertising Executive; Art Director; Computer Support Technician; Computer Technician; Copywriter; Customer Service Rep.; Editor; Human Resources Manager; MIS Specialist; Secretary. **Educational backgrounds include:** Art/Design; Biology; Chemistry; Communications; Health Care; Liberal Arts; Marketing. **Benefits:** 401(k); Bonus Award/Plan; Casual Dress - Fridays; Daycare Assistance; Dental Insurance; Disability Coverage; Life Insurance; Medical Insurance; Pension Plan; Profit Sharing; Tuition Assistance. **Special programs:** Summer Jobs. **Office hours:** Monday - Friday, 9:00 a.m. - 5:00 p.m. **Parent company:** Omnicom Group, Inc. **President:** Al Nickel. **Number of employees at this location:** 200.

MBI, INC.
47 Richards Avenue, Norwalk CT 06857. 203/853-2000. **Contact:** Tom Reese, Personnel Manager.

Description: A direct marketing firm for collectibles including coin and stamp sets, porcelain dolls, porcelain plates, and die-cast vehicles. **Common positions include:** Product Manager. **Educational backgrounds include:** Business Administration; Finance; Liberal Arts; Marketing. **Benefits:** Bonus Award/Plan; Dental Insurance; Disability Coverage; Employee Discounts; Life Insurance; Medical Insurance; Pension Plan; Profit Sharing; Tuition Assistance. **Special programs:** Internships. **Corporate headquarters location:** This Location. **Number of employees at this location:** 700.

MZD (MONTGOMERY ZUKERMAN DAVIS)
1800 North Meridian Street, 2nd Floor, Indianapolis IN 46202. 317/924-6271. **Fax:** 317/925-3854. **Contact:** Personnel. **World Wide Web address:** http://www.mzd.com. **Description:** An advertising, strategic marketing, and public relations agency, offering creative planning, Website development, market research, promotional assistance, and a variety of marketing services. MZD also owns Telematrix, an audio and video production company, and offers computer graphics development. **Corporate headquarters location:** This Location. **Other U.S. locations:** Chicago IL.

MARTIN WILLIAMS ADVERTISING INC.
60 South Sixth Street, Suite 2800, Minneapolis MN 55402. 612/340-0800. **Contact:** Tena Murphy, Personnel Director. **World Wide Web address:** http://www.martinwilliams.com. **Description:** An advertising agency. **Common positions include:** Marketing Specialist. **Educational backgrounds include:** Communications; Marketing. **Benefits:** Daycare Assistance; Dental Insurance; Disability Coverage; Life Insurance; Medical Insurance; Profit Sharing; Tuition Assistance. **Special programs:** Internships. **Corporate headquarters location:** This Location.

McCANN-ERICKSON WORLDWIDE
750 Third Avenue, New York NY 10017. 212/697-6000. **Contact:** Donna Borseso, Human Resources. **Description:** An advertising agency. **Corporate headquarters location:** This Location. **Other U.S. locations:** Atlanta GA; Chicago IL; Louisville KY; Houston TX; Seattle WA. **Parent company:** The Interpublic Group of Companies, Inc.

THE MEDICUS GROUP
1675 Broadway, New York NY 10019-5809. 212/468-3100. **Fax:** 212/468-3208. **Contact:** Emilie Schaum, Director of Human Resources. **World Wide Web address:** http://www.medicusgroup.com. **Description:** Markets a wide range of pharmaceutical and consumer health products and services to health care professionals, patients, and consumers. Services include advertising and promotions, direct-to-consumer marketing, interactive media, medical education, public relations, publication planning, and sales training. **NOTE:** Entry-level positions are offered. **Common positions include:** Administrative Assistant; Advertising Executive; Art Director; Copywriter; Graphic Artist; Public Relations Specialist; Technical Writer. **Educational backgrounds include:** Advertising; Art/Design; Biology; Communications; Health Care; Liberal Arts; Marketing; Public Relations. **Benefits:** 401(k); Dental Insurance; Disability Coverage; Life Insurance; Medical Insurance; Pension Plan. **Special programs:** Internships. **Corporate headquarters location:** This Location. **International locations:** Worldwide. **Parent company:** D'Arcy Masius Benton & Bowles (also at this location, 212/468-3622) is an international advertising agency whose other subsidiaries include Brainwaves; Highway

One; Telewest. **Operations at this facility include:** Administration; Regional Headquarters. **Listed on:** Privately held. **CEO:** Glenn DeSimone. **Facilities Manager:** Sandy Smith. **Annual sales/revenues:** $51 - $100 million. **Number of employees worldwide:** 530.

MERCURY PRINT & MAIL
1110 Central Avenue, Pawtucket RI 02861. 401/724-7600. **Fax:** 401/724-9920. **Contact:** Personnel. **World Wide Web address:** http://www.mpmri.com. **Description:** Provides printing and direct mail advertising services. **President/CEO/Owner:** Peter Ottmar. **Facilities Manager:** Dennis Dress. **Information Systems Manager:** Scott Machado.

MILES ADVERTISING, INC.
1936 Market Street, Denver CO 80202. 303/293-9191. **Toll-free phone:** 800/342-8978. **Contact:** Annie Fisher, Controller. **Description:** A full-service advertising agency specializing in residential real estate. Founded in 1986. **NOTE:** Entry-level positions are offered. **Common positions include:** Account Manager; Advertising Executive; Graphic Designer. **Educational backgrounds include:** Art/Design; Marketing; QuarkXPress. **Benefits:** 401(k); Life Insurance; Medical Insurance; Sick Days (1 - 5); Vacation Days (6 - 10). **Special programs:** Internships. **Corporate headquarters location:** This Location. **CEO:** David R. Miles. **Annual sales/revenues:** $11 - $20 million.

MILLWARD BROWN
425 Post Road, Fairfield CT 06430. 203/255-1222. **Fax:** 203/256-5470. **Contact:** Karen Maintanis, Human Resources Manager. **E-mail address:** karen.maintanis@us.millwardbrown.com. **World Wide Web address:** http://www.millwardbrown.com. **Description:** Provides research-based marketing consultancy to assist clients in building profitable brands and e-brands. **President/CEO/Owner:** Rosi Ware. **Facilities Manager:** Terri Leopold. **Sales Manager:** Philip Herr.

MINTZ & HOKE INC.
40 Tower Lane, Avon CT 06001. 860/678-0473. **Fax:** 860/679-9750. **Contact:** Dawn Hassan, Manager of Personnel. **E-mail address:** jobs@mintz-hoke.com. **World Wide Web address:** http://www.mintz-hoke.com. **Description:** An advertising and public relations firm providing advertising creative development and execution; collateral materials development including brochures, packaging, and signage; direct mail/direct marketing; Internet services; market research; marketing communications planning; media planning, negotiating, and trafficking; positioning strategy development; and public relations services. Founded in 1971. **Company slogan:** The Street Smart Agency. **Common positions include:** Administrative Assistant; Advertising Executive; Computer Support Technician; Finance Director; Graphic Artist; Graphic Designer; Human Resources Manager; Market Research Analyst; Public Relations Specialist; Secretary; Systems Manager; Webmaster. **Educational backgrounds include:** Accounting; Art/Design; Business Administration; CGI; Communications; Finance; HTML; Internet; Java; Marketing; Microsoft Word; Novell; Public Relations; QuarkXPress; Software Tech. Support; Spreadsheets. **Benefits:** 401(k); Casual Dress - Daily; Dental Insurance; Disability Coverage; Employee Discounts; Financial Planning Assistance; Flexible Schedule; Life Insurance; Medical Insurance; Pension Plan; Profit Sharing; Telecommuting. **Special programs:** Internships. **Internship information:** Internships are offered for

school credit only in the areas of public relations, graphic design, new business development, and media. **Corporate headquarters location:** This Location. **President:** Chris Knopf. **Number of employees at this location:** 70.

NFO WORLDWIDE, INC.
2 Pickwick Plaza, Greenwich CT 06830. 203/629-8888. **Contact:** Human Resources. **World Wide Web address:** http://www.nfow.com. **Description:** Provides custom and syndicated market research services, primarily using a proprietary panel of pre-recruited consumer households throughout the country. NFO also offers Internet-based custom marketing research. **Benefits:** 401(k); Pension Plan; Retirement Plan. **Corporate headquarters location:** This Location. **Other U.S. locations:** Toledo OH. **Subsidiaries include:** Advanced Marketing Solutions, Inc. (CT) provides custom computer software systems used by clients to quickly access and analyze complex business and consumer information; Payment Systems, Inc. (FL) is a leading supplier of information to the financial services industry in the United States. **Parent company:** The Interpublic Group of Companies, Inc. **Number of employees nationwide:** 770.

THE NPD GROUP, INC.
900 West Shore Road, Port Washington NY 11050. 516/625-0700. **Fax:** 516/625-4866. **Contact:** Personnel. **E-mail address:** hr@npd.com. **World Wide Web address:** http://www.npd.com. **Description:** A market research firm offering a full line of custom and syndicated consumer research services including point-of-sale computerized audits, purchase panels, mail panels, telephone research, mathematical modeling, and consulting. Industries covered include consumer packaged goods, apparel, toys, electronics, automotive, sports, books, and food consumption. **Common positions include:** Account Manager; Administrative Assistant; Administrative Manager; Computer Programmer; Data Entry Clerk; Economist; Researcher; Statistician; Technical Writer/Editor. **Educational backgrounds include:** Business Administration; Computer Science; Data Processing; Liberal Arts; Marketing; Mathematics; Psychology. **Benefits:** Dental Insurance; Disability Coverage; Life Insurance; Medical Insurance; Profit Sharing; Tuition Assistance. **Special programs:** Internships. **Corporate headquarters location:** This Location. **Other U.S. locations:** Chicago IL; Greensboro NC; Cincinnati OH; Houston TX.

NATIONAL FULFILLMENT SERVICES
100 Pine Avenue, Building 4, Holmes PA 19043. 610/532-4700. **Contact:** Personnel. **Description:** A direct marketing service bureau that provides automated fulfillment services. **Common positions include:** Customer Service Rep. **Educational backgrounds include:** Computer Science. **Benefits:** Dental Insurance; Life Insurance; Medical Insurance. **Corporate headquarters location:** This Location. **Operations at this facility include:** Administration; Sales; Service. **Listed on:** Privately held. **Number of employees at this location:** 110.

NIEHAUS RYAN WONG INC.
601 Gateway Boulevard, 9th Floor, South San Francisco CA 94080. 650/615-7900. **Fax:** 650/827-7000. **Contact:** Personnel. **World Wide Web address:** http://www.nrwpr.com. **Description:** A public relations firm that primarily serves high-tech companies. **NOTE:** Entry-level positions are offered. **Common positions include:** Account Manager; Administrative Manager; Operations Manager; Public Relations Specialist. **Educational backgrounds include:** Business Administration; Communications; Computer Science; Liberal Arts;

Marketing; Public Relations. **Benefits:** 401(k); Dental Insurance; Disability Coverage; Life Insurance; Medical Insurance; Tuition Assistance. **Special programs:** Internships; Summer Jobs. **Corporate headquarters location:** This Location. **Number of employees at this location:** 80.

OLSON & COMPANY
126 North Third Street, Suite 200, Minneapolis MN 55401. 612/215-9800. **Contact:** Human Resources. **World Wide Web address:** http://www.oco.com. **Description:** An advertising agency focusing on corporate advertising.

PAN COMMUNICATIONS INC.
300 Brickstone Square, Andover MA 01810. 978/474-1900. **Fax:** 978/474-1903. **Contact:** Personnel Manager. **World Wide Web address:** http://www.pancommunications.com. **Description:** A full-service public relations agency specializing in four portfolios: business-to-business, high-technology, fashion and consumer products, and trade shows. **NOTE:** Entry-level positions offered. **Company slogan:** Partners in public relations. **Common positions include:** Account Manager. **Educational backgrounds include:** Internet; Marketing; Microsoft Office; Microsoft Word; Public Relations. **Benefits:** 401(k); Casual Dress - Daily; Dental Insurance; Disability Coverage; Medical Insurance; Profit Sharing; Tuition Assistance. **Special programs:** Internships. **Corporate headquarters location:** This Location. **President:** Philip A. Nardone, Jr. **Number of employees at this location:** 45.

PORTER NOVELLI CONVERGENCE GROUP
100 First Street, Suite 2600, San Francisco CA 94105. 415/284-5200. **Fax:** 415/975-2285. **Contact:** Personnel. **World Wide Web address:** http://www.pnicg.com. **Description:** A public relations firm primarily serving the high-tech and consumer electronics industries. **Corporate headquarters location:** This Location. **Other U.S. locations:**
• 855 Boylston Street, 8th Floor, Boston MA 02116. 617/450-4300.

PRICEWEBER MARKETING COMMUNICATIONS
2101 Production Drive, Louisville KY 40299. 502/499-9220. **Fax:** 502/491-5593. **Contact:** Personnel. **Description:** An advertising agency.

PUBLISHERS CLEARING HOUSE
382 Channel Drive, Port Washington NY 11050. 516/883-5432. **Contact:** Human Resources. **World Wide Web address:** http://www.pch.com. **Description:** A direct mail marketing company. Publishers Clearing House is one of the largest sources of new magazine subscribers. The company also conducts continuing research to develop effective promotions for other products and services. **Common positions include:** Accountant; Advertising Clerk; Computer Programmer; Customer Service Rep.; Financial Analyst; Industrial Engineer; Marketing Specialist; Systems Analyst. **Educational backgrounds include:** Accounting; Business Administration; Computer Science; Marketing. **Benefits:** Dental Insurance; Disability Coverage; Life Insurance; Medical Insurance; Pension Plan; Tuition Assistance. **Corporate headquarters location:** This Location. **Subsidiaries include:** Campus Subscriptions.

RED7E
637 West Main Street, Louisville KY 40202. 502/585-3403. **Contact:** Personnel. **Description:** Red7e provides a broad range of planning, creative, direct marketing, public relations, sales promotion, production, and media services. Services are

provided to the construction, health care, restaurant, business, financial, and manufacturing industries. **Common positions include:** Accountant/Auditor; Advertising Clerk; Buyer; Public Relations Specialist; Services Sales Representative. **Benefits:** 401(k); Disability Coverage; ESOP; Life Insurance; Medical Insurance. **Special programs:** Internships. **Corporate headquarters location:** This Location. **Number of employees at this location:** 40.

ROBLEY MARKETING INC.
700 SW Taylor, Suite 400, Portland OR 97205. 503/279-4000. **Fax:** 503/279-4066. **Contact:** Personnel. **World Wide Web address:** http://www. robleymarketing.com. **Description:** An advertising, marketing, and public relations agency focusing on a wide range of industries including cable television, retirement homes, and technical services. **Common positions include:** Commercial Artist; Copywriter; Marketing Specialist; Media Buyer; Operations/Production Manager; Public Relations Specialist. **Educational backgrounds include:** Art/Design; Business Administration; Marketing; Public Relations. **Benefits:** 401(k); Dental Insurance; Disability Coverage; Life Insurance; Medical Insurance. **Special programs:** Internships. **Corporate headquarters location:** This Location.

SMZ ADVERTISING
900 Wilshire Drive, Suite 102, Troy MI 48084. 248/362-4242. **Fax:** 248/362-2014. **Contact:** Personnel. **World Wide Web address:** http://www. smz.com. **Description:** Develops and produces advertising and marketing communications materials. **Common positions include:** Account Manager; Account Rep.; Advertising Clerk; Copywriter; Designer; Market Research Analyst; Public Relations Specialist; Typist/Word Processor; Video Production Coordinator. **Educational backgrounds include:** Communications; Liberal Arts; Marketing. **Benefits:** 401(k); Medical Insurance; Profit Sharing. **Special programs:** Internships. **Corporate headquarters location:** This Location. **Operations at this facility include:** Administration; Sales; Service. **Listed on:** Privately held. **Annual sales/revenues:** $21 - $50 million. **Number of employees at this location:** 60.

SAATCHI & SAATCHI ADVERTISING
375 Hudson Street, New York NY 10014. 212/463-2304. **Contact:** Human Resources. **World Wide Web address:** http://www.saatchi-saatchi.com. **Description:** An advertising agency. **Company slogan:** Nothing is impossible. **Office hours:** Monday - Friday, 9:00 a.m. - 5:00 p.m. **Corporate headquarters location:** This Location. **Other U.S. locations:** Nationwide. **Number of employees at this location:** 500.

SADDLE CREEK COPAK CORPORATION
9801 Twin Lakes Parkway, Charlotte NC 28269. 704/875-1996. **Contact:** Human Resources. **Description:** A direct mail advertising agency with a broad range of clients.

SAXTON FERRIS
11900 Wayzata Boulevard, Suite 114, Minnetonka MN 55305. 612/544-9300. **Contact:** June Ferris, General Manager. **World Wide Web address:** http://www.saxton-ferris.com. **Description:** A national Yellow Pages advertising agency. **NOTE:** Entry-level positions are offered. **Common positions include:** Administrative Assistant; Advertising Clerk; Advertising Executive; Customer Service Representative. **Benefits:** 401(k); Casual Dress - Daily; Dental Insurance; Flexible Schedule; Life Insurance; Medical Insurance; Sick Days (1 - 5); Vacation Days (10 - 20). **Corporate headquarters location:** This Location. **Parent**

company: Ferris Marketing, Inc. **Operations at this facility include:** Service. **Number of employees at this location:** 15.

THE SMITH COMPANY
4455 Connecticut Avenue NW, Suite B600, Washington DC 20008. 202/895-0900. **Contact:** Personnel. **Description:** Provides telemarketing services.

SOLEM & ASSOCIATES
550 Kearny Street, Suite 1010, San Francisco CA 94108. 415/788-7788. **Fax:** 415/788-7858. **Contact:** Personnel. **World Wide Web address:** http://www.solem.com. **Description:** A public relations firm that primarily serves the health care, transportation, and government advocacy industries. **Corporate headquarters location:** This Location.

STERLING COMMUNICATIONS, INC.
100 Century Center Court, Suite 400, San Jose CA 95112. 408/441-4100. **Contact:** Personnel. **World Wide Web address:** http://www.sterlingpr.com. **Description:** A public relations firm that provides services to technology-based companies. **Corporate headquarters location:** This Location.

STIRLING & KARBO INC.
110 Marsh Drive, Suite 105, Foster City CA 94404. 650/513-0970. **Fax:** 650/513-0985. **Contact:** Human Resources. **World Wide Web address:** http://www.skco.com. **Description:** A public relations firm. **Corporate headquarters location:** This Location. **President/CEO:** Cynthia L. Stirling.

STONE AND SIMONS ADVERTISING INC.
24245 Northwestern Highway, Southfield MI 48075. 248/358-4800. **Contact:** Human Resources. **Description:** An advertising agency. **Common positions include:** Advertising Clerk; Commercial Artist; Marketing Specialist; Public Relations Specialist. **Educational backgrounds include:** Accounting; Art/Design; Business Administration; Communications; Marketing. **Benefits:** Life Insurance; Medical Insurance; Profit Sharing. **Corporate headquarters location:** This Location. **Operations at this facility include:** Service. **Listed on:** Privately held. **Number of employees at this location:** 40.

SUDLER & HENNESSEY INC.
230 Park Avenue South, New York NY 10003. 212/614-4100. **Contact:** Human Resources. **Description:** An advertising agency. **Corporate headquarters location:** This Location.

SYSTEMAX, INC.
22 Harbor Park Drive, Port Washington NY 11050. 516/625-1555. **Fax:** 516/608-7111. **Contact:** Karen Center, Corporate Recruiter. **World Wide Web address:** http://www.systemax.com. **Description:** A direct marketer of brand name and private label computer, office, and industrial products targeting mid-range and major corporate accounts, small office/home customers, and value-added resellers. Founded in 1949. **NOTE:** Entry-level positions are offered. **Common positions include:** Account Rep.; Accountant; Administrative Assistant; Advertising Executive; Applications Engineer; Auditor; Buyer; Computer Operator; Computer Programmer; Computer Support Technician; Computer Technician; Customer Service Rep.; Database Administrator; Database Manager; Desktop Publishing Specialist; Graphic Artist; Industrial Engineer; Internet Services Manager; Market Research Analyst; Marketing Manager; Marketing Specialist; MIS Specialist; Network Administrator; Sales Representative; Software Engineer; Systems Analyst; Technical Writer; Transportation

Specialist; Webmaster. **Educational backgrounds include:** Accounting; Art/Design; Business Administration; Computer Science; HTML; Java; Marketing; MCSE; Microsoft Word; QuarkXPress; Software Development; Software Tech. Support; Spreadsheets. **Benefits:** 401(k); Casual Dress - Fridays; Dental Insurance; Disability Coverage; Employee Discounts; Flexible Schedule; Life Insurance; Medical Insurance. **Special programs:** Internships; Summer Jobs. **Corporate headquarters location:** This Location. **Other U.S. locations:** CA; FL; GA; IL; NC; NJ; OH. **Subsidiaries include:** Global Computer Supplies; Midwest Micro Corp.; Misco America, Inc.; Misco Canada Inc.; TigerDirect Inc. **Listed on:** New York Stock Exchange. **Annual sales/revenues:** More than $100 million. **Number of employees at this location:** 500. **Number of employees nationwide:** 2,000. **Number of employees worldwide:** 4,200.

J. WALTER THOMPSON COMPANY
466 Lexington Avenue, New York NY 10017. 212/210-7000. **Contact:** Personnel. **World Wide Web address:** http://www.jwt.com. **Description:** A full-service advertising agency. **Corporate headquarters location:** This Location. **Other U.S. locations:** Nationwide. **International locations:** Worldwide. **Parent company:** WPP Group.

TOTAL RESEARCH CORPORATION
5 Independence Way, Princeton NJ 08543. 609/520-9100. **Fax:** 609/987-8839. **Contact:** Jane Giles, Personnel Manager. **E-mail address:** trc@totalres. com. **World Wide Web address:** http://www. totalres.com. **Description:** A full-service marketing research firm that provides information for use in strategic and tactical marketing decisions. **Common positions include:** Administrative Assistant; Applications Engineer; Computer Programmer; Market Research Analyst; Network/Systems Administrator. **Educational backgrounds include:** Marketing; Mathematics. **Benefits:** 401(k); Casual Dress - Daily; Dental Insurance; Disability Coverage; Flexible Schedule; Life Insurance; Medical Insurance; Telecommuting; Tuition Assistance. **Special programs:** Internships. **Corporate headquarters location:** This Location. **Other U.S. locations:** Tampa FL; Chicago IL; Detroit MI; Minneapolis MN; Poughkeepsie NY. **International locations:** London, England. **Listed on:** NASDAQ. **Stock exchange symbol:** TOTL. **Annual sales/revenues:** $21 - $50 million. **Number of employees at this location:** 150. **Number of employees nationwide:** 200. **Number of employees worldwide:** 250.

TULLY-MENARD, INC.
4919 Bayshore Boulevard, Tampa FL 33611. 813/832-6602. **Contact:** Mr. J.E. Tully, President. **Description:** An advertising agency. **NOTE:** Part-time jobs are offered. **Common positions include:** Advertising Executive; Secretary. **Benefits:** Casual Dress - Fridays; Medical Insurance; Sick Days (1 - 5); Vacation Days (6 - 10). **Office hours:** Monday - Friday, 8:30 a.m. - 5:00 p.m. **Corporate headquarters location:** This Location. **Annual sales/revenues:** Less than $5 million.

UPSTART COMMUNICATIONS
6425 Christie Avenue, Suite 300, Emeryville CA 94608. 510/457-3000. **Fax:** 510/457-3010. **Contact:** Human Resources. **World Wide Web address:** http://www.upstart.com. **Description:** A public relations firm. **Corporate headquarters location:** This Location.

UTAH WOOL MARKETING ASSOCIATION
855 South 500 West, Salt Lake City UT 84101. 801/328-1507. **Contact:** James Elliott, Manager.

Description: Provides a variety of marketing and related business and financial services to ranchers, processors, and retailers involved in the production and sale of wool and related products. **Corporate headquarters location:** This Location.

VAL-PAK DIRECT MARKETING
8575 Largo Lakes Drive, Largo FL 33773. 727/399-3189. **Toll-free phone:** 800/237-2871. **Fax:** 727/399-3085. **Recorded jobline:** 727/399-3012. **Contact:** LaToy Black, Recruiting Specialist. **E-mail address:** latoy_black@valpak.com. **World Wide Web address:** http://www.valpak.com. **Description:** An international direct mail advertising company which designs, prints, and mails more than 15 billion coupons annually. **NOTE:** Entry-level positions and second and third shifts are offered. **Common positions include:** Account Manager; Account Rep.; Accountant; Administrative Assistant; Blue-Collar Worker Supervisor; Buyer; Chief Financial Officer; Computer Operator; Computer Programmer; Computer Support Technician; Computer Technician; Controller; Credit Manager; Customer Service Rep.; Database Administrator; Database Manager; Desktop Publishing Specialist; Financial Analyst; Graphic Artist; Graphic Designer; Human Resources Manager; Internet Services Manager; Market Research Analyst; Marketing Manager; MIS Specialist; Network Administrator; Paralegal; Production Manager; Project Manager; Purchasing Agent/Manager; Registered Nurse; Sales Representative; Secretary; Systems Analyst; Systems Manager; Technical Writer/Editor. **Educational backgrounds include:** Accounting; Art; Business Administration; Communications; Computer Science; Finance; HTML; Internet; Java; Liberal Arts; Marketing; MCSE; Microsoft Word; Public Relations; QuarkXPress; Software Tech. Support; Spreadsheets; Visual Basic. **Benefits:** 401(k); Casual Dress - Daily; Dental Insurance; Disability Coverage; Employee Discounts; Financial Planning Assistance; Flexible Schedule; Life Insurance; Medical Insurance; Pension Plan; Public Transit Available; Savings Plan; Sick Days (6 - 10); Tuition Assistance; Vacation Days (6 - 10). **Special programs:** Internships. **Office hours:** Monday - Friday, 8:00 a.m. - 5:00 p.m. **Corporate headquarters location:** This Location. **Parent company:** Cox Enterprises, Inc. is one of the nation's largest privately held media companies with major holdings in newspaper, television, radio, and cable industries. **Listed on:** Privately held. **President:** Joseph Bourdow. **Annual sales/revenues:** More than $100 million. **Number of employees at this location:** 1,100. **Number of employees nationwide:** 1,500.

WATT/FLEISHMAN-HILLARD
Key Center, Suite 5200, 127 Public Square, Cleveland OH 44114. 216/566-7019. **Contact:** Human Resources. **Description:** A public relations and marketing firm.

WAYPOINT GROUP
715 Orange Street, Wilmington DE 19801. 302/654-6146. **Contact:** Human Resources Manager. **World Wide Web address:** http://www.waypointgroup. com. **Description:** An advertising agency.

JANE WESMAN PUBLIC RELATIONS
928 Broadway, New York NY 10010. 212/598-4440. **Fax:** 212/598-4590. **Contact:** Human Resources. **Description:** Jane Wesman Public Relations provides book publicity services including press kits, author tours, radio and print publicity, and media training. **Corporate headquarters location:** This Location.

WEST WAYNE
1100 Peachtree Street NE, Suite 1800, Atlanta GA 30309. 404/347-8700. **Contact:** Cristi Axon, Human Resources Director. **World Wide Web address:** http://www.westwayne.com. **Description:** An advertising agency. **NOTE:** Please contact the appropriate department head for the position for which you are applying. **Common positions include:** Account Representative; Art Director; Commercial Artist; Copywriter; Media Specialist; Production Coordinator; Secretary. **Benefits:** Dental Insurance; Eye Care; Life Insurance; Medical Insurance; Profit Sharing. **Number of employees at this location:** 200.

WHIPPLE, SARGENT & ASSOCIATES
37 Derby Street, Suite 7B, Hingham MA 02043. 781/740-4025. **Fax:** 781/749-9474. **Contact:** Human Resources. **World Wide Web address:** http://www.whipplesargent.com. **Description:** An advertising and marketing consulting firm. **Common positions include:** Administrative Assistant; Advertising Executive; Computer Operator; Desktop Publishing Specialist; Graphic Artist; Graphic Designer; Market Research Analyst; Marketing Manager; Marketing Specialist; Secretary; Typist/Word Processor; Webmaster. **Educational backgrounds include:** Art/Design; Business Administration; Communications; Computer Science; Economics; IBM Mainframe; Marketing. **Special programs:** Internships. **Corporate headquarters location:** This Location. **Operations at this facility include:** Research and Development; Service. **Annual sales/revenues:** Less than $5 million.

WHITERUNKLE ASSOCIATES
505 West Riverside, Suite 300, Spokane WA 99201. 509/747-6767. **Contact:** Human Resources. **World Wide Web address:** http://www.whiterunkle.com. **Description:** A full-service advertising, marketing, and public relations firm serving clients throughout the Northwest. Founded in 1980. **Common positions include:** Accountant/Auditor; Advertising Clerk; Advertising Executive; Commercial Artist; Marketing Specialist; Technical Writer/Editor. **Educational backgrounds include:** Accounting; Art/Design; Communications; Liberal Arts; Marketing. **Benefits:** Dental Insurance; Medical Insurance; Profit Sharing. **Special programs:** Internships. **Corporate headquarters location:** This Location. **Operations at this facility include:** Administration; Service. **Number of employees at this location:** 20.

WITHERSPOON ADVERTISING & PUBLIC RELATIONS
1000 West Weatherford, Fort Worth TX 76102. 817/335-1373. **Contact:** Mike Wilie, Senior Vice President. **World Wide Web address:** http://www.witherspoon.com. **Description:** A national advertising and public relations agency. **Common positions include:** Graphic Artist. **Educational**

backgrounds **include:** Art/Design; Business Administration; Marketing. **Benefits:** Life Insurance; Medical Insurance. **Corporate headquarters location:** This Location. **Operations at this facility include:** Service. **Number of employees at this location:** 35.

WOLF GROUP
1350 Euclid Avenue, Cleveland OH 44115. 216/241-2141. **Fax:** 216/479-2438. **Contact:** Human Resources. **Description:** An advertising agency. **Common positions include:** Account Manager; Artist; Copywriter; Marketing Manager. **Educational backgrounds include:** Advertising; Business Administration. **Benefits:** 401(k); Dental Insurance; Employee Discounts; Life Insurance; Medical Insurance; Profit Sharing. **Corporate headquarters location:** This Location. **Number of employees at this location:** 150.

YESAWICH, PEPPERDINE AND BROWN
1900 Summit Tower Boulevard, Suite 600, Orlando FL 32810. 407/875-1111. **Contact:** Julie Gochnour, Director of Human Resources. **World Wide Web address:** http://www.ypb.com. **Description:** An advertising agency. **Corporate headquarters location:** This Location.

YOUNG & RUBICAM, INC.
285 Madison Avenue, New York NY 10017. 212/210-3000. **Contact:** Human Resources Associate. **World Wide Web address:** http://www.yandr.com. **Description:** Young & Rubicam is an international advertising agency. The company operates through three divisions: Young & Rubicam International; Marsteller Inc., a worldwide leader in business-to-business and consumer advertising; and Young & Rubicam USA, with consumer advertising agencies operating through four regional groups, and five specialized advertising and marketing agencies. **Common positions include:** Advertising Clerk; Financial Analyst; Human Resources Manager; Market Research Analyst; Systems Analyst. **Educational backgrounds include:** Business Administration; Communications. **Benefits:** 401(k); Dental Insurance; Disability Coverage; Employee Discounts; Life Insurance; Medical Insurance; Pension Plan; Savings Plan. **Special programs:** Internships. **Corporate headquarters location:** This Location. **International locations:** Worldwide. **Subsidiaries include:** Burson-Marsteller provides public relations services throughout the world. **Listed on:** New York Stock Exchange. **Stock exchange symbol:** YNR. **President:** Mike Webster. **Number of employees nationwide:** 10,000.
Other U.S. locations:
- 550 Town Center Drive, Suite 300, Dearborn MI 48126. 313/583-8000.
- 233 North Michigan Avenue, Suite 1600, Chicago IL 60601. 312/596-3000.

For more information on career opportunities in advertising, marketing, and public relations:

Associations

ADVERTISING RESEARCH FOUNDATION
641 Lexington Avenue, 11th Floor, New York NY 10022. 212/751-5656. Fax: 212/319-5265. E-mail address: email@arfsite.org. World Wide Web address: http://www.arfsite.org. A nonprofit organization comprised of advertising, marketing, and media research companies.

AMERICAN ASSOCIATION OF ADVERTISING AGENCIES
405 Lexington Avenue, 18th Floor, New York NY 10174. 212/682-2500. World Wide Web address: http://www.aaaa.org. Offers educational and enrichment benefits such as publications, videos, and conferences.

AMERICAN MARKETING ASSOCIATION
311 South Wacker Drive, Suite 5800, Chicago IL 60606. 312/542-9000. Toll-free phone: 800/AMA-1150. World Wide Web address: http://www.ama.org. An association with nearly 45,000 members worldwide. Offers a reference center, 25 annual conferences, and eight publications for marketing professionals and students.

THE DIRECT MARKETING ASSOCIATION
1120 Avenue of the Americas, New York NY 10036-6700. 212/768-7277. World Wide Web address: http://www.the-dma.org. This association offers monthly newsletters, seminars, and an annual telephone marketing conference.

MARKETING RESEARCH ASSOCIATION
1344 Silas Deane Highway, Suite 306, Rocky Hill CT 06067. 860/257-4008. World Wide Web address: http://www.mra-net.org. Publishes several magazines and newsletters.

PUBLIC RELATIONS SOCIETY OF AMERICA
33 Irving Place, New York NY 10003-2376. 212/995-2230. World Wide Web address: http://www.prsa.org. Publishes books and magazines for public relations professionals.

Directories

AAAA ROSTER AND ORGANIZATION
American Association of Advertising Agencies, 405 Lexington Avenue, 18th Floor, New York NY 10147. 212/682-2500.

DIRECTORY OF MINORITY PUBLIC RELATIONS PROFESSIONALS
Public Relations Society of America, 33 Irving Place, New York NY 10003-2376. 212/995-2230.

O'DWYER'S DIRECTORY OF PUBLIC RELATIONS FIRMS
J.R. O'Dwyer Company, 271 Madison Avenue, Room 600, New York NY 10016. 212/679-2471.

PUBLIC RELATIONS CONSULTANTS DIRECTORY
American Business Directories, Division of American Business Lists, 5711 South 86th Circle, Omaha NE 68137. 402/593-4500.

STANDARD DIRECTORY OF ADVERTISING AGENCIES
Reed Elsevier New Providence, 121 Chanlon Road, New Providence NJ 07974. 908/665-6775. Toll-free phone: 800/521-8110. World Wide Web address: http://www.reedref.com.

Magazines

ADVERTISING AGE
Crain Communications Inc., 220 East 42nd Street, New York NY 10017-5846. 212/210-0100. World Wide Web address: http://www.adage.com.

ADWEEK
BPI Communications, 1515 Broadway, 12th Floor, New York NY 10036-8986. 212/764-7300. World Wide Web address: http://www.adweek.com.

BUSINESS MARKETING
Crain Communications Inc., 220 East 42nd Street, New York NY 10017-5846. 212/210-0100. World Wide Web address: http://www.businessmarketing. com.

JOURNAL OF MARKETING
American Marketing Association, 250 South Wacker Drive, Suite 200, Chicago IL 60606. 312/648-0536.

THE MARKETING NEWS
American Marketing Association, 250 South Wacker Drive, Suite 200, Chicago IL 60606. 312/648-0536. A biweekly magazine offering new ideas and developments in marketing.

PR REPORTER
PR Publishing Company, P.O. Box 600, Exeter NH 03833. 603/778-0514. World Wide Web address: http://www.prpublishing.com.

PUBLIC RELATIONS NEWS
Phillips Business Information, Inc., 1201 Seven Locks Road, Suite 300, Potomac MD 20854. 301/424-3338. Fax: 301/309-3847. World Wide Web address: http://www.phillips.com.

Newsletters

PUBLIC RELATIONS CAREER OPPORTUNITIES
101 South Whiting Street, Suite 305, Alexandria VA 22304. 703/823-4094. Fax: 703/823-5352. World Wide Web address: http://www.careeropps. com/prcareer1. A newsletter listing public relations, public affairs, special events, and investor positions nationwide compensating above $35,000 annually. Available on a subscription basis, published 24 times a year. Produced by the Public Relations Society of America, which also publishes other newsletters including *CEO Job Opportunities Update* and *ASAE Career Opportunities* (for the American Society of Association Executives).

Online Services

ADVERTISING & MEDIA JOBS PAGE
World Wide Web address: http://www.nationjob. com/media. This Website offers advertising and media job openings that can be searched by a variety of criteria including location, type of position, and salary. This site also offers a service that will perform the search for you.

DIRECT MARKETING WORLD'S JOB CENTER
World Wide Web address: http://www.dmworld. com. Posts professional job openings for the direct marketing industry. This site also provides a career reference library, a list of direct marketing professionals, and a list of events within the industry.

MARKETING CLASSIFIEDS ON THE INTERNET
World Wide Web address: http://www. marketingjobs.com. Offers job listings by state, resume posting, discussions with other marketing professionals, and links to other career sites and company home pages.

Aerospace

You can expect to find the following types of companies in this chapter:
Aerospace Products and Services • Aircraft Equipment and Parts

Some helpful information: *Salaries in parts manufacturing are normally concurrent with other manufacturing jobs (running approximately $21,000 - $35,000 per year), while aeronautical and astronautical engineers with a reasonable amount of experience (5 - 10 years) can earn over $50,000 annually.*

AEROFLEX LABORATORIES, INC.
35 Service Road, Plainview NY 11803. 516/293-8686. **Contact:** Jane Brady, Vice President of Personnel. **World Wide Web address:** http://www. aeroflex.com. **Description:** Manufactures custom-designed hybrid microcircuits for use in applications including electrical systems used in aircraft maintenance, flight and navigational systems, sonar systems, satellite experimentation systems, missile firing systems, power supply systems, computer testing systems, television camera and radio receiver systems, and other applications using miniaturized components. **Common positions include:** Electrical Engineer; Mechanical Engineer. **Corporate headquarters location:** This Location. **Parent company:** ARX, Inc. **Listed on:** NASDAQ.

AEROJET
P.O. Box 13222, Sacramento CA 95813-6000. 916/355-4000. **Contact:** Human Resources. **World Wide Web address:** http://www.aerojet.com. **Description:** Engaged in the research, development, testing, and production of liquid propellant rocket engines, solid rocket motors, sounding rockets, defense and aerospace systems, and waterjet propulsion systems. **Common positions include:** Aerospace Engineer; Mechanical Engineer. **Benefits:** Dental Insurance; Disability Coverage; Life Insurance; Medical Insurance; Pension Plan; Savings Plan; Tuition Assistance. **Corporate headquarters location:** This Location. **Parent company:** GenCorp, through its subsidiaries, manufactures products for the aerospace, pharmaceutical, fine chemical, and automotive industries. **Listed on:** New York Stock Exchange.

AEROSONIC CORPORATION
1212 North Hercules Avenue, Clearwater FL 33765. 727/461-3000. **Fax:** 727/447-5926. **Contact:** Personnel. **World Wide Web address:** http://www. aerosonic.com. **Description:** Manufactures mechanical and microprocessor-based aircraft instruments. **Common positions include:** Accountant; Administrative Assistant; Aerospace Engineer; Blue-Collar Worker Supervisor; Buyer; Computer Programmer; Controller; Customer Service Rep.; Draftsperson; Human Resources Manager; Industrial Engineer; Machinist; Mechanical Engineer; MIS Specialist; Production Manager; Purchasing Agent; Quality Control Supervisor; Sales Executive; Services Sales Rep.; Software Engineer; Systems Analyst; Technical Writer. **Educational backgrounds include:** Accounting; Engineering; Finance; Marketing. **Benefits:** 401(k); Dental Insurance; Disability Coverage; Life Insurance; Medical Insurance. **Corporate headquarters location:** This Location. **Other U.S. locations:** Wichita KS; Charlottesville VA. **Operations at this facility include:** Manufacturing; Research and Development; Sales; Service. **Number of employees at this location:** 140. **Number of employees nationwide:** 250.

THE AEROSPACE CORPORATION
P.O. Box 92957, MS1/050, Los Angeles CA 90009-2957. 310/336-1614. **Fax:** 310/336-7933. **Contact:** Walter L. Caldwell, Manager of Staffing Resources. **World Wide Web address:** http://www.aero.org. **Description:** A nonprofit corporation engaged in space systems architecture, engineering, planning, analysis, and research, predominantly for programs managed by the Space and Missile Systems Center of the Air Force Material Command. **Common positions include:** Aerospace Engineer; Chemical Engineer; Computer Programmer; Electrical Engineer; Industrial Engineer; Mathematician; Mechanical Engineer; Physicist; Software Engineer; Structural Engineer; Systems Analyst. **Educational backgrounds include:** Chemistry; Computer Science; Engineering; Mathematics; Physics. **Benefits:** 401(k); Dental Insurance; Disability Coverage; Employee Discounts; Life Insurance; Medical Insurance; Pension Plan; Savings Plan; Tuition Assistance. **Corporate headquarters location:** This Location. **Other U.S. locations:** Colorado Springs CO; Kennedy Space Center FL; Columbia MD; Albuquerque NM; Houston TX; Crystal City VA; Chantilly VA. **Operations at this facility include:** Research and Development. **Number of employees at this location:** 3,000.

AEROSPACE INDUSTRIES ASSOCIATION OF AMERICA
1250 Eye Street NW, 12th Floor, Washington DC 20005. 202/371-8400. **Fax:** 202/371-8470. **Contact:** Jane Weeden, Personnel Manager. **World Wide Web address:** http://www.aia-aerospace.org. **Description:** An organization representing companies involved in aerospace research, development, and manufacturing. The association consists of the Civil Aviation, Government, and International divisions. **Common positions include:** Accountant; Aerospace Engineer; Ceramics Engineer; Computer Programmer; Economist; Editor; Electrical Engineer; Librarian; Materials Engineer; Metallurgical Engineer; Operations Manager; Secretary; Statistician; Systems Analyst; Technical Writer. **Educational backgrounds include:** Accounting; Art; Business Administration; Communications; Computer Science; Engineering; Finance; Liberal Arts. **Benefits:** Life Insurance; Medical Insurance; Pension Plan. **Corporate headquarters location:** This Location. **Number of employees at this location:** 60.

ALL AMERICAN AVIATION
590 West Clearwater Loop, Post Falls ID 83854. 208/773-6083. **Fax:** 208/773-6014. **Contact:** Personnel. **Description:** Manufactures airplane parts. **Common positions include:** Computer Programmer; Manufacturing Engineer. **Benefits:** Medical Insurance. **President:** George Bekessy. **Information Systems Manager:** Jim Moser. **Number of employees at this location:** 25.

ANSER (ANALYTIC SERVICES INC.)
1215 Jefferson Davis Highway, Suite 800, Arlington VA 22202. 703/416-3093. **Contact:** Human Resources. **World Wide Web address:** http://www. anser.org. **Description:** An independent, nonprofit, public research institute that performs studies for the development and acquisition of weapons systems. ANSER's clients are the U.S. Air Force and other aerospace-related federal agencies. Founded in 1958. **Common positions include:** Accountant; Aerospace Engineer; Biological Scientist; Budget Analyst; Chemical Engineer; Chemist; Civil Engineer; Computer Programmer; Cost Estimator; Economist; Electrical Engineer; Environmental Engineer; Financial Analyst; Geologist; Human Resources Manager; Industrial Engineer; Mathematician; Mechanical Engineer; Metallurgical Engineer; Physicist; Science Technologist; Software Engineer; Statistician; Systems Analyst; Technical Writer. **Educational backgrounds include:** Accounting; Computer Science; Economics; Engineering; Mathematics; Physics. **Benefits:** 401(k); Dental Insurance; Disability Coverage; Life Insurance; Medical Insurance; Pension Plan; Tuition Assistance. **Special programs:** Internships. **Corporate headquarters location:** This Location. **Other U.S. locations:** Colorado Springs CO; Stoneham MA; Albuquerque NM; Newport News VA; Fairmont VA. **Operations at this facility include:** Research and Development. **Number of employees at this location:** 480.

APPLIED AEROSPACE STRUCTURES CORP.
P.O. Box 6189, Stockton CA 95206-0189. 209/983-3279. **Fax:** 209/983-3375. **Contact:** Human Resources Manager. **World Wide Web address:** http://www.aascworld.com. **Description:** Provides designing, engineering, and manufacturing services internationally to private and government clients in the aerospace industry. **Common positions include:** Accountant; Aerospace Engineer; Blue-Collar Worker Supervisor; Buyer; Chemist; Computer Programmer; Cost Estimator; Designer; Draftsperson; Electrician; Environmental Engineer; Financial Analyst; General Manager; Industrial Engineer; Manufacturing Engineer; Materials Engineer; Mechanical Engineer; Operations Manager; Program Manager; Quality Control Supervisor. **Educational backgrounds include:** Accounting; Engineering; Marketing. **Benefits:** 401(k); Dental Insurance; Disability Coverage; Life Insurance; Medical Insurance; Tuition Assistance. **Special programs:** Internships. **Corporate headquarters location:** This Location. **Operations at this facility include:** Administration; Manufacturing; Sales. **Listed on:** Privately held. **Number of employees nationwide:** 270.

B & E TOOL COMPANY, INC.
P.O. Box 40, Southwick MA 01077. 413/569-5585. **Physical address:** 10 Hudson Drive, Southwick MA. **Fax:** 413/569-6543. **Contact:** Personnel. **World Wide Web address:** http://www.betool. com. **Description:** Manufactures components for aircraft engines and controls. **Corporate headquarters location:** This Location.

B/E AEROSPACE, INC.
1400 Corporate Center Way; Wellington FL 33414. 561/791-5000. **Fax:** 561/791-7900. **Contact:** Joseph A. Piegari, Vice President of Personnel. **World Wide Web address:** http://www. beaerospace.com. **Description:** Manufactures, sells, and supports a broad range of commercial aircraft cabin interior products including seats, passenger entertainment and service systems, lighting products, oxygen products, and galley structures and inserts. The company supplies commercial airlines and airframe manufacturers. **Common positions include:** Accountant; Attorney; Credit Manager; Designer; Electrical Engineer; Industrial Engineer; Paralegal; Personnel Manager; Purchasing Agent; Technical Writer. **Educational backgrounds include:** Accounting; Engineering; Finance. **Benefits:** 401(k); Dental Insurance; Disability Coverage; Life Insurance; Medical Insurance; Profit Sharing; Stock Option; Tuition Assistance. **Special programs:** Internships. **Corporate headquarters location:** This Location. **International locations:** England; Singapore; Wales. **Subsidiaries include:** Aerospace Lighting Corporation; Aircraft Modular Products; Puritan-Bennett Aero Systems; SMR Aerospace; Sextant In-Flight Systems; C.F. Taylor. **Operations at this facility include:** Administration; Sales. **CEO:** Robert J. Khoury. **Annual sales/revenues:** More than $100 million. **Other U.S. locations:**
- 1455 Fairchild Road, Winston-Salem NC 27105. 336/767-2000.
- Galley Products Division, 11710 Central Parkway, Jacksonville FL 32224-7626. 904/996-3800.

BAE SYSTEMS
4908 Tampa West Boulevard, MS 114, Tampa FL 33634. 813/885-7481. **Contact:** Personnel. **World Wide Web address:** http://www.baesystems.com. **Description:** Designs, manufactures, and sells flight simulators, weapon systems, tactical air defense systems, small arms, and training devices for the U.S. government, as well as commercial and international customers. BAE Systems also develops simulation-based devices for the entertainment industry. The company also provides a variety of simulator-related training services at customer-owned facilities, its Tampa training center, and the British Aerospace-owned Dulles training facility. BAE Systems conducts business through its three primary operating segments: Training Devices, Training Services, and Systems Management. **Common positions include:** Accountant; Administrator; Aerospace Engineer; Buyer; Draftsperson; Electrical Engineer; Industrial Designer; Mechanical Engineer; Purchasing Agent; Quality Control Supervisor. **Educational backgrounds include:** Accounting; Engineering; Finance; Marketing; Mathematics; Physics. **Benefits:** Dental Insurance; Disability Coverage; Employee Discounts; Life Insurance; Medical Insurance; Pension Plan; Profit Sharing; Savings Plan; Stock Option; Tuition Assistance. **Corporate headquarters location:** This Location. **Subsidiaries include:** Reflectone UK Limited. **Number of employees worldwide:** 100,000.

BALL CORPORATION
10 Longs Peak Drive, Broomfield CO 80021. 303/469-3131. **Contact:** Human Resources. **World Wide Web address:** http://www.ball.com. **Description:** Produces metal and glass packaging products for foods and beverages, and provides aerospace and communications products and services to government and commercial customers. **Corporate headquarters location:** This Location.

BELL HELICOPTER TEXTRON
P.O. Box 482, Fort Worth TX 76101. 817/280-2011. **Contact:** Employment Department. **World Wide Web address:** http://www.bellhelicopter.textron. com. **Description:** Manufactures a variety of commercial and civilian helicopters and also conducts extensive research and development activities. **Corporate headquarters location:** This Location. **Parent company:** Textron Inc.

BFGOODRICH
4 Coliseum Centre, 2730 West Tyvola Road, Charlotte NC 28217-4578. 704/423-7000. **Fax:**

704/423-7069. **Contact:** Human Resources. **World Wide Web address:** http://www.bfgoodrich.com. **Description:** Provides components and systems for general aviation, regional, business, commercial, and military aircraft and space vehicles. The company also manufactures performance polymer systems and additives. **Corporate headquarters location:** This Location.

THE BOEING COMPANY
P.O. Box 3707, Mail Stop 6H-PL, Seattle WA 98124-2207. 206/655-1131. **Contact:** Employment Office. **World Wide Web address:** http://www. boeing.com. **Description:** An aerospace firm. The company is a major U.S. government contractor, with capabilities in missiles and space, electronic systems, military aircraft, helicopters, and information systems management. The Boeing Company is divided into four business segments: Commercial Aircraft, Space and Communications, Military Aircraft and Missiles, and Shared Services. The Commercial Aircraft Group is the company's largest operating unit. **Common positions include:** Accountant; Aerospace Engineer; Electrical Engineer; Mechanical Engineer. **Corporate headquarters location:** This Location. **Subsidiaries include:** Boeing Information Services, Inc. (Vienna VA) develops and manages large-scale information systems for selected agencies of the federal government. **Annual sales/revenues:** More than $100 million.

BOEING DEFENSE & SPACE GROUP
767 Boeing Road, Oak Ridge TN 37831. 865/481-7100. **Contact:** Personnel. **World Wide .Web address:** http://www.boeing.com. **Description:** Operates a manufacturing plant which primarily works on subassemblies for commercial jetliners built by the Boeing Commercial Airplane Group. The company primarily works on defense projects including building components and supplying the turret for the U.S. Army's Pedestal Mounted Stinger/Avenger air defense system. **Corporate headquarters location:** Seattle WA. **Parent company:** Boeing Company is one of the largest aerospace firms in the United States and one of the world's leading manufacturers of commercial jet transports. The company is a major U.S. government contractor with capabilities in missile and space, electronic systems, military aircraft, helicopters, and information systems management. The Boeing Company is divided into four business segments: Commercial Aircraft, Space and Communications, Military Aircraft and Missiles, and Shared Services. The Commercial Aircraft Group is the company's largest operating unit. **Number of employees at this location:** 780.

BREEZE-EASTERN
700 Liberty Avenue, Union NJ 07083. 908/686-4000. **Fax:** 908/686-4279. **Contact:** Personnel. **Description:** Designs, develops, manufactures, and services sophisticated lifting and restraining products, principally helicopter rescue hoist and cargo hook systems; winches and hoists for aircraft and weapon systems; and aircraft cargo tie-down systems. **Corporate headquarters location:** This Location. **Parent company:** TransTechnology designs, manufactures, sells, and distributes specialty fasteners through several other subsidiaries including Breeze Industrial Products (Saltsburg PA), manufactures a complete line of standard and specialty gear-driven band fasteners in high-grade stainless steel for use in highly engineered applications; The Palnut Company (Mountainside NJ), manufactures light- and heavy-duty single and multithread specialty fasteners; Industrial Retaining Ring (Irvington NJ), manufactures a variety of retaining rings made of

carbon steel, stainless steel, and beryllium copper; The Seeger Group (Somerville NJ) manufactures retaining clips, circlips, and spring pins.

C&D AEROSPACE, INC.
5412 Argosy Drive, Huntington Beach CA 92649. 714/891-1906. **Fax:** 714/891-6497. **Contact:** Sally Hicks, Human Resources Manager. **Description:** Designs and manufactures aircraft interiors for commercial airlines and for various governments. **Common positions include:** Accountant; Aerospace Engineer; Blue-Collar Worker Supervisor; Computer Programmer; Designer; Electrical Engineer; Human Resources Manager; Mechanical Engineer; Purchasing Agent; Quality Control Supervisor; Structural Engineer. **Educational backgrounds include:** Accounting; Business Administration; Engineering; Marketing. **Benefits:** Dental Insurance; Disability Coverage; Life Insurance; Medical Insurance; Savings Plan. **Special programs:** Internships. **Corporate headquarters location:** Garden Grove CA. **Other area locations:** La Palma CA; Ontario CA; Santa Maria CA. **Other U.S. locations:** Marysville WA. **Operations at this facility include:** Administration; Manufacturing; Research and Development; Sales. **Listed on:** Privately held. **Number of employees at this location:** 550. **Number of employees nationwide:** 2,500.

J.C. CARTER COMPANY, INC.
671 West 17th Street, Costa Mesa CA 92627-3605. 949/548-3421. **Contact:** Human Resources. **World Wide Web address:** http://www.jccarter.com. **Description:** Designs and manufactures pumps, valves, and pressure regulators used in aircraft fuel systems. **Common positions include:** Accountant; Aerospace Engineer; Buyer; Computer Programmer; Draftsperson; Human Resources Manager; Industrial Engineer; Manufacturer's Sales Rep.; Marketing Specialist; Mechanical Engineer; Operations Manager; Purchasing Agent; Quality Control Supervisor. **Educational backgrounds include:** Engineering; Finance; Marketing. **Benefits:** Dental Insurance; Disability Coverage; Employee Discounts; Life Insurance; Medical Insurance; Savings Plan; Tuition Assistance. **Corporate headquarters location:** This Location. **Parent company:** Argo-Tech Corp. **Operations at this facility include:** Manufacturing; Research and Development; Sales; Service.

CESSNA AIRCRAFT COMPANY
One Cessna Boulevard, Wichita KS 67215-1424. 316/517-6000. **Contact:** Bill Quattlebaum, Employment Director . **World Wide Web address:** http://www.cessna.textron.com. **Description:** Engaged in the engineering, fabrication, assembly, and marketing of commercial and business aircraft. Primary customers are corporations. **NOTE:** Applications for employment will remain on file for one year. **Common positions include:** Accountant; Aerospace Engineer; Buyer; Computer Programmer; Draftsperson; Electrical Engineer; Human Resources Manager; Industrial Engineer; Mechanical Engineer; Systems Analyst; Technical Writer. **Educational backgrounds include:** Accounting; Computer Science; Engineering; Marketing. **Benefits:** Dental Insurance; Disability Coverage; Life Insurance; Medical Insurance; Pension Plan; Savings Plan; Tuition Assistance. **Corporate headquarters location:** This Location. **Parent company:** Textron Inc. **Operations at this facility include:** Administration; Manufacturing; Research and Development; Sales; Service.

CHROMALLOY FLORIDA
630 Anchors Street NW, Fort Walton Beach FL 32548. 850/244-7684. **Contact:** Human Resources.

Description: Repairs turbine jet engine component parts. **Common positions include:** Mechanical Engineer; Metallurgical Engineer. **Operations at this facility include:** Manufacturing.

C.R. DANIELS, INC.
3451 Ellicott Center Drive, Ellicott City MD 21043. 410/461-2100. **Fax:** 410/461-2987. **Contact:** Personnel. **World Wide Web address:** http://www.crdaniels.com. **Description:** Produces a wide range of aviation products including seats, nets, and cushions; material handling containers; industrial and other premium fabric products; canvas and synthetic tarpaulins; and conveyor belts. **Common positions include:** Accountant; Administrator; Blue-Collar Worker Supervisor; Buyer; Credit Manager; Customer Service Rep.; Draftsperson; Industrial Engineer; Industrial Production Manager; Manufacturer's Sales Rep.; Mechanical Engineer; Purchasing Agent; Quality Control Supervisor. **Educational backgrounds include:** Business Administration; Engineering. **Benefits:** Dental Insurance; Disability Coverage; Life Insurance; Medical Insurance; Pension Plan; Profit Sharing. **Corporate headquarters location:** This Location. **Other U.S. locations:** Rutledge TN. **Operations at this facility include:** Administration; Manufacturing; Research and Development; Sales. **Number of employees at this location:** 170.

DASSAULT FALCON JET CORPORATION
P.O. Box 967, Little Rock AR 72203. 501/372-5254. **Toll-free phone:** 800/643-9511. **Recorded jobline:** 501/210-0454. **Contact:** Julie Milinowski, Personnel Administrator. **World Wide Web address:** http://www.falconjet.com. **Description:** This location is a completion and service center for Falcon Jet Aircraft. Overall, Dassault Falcon Jet Corporation manufactures and sells a line of two- and three-engine business aircraft. Dassault Falcon Jet also operates international jet aircraft service and maintenance centers (Falcon Jet Service Centers), engaged in a wide range of jet aircraft engine, airframe, avionics, instruments, and accessories service, repair, and maintenance. **Common positions include:** Accountant; Administrative Manager; Aerospace Engineer; Aircraft Mechanic; Assistant Manager; Budget Analyst; Buyer; Computer Operator; Computer Programmer; Cost Estimator; Customer Service Rep.; Electrical Engineer; Electrician; Employment Interviewer; Financial Manager; General Manager; Heating Technician; Human Resources Manager; Industrial Engineer; Machinist; Marketing Manager; Mechanical Engineer; Millwright; Payroll Clerk; Purchasing Agent; Quality Control Supervisor; Receptionist; Registered Nurse; Services Sales Rep.; Sheet-Metal Worker; Stock Clerk; Structural Engineer; Systems Analyst; Technical Writer; Typist; Welder. **Educational backgrounds include:** Accounting; Business Administration; Chemistry; Computer Science; Economics; Engineering; Finance; Liberal Arts; Marketing. **Benefits:** Dental Insurance; Disability Coverage; Life Insurance; Medical Insurance; Pension Plan; Savings Plan; Tuition Assistance. **Corporate headquarters location:** South Hackensack NJ. **Parent company:** Dassault Aviation. **Operations at this facility include:** Administration; Manufacturing; Sales; Service. **Number of employees at this location:** 1,300. **Number of employees nationwide:** 1,550.

DAYTON-GRANGER, INC.
3299 SW Ninth Avenue, Fort Lauderdale FL 33315. 954/463-3451. **Fax:** 954/761-3172. **Contact:** Personnel Manager. **World Wide Web address:** http://www.daytongranger.com. **Description:** A manufacturer of aviation communications products.

NOTE: Entry-level positions are offered. **Common positions include:** Accountant; Electrical Engineer; Mechanical Engineer; MIS Specialist; Purchasing Agent; Quality Control Supervisor; Technical Writer. **Educational backgrounds include:** Accounting; Computer Science; Engineering; Marketing. **Benefits:** 401(k); Dental Insurance; Disability Coverage; Employee Discounts; Life Insurance; Medical Insurance; Tuition Assistance. **Corporate headquarters location:** This Location. **Operations at this facility include:** Administration; Manufacturing; Research and Development; Sales; Service. **Listed on:** Privately held. **Number of employees at this location:** 220.

DERCO AEROSPACE INC.
8000 West Tower, P.O. Box 25549, Milwaukee WI 53223. 414/355-3066. **Fax:** 414/365-4686. **Contact:** Mike Krier, Hiring Manager. **World Wide Web address:** http://www.dercoaerospace.com. **Description:** Distributes OEM spares, components, and ground support equipment for aircraft. **NOTE:** Entry-level positions are offered. **Common positions include:** Administrative Assistant; Cost Estimator; Customer Service Rep.; Industrial Engineer; Manufacturing Engineer; Mechanical Engineer; Purchasing Agent; Quality Assurance Engineer; Sales Executive; Sales Rep.; Technical Writer; Typist. **Educational backgrounds include:** Accounting; Business Administration; Computer Science; Engineering; Marketing; Public Relations. **Benefits:** 401(k); Daycare Assistance; Dental Insurance; Disability Coverage; Financial Planning Assistance; Life Insurance; Medical Insurance; Profit Sharing; Tuition Assistance. **Corporate headquarters location:** This Location. **Listed on:** Privately held. **Annual sales/revenues:** $51 - $100 million. **Number of employees at this location:** 300. **Number of projected hires for 2000 - 2001 at this location:** 100.

DOWTY AEROSPACE
1700 Business Center Drive, Duarte CA 91010. 626/359-9211. **Fax:** 626/357-0069. **Contact:** Cathy Herrera, Human Resources Representative. **World Wide Web address:** http://www.dowty.com. **Description:** This location manufactures propellers and hydraulic engines. Overall, Dowty Aerospace is a diversified manufacturing firm which conducts business in four major industrial segments: Aerospace, Metals, Packaged Products, and Aviation. Aerospace consists of hydraulic and pneumatic valves used in military and commercial fixed-wing aircraft and helicopters, tanks, and the national aerospace program. Metals includes the production of flints and various extruded metals. Packaged Products consists principally of packaged fuels and flints. Aviation includes the chartering, servicing, and sales of helicopters and fixed-wing aircraft. **Common positions include:** Accountant; Buyer; Industrial Engineer; Manufacturing Engineer; Mechanical Engineer; MIS Specialist; Systems Analyst. **Educational backgrounds include:** Accounting; Engineering; Software Tech. Support. **Benefits:** 401(k); Dental Insurance; Disability Coverage; Employee Discounts; Life Insurance; Medical Insurance; Pension Plan; Profit Sharing; Tuition Assistance. **Parent company:** TI Group plc. **Listed on:** New York Stock Exchange. **Number of employees at this location:** 295. **Other U.S. locations:**
- P.O. Box 9907, Yakima WA 98909. 509/248-5000.

DYNAMICS RESEARCH CORPORATION
60 Frontage Road, Andover MA 01810. 978/475-9090. **Fax:** 978/470-0201. **Contact:** Personnel. **World Wide Web address:** http://www.drc.com. **Description:** Provides systems engineering and

analysis, operations research, logistics, and database systems support for the Department of Defense. Applications include acquisition management, inertial navigation and guidance, human resources requirements analyses, software systems, and logistic support analyses. The company also manufactures rotary and linear optical incremental encoders and precision patterned glass and metal products including precision measuring scales, reticles, and optical pick-offs for computer peripheral and optical equipment OEMs. **Common positions include:** Communications Engineer; Computer Programmer; Electrical Engineer; Logistics Support Worker; Software Engineer; Systems Analyst. **Educational backgrounds include:** Communications; Computer Science; Engineering; Mathematics; Physics. **Benefits:** 401(k); Dental Insurance; Disability Coverage; Life Insurance; Medical Insurance; Pension Plan; Referral Bonus Plan; Relocation Assistance; Savings Plan; Tuition Assistance. **Corporate headquarters location:** This Location. **Other U.S. locations:** Nationwide. **Operations at this facility include:** Research and Development; Sales; Service.

ELLANEF MANUFACTURING CORP.
97-11 50th Avenue, Corona NY 11368. 718/699-4000x227. **Contact:** Ernest Constantine, Human Resources Manager. **Description:** Manufactures a wide range of aircraft components for major aerospace OEMs and airlines operating nationwide. **Common positions include:** Accountant/Auditor; Aerospace Engineer; Cost Estimator; Customer Service Rep.; Electrician; General Manager; Industrial Production Manager; Machinist; Operations Manager; Purchasing Agent; Quality Control Supervisor. **Educational backgrounds include:** Mathematics. **Benefits:** Dental Insurance; Disability Coverage; Life Insurance; Medical Insurance; Pension Plan; Profit Sharing; Tuition Assistance. **Corporate headquarters location:** This Location. **Operations at this facility include:** Manufacturing. **Listed on:** Privately held. **Number of employees at this location:** 500.

ENGINE COMPONENTS INC.
9503 Middlex Drive, San Antonio TX 78217. 210/828-3131. **Contact:** Personnel. **Description:** Manufactures engine components for aircraft. **Corporate headquarters location:** This Location. **Other U.S. locations:** Bradenton FL; Aurora OR. **Number of employees at this location:** 170.

ENGINEERING SERVICE, INC.
21556 Telegraph Road, Southfield MI 48034. 248/357-3800. **Contact:** Personnel. **Description:** An engineering firm specializing in CAD design for powertrain, electrical, and tooling applications in the automotive and aerospace industries. Engineering Service also offers project management services. **Common positions include:** Accountant; Computer-Aided Designer; Draftsperson; Industrial Designer; Manufacturer's/Wholesaler's Sales Rep. **Educational backgrounds include:** Art/Design; Computer-Aided Design; Drafting. **Benefits:** Dental Insurance; Disability Coverage; Life Insurance; Medical Insurance; Prescription Drugs; Savings Plan. **Corporate headquarters location:** This Location. **Other U.S. locations:** Dearborn MI. **Number of employees nationwide:** 200.

ESTERLINE TECHNOLOGIES
10800 NE Eighth Street, Suite 600, Bellevue WA 98004. 425/453-9400. **Fax:** 425/519-1895. **Contact:** Personnel Department. **World Wide Web address:** http://www.esterline.com. **Description:** A manufacturing company serving several market areas including commercial aerospace, the defense, and the electronics industries. The company is

divided into three business groups: Advanced Materials, Aerospace, and Automation. **Corporate headquarters location:** This Location. **Subsidiaries include:** Armtec Defense Products Co., 85-901 Avenue 53, Coachella CA 92236; Excellon Automation Co., 24751 Crenshaw Boulevard, Torrance CA 90505; Korry Electronics Co., 901 Dexter Avenue North, Seattle WA 98109; W.A. Whitney Co., 650 Race Street, Rockford IL 61105. **Listed on:** New York Stock Exchange.

EVERGREEN INTERNATIONAL AVIATION
3850 Three Mile Lane, McMinnville OR 97128. 503/472-9361. **Contact:** Mike McClure, Recruiting Manager. **World Wide Web address:** http://www.evergreenaviation.com. **Description:** A holding company. **Common positions include:** Accountant; Aircraft Mechanic; Attorney; Computer Programmer; Dispatcher; Flight Attendant; Manufacturer's Sales Rep.; Receptionist; Travel Agent; Typist. **Educational backgrounds include:** Accounting; Business Administration; Engineering; Marketing. **Benefits:** 401(k); Dental Insurance; Disability Coverage; Employee Discounts; Life Insurance; Medical Insurance; Pension Plan. **Corporate headquarters location:** This Location. **Other U.S. locations:** Marana AZ; Los Angeles CA; New York NY. **Subsidiaries include:** Evergreen International Airlines; Evergreen Aircraft Sales & Leasing Co.; Evergreen Helicopters; Evergreen Air Center; Evergreen Aviation Ground Logistics Enterprises; Quality Aviation Services; Evergreen Agricultural Enterprises. **Operations at this facility include:** Administration; Sales. **Number of employees worldwide:** 2,200.

FAIRCHILD AEROSPACE CORPORATION
P.O. Box 790490, San Antonio TX 78279-0490. 210/824-9421. **Fax:** 210/824-9476. **Contact:** Personnel. **World Wide Web address:** http://www.faidor.com. **Description:** Manufactures aircraft and provides a wide range of aviation services. **Corporate headquarters location:** This Location.

FAIRCHILD FASTENERS - U.S.
800 South State College Boulevard, Fullerton CA 92831. 714/871-1550. **Contact:** Personnel Manager. **Description:** Manufactures and supplies precision fastening systems and components and latching devices for aerospace and industrial applications. Fairchild Fasteners - U.S. was established to collectively manage all of Fairchild's fastener operations in the United States. Fairchild Fasteners - Europe (Germany) is its sister company. **Common positions include:** Aerospace Engineer; Computer Programmer; Customer Service Rep.; Draftsperson; Industrial Engineer; Machinist; Manufacturer's Sales Rep.; Mechanical Engineer; Metallurgical Engineer. **Educational backgrounds include:** Business Administration; Engineering. **Benefits:** 401(k); Dental Insurance; Life Insurance; Medical Insurance; Profit Sharing; Savings Plan; Tuition Assistance. **Corporate headquarters location:** This Location. **Parent company:** The Fairchild Corporation (Chantilly VA). **Operations at this facility include:** Manufacturing; Research and Development; Sales; Service. **Listed on:** Privately held. **Number of employees at this location:** 600.

THE FLIGHT INTERNATIONAL GROUP
Newport News/Williamsburg International Airport, One Lear Drive, Newport News VA 23602. 757/886-5500. **Fax:** 757/874-7481. **Contact:** Personnel. **World Wide Web address:** http://www.fltintl.com. **Description:** An aviation services company that performs military training services using specially-modified commercial aircraft, principally under contracts with the U.S. Department of Defense, other government agencies,

and foreign countries. The company also operates a fixed-base operation and owns a flight school at the Newport News/Williamsburg International Airport. **Corporate headquarters location:** This Location. **Other U.S. locations:** Anchorage AK; Yuma AZ; China Lake CA; Inyokern CA; San Diego CA. **Subsidiaries include:** Flight International Aviation Training Center, Inc.; Flight International of Alaska, Inc.; Flight International, Inc. **Chairman of the Board:** David E. Sandlin.

FLIGHTLINE ELECTRONICS
P.O. Box 750, Fishers NY 14453-0750. 716/924-4000. **Physical address:** 7525 County Road 42, Fishers NY 14453. **Contact:** Human Resources. **Description:** A defense contractor involved with the design, development, and manufacture of airborne military communications equipment. **NOTE:** Entry-level positions are offered. **Common positions include:** Accountant; Administrative Assistant; Blue-Collar Worker Supervisor; Controller; Design Engineer; Draftsperson; Electrical Engineer; Human Resources Manager; Manufacturing Engineer; Marketing Specialist; Network Administrator; Production Manager; Purchasing Agent; Quality Assurance Engineer; Quality Control Supervisor; Software Engineer. **Educational backgrounds include:** Accounting; C/C++; Computer Science; Engineering; Finance; Microsoft Word; Software Development; Spreadsheets; Visual Basic. **Benefits:** 401(k); Casual Dress - Fridays; Dental Insurance; Disability Coverage; Life Insurance; Medical Insurance; Profit Sharing; Savings Plan; Sick Days (1 - 5); Tuition Assistance; Vacation Days (10 - 20). **Corporate headquarters location:** Greenford, England. **Parent company:** Ultra Electronics. **Operations at this facility include:** Manufacturing; Research and Development.

FUTRON CORPORATION
7315 Wisconsin Avenue, Suite 900W, Bethesda MD 20814-3202. 301/347-3403. **Fax:** 301/913-9475. **Contact:** Robin Andrusko, Personnel Director. **E-mail address:** resume@futron.com. **World Wide Web address:** http://www.futron.com. **Description:** Provides management consulting to the aerospace industry. Services focus on information technology and management; space market forecasting; risk-based decision support; education and outreach; and aerospace safety, reliability management, and quality assurance. **NOTE:** Entry-level positions and part-time jobs are offered. **Common positions include:** Administrative Assistant; Administrative Manager; Applications Engineer; Computer Engineer; Computer Programmer; Computer Scientist; Computer Support Technician; Database Administrator; Database Manager; Desktop Publishing Specialist; Finance Director; Graphic Artist; Internet Services Manager; MIS Specialist; Multimedia Designer; Network Administrator; Quality Assurance Engineer; Software Engineer; SQL Programmer; Systems Analyst; Technical Writer/Editor. **Educational backgrounds include:** Biology; Computer Science; Engineering; MCSE; QuarkXPress; Software Development; Visual Basic. **Benefits:** 401(k); Casual Dress - Fridays; Dental Insurance; Disability Coverage; Flexible Schedule; Life Insurance; Medical Insurance; Public Transit Available; Sick Days (1 - 5); Tuition Assistance; Vacation Days (10 - 20). **Special programs:** Internships; Training. **Corporate headquarters location:** This Location. **Other U.S. locations:** Washington DC; Houston TX. **President:** Joseph Fuller, Jr. **Number of employees at this location:** 35. **Number of employees nationwide:** 85.

GB TECH INC.
2200 Space Park Drive, Suite 400, Houston TX 77058. 281/333-3703. **Contact:** Human Resources.

World Wide Web address: http://www.gbtech.net. **Description:** Performs aerospace and computer engineering services for several organizations including NASA. **Corporate headquarters location:** This Location.

GE AIRCRAFT ENGINES
One Neumann Way, Mail Drop B-5, Cincinnati OH 45215. 513/243-3614. **Fax:** 513/243-9481. **Contact:** Recruiting Office. **Description:** Manufactures jet engine parts. **Common positions include:** Aerospace Engineer; Aircraft Mechanic Specialist; Attorney; Blue-Collar Worker Supervisor; Buyer; Chemical Engineer; Computer Programmer; Designer; Draftsperson; Electrical Engineer; Electrician; Human Resources Manager; Librarian; Mechanical Engineer; Metallurgical Engineer; Paralegal; Software Engineer; Systems Analyst. **Educational backgrounds include:** Business Administration; Engineering; Finance. **Benefits:** Dental Insurance; Disability Coverage; Employee Discounts; Life Insurance; Medical Insurance; Pension Plan; Savings Plan; Tuition Assistance. **Corporate headquarters location:** This Location. **Parent company:** General Electric (GE) operates in the following areas: aircraft engines (jet engines, replacement parts, and repair services for commercial, military, executive, and commuter aircraft); appliances; broadcasting (NBC); industrial (lighting products, electrical distribution and control equipment, transportation systems products, electric motors and related products, electrical and electronic industrial automation products, and a network of electrical supply houses); materials (plastics, ABS resins, silicones, superabrasives, and laminates); power systems (products for the generation, transmission, and distribution of electricity); technical products and systems (medical systems and equipment, as well as a full range of computer-based information and data interchange services for both internal use and external commercial and industrial customers); and capital services (consumer services, financing, and specialty insurance). **Operations at this facility include:** Divisional Headquarters; Manufacturing; Research and Development; Sales; Service. **Number of employees worldwide:** 230,000.

GKN AEROSPACE CHEM-TRONICS INC.
1150 West Bradley Avenue, El Cajon CA 92020. 619/448-2320. **Contact:** Personnel. **World Wide Web address:** http://www.chem-tronics.com. **Description:** Manufactures aerospace component and repairs for business and defense clients.

GABLES ENGINEERING, INC.
247 Greco Avenue, Coral Gables FL 33146. 305/442-2578. **Fax:** 305/446-5902. **Contact:** Cary Reyes, Personnel Manager. **Description:** Engineers, designs, configures, and manufactures aircraft communications and navigation control systems. **Common positions include:** Electrical Engineer; Electronics Technician; Software Engineer; Technical Writer. **Educational backgrounds include:** Engineering. **Benefits:** 401(k); Dental Insurance; Disability Coverage; Life Insurance; Medical Insurance. **Corporate headquarters location:** This Location. **Operations at this facility include:** Manufacturing; Research and Development.

GROS-ITE INDUSTRIES
1790 New Britain Avenue, Farmington CT 06032. 860/677-2603. **Contact:** Bev Mylen-Kelly, Human Resources Manager. **World Wide Web address:** http://www.grosite.com. **Description:** Offers design and manufacturing services in areas such as jet engine parts, special tooling, equipment and gauges, and components used in the manufacture, assembly,

and inspection of jet engines. **Benefits:** 401(k); ESOP; Pension Plan; Stock Option. **Corporate headquarters location:** This Location. **Subsidiaries include:** American Research offers environmental test chambers which duplicate hostile conditions such as high altitude, wind and dust, compression, humidity, decompression, temperature, and explosions; Gros-Ite Spindle specializes in the design, manufacture, and repair of precision spindles. **Parent company:** Edac Technologies offers design and manufacturing services for the medical instruments industry. Edac also maintains manufacturing and design facilities with computerized, numerically controlled machining centers; grinding, welding, and sheet metal fabrication; and painting and assembly capabilities.

GULFSTREAM AEROSPACE CORP.
P.O. Box 2206, Savannah GA 31402. 912/965-3000. **Contact:** Fred Fretto, Vice President of Personnel. **World Wide Web address:** http://www. gulfstream.com. **Description:** Manufactures corporate and private executive aircraft. **Corporate headquarters location:** This Location. **Parent company:** General Dynamics.

HAMILTON SUNDSTRAND CORP.
4747 Harrison Avenue, P.O. Box 7002, Rockford IL 61125-7002. 815/226-6000. **Contact:** Personnel. **World Wide Web address:** http://www. hamiltonsundstrandcorp.com. **Description:** Makes aeronautics and aviation equipment and parts. Sundstrand designs and develops high-tech components for aerospace, aviation, power transmission, and fluid and heat transfer products.

HOOVER INDUSTRIES INC.
7260 NW 68th Street, Miami FL 33166-2014. 305/888-9791. **Fax:** 305/887-4632. **Contact:** Personnel. **Description:** Manufactures seat covers, cushions, and inflatable survival equipment for the aerospace industry. **Common positions include:** Accountant; Blue-Collar Worker Supervisor; Buyer; Cost Estimator; Draftsperson; Human Resources Manager; Purchasing Agent/Manager; Quality Control Supervisor; Software Engineer; Systems Analyst; Transportation/Traffic Specialist. **Educational backgrounds include:** Accounting; Business Administration; Computer Science; Engineering; Finance; Marketing. **Benefits:** Dental Insurance; Disability Coverage; Life Insurance; Medical Insurance. **Corporate headquarters location:** This Location. **Listed on:** Privately held. **Number of employees at this location:** 200.

HOWMET CORPORATION
475 Steamboat Road, Greenwich CT 06830. 203/661-4600. **Contact:** Human Resources. **World Wide Web address:** http://www.howmet.com. **Description:** Manufactures airfoils, structural castings, and gas and turbine engines for the aerospace industry. **Corporate headquarters location:** This Location.

INTERNATIONAL AVIATION COMPOSITES
P.O. Box 376, Haslet TX 76052-0376. 817/491-6755. **Contact:** Human Resources. **Description:** Repairs main and tail rotor blades on helicopters. **Common positions include:** Accountant/Auditor; Aerospace Engineer; Aircraft Mechanic/Engine Specialist; General Manager; Mechanical Engineer; Typist/Word Processor. **Educational backgrounds include:** Engineering. **Benefits:** Medical Insurance. **Special programs:** Apprenticeships. **Corporate headquarters location:** This Location. **Operations at this facility include:** Administration; Manufacturing; Research and Development; Sales; Service. **Number of employees at this location:** 10.

KAMAN CORPORATION
1332 Blue Hills Avenue, P.O. Box One, Bloomfield CT 06002. 860/243-8311. **Contact:** Personnel. **World Wide Web address:** http://www.kaman. com. **Description:** This location manufactures helicopters. Overall, Kaman is a highly-diversified *Fortune* International 500 company with two segments providing products and services in five functional areas. The Diversified Technology segment includes Kaman Instrumentation Corporation, offering value-added products that solve problems in niche markets for military and industrial customers; Kamatics Corporation offers advanced information technologies and high-technology science and engineering products and services including artificial intelligence systems, advanced technology systems, and other technical professional services; and Kaman Aerospace Corporation offers commercial and military helicopter programs, components for commercial airliners, military subcontract programs, and laser optics systems. The Distribution Segment includes Kaman Industrial Technologies Corporation, involving the distribution of nearly 800,000 repair and replacement products and services to nearly every sector of heavy and light industry; Kaman Music Corporation sells over 13,000 musical products and instruments. **Corporate headquarters location:** This Location.

LEONARDS METAL INC.
P.O. Box 900, 3600 Mueller Road, St. Charles MO 63302. 636/946-6525. **Fax:** 636/916-2127. **Contact:** Recruiting Coordinator. **Description:** Manufactures a broad range of metal components for the aerospace industry. **Common positions include:** Accountant; Administrative Manager; Aerospace Engineer; Clerical Supervisor; Computer Programmer; General Manager; Human Resources Manager; Industrial Engineer; Industrial Production Manager; Materials Engineer; Mechanical Engineer; MIS Specialist; Operations Manager; Purchasing Agent; Quality Control Supervisor; Systems Analyst. **Benefits:** 401(k); Dental Insurance; Disability Coverage; Life Insurance; Medical Insurance; Profit Sharing; Tuition Assistance. **Corporate headquarters location:** This Location. **Other U.S. locations:** Wichita KS; Tulsa OK; Seattle WA. **Operations at this facility include:** Administration; Manufacturing. **Listed on:** Privately held. **Annual sales/revenues:** $21 - $50 million. **Number of employees at this location:** 260. **Number of employees nationwide:** 490.

LOCKHEED MARTIN CORPORATION
6801 Rockledge Drive, Bethesda MD 20817. 301/897-6000. **Contact:** Human Resources. **World Wide Web address:** http://www.lmco.com. **Description:** This location houses administrative offices. Overall, Lockheed Martin is an aerospace and technology company engaged in the design, manufacture, and management of systems and products for the space, defense, electronics, communications, information management, energy, and materials fields. **Corporate headquarters location:** This Location. **Number of employees worldwide:** 149,000.
Other U.S. locations:
- Lockheed Martin Aeroparts, Inc., 221 Industrial Park Road, Johnstown PA 15904. 814/262-3000.
- Lockheed Martin Missiles & Fire Control, P.O. Box 650003, Mail Stop LHR-PE, Dallas TX 75265-0003. 972/603-1000.

LUMINATOR
1200 East Plano Parkway, Plano TX 75074. 972/424-6511. **Contact:** Denise Boyd, Personnel Manager. **World Wide Web address:** http://www. luminatorusa.com. **Description:** Manufactures

aircraft parts, bus products, and rail products. Luminator aircraft products include batteries, lamps, search lights, interiors, and crew stations. Bus products include flip-out signs and voice systems. Rail products include various types of lighting, flip dot sign systems, voice systems, and air diffusers. **Corporate headquarters location:** This Location. **Parent company:** Mark IV Industries.

LYNTON AVIATION
3 Airport Road, Morristown Municipal Airport, Morristown NJ 07960-4624. 973/292-9000. **Fax:** 973/292-1497. **Contact:** Personnel. **Description:** Performs aviation services including the management, charter, maintenance, and refueling of corporate helicopters and fixed-wing aircraft, and helicopter support services for industrial applications. Lynton also provides aircraft sales and brokerage services to customers worldwide. **Corporate headquarters location:** This Location.

MRC BEARINGS
402 Chandler Street, Jamestown NY 14702-0280. 716/661-2600. **Contact:** Mike Mistretta, Human Resources Department. **Description:** Produces custom-engineered, anti-friction ball and roller bearings for use in aerospace and special industrial applications. The MRC product range includes bearings for helicopters, jet engine mainshafts and gearboxes, and bearings for all types of aircraft power transmission assemblies as well as other types of specialty applications. **Corporate headquarters location:** This Location. **Other U.S. locations:** Winsted CT; Falconer NY.

MARATHON POWER TECHNOLOGIES CO.
P.O. Box 8233, Waco TX 76714-8233. 254/776-0650. **Fax:** 254/776-1309. **Contact:** Jeff Oliver, Personnel Manager. **Description:** Manufactures nickel-cadmium aircraft batteries and electronic assemblies. **Common positions include:** Accountant; Blue-Collar Worker Supervisor; Buyer; Chemical Engineer; Chemist; Clinical Lab Technician; Computer Programmer; Draftsperson; Electrical Engineer; Electrician; General Manager; Human Resources Manager; Industrial Engineer; Industrial Production Manager; Mechanical Engineer; Purchasing Agent; Quality Control Supervisor; Services Sales Rep. **Educational backgrounds include:** Accounting; Business Administration; Chemistry; Engineering; Liberal Arts; Marketing. **Benefits:** 401(k); Dental Insurance; Disability Coverage; Life Insurance; Medical Insurance; Tuition Assistance. **Corporate headquarters location:** This Location. **Parent company:** Metapoint Partners. **Operations at this facility include:** Administration; Manufacturing; Research and Development; Sales; Service. **Number of employees at this location:** 190.

MERCURY AIR GROUP, INC.
5456 McConnell Avenue, Los Angeles CA 90066. 310/827-2737. **Contact:** Rae Beth Stroud, Personnel Manager. **World Wide Web address:** http://www.mercuryairgroup.com. **Description:** Engaged primarily in ground support services for passenger and freight air carriers and also in the manufacturing of electronic components. Support services include aircraft refueling and maintenance. Electronic components and parts include resistors, fusing devices, circuit breakers, audio accessories, service accessories, and electrical modules. **Corporate headquarters location:** This Location. **Listed on:** American Stock Exchange.

METRIC SYSTEMS CORPORATION
645 Anchors Street, Fort Walton Beach FL 32548. 850/302-3000. **Fax:** 850/302-3475. **Contact:** Barbara Fallin, Director of Human Resources.

World Wide Web address: http://www.metricsys.com. **Description:** Provides engineering and manufacturing services to produce air, land, and sea systems for the commercial and defense industries. **Common positions include:** Account Manager; Accountant; Administrative Assistant; Attorney; Blue-Collar Worker Supervisor; Clerical Supervisor; Computer Engineer; Computer Operator; Computer Programmer; Computer Technician; Controller; Cost Estimator; Database Administrator; Design Engineer; Draftsperson; Electrical Engineer; Environmental Engineer; Graphic Artist; Graphic Designer; Human Resources Manager; Industrial Engineer; Manufacturing Engineer; Mechanical Engineer; Operations Manager; Production Manager; Project Manager; Purchasing Agent; Quality Assurance Engineer; Quality Control Supervisor; Secretary; Software Engineer; Systems Analyst; Technical Writer; Vice President. **Educational backgrounds include:** Accounting; AS400 Certification; C/C++; Computer Science; Engineering; Finance; Internet; Java; Marketing; Mathematics; Microsoft Word; Novell; Software Development; Software Tech. Support; Spreadsheets; Visual Basic. **Benefits:** 401(k); Daycare Assistance; Dental Insurance; Disability Coverage; Employee Discounts; Life Insurance; Medical Insurance; Pension Plan; Tuition Assistance. **Corporate headquarters location:** Houston TX. **Parent company:** Tech-Sym Corporation. **Operations at this facility include:** Administration; Manufacturing; Research and Development; Sales; Service. **Listed on:** New York Stock Exchange. **Stock exchange symbol:** TSY. **President:** Charles Johnson. **Information Systems Manager:** Jay Busch. **Annual sales/revenues:** $51 - $100 million. **Number of employees at this location:** 560.

MICRO CRAFT, INC.
P.O. Box 370, Tullahoma TN 37388. 931/455-2664. **Contact:** Human Resources. **World Wide Web address:** http://www.microcraft.com. **Description:** Manufactures aerospace models and provides aerospace engineering services. **Corporate headquarters location:** This Location. **Other U.S. locations:** Houston TX.

MIDDLETON AEROSPACE CORP.
206 South Main Street, Middleton MA 01949. 978/774-6000. **Contact:** Personnel. **Description:** Manufactures aircraft engine components.

MOOG INC.
P.O. Box 18, East Aurora NY 14052-0018. 716/652-2000. **Fax:** 716/687-4457. **Contact:** Jack Keebler, Director of Human Resources. **World Wide Web address:** http://www.moog.com. **Description:** A manufacturer of motion control components and systems. Moog actuation devices control high-performance aircraft, satellites and space vehicles, strategic and tactical missiles, and automated industrial machinery. **Common positions include:** Mechanical Engineer. **Educational backgrounds include:** Engineering. **Benefits:** 401(k); Dental Insurance; Disability Coverage; Employee Discounts; Life Insurance; Medical Insurance; Pension Plan; Profit Sharing; Savings Plan; Tuition Assistance. **Corporate headquarters location:** This Location. **Other U.S. locations:** Torrance CA. **International locations:** Worldwide. **Operations at this facility include:** Administration; Divisional Headquarters; Manufacturing; Research and Development; Sales; Service. **Number of employees nationwide:** 2,000.

THE NEW PIPER AIRCRAFT, INC.
2926 Piper Drive, Vero Beach FL 32960. 561/567-4361. **Fax:** 561/778-2144. **Contact:** Patrick Faller,

Vice President of Personnel. **World Wide Web address:** http://www.newpiper.com. **Description:** Manufactures personal and business aircraft including the Saratoga II TC, Warrior III, Arrow, Seminole, Saratoga II HP, Archer III, Malibu Mirage, Malibu Meridian, and Seneca V. **Corporate headquarters location:** This Location. **Subsidiaries include:** Piper Financial Services, Inc. provides aircraft financing and leasing services.

THE NORDAM GROUP
P.O. Box 3365, Tulsa OK 74101-3365. 918/560-8612. **Contact:** Personnel. **World Wide Web address:** http://www.nordam.com. **Description:** Conducts manufacturing, repair, and overhaul services for the air transportation industry. The Nordam Group is one of the world's largest privately-held, FAA-certified repair stations. **Common positions include:** Accountant; Aerospace Engineer; Aircraft Mechanic; Buyer; Computer Programmer; Customer Service Rep.; Design Engineer; Human Resources Manager; Mechanical Engineer; Metallurgical Engineer; Purchasing Agent; Technical Writer. **Educational backgrounds include:** Engineering; Marketing. **Benefits:** 401(k); Dental Insurance; Disability Coverage; Life Insurance; Medical Insurance; Pension Plan. **Corporate headquarters location:** This Location. **Operations at this facility include:** Administration; Manufacturing; Research and Development; Sales; Service. **Listed on:** Privately held. **Annual sales/revenues:** More than $100 million. **Number of employees at this location:** 1,500. **Number of employees nationwide:** 1,900.

NORTHROP GRUMMAN CORPORATION
1840 Century Park East, Los Angeles CA 90067. 310/553-6262. **Contact:** Human Resources. **World Wide Web address:** http://www.northgrum.com. **Description:** Manufactures military aircraft, commercial aircraft parts, radar equipment, and electronic systems. Northrop Grumman develops the B-2 Spirit Stealth Bomber, as well as parts for the F/A-18 and the Boeing 747. Other operations include computer systems development for management and scientific applications. **Corporate headquarters location:** This Location. **Other U.S. locations:** Nationwide.

OEA, INC.
P.O. Box 100488, Denver CO 80250. 303/693-1248. **Contact:** James H. Welsh, Director of Personnel. **Description:** A manufacturer of aircraft crew escape systems. **Common positions include:** Aerospace Engineer; Draftsperson; Electrical Engineer; General Manager; Mechanical Engineer; Operations Manager; Quality Control Supervisor. **Educational backgrounds include:** Engineering. **Benefits:** Dental Insurance; Disability Coverage; Life Insurance; Medical Insurance; Pension Plan; Prescription Drugs; Savings Plan; Tuition Assistance. **Corporate headquarters location:** This Location. **Operations at this facility include:** Manufacturing.

ORBITAL SCIENCES CORPORATION
21700 Atlantic Boulevard, Dulles VA 20166. 703/406-5000. **Fax:** 703/406-5511. **Contact:** Emily Bender, Employment Manager. **E-mail address:** staffing@orbital.com. **World Wide Web address:** http://www.orbital.com. **Description:** Designs, manufactures, operates, and markets a broad range of space and ground infrastructure systems, satellite access products, and satellite services. These include launch vehicles, satellites, space and sensor electronics, satellite ground systems and software, satellite-based navigation and communications products, and satellite-delivered communications and Earth-imaging services. Founded in 1982.

Common positions include: Account Manager; Account Representative; Accountant/Auditor; Administrative Assistant; Applications Engineer; Attorney; Controller; Design Engineer; Electrical/Electronics Engineer; Human Resources Manager; Marketing Manager; Marketing Specialist; Mechanical Engineer; Secretary; Software Engineer; Systems Analyst. **Educational backgrounds include:** Computer Science; Engineering; Finance. **Benefits:** 401(k); Dental Insurance; Disability Coverage; Job Sharing; Life Insurance; Medical Insurance; Profit Sharing; Tuition Assistance. **Special programs:** Internships. **Internship information:** Internships are offered to undergraduate and graduate students in the areas of computer science, electrical, mechanical, and systems engineering. Resumes must be received by March 15. **Corporate headquarters location:** This Location. **Listed on:** New York Stock Exchange. **Number of employees worldwide:** 5,500.

OZONE INDUSTRIES, INC.
29 Industrial Park Road, P.O. Box 219, East Lyme CT 06333. 860/739-4926. **Fax:** 860/691-2321. **Contact:** Donald W. Miner, Human Resources Manager. **E-mail address:** info@ozone-ind.com. **World Wide Web address:** http://www.ozone-ind.com. **Description:** This location houses manufacturing, engineering, quality control, marketing, and administrative offices. Overall, Ozone Industries Inc. designs, develops, and manufactures hydraulics for the aerospace and industrial markets. Products include landing gear, aircraft steering systems, and hydraulic power, control, and storage devices. **Common positions include:** Accountant; Aerospace Engineer; Electrical Engineer; Mechanical Engineer. **Educational backgrounds include:** Engineering. **Benefits:** 401(k); Dental Insurance; Disability Coverage; Life Insurance; Medical Insurance; Pension Plan; Profit Sharing. **Office hours:** Monday - Friday, 8:00 a.m. - 5:00 p.m. **Corporate headquarters location:** United Kingdom. **Parent company:** BBA Group, plc. **Operations at this facility include:** Administration; Manufacturing; Sales. **Annual sales/revenues:** $11 - $20 million. **Number of employees at this location:** 130.

PTI TECHNOLOGIES, INC.
950 Rancho Conejo Boulevard, Newbury Park CA 91320. 805/499-2661. **Fax:** 805/375-2417. **Contact:** Employment. **World Wide Web address:** http://www.ptitechnologies.com. **Description:** PTI Technologies designs, manufactures, and markets filtration and coupling equipment that is used in most commercial, military, and general aviation aircraft. The company also produces and markets filters for use in fluid power systems in heavy equipment, industrial machinery, and energy extraction applications. **Common positions include:** Accountant; Aerospace Engineer; Blue-Collar Worker Supervisor; Buyer; Computer Programmer; Credit Manager; Draftsperson; Industrial Engineer; Mechanical Engineer; Operations Manager; Purchasing Agent; Quality Control Supervisor. **Educational backgrounds include:** Accounting; Engineering. **Benefits:** Dental Insurance; Disability Coverage; Employee Discounts; Life Insurance; Medical Insurance; Pension Plan; Savings Plan; Tuition Assistance. **Special programs:** Summer Jobs. **Parent company:** ESCO Electronics Corporation is a diversified producer of defense systems and commercial products including valves and filters, mobile tactical systems, armament systems, automatic test equipment, utility load management equipment, and anechoic/shielding systems. ESCO's other operating subsidiaries include EMC Test Systems, L.P.; VACCO Industries; Comtrak

Technologies, Inc.; Filtertek Inc.; Lindgren RF Enclosures; Distribution Control Systems, Inc.; Rantec Microwave & Electronics. **Operations at this facility include:** Manufacturing; Research and Development; Sales.

PEMCO AEROPLEX, INC.
P.O. Box 2287, Birmingham AL 35201. 205/592-0011. **Contact:** Brian Cameron, Human Resources Director. **World Wide Web address:** http://www.pemcoair.com. **Description:** Engaged in the maintenance, modification, overhaul, and repair of military and commercial multi-engine aircraft and components. **Common positions include:** Accountant; Aerospace Engineer; Biomedical Engineer; Blue-Collar Worker Supervisor; Buyer; Chemist; Civil Engineer; Commercial Artist; Computer Programmer; Draftsperson; Financial Manager; Human Resources Manager; Industrial Engineer; Marketing Manager; Mechanical Engineer; Metallurgical Engineer; Production Manager; Purchasing Agent; Quality Control Supervisor; Services Sales Rep.; Statistician; Systems Analyst; Technical Writer. **Educational backgrounds include:** Accounting; Business Administration; Chemistry; Communications; Computer Science; Engineering; Finance; Marketing; Mathematics; Physics. **Benefits:** Dental Insurance; Disability Coverage; Life Insurance; Medical Insurance; Pension Plan; Savings Plan; Tuition Assistance. **Special programs:** Internships. **Corporate headquarters location:** This Location. **Parent company:** Precision Standard, Inc. **Operations at this facility include:** Manufacturing; Research and Development; Sales; Service. **Listed on:** New York Stock Exchange.

PHAOSTRON INSTRUMENT & ELECTRONICS
717 North Coney Avenue, Azusa CA 91702. 626/969-6801. **Fax:** 626/334-8057. **Contact:** Ms. Jackie Cangialosi, Human Resources Manager. **World Wide Web address:** http://www.phaostron.com. **Description:** Primarily engaged in the manufacture and sale of panel meters, avionic mechanisms, and edge-lighted plastic panels for a variety of aircraft. **Common positions include:** Aerospace Engineer; Industrial Engineer; Machinist; Mechanical Engineer; Precision Assembler; Quality Control Supervisor; Receptionist; Tool and Die Maker. **Educational backgrounds include:** Business Administration; Engineering. **Benefits:** Life Insurance; Medical Insurance. **Operations at this facility include:** Manufacturing.

PIONEER INDUSTRIES
7000 Highland Parkway SW, Seattle WA 98106. 206/762-7737. **Contact:** Human Resources. **Description:** A contract manufacturer of aircraft components and sheet metal products for a variety of industrial uses. Founded in 1966. **NOTE:** Second and third shifts are offered. **Common positions include:** Blue-Collar Worker Supervisor; Cost Estimator; Production Manager; Quality Control Supervisor; Teacher. **Benefits:** 403(b); Dental Insurance; Disability Coverage; Employee Discounts; Life Insurance; Medical Insurance; Pension Plan; Public Transit Available; Tuition Assistance. **Special programs:** Training. **Corporate headquarters location:** This Location. **Parent company:** Pioneer Human Services operates rehabilitation and job training programs for work-release prisoners and people recovering from addictions.

PRATT & WHITNEY
400 Main Street, East Hartford CT 06108. 860/565-4321. **Contact:** John Leary, Vice President of Personnel. **World Wide Web address:** http://www.pratt-whitney.com. **Description:** Pratt & Whitney manufactures aircraft engine parts and blades for commercial and military engines. **Corporate headquarters location:** This Location. **Parent company:** United Technologies Corporation designs and manufactures engines and space propulsion systems for commercial and general aviation. Products include large jet engines, temperature control systems, elevators and escalators, helicopters, and flight systems. The company markets its products under a variety of brand names including Carrier heating and air-conditioning systems, Hamilton Sundstrand aerospace systems, Otis elevators, Pratt & Whitney engines, and Sikorsky helicopters.
Other U.S. locations:
- 1177 Great Southwest Parkway, Grand Prairie TX 75050. 972/647-7800.

THE PURDY CORPORATION
586 Hillard Street, P.O. Box 1898, Manchester CT 06045-1898. 860/649-0000. **Contact:** Personnel. **World Wide Web address:** http://www.purdytransmissions.com. **Description:** The Purdy Corporation manufactures major parts for helicopters and other aircraft including gear box housings and components. Founded in 1946. **NOTE:** Employees are trained in advanced machining and are offered courses in computers, electronics, engineering, and mathematics. **Corporate headquarters location:** This Location.

ROCKWELL COLLINS
P.O. Box 833807, Richardson TX 75083-3807. 972/705-3598. **Fax:** 972/705-1124. **Recorded jobline:** 972/705-1870. **Contact:** Personnel. **E-mail address:** careers@collins.rockwell.com. **World Wide Web address:** http://www.collins.rockwell.com. **Description:** Manufactures electronic aviation systems for use in both commercial and military aircraft. **NOTE:** Entry-level positions are offered. Please call the jobline for a listing of open positions. **Common positions include:** Administrative Assistant; Electrical Engineer; Mechanical Engineer; Secretary; Software Engineer. **Educational backgrounds include:** Engineering. **Benefits:** 401(k); Casual Dress - Daily; Dental Insurance; Disability Coverage; Employee Discounts; Flexible Schedule; Life Insurance; Medical Insurance; Pension Plan; Profit Sharing; Savings Plan; Tuition Assistance. **Special programs:** Co-ops; Internships; Summer Jobs. **Corporate headquarters location:** Cedar Rapids IA. **Other U.S. locations:** Pomona CA; Melbourne FL. **International locations:** Worldwide. **Operations at this facility include:** Administration; Manufacturing; Research and Development. **Listed on:** New York Stock Exchange. **Annual sales/revenues:** More than $100 million. **Number of employees at this location:** 750. **Number of employees worldwide:** 40,000.

ROLLS ROYCE ENGINE SERVICES
7200 Earhart Road, Oakland CA 94621. 510/613-1000. **Fax:** 510/635-6911. **Recorded jobline:** 510/613-1011. **Contact:** Cheryl Williams, Human Resources Manager. **Description:** Engaged in the maintenance, repair, and overhaul of aviation and industrial gas turbine engines. Founded in 1960. **NOTE:** Entry-level positions and part-time jobs are offered. **Company slogan:** Engines fueled by people. **Common positions include:** Account Manager; Administrative Assistant; Blue-Collar Worker Supervisor; Computer Support Technician; Computer Technician; Customer Service Rep.; Database Administrator; Financial Analyst; Mechanical Engineer; Metallurgical Engineer; Network Administrator; Sales Executive; Technical Writer. **Educational backgrounds include:** C/C++; Engineering; MCSE; Novell. **Benefits:** 401(k);

Casual Dress - Daily; Dental Insurance; Disability Coverage; Flexible Schedule; Life Insurance; Medical Insurance; Profit Sharing; Public Transit Available; Savings Plan; Sick Days (6 - 10); Tuition Assistance; Vacation Days (10 - 20). **Special programs:** Apprenticeships; Co-ops; Internships; Training. **Corporate headquarters location:** This Location. **Parent company:** First Aviation Services, Inc. **Operations at this facility include:** Administration; Manufacturing; Sales; Service. **President/CEO:** Raj Sharma. **Purchasing Manager:** Barry Lynch. **Sales Manager:** Joe Ghantous. **Annual sales/revenues:** More than $100 million. **Number of employees at this location:** 340. **Number of employees nationwide:** 360.

SIMULA GOVERNMENT PRODUCTS, INC.
7414 South Harl, Tempe AZ 85283. 480/730-4338. **Fax:** 480/756-2737. **Contact:** Human Resources. **World Wide Web address:** http://www.simula. com. **Description:** Researches, develops, and manufactures crash-worthy aircraft components and related structural products for the U.S. military and prime defense contractors. **Company slogan:** Protecting people in motion. **Common positions include:** Designer; Industrial Engineer; Manufacturing Engineer; Mechanical Engineer; Quality Assurance Engineer. **Benefits:** 401(k); Dental Insurance; Disability Coverage; Employee Discounts; Life Insurance; Medical Insurance; Tuition Assistance. **Corporate headquarters location:** Phoenix AZ. **Parent company:** Simula, Inc. **Operations at this facility include:** Manufacturing. **Number of employees at this location:** 240.

SKYLINE INDUSTRIES, INC.
P.O. Box 821, Fort Worth TX 76101. 817/551-1967. **Contact:** Personnel Department. **World Wide Web address:** http://www.skyline-usa.com. **Description:** A manufacturer of aircraft parts including armored pilot seats, floor armor, seat covers, ground handling equipment, and aerospace fasteners. **Corporate headquarters location:** This Location.

SMITHS INDUSTRIES AEROSPACE
255 Great Valley Parkway, Malvern PA 19355. 610/296-5000. **Fax:** 610/296-0912. **Contact:** Anita Schweiger, Human Resources. **E-mail address:** schweigeranita@si.com. **World Wide Web address:** http://www.smithsind-aerospace.com. **Description:** Develops and manufactures avionics instruments and fuel systems. **Common positions include:** Accountant; Administrative Assistant; Computer Support Technician; Computer Technician; Controller; Customer Service Representative; Database Administrator; Database Manager; Editorial Assistant; Finance Director; Financial Analyst; General Manager; Graphic Artist; Human Resources Manager; Industrial Production Manager; Internet Services Manager; Managing Editor; Marketing Manager; Marketing Specialist; MIS Specialist; Operations Manager; Production Manager; Purchasing Agent/Manager; Quality Control Supervisor; Vice President. **Educational backgrounds include:** Microsoft Word; Novell; Software Development; Spreadsheets; Visual Basic. **Benefits:** 401(k); Casual Dress - Fridays; Dental Insurance; Disability Coverage; Flexible Schedule; Life Insurance; Medical Insurance; Pension Plan; Profit Sharing; Savings Plan; Sick Days (6 - 10); Tuition Assistance; Vacation Days (6 - 10). **Special programs:** Co-ops; Internships. **Internship information:** Internships are available in engineering, manufacturing, and marketing. **Corporate headquarters location:** London, England. **International locations:** France; Germany; South America. **Parent company:** Smiths Industries, plc. **Listed on:** European Bourse. **CEO:**

Keith Butler-Wheelhouse. **Facilities Manager:** Lee Barthold. **Information Systems Manager:** Raymond Ray. **Purchasing Manager:** Carol Festa. **Number of employees at this location:** 165. **Number of employees nationwide:** 2,500. **Number of employees worldwide:** 15,000. **Other U.S. locations:**
- Smiths Industries Aerospace, DCS - Leland, 740 East National Road, Vandalia OH 45377. 937/898-5881.

SPACEHAB, INC.
300 D Street SW, Suite 814, Washington DC 20024. 202/488-3500. **Contact:** Human Resources. **World Wide Web address:** http://www.spacehab.com. **Description:** Manufactures modules used by NASA to carry experiments, equipment, and supplies to space stations. **Corporate headquarters location:** This Location. **Listed on:** NASDAQ.

STANLEY AVIATION CORPORATION
2501 Dallas Street, Aurora CO 80010. 303/340-5200. **Contact:** Jim Sexton, Vice President of Human Resources. **Description:** Manufactures structural sheet metal and metal tube fabrications for the aircraft industry, couplings used in aircraft and missiles, structural ground support equipment for airlines, and large metal containers. **Common positions include:** Accountant; Buyer; Cost Estimator; Department Manager; Draftsperson; Manufacturer's Sales Rep.; Marketing Specialist; Mechanical Engineer; Systems Analyst. **Educational backgrounds include:** Accounting; Business Administration; Engineering; Marketing. **Benefits:** 401(k); Daycare Assistance; Dental Insurance; Disability Coverage; Life Insurance; Medical Insurance; Pension Plan; Profit Sharing; Savings Plan; Tuition Assistance. **Corporate headquarters location:** This Location. **Parent company:** Flight Refueling Ltd. **Operations at this facility include:** Administration; Manufacturing; Research and Development; Sales. **Number of employees at this location:** 180.

STELLEX MONITOR AEROSPACE CORP.
1000 New Horizons Boulevard, Amityville NY 11701-1181. 631/957-2300. **Contact:** Human Resources. **World Wide Web address:** http://www. monair.com. **Description:** Manufactures precision structural aerospace parts and assemblies for commercial and military aircraft.

SVERDRUP TECHNOLOGY, INC.
600 William Northern Boulevard, Tullahoma TN 37388. 931/455-6400. **Fax:** 931/393-6394. **Contact:** Alexis Walker, Employment Specialist. **E-mail address:** walkeras@sverdrup.com. **World Wide Web address:** http://www.sverdrup.com. **Description:** A professional and engineering services firm supporting NASA, U.S. Department of Defense entities, and private companies. **Common positions include:** Accountant; Administrative Assistant; Auditor; Chemical Engineer; Civil Engineer; Computer Programmer; Computer Support Technician; Design Engineer; Draftsperson; Electrical Engineer; Environmental Engineer; Financial Analyst; Graphic Designer; Intranet Developer; Mechanical Engineer; Network Administrator; Secretary; Technical Writer; Website Developer. **Educational backgrounds include:** Accounting; Business Administration; C/C++; Computer Science; Engineering; Finance; HTML; Internet Development; Marketing; MBA; MCSE; Microsoft Office; Microsoft Word; Novell; Spreadsheets. **Benefits:** 401(k); Casual Dress - Fridays; Dental Insurance; Disability Coverage; Flexible Schedule; Life Insurance; Medical Insurance; Relocation Assistance; Telecommuting; Tuition Assistance. **Corporate headquarters**

location: This Location. **Parent company:** Sverdrup Corporation. **Number of employees worldwide:** 4,000.

TRW SPACE & ELECTRONICS GROUP
One Space Park, Building E-1, Room 2012, Redondo Beach CA 90278. 310/812-4321. **Contact:** Recruiting Department. **World Wide Web address:** http://www.trw.com. **Description:** Designs and develops space systems, microelectronics, and aircraft avionics for worldwide government and commercial use. TRW Space & Electronics Group's technologies are employed in several national security, communications, and science program projects. **Corporate headquarters location:** Cleveland OH. **Parent company:** TRW Inc. **Listed on:** New York Stock Exchange.

TECH-SYM CORPORATION
10500 Westoffice Drive, Suite 200, Houston TX 77042. 713/785-7790. **Contact:** Human Resources. **World Wide Web address:** http://www.tech-sym.com. **Description:** A holding company that provides administrative support for its various subsidiaries that manufacture aerospace products including microwave subsystems, defense products, and radio transmitters. **Corporate headquarters location:** This Location. **International locations:** Chile; Germany; Scotland. **Subsidiaries include:** Continental Electronics Corporation, 4212 South Buckner Boulevard, Dallas TX 75227, 214/381-7161; Enterprise Electronics Corporation, 128 South Industrial Boulevard, Enterprise AL 36330, 334/347-3478; Metric Systems Corporation, 645 Anchors Street, Fort Walton Beach FL 32548, 850/302-3000; TRAK Microwave Corporation, 4726 Eisenhower Boulevard, Tampa FL 33634, 813/901-7200.

TELEPHONICS CORPORATION
815 Broad Hollow Road, Farmingdale NY 11735. 516/755-7000. **Fax:** 516/755-7409. **Contact:** Mrs. Winsome Foulkes, Director of Human Resources. **World Wide Web address:** http://www.telephonics.com. **Description:** Supplies advanced engineering products for industrial, military, and aerospace applications. Telephonics Corporation supplies cabin and flight deck avionics for the commercial airline industry with systems in use by more than 60 different airlines. The company also serves the military and aerospace markets by offering a complete line of secure communications systems, advanced avionics, and sonar support systems. The company offers commercial acoustics field products ranging from lightweight telephone headsets to highly-sensitive earphones used for clinical hearing analysis, as well as the company's traditional line of aircraft microphones and headsets. **Common positions include:** Accountant; Buyer; Computer Operator; Computer Programmer; Cost Estimator; Draftsperson; Electrical Engineer; Electrician; Financial Manager; Human Resources Manager; Mechanical Engineer; Purchasing Agent; Receptionist; Secretary; Software Engineer; Systems Analyst; Technical Writer/Editor; Typist/Word Processor. **Educational backgrounds include:** Accounting; Business Administration; Communications; Engineering; Finance; Liberal Arts. **Benefits:** Dental Insurance; Disability Coverage; Life Insurance; Medical Insurance; Pension Plan; Profit Sharing; Tuition Assistance. **Corporate headquarters location:** This Location. **Other U.S. locations:** Gardena CA; Boston MA; Huntington NY. **Parent company:** Griffon Corporation. **Operations at this facility include:** Administration; Manufacturing; Research and Development. **Listed on:** American Stock Exchange. **Number of employees nationwide:** 900.

TEXTRON INC.
40 Westminster Street, Providence RI 02903. 401/421-2800. **Fax:** 401/457-3599. **Recorded jobline:** 877/4-TEXTRON. **Contact:** Lisa Whiting, Manager of Employment. **World Wide Web address:** http://www.textron.com. **Description:** A diversified conglomerate with over 30 separate companies in four primary areas: Aerospace and Defense Technology; Financial Services; Industrial; and Automotive. **NOTE:** Entry-level positions are offered. **Common positions include:** Accountant; Administrative Manager; Attorney; Auditor; Budget Analyst; Financial Analyst; Human Resources Manager; Marketing Manager; Marketing Specialist; Paralegal; Public Relations Specialist; Telecommunications Manager. **Educational backgrounds include:** Accounting; Business Administration; Communications; Economics; Finance; Liberal Arts; Marketing; Microsoft Word; Public Relations; Spreadsheets. **Benefits:** 401(k); Casual Dress - Fridays; Dental Insurance; Disability Coverage; Employee Discounts; Financial Planning Assistance; Flexible Schedule; Job Sharing; Life Insurance; Medical Insurance; Pension Plan; Profit Sharing; Public Transit Available; Savings Plan; Sick Days (6 - 10); Telecommuting; Tuition Assistance; Vacation Days (16+). **Special programs:** Co-ops; Internships; Summer Jobs; Training. **Corporate headquarters location:** This Location. **International locations:** Worldwide. **Subsidiaries include:** Bell Helicopter; Cessna Aircraft Company. **Chairman/CEO:** Lewis Campbell. **Annual sales/revenues:** More than $100 million. **Number of employees worldwide:** 68,000. **Other U.S. locations:**
- H.R. Textron, Inc., 25200 West Rye Canyon Road, Santa Clarita CA 91355. 661/294-6000.

UNITED TECHNOLOGIES CORP.
One Financial Plaza, Hartford CT 06101. 860/728-7000. **Contact:** Human Resources Manager. **World Wide Web address:** http://www.utc.com. **Description:** A *Fortune* 500 company that provides high-tech products and support services to customers in the aerospace, building, military, and automotive industries worldwide. Products include large jet engines, temperature control systems, elevators and escalators, helicopters, and flight systems. The company markets its products under a variety of brand names including Carrier, International Fuel Cells, Hamilton Sundstrand, Otis, Pratt & Whitney, and Sikorsky. **Corporate headquarters location:** This Location. **International locations:** Asia; Australia; Canada; Europe; Latin America; Mexico.

VERIDIAN ENGINEERING
5200 Springfield Pike, Suite 200, Dayton OH 45431. 937/253-4770. **Fax:** 937/476-2900. **Contact:** JoAnne Henry, Personnel Manager. **E-mail address:** personnel@dytn.veridian.com. **World Wide Web address:** http://www.veridian.com. **Description:** Researches, develops, and tests major U.S. aircraft and spacecraft. Veridian Engineering operates through three groups. The Flight Research Group operates in-flight simulators. The Transportation Group focuses on vehicle transportation safety. The Systems Analysis and Research Group supplies human systems technology services to the U.S. Department of Defense. **Common positions include:** Accountant; Administrative Assistant; Administrative Manager; Biological Scientist; Buyer; Chemist; CFO; Computer Operator; Computer Programmer; Cost Estimator; Design Engineer; Draftsperson; Editor; Electrical Engineer; Electrician; Environmental Engineer; General Manager; Graphic Artist; Graphic Designer; Human Resources Manager; Market Research Analyst; Marketing Manager; Marketing

Specialist; Mechanical Engineer; MIS Specialist; Project Manager; Psychologist; Quality Control Supervisor; Software Engineer; Statistician; Systems Analyst; Systems Manager; Technical Writer; Typist. **Educational backgrounds include:** Chemistry; Computer Science; Engineering. **Benefits:** 401(k); Dental Insurance; Disability Coverage; Employee Discounts; Life Insurance; Medical Insurance; Tuition Assistance. **Number of employees at this location:** 425.

WORLD FUEL SERVICES, INC.
700 South Royal Poinciana Boulevard, Suite 800, Miami Springs FL 33166. 305/884-2001. **Contact:** Ileana Garcia, Director of Human Resources. **Description:** Engaged in aviation fuel services for air carriers and provides used oil recycling services in the southeastern United States. **Common positions include:** Accountant; Biological Scientist; Chemist; Credit Manager; Geologist/Geophysicist; Petroleum Engineer; Services Sales Representative. **Educational backgrounds include:** Accounting; Business Administration; Chemistry. **Benefits:** Dental Insurance; Life Insurance; Medical Insurance. **Corporate headquarters location:** This Location.

WYMAN-GORDON COMPANY
244 Worcester Street, Box 8001, North Grafton MA 01536-8001. 508/839-4441. **Contact:** Human Resources. **World Wide Web address:** http://www. wyman-gordon.com. **Description:** This location manufactures metal components for aerospace applications. Overall, Wyman-Gordon uses forging and investment casting technologies to produce components for applications such as jet turbine engines and airframes, and designs and produces prototype products using composite technologies. The Forging Division melts titanium into ingot; converts ingot to billet in its cogging presses; produces superalloy metal powders; and consolidates and extrudes these powders into billets. Founded in 1883. **Common positions include:** Design Engineer; Designer; Environmental Engineer; Manufacturing Engineer. **Educational backgrounds include:** Accounting; Computer Science; Engineering; Finance; Liberal Arts; Marketing; Mathematics; Physics. **Benefits:** Dental Insurance; Disability Coverage; Life Insurance; Medical Insurance; Pension Plan; Savings Plan; Tuition Assistance. **Corporate headquarters location:** This Location. **Subsidiaries include:** Wyman-Gordon Investment Castings, Inc. (WGIC) uses automated, high-volume, production equipment and both air-melt and vacuum-melt furnaces to produce a wide variety of complex investment castings. WGIC investment castings are made from a range of metal alloys including aluminum and magnesium, steel, titanium, and high temperature-based alloys. The company's composites operation, Scaled Composites, Inc., plans, proposes, designs, fabricates, and tests prototypes for aerospace, automotive, and other customers. **Parent company:** Precision Castparts Corporation. **Listed on:** NASDAQ. **Number of employees at this location:** 725. **Number of employees nationwide:** 2,600. **Number of employees worldwide:** 3,000.

For more information on career opportunities in aerospace:

Associations

AHS INTERNATIONAL -- THE VERTICAL FLIGHT SOCIETY
217 North Washington Street, Alexandria VA 22314. 703/684-6777. Fax: 703/739-9279. E-mail address: ahs703@aol.com. World Wide Web address: http://www.vtol.org. Promotes the advancement of vertical flight technology.

AMERICAN ASTRONAUTICAL SOCIETY
6352 Rolling Mill Place, Suite 102, Springfield VA 22152-2354. 703/866-0020. Fax: 703/866-3526. E-mail address: info@astronautical.org. World Wide Web address: http://www.astronautical.org. Offers conferences and scholarships for students.

AMERICAN INSTITUTE OF AERONAUTICS AND ASTRONAUTICS, INC.
1801 Alexander Bell Drive, Suite 500, Reston VA 20191-4344. 703/264-7500. Toll-free phone: 800/NEW-AIAA. Fax: 703/264-7551. World Wide Web address: http://www.aiaa.org. Membership required. Publishes 10 journals and books. The Website provides information on employment opportunities, resume services, aerospace news, career placement services, continuing education resources, and a mentor program.

NATIONAL AERONAUTIC ASSOCIATION
1815 North Fort Myer Drive, Suite 700, Arlington VA 22209. 703/527-0226. World Wide Web address: http://www.naa.ycg.org. Publishes a magazine. Membership required.

PROFESSIONAL AVIATION MAINTENANCE ASSOCIATION
1707 H Street NW, Suite 700, Washington DC 20006-3915.202/730-0260. World Wide Web address: http://www.pama.org. Conducts local and national seminars; publishes industry news journals; and addresses government issues. Members have access to the Worldwide Membership Directory.

Newsletters

AIR JOBS DIGEST
World Air Data, Department 700, P.O. Box 42360, Washington DC 20015. This monthly resource provides current job openings in aerospace, space, and aviation industries. Subscription rates: $96.00 annually, $69.00 for six months, and $49.00 for three months.

Online Services

AVIATION EMPLOYMENT.COM
World Wide Web address: http://www. aviationemployment.com. Offers employer profiles and job listings.

SPACE JOBS
World Wide Web address: http://www.spacejobs. com. Provides national and international job listings in the aerospace field. Includes an e-mail service that notified jobseekers of opportunities that match their criteria.

Apparel, Fashion, and Textiles

You can expect to find the following types of companies in this chapter:
*Broadwoven Fabric Mills • Knitting Mills • Curtains and Draperies • Footwear
Nonwoven Fabrics • Textile Goods and Finishing • Yarn and Thread Mills*

....

Some helpful information: *The average salary for machine operators and other apparel
and textile production workers is normally under $25,000 yearly but can increase based
on experience, particularly for workers who attain supervisory positions. Upholsterers
earn, on average, $18,000 - $22,000 per year.*

....

ABERDEEN SPORTSWEAR, INC.
350 Fifth Avenue, Suite 2828, New York NY
10118. 212/244-5100. **Contact:** Thomas Jackson,
Controller. **Description:** Produces sport jackets.
Corporate headquarters location: This Location.

ACE TEX ENTERPRISES
7601 Central Avenue, Detroit MI 48210. 313/834-
4000. **Contact:** Personnel. **World Wide Web
address:** http://www.ace-tex.com. **Description:**
Manufactures textile goods including cotton wiping
cloths. **Common positions include:** Accountant;
Administrator; Blue-Collar Worker Supervisor;
Branch Manager; Customer Service Rep.;
Department Manager; Financial Analyst; Human
Resources Manager; Management Trainee;
Manufacturer's Sales Rep.; Operations Manager;
Purchasing Agent; Quality Control Supervisor;
Transportation. **Educational backgrounds include:**
Accounting; Finance; Liberal Arts; Marketing.
Benefits: Dental Insurance; Disability Coverage;
Life Insurance; Medical Insurance; Pension Plan;
Profit Sharing. **Corporate headquarters location:**
This Location. **Operations at this facility include:**
Administration; Manufacturing; Sales; Service.
Number of employees nationwide: 650.

ADIDAS AMERICA
P.O. Box 4015, Beaverton OR 97076. 503/972-
2300. **Contact:** Personnel. **World Wide Web
address:** http://www.adidas.com. **Description:** This
location houses administrative offices. Overall,
Adidas America manufactures athletic wear.
Corporate headquarters location: This Location.

ALBA-WALDENSIAN, INC.
P.O. Box 100, Valdese NC 28690. 828/874-2191.
Physical address: 201 St. Germain Avenue SW,
Valdese NC. **Toll-free phone:** 800/554-2522.
Contact: Human Resources Manager. **World Wide
Web address:** http://www.alba1.com. **Description:**
A national, multifacility apparel manufacturing
company offering a variety of knit products. The
company primarily produces women's knit hosiery
and stretch panties. Alba-Waldensian also produces
knit health care products, which are used in
hospitals and nursing homes, and are distributed
throughout the United States, Canada, England,
Europe, and the Middle East. Founded in 1901.
Corporate headquarters location: This Location.
President/CEO: Lee N. Mortenson. **Number of
employees nationwide:** 850.

AMERICAN IDENTITY
1520 Albany Place SE, Orange City IA 51041.
712/737-4925. **Toll-free phone:** 800/369-4670.
Contact: Deb Sandbulte, Employment Coordinator.
World Wide Web address: http://www.americanid.
com. **Description:** A full-line, promotional products
supplier offering wearables, caps, and specialty
products for men, women, and children. This
location also hires seasonally. **NOTE:** Second and
third shifts are offered. **Common positions include:**
Accountant; Apparel Worker; Bindery Worker;
Blue-Collar Worker Supervisor; Branch Manager;
Buyer; Chef; Commercial Artist; Computer
Operator; Computer Programmer; Computer
Support Technician; Computer Technician;
Construction Trade Worker; Credit Clerk and
Authorizer; Credit Manager; Customer Service
Rep.; Department Manager; Economist; Editor;
Electrician; Employment Interviewer; Food and
Beverage Service Worker; General Manager;
Graphic Artist; Heating Technician; Human
Resources Manager; Industrial Engineer; Industrial
Production Manager; Inspector; Machinist;
Manufacturer's Sales Rep.; Market Research
Analyst; Marketing Manager; Network
Administrator; Payroll Clerk; Photographer
Operator; Photographic Process Worker; Printing
Press Operator; Purchasing Agent; Quality Control
Supervisor; Receptionist; Registered Nurse; Sales
Rep.; Services Sales Rep.; Stock Clerk; Systems
Analyst; Tool and Die Maker; Truck Driver; Typist;
Welder. **Educational backgrounds include:**
Accounting; Art/Design; Business Administration;
Communications; Computer Science; Economics;
Engineering; Finance; Liberal Arts; Marketing;
Mathematics; MBA; MCSE; Spreadsheets.
Benefits: 401(k); Casual Dress - Daily; Dental
Insurance; Disability Coverage; Employee
Discounts; Flexible Schedule; Job Sharing; Life
Insurance; Medical Insurance; Profit Sharing;
Relocation Assistance; Savings Plan. **Office hours:**
Monday - Friday, 7:30 a.m. - 4:30 p.m. **Corporate
headquarters location:** Kansas City MO. **Other
U.S. locations:** Hawarden IA; Marcus IA; Rock
Rapids IA; Bonner Springs KS; Shawnee KS; Ocean
Springs MS; Fairbury NE; Canton SD. **Parent
company:** AMI. **Operations at this facility
include:** Administration; Divisional Headquarters;
Manufacturing; Sales. **President:** Roger Henry.
Facilities Manager: Wally Boogerd. **Information
Systems Manager:** Randy Kirsch. **Purchasing
Manager:** Gerry Korver. **Annual sales/revenues:**
More than $100 million. **Number of employees at
this location:** 650. **Number of employees
nationwide:** 2,400.

ANGELICA CORPORATION
424 South Woods Mill Road, Suite 300,
Chesterfield MO 63017-3406. 314/854-3800.
Contact: Personnel. **World Wide Web address:**
http://www.angelica-corp.com. **Description:** This
location houses the general offices for the Angelica
Healthcare Services Group, Inc., a health care
uniform rental store. Overall, Angelica Corporation
provides textile rental and laundry services;
manufactures and markets uniform and business
career apparel; and operates specialty retail stores
primarily for nurses and other health care
professionals. Angelica's principal markets include

health service networks and institutions (such as hospitals, nursing homes, outpatient service centers, health maintenance organizations, medical clinics, and laboratories) and health service personnel (such as doctors, dentists, and nurses); the hospitality market including lodging establishments (such as resorts, hotels and motels, and gaming establishments) and food service establishments (such as fast food, dinner and cafeteria chains, restaurants, food service management companies, amusement parks, clubs, and other eating and drinking places); other service industries including retailers (such as supermarkets and other food stores), drug and discount stores, financial institutions, transportation companies (such as car rental, cruise line, airline, bus, and other public transportation companies); manufacturers (such as food processors, drug and pharmaceutical, high-technology, and automotive companies); law enforcement and security companies; and educational and government institutions. **Common positions include:** Accountant; Credit Manager; Customer Service Rep.; Industrial Designer; Manufacturer's Sales Rep.; Marketing Specialist; Operations Manager; Quality Control Supervisor; Systems Analyst. **Educational backgrounds include:** Accounting; Art/Design; Business Administration; Computer Science; Liberal Arts; Marketing. **Benefits:** Dental Insurance; Disability Coverage; Employee Discounts; Life Insurance; Medical Insurance; Pension Plan; Savings Plan; Tuition Assistance. **Corporate headquarters location:** This Location. **Operations at this facility include:** Administration; Manufacturing; Sales; Service. **Number of employees nationwide:** 9,500.

ALFRED ANGELO, INC.
116 Welsh Road, Horsham PA 19044. 215/659-5300. **Contact:** Personnel. **Description:** Designs, manufactures, and wholesales bridal gowns, special occasion dresses, and a wide range of related accessories. **Common positions include:** Accountant; Computer Programmer; Credit Manager; Customer Service Rep.; Department Manager; Designer; Financial Analyst; Manufacturer's Sales Rep.; Marketing Specialist; Operations Manager; Purchasing Agent; Systems Analyst; Warehouse Worker. **Educational backgrounds include:** Accounting; Business Administration; Communications; Computer Science; Finance; Liberal Arts; Marketing. **Benefits:** Dental Insurance; Disability Coverage; Flexible Benefits; Life Insurance; Medical Insurance; Profit Sharing; Tuition Assistance. **Corporate headquarters location:** This Location. **Operations at this facility include:** Administration; Design; Manufacturing; Sales; Service.

ARROWOOD MILLS, INC.
P.O. Box 908, Mount Pleasant NC 28124. 704/436-9351. **Contact:** Linda Bridges, Personnel Director. **Description:** A manufacturer and wholesaler of women's sheer hosiery. **Benefits:** Dental Insurance; Employee Discounts; Life Insurance; Medical Insurance; Pension Plan; Savings Plan. **Corporate headquarters location:** This Location. **Operations at this facility include:** Manufacturing; Sales. **Number of employees at this location:** 200.

ASHLEY MANUFACTURING INC.
P.O. Box 1357, Jesup GA 31545. 912/427-8734. **Fax:** 912/427-0321. **Contact:** Art Stone, President. **Description:** Manufactures Halloween costumes, as well as tap, jazz, and ballet clothing. **Common positions include:** Accountant; Blue-Collar Worker Supervisor; Clerical Supervisor; Designer; Industrial Production Manager; Operations Manager. **Educational backgrounds include:** Accounting; Art/Design. **Benefits:** Life Insurance;

Medical Insurance; Profit Sharing. **Special programs:** Internships. **Corporate headquarters location:** This Location. **Operations at this facility include:** Administration; Divisional Headquarters; Manufacturing. **Number of employees at this location:** 600.

ASHWORTH, INC.
2791 Loker Avenue West, Carlsbad CA 92008. 760/438-6610. **Contact:** Human Resources. **World Wide Web address:** http://www.ashworthinc.com. **Description:** Designs, manufactures, and markets golf apparel including men's and women's cotton shirts, pullovers, sweaters, shorts, pants, and jackets. **Corporate headquarters location:** This Location.

BARCO OF CALIFORNIA
350 West Rosecrans Avenue, Gardena CA 90248. 310/323-7315. **Contact:** Human Resources. **Description:** Manufactures and markets uniforms for health care and fast-food companies. **Corporate headquarters location:** This Location. **Number of employees at this location:** 250.

G.H. BASS & COMPANY
P.O. Box 9431, South Portland ME 04116-9431. 207/791-4000. **Fax:** 207/791-4905. **Contact:** Human Resources. **World Wide Web address:** http://www.ghbass.com. **Description:** Manufactures and retails men's and women's casual footwear and apparel. **Common positions include:** Accountant; Computer Operator; Computer Programmer; Customer Service Rep.; Retail Sales Worker; Secretary; Systems Analyst; Wholesale and Retail Buyer. **Benefits:** Daycare Assistance; Disability Coverage; Employee Discounts; Life Insurance; Medical Insurance; Pension Plan; Savings Plan; Tuition Assistance. **Corporate headquarters location:** This Location. **Parent company:** Phillips-Van Heusen Corporation.

BATA SHOE COMPANY, INC.
4501 Pulaski Highway, Belcamp MD 21017. 410/272-2000. **Fax:** 410/272-3346. **Contact:** Lisa Staudenecker, Director of Human Resources. **Description:** A manufacturer and marketer of industrial protective footwear, safety boots, and related products. **Common positions include:** Accountant; Blue-Collar Worker Supervisor; Buyer; Cashier; Chemist; Clinical Lab Technician; Computer Operator; Computer Programmer; Cost Estimator; Credit Manager; Customer Service Rep.; Electrical Engineer; Electrician; Financial Manager; Human Resources Manager; Industrial Engineer; Industrial Production Manager; Machinist; Manufacturer's Sales Rep.; Mechanical Engineer; Order Clerk; Payroll Clerk; Purchasing Agent; Receptionist; Secretary; Stock Clerk; Transportation. **Educational backgrounds include:** Chemistry; Engineering. **Benefits:** Dental Insurance; Disability Coverage; Employee Discounts; Life Insurance; Medical Insurance; Pension Plan; Tuition Assistance. **Corporate headquarters location:** Toronto, Canada. **Operations at this facility include:** Administration; Manufacturing; Sales. **Listed on:** Privately held. **Number of employees at this location:** 170.

BEACH PATROL INC.
1165 East 230th Street, Carson CA 90745. 310/952-8400. **Contact:** Controller. **Description:** Designs swimwear and other apparel. **Corporate headquarters location:** This Location.

BEACON LOOMS, INC.
411 Alfred Avenue, Teaneck NJ 07666. 201/833-1600. **Contact:** Personnel. **Description:** Produces a wide range of textiles, primarily for sale to retailers.

Corporate headquarters location: This Location.
Other U.S. locations: Englewood NJ.

BEST MANUFACTURING, INC.
1633 Broadway, 18th Floor, New York NY 10019.
212/974-1100. **Fax:** 212/245-0385. **Contact:** Gary
C. Wool, Controller. **Description:** A manufacturer
of textiles and washable service apparel. **Common
positions include:** Customer Service Rep.;
Management Trainee. **Educational backgrounds
include:** Liberal Arts. **Benefits:** 401(k); Disability
Coverage; Life Insurance; Medical Insurance;
Pension Plan. **Corporate headquarters location:**
This Location. **Other U.S. locations:** Nationwide.
Operations at this facility include: Administration.
Number of employees at this location: 85.
Number of employees nationwide: 1,100.

BETLIN, INC.
1445 Marion Road, Columbus OH 43207. 614/443-
0248. **Fax:** 614/443-4658. **Contact:** Human
Resources. **Description:** Manufactures customized
athletic uniforms. **Common positions include:**
Accountant; Administrative Manager; Credit
Manager; Human Resources Manager; Purchasing
Agent/Manager. **Educational backgrounds
include:** Accounting; Business Administration.
Benefits: Dental Insurance; Employee Discounts;
Life Insurance; Medical Insurance. **Corporate
headquarters location:** This Location. **Operations
at this facility include:** Administration;
Manufacturing. **Listed on:** Privately held. **Number
of employees at this location:** 100.

BILJO INC.
P.O. Box 609, Dublin GA 31040. 912/272-6935.
Contact: Margaret Crabb, Plant Superintendent.
Description: Manufactures men's trousers.
Corporate headquarters location: This Location.

BOGNER OF AMERICA
P.O. Box 644, Newport VT 05855. 802/334-6507.
Contact: Personnel. **World Wide Web address:**
http://www.bogner-america.com. **Description:**
Manufactures ski and golf clothing. **Corporate
headquarters location:** This Location.

BOLLMAN HAT COMPANY
P.O. Box 517, Adamstown PA 19501. 717/484-
4361. **Physical address:** 110 East Main Street,
Adamstown PA. **Contact:** Denise Koval, Human
Resources Manager. **Description:** A manufacturer
of wool felt, fur felt, cloth, and straw hats. Bollman
Hat Company also cleans and processes wool.
Common positions include: Accountant;
Administrator; Blue-Collar Worker Supervisor;
Buyer; Chemical Engineer; Chemist; Department
Manager; Electrical Engineer; General Manager;
Human Resources Manager; Industrial Designer;
Industrial Engineer; Management Trainee;
Mechanical Engineer; Operations Manager.
Benefits: Daycare Assistance; Dental Insurance;
Disability Coverage; Employee Discounts; Life
Insurance; Medical Insurance; Pension Plan;
Savings Plan; Stock Option; Tuition Assistance.
Corporate headquarters location: This Location.
Operations at this facility include: Manufacturing;
Research and Development; Sales.

BROWN SHOE COMPANY
8300 Maryland Avenue, St. Louis MO 63105.
314/854-4000. **Contact:** Director of Human
Resources. **World Wide Web address:** http://www.
browngroup.com. **Description:** A footwear
company with worldwide operations in the
manufacturing, marketing, and retailing of footwear
for women, men, and children. The company's
Footwear Retail Operations include Famous
Footwear, one of the nation's largest chains of
branded family shoe stores. Brown Shoe also owns
and operates the Naturalizer brand in the United
States and Canada, and the F.X. LaSalle chain of
shoe stores in Canada. Footwear Wholesale
Operations include Pagoda, one of the leading
marketers of brand name footwear throughout the
world. Major brand names include Naturalizer, Life
Stride, NaturalSport, Penaljo, Air Step, and Connie
for women; Dr. Scholl's for men and women; and a
wide variety of children's brands including Disney,
Barbie, Buster Brown, Playskool, and Candie's.
Corporate headquarters location: This Location.
Number of employees nationwide: 14,500.

BROWNWOOD MANUFACTURING CO.
1600 Custer Road, Brownwood TX 76801-6496.
915/646-9505. **Contact:** Personnel. **Description:** A
manufacturer of military raincoats, Navy uniforms,
and Cripple Creek brand jackets. **Corporate
headquarters location:** This Location.

BURKE MILLS, INC.
P.O. Box 190, Valdese NC 28690. 828/874-6341.
Contact: Maggie Hughes, Human Resources
Manager. **Description:** Engaged in twisting,
texturing, winding, dyeing, processing, and selling
filament, novelty, and spun yarns and also in the
dyeing and processing of these yarns for others on a
commission basis. The company's products have
upholstery, apparel, and industrial uses for the
knitting and weaving industry. **Corporate
headquarters location:** This Location.

BURLINGTON INDUSTRIES
3330 West Friendly Avenue, Greensboro NC 27410.
336/379-2000. **Contact:** Jim Guin, Vice President
of Human Resources. **World Wide Web address:**
http://www.burlingtonindustries.com. **Description:**
A major producer of textiles including apparel and
interior furnishings. Apparel products, which are
designed, manufactured, and sold by five divisions
within the company include yarns, wools, woven
synthetics, clothes, denims, industrial uniforms, and
sportswear. The interior furnishings division
includes Burlington House, which manufactures
drapes, upholstery, and bedroom ensembles; the
carpet division, which uses the Lees brand name;
and the Burlington House Area Rugs unit.
Educational backgrounds include: Computer
Science; Engineering; Finance; Manufacturing
Management; Marketing. **Corporate headquarters
location:** This Location.

CHF INDUSTRIES, INC.
8701 Red Oak Boulevard, Charlotte NC 28217.
704/522-5000. **Contact:** Garry Farmer, Director of
Human Resources. **Description:** Designs and
manufactures curtains, draperies, bedspreads,
comforters, and shower curtains. **Common
positions include:** Accountant; AS400 Programmer
Analyst; CFO; Computer Programmer; Controller;
Credit Manager; Financial Analyst; Purchasing
Agent; Systems Manager. **Benefits:** 401(k); Casual
Dress - Daily; Dental Insurance; Disability
Coverage; Life Insurance; Medical Insurance;
Tuition Assistance. **Corporate headquarters
location:** This Location. **Other U.S. locations:** New
York NY. **Listed on:** Privately held.
President/CEO/Owner: Frank Foley. **Information
Systems Manager:** Joe Porto. **Annual
sales/revenues:** More than $100 million. **Number
of employees nationwide:** 1,140.

CARHARTT INC.
P.O. Box 600, Dearborn MI 48121. 313/271-8460.
Contact: Personnel. **Description:** Manufactures
casual and work clothing for men, women, and
children. **Corporate headquarters location:** This
Location.

CARRIAGE INDUSTRIES, INC.
P.O. Box 12542, Calhoun GA 30703. 706/629-9234. **Contact:** Gary Penn, Director of Human Resources. **Description:** A vertically-integrated manufacturer of carpet for the manufactured housing, recreational vehicle, exposition, contract/residential, hospitality/commercial, and home center markets. **Common positions include:** Accountant; Blue-Collar Worker Supervisor; Computer Programmer; Credit Clerk and Authorizer; Customer Service Rep.; Management Trainee; Manufacturer's Sales Rep.; Typist/Word Processor. **Educational backgrounds include:** Accounting; Art/Design; Business Administration; Computer Science; Marketing. **Benefits:** 401(k); Dental Insurance; Disability Coverage; Employee Discounts; Life Insurance; Medical Insurance; Profit Sharing; Retirement Plan; Savings Plan; Tuition Assistance. **Special programs:** Internships. **Other U.S. locations:** CA; IN; TX. **Parent company:** Dixie Group, Inc. **Operations at this facility include:** Administration; Manufacturing; Research and Development; Sales; Service. **Listed on:** NASDAQ. **Number of employees at this location:** 950. **Number of employees nationwide:** 1,010.

CHAMBERS BELT COMPANY
P.O. Box 20367, Phoenix AZ 85036-0367. 602/276-0016. **Physical address:** 2920 East Chambers Street, Phoenix AZ. **Contact:** Personnel. **Description:** Produces leather belts and related leather products. **Common positions include:** Accountant; Blue-Collar Worker Supervisor; Buyer; Chemical Engineer; Computer Programmer; Customer Service Rep.; Human Resources Manager; Manufacturer's Sales Rep.; Mechanical Engineer; Operations Manager; Purchasing Agent. **Educational backgrounds include:** Accounting; Business Administration; Economics; Marketing; Mathematics. **Benefits:** Dental Insurance; Life Insurance; Medical Insurance; Pension Plan; Profit Sharing. **Corporate headquarters location:** This Location. **Operations at this facility include:** Manufacturing; Research and Development.

CHARLES CRAFT
P.O. Box 370, Wadesboro NC 28170. 704/694-5121. **Contact:** Human Resources. **Description:** Charles Craft manufactures and wholesales cotton yarn. **Common positions include:** Accountant; Administrator; Attorney; Blue-Collar Worker Supervisor; Buyer; Computer Programmer; Customer Service Rep.; Department Manager; Financial Analyst; General Manager; Human Resources Manager; Industrial Engineer; Manufacturer's Sales Rep.; Mechanical Engineer; Operations Manager; Purchasing Agent; Quality Control Supervisor. **Educational backgrounds include:** Accounting; Business Administration; Computer Science; Engineering. **Benefits:** Life Insurance; Medical Insurance; Pension Plan; Savings Plan. **Corporate headquarters location:** This Location. **Operations at this facility include:** Manufacturing; Sales; Service.

CHICO'S
11215 Metro Parkway, Fort Myers FL 33912. 941/277-6200. **Fax:** 941/277-5237. **Contact:** Human Resources. **Description:** A manufacturer and retailer of women's apparel. **Corporate headquarters location:** This Location.

CHIPMAN-UNION INC.
500 Sibley Avenue, Union Point GA 30669. 706/486-2112. **Contact:** Human Resources. **Description:** Manufactures textile mill products including women's full-length and knee-length hosiery. **Corporate headquarters location:** This Location.

CLIFTEX CORPORATION
194 Riverside Avenue, New Bedford MA 02746. 508/999-1311. **Contact:** Personnel Manager. **Description:** A manufacturer of men's tailored suits and sportcoats, and ladies' sportswear. **Common positions include:** Accountant; Blue-Collar Worker Supervisor; Buyer; Computer Programmer; Customer Service Rep.; Department Manager; Industrial Engineer; Purchasing Agent/Manager. **Educational backgrounds include:** Accounting; Business Administration; Computer Science; Engineering. **Benefits:** Disability Coverage; Employee Discounts; Life Insurance; Medical Insurance; Savings Plan. **Corporate headquarters location:** This Location. **Operations at this facility include:** Administration; Manufacturing; Service.

COATS NORTH AMERICA
4135 South Stream Boulevard, Charlotte NC 28217. 704/329-5800. **Contact:** Human Resources. **Description:** A manufacturer and supplier of sewing thread and associated products for the industrial and consumer markets. The company is also engaged in manufacturing cotton and synthetic thread and yarn; metal and coil slide fasteners, tapes, trimmings, and small diecastings; wood turnings and novelties; and special machinery spools, nylon travelers, and other plastic injection moldings. **Common positions include:** Accountant; Chemical Engineer; Computer Programmer; Credit Manager; Customer Service Rep.; Economist; Human Resources Manager; Industrial Production Manager; Manufacturer's Sales Rep.; Purchasing Agent/Manager; Quality Control Supervisor; Systems Analyst. **Educational backgrounds include:** Accounting; Business Administration; Chemistry; Marketing. **Benefits:** 401(k); Dental Insurance; Disability Coverage; Life Insurance; Matching Gift; Medical Insurance; Pension Plan; Tuition Assistance. **Corporate headquarters location:** This Location. **Other area locations:** Gastonia NC; Marble NC; Marlon NC; Old Fort NC; Rosman NC; Stanley NC. **Other U.S. locations:** Acworth GA; Albany GA; Cleveland GA; Rossville GA; Thomasville GA; Toccoa GA; New York NY; Bristol RI; Greer SC; Lake City SC. **Subsidiaries include:** Coats & Clark, Inc., Greenville SC. **Operations at this facility include:** Administration; Sales; Service. **Number of employees at this location:** 215. **Number of employees nationwide:** 6,700.

COLLINS & AIKMAN HOLDINGS CORP.
P.O. Box 32665, Charlotte NC 28232. 704/548-2350. **Contact:** Manager of Personnel. **Description:** Collins & Aikman Holdings Corporation and its subsidiaries manufacture home furnishings and hosiery products, as well as textile products for major automobile manufacturers. The home furnishings division produces and sells decorative upholstery fabrics through 15 manufacturing facilities and 11 showrooms across the nation. Consumer legwear includes the brand name No-Nonsense. **Corporate headquarters location:** This Location. **Listed on:** American Stock Exchange.

CONCORD FABRICS INC.
1359 Broadway, 3rd Floor, New York NY 10018. 212/760-0300. **Contact:** Personnel. **Description:** Designs, develops, and manufactures woven and knitted fabrics for sale to manufacturers and retailers. Concord Fabrics is one of the nation's largest independent textile converters. **Common positions include:** Clerical Supervisor; Computer Programmer; Designer; Systems Analyst. **Educational backgrounds include:** Accounting; Business Administration; Computer Science; Marketing. **Benefits:** 401(k); Disability Coverage; Life Insurance; Medical Insurance; Profit Sharing. **Special programs:** Internships. **Corporate**

headquarters location: This Location. **Other U.S. locations:** CA; GA. **Operations at this facility include:** Administration; Sales. **Number of employees at this location:** 200. **Number of employees nationwide:** 700.

CONE MILLS
3101 North Elm Street, Greensboro NC 27415. 336/379-6220. **Contact:** Dan Minnis, Director of Human Resources. **World Wide Web address:** http://www.cone.com. **Description:** Cone Mills is a major manufacturer of denim and home furnishing fabrics. The denim division produces about 400 styles and is one of the largest suppliers for Levi Strauss & Company. The division also manufactures specialty fabrics including plaids, chamois flannel, and uniform and sportswear fabrics. **Corporate headquarters location:** This Location. **Subsidiaries include:** Carlisle Finishing Company, one of the largest U.S. commission printers of home furnishing fabrics; John Wolf Decorative Fabrics, a maker of fabrics for upholstery, drapes, and bedroom products; Olympic Products Company, which manufactures foams for beds, carpets, and furniture used in the medical and consumer markets.

CONGOLEUM CORPORATION
P.O. Box 3127, Mercerville NJ 08619. 609/584-3000. **Fax:** 609/584-3522. **Contact:** Human Resources. **World Wide Web address:** http://www.congoleum.com. **Description:** This location distributes vinyl floor products to wholesalers worldwide. Overall, Congoleum Corporation is a diversified manufacturer and distributor, operating in the areas of home furnishings, shipbuilding, and automotive and industrial distribution. The company developed one of the first no-wax floors, one of the first chemically embossed sheet vinyl floors, and one of the first types of domestically produced sheet vinyl to use environmentally safe, water-based inks. **Common positions include:** Accountant; Claim Representative; Customer Service Representative; Secretary. **Benefits:** 401(k); Dental Insurance; Employee Discounts; Life Insurance; Medical Insurance; Pension Plan; Tuition Assistance. **Corporate headquarters location:** This Location. **Other area locations:** Cedarhurst NJ; Trenton NJ.

CONSO PRODUCTS COMPANY, INC.
P.O. Box 326, Union SC 29379. 864/427-9004. **Fax:** 864/429-0290. **Contact:** Jim Bellune, Human Resources Manager. **Description:** Manufactures decorative accessories and trimmings including tassels, tiebacks, braids, and fringes. **Common positions include:** Accountant; Blue-Collar Worker Supervisor; Computer Programmer; Credit Manager; Customer Service Rep.; Designer; Electrician; Industrial Engineer; Industrial Production Manager; Operations Manager; Purchasing Agent; Systems Analyst. **Educational backgrounds include:** Accounting; Marketing. **Benefits:** 401(k); Dental Insurance; Disability Coverage; Life Insurance; Medical Insurance; Tuition Assistance. **Corporate headquarters location:** This Location. **Subsidiaries include:** British Trimmings. **Operations at this facility include:** Administration; Manufacturing; Sales. **Listed on:** NASDAQ. **Annual sales/revenues:** $51 - $100 million. **Number of employees at this location:** 730.

CONVERSE, INC.
One Fordham Road, North Reading MA 01864. 978/664-1100. **Contact:** Recruiting Representative. **World Wide Web address:** http://www.converse.com. **Description:** Manufactures men's, women's, and children's footwear. **Common positions include:** Accountant; Administrative Manager;

Advertising Clerk; Attorney; Budget Analyst; Buyer; Chemical Engineer; Computer Operator; Credit Manager; Customer Service Rep.; Designer; Economist; Financial Analyst; General Manager; Human Resources Manager; Industrial Engineer; Management Trainee; Manufacturer's Sales Rep.; Materials Engineer; Operations Manager; Paralegal; Public Relations Specialist; Purchasing Agent; Quality Control Supervisor; Services Sales Rep.; Systems Analyst; Transportation; Wholesale and Retail Buyer. **Educational backgrounds include:** Accounting; Art; Biology; Business Administration; Chemistry; Communications; Computer Science; Economics; Energy; Finance; Liberal Arts; Marketing. **Benefits:** 401(k); Dental Insurance; Disability Coverage; Employee Discounts; Life Insurance; Medical Insurance; Pension Plan; Savings Plan; Stock Option; Tuition Assistance. **Special programs:** Internships. **Corporate headquarters location:** This Location. **Other U.S. locations:** Nationwide. **Operations at this facility include:** Administration; Research and Development; Sales; Service. **Number of employees at this location:** 400. **Number of employees nationwide:** 2,000.

CORBIN, LTD.
P.O. Box 7000, 151 West Lynn Avenue, Ashland KY 41105-7000. 606/928-3333. **Contact:** Ron Dyke, Operations Manager. **Description:** Manufactures fine tailored men's and women's apparel. **Common positions include:** Accountant; Administrator; Blue-Collar Worker Supervisor; Computer Programmer; Credit Manager; Customer Service Rep.; Department Manager; Financial Analyst; General Manager; Human Resources Manager; Industrial Engineer; Industrial Production Manager; Instructor; Management Trainee; Operations Manager; Purchasing Agent; Quality Control Supervisor; Scheduler; Systems Analyst. **Educational backgrounds include:** Accounting; Business Administration; Communications; Computer Science; Economics; Engineering; Finance; Liberal Arts; Marketing; Mathematics. **Benefits:** Disability Coverage; Employee Discounts; Life Insurance; Medical Insurance; Pension Plan; Savings Plan; Tuition Assistance. **Corporate headquarters location:** This Location. **Operations at this facility include:** Administration; Manufacturing. **Number of employees at this location:** 525.

CRAFTEX MILLS INC.
450 Sentry Parkway East, Blue Bell PA 19422. 610/941-1212. **Contact:** Human Resources. **Description:** Produces upholstery fabrics for furniture manufacturers. **Corporate headquarters location:** This Location.

CRANSTON PRINT WORKS COMPANY
1381 Cranston Street, Cranston RI 02920. 401/943-4800. **Contact:** Herbert J. Gray, Vice President of Human Resources. **World Wide Web address:** http://www.cpw.com. **Description:** A finisher, converter, and printer of textiles. **Common positions include:** Accountant; Blue-Collar Worker Supervisor; Buyer; Chemical Engineer; Chemist; Credit Manager; Customer Service Rep.; Department Manager; Financial Analyst; General Manager; Human Resources Manager; Industrial Engineer; Management Trainee; Manufacturer's Sales Rep.; Mechanical Engineer; Operations Manager; Purchasing Agent; Quality Control Supervisor; Systems Analyst. **Educational backgrounds include:** Accounting; Art/Design; Business Administration; Chemistry; Computer Science; Finance. **Benefits:** Dental Insurance; Life Insurance; Medical Insurance; Pension Plan; Profit Sharing; Tuition Assistance. **Corporate**

CRAZY SHIRTS
99-969 Iwaena Street, Aiea HI 96701. 808/487-9919. **Fax:** 808/486-1276. **Recorded jobline:** 808/486-6312. **Contact:** Human Resources. **E-mail address:** info@crazyshirts.com. **World Wide Web address:** http://www.crazyshirts.com. **Description:** Manufactures and sells custom-imprinted or embroidered sportswear apparel. Founded in 1964. **Common positions include:** Retail Manager; Retail Sales Worker. **Benefits:** 401(k); Dental Insurance; Disability Coverage; Employee Discounts; Financial Planning Assistance; Flexible Schedule; Life Insurance; Medical Insurance; Profit Sharing. **Office hours:** Monday - Friday, 8:00 a.m. - 5:00 p.m. **Corporate headquarters location:** This Location. **Other U.S. locations:** CO; FL; NV; NY; UT. **International locations:** Guam. **Listed on:** Privately held. **Annual sales/revenues:** $51 - $100 million. **Number of employees nationwide:** 1,000.

CROWNTEX
P.O. Box 47, Wrightsville GA 31096. 912/864-2704. **Contact:** Human Resources. **Description:** Manufactures men's and women's pants and slacks. Crowntex works on a contract-only basis for several companies nationwide. **Corporate headquarters location:** This Location.

DALLCO INDUSTRIES INC.
P.O. Box 2727, York PA 17405-2727. 717/854-7875. **Fax:** 717/845-5283. **Contact:** Personnel. **Description:** Manufactures sleepwear and loungewear for women and children. **Common positions include:** Accountant; Administrative Manager; Blue-Collar Worker Supervisor; Cost Estimator; Customer Service Representative; Designer; Electrician; General Manager; Human Resources Manager; Industrial Production Manager; Management Analyst; Management Trainee; Operations Manager; Quality Control Supervisor; Transportation. **Educational backgrounds include:** Business Administration; Marketing. **Benefits:** Disability Coverage; Employee Discounts; Life Insurance; Medical Insurance; Profit Sharing. **Corporate headquarters location:** This Location. **Number of employees at this location:** 300.

DAN RIVER, INC.
P.O. Box 261, Danville VA 24543. 804/799-7000. **Contact:** Joe Bouknight, Vice President of Human Resources. **World Wide Web address:** http://www.danriver.com. **Description:** A manufacturer and marketer of textile products for the home fashions and apparel fabrics markets. Dan River manufactures a coordinated line of home fashions products consisting of packaged bedroom furnishings such as comforters, sheets, pillowcases, shams, bedskirts, decorative pillows, and draperies. The company also manufactures a broad range of woven and knit cotton and cotton-blend apparel fabrics, and is a leading domestic supplier of men's dress shirt fabrics, primarily oxford and pinpoint oxford cloth. **Benefits:** Retirement Plan. **Corporate headquarters location:** This Location. **Other U.S. locations:** Nationwide. **Subsidiaries include:** Dan River Factory Stores, Inc. operates 12 factory outlet stores in the Midwest and Southeast. **Parent company:** Braelan Corp. **Listed on:** Privately held.

DANSKIN INC.
530 Seventh Avenue, New York NY 10018. 212/764-4630. **Contact:** Personnel. **Description:** Danskin designs, manufactures, and markets several brands of women's activewear, dancewear, tights, and sheer hosiery. Brand names include Danskin, Dance France, Round-the-Clock, Givenchy, and Anne Klein. **Corporate headquarters location:** This Location. **Other U.S. locations:** Nationwide. **Subsidiaries include:** Pennaco (Grenada MS). **Number of employees nationwide:** 1,550.

DECKERS OUTDOOR CORPORATION
495-A South Fairview Avenue, Goleta CA 93117. 805/967-7611. **Contact:** Personnel. **Description:** Designs, manufactures, and markets footwear developed for high-performance outdoor, recreational, and sports activities, as well as casual wear. Deckers Outdoor's products are sold under the Teva, Simple, Sensi, and Picante brand names and are marketed through leading outdoor retailers, athletic footwear stores, specialty retailers, and department stores throughout the U.S. **Corporate headquarters location:** This Location.

DELONG
P.O. Box 189, Grinnell IA 50112-0189. 515/236-3106. **Contact:** Becky Harter, Personnel Manager. **Description:** A manufacturer of sports and leisure apparel. **Common positions include:** Accountant; Computer Programmer; Industrial Engineer; Manufacturer's Sales Rep.; Marketing Specialist; Systems Analyst. **Educational backgrounds include:** Accounting; Business Administration; Engineering. **Benefits:** 401(k); Disability Coverage; Employee Discounts; Life Insurance; Medical Insurance; Savings Plan; Tuition Assistance. **Corporate headquarters location:** This Location. **Operations at this facility include:** Customer Service; Manufacturing; Marketing; Sales.

DEXTER SHOE COMPANY
1230 Washington Street, West Newton MA 02465-2129. 617/332-4300. **Contact:** Office Manager. **World Wide Web address:** http://www.dextershoe.com. **Description:** Manufactures men's and women's footwear. **Common positions include:** Advertising Clerk; Computer Programmer; Credit Manager; Economist; Systems Analyst. **Benefits:** Employee Discounts; Life Insurance; Medical Insurance; Pension Plan; Savings Plan. **Corporate headquarters location:** Dexter ME. **Parent company:** Berkshire Hathaway. **Operations at this facility include:** Administration.

DICKSON FABRICS
P.O. Box 6107, Alberton GA 30635. 706/283-3721. **Contact:** Human Resources. **World Wide Web address:** http://www.dickson-us.com. **Description:** Produces industrial fabrics including furniture upholstery fabrics, outdoor canvasses for umbrellas, casual patio furniture, and marine applications. **Common positions include:** Accountant; Computer Programmer; Customer Service Rep.; Designer; Electrician; Financial Manager; Industrial Production Manager; Manufacturer's Sales Rep.; Marketing Manager; Purchasing Agent; Quality Control Supervisor; Textile Technologist; Weaver. **Educational backgrounds include:** Accounting; Art/Design. **Benefits:** Dental Insurance; Life Insurance; Medical Insurance; Savings Plan. **Corporate headquarters location:** This Location. **Parent company:** Dickson Constant (France). **Operations at this facility include:** Administration; Manufacturing; Research and Development; Sales.

DONNKENNY, INC.
1411 Broadway, 10th Floor, New York NY 10018. 212/730-7770. **Contact:** Human Resources. **Description:** A sportswear manufacturer that operates through three divisions: Donnkenny Classics, Mickey & Co., and Lewis Frimel/Flirts. **NOTE:** Please send resumes to Barbara Collins,

Director of Human Resources, Donnkenny, Inc., 995 Industry Road, Wytheville VA 24382. **Corporate headquarters location:** This Location. **Listed on:** NASDAQ.

DREXEL SHIRT COMPANY
402-412 Route 23, Franklin NJ 07416. 973/827-9135. **Contact:** Mrs. Pat Ward, Personnel Manager. **Description:** Manufactures men's shirts. **Corporate headquarters location:** This Location.

ECOLOGY KIDS
25 Kay Fries Drive, Stony Point NY 10980. 914/786-5552. **Contact:** Personnel. **Description:** Ecology Kids manufactures, markets, and distributes infantwear and care products, nursery accessories, and other products for infant and toddler comfort and care. The company's products include infant clothing, cloth diapers, diaper covers, bedding, furniture covers, layettes, infant and child travel products, and other accessories. **Corporate headquarters location:** This Location.

ESPRIT DE CORP
900 Minnesota Street, San Francisco CA 94107. 415/648-6900. **Recorded jobline:** 415/550-3998. **Contact:** Recruiter. **World Wide Web address:** http://www.esprit.com. **Description:** Esprit is a manufacturer and retailer of clothing, footwear, eyewear, bath and bed accessories, and watches. Founded in 1968. **NOTE:** Entry-level positions are offered. **Common positions include:** Account Manager; Account Rep.; Accountant; Administrative Assistant; Assistant Manager; Budget Analyst; Buyer; CFO; Controller; Credit Manager; Customer Service Rep.; Finance Director; Financial Analyst; Human Resources Manager; Marketing Manager; Operations Manager; Production Manager; Project Manager; Public Relations Specialist; Purchasing Agent; Quality Control Supervisor; Sales Executive; Sales Manager; Sales Rep.; Systems Analyst; Systems Manager; Technical Writer; Transportation; Webmaster. **Educational backgrounds include:** Accounting; Art/Design; Business Administration; Communications; Finance; Liberal Arts; Marketing; Mathematics; Public Relations; Software Development. **Benefits:** 401(k); Dental Insurance; Disability Coverage; Employee Discounts; Financial Planning Assistance; Life Insurance; Medical Insurance; Pension Plan; Profit Sharing; Public Transit Available; Savings Plan; Tuition Assistance. **Special programs:** Summer Jobs. **Office hours:** Monday - Friday, 8:00 a.m. - 6:00 p.m. **Corporate headquarters location:** This Location. **Other U.S. locations:** Nationwide. **Listed on:** Privately held. **CEO:** Jay Margolis. **Number of employees at this location:** 350. **Number of employees nationwide:** 1,400. **Number of employees worldwide:** 5,000.

FARLEY INDUSTRIES
FRUIT OF THE LOOM, INC.
233 South Wacker Drive, Suite 5000, Chicago IL 60606. 312/876-1724. **Contact:** Human Resources. **Description:** Farley Industries is the holding company for Fruit of the Loom. Fruit of the Loom produces clothes for adults and children. Products are primarily underwear, T-shirts, socks, activewear, casualwear, and licensed sports clothing, manufactured under the brand names BVD, Fruit of the Loom, Gitano, Best, and Screen Stars. Fruit of the Loom also has licenses with companies including Wilson and Munsingwear. **Corporate headquarters location:** This Location. **Listed on:** New York Stock Exchange.

THE WARREN FEATHERBONE CO.
P.O. Box 383, Gainesville GA 30503. 770/535-3000. **Contact:** William T. Holbrook, Director of Personnel. **World Wide Web address:** http://www. alexisusa.com. **Description:** Manufactures and markets infant clothing and related infant care products under the brand name Alexis. **Common positions include:** Accountant; Computer Programmer; Department Manager; Industrial Engineer; Manufacturer's Sales Rep.; Mechanical Engineer; Quality Control Supervisor. **Educational backgrounds include:** Accounting; Computer Science; Engineering; Marketing. **Benefits:** 401(k); Dental Insurance; Disability Coverage; Employee Discounts; Life Insurance; Medical Insurance; Profit Sharing; Savings Plan. **Corporate headquarters location:** This Location.

FIELDCREST CANNON, INC.
326 East Stadium Drive, Eden NC 27288. 336/627-3000. **Contact:** Employment Office. **Description:** An international manufacturer of home textiles that distributes its products through department stores, catalog merchandisers, specialty stores, and mass retailers, and also has institutional, government, and corporate clients. The company's rugs and carpets segment makes products under brand names including Fieldcrest, Royal Velvet, Touch of Class, Cannon, and Monicello. The bath segment manufactures bath towels, rugs, and kitchen products, while the bed segment produces blankets, throws, bedding, and decorative window treatments. **Common positions include:** Accountant; Chemist; Computer Programmer; Electrical Engineer; Industrial Agent; Management Trainee; Manufacturer's Sales Rep.; Mechanical Engineer; Operations Manager; Textile Manager. **Educational backgrounds include:** Accounting; Business Administration; Chemistry; Computer Science; Engineering; Liberal Arts; Management/Planning; Marketing; Textiles. **Benefits:** Dental Insurance; Disability Coverage; Employee Discounts; Life Insurance; Medical Insurance; Pension Plan; Savings Plan; Tuition Assistance. **Special programs:** Internships. **Corporate headquarters location:** This Location. **Operations at this facility include:** Administration; Manufacturing; Service.

M. FINE & SONS MANUFACTURING CO.
350 Fifth Avenue, Suite 4310, New York NY 10118. 212/239-1111. **Contact:** Stephen L. Fine, Co-President. **Description:** Manufactures and distributes men's work clothes and leisure apparel. **Common positions include:** Bookkeeper; Manufacturer's Sales Rep.; Merchandiser; Production Manager. **Corporate headquarters location:** This Location.

FLINT RIVER TEXTILES, INC.
P.O. Box 489, Albany GA 31702. 912/435-1495. **Contact:** Dave McEwen, Personnel Director. **Description:** Produces and markets cotton and polyester fabrics and blends. **Corporate headquarters location:** This Location.

S.B. FOOT TANNING COMPANY
805 Bench Street, Red Wing MN 55066. 651/388-4731. **Contact:** Jerry Dietzman, Personnel Vice President. **Description:** A leather tanning and finishing company. **Common positions include:** Accountant; Blue-Collar Worker Supervisor; Customer Service Rep.; Industrial Production Manager; Purchasing Agent. **Educational backgrounds include:** Business Administration; Chemistry; Liberal Arts. **Benefits:** 401(k); Disability Coverage; Investment Plan; Life Insurance; Medical Insurance; Pension Plan; Savings Plan; Tuition Assistance. **Special programs:** Internships. **Corporate headquarters location:** This Location. **Parent company:** Red Wing Shoe Company.

FREUDENBERG SPUNWEB COMPANY
P.O. Box 15910, Durham NC 27704. 919/479-7226.
Fax: 919/471-2516. **Contact:** Personnel.
Description: Manufactures nonwoven fabrics.
Common positions include: Accountant; Electrical
Engineer; Mechanical Engineer. **Educational
backgrounds include:** Accounting; Engineering;
Finance; Marketing. **Benefits:** Dental Insurance;
Disability Coverage; Life Insurance; Medical
Insurance; Pension Plan; Savings Plan; Tuition
Assistance. **Corporate headquarters location:**
This Location. **Operations at this facility include:**
Administration; Manufacturing; Research and
Development; Sales. **Number of employees at this
location:** 145.

FRITZI CALIFORNIA
13071 East Temple, City of Industry CA 91746.
213/680-0154. **Contact:** Human Resources. **World
Wide Web address:** http://www.fritzi.com.
Description: Designs, manufactures, and distributes
moderately-priced misses', juniors', and girls'
apparel, sold under a variety of labels. **Benefits:**
401(k); Dental Insurance; Employee Discounts; Life
Insurance; Medical Insurance; Profit Sharing; Public
Transit Available. **Corporate headquarters
location:** This Location. **Other U.S. locations:** Los
Angeles CA; New York NY; Dallas TX. **Parent
company:** Kellwood Company (Chesterfield MO).
Annual sales/revenues: More than $100 million.
Number of employees at this location: 375.
Number of employees nationwide: 450.

GALEY & LORD, INC.
980 Avenue of the Americas, 4th Floor, New York
NY 10018-5401. 212/465-3000. **Fax:** 212/465-
3025. **Contact:** Human Resources. **Description:**
This location houses executive offices. Overall,
Galey & Lord is a leading manufacturer and
marketer of apparel fabric sold to clothing
manufacturers. The company is a major producer of
wrinkle-free cotton fabrics for uniforms and for
sportswear manufacturers and printed fabrics for the
home. Galey & Lord also manufactures denim.
Corporate headquarters location: This Location.
Other U.S. locations: Greensboro NC.
Subsidiaries include: G&L Service Company
provides marketing services for Galey & Lord.
Galey & Lord Home Fashion Fabrics manufactures
and distributes fabrics used in home decorating and
furnishing. Klopman International is a supplier of
fabrics used in career wear. Swift Denim
manufactures and distributes a wide variety of
denim products. **President/CEO:** Arthur C. Wiener.

GARAN INC.
350 Fifth Avenue, 19th Floor, New York NY 10118.
212/563-2000. **Contact:** Ms. Dana Gleason,
Personnel Manager. **Description:** Garan designs,
manufactures, and sells apparel for children,
women, and men. Products include shirts,
sweatshirts, sweaters, trousers, skirts, shorts, and
overalls. Tradenames, trademarks, and licensed
names include Garanimals, Garan by Marita, Bobbie
Brooks, Garan Mountain Lion, Long Gone, Team
Rated, National Football League, National
Basketball Association, National Hockey League,
Major League Baseball, and Disney. **Corporate
headquarters location:** This Location.

GENESCO, INC.
Genesco Administration Building, P.O. Box 731,
Nashville TN 37202-0731. 615/367-7000. **Contact:**
Personnel. **Description:** Markets, distributes, and
manufactures men's footwear. The company owns
and licenses footwear brands, sold through both
wholesale and retail channels, including Johnston &
Murphy, Dockers, Nautica, and Jarman. Genesco
products are sold at wholesale to a number of

leading department, specialty, and discount stores.
Products are sold at retail through the company's
own network of retail shoe stores including
Johnston & Murphy, Jarman, and Journeys.
Corporate headquarters location: This Location.

GLOBE MANUFACTURING COMPANY
456 Bedford Street, Fall River MA 02720. 508/674-
3585. **Fax:** 508/674-3580. **Contact:** Personnel.
Description: Manufactures and markets rubber
threads and synthetic spandex fibers. Customers
include apparel, textile, and nonwoven
manufacturers. **Common positions include:**
Accountant; Administrative Manager; Blue-Collar
Worker Supervisor; Chemical Engineer; Chemist;
Credit Manager; Electrical Engineer; Electrician;
General Manager; Human Resources Manager;
Industrial Production Manager; Manufacturer's
Sales Rep.; Mechanical Engineer; Operations
Manager; Purchasing Agent; Quality Control
Supervisor. **Educational backgrounds include:**
Accounting; Business Administration; Chemistry;
Engineering; Finance; Marketing. **Benefits:** 401(k);
Disability Coverage; Life Insurance; Medical
Insurance; Pension Plan; Tuition Assistance.
Corporate headquarters location: This Location.
Other U.S. locations: Tuscaloosa AL; Gastonia
NC. **Operations at this facility include:**
Manufacturing; Research and Development; Sales.
Number of employees at this location: 650.
Number of employees nationwide: 1,000.

GOLD BUG INC.
4999 Oakland Street, Denver CO 80239. 303/371-
2885. **Fax:** 303/373-8131. **Contact:** Personnel.
Description: Distributes children's apparel and
accessories. **NOTE:** Entry-level positions and
second and third shifts are offered. **Common
positions include:** Account Rep.; Administrative
Assistant; Buyer; CFO; Clerical Supervisor;
Computer Operator; Controller; Credit Manager;
Customer Service Rep.; Graphic Artist; Graphic
Designer; Human Resources Manager; Marketing
Manager; MIS Specialist; Production Manager;
Sales Executive; Sales Manager; Sales Rep.;
Secretary. **Educational backgrounds include:**
Accounting; Art; Business Administration;
Computer Science; Finance; Marketing. **Benefits:**
401(k); Dental Insurance; Disability Coverage;
Employee Discounts; Job Sharing; Medical
Insurance; Profit Sharing. **Special programs:**
Internships; Summer Jobs. **Corporate
headquarters location:** This Location. **Annual
sales/revenues:** $21 - $50 million. **Number of
employees at this location:** 120.

S. GOLDBERG & COMPANY, INC.
20 East Broadway, Hackensack NJ 07601. 201/342-
1200. **Contact:** Personnel Manager. **Description:**
Manufactures house slippers. **Common positions
include:** Industrial Engineer. **Benefits:** Disability
Coverage; Employee Discounts; Life Insurance;
Medical Insurance; Pension Plan; Profit Sharing;
Tuition Assistance. **Corporate headquarters
location:** This Location. **Operations at this facility
include:** Manufacturing.

W.L. GORE & ASSOCIATES, INC.
P.O. Box 9206, Newark DE 19714-9206. 302/738-
4880. **Physical address:** 551 Paper Mill Road,
Newark DE. **Contact:** Barbara Pizzala, Recruiter.
World Wide Web address: http://www.gore.com.
Description: Manufactures dental floss, guitar
strings, bicycle cable systems, vacuum filters, and
water/stain repellent. The company also produces
electronic products including copper and optical
signal transmission products, digital and analog
cable assemblies, circuit chips and related products;
chemical products including a chemical polymer

used to repair diseased arteries and also as an industrial sealant; and GORE-TEX fabric. **Common positions include:** Attorney; Chemical Engineer; Chemist; Electrical Engineer; Mechanical Engineer; Metallurgical Engineer; Sales Engineer. **Educational backgrounds include:** Chemistry; Engineering. **Benefits:** Dental Insurance; Disability Coverage; Employee Discounts; Fitness Program; Life Insurance; Medical Insurance; Profit Sharing. **Special programs:** Internships. **Corporate headquarters location:** This Location. **Operations at this facility include:** Manufacturing; Research and Development; Sales; Service. **Number of employees nationwide:** 5,800.

GRANITE KNITWEAR, INC.
P.O. Box 498, Granite Quarry NC 28072-0498. 704/279-5526. **Contact:** Personnel Manager. **Description:** A sportswear and fleecewear apparel manufacturer. **Common positions include:** Credit Manager; Customer Service Rep.; Human Resources Manager; Industrial Engineer. **Benefits:** Disability Coverage; Employee Discounts; Life Insurance; Medical Insurance; Profit Sharing; Tuition Assistance. **Corporate headquarters location:** This Location. **Parent company:** Cal Cru Company Inc. **Number of employees at this location:** 170.

GUESS? INC.
1444 South Alameda Street, Los Angeles CA 90021. 213/765-3100. **Contact:** Personnel. **World Wide Web address:** http://www.guess.com. **Description:** Designs, develops, and markets jeans and other casualwear for men and women. **Corporate headquarters location:** This Location.

GUILFORD MILLS, INC.
P.O. Box 26969, Greensboro NC 27419-6969. 336/316-4000. **Contact:** Personnel. **Description:** A manufacturer, processor, and marketer of warp knit fabrics for the apparel, automotive, home furnishing, swimwear, dress, and sportswear industries. **Corporate headquarters location:** This Location. **Other U.S. locations:** Nationwide. **International locations:** United Kingdom.

HAGGAR CLOTHING COMPANY
6113 Lemmon Avenue, Dallas TX 75209. 214/956-4235. **Fax:** 214/956-4419. **Contact:** Human Resources. **Description:** Manufactures men's dress and casual clothing. **Common positions include:** Accountant; Blue-Collar Worker Supervisor; Computer Programmer; Industrial Engineer; Management Trainee; Operations Manager; Systems Analyst. **Educational backgrounds include:** Accounting; Business Administration; Communications; Computer Science; Engineering; Marketing. **Benefits:** 401(k); Daycare Assistance; Dental Insurance; Disability Coverage; Employee Discounts; Life Insurance; Medical Insurance; Profit Sharing; Tuition Assistance. **Special programs:** Internships. **Corporate headquarters location:** This Location. **Operations at this facility include:** Research and Development; Service. **Number of employees at this location:** 800.

HAMPSHIRE DESIGNERS, INC.
215 Commerce Boulevard, Anderson SC 29625. 864/225-6232. **Contact:** Human Resources. **World Wide Web address:** http://www.hamp.com. **Description:** One of the largest manufacturers of full-fashion sweaters in the United States. The company designs, manufactures, and markets sweaters under the brand name Designers Originals. **Corporate headquarters location:** This Location.

HAMPTON INDUSTRIES, INC.
P.O. Box 614, Kinston NC 28502-0614. 252/527-8011. **Contact:** Human Resources. **World Wide**

Web address: http://www.hamptonindustries.com. **Description:** Hampton Industries, Inc. manufactures and sells apparel, principally under private or store labels, to national and regional chain and department stores. The company's products include sportswear, activewear, and loungewear. The company's products are sold under the brand names Bugle Boy, Dickies, Joe Boxer, Nautica, Rawlings, and Spaulding. **Corporate headquarters location:** This Location. **Other U.S. locations:** New York NY. **Listed on:** American Stock Exchange.

HANCOCK FABRICS, INC.
P.O. Box 2400, Tupelo MS 38803-2400. 662/842-2834. **Contact:** Personnel Department. **World Wide Web address:** http://www.hancockfabrics.com. **Description:** Operates retail and wholesale fabric businesses offering a wide selection of clothing fabrics, notions, patterns, decorative fabrics, craft items, and related supplies. **Corporate headquarters location:** This Location. **Subsidiaries include:** Minnesota Fabrics, Inc. **Number of employees nationwide:** 7,000.

THE HARODITE FINISHING COMPANY
66 South Street, North Dighton MA 02764. 508/824-6961. **Contact:** Personnel. **Description:** One of the oldest textile manufacturing companies in New England. Products include a complete range of woven and nonwoven fabrics. Founded in 1908. **Common positions include:** Accountant; Buyer; Chemist; Customer Service Rep.; Financial Analyst; Human Resources Manager; Purchasing Agent. **Educational backgrounds include:** Accounting; Business Administration; Chemistry; Finance; Marketing. **Benefits:** 401(k); Life Insurance; Medical Insurance; Pension Plan; Profit Sharing; Tuition Assistance. **Corporate headquarters location:** This Location. **Other U.S. locations:** Taylors SC. **Operations at this facility include:** Administration; Manufacturing. **Listed on:** Privately held. **Number of employees at this location:** 130.

HARTMARX CORPORATION
101 North Wacker Drive, Chicago IL 60606. 312/372-6300. **Fax:** 312/444-2679. **Contact:** Susan Klawitter, Director of Human Resources. **World Wide Web address:** http://www.hartmarx.com. **Description:** A manufacturer of men's tailored clothing and women's clothing and sportswear. Brand names include Hart Schaffner & Marx, Sansabelt, Palm Beach, Barrie Pace, and Hickey-Freeman. The company conducts direct marketing and catalog sales operations worldwide. **Common positions include:** Accountant; Blue-Collar Worker Supervisor; Clerical Supervisor; Computer Programmer; Credit Manager; Customer Service Rep.; Industrial Engineer; Industrial Production Manager; Management Trainee; Manufacturer's Sales Rep.; Systems Analyst. **Educational backgrounds include:** Accounting; Business Administration; Liberal Arts. **Benefits:** 401(k); Dental Insurance; Disability Coverage; Employee Discounts; Life Insurance; Medical Insurance; Pension Plan; Savings Plan; Tuition Assistance. **Corporate headquarters location:** This Location. **Other U.S. locations:** Des Plaines IL; Rock Island IL; Rochester IN; Winchester KY; Cape Girardeau MO; New York NY. **Operations at this facility include:** Administration; Manufacturing; Sales; Service. **Listed on:** New York Stock Exchange. **Number of employees at this location:** 400. **Number of employees nationwide:** 10,000.

HARTZ & COMPANY, INC.
1341 Hughes Ford Road, Frederick MD 21701. 301/662-7500. **Fax:** 301/662-0461. **Contact:** Jane L. Wilcom, Director of Human Resources.

Description: A manufacturer of men's clothing. **Common positions include:** Accountant; Clerical Supervisor; Computer Programmer; Cost Estimator; Credit Manager; Customer Service Rep.; Designer; Draftsperson; Electrician; Financial Analyst; General Manager; Human Resources Manager; Industrial Engineer; Industrial Production Manager; Management Analyst; Operations Manager; Purchasing Agent; Quality Control Supervisor; Restaurant Manager; Services Sales Rep.; Systems Analyst; Wholesale and Retail Buyer. **Educational backgrounds include:** Art/Design; Business Administration; Engineering; Liberal Arts. **Benefits:** 401(k); Dental Insurance; Disability Coverage; Employee Discounts; Life Insurance; Medical Insurance. **Corporate headquarters location:** This Location. **Other U.S. locations:** New York NY; Broadway VA. **Operations at this facility include:** Administration; Manufacturing. **Number of employees at this location:** 350. **Number of employees nationwide:** 850.

HATCO
601 Marion Drive, Garland TX 75042. 972/494-0511. **Contact:** Personnel Manager. **Description:** Manufactures a variety of men's weather-resistant hats and headgear. **Corporate headquarters location:** This Location.

HICKORY SPRINGS INC.
3900 NE 158th Avenue, Portland OR 97230-5002. 503/255-5850. **Contact:** Human Resources. **Description:** Manufactures carpet padding. **Corporate headquarters location:** This Location. **Number of employees at this location:** 100.

HOLLANDER HOME FASHIONS CORP.
6560 West Rogers Circle, Suite 19, Boca Raton FL 33487. 561/997-6900. **Fax:** 561/997-8738. **Contact:** Personnel. **Description:** Manufactures bed pillows, comforters, mattress pads, comforter sets, and specialty bedding products. **Common positions include:** Accountant; Administrative Manager; Blue-Collar Worker Supervisor; Clerical Supervisor; Computer Programmer; Credit Manager; Customer Service Rep.; Designer; Financial Analyst; General Manager; Human Resources Manager; Industrial Engineer; Industrial Production Manager; Manufacturer's Sales Rep.; Mechanical Engineer; Purchasing Agent; Quality Control Supervisor. **Educational backgrounds include:** Accounting; Art/Design; Business Administration; Computer Science; Engineering; Liberal Arts; Marketing. **Benefits:** 401(k); Disability Coverage; Life Insurance; Medical Insurance. **Corporate headquarters location:** This Location. **Other U.S. locations:** Nationwide. **Operations at this facility include:** Administration; Manufacturing; Research and Development; Sales. **Number of employees nationwide:** 1,200.

HOLLOWAY SPORTSWEAR
P.O. Box 4489, Sidney OH 45365. 937/596-6193. **Physical address:** 2633 Cambell Road, Sidney OH. **Contact:** Human Resources. **Description:** This location houses administrative offices. Overall, Holloway Sportswear manufactures jackets, sweatshirts, sweatsuits, golf shirts, and golf hats. **Corporate headquarters location:** This Location. **Other U.S. locations:** Jackson Center OH.

HOLLYTEX CARPET MILL INC.
P.O. Box 369, Anadarko OK 73005. 405/247-7453. **Physical address:** 505 NE Seventh Street, Anadarko OK 73005. **Contact:** Personnel. **Description:** A national tufted carpet manufacturer. **Common positions include:** Accountant; Advertising Clerk; Blue-Collar Worker Supervisor;

Computer Programmer; Customer Service Rep.; Human Resources Manager; Management Trainee; Purchasing Agent; Systems Analyst. **Educational backgrounds include:** Accounting; Business Administration; Computer Science; Engineering; Liberal Arts. **Benefits:** 401(k); Dental Insurance; Disability Coverage; Employee Discounts; Life Insurance; Medical Insurance; Tuition Assistance. **Corporate headquarters location:** This Location. **Operations at this facility include:** Administration; Manufacturing.

HOUSTON WIPER & MILL SUPPLY CO.
P.O. Box 24962, Houston TX 77229-4962. 713/672-0571. **Toll-free phone:** 800/633-5968. **Fax:** 713/673-7637. **Contact:** Jay Grossman, Controller. **E-mail address:** howmisco@msn.com. **World Wide Web address:** http://www.houstonwiper.com. **Description:** A secondary textile recycler. Founded in 1954. **Common positions include:** Administrative Assistant; Applications Engineer; Customer Service Rep.; Transportation. **Corporate headquarters location:** This Location. **Operations at this facility include:** Manufacturing. **Listed on:** Privately held. **President:** Michael J. Brown. **Facilities Manager:** Barry H. Brown. **Number of employees at this location:** 70.

HUTSPAH SHIRTS
185 West Wyoming Avenue, Philadelphia PA 19140-1691. 215/329-7700. **Fax:** 215/329-4650. **Contact:** Ken Williams, Personnel Director. **Description:** An apparel manufacturer specializing in shirts and nightwear. **Common positions include:** Accountant/Auditor; Clerical Supervisor; Computer Operator; Credit Manager; Order Clerk; Receptionist; Secretary; Stock Clerk. **Corporate headquarters location:** This Location. **Operations at this facility include:** Administration.

INJECTION FOOTWEAR CORPORATION
8730 NW 36th Avenue, Miami FL 33147. 305/696-4611. **Contact:** Human Resources. **Description:** Manufactures shoes. **Common positions include:** Accountant; Administrator; Computer Programmer; Credit Manager; Customer Service Rep.; General Manager; Industrial Designer; Manufacturer's Sales Rep.; Marketing Specialist; Purchasing Agent; Quality Control Supervisor; Systems Analyst. **Educational backgrounds include:** Accounting; Business Administration; Computer Science; Engineering; Marketing. **Benefits:** Employee Discounts; Life Insurance; Tuition Assistance. **Corporate headquarters location:** This Location. **Operations at this facility include:** Manufacturing; Sales.

INTERFACE, INC.
2859 Paces Ferry Road, Suite 2000, Atlanta GA 30339. 770/437-6800. **Contact:** Human Resources. **World Wide Web address:** http://www.interfaceinc.com. **Description:** Manufacturer and seller of modular and broadloom carpeting to commercial, residential, and institutional markets. The company also produces chemicals and designs, manufactures, and markets interior fabrics including upholstery and decorative window treatments. **Educational backgrounds include:** Accounting; Business Administration; English; Finance; Marketing. **Corporate headquarters location:** This Location. **Other U.S. locations:** Los Angeles CA; San Diego CA; San Francisco CA; Washington DC; LaGrange GA; Chicago IL; Boston MA; Detroit MI; St. Louis MO; New York NY; Philadelphia PA; Dallas TX; Houston TX; Seattle WA. **Subsidiaries include:** Guilford of Maine manufactures wall and ceiling covering fabrics; Interface Flooring Systems, Inc. manufactures broadloom carpeting; Pandel

manufactures vinyl carpet tile backing, specialty mats, and foam. **Listed on:** NASDAQ.

IRWIN MANUFACTURING GROUP
P.O. Box 507, Ocilla GA 31774. 912/468-9481. **Contact:** Personnel. **Description:** Manufactures and retails children's sleepwear products. **Corporate headquarters location:** This Location.

JPS INDUSTRIES
555 North Pleasantburg Drive, Suite 202, Greenville SC 29607. 864/239-3900. **Contact:** Monnie Broome, Human Resources Manager. **Description:** A holding company whose companies are engaged in the following areas of business: manufacturing and marketing a broad range of unfinished fabrics used in men's, women's, and children's apparel; automotive products; home furnishings; and residential and commercial carpets. **Corporate headquarters location:** This Location. **Number of employees nationwide:** 6,000.

JACLYN, INC.
5801 Jefferson Street, West New York NJ 07093. 201/868-9400. **Contact:** Personnel. **Description:** Designs, manufactures, and sells women's and children's handbag fashions, accessories, specialty items, and ready-to-wear apparel. **Common positions include:** Accountant; Administrator; Blue-Collar Worker Supervisor; Buyer; Computer Programmer; Credit Manager; Department Manager; Financial Analyst; General Manager; Human Resources Manager; Operations Manager; Purchasing Agent; Sales Executive; Transportation. **Educational backgrounds include:** Accounting; Business Administration; Economics; Finance. **Benefits:** Disability Coverage; Employee Discounts; Life Insurance; Medical Insurance; Pension Plan; Profit Sharing. **Corporate headquarters location:** This Location. **Operations at this facility include:** Administration; Manufacturing; Research and Development; Sales; Service. **Listed on:** American Stock Exchange.

JOAN FABRICS CORPORATION
100 Vesper Executive Park, Tyngsboro MA 01879-2710. 978/649-5626. **Contact:** Director of Human Resources. **Description:** Engaged in the manufacturing of woven and knitted fabrics for furniture and automotive manufacturers. The company also operates retail fabric stores nationwide. **Common positions include:** Accountant; Blue-Collar Worker Supervisor; Computer Programmer; Credit Manager; Customer Service Rep.; Department Manager; Financial Analyst; Human Resources Manager; Industrial Engineer; Operations Manager; Purchasing Agent; Quality Control Supervisor; Systems Analyst. **Educational backgrounds include:** Accounting; Business Administration; Computer Science; Engineering; Finance; Textiles. **Benefits:** 401(k); Disability Coverage; Life Insurance; Medical Insurance; Pension Plan; Tuition Assistance. **Corporate headquarters location:** This Location. **Other U.S. locations:** Fall River MA; Lowell MA; Hickory NC. **Operations at this facility include:** Administration.

JOCKEY INTERNATIONAL, INC.
P.O. Box 1417, Kenosha WI 53141-1417. 262/658-8111. **Fax:** 262/658-0036. **Contact:** Karen Fischer, Employment Supervisor. **World Wide Web address:** http://www.jockey.com. **Description:** One of the world's largest privately-owned underwear, sportswear, and hosiery companies. Founded in 1876. **NOTE:** Entry-level positions are offered. **Common positions include:** Accountant; Administrative Assistant; Advertising Clerk; Assistant Manager; Attorney; Auditor; Budget Analyst; Buyer; CFO; Computer Operator; Computer Programmer; Controller; Credit Manager; Customer Service Rep.; Database Manager; Designer; Editor; Environmental Engineer; Finance Director; Food Scientist; Human Resources Manager; Industrial Engineer; Industrial Production Manager; Manufacturing Engineer; Market Research Analyst; Marketing Manager; MIS Specialist; Operations Manager; Paralegal; Production Manager; Quality Control Supervisor; Registered Nurse; Sales Manager; Sales Rep.; Secretary; Systems Analyst; Systems Manager; Transportation. **Educational backgrounds include:** Accounting; Art/Design; Business Administration; Communications; Computer Science; Economics; Engineering; Finance; Liberal Arts; Marketing; Mathematics; Public Relations. **Benefits:** 401(k); Dental Insurance; Disability Coverage; Employee Discounts; Financial Planning Assistance; Life Insurance; Medical Insurance; Pension Plan; Savings Plan; Tuition Assistance. **Special programs:** Internships. **Corporate headquarters location:** This Location. **Other U.S. locations:** Nationwide. **International locations:** Canada; Hong Kong; the United Kingdom. **Number of employees worldwide:** 5,600.

JOHNSTON INDUSTRIES, INC.
105 13th Street, Columbus GA 31901. 706/641-3140. **Contact:** Personnel. **World Wide Web address:** http://www.johnstonind.com. **Description:** Manufactures woven and nonwoven textile fabrics for the industrial, home use, and apparel markets. **Corporate headquarters location:** This Location. **Subsidiaries include:** Johnston Industries Composite Reinforcements.

JONES APPAREL GROUP, INC.
250 Rittenhouse Circle, Bristol PA 19007. 215/785-4000. **Fax:** 215/785-5136. **Contact:** Aida Decolli, Personnel Director. **World Wide Web address:** http://www.jny.com. **Description:** Designs, manufactures, and markets a broad range of women's sportswear, suits, and dresses. Jones Apparel Group markets its products under the brand names Jones New York, Jones*Wear, Saville, Rena Rowan for Saville, Evan-Picone, Ellen Kaye, and under the licensed name Christian Dior. The company also has licenses for the Jones New York and Evan-Picone brand names with selected manufacturers of related apparel and accessories such as women's rainwear, coats, footwear, intimate apparel, hosiery, handbags, belts, men's tailored clothing, and eyewear. **Common positions include:** Accountant; Adjuster; Blue-Collar Worker Supervisor; Budget Analyst; Buyer; Clerical Supervisor; Computer Programmer; Credit Manager; Customer Service Rep.; Designer; Electrician; Financial Analyst; General Manager; Human Resources Manager; Operations Manager; Systems Analyst. **Educational backgrounds include:** Accounting; Art/Design; Business Administration; Finance. **Benefits:** 401(k); Dental Insurance; Disability Coverage; Employee Discounts; Life Insurance; Medical Insurance; Tuition Assistance. **Corporate headquarters location:** This Location. **Other U.S. locations:** Los Angeles CA; Atlanta GA; Chicago IL; New York NY; Lawrenceburg TN; Dallas TX; Seattle WA. **International locations:** Ciudad Juarez, Mexico; Kowloon, Hong Kong; Toronto, Canada. **Operations at this facility include:** Administration; Research and Development; Service. **Number of employees at this location:** 1,000. **Number of employees nationwide:** 2,000.

KL MANUFACTURING COMPANY
2726 North Monroe Street, Spokane WA 99205-3355. 509/326-2350. **Fax:** 509/326-2032. **Contact:**

Christine M. Green, Personnel Manager. **Description:** A garment mill engaged in the manufacture of clothing and backpacks. **NOTE:** Entry-level positions are offered. **Common positions include:** Administrative Assistant; Administrative Manager; Branch Manager; Human Resources Manager; Production Manager; Secretary. **Educational backgrounds include:** Accounting; Business Administration. **Benefits:** Life Insurance; Medical Insurance; Profit Sharing. **Special programs:** Apprenticeships. **Corporate headquarters location:** This Location. **Other area locations:** Chewelah WA. **Facilities Manager:** Michael E. Doohan. **Number of employees at this location:** 135. **Number of employees nationwide:** 225.

KAST FABRICS
P.O. Box 1660, Pasadena TX 77501. 713/473-4848. **Fax:** 713/473-3130. **Contact:** Human Resources. **World Wide Web address:** http://www.kastfabrics.com. **Description:** A wholesale distributor of decorative fabrics for drapes and upholstery. The company also manufactures bedding products such as quilts, bedspreads, and dust ruffles. **Corporate headquarters location:** This Location.

KENNETH COLE PRODUCTIONS
152 West 57th Street, 9th Floor, New York NY 10019. 212/265-1500. **Contact:** Human Resources. **Description:** Manufactures men's and women's shoes, bags, scarves, watches, belts, and other accessories. **NOTE:** Resumes should be sent to Human Resources, 2 Emerson Lane, Secaucus NJ 07094. 201/864-8080. **Corporate headquarters location:** This Location.

KENTUCKY APPAREL & LAUNDRY CO.
P.O. Box 368, Tompkinsville KY 42167. 270/487-6723. **Contact:** Linda Fraley, Director of Human Resources. **Description:** A manufacturer of jeans. **Corporate headquarters location:** This Location.

KLEINERT'S INC.
120 West Germantown Pike, Suite 100, Plymouth Meeting PA 19462-1420. 610/828-7261. **Fax:** 610/828-4589. **Contact:** Denise Hale, Vice President of Human Resources. **Description:** Manufactures children's sportswear and sleepwear. The company is also engaged in knitting polyester, cotton/polyester blends, and acrylic fabrics for a variety of uses. Founded in 1869. **Educational backgrounds include:** Accounting; Art/Design; Liberal Arts. **Benefits:** Disability Coverage; Life Insurance; Medical Insurance; Pension Plan. **Corporate headquarters location:** This Location. **Other U.S. locations:** Elba AL; Wilmington DE; Gastonia NC; New York NY. **International locations:** San Pedro Sula, Honduras. **Operations at this facility include:** Administration. **President/CEO:** Jack Brier. **Number of employees worldwide:** 1,000.

KNAPP SHOE
One Keuka Business Park, Suite 300, Penn Yan NY 14527. 315/536-8865. **Contact:** Human Resources. **Description:** Manufactures and retails shoes. **Corporate headquarters location:** This Location.

KRAEMER TEXTILES, INC.
P.O. Box 72, Nazareth PA 18064. 610/759-4030. **Contact:** Employment. **Description:** Manufactures spun yarns for the apparel, home furnishings, and crafts markets. **Corporate headquarters location:** This Location.

LaCROSSE FOOTWEAR, INC.
P.O. Box 1328, 1407 St. Andrew Street, La Crosse WI 54602-1328. 608/782-3020. **Fax:** 608/782-1318. **Contact:** Personnel. **World Wide Web address:** http://www.lacrosse-outdoors.com. **Description:** A leading producer of protective footwear for the sporting, occupational, and recreational markets. **Benefits:** 401(k); Disability Coverage; Employee Discounts; Life Insurance; Medical Insurance; Pension Plan; Tuition Assistance. **Corporate headquarters location:** This Location. **Operations at this facility include:** Administration; Manufacturing; Sales; Service. **President/CEO:** Patrick K. Gantert. **Annual sales/revenues:** $51 - $100 million. **Number of employees at this location:** 800. **Number of employees nationwide:** 1,300.
Other U.S. locations:
• P.O. Box 1380, Claremont NH 03743-1380. 603/543-1266.

LANDAU UNIFORMS, INC.
P.O. Box 516, Olive Branch MS 38654. 662/895-7200. **Physical address:** 8410 Sandidge Road, Olive Branch MS 38654. **Fax:** 662/893-2205. **Contact:** Sandra Dodd, Human Resources Manager. **World Wide Web address:** http://www.landau.com. **Description:** A manufacturer of health care uniforms. **Common positions include:** Accountant; Advertising Clerk; Blue-Collar Worker Supervisor; Buyer; Clerical Supervisor; Computer Programmer; Credit Manager; Customer Service Rep.; Designer; Draftsperson; Electrical Engineer; Human Resources Manager; Industrial Engineer; Mechanical Engineer; Operations Manager; Purchasing Agent; Quality Control Supervisor; Systems Analyst. **Educational backgrounds include:** Accounting. **Benefits:** 401(k); Dental Insurance; Disability Coverage; Life Insurance; Medical Insurance; Profit Sharing; Tuition Assistance. **Corporate headquarters location:** This Location. **Other U.S. locations:** New Albany MS. **Operations at this facility include:** Administration; Manufacturing; Sales. **Number of employees at this location:** 400. **Number of employees nationwide:** 600.

THE LESLIE FAY COMPANIES, INC.
1412 Broadway, 2nd Floor, New York NY 10018. 212/221-4000. **Contact:** Personnel. **Description:** Engaged in the design, manufacture, and sale of a diversified line of women's dresses, sportswear, blouses, and intimate apparel. **Corporate headquarters location:** This Location.

LEVI STRAUSS & COMPANY
1155 Battery Street, San Francisco CA 94111. 415/501-6000. **Contact:** Human Resources. **World Wide Web address:** http://www.levi.com. **Description:** Designs, manufactures, and markets a diversified line of apparel, primarily jeans and jeans-related products under the Levi's and Brittania brand names. The company also makes the Dockers line of clothing for U.S. markets. **Common positions include:** Accountant; Administrator; Advertising Clerk; Attorney; Blue-Collar Worker Supervisor; Claim Rep.; Computer Programmer; Customer Service Rep.; Department Manager; Financial Analyst; Human Resources Manager; Industrial Designer; Industrial Engineer; Manufacturer's Sales Rep.; Marketing Specialist; Operations Manager; Public Relations Specialist; Quality Control Supervisor; Statistician; Systems Analyst. **Educational backgrounds include:** Accounting; Art/Design; Business Administration; Communications; Computer Science; Economics; Engineering; Finance; Marketing. **Benefits:** Dental Insurance; Disability Coverage; Employee Discounts; Life Insurance; Medical Insurance; Pension Plan; Profit Sharing; Savings Plan; Tuition Assistance. **Corporate headquarters location:** This Location.

LIBERTY FABRICS, INC.
295 Fifth Avenue, New York NY 10016. 212/684-3100. **Contact:** Human Resources. **Description:** A manufacturer of knitted lace and elastic fabrics used by producers of lingerie, sportswear, swimwear, and home furnishings. **Common positions include:** Accountant; Administrator; Credit Manager; Customer Service Rep.; Marketing Specialist; Quality Control Supervisor. **Educational backgrounds include:** Accounting; Art/Design; Communications. **Benefits:** Disability Coverage; Life Insurance; Medical Insurance; Profit Sharing; Tuition Assistance. **Corporate headquarters location:** This Location. **Other U.S. locations:** Jamesville NC; North Bergen NJ; Gordonsville VA; Woolwine VA. **Parent company:** Courtaulds Textiles. **Operations at this facility include:** Administration; Sales. **Number of employees nationwide:** 1,400.

S. LICHTENBERG & CO. INC.
231 East 13th Street, P.O. Box 807, Waynesboro GA 30830. **Toll-free phone:** 800/682-1959. **Fax:** 706/554-6857. **Contact:** Human Resources. **World Wide Web address:** http://www.lichtenberg.com. **Description:** Manufactures draperies and curtains. **NOTE:** Entry-level positions are offered. **Common positions include:** Administrative Assistant; Administrative Manager; Assistant Manager; Blue-Collar Worker Supervisor; Computer Programmer; Computer Support Technician; Computer Technician; Customer Service Rep.; General Manager; Human Resources Manager; Industrial Engineer; Industrial Production Manager; Management Trainee; Production Manager; Quality Control Supervisor. **Benefits:** 401(k); Casual Dress - Daily; Dental Insurance; Disability Coverage; Life Insurance; Medical Insurance; Vacation Days (10 - 20). **Corporate headquarters location:** New York NY. **Other area locations:** Louisville GA. **President/CEO/Owner:** Ric Lichtenberg. **Number of employees at this location:** 550.

LIZ CLAIBORNE
1441 Broadway, New York NY 10018. 212/354-4900. **Contact:** Jorge Figueredo, Human Resources Director. **World Wide Web address:** http://www.lizclaiborne.com. **Description:** One of America's leading apparel companies. Liz Claiborne is comprised of 18 apparel and accessories divisions and several licenses. Products are sold under the company brand names and private labels. **NOTE:** Entry-level positions are offered. **Common positions include:** Account Manager; Account Rep.; Administrative Assistant. **Educational backgrounds include:** Business Administration; Marketing; Microsoft Word. **Benefits:** 401(k); Casual Dress - Daily; Dental Insurance; Disability Coverage; Employee Discounts; Life Insurance; Medical Insurance; Profit Sharing; Tuition Assistance. **Special programs:** Internships. **Corporate headquarters location:** This Location. **CEO:** Paul Charron. **Number of employees worldwide:** 7,000.

LONDON FOG INDUSTRIES
1332 Londontown Boulevard, Eldersburg MD 21784. 410/795-5900. **Contact:** Human Resources. **Description:** London Fog is a manufacturer and retailer of traditional and contemporary men's and women's rainwear; and of men's, women's, and children's outerwear and sportswear. Founded in 1923. **NOTE:** Entry-level positions are offered. **Common positions include:** Accountant; Adjuster; Administrative Manager; Attorney; Blue-Collar Worker Supervisor; Budget Analyst; Computer Programmer; Credit Manager; Customer Service Representative; Financial Analyst; Management Trainee; MIS Specialist; Systems Analyst;

Transportation. **Educational backgrounds include:** Accounting; Art/Design; Business Administration; Computer Science; Finance; Marketing. **Benefits:** 401(k); Dental Insurance; Disability Coverage; Employee Discounts; Life Insurance; Medical Insurance; Savings Plan; Tuition Assistance. **Corporate headquarters location:** This Location. **Other U.S. locations:** Nationwide. **Subsidiaries include:** Pacific Trail (Seattle WA). **Operations at this facility include:** Administration. **Listed on:** Privately held. **Annual sales/revenues:** More than $100 million. **Number of employees at this location:** 400. **Number of employees nationwide:** 2,400.

LOOKOUT KNITWEAR
2739 Cummings Highway, Chattanooga TN 37419. 423/825-6690. **Contact:** Personnel Manager. **Description:** Manufactures undyed hosiery and socks. **Common positions include:** Accountant; Human Resources Manager; Quality Control Supervisor. **Benefits:** Dental Insurance; Disability Coverage; Employee Discounts; Life Insurance; Medical Insurance. **Corporate headquarters location:** This Location. **Operations at this facility include:** Administration; Manufacturing; Research and Development; Sales. **Number of employees at this location:** 450.

LOUISVILLE BEDDING COMPANY
10400 Bunsen Way, Louisville KY 40299. 502/491-3370. **Fax:** 502/495-5346. **Contact:** Human Resources. **Description:** A manufacturer of bed pillows, mattress pads, and chair pads. **Corporate headquarters location:** This Location.

MALLORY AND CHURCH CORP.
676 South Industrial Way, Seattle WA 98108. 206/587-2100. **Toll-free phone:** 800/255-TIES. **Fax:** 206/587-2971. **Contact:** Human Resources. **World Wide Web address:** http://www.malloryandchurch.com. **Description:** One of the world's largest manufacturers of neckties. Founded in 1908. **Corporate headquarters location:** This Location. **Other U.S. locations:** Corona CA; Roswell GA; New York NY; Pittsburgh PA.

J.B. MARTIN COMPANY
10 East 53rd Street, Suite 3100, New York NY 10022. 212/421-2020. **Contact:** David Budd, Director of Sales. **Description:** Manufactures velvet. **Corporate headquarters location:** This Location.

MAXWELL SHOE COMPANY INC.
P.O. Box 37, Readville MA 02137-0037. 617/364-5090. **Physical address:** 101 Sprague Street, Hyde Park MA 02136. **Fax:** 617/333-4033. **Contact:** Personnel. **World Wide Web address:** http://www.maxwellshoe.com. **Description:** Designs, develops, and markets moderately priced casual and dress footwear for women under the Mootsies Tootsies brand name and for children under the Mootsies Kids brand name. The company has also entered an exclusive license agreement to design, develop, and market casual and dress footwear under the Jones New York and Jones New York Sport brand names. In addition, the company designs and develops private label footwear for selected retailers under the retailers' brand names. **Corporate headquarters location:** This Location. **Chairman and CEO:** Mark Cocozza.

MILLER INTERNATIONAL, INC.
8500 Zuni Street, Denver CO 80260-5007. 303/428-5696. **Contact:** Employment Manager. **Description:** Manufactures, wholesales, and retails Western wear through its two divisions, Rocky Mountain Clothing Company and Miller Stockman.

Common positions include: Accountant; Administrative Manager; Advertising Clerk; Buyer; Credit Manager; Customer Service Rep.; Human Resources Manager; Instructor; Operations Manager; Public Relations Specialist; Services Sales Rep.; Systems Analyst; Warehouse Worker. **Educational backgrounds include:** Art/Design; Business Administration; Computer Science; Marketing. **Benefits:** 401(k); Daycare Assistance; Disability Coverage; Employee Discounts; ESOP; Life Insurance; Medical Insurance; Tuition Assistance. **Special programs:** Internships. **Corporate headquarters location:** This Location. **Other U.S. locations:** GA. **Operations at this facility include:** Administration; Research and Development; Sales; Service. **Number of employees at this location:** 300. **Number of employees nationwide:** 800.

MITCHELLACE INC.
P.O. Box 89, Portsmouth OH 45662. 740/354-2813. **Physical address:** 830 Murray Street, Portsmouth OH. **Contact:** Personnel Manager. **Description:** Develops, manufactures, markets, and distributes shoelaces and other braided and woven products. **Common positions include:** Accountant; Administrator; Blue-Collar Worker Supervisor; Computer Programmer; Customer Service Rep.; Department Manager; Electrical Engineer; General Manager; Human Resources Manager; Industrial Engineer; Marketing Specialist; Operations Manager; Purchasing Agent; Quality Control Supervisor; Sales Executive. **Educational backgrounds include:** Accounting; Art/Design; Business Administration; Engineering; Marketing. **Benefits:** Disability Coverage; Life Insurance; Medical Insurance. **Corporate headquarters location:** This Location. **Operations at this facility include:** Administration; Manufacturing; Research and Development; Sales; Service.

MOHAWK INDUSTRIES
P.O. Box 12069, Calhoun GA 30703. 706/629-7721. **Physical address:** 160 South Industrial Boulevard, Calhoun GA 30701. **Contact:** L.C. Crane, Director of Human Resources. **World Wide Web address:** http://www.mohawkind.com. **Description:** A carpet mill and a leading producer of area rugs and mats for both the residential and commercial markets. Mohawk manufactures and markets broadloom carpet, area and accent rugs, and indoor and outdoor mats, covering all significant market segments, distribution channels, and price points. Brand names include Aladdin, Alexander Smith, American Rug Craftsmen, Galaxy, Harbinger, Horizon, Karastan, and Mohawk. **Common positions include:** Accountant; Advertising Clerk; Architectural Engineer; Assistant Manager; Blue-Collar Worker Supervisor; Buyer; Chemical Engineer; Chemist; Civil Engineer; Claim Rep.; Credit Manager; Customer Service Rep.; Department Manager; Draftsperson; Editor; Electrical Engineer; Financial Analyst; General Manager; Human Resources Manager; Industrial Engineer; Industrial Production Manager; Instructor; Management Trainee; Manufacturer's Sales Rep.; Mechanical Engineer; Operations Manager; Public Relations Specialist; Purchasing Agent; Quality Control Supervisor; Reporter; Systems Analyst. **Educational backgrounds include:** Accounting; Business Administration; Chemistry; Communications; Computer Science; Engineering; Finance; Marketing; Mathematics. **Benefits:** Dental Insurance; Disability Coverage; Employee Discounts; Life Insurance; Medical Insurance; Pension Plan; Profit Sharing; Savings Plan; Stock Option; Tuition Assistance. **Special programs:** Internships. **Corporate headquarters location:** This Location. **Other U.S. locations:** Los Angeles CA; Bennett SC; Dillon SC; Liberty SC; Seattle WA. **Operations at this facility include:** Administration; Manufacturing; Research and Development; Sales; Service. **Listed on:** NASDAQ.

MOUNT VERNON MILLS
P.O. Box 700, Commerce GA 30529. 706/335-3171. **Contact:** Human Resources. **Description:** Produces and distributes cotton fabrics to clothing and other textile manufacturers. **Corporate headquarters location:** This Location.

MOVIE STAR, INC.
136 Madison Avenue, 4th Floor, New York NY 10016. 212/684-3400. **Contact:** Human Resources Department. **Description:** A diversified apparel manufacturer. The company operates through four divisions. The largest division, Sanmark, designs, manufactures, and sells private label sleepwear, robes, loungewear, leisurewear, daywear, and undergarments to mass merchants, as well as to national and regional chains. Cinema Etoile is also an intimate apparel producer. The Irwin B. Schwabe division produces private label work and leisure shirts for chain stores and mail order catalogs as well as shirts that are sold under the Private Property brand name. The 25 Movie Star factory stores carry an assortment of merchandise, some of which is supplied by the three manufacturing divisions, as well as sportswear and accessories. **Corporate headquarters location:** This Location. **Other U.S. locations:** GA; MI. **Listed on:** American Stock Exchange.

NATIONAL NONWOVENS
180 Pleasant Street, Easthampton MA 01027. 413/527-3445. **Toll-free phone:** 800/333-3469. **Fax:** 413/527-9570. **Contact:** Human Resources. **Description:** Develops, markets, and manufactures needle punch and other nonwoven textiles. **Common positions include:** Accountant; Blue-Collar Worker Supervisor; Credit Manager; Customer Service Rep.; Electrician; Human Resources Manager; Industrial Production Manager; Manufacturer's Sales Rep.; Operations Manager; Quality Control Supervisor; Systems Analyst. **Educational backgrounds include:** Accounting; Business Administration; Chemistry; Engineering; Marketing; Textiles. **Benefits:** Dental Insurance; Disability Coverage; Life Insurance; Medical Insurance; Pension Plan; Tuition Assistance. **Corporate headquarters location:** This Location. **Operations at this facility include:** Administration; Manufacturing; Research and Development; Sales. **Annual sales/revenues:** $21 - $50 million. **Number of employees at this location:** 200.

NATIONAL SPINNING COMPANY INC.
111 West 40th Street, 28th Floor, New York NY 10018. 212/382-6400. **Contact:** Personnel Director. **World Wide Web address:** http://www.natspin.com. **Description:** Manufactures, markets, and distributes yarn products to knitwear manufacturers. The company also produces hand-knitting yarn and rug kits for distribution to retail chains throughout the United States. **Corporate headquarters location:** This Location.

NATIVE TEXTILES INC.
16 East 34th Street, 12th Floor, New York NY 10016. 212/951-5100. **Contact:** Personnel. **Description:** Manufactures lace and other fabrics for distribution throughout the United States. **Corporate headquarters location:** This Location.

NEW BALANCE ATHLETIC SHOE INC.
61 North Beacon Street, Boston MA 02134. 617/783-4000. **Contact:** Personnel Department.

World Wide Web address: http://www. newbalance.com. **Description:** Manufactures and distributes running and other athletic shoes. **Common positions include:** Accountant/Auditor; Administrator; Computer Programmer; Credit Clerk and Authorizer; Customer Service Representative; Human Resources Manager; Marketing Specialist; Systems Analyst. **Educational backgrounds include:** Accounting; Business Administration; Liberal Arts; Marketing. **Benefits:** Dental Insurance; Disability Coverage; Employee Discounts; Life Insurance; Medical Insurance; Tuition Assistance. **Corporate headquarters location:** This Location. **Operations at this facility include:** Manufacturing.

NEW ERA CAP COMPANY, INC.
8061 Erie Road, Derby NY 14047. 716/549-0445. **Contact:** Mary Farallo, Human Resources Manager. **Description:** Manufactures baseball caps. Founded in 1920. **Corporate headquarters location:** This Location. **Other area locations:** Blasdell NY; Buffalo NY.

NIKE, INC.
One Bowerman Drive, Beaverton OR 97005. 503/671-6453. **Fax:** 503/671-6300. **Contact:** Recruiter. **World Wide Web address:** http://www. nike.com. **Description:** Develops, manufactures, and markets a line of athletic shoes, casual shoes, accessories, and athletic apparel. Founded in 1964. **Common positions include:** Marketing Specialist. **Special programs:** Internships. **Corporate headquarters location:** This Location. **International locations:** Brazil; Hong Kong; Mexico; the Netherlands.

OAK HILL SPORTSWEAR CORP.
1411 Broadway, 10th Floor, New York NY 10018. 212/789-8900. **Contact:** Human Resources. **Description:** Oak Hill Sportswear is a diversified apparel company with sportswear, manufacturing, and accessory divisions that design, import, manufacture, and market a wide range of women's apparel and accessories. The sportswear division has several lines that are marketed under the Victoria Jones, Victoria Sport, and Casey & Max labels. Product lines include sweaters, cotton knits, woven shirts, and two-piece sets. The Marietta Manufacturing Division produces a portion of the products and provides all warehousing services for the sportswear division. The Accessories Division manufactures, imports, and markets several product lines, mainly under the Harmal label, consisting of belts and various accessory items. Principal customers include chain stores, discounters, and specialty retailers. **Corporate headquarters location:** This Location. **Other U.S. locations:** Marietta MS; Long Island City NY.

O'BRYAN BROTHERS
4256 West Belmont Avenue, Chicago IL 60641. 773/283-3000. **Contact:** Carroll Brahm, Human Resources Director. **Description:** Manufactures ladies' loungewear and lingerie. **Corporate headquarters location:** This Location.

OLD DEERFIELD FABRICS INC.
99 Commerce Road, Cedar Grove NJ 07009. 973/239-6600. **Contact:** Personnel. **Description:** Manufactures decorative fabrics and other household decorations. **Corporate headquarters location:** This Location.

OSBORN APPAREL MANUFACTURING CO.
7095 West 3500 South, West Valley City UT 84128. 801/250-6307. **Contact:** Personnel. **World Wide Web address:** http://www.cobblestones.com. **Description:** Manufactures a wide range of sportswear and activewear under the trade name Cobblestones Activewear. **Benefits:** 401(k); Dental Insurance; Employee Discounts; Life Insurance; Medical Insurance; Tuition Assistance. **Corporate headquarters location:** This Location.

OSHKOSH B'GOSH INC.
P.O. Box 300, Oshkosh WI 54902. 920/231-8800. **Physical address:** 112 Otter Avenue, Oshkosh WI. **Recorded jobline:** 920/232-4410. **Contact:** Human Resources. **World Wide Web address:** http://www. oshkoshbgosh.com. **Description:** A manufacturer of rugged adult workwear for farmers and railroad workers. The company also manufactures children's wear, bib overalls, shorts, shirts, dresses, activewear, swimwear, and accessories sold under the OshKosh B'Gosh and Baby B'Gosh labels; and youthwear under the Genuine Girl and Genuine Blues labels. The company also manufactures footwear, bedding, outerwear, and eyewear. **NOTE:** Please call the jobline for current openings and information necessary for sending a resume. **Corporate headquarters location:** This Location. **International locations:** Worldwide.

L.W. PACKARD & COMPANY
6 Mill Street, P.O. Box 515, Ashland NH 03217. 603/968-3351. **Fax:** 603/968-7649. **Contact:** Dan Brown, Director of Human Resources. **Description:** Manufactures woolen fabric for the apparel industry. L.W. Packard's manufacturing processes include blending, carding, rewinding, spinning, and weaving. **Common positions include:** Accountant; Buyer; Chemical Engineer; Computer Programmer; Electrician; General Manager; Human Resources Manager; Industrial Engineer; Management Trainee; Mechanical Engineer; Operations Manager; Systems Analyst. **Educational backgrounds include:** Accounting; Business Administration; Chemistry; Computer Science; Engineering; Finance. **Benefits:** 401(k); Disability Coverage; Employee Discounts; Life Insurance; Medical Insurance; Profit Sharing. **Special programs:** Internships. **Corporate headquarters location:** This Location. **Operations at this facility include:** Manufacturing; Research and Development. **Listed on:** Privately held. **Number of employees at this location:** 300.

PAPERPACK PRODUCTS
100 Readington Road, Somerville NJ 08876. 908/707-1800. **Contact:** Lisa Stewart, Personnel Coordinator. **Description:** Manufactures disposable underpads, cloths, and wipes for the health care, industrial, food service, and janitorial markets.

PHILLIPS-VAN HEUSEN CORPORATION
200 Madison Avenue, 10th Floor, New York NY 10016-3908. 212/381-3500. **Contact:** Betty Chaves, Director of Human Resources. **Description:** Manufactures, wholesales, and retails men's and women's apparel. **Common positions include:** Accountant; Buyer; Computer Programmer; Designer; Human Resources Manager; Manufacturer's Sales Rep.; Purchasing Agent; Systems Analyst. **Educational backgrounds include:** Accounting; Art/Design; Computer Science; Finance; Liberal Arts; Marketing. **Benefits:** 401(k); Disability Coverage; Employee Discounts; Life Insurance; Medical Insurance; Pension Plan; Tuition Assistance. **Corporate headquarters location:** This Location. **Other U.S. locations:** AL; NJ. **Operations at this facility include:** Design; Sales. **Number of employees nationwide:** 14,000.

PILLOWTEX CORPORATION
4111 Mint Way, Dallas TX 75237. 214/333-3225x114. **Fax:** 214/337-8398. **Contact:** Personnel Director. **World Wide Web address:** http://www. pillowtex.com. **Description:** A manufacturer of bed pillows, comforters, and mattress pads. **Common**

positions include: Manufacturer's Sales Rep. **Benefits:** Dental Insurance; Disability Coverage; Employee Discounts; Life Insurance; Medical Insurance; Pension Plan; Tuition Assistance. **Corporate headquarters location:** This Location. **Other U.S. locations:** Monroe NC; Lando SC. **Operations at this facility include:** Administration.

PLAYTEX PRODUCTS, INC.
P.O. Box 7016, 50 North DuPont Highway, Dover DE 19903. 302/678-6000. **Fax:** 302/678-6200. **Contact:** Donna M. Griffith, Director of Human Resources. **Description:** Manufactures intimate apparel. **Common positions include:** Accountant; Administrator; Blue-Collar Worker Supervisor; Buyer; Chemist; Computer Programmer; Credit Manager; Customer Service Rep.; Department Manager; Draftsperson; Electrical Engineer; Financial Analyst; General Manager; Human Resources Manager; Industrial Engineer; Mechanical Engineer; Operations Manager; Purchasing Agent; Quality Control Supervisor; Systems Analyst; Transportation. **Educational backgrounds include:** Accounting; Business Administration; Chemistry; Computer Science; Engineering; Finance; Human Resources; Liberal Arts; Marketing. **Benefits:** 401(k); Dental Insurance; Disability Coverage; Employee Discounts; Life Insurance; Medical Insurance; Pension Plan; Profit Sharing; Savings Plan; Tuition Assistance. **Special programs:** Internships. **Corporate headquarters location:** Westport CT. **Other U.S. locations:** Paramus NJ; Watervliet NY. **Operations at this facility include:** Administration; Distribution; Manufacturing; Research and Development; Service. **Number of employees nationwide:** 1,500.

PRESTIGE LEATHER INC.
5445 Jillson Street, City of Commerce CA 90040. 323/726-2109. **Contact:** Personnel. **Description:** A manufacturer of leather belts for men and women. **Corporate headquarters location:** This Location.

PRINTED FABRICS CORPORATION
P.O. Box 220, Carrollton GA 30117. 770/832-3561. **Fax:** 770/832-9658. **Contact:** Human Resources. **Description:** This location dyes, finishes, and cuts fabric. Overall, Printed Fabrics Corporation produces printed and finished upholstery materials. Founded in 1954. **NOTE:** Entry-level positions and second and third shifts are offered. **Common positions include:** Account Manager; Administrative Assistant; Electrician; Purchasing Agent; Secretary; Typist. **Educational backgrounds include:** Accounting; Business Administration; Health Care. **Benefits:** Life Insurance; Medical Insurance. **Corporate headquarters location:** This Location. **President:** Bernard Kress.

QUAKER FABRIC CORPORATION
941 Grinnell Street, Fall River MA 02721. 508/678-1951. **Fax:** 508/646-2429. **Contact:** Rose Pedro, Personnel Manager. **Description:** Manufactures textile upholstery fabrics and yarn. **Common positions include:** Accountant; Budget Analyst; Buyer; Clerical Supervisor; Computer Operator; Computer Programmer; Designer; Draftsperson; Editor; Electrician; Employment Interviewer; Financial Manager; General Manager; Human Resources Manager; Industrial Engineer; Inspector; Interviewing Clerk; Licensed Practical Nurse; Machinist; Management Trainee; Manufacturer's Sales Rep.; Mechanical Engineer; Millwright; New Accounts Clerk; Paralegal; Payroll Clerk; Purchasing Agent; Quality Control Supervisor; Receptionist; Secretary; Systems Analyst; Travel Agent; Truck Driver; Typist; Welder. **Benefits:**

Disability Coverage; Employee Discounts; Life Insurance; Medical Insurance; Pension Plan; Savings Plan; Tuition Assistance. **Corporate headquarters location:** This Location. **Operations at this facility include:** Administration; Manufacturing; Research and Development; Service. **Listed on:** NASDAQ. **Number of employees at this location:** 1,500.

QUEEN CARPET CORPORATION
P.O. Box 1527, Dalton GA 30722-1527. 706/277-1900. **Contact:** Jim Cobb, Personnel Director. **Description:** A manufacturer and international distributor of carpeting. **Common positions include:** Account Manager; Administrative Manager; Blue-Collar Worker Supervisor; Buyer; Chemical Engineer; Chemist; Claim Rep.; Clerical Supervisor; Computer Operator; Computer Programmer; Credit Manager; Customer Service Rep.; Electrician; Graphic Designer; Human Resources Manager; Industrial Engineer; Industrial Production Manager; Licensed Practical Nurse; Management Trainee; Manufacturing Engineer; Marketing Manager; MIS Specialist; Operations Manager; Production Manager; Purchasing Agent; Quality Control Supervisor; Sales Executive; Sales Manager; Sales Rep.; Systems Analyst; Systems Manager; Transportation. **Educational backgrounds include:** Business Administration; Computer Science; Engineering. **Benefits:** 401(k); Dental Insurance; Disability Coverage; Employee Discounts; Life Insurance; Medical Insurance; Tuition Assistance. **Corporate headquarters location:** This Location. **Listed on:** Privately held. **Number of employees nationwide:** 4,500.

REEBOK INTERNATIONAL LTD.
100 Technology Center Drive, Stoughton MA 02072. 781/401-5000. **Contact:** Personnel. **World Wide Web address:** http://www.reebok.com. **Description:** Reebok International is a leading worldwide designer, marketer, and distributor of sports, fitness, and casual footwear, apparel, and equipment. Principal operating units include the Reebok Division, Avia Group International, Inc., and The Rockport Company, Inc. **Corporate headquarters location:** This Location.

REGAL MANUFACTURING COMPANY
P.O. Box 2363, Hickory NC 28603. 828/328-5381. **Contact:** Betty Jo Pierce, Personnel Manager. **Description:** Develops, manufactures, and markets elastic yarn for the garment industry. **Common positions include:** Blue-Collar Worker Supervisor; Buyer; Computer Programmer; General Manager; Human Resources Manager; Industrial Engineer; Operations Manager; Quality Control Supervisor. **Benefits:** 401(k); Credit Union; Disability Coverage; Life Insurance; Medical Insurance; Profit Sharing; Savings Plan; Tuition Assistance. **Corporate headquarters location:** This Location. **Parent company:** Worldtex, Inc. **Operations at this facility include:** Administration; Manufacturing; Research and Development; Sales; Service. **Listed on:** New York Stock Exchange.

RIVERSIDE MANUFACTURING CO.
P.O. Box 460, Moultrie GA 31776. 912/985-5210. **Contact:** Personnel Manager. **Description:** Manufactures industrial uniforms and work clothing including shirts, aprons, and other careerwear. The company also produces a line of apparel products including men's blazers and dress pants. **Corporate headquarters location:** This Location.

THE ROCKPORT COMPANY, INC.
220 Donald Lynch Boulevard, Marlborough MA 01752. 508/485-2090. **Toll-free phone:** 800/ROCKPORT. **Fax:** 508/480-5763. **Contact:**

Human Resources. **World Wide Web address:** http://www.rockport.com. **Description:** Designs, markets, and sells men's and women's shoes. **Common positions include:** Accountant; Administrator; Advertising Clerk; Apparel Worker; Budget Analyst; Buyer; Computer Programmer; Credit Manager; Customer Service Rep.; Designer; Financial Analyst; General Manager; Human Resources Manager; Management Analyst; Manufacturer's Sales Rep.; Marketing Specialist; Operations Manager; Public Relations Specialist; Software Engineer; Systems Analyst; Transportation. **Educational backgrounds include:** Accounting; Art/Design; Business Administration; Communications; Computer Science; Finance; Liberal Arts; Marketing. **Benefits:** 401(k); Daycare Assistance; Dental Insurance; Disability Coverage; Employee Discounts; Life Insurance; Medical Insurance; Profit Sharing; Tuition Assistance. **Corporate headquarters location:** This Location. **Parent company:** Reebok International Ltd. (Stoughton MA). **Operations at this facility include:** Administration; Research and Development; Sales; Service. **Number of employees at this location:** 300. **Number of employees nationwide:** 425. **Number of employees worldwide:** 550.

ROCKY MOUNT CORD COMPANY
P.O. Drawer 4304, Rocky Mount NC 27803-0304. 252/977-9130. **Contact:** Personnel Director. **Description:** Manufactures braided cord and twisted rope. **Benefits:** Disability Coverage; Life Insurance; Medical Insurance. **Corporate headquarters location:** This Location. **Operations at this facility include:** Administration; Manufacturing; Research and Development; Sales; Service.

ROPER APPAREL AND FOOTWEAR
14707 East Second Avenue, Aurora CO 80011. 303/893-2320. **Contact:** Human Resources. **World Wide Web address:** http://www.roperusa.com. **Description:** Manufactures Western apparel. **Corporate headquarters location:** This Location.

ROYAL HOME FASHIONS INC.
P.O. Box 930, Durham NC 27702. 919/683-8011. **Fax:** 919/682-2997. **Contact:** Human Resources. **Description:** Manufactures home furnishings such as window treatments, comforters, sheets, and pillows. **Common positions include:** Accountant; Administrator; Blue-Collar Worker Supervisor; Buyer; Computer Programmer; Credit Manager; Customer Service Rep.; Department Manager; Human Resources Manager; Industrial Engineer; Industrial Production Manager; Instructor; Management Trainee; Operations Manager; Purchasing Agent; Quality Control Supervisor; Teacher. **Educational backgrounds include:** Business Administration; Engineering. **Benefits:** 401(k); Disability Coverage; Employee Discounts; Life Insurance; Medical Insurance; Pension Plan; Tuition Assistance. **Corporate headquarters location:** This Location. **Other U.S. locations:** Henderson NC. **Parent company:** Croscill Home Fashions. **Operations at this facility include:** Administration; Manufacturing. **Listed on:** Privately held. **Number of employees nationwide:** 1,500.

RUSSELL CORPORATION
P.O. Box 272, Alexander City AL 35011. 256/329-4000. **Contact:** Mike Hager, Vice President of Human Resources. **World Wide Web address:** http://www.russell.com. **Description:** A vertically-integrated international designer, manufacturer, and marketer of activewear, athletic uniforms, knit shirts, leisure apparel, licensed sports apparel, sports and casual socks, and a comprehensive line of lightweight, yarn-dyed woven fabrics. Russell's products are marketed principally through five sales divisions: Knit Apparel, Athletic, Licensed Products, International, and Fabrics. Products are marketed to sporting goods dealers, department and specialty stores, mass merchandisers, golf pro shops, college bookstores, screen printers, distributors, mail-order houses, and other apparel manufacturers. Major brand names include Jerzee's (knit apparel) and Russell Athletic (teamwear and knit activewear). **Corporate headquarters location:** This Location. **Other U.S. locations:** Crestview FL; Marianna FL; Niceville FL. **Subsidiaries include:** DeSoto Mills, Inc.; Fabrics Cross Creek Apparel, Inc. **Number of employees nationwide:** 16,640.

SALANT CORPORATION
1114 Avenue of the Americas, 34th Floor, New York NY 10036. 212/221-7500. **Contact:** Human Resources. **Description:** Designs, manufactures, imports, and markets a broad line of men's, children's, and women's apparel and accessories to retailers. Menswear is the company's largest sales category, with a focus on sportswear, dress shirts, neckwear, slacks, and jeans marketed under the Perry Ellis, J.J. Farmer, Thomson, John Henry, Gant, Manhattan, AXXA, Liberty of London, UNICEF, Peanuts, and Save the Children brand names. Women's wear includes sportswear marketed under the Made in the Shade brand name. The company's products are sold through department and specialty stores, major discounters, and mass volume retailers. **Corporate headquarters location:** This Location. **Number of employees worldwide:** 4,200.

F. SCHUMACHER & COMPANY
79 Madison Avenue, New York NY 10016. 212/213-7900. **Contact:** Gail Maddox, Personnel Director. **Description:** A textile wholesaler specializing in rug and fabric trading. **Corporate headquarters location:** This Location. **Other U.S. locations:** Nationwide.

SETON COMPANY
849 Broadway, Newark NJ 07104. 973/485-4800. **Contact:** Frank Quintiliani, Human Resources. **Description:** Company operations are conducted primarily through two business segments. The Leather Division's operations include tanning, finishing, and distributing whole-hide cattle leathers for the automotive and furniture upholstery industries, cattle hide side leathers for footwear, handbag, and other markets, and cattle products for collagen, rawhide pet items, and other applications. The Chemicals and Coated Products Division is engaged in the manufacture and distribution of epoxy and urethane chemicals, specialty leather finishes, industrial and medical tapes, foams, films, and laminates. Other manufacturing facilities are located in Wilmington DE (epoxy, urethane chemicals, leather finishes); Toledo OH (cattle hide processing); Malvern PA (industrial coated products); and Saxton PA (cutting of finished leathers). **Corporate headquarters location:** This Location. **Subsidiaries include:** Radel Leather Manufacturing Company; Seton Leather Company.

SHADOWLINE INC.
550 Lenoir Road, Morganton NC 28655. 828/437-3821. **Fax:** 828/437-8423. **Contact:** Judy B. Fisher, Personnel Manager. **Description:** A manufacturer of lingerie. **Common positions include:** Accountant; Blue-Collar Worker Supervisor; Clerical Supervisor; Computer Programmer; Cost Estimator; Credit Manager; Customer Service Rep.; Designer; Human Resources Manager; Industrial Engineer; Operations Manager; Purchasing Agent; Quality

Control Supervisor; Services Sales Rep.; Systems Analyst. **Educational backgrounds include:** Accounting; Art/Design; Business Administration; Computer Science; Finance; Marketing. **Benefits:** Dental Insurance; Disability Coverage; Employee Discounts; Life Insurance; Medical Insurance; Pension Plan. **Special programs:** Internships. **Corporate headquarters location:** This Location. **Other area locations:** Boone NC; Fallston NC; Mars Hill NC. **Operations at this facility include:** Administration; Manufacturing; Research and Development; Sales; Service. **Number of employees nationwide:** 500.

SHAER SHOE CORPORATION
P.O. Box 10600, Bedford NH 03110. 603/625-8566. **Contact:** Office Manager. **Description:** A manufacturer of women's clothing and casual shoes. **Corporate headquarters location:** This Location.

SHAW INDUSTRIES, INC.
P.O. Drawer 2128, Dalton GA 30722. 706/278-3812. **Contact:** Personnel. **World Wide Web address:** http://www.shawinc.com. **Description:** The company manufactures tufted floor coverings and related products. The company manufactures and sells tufted carpet for both residential and commercial use. All products are marketed through retailers, distributors, and other end-users and are exported to over 150 countries. Brand names include Philadelphia Carpet Company, Expressive Designs, Sutton, Shaw Commercial Carpets, and Salemcarpets. **Corporate headquarters location:** This Location.

SIGNAL APPAREL COMPANY
200A Manufacturers Road, P.O. Box 4296, Chattanooga TN 37405. 423/266-2175. **Contact:** Personnel. **Description:** Manufactures fabric and produces T-shirts, fleece garments, and other sportswear. Products are sold primarily to wholesalers, distributors, screen printers, and certain retail locations. **Corporate headquarters location:** This Location. **Other U.S. locations:** Bean Station TN; New Tazewell TN.

SIOUX MANUFACTURING CORP.
P.O. Box 400, Fort Totten ND 58335. 701/766-4211. **Fax:** 701/766-4359. **Contact:** Bernadette Brown, Human Resources Supervisor. **Description:** A textile manufacturer. Products include structural and ballistic composites and camouflage netting systems. **Common positions include:** Accountant; Aerospace Engineer; Blue-Collar Worker Supervisor; Buyer; Chemist; Computer Programmer; Department Manager; Draftsperson; Industrial Engineer; Manufacturer's Sales Rep.; Marketing Specialist; Mechanical Engineer; Operations Manager; Purchasing Agent; Quality Control Supervisor; Systems Analyst; Technical Writer. **Educational backgrounds include:** Business Administration; Computer Science; Engineering. **Benefits:** Dental Insurance; Life Insurance; Medical Insurance; Pension Plan; Profit Sharing; Tuition Assistance. **Corporate headquarters location:** This Location. **Operations at this facility include:** Administration; Manufacturing; Research and Development.

SOUTHERN MILLS
P.O. Box 289, Union City GA 30291. 770/969-1000. **Contact:** Personnel. **World Wide Web address:** http://www.somills.com. **Description:** Manufactures industrial fabrics for use by other manufacturing companies. Southern Mills also manufactures press pads and covers for dry cleaning and laundry services. **Corporate headquarters location:** This Location.

SPRINGS INDUSTRIES, INC.
P.O. Box 70, Fort Mill SC 29716. 803/547-1500. **Physical address:** 205 North White Street, Fort Mill SC 29715. **Contact:** Human Resources. **Description:** A producer of home furnishings, finished fabrics, and other fabrics for industrial uses. Products include bedroom accessories, bath products, novelties, window treatments, and specialty fabrics for the apparel, home furnishing, home sewing, and sporting good industries. **Corporate headquarters location:** This Location.

STARTER CORPORATION
370 James Street, New Haven CT 06513. 203/781-4000. **Contact:** Human Resources. **World Wide Web address:** http://www.starter.com. **Description:** This location houses administrative offices. Overall, Starter Corporation is a manufacturer of brand-name sporting apparel for professional sports teams as well as for consumers. The company also operates a chain of retail fashion outlets. **Corporate headquarters location:** This Location.

STEVENS LINEN ASSOCIATES, INC.
137 Scofield Avenue, P.O. Box 95, Dudley MA 01571. 508/943-0813x38. **Fax:** 800/339-6569. **Contact:** Terri Colognesi, Personnel. **Description:** Engaged in linen screen printing. Products include calendar towels, tea towels, pot holders, and other domestic goods. Founded in 1846. **NOTE:** Entry-level positions are offered. **Common positions include:** Administrative Assistant; Credit Manager; Customer Service Representative; Database Manager. **Educational backgrounds include:** Art/Design. **Benefits:** 401(k); Dental Insurance; Disability Coverage; Employee Discounts; Flexible Schedule; Life Insurance; Medical Insurance; Savings Plan; Tuition Assistance. **Corporate headquarters location:** This Location.

STITCHES INC.
1144 Vista De Oro Drive, El Paso TX 79935. 915/593-2990. **Contact:** Personnel. **Description:** A textile sewing and cutting contractor. **Corporate headquarters location:** This Location.

STRIDE-RITE CORPORATION
191 Spring Street, P.O. Box 9191, Lexington MA 02421. 617/824-6000. **Contact:** Mary Kuconis, Human Resources Director. **World Wide Web address:** http://www.striderite.com. **Description:** Manufactures and distributes a wide range of children's footwear products. The company also operates retail stores. **Corporate headquarters location:** This Location.

SUPERIOR UNIFORM GROUP
10099 Seminole Boulevard, Seminole FL 33772. 727/397-9611. **Contact:** Terry Lupo, Corporate Manager of Human Resources. **Description:** A manufacturer and wholesale distributor of uniforms, career apparel, and accessories for the hospital and health care fields, hotels and restaurants, and the public safety, industrial, transportation, and commercial markets. Fashion Seal Uniforms is the company's largest division and a prime supplier to the health care market. Other divisions include Worklon, Martin's Uniforms, Appel Uniforms, Universal Laundry Bags, Lamar Caribbean Sales, D'Armigene Design Center, and Superior Surgical International. **Common positions include:** Accountant; Buyer; Commercial Artist; Computer Programmer; Credit Manager; Customer Service Rep.; Human Resources Manager; Industrial Engineer; Industrial Production Manager; Manufacturer's Sales Rep.; Quality Control Supervisor; Systems Analyst. **Educational backgrounds include:** Accounting; Business Administration; Computer Science; Marketing.

Benefits: Disability Coverage; Life Insurance; Medical Insurance; Pension Plan. **Corporate headquarters location:** This Location.

SURE FIT INC.
939 Marcon Boulevard, Allentown PA 18103. 610/264-7300. **Contact:** Kenneth J. Guerin, Director of Human Resources. **Description:** Manufactures decorative home textiles including furniture covers and throw pillows. **Common positions include:** Accountant; Blue-Collar Worker Supervisor; Computer Programmer; Customer Service Rep.; Industrial Engineer; Systems Analyst. **Educational backgrounds include:** Accounting; Business Administration; Computer Science; Textiles. **Benefits:** 401(k); Employee Discounts; Life Insurance; Medical Insurance. **Corporate headquarters location:** New York NY.

TAOS MOCCASIN COMPANY
P.O. Box 708, Taos NM 87571. 505/758-4276. **Contact:** Tom Powell, General Manager. **Description:** Manufactures a wide variety of Native American leathercraft products. **Corporate headquarters location:** This Location.

THOMASTON MILLS INC.
P.O. Box 311, Thomaston GA 30286. 706/647-7131. **Contact:** Personnel Director. **World Wide Web address:** http://www.thomastonmills.com. **Description:** Manufactures textile mill products in four divisions: consumer products, which includes fabrics used in home furnishings such as comforters, pillow cases, and sheets; industrial grade products, which includes yarns; fabrication products, which includes camouflage materials; and apparel products, which includes denim. **Corporate headquarters location:** This Location.

THE TIMBERLAND COMPANY
200 Domain Drive, Stratham NH 03885. 603/772-9500. **Recorded jobline:** 603/772-9500x6802. **Contact:** Human Resources Department. **World Wide Web address:** http://www.timberland.com. **Description:** The Timberland Company designs, manufactures, and markets footwear, apparel, and accessories under the Timberland brand name. Timberland products for men and women include boots, casual shoes, boat shoes, and accessories. Timberland products are sold primarily through Timberland stores, other retail specialty stores, department stores, athletic stores, and shoe stores worldwide. **Common positions include:** Accountant; Attorney; Computer Programmer; Customer Service Rep.; Designer; Financial Analyst; Operations Manager; Systems Analyst. **Benefits:** 401(k); Dental Insurance; Disability Coverage; Employee Discounts; Life Insurance; Medical Insurance; Tuition Assistance. **Corporate headquarters location:** This Location. **Operations at this facility include:** Administration.

TRADE APPAREL INC.
6969-B Industrial Drive, El Paso TX 79915. 915/772-7170. **Contact:** Personnel. **Description:** Manufactures jeans. **Corporate headquarters location:** This Location.

TRANS-APPAREL GROUP
5000 South Ohio Street, Michigan City IN 46360. 219/879-7341. **Contact:** Personnel. **Description:** A manufacturer of men's slacks. **Common positions include:** Accountant; Advertising Clerk; Blue-Collar Worker Supervisor; Customer Service Rep.; Financial Analyst; Industrial Engineer. **Educational backgrounds include:** Accounting; Business Administration; Computer Science; Finance. **Benefits:** Disability Coverage; Employee Discounts; Life Insurance; Medical Insurance;

Tuition Assistance. **Corporate headquarters location:** This Location. **Operations at this facility include:** Manufacturing.

TROPICAL SPORTSWEAR INTERNATIONAL
4902 West Waters Avenue, Tampa FL 33634. 813/249-4900. **Contact:** Recruiting Department. **Description:** Manufactures men's and women's denim, twill, and corduroy casual clothing. Brand names include Savane and Bill Blass. **NOTE:** Entry-level positions and second and third shifts are offered. **Common positions include:** Administrative Assistant; Blue-Collar Worker Supervisor; Controller; Cost Estimator; Education Administrator; Financial Analyst; Human Resources Manager; Manufacturing Engineer; Quality Control Supervisor; Sales Manager; Systems Manager. **Educational backgrounds include:** Accounting; Computer Science; Finance; Public Relations. **Benefits:** 401(k); Dental Insurance; Disability Coverage; Employee Discounts; Medical Insurance; On-Site Exercise Facility; Tuition Assistance. **Special programs:** Internships. **Corporate headquarters location:** This Location. **Other U.S. locations:** NY. **International locations:** Dominican Republic; Mexico.

TRU-STITCH FOOTWEAR
123 Catherine Street, Malone NY 12953. 518/483-6300. **Fax:** 518/483-8233. **Contact:** Gary Buck, Personnel Manager. **Description:** Manufactures slippers and moccasins. **Parent company:** Wolverine Worldwide (Rockford MI). **Operations at this facility include:** Divisional Headquarters.

UNIFI, INC.
P.O. Box 19109, Greensboro NC 27419-9109. 336/294-4410. **Fax:** 336/316-5422. **Contact:** Human Resources Director. **World Wide Web address:** http://www.unifi-inc.com. **Description:** Unifi, Inc. and its subsidiaries are engaged in the processing of yarns by texturing synthetic filament polyester and nylon fibers and spinning cotton and cotton-blend fibers. The company supplies knitters and weavers for apparel, industrial hosiery, home furnishing, automotive upholstery, and other end use markets. Women's and men's hosiery, high-performance stretch activewear, and medical products including tape and bandages that contain the company's textured nylon and covered lycra and rubber products. **Corporate headquarters location:** This Location. **International locations:** Letterkenny, Ireland. **Subsidiaries include:** Unifi Spun Yarns, Inc.; Vintage Yarns, Inc.

UNIFORMS TO YOU
5600 West 73rd Street, Chicago IL 60638. 708/563-4913. **Fax:** 708/563-4360. **Contact:** Amy Kitzmiller, Personnel Manager. **Description:** Designs, manufactures, and markets specialty apparel for the hospitality, restaurant, and entertainment industries. **Common positions include:** Accountant; Blue-Collar Worker Supervisor; Buyer; Computer Programmer; Customer Service Rep.; Human Resources Manager; Systems Analyst. **Educational backgrounds include:** Accounting; Art/Design; Business Administration; Communications; Computer Science; Marketing. **Benefits:** 401(k); Dental Insurance; Disability Coverage; Life Insurance; Medical Insurance; Tuition Assistance. **Corporate headquarters location:** This Location. **International locations:** Canada; Mexico; Puerto Rico. **Operations at this facility include:** Research and Development; Sales; Service.

UNITY KNITTING MILLS INC.
P.O. Box 827, Wadesboro NC 28170. 704/694-6544. **Contact:** Personnel Director. **Description:**

Manufactures thermal underwear. **Common positions include:** Accountant; Computer Programmer; Operations Manager; Purchasing Agent; Quality Control Supervisor. **Educational backgrounds include:** Business Administration; Communications; Finance; Mathematics. **Benefits:** Disability Coverage; Employee Discounts; Life Insurance; Medical Insurance. **Corporate headquarters location:** This Location.

VF CORPORATION
628 Green Valley Road, Suite 500, Greensboro NC 27408. 336/547-6000. **Fax:** 336/547-7696. **Contact:** Susan Williams, Vice President of Personnel. **World Wide Web address:** http://www.vfc.com. **Description:** Manufactures jeanswear, decorative knitwear, intimate apparel, playwear, and specialty apparel. The company markets its products under the brand names Vanity Fair, Barbizon, JanSport, Rustler, Girbaud, Lee, and Wrangler. **Educational backgrounds include:** Accounting; Finance; Marketing. **Corporate headquarters location:** This Location. **Subsidiaries include:** Red Kap Industries; VF Workwear.

VF WORKWEAR
545 Marriott Drive, P.O. Box 140995, Nashville TN 37214. 615/391-1200. **Contact:** Human Resources. **Description:** Manufactures occupational apparel. Specialties include safety and flame-resistant products including high-visibility and reflective trim garments, as well as fluid-resistant and other protective apparel. The company also produces durable press, easy-care, 100 percent cotton products. Brand names of work utility wear include Big Ben and WorkWear. **Corporate headquarters location:** This Location. **Other U.S. locations:** Dickson TN; Harriman TN; Wartburg TN. **Parent company:** VF Corporation (Greensboro NC).

VENATOR GROUP
112 West 34th Street, New York NY 10120. 212/720-3700. **Contact:** Human Resources. **World Wide Web address:** http://www.venator.com. **Description:** Manufactures men's, women's, and children's sportswear under the brand names Champs Sports, Eastbay, Foot Locker, Northern Elements, Northern Getaway, Northern Reflections, and Northern Traditions. **Corporate headquarters location:** This Location.

VISION LEGWEAR LLC
P.O. Box 528, Spruce Pine NC 28777. 828/765-9011. **Fax:** 828/765-0526. **Contact:** Human Resources Manager. **World Wide Web address:** http://www.visionlegwear.com. **Description:** Vision Legwear manufactures women's sheer hosiery.

WALLS INDUSTRIES, INC.
P.O. Box 18, Gatesville TX 76528. 254/865-7215. **Physical address:** 1501 West Main, Gatesville TX 76528. **Contact:** Human Resources. **World Wide Web address:** http://www.wallsoutdoors.com. **Description:** Manufactures outerwear for men, women, and children. **Corporate headquarters location:** This Location.

WALTON FABRICS, INC.
P.O. Box 1046, Monroe GA 30655. 770/267-9411. **Contact:** Carol Johnson, Employment Manager. **Description:** Manufactures woven textiles and other piece-goods. **Corporate headquarters location:** This Location.

THE WARNACO GROUP, INC.
90 Park Avenue, New York NY 10016. 212/661-1300. **Contact:** Human Resources Department. **Description:** A manufacturer, designer, and marketer of women's intimate apparel, menswear, and men's accessories under brand names including Calvin Klein, Fruit of the Loom, Warner's, Olga, and Chaps by Ralph Lauren. Warnaco markets its products through a chain of 48 retail outlets, as well as department stores and mass merchandisers. **Corporate headquarters location:** This Location. **Other U.S. locations:**
- 470 Wheelers Farms Road, Milford CT 06460. 203/301-7000.

WELLINGTON LEISURE PRODUCTS INC.
P.O. Box 244, Madison GA 30650. 706/342-1916. **Contact:** Thomas Little, Director of Human Resources. **World Wide Web address:** http://www.wellingtoninc.com. **Description:** Manufactures cordage and twine which is used in water and outdoor sport equipment. **Corporate headquarters location:** This Location.

WELLMAN, INC.
1040 Broad Street, Suite 302, Shrewsbury NJ 07702. 732/542-7300. **Contact:** Personnel. **World Wide Web address:** http://www.wellmanwlm.com. **Description:** This location houses the company's executive offices. Overall, Wellman manufactures polyester fibers and a recycler of fibers, resins, and plastics. **Corporate headquarters location:** This Location. **Other U.S. locations:** Commerce CA; Rolling Meadows IL; Chelmsford MA; Bloomfield Hills MI; Charlotte NC; Bridgeport NJ; New York NY; Medina OH; Pawtucket RI; Florence SC; Johnsonville SC; Marion SC; Ripon WI.

WESCO FABRICS INC.
4001 Forest Street, Denver CO 80216. 303/388-4101. **Contact:** Human Resources. **Description:** Wholesales drapery fabrics and distributes window coverings and bedspreads on a wholesale trade basis. Wesco Fabrics also manufactures bedspreads. **Corporate headquarters location:** This Location.

WEST MILL CLOTHES INC.
57-07 31st Avenue, Woodside NY 11377. 718/204-6640. **Contact:** Clifford Goodman, Personnel Officer. **Description:** Manufactures formalwear. **Corporate headquarters location:** This Location.

WHITE SWAN META UNIFORM CO.
14044 West Petronella, Suite 1, Libertyville IL 60048. 847/247-0380. **Contact:** Human Resources. **Description:** This location is the sales and service office. Overall, White Swan Meta Uniform Company manufactures uniforms.

WILLIAMSON-DICKIE MANUFACTURING CO.
P.O. Box 1779, Fort Worth TX 76101. 817/336-7201. **Contact:** Estelle Lewis, Director of Human Resources. **World Wide Web address:** http://www.dickies.com. **Description:** Manufactures apparel for men and boys including casual slacks and work pants. **Corporate headquarters location:** This Location.

WONALANCET COMPANY
1711 Tullie Circle NE, Suite 104, Atlanta GA 30329-2391. 404/633-4551. **Contact:** Treasurer. **Description:** A small dealer of textile fibers. **Common positions include:** Services Sales Representative. **Educational backgrounds include:** Business Administration. **Benefits:** Dental Insurance; Life Insurance; Medical Insurance; Profit Sharing; Savings Plan. **Corporate headquarters location:** This Location. **Operations at this facility include:** Administration; Sales; Service.

WOOLRICH, INC.
One Mill Street, Woolrich PA 17779. 570/769-6464. **Contact:** Roger Sheets, Director of Personnel. **World Wide Web address:** http://www.woolrich.

com. **Description:** Manufactures a wide variety of outerwear and sweaters for men and women. **Corporate headquarters location:** This Location.

WORKRITE UNIFORM COMPANY, INC.
P.O. Box 1192, Oxnard CA 93032. 805/483-0175. **Physical address:** 500 East Third Street, Oxnard CA. **Fax:** 805/483-7622. **Contact:** Personnel. **Description:** An apparel manufacturer specializing in flame-retardant garments. This location also hires seasonally. **NOTE:** Workrite Uniform Company primarily hires sewing machine operators. Entry-level positions are offered. **Common positions include:** Account Manager; Administrative Assistant; AS400 Programmer Analyst; CFO; Customer Service Rep.; Draftsperson; Human Resources Manager; Industrial Designer; Industrial Engineer; Marketing Manager; MIS Specialist; Network Administrator; Operations Manager; Production Manager; Purchasing Agent; Quality Assurance Engineer; Quality Control Supervisor; Sales Manager; Typist. **Educational backgrounds include:** Accounting; AS400 Certification; Business Administration; Computer Science; Engineering; Marketing; MBA; MCSE; Microsoft Office; Novell;

Sales; Spreadsheets; SQL. **Benefits:** 401(k); Dental Insurance; Disability Coverage; Life Insurance; Medical Insurance; Public Transit Available; Tuition Assistance. **Corporate headquarters location:** This Location. **Parent company:** Williamson-Dickie Manufacturing Company. **Operations at this facility include:** Administration; Manufacturing; Sales; Service.

ZEEMAN
dba BARRY MANUFACTURING
2303 John Glenn Drive, Chamblee GA 30341. 770/451-5476. **Fax:** 770/451-8095. **Contact:** Sean Whiteman, Vice President. **Description:** Manufactures and sells suits in 38 retail stores throughout the Southeast. **Common positions include:** Administrative Assistant; Advertising Executive; Buyer; Operations Manager; Production Manager; Sales Manager; Sales Representative. **Educational backgrounds include:** Business Administration; Marketing. **Benefits:** Employee Discounts; Profit Sharing. **Corporate headquarters location:** This Location. **Other U.S. locations:** Charlotte NC; Dallas TX; Norfolk VA.

For more information on career opportunities in the apparel, fashion, and textiles industries:

Associations

AMERICAN APPAREL MANUFACTURERS ASSOCIATION
2500 Wilson Boulevard, Suite 301, Arlington VA 22201. 703/524-1864. World Wide Web address: http://www.americanapparel.org. Publishes magazines, newsletters, and bulletins for the benefit of employees in the apparel manufacturing industry.

AMERICAN TEXTILE MANUFACTURERS INSTITUTE
Office of the Chief Economist, 1130 Connecticut Avenue NW, Suite 1200, Washington DC 20036. 202/862-0500. Fax: 202/862-0570. World Wide Web address: http://www.atmi.org. The national trade association for the domestic textile industry. Members are corporations only.

THE FASHION GROUP INTERNATIONAL, INC.
597 Fifth Avenue, 8th Floor, New York NY 10017. 212/593-1715. World Wide Web address: http://www.fgi.org. A nonprofit organization for professionals in the fashion industries (apparel, accessories, beauty, and home).

INTERNATIONAL ASSOCIATION OF CLOTHING DESIGNERS
475 Park Avenue South, 9th Floor, New York NY 10016. 212/685-6602. Fax: 212/545-1709.

Directories

AAMA DIRECTORY
American Apparel Manufacturers Association, 2500 Wilson Boulevard, Suite 301, Arlington VA 22201. 703/524-1864. A directory of publications.

APPAREL TRADES BOOK
Dun & Bradstreet Inc., One Diamond Hill Road, Murray Hill NJ 07974. 908/665-5000.

FAIRCHILD'S MARKET DIRECTORY OF WOMEN'S AND CHILDREN'S APPAREL
Fairchild Publications, 7 West 34th Street, New York NY 10001. 212/630-4000. World Wide Web address: http://www.fairchildpub.com.

Magazines

ACCESSORIES
Business Journals Inc., 50 Day Street, Norwalk CT 06854. 203/853-6015.

AMERICA'S TEXTILES INTERNATIONAL
Billiam Publishing, 555 North Pleasantburg Drive, Suite 132, Greenville SC 29607. 864/242-5300.

APPAREL INDUSTRY MAGAZINE
Bill Communications, 1115 Northmeadow Parkway, Roswell GA 30046. 770/569-1540. Toll-free phone: 800/241-9034. Fax: 770/569-5105. World Wide Web address: http://www.aimagazine.com.

BOBBIN MAGAZINE
Bobbin Publishing, P.O. Box 1986, 1500 Hampton Street, Columbia SC 29201. 803/771-7500.

TEXTILE HILIGHTS
American Textile Manufacturers Institute, Office of the Chief Economist, 1130 Connecticut Avenue NW, Washington DC 20036. A quarterly publication. Subscriptions: $125.00 per year.

WOMEN'S WEAR DAILY (WWD)
Fairchild Publications, 7 West 34th Street, New York NY 10001. 212/630-4000. World Wide Web address: http://www.fairchildpub.com.

Online Services

THE INTERNET FASHION EXCHANGE
World Wide Web address: http://www.fashionexch.com. An excellent site for those industry professionals interested in apparel and retail. The extensive search engine allows you to search by job title, location, salary, product line, industry, and whether you want a permanent, temporary, or freelance position. The site also offers career services such as recruiting and outplacement firms that place fashion and retail professionals.

Architecture, Construction, and Engineering

You can expect to find the following types of companies in this chapter:
*Architectural and Engineering Services • Civil and Mechanical Engineering Firms
Construction Products, Manufacturers, and Wholesalers • General Contractors/
Specialized Trade Contractors*

Some helpful information: *The average salary for an entry-level architect is $20,000 -
$30,000, with licensed, experienced architects earning $33,000 - $45,000 and firm
partners earning as much as $80,000. Construction workers' salaries depend heavily on
the season and the housing economy; on average, experienced workers earn around
$25,000. Engineers with strong academic backgrounds can earn as much as $40,000
initially. Salary increases are largely dependent upon performance in this field, and
talented, experienced engineers frequently earn over $75,000 annually. In particular,
chemical and electrical engineers are in considerable demand.*

ABB INC.
P.O. Box 5308, Norwalk CT 06856-5308. 203/750-2200. **Fax:** 203/750-2295. **Contact:** Human
Resources. **World Wide Web address:** http://www.abb.com/usa. **Description:** Provides engineering,
construction, and sales support services as part of a
worldwide engineering firm. Internationally, the
company operates in five business segments: oil
field equipment and services; power systems;
engineering and construction; process equipment;
and industrial products. **Corporate headquarters
location:** This Location. **Subsidiaries include:**
ABB Lumus Global Inc. (Bloomfield NJ); ABB
Simcon (Broomfield NJ); ABB Susa (North
Brunswick NJ). **Parent company:** ABB Asea
Brown Boveri Ltd. (Baden, Switzerland). **Number
of employees worldwide:** 220,000.
Other U.S. locations:
• P.O. Box 6005, North Brunswick NJ 08902-6005. 732/932-6000.

ABTCO, INC.
3250 West Big Beaver Road, Suite 200, Troy MI
48084. 248/649-3300. **Contact:** Arlene Appleman,
Personnel Director. **World Wide Web address:**
http://www.abtco.com. **Description:** Engaged in the
research, design, manufacturing, and marketing of
building products such as architectural trim, siding,
paneling, molding, and shutters. ABTCO is an
operating division of ABT Building Products
Corporation, and part of the corporation's
Hardboard/Plastic Division. **Common positions
include:** Accountant/Auditor; Chemical Engineer;
Computer Programmer; Credit Manager; Customer
Service Rep.; Draftsperson; Electrical/Electronics
Engineer; Financial Analyst; Forester/Conservation
Scientist; Human Resources Manager; Industrial
Designer; Management Trainee; Manufacturer's/
Wholesaler's Sales Rep.; Mechanical Engineer;
Purchasing Agent/Manager; Quality Control
Supervisor; Transportation/Traffic Specialist.
Educational backgrounds include: Accounting;
Business Administration; Computer Science;
Engineering; Finance; Marketing. **Benefits:** Dental
Insurance; Disability Coverage; Employee
Discounts; Life Insurance; Medical Insurance;
Pension Plan; Savings Plan; Tuition Assistance.
Corporate headquarters location: This Location.
Other U.S. locations: Middlebury IN; Alpena MI;
Roaring River NC; Toledo OH. **Parent company:**
ABT Building Products Corporation. **Listed on:**
NASDAQ.

ACR GROUP, INC.
3200 Wilcrest Drive, Suite 440, Houston TX 77042-6019. 713/780-8532. **Fax:** 713/780-4067. **Contact:**
Personnel. **World Wide Web address:** http://www.acrgroup.com. **Description:** A wholesale distributor
of heating, ventilation, air conditioning, and
refrigeration equipment, parts, and supplies. ACR
Group's products include motors, fiberglass air
handling products, sheet metal products, copper
tubing, flexible duct, controls, grilles, registers, and
pipe vents. The company has 18 distribution outlets
in the United States. Founded in 1990. **Subsidiaries
include:** ACR Supply, Inc. (TX and LA); Beaumont
A/C Supply, Inc. (TX); Contractors Heating &
Supply, Inc. (CO and NM); Ener-Tech Industries,
Inc. (TN); Florida Cooling Supply, Inc. (FL);
Heating and Cooling Supply, Inc. (NV); Lifetime
Filter, Inc. (TX); Total Supply, Inc. (GA); Valley
Supply, Inc. (TN); West Coast HVAC Supply, Inc.
(CA). **Corporate headquarters location:** This
Location. **Listed on:** NASDAQ. **Stock exchange
symbol:** ACRG. **President/CEO:** Alex Trevino, Jr.
Annual sales/revenues: More than $100 million.

AEPA ARCHITECTS ENGINEERS PC
2421 Pennsylvania Avenue NW, Washington DC
20037. 202/822-8320. **Fax:** 202/457-0908.
Contact: Director of Operations. **World Wide Web
address:** http://www.aepa.com. **Description:** An
architectural firm that designs and builds biomedical
research facilities. **Corporate headquarters
location:** This Location.

AAVID THERMAL PRODUCTS INC.
P.O. Box 400, Laconia NH 03247. 603/528-3400.
Physical address: One Kool Path, Laconia NH.
Fax: 603/527-2369. **Contact:** Deborah Lacey,
Recruiter. **E-mail address:** lacey@aavid.com.
World Wide Web address: http://www.aavid.com.
Description: A thermal engineering and
management company that develops and markets
solutions to heat-related problems. **NOTE:** Entry-
level positions are offered. **Common positions
include:** Applications Engineer; Computer
Operator; Computer Programmer; Industrial
Engineer; Mechanical Engineer; Production
Manager; Sales Engineer; Sales Rep.; Systems
Analyst. **Educational backgrounds include:**
Engineering; Marketing; Microsoft Word;
Spreadsheets. **Benefits:** 401(k); Dental Insurance;
Disability Coverage; Employee Discounts; Life
Insurance; Medical Insurance; Profit Sharing;
Tuition Assistance. **Corporate headquarters**

location: This Location. **Other U.S. locations:**
Santa Ana CA; Terrell TX. **Parent company:** Aavid
Thermal Technologies Inc. **Number of employees
at this location:** 700. **Number of employees
nationwide:** 1,500.

ABCO BUILDERS INC.
2680 Abco Court, Lithonia GA 30058. 770/981-
0350. **Contact:** Mr. Lynn Bledsoe, Vice President.
Description: A commercial construction firm.
Corporate headquarters location: This Location.

J.D. ABRAMS INTERNATIONAL INC.
111 Congress Avenue, Suite 2400, Austin TX
78701. 512/322-4000. **Fax:** 512/322-4012.
Contact: Mr. Dean Bernal, Vice President of
Human Resources. **E-mail address:** hr@
jdabrams.com. **World Wide Web address:**
http://www.jdabrams.com. **Description:** A heavy
civil construction company specializing in public
works infrastructure projects. **Corporate
headquarters location:** This Location.

ACORN WINDOW SYSTEMS
42 Cole Street, Quincy MI 49082. 517/639-8731.
Contact: Human Resources Department.
World Wide Web address: http://www.
acornwindows.com. **Description:** Manufactures
metal doors, frames, and windows. **Benefits:** Dental
Insurance; Life Insurance; Medical Insurance; Profit
Sharing; Tuition Assistance. **Corporate
headquarters location:** This Location. **Number of
employees nationwide:** 600.

ADOBEAIR, INC.
500 South 15th Street, Phoenix AZ 85034. 602/257-
0060. **Fax:** 602/257-1349. **Contact:** Human
Resources. **World Wide Web address:** http://www.
adobeair.com. **Description:** A manufacturer of
portable electric heaters and evaporative coolers.
Common positions include: Accountant/Auditor;
Advertising Clerk; Customer Service Rep.;
Industrial Engineer; Mechanical Engineer. **Benefits:**
Dental Insurance; Employee Discounts; Life
Insurance; Medical Insurance; Pension Plan;
Savings Plan; Tuition Assistance. **Corporate
headquarters location:** This Location. **Number of
employees at this location:** 500.

AIR CONDITIONING COMPANY, INC.
6265 San Fernando Road, Glendale CA 91201.
818/244-6571. **Fax:** 818/549-0120. **Contact:**
Roberta Kessler, Human Resources Director. **E-mail
address:** acco@accoair.com. **World Wide Web
address:** http://www.accoair.com. **Description:**
Provides heating and air conditioning services for
both commercial and industrial customers.
Common positions include: Accountant; Buyer;
CADD Operator; Design Engineer; Mechanical
Engineer; Project Manager. **Educational
backgrounds include:** Engineering. **Benefits:**
401(k); Life Insurance; Medical Insurance; Profit
Sharing; Tuition Assistance. **Corporate
headquarters location:** This Location. **Other area
locations:** Concord CA; Sacramento CA; San
Carlos CA; San Diego CA; Tustin CA. **Other U.S.
locations:** Kent WA. **Listed on:** Privately held.
Annual sales/revenues: More than $100 million.
Number of employees at this location: 300.
Number of employees nationwide: 1,200.

AMBITECH ENGINEERING CORPORATION
1333 Butterfield Road, Suite 200, Downers Grove
IL 60515. 630/963-5800. **Fax:** 630/963-8099.
Contact: Elizabeth A. Smith, Manager of Human
Resources. **E-mail address:** b.smith@
ambitech.com. **World Wide Web address:**
http://www.ambitech.com. **Description:** A
consulting and engineering firm engaged in the
engineering and design of petroleum refineries,
chemical plants, and petrochemical plants.
Common positions include: Architect; Chemical
Engineer; Civil Engineer; Construction Contractor;
Cost Estimator; Design Engineer; Designer;
Draftsperson; Electrical/Electronics Engineer;
Mechanical Engineer; Petroleum Engineer;
Structural Engineer. **Educational backgrounds
include:** Drafting; Engineering. **Benefits:** 401(k);
Dental Insurance; Disability Coverage; Life
Insurance; Medical Insurance; Tuition Assistance.
Corporate headquarters location: This Location.
Listed on: Privately held. **Annual sales/revenues:**
$11 - $20 million. **Number of employees at this
location:** 190.

AMERICAN HOMESTAR CORPORATION
2450 South Shore Boulevard, Suite 300, League
City TX 77573. 281/334-9700. **Contact:** Human
Resources. **World Wide Web address:** http://www.
americanhomestar.com. **Description:** Designs,
manufactures, and sells houses nationwide.
Corporate headquarters location: This Location.
Other U.S. locations: AK; CO; KS; LA; MO; NM.
Listed on: NASDAQ. **Stock exchange symbol:**
HSTR.

AMERICAN PINE PRODUCTS
P.O. Box 687, Prineville OR 97754-0685. 541/447-
4177. **Contact:** Human Resources. **Description:**
Manufactures moldings, door frames, and window
frames. **Corporate headquarters location:**
Chesterfield MO. **Parent company:** Huttig Building
Products. **Number of employees at this location:**
400.

AMERICAN SHOWER AND BATH
693 South Court Street, Lapeer MI 48446. 810/664-
8501. **Contact:** Human Resources. **Description:**
Manufactures wall surrounds for showers and
bathtubs. **Common positions include:** Blue-Collar
Worker Supervisor; Draftsperson; General Manager;
Human Resources Manager; Industrial Production
Manager; Manufacturer's/Wholesaler's Sales Rep.;
Mechanical Engineer; Operations/Production
Manager; Purchasing Agent/Manager; Quality
Control Supervisor. **Educational backgrounds
include:** Business Administration; Engineering;
Marketing. **Benefits:** Dental Insurance; Disability
Coverage; Employee Discounts; Life Insurance;
Medical Insurance; Pension Plan; Profit Sharing;
Savings Plan. **Special programs:** Internships.
Corporate headquarters location: This Location.
Parent company: Masco Corporation. **Number of
employees at this location:** 100.

AMERICAN STANDARD COMPANIES INC.
One Centennial Avenue, Piscataway NJ 08855.
732/980-6000. **Contact:** Human Resources.
World Wide Web address: http://www.
americanstandard.com. **Description:** A global,
diversified manufacturer. The company's operations
are comprised of four segments: air conditioning
products, plumbing products, automotive products,
and medical systems. The air conditioning products
segment (through subsidiary The Trane Company)
develops and manufactures Trane and American
Standard air conditioning equipment for use in
central air conditioning systems for commercial,
institutional, and residential buildings. The
plumbing products segment develops and
manufactures American Standard, Ideal Standard,
Porcher, Armitage Shanks, Dolomite, and Standard
bathroom and kitchen fixtures and fittings. The
automotive products segment develops and
manufactures truck, bus, and utility vehicle braking
and control systems under the WABCO and Perrot
brands. The medical systems segment manufactures
Copalis, DiaSorin, and Pylori-Chek medical

diagnostic products and systems for a variety of diseases including HIV, osteoporosis, and renal disease. **Corporate headquarters location:** This Location. **International locations:** Worldwide. **Listed on:** New York Stock Exchange. **Chairman/CEO:** Frederic M. Poses. **Number of employees worldwide:** 57,000.

AMERICAN WOODMARK CORPORATION
P.O. Box 1980, Winchester VA 22604. 540/665-9100. **Physical address:** 3102 Shawnee Drive, Winchester VA 22601. **Contact:** Rick Hardy, Human Resources Manager. **World Wide Web address:** http://www.americanwoodmark.com. **Description:** Manufactures and distributes kitchen cabinets and vanities. The company's products are sold nationally through a network of independent distributors, home centers, major builders, and home manufacturers. **NOTE:** Entry-level positions and part-time jobs are offered. **Company slogan:** Creating value through people. **Common positions include:** Account Manager; Account Rep.; Accountant; Administrative Assistant; Auditor; Chief Financial Officer; Computer Operator; Computer Programmer; Computer Support Technician; Controller; Customer Service Rep.; Database Administrator; Database Manager; Design Engineer; Draftsperson; Human Resources Manager; Industrial Engineer; Manufacturing Engineer; Marketing Manager; Marketing Specialist; MIS Specialist; Operations Manager; Quality Control Supervisor; Sales Manager; Sales Representative; Systems Analyst; Systems Manager; Transportation/Traffic Specialist; Vice President of Operations. **Educational backgrounds include:** Accounting; Business Administration; Engineering; Finance; Marketing; Microsoft Word; Spreadsheets. **Benefits:** 401(k); Casual Dress - Daily; Dental Insurance; Disability Coverage; Life Insurance; Medical Insurance; Pension Plan; Profit Sharing; Savings Plan; Sick Days (11+); Tuition Assistance; Vacation Days (11 - 15). **Corporate headquarters location:** This Location. **Other U.S. locations:** AZ; GA; IN; KY; MN; VA; WV. **Listed on:** NASDAQ. **Stock exchange symbol:** AMWD. **Annual sales/revenues:** More than $100 million. **Number of employees at this location:** 220. **Number of employees nationwide:** 2,600.

AMSCO WINDOWS
P.O. Box 25368, Salt Lake City UT 84125. 801/972-6441. **Recorded jobline:** 801/978-5011. **Contact:** Personnel. **World Wide Web address:** http://www.amscowindows.com. **Description:** A window manufacturer. **Common positions include:** Accountant; Controller; General Manager; Marketing Manager; Production Manager; Project Manager. **Benefits:** Profit Sharing. **Corporate headquarters location:** This Location.

ANCO INDUSTRIES
15981 Airline Highway, Baton Rouge LA 70884-3730. 225/752-2000. **Fax:** 225/756-7678. **Contact:** Human Resources. **Description:** Engaged in industrial insulating, painting, and asbestos abatement. **Common positions include:** Account Manager; Administrative Assistant; Biomedical Engineer; Blue-Collar Worker Supervisor; Clerical Supervisor; Clinical Lab Technician; Computer Operator; Computer Programmer; Cost Estimator; Customer Service Rep.; Human Resources Manager; Industrial Engineer; Project Manager; Purchasing Agent/Manager; Quality Control Supervisor; Sales Engineer; Sales Manager; Secretary. **Benefits:** 401(k); Dental Insurance; Disability Coverage; Employee Discounts; Flexible Schedule; Life Insurance; Medical Insurance; Profit Sharing; Savings Plan. **Special programs:** Apprenticeships; Training. **Corporate headquarters location:** This

Location. **Other U.S. locations:** AL; NC; TX. **Subsidiaries include:** Amspec; Basic Industries. **Parent company:** Anco Insulation. **Listed on:** Privately held. **Owner:** R.L. Anderson. **Facilities Manager:** Billy Sanders. **Number of employees at this location:** 150. **Number of employees nationwide:** 7,000. **Number of employees worldwide:** 7,500.

ANDERSON INDUSTRIES, INC.
12457 Montego Plaza, Dallas TX 75230. 972/233-1805. **Contact:** Personnel Department. **Description:** Produces pre-fabricated building materials. **Corporate headquarters location:** This Location.

ANNING-JOHNSON COMPANY
1959 Anson Drive, Melrose Park IL 60160. 708/681-1300. **Contact:** Human Resources Director. **World Wide Web address:** http://www.anningjohnson.com. **Description:** Engaged in contract work in a variety of areas including acoustical ceiling, drywall, fireproofing, metal floor decks, metal siding, roofing, and geotechnical fill. **Corporate headquarters location:** This Location. **Parent company:** Anson Industries Inc. **Number of employees nationwide:** 750.

APAC, INC.
900 Ashwood Parkway, Suite 700, Atlanta GA 30338. 770/392-5300. **Contact:** Personnel. **World Wide Web address:** http://www.apac.com. **Description:** Provides a variety of construction services including asphalt and concrete paving and the excavation and construction of bridges and other structures. **Common positions include:** Accountant/Auditor; Attorney; Systems Analyst. **Educational backgrounds include:** Accounting; Computer Science; Finance. **Benefits:** Dental Insurance; Disability Coverage; Life Insurance; Medical Insurance; Pension Plan; Savings Plan; Tuition Assistance. **Corporate headquarters location:** This Location. **Listed on:** New York Stock Exchange.

APEX SUPPLY COMPANY, INC.
2500 Button Gwinnett Drive, Atlanta GA 30340. 770/449-7000. **Fax:** 770/441-8674. **Contact:** Human Resources. **World Wide Web address:** http://www.apexsupply.com. **Description:** A wholesale distributor of plumbing, heating, air conditioning, industrial piping products, cabinetry, appliances, and tools. The company's three major businesses are plumbing, heating and air conditioning, and building specialty products. The company makes a number of products including brand names Kohler, Price-Pfister, Jacuzzi, Delta, and State (plumbing products); Trane, Honeywell, and Reznor (heating and air conditioning equipment and parts); Jamesbury, Sarco, Nibco, Asahi, Weldbend, and US Pipe (pipes, valves, and fittings); Timberlake, Millbrook, and Plato (cabinetry and counter surfaces); GE, Magic-Chef, Kitchen Aid, and Sub Zero (appliances); and Makita and Ridgid (tools). **NOTE:** Entry-level positions are offered. **Common positions include:** Account Rep.; Administrative Assistant; Customer Service Rep.; Management Trainee; Purchasing Agent/Manager; Sales Manager; Sales Rep.; Secretary. **Educational backgrounds include:** Accounting; Business Administration; Communications; Economics; Finance; Marketing. **Benefits:** 401(k); Dental Insurance; Disability Coverage; Employee Discounts; Life Insurance; Medical Insurance; Pension Plan. **Special programs:** Internships; Co-ops. **Corporate headquarters location:** This Location. **Other U.S. locations:** Cartersville GA; Douglasville GA; Forest Park GA; Gainesville GA; Lawrenceville GA; Lilburn GA; Macon GA; Marietta GA; Roswell GA; Cookeville TN;

Dyersburg TN; Knoxville TN; Memphis TN. **Listed on:** Privately held. **Number of employees at this location:** 200. **Number of employees nationwide:** 450.

ARCADIS GIFFELS
P.O. Box 5025, Southfield MI 48086. 248/936-8000. **Contact:** Ed Dodge, Human Resources Administrator. **Description:** An engineering, architectural, and surveying firm. **Common positions include:** Architect; Civil Engineer; Draftsperson; Electrical/Electronics Engineer; Industrial Designer; Industrial Engineer; Mechanical Engineer. **Educational backgrounds include:** Architecture; Engineering. **Benefits:** Dental Insurance; Disability Coverage; Employee Discounts; Life Insurance; Medical Insurance; Profit Sharing; Savings Plan; Tuition Assistance. **Corporate headquarters location:** This Location. **Number of employees at this location:** 500.

ARINC INCORPORATED
2551 Riva Road, Annapolis MD 21401-7465. 410/266-4000. **Fax:** 410/266-4040. **Contact:** Human Resources. **World Wide Web address:** http://www.arinc.com. **Description:** An engineering and management consulting firm providing technical studies, analyses, and evaluations of aircraft and ship communication and information systems. Customers of ARINC include the Department of Defense, the Department of Energy, the Department of Transportation, and the Federal Aviation Administration. **Common positions include:** Aerospace Engineer; Budget Analyst; Ceramics Engineer; Computer Programmer; Draftsperson; Electrical/Electronics Engineer; Financial Analyst; Materials Engineer; Mechanical Engineer; Metallurgical Engineer; Software Engineer; Systems Analyst; Technical Writer/Editor. **Educational backgrounds include:** Communications; Computer Science; Engineering; Mathematics; Physics. **Benefits:** 401(k); Daycare Assistance; Dental Insurance; Disability Coverage; Employee Discounts; Life Insurance; Medical Insurance; Pension Plan; Tuition Assistance. **Special programs:** Internships. **Corporate headquarters location:** This Location. **Other U.S. locations:** Nationwide. **Listed on:** Privately held. **Number of employees at this location:** 2,600.

ARROW GROUP INDUSTRIES, INC.
1680 Route 23 North, P.O. Box 928, Wayne NJ 07474-0928. 973/696-6900. **Fax:** 973/696-8539. **Contact:** Joanne Trezza, Human Resources Director. **Description:** Manufactures steel storage buildings. **Corporate headquarters location:** This Location. **Other U.S. locations:** Breese IL. **Number of employees at this location:** 115. **Number of employees nationwide:** 330.

ARVADA HARDWOOD FLOOR COMPANY
3301 Lewiston Street, Aurora CO 80011. 303/343-9000. **Contact:** Paula Bardon, Human Resources Manager. **World Wide Web address:** http://www.arvadahardwood.com. **Description:** Engaged in the installation and refinishing of hardwood floors. The company is also engaged in the installation of carpet, vinyl, ceramic tile, and related floor coverings. **Common positions include:** Administrative Worker/Clerk; Installer. **Corporate headquarters location:** This Location. **Number of employees at this location:** 150.

ASCHINGER ELECTRIC COMPANY
P.O. Box 26322, Fenton MO 63026. 636/343-1211. **Fax:** 636/343-9658. **Contact:** Donna L. Kebel, Controller/Office Manager. **World Wide Web address:** http://www.aschinger.com. **Description:** An electrical contracting firm specializing in industrial and commercial applications. **Common positions include:** Administrative Assistant; Cost Estimator; Customer Service Representative; Draftsperson; Electrical/Electronics Engineer; Electrician; Secretary. **Educational backgrounds include:** Engineering. **Benefits:** 401(k); Dental Insurance; Disability Coverage; Life Insurance; Medical Insurance; Pension Plan. **Office hours:** Monday - Friday, 8:00 a.m. - 5:00 p.m. **Corporate headquarters location:** This Location. **Listed on:** Privately held. **President:** Eric D. Aschinger. **Annual sales/revenues:** $21 - $50 million. **Number of employees at this location:** 200.

THE AUSTIN COMPANY
3650 Mayfield Road, Cleveland OH 44121-1734. 216/382-6600. **Fax:** 216/291-6684. **Contact:** Dennis M. Raymond, Vice President of Human Resources. **E-mail address:** humanres@theaustin.com. **World Wide Web address:** http://www.theaustin.com. **Description:** An engineering and architectural design firm concentrating on industrial, commercial, and government projects. **Common positions include:** Architect; Civil Engineer; Construction Superintendent; Draftsperson; Electrical/Electronics Engineer; Graphic Designer; Mechanical Engineer; Project Manager. **Educational backgrounds include:** Construction; Engineering. **Benefits:** 401(k); Dental Insurance; Disability Coverage; Life Insurance; Medical Insurance; Pension Plan. **Corporate headquarters location:** This Location. **Other U.S. locations:** Nationwide. **International locations:** London, England. **Subsidiaries include:** Ragnor Benson. **President/CEO:** J. William Melsop. **Number of employees nationwide:** 610.

AXIS INC.
2201 West Townline Road, Peoria IL 61615. 309/691-3988. **Contact:** Human Resources. **World Wide Web address:** http://www.axis-inc.com. **Description:** Engaged in civil and mechanical engineering, information technology, and client-site technical services. Founded in 1987. **Subsidiaries include:** Axis Software, Inc. (Indianapolis IN); Axis Computers Ltd. (New Delhi, India); Axis EU Ltd. (London, England). **Other U.S. locations:** Joliet IL; Indianapolis IN.

THE BSC GROUP, INC.
425 Summer Street, Boston MA 02210. 617/330-5300. **Toll-free phone:** 800/288-8123. **Fax:** 617/345-8008. **Contact:** Alison Hunt, Human Resources. **E-mail address:** hrdept@bscgroup.com. **World Wide Web address:** http://www.bscgroup.com. **Description:** A land resource and consulting engineering firm providing a variety of consulting services in the fields of land surveying and mapping, geographic information systems, civil engineering, environmental engineering, planning, and landscape architecture. The BSC Group focuses on coastal, land development, and transportation projects. Founded in 1965. **Common positions include:** Biological Scientist; Civil Engineer; Draftsperson; Environmental Engineer; Software Engineer; Surveyor; Transportation/Traffic Specialist. **Educational backgrounds include:** Biology; Computer Science; Engineering; Surveying/Mapping. **Benefits:** 401(k); Dental Insurance; Disability Coverage; Life Insurance; Medical Insurance; Profit Sharing; Tuition Assistance. **Corporate headquarters location:** This Location. **Parent company:** BSC Companies. **Number of employees at this location:** 90. **Number of employees nationwide:** 120.

BSI CONSTRUCTORS INC.
6767 Southwest Avenue, St. Louis MO 63143. 314/781-7820. **Contact:** Joseph M. Kaiser,

Executive Vice President. **Description:** A general contracting and construction management firm. **Common positions include:** Civil Engineer; Construction Contractor. **Educational backgrounds include:** Construction; Engineering. **Benefits:** Dental Insurance; Disability Coverage; Life Insurance; Medical Insurance; Pension Plan; Profit Sharing; Tuition Assistance. **Corporate headquarters location:** This Location. **Number of employees at this location:** 100.

MICHAEL BAKER CORPORATION
Airport Office Park, Building 3, 420 Rouser Road, Coraopolis PA 15108. 412/269-6300. **Contact:** Human Resources. **World Wide Web address:** http://www.mbakercorp.com. **Description:** Provides engineering and management operations services to the construction, energy, environmental, and transportation markets. **NOTE:** All interested jobseekers should address resumes to Ann Michalski, Human Resources Manager, P.O. Box 12259, Pittsburgh PA 15221. **Common positions include:** Architect; Civil Engineer; Environmental Engineer; Industrial Engineer; Mechanical Engineer; Structural Engineer. **Corporate headquarters location:** This Location.

BALCO INC.
306 Northern Avenue, Boston MA 02205. 617/482-0100. **Contact:** Personnel Manager. **Description:** A heating, ventilation, air conditioning, and refrigeration contractor engaged in construction and maintenance services. **Common positions include:** Accountant/Auditor; Financial Analyst; Marketing Specialist; Mechanical Engineer; Purchasing Agent/Manager. **Benefits:** Dental Insurance; Disability Coverage; Life Insurance; Medical Insurance; Pension Plan; Savings Plan; Tuition Assistance. **Corporate headquarters location:** This Location. **Other U.S. locations:** Birmingham AL; Rockville MD; Harrisburg PA. **Parent company:** Energy Systems, Inc. **Number of employees at this location:** 500.

BARBER & ROSS COMPANY
P.O. Box 1294, Leesburg VA 20177. 703/478-1970. **Contact:** Dan Reeves, Controller. **Description:** Manufactures window units, interior and exterior door units, door entrance products, and other door and sash products. **Corporate headquarters location:** This Location.

BARGE, WAGGONER, SUMNER & CANNON
162 Third Avenue North, Nashville TN 37201. 615/254-1500. **Contact:** Director of Human Resources. **World Wide Web address:** http://www.bargewaggoner.com. **Description:** An employee-owned design firm offering services in engineering, architecture, planning, landscape architecture, and surveying. Civil engineering services include site engineering and utilities design, grading, drainage, traffic impact studies, traffic signal system design, and transportation facility planning and design. Planning services are used by city, county, and regional authorities. Barge, Waggoner, Sumner & Cannon is supported by in-house engineers, architects, planners, and landscape architects providing services to private developers on projects ranging from small residential developments to mixed-use projects of more than 6,000 acres. Services include zoning and land use controls, airport master planning, housing and community development, environmental assessments, feasibility analyses, grant program administration, recreation facilities, and park design. Architectural services are used in office buildings, multilevel parking garages, historic restoration, and commercial, institutional, and recreational facilities. The engineering and architectural staff offer services in industrial buildings and facilities design as well. The firm also provides environmental engineering services for water treatment and distribution systems, wastewater collection and treatment systems, and solid and hazardous waste projects. **Corporate headquarters location:** This Location. **Other U.S. locations:** AL; KY; OH; TN.

BARTON MALOW COMPANY
27777 Franklin Road, Suite 800, Southfield MI 48034. 248/351-4500. **Contact:** Judy Willard, Human Resources Director. **World Wide Web address:** http://www.bmco.com. **Description:** A construction management, program management, and general contracting company engaged in the construction of health facilities and commercial and industrial buildings. **Common positions include:** Architect; Civil Engineer; Electrical/Electronics Engineer; Industrial Engineer; Mechanical Engineer. **Educational backgrounds include:** Engineering. **Benefits:** Dental Insurance; Disability Coverage; Life Insurance; Medical Insurance; Profit Sharing; Savings Plan; Tuition Assistance. **Special programs:** Internships. **Corporate headquarters location:** This Location. **Number of employees nationwide:** 1,200.

BEAZER HOMES USA, INC.
5775 Peachtree Dunwoody Road, Suite B-200, Atlanta GA 30342. 404/250-3420. **Fax:** 404/250-3428. **Contact:** Jennifer Jones, Benefits Manager. **World Wide Web address:** http://www.beazer.com. **Description:** One of the nation's largest homebuilders. **Corporate headquarters location:** This Location. **Other U.S. locations:** Phoenix AZ; Los Angeles CA; San Diego CA; Jacksonville FL; Stuart FL; Charlotte NC; Raleigh NC; Clifton NJ; Las Vegas NV; Charleston SC; Columbia SC; Nashville TN; Dallas TX; Houston TX. **Listed on:** New York Stock Exchange.

BECHTEL CORPORATION
P.O. Box 193965, San Francisco CA 94119-3965. 415/768-1234. **Physical address:** 50 Beale Street, San Francisco CA 94105-1895. **Contact:** Employment Department. **World Wide Web address:** http://www.bechtel.com. **Description:** Operations focus on engineering, construction, financing operations and maintenance, electricity, nuclear fuel, metals, minerals, procurement management, transportation, and pollution control. **NOTE:** Resumes should be sent to Bechtel Staffing Support Center-SF, P.O. Box 36359, Phoenix AZ 85067-6359. All resumes should be in a scannable format. **Educational backgrounds include:** Computer Science; Engineering; Environmental Science. **Corporate headquarters location:** This Location. **Listed on:** American Stock Exchange.

R.W. BECK, INC.
1001 Fourth Avenue, Suite 2500, Seattle WA 98154. 206/695-4700. **Contact:** Mr. Van Finger, Director of Human Resources. **World Wide Web address:** http://www.rwbeck.com. **Description:** Provides professional, technical, and management consulting services to electric utilities and other energy-intensive industries. R.W. Beck operates 10 regional offices. **Common positions include:** Civil Engineer; Designer; Economist; Electrical/Electronics Engineer; Financial Analyst; Management Analyst/Consultant; Mechanical Engineer; Technical Writer/Editor. **Educational backgrounds include:** Economics; Engineering; Finance. **Benefits:** 401(k); Dental Insurance; Disability Coverage; Life Insurance; Medical Insurance; Pension Plan; Tuition Assistance. **Corporate headquarters location:** This Location. **Number of employees at this location:** 175. **Number of employees nationwide:** 500.

BEERS CONSTRUCTION COMPANY
70 Ellis Street NE, Atlanta GA 30303. 404/659-1970. **Contact:** Ted Hudgins, President. **World Wide Web address:** http://www.beersconstruction.com. **Description:** A construction firm primarily engaged in large-scale commercial and industrial construction projects. **Common positions include:** Project Engineer; Project Manager; Superintendent. **Educational backgrounds include:** Construction; Marketing. **Benefits:** Bonus Award/Plan; Dental Insurance; Disability Coverage; Life Insurance; Medical Insurance; Profit Sharing; Tuition Assistance. **Special programs:** Internships. **Corporate headquarters location:** This Location.

BELCAN CORPORATION
10200 Anderson Way, Cincinnati OH 45242-4700. 513/891-0972. **Fax:** 513/793-8618. **Contact:** Human Resources. **World Wide Web address:** http://www.belcan.com. **Description:** An engineering consulting company. Founded in 1958. **Common positions include:** Architect; Chemical Engineer; Civil Engineer; Design Engineer; Draftsperson; Electrical/Electronics Engineer; Environmental Engineer; Industrial Engineer; Manufacturing Engineer; Marketing Manager; Marketing Specialist; Mechanical Engineer; Project Manager; Sales Engineer; Sales Manager; Sales Rep.; Software Engineer; Systems Analyst; Systems Manager. **Educational backgrounds include:** Computer Science; Engineering; Marketing. **Benefits:** 401(k); Dental Insurance; Disability Coverage; Employee Discounts; Financial Planning Assistance; Flexible Schedule; Life Insurance; Medical Insurance; Public Transit Available; Tuition Assistance; Vision Insurance. **Corporate headquarters location:** This Location. **Other U.S. locations:** Mobile AL; Phoenix AZ; East Hartford CT; St. Louis MO; Cleveland OH; Pittsburgh PA; Houston TX. **Subsidiaries include:** Belcan Engineering Group; Belcan Services Group. **Annual sales/revenues:** More than $100 million. **Number of employees at this location:** 400.

BELDON ROOFING COMPANY
P.O. Box 13380, San Antonio TX 78213. 210/341-3100. **Toll-free phone:** 800/688-7663. **Fax:** 210/341-2959. **Contact:** Personnel. **World Wide Web address:** http://www.beldon.com. **Description:** A construction company that specializes in roofing and sheet metal work for all types of buildings. Founded in 1946. **Common positions include:** Supervisor. **Office hours:** Monday - Friday, 8:00 a.m. - 5:00 p.m. **President:** Michael D. Beldon.

THE LOUIS BERGER GROUP, INC.
100 Halsted Street, East Orange NJ 07018. 973/678-1960. **Fax:** 973/672-4284. **Contact:** Terry Williams, Human Resources Manager. **E-mail address:** hr@louisberger.com. **World Wide Web address:** http://www.louisberger.com. **Description:** A diversified consulting firm. The company provides cultural, environmental, and transportation-related engineering and planning services in the United States. Louis Berger also aids in urban and rural development projects in Africa, Asia, Latin America, and the Middle East. This location also hires seasonally. Founded in 1940. **NOTE:** Please do not contact by fax or phone. Send a scannable resume by regular mail or in ASCII format by e-mail. Entry-level positions and part-time jobs are offered. **Common positions include:** Accountant; Administrative Assistant; Biological Scientist; Chemical Engineer; Civil Engineer; Design Engineer; Economist; Electrical/Electronics Engineer; Environmental Engineer; Financial Analyst; Geographer; Geologist/Geophysicist; Transportation/Traffic Specialist. **Educational backgrounds include:** Accounting; Biology; Business Administration; Chemistry; Economics; Engineering; Finance; Geology; Mathematics; Visual Basic. **Benefits:** 401(k); Dental Insurance; Disability Coverage; Life Insurance; Medical Insurance; Public Transit Available; Relocation Assistance; Sick Days (1 - 5); Tuition Assistance; Vacation Days (6 - 10). **Special programs:** Summer Jobs. **Office hours:** Monday - Friday, 8:30 a.m. - 5:15 p.m. **Corporate headquarters location:** This Location. **Other U.S. locations:** Washington DC; Chicago IL; Needham MA; Las Vegas NV. **International locations:** Worldwide. **Listed on:** Privately held. **President:** Derish Wolff. **Information Systems Manager:** Michael Stern. **Annual sales/revenues:** More than $100 million. **Number of employees at this location:** 270. **Number of employees nationwide:** 900. **Number of employees worldwide:** 2,000.

BERGER/ABAM ENGINEERS INC.
33301 Ninth Avenue South, Suite 300, Federal Way WA 98003-2600. 253/952-6100. **Contact:** Personnel. **World Wide Web address:** http://www.abam.com. **Description:** A civil engineering and consulting firm specializing in the design of piers and waterfront structures, tanks and reservoirs, bridges, transit guideways, buildings, floating structures, and offshore drilling platforms. Berger/Abam Engineers Inc. also performs concrete material research, advanced computer design analysis, and construction management services. **Common positions include:** Accountant/Auditor; Civil Engineer; Draftsperson; Marketing Specialist; Structural Engineer. **Educational backgrounds include:** Accounting; Business Administration; Computer Science; Engineering; Marketing. **Benefits:** Dental Insurance; Disability Coverage; Life Insurance; Medical Insurance; Tuition Assistance. **Corporate headquarters location:** This Location.

BERNARD JOHNSON YOUNG, INC.
100 Congress Avenue, Suite 1800, Austin TX 78701-4072. 512/338-1000. **Contact:** Human Resources. **World Wide Web address:** http://www.bjy.com. **Description:** An architectural engineering firm. The company also provides technical services using the Internet to provide a full-time video link to customers. **Common positions include:** Accountant; Architect; Broadcast Technician; Civil Engineer; Computer Programmer; Cost Estimator; Draftsperson; Electrical/Electronics Engineer; Environmental Engineer; Landscape Architect; Librarian; Software Engineer; Structural Engineer; Surveyor; Technical Writer/Editor; Transportation/Traffic Specialist. **Educational backgrounds include:** Accounting; Computer Science; Engineering; Marketing. **Benefits:** 401(k); Dental Insurance; Disability Coverage; Employee Discounts; Life Insurance; Medical Insurance; Pension Plan; Tuition Assistance. **Special programs:** Internships. **Corporate headquarters location:** This Location. **Listed on:** Privately held. **Number of employees at this location:** 150.

BLACK & VEATCH
8400 Ward Parkway, Kansas City MO 64114. 913/458-2000. **Contact:** Hiring Manager. **World Wide Web address:** http://www.bv.com. **Description:** An environmental/civil engineering and construction firm serving utilities, commerce, and government agencies in more than 40 countries worldwide. Black & Veatch provides a broad range of study, design, construction management, and turnkey capabilities to clients in the water and wastewater fields. The firm is one of the leading authorities on drinking water treatment through the

use of activated carbon, ozone, and other processes. Black & Veatch is also engaged in wastewater treatment work, including reclamation and reuse projects and the beneficial use of wastewater residuals. Black & Veatch's capabilities also include nuclear power projects, advanced technology, air quality control, performance monitoring, plant life management, and facilities modification. In addition, Black & Veatch operates in the transmission and distribution field. In the industrial sector, Black & Veatch focuses on projects involving cleanrooms, industrial processes and planning, utility systems, and cogeneration. **NOTE:** All hiring for engineering positions is done through the Overland Park KS location. Interested jobseekers should direct resumes to Skip Gast, Human Resources, 11401 Lamar, Overland Park KS 66211. **Common positions include:** Chemical Engineer; Civil Engineer; Computer Scientist; Electrical/Electronics Engineer; Mechanical Engineer. **Corporate headquarters location:** This Location.

BONNAVILLA HOMES
P.O. Box 127, Aurora NE 68818. 402/694-5250. **Fax:** 402/694-5872. **Contact:** Human Resources. **Description:** A housing manufacturer. **NOTE:** Entry-level positions are offered. **Common positions include:** Design Engineer; Draftsperson; Electrician. **Educational backgrounds include:** Construction. **Benefits:** 401(k); Casual Dress - Daily; Dental Insurance; Disability Coverage; Employee Discounts; Life Insurance; Medical Insurance; Tuition Assistance. **Special programs:** Summer Jobs. **Office hours:** Monday - Friday, 8:00 a.m. - 5:00 p.m. **Parent company:** Chief Industries Inc. (Grand Island NE). **Purchasing Manager:** Roger Scott. **Sales Manager:** Mike Newman. **Number of employees at this location:** 350.

BOYLE ENGINEERING CORPORATION
P.O. Box 3030, Newport Beach CA 92660. 949/476-3400. **Contact:** Connie McCafferty, Personnel Manager. **World Wide Web address:** http://www.boyleengineering.com. **Description:** Provides comprehensive services ranging from project planning and feasibility studies to design and construction phases. The company specializes in the fields of water resources; water treatment and distribution; wastewater collection, treatment, and reuse; streets, highways, and bridges; light and heavy rail; drainage and flood control; and land planning. **Common positions include:** Agricultural Scientist; Architect; Civil Engineer; Designer; Electrical/Electronics Engineer; Mechanical Engineer; Structural Engineer. **Educational backgrounds include:** Architecture; Engineering. **Benefits:** Dental Insurance; Disability Coverage; Life Insurance; Medical Insurance; Profit Sharing. **Corporate headquarters location:** This Location.

BRIGGS PLUMBING PRODUCTS
4350 West Cypress Street, Suite 800, Tampa FL 33607. 813/878-0178. **Contact:** Personnel Manager. **Description:** A manufacturer of bathtubs, sinks, and other related plumbing accessories and tools. **Corporate headquarters location:** This Location.

BRONZE CRAFT CORPORATION
P.O. Box 788, Nashua NH 03061-0788. 603/883-7747. **Physical address:** 37 Will Street, Nashua NH 03060. **Fax:** 603/883-0222. **Contact:** Douglas MacLeod, Personnel Director. **World Wide Web address:** http://www.bronzecraft.com. **Description:** A sand-cast foundry, Bronze Craft Corporation manufactures architectural products including window and door hardware. The company also supplies finished products to companies like Steinway, GE, and Westinghouse. Functions at this location include machining, polishing, finishing, and assembly. Bronze Craft Corporation also provides customer support including engineering, pattern making, tooling, and repairing. **Corporate headquarters location:** This Location. **Number of employees at this location:** 150.

BURGESS & NIPLE, LTD.
5085 Reed Road, Columbus OH 43220. 614/459-2050. **Fax:** 614/451-1385. **Contact:** Ms. Pat Forster, Director of Human Resources. **World Wide Web address:** http://www.burgessniple.com. **Description:** An engineering and architecture firm engaged in study, analysis, and design services. Programs include waterworks, wastewater, industrial services, hydropower, energy conservation, transportation, systems analysis, HVAC, and geotechnical. **Common positions include:** Architect; Civil Engineer; Electrical/Electronics Engineer; Mechanical Engineer; Transportation/Traffic Specialist. **Benefits:** 401(k); Dental Insurance; Disability Coverage; Life Insurance; Medical Insurance; Profit Sharing; Tuition Assistance. **Corporate headquarters location:** This Location. **Other area locations:** Akron OH; Cincinnati OH; Painesville OH. **Other U.S. locations:** Payson AZ; Phoenix AZ; Indianapolis IN; Lexington KY; Charleston WV; Parkersburg WV. **Listed on:** Privately held. **Number of employees at this location:** 275. **Number of employees nationwide:** 480.

BURN CONSTRUCTION COMPANY, INC.
P.O. Drawer 1869, Las Cruces NM 88004. 505/526-4421. **Fax:** 505/526-1714. **Contact:** Barbara Burks, Personnel Director. **Description:** Provides a variety of services including dirt work, paving, and concrete services. **Corporate headquarters location:** This Location.

BURNS AND ROE ENTERPRISES, INC.
800 Kinderkamack Road, Oradell NJ 07649. 201/265-2000. **Contact:** Human Resources. **Description:** Engaged in construction, engineering, maintenance, and operations services. The company specializes in the design and engineering of complex facilities. **NOTE:** Entry-level positions are offered. **Common positions include:** Electrical/Electronics Engineer; Environmental Engineer; Industrial Engineer; Manufacturing Engineer; Marketing Manager; Marketing Specialist; Mechanical Engineer; Metallurgical Engineer; MIS Specialist; Project Manager; Purchasing Agent/Manager; Quality Control Supervisor; Secretary; Systems Analyst; Technical Writer/Editor; Transportation/Traffic Specialist. **Educational backgrounds include:** Computer Science; Engineering; Marketing. **Benefits:** 401(k); Dental Insurance; Disability Coverage; Life Insurance; Medical Insurance; Pension Plan; Tuition Assistance. **Special programs:** Internships. **Corporate headquarters location:** This Location. **Number of employees at this location:** 600. **Number of employees nationwide:** 1,200. **Number of employees worldwide:** 1,250.

C/S GROUP
3 Werner Way, Lebanon NJ 08833. 908/236-0800. **Fax:** 908/236-0604. **Contact:** Mr. Lee DiRubbo, Director of Human Resources. **E-mail address:** careerops@c-sgroup.com. **World Wide Web address:** http://www.c-sgroup.com. **Description:** Manufactures building materials including wall protection products, sun controls, and fire vents. **NOTE:** Entry-level positions and part-time jobs are offered. **Common positions include:** Accountant; Computer Support Technician; Computer Technician; Database Administrator; Draftsperson; Mechanical Engineer; Sales Manager; Sales

Representative. **Educational backgrounds include:** Accounting; Business Administration; Computer Science; Engineering; Microsoft Word; Novell; Software Tech. Support; Spreadsheets; Visual Basic. **Benefits:** 401(k); Casual Dress - Fridays; Dental Insurance; Disability Coverage; Life Insurance; Medical Insurance; Profit Sharing; Savings Plan; Tuition Assistance; Vacation Days (6 - 10). **Corporate headquarters location:** This Location. **Other U.S. locations:** Garden Grove CA; Muncy PA. **International locations:** France; Spain; United Kingdom. **Listed on:** Privately held. **Annual sales/revenues:** More than $100 million.

CH2M HILL
P.O. Box 22111, Denver CO 80222. 303/771-0900. **Fax:** 303/754-0199. **Contact:** Human Resources. **World Wide Web address:** http://www.ch2m.com. **Description:** Provides mechanical, structural, and environmental engineering services through its operating divisions. **Subsidiaries include:** CH2M Hill Engineering; Industrial Design Corporation; and Operating Management International. **Common positions include:** Agricultural Engineer; Architect; Chemical Engineer; Chemist; Civil Engineer; Computer Programmer; Draftsperson; Electrical/Electronics Engineer; Geologist/Geophysicist; Human Resources Manager; Mechanical Engineer; Sanitary Engineer; Structural Engineer; Systems Analyst; Technical Writer/Editor; Transportation/Traffic Specialist. **Educational backgrounds include:** Business Administration; Chemistry; Computer Science; Engineering. **Benefits:** Dental Insurance; Disability Coverage; Life Insurance; Medical Insurance; Pension Plan; Profit Sharing; Stock Option; Tuition Assistance. **Corporate headquarters location:** This Location.

CRA SERVICES
4915 South Sherwood Forest Boulevard, Baton Rouge LA 70816. 225/292-9007. **Fax:** 225/292-3614. **Contact:** Human Resources. **E-mail address:** info@rovers.com. **World Wide Web address:** http://www.rovers.com. **Description:** Provides engineering, environmental, and construction services. **NOTE:** Entry-level positions and part-time jobs are offered. **Common positions include:** Accountant; Administrative Assistant; Business Development Manager; Chemical Engineer; Civil Engineer; Computer Engineer; Computer Scientist; Computer Support Technician; Design Engineer; Draftsperson; Environmental Engineer; Human Resources Rep.; Librarian; Mechanical Engineer; Network/Systems Administrator; Sales Manager. **Educational backgrounds include:** Accounting; Biology; Computer Science; Engineering; Geology; Microsoft Word; Novell; Software Tech. Support; Spreadsheets. **Benefits:** 401(k); Casual Dress - Daily; Dental Insurance; Disability Coverage; Life Insurance; Medical Insurance; Vacation Days (10 - 20). **Office hours:** Monday - Friday, 7:30 a.m. - 5:00 p.m. **Corporate headquarters location:** Niagara Falls NY. **Other U.S. locations:** Nationwide. **International locations:** Canada; Mexico; UK. **Subsidiaries include:** CNA Services; Inspec-Sol, Inc.; Soil Enrichment Systems. **Parent company:** Conestoga Rovers & Assoc. **Listed on:** Privately held. **President/CEO/Owner:** Anthony Ying. **Facilities Manager:** Kenneth Turpin. **Information Systems Manager:** Linda McConnell. **Sales Manager:** Sue Lokay. **Annual sales/revenues:** $21 - $50 million. **Number of employees at this location:** 75. **Number of employees nationwide:** 250. **Number of employees worldwide:** 800.

CALPROP CORPORATION
13160 Mindanao Way, Suite 180, Marina Del Rey CA 90292-7903. 310/306-4314. **Contact:** Dori Baron, Personnel Manager. **World Wide Web address:** http://www.clpo.com. **Description:** Builds and sells single-family homes and condominiums in California. **Corporate headquarters location:** This Location. **Listed on:** American Stock Exchange.

CARLSON ASSOCIATES, INC.
959 Concord Street, 2nd Floor, Framingham MA 01701. 508/370-0100. **Fax:** 508/626-2390. **Contact:** Ms. Saroj Patel, Personnel Manager. **Description:** Provides a variety of architectural services. **Common positions include:** Architect; Civil Engineer; Designer; Draftsperson; Electrical/Electronics Engineer; Mechanical Engineer; Structural Engineer. **Educational backgrounds include:** Accounting; Engineering; Marketing. **Benefits:** 401(k); Dental Insurance; Disability Coverage; Life Insurance; Medical Insurance; Tuition Assistance. **Corporate headquarters location:** This Location. **Other U.S. locations:** CA; FL; NC. **Subsidiaries include:** Carlson Design/Construction Corporation. **Parent company:** Carlson Holdings Company. **Number of employees at this location:** 40. **Number of employees nationwide:** 95.

CAVALIER HOMES, INC.
CAVALIER HOMES OF ALABAMA, INC.
P.O. Box 300, Addison AL 35540. 256/747-1575. **Fax:** 256/747-8019. **Contact:** Sherry Jones, Personnel Director. **Description:** This location houses executive offices and operates two manufacturing facilities, which function under the name Cavalier Homes of Alabama, Inc. Overall, Cavalier Homes designs, produces, and sells prefabricated mobile homes. The company markets homes through approximately 500 independent dealers located in 32 states. **Corporate headquarters location:** This Location. **Other area locations:** Hamilton AL; Winfield AL. **Other U.S. locations:** Cordele GA; Nashville NC; Robbins NC; Shippenville PA; Fort Worth TX. **Number of employees nationwide:** 1,490.

CAVCO INDUSTRIES
1001 North Central Avenue, Suite 800, Phoenix AZ 85004. 602/256-6263. **Contact:** Human Resources. **World Wide Web address:** http://www.cavco.com. **Description:** A manufacturer of mobile homes and recreational vehicles. **Benefits:** Dental Insurance; Disability Coverage; Employee Discounts; Life Insurance; Medical Insurance; Pension Plan. **Corporate headquarters location:** This Location. **Operations at this facility include:** Administration. **Listed on:** NASDAQ. **Number of employees at this location:** 420.

CELOTEX CORPORATION
4010 Boy Scout Boulevard, Tampa FL 33631. 813/873-4252. **Fax:** 813/873-4430. **Recorded jobline:** 813/873-1700. **Contact:** Human Resources. **E-mail address:** hr@celotex.com. **World Wide Web address:** http://www.celotex.com. **Description:** Manufactures building products and acoustical ceiling systems. **Common positions include:** Accountant/Auditor; Assistant Manager; Attorney; Budget Analyst; Buyer; Chemical Engineer; Chemist; Clerical Supervisor; Computer Operator; Computer Programmer; Credit Manager; Department Manager; Economist; Employment Interviewer; Human Resources Manager; Market Research Analyst; Marketing Manager; Paralegal; Payroll Clerk; Purchasing Agent/Manager; Quality Control Supervisor; Sales and Marketing Manager; Secretary; Systems Analyst; Transportation/Traffic Specialist; Typist/Word Processor. **Educational backgrounds include:** Accounting; Business Administration; Chemistry; Computer Science; Economics;

Engineering; Finance; Liberal Arts; Marketing; MBA. **Benefits:** Daycare Assistance; Dental Insurance; Disability Coverage; Employee Discounts; Life Insurance; Medical Insurance; Pension Plan; Retirement Plan; Savings Plan; Tuition Assistance. **Corporate headquarters location:** This Location. **Other U.S. locations:** Nationwide. **Number of employees at this location:** 265. **Number of employees nationwide:** 2,500.

CENTEX CONSTRUCTION COMPANY
10150 Monroe Drive, Dallas TX 75229. 214/357-1891. **Fax:** 214/902-6391. **Contact:** David Preston, Vice President of Administration. **World Wide Web address:** http://www.centex-construction.com. **Description:** A commercial general contractor providing pre-construction, construction, management, and general contracting services. **Common positions include:** Civil Engineer; Construction Contractor; Cost Estimator; Project Manager; Purchasing Agent/Manager; Quality Control Supervisor. **Educational backgrounds include:** Construction. **Benefits:** 401(k); Dental Insurance; Disability Coverage; Life Insurance; Medical Insurance; Profit Sharing. **Corporate headquarters location:** This Location. **Other U.S. locations:** Fairfax VA. **Subsidiaries include:** Centex Landis (New Orleans LA). **Parent company:** Centex Corporation. **Listed on:** New York Stock Exchange. **Number of employees at this location:** 220.

CENTEX CORPORATION
P.O. Box 199000, Dallas TX 75219. 214/981-5000. **Contact:** Human Resources. **World Wide Web address:** http://www.centex.com. **Description:** Provides home building, mortgage banking, contracting, and construction products and services. **Corporate headquarters location:** This Location. **Subsidiaries include:** Centex Homes is one of America's largest home builders. CTX Mortgage Company is among the top retail originators of single-family home mortgages. Centex Construction Company, Inc. is one of the largest general building contractors in the U.S., as well as one of the largest constructors of health care facilities. Centex Construction Products, Inc., which manufactures and distributes cement, ready-mix concrete, aggregates, and gypsum wallboard, is one of the largest U.S.-owned cement producers. Centex Development Company, LP conducts real estate development activities. **Listed on:** New York Stock Exchange. **Annual sales/revenues:** More than $100 million.

CENTEX HOMES
9250 East Costilla Avenue, Suite 110, Englewood CO 80112. 303/792-9810. **Contact:** Human Resources. **World Wide Web address:** http://www.centexhomes.com. **Description:** Builds and sells residential homes nationwide. **Corporate headquarters location:** This Location. **Parent company:** Centex Corporation.

CERTAINTEED CORPORATION
P.O. Box 860, Valley Forge PA 19482. 610/341-7000. **Contact:** Kenneth Chiarello, Human Resources Manager. **World Wide Web address:** http://www.certainteed.com. **Description:** Manufactures and distributes building materials, fiberglass products, and piping products. Principal products are used in residential, commercial, and industrial construction; repair and remodeling; fiberglass reinforcement applications; water and sewer systems; and other underground utility systems. Other products include roofing, acoustical insulation, fiberglass thermal insulation, air handling products, glass fiber, vinyl siding, and PVC piping. **Common positions include:** Accountant/Auditor; Financial Analyst; Human Resources Manager; Technical Writer/Editor. **Educational backgrounds include:** Accounting; Business Administration; Finance. **Corporate headquarters location:** This Location. **Other U.S. locations:** Nationwide. **Parent company:** Compagnie de Saint-Gobain. The U.S. and Canadian operations of four of the company's worldwide branches are Abrasives, Construction Materials, Industrial Ceramics, and Insulation and Reinforcements. The Saint-Gobain companies based in North America are organized under the umbrella of the Saint-Gobain Corporation, which includes the Certainteed Corporation, Norton Company, and all of their subsidiaries. **Number of employees at this location:** 450. **Number of employees nationwide:** 8,000.

CIANBRO CORPORATION
P.O. Box 1000, Hunnewell Square, Pittsfield ME 04967. 207/487-3311. **Contact:** Alan Burton, Human Resources Director. **World Wide Web address:** http://www.cianbro.com. **Description:** A diversified, heavy construction company that serves the East Coast. **Common positions include:** Civil Engineer; Construction Contractor; Cost Estimator; Draftsperson; Electrical/Electronics Engineer; Mechanical Engineer; Nuclear Engineer; Structural Engineer. **Educational backgrounds include:** Business Administration; Engineering; Liberal Arts. **Benefits:** 401(k); Dental Insurance; Disability Coverage; Life Insurance; Medical Insurance; Profit Sharing; Tuition Assistance. **Corporate headquarters location:** This Location. **Number of employees at this location:** 150. **Number of employees nationwide:** 1,200.

CLAYTON HOMES, INC.
500 Alcoa Trail, Maryville TN 37802. 865/380-3000. **Contact:** Human Resources. **World Wide Web address:** http://www.clayton.net. **Description:** A vertically-integrated builder and seller of low- to medium-priced manufactured homes. The company provides financing and insurance services to its retail customers and develops communities for manufactured housing. **Common positions include:** Accountant/Auditor; Adjuster; Collector; Computer Programmer; Credit Manager; Customer Service Rep.; Financial Analyst; Investigator; Systems Analyst. **Educational backgrounds include:** Accounting; Business Administration; Computer Science; Finance; Mathematics. **Benefits:** 401(k); Dental Insurance; Disability Coverage; Employee Discounts; Life Insurance; Medical Insurance; Savings Plan. **Corporate headquarters location:** This Location. **Listed on:** New York Stock Exchange.

COAST FOUNDRY AND MANUFACTURING CO.
P.O. Box 1788, Pomona CA 91769. 909/596-1883. **Contact:** Human Resources. **Description:** A manufacturer of plumbing supplies. **Common positions include:** Accountant/Auditor; Administrative Manager; Blue-Collar Worker Supervisor; Computer Programmer; Human Resources Manager; Operations/Production Manager; Purchasing Agent/Manager; Quality Control Supervisor. **Educational backgrounds include:** Accounting; Business Administration; Engineering; Finance. **Benefits:** 401(k); Dental Insurance; Disability Coverage; Employee Discounts; Medical Insurance. **Corporate headquarters location:** This Location. **Number of employees at this location:** 300.

CONDAIRE INC.
1141 Reco Drive, St. Louis MO 63126. 314/821-8388. **Fax:** 314/821-6530. **Contact:** Malcolm J.

Sweet, Jr., President. **E-mail address:** cndaire1@ il.net. **World Wide Web address:** http://www. condaire.com. **Description:** A mechanical contracting firm engaged in a variety of heating, ventilating, air conditioning, plumbing, and industrial piping services. Founded in 1946. **Common positions include:** Cost Estimator; Draftsperson; Mechanical Engineer; Project Manager. **Benefits:** Life Insurance; Medical Insurance. **Corporate headquarters location:** This Location. **Listed on:** Privately held. **Number of employees at this location:** 100.

THE CONDUIT AND FOUNDATION CORP.
33 Rock Hill Road, Bala-Cynwyd PA 19004. 610/668-8400. **Contact:** Employment. **Description:** A general construction firm engaged in large project construction including highways, bridges, tunnels, wastewater treatment plants, dams, and power generation stations. **Common positions include:** Accountant; Civil Engineer; Computer Programmer; Construction Superintendent; Management Trainee; Mechanical Engineer; Purchasing Agent/Manager. **Educational backgrounds include:** Accounting; Business Administration; Computer Science; Engineering; Mathematics. **Benefits:** Disability Coverage; Life Insurance; Medical Insurance; Pension Plan; Profit Sharing; Tuition Assistance. **Special programs:** Internships. **Corporate headquarters location:** This Location. **Other U.S. locations:** Orlando FL; Parsippany NJ.

CONESTOGA WOOD SPECIALTIES, INC.
P.O. Box 158, East Earl PA 17519. 717/445-6701. **Physical address:** 245 Reading Road, East Earl PA. **Fax:** 717/445-3422. **Contact:** Elizabeth Ford, Personnel Supervisor. **Description:** Produces millwork including panel doors, components, and moldings. **Common positions include:** Accountant/ Auditor; Blue-Collar Worker Supervisor; Computer Programmer; Customer Service Rep.; Department Manager; Draftsperson; Electrical/Electronics Engineer; Financial Analyst; General Manager; Human Resources Manager; Industrial Engineer; Industrial Production Manager; Marketing Specialist; Mechanical Engineer; Operations/ Production Manager; Public Relations Specialist; Purchasing Agent/Manager; Quality Control Supervisor; Sales Executive; Systems Analyst; Transportation/Traffic Specialist. **Educational backgrounds include:** Accounting; Business Administration; Communications; Economics; Engineering; Finance; Marketing; Mathematics. **Benefits:** 401(k); Adoption Assistance; Credit Union; Dental Insurance; Disability Coverage; Employee Discounts; Eye Care; Life Insurance; Medical Insurance; Profit Sharing; Savings Plan; Scholarship Program; Tuition Assistance. **Special programs:** Internships. **Corporate headquarters location:** This Location. **Other U.S. locations:** Jacksonville AR; Darlington MD; Kenlet NC; Kramer PA. **Listed on:** Privately held. **Number of employees at this location:** 675. **Number of employees nationwide:** 1,200.

CONTECH CONSTRUCTION PRODUCTS
P.O. Box 800, Middletown OH 45042. 513/425-2019. **Physical address:** 1001 Grove Street, Middletown OH 45044. **Fax:** 513/425-5689. **Contact:** Michael Ongkiko, Recruiting Representative. **World Wide Web address:** http://www.contech-cpi.com. **Description:** A leader in the manufacture and sale of steel, aluminum, geosynthetic, and plastic construction products for the civil construction market. **Common positions include:** Civil Engineer; Production Manager; Sales Engineer. **Educational backgrounds include:** Engineering. **Corporate headquarters location:** This Location. **Listed on:** Privately held.

CREARE INC.
P.O. Box 71, Etna Road, Hanover NH 03755. 603/643-3800. **Fax:** 603/643-4657. **Contact:** Kelly Koloski, Human Resources Assistant. **E-mail address:** recruit@creare.com. **World Wide Web address:** http://www.creare.com. **Description:** Provides engineering services to customers worldwide. Services range from basic research to the development of prototype products. **Common positions include:** Aerospace Engineer; Biomedical Engineer; Electrical/Electronics Engineer; Mechanical Engineer; Nuclear Engineer; Software Engineer. **Educational backgrounds include:** C/C++; Engineering; Java; Visual Basic. **Benefits:** 401(k); Casual Dress - Daily; Employee Discounts; Flexible Schedule; Life Insurance; Medical Insurance; Profit Sharing; Savings Plan; Tuition Assistance. **Office hours:** Monday - Friday, 8:00 a.m. - 5:00 p.m. **Corporate headquarters location:** This Location. **Number of employees at this location:** 100.

CRISPELL-SNYDER, INC.
114 West Court Street, P.O. Box 320, Elkhorn WI 53121. 262/723-5600. **Toll-free phone:** 800/203-7700. **Fax:** 262/723-5106. **Contact:** Maggie Mentel, Human Resources Director. **World Wide Web address:** http://www.crispell-snyder.com. **Description:** Consulting engineers specializing in civil engineering for small municipalities in southeastern and eastern Wisconsin. Crispell-Snyder provides services in the areas of transportation, water resources, wastewater treatment, general public works engineering, studies, grant writing, and structural engineering. **NOTE:** Entry-level positions and part-time jobs are offered. **Common positions include:** Administrative Assistant; Administrative Manager; Branch Manager; Civil Engineer; Controller; Desktop Publishing Specialist; Environmental Engineer; Financial Analyst; Geologist/Geophysicist; Human Resources Manager; Marketing Manager. **Educational backgrounds include:** Accounting; Engineering; Excel; Geology; Marketing; Microsoft Word; Spreadsheets. **Benefits:** 401(k); Dental Insurance; Disability Coverage; Flexible Schedule; Life Insurance; Medical Insurance; Profit Sharing; Sick Days (6 - 10); Tuition Assistance; Vacation Days (6 - 10). **Special programs:** Internships; Co-ops; Summer Jobs. **Corporate headquarters location:** This Location. **Other area locations:** Racine WI; Sheboygan WI. **Listed on:** Privately held. **President:** Douglas Mushel. **Annual sales/revenues:** Less than $5 million. **Number of employees at this location:** 45. **Number of employees nationwide:** 75.

CROFT METALS INC.
107 Oliver Emmerich Drive, McComb MS 39648. 601/684-6121. **Toll-free phone:** 800/222-3195. **Fax:** 601/684-1378. **Contact:** Victor C. Donati, Jr., Corporate Human Resources Director. **Description:** A national manufacturer of aluminum and vinyl building products. Products include windows, doors, patio doors, and bath and shower enclosures. **Common positions include:** Accountant/Auditor; Administrative Manager; Attorney; Blue-Collar Worker Supervisor; Buyer; Clerical Supervisor; Computer Programmer; Customer Service Rep.; Designer; Draftsperson; Electrician; Human Resources Manager; Industrial Engineer; Industrial Production Manager; Licensed Practical Nurse; Management Trainee; Manufacturer's/Wholesaler's Sales Rep.; Mechanical Engineer; Purchasing Agent/Manager; Technical Writer/Editor; Transportation/Traffic Specialist. **Educational backgrounds include:** Accounting; Art/Design; Business Administration; Computer Science; Engineering; Marketing. **Benefits:** Dental

Insurance; Disability Coverage; Employee Discounts; Life Insurance; Medical Insurance; Profit Sharing; Tuition Assistance. **Corporate headquarters location:** This Location. **Other U.S. locations:** Oviedo FL; Newton MS; Lumber Bridge NC. **Number of employees at this location:** 105. **Number of employees nationwide:** 2,500.

DLR GROUP
508 West Arrington, Farmington NM 87401. 505/327-6068. **Contact:** George Trosky, Partner. **World Wide Web address:** http://www. dlrgroup.com. **Description:** An architectural design firm that specializes in educational, medical, judicial, and recreational projects. Founded in 1977. **Office hours:** Monday - Friday, 8:00 a.m. - 5:00 p.m. **Number of employees nationwide:** 600.

DANIEL, MANN, JOHNSON & MENDENHALL
3250 Wilshire Boulevard, Los Angeles CA 90010. 213/381-3663. **Contact:** John Dyer, Personnel Recruiter. **World Wide Web address:** http://www. dmjm.com. **Description:** Provides a wide range of architectural/engineering services to the public and private sectors. Operations include transportation, public works, and commercial architecture. **Common positions include:** Architect; Civil Engineer; Electrical/Electronics Engineer; Mechanical Engineer. **Educational backgrounds include:** Architecture; Engineering. **Benefits:** 401(k); Dental Insurance; Disability Coverage; Employee Discounts; Life Insurance; Medical Insurance; Pension Plan; Savings Plan; Tuition Assistance. **Special programs:** Internships. **Corporate headquarters location:** This Location. **Other U.S. locations:** San Bernardino CA; San Francisco CA; Santa Monica CA.

DEWBERRY & DAVIS
8401 Arlington Boulevard, Fairfax VA 22031. 703/849-0525. **Fax:** 703/849-0185. **Contact:** Richard A. Penner, Director of Human Resources. **E-mail address:** dhr@dewberry.com. **World Wide Web address:** http://www.dewberryanddavis.com. **Description:** A full-service architectural and engineering firm. Operations include water resources, environmental engineering, transportation engineering, mechanical/electrical and structural engineering, planning, landscape architecture, architecture, program management, and digital mapping services, as well as land design and surveying. Founded in 1956. **NOTE:** Entry-level positions are offered. **Common positions include:** Accountant; Administrative Assistant; Architect; Civil Engineer; Computer Technician; Construction Contractor; Design Engineer; Draftsperson; Electrical/Electronics Engineer; Environmental Engineer; Geographer; Landscape Architect; Mechanical Engineer; Surveyor. **Educational backgrounds include:** Accounting; Engineering; Environmental Science; Geography; Microsoft Office; Microsoft Word; Spreadsheets. **Benefits:** 401(k); Casual Dress - Fridays; Dental Insurance; Disability Coverage; Employee Discounts; Life Insurance; Medical Insurance; Profit Sharing; Public Transit Available; Relocation Assistance; Tuition Assistance. **Special programs:** Internships. **Office hours:** Monday - Friday, 8:00 a.m. - 5:00 p.m. **Corporate headquarters location:** This Location. **Other U.S. locations:** Nationwide. **Subsidiaries include:** Dewberry Design Group; Dewberry Technologies Inc.; Goodkind & O'Dea; TOLK. **Listed on:** Privately held. **Owner:** Sidney Dewberry. **Facilities Manager:** Jean Atkinson Mitchell. **Information Systems Manager:** Henry Tyler. **Annual sales/revenues:** More than $100 million. **Number of employees at this location:** 600. **Number of employees nationwide:** 1,400.

DUALSTAR TECHNOLOGIES CORP.
13-15 Jackson Avenue, Long Island City NY 11101. 718/340-6600. **Contact:** Human Resources. **World Wide Web address:** http://www.dualstar.com. **Description:** Operates through its subsidiaries to provide heating, ventilation, air conditioning, electrical, security, and communications (Internet access, cable television, satellite broadcasting) services for commercial and residential buildings. **Common positions include:** Accountant; Computer Programmer; Cost Estimator; Design Engineer; Draftsperson; Electrical/Electronics Engineer; Electrician; Environmental Engineer; Internet Services Manager; Mechanical Engineer; MIS Specialist; Multimedia Designer; Public Relations Specialist; Software Engineer; Systems Analyst; Technical Writer/Editor; Telecommunications Manager; Typist/Word Processor. **Educational backgrounds include:** Accounting; Computer Science; Engineering; Telecommunications. **Benefits:** 401(k); Medical Insurance. **Corporate headquarters location:** This Location. **Other U.S. locations:** New York NY. **Listed on:** NASDAQ. **Stock exchange symbol:** DSTR. **Annual sales/revenues:** $51 - $100 million. **Number of employees nationwide:** 300.

DURA SUPREME
300 Dura Drive, Howard Lake MN 55349. 320/543-3872. **Contact:** Louise Erickson, Human Resources Manager. **Description:** Manufactures cabinets. **Common positions include:** Accountant/Auditor; Buyer; Computer Programmer; Credit Manager; Draftsperson; Electrician; Human Resources Manager; Industrial Engineer; Industrial Production Manager; Quality Control Supervisor. **Educational backgrounds include:** Engineering; Marketing. **Benefits:** 401(k); Dental Insurance; Disability Coverage; Employee Discounts; Life Insurance; Medical Insurance. **Special programs:** Internships. **Corporate headquarters location:** This Location. **Listed on:** Privately held. **Number of employees at this location:** 300.

ERB LUMBER, INC.
375 South Eton Road, Birmingham MI 48009. 248/644-5300. **Contact:** Human Resources. **Description:** A distributor of lumber and other building materials including tools, screws, windows, doors, and nails. **Common positions include:** Accountant/Auditor; Actuary; Administrative Manager; Advertising Clerk; Assistant Manager; Attorney; Budget Analyst; Buyer; Cashier; Clerical Supervisor; Computer Operator; Computer Programmer; Construction Contractor; Construction Trade Worker; Cost Estimator; Credit Clerk and Authorizer; Credit Manager; Editor; Employment Interviewer; Financial Manager; Health Services Manager; Management Trainee; Payroll Clerk; Receptionist; Sales Executive; Secretary; Systems Analyst; Teacher/Professor; Typist/Word Processor. **Benefits:** Dental Insurance; Disability Coverage; Employee Discounts; Life Insurance; Medical Insurance; Pension Plan; Profit Sharing; Savings Plan; Tuition Assistance. **Corporate headquarters location:** This Location. **Parent company:** Woslzy (Great Britain). **Number of employees at this location:** 300.

MARTIN K. EBY CONSTRUCTION
P.O. Box 1679, Wichita KS 67201-1679. 316/268-3500. **Fax:** 316/268-3665. **Contact:** Larry Cheatham, Vice President of Corporate Services. **E-mail address:** information@ebycorp.com. **World Wide Web address:** http://www.ebycorp.com. **Description:** A general contractor for commercial buildings, treatment plants, pipelines, heavy highways, locks, dams, and power plants. Founded in 1937. **NOTE:** Entry-level positions are offered.

Common positions include: Civil Engineer; Estimator; Project Manager; Superintendent. **Educational backgrounds include:** Engineering. **Benefits:** 401(k); Dental Insurance; Disability Coverage; Life Insurance; Medical Insurance; Savings Plan; Tuition Assistance. **Special programs:** Internships; Co-ops. **Corporate headquarters location:** This Location. **Other U.S. locations:** Phoenix AZ; Orlando FL; Fort Worth TX; Austin TX. **Listed on:** Privately held. **President:** Rich Bean. **Annual sales/revenues:** More than $100 million. **Number of employees nationwide:** 1,000.

EDWARDS AND KELCEY INC.
299 Madison Avenue, Morristown NJ 07962. 973/267-8830. **Contact:** Harry P. Daley, Human Resources Director. **E-mail address:** ekresume@ webhire.com. **World Wide Web address:** http://www.ekcorp.com. **Description:** A consulting, engineering, planning, and communications organization whose range of services includes location and economic feasibility studies; valuations and appraisals; cost analyses; computer technology; marketing studies; traffic and transportation studies; soils and foundation analyses; environmental impact studies; master planning; structural surveys; and preliminary and final designs. Services also include preparation of contract documents and observation of construction operations for public transit systems, terminals, railroads, bus depots, parking garages, airports, ports, highways, streets, bridges, tunnels, traffic control systems, military facilities, communications systems, storm and sanitary sewers, water supply and distribution, flood control, and land development. Founded in 1946. **NOTE:** Entry-level positions are offered. **Common positions include:** Accountant; Civil Engineer; Construction Engineer; Cost Estimator; Draftsperson; Electrical/Electronics Engineer; Market Research Analyst; Marketing Specialist; Transportation/Traffic Specialist. **Educational backgrounds include:** Accounting; Engineering; Marketing. **Benefits:** 401(k); Casual Dress - Fridays; Daycare Assistance; Dental Insurance; Disability Coverage; Life Insurance; Medical Insurance; Pension Plan; Public Transit Available; Savings Plan; Sick Days (1 - 5); Tuition Assistance; Vacation Days (10 - 20). **Special programs:** Internships. **Corporate headquarters location:** This Location. **Other U.S. locations:** Atlanta GA; Chicago IL; Boston MA; Baltimore MD; Minneapolis MN; Manchester NH; New York NY; Saratoga Springs NY; Cincinnati OH; Chadds Ford PA; West Chester PA; Providence RI; Dallas TX; Houston TX; Leesburg VA; Milwaukee WI. **International locations:** Carolina, Puerto Rico. **Listed on:** Privately held. **Information Systems Manager:** Sandra Currin. **Annual sales/revenues:** More than $100 million. **Number of employees at this location:** 200. **Number of employees nationwide:** 730.

ELCOR CORPORATION
14643 Dallas Parkway, Suite 1000, Dallas TX 75240-8871. 972/851-0500. **Contact:** Human Resources. **World Wide Web address:** http://www.elcor.com. **Description:** Manufactures roofing products including fiberglass asphalt shingles. **Corporate headquarters location:** This Location. **Subsidiaries include:** Elk Corporation of Texas.

ELIXIR INDUSTRIES
17905 South Broadway, Gardena CA 90247. 310/767-3400. **Contact:** Human Resources. **Description:** Manufactures metal siding, roofing, doors, frame parts, roof vents, roof domes, and related mobile home products. **Corporate headquarters location:** This Location.

ELKAY MANUFACTURING COMPANY
2222 Camden Court, Oak Brook IL 60523. 630/574-8484. **Fax:** 630/574-4504. **Contact:** Human Resources. **World Wide Web address:** http://www.elkay.com. **Description:** Manufactures stainless steel sinks, faucets, water coolers, and kitchen cabinets. **NOTE:** Entry-level positions are offered. **Common positions include:** Accountant/Auditor; Buyer; Computer Programmer; Credit Manager; Customer Service Representative; Design Engineer; Draftsperson; Financial Analyst; Mechanical Engineer; Systems Analyst; Typist/Word Processor. **Educational backgrounds include:** Accounting; Business Administration; Computer Science; Engineering; Finance; Marketing. **Benefits:** 401(k); Dental Insurance; Disability Coverage; Employee Discounts; Life Insurance; Medical Insurance; Pension Plan; Profit Sharing; Tuition Assistance. **Corporate headquarters location:** This Location. **Listed on:** Privately held. **Annual sales/revenues:** More than $100 million. **Number of employees at this location:** 175. **Number of employees nationwide:** 3,500.

ELLERBE BECKET
800 LaSalle Avenue, Minneapolis MN 55402-2014. 612/376-2000. **Fax:** 612/376-2390. **Recorded jobline:** 612/376-2069. **Contact:** Human Resources. **World Wide Web address:** http://www.ellerbebecket.com. **Description:** An architectural and engineering firm engaged in the design of industrial, commercial, corporate, public assembly, educational, and medical buildings nationwide. Founded in 1908. **NOTE:** Entry-level positions are offered. **Common positions include:** Administrative Assistant; Architect; Civil Engineer; Draftsperson; Electrical/Electronics Engineer; Mechanical Engineer. **Educational backgrounds include:** Architecture; Engineering. **Benefits:** 401(k); Dental Insurance; Disability Coverage; Employee Discounts; Life Insurance; Medical Insurance. **Corporate headquarters location:** This Location. **Annual sales/revenues:** More than $100 million. **Number of employees at this location:** 425. **Number of employees nationwide:** 700.

DAVIS H. ELLIOT COMPANY INC.
P.O. Box 12707, Roanoke VA 24027. 540/992-2865. **Contact:** Karen Cobble, Human Resources Director. **World Wide Web address:** http://www.davishelliot.com. **Description:** Specializes in commercial and industrial electrical construction; the design and manufacture of control panels; and transmission and distribution line construction and repair. Founded in 1946. **NOTE:** Entry-level positions are offered. **Benefits:** Disability Coverage; Life Insurance; Medical Insurance; Profit Sharing; Tuition Assistance. **Special programs:** Apprenticeships. **Office hours:** Monday - Friday, 8:00 a.m. - 5:00 p.m. **Corporate headquarters location:** This Location. **Other U.S. locations:** Lexington KY; Lebanon MO; Broken Arrow OK. **Number of employees at this location:** 200. **Number of employees nationwide:** 700.

ENVIRONMENTAL MONITORING & TESTING CORPORATION
825 Main Street South, New Ellenton SC 29809. 803/652-2718. **Contact:** Human Resources. **Description:** A diversified drilling company with expertise in environmental drilling; industrial water wells; recovery wells as related to environmental requirements; construction drilling and grouting for piling; and stabilization drilling and grouting core drilling, as well as angle coring drilling and grouting for dams and other similar structures. The company operates as a subcontractor within the construction industry rather than as a prime or general contractor. **Corporate headquarters**

location: This Location. **Number of employees at this location:** 20.

MARSHALL ERDMAN AND ASSOCIATES
5117 University Avenue, Madison WI 53705. 608/238-0211. **Fax:** 608/238-5604. **Contact:** Personnel. **World Wide Web address:** http://www. erdman.com. **Description:** Designs and constructs medical outpatient facilities nationwide and specializes in ambulatory healthcare facilities. **NOTE:** Entry-level positions and second and third shifts are offered. **Common positions include:** Administrative Assistant; Architect; Blue-Collar Worker Supervisor; Buyer; Civil Engineer; Computer Programmer; Construction Contractor; Controller; Cost Estimator; Credit Manager; Design Engineer; Draftsperson; Electrical/Electronics Engineer; Financial Analyst; Human Resources Manager; Industrial Production Manager; Internet Services Manager; Manufacturing Engineer; Marketing Manager; Marketing Specialist; Mechanical Engineer; MIS Specialist; Operations/ Production Manager; Project Manager; Purchasing Agent/Manager; Quality Control Supervisor; Sales Executive; Sales Manager; Sales Representative; Secretary; Structural Engineer; Systems Analyst; Transportation/Traffic Specialist. **Educational backgrounds include:** Accounting; Art/Design; Business Administration; Engineering; Finance; Marketing. **Benefits:** Disability Coverage; Employee Discounts; Life Insurance; Medical Insurance; Profit Sharing; Public Transit Available; Savings Plan; Tuition Assistance. **Special programs:** Internships. **Corporate headquarters location:** This Location. **Other U.S. locations:** San Jose CA; Denver CO; Hartford CT; Washington DC; Atlanta GA; Dallas TX. **Subsidiaries include:** Techline Furniture is a manufacturer of a line of modular laminate furniture for the home and office. **Listed on:** Privately held. **Annual sales/revenues:** More than $100 million. **Number of employees at this location:** 250. **Number of employees nationwide:** 700.

J.C. EVANS CONSTRUCTION COMPANY
P.O. Box 9647, Austin TX 78766. 512/244-1400. **Contact:** Human Resources. **World Wide Web address:** http://www.jcevans.com. **Description:** A general contracting company. **Corporate headquarters location:** This Location.

EXPONENT FAILURE ANALYSIS ASSOCIATES
149 Commonwealth Drive, Menlo Park CA 94025. 650/326-9400. **Fax:** 650/328-3049. **Contact:** Recruiter. **E-mail address:** hr@exponent.com. **World Wide Web address:** http://www. exponent.com. **Description:** A technical consulting firm dedicated to the investigation, analysis and prevention of accidents and failures of an engineering or scientific nature. The company provides a multidisciplinary approach to analyze how failures occur. The company specializes in accident reconstruction, biomechanics, construction/ structural engineering, aviation and marine investigations, environmental assessment, materials and product testing, warning and labeling issues, accident statistical data analysis, and risk prevention/mitigation. Founded in 1967. **NOTE:** Only candidates holding a master's or doctorate degree in a suitable background will be considered. **Common positions include:** Biomedical Engineer; Chemical Engineer; Civil Engineer; Electrical/ Electronics Engineer; Environmental Engineer; Geologist/Geophysicist; Mechanical Engineer; Metallurgical Engineer. **Educational backgrounds include:** Engineering. **Benefits:** 401(k); Daycare Assistance; Dental Insurance; Disability Coverage; Life Insurance; Medical Insurance; Pension Plan; Tuition Assistance. **Special programs:** Internships.

Office hours: Monday - Friday, 8:00 a.m. - 5:00 p.m. **Corporate headquarters location:** This Location. **Other U.S. locations:** Nationwide. **Subsidiaries include:** Exponent Environmental Group; Exponent Failure Analysis; Exponent Health Group. **Listed on:** NASDAQ. **Stock exchange symbol:** EXPO. **CEO:** Michael Gaulke. **Annual sales/revenues:** $51 - $100 million. **Number of employees at this location:** 600.

FM GLOBAL
1301 Atwood Avenue, Johnston RI 02919. 401/275-3000. **Toll-free phone:** 800/343-7722. **Fax:** 401/464-8931. **Contact:** Michele Wilson-Skarr, Staffing Manager. **E-mail address:** jobs@ fmglobal.com. **World Wide Web address:** http://www.fmglobal.com. **Description:** A loss-control services organization. FM Global's primary objective is to help owner/company policyholders protect their properties and occupancies from damage from fire, wind, flood, and explosion; boiler, pressure vessel, and machinery accidents; and from many other insured hazards. **Common positions include:** Account Manager; Accountant; Administrative Assistant; Applications Engineer; Attorney; Auditor; Chemical Engineer; Civil Engineer; Computer Programmer; Computer Support Technician; Computer Technician; Controller; Database Administrator; Database Manager; Desktop Publishing Specialist; Draftsperson; Editor; Editorial Assistant; Electrical/Electronics Engineer; Financial Analyst; Graphic Artist; Graphic Designer; Help-Desk Technician; Human Resources Manager; Intranet Developer; Managing Editor; Mechanical Engineer; Multimedia Designer; Network Engineer; Network/Systems Administrator; Quality Assurance Engineer; Software Engineer; SQL Programmer; Systems Analyst; Technical Writer/Editor; Underwriter/Assistant Underwriter; Webmaster; Website Developer. **Educational backgrounds include:** Accounting; Business Administration; Cold Fusion; Computer Science; Engineering; Finance; HTML; Internet Development; MBA; Microsoft Office; Microsoft Word; Publishing; QuarkXPress; Software Development; SQL; Visual Basic. **Benefits:** 401(k); Casual Dress - Daily; Daycare Assistance; Dental Insurance; Disability Coverage; Employee Discounts; Flexible Schedule; Life Insurance; Medical Insurance; On-Site Daycare; Pension Plan; Public Transit Available; Relocation Assistance; Savings Plan; Sick Days (6 - 10); Tuition Assistance; Vacation Days (10 - 20). **Corporate headquarters location:** This Location. **Other U.S. locations:** Nationwide. **International locations:** Worldwide. **Number of employees at this location:** 700. **Number of employees worldwide:** 4,000.

FAIRMONT HOMES, INC.
P.O. Box 27, Nappanee IN 46550. 219/773-7941. **Contact:** Personnel. **World Wide Web address:** http://www.fairmonthomes.com. **Description:** Manufactures sectional housing, modular homes, and recreational vehicles. **Common positions include:** Accountant/Auditor; Advertising Clerk; Blue-Collar Worker Supervisor; Buyer; Computer Programmer; Construction and Building Inspector; Customer Service Rep.; Draftsperson; Electrical/ Electronics Engineer; Electrician; Financial Analyst; General Manager; Industrial Engineer; Industrial Production Manager; Management Trainee; Manufacturer's/Wholesaler's Sales Rep.; Mechanical Engineer; Operations/Production Manager; Purchasing Agent/Manager; Quality Control Supervisor; Software Engineer; Systems Analyst. **Benefits:** 401(k); Life Insurance; Medical Insurance; Savings Plan. **Corporate headquarters location:** This Location. **Other U.S. locations:**

Montevideo MN. **Listed on:** Privately held. **Number of employees at this location:** 2,400. **Number of employees nationwide:** 2,700.

FAY, SPOFFORD & THORNDIKE, INC.
5 Burlington Woods, Burlington MA 01803. 781/221-1000. **Fax:** 781/229-1115. **Contact:** Human Resources Department. **World Wide Web address:** http://www.fstinc.com. **Description:** Engaged in civil, electrical, environmental, and mechanical engineering. **Common positions include:** Civil Engineer; Structural Engineer. **Corporate headquarters location:** This Location. **Number of employees at this location:** 175.

FLORIDA ENGINEERED CONSTRUCTION PRODUCTS
P.O. Box 24567, Tampa FL 33623. 813/621-4641. **Fax:** 813/621-0671. **Contact:** Larry Toll, Personnel Director. **Description:** A manufacturer of building materials including precast lintels and sills, prestressed concrete beams and joints, roof trusses, and architectural precast slabs. **Common positions include:** Accountant/Auditor; Civil Engineer; Draftsperson; Management Trainee; Manufacturer's/Wholesaler's Sales Rep.; Operations/Production Manager; Quality Control Supervisor. **Educational backgrounds include:** Business Administration; Engineering; Finance; Marketing. **Benefits:** Dental Insurance; Life Insurance; Medical Insurance; Savings Plan. **Corporate headquarters location:** This Location. **Other U.S. locations:** Kissimmee FL; Odessa FL; Sarasota FL; West Palm Beach FL; Winter Springs FL. **Listed on:** Privately held. **Number of employees at this location:** 250. **Number of employees nationwide:** 350.

FLUOR CORPORATION
One Enterprise Drive, Aliso Viejo CA 92698-0001. 949/349-2000. **Contact:** Human Resources. **World Wide Web address:** http://www.fluor.com. **Description:** Operates within the fields of engineering, global services, coal production, procurement, and construction services. Fluor Global Services provides a wide range of products and services including consulting, equipment rental, sales, and maintenance services. Fluor Signature Services provides business support services to Fluor Corporation. A.T. Massey Coal Group produces coal for the steel industry. **Common positions include:** Accountant/Auditor; Architect; Attorney; Buyer; Chemical Engineer; Civil Engineer; Computer Programmer; Draftsperson; Electrical/Electronics Engineer; Financial Analyst; Geologist/Geophysicist; Industrial Engineer; Mechanical Engineer; Purchasing Agent/Manager; Systems Analyst. **Educational backgrounds include:** Business Administration; Computer Science; Engineering; Environmental Science; Finance; Marketing; Telecommunications. **Benefits:** Dental Insurance; Disability Coverage; Employee Discounts; Life Insurance; Medical Insurance; Pension Plan; Savings Plan; Tuition Assistance. **Corporate headquarters location:** This Location. **Listed on:** New York Stock Exchange. **Number of employees at this location:** 56,885.

FRU-CON CONSTRUCTION CORPORATION
P.O. Box 100, 15933 Clayton Road, Ballwin MO 63022. 636/391-6700. **Contact:** Human Resources. **Description:** An international construction and engineering firm. **Common positions include:** Civil Engineer; Electrical/Electronics Engineer; Mechanical Engineer. **Educational backgrounds include:** Accounting; Business Administration; Engineering; Finance. **Benefits:** Dental Insurance; Disability Coverage; Life Insurance; Medical Insurance; Pension Plan; Savings Plan; Tuition Assistance. **Corporate headquarters location:**

This Location. **Number of employees at this location:** 1,000.

FUELLGRAF ELECTRIC COMPANY
600 South Washington Street, Butler PA 16001. 724/282-4800. **Fax:** 724/282-1926. **Contact:** Claudia Fischer, Human Resources. **E-mail address:** feco@fuellgraf.com. **World Wide Web address:** http://www.fuellgraf.com. **Description:** A full-service electrical/teledata construction and engineering firm. Founded in 1946. **NOTE:** Entry-level positions are offered. **Common positions include:** Administrative Assistant; Administrative Manager; Construction Contractor; Electrical/Electronics Engineer; Electrician; Secretary. **Benefits:** 401(k); Casual Dress - Daily; Disability Coverage; Life Insurance; Medical Insurance; Sick Days (1 - 5); Vacation Days (10 - 20). **Office hours:** Monday - Friday, 7:00 a.m. - 5:00 p.m. **Corporate headquarters location:** This Location. **Other U.S. locations:** Williamsport PA. **Annual sales/revenues:** $11 - $20 million. **Number of employees at this location:** 100.

FUGRO GEOSCIENCES
6105 Rookin, Houston TX 77074. 713/778-5580. **Contact:** Director of Personnel. **Description:** An international engineering and geoscience consulting firm serving the offshore, industrial, public works, and commercial industries. The firm offers geosciences, earth sciences, and waste management services. **Common positions include:** Accountant/Auditor; Civil Engineer; Computer Programmer; Draftsperson; Geologist/Geophysicist; Systems Analyst. **Educational backgrounds include:** Geology. **Benefits:** 401(k); Dental Insurance; Life Insurance; Medical Insurance; Tuition Assistance. **Corporate headquarters location:** This Location. **Number of employees at this location:** 200.

GALE ASSOCIATES, INC.
33 Riverside Drive, Pembroke MA 02359-1938. 781/829-2000. **Toll-free phone:** 800/659-4753. **Fax:** 781/829-2007. **Contact:** Kathleen A. Forrand, Human Resources Manager. **E-mail address:** gale@gainc.com. **World Wide Web address:** http://www.gainc.com. **Description:** A national architecture and engineering firm that specializes in the improvement of existing buildings, sites, and infrastructures for both public and private clients. This location also hires seasonally. Founded in 1964. **NOTE:** Entry-level positions and part-time jobs are offered. **Common positions include:** Administrative Assistant; Architect; CADD Operator; Civil Engineer; Design Engineer; Draftsperson; Environmental Engineer; Finance Director; Graphic Designer; Human Resources Manager; Marketing Specialist; Operations Manager; Secretary; Structural Engineer; Transportation/Traffic Specialist; Typist/Word Processor. **Educational backgrounds include:** Architecture; Engineering; Microsoft Office. **Benefits:** 401(k); Casual Dress - Daily; Disability Coverage; Flexible Schedule; Life Insurance; Medical Insurance; Sick Days (6 - 10); Tuition Assistance; Vacation Days (10 - 20). **Special programs:** Training; Co-ops; Summer Jobs. **Office hours:** Monday - Friday, 8:00 a.m. - 5:00 p.m. **Corporate headquarters location:** This Location. **Other U.S. locations:** San Francisco CA; Orlando FL; Baltimore MD. **Operations at this facility include:** Divisional Headquarters. **Listed on:** Privately held. **President:** Harold E. Flight. **Facilities Manager:** Bruce P. White. **Information Systems Manager:** Christopher L. Collins. **Annual sales/revenues:** $5 - $10 million. **Number of employees at this location:** 60. **Number of employees nationwide:** 100.

THE GARDNER-ZEMKE COMPANY
6100 Indian School Road, Albuquerque NM 87110.
505/881-0555. **Fax:** 505/884-2191. **Contact:** Nancy
Reisbeck, Personnel Manager. **Description:** An
electrical and mechanical contractor for commercial
buildings. **Corporate headquarters location:** This
Location.

GENERAL PHYSICS CORPORATION
6700 Alexander Bell Drive, Suite 400, Columbia
MD 21046. 410/290-2300. **Toll-free phone:**
800/727-6677. **Fax:** 410/290-2501. **Contact:**
Human Resources. **E-mail address:** hr@
genphysics.com. **World Wide Web address:**
http://www.gpworldwide.com. **Description:** A
performance improvement firm that provides
training, engineering, and technical services to
clients in the aerospace, automotive, defense,
government, manufacturing, utility, independent
power, pharmaceutical, and process industries.
Founded in 1966. **NOTE:** Entry-level positions are
offered. **Company slogan:** Leading the world to
better performance. **Common positions include:**
Account Manager; Account Rep.; Accountant;
Administrative Assistant; Attorney; Chief Financial
Officer; Civil Engineer; Computer Programmer;
Controller; Design Engineer; Desktop Publishing
Specialist; Electrical/Electronics Engineer;
Electrician; Environmental Engineer; Finance
Director; Financial Analyst; Graphic Artist; Graphic
Designer; Help-Desk Technician; Human Resources
Manager; Industrial Engineer; Instructional
Technologist; Intranet Developer; Manufacturing
Engineer; Market Research Analyst; Marketing
Manager; Marketing Specialist; Mechanical
Engineer; Multimedia Designer; Network/Systems
Administrator; Project Manager; Purchasing Agent/
Manager; Quality Assurance Engineer; Sales
Engineer; Sales Manager; Secretary; Software
Engineer; Systems Analyst; Technical Writer/
Editor; Webmaster; Website Developer.
Educational backgrounds include: Accounting;
Business Administration; Computer Science;
Education; Engineering; Finance; HTML; Internet
Development; Marketing; MBA; MCSE; Microsoft
Office; Microsoft Word; Software Development;
SQL; Visual Basic. **Benefits:** 401(k); Casual Dress -
Fridays; Dental Insurance; Disability Coverage; Life
Insurance; Medical Insurance; Relocation
Assistance; Tuition Assistance. **Special programs:**
Internships; Training. **Office hours:** Monday -
Friday, 8:30 a.m. - 5:00 p.m. **Corporate
headquarters location:** This Location. **Other U.S.
locations:** Nationwide. **International locations:**
Brazil; Canada; Malaysia; Mexico. **Parent
company:** GP Strategies. **Listed on:** New York
Stock Exchange. **Stock exchange symbol:** GPX.
Annual sales/revenues: More than $100 million.
Number of employees at this location: 200.
Number of employees nationwide: 1,400. **Number
of employees worldwide:** 2,200.

GENERAL RESOURCE CORPORATION
201 Third Street South, Hopkins MN 55343.
952/933-7474. **Fax:** 952/933-9777. **Contact:** Ms.
C.J. Bollhoefer, Personnel Director. **Description:**
Manufactures ventilation, dust collecting, and
heating equipment. **Common positions include:**
Accountant/Auditor; Administrative Worker/Clerk;
Advertising Clerk; Applications Engineer; Buyer;
Computer Operator; Designer; Draftsperson; Food
Scientist/Technologist; Machinist; Mechanical
Engineer; Purchasing Agent/Manager; Receptionist;
Sales Engineer; Secretary; Sheet-Metal Worker;
Technician; Transportation/Traffic Specialist;
Typist/Word Processor; Welder. **Educational
backgrounds include:** Accounting; Business
Administration; Communications; Engineering;
Finance; Marketing. **Benefits:** Disability Coverage;

Life Insurance; Medical Insurance; Profit Sharing;
Tuition Assistance. **Corporate headquarters
location:** This Location. **Subsidiaries include:** Air
Purification Methods, Inc. produces air pollution
control systems; Fluidizer, Inc. designs and
manufactures systems and equipment for the
conveying, storage, vacuum clean up, and ship and
barge loading and unloading of bulk materials and
commodities; Ammerman, Inc. produces roof
ventilators, industrial fans, and auto exhaust
ventilator systems; Isomatic Corporation produces
standard and custom industrial components; and
Marshall Labs Inc. spray-dries food products and
pharmaceutical products.

GENSLER
600 California Street, 10th Floor, San Francisco CA
94108. 415/433-3700. **Contact:** Human Resources.
World Wide Web address: http://www.
gensler.com. **Description:** Provides architectural
space planning, graphics, and interior design
services nationwide. **Common positions include:**
Accountant/Auditor; Administrative Manager;
Architect; Computer Programmer; Draftsperson;
Human Resources Manager; Librarian; Systems
Analyst. **Educational backgrounds include:**
Accounting; Art/Design; Business Administration;
Computer Science; Finance; Interior Design; Liberal
Arts; Marketing. **Benefits:** Dental Insurance;
Disability Coverage; Life Insurance; Medical
Insurance; Profit Sharing; Tuition Assistance.
Special programs: Internships. **Corporate
headquarters location:** This Location. **Other U.S.
locations:** Irvine CA; Los Angeles CA; Denver CO;
Washington DC; Atlanta GA; Boston MA; Detroit
MI; New York NY; Houston TX. **Listed on:**
Privately held. **Number of employees at this
location:** 175. **Number of employees nationwide:**
800.

GERBER PLUMBING FIXTURES CORP.
4600 West Touhy Avenue, Lincolnwood IL 60712.
847/675-6570. **Contact:** Human Resources. **World
Wide Web address:** http://www.gerberonline.com.
Description: A manufacturer of a variety of
bathroom and kitchen plumbing products including
faucets, valves, lavatories, and vanities. **Corporate
headquarters location:** This Location.

GEUPEL DEMARS HAGERMAN
7930 Castleway Drive, Indianapolis IN 46250.
317/924-9192. **Contact:** Human Resources.
Description: Engaged in construction management
and general contracting services. **NOTE:** All
resumes should be sent to Human Resources, 510
West Washington Boulevard, Fort Wayne IN 46853.
Common positions include: Accountant/Auditor;
Civil Engineer; Construction Contractor; Cost
Estimator; Electrical/Electronics Engineer;
Mechanical Engineer. **Educational backgrounds
include:** Accounting; Engineering. **Benefits:**
401(k); Dental Insurance; Disability Coverage; Life
Insurance; Medical Insurance; Pension Plan; Tuition
Assistance. **Corporate headquarters location:**
This Location. **Number of employees at this
location:** 100.

GILBANE BUILDING COMPANY
7 Jackson Walkway, Providence RI 02903. 401/456-
5800. **Fax:** 401/456-5936. **Contact:** Human
Resources. **World Wide Web address:** http://www.
gilbaneco.com. **Description:** A full-service
construction and real estate development company
offering services in site selection, financing,
programming, and construction. The company is
involved in all major construction markets including
industrial, corporate, health care, education,
airports, convention centers, and correctional
facilities. **Common positions include:** Accountant;

Biomedical Engineer; Civil Engineer; Computer Animator; Computer Operator; Computer Programmer; Construction Contractor; Controller; Cost Estimator; Database Manager; Design Engineer; Internet Services Manager; Management Trainee; Manufacturing Engineer; Mechanical Engineer; MIS Specialist; Multimedia Designer; Online Content Specialist; Operations Manager; Project Manager; Quality Control Supervisor; Webmaster. **Educational backgrounds include:** Accounting; Business Administration; Computer Science; Engineering; Software Tech. Support. **Benefits:** 401(k); Dental Insurance; Disability Coverage; Life Insurance; Medical Insurance; Pension Plan; Profit Sharing; Tuition Assistance. **Office hours:** Monday - Friday, 8:00 a.m. - 5:00 p.m. **Corporate headquarters location:** This Location. **Other U.S. locations:** Nationwide. **Annual sales/revenues:** More than $100 million. **Number of employees at this location:** 200. **Number of employees nationwide:** 1,000.

GLASGOW, INC.
P.O. Box 1089, Glenside PA 19038-1089. 215/884-8800. **Contact:** Human Resources. **World Wide Web address:** http://www.glasgowinc.com. **Description:** A construction firm. **Common positions include:** Civil Engineer; Construction Contractor; Cost Estimator. **Educational backgrounds include:** Engineering. **Benefits:** Dental Insurance; Life Insurance; Medical Insurance; Pension Plan; Tuition Assistance. **Corporate headquarters location:** This Location. **Listed on:** Privately held. **President:** Bruce Rambo.

GOEDECKE COMPANY INC.
4101 Clayton Avenue, St. Louis MO 63110. 314/652-1810. **Contact:** Human Resources. **Description:** This location houses administrative offices only. Overall, Goedecke Company provides construction services including insulation, hard board for industrial buildings, wall systems, sealants, insulation, adhesives, waterproofing, and scaffold rental and erection. **Common positions include:** Accountant/Auditor; Branch Manager; Buyer; Credit Manager; Draftsperson; Mechanical Engineer; Purchasing Agent/Manager. **Educational backgrounds include:** Accounting; Business Administration; Marketing. **Benefits:** 401(k); Disability Coverage; Employee Discounts; Life Insurance; Medical Insurance. **Special programs:** Internships. **Corporate headquarters location:** This Location. **Other U.S. locations:** Decatur IL; Evansville IN; Indianapolis IN; Louisville KY; Kansas City MO; Springfield MO. **Listed on:** Privately held. **Number of employees at this location:** 100.

GOETTL AIR CONDITIONING INC.
3830 East Wier Avenue, Phoenix AZ 85040. 602/275-1515. **Contact:** Personnel. **World Wide Web address:** http://www.goettl.com. **Description:** Manufactures a broad range of air conditioning, heating, and air distribution products including air conditioning systems and components, heat pumps, and evaporative coolers. **Common positions include:** Accountant; Administrator; Buyer; Credit Manager; Customer Service Rep.; Manufacturer's/ Wholesaler's Sales Rep.; Mechanical Engineer; Purchasing Agent/Manager. **Benefits:** Dental Insurance; Employee Discounts; Life Insurance; Medical Insurance; Pension Plan; Tuition Assistance. **Corporate headquarters location:** This Location.

GOLDEN WEST & ASSOCIATES
4711 East Falcon Drive, Suite 222, Mesa AZ 85215. 480/396-4653. **Contact:** Personnel. **Description:** Designs and produces manufactured homes.

Products are sold through 190 independent retailers. **Corporate headquarters location:** This Location.

GREENHECK FAN CORPORATION
P.O. Box 410, Schofield WI 54476. 715/359-6171. **Fax:** 715/355-2444. **Contact:** Human Resources. **World Wide Web address:** http://www.greenheck.com. **Description:** Manufactures rooftop ventilators, sidewall fans, centrifugal fans, and kitchen ventilation systems. **Common positions include:** Accountant/Auditor; Buyer; Computer Operator; Computer Programmer; Credit Manager; Designer; Draftsperson; Financial Manager; Human Resources Manager; Industrial Designer; Industrial Production Manager; Manufacturer's/Wholesaler's Sales Rep.; Market Research Analyst; Mechanical Engineer; Order Clerk; Payroll Clerk; Purchasing Agent/Manager; Receptionist; Registered Nurse; Secretary; Sheet-Metal Worker; Stock Clerk; Systems Analyst; Tool and Die Maker; Welder. **Educational backgrounds include:** Accounting; Business Administration; Computer Science; Engineering; Finance; Marketing. **Special programs:** Internships. **Corporate headquarters location:** This Location. **Other U.S. locations:** Sacramento CA; Frankfort KY. **Annual sales/revenues:** More than $100 million. **Number of employees nationwide:** 1,400.

GREENHORNE & O'MARA, INC.
2211 New Market Parkway, Suite 104, Marietta GA 30067. 770/988-9555. **Toll-free phone:** 800/463-3455. **Contact:** Human Resources Department. **World Wide Web address:** http://www.g-and-o.com. **Description:** Provides civil/site, environmental, transportation, and geosciences engineering services. Founded in 1950. **Common positions include:** Archaeologist; Architect; Civil Engineer; Environmental Engineer; Geographer; Surveyor. **Educational backgrounds include:** Engineering. **Benefits:** 401(k); Casual Dress - Fridays; Dental Insurance; Life Insurance; Medical Insurance; Pension Plan; Profit Sharing; Tuition Assistance. **Special programs:** Internships. **Corporate headquarters location:** Greenbelt MD. **Other U.S. locations:** FL; MD; NC; VA. **Number of employees at this location:** 50. **Number of employees nationwide:** 700.

GULF STATES INC. (GSI)
P.O. Box 856, Freeport TX 77542. 979/233-5555. **Toll-free phone:** 800/231-9849. **Fax:** 979/265-3223. **Contact:** Steve Oler, Corporate Human Resources Manager. **World Wide Web address:** http://www.gsiusa.com. **Description:** Engaged in construction, maintenance, and heavy industrial work. **Common positions include:** Accountant; Administrative Assistant; Blue-Collar Worker Supervisor; Civil Engineer; Computer Support Technician; Electrician; Marketing Specialist; Mechanical Engineer; MIS Specialist; Project Manager. **Educational backgrounds include:** Accounting; Business Administration; Computer Science; Engineering; Marketing. **Benefits:** 401(k); Casual Dress - Daily; Dental Insurance; Disability Coverage; Life Insurance; Medical Insurance; Profit Sharing; Relocation Assistance; Tuition Assistance; Vacation Days (6 - 10). **Office hours:** Monday - Friday, 7:00 a.m. - 5:00 p.m. **Corporate headquarters location:** This Location. **Other U.S. locations:** AL; CA; UT. **Operations at this facility include:** Administration; Divisional Headquarters; Sales. **Listed on:** NASDAQ. **CEO:** Joe Ivey. **Facilities Manager:** Larry Peel. **Information Systems Manager:** Bryan Roberts. **Purchasing Manager:** Elmer Burch. **Annual sales/revenues:** More than $100 million. **Number of employees at this location:** 700. **Number of employees worldwide:** 1,700.

GULF STATES MANUFACTURERS
P.O. Box 1128, Starkville MS 39760. 662/323-8021. **Fax:** 662/324-9695. **Contact:** Gary Mitchell, Director of Human Resources. **World Wide Web address:** http://www.gulfstates-abs.com. **Description:** A manufacturer of pre-engineered metal buildings. **Common positions include:** Civil Engineer; Credit Manager; Customer Service Representative; Draftsperson; Electrician; Human Resources Manager; Structural Engineer. **Educational backgrounds include:** Engineering. **Benefits:** Life Insurance; Medical Insurance; Pension Plan. **Corporate headquarters location:** This Location. **Listed on:** Privately held. **Number of employees at this location:** 400.

H.B.D. CONTRACTING INC.
5517 Manchester Avenue, St. Louis MO 63110. 314/781-8000. **Contact:** Human Resources. **World Wide Web address:** http://www.hbdcontracting.com. **Description:** A general contracting firm specializing in commercial engineering. **Common positions include:** Civil Engineer. **Educational backgrounds include:** Engineering. **Benefits:** Dental Insurance; Disability Coverage; Life Insurance; Medical Insurance; Pension Plan; Profit Sharing. **Corporate headquarters location:** This Location. **Number of employees at this location:** 100.

HBE CORPORATION
11330 Olive Boulevard, St. Louis MO 63141. 314/567-9000. **Contact:** Personnel. **Description:** Engaged in the design and construction of hospitals, financial institutions, and hotels. HBE Corporation also operates and manages hotels. **Common positions include:** Accountant/Auditor; Architect; Civil Engineer; Credit Manager; Draftsperson; Electrical/Electronics Engineer; General Manager; Hotel Manager; Human Resources Manager; Manufacturer's/Wholesaler's Sales Rep.; Mechanical Engineer; Purchasing Agent/Manager. **Educational backgrounds include:** Accounting; Art/Design; Engineering. **Benefits:** Dental Insurance; Disability Coverage; Employee Discounts; Life Insurance; Medical Insurance; Savings Plan. **Corporate headquarters location:** This Location.

HDR, INC.
8404 Indian Hills Drive, Omaha NE 68114. 402/399-1000. **Fax:** 402/548-5015. **Contact:** Richard A. O'Gara, Director of Employment. **E-mail address:** careers@hdrinc.com. **World Wide Web address:** http://www.hdrinc.com. **Description:** A holding company for two operating companies. Founded in 1917. **NOTE:** Entry-level positions and part-time jobs are offered. **Common positions include:** Accountant; Administrative Assistant; Advertising Clerk; Architect; Attorney; Budget Analyst; Chief Financial Officer; Civil Engineer; Computer Operator; Computer Programmer; Computer Support Technician; Computer Technician; Controller; Customer Service Rep.; Database Administrator; Database Manager; Design Engineer; Desktop Publishing Specialist; Draftsperson; Electrical/Electronics Engineer; Environmental Engineer; Finance Director; Graphic Artist; Graphic Designer; Human Resources Manager; Internet Services Manager; Management Analyst/Consultant; Marketing Manager; Marketing Specialist; Mechanical Engineer; MIS Specialist; Network/Systems Administrator; Project Manager; Public Relations Specialist; Secretary; Software Engineer; Systems Analyst; Systems Manager; Webmaster. **Educational backgrounds include:** Accounting; Business Administration; Computer Science; Engineering; Finance; Health Care; Internet; Liberal Arts; Marketing; Microsoft Word; Public Relations; QuarkXPress; Software

Development; Software Tech. Support; Spreadsheets; Visual Basic. **Benefits:** 401(k); Casual Dress - Fridays; Dental Insurance; Disability Coverage; ESOP; Flexible Schedule; Life Insurance; Medical Insurance; Public Transit Available; Telecommuting; Tuition Assistance. **Special programs:** Internships; Co-ops; Summer Jobs. **Corporate headquarters location:** This Location. **Other U.S. locations:** Nationwide. **Subsidiaries include:** HDR Architecture, Inc. specializes in the architectural design of health care facilities (hospitals and integrated health care networks, ambulatory care centers, oncology and cardiology centers, diagnostic and treatment centers, and strategic facilities assessment); justice facilities (courthouse and administrative facilities, adult and juvenile detention facilities, and state correctional facilities); and science and technology facilities (research facilities, advanced technology facilities, telecommunications, university science facilities, and manufacturing facilities). HDR Engineering, Inc. provides water, transportation, waste, and energy services including studies, design, and implementation for complex projects. **Listed on:** Privately held. **Chairman/CEO:** Dick Bell. **Information Systems Manager:** Angelo Privetera. **Number of employees at this location:** 450. **Number of employees nationwide:** 2,000.

HRI INC.
1750 West College Avenue, State College PA 16804. 814/238-5071. **Contact:** Dan Cornali, Human Resources. **Description:** A road construction company.

HALLIBURTON
3600 Lincoln Plaza, Dallas TX 75201. 214/978-2600. **Fax:** 214/978-2611. **Contact:** Human Resources. **World Wide Web address:** http://www.halliburton.com. **Description:** A leading diversified energy services, engineering, construction, maintenance, and energy equipment company. **Corporate headquarters location:** This Location. **Subsidiaries include:** Brown & Root Energy Services; Brown & Root Services; Dresser Equipment Company; Halliburton Energy Services; Kellogg Brown & Root; Landmark Graphics.

HANSON ENGINEERS
1525 South Sixth Street, Springfield IL 62703. 217/788-2450. **Fax:** 217/788-2503. **Contact:** Human Resources. **World Wide Web address:** http://www.hansonengineers.com. **Description:** A consulting firm that provides a variety of architectural, engineering, and scientific services. Founded in 1954. **Corporate headquarters location:** This Location. **Other U.S. locations:** Pleasanton CA; Orlando FL; West Palm Beach FL; Atlanta GA; Oak Brook IL; Peoria IL; Rockford IL; Kansas City MO; Wayne NJ; Herndon VA; Bellevue WA.

HARDAWAY GROUP, INC.
615 Main Street, P.O. Box 60429, Nashville TN 37206. 615/254-5461. **Fax:** 615/254-4518. **Contact:** Randy Swinehart, Human Resources Director. **E-mail address:** rswinehart@hardaway.net. **World Wide Web address:** http://www.hardaway.net. **Description:** A general contractor engaged in residential and commercial property management and real estate sales. Founded in 1924. **NOTE:** Entry-level positions are offered. **Common positions include:** Accountant; Administrative Assistant; Architect; Chief Financial Officer; Civil Engineer; Computer Programmer; Construction Contractor; Cost Estimator; Design Engineer; Draftsperson; Human Resources Manager; Marketing Specialist; Project Manager; Real Estate Agent; Secretary. **Educational**

backgrounds include: Accounting; Business Administration; Engineering. **Benefits:** 401(k); Dental Insurance; Disability Coverage; Life Insurance; Medical Insurance; Savings Plan. **Special programs:** Internships; Apprenticeships. **Corporate headquarters location:** This Location. **Subsidiaries include:** Hardaway Construction Corporation of Tennessee; Hardaway Management Company, Inc.; Hardaway Realty, Inc. **Number of employees at this location:** 400. **Number of employees nationwide:** 500.

HARLEYELLIS
26913 Northwestern Highway, Suite 200, Southfield MI 48034. 248/262-1500. **Contact:** Vice President of Operations. **Description:** A multidivisional architectural and engineering firm providing comprehensive planning, design, and problem-solving services to commercial, governmental, industrial, and institutional clients. Founded in 1962. **Common positions include:** Architect; Civil Engineer; Electrical/Electronics Engineer; Facilities Engineer; Interior Designer; Mechanical Engineer; MIS Specialist. **Educational backgrounds include:** Architecture; Engineering; Interior Design. **Benefits:** 401(k); Dental Insurance; Disability Coverage; Flextime Plan; Life Insurance; Medical Insurance; Tuition Assistance. **Corporate headquarters location:** This Location. **Subsidiaries include:** ENG/6A. **Listed on:** Privately held. **Annual sales/revenues:** $5 - $10 million. **Number of employees at this location:** 100. **Number of employees nationwide:** 140.

HARSCO CORPORATION
P.O. Box 8888, Camp Hill PA 17001-8888. 717/763-7064. **Fax:** 717/612-5619. **Contact:** Jerry Vinci, Director of Human Resources. **World Wide Web address:** http://www.harsco.com. **Description:** A diversified industrial manufacturing and service company which conducts business through 10 divisions and has 16 classes of products and services. Operations fall into three groups: Metal Reclamation and Mill Services includes scrap management, slab management systems, iron making, materials handling, equipment rental, recycling technology, aggregate marketing, and nonferrous metallurgical industry services; Infrastructure and Construction includes railway maintenance equipment, industrial grating products, and scaffolding, shoring, and concrete forming equipment; and Process Industry Products includes industrial pipe fittings, process equipment, and gas control and containment equipment. **Common positions include:** Accountant/Auditor; Attorney; Buyer; Computer Programmer; Draftsperson; Editor; Environmental Engineer; Financial Analyst; Human Resources Manager; Industrial Production Manager; Mechanical Engineer; Public Relations Specialist; Purchasing Agent/Manager; Quality Control Supervisor; Structural Engineer; Systems Analyst. **Educational backgrounds include:** Accounting; Business Administration; Computer Science; Engineering; Finance. **Benefits:** 401(k); Dental Insurance; Disability Coverage; Life Insurance; Medical Insurance; Pension Plan; Profit Sharing; Tuition Assistance. **Special programs:** Internships. **Corporate headquarters location:** This Location. **Other U.S. locations:** Nationwide. **Listed on:** New York Stock Exchange. **Number of employees at this location:** 90. **Number of employees worldwide:** 13,000.

HARTRAMPF, INC.
180 Allen Road, Suite 217N, Atlanta GA 30328. 404/252-2063. **Contact:** Carol Lathem, Office Manager. **Description:** A full-service engineering and architectural firm. Services provided include architectural, structural, mechanical, electrical, civil, environmental, and municipal engineering; surveying and energy conservation; and economic and technical feasibility studies and reports. **Common positions include:** Accountant/Auditor; Administrator; Architect; Civil Engineer; Electrical/Electronics Engineer; Mechanical Engineer; Technical Writer/Editor. **Educational backgrounds include:** Architecture; Engineering. **Benefits:** Dental Insurance; Life Insurance; Medical Insurance; Pension Plan; Savings Plan. **Special programs:** Internships. **Corporate headquarters location:** This Location. **Number of employees at this location:** 25.

HARVEY INDUSTRIES, INC.
43 Emerson Road, Waltham MA 02451-9180. 781/899-3500. **Contact:** Human Resources. **E-mail address:** jobs@harveyind.com. **World Wide Web address:** http://www.harveyind.com. **Description:** Manufactures windows and doors, and is a wholesale distributor of building materials.

THE HASKELL COMPANY
111 Riverside Avenue, Jacksonville FL 32202. 904/791-4500. **Contact:** Richard Evans, Director of Human Resources. **World Wide Web address:** http://www.thehaskellco.com. **Description:** A design-build company that provides architectural, construction, engineering, and real estate services. **Common positions include:** Accountant/Auditor; Administrator; Architect; Civil Engineer; Computer Programmer; Draftsperson; Electrical/Electronics Engineer; Human Resources Manager; Management Trainee; Mechanical Engineer; Operations/Production Manager; Quality Control Supervisor; Systems Analyst. **Educational backgrounds include:** Accounting; Business Administration; Engineering; Finance; Marketing. **Benefits:** Dental Insurance; Disability Coverage; Employee Discounts; Life Insurance; Medical Insurance; Pension Plan; Profit Sharing; Savings Plan; Tuition Assistance. **Corporate headquarters location:** This Location.

GLENN O. HAWBAKER, INC.
P.O. Box 135, State College PA 16804-0135. 814/237-1444. **Toll-free phone:** 800/350-5078. **Fax:** 814/235-3654. **Contact:** Mr. Page L. Gaddis, Personnel Manager. **E-mail address:** plg@goh-inc.com. **World Wide Web address:** http://www.goh-inc.com. **Description:** Engaged in heavy construction services including paving, road construction, bridge construction, and other related services. **Common positions include:** Accountant; Administrative Assistant; Controller; Cost Estimator; Credit Manager; Customer Service Rep.; Electrician; General Manager; Human Resources Manager; MIS Specialist; Project Manager; Quality Control Supervisor; Sales Rep. **Educational backgrounds include:** Accounting; Business Administration; Communications; Computer Science; Engineering; Marketing. **Benefits:** 401(k); Dental Insurance; Disability Coverage; Financial Planning Assistance; Flexible Schedule; Life Insurance; Medical Insurance; Pension Plan; Profit Sharing; Tuition Assistance. **Special programs:** Internships; Summer Jobs. **Office hours:** Monday - Friday, 8:00 a.m. - 5:00 p.m. **Corporate headquarters location:** This Location. **Other area locations:** DuBois PA; Montoursville PA; Turtlepoint PA. **Listed on:** Privately held. **Annual sales/revenues:** $21 - $50 million. **Number of employees at this location:** 600.

HEAT-N-GLO CORPORATION
20802 Kensington Boulevard, Lakeville MN 55044-8052. 952/985-6000. **Contact:** Human Resources. **World Wide Web address:** http://www.heatnglo.com. **Description:** Manufactures and

installs gas, wood, and electric fireplaces, stoves, and related accessories. **Corporate headquarters location:** This Location.

HEERY INTERNATIONAL, INC.
999 Peachtree Street NE, Atlanta GA 30367-5401. 404/881-9880. **Toll-free phone:** 800/500-1730. **Fax:** 404/875-1283. **Contact:** Dan Wise, Director. **World Wide Web address:** http://www.heery.com. **Description:** An architectural, engineering, and construction program management firm. The company specializes in industrial facilities and other commercial buildings. **Common positions include:** Architect; Civil Engineer; Electrical/Electronics Engineer; Mechanical Engineer. **Educational backgrounds include:** Construction; Engineering. **Benefits:** Dental Insurance; Disability Coverage; Medical Insurance; Savings Plan. **Office hours:** Monday - Friday, 8:30 a.m. - 5:30 p.m. **Corporate headquarters location:** This Location. **Subsidiaries include:** Heery, Architects & Engineers, Inc.; Heery Program Management, Inc. (building program management services); Heery Energy Consultants (consultants in the areas of energy conservation and alternative energy sources); Heery Interiors, Inc. (interior design); Heery Graphics, Inc. (comprehensive visual communications services); Heery Engineering, Inc. (civil engineering and landscape architecture). Heery International operates six other United States offices, as well as several branches in Europe. **President/CEO/Owner:** James Moynihan.

JAY HENGES ENTERPRISES, INC.
4133 Shoreline Drive, Earth City MO 63045. 314/291-6600. **Contact:** Personnel. **Description:** Engaged in the installation of carpet, wood, and vinyl floors; insulation and acoustical ceiling work; and the manufacture of portable buildings. **Corporate headquarters location:** This Location.

HENKELS & McCOY, INC.
985 Jolly Road, Blue Bell PA 19422-0900. 215/283-7688. **Contact:** Vincent Benedict, Director of Human Resources. **World Wide Web address:** http://www.henkelsandmccoy.com. **Description:** An engineering and construction firm that specializes in designing, building, and maintaining infrastructure. **Common positions include:** Accountant/Auditor; Administrator; Architect; Buyer; Civil Engineer; Computer Programmer; Credit Manager; Department Manager; Draftsperson; Editor; Electrical/Electronics Engineer; Financial Analyst; General Manager; Human Resources Manager; Management Trainee; Marketing Specialist; Mechanical Engineer; Purchasing Agent/Manager; Reporter; Sales Executive; Technical Writer/Editor. **Educational backgrounds include:** Accounting; Business Administration; Computer Science; Engineering; Finance; Liberal Arts; Marketing. **Benefits:** Disability Coverage; Life Insurance; Medical Insurance; Profit Sharing; Savings Plan; Tuition Assistance. **Corporate headquarters location:** This Location. **Other U.S. locations:** Nationwide. **Listed on:** Privately held. **Number of employees nationwide:** 5,000.

HIGH INDUSTRIES, INC.
P.O. Box 10008, Lancaster PA 17605-0008. 717/293-4486. **Contact:** Vincent F. Mizeras, Director of Human Resources. **World Wide Web address:** http://www.high.net. **Description:** Products and services include design and construction, food services, hotel management, prestress/precast concrete products, real estate development and management, and steel fabrication. **Common positions include:** Accountant/Auditor; Architect; Civil Engineer; Computer Programmer;

Customer Service Representative; Draftsperson; Hotel Manager; Human Resources Manager; Services Sales Representative; Systems Analyst. **Educational backgrounds include:** Accounting; Business Administration; Computer Science; Engineering; Finance; Marketing. **Benefits:** Credit Union; Dental Insurance; Disability Coverage; Life Insurance; Medical Insurance; Pension Plan; Profit Sharing; Savings Plan; Tuition Assistance. **Corporate headquarters location:** This Location.

HORNING BROTHERS
1350 Connecticut Avenue NW, Suite 800, Washington DC 20036. 202/659-0700. **Contact:** Human Resources. **Description:** A residential and commercial development, construction, and management company. **Common positions include:** Accountant/Auditor; Construction Contractor; Groundskeeper; Maintenance Technician; Property and Real Estate Manager. **Educational backgrounds include:** Business Administration; Marketing. **Benefits:** 401(k); Dental Insurance; Disability Coverage; Life Insurance; Pension Plan; Profit Sharing; Tuition Assistance. **Corporate headquarters location:** This Location. **Number of employees at this location:** 15. **Number of employees nationwide:** 100.

K. HOVNANIAN COMPANIES
10 Highway 35, Red Bank NJ 07701. 732/747-7800. **Contact:** Human Resources. **World Wide Web address:** http://www.khov.com. **Description:** Designs, constructs, and sells condominium apartments, townhouses, and single-family homes in planned residential communities. The company is also engaged in mortgage banking. Founded in 1959. **NOTE:** Entry-level positions are offered. **Common positions include:** Accountant; Administrative Assistant; Architect; Attorney; Auditor; Civil Engineer; Computer Operator; Computer Programmer; Controller; Financial Analyst; Human Resources Manager; Market Research Analyst; Marketing Manager; Marketing Specialist; MIS Specialist; Online Content Specialist; Real Estate Agent; Sales Manager; Secretary; Systems Analyst; Systems Manager; Technical Writer/Editor; Webmaster. **Educational backgrounds include:** Accounting; Business Administration; Computer Science; Engineering; Marketing. **Benefits:** 401(k); Dental Insurance; Disability Coverage; Life Insurance; Medical Insurance; Profit Sharing; Tuition Assistance. **Corporate headquarters location:** This Location. **Other U.S. locations:** CA; FL; NC; NY; PA; VA. **Subsidiaries include:** New Fortis Homes. **Listed on:** American Stock Exchange. **Stock exchange symbol:** HOV. **Number of employees at this location:** 90. **Number of employees nationwide:** 1,150.

HUBBARD CONSTRUCTION COMPANY
P.O. Box 547217, Orlando FL 32854-7217. 407/645-5500. **Contact:** Margaret Collins, Director of Personnel. **Description:** A general construction contractor that specializes in paving, bridge building, and highway construction. **Common positions include:** Blue-Collar Worker Supervisor; Civil Engineer; Estimator. **Educational backgrounds include:** Engineering. **Benefits:** 401(k); Dental Insurance; Disability Coverage; Life Insurance; Medical Insurance; Profit Sharing; Tuition Assistance. **Corporate headquarters location:** This Location. **Number of employees at this location:** 750. **Number of employees nationwide:** 1,000.

HUBER, HUNT & NICHOLS, INC.
P.O. Box 128, Indianapolis IN 46206. 317/241-6301. **Physical address:** 2450 South Tibbs Avenue,

Indianapolis IN 46241. **Contact:** Human Resources. **World Wide Web address:** http://www. huberhuntnichols.com. **Description:** Provides contract construction services. **NOTE:** Please direct resumes to the department in which you are seeking employment. **Common positions include:** Civil Engineer; Construction Contractor; Electrical/ Electronics Engineer; Industrial Engineer; Mechanical Engineer. **Educational backgrounds include:** Construction; Engineering. **Corporate headquarters location:** This Location.

HUDSON-SHATZ PAINTING COMPANY
429 West 53rd Street, New York NY 10019. 212/757-6363. **Contact:** Lynn Kazimir, Personnel Department. **Description:** A painting contractor. **Corporate headquarters location:** This Location.

INDUSTRIAL BUILDERS, INC.
P.O. Box 406, Fargo ND 58107. 701/282-4977. **Contact:** Paul Diederich, President. **World Wide Web address:** http://www.industrialbuilders.com. **Description:** General contractors engaged in road and building construction.

INNOVATIVE TECHNOLOGIES CORP.
1020 Woodman Drive, Dayton OH 45432-1410. 937/252-2145. **Contact:** Human Resources. **World Wide Web address:** http://www.itc-1.com. **Description:** A general contractor and engineering services firm. The company specializes in defense contracting. **Corporate headquarters location:** This Location.

INTEGRATED ELECTRICAL SERVICES
515 Post Oak Boulevard, Suite 450, Houston TX 77027-9408. 713/860-1500. **Toll-free phone:** 800/696-1044. **Fax:** 713/860-1599. **Contact:** Kent M. Edwards, Vice President of Human Resources. **E-mail address:** kedwards@ielectric.com. **World Wide Web address:** http://www.ielectric.com. **Description:** An electrical contractor providing construction and maintenance work to a variety of business segments. The company's services include design and installation work for new and renovation projects, preventative maintenance, and emergency repair work. **Company slogan:** The power of partnership. **Common positions include:** Accountant; Administrative Assistant; Administrative Manager; Applications Engineer; Chief Financial Officer; Computer Operator; Computer Programmer; Computer Support Technician; Controller; Database Administrator; Database Manager; Electrician; Help-Desk Technician; Internet Services Manager; Intranet Developer; Marketing Manager; MIS Specialist; Public Relations Specialist; Secretary; Systems Analyst. **Benefits:** 401(k); Casual Dress - Daily; Dental Insurance; Disability Coverage; Flexible Schedule; Life Insurance; Medical Insurance; Telecommuting; Vacation Days (10 - 20). **Office hours:** Monday - Friday, 8:00 a.m. - 5:00 p.m. **Corporate headquarters location:** This Location. **Other U.S. locations:** Nationwide. **Listed on:** New York Stock Exchange. **Stock exchange symbol:** IEE. **Annual sales/revenues:** More than $100 million. **Number of employees at this location:** 40. **Number of employees nationwide:** 13,000.

INTERNATIONAL SPECIALTY PRODUCTS
1361 Alps Road, Wayne NJ 07470. 973/628-4000. **Contact:** Gary Schneid, Director of Employee Selection. **World Wide Web address:** http://www. ispcorp.com. **Description:** Manufactures specialty chemicals and building materials. Chemicals include high-pressure acetylene derivatives, industrial organic and inorganic chemicals, GAF filter systems, and GAF mineral products. Building materials include prepared roofing, roll roofing,

built-up roofing systems, and single-ply roofing. The company maintains active research and development facilities worldwide. **Common positions include:** Accountant/Auditor; Advertising Clerk; Attorney; Biological Scientist; Biomedical Engineer; Budget Analyst; Buyer; Chemical Engineer; Chemist; Computer Programmer; Financial Analyst; General Manager; Paralegal; Pharmacist; Systems Analyst. **Educational backgrounds include:** Chemistry; Engineering. **Benefits:** 401(k); Dental Insurance; Disability Coverage; Life Insurance; Medical Insurance; Savings Plan; Tuition Assistance. **Corporate headquarters location:** This Location. **Listed on:** New York Stock Exchange. **Number of employees at this location:** 700. **Number of employees nationwide:** 4,300.

INTERNATIONAL STEEL REVOLVING DOOR COMPANY
2124 North Sixth Avenue, Evansville IN 47710. 812/425-3311. **Toll-free phone:** 800/745-4726. **Fax:** 812/426-2682. **Contact:** Personnel. **Description:** Designs and builds custom revolving doors. The company also performs metal stamping. Founded in 1963. **Common positions include:** Account Manager; Administrative Assistant; Chief Financial Officer; Controller; Cost Estimator; Database Manager; Design Engineer; Draftsperson; Electrician; Financial Analyst; Industrial Production Manager; Sales Representative. **Educational backgrounds include:** Business Administration; Computer Science; Engineering. **Benefits:** Life Insurance; Medical Insurance; Savings Plan; Tuition Assistance. **Special programs:** Internships; Apprenticeships. **Corporate headquarters location:** This Location. **Parent company:** Evansville Metal Products. **Listed on:** Privately held. **Annual sales/revenues:** $5 - $10 million. **Number of employees at this location:** 100.

IVEY MECHANICAL COMPANY
P.O. Box 610, Kosciusko MS 39090. **Toll-free phone:** 800/688-4839. **Fax:** 662/289-8602. **Contact:** Personnel. **World Wide Web address:** http://www.iveymechanical.com. **Description:** A mechanical contracting company that provides piping, plumbing, and HVAC services primarily to the correctional, health care, commercial, entertainment, industrial, and manufacturing industries. **Common positions include:** Construction Superintendent; Construction Trade Worker; Management Trainee; Project Manager. **Educational backgrounds include:** Business Administration; Engineering. **Benefits:** Dental Insurance; Life Insurance; Medical Insurance. **Corporate headquarters location:** This Location. **Number of employees at this location:** 960.

J.C.J. INC.
P.O. Box 688, Bladensburg MD 20710. 301/322-3150. **Contact:** Owner. **Description:** A sheet metal and roofing contractor. The company is also engaged in stainless steel fabrication. **Corporate headquarters location:** This Location.

JACOBSEN CONSTRUCTION COMPANY
P.O. Box 27608, Salt Lake City UT 84127. 801/973-0500. **Fax:** 801/973-7496. **Contact:** Holly Lehigh, Director of Human Resources. **World Wide Web address:** http://www.jacobsen-const.com. **Description:** A general contractor involved in large commercial, industrial, and institutional projects. **NOTE:** Entry-level positions are offered. **Common positions include:** Blue-Collar Worker Supervisor; Carpenter; Civil Engineer; Superintendent. **Educational backgrounds include:** Construction; Engineering. **Benefits:** 401(k); Casual Dress - Fridays; Dental Insurance; Life Insurance; Medical

Insurance; Pension Plan; Profit Sharing. **Special programs:** Apprenticeships; Training; Summer Jobs. **Corporate headquarters location:** This Location. **Subsidiaries include:** Jacobsen Construction Services. **Listed on:** Privately held. **President:** Lonnie Bullard. **Facilities Manager:** Mike Argyle. **Information Systems Manager:** Richard Kirkham. **Purchasing Manager:** Mike Argyle. **Sales Manager:** Jack Wixom. **Annual sales/revenues:** More than $100 million. **Number of employees at this location:** 45. **Number of employees nationwide:** 450.

J.A. JONES CONSTRUCTION COMPANY
J.A. Jones Drive, Charlotte NC 28287. 704/553-3000. **Contact:** Employment Manager. **World Wide Web address:** http://www.jajones.com. **Description:** A general contractor involved in the construction of commercial and institutional facilities, heavy and marine structures, process and industrial facilities, and energy facilities both domestically and internationally. **Common positions include:** Civil Engineer; Electrical/Electronics Engineer; Mechanical Engineer. **Educational backgrounds include:** Engineering. **Benefits:** Dental Insurance; Disability Coverage; Employee Discounts; Life Insurance; Medical Insurance; Pension Plan; Profit Sharing; Savings Plan; Tuition Assistance. **Corporate headquarters location:** This Location. **Parent company:** Philipp Holzmann USA, Inc. is the holding company for the American construction and engineering operations of The Holzmann Group of Germany. The Holzmann Group operates in three segments: general construction, construction of transportation systems, and energy and environmental technology.

KCI TECHNOLOGIES, INC.
10 North Park Drive, Hunt Valley MD 21050. 410/316-7800. **Contact:** Eileen Edwards, Director of Human Resources. **World Wide Web address:** http://www.kci.com/tech. **Description:** Provides planning, engineering, surveying, geotechnical testing, and construction inspection services. **Common positions include:** Accountant/Auditor; Architect; Civil Engineer; Computer Programmer; Credit Manager; Draftsperson; Electrical/Electronics Engineer; Industrial Engineer; Mechanical Engineer; Technical Writer/Editor. **Educational backgrounds include:** Accounting; Computer Science; Engineering. **Benefits:** Dental Insurance; Disability Coverage; Employee Discounts; Life Insurance; Medical Insurance; Pension Plan; Profit Sharing; Savings Plan; Tuition Assistance. **Corporate headquarters location:** This Location.

KSW MECHANICAL SERVICES
3716 23rd Street, Long Island City NY 11101. 718/361-6500. **Contact:** Personnel. **Description:** A mechanical contracting firm engaged in the installation of heating, ventilation, and air conditioning systems in commercial buildings. **Corporate headquarters location:** This Location.

KEATING BUILDING CORPORATION
One Bala Avenue, Suite 400, Bala-Cynwyd PA 19004. 610/668-4100. **Fax:** 610/660-4062. **Contact:** Tim Clippinger, Director of Construction Operations. **World Wide Web address:** http://www.keatingweb.com. **Description:** A general construction firmt that specializes in development, emissions, construction, and housing programs. **NOTE:** Entry-level positions are offered. **Common positions include:** Civil Engineer; Construction Contractor; Cost Estimator; Structural Engineer; Typist/Word Processor. **Educational backgrounds include:** Engineering. **Benefits:** 401(k); Daycare Assistance; Dental Insurance; Disability Coverage; Life Insurance; Medical

Insurance; Public Transit Available; Tuition Assistance. **Special programs:** Internships. **Corporate headquarters location:** This Location. **Other U.S. locations:** CT; FL; NJ; OH. **Listed on:** Privately held. **Annual sales/revenues:** More than $100 million. **Number of employees at this location:** 100. **Number of employees nationwide:** 175.

KELLY CABLE CORPORATION OF NEW MEXICO
3744 Hawkins Street NE, Albuquerque NM 87109. 505/343-1144. **Contact:** Personnel. **World Wide Web address:** http://www.kellycablenm.com. **Description:** A cable television contractor. Kelly Cable Corporation specializes in burying phone cable, as well as installing aerial phone cable. The company also provides construction contracting for utilities. **Common positions include:** Construction Contractor. **Benefits:** 401(k); Dental Insurance; Medical Insurance. **Corporate headquarters location:** Denver CO. **Listed on:** Privately held. **Number of employees at this location:** 70.

THE KIEWIT COMPANIES
1000 Kiewit Plaza, Omaha NE 68131. 402/342-2052. **Contact:** Dee Uecker, Human Resources Generalist. **World Wide Web address:** http://www.kiewit.com. **Description:** One of the largest construction companies in the country. Kiewit's primary markets are building, power, transportation, water resources, and mining industries. Projects include highways, bridges, high-rise buildings, office complexes, railroads, tunnels, subways, dams, airports, power plants, canals, water treatment facilities, offshore petroleum platforms, and other heavy civil projects. The company has district offices throughout North America. **Common positions include:** Civil Engineer. **Educational backgrounds include:** Engineering. **Benefits:** 401(k); Dental Insurance; Disability Coverage; Life Insurance; Medical Insurance; Profit Sharing; Public Transit Available; Tuition Assistance. **Corporate headquarters location:** This Location. **Other U.S. locations:** Nationwide. **Listed on:** Privately held. **Annual sales/revenues:** More than $100 million. **Number of employees at this location:** 300. **Number of employees nationwide:** 3,000.

L. ROBERT KIMBALL & ASSOCIATES
615 West Highland Avenue, P.O. Box 1000, Ebensburg PA 15931. 814/472-7700. **Fax:** 814/472-7712. **Contact:** Karen Maul, Vice President, Human Resources. **E-mail address:** hmnres@lrkimball.com. **World Wide Web address:** http://www.lrkimball.com. **Description:** A national, full-service consulting firm specializing in engineering, architecture, mapping sciences, and environmental services. **NOTE:** Entry-level positions are offered. **Common positions include:** Architect; Biological Scientist; Chemical Engineer; Chemist; Civil Engineer; Construction Contractor; Design Engineer; Draftsperson; Geographer; Geologist/Geophysicist; Mechanical Engineer; Science Technologist; Structural Engineer; Surveyor; Telecommunications Manager; Urban/Regional Planner. **Educational backgrounds include:** Architecture; Biology; Chemistry; Computer Science; Engineering; Environmental Science; Geology. **Benefits:** 401(k); Disability Coverage; Employee Discounts; Life Insurance; Medical Insurance; Section 125 Plan; Tuition Assistance. **Special programs:** Training. **Corporate headquarters location:** This Location. **Other area locations:** Harrisburg PA; Philadelphia PA; Pittsburgh PA; State College PA. **Other U.S. locations:** Raleigh NC; Cranford NJ; Syracuse NY; Richmond VA. **Annual sales/revenues:** $21 - $50

million. **Number of employees at this location:** 350. **Number of employees nationwide:** 500.

KIT MANUFACTURING COMPANY
P.O. Box 990, Caldwell ID 83606. 208/454-9291. **Physical address:** 412 South Kit Avenue, Caldwell ID 83605. **Contact:** Human Resources. **Description:** One of the largest manufacturers of travel trailers and trucks in the United States. The company also manufactures a wide range of recreational vehicle (RV) products. Products are sold under the Road Ranger, Companion, and Sportsmaster brand names. KIT manufactured homes are distributed through a network of approximately 60 dealers located in seven western states and are marketed in six product lines.

KLING LINDQUIST
2301 Chestnut Street, Philadelphia PA 19103. 215/569-2900. **Fax:** 215/569-5963. **Contact:** Steve Huston, Technical Recruiter. **E-mail address:** shuston@tklp.com. **World Wide Web address:** http://www.tklp.com. **Description:** Provides architectural, engineering, and interior design services. **NOTE:** Entry-level positions are offered. **Common positions include:** Accountant; Administrative Assistant; Administrative Manager; Architect; Chief Financial Officer; Civil Engineer; Computer Animator; Computer Engineer; Computer Operator; Computer Programmer; Computer Support Technician; Computer Technician; Computer-Aided Designer; Database Administrator; Database Manager; Design Engineer; Desktop Publishing Specialist; Draftsperson; Electrical/ Electronics Engineer; Human Resources Manager; Instrument Engineer; Interior Designer; Librarian; Marketing Manager; Mechanical Engineer; MIS Specialist; Network/Systems Administrator; Operations Manager; Project Manager; Public Relations Specialist; Purchasing Agent/Manager; Secretary; Software Engineer; Structural Engineer; Technical Writer/Editor; Typist/Word Processor. **Educational backgrounds include:** Architecture; Computer Science; Engineering; Interior Design; Microsoft Word; Novell; Spreadsheets; Visual Basic. **Benefits:** 401(k); Casual Dress - Fridays; Dental Insurance; Disability Coverage; Life Insurance; Medical Insurance; Public Transit Available; Savings Plan; Sick Days (6 - 10); Tuition Assistance; Vacation Days (6 - 10). **Special programs:** Internships; Training; Co-ops; Summer Jobs. **Office hours:** Monday - Friday, 8:30 a.m. - 5:30 p.m. **Corporate headquarters location:** This Location. **Other U.S. locations:** Washington DC; Fort Meade MD. **Listed on:** Privately held. **CEO:** Mel Sotnick. **Facilities Manager:** Bill Daly. **Information Systems Manager:** Sri Sagaram. **Purchasing Manager:** Pat McGuire. **Annual sales/revenues:** $21 - $50 million. **Number of employees at this location:** 350. **Number of employees nationwide:** 400.

LESTER B. KNIGHT & ASSOCIATES, INC.
549 West Randolph Street, Chicago IL 60661. 312/346-2100. **Contact:** Barb Maier, Manager of Human Resources. **Description:** An architectural and engineering firm. Founded in 1945. **Common positions include:** Architect; Civil Engineer; Electrical/Electronics Engineer; Industrial Engineer; Mechanical Engineer; Secretary. **Educational backgrounds include:** Engineering. **Benefits:** 401(k); Dental Insurance; Disability Coverage; Employee Discounts; Flexible Schedule; Life Insurance; Medical Insurance; Public Transit Available; Tuition Assistance. **Corporate headquarters location:** This Location. **Other U.S. locations:** Phoenix AZ; San Francisco CA. **Number of employees at this location:** 200. **Number of employees worldwide:** 800.

KOKOSING CONSTRUCTION COMPANY
17531 Waterford Road, P.O. Box 226, Fredericktown OH 43019. 740/694-6315. **Contact:** Human Resources. **World Wide Web address:** http://www.kokosing-inc.com. **Description:** A general contracting firm engaged in engineering, manufacturing, and construction. **Corporate headquarters location:** This Location.

KOLBE & KOLBE MILLWORK
1323 South 11th Avenue, Wausau WI 54401. 715/842-5666. **Contact:** Human Resources. **World Wide Web address:** http://www.kolbe-kolbe.com. **Description:** Manufactures wooden doors and wood-framed windows. **Corporate headquarters location:** This Location. **Subsidiaries include:** K-K Sales distributes products throughout the Midwest; K-K Way transports products throughout the Midwest; KVW manufactures vinyl windows and doors. **Number of employees at this location:** 1,300.

KRAFTMAID CABINETRY, INC.
P.O. Box 1055, Middlefield OH 44062. 440/632-1833. **Physical address:** 15535 South State Avenue, Middlefield OH. **Fax:** 440/632-0032. **Contact:** Deborah L. Keene, Human Resources/Recruiter. **World Wide Web address:** http://www.kraftmaid.com. **Description:** A cabinet manufacturer. **Common positions include:** Account Representative; Customer Service Representative. **Benefits:** 401(k); Dental Insurance; Life Insurance; Medical Insurance; Profit Sharing. **Parent company:** MASCO. **Number of employees nationwide:** 3,000.

LARSON MANUFACTURING COMPANY
2333 Eastbrook Drive, Brookings SD 57006. 605/692-6115. **Contact:** Human Resources. **Description:** Manufactures storm doors and storm windows. **Corporate headquarters location:** This Location. **Other U.S. locations:** Lake Mills IA.

LATHROP CONSTRUCTION COMPANY
4001 Park Road, Benicia CA 94510. 707/746-8000. **Contact:** Olaf Lyssand, Treasurer. **World Wide Web address:** http://www.lathropconstruction.com. **Description:** A general contractor that offers a variety of services including construction management, budget development, document review, and cost estimation. **Corporate headquarters location:** This Location.

ANDREW LAUREN INTERIORS
2245 West University Drive, Suite 9, Tempe AZ 85281. 480/829-0054. **Contact:** Human Resources. **Description:** Engaged in commercial and residential interior decorating and design. **Corporate headquarters location:** This Location.

LENNOX INTERNATIONAL, INC.
P.O. Box 799900, Dallas TX 75379. 972/497-5000. **Physical address:** 2100 Lake Park Boulevard, Dallas TX. **Fax:** 972/497-5476. **Contact:** Human Resources. **Description:** Produces Lennox brand heating and air conditioning equipment. **Common positions include:** Accountant/Auditor; Buyer; Computer Programmer; Customer Service Rep.; Manufacturing Engineer; Mechanical Engineer; Sales Rep.; Systems Analyst. **Educational backgrounds include:** Accounting; Business Administration; Computer Science; Engineering; Finance; Liberal Arts; Marketing. **Benefits:** 401(k); Dental Insurance; Disability Coverage; Employee Discounts; Life Insurance; Medical Insurance; Pension Plan; Profit Sharing; Tuition Assistance. **Special programs:** Internships. **Corporate headquarters location:** This Location. **Subsidiaries include:** Armstrong; Heatcraft Inc.;

Lennox Industries. **Listed on:** Privately held. **Annual sales/revenues:** More than $100 million. **Number of employees at this location:** 1,000. **Number of employees nationwide:** 9,000. **Number of employees worldwide:** 10,000.

LESTER BUILDING SYSTEMS
1111 Second Avenue South, Lester Prairie MN 55354. 320/395-2531. **Fax:** 320/395-5380. **Contact:** Human Resources Department. **World Wide Web address:** http://www. lesterbuildings.com. **Description:** A manufacturer and retailer of pre-engineered wood-frame buildings. **NOTE:** Entry-level positions are offered. **Common positions include:** Administrative Assistant; Construction Contractor; Draftsperson; Marketing Manager; Marketing Specialist; Sales Rep. **Educational backgrounds include:** Business Administration; Construction; Engineering; Management/Planning. **Benefits:** 401(k); Casual Dress - Daily; Dental Insurance; Disability Coverage; Employee Discounts; Life Insurance; Medical Insurance; Pension Plan; Profit Sharing; Relocation Assistance; Tuition Assistance. **Corporate headquarters location:** This Location. **Parent company:** Butler Manufacturing Company.

LIFETIME DOORS INC.
30700 Northwestern Highway, Farmington Hills MI 48334. 248/851-7700. **Fax:** 248/851-8534. **Contact:** Administration. **World Wide Web address:** http://www.lifetimedoors.com. **Description:** A manufacturer of wooden interior doors. Founded in 1947.

LINDAL CEDAR HOMES INC.
P.O. Box 24426, Seattle WA 98124. 206/725-0900. **Contact:** Personnel Department. **World Wide Web address:** http://www.lindal.com. **Description:** Manufactures precut cedar homes and wholesales lumber and other building materials. **Corporate headquarters location:** This Location.

LIPINSKI LANDSCAPING
180 Elbow Lane, Mount Laurel NJ 08054. 856/231-7941. **Contact:** Human Resources. **World Wide Web address:** http://www.lipinskiland.com. **Description:** Provides landscaping services to commercial and residential clients. This location also hires seasonally. **NOTE:** Entry-level positions are offered. **Common positions include:** Accountant; Administrative Assistant; Architect; Blue-Collar Worker Supervisor; Construction Contractor; Design Engineer; Draftsperson; Engineer; Horticulturist; Landscape Architect; Management Trainee; Operations Manager; Production Manager; Project Manager; Sales Manager; Sales Rep.; Seasonal Worker; Secretary; Transportation/Traffic Specialist. **Educational backgrounds include:** Microsoft Office; Microsoft Word. **Benefits:** 401(k); Casual Dress - Daily; Dental Insurance; Medical Insurance; Profit Sharing; Sick Days (6 - 10); Vacation Days (1 - 5). **Special programs:** Internships; Apprenticeships; Summer Jobs. **Corporate headquarters location:** This Location. **Other U.S. locations:** Princeton NJ. **Annual sales/revenues:** $21 - $50 million. **Number of employees at this location:** 320.

LOCKWOOD GREENE ENGINEERS, INC.
P.O. Box 491, Spartanburg SC 29304. 864/578-2000. **Contact:** Trudy Wofford, Personnel Manager. **World Wide Web address:** http://www.lg.com. **Description:** A consulting firm providing engineering and architectural design for industrial and commercial clients. Specifically, the company is involved in the planning and project management of industrial plants and production facilities. **Common positions include:** Architect; Architectural Engineer; Chemical Engineer; Civil Engineer; Computer Programmer; Draftsperson; Electrical/Electronics Engineer; Industrial Engineer; Mechanical Engineer; Systems Analyst. **Educational backgrounds include:** Architecture; Computer Science; Engineering. **Benefits:** Dental Insurance; Disability Coverage; Life Insurance; Medical Insurance; Pension Plan; Profit Sharing. **Corporate headquarters location:** This Location. **Parent company:** Philipp Holzmann USA is the holding company of the American design and construction operations of The Holzmann Group of Germany. The group operates in three segments: general construction, construction of transportation systems, and energy and environmental technology. **Other U.S. locations:**
• 250 Williams Street, Suite 4000, Atlanta GA 30303. 404/818-8585.

LOCKWOOD, ANDREWS & NEWNAM
1500 City West Boulevard, Houston TX 77042. 713/266-6900. **Fax:** 713/266-7191. **Contact:** Linda Garnett, Human Resources Coordinator. **World Wide Web address:** http://www.lan-inc.com. **Description:** Provides complete architectural, construction management, engineering, planning, and project management services. The company also operates within the fields of infrastructure, thermal energy, and transportation. **NOTE:** Part-time jobs are offered. **Common positions include:** Accountant; Administrative Assistant; Architect; Construction Contractor; Design Engineer; Draftsperson; Electrical/Electronics Engineer; Environmental Engineer; Marketing Specialist; Mechanical Engineer; Secretary; Transportation/Traffic Specialist; Typist/Word Processor. **Educational backgrounds include:** Accounting; Engineering; Finance; Marketing. **Benefits:** 401(k); Dental Insurance; Disability Coverage; Employee Discounts; Life Insurance; Medical Insurance; Savings Plan. **Special programs:** Internships; Summer Jobs. **Office hours:** Monday - Friday, 7:30 a.m. - 4:30 p.m. **Corporate headquarters location:** This Location. **Other U.S. locations:** Omaha NE; Dallas TX; San Antonio TX. **Subsidiaries include:** Geogram. **Parent company:** Leo A. Daly Company. **President/CEO:** Dennis W. Petersen. **Information Systems Manager:** Elizabeth Zamudio. **Annual sales/revenues:** $11 - $20 million. **Number of employees at this location:** 150. **Number of employees nationwide:** 220.

LUDWIG BUILDING SYSTEMS
P.O. Box 23134, Harahan LA 70183. 504/733-6260. **Contact:** Human Resources. **Description:** Engaged in the manufacture and construction of commercial, retail, industrial, and steel buildings. **Common positions include:** Architect; Buyer; Civil Engineer; Customer Service Representative; Draftsperson; Manufacturer's/Wholesaler's Sales Rep.; Purchasing Agent/Manager. **Educational backgrounds include:** Engineering. **Benefits:** Disability Coverage; Life Insurance; Medical Insurance. **Corporate headquarters location:** This Location.

MAGUIRE GROUP, INC.
225 Foxboro Boulevard, Foxboro MA 02035. 508/543-1700. **Contact:** Jan Washburn, Human Resources Manager. **World Wide Web address:** http://www.maguiregroup.com. **Description:** A multidisciplined architectural, engineering, and planning firm, serving domestic and international clients. Maguire Group, Inc. is engaged in the design and construction management of industrial commercial buildings; environmental facilities including sewers and treatment plants; hydroelectric power plants; highways; bridges; airports, and mass transit projects; and port and marine facilities. **Common positions include:** Architect; Civil

Engineer; Designer; Draftsperson; Electrical/ Electronics Engineer; Mechanical Engineer; Structural Engineer. **Educational backgrounds include:** Engineering. **Benefits:** Daycare Assistance; Dental Insurance; Disability Coverage; Life Insurance; Medical Insurance; Savings Plan; Tuition Assistance. **Corporate headquarters location:** This Location. **Other U.S. locations:** New Britain CT; Providence RI.

MANUFACTURED HOUSING ENTERPRISES
9302 State Route 6, Bryan OH 43506. 419/636-4511. **Toll-free phone:** 800/821-0220. **Fax:** 419/636-6521. **Contact:** Sheryl Steele, Human Resources Manager. **E-mail address:** mhe@ bright.net. **World Wide Web address:** http://www.mheinc.com. **Description:** Manufactures single-wide, double-wide, and modular homes. The company also provides the chassis and components for its homes including cabinets, countertops, carpeting, and a variety of custom options. **Common positions include:** Blue-Collar Worker Supervisor; Customer Service Rep.; Design Engineer; Draftsperson; Electrician; Human Resources Manager; Industrial Production Manager; Production Manager; Purchasing Agent/Manager; Quality Control Supervisor; Sales Rep.; Secretary. **Educational backgrounds include:** Accounting; Business Administration; Computer Science; Engineering; Microsoft Word. **Benefits:** 401(k); Employee Discounts; Life Insurance; Medical Insurance. **Corporate headquarters location:** This Location. **Owner:** James Newman. **Information Systems Manager:** Dennis Schall. **Purchasing Manager:** Nick Newcomb. **Number of employees at this location:** 350.

MATICH CORPORATION
P.O. Box 50000, San Bernardino CA 92412. 909/825-9100. **Fax:** 909/824-2360. **Contact:** Human Resources. **World Wide Web address:** http://www.matichicm.com. **Description:** An asphalt paving and manufacturing company. Matich Corporation is also a highway contractor and construction management firm. Founded in 1918. **Common positions include:** Accountant; Administrative Assistant; Chief Financial Officer; Civil Engineer; Claim Rep.; Construction Contractor; Controller; Human Resources Manager; Quality Assurance Engineer; Sales Manager; Sales Rep.; Secretary. **Educational backgrounds include:** Accounting; Engineering; Microsoft Word; Spreadsheets. **Benefits:** 401(k); Casual Dress - Daily; Life Insurance; Medical Insurance. **Corporate headquarters location:** Colton CA. **Number of employees at this location:** 20. **Number of employees nationwide:** 115.

McBRIDE & SON
One McBride & Son Center Drive, Chesterfield MO 63005. 636/537-2000. **Contact:** Ms. Faye Peats, Director of Human Resources. **Description:** A construction company engaged in concrete foundation work, carpentry work, home building, general contracting, real estate sales, property management, and remodeling. **Common positions include:** Accountant; Construction Contractor; Cost Estimator; Credit Manager; Customer Service Representative; Draftsperson; Human Resources Manager; Paralegal; Property and Real Estate Manager; Purchasing Agent/Manager. **Educational backgrounds include:** Accounting; Business Administration; Finance; Marketing. **Benefits:** 401(k); Daycare Assistance; Dental Insurance; Disability Coverage; Employee Discounts; Life Insurance; Medical Insurance; Pension Plan; Tuition Assistance. **Corporate headquarters location:** This Location. **Number of employees at this location:** 400.

McCARTHY CONSTRUCTION COMPANY
1341 North Rock Hill Road, St. Louis MO 63124. 314/968-3300. **Fax:** 314/968-3037. **Contact:** Jim Faust, Personnel Office. **World Wide Web address:** http://www.mccarthy.com. **Description:** One of the nation's oldest privately held construction firms. The company provides a wide range of construction-related services under construction management, general contract, and design and building contractual arrangements, and operates a separate division for work on bridges. **Common positions include:** Accountant; Administrative Assistant; Administrative Manager; AS400 Programmer Analyst; Attorney; Civil Engineer; Computer Operator; Construction Contractor; Controller; Cost Estimator; Design Engineer; Fund Manager; General Manager; Human Resources Manager; Internet Services Manager; Network/Systems Administrator; Secretary; Systems Analyst. **Educational backgrounds include:** Accounting; AS400 Certification; Business Administration; Computer Science; Engineering; Finance; Internet; Software Development; Software Tech. Support. **Benefits:** 401(k); Casual Dress - Daily; Dental Insurance; Disability Coverage; Life Insurance; Medical Insurance; Profit Sharing; Tuition Assistance. **Special programs:** Internships. **Corporate headquarters location:** This Location. **Other U.S. locations:** Phoenix AZ; Newport Beach CA; Sacramento CA; San Francisco CA; Las Vegas NV; Portland OR; Dallas TX; Seattle WA. **Subsidiaries include:** SDL Corporation (Seattle WA) provides commercial and industrial construction services in the Puget Sound region. **President:** Mike Hurst. **Information Systems Manager:** Mike Oster. **Sales Manager:** Kris Anderson. **Annual sales/revenues:** More than $100 million. **Number of employees at this location:** 150. **Number of employees nationwide:** 625.

McNAMEE, PORTER, AND SEELEY, INC.
3131 South State Street, Ann Arbor MI 48108. 734/665-6000. **Fax:** 734/665-2570. **Contact:** Human Resources. **World Wide Web address:** http://www.mcnamee.com. **Description:** An engineering, architectural, and surveying firm. **Common positions include:** Civil Engineer; Electrical/Electronics Engineer; Environmental Engineer; Mechanical Engineer; Structural Engineer. **Educational backgrounds include:** Engineering. **Benefits:** 401(k); Dental Insurance; Disability Coverage; Life Insurance; Medical Insurance; Pension Plan; Profit Sharing. **Special programs:** Internships. **Corporate headquarters location:** This Location. **Subsidiaries include:** McNamee Industrial Services, Inc. **Annual sales/revenues:** $11 - $20 million. **Number of employees at this location:** 300.

MELARD MANUFACTURING CORP.
2 Paulison Avenue, Passaic NJ 07055. 973/472-8888. **Contact:** Human Resources. **Description:** Manufactures a broad range of hardware products including bath accessories and plumbing equipment. **Corporate headquarters location:** This Location. **Parent company:** Masco Corporation.

MERRICK & COMPANY
P.O. Box 22026, Denver CO 80222. 303/751-0741. **Contact:** Personnel Manager. **World Wide Web address:** http://www.merrick.com. **Description:** A full-service, multi-disciplinary engineering and architectural firm. The company specializes in advanced technology, civil infrastructure, government, heavy industrial, and land development services. **Common positions include:** Architect; Chemical Engineer; Civil Engineer; Design Engineer; Designer; Draftsperson; Electrical/ Electronics Engineer; Industrial Engineer;

Mechanical Engineer; Structural Engineer. **Educational backgrounds include:** Architecture; Engineering. **Benefits:** 401(k); Dental Insurance; Disability Coverage; Life Insurance; Medical Insurance; Profit Sharing. **Corporate headquarters location:** This Location. **Other U.S. locations:** Phoenix AZ; Albuquerque NM; Los Alamos NM. **Listed on:** Privately held. **Number of employees at this location:** 270. **Number of employees nationwide:** 460.

C.R. MEYER AND SONS COMPANY
895 West 20th Street, P.O. Box 2157, Oshkosh WI 54903. 920/235-3350. **Contact:** Human Resources. **Description:** A full-service construction company. **Corporate headquarters location:** This Location. **Other U.S. locations:** Kalamazoo MI; Rhinelander WI.

MILLER & LONG COMPANY, INC.
4824 Rugby Avenue, Bethesda MD 20814. 301/657-8000. **Contact:** Miles Gladstone, Personnel Director. **World Wide Web address:** http://www.millerandlong.com. **Description:** A construction firm specializing in high-rise concrete construction. **Corporate headquarters location:** This Location.

THE MILLGARD CORPORATION
12822 Stark Road, Livonia MI 48150. 734/425-8550. **Fax:** 734/425-0624. **Contact:** David B. Coleman, Vice President. **World Wide Web address:** http://www.millgard.com. **Description:** A contractor specializing in caissons, piles, and slurrywall construction. **Common positions include:** Cost Estimator. **Educational backgrounds include:** Business Administration; Engineering; Marketing. **Benefits:** 401(k); Medical Insurance. **Corporate headquarters location:** This Location. **Other U.S. locations:** Boston MA. **Listed on:** Privately held. **Number of employees at this location:** 100.

MISENER MARINE CONSTRUCTION INC.
5440 West Tyson Avenue, Tampa FL 33612. 813/839-8441. **Contact:** Cindy Pierce, Personnel. **World Wide Web address:** http://www.misenermarine.com. **Description:** Engaged in the heavy marine construction of bridges, docks, piers, underwater pipeline and cable, and foundation piling. **Common positions include:** Accountant/Auditor; Civil Engineer; Computer Programmer; Draftsperson; Geologist/Geophysicist; Purchasing Agent/Manager. **Educational backgrounds include:** Accounting; Business Administration; Engineering. **Benefits:** Disability Coverage; Life Insurance; Medical Insurance; Profit Sharing; Tuition Assistance. **Corporate headquarters location:** This Location.

MODERN TECHNOLOGIES CORPORATION
4032 Linden Avenue, Dayton OH 45432. 937/252-9199. **Contact:** Human Resources. **World Wide Web address:** http://www.modtechcorp.com. **Description:** Provides engineering, system support, and management solutions to engineering, manufacturing, technical, and government industries. **Common positions include:** Accountant/Auditor; Aerospace Engineer; Budget Analyst; Buyer; Ceramics Engineer; Chemical Engineer; Chemist; Computer Programmer; Cost Estimator; Electrical/Electronics Engineer; Financial Analyst; Human Resources Manager; Industrial Engineer; Materials Engineer; Mechanical Engineer; Metallurgical Engineer; Software Engineer; Systems Analyst; Technical Writer/Editor. **Benefits:** 401(k); Dental Insurance; Disability Coverage; Life Insurance; Medical Insurance; Tuition Assistance. **Corporate headquarters location:** This Location. **Subsidiaries include:** Composite Technologies

Corporation. **Listed on:** Privately held. **Number of employees at this location:** 350. **Number of employees nationwide:** 780.

F.E. MORAN
2265 Carlson Drive, Northbrook IL 60062. 847/498-4800. **Contact:** Richard Maloni, President. **Description:** An mechanical contracting company specializing in fire detection, heating, air conditioning, plumbing, and ventilation systems. **Corporate headquarters location:** This Location.

MORGAN BUILDING & SPAS, INC.
P.O. Box 660280, Dallas TX 75266. 972/840-1200. **Physical address:** 2800 McCree Road, Garland TX 75041. **Fax:** 972/864-7316. **Contact:** Leslie McLeod, Personnel Coordinator. **World Wide Web address:** http://www.morgandallastx.com. **Description:** Manufactures, transports, and retails relocatable buildings, spas, recreational vehicles, swimming pools, and decks to consumers, businesses, government buyers, and institutional buyers. **Common positions include:** Accountant/Auditor; Advertising Clerk; Architect; Attorney; Blue-Collar Worker Supervisor; Branch Manager; Budget Analyst; Buyer; Clerical Supervisor; Computer Programmer; Cost Estimator; Draftsperson; Financial Analyst; Human Resources Manager; Management Trainee; Manufacturer's/Wholesaler's Sales Rep.; Operations/Production Manager; Paralegal; Purchasing Agent/Manager; Quality Control Supervisor; Structural Engineer; Systems Analyst; Wholesale and Retail Buyer. **Educational backgrounds include:** Accounting; Art/Design; Business Administration; Computer Science; Engineering; Mathematics. **Benefits:** Dental Insurance; Disability Coverage; Employee Discounts; Life Insurance; Medical Insurance; Tuition Assistance. **Corporate headquarters location:** This Location. **Other U.S. locations:** AL; AR; CO; GA; LA; MO; MS; NM; OK; TN. **Listed on:** Privately held. **Number of employees at this location:** 120.

MORGAN WIGHTMAN SUPPLY COMPANY
10199 Woodfield Lane, Suite 300, St. Louis MO 63132. 314/995-9990. **Fax:** 314/995-9781. **Contact:** Sandy Brewer, Personnel Director. **Description:** A distributor of wholesale building materials including windows, doors, moldings, and cabinets. **Common positions include:** Buyer; Credit Manager; Manufacturer's/Wholesaler's Sales Rep.; Operations/Production Manager. **Benefits:** Dental Insurance; Disability Coverage; Employee Discounts; Life Insurance; Medical Insurance; Pension Plan; Tuition Assistance. **Corporate headquarters location:** This Location.

MORRISON KNUDSEN CORPORATION
P.O. Box 73, Boise ID 83729. 208/386-5000. **Fax:** 208/386-6425. **Recorded jobline:** 208/386-6966. **Contact:** Stacie L. Farnham, Human Resources Specialist/Recruiter. **E-mail address:** stacie-farnham@mk.com. **World Wide Web address:** http://www.mk.com. **Description:** Provides construction, engineering, environmental, and mining services. The company works through four major divisions: Engineering & Construction Group, Environmental/Government Group, Heavy Civil Construction Group, and the Mining Group. Founded in 1912. **NOTE:** Entry-level positions are offered. **Common positions include:** Accountant; Architect; Biological Scientist; Chemical Engineer; Civil Engineer; Electrical/Electronics Engineer; Environmental Engineer; Financial Analyst; Geologist/Geophysicist; Human Resources Manager; Industrial Engineer; Mechanical Engineer; Operations Manager; Project Manager; Quality Control Supervisor. **Educational backgrounds**

include: Accounting; Economics; Engineering. **Benefits:** 401(k); Dental Insurance; Disability Coverage; Life Insurance; Medical Insurance; Tuition Assistance. **Special programs:** Internships; Co-ops; Summer Jobs. **Corporate headquarters location:** This Location. **Other U.S. locations:** San Francisco CA; Denver CO; Cleveland OH; San Antonio TX. **International locations:** Worldwide. **Listed on:** New York Stock Exchange. **Stock exchange symbol:** MK. **Number of employees worldwide:** 8,500.

JAMES D. MORRISSEY, INC.
9119 Frankford Avenue, Philadelphia PA 19114. 215/333-8000. **Contact:** Human Resources. **World Wide Web address:** http://www.jdm-inc.com. **Description:** A heavy construction firm working on large-scale projects such as highways and commercial buildings. **Common positions include:** Civil Engineer; Computer Programmer; Draftsperson; Management Trainee; Mining Engineer; Purchasing Agent/Manager; Systems Analyst. **Educational backgrounds include:** Engineering. **Benefits:** Dental Insurance; Life Insurance; Medical Insurance; Pension Plan; Tuition Assistance. **Corporate headquarters location:** This Location.

MORSE DIESEL INTERNATIONAL, INC.
1633 Broadway, 24th Floor, New York NY 10019. 212/484-0300. **Fax:** 212/484-0580. **Contact:** Irwin R. Wecker, Senior Vice President of Human Resources. **World Wide Web address:** http://www.morsediesel.com. **Description:** One of the largest construction management companies in the world offering a wide range of services including construction management, contracting program management, consulting, and design/construction. **Common positions include:** Accountant/Auditor; Attorney; Civil Engineer; Claim Representative; Computer Programmer; Construction and Building Inspector; Construction Contractor; Cost Estimator; Human Resources Manager; Mechanical Engineer; MIS Specialist; Paralegal; Structural Engineer; Systems Analyst; Technical Writer/Editor. **Educational backgrounds include:** Accounting; Computer Science; Engineering; Finance; Marketing. **Benefits:** 401(k); Dental Insurance; Disability Coverage; EAP; Life Insurance; Medical Insurance; Pension Plan; Public Transit Available; Savings Plan; Tuition Assistance. **Special programs:** Internships. **Corporate headquarters location:** This Location. **Parent company:** AMEC Holdings, Inc. **Number of employees at this location:** 140.

M.A. MORTENSON COMPANY
P.O. Box 710, Minneapolis MN 55440. 612/522-2100. **Fax:** 612/522-2278. **Contact:** Dan Haag, Human Services Director. **World Wide Web address:** http://www.mortenson.com **Description:** A general construction firm that provides construction management, design-build, general contracting, maintenance, operations, turnkey construction, and project development services. **Common positions include:** Accountant/Auditor; Attorney; Blue-Collar Worker Supervisor; Construction and Building Inspector; Construction Contractor; Cost Estimator; Systems Analyst. **Educational backgrounds include:** Accounting; Business Administration; Computer Science; Engineering; Marketing. **Benefits:** 401(k); Dental Insurance; Disability Coverage; Life Insurance; Medical Insurance; Pension Plan; Profit Sharing; Tuition Assistance. **Special programs:** Internships. **Corporate headquarters location:** This Location. **Other U.S. locations:** CA; CO; HI; WI. **Operations at this facility include:** Administration. **Number of employees nationwide:** 1,600.

THE MOSSER GROUP
122 South Wilson Avenue, P.O. Drawer D, Fremont OH 43420. 419/334-3801. **Contact:** Employment. **World Wide Web address:** http://www.mossergrp.com. **Description:** A general construction firm that specializes in masonry, pre-engineered steel buildings, precast concret construction, and renovations. **Common positions include:** Civil Engineer; Cost Estimator; Draftsperson. **Educational backgrounds include:** Engineering. **Benefits:** ESOP; Life Insurance; Medical Insurance. **Special programs:** Internships. **Corporate headquarters location:** This Location. **Other U.S. locations:** Toledo OH. **Number of employees at this location:** 60.

JOS. L. MUSCARELLE, INC.
99 Essex Street, Maywood NJ 07607. 201/845-8100. **Contact:** Joseph Muscarelle, Jr., President. **Description:** Engaged in construction and real estate development. **Common positions include:** Civil Engineer; Cost Estimator; Credit Manager; Draftsperson; Electrical/Electronics Engineer; General Manager; Human Resources Manager; Operations/Production Manager; Project Manager; Purchasing Agent/Manager; Real Estate Agent; Sales Executive; Scheduler. **Educational backgrounds include:** Accounting; Business Administration; Engineering; Finance; Marketing. **Benefits:** Dental Insurance; Life Insurance; Medical Insurance; Tuition Assistance.

MUSTANG ENGINEERING
16001 Park Ten Place, Houston TX 77084. 713/215-8000. **Fax:** 713/215-8506. **Contact:** Marty J. Kunz, Employee Relations Manager. **E-mail address:** human.resources@mustangeng.com. **World Wide Web address:** http://www.mustangeng.com. **Description:** An engineering firm specializing in offshore production platforms and pipelines. Founded in 1987. **NOTE:** Entry-level positions are offered. **Common positions include:** Administrative Assistant; Civil Engineer; Computer Support Technician; Computer Technician; Cost Estimator; Design Engineer; Draftsperson; Electrical/Electronics Engineer; Environmental Engineer; Help-Desk Technician; Human Resources Manager; Librarian; Mechanical Engineer; Network/Systems Administrator; Project Manager; Purchasing Agent/Manager; Sales Executive; Secretary; Technical Writer/Editor. **Educational backgrounds include:** Engineering; Microsoft Office; Microsoft Word; Spreadsheets. **Benefits:** 401(k); Casual Dress - Daily; Dental Insurance; Disability Coverage; Employee Discounts; Flexible Schedule; Life Insurance; Medical Insurance; Profit Sharing; Tuition Assistance; Vacation Days (10 - 20). **Special programs:** Summer Jobs. **Office hours:** Monday - Friday, 7:30 a.m. - 4:30 p.m. **Corporate headquarters location:** This Location. **Other U.S. locations:** Monroe LA. **Listed on:** Privately held. **President:** Paul E. Redmon. **Facilities Manager:** Tracey Bayles. **Information Systems Manager:** Gene Atteberry. **Purchasing Manager:** Ted Kelly. **Sales Manager:** William G. Higgs. **Annual sales/revenues:** More than $100 million. **Number of employees at this location:** 650. **Number of employees nationwide:** 1,000.

NVR, INC.
7601 Lewinsville Road, Suite 300, McLean VA 22102. 703/761-2000. **Fax:** 703/761-2259. **Contact:** Human Resources. **World Wide Web address:** http://www.nvrinc.com. **Description:** A national home builder and mortgage company. Founded in 1948. **NOTE:** Entry-level positions and part-time jobs are offered. **Common positions include:** Accountant; Architect; Auditor; Civil Engineer; Construction Contractor; Draftsperson;

Financial Analyst; Management Trainee; Production Manager; Project Manager; Sales Executive; Sales Manager; Sales Rep. **Educational backgrounds include:** Accounting; Business Administration; Computer Science; Engineering; Finance; Marketing; MBA; Microsoft Office; Microsoft Word; Spreadsheets. **Benefits:** 401(k); Casual Dress - Daily; Dental Insurance; Disability Coverage; Employee Discounts; Life Insurance; Medical Insurance; Pension Plan; Profit Sharing; Relocation Assistance; Savings Plan; Sick Days; Tuition Assistance; Vacation Days (10 - 20). **Special programs:** Internships; Training; Co-ops; Summer Jobs. **Office hours:** Monday - Friday, 8:00 a.m. - 5:00 p.m. **Corporate headquarters location:** This Location. **Other U.S. locations:** DE; MD; NC; NJ; NY; OH; PA; SC; TN. **Listed on:** American Stock Exchange. **Stock exchange symbol:** NVR. **Annual sales/revenues:** More than $100 million. **Number of employees at this location:** 75. **Number of employees nationwide:** 3,500.

NANTICOKE HOMES, INC.

P.O. Box F, Greenwood DE 19950. 302/349-4561. **Contact:** Personnel Manager. **World Wide Web address:** http://www.nanticoke.com. **Description:** Manufactures and builds residential homes, townhouses, apartments, and some comemercial buildings. **Common positions include:** Accountant/ Auditor; Administrator; Architect; Blue-Collar Worker Supervisor; Buyer; Computer Programmer; Customer Service Rep.; Department Manager; Draftsperson; General Manager; Human Resources Manager; Industrial Engineer; Mechanical Engineer; Operations/Production Manager; Purchasing Agent/ Manager; Quality Control Supervisor; Services Sales Representative. **Educational backgrounds include:** Accounting; Business Administration; Engineering; Sales. **Benefits:** Disability Coverage; Employee Discounts; Eye Care; Life Insurance; Medical Insurance; Pension Plan; Profit Sharing; Savings Plan; Tuition Assistance. **Corporate headquarters location:** This Location.

NATKIN CONTRACTING

2775 South Vallejo Street, Englewood CO 80110. 303/783-7500. **Contact:** Human Resources. **World Wide Web address:** http://www.natkin.com. **Description:** A mechanical contractor specializing in air conditioning, heating, piping, and plumbing. **Common positions include:** Accountant; Administrative Assistant; Controller; Draftsperson; Estimator; Human Resources Manager; Project Manager; Secretary. **Educational backgrounds include:** Accounting; Business Administration; Engineering. **Benefits:** 401(k); Dental Insurance; Life Insurance; Medical Insurance; Tuition Assistance. **Office hours:** Monday - Friday, 8:00 a.m. - 5:00 p.m. **Corporate headquarters location:** This Location. **Other U.S. locations:** Nationwide. **Number of employees at this location:** 60. **Number of employees nationwide:** 100.

NESCO INC.

6140 Parkland Boulevard, Mayfield Heights OH 44124. 440/461-6000. **Contact:** Human Resources. **World Wide Web address:** http://www. nescoinc.com. **Description:** A holding company that operates through three major groups. The Industrial Group builds process automation and material handling systems. The Service Group specializes in engineering, design, in-house drafting, and documentation. The Real Estate Group owns and manages a variety of commercial and residential buildings. **Common positions include:** Accountant/ Auditor; Attorney; Blue-Collar Worker Supervisor; Buyer; Computer Programmer; Draftsperson; Financial Analyst; General Manager; Human Resources Manager; Industrial Engineer; Industrial

Production Manager; Manufacturer's/Wholesaler's Sales Rep.; Mechanical Engineer; Metallurgical Engineer; Operations/Production Manager; Purchasing Agent/Manager; Quality Control Supervisor; Systems Analyst. **Educational backgrounds include:** Accounting; Business Administration; Engineering; Marketing. **Benefits:** Dental Insurance; Disability Coverage; Life Insurance; Medical Insurance. **Corporate headquarters location:** This Location. **Number of employees at this location:** 4,000.

NIELSEN DILLINGHAM BUILDERS

3127 Jefferson Street, San Diego CA 92110. 619/291-6330. **Fax:** 619/291-9940. **Contact:** Denise M. Howe, Human Resources Manager. **World Wide Web address:** http://www. nielsendillingham.com. **Description:** A multifaceted construction firm specializing in commercial, industrial, medical/health care, engineering, retail, and hospitality projects. Founded in 1945. **NOTE:** Entry-level positions and part-time jobs are offered. **Common positions include:** Accountant; Administrative Assistant; Administrative Manager; AS400 Programmer Analyst; Attorney; Civil Engineer; Computer Support Technician; Computer Technician; Controller; Cost Estimator; Human Resources Manager; Marketing Manager; Mechanical Engineer; MIS Specialist; Operations Manager; Paralegal; Project Manager; Secretary. **Educational backgrounds include:** AS400 Certification; Engineering; Microsoft Office; Microsoft Word; Spreadsheets. **Benefits:** 401(k); Casual Dress - Fridays; Dental Insurance; Disability Coverage; Employee Discounts; Life Insurance; Medical Insurance; Profit Sharing; Relocation Assistance; Savings Plan; Sick Days (1 - 5); Tuition Assistance; Vacation Days (6 - 10). **Special programs:** Internships. **Office hours:** Monday - Friday, 8:00 a.m. - 5:00 p.m. **Corporate headquarters location:** This Location. **Other area locations:** Long Beach CA; Pleasanton CA. **Other U.S. locations:** Las Vegas NV; Portland OR. **Parent company:** Dillingham, Inc. **Listed on:** Privately held. **President:** Larry M. Geiser. **Number of employees at this location:** 250. **Number of employees nationwide:** 350.

NOBILITY HOMES, INC.

3741 SW Seventh Street, Ocala FL 34474. 352/732-5157. **Contact:** Human Resources. **World Wide Web address:** http://www.nobilityhomes.com. **Description:** Designs and manufactures factory-constructed homes. The company also operates real estate sales centers. **Corporate headquarters location:** This Location.

NORCRAFT COMPANIES, INC.

3020 Denmark Avenue, Suite 100, Eagan MN 55121. 651/234-3300. **Contact:** Brenda Lee Lally, Manager of Benefits & Payroll. **Description:** Manufactures wooden kitchen cabinets. **Corporate headquarters location:** This Location. **Other U.S. locations:** Newton KS; Cottonwood MN. **Number of employees at this location:** 50. **Number of employees nationwide:** 735.

NORTEK, INC.

50 Kennedy Plaza, Providence RI 02903. 401/751-1600. **Fax:** 401/751-4724. **Contact:** Jane White, Personnel Manager. **World Wide Web address:** http://www.nortek-inc.com. **Description:** A diversified manufacturer of residential and commercial building products operating within three principal product groups: Residential Building Products; Air Conditioning and Heating Products; and Plumbing Products. Through these groups, the company manufactures and sells products for the residential and commercial construction,

manufactured housing, and the do-it-yourself and professional remolding and renovation markets primarily in the U.S. and Canada. Products include furnaces, ventilation systems, cabinets, security products, garage door openers, heat pumps, and energy management systems under the brand names Braun, Nautilus, and Air Care. Plumbing products include faucets, fixtures, vanities, spas, whirlpools, shower components, tubs, and other accessories. **Corporate headquarters location:** This Location. **Listed on:** New York Stock Exchange.

NORTH AMERICAN MECHANICAL, INC.
6135 North American Lane, Deforest WI 53532. 608/241-4328. **Fax:** 608/241-2710. **Contact:** Janice Ross, Human Resources Director. **E-mail address:** jross@naminc.com. **World Wide Web address:** http://www.naminc.com. **Description:** A commercial HVAC contractor. **NOTE:** Entry-level positions and part-time jobs are offered. **Common positions include:** Administrative Assistant; Mechanical Engineer; Project Manager. **Educational backgrounds include:** Engineering; Mathematics. **Benefits:** 401(k); Casual Dress - Fridays; Dental Insurance; Disability Coverage; Flexible Schedule; Life Insurance; Medical Insurance; Profit Sharing; Sick Days; Vacation Pay; Vision Insurance. **Special programs:** Internships; Apprenticeships; Summer Jobs. **Corporate headquarters location:** This Location. **Parent company:** Comfort Systems USA, Inc. **Listed on:** New York Stock Exchange. **Stock exchange symbol:** FIX. **Number of employees at this location:** 165.

O&G INDUSTRIES INC.
112 Wall Street, Torrington CT 06790. 860/489-9261. **Contact:** Sharon Okraska, Human Resources. **World Wide Web address:** http://www.ogindustries.com. **Description:** A construction firm providing building construction management, design services, heavy civil construction, environmental remediation, and construction materials. **Corporate headquarters location:** This Location.

OAKWOOD HOMES
P.O. Box 27081, Greensboro NC 27425-7081. 336/664-2400. **Contact:** Paul Macksood, Director of Human Resources. **World Wide Web address:** http://www.oakwoodhomes.com. **Description:** Manufactures and sells prefabricated housing under the Oakwood and Freedom brand names. Oakwood Homes also finances a portion of its installment contracts through its finance unit. **Common positions include:** Accountant/Auditor; Credit Manager; Customer Service Rep.; Management Trainee; Operations/Production Manager; Sales Representative. **Educational backgrounds include:** Accounting; Finance; Liberal Arts. **Benefits:** 401(k); Dental Insurance; Disability Coverage; Life Insurance; Medical Insurance; Pension Plan; Profit Sharing; Tuition Assistance. **Special programs:** Internships. **Corporate headquarters location:** This Location. **Other U.S. locations:** Nationwide.

W.E. O'NEIL CONSTRUCTION COMPANY
2751 North Clybourn Avenue, Chicago IL 60614. 773/755-1611. **Contact:** Employment. **World Wide Web address:** http://www.oneilind.com. **Description:** A general construction company specializing in commercial projects. **NOTE:** Jobseekers should indicate the department in which they are interested in a cover letter. **Common positions include:** Civil Engineer; Construction Engineer; Electrical/Electronics Engineer; Mechanical Engineer. **Educational backgrounds include:** Engineering. **Benefits:** Dental Insurance; Disability Coverage; Life Insurance; Medical

Insurance; Profit Sharing; Savings Plan. **Corporate headquarters location:** This Location.

OPTIMIZED PROCESS DESIGNS (OPD)
P.O. Box 810, Katy TX 77493. 281/371-7500. **Physical address:** 25610 Clay Road, Katy TX 77493. **Fax:** 281/371-0132. **Contact:** Human Resources. **World Wide Web address:** http://www.opd-inc.com. **Description:** Designs, engineers, and constructs natural gas treatment facilities. **Common positions include:** Accountant; Administrative Assistant; Chemical Engineer; Civil Engineer; Clerical Supervisor; Construction Superintendent; Controller; Draftsperson; Electrical/Electronics Engineer; Human Resources Manager; Mechanical Engineer; Painter; Pipe Fitter; Project Manager; Purchasing Agent/Manager; Quality Control Supervisor; Sales Executive; Secretary; Welder. **Educational backgrounds include:** Business Administration; Chemistry; Engineering; Microsoft Office; Microsoft Word; Spreadsheets. **Benefits:** 401(k); Casual Dress - Daily; Dental Insurance; Disability Coverage; Flexible Schedule; Life Insurance; Medical Insurance; Pension Plan; Savings Plan; Sick Days (6 - 10); Tuition Assistance; Vacation Days. **Parent company:** Koch Industries, Inc. **Listed on:** Privately held.

OVERHEAD DOOR CORPORATION OF TEXAS
6750 LBJ Freeway, Suite 1200, Dallas TX 75240. 972/233-6611. **Contact:** Human Resources. **World Wide Web address:** http://www.overheaddoor.com. **Description:** Manufactures aluminum, steel, fiberglass, and wooden overhead doors, rolling steel fire doors, grilles, and metal insulated entrance doors. Products are distributed through a network of more than 400 authorized distributors in the United States and Canada. The company also manufactures truck and trailer doors. **Corporate headquarters location:** This Location. **Other area locations:** Carrollton TX; Corpus Christi TX; Fort Worth TX; Houston TX; Mount Pleasant TX; Richardson TX.

PACKER ENGINEERING INC.
1950 North Washington Street, Naperville IL 60563. 630/505-5722. **Toll-free phone:** 800/323-0114. **Fax:** 630/505-1986. **Contact:** Human Resources. **World Wide Web address:** http://www.packereng.com. **Description:** A multidisciplinary engineering, consulting, and technical services company. The practice includes failure analysis; accident investigation and reconstruction; fire/explosion cause and origin studies; product design evaluations; process design assessments; customized and routine testing; applied research; commercial product development; and litigation support. **NOTE:** Entry-level positions are offered. **Common positions include:** Biochemist; Biomedical Engineer; Chemist; Civil Engineer; Computer Animator; Electrical/Electronics Engineer; Environmental Engineer; Industrial Engineer; Marketing Manager; Mechanical Engineer; Metallurgical Engineer. **Educational backgrounds include:** Chemistry; Engineering. **Benefits:** 401(k); Dental Insurance; Disability Coverage; Life Insurance; Medical Insurance; Pension Plan. **Special programs:** Internships. **Internship information:** Paid summer internships are available through The Packer Foundation. Candidates should send a letter of application and a resume by February 1st. **Corporate headquarters location:** This Location. **Other U.S. locations:** Nationwide. **Parent company:** The Packer Group. **Number of employees at this location:** 75.

PARAMOUNT ELECTRONICS COMPANY
57 Willoughby Street, Brooklyn NY 11201. 718/237-8730. **Contact:** Personnel Manager.

Description: Provides contract drafting services. **Corporate headquarters location:** This Location.

PARSONS BRINCKERHOFF INC.
One Penn Plaza, New York NY 10119. 212/465-5000. **Contact:** Ed Swartz, Vice President of Personnel. **World Wide Web address:** http://www.pbworld.com. **Description:** Provides total engineering and construction management services, including the development of major bridges, tunnels, highways, marine facilities, buildings, industrial complexes, and railroads. **Corporate headquarters location:** This Location.

PATRICK ENGINEERING
22 West 600 Butterfield Road, Glen Ellyn IL 60137. 630/790-7600. **Fax:** 630/790-7612. **Contact:** Jay Weiss, Vice President. **E-mail address:** jweiss@patrickengineering.com. **World Wide Web address:** http://www.patrickengineering.com. **Description:** Offers solid waste planning, architecture, surveying, and engineering services in the civil, transportation, environmental, geotechnical, hydraulic, water resources, structural, and electrical sectors. **Common positions include:** Administrative Assistant; Architect; Civil Engineer; Design Engineer; Draftsperson; Electrical/Electronics Engineer; Environmental Engineer; Industrial Engineer; Mechanical Engineer. **President:** Daniel P. Dietzler. **Information Systems Manager:** Michael Racki. **Purchasing Manager:** Teri Deddo. **Sales Manager:** Steven Luetkehans.

PERINI BUILDING COMPANY
P.O. Box 33730, Phoenix AZ 85067-3730. 602/256-6777. **Contact:** Joseph Schindler, Operations Manager. **Description:** Provides general contracting and construction management services. **Common positions include:** Civil Engineer. **Educational backgrounds include:** Engineering. **Benefits:** Dental Insurance; Life Insurance; Medical Insurance; Pension Plan; Tuition Assistance. **Corporate headquarters location:** This Location. **Listed on:** New York Stock Exchange.

PERINI CORPORATION
73 Mount Wayte Avenue, Framingham MA 01701. 508/628-2000. **Fax:** 508/628-2960. **Contact:** Human Resources. **Description:** One of the largest heavy and building construction firms in the United States. Worldwide projects include bridges and roads, mass transportation and airport construction, and commercial building construction. Perini also provides engineering and consulting services. **Common positions include:** Accountant/Auditor; Civil Engineer. **Educational backgrounds include:** Accounting; Computer Science; Engineering. **Benefits:** Dental Insurance; Disability Coverage; Life Insurance; Medical Insurance; Pension Plan; Profit Sharing; Savings Plan; Tuition Assistance. **Corporate headquarters location:** This Location.

PERKINS & WILL
330 North Wabash Avenue, Suite 3600, Chicago IL 60611. 312/755-0770. **Toll-free phone:** 800/837-9455. **Fax:** 312/755-0775. **Contact:** Human Resources. **E-mail address:** hr@perkinswill.com. **World Wide Web address:** http://www.perkinswill.com. **Description:** An architectural, interior design and planning firm that serves both commercial and industrial companies. The company also provides an IDP/IDEP program for unlicensed designers. This location also hires seasonally. Founded in 1935. **NOTE:** Entry-level positions and part-time jobs are offered. **Company slogan:** Design excellence. **Common positions include:** Accountant; Architect; Database Administrator; Draftsperson; Environmental Engineer; Financial

Analyst; Graphic Artist; Graphic Designer; Help-Desk Technician; Human Resources Manager; Intranet Developer; Multimedia Designer; Sales Representative; SQL Programmer; Webmaster; Website Developer. **Educational backgrounds include:** Accounting; Art/Design; Business Administration; Computer Science; Engineering; Finance; HTML; Liberal Arts; Marketing; Mathematics; MBA; Microsoft Office; Microsoft Word; Public Relations; Spreadsheets. **Benefits:** 401(k); Casual Dress - Daily; Dental Insurance; Financial Planning Assistance; Flexible Schedule; Life Insurance; Medical Insurance; Public Transit Available; Relocation Assistance; Savings Plan; Sick Days (6 - 10); Vacation Days (10 - 20). **Special programs:** Internships; Training; Co-ops; Summer Jobs. **Office hours:** Monday - Friday, 8:00 a.m. - 5:00 p.m. **Corporate headquarters location:** This Location. **Other U.S. locations:** Los Angeles CA; Miami FL; Atlanta GA; Minneapolis MN; Charlotte NC; New York NY. **International locations:** Paris, France. **Subsidiaries include:** TY Lin, Inc. **Parent company:** Dar Al Handesah. **President:** Henry Mann. **Annual sales/revenues:** $21 - $50 million. **Number of employees at this location:** 150.

PHILLIPS, GETSCHOW COMPANY
1913 South Briggs Street, Joliet IL 60433. 815/727-4624. **Fax:** 815/727-4624. **Contact:** Human Resources. **World Wide Web address:** http://www.phillipsgetschow.com. **Description:** A mechanical engineering company that provides a variety of services including HVAC, power piping, fabrication, and plumbing. **Common positions include:** Accountant/Auditor; Blue-Collar Worker Supervisor; Management Trainee; Mechanical Engineer. **Educational backgrounds include:** Accounting; Engineering. **Benefits:** Dental Insurance; Disability Coverage; Life Insurance; Medical Insurance; Pension Plan; Profit Sharing; Savings Plan. **Special programs:** Internships. **Corporate headquarters location:** Oconto Falls WI. **Other U.S. locations:** Cloquet MN; Green Bay WI. **Number of employees nationwide:** 500.

GERALD H. PHIPPS, INC.
1530 West 13th Avenue, Denver CO 80204-2400. 303/571-5377. **Fax:** 303/629-7467. **Contact:** Human Resources. **World Wide Web address:** http://www.geraldhphipps.com. **Description:** A general contractor/construction manager for commercial buildings. Gerald H. Phipps, Inc. specializes in building medical complexes, high-tech buildings, universities, schools, offices that tenants finish, public facilities, biotechnology labs, and retail projects. Founded in 1952. **NOTE:** Entry-level positions are offered. **Common positions include:** Construction Contractor; Cost Estimator; Project Manager. **Educational backgrounds include:** Construction; Engineering. **Benefits:** Dental Insurance; Disability Coverage; Life Insurance; Medical Insurance; Pension Plan; Profit Sharing; Savings Plan; Tuition Assistance. **Special programs:** Apprenticeships. **Corporate headquarters location:** This Location. **Annual sales/revenues:** More than $100 million. **Number of employees at this location:** 250.

PIERCE ASSOCIATES
4216 Wheeler Avenue, Alexandria VA 22304. 703/751-2400. **Fax:** 703/751-2479. **Contact:** John Dunleavy, Senior Vice President. **Description:** A contractor specializing in mechanical construction (HVAC, plumbing, and fire protection). **Common positions include:** Mechanical Engineer. **Benefits:** 401(k); Dental Insurance; Life Insurance; Medical Insurance. **Corporate headquarters location:** This Location. **Listed on:** Privately held. **Number of employees at this location:** 40.

PIZZAGALLI CONSTRUCTION COMPANY
50 Joy Drive, South Burlington VT 05403. 802/658-4100. **Contact:** Gary Warner, Vice President of Administration. **World Wide Web address:** http://www.pizzagalli.com. **Description:** A general contractor that handles projects including water and wastewater treatment plants; government work including army barracks and prisons; and high school renovations and additions. **Corporate headquarters location:** This Location. **Other U.S. locations:** Tempe AZ; Raleigh NC. **Number of employees at this location:** 95. **Number of employees nationwide:** 1,200.

PORTER-HUGGINS INC.
P.O. Box 2246, Savannah GA 31402. 912/232-1255. **Contact:** Ms. Renee Huggins, Vice President. **Description:** Provides a variety of services for the construction industry including the rental of backhoes, cranes, and tractors. The company is also engaged in large-scale construction and the fabrication of pipes used in the process control industries. **Corporate headquarters location:** This Location.

J.D. POSILLICO INC.
1610 New Highway, Farmingdale NY 11735. 516/249-1872. **Contact:** Anne M. Seeley, Secretary. **Description:** A heavy construction firm whose projects include sewage systems, drainage, and road work. **Corporate headquarters location:** This Location.

TRAVIS PRUITT & ASSOCIATES, P.C.
5555 Oakbrook Parkway, Suite 280, Norcross GA 30093. 770/416-7511. **Fax:** 770/416-6759. **Contact:** Ann Poole, Human Resources Representative. **E-mail address:** ann@travispruitt.com. **World Wide Web address:** http://www.travispruitt.com. **Description:** A consulting firm specializing in civil engineering, land surveys, and landscape architecture. The company also offers environmental engineering services. **Common positions include:** Biological Scientist; Civil Engineer; Draftsperson; Landscape Architect; Surveyor. **Educational backgrounds include:** Biology; Computer Science; Engineering. **Benefits:** 401(k); Dental Insurance; Medical Insurance; Profit Sharing. **Office hours:** Monday - Friday, 8:00 a.m. - 5:00 p.m. **Corporate headquarters location:** This Location. **President:** Travis Pruitt, Sr. **Number of employees at this location:** 70.

PULTE HOME CORPORATION
33 Bloomfield Hills Parkway, Suite 200, Bloomfield Hills MI 48304. 248/644-7300. **Contact:** Kathy McGuire, Human Resources Manager. **World Wide Web address:** http://www.pulte.com. **Description:** One of the largest independent, publicly-owned, home-building companies in the United States. The principal business of Pulte Home Corporation is the construction and sale of moderately-priced, single-family homes. **Benefits:** 401(k); Dental Insurance; Disability Coverage; Life Insurance; Medical Insurance; Profit Sharing; Tuition Assistance. **Corporate headquarters location:** This Location. **Subsidiaries include:** Builders Supply and Lumber; ICM Mortgage Corporation. **Parent company:** Pulte Corporation. **Listed on:** New York Stock Exchange. **Number of employees at this location:** 90. **Number of employees nationwide:** 4,000.

RANDERS ENGINEERS AND CONSTRUCTORS
570 Seminole Road, Muskegon MI 49444. 231/733-0036. **Fax:** 231/733-8137. **Contact:** Human Resources. **World Wide Web address:** http://www.randers.com. **Description:** A full-service architectural, construction, development,

engineering, and environmental firm. The company also provides turnkey modular systems for complex process operations. **Corporate headquarters location:** This Location. **Other area locations:** Detroit MI; Lansing MI. **Other U.S. locations:** Chicago IL; Cincinnati OH; Charleston WV. **Subsidiaries include:** Clark-Trombley Consulting Engineers, Inc.; Randers Engineering, Inc.; Randers Group Property Corporation; Randers-EPC Inc.; Redeco Inc.

RIZZO ASSOCIATES, INC.
235 West Central Street, Natick MA 01760. 508/903-2401. **Fax:** 508/903-2001. **Contact:** Human Resources. **E-mail address:** hr@rizzo.com. **World Wide Web address:** http://www.rizzo.com. **Description:** An engineering and environmental consulting firm. **NOTE:** Entry-level positions and part-time jobs are offered. **Common positions include:** Chemical Engineer; Civil Engineer; Design Engineer; Draftsperson; Environmental Engineer; Mechanical Engineer; Technical Writer/Editor. **Educational backgrounds include:** Biology; Engineering; Geology. **Benefits:** 401(k); Casual Dress - Fridays; Dental Insurance; Disability Coverage; ESOP; Flexible Schedule; Life Insurance; Medical Insurance; On-Site Daycare; Sick Days (6 - 10); Tuition Assistance. **Special programs:** Internships; Co-ops. **Office hours:** Monday - Friday, 9:00 a.m. - 5:30 p.m. **Corporate headquarters location:** This Location. **Parent company:** Tetra Tech. **Listed on:** Privately held.

J.B. RODGERS KINETICS
P.O. Box 52147, Phoenix AZ 85072. 602/685-2000. **Contact:** Kathy Littler, Human Resources Manager. **World Wide Web address:** http://www.jbrodgers.com. **Description:** One of the largest mechanical contracting firms in Arizona, and one of the top 100 in the country. J.B. Rodgers Mechanical Contractors provides a wide array of commercial and industrial services including process piping, heating, ventilating, air conditioning, control systems, ultra-high-purity process piping, plumbing, special projects services, energy audits and retrofits, performance contracting, air and water balance, and back flow prevention. **Common positions include:** Accountant/Auditor; Administrative Manager; Buyer; Clerical Supervisor; Computer Programmer; Construction Contractor; Cost Estimator; Customer Service Rep.; Draftsperson; Human Resources Manager; Management Trainee; Market Research Analyst; Mechanical Engineer; Project Manager; Public Relations Specialist; Purchasing Agent/Manager; Systems Analyst. **Educational backgrounds include:** Accounting; Business Administration; Computer Science; Engineering; Finance; Marketing. **Benefits:** 401(k); Dental Insurance; Disability Coverage; Employee Discounts; Life Insurance; Medical Insurance; Pension Plan; Profit Sharing; Public Transit Available; Telecommuting; Tuition Assistance. **Special programs:** Training. **Corporate headquarters location:** This Location. **Annual sales/revenues:** $51 - $100 million. **Number of employees at this location:** 135. **Number of employees nationwide:** 600.

ROEL CONSTRUCTION COMPANY
P.O. Box 80216, San Diego CA 92138. 619/297-4156. **Contact:** Personnel Director. **Description:** A commercial and residential construction company. Roel Construction also provides tenant improvements, structural concrete construction, construction forensic services, and surety claim services. **Corporate headquarters location:** This Location. **Other U.S. locations:** AZ; NV. **President/CEO:** Stephen Roel.

ROSSER INTERNATIONAL, INC.
524 West Peachtree Street NW, Atlanta GA 30308. 404/888-6843. **Fax:** 404/888-6863. **Contact:** Sandra Kuzma, Vice President of Human Resources. **World Wide Web address:** http://www.rosser.com. **Description:** An architectural and engineering design firm. Projects include prisons, stadiums, hangars, commercial retail space, and other facilities. **Common positions include:** Accountant; Architect; Civil Engineer; Designer; Draftsperson; Electrical/Electronics Engineer; Landscape Architect; Marketing Specialist; Mechanical Engineer; Structural Engineer. **Educational backgrounds include:** Accounting; Architecture; Business Administration; Computer Science; Engineering; Finance; Marketing. **Office hours:** Monday - Friday, 8:00 a.m. - 5:00 p.m. **Corporate headquarters location:** This Location. **Other U.S. locations:** Savannah GA. **Listed on:** Privately held. **Number of employees at this location:** 150. **Number of employees nationwide:** 235.

RUDOLPH/LIBBE, INC.
6494 Latcha Road, Walbridge OH 43465-9738. 419/241-5000. **Contact:** Human Resources. **Description:** A general contractor and construction management firm. **Corporate headquarters location:** This Location.

RUST CONSTRUCTORS, INC.
RAYTHEON ENGINEERS & CONSTRUCTORS
100 Corporate Parkway, Birmingham AL 35242-2928. 205/995-3540. **Fax:** 205/995-6691. **Contact:** Edward Wick, Human Resources. **E-mail address:** edward_wick@rec.raytheon.com. **World Wide Web address:** http://www.rayjobs.com. **Description:** Sells and manages industrial maintenance contracts. Raytheon Engineers & Constructors (also at this location, 205/995-7878) is an environmental and industrial consulting engineering firm offering scientific services in the areas of solid waste, hazardous waste, wastewater, and water resources. The company's construction projects include industrial plants, pulp and paper mills, steel mills, chemical plants, and other energy-related construction projects. Founded in 1905. **NOTE:** Entry-level positions are offered. **Common positions include:** Accountant; Administrative Assistant; Administrative Manager; Assistant Manager; Blue-Collar Worker Supervisor; Buyer; Civil Engineer; Claim Rep.; Computer Operator; Computer Programmer; Computer Support Technician; Computer Technician; Construction Contractor; Controller; Cost Estimator; Customer Service Rep.; Design Engineer; Electrical/Electronics Engineer; Electrician; Environmental Engineer; General Manager; Human Resources Manager; Mechanical Engineer; Operations Manager; Project Manager; Quality Assurance Engineer; Quality Control Supervisor; Sales Executive; Sales Manager; Sales Representative; Secretary; Typist/Word Processor. **Educational backgrounds include:** Accounting; Business Administration; Chemistry; Computer Science; Engineering; Finance; Marketing; Mathematics; MBA; Microsoft Office; Physics. **Benefits:** 401(k); Casual Dress - Daily; Dental Insurance; Employee Discounts; Life Insurance; Medical Insurance; Pension Plan; Relocation Assistance; Tuition Assistance. **Special programs:** Apprenticeships; Training; Co-ops. **Office hours:** Monday - Friday, 7:30 a.m. - 4:30 p.m. **Corporate headquarters location:** Lexington MA. **Other U.S. locations:** Nationwide. **International locations:** Worldwide. **Parent company:** Raytheon Company. **Listed on:** New York Stock Exchange. **President:** Monty Glover. **Vice President of Business Development:** Jerry Purcell. **Annual sales/revenues:** More than $100 million. **Number of employees at this location:** 560. **Number of employees nationwide:** 7,200. **Number of employees worldwide:** 8,700.

RYAN COMPANIES U.S., INC.
900 Second Avenue South, Suite 700, Minneapolis MN 55402. 612/336-1200. **Recorded jobline:** 612/336-1200x360. **Contact:** James Nahrgang, Director of Human Resources. **World Wide Web address:** http://www.ryancompanies.com. **Description:** Engaged in the design and construction of commercial projects including corporate office, manufacturing, industrial, product distribution, high-tech, medical and retail buildings. The company also provides property management and development services. **NOTE:** Entry-level positions and part-time jobs are offered. **Company slogan:** Building lasting relationships. **Common positions include:** Administrative Assistant; Architect; Civil Engineer; Computer Programmer; Computer Support Technician; Construction Contractor; Content Developer; Finance Director; Financial Analyst; Marketing Manager; Marketing Specialist; MIS Specialist; Network/Systems Administrator; Project Manager; Secretary; Systems Analyst. **Educational backgrounds include:** Accounting; Computer Science; Engineering; Finance. **Benefits:** 401(k); Casual Dress - Fridays; Dental Insurance; Disability Coverage; Employee Discounts; Flexible Schedule; Life Insurance; Medical Insurance; Profit Sharing; Tuition Assistance. **Special programs:** Internships; Training; Co-ops. **Corporate headquarters location:** This Location. **Other U.S. locations:** Phoenix AZ; Cedar Rapids IA. **Listed on:** Privately held. **Number of employees nationwide:** 300.

SHG
500 Griswold Street, Suite 200, Detroit MI 48226. 313/983-3600. **Contact:** Human Resources. **World Wide Web address:** http://www.smithgroup.com. **Description:** A multi-faceted architectural and engineering firm engaged in construction, facility management, historic preservation, landscaping, telecommunications, and real estate consulting. **Common positions include:** Architect; Electrical/Electronics Engineer; Mechanical Engineer; Structural Engineer. **Educational backgrounds include:** Architecture; Engineering. **Benefits:** 401(k); Dental Insurance; Disability Coverage; Life Insurance; Medical Insurance; Profit Sharing; Tuition Assistance. **Corporate headquarters location:** This Location. **Other U.S. locations:** Phoenix AZ; San Francisco CA; Santa Monica CA; Washington DC; Miami FL; Chicago IL. **Parent company:** The SmithGroup Incorporated. **Number of employees at this location:** 250.

SNE ENTERPRISES, INC.
888 Southview Drive, Mosinee WI 54455. 715/693-7000. **Fax:** 715/693-8505. **Contact:** Human Resources. **World Wide Web address:** http://www.crestlineonline.com. **Description:** A manufacturer of windows, patio doors, and skylights under the Vetter and Crestline labels. **NOTE:** Entry-level positions are offered. **Common positions include:** Blue-Collar Worker Supervisor; Buyer; Computer Programmer; Customer Service Representative; Design Engineer; Draftsperson; Industrial Engineer; Manufacturing Engineer; Sales Representative; Systems Analyst. **Educational backgrounds include:** Business Administration; Computer Science; Engineering; Mathematics. **Benefits:** 401(k); Dental Insurance; Disability Coverage; Employee Discounts; Life Insurance; Medical Insurance; Profit Sharing; Tuition Assistance. **Corporate headquarters location:** This Location. **Parent company:** Nortek Inc. **Annual sales/revenues:** More than $100 million. **Number of employees nationwide:** 2,000.

STV GROUP
21 Governor's Court, Suite 200, Baltimore MD 21244. 410/944-9112. **Contact:** Human Resources. **E-mail address:** info@stvinc.com. **World Wide Web address:** http://www.stvinc.com. **Description:** STV Group provides engineering and architectural consulting and design services for a variety of projects, as well as construction inspection services. The company operates four business segments including civil engineering, which provides services for the construction of highways, bridges, airports, and marine ports; defense systems engineering, which serves the U.S. Department of Defense regarding the development of equipment and special hardware; industrial process engineering, which consists of services for the development of manufacturing equipment and process systems; and transportation engineering, which involves consulting, design, and construction supervision services for transportation facilities. **Common positions include:** Architect; Civil Engineer; Computer Programmer; Construction and Building Inspector; Construction Contractor; Cost Estimator; Designer; Draftsperson; Electrical/Electronics Engineer; Environmental Engineer; Geologist/ Geophysicist; Landscape Architect; Materials Engineer; Mechanical Engineer; Network/Systems Administrator; Planner; Planning Technician; Program Manager; Structural Engineer; Systems Analyst; Technical Writer/Editor; Transportation/ Traffic Specialist; Typist/Word Processor; Urban/Regional Planner. **Educational backgrounds include:** Engineering. **Benefits:** 401(k); Casual Dress - Fridays; Dental Insurance; Employee Discounts; Life Insurance; Medical Insurance; Pension Plan; Tuition Assistance. **Subsidiaries include:** STV Environmental; STV International; STV Architects; STV Inc. **Listed on:** NASDAQ. **Number of employees at this location:** 120. **Number of employees nationwide:** 1,000.
Other U.S. locations:
- 205 West Welsh Drive, Douglasville PA 19518. 610/385-8213.

GEORGE T. SANDERS COMPANY
10201 West 49th Avenue, Wheat Ridge CO 80033. 303/423-9660. **Toll-free phone:** 800/284-0400. **Fax:** 303/420-8737. **Contact:** Thomas C. Tooley, Vice President. **Description:** An independent wholesale distributor of plumbing and heating supplies. George T. Sanders Company operates seven locations in Colorado. **NOTE:** Entry-level positions and part-time jobs are offered. **Common positions include:** Accountant; Administrative Assistant; Administrative Manager; Branch Manager; Buyer; Claim Rep.; Clerical Supervisor; Computer Operator; Computer Programmer; Computer Technician; Credit Manager; Customer Service Rep.; Database Manager; Driver; General Manager; Human Resources Manager; Marketing Manager; MIS Specialist; Operations Manager; Public Relations Specialist; Purchasing Agent/ Manager; Sales Rep.; Secretary; Systems Manager; Transportation/Traffic Specialist; Typist/Word Processor. **Benefits:** Casual Dress - Fridays; Disability Coverage; Employee Discounts; Job Sharing; Life Insurance; Medical Insurance; Profit Sharing; Public Transit Available; Sick Days (1 - 5). **Office hours:** Monday - Friday, 7:00 a.m. - 5:00 p.m. **Corporate headquarters location:** This Location. **Listed on:** Privately held. **President:** Gary T. Sanders. **Purchasing Manager:** Kirk Anderson.

SARGENT & LUNDY
55 East Monroe Street, Chicago IL 60603. 312/269-2000. **Fax:** 312/269-2617. **Contact:** Carol Talaronek, Employee Relations Division. **E-mail address:** carol.talaronek@slchicago.infonet.com.

World Wide Web address: http://www.sargentlundy.com. **Description:** Provides a broad range of engineering services. **NOTE:** Entry-level positions are offered. **Common positions include:** Civil Engineer; Design Engineer; Draftsperson; Electrical/Electronics Engineer; Mechanical Engineer. **Educational backgrounds include:** Engineering. **Benefits:** 401(k); Dental Insurance; Disability Coverage; Life Insurance; Medical Insurance; Pension Plan; Relocation Assistance; Savings Plan; Tuition Assistance. **Corporate headquarters location:** This Location. **Other U.S. locations:** Wilmington DE.

SASAKI ASSOCIATES, INC.
64 Pleasant Street, Watertown MA 02472. 617/926-3300. **Contact:** Human Resources. **World Wide Web address:** http://www.sasaki.com. **Description:** Offers architectural design and planning services including civil engineering, graphic design, interior design, and landscape architecture. Founded in 1953. **Common positions include:** Architect; Civil Engineer; Designer; Draftsperson; Graphic Designer; Interior Designer; Landscape Architect; Planner. **Educational backgrounds include:** Architecture; Art/Design; Engineering; Landscape Architecture. **Benefits:** 401(k); Daycare Assistance; Dental Insurance; Disability Coverage; Medical Insurance; Profit Sharing; Tuition Assistance. **Corporate headquarters location:** This Location. **Other U.S. locations:** San Francisco CA; Dallas TX. **Number of employees at this location:** 155. **Number of employees nationwide:** 200.

SCOTTY'S, INC.
5300 North Recker Highway, Winter Haven FL 33880. 941/299-1111. **Contact:** Human Resources. **World Wide Web address:** http://www.scottys.com. **Description:** A wholesale construction supply company. **Corporate headquarters location:** This Location.

SERVIDYNE SYSTEMS, INC.
P.O. Box 93846, Atlanta GA 30377. 404/352-2050. **Fax:** 404/352-2827. **Contact:** Corporate Recruiter. **World Wide Web address:** http://www.servidyne.com. **Description:** Provides facilities performance management consulting. Servidyne Systems utilizes systematic engineering processes to prevent and solve building operations problems in order to enhance energy efficiency and labor productivity. **NOTE:** Entry-level positions are offered. **Common positions include:** Account Manager; Database Manager; Mechanical Engineer; Network/Systems Administrator; Sales Engineer. **Educational backgrounds include:** Computer Science; Engineering. **Benefits:** 401(k); Casual Dress - Fridays; Dental Insurance; Disability Coverage; Life Insurance; Medical Insurance. **Corporate headquarters location:** This Location. **Other U.S. locations:** Baton Rouge LA. **Listed on:** Privately held. **Number of employees at this location:** 30.

SLANT/FIN CORPORATION
100 Forest Drive, Greenvale NY 11548. 516/484-2600. **Contact:** Edward F. Sliwinski, Personnel Manager. **Description:** Engaged in the manufacture and sale of heating and cooling equipment for both domestic and foreign markets. **NOTE:** Edward F. Sliwinski is the Personnel Manager for the factory. Contact the company regarding employment in other departments. **Corporate headquarters location:** This Location.

SLATTERY SKANSKA INC.
16-16 Whitestone Expressway, Whitestone NY 11357. 718/767-2600. **Contact:** Larry Bolyard, Director of Human Resources. **E-mail address:**

larry.bolyard@slatteryny.com. **World Wide Web address:** http://www.slatteryskanska.com. **Description:** A heavy construction firm engaged in large-scale projects such as mass transit, sewage treatment plants, highways, bridges, and tunnels. **Common positions include:** Accountant/Auditor; Civil Engineer; Cost Estimator; Draftsperson; Environmental Engineer; Mechanical Engineer; Structural Engineer. **Educational backgrounds include:** Accounting; Business Administration; Engineering. **Benefits:** 401(k); Bonus Award/Plan; Dental Insurance; Disability Coverage; Life Insurance; Medical Insurance; Pension Plan. **Office hours:** Monday - Friday, 8:00 a.m. - 4:30 p.m. **Corporate headquarters location:** This Location. **Parent company:** Skanska USA. **Listed on:** Privately held. **Number of employees at this location:** 1,000.

SLETTEN CONSTRUCTION COMPANY
1000 25th Street North, Great Falls MT 59401. 406/761-7920. **Fax:** 406/761-0923. **Contact:** Fred Dahlman, Personnel Director. **World Wide Web address:** http://www.sletten-inc.com. **Description:** Sletten Construction Company is a general construction contractor with operations in bridge, dam, medical center, light and heavy industrial, and multi-unit housing construction. Sletten Construction is licensed to perform construction in Montana, Wyoming, Washington, Idaho, Nevada, Oregon, California, Arizona, Utah, North and South Dakota, and Colorado. **Common positions include:** Construction Contractor; Cost Estimator. **Educational backgrounds include:** Engineering. **Benefits:** 401(k); Dental Insurance; Disability Coverage; Life Insurance; Medical Insurance; Profit Sharing. **Special programs:** Internships. **Corporate headquarters location:** This Location. **Other U.S. locations:** Phoenix AZ; Las Vegas NV; Sheridan WY. **Subsidiaries include:** Westates Construction Company. **Number of employees at this location:** 30. **Number of employees nationwide:** 350.

WILLIAM A. SMITH CONSTRUCTION COMPANY, INC.
6060 Armour Drive, Houston TX 77020. 713/673-6208. **Contact:** Dan Burg, Controller. **Description:** A railroad construction contractor. **Corporate headquarters location:** This Location. **Listed on:** Privately held.

GEORGE SOLLITT CONSTRUCTION CO.
790 North Central, Wood Dale IL 60191. 630/860-7333. **Fax:** 630/860-7347. **Contact:** Howard Strong, Vice President of Operations. **Description:** A leading general contractor/construction management firm. Clients include hospitals, schools, and major corporations. Founded in 1838. **NOTE:** Entry-level positions are offered. **Common positions include:** Construction Contractor; Cost Estimator. **Educational backgrounds include:** Construction. **Benefits:** ESOP; Medical Insurance; Profit Sharing. **Special programs:** Training. **Corporate headquarters location:** This Location. **Annual sales/revenues:** $51 - $100 million. **Number of employees at this location:** 150.

SOUTHERN INVESTORS SERVICE CO.
2727 North Loop West, Suite 200, Houston TX 77008. 713/869-7800. **Contact:** Human Resources. **Description:** Offers commercial construction, real estate development, distribution and installation of construction products, and savings and loan services. **Corporate headquarters location:** This Location.

SPAWGLASS CONSTRUCTION INC.
13603 Westland East Boulevard, Houston TX 77041. 281/970-5300. **Contact:** Human Resources.

World Wide Web address: http://www.spawglass.com. **Description:** A general construction contractor. **Common positions include:** Civil Engineer; Computer Programmer; Electrical/Electronics Engineer; Industrial Engineer; Mechanical Engineer; Systems Analyst. **Educational backgrounds include:** Accounting; Business Administration; Engineering; Finance. **Benefits:** Dental Insurance; Disability Coverage; Life Insurance; Medical Insurance. **Corporate headquarters location:** This Location.

STROBER ORGANIZATION, INC.
Pier 3, Furman Street, Brooklyn NY 11201. 718/832-1212. **Fax:** 718/246-3080. **Contact:** Human Resources. **Description:** Supplies building materials to professional building contractors in the residential, commercial, and renovation construction markets. The company operates 10 building centers across four states, offering a broad selection of gypsum wallboard and other drywall products, lumber, roofing, insulation and acoustical materials, plywood, siding products, metal specialties, hardware and tools, waterproofing, masonry, and steel decking products. The building centers also offer a full spectrum of millwork. **Corporate headquarters location:** This Location.

SVERDRUP CRSS
DIVISION OF JACOBS FACILITIES INC.
400 South Fourth Street, St. Louis MO 63102. 314/552-8025. **Fax:** 314/552-8289. **Contact:** Theresa Czolgosz, Recruiting Manager. **E-mail address:** czolgotb@sverdrup.com. **World Wide Web address:** http://www.sverdrup.com. **Description:** An engineering, architectural, and construction firm that provides consulting services, design services, construction management, and construction services. **NOTE:** Entry-level positions are offered. **Common positions include:** Architect; Design Engineer; Draftsperson; Electrical/Electronics Engineer; Human Resources Manager; Landscape Architect; Mechanical Engineer; Project Manager. **Educational backgrounds include:** Engineering. **Benefits:** 401(k); Casual Dress - Fridays; Dental Insurance; Disability Coverage; Life Insurance; Medical Insurance. **Special programs:** Internships; Summer Jobs. **Corporate headquarters location:** Pasadena CA. **Other U.S. locations:** Costa Mesa CA; Orlando FL; Chicago IL; Arlington VA. **International locations:** Worldwide. **Parent company:** Jacobs Engineering. **Listed on:** New York Stock Exchange. **Annual sales/revenues:** More than $100 million. **Number of employees at this location:** 580.

SWINERTON AND WALBERG BUILDERS
580 California Street, 12th Floor, San Francisco CA 94104. 415/984-1322. **Fax:** 415/984-1306. **Contact:** Dave Ferretti, Director of Employment and Staffing. **Description:** A general construction firm that specializes in consulting, value management, and conceptual design. The company's expertise lies in the assisted living, health care, renovation/restoration, tenant improvement, and transportation markets. **Common positions include:** Accountant/Auditor; Administrative Manager; Civil Engineer; Computer Programmer; Cost Estimator; Mechanical Engineer; Quality Control Supervisor; Systems Analyst. **Educational backgrounds include:** Accounting; Business Administration; Liberal Arts; Marketing. **Special programs:** Internships. **Corporate headquarters location:** This Location. **Other U.S. locations:** Tucson AZ; Los Angeles CA; Denver CO; Portland OR. **Listed on:** Privately held. **Number of employees at this location:** 100. **Number of employees nationwide:** 500.

TD INDUSTRIES, INC.
P.O. Box 819060, Dallas TX 75381-9060. 972/888-9505. **Physical address:** 13850 Diplomat Drive, Dallas TX 75234. **Fax:** 972/888-9507. **Contact:** Ms. Jessie McCain, Vice President of Administration. **E-mail address:** jessie.mccain@tdindustries.com. **World Wide Web address:** http://www.tdindustries.com. **Description:** A national construction and service company that designs, installs, and repairs HVAC, plumbing, high-purity process piping, and energy management systems in commercial and industrial markets. Founded in 1946. **NOTE:** Entry-level positions are offered. **Common positions include:** Electrical/Electronics Engineer; Mechanical Engineer; Project Manager. **Educational backgrounds include:** Engineering. **Benefits:** Tuition Assistance; Vacation Days (10 - 20). **Special programs:** Internships; Apprenticeships; Co-ops; Summer Jobs. **Corporate headquarters location:** This Location. **Other U.S. locations:** Houston TX; San Antonio TX. **Listed on:** Privately held. **CEO:** Jack Lowe. **Annual sales/revenues:** More than $100 million. **Number of employees at this location:** 800. **Number of employees nationwide:** 1,150.

TPI CORPORATION
P.O. Box 4973, Johnson City TN 37602-4973. 423/477-4131. **Contact:** Margie Bowling, Director of Human Resources. **World Wide Web address:** http://www.tpicorp.com. **Description:** Manufactures electric heating and air ventilation products. **Common positions include:** Accountant/Auditor; Blue-Collar Worker Supervisor; Buyer; Credit Manager; Customer Service Rep.; Draftsperson; Electrical/Electronics Engineer; Electrician; Human Resources Manager; Industrial Engineer; Industrial Production Manager; Manufacturer's/Wholesaler's Sales Rep.; Mechanical Engineer; Purchasing Agent/Manager; Quality Control Supervisor. **Educational backgrounds include:** Business Administration; Engineering. **Benefits:** 401(k); Disability Coverage; Life Insurance. **Corporate headquarters location:** This Location. **Other U.S. locations:** Nationwide. **Subsidiaries include:** Columbus Electric; Fostoria Industries. **Listed on:** Privately held. **Number of employees at this location:** 425.

TARLTON CORPORATION
5500 West Park Avenue, St. Louis MO 63110. 314/647-6000. **Contact:** Patricia Allers, Personnel Manager. **World Wide Web address:** http://www.tarltoncorp.com. **Description:** A general contractor and construction company. **Common positions include:** Accountant/Auditor; Civil Engineer; Human Service Worker; Mechanical Engineer. **Educational backgrounds include:** Accounting; Engineering. **Benefits:** 401(k); Dental Insurance; Disability Coverage; Life Insurance; Medical Insurance; Profit Sharing; Tuition Assistance. **Special programs:** Internships. **Corporate headquarters location:** This Location. **Listed on:** Privately held. **Number of employees at this location:** 45.

TATE ACCESS FLOORS, INC.
7510 Montevideo Road, Jessup MD 20794. 410/799-4200. **Contact:** Human Resources. **Description:** Manufactures access flooring and accessories. **Common positions include:** Accountant; Blue-Collar Worker Supervisor; Computer Programmer; Customer Service Rep.; Department Manager; Draftsperson; Electrical/Electronics Engineer; Human Resources Manager; Industrial Engineer; Marketing Specialist; Mechanical Engineer; Operations/Production Manager; Quality Control Supervisor. **Educational backgrounds include:** Accounting; Business

TESTWELL LABORATORIES, INC.
47 Hudson Street, Ossining NY 10562. 914/762-9000. **Fax:** 914/762-9638. **Contact:** Operations/Personnel Director. **World Wide Web address:** http://www.testwelllabs.com. **Description:** Provides construction materials and environmental testing, inspection, and construction services for the construction, environmental, and real estate industries. **Common positions include:** Chemical Engineer; Chemist; Civil Engineer; Clerical Supervisor; Geologist/Geophysicist; Services Sales Representative; Structural Engineer. **Educational backgrounds include:** Accounting; Biology; Chemistry; Economics; Engineering; Finance; Mathematics; Physics. **Benefits:** Dental Insurance; Disability Coverage; Medical Insurance; Profit Sharing. **Corporate headquarters location:** This Location. **Other U.S. locations:** Miami FL; Mays Landing NJ; Albany NY. **Listed on:** Privately held. **Number of employees at this location:** 90. **Number of employees nationwide:** 400.

THERMA-TRU CORPORATION
P.O. Box 8780, Maumee OH 43537. 419/891-7400. **Contact:** Human Resources. **World Wide Web address:** http://www.thermatru.com. **Description:** A leading manufacturer of fiberglass and steel doors. **Corporate headquarters location:** This Location.

R&D THIEL INC.
2340 Newburg Road, Belvidere IL 61008. 815/544-1699. **Contact:** Human Resources. **World Wide Web address:** http://www.rdthiel.com. **Description:** Provides a variety of construction services ranging from carpentry to completed residential housing. **Corporate headquarters location:** This Location.

THORPE CORPORATION
6833 Kirbyville Street, Houston TX 77033. 713/644-1247. **Fax:** 713/644-3011. **Contact:** Human Resources. **Description:** An engineering, construction, and refractory company. **NOTE:** Entry-level positions are offered. **Common positions include:** Branch Manager; Buyer; Computer Programmer; Construction Contractor; Cost Estimator; Design Engineer; Designer; Draftsperson; Human Resources Manager; Mechanical Engineer; Purchasing Agent/Manager. **Educational backgrounds include:** Accounting; Business Administration; Engineering; Finance; Industrial Technology; Marketing; Mathematics. **Benefits:** 401(k); Dental Insurance; Disability Coverage; Life Insurance; Medical Insurance; Pension Plan; Profit Sharing; Tuition Assistance. **Corporate headquarters location:** This Location. **Other area locations:** Beaumont TX; Dallas TX. **Other U.S. locations:** Gonzales LA. **Subsidiaries include:** J.T. Thorpe (also at this location); Leacon-Sunbelt, Inc.; Thorpe Products. **Listed on:** Privately held. **Annual sales/revenues:** $21 - $50 million. **Number of employees at this location:** 90. **Number of employees nationwide:** 150.

3D/INTERNATIONAL
1900 West Loop South, Suite 600, Houston TX 77027. 713/871-7000. **Contact:** Personnel. **World Wide Web address:** http://www.3di.com. **Description:** An architectural and interior design firm. The company also provides construction management, engineering, environmental consulting, and program management services.

Common positions include: Accountant/Auditor; Architect; Civil Engineer; Computer Programmer; Draftsperson; Electrical/Electronics Engineer; Interior Designer; Mechanical Engineer. **Educational backgrounds include:** Accounting; Art/Design; Engineering. **Benefits:** Dental Insurance; Disability Coverage; Life Insurance; Medical Insurance; Pension Plan; Profit Sharing. **Corporate headquarters location:** This Location.

TIDEWATER CONSTRUCTION CORP.
P.O. Box 57, Norfolk VA 23501. 757/420-4140. **Fax:** 757/420-3551. **World Wide Web address:** http://www.tidewater-construction.com. **Contact:** Paul Rose, Vice President of Human Resources & Administration. **Description:** A heavy industrial, highway, and bridge contractor with primary operations in the Southeast. **Common positions include:** Account Manager; Accountant; Blue-Collar Worker Supervisor; Chief Financial Officer; Civil Engineer; Computer Programmer; Construction Contractor; Controller; Cost Estimator; Human Resources Manager. **Educational backgrounds include:** Accounting; Engineering. **Benefits:** 401(k); Dental Insurance; Disability Coverage; Life Insurance; Medical Insurance; Pension Plan; Profit Sharing. **Corporate headquarters location:** This Location. **Parent company:** Hanson, plc. **Listed on:** Privately held. **Number of employees at this location:** 90. **Number of employees nationwide:** 600.

TOLL BROTHERS, INC.
3103 Philmont Avenue, Huntingdon Valley PA 19006. 215/938-8000. **Fax:** 215/938-8291. **Contact:** Jay Lehman, Recruiting Specialist. **E-mail address:** recruiting@tollbrothersinc.com. **World Wide Web address:** http://www.tollbrothers.com. **Description:** One of the nation's leading builders of luxury homes. Founded in 1967. **Common positions include:** Accountant; Administrative Assistant; Applications Engineer; Architect; Attorney; Computer Support Technician; Computer Technician; Construction Contractor; Draftsperson; Financial Analyst; Graphic Artist; Graphic Designer; Insurance Agent/Broker; Management Trainee; MIS Specialist; Network/Systems Administrator; Sales Manager; Sales Rep.; Secretary; Systems Analyst; Systems Manager; Typist/Word Processor; Underwriter/Assistant Underwriter. **Educational backgrounds include:** Accounting; Business Administration; Construction; MCSE; Microsoft Word; Novell; Real Estate; Spreadsheets. **Benefits:** 401(k); Casual Dress - Fridays; Dental Insurance; Disability Coverage; Employee Discounts; Life Insurance; Medical Insurance; Profit Sharing; Stock Purchase; Tuition Assistance. **Corporate headquarters location:** This Location. **Other U.S. locations:** Nationwide. **Subsidiaries include:** Coleman Homes; Geoffrey Edmonds & Associates. **Listed on:** New York Stock Exchange. **Stock exchange symbol:** TOL. **Number of employees at this location:** 200. **Number of employees nationwide:** 2,000.

TOWN & COUNTRY ELECTRIC INC.
2662 American Drive, Appleton WI 54915. 920/738-1500. **Toll-free phone:** 800/677-1506. **Fax:** 920/738-8984. **Contact:** Human Resources. **World Wide Web address:** http://www.tandcelec.com. **Description:** A commercial and industrial electrical contractor. **Common positions include:** Cost Estimator; Electrician. **Benefits:** 401(k); Dental Insurance; Disability Coverage; Life Insurance; Medical Insurance; Tuition Assistance. **Corporate headquarters location:** This Location. **Listed on:** NASDAQ. **Annual sales/revenues:** $21 - $50 million. **Number of employees nationwide:** 600.

TRANE COMPANY
101 William White Boulevard, Pueblo CO 81001. 719/585-3800. **Contact:** Paul Read, Manager of Human Resources. **World Wide Web address:** http://www.trane.com. **Description:** Develops, manufactures, and sells air conditioning equipment. **Corporate headquarters location:** La Crosse WI.

TRI-PHASE AUTOMATION, INC.
West 232 North 2885 Roundy Circle East, Suite 400, Pewaukee WI 53072. 262/542-0650. **Fax:** 262/542-0710. **Contact:** Human Resources. **World Wide Web address:** http://www.tri-phase.com. **Description:** A distributor of mechanical engineering products. **Corporate headquarters location:** This Location.

TURNER CORPORATION
375 Hudson Street, New York NY 10014. 212/229-6000. **Contact:** Human Resources. **World Wide Web address:** http://www.turnerconstruction.com. **Description:** A holding company involved in construction, general building, contract management, and real estate development. **Corporate headquarters location:** This Location. **Subsidiaries include:** Turner Construction Company; Turner Medical Building Services. **Listed on:** New York Stock Exchange.

TURNER, COLLIE & BRADEN, INC.
P.O. Box 130089, Houston TX 77219. 713/780-4100. **Fax:** 713/784-1546. **Contact:** Todd Davis, Human Resources Specialist. **E-mail address:** tcbhr@tcbhou.com. **World Wide Web address:** http://www.tcandb.com. **Description:** A consulting firm providing technical services including engineering and design for the transportation, public works, environmental, and land development industries; and engineering economics and feasibility studies. Founded in 1946. **NOTE:** Entry-level positions and part-time jobs are offered. **Common positions include:** Civil Engineer; Environmental Engineer; Geologist/Geophysicist; Transportation/Traffic Specialist. **Educational backgrounds include:** Engineering. **Benefits:** 401(k); Casual Dress - Fridays; Dental Insurance; Disability Coverage; Life Insurance; Medical Insurance; Relocation Assistance; Tuition Assistance. **Special programs:** Internships; Co-ops; Summer Jobs. **Office hours:** Monday - Friday, 7:30 a.m. - 4:30 p.m. **Corporate headquarters location:** This Location. **Other area locations:** Austin TX; Dallas TX; San Antonio TX. **Other U.S. locations:** Denver CO. **Parent company:** AECOM. **Listed on:** Privately held. **President/CEO/Owner:** Jim Royer. **Number of employees at this location:** 275. **Number of employees nationwide:** 6,000.

U.S. ENGINEERING COMPANY
P.O. Box 905, Loveland CO 80539-0905. 970/669-1666. **Physical address:** 729 SE Eighth Street, Loveland CO. **Contact:** Human Resources Department. **Description:** A contracting company that installs heating, air conditioning, piping, and sprinkler systems for businesses. **Educational backgrounds include:** Engineering. **Benefits:** 401(k); Casual Dress - Fridays; Dental Insurance; Disability Coverage; Flexible Benefits; Life Insurance; Medical Insurance; Pension Plan; Profit Sharing; Sick Days (1 - 5); Tuition Assistance; Vacation Days (6 - 10). **Corporate headquarters location:** Kansas City MO. **Listed on:** Privately held. **Annual sales/revenues:** More than $100 million. **Number of employees at this location:** 300. **Number of employees nationwide:** 600.

U.S. HOME CORPORATION
P.O. Box 2863, Houston TX 77252-2863. 713/877-2311. **Physical address:** 10707 Clay Road, Houston

TX 77041. **Contact:** Human Resources. **World Wide Web address:** http://www.ushome.com. **Description:** Builds and sells single-family houses. **Number of employees at this location:** 90. **Number of employees nationwide:** 2,500.

U.S. INDUSTRIES
101 Wood Avenue, Iselin NJ 08830. 732/767-0700. **Contact:** Human Resources. **Description:** A holding company for four categories of manufacturing companies: bath and plumbing products, hardware and non-electric tools, commercial and residential lighting, and a variety of consumer products ranging from vacuum cleaners to toys. **Corporate headquarters location:** This Location. **Subsidiaries include:** Jacuzzi; Lighting Corporation of America; Selkirk; Spaulding.

UNDERWRITERS LABORATORIES INC.
333 Pfingsten Road, Northbrook IL 60062. 847/272-8800. **Fax:** 847/509-6300. **Contact:** Charmaine Williams, Human Resources Supervisor. **E-mail address:** williamsc@ul.com. **World Wide Web address:** http://www.ul.com. **Description:** An independent, nonprofit corporation established to help reduce or prevent bodily injury, loss of life, and property damage. Engineering functions are divided between six departments: Electrical Department; Burglary Protection and Signaling Department; Casualty and Chemical Hazards Department; Fire Protection Department; Heating, Air Conditioning, and Refrigeration Department; and Marine Department. The company also provides factory inspection services through offices in the United States and 54 other countries. **Common positions include:** Electrical/Electronics Engineer; Mechanical Engineer; MIS Specialist. **Educational backgrounds include:** Computer Science; Engineering. **Benefits:** 401(k); Dental Insurance; Disability Coverage; Employee Discounts; Life Insurance; Medical Insurance; Pension Plan; Public Transit Available; Tuition Assistance. **Corporate headquarters location:** This Location. **Other U.S. locations:** CA; NC; NY; WA. **Listed on:** Privately held. **Number of employees at this location:** 1,800. **Number of employees worldwide:** 4,100.

UNITED DOMINION INDUSTRIES, INC.
2300 One First Union Center, Charlotte NC 28202-6039. 704/347-6800. **Contact:** Human Resources. **World Wide Web address:** http://www.uniteddominion.com. **Description:** This location houses the executive offices. Overall, the company operates in three segments: industrial products, building products, and engineering. The industrial products segment produces sanitary pumps for the food and industrial processing industries; submersible water and petroleum pumps; petroleum leak detection equipment; compacting equipment for soil, asphalt, and refuse applications; cooling towers for power generation, industrial, and heating and cooling applications; cast-iron boilers and electrical resistance heaters for industrial and residential customers; industrial machinery and process equipment; and aerospace components. The building products segment manufactures complementary products that encompass architectural metal roofing; side-hinged and rolling steel doors; residential garage doors; pre-engineered metal buildings; loading dock systems and related equipment; and wall, roof, floor, and window systems. It also provides general and specialized contractor services. The engineering segment is comprised of the Litwin companies which provide worldwide engineering and construction services for the refining and petrochemical, polymers, specialty chemicals, and environmental control markets. Litwin also provides advanced process control and instrumentation capabilities. **Corporate**

headquarters location: This Location. **Listed on:** New York Stock Exchange. **Number of employees nationwide:** 12,000.

UNITED McGILL CORPORATION
One Mission Park, Groveport OH 43125. 614/836-9981. **Fax:** 614/836-9843. **Contact:** Kathleen Cauley, Personnel Services Director. **E-mail address:** unitedmcgillpers@compuserve.com. **World Wide Web address:** http://www.unitedmcgill.com. **Description:** An engineering, manufacturing, and construction firm. Products include spiral and rectangular ducts and fittings for HVAC, acoustical equipment, vacuum drying systems, pressure vessels, and air pollution control systems. Founded in 1951. **NOTE:** Entry-level positions are offered. **Common positions include:** Draftsperson; Industrial Engineer; Industrial Production Manager; Manufacturing Engineer; Mechanical Engineer; Sales Manager; Secretary. **Educational backgrounds include:** Business Administration; Engineering. **Benefits:** 401(k); Dental Insurance; Disability Coverage; Life Insurance; Medical Insurance; Relocation Assistance; Tuition Assistance. **Special programs:** Training. **Office hours:** Monday - Friday, 8:00 a.m. - 5:00 p.m. **Corporate headquarters location:** This Location. **Other U.S. locations:** Nationwide. **Annual sales/revenues:** $51 - $100 million. **Number of employees nationwide:** 600.

UNIVERSAL ENGINEERING CORPORATION
100 Boylston Street, Suite 500, Boston MA 02116. 617/542-8216. **Fax:** 617/423-0373. **Contact:** Human Resources Director. **Description:** A civil engineering firm. **Common positions include:** Civil Engineer; Controller; Draftsperson; Environmental Engineer. **Educational backgrounds include:** Engineering. **Benefits:** 401(k); Casual Dress - Fridays; Disability Coverage; Life Insurance; Medical Insurance; Sick Days (6 - 10); Tuition Assistance; Vacation Days (6 - 10). **Office hours:** Monday - Friday, 8:00 a.m. - 5:00 p.m. **Corporate headquarters location:** This Location. **Other U.S. locations:** RI. **Parent company:** Davis and Floyd. **Listed on:** Privately held. **Annual sales/revenues:** Less than $5 million. **Number of employees at this location:** 15. **Number of employees nationwide:** 20.

UNIVERSAL SYSTEMS
1401 East Stewart Avenue, Flint MI 48505-3698. 810/785-7970. **Contact:** Human Resources. **World Wide Web address:** http://www.universalsys.com. **Description:** Provides industrial control engineering and industrial electrical construction nationwide. **Common positions include:** Electrical/Electronics Engineer. **Benefits:** Dental Insurance; Life Insurance; Medical Insurance; Pension Plan; Savings Plan. **Corporate headquarters location:** This Location.

UTILX CORPORATION
P.O. Box 97009, Kent WA 98064-9709. 253/395-0200. **Fax:** 253/395-1040. **Contact:** Personnel Department. **Description:** Provides installation and maintenance services for underground utilities including electricity, water, gas, and telephone. UTILX's technologies include the FlowMole guided drilling system and the CableCure service for injecting silicon fluids into utility cables to repair damage from water. The company's services are marketed domestically while their products are sold primarily in international markets. **Corporate headquarters location:** This Location. **Subsidiaries include:** Flow Mole Limited (UK). **Listed on:** NASDAQ. **Number of employees at this location:** 100. **Number of employees nationwide:** 500.

VP BUILDINGS
3200 Players Club Circle, Memphis TN 38125. 901/748-8000. **Contact:** Human Resources. **World Wide Web address:** http://www.vp.com. **Description:** Designs and manufactures pre-engineered metal building systems. **Common positions include:** Civil Engineer; Draftsperson. **Educational backgrounds include:** Engineering. **Benefits:** Dental Insurance; Disability Coverage; Life Insurance; Medical Insurance; Pension Plan; Savings Plan; Tuition Assistance. **Corporate headquarters location:** This Location. **Other U.S. locations:** Pine Bluff AR; Turlock CA; St. Joseph MO; Kernersville NC; Evansville WI. **Parent company:** United Dominion Industries. **Listed on:** New York Stock Exchange. **Number of employees nationwide:** 10,300.

VANGUARD RESEARCH, INC.
1330 Inverness Drive, Suite 450, Colorado Springs CO 80910. 719/596-1174. **Contact:** Lee Morgan, General Manager. **World Wide Web address:** http://www.vriffx.com. **Description:** Provides engineering and technical support services. **Common positions include:** Aerospace Engineer; Communications Engineer; Computer Engineer; Computer Programmer; Computer Scientist; Database Manager; General Manager; Management Analyst/Consultant; Mathematician; Network/Systems Administrator; Operations Research Analyst; Secretary; Software Engineer; Systems Analyst; Systems Engineer; Systems Manager; Test Engineer. **Educational backgrounds include:** Business Administration; Computer Science; Engineering; Mathematics. **Benefits:** 401(k); Dental Insurance; Life Insurance; Medical Insurance; Sick Days (11+); Tuition Assistance; Vacation Days (11 - 15). **Corporate headquarters location:** Fairfax VA. **Other U.S. locations:** Omaha NE. **President/CEO:** Mel Chaskin. **Facilities Manager:** Lee Morgan. **Number of employees at this location:** 30.

THE WALDINGER CORPORATION
P.O. Box 1612, Des Moines IA 50306. 515/284-1911. **Contact:** Personnel. **World Wide Web address:** http://www.waldinger.com. **Description:** Engaged in mechanical and sheet metal construction. The company also designs, manufactures, and installs HVAC and plumbing systems. **Common positions include:** Accountant; Computer Programmer; Draftsperson; Mechanical Engineer. **Educational backgrounds include:** Engineering. **Benefits:** 401(k); Disability Coverage; Flexible Benefits; Life Insurance; Medical Insurance; Profit Sharing; Savings Plan; Tuition Assistance. **Office hours:** Monday - Friday, 8:00 a.m. - 5:00 p.m. **Corporate headquarters location:** This Location.

WALK, HAYDEL & ASSOCIATES, INC.
600 Carondelet Street, New Orleans LA 70130. 504/586-8111. **Fax:** 504/522-0554. **Contact:** Maria Babb, Human Resources Associate. **Description:** A fully-integrated engineering and architectural organization that specializes in the project management, design, and construction management of industrial, private, and government facilities. Walk, Haydel & Associates also provides process and environmental engineering, architectural design, and total support services. **Corporate headquarters location:** This Location. **Other U.S. locations:** Mobile AL; Baton Rouge LA; Lake Charles LA. **International locations:** Saudi Arabia. **Number of employees at this location:** 400.

WALT DISNEY IMAGINEERING
200 Celebration Place, Celebration FL 34747. 407/566-1900. **Fax:** 407/566-4220. **Contact:** Professional Staffing. **World Wide Web address:** http://www.disney.com. **Description:** Responsible for the design, development, and construction of The Walt Disney Company's premiere attractions, resorts, and entertainment venues. **NOTE:** Entry-level positions are offered. **Company slogan:** We make the magic! **Common positions include:** Accountant; Administrative Assistant; Architect; Civil Engineer; Computer Engineer; Computer Programmer; Computer Support Technician; Computer Technician; Cost Estimator; Design Engineer; Electrical/Electronics Engineer; Financial Analyst; Mechanical Engineer; MIS Specialist; Network/Systems Administrator; Secretary; Software Engineer; Systems Analyst. **Educational backgrounds include:** Accounting; Art/Design; Business Administration; Computer Science; Engineering; Finance; HTML; Java; MCSE; Microsoft Word; Novell; Software Tech. Support. **Benefits:** 401(k); Casual Dress - Daily; Dental Insurance; Disability Coverage; Employee Discounts; Life Insurance; Medical Insurance; Pension Plan; Sick Days; Tuition Assistance; Vacation Days (6 - 10). **Special programs:** Internships. **Corporate headquarters location:** Glendale CA. **Other U.S. locations:** Orlando FL. **Parent company:** The Walt Disney Company. **Listed on:** New York Stock Exchange. **Number of employees at this location:** 400. **Number of employees nationwide:** 50,000. **Number of employees worldwide:** 60,000.

WAUSAU HOMES, INC.
P.O. Box 8005, Wausau WI 54402. 715/359-7272. **Contact:** Human Resources. **World Wide Web address:** http://www.wausauhomes.com. **Description:** A builder of custom-designed residential homes. **Corporate headquarters location:** This Location. **Number of employees at this location:** 500.

WAXMAN INDUSTRIES, INC.
24460 Aurora Road, Bedford Heights OH 44146. 440/439-1830. **Fax:** 440/439-8678. **Contact:** Personnel Director. **World Wide Web address:** http://www.waxmanind.com. **Description:** One of the largest distributors of plumbing and electrical supplies in the United States and Canada. **Common positions include:** Accountant/Auditor; Computer Programmer; Credit Manager; Customer Service Representative; Manufacturer's/Wholesaler's Sales Rep.; Marketing Specialist; Operations/Production Manager; Purchasing Agent/Manager; Quality Control Supervisor. **Educational backgrounds include:** Accounting; Business Administration; Computer Science; Marketing. **Benefits:** Dental Insurance; Disability Coverage; Life Insurance; Medical Insurance; Profit Sharing; Stock Option. **Corporate headquarters location:** This Location.

WEATHERLY INC.
1100 Spring Street NW, Suite 800, Atlanta GA 30309. 404/873-5030. **Fax:** 404/873-1303. **Contact:** Ms. G.C. Bailey, Executive Assistant. **Description:** Designs, engineers, and constructs chemical process plants. **Common positions include:** Chemical Engineer; Draftsperson; Electrical/Electronics Engineer; Instrument Engineer; Mechanical Engineer. **Educational backgrounds include:** Engineering. **Benefits:** Dental Insurance; Disability Coverage; Life Insurance; Medical Insurance; Tuition Assistance. **Corporate headquarters location:** This Location. **Number of employees at this location:** 30.

WELDING SERVICES, INC.
2225 Skyland Court, Norcross GA 30071. 770/452-0005. **Contact:** Human Resources. **Description:** Provides repair welding at nationwide nuclear and

fossil fuel power plants. **Common positions include:** Construction Contractor; Mechanical Engineer. **Educational backgrounds include:** Construction; Engineering. **Benefits:** Dental Insurance; Disability Coverage; Life Insurance; Medical Insurance; Pension Plan; Profit Sharing; Tuition Assistance. **Corporate headquarters location:** This Location. **Number of employees at this location:** 100.

WELSBACH ELECTRIC CORPORATION
P.O. Box 560252, 111-01 14th Avenue, College Point NY 11356-0252. 718/670-7900. **Contact:** Human Resources. **Description:** An electrical contractor engaged in the installation and maintenance of street lights and traffic signals. **Corporate headquarters location:** This Location. **Parent company:** EMCOR Corporation. **President:** Fred Goodman.

L.E. WENTZ COMPANY
P.O. Box 610, San Carlos CA 94070. 650/592-3950. **Contact:** Bradley W. Wentz, Vice President. **Description:** Provides general construction services. **Common positions include:** Accountant/Auditor; Branch Manager; Construction Contractor; Cost Estimator. **Benefits:** 401(k); Dental Insurance; Disability Coverage; Life Insurance; Medical Insurance; Profit Sharing. **Corporate headquarters location:** This Location. **Other U.S. locations:** Los Angeles CA. **Listed on:** Privately held. **Number of employees at this location:** 30.

WESTMINSTER HOMES
2706 North Church Street, Greensboro NC 27405. 336/375-6200. **Fax:** 336/375-6355. **Contact:** Human Resources Department. **World Wide Web address:** http://www.greensboro.com/westminster. **Description:** A real estate and construction company. Westminster Homes specializes in single-family home development and sales in North Carolina. **Common positions include:** Accountant/Auditor; Computer Programmer; Customer Service Representative; Draftsperson; Human Resources Manager; Manufacturer's/Wholesaler's Sales Rep.; Marketing Specialist; Operations/Production Manager; Purchasing Agent/Manager; Quality Control Supervisor. **Educational backgrounds include:** Accounting; Business Administration; Computer Science; Marketing. **Benefits:** Dental Insurance; Disability Coverage; Employee Discounts; Life Insurance; Medical Insurance; Pension Plan; Profit Sharing; Savings Plan; Stock Option; Tuition Assistance. **Corporate headquarters location:** This Location. **Other U.S. locations:** Cary NC. **Parent company:** Washington Homes, Inc. **Listed on:** New York Stock Exchange. **Number of employees at this location:** 60. **Number of employees nationwide:** 100.

WHITE CONTRACTING COMPANY
4708 South Old Peachtree Road, Suite 100A, Norcross GA 30071-1578. 770/452-8778. **Fax:** 770/613-0501. **Contact:** Barry D. White, Vice President. **World Wide Web address:** http://www.whitecontracting.com. **Description:** A general contracting company specializing in fire damage repairs. Founded in 1960. **NOTE:** Entry-level positions are offered. **Common positions include:** Account Representative; Construction Contractor; Cost Estimator; Marketing Specialist; Sales Representative. **Benefits:** 401(k); Medical Insurance; Profit Sharing. **Special programs:** Internships; Apprenticeships. **Office hours:** Monday - Friday, 7:00 a.m. - 7:00 p.m. **Corporate headquarters location:** This Location. **Listed on:** Privately held. **Annual sales/revenues:** Less than $5 million. **Number of employees at this location:** 15.

WICKES INC.
706 Deerpath Drive, Vernon Hills IL 60061. **Contact:** Human Resources. **World Wide Web address:** http://www.wickes.com. **Description:** One of the largest suppliers of building materials in the United States. Wickes's manufacturing facilities produce prehung door units, window assemblies, roof and floor trusses, and framed wall panels. **Corporate headquarters location:** This Location. **Other U.S. locations:** Denver CO; Elwood IN; Ocean Springs MS; Lomira WI. **Listed on:** NASDAQ. **Stock exchange symbol:** WIKS.

WILLIAMS INDUSTRIES INC.
2849 Meadow View Road, Falls Church VA 22042. 703/560-5196. **Fax:** 703/280-9082. **Contact:** Marianna V. Pastor, Director of Administration. **World Wide Web address:** http://www.wmsi.com. **Description:** A general construction company. Founded in 1970. **NOTE:** Entry-level positions and second and third shifts are offered. **Common positions include:** Accountant/Auditor; Adjuster; Administrative Assistant; Attorney; Civil Engineer; Communications Engineer; Computer Programmer; Construction and Building Inspector; Construction Contractor; Cost Estimator; Customer Service Representative; Draftsperson; Industrial Engineer; Manufacturing Engineer; Production Manager; Project Manager; Quality Assurance Engineer; Secretary. **Educational backgrounds include:** Accounting; Energy. **Benefits:** 401(k); Casual Dress - Daily; Dental Insurance; Employee Discounts; Life Insurance; Medical Insurance; Sick Days; Vacation Days. **Special programs:** Apprenticeships. **Office hours:** Monday - Friday, 8:30 a.m. - 4:30 p.m. **Corporate headquarters location:** This Location. **Subsidiaries include:** Greenway Crane; Piedmont Metal Products; Williams Bridge Co.;Williams Equipment Co.; Williams Steel Erection. **Listed on:** NASDAQ. **Stock exchange symbol:** WMSI. **Number of employees nationwide:** 600.

WILLIARD INC.
375 Highland Avenue, Jenkintown PA 19046. 215/885-5000. **World Wide Web address:** http://www.williard.com. **Contact:** Sue Melia, Human Resources Manager. **Description:** A mechanical/electrical construction firm specializing in HVAC, sheet metal, and water treatment. **Corporate headquarters location:** This Location.

GEORGE H. WILSON, INC.
MECHANICAL CONTRACTORS
P.O. Box 1140, Santa Cruz CA 95061-1140. 831/423-9522. **Contact:** Thomas E. Wilson, Administrative Manager. **Description:** Provides plumbing, heating, air conditioning, and metal fabrication services. **Common positions include:** Industrial Engineer; Mechanical Engineer. **Educational backgrounds include:** Engineering; Liberal Arts. **Benefits:** Dental Insurance; Medical Insurance; Profit Sharing. **Corporate headquarters location:** This Location. **Operations at this facility include:** Administration; Manufacturing.

WINTER CONSTRUCTION COMPANY
1330 Spring Street, Atlanta GA 30309. 404/588-3300. **Fax:** 404/946-6494. **Contact:** Marketing Director. **World Wide Web address:** http://www.wintercompanies.com. **Description:** A general contractor engaged in commercial construction. **Common positions include:** Accountant/Auditor; Blue-Collar Worker Supervisor; Civil Engineer; Computer Programmer; Department Manager; Operations/Production Manager; Quality Control Supervisor. **Educational backgrounds include:** Construction; Engineering; Finance; Marketing; Physics. **Benefits:** Dental Insurance; Disability

Coverage; Life Insurance; Medical Insurance; Tuition Assistance. **Special programs:** Internships. **Corporate headquarters location:** This Location. **Parent company:** The Winter Companies (also at this location).

WRIGHT-PIERCE ENGINEERS
99 Main Street, Topsham ME 04086. 207/725-8721. **World Wide Web address:** http://www.wright-pierce. com. **Contact:** Human Resources. **Description:** A full-service civil and environmental engineering firm. The company specializes in civil and transportation engineering, environmental laboratory services, and water treatment. **Common positions include:** Civil Engineer. **Educational backgrounds include:** Engineering. **Benefits:** 401(k); Dental Insurance; Disability Coverage; Life Insurance; Medical Insurance; Tuition Assistance. **Corporate headquarters location:** This Location. **Number of employees at this location:** 95.

YORK INTERNATIONAL CORPORATION
P.O. Box 1592-36BH, York PA 17405-1592. 717/771-6578. **Contact:** Diane Yerkey, Corporate Employment Recruiter. **World Wide Web address:** http://www.york.com. **Description:** Manufactures a full line of residential, commercial, and industrial air conditioning and refrigeration equipment and systems, heating systems, and food refrigeration systems. **Common positions include:** Accountant/Auditor; Electrical/Electronics Engineer; Mechanical Engineer; MIS Specialist; Software Engineer. **Educational backgrounds include:** Accounting; Business Administration; Computer Science; Economics; Engineering; Finance; Marketing; Mathematics; Physics. **Benefits:** 401(k); Dental Insurance; Disability Coverage; Employee Discounts; Life Insurance; Medical Insurance; Pension Plan; Profit Sharing; Savings Plan. **Special programs:** Internships. **Corporate headquarters location:** This Location. **International locations:** Worldwide. **Subsidiaries include:** York Engineered Systems; York Refrigeration; York Unitary Products. **Listed on:** New York Stock Exchange. **Annual sales/revenues:** More than $100 million. **Number of employees worldwide:** 25,000.

H.B. ZACHRY COMPANY
527 Logwood, San Antonio TX 78221. 210/475-8000. **Fax:** 210/475-8775. **Recorded jobline:** 800/JOB-SUSA. **Contact:** Professional Recruiting. **World Wide Web address:** http://www.zachry.com. **Description:** A construction management company operating through the following seven divisions: Process, Power, Heavy, Maintenance & Service, Commercial, International, and Pipeline. The company primarily builds power plants, highways, and pipelines in the southern United States, as well as in foreign countries. H.B. Zachry Company does not handle residential construction contracts. Founded in 1923. **NOTE:** Entry-level positions are offered. **Common positions include:** Accountant; Administrative Assistant; Civil Engineer; Cost Estimator; Financial Analyst; Industrial Engineer; Management Trainee; Mechanical Engineer; Project Manager; Quality Assurance Engineer; Secretary. **Benefits:** 401(k); Casual Dress - Fridays; Dental Insurance; Disability Coverage; Life Insurance; Medical Insurance; Profit Sharing; Sick Days (6 - 10); Tuition Assistance; Vacation Days (6 - 10). **Special programs:** Summer Jobs. **Corporate headquarters location:** This Location. **Listed on:** Privately held. **Owner:** Bartel Zachry. **Information Systems Manager:** Jerry Wiggins. **Annual sales/revenues:** More than $100 million. **Number of employees nationwide:** 10,000. **Number of employees worldwide:** 14,000.

ZURHEIDE-HERRMANN INC.
4333 Clayton Avenue, St. Louis MO 63110. 314/652-6805. **Contact:** Ronald Bahman, President. **Description:** Provides engineering and architectural services. **Common positions include:** Accountant/Auditor; Architect; Architectural Engineer; Civil Engineer; Electrical/Electronics Engineer; Financial Analyst; Industrial Engineer; Mechanical Engineer. **Educational backgrounds include:** Engineering; Marketing. **Benefits:** 401(k); Life Insurance; Medical Insurance. **Special programs:** Internships. **Corporate headquarters location:** This Location. **Other U.S. locations:** Champaign IL. **Operations at this facility include:** Service. **Number of employees at this location:** 35.

For more information on career opportunities in architecture, construction, and engineering:

Associations

AACE INTERNATIONAL: THE ASSOCIATION FOR ADVANCEMENT OF COST ENGINEERING
209 Prairie Avenue, Suite 100, Morgantown WV 26501. 304/296-8444. Toll-free phone: 800/858-2678. Fax: 304/291-5728. World Wide Web address: http://www.aacei.org. A membership organization which offers *Cost Engineering*, a monthly magazine; employment referral services; technical reference information and assistance; insurance; and a certification program accredited by the Council of Engineering Specialty Boards. Toll-free number provides information on scholarships for undergraduates.

ASM INTERNATIONAL: THE MATERIALS INFORMATION SOCIETY
9639 Kinsman Road, Materials Park OH 44073. 440/338-5151. World Wide Web address: http://www.asm-intl.org. Gathers, processes, and disseminates technical information to foster the understanding and application of engineered materials.

ACOUSTICAL SOCIETY OF AMERICA
2 Huntington Quadrangle, Suite 1NO1, Melville NY 11747. 516/576-2360. Fax: 516/576-2377. E-mail address: asa@aip.org. World Wide Web address: http://asa.aip.org.

AMERICAN ASSOCIATION OF ENGINEERING SOCIETIES
1111 19th Street NW, Suite 403, Washington DC 20036-3690. 202/296-2237. Fax: 202/296-1151. World Wide Web address: http://www.aaes.org. A multidisciplinary organization of professional engineering societies. Publishes reference works, including *Who's Who in Engineering, International Directory of Engineering Societies*, and the *Thesaurus of Engineering and Scientific Terms*, as well as statistical reports from studies conducted by the Engineering Workforce Commission.

AMERICAN CONGRESS ON SURVEYING AND MAPPING
5410 Grosvenor Lane, Suite 100, Bethesda MD 20814. 301/493-0200. Publishes *Cartography and Geographic Information Systems: A Career Guide*, which includes educational and government information.

AMERICAN CONSULTING ENGINEERS COUNCIL
1015 15th Street NW, Suite 802, Washington DC 20005. 202/347-7474. Fax: 202/898-0068. World Wide Web address: http://www.acec.org. A national organization of more than 5,000 member firms.

Offers *Last Word,* a weekly newsletter; *American Consulting Engineer* magazine; life and health insurance programs; books, manuals, video- and audiotapes, and contract documents; conferences and seminars; and voluntary peer reviews.

AMERICAN DESIGN DRAFTING ASSOCIATION
P.O. Box 11937, Columbia SC 29211. 803/771-0008. Fax: 803/771-4272. World Wide Web address: http://www.adda.org.

AMERICAN INSTITUTE OF ARCHITECTS
1735 New York Avenue NW, Washington DC 20006. 202/626-7300. Toll-free phone: 800/365-2724. World Wide Web address: http://www.aiaonline.org.

AMERICAN INSTITUTE OF CONSTRUCTORS
1300 North 17th Street, Suite 830, Arlington VA 22209. 703/812-2021. World Wide Web address: http://www.aicnet.org.

AMERICAN SOCIETY FOR ENGINEERING EDUCATION
1818 N Street NW, Suite 600, Washington DC 20036. 202/331-3500. World Wide Web address: http://www.asee.org. Publishes magazines and journals including the *Journal of Engineering Education.*

AMERICAN SOCIETY OF CIVIL ENGINEERS
1801 Alexander Bell Drive, Reston VA 20191-4400. 703/295-6300. World Wide Web address: http://www.asce.org. A membership organization which offers subscriptions to *Civil Engineering* magazine and *ASCE News,* discounts on various other publications, seminars, video- and audiotapes, specialty conferences, an annual convention, group insurance programs, and pension plans.

AMERICAN SOCIETY OF HEATING, REFRIGERATING AND AIR CONDITIONING ENGINEERS
1791 Tullie Circle NE, Atlanta GA 30329. 404/636-8400. Fax: 404/321-5478. World Wide Web address: http://www.ashrae.org. A society of 50,000 members which offers handbooks, a monthly journal, a monthly newspaper, discounts on other publications, group insurance, continuing education, and registration discounts for meetings, conferences, seminars, and expositions.

AMERICAN SOCIETY OF LANDSCAPE ARCHITECTS
636 Eye Street NW, Washington DC 20001. 202/898-2444. World Wide Web address: http://www.asla.org. Check out the Website's Joblink for listings of employment opportunities.

AMERICAN SOCIETY OF MECHANICAL ENGINEERS
3 Park Avenue, New York NY 10016. 212/591-7722. World Wide Web address: http://www.asme.org. Provides educational materials and scholarships for certified engineers.

AMERICAN SOCIETY OF NAVAL ENGINEERS
1452 Duke Street, Alexandria VA 22314. 703/836-6727. World Wide Web address: http://www.navalengineers.org. Holds symposiums based on technical papers. Publishes a journal and newsletter bimonthly.

AMERICAN SOCIETY OF PLUMBING ENGINEERS
3617 Thousand Oaks Boulevard, Suite 210,

Westlake CA 91362. 805/495-7120. Provides technical and educational information.

AMERICAN SOCIETY OF SAFETY ENGINEERS
1800 East Oakton Street, Des Plaines IL 60018-2187. 847/699-2929. Jobline service available at ext. 243. Fax: 847/768-3434. World Wide Web address: http://www.asse.org. A membership organization offering *Professional Safety,* a monthly journal; educational seminars; technical publications; certification preparation programs; career placement services; and group and liability insurance programs.

ASSOCIATED BUILDERS & CONTRACTORS
1300 North 17th Street, 8th Floor, Rosslyn VA 22209. 703/812-2000. World Wide Web address: http://www.abc.org. Sponsors annual career fair.

ASSOCIATED GENERAL CONTRACTORS OF AMERICA, INC.
333 John Carlyle Street, Suite 200, Alexandria VA 22314. 202/393-2040. World Wide Web address: http://www.agc.org. A full-service construction association of subcontractors, specialty contractors, suppliers, equipment manufacturers, and professional firms. Services include government relations, education and training, jobsite services, legal services, and information services.

THE ENGINEERING CENTER (TEC)
One Walnut Street, Boston MA 02108-3616. 617/227-5551. Contact: Abbie Goodman. World Wide Web address: http://www.engineers.org. An association that provides services for many engineering membership organizations.

ILLUMINATING ENGINEERING SOCIETY OF NORTH AMERICA
120 Wall Street, 17th Floor, New York NY 10005-4001. 212/248-5000. World Wide Web address: http://www.iesna.org. An organization for industry professionals involved in the manufacturing, design, specification, and maintenance of lighting systems. Conference held annually. Offers a Technical Knowledge Examination.

JUNIOR ENGINEERING TECHNICAL SOCIETY
1420 King Street, Suite 405, Alexandria VA 22314-2794. 703/548-JETS. Fax: 703/548-0769. E-mail address: jets@nae.edu. World Wide Web address: http://www.jets.org. A nonprofit, educational society promoting interest in engineering, technology, mathematics, and science. Provides information to high school students and teachers regarding careers in engineering and technology.

NATIONAL ACTION COUNCIL FOR MINORITIES IN ENGINEERING
350 Fifth Avenue, Suite 2212, New York NY 10118. 212/279-2626. World Wide Web address: http://www.nacme.org. Offers scholarship programs for students.

NATIONAL ASSOCIATION OF HOME BUILDERS
1201 15th Street NW, Washington DC 20005. 202/822-0200. World Wide Web address: http://www.nahb.com. A trade association promoting safe and affordable housing. The association provides management services and education for members.

NATIONAL ASSOCIATION OF MINORITY ENGINEERING PROGRAM ADMINISTRATORS, INC.
1133 West Morse Boulevard, Suite 201, Winter

Park FL 32789. 407/647-8839. World Wide Web address: http://www.namepa.org.

NATIONAL ELECTRICAL CONTRACTORS ASSOCIATION
3 Bethesda Metro Center, Suite 1100, Bethesda MD 20814. 301/657-3110. World Wide Web address: http://www.necanet.org. Provides information on hiring and trade shows. The association also publishes a magazine called *Electrical Contractor*.

NATIONAL SOCIETY OF BLACK ENGINEERS
1454 Duke Street, Alexandria VA 22314. 703/549-2207. World Wide Web address: http://www.nsbe.org. A nonprofit organization run by college students. Offers scholarships, editorials, and magazines.

NATIONAL SOCIETY OF PROFESSIONAL ENGINEERS
1420 King Street, Alexandria VA 22314-2794. 703/684-2800. Call 703/684-2830 for scholarship information for students. Fax: 703/836-4875. World Wide Web address: http://www.nspe.org. A society of over 73,000 engineers. Membership includes the monthly magazine *Engineering Times;* continuing education; scholarships and fellowships; discounts on publications; and health and life insurance programs.

SOCIETY OF AMERICAN REGISTERED ARCHITECTS (SARA)
305 East 64th Street, New York NY 10017. 212/759-2007. Toll-free phone: 888/385-7272. World Wide Web address: http://www.sara-national.org.

SOCIETY OF FIRE PROTECTION ENGINEERS
7315 Wisconsin Avenue, Suite 1225W, Bethesda MD 20814. 301/718-2910. Fax: 301/718-2242. World Wide Web address: http://www.sfpe.org. A professional society which offers members reports, newsletters, *Journal of Fire Protecting Engineering*, insurance programs, short courses, symposiums, tutorials, an annual meeting, and engineering seminars.

Directories

DIRECTORY OF ENGINEERING SOCIETIES
American Association of Engineering Societies, 1111 19th Street NW, Suite 403, Washington DC 20036. 202/296-2237. World Wide Web address: http://www.aaes.org. $185.00. Lists other engineering association members, publications, and convention exhibits.

DIRECTORY OF ENGINEERS IN PRIVATE PRACTICE
National Society of Professional Engineers, 1420 King Street, Alexandria VA 22314-2794. 703/684-2800. World Wide Web address: http://www.nspe.org. $50.00. Lists members and companies.

Magazines

THE CAREER ENGINEER
National Society of Black Engineers, 1454 Duke Street, Alexandria VA 22314. 703/549-2207. World Wide Web address: http://www.nsbe.org.

CHEMICAL & ENGINEERING NEWS
American Chemical Society, 1155 16th Street NW, Washington DC 20036. 202/872-4600. World Wide Web address: http://www.acs.org.

EDN CAREER NEWS
Cahners Business Information, 275 Washington Street, Newton MA 02458. 617/964-3030. World Wide Web address: http://www.cahners.com.

ENGINEERING TIMES
National Society of Professional Engineers, 1420 King Street, Alexandria VA 22314. 703/684-2800. World Wide Web address: http://www.nspe.org.

NAVAL ENGINEERS JOURNAL
American Society of Naval Engineers, 1452 Duke Street, Alexandria VA 22314. 703/836-6727. World Wide Web address: http://www.navalengineers.org/services.htm#journal. Subscription: $48.00.

Online Services

ARCHITECTURE & BUILDING FORUM
Go: Arch. A CompuServe discussion group for architectural professionals.

ENGINEERJOBS.COM
World Wide Web address: http://www.engineerjobs.com. This site caters to engineering positions in the Great Lakes area. Detailed job descriptions are provided as well as links to other related sites.

HOT JOBS! - CONSTRUCTION
World Wide Web address: http://www.kbic.com/construction.htm. Provides construction employment opportunities organized by job title.

P.L.A.C.E.S. FORUM
Keyword: places. A discussion group available to America Online subscribers who are professionals in the fields of architecture, construction, and engineering.

Arts, Entertainment, Sports, and Recreation

You can expect to find the following types of companies in this chapter:
Botanical and Zoological Gardens • Entertainment Groups • Motion Picture and Video Tape Production and Distribution • Museums and Art Galleries • Physical Fitness Facilities • Professional Sports Clubs • Public Golf Courses • Racing and Track Operations • Sporting and Recreational Camps • Theatrical Producers

Some helpful information: *Salaries in the entertainment industry vary widely. Scientists hired to work in public zoos and gardens can make $30,000 - $40,000 per year (at the upper end of the range, advanced degrees are required). Experienced museum curators make, on average, $50,000 per year. In theater, the payscale of directors depends partly upon the success of the production. A director can expect a fee, which can be as low as a $5,000 at a small theater or over $40,000 for a Broadway production, as well as a percentage of the box office profits. In sports, athletic directors at competitive universities earn $50,000 on average.*

A&E TELEVISION NETWORKS
235 East 45th Street, New York NY 10017. 212/210-1400. **Contact:** Human Resources. **World Wide Web address:** http://www.aande.com/corporate. **Description:** A media corporation providing magazine publishing, Websites, books, home videos, and operating A&E and The History Channel cable stations. **Corporate headquarters location:** This Location.

AMC ENTERTAINMENT INC.
P.O. Box 219615, Kansas City MO 64121-9615. 816/221-4000. **Contact:** Vice President of Human Resources. **World Wide Web address:** http://www.amctheatres.com. **Description:** AMC Entertainment Inc. is one of the largest motion picture exhibitors in the United States. AMC's theater technology ranges from computerized box offices to High Impact Theatre Systems. The company operates 214 theaters with 2,906 screens in 23 states and the District of Columbia. **Corporate headquarters location:** This Location. **Subsidiaries include:** American Multi-Cinema Inc.

THE ACKERLEY GROUP, INC.
1301 Fifth Avenue, Suite 4000, Seattle WA 98101. 206/624-2888. **Contact:** Personnel. **World Wide Web address:** http://www.ackerley.com. **Description:** Operates a group of media and entertainment companies. The Ackerley Group's national operations include an outdoor advertising agency, 17 television stations, five radio stations, and a sports/entertainment division that operates the NBA's Seattle SuperSonics and the WNBA's Seattle Storm. **Corporate headquarters location:** This Location. **Subsidiaries include:** AKMedia/Massachusetts; AKMedia/Northwest; Full House Sports & Entertainment. **Listed on:** New York Stock Exchange. **Stock exchange symbol:** AK.

ADLER PLANETARIUM & ASTRONOMY MUSEUM
1300 South Lake Shore Drive, Chicago IL 60605. 312/322-0591. **Fax:** 312/322-9909. **Contact:** Marguerite E. Dawson, Human Resources Manager. **E-mail address:** mdawson@adlernet.org. **World Wide Web address:** http://www.adlerplanetarium. org. **Description:** A planetarium and science museum focusing on astronomy. Founded in 1930. **NOTE:** Entry-level positions are offered. **Common positions include:** Librarian; Operations/Production Manager; Physicist; Public Relations Specialist;

Systems Analyst. **Educational backgrounds include:** Education; Physics. **Benefits:** Dental Insurance; Disability Coverage; Employee Discounts; Life Insurance; Medical Insurance; Pension Plan; Public Transit Available; Savings Plan. **Special programs:** Internships; Training. **Corporate headquarters location:** This Location. **Number of employees at this location:** 185.

ALBUQUERQUE INTERNATIONAL BALLOON FIESTA
8309 Washington Place NE, Albuquerque NM 87113. 505/821-1000. **Fax:** 505/828-2887. **Contact:** Human Resources. **E-mail address:** balloons@aibf.org. **World Wide Web address:** http://www.aibf.org. **Description:** Held annually during the first week of October. The Fiesta is one of the largest hot air ballooning events in the world with attendance reaching totals of over 1 million.

ALLIANCE ENTERTAINMENT CORPORATION
4250 Coral Ridge Drive, Coral Springs FL 33065. 954/346-0110. **Fax:** 954/255-4078. **Contact:** Human Resources. **World Wide Web address:** http://www.aent.com. **Description:** Alliance Entertainment operates in two segments of the entertainment industry including the sale and distribution of pre-recorded music and related products and the acquisition and exploration of proprietary rights to recorded music, video, television, CD-ROMs, and books. **Corporate headquarters location:** This Location.

ALLIED DIGITAL TECHNOLOGIES CORPORATION
15 Gilpin Avenue, Hauppauge NY 11788. 631/234-0200. **Contact:** Personnel Manager. **World Wide Web address:** http://www.allied-digital.com. **Description:** An independent multimedia manufacturing companies offering CD-audio and CD-ROM mastering and replication; videocassette and audiocassette duplication; laser video disc recording; off-line and online video editing; motion picture film processing; film-to-tape and tape-to-film transfers; and finishing, packaging, warehousing, and fulfillment services. **Corporate headquarters location:** This Location.

AMERICAN BINGO & GAMING CORPORATION
1440 Charleston Highway, West Columbia SC 29169. 803/796-7875. **Contact:** Personnel. **World Wide Web address:** http://www.ambingo.com.

Description: Through its subsidiaries, American Bingo & Gaming Corporation provides set up, maintenance, and management support for charities which use bingo events as fund-raisers. The company currently operates eight centers containing more than 3,000 seats. The company also operates vending and concession outlets, and sells bingo paper, daubers, and other supplies. **Corporate headquarters location:** This Location. **Subsidiaries include:** B/J Charity Bingo Inc.; Bing-O-Rama, Inc.; Charity Bingo of Texas, Inc.; Charity Bingo, Inc.; Charity Bingo-Birmingham; SA Charities Inc.; Texas Charities Inc. **Listed on:** NASDAQ. **Stock exchange symbol:** BNGO.

THE AMERICAN KENNEL CLUB
260 Madison Avenue, 4th Floor, New York NY 10016. 212/696-8304. **Fax:** 212/696-8367. **Contact:** Susan Maples, Human Resources Administrator. **World Wide Web address:** http://www.akc.org. **Description:** An independent, nonprofit organization devoted to the advancement of purebred dogs. The American Kennel Club adopts and enforces rules and regulations governing dog shows, obedience trials, and field trials, and fosters and encourages interest in the health and welfare of purebred dogs. Founded in 1884. **NOTE:** Entry-level positions are offered. **Common positions include:** Accountant; Administrative Assistant; Desktop Publishing Specialist; Editor; Editorial Assistant; Financial Analyst; Graphic Designer. **Educational backgrounds include:** Accounting; Art/Design; Business Administration; Liberal Arts; MBA; Microsoft Office; Microsoft Word; Photoshop; Public Relations; QuarkXPress; Spreadsheets. **Benefits:** 401(k); Casual Dress - Fridays; Dental Insurance; Disability Coverage; Life Insurance; Medical Insurance; Pension Plan; Tuition Assistance. **Office hours:** Monday - Friday, 8:30 a.m. - 4:15 p.m. **Corporate headquarters location:** This Location. **Other U.S. locations:** Raleigh NC. **Listed on:** Privately held. **President/CEO:** Al Cheaure. **Annual sales/revenues:** $21 - $50 million. **Number of employees at this location:** 75. **Number of employees nationwide:** 450.

AMERICAN MEDIA INC.
4900 University Avenue, West Des Moines IA 50266. 515/224-0919. **Toll-free phone:** 800/262-2557. **Fax:** 515/224-0256. **Contact:** Human Resources. **World Wide Web address:** http://www.ammedia.com. **Description:** A leading producer of corporate training products and services. The company offers audio, interactive multimedia, and video products. **Common positions include:** Account Manager; Multimedia Designer. **Benefits:** 401(k); Casual Dress - Daily; Dental Insurance; Disability Coverage; Flexible Schedule; Life Insurance; Medical Insurance; Profit Sharing; Sick Days (6 - 10).

AMERICAN MUSEUM OF NATURAL HISTORY
175-208 Central Park West, New York NY 10024. 212/769-5000. **Contact:** Richard MacKewice, Director of Human Resources. **World Wide Web address:** http://www.amnh.org. **Description:** A museum of anthropology, astronomy, mineralogy, and zoology. The museum has a research library and 38 exhibition halls. The museum offers educational and research programs. The museum also publishes several in-house and nationally-distributed magazines based on research conducted there. Founded in 1869. **Corporate headquarters location:** This Location.

AMERICAN PRODUCTION SERVICES
2247 15th Avenue West, Seattle WA 98119. 206/282-1776. **Fax:** 206/282-3535. **Contact:** Human Resources. **World Wide Web address:** http://www.apsnw.com. **Description:** Provides video duplication, audio and editing services, and computer graphics services. **Common positions include:** Customer Service Representative; Electrical/Electronics Engineer; Video Editor; Video Production Coordinator. **Educational backgrounds include:** Art/Design; Computer Science; Electronics; Engineering; Liberal Arts; Marketing. **Corporate headquarters location:** This Location. **Other area locations:** North Hollywood CA. **Annual sales/revenues:** $5 - $10 million. **Number of employees at this location:** 50. **Number of employees nationwide:** 75.

AMERICAN REPERTORY THEATRE
Loeb Drama Center, 64 Brattle Street, Cambridge MA 02138. 617/495-2668. **Contact:** Robert Orchard, Managing Director. **World Wide Web address:** http://www.amrep.org. **Description:** A nonprofit theater. **Special programs:** Internships. **Office hours:** Monday - Friday, 9:00 a.m. - 5:00 p.m.

AMERICAN SYMPHONY ORCHESTRA LEAGUE
33 West 60th Street, 5th Floor, New York NY 10023. 212/262-5161. **Fax:** 212/262-5298. **Contact:** Lisa Morton, Director of Human Resources. **E-mail address:** hr@symphony.org. **World Wide Web address:** http://www.symphony.org. **Description:** A national service organization for America's professional symphony, chamber, youth, and college orchestras. Founded in 1942. **NOTE:** Resumes can also be sent to the attention of Nicole M. Kelley, Human Resources Assistant. **Common positions include:** Marketing Manager; Marketing Specialist; Network/Systems Administrator; Public Relations Specialist; Web Advertising Specialist; Webmaster; Website Developer. **Educational backgrounds include:** Business Administration; C/C++; Communications; Computer Science; HTML; Marketing; Microsoft Office; Microsoft Word; Novell; Public Relations; QuarkXPress; Visual Basic. **Office hours:** Monday - Friday, 9:00 a.m. - 5:30 p.m.

ARENA STAGE
1101 Sixth Street SW, Washington DC 20024-2691. 202/554-9066. **Fax:** 202/488-4056. **Contact:** Administrative Director. **World Wide Web address:** http://www.arenastage.org. **Description:** A nonprofit theater company. **NOTE:** Entry-level positions are offered. **Common positions include:** Customer Service Representative; Developmental Specialist; Graphic Artist; Marketing Specialist; Public Relations Specialist; Systems Manager; Webmaster. **Educational backgrounds include:** Art/Design; Business Administration; Communications; Computer Science; Finance; Liberal Arts; Marketing; Public Relations; Theater. **Benefits:** Disability Coverage; Life Insurance; Medical Insurance; Pension Plan. **Special programs:** Internships; Apprenticeships. **Number of employees at this location:** 200.

ARISTA RECORDS, INC.
6 West 57th Street, New York NY 10019. 212/489-7400. **Contact:** Yvonne Lung, Director of Personnel. **World Wide Web address:** http://www.arista.com. **Description:** Provides sales, promotional, and artist and repertoire activities for Arista Records and its contracted artists. **Corporate headquarters location:** This Location. **Parent company:** BMG Music.

ARIZONA ED-VENTURE TOURS
P.O. Box 4137, Prescott AZ 86302-4137. 520/541-0734. **Contact:** Rich Holtzin, Owner. **E-mail**

address: azedtours@yahoo.com. **Description:** Offers sightseeing, educational, and historical tours throughout the Southwest. The company specializes in environmental, cultural, and historical sights. Founded in 1997.

ARTISAN ENTERTAINMENT
2700 Colorado Avenue, 2nd Floor, Santa Monica CA 90404. 310/449-9200. **Contact:** Human Resources. **World Wide Web address:** http://www.artisanent.com. **Description:** Produces, markets, and distributes motion pictures. **Listed on:** Privately held. **Annual sales/revenues:** More than $100 million.

ASH LAWN-HIGHLAND SUMMER FESTIVAL
1941 James Monroe Parkway, Charlottesville VA 22902. 804/293-4500. **Fax:** 804/293-0736. **Contact:** Judith Walker, General Manager. **World Wide Web address:** http://www.avenue.org/summerfestival. **Description:** A summer festival that produces two operas and one musical theatrical production each season. Ash Lawn-Highland Summer Festival offers pre-performance lectures; presents Music at Twilight (including classical and contemporary programs); and offers Summer Saturdays, a theater and music production for children. **Special programs:** Internships; Apprenticeships. **Internship information:** There are two summer internships available in Production and Arts Management/Production. There are four summer and academic year internships available in Press, Development, Marketing, and Administration. For more information or to apply, please contact Saskia Santen-Arts, Intern Coordinator. **Corporate headquarters location:** This Location. **Annual sales/revenues:** Less than $5 million.

BALLET INTERNATIONALE
502 North Capitol Avenue, Suite B, Indianapolis IN 46204. 317/637-8979. **Fax:** 317/637-1637. **Contact:** Barbara Turner, Managing Director. **Description:** A professional ballet company that performs nationally. **Special programs:** Internships. **Corporate headquarters location:** This Location. **Number of employees at this location:** 45.

BALLETMET COLUMBUS
BALLETMET DANCE ACADEMY
322 Mt. Vernon Avenue, Columbus OH 43215. 614/229-4860. **Fax:** 614/229-4858. **Contact:** Human Resources Department. **World Wide Web address:** http://www.balletmet.org. **Description:** A nonprofit professional dance company. The BalletMet Dance Academy (also at this location) currently ranks as one of the top five professional dance schools in the country. Founded in 1978. **Educational backgrounds include:** Business Administration; Liberal Arts; Marketing. **Benefits:** 403(b); Dental Insurance; Employee Discounts; Life Insurance; Medical Insurance. **Corporate headquarters location:** This Location. **Annual sales/revenues:** Less than $5 million. **Number of employees at this location:** 100.

BALLY TOTAL FITNESS CORPORATION
8700 West Bryn Mawr Avenue, Chicago IL 60631. 773/399-1300. **Contact:** Personnel Director. **World Wide Web address:** http://www.ballyfitness.com. **Description:** Bally Total Fitness operates 360 fitness centers located in 27 states with approximately 4.2 million members. The fitness centers operate under the Bally name in conjunction with various others including Holiday Health, Jack LaLanne, Holiday Spa, Chicago Health Clubs, Scandinavian, President's First Lady, Vic Tanny and Aerobics Plus, and The Vertical Clubs. In addition, the company operates four fitness centers in Canada.

Special programs: Internships. **Corporate headquarters location:** This Location. **Other U.S. locations:** Nationwide. **Listed on:** New York Stock Exchange. **Stock exchange symbol:** BFT.

BALTIMORE ORIOLES
333 West Camden Street, Baltimore MD 21201-2435. 410/685-9800. **Contact:** Human Resources. **Description:** Administrative offices for the Major League Baseball team. **Corporate headquarters location:** This Location.

BAY MEADOWS COMPANY
P.O. Box 5050, San Mateo CA 94402. 650/574-7223. **Contact:** Human Resources. **Description:** Operates Bay Meadows Race Track on the San Francisco Peninsula, and California Jockey Club, an equity real estate investment trust whose principal asset is Bay Meadows Race Track. **Corporate headquarters location:** This Location.

THE BIG MOUNTAIN SKI & SUMMER RESORT
WINTER SPORTS, INC. (WSI)
P.O. Box 1400, Whitefish MT 59937. 406/862-1936. **Fax:** 406/862-2955. **Contact:** Director of Human Resources. **E-mail address:** jobs@bigmtn.com. **World Wide Web address:** http://www.bigmtn.com. **Description:** The Big Mountain Ski & Summer Resort operates 10 ski lifts covering nearly 4,000 acres of land. The Summit House is a mountaintop cafeteria, restaurant, and lounge located on U.S. Forest Service land. Base facilities including lodging, a cafeteria, restaurants and lounges, a daycare center, a ski school, a rental shop, and other related services located on land owned by WSI. **NOTE:** Entry-level positions are offered. **Common positions include:** Account Manager; Accountant; Administrative Assistant; Advertising Clerk; Advertising Executive; Blue-Collar Worker Supervisor; General Manager; Human Resources Manager; Marketing Manager; Marketing Specialist; MIS Specialist; Public Relations Manager; Public Relations Specialist; Real Estate Agent; Sales Representative; Secretary; Transportation/Traffic Specialist; Vice President of Marketing. **Educational backgrounds include:** Accounting; Computer Science; Marketing; Public Relations. **Benefits:** 401(k); Dental Insurance; Employee Discounts; Life Insurance; Medical Insurance; Tuition Assistance. **Special programs:** Internships. **Office hours:** Monday - Friday, 8:00 a.m. - 4:30 p.m. **Corporate headquarters location:** This Location. **Subsidiaries include:** Big Mountain Water Company furnishes the domestic water supply to the resort and adjacent properties. Big Mountain Development Corporation oversees and coordinates the planning and development of certain parcels owned by Winter Sports, Inc. **Annual sales/revenues:** $11 - $20 million. **Number of employees at this location:** 450.

BOSTON BRUINS
One Fleet Center, Boston MA 02114. 617/624-1050. **Contact:** Human Resources. **Description:** Administrative and publicity offices for the National Hockey League team. **Corporate headquarters location:** This Location.

BOWL AMERICA INC.
6446 Edsall Road, Alexandria VA 22312. 703/941-6300. **Contact:** Human Resources. **Description:** Engaged in the operation of 25 bowling centers. **Benefits:** ESOP; Profit Sharing. **Corporate headquarters location:** This Location. **Other area locations:** Richmond VA. **Other U.S. locations:** Washington DC; Jacksonville FL; Orlando FL; Baltimore MD. **Listed on:** American Stock Exchange. **Number of employees nationwide:** 800.

BRECKENRIDGE OUTDOOR EDUCATION CENTER
P.O. Box 697, Breckenridge CO 80424. 970/453-6422. **Fax:** 970/453-4676. **Contact:** Human Resources. **World Wide Web address:** http://www.boec.org. **Description:** A nonprofit organization offering year-round wilderness and adventure programs and adaptive skiing opportunities for people with disabilities and other special needs. Activities include downhill and cross-country skiing, ropes courses, rafting, rock climbing, camping, and fishing. Founded in 1976. **Educational backgrounds include:** Education; Geology; Health Care; Liberal Arts. **Special programs:** Internships. **Corporate headquarters location:** This Location.

BROADVIEW MEDIA
142 East Ontario, Chicago IL 60611. 312/337-6000. **Contact:** Human Resources. **World Wide Web address:** http://www.broadviewmedia.com. **Description:** A full-service film and video production company involved in production, editing, audio, servicing broadcast, consumer graphics, and distribution.

BROADWAY VIDEO INC.
1619 Broadway, 10th Floor, New York NY 10019. 212/265-7600. **Contact:** Vice President of Operations. **World Wide Web address:** http://www.broadwayvideo.com. **Description:** An entertainment production company offering editing, design, sound, and related services for all types of media. **Corporate headquarters location:** This Location. **Founder:** Mr. Lorne Michaels.

BROOKLYN ACADEMY OF MUSIC
30 Lafayette Avenue, Brooklyn NY 11217. 718/636-4111. **Contact:** Katina Jackson, Human Resources Director. **World Wide Web address:** http://www.bam.org. **Description:** A nonprofit arts showcase offering dance, opera, and theatrical performances, as well as performances by the Brooklyn Philharmonic Orchestra. Founded in 1859. **Educational backgrounds include:** Microsoft Word. **Special programs:** Internships.

CNBC
MSNBC
2200 Fletcher Avenue, Fort Lee NJ 07024. 201/585-2622. **Contact:** Human Resources. **World Wide Web address:** http://www.cnbc.com. **Description:** Operates all-news networks offering current business and finance news. CNBC and MSNBC are both updated 24 hours a day, seven days a week. **Corporate headquarters location:** This Location. **Parent company:** NBC.

THE CAPITAL CHILDREN'S MUSEUM
800 Third Street NE, Washington DC 20002. 202/675-4121. **Contact:** Personnel. **World Wide Web address:** http://www.ccm.org. **Description:** A hands-on, interactive museum with several other divisions which include Options School (alternative seventh grade), Community Access Computer Center, and Media Arts Center (film and animation). Founded in 1979. **Common positions include:** Blue-Collar Worker Supervisor; Counselor; Management Trainee; Preschool Worker; Teacher/Professor. **Educational backgrounds include:** Art/Design; Business Administration; Finance; Liberal Arts; Marketing. **Benefits:** Dental Insurance; Medical Insurance. **Special programs:** Internships. **Corporate headquarters location:** This Location.

CARMIKE CINEMAS
P.O. Box 391, Columbus GA 31902. 706/576-3400. **Contact:** Human Resources. **Description:** One of the largest operators of motion picture theaters in the United States. **Corporate headquarters location:** This Location. **Listed on:** New York Stock Exchange.

CHICAGO SYMPHONY ORCHESTRA
220 South Michigan Avenue, Chicago IL 60604. 312/294-3000. **Recorded jobline:** 312/294-3326. **Contact:** Director of Human Resources. **World Wide Web address:** http://www.chicagosymphony. org. **Description:** One of the nation's most prestigious orchestras. **Common positions include:** Accountant/Auditor; Editor; Education Administrator; Financial Analyst; General Manager; Human Resources Manager; Systems Analyst; Technical Writer/Editor. **Educational backgrounds include:** Accounting; Communications; Liberal Arts; Music. **Benefits:** 403(b); Dental Insurance; Disability Coverage; Life Insurance; Medical Insurance; Pension Plan. **Corporate headquarters location:** This Location.

CHICAGO TOUR GUIDES INSTITUTE EUROPEAN LANGUAGE CENTER INC.
101 North Wacker Drive, Suite CM-285, Chicago IL 60606. 773/276-6683. **Fax:** 773/252-3729. **Contact:** Human Resources. **E-mail address:** chitourint@aol.com. **World Wide Web address:** http://www.chicago.guide.net. **Description:** Offers tours of Chicago. The European Language Center (also at this location) hires part-time and full-time foreign language interpreters for U.S. and foreign companies. **NOTE:** Guides earn $15 to $25 per hour and need to have a comprehensive knowledge of the city including local museums, architecture, art, and city history. **Common positions include:** Tour Guide. **Educational backgrounds include:** Architecture; Art/Design; Business Administration; Communications; Foreign Languages; Liberal Arts. **Corporate headquarters location:** This Location.

THE CHILDREN'S MUSEUM OF INDIANAPOLIS
P.O. Box 3000, Indianapolis IN 46206. 317/924-5431. **Toll-free phone:** 800/826-5431. **Fax:** 317/921-4019. **Contact:** Suzanne Mandel, Manager of Recruiting Services. **E-mail address:** suzannem@childrensmuseum.org. **World Wide Web address:** http://www.childrensmuseum.org. **Description:** A nonprofit, interactive museum for children. The Children's Museum of Indianapolis is one of the largest and fourth oldest children's museum in the world. Founded in 1925. **NOTE:** Entry-level positions, part-time jobs, and second and third shifts are offered. **Common positions include:** Administrative Assistant; Administrative Manager; Assistant Manager; Biochemist; Biological Scientist; Buyer; Chemical Engineer; Chemist; Chief Financial Officer; Controller; Customer Service Representative; Database Administrator; Editor; Education Administrator; Electrician; Electronics Technician; Geologist/ Geophysicist; Graphic Artist; Graphic Designer; Human Resources Manager; Librarian; Marketing Specialist; Network/Systems Administrator; Preschool Worker; Public Relations Specialist; Purchasing Agent/Manager; Sales Manager; Sales Representative; Teacher/Professor; Technical Writer/Editor; Typist/Word Processor. **Educational backgrounds include:** Accounting; Art/Design; Biology; Business Administration; Chemistry; Communications; Computer Science; Economics; Education; Finance; Geology; Liberal Arts; Macintosh Computer; Marketing; Microsoft Word; Physics; Public Relations. **Benefits:** 403(b); Casual Dress - Fridays; Daycare Assistance; Dental Insurance; Disability Coverage; Employee Discounts; Financial Planning Assistance; Flexible Schedule; Job Sharing; Life Insurance; Medical Insurance; Public Transit Available; Sick Days;

Tuition Assistance; Vacation Pay. **Special programs:** Internships; Training; Summer Jobs. **Office hours:** Monday - Friday, 9:00 a.m. - 5:00 p.m. **Corporate headquarters location:** This Location. **Listed on:** Privately held. **President:** Peter Sterling. **Number of employees at this location:** 425.

CINE MAGNETICS VIDEO & DIGITAL LABORATORIES
100 Business Park Drive, Armonk NY 10504-1750. 914/273-7600. **Contact:** Ms. Van Arone, Personnel Manager. **World Wide Web address:** http://www.cinemagnetics.com. **Description:** Cine Magnetics is involved in video and film duplication and photo finishing. **Benefits:** Cafeteria Plan; Life Insurance; Medical Insurance. **Corporate headquarters location:** This Location. **Other U.S. locations:** Culver City CA.

CIRCA '21 DINNER PLAYHOUSE
1828 Third Avenue, Rock Island IL 61201. 309/786-2667. **Fax:** 309/786-4119. **Contact:** Dennis Hitchcock, Producer. **World Wide Web address:** http://www.circa21.com. **Description:** Produces musicals and modern comedies, as well as a series of children's plays and concerts year-round. Circa '21 Dinner Playhouse has produced numerous national tours. Founded in 1977. **NOTE:** Part-time jobs are offered. **Common positions include:** Accountant; Administrative Assistant; Marketing Specialist; Sales Manager; Sales Representative. **Educational backgrounds include:** Marketing; Microsoft Word; Spreadsheets; Theater. **Benefits:** Casual Dress - Daily; Employee Discounts; Medical Insurance. **Special programs:** Internships. **Listed on:** Privately held. **President/CEO/Owner:** Dennis Hitchcock. **Annual sales/revenues:** Less than $5 million.

CITY CENTER OF MUSIC AND DRAMA INC.
70 Lincoln Center Plaza, 4th Floor, New York NY 10023-6580. 212/870-4266. **Fax:** 212/870-4286. **Contact:** Cynthia Herzegovitch, Human Resources Administrator. **Description:** Organizational and management offices for the nonprofit cultural organization whose activities include plays, ballets, and operas. The center operates the New York State Theater, the New York City Opera, the New York Ballet, and City Center Special Productions. **Common positions include:** Accountant/Auditor; Clerical Supervisor; Computer Programmer; Health Services Manager; Human Resources Manager; MIS Specialist. **Educational backgrounds include:** Accounting; Computer Science. **Benefits:** Dental Insurance; Disability Coverage; Life Insurance; Medical Insurance; Pension Plan; Tuition Assistance. **Corporate headquarters location:** This Location. **Number of employees nationwide:** 2,000.

THE COLONIAL WILLIAMSBURG FOUNDATION
P.O. Box 1776, Williamsburg VA 23187. 757/229-1000. **Toll-free phone:** 800/HISTORY. **Fax:** 757/220-7259. **Recorded jobline:** 757/220-7129. **Contact:** Sherri Ashby, Human Resources Representative. **E-mail address:** sashby@cwf.org. **World Wide Web address:** http://www.history.org. **Description:** A nonprofit educational organization that acts to preserve and restore 18th-century Williamsburg through historical interpretation. Founded in 1926. **NOTE:** Entry-level positions, part-time jobs, and second and third shifts are offered. **Common positions include:** Account Representative; Accountant; Administrative Assistant; Administrative Manager; Advertising Executive; AS400 Programmer Analyst; Assistant Manager; Auditor; Budget Analyst; Clerical Supervisor; Computer Support Technician;

Computer Technician; Controller; Cost Estimator; Customer Service Representative; Database Administrator; Database Manager; Economist; Editorial Assistant; Finance Director; Financial Analyst; General Manager; Human Resources Manager; Market Research Analyst; Marketing Manager; Marketing Specialist; MIS Specialist; Public Relations Specialist; Sales Representative; Secretary; Typist/Word Processor. **Educational backgrounds include:** Accounting; AS400 Certification; Business Administration; Computer Science; Engineering; Finance; HTML; Internet; Marketing; Mathematics; MCSE; Microsoft Word; Novell; Public Relations; Software Development; Software Tech. Support; Spreadsheets. **Benefits:** 401(k); Casual Dress - Fridays; Employee Discounts; Financial Planning Assistance; Life Insurance; Medical Insurance; Pension Plan; Profit Sharing; Savings Plan; Tuition Assistance. **Special programs:** Internships; Apprenticeships; Summer Jobs. **Corporate headquarters location:** This Location.

COLORADO HISTORICAL SOCIETY
1300 Broadway, Denver CO 80203. 303/866-2136. **Fax:** 303/866-4464. **Contact:** Ms. C.J. Williams, Personnel Officer. **Description:** A nonprofit organization that collects, preserves, and interprets the history and prehistory of Colorado and the West through educational programs and museum exhibits. Founded in 1879. **Common positions include:** Administrative Assistant; Archaeologist; Controller; Curatorial Specialist; Database Manager; Editor; Editorial Assistant; Education Administrator; Graphic Artist; Graphic Designer; Historical Preservation Specialist; Human Resources Manager; Librarian; Marketing Manager; Photographer; Public Relations Specialist; Sales Manager; Secretary. **Educational backgrounds include:** Archaeology; Art/Design; Education; History; Liberal Arts; Marketing; Museum Studies; Public Relations; Sales. **Benefits:** 401(k); 403(b); Dental Insurance; Disability Coverage; Employee Discounts; Flexible Schedule; Life Insurance; Medical Insurance; Pension Plan; Public Transit Available. **Special programs:** Internships; Summer Jobs. **Corporate headquarters location:** This Location. **Operations at this facility include:** Administration; Sales. **President:** Georgianna Contiguglia. **Facilities Manager:** Joseph Dean. **Information Systems Director:** Diane Huling. **Facilities Director:** Joseph Bell. **Number of employees at this location:** 95. **Number of employees nationwide:** 115.

COMCAST-SPECTACOR, LP
3601 South Broad Street, Philadelphia PA 19148. 215/336-3600. **Fax:** 215/389-9413. **Recorded jobline:** 215/952-4180. **Contact:** Curt Wilson, Recruiter. **World Wide Web address:** http://www.comcast-spectacor.com. **Description:** A sports/entertainment firm managing the Philadelphia Flyers, 76ers, Kixx, and Phantoms; Comcast SportsNet; the First Union Spectrum; and the First Union Center. The First Union Spectrum and Center are host to Flyers and Phantoms hockey, 76ers basketball, Kixx soccer, and over 500 other sporting, musical, and entertainment events each year. Comcast SportsNet is a 24-hour network dedicated to the Philadelphia-area sports world. **Common positions include:** Accountant/Auditor; Administrative Assistant; Administrator; Blue-Collar Worker Supervisor; Customer Service Representative; General Manager; Human Resources Manager; Marketing Specialist; MIS Specialist; Network/Systems Administrator; Operations/Production Manager; Public Relations Specialist; Radio/TV Announcer/Broadcaster; Sales Executive; Sales Representative; Services Sales

Representative; Technical Writer/Editor. **Educational backgrounds include:** Accounting; Business Administration; Communications; Finance; Marketing; Sports Management. **Benefits:** 401(k); Casual Dress - Fridays; Dental Insurance; Disability Coverage; Life Insurance; Medical Insurance; Profit Sharing; Public Transit Available; Tuition Assistance. **Special programs:** Internships. **Internship information:** A variety of internship opportunities are available to college students during the fall, spring, and summer semesters. **Corporate headquarters location:** This Location. **Number of employees at this location:** 800.

COMEDY CENTRAL
1775 Broadway, 9th Floor, New York NY 10019. 212/767-8600. **Contact:** Human Resources. **World Wide Web address:** http://www.comcentral.com. **Description:** Operates the Comedy Central network, which produces such shows as *The Daily Show, South Park,* and *Dr. Katz.* **Corporate headquarters location:** This Location.

COURT TV
600 Third Avenue, 2nd Floor, New York NY 10016. 212/973-2800. **Contact:** Human Resources. **World Wide Web address:** http://www.courttv.com. **Description:** A cable network providing coverage of some of the country's most widely-publicized legal battles. **Corporate headquarters location:** This Location.

CREEDE REPERTORY THEATRE
P.O. Box 269, Creede CO 81130. 719/658-2541. **Fax:** 719/658-2343. **Contact:** Human Resources. **E-mail address:** crt@creederep.com. **World Wide Web address:** http://www.creederep.com. **Description:** A nonprofit theater producing eight plays annually. This location also hires seasonally. Founded in 1969. **Special programs:** Internships. **CEO:** Richard Baxter. **Number of employees at this location:** 40.

DALLAS COWBOYS
One Cowboys Parkway, Irving TX 75063-4945. 972/556-9900. **Fax:** 972/556-9304. **Contact:** Human Resources. **Description:** Administrative offices for the National Football League team. **Corporate headquarters location:** This Location.

DAVE & BUSTER'S, INC.
2481 Manana Drive, Dallas TX 75220. 214/357-9588. **Contact:** Human Resources. **World Wide Web address:** http://www.daveandbusters.com. **Description:** An operator of 20 restaurant/entertainment complexes. Each location houses eating venues and amusement facilities including billiards, video games, and virtual reality games. Founded in 1982. **Corporate headquarters location:** This Location. **Other area locations:** Houston TX. **Other U.S. locations:** Ontario CA; Denver CO; Hollywood FL; Atlanta GA; Chicago IL; North Bethesda MD; Utica MI; Cincinnati OH; Philadelphia PA. **International locations:** Birmingham, England. **Listed on:** New York Stock Exchange. **Stock exchange symbol:** DAB.

DELUXE LABORATORIES, INC.
1377 North Serrano Avenue, Hollywood CA 90027. 323/462-6171. **Contact:** Human Resources. **Description:** A motion picture film developer. **Benefits:** Dental Insurance; Life Insurance; Medical Insurance.

DENON DIGITAL INDUSTRIES INC.
1380 Monticello Road, Madison GA 30650. 706/342-3425. **Contact:** Foss Hodges, Personnel Manager. **World Wide Web address:** http://www.denon.com. **Description:** Manufactures prerecorded compact discs.

DENVER CENTER THEATRE COMPANY
1245 Champa, Denver CO 80204. 303/893-4000. **Contact:** Barbara Sellers, Production Director. **World Wide Web address:** http://www. denvercenter.org. **Description:** A professional acting troupe that performs a broad range of theatrical productions year-round. Founded in 1978. **Parent company:** Denver Center for the Performing Arts. **Number of employees at this location:** 300.

THE DENVER ZOO
2300 Steele Street, Denver CO 80205. 303/376-4800. **Contact:** Human Resources. **World Wide Web address:** http://www.denverzoo.org. **Description:** A zoo featuring year-round exhibits including Bird World and Tropical Discovery. **Corporate headquarters location:** This Location.

DIAMOND ENTERTAINMENT CORPORATION
800 Tucker Lane, Walnut CA 91789. 909/839-1989. **Contact:** Human Resources. **Description:** A full-service video product duplicating, manufacturing, packaging, and distribution company. Through its Custom Duplication Division, the company duplicates and packages videocassettes on a custom-made basis. Customers for this service include companies and individuals within the multilevel marketing industry who use videocassettes for product information, business recruitment, training, or sales and marketing purposes. The Entertainment Division markets and sells a variety of videocassette titles to the budget home video market. The company's inventory of programs consists of more than 675 titles including children's cartoons, motion pictures, sports highlights, educational, and exercise programs. The feature motion pictures offered by the company include such film classics as *Life with Father* and *It's a Wonderful Life.* **Corporate headquarters location:** This Location.

THE WALT DISNEY COMPANY
500 South Buena Vista Street, Burbank CA 91521-7235. 818/560-6335. **Contact:** Staffing Services. **World Wide Web address:** http://disney.go.com. **Description:** One of the nation's top film studios. **Common positions include:** Accountant/Auditor; Budget Analyst; Computer Programmer; Economist; Financial Manager; Market Research Analyst; Marketing Manager; Secretary; Software Engineer; Systems Analyst. **Educational backgrounds include:** Accounting; Business Administration; Engineering; Finance; Marketing. **Benefits:** Dental Insurance; Life Insurance; Medical Insurance. **Corporate headquarters location:** This Location.

E! ENTERTAINMENT TELEVISION NETWORKS
5750 Wilshire Boulevard, Los Angeles CA 90036. **Recorded jobline:** 323/954-2666. **Contact:** Human Resources. **E-mail address:** hr@eentertainment. com. **World Wide Web address:** http://www. eonline.com. **Description:** Operates a cable network dedicated to the entertainment and fashion industries. **Corporate headquarters location:** This Location.

ESPN INC.
935 Middle Street, Bristol CT 06010. 860/585-2000. **Contact:** Human Resources. **World Wide Web address:** http://espn.go.com. **Description:** Operates the ESPN, ESPN2, and ESPN Classic all-sports networks. **Corporate headquarters location:** This Location.

FAMILY GOLF CENTERS, INC.
538 Broadhollow Road, Suite 410E, Melville NY 11747. 516/694-1666. **Contact:** Human Resources.

E-mail address: corp@familygolf.com. **World Wide Web address:** http://www.familygolf.com. **Description:** Owns, operates, and manages over 121 recreational golf centers, 30 ice rinks, and family entertainment centers nationwide. Some of the facilities operate under the name Golden Bear Golf Centers. The centers offer golf lessons and facilities for practicing driving, pitching, putting, chipping, and sand play, as well as miniature golf courses and snack bars. **Corporate headquarters location:** This Location. **Other U.S. locations:** Nationwide. **International locations:** Canada. **Subsidiaries include:** EagleQuest Golf Centers (Canada). **Listed on:** NASDAQ. **Stock exchange symbol:** FGCI.

FELD ENTERTAINMENT, INC.
8607 Westwood Center Drive, Vienna VA 22182. 703/448-4000. **Contact:** Gary Baron, Office Manager. **World Wide Web address:** http://www.ringling.com. **Description:** Operates circuses including Ringling Bros. and Barnum & Bailey Circus, television productions, and ice shows including Walt Disney's World on Ice. **Corporate headquarters location:** This Location.

THE FIELD MUSEUM OF NATURAL HISTORY
1400 South Lake Shore Drive, Chicago IL 60605. 312/922-9410. **Fax:** 312/922-0254. **Contact:** Shawn VanDerziel, Human Resources Representative. **E-mail address:** hr@fmnh.org. **World Wide Web address:** http://www.fmnh.org. **Description:** A natural history museum. The museum provides both formal and informal educational opportunities for the public, and conducts its own research in the fields of anthropology, geology, zoology, and biology. Founded in 1893. **NOTE:** Entry-level positions are offered. **Common positions include:** Accountant/Auditor; Anthropologist; Biological Scientist; Botanist; Budget Analyst; Customer Service Representative; Designer; Electrician; Financial Analyst; Forester/Conservation Scientist; Geologist/Geophysicist; Human Resources Manager; Librarian; Meteorologist; Public Relations Specialist; Purchasing Agent/Manager; Science Technologist; Systems Analyst; Teacher/Professor. **Educational backgrounds include:** Anthropology; Art/Design; Biology; Botany; Business Administration; Communications; Geology; Marketing. **Benefits:** 403(b); Dental Insurance; Disability Coverage; Employee Discounts; Life Insurance; Medical Insurance; Pension Plan; Savings Plan. **Special programs:** Internships. **Corporate headquarters location:** This Location. **Listed on:** Privately held. **Number of employees at this location:** 470.

FRIENDS OF THE NATIONAL ZOO
3001 Connecticut Avenue NW, Washington DC 20008. 202/673-4640. **Fax:** 202/673-0289. **Contact:** Human Resources. **World Wide Web address:** http://www.fonz.org. **Description:** In support of the mission of the Smithsonian National Zoological Park, Friends of the National Zoo is a nonprofit corporation that provides biological education and environmental protection. Founded in 1958. **NOTE:** Entry-level positions and part-time jobs are offered. **Common positions include:** Accountant; Administrative Assistant; Management Trainee; Marketing Specialist; Public Relations Specialist; Sales Representative; Webmaster. **Educational backgrounds include:** Accounting; Art/Design; Biology; Business Administration; Communications; Finance; HTML; Marketing; Microsoft Word; Public Relations; Spreadsheets. **Benefits:** Employee Discounts; Flexible Schedule; Public Transit Available. **Special programs:** Internships; Co-ops; Summer Jobs. **Office hours:** Monday - Friday, 9:00 a.m. - 4:00 p.m. **Corporate**

headquarters location: This Location. **Listed on:** Privately held. **Annual sales/revenues:** $5 - $10 million.

GLOBAL OUTDOORS INC.
GOLD PROSPECTOR'S ASSOCIATION OF AMERICA, INC.
43445 Business Park Drive, Temecula CA 92590. 909/699-4749. **Contact:** Human Resources. **Description:** A leisure and entertainment company that owns and operates The Outdoor Channel, a national television network; Gold Prospector's Association of America, Inc. (also at this location); and the Lost Dutchman's Mining Association, a recreational mining club. **Corporate headquarters location:** This Location. **Listed on:** NASDAQ. **Stock exchange symbol:** GLRS.

GOLDEN BEAR GOLF INC.
11780 U.S. Highway One, North Palm Beach FL 33408. 561/626-3900. **Contact:** Sandy Zurnen, Personnel Administrator. **World Wide Web address:** http://www.nicklaus.com/gbg. **Description:** Franchises golf practice and instruction facilities, operates golf schools, constructs golf courses through Weitz Golf International (also at this location), and sells consumer golf products and apparel. **Common positions include:** Accountant/Auditor; Administrator; Architect; Civil Engineer; Marketing Specialist. **Educational backgrounds include:** Accounting; Art/Design; Business Administration; Finance; Marketing. **Benefits:** Dental Insurance; Disability Coverage; Life Insurance; Medical Insurance; Profit Sharing. **Corporate headquarters location:** This Location. **Listed on:** NASDAQ.

GOLD'S GYM
4070 Airport Center Drive, Palm Springs CA 92262. 760/322-4653. **Contact:** Manager. **World Wide Web address:** http://www.goldsgym.com. **Description:** A full-service health and fitness club. Each club is complete with weights and cardiovascular equipment, fitness and aerobic classes, tanning, personal training, and childcare facilities. Gold's Gym is one of the world's largest health club chains, with 500 locations. Founded in 1986. **NOTE:** Part-time jobs are offered. **Common positions include:** Account Representative; Administrative Manager; Assistant Manager; Child Care Worker; Computer Operator; Customer Service Representative; Fitness Professional; Operations Manager; Sales Representative; Secretary. **Corporate headquarters location:** This Location. **Parent company:** Neste Development.
Other U.S. locations:
- 1046 South Country Club Drive, Mesa AZ 85210. 480/833-0099.
- 2156 East Baseline Road, Mesa AZ 85204. 480/497-8686.
- 39605 Entrepreneur Lane, Palm Desert CA 92211. 760/360-0565.
- 26201 Ynez Road, Suite 1318, Temecula CA 92591. 909/699-5432.
- 13785 Park Avenue, Victorville CA 92392. 760/243-4653.
- 9310 South Eastern Avenue, Suite 110, Henderson NV 89009. 702/914-5885.
- 3750 East Flamingo Road, Las Vegas NV 89121. 702/451-4222.
- 4720 West Sahara Boulevard, Las Vegas NV 89102. 702/877-6966.
- 7501 West Lake Mead Boulevard, Suite 109, Las Vegas NV 89128. 702/360-8205.

SAMUEL GOLDWYN COMPANY
9750 West Pico Boulevard, Suite 400, Los Angeles CA 90035. 310/860-3100. **Contact:** Human Resources. **Description:** Engaged primarily in the

financing, production, and distribution of feature-length motion pictures. Samuel Goldwyn Company also finances and distributes television programs intended for licensing to cable and first-run syndication markets, and to U.S. and foreign television networks. **Common positions include:** Accountant/Auditor; Administrative Manager. **Educational backgrounds include:** Accounting; Entertainment/Film; Television. **Benefits:** 401(k); Daycare Assistance; Dental Insurance; Disability Coverage; Employee Discounts; Life Insurance; Medical Insurance; Pension Plan; Savings Plan; Tuition Assistance. **Special programs:** Internships. **Corporate headquarters location:** This Location. **Other U.S. locations:** New York NY. **Number of employees at this location:** 260.

GREEN BAY PACKERS
1265 Lombardi Avenue, Green Bay WI 54304. 920/496-5700. **Contact:** Human Resources. **World Wide Web address:** http://www.packer.com. **Description:** The administrative offices for the National Football League team. **Corporate headquarters location:** This Location.

HARTFORD CIVIC CENTER
One Civic Center Plaza, Hartford CT 06103. 860/249-6333. **Contact:** Pamela Marquis, Director of Human Resources. **World Wide Web address:** http://www.hartfordciviccenter.com. **Description:** Business offices for the civic center, which is host to numerous concerts, sporting events, and entertainers year-round. Hartford Civic Center is managed by Madison Square Garden. **Special programs:** Internships. **Corporate headquarters location:** This Location.

HARTFORD SYMPHONY ORCHESTRA
228 Farmington Avenue, Hartford CT 06105. 860/246-8742. **Contact:** Human Resources. **Description:** Business offices for the symphony orchestra. **Corporate headquarters location:** This Location.

HORSE CAVE THEATRE
P.O. Box 215, Horse Cave KY 42749. 270/786-1200. **Contact:** Warren Hammack, Executive Director. **World Wide Web address:** http://www.horsecavetheatre.org. **Description:** A nonprofit repertory theater promoting professional and educational theater programs. **Common positions include:** Marketing Manager; Secretary. **Educational backgrounds include:** Art/Design; Business Administration; Communications; Liberal Arts; Marketing. **Benefits:** Employee Discounts; Pension Plan. **Special programs:** Internships. **Corporate headquarters location:** This Location. **Number of employees at this location:** 10.

INDIANAPOLIS COLTS
P.O. Box 535000, Indianapolis IN 46253. 317/297-7000. **Fax:** 317/297-8971. **Contact:** EVP of Operations. **E-mail address:** info@colts.com. **World Wide Web address:** http://www.colts.com. **Description:** Administrative offices for the National Football League team. **Special programs:** Internships. **Internship information:** Please check the Website for specific internship information. **Corporate headquarters location:** This Location.

IWERKS ENTERTAINMENT, INC.
4540 West Valerio Street, Burbank CA 91505. 818/841-7766. **Contact:** Karen Bermeo, Human Resources. **World Wide Web address:** http://www.iwerks.com. **Description:** Designs, manufactures, installs, and services high-resolution, proprietary motion picture theater attractions in museums, visitor centers, casinos, and newly emerging entertainment venues. The company's attractions are built around a variety of theater systems including fixed and portable simulators, giant screen, 360-degree, and virtual reality theater systems. Business segments include Iwerks Attractions and Technologies, Iwerks Studios, Iwerks Cinetropolis, Iwerks Touring Technologies, and Omni Films International. **NOTE:** Entry-level positions are offered. **Common positions include:** Accountant; Administrative Assistant; Chief Financial Officer; Controller; Electrician; Financial Analyst; Human Resources Manager; Marketing Manager; Public Relations Specialist; Sales Executive; Sales Representative. **Educational backgrounds include:** ASP; C/C++; MCSE; Microsoft Office; Microsoft Word; SQL. **Benefits:** 401(k); Casual Dress - Fridays; Dental Insurance; Disability Coverage; Life Insurance; Medical Insurance; Sick Days (6 - 10); Tuition Assistance; Vacation Days (6 - 10). **Special programs:** Internships. **Corporate headquarters location:** This Location. **Listed on:** NASDAQ. **Stock exchange symbol:** IWRK. **President/CEO:** Chuck Goldwater. **Sales Manager:** Don Savant. **Number of employees at this location:** 90. **Number of employees nationwide:** 95. **Number of employees worldwide:** 100.

JACOB'S PILLOW DANCE FESTIVAL
P.O. Box 287, Lee MA 01238. 413/637-1322. **Fax:** 413/243-4744. **Contact:** Debbie Markowitz, Company Manager. **E-mail address:** jacobspillow@taconic.net. **World Wide Web address:** http://www.jacobspillow.org. **Description:** One of America's oldest dance festivals, presenting 10 weeks of dance performances and conducting a professional dance school each summer. Founded in 1942. **Educational backgrounds include:** Arts Administration; Business Administration; Mathematics; Public Relations; Theater. **Benefits:** Employee Discounts. **Special programs:** Internships. **Internship information:** Internships are offered in the following areas: archives/preservation; business office; development; documentation; education; marketing/press; operations; programming; technical/theatre production; and ticket services. The internships run from May 24 through August 31, during which time the intern is provided with a $300 stipend and room and board.

JUNIPER GROUP, INC.
111 Great Neck Road, Suite 604, Great Neck NY 11021. 516/829-4670. **Fax:** 516/829-4691. **Contact:** Human Resources. **Description:** Juniper Group operates in two segments: health care and entertainment. The company's principal revenues are generated from health care, which consists of management for hospitals and health care cost containment for health care payers. The entertainment segment acquires and distributes film rights to various media including home video, pay-per-view, pay television, cable television, networks, ad-hoc networks, and independent syndicated television stations. **Corporate headquarters location:** This Location. **Subsidiaries include:** Juniper Medical Systems, Inc. whose subsidiaries include Diversified Health Affiliates, Inc. and Juniper Healthcare Containment Systems, Inc. Diversified Health Affiliates operates Juniper Group's management business while Juniper Healthcare Containment Systems conducts health care cost containment service operations.

K-TEL INTERNATIONAL (USA), INC.
2605 Fernbrook Lane North, Plymouth MN 55447. 763/559-6800. **Contact:** Manager of Human Resources. **World Wide Web address:** http://www.k-tel.com. **Description:** Distributes recorded music products. **Common positions**

include: Accountant/Auditor; Administrative Assistant; Blue-Collar Worker Supervisor; Chief Financial Officer; Computer Operator; Controller; Customer Service Representative; General Manager; Graphic Artist; Human Resources Manager; Marketing Manager; Network/Systems Administrator; Purchasing Agent/Manager; Sales Executive; Sales Manager; Sales Representative; Systems Analyst. **Educational backgrounds include:** Accounting; Art/Design; Business Administration; Computer Science; Finance; Marketing; Microsoft Office; Microsoft Word. **Benefits:** 401(k); Dental Insurance; Disability Coverage; Employee Discounts; Life Insurance; Medical Insurance; Tuition Assistance. **Corporate headquarters location:** This Location.

KILLINGTON LTD.
4763 Killington Road, Killington VT 05751. 802/422-3333. **Contact:** Personnel. **World Wide Web address:** http://www.killington.com. **Description:** A resort located in central Vermont with an 18-hole golf course, a tennis school, and winter skiing. **Common positions include:** Accountant/Auditor; Computer Programmer; Customer Service Representative; Services Sales Representative; Systems Analyst. **Benefits:** Daycare Assistance; Employee Discounts; Life Insurance; Medical Insurance; Savings Plan. **Special programs:** Internships. **Corporate headquarters location:** This Location.

KNOTT'S BERRY FARM
8039 Beach Boulevard, Buena Park CA 90620. 714/827-1776. **Contact:** Staffing. **World Wide Web address:** http://www.knotts.com. **Description:** This location is an amusement park. Overall, Knott's Berry Farm is engaged in the development and management of family restaurants, retail operations, and specialty food products manufacturing. **Common positions include:** Accountant/Auditor; Buyer; Computer Programmer; Food Scientist/Technologist; Restaurant/Food Service Manager; Services Sales Representative; Store Manager; Systems Analyst. **Educational backgrounds include:** Architecture; Business Administration; Finance; Hospitality; Liberal Arts. **Benefits:** Dental Insurance; Disability Coverage; Employee Discounts; Life Insurance; Medical Insurance; Profit Sharing. **Special programs:** Internships. **Corporate headquarters location:** This Location. **Other U.S. locations:** Irvine CA; Moreno Valley CA; Placentia CA; Bloomington MN.

KOHL CHILDREN'S MUSEUM
165 Green Bay Road, Wilmette IL 60091. 847/256-6056. **Fax:** 847/853-9154. **Contact:** Human Resources. **World Wide Web address:** http://www.kohlchildrensmuseum.org. **Description:** A children's museum with multisensory exhibits and programs intended to enhance children's understanding of themselves and the world around them. **Common positions include:** Developmental Specialist; Education Administrator; Marketing Specialist; Public Relations Specialist. **Special programs:** Internships. **Corporate headquarters location:** This Location.

LADY BIRD JOHNSON WILDFLOWER CENTER
4801 La Crosse Avenue, Austin TX 78739. 512/292-4200. **Contact:** Human Resources. **World Wide Web address:** http://www.wildflower.org. **Description:** A nonprofit organization that educates people on the value and beauty of native plants. Lady Bird Johnson Wildflower Center also houses Wild Ideas: The Store, a retail store offering books, art, and clothing dedicated to generating an interest in plant life; and The Wildflower Cafe, a coffee shop and eatery. **Special programs:** Internships. **Corporate headquarters location:** This Location.

LASERPACIFIC MEDIA CORPORATION
809 North Cahuenga Boulevard, Hollywood CA 90038. 323/462-6266. **Fax:** 323/464-3233. **Contact:** Human Resources. **World Wide Web address:** http://www.laserpacific.com. **Description:** A major supplier of film, videotape, digital sound post-production, and multimedia services to prime-time television shows. **Corporate headquarters location:** This Location. **Listed on:** NASDAQ. **Stock exchange symbol:** LPAC. **Annual sales/revenues:** $21 - $50 million.

LIEBERMAN COMPANIES, INC.
9549 Penn Avenue South, Bloomington MN 55431. 952/887-5299. **Contact:** Human Resources. **World Wide Web address:** http://www.liebermanmusic. com. **Description:** A wholesale record and tape distributor. **Common positions include:** Accountant/Auditor; Branch Manager; Credit Manager; Customer Service Representative; Manufacturer's/Wholesaler's Sales Rep.; Operations/Production Manager. **Educational backgrounds include:** Accounting. **Benefits:** 401(k); Dental Insurance; Disability Coverage; Life Insurance; Medical Insurance; Savings Plan. **Special programs:** Internships. **Corporate headquarters location:** This Location. **Parent company:** LIVE. **Listed on:** Privately held. **Number of employees at this location:** 60.

LOS ANGELES ATHLETIC CLUB
431 West Seventh Street, Los Angeles CA 90014. 213/625-2211. **Contact:** Stuart Lava, Director of Human Resources. **Description:** Operates an athletic facility with programs in virtually every sport, as well as concession, banquet, and guest hotel facilities. **Common positions include:** Accountant/Auditor; Assistant Manager; Customer Service Representative. **Educational backgrounds include:** Accounting; Communications; Marketing. **Benefits:** Dental Insurance; Disability Coverage; Life Insurance; Medical Insurance; Pension Plan; Tuition Assistance. **Corporate headquarters location:** This Location. **Other U.S. locations:** Marina del Rey CA; Orange CA. **Listed on:** Privately held. **Number of employees at this location:** 240. **Number of employees nationwide:** 370.

LOS ANGELES COUNTY MUSEUM OF ART
5905 Wilshire Boulevard, Los Angeles CA 90036. 323/857-6000. **Fax:** 323/857-4720. **Recorded jobline:** 323/857-6069. **Personnel phone:** 323/857-4745. **Contact:** Adam Kaplan, Employment Administrator. **E-mail address:** jobs@lacma.org. **World Wide Web address:** http://www.lacma.org. **Description:** A premier visual arts museum. The museum's collection expresses the creativity of cultures from all over the world. This is a nonprofit company. Founded in 1938. **NOTE:** Entry-level positions and part-time jobs are offered. **Common positions include:** Accountant; Administrative Assistant; Attorney; Budget Analyst; Chief Financial Officer; Computer Programmer; Computer Support Technician; Computer Technician; Controller; Customer Service Representative; Database Administrator; Editor; Electrician; Event Planner; Financial Analyst; Graphic Artist; Graphic Designer; Help-Desk Technician; Human Resources Manager; Internet Services Manager; Intranet Developer; Librarian; Managing Editor; Marketing Manager; Marketing Specialist; Media Planner; Network Administrator; Operations Manager; Paralegal; Secretary; Systems Analyst; Technical Support Engineer; Telecommunications Manager;

Video Production Coordinator; Website Developer. **Educational backgrounds include:** Art/Design; Communications; Computer Science; Finance; Liberal Arts; Marketing; Public Relations. **Benefits:** 403(b); Casual Dress - Fridays; Dental Insurance; Disability Coverage; Employee Discounts; Financial Planning Assistance; Flexible Schedule; Life Insurance; Medical Insurance; Pension Plan; Public Transit Available; Savings Plan. **Special programs:** Internships. **Office hours:** Monday - Friday, 8:00 a.m. - 5:00 p.m. **Corporate headquarters location:** This Location. **Listed on:** Privately held. **President/CEO:** Dr. Andrea Rich. **Facilities Manager:** Donald Battjes. **Information Systems Manager:** Peter Bodell. **Sales Manager:** Keith McKeown. **Annual sales/revenues:** $21 - $50 million.

LUCAS DIGITAL LTD. LLC
P.O. Box 2459, San Rafael CA 94912. 415/258-2200. **Recorded jobline:** 415/448-2100. **Contact:** Recruitment Department. **World Wide Web address:** http://www.ilm.com. **Description:** A digital effects company engaged in motion picture film production. The company is comprised of Industrial Light & Magic (ILM), a visual effects company; and Skywalker Sound, a state-of-the-art audio facility. **Common positions include:** Database Manager; Network Administrator; Software Engineer; Systems Specialist; Technician; Video Maintenance Engineer. **Corporate headquarters location:** This Location.

LUCASFILM LTD.
P.O. Box 2009, San Rafael CA 94912-2009. 415/662-1700. **Contact:** Human Resources. **World Wide Web address:** http://www.lucasfilm.com. **Description:** A leading film production company specializing in visual and sound effects. **Educational backgrounds include:** Database Software; Spreadsheets. **Special programs:** Internships. **Corporate headquarters location:** This Location.

LYRIC OPERA OF CHICAGO
20 North Wacker Drive, Chicago IL 60606. 312/332-2244. **Fax:** 312/419-1082. **Contact:** Human Resources. **E-mail address:** jobs@lyricopera.org. **World Wide Web address:** http://www.lyricopera.org. **Description:** Engaged in the study of opera, music, and the fine arts. Lyric Opera is a nonprofit organization that sponsors, produces, and encourages opera and musical performances in Chicago and the surrounding areas. Founded in 1954. **NOTE:** Entry-level positions are offered. **Common positions include:** Accountant/Auditor; Administrative Assistant; Administrative Manager; Budget Analyst; Computer Programmer; Customer Service Representative; Fundraising Specialist; Human Resources Manager; Management Trainee; Public Relations Specialist; Systems Analyst. **Educational backgrounds include:** Business Administration; Communications; Liberal Arts; Music; Theater. **Benefits:** Dental Insurance; Disability Coverage; Life Insurance; Medical Insurance; Pension Plan. **Special programs:** Internships. **Corporate headquarters location:** This Location.

M.E. PRODUCTIONS
2000 SW 30th Avenue, Pembroke Park FL 33009. 954/458-4000. **Fax:** 954/458-4003. **Contact:** Jim Etkin, Vice President. **World Wide Web address:** http://www.meproductions.com. **Description:** A production corporation providing sets, lighting, staging, floral arrangements, decor, audio/visual, entertainment, and music services. **Common positions include:** Commercial Artist; Computer Programmer; Construction Contractor; Cost Estimator; Department Manager; Designer; Draftsperson; Electrician; General Manager; Manufacturer's/Wholesaler's Sales Rep.; Marketing Manager; Public Relations Specialist; Secretary; Sheet-Metal Worker; Travel Agent; Typist/Word Processor. **Educational backgrounds include:** Accounting; Art/Design; Business Administration; Communications; Computer Science; Marketing. **Benefits:** Disability Coverage; Medical Insurance. **Special programs:** Internships. **Corporate headquarters location:** This Location. **Number of employees at this location:** 60.

MGM/UNITED ARTISTS
ORION PICTURES CORPORATION
1350 Avenue of the Americas, 24th Floor, New York NY 10010. 212/708-0300. **Contact:** Human Resources. **World Wide Web address:** http://www.mgm.com. **Description:** One of the nation's largest film distribution companies. **Common positions include:** Attorney; Branch Manager; Computer Programmer; Customer Service Representative; Department Manager; Human Resources Manager; Public Relations Specialist; Systems Analyst. **Educational backgrounds include:** Marketing. **Benefits:** Dental Insurance; Disability Coverage; Employee Discounts; Life Insurance; Medical Insurance; Tuition Assistance. **Special programs:** Internships. **Corporate headquarters location:** This Location. **Other U.S. locations:** Los Angeles CA. **Number of employees at this location:** 250.

MADISON CIVIC CENTER
MADISON REPERTORY THEATRE
211 State Street, Desk 2287, Madison WI 53703-2287. 608/266-6550. **Contact:** Human Resources Department. **Description:** Offers performances by the Madison Symphony Orchestra, the Madison Opera, the Madison Repertory Theatre (also at this location), and the Children's Theatre of Madison. **Corporate headquarters location:** This Location.

MADISON OPERA & GUILD
333 Glenway Street, Madison WI 53705. 608/238-8085. **Contact:** Human Resources. **Description:** Holds performances throughout the year at the Madison Civic Center. **Corporate headquarters location:** This Location.

MADISON SQUARE GARDEN CORPORATION
2 Penn Plaza, 16th Floor, New York NY 10121. 212/465-6330. **Fax:** 212/465-6026. **Recorded jobline:** 212/465-6335. **Contact:** Human Resources. **E-mail address:** msghr@thegarden.com. **World Wide Web address:** http://www.thegarden.com. **Description:** Operates sports and entertainment events in the Arena, Rotunda, and Paramount Theatre. Professional sports teams include the NBA's New York Knicks basketball team, the WNBA's New York Liberty, and the New York Rangers hockey team. Madison Square Garden also operates the MSG Network (one of the nation's oldest regional cable television sports networks). In addition, Madison Square Garden operates its own restaurants, catering, fast food, and merchandise divisions. **NOTE:** Part-time jobs are offered. **Common positions include:** Budget Analyst; Computer Programmer; Customer Service Representative; Financial Analyst; Human Resources Manager; MIS Specialist; Public Relations Specialist; Radio/TV Announcer/Broadcaster; Restaurant/Food Service Manager; Systems Analyst; Typist/Word Processor. **Educational backgrounds include:** Accounting; Communications; Marketing. **Benefits:** Dental Insurance; Disability Coverage; Employee Discounts; Life Insurance; Medical Insurance; Pension Plan; Savings Plan; Tuition Assistance.

Special programs: Internships. **Internship information:** Madison Square Garden has a college internship program that runs during the fall, spring, and summer semesters. For application information, call 212/465-6258. **Corporate headquarters location:** This Location. **Operations at this facility include:** Administration; Sales.

MAINE STATE MUSIC THEATRE, INC.
14 Maine Street, Suite 109, Brunswick ME 04011. 207/725-8769. **Fax:** 207/725-1199. **Contact:** Kathy Kacinski, Company Manager. **World Wide Web address:** http://www.msmt.org. **Description:** A nonprofit music theater company that produces five shows per summer. Maine State Music Theatre also trains theater professionals. **Common positions include:** Actor/Actress/Performer; Administrator; Management Trainee; Musician/Musical Arranger; Public Relations Specialist; Technician. **Educational backgrounds include:** Art/Design; Communications; Liberal Arts; Music. **Benefits:** Medical Insurance. **Special programs:** Internships. **Office hours:** Monday - Saturday, 9:00 a.m. - 5:00 p.m. **Corporate headquarters location:** This Location. **Managing Director:** Steven C. Peterson.

MALIBU ENTERTAINMENT WORLDWIDE
717 North Harwood Street, Suite 1650, Dallas TX 75201. 214/210-8701. **Contact:** Human Resources. **Description:** Develops, owns, and operates 25 entertainment centers called SpeedZone, Malibu, Grand Prix, and Mountasia Family FunCenters. FunCenters are located in suburban communities and feature miniature golf courses, state-of-the-art video and skill game rooms, go-cart raceways, bumper boats, batting cages, and roller skating arenas. Founded in 1986. **Corporate headquarters location:** This Location.

MANHATTAN TRANSFER, INC.
545 Fifth Avenue, New York NY 10017. 212/687-4000. **Contact:** Human Resources. **World Wide Web address:** http://www.mte.com. **Description:** Produces television commercials. **Corporate headquarters location:** This Location. **Parent company:** International Post Ltd., through its operating subsidiaries Audio Plus Video International, Inc., Big Picture/Even Time Limited, Cabana, and The Post Edge, Inc., is a provider of a wide range of post-production services primarily to the television advertising industry, and a distributor of television programming to the international market. The company's services include creative editorial services; film-to-tape transfer; electronic video editing; computer-generated graphics, duplication, and audio services, all in multiple standards and formats; as well as network playback operations. The company's services are provided in both the New York metropolitan area and South Florida.

MANN THEATRES
711 Hennepin Avenue, Minneapolis MN 55403. 612/332-3303. **Contact:** Human Resources. **Description:** Operates a chain of movie theaters throughout Minnesota. **Corporate headquarters location:** This Location.

McCARTER THEATRE
91 University Place, Princeton NJ 08540. 609/258-6500. **Fax:** 609/497-0369. **Contact:** General Manager. **Description:** A performing arts center which produces and presents artists in dramatic, musical, dance, and special events. Established in 1963. **Common positions include:** Actor/Actress/Performer; Artist; Designer; Painter; Tailor. **Educational backgrounds include:** Art/Design; Business Administration; Communications; Liberal Arts; Marketing. **Benefits:** Dental Insurance; Life

Insurance; Medical Insurance; Pension Plan. **Special programs:** Internships. **Corporate headquarters location:** This Location. **Number of employees at this location:** 200.

THE METROPOLITAN OPERA
Lincoln Center, New York NY 10023. 212/799-3100. **Fax:** 212/870-7405. **Contact:** Adrienne Selan, Human Resources Associate. **E-mail address:** resumes@mail.metopera.org. **World Wide Web address:** http://www.metopera.org. **Description:** One of the world's largest nonprofit arts organizations, producing approximately 25 operas per year. The opera tours internationally and performs free outdoor concerts in New York area parks. **NOTE:** Entry-level positions, part-time jobs, and second and third shifts are offered. **Common positions include:** Accountant; Actor/Actress/Performer; Administrative Assistant; Administrative Manager; Applications Engineer; Blue-Collar Worker Supervisor; Budget Analyst; Cashier; Commercial Artist; Computer Programmer; Computer Technician; Customer Service Representative; Database Administrator; Department Manager; Designer; Electrical/Electronics Engineer; Employment Interviewer; Financial Analyst; Help-Desk Technician; Human Resources Manager; Marketing Manager; Mechanical Engineer; Operations Manager; Secretary; Telecommunications Manager. **Educational backgrounds include:** Accounting; Business Administration; Communications; Economics; Finance; Liberal Arts; Marketing; MBA; Microsoft Office; Microsoft Word; Public Relations. **Benefits:** 403(b); Casual Dress - Daily; Dental Insurance; Life Insurance; Medical Insurance; Pension Plan; Vacation Days (6 - 10). **Corporate headquarters location:** This Location. **Operations at this facility include:** Administration; Manufacturing; Sales; Service. **Number of employees at this location:** 1,000.

MGM INC.
2500 Broadway Street, Santa Monica CA 90404. 310/449-3560. **Contact:** Human Resources. **World Wide Web address:** http://www.mgm.com. **Description:** A fully-integrated media company providing entertainment through the production and distribution of feature films, television programs, animation, music, and interactive games. **Corporate headquarters location:** New York NY.

MILWAUKEE BALLET COMPANY, INC.
504 West National Avenue, Milwaukee WI 53204. 414/643-7677. **Fax:** 414/649-4066. **Contact:** Controller. **Description:** A nonprofit professional dance company. Milwaukee Ballet Company also operates a ballet school with over 800 students. The ballet has five series of performances each year and over 25 performances of *The Nutcracker* each December. **Common positions include:** Administrative Assistant; Administrative Manager; Controller; Education Administrator; Marketing Manager; Musician/Musical Arranger; Operations/Production Manager; Public Relations Specialist; Sales Manager; Teacher/Professor; Typist/Word Processor. **Educational backgrounds include:** Accounting; Art/Design; Business Administration; Communications; Computer Science; Finance; Liberal Arts; Marketing; Public Relations. **Benefits:** 403(b); Dental Insurance; Disability Coverage; Employee Discounts; Financial Planning Assistance; Life Insurance; Medical Insurance; Public Transit Available. **Special programs:** Apprenticeships. **Corporate headquarters location:** This Location. **Subsidiaries include:** Milwaukee Ballet Orchestra. **Annual sales/revenues:** Less than $5 million. **Number of employees at this location:** 250.

MILWAUKEE PUBLIC MUSEUM
800 West Wells Street, Milwaukee WI 53233. 414/278-2700. **Contact:** Human Resources Department. **World Wide Web address:** http://www.mpm.edu. **Description:** A museum open to the public year-round. Exhibits include "The Streets of Old Milwaukee," "Third Planet," and "Rain Forest: Exploring Life on Earth." The museum operates the Humphrey IMAX Dome Theater. The museum also offers weekend family programs called "Afternoon Adventures." **Corporate headquarters location:** This Location.

MINNESOTA VIKINGS
9520 Viking Drive, Eden Prairie MN 55344. 952/828-6500. **Contact:** Senior Vice President of Football Operations. **Description:** Operates an NFL football team. **Benefits:** 401(k); Dental Insurance; Disability Coverage; Employee Discounts; Life Insurance; Medical Insurance; Pension Plan. **Corporate headquarters location:** This Location.

MISSOURI ATHLETIC CLUB
405 Washington Avenue, St. Louis MO 63102. 314/231-7220. **Recorded jobline:** 314/539-4437. **Contact:** Human Resources. **World Wide Web address:** http://www.mac-stl.com. **Description:** A private club offering a full gymnasium, heated swimming pool and solarium, multiple private dining rooms, a pro shop, and overnight guest accommodations. This location also hires seasonally. Founded in 1903. **NOTE:** Entry-level positions and second and third shifts are offered. **Common positions include:** Assistant Manager; Chef/Cook/Kitchen Worker; Chief Financial Officer; Editor; Food and Beverage Service Worker; Graphic Artist; Hotel Manager; Human Resources Manager; Operations Manager; Purchasing Agent/Manager; Sales Executive; Secretary; Systems Manager. **Educational backgrounds include:** Accounting; Business Administration; Communications; Computer Science; Hotel Administration; Restaurant Management. **Benefits:** 401(k); Dental Insurance; Disability Coverage; Free Meals; Life Insurance; Medical Insurance; Pension Plan; Savings Plan; Tuition Assistance. **Special programs:** Apprenticeships; Summer Jobs. **Office hours:** Monday - Friday, 8:00 a.m. - 4:30 p.m. **Corporate headquarters location:** This Location. **Number of employees at this location:** 235. **Number of employees nationwide:** 310.

MISSOURI BOTANICAL GARDEN
P.O. Box 299, St. Louis MO 63166. 314/577-5100. **Physical address:** 4344 Shaw Boulevard, St. Louis MO. **Fax:** 314/577-9597. **Recorded jobline:** 314/577-9401. **Contact:** Human Resources. **E-mail address:** jobs@mobot.org. **World Wide Web address:** http://www.mobot.org. **Description:** A nonprofit cultural organization that promotes the preservation and enrichment of plant life and the environment. Missouri Botanical Garden has been internationally recognized for its botanical research, education programs, and horticulture display. Founded in 1859. **NOTE:** Part-time jobs are offered. **Common positions include:** Accountant; Administrative Assistant; Administrative Manager; Biological Scientist; Botanist; Buyer; Content Developer; Controller; Curator; Customer Service Representative; Database Administrator; Editor; Editorial Assistant; Education Administrator; Electrician; Fundraising Specialist; General Manager; Horticulturist; Human Resources Manager; Instructional Technologist; Librarian; Maintenance Technician; Managing Editor; Marketing Manager; MIS Specialist; Network/Systems Administrator; Public Relations Specialist; Researcher; Sales Representative; Secretary; Teacher/Professor; Technical Writer/Editor; Tour Guide; Typist/Word Processor; Webmaster. **Educational backgrounds include:** Biology; Botany; Business Administration; Computer Science; Education; Horticulture; HTML; Java; Liberal Arts; Marketing; Microsoft Word; Novell; Public Relations; Software Tech. Support; Spreadsheets. **Benefits:** 403(b); Dental Insurance; Disability Coverage; Employee Discounts; Flexible Schedule; Life Insurance; Medical Insurance; Pension Plan; Public Transit Available. **Special programs:** Internships; Summer Jobs. **Office hours:** Monday - Friday, 9:00 a.m. - 5:00 p.m. **Corporate headquarters location:** This Location. **Director:** Dr. Peter H. Raven. **Number of employees at this location:** 370.

MULTIMEDIA TUTORIAL
205 Kings Highway, Brooklyn NY 11223. 718/234-0404. **Contact:** Human Resources. **Description:** Produces and markets tutorial education programs, primarily in videotape and also CD-ROM formats, for use by adults and children in homes, work, schools, libraries, and other locales. Principal products consist of a series of 92 videotapes and supplemental materials on mathematics and an interactive, audio-visual, CD-ROM based system for language instruction. The company's videotapes include colorful computer graphics and real life vignettes. **Corporate headquarters location:** This Location.

MUNICIPAL THEATRE ASSOCIATION OF ST. LOUIS
Forest Park, St. Louis MO 63112-1098. 314/361-1900. **Contact:** Barbara Echele, Assistant to the General Manager and CEO. **Description:** A nonprofit theatrical production company that operates a large outdoor theater. Founded in 1919. **Common positions include:** Accountant/Auditor; Advertising Clerk; Customer Service Representative; Department Manager; Marketing Specialist; Operations/Production Manager; Public Relations Specialist. **Educational backgrounds include:** Accounting; Art/Design; Business Administration; Communications; Finance; Liberal Arts; Marketing. **Special programs:** Internships; Summer Jobs. **Corporate headquarters location:** This Location. **Operations at this facility include:** Sales. **Number of employees at this location:** 20.

MUSEUM OF CONTEMPORARY ART
220 East Chicago Avenue, Chicago IL 60611. 312/397-3819. **Toll-free phone:** 800/MCA-7858. **Fax:** 312/397-4095. **Recorded jobline:** 312/397-4050. **Contact:** Susan Kieffer, Human Resources Manager. **E-mail address:** skieffer@mcachicago.org. **World Wide Web address:** http://www.mcachicago.org. **Description:** A nonprofit, contemporary art museum offering exhibitions of international works from 1945 to the present, with a permanent collection of over 1,500 works. **NOTE:** Entry-level positions, part-time jobs, and second and third shifts are offered. **Common positions include:** Accountant; Administrative Assistant; Chief Financial Officer; Controller; Editor; Graphic Designer; Librarian; Marketing Manager; MIS Specialist; Multimedia Designer; Network/Systems Administrator; Systems Analyst. **Educational backgrounds include:** Accounting; Art/Design; Excel; Marketing; Microsoft Word; Public Relations. **Benefits:** Employee Discounts; Medical Insurance; Pension Plan; Vacation Days (11 - 15). **Special programs:** Internships; Summer Jobs. **Office hours:** Monday - Friday, 10:00 a.m. - 5:00 p.m.

MUSEUM OF FINE ARTS - BOSTON
465 Huntington Avenue, Boston MA 02115. 617/267-9300. **Contact:** Sandra Matthews,

Employment Manager. **World Wide Web address:** http://www.mfa.org. **Description:** One of the largest museums in New England, with a wide spectrum of permanent and featured exhibits. **Educational backgrounds include:** Art History; Liberal Arts. **Corporate headquarters location:** This Location.

THE MUSEUM OF FINE ARTS - HOUSTON
1001 Bissonnet, Houston TX 77005. 713/639-7560. **Fax:** 713/639-7597. **Contact:** Marilyn Fisher, Employment Manager. **World Wide Web address:** http://www.mfah.org. **Description:** An art museum with exhibits including "The Glassell Collection of African Gold," "Art of Asia," and "Modern and Contemporary Art." **Common positions include:** Accountant/Auditor; Administrator; Advertising Clerk; Blue-Collar Worker Supervisor; Curatorial Specialist; Department Manager; Editor; Education Administrator; Food Scientist/Technologist; Fundraising Specialist; Grant Writer; Graphic Artist; Human Resources Manager; Librarian; Marketing Specialist; Public Relations Specialist; Reporter; Security Manager. **Educational backgrounds include:** Accounting; Art History; Art/Design; Business Administration; Communications; Computer Science; Education; Finance; Liberal Arts; Marketing. **Benefits:** Credit Union; Disability Coverage; Employee Discounts; Life Insurance; Medical Insurance; Pension Plan; Tuition Assistance. **Special programs:** Internships. **Corporate headquarters location:** This Location. **Number of employees at this location:** 500.

MUSEUM OF MODERN ART
11 West 53rd Street, New York NY 10019. 212/708-9400. **Contact:** Human Resources Manager. **World Wide Web address:** http://www.moma.org. **Description:** Houses one of the world's foremost collections of modern art. **Common positions include:** Administrative Worker/Clerk; Secretary. **Educational backgrounds include:** Art/Design; Liberal Arts. **Benefits:** Dental Insurance; Disability Coverage; Employee Discounts; Life Insurance; Medical Insurance; Pension Plan; Tuition Assistance. **Special programs:** Internships. **Corporate headquarters location:** This Location. **Number of employees at this location:** 550.

MUSEUM OF SCIENCE & INDUSTRY
57th Street & Lake Shore Drive, Chicago IL 60637. 773/684-9844. **Fax:** 773/684-7107. **Contact:** Human Resources. **E-mail address:** humanresources@msichicago.org. **World Wide Web address:** http://www.msichicago.org. **Description:** One of the largest science museums in the world. Museum of Science & Industry offers over 800 exhibits including hands-on interactive exhibits. Founded in 1933. **Common positions include:** Administrative Assistant; Blue-Collar Worker Supervisor; Buyer; Chief Financial Officer; Clerical Supervisor; Computer Programmer; Controller; Customer Service Representative; Education Administrator; Electrician; Finance Director; Graphic Artist; Graphic Designer; Human Resources Manager; Internet Services Manager; Marketing Manager; Marketing Specialist; Operations Manager; Project Manager; Public Relations Specialist; Purchasing Agent/Manager; Secretary. **Educational backgrounds include:** Accounting; Art/Design; Biology; Business Administration; Chemistry; Communications; Finance; Liberal Arts; Marketing; Mathematics; Public Relations. **Benefits:** 403(b); Dental Insurance; Disability Coverage; Employee Discounts; Life Insurance; Medical Insurance; Pension Plan; Public Transit Available. **Special programs:** Internships. **Corporate headquarters**

location: This Location. **Number of employees at this location:** 460.

MYSTIC AQUARIUM INSTITUTE FOR EXPLORATION
55 Coogan Boulevard, Mystic CT 06355. 860/572-5955. **Fax:** 860/572-5984. **Contact:** Recruitment. **E-mail address:** humanresources@mysticaquarium.org. **World Wide Web address:** http://www.mysticaquarium.org. **Description:** A nonprofit organization that promotes awareness of the aquatic world through an integration of educational programs, marine-life exhibits, research and development, and ocean exploration. Mystic Aquarium's exhibits include a variety of fish and invertebrates, African black-footed penguins, beluga whales, Stellar's sea lions, northern fur seals, harbor seals, and Atlantic bottlenose dolphins. Mystic Aquarium also offers the Education Center in Hartford, which provides live animal exhibits, classrooms, and a resource center. This location also hires seasonally. Founded in 1973. **NOTE:** Entry-level positions, part-time jobs, and second and third shifts are offered. **Common positions include:** Accountant; Administrative Assistant; Administrative Manager; Biological Scientist; Broadcast Technician; Buyer; Carpenter; Chief Financial Officer; Clinical Lab Technician; Computer Support Technician; Construction Contractor; Controller; Draftsperson; Event Planner; Graphic Artist; Graphic Designer; Housekeeper; Human Resources Manager; Insurance Agent/Broker; Marine Scientist; Marketing Manager; MIS Specialist; Network/Systems Administrator; Operations Manager; Public Relations Specialist; Sales Executive; Sales Representative; Secretary; Teacher/Professor; Technical Support Manager; Technical Writer/Editor; Technician; Veterinarian; Vice President of Finance; Vice President of Operations; Vice President of Project Development; Webmaster. **Educational backgrounds include:** Animal Science; ASP; Biology; Communications; Computer Science; Education; Environmental Science; HTML; Internet Development; Java; Marine Science; MCSE; Microsoft Office; Microsoft Word; Novell; Public Relations; Software Tech. Support; Spreadsheets; SQL; Visual Basic. **Benefits:** 401(k); Disability Coverage; Employee Discounts; Financial Planning Assistance; Flexible Schedule; Life Insurance; Medical Insurance; Profit Sharing; Sick Days (6 - 10); Tuition Assistance; Vacation Days (10 - 20). **Special programs:** Internships. **Corporate headquarters location:** This Location. **Parent company:** Sea Research Foundation, Inc. **Annual sales/revenues:** Less than $5 million. **Number of employees at this location:** 225.

NYS THEATRE INSTITUTE
P.O. Box 28, Troy NY 12181-0028. 518/274-3200. **Physical address:** 155 River Street, Troy NY 12180. **Fax:** 518/274-3815. **Contact:** Arlene Leff, Intern Program Director. **World Wide Web address:** http://www.nysti.org. **Description:** A professional resident theater company that specializes in theater for family audiences with a strong arts and education approach.

NATIONAL MUSEUM OF AMERICAN HISTORY
14th Street & Constitution Avenue NW, Room A-1040, MRC 605, Washington DC 20560-0605. 202/357-1606. **Fax:** 202/786-2851. **Contact:** Internship/Fellowship Coordinator. **World Wide Web address:** http://americanhistory.si.edu. **Description:** A museum that investigates, interprets, collects, preserves, exhibits, and honors the heritage of America. Founded in 1846. **NOTE:** For permanent employment, please send resumes to Human Resources, 955 L'Enfant Plaza SW, Suite

2100, Washington DC 20560. **Company slogan:** The increase and diffusion of knowledge. **Special programs:** Internships. **Internship information:** The museum's internship program is open to persons enrolled in their final two years of high school and through retirement. Please contact the Office of Internships and Fellowships to receive an application packet. **Corporate headquarters location:** This Location.

NATIONAL SPORTS CENTER FOR THE DISABLED
P.O. Box 1290, Winter Park CO 80482. 970/726-1540. **Contact:** Georgianne Dominguez, Assistant Director. **World Wide Web address:** http://www.nscd.org. **Description:** A nonprofit organization that provides outdoor mountain recreational services to children and adults with disabilities. Founded in 1970. **Common positions include:** Accountant/Auditor; Recreational Therapist; Teacher/Professor. **Educational backgrounds include:** Accounting; Business Administration; Education; Health Care; Recreation. **Benefits:** 401(k); Daycare Assistance; Dental Insurance; Job Sharing; Life Insurance; Medical Insurance; Pension Plan; Public Transit Available; Tuition Assistance. **Special programs:** Internships. **Corporate headquarters location:** This Location. **Parent company:** Winter Park Recreation Association. **Annual sales/revenues:** Less than $5 million. **Number of employees at this location:** 55.

NEW HAVEN RAVENS
252 Derby Avenue, West Haven CT 06516. 203/782-1666. **Fax:** 203/782-3150. **Contact:** Human Resources. **World Wide Web address:** http://www.ravens.com. **Description:** Administrative offices for the minor league baseball team. **Corporate headquarters location:** This Location.

NEW JERSEY SPORTS & EXPOSITION AUTHORITY
50 Route 120, East Rutherford NJ 07073. 201/935-8500. **Contact:** Gina Klein, Assistant Director of Human Resources. **World Wide Web address:** http://www.njsea.com. **Description:** A state-appointed agency responsible for coordinating and running sports and entertainment activities at the Meadowlands Sports Complex, which includes Meadowlands Racetrack (harness and thoroughbred racing, as well as other events), Giants Stadium (New York Giants, New York Jets, concerts, and other events), and Continental Airlines Arena (New Jersey Nets, New Jersey Devils, tennis, track, concerts, and other events). **Corporate headquarters location:** This Location.

NEW LINE CINEMA
116 North Robertson Boulevard, Suite 200, Los Angeles CA 90048. 310/854-5811. **Fax:** 310/659-8145. **Recorded jobline:** 310/967-6553. **Contact:** Personnel. **World Wide Web address:** http://www.newline.com. **Description:** Produces and distributes motion pictures (generally action/adventure and comedy films for the younger market). New Line Cinema also acquires distribution rights to films produced by others, and has agreements with distributors in ancillary markets such as home video, pay television, and free television. **NOTE:** Entry-level positions are offered. **Common positions include:** Administrative Assistant; Network/Systems Administrator; Paralegal; Secretary. **Benefits:** 401(k); Casual Dress - Daily; Dental Insurance; Disability Coverage; Employee Discounts; Medical Insurance; Sick Days (6 - 10); Vacation Days (6 - 10). **Special programs:** Internships. **Corporate headquarters location:** New York NY. **Other U.S.**

locations: Chicago IL; Dallas TX. **International locations:** United Kingdom. **Parent company:** Time Warner. **Number of employees at this location:** 300.

THE NEW YORK BOTANICAL GARDEN
200th Street & Kazimiroff Boulevard, Bronx NY 10458-5126. 718/817-8744. **Fax:** 718/220-6504. **Contact:** Human Resources. **World Wide Web address:** http://www.nybg.org. **Description:** An internationally recognized center for botanical research offering 47 gardens and plant collections. The New York Botanical Garden is dedicated to environmental education and the conservation of plant diversity. Founded in 1891. **Common positions include:** Administrator; Fundraising Specialist. **Educational backgrounds include:** Education; Horticulture; Marketing; Science. **Special programs:** Internships. **Corporate headquarters location:** This Location.

THE OAKLAND ATHLETICS (A'S)
7677 Oakport Street, Suite 200, Oakland CA 94621. 510/638-4900. **Recorded jobline:** 510/638-4900x2817. **Contact:** Human Resources. **E-mail address:** info@oaklandathletics.com. **World Wide Web address:** http://www.oaklandathletics.com. **Description:** Business offices for the Major League Baseball team. **NOTE:** Entry-level positions and part-time jobs are offered. **Common positions include:** Account Representative; Accountant; Administrative Assistant; Advertising Executive; Marketing Manager; MIS Specialist; Public Relations Specialist. **Educational backgrounds include:** Accounting; Business Administration; Computer Science; Finance; Marketing; Public Relations. **Benefits:** 401(k); Casual Dress - Daily; Dental Insurance; Disability Coverage; Employee Discounts; Life Insurance; Medical Insurance; Pension Plan; Public Transit Available. **Special programs:** Internships. **Office hours:** Monday - Friday, 8:00 a.m. - 5:00 p.m. **Corporate headquarters location:** This Location. **Listed on:** Privately held.

OREGON COAST AQUARIUM
2820 SE Ferry Slip Road, Newport OR 97365. 541/867-3474. **Fax:** 541/867-6846. **Contact:** Lou Willcox, Human Resources Administrator. **World Wide Web address:** http://www.aquarium.org. **Description:** A nonprofit aquarium offering a variety of special events including an annual music festival, whale watching cruises, artist workshops, bay cruises, and "Breakfast with the Animals." The aquarium focuses on education and features fish and animal species found off the Oregon coast. **NOTE:** Entry-level positions are offered. **Benefits:** 403(b); Dental Insurance; Employee Discounts; Life Insurance; Medical Insurance; Pension Plan; Sick Days (6 - 10); Vacation Days (10 - 20). **Special programs:** Internships; Summer Jobs. **Office hours:** Monday - Friday, 9:00 a.m. - 6:00 p.m. **Corporate headquarters location:** This Location. **President:** Phyllis Bell. **Number of employees at this location:** 90.

OXYGEN MEDIA, INC.
75 9th Avenue, 7th Floor, New York City NY 10011. 212/651-2000. **Contact:** Human Resources. **E-mail address:** resumes@oxygen.com. **World Wide Web address:** http://www.oxygen.com. **Description:** Produces and broadcasts television programs and Websites geared towards women viewers.

PPI ENTERTAINMENT
88 St. Francis Street, Newark NJ 07105. 973/344-4214. **Contact:** Personnel. **World Wide Web address:** http://www.peterpan.com. **Description:**

Manufactures and distributes records, tapes, videos, and CD-ROMs. **Common positions include:** Accountant; Advertising Executive; Editorial Assistant; Graphic Artist; Graphic Designer; Marketing Manager; Production Manager; Public Relations Specialist; Purchasing Agent/Manager; Sales Manager; Sales Representative; Secretary; Video Production Coordinator. **Educational backgrounds include:** Accounting; Art/Design; Communications; Marketing. **Benefits:** 401(k); Employee Discounts; Life Insurance; Medical Insurance; Public Transit Available. **Corporate headquarters location:** This Location. **Listed on:** Privately held.

PEARSON TELEVISION
2700 Colorado Avenue, Suite 450, Santa Monica CA 90404. 310/656-1100. **Contact:** Human Resources. **World Wide Web address:** http://www.pearsontv.com. **Description:** Produces, distributes, markets, and promotes television programs and recorded music both domestically and internationally. The company's television operations include the production and domestic distribution of *The Price is Right* and *Family Feud,* both of which are popular television game shows. The company is a leading distributor of television programming in the first-run syndication and distributes, represents, or owns participations in more than 160 television series, over 250 motion pictures, a variety of children's programming, and live-event specials. **Corporate headquarters location:** This Location. **Number of employees at this location:** 125.

PHOENIX ART MUSEUM
1625 North Central Avenue, Phoenix AZ 85004-1685. 602/257-2121. **Fax:** 602/253-8662. **Recorded jobline:** 602/307-2010. **Contact:** Mary Anderson, Human Resources Manager. **World Wide Web address:** http://www.phxart.org. **Description:** A nonprofit, visual arts museum with collections including Asian art, European art, Latin American art, decorative art, and fashion design. This location also hires seasonally. Founded in 1949. **NOTE:** Entry-level positions, part-time jobs, and second and third shifts are offered. **Common positions include:** Accounting Clerk; Administrative Assistant; Clerk; Computer Support Technician; Controller; Curator; Development Officer; Education Administrator; Human Resources Manager; Librarian; Network/Systems Administrator; Public Relations Specialist; Visitor Services. **Educational backgrounds include:** Accounting; Art/Design; Business Administration; Communications; Education; Finance; Liberal Arts; Marketing; Microsoft Office; Microsoft Word; Public Relations; Spreadsheets; SQL. **Benefits:** 403(b); Dental Insurance; Disability Coverage; Employee Discounts; Flexible Schedule; Life Insurance; Medical Insurance; Pension Plan; Public Transit Available; Sick Days (6 - 10); Vacation Days (10 - 20). **Special programs:** Internships. **Corporate headquarters location:** This Location. **Listed on:** Privately held. **CEO:** Michael Greenbaum. **Facilities Manager:** Sherwood Spivey. **Information Systems Manager:** Mary Anderson. **Sales Manager:** Carla Foster. **Number of employees at this location:** 110.

PHOENIX SUNS
201 East Jefferson Street, Phoenix AZ 85004. 602/379-7900. **Contact:** Human Resources. **World Wide Web address:** http://www.suns.com. **Description:** Offices for the NBA team. **Corporate headquarters location:** This Location.

PORTLAND SEA DOGS
P.O. Box 636, Portland ME 04104. 207/874-9300. **Contact:** Personnel. **World Wide Web address:** http://www.portlandseadogs.com. **Description:** A minor league baseball franchise. The Portland Sea Dogs are the AA affiliate of the Florida Marlins Major League Baseball franchise. **Corporate headquarters location:** This Location.

PORTLAND STAGE COMPANY
P.O. Box 1458, Portland ME 04104. 207/774-1043. **Contact:** Steve Smith, Technical Director. **Description:** A nonprofit professional theater. **Common positions include:** Accountant/Auditor; Administrative Manager; Designer; General Manager. **Educational backgrounds include:** Theater. **Benefits:** Medical Insurance. **Special programs:** Internships. **Corporate headquarters location:** This Location. **Number of employees at this location:** 30.

THE PRINCE GEORGE'S PUBLICK PLAYHOUSE FOR THE PERFORMING ARTS
5445 Landover Road, Hyattsville MD 20784-1225. 301/277-1711. **Contact:** Hiring Manager. **Description:** A theater offering dramatic, dance, and musical performances year-round. **Corporate headquarters location:** This Location.

RADIO CITY ENTERTAINMENT
1260 Avenue of the Americas, New York NY 10020. 212/247-4777. **Contact:** Human Resources. **World Wide Web address:** http://www.radiocity.com. **Description:** A diversified entertainment production company. **Common positions include:** Advertising Manager; Attorney; Customer Service Representative; Emergency Medical Technician; Human Resources Manager; Operations/Production Manager; Public Relations Specialist; Purchasing Agent/Manager; Systems Analyst. **Special programs:** Internships. **Corporate headquarters location:** This Location. **Parent company:** Cablevision.

RAINBOW MEDIA AMC (AMERICAN MOVIE CLASSICS)
1111 Stewart Avenue, Bethpage NY 11714. 516/364-2222. **Contact:** Human Resources. **World Wide Web address:** http://www.amctv.com. **Description:** Operates the AMC network (also at this location), dedicated to the preservation of classic cinema, and Bravo, a cable network dedicated to the arts and entertainment industry. **Corporate headquarters location:** This Location.

REGAL CINEMAS, INC.
7132 Commercial Park Drive, Knoxville TN 37918. 865/922-1123. **Contact:** Debbie Robertson, Director of Employee Relations. **World Wide Web address:** http://www.regalcinemas.com. **Description:** A leading motion picture exhibitor in the eastern United States. The company primarily shows first-run movies at its 422 multiscreen theaters, with an aggregate of more than 4,455 screens in 32 states. Founded in 1989. **Corporate headquarters location:** This Location.

SCIENCE MUSEUM OF MINNESOTA
120 West Kellogg Boulevard, St. Paul MN 55102. 651/221-2532. **Fax:** 651/221-4777. **Recorded jobline:** 651/221-4548. **Contact:** Human Resources. **World Wide Web address:** http://www.smm.org. **Description:** Science Museum of Minnesota is a private, nonprofit, educational and research institution organized to collect, study, and preserve objects of scientific significance and to interpret the objects, discoveries, and insights of science for the general public through its exhibits and education programs. The museum has exhibits in anthropology, biology, geography, paleontology, technology, cultural history, and natural history. Additionally, the museum houses a collection of

over 1.5 million scientific objects and an Omnitheater that produces and distributes OMNIMAX films shown around the world. **NOTE:** Advanced degrees in the natural sciences are required for curatorial positions. **Common positions include:** Biological Scientist; Buyer; Curatorial Specialist; Customer Service Representative; Designer; Editor; Education Administrator; Exhibit Designer; Financial Analyst; Fundraising Specialist; Geographer; Graphic Artist; Human Resources Manager; Interpreter; Library Technician; Marketing Specialist; Public Relations Specialist; Services Sales Representative; Teacher/Professor; Technical Writer/Editor; Wholesale and Retail Buyer; Writer. **Educational backgrounds include:** Accounting; Anthropology; Art/Design; Business Administration; Communications; Computer Science; Finance; Geology; Liberal Arts; Marketing; Mathematics; Paleontology; Physics. **Benefits:** Dental Insurance; Employee Discounts; Life Insurance; Medical Insurance; Pension Plan; Section 125 Plan. **Corporate headquarters location:** This Location. **Number of employees at this location:** 600.

SEA PINES ASSOCIATES, INC.
P.O. Box 7000, Hilton Head Island SC 29938. 843/785-3333. **Fax:** 843/842-1412. **Contact:** Monica Nash, Director of Human Resources. **World Wide Web address:** http://www.seapines.com. **Description:** A holding company. **Corporate headquarters location:** This Location. **Subsidiaries include:** Sea Pines Company, Inc. (also at this location) operates resort assets including three golf courses, a 28-court racquet club, a home and villa rental management business, retail sales outlets, food services operations, and other resort recreational facilities. Sea Pines Real Estate Company, Inc. is an independent real estate brokerage firm with 18 offices. Sea Pines Country Club, Inc. owns and operates a full-service private country club providing golf, tennis, and clubhouse facilities for approximately 1,500 club members. **Number of employees at this location:** 250.

SEATTLE CHORAL COMPANY
1518 NE 143rd Street, Seattle WA 98125. 206/365-8765. **Fax:** 206/365-8714. **Contact:** Fred Coleman, Artistic Director. **Description:** An oratorio society performing symphonic and a cappella masterworks. Founded in 1980. **Corporate headquarters location:** This Location.

SHEDD AQUARIUM
1200 South Lake Shore Drive, Chicago IL 60605. 312/939-2426. **Contact:** Human Resources. **E-mail address:** jobs@sheddaquarium.org. **World Wide Web address:** http://www.shedd.org. **Description:** An aquarium and oceanarium offering a wide range of exhibits, outreach programs, and educational workshops. **Corporate headquarters location:** This Location.

SHOWTIME NETWORKS INC.
1633 Broadway, New York NY 10019. 212/708-1600. **Contact:** Human Resources. **World Wide Web address:** http://www.showtimeonline.com. **Description:** Operates a number of premium cable networks including SHOWTIME, SHO2, SHO3, Showtime Extreme, Showtime Beyond, The Movie Channel, The Movie Channel 2, Sundance, and FLIX. **Corporate headquarters location:** This Location. **Parent company:** Viacom Company.

SHUBERT ORGANIZATION, INC.
234 West 44th Street, New York NY 10036. 212/944-3700. **Contact:** Elliot H. Greene, Vice President of Finance. **Description:** Owns 16 Broadway theatres, the National Theatre in Washington DC, and the Shubert Theatre in Los Angeles CA. The Shubert Organization also produces plays. **Common positions include:** Accountant/Auditor; Administrative Worker/Clerk; Management Trainee. **Educational backgrounds include:** Accounting; Business Administration; Liberal Arts. **Benefits:** Dental Insurance; Disability Coverage; Life Insurance; Medical Insurance; Pension Plan. **Corporate headquarters location:** This Location.

SIX FLAGS HOUSTON
SIX FLAGS ASTROWORLD
9001 Kirby Drive, Houston TX 77054. 713/794-3217. **Fax:** 713/799-1030. **Contact:** Charity Melton, Human Resources Supervisor. **E-mail address:** cmelton@sftp.com. **World Wide Web address:** http://www.sixflags.com. **Description:** An amusement and theme park. Six Flags AstroWorld offers seven theme lands based on the nations of the world, past and present. Six Flags AstroWorld has 11 roller coasters and also offers Wonderland, filled with rides and activities for younger children. The park also offers entertainment including shows and concerts. Six Flags WaterWorld (also at this location) offers water slides, waterfalls, a fantasy water playground for kids, a game room, specialty shops, a restaurant, and food stands. Six Flags SplashTown (also at this location) is a family-oriented water park. **NOTE:** Jobseekers should apply in person, if possible. Six Flags Houston hires over 3,000 employees each season. Entry-level positions, part-time jobs, and second and third shifts are offered. **Common positions include:** Accountant; Administrative Assistant; Blue-Collar Worker Supervisor; Controller; Electrician; MIS Specialist; Sales Representative. **Educational backgrounds include:** Business Administration; Marketing. **Benefits:** 401(k); Dental Insurance; Employee Discounts; Medical Insurance; Pension Plan; Tuition Assistance. **Special programs:** Internships; Training; Summer Jobs. **Internship information:** Some paid summer internships are offered and housing is available. For more information, e-mail or write to the Recruitment Coordinator at the above address. **Office hours:** Monday - Friday, 9:00 a.m. - 12:00 p.m., 1:00 p.m. - 6:00 p.m. **Parent company:** Premier Parks (OK) owns and operates 35 theme parks nationwide.

SMITHSONIAN INSTITUTION
955 L'Enfant Plaza SW, Suite 2100, Washington DC 20560. 202/287-3102. **Fax:** 202/287-3088. **Contact:** Human Resources. **World Wide Web address:** http://www.si.edu. **Description:** An independent, federal establishment devoted to research, public education, and national service in the arts, sciences, and history. The Smithsonian Institution consists of 16 museums and galleries and one national zoo. Founded in 1846. **Common positions include:** Accountant/Auditor; Administrative Manager; Advertising Clerk; Aerospace Engineer; Agricultural Engineer; Agricultural Scientist; Architect; Attorney; Biological Scientist; Biomedical Engineer; Blue-Collar Worker Supervisor; Budget Analyst; Chemist; Civil Engineer; Clerical Supervisor; Clinical Lab Technician; Computer Programmer; Construction and Building Inspector; Construction Contractor; Cost Estimator; Counselor; Designer; Draftsperson; Editor; Education Administrator; Electrical/Electronics Engineer; Electrician; Financial Analyst; General Manager; Geographer; Geologist/Geophysicist; Health Services Manager; Human Resources Manager; Human Service Worker; Industrial Engineer; Landscape Architect; Librarian; Library Technician; Management Analyst/Consultant; Mathematician; Mechanical Engineer; Meteorologist; Paralegal; Physicist;

Public Relations Specialist; Reporter; Restaurant/Food Service Manager; Science Technologist; Sociologist; Statistician; Structural Engineer; Systems Analyst; Teacher/Professor; Technical Writer/Editor. **Educational backgrounds include:** Accounting; Art/Design; Biology; Business Administration; Chemistry; Communications; Computer Science; Engineering; Geology; Liberal Arts; Marketing. **Benefits:** Daycare Assistance; Dental Insurance; Disability Coverage; Employee Discounts; Life Insurance; Medical Insurance; Pension Plan; Savings Plan. **Special programs:** Internships. **Corporate headquarters location:** This Location. **Number of employees at this location:** 6,000.

SONY PICTURES ENTERTAINMENT
10202 West Washington Boulevard, Suite 3900, Culver City CA 90232. **Contact:** Personnel. **E-mail address:** resumes@spe.sony.com. **World Wide Web address:** http://www.spe.sony.com. **Description:** Sony Pictures is involved in motion pictures, television, theatrical exhibitions, and studio facilities and technology. The motion picture business distributes movies produced by Columbia TriStar Pictures. The television business, which encompasses Columbia TriStar Television, Columbia TriStar Television Distribution, and Columbia TriStar International Television, is involved with numerous cable channels and distributes and syndicates television programs such as *Days of Our Lives* and *Dawson's Creek.* Loews Cineplex Entertainment operates state-of-the-art theaters in 385 locations with 2,926 screens in 15 states. Sony Pictures Imageworks specializes in motion picture special effects and production planning through previsualization sequences. **Corporate headquarters location:** This Location. **Parent company:** Sony Corporation of America. **Listed on:** New York Stock Exchange. **Other U.S. locations:**
- 550 Madison Avenue, 7th Floor, New York NY 10022. 212/833-8500.

SOUTH CAROLINA STATE MUSEUM
P.O. Box 100107, Columbia SC 29202-3107. 803/898-4921. **Physical address:** 301 Gervais Street, Columbia SC 29201. **Contact:** Charles Lee, Director of Human Resources. **World Wide Web address:** http://www.museum.state.sc.us. **Description:** A museum featuring art, history, natural history, and science and technology. **Corporate headquarters location:** This Location.

SOUTH STREET SEAPORT MUSEUM
207 Front Street, New York NY 10038. 212/748-8600. **Fax:** 212/748-8610. **Contact:** Melissa Clark, Human Resources Director. **World Wide Web address:** http://www.southstseaport.org. **Description:** A maritime history museum. Through educational programs, exhibitions, and the preservation of buildings and ships, the museum interprets the role of the seaport in the development of the city, state, and nation. Founded in 1967.

SPEEDWAY MOTORSPORTS, INC.
P.O. Box 600, Concord NC 28026. 704/455-3239. **Fax:** 704/455-2168. **Contact:** Cynthia Mankus, Personnel. **World Wide Web address:** http://www.gospeedway.com. **Description:** Promotes, markets, and sponsors motorsport activities including eight racing events annually sanctioned by NASCAR, five of which are associated with the Winston Cup professional stock car racing circuit and three of which are associated with the Busch Grand National circuit. The company also operates, sanctions, and promotes its Legends Cars, 5/8-scale modified cars, modeled after those driven by legendary NASCAR racers, for use on its Legends Car Racing Circuit,

which is an entry-level stock car racing series. Other Speedway Motorsports operations include two ARCA annual stock car races. **Common positions include:** Accountant; Administrative Assistant; Advertising Clerk; Advertising Executive; Architect; Attorney; Chief Financial Officer; Civil Engineer; Communications Engineer; Construction Contractor; Design Engineer; Draftsperson; Electrical/Electronics Engineer; Electrician; Emergency Medical Technician; Environmental Engineer; Event Planner; General Manager; Human Resources Manager; Industrial Designer; Industrial Engineer; Landscape Architect; Manufacturing Engineer; Market Research Analyst; Marketing Manager; Marketing Specialist; Mechanical Engineer; Media Planner; Metallurgical Engineer; Paralegal; Public Relations Specialist; Quality Assurance Engineer; Web Advertising Specialist. **Educational backgrounds include:** Accounting; Business Administration; Communications; Finance; Marketing; Public Relations. **Benefits:** 401(k); Dental Insurance; Life Insurance; Medical Insurance. **Special programs:** Internships. **Office hours:** Monday - Friday, 9:00 a.m. - 5:00 p.m. **Corporate headquarters location:** This Location. **Subsidiaries include:** Atlanta Motor Speedway; Bristol Motor Speedway; Finish Line Events; Las Vegas Motor Speedway; Lowe's Motor Speedway; Performance Racing Network; Sears Point Raceway; Texas Motor Speedway. **Listed on:** New York Stock Exchange. **Stock exchange symbol:** TRK. **Information Systems Manager:** Chip Long. **Purchasing Manager:** Roger Neale. **Sales Manager:** Jim Dunean. **Number of employees at this location:** 255.

SPELLING ENTERTAINMENT INC.
5700 Wilshire Boulevard, Suite 575, Los Angeles CA 90036. 323/965-5700. **Contact:** Human Resources. **Description:** A leading producer and distributor of television, film, and interactive entertainment. The company comprises Spelling Television, which produces made-for-television movies, miniseries, and one-hour series including *Seventh Heaven;* Big Ticket Television, which produces sitcoms for the broadcast and first-run markets; Spelling Films, which produces and distributes feature films; Worldwide Vision, which syndicates the Spelling Entertainment library of more than 20,000 hours of television programming and thousands of feature films; Republic Entertainment, a distributor of home videos for the rental and sell-through markets; Virgin Interactive Entertainment, a developer and publisher of interactive games; and Hamilton products, a licensing and merchandising company that handles Spelling Properties. **Corporate headquarters location:** This Location. **Parent company:** Viacom, Inc. **Listed on:** New York Stock Exchange. **Stock exchange symbol:** SP. **Number of employees worldwide:** 1,000.

THE SPORTS CLUB COMPANY
11100 Santa Monica Boulevard, Suite 300, Los Angeles CA 90025. 310/479-5200. **Fax:** 310/479-8350. **Contact:** Human Resources. **Description:** Owns and operates several health clubs throughout California under the names Sports Club and Spectrum Club. **Corporate headquarters location:** This Location. **Listed on:** American Stock Exchange. **Stock exchange symbol:** SCY.

SUGARLOAF/USA
Rural Route 1, Box 5000, Kingfield ME 04947. 207/237-2000. **Fax:** 207/237-2718. **Contact:** Personnel. **E-mail address:** info@sugarloaf.com. **World Wide Web address:** http://www.sugarloaf.com. **Description:** An operator of a ski mountain and resort. Races and other events are held year-

round. Features at Sugarloaf include a number of cross-country trails, an Olympic-sized ice skating rink, and an 18-hole golf course. **Common positions include:** Customer Service Representative; Driver; Food and Beverage Service Worker; Resort Staff; Teacher/Professor. **Benefits:** 401(k); Daycare Assistance; Dental Insurance; Disability Coverage; Employee Discounts; Life Insurance; Medical Insurance; Season Pass. **Special programs:** Internships. **Corporate headquarters location:** This Location. **Number of employees at this location:** 750.

THE SUMMIT AT SNOQUALMIE
P.O. Box 1068, Snoqualmie Pass WA 98068. 425/434-7669. **Contact:** Human Resources. **World Wide Web address:** http://www.summit-at-snoqualmie.com. **Description:** Operates four ski areas in the metropolitan Seattle area. This location also hires seasonally. **Common positions include:** Accountant/Auditor; Automotive Mechanic; Customer Service Representative; Electrician; Food and Beverage Service Worker; Seasonal Worker. **Benefits:** Season Pass. **Corporate headquarters location:** This Location. **Number of employees at this location:** 1,200.

SWANK AUDIO VISUALS INC.
2720 Walnut Place, St. Louis MO 63103. 314/534-1940. **Contact:** Human Resources. **Description:** A non-theatrical film distribution and audio visual equipment rental company. **Common positions include:** Computer Programmer; Management Trainee; Services Sales Representative; Systems Analyst. **Educational backgrounds include:** Business Administration; Communications; Liberal Arts. **Benefits:** 401(k); Dental Insurance; Disability Coverage; Flexible Benefits; Life Insurance; Medical Insurance; Savings Plan; Tuition Assistance. **Special programs:** Internships. **Corporate headquarters location:** This Location. **Other U.S. locations:** Phoenix AZ; CA; Washington DC; Chicago IL; New York NY; Tulsa OK; Philadelphia PA; Austin TX; Corpus Christi TX; Houston TX. **Listed on:** Privately held. **Number of employees at this location:** 100. **Number of employees nationwide:** 500.

THE THEATER AT MONMOUTH
P.O. Box 385, Monmouth ME 04259-0385. 207/933-2952. **Contact:** David Greenham, Managing Director. **Description:** A small, professional, summer theater in central Maine, performing in a national historic landmark Victorian opera house. **NOTE:** The theater offers seasonal employment for professionals in the technical, costume, administrative, and performance departments. **Common positions include:** Actor/Actress/Performer; Assistant Manager; Chef/Cook/Kitchen Worker. **Educational backgrounds include:** Accounting; Business Administration; Liberal Arts. **Benefits:** Employee Discounts; Room and Board. **Special programs:** Internships. **Office hours:** Monday - Friday, 9:00 a.m. - 5:00 p.m. **Corporate headquarters location:** This Location. **Number of employees at this location:** 40.

TIME WARNER INC.
75 Rockefeller Plaza, New York NY 10019. 212/484-8000. **Contact:** Human Resources. **World Wide Web address:** http://www.timewarner.com. **Description:** Publishes and distributes books and magazines including the weekly *Time* magazine. Time Warner also produces, distributes, licenses, and publishes recorded music; owns and administers music copyrights; produces, finances, and distributes motion pictures and television programming; distributes videocassettes; produces and distributes pay television and cable programming; and operates and manages cable television systems. **NOTE:** In January 2000, America Online, Inc. and Time Warner, Inc. announced plans to merge. The new company will be named AOL Time Warner Inc. Also in January 2000, EMI Group PLC and Time Warner, Inc. announced plans to merge their music businesses. Companies affected by this merger will be named Warner EMI Music. Please contact this location for more information. **Corporate headquarters location:** This Location.

TRANS-LUX CORPORATION
110 Richards Avenue, Norwalk CT 06854. 203/853-4321. **Contact:** Human Resources Department. **World Wide Web address:** http://www.trans-lux.com. **Description:** Designs, produces, leases, sells, and services large-scale, multicolor, real-time electronic information displays for both indoor and outdoor use. These displays are used primarily in applications for the financial, banking, gaming, corporate, retail, healthcare, transportation, and sports markets. The company also owns an expanding chain of movie theaters in the western region of the United States and owns real estate in the U.S. and Canada. **Corporate headquarters location:** This Location. **Listed on:** American Stock Exchange. **Stock Exchange Symbol:** TLX.

TURF PARADISE INC.
1501 West Bell Road, Phoenix AZ 85023. 602/942-1101. **Contact:** Human Resources. **World Wide Web address:** http://www.turfparadise.com. **Description:** Conducts an annual thoroughbred race at its 220-acre facility in Phoenix. Turf Paradise also operates a 14-acre mobile home park. **Corporate headquarters location:** This Location.

USA NETWORKS, INC.
152 West 57th Street, New York NY 10019. 212/314-7300. **Contact:** Human Resources. **World Wide Web address:** http://www.usanetwork.com. **Description:** An e-commerce and entertainment company operating one of the nation's largest cable television networks. **Corporate headquarters location:** This Location.

UNITED ARTISTS THEATRE CIRCUIT
9110 East Nichols Avenue, Suite 200, Englewood CO 80112. 303/792-8613. **Fax:** 303/792-8221. **Contact:** Human Resources. **World Wide Web address:** http://www.uatc.com. **Description:** Operates 300 movie theaters with 2,000 screens in 23 states. Founded in 1926. **Common positions include:** Administrative Assistant; Auditor; Chief Financial Officer; Graphic Artist; Graphic Designer; Marketing Manager; Paralegal; Project Manager; Sales Manager; Secretary. **Educational backgrounds include:** Accounting; Business Administration; Communications; Computer Science; Finance; Liberal Arts; Marketing; Public Relations. **Benefits:** 401(k); Dental Insurance; Disability Coverage; Life Insurance; Medical Insurance; Tuition Assistance. **Corporate headquarters location:** This Location. **Other U.S. locations:** Nationwide. **International locations:** Worldwide. **Number of employees at this location:** 200. **Number of employees nationwide:** 11,000.

UNIVERSAL STUDIOS, INC.
100 Universal City Plaza, Universal City CA 91608. 818/777-1000. **Recorded jobline:** 818/777-JOBS. **Contact:** Corporate Workforce Planning & Strategic Staffing. **E-mail address:** jobs@unistudios.com. **World Wide Web address:** http://www.universalstudios.com. **Description:** A diversified entertainment company and a worldwide leader in motion pictures, television, music, and home and location-based themed entertainment. The

company's main operating divisions include Universal Studios, Universal Studios Recreation Group, Universal Studios Information Technology, Universal Studios Operations Group, Universal Music Group, Universal Pictures, Universal Networks & Worldwide Television Distribution, Universal Studios Consumer Products Group, Universal Studios Online, and Spencer Gifts. **NOTE:** Entry-level positions are offered. **Common positions include:** Accountant; Administrative Assistant; Administrative Manager; Architect; Attorney; Auditor; Budget Analyst; Buyer; Chief Financial Officer; Civil Engineer; Computer Animator; Computer Operator; Computer Programmer; Controller; Cost Estimator; Design Engineer; Draftsperson; Editor; Editorial Assistant; Electrical/Electronics Engineer; Electrician; Finance Director; Financial Analyst; General Manager; Graphic Artist; Graphic Designer; Human Resources Manager; Industrial Engineer; Intellectual Property Lawyer; Internet Services Manager; Management Analyst/Consultant; Market Research Analyst; Marketing Manager; Marketing Specialist; Mechanical Engineer; MIS Specialist; Multimedia Designer; Online Content Specialist; Operations Manager; Paralegal; Project Manager; Public Relations Specialist; Purchasing Agent/Manager; Sales Executive; Sales Manager; Sales Representative; Secretary; Systems Analyst; Systems Manager; Technical Writer/Editor; Video Production Coordinator. **Educational backgrounds include:** Accounting; Art/Design; Business Administration; Communications; Engineering; Finance; Liberal Arts; Marketing; Public Relations. **Benefits:** 401(k); Dental Insurance; Disability Coverage; Employee Discounts; Life Insurance; Medical Insurance; On-Site Daycare; Profit Sharing; Public Transit Available; Tuition Assistance. **Special programs:** Internships; Training; Co-ops; Summer Jobs. **Corporate headquarters location:** This Location. **International locations:** Worldwide. **Parent company:** The Seagram Co. Ltd. **Listed on:** New York Stock Exchange. **Stock exchange symbol:** VOX. **Annual sales/revenues:** More than $100 million.

Other U.S. locations:
- 1000 Universal Studios Plaza, Orlando FL 32819. 407/363-8000.

UTAH ZOOLOGICAL SOCIETY
2600 East Sunnyside Avenue, Salt Lake City UT 84108. 801/582-1631. **Fax:** 801/584-1771. **Contact:** Bonnie Thomas, Human Resources Coordinator. **World Wide Web address:** http://www.hoglezoo.org/zoosocty.htm. **Description:** A nonprofit organization that operates the Hogle Zoo. This location also hires seasonally. Founded in 1912. **NOTE:** The society offers volunteer opportunities. Entry-level positions and part-time jobs are offered. **Common positions include:** Accountant; Administrative Assistant; Administrative Manager; Advertising Executive; Blue-Collar Worker Supervisor; Chief Financial Officer; Clerical Supervisor; Computer Technician; Construction Contractor; Controller; Education Administrator; Event Planner; Executive Director; Finance Director; General Manager; Graphic Artist; Graphic Designer; Human Resources Manager; Industrial Designer; Landscape Architect; Marketing Manager; Marketing Specialist; Public Relations Specialist; Secretary; Surgical Technician; Typist/Word Processor; Veterinarian; Vice President; Website Developer. **Educational backgrounds include:** Accounting; Animal Science; Art/Design; Business Administration; Liberal Arts; Marketing; Microsoft Word; Public Relations; Software Tech. Support; Spreadsheets; Visual Basic. **Benefits:** 401(k); Casual Dress - Daily; Dental Insurance; Disability Coverage;

Employee Discounts; Life Insurance; Medical Insurance; Pension Plan; Public Transit Available; Sick Days (1 - 5); Vacation Days (10 - 20). **Special programs:** Internships; Summer Jobs. **Corporate headquarters location:** This Location. **Annual sales/revenues:** $5 - $10 million. **Number of employees at this location:** 110.

WALKER ART CENTER
725 Vineland Place, Minneapolis MN 55403. 612/375-7600. **Fax:** 612/375-7590. **Recorded jobline:** 612-375-7588. **Contact:** Gary A. White, Director of Human Resources. **E-mail address:** work@walkerart.org. **World Wide Web address:** http://www.walkerart.org. **Description:** An international contemporary art museum with exhibition, film/video, and performing arts programming. **Common positions include:** Accountant/Auditor; Administrator; Carpenter; Curatorial Specialist; Editor; Educational Specialist; Graphic Artist; Human Resources Manager; Marketing Specialist; Program Manager; Secretary; Technician; Visitor Services. **Educational backgrounds include:** Accounting; Art History; Art/Design; Business Administration; Communications; Liberal Arts; Marketing. **Benefits:** Dental Insurance; Disability Coverage; Employee Discounts; Life Insurance; Medical Insurance; Pension Plan. **Special programs:** Internships. **Corporate headquarters location:** This Location. **Number of employees at this location:** 150.

WILLIAM MORRIS AGENCY, INC.
1325 Avenue of the Americas, New York NY 10019. 212/903-1110. **Fax:** 212/903-1474. **Contact:** Ms. Pat Galloway, Director of Human Resources. **Description:** One of the largest talent and literary agencies in the world. Founded in 1898. **NOTE:** Entry-level positions are offered. **Common positions include:** Administrative Assistant; Agent Trainee. **Educational backgrounds include:** Business Administration; Communications; Film; Liberal Arts; Theater. **Benefits:** Daycare Assistance; Dental Insurance; Disability Coverage; Life Insurance; Medical Insurance; Profit Sharing; Public Transit Available; Sick Days (6 - 10); Vacation Days (6 - 10). **Special programs:** Training. **Corporate headquarters location:** 151 El Camino Drive, Beverly Hills CA. 310/859-4000. **Other U.S. locations:** Nashville TN. **Listed on:** Privately held. **Number of employees at this location:** 200. **Number of employees nationwide:** 700. **Number of employees worldwide:** 750.

WOLF PARK
Battle Ground IN 47920. 765/567-2265. **Fax:** 765/567-4299. **Contact:** Manager. **World Wide Web address:** http://www.wolfpark.org. **Description:** A nonprofit research organization focusing on wolf behavior and preservation. The park offers walking tours, lectures, and seminars to the public. **Special programs:** Internships; Co-ops. **Corporate headquarters location:** This Location.

WORLD WRESTLING FEDERATION ENTERTAINMENT, INC.
1241 East Main Street, P.O. Box 3857, Stamford CT 06902. 203/352-8600. **Contact:** Human Resources. **World Wide Web address:** http://www.wwf.com. **Description:** Develops and markets television programming and pay-per-view broadcasting for the World Wrestling Federation. The company also produces and manages live wrestling events. **Corporate headquarters location:** This Location.

YONKERS RACEWAY
810 Central Park Avenue, Yonkers NY 10704. 914/968-4200. **Contact:** Anita Tripo, Director of

Personnel. **Description:** Operates a major harness racing facility, as well as a convention and meeting facility. **Common positions include:** Accountant/Auditor; Food and Beverage Service Worker; Market Research Analyst; Public Relations Specialist; Services Sales Representative. **Corporate headquarters location:** This Location.

For more information on career opportunities in arts, entertainment, sports, and recreation:

Associations

AMERICAN ASSOCIATION OF MUSEUMS
1575 Eye Street NW, Suite 400, Washington DC 20005. 202/289-1818. Fax: 202/289-6578. World Wide Web address: http://www.aam-us.org. Publishes *Aviso*, a monthly newsletter containing employment listings for the entire country.

AMERICAN CAMPING ASSOCIATION
5000 State Road 67 North, Martinsville IN 46151. 765/342-8456. World Wide Web address: http://www.aca-camps.org. Provides information on job opportunities at day and overnight camps for children and adults with special needs.

AMERICAN CRAFTS COUNCIL
72 Spring Street, New York NY 10012-4019. 212/274-0630. Operates a research library. Publishes *American Crafts* magazine.

AMERICAN DANCE GUILD
P.O. Box 2006, Lenox Hill Station, New York NY 10021. World Wide Web address: http://www. americandanceguild.org. Holds an annual conference with panels, performances, and workshops. Operates a job listings service (available at a discount to members).

AMERICAN FEDERATION OF MUSICIANS
1501 Broadway, Suite 600, New York NY 10036. 212/869-1330. World Wide Web address: http://www.afm.org.

AMERICAN FILM INSTITUTE
2021 North Western Avenue, Los Angeles CA 90027. 323/856-7600. Toll-free phone: 800/774-4AFI. World Wide Web address: http://www. afionline.org. Membership is required, and includes a newsletter; and members-only discounts on events, seminars, workshops, and exhibits.

AMERICAN MUSIC CENTER
30 West 26th Street, Suite 1001, New York NY 10010-2011. 212/366-5260. Fax: 212/366-5265. World Wide Web address: http://www.amc.net. A nonprofit research and information center for contemporary music and jazz. Provides information services and grant programs.

AMERICAN SOCIETY OF COMPOSERS, AUTHORS, AND PUBLISHERS (ASCAP)
One Lincoln Plaza, New York NY 10023. 212/621-6000. World Wide Web address: http://www.ascap. com. A membership association which licenses members' work and pays members' royalties. Offers showcases and educational seminars and workshops. The society also has an events hotline: 212/621-6485.

AMERICAN SYMPHONY ORCHESTRA LEAGUE
33 West 60th Street, 5th Floor, New York NY 10023-7905. 212/262-5161. Fax: 212/262-5198. World Wide Web address: http://www.symphony. org.

AMERICAN ZOO AND AQUARIUM ASSOCIATION
8403 Colesville Road, Suite 710, Silver Spring MD 20910. 301/562-0777. E-mail address: azaoms@ aol.com. World Wide Web address: http://www.aza.org. Publishes a monthly newspaper with employment opportunities for members.

AMERICANS FOR THE ARTS
One East 53rd Street, New York NY 10022. 212/223-2787. World Wide Web address: http://www.artsusa.org. A nonprofit organization for the literary, visual, and performing arts. Supports K-12 education and promotes public policy through meetings, forums, and seminars.

ASSOCIATION OF INDEPENDENT VIDEO AND FILMMAKERS
304 Hudson Street, 6th Floor, New York NY 10013. 212/807-1400. World Wide Web address: http://www.aivf.org.

THE CENTER FOR THE STUDY OF SPORT IN SOCIETY
Northeastern University, 360 Huntington Avenue, Suite 161CP, Boston MA 02120. 617/373-4025. World Wide Web address: http://www. sportinsociety.org. Develops programs and provides publications on the interaction of sports and society.

NATIONAL ARTISTS' EQUITY ASSOCIATION
P.O. Box 28068, Central Station, Washington DC 20038-8068. 202/628-9633. A national, nonprofit organization dedicated to improving economic, health, and legal conditions for visual artists.

NATIONAL ENDOWMENT FOR THE ARTS
1100 Pennsylvania Avenue NW, Washington DC 20506. 202/682-5400. World Wide Web address: http://www.arts.endow.gov.

NATIONAL RECREATION AND PARK ASSOCIATION
22377 Belmont Ridge Road, Ashburn VA 20148. 703/858-0784. Fax: 703/858-0794. World Wide Web address: http://www.nrpa.org. A national, nonprofit service organization. Offers professional development and training opportunities in recreation, parks, and leisure services. Publishes a newsletter and magazine that offer employment opportunities for members only.

PRODUCERS GUILD OF AMERICA
400 South Beverly Drive, Suite 211, Beverly Hills CA 90212. 310/557-0807. Fax: 310/557-0436. World Wide Web address: http://www. producersguild.com. Membership is required, and includes credit union access; subscription to *P.O.V. Magazine* and the association newsletter; attendance at the organization's annual Golden Laurel Awards and other events; and special screenings of motion pictures at the time of the Academy Awards.

Directories

ARTIST'S AND GRAPHIC DESIGNER'S MARKET
Writer's Digest Books, 1507 Dana Avenue, Cincinnati OH 45207. 513/531-2222.

BLACK BOOK ILLUSTRATION
The Black Book, 10 Astor Place, 6th Floor, New York NY 10003. 212/539-9800. World Wide Web address: http://www.blackbook.com.

BLACK BOOK PHOTOGRAPHY
The Black Book, 10 Astor Place, 6th Floor, New York NY 10003. 212/539-9800. World Wide Web address: http://www.blackbook.com.

ROSS REPORTS TELEVISION AND FILM
BPI Communications, Inc., 1515 Broadway, 14th Floor, New York NY 10036-8986. 212/764-7300.

Magazines

AMERICAN CINEMATOGRAPHER
American Society of Cinematographers, 1782 North Orange Drive, Hollywood CA 90028. Toll-free phone: 800/448-0154. World Wide Web address: http://www.cinematographer.com.

ARTFORUM
65 Bleecker Street, 13th Floor, New York NY 10012. 212/475-4000. World Wide Web address: http://www.artforum.com.

AVISO
American Association of Museums, 1575 Eye Street NW, Suite 400, Washington DC 20005. 202/289-1818.

BACK STAGE
BPI Communications, Inc., 1515 Broadway, New York NY 10036-8986. 212/764-7300. World Wide Web address: http://www.backstage.com.

BILLBOARD
BPI Communications, Inc., 1515 Broadway, New York NY 10036-8986. 212/764-7300. World Wide Web address: http://www.billboard.com.

CRAFTS REPORT
300 Water Street, Box 1992, Wilmington DE 19899. 302/656-2209. World Wide Web address: http://www.craftsreport.com.

DRAMA-LOGUE
P.O. Box 38771, Los Angeles CA 90038. 213/464-5079.

HOLLYWOOD REPORTER
BPI Communications, Inc., 5055 Wilshire Boulevard, 6th Floor, Los Angeles CA 90036. 213/525-2000. World Wide Web address: http://www.hollywoodreporter.com.

VARIETY
245 West 17th Street, 5th Floor, New York NY 10011. 212/337-7001. Toll-free phone: 800/323-4345.

WOMEN ARTIST NEWS
300 Riverside Drive, New York NY 10025. 212/666-6990.

Online Services

ARTJOB
Gopher://gopher.tmn.com/11/Artswire/artjob. Provides information on jobs, internships, and conferences in theater, dance, opera, and museums. This site is only accessible through America Online.

COOLWORKS
World Wide Web address: http://www.coolworks.com. Provides links to 22,000 job openings in national parks, summer camps, ski areas, river areas, ranches, fishing areas, cruise ships, and resorts. This site also includes information on volunteer openings.

THE INTERNET MUSIC PAGES
World Wide Web address: http://www.musicpages.com. Offers job listings at well-known companies such as Dolby, Microsoft, and Fender and also provides links to music-related newsgroups.

JOBS IN SPORTS CAREEREXPERIENCE.COM
World Wide Web address: http://careerexperience.com. Offers members direct access to full contact information for hundreds of jobs in sports and recreation. Fees are $9.95 for one day; $49.00 for one month; $399.00 for a year.

VISUAL NATION ARTS JOBS LINKS
World Wide Web address: http://www.visualarts.com. Provides links to other sites that post arts and academic job openings and information.

Automotive

You can expect to find the following types of companies in this chapter:
*Automotive Repair Shops • Automotive Stampings • Industrial Vehicles and Moving
Equipment • Motor Vehicles and Equipment • Travel Trailers and Campers*

Some helpful information: *The average salary range for automotive mechanics and
servicers is approximately $25,000 - $35,000 per year. Commissioned mechanics, as well
as specialist mechanics, can earn considerably more.*

A.M.P. INDUSTRIES
42050 Executive Drive, Harrison Township MI
48045-1311. 810/469-4100. **Fax:** 810/463-8650.
Contact: Stephen Mann, Human Resources
Manager. **Description:** Supplies plastic injection
molding and tool building for OEM automotive and
recreational vehicle manufacturers. **Common
positions include:** Accountant/Auditor; Blue-Collar
Worker Supervisor; Budget Analyst; Buyer; Cost
Estimator; Designer; Financial Analyst; Human
Resources Manager; Operations/Production
Manager; Plastics Engineer; Process Engineer;
Purchasing Agent/Manager; Quality Control
Supervisor. **Educational backgrounds include:**
Accounting; Business Administration; Engineering;
Marketing. **Benefits:** 401(k); Casual Dress -
Fridays; Dental Insurance; Disability Coverage; Life
Insurance; Medical Insurance; Profit Sharing;
Tuition Assistance; Vacation Days (11 - 15).
Special programs: Internships. **Corporate
headquarters location:** This Location. **President:**
Karl Blankenburg. **Information Systems Manager:**
Mike Aiuto. **Sales Manager:** Mike Orlos. **Number
of employees at this location:** 260.

ASC INC.
18640 Walnut, Southgate MI 48195. 734/285-4911.
Fax: 734/246-2609. **World Wide Web address:**
http://www.acsglobal.com. **Contact:** Human
Resources/Staffing. **Description:** An original
equipment manufacturer that engineers and
develops convertible systems, exterior enhancement
programs, sunroofs, and interior trim for cars and
trucks. ASC Inc. also converts imported and
domestic sedans into convertibles. Founded in 1965.
Common positions include: Accountant; Buyer;
Computer Programmer; Electrical/Electronics
Engineer; Financial Analyst; Human Resources
Manager; Industrial Engineer; Mechanical Engineer;
Product Engineer; Purchasing Agent/Manager;
Quality Control Supervisor; Structural Engineer;
Systems Analyst. **Educational backgrounds
include:** Accounting; Business Administration;
Engineering. **Benefits:** 401(k); Car Purchase Plan;
Dental Insurance; Disability Coverage; Employee
Discounts; Life Insurance; Medical Insurance;
Pension Plan; Profit Sharing; Savings Plan; Tuition
Assistance; Vision Insurance. **Special programs:**
Internships. **Corporate headquarters location:**
This Location. **Other area locations:** Gibraltar MI;
Lansing MI; Livonia MI. **Other U.S. locations:**
Long Beach CA; Bowling Green KY; Statesville
NC; Columbus OH; Dublin VA; Vancouver WA.
International locations: Germany; Japan; Korea.
Listed on: Privately held. **Annual sales/revenues:**
More than $100 million. **Number of employees at
this location:** 500. **Number of employees
nationwide:** 2,500.

ACCURIDE CORPORATION
2315 Adams Lane, Henderson KY 42420. 270/826-
5000. **Contact:** Human Resources. **World Wide
Web address:** http://www.accuridecorp.com.
Description: Manufactures rims and wheels for cars
and semi-tractor trailers. **Common positions
include:** Accountant/Auditor; Blue-Collar Worker
Supervisor; Buyer; Chemist; Computer
Programmer; Customer Service Rep.; Designer;
Draftsperson; Electrical/Electronics Engineer;
Electrician; Human Resources Manager; Industrial
Engineer; Mechanical Engineer; Metallurgical
Engineer; Quality Control Supervisor; Registered
Nurse; Safety Specialist; Systems Analyst.
Educational backgrounds include: Accounting;
Business Administration; Computer Science;
Engineering; Marketing. **Benefits:** 401(k); Dental
Insurance; Disability Coverage; Medical Insurance;
Pension Plan; Prescription Drugs; Tuition
Assistance. **Special programs:** Internships.
Corporate headquarters location: This Location.
Parent company: Phelps Dodge Corporation.
Number of employees at this location: 650.

ADAPTO, INC.
122 South Litchfield Road, Goodyear AZ 85338.
623/935-2681. **Fax:** 623/932-0939. **Contact:**
Human Resources. **E-mail address:** adapto@
syspac.com. **Description:** This location
manufactures metal components for air bag systems.
Overall, Adapto manufactures automotive parts.
NOTE: Entry-level positions and second and third
shifts are offered. **Common positions include:**
Account Manager; Account Rep.; Accountant;
Administrative Assistant; Blue-Collar Worker
Supervisor; Buyer; Chief Financial Officer;
Controller; Human Resources Manager;
Manufacturing Engineer; MIS Specialist;
Production Manager; Project Manager; Purchasing
Agent/Manager; Quality Control Supervisor; Sales
Executive; Secretary; Typist/Word Processor.
Educational backgrounds include: Accounting;
Business Administration; Engineering; Finance;
Marketing. **Benefits:** 401(k); Dental Insurance;
Disability Coverage; Flexible Schedule; Life
Insurance; Medical Insurance; Profit Sharing;
Tuition Assistance. **Special programs:** Training.
Corporate headquarters location: This Location.
Other U.S. locations: South Bend IN. **Parent
company:** SOCOR. **President:** Tom Schoaf.
Facilities Manager: Robert Gordon. **Number of
employees at this location:** 185.

ADESA BOSTON
63 Western Avenue, Framingham MA 01702.
508/626-7000. **Contact:** Human Resources.
Description: Auctions used cars and other vehicles
to franchised auto dealerships. Adesa also provides
auto reconditioning and vehicle transport services.
NOTE: Entry-level positions and part-time jobs are
offered. **Common positions include:** Automotive
Mechanic; Light Industrial Worker. **Benefits:**
401(k); Dental Insurance; Disability Coverage; Life
Insurance; Medical Insurance; Profit Sharing. **Office
hours:** Monday - Friday, 8:30 a.m. - 5:00 p.m.
Number of employees at this location: 380.
Number of employees nationwide: 4,000.

ALFA LEISURE INC.
13501 Fifth Street, Chino CA 91710. 909/628-5574. **Fax:** 909/591-7902. **Contact:** Human Resources. **E-mail address:** info@alfaleisure.com. **World Wide Web address:** http://www.alfaleisure.com. **Description:** Manufactures high-end, fifth wheel recreation trailers designed to be pulled by pickup trucks. Founded in 1973. **Common positions include:** Accountant; Administrative Assistant; Blue-Collar Worker Supervisor; Buyer; Chief Financial Officer; Claim Rep.; Computer Operator; Computer Programmer; Computer Technician; Customer Service Representative; Design Engineer; Draftsperson; Industrial Engineer; Industrial Production Manager; Manufacturing Engineer; Marketing Specialist; Mechanical Engineer; Production Manager; Project Manager; Quality Control Supervisor; Sales Executive; Sales Manager; Sales Rep.; Typist/Word Processor; Vice President. **Educational backgrounds include:** Accounting; Engineering; Finance; Marketing; Microsoft Word; Spreadsheets. **Benefits:** 401(k); Casual Dress - Daily; Dental Insurance; Life Insurance; Medical Insurance; Vacation Pay. **Office hours:** Monday - Friday, 8:00 a.m. - 5:00 p.m. **Corporate headquarters location:** This Location. **Annual sales/revenues:** $21 - $50 million. **Number of employees at this location:** 330.

AMERICAN HONDA MOTOR COMPANY
1919 Torrance Boulevard, Torrance CA 90501-2746. 310/783-2000. **Fax:** 310/783-2110. **Contact:** Rex Simpson, Manager of Employment Relations. **World Wide Web address:** http://www.honda.com. **Description:** Distributes Honda automotive, motorcycle, and power equipment parts throughout the U.S. **Common positions include:** Account Rep.; Accountant/Auditor; Administrative Assistant; Administrative Manager; Assistant Manager; Budget Analyst; Buyer; Computer Operator; Credit Manager; Customer Service Rep.; Financial Analyst; Management Trainee; Marketing Specialist; Public Relations Specialist; Sales Rep.; Systems Analyst; Transportation/Traffic Specialist. **Educational backgrounds include:** Accounting; Business Administration; Marketing. **Benefits:** 401(k); Dental Insurance; Disability Coverage; Employee Discounts; Life Insurance; Medical Insurance; Pension Plan. **Special programs:** Internships; Training. **Corporate headquarters location:** This Location. **Other U.S. locations:** Nationwide. **Subsidiaries include:** American Honda Finance Co. **Parent company:** Honda Motors Ltd. **Listed on:** American Stock Exchange. **Number of employees at this location:** 1,800. **Number of employees nationwide:** 3,500.

AMERICAN STANDARD COMPANIES INC.
One Centennial Avenue, Piscataway NJ 08855. 732/980-6000. **Contact:** Human Resources. **World Wide Web address:** http://www.americanstandard.com. **Description:** A global, diversified manufacturer. The company's operations are comprised of four segments: air conditioning products, plumbing products, automotive products, and medical systems. The air conditioning products segment (through subsidiary The Trane Company) develops and manufactures Trane and American Standard air conditioning equipment for use in central air conditioning systems for commercial, institutional, and residential buildings. The plumbing products segment develops and manufactures American Standard, Ideal Standard, Porcher, Armitage Shanks, Dolomite, and Standard bathroom and kitchen fixtures and fittings. The automotive products segment develops and manufactures truck, bus, and utility vehicle braking and control systems under the WABCO and Perrot brands. The medical systems segment manufactures Copalis, DiaSorin, and Pylori-Chek medical diagnostic products and systems for a variety of diseases including HIV, osteoporosis, and renal disease. **Corporate headquarters location:** This Location. **International locations:** Worldwide. **Listed on:** New York Stock Exchange. **Stock exchange symbol:** ASD. **Chairman/CEO:** Frederic M. Poses. **Number of employees worldwide:** 57,000.

ARMATRON INTERNATIONAL INC.
2 Main Street, Melrose MA 02176. 781/321-2300. **Contact:** Cindie McCue, Human Resources Director. **Description:** Operates through two segments: The Consumer Products segment manufactures and distributes bug killers, chipper/shredders, and leaf-eaters; and The Industrial Products segment imports and sells radios to a large automobile manufacturer. **Common positions include:** Accountant/Auditor; Administrator; Blue-Collar Worker Supervisor; Buyer; Computer Programmer; Credit Manager; Customer Service Representative; Department Manager; Draftsperson; Human Resources Manager; Industrial Engineer; Mechanical Engineer; Public Relations Specialist; Purchasing Agent/Manager; Quality Control Supervisor. **Educational backgrounds include:** Accounting; Business Administration; Computer Science; Engineering; Finance; Liberal Arts; Marketing; Mathematics. **Benefits:** 401(k); Dental Insurance; Disability Coverage; Employee Discounts; Life Insurance; Medical Insurance; Savings Plan; Tuition Assistance. **Corporate headquarters location:** This Location.

AUDIOVOX CORPORATION
150 Marcus Boulevard, Hauppauge NY 11788. 631/231-7750. **Contact:** Elizabeth O'Connell, Manager of Employee Services. **World Wide Web address:** http://www.audiovox.com. **Description:** Engaged in the sale and distribution of a variety of automotive electronic components including car radios, speakers, alarm systems, and cellular phones. **Common positions include:** Accountant/Auditor; Branch Manager; Budget Analyst; Computer Programmer; Credit Manager; Customer Service Rep.; Draftsperson; Electrical/Electronics Engineer; Financial Analyst; Marketing Manager; Mechanical Engineer; Payroll Clerk; Purchasing Agent/Manager; Quality Control Supervisor; Secretary; Services Sales Rep.; Stock Clerk; Systems Analyst; Travel Agent. **Educational backgrounds include:** Accounting; Business Administration; Engineering; Finance; Marketing. **Benefits:** 401(k); Disability Coverage; Employee Discounts; Life Insurance; Medical Insurance; Pension Plan; Profit Sharing; Savings Plan; Stock Option. **Special programs:** Internships. **Corporate headquarters location:** This Location. **Other U.S. locations:** Nationwide. **Subsidiaries include:** Quintex Mobile Communications. **Listed on:** American Stock Exchange. **Number of employees at this location:** 350.

AUTOALLIANCE INTERNATIONAL, INC.
One International Drive, Flat Rock MI 48134-9401. 734/782-7800. **Contact:** Human Resources. **Description:** A manufacturer of automobiles. AutoAlliance International is a joint venture between the Ford and Mazda motor companies. **Common positions include:** Buyer; Electrical/Electronics Engineer; Financial Analyst; Human Resources Manager; Industrial Engineer; Manufacturing Manager; Mechanical Engineer; Purchasing Agent/Manager; Quality Control Supervisor; Transportation/Traffic Specialist. **Educational backgrounds include:** Bachelor of Arts; Business Administration; Engineering.

Benefits: 401(k); Dental Insurance; Disability Coverage; Life Insurance; Medical Insurance; Pension Plan; Tuition Assistance. **Corporate headquarters location:** This Location. **Number of employees at this location:** 3,500.

AUTOLIV
AUTOMOTIVE SAFETY PRODUCTS
3350 Airport Road, Ogden UT 84405. 801/625-4800. **Contact:** Human Resources. **World Wide Web address:** http://www.autoliv.com. **Description:** Manufactures air bags, anti-whiplash seats, child restraints, and leg protection products for automotive manufacturers. **Corporate headquarters location:** This Location.

BEAVER MOTOR COACHES
P.O. Box 6089, Bend OR 97708. 541/389-1144. **Contact:** Human Resources. **World Wide Web address:** http://www.beavermotorcoaches.com. **Description:** Designs, manufactures, and markets Class A motor coaches, which incorporate living, dining, sleeping, and bathing facilities on a specially-designed motor vehicle chassis. Beaver models include The Patriot, The Marquis, The Contessa, The Monterey, and The Solitaire. **Parent company:** SMC Corporation.

BESTOP, INC.
P.O. Box 307, Broomfield CO 80038. 303/465-1755. **Physical address:** 2100 West Midway Boulevard, Broomfield CO 80020. **Toll-free phone:** 800/845-3567. **Fax:** 303/464-2696. **Recorded jobline:** 303/464-2562. **Contact:** Andrea McFarlane, Human Resources Manager. **World Wide Web address:** http://www.bestop.com. **Description:** Designs and manufactures automotive soft tops and accessories for sports-utility vehicles. **NOTE:** Entry-level positions and second and third shifts are offered. **Common positions include:** Blue-Collar Worker Supervisor; Customer Service Representative. **Educational backgrounds include:** Microsoft Office; Microsoft Word; Spreadsheets. **Benefits:** 401(k); Casual Dress - Fridays; Dental Insurance; Life Insurance; Medical Insurance; Profit Sharing; Tuition Assistance. **Office hours:** Monday - Friday, 7:30 a.m. - 5:00 p.m. **Corporate headquarters location:** This Location. **Other U.S. locations:** Eastman GA. **International locations:** Ontario, Canada. **President:** Ross MacLean. **Annual sales/revenues:** More than $100 million. **Number of employees at this location:** 500. **Number of employees nationwide:** 630.

BLUE BIRD CORPORATION
P.O. Box 7839, Macon GA 31210. 912/757-7100. **Contact:** Human Resources Department. **World Wide Web address:** http://www.blue-bird.com. **Description:** A holding company for manufacturers of school buses, motorcoach, and commercial vehicles. **Corporate headquarters location:** This Location. **Other U.S. locations:** Mount Pleasant IA. **Subsidiaries include:** Blue Bird Body Company (Fort Valley GA) manufactures commercial and school buses and recreational vehicles. The company also provides financial services in the form of leasing agreements to its customers. **Number of employees at this location:** 2,200. **Number of employees nationwide:** 2,330.

BORG INDAK, INC.
701 Enterprise Drive, Delavan WI 53115. 262/728-5531. **Fax:** 262/728-3788. **Contact:** Human Resources. **E-mail address:** info@borgindak.com. **World Wide Web address:** http://www.borgindak.com. **Description:** A manufacturer and designer of electrical/electronic devices for the automotive and appliance industry. **Common positions include:** Electrical/Electronics Engineer;

Quality Assurance Engineer. **Educational backgrounds include:** Business Administration; Engineering. **Benefits:** 401(k); Dental Insurance; Disability Coverage; Flexible Schedule; Life Insurance; Medical Insurance; Pension Plan; Profit Sharing; Tuition Assistance. **Special programs:** Internships; Co-ops. **Corporate headquarters location:** This Location. **Listed on:** Privately held. **Number of employees at this location:** 250.

BORG-WARNER AUTOMOTIVE
200 South Michigan Avenue, Chicago IL 60604. 312/322-8500. **Contact:** Director of Human Resources. **World Wide Web address:** http://www.bwauto.com. **Description:** Manufactures powertrain components for original equipment manufacturers and original equipment suppliers in the automobile and aerospace industries. **Common positions include:** Accountant/Auditor; Attorney; Computer Programmer; Human Resources Manager; Systems Analyst. **Educational backgrounds include:** Accounting; Business Administration; Computer Science; Economics; Finance. **Benefits:** Dental Insurance; Disability Coverage; Life Insurance; Medical Insurance; Pension Plan; Savings Plan; Tuition Assistance. **Corporate headquarters location:** This Location.

BOSCH AUTOMATION TECHNOLOGY
7505 Durand Avenue, Racine WI 53406. 262/554-8595x243. **Fax:** 262/554-7214. **Contact:** Bill Widen, Director of Human Resources. **World Wide Web address:** http://www.boschat.com. **Description:** Designs, develops, manufactures, and markets hydraulic components to various OEMs. **NOTE:** Entry-level positions are offered. **Common positions include:** Account Manager; AS400 Programmer Analyst; Design Engineer; Electrical/Electronics Engineer; Financial Analyst; Manufacturing Engineer; Mechanical Engineer; Production Manager; Project Manager; Purchasing Agent/Manager; Quality Assurance Engineer; Quality Control Supervisor. **Benefits:** 401(k); Casual Dress - Daily; Dental Insurance; Disability Coverage; Employee Discounts; Life Insurance; Medical Insurance; Pension Plan; Savings Plan; Tuition Assistance. **Information Systems Manager:** Chuck Olin. **Annual sales/revenues:** More than $100 million.

ROBERT BOSCH CORPORATION
P.O. Box 4601, Carol Stream IL 60197. 708/865-5200. **Physical address:** 2800 South 25th Avenue, Broadview IL 60153. **Fax:** 708/865-6448. **Contact:** Robert Cummins, Vice President of Human Resources. **World Wide Web address:** http://www.bosch.com. **Description:** Robert Bosch Corporation operates through three groups: Automotive-Original Equipment, Industrial Group, and Sales-Automotive Aftermarket. The largest segment of the company's business is the Automotive Group, which includes products such as anti-lock braking systems, airbag electronics, fuel injectors, and oxygen sensors. The Industrial Group consists of the Packaging Machinery Division, which sells high-tech packaging equipment, primarily to the food processing and pharmaceutical industries; the Surftran Division, which offers a range of deburring services, as well as manufacturing, selling, and servicing cleaning equipment; and Weldun International, Inc., which manufactures flexible assembly systems and automation products and assembles machinery for the Packaging Machinery Division. The Sales Group handles mobile communications, the automotive aftermarket, and household goods. Robert Bosch Corporation also participates in three joint ventures. Diessel Technology Company produces electronic and mechanical unit injectors. S-B Power Tool

Company markets portable electric power tools and accessories to the industrial, contractor, and do-it-yourself markets. Automotive Electronic Controls Systems, Inc. manufactures parts for fuel injection systems and automotive transmissions. **Corporate headquarters location:** This Location. **Subsidiaries include:** Robert Bosch Fluid Power Corporation designs, produces, and markets hydraulic pumps, valves, and power units, and offers a full line of pneumatic products. **President/CEO:** Robert S. Oswald. **Annual sales/revenues:** More than $100 million.

BREED TECHNOLOGIES, INC.

P.O. Box 33050, Lakeland FL 33807. 941/668-6000. **Contact:** Human Resources. **World Wide Web address:** http://www.breedtech.com. **Description:** Designs, develops, and manufactures automotive restraint systems and components including air bags, electronics, seat belts, and steering wheels. **Common positions include:** Buyer; Chemical Engineer; Chemist; Designer; Draftsperson; Electrical/Electronics Engineer; Financial Analyst; Mechanical Engineer; Systems Analyst. **Educational backgrounds include:** Business Administration; Chemistry; Computer Science; Engineering. **Benefits:** 401(k); Dental Insurance; Disability Coverage; EAP; Life Insurance; Medical Insurance; Stock Option; Tuition Assistance. **Corporate headquarters location:** This Location. **Listed on:** New York Stock Exchange. **Number of employees at this location:** 600.
Other U.S. locations:
- 1644 Mustang Drive, Maryville TN 37801. 865/984-5007.

BURNS BROTHERS INC.

4800 SW Meadows Road, Suite 475, Lake Oswego OR 97035. 503/697-0666. **Contact:** Stephen M. Gross, CFO. **Description:** A diversified manufacturer, wholesaler, and retailer of truck and auto parts, accessories, and fuel. Other activities include real estate development and the wholesaling of battery-powered lighting products. **Common positions include:** Accountant/Auditor; Blue-Collar Worker Supervisor; Computer Programmer; Customer Service Representative. **Educational backgrounds include:** Accounting; Computer Science. **Benefits:** Dental Insurance; Employee Discounts; Medical Insurance; Profit Sharing. **Corporate headquarters location:** This Location.

CARRON INDUSTRIES

26700 Princeton Street, Inkster MI 48141. 313/274-2300. **Contact:** Human Resources Manager. **World Wide Web address:** http://www.carronind.com. **Description:** An engineering service provider to the automotive industry. Services include design analysis, engineering, parts fabrications, testing, and vehicle assembly. **Common positions include:** Computer-Aided Designer; Draftsperson. **Educational backgrounds include:** Engineering. **Benefits:** Dental Insurance; Disability Coverage; Life Insurance; Medical Insurance; Pension Plan; Tuition Assistance. **Corporate headquarters location:** This Location. **Number of employees at this location:** 600.

CAVCO INDUSTRIES

1001 North Central Avenue, Suite 800, Phoenix AZ 85004. 602/256-6263. **Contact:** Human Resources. **World Wide Web address:** http://www.cavco.com. **Description:** Builds manufactured homes and recreational vehicles. **Benefits:** Dental Insurance; Disability Coverage; Employee Discounts; Life Insurance; Medical Insurance; Pension Plan. **Corporate headquarters location:** This Location.

Listed on: NASDAQ. **Number of employees at this location:** 420.

CHIVAS INDUSTRIES

42555 Merrill Road, Sterling Heights MI 48314. 810/254-3535. **Contact:** Gary D. Celestini, Corporate Personnel Director. **World Wide Web address:** http://www.chivasind.com. **Description:** Manufactures interior automotive parts including lighting systems, instrument panels, floor consoles, and overhead systems components. **Common positions include:** Buyer; Mechanical Engineer; Operations/Production Manager; Quality Control Supervisor. **Educational backgrounds include:** Engineering. **Benefits:** 401(k); Bonus Award/Plan; Dental Insurance; Disability Coverage; Life Insurance; Medical Insurance; Prescription Drugs; Tuition Assistance. **Corporate headquarters location:** This Location. **Listed on:** Privately held. **Number of employees at this location:** 450.

CLAYTON INDUSTRIES

P.O. Box 5530, El Monte CA 91734. 626/443-9381. **Physical address:** 4213 North Temple City Boulevard, El Monte CA 91731. **Fax:** 626/442-3787. **World Wide Web address:** http://www.claytonindustries.com. **Contact:** Human Resources. **Description:** Manufactures a broad range of industrial and automotive equipment for a variety of commercial and government customers. Products include steam generators, dynamometers, and a number of automotive diagnostic components. **Common positions include:** Accountant/Auditor; Administrative Manager; Advertising Clerk; Blue-Collar Worker Supervisor; Buyer; Chemical Engineer; Computer Programmer; Customer Service Rep.; Designer; Electrical/Electronics Engineer; Financial Analyst; General Manager; Industrial Engineer; Industrial Production Manager; Mechanical Engineer; Operations/Production Manager; Purchasing Agent/Manager; Quality Control Supervisor; Services Sales Representative; Software Engineer; Systems Analyst; Technical Writer/Editor; Transportation/Traffic Specialist. **Educational backgrounds include:** Accounting; Business Administration; Computer Science; Engineering; Marketing. **Benefits:** 401(k); Dental Insurance; Life Insurance; Medical Insurance; Pension Plan; Profit Sharing; Savings Plan; Tuition Assistance. **Special programs:** Internships. **Corporate headquarters location:** This Location. **Other U.S. locations:** DE; GA; IL; KY; MA; MI; MO; MS; NE; NJ; NY; OH; TX. **International locations:** Belgium; Mexico. **Listed on:** Privately held. **Number of employees at this location:** 135.

CLUB CAR, INC.

P.O. Box 204658, Augusta GA 30917-4658. 706/863-3000. **Fax:** 706/869-9864. **Recorded jobline:** 706/868-3890. **Contact:** Staffing Coordinator. **World Wide Web address:** http://www.clubcar.com. **Description:** This location serves as the divisional headquarters. Overall, Club Car, Inc. manufactures and markets four-wheel gasoline- and electric-powered golf carts and utility vehicles. **NOTE:** Entry-level positions and second and third shifts are offered. **Common positions include:** Accountant; Administrative Assistant; Blue-Collar Worker Supervisor; Buyer; Controller; Credit Manager; Design Engineer; Draftsperson; Human Resources Manager; Industrial Engineer; Manufacturing Engineer; MIS Specialist; Purchasing Agent/Manager; Quality Control Supervisor; Sales Representative; Secretary; Systems Analyst; Technical Writer/Editor. **Educational backgrounds include:** Accounting; Business Administration; Engineering; Finance; Marketing. **Benefits:** 401(k); Dental Insurance; Disability Coverage; Employee Discounts; Life

Insurance; Medical Insurance; Tuition Assistance. **Corporate headquarters location:** This Location. **Parent company:** Ingersoll-Rand. **Listed on:** NASDAQ. **Annual sales/revenues:** More than $100 million. **Number of employees at this location:** 850. **Number of employees nationwide:** 1,000.

COACHMEN INDUSTRIES, INC.
P.O. Box 3300, Elkhart IN 46515. 219/262-0123. **Contact:** Human Resources. **World Wide Web address:** http://www.coachmen.com. **Description:** This location houses corporate offices. Overall, Coachmen Industries manufactures recreational vehicles such as motor homes, travel trailers, camping trailers, truck campers, and van campers. The company also manufactures parts and supplies for all of these vehicles. **NOTE:** Please send resumes to Human Resources, 423 North Main Street, P.O. Box 30, Middlebury IN 46540, 219/825-8258. **Corporate headquarters location:** This Location. **Subsidiaries include:** Coachmen Recreational Vehicles, Inc.

COOPER-STANDARD AUTOMOTIVE
2401 South Gulley Road, Dearborn MI 48124. 313/561-1100. **Contact:** Karen Laskowski, Human Resources Manager. **World Wide Web address:** http://www.cooperstandard.com. **Description:** Manufactures sealing, trimming, and vibration control systems for the automotive original equipment industry. **NOTE:** Entry-level positions and part-time jobs are offered. **Common positions include:** Account Manager; Accountant; Administrative Assistant; Applications Engineer; Attorney; Auditor; Buyer; Chief Financial Officer; Cost Estimator; Design Engineer; Draftsperson; Environmental Engineer; Financial Analyst; Human Resources Manager; Market Research Analyst; Mechanical Engineer; Network/Systems Administrator; Paralegal; Quality Assurance Engineer; Sales Rep.; Transportation/Traffic Specialist; Vice President of Sales. **Educational backgrounds include:** Accounting; AS400 Certification; Business Administration; Engineering; Finance; Marketing; Novell; Spreadsheets. **Benefits:** 401(k); Casual Dress - Daily; Dental Insurance; Disability Coverage; Flexible Schedule; Life Insurance; Medical Insurance; Pension Plan; Tuition Assistance. **Special programs:** Internships; Co-ops; Summer Jobs. **Corporate headquarters location:** This Location. **Other U.S. locations:** Nationwide. **International locations:** Worldwide. **Subsidiaries include:** Helen Industries; Oliver Rubber. **Listed on:** New York Stock Exchange. **CEO:** Ron Roudebush. **Number of employees at this location:** 400. **Number of employees nationwide:** 10,000.

THE CROWN GROUP, INC.
2111 Walter Reuther Drive, Warren MI 48091. 810/575-9800. **Contact:** Personnel. **Description:** An automotive manufacturing company specializing in electroplating. **Common positions include:** Accountant; Administrator; Computer Programmer; Credit Manager; Department Manager; General Manager; Industrial Engineer; Manufacturer's/ Wholesaler's Sales Rep.; Operations/Production Manager; Quality Control Supervisor. **Educational backgrounds include:** Accounting; Business Administration; Computer Science; Economics; Engineering; Finance; Liberal Arts. **Benefits:** Disability Coverage; Life Insurance; Medical Insurance; Profit Sharing; Tuition Assistance. **Corporate headquarters location:** This Location.

CUMMINS ENGINE COMPANY, INC.
P.O. Box 3005, Columbus IN 47202. 812/377-5000. **Contact:** Human Resources. **World Wide Web address:** http://www.cummins.com. **Description:** One of the world's leading producers of diesel engines for heavy-duty trucks, engine parts, and powertrain systems for the mining, military, construction, transportation, agricultural, and industrial vehicle markets. **Corporate headquarters location:** This Location. **Listed on:** New York Stock Exchange. **Number of employees nationwide:** 26,000.

CUSTOM CHROME, INC.
16100 Jacqueline Court, Morgan Hill CA 95037. 408/778-0500. **Fax:** 408/778-0530. **Contact:** Human Resources. **World Wide Web address:** http://www.customchrome.com. **Description:** A leading independent supplier of aftermarket parts and accessories for Harley-Davidson motorcycles. Custom Chrome distributes its own products under brand names including Rev Tech, Premium, Dyno Power, and C.C. Rider. The company also supplies products by manufacturers such as Dunlop, Champion, Hastings, and Accel. Founded in 1970. **Corporate headquarters location:** This Location. **Parent company:** Global Motorsport Group Inc. **Listed on:** NASDAQ. **Stock exchange symbol:** CSTM.

DAIMLERCHRYSLER CORPORATION
1000 Chrysler Drive, Auburn Hills MI 48326. **Contact:** Employment Operations. **World Wide Web address:** http://www.daimlerchrysler.com. **Description:** Manufactures cars, trucks, minivans, and sport-utility vehicles for customers in more than 100 countries. **Common positions include:** Accountant; Blue-Collar Worker Supervisor; Buyer; Computer Programmer; Draftsperson; Electrical/ Electronics Engineer; Financial Analyst; Human Resources Manager; Industrial Engineer; Management Trainee; Mechanical Engineer; Operations/Production Manager; Public Relations Specialist; Purchasing Agent/Manager; Quality Control Supervisor; Sales Executive; Systems Analyst; Transportation/Traffic Specialist. **Educational backgrounds include:** Accounting; Business Administration; Computer Science; Economics; Engineering; Finance; Marketing. **Benefits:** Dental Insurance; Disability Coverage; Employee Discounts; Life Insurance; Medical Insurance; Pension Plan; Savings Plan; Tuition Assistance. **Corporate headquarters location:** This Location.

DELPHI AUTOMOTIVE SYSTEMS CORP.
5725 Delphi Drive, Troy MI 48098-2815. 248/813-2000. **Fax:** 248/813-2670. **Contact:** Human Resources. **World Wide Web address:** http://www.delphiauto.com. **Description:** This location is the world headquarters for Delphi Automotive Systems Corporation, an independent spin-off of General Motors Corporation. Delphi is one of the world's largest suppliers of automotive components and parts. **Corporate headquarters location:** This Location. **Number of employees worldwide:** 198,000.

DELPHI DELCO ELECTRONIC SYSTEMS
One Corporate Center, P.O. Box 9005, Kokomo IN 46904-9005. 765/451-5011. **Contact:** Personnel. **World Wide Web address:** http://www.delphiauto.com. **Description:** Produces automotive starting, generating, ignition systems, and a wide variety of related parts and systems. **Corporate headquarters location:** This Location.

E&G CLASSICS, INC.
8910 McGaw Court, Columbia MD 21045. 410/381-4900. **Contact:** Human Resources. **World Wide Web address:** http://www.egclassic.com. **Description:** Manufactures automotive restyling products including convertible tops, gold and silver

grilles, classic spares, sunroofs, leather interiors, smoothie bumpers, and roll pans. **Corporate headquarters location:** This Location. **Other U.S. locations:** Gardena CA; Oakland Park FL; Wood Dale IL.

EAST PENN MANUFACTURING COMPANY INC.

P.O. Box 147, Lyon Station PA 19536. 610/682-6361. **Contact:** Alan Hohl, Vice President of Personnel. **Description:** Produces automotive and industrial batteries. **Common positions include:** Accountant/Auditor; Administrator; Advertising Clerk; Blue-Collar Worker Supervisor; Buyer; Chemical Engineer; Chemist; Computer Programmer; Draftsperson; Electrical/Electronics Engineer; Industrial Designer; Industrial Engineer; Marketing Specialist; Mechanical Engineer; Operations/Production Manager; Purchasing Agent/Manager; Quality Control Supervisor; Sales Executive; Transportation/Traffic Specialist. **Educational backgrounds include:** Accounting; Business Administration; Chemistry; Computer Science; Engineering; Marketing. **Benefits:** Dental Insurance; Disability Coverage; Employee Discounts; Life Insurance; Medical Insurance; Pension Plan; Profit Sharing; Savings Plan; Tuition Assistance. **Corporate headquarters location:** This Location.

EFFICIENT ENGINEERING COMPANY, INC.

130 Town Center Drive, Troy MI 48084. 248/528-2888. **Fax:** 248/689-2117. **Contact:** Human Resources. **World Wide Web address:** http://www.efficient-eng.com. **Description:** A full-service design engineering firm primarily serving the automotive industry. Founded in 1939. **NOTE:** Entry-level positions are offered. **Common positions include:** Computer Operator; Design Engineer; Draftsperson; Mechanical Engineer; Sales Engineer; Sales Representative. **Educational backgrounds include:** Engineering. **Benefits:** 401(k); Dental Insurance; Disability Coverage; Life Insurance; Medical Insurance. **Special programs:** Apprenticeships. **Corporate headquarters location:** This Location. **Other area locations:** Warren MI. **Listed on:** Privately held. **Annual sales/revenues:** $21 - $50 million. **Number of employees at this location:** 400.

ENGINEERING SERVICE, INC.

21556 Telegraph Road, Southfield MI 48034. 248/357-3800. **Contact:** Human Resources. **Description:** An engineering firm specializing in CAD design for powertrain, electrical, and tooling applications in the automotive and aerospace industries. Engineering Service also offers full-service project management. **Common positions include:** Accountant; Computer-Aided Designer; Draftsperson; Industrial Designer; Manufacturer's/Wholesaler's Sales Rep. **Educational backgrounds include:** Art/Design; Computer-Aided Design; Drafting. **Benefits:** Dental Insurance; Disability Coverage; Life Insurance; Medical Insurance; Prescription Drugs; Savings Plan. **Corporate headquarters location:** This Location. **Other U.S. locations:** Dearborn MI. **Number of employees nationwide:** 200.

EXIDE CORPORATION

P.O. Box 14205, Reading PA 19612. 610/378-0500. **Contact:** Jack Sosiak, Executive Director, Human Resources. **World Wide Web address:** http://www.exideworld.com. **Description:** Produces lead acid storage batteries for a wide variety of uses including consumer, industrial, and automotive. **Common positions include:** Accountant/Auditor; Computer Programmer; Credit Manager; Customer Service Rep.; Designer; Environmental Engineer; Financial Analyst; Human Resources Manager; Industrial Engineer; Mechanical Engineer; Metallurgical Engineer; Operations/Production Manager; Production Manager; Quality Control Supervisor; Systems Analyst. **Educational backgrounds include:** Accounting; Business Administration; Communications; Computer Science; Engineering; Liberal Arts. **Benefits:** 401(k); Dental Insurance; Disability Coverage; Life Insurance; Medical Insurance; Pension Plan; Tuition Assistance. **Corporate headquarters location:** This Location. **Other U.S. locations:** Nationwide. **Listed on:** New York Stock Exchange. **Number of employees at this location:** 300. **Number of employees nationwide:** 6,500.

FWD/SEAGRAVE

105 East 12th Street, Clintonville WI 54929. 715/823-2141. **Fax:** 715/823-5474. **Contact:** Industrial Relations. **World Wide Web address:** http://www.seagrave.com. **Description:** This location manufactures fire trucks. Overall, FWD/Seagrave is engaged principally in the design and manufacture of heavy-duty, on/off-highway, all-wheel drive trucks, as well as Seagrave firefighting apparatus including components and service parts for all units. Founded in 1908. **Common positions include:** Accountant/Auditor; Buyer; Computer Programmer; Cost Estimator; Draftsperson; Electrical/Electronics Engineer; Electrician; Human Resources Manager; Industrial Engineer; Mechanical Engineer; Purchasing Agent/Manager; Quality Control Supervisor; Systems Analyst. **Educational backgrounds include:** Accounting; Business Administration; Computer Science; Engineering; Marketing. **Benefits:** 401(k); Dental Insurance; Disability Coverage; Life Insurance; Medical Insurance; Pension Plan; Tuition Assistance. **Corporate headquarters location:** This Location. **Listed on:** Privately held. **Number of employees at this location:** 400.

FEDERAL-MOGUL CORPORATION

26555 Northwestern Highway, Southfield MI 48034. 248/354-7700. **Contact:** Human Resources. **World Wide Web address:** http://www.federal-mogul.com. **Description:** Manufactures engine components and transportation products. **Common positions include:** Accountant; Administrator; Advertising Clerk; Computer Programmer; Customer Service Rep.; Financial Analyst; General Manager; Human Resources Manager; Manufacturer's/Wholesaler's Sales Rep.; Marketing Specialist; Systems Analyst. **Educational backgrounds include:** Accounting; Business Administration; Communications; Computer Science; Finance; Liberal Arts; Marketing. **Benefits:** Dental Insurance; Disability Coverage; Employee Discounts; Life Insurance; Medical Insurance; Pension Plan; Profit Sharing; Savings Plan; Tuition Assistance. **Corporate headquarters location:** This Location.

FENDERS & MORE, INC.

500 Wilson Pike Circle, Suite 115, Brentwood TN 37027. 615/373-2050. **Contact:** Alison Franks, Director of Human Resources. **World Wide Web address:** http://www.republicauto.com. **Description:** Distributes a line of automobile replacement parts. The company also distributes a number of replacement parts for heavy-duty trucks, snowmobiles, motorcycles, farm and marine equipment, and other types of machinery through its automotive distribution centers and stores; and new replacement parts to repair vehicles damaged in collisions. Distribution centers located in Nashville and Atlanta sell products to automotive collision repair shops and smaller parts distributors. **Corporate headquarters location:** This Location.

FLEETWOOD ENTERPRISES, INC.
P.O. Box 7638, Riverside CA 92513. 909/351-3500.
Physical address: 3125 Myers Street, Riverside CA
92503. **Contact:** Human Resources. **World Wide
Web address:** http://www.fleetwood.com.
Description: Manufactures recreational vehicles
with operations in the U.S., Canada, and Germany.
The company's recreational vehicles are primarily
motor homes sold under brand names including
American Eagle, Coronado, Bounder, Flair, and
PaceArrow. Fleetwood Enterprises also
manufactures a variety of trailers and campers and
owns subsidiaries which offer financial services and
supplies. **Corporate headquarters location:** This
Location. **Listed on:** New York Stock Exchange.

FORD MOTOR COMPANY
P.O. Box 0520, Allen Park MI 48101-0520.
313/322-7500. **Physical address:** The American
Road, Building 49, Dearborn MI 48121. **Toll-free
phone:** 800/248-4444. **Contact:** Salaried Recruiting
ATS. **World Wide Web address:** http://www.
ford.com. **Description:** Engaged in the design,
development, manufacture, and sale of cars, trucks,
tractors, and related components and accessories.
Ford Motor Company is also one of the largest
providers of financial services in the United States.
The company has manufacturing, assembly, and
sales affiliates in 29 countries outside of the United
States. The company's two core businesses are the
Automotive Group and the Financial Services
Group (Ford Credit, The Associates, USL Capital,
and First Nationwide). Ford is also engaged in other
businesses including electronics, glass, electrical
and fuel-handling products, plastics, climate-control
systems, automotive service and replacement parts,
vehicle leasing and rental, and land development.
Common positions include: Accountant/Auditor;
Buyer; Computer Programmer; Customer Service
Representative; Electrical/Electronics Engineer;
Financial Analyst; Human Resources Manager;
Manufacturer's/Wholesaler's Sales Rep.; Marketing
Specialist; Mechanical Engineer; Purchasing
Agent/Manager; Systems Analyst. **Educational
backgrounds include:** Accounting; Business
Administration; Computer Science; Engineering;
Finance; Marketing. **Benefits:** Dental Insurance;
Disability Coverage; Employee Discounts; Life
Insurance; Medical Insurance; Pension Plan; Profit
Sharing; Savings Plan; Tuition Assistance. **Special
programs:** Internships. **Corporate headquarters
location:** This Location. **Listed on:** New York
Stock Exchange. **Number of employees
nationwide:** 150,000.

FORETRAVEL, INC.
1221 NW Stallings Drive, Nacogdoches TX 75961.
936/569-7906. **Contact:** Human Resources. **World
Wide Web address:** http://www.foretravel.com.
Description: Manufactures and sells motor homes.
Corporate headquarters location: This Location.

GARDEN STATE TANNING
15717 Clear Springs Road, Williamsport MD
21795-1010. 301/223-7500. **Fax:** 301/223-5420.
Contact: Jeff Rowland, Assistant Human Resources
Manager. **World Wide Web address:** http://www.
gstleather.com. **Description:** Produces leather for
use in the manufacture of automobile upholstery.
Founded in 1933. **NOTE:** Entry-level positions and
second and third shifts are offered. **Common
positions include:** Administrative Assistant; AS400
Programmer Analyst; Blue-Collar Worker
Supervisor; Chemist; Computer Operator; Network/
Systems Administrator; Quality Assurance
Engineer. **Educational backgrounds include:**
Accounting; AS400 Certification; Business
Administration; Chemistry; Computer Science;
Engineering; Finance; Marketing; MCSE; Novell;

Spreadsheets. **Benefits:** 401(k); Casual Dress -
Daily; Dental Insurance; Disability Coverage; Life
Insurance; Medical Insurance; Pension Plan; Tuition
Assistance. **Special programs:** Internships.
Corporate headquarters location: King of Prussia
PA. **Other U.S. locations:** Adrian MI; Fleetwood
PA; Reading PA. **International locations:** Mexico.
Parent company: US Industries is an industrial
management company with four principal divisions:
USI Bath and Plumbing Products; Lighting
Corporation of America; USI Hardware and Tools;
and USI Diversified. **President/CEO/Owner:** Ernst
Inmon, Jr.

GAS-N-GO
P.O. Box 1903, Provo UT 84603. 801/375-1412.
Contact: Human Resources. **Description:** Operates
a chain of automotive service stations that includes
gas stations, car washes, and oil change stations.
Corporate headquarters location: This Location.

GECOM CORPORATION
1025 Barachel Lane, Greensburg IN 47240.
812/663-2270. **Fax:** 812/663-1781. **Contact:** Amy
Bray, Recruiting Manager. **Description:** A QS-9000
certified automotive parts supplier to Honda,
Toyota, Mazda, Isuzu, and other OEMs. GECOM
manufactures opener and latch assemblies. Founded
in 1987. **NOTE:** Entry-level positions are offered.
Common positions include: AS400 Programmer
Analyst; Assistant Manager; Blue-Collar Worker
Supervisor; Electrical/Electronics Engineer;
Manufacturing Engineer; Marketing Specialist;
Production Manager; Quality Assurance Engineer;
Quality Control Supervisor. **Educational
backgrounds include:** Engineering. **Benefits:**
401(k); Daycare Assistance; Dental Insurance;
Disability Coverage; Life Insurance; Medical
Insurance; On-Site Daycare; Tuition Assistance.
Special programs: Apprenticeships. **Corporate
headquarters location:** This Location. **Other U.S.
locations:** Southfield MI. **International locations:**
China; England; Japan; Thailand. **Subsidiaries
include:** NAC, Inc. **Parent company:** Mitsui
Kinzoku. **Listed on:** Privately held. **Annual
sales/revenues:** More than $100 million. **Number
of employees at this location:** 1,700. **Number of
employees nationwide:** 2,200. **Number of
employees worldwide:** 15,000.

GENERAL HOSE PRODUCTS INC.
30 Sherwood Lane, Fairfield NJ 07004. 973/228-
0500. **Contact:** Diana Taylor, Office Manager.
Description: Manufactures heavy-duty hose
products used by automobile manufacturers in air
conditioning systems. General Hose is also engaged
in tube fabrication and assemblies. **Common
positions include:** Accountant/Auditor; Blue-Collar
Worker Supervisor; Manufacturer's/Wholesaler's
Sales Rep.; Mechanical Engineer; Operations/
Production Manager. **Benefits:** Life Insurance;
Medical Insurance. **Corporate headquarters
location:** This Location. **Number of employees at
this location:** 25.

GENERAL MOTORS CORPORATION
100 Renaissance Center, Detroit MI 48265.
313/556-5000. **Contact:** Human Resources. **World
Wide Web address:** http://www.gm.com.
Description: This location houses the
administrative offices, as well as a metal fabrication
plant that manufactures stampings for General
Motors auto body parts. Overall, General Motors
Corporation is one of the world's largest full-line
vehicle manufacturers, and has substantial interests
in information technology, electronics, and finance.
GM conducts business through the following
sectors: North American Automotive Operations,
International Operations, General Motors

Acceptance Corporation (GMAC), Electronic Data Systems Corporation (EDS), and GM Hughes Electronics Corporation. North American Automotive Operations includes Sales/Service Groups (Buick, Cadillac, Chevrolet, GMC Truck, Oldsmobile, Pontiac, and Saturn) and Vehicle Development Groups (Powertrain, Truck Group, Small Car Group, and Midsize/Luxury Car Group). International Operations includes GM Europe; Asia Pacific Operations; and Latin America, Africa, Middle East Operations. GMAC, which provides financing and insurance to GM customers and dealers, consists of North American Operations, International Operations, Motors Insurance Corporation, and GMAC Mortgage Group. EDS applies information technologies to customers globally in the communications, energy/chemical, insurance, public sector, travel and transportation, financial services, manufacturing, and retail industries. GM Hughes Electronics Corporation is involved in automotive electronics, telecommunications and space electronics, and defense electronics. Founded in 1908. **Corporate headquarters location:** This Location. **Listed on:** New York Stock Exchange.

GENUINE PARTS COMPANY
2999 Circle 75 Parkway, Atlanta GA 30339. 770/953-1700. **Contact:** Director of Personnel. **World Wide Web address:** http://www.genpt.com. **Description:** A service organization engaged in the distribution of automotive replacement parts, industrial replacement parts, and office products. The company serves customers through more than 1,200 operations and is a member of the National Automotive Parts Association (NAPA). The company operates in three major divisions. The Automotive Parts Group, the largest division of the company, distributes automotive replacement parts and accessory items. The Industrial Parts Group distributes industrial replacement parts and related supplies through Motion Industries, Berry Bearing Company, and Oliver Industrial Supply. The Office Products Group distributes a broad line of office products ranging from furniture to computer supplies, through S.P. Richards Company. Brand name products include Sparco office supplies and Nature Saver recycled and recyclable products. Founded in 1928. **Common positions include:** Assistant Manager; Branch Manager; Cashier; Computer Programmer; Management Trainee; Manufacturer's/Wholesaler's Sales Rep.; Order Clerk; Retail Sales Worker; Services Sales Rep.; Stock Clerk; Truck Driver; Typist/Word Processor. **Educational backgrounds include:** Accounting; Business Administration; Economics; Finance; Liberal Arts; Marketing. **Benefits:** Accident/ Emergency Insurance; Dental Insurance; Disability Coverage; Employee Discounts; Life Insurance; Medical Insurance; Pension Plan; Savings Plan. **Special programs:** Internships. **Corporate headquarters location:** This Location. **Listed on:** New York Stock Exchange. **Number of employees at this location:** 150. **Number of employees nationwide:** 21,000.

GOERLICH'S EXHAUST SYSTEMS
300 Dixie Trail, Goldsboro NC 27530. 919/735-2030. **Contact:** David Mozingo, Human Resources Director. **Description:** Manufactures motor vehicle parts and accessories. **Corporate headquarters location:** This Location.

GREASE MONKEY INTERNATIONAL, INC.
633 17th Street, Suite 400, Denver CO 80202. 303/308-1660. **Contact:** Human Resources. **World Wide Web address:** http://www. greasemonkeyintl.com. **Description:** This location provides sales, management, marketing,

administrative, accounting, MIS, human resource, franchise support, and real estate services to the organization. Overall, the company is a franchiser, owner, and operator of retail quick lube centers. Grease Monkey centers provide customer service and preventive maintenance services for motor vehicles. **NOTE:** Entry-level positions are offered. **Common positions include:** Accountant/Auditor; Administrative Assistant; Assistant Manager; Branch Manager; Marketing Specialist; Operations Manager. **Educational backgrounds include:** Accounting; Business Administration; Computer Science; Finance; Marketing. **Benefits:** 401(k); Cafeteria; Credit Union; Dental Insurance; Disability Coverage; Employee Discounts; Fitness Program; Life Insurance; Medical Insurance; Public Transit Available; Tuition Assistance. **Special programs:** Internships. **Corporate headquarters location:** This Location. **Other U.S. locations:** Nationwide. **International locations:** Mexico. **Number of employees at this location:** 50. **Number of employees nationwide:** 350.

GREAT DANE TRAILERS, INC.
P.O. Box 67, Savannah GA 31402-0067. 912/232-4471. **Contact:** Ronald Wormack, Industrial Relations Manager. **World Wide Web address:** http://www.greatdanetrailers.com. **Description:** Engaged in the manufacture and distribution of a line of flatbed and refrigerated trailers. The company also manufactures and distributes truck van bodies. **Common positions include:** Accountant/Auditor; Administrator; Computer Programmer; Customer Service Rep.; Draftsperson; Industrial Engineer; Mechanical Engineer; Systems Analyst; Transportation/Traffic Specialist. **Educational backgrounds include:** Accounting; Business Administration; Computer Science; Engineering; Finance; Marketing. **Benefits:** Dental Insurance; Disability Coverage; Employee Discounts; Life Insurance; Medical Insurance; Pension Plan; Savings Plan; Tuition Assistance. **Corporate headquarters location:** This Location.

HACKNEY & SONS INC.
P.O. Box 880, Washington NC 27889. 252/946-6521. **Fax:** 252/975-8340. **Contact:** Sara Hampton, Corporate Human Resources Director. **Description:** One of the world's largest manufacturers of trucks and trailers for the beverage industry. Hackney & Sons also manufactures emergency service vehicles. **Common positions include:** Accountant/Auditor; Buyer; Computer Programmer; Credit Manager; Draftsperson; Electrical/Electronics Engineer; Electrician; Financial Analyst; General Manager; Industrial Engineer; Industrial Production Manager; Mechanical Engineer; Operations/Production Manager; Purchasing Agent/Manager. **Educational backgrounds include:** Business Administration; Engineering; Management/Planning. **Benefits:** 401(k); Dental Insurance; Disability Coverage; Life Insurance; Medical Insurance; Tuition Assistance. **Corporate headquarters location:** This Location. **Other U.S. locations:** KS; NV. **Listed on:** Privately held. **Number of employees at this location:** 250. **Number of employees nationwide:** 500.

HAHN AUTOMOTIVE WAREHOUSE, INC.
415 West Main Street, Rochester NY 14608. 716/235-1595. **Fax:** 716/235-3108. **Contact:** Human Resources. **Description:** Hahn Automotive Warehouse is a regional distributor of automotive aftermarket parts to commercial jobbers and retail stores. The company purchases its products from auto parts, accessory, and chemical suppliers and distributes them through 17 distribution centers located in New York and Kentucky. **Corporate headquarters location:** This Location. **Listed on:** NASDAQ.

HARLEY-DAVIDSON, INC.
P.O. Box 653, Milwaukee WI 53201. 414/342-4680.
Fax: 414/343-8230. **Contact:** Personnel. **World Wide Web address:** http://www.harley-davidson.com. **Description:** Manufactures heavyweight motorcycles, markets its merchandised trademarks, and manufactures and supplies motorcycle replacement parts and accessories. The company also produces recreational vehicles such as motor homes and specialized commercial vehicles through its subsidiary, Harley Rambler. **NOTE:** Interested applicants should call and ask for the jobline for current openings. **Common positions include:** Accountant/Auditor; Buyer; Claim Rep.; Computer Programmer; Customer Service Rep.; Department Manager; Designer; Draftsperson; Electrical/Electronics Engineer; Financial Analyst; General Manager; Human Resources Manager; Manufacturer's/Wholesaler's Sales Rep.; Marketing Specialist; Mechanical Engineer; Technical Writer/ Editor. **Educational backgrounds include:** Accounting; Business Administration; Engineering; Finance; Marketing. **Benefits:** Dental Insurance; Disability Coverage; Employee Discounts; Life Insurance; Medical Insurance; Pension Plan; Savings Plan; Tuition Assistance. **Corporate headquarters location:** This Location. **Other U.S. locations:** Talladega AL; York PA; Tomahawk WI. **Listed on:** New York Stock Exchange.

HAWTAL WHITING, INC.
600 Stephenson Highway, Troy MI 48083. 248/597-7777. **Fax:** 248/597-7818. **Contact:** Recruiter. **E-mail address:** hwrec@hawtal.com. **World Wide Web address:** http://www.hawtalwhiting.com. **Description:** Provides automotive design and engineering services. **Common positions include:** Design Engineer; Designer; Draftsperson; Electrical/Electronics Engineer; Mechanical Engineer; Structural Engineer. **Educational backgrounds include:** Engineering. **Benefits:** 401(k); Dental Insurance; Disability Coverage; Life Insurance; Medical Insurance; Tuition Assistance. **Corporate headquarters location:** This Location. **Parent company:** Hawtal Whiting, Ltd. **Listed on:** Privately held. **Annual sales/revenues:** $21 - $50 million. **Number of employees at this location:** 250. **Number of employees nationwide:** 875.

HENDRICKSON INTERNATIONAL
800 South Frontage Road, Woodridge IL 60517. 630/910-2800. **Fax:** 630/910-2899. **Contact:** Human Resources. **World Wide Web address:** http://www.hendrickson-intl.com. **Description:** A worldwide supplier of engineered products for the truck and automotive industries. Hendrickson International designs, develops, and manufactures suspension systems, leaf springs, and heavy stampings primarily for heavy-duty trucks. **Common positions include:** Accountant/Auditor; Buyer; Human Resources Manager; Industrial Engineer; Mechanical Engineer. **Educational backgrounds include:** Accounting; Business Administration; Engineering; Marketing. **Benefits:** 401(k); Dental Insurance; Disability Coverage; Life Insurance; Medical Insurance; Pension Plan; Savings Plan; Tuition Assistance. **Corporate headquarters location:** This Location. **Other U.S. locations:** IN; OH. **Parent company:** The Boler Company. **Listed on:** Privately held. **Number of employees at this location:** 90. **Number of employees nationwide:** 1,500.

HENNESSY INDUSTRIES INC.
1601 J.P. Hennessy Drive, La Vernge TN 37086. 615/641-7533. **Contact:** Teena Welch, Human Resources Manager. **World Wide Web address:** http://www.hennessy-ind.com. **Description:** Manufactures automotive equipment including AMMCO brake lathes and lifts; BADA wheel balancing weights; and COATS tire changers and wheel balancers. **Parent company:** Danaher Corp.

HI-STAT MANUFACTURING COMPANY
7290 26th Court East, Sarasota FL 34243. 941/355-9761. **Fax:** 941/351-8342. **Contact:** Human Resources. **World Wide Web address:** http://www.histat.com. **Description:** Manufactures and distributes automotive sensors. The company's product line includes speed, temperature, ABS, and pressure sensors. **NOTE:** Entry-level positions and second and third shifts are offered. **Common positions include:** Blue-Collar Worker Supervisor; Computer Programmer; Electrician; Industrial Engineer; Manufacturing Engineer; Project Manager; Quality Control Supervisor. **Educational backgrounds include:** Chemistry; Engineering. **Benefits:** 401(k); Dental Insurance; Disability Coverage; Employee Discounts; Life Insurance; Medical Insurance; Tuition Assistance. **Corporate headquarters location:** This Location. **Other U.S. locations:** Lexington OH. **Listed on:** Privately held. **Number of employees at this location:** 650. **Number of employees nationwide:** 1,500.

HONEYWELL
FRICTION MATERIALS
105 Pawtucket Avenue, Rumford RI 02916-2422. 401/434-7000. **Contact:** Human Resources. **World Wide Web address:** http://www.honeywell.com. **Description:** Manufactures Bendix brakes. **Common positions include:** Accountant/Auditor; Administrator; Claim Rep.; Customer Service Rep.; Instructor/Trainer; Manufacturer's/Wholesaler's Sales Rep.; Marketing Specialist; Purchasing Agent/Manager; Systems Analyst. **Educational backgrounds include:** Accounting; Business Administration; Communications; Computer Science; Finance; Marketing; Mathematics. **Benefits:** Dental Insurance; Disability Coverage; Life Insurance; Medical Insurance; Pension Plan; Profit Sharing; Savings Plan; Tuition Assistance. **Special programs:** Internships. **Corporate headquarters location:** Morristown NJ. **Listed on:** New York Stock Exchange.

JANESVILLE PRODUCTS
P.O. Box 349, Norwalk OH 44857. 419/668-4474. **Physical address:** 156 South Norwalk Road, Norwalk OH. **Contact:** Personnel. **World Wide Web address:** http://www.janesvilleproducts.com. **Description:** Manufactures insulation for automobiles. **Corporate headquarters location:** This Location. **Number of employees at this location:** 40.

JIFFY LUBE INTERNATIONAL, INC.
P.O. Box 2967, Houston TX 77252. 713/546-4100. **Contact:** Human Resources. **World Wide Web address:** http://www.jiffylube.com. **Description:** Provides automobile maintenance services including oil changes, tire rotations, and wheel balancing. **Corporate headquarters location:** This Location. **Parent company:** Pennzoil Products.

JOHNSON CONTROLS, INC.
P.O. Box 989, Athens TN 37371. 423/745-5807. **Physical address:** 1210 East Madison, Athens TN 37303. **Contact:** Charlotta Pickens, Human Resources Manager. **World Wide Web address:** http://www.johnsoncontrols.com. **Description:** This location manufactures metal seat framing for Ford, General Motors, and DaimlerChrysler. Overall, Johnson Controls is a global market leader in automotive seating, facility services and control systems, and automotive batteries. These industries make up the three business units of the company: Automotive, Controls, and Battery. Automotive

produces complete seat systems, seating components, and interior trim systems for cars, light trucks, and vans. Controls is involved in the installation and service of facility management and control systems, the retrofit and service of mechanical equipment and lighting systems in non-residential buildings, and on-site management of facility operations and maintenance. Battery manufactures automotive batteries for the replacement and original equipment markets and specialty batteries for telecommunications and uninterruptible power supply (UPS) applications. Founded in 1885. **Corporate headquarters location:** Milwaukee WI.

JOHNSON MATTHEY INC.
456 Devon Park Drive, Wayne PA 19087. 610/341-8300. **Fax:** 610/341-8259. **Contact:** Human Resources. **World Wide Web address:** http://www.matthey.com. **Description:** Manufactures automotive catalytic systems. **NOTE:** Entry-level positions and second and third shifts are offered. **Common positions include:** Chemical Engineer; Chemist; Manufacturing Engineer; Mechanical Engineer. **Benefits:** 401(k); Dental Insurance; Disability Coverage; Life Insurance; Medical Insurance; Pension Plan; Tuition Assistance. **Special programs:** Summer Jobs.

KEM MANUFACTURING COMPANY INC.
18-35 River Road, Fair Lawn NJ 07410. 201/796-8000. **Contact:** Personnel. **World Wide Web address:** http://www.kemparts.com. **Description:** Manufactures and markets a wide range of products for sale to the automotive aftermarket. **Common positions include:** Accountant; Administrator; Advertising Clerk; Blue-Collar Worker Supervisor; Buyer; Computer Programmer; Credit Manager; Customer Service Rep.; Department Manager; Draftsperson; General Manager; Human Resources Manager; Manufacturer's/Wholesaler's Sales Rep.; Mechanical Engineer; Operations/Production Manager; Purchasing Agent/Manager; Quality Control Supervisor. **Educational backgrounds include:** Accounting; Business Administration; Computer Science; Engineering; Liberal Arts; Marketing. **Benefits:** Disability Coverage; Employee Discounts; Life Insurance; Medical Insurance; Pension Plan; Tuition Assistance. **Corporate headquarters location:** This Location.

KIT MANUFACTURING COMPANY
P.O. Box 848, Long Beach CA 90801-0848. 562/595-7451. **Contact:** Human Resources. **Description:** One of the largest manufacturers of travel trailers and fifth-wheels in the United States. The company produces its travel trailers and fifth-wheels under the brand names of Road Ranger, Companion, and Sportsmaster. **Corporate headquarters location:** This Location.

KRACO PRODUCTS INC.
505 East Euclid Avenue, Compton CA 90224. 310/639-0666. **Contact:** Human Resources. **Description:** Manufactures automotive accessories including car stereos, floor mats, and car security alarms. **Common positions include:** Art Director; Buyer; Chemist; Operations/Production Manager. **Educational backgrounds include:** Art/Design. **Benefits:** Dental Insurance; Employee Discounts; Life Insurance; Medical Insurance; Tuition Assistance. **Corporate headquarters location:** This Location. **Listed on:** New York Stock Exchange. **Number of employees nationwide:** 450.

LAND ROVER NORTH AMERICA, INC.
4371 Parliament Place, Lanham MD 20706. 301/731-9040. **Fax:** 301/731-9054. **Contact:** Human Resources. **World Wide Web address:** http://www.best4x4.landrover.com. **Description:** Manufactures 4-wheel drive, sport-utility vehicles under the names Land Rover and Range Rover. Founded in 1948. **Corporate headquarters location:** This Location. **Parent company:** BMW Group (Munich, Germany). **President:** Charles R. Hughes.

LEAR CORPORATION
21557 Telegraph Road, Southfield MI 48086. 248/447-1500. **Contact:** Human Resources. **World Wide Web address:** http://www.lear.com. **Description:** A worldwide supplier of automotive seat systems; floor and acoustic systems; instrument panel systems; overhead systems; and interior trim systems. Founded in 1917. **Common positions include:** Accountant/Auditor; Budget Analyst; Buyer; Computer Programmer; Cost Estimator; Designer; Draftsperson; Electrical/Electronics Engineer; Financial Analyst; General Manager; Human Resources Manager; Industrial Engineer; Librarian; Materials Engineer; Mechanical Engineer; Operations/Production Manager; Public Relations Specialist; Purchasing Agent/Manager; Quality Control Supervisor; Services Sales Representative; Software Engineer; Statistician; Systems Analyst; Technical Writer/Editor; Transportation/Traffic Specialist; Travel Agent. **Educational backgrounds include:** Accounting; Business Administration; Computer Science; Economics; Engineering; Finance; Marketing; Mathematics; MBA; Physics. **Benefits:** 401(k); Daycare Assistance; Dental Insurance; Disability Coverage; Life Insurance; Medical Insurance; Pension Plan; Profit Sharing; Savings Plan; Tuition Assistance. **Special programs:** Internships. **Corporate headquarters location:** This Location. **Other U.S. locations:** GA; IL; OH; SC; TN; WI. **Listed on:** New York Stock Exchange. **Stock exchange symbol:** LEA. **Annual sales/revenues:** More than $100 million. **Number of employees nationwide:** 35,555.

LIBRALTER PLASTICS, INC.
3175 Martin Road, Walled Lake MI 48390. 248/669-4900. **Fax:** 248/669-5372. **Contact:** Human Resources. **Description:** Manufactures injection molding for the automotive industry. **Common positions include:** Accountant/Auditor; Administrative Manager; Blue-Collar Worker Supervisor; Computer Programmer; Cost Estimator; Customer Service Representative; Education Administrator; General Manager; Purchasing Agent/Manager; Quality Control Supervisor; Services Sales Representative; Systems Analyst. **Educational backgrounds include:** Accounting; Business Administration; Engineering; Finance; Marketing. **Benefits:** 401(k); Dental Insurance; Disability Coverage; Life Insurance; Medical Insurance; Pension Plan; Profit Sharing; Tuition Assistance. **Special programs:** Internships. **Corporate headquarters location:** This Location. **Other area locations:** Howell MI; Westland MI. **Listed on:** Privately held. **Number of employees at this location:** 200. **Number of employees nationwide:** 500.

LOWELL ENGINEERING
6151 Bancroft Avenue, Alto MI 49302. 616/868-6122. **Fax:** 616/868-0084. **Contact:** Connie Taber, Human Resources Manager. **Description:** Manufactures exterior automobile mirrors. **NOTE:** Second and third shifts are offered. **Common positions include:** Accountant; Computer Support Technician; Cost Estimator; Database Administrator; Electrician; General Manager; Human Resources Manager; Manufacturing Engineer; Production Manager; Quality Assurance Engineer. **Educational backgrounds include:**

Accounting; Communications; Engineering; Microsoft Word; Software Tech. Support. **Benefits:** 401(k); Casual Dress - Fridays; Dental Insurance; Disability Coverage; Life Insurance; Medical Insurance; Profit Sharing; Tuition Assistance. **Special programs:** Training. **Corporate headquarters location:** Toronto, Canada. **Other U.S. locations:** Nationwide. **International locations:** Worldwide. **Parent company:** Magna International Inc. **Listed on:** New York Stock Exchange. **Information Systems Manager:** Eric Hornsby. **Purchasing Manager:** Clark Schviteman. **Number of employees at this location:** 700. **Number of employees worldwide:** 49,000.

LUSTINE GM PARTS DISTRIBUTORS
5710 Baltimore Avenue, Hyattsville MD 20781. 301/927-4455. **Contact:** Human Resources. **World Wide Web address:** http://www.lustineparts.com. **Description:** A wholesale distributor of new and remanufactured Genral Motors automotive parts, engines, and transmissions. **Office hours:** Monday - Friday, 8:00 a.m. - 5:30 p.m. **Corporate headquarters location:** This Location.

MACK TRUCKS INC.
P.O. Box M, Allentown PA 18105-5000. 610/709-3011. **Contact:** Tim Mulchaney, Employment Manager. **World Wide Web address:** http://www.macktrucks.com. **Description:** Manufactures and sells heavy-duty trucks, truck tractors, and truck replacement parts. The company also provides repair and maintenance services for these products. **Common positions include:** Accountant/Auditor; Attorney; Blue-Collar Worker Supervisor; Branch Manager; Buyer; Computer Programmer; Department Manager; Draftsperson; Electrical/Electronics Engineer; General Manager; Human Resources Manager; Industrial Engineer; Manufacturer's/Wholesaler's Sales Rep.; Mechanical Engineer; Operations/Production Manager; Purchasing Agent/Manager; Quality Control Supervisor; Systems Analyst. **Educational backgrounds include:** Accounting; Business Administration; Communications; Computer Science; Economics; Engineering; Finance; Liberal Arts; Marketing. **Benefits:** Dental Insurance; Disability Coverage; Life Insurance; Medical Insurance; Pension Plan; Savings Plan; Tuition Assistance. **Corporate headquarters location:** This Location. **Number of employees at this location:** 5,400.

MARK IV AUTOMOTIVE
6120 South Yale Avenue, Tulsa OK 74136. 918/481-2500. **Contact:** Human Resources. **Description:** Produces automotive filters, fuel systems, and power transmission systems. Mark IV Automotive also manufactures automotive belts and hoses under the brand name Dayco. **Common positions include:** Accountant; Administrator; Advertising Clerk; Computer Programmer; Credit Manager; Customer Service Rep.; Draftsperson; Financial Analyst; Industrial Engineer; Industrial Production Manager; Management Trainee; Manufacturer's/Wholesaler's Sales Rep.; Marketing Specialist; Mechanical Engineer; Petroleum Engineer; Purchasing Agent/Manager; Systems Analyst. **Educational backgrounds include:** Accounting; Art/Design; Business Administration; Computer Science; Engineering; Liberal Arts; Marketing. **Benefits:** Daycare Assistance; Dental Insurance; Disability Coverage; Employee Discounts; Life Insurance; Medical Insurance; Pension Plan; Savings Plan; Tuition Assistance. **Special programs:** Internships. **Corporate headquarters location:** This Location. **Parent company:** Mark IV Industries, Inc.

MARK IV INDUSTRIES, INC.
One Towne Center, 501 J.J. Audubon Parkway, Amherst NY 14228. 716/689-4972. **Contact:** Ms. Chris Werth, Human Resources. **World Wide Web address:** http://www.mark-iv.com. **Description:** Produces power transfer/fluid handling, mass transit/traffic control, and professional audio equipment and components for the automotive, industrial, transportation, and music aftermarket and original equipment manufacturers. **Corporate headquarters location:** This Location. **Subsidiaries include:** Mark IV Automotive. **Listed on:** New York Stock Exchange.

MERCEDES-BENZ OF NORTH AMERICA
One Mercedes Drive, Montvale NJ 07645. 201/573-2530. **Contact:** Staffing/Employee Relations. **Description:** An importer of the complete line of Mercedes-Benz automobiles and related components. Mercedes-Benz of North America distributes Mercedes products to dealers throughout the United States. **Common positions include:** Accountant; Automotive Engineer; Computer Programmer; Customer Service Rep.; Financial Analyst; Instructor/Trainer; Marketing Specialist; Systems Analyst; Technical Writer/Editor. **Educational backgrounds include:** Accounting; Computer Science; Engineering; Finance; Marketing. **Benefits:** Dental Insurance; Disability Coverage; Employee Discounts; Life Insurance; Medical Insurance; Pension Plan; Savings Plan; Tuition Assistance. **Corporate headquarters location:** This Location. **Parent company:** DaimlerChrysler. **Number of employees nationwide:** 1,500.

MERITOR AUTOMOTIVE INC.
2135 West Maple Road, Troy MI 48084. 248/435-1000. **Contact:** Human Resources. **World Wide Web address:** http://www.meritorauto.com. **Description:** Operates in two segments: Heavy Vehicle Systems and Light Vehicle Systems. Heavy Vehicle Systems supplies drivetrain components and systems for commercial vehicles. Light Vehicle Systems's products include automotive electronic controls, electric motors, and suspension systems for light trucks and passenger cars. **Common positions include:** Financial Analyst; Industrial Engineer; Mechanical Engineer. **Educational backgrounds include:** Engineering; Finance. **Benefits:** Dental Insurance; Disability Coverage; Life Insurance; Medical Insurance; Pension Plan; Savings Plan; Tuition Assistance. **Corporate headquarters location:** This Location. **Listed on:** New York Stock Exchange.

MOTORCAR PARTS & ACCESSORIES, INC.
2727 Maricopa Street, Torrance CA 90503. 310/212-7910. **Contact:** Human Resources. **Description:** Remanufactures alternators and starters for import cars and light trucks, as well as for domestic vehicles originally equipped with Japanese-made units. The company also produces spark plug wire sets for both domestic and import cars. The company distributes its products to automotive retail chain stores and warehouse distributors. **Corporate headquarters location:** This Location. **Other U.S. locations:** Woodbury NY; Nashville TN. **Listed on:** NASDAQ. **Stock exchange symbol:** MPAA. **Number of employees nationwide:** 400.

MYERS INDUSTRIES INC.
1293 South Main Street, Akron OH 44301. 330/253-5592. **Contact:** Personnel Specialist. **Description:** An international wholesale distributor of retread equipment, supplies, and undercar service equipment. Myers Industries also manufactures plastic and metal storage organizers. **Common**

positions include: Accountant/Auditor; Advertising Clerk; Blue-Collar Worker Supervisor; Branch Manager; Computer Programmer; Customer Service Representative; Department Manager; Draftsperson; Financial Analyst; Human Resources Manager; Industrial Designer; Management Trainee; Manufacturer's/Wholesaler's Sales Rep.; Marketing Specialist; Mechanical Engineer; Systems Analyst. **Educational backgrounds include:** Accounting; Art/Design; Business Administration; Computer Science; Marketing. **Benefits:** Disability Coverage; Employee Discounts; Life Insurance; Medical Insurance; Profit Sharing; Savings Plan; Tuition Assistance. **Corporate headquarters location:** This Location. **Other U.S. locations:** Nationwide. **Listed on:** American Stock Exchange.

NAVISTAR INTERNATIONAL
455 North Cityfront Plaza Drive, Chicago IL 60611. 312/836-2000. **Contact:** Pam Hamilton, Senior Vice President of Employee Relations. **World Wide Web address:** http://www.navistar.com. **Description:** Manufactures heavy-duty trucks, severe service trucks, and school buses. **Corporate headquarters location:** This Location. **Listed on:** New York Stock Exchange.

NEAPCO, INC.
740 Queen Street, Pottstown PA 19464. 610/323-6000. **Contact:** Human Resources. **World Wide Web address:** http://www.neapco.com. **Description:** Operates in the OEM and aftermarket areas with customers in the automotive, heavy-duty, and agricultural lines. **Common positions include:** Customer Service Rep.; Manufacturer's/Wholesaler's Sales Rep.; Mechanical Engineer. **Educational backgrounds include:** Accounting; Business Administration; Engineering. **Benefits:** Dental Insurance; Disability Coverage; Life Insurance; Medical Insurance; Pension Plan; Tuition Assistance. **Corporate headquarters location:** This Location. **Other U.S. locations:** CA; MO; NE. **Parent company:** UIS, Inc. (New York NY).

NEOPLAN USA CORPORATION
700 Gottlob Auwaeter Drive, Lamar CO 81052. 719/336-3256. **Contact:** Ms. Pat Robinette, Personnel Director. **Description:** Produces and markets buses for international distribution. **Common positions include:** Accountant/Auditor; Administrator; Blue-Collar Worker Supervisor; Computer Programmer; Customer Service Rep.; Department Manager; Draftsperson; Electrical/Electronics Engineer; Financial Analyst; General Manager; Human Resources Manager; Industrial Engineer; Management Trainee; Mechanical Engineer; Operations/Production Manager; Purchasing Agent/Manager; Quality Control Supervisor; Technical Representative. **Educational backgrounds include:** Accounting; Business Administration; Communications; Computer Science; Economics; Engineering; Finance. **Benefits:** Disability Coverage; Life Insurance; Medical Insurance; Tuition Assistance. **Corporate headquarters location:** This Location.

NEW UNITED MOTOR MANUFACTURING
45500 Fremont Boulevard, Fremont CA 94538. 510/498-5500. **Fax:** 510/770-4116. **Contact:** Human Resources Department. **World Wide Web address:** http://www.nummi.com. **Description:** Through a joint venture between General Motors Corporation and Toyota Motor Corporation, New United Motor Manufacturing manufactures Chevrolet Prizms for the Chevrolet Motor Division of General Motors and Toyota Corolla sedans and Tacoma pickup trucks for Toyota. Founded in 1984. **NOTE:** Entry-level positions are offered. **Common positions include:** Accountant; Administrative

Assistant; Assistant Manager; Blue-Collar Worker Supervisor; Budget Analyst; Buyer; Chemical Engineer; Computer Programmer; Financial Analyst; General Manager; Human Resources Manager; Industrial Engineer; Manufacturing Engineer; Mechanical Engineer; MIS Specialist; Operations Manager; Paralegal; Production Manager; Project Manager; Public Relations Specialist; Purchasing Agent/Manager; Quality Control Supervisor; Secretary; Systems Analyst. **Educational backgrounds include:** Accounting; Business Administration; Communications; Computer Science; Engineering; Finance. **Benefits:** 401(k); Dental Insurance; Disability Coverage; Employee Discounts; Life Insurance; Medical Insurance; Pension Plan; Public Transit Available; Tuition Assistance. **Special programs:** Co-ops. **Internship information:** The company offers a six-month cooperative education program. **Corporate headquarters location:** This Location. **Number of employees at this location:** 4,800.

NISSAN MOTOR MANUFACTURING CORP.
983 Nissan Drive, Smyrna TN 37167. 615/459-1400. **Contact:** Employment Department. **World Wide Web address:** http://www.nissan-plant.com. **Description:** Operates the automobile manufacturing division of Nissan. **NOTE:** The Employment Department only accepts applications for professional positions. **Corporate headquarters location:** This Location.

NORTH AMERICAN ROYALTIES
200 East Eighth Street, Chattanooga TN 37402. 423/265-3181. **Fax:** 423/266-5669. **Contact:** Rick Roberts, Labor Relations Manager. **Description:** One of the largest independent producers of cast iron automotive brake components in the United States. Founded in 1866. **Common positions include:** Accountant/Auditor; Civil Engineer; Computer Programmer; Electrical/Electronics Engineer; Electrician; Financial Analyst; General Manager; Human Resources Manager; Industrial Engineer; Management Trainee; Mechanical Engineer; Metallurgical Engineer; Purchasing Agent/Manager; Registered Nurse; Systems Analyst. **Educational backgrounds include:** Business Administration; Engineering. **Benefits:** 401(k); Dental Insurance; Disability Coverage; Life Insurance; Medical Insurance; Pension Plan; Tuition Assistance. **Corporate headquarters location:** This Location. **Other U.S. locations:** Warrenton GA. **Listed on:** Privately held. **Number of employees at this location:** 250. **Number of employees nationwide:** 1,450.

OEA, INC.
1360 North 1000 West, Tremonton UT 84337. 435/257-1007. **Fax:** 435/257-1010. **Contact:** Trish Valcarce, Personnel Administrator. **E-mail address:** oeahr@utahlinx.com. **World Wide Web address:** http://www.oeainc.com. **Description:** Manufactures air bag initiators for the automotive industry. The company also designs and manufactures personal escape systems for military aircraft and specialty products for missile and aerospace applications. **NOTE:** Entry-level positions and second and third shifts are offered. **Common positions include:** Buyer; Design Engineer; Draftsperson; Machine Operator; Manufacturing Engineer; MIS Specialist; Quality Assurance Engineer; Registered Nurse; Secretary. **Educational backgrounds include:** Engineering. **Benefits:** 401(k); Dental Insurance; Disability Coverage; Employee Discounts; Flexible Schedule; Life Insurance; Medical Insurance; Pension Plan; Profit Sharing; Sick Days (6 - 10); Tuition Assistance; Vacation Days (10 - 20). **Special programs:** Training. **Corporate headquarters location:** Denver CO. **Other U.S.**

locations: Fairfield CA. International locations: Paris, France. Number of employees at this location: 300.

OSHKOSH TRUCK CORPORATION

2307 Oregon Street, P.O. Box 2566, Oshkosh WI 54903-2566. 920/235-9151. Contact: Human Resources. World Wide Web address: http://www.oshkoshtruck.com. Description: Manufactures a wide variety of specialized vehicles and transport equipment. The company's major product categories include specialized trucks, proprietary automotive components, service parts, trailers, and motorized chassis. The company's products are primarily produced for the construction, earthmoving, defense, motor home, bus, and delivery step van markets. Corporate headquarters location: This Location. Listed on: NASDAQ.

OXFORD AUTOMOTIVE

P.O. Box 129, Alma MI 48801-2659. 517/463-3151. Physical address: 520 Republic Street, Troy MI. Contact: Manager of Human Resources. World Wide Web address: http://www.oxauto.com. Description: A full-service supplier of metal stampings and welded assemblies, primarily to the automotive industry. Common positions include: Accountant/Auditor; Budget Analyst; Computer Programmer; Cost Estimator; Financial Analyst; Industrial Engineer; Mechanical Engineer; Systems Analyst. Educational backgrounds include: Engineering; Finance; Liberal Arts. Benefits: 401(k); Dental Insurance; Disability Coverage; Life Insurance; Medical Insurance; Pension Plan; Tuition Assistance. Special programs: Internships. Corporate headquarters location: This Location. Other U.S. locations: Argos IN; Corydon IN; Greencastle IN; Winchester IN. Subsidiaries include: Winchester Fabrication. Listed on: Privately held. Number of employees at this location: 100.

PACCAR INC.

P.O. Box 1518, Bellevue WA 98009. 425/468-7400. Fax: 425/468-8206. Recorded jobline: 425/468-7011. Contact: Human Resources. World Wide Web address: http://www.paccar.com. Description: Manufactures, leases, and finances heavy duty on- and off-road trucks and industrial winches for industrial and commercial use. Brand names include Peterbilt, Foden, DAF, and Kenworth. Common positions include: Accountant/Auditor; Buyer; Computer Operator; Computer Programmer; Design Engineer; Industrial Engineer; Manufacturing Engineer; Mechanical Engineer; Purchasing Agent/Manager; Sales Representative. Educational backgrounds include: Accounting; Business Administration; Computer Science; Engineering; Finance. Benefits: 401(k); Dental Insurance; Disability Coverage; Life Insurance; Medical Insurance; Pension Plan; Savings Plan; Tuition Assistance. Special programs: Internships. Corporate headquarters location: This Location. Other U.S. locations: Nationwide. International locations: Australia; Canada; Mexico; the Netherlands; the United Kingdom. Annual sales/revenues: More than $100 million. Number of employees at this location: 425. Number of employees nationwide: 10,000.

PAK-MOR MANUFACTURING CO.

P.O. Box 14147, San Antonio TX 78214. 210/923-4317. Contact: Personnel Director. Description: A manufacturer of refuse trucking equipment. Corporate headquarters location: This Location.

PAM COMPANIES

P.O. Box 5200, Sioux Falls SD 57117. 605/336-1788. Fax: 605/367-6511. Contact: Human Resources. World Wide Web address: http://www.pam-companies.com. Description: This location is a distribution center. Overall, Pam is an automotive oil wholesaler. Common positions include: Automotive Mechanic; Bindery Worker; Branch Manager; Buyer; Computer Operator; Credit Manager; Customer Service Representative; Dispatcher; Manufacturer's/Wholesaler's Sales Rep.; Payroll Clerk; Printing Press Operator; Secretary; Systems Analyst; Truck Driver; Wholesale and Retail Buyer. Benefits: 401(k); Dental Insurance; Disability Coverage; Employee Discounts; Life Insurance; Medical Insurance; Pension Plan; Profit Sharing; Tuition Assistance. Corporate headquarters location: This Location. Other U.S. locations: Denver CO; Council Bluffs IA; Boise ID; Plymouth MN; Fargo ND; Salt Lake City UT. Listed on: Privately held. Number of employees at this location: 195. Number of employees nationwide: 325.

PILOT INDUSTRIES, INC.

2319 Bishop Circle East, Dexter MI 48130. 734/426-4376. Fax: 734/426-8160. Contact: Human Resources. Description: Manufactures automotive and non-automotive components, primarily focusing on the development of fuel-carrying systems. Founded in 1977. Common positions include: Accountant/Auditor; Automotive Engineer; Automotive Mechanic; Blue-Collar Worker Supervisor; Buyer; Chemical Engineer; Chemist; Clinical Lab Technician; Computer Programmer; Cost Estimator; Draftsperson; Electrical/Electronics Engineer; Environmental Engineer; Financial Analyst; General Manager; Human Resources Manager; Industrial Engineer; Industrial Production Manager; Management Analyst/Consultant; Manufacturer's/Wholesaler's Sales Rep.; Materials Engineer; Mechanical Engineer; Metallurgical Engineer; Operations/Production Manager; Quality Control Supervisor; Systems Analyst; Technical Writer/Editor; Transportation/Traffic Specialist. Educational backgrounds include: Accounting; Business Administration; Chemistry; Communications; Computer Science; Engineering; Finance; Marketing; Physics. Benefits: 401(k); Disability Coverage; Life Insurance; Medical Insurance; Profit Sharing; Tuition Assistance. Corporate headquarters location: This Location. Other area locations: Sterling Heights MI. Other U.S. locations: North Vernon IN. Listed on: Privately held. Number of employees at this location: 150.

PRESTIGE STAMPING, INC.

23513 Groesbeck Highway, P.O. Box 1086, Warren MI 48090-1086. 810/773-2700. Fax: 810/773-2298. Contact: James Leo; Human Resources Manager. World Wide Web address: http://www.prestigestamping.com. Description: A manufacturer of washers and shims, primarily for the automotive industry. Common positions include: Automotive Mechanic; Blue-Collar Worker Supervisor; Cost Estimator; Manufacturer's/Wholesaler's Sales Rep. Benefits: 401(k); Dental Insurance; EAP; Life Insurance; Medical Insurance; Savings Plan; Tuition Assistance. Corporate headquarters location: This Location. Listed on: Privately held. Number of employees at this location: 100.

RED DOT CORPORATION

P.O. Box 58270, Seattle WA 98138. 206/575-3840. Contact: Human Resources. World Wide Web address: http://www.reddotcom. Description: A manufacturer and wholesaler of heating and air conditioning equipment for heavy vehicles such as semi-trucks and off-road vehicles. Office hours: Monday - Friday, 7:45 a.m. - 4:30 p.m. Corporate headquarters location: This Location.

RENOSOL CORPORATION

1512 Woodland Avenue, Saline MI 48176. 734/429-5418. **Contact:** Personnel. **Description:** Manufactures polyurethane products and vinyl products, as well as liquid systems primarily for the automotive industry. **Common positions include:** Accountant/Auditor; Administrative Manager; Blue-Collar Worker Supervisor; Budget Analyst; Buyer; Computer Programmer; Cost Estimator; Credit Manager; Customer Service Representative; Financial Analyst; Human Resources Manager; Market Research Analyst; Materials Engineer; MIS Specialist; Systems Analyst; Typist/Word Processor. **Educational backgrounds include:** Accounting; Business Administration; Chemistry; Computer Science; Engineering; Finance; Marketing. **Benefits:** 401(k); Dental Insurance; Disability Coverage; Life Insurance; Medical Insurance; Pension Plan; Profit Sharing; Tuition Assistance. **Corporate headquarters location:** This Location. **Other U.S. locations:** Nationwide. **Annual sales/revenues:** $21 - $50 million. **Number of employees at this location:** 25. **Number of employees nationwide:** 250.

RIETER AUTOMOTIVE NORTH AMERICA

38555 Hills Tech Drive, Farmington Hills MI 48331. 248/848-0100. **Contact:** Human Resources. **Description:** Manufactures sound-deadening materials for the automotive industry. **Corporate headquarters location:** This Location. **Other area locations:** Troy MI. **Other U.S. locations:** Lowell IN; Oregon OH.

SCS-FRIGETTE CORPORATION

P.O. Box 40550, Fort Worth TX 76140. 817/293-5313. **Contact:** Human Resources. **World Wide Web address:** http://www.scsfrigette.com. **Description:** A manufacturer of automobile air conditioning and heating systems, cruise control, security systems, and accessories. **Common positions include:** Accountant/Auditor; Buyer; Clerical Supervisor; Credit Manager; Customer Service Rep.; Designer; Draftsperson; Electrical/Electronics Engineer; Manufacturer's/Wholesaler's Sales Rep.; Materials Engineer; Mechanical Engineer; Purchasing Agent/Manager; Quality Control Supervisor; Services Sales Representative. **Educational backgrounds include:** Accounting; Art/Design; Business Administration; Engineering; Finance; Marketing. **Benefits:** 401(k); Dental Insurance; Life Insurance; Medical Insurance; Savings Plan. **Corporate headquarters location:** This Location. **Listed on:** Privately held.

SMC CORPORATION

SAFARI MOTOR COACHES

P.O. Box 5639, Bend OR 97708. 541/389-1144. **Physical address:** 30725 Diamond Hill Road, Harrisburg OR. **Contact:** Human Resources. **World Wide Web address:** http://www.smccorporation.com. **Description:** One of the largest designers, manufacturers, and marketers of high-line, Class A motor coaches, which incorporate living, dining, sleeping, and bathing facilities. **Corporate headquarters location:** This Location. **International locations:** Barbados. **Subsidiaries include:** Beaver Motor Coaches, Inc. (Bend OR) manufactures luxury motor coaches; Composite Technologies, Inc. (Hines OR) manufactures fiberglass; Electronic Design & Assembly, Inc. (Bend OR) manufactures electronic systems for motor coaches; Harney County Operations, Inc. (Hines OR) manufactures Class C motor coaches; Magnum Manufacturing, Inc. (Harrisburg OR) manufactures RV chassis; SMC Midwest, Inc. (Minneapolis KS) manufactures Honorbuilt motor homes; Safari Motor Coaches (also at this location, http://www.safarimotorcoaches.com) manufactures luxury motor coaches. **Listed on:** NASDAQ. **Chairman/CEO:** Mathew M. Perlot. **Number of employees nationwide:** 1,400.

SPX CORPORATION

700 Terrace Point Drive, P.O. Box 3301, Muskegon MI 49443. 231/724-5000. **Contact:** Human Resources. **World Wide Web address:** http://www.spx.com. **Description:** Manufactures specialty tools and components for the automotive industry. Products include gauges, hand tools, battery testers, air conditioning and anti-freeze recycling systems, and diagnostic and emissions testing equipment. Subsidiaries are involved in the production of valves, die casting, filters, piston rings, and cylinder liners for the automotive, commercial, and manufacturing industries. Founded in 1925. **Corporate headquarters location:** This Location. **International locations:** Worldwide. **Listed on:** New York Stock Exchange. **Stock exchange symbol:** SPW. **Annual sales/revenues:** $51 - $100 million. **Number of employees nationwide:** 1,000. **Other U.S. locations:**

- 28635 Mound Road, Warren MI 48092-3499. 810/574-2332.

SST TRUCK COMPANY

4030 Forest Lane, Garland TX 75042. 972/276-5121. **Contact:** Human Resources. **Description:** Manufactures trucks for Navistar. **Corporate headquarters location:** This Location. **Listed on:** Privately held.

SW MANUFACTURING, INC.

1111 West Broad Street, Smithville TN 37166. 615/597-8870. **Fax:** 615/597-8635. **Contact:** Personnel. **Description:** Supplies and manufactures automobile window regulators and seat adjusters. **Common positions include:** Accountant; Electrical/Electronics Engineer; Electrician; Human Resources Manager; Industrial Engineer; Mechanical Engineer; Purchasing Agent/Manager; Quality Control Supervisor; Systems Analyst. **Educational backgrounds include:** Accounting; Computer Science; Engineering; Finance; Marketing. **Benefits:** 401(k); Dental Insurance; Disability Coverage; Life Insurance; Medical Insurance; Tuition Assistance. **Corporate headquarters location:** This Location. **Parent company:** Shiroki Corporation (Japan). **Listed on:** Privately held. **Number of employees at this location:** 450.

SADDLEMAN, INC.

80 West 900 South, Logan UT 84321. 435/752-1000. **Contact:** Human Resources. **World Wide Web address:** http://www.saddleman.com. **Description:** A manufacturer and distributor of automotive aftermarket products including car seat covers and front-end covers. **NOTE:** Entry-level positions are offered. **Common positions include:** Computer Operator; Computer Programmer; Customer Service Rep.; Market Research Analyst; Marketing Manager; Marketing Specialist; Systems Analyst. **Educational backgrounds include:** Accounting; Business Administration; Computer Science; Finance; Marketing. **Benefits:** 401(k); Dental Insurance; Disability Coverage; Employee Discounts; Life Insurance; Medical Insurance; Pension Plan. **Corporate headquarters location:** This Location. **Other U.S. locations:** Fremont OH; Anderson SC. **Annual sales/revenues:** $21 - $50 million. **Number of employees at this location:** 100. **Number of employees nationwide:** 800.

SATURN CORPORATION

P.O. Box 7025, Troy MI 48007. 248/524-5000. **Contact:** Human Resources. **World Wide Web address:** http://www.saturn.com. **Description:**

Develops, manufactures, and sells cars. **NOTE:** Please send resumes to Human Resources, Saturn Corporation, 100 Saturn Parkway, Mail Drop 371999E21, P.O. Box 1500, Spring Hill TN 37174. **Common positions include:** Designer; Draftsperson; Electrical/Electronics Engineer; Mechanical Engineer. **Educational backgrounds include:** Engineering. **Benefits:** 401(k); Dental Insurance; Disability Coverage; Employee Discounts; Life Insurance; Medical Insurance; Pension Plan; Profit Sharing; Savings Plan; Tuition Assistance. **Corporate headquarters location:** This Location. **Other U.S. locations:** Springhill TN. **Parent company:** General Motors Corporation. **Listed on:** New York Stock Exchange. **Number of employees at this location:** 900. **Number of employees nationwide:** 9,200.

SAUER-SUNDSTRAND
2800 East 13th Street, Ames IA 50010. 515/239-6000. **Fax:** 515/239-6318. **Contact:** Human Resources. **World Wide Web address:** http://www. sauer.com. **Description:** Sauer-Sundstrand provides controlled hydraulic power systems and components to manufacturers of off-highway vehicles throughout the world. Products include hydrostatic transmissions, piston pumps and motors, gear pumps and motors, mechanical gear boxes, and electronic and electrohydraulic controls. **Common positions include:** Accountant; Agricultural Engineer; Designer; Draftsperson; Electrician; Financial Analyst; General Manager; Industrial Engineer; Mechanical Engineer; Purchasing Agent/Manager; Services Sales Rep.; Technical Writer/Editor. **Educational backgrounds include:** Engineering. **Benefits:** 401(k); Dental Insurance; Disability Coverage; Life Insurance; Medical Insurance; Pension Plan; Profit Sharing; Tuition Assistance. **Special programs:** Internships. **Corporate headquarters location:** This Location. **Other area locations:** West Branch IA. **Other U.S. locations:** Freeport IL; LaSalle IL; Lawrence KS; Plymouth MN. **Listed on:** NASDAQ. **Number of employees at this location:** 600. **Number of employees nationwide:** 1,700. **Number of employees worldwide:** 3,600.

EARL SCHEIB, INC.
8737 Wilshire Boulevard, Beverly Hills CA 90211. 310/652-4880. **Contact:** Human Resources. **World Wide Web address:** http://www.earlscheib.com. **Description:** Operates a chain of automobile paint centers throughout the United States which offer painting and light body and fender repair services. **Corporate headquarters location:** This Location. **Other U.S. locations:** Tampa FL; Evergreen Park IL; Springfield MO.

SKYLINE CORPORATION
2520 Bypass Road, Elkhart IN 46514. 219/294-6521. **Contact:** Human Resources. **World Wide Web address:** http://www.skylinecorp.com. **Description:** Designs, produces, and distributes mobile homes and recreational vehicles such as travel trailers, park models, mini motor homes, and fifth wheels. **Corporate headquarters location:** This Location. **Listed on:** New York Stock Exchange.

SPARTAN MOTORS
1000 Reynolds Road, Charlotte MI 48813. 517/543-6400. **Contact:** Human Resources. **World Wide Web address:** http://www.spartanmotors.com. **Description:** Produces custom-designed heavy truck chassis for specialized applications. **Corporate headquarters location:** This Location. **Listed on:** NASDAQ. **Stock exchange symbol:** SPAR. **Number of employees at this location:** 420.

STANDARD MOTOR PRODUCTS INC.
37-18 Northern Boulevard, Long Island City NY 11101. 718/392-0200. **Contact:** Vincent Ruggiero, Employment Manager. **World Wide Web address:** http://www.smpcorp.com. **Description:** Engaged primarily in the manufacture of electrical and fuel system automotive replacement parts sold internationally under the Standard Blue Streak, Hygrade, Champ, and Four Seasons brand names. Products include ignition parts, automotive wire and cable parts, carburetor parts and kits, general service auto parts (radio antennas, gasoline cans, brooms and brushes, polishing cloths, fuses, and other auto accessories), and automotive heating and air conditioning systems. **Common positions include:** Accountant/Auditor; Buyer; Computer Programmer; Draftsperson; Electrical/Electronics Engineer; Financial Analyst; Industrial Designer; Industrial Engineer; Mechanical Engineer; Purchasing Agent/Manager; Quality Control Supervisor; Statistician; Systems Analyst; Technical Writer/Editor. **Educational backgrounds include:** Business Administration; Computer Science; Engineering; Finance; Marketing. **Benefits:** Dental Insurance; Disability Coverage; Life Insurance; Medical Insurance; Pension Plan; Profit Sharing; Tuition Assistance. **Corporate headquarters location:** This Location. **International locations:** Canada; Hong Kong; Puerto Rico. **Listed on:** New York Stock Exchange. **Number of employees worldwide:** 3,500.

STARCRAFT AUTOMOTIVE GROUP, INC.
2703 College Avenue, Goshen IN 46528. 219/533-1105. **Contact:** Human Resources. **World Wide Web address:** http://www.starcraftcorp.com. **Description:** Specializes in upscale, custom vehicles and is one of the largest conversion van manufacturers in the United States. In addition to converting full-size vans and minivans, the company customizes pick-up trucks and sport-utility vehicles. Starcraft Automotive Group sells its products through a network of approximately 900 authorized automotive dealers worldwide. **Corporate headquarters location:** This Location. **Listed on:** NASDAQ.

STELLAR ENGINEERING INC.
5505 Thirteen Mile Road, Warren MI 48092. 810/978-8444. **Fax:** 810/978-2315. **Contact:** Human Resources Manager. **World Wide Web address:** http://www.stellar-eng.com. **Description:** Designs automated assembly and welding systems for the automotive industry. **Common positions include:** Ceramics Engineer; Chemical Engineer; Civil Engineer; Cost Estimator; Designer; Draftsperson; Electrical/Electronics Engineer; Industrial Engineer; Materials Engineer; Mechanical Engineer; Metallurgical Engineer; Software Engineer; Technical Writer/Editor. **Educational backgrounds include:** Engineering. **Benefits:** 401(k); Dental Insurance; Disability Coverage; Employee Discounts; Life Insurance; Medical Insurance; Pension Plan; Savings Plan. **Corporate headquarters location:** This Location. **Other area locations:** Sterling Heights MI. **Listed on:** Privately held. **Number of employees at this location:** 300. **Number of employees nationwide:** 500.

STRICK CORPORATION
225 Lincoln Highway, Fairless Hills PA 19030. 215/949-3600. **Fax:** 215/949-4766. **Contact:** Maureen Arnoldy, Assistant Human Resource Manager. **World Wide Web address:** http://www.strickcorp.com. **Description:** A manufacturer of trailers, flatbeds, and chassis. **Common positions include:** Accountant/Auditor; Buyer; Computer Programmer; Designer; Human Resources Rep.; Industrial Engineer; Industrial

Production Manager; Materials Engineer; Mechanical Engineer; Operations/Production Manager; Purchasing Agent/Manager; Quality Control Supervisor; Structural Engineer; Systems Analyst. **Educational backgrounds include:** Accounting; Business Administration; Engineering. **Benefits:** 401(k); Dental Insurance; Disability Coverage; Life Insurance; Medical Insurance; Tuition Assistance. **Corporate headquarters location:** This Location. **Other U.S. locations:** IN. **Listed on:** Privately held. **Number of employees at this location:** 65. **Number of employees nationwide:** 1,000.

SUPERIOR INDUSTRIES INTERNATIONAL
7800 Woodley Avenue, Van Nuys CA 91406. 818/781-4973. **Contact:** Human Resources. **World Wide Web address:** http://www.supind.com. **Description:** Produces cast aluminum road wheels for original equipment manufacturers and a variety of automotive aftermarket products. **NOTE:** Entry-level positions are offered. **Common positions include:** Accountant/Auditor; Design Engineer; Mechanical Engineer; Systems Analyst. **Educational backgrounds include:** Accounting; Engineering. **Benefits:** 401(k); Dental Insurance; Disability Coverage; Employee Discounts; Life Insurance; Medical Insurance; Tuition Assistance. **Corporate headquarters location:** This Location. **Other U.S. locations:** AR; KS; TN. **Listed on:** New York Stock Exchange. **Annual sales/revenues:** More than $100 million. **Number of employees at this location:** 900. **Number of employees nationwide:** 4,500.

TI GROUP AUTOMOTIVE SYSTEMS
2660 Jewett Lane, Sanford FL 32771. 407/323-2780. **Contact:** Human Resources. World Wide Web address: http://www.bundy.com. **Description:** Manufactures a variety of internal automotive equipment including brake fluid carrying systems; fuel storage and delivery systems; bellows for exhaust systems; and hoses for air conditioning, heating, and exhaust systems. The company also manufactures engine management products for chain saws, industrial engines, marine engines, and recreational vehicles.

TRW
FASTENERS DIVISION
180 State Road East, Westminster MA 01473. 978/874-5008. **Fax:** 978/874-5163. **Contact:** Janis Pollock, Human Resources Manager. **World Wide Web address:** http://www.trw.com. **Description:** Manufactures systems-engineered automotive electrical and electronic controls and specialty fasteners. **Common positions include:** Accountant; Blue-Collar Worker Supervisor; Buyer; Computer Programmer; Customer Service Rep.; Financial Analyst; Industrial Engineer; Mechanical Engineer; Operations/Production Manager; Production Manager; Quality Control Supervisor; Systems Analyst. **Educational backgrounds include:** Accounting; Business Administration; Computer Science; Engineering; Finance; Marketing; Mathematics. **Special programs:** Internships. **Corporate headquarters location:** Cleveland OH. **Number of employees at this location:** 105.

TEKSID ALUMINUM FOUNDRY INC.
1635 Old Columbia Road, Dickson TN 37055. 615/446-8110. **Fax:** 615/446-0852. **Contact:** Lori Donegan, Employment Manager. **Description:** Manufactures aluminum cylinder heads for Ford, GM, and DaimlerChrysler. Founded in 1987. **NOTE:** Entry-level positions are offered. **Common positions include:** Accountant; Administrative Assistant; Blue-Collar Worker Supervisor; Computer Support Technician; Draftsperson;

Electrical/Electronics Engineer; Management Trainee; Mechanical Engineer; Production Manager. **Educational backgrounds include:** Accounting; Business Administration; Chemistry; Engineering; Microsoft Office; Microsoft Word; Physics; Spreadsheets. **Benefits:** 401(k); Casual Dress - Daily; Dental Insurance; Disability Coverage; Employee Discounts; Life Insurance; Medical Insurance; Relocation Assistance; Sick Days (1 - 5); Tuition Assistance; Vacation Days (11 - 15). **Special programs:** Training. **Office hours:** Monday - Friday, 8:00 a.m. - 5:00 p.m. **Corporate headquarters location:** This Location. **Parent company:** Fiat USA. **Listed on:** New York Stock Exchange. **CEO:** Leon Cueto. **Facilities Manager:** Walter Devietti. **Information Systems Manager:** Ed Brown. **Purchasing Manager:** Pete McKee. **Number of employees at this location:** 650.

TENNECO AUTOMOTIVE
500 North Field Drive, Lake Forest IL 60045. 847/482-5000. **Contact:** Human Resources. **World Wide Web address:** http://www.tenneco-automotive.com. **Description:** Develops and manufactures suspension and engine mounting systems providing noise, shock, and vibration control for the transportation industry. **Corporate headquarters location:** This Location. **Parent company:** Tenneco (Greenwich CT).

TESCO WILLIAMSEN
P.O. Box 26864, Salt Lake City UT 84126. 801/973-9400. **Contact:** Skip Musgraves, Vice President of Finance. **Description:** Manufactures truck and bus bodies. **Corporate headquarters location:** This Location.

TOLEDO MOLDING & DIE INC.
1429 Coining Drive, Toledo OH 43612. 419/470-3950. **Contact:** Joseph Straka, Director of Corporate Human Resources. **World Wide Web address:** http://www.tmdinc.com. **Description:** Designs, engineers, and manufactures injection-molded plastic products, primarily for the automotive industry. **Corporate headquarters location:** This Location.

TRANSPRO, INC.
100 Gando Drive, New Haven CT 06513. 203/401-6450. **Fax:** 203/865-0803. **Contact:** Melissa Chambrelli, Human Resources Manager. **World Wide Web address:** http://www.transpro.com. **Description:** A holding company. **Common positions include:** Accountant; Administrative Assistant; AS400 Programmer Analyst; Chief Financial Officer; Computer Programmer; Controller; Credit Manager; Customer Service Rep.; Design Engineer; Financial Analyst; Marketing Manager; Mechanical Engineer; Purchasing Agent/Manager; Sales Executive; Sales Manager; Secretary. **Educational backgrounds include:** Accounting; Engineering; Finance; Marketing. **Special programs:** Co-ops; Summer Jobs. **Corporate headquarters location:** This Location. **Other U.S. locations:** Nationwide. **Subsidiaries include:** A/C Plus, Inc. remanufactures automotive air conditioning compressors; Crown Industries produces specialty van interiors; Evap, Inc. distributes a variety of automotive components including compressors, evaporators, and hose assemblies; G&O Manufacturing produces automotive radiators; GO/DAN Industries (also at this location) manufactures automotive heat transfer products. **Listed on:** New York Stock Exchange. **Stock exchange symbol:** TPR. **President/CEO:** Hank McHale. **Information Systems Manager:** Mike Shook. **Sales Manager:** Kevin O'Connor. **Number of employees at this location:** 150. **Number of employees nationwide:** 2,300.

TRICO TECHNOLOGIES
1995 Billy Mitchell Boulevard, Brownsville TX 78521. 956/544-2722. **Contact:** Human Resources. **World Wide Web address:** http://www. tricoproducts.com. **Description:** A manufacturer of windshield wipers. **Corporate headquarters location:** Rochester Hills MI.

TRUCK-LITE COMPANY INC.
310 East Elmwood Avenue, Falconer NY 14733. 716/665-6214. **Wide Web address:** http://www. trucklite.net. **Contact:** Joe Zeman, Human Resources Manager. **Description:** Manufactures vehicular safety lights. Truck-Lite's products are distributed worldwide. **Corporate headquarters location:** This Location. **Number of employees at this location:** 250.

U.S. MANUFACTURING CORPORATION
17717 Masonic, Fraser MI 48026. 810/293-8744. **Contact:** Human Resources. **Description:** Manufactures axles for the automotive industry. **Common positions include:** Draftsperson; Industrial Engineer; Mechanical Engineer. **Educational backgrounds include:** Engineering. **Benefits:** Dental Insurance; Disability Coverage; Life Insurance; Medical Insurance; Pension Plan; Tuition Assistance. **Corporate headquarters location:** This Location. **Number of employees at this location:** 700.

UNIQUE FABRICATING INC.
1601 West Hamlin Road, Rochester Hills MI 48309. 248/853-2333. **Fax:** 248/853-7720. **Contact:** Human Resources. **World Wide Web address:** http://www.uniquefab.com. **Description:** Manufactures gaskets and seals for General Motors and Ford. **NOTE:** Entry-level positions are offered. **Common positions include:** Administrative Manager; Blue-Collar Worker Supervisor; Clerical Supervisor; Computer Programmer; Customer Service Rep.; Human Resources Manager; Manufacturer's/Wholesaler's Sales Rep.; Mechanical Engineer; MIS Specialist; Operations/Production Manager; Purchasing Agent/Manager; Quality Control Supervisor; Systems Analyst. **Educational backgrounds include:** Business Administration; Computer Science; Engineering; Marketing. **Benefits:** 401(k); Dental Insurance; Disability Coverage; Medical Insurance. **Special programs:** Internships. **Corporate headquarters location:** This Location. **Listed on:** Privately held. **Annual sales/revenues:** $21 - $50 million. **Number of employees at this location:** 500.

UNITED ENGINE & MACHINE COMPANY
4909 Goni Road, Carson City NV 89706. 775/882-7790. **Contact:** Nancy Weaver, Personnel Manager. **Description:** Manufactures aluminum pistons for automotive engines. **Corporate headquarters location:** This Location.

VOLVO CARS OF NORTH AMERICA, INC.
6 Volvo Drive, Rockleigh NJ 07647. 201/767-4715. **Contact:** Ellen Andretta, Human Resources Services Representative. **Wide Web address:** http://www.volvo.com. **Description:** Supports the sale and service of Volvo automobiles and related parts and accessories for approximately 400 dealers. **Common positions include:** Automotive Engineer. **Corporate headquarters location:** This Location.

WABASH NATIONAL CORPORATION
P.O. Box 6129, Lafayette IN 47903. 765/771-5300. **Contact:** Chuck Fish, Vice President of Human Resources. **World Wide Web address:** http://www. wabashnational.com. **Description:** Designs, manufactures, and markets standard and customized truck trailers including dry freight vans, refrigerated trailers, and bimodal vehicles, as well as parts and related equipment. Wabash National markets its products through dealers to truckload and less-than-truckload common carriers, private fleet operators, household moving and storage companies, package carriers, and intermodal carriers including railroads. **Common positions include:** Accountant/Auditor; Blue-Collar Worker Supervisor; Buyer; Computer Programmer; Draftsperson; Electrical/Electronics Engineer; Human Resources Manager; Industrial Engineer; Licensed Practical Nurse; Mechanical Engineer; Purchasing Agent/Manager; Systems Analyst; Transportation/Traffic Specialist. **Educational backgrounds include:** Accounting; Computer Science; Engineering. **Benefits:** 401(k); Dental Insurance; Disability Coverage; Life Insurance; Medical Insurance; Pension Plan; Profit Sharing; Tuition Assistance. **Corporate headquarters location:** This Location. **Listed on:** New York Stock Exchange. **Number of employees at this location:** 2,700.

WHITMAN GENERAL BOTTLERS
3501 Algonquin Road, Rolling Meadows IL 60008. 847/818-5000. **Contact:** Human Resources. **World Wide Web address:** http://www.whitmancorp.com. **Description:** This location houses administrative offices. Overall, Whitman Corporation is a holding company for diverse industrial interests including automotive and food and beverages. **Corporate headquarters location:** This Location. **Subsidiaries include:** Pepsi-Cola General Bottlers (also at this location) is a producer and distributor of soft drinks and nonalcoholic beverages in 12 states; Midas International provides automobile suspension systems, exhaust systems, and brake services through 2,525 outlets across the U.S.; and Hussmann Corporation manufactures refrigeration systems and related components for the food industry. **Listed on:** New York Stock Exchange.

WILLIAMS CONTROLS, INC.
14100 SW 72nd Avenue, Portland OR 97224. 503/684-8600. **Fax:** 503/684-8675. **Contact:** Human Resources. **World Wide Web address:** http://www.wmco.com. **Description:** A diversified manufacturer and distributor operating through its subsidiaries. Founded in 1937. **NOTE:** Entry-level positions and second and third shifts are offered. **Common positions include:** Account Manager; Accountant; Administrative Assistant; Controller; Customer Service Representative; Design Engineer; Draftsperson; Electrician; General Manager; Human Resources Manager; Industrial Engineer; Manufacturing Engineer; Marketing Manager; MIS Specialist; Production Manager; Sales Manager; Secretary; Technical Writer/Editor. **Educational backgrounds include:** Accounting; Business Administration; Engineering; Marketing. **Benefits:** 401(k); Dental Insurance; Disability Coverage; Life Insurance; Medical Insurance; Pension Plan; Profit Sharing; Tuition Assistance. **Corporate headquarters location:** This Location. **Subsidiaries include:** Williams Controls Industries, Inc. designs, engineers, manufactures, and distributes electronic, pneumatic, and hydraulic controls for heavy-duty vehicles and equipment. Distribution of products includes OEMs, dealers, and selected distributors. Kenco Williams, Inc. is a manufacturer and distributor of light truck, van, and sport-utility vehicle accessories. An extensive distribution system includes mass merchants, installers, and auto dealers. NESC Williams, Inc. manufactures compressed natural gas conversion kits for gasoline engines, as well as natural gas monitoring equipment and services. The company's other wholly-owned subsidiaries are Williams Technologies, Inc. for research and development activities, and Williams World Trade, Inc. for

foreign sourcing activities. **Listed on:** NASDAQ. **Number of employees at this location:** 180.

WINNEBAGO INDUSTRIES, INC.
605 West Crystal Lake Road, Forest City IA 50436. 515/582-3535. **Contact:** Larry Kluckhohn, Director of Personnel. **World Wide Web address:** http://www.winnebagoind.com. **Description:** A manufacturer and distributor of recreational and camping vehicles. **Common positions include:** Accountant/Auditor; Administrator; Advertising Clerk; Attorney; Blue-Collar Worker Supervisor; Branch Manager; Buyer; Civil Engineer; Computer Programmer; Credit Manager; Customer Service Rep.; Department Manager; Draftsperson; Editor; Electrical/Electronics Engineer; Financial Analyst; General Manager; Human Resources Manager; Industrial Engineer; Manufacturer's/Wholesaler's Sales Rep.; Mechanical Engineer; Operations/Production Manager; Public Relations Specialist; Purchasing Agent/Manager; Quality Control Supervisor; Systems Analyst; Transportation/Traffic Specialist. **Educational backgrounds include:** Accounting; Business Administration; Computer Science; Engineering; Finance; Marketing. **Benefits:** Dental Insurance; Disability Coverage; Employee Discounts; Life Insurance; Medical Insurance; Profit Sharing; Savings Plan; Tuition Assistance. **Special programs:** Internships. **Corporate headquarters location:** This Location. **Listed on:** New York Stock Exchange.

YAMAHA MOTOR CORPORATION U.S.A.
6555 Katella Avenue, Cypress CA 90630. 714/761-7300. **Contact:** Personnel Department. **World Wide Web address:** http://www.yamaha-motor.com. **Description:** Distributes motorized products including motorcycles, ATVs, snowmobiles, golf carts, outboards, and power products. **Corporate headquarters location:** This Location.

ZIEBART INTERNATIONAL CORPORATION
P.O. Box 1290, Troy MI 48007. 248/588-4100. **Contact:** Personnel. **World Wide Web address:** http://www.ziebart.com. **Description:** Operates a network of franchised automotive service locations. **Common positions include:** Administrator; Advertising Clerk; Chemist; Credit Clerk and Authorizer; Customer Service Representative; Human Resources Manager; Public Relations Specialist; Purchasing Agent/Manager; Services Sales Representative. **Educational backgrounds include:** Business Administration; Chemistry; Liberal Arts; Marketing. **Benefits:** Dental Insurance; Disability Coverage; Employee Discounts; Life Insurance; Medical Insurance; Pension Plan; Profit Sharing; Savings Plan; Tuition Assistance. **Corporate headquarters location:** This Location. **Operations at this facility include:** Administration; Sales; Service. **Number of employees at this location:** 250.

For more information on career opportunities in the automotive industry:

Associations

ALLIANCE OF AUTOMOBILE MANUFACTURERS
1401 H Street NW, Suite 900, Washington DC 20005. 202/326-5500. Fax: 202/326-5567. World Wide Web address: http://www.autoalliance.org. A trade association. Reviews social and public policies pertaining to the motor vehicle industry and its customers.

AUTOMOTIVE AFTERMARKET INDUSTRY ASSOCIATION
25 Northwest Point Boulevard, Suite 425, Elk Grove Village IL 60007-1035. 847/228-1310. World Wide Web address: http://www.aftmkt.com/asia. Members are manufacturers and distributors of automobile replacement parts. Sponsors a trade show. Publishes educational guidebooks and training manuals.

AUTOMOTIVE SERVICE ASSOCIATION
P.O. Box 929, Bedford TX 76095. 817/283-6205. World Wide Web address: http://www.asashop.org. Works with shops to find workers. Publishes a monthly magazine with classified advertisements.

Directories

AUTOMOTIVE NEWS MARKET DATA BOOK
Crain Communications, Automotive News, 1400 Woodbridge Avenue, Detroit MI 48207-3187. 313/446-6000.

WARD'S AUTOMOTIVE YEARBOOK
Ward's Communications, Inc., 3000 Town Center, Suite 2750, Southville MI 48075. 248/357-0800. World Wide Web address: http://www.wardsauto.com.

Magazines

AUTOMOBILE MAGAZINE
PRIMEDIA, Inc., 120 East Liberty Street, Ann Arbor MI 48104. 734/994-3500. World Wide Web address: http://www.automobilemag.com. A monthly magazine covering all facets of automobile buying.

AUTOMOTIVE INDUSTRIES
Cahners Business Information, 201 King of Prussia Road, Radnor PA 19089. 610/964-4000.

AUTOMOTIVE NEWS
Crain Communications, 1400 Woodbridge Avenue, Detroit MI 48207-3187. 313/446-6000.

WARD'S AUTO WORLD
WARD'S AUTOMOTIVE REPORTS
Ward's Communications, Inc., 3000 Town Center, Suite 2750, Southville MI 48075. 248/357-0800. World Wide Web address: http://www.wardsauto.com.

Banking/Savings and Loans

You can expect to find the following types of companies in this chapter:
Banks • Bank Holding Companies and Associations
• Lending Firms/Financial Services Institutions

Some helpful information: *The average salary range for entry-level bank and loan officers is approximately $30,000 - $40,000 annually. Senior officers and directors can earn over $50,000, and executives often top $100,000. Tellers and clerks' salaries are usually under $20,000. Loan officers generally earn between $30,000 and $70,000, depending upon their specialty (in particular, commercial real estate mortgage loan officers earn salaries at the upper end of the range).*

ABINGTON SAVINGS BANK
538 Bedford Street, Abington MA 02351. 781/982-3200. **Contact:** Human Resources Department. **Description:** A full-service bank. **Corporate headquarters location:** This Location. **Other U.S. locations:** Halifax MA; Hull MA; Kingston MA; Pembroke MA; Whitman MA.

THE ACACIA GROUP
7315 Wisconsin Avenue, Bethesda MD 20814. 301/280-1000. **Contact:** Karen Mayo, Manager of Recruitment. **World Wide Web address:** http://www.acaciagroup.com. **Description:** Provides diversified financial services through its operating companies. **Common positions include:** Accountant Actuary; Attorney; Bank Officer/Manager; Branch Manager; Brokerage Clerk; Claim Rep.; Customer Service Rep.; Financial Analyst; Human Resources Manager; Insurance Agent/Broker; Paralegal; Securities Sales Rep.; Systems Analyst. **Educational backgrounds include:** Accounting; Business Administration; Finance; Liberal Arts; Marketing. **Benefits:** 401(k); Daycare Assistance; Dental Insurance; Disability Coverage; Employee Discounts; Job Sharing; Life Insurance; Medical Insurance; Profit Sharing; Public Transit Available; Telecommuting; Tuition Assistance. **Corporate headquarters location:** This Location. **Subsidiaries include:** Acacia Life and Acacia National Life offer life insurance policies. The Advisors Group provides investment management services. The Calvert Group, Ltd. offers mutual fund management services. Acacia Federal Savings Bank provides traditional savings and loan services. **Parent company:** Ameritas Acacia Mutual Holding Company.

AGFIRST FARM CREDIT BANK
P.O. Box 1499, Columbia SC 29202. 803/799-5000. **Physical address:** 1401 Hampton Street, Columbia SC 29201. **Contact:** Recruiter. **World Wide Web address:** http://www.agfirst.com. **Description:** An agricultural lender in the United States and Puerto Rico. The company provides more than $10 billion in loans to farmers, ranchers, and rural homeowners through affiliated agricultural credit associations. **NOTE:** Entry-level positions are offered. **Common positions include:** Accountant; Administrative Assistant; Customer Service Rep.; Loan Officer; Systems Analyst. **Educational backgrounds include:** Accounting; Business Administration; Computer Science; Economics; Finance. **Benefits:** 401(k); Dental Insurance; Flexible Schedule; Life Insurance; Medical Insurance; Pension Plan. **Corporate headquarters location:** This Location.

AGRIBANK, FCB
375 Jackson Street, St. Paul MN 55101. 651/282-8800. **Contact:** Human Resources Manager. **World**

Wide Web address: http://www.farmcredit.com. **Description:** A banking institution providing mortgage loans to farmers. **Common positions include:** Accountant/Auditor; Attorney; Financial Analyst. **Benefits:** Dental Insurance; Disability Coverage; Life Insurance; Medical Insurance; Pension Plan; Savings Plan; Tuition Assistance. **Corporate headquarters location:** This Location. **Other U.S. locations:** Nationwide.

AMERIANA BANK
P.O. Box H, New Castle IN 47362. 765/529-2230. **Contact:** Jane K. Moyer, AVP Personnel and Administrative Services. **Description:** A savings and loan bank. **Parent company:** Ameriana Bancorp.

AMERICAN NATIONAL BANKSHARES
P.O. Box 191, Danville VA 24543. 804/792-5111. **Contact:** Donna Hankins, Human Resources Administrator. **World Wide Web address:** http://www.amnb.com. **Description:** A bank holding company. **Corporate headquarters location:** This Location. **Subsidiaries include:** American National Bank and Trust Company (Danville VA) offers a wide variety of retail, commercial, and trust banking services.

AmSOUTH BANCORPORATION
P.O. Box 11007, AHP7, Birmingham AL 35288. 205/326-5476. **Contact:** Corporate Staffing. **E-mail address:** career@amsouth.com. **World Wide Web address:** http://www.amsouth.com. **Description:** One of the nation's largest banking institutions with more than 300 locations. AmSouth provides commercial, electronic, and telephone banking services. **Common positions include:** Accountant/Auditor; Branch Manager; Computer Programmer; Credit Manager. **Educational backgrounds include:** Accounting; Business Administration; Computer Science; Finance; Marketing. **Benefits:** Daycare Assistance; Disability Coverage; Employee Discounts; Life Insurance; Medical Insurance; Profit Sharing; Savings Plan; Tuition Assistance. **Corporate headquarters location:** This Location. **Other U.S. locations:** FL; GA. **Number of employees at this location:** 5,000.

AmSOUTH BANK
300 Union Street, Nashville TN 37237-0102. 615/748-2000. **Contact:** Human Resources. **World Wide Web address:** http://www.amsouth.com. **Description:** A commercial bank. **Corporate headquarters location:** Birmingham AL. **Parent company:** AmSouth Bancorporation.

ANDREWS FEDERAL CREDIT UNION
P.O. Box 4000, Clemson MD 20735. 301/702-5500. **Physical address:** 5711 Allentown Road, Suitland

MD 20746. **Contact:** Human Resources. **World Wide Web address:** http://www.andrews.fcu.org. **Description:** This location houses the administrative offices and a credit union. Overall, Andrews Federal Credit Union provides financial services to members of the military and their families. **Corporate headquarters location:** This Location. **Other U.S. locations:** Burlington NJ; Wrightstown NJ; Falls Church VA; Rockville VA; Springfield VA.

APPLE BANK FOR SAVINGS

277 Park Avenue, New York NY 10172. 212/224-6400. **Toll-free phone:** 800/722-6888. **Fax:** 212/224-6592. **Contact:** Human Resources. **World Wide Web address:** http://www.theapplebank.com. **Description:** Operates a full-service savings bank serving New York City, Long Island, and Westchester with a total of 43 branches. **NOTE:** Entry-level positions are offered. Interested jobseekers should fax resumes and indicate department of interest. **Common positions include:** Account Representative; Administrative Assistant; Advertising Clerk; Assistant Manager; Auditor; Bank Officer/Manager; Bank Teller; Computer Operator; Computer Programmer; Customer Service Representative; Insurance Agent/Broker; Marketing Specialist; MIS Specialist; Sales Executive; Sales Manager; Sales Rep.; Secretary. **Educational backgrounds include:** Accounting; Business Administration; Computer Science; Finance; Liberal Arts; Marketing. **Benefits:** 401(k); Dental Insurance; Disability Coverage; Employee Discounts; Life Insurance; Medical Insurance; Pension Plan; Tuition Assistance. **Corporate headquarters location:** This Location. **Annual sales/revenues:** More than $100 million. **Number of employees at this location:** 900.

ASSOCIATED BANC-CORP

1200 Hansen Road, Green Bay WI 54304. 920/433-3166. **Contact:** Robert J. Johnson, Director of Human Resources. **World Wide Web address:** http://www.assocbank.com. **Description:** A diversified, multibank holding company providing a complete range of business, retail, trust/asset management, correspondent, leasing, insurance, mortgage banking, real estate, and investment services. Founded in 1970. **Corporate headquarters location:** This Location. **Other U.S. locations:** IL; MN. **Listed on:** NASDAQ.

ASTORIA FINANCIAL CORPORATION
ASTORIA FEDERAL SAVINGS & LOAN ASSOCIATION

One Astoria Federal Plaza, Lake Success NY 11042-1085. 516/327-3000. **Toll-free phone:** 800/AST-ORIA. **Fax:** 516/327-7610. **Contact:** Manager of Recruiting and Employee Relations. **E-mail address:** hr@astoriafederal.com. **World Wide Web address:** http://www.astoriafederal.com. **Description:** A bank holding company. Founded in 1888. **Common positions include:** Accountant; Adjuster; Assistant Manager; Auditor; Branch Manager; Customer Service Rep.; Management Trainee; Typist/Word Processor. **Educational backgrounds include:** Accounting; Business Administration. **Benefits:** 401(k); Dental Insurance; Disability Coverage; Employee Discounts; Life Insurance; Medical Insurance; Pension Plan; Tuition Assistance. **Corporate headquarters location:** This Location. **Subsidiaries include:** With 87 banking offices, Astoria Federal Savings & Loan Association provides a range of financial services and products to over 700,000 customers throughout the Long Island and New York City metropolitan areas. **Listed on:** NASDAQ. **CEO:** George L. Engelke, Jr. **Number of employees at this location:** 400. **Number of employees nationwide:** 2,000.

BB&T CORPORATION

P.O. Box 1215, Winston-Salem NC 27102. 336/733-2000. **Contact:** Human Resources. **World Wide Web address:** http://www.bbandt.com. **Description:** A multi-bank holding company. Founded in 1872. **NOTE:** Entry-level positions and part-time jobs are offered. **Company slogan:** Respect the individual. Value the relationship. **Benefits:** 401(k); Casual Dress - Fridays; Daycare Assistance; Dental Insurance; Disability Coverage; Employee Discounts; Life Insurance; Medical Insurance; Pension Plan; Savings Plan; Sick Days; Tuition Assistance; Vacation Days (10 - 20). **Special programs:** Internships; Training; Summer Jobs. **Office hours:** Monday - Friday, 8:30 a.m. - 5:00 p.m. **Corporate headquarters location:** This Location. **Other U.S. locations:** DC; MD; SC; VA. **Subsidiaries include:** BB&T of North Carolina, which offers full-service commercial and retail banking and additional financial services such as investments, leasing, factoring, and trust. **Listed on:** New York Stock Exchange. **Stock exchange symbol:** BBT. **CEO:** John Allison. **Facilities Manager:** Gary Scott. **Information Systems Manager:** Leon Wilson. **Purchasing Manager:** Steve Paige. **Sales Manager:** Kelly King. **Number of employees at this location:** 750. **Number of employees nationwide:** 11,120.

BSB BANCORP INC.
BSB BANK & TRUST

58-68 Exchange Street, Binghamton NY 13901. 607/779-3542. **Contact:** Ruth Rudball, Human Resources. **World Wide Web address:** http://www.bsbbank.com. **Description:** A bank holding company. **NOTE:** In April 2000, NBT Bancorp Inc. and BSB Bancorp, Inc. announced plans to merge. Please contact this location for more information. **Corporate headquarters location:** This Location. **Subsidiaries include:** BSB Bank & Trust provides diversified financial services to individuals and businesses throughout Broome County and surrounding areas of New York state. Services include retail banking; commercial, mortgage, and consumer loans; and investment banking.

BT FINANCIAL CORPORATION

BT Financial Plaza, 551 Main Street, Johnstown PA 15901. 814/532-3801. **Contact:** Betsy Zipf, Vice President of Human Resources. **World Wide Web address:** http://www.btfinancial.com. **Description:** A bank holding company. **Corporate headquarters location:** This Location. **Subsidiaries include:** Bedford Associates, Inc.; Laurel Trust Company; Laurel Bank. **Listed on:** NASDAQ.

BWC FINANCIAL CORPORATION
BANK OF WALNUT CREEK

1400 Civic Drive, Walnut Creek CA 94596. 925/932-5353. **Contact:** Donna Schneider, Vice President of Human Resources. **World Wide Web address:** http://www.bowc.com. **Description:** A holding company. **Corporate headquarters location:** This Location. **Subsidiaries include:** Bank of Walnut Creek (also at this location); BWC Real Estate. **Number of employees at this location:** 55.

BANCORP SOUTH BANK

P.O. Box 55338, Birmingham AL 35255. 205/933-8080. **Recorded jobline:** 205/939-4220. **Contact:** Personnel. **Description:** A bank. **Corporate headquarters location:** This Location.

BANGOR SAVINGS BANK

P.O. Box 930, Bangor ME 04402-0930. 207/942-5211. **Contact:** Human Resources. **Description:** A mutual savings institution with 14 branch locations throughout the state of Maine. The bank holds accounts for Maine residents only. **Corporate headquarters location:** This Location.

BANK OF AMERICA
401 North Tryon Street, Charlotte NC 28255. **Toll-free phone:** 888/279-3457. **Recorded jobline:** 800/587-JOBS. **Contact:** Manager of Recruiting. **World Wide Web address:** http://www.bankofamerica.com. **Description:** A bank offering commercial lending, consumer banking, trust accounts, mortgage banking, corporate banking, sales, trading, investment banking, operations and systems, audit services, control services, dealer financial services, and bankcards. **Corporate headquarters location:** This Location.
Other U.S. locations:
• 800 Fifth Avenue, 33rd Floor, Seattle WA 98104. 206/461-0800.

THE BANK OF CHERRY CREEK
3033 East First Avenue, Denver CO 80206. 303/394-5100. **Contact:** Eileen Terrell, Human Resources Director. **Description:** Operates a commercial bank with a complete range of services for private, commercial, and institutional customers. **Common positions include:** Bank Officer/Manager; Branch Manager; Credit Manager; Customer Service Rep.; Department Manager; General Manager; Operations/Production Manager. **Educational backgrounds include:** Accounting; Business Administration; Economics; Finance; Marketing. **Benefits:** Dental Insurance; Disability Coverage; Employee Discounts; Life Insurance; Medical Insurance; Pension Plan; Profit Sharing. **Corporate headquarters location:** This Location.

BANK OF CLARKE COUNTY
EAGLE FINANCIAL SERVICES, INC.
P.O. Box 391, Berryville VA 22611. 540/955-2510. **Physical address:** 2 East Main Street, Berryville VA. **Contact:** Daisy McDonald, Vice President of Human Resources. **World Wide Web address:** http://www.bankofclarke.com. **Description:** Eagle Financial Services (also at this location) is a bank holding company for Bank of Clarke County. Both Bank of Clarke County and Eagle Financial Services grant commercial, financial, agricultural, residential, and consumer loans to customers in Virginia and eastern West Virginia. Bank of Clarke County also provides general banking services. **Benefits:** Pension Plan; Retirement Plan. **Corporate headquarters location:** This Location. **Number of employees nationwide:** 65.

BANK OF GLOUCESTER COUNTY
100 Park Avenue, Woodbury NJ 08096. 856/845-0700. **Fax:** 856/845-1436. **Contact:** Kathleen Hoffman, Human Resources Officer. **E-mail address:** humanresources@thebankofgc.com. **World Wide Web address:** http://www.thebankofgc.com. **Description:** A bank. Founded in 1989. **Common positions include:** Administrative Assistant; Assistant Manager; Bank Officer/Manager; Bank Teller; Branch Manager; Credit Manager; Customer Service Rep.; Financial Analyst; Management Trainee. **Educational backgrounds include:** Banking; Business Administration; Economics; Finance; Microsoft Office; Microsoft Word; Spreadsheets. **Benefits:** 401(k); Casual Dress - Fridays; Dental Insurance; Disability Coverage; Life Insurance; Medical Insurance; Profit Sharing; Tuition Assistance. **Office hours:** Monday - Friday, 8:30 a.m. - 5:00 p.m. **Corporate headquarters location:** This Location. **Parent company:** Fulton Financial Corporation. **CEO:** W. Knobe. **Facilities Manager:** A. Berry. **Information Systems Manager:** R. Bukunus. **Number of employees at this location:** 200.

BANK OF LODI, N.A.
FIRST FINANCIAL BANCORP
Call Box 3009, Lodi CA 95241. 209/367-2000. **Physical address:** 701 South Ham Lane, Lodi CA 95242. **Contact:** Human Resources. **World Wide Web address:** http://www.banklodi.com. **Description:** A full-service commercial bank providing depository accounts including checking, money market, and passbook savings accounts; and a full range of lending activities, with an emphasis on providing the agricultural, business, and professional communities with short-term commercial loans with interest rates tied to prevailing rates in the current money market. Bank of Lodi lends to light industrial, manufacturing, agricultural concerns, and professional organizations in the city of Lodi and the surrounding area. It also offers a full line of residential mortgage products and engages in limited consumer lending activities. **Corporate headquarters location:** This Location. **Number of employees at this location:** 75.

BANK OF NEW YORK
101 Barclay Street, Floor 1-E, New York NY 10286. 212/815-4984. **Contact:** Personnel. **World Wide Web address:** http://www.bankofny.com. **Description:** A bank that serves individuals, corporations, foreign and domestic banks, governments, and other institutions through banking offices in New York City and foreign branches, representative offices, subsidiaries, and affiliates. **Common positions include:** Bank Officer/Manager. **Educational backgrounds include:** Economics; Finance. **Corporate headquarters location:** This Location. **Parent company:** The Bank of New York Company, Inc. **Listed on:** New York Stock Exchange. **Number of employees nationwide:** 12,000.

BANK OF NORTH DAKOTA
P.O. Box 5509, Bismarck ND 58506. 701/328-5600. **Fax:** 701/328-5716. **Contact:** Human Resources. **World Wide Web address:** http://www.banknd.com. **Description:** Bank of North Dakota offers financial services to promote the development of agriculture, commerce, and industry in North Dakota, and provides loans to individuals who want to pursue post-secondary educational opportunities. **Common positions include:** Accountant/Auditor; Bank Officer/Manager; Computer Programmer; Customer Service Rep.; Financial Analyst; Marketing Specialist; Public Relations Specialist; Systems Analyst. **Educational backgrounds include:** Accounting; Business Administration; Computer Science; Finance; Marketing. **Benefits:** Disability Coverage; Life Insurance; Medical Insurance; Pension Plan; Tuition Assistance. **Special programs:** Internships. **Corporate headquarters location:** This Location. **Number of employees at this location:** 175.

THE BANK OF SANTA FE
P.O. Box 2027, Santa Fe NM 87504. 505/984-0500. **Contact:** Human Resources. **Description:** A full-service commercial bank. The Bank of Santa Fe offers consumer banking services, foreign currency services, notary public services, registered key ring services, research services, travelers checks, wire transfers, and TellerFone Banking. **Common positions include:** Bank Teller. **Corporate headquarters location:** This Location.

BANK OF TOKYO MITSUBISHI
1251 Avenue of the Americas, New York NY 10020. 212/766-3400. **Contact:** Recruitment. **Description:** One of the 50 largest commercial banks in the United States. The company operates five offices throughout the New York metropolitan

area, as well as in London and the Bahamas. **Corporate headquarters location:** This Location. **Parent company:** The Bank of Tokyo Ltd. (Tokyo, Japan).

BANK OF UTAH
2605 Washington Boulevard, Ogden UT 84401. 801/409-5000. **Contact:** Personnel. **E-mail address:** info@bankofutah.com. **World Wide Web address:** http://www.bankofutah.com. **Description:** Operates a full-service commercial bank with a wide range of traditional banking services including online and telephone banking. **Corporate headquarters location:** This Location. **Other U.S. locations:** Roy UT; Salt Lake City UT.

BANK ONE COLUMBUS N.A.
P.O. Box 710610, Columbus OH 43271. 614/248-8820. **Contact:** Employment Office. **World Wide Web address:** http://www.bankone.com. **Description:** A bank. **Common positions include:** Accountant; Adjuster; Assistant Manager; Bank Officer/Manager; Branch Manager; Budget Analyst; Claim Rep.; Computer Programmer; Credit Manager; Customer Service Rep.; Department Manager; Economist; Financial Analyst; General Manager; Human Resources Manager; Management Analyst/Consultant; Management Trainee; Marketing Specialist; Operations/Production Manager; Quality Control Supervisor; Services Sales Rep.; Systems Analyst. **Educational backgrounds include:** Accounting; Business Administration; Communications; Computer Science; Economics; Finance; Liberal Arts; Marketing. **Benefits:** Dental Insurance; Disability Coverage; Employee Discounts; Life Insurance; Medical Insurance; Pension Plan; Savings Plan; Tuition Assistance. **Corporate headquarters location:** Chicago IL. **Other U.S. locations:** AZ; CA; CO; IN; KY; MI; TX; UT; WI; WV. **Parent company:** Bank One Corporation is one of the nation's largest bank holding companies. Bank One operates an affiliate network of over 1,800 banks in 14 states. In addition, Bank One operates corporations involved in data processing, venture capital, investment and merchant banking, trust, brokerage, investment management, leasing, mortgage banking, consumer finance, and insurance. **Listed on:** New York Stock Exchange. **Number of employees at this location:** 8,500. **Number of employees nationwide:** 86,200.

BANK ONE CORPORATION
One Bank One Plaza, Chicago IL 60670. 312/732-4000. **Contact:** Human Resources. **World Wide Web address:** http://www.bankone.com. **Description:** A bank holding company that provides a broad range of commercial and investment banking, trust services, and financial and other services on a worldwide basis to individuals, businesses, and governmental units. **Corporate headquarters location:** This Location.

BANKATLANTIC
1750 East Sunrise Boulevard, Fort Lauderdale FL 33304. 954/760-5480. **Fax:** 954/760-5489. **Recorded jobline:** 954/760-5550. **Contact:** Employment Department. **Description:** A federal savings and loan bank. **Common positions include:** Accountant/Auditor; Branch Manager; Customer Service Rep.; Securities Sales Rep. **Benefits:** 401(k); Bonus Award/Plan; Dental Insurance; Disability Coverage; Employee Discounts; Life Insurance; Medical Insurance; Pension Plan; Tuition Assistance. **Corporate headquarters location:** This Location. **Parent company:** BankAtlantic Financial Corporation. **Listed on:** NASDAQ. **Number of employees at this location:** 640.

BANKNORTH GROUP, INC.
P.O. Box 366, Burlington VT 05401-0366. 802/860-3100. **Physical address:** 161 St. Paul Street, Burlington VT. **Fax:** 802/860-5548. **Recorded jobline:** 800/462-1943. **Contact:** Michael New, Human Resources Manager. **World Wide Web address:** http://www.banknorth.com. **Description:** A multibank holding company comprised of seven community banks, a mortgage company, and a financial asset management group. Banknorth is one of Vermont's largest banking companies with $18.4 billion in assets. **NOTE:** Applications may be obtained by calling the jobline or by visiting any subsidiary branch location. Entry-level positions, part-time jobs, and second and third shifts are offered. **Common positions include:** Account Rep.; Accountant; Adjuster; Administrative Assistant; Advertising Clerk; Auditor; Bank Officer/Manager; Branch Manager; Budget Analyst; Chief Financial Officer; Controller; Credit Manager; Customer Service Rep.; Database Administrator; Database Manager; Financial Analyst; Fund Manager; Human Resources Manager; Marketing Manager; Marketing Specialist; Public Relations Specialist; Purchasing Agent/Manager; Sales Executive; Sales Manager; Secretary; SQL Programmer; Systems Analyst; Systems Manager; Typist/Word Processor. **Educational backgrounds include:** Accounting; Business Administration; Communications; Computer Science; Excel; Finance; Marketing; Microsoft Word; Novell; Software Development; Software Tech. Support; Spreadsheets. **Benefits:** 401(k); Dental Insurance; Disability Coverage; Employee Discounts; Life Insurance; Medical Insurance; Pension Plan; Profit Sharing; Tuition Assistance. **Special programs:** Internships; Training; Summer Jobs. **Corporate headquarters location:** Portland ME. **Subsidiaries include:** Evergreen Bank; First Vermont Bank and Trust Company; Franklin Lamoille Bank; Granite Savings Bank and Trust Company; First Massachusetts Bank; The Stratevest Group, N.A. These subsidiaries serve consumers throughout Vermont, New Hampshire, Maine, central and western Massachusetts, and northwestern New York. Services offered include a full range of loan, deposit, investment, and trust services designed to meet the financial needs of individual consumers, businesses, and municipalities. Mortgage banking services are also provided. **Listed on:** NASDAQ. **Annual sales/revenues:** More than $100 million.

BARCLAYS BANK
222 Broadway, 10th Floor, New York NY 10038. 212/412-4000. **Contact:** Human Resources. **World Wide Web address:** http://www.barclays.co.uk. **Description:** An international banking institution with more than 5,000 offices in 60 countries including most international trade centers. International banking services include commercial loans, foreign exchange services, drafts and money transfers, foreign collections, leasing, stock and security custodial services, and economic information and publications. Barclays Bank also operates a global investment bank through its BZW Group subsidiary. **Corporate headquarters location:** This Location.

BAY BANK OF COMMERCE
1495 East 14th Street, San Leandro CA 94577. 510/357-2265. **Contact:** Human Resources. **Description:** A full-service bank. The bank's Construction Lending Division provides residential construction financing to individuals and builders throughout the East Bay area. **Corporate headquarters location:** This Location. **Parent company:** Bay Commercial Services. **Number of employees at this location:** 60.

BAY VIEW BANK
136 Second Avenue, San Mateo CA 94401.
650/312-7200. **Contact:** Human Resources. **World Wide Web address:** http://www.bayviewbank.com. **Description:** A commercial bank. Founded in 1911. **NOTE:** Please send resumes to Human Resources, Bay View Capital Corporation, 1840 Gateway Drive, San Mateo CA 94404. **Parent company:** Bay View Capital Corporation is a diversified financial institution.

BENCHMARK BANKSHARES, INC.
BENCHMARK COMMUNITY BANK
P.O. Box 569, Kenbridge VA 23944. 804/676-8444. **Fax:** 804/676-4603. **Contact:** Jennifer Clarke, Human Resources Officer. **Description:** A holding company for Benchmark Community Bank, a savings and loan institution with six branch offices located in southern Virginia. **Corporate headquarters location:** This Location.

BERKSHIRE COUNTY SAVINGS BANK
P.O. Box 1308, Pittsfield MA 01202. 413/443-5601. **Contact:** Human Resources. **Description:** A full-service mutual savings bank. **Common positions include:** Accountant; Bank Officer/Manager; Branch Manager; Credit Manager; Customer Service Rep.; Human Resources Manager; Systems Analyst. **Educational backgrounds include:** Accounting; Business Administration; Finance. **Benefits:** 401(k); Daycare Assistance; Dental Insurance; Disability Coverage; Life Insurance; Medical Insurance; Pension Plan; Tuition Assistance. **Corporate headquarters location:** This Location. **Number of employees at this location:** 150.

BOLLING FEDERAL CREDIT UNION
Chappie James Boulevard, Building 4447, Washington DC 20336. 202/562-5385. **Fax:** 202/562-8210. **Contact:** Human Resources. **Description:** A credit union for Air Force personnel. **Common positions include:** Accountant; Bank Teller; Services Sales Rep. **Benefits:** Disability Coverage; Medical Insurance; Pension Plan; Tuition Assistance. **Corporate headquarters location:** This Location. **Number of employees at this location:** 20.

BOSTON FEDERAL SAVINGS BANK
17 New England Executive Park, Burlington MA 01803. 781/273-0300. **Contact:** Scott Flagg, Vice President of Human Resources. **World Wide Web address:** http://www.bostonfed.com. **Description:** A full-service federal savings bank with several branch locations throughout the greater Boston area. **Common positions include:** Bank Teller; Customer Service Rep. **Benefits:** Dental Insurance; Disability Coverage; Life Insurance; Medical Insurance; Pension Plan; Profit Sharing; Tuition Assistance. **Corporate headquarters location:** This Location.

BRENTON BANK
13621 University Avenue, Clive IA 50325. 515/237-5194. **Contact:** Pat Ogier, Senior Human Resources Officer. **E-mail address:** pat.ogier@brentonbank.com. **World Wide Web address:** http://www.brentonbank.com. **Description:** A multibank holding company with 46 locations. Assets total $1.6 billion with an additional $600 million under trust agreement and $200 million in investment brokerage accounts. Founded in 1881. **Common positions include:** Account Rep.; Accountant/Auditor; Administrative Assistant; Bank Teller; Clerk; Financial Analyst; Help-Desk Technician; Mortgage Banker; Network Administrator; Operations Manager; Telephone Service Rep. **Educational backgrounds include:** Accounting; Business Administration; Finance;

Information Systems; Liberal Arts; Marketing. **Benefits:** 401(k); Casual Dress - Daily; Dental Insurance; Disability Coverage; Life Insurance; Medical Insurance; Profit Sharing; Tuition Assistance. **Office hours:** Monday - Friday, 8:00 a.m. - 5:00 p.m. **Corporate headquarters location:** This Location. **Listed on:** NASDAQ. **CEO:** Bob DeMeulenaere. **Number of employees at this location:** 300.

BRITTON & KOONTZ CAPITAL CORP.
P.O. Box 1407, Natchez MS 39121. 601/445-5576. **Contact:** Personnel. **World Wide Web address:** http://www.bkbank.com. **Description:** A bank holding company. **Corporate headquarters location:** This Location. **Subsidiaries include:** Britton & Koontz First National Bank performs commercial banking operations and other related financial services. **Number of employees at this location:** 70.

BROOKLINE SAVINGS BANK
P.O. Box 470469, Brookline MA 02477. 617/730-3500. **Physical address:** 24 Webster Place, Brookline MA. **Contact:** Jack Nealon, Personnel Director. **World Wide Web address:** http://www.brooklinesavings.com. **Description:** A full-service savings bank. **Common positions include:** Accountant/Auditor; Bank Officer/Manager; Bank Teller; Branch Manager; Customer Service Rep. **Educational backgrounds include:** Business Administration. **Benefits:** Disability Coverage; Medical Insurance; Pension Plan; Tuition Assistance. **Corporate headquarters location:** This Location.

CCB FINANCIAL CORPORATION
P.O. Box 931, Durham NC 27702. 919/683-7621. **Physical address:** 111 Corcoran Street, Durham NC. **Fax:** 919/683-7662. **Contact:** Human Resources. **E-mail address:** human_resources@ccbf.com. **World Wide Web address:** http://www.ccbonline.com. **Description:** A bank holding company offering a complete line of traditional banking services, as well as a full array of financial products such as investments, insurance, and trust services. This location also hires seasonally. Founded in 1903. **NOTE:** Entry-level positions and part-time jobs are offered. **Common positions include:** Accountant; Administrative Assistant; Applications Engineer; Assistant Manager; Auditor; Bank Officer/Manager; Branch Manager; Computer Programmer; Credit Manager; Customer Service Rep.; Financial Analyst; Insurance Agent/Broker; Internet Services Manager; Marketing Specialist; Network/Systems Administrator; Sales Rep.; Secretary; Systems Analyst; Technical Writer/Editor; Typist/Word Processor; Website Developer. **Educational backgrounds include:** Accounting; Business Administration; C/C++; Communications; Economics; Finance; HTML; Internet Development; Java; Marketing; MBA; Microsoft Office; SQL. **Benefits:** 401(k); Dental Insurance; Employee Discounts; Life Insurance; Medical Insurance; Savings Plan. **Special programs:** Summer Jobs. **Corporate headquarters location:** This Location. **Listed on:** New York Stock Exchange. **CEO:** Ernest C. Roessler. **Information Systems Manager:** Jim Koontz. **Number of employees nationwide:** 3,000.

CPB INC.
CENTRAL PACIFIC BANK
220 South King Street, Honolulu HI 96813. 808/544-0762. **Fax:** 808/544-0736. **Contact:** Rita Flynn, Vice President/Manager. **World Wide Web address:** http://www.cpbi.com. **Description:** This location houses administrative offices as well as a bank. Overall, CPB Inc. is a bank holding company

whose subsidiary, Central Pacific Bank, is a full-service commercial bank with 26 banking offices located throughout the state of Hawaii. Central Pacific Bank is also a member of the Federal Home Loan Bank of Seattle and the FDIC. **Common positions include:** Management Trainee. **Educational backgrounds include:** Accounting; Business Administration; Finance; Management/ Planning; Mathematics. **Benefits:** 401(k); Bonus Award/Plan; Dental Insurance; Disability Coverage; Employee Discounts; ESOP; Life Insurance; Medical Insurance; Pension Plan; Profit Sharing; Savings Plan; Tuition Assistance. **Special programs:** Internships. **Corporate headquarters location:** This Location. **Listed on:** NASDAQ. **Number of employees at this location:** 555.

CAMBRIDGE SAVINGS BANK
1374 Massachusetts Avenue, Cambridge MA 02138. 617/864-8700. **Fax:** 617/441-4171. **Contact:** Charlene Apidianakis, Human Resources Manager. **World Wide Web address:** http://www.cambridgesavings.com. **Description:** Operates a full-service savings bank. **Common positions include:** Bank Teller; Customer Service Representative; New Accounts Clerk. **Educational backgrounds include:** Business Administration; Communications; Finance; Liberal Arts. **Benefits:** Daycare Assistance; Dental Insurance; Disability Coverage; Employee Discounts; Life Insurance; Medical Insurance; Pension Plan; Savings Plan; Tuition Assistance. **Special programs:** Internships. **Corporate headquarters location:** This Location. **Number of employees at this location:** 265.

CAMBRIDGEPORT BANK
689 Massachusetts Avenue, Cambridge MA 02139. 617/661-4900. **Contact:** Human Resources. **Description:** Operates full-service community banks in Middlesex County. **NOTE:** Entry-level positions are offered. **Common positions include:** Accountant/Auditor; Bank Officer/Manager; Branch Manager; Computer Programmer; Credit Manager; Customer Service Rep.; Financial Analyst; Human Resources Manager; MIS Specialist; Services Sales Rep.; Systems Analyst; Underwriter/Assistant Underwriter. **Educational backgrounds include:** Accounting; Business Administration; Computer Science; Economics; Finance; Liberal Arts; Marketing. **Benefits:** 401(k); Dental Insurance; Disability Coverage; Employee Discounts; Life Insurance; Medical Insurance; Pension Plan; Public Transit Available; Sick Days; Tuition Assistance; Vacation Days. **Corporate headquarters location:** This Location. **Listed on:** Privately held. **Number of employees at this location:** 95. **Number of employees nationwide:** 165.

CARROLLTON BANK
1589 Sulphur Spring Road, Suite 102, Arbutus MD 21227. 410/536-4600. **Contact:** Colleen Hedges, Recruiter. **Description:** Operates a full-service commercial bank. **Common positions include:** Bank Officer/Manager; Bank Teller; Branch Manager; Clerical Supervisor; Customer Service Representative. **Educational backgrounds include:** Accounting; Finance. **Benefits:** Dental Insurance; Disability Coverage; Life Insurance; Medical Insurance; Pension Plan; Savings Plan; Tuition Assistance. **Corporate headquarters location:** This Location.

CATHAY BANCORP, INC.
CATHAY BANK
777 North Broadway, Los Angeles CA 90012. 213/625-4700. **Contact:** Personnel. **World Wide Web address:** http://www.cathaybank.com. **Description:** A commercial bank. Founded in 1962. **NOTE:** Part-time positions are offered. **Common**

positions include: Bank Teller; Software Engineer. **Educational backgrounds include:** Microsoft Word. **Benefits:** 401(k); Dental Insurance; Disability Coverage; Life Insurance; Medical Insurance; Pension Plan; Vacation Days (6 - 10). **Corporate headquarters location:** This Location. **Listed on:** NASDAQ. **Stock exchange symbol:** CATY. **Number of employees nationwide:** 500.

CENIT BANCORP, INC.
CENIT BANK, FSB
P.O. Box 1811, Norfolk VA 23501. 757/446-6600. **Physical address:** 225 West Olney Road, Norfolk VA 23510. **Contact:** Mary Anderson, Human Resources Manager. **Description:** CENIT Bancorp, Inc. is the holding company for CENIT Bank, FSB (also at this location), a federal stock savings bank. Through its branches, the bank offers retail deposit services. CENIT Bank also offers permanent and construction residential loans, consumer loans, and commercial real estate and business loans. **Benefits:** 401(k); ESOP; Retirement Plan; Stock Option. **Corporate headquarters location:** This Location. **Other U.S. locations:** Norfolk PA; Portsmouth PA; Chesapeake VA; Hampton VA; Virginia Beach VA; York County VA. **Listed on:** NASDAQ. **Number of employees nationwide:** 170.

CENTENNIAL BANCORP
CENTENNIAL BANK
P.O. Box 1560, Eugene OR 97440. 541/342-3970. **Physical address:** 675 Oak Street, Eugene OR 97401. **Contact:** Human Resources. **Description:** A holding company. **Corporate headquarters location:** This Location. **Subsidiaries include:** Centennial Bank (also at this location) provides commercial and consumer banking services. **Number of employees at this location:** 135.

CENTRAL VIRGINIA BANKSHARES, INC.
CENTRAL VIRGINIA BANK
P.O. Box 39, Powhatan VA 23139. 804/598-4216. **Physical address:** 2501 Anderson Highway, Powhatan VA. **Contact:** Shirley G. Boelt, Assistant Vice President of Human Resources. **World Wide Web address:** http://www.centralvabank.com. **Description:** Central Virginia Bankshares, Inc. is the holding company for Central Virginia Bank(also at this location). Central Virginia Bank offers a wide range of services including checking and savings accounts, certificates of deposit, and installment, construction, and permanent residential mortgage loans and other consumer lending services. The bank also offers related services such as travelers checks, safe deposit, deposit transfer, customer note payment, collections, notary public, and escrow. **NOTE:** Entry-level positions and part-time jobs are offered. **Common positions include:** Accountant; Adjuster; Administrative Assistant; Assistant Manager; Bank Officer/Manager; Bank Teller; Branch Manager; Chief Financial Officer; Computer Operator; Credit Manager; Customer Service Representative; Human Resources Manager; Operations Manager; Secretary; Vice President. **Educational backgrounds include:** AS400 Certification; Business Administration; Economics; Finance; Microsoft Word; PC; Spreadsheets. **Benefits:** Casual Dress - Fridays; Dental Insurance; Disability Coverage; Employee Discounts; Flexible Benefits; Flexible Schedule; Job Sharing; Life Insurance; Medical Insurance; Pension Plan; Retirement Plan; Sick Days; Stock Option; Tuition Assistance; Vacation Days (11 - 15). **Special programs:** Summer Jobs. **Corporate headquarters location:** This Location. **Other U.S. locations:** Brandermill VA; Cartersville VA; Midlothian VA. **Listed on:** NASDAQ. **Annual sales/revenues:** $11 - $20 million. **Number of employees nationwide:** 90.

CENTURA BANKS, INC.
P.O. Box 1220, Rocky Mount NC 27802. 252/454-4400. **Contact:** Personnel. **Description:** A bank holding company that provides a full range of banking, investment, and insurance services for individuals and businesses. **Corporate headquarters location:** This Location. **Subsidiaries include:** Centura Bank; Centura Securities; Cleveland Federal Bank (Shelby NC); First Southern Bancorp Inc. (Asheboro NC); Triangle Bancorp Inc. (Raleigh NC). **Listed on:** New York Stock Exchange. **CEO:** Cecil Sewell. **Number of employees nationwide:** 1,870.

CENTURY BANCORP, INC.
400 Mystic Avenue, Medford MA 02155. 781/391-4000. **Toll-free phone:** 800/442-1859. **Fax:** 781/393-4613. **Contact:** Jill K. MacCully, Senior Human Resources Representative. **E-mail address:** jmaccully@century-bank.com. **World Wide Web address:** http://www.century-bank.com. **Description:** A bank holding company. This location also hires seasonally. Founded in 1969. **NOTE:** Entry-level positions and part-time jobs are offered. **Common positions include:** Account Manager; Accountant; Administrative Assistant; AS400 Programmer Analyst; Assistant Manager; Auditor; Bank Officer/Manager; Branch Manager; Budget Analyst; Chief Financial Officer; Clerical Supervisor; Computer Operator; Computer Support Technician; Controller; Credit Manager; Customer Service Rep.; Financial Analyst; Marketing Manager; Marketing Specialist; Network/Systems Administrator; Operations Manager; Purchasing Agent/Manager; Secretary; Systems Analyst; Webmaster. **Educational backgrounds include:** Accounting; AS400 Certification; Business Administration; Finance; Marketing; Microsoft Office; Microsoft Word; Spreadsheets. **Benefits:** 401(k); Dental Insurance; Disability Coverage; Employee Discounts; Life Insurance; Medical Insurance; Pension Plan; Sick Days (6 - 10); Tuition Assistance; Vacation Days (10 - 20). **Office hours:** Monday - Friday, 8:30 a.m. - 5:00 p.m. **Corporate headquarters location:** This Location. **Other U.S. locations:** Beverly MA; Boston MA; Braintree MA; Brighton MA; Burlington MA; Cambridge MA; Everett MA; Lynn MA; Malden MA; Peabody MA; Quincy MA; Salem MA; Somerville MA. **Subsidiaries include:** Century Bank and Trust Company offers a full range of banking services to individuals, businesses, and municipal customers. The bank operates through 16 branches in the greater Boston area. **Listed on:** NASDAQ. **Chairman and CEO:** Marshall Sloane. **Facilities Manager:** Joe Chapman. **Information Systems Manager:** Philip Gannon. **Number of employees at this location:** 150. **Number of employees nationwide:** 300.

CHARTER ONE BANK
1215 Superior Avenue, Mezzanine Level, Cleveland OH 44114. 216/566-5300. **Fax:** 216/566-1038. **Recorded jobline:** 216/566-0253. **Contact:** Human Resources. **Description:** Charter One Bank has 95 full-service banking offices located throughout the state. **Common positions include:** Accountant/Auditor; Bank Officer/Manager; Branch Manager; Clerical Supervisor; Collector; Customer Service Rep.; Securities Sales Rep.; Services Sales Rep. **Educational backgrounds include:** Accounting; Business Administration; Finance. **Benefits:** 401(k); Disability Coverage; Employee Discounts; Life Insurance; Medical Insurance; Profit Sharing; Tuition Assistance. **Corporate headquarters location:** This Location. **Subsidiaries include:** First Northern Insurance Company; Real Estate Appraisal Services. **Listed on:** NASDAQ. **Number of employees at this location:** 1,300.

CHASE BANK OF TEXAS
712 Main Street, Houston TX 77002. 713/216-7000. **Contact:** Human Resources. **Description:** A banking organization, operating through a network of 40 member banks in Texas. Operations include energy, commercial, real estate, and international banking. **Corporate headquarters location:** This Location. **Other U.S. locations:** Denver CO; New York NY. **International locations:** Worldwide.

CHASE MANHATTAN BANK, N.A.
270 Park Avenue, New York NY 10017. 212/270-6000. **Contact:** Employment Office. **World Wide Web address:** http://www.chase.com. **Description:** A full-service bank with 54 branches. **Corporate headquarters location:** This Location. **Other area locations:** Dutchess NY; Orange NY; Rockland NY; Westchester NY. **Listed on:** New York Stock Exchange.

CHITTENDEN BANK
P.O. Box 804, Brattleboro VT 05302. 802/257-7151. **Contact:** Human Resources. **World Wide Web address:** http://www.chittenden.com. **Description:** A full-service bank. **Corporate headquarters location:** Burlington VT.

CITIZENS AND FARMERS BANK
C&F FINANCIAL CORPORATION
P.O. Box 391, West Point VA 23181. 804/843-2360. **Physical address:** 802 Main Street, West Point VA. **Contact:** Laura Shreaves, Personnel. **Description:** C&F Financial Corporation is the holding company for Citizens and Farmers Bank (also at this location). The bank is a savings and loan institution with 10 branch locations in Virginia. Other subsidiaries of C&F Financial Corporation include C&F Mortgage Corporation, which originates and sells mortgages; and C&F Investment Services, Inc., which offers brokerage services. **Benefits:** Incentive Plan; Pension Plan; Profit Sharing; Stock Option. **Corporate headquarters location:** This Location. **Other U.S. locations:** Norge VA; Providence Forge VA; Quinton VA; Richmond VA; Saluda VA; Tappahannock VA; Williamsburg VA. **Listed on:** NASDAQ. **Stock exchange symbol:** CFFI. **President/CEO:** Larry Dillon. **Number of employees nationwide:** 95.

CITIZENS BANKING CORPORATION
CITIZENS BANK
328 South Saginaw Street, Flint MI 48502. 810/766-7500. **Contact:** Human Resources. **Description:** Overall, Citizens Banking Corporation is the holding company for Citizens Bank (also at this location), a full-service banking institution. **Corporate headquarters location:** This Location.

CITIZENS NATIONAL BANK
517 Main Street, Laurel MD 20707. 301/725-3100. **Contact:** Human Resources. **World Wide Web address:** http://www.mercantile.net/citizens. **Description:** Operates a full-service commercial bank with 18 offices. **Corporate headquarters location:** This Location. **Parent company:** Mercantile Bankshares Corporation (Baltimore MD).

CITY NATIONAL BANK
400 North Roxbury Drive, Beverly Hills CA 90210. 310/888-6000. **Contact:** Personnel. **World Wide Web address:** http://www.cityntl.com. **Description:** A commercial bank with 50 offices in California. **NOTE:** Jobseekers should send resumes to Personnel, City National Bank, 633 West Fifth Street, 10th Floor, Los Angeles CA 90071. 213/553-8272. **Common positions include:** Accountant/Auditor; Bank Teller; Credit Manager; Customer Service Rep.; Management Trainee; Secretary.

Educational backgrounds include: Accounting; Business Administration; Finance. **Benefits:** Dental Insurance; Disability Coverage; Employee Discounts; Life Insurance; Medical Insurance; Profit Sharing; Tuition Assistance. **Corporate headquarters location:** This Location.

COBANK
P.O. Box 5110, Denver CO 80217. 303/740-4000. **Contact:** Larry E. Williams, Senior Vice President of Human Resources. **World Wide Web address:** http://www.cobank.com. **Description:** A full-service cooperative bank. The bank specializes in cooperative, agribusiness, rural utility, and agricultural export financing. Founded in 1916. **Corporate headquarters location:** This Location.

COMERICA INC.
P.O. Box 75000, Detroit MI 48275-3121. **Toll-free phone:** 800/521-1190. **Recorded jobline:** 313/222-4610. **Contact:** Staffing. **World Wide Web address:** http://www.comerica.com. **Description:** A bank holding company. The company's primary businesses include individual banking, which consists of consumer banking and lending, mortgage banking, small business banking, and private banking; investment banking, which offers investment services; and business banking, which provides corporate, global, and asset-based banking. Comerica Inc. operates a network of 350 branch offices and 770 ATMs, supermarket branches, and PC and telephone banking services. Founded in 1849. **NOTE:** Entry-level positions and part-time jobs are offered. **Company slogan:** We listen, we understand, we make it work. **Common positions include:** Account Rep.; Accountant/Auditor; Administrative Assistant; Assistant Manager; Auditor; Computer Programmer; Customer Service Rep.; Financial Analyst; Insurance Agent/Broker; Management Trainee; MIS Specialist; Sales Rep.; Secretary; Systems Analyst. **Educational backgrounds include:** Accounting; Business Administration; Computer Science; Economics; Finance; Liberal Arts; Marketing; Microsoft Word; Software Tech. Support. **Benefits:** 401(k); Dental Insurance; Disability Coverage; Employee Discounts; Life Insurance; Medical Insurance; Pension Plan; Profit Sharing; Tuition Assistance. **Special programs:** Internships; Summer Jobs. **Corporate headquarters location:** This Location. **Other U.S. locations:** CA; CO; FL; IL; IN; NY; TN; TX. **International locations:** Canada; Mexico. **Subsidiaries include:** Comerica Community Development Corporation; Comerica Investment Services, Inc.; Comerica Corporate Banking. **Listed on:** New York Stock Exchange. **Stock exchange symbol:** CMA. **CEO:** Eugene Miller. **Annual sales/revenues:** More than $100 million. **Number of employees nationwide:** 11,000.

COMMERCIAL FEDERAL BANK, FSB
COMMERCIAL FEDERAL CORP.
2120 South 72nd Street, 14th Floor, Omaha NE 68124. 402/390-5200. **Contact:** Human Resources. **World Wide Web address:** http://www.comfedbank.com. **Description:** Commercial Federal Bank is a federal savings bank offering all financial services. **Common positions include:** Accountant/Auditor; Administrator; Bank Officer/Manager; Branch Manager; Broker; Credit Manager; Customer Service Rep.; Department Manager; Financial Analyst; General Manager; Human Resources Manager; Manufacturer's/Wholesaler's Sales Rep.; Underwriter/Assistant Underwriter. **Educational backgrounds include:** Accounting; Business Administration; Communications; Computer Science; Economics; Finance; Liberal Arts; Marketing. **Benefits:** 401(k); Dental Insurance; Disability Coverage; Employee

Discounts; Life Insurance; Medical Insurance; Savings Plan; Tuition Assistance. **Corporate headquarters location:** This Location. **Parent company:** Commercial Federal Corporation (also at this location).

COMMONWEALTH BANK
2 West Lafayette Street, Norristown PA 19401. **Toll-free phone:** 800/327-9885. **Fax:** 610/313-1509. **Contact:** Human Resources Department. **E-mail address:** hrrecruit@commonwealthbank.com. **World Wide Web address:** http://www.commonwealthbank.com. **Description:** A full-service community bank serving retail and small business customers in northeast Pennsylvania, and Bucks, Berks, Delaware, Montgomery, Chester, and Lehigh Counties. The company operates over 60 traditional and supermarket branches and mortgage offices. Founded in 1924. **NOTE:** Part-time jobs are offered. **Common positions include:** Accountant; Assistant Manager; Auditor; Bank Officer/Manager; Branch Manager; Customer Service Representative; Sales Manager; Sales Representative. **Educational backgrounds include:** Accounting; Bachelor of Arts; Bachelor of Science; Finance; Microsoft Office. **Benefits:** 401(k); Dental Insurance; Disability Coverage; Life Insurance; Medical Insurance; Profit Sharing; Sick Days; Tuition Assistance; Vacation Days. **Special programs:** Training; Summer Jobs. **Corporate headquarters location:** This Location. **Listed on:** NASDAQ. **Stock exchange symbol:** CMSB.

COMMONWEALTH BANKSHARES, INC.
BANK OF THE COMMONWEALTH
P.O. Box 1177, Norfolk VA 23501-1177. 757/446-6900. **Physical address:** 403 Boush Street, Norfolk VA 23510. **Fax:** 757/446-6929. **Contact:** Human Resources. **World Wide Web address:** http://www.pilotonline.com/boc. **Description:** A bank holding company whose subsidiary, Bank of the Commonwealth (also at this location), provides a complete line of banking, investment, and trust services to businesses and individuals. The bank operates seven branch offices. Founded in 1971. **Corporate headquarters location:** This Location. **Other U.S. locations:** Virginia Beach VA. **Listed on:** NASDAQ. **Stock exchange symbol:** CWBS. **Chairman of the Board:** E.J. Woodard.

COMMUNITY BANK
100 East Corson Street, Pasadena CA 91103-3839. 626/568-2067. **Fax:** 626/568-2299. **Contact:** Human Resources. **Description:** A commercial bank. **Common positions include:** Accountant/Auditor; Bank Teller; Branch Manager; Customer Service Rep.; Financial Analyst; Loan Officer. **Educational backgrounds include:** Accounting; Business Administration; Finance; Liberal Arts. **Benefits:** 401(k); Dental Insurance; Disability Coverage; Employee Discounts; Life Insurance; Medical Insurance; Profit Sharing; Savings Plan; Tuition Assistance. **Corporate headquarters location:** This Location. **Other area locations:** Anaheim CA; Huntington Park CA; Inland CA. **Number of employees at this location:** 370.

COMMUNITY BANK
COMMUNITY BANK SHARES OF INDIANA
P.O. Box 939, New Albany IN 47151. 812/944-2224. **Contact:** Diane Murphy, Human Resources Director. **Description:** A full-service savings and loan bank. **Corporate headquarters location:** This Location. **Parent company:** Community Bank Shares of Indiana, Inc. (also at this location).

COMMUNITY FIRST BANKSHARES, INC.
520 Main Avenue, 7th Floor, Fargo ND 58124. 701/293-2200. **Contact:** Human Resources. **World**

Wide Web address: http://www.cfbx.com. **Description:** A multibank holding company offering a full-line of banking, investment, trust and insurance services. **Corporate headquarters location:** This Location. **Other U.S. locations:** AZ; CA; CO; IA; MN; NE; NM; SD; UT; WI; WY. **Subsidiaries include:** Community First National Bank. **Listed on:** NASDAQ. **Stock exchange symbol:** CFBX.

COMMUNITY FIRST NATIONAL BANK
2020 North Central Avenue, Phoenix AZ 85002. 602/258-5555. **Contact:** Personnel. **World Wide Web address:** http://www.cfbx.com. **Description:** A commercial bank which provides a full range of domestic and international banking services. **Corporate headquarters location:** Fargo ND.

COMPASS BANCSHARES, INC.
P.O. Box 10566, Birmingham AL 35296. 205/933-3000. **Contact:** Staff Recruiting. **World Wide Web address:** http://www.compassweb.com. Description: A bank holding company. **Common positions include:** Accountant; Bank Officer/ Manager; Computer Programmer; Customer Service Rep.; Financial Manager; Financial Services Sales Rep.; Marketing Manager. **Benefits:** Disability Coverage; Life Insurance; Medical Insurance; Pension Plan; Profit Sharing; Savings Plan; Tuition Assistance. **Corporate headquarters location:** This Location. **Subsidiaries include:** Compass Bank; Compass Bank-Florida (Jacksonville FL); Central Bank of the South (Anniston AL); and Compass Banks of Texas, Inc., a bank holding company which owns Compass Bank-Houston in Houston Texas and Compass Bank-Dallas in Dallas Texas. Compass Banks of Texas also owns River Oaks Trust Company with offices in Houston and Dallas. Services of these subsidiaries include receiving demand and time deposit accounts, making personal and commercial loans, and furnishing personal and commercial checking accounts. Certain subsidiaries also offer trust and insurance services. Compass Bank conducts general commercial banking and trust business from 88 locations in 47 communities in Alabama; 50 locations in Arizona; nine locations in Colorado; nine locations in New Mexico; Compass Bank-Houston operates from 38 locations in Houston and San Antonio; Compass Bank-Dallas operates from 21 banking offices in Dallas and Collins Counties; and Compass Bank-Florida operates from 41 locations. **Number of employees nationwide:** 4,100.

COOPERATIVE BANKSHARES, INC.
P.O. Box 600, Wilmington NC 28402. 910/343-0181. **Contact:** Ms. Dare Rhodes, Vice President of Human Resources. **Description:** A savings bank holding company. **Corporate headquarters location:** This Location. **Other area locations:** Beaufort NC; Belhaven NC; Corolla NC; Elizabethtown NC; Jacksonville NC; Kill Devil Hills NC; Morehead City NC; Robersonville NC; Tabor City NC; Wallace NC; Washington NC; Wilmington NC. **Subsidiaries include:** Cooperative Bank For Savings, Inc., SSB is engaged in general banking activities. **Listed on:** NASDAQ.

CUPERTINO NATIONAL BANK & TRUST
20230 Stevens Creek Boulevard, Cupertino CA 95014. 408/996-1144. **Fax:** 408/843-1287. **Contact:** Human Resources. **Description:** A bank offering a variety of services including corporate and personal relationship banking, residential lending, SBA lending, and personal and corporate trust services. **Corporate headquarters location:** This Location. **Other U.S. locations:** Palo Alto CA; San Jose CA.

DAI-ICHI KANGYO BANK OF CALIFORNIA
555 West Fifth Street, Los Angeles CA 90013. 213/612-2700. **Fax:** 213/347-2927. **Contact:** Marybeth Literatus-Sosa, Assistant Vice President. **World Wide Web address:** http://www.dkbca.com. **Description:** A full-service commercial bank. Founded in 1974. **NOTE:** Entry-level positions and part-time jobs are offered. **Common positions include:** Accountant; Administrative Assistant; Auditor; Bank Officer/Manager; Branch Manager; Clerical Supervisor; Computer Operator; Customer Service Representative; Human Resources Manager; Loan Officer; Management Analyst/Consultant; Market Research Analyst; Marketing Specialist; Network/Systems Administrator; Operations Manager; Sales Executive; Secretary; Trust Officer. **Educational backgrounds include:** Accounting; Business Administration; Finance; Marketing; Microsoft Office; Microsoft Word; Public Relations; Spreadsheets. **Benefits:** 401(k); Casual Dress - Fridays; Dental Insurance; Flexible Schedule; Life Insurance; Medical Insurance; Profit Sharing; Tuition Assistance. **Special programs:** Summer Jobs. **Office hours:** Monday - Friday, 8:00 a.m. - 5:00 p.m. **Corporate headquarters location:** This Location. **International locations:** Worldwide. **Parent company:** The Dai-Ichi Kangyo Bank, Ltd. (Tokyo, Japan). **Listed on:** New York Stock Exchange. **President/CEO:** Takuo Yoshida. **Information Systems Manager:** Rick Richardson. **Purchasing Manager:** Stanley Takaki. **Number of employees at this location:** 90.

DELAWARE NATIONAL BANK
P.O. Box 520, Georgetown DE 19947. 302/855-2400. **Contact:** Jeanne Dallas, Human Resources Director. **Description:** A full-service commercial bank offering a variety of services to commercial and retail customers. Large business customers use the bank's demand and time deposit services; commercial, industrial, and real estate loans; and financing services. Retail banking services are furnished to individuals, small businesses, nonprofit organizations, and municipal units. These services include checking and savings accounts, savings certificates, personal loans, mortgage loans, and safe deposit boxes. The bank conducts its business through six branch offices in Georgetown, Fenwick Island, Laurel, Ocean View, Pike Creek, and Rehoboth Beach. **Corporate headquarters location:** This Location. **Parent company:** Delaware National Bankshares Corporation.

DIME SAVINGS BANK OF NEW YORK
EAB Plaza, 14th Floor, Uniondale NY 11556. 516/745-2980. **Contact:** Denise Barnes, Human Resources. **E-mail address:** barnesd@dime.com. **World Wide Web address:** http://www.dime.com. **Description:** A full-service bank. **Common positions include:** Account Rep.; Accountant/ Auditor; Bank Officer/Manager; Branch Manager; Computer Programmer; Credit Manager; Customer Service Rep.; Financial Analyst; Sales Executive; Services Sales Rep.; Systems Analyst. **Educational backgrounds include:** Computer Science; Finance. **Benefits:** Dental Insurance; Disability Coverage; Employee Discounts; Life Insurance; Medical Insurance; Pension Plan; Savings Plan; Stock Option; Tuition Assistance. **Corporate headquarters location:** New York NY. **Parent company:** Dime Bancorp, Inc. is the holding company for Dime Savings Bank of New York. The company operates 127 branches in the New York metropolitan area including Long Island, Westchester, and Rockland Counties in New York, and also in northern New Jersey. Dime Bancorp provides a broad range of consumer financial services through its branch banking network and provides residential and other loans through the

North American Mortgage Company. **Listed on:** New York Stock Exchange.

EASTERN BANK
270 Union Street, Lynn MA 01901. 781/598-7899. **Contact:** Personnel. **World Wide Web address:** http://www.easternbank.com. **Description:** Operates a full-service savings bank. **Corporate headquarters location:** This Location.

EMIGRANT SAVINGS BANK
5 East 42nd Street, New York NY 10017. 212/850-4000. **Contact:** Edward Tully, Senior Vice President of Human Resources. **Description:** Offers a wide range of traditional banking services. Emigrant Savings Bank has locations in Manhattan, Brooklyn, and Queens, as well as in Nassau, Suffolk, and Westchester Counties. **Corporate headquarters location:** This Location.

EXCHANGE NATIONAL BANCSHARES
132 East High Street, Jefferson City MO 65101. 573/761-6100. **Toll-free phone:** 800/761-8362. **Fax:** 573/761-6272. **Contact:** Lori K. Lock, Human Resources Director. **E-mail address:** employment@exchangebk.com. **World Wide Web address:** http://www.exchangebk.com. **Description:** A bank holding company that performs commercial banking operations and other related financial activities. Founded in 1865. **NOTE:** Entry level positions and part-time jobs are offered. **Common positions include:** Accountant/Auditor; Administrative Assistant; Bank Officer/Manager; Branch Manager; Chief Financial Officer; Computer Operator; Computer Support Technician; Controller; Customer Service Rep.; Human Resources Manager; Marketing Manager; Network/Systems Administrator; Operations Manager; Secretary; Systems Manager; Underwriter/Assistant Underwriter. **Educational backgrounds include:** Accounting; Business Administration; Finance; Microsoft Office; Microsoft Word; Novell; Software Tech. Support; Spreadsheets. **Benefits:** Dental Insurance; Disability Coverage; Employee Discounts; Financial Planning Assistance; Flexible Schedule; Life Insurance; Medical Insurance; Pension Plan; Profit Sharing; Sick Days (6 - 10); Tuition Assistance; Vacation Days (10 - 20). **Special programs:** Internships; Summer Jobs. **Office hours:** Monday - Friday, 8:00 a.m. - 5:00 p.m. **Corporate headquarters location:** This Location. **Listed on:** New York Stock Exchange. **CEO:** Donald L. Campbell. **Information Systems Manager:** Duane Muck. **Number of employees at this location:** 130.

EXPORT-IMPORT BANK OF THE UNITED STATES
811 Vermont Avenue NW, Room 771, Washington DC 20571. 202/565-3329. **Fax:** 202/565-3627. **Contact:** Human Resources. **World Wide Web address:** http://www.exim.gov. **Description:** As an agency of the federal government, the bank provides assistance to American exporters through loans, guarantees, and insurance programs. **NOTE:** This firm does not accept unsolicited resumes. Please contact the office for information about application procedures. **Common positions include:** Accountant/Auditor; Computer Programmer; Economist; Financial Analyst. **Educational backgrounds include:** Accounting; Economics; Finance. **Benefits:** Life Insurance; Medical Insurance; Pension Plan. **Special programs:** Internships. **Corporate headquarters location:** This Location.

FAR EAST NATIONAL BANK
350 South Grand Avenue, 41st Floor, Los Angeles CA 90071. 213/687-1200. **Fax:** 213/687-8511.

Contact: Human Resources. **Description:** Offers commercial banking services. **Corporate headquarters location:** This Location.

FARMERS AND MERCHANTS BANK
302 Pine Avenue, Long Beach CA 90802. 562/437-0011. **Fax:** 562/436-5048. **Contact:** Sheri Mallon, Vice President. **Description:** A commercial bank offering a wide range of services through 16 local offices. **Common positions include:** Bank Teller. **Educational backgrounds include:** Accounting; Business Administration; Economics; Finance; Liberal Arts; Mathematics. **Benefits:** Life Insurance; Medical Insurance; Profit Sharing; Tuition Assistance. **Corporate headquarters location:** This Location. **Other U.S. locations:** Fullerton CA; Garden Grove CA; Lake Forest CA; Lakewood CA; Orange CA; San Juan Capistrano CA; Santa Ana CA; Seal Beach CA. **Number of employees at this location:** 100.

FEDERAL RESERVE BANK OF CHICAGO
230 South LaSalle Street, Chicago IL 60604. 312/322-5490. **Fax:** 312/322-5332. **Contact:** Staffing Division. **E-mail address:** hrs.chi@chi.frb.org. **World Wide Web address:** http://www.frbchi.org. **Description:** One of 12 regional Federal Reserve banks that, along with the Federal Reserve Board of Governors in Washington DC and the Federal Open Market Committee, comprise the Federal Reserve System (the nation's central bank). As the nation's central bank, Federal Reserve is charged with three major responsibilities: setting monetary policy, banking supervision and regulation, and payment processing. **NOTE:** Entry-level positions and second and third shifts are offered. **Common positions include:** Accountant/Auditor; Bank Officer/Manager; Budget Analyst; Computer Programmer; Economist; Editor; Financial Analyst; Human Resources Manager; Instructor/Trainer; Management Analyst/Consultant; Management Trainee; Operations/Production Manager; Reporter; Systems Analyst; Technical Writer/Editor. **Educational backgrounds include:** Accounting; Business Administration; C/C++; Communications; Computer Science; Economics; Finance; HTML; Internet; Java; Liberal Arts; Novell. **Benefits:** 401(k); Casual Dress - Daily; Daycare Assistance; Dental Insurance; Disability Coverage; Life Insurance; Medical Insurance; Pension Plan; Savings Plan; Sick Days (6 - 10); Tuition Assistance; Vacation Days (11 - 15). **Special programs:** Internships. **Office hours:** Monday - Friday, 8:15 a.m. - 5:00 p.m. **Corporate headquarters location:** Washington DC. **Number of employees at this location:** 2,100.

FEDERAL RESERVE BANK OF ST. LOUIS
411 Locust Street, P.O. Box 442, St. Louis MO 63102. 314/444-8444. **Contact:** Personnel. **World Wide Web address:** http://www.stls.frb.org. **Description:** One of 12 regional Federal Reserve banks that, along with the Federal Reserve Board of Governors in Washington DC and the Federal Open Market Committee, comprise the Federal Reserve System, the nation's central bank. As the nation's central bank, the Federal Reserve is charged with three major responsibilities: monetary policy, banking supervision and regulation, and processing payments. **Common positions include:** Accountant/Auditor; Attorney; Bank Officer/Manager; Budget Analyst; Clerical Supervisor; Computer Programmer; Economist; Editor; Electrician; Financial Analyst; General Manager; Human Resources Manager; Librarian; Management Analyst/Consultant; Systems Analyst; Technical Writer/Editor. **Educational backgrounds include:** Accounting; Business Administration; Computer Science; Economics; Finance. **Benefits:** Dental

Insurance; Disability Coverage; Life Insurance; Medical Insurance; Pension Plan; Savings Plan; Tuition Assistance. **Number of employees at this location:** 800.

FEDERAL RESERVE BANK OF SAN FRANCISCO
101 Market Street, San Francisco CA 94105. 415/974-2000. **Contact:** Human Resources. **World Wide Web address:** http://www.frbsf.org. **Description:** One of 12 regional Federal Reserve banks that, along with the Federal Reserve Board of Governors in Washington DC, and the Federal Open Market Committee (FOMC), comprise the Federal Reserve System, the nation's central bank. As the nation's central bank, Federal Reserve is charged with three major responsibilities: setting monetary policy, banking supervision and regulation, and payment processing. **NOTE:** Entry-level positions and second and third shifts are offered. **Common positions include:** Account Manager; Account Rep.; Administrative Assistant; Applications Engineer; AS400 Programmer Analyst; Assistant Manager; Auditor; Bank Officer/Manager; Blue-Collar Worker Supervisor; Computer Programmer; Database Administrator; Economist; Financial Analyst; Help-Desk Technician; Intranet Developer; Network Engineer; Network/Systems Administrator; Operations Manager; Project Manager; Public Relations Specialist; SQL Programmer; Systems Analyst; Website Developer. **Educational backgrounds include:** AS400 Certification; Business Administration; Economics; Finance; HTML; Internet Development; Java; MBA; MCSE; Microsoft Office; Microsoft Word; Novell; QuarkXPress; SQL; Visual Basic. **Benefits:** 401(k); Casual Dress - Daily; Dental Insurance; Disability Coverage; Flexible Schedule; Life Insurance; Medical Insurance; Pension Plan; Public Transit Available; Relocation Assistance; Savings Plan; Telecommuting; Tuition Assistance.

FIDELITY FEDERAL BANK & TRUST
200 Datura Street, West Palm Beach FL 33401. 561/659-9900. **Contact:** Michele L. Dobos, Staffing Coordinator. **World Wide Web address:** http://www.fidfed.com. **Description:** A savings bank. Founded in 1952. **NOTE:** Entry-level positions and part-time jobs are offered. **Company slogan:** Count on us! **Common positions include:** Assistant Manager; Bank Teller; Branch Manager; Financial Services Sales Rep.; Management Trainee; Sales Rep. **Educational backgrounds include:** Business Administration; Finance; High School Diploma/GED; Microsoft Word; Spreadsheets. **Benefits:** 401(k); Casual Dress - Fridays; Dental Insurance; Disability Coverage; Employee Discounts; Life Insurance; Medical Insurance; Pension Plan; Sick Days (6 - 10); Tuition Assistance; Vacation Days (6 - 10). **Corporate headquarters location:** This Location. **Number of employees at this location:** 410.

FIFTH THIRD BANCORP
FIFTH THIRD BANK
38 Fountain Square Plaza, Cincinnati OH 45263. 513/579-5300. **Contact:** Human Resources. **World Wide Web address:** http://www.fifththird.com. **Description:** A regional bank holding company. **Corporate headquarters location:** This Location. **Other U.S. locations:** IN; KY. **Subsidiaries include:** Fifth Third Bank (also at this location) is a full-service banking institution. **Listed on:** NASDAQ.

FIRST BANCORP
FIRST BANK
P.O. Box 508, Troy NC 27371. 910/576-6171. **Physical address:** 341 North Main Street, Troy NC 27341. **Fax:** 910/576-1070. **Contact:** Patricia McCormick, Human Resources Director. **World Wide Web address:** http://www.firstbancorp.com. **Description:** First Bancorp is a bank holding company, which owns and operates First Bank (also at this location). **Corporate headquarters location:** This Location. **Subsidiaries include:** First Recovery Montgomery Data Services, Inc. provides data processing services to financial institutions; First Bank Insurance Services, Inc.; First Bank operates through 35 branches located within a 60-mile radius of Troy NC. The bank provides a full range of banking services including the accepting of demand and time deposits, the granting of secured and unsecured loans to individuals and businesses, trust services, discount brokerage services, and self-directed IRAs. **Listed on:** NASDAQ.

FIRST BANK
11901 Olive Boulevard, Creve Coeur MO 63141. 314/995-8700. **Contact:** Human Resources Manager. **Description:** A full-service bank. **Common positions include:** Accountant/Auditor; Administrator; Bank Officer/Manager; Branch Manager; Computer Programmer; Customer Service Rep.; Department Manager; Insurance Agent/Broker; Marketing Specialist; Operations/Production Manager; Systems Analyst. **Educational backgrounds include:** Business Administration; Finance; Liberal Arts. **Benefits:** Dental Insurance; Disability Coverage; Employee Discounts; Life Insurance; Medical Insurance; Pension Plan; Savings Plan. **Corporate headquarters location:** This Location. **Other U.S. locations:** CA; IL; TX. **Listed on:** Privately held. **Number of employees at this location:** 100.

FIRST BANK TEXAS, N.A.
8820 Westheimer, Houston TX 77063. 713/781-7171. **Contact:** Human Resources. **Description:** Operates full-service banks. **Common positions include:** Bank Officer/Manager; Branch Manager; Credit Manager; Customer Service Rep.; Financial Analyst. **Educational backgrounds include:** Accounting; Business Administration; Economics; Finance. **Benefits:** Dental Insurance; Life Insurance; Medical Insurance; Pension Plan; Tuition Assistance. **Corporate headquarters location:** This Location.

FIRST CHARTER CORPORATION
FIRST CHARTER NATIONAL BANK
P.O. Box 228, Concord NC 28026. 704/782-1193. **Contact:** Human Resources Director. **World Wide Web address:** http://www.firstcharter.com. **Description:** First Charter Corporation is a holding company that operates 50 banks throughout the greater Charlotte metropolitan area. Assets total $2.7 billion. **Corporate headquarters location:** This Location. **Subsidiaries include:** First Charter National Bank provides businesses and individuals with a broad range of financial services including banking, financial planning, funds management, investments, insurance mortgages, and employee benefits programs.

FIRST CITIZENS BANCORPORATION OF SOUTH CAROLINA, INC.
P.O. Box 29, Columbia SC 29202. 803/771-8700. **Contact:** Human Resources. **World Wide Web address:** http://www.fcbsc.com. **Description:** A bank holding company with statewide subsidiaries engaged in commercial banking, credit card services, and mortgage banking. **Corporate headquarters location:** This Location. **Subsidiaries include:** First Citizens Bank & Trust Company of South Carolina. **Number of employees nationwide:** 1,000.

FIRST CITIZENS BANK
P.O. Box 400, Newnan GA 30264. 770/253-5017.
Contact: Human Resources. **Description:** A bank.
Corporate headquarters location: This Location.

FIRST CITIZENS BANK & TRUST
P.O. Box 27131, Raleigh NC 27611. 919/755-7000.
Fax: 919/716-7085. **Recorded jobline:** 919/755-2070. **Contact:** Roberta Anderson, Corporate Recruiting & Development. **World Wide Web address:** http://www.firstcitizens.com. **Description:** A bank. Founded in 1898. **NOTE:** This bank only accepts resumes for open positions. Please call the jobline for a list of available jobs and instructions on how to apply. Entry-level positions and second and third shifts are offered. **Common positions include:** Adjuster; Administrative Assistant; Auditor; Bank Officer/Manager; Branch Manager; Computer Operator; Computer Programmer; Customer Service Rep.; Financial Analyst; Insurance Agent/Broker; Management Trainee; Sales Rep.; Systems Analyst; Technical Writer/Editor; Typist/Word Processor; Underwriter/Assistant Underwriter. **Educational backgrounds include:** Accounting; Business Administration; Computer Science; Finance; Mathematics; Software Tech. Support. **Benefits:** 401(k); Dental Insurance; Disability Coverage; Employee Discounts; Financial Planning Assistance; Life Insurance; Medical Insurance; Pension Plan; Savings Plan. **Special programs:** Training; Summer Jobs. **Office hours:** Monday - Friday, 9:00 a.m. - 5:00 p.m. **Corporate headquarters location:** This Location. **Annual sales/revenues:** $5 - $10 million. **Number of employees nationwide:** 4,000.

FIRST CITIZENS BANK, N.A.
P.O. Box 976, Talladega AL 35161. 256/362-8784.
Fax: 256/761-2153. **Contact:** Human Resources.
Description: A bank. **Common positions include:** Accountant/Auditor. **Educational backgrounds include:** Accounting; Business Administration; Computer Science. **Benefits:** Dental Insurance; Life Insurance; Medical Insurance. **Corporate headquarters location:** This Location. **Number of employees at this location:** 20.

FIRST COMMUNITY BANCSHARES, INC.
FIRST COMMUNITY BANK
P.O. Box 5939, Princeton WV 24740. 304/487-9000. **Contact:** Human Resources. **World Wide Web address:** http://www.fcbinc.com. **Description:** A holding company whose subsidiaries operate 31 banks. **NOTE:** Entry-level positions are offered. **Common positions include:** Administrative Assistant; Auditor; Chief Financial Officer; Computer Animator; Computer Programmer; Controller; Customer Service Rep.; Human Resources Manager; Marketing Specialist; Purchasing Agent/Manager; Secretary. **Educational backgrounds include:** Accounting; Business Administration; Finance; Marketing; Software Tech. Support. **Benefits:** 401(k); Dental Insurance; Disability Coverage; ESOP; Life Insurance; Medical Insurance; Tuition Assistance. **Special programs:** Internships; Summer Jobs. **Corporate headquarters location:** This Location. **Subsidiaries include:** Blue Ridge Bank; FCBank of Mercer County, Inc.; FCBank of Southwest Virginia, Inc.; FCBank, Inc.; First Community Bank (also at this location). **Number of employees at this location:** 85. **Number of employees nationwide:** 530.

FIRST CONSUMERS NATIONAL BANK
9300 SW Gemini Drive, Beaverton OR 97008.
503/520-8550. **Recorded jobline:** 503/520-8464.
Contact: Joyce Teufel, Recruiting & Employment.
Description: A bank providing credit card services.

NOTE: Entry-level positions and second and third shifts are offered. **Common positions include:** Account Manager; Administrative Assistant; Clerical Supervisor; Computer Operator; Credit Manager; Customer Service Rep.; Operations Manager; Secretary; Typist/Word Processor. **Educational backgrounds include:** Business Administration; Communications; Finance; Marketing. **Benefits:** 401(k); Dental Insurance; Disability Coverage; Employee Discounts; Flexible Schedule; Life Insurance; Medical Insurance; Profit Sharing; Savings Plan; Tuition Assistance. **Special programs:** Training. **Corporate headquarters location:** This Location. **Parent company:** Spiegel Inc. **Number of employees at this location:** 800.

FIRST FEDERAL CREDIT UNION
1232 East Baseline Road, Tempe AZ 85283.
480/831-2645. **Toll-free phone:** 800/732-6986.
Fax: 480/345-2130. **Contact:** Human Resources.
World Wide Web address: http://www.firstfederalcu.org. **Description:** A nonprofit credit union serving more than 50,000 members. **Corporate headquarters location:** This Location. **Other area locations:** Chandler AZ; Glendale AZ; Phoenix AZ; Tucson AZ.

FIRST FEDERAL SAVINGS & LOAN ASSOCIATION OF EAST HARTFORD
1137 Main Street, East Hartford CT 06108.
860/289-6401. **Fax:** 860/289-8548. **Contact:** Andrea Squires, Human Resources Representative. **Description:** First Federal Savings & Loan Association is a stock-chartered federal savings and loan institution. The company serves the retail financial market as a savings and mortgage loan specialist with 12 full-service offices east of the Connecticut River. The bank offers multifamily residential mortgage loans, equity loans, commercial real estate loans, business loans, and consumer loans. **Corporate headquarters location:** This Location.

FIRST FINANCIAL HOLDINGS, INC.
P.O. Box 118068, Charleston SC 29423. 843/529-5800. **Contact:** Human Resources. **Description:** A multiple thrift holding company serving retail banking markets. **Corporate headquarters location:** This Location. **Subsidiaries include:** First Federal Savings and Loan Association of Charleston; Peoples Federal Savings and Loan Association. **Listed on:** NASDAQ. **Number of employees at this location:** 565.

FIRST HAWAIIAN BANK
P.O. Box 3200, Honolulu HI 96847. 808/525-7000.
Physical address: 999 Bishop Street, 29th Floor, Honolulu HI. **Fax:** 808/525-8192. **Contact:** Human Resources. **World Wide Web address:** http://www.fhb.com. **Description:** A bank with 59 branch locations throughout the state of Hawaii, two locations in Guam, and one in Saipan. **Common positions include:** Bank Officer/Manager. **Educational backgrounds include:** Business Administration; Economics. **Benefits:** Daycare Assistance; Dental Insurance; Disability Coverage; Employee Discounts; Life Insurance; Medical Insurance; Pension Plan; Profit Sharing; Savings Plan; Tuition Assistance. **Corporate headquarters location:** This Location. **Listed on:** American Stock Exchange. **Number of employees at this location:** 400. **Number of employees nationwide:** 2,800.

FIRST INDIANA BANK
FIRST INDIANA CORPORATION
135 North Pennsylvania Street, Indianapolis IN 46204. 317/269-1304. **Contact:** Human Resources. **World Wide Web address:** http://www.firstindiana.com. **Description:** A full-service bank.

Common positions include: Accountant/Auditor; Bank Officer/Manager; Branch Manager; Credit Manager; Securities Sales Rep. **Educational backgrounds include:** Accounting; Business Administration; Finance; Marketing. **Benefits:** Dental Insurance; Disability Coverage; Employee Discounts; Life Insurance; Medical Insurance; Pension Plan. **Corporate headquarters location:** This Location. **Parent company:** First Indiana Corporation (also at this location) is a holding company whose principal subsidiary is First Indiana Bank. The corporation is engaged primarily in retail banking and lending through 29 banking centers including Mid-West Federal Savings Bank, First Federal Savings and Loan of Rushville, and Mooresville Savings Bank. In addition, the corporation operates six mortgage services offices in central Indiana. One Mortgage Corporation, a subsidiary, operates offices in Florida and North Carolina. First Indiana Corporation's other subsidiaries, One Insurance Agency, One Investment Corporation, and One Property Corporation, are engaged in insurance sales, investments, and full-service securities brokerage. **Listed on:** NASDAQ. **Number of employees at this location:** 450. **Number of employees nationwide:** 550.

FIRST MASSACHUSETTS BANK
153 Merrimack Street, Haverhill MA 01831. 978/374-1911. **Contact:** Human Resources. **Description:** Operates a full-service bank providing residential mortgage lending, commercial lending, construction lending, and savings.

FIRST MERIT BANK
3 Cascade Plaza, 1st Floor, Akron OH 44308. 330/384-7107. **Contact:** Human Resources. **Description:** A full-service commercial bank. **Corporate headquarters location:** This Location.

FIRST MIDWEST BANK, N.A.
50 West Jefferson Street, Joliet IL 60432. 815/727-5222. **Fax:** 815/774-2295. **Contact:** Elaine B. Aspel, Recruitment Officer. **World Wide Web address:** http://www.firstmidwest.com. **Description:** A full-service bank offering online banking, trust services, and other financial services. **NOTE:** Entry-level positions and part-time jobs are offered. **Common positions include:** Bank Officer/Manager; Human Resources Manager. **Educational backgrounds include:** Computer Science; Economics; Education; Internet Development; Spreadsheets. **Benefits:** 401(k); Casual Dress - Fridays; Daycare Assistance; Dental Insurance; Disability Coverage; Financial Planning Assistance; Life Insurance; Medical Insurance; Pension Plan; Profit Sharing; Public Transit Available; Savings Plan; Sick Days (1 - 5); Tuition Assistance; Vacation Days (10 - 20). **Special programs:** Co-ops. **Listed on:** NASDAQ. **Number of employees at this location:** 500. **Number of employees nationwide:** 1,700.

FIRST MUTUAL BANK
P.O. Box 1647, Bellevue WA 98009. 425/455-7300. **Contact:** Paulette O'Connell, Vice President of Human Resources. **World Wide Web address:** http://www.firstmutual.com. **Description:** A savings bank. The bank primarily offers real estate loan services. The company also offers a variety of depository and banking services. Founded in 1953. **Corporate headquarters location:** This Location. **Other area locations:** Issaquah WA; Monroe WA; Redmond WA; Seattle WA. **Listed on:** NASDAQ.

FIRST NATIONAL BANK NORTH DAKOTA
P.O. Box 6001, Grand Forks ND 58206. 701/795-3200. **Fax:** 701/795-3355. **Contact:** Human Resources. **World Wide Web address:** http://www.fnbnd.com. **Description:** A bank. **Common positions include:** Bank Officer/Manager; Credit Manager; Customer Service Rep. **Educational backgrounds include:** Business Administration; Finance. **Benefits:** 401(k); Dental Insurance; Disability Coverage; Life Insurance; Medical Insurance; Profit Sharing; Tuition Assistance. **Special programs:** Internships. **Corporate headquarters location:** This Location. **Other area locations:** Casselton ND; Fargo ND; Hankinson ND; Northwood ND; West Fargo ND. **Number of employees at this location:** 250.

FIRST NATIONAL BANK OF ABILENE
P.O. Box 701, Abilene TX 79604. 915/627-7000. **Contact:** Pam Mann, Director of Human Resources. **World Wide Web address:** http://www.fnbabilene.com. **Description:** A full-service bank that offers online banking, loan, and investment services.

FIRST NATIONAL BANK OF DAMARISCOTTA
Main Street, P.O. Box 940, Damariscotta ME 04543. 207/563-3195. **Contact:** Joyce Dexter, Personnel Director. **World Wide Web address:** http://www.the1st.com. **Description:** A bank providing a full range of banking services to individual and corporate customers in Maine. **Corporate headquarters location:** This Location.

FIRST NATIONAL BANK OF OMAHA
1620 Dodge Street, Omaha NE 68102. 402/341-0500. **Fax:** 402/633-3019. **Contact:** Human Resources. **World Wide Web address:** http://www.fnbo.com. **Description:** A commercial bank and financial services company. **Common positions include:** Accountant; Adjuster; Bank Officer/Manager; Branch Manager; Budget Analyst; Computer Programmer; Credit Manager; Customer Service Rep.; Financial Analyst; Human Resources Manager; Management Trainee; Software Engineer; Systems Analyst. **Educational backgrounds include:** Accounting; Business Administration; Communications; Computer Science; Economics; Engineering; Finance; Liberal Arts; Marketing; Mathematics; Physics. **Benefits:** 401(k); Daycare Assistance; Dental Insurance; Disability Coverage; Employee Discounts; Life Insurance; Medical Insurance; Pension Plan; Savings Plan; Tuition Assistance. **Corporate headquarters location:** This Location. **Other U.S. locations:** Fort Collins CO; Greeley CO; Kansas City MO. **Parent company:** First National of Nebraska. **Listed on:** NASDAQ. **Number of employees at this location:** 2,500. **Number of employees nationwide:** 3,700.

FIRST NATIONAL BANK OF PENNSYLVANIA
3320 East State Street, Hermitage PA 16148. 724/983-3449. **Fax:** 724/983-3509. **Contact:** Employment Office. **Description:** A banking corporation with 31 branches located throughout Pennsylvania. **NOTE:** Entry-level positions are offered. **Common positions include:** Accountant; Administrative Assistant; Assistant Manager; Auditor; Bank Officer/Manager; Branch Manager; Controller; Credit Manager; Financial Analyst; Human Resources Manager; Marketing Manager; Marketing Specialist; Public Relations Specialist; Purchasing Agent/Manager; Sales Executive; Sales Manager; Secretary; Underwriter/Assistant Underwriter. **Educational backgrounds include:** Accounting; Business Administration; Economics; Finance; Marketing. **Benefits:** 401(k); Dental Insurance; Disability Coverage; Life Insurance; Medical Insurance; Pension Plan; Profit Sharing; Tuition Assistance. **Office hours:** Monday - Friday, 8:30 a.m. - 5:00 p.m. **Corporate headquarters**

location: This Location. **Parent company:** FNB Corporation is a holding company which, in addition to performing savings bank operations, also provides mortgage banking and leasing services, real estate activities, insurance services, and other financial activities. **Stock exchange symbol:** FNB. **President/CEO:** Steve Gurgovits. **Annual sales/revenues:** More than $100 million. **Number of employees at this location:** 510. **Number of employees nationwide:** 1,300.

FIRST NATIONAL CORPORATION
P.O. Box 1287, Orangeburg SC 29116-1287. 803/534-2175. **Contact:** Human Resources. **Description:** A bank holding company whose subsidiaries perform commercial banking operations and provide other financial services. **Corporate headquarters location:** This Location. **Subsidiaries include:** First National Bank; National Bank of York County. **Number of employees at this location:** 150. **Number of employees nationwide:** 350.

FIRST REPUBLIC BANCORP INC.
111 Pine Street, San Francisco CA 94111-5602. 415/392-1400. **Contact:** Human Resources. **Description:** A leading banking and mortgage institution with growing operations in San Francisco, Los Angeles, San Diego, and Las Vegas. **Corporate headquarters location:** This Location.

FIRST SIGNATURE BANK & TRUST
P.O. Box 7090, Portsmouth NH 03802-7090. 603/433-3700. **Physical address:** 100 Arboretum Drive, Portsmouth NH. **Contact:** Pamela Howell, Human Resources. **Description:** A state commercial bank offering money market accounts, certificates of deposit, IRAs, NOW accounts, instant credit, home mortgages, home equity lines of credit, and consumer loans. **Parent company:** John Hancock Financial Services (Boston MA).

FIRST TENNESSEE NATIONAL CORP.
FIRST TENNESSEE BANK
P.O. Box 84, Memphis TN 38101-8416. 901/523-5308. **Physical address:** 300 Court Street, Memphis TN 38103. **Fax:** 901/523-5303. **Recorded jobline:** 901/523-5056. **Contact:** Employment Services Department. **World Wide Web address:** http://www.ftb.com. **Description:** This location houses both the parent company and a branch of the bank. Overall, First Tennessee National Corporation (FTNC) is one of the nation's largest banking companies with assets of over $12 billion. FTNC, whose principal subsidiary is First Tennessee Bank National Association (FTBNA), is one of the largest Tennessee-based bank holding companies. FTBNA offers general banking products through 289 locations which serve Tennessee, Arkansas, and Mississippi. Mortgage banking services are provided through 148 offices in 30 states. In addition, consumer lending services are offered at 10 offices in five states. FTBNA also offers related financial services including bond broker/agency services, mortgage banking, merchant credit card processing, nationwide check clearing, integrated check processing solutions, trust services, brokerage, venture capital, and credit life insurance. **Common positions include:** Accountant/Auditor; Attorney; Bank Officer/Manager; Branch Manager; Brokerage Clerk; Budget Analyst; Buyer; Clerical Supervisor; Computer Programmer; Cost Estimator; Financial Analyst; Human Resources Manager; Management Trainee; MIS Specialist; Paralegal; Quality Control Supervisor; Registered Nurse; Software Engineer; Systems Analyst; Telecommunications Manager; Typist/Word Processor; Underwriter/Assistant Underwriter. **Educational backgrounds include:** Accounting;

Business Administration; Communications; Computer Science; Economics; Finance; Liberal Arts. **Benefits:** 401(k); Daycare Assistance; Dental Insurance; Disability Coverage; Employee Discounts; Job Sharing; Life Insurance; Medical Insurance; Pension Plan; Profit Sharing; Savings Plan; Telecommuting; Tuition Assistance. **Corporate headquarters location:** This Location. **Subsidiaries include:** Cleveland Bank & Trust Company (Cleveland TN); Planters Bank (Tunica MS); SNMC Management Corporation (Dallas TX). **Listed on:** New York Stock Exchange. **Annual sales/revenues:** More than $100 million. **Number of employees at this location:** 3,000. **Number of employees nationwide:** 8,000.

FIRST UNION CORPORATION
FIRST UNION MORTGAGE CORP.
301 South College Street, Suite 4000, Charlotte NC 28288. 704/374-6565. **Contact:** Human Resources. **World Wide Web address:** http://www.firstunion.com. **Description:** One of the nation's largest bank holding companies with subsidiaries that operate over 2,300 full-service bank branches in the Southeast. These branches provide retail banking, retail investment, and commercial banking services. The corporation provides other financial services including mortgage banking, home equity lending, leasing, insurance, and securities brokerage services from 222 branch locations. First Union also operates 3,800 ATMs. **NOTE:** Resumes can also be sent to Human Resources, First Union Corporation, 1525 West W.T. Harris Boulevard, Building 3A2, Charlotte NC 28288. **Corporate headquarters location:** This Location. **International locations:** Worldwide. **Subsidiaries include:** First Union Brokerage Services Inc.; First Union Capital Markets Corporation; First Union Home Equity Bank, N.A.; First Union Mortgage Corporation (also at this location); First Union National Bank of Florida; First Union National Bank of Georgia; First Union National Bank of Maryland; First Union National Bank of North Carolina; First Union National Bank of South Carolina; First Union National Bank of Tennessee; First Union National Bank of Virginia; First Union National Bank of Washington DC; Money Store; First Union Pennsylvania. **Listed on:** New York Stock Exchange. **Number of employees nationwide:** 71,660.

FIRST UNION NATIONAL BANK
1500 Market Street, Philadelphia PA 19102. 215/786-5980. **Contact:** Human Resources. **World Wide Web address:** http://www.firstunion.com. **Description:** A full-service commercial bank providing corporate and consumer services. **Parent company:** First Union Corporation (Charlotte NC) is one of the nation's largest bank holding companies with subsidiaries that operate over 2,300 full-service bank branches in the Southeast. These branches provide retail banking, retail investment, and commercial banking services. The corporation provides other financial services including mortgage banking, home equity lending, leasing, insurance, and securities brokerage services from 222 branch locations. First Union also operates 3,800 ATMs.

FIRST UNION NATIONAL BANK OF SOUTH CAROLINA
P.O. Box 1329, Greenville SC 29602. 864/255-8000. **Contact:** Human Resources. **World Wide Web address:** http://www.firstunion.com. **Description:** A full-service commercial bank providing corporate and consumer services. First Union National Bank of South Carolina operates more than 65 offices. **Corporate headquarters location:** This Location. **Parent company:** First Union Corporation (Charlotte NC) is one of the

nation's largest bank holding companies with subsidiaries that operate over 2,300 full-service bank branches in the Southeast. These branches provide retail banking, retail investment, and commercial banking services. The corporation provides other financial services including mortgage banking, home equity lending, leasing, insurance, and securities brokerage services from 222 branch locations. First Union also operates 3,800 ATMs. **Listed on:** New York Stock Exchange. **Number of employees nationwide:** 71,660.

FIRST UNION NATIONAL BANK OF TENNESSEE
150 Fourth Avenue North, Nashville TN 37219. 615/251-9200. **Contact:** Human Resources. **E-mail address:** jobs@firstunion.com. **World Wide Web address:** http://www.firstunion.com. **Description:** A full-service commercial bank providing corporate and consumer services. First Union National Bank of Tennessee operates 54 offices. **Corporate headquarters location:** This Location. **Parent company:** First Union Corporation (Charlotte NC) is one of the nation's largest bank holding companies with subsidiaries that operate over 2,300 full-service bank branches in the Southeast. These branches provide retail banking, retail investment, and commercial banking services. The corporation provides other financial services including mortgage banking, home equity lending, leasing, insurance, and securities brokerage services from 222 branch locations. First Union also operates 3,800 ATMs. **Listed on:** New York Stock Exchange. **Number of employees nationwide:** 71,660.

FIRST UNION NATIONAL BANK OF VIRGINIA
P.O. Box 13327, Roanoke VA 24040-7366. 540/563-6393. **Contact:** Human Resources. **World Wide Web address:** http://www.firstunion.com. **Description:** A full-service bank providing corporate and consumer services. First Union National Bank of Virginia operates 177 offices. **Common positions include:** Account Manager; Accountant/Auditor; Bank Officer/Manager; Branch Manager; Customer Service Rep.; Financial Analyst; Human Resources Manager; Instructor/Trainer. **Educational backgrounds include:** Accounting; Business Administration; Economics; Finance; Liberal Arts. **Benefits:** 401(k); Daycare Assistance; Disability Coverage; Employee Discounts; Life Insurance; Medical Insurance; Pension Plan; Savings Plan; Stock Option; Tuition Assistance. **Corporate headquarters location:** This Location. **Parent company:** First Union Corporation (Charlotte NC) is one of the nation's largest bank holding companies with subsidiaries that operate over 2,300 full-service bank branches in the Southeast. These branches provide retail banking, retail investment, and commercial banking services. The corporation provides other financial services including mortgage banking, home equity lending, leasing, insurance, and securities brokerage services from 222 branch locations. First Union also operates 3,800 ATMs. **Listed on:** New York Stock Exchange. **Number of employees at this location:** 2,200. **Number of employees nationwide:** 71,660.

FIRST VIRGINIA BANKS, INC.
One First Virginia Plaza, 6400 Arlington Boulevard, Falls Church VA 22042-2336. 703/241-3657. **Contact:** Human Resources. **World Wide Web address:** http://www.firstvirginia.com. **Description:** A bank holding company. First Virginia Banks, Inc., with assets of $7.8 billion, is one of the oldest banks headquartered in Virginia. The company has a network of six Virginia member banks with over 305 offices; two banks in Maryland operating 60 offices; and two banks in Tennessee that operate 26 offices. The company also owns several firms that

are engaged in financially-related activities such as mortgage banking and insurance in seven states. **Corporate headquarters location:** This Location. **Subsidiaries include:** First Virginia Bank (306 offices); Atlantic Bank (five offices); Farmers Bank of Maryland (22 offices); Tri-City Bank and Trust Company (12 offices); First Virginia Mortgage Company; First General Mortgage Company; First Virginia Life Insurance Company; First Virginia Insurance Services, Inc.; First Virginia Credit Services, Inc.; First Virginia Services, Inc.; Springdale Advertising Agency, Inc. **Number of employees nationwide:** 5,680.

FIRSTAR BANK
P.O. Box 524, St. Louis MO 63166. 314/425-2525. **Contact:** Human Resources. **World Wide Web address:** http://www.firstar.com. **Description:** A commercial bank.

FIRSTAR CORPORATION
777 East Wisconsin Avenue, Milwaukee WI 53202. 414/765-4321. **Contact:** Human Resources. **World Wide Web address:** http://www.firstar.com. **Description:** A holding company. The company's banks offer banking and related financial services to business, financial institutions, the government, and non-profit organizations.

FIRSTFED FINANCIAL CORPORATION
FIRST FEDERAL BANK OF CALIFORNIA
401 Wilshire Boulevard, Santa Monica CA 90401. 310/319-6000. **Contact:** Human Resources. **Description:** A bank holding company. **Corporate headquarters location:** This Location. **Subsidiaries include:** First Federal Bank of California (also at this location).

FLEET BANK OF MASSACHUSETTS, N.A.
100 Federal Street, Boston MA 02110. 617/434-2200. **Fax:** 617/434-0532. **Contact:** Human Resources. **World Wide Web address:** http://www.fleet.com. **Description:** Operates a full-service bank, serving the commercial and consumer banking needs of individuals, corporations, institutions, and government in the Northeast.

FRANKLIN BANK, N.A.
24725 West Twelve Mile Road, Southfield MI 48034. **Contact:** Human Resources. **World Wide Web address:** http://www.franklinbank.com. **Description:** An independently-owned commercial bank. **Corporate headquarters location:** This Location. **Other area locations:** Birmingham MI; Grosse Pointe Woods MI. **Subsidiaries include:** Franklin Finance Corporation; Franklin Home Lending Group. **Listed on:** NASDAQ. **Stock exchange symbol:** FSVB. **CEO:** Read P. Dunn.

FROST NATIONAL BANK
CULLEN/FROST BANKERS, INC.
P.O. Box 1600, San Antonio TX 78296-1400. 210/220-4011. **Recorded jobline:** 210/220-5627. **Contact:** Human Resources. **World Wide Web address:** http://www.frostbank.com. **Description:** A bank that offers online banking, financial management, and loan services. **Corporate headquarters location:** This Location. **Parent company:** Cullen/Frost Bankers, Inc. (also at this location) is a multibank holding company with 80 offices in Texas. In addition to Frost National, Cullen/Frost also operates United States National Bank (Galveston TX).

FULTON FINANCIAL CORPORATION
FULTON BANK
One Penn Square, Lancaster PA 17602. 717/291-2467. **Fax:** 717/295-4783. **Contact:** Craig Hill, Director of Human Resources. **World Wide Web**

address: http://www.fult.com. **Description:** A multi-bank holding company. **Common positions include:** Bank Officer/Manager; Branch Manager; Management Trainee. **Educational backgrounds include:** Accounting; Business Administration; Finance. **Benefits:** Dental Insurance; Disability Coverage; Employee Discounts; Life Insurance; Medical Insurance; Pension Plan; Profit Sharing; Tuition Assistance. **Corporate headquarters location:** This Location. **Subsidiaries include:** Fulton Bank (also at this location). **Number of employees at this location:** 900.

GOLDEN STATE BANCORP
CALIFORNIA FEDERAL BANK
135 Main Street, San Francisco CA 94105. 415/904-1100. **Contact:** Human Resources. **World Wide Web address:** http://www.calfed.com. **Description:** Golden State Bancorp is a holding company. **Corporate headquarters location:** This Location. **Subsidiaries include:** California Federal Bank (also at this location) offers mortgage services, consumer and business banking products, and automobile financing. **Stock exchange symbol:** GSB. **Annual sales/revenues:** More than $100 million.

GREENVILLE NATIONAL BANK
P.O. Box 190, Greenville OH 45331. 937/548-1114. **Physical address:** 446 South Broadway, Greenville OH. **Fax:** 937/548-0650. **Contact:** Gloria Harpest, Personnel Director. **World Wide Web address:** http://www.greenvillenationalbank.com. **Description:** A full-service bank.

GUARANTY SAVINGS AND LOAN, F.A.
1658 State Farm Boulevard, Charlottesville VA 22911. 804/974-1100. **Contact:** Human Resources. **Description:** A federally chartered savings association. The principal business of Guaranty Savings and Loan is attracting deposits and originating, servicing, investing in, and selling loans secured by first mortgage liens on single family dwellings. Guaranty also provides home equity and installment loans, and originates loans secured by commercial property. **Corporate headquarters location:** This Location. **Subsidiaries include:** GMSC, Inc.; Guaranty Investments Corporation.

HSBC BANK
140 Broadway, 20th Floor, New York NY 10005. 212/658-1000. **Contact:** Personnel. **Description:** An international banking institution which provides a wide range of individual and commercial services.

HIBERNIA NATIONAL BANK
P.O. Box 3402, Lake Charles LA 70602-3402. 337/494-3396. **Contact:** Human Resources. **Description:** A commercial bank. **Corporate headquarters location:** This Location. **Parent company:** Hibernia Corporation offers consumer banking, commercial middle market and small business lending, and trust services in Louisiana.

HOMETOWN BANK OF GALVESTON
1801 45th Street, Galveston TX 77550. 409/763-1271. **Contact:** Human Resources. **World Wide Web address:** http://www.bankofgalveston.com. **Description:** A full-service bank. **Corporate headquarters location:** This Location. **Other area locations:** 4424 Seawall Boulevard, Galveston TX 77550, 409/763-5252. **Parent company:** Hometown Bank, N.A.

HUDSON UNITED BANK
1500 Route 202, Harding Township NJ 07920. **Contact:** Human Resources. **Description:** A bank. **NOTE:** Please send resumes to 1000 MacArthur Boulevard, Mahwah NJ 07430. 201/236-2600. **Corporate headquarters location:** This Location.

HUNTINGTON BANCSHARES INC.
41 South High Street, 3rd Floor, Columbus OH 43287. 614/480-4639. **Contact:** Carol Powers, Assistant Vice President. **World Wide Web address:** http://www.huntington.com. **Description:** A bank and financial services holding company. **Common positions include:** Accountant/Auditor; Bank Officer/Manager; Financial Analyst; Securities Sales Rep. **Corporate headquarters location:** This Location. **Subsidiaries include:** The Huntington National Bank (also at this location); The Huntington National Life Insurance Agency, Inc.; The Huntington Financial Services Company.

INDEPENDENCE COMMUNITY BANK
195 Montague Street, Brooklyn NY 11201. 718/722-5300. **Contact:** Personnel Department. **World Wide Web address:** http://www.icbny.com. **Description:** A savings bank that offers a wide range of traditional banking services as well as specialized financial services, loans, and insurance services. **Corporate headquarters location:** This Location.

INDEPENDENT BANKSHARES, INC.
P.O. Box 3296, Abilene TX 79604. 915/677-5550. **Fax:** 915/677-5943. **Contact:** Human Resources. **Description:** A bank holding company. Founded in 1981. **Common positions include:** Accountant/Auditor; Administrative Assistant; Bank Officer/Manager; Chief Financial Officer; Controller; Operations/Production Manager; Secretary. **Educational backgrounds include:** Accounting; Business Administration; Finance. **Benefits:** 401(k); Dental Insurance; Disability Coverage; Employee Discounts; ESOP; Life Insurance; Medical Insurance. **Corporate headquarters location:** This Location. **Subsidiaries include:** Independent Financial Corporation (Abilene TX) owns First State Bank, N.A. **Listed on:** American Stock Exchange. **Stock exchange symbol:** IBK. **Number of employees at this location:** 20. **Number of employees nationwide:** 125.

INTERWEST BANK
INTERWEST BANCORP, INC.
P.O. Box 1649, Oak Harbor WA 98277. 360/675-0788. **Toll-free phone:** 800/321-8592. **Fax:** 360/675-8860. **Recorded jobline:** 800/321-8592x1605. **Contact:** Human Resources. **World Wide Web address:** http://www.interwestbank.com. **Description:** A full-service bank with 55 offices in Washington state. **NOTE:** Entry-level positions and part-time jobs are offered. **Common positions include:** Accountant; Administrative Assistant; Administrative Manager; Advertising Clerk; Advertising Executive; Assistant Manager; Auditor; Bank Officer/Manager; Branch Manager; Chief Financial Officer; Clerical Supervisor; Computer Programmer; Computer Support Technician; Computer Technician; Content Developer; Controller; Credit Manager; Customer Service Rep.; Database Administrator; Database Manager; Finance Director; Financial Analyst; Fund Manager; General Manager; Human Resources Manager; Insurance Agent/Broker; Internet Services Manager; Management Trainee; Marketing Manager; Marketing Specialist; Network/Systems Administrator; Operations Manager; Project Manager; Public Relations Specialist; Purchasing Agent/Manager; Quality Control Supervisor; Secretary; SQL Programmer; Systems Analyst; Systems Manager; Typist/Word Processor; Vice President. **Educational backgrounds include:** Accounting; Business Administration; Computer Science; Economics; Finance; Marketing; MCSE; Microsoft Word; Novell; Software Tech. Support; Spreadsheets. **Benefits:** 401(k); Casual Dress - Fridays; Dental Insurance; Disability Coverage;

Employee Discounts; Life Insurance; Medical Insurance. **Special programs:** Internships. **Corporate headquarters location:** This Location. **Subsidiaries include:** InterWest Financial Services; Interwest Insurance Agency. **Parent company:** Interwest Bancorp, Inc. (also at this location) is a bank holding company. **Listed on:** NASDAQ. **Number of employees at this location:** 935.

JEFFERSONVILLE BANCORP
THE FIRST NATIONAL BANK OF JEFFERSONVILLE
P.O. Box 398, Jeffersonville NY 12748. 914/482-4000. **Physical address:** 300 Main Street, Jeffersonville NY. **Contact:** Human Resources. **E-mail address:** jeffbank@jeffbank.com. **World Wide Web address:** http://www.jeffbank.com. **Description:** Owns and operates full-service banks. Founded in 1913. **Corporate headquarters location:** This Location. **Other U.S. locations:** Eldred NY; Liberty NY; Loch Sheldrake NY; Monticello NY. **Subsidiaries include:** The First National Bank of Jeffersonville (also at this location). **Listed on:** NASDAQ.

KEYBANK OF IDAHO
702 West Idaho, Boise ID 83702. 208/364-8703. **Contact:** Paula Barber, Manager of Human Resources. **World Wide Web address:** http://www.keybank.com. **Description:** Provides banking services. **Common positions include:** Bank Officer/Manager; Branch Manager; Client Services Rep.; Credit Clerk and Authorizer; Credit Manager; Customer Service Rep.; Department Manager; Financial Analyst; Management Trainee; Sales Manager; Sales Rep. **Educational backgrounds include:** Accounting; Business Administration; Communications; Economics; Finance; Marketing. **Benefits:** Dental Insurance; Disability Coverage; Employee Discounts; Life Insurance; Medical Insurance; Pension Plan; Profit Sharing; Savings Plan; Tuition Assistance. **Corporate headquarters location:** Cleveland OH. **Parent company:** KeyCorp. **President:** Mike Mooney.

KEYSTONE FINANCIAL
601 Dresher Road, Horsham PA 19044. 215/956-7001. **Contact:** Human Resources. **World Wide Web address:** http://www.keyfin.com. **Description:** A full-service banking institution. **Common positions include:** Accountant/Auditor; Bank Officer/Manager; Customer Service Rep. **Educational backgrounds include:** Accounting; Finance. **Benefits:** Employee Discounts; Life Insurance; Medical Insurance; Pension Plan; Tuition Assistance. **Corporate headquarters location:** This Location.

LEBANON VALLEY FARMERS BANK
P.O. Box 1285, Lebanon PA 17042. 717/274-6871. **Fax:** 717/274-6838. **Contact:** Human Resources. **E-mail address:** lvnb@nbn.net. **Description:** A bank. **Common positions include:** Accountant; Bank Officer/Manager; Branch Manager; Computer Programmer; Financial Analyst; Management Trainee; Systems Analyst; Underwriter/Assistant Underwriter. **Educational backgrounds include:** Accounting; Communications; Computer Science; Finance; Mathematics. **Benefits:** 401(k); Disability Coverage; Life Insurance; Medical Insurance; Pension Plan; Tuition Assistance. **Special programs:** Internships. **Corporate headquarters location:** This Location. **Parent company:** Keystone Heritage Group, Inc. **Number of employees at this location:** 325.

MANUFACTURERS BANK
515 South Figueroa Street, 2nd Floor, Los Angeles CA 90071. 213/489-6200. **Contact:** Mike Moore,

Director of Human Resources. **Description:** A banking institution offering a wide range of services including checking and savings accounts; certificates of deposit; commercial, industrial, real estate, and installment loans; direct and leveraged leases; collections; escrow services; and letters of credit. **Common positions include:** Accountant/Auditor; Bank Officer/Manager; Bank Teller; Customer Service Rep.; Loan Officer. **Benefits:** Dental Insurance; Disability Coverage; Employee Discounts; Life Insurance; Medical Insurance; Pension Plan; Profit Sharing; Tuition Assistance; Vacation Days. **Corporate headquarters location:** This Location. **Other U.S. locations:** Beverly Hills CA; Newport Beach CA. **Parent company:** Mitsui Bank, Ltd.

MARQUETTE BANK
1650 West 82nd Street, Suite 400, Bloomington MN 55431. 952/948-5800. **Fax:** 952/948-5619. **Recorded jobline:** 952/948-5668. **Contact:** Human Resources. **E-mail address:** hr@marquette.com. **World Wide Web address:** http://www.marquette.com. **Description:** A full-service bank. **NOTE:** Entry-level positions, part-time jobs, and second and third shifts are offered. **Common positions include:** Accountant; Administrative Assistant; Bank Officer/Manager; Bank Teller; Customer Service Rep.; Help-Desk Technician; Human Resources Manager; Market Research Analyst; Marketing Specialist; Operations Manager; Project Manager; Secretary. **Educational backgrounds include:** Accounting; Business Administration; Finance; Liberal Arts; Microsoft Office; Microsoft Word; Spreadsheets. **Benefits:** 401(k); Casual Dress - Fridays; Daycare Assistance; Dental Insurance; Disability Coverage; Employee Discounts; Flexible Schedule; Job Sharing; Life Insurance; Medical Insurance; Tuition Assistance; Vacation Days (10 - 20). **Special programs:** Internships; Training; Summer Jobs. **Corporate headquarters location:** This Location. **Parent company:** Marquette Financial Companies. **Number of employees at this location:** 200. **Number of employees nationwide:** 3,000.

MATEWAN BANK
P.O. Box 100, Williamson WV 25661. 304/235-1544. **Contact:** Human Resources. **Description:** A bank holding company. **Corporate headquarters location:** This Location. **Subsidiaries include:** A commercial bank with eight full-service offices and one loan office providing services to customers in southern West Virginia and eastern Kentucky. Matewan Bank, FSB is a savings bank with two offices in eastern Kentucky.

MEDFORD SAVINGS BANK
5 High Street, Suite 205, Medford MA 02155. 781/395-7700. **Contact:** Personnel Officer. **World Wide Web address:** http://www.medfordbank.com. **Description:** A bank. **NOTE:** Entry-level positions are offered. **Common positions include:** Accountant; Bank Officer/Manager; Bank Teller; Branch Manager; Customer Service Rep.; Financial Analyst; Human Resources Manager; Payroll Clerk; Typist/Word Processor. **Educational backgrounds include:** Accounting; Business Administration; Economics; Finance; Marketing. **Benefits:** 401(k); Dental Insurance; Disability Coverage; Life Insurance; Medical Insurance; Pension Plan; Public Transit Available; Tuition Assistance. **Corporate headquarters location:** This Location. **Listed on:** NASDAQ. **Number of employees at this location:** 110. **Number of employees nationwide:** 315.

MERCANTILE BANKSHARES CORP.
2 Hopkins Plaza, Baltimore MD 21201. 410/237-5900. **Contact:** Human Resources Manager.

Description: A multibank holding company. Affiliates of Mercantile Bankshares Corporation include 20 banks and a mortgage banking company. The affiliated banks are engaged in general, personal, and corporate banking. Mercantile Bankshares Corporation's largest bank, Mercantile Safe Deposit & Trust Company, also provides a full range of trust services. The banking affiliates have 155 retail banking offices located in Maryland, Delaware, and Virginia providing personal banking services including deposit vehicles such as checking accounts, NOW accounts, money market deposit accounts, certificates of deposit, and individual retirement accounts. **NOTE:** Please send resumes to Mercantile Safe Deposit & Trust Company, Human Resources Manager, 750 Old Hammonds Ferry Road, Linthicum MD 21090. **Benefits:** 401(k); Pension Plan; Retirement Plan; Stock Option. **Corporate headquarters location:** This Location. **Listed on:** NASDAQ.

MERCANTILE NATIONAL BANK
1840 Century Park East, 2nd Floor, Los Angeles CA 90067. 310/277-2265. **Contact:** Trudy Bakalyan, Director of Human Resources. **Description:** A commercial bank. **Common positions include:** Accountant/Auditor; Customer Service Rep.; Loan Officer. **Educational backgrounds include:** Accounting; Business Administration; Economics; Finance. **Benefits:** 401(k); Employee Discounts; Life Insurance; Medical Insurance; Tuition Assistance. **Corporate headquarters location:** This Location.

MIDAMERICA BANK
55th and Holmes, Clarendon Hills IL 60514. 630/325-7300. **Contact:** Teresa Colson, Human Resources Manager. **Description:** A full-service bank. **Common positions include:** Bank Officer/Manager; Branch Manager. **Benefits:** 401(k); Daycare Assistance; Dental Insurance; Employee Discounts; Life Insurance; Meal Plan; Pension Plan; Profit Sharing; Savings Plan; Tuition Assistance. **Corporate headquarters location:** This Location. **Other U.S. locations:** Cicero IL; La Grange Park IL; Naperville IL; Riverside IL; St. Charles IL; Wheaton IL. **Listed on:** NASDAQ.

MIDDLESEX SAVINGS BANK
6 Main Street, Natick MA 01760. 508/653-0300. **Contact:** Human Resources. **World Wide Web address:** http://www.middlesexbank.com. **Description:** A savings bank. **Corporate headquarters location:** This Location. **Other U.S. locations:** Framingham MA.

NATIONAL CITY CORPORATION
1900 East Ninth Street, 4th Floor, Cleveland OH 44114-3484. 216/575-3000. **Contact:** Human Resources. **World Wide Web address:** http://www. national-city.com. **Description:** A major bank holding company. **Common positions include:** Accountant; Attorney; Bank Officer/Manager; Branch Manager; Brokerage Clerk; Budget Analyst; Computer Programmer; Credit Manager; Customer Service Rep.; Human Resources Manager; Management Trainee; Paralegal; Purchasing Agent/ Manager; Securities Sales Rep.; Software Engineer; Systems Analyst. **Educational backgrounds include:** Accounting; Business Administration; Communications; Computer Science; Economics; Finance; Marketing. **Benefits:** 401(k); Dental Insurance; Disability Coverage; Employee Discounts; Life Insurance; Medical Insurance; Pension Plan; Tuition Assistance. **Corporate headquarters location:** This Location. **Other U.S. locations:** IN; KY. **Listed on:** New York Stock Exchange. **Number of employees at this location:** 4,300. **Number of employees nationwide:** 25,000.

NATIONAL PENN BANK
P.O. Box 547, Boyertown PA 19512. 610/367-6001. **Toll-free phone:** 800/822-3321. **Fax:** 610/369-6676. **Contact:** Human Resources. **World Wide Web address:** http://www.natpennbank.com. **Description:** A bank. **Parent company:** National Penn Bancshares, Inc. is a $2.1 billion bank holding company. Other subsidiaries of National Penn Bancshares include Investors Trust Company.

NAZARETH NATIONAL BANK AND TRUST CO.
3864 Adler Place, Bethlehem PA 18017. 610/746-7300. **Contact:** Human Resources. **World Wide Web address:** http://www.nazbank.com. **Description:** An independent community bank providing financial services at 14 local branches. **Corporate headquarters location:** This Location. **Parent company:** First Colonial Group is a bank holding company. The company also operates First C.G. Company, Inc. (Wilmington DE), established to invest in various types of securities.

NORTH COUNTY BANCORP
NORTH COUNTY BANK
444 South Escondido Boulevard, Escondido CA 92025. 760/743-2200. **Contact:** Lori Wolf, Human Resources Manager. **Description:** A bank holding company with nine branches located throughout California and a loan production office in Washington. **Corporate headquarters location:** This Location. **Other area locations:** 1735 West Ramsey Street, Banning CA 92220, 909/849-5605; 499 East Sixth Street, Beaumont CA 92223, 909/845-2605; 2025 Vineyard Avenue, Escondido CA 92029, 760/741-8333; 41500 Ivy Street, Murrieta CA 92562, 909/304-0026; 13436 Poway Road, Poway CA 92064, 619/748-1557; 8085 Clairemont Mesa Boulevard, San Diego CA 92111, 619/278-3445; 1000 West San Marcos Boulevard, San Marcos CA 92069, 760/744-8290; 27425 Ynez Road, Temecula CA 92591, 909/676-6500. **Other U.S. locations:** Renton WA. **Subsidiaries include:** North County Bank (also at this location). **Listed on:** NASDAQ. **Stock exchange symbol:** NCBH.

NORTH FORK BANCORPORATION, INC.
NORTH FORK BANK
275 Broad Hollow Road, Melville NY 11747. 631/298-5000. **Contact:** Human Resources. **World Wide Web address:** http://www. northforkbank.com. **Description:** A commercial bank holding company whose principal subsidiary, North Fork Bank (also at this location), is one of the largest independent commercial banks headquartered on Long Island. **Corporate headquarters location:** This Location.

THE NORTHERN TRUST COMPANY
50 South LaSalle Street, Chicago IL 60675. 312/630-6000. **Contact:** Human Resources. **Description:** A full-service bank engaged in commercial lending services, trust services, financial services, bond services, financial management, and other related services. **Common positions include:** Accountant/Auditor; Lender; Trust Officer. **Educational backgrounds include:** Accounting; Economics; Finance; Liberal Arts. **Benefits:** Daycare Assistance; Dental Insurance; Disability Coverage; Employee Discounts; Life Insurance; Medical Insurance; Pension Plan; Profit Sharing; Savings Plan; Stock Option; Tuition Assistance. **Special programs:** Internships. **Corporate headquarters location:** This Location. **Number of employees nationwide:** 6,300.

THE OHIO BANK
P.O. Box 300, Findlay OH 45839. 419/424-4000. **Physical address:** 236 South Main Street, Findlay OH. **Contact:** Francine Wahrman, Human

Resources Manager. **World Wide Web address:** http://www.ohiobank.com. **Description:** An independent commercial bank. **Common positions include:** Accountant; Customer Service Rep.; Financial Analyst; MIS Specialist; Typist/Word Processor. **Educational backgrounds include:** Accounting; Business Administration; Finance; Mathematics. **Benefits:** 401(k); Dental Insurance; Life Insurance; Medical Insurance; Profit Sharing; Tuition Assistance. **Special programs:** Internships. **Corporate headquarters location:** This Location. **Listed on:** Privately held. **Number of employees nationwide:** 260.

OLD KENT FINANCIAL CORPORATION
1830 East Paris SE, Grand Rapids MI 49546. 616/771-5812. **Fax:** 616/771-6992. **Recorded jobline:** 800/552-4350. **Contact:** Human Resources. **E-mail address:** careers@oldkent.com. **World Wide Web address:** http://www. oldkent.com. **Description:** A financial services institution which, through its subsidiaries, provides mortgage loans and traditional banking services. Founded in 1853. **NOTE:** Entry-level positions, part-time jobs, and second and third shifts are offered. **Common positions include:** Administrative Assistant; Assistant Manager; Bank Officer/Manager; Branch Manager; Computer Programmer; Credit Manager; Customer Service Rep.; Database Administrator; Database Manager; Financial Analyst; Help-Desk Technician; Intranet Developer; Management Trainee; Marketing Specialist; Sales Manager; Sales Rep.; Secretary; Underwriter/Assistant Underwriter; Webmaster; Website Developer. **Educational backgrounds include:** Accounting; Business Administration; Communications; Computer Science; Economics; Finance; Marketing; MBA; Microsoft Office; Microsoft Word; Spreadsheets. **Benefits:** 401(k); Dental Insurance; Disability Coverage; Employee Discounts; Financial Planning Assistance; Life Insurance; Medical Insurance; Pension Plan; Profit Sharing; Relocation Assistance; Sick Days (6 - 10); Tuition Assistance; Vacation Days. **Special programs:** Internships; Training. **Corporate headquarters location:** This Location. **Other area locations:** Southfield MI. **Other U.S. locations:** Elmhurst IL. **Subsidiaries include:** Old Kent Bank; Old Kent Mortgage Company. **Listed on:** New York Stock Exchange. **Stock exchange symbol:** OK. **CEO:** David Wagner. **Number of employees at this location:** 4,500. **Number of employees nationwide:** 9,000.

OLD NATIONAL BANCORP
420 Main Street, 10th Floor, Evansville IN 47708. 812/464-1434. **Contact:** Human Resources. **World Wide Web address:** http://www.oldnational.com. **Description:** A multibank holding company. The company provides a comprehensive range of financial services including commercial and retail banking, trust, brokerage, correspondent banking, and insurance. **Corporate headquarters location:** This Location. **Annual sales/revenues:** More than $100 million.

ONE VALLEY BANCORP OF WEST VIRGINIA, INC.
P.O. Box 1793, Charleston WV 25326. 304/348-7039. **Contact:** Human Resources. **Description:** A multibank holding company. One Valley Bancorp owns 11 banking subsidiaries operating in 50 cities with full-service banking operations in 79 locations statewide. **Common positions include:** Accountant; Administrator; Bank Officer/Manager; Branch Manager; Credit Manager; Customer Service Rep.; Department Manager; Financial Analyst; General Manager; Human Resources Manager; Management Trainee; Marketing Specialist; Operations/

Production Manager; Public Relations Specialist; Systems Analyst. **Educational backgrounds include:** Accounting; Business Administration; Finance. **Benefits:** Dental Insurance; Disability Coverage; Life Insurance; Medical Insurance; Pension Plan; Savings Plan; Tuition Assistance. **Corporate headquarters location:** This Location.

ONE VALLEY BANK
P.O. Box 340, Lynchburg VA 24505. 804/847-3800. **Physical address:** 2120 Langhorne Road, Lynchburg VA. **Fax:** 804/846-7502. **Contact:** Ann Hicks, Human Resources. **Description:** A bank. **Benefits:** 401(k); ESOP; Incentive Plan; Pension Plan. **Corporate headquarters location:** Charlestown WV. **Listed on:** NASDAQ.

PATRIOT NATIONAL BANK
900 Bedford Street, Stamford CT 06901. 203/324-7500. **Fax:** 203/324-8877. **Contact:** Human Resources. **Description:** A full-service banking institution offering a broad range of consumer and commercial banking services. Founded in 1994. **Corporate headquarters location:** This Location.

PEMCO FINANCIAL SERVICES
P.O. Box 778, Seattle WA 98111. 206/628-4090. **Toll-free phone:** 800/552-7430. **Fax:** 206/628-6072. **Recorded jobline:** 206/628-8740. **Contact:** Human Resources. **E-mail address:** jobs@ pfcenter.com. **World Wide Web address:** http://www.pemco.com. **Description:** Provides insurance, banking, and credit union services through its subsidiaries. Founded in 1936. **NOTE:** Entry-level positions and second and third shifts are offered. **Common positions include:** Adjuster; Claim Rep.; Customer Service Rep.; Sales Rep. **Benefits:** 401(k); Dental Insurance; Disability Coverage; Employee Discounts; Life Insurance; Medical Insurance. **Special programs:** Training. **Corporate headquarters location:** This Location. **Number of employees at this location:** 800. **Number of employees nationwide:** 1,030.

PEOPLE'S BANK
850 Main Street, Bridgeport CT 06604. 203/338-7171. **Contact:** Executive Administrator. **World Wide Web address:** http://www.peoples.com. **Description:** Conducts business through more than 100 banking offices and one loan office in Fairfield, Hartford, Litchfield, Middlesex, New Haven, New London, Tolland and Windham Counties of Connecticut. People's Bank is one of the largest residential mortgage originators in Connecticut. Founded in 1842. **Corporate headquarters location:** This Location. **Parent company:** People's Mutual Holdings.

PLYMOUTH SAVINGS BANK
95 Bedford Street, P.O. Box 1439, Middleborough MA 02346. 508/946-3000. **Contact:** Susan R. White, Senior Vice President of Human Resources. **World Wide Web address:** http://www. plymouthsavings.com. **Description:** A full-service savings bank with 17 branch offices. **Common positions include:** Accountant; Administrative Assistant; Bank Teller; Branch Manager; Commercial Lending Officer; Customer Service Rep.; Financial Analyst; Loan Processor; Mortgage Originator; Underwriter/Assistant Underwriter. **Educational backgrounds include:** Accounting; Business Administration; Computer Science; Finance; Liberal Arts; Marketing; Mathematics. **Benefits:** 401(k); Dental Insurance; Life Insurance; Medical Insurance; Pension Plan; Tuition Assistance. **Corporate headquarters location:** This Location. **Other area locations:** Duxbury MA; Falmouth MA; Lakeville MA; Marion MA;

Mashpee MA; Mattapoisett MA; Raynham MA; Sandwich MA.

PROVIDENT BANK
One East Fourth Street, Mail Stop 550E, Cincinnati OH 45202. 513/579-2205. **Fax:** 513/345-7190. **Recorded jobline:** 513/345-7272. **Contact:** Human Resources. **World Wide Web address:** http://www.provident-bank.com. **Description:** A full-service commercial bank. **NOTE:** This firm does not accept unsolicited resumes. Please call the jobline before applying so that the appropriate job code can be submitted with your resume. **Common positions include:** Accountant; Adjuster; Administrative Manager; Advertising Clerk; Assistant Manager; Attorney; Bank Officer/Manager; Bank Teller; Branch Manager; Clerical Supervisor; Computer Operator; Computer Programmer; Credit Clerk and Authorizer; Credit Manager; Customer Service Representative; Department Manager; Employment Interviewer; Financial Manager; Financial Services Sales Representative; General Manager; Human Resources Manager; Interviewing Clerk; Lender; Management Trainee; Marketing Manager; New Accounts Clerk; Payroll Clerk; Property and Real Estate Manager; Public Relations Specialist; Purchasing Agent/Manager; Receptionist; Securities Sales Representative; Services Sales Rep.; Systems Analyst; Trust Officer; Typist/Word Processor. **Educational backgrounds include:** Accounting; Business Administration; Communications; Computer Science; Economics; Finance; Liberal Arts; Marketing. **Benefits:** Dental Insurance; Disability Coverage; Life Insurance; Medical Insurance; Pension Plan; Profit Sharing; Savings Plan; Tuition Assistance. **Special programs:** Internships. **Corporate headquarters location:** This Location. **Other area locations:** Cleveland OH; Columbus OH; Dayton OH. **Other U.S. locations:** KY. **Parent company:** Provident Financial Group, Inc. **Listed on:** NASDAQ. **Number of employees at this location:** 1,600. **Number of employees nationwide:** 1,700.

PROVIDENT BANK OF MARYLAND
114 East Lexington Street, Baltimore MD 21202. 410/576-2872. **Contact:** Human Resources. **Description:** A full-service, commercial bank. Founded in 1886. **Corporate headquarters location:** This Location. **Parent company:** Provident Bankshares Corporation.

THE PUTNAM TRUST COMPANY
10 Mason Street, Greenwich CT 06830. 203/869-3000. **Contact:** Personnel. **Description:** Operates a full-service bank providing traditional banking and trust services for individuals and businesses. The six branch offices are located in Greenwich. **Corporate headquarters location:** This Location. **Subsidiaries include:** Ten Mason Realty Corporation operates bank properties.

QUEENS COUNTY SAVINGS BANK
38-25 Main Street, Flushing NY 11354. 718/359-6400. **Contact:** Human Resources. **World Wide Web address:** http://www.qcsb.com. **Description:** Operates a mutual savings bank. Founded in 1859. **Corporate headquarters location:** This Location. **Other area locations:** Corona NY; Kew Gardens Hills NY; Little Neck NY; Plainview NY.

REDWOOD BANCORP
735 Montgomery Street, San Francisco CA 94111. 415/788-3700. **Fax:** 415/391-9090. **Contact:** Sue Allen, Assistant Vice President. **Description:** A bank holding company. **Common positions include:** Bank Officer/Manager; Customer Service Rep. **Educational backgrounds include:** Business Administration; Finance. **Benefits:** 401(k); Dental Insurance; Disability Coverage; Life Insurance; Medical Insurance; Profit Sharing. **Corporate headquarters location:** This Location. **Subsidiaries include:** Redwood Bank (also at this location) offers full banking services at four area locations. **Listed on:** Privately held. **Number of employees at this location:** 40.

REGIONS BANK
P.O. Box 11240, New Iberia LA 70562-1240. 337/365-6761. **Contact:** Beth Broussard, Director of Human Resources. **Description:** A full-service bank. **Corporate headquarters location:** This Location.

REGIONS FINANCIAL CORPORATION
417 North 20th Street, Birmingham AL 35203. 205/944-1300. **Recorded jobline:** 888/650-TEAM. **Contact:** Human Resources. **World Wide Web address:** http://www.regionsbank.com. **Description:** A multibank holding company with 700 offices. **NOTE:** Entry-level positions, part-time jobs, and second and third shifts are offered. **Common positions include:** Account Manager; Account Rep.; Accountant; Administrative Assistant; Advertising Clerk; Advertising Executive; Applications Engineer; AS400 Programmer Analyst; Assistant Manager; Attorney; Auditor; Bank Officer/Manager; Branch Manager; Budget Analyst; Chief Financial Officer; Clerical Supervisor; Computer Engineer; Computer Operator; Computer Programmer; Computer Support Technician; Computer Technician; Controller; Customer Service Rep.; Finance Director; Financial Analyst; Graphic Artist; Graphic Designer; Human Resources Manager; Management Trainee; Market Research Analyst; Marketing Manager; Marketing Specialist; Network/Systems Administrator; Operations Manager; Paralegal; Project Manager; Public Relations Specialist; Purchasing Agent/Manager; Quality Control Supervisor; Sales Manager; Sales Representative; Secretary; Software Engineer; SQL Programmer; Systems Analyst; Technical Writer/Editor; Telecommunications Manager; Vice President. **Educational backgrounds include:** Accounting; Business Administration; C/C++; COBOL; Computer Science; Finance; Marketing; Mathematics; MCSE; Microsoft Word; Novell; Visual Basic. **Benefits:** 401(k); Casual Dress - Fridays; Dental Insurance; Disability Coverage; Employee Discounts; Flexible Schedule; Life Insurance; Medical Insurance; Pension Plan; Profit Sharing; Savings Plan; Sick Days (6 - 10); Telecommuting; Tuition Assistance; Vacation Days (6 - 10). **Special programs:** Training; Summer Jobs. **Corporate headquarters location:** This Location. **Other U.S. locations:** AK; FL; GA; LA; SC; TN; TX. **Subsidiaries include:** Regions Bank of Alabama, Regions Bank of Louisiana, Regions Bank of New Roads (Louisiana), Regions Bank of Florida, Regions Bank of Tennessee, Regions Bank of Georgia, First Bank of Rome (Georgia). The primary business of the subsidiaries is commercial banking. The banks also provide services in the fields of mortgage banking, leasing, credit life insurance, securities brokerage, and credit card services. **Listed on:** NASDAQ. **President/CEO:** Carl Jones, Jr.. **Information Systems Manager:** William S. Ringler. **Annual sales/revenues:** More than $100 million. **Number of employees at this location:** 2,000. **Number of employees nationwide:** 15,000.

REPUBLIC SECURITY FINANCIAL CORP.
REPUBLIC SECURITY BANK
450 Australian Avenue, West Palm Beach FL 33401. 561/840-1200. **Contact:** Human Resources. **Description:** Republic Security Financial

Corporation is a bank holding company. **Corporate headquarters location:** This Location. **Subsidiaries include:** Republic Security Bank (also at this location) is a savings and mortgage bank.

RIDGEWOOD SAVINGS BANK
71-02 Forest Avenue, Ridgewood NY 11385. 718/240-4800. **Contact:** Norman McNamee, Vice President. **Description:** A full-service savings bank. **Common positions include:** Accountant/Auditor; Assistant Manager; Bank Officer/Manager; Branch Manager; Credit Manager; Customer Service Rep.; Department Manager; Instructor/Trainer; Insurance Agent/Broker; Management Trainee; Marketing Specialist; Purchasing Agent/Manager; Systems Analyst. **Educational backgrounds include:** Accounting; Business Administration; Computer Science; Finance; Marketing. **Benefits:** Dental Insurance; Disability Coverage; Life Insurance; Medical Insurance; Pension Plan; Profit Sharing; Savings Plan; Tuition Assistance. **Corporate headquarters location:** This Location.

ROCKLAND TRUST COMPANY
288 Union Street, Rockland MA 02370. 781/878-6100. **Fax:** 781/982-6424. **Contact:** Paul McDonough, Employment Manager. **World Wide Web address:** http://www.rockland-trust.com. **Description:** A commercial bank with 44 offices offering retail and commercial banking services, trust and estate planning, investment, and employee benefit services. **NOTE:** Entry-level positions are offered. **Common positions include:** Accountant; Administrative Assistant; Bank Officer/Manager; Branch Manager; Budget Analyst; Controller; Credit Analyst; Customer Service Rep.; Typist/Word Processor. **Educational backgrounds include:** Accounting; Economics; Finance; Liberal Arts; Marketing; Mathematics. **Benefits:** 401(k); Daycare Assistance; Dental Insurance; Disability Coverage; Employee Discounts; Life Insurance; Medical Insurance; Pension Plan; Tuition Assistance. **Special programs:** Training. **Corporate headquarters location:** This Location. **Parent company:** Independent Bank Corp. **Number of employees at this location:** 570.

ROOSEVELT SAVINGS BANK
1122 Franklin Avenue, Garden City NY 11530. 516/742-9300. **Contact:** Human Resources. **Description:** Operates a full-service mutual savings bank. Roosevelt Savings offers a full range of commercial and savings bank services through 12 offices including locations in Brooklyn, Queens, Deer Park, and Nassau County. Founded in 1895. **Corporate headquarters location:** This Location.

RUSHMORE BANK & TRUST
P.O. Box 2290, Rapid City SD 57709-2290. 605/343-9230. **Physical address:** 14 St. Joseph Street, Rapid City SD. **Fax:** 605/343-8418. **Contact:** Peggy Palmer, Vice President of Human Resources. **World Wide Web address:** http://www.rushmorebank.com. **Description:** A bank. **NOTE:** Part-time jobs are offered. **Common positions include:** Accountant; Bank Officer/Manager; Budget Analyst; Chief Financial Officer; Customer Service Rep.; Human Resources Manager; Insurance Agent/Broker; Internet Services Manager; Marketing Manager; Network/Systems Administrator. **Educational backgrounds include:** Accounting; AS400 Certification; Business Administration; Finance; Marketing; Microsoft Word; Public Relations. **Benefits:** 401(k); Casual Dress - Fridays; Dental Insurance; Disability Coverage; Life Insurance; Medical Insurance; Pension Plan; Profit Sharing; Sick Days (1 - 5); Vacation Days (10 - 20). **Special programs:** Summer Jobs.

ST. FRANCIS BANK, F.S.B.
3545 South Kinnickinnic Avenue, St. Francis WI 53235-3700. 414/744-8600. **Contact:** Human Resources. **Description:** A federally chartered savings bank. The company operates 11 full-service and two limited-service retail banking offices in Milwaukee. The company provides a wide range of personal financial services, and is one of the largest thrift companies headquartered in the greater Milwaukee area. The company offers a number of retail banking products and services including savings, checking, and money market accounts; home mortgage loans; home equity and other types of consumer loans; annuities; and related financial services. **Corporate headquarters location:** This Location. **Subsidiaries include:** St. Francis Insurance Corporation offers annuities sold exclusively through licensed agents who are also employees of the bank. St. Francis Development Corporation develops and invests in real estate. St. Francis Equity Properties, Inc. develops, invests in, and operates a multifamily rental property, primarily as a limited partner. S-F Mortgage Corporation is a mortgage company. **Parent company:** St. Francis Capital Corporation. **Listed on:** NASDAQ.

ST. PAUL FEDERAL BANK FOR SAVINGS
6700 West North Avenue, Chicago IL 60707. 773/622-5000. **Contact:** Human Resources. **Description:** A federally-chartered savings and loan bank. **Common positions include:** Accountant/Auditor; Customer Service Rep.; Services Sales Representative. **Educational backgrounds include:** Accounting; Finance. **Benefits:** Dental Insurance; Disability Coverage; Employee Discounts; Life Insurance; Medical Insurance; Pension Plan; Profit Sharing; Savings Plan; Tuition Assistance. **Corporate headquarters location:** This Location.

SLADE'S FERRY BANCORP
SLADE'S FERRY BANK
P.O. Box 390, Somerset MA 02726. 508/675-2121. **Physical address:** 100 Slade's Ferry Avenue, Somerset MA. **Fax:** 508/675-1751. **Contact:** Charlene Jarest, Vice President of Human Resources. **Description:** A holding company. This location also houses a branch of Slade's Ferry Bank. Founded in 1989. **Corporate headquarters location:** This Location. **Other U.S. locations:** Fairhaven MA; Fall River MA; New Bedford MA; Seekonk MA; Swansea MA. **Subsidiaries include:** Slade's Ferry Trust Company. **Listed on:** NASDAQ. **Stock exchange symbol:** SFBC. **President/CEO:** James Carey. **Number of employees nationwide:** 250.

SOUTHERN BANK OF COMMERCE
P.O. Drawer 1269, Eufaula AL 36072-1269. 334/687-3581. **Contact:** Human Resources. **Description:** A bank holding company. **Corporate headquarters location:** This Location. **Number of employees at this location:** 50.

SOUTHTRUST CORPORATION
P.O. Box 2554, Birmingham AL 35290. 205/254-5000. **Contact:** Chuck Whitfield, Human Resources Manager. **World Wide Web address:** http://www.southtrust.com. **Description:** A bank holding company. **Corporate headquarters location:** This Location. **Other U.S. locations:** FL; GA; MS; NC; SC; TN; TX. **Subsidiaries include:** SouthTrust Bank, N.A., is a regional bank operating through more than 600 offices and more than 700 ATMs in the Southeastern region; SouthTrust Securities Inc.; SouthTrust Mortgage Corporation; SouthTrust Data Services. **Listed on:** NASDAQ. **Chairman/CEO/President:** Wallace D. Malone, Jr. **Annual sales/revenues:** More than $100 million. **Number of employees nationwide:** 12,500.

SOUTHWEST BANK
2301 South Kings Highway Boulevard, St. Louis MO 63110. 314/776-5200. **Contact:** Human Resources. **Description:** A bank. **Common positions include:** Customer Service Rep.; Management Trainee. **Educational backgrounds include:** Accounting; Business Administration; Communications; Economics; Finance. **Benefits:** Dental Insurance; Disability Coverage; Life Insurance; Medical Insurance; Pension Plan; Savings Plan; Tuition Assistance. **Special programs:** Internships. **Corporate headquarters location:** This Location. **Number of employees at this location:** 190.

SOUTHWEST NATIONAL CORPORATION SOUTHWEST BANK
111 South Main Street, P.O. Box 760, Greensburg PA 15601. 724/834-2310. **Contact:** Human Resources. **Description:** A commercial bank holding company. **Corporate headquarters location:** This Location. **Subsidiaries include:** Southwest Bank (also at this location) is a commercial bank.

SOVEREIGN BANCORP, INC.
P.O. Box 12646, Reading PA 19612. 610/320-8400. **Physical address:** 1130 Berkshire Boulevard, Wyomissing PA 19610. **Fax:** 610/376-8379. **Contact:** Recruiting. **World Wide Web address:** http://www.sovereignbank.com. **Description:** A $20 billion thrift holding company. **NOTE:** Entry-level positions and second and third shifts are offered. **Common positions include:** Accountant; Administrative Assistant; Attorney; Auditor; Bank Officer/Manager; Branch Manager; Budget Analyst; Chief Financial Officer; Computer Engineer; Controller; Customer Service Rep.; Database Manager; Editorial Assistant; Finance Director; Financial Analyst; Fund Manager; Graphic Artist; Graphic Designer; Human Resources Manager; Internet Services Manager; Management Trainee; Market Research Analyst; Marketing Manager; Marketing Specialist; Network/Systems Administrator; Paralegal; Purchasing Agent/Manager; Secretary; Systems Analyst; Systems Manager; Webmaster. **Educational backgrounds include:** Accounting; Business Administration; Economics; Finance; Marketing; Microsoft Word; Novell; QuarkXPress; Spreadsheets. **Benefits:** 401(k); Dental Insurance; Disability Coverage; Employee Discounts; Financial Planning Assistance; Flexible Schedule; Life Insurance; Medical Insurance; Pension Plan; Profit Sharing; Public Transit Available; Sick Days; Tuition Assistance; Vacation Pay. **Special programs:** Internships; Training; Summer Jobs. **Corporate headquarters location:** This Location. **Other U.S. locations:** DE; NJ. **Subsidiaries include:** Main Line Bank; Sovereign Bank, FSB operates more than 300 branches in Pennsylvania, Delaware, and New Jersey. **Listed on:** NASDAQ. **Number of employees nationwide:** 4,500.

STANDARD CHARTERED BANK
7 World Trade Center, New York NY 10048. 212/667-0700. **Contact:** Mary Casey, Vice President of Human Resources. **Description:** This location houses executive offices. Overall, Standard Chartered Bank is an international bank. **Common positions include:** Accountant/Auditor; Bank Officer/Manager; Credit Manager; Customer Service Rep.; Financial Analyst; General Manager; Human Resources Manager; Systems Analyst. **Educational backgrounds include:** Accounting; Business Administration; Communications; Finance; Marketing. **Benefits:** 401(k); Dental Insurance; Disability Coverage; Life Insurance; Medical Insurance; Pension Plan; Savings Plan;

Tuition Assistance. **Corporate headquarters location:** This Location. **Other U.S. locations:** Los Angeles CA; Miami FL; Atlanta GA; Chicago IL; Houston TX.

STERLING NATIONAL BANK & TRUST CO.
355 Lexington Avenue, New York NY 10017. 212/490-9809. **Contact:** Human Resources. **Description:** A full-service commercial bank offering a complete range of corporate and individual services. **Corporate headquarters location:** This Location.

STERLING SAVINGS ASSOCIATION
111 North Wall Street, Spokane WA 99201. 509/458-2711. **Fax:** 509/358-6161. **Contact:** Human Resources. **Description:** Provides full-service banking services including deposits and originating consumer, business banking, commercial real estate, and residential construction loans. **Subsidiaries include:** Action Mortgage Company operates residential loan production offices. Harbor Financial Services provides nonbank investments including mutual funds, variable annuities, and tax-deferred annuities to clients through regional representatives. INTERVEST-Mortgage Investment Company provides commercial real estate lending. **Number of employees nationwide:** 860.

SUMMIT BANK
301 Carnegie Center, Princeton NJ 08540. 609/987-3200. **Contact:** James N. Ferrier, Staffing Manager. **World Wide Web address:** http://www.summitbank.com. **Description:** A bank. **Corporate headquarters location:** This Location.
Other U.S. locations:
- 55 Main Street, New Milford CT 06776-2400. 860/210-0391.

SUNTRUST BANK, ATLANTA, N.A.
SUNTRUST BANKS, INC.
P.O. Box 4418, Atlanta GA 30302. 404/588-7119. **Fax:** 404/827-6934. **Contact:** Human Resources. **World Wide Web address:** http://www.suntrust.com. **Description:** A full-service bank. **Common positions include:** Accountant/Auditor; Adjuster; Bank Officer/Manager; Branch Manager; Brokerage Clerk; Clerical Supervisor; Computer Programmer; Credit Manager; Customer Service Rep.; Draftsperson; Financial Analyst; Financial Services Sales Representative; Human Resources Manager; Human Service Worker; Management Trainee; Operations/Production Manager; Property and Real Estate Manager; Securities Sales Rep.; Systems Analyst. **Educational backgrounds include:** Accounting; Business Administration; Computer Science; Finance. **Benefits:** 401(k); Dental Insurance; Disability Coverage; Employee Discounts; Life Insurance; Medical Insurance; Pension Plan; Profit Sharing; Tuition Assistance. **Corporate headquarters location:** This Location. **Parent company:** SunTrust Banks, Inc. (also at this location) is a financial services company. The company's primary businesses include traditional deposit and credit services, as well as trust and investment services. Additionally, SunTrust Banks, Inc. provides corporate finance, mortgage banking, factoring, credit cards, discount brokerage, credit-related insurance, and data processing and information services. **Listed on:** New York Stock Exchange. **Number of employees at this location:** 5,000. **Number of employees nationwide:** 19,530.

SUNTRUST BANKS, INC.
1001 Semmes Avenue, Richmond VA 23261. 804/319-1798. **Contact:** Human Resources. **World Wide Web address:** http://www.suntrust.com. **Description:** SunTrust Banks is a bank holding

company with 1,100 subsidiary banking offices. **Subsidiaries include:** SunTrust Bank.

SYNOVUS FINANCIAL CORPORATION
P.O. Box 120, Columbus GA 31902. 706/649-4545. **Fax:** 706/649-5797. **Recorded jobline:** 706/649-4758. **Contact:** Mrs. Danni Harris, Director of Employment Services. **E-mail address:** careers@synovus.com. **World Wide Web address:** http://www.synovus.com. **Description:** A multiservice financial company. Synovus Financial owns 80 percent of Total Systems Services, Inc. (also at this location, 706/649-2310, http://www.totalsystem.com), one of the largest credit, debit, commercial, and private label processing companies in the world. Synovus Financial Corporation also operates 38 banks in the Southeast. **NOTE:** All applicants should contact the jobline for available positions. Entry-level positions and second and third shifts are offered. **Common positions include:** Administrative Assistant; Assistant Manager; Auditor; Bank Officer/Manager; Blue-Collar Worker Supervisor; Branch Manager; Computer Operator; Computer Programmer; Customer Service Rep.; Editor; Financial Analyst; Management Trainee; Marketing Specialist; Project Manager; Sales Rep.; Software Engineer; Systems Analyst; Technical Writer/Editor. **Educational backgrounds include:** Accounting; Business Administration; Communications; Computer Science; Finance; M.I.S.; Marketing; Software Development. **Benefits:** 401(k); Dental Insurance; Disability Coverage; Employee Discounts; Fitness Program; Life Insurance; Medical Insurance; Pension Plan; Profit Sharing; Tuition Assistance. **Special programs:** Internships; Training; Summer Jobs. **Corporate headquarters location:** This Location. **Other U.S. locations:** AL; FL; SC. **Subsidiaries include:** Columbus Bank & Trust Company; Synovus Securities, Inc. is a full-service brokerage firm; Synovus Trust Company is one of the Southeast's largest providers of trust services; Synovus Mortgage Corporation offers mortgage servicing throughout the Southeast; Synovus Leasing Company offers equipment leasing; Synovus Insurance Services offers insurance services; Synovus Technologies Inc. **President/CEO/Owner:** James H. Blanchard. **Number of employees at this location:** 8,100.

TCF BANK
401 East Liberty Street, Ann Arbor MI 48104. 734/769-8300. **Contact:** Human Resources. **World Wide Web address:** http://www.tcfbank.com. **Description:** A bank holding company with 63 branches in Michigan. **Parent company:** TCF Financial Corporation (MN).

TCF FINANCIAL CORPORATION
TCF BANK
801 Marquette Avenue South, Minneapolis MN 55402. 612/661-8450. **Fax:** 612/661-8277. **Contact:** Human Resources. **World Wide Web address:** http://www.tcfbank.com. **Description:** A bank holding company. **Common positions include:** Accountant/Auditor; Branch Manager; Clerical Supervisor; Computer Programmer; Customer Service Rep.; Financial Services Sales Rep.; Insurance Agent/Broker; Securities Sales Rep.; Services Sales Rep.; Systems Analyst; Underwriter/Assistant Underwriter. **Educational backgrounds include:** Accounting; Business Administration; Communications; Computer Science; Finance; Liberal Arts. **Benefits:** 401(k); Daycare Assistance; Dental Insurance; Disability Coverage; Life Insurance; Medical Insurance; Pension Plan; Tuition Assistance. **Corporate headquarters location:** This Location. **Other U.S. locations:** Oakbrook IL; Ann Arbor MI; Pontiac MI; Milwaukee WI. **Subsidiaries include:** TCF Bank (also at this location) is a thrift and banking institution that operates 342 retail branches in Colorado, Illinois, Minnesota, Wisconsin, and Michigan. Other subsidiaries provide consumer lending, insurance, mutual funds, title insurance, and mortgage banking products and services. **Listed on:** New York Stock Exchange. **Number of employees at this location:** 2,500. **Number of employees nationwide:** 3,500.

TUCKER FEDERAL BANK
P.O. Box 86, Tucker GA 30084-0086. 770/908-6600. **Fax:** 770/908-6655. **Recorded jobline:** 770/908-6608. **Contact:** Human Resources. **Description:** A bank. **NOTE:** Entry-level positions are offered. **Common positions include:** Bank Teller. **Benefits:** 401(k); Dental Insurance; Disability Coverage; Employee Discounts; Life Insurance; Medical Insurance; Pension Plan; Profit Sharing; Tuition Assistance. **Corporate headquarters location:** This Location. **Parent company:** Eagle Bancshares. **Number of employees at this location:** 300.

U.S. BANCORP
U.S. BANK
601 Second Avenue South, Minneapolis MN 55402. 612/973-1111. **Contact:** Robert Sayer, Human Resources Director. **World Wide Web address:** http://www.usbank.com. **Description:** U.S. Bancorp is one of the largest bank holding companies in the Northwest. **Corporate headquarters location:** This Location. **Subsidiaries include:** U.S. Bank (also at this location).

UNION BANK & TRUST COMPANY
100 Broadway, Denver CO 80203. 303/744-3221. **Contact:** Patricia Ludwig, Director of Human Resources. **Description:** Offers a wide range of banking and other financial services. **Corporate headquarters location:** This Location.

UNION BANK OF CALIFORNIA, N.A.
400 California Street, 10th Floor, San Francisco CA 94104. 415/765-2147. **Fax:** 415/765-2202. **Contact:** Corporate Staffing. **World Wide Web address:** http://www.uboc.com. **Description:** One of the largest, full-service commercial banks providing a broad mix of financial services including retail and small business banking, middle market banking, personal and business trust services, real estate finance, corporate banking, trade finance (with a focus on the Pacific Rim), and financial management services. **Common positions include:** Branch Manager; Credit Manager; Customer Service Rep.; Financial Analyst; Financial Services Sales Rep.; Management Trainee; Paralegal; Securities Sales Rep. **Educational backgrounds include:** Economics; Finance; Marketing. **Benefits:** 401(k); Dental Insurance; Disability Coverage; Employee Discounts; Life Insurance; Medical Insurance; Pension Plan; Profit Sharing; Savings Plan; Tuition Assistance. **Subsidiaries include:** U.S. Investment Services, Inc. **Parent company:** UnionBanCal Corporation (San Francisco CA). **Number of employees at this location:** 3,500.

UNITED NATIONAL BANK
P.O. Box 6000, Bridgewater NJ 08807. 908/429-2200. **Physical address:** 1130 Route 22 East, Bridgewater NJ. **Contact:** Human Resources. **World Wide Web address:** http://www.united-national.com. **Description:** Operates a full-service commercial bank offering a wide range of traditional banking, trust, and other financial services. **Corporate headquarters location:** This Location.

UNITED SAVINGS AND LOAN BANK
601 South Jackson Street, Seattle WA 98104. 206/624-7581. **Contact:** Personnel. **Description:** A full-service bank. **Common positions include:** Customer Service Rep.; Management Trainee. **Educational backgrounds include:** Accounting; Finance. **Benefits:** Dental Insurance; Life Insurance; Medical Insurance; Savings Plan. **Corporate headquarters location:** This Location. **Number of employees at this location:** 50.

UNITED SECURITY BANCORPORATION
9506 North Newport Highway, Spokane WA 99218. 509/467-6949. **Contact:** Human Resources. **Description:** A bank holding company. **Corporate headquarters location:** This Location. **Subsidiaries include:** United Security Bank; Home Security Bank.

UNIVEST CORPORATION
14 North Main Street, Souderton PA 18964. 215/721-2400. **Fax:** 215/721-2427. **Contact:** Lewis R. Keel, Human Resources Officer. **World Wide Web address:** http://www.univest-corp.com. **Description:** A bank holding company. **Common positions include:** Account Manager; Account Rep.; Accountant; Administrative Assistant; Administrative Manager; Advertising Clerk; Advertising Executive; AS400 Programmer Analyst; Assistant Manager; Auditor; Bank Officer/ Manager; Chief Financial Officer; Clerical Supervisor; Computer Operator; Computer Programmer; Computer Support Technician; Controller; Credit Manager; Customer Service Rep.; Economist; Event Planner; Finance Director; Financial Analyst; General Manager; Human Resources Manager; Management Analyst/ Consultant; Management Trainee; Marketing Manager; Marketing Specialist; MIS Specialist; Operations Manager; Public Relations Specialist; Sales Executive; Sales Manager; Sales Rep.; Secretary. **Educational backgrounds include:** Accounting; AS400 Certification; Business Administration; C/C++; Communications; Computer Science; Economics; Finance; HTML; Liberal Arts; Marketing; Mathematics; MBA; Microsoft Office; Microsoft Word; Public Relations; Spreadsheets. **Benefits:** 401(k); Dental Insurance; Disability Coverage; Employee Discounts; Life Insurance; Medical Insurance; Pension Plan; Savings Plan; Sick Days (6 - 10); Tuition Assistance; Vacation Days (10 - 20). **Special programs:** Summer Jobs. **Subsidiaries include:** Union National Bank; Pennview Savings Bank; Fin-Plan Group. **Number of employees at this location:** 455.

VALLEY NATIONAL BANK
1445 Valley Road, Wayne NJ 07470. 973/696-4020. **Contact:** Peter Verbout, Director of Human Resources. **Description:** Operates a commercial bank offering a wide range of traditional banking services. **Common positions include:** Bank Officer/Manager; Branch Manager; Computer Programmer; Credit Manager; Customer Service Rep.; Department Manager; Financial Analyst; General Manager; Human Resources Manager; Management Trainee. **Educational backgrounds include:** Accounting; Business Administration; Computer Science; Economics; Finance; Mathematics. **Benefits:** Dental Insurance; Disability Coverage; Life Insurance; Medical Insurance; Pension Plan; Profit Sharing; Tuition Assistance. **Corporate headquarters location:** This Location. **Parent company:** Valley National Bancorp.

WACHOVIA CORPORATION
100 North Main Street, NC37172, Winston-Salem NC 27101. 336/770-5000. **Fax:** 336/732-5226.

Recorded jobline: 888/WC-EMPLOYS. **Contact:** Patti L. Tuten, Employment Manager. **E-mail address:** apply.careers@wachovia.com. **World Wide Web address:** http://www.wachovia.com. **Description:** A holding company whose member companies provide a variety of banking and financial services. **NOTE:** Entry-level positions, part-time jobs, and second and third shifts are offered. **Common positions include:** Account Manager; Account Representative; Accountant; Administrative Assistant; Applications Engineer; AS400 Programmer Analyst; Auditor; Bank Officer/ Manager; Branch Manager; Budget Analyst; Computer Engineer; Computer Operator; Computer Programmer; Computer Support Technician; Computer Technician; Content Developer; Credit Manager; Customer Service Rep.; Database Administrator; Database Manager; Desktop Publishing Specialist; Financial Analyst; Fund Manager; Human Resources Manager; Internet Services Manager; Management Trainee; Market Research Analyst; Marketing Specialist; MIS Specialist; Network/Systems Administrator; Operations Manager; Paralegal; Project Manager; Sales Manager; Sales Rep.; Secretary; Software Engineer; SQL Programmer; Systems Analyst; Systems Manager; Technical Writer/Editor; Webmaster. **Educational backgrounds include:** Accounting; AS400 Certification; Business Administration; Communications; Computer Science; Economics; Finance; HTML; Internet; Java; Liberal Arts; Marketing; Master of Arts; Mathematics; MCSE; Microsoft Word; Novell; Public Relations; Software Development; Software Tech. Support; Spreadsheets; Visual Basic. **Benefits:** 401(k); Dental Insurance; Disability Coverage; Employee Discounts; Financial Planning Assistance; Flexible Schedule; Life Insurance; Medical Insurance; Pension Plan; Profit Sharing; Savings Plan; Tuition Assistance. **Special programs:** Internships; Training; Co-ops; Summer Jobs. **Corporate headquarters location:** This Location. **Other U.S. locations:** GA. **Subsidiaries include:** Wachovia Bank, N.A. has 700 banking branches in Florida, Georgia, North Carolina, South Carolina, and Virginia. Wachovia Corporate Services Inc. provides business consulting services to corporate and institutional clients. Wachovia Investments provides investment services to individuals. Wachovia Operational Services Corporation provides payment processing services for client companies. Wachovia also provides trust banking, credit card operations, deposit banking, and mortgage banking services. **Listed on:** New York Stock Exchange. **Stock exchange symbol:** WB. **Number of employees at this location:** 3,500.

WASHINGTON FEDERAL SAVINGS & LOAN ASSOCIATION
425 Pike Street, Seattle WA 98101. 206/624-7930. **Contact:** Human Resources. **Description:** Offers a full range of banking services through 85 branch offices. Subsidiaries of the company are also involved in real estate development and insurance brokerage operations. **Corporate headquarters location:** This Location. **Other U.S. locations:** AZ; ID; OR; UT. **Listed on:** NASDAQ.

WASHINGTON MUTUAL
17877 Von Karman Avenue, Irvine CA 92614. 949/252-7000. **Fax:** 949/833-4104. **Contact:** Human Resources. **Description:** A bank offering a full range of products and services throughout California including 24-hour convenience checking and mortgage loans. **Common positions include:** Financial Analyst; Securities Sales Rep.; Systems Analyst. **Educational backgrounds include:** Accounting; Finance. **Benefits:** 401(k); Dental Insurance; Disability Coverage; Employee

Discounts; Life Insurance; Medical Insurance; Tuition Assistance. **Corporate headquarters location:** This Location. **Subsidiaries include:** ASB Financial Services. **Listed on:** Privately held. **Number of employees at this location:** 300.

WASHINGTON MUTUAL SAVINGS BANK

P.O. Box 834, Seattle WA 98111. 206/461-6400. **Recorded jobline:** 800/952-0787. **Contact:** Human Resources Staffing. **World Wide Web address:** http://www.wamu.com. **Description:** One of the largest independently-owned and locally-managed banks in Washington state. Washington Mutual offers a wide array of financial products and services through the bank and its affiliates including traditional and innovative deposit accounts and loans, annuities, mutual funds, full-service securities brokerage, and travel services. **Common positions include:** Accountant; Adjuster; Administrative Manager; Bank Officer/Manager; Branch Manager; Brokerage Clerk; Budget Analyst; Clerical Supervisor; Computer Programmer; Credit Manager; Customer Service Rep.; Economist; Insurance Agent/Broker; Management Analyst/ Consultant; Management Trainee; Operations/ Production Manager; Property and Real Estate Manager; Securities Sales Rep.; Services Sales Rep.; Systems Analyst; Travel Agent; Underwriter/ Assistant Underwriter. **Educational backgrounds include:** Accounting; Business Administration; Computer Science; Finance; Liberal Arts. **Benefits:** 401(k); Dental Insurance; Disability Coverage; Employee Discounts; Life Insurance; Medical Insurance; Pension Plan; Profit Sharing; Savings Plan; Tuition Assistance. **Special programs:** Internships. **Corporate headquarters location:** This Location. **Other U.S. locations:** ID; OR; UT. **Subsidiaries include:** Composite Research & Management Company; Murphey Favre; Mutual Travel; WM Insurance Services; WM Life Insurance. **Listed on:** American Stock Exchange; NASDAQ; New York Stock Exchange. **Annual sales/revenues:** More than $100 million. **Number of employees at this location:** 2,000. **Number of employees nationwide:** 30,000.

WASHINGTON TRUST BANCORP, INC.

23 Broad Street, Westerly RI 02891. 401/348-1200. **Contact:** Vernon Bliven, Human Resources Director. **Description:** The holding company of The Washington Trust Company. **Subsidiaries include:** The Washington Trust Company a bank that offers a wide variety of financial services including home equity loans, credit cards, commercial mortgages, trust services, and is toll-free telephone banking service. Eleven branch offices are located in southern Rhode Island and southeastern Connecticut. **Listed on:** NASDAQ.

WEBSTER BANK

Webster Plaza, Waterbury CT 06702. 203/753-2921. **Contact:** Human Resources Department. **World Wide Web address:** http://www.websterbank.com. **Description:** Webster Bank is primarily involved in attracting deposits from the general public and investing these funds in mortgage loans for the purchase, construction, and refinancing of one- to four-family homes. Webster Bank also provides commercial banking services to businesses. **Benefits:** 401(k); Pension Plan. **Corporate headquarters location:** This Location.

WELLS FARGO

420 Montgomery Street, 11th Floor, San Francisco CA 94104. 415/396-3849. **Contact:** Recruitment Services. **World Wide Web address:** http://www.wellsfargo.com. **Description:** A bank providing a wide variety of financial services. Founded in 1852. **Company slogan:** Fast then. Fast now. **Common positions include:** Account Manager; Account Representative; Accountant/Auditor; Administrative Assistant; Applications Engineer; Assistant Manager; Auditor; Bank Officer/Manager; Branch Manager; Computer Programmer; Credit Manager; Customer Service Rep.; Database Administrator; Financial Analyst; Fund Manager; General Manager; Human Resources Manager; Industrial Engineer; Management Trainee; Market Research Analyst; Marketing Manager; Marketing Specialist; MIS Specialist; Network/Systems Administrator; Operations/Production Manager; Project Manager; Sales Manager; Sales Representative; Secretary; Services Sales Rep.; Software Engineer; Systems Analyst; Webmaster. **Educational backgrounds include:** Accounting; Business Administration; C/C++; Computer Science; Economics; Engineering; Finance; HTML; Internet; Java; Marketing; Mathematics; Microsoft Word; Novell; Spreadsheets. **Benefits:** 401(k); Dental Insurance; Disability Coverage; Employee Discounts; Life Insurance; Medical Insurance; Pension Plan; Tuition Assistance. **Special programs:** Internships; Training; Summer Jobs. **Internship information:** The company offers summer internships only. **Corporate headquarters location:** This Location. **Other U.S. locations:** Nationwide. **International locations:** Asia; Cambodia; Caribbean; South America. **Parent company:** Wells Fargo & Company is one of the largest bank holding companies in the United States with 5,000 branch locations. **Listed on:** Frankfurt Stock Exchange; London Stock Exchange; New York Stock Exchange. **President/CEO:** Dick Kovacevich. **Number of employees nationwide:** 103,050.

WEST COAST BANK

P.O. Box 428, Salem OR 97308. 503/315-2836. **Contact:** Human Resources. **World Wide Web address:** http://www.westcoastbancorp.com. **Description:** An association of community banks and closely related businesses. In total, West Coast Bank operates 41 branch locations. **Corporate headquarters location:** This Location. **Parent company:** West Coast Bancorp. **Number of employees at this location:** 135.

WESTAMERICA BANK

540 Wall Street, Auburn CA 95603. 530/823-1144. **Contact:** Human Resources. **Description:** Offers a wide range of general commercial banking services including money market accounts, NOW accounts, checking accounts, savings accounts, and certificates of deposit. The bank also offers night depository and bank-by-mail services. The bank sells traveler's checks, cashier's checks, and money orders. In addition, it provides bank note and collection services. The bank engages in a full complement of lending activities including commercial, consumer/installment, and real estate loans, with particular emphasis on short- and medium-term loans. **Corporate headquarters location:** This Location.

WESTERN SECURITY BANK

P.O. Box 4547, Missoula MT 59806. 406/721-3700. **Fax:** 406/543-1409. **Contact:** Personnel Manager. **World Wide Web address:** http://www.westernsecuritybank.com. **Description:** A full-service bank. **Common positions include:** Accountant; Auditor; Bank Officer/Manager; Branch Manager; Chief Financial Officer; Computer Technician; Controller; Customer Service Rep.; Human Resources Manager; Network Engineer; Network/Systems Administrator; Operations Manager. **Educational backgrounds include:** Accounting; Business Administration; Finance. **Other area locations:** Billings MT; Bozeman MT; Conrad MT; East Helena MT; Great Falls MT;

Hamilton MT; Hardin MT; Helena MT; Lewistown MT; Miles City MT. **Listed on:** NASDAQ. **Stock exchange symbol:** WSTR. **Number of employees at this location:** 350.

WILMINGTON SAVINGS FUND SOCIETY
838 Market Street, Wilmington DE 19801. 302/571-7223. **Contact:** Human Resources. **World Wide Web address:** http://www.wsfsbank.com. **Description:** A savings bank. **Common positions include:** Accountant/Auditor; Administrator; Bank Officer/Manager; Branch Manager; Credit Manager; Customer Service Rep.; Department Manager; General Manager; Purchasing Agent/Manager; Services Sales Rep. **Educational backgrounds include:** Accounting; Business Administration; Communications; Economics; Liberal Arts. **Benefits:** 401(k); Daycare Assistance; Dental Insurance; Disability Coverage; Life Insurance; Medical Insurance; Tuition Assistance. **Corporate headquarters location:** This Location. **Parent company:** WSFS Financial Corporation. **Listed on:** NASDAQ. **Number of employees nationwide:** 430.

WORLD SAVINGS & LOAN ASSOCIATION
1901 Harrison Street, Oakland CA 94612. 510/446-6000. **Contact:** Human Resources. **Description:** One of the largest savings and loan associations in the United States, with more than 50 locations nationwide. **Common positions include:** Accountant; Administrator; Advertising Clerk; Bank Officer/Manager; Branch Manager; Computer Programmer; Credit Manager; Customer Service Rep.; Department Manager; Financial Analyst; General Manager; Human Resources Manager; Insurance Agent/Broker; Management Trainee; Marketing Specialist; Purchasing Agent/Manager; Systems Analyst; Technical Writer/Editor; Transportation/Traffic Specialist. **Educational backgrounds include:** Accounting; Business Administration; Computer Science; Economics; Finance; Marketing. **Benefits:** Dental Insurance; Disability Coverage; Employee Discounts; Life Insurance; Medical Insurance; Pension Plan; Savings Plan; Tuition Assistance. **Corporate headquarters location:** This Location. **Other area locations:** Sacramento CA; San Francisco CA; Walnut Creek CA. **Other U.S. locations:** Nationwide. **Parent company:** Golden West Financial (also at this location). **Listed on:** New York Stock Exchange.

YORK FEDERAL SAVINGS & LOAN ASSOCIATION
101 South George Street, York PA 17401. 717/846-8777. **Toll-free phone:** 800/222-YFED. **Fax:** 717/845-4124. **Contact:** Cindy Foor, Employment and Recruiting Coordinator. **E-mail address:** cfloor@yorkfed.com. **World Wide Web address:** http://www.yorkfed.com. **Description:** A savings and loan association. **Common positions include:** Accountant/Auditor; Bank Officer/Manager; Branch Manager; Customer Service Rep.; Human Resources Manager; Underwriter/Assistant Underwriter. **Educational backgrounds include:** Accounting; Business Administration; Finance. **Benefits:** Dental Insurance; Disability Coverage; Employee Discounts; ESOP; Life Insurance; Medical Insurance; Pension Plan. **Corporate headquarters location:** This Location. **Other U.S. locations:** MD. **Parent company:** York Financial Corporation. **Number of employees at this location:** 270. **Number of employees nationwide:** 480.

ZIONS FIRST NATIONAL BANK
One South Main Street, Suite 800, Salt Lake City UT 84111. 801/524-4690. **Contact:** Director of Human Resources. **Description:** A national bank engaged in a wide range of commercial banking and trust activities including checking and savings accounts, loan services, credit services, trust services, and other traditional banking services. Zions First National Bank operates more than 70 banking offices. **Common positions include:** Accountant; Administrator; Advertising Clerk; Attorney; Bank Officer/Manager; Blue-Collar Worker Supervisor; Branch Manager; Buyer; Claim Rep.; Computer Programmer; Credit Manager; Customer Service Rep.; Department Manager; Economist; Editor; Financial Analyst; Human Resources Manager; Insurance Agent/Broker; Marketing Specialist; Operations/Production Manager; Public Relations Specialist; Reporter; Services Sales Rep.; Systems Analyst; Underwriter/Assistant Underwriter. **Educational backgrounds include:** Accounting; Business Administration; Communications; Computer Science; Economics; Finance; Liberal Arts; Marketing; Mathematics. **Benefits:** Dental Insurance; Disability Coverage; Employee Discounts; Life Insurance; Medical Insurance; Pension Plan; Savings Plan; Stock Option; Tuition Assistance. **Corporate headquarters location:** This Location. **Parent company:** Zions Bancorporation.

For more information on career opportunities in the banking/savings and loans industry:

Associations

AMERICA'S COMMUNITY BANKERS
900 19th Street NW, Suite 400, Washington DC 20006. 202/857-3100. World Wide Web address: http://www.acbankers.org. A trade association representing the expanded thrift industry. Membership is limited to institutions.

AMERICAN BANKERS ASSOCIATION
1120 Connecticut Avenue NW, Washington DC 20036. 202/663-5221. World Wide Web address: http://www.aba.com. Provides banking education and training services, sponsors industry programs and conventions, and publishes articles, newsletters, and the *ABA Service Member Directory.*

Career Fairs

CAREER FAIRS INTERNATIONAL
World Wide Web address: http://www.career-fairs.com. Organizes career fairs in the fields of accounting, banking, finance, and insurance.

Directories

AMERICAN FINANCIAL DIRECTORY
Thomson Financial Publications, 4709 West Golf Road, Skokie IL 60076. Toll-free phone: 800/321-3373.

AMERICAN SAVINGS DIRECTORY
Thomson Financial Publications, 4709 West Golf Road, Skokie IL 60076. Toll-free phone: 800/321-3373.

MOODY'S BANK AND FINANCE MANUAL
Moody's Investors Service, Inc., 99 Church Street, 1st Floor, New York NY 10007-2701. 212/553-0300. World Wide Web address: http://www.moodys.com.

RANKING THE BANKS
American Banker, Inc., One State Street Plaza, New York NY 10004. 212/803-6700. World Wide Web address: http://www.americanbanker.com.

Magazines

ABA BANKING JOURNAL
American Bankers Association, 1120 Connecticut Avenue NW, Washington DC 20036. 202/663-5221. World Wide Web address: http://www.aba.com.

BANKERS MAGAZINE
Faulkner & Gray, 11 Penn Plaza, New York NY 10001. Toll-free phone: 800/200-8963.

BANKING STRATEGIES
Bank Administrators Institute, One North Franklin, Suite 1000, Chicago IL 60606. Toll-free phone: 800/224-9889. World Wide Web address: http://www.bai.org.

JOURNAL OF LENDING AND CREDIT RISK MANAGEMENT
Robert Morris Associates, 1650 Market Street, Suite 2300, Philadelphia PA 19103. 215/446-4000.

Online Services

AMERICAN BANKER ONLINE'S CAREERZONE
World Wide Web address: http://www.americanbanker.com. Provides listings of financial job openings, updated daily.

JOBS FOR BANKERS
World Wide Web address: http://www.bankjobs.com. This site provides access to a database of over 15,000 banking-related job openings. Jobs for Bankers is run by Careers, Inc. This Website also includes a resume database.

JOBS IN COMMERCIAL BANKING
World Wide Web address: http://www.cob.ohio-state.edu/dept/fin/jobs/commbank.htm. Provides information and resources for jobseekers looking to work in the field of commercial banking.

Biotechnology, Pharmaceuticals, and Scientific R&D

You can expect to find the following types of companies in this chapter:
Clinical Labs • Lab Equipment Manufacturers
Pharmaceutical Manufacturers and Distributors

Some helpful information: *The average salary for entry-level biological scientists with bachelor's degrees depends largely on the industry in which they work, but on average they earn approximately $25,000 - $30,000 (scientists with advanced degrees can earn more). Laboratory technicians earn between $20,000 and $40,000 on average. Experienced scientists, such as pharmacologists, may earn more, particularly if they produce for a large company. Research scientists generally earn less than those in the private sector.*

ABS GLOBAL
1525 River Road, De Forest WI 53532. 608/846-3721. **Toll-free phone:** 800/356-5331. **Fax:** 608/846-6442. **Contact:** Human Resources. **World Wide Web address:** http://www.absglobal.com. **Description:** Manufactures artificial insemination products for cattle. The company is a world leader in bovine DNA, in vitro fertilization, and cell cloning research.

ARUP LABORATORIES
500 Chipeta Way, Salt Lake City UT 84108. **Toll-free phone:** 800/242-2787. **Fax:** 801/584-5218. **Contact:** Recruitment. **World Wide Web address:** http://www.arup-lab.com. **Description:** Performs esoteric and general laboratory testing for hospitals, reference laboratories, and independent laboratory clients. ARUP Laboratories provides a broad range of tests including analytical determinations on biological fluids and tissues. **Common positions include:** Biological Scientist; Chemist; Clinical Lab Technician; Computer Programmer; Customer Service Rep.; Human Resources Manager; Licensed Practical Nurse; Science Technologist; Systems Analyst. **Educational backgrounds include:** Chemistry; Computer Science; Marketing; Medical Technology. **Benefits:** 401(k); Dental Insurance; Disability Coverage; Employee Discounts; Life Insurance; Medical Insurance; Pension Plan; Profit Sharing; Tuition Assistance. **Corporate headquarters location:** This Location. **Operations at this facility include:** Administration; Research and Development; Sales; Service. **Number of employees at this location:** 700.

ABAXIS, INC.
1320 Chesapeake Terrace, Sunnyvale CA 94089. 408/734-0200. **Contact:** Human Resources. **World Wide Web address:** http://www.abaxis.com. **Description:** A research and development firm. Abaxis, Inc. is focused on the commercialization of the Piccolo System, which consists of a small, whole-blood analyzer and blood chemistry reagent rotors. The company developed Primary Health Profile, a nine-test reagent rotor marketed to veterinarians. Founded in 1989. **Corporate headquarters location:** This Location. **Number of employees at this location:** 75.

ABBOTT LABORATORIES
100 Abbott Park Road, Abbott Park IL 60064-3500. 847/937-6100. **Contact:** Staffing Department. **World Wide Web address:** http://www. abbott.com. **Description:** Manufactures pharmaceuticals and liquid nutrition products including Similac, Pedialyte, and Ensure. The company also manufactures anesthetics, blood pressure monitors, and intravenous systems. **Common positions include:** Attorney; Biological Scientist; Biomedical Engineer; Chemical Engineer; Chemist; Civil Engineer; Computer Programmer; Electrical/Electronics Engineer; Financial Analyst; Human Resources Manager; Mechanical Engineer; Systems Analyst. **Educational backgrounds include:** Accounting; Biology; Business Administration; Chemistry; Computer Science; Engineering; Industrial Relations; Personnel Relations. **Benefits:** Dental Insurance; Disability Coverage; Employee Discounts; Life Insurance; Medical Insurance; Pension Plan; Profit Sharing; Savings Plan; Tuition Assistance. **Corporate headquarters location:** This Location. **Listed on:** New York Stock Exchange. **Number of employees worldwide:** 52,000.

ACCUTECH
2641 La Mirada Drive, Vista CA 92083. 760/602-9130. **Contact:** Human Resources. **World Wide Web address:** http://www.accutechllc.com. **Description:** Develops, manufactures, and markets disposable diagnostic tests. **Corporate headquarters location:** This Location.

ACCUWEATHER, INC.
385 Science Park Road, State College PA 16803. 814/237-0309. **Fax:** 814/235-8599. **Contact:** Richard Cooper, Human Resources Manager. **World Wide Web address:** http://www. accuweather.com. **Description:** One of the world's leading commercial weather services providing information and products to customers nationwide. Founded in 1962. **NOTE:** Entry-level positions and second and third shifts are offered. **Common positions include:** Administrative Assistant; Computer Programmer; Customer Service Representative; Editor; Graphic Artist; Graphic Designer; Human Resources Manager; Meteorologist; Radio/TV Announcer/Broadcaster; Sales Representative; Secretary; Software Engineer; Systems Analyst; Systems Manager; Technical Writer/Editor; Webmaster. **Educational backgrounds include:** Accounting; Business Administration; Computer Science; Engineering; Meteorology. **Benefits:** 401(k); Disability Coverage; Employee Discounts; Flexible Schedule; Life Insurance; Medical Insurance; Profit Sharing; Public Transit Available. **Special programs:** Internships. **Corporate headquarters location:** This Location. **Subsidiaries include:** Perfect Date. **Number of employees at this location:** 320.

ADVANCED POLYMER SYSTEMS INC.
123 Saginaw Drive, Redwood City CA 94063. 650/366-2626. **Contact:** Shelly Howell, Human Resources Administrator. **World Wide Web address:** http://www.advancedpolymer.com. **Description:** A leader in polymer-based delivery systems and related technologies for use in pharmaceuticals, over-the-counter drugs, toiletries, and specialty applications. **Common positions include:** Chemical Engineer; Chemist. **Educational backgrounds include:** Chemistry. **Benefits:** 401(k); Dental Insurance; Disability Coverage; Life Insurance; Medical Insurance; Tuition Assistance. **Corporate headquarters location:** This Location. **Other U.S. locations:** Greenwich CT; Lafayette LA. **Operations at this facility include:** Administration; Research and Development; Sales. **Listed on:** NASDAQ. **Stock exchange symbol:** APOS. **President/CEO:** John J. Meakem, Jr. **Number of employees at this location:** 45.

ADVANCED TISSUE SCIENCES
10933 North Torrey Pines Road, La Jolla CA 92037-1005. 858/713-7300. **Fax:** 858/713-7400. **Contact:** Recruiter. **World Wide Web address:** http://www.advancedtissue.com. **Description:** Develops products for tissue and organ replacement by simulating the natural growth conditions that exist in the human body. Advanced Tissue Sciences is able to grow cells that develop and assemble into functional tissue masses. **Corporate headquarters location:** This Location. **Number of employees at this location:** 145.

AGOURON PHARMACEUTICALS, INC.
10357 North Torrey Pines Road, La Jolla CA 92037. 858/622-3000. **Contact:** Human Resources. **World Wide Web address:** http://www. agouron.com. **Description:** Researches and develops human pharmaceuticals utilizing protein structure-based drug design. The company has developed engineering technology that permits the design of new molecules that are active against cancer, viruses, and inflammatory disease. Founded in 1984. **NOTE:** In February 2000, Pfizer Inc. announced plans to acquire Warner Lambert Company. The new company will be named Pfizer Inc. and will be headquartered in New York. Please contact this location for more information. **Corporate headquarters location:** This Location. **Parent company:** Warner-Lambert Company (Morris Plains NJ). **Number of employees at this location:** 220.

ALKERMES, INC.
64 Sidney Street, Cambridge MA 02139. 617/494-0171. **Contact:** Peter Maguire, Director of Human Resources. **World Wide Web address:** http://www. alkermes.com. **Description:** A pharmaceutical company that produces drug delivery systems for pharmaceutical agents. Alkermes reproduces four proprietary delivery systems: Cereport blood-brain permeabilizers; ProLease and Medisorb injectable sustained-release systems; RingCap and Dose Sipping oral delivery systems; and AIR pulmonary delivery systems. **Corporate headquarters location:** This Location.

ALLERGAN, INC.
2525 DuPont Drive, P.O. Box 19534, Irvine CA 92623-9534. 714/246-4500. **Contact:** Human Resources. **World Wide Web address:** http://www. allergan.com. **Description:** Develops, manufactures, and distributes prescription and nonprescription pharmaceutical products in the specialty fields of ophthalmology and dermatology. Allergan, Inc.'s products are designed to treat eye and skin disorders, and to aid contact lens wearers. **Common positions include:** Accountant/Auditor; Biological Scientist; Biomedical Engineer; Buyer; Chemist; Computer Programmer; Customer Service Representative; Financial Analyst; Manufacturer's/Wholesaler's Sales Rep.; Operations/Production Manager; Quality Control Supervisor. **Educational backgrounds include:** Biology; Business Administration; Chemistry; Computer Science; Finance; Marketing. **Benefits:** Dental Insurance; Disability Coverage; EAP; Employee Discounts; Life Insurance; Medical Insurance; Pension Plan; Profit Sharing; Savings Plan; Tuition Assistance. **Corporate headquarters location:** This Location. **Operations at this facility include:** Administration; Divisional Headquarters; Manufacturing; Research and Development; Sales.

ALPHARMA INC.
One Executive Drive, Fort Lee NJ 07024. 201/947-7774. **Fax:** 201/947-6145. **Contact:** Nancy Ryan, Vice President of Human Resources. **World Wide Web address:** http://www.alpharma.com. **Description:** A multinational pharmaceutical company which develops, manufactures, and markets specialty generic and proprietary human pharmaceuticals and animal health products. The U.S. Pharmaceuticals Division is a market leader in liquid pharmaceuticals and a prescription market leader in creams and ointments. The International Pharmaceuticals Division manufactures generic pharmaceuticals and OTC products. Other divisions include the Animal Health Division, which manufactures and markets antibiotics and other feed additives for the poultry and swine industries; the Aquatic Animal Health Division, which serves the aquaculture industry and is a manufacturer and marketer of vaccines for farmed fish; and the Fine Chemicals Division, which is a basic producer of specialty bulk antibiotics. **Corporate headquarters location:** This Location. **Listed on:** NASDAQ. **Stock exchange symbol:** ALO.

ALPINE HEALTH INDUSTRIES
1525 West Business Park Drive, Orem UT 84058. 801/225-5525x123. **Toll-free phone:** 800/572-5076. **Fax:** 801/225-0956. **Contact:** Gary Dastrup, Director. **World Wide Web address:** http://www. alpinehi.com. **Description:** A contract manufacturer for the pharmaceutical industry. The company provides convenience packet filling, substantial mixing capacity, encapsulating and tableting, and multiple packaging services. **NOTE:** Part-time jobs and second and third shifts are offered. **Common positions include:** Account Manager; Accountant; Administrative Assistant; Chemist; Controller; Customer Service Rep.; Graphic Designer; Human Resources Manager; Marketing Manager; Marketing Specialist; Production Manager; Purchasing Agent/Manager; Quality Control Supervisor; Sales Executive; Sales Rep.; Systems Manager; Vice President of Operations. **Educational backgrounds include:** Accounting; Marketing; Microsoft Word. **Benefits:** 401(k); Casual Dress - Fridays; Dental Insurance; Disability Coverage; Employee Discounts; Life Insurance; Medical Insurance; Sick Days (1 - 5); Tuition Assistance; Vacation Days (1 - 5). **Special programs:** Summer Jobs. **Office hours:** Monday - Friday, 8:00 a.m. - 5:00 p.m. **Corporate headquarters location:** Texarkana TX. **Parent company:** Humco Holding Group, International. **Listed on:** Privately held. **President:** Derek Hall. **Annual sales/revenues:** $11 - $20 million. **Number of employees at this location:** 100. **Number of employees nationwide:** 225.

ALRA LABORATORIES, INC.
3850 Clearview Court, Gurnee IL 60031. 847/244-9440. **Toll-free phone:** 800/248-ARLA. **Fax:** 847/244-9464. **Contact:** Human Resources. **Description:** Researches, develops, and

manufactures generic pharmaceuticals. Products include eryzole, gelpirin, multivitamins, and methalgen cream. Founded in 1982. **Corporate headquarters location:** This Location.

ALZA CORPORATION
P.O. Box 7210, Mountain View CA 94039. 650/494-5000. **Physical address:** 1900 Charlestown Road, Mountain View CA 94043. **Fax:** 650/494-5656. **Recorded jobline:** 650/494-5319. **Contact:** Darlene Markovitch, Human Resources Director. **World Wide Web address:** http://www.alza.com. **Description:** Develops, manufactures, and markets therapeutic systems for both humans and animals. Products include transdermal drug delivery patches and OROS drug delivery technology which are used for the treatment of angina, chronic pain, respiratory diseases, motion sickness, periodontal disease, and nicotine withdrawal. Founded in 1968. **Common positions include:** Accountant/Auditor; Attorney; Biological Scientist; Biomedical Engineer; Buyer; Chemical Engineer; Chemist; Clinical Lab Technician; Computer Programmer; Designer; Economist; Financial Analyst; Industrial Engineer; Industrial Production Manager; Insurance Agent/Broker; Librarian; Library Technician; Materials Engineer; Mechanical Engineer; Physician Assistant; Public Relations Specialist; Quality Control Supervisor; Registered Nurse; Statistician. **Educational backgrounds include:** Biology; Chemistry; Engineering; Health Care. **Benefits:** 401(k); Dental Insurance; Disability Coverage; Employee Discounts; Life Insurance; Medical Insurance; Pension Plan; Profit Sharing; Tuition Assistance. **Special programs:** Internships. **Corporate headquarters location:** This Location. **Other U.S. locations:** Vacaville CA; Minneapolis MN. **Operations at this facility include:** Administration; Divisional Headquarters; Manufacturing; Research and Development. **Listed on:** New York Stock Exchange. **Number of employees at this location:** 1,000. **Number of employees nationwide:** 1,370.

AMBI, INC.
4 Manhattanville Road, Purchase NY 10577. 914/701-4500. **Fax:** 914/701-0860. **Contact:** Nancy Hutter, Human Resources Director. **World Wide Web address:** http://www.ambiinc.com. **Description:** Develops and markets nutrition products. The company focuses on products with medical value for consumers concerned with cardiovascular health and diabetes. Founded in 1982. **Common positions include:** Chemist; Customer Service Representative; Food Scientist/Technologist; Marketing Manager; Nutritionist; Product Manager. **Educational backgrounds include:** Biology; Business Administration; Chemistry; Marketing. **Benefits:** 401(k); Dental Insurance; Disability Coverage; Life Insurance; Medical Insurance; Pension Plan; Public Transit Available; Stock Option. **Corporate headquarters location:** This Location. **Listed on:** NASDAQ.

AMERICAN AG-TEC INTERNATIONAL, LTD.
P.O. Box 569, Delavan WI 53115-0569. 262/728-8815. **Fax:** 262/728-8131. **Contact:** Human Resources. **E-mail address:** info@ag-tec.com. **World Wide Web address:** http://www.ag-tec.com. **Description:** Works within the agriculture industry, focusing primarily on genetic development and biotechnology, technology transfers, and seeds and seed production.

AMERICAN HOME PRODUCTS CORP.
5 Giralda Farms, Madison NJ 07940. 973/660-5000. **Contact:** Human Resources. **World Wide Web address:** http://www.ahp.com. **Description:** Manufactures and markets prescription drugs and medical supplies, packaged medicines, food products, household products, and housewares. Each division operates through one or more of American Home Products Corporation's subsidiaries. Prescription Drugs and Medical Supplies operates through: Wyeth-Ayerst Laboratories (produces ethical pharmaceuticals, biologicals, nutritional products, over-the-counter antacids, vitamins, and sunburn remedies); Fort Dodge Animal Health (veterinary pharmaceuticals and biologicals); Sherwood Medical (medical devices, diagnostic instruments, test kits, and bacteria identification systems); and Corometrics Medical Systems (medical electronic instrumentation for obstetrics and neonatology). The Packaged Medicines segment operates through Whitehall-Robins Healthcare (produces analgesics, cold remedies, and other packaged medicines). The Food Products segment operates through American Home Foods (canned pasta, canned vegetables, specialty foods, mustard, and popcorn). The Household Products and Housewares segment operates through: Boyle-Midway (cleaners, insecticides, air fresheners, waxes, polishes, and other items for home, appliance, and apparel care); Dupli-Color Products (touch-up, refinishing, and other car care and shop-use products); Ekco Products (food containers, commercial baking pans, industrial coatings, food-handling systems, foilware, and plasticware); Ekco Housewares (cookware, cutlery, kitchen tools, tableware and accessories, and padlocks); and Prestige Group (cookware, cutlery, kitchen tools, carpet sweepers, and pressure cookers). **Corporate headquarters location:** This Location. **Number of employees worldwide:** 53,000.

AMERICAN STANDARDS TESTING BUREAU
40 Water Street, New York NY 10004. 212/943-3160. **Fax:** 212/825-2250. **Contact:** John Zimmerman, Director, Professional Staffing. **Description:** Offers lab consulting and forensic services to the government and various industries. The company specializes in biotechnology, environmental sciences, forensics, engineering, failure analysis, and products liability. **Common positions include:** Administrative Manager; Aerospace Engineer; Agricultural Engineer; Architect; Attorney; Biomedical Engineer; Chemical Engineer; Chemist; Civil Engineer; Clerical Supervisor; Construction Contractor; Credit Manager; Editor; Electrical/Electronics Engineer; Environmental Engineer; Financial Analyst; Food Scientist/Technologist; General Manager; Industrial Engineer; Management Analyst/Consultant; Management Trainee; Manufacturer's/Wholesaler's Sales Rep.; Materials Engineer; Mechanical Engineer; Metallurgical Engineer; MIS Specialist; Paralegal; Petroleum Engineer; Public Relations Specialist; Science Technologist; Services Sales Representative; Structural Engineer; Technical Writer/Editor; Typist/Word Processor; Video Production Coordinator. **Educational backgrounds include:** Accounting; Biology; Business Administration; Chemistry; Communications; Computer Science; Economics; Engineering; Finance; Geology; Marketing; Mathematics; Physics. **Benefits:** Dental Insurance; Life Insurance; Medical Insurance; Tuition Assistance. **Corporate headquarters location:** This Location. **Other U.S. locations:** Nationwide. **Listed on:** Privately held. **Annual sales/revenues:** More than $100 million. **Number of employees at this location:** 470.

AMERISOURCE HEALTH CORPORATION
300 Chesterfield Parkway, Malvern PA 19355. 610/296-4480. **Fax:** 610/647-0141. **Contact:** Lisa Hickman, Human Resources Manager. **World Wide Web address:** http://www.amerisource.com.

Description: A large pharmaceutical distribution company serving hospitals, nursing homes, clinics, and pharmacy chains. The company also provides health and beauty aids, general merchandise, inventory control, emergency delivery, and marketing and promotional services. **Corporate headquarters location:** This Location. **Listed on:** New York Stock Exchange. **Stock exchange symbol:** AAS. **Annual sales/revenues:** More than $100 million.

AMGEN INC.
One Amgen Center Drive, Thousand Oaks CA 91320-1789. 805/447-1000. **Fax:** 805/499-3507. **Recorded jobline:** 800/446-4007. **Contact:** Human Resources. **World Wide Web address:** http://www.amgen.com. **Description:** Researches, develops, manufactures, and markets human therapeutics based on advanced cellular and molecular biology. Products include EPOGEN (Epoetin Alfa), which counteracts the symptoms of renal failure experienced by kidney dialysis patients; INFERGEN (Interferon alfacon-1); and NEUPOGEN (Filgrastim), which reduces the incidence of infection in cancer patients who receive chemotherapy. When used in conjunction with chemotherapy, NEUPOGEN selectively stimulates the bone marrow to produce neutrophil cells, accelerating the return of the patient's antibacterial defense system. **Common positions include:** Accountant/Auditor; Attorney; Biological Scientist; Buyer; Chemical Engineer; Chemist; Computer Programmer; Customer Service Representative; Financial Analyst; Systems Analyst. **Educational backgrounds include:** Biology; Business Administration; Finance; Law/Pre-Law; Marketing. **Special programs:** Internships. **Corporate headquarters location:** This Location. **Other U.S. locations:** Nationwide. **Listed on:** NASDAQ. **Stock exchange symbol:** AMGN. **Annual sales/revenues:** More than $100 million. **Number of employees at this location:** 2,280. **Number of employees worldwide:** 5,600.

AMYLIN PHARMACEUTICALS, INC.
9373 Towne Centre Drive, Suite 250, San Diego CA 92121. 858/552-2200. **Fax:** 858/552-2212. **Contact:** Human Resources. **World Wide Web address:** http://www.amylin.com. **Description:** Researches the hormone amylin, which provides drug strategies for treating juvenile- and maturity-onset diabetes, insulin resistance syndrome, hypertension, and obesity. **Corporate headquarters location:** This Location. **Number of employees at this location:** 100.

ANESTA CORPORATION
4745 Wiley Post Way, Plaza 6, Suite 650, Salt Lake City UT 84116. 801/595-1405. **Contact:** Human Resources. **World Wide Web address:** http://www.anesta.com. **Description:** A biotechnology company specializing in the manufacture of pain relievers and cancer treatments. **Corporate headquarters location:** This Location.

ANIKA THERAPEUTICS
236 West Cummings Park, Woburn MA 01801. 781/932-6616. **Fax:** 781/935-4120. **Contact:** Personnel. **World Wide Web address:** http://www.anikatherapeutics.com. **Description:** Develops and commercializes hyaluronic acid (HA)-based products for use in medical and therapeutic applications. Products include AMVISC, a high molecular weight HA product that is used as a viscoelastic agent in ophthalmic surgical procedures including cataract extraction and intraocular lens implantation; HYVISC, a high molecular weight HA product used for the treatment of joint dysfunction in horses due to non-infectious synovitis associated with equine osteoarthritis; ORTHOVISC, a high molecular weight, injectable HA product for the symptomatic treatment of osteoarthritis of the knee; and INCERT, a chemically-modified, cross-linked form of HA designed to prevent the formation of post-surgical wound adhesions. Founded in 1993. **NOTE:** Entry-level positions and second and third shifts are offered. **Common positions include:** Accountant; Biochemist; Biological Scientist; Chemical Engineer; Chemist; Clinical Lab Technician; Secretary. **Educational backgrounds include:** Accounting; Biology; Business Administration; Chemistry; Engineering. **Benefits:** 401(k); Dental Insurance; Disability Coverage; Life Insurance; Medical Insurance. **Special programs:** Internships. **Corporate headquarters location:** This Location. **Listed on:** NASDAQ. **Stock exchange symbol:** ANIK. **President/CEO:** J. Melville Engle.. **Annual sales/revenues:** $21 - $50 million. **Number of employees at this location:** 55.

APPLIED SCIENCE LABORATORIES
175 Middlesex Turnpike, Bedford MA 01730. 781/275-4000. **Contact:** Human Resources. **E-mail address:** asl@a-s-l.com. **World Wide Web address:** http://www.a-s-l.com. **Description:** A research, development, and manufacturing facility concentrating on eye tracking technology and systems. **Common positions include:** Computer Programmer; Electrical/Electronics Engineer. **Educational backgrounds include:** Computer Science; Engineering; Optometry. **Benefits:** Disability Coverage; Life Insurance; Medical Insurance; Profit Sharing; Tuition Assistance. **Corporate headquarters location:** This Location. **Parent company:** Applied Science Group, Inc. **Operations at this facility include:** Administration; Manufacturing; Research and Development; Sales.

ARETE ASSOCIATES
P.O. Box 6024, Sherman Oaks CA 91413. 818/501-2880x432. **Fax:** 818/501-2905. **Contact:** Nancy Balbuena, Assistant Manager of Human Resources. **E-mail address:** personnel@arete.com. **World Wide Web address:** http://www.arete.com. **Description:** Provides research and development in the area of signal processing as it applies to atmospheric, oceanographic, and related areas. The company is involved in the mathematical modeling of physical processes, signal and image processing, remote sensing and phenomenology, electro-optics, lidar, radar, and acoustics. Founded in 1976. **NOTE:** U.S. citizenship, a drug test, and a security investigation are required to meet position eligibility. Entry-level positions are offered. **Common positions include:** Electrical/Electronics Engineer; Geologist/Geophysicist; Mathematician; Physicist; Researcher; Scientist; Systems Analyst. **Educational backgrounds include:** Engineering; Mathematics; Physics. **Benefits:** 401(k); Dental Insurance; Disability Coverage; Fitness Program; Life Insurance; Medical Insurance; Pension Plan; Tuition Assistance; Vision Insurance. **Corporate headquarters location:** This Location. **Other U.S. locations:** Nationwide. **Operations at this facility include:** Administration; Research and Development. **Listed on:** Privately held. **Number of employees at this location:** 95. **Number of employees nationwide:** 125.

ARIAD PHARMACEUTICALS, INC.
26 Landsdowne Street, Cambridge MA 02139. 617/494-0400. **Contact:** Human Resources. **World Wide Web address:** http://www.ariad.com. **Description:** Develops pharmaceuticals for the purpose of fighting diseases. The company focuses on developing treatments for four distinct areas:

allergy/asthma, gene therapy, immune-related disorders, and osteoporosis. Founded in 1991. **Corporate headquarters location:** This Location.

AVANT IMMUNOTHERAPEUTICS, INC.
119 Fourth Avenue, Needham MA 02194-2725. 781/433-0771. **Fax:** 781/433-0262. **Contact:** Human Resources. **E-mail address:** info@ avantimmune.com. **World Wide Web address:** http://www.avantimmune.com. **Description:** A biopharmaceutical company specializing in the understanding and treatment of diseases caused by misregulation of the body's natural defense systems. **Benefits:** 401(k); Incentive Plan; Stock Option. **Corporate headquarters location:** This Location. **Listed on:** NASDAQ.

AVENTIS PHARMACEUTICALS
500 Arcola Road, Collegeville PA 19426. 610/454-8000. **Contact:** Human Resources. **Description:** A major manufacturer of a wide variety of prescription and over-the-counter drugs. **Special programs:** Internships. **Corporate headquarters location:** This Location.

AXYS PHARMACEUTICALS
180 Kimball Way, South San Francisco CA 94080. 650/829-1000. **Contact:** Human Resources. **E-mail address:** hr@axyspharm.com. **World Wide Web address:** http://www.axyspharm.com. **Description:** Engaged in the discovery and development of innovative drugs, with a focus in oncology. **Corporate headquarters location:** This Location. **Listed on:** NASDAQ. **Stock exchange symbol:** AXPH.

BASF CORPORATION
KNOLL PHARMACEUTICALS
3000 Continental Drive North, Mount Olive NJ 07828-1234. 973/426-2600. **Contact:** Robert Stein, Director of Human Resources. **World Wide Web address:** http://www.basf.com. **Description:** This location serves as the United States headquarters and houses management offices and the pharmaceutical division, Knoll Pharmaceuticals. Overall, BASF Corporation is an international chemical products organization, doing business in five operating groups: Chemicals; Coatings and Colorants; Consumer Products and Life Sciences; Fiber Products; and Polymers. **Common positions include:** Accountant/Auditor; Chemical Engineer; Computer Programmer; Financial Analyst; Marketing Specialist. **Benefits:** Dental Insurance; Disability Coverage; Life Insurance; Medical Insurance; Pension Plan; Savings Plan; Tuition Assistance. **Corporate headquarters location:** This Location. **Operations at this facility include:** Administration; Divisional Headquarters; Sales. **Number of employees worldwide:** 125,000.

BD BIOSCIENCES
2350 Qume Drive, San Jose CA 95131. 408/432-9475. **Contact:** Tim Outman, Recruiter. **Word Wide Web address:** http://www.bdbiosciences.com. **Description:** BD Biosciences serves laboratories worldwide with research and clinical applications in immunology, hematology, and cell biology. The company also provides products and instruments for infectious disease diagnosis, which screen for microbial presence; grow and identify organisms; and test for antibiotic susceptibility. Products for the industrial microbiology market are used for food testing, environmental monitoring, and biopharmaceutical fermentation media. Tissue culture products help advance the understanding of diseases and potential therapies. **Common positions include:** Accountant; Biological Scientist; Biomedical Engineer; Budget Analyst; Buyer; Chemist; Computer Programmer;

Customer Service Rep.; Designer; Draftsperson; Electrical/Electronics Engineer; Financial Analyst; Industrial Engineer; Mechanical Engineer; Purchasing Agent/Manager; Quality Control Supervisor; Scientist; Software Engineer; Statistician; Systems Analyst; Technical Writer/ Editor. **Educational backgrounds include:** Biology; Chemistry; Computer Science; Engineering. **Benefits:** 401(k); Daycare Assistance; Dental Insurance; Disability Coverage; Education Assistance; Life Insurance; Medical Insurance; Pension Plan; Profit Sharing; Savings Plan. **Corporate headquarters location:** Franklin Lakes NJ. **Other U.S. locations:** Mansfield MA. **Operations at this facility include:** Manufacturing; Research and Development; Sales; Service. **Listed on:** New York Stock Exchange. **Number of employees at this location:** 500. **Number of employees nationwide:** 600.

BATTELLE
505 King Avenue, Columbus OH 43201-2693. 614/424-6322. **Contact:** Employment Advisor. **E-mail address:** employment@battelle.org. **World Wide Web address:** http://www. battelle.org/careers. **Description:** An international technology organization that serves industry and government by generating, applying, and commercializing technology through research and development. With a wide range of scientific and technical capabilities, Battelle serves clients worldwide. **NOTE:** Resumes are only accepted for advertised positions and a specific job reference number must accompany every resume. Available positions are listed on the company's Website. Interested jobseekers are encouraged to apply using the online form available on Battelle's Website. **Common positions include:** Biological Scientist; Chemical Engineer; Chemist; Computer Programmer; Electrical/Electronics Engineer; Management Analyst/Consultant; Mechanical Engineer; Software Engineer; Statistician; Systems Analyst; Transportation/Traffic Specialist. **Educational backgrounds include:** Biology; Chemistry; Computer Science; Engineering. **Benefits:** 401(k); Dental Insurance; Disability Coverage; Life Insurance; Medical Insurance; Pension Plan; Tuition Assistance. **Special programs:** Internships. **Corporate headquarters location:** This Location. **Operations at this facility include:** Administration; Research and Development. **Number of employees at this location:** 2,000. **Number of employees nationwide:** 8,000.

BAYER DIAGNOSTICS
63 North Street, Medfield MA 02052. 508/359-7711. **Contact:** Human Resources Department. **World Wide Web address:** http://www. bayerds.com. **Description:** Develops and manufactures medical diagnostic systems. **Corporate headquarters location:** This Location. **International locations:** Worldwide.

BECKMAN COULTER, INC.
4300 North Harbor Boulevard, Fullerton CA 92834. 714/993-8584. **Contact:** Employment. **World Wide Web address:** http://www.beckman.com. **Description:** Sells and services a diverse range of scientific instruments, reagents, and related equipment. Products include DNA synthesizers, robotic workstations, centrifuges, electrophoresis systems, detection and measurement equipment, data processing software, and specialty chemical and automated general chemical systems. Many of the company's products are used in research, development, and diagnostic analysis. **NOTE:** Second and third shifts are offered. **Common positions include:** Accountant; Administrative

Assistant; Applications Engineer; Biochemist; Biological Scientist; Chemical Engineer; Computer Programmer; Computer Support Technician; Customer Service Rep.; Database Administrator; Database Manager; Financial Analyst; Librarian; Marketing Specialist; Mechanical Engineer; MIS Specialist; Network/Systems Administrator; Sales Representative; Secretary; Software Engineer. **Educational backgrounds include:** Accounting; Biology; Business Administration; C/C++; Chemistry; Communications; Computer Science; Engineering; Finance; HTML; Marketing; Microsoft Word; Software Development; Spreadsheets. **Benefits:** 401(k); Dental Insurance; Disability Coverage; Employee Discounts; Life Insurance; Medical Insurance; Pension Plan; Savings Plan; Tuition Assistance. **Corporate headquarters location:** This Location. **Parent company:** Beckman Instruments, Inc. **Operations at this facility include:** Administration; Manufacturing; Research and Development. **Listed on:** New York Stock Exchange. **CEO:** Jack Wareham. **Annual sales/revenues:** More than $100 million. **Number of employees worldwide:** 11,000.

BERGEN BRUNSWIG CORPORATION
4000 Metropolitan Drive, Orange CA 92868. 714/385-4000. **Fax:** 714/385-8877. **Recorded jobline:** 714/385-HIRE. **Contact:** Personnel. **E-mail address:** bbcjobs@deltanet.com. **World Wide Web address:** http://www.bergenbrunswig.com. **Description:** One of the nation's leading distributors of pharmaceuticals and medical-surgical supplies. Bergen Brunswig Corporation is a *Fortune* 500 company. **Common positions include:** Accountant; Administrative Assistant; Budget Analyst; Buyer; Computer Programmer; Consultant; Data Entry Clerk; Financial Analyst; Marketing Specialist; Project Manager; Secretary; Systems Analyst; Technical Writer/Editor; Telecommunications Manager; Typist/Word Processor. **Educational backgrounds include:** Accounting; Business Administration; Communications; Computer Science; Finance; Marketing. **Benefits:** 401(k); Daycare Assistance; Dental Insurance; Disability Coverage; Financial Planning Assistance; Life Insurance; Medical Insurance; On-Site Exercise Facility; Public Transit Available; Savings Plan; Tuition Assistance. **Office hours:** Monday - Friday, 7:30 a.m. - 4:30 p.m. **Corporate headquarters location:** This Location. **Other U.S. locations:** Nationwide. **Subsidiaries include:** Bergen Brunswig Drug Company; Bergen Brunswig Medical Corporation; Bergen Brunswig Specialty Company. **Listed on:** New York Stock Exchange. **Stock exchange symbol:** BBC. **CEO:** Donald R. Roden. **Annual sales/revenues:** More than $100 million. **Number of employees nationwide:** 5,400.

BERLEX LABORATORIES, INC.
300 Fairfield Road, Wayne NJ 07470. 973/694-4100. **Contact:** Human Resources. **World Wide Web address:** http://www.berlex.com. **Description:** Researches, manufactures, and markets ethical pharmaceutical products in the fields of cardiovascular medicine, endocrinology and fertility control, diagnostic imaging, oncology, and central nervous system disorders. Berlex Laboratories has three strategic units: Berlex Drug Development & Technology, Oncology/Central Nervous System, and Berlex Biosciences. The company also owns Berlex Drug Development and Technology and operates a national sales force. The sales force, which is divided into three geographic regions, markets the complete line of Berlex products including BETASERON, which is used to treat multiple sclerosis. **Corporate headquarters location:** This Location. **Parent company:** Schering AG (Germany).

BINDLEY WESTERN INDUSTRIES, INC.
8909 Purdue Road, Indianapolis IN 46268. 317/704-4000. **Contact:** Thomas J. Weakley, Human Resources Director. **World Wide Web address:** http://www.bindley.com. **Description:** Distributes prescription pharmaceuticals to drug stores, hospitals, clinics, and other health care providers. The company also distributes non-pharmaceutical products including health and beauty aids. **Corporate headquarters location:** This Location.

BIO-RAD LABORATORIES
1000 Alfred Noble Drive, Hercules CA 94547. 510/724-7000. **Contact:** Human Resources. **World Wide Web address:** http://www.bio-rad.com. **Description:** Develops, manufactures, and markets diagnostic test kits, specialty chemicals, and related equipment used for separating complex mixtures. Bio-Rad Laboratories also produces analytical instruments used to detect and measure chemical components in minute quantities, as well as products for electron microscopy. **NOTE:** For positions in the Diagnostics division, send resumes to Bio-Rad Laboratories, Human Resources Department, 4000 Alfred Noble Drive, Hercules CA 94547. For positions in the Life Sciences division, send resumes to Bio-Rad Laboratories, Human Resources Department, 2000 Alfred Noble Drive, Hercules CA 94547. **Common positions include:** Accountant/Auditor; Advertising Clerk; Biological Scientist; Biomedical Engineer; Buyer; Chemical Engineer; Chemist; Computer Programmer; Customer Service Representative; Department Manager; Electrical/Electronics Engineer; Financial Analyst; General Manager; Human Resources Manager; Mechanical Engineer; Medical Records Technician; Medical Technologist; Operations/Production Manager; Purchasing Agent/Manager; Quality Control Supervisor; Systems Analyst; Transportation/Traffic Specialist. **Educational backgrounds include:** Accounting; Biology; Business Administration; Chemistry; Computer Science; Engineering; Finance; Marketing; Mathematics. **Benefits:** Dental Insurance; Disability Coverage; Life Insurance; Medical Insurance; Pension Plan; Profit Sharing; Savings Plan; Tuition Assistance. **Corporate headquarters location:** This Location. **Operations at this facility include:** Administration; Manufacturing; Research and Development; Service. **Listed on:** American Stock Exchange.

BIO-REFERENCE LABORATORIES
481B Edward H. Ross Drive, Elmwood Park NJ 07407. 201/791-2600. **Contact:** Human Resources. **Description:** Operates a clinical laboratory serving the metropolitan New York area. Bio-Reference offers a list of chemical diagnostic tests including blood and urine analysis, blood chemistry, hematology services, serology, radioimmunological analysis, toxicology (including drug screening), Pap smears, tissue pathology (biopsies), and other tissue analyses. Bio-Reference markets its services directly to physicians, hospitals, clinics, and other health facilities. **Corporate headquarters location:** This Location.

BIO-TECHNOLOGY GENERAL CORP.
70 Wood Avenue South, Iselin NJ 08830. 732/632-8800. **Contact:** Human Resources Department. **World Wide Web address:** http://www.btgc.com. **Description:** Manufactures, and markets novel therapeutic products. The company specializes in pre-clinical studies, research and development, and biotechnology products. **Corporate headquarters location:** This Location. **International locations:** Rehovot, Israel. **Listed on:** NASDAQ. **Stock exchange symbol:** BTGC.

BIOGEN CORPORATION

14 Cambridge Center, Cambridge MA 02142. 617/252-9200. **Fax:** 617/679-2546. **Contact:** Personnel. **World Wide Web address:** http://www. biogen.com. **Description:** Develops and markets drugs produced by genetic engineering. Biogen Corporation's products include alpha interferon, sold by Schering-Plough, and Hepatitis B vaccines, sold by Merck and SmithKline Beecham. **Common positions include:** Biological Scientist; Biomedical Engineer; Chemist; Statistician. **Educational backgrounds include:** Biology; Chemistry. **Benefits:** 401(k); Dental Insurance; Disability Coverage; Employee Discounts; Life Insurance; Medical Insurance; Pension Plan; Savings Plan; Tuition Assistance. **Corporate headquarters location:** This Location. **Operations at this facility include:** Administration; Manufacturing; Research and Development. **Listed on:** NASDAQ. **Stock exchange symbol:** BGEN. **Number of employees nationwide:** 430.

BIORELIANCE

14920 Broschart Road, Rockville MD 20850-3349. 301/738-1000. **Contact:** Human Resources. **World Wide Web address:** http://www.bioreliance.com. **Description:** A contract service organization that provides development and nonclinical services to biotechnology and pharmaceutical companies. BioReliance provides development, testing, and manufacturing services that cover the product from preclinical development to production. **Common positions include:** Animal Handler; Biological Scientist; Maintenance Technician; Secretary; Technical Writer/Editor; Technician. **Educational backgrounds include:** Biology; Immunology; Microbiology; Virology. **Benefits:** 401(k); Credit Union; Dental Insurance; Disability Coverage; Life Insurance; Medical Insurance; Savings Plan; Tuition Assistance. **Corporate headquarters location:** This Location. **Other U.S. locations:** Bethesda MD.

BIOSIS

2 Commerce Square, 2001 Market Street, Suite 700, Philadelphia PA 19103-7095. 215/587-4800. **Fax:** 215/587-2041. **Contact:** Human Resources. **World Wide Web address:** http://www.biosis.org. **Description:** A nonprofit educational organization that fosters the growth, communication, and use of biological knowledge. The organization offers one of the world's largest collections of abstracts and bibliographical references of biological and medical literature available for public use. Founded in 1926. **NOTE:** Entry-level positions are offered. **Common positions include:** Biological Scientist; Computer Programmer; Marketing Specialist; MIS Specialist; Systems Analyst; Technical Writer/Editor. **Educational backgrounds include:** Biology; Chemistry; Communications; Computer Science; Geology; Health Care; Marketing. **Benefits:** 403(b); Dental Insurance; Disability Coverage; Flextime Plan; Life Insurance; Medical Insurance; Public Transit Available; Tuition Assistance. **Special programs:** Training. **Corporate headquarters location:** This Location. **Subsidiaries include:** BIOSIS, UK. **Operations at this facility include:** Administration; Marketing; Production; Sales. **President:** John Anderson. **Number of employees at this location:** 250.

BIOSOURCE INTERNATIONAL, INC.

820 Flynn Road, Camarillo CA 93012. 805/987-0086. **Toll-free phone:** 800/242-0607. **Fax:** 805/383-0176. **Contact:** Human Resources. **E-mail address:** hr.dept@biosource.com. **World Wide Web address:** http://www.biosource.com. **Description:** Licenses, develops, manufactures, markets, and distributes immunological reagents and enzyme-linked immunosorbent assay (ELISA)

test kits used in biomedical research. BioSource International offers over 700 products for the study of cell biology and immunology research. The ELISA test kits are used by researchers and scientists to detect various immunological molecules in biological fluids found in humans, mice, rats, and primates. **NOTE:** Entry-level positions and part-time jobs are offered. **Common positions include:** Accountant; Administrative Assistant; Advertising Executive; Biochemist; Biological Scientist; Chemist; Controller; Customer Service Rep.; Financial Analyst; Human Resources Manager; Market Research Analyst; Marketing Manager; Marketing Specialist; MIS Specialist; Network/Systems Administrator; Purchasing Agent/Manager; Quality Control Supervisor; Sales Executive; Sales Manager; Sales Representative. **Educational backgrounds include:** Accounting; Biology; Business Administration; Chemistry; Finance; Marketing; Microsoft Word; Spreadsheets. **Benefits:** 401(k); Casual Dress - Daily; Dental Insurance; Disability Coverage; Flexible Schedule; Life Insurance; Medical Insurance; Profit Sharing; Vacation Days (16+). **Corporate headquarters location:** This Location. **Other area locations:** Foster City CA. **Other U.S. locations:** Hopkinton MA; Rockville MD. **International locations:** Belgium. **Listed on:** NASDAQ. **Stock exchange symbol:** BIOI. **Number of employees at this location:** 75. **Number of employees nationwide:** 145. **Number of employees worldwide:** 190.

BIOSPECIFICS TECHNOLOGIES CORP.

35 Wilbur Street, Lynbrook NY 11563. 516/593-7000. **Fax:** 516/593-7039. **Contact:** Department of Human Resources. **World Wide Web address:** http://www.biospecifics.com. **Description:** A leader in the production and development of enzyme pharmaceuticals used for wound healing, tissue regeneration, and tissue remodeling. Biospecifics Technologies Corporation produces Collagenase Santyl ointment, an enzyme used for the treatment of chronic wounds and dermal ulcers. **NOTE:** Part-time jobs are offered. **Common positions include:** Accountant; Administrative Assistant; Biochemist; Biological Scientist; Chemical Engineer; Chemist; Chief Financial Officer; Clinical Lab Technician; Human Resources Manager; Secretary; Statistician. **Benefits:** 401(k); Dental Insurance; Medical Insurance. **President/CEO:** Edwin H. Wegman.

BLOOD SYSTEMS

6210 East Oak Street, Scottsdale AZ 85257. **Fax:** 480/675-5780. **Recorded jobline:** 888/892-7598. **Contact:** Personnel. **Description:** One of the largest nonprofit blood service providers in the country. Blood Systems collects 800,000 blood donations annually. Founded in 1943. **NOTE:** Entry-level positions and second and third shifts are offered. **Corporate headquarters location:** This Location. **Other U.S. locations:** Blood Systems Laboratories, 2424 West Erie Drive, Tempe AZ 85282. 480/675-7000.

BRADLEY PHARMACEUTICALS, INC.

383 Route 46 West, Fairfield NJ 07004. 973/882-1505. **Fax:** 973/575-5366. **Contact:** Human Resources. **World Wide Web address:** http://www.bradpharm.com. **Description:** Manufactures and markets over-the-counter and prescription drugs, and other health-related products. Founded in 1985. **Corporate headquarters location:** This Location. **Subsidiaries include:** Doak Dermatologics Co. Inc; Kenwood Therapeutics. **Listed on:** NASDAQ. **Stock exchange symbol:** BPRX.

BRISTOL-MYERS SQUIBB COMPANY

345 Park Avenue, New York NY 10154. 212/546-4000. **Contact:** Human Resources. **World Wide**

Web address: http://www.bms.com. **Description:** Manufactures and markets pharmaceuticals. Overall, Bristol-Myers Squibb is a manufacturer of pharmaceuticals, medical devices, nonprescription drugs, toiletries, and beauty aids. The company's pharmaceutical products include cardiovascular drugs, anti-infective agents, anti-cancer agents, AIDS therapy treatments, central nervous system drugs, diagnostic agents, and other drugs. The company's line of nonprescription products includes formulas, vitamins, analgesics, remedies, and skin care products sold under the brand names Bufferin, Excedrin, Nuprin, and Comtrex. Beauty aids include Clairol and Ultress hair care, Nice 'n Easy hair colorings, hair sprays, gels, and deodorants. **Common positions include:** Biological Scientist; Chemical Engineer; Chemist; Financial Analyst; Mechanical Engineer. **Corporate headquarters location:** This Location. **Listed on:** New York Stock Exchange. **Stock exchange symbol:** BMY. **Other U.S. locations:** Buffalo Technical Operations, 100 Forest Avenue, Buffalo NY 14213. 716/887-3400.

CALGENE, INC.
1920 Fifth Street, Davis CA 95616. 530/753-6313. **Fax:** 530/792-2453. **Contact:** Human Resources. **Description:** Develops genetically-engineered plants and plant products for the food and seed industries. The company's research and business efforts are focused in three main crop areas: fresh market tomato, edible and industrial plant oils, and cotton. **Corporate headquarters location:** This Location.

CALYPTE BIOMEDICAL
1500 East Gude Drive, Rockville MD 20850. 301/251-0800. **Toll-free phone:** 800/327-2747. **Fax:** 301/251-2677. **Contact:** Nancy Yu, Human Resources Manager. **World Wide Web address:** http://www.calypte.com. **Description:** A worldwide manufacturer of diagnostic test kits for human viral diseases including HIV and HTLV. **Common positions include:** Account Manager; Accountant; Administrative Assistant; Administrative Manager; Biochemist; Biological Scientist; Buyer; Clinical Lab Technician; Controller; Customer Service Manager; General Manager; Human Resources Manager; Industrial Engineer; Industrial Production Manager; Marketing Manager; Molecular Biologist; Operations Manager; Product Manager; Quality Assurance Engineer; Quality Control Supervisor; Sales Executive; Secretary; Statistician; Systems Manager. **Educational backgrounds include:** Biology; Business Administration; Chemistry; Computer Science; Engineering; Microsoft Office; Microsoft Word; Spreadsheets. **Benefits:** 401(k); Casual Dress - Daily; Daycare Assistance; Dental Insurance; Disability Coverage; Flexible Schedule; Life Insurance; Medical Insurance; Relocation Assistance; Sick Days (6 - 10); Stock Option; Tuition Assistance; Vacation Days (10 - 20). **Corporate headquarters location:** Alameda CA. **Listed on:** NASDAQ. **Stock exchange symbol:** CALY. **General Manager:** Jim Tuite. **Facilities Manager:** Dan Campbell. **Information Systems Manager:** Chris McGrath. **Purchasing Manager:** Jason Hightower. **Sales Manager:** Dick Van Maanen. **Annual sales/revenues:** $5 - $10 million. **Number of employees at this location:** 30. **Number of employees nationwide:** 70.

CAMBRIDGE NEUROSCIENCE, INC.
One Kendall Square, Building 700, Cambridge MA 02139. 617/225-0600. **Fax:** 617/225-2741. **Contact:** Human Resources. **E-mail address:** info@cambneuro.com. **World Wide Web address:** http://www.cambneuro.com. **Description:** Develops pharmaceuticals to treat severe neurological

disorders. The company specializes in products designed to treat stroke, Alzheimer's Disease, glaucoma, multiple sclerosis, and neuropathic pain. **Corporate headquarters location:** This Location.

CARDINAL HEALTH, INC.
7000 Cardinal Place, Dublin OH 43017. 614/717-5000. **Recorded jobline:** 614/757-JOBS. **Contact:** Human Resources Department. **World Wide Web address:** http://www.cardhealth.com. **Description:** A wholesale distributor of pharmaceuticals, medical and surgical products, and related health supplies. The company also distributes merchandise typically sold in retail drug stores, hospitals, and health care provider facilities. In addition, Cardinal Health provides specialized support services such as order-entry and confirmation, inventory control, monitoring pricing strategies, and financial reporting. The company has also developed an in-pharmacy computer system which provides prices, patient profiles, financial data, and management services. **NOTE:** Entry-level positions and part-time jobs are offered. **Common positions include:** Account Manager; Account Rep.; Accountant; Administrative Assistant; Administrative Manager; AS400 Programmer Analyst; Auditor; Budget Analyst; Buyer; Computer Operator; Computer Programmer; Computer Support Technician; Controller; Credit Manager; Customer Service Representative; Database Administrator; Database Manager; Finance Director; Financial Analyst; General Manager; Graphic Designer; Help-Desk Technician; Human Resources Manager; Market Research Analyst; Marketing Manager; Marketing Specialist; MIS Specialist; Network Engineer; Sales Executive; Sales Manager; Sales Representative; Systems Analyst; Systems Manager. **Educational backgrounds include:** Accounting; AS400 Certification; Business Administration; C/C++; Computer Science; Finance; HTML; Internet Development; Marketing; MCSE; Microsoft Office; Microsoft Word; Novell; Visual Basic. **Benefits:** 401(k); 403(b); Casual Dress - Daily; Dental Insurance; Disability Coverage; Employee Discounts; Life Insurance; Medical Insurance; Profit Sharing; Public Transit Available; Relocation Assistance; Savings Plan; Tuition Assistance. **Corporate headquarters location:** This Location. **Subsidiaries include:** Medicine Shoppe International; National PharmPak Services Inc.; PCI Services, Inc.; ScriptLINE. **Listed on:** New York Stock Exchange. **Stock exchange symbol:** CAH. **Annual sales/revenues:** $21 - $50 million. **Number of employees at this location:** 1,300. **Number of employees nationwide:** 30,000. **Number of employees worldwide:** 36,000.

CARRINGTON LABORATORIES
P.O. Box 168128, 2001 Walnut Hill, Irving TX 75016-8128. 972/518-1300. **Contact:** Human Resources. **World Wide Web address:** http://www.carringtonlabs.com. **Description:** Manufactures, and markets a number of wound care products, pharmaceutical products, and veterinary products, all of which are based on complex carbohydrates derived from aloe vera. Products include Carrasyn Hydrogel Wound Dressing; CarraSorb H Calcium Alginate Wound Dressing; CarraFilm Transparent Film Dressing; CarraSorb M Freeze-Dried Gel; DiaB, a line of wound care products for diabetics; and RadiaCare, a line of products to treat radiation dermatitis. **Corporate headquarters location:** This Location. **Subsidiaries include:** Caraloe, Inc. manufactures and markets nutritional aloe drinks.

CEL-SCI CORPORATION
8229 Boone Boulevard, Suite 802, Vienna VA 22182. 703/506-9460. **Fax:** 703/506-9471. **Contact:** Department of Human Resources. **World

Wide Web address: http://www.cel-sci.com. **Description:** Cel-Sci Corporation researches and develops products for the treatment of diseases which affect the immune system. The company is involved in the research and development of natural human interleukin-2 and cytokine-related products and processes using proprietary cell culture technologies. Founded in 1983. **Common positions include:** Administrative Assistant; Biological Scientist. **Educational backgrounds include:** Biology; Business Administration. **Benefits:** 401(k); Dental Insurance; Disability Coverage; Life Insurance; Medical Insurance; Tuition Assistance; Vision Insurance. **Corporate headquarters location:** This Location. **Subsidiaries include:** Viral Technologies, Inc. is a privately-held company engaged in the development of a vaccine for AIDS. **Listed on:** American Stock Exchange. **Number of employees at this location:** 10. **Number of employees nationwide:** 30.

CELGENE CORPORATION
7 Powder Horn Drive, Warren NJ 07059. 732/271-1001. **Contact:** Personnel. **World Wide Web address:** http://www.celgene.com. **Description:** Engaged in the development and commercialization of a broad range of immunotherapeutic drugs designed to control serious disease states. Celgene also manufactures and sells chiral intermediates, key building blocks in the production of advanced therapeutic compounds and certain agrochemical and food-related products. The focus of Celgene's immunotherapeutics program is the development of small molecule compounds that modulate bodily production of tumor necrosis factor alpha, a hormone-like protein. Elevated levels of this cytokine are believed to cause symptoms associated with several debilitating diseases such as HIV and AIDS-related conditions, sepsis, and inflammatory bowel disease. **Corporate headquarters location:** This Location.

CELL GENESYS, INC.
342 Lakeside Drive, Foster City CA 94404. 650/358-9600. **Contact:** Human Resources. **World Wide Web address:** http://www.cellgenesys.com. **Description:** Develops and commercializes gene therapies to treat major, life-threatening diseases including cancer and cardiovascular disease. The company is conducting two multicenter Phase II human clinical trials for its GVAX cancer vaccine in prostate cancer and plans to initiate a multicenter Phase I/II trial of GVAX vaccine in lung cancer. Preclinical stage programs include gene therapy for cancer, cardiovascular disorders, hemophilia, and Parkinson's disease. **Corporate headquarters location:** This Location.

CELL THERAPEUTICS, INC.
201 Elliott Avenue, Suite 400, Seattle WA 98119. 206/282-7100. **Fax:** 206/284-6206. **Recorded jobline:** 800/656-2355. **Contact:** Personnel. **E-mail address:** resume@ctiseattle.com. **World Wide Web address:** http://www.cticseattle.com. **Description:** Researches, and develops oncology products that are designed to manage cancer. The company also specializes in the reduction of cancer treatment side effects. **Common positions include:** Accountant; Attorney; Biochemist; Biological Scientist; Chemist; Computer Programmer; Paralegal; Physician; Secretary; Statistician; Webmaster. **Educational backgrounds include:** Accounting; Biology; Business Administration; Chemistry. **Benefits:** 401(k); Dental Insurance; Disability Coverage; Life Insurance; Medical Insurance. **Corporate headquarters location:** This Location. **Listed on:** NASDAQ. **Stock exchange symbol:** CTIC. **Number of employees at this location:** 190.

CELLOMICS, INC.
635 William Pitt Way, Pittsburgh PA 15238. 412/826-3600. **Fax:** 412/826-3850. **Contact:** Human Resources. **World Wide Web address:** http://www.cellomics.com. **Description:** Develops components for pharmaceutical and biotechnology companies to aid in faster, more efficient drug discovery processes. Cellomics, Inc. delivers genomic- and cell-based solutions. Founded in 1996. **Common positions include:** Scientist; Software Developer; Systems Specialist. **Corporate headquarters location:** This Location. **Listed on:** Privately held.

CELTRIX PHARMACEUTICALS INC.
2033 Gateway Place, Suite 600, San Jose CA 95110. 408/988-2500. **Fax:** 408/573-6228. **Contact:** Human Resources. **Description:** Develops pharmaceutical products for the treatment of degenerative diseases associated with aging and autoimmune conditions. The most advanced product candidate is BetaKine, used for the treatment of potentially blinding ophthalmic diseases. Other product development programs focus on the treatment of chronic dermal ulcers, localized tissue damage, and systemic, degenerative diseases such as multiple sclerosis and osteoporosis. **Corporate headquarters location:** This Location.

CENTER FOR BLOOD RESEARCH LABORATORIES, INC.
800 Huntington Avenue, Boston MA 02115. 617/278-3000. **Contact:** Paula Muccini, Human Resources Generalist. **Description:** Provides commercial testing services and contract research for the industry and federal agencies. The main laboratories are housed in two locations at Harvard University's medical community in Boston. Center for Blood Research Laboratories provides molecular diagnostic and genetic typing services for the purpose of identity testing, matching potential donors for patients, and diagnosis of inherited diseases. The company also provides blood testing services to detect diseases for early treatment, as well as the testing of new medical treatments and diagnostic products. **Common positions include:** Accountant/Auditor; Biological Scientist; Clinical Lab Technician; Purchasing Agent/Manager. **Educational backgrounds include:** Biology; Chemistry. **Benefits:** 403(b); Dental Insurance; Disability Coverage; Life Insurance; Medical Insurance; Pension Plan; Savings Plan; Tuition Assistance. **Special programs:** Internships. **Corporate headquarters location:** This Location. **Parent company:** The Center for Blood Research (CBR) is a nonprofit organization affiliated with Harvard Medical School that conducts research on the functions and uses of components of blood and other tissue and trains medical and scientific personnel in research.

CENTOCOR, INC.
200 Great Valley Parkway, Malvern PA 19355-1307. 610/651-6000. **Fax:** 610/651-6330. **Contact:** Tim Shanahan, Human Resources Coordinator. **World Wide Web address:** http://www.centocor.com. **Description:** Develops and markets biopharmaceutical therapeutics and diagnostic products for cardiovascular, inflammatory, and infectious diseases, and cancer. Centocor concentrates on research, development, and manufacturing with a technological focus on monoclonal antibodies, peptides, and nucleic acids. **Corporate headquarters location:** This Location. **Subsidiaries include:** Centocor B.V. (the Netherlands); Centocor U.K. Limited (England); and Nippon Centocor K.K. (Japan). **Parent company:** Johnson & Johnson.

CEPHALON, INC.
145 Brandywine Parkway, West Chester PA 19380. 610/344-0200. **Contact:** Human Resources. **World Wide Web address:** http://www.cephalon.com. **Description:** Researches, develops, and markets products to treat neurological disorders including amyotrophic lateral sclerosis, narcolepsy, peripheral neuropathies, Alzheimer's disease, head and spinal injury, and stroke. **Benefits:** 401(k); Stock Option. **Corporate headquarters location:** This Location. **Subsidiaries include:** Cephalon Development Corporation; Cephalon International Holdings, Inc.; Cephalon Investments, Inc.; Cephalon Property Management, Inc.; Cephalon Technology, Inc. **Listed on:** NASDAQ. **Stock exchange symbol:** CEPH.

CHARLES RIVER LABORATORIES
251 Ballardvale Street, Wilmington MA 01887. 978/658-6000. **Contact:** Human Resources. **World Wide Web address:** http://www.criver.com. **Description:** A commercial supplier of laboratory animals including mice, rats, and guinea pigs for use in medical and scientific research. Primary buyers include chemical and pharmaceutical companies, government agencies, universities, commercial testing laboratories, and research hospitals **Common positions include:** Accountant/Auditor; Administrator; Agricultural Engineer; Attorney; Biological Scientist; Biomedical Engineer; Blue-Collar Worker Supervisor; Buyer; Computer Programmer; Credit Manager; Customer Service Rep.; Draftsperson; Electrical/Electronics Engineer; Financial Analyst; General Manager; Industrial Designer; Industrial Engineer; Mechanical Engineer; Operations/Production Manager; Quality Control Supervisor; Services Sales Rep.; Systems Analyst; Technical Writer/Editor; Transportation/ Traffic Specialist. **Educational backgrounds include:** Accounting; Animal Science; Art/Design; Biology; Business Administration; Computer Science; Engineering; Finance; Liberal Arts; Marketing. **Benefits:** 401(k); Credit Union; Dental Insurance; Disability Coverage; Employee Discounts; Life Insurance; Medical Insurance; Pension Plan; Savings Plan; Tuition Assistance. **Corporate headquarters location:** This Location. **Parent company:** Bausch & Lomb. **Number of employees nationwide:** 1,100.

CHIREX, INC.
300 Atlantic Street, Suite 402, Stamford CT 06901. 203/356-9054. **Contact:** Human Resources. **World Wide Web address:** http://www.chirex.com. **Description:** Manufactures active pharmaceutical ingredients, intermediates, and catalysts. Chirex also provides drug research and clinical trial testing. **Corporate headquarters location:** This Location. **Other U.S. locations:** Boston MA; Malvern PA. **International locations:** England; Scotland. **CEO:** Michael A. Griffith.

CHIRON CORPORATION
4560 Horton Street, Emeryville CA 94608-2916. 510/655-8730. **Fax:** 510/655-9910. **Contact:** Human Resources Department. **World Wide Web address:** http://www.chiron.com. **Description:** A biotechnology company that operates within three global health care sectors: biopharmaceuticals, blood testing, and vaccines. Chiron Corporation specializes in products designed to prevent and treat cancer, cardiovascular disease, and infectious diseases. **Corporate headquarters location:** This Location. **Subsidiaries include:** IOLAB. **Listed on:** NASDAQ. **Stock exchange symbol:** CHIR.

CHOLESTECH CORPORATION
3347 Investment Boulevard, Hayward CA 94545. 510/732-7200. **Fax:** 510/732-7227. **Contact:** Human Resources. **World Wide Web address:** http://www.cholestech.com. **Description:** Develops and manufactures diagnostics systems that measure cholesterol. **Corporate headquarters location:** This Location. **Listed on:** NASDAQ. **Stock exchange symbol:** CTEC.

CIMA LABS INC.
10000 Valley View Road, Eden Prairie MN 55344. 952/947-8725. **Fax:** 952/947-8770. **Contact:** Human Resources Department. **World Wide Web address:** http://www.cimalabs.com. **Description:** Develops and manufactures a pharmaceutical drug delivery system. CIMA LABS INC.'s main product is a fast-dissolving tablet for individuals who have difficulty swallowing pills. Founded in 1986. **NOTE:** Entry-level positions are offered. **Common positions include:** Accountant; Administrative Assistant; Chemist; Purchasing Agent/Manager. **Educational backgrounds include:** Chemistry; Microsoft Word; Novell; Spreadsheets. **Benefits:** 401(k); Casual Dress - Daily; Dental Insurance; Disability Coverage; Financial Planning Assistance; Flexible Schedule; Life Insurance; Medical Insurance; Tuition Assistance; Vacation Days (11 - 15). **Corporate headquarters location:** This Location. **Listed on:** NASDAQ. **Stock exchange symbol:** CIMA. **President/CEO:** John Siebert, Ph.D. **Annual sales/revenues:** Less than $5 million. **Number of employees at this location:** 70.

COCENSYS, INC.
213 Technology Drive, Irvine CA 92618. 949/753-6100. **Contact:** Personnel. **World Wide Web address:** http://www.cocensys.com. **Description:** Engaged in the development of pharmaceuticals to treat problems affecting the central nervous system such as anxiety, epilepsy, insomnia, migraine, and stroke. **Corporate headquarters location:** This Location.

CORIXA CORPORATION
553 Old Corvallis Road, Hamilton MT 59840. 406/363-6214. **Contact:** Human Resources. **World Wide Web address:** http://www.corixa.com. **Description:** Involved in the research and development of biopharmaceuticals to prevent or treat various diseases including cancer, autoimmune diseases, and infectious diseases. **Corporate headquarters location:** This Location.

CORVAS INTERNATIONAL, INC.
3030 Science Park Road, San Diego CA 92121-1102. 858/455-9800. **Fax:** 858/455-5169. **Contact:** Mary Anne Obedoza, Human Resources. **World Wide Web address:** http://www.corvas.com. **Description:** Designs and develops therapeutic agents for the prevention and treatment of major cardiovascular and inflammatory diseases. The company also develops drugs that block the initiation of blood clot formation (thrombosis) and white blood cell activation (inflammation), two closely linked and potentially damaging processes. Founded in 1987. **NOTE:** Entry-level positions are offered. **Common positions include:** Accountant; Biochemist; Biological Scientist; Buyer; Chemist; Computer Programmer; Controller; Human Resources Manager; Intellectual Property Lawyer; Paralegal. **Educational backgrounds include:** Accounting; Biology; Business Administration; Chemistry. **Benefits:** 401(k); Dental Insurance; Disability Coverage; Employee Discounts; Life Insurance; Medical Insurance; Tuition Assistance. **Special programs:** Internships. **Internship information:** Summer interns are hired annually. Applicants are encouraged to send resumes beginning May 1st. **Corporate headquarters location:** This Location. **Operations at this facility include:** Divisional Headquarters. **Listed on:**

NASDAQ. **Annual sales/revenues:** Less than $5 million. **Number of employees at this location:** 80.

COVANCE INC.
210 Carnegie Center, Princeton NJ 08540. 609/452-4440. **Toll-free phone:** 888/COV-ANCE. **Fax:** 609/452-9375. **Contact:** Human Resources. **E-mail address:** info@covance.com. **World Wide Web address:** http://www.covance.com. **Description:** One of the world's largest and most comprehensive drug development services companies. Covance Inc. provides preclinical testing, health economics consulting, biomanufacturing, and clinical support services. **NOTE:** Entry-level positions are offered. **Common positions include:** Administrative Assistant; Computer Support Technician; Data Analyst; Database Administrator; Network/Systems Administrator; Registered Nurse; Research Scientist; Statistician. **Educational backgrounds include:** Health Care. **Benefits:** 401(k); Casual Dress - Daily; Flexible Schedule; Tuition Assistance. **Office hours:** Monday - Friday, 8:30 a.m. - 5:00 p.m. **Corporate headquarters location:** This Location. **Other U.S. locations:** Berkeley CA; Richmond CA; Walnut Creek CA; Washington DC; Tampa FL; Indianapolis IN; Kalamazoo MI; Research Triangle Pa NC; Reno NV; Allentown PA; Denver PA; Radnor PA; Nashville TN; Alice TX; Cumberland VA; Vienna VA; Madison WI. **Subsidiaries include:** Berkeley Antibody Company, Inc. provides preclinical services. GDXI, Inc. provides electrocardiogram analysis for clinical trials. **President/CEO:** Christopher Kuebler. **Annual sales/revenues:** More than $100 million. **Number of employees at this location:** 1,000. **Number of employees worldwide:** 7,700.

CRYOLIFE
1655 Roberts Boulevard NW, Kennesaw GA 30144. 770/419-3355. **Toll-free phone:** 800/438-8285. **Fax:** 770/590-3741. **Contact:** Human Resources. **E-mail address:** schoenberg.marion@cryolife.com. **World Wide Web address:** http://www.cryolife.com. **Description:** A biomedical laboratory specializing in cryopreserved transplantable human tissues as well as the development and production of bio-adhesives. Founded in 1984. **Educational backgrounds include:** Biology; Chemistry; Engineering; Lotus. **Benefits:** 401(k); Casual Dress - Daily; Dental Insurance; Disability Coverage; Life Insurance; Medical Insurance; Tuition Assistance; Vacation Days (10 - 20). **Office hours:** Monday - Friday, 9:00 a.m. - 6:00 p.m. **Corporate headquarters location:** This Location.

CYANOTECH CORPORATION
73-4460 Queen Kaahumanu Highway, Suite 102, Kailua-Kona HI 96740. 808/326-1353. **Fax:** 808/334-9405. **Contact:** Human Resources Manager. **World Wide Web address:** http://www.cyanotech.com. **Description:** Develops, produces, and markets natural products from microalgae. The company manufactures products for nutritional supplement and immunological diagnostics. **Corporate headquarters location:** This Location. **Other U.S. locations:** NV. **Subsidiaries include:** Cyanotech International FSC, Inc.; Nutrex, Inc. **Listed on:** NASDAQ. **Stock exchange symbol:** CYAN. **President/CEO:** Gerald E. Cysewski. **Number of employees at this location:** 80.

CYGNUS, INC.
400 Penobscot Drive, Redwood City CA 94063. 650/369-4300. **Fax:** 650/599-3938. **Contact:** Personnel. **E-mail address:** recruiting@cygn.com. **World Wide Web address:** http://www.cygn.com. **Description:** Develops and manufactures diagnostic medical devices. **Corporate headquarters location:** This Location.

CYTOGEN CORPORATION
600 College Road East, Princeton NJ 08540. 609/987-8200. **Fax:** 609/452-2975. **Contact:** Human Resources Manager. **World Wide Web address:** http://www.cytogen.com. **Description:** Develops products for the targeted delivery of diagnostic and therapeutic substances directly to sites of disease, using monoclonal antibodies. Proprietary antibody linking technology is used primarily to develop specific cancer diagnostic imaging and therapeutic products. Founded in 1981. **Common positions include:** Accountant/Auditor; Biological Scientist; Chemist; Systems Analyst. **Educational backgrounds include:** Business Administration; Communications; Health Care; Liberal Arts; M.D./Medicine. **Benefits:** 401(k); Dental Insurance; Disability Coverage; Life Insurance; Medical Insurance; Pension Plan; Tuition Assistance. **Corporate headquarters location:** This Location. **Operations at this facility include:** Administration; Sales. **Listed on:** NASDAQ. **Number of employees at this location:** 120.

D&K HEALTHCARE RESOURCES
8000 Maryland Avenue, Suite 920, Clayton MO 63105. 314/727-3485. **Fax:** 314/727-5759. **Contact:** Human Resources Manager. **World Wide Web address:** http://www.dkwd.com. **Description:** Distributes pharmaceuticals and health and beauty aids to retail companies and hospitals. **Corporate headquarters location:** This Location. **Listed on:** NASDAQ. **Stock exchange symbol:** DKWD.

DNA PLANT TECHNOLOGY CORPORATION
6701 San Pablo Avenue, Oakland CA 94608. 510/547-2395. **Contact:** Human Resources. **World Wide Web address:** http://www.dnap.com. **Description:** A leading agribusiness biotechnology company focused on developing and marketing premium, fresh, and processed fruits and vegetables, using advanced breeding, genetic engineering, and other biotechniques. **Corporate headquarters location:** This Location. **Subsidiaries include:** FreshWorld Farms markets a line of premium vegetables under the FreshWorld Farms brand name including tomatoes, carrot bites, sweet red mini-peppers, and carrot sticks.

DSM DESOTECH INC.
1122 St. Charles Street, Elgin IL 60120. 847/697-0400. **Toll-free phone:** 800/223-7191. **Fax:** 847/468-7795. **Contact:** Human Resources. **World Wide Web address:** http://www.dsmdesotech.com. **Description:** Researches, formulates, manufactures, and sells ultraviolet and electron beam curable materials and technology. **Corporate headquarters location:** This Location.

DARBY GROUP COMPANIES
865 Merrick Avenue, Westbury NY 11590. 516/536-3000. **Contact:** Human Resources. **World Wide Web address:** http://www.darbygroup.com. **Description:** Manufactures and distributes over-the-counter pharmaceuticals, and vitamins. **Corporate headquarters location:** This Location.

DAXOR CORPORATION
The Empire State Building, 350 Fifth Avenue, Suite 7120, New York NY 10118. 212/244-0555. **Fax:** 212/244-0806. **Contact:** Human Resources. **World Wide Web address:** http://www.daxor.com. **Description:** Researches cryobiology for artificial insemination purposes. The company also operates one of the largest sperm banks in the U.S. **Corporate headquarters location:** This Location.

DEL LABORATORIES, INC.
178 EAB Plaza, West Tower, 8th Floor, Uniondale NY 11556. 516/844-2020. **Fax:** 516/577-1035.

Contact: Human Resources. **E-mail address:** resumes@dellabs.com. **World Wide Web address:** http://www.dellabs.com. **Description:** A fully-integrated manufacturer and marketer of packaged consumer products including cosmetics, toiletries, beauty aids, and proprietary pharmaceuticals. Products are distributed to chain and independent drug stores, mass merchandisers, and supermarkets. Divisions include Commerce Drug Company, Del International, Natural Glow, La Cross, La Salle Laboratories, Nutri-Tonic, Naturistics, Rejuvia, and Sally Hansen. **NOTE:** Entry-level positions and second and third shifts are offered. **Common positions include:** Account Manager; Account Rep.; Accountant; Administrative Assistant; Advertising Clerk; AS400 Programmer Analyst; Blue-Collar Worker Supervisor; Budget Analyst; Buyer; Chemist; Clerical Supervisor; Computer Operator; Customer Service Representative; Database Administrator; Electrician; Environmental Engineer; Event Planner; Financial Analyst; Graphic Artist; Help-Desk Technician; Industrial Engineer; Internet Services Manager; Intranet Developer; Manufacturing Engineer; Marketing Manager; Media Planner; MIS Specialist; Network/Systems Administrator; Production Manager; Public Relations Specialist; Quality Control Supervisor; Sales Manager; Sales Representative; Secretary; Systems Analyst; Systems Manager; Webmaster; Website Developer. **Educational backgrounds include:** Accounting; Art/Design; AS400 Certification; Business Administration; Chemistry; Communications; Computer Science; Engineering; Finance; Marketing; MBA; Microsoft Office; Microsoft Word; Public Relations; Spreadsheets. **Benefits:** 401(k); Casual Dress - Fridays; Dental Insurance; Disability Coverage; ESOP; Life Insurance; Medical Insurance; Pension Plan; Sick Days (6 - 10); Tuition Assistance; Vacation Days (6 - 10). **Corporate headquarters location:** This Location. **Other area locations:** Farmingdale NY. **Other U.S. locations:** Rocky Point NC. **Listed on:** American Stock Exchange. **Stock exchange symbol:** OLI. **Annual sales/revenues:** More than $100 million.

DIACRIN, INC.
Building 96, 13th Street, Charlestown Navy Yard, Charlestown MA 02129. 617/242-9100. **Fax:** 617/242-0070. **Contact:** Human Resources. **E-mail address:** info@diacrin.com. **World Wide Web address:** http://www.diacrin.com. **Description:** A biotechnology company that specializes in cell transplantation technolgy designed to treat diseases characterized by cell dysfunction or cell death. Founded in 1989. **Common positions include:** Administrative Assistant; Biochemist; Biological Scientist; Molecular Biologist. **Benefits:** 401(k); Dental Insurance; Disability Coverage; Life Insurance; Medical Insurance; Public Transit Available; Sick Days (11+); Tuition Assistance; Vacation Days (11 - 15). **Special programs:** Co-ops. **Office hours:** Monday - Friday, 8:00 a.m. - 5:30 p.m. **Corporate headquarters location:** This Location. **Listed on:** NASDAQ. **Stock exchange symbol:** DCRN. **President/CEO:** Thomas H. Fraser, Ph.D. **Annual sales/revenues:** Less than $5 million. **Number of employees at this location:** 40.

DIAGNOSTIC PRODUCTS CORPORATION
5700 West 96th Street, Los Angeles CA 90045. 310/645-8200. **Contact:** Personnel Department. **World Wide Web address:** http://www.dpcweb.com. **Description:** Manufactures medical immunodiagnostic test kits that are used to diagnose and treat a variety of medical conditions such as allergies, anemia, cancer, diabetes, infectious diseases, reproductive disorders, thyroid disorders, and veterinary applications. **Common positions**

include: Biological Scientist; Chemist; Clinical Lab Technician. **Educational backgrounds include:** Biology; Chemistry. **Benefits:** Dental Insurance; Disability Coverage; Employee Discounts; Life Insurance; Medical Insurance; Pension Plan; Profit Sharing; Tuition Assistance. **Corporate headquarters location:** This Location. **Listed on:** New York Stock Exchange. **Number of employees at this location:** 430.

DIANON SYSTEMS, INC.
200 Watson Boulevard, Stratford CT 06615. 203/381-4000. **Contact:** Human Resources. **World Wide Web address:** http://www.dianon.com. **Description:** A provider of testing services and diagnostic information to focused physician audiences in the United States and Europe. A wide range of laboratory tests are offered, with applications in the screening, diagnosis, prognosis, and monitoring of cancer and genetic disorders. Screening tests include those for congenital abnormalities; prostate, bladder, and ovarian cancer; and kidney disease. Prognostic testing is available for patients for whom a diagnosis has already been made regarding prostate cancer, bladder cancer, breast cancer, colon cancer, leukemia, and lymphoma. Monitoring tests are used to detect recurrent tumors and to estimate the response to therapy. **Corporate headquarters location:** This Location. **Other U.S. locations:** AZ; GA; MD; OH; TX. **International locations:** Amsterdam; France; Germany. **Listed on:** NASDAQ. **Number of employees nationwide:** 300.

DIASORIN INC.
1990 Industrial Boulevard, P.O. Box 285, Stillwater MN 55082-0285. 651/439-9710. **Contact:** Human Resources Department. **E-mail address:** hr@diasorin.com. **World Wide Web address:** http://www.diasorin.com. **Description:** Diasonin, Inc. manufactures and markets medical testing kits. **Common positions include:** Account Manager; Account Rep.; Accountant; Administrative Assistant; Administrative Manager; Applications Engineer; Attorney; Biochemist; Biological Scientist; Biomedical Engineer; Blue-Collar Worker Supervisor; Chemist; Clinical Lab Technician; Computer Engineer; Computer Programmer; Computer Scientist; Computer Support Technician; Computer Technician; Controller; Credit Manager; Customer Service Rep.; Database Administrator; Design Engineer; Desktop Publishing Specialist; Draftsperson; Electrical/Electronics Engineer; Event Planner; Help-Desk Technician; Human Resources Manager; Intranet Developer; Market Research Analyst; Marketing Manager; Marketing Specialist; Media Planner; Molecular Biologist; Network/Systems Administrator; Operations Manager; Production Manager; Purchasing Agent/Manager; Sales Executive; Sales Manager; Sales Representative; Software Engineer; Technical Writer/Editor. **Educational backgrounds include:** Accounting; Biology; Chemistry; Computer Science; Engineering; Finance. **Benefits:** 401(k); Casual Dress - Daily; Dental Insurance; Disability Coverage; Employee Discounts; Flexible Schedule; Job Sharing; Life Insurance; Medical Insurance; Public Transit Available; Savings Plan; Tuition Assistance. **Special programs:** Internships; Summer Jobs. **Office hours:** Monday - Friday, 8:00 a.m. - 5:00 p.m. **Corporate headquarters location:** This Location. **Facilities Manager:** Ross Buschman. **Purchasing Manager:** Cathy Bygd. **Number of employees at this location:** 325.

CHARLES STARK DRAPER LABORATORY
555 Technology Square, Mail Stop 44, Cambridge MA 02139. 617/258-1000. **Contact:** Professional Employment. **World Wide Web address:**

http://www.draper.com. **Description:** A private, nonprofit corporation that specializes in scientific research, development, and education. **Common positions include:** Aerospace Engineer; Ceramics Engineer; Chemical Engineer; Electrical/Electronics Engineer; Mechanical Engineer; Metallurgical Engineer; Physicist; Technical Writer/Editor. **Educational backgrounds include:** Chemistry; Computer Science; Engineering; Mathematics; Physics. **Benefits:** Dental Insurance; Disability Coverage; Employee Discounts; Life Insurance; Medical Insurance; Pension Plan; Savings Plan; Tuition Assistance. **Corporate headquarters location:** This Location.

DURA PHARMACEUTICALS, INC.
7475 Lusk Boulevard, San Diego CA 92121. 858/457-2553. **Fax:** 858/457-2555. **Contact:** Vice President of Human Resources . **World Wide Web address:** http://www.durapharm.com. **Description:** Develops and markets prescription pharmaceutical products and pulmonary drug delivery systems for the treatment of allergies, asthma, and related respiratory conditions. **Corporate headquarters location:** This Location. **Subsidiaries include:** DJ Pharma, Inc. develops and sells generic prescription pharmaceuticals. **Listed on:** NASDAQ. **Stock exchange symbol:** DURA. **Chairman and CEO:** Cam L. Garner. **Annual sales/revenues:** More than $100 million.

ELAN PHARMACEUTICALS, INC.
800 Gateway Boulevard, South San Francisco CA 94080. 650/614-1029. **Fax:** 650/553-7138. **Contact:** Personnel Director. **E-mail address:** careers@elanpharma.com. **World Wide Web address:** http://www.elanpharma.com. **Description:** A research-based pharmaceutical company that specializes in the field of neurology. **Common positions include:** Account Manager; Account Rep; Accountant; Administrative Assistant; Attorney; Biochemist; Biological Scientist; Biomedical Engineer; Budget Analyst; Buyer; Chemist; Chief Financial Officer; Clinical Lab Technician; Computer Engineer; Computer Support Technician; Computer Technician; Construction Contractor; Controller; Customer Service Representative; Database Administrator; Database Manager; Desktop Publishing Specialist; Draftsperson; Editor; Editorial Assistant; Electrical/Electronics Engineer; Electrician; Finance Director; Financial Analyst; Graphic Designer; Human Resources Manager; Intellectual Property Lawyer; Internet Services Manager; Librarian; Market Research Analyst; Marketing Manager; Marketing Specialist; MIS Specialist; Network/Systems Administrator; Occupational Therapist; Pharmacist; Physician; Purchasing Agent/Manager; Registered Nurse; Sales Executive; Sales Manager; Sales Representative; Secretary; Statistician; Systems Manager; Technical Writer/Editor; Typist/Word Processor; Webmaster. **Educational backgrounds include:** Accounting; Biology; Business Administration; Chemistry; Communications; Computer Science; Economics; Finance; Health Care; Liberal Arts; Marketing; Mathematics; Microsoft Word; Spreadsheets. **Benefits:** 401(k); Casual Dress - Fridays; Dental Insurance; Disability Coverage; Employee Discounts; Life Insurance; Medical Insurance; Vacation Days (10 - 20). **Corporate headquarters location:** This Location. **Parent company:** Elan Corporation. **Stock exchange symbol:** ELN. **Number of employees at this location:** 1,000.

ELI LILLY AND COMPANY
Lilly Corporate Center, Indianapolis IN 46285. 317/277-7731. **Contact:** Human Resources. **World Wide Web address:** http://www.lilly.com. **Description:** Discovers, develops, manufactures,

and sells a broad line of human health products and pharmaceuticals including diagnostic products; monoclonal antibody-based diagnostic tests for colon, prostate, and testicular cancer; medical devices; patient vital-signs measurement and electrocardiograph systems; implantable cardiac pacemakers and related medical systems; and anti-infectives and diabetic care products. The company also produces animal health products. **Common positions include:** Biological Scientist; Biomedical Engineer; Chemical Engineer; Chemist; Civil Engineer; Computer Programmer; Electrical/Electronics Engineer; Financial Analyst; Industrial Engineer; Mechanical Engineer; Statistician; Systems Analyst. **Educational backgrounds include:** Biology; Chemistry; Computer Science; Economics; Engineering; Finance; Marketing. **Benefits:** Dental Insurance; Disability Coverage; Life Insurance; Medical Insurance; Pension Plan; Profit Sharing; Savings Plan. **Corporate headquarters location:** This Location. **Listed on:** New York Stock Exchange. **Number of employees nationwide:** 30,000.

EMBREX INC.
P.O. Box 13989, Research Triangle Park NC 27709-3989. 919/941-5185. **Fax:** 919/941-5186. **Contact:** Human Resources. **World Wide Web address:** http://www.embrex.com. **Description:** Develops and manufactures an automated egg-injection system, eliminating the need for manual vaccination of newly hatched broiler chicks. Its patented INOVOJECT system inoculates up to 50,000 eggs per hour. The company's research also includes viral neutralizing factors, immunomodulators, gene vaccines, and performance enhancement products which alter bird physiology for early delivery. **Corporate headquarters location:** This Location. **Subsidiaries include:** Embrex Europe Ltd. **Listed on:** NASDAQ. **Stock exchange symbol:** EMBX. **Number of employees nationwide:** 100.

EMISPHERE TECHNOLOGIES INC.
765 Old Saw Mill River Road, Tarrytown NY 10591. 914/347-2220. **Fax:** 914/347-0108. **Contact:** Human Resources. **World Wide Web address:** http://www.emisphere.com. **Description:** Researches and develops oral drug delivery systems. **Corporate headquarters location:** This Location.

ENDOGEN, INC.
30 Commerce Way, Woburn MA 01801-1059. 781/937-0890. **Fax:** 781/937-3096. **Contact:** Human Resources. **World Wide Web address:** http://www.endogen.com. **Description:** Develops, manufactures, and markets diagnostic test kits that test for HIV and cancer. Products are sold in the United States to private and government institutions, university hospitals, medical centers, and large commercial laboratories via a direct sales force. **Benefits:** 401(k); Incentive Plan; Stock Option. **Corporate headquarters location:** This Location. **Listed on:** NASDAQ.

EPIMMUNE INC.
5820 Nancy Ridge Drive, San Diego CA 92121. 858/552-3000. **Contact:** Human Resources. **World Wide Web address:** http://www.epimmune.com. **Description:** Researches and develops vaccines to prevent and treat infectious diseases and cancer. **Corporate headquarters location:** This Location. **Listed on:** NASDAQ.

EPITOPE, INC.
8505 SW Creekside Place, Beaverton OR 97008. 503/641-6115. **Fax:** 503/643-2781. **Contact:** Ms. Anshu Kane, Human Resources. **E-mail address:** jobs@epitopeinc.com. **World Wide Web address:** http://www.epitope.com. **Description:** Develops

and markets oral fluid diagnostic tests for the public and private sectors. The company focuses on the detection of HIV and substance abuse. Founded in 1987. **Common positions include:** Accountant; Administrative Assistant; Biological Scientist; Chief Financial Officer; Clinical Lab Technician; Computer Operator; Controller; Database Manager; Human Resources Manager; Marketing Specialist; MIS Specialist; Operations Manager; Public Relations Specialist; Purchasing Agent/Manager; Quality Control Supervisor; Sales Executive; Sales Manager; Sales Rep.; Secretary; Typist/Word Processor. **Educational backgrounds include:** Accounting; Biology; Business Administration; Health Care; Marketing. **Benefits:** 401(k); Dental Insurance; Disability Coverage; Life Insurance; Medical Insurance; Public Transit Available. **Corporate headquarters location:** This Location. **Listed on:** NASDAQ. **Stock exchange symbol:** EPTO. **President:** John Morgan. **Number of employees at this location:** 85.

THE FEMALE HEALTH COMPANY
875 North Michigan Avenue, Suite 3660, Chicago IL 60611. 312/280-1119. **Contact:** Human Resources. **World Wide Web address:** http://www. femalehealth.com. **Description:** Manufactures and markets a proprietary female barrier contraceptive product known as the Reality female condom. **Corporate headquarters location:** This Location. **Parent company:** Wisconsin Pharmacal Company, Inc. (Jackson WI).

FISHER SCIENTIFIC INTERNATIONAL
Liberty Lane, Hampton NH 03842. 603/926-5911. **Contact:** Personnel Department. **World Wide Web address:** http://www.fishersci.com. **Description:** One of the largest providers of instruments, equipment, and other products to the scientific community. The company offers a selection of products and services to research centers and industrial customers worldwide. Fisher Scientific serves scientists engaged in biomedical, biotechnology, pharmaceutical, chemical, and other fields of research and development in corporations, the educational and research institutions, and government agencies. The company also supplies clinical laboratories, hospitals, environmental testing centers, remediation companies, quality control laboratories, and other industrial facilities. In addition, Fisher Scientific represents its customers as a third-party purchaser of maintenance materials and other basic supplies. **Common positions include:** Financial Analyst; General Manager; Human Resources Manager; MIS Specialist; Typist/Word Processor. **Educational backgrounds include:** Accounting; Computer Science; Economics; Finance; Marketing. **Benefits:** 401(k); Dental Insurance; Disability Coverage; Employee Discounts; Life Insurance; Medical Insurance. **Corporate headquarters location:** This Location. **Listed on:** New York Stock Exchange. **Annual sales/revenues:** More than $100 million. **Number of employees at this location:** 110.

FOLEY LABORATORY SERVICES, INC.
124 Hebron Avenue, Glastonbury CT 06033. 860/633-2660. **Fax:** 860/652-3259. **Contact:** Human Resources. **World Wide Web address:** http://www.dotdrugtest.com. **Description:** Provides alcohol and drug testing services. **Corporate headquarters location:** This Location.

FOREST LABORATORIES, INC.
909 Third Avenue, New York NY 10022. 212/224-6741. **Toll-free phone:** 800/947-5227. **Fax:** 212/750-9152. **Contact:** Bernard McGovern, Vice President of Human Resources. **E-mail address:** staffing@frx.com. **World Wide Web address:**

http://www.frx.com. **Description:** Manufactures and sells branded and generic prescription drugs for the treatment of cardiovascular, central nervous system, pulmonary, and women's health problems. In the United States, Forest Laboratories' ethical specialty products and generics are marketed directly by the company's subsidiaries Forest Pharmaceuticals and Inwood Laboratories. In the United Kingdom, Ireland, and certain export markets, Forest Laboratories products are marketed directly by the company's subsidiaries, Pharmax Ltd. and Tosara Group. **NOTE:** Entry-level positions are offered. **Common positions include:** Analytical Engineer; Biochemist; Biological Scientist; Business Development Manager; Clinical Applications Specialist; Clinical Lab Technician; Contract/ Grant Administrator; Financial Analyst; Market Research Analyst; Marketing Manager; Pharmacist; Product Manager; Quality Assurance Engineer; Regulatory Affairs Director; Research and Development Engineer; Research Scientist; Safety Specialist; Sales Representative; Technical Writer/ Editor; Toxicologist. **Educational backgrounds include:** Accounting; Bachelor of Arts; Bachelor of Science; Biology; Business Administration; Chemistry; Computer Science; Finance; Master of Arts; Master of Sciences; Ph.D. **Benefits:** 401(k); Dental Insurance; Disability Coverage; Life Insurance; Medical Insurance; Pension Plan. **Special programs:** Co-ops; Internships; Summer Jobs. **Corporate headquarters location:** This Location. **Other U.S. locations:** St. Louis MO; Jersey City NJ; Commack NY; Farmingdale NY; Inwood NY; Cincinnati OH. **International locations:** Ireland; United Kingdom. **Subsidiaries include:** Forest Pharmaceuticals; Inwood Laboratories, Inc.; Pharmax Ltd.; Tosara Group. **Listed on:** New York Stock Exchange. **Stock exchange symbol:** FRX. **Annual sales/revenues:** More than $100 million. **Number of employees at this location:** 250. **Number of employees nationwide:** 1,700.

E. FOUGERA & COMPANY
SAVAGE LABORATORIES
60 Baylis Road, Melville NY 11747. 631/454-6996. **Contact:** Human Resources. **World Wide Web address:** http://www.fougera.com. **Description:** Manufactures and markets various multisource topicals and ophthalmics. The company's products include surgical lubricants, antifungal creams, and hydrocortisone ointments. **Corporate headquarters location:** This Location. **Parent company:** Altana, Inc. also owns Savage Laboratories (also at this location), which manufactures and markets ethical pharmaceuticals.

FUJISAWA HEALTHCARE, INC.
3 Parkway North, Deerfield IL 60015. 847/317-8800. **Contact:** Personnel. **World Wide Web address:** http://www.fujisawausa.com. **Description:** A pharmaceutical company that markets products to the anti-infective, cardiovascular, transplantation, and dermatology markets. **Corporate headquarters location:** This Location. **Parent company:** Fujisawa Company Ltd.

GPC BIOTECH
One Kendall Square, Building 600, Cambridge MA 02139. 617/225-0001. **Fax:** 617/225-0005. **Contact:** Human Resources. **World Wide Web address:** http://www.gpc-biotech.com. **Description:** A genomics drug discovery company that specializes in proprietary technologies designed to improve the process of drug development. Founded in 1992. **Common positions include:** Chemist. **Educational backgrounds include:** Biology; Chemistry. **Benefits:** 401(k); Casual Dress - Daily; Dental Insurance; Disability Coverage; Life Insurance; Medical Insurance; Tuition Assistance.

Office hours: Monday - Friday, 8:30 a.m. - 5:00 p.m. **Listed on:** Privately held. **Facilities Manager:** Pat Marolda. **Information Systems Manager:** James Schultz. **Purchasing Manager:** Bonnie Grassley.

GENENTECH, INC.
One DNA Way, South San Francisco CA 94080. 650/225-1000. **Contact:** Human Resources Department. **E-mail address:** genentechjobpost@ webhirepc.com. **World Wide Web address:** http://www.gene.com. **Description:** Develops and markets pharmaceuticals using human genetic information. Genentech specializes in products designed to treat growth deficiencies, breast cancer, and AMI. **NOTE:** If sending a hard copy of your resume, please make sure that it is in a scannable format and mail to Genentech, Inc., Human Resources, P.O. Box 1950, South San Francisco CA 94083-1950. **Corporate headquarters location:** This Location. **Listed on:** New York Stock Exchange. **Stock exchange symbol:** GNE.

GENE-TRAK SYSTEMS
94 South Street, Hopkinton MA 01748. 508/435-7400. **Fax:** 508/435-0025. **Contact:** Human Resources. **Description:** Develops, manufactures, and distributes innovative biotechnology-based products for genetic disease, food pathogen testing, and clinical diagnostics. Utilizing DNA probe-based technology, the company has introduced products for cytogenetic analysis and chromosome enumeration that are used in cancer research, as well as tests which detect the presence of pathogens in food products. **Common positions include:** Biological Scientist; Biomedical Engineer; Chemist; Clinical Lab Technician; Electrical/ Electronics Engineer; Food Scientist/Technologist; Manufacturing Engineer; Medical Technologist; Quality Assurance Engineer; Quality Control Supervisor. **Educational backgrounds include:** Biology; Chemistry; Engineering. **Benefits:** 401(k); Daycare Assistance; Dental Insurance; Disability Coverage; Employee Discounts; Life Insurance; Medical Insurance; Tuition Assistance. **Corporate headquarters location:** This Location. **Other U.S. locations:** Naperville IL. **Operations at this facility include:** Administration; Manufacturing; Research and Development; Sales; Service. **Number of employees at this location:** 190. **Number of employees nationwide:** 235.

GENETIC THERAPY INC.
9 West Watkins Mill Road, Gaithersburg MD 20878. 301/258-4600. **Fax:** 301/258-4605. **Contact:** Human Resources. **E-mail address:** gtijobs@pharma.novartis.com. **World Wide Web address:** http://www.novartis.com. **Description:** Engaged in genetic and cancer research. **Common positions include:** Administrative Assistant; Biochemist; Biological Scientist; Molecular Biologist. **Educational backgrounds include:** Biology; Chemistry; Microsoft Office; Spreadsheets. **Benefits:** 401(k); Casual Dress - Daily; Dental Insurance; Disability Coverage; Financial Planning Assistance; Life Insurance; Medical Insurance; Pension Plan; Sick Days (11+); Tuition Assistance; Vacation Days (10 - 20). **Corporate headquarters location:** Palo Alto CA. **International locations:** Worldwide. **Parent company:** Novartis. **Listed on:** Swiss Stock Exchange. **CEO:** Michael Perry. **Number of employees at this location:** 130.

GENEVA PHARMACEUTICALS
2655 West Midway Boulevard, Broomfield CO 80038. 303/466-2400. **Contact:** Personnel. **World Wide Web address:** http://www.genevarx.com. **Description:** Manufactures and distributes generic pharmaceutical products. **Corporate headquarters location:** This Location. **Parent company:** Novartis Corporation.

GENOME THERAPEUTICS CORPORATION
100 Beaver Street, Waltham MA 02453-8443. 781/398-2300. **Fax:** 781/893-9535. **Contact:** Human Resources. **World Wide Web address:** http://www.genomecorp.com. **Description:** Focuses on the research, analysis, and commercial development of genetic information. Founded in 1961. **NOTE:** Entry-level positions and second and third shifts are offered. **Common positions include:** Accountant; Administrative Assistant; Applications Engineer; Biochemist; Biological Scientist; Chemist; Computer Programmer; Computer Support Technician; Controller; Database Administrator; Help-Desk Technician; Human Resources Manager; Intellectual Property Lawyer; Intranet Developer; Molecular Biologist; Public Relations Specialist; Quality Control Supervisor; Secretary; Software Engineer; Statistician; Webmaster. **Educational backgrounds include:** Biology; Chemistry; Computer Science; MBA. **Benefits:** 401(k); Casual Dress - Daily; Dental Insurance; Disability Coverage; Flexible Schedule; Life Insurance; Medical Insurance; Relocation Assistance; Sick Days (1 - 5); Tuition Assistance; Vacation Days (10 - 20). **Office hours:** Monday - Friday 8:30 a.m. - 5:00 p.m. **Corporate headquarters location:** This Location. **Listed on:** NASDAQ; New York Stock Exchange. **Stock exchange symbol:** GENE. **President:** Richard Gill. **Facilities Manager:** James O'Connell. **Information Systems Manager:** Derek Kelly. **Purchasing Manager:** Kurt Hentschel. **Annual sales/revenues:** $21 - $50 million. **Number of employees at this location:** 185.

GENZYME CORPORATION
One Kendall Square, Building 1400, Cambridge MA 02139-1562. 617/252-7500. **Contact:** Human Resources. **World Wide Web address:** http://www.genzyme.com. **Description:** An international, diversified health care products company focused on developing and delivering practical solutions to specific medical needs. The company's activities and products are organized into six primary business areas: Therapeutics, Surgical Products, Genetics, Pharmaceuticals, Diagnostic Services, and Tissue Repair. **Common positions include:** Accountant; Administrative Assistant; Auditor; Biochemist; Biological Scientist; Biomedical Engineer; Chemist; Clinical Lab Technician; Cost Estimator; Database Administrator; Database Manager; Environmental Engineer; Financial Analyst; Geneticist; Intellectual Property Lawyer; Librarian; Licensed Practical Nurse; Manufacturing Engineer; Market Research Analyst; Molecular Biologist; Network Engineer; Network/Systems Administrator; Pharmacist; Purchasing Agent/ Manager; Quality Assurance Engineer; Secretary; Social Worker; Statistician; Systems Analyst; Veterinarian. **Educational backgrounds include:** Accounting; Biology; Business Administration; Chemistry; Computer Science; Engineering; Health Care; Marketing; MBA; Microsoft Office; Microsoft Word; SQL. **Benefits:** 401(k); Casual Dress - Fridays; Dental Insurance; Disability Coverage; Flexible Schedule; Life Insurance; Medical Insurance; Profit Sharing; Public Transit Available; Relocation Assistance; Sick Days (6 - 10); Tuition Assistance; Vacation Days (10 - 20). **Special programs:** Internships; Co-ops; Summer Jobs. **Office hours:** Monday - Friday, 8:30 a.m. - 5:00 p.m. **Corporate headquarters location:** This Location. **Listed on:** NASDAQ. **Annual sales/revenues:** $51 - $100 million. **Number of employees nationwide:** 3,140. **Number of employees worldwide:** 3,700.

GILEAD SCIENCES
333 Lakeside Drive, Foster City CA 94404. 650/574-3000. **Fax:** 650/522-5800. **Contact:** Human Resources Department. **World Wide Web address:** http://www.gilead.com. **Description:** A biopharmaceutical company dedicated to the discovery, development, and commercialization of treatments for human diseases. The company's business is focused on making new therapies available to patients, physicians, and health care systems. The company has developed treatments for diseases caused by HIV, the Hepatitis B virus, the Herpes simplex virus, human papillomavirus, and the influenza virus. **NOTE:** Entry-level positions are offered. **Common positions include:** Biochemist; Biological Scientist; Chemist; Clinical Lab Technician; Research Scientist; Statistician. **Educational backgrounds include:** Biology; Chemistry; Health Care. **Benefits:** 401(k); Daycare Assistance; Dental Insurance; Disability Coverage; Financial Planning Assistance; Flexible Schedule; Life Insurance; Medical Insurance; Public Transit Available. **Corporate headquarters location:** This Location. **Listed on:** NASDAQ. **Stock exchange symbol:** GILD. **Annual sales/revenues:** $11 - $20 million. **Number of employees at this location:** 270.

GLAXO WELLCOME
5 Moore Drive, P.O. Box 13398, Research Triangle Park NC 27709-3398. 919/248-2100. **Contact:** Human Resources. **World Wide Web address:** http://www.glaxowellcome.com. **Description:** A pharmaceutical preparations company whose products include AZT, an AIDS treatment drug; Zantac; and Malarone, a medication for malaria. **NOTE:** In January 2000, Glaxo Wellcome and SmithKline Beecham announced plans to merge. The new company will be named Glaxo SmithKline. Please contact this location for more information. **Common positions include:** Accountant/Auditor; Biological Scientist; Chemist; Clinical Lab Technician; Computer Programmer; Data Processor; Pharmacist; Research Scientist; Systems Analyst. **Educational backgrounds include:** Biology; Chemistry; Computer Science. **Benefits:** 401(k); Daycare Assistance; Dental Insurance; Disability Coverage; Employee Discounts; Life Insurance; Medical Insurance; Pension Plan; Profit Sharing; Savings Plan; Tuition Assistance. **Special programs:** Internships. **Corporate headquarters location:** London, England. **Other U.S. locations:** Zebulon NC. **International locations:** Worldwide. **Listed on:** New York Stock Exchange.

THE HACH COMPANY
P.O. Box 389, Loveland CO 80539-0389. 970/669-3050. **Recorded jobline:** 970/962-6720. **Contact:** Human Resources. **World Wide Web address:** http://www.hach.com. **Description:** Manufactures and sells laboratory instruments, process analyzers, and test kits that analyze the chemical content and other properties of water and other aqueous solutions. The company also produces chemicals for use with its manufactured instruments and test kits. **Common positions include:** Accountant/Auditor; Chemist; Computer Programmer; Electrical/Electronics Engineer; Industrial Engineer; Marketing Specialist; Mechanical Engineer; Systems Analyst; Technical Writer/Editor. **Educational backgrounds include:** Accounting; Chemistry; Communications; Computer Science; Engineering; Marketing. **Benefits:** 401(k); Dental Insurance; Disability Coverage; Life Insurance; Medical Insurance; Pension Plan; Profit Sharing; Savings Plan; Tuition Assistance. **Corporate headquarters location:** This Location. **Other U.S. locations:** Ames IA. **Parent company:** Danaher Corporation. **Listed on:** NASDAQ.

HEALTH-CHEM COMPANIES
460 Park Avenue, New York NY 10022. 212/751-5600. **Contact:** Human Resources. **Description:** Manufactures transdermal pharmaceuticals and protective coatings. Through its subsidiaries, Health-Chem applies its technologies to a variety of products such as mattress ticking, transdermal nitroglycerin patches, insect traps, baseball stadium tarps, livestock curtains, and nuclear power plant fabrics. Health-Chem Companies' products serve the agricultural, environmental, health care, and pharmaceutical industries. **Corporate headquarters location:** This Location. **Subsidiaries include:** Hercon Environmental Corp. (also at this location); Hercon Laboratories Corporation (also at this location); Herculite Products, Inc. (Los Angeles CA); Pacific Combining Corporation (also at this location).

HEMACARE CORPORATION
4954 Van Nuys Boulevard, Sherman Oaks CA 91403. 818/986-3883. **Fax:** 818/986-1417. **Contact:** Human Resources Department. **World Wide Web address:** http://www.hemacare.com. **Description:** Provides blood management programs such as plasma exchange and bone marrow transplantation. The company also operates a donor center. **Corporate headquarters location:** This Location. **Subsidiaries include:** HemaBiologics, Inc. conducts research on anti-HIV pharmaceuticals. **Listed on:** NASDAQ. **Stock exchange symbol:** HEMA.

HEMAGEN DIAGNOSTICS, INC.
40 Bear Hill Road, Waltham MA 02451. 781/890-3766. **Fax:** 781/890-3748. **Contact:** Human Resources. **World Wide Web address:** http://www.hemagen.com. **Description:** Manufactures, and markets proprietary medical diagnostic kits used to aid in the diagnosis of several autoimmune diseases. The kits include several in vitro products as well as cardiovascular tests. **Corporate headquarters location:** This Location. **Listed on:** NASDAQ. **Stock exchange symbol:** HMGN.

HI-TECH PHARMACAL CO., INC.
369 Bayview Avenue, Amityville NY 11701. 631/789-8228. **Contact:** Human Resources. **Description:** Develops, manufactures, and markets generic pharmaceuticals. **Corporate headquarters location:** This Location. **Subsidiaries include:** Health Care Products manufactures branded items marketed under the H-T, Sooth-It, and Diabetic Tussin brands. **Listed on:** NASDAQ. **Stock exchange symbol:** HITK.

HOFFMANN-LA ROCHE INC.
340 Kingsland Street, Nutley NJ 07110. 973/235-5000. **Contact:** Personnel. **World Wide Web address:** http://www.rocheusa.com. **Description:** A health care organization that develops, and manufactures pharmaceuticals, diagnostics, and vitamins. **NOTE:** Entry-level positions, part-time jobs, and second and third shifts are offered. **Common positions include:** Accountant; Auditor; Computer Programmer; Database Administrator; Financial Analyst; Manufacturing Engineer; Market Research Analyst; Marketing Manager; Network Engineer; Public Relations Specialist; Systems Analyst; Website Developer. **Educational backgrounds include:** Accounting; Biology; Chemistry; Computer Science; Engineering; Finance; Marketing; MBA. **Benefits:** 401(k); Casual Dress - Fridays; Daycare Assistance; Dental Insurance; Employee Discounts; Fitness Program; Flexible Schedule; Job Sharing; Life Insurance; Medical Insurance; On-Site Daycare; Pension Plan; Relocation Assistance; Savings Plan; Tuition Assistance. **Special programs:** Co-ops; Internships;

Training. **Corporate headquarters location:** This Location. **Other U.S. locations:** Nationwide. **International locations:** Worldwide. **Subsidiaries include:** Roche Biomedical Laboratories; Roche Diagnostics (ethical pharmaceuticals); Roche Vitamins Inc. **Parent company:** F. Hoffmann-La Roche Ltd. **Listed on:** Privately held. **Annual sales/revenues:** More than $100 million. **Number of employees at this location:** 6,000. **Number of employees nationwide:** 20,000. **Number of employees worldwide:** 80,000.

HUNTINGDON LIFE SCIENCES
P.O. Box 2360, Mettlers Road, East Millstone NJ 08875. 732/873-2550. **Fax:** 732/873-8513. **Contact:** Cathy Brower, Assistant to the President. **E-mail address:** browerc@huntingdon.com. **World Wide Web address:** http://www.huntingdon.com. **Description:** Provides contract biological safety (toxicological) testing services on a worldwide basis through two laboratories in the United States and the United Kingdom. The toxicology divisions of Huntington Life Sciences conduct studies designed to test pharmaceutical products, biologicals, chemical compounds, and other substances in order to produce the data required to identify, quantify, and evaluate the risks to humans and the environment resulting from the manufacture or use of these substances. These divisions also perform analytical and metabolic chemistry services. Huntington Life Sciences also performs clinical trials of new and existing pharmaceutical and biotechnology products and medical devices. The company is engaged in the clinical development process including analytical chemistry, evaluation of clinical data, data processing, biostatistical analysis, and the preparation of supporting documentation for compliance with regulatory requirements. Founded in 1952. **NOTE:** Entry-level positions, part-time jobs, and second and third shifts are offered. **Common positions include:** Accountant; Administrative Assistant; Advertising Executive; Biochemist; Chemist; Computer Engineer; Computer Support Technician; Computer Technician; Finance Director; Help-Desk Technician; Human Resources Manager; Internet Services Manager; Network/Systems Administrator; Purchasing Agent/Manager; Sales Manager; Sales Rep.; Secretary; Systems Analyst; Veterinarian; Vice President. **Educational backgrounds include:** Biology; Business Administration; Chemistry; Computer Science; Marketing; MBA; Microsoft Office; Microsoft Word; Novell. **Benefits:** 401(k); Casual Dress - Fridays; Dental Insurance; Disability Coverage; Flexible Schedule; Life Insurance; Medical Insurance; Relocation Assistance; Sick Days (1 - 5); Tuition Assistance; Vacation Days (10 - 20). **Special programs:** Summer Jobs. **Corporate headquarters location:** Cambridgeshire, UK. **Parent company:** Huntingdon Life Sciences, Ltd. **Listed on:** American Stock Exchange. **Stock exchange symbol:** HTD. **President:** Alan Staple. **Facilities Manager:** Dirk Moedt. **Information Systems Manager:** Donald Wagner. **Purchasing Manager:** Janice Hanas. **Annual sales/revenues:** $51 - $100 million. **Number of employees at this location:** 200. **Number of employees worldwide:** 1,500.

HYCLONE LABORATORIES
1725 South Hyclone Road, Logan UT 84321. 435/753-4584. **Contact:** Human Resources. **World Wide Web address:** http://www.hyclone.com. **Description:** Involved in the extraction of serum from the blood of fetal bovines, equines, and calves which is used to grow new cells. The company also manufactures cell culture media, which promote the growth of these new cells, and BioProcessing Containers, which are sterile plastic containers for storing the serum solutions. **Corporate headquarters location:** This Location.

HYCOR BIOMEDICAL INC.
7272 Chapman Avenue, Garden Grove CA 92841. 714/895-9558. **Contact:** Human Resources. **Description:** Develops, produces, and markets a broad range of diagnostic and medical products. The company's focus is on allergy diagnostics and therapy, microscopic urinalysis, specialized immunodiagnostics, and laboratory controls. **Corporate headquarters location:** This Location.

I-STAT CORPORATION
104 Windsor Center Drive, East Windsor NJ 08520. 609/443-9300. **Fax:** 609/443-9310. **Contact:** Human Resources Department. **E-mail address:** hr_usa@i-stat.com. **World Wide Web address:** http://www.i-stat.com. **Description:** Develops, manufactures, and markets medical diagnostic products for blood analysis. Products of i-Stat provide health care professionals with diagnostic information at the point of patient care. **NOTE:** Entry-level positions and part-time jobs are offered. **Common positions include:** Electrical/Electronics Engineer; Electronics Technician; Mechanical Engineer; Software Engineer. **Educational backgrounds include:** C/C++; Engineering. **Benefits:** 401(k); Casual Dress - Daily; Dental Insurance; Disability Coverage; Life Insurance; Medical Insurance; Vacation Days (6 - 10). **Corporate headquarters location:** This Location. **International locations:** Ontario, Canada. **Listed on:** NASDAQ. **Number of employees at this location:** 120.

IGI, INC.
Wheat Road and Lincoln Avenue, P.O. Box 687, Buena NJ 08310. 856/697-1441. **Contact:** Human Resources. **World Wide Web address:** http://www.askigi.com. **Description:** A diversified company engaged in three business segments: animal health products, cosmetic and consumer products, and biotechnology. The animal health products business produces and markets poultry vaccines, veterinary products, nutritional supplements, and grooming aids. The cosmetic and consumer products business produces and markets dermatologic, cosmetic, and consumer products. The biotechnology business develops and markets various applications of IGI's lipid encapsulation technology, primarily for human medicines and vaccines. **Corporate headquarters location:** This Location.

IVC INDUSTRIES, INC.
500 Halls Mill Road, Freehold NJ 07728. 732/308-3000. **Fax:** 732/308-9793. **Contact:** Human Resources. **World Wide Web address:** http://www.ivcinc.com. **Description:** Manufactures and sells vitamins, herbs, nonprescription pharmaceuticals, and nutritional supplements under the brand names Fields of Nature, Pine Brothers throat drops, Rybutol, Nature's Wonder, Synergy Plus, and Liquafil vitamin supplements. **Corporate headquarters location:** This Location. **Listed on:** NASDAQ. **Stock exchange symbol:** IVCO.

ICOS CORPORATION
22021 20th Avenue SE, Bothell WA 98021. 425/485-1900. **Fax:** 425/489-0356. **Recorded jobline:** 425/485-1900x2032. **Contact:** Human Resources Manager. **E-mail address:** hr@icos.com. **World Wide Web address:** http://www.icos.com. **Description:** Discovers and develops new drugs by targeting early stages of the chronic inflammatory process and by seeking points of intervention that may lead to more specific and efficacious drugs. ICOS scientists are developing pharmaceutical products that address important cellular and

molecular mechanisms in three separate yet interrelated parts of the inflammatory process: directed cell movement, the inhibition of pro-inflammatory mediators, and intracellular signal transduction. ICOS's signal transduction programs in PDE inhibitors and cell cycle checkpoint modulators have yielded additional approaches to treating inflammatory conditions, as well as male erectile dysfunction, cardiovascular diseases, and cancer. **Corporate headquarters location:** This Location.

IDEC PHARMACEUTICALS CORPORATION
11011 Torreyana Road, San Diego CA 92121. 858/550-8500. **Contact:** Human Resources. **World Wide Web address:** http://www.idecpharm.com. **Description:** Manufactures chemotherapeutic drugs for the treatment of lymphoma. The company is also in the clinical trial phase of drug development for diseases such as arthritis. **Corporate headquarters location:** This Location.

IGEN INTERNATIONAL
16020 Industrial Drive, Gaithersburg MD 20877. 301/984-8000. **Fax:** 301/947-6998. **Contact:** Personnel. **E-mail address:** humanresources@igen.com. **World Wide Web address:** http://www.igen.com. **Description:** Develops, and markets diagnostic products used to detect and measure biological substances. The company uses its patented ORIGEN technology to develop these products. The company tests within three markets: the clinical testing market, the industrial market, and the life sciences market. **NOTE:** Entry-level positions are offered. **Common positions include:** Administrative Assistant; Biochemist; Biological Scientist; Chemist; Electrical/Electronics Engineer; Manufacturing Engineer; Marketing Specialist; Mechanical Engineer; Sales Representative. **Educational backgrounds include:** Biology; Chemistry; Engineering. **Benefits:** 401(k); Dental Insurance; Disability Coverage; Life Insurance; Medical Insurance; Tuition Assistance. **Corporate headquarters location:** This Location. **Listed on:** NASDAQ. **Stock exchange symbol:** IGEN.

IMMUCOR
P.O. Box 5625, Norcross GA 30091. 770/441-2051. **Physical address:** 3130 Gateway Drive, Norcross GA. **Toll-free phone:** 800/829-2553. **Fax:** 770/441-3807. **Contact:** Human Resources. **E-mail address:** hr@immucor.com. **World Wide Web address:** http://www.immucor.com. **Description:** An invitro diagnostic company that develops, manufactures, and markets products used by blood banks, hospitals, and clinical laboratories to test, detect, and identify properties of the human blood. **NOTE:** Entry-level positions are offered. **Common positions include:** Biomedical Engineer; Customer Service Representative; Medical Technologist; MIS Specialist; Sales Representative; Software Engineer. **Educational backgrounds include:** Biology; Computer Science; Engineering; Health Care; Marketing. **Benefits:** 401(k); Dental Insurance; Disability Coverage; Life Insurance; Medical Insurance. **Corporate headquarters location:** This Location.

IMMUDYNE, INC.
11200 Wilcrest Green Drive, Houston TX 77042. 713/783-7034. **Contact:** Human Resources. **World Wide Web address:** http://www.immudyne.com. **Description:** Develops, manufactures, and markets dietary supplements and skin care products. **Corporate headquarters location:** This Location.

IMMULOGIC PHARMACEUTICAL CORP.
610 Lincoln Street, Waltham MA 02451. 781/466-6000. **Fax:** 781/466-6010. **Contact:** Human Resources. Department. **Description:** Manufactures and markets peptide immunotherapeutics to treat allergies and autoimmune diseases. **Common positions include:** Biochemist; Biological Scientist; Chemist. **Educational backgrounds include:** Biology; Chemistry. **Benefits:** 401(k); Dental Insurance; Disability Coverage; Life Insurance; Medical Insurance; Tuition Assistance. **Corporate headquarters location:** This Location. **Listed on:** NASDAQ. **Stock exchange symbol:** IMUL. **Annual sales/revenues:** Less than $5 million. **Number of employees at this location:** 155.

IMMUNEX CORPORATION
Immunex Building, 51 University Street, Seattle WA 98101. 206/587-0430. **Contact:** Human Resources. **World Wide Web address:** http://www.immunex.com. **Description:** Researches, discovers, manufactures, and markets products that treat immune system disorders. **Common positions include:** Biological Scientist; Chemist; Clinical Lab Technician; Medical Records Technician; Pharmacist; Physician; Statistician; Systems Analyst. **Educational backgrounds include:** Biology; Business Administration; Chemistry; Mathematics. **Benefits:** Dental Insurance; Disability Coverage; Life Insurance; Medical Insurance; Pension Plan; Savings Plan; Tuition Assistance. **Corporate headquarters location:** This Location. **Other area locations:** Bothell WA. **Listed on:** NASDAQ. **Number of employees at this location:** 800.

IMMUNOCHEMISTRY TECHNOLOGIES
9401 James Avenue South, Suite 155, Bloomington MN 55431. 952/888-8788. **Contact:** Vice President of Marketing. **World Wide Web address:** http://www.mm.com/ichem. **Description:** Develops, and manufactures custom-designed immunoassays in kit form. The company also provides protein purification, modification, and conjugation services, as well as antibody production. Founded in 1994. **NOTE:** Entry-level positions are offered. **Common positions include:** Biochemist; Biological Scientist; Chemist; Clinical Lab Technician; Market Research Analyst. **Educational backgrounds include:** Biology; Business Administration; Chemistry; Marketing. **Benefits:** Medical Insurance. **Corporate headquarters location:** This Location. **Listed on:** Privately held. **President:** Gary L. Johnson. **Annual sales/revenues:** Less than $5 million. **Number of employees at this location:** 15.

IMMUNOGEN INC.
333 Providence Highway, Norwood MA 02062. 781/769-4242. **Contact:** Human Resources. **World Wide Web address:** http://www.immunogen.com. **Description:** ImmunoGen is engaged in the research and development of pharmaceuticals, primarily for the treatment of cancer. The company's product line consists of proprietary toxins or drugs coupled with highly-specific targeting agents. The drugs, called immunoconjugates, are designed to identifyand destroy target cells. **Corporate headquarters location:** This Location. **Other U.S. locations:** Cambridge MA.

INHALE THERAPEUTIC SYSTEMS, INC.
150 Industrial Road, San Carlos CA 94070. 650/631-3100. **Fax:** 650/631-3150. **Contact:** Human Resources. **World Wide Web address:** http://www.inhale.com. **Description:** Researches, develops, and manufactures aerosol drug delivery systems for the treatment of lung diseases. The system allows macromolecules of drug powder particles to be absorbed by alveoli in the lungs. **Corporate headquarters location:** This Location.

INSITE VISION
965 Atlantic Avenue, Alameda CA 94501. 510/865-8800. **Fax:** 510/865-5700. **Contact:** Human Resources. **World Wide Web address:** http://www.insitevision.com. **Description:** Develops and manufactures ophthalmic pharmaceuticals. The company is responsible for the development of the DuraSite eye drop-based drug delivery system, which provides a steady drug flow to the eye over an elapsed period of time. **Corporate headquarters location:** This Location.

INTERNEURON PHARMACEUTICALS
One Ledgemont Center, 99 Hayden Avenue, Lexington MA 02421. 781/861-8444. **Contact:** Personnel. **World Wide Web address:** http://www.interneuron.com. **Description:** Develops medical products to treat neurological and behavioral disorders. **Corporate headquarters location:** This Location. **Subsidiaries include:** Intercardia, Inc.; Progenitor, Inc.; and Transcell Technologies, Inc. develop products and technologies that treat cardiovascular disease, and are used for gene therapy, stem cell production, oligosaccharide synthesis, and drug transport.

IRWIN NATURALS FOR HEALTH NATURE'S SECRET
5310 Beethoven Street, Los Angeles CA 90066. 310/253-5305. **Contact:** Human Resources. **Description:** Develops herbal remedies and nutritional products. Nature's Secret is the brand name of the company's line of vitamins. **Common positions include:** Sales Executive; Sales Rep.. **Parent company:** OMNI Neutraceuticals. **Annual sales/revenues:** $21 - $50 million.

IVAX CORPORATION
4400 Biscayne Boulevard, Miami FL 33137. 305/575-6000. **Contact:** Director of Human Resources. **World Wide Web address:** http://www.ivax.com. **Description:** IVAX Corporation is a holding company with subsidiaries involved in specialty chemicals, pharmaceuticals, personal care products, and medical diagnostics. The company's principal business is the research, development, manufacture, marketing, and distribution of health care products. Brand name products, marketed under the Baker Norton trade name, include the urological medications Bicitra, Polycitra, Polycitra-K, Polycitra-LC, Neutra-Phos, Neutra-Phos-K, Prohim, Urotrol, Lubraseptic Jelly, and Pro-Banthine; and cardiovascular medicines Cordilox, Triam-Co, Amil-Co, Spiro-Co, and Fru-Co. Other drugs include Proglycem, used to treat hyperinsulinism; Serenance, a neuroleptic used for psychiatric disorders; the respiratory medications Cromogen, Salamol, and Beclazone metered dose inhalers; the Steri-Nebs line of nebulization products; and Eye-Crom and Glaucol. IVAX also markets generic drugs. Through DVM Pharmaceuticals, Inc., IVAX formulates, packages, and distributes veterinary products including DermCaps, a daily dietary supplement; a line of topical therapeutics including ChlorhexiDerm Flush and shampoo, OxyDex shampoo and gel, HyLyt shampoo and rinse, and Relief shampoo, rinse, and spray; two groups of optic products known as Clear and OtiCalm; the DuraKyl and SynerKyl line of ectoparasiticidals; and the wound dressing BioDres. **Corporate headquarters location:** This Location. **Listed on:** American Stock Exchange. **Stock exchange symbol:** IVX. **Number of employees nationwide:** 2,910.

THE JACKSON LABORATORY
600 Main Street, Bar Harbor ME 04609. 207/288-6000. **Contact:** Joanne Bradt, Employment Specialist. **World Wide Web address:** http://www.jax.org. **Description:** The Jackson Laboratory is an independent, nonprofit institution. A staff of more than 30 scientists conducts research directed toward two general goals: the development of new knowledge of mammalian genetics through the use of inbred and mutant mice; and the investigation of basic biological processes and their relationships to human diseases by combining genetic knowledge with that of other disciplines. In addition to research, the laboratory offers research training programs. **Common positions include:** Biological Scientist; Computer Programmer; Systems Analyst. **Educational backgrounds include:** Biology; Computer Science. **Benefits:** Dental Insurance; Disability Coverage; Life Insurance; Medical Insurance; Pension Plan. **Corporate headquarters location:** This Location. **Number of employees at this location:** 650.

JAYCOR
9775 Towne Centre Drive, San Diego CA 92186. 858/453-6580. **Fax:** 858/457-5190. **Contact:** Human Resources Administrator. **World Wide Web address:** http://www.jaycor.com. **Description:** Provides scientific, high-tech research and development for public and private companies as well as the U.S. Department of Defense. Jaycor specializes in civil engineering, communications, and biological defense systems. **NOTE:** Entry-level positions are offered. **Common positions include:** Accountant; Computer Programmer; Electrical/Electronics Engineer; Physicist; Secretary; Technical Writer/Editor. **Educational backgrounds include:** Accounting; Computer Science; Engineering. **Benefits:** 401(k); Daycare Assistance; Dental Insurance; Disability Coverage; Employee Discounts; Life Insurance; Medical Insurance; Pension Plan; Profit Sharing; Tuition Assistance; Vision Plan. **Special programs:** Internships. **Corporate headquarters location:** This Location. **Other U.S. locations:** Nationwide. **Listed on:** Privately held. **Number of employees at this location:** 120. **Number of employees nationwide:** 500.

JONES PHARMA, INC.
1945 Craig Road, St. Louis MO 63146. 314/576-6100. **Fax:** 314/682-3118. **Contact:** Human Resources. **World Wide Web address:** http://www.jmedpharma.com. **Description:** A pharmaceutical manufacturer that focuses on three specialties. The company produces endocrine products for the treatment of thyroid disease; manufactures and markets a variety of veterinary pharmaceuticals; and markets pharmaceuticals used in hospitals. **Corporate headquarters location:** This Location. **Subsidiaries include:** GenTrac; JMI Phoenix Laboratories, Inc.; JMI-Canton Pharmaceuticals, Inc. **Listed on:** NASDAQ. **Stock exchange symbol:** JMED.

KV PHARMACEUTICAL COMPANY
10888 Metro Court, St. Louis MO 63043. 314/645-6600. **Fax:** 314/567-1096. **Contact:** Staffing Department. **Description:** Researches, develops, produces, and sells drug delivery products. **NOTE:** Second and third shifts are offered. **Common positions include:** Account Manager; Account Representative; Accountant; Administrative Assistant; AS400 Programmer Analyst; Assistant Manager; Biochemist; Budget Analyst; Chemical Engineer; Chemist; Customer Service Rep.; Financial Analyst; Industrial Production Manager; Manufacturing Engineer; Mechanical Engineer; Network/Systems Administrator; Operations Manager; Production Manager; Quality Control Supervisor; Sales Rep.; Secretary; Statistician; Website Developer. **Educational backgrounds include:** Accounting; AS400 Certification; Biology;

Business Administration; Chemistry; Computer Science; Engineering; Finance; Marketing; MBA; MCSE; Microsoft Office; Microsoft Word; Public Relations; Spreadsheets. **Benefits:** 401(k); Casual Dress - Daily; Dental Insurance; Disability Coverage; Life Insurance; Medical Insurance; Profit Sharing; Relocation Assistance; Stock Option; Tuition Assistance; Vacation Days (11 - 15). **Office hours:** Monday - Friday, 8:00 a.m. - 4:30 p.m. **Corporate headquarters location:** This Location. **Listed on:** New York Stock Exchange. **Number of employees nationwide:** 550.

LA JOLLA PHARMACEUTICAL COMPANY
6455 Nancy Ridge Drive, San Diego CA 92121. 858/452-6600. **Fax:** 858/625-0155. **Contact:** Human Resources. **E-mail address:** hr@ljpc.com. **World Wide Web address:** http://www.ljpc.com. **Description:** Develops highly specific therapeutics to treat antibody-mediated and inflammatory diseases. The company develops therapeutics for recurrent fetal loss, autoimmune stroke, Rh hemolytic disease of the newborn, myasthenia gravis, and Graves' disease. The company also develops compounds that control inflammation. **Corporate headquarters location:** This Location. **Listed on:** NASDAQ. **Stock exchange symbol:** LJPC.

LABORATORY CORPORATION OF AMERICA (LABCORP)
P.O. Box 2230, Burlington NC 27216. 336/229-1127. **Physical address:** 358 South Main Street, Burlington NC 27215. **Contact:** Human Resources. **World Wide Web address:** http://www.labcorp.com. **Description:** One of the nation's leading clinical laboratory companies, providing services primarily to physicians, as well as to hospitals, clinics, nursing homes, and other clinical labs nationwide. LabCorp performs tests on blood, urine, and other body fluids and tissue, aiding in the diagnosis of diseases. **Common positions include:** Biological Scientist; Chemist; Manufacturer's/Wholesaler's Sales Rep.; Technician. **Educational backgrounds include:** Biology; Chemistry; Medical Technology; Sales. **Benefits:** Stock Purchase. **Special programs:** Internships. **Corporate headquarters location:** This Location. **Other U.S. locations:** Nationwide. **Listed on:** American Stock Exchange; NASDAQ; New York Stock Exchange. **Stock exchange symbol:** LH. **Number of employees nationwide:** 18,000.

ERNEST ORLANDO LAWRENCE BERKELEY NATIONAL LABORATORY
2120 University Avenue, Berkeley CA 94720. 510/486-7950. **Fax:** 510/486-5870. **Contact:** Human Resources. **E-mail address:** employment@lbl.gov. **World Wide Web address:** http://www.lbl.gov. **Description:** A multiprogram national research facility operated by the University of California for the Department of Energy. The company's major activities include the Advanced Light Source, Human Genome Center, California Institute for Energy Efficiency, and the Center for Advanced Materials. **Common positions include:** Biological Scientist; Chemical Engineer; Chemist; Electrical/Electronics Engineer; Environmental Engineer; Geologist/Geophysicist; Mathematician; Mechanical Engineer; Physicist; Science Technologist; **Educational backgrounds include:** Biology; Chemistry; Engineering; Mathematics; Physics. **Benefits:** 401(k); Dental Insurance; Disability Coverage; Employee Discounts; Life Insurance; Medical Insurance; Pension Plan; Public Transit Available; Savings Plan; Telecommuting; Tuition Assistance. **Special programs:** Internships. **Corporate headquarters location:** This Location. **Number of employees at this location:** 3,000.

LIFE MEDICAL SCIENCES, INC.
379 Thornall Street, Edison NJ 08837-2227. 732/494-0444. **Fax:** 732/494-6252. **Contact:** Personnel. **World Wide Web address:** http://www.lifemed.com. **Description:** Develops and markets medical products for use in a variety of therapeutic applications. Products include REPEL, to prevent surgical scars; REPEL-CV, to prevent scars as a result of cardiovascular surgery; RESOLVE, for the reduction of surgical scars; and CLINICEL, a scar management product. **Corporate headquarters location:** This Location. **Listed on:** NASDAQ. **Stock exchange symbol:** CHAI. **President:** Robert P. Hickey.

LIFE TECHNOLOGIES, INC.
9800 Medical Center Drive, Rockville MD 20850. 301/840-4000. **Fax:** 301/610-8020. **Recorded jobline:** 301/610-8022. **Contact:** Human Resources. **World Wide Web address:** http://www.lifetech.com. **Description:** Develops, manufactures, and markets products used principally in life sciences research and the commercial manufacture of genetically engineered products. The company is also a supplier of sera and cell growth media, as well as enzymes and other biological products necessary for recombinant DNA procedures. **Common positions include:** Associate Scientist; Biological Scientist; Chemical Engineer; Chemist; Graphic Artist; Scientist; Technical Writer/Editor. **Educational backgrounds include:** Biology; Engineering; M.I.S. **Benefits:** 401(k); Daycare Assistance; Dental Insurance; Disability Coverage; Employee Discounts; Life Insurance; Medical Insurance; Pension Plan; Profit Sharing; Stock Option; Tuition Assistance. **Special programs:** Internships. **Corporate headquarters location:** This Location. **International locations:** Worldwide.

LIFECELL CORPORATION
One Millennium Way, Branchburg NJ 08876. 908/947-1100. **Contact:** Human Resources. **World Wide Web address:** http://www.lifecell.com. **Description:** Designs, manufactures, and produces products dealing with skin grafts for burn patients and with the preservation of transfusable blood platelets (blood cells that control clotting). LifeCell's main product, AlloDerm, removes the cells in allograft skin (from a cadaveric donor) that the patient's own immune system would normally reject. This technology enables the AlloDerm to become populated with the patient's own skin cells and blood vessels. Founded in 1986.

LIGAND PHARMACEUTICALS INC.
10275 Science Center Drive, San Diego CA 92121. 858/550-7500. **Contact:** Personnel. **World Wide Web address:** http://www.ligand.com. **Description:** A biopharmaceutical company that researches, develops, manufactures, and sells small molecule pharmaceutical products that address the medical needs of patients with cancer, cardiovascular and inflammatory diseases, osteoporosis, and matabolic disorders. **Corporate headquarters location:** This Location. **Listed on:** NASDAQ. **Stock exchange symbol:** LGND.

THE LIPOSOME COMPANY, INC.
One Research Way, Princeton Forrestal Center, Princeton NJ 08540-6619. 609/452-7060. **Contact:** Human Resources. **World Wide Web address:** http://www.lipo.com. **Description:** Develops liposome-based pharmaceuticals for the treatment, prevention, and diagnosis of cancer, systemic fungal infections, and inflammatory and vaso-occlusive diseases. **Corporate headquarters location:** This Location.

LOVELACE RESPIRATORY RESEARCH INSTITUTE
2425 Ridgecrest Drive SE, Albuquerque NM 87108. 505/262-7155. **Contact:** Personnel. **World Wide Web address:** http://www.lrri.org. **Description:** A private biomedical research institute that is focused solely on respiratory disease research. **NOTE:** Entry-level positions are offered. **Common positions include:** Biochemist; Biological Scientist; Chemist; Secretary; Veterinarian. **Educational backgrounds include:** Biology; Chemistry; Physics; Toxicology. **Benefits:** Dental Insurance; Disability Coverage; EAP; Life Insurance; Medical Insurance; Pension Plan; Tuition Assistance. **Internship information:** Post-doctoral positions are available year-round. Please call for more information. **Corporate headquarters location:** This Location. **Number of employees at this location:** 150. **Number of employees nationwide:** 310.

LYNNTECH INC.
7610 Eastmark Drive, Suite 202, College Station TX 77840. 979/693-0017. **Contact:** Human Resources. **World Wide Web address:** http://www.lynntech.com. **Description:** Offers a broad range of research services including environmental and genetic research. Lynntech receives most of its business from government contracts. **Corporate headquarters location:** This Location.

MDS HARRIS
P.O. Box 80837, Lincoln NE 68501. 402/476-2811. **Contact:** Human Resources. **World Wide Web address:** http://www.mdsharris.com. **Description:** Offers a complete range of clinical trials, analytical and statistical services, and consumer product research. These services are provided from facilities and offices in the United States, Europe, and Japan, and in more than 1,000 clinical investigation sites. MDS Harris performs all types of Phase I studies including complete bioavailability and bioequivalence studies and pharmacokinetic/ pharmacodynamic clinical studies with healthy and special populations, as well as offering data analysis and customized reporting. MDS Harris also designs and manages complete Phase II, III, and IV multi-center clinical studies. MDS Harris associates have extensive expertise in a wide range of therapeutic areas including oncology, CNS, anti-infectives, dermatology, inflammation and tissue repair, cardiopulmonary conditions, and vaccines. **Corporate headquarters location:** This Location. **Other area locations:** Omaha NE. **Other U.S. locations:** Phoenix AZ.

M.I.T. LINCOLN LABORATORY
244 Wood Street, Lexington MA 02420-9108. 781/981-7066. **Fax:** 781/981-2011. **Contact:** Human Resources. **E-mail address:** resume@ ll.mit.edu. **World Wide Web address:** http://www. ll.mit.edu. **Description:** A federally-funded, non-profit research center of the Massachusetts Institute of Technology (M.I.T.). Lincoln Laboratory applies science, by means of advanced technology, to critical problems of national security such as space surveillance, tactical systems, free space and terrestrial optical communications, and air traffic control systems. Founded in 1951. **NOTE:** Resumes must be in a scannable format and may be e-mailed (ASCII text file) or faxed. **Common positions include:** Applications Engineer; Computer Engineer; Computer Programmer; Computer Scientist; Computer Support Technician; Computer Technician; Electrical/Electronics Engineer; Electrician; Mechanical Engineer; Network/ Systems Administrator; Software Engineer; SQL Programmer; **Educational backgrounds include:** Computer Science; Engineering; Mathematics;

Physics. **Benefits:** 401(k); 403(b); Life Insurance; Medical Insurance; On-Site Daycare; Pension Plan; Tuition Assistance. **Office hours:** Monday - Friday, 8:30 a.m. - 5:00 p.m. **Corporate headquarters location:** This Location. **Number of employees at this location:** 2,200.

MACROCHEM CORPORATION
110 Hartwell Avenue, Lexington MA 02421-3123. 781/862-4003. **Fax:** 781/862-4338. **Contact:** Human Resources. **World Wide Web address:** http://www.mchm.com. **Description:** Develops and commercializes advanced drug delivery systems for the transdermal delivery of enzyme, protein, and drug compounds for therapeutic, over-the-counter, and cosmetic applications. SEPA, MacroChem's worldwide patented compound, accelerates the passage of drugs through the skin and other biomembranes. MacroDerm, the company's topical polymer, provides a broad range of benefits to cosmetic and OTC formulators. MacroChem also provides broad benefits to the biomedical industry by creating safe and stable protein formulations for therapeutic use. **Corporate headquarters location:** This Location.

MAGAININ PHARMACEUTICALS INC.
5110 Campus Drive, Plymouth Meeting PA 19462. 610/941-4020. **Fax:** 610/941-5399. **Contact:** Human Resources. **World Wide Web address:** http://www.magainin.com. **Description:** Engaged in the development of medicine for serious diseases. The company's clinical development efforts are focused on oncology with ongoing research efforts in respiratory and infectious diseases. **Benefits:** 401(k); Casual Dress - Daily; Dental Insurance; Disability Coverage; Life Insurance; Medical Insurance; Tuition Assistance.

MALLINCKRODT, INC.
3600 North Second Street, St. Louis MO 63147. 314/654-2000. **Contact:** Human Resources. **World Wide Web address:** http://www.mallinckrodt.com. **Description:** Manufactures and markets healthcare products through three main specialty groups. The Imaging Group provides magnetic resonance, nuclear medicine, and X-ray products. The Pharmaceuticals group provides pharmaceutical products for addiction therapy and pain relief. The Respiratory Group designs airway management systems and respiratory devices. **NOTE:** Jobseekers should send resumes to Corporate Employment, 675 McDonnell Boulevard, P.O. Box 5840, St. Louis MO 63134. **Common positions include:** Accountant; Attorney; Computer Programmer; Financial Analyst. **Educational backgrounds include:** Accounting; Business Administration; Computer Science; Finance. **Benefits:** Dental Insurance; Life Insurance; Medical Insurance; Pension Plan; Tuition Assistance. **Corporate headquarters location:** This Location.

MARTEK BIOSCIENCES CORPORATION
6480 Dobbin Road, Columbia MD 21045. 410/740-0081. **Contact:** Human Resources Manager. **World Wide Web address:** http://www.martekbio.com. **Description:** Engaged in the research, development, and production of nutritional supplements, food ingredients, reagents, and pharmaceuticals drawn from the ocean's microalgae supply. Founded in 1985. **Corporate headquarters location:** This Location. **Listed on:** NASDAQ. **Stock exchange symbol:** MATK.

MATRITECH, INC.
330 Nevada Street, Newton MA 02460. 617/928-0820. **Toll-free phone:** 800/320-2521. **Contact:** Human Resources Department. **World Wide Web address:** http://www.matritech.com. **Description:** A

biotechnology company that uses proprietary, nuclear matrix protein technology to develop and commercialize innovative serum-, cell-, and urine-based NMP diagnostics that enable physicians to detect and monitor the presence of bladder, breast, colorectal, cervical, and prostate cancers. The company's other primary focus is the development of additional serum assays for lung, liver, pancreatic, stomach, and renal cancer. Founded in 1987. **NOTE:** Entry-level positions are offered. **Common positions include:** Biochemist; Research Assistant. **Educational backgrounds include:** Biology; Chemistry. **Benefits:** 401(k); Life Insurance; Medical Insurance; Tuition Assistance. **Corporate headquarters location:** This Location. **Listed on:** NASDAQ. **CEO:** Stephen D. Chubb. **Annual sales/revenues:** Less than $5 million. **Number of employees at this location:** 55.

MATRIX PHARMACEUTICAL, INC.
34700 Campus Drive, Fremont CA 94555. 510/742-9900. **Fax:** 510/742-8510. **Contact:** Human Resources. **World Wide Web address:** http://www.matx.com. **Description:** Develops and manufactures treatments for cancer that can be delivered through intratumoral delivery systems or intravenous injection. **Corporate headquarters location:** This Location. **Listed on:** NASDAQ. **Stock exchange symbol:** MATX. **Number of employees at this location:** 105.

McGHAN MEDICAL
48490 Milmont Drive, Fremont CA 94538. 510/623-2400. **Contact:** Personnel. **Description:** A world leader in the development of collagen-based biomaterials. **Corporate headquarters location:** This Location.

MERCK & COMPANY, INC.
P.O. Box 100, One Merck Drive, Whitehouse Station NJ 08889-0100. 908/423-1000. **Contact:** Human Resources. **World Wide Web address:** http://www.merck.com. **Description:** A worldwide organization engaged in discovering, developing, producing, and marketing products for health care and the maintenance of the environment. Products include human and animal pharmaceuticals and chemicals sold to the health care, oil exploration, food processing, textile, paper, and other industries. Merck also runs an ethical drug mail-order marketing business. **Corporate headquarters location:** This Location.

MICROMERITICS INSTRUMENT CORP.
One Micromeritics Drive, Norcross GA 30093. 770/662-3678. **Contact:** Director of Human Resources. **World Wide Web address:** http://www.micromeritics.com. **Description:** Produces and distributes laboratory analysis equipment used in various health care and scientific applications including liquid chromatographs. **Benefits:** Dental Insurance; Disability Coverage; Life Insurance; Medical Insurance; Savings Plan. **Corporate headquarters location:** This Location. **Operations at this facility include:** Manufacturing; Research and Development.

MILLIPORE CORPORATION
80 Ashby Road, Bedford MA 01730. 781/533-6000. **Contact:** Employment Manager. **World Wide Web address:** http://www.millipore.com. **Description:** Manufactures microporous filters and filtration devices used for the analysis, separation, and purification of fluids. Products are used in the fields of health care, pharmaceuticals, micro-electronics, biological sciences, and genetic engineering. **Common positions include:** Accountant/Auditor; Biological Scientist; Biomedical Engineer; Blue-Collar Worker Supervisor; Buyer; Chemical Engineer; Chemist; Computer Programmer; Credit Manager; Customer Service Rep.; Department Manager; Draftsperson; Financial Analyst; General Manager; Human Resources Manager; Industrial Engineer; Manufacturer's/Wholesaler's Sales Rep.; Marketing Specialist; Mechanical Engineer; Operations/Production Manager; Quality Control Supervisor; Systems Analyst; Transportation/Traffic Specialist. **Educational backgrounds include:** Accounting; Biochemistry; Biology; Business Administration; Chemistry; Engineering; Finance. **Benefits:** Dental Insurance; Disability Coverage; Employee Discounts; Life Insurance; Medical Insurance; Pension Plan; Profit Sharing; Savings Plan; Stock Option; Tuition Assistance. **Corporate headquarters location:** This Location.

THE MONTICELLO COMPANY
1604 Stockton Street, Jacksonville FL 32204. 904/384-3666. **Contact:** Personnel. **Description:** This location provides administrative services. Overall, The Monticello Company manufactures and sells over-the-counter pharmaceuticals produced at the company's plant in Mexico. **Corporate headquarters location:** This Location. **Parent company:** Monticello Companies.

MOORE MEDICAL CORPORATION
389 John Downey Drive, New Britain CT 06050. 860/826-3600. **Contact:** Human Resources Manager. **World Wide Web address:** http://www.mooremedical.com. **Description:** A distributor of pharmaceuticals and medical supplies. Primary customers include pharmacies, physicians, dentists, veterinarians, emergency medical services, school systems, and correctional facilities. **Common positions include:** Administrative Worker/Clerk; Buyer; Computer Programmer; Customer Service Rep.; Department Manager; Manufacturer's/Wholesaler's Sales Rep.; Secretary; Warehouse/Distribution Worker. **Educational backgrounds include:** Accounting; Business Administration; Communications; Computer Science; Liberal Arts; Marketing. **Benefits:** 401(k); Dental Insurance; Disability Coverage; Employee Discounts; Life Insurance; Medical Insurance; Pension Plan; Tuition Assistance. **Corporate headquarters location:** This Location. **Other U.S. locations:** Hayward CA; Visalia CA; Lemont IL. **Operations at this facility include:** Administration; Sales; Service. **Listed on:** American Stock Exchange. **Number of employees nationwide:** 425.

MYLAN LABORATORIES INC.
1030 Century Building, 130 Seventh Street, Pittsburgh PA 15222. 412/232-0100. **Contact:** Human Resources. **World Wide Web address:** http://wwwmylan.com. **Description:** Manufactures generic pharmaceutical products in finished tablet, capsule, and powder dosage forms for resale by others under their own labels. Mylan Laboratories, through its subsidiaries, also develops and manufactures wound care products. **Corporate headquarters location:** This Location. **Number of employees nationwide:** 1,240.

NAPP TECHNOLOGIES
299 Market Street, 4th Floor, Saddle Brook NJ 07663. 201/843-4664. **Contact:** Personnel. **World Wide Web address:** http://www.napptech.com. **Description:** Manufactures bulk pharmaceuticals, cosmetic materials, and fine chemicals. **Corporate headquarters location:** This Location.

NATIONAL INSTITUTE OF ENVIRONMENTAL HEALTH SCIENCES
P.O. Box 12233, Mail Drop EC - 11, Research Triangle Park NC 27709. 919/541-0218. **Contact:** Human Resources. **World Wide Web address:**

http://www.niehs.nih.gov. **Description:** Specializes in biomedical research programs, communication strategies, and prevention and intervention efforts. The focus of the Institute is to reduce human illness and dysfunction caused by the environment.

NATIONAL OPTICAL ASTRONOMY OBSERVATORIES
P.O. Box 26732, Tucson AZ 85726. 520/318-8386. **Fax:** 520/318-8560. **Contact:** Human Resources. **E-mail address:** hrnoao@noao.edu. **World Wide Web address:** http://www.noao.edu. **Description:** Responsible for the development and continuing operation of the Kitt Peak National Observatory, which provides observational frontier research in optical astronomy. **Common positions include:** Astronomer; Electrical/Electronics Engineer; Mechanical Engineer; Physicist. **Educational backgrounds include:** Computer Science; Engineering; Physics. **Benefits:** 401(k); 403(b); Casual Dress - Daily; Dental Insurance; Disability Coverage; Flexible Schedule; Life Insurance; Medical Insurance; Sick Days; Telecommuting; Tuition Assistance; Vacation Days (20+). **Other U.S. locations:** Hilo HI; Baltimore MD; Sunspot NM. **International locations:** Worldwide. **Parent company:** AURA. **Director:** Dr. Sidney Wolff. **Number of employees at this location:** 330. **Number of employees worldwide:** 500.

NATURE'S SUNSHINE
75 East 1700 South, Provo UT 84606. 801/342-4300. **Contact:** Human Resources. **World Wide Web address:** http://www.naturessunshine.com. **Description:** Produces herbs and vitamins in capsule form. Nature's Sunshine manufactures over 200 vitamin and health products. **Corporate headquarters location:** This Location.

NATURE'S WAY
10 Mountain Springs Parkway, Springville UT 84663. 801/489-1483. **Toll-free phone:** 800/962-8873. **Fax:** 801/489-1484. **Recorded jobline:** 801/489-1501. **Contact:** Human Resources **E-mail address:** andreacl@naturesway.com. **World Wide Web address:** http://www.naturesway.com. **Description:** Manufactures health foods including herbs and vitamins. **NOTE:** Entry-level positions and second and third shifts are offered. This firm does not accept unsolicited resumes. Please call the jobline for a list of available positions. Founded in 1969. **Company slogan:** To advance healthy living through natural choices. **Common positions include:** Account Manager; Account Rep.; Accountant; Administrative Assistant; Biochemist; Blue-Collar Worker Supervisor; Chemist; Chief Financial Officer; Computer Programmer; Computer Support Technician; Computer Technician; Controller; Customer Service Rep.; Dietician/Nutritionist; Electrician; Graphic Artist; Graphic Designer; Human Resources Manager; Librarian; Marketing Manager; Marketing Specialist; Network/Systems Administrator; Operations Manager; Production Manager; Purchasing Agent/Manager; Quality Control Supervisor; Sales Representative; Systems Analyst; Technical Writer/Editor. **Educational backgrounds include:** Accounting; Art/Design; Business Administration; C/C++; Chemistry; Computer Science; Finance; Marketing; MCSE; Microsoft Word; QuarkXPress; Software Development; Software; Support; Spreadsheets. **Benefits:** 401(k); Casual Dress - Fridays; Dental Insurance; Disability Coverage; Employee Discounts; Life Insurance; Medical Insurance; Savings Plan; Sick Days (6 - 10); Tuition Assistance; Vacation Days (6 - 10). **Corporate headquarters location:** This Location. **Parent company:** Murdock Madaus Schwabe. **Listed on:** Privately held.

NEIGHBORCARE
1250 East Diehl Road, Suite 208, Naperville IL 60563. 630/245-4800. **Fax:** 630/505-1319. **Contact:** Human Resources Manager. **World Wide Web address:** http://www.neighborcare.com. **Description:** An institutional pharmacy provider that offers services such as infusion therapy, drug distribution, patient management, educational services, and consulting services for managing health care costs. **Common positions include:** Account Manager; Accountant; Budget Analyst; Controller; Financial Analyst; Human Resources Manager; Marketing Manager; Marketing Specialist; MIS Specialist; Pharmacist; Purchasing Agent/Manager; Registered Nurse; Secretary; Systems Analyst; Systems Manager; Transportation/Traffic Specialist. **Educational backgrounds include:** Pharmacology. **Office hours:** Monday - Friday, 8:30 a.m. - 5:00 p.m. **Other U.S. locations:** Nationwide. **Annual sales/revenues:** More than $100 million. **Number of employees at this location:** 100.

NEORX CORPORATION
410 West Harrison Street, Seattle WA 98119. 206/281-7001. **Fax:** 206/284-7112. **Contact:** Personnel. **World Wide Web address:** http://www.neorx.com. **Description:** Develops treatments for cancer and cardiovascular disease. The company's focus is on targeting therapeutic agents on diseased or injured cells, while sparing normal tissues the full impact of these treatments. The company's cardiovascular program is focused primarily on reducing reclosure of coronary arteries following balloon angioplasty. **Common positions include:** Accountant/Auditor; Attorney; Biological Scientist; Buyer; Chemist; Computer Programmer; Human Resources Manager; Statistician. **Educational backgrounds include:** Biology; Chemistry. **Benefits:** 401(k); Dental Insurance; Disability Coverage; Life Insurance; Medical Insurance; Tuition Assistance. **Corporate headquarters location:** This Location. **Listed on:** NASDAQ. **Number of employees at this location:** 80.

NEUREX CORPORATION
800 Gateway Boulevard, South San Francisco CA 94080. 650/853-1500. **Contact:** Human Resources. **Description:** Manufactures and markets acute care pharmaceuticals. Products include Corlopam, which is used in hospitals to lower blood pressure; and Ziconotide, which is used to treat pain and neurodegeneration caused by head injuries or strokes. **Corporate headquarters location:** This Location.

NEUROGEN CORPORATION
35 NE Industrial Road, Branford CT 06405. 203/488-8201. **Fax:** 203/481-8683. **Contact:** Human Resources Manager. **World Wide Web address:** http://www.neurogen.com. **Description:** Manufactures and markets neuropharmaceuticals for the treatment of psychiatric and neurological disorders through research involving molecular biology, medicinal chemistry, genetic engineering, and neurobiology. Development has also begun on new psychotherapeutic drugs to aid in treating a wide range of neuropsychiatric disorders including anxiety, psychosis, epilepsy, dementia, sleep- and stress-related disorders, and depression. **Common positions include:** Biological Scientist; Chemist; Pharmacist. **Educational backgrounds include:** Biology; Chemistry. **Benefits:** 401(k); Dental Insurance; Disability Coverage; Life Insurance; Medical Insurance; Stock Option; Tuition Assistance. **Corporate headquarters location:** This Location. **Listed on:** NASDAQ. **Stock exchange symbol:** NRGN. **Number of employees at this location:** 80.

NEXELL THERAPEUTICS

9 Parker, Irvine CA 92618. 949/470-9011. **Contact:** Human Resources. **World Wide Web address:** http://www.nexellinc.com. **Description:** Develops and sells diagnostics and cell therapies for autoimmune, genetic, and metabolic diseases, and cancer. Nexell Therapeutics' products include the Isolex Cell Selection System, Cryocyte, and Lifecell. **Corporate headquarters location:** This Location.

NORTH AMERICAN BIOLOGICALS, INC.

5800 Park of Commerce Boulevard NW, Boca Raton FL 33487. 561/989-5800x5511. **Fax:** 561/989-5874. **Contact:** Jan Cameron, Human Resources Manager. **Description:** Provides plasma and plasma-based products which aid in the prevention and treatment of diseases and disorders. **Corporate headquarters location:** This Location. **Listed on:** NASDAQ. **Stock exchange symbol:** NBIO.

NOVARTIS PHARMACEUTICALS CORP.

59 Route 10, East Hanover NJ 07936. 973/503-7500. **Contact:** Human Resources Manager. **World Wide Web address:** http://www.novartis.com. **Description:** This location houses administrative offices and Novartis Pharmaceuticals's primary research facility. Overall, Novartis Pharmaceuticals Corporation is one of the largest life science companies in the world. The company has three major divisions: health care, agribusiness, and nutrition. The health care division specializes in pharmaceuticals, both proprietary and generic, and ophthalmic health care. The agribusiness division is involved in seed technology, animal health, and crop protection. The nutrition sector includes medical, health, and infant nutrition. **Corporate headquarters location:** This Location.

NUTRACEUTICAL CORPORATION

1104 Country Hills Drive, Suite 300, Ogden UT 84403. 801/626-4900. **Toll-free phone:** 800/669-3009. **Fax:** 801/626-4949. **Contact:** Human Resources. **E-mail address:** jobs@nutracorp.com. **World Wide Web address:** http://www.nutraceutical.com. **Description:** Manufactures and markets nutritional and herbal supplements. **NOTE:** Entry-level positions, part-time jobs, and second and third shifts are offered. **Common positions include:** Accountantr; Administrative Assistant; AS400 Programmer Analyst; Assistant Manager; Biochemist; Buyer; Chemical Engineer; Chemist; Chief Financial Officer; Clinical Lab Technician; Computer Operator; Computer Support Technician; Computer Technician; Construction Contractor; Controller; Credit Manager; Customer Service Rep.; Database Administrator; Database Manager; Education Administrator; Financial Analyst; Food Scientist/Technologist; General Manager; Graphic Artist; Help-Desk Technician; Human Resources Manager; Industrial Production Manager; Internet Services Manager; Intranet Developer; Librarian; Manufacturing Engineer; Market Research Analyst; Marketing Manager; Marketing Specialist; MIS Specialist; Network Engineer; Network/Systems Administrator; Operations/Production Manager; Paralegal; Pharmacist; Production Manager; Project Manager; Public Relations Specialist; Purchasing Agent/Manager; Quality Assurance Engineer; Quality Control Supervisor; Sales Manager; Sales Rep.; Secretary; Software Engineer; Statistician; Webmaster; Website Developer. **Educational backgrounds include:** Accounting; AS400 Certification; Biology; Business Administration; C/C++; Chemistry; Communications; Computer Science; Engineering; Finance; HTML; Internet; Java; Marketing; Mathematics; MBA; MCSE; Microsoft Office; Microsoft Word; Public Relations; Publishing; QuarkXPress; Spreadsheets; Visual Basic. **Benefits:** 401(k); Casual Dress - Daily; Dental Insurance; Disability Coverage; Employee Discounts; Life Insurance; Medical Insurance; Profit Sharing; Tuition Assistance. **Special programs:** Internships; Summer Jobs. **Corporate headquarters location:** This Location. **Subsidiaries include:** Au Naturel; Monarch Labs. **Listed on:** Privately held. **Annual sales/revenues:** $51 - $100 million. **Number of employees at this location:** 50. **Number of employees nationwide:** 600.

NUTRAMAX PRODUCTS INC.

51 Blackburn Drive, Gloucester MA 01930. 978/283-1800. **Fax:** 978/282-3794. **Contact:** Carol Wollos, Manager of Human Resources. **World Wide Web address:** http://www.nutramax.com. **Description:** Manufactures pharmaceutical and personal care products. **Common positions include:** Biological Scientist; Blue-Collar Worker Supervisor; Buyer; Chemist; Computer Programmer; Customer Service Rep.; Electrician; Human Resources Manager; Industrial Engineer; Industrial Production Manager; Operations/Production Manager; Quality Control Supervisor; Transportation/Traffic Specialist. **Educational backgrounds include:** Biology; Business Administration; Chemistry. **Benefits:** 401(k); Dental Insurance; Disability Coverage; Life Insurance; Medical Insurance; Profit Sharing; Tuition Assistance. **Corporate headquarters location:** This Location. **Other area locations:** Brockton MA. **Other U.S. locations:** Fairton NJ. **Listed on:** NASDAQ. **Number of employees at this location:** 250. **Number of employees nationwide:** 525.

OSI PHARMACEUTICALS, INC.

106 Charles Lindbergh Boulevard, Uniondale NY 11553-3649. 516/222-0023. **Fax:** 516/222-0114. **Contact:** Ann McDermott-Kave, Human Resources Director. **E-mail address:** amcdermott@osip.com. **World Wide Web address:** http://www.osip.com. **Description:** A biopharmaceutical company utilizing proprietary technologies to discover and develop products for the treatment and diagnosis of human diseases. The company conducts a full range of drug discovery activities for its own products and in collaboration with other major pharmaceutical companies. **Corporate headquarters location:** This Location. **President:** Dr. Colin Goddard.

ONYX PHARMACEUTICALS, INC.

3031 Research Drive, Building A, Richmond CA 94806. 510/222-9700. **Contact:** Human Resources. **World Wide Web address:** http://www.onyx-pharm.com. **Description:** Engaged in cancer treatment research. **Corporate headquarters location:** This Location.

ORAVAX, INC.

38 Sidney Street, 4th Floor, Cambridge MA 02139. 617/494-1339. **Contact:** Human Resources. **World Wide Web address:** http://www.oravax.com. **Description:** Discovers and develops oral vaccines and noninjected antibody products to prevent and treat diseases that infect the human body at its mucous membranes. These tissues include the linings of the gastrointestinal, respiratory, and genitourinary tracts and the surfaces of the eyes. OraVax is pursuing three principal product development programs which target diseases that have high rates of incidence including viral pneumonia in children, peptic ulcer disease, and antibiotic-associated diarrhea and colitis. **Corporate headquarters location:** This Location.

ORGANOGENESIS INC.
150 Dan Road, Canton MA 02021. 781/575-0775. **Contact:** Human Resources Manager. **World Wide Web address:** http://www.organogenesis.com. **Description:** Designs, develops, and manufactures medical therapeutics containing living cells and/or natural connective tissue components. The company's products are designed to promote the establishment and growth of new tissues to restore, maintain, or improve biological function. Organogenesis's product development focus includes living tissue replacements, organ assist treatments, and guided tissue regeneration scaffolds. **Corporate headquarters location:** This Location.

ORGANON INC.
375 Mount Pleasant Avenue, West Orange NJ 07052. 973/325-4500. **Fax:** 973/669-6143. **Contact:** Human Resources. **E-mail address:** wohr@organoninc.com. **World Wide Web address:** http://www.organoninc.com. **Description:** Organon is an international leader in pharmaceutical research and development in the fields of reproductive medicine, anesthesiology, central nervous system disorders, thrombosis, and immunology. **NOTE:** Entry-level positions and part-time jobs are offered. **Common positions include:** Accountant; Administrative Assistant; Biochemist; Biological Scientist; Chemical Engineer; Chemist; Computer Programmer; Computer Support Technician; Customer Service Rep.; Market Research Analyst; Mechanical Engineer; MIS Specialist; Pharmacist; Physician; Public Relations Specialist; Quality Assurance Engineer; Sales Rep.; Secretary; SQL Programmer; Statistician; Systems Analyst; Technical Writer/Editor. **Educational backgrounds include:** Accounting; Biology; Business Administration; Chemistry; Communications; Computer Science; Engineering; Finance; Health Care; Marketing; Mathematics; Microsoft Word; Nutrition; Spreadsheets. **Benefits:** 401(k); Casual Dress - Daily; Dental Insurance; Disability Coverage; Flexible Schedule; Life Insurance; Medical Insurance; Pension Plan; Tuition Assistance; Vacation Days. **Special programs:** Internships; Summer Jobs. **Office hours:** Monday - Friday, 8:00 a.m. - 4:30 p.m. **Corporate headquarters location:** This Location. **Parent company:** Akzo Nobel. **Annual sales/revenues:** More than $100 million. **Number of employees at this location:** 1,200.

ORTHO-McNEIL PHARMACEUTICAL
Welsh Road at McKean Road, Spring House PA 19477-0776. 215/628-5000. **Contact:** Human Resources. **World Wide Web address:** http://www.ortho-mcneil.com. **Description:** Develops and sells pharmaceutical products including women's health, infectious disease, and wound healing products. **Common positions include:** Accountant/Auditor; Chemical Engineer; Computer Programmer; Electrical/Electronics Engineer; Financial Analyst; Human Resources Manager; Industrial Engineer; Manufacturer's/Wholesaler's Sales Rep.; Mechanical Engineer; Statistician; Technical Writer/Editor. **Educational backgrounds include:** Accounting; Business Administration; Computer Science; Engineering; Finance. **Benefits:** 401(k); Dental Insurance; Disability Coverage; Employee Discounts; Life Insurance; Medical Insurance; Pension Plan; Savings Plan; Tuition Assistance. **Corporate headquarters location:** This Location. **Parent company:** Johnson & Johnson (New Brunswick NJ).

OSTEOTECH INC.
51 James Way, Eatontown NJ 07724. 732/542-2800. **Fax:** 732/542-9312. **Contact:** Human Resources Director. **World Wide Web address:** http://www.osteotech.com. **Description:** Develops and manufactures biomaterial and device systems for musculoskeletal surgery. The company also processes human bone and connective tissue for transplantation. Osteotech is a leader in volume and quality of tissue processing for the American Red Cross and the Musculoskeletal Tissue Foundation. Founded in 1986. **NOTE:** Entry-level positions and second and third shifts are offered. **Common positions include:** Accountant; Administrative Assistant; Biochemist; Biological Scientist; Biomedical Engineer; Buyer; Chemist; Database Manager; Environmental Engineer; Librarian; Marketing Specialist; Operations Manager; Pharmacist; Physician; Production Manager; Quality Control Supervisor; Sales Executive; Sales Repr.; Secretary; Surgical Technician; Systems Analyst; Technical Editor; Technical Writer. **Educational backgrounds include:** Accounting; Biology; Chemistry; Computer Science; Finance; Health Care; Marketing; Physics. **Benefits:** 401(k); Dental Insurance; Disability Coverage; Employee Discounts; Life Insurance; Medical Insurance; Savings Plan; Tuition Assistance. **Corporate headquarters location:** This Location. **Other U.S. locations:** Nationwide. **International locations:** The Netherlands. **Listed on:** NASDAQ. **Stock exchange symbol:** OSTE. **President:** Richard Bauer. **Annual sales/revenues:** $21 - $50 million. **Number of employees at this location:** 180. **Number of employees nationwide:** 200. **Number of employees worldwide:** 225.

PE BIOSYSTEMS, INC.
500 Old Connecticut Path, Framingham MA 01701. 508/383-7700. **Fax:** 508/383-7833. **Contact:** Human Resources Department. **World Wide Web address:** http://www.pbio.com. **Description:** Designs, manufactures, and markets diagnostic systems. **Corporate headquarters location:** This Location. **International locations:** France; Germany; Japan; United Kingdom. **Listed on:** NASDAQ. **Stock exchange symbol:** PBIO.

PE CORPORATION
761 Main Avenue, Norwalk CT 06859. 203/762-1000. **Fax:** 203/762-6000. **Contact:** Director of Human Resources. **World Wide Web address:** http://www.pecorporation.com. **Description:** A worldwide leader in the development, manufacture, and distribution of analytical and life science systems for use in environmental technology, pharmaceuticals, biotechnology, chemicals, plastics, food, agriculture, and scientific research. **Common positions include:** Chemical Engineer; Computer Programmer; Designer; Draftsperson; Electrical/Electronics Engineer; Mechanical Engineer; Systems Analyst. **Educational backgrounds include:** Accounting; Chemistry; Computer Science; Engineering; Mathematics; Physics. **Benefits:** 401(k); Dental Insurance; Disability Coverage; Employee Discounts; Life Insurance; Medical Insurance; Pension Plan; Profit Sharing; Savings Plan; Tuition Assistance. **Corporate headquarters location:** This Location. **Subsidiaries include:** Celera Genomics Group; PE Biosystems Group. **Number of employees at this location:** 1,800. **Number of employees worldwide:** 5,700.

PACKARD INSTRUMENT COMPANY
800 Research Parkway, Meriden CT 06450. 203/238-2351. **Toll-free phone:** 800/323-1891. **Fax:** 203/639-2331. **Contact:** Human Resources Department. **World Wide Web address:** http://www.packardinstrument.com. **Description:** Develops and sells radioisotopic and nonisotopic instruments to the life sciences market. **Corporate headquarters location:** This Location.

International locations: Worldwide. **Parent company:** Canberra (also at this location).

PARACELSIAN
Langmuir Laboratories, 95 Brown Road #1005, Ithaca NY 14850. 607/257-4224. **Fax:** 607/257-2734. **Contact:** Human Resources. **World Wide Web address:** http://www.paracelsian.com. **Description:** Uses Asian herbal medicines to develop assay and molecular instruments for improved cancer diagnosis and to discover anti-cancer drugs. **Corporate headquarters location:** This Location.

PATHOLOGY ASSOCIATES MEDICAL LABORATORIES
P.O. Box 2687, Spokane WA 99220. 509/926-2400. **Contact:** Human Resources. **World Wide Web address:** http://www.paml.com. **Description:** A laboratory which performs blood, tissue, and drug tests. **Corporate headquarters location:** This Location.

PERRIGO COMPANY
117 Water Street, Allegan MI 49010. 616/673-8451. **Contact:** Human Resources **World Wide Web address:** http://www.perrigo.com. **Description:** Manufactures and sells pharmaceuticals, vitamins, and personal care products. These products are sold under individual store brand names. **Common positions include:** Accountant; Budget Analyst; Buyer; Chemist; Compliance Analyst; Computer Programmer; Customer Service Representative; Draftsperson; Electrician; General Manager; Human Resources Manager; Industrial Engineer; Industrial Production Manager; Mechanical Engineer; Operations/Production Manager; Public Relations Specialist; Purchasing Agent/Manager; Quality Control Supervisor; Regulatory Affairs Director; Systems Analyst. **Educational backgrounds include:** Accounting; Art/Design; Business Administration; Chemistry; Engineering; Liberal Arts; Marketing. **Benefits:** 401(k); Dental Insurance; Disability Coverage; Employee Discounts; Life Insurance; Medical Insurance; Profit Sharing; Savings Plan; Tuition Assistance. **Special programs:** Internships. **Corporate headquarters location:** This Location. **Other U.S. locations:** Greenville SC; TN. **Listed on:** NASDAQ. **Number of employees at this location:** 2,500.

PFANSTIEHL LABORATORIES, INC.
1219 Glen Rock Avenue, Waukegan IL 60085. 847/623-0370. **Fax:** 847/623-9173. **Contact:** Human Resources Department. **World Wide Web address:** http://www.pfanstiehl.com. **Description:** A chemical laboratory that specializes in the production of carbohydrates and biological chemicals. **NOTE:** Entry-level positions and second and third shifts are offered. **Common positions include:** Administrative Assistant; Customer Service Rep. **Benefits:** 401(k); Dental Insurance; Disability Coverage; Life Insurance; Medical Insurance; Profit Sharing; Tuition Assistance. **Corporate headquarters location:** This Location. **Subsidiaries include:** Pfanstiehl Europe, Ltd., (Cheshire, England). **Listed on:** Privately held.

PFIZER
201 Tabor Road, Morris Plains NJ 07950. 973/540-2000. **Contact:** Human Resources. **World Wide Web address:** http://www.pfizer.com. **Description:** A leading pharmaceutical company that distributes products concerning cardiovascular health, central nervous system disorders, infectious diseases, and women's health worldwide. The company's brand-name products include Benadryl, Ben Gay, Cortizone, Desitin, Halls, Listerine, Sudafed, and Zantac 75.

PHARMACEUTICAL FORMULATIONS
460 Plainfield Avenue, Edison NJ 08818. 732/819-3308. **Fax:** 732/819-4264. **Contact:** Human Resources. **World Wide Web address:** http://www.pfiotc.com. **Description:** Manufactures and markets over-the-counter, solid dosage pharmaceutical products in tablet, caplet, and capsule forms. **Common positions include:** Accountant/Auditor; Buyer; Chemical Engineer; Chemist; Customer Service Rep.; Electrician; General Manager; Human Resources Manager; Purchasing Agent/Manager; Science Technologist; Services Sales Rep.; Transportation/Traffic Specialist. **Educational backgrounds include:** Accounting; Business Administration; Chemistry; Computer Science; Engineering; Finance; Marketing. **Benefits:** 401(k); Dental Insurance; Disability Coverage; Employee Discounts; Life Insurance; Medical Insurance; Profit Sharing. **Corporate headquarters location:** This Location. **Number of employees at this location:** 320.

PHARMACIA CORPORATION
100 Route 206 North, Peapack NJ 07977. 908/901-8000. **Contact:** Personnel. **World Wide Web address:** http://www.pharmacia.com. **Description:** This location houses administrative offices. Overall, Pharmacia manufactures and markets agricultural products, performance chemicals used in consumer products, prescription pharmaceuticals, and food ingredients. **Corporate headquarters location:** This Location. **Listed on:** European Bourse. **Number of employees worldwide:** 60,000.

PHARMCHEM LABORATORIES INC.
1505-A O'Brien Drive, Menlo Park CA 94025. 650/328-6200. **Contact:** Human Resources. **World Wide Web address:** http://www.pharmchem.com. **Description:** A forensic drug testing laboratory. **Common positions include:** Laboratory Technician. **Educational backgrounds include:** Biology; Chemistry. **Benefits:** 401(k); Dental Insurance; Employee Discounts; Life Insurance; Medical Insurance; Savings Plan; Tuition Assistance. **Special programs:** Internships. **Corporate headquarters location:** This Location. **Listed on:** NASDAQ. **Number of employees at this location:** 260.

PHARMERICA
PHARMACY MANAGEMENT SERVICES (PMSI)
175 Kelsey Lane, Tampa FL 33619. 813/626-7788. **Contact:** Director of Human Resources. **World Wide Web address:** http://www.pharmerica.com. **Description:** Supplies pharmaceuticals and related products to a range of health care companies including assisted-living facilities and nursing homes. PMSI (also at this location) offers medical equipment and supplies through mail-order delivery. **Corporate headquarters location:** This Location. **Number of employees at this location:** 985.

PHYSICAL SCIENCE LABORATORY
P.O. Box 30002, Las Cruces NM 88003-8002. 505/522-9100. **Contact:** Regina Galvan, Personnel Manager. **Description:** Provides a wide range of research and development services in geothermal and wind energy, as well as providing contract services to the Department of Defense. **Corporate headquarters location:** This Location.

PIONEER HI-BRED INTERNATIONAL
400 Locust Street, Suite 700, Des Moines IA 50306-3454. 515/270-4000. **Toll-free phone:** 800/247-Fax: 515/334-6555. **Recorded jobline:** 800/247-6803x4000. **Contact:** Human Resources. **E-mail address:** jobs@phibred.com. **World Wide Web address:** http://www.pioneer.com. **Description:** A world leader in the discovery, development, and

delivery of elite crop genetics. Founded in 1926. **NOTE:** Entry-level positions and part-time jobs are offered. **Common positions include:** Accountant; Administrative Assistant; Auditor; Biochemist; Chemist; Computer Engineer; Computer Operator; Computer Programmer; Computer Scientist; Computer Support Technician; Content Developer; Database Administrator; Financial Analyst; Intellectual Property Lawyer; Management Trainee; Market Research Analyst; MIS Specialist; Software Engineer; Statistician; Systems Analyst. **Educational backgrounds include:** Accounting; Biology; Business Administration; C/C++; Chemistry; Communications; Computer Science; Economics; Engineering; Finance; HTML; Internet; Java; Marketing; MCSE; Microsoft Word; Software Development; Software Tech. Support; Spreadsheets; Visual Basic. **Benefits:** 401(k); Dental Insurance; Disability Coverage; Flexible Schedule; Life Insurance; Medical Insurance; Pension Plan; Profit Sharing; Savings Plan; Tuition Assistance. **Special programs:** Internships; Summer Jobs. **Corporate headquarters location:** This Location. **Other U.S. locations:** Nationwide. **International locations:** Worldwide. **Listed on:** NASDAQ. **Stock exchange symbol:** PHB. **President/CEO:** Charles Johnson. **Information Systems Manager:** Tom Hanigan. **Sales Manager:** Bob Wichman. **Annual sales/revenues:** More than $100 million. **Number of employees at this location:** 1,200. **Number of employees worldwide:** 5,000.

PROTEIN DESIGN LABS, INC.

34801 Campus Drive, Fremont CA 94555. 510/574-1400. **Contact:** Human Resources. **World Wide Web address:** http://www.pdl.com. **Description:** A research and development company focused on the development of humanized and human monoclonal antibodies for the treatment and prevention of various diseases. **Corporate headquarters location:** This Location.

PSYCHEMEDICS CORPORATION

1280 Massachusetts Avenue, Suite 200, Cambridge MA 02138. 617/868-7455. **Fax:** 617/864-1639. **Contact:** Personnel. **World Wide Web address:** http://www.psychemedics.com. **Description:** A biotechnology company that focuses on the detection and measurement of substances in the body by using hair samples. The first commercial product, a testing service for the detection of drugs, is provided principally to private sector companies. This test identifies traces various illegal drugs. Psychemedics's testing methods use patented technology for performing immunoassays on enzymatically-dissolved hair samples with confirmation testing by gas chromatography or mass spectrometry. **Corporate headquarters location:** This Location. **Other U.S. locations:** Los Angeles CA; Fort Lauderdale FL; Atlanta GA; Chicago IL; Las Vegas NV; Dallas TX. **Listed on:** American Stock Exchange. **Stock exchange symbol:** PMD. **Number of employees nationwide:** 95.

THE PSYCHOLOGICAL CORPORATION

555 Academic Court, San Antonio TX 78204. 210/299-3616. **Fax:** 210/299-3662. **Recorded jobline:** 210/299-2700. **Contact:** Recruiter. **World Wide Web address:** http://www.hbtpc.com. **Description:** One of the oldest and largest commercial test publishers in the nation. The company provides tests and related services to schools and colleges, clinicians and professional organizations, businesses, and public entities. The company's services include test research and development, printing, marketing, distribution, administration, and scoring. The company has three divisions: an educational measurement division; a psychological measurement and communications division; and a division that awards licenses and credentials. **NOTE:** Entry-level positions and second and third shifts are offered. **Common positions include:** Accountant; Administrative Assistant; Computer Operator; Computer Programmer; Customer Service Representative; Database Manager; Desktop Publishing Specialist; Editor; Financial Analyst; Graphic Designer; Human Resources Manager; Managing Editor; Market Research Analyst; Marketing Specialist; Occupational Therapist; Psychologist; Purchasing Agent/Manager; Research Assistant; Sales Rep.; Speech-Language Pathologist; Statistician; Systems Analyst; Teacher/Professor; Warehouse Manager. **Educational backgrounds include:** Business Administration; Computer Science; Psychology. **Benefits:** 401(k); Dental Insurance; Disability Coverage; Employee Discounts; Financial Planning Assistance; Flexible Schedule; Life Insurance; Medical Insurance; Pension Plan; Public Transit Available; Savings Plan; Tuition Assistance. **Corporate headquarters location:** Orlando FL. **Parent company:** Harcourt Brace & Company. **Annual sales/revenues:** More than $100 million. **Number of employees at this location:** 1,000. **Number of employees nationwide:** 2,000.

QUEST DIAGNOSTICS INCORPORATED

One Malcolm Avenue, Teterboro NJ 07608. 201/393-5211. **Contact:** Personnel. **World Wide Web address:** http://www.questdiagnostics.com. **Description:** One of the largest clinical laboratories in North America, providing a broad range of clinical laboratory services to health care clients which include physicians, hospitals, clinics, dialysis centers, and pharmaceutical companies. The company offers and performs tests on blood, urine, and other bodily fluids and tissues to provide information for health and well-being. **Corporate headquarters location:** This Location. **Other U.S. locations:** Nationwide.

QUESTCOR PHARMACEUTICALS CORP.

2714 Loker Avenue West, Carlsbad CA 92008. 760/929-9500. **Contact:** Human Resources. **World Wide Web address:** http://www.questcor.com. **Description:** Researches, develops, and markets a variety of pharmaceuticals to the health care industry. The company's products include Emitasol, Ethamolin, Inulin, Glofil-125, and NeoFlo.**NOTE:** Interested jobseekers should send their resumes to Questcor Pharmaceuticals Corporation, Human Resources Department, 26118 Research Road, Hayward CA 94545. **Corporate headquarters location:** This Location. **Listed on:** NASDAQ. **Stock exchange symbol:** CYPR.

QUIDEL CORPORATION

10165 McKellar Court, San Diego CA 92121. 858/552-1100. **Toll-free phone:** 800/874-1517. **Fax:** 858/453-4338. **Contact:** Human Resources. **World Wide Web address:** http://www. quidel.com. **Description:** Researches, develops, and manufactures immunodiagnostic products designed to provide accurate testing for acute and chronic human illnesses. **Corporate headquarters location:** This Location. **Subsidiaries include:** VHA Inc. **Listed on:** NASDAQ. **Stock exchange symbol:** QDEL. **President/CEO:** Andre de Bruin, President/CEO.

R&D SYSTEMS
TECHNE CORPORATION

614 McKinley Place NE, Minneapolis MN 55413. 612/379-2956. **Toll-free phone:** 800/328-2400. **Contact:** Human Resources. **World Wide Web address:** http://www.rndsystems.com. **Description:** Supplies cytokine and related reagents to research

institutions. **Corporate headquarters location:** This Location. **Subsidiaries include:** Nalge Company develops, manufactures, and markets a diversified line of reusable and disposable plastic labware, biopharmaceutical packaging products, recreational containers, and environmental testing containers. Erie Scientific Company develops, manufactures, and markets microscope slides and cover glass. Barnstead Thermolyne Corporation develops, manufactures, and markets precision heating, stirring, and temperature control apparatus and water purification systems to industrial, clinical, academic, governmental, and biotechnological laboratories. Sybron Dental Specialties, Inc. (Sybron International's orthodontic and dental business), has two operating subsidiaries: Ormco Corporation develops, manufactures, and markets a broad line of orthodontic appliances including bands, brackets, wire, adhesives, and ancillary equipment used during the course of orthodontic treatment; and Kerr Corporation develops, manufactures, and markets a broad range of consumable products for use in restorative, prosthetic, and endodontic dentistry. Techne Corporation (also at this location) is a holding company whose subsidiaries manufacture hematology control products, biotech products, and biological products. **Number of employees at this location:** 190.

REGENERON PHARMACEUTICALS, INC.
777 Old Saw Mill River Road, Suite 10, Tarrytown NY 10591. 914/345-7400. **Fax:** 914/345-7685. **Contact:** Human Resources. **World Wide Web address:** http://www.regeneron.com. **Description:** Develops pharmaceuticals to treat neurological, oncological, inflammatory, allergic, and bone disorders as well as muscle atrophy. **Corporate headquarters location:** This Location. **Listed on:** NASDAQ. **Stock exchange symbol:** REGN.

RESEARCH TRIANGLE INSTITUTE (RTI)
P.O. Box 12194, Research Triangle Park NC 27709. 919/541-6000. **Physical address:** 3040 Cornwallis Road, RTP NC. **Contact:** Supervisor/Employment Services. **World Wide Web address:** http://www.rti.org. **Description:** A nonprofit, independent research organization involved in many scientific fields, under contract to business; industry; government; industrial associations; and public service agencies. The institute was created as an independent entity by the joint action of North Carolina State University, Duke University, and the University of North Carolina at Chapel Hill; however, close ties are maintained with the universities' scientists, both through the active research community of the Research Triangle Park region and through collaborative research for government and industry clients. RTI responds to national priorities in health, the environment, advanced technology, and social policy with contract research for the U.S. government including applications in statistics, social sciences, chemistry, life sciences, environmental sciences, engineering, and electronics. **NOTE:** Entry-level positions are offered. **Common positions include:** Chemist; Computer Programmer; Database Manager; Economist; MIS Specialist; Statistician; Systems Analyst. **Educational backgrounds include:** Chemistry; Computer Science; Economics; Software Development. **Benefits:** 403(b); Daycare Assistance; Dental Insurance; Disability Coverage; Life Insurance; Medical Insurance; On-Site Daycare; Pension Plan; Public Transit Available; Savings Plan; Tuition Assistance. **Corporate headquarters location:** This Location. **Other U.S. locations:** Washington DC; Cocoa Beach FL; Hampton VA. **Listed on:** Privately held. **Annual sales/revenues:** More than $100 million. **Number of employees at this location:** 1,400.

RICERCA, INC.
7528 Auburn Road, Painesville OH 44077. 440/357-3300. **Fax:** 440/354-6276. **Contact:** Human Resources. **World Wide Web address:** http://www.ricerca.com. **Description:** Provides research and development services on a contract basis to clients primarily in the agricultural, pharmaceutical, and specialty chemicals industries. The company also helps clients develop new products, improve existing products, and support the registration of products for regulatory compliance. Founded in 1961. **Common positions include:** Agricultural Scientist; Biological Scientist; Chemical Engineer; Chemist. **Educational backgrounds include:** Biology; Chemistry; Engineering. **Benefits:** 401(k); Dental Insurance; Disability Coverage; Life Insurance; Medical Insurance; Pension Plan; Tuition Assistance. **Corporate headquarters location:** This Location. **Parent company:** Ishihara Sangyo Kaisha, Ltd. (Japan).

ROBERTS PHARMACEUTICAL CORP.
Meridian Center II, 4 Industrial Way West, Eatontown NJ 07724. 732/389-1182. **Fax:** 732/389-1014. **Contact:** Human Resources Director. **World Wide Web address:** http://www.robertspharm.com. **Description:** An international pharmaceutical company focused on acquiring, developing, and bringing new prescription products to the market. Founded in 1983. **Corporate headquarters location:** This Location. **International locations:** Canada; United Kingdom. **Listed on:** American Stock Exchange. **Stock exchange symbol:** RPC. **President/CEO:** John Spitznagel, President/CEO. **Annual sales/revenues:** More than $100 million.

ROCHE VITAMINS INC.
45 Waterview Boulevard, Parsippany NJ 07054-1298. 973/257-1063. **Contact:** Human Resources. **Description:** A pharmaceutical company which manufactures pharmaceutical drugs, diagnostic kits, and vitamins for dietary, pharmaceutical, and cosmetic use. **Corporate headquarters location:** This Location.

SGS U.S. TESTING COMPANY INC.
291 Fairfield Avenue, Fairfield NJ 07004. 973/575-5252. **Toll-free phone:** 800/777-8378. **Fax:** 973/575-1071. **Contact:** Personnel. **World Wide Web address:** http://www.ustesting.sgsna.com. **Description:** Specializes in the testing of a variety of industrial and consumer products. Services include biological, chemical, engineering/materials, environmental, electrical, paper/packaging, textiles, certification programs, and inspections. **Common positions include:** Account Rep.; Administrative Assistant; Administrative Manager; Biological Scientist; Chemist; Civil Engineer; Clinical Lab Technician; Customer Service Representative; Electrical/Electronics Engineer; Industrial Engineer; Manufacturing Engineer; Marketing Manager; Marketing Specialist; Mechanical Engineer; Sales Rep. **Educational backgrounds include:** Biology; Chemistry; Engineering. **Benefits:** 401(k); Dental Insurance; Disability Coverage; Flexible Schedule; Life Insurance; Medical Insurance; Pension Plan; Tuition Assistance. **Corporate headquarters location:** This Location. **Other U.S. locations:** Los Angeles CA; Tulsa OK. **Parent company:** SGS North America.

SRI INTERNATIONAL
333 Ravenswood Avenue, Menlo Park CA 94025. 650/326-6200. **Contact:** Human Resources. **E-mail address:** careers@sri.com. **World Wide Web address:** http://www.sri.com. **Description:** A research, development, and consulting organization engaged in government and private industry

research. SRI International provides solutions in several areas including pharmaceutical discovery; biopharmaceutical discovery and development; engineering sciences; and systems development. **Common positions include:** Biological Scientist; Biomedical Engineer; Chemist; Economist; Electrical/Electronics Engineer; Financial Analyst; Human Resources Manager; Mechanical Engineer; Physicist; Systems Analyst; Technical Writer/ Editor. **Educational backgrounds include:** Biology; Business Administration; Chemistry; Communications; Computer Science; Economics; Engineering; Finance; Mathematics; Physics. **Benefits:** Dental Insurance; Disability Coverage; Employee Discounts; Life Insurance; Medical Insurance; Pension Plan; Tuition Assistance. **Corporate headquarters location:** This Location.

SALIVA DIAGNOSTIC SYSTEMS INC.
11719 NE 95th Street, Suite G, Vancouver WA 98682. 360/696-4800. **Contact:** Human Resources. **World Wide Web address:** http://www.salv.com. **Description:** Develops, manufactures, and markets bodily fluid specimen diagnostic devices for use in the detection of HIV antibodies, other viruses and diseases, and drug testing. **Corporate headquarters location:** This Location.

SANGSTAT MEDICAL CORPORATION
6300 Dumbarton Circle, Fremont CA 94555. 510/789-4300. **Contact:** Human Resources. **World Wide Web address:** http://www.sangstat.com. **Description:** Produces diagnostic and therapeutic pharmaceutical products for use in organ transplantation. **Corporate headquarters location:** This Location.

SCHEIN PHARMACEUTICAL
100 Campus Drive, Florham Park NJ 07932. 973/593-5500. **Contact:** Human Resources. **World Wide Web address:** http://www.schein-rx.com. **Description:** Manufactures and markets generic pharmaceuticals **Corporate headquarters location:** This Location. **Listed on:** New York Stock Exchange. **Number of employees nationwide:** 1,500.

SCHERING-PLOUGH CORPORATION
One Giralda Farms, Madison NJ 07940-1000. 973/822-7000. **Contact:** Personnel. **World Wide Web address:** http://www.schering-plough.com. **Description:** Discover, develops, manufactures and markets pharmaceuticals and consumer products. Pharmaceutical products include prescription drugs, over-the-counter medicines, eye care products, and animal health products. The consumer products group consists of proprietary medicines, toiletries, cosmetics, and foot care products. Brand names include Coricidin, Maybelline, Claritin, Coppertone, and Dr. Scholl's. **Corporate headquarters location:** This Location. **Other U.S. locations:** Miami FL; Kenilworth NJ; Union NJ; Memphis TN.

SCIENCE & TECHNOLOGY CORPORATION
10 Basil Sawyer Drive, Hampton VA 23666. 757/766-5800. **Fax:** 757/865-1294. **Contact:** Director of Human Resources. **E-mail address:** jobs@stcnet.com. **World Wide Web address:** http://www.stcnet.com. **Description:** A research and development government contractor engaged in atmospheric sciences and meteorology, remote sensing, scientific data processing and modeling, chemical and biological defense, evaluation, and programming support. **Common positions include:** Biochemist; Biological Scientist; Biomedical Engineer; Computer Programmer; Editor; Electrical/ Electronics Engineer; Environmental Engineer; Mechanical Engineer; Meteorologist; MIS Specialist; Physicist; Systems Analyst; Systems

Manager; Technical Writer/Editor. **Educational backgrounds include:** Business Administration; Mathematics; Physics. **Benefits:** 401(k); Dental Insurance; Disability Coverage; Life Insurance; Medical Insurance; Pension Plan; Profit Sharing; Tuition Assistance. **Corporate headquarters location:** This Location. **Other U.S. locations:** Nationwide. **Operations at this facility include:** Administration; Divisional Headquarters. **Listed on:** Privately held. **Annual sales/revenues:** $21 - $50 million. **Number of employees at this location:** 65.

SCIENTIFIC INDUSTRIES, INC.
70 Orville Drive, Airport International Plaza, Bohemia NY 11716. 631/567-4700. **Contact:** Human Resources. **World Wide Web address:** http://www.scientificindustries.com. **Description:** Manufactures and markets laboratory equipment including vortex mixers and miscellaneous laboratory apparatuses including timers, rotators, and pumps. The company develops and sells computerized control and data logging systems for sterilizers and autoclaves. Scientific Industries' products are used by hospital laboratories, clinics, research laboratories, pharmaceutical manufacturers, and medical device manufacturers. **Corporate headquarters location:** This Location.

SCIOS INC.
820 West Maude Avenue, Sunnyvale CA 94086. 408/616-8200. **Contact:** Department of Human Resources. **World Wide Web address:** http://www. sciosinc.com. **Description:** Researches, develops and markets pharmaceuticals for the treatment of cardiovascular and neurological disorders. Founded in 1981. **Common positions include:** Biochemist; Biological Scientist. **Benefits:** 401(k); Dental Insurance; Disability Coverage; Life Insurance; Medical Insurance; Tuition Assistance. **Corporate headquarters location:** This Location. **Listed on:** NASDAQ. **Stock exchange symbol:** SCIO. **Number of employees at this location:** 240. **Number of employees nationwide:** 340.

SEARLE & COMPANY
5200 Old Orchard Road, Skokie IL 60077. 847/982-7000. **Contact:** Human Resources. **World Wide Web address:** http://www.searlehealthnet.com. **Description:** Engaged in the research, development, and marketing of prescription pharmaceuticals and other health care products worldwide. **Corporate headquarters location:** This Location. **Parent company:** Monsanto Company.

SEPRACOR INC.
111 Locke Drive, Marlborough MA 01752. 508/481-6700. **Fax:** 508/357-7596. **Contact:** Personnel. **World Wide Web address:** http://www. sepracor.com. **Description:** Develops new and improved versions of prescription drugs. Sepracor's products are known as Improved Chemical Entities (ICE Pharmaceuticals) and are used in the allergy, asthma, gastroenterology, neurology, psychiatry, and urology markets. **Corporate headquarters location:** This Location. **Listed on:** NASDAQ.

SERADYN INC.
7998 Georgetown Road, Suite 1000, Indianapolis IN 46268. 317/610-3800. **Contact:** Personnel. **World Wide Web address:** http://www.seradyn.com. **Description:** This location manufactures medical test kits. Overall, Seradyn consists of three distinct divisions: Diagnostics, Particle Technology, and Photovolt. Products include diagnostic instruments, as well as a full line of medical diagnostic reagents. **Common positions include:** Accountant/Auditor; Biological Scientist; Buyer; Chemist; Computer Programmer; Customer Service Rep; Department

Manager; Electrical Engineer; Electronics Engineer; Manufacturer's/Wholesaler's Sales Rep.; Mechanical Engineer; Quality Control Supervisor. **Educational backgrounds include:** Biochemistry; Biology; Chemistry; Engineering; Immunology; Marketing. **Benefits:** Dental Insurance; Disability Coverage; Life Insurance; Medical Insurance; Savings Plan; Tuition Assistance. **Parent company:** Mitsubishi Chemical Corporation. **Number of employees nationwide:** 150.

SERONO LABORATORIES, INC.
100 Longwater Circle, Norwell MA 02061. 781/982-9000. **Fax:** 781/982-9612. **Contact:** Human Resources. **World Wide Web address:** http://www.seronousa.com. **Description:** Develops prescription pharmaceuticals for the treatment of a variety of diseases including multiple sclerosis and cancer. **Common positions include:** Accountant; Biological Scientist; Clinical Lab Technician; Financial Analyst; Industrial Production Manager; Systems Analyst. **Educational backgrounds include:** Biology; Chemistry; Engineering. **Benefits:** 401(k); Dental Insurance; Disability Coverage; Employee Discounts; Life Insurance; Medical Insurance; Pension Plan; Savings Plan; Tuition Assistance. **Corporate headquarters location:** This Location. **Operations at this facility include:** Administration; Manufacturing; Research and Development; Sales; Service. **Listed on:** Privately held. **Number of employees at this location:** 150. **Number of employees nationwide:** 370.

SILLIKER LABORATORIES GROUP, INC.
900 Maple Road, Homewood IL 60430. 708/957-7878. **Fax:** 708/957-3798. **Contact:** Margo Neetz, Human Resources Generalist. **E-mail address:** human.resources@silliker.com. **World Wide Web address:** http://www.silliker.com. **Description:** Operates a network of food testing laboratories. The labs test for pathogens and microbes, and serve to verify the accuracy of nutritional labeling. **NOTE:** Entry-level positions and part-time jobs are offered. **Common positions include:** Biological Scientist; Chemist; Computer Programmer; Food Scientist/Technologist; Secretary. **Educational backgrounds include:** Biology; Chemistry; Microsoft Office. **Benefits:** 401(k); Casual Dress - Daily; Dental Insurance; Disability Coverage; Life Insurance; Medical Insurance; Sick Days; Tuition Assistance; Vacation Days. **Special programs:** Summer Jobs. **Corporate headquarters location:** This Location. **International locations:** Worldwide. **Operations at this facility include:** Administration; Service. **Listed on:** Privately held. **Number of employees at this location:** 60. **Number of employees nationwide:** 530.

SKYEPHARMA
10450 Science Center Drive, San Diego CA 92121. 858/625-2424. **Fax:** 858/625-2439. **Contact:** Personnel. **World Wide Web address:** http://www.skyepharma.com. **Description:** Researches develops proprietary, injectable material that can encapsulate a wide variety of drugs to provide sustained and controlled delivery. **Corporate headquarters location:** This Location. **Number of employees at this location:** 60.

SMITHKLINE BEECHAM CORPORATION
One Franklin Plaza, P.O. Box 7929, Philadelphia PA 19101-7929. 215/751-4000. **Physical address:** 200 North 16th Street, Philadelphia PA 19102-1282. **Contact:** Personnel Department. **World Wide Web address:** http://www.sb.com. **Description:** A health care corporation that specializes in the research, development, manufacture, and marketing of ethical pharmaceuticals, animal health products, ethical and proprietary medicines, and eye care products. The company's principal divisions include SmithKline Beecham Pharmaceuticals, SmithKline Beecham Animal Health, and SmithKline Beecham Consumer Healthcare. The company is also engaged in many other aspects of the health care field including the production of medical and electronic instruments. **NOTE:** In January 2000, Glaxo Wellcome and SmithKline Beecham announced plans to merge. The new company will be named Glaxo SmithKline. Please contact this location for more information. **Corporate headquarters location:** This Location. **Number of employees nationwide:** 20,000.

SNYDER MEMORIAL RESEARCH FOUNDATION
1407 Wheat Road, Winfield KS 67156. 316/221-4080. **Contact:** Human Resources. **Description:** A nonprofit foundation specializing in cancer research. **Common positions include:** Biological Scientist. **Educational backgrounds include:** Biology; Chemistry. **Benefits:** Medical Insurance; Pension Plan. **Corporate headquarters location:** This Location. **Listed on:** Privately held.

SOUTHERN RESEARCH INSTITUTE
P.O. Box 55305, Birmingham AL 35255-5305. 205/581-2000. **Physical address:** 3000 Ninth Avenue South, Birmingham AL. **Recorded jobline:** 205/581-2609. **Contact:** Human Resources Manager. **World Wide Web address:** http://www.sri.org. **Description:** A contract, research institute that specializes in diversified areas of science and engineering including health, pollution control, chemistry, and combustion. **Common positions include:** Biological Scientist; Chemist; Mechanical Engineer; Metallurgical Engineer. Physicist. **Educational backgrounds include:** Biology; Chemistry; Engineering; Environmental Science; Physics. **Benefits:** Dental Insurance; Disability Coverage; Employee Discounts; Life Insurance; Medical Insurance; Pension Plan; Tuition Assistance. **Corporate headquarters location:** This Location.

SOUTHWEST RESEARCH INSTITUTE
6220 Culebre Road, San Antonio TX 78228. 210/522-2223. **Fax:** 210/522-3990. **Contact:** Human Resources. **E-mail address:** personnel@swri.org. **World Wide Web address:** http://www.swri.org. **Description:** An independent, nonprofit, applied engineering and physical science research organization. Research is conducted in areas such as automation, intelligent systems, and advanced computer technology; biosciences/bioengineering; nuclear waste regulatory analyses; electronic systems and instrumentation; encapsulation and polymer research; engines, fuels, and lubricants; environmental science; fire technology; fluid and machinery dynamics; engineering and materials sciences; nondestructive evaluation research and development; and space sciences. **Common positions include:** Chemist; Electrical/Electronics Engineer; Mechanical Engineer; Software Engineer. **Educational backgrounds include:** Chemistry; Computer Science; Engineering. **Benefits:** Dental Insurance; Disability Coverage; Life Insurance; Medical Insurance; Pension Plan; Retirement Plan; Tuition Assistance. **Special programs:** Internships. **Corporate headquarters location:** This Location. **Listed on:** Privately held. **Number of employees at this location:** 2,600.

SUGEN, INC.
230 East Grand Avenue, South San Francisco CA 94080. 650/553-8300. **Fax:** 650/553-8301. **Contact:** Human Resources Manager. **Description:** A leading biopharmaceutical company engaged in the discovery and development of small molecule

drugs. **Corporate headquarters location:** This Location. **Parent company:** Pharmacia.

SYBRON INTERNATIONAL CORPORATION
411 East Wisconsin Avenue, 24th Floor, Milwaukee WI 53202. 414/274-6600. **Contact:** Human Resources. **World Wide Web address:** http://www.sybron.com. **Description:** Owns and operates orthodontic and dental equipment manufacturing companies. **Corporate headquarters location:** This Location. **Subsidiaries include:** Nalge Company develops, manufactures, and markets a diversified line of reusable and disposable plastic labware, biopharmaceutical packaging products, and environmental testing containers. Erie Scientific Company develops, manufactures, and markets microscope slides and cover glass. Barnstead Thermolyne Corporation develops, manufactures, and markets heating, stirring, and temperature control apparatus and water purification systems to industrial, governmental, and biotechnological laboratories. Sybron Dental Specialties, Inc. (Sybron International's orthodontic and dental business), has two operating subsidiaries: Ormco Corporation develops, manufactures, and markets a broad line of orthodontic appliances including bands, brackets, wire, adhesives, and ancillary equipment used during the course of orthodontic treatment; and Kerr Corporation develops, manufactures, and markets a broad range of consumable products for use in restorative, prosthetic, and endodontic dentistry.

SYNAPTIC PHARMACEUTICAL CORP.
215 College Road, Paramus NJ 07652. 201/261-1331. **Contact:** Human Resources. **Description:** This location houses administrative offices and is not involved in the manufacturing process. Overall, Synaptic Pharmaceutical Corporation researches and develops pharmaceuticals. **NOTE:** Part-time jobs are offered. **Common positions include:** Biochemist; Biological Scientist; Chemist; Clinical Lab Tech. **Educational backgrounds include:** Biology; Chemistry. **Benefits:** 401(k); Casual Dress - Daily; Dental Insurance; Disability Coverage; Life Insurance; Medical Insurance; Tuition Assistance. **Corporate headquarters location:** This Location. **Listed on:** NASDAQ. **Stock exchange symbol:** SNAP. **Number of employees at this location:** 130.

SYNCOR INTERNATIONAL CORPORATION
6464 Canoga Avenue, Woodland Hills CA 91367-2407. 818/737-4000. **Toll-free phone:** 800/999-9098. **Contact:** Human Resources Manager. **World Wide Web address:** http://www.syncor.com. **Description:** Compounds, dispenses, and distributes patient-specific intravenous drugs and solutions for use in diagnostic imaging and offers a complete range of pharmacy services. **Common positions include:** Account Manager; Accountant/Auditor; Administrative Manager; Computer Programmer; Marketing Manager; Pharmacist; Sales Manager. **Educational backgrounds include:** Accounting; Business Administration; Computer Science; Finance; Marketing; Pharmacology; Physics. **Benefits:** Dental Insurance; Disability Coverage; Life Insurance; Medical Insurance; Savings Plan; Tuition Assistance; Vision Insurance. **Special programs:** Internships. **Corporate headquarters location:** This Location.

SYSTEMIX INC.
3155 Porter Drive, Palo Alto CA 94304. 650/856-4901. **Contact:** Human Resources. **World Wide Web address:** http://www.stem.com. **Description:** A research facility specializing in the development of therapies for illnesses of the blood and immune system. The company is focused primarily on discovering therapies for cancer and AIDS patients. **Corporate headquarters location:** This Location.

TARGETED GENETICS CORPORATION
1100 Olive Way, Suite 100, Seattle WA 98101. 206/623-7612. **Fax:** 206/521-7872. **Contact:** Department of Human Resources. **World Wide Web address:** http://www.targen.com. **Description:** gene therapy products for the treatment of certain acquired and inherited diseases. The principal focus is, on three product development programs that address high-risk diseases for which there are no known cures: cytoxic T lymphocyte (CTL)-based immunotherapy for infectious diseases and cancer; in vivo adeno-associated virus (AAV)-based therapy for cystic fibrosis and other diseases; and stem cell therapy. The company is approaching gene therapy through multiple delivery systems including retroviral vector delivery, AAV vector delivery, and nonviral vector delivery. **NOTE:** Entry-level positions are offered. **Common positions include:** Accountant/Auditor; Attorney; Biological Scientist; Biomedical Engineer; Buyer; Chemical Engineer; Clinical Lab Technician; Human Resources Manager; Systems Analyst; Typist/Word Processor. **Educational backgrounds include:** Biology. **Benefits:** 401(k); Dental Insurance; Disability Coverage; Life Insurance; Medical Insurance; Public Transit Available. **Special programs:** Internships. **Corporate headquarters location:** This Location. **Listed on:** NASDAQ. **Number of employees at this location:** 80.

TEVA PHARMACEUTICALS USA
18-01 River Road, Fair Lawn NJ 07410. 201/703-0400. **Fax:** 201/703-9491. **Contact:** Human Resources. **World Wide Web address:** http://www.tevapharmusa.com. **Description:** Manufactures and markets generic pharmaceuticals. The company focuses on therapeutic medicines for the analgesic, dermatological, and anti-inflammatory markets. **Corporate headquarters location:** This Location. **Other U.S. locations:** Mexico MO; Elmwood Park NJ; Fairfield NJ; Paterson NJ; Waldwick NJ. **Number of employees nationwide:** 790.

TEXAS BIOTECHNOLOGY CORPORATION
7000 Fannin, Suite 1920, Houston TX 77030. 713/796-8822. **Fax:** 713/796-8232. **Contact:** Human Resources. **World Wide Web address:** http://www.tbc.com. **Description:** A pharmaceutical research and development firm that specializes in treatment of cardiovascular conditions. **Corporate headquarters location:** This Location. **Listed on:** American Stock Exchange. **Stock exchange symbol:** TXB.

TEXAS VETERINARY MEDICAL DIAGNOSTIC LABORATORY
P.O. Box 3200, Amarillo TX 79116. 806/353-7478. **Physical address:** 6610 Amarillo Boulevard West, Amarillo TX. **Toll-free phone:** 888/646-5624. **Fax:** 806/359-0636. **Contact:** Human Resources. **World Wide Web address:** http://www.tvmdl.tamu.edu. **Description:** Performs medical testing on animals to assist veterinarians with diagnosis and prognosis. The laboratory's test fields include chemistry, hematology, urology, toxicology, serology, histology, bacteriology, and necropsies. **Common positions include:** Chemist; Clinical Lab Technician; Computer Operator; Human Resources Manager; Microbiologist; Pathologist; Toxicologist. **Educational backgrounds include:** Chemistry; Veterinary Medicine. **Benefits:** 401(k); Dental Insurance; Life Insurance; Medical Insurance; Pension Plan. **Other U.S. locations:** College Station TX. **Executive Director:** A. Konrad Eugster.

TRIPATH, INC.
8271 154th Avenue NE, Redmond WA 98052. 425/869-7284. **Contact:** Human Resources. **Description:** Engaged in the research and

development of technologies to automate the interpretation of medical images. The company's initial products are automated screening systems that are used to analyze and classify Pap smears. These screening systems use high-speed video microscopes, image interpretation software, and field-of-view computers to recognize, analyze, and classify individual cells within the complex images on a Pap smear. These products include the AutoPap QC and the AutoPap Screener. **Corporate headquarters location:** This Location. **Number of employees at this location:** 100.

UNDERWRITERS LABORATORIES INC.
1285 Walt Whitman Road, Melville NY 11747. 631/271-6200. **Fax:** 631/271-8259. **Contact:** Human Resources. **World Wide Web address:** http://www.ul.com. **Description:** An independent, nonprofit organization that specializes in product safety testing and certification. **Common positions include:** Clerk; Computer Programmer; Electrical/ Electronics Engineer; Electronics Technician. **Educational backgrounds include:** Business Administration; Engineering. **Benefits:** 401(k); 403(b); Dental Insurance; Disability Coverage; Flexible Schedule; Life Insurance; Medical Insurance; Pension Plan; Tuition Assistance. **Special programs:** Summer Jobs. **Corporate headquarters location:** Northbrook IL. **Other U.S. locations:** Santa Clara CA; Research Triangle Pk NC; Camas WA. **Number of employees at this location:** 800. **Number of employees worldwide:** 4,000.

UNIGENE LABORATORIES, INC.
110 Little Falls Road, Fairfield NJ 07004. 973/882-0860. **Fax:** 973/227-6088. **Contact:** Human Resources. **World Wide Web address:** http://www. unigene.com. **Description:** A biopharmaceutical research and manufacturing company that has developed a patented method to produce calcitonin, a leading drug for treating osteoporosis. Founded in 1980. **Benefits:** 401(k). **Corporate headquarters location:** This Location. **Other U.S. locations:** Boonton NJ. **Listed on:** NASDAQ. **Stock exchange symbol:** UGNE. **President:** Warren P. Levy, Ph.D.

UNILAB CORPORATION
18408 Oxnard Street, Tarzana CA 91356-1504. 818/996-7300. **Contact:** Human Resources. **World Wide Web address:** http://www.unilab.com. **Description:** A clinical laboratory that analyzes a wide variety of medical tests. Unilab also performs drug testing. **Corporate headquarters location:** This Location.

UNILEVER HOME & PERSONAL CARE USA
45 River Road, Edgewater NJ 07020. 201/943-7100. **Contact:** Ms. Mikel Gittens, Manager of Human Resources. **Description:** Researches and develops household and personal care products. **Common positions include:** Chemical Engineer; Chemist. **Educational backgrounds include:** Chemistry. **Benefits:** 401(k); Casual Dress - Daily; Daycare Assistance; Dental Insurance; Disability Coverage; Employee Discounts; Life Insurance; Medical Insurance; On-Site Daycare; Pension Plan; Savings Plan; Tuition Assistance. **Corporate headquarters location:** Greenwich CT. **Annual sales/revenues:** More than $100 million. **Number of employees at this location:** 500.

UROCOR INC.
840 Research Parkway, Oklahoma City OK 73104. 405/290-4000. **Fax:** 405/290-4413. **Contact:** Human Resources Director. **World Wide Web address:** http://www.urocor.com. **Description:** Provides urological diagnostic testing services. **Corporate headquarters location:** This Location.

V.I. TECHNOLOGIES, INC.
155 Duryea Road, Melville NY 11747. 516/752-7314. **Fax:** 631/752-7367. **Contact:** Department of Human Resources. **E-mail address:** hr@ vitechnologies.com. **World Wide Web address:** http://www.vitechnologies.com. **Description:** A leader in the field of pathogen inactivation of blood products. The company's technologies are designed to address the risk of viral contamination of blood products. Founded in 1995. **NOTE:** Second and third shifts are offered. **Common positions include:** Accountant; Administrative Assistant; Biochemist; Biological Scientist; Budget Analyst; Chemical Engineer; Computer Support Technician; Database Manager; Financial Analyst; Help-Desk Technician; Human Resources Manager; Manufacturing Engineer; Production Manager; Purchasing Agent/ Manager; Quality Assurance Engineer; Quality Control Supervisor; Sales Manager; Secretary. **Educational backgrounds include:** Accounting; Biology; Chemistry; Engineering; Finance; MBA; Microsoft Office. **Benefits:** 401(k); Dental Insurance; Disability Coverage; Flexible Schedule; Life Insurance; Medical Insurance; Pension Plan; Relocation Assistance; Savings Plan; Tuition Assistance; Vision Insurance. **Office hours:** Monday - Friday, 8:00 a.m. - 5:30 p.m. **Corporate headquarters location:** This Location. **Other U.S. locations:** Cambridge MA. **Listed on:** Privately held. **Stock exchange symbol:** VITX. **CEO:** John Barr. **Information Systems Manager:** Rose Mattice. **Purchasing Manager:** Tom McKeefrey. **Annual sales/revenues:** $21 - $50 million. **Number of employees at this location:** 125. **Number of employees nationwide:** 185.

VWR SCIENTIFIC PRODUCTS
1310 Goshen Parkway, West Chester PA 19380. 610/431-1700. **Contact:** Human Resources. **World Wide Web address:** http://www.vwrsp.com. **Description:** Provides laboratory equipment, chemicals, and supplies to the scientific marketplace through five operating units worldwide. VWR Scientific, the company's main domestic operating unit, is a full-line distributor of scientific supplies, laboratory chemicals and apparatus, and research equipment. VWR Canada provides the Canadian marketplace with a single coast-to-coast supplier. VWR International exports scientific equipment and supplies to more than 54 countries worldwide. Bender & Hobein is a joint venture with E. Merck of Germany and is one of the largest scientific distributors in the German marketplace. Sargent-Welch Scientific sells scientific instruments to the education market for the teaching of science in public and private schools throughout the U.S. **Corporate headquarters location:** This Location. **Number of employees nationwide:** 1,635.

VERTEX PHARMACEUTICALS INC.
130 Waverly Street, Cambridge MA 02139-4242. 617/576-3111. **Fax:** 617/577-6645. **Contact:** Human Resources. **World Wide Web address:** http://www.vpharm.com. **Description:** Develops drugs for viral, autoimmune, inflammatory, and neurodegenerative diseases. Vertex Pharmaceuticals also develops oral active pharmaceuticals for drug-resistant cancer and hemoglobin disorders. **Corporate headquarters location:** This Location. **Subsidiaries include:** Altus Biologics Inc., Cambridge MA; Versal Technologies, Inc., Cambridge MA; Vertex Pharmaceuticals (Europe) Limited, United Kingdom; Vertex Securities Corporation, Cambridge MA. **Listed on:** NASDAQ. **Stock exchange symbol:** VRTX.

VI-JON LABORATORIES, INC.
8515 Page Avenue, St. Louis MO 63133. 314/721-2991. **Fax:** 314/721-0455. **Contact:** Edward

Sander, Human Resources Manager. **Description:** Wholesalers of a variety of pharmaceuticals and cosmetics. **Common positions include:** Accountant/Auditor; Budget Analyst; Buyer; Chemist; Computer Programmer; Customer Service Representative; Human Resources Manager; Industrial Production Manager; Operations/Production Manager; Purchasing Agent/Manager; Quality Control Supervisor; Services Sales Representative; Systems Analyst; Transportation/Traffic Specialist. **Educational backgrounds include:** Accounting; Chemistry; Computer Science. **Benefits:** 401(k); Dental Insurance; Disability Coverage; Life Insurance; Medical Insurance; Tuition Assistance. **Corporate headquarters location:** This Location. **Listed on:** Privately held. **Number of employees at this location:** 100.

VICAL INC.
9373 Towne Center Drive, Suite 100, San Diego CA 92121. 858/453-9900. **Contact:** Human Resources. **World Wide Web address:** http://www.vical.com. **Description:** Provides research and development services for DNA, gene therapy, cancer, AIDS, and malaria. **Corporate headquarters location:** This Location.

WATERS CORPORATION
34 Maple Street, Milford MA 01757. 508/478-2000. **Fax:** 508/482-2413. **Recorded jobline:** 508/482-3332. **Contact:** Human Resources Representative. **World Wide Web address:** http://www.waters.com. **Description:** Produces a range of instruments, information management systems, and chromatography products for high-performance liquid chromatography and related applications. Waters Corporation's products are also used in fundamental research directed toward a better understanding of the chemical, physical, and biological composition of compounds, as well as in the detection, measurement, and identification of compounds of interest across a wide range of industries. Founded in 1958. **NOTE:** Entry-level positions and second and third shifts are offered. **Common positions include:** Buyer; Chemical Engineer; Chemist; Customer Service Rep.; Electrical/Electronics Engineer; Financial Analyst; Human Resources Manager; Manufacturing Engineer; Marketing Manager; Marketing Specialist; Mechanical Engineer; MIS Specialist; Purchasing Agent/Manager; Sales Engineer; Sales Rep.; Secretary; Systems Analyst; Technical Writer/Editor. **Educational backgrounds include:** Accounting; Biology; Business Administration; Chemistry; Computer Science; Engineering; Finance; Marketing; Mathematics; Software Development; Software Tech. Support. **Benefits:** 401(k); Dental Insurance; Disability Coverage; Employee Discounts; Flexible Schedule; Job Sharing; Life Insurance; Medical Insurance; Pension Plan; Profit Sharing; Savings Plan; Tuition Assistance. **Special programs:** Co-ops; Internships; Summer Jobs. **Office hours:** Monday - Friday, 8:00 a.m. - 4:30 p.m. **Corporate headquarters location:** This Location. **Other U.S. locations:** Nationwide. **International locations:** Worldwide. **Listed on:** New York Stock Exchange. **President/CEO:** Douglas Berthiaume. **Facilities Manager:** William Stares. **Annual sales/revenues:** More than $100 million. **Number of employees at this location:** 950. **Number of employees worldwide:** 2,000.

WATSON PHARMACEUTICALS, INC.
311 Bonnie Circle, Corona CA 92880. 909/270-1400x4299. **Fax:** 909/898-0926. **Contact:** Human Resources. **World Wide Web address:** http://www.watsonpharm.com. **Description:** Produces and distributes proprietary pharmaceuticals such as analgesics, dermatological, primary care, antihypertensive, hormonal, generic, and central nervous system treatments. **Common positions include:** Budget Analyst; Computer Programmer; Intellectual Property Lawyer; Manufacturing Engineer; Paralegal; Quality Assurance Engineer; Quality Control Supervisor. **Educational backgrounds include:** Biology; Chemistry; Engineering; Mathematics; Physics. **Benefits:** 401(k); Dental Insurance; Disability Coverage; Employee Discounts; Medical Insurance; Tuition Assistance. **Corporate headquarters location:** This Location. **Subsidiaries include:** Circa Pharmaceuticals, Inc.; Oclassen Pharmaceuticals, Inc.; Watson Laboratories, Inc. **Listed on:** New York Stock Exchange. **Stock exchange symbol:** WPI. **CEO:** Dr. Allen Chao. **Facilities Manager:** Bill Liberty. **Information Systems Manager:** Frank Chen. **Purchasing Manager:** Linda Childs. **Sales Manager:** Jesse Childs.

WEST PHARMACEUTICAL SERVICES
101 Gordon Drive, Lionville PA 19341. 610/594-2900. **Fax:** 610/594-3000. **Contact:** Employment Specialist. **World Wide Web address:** http://www.westpharma.com. **Description:** Researches and develops drug molecule delivery systems; designs and manufactures packaging components, systems, and devices that deliver and differentiate drugs and health care products; provides contract laboratory services; and performs commercialization processes for the manufacturing, filling, and packaging of health care products. **Common positions include:** Account Manager; Account Rep.; Administrative Assistant; Auditor; Chemist; Computer Operator; Customer Service Rep.; Financial Analyst; Market Research Analyst; Mechanical Engineer; Network/Systems Administrator; Purchasing Agent/Manager. **Educational backgrounds include:** C/C++; Chemistry; Engineering; Finance; Microsoft Word; Novell. **Benefits:** 401(k); Casual Dress - Fridays; Dental Insurance; Disability Coverage; Life Insurance; Medical Insurance; Pension Plan; Tuition Assistance. **Corporate headquarters location:** This Location. **International locations:** Worldwide. **Listed on:** New York Stock Exchange. **Stock exchange symbol:** WST. **Annual sales/revenues:** More than $100 million. **Number of employees at this location:** 300. **Number of employees nationwide:** 2,500. **Number of employees worldwide:** 5,000.

WHITEHEAD INSTITUTE FOR BIOMEDICAL RESEARCH
9 Cambridge Center, Cambridge MA 02142-1479. 617/258-5000. **Fax:** 617/258-6294. **Contact:** Lisa Heisterkamp, Employment Manager. **World Wide Web address:** http://www.wi.mit.edu. **Description:** A nonprofit research and teaching institution that specializes in programs regarding AIDS and cancer research, developmental biology, infectious disease, and structural biology. **Educational backgrounds include:** Biology; Business Administration; Chemistry; Computer Science; Finance; Liberal Arts. **Benefits:** Dental Insurance; Disability Coverage; Life Insurance; Medical Insurance; Pension Plan; Tuition Assistance. **Corporate headquarters location:** This Location.

WHOLEPEOPLE.COM
1500 East 128th Avenue, Thornton CO 80241. 303/474-2300. **Fax:** 303/474-2715. **Recorded jobline:** 303/474-3094. **Contact:** Personnel. **Description:** Markets and sells vitamins, nutritional supplements, and personal health care products. WholePeople.com operates as part of Whole Foods Markets. **Common positions include:** Account Manager; Account Representative; Accountant; Administrative Assistant; Administrative Manager;

Buyer; Computer Programmer; Content Developer; Customer Service Representative; Database Administrator; Financial Analyst; General Manager; Graphic Artist; Graphic Designer; Help-Desk Technician; Internet Services Manager; Market Research Analyst; Marketing Manager; Marketing Specialist; MIS Manager; Online Sales Manager; Operations Manager; Production Manager; Project Manager; Sales Representative; Systems Analyst; Systems Manager; Web Advertising Specialist; Webmaster; Website Developer. **Educational backgrounds include:** HTML; Internet Development; Java; MCSE; Oracle; SQL. **Benefits:** 401(k); Casual Dress - Daily; Daycare Assistance; Dental Insurance; Disability Coverage; Employee Discounts; Financial Planning Assistance; Flexible Schedule; Life Insurance; Medical Insurance; Public Transit Available; Savings Plan; Sick Days; Vacation Days. **Listed on:** Privately held. **Annual sales/revenues:** $51 - $100 million. **Number of employees at this location:** 400. **Number of employees nationwide:** 500.

WYETH-AYERST PHARMACEUTICALS
611 East Nield Street, West Chester PA 19382. 610/696-3100. **Contact:** Personnel. **Description:** Produces a wide range of pharmaceutical products and proprietary medicines. **NOTE:** Entry-level positions are offered. **Common positions include:** Accountant; Administrative Assistant; Biochemist; Chemist; Controller; Draftsperson; Electrician; Environmental Engineer; Human Resources Manager; Licensed Practical Nurse; Mechanical Engineer; Network Engineer; Network/Systems Administrator; Operations Manager; Production Manager; Project Manager; Purchasing Agent/Manager; Quality Assurance Engineer; Systems Analyst. **Educational backgrounds include:** Accounting; Biology; Chemistry; Computer

Science; Engineering; Finance; Health Care; Microsoft Office; Microsoft Word; Novell. **Benefits:** 401(k); Casual Dress - Fridays; Daycare Assistance; Dental Insurance; Disability Coverage; Life Insurance; Medical Insurance; Relocation Assistance; Savings Plan; Tuition Assistance. **Special programs:** Summer Jobs. **Corporate headquarters location:** Radnor PA.

ZENITH GOLDLINE PHARMACEUTICALS
140 LeGrand Avenue, Northvale NJ 07647. 201/767-1700. **Contact:** Director of Personnel. **Description:** Produces ethical pharmaceuticals for cardiovascular, nervous, digestive, and respiratory systems. **Corporate headquarters location:** This Location.

ZILA PHARMACEUTICALS
5227 North Seventh Street, Phoenix AZ 85014-2800. 602/266-6700. **Contact:** Mr. Marlin Steele, Human Resources. **World Wide Web address:** http://www.zila.com. **Description:** Manufactures treatments for cold sores and fever blisters. **Common positions include:** Accountant/Auditor. **Corporate headquarters location:** This Location. **Parent company:** Zila Inc. **Operations at this facility include:** Administration; Research and Development; Sales; Service. **Listed on:** NASDAQ. **Number of employees at this location:** 20.

ZONAGEN INC.
2408 Timberloch Place, Suite B-4, The Woodlands TX 77380. 281/367-5892. **Contact:** Human Resources. **World Wide Web address:** http://www.zonagen.com. **Description:** Researches, develops, and markets biopharmaceutical products that deal with sexual dysfunction, urology, fertility, and contraception. **Corporate headquarters location:** This Location.

For more information on career opportunities in biotechnology, pharmaceuticals, and scientific R&D:

Associations

AMERICAN ASSOCIATION FOR CLINICAL CHEMISTRY
2101 L Street NW, Suite 202, Washington DC 20037-1526. 202/857-0717. Toll-free phone: 800/892-1400. World Wide Web address: http://www.aacc.org. International scientific/medical society of individuals involved with clinical chemistry and other clinical lab science-related disciplines.

AMERICAN ASSOCIATION OF COLLEGES OF PHARMACY
1426 Prince Street, Alexandria VA 22314-2841. 703/739-2330. World Wide Web address: http://www.aacp.org. An organization composed of all U.S. pharmacy colleges and over 2,000 school administrators and faculty members. Career publications include *Shall I Study Pharmacy?*, *Pharmacy: A Caring Profession*, and *A Graduate Degree in the Pharmaceutical Sciences: An Option For You?*

AMERICAN ASSOCIATION OF PHARMACEUTICAL SCIENTISTS
1650 King Street, Suite 200, Alexandria VA 22314-2747. 703/548-3000. World Wide Web address: http://www.aaps.org.

THE AMERICAN COLLEGE OF CLINICAL PHARMACY (ACCP)
3101 Broadway, Suite 380, Kansas City MO 64111. 816/531-2177. World Wide Web address: http://www.accp.com. Operates ClinNet jobline at 412/648-7893 for members only.

AMERICAN INSTITUTE OF BIOLOGICAL SCIENCES
1444 I Street NW, Suite 200, Washington DC 20005. 202/628-1500. Fax: 202/628-1509. Offers *Careers in Biology*, which details various science-related careers.

AMERICAN PHARMACEUTICAL ASSOCIATION
2215 Constitution Avenue NW, Washington DC 20037-2985. 202/628-4410. World Wide Web address: http://www.aphanet.org.

AMERICAN SOCIETY FOR BIOCHEMISTRY AND MOLECULAR BIOLOGY
9650 Rockville Pike, Bethesda MD 20814-3996. 301/530-7145. Fax: 301/571-1824. World Wide Web address: http://www.faseb.org/asbmb. A nonprofit scientific and educational organization whose primary scientific activities are in the publication of the *Journal of Biological Chemistry* and holding an annual scientific meeting. Also publishes a career brochure entitled *Unlocking Life's Secrets: Biochemistry and Molecular Biology.*

AMERICAN SOCIETY FOR CELL BIOLOGY
9650 Rockville Pike, Bethesda MD 20814-3992. 301/530-7153. Fax: 301/530-7139. World Wide Web address: http://www.ascb.org/ascb. Publishes numerous career guides such as *Opportunity and Adventure in Cell Biology* and *How to Get a Research Job in Academia and Industry.*

AMERICAN SOCIETY FOR CLINICAL LABORATORY SCIENCE
7910 Woodmont Avenue, Suite 530, Bethesda MD

20814. 301/657-2768. Fax: 301/657-2909. World Wide Web address: http://www.ascls.org.

AMERICAN SOCIETY OF HEALTH-SYSTEM PHARMACISTS
7272 Wisconsin Avenue, Bethesda MD 20814. 301/657-3000. World Wide Web address: http://www.ashp.org. Provides pharmaceutical education. Updates pharmacies on current medical developments. Offers a service for jobseekers for a fee.

BIOTECHNOLOGY INDUSTRY ORGANIZATION (BIO)
1625 K Street NW, Suite 1100, Washington DC 20006-1604. 202/857-0244. Fax: 202/857-0237. World Wide Web address: http://www.bio.org. Represents agriculture, biomedical, diagnostic, food, energy, and environmental companies. Publishes a profile of the U.S. biotechnology industry.

INTERNATIONAL SOCIETY FOR PHARMACEUTICAL ENGINEERING
3816 West Linebaugh Avenue, Suite 412, Tampa FL 33624. 813/960-2105. World Wide Web address: http://www.ispe.org.

NATIONAL PHARMACEUTICAL COUNCIL
1894 Preston White Drive, Reston VA 20191. 703/620-6390. Fax: 703/476-0904. An organization of research-based pharmaceutical companies.

Directories

DRUG TOPICS RED BOOK
Medical Economics Company, 5 Paragon Drive, Montvale NJ 07645. 201/358-7200.

Magazines

DRUG TOPICS
Medical Economics Company, 5 Paragon Drive, Montvale NJ 07645. 201/358-7200.

PHARMACEUTICAL ENGINEERING
International Society for Pharmaceutical Engineering, 3816 West Linebaugh Avenue, Suite 412, Tampa FL 33624. 813/960-2105. World Wide Web address: http://www.ispe.org.

Online Services

BIO ONLINE
World Wide Web address: http://www.bio.com. Offers links to industry news and educational resources.

MEDZILLA
E-mail address: info@medzilla.com. World Wide Web address: http://www.medzilla.com. Lists job openings for professionals in the fields of biotechnology, health care, medicine, and science related industries.

Charities and Social Services

You can expect to find the following types of organizations in this chapter:
Social and Human Service Agencies • Job Training and Vocational Rehabilitation Services • Nonprofit Organizations

Some helpful information: *The average annual salary range for social workers is approximately $25,000 - $35,000, with casework supervisors and managers earning $30,000 - $40,000. Salaries are similar or lower for workers in charitable organizations, although executives may earn a great deal more ($75,000 or higher would not be uncommon).*

ACTION FOR BOSTON COMMUNITY DEVELOPMENT (ABCD)
178 Tremont Street, Boston MA 02111. 617/357-6000. **Contact:** Personnel.. **World Wide Web address:** http://www.bostonabcd.org. **Description:** A nonprofit, community action, human services agency that helps low-income residents. The agency provides programs and services including job training, education, housing services, fuel assistance, the Urban College Program, child care; and elder service programs. **Common positions include:** Accountant/Auditor; Administrator; Health Services Worker; Human Service Worker. **Educational backgrounds include:** Accounting; Business Administration; Computer Science; Human Services; Liberal Arts; Political Science; Public Administration; Public Policy. **Benefits:** Dental Insurance; Disability Coverage; Life Insurance; Medical Insurance; Pension Plan; Tuition Assistance. **Corporate headquarters location:** This Location.

AIDS ACTION COMMITTEE
Box WS, 131 Clarendon Street, Boston MA 02116. 617/437-6200. **Fax:** 617/437-6445. **Recorded jobline:** 617/450-1435. **Contact:** Personnel. **World Wide Web address:** http://www.aac.org. **Description:** A nonprofit organization providing services to people living with HIV, and their families; combating the AIDS epidemic through education; and advocating fair and effective AIDS policy and funding. The AIDS Action Committee is the largest AIDS service organization in New England. Founded by a small group of volunteers, the organization now includes a full-time professional staff supported by several thousand volunteers. The group operates through several segments including clinical services, housing, financial and legal, counseling, education, training, development, fundraising, public policy, government relations, grant writing, administration and finance, AR/AP, human resources, MIS, computer operations, and facilities. **NOTE:** Please call the jobline for current openings. **Common positions include:** Case Manager; Counselor; Education Administrator; Health Services Worker; Social Worker; Systems Analyst. **Educational backgrounds include:** Business Administration; Communications; Education; Health Care; Public Health; Social Work. **Benefits:** 403(b); Dental Insurance; Disability Coverage; Life Insurance; Medical Insurance. **Special programs:** Internships. **Corporate headquarters location:** This Location. **Operations at this facility include:** Administration. **Number of employees at this location:** 100.

ALCOHOLICS ANONYMOUS (A.A.)
475 Riverside Drive, New York NY 10115. 212/870-3400. **Contact:** Human Resources. **World Wide Web address:** http://www.aa.org. **Description:** Alcoholics Anonymous (A.A.) is a fellowship of men and women who share their experiences with each other so that they may work on their common problems and help others to recover from alcoholism. Founded in 1935. **Corporate headquarters location:** This Location. **Subsidiaries include:** A.A. World Services, Inc. operates at this location with 100 employees coordinating with local groups, with A.A. groups in treatment and correctional facilities, and with members and groups overseas. A.A. literature is prepared, published, and distributed through this office. The A.A. Grapevine, Inc. publishes the *A.A. Grapevine*, the fellowship's monthly international journal. The magazine has a circulation of about 119,000 in the U.S., Canada, and other countries. A.A. Grapevine, Inc. also produces a selection of cassette tapes and anthologies of magazine articles.

AMERICAN CANCER SOCIETY
1599 Clifton Road NE, Atlanta GA 30329. 404/320-3333. **Fax:** 404/982-3677. **Contact:** Recruiter. **World Wide Web address:** http://www.cancer.org. **Description:** A nationwide, nonprofit, voluntary health organization dedicated to eliminating cancer as a major health problem. The organization helps fund cancer research and public education. Services include research, education, advocacy, and public service. **Common positions include:** Accountant; Administrative Assistant; Computer Programmer; Computer Support Technician; Content Developer; Database Administrator; Database Manager; Help-Desk Technician; Market Research Analyst; Marketing Manager; Network Engineer; Network/ Systems Administrator; Paralegal; Project Manager; Secretary; Systems Analyst; Webmaster; Website Developer. **Educational backgrounds include:** Communications; Computer Science; HTML; MCSE; Microsoft Office; Public Relations; Software Development; Software Tech. Support; Spreadsheets. **Benefits:** 403(b); Casual Dress - Fridays; Dental Insurance; Disability Coverage; Life Insurance; Medical Insurance; Pension Plan. **Special programs:** Internships. **Corporate headquarters location:** This Location. **Number of employees at this location:** 485.

AMERICAN COUNCIL OF THE BLIND
1155 15th Street NW, Suite 1004, Washington DC 20005. 202/467-5081. **Toll-free phone:** 800/424-8666. **Fax:** 202/467-5085. **Contact:** Human Resources Department. **E-mail address:** info@acb.org. **World Wide Web address:** http://www.acb.org. **Description:** The American Council of the Blind (ACB) is a national membership organization established to promote the independence, dignity, and well-being of blind and visually-impaired people. ACB is one of the largest organizations of blind people in the U.S. with over 70 state and special interest affiliates and a national network of chapters and members. By providing numerous programs and services, ACB enables blind people to

live and work independently and to advocate for their rights. **Corporate headquarters location:** This Location.

AMERICAN HEART ASSOCIATION (AHA)
7272 Greenville Avenue, Dallas TX 75231. 214/373-6300. **Fax:** 214/706-1191. **Contact:** Human Resources. **World Wide Web address:** http://www.americanheart.org. **Description:** One of the oldest and largest national, nonprofit, voluntary health associations dedicated to reducing disability and death from cardiovascular diseases and stroke. AHA-funded research has yielded such discoveries as CPR, bypass surgery, pacemakers, artificial heart valves, microsurgery, life-extending drugs, and new surgical techniques to repair heart defects. The AHA's interactive public education programs emphasize quitting smoking, controlling high blood pressure, eating a low-fat, low-cholesterol diet, and being physically active. The AHA also teaches the warning signs of heart attack and stroke and what to do if they occur. The association trains about 5 million Americans per year in emergency care procedures; these training systems are used by millions worldwide. Founded in 1924. **Special programs:** Internships. **Corporate headquarters location:** This Location. **Other U.S. locations:** Nationwide.

AMERICAN RED CROSS
2131 K Street NW, Washington DC 20037. 202/728-6400. **Contact:** Human Resources. **World Wide Web address:** http://www.redcross.org. **Description:** A humanitarian organization that aids disaster victims, gathers blood for distribution in crisis situations, and provides a variety of other social services including training individuals to respond to emergencies, educating them on various diseases, and raising funds for other charitable establishments. **Corporate headquarters location:** This Location.

ARTHRITIS FOUNDATION
1330 West Peachtree Street, Atlanta GA 30309. 404/872-7100. **Fax:** 404/872-0457. **Contact:** Human Resources. **World Wide Web address:** http://www.arthritis.org. **Description:** Engaged in research to find a cure for arthritis and provides information to educate those who have the disease. **Corporate headquarters location:** This Location.

ASHLAND NATURE CENTER
P.O. Box 700, Hockessin DE 19707. 302/239-2334. **Contact:** Human Resources. **Description:** A private, nonprofit, membership organization dedicated to environmental education and the preservation of natural areas. **Parent company:** Delaware Nature Society operates Ashland Nature Center and Abbott's Mill, offering year-round programming for all age groups.

BLACK HILLS NATIONAL FOREST
Rural Route 2, Box 200, Custer SD 57730. 605/673-2251. **Contact:** Human Resources. **Description:** An organization that protects the Black Hills National Forest. **Common positions include:** Computer Technician; Forester/Conservation Scientist. **Benefits:** Casual Dress - Daily; Flexible Schedule; Life Insurance. **Special programs:** Summer Jobs.

B'NAI B'RITH INTERNATIONAL
1640 Rhode Island Avenue NW, Washington DC 20036. 202/857-6600. **Contact:** Director of Human Resources. **Description:** A Jewish social services and political action organization. B'Nai B'Rith has seven district offices located across the United States. **Common positions include:** Fundraising Specialist; Social Worker. **Benefits:** Life Insurance; Medical Insurance; Pension Plan; Savings Plan.

Special programs: Internships. **Corporate headquarters location:** This Location.

BOY SCOUTS OF AMERICA
1325 West Walnut Hill Lane, P.O. Box 152079, Irving TX 75015-2079. 972/580-2000. **Contact:** Human Resources. **World Wide Web address:** http://www.bsa.scouting.org. **Description:** The national scouting organization for young men. **Common positions include:** Administrator; Customer Service Rep.; Human Service Worker; Sales Rep. **Educational backgrounds include:** Bachelor of Arts; Business Administration; College Degree; Liberal Arts; Management/Planning; Master of Arts; MBA; Ph.D.; Social Science. **Benefits:** 401(k); Dental Insurance; Disability Coverage; Life Insurance; Medical Insurance; Pension Plan. **Special programs:** Internships. **Corporate headquarters location:** This Location. **Other U.S. locations:** Nationwide. **Listed on:** Privately held. **Number of employees nationwide:** 4,000.

BOYS & GIRLS CLUBS OF AMERICA
1230 West Peachtree Street NW, Atlanta GA 30309. 404/815-5700. **Contact:** Human Resources. **World Wide Web address:** http://www.bgca.org. **Description:** One of the nation's largest, private, nonprofit organizations providing developmental programs for disadvantaged young people. **Corporate headquarters location:** This Location. **Other U.S. locations:** Nationwide.

THE BOYS' CLUB OF NEW YORK (BCNY)
287 East 10th Street, New York NY 10009. 212/677-1109. **Contact:** Hiring. **Description:** Provides a variety of services to young men in the New York City area. BCNY's educational program has helped hundreds of young men to attend leading prep schools and colleges, offering support and counseling to help them succeed. BCNY's job training program offers teenage members their first work experience in top-flight New York companies. The club offers a year-round program serving boys between six and 17 years old. Founded in 1876. **Corporate headquarters location:** This Location. **Parent company:** Boys Club of America.

CABBAGE PATCH SETTLEMENT HOUSE
1413 South Sixth Street, Louisville KY 40208. 502/634-0811. **Contact:** Human Resources. **Description:** An independently-funded, nonprofit, Christian charity assisting underprivileged, inner-city individuals through daycare, family services, and recreational/educational programs. Services include youth activities; teaching children and teens gardening, culinary arts, nutrition, and food economics; the distribution of Christmas baskets; and other family services. Founded in 1910. **Common positions include:** Recreation Worker; Social Worker. **Educational backgrounds include:** Social Science. **Benefits:** Life Insurance; Medical Insurance; Pension Plan. **Corporate headquarters location:** This Location. **Number of employees at this location:** 30.

CARDINAL RITTER INSTITUTE
4483 Lindell Boulevard, St. Louis MO 63108. 314/652-3600. **Contact:** Personnel. **Description:** An organization that specializes in providing home health care, housing, social services, employment programs, and volunteer programs to the elderly. **Common positions include:** Human Service Worker; Social Worker. **Educational backgrounds include:** Accounting; Liberal Arts; Nursing; Social Work. **Benefits:** 403(b); Dental Insurance; Disability Coverage; Life Insurance; Medical Insurance; Pension Plan; Savings Plan. **Corporate headquarters location:** This Location.

CARE USA
151 Ellis Street, Atlanta GA 30303. 404/681-2552.
Fax: 404/577-9814. Contact: Human Resources.
World Wide Web address: http://www.care.org.
Description: CARE USA is a member of CARE
International, an umbrella organization which
coordinates the program activities of the member
organizations. CARE's purpose is to help the
developing world's poor in their efforts to achieve
social and economic well-being. CARE offers
disaster relief, technical assistance, training, food,
and other material resources and management in
combinations appropriate to local needs and
priorities. CARE also advocates public policies and
programs that support these services. Founded in
1945. Corporate headquarters location: This
Location. President: Peter Bell.

CATHOLIC CHARITIES
P.O. Box 4900, Santa Rosa CA 95402. 707/528-
8712. Fax: 707/575-4910. Contact: Personnel
Director. World Wide Web address: http://www.
srcharities.org. Description: Provides social service
programs for the needy and vulnerable in several
counties of California.

CHILD AND FAMILY SERVICES, INC. OF
LEA COUNTY
950 East Snyder Street, Hobbs NM 88240. 505/397-
7336. Fax: 505/393-0420. Contact: Human
Resources. Description: A nonprofit, full-service,
Head Start preschool and daycare program that
sponsors the summer food program in Lea County
and coordinates with the Foster Grandparent
Program. NOTE: Entry-level positions are offered.
Common positions include: Administrative
Assistant; Computer Operator; Daycare Worker;
Education Administrator; Librarian; Preschool
Worker; Registered Nurse; Secretary; Social
Worker; Teacher/Professor; Transportation/Traffic
Specialist; Typist/Word Processor. Educational
backgrounds include: Liberal Arts; Nutrition.
Benefits: 401(k); Daycare Assistance; Dental
Insurance; Disability Coverage; Employee
Discounts; Financial Planning Assistance; Flexible
Schedule; Life Insurance; Medical Insurance; On-
Site Daycare; Savings Plan; Tuition Assistance.
Special programs: Apprenticeships; Internships;
Training. Corporate headquarters location: This
Location. Other U.S. locations: Lovington NM.

CHILDREN'S AID SOCIETY
105 East 22nd Street, New York NY 10010.
212/949-4800. Contact: Human Resources.
Description: Provides early, intensive, and long-
term support to thousands of city children and their
families through various programs and services
including medical and dental care, foster care, group
homes, adoption, homemakers, emergency
assistance, food distribution, Head Start, tutoring,
mentors, community centers, community schools,
counseling, court diversion programs, camps,
sports, arts, dance, theater, chorus, internships, jobs,
teen pregnancy prevention, leadership projects,
college and prep/college scholarships, and services
to the homeless. Founded in 1853. Corporate
headquarters location: This Location.

CHILDREN'S VILLAGE
Dobbs Ferry NY 10522. 914/693-0600. Contact:
Director of Personnel. World Wide Web address:
http://www.childrensvillage.org. Description: A
nonprofit organization that operates a residential
treatment center for emotionally disturbed children.
Corporate headquarters location: This Location.

THE CHIMES, INC.
4815 Seton Drive, Baltimore MD 21215. 410/358-
6400. Toll-free phone: 800/CHIMES1. Fax:

410/358-6038. Recorded jobline: 410/358-6006.
Contact: Human Resources. World Wide Web
address: http://www.chimes.org. Description: A
nonprofit agency that offers a broad range of
vocational, rehabilitative, residential, educational,
and support services for 1,000 individuals in central
Maryland, northern Virginia, and Washington DC.
The Chimes helps children, adults, and senior
citizens with mental and related disabilities to lead
more independent lives. Founded in 1947. Common
positions include: Counselor; Human Service
Worker. Educational backgrounds include:
Human Services; Psychology; Sociology. Benefits:
403(b); Credit Union; Dental Insurance; Disability
Coverage; Employee Discounts; Life Insurance;
Medical Insurance; Pension Plan; Tuition
Assistance. Corporate headquarters location:
This Location. Other U.S. locations: CA; DC; DE;
IA; VA.

CHRISTIAN CITY
7290 Lester Road, Union City GA 30291. 770/964-
3301. Fax: 770/964-7041. Contact: Human
Resources. Description: A nonprofit company
operating a home for children, retirement homes, a
retirement center, a convalescent center, and an
Alzheimer's care center. Founded in 1964. NOTE:
Entry-level positions and second and third shifts are
offered. Common positions include: Accountant;
Administrative Assistant; Certified Nurses Aide;
Controller; Daycare Worker; Dietician/Nutritionist;
Electrician; Emergency Medical Technician; Human
Resources Manager; Licensed Practical Nurse;
Medical Records Technician; Pharmacist; Public
Relations Specialist; Registered Nurse; Secretary;
Social Worker. Educational backgrounds include:
Business Administration; Health Care; Nutrition;
Public Relations. Benefits: 403(b); Daycare
Assistance; Dental Insurance; Disability Coverage;
Employee Discounts; Life Insurance; Medical
Insurance; On-Site Daycare. Special programs:
Summer Jobs. Corporate headquarters location:
This Location.

CONNECTIONS COMMUNITY SUPPORT
PROGRAMS, INC.
500 West 10th Street, Wilmington DE 19801.
302/984-3380. Fax: 302/984-3385. Contact: Staff
Development. Description: Provides a full range of
residential, case management, medical, educational,
vocational, and recreational services to persons who
are both mentally ill and addicted to drugs or
alcohol, homeless mentally ill persons, homeless
families, elderly persons with mental illness, and
persons who are both mentally ill and physically
handicapped. Founded in 1985. NOTE: Entry-level
positions are offered. Common positions include:
Counselor; Licensed Practical Nurse; Psychiatrist;
Registered Nurse; Social Worker. Educational
backgrounds include: Counseling; Education;
Health Care; Human Services; Liberal Arts;
Psychology; Social Work; Sociology. Benefits:
403(b); Dental Insurance; Disability Coverage; Life
Insurance; Savings Plan; Tuition Assistance.
Special programs: Internships. Corporate
headquarters location: This Location.

CREATIVE COMMUNITY LIVING
SERVICES, INC.
P.O. Box 260, Watertown WI 53094. Toll-free
phone: 800/236-2257. Recorded jobline: 888/843-
8183. Contact: Recruiting. Description: An
organization providing residential and community
services to adults with disabilities. Founded in 1973.
NOTE: Entry-level positions, part-time jobs, and
second and third shifts are offered. Common
positions include: Program Manager. Educational
backgrounds include: Health Care; Human
Services. Benefits: 401(k); Casual Dress - Daily;

Dental Insurance; Disability Coverage; Life Insurance; Medical Insurance; Profit Sharing; Sick Days). **Corporate headquarters location:** This Location. **Other U.S. locations:** Madison WI; Milwaukee WI; Waukesha WI.

DECI (DURHAM EXCHANGE CLUB INDUSTRY, INC.)
1717 Lawson Street, Durham NC 27703. 919/596-1341. **Fax:** 919/596-6380. **Recorded jobline:** 919/596-1346x501. **Contact:** Human Resources. **E-mail address:** deci@deci.org. **World Wide Web address:** http://www.deci.org. **Description:** A private, nonprofit, community-based, vocational rehabilitation facility. **NOTE:** Entry-level positions are offered. **Common positions include:** Administrative Assistant; Certified Occupational Therapy Assistant; Computer Support Technician; Counselor; Special Education Teacher. **Educational backgrounds include:** AS400 Certification; Business Administration; Liberal Arts; Microsoft Office. **Benefits:** 403(b); Bonus Award/Plan; Dental Insurance; Disability Coverage; Life Insurance; Medical Insurance; Pension Plan; Public Transit Available; Tuition Assistance; Vacation Days (10 - 20). **Special programs:** Internships; Summer Jobs. **Corporate headquarters location:** This Location.

EDUCATION DEVELOPMENT CENTER
55 Chapel Street, Newton MA 02458. 617/969-7100. **Contact:** Director of Human Resources. **World Wide Web address:** http://www.edc.org. **Description:** One of the world's leading educational nonprofit research and development firms specializing in early childhood development, K-12 education, health promotion, learning technologies, and institutional reform. Founded in 1958. **Common positions include:** Administrative Assistant; Research Assistant; Teacher/Professor. **Educational backgrounds include:** Education; Health Care; Mathematics. **Benefits:** Dental Insurance; Disability Coverage; EAP; Life Insurance; Medical Insurance; Tuition Assistance; Vacation Days. **Corporate headquarters location:** This Location. **Other U.S. locations:** Washington DC; New York NY.

FAMILY AND CHILD SERVICES OF WASHINGTON DC
929 L Street NW, Washington DC 20001. 202/289-1510. **Contact:** Executive Director. **Description:** A private, nonprofit, social services organization offering a broad range of services including counseling, adoption, family daycare, foster care, and summer and winter camping for children, as well as services for the elderly. **Common positions include:** Administrative Worker/Clerk; Counselor; Social Worker. **Benefits:** Disability Coverage; Life Insurance; Medical Insurance; Pension Plan. **Special programs:** Internships. **Corporate headquarters location:** This Location.

FAMILY SERVICE & CONSUMER CREDIT COUNSELING SERVICE
128 East Olin Avenue, Suite 100, Madison WI 53713. 608/252-1325x1147. **Fax:** 608/251-4665. **Contact:** Human Resources Manager. **Description:** A private, nonprofit mental health agency whose programs include ATA (Alternatives to Aggression), SAH (Safe at Home), FIT (Families in Transition), and CCCS (Consumer Credit Counseling Services). **Common positions include:** Counselor; Psychologist; Social Worker; Therapist. **Educational backgrounds include:** Human Services. **Benefits:** 401(k); Daycare Assistance; Dental Insurance; Disability Coverage; Life Insurance; Medical Insurance. **Special programs:** Internships. **Other U.S. locations:** Nationwide.

FEDERATED DORCHESTER NEIGHBORHOOD HOUSES
450 Washington Street, Dorchester MA 02124. 617/282-5034. **Fax:** 617/265-6020. **Contact:** Human Resources. **E-mail address:** hrfdnh@ thecia.net. **Description:** A nonprofit, human service agency with eight locations. **NOTE:** Entry-level positions and part-time jobs are offered. **Common positions include:** Accountant; Administrative Assistant; Administrative Manager; Certified Nurses Aide; Certified Occupational Therapy Assistant; Clerical Supervisor; Education Administrator; ESL Teacher; Home Health Aide; Licensed Practical Nurse; Marketing Specialist; MIS Specialist; Occupational Therapist; Physical Therapist; Physical Therapy Assistant; Preschool Worker; Public Relations Specialist; Secretary; Social Worker; Special Education Teacher; Teacher /Professor; Typist/Word Processor. **Educational backgrounds include:** Accounting; Finance. **Benefits:** Daycare Assistance; Dental Insurance; Life Insurance; Medical Insurance; Pension Plan; Public Transit Available; Savings Plan; Sick Days (6 - 10); Vacation Days (11 - 15). **Special programs:** Internships; Summer Jobs. **Corporate headquarters location:** This Location. **Executive Director:** Linda Mayo-Perez.

THE FORD FOUNDATION
320 East 43rd Street, New York NY 10017. 212/573-5000. **Fax:** 212/351-3677. **Contact:** Employment. **World Wide Web address:** http://www.fordfound.org. **Description:** One of the largest philanthropic organizations in the United States. This private, nonprofit institution gives funds for educational, developmental, research, and experimental efforts designed to produce significant advances in a wide range of social problems. The company also operates several overseas field offices. **Common positions include:** Accountant/ Auditor; Administrator; Assistant Program Officer; Attorney; Economist; Human Resources Manager; Program Officer; Systems Analyst. **Educational backgrounds include:** Agricultural Science; Anthropology; Economics; International Relations; Political Science; Social Science. **Benefits:** Dental Insurance; Disability Coverage; Life Insurance; Medical Insurance; Retirement Plan; Savings Plan; Tuition Assistance. **Corporate headquarters location:** This Location.

FOSTER HOME SERVICES
JEWISH CHILD CARE ASSOCIATION
120 Wall Street, 12th Floor, New York NY 10005. 212/558-9943. **Contact:** Human Resources. **Description:** Provides social services for children including the placement of abused children in foster homes, as well as training programs for future foster parents. **Common positions include:** Registered Nurse; Social Worker. **Educational backgrounds include:** Nursing; Psychology; Social Work. **Benefits:** Dental Insurance; Disability Coverage; Life Insurance; Medical Insurance; Pension Plan; Tuition Assistance. **Corporate headquarters location:** This Location.

GATEWAY
P.O. Box 272, Berrien Springs MI 49103. 616/471-2897. **Contact:** Human Resources. **Description:** A nonprofit organization that provides employment, rehabilitation services, testing, and training for persons with vocational disabilities. **Corporate headquarters location:** This Location. **Parent company:** United Way of America.

GEMINUS CORPORATION
5281 Fountain Drive, Crown Point IN 46307. 219/791-2300. **Contact:** Human Resources. **World Wide Web address:** http://www.geminus.org.

Description: Operates Head Start programs and performs accounting, marketing, and human resource functions for Southlake Center for Mental Health, an inpatient and outpatient mental health center, and Tri-City Mental Health, an outpatient mental health center. **Common positions include:** Claim Representative; Counselor; Medical Records Technician; Physician; Psychologist; Recreational Therapist; Registered Nurse; Social Worker; Teacher/Professor. **Benefits:** Dental Insurance; Disability Coverage; Employee Discounts; Life Insurance; Medical Insurance; Pension Plan; Tuition Assistance. **Special programs:** Internships. **Corporate headquarters location:** This Location.

GIRL SCOUTS OF THE UNITED STATES OF AMERICA
420 Fifth Avenue, New York NY 10018-2798. 212/852-8000. **Toll-free phone:** 800/GSUSA-4-U. **Contact:** Staffing. **World Wide Web address:** http://www.gsusa.org. **Description:** Girl Scouts is a national scouting organization for girls. **Corporate headquarters location:** This Location.

RAY GRAHAM ASSOCIATION
2801 Finley Road, Downers Grove IL 60515. 630/620-2222. **Contact:** Human Resources. **Description:** A consumer-driven organization that responds to the needs of people with disabilities and their families. **Common positions include:** Abstractor/Indexer; Accountant/Auditor; Budget Analyst; Clerical Supervisor; Counselor; Dietician/Nutritionist; Financial Analyst; Human Service Worker; Licensed Practical Nurse; Occupational Therapist; Physical Therapist; Preschool Worker; Public Relations Specialist; Recreational Therapist; Registered Nurse; Social Worker; Speech-Language Pathologist. **Educational backgrounds include:** Human Services. **Benefits:** 401(k); Dental Insurance; Life Insurance; Medical Insurance. **Corporate headquarters location:** This Location.

HABITAT FOR HUMANITY INTERNATIONAL
322 West Lamar Street, Americus GA 31709. 912/924-6935. **Toll-free phone:** 800/422-4828. **Contact:** Human Resources. **E-mail address:** hrstaffing@habitat.org. **World Wide Web address:** http://www.habitat.org. **Description:** A nonprofit, ecumenical, Christian housing ministry whose mission is to build housing for the poor around the world. **Corporate headquarters location:** This Location. **Other U.S. locations:** Nationwide.

H.O.M.E., INC.
P.O. Box 10, Orland ME 04472. 207/469-7961. **Contact:** Father Randy Eldridge, Internship Coordinator. **Description:** Provides self-sufficiency instruction to individuals. In addition, this nonprofit company provides education, an outlet for people to sell their crafts, and health care for low-income individuals. H.O.M.E., Inc. also gives job training workshops and provides housing. Founded in 1970. **Common positions include:** Computer Operator; Editor; Education Administrator; Secretary; Social Worker; Teacher Aide; Teacher/Professor; Typist/Word Processor. **Benefits:** Casual Dress - Daily; Employee Discounts; On-Site Daycare. **Special programs:** Internships. **Internship information:** Interns receive training, room and board, and a stipend. **Corporate headquarters location:** This Location.

HUMANE SOCIETY OF MISSOURI
1201 Macklind Avenue, St. Louis MO 63110. 314/647-8800. **Contact:** Director of Personnel. **Description:** One of the oldest and largest humane societies in the U.S., providing emergency field services in St. Louis County. The organization investigates cruelty and neglect to animals statewide, operates two animal shelters, and operates two veterinary clinics. The society also operates a rehabilitation farm for large animals. **Common positions include:** Accountant/Auditor; Administrator; Animal Health Technician; Branch Manager; Director of Development; General Manager; Kennel Worker; Secretary; Veterinarian. **Educational backgrounds include:** Accounting; Animal Science; Business Administration; Management/Planning; Veterinary Medicine. **Benefits:** Dental Insurance; Disability Coverage; Employee Discounts; Life Insurance; Medical Insurance; Pension Plan; Tuition Assistance. **Corporate headquarters location:** This Location.

HUNT'S POINT MULTI-SERVICE CENTER INC.
2804 Third Avenue, 3rd Floor, Bronx NY 10455. 718/402-8899. **Contact:** Personnel Director. **Description:** A private, nonprofit organization which operates a multi-service program center with facilities that include a general health center, six mental health centers, and community advocacy organizations. **Corporate headquarters location:** This Location.

INDIANHEAD COMMUNITY ACTION AGENCY
P.O. Box 40, Ladysmith WI 54848. 715/532-5594x48. **Fax:** 715/532-7808. **Contact:** Personnel Director. **E-mail address:** georgettebembenek@usa.net. **World Wide Web address:** http://www.icaaheadstart.com. **Description:** A nonprofit agency providing a variety of social services including home health care, Head Start programs, a home weatherization program, and a clothing center. **NOTE:** Entry-level positions and part-time jobs are offered. **Company slogan:** People helping people help themselves. **Common positions include:** Accountant; Administrative Assistant; Human Resources Manager; Preschool Worker; Secretary; Teacher/Professor. **Educational backgrounds include:** Carpentry; Finance; Health Care; Microsoft Word; Spreadsheets. **Benefits:** Casual Dress - Fridays; Dental Insurance; Life Insurance; Medical Insurance; Pension Plan; Public Transit Available; Savings Plan. **Corporate headquarters location:** This Location. **Executive Director:** Jerome Drahos.

JANE ADDAMS HULL HOUSE ASSOCIATION
10 South Riverside Plaza, Suite 1720, Chicago IL 60606. 312/906-8600. **Contact:** Staffing. **World Wide Web address:** http://www.hullhouse.org. **Description:** A nonprofit, multiservice social agency dedicated to helping people build better lives for themselves and their families. Jane Addams Hull House Association has six community centers and 35 satellite locations throughout metropolitan Chicago. The organization serves approximately 225,000 people from geographically, culturally, and economically diverse backgrounds each year. **Common positions include:** Accountant/Auditor; Counselor; Education Administrator; Health Services Manager; Human Service Worker; Preschool Worker; Psychologist; Recreational Therapist; Social Worker; Teacher/Professor; Typist/Word Processor. **Educational backgrounds include:** Accounting; Child Development; Education; Human Services; Marketing; Psychology; Social Work. **Benefits:** 403(b); Dental Insurance; Disability Coverage; Life Insurance; Medical Insurance; Pension Plan; Public Transit Available; Savings Plan. **Corporate headquarters location:** This Location.

JUST ONE BREAK, INC.
120 Wall Street, 20th Floor, New York NY 10005. 212/785-7300. **Fax:** 212/785-4513. **Contact:** Recruiter. **E-mail address:** justonebreak@interactive.net. **World Wide Web address:**

http://www.justonebreak.com. **Description:** A nonprofit organization that helps people with disabilities find employment. **Common positions include:** Accountant; Administrative Assistant; Bank Officer/Manager; Clerical Supervisor; Computer Operator; Counselor; Customer Service Manager; Database Manager; Graphic Artist; Management Trainee; MIS Specialist; Operations Manager; Paralegal; Project Manager; Sales Representative; Secretary; Social Worker; Systems Analyst; Systems Manager; Telecommunications Manager.

KNOX COUNTY COUNCIL FOR DEVELOPMENTAL DISABILITIES
2015 Windish Drive, Galesburg IL 61401. 309/344-2600. **Contact:** Human Resources. **Description:** A nonprofit agency that serves people with developmental disabilities. **Common positions include:** Accountant; Administrator; Assistant Manager; Blue-Collar Worker Supervisor; Branch Manager; Counselor; Department Manager; General Manager; Instructor/Trainer; Marketing Specialist; Operations/Production Manager. **Educational backgrounds include:** Human Services; Nursing; Occupational Therapy; Social Work; Teaching. **Benefits:** Disability Coverage; Life Insurance; Medical Insurance; Pension Plan; Savings Plan; Tuition Assistance. **Corporate headquarters location:** This Location.

LA FRONTERA CENTER, INC.
502 West 29th Street, Tucson AZ 85713. 520/884-9920. **Contact:** Human Resources. **Description:** A nonprofit, community-based, behavioral health center that provides mental health and chemical dependency services to residents of Pima County. The center operates 30 programs in 23 different facilities throughout Pima County. La Frontera Center provides services for infants born to addicted mothers; children with developmental disabilities; chemically-dependent adults; and homeless adults with mental illnesses. The center also provides outreach, rehabilitation, and substance abuse recovery programs. Founded in 1968. **Common positions include:** Accountant; Administrative Assistant; Administrative Manager; Budget Analyst; Certified Nurses Aide; Chief Financial Officer; Child Care Center Director; Claim Representative; Controller; Counselor; Customer Service Rep.; Database Administrator; Human Resources Manager; Licensed Practical Nurse; Medical Records Technician; MIS Manager; Network/ Systems Administrator; Nurse Practitioner; Pharmacist; Physician; Preschool Worker; Psychologist; Registered Nurse; Secretary; Social Worker; Special Education Teacher; Systems Analyst. **Educational backgrounds include:** Accounting; Communications; Finance; Microsoft Office; Microsoft Word; Novell; Spreadsheets. **Benefits:** 403(b); Casual Dress - Fridays; Dental Insurance; Disability Coverage; Flexible Schedule; Life Insurance; Medical Insurance; Sick Days (11+); Vacation Days (10 - 20).

LIGHTHOUSE INTERNATIONAL
111 East 59th Street, New York NY 10022. 212/821-9200. **Toll-free phone:** 800/829-0500. **Contact:** Recruiting. **World Wide Web address:** http://www.lighthouse.org. **Description:** Enables people who are blind or partially blind to lead independent lives through education, research, information, career and social services, and vision rehabilitation. **Common positions include:** Accountant; Accounting Clerk; Administrative Assistant; Development Officer; Early Childhood Teacher; Mail Distributor; Optician; Physical Therapist; Public Relations Specialist; Registered Nurse; Rehabilitation Teacher; Social Worker;

Speech-Language Pathologist; Teacher Aide; Teacher/Professor. **Educational backgrounds include:** Communications; Rehabilitative Teaching; Social Work; Special Education. **Benefits:** Dental Insurance; Disability Coverage; Life Insurance; Medical Insurance; Pension Plan; Tax-Deferred Annuity. **Special programs:** Internships. **Other U.S. locations:** Medford NY; Poughkeepsie NY; Queens NY; White Plains NY.

LITTLE FLOWER CHILDREN'S SERVICES OF NEW YORK
186 Remsen Street, Brooklyn NY 11201. 718/260-8840. **Contact:** Carol A. Huck, Human Resources Director. **Description:** Provides foster care and adoption services, group homes, residential treatment units, shelter cottages, intermediate care facilities for mentally handicapped children, and therapeutic foster boarding homes. Little Flower Children's Services cares for approximately 2,600 children annually. **NOTE:** Resumes should be sent to Human Resources, Little Flower Children's Services of New York, P.O. Box 9000, Wading River NY 11792. **Educational backgrounds include:** Accounting; Business Administration; Computer Science; Social Work; Sociology. **Benefits:** 403(b); Daycare Assistance; Disability Coverage; Life Insurance; Medical Insurance; Pension Plan; Savings Plan; Tuition Assistance. **Corporate headquarters location:** This Location.

LOWER WEST SIDE HOUSEHOLD SERVICES CORPORATION
250 West 57th Street, Suite 1511, New York NY 10107. 212/307-7107. **Fax:** 212/956-2308. **Contact:** Assistant Program Manager. **Description:** A nonprofit company which provides home health care services to the elderly, infants, toddlers, and adults living in the five boroughs of New York City and Westchester County. Services include nursing, custodial care, nutrition, social work, and arrangements for medical equipment. The agency also provides free custodial care for individuals and families infected with HIV/AIDS. Founded in 1969. **NOTE:** Second and thirds shifts are offered. **Common positions include:** Accountant; Administrative Assistant; Computer Scientist; Home Health Aide; Licensed Practical Nurse; Marketing Specialist; Occupational Therapist; Physical Therapist; Social Worker; Speech-Language Pathologist; Web Advertising Specialist; Website Developer. **Educational backgrounds include:** Education; Health Care; Microsoft Office; Microsoft Word. **Benefits:** 403(b); Casual Dress - Daily; Dental Insurance; Disability Coverage; Life Insurance; Medical Insurance; Public Transit Available; Sick Days (11+); Vacation Days (10 - 20). **Special programs:** Training. **Corporate headquarters location:** This Location. **Other U.S. locations:** Scarsdale NY.

MADISON AREA REHABILITATION CENTERS, INC.
2001 West Broadway, Madison WI 53713. 608/223-9110. **Fax:** 608/273-4638. **Contact:** Human Resources Department. **Description:** A nonprofit rehabilitation center geared towards adults with developmental disabilities. **NOTE:** Entry-level positions are offered. **Common positions include:** Certified Nurses Aide. **Educational backgrounds include:** Human Services. **Benefits:** Dental Insurance; Disability Coverage; Life Insurance; Medical Insurance; Pension Plan; Tuition Assistance. **Corporate headquarters location:** This Location.

MAINSTREAM, INC.
6930 Carroll Avenue, Suite 240, Takoma Park MD 20912. 301/891-8777. **Fax:** 301/891-8778.

Contact: Staffing **E-mail address:** info@ mainstreaminc.org. **World Wide Web address:** http://www.mainstreaminc.org. **Description:** Offers employment options and job placement services for people with physical, mental, emotional, or psychological disabilities. Mainstream also provides seminars and training for employers and service providers; and links employers, disability organizations, service providers, and people with disabilities. **Corporate headquarters location:** This Location.

MARCH OF DIMES
1275 Mamaroneck Avenue, White Plains NY 10605. 914/428-7100. **Contact:** Human Resources. **World Wide Web address:** http://www.modimes.org. **Description:** The organization operates the Campaign for Healthier Babies, which includes programs of research, community service, education, and advocacy. Birth defects are the primary focus of March of Dimes research efforts. March of Dimes chapters across the country work with their communities to determine and meet the needs of women, children, and families. Through specially designed programs, women are provided with access to prenatal care. **Corporate headquarters location:** This Location.

MARYKNOLL FATHERS AND BROTHERS
Price Building, 85 Ryder Road, Ossining NY 10562-0302. 914/941-7590. **Fax:** 914/941-4113. **Contact:** Director of Personnel. **E-mail address:** aglass@maryknoll.org. **World Wide Web address:** http://www.maryknoll.org. **Description:** This location houses administrative and fundraising offices. Overall, Maryknoll Fathers and Brothers is an international order of religious missionaries. **NOTE:** Entry-level positions and part-time jobs are offered. **Common positions include:** Controller; Graphic Artist; Help-Desk Technician; Internet Services Manager; Managing Editor; Network/ Systems Administrator; Radio/TV Announcer/ Broadcaster; Registered Nurse; Reporter; Technical Writer/Editor; Video Production Coordinator; Webmaster. **Educational backgrounds include:** Accounting; AS400 Certification; Business Administration; Computer Science; Health Care; Microsoft Office; Microsoft Word; Novell; Publishing; QuarkXPress; Software Tech. Support; Spreadsheets. **Benefits:** Dental Insurance; Disability Coverage; Employee Discounts; Financial Planning Assistance; Life Insurance; Medical Insurance; Pension Plan; Savings Plan; Sick Days; Tuition Assistance; Vacation Days. **Special programs:** Summer Jobs. **Corporate headquarters location:** This Location.

MARYVILLE ACADEMY
1150 North River Road, Des Plaines IL 60016. 847/824-6126. **Fax:** 847/824-7190. **Contact:** Personnel. **Description:** A residential home for orphaned and homeless children. Founded in 1882. **Corporate headquarters location:** This Location.

MELWOOD TRAINING CENTER
5606 Dower House Road, Upper Marlboro MD 20772. 301/599-8000. **Fax:** 301/599-0180. **Contact:** Corporate Recruiting Manager. **E-mail address:** klong@melwood.org. **World Wide Web address:** http://www.melwood.org. **Description:** A private, nonprofit agency providing services for individuals with disabilities. This location also hires seasonally.Founded in 1963. **NOTE:** Entry-level positions, part-time jobs, and second and third shifts are offered. **Company slogan:** Growing together. **Common positions include:** Accountant; Administrative Assistant; Blue-Collar Worker Supervisor; Certified Nurses Aide; Computer Support Technician; Counselor; Customer Service

Representative; Finance Director; Home Health Aide; Human Resources Manager; Marketing Manager; Marketing Specialist; Network/Systems Administrator; Operations Manager; Project Manager; Public Relations Specialist; Quality Control Supervisor; Registered Nurse; Secretary; Social Worker; Vice President of Finance; Vice President of Operations. **Educational backgrounds include:** Accounting; Education; Finance; Health Care; Microsoft Office; Microsoft Word; Public Relations; Spreadsheets. **Benefits:** 401(k); Casual Dress - Fridays; Dental Insurance; Disability Coverage; Employee Discounts; Flexible Schedule; Life Insurance; Medical Insurance; Public Transit Available; Tuition Assistance. **Special programs:** Internships; Summer Jobs; Training. **Corporate headquarters location:** This Location.

METROPOLITAN FAMILY SERVICES
14 East Jackson Boulevard, 14th Floor, Chicago IL 60604. 312/986-4000. **Fax:** 312/986-4347. **Contact:** Human Resources. **World Wide Web address:** http://www.cccsmetro.com. **Description:** A nonprofit, social services agency that provides counseling and support services to low-income families and individuals. The agency operates 23 other locations in the Chicago area. **Common positions include:** Accountant; Attorney; Computer Programmer; Counselor; Human Resources Manager; Paralegal. **Educational backgrounds include:** Accounting; Business Administration; Communications; Computer Science. **Benefits:** Dental Insurance; Disability Coverage; Life Insurance; Medical Insurance; Pension Plan; Tuition Assistance. **Special programs:** Internships. **Corporate headquarters location:** This Location.

MILE HIGH UNITED WAY
2505 East 18th Street, Denver CO 80211. 303/433-8383. **Fax:** 303/561-2202. **Contact:** Human Resources. **World Wide Web address:** http://www.unitedwaydenver.org. **Description:** A nonprofit organization made up of volunteers and human service professionals. Mile High United Way provides disaster relief, emergency food and shelter, and rehabilitation and development services to needy individuals. Founded in 1887. **NOTE:** Entry-level positions are offered. **Common positions include:** Accountant; Administrative Assistant; Chief Financial Officer; Controller; Database Manager; Event Planner; Graphic Designer; Human Resources Manager; Marketing Manager; Secretary. **Educational backgrounds include:** Accounting; Business Administration; Liberal Arts; Marketing; MBA; Microsoft Office; Microsoft Word. **Benefits:** 403(b); Casual Dress - Fridays; Dental Insurance; Disability Coverage; Life Insurance; Medical Insurance; Sick Days (11+); Tuition Assistance; Vacation Days (10 - 20).

NASHVILLE SANCTION CENTER
652 West Iris Drive, Nashville TN 37204. 615/292-1657. **Contact:** Human Resources. **Description:** A half-way house for convicted felons. **NOTE:** Entry-level positions, part-time jobs, and second and third shifts are offered. **Common positions include:** Administrative Assistant; Counselor. **Benefits:** 401(k); Casual Dress - Fridays; Flexible Schedule; Life Insurance; Medical Insurance; Sick Days; Vacation Days. **Special programs:** Internships. **Corporate headquarters location:** Lynn Haven FL. **Other U.S. locations:** AL; FL; KY. **Listed on:** Privately held.

NATIONAL ASSISTANCE LEAGUE
5627 Fernwood Avenue, Los Angeles CA 90028. 323/469-5897. **Fax:** 323/469-0669. **Contact:** Human Resources. **Description:** This location houses administrative offices. Overall, the National

Assistance League was one of the first nonprofit, nonpolitical, nonsectarian organizations founded in the West to have volunteers help those less fortunate to attain better lives. Volunteers raise funds in order to provide services to those in need. Services include supplying clothing to children and sponsoring reading programs. Founded in 1935. **Corporate headquarters location:** This Location.

NATIONAL PARK SERVICE
Rural Route 1, Box 190, Hot Springs SD 57747. 605/745-4600. **Contact:** Human Resources. **World Wide Web address:** http://www.nps.gov/wica. **Description:** Protects and preserves caves in the national park and maintains the park's natural resources.

NATIONAL WILDLIFE FEDERATION
WINDCAVE NATIONAL PARK
8925 Leesburg Pike, Vienna VA 22184-0001. 703/790-4248. **Fax:** 703/790-4039. **Recorded jobline:** 703/790-4522. **Contact:** Human Resources. **E-mail address:** jobopp@nwf.org. **World Wide Web address:** http://www.nwf.org. **Description:** A nonprofit, conservation society dedicated to preserving the nation's wildlife. Founded in 1936. **Common positions include:** Accountant; Administrative Assistant; Attorney; Buyer; Customer Service Representative; Editor; Finance Director; Financial Analyst; Graphic Artist; Human Resources Manager; Market Research Analyst; Secretary; Vice President. **Educational backgrounds include:** Accounting; Art/ Design; Business Administration; Communications; Computer Science; Finance; Marketing; Public Relations. **Benefits:** 403(b); Dental Insurance; Disability Coverage; Employee Discounts; Flexible Schedule; Life Insurance; Medical Insurance; Pension Plan; Tuition Assistance. **Special programs:** Internships. **Internship information:** Cover letters and resumes should be directed to 1400 16th Street NW, Washington DC 20036. **Corporate headquarters location:** This Location. **Other U.S. locations:** Washington DC; Atlanta GA; Winchester VA.

NEW HAMPSHIRE VOCATIONAL REHABILITATION OFFICE
DEPARTMENT OF EDUCATION
78 Regional Drive, Building 2, Concord NH 03301. 603/271-3471. **Fax:** 603/271-1953. **Contact:** Personnel. **Description:** Assists disabled persons in obtaining or maintaining employment. **Corporate headquarters location:** This Location.

PARC
9901 Derby Lane, Westchester IL 60154. 708/547-3550. **Fax:** 708/547-4067. **Contact:** Christine Hunt, Human Resources Manager. **Description:** A private, nonprofit agency serving the developmental, residential, and vocational needs of adults and children with developmental and mental disabilities. P**Common positions include:** Occupational Therapist; Physical Therapist; Preschool Worker; Psychologist; Recreational Therapist; Social Worker; Speech-Language Pathologist; Teacher/ Professor; Typist/Word Processor. **Educational backgrounds include:** Health Care; Liberal Arts; Psychology. **Benefits:** 401(k); Dental Insurance; Disability Coverage; Life Insurance; Medical Insurance; Public Transit Available; Savings Plan; Vision Insurance. **Special programs:** Internships. **Corporate headquarters location:** This Location.

PROJECT BREAD
WALK FOR HUNGER
160 North Washington Street, 5th Floor, Boston MA 02114. 617/723-5000. **Contact:** Human Resources. **World Wide Web address:** http://www. projectbread.org. **Description:** Supports nearly 500 food pantries, soup kitchens, homeless shelters, food banks, and other emergency feeding programs in 119 Massachusetts communities. Project Bread's Technical Assistance Program trains over 200 volunteers and staff, provides over 100 programs with one-on-one management assistance, and holds training series. Project Bread's transportation program, Food Drive for the Hungry, operated jointly with the American Red Cross, provides transportation to pick up low-cost or donated food. Since it began in 1969, the Walk for Hunger has become one of the nation's largest annual, one-day fund-raisers for the hungry.

RANCH COMMUNITY SERVICES
West 187 North 8661 Maple Road, Menomonee Falls WI 53051. 262/251-8670. **Fax:** 262/251-8878. **Contact:** Human Resources. **Description:** A nonprofit human services organization devoted to assisting adults with developmental disabilities by helping them to find jobs and providing them with community activities. There are additional locations in Waukesha and Milwaukee Counties. Founded in 1960. **NOTE:** Entry-level positions and second and third shifts are offered. **Common positions include:** Certified Nurses Aide. **Educational backgrounds include:** Human Services; Sociology. **Benefits:** Dental Insurance; Life Insurance; Medical Insurance; Pension Plan; Vacation Days. **Special programs:** Internships; Training. **Corporate headquarters location:** This Location. **Annual sales/revenues:** Less than $5 million.

REGIONAL CENTER OF ORANGE COUNTY
P.O. Box 22010, Santa Ana CA 92702-2010. 714/796-5100. **Contact:** Personnel. **Description:** A nonprofit organization dedicated to helping individuals with all types of learning disabilities ranging from mental retardation to cerebral palsy. **Common positions include:** Social Worker. **Educational backgrounds include:** Social Work. **Benefits:** 401(k); Daycare Assistance; Dental Insurance; Disability Coverage; Employee Discounts; Life Insurance; Medical Insurance; Pension Plan; Savings Plan. **Corporate headquarters location:** This Location.

RIVERBEND COMMUNITY MENTAL HEALTH
P.O. Box 2032, Concord NH 03302-2032. 603/228-1551. **Contact:** Human Resources Coordinator. **E-mail address:** hr@riverbendcmhc.org. **World Wide Web address:** http://www.riverbendcmhc.org. **Description:** An organization providing outpatient, group, and family therapy; case management; psychiatric treatment; 24-hour emergency and assessment services; a crisis intervention program; and supervised residential living. **NOTE:** Entry-level positions and second and third shifts are offered. **Common positions include:** Accountant; Administrative Assistant; Certified Nurses Aide; Counselor; Nurse Practitioner; Psychologist; Registered Nurse; Secretary; Social Worker. **Educational backgrounds include:** Accounting; Business Administration; Computer Science; Health Care. **Benefits:** 403(b); Dental Insurance; Disability Coverage; Flexible Schedule; Life Insurance; Medical Insurance; Tuition Assistance. **Special programs:** Internships; Training. **Corporate headquarters location:** This Location. **Other U.S. locations:** Franklin NH; Henniker NH; New London NH. **President:** Dale K. Klatzker. **Annual sales/revenues:** $11 - $20 million.

ROTARY INTERNATIONAL
One Rotary Center, 1560 Sherman Avenue, Evanston IL 60201. 847/866-3000. **Fax:** 847/866-5766. **Contact:** Human Resources. **World Wide Web address:** http://www.rotary.org. **Description:**

This location provides administrative services to Rotary clubs including publicity and the administration of humanitarian and scholarship programs funded by the Rotary Foundation. Overall, Rotary International is one of the largest international, nonprofit, service organizations in the world. **Common positions include:** Accountant/Auditor; Administrative Assistant; Applications Engineer; Attorney; Budget Analyst; Commercial Artist; Computer Programmer; Controller; Customer Service Rep.; Database Manager; Editor; Editorial Assistant; Education Administrator; Financial Analyst; Fund Manager; Graphic Designer; Human Resources Manager; Managing Editor; Marketing Specialist; MIS Specialist; Production Manager; Public Relations Specialist; Purchasing Agent/Manager; Secretary; Software Engineer; Systems Analyst; Systems Manager; Technical Writer/Editor; Typist/Word Processor; Webmaster. **Educational backgrounds include:** Accounting; Business Administration; Communications; Computer Science; Finance; International Relations; Liberal Arts; Marketing; Public Relations. **Benefits:** 401(k); Dental Insurance; Disability Coverage; Life Insurance; Medical Insurance; Pension Plan; Public Transit Available; Tuition Assistance. **Special programs:** Internships. **Corporate headquarters location:** This Location.

SAVE THE CHILDREN
54 Wilton Road, Westport CT 06880. 203/221-4000. **Contact:** Human Resources. **World Wide Web address:** http://www.savethechildren.org. **Description:** A nonprofit organization that works to raise funds for disadvantaged children worldwide. **Corporate headquarters location:** This Location.

SELFHELP COMMUNITY SERVICES, INC.
440 Ninth Avenue, New York NY 10001. 212/971-7600. **Fax:** 212/695-0941. **Contact:** Human Resources. **Description:** Operates a nonprofit social services organization providing a broad range of housing, home care, food and outreach social services, primarily for the elderly and children. **Common positions include:** Accountant/Auditor; Administrative Worker/Clerk; Chef/Cook/Kitchen Worker; Computer Programmer; Department Manager; Human Resources Manager; Registered Nurse; Social Worker. **Educational backgrounds include:** Accounting; Business Administration; Counseling; Nursing; Psychology; Social Work. **Corporate headquarters location:** This Location.

SENIORS! INC.
777 Grant Street, Suite 603, Denver CO 80203. 303/832-5565. **Fax:** 303/839-1086. **Contact:** Human Resources. **Description:** Provides programs and services for older persons which promote and enhance independent living. **Common positions include:** Accountant; Customer Service Rep.; General Manager; Gerontologist; Human Service Worker; Public Relations Specialist; Sociologist. **Educational backgrounds include:** Business Administration; Liberal Arts; Marketing. **Benefits:** Medical Insurance; Pension Plan. **Special programs:** Internships. **Corporate headquarters location:** This Location.

SIERRA CLUB
85 Second Street, 2nd Floor, San Francisco CA 94105. 415/977-5500. **Recorded jobline:** 415/977-5744. **Contact:** Personnel. **World Wide Web address:** http://www.sierraclub.org. **Description:** A volunteer-based, nonprofit company chiefly concerned with the maintenance and preservation of national natural resources, wildlife, and wildlands. **NOTE:** Please call the jobline for a listing of available positions before sending a resume. **Corporate headquarters location:** This Location.

SOCIETY FOR THE PRESERVATION OF NEW ENGLAND ANTIQUITIES
141 Cambridge Street, Boston MA 02114. 617/227-3956. **Fax:** 617/227-9204. **Contact:** Personnel. **Description:** A nonprofit society founded to preserve New England's domestic buildings and artifacts. It is among the country's largest regional preservation organizations, owning 43 historic properties, 34 of which are open as house museums. **Benefits:** Daycare Assistance; Dental Insurance; Disability Coverage; Employee Discounts; Life Insurance; Medical Insurance; Pension Plan. **Special programs:** Internships. **Corporate headquarters location:** This Location. **Other U.S. locations:** CT; ME; NH; RI.

SOUTHWEST BUSINESS INDUSTRY & REHABILITATION ASSOCIATION
4435 North Buckboard Trail, Scottsdale AZ 85251. 480/949-0135. **Contact:** Personnel Department. **Description:** Provides employment counseling and training to people with disabilities. **Common positions include:** Employment Interviewer; Social Worker. **Educational backgrounds include:** Social Science. **Corporate headquarters location:** This Location.

TACOMA GOODWILL INDUSTRIES REHABILITATION CENTER INC.
714 South 27th Street, Tacoma WA 98409. 253/272-5166. **Fax:** 253/428-4162. **Contact:** Personnel. **World Wide Web address:** http://www.tacomagoodwill.org. **Description:** Offers vocational rehabilitation programs. **Common positions include:** Blue-Collar Worker Supervisor; Cashier; Payroll Clerk; Retail Manager; Retail Sales Worker. **Educational backgrounds include:** Business Administration; Marketing. **Benefits:** Dental Insurance; Life Insurance; Medical Insurance. **Corporate headquarters location:** Bethesda MD.

TECHNOSERVE INC.
49 Day Street, Norwalk CT 06854. 203/852-0377. **Fax:** 203/838-6717. **Contact:** Human Resources. **Description:** A private, nonprofit development aid organization that works with low-income people and development institutions in Africa, Latin America, and Eastern Europe to help establish or strengthen self-help enterprises. **Common positions include:** Accountant; Administrator; Financial Analyst; Fundraising Specialist; Instructor/Trainer; Project Manager; Supervisor. **Educational backgrounds include:** Accounting; Business Administration; Finance. **Benefits:** Dental Insurance; Disability Coverage; Life Insurance; Medical Insurance; Pension Plan; Savings Plan. **Special programs:** Internships. **Corporate headquarters location:** This Location.

U.S. FUNDS FOR UNICEF
333 East 38th Street, Sixth Floor, New York NY 10016. 212/686-5522. **Contact:** Director of Human Resources. **World Wide Web address:** http://www.unicefusa.org. **Description:** Organized for educational and charitable purposes, U.S. Funds for UNICEF aims to increase awareness of the needs of children around the world. **Common positions include:** Accountant; Administrator; Budget Analyst; Computer Programmer; Customer Service Rep.; Editor; Education Administrator; Financial Analyst; Marketing Specialist; Public Relations Specialist; Purchasing Agent/Manager; Systems Analyst. **Educational backgrounds include:** Business Administration; Communications; Computer Science; Finance; Liberal Arts; Marketing. **Benefits:** 403(b); Dental Insurance; Disability Coverage; Employee Discounts; Life Insurance; Medical Insurance; Tuition Assistance. **Special programs:** Internships. **Corporate**

headquarters location: This Location. **Other U.S. locations:** Los Angeles CA; Washington DC; Atlanta GA; Chicago IL; Boston MA; Houston TX.

UNITED CEREBRAL PALSY OF COLORADO, INC.
2200 South Jasmine Street, Denver CO 80222. 303/691-9339. **Contact:** Personnel. **Description:** A nonprofit organization that provides education, childcare, and employment services, as well as information and referrals. The organization is also engaged in donation pickup. **Benefits:** 403(b); Dental Insurance; Employee Discounts; Health Benefits; Life Insurance; Vision Insurance. **Corporate headquarters location:** This Location. **Annual sales/revenues:** $5 - $10 million.

UNITED MIGRANT OPPORTUNITY SERVICES,
P.O. Box 04129, Milwaukee WI 53204. 414/671-5700x3007. **Physical address:** 929 West Mitchell Street, Milwaukee WI. **Toll-free phone:** 800/279-8667. **Fax:** 414/671-4833. **Contact:** Human Resources. **Description:** A nonprofit company offering a wide range of employment, training, and educational programs and services statewide to enable migrant, seasonal farm workers and other disadvantaged clients to obtain full employment and to increase their marketable skills. **NOTE:** Entry-level positions are offered. **Common positions include:** Administrative Assistant; Daycare Worker; ESL Teacher; Secretary; Social Worker; Teacher/Professor; Typist/Word Processor. **Educational backgrounds include:** Accounting; Public Relations; Social Work. **Benefits:** 401(k); Dental Insurance; Disability Coverage; Life Insurance; Medical Insurance; Public Transit Available. **Corporate headquarters location:** This Location.

UNITED WAY OF AMERICA
701 North Fairfax Street, Alexandria VA 22314. 703/836-7100. **Contact:** Human Resources Director. **World Wide Web address:** http://www.unitedway.org. **Description:** This location is the national service and training center, supporting its members with services that include advertising, training, corporate relations, research, networks, and government relations. Overall, through a vast network of volunteers and local charities, local United Way organizations throughout America help meet the health needs of millions. United Way's history is built on local organizations helping people in their communities. The United Way system includes approximately 1,900 community-based organizations. **Corporate headquarters location:** This Location.
Other U.S. locations:
* 901 Ross Avenue, Dallas TX 75202. 214/978-0000.

THE URBAN LEAGUE OF METROPOLITAN DENVER
5900 East 39th Avenue, Denver CO 80207. 303/388-5861. **Fax:** 303/388-3523. **Contact:** Human Resources. **World Wide Web address:** http://www.denverurbanleague.org. **Description:** A nonprofit organization that sponsors a variety of social programs including employment services and career and outplacement counseling. **Common positions include:** Accountant; Administrative Manager; Automotive Mechanic; Branch Manager; Buyer; Clerical Supervisor; Clinical Lab Technician; Computer Programmer; Construction Contractor; Counselor; Credit Manager; Customer Service Rep.; Dental Assistant/Dental Hygienist; Education Administrator; Electrician; Emergency Medical Technician; Financial Analyst; General Manager; Health Services Manager; Human Resources Specialist; Licensed Practical Nurse; Management Trainee; Market Research Analyst; Paralegal; Physical Therapist; Preschool Worker; Psychologist; Purchasing Agent/Manager; Quality Control Supervisor; Broadcaster; Registered Nurse; Reporter; Respiratory Therapist; Restaurant/Food Service Manager; Securities Sales Rep.; Services Sales Representative; Social Worker; Software Engineer; Systems Analyst; Teacher/Professor; Technical Writer/Editor; Telecommunications Manager; Transportation/Traffic Specialist; Travel Agent; Typist/Word Processor; Underwriter; Urban/Regional Planner. **Corporate headquarters location:** This Location.

VALLEY PACKAGING INDUSTRIES, INC.
1325 South Perkins Street, Appleton WI 54914. 920/749-5840x137. **Fax:** 920/749-5850. **Contact:** Cynthia Krzewina, Human Resources Director. **E-mail address:** ckrzewina@vpind.com. **Description:** A nonprofit corporation that provides a broad range of vocational rehabilitation services for disabled persons. The majority of participants are engaged in production line packaging and product assembly. The corporation also offers an Early Intervention Program for children with developmental delays; vocational evaluations; work adjustment training; extended employment; transitional employment; vocational support programs; and a School-To-Work Program. Founded in 1956. **Common positions include:** Assembly Worker; Human Service Worker; Production Worker. **Benefits:** 403(b); Dental Insurance; Disability Coverage; Flexible Schedule; Life Insurance; Medical Insurance; Pension Plan; Tuition Assistance. **Special programs:** Internships. **Corporate headquarters location:** This Location. **Other area locations:** 2730 North Roemer Road, Appleton WI 54911, 920/749-5859; 3375 West Brewster Street, Appleton WI 54914, 920/749-5870. **Subsidiaries include:** Madison Packaging & Assembly, 2841 Index Road, Madison WI 53713. **Executive Director:** Robert Russo.

VERMONT NETWORK AGAINST DOMESTIC VIOLENCE AND SEXUAL ASSAULT
P.O. Box 405, Montpelier VT 05601. 802/223-1302. **Contact:** Coordinator. **World Wide Web address:** http://www.vnadvsa.together.com. **Description:** A nonprofit, public education and advocacy organization composed of 16 member organizations offering services to battered women and their children. Activities of the coalition include public education and advocacy; technical assistance to member groups; information and technical assistance to public agencies and legislative committees; and professional training for law enforcement and human service workers. In addition, the coalition staff prepares policy statements and offers assistance and expertise in the preparation of protocols and practices for a wide variety of public and private entities. **Corporate headquarters location:** This Location.

VISIONQUEST
P.O. Box 12906, Tucson AZ 85732. 520/881-3950. **Toll-free phone:** 800/523-5976. **Fax:** 520/881-3269. **Contact:** Recruiting. **World Wide Web address:** http://www.vq.com. **Description:** A social service organization providing troubled kids and teens with recreational alternatives. VisionQuest allows participants to engage in such outdoor activities as camping and sailing. **Common positions include:** Accountant/Auditor; Counselor; Emergency Medical Technician; Human Service Worker; Licensed Practical Nurse; Psychologist; Recreational Therapist; Registered Nurse; Social Worker; Sociologist; Teacher Aide; Teacher/Professor. **Educational backgrounds include:** Health Care; Social Work. **Benefits:** 401(k); Dental Insurance; Disability Coverage; Employee

Discounts; Life Insurance; Medical Insurance. **Corporate headquarters location:** This Location. **Other U.S. locations:** PA; TX. **Subsidiaries include:** Lodgemakers.

WESTCHESTER COMMUNITY OPPORTUNITY PROGRAM
2269 Saw Mill River Road, Building 3, Elmsford NY 10523-3833. 914/592-5600. **Contact:** Paulette Warren, Personnel Director. **Description:** A county-sponsored, nonprofit social services agency operating through numerous community action programs which provide clinical services, employment training programs, energy programs, and a wide range of other community services. **Corporate headquarters location:** This Location.

AMHERST H. WILDER FOUNDATION
919 Lafond Avenue, St. Paul MN 55104. 651/642-4000. **Fax:** 651/642-4068. **Contact:** Human Resources. **World Wide Web address:** http://www.wilder.org. **Description:** A nonprofit, human services foundation. **NOTE:** Entry-level positions are offered. **Common positions include:** Counselor; Human Service Worker; Licensed Practical Nurse; Occupational Therapist; Physical Therapist; Preschool Worker; Psychologist; Registered Nurse; Social Worker; Teacher Aide. **Educational backgrounds include:** Social Work. **Benefits:** Dental Insurance; Disability Coverage; Life Insurance; Medical Insurance; Pension Plan; Savings Plan; Tuition Assistance. **Special programs:** Internships. **Corporate headquarters location:** This Location.

WINSTON-SALEM INDUSTRIES FOR THE BLIND
7730 North Point Drive, Winston-Salem NC 27106-3310. 336/759-0551. **Contact:** Sharon Peters, Human Resources Manager. **Description:** Provides training and employment workshops for the blind. **Corporate headquarters location:** This Location.

WISCONSIN HUMANE SOCIETY
4500 West Wisconsin Avenue, Milwaukee WI 53208. 414/264-6257. **Contact:** Human Resources. **World Wide Web address:** http://www.humane.mil.wi.us. **Description:** A nonprofit, organization that provides shelter and veterinary care for stray, unwanted, feral, and wild animals, and prevents the mistreatment of animals through education and law enforcement. Founded in 1879. **NOTE:** Entry-level positions, part-time jobs, and second and third shifts are offered. **Company slogan:** A community where people value animals and treat them with respect and kindness. **Common positions include:** Animal Handler; Customer Service Rep. **Educational backgrounds include:** Business Administration; Communications; Liberal Arts; Marketing; Microsoft Word; Public Relations; Spreadsheets. **Benefits:** 403(b); Casual Dress - Daily; Dental Insurance; Disability Coverage; Employee Discounts; Life Insurance; Medical Insurance; Public Transit Available; Savings Plan; Sick Days (1 - 5). **Special programs:** Internships; Summer Jobs.

WOLF PARK
Battle Ground IN 47920. 765/567-2265. **Fax:** 765/567-4299. **Contact:** Human Resources. **World Wide Web address:** http://www.wolfpark.org. **Description:** A nonprofit research organization focusing on wolf behavior and preservation. The park offers walking tours, lectures, and seminars to the public. Founded in 1972. **Special programs:** Co-ops; Internships. **Corporate headquarters location:** This Location. **Parent company:** North American Wildlife Park Foundation, Inc.

THE WOODLAWN ORGANIZATION
6040 South Harper Avenue, Chicago IL 60637. 773/288-5840. **Contact:** Director of Personnel. **Description:** Provides social services including a detoxification center, a child abuse treatment center, mental health facilities, two early childhood development programs, secretarial and word-processing training programs, a youth try-out employment project, and HUD real estate management services. **Common positions include:** Accountant; Administrator; Computer Programmer; Counselor; Department Manager; Financial Analyst; Purchasing Agent/Manager; Registered Nurse; Social Worker; Teacher/Professor. **Educational backgrounds include:** Accounting; Business Administration; Computer Science; Finance; Liberal Arts. **Benefits:** Dental Insurance; Life Insurance; Medical Insurance; Tuition Assistance. **Corporate headquarters location:** This Location.

YMCA CAMP POTAWOTAMI
P.O. Box 38, South Milford IN 46786. 219/351-2525. **Toll-free phone:** 800/966-9622. **Fax:** 219/351-3915. **Contact:** Executive Director. **E-mail address:** ymcacamp@kuntrynet.com. **World Wide Web address:** http://www.camp-potawotami.org. **Description:** Provides educational opportunities in a Christian environment. The camp operates as a branch of the YMCA of greater Fort Wayne. This location also hires seasonally. **Common positions include:** Counselor. **Special programs:** Internships; Summer Jobs.

YMCA OF CENTRAL OHIO
40 West Long Street, Columbus OH 43215. 614/224-1142. **Fax:** 614/224-0639. **Contact:** Lori Leist, Human Resources Director. **World Wide Web address:** http://www.ymcacolumbus.com. **Description:** One of the nation's largest and most comprehensive nonprofit service organizations. The YMCA provides health and fitness; social and personal development; sports and recreation; education and career development; and camps and conferences to children, youths, adults, the elderly, families, disabled individuals, refugees and foreign nationals, YMCA residents, and community residents through a broad range of specific programs. This location also hires seasonally. **NOTE:** Entry-level positions and part-time jobs are offered. **Company slogan:** We build strong kids, strong families, strong communities. **Common positions include:** Administrative Assistant; Child Care Center Director; Preschool Worker; Social Worker. **Educational backgrounds include:** Business Administration; Education. **Benefits:** 403(b); Casual Dress - Daily; Daycare Assistance; Dental Insurance; Disability Coverage; Employee Discounts; Life Insurance; Medical Insurance; On-Site Daycare; Pension Plan; Public Transit Available; Sick Days (11+); Vacation Days. **Special programs:** Summer Jobs. **Corporate headquarters location:** This Location. **Other U.S. locations:** Nationwide. **International locations:** Worldwide. **President/CEO:** John Bickley. **Facilities Manager:** Ray Moore. **Information Systems Manager:** Carla Sesser. **Annual sales/revenues:** $11 - $20 million. **Number of employees at this location:** 800.

YWCA
610 Lexington Avenue, New York NY 10022. 212/755-4500. **Contact:** Human Resources Department. **Description:** The YWCA provides counseling, physical fitness activities and daycare facilities for women and their children. The organization also provides a shelter. **Corporate headquarters location:** This Location. **Other U.S. locations:** Nationwide.

For more information on career opportunities in charities and social services:

Associations

ADVOCACY INSTITUTE
1707 L Street NW, Suite 400, Washington DC
20036. 202/659-8475.

ALLIANCE FOR CHILDREN AND FAMILIES
11700 West Lake Park Drive, Milwaukee WI
53224. 414/359-1040. World Wide Web address:
http://www.alliance1.org. Membership required.

AMERICAN LUNG ASSOCIATION
1740 Broadway, New York NY 10019. Toll-free
phone: 800/586-4872. World Wide Web address:
http://www.lungusa.org. Focused on preventing and
curing lung disease through research, education, and
fundraising.

CATHOLIC CHARITIES USA
1731 King Street, Suite 200, Alexandria VA 22314.
703/549-1390. World Wide Web address:
http://www.catholiccharitiesusa.org. Membership
required.

CLINICAL SOCIAL WORK FEDERATION
P.O. Box 3740, Arlington VA 22203. 703/522-
3866. A lobbying organization. Offers newsletters
and a conference every two years to member
organizations.

**NATIONAL ASSOCIATION OF SOCIAL
WORKERS**
750 First Street NE, Suite 700, Washington DC
20002-4241. 202/408-8600. World Wide Web
address: http://www.socialworkers.org.

**NATIONAL COUNCIL ON ALCOHOLISM
AND DRUG DEPENDENCE**
12 West 21st Street, New York NY 10010. 212/206-
6770. Toll-free phone: 800/622-2255. Fax: 212/645-
1690. Provides counseling and treatment for those
suffering from alcohol and drug addictions. The
association also educates the public in an attempt to
prevent addictions.

**NATIONAL COUNCIL ON FAMILY
RELATIONS**
3989 Central Avenue NE, Suite 550, Minneapolis
MN 55421. 612/781-9331. Fax: 612/781-9348.
Membership required. Publishes two quarterly
journals. Offers an annual conference and
newsletters.

THE NATIONAL COUNCIL ON THE AGING
409 Third Street SW, Suite 200, Washington DC
20024. Toll-free phone: 800/424-9046. World Wide
Web address: http://www.ncoa.org. Ensures the
well-being of the nation's elderly by improving both
public and private policies and educating the public.

NATIONAL FEDERATION OF THE BLIND
1800 Johnson Street, Baltimore MD 21230.

410/659-9314. World Wide Web address:
http://www.nfb.org. Membership of 50,000 in 600
local chapters. Publishes a quarterly magazine.

**NATIONAL MULTIPLE SCLEROSIS
SOCIETY**
733 Third Avenue, New York NY 10017. 212/986-
3240. Toll-free phone: 800/344-4867. World Wide
Web address: http://www.nmss.org. Publishes
InsideMS magazine.

**NATIONAL ORGANIZATION FOR HUMAN
SERVICE EDUCATION**
Brookdale Community College, 765 Newman
Springs Road, Lyncroft NJ 07738. 732/842-
1900x546.

Directories

**NON-PROFITS AND EDUCATION JOB
FINDER**
Planning/Communications, 7215 Oak Avenue,
River Forest IL 60305. 708/366-5200. World Wide
Web address: http://www.jobfindersonline.com.
Provides over 2,200 sources with which to find a
job in the competitive nonprofit/education sectors.
Sources include online job and resume databases,
directories, mailing lists, job matching services, and
salary negotiation surveys. Organized by profession
and state.

Newsletters

CEO UPDATE
101 South Whiting Street, Suite 305, Alexandria
VA 22304. 703/370-6700. World Wide Web
address: http://www.associationjobs.com. A
bimonthly newsletter which lists job openings at
associations and nonprofit organizations, with
salaries of at least $50,000 per year.

Online Services

COOLWORKS
World Wide Web address:
http://www.coolworks.com. This Website includes
information on volunteer openings. The site also
provides links to 22,000 job openings in national
parks, summer camps, ski areas, river areas,
ranches, fishing areas, cruise ships, and resorts.

NONPROFIT JOBS
World Wide Web address: http://www.philanthropy-
journal.org. The *Philanthropy Journal*'s site lists
jobs in nonprofit associations and philanthropic
occupations.

SOCIALSERVICE.COM
World Wide Web address:
http://www.socialservice.com. Provides links to
local job sites as well as detailed job listings
searchable by geographic area.

Chemicals/Rubber and Plastics

You can expect to find the following types of companies in this chapter:
*Adhesives, Detergents, Inks, Paints, Soaps, Varnishes • Agricultural Chemicals
and Fertilizers • Carbon and Graphite Products • Chemical Engineering Firms
Industrial Gases*

*Some helpful information: The average salary for rubber and plastics manufacturing
workers is approximately $20,000 - $25,000 annually. Entry-level chemists generally earn
between $20,000 and $30,000, and chemists with advanced degrees can earn over $50,000
annually in the private sector.*

AC MOLDING COMPOUND
2700 South Westmoreland Road, Dallas TX 75233.
214/330-8671. **Contact:** General Manager.
Description: Manufactures a wide variety of resins,
plastics, and glass-reinforced plastics for use in the
electronics industry, as well as plastic tableware
products used in the food service industry. A second
Dallas location produces other plastic products for
use in the construction and food service industries.
Corporate headquarters location: This Location.

ACE HARDWARE CORPORATION
2200 Kensington Court, Oak Brook IL 60523.
630/990-6600. **Contact:** Director of Human
Resources. **World Wide Web address:** http://www.
acehardware.com. **Description:** A dealer-owned
cooperative operating through 5,100 hardware
retailers in 62 countries. Ace Hardware Corporation
also produces a line of hand and power tools,
plumbing products, lawn and garden products,
cleaning supplies, and manufactures a line of paint.
Corporate headquarters location: This Location.

ADVANCE DIAL COMPANY
940 Industrial Drive, Elmhurst IL 60126. 630/993-
1700. **Fax:** 630/993-0372. **Contact:** Human
Resources Department. **World Wide Web address:**
http://www.advance-dial.com. **Description:** A
manufacturer of custom, injection-molded plastics.
Common positions include: Accountant/Auditor;
Customer Service Representative; Human Resources
Manager; Production Manager; Purchasing Agent/
Manager. **Educational backgrounds include:**
Engineering. **Benefits:** 401(k); Dental Insurance;
Disability Coverage; Life Insurance; Medical
Insurance; Profit Sharing; Tuition Assistance.
Corporate headquarters location: This Location.
Other U.S. locations: Boca Raton FL; Addison IL;
Huntley IL. **Parent company:** Anderson Industries.

AIR PRODUCTS AND CHEMICALS, INC.
7201 Hamilton Boulevard, Allentown PA 18195-
1501. 610/481-7050. **Contact:** Human Resources
Manager. **World Wide Web address:** http://www.
airproducts.com. **Description:** A manufacturer of
industrial gases, process equipment, and chemicals.
Products include cryogenic equipment, air
separation systems, hydrogen purification devices,
and nitrogen rejection equipment. In addition, the
company is a provider of engineering services, and
is involved in landfill gas recovery, waste-to-energy
ventures, flue gas desulfurization, and cogeneration
operations. **Common positions include:** Chemical
Engineer; Financial Analyst; Mechanical Engineer.
Educational backgrounds include: Engineering;
Finance; Marketing; MBA. **Benefits:** Dental
Insurance; Disability Coverage; Life Insurance;
Pension Plan; Savings Plan; Stock Option; Tuition
Assistance. **Special programs:** Internships.
Corporate headquarters location: This Location.

AIRGAS CARBONIC
3700 Crestwood Parkway, Suite 200, Duluth GA
30096. 770/717-2200. **Contact:** Human Resources.
World Wide Web address: http://www.airgas.com.
Description: Manufactures and markets liquid
carbon dioxide and related handling equipment.
Corporate headquarters location: Radnor PA.
Parent company: Airgas.

AKZO NOBEL CHEMICALS
300 South Riverside Plaza, Suite 2200, Chicago IL
60606. 312/906-7500. **Contact:** Director of Human
Resources. **World Wide Web address:** http://www.
akzo-nobel.com. **Description:** Produces salt and
chemicals, coatings, health care products, and
fibers. Business activities are conducted in four
units: Chemicals, Coatings, Pharma, and Fibers. The
Chemicals Group produces polymer chemicals,
rubber chemicals, catalysts, detergents, surfactants,
functional chemicals, salt, chlor-alkali, and
industrial chemicals. The Coatings Group produces
decorative coatings, car refinishes, industrial
coatings, industrial wood finishes, aerospace
finishes, automotive finishes, and resins. The
Pharma Group includes the production of ethical
drugs, hospital supplies, nonprescription products,
raw materials for the pharmaceutical industry,
generics, and veterinary products. The Fibers Group
produces textile, industrial, and high-performance
fibers; industrial nonwovens; and membranes for
medical, technical, and industrial uses. **Common
positions include:** Accountant; Chemical Engineer;
Computer Scientist; Financial Analyst. **Educational
backgrounds include:** Accounting; Chemistry;
Computer Science; Data Processing; Engineering;
Finance; Law/Pre-Law. **Corporate headquarters
location:** This Location. **International locations:**
Worldwide.
Other U.S. locations:
• 3492 East 26th Street, Los Angeles CA
90023. 323/260-8894.
• Akzo Nobel Coatings, P.O. Box 669,
Bloomfield Hills MI 48303-0669. 248/253-
2562.

ALCIDE CORPORATION
8561 154th Avenue NE, Redmond WA 98052.
425/882-2555. **Fax:** 425/861-0173. **Contact:**
Personnel. **World Wide Web address:** http://www.
alcide.com. **Description:** Researches, develops, and
markets antimicrobial products for industrial,
human and animal health uses; and for direct
application to food in order to control food borne
pathogens. Alcide has developed several
disinfectants and a sterilant to kill microorganisms
on surface areas and to reduce the threat of disease
transmission in health care facilities. In the animal
health field, the company has marketed technology
to prevent mastitis in dairy cattle. **Corporate
headquarters location:** This Location. **Listed on:**
NASDAQ.

ALLTRISTA CORPORATION
5875 Castle Creek Parkway, Suite 440, Indianapolis IN 46250. 317/577-5000. **Contact:** Human Resources. **World Wide Web address:** http://www. alltrista.com. **Description:** A manufacturer that operates in a number of product and service areas such as high-barrier, multilayer, co-extruded plastic products including sheet-formed containers and retort containers; copper-plated zinc penny blanks, cans for use in zinc/carbon batteries, and other industrial zinc products; protective coating application and decorative lithography services; tin-plated steel aluminum and light-gauge rolled products; thermoformed plastic refrigerator door liners, separators, and evaporator trays; injection molded plastics products; and software and hardware for non-destructive inspection systems. **Corporate headquarters location:** This Location.

AMERICAN PRIDE
P.O. Box 98, Henderson CO 80640. 303/659-3640. **Contact:** Human Resources Manager. **Description:** Markets bulk and bagged fertilizer, agricultural chemicals, seeds, feed, and veterinary supplies. **Common positions include:** Agricultural Scientist. **Educational backgrounds include:** Business Administration; Marketing. **Benefits:** Dental Insurance; Disability Coverage; Life Insurance; Medical Insurance; Pension Plan; Savings Plan; Tuition Assistance. **Corporate headquarters location:** This Location.

AMERICAN VANGUARD CORPORATION
2110 Davie Avenue, City of Commerce CA 90040. 323/264-3910. **Contact:** Human Resources Department. **Description:** A holding company. **Corporate headquarters location:** This Location. **Subsidiaries include:** AMVAC manufactures and formulates chemicals for crop, human, and animal health protection. These chemicals, which include insecticides, fungicides, plant growth regulators, and soil fumigants, are marketed in liquid, powder, and granular forms.

AMOCO CHEMICAL COMPANY
P.O. Box 941, Joliet IL 60434. 815/467-3293. **Fax:** 815/467-3425. **Contact:** Manager of Human Resources. **Description:** Manufactures industrial intermediate petrochemicals. **Common positions include:** Accountant/; Buyer; Chemical Engineer; Chemist; Civil Engineer; Computer Programmer; Draftsperson; Electrician; Human Resources Manager; Mechanical Engineer; Purchasing Agent/Manager; Systems Analyst. **Educational backgrounds include:** Accounting; Business Administration; Chemistry; Computer Science; Engineering. **Benefits:** 401(k); Dental Insurance; Disability Coverage; Life Insurance; Medical Insurance; Pension Plan; Profit Sharing; Tuition Assistance. **Special programs:** Internships. **Corporate headquarters location:** This Location.

APPLIED COMPOSITES
333 North Sixth Street, St. Charles IL 60174. 630/584-3130. **Fax:** 630/584-0659. **Contact:** Personnel. **Description:** Manufactures fiber-reinforced plastic. **Common positions include:** Accountant; Blue-Collar Worker Supervisor; Buyer; Chemist; Computer Programmer; Manufacturer's/Wholesaler's Sales Representative; Quality Control Supervisor. **Educational backgrounds include:** Accounting; Chemistry; Finance; Marketing. **Benefits:** Dental Insurance; Disability Coverage; Life Insurance; Medical Insurance; Savings Plan. **Corporate headquarters location:** This Location.

APPLIED EXTRUSION TECHNOLOGIES
3 Centennial Drive, Peabody MA 01960. 978/538-1500. **Contact:** Human Resources. **Description:** A leading manufacturer of a broad range of plastic films, nets, and webs used primarily in packaging, health care, and environmental settings. The Packaging Films Division develops, manufactures, and sells oriented polypropylene film for flexible packaging applications, primarily for the snack food, soft drink, and confectionery markets. The Specialty Nets and Profiles Divisions develop, manufacture, and sell oriented aperture film or nets, as well as non-net thermoplastic products to a number of markets such as health care, environmental, packaging, and home products. **Corporate headquarters location:** This Location.

ARISTECH CHEMICAL CORPORATION
600 Grant Street, Pittsburgh PA 15219-2704. 412/433-2747. **Contact:** Director of Human Resources. **World Wide Web address:** http://www. aristechchem.com. **Description:** A diversified worldwide chemicals and polymers manufacturer, marketing a broad range of products that are converted into consumer items. Markets served include automotive, construction, marine, and recreational. Products include phenol, bisphenol-A, polypropylene, acrylic sheet, coal chemicals, dibasic acids, 2-ethylhexanol, cumene, plasticizers, and unsaturated polyester resins. Aristech operates 10 plants and 10 distribution centers nationwide. **Educational backgrounds include:** Chemistry; Engineering. **Corporate headquarters location:** This Location. **Other U.S. locations:** KY; OH; TX; WV. **Number of employees nationwide:** 1,400.

ASEC MANUFACTURING
P.O. Box 580970, Tulsa OK 74158-0970. 918/266-4838. **Fax:** 918/266-4987. **Recorded jobline:** 918/266-8045. **Contact:** Personnel. **Description:** ASEC Manufacturing is primarily a chemical coating company, and focuses on developing innovative technology to be used in the manufacture of emission control catalysts. **NOTE:** Entry-level positions and second and third shifts are offered. **Common positions include:** Accountant; Auditor; Blue-Collar Worker Supervisor; Chemical Engineer; Chemist; Chief Financial Officer; Clinical Lab Technician; Computer Operator; Computer Programmer; Controller; Financial Analyst; General Manager; Human Resources Manager; Operations Manager; Production Manager; Project Manager; Purchasing Manager. **Educational backgrounds include:** Chemistry; Engineering. **Benefits:** 401(k); Dental Insurance; Disability Coverage; Employee Discounts; Life Insurance; Medical Insurance; Pension Plan; Savings Plan; Sick Days; Spending Account; Tuition Assistance; Vacation Days (6 - 10). **Corporate headquarters location:** Flint MI. **Parent company:** General Motors Delphi Energy and Engine Management Systems. **Annual sales/revenues:** $5 - $10 million.

ASHLAND DISTRIBUTION & SPECIALTY CHEMICAL COMPANY
P.O. Box 2219, Columbus OH 43216. 614/790-3333. **Contact:** Human Resources Manager. **World Wide Web address:** http://www.ashchem.com. **Description:** Manufactures, markets, and distributes a wide variety of chemical products through facilities in 33 states and 46 foreign countries. **NOTE:** Entry-level positions are offered. **Common positions include:** Chemical Engineer; Chemist; Customer Service Rep.; Environmental Engineer; Sales Rep. **Educational backgrounds include:** Accounting; Business Administration; Chemistry; Communications; Computer Science; Engineering. **Benefits:** 401(k); Credit Union; Dental Insurance; Disability Coverage; Life Insurance; Medical Insurance; Pension Plan; Savings Plan; Thrift Plan; Tuition Assistance. **Special programs:** Co-ops; Training, **Internship information:** The company

hires chemical engineering students to participate in a co-op program to work one rotation in Dublin OH and other rotations at different plants. Ashland Chemical prefers to hire students in their sophomore year of college. **Corporate headquarters location:** This Location. **Other U.S. locations:** Nationwide. **International locations:** Worldwide. **Parent company:** Ashland, Inc.

AVON RUBBER & PLASTICS, INC.
805 West 13th Street, Cadillac MI 49601-9282. 231/779-1178. **Contact:** Dale Rosser, Corporate Human Resources. **Description:** Produces rubber extrusions and profiles. Another manufacturing facility in Manton MI produces plastic injection-molded components and assembles vacuum emission harnesses for the automotive industry. **Common positions include:** Blue-Collar Worker Supervisor; Buyer; Chemical Engineer; Chemist; Computer Programmer; Customer Service Rep.; Department Manager; Draftsperson; Financial Analyst; General Manager; Human Resources Manager; Industrial Designer; Mechanical Engineer; Operations Manager; Product Engineer; Purchasing Agent/Manager; Quality Control Supervisor. **Educational backgrounds include:** Business Administration; Chemistry; Computer Science; Engineering. **Benefits:** Dental Insurance; Disability Coverage; Life Insurance; Medical Insurance; Pension Plan; Profit Sharing; Tuition Assistance. **Corporate headquarters location:** This Location.

BASF CORPORATION
KNOLL PHARMACEUTICALS
3000 Continental Drive North, Mount Olive NJ 07828-1234. 973/426-2600. **Contact:** Human Resources. **World Wide Web address:** http://www.basf.com. **Description:** This location serves as the United States headquarters and houses management offices as well as the pharmaceutical division, Knoll Pharmaceuticals. Overall, BASF Corporation is an international chemical products organization, doing business in five operating groups: Chemicals; Coatings and Colorants; Consumer Products and Life Sciences; Fiber Products; and Polymers. **Common positions include:** Accountant/Auditor; Chemical Engineer; Computer Programmer; Financial Analyst; Marketing Specialist. **Benefits:** Dental Insurance; Disability Coverage; Life Insurance; Medical Insurance; Pension Plan; Savings Plan; Tuition Assistance. **Corporate headquarters location:** This Location..

BOC GASES
575 Mountain Avenue, Murray Hill NJ 07974. 908/464-8100. **Contact:** Personnel Director **World Wide Web address:** http://www.boc.com/gases. **Description:** Manufactures and markets industrial gases and related products. BOC Gases also provides full engineering and technical services. **Corporate headquarters location:** This Location. **Other U.S. locations:** Nationwide.

BAKER PETROLITE
P.O. Box 5050, Sugar Land TX 77487. 281/276-5400. **Physical address:** 12645 West Airport Boulevard, Sugar Land TX 77478. **Fax:** 281/275-7392. **Contact:** Human Resources. **World Wide Web address:** http://www.bakerhughes.com/bapt. **Description:** Engaged in the manufacture and sale of chemicals. **Common positions include:** Accountant; Auditor; Chemical Engineer; Chemist; Clerical Supervisor; Computer Programmer; Credit Manager; Customer Service Rep.; Financial Analyst; Human Resources Manager; Petroleum Engineer; Systems Analyst; Technical Writer/Editor; Transportation/Traffic Specialist. **Corporate headquarters location:** This Location. **Other U.S. locations:** Anchorage AK; Bakersfield CA; Los

Angeles CA; Tulsa OK. **International locations:** Caracas, Venezuela; Liverpool, England. **Parent company:** Baker Hughes Inc. **Listed on:** Privately held. **President:** Glen Bassett.

BALCHEM CORPORATION
P.O. Box 175, Slate Hill NY 10973. 914/355-5300. **Contact:** Human Resources. **World Wide Web address:** http://www.balchem.net. **Description:** A leader in the manufacturing and marketing of encapsulated food ingredients for a variety of industries. The company is also a leading supplier of ethylene oxide, a packaging sterilant. Founded in 1967. **Corporate headquarters location:** This Location. **Listed on:** American Stock Exchange. **Stock exchange symbol:** BCP.

BENJAMIN MOORE & COMPANY
51 Chestnut Ridge Road, Montvale NJ 07645. 201/573-9600. **Fax:** 201/573-6631. **Contact:** Personnel. **World Wide Web address:** http://www.benjaminmoore.com. **Description:** Manufactures and markets paints, varnishes, and other coatings. **Common positions include:** Accountant/Auditor; Administrative Manager; Advertising Clerk; Attorney; Budget Analyst; Buyer; Chemist; Computer Programmer; Credit Manager; Customer Service Rep.; Economist; Financial Analyst; Human Resources Manager; Human Service Worker; Manufacturer's/Wholesaler's Sales Rep.; Paralegal; Public Relations Specialist; Purchasing Agent/Manager; Systems Analyst; Transportation/Traffic Specialist. **Benefits:** 401(k); Dental Insurance; Disability Coverage; Employee Discounts; Life Insurance; Medical Insurance; Pension Plan; Tuition Assistance. **Corporate headquarters location:** This Location. **Other U.S. locations:** Nationwide. **Listed on:** Privately held.

BETZDEARBORN
4636 Somerton Road, Trevose PA 19053. 215/355-3300. **Contact:** Human Resources. **World Wide Web address:** http://www.betzdearborn.com. **Description:** Manufactures and markets a wide variety of specialty chemical products used in the chemical treatment of water, wastewater, and process systems. BetzDearborn operates in a wide variety of industrial and commercial applications, with particular emphasis on the chemical, petroleum refining, paper, automotive, electrical utility, and steel industries. The company's chemical treatment programs are used in boilers, cooling towers, heat exchangers, paper and petroleum process streams, and both influent and effluent systems. **Common positions include:** Chemical Engineer; Chemist; Electrical/Electronics Engineer; Research Scientist. **Corporate headquarters location:** This Location. **Parent company:** Hercules Inc.

BIO-LAB INC.
P.O. Box 1489, Decatur GA 30031-1489. 404/378-1753. **Contact:** Human Resources Department. **World Wide Web address:** http://www.biolabinc.com. **Description:** A producer of alkalis and chlorine. **Common positions include:** Account Manager; Administrative Assistant; Advertising Clerk; Applications Engineer; Biochemist; Biological Scientist; Chemical Engineer; Chemist; Clinical Lab Technician; Computer Operator; Computer Programmer; Controller; Credit Manager; Customer Service Rep.; Financial Analyst; Graphic Artist; Human Resources Manager; Sales Manager; Sales Rep.; Systems Analyst; Telecommunications Manager. **Educational backgrounds include:** Accounting; Biology; Chemistry; Marketing. **Benefits:** 401(k); Dental Insurance; Disability Coverage; Flexible Schedule; Life Insurance; Medical Insurance; Pension Plan. **Corporate headquarters location:** This Location. **Other area**

locations: Conyers GA. **Other U.S. locations:** Lake Charles LA; Adrian MI. **Parent company:** Great Lakes Chemical. **Annual sales/revenues:** More than $100 million.

BIO-RAD LABORATORIES
1000 Alfred Noble Drive, Hercules CA 94547. 510/724-7000. **Contact:** Human Resources. **World Wide Web address:** http://www.bio-rad.com. **Description:** Develops, manufactures, and markets diagnostic test kits, specialty chemicals, and related equipment used for separating complex mixtures. The company also produces analytical instruments used to detect and measure chemical components in minute quantities, as well as products for electron microscopy. **NOTE:** Resumes should be sent to the location that specializes in the area of interest. For Diagnostics, resumes should be sent to Bio-Rad Laboratories, Human Resources Department, 4000 Alfred Noble Drive, Hercules CA 94547; for Life Sciences, resumes should be sent to Bio-Rad Laboratories, Human Resources Department, 2000 Alfred Noble Drive, Hercules CA 94547. **Common positions include:** Accountant/Auditor; Advertising Clerk; Biological Scientist; Biomedical Engineer; Buyer; Chemical Engineer; Chemist; Computer Programmer; Customer Service Rep.e; Department Manager; Electrical/Electronics Engineer; Financial Analyst; General Manager; Human Resources Manager; Mechanical Engineer; Medical Records Technician; Medical Technologist; Operations/Production Manager; Purchasing Agent/Manager; Quality Control Supervisor; Systems Analyst; Transportation/Traffic Specialist. **Educational backgrounds include:** Accounting; Biology; Business Administration; Chemistry; Computer Science; Engineering; Marketing; Mathematics. **Benefits:** Dental Insurance; Disability Coverage; Life Insurance; Medical Insurance; Pension Plan; Profit Sharing; Savings Plan; Tuition Assistance. **Corporate headquarters location:** This Location. **Listed on:** American Stock Exchange.

BORDEN COATINGS & GRAPHICS
630 Glendale-Milford Road, Cincinnati OH 45215. 513/782-6309. **Fax:** 513/782-6342. **Contact:** Human Resources. **Description:** Manufactures inks and related coatings for commercial use. **NOTE:** Entry-level positions and second and third shifts are offered. **Common positions include:** Accountant; Administrative Assistant; Budget Analyst; Buyer; Chemical Engineer; Chemist; Clinical Lab Technician; Computer Operator; Computer Programmer; Controller; Credit Manager; Customer Service Representative; General Manager; Human Resources Manager; Manufacturing Engineer; Marketing Manager; Purchasing Agent/Manager; Quality Control Supervisor; Sales Engineer; Sales Executive; Sales Manager; Sales Rep.; Secretary; Systems Manager. **Educational backgrounds include:** Accounting; Business Administration; Chemistry; Computer Science; Engineering; Marketing. **Benefits:** 401(k); Dental Insurance; Disability Coverage; Financial Planning Assistance; Life Insurance; Medical Insurance; Pension Plan; Savings Plan; Tuition Assistance. **Corporate headquarters location:** Columbus OH. **Parent company:** Borden Chemical. **Listed on:** Privately held.

BROOKDALE PLASTICS INC.
9909 South Shore Drive, Plymouth MN 55441. 612/797-1000. **Toll-free phone:** 800/475-7092. **Fax:** 612/797-5252. **Contact:** Personnel. **E-mail address:** bpi@brookdaleplastics.com. **World Wide Web address:** http://www.brookdaleplastics.com. **Description:** Manufactures and markets plastic packing and display products. Founded in 1963. **NOTE:** Entry-level positions are offered. **Common**

positions include: Accountant; Administrative Assistant; Applications Engineer; Blue-Collar Worker Supervisor; Computer Support Technician; Marketing Specialist; Project Manager; Purchasing Agent/Manager; Sales Representative. **Educational backgrounds include:** Accounting; Business Administration; Communications; Engineering; Finance; Marketing; Microsoft Office; Spreadsheets. **Benefits:** 401(k); Casual Dress - Fridays; Dental Insurance; Disability Coverage; Life Insurance; Medical Insurance; Pension Plan; Profit Sharing; Public Transit Available; Sick Days; Tuition Assistance. **Special programs:** Internships. **Corporate headquarters location:** This Location. **Parent company:** Ameristar Packaging. **Listed on:** Privately held. **Annual sales/revenues:** $5 - $10 million.

M.A. BRUDER & SONS INC.
600 Reed Road, Broomall PA 19008. 610/353-5100. **Toll-free phone:** 800/MAB-1899. **Fax:** 610/325-2718. **Contact:** Human Resources Manager. **World Wide Web address:** http://www.mabpaints.com. **Description:** A manufacturer and marketer of paint, operating over 250 retail and wholesale locations. Founded in 1899. **Corporate headquarters location:** This Location.

CF INDUSTRIES, INC.
One Salem Lake Drive, Long Grove IL 60047-8402. 847/438-9500. **Contact:** Human Resources. **World Wide Web address:** http://www.cfindustries.com. **Description:** One of North America's largest manufacturers and distributors of fertilizer products. **NOTE:** Entry-level positions are offered. **Common positions include:** Accountant; Administrative Assistant; Computer Programmer; Mechanical Engineer; Systems Analyst; Typist/Word Processor. **Educational backgrounds include:** Accounting; Computer Science; Engineering; Liberal Arts; Marketing. **Benefits:** 401(k); Dental Insurance; Disability Coverage; Financial Planning Assistance; Life Insurance; Medical Insurance; On-Site Exercise Facility; Pension Plan; Profit Sharing; Tuition Assistance. **Corporate headquarters location:** This Location. **Operations at this facility include:** Administration; Research and Development; Sales; Service. **Listed on:** Privately held. **Annual sales/revenues:** More than $100 million.

CK WITCO CORPORATION
199 Benson Road, Middlebury CT 06749. 203/573-2000. **Contact:** Human Resources Department. **World Wide Web address:** http://www.ckwitco.com. **Description:** CK Witco is a manufacturer of specialty chemical and petroleum products. CK Witco's products are used primarily as intermediates by other manufacturers in hundreds of industries such as personal care and household products, agricultural, automotive, housing and construction, packaging, food, and textiles. **Corporate headquarters location:** This Location. **Other U.S. locations:** Greenwich CT. **Subsidiaries include:** Oleo/Surfactants, a supplier of specialty surfactants and oleochemicals to manufacturers of personal care, cosmetics, and laundry products; Polymer Additives, a supplier of additives including stabilizers for vinyl plastics used in pipe, siding, and other building applications, as well as flexible wall and floor coverings, and wire and cable insulation; Resins, a supplier of saturated polyesters to manufacturers of cellular products such as flexible foam used in furniture, automobiles, and textiles; Petroleum Specialties, a supplier of white oils and petrolatums used in cosmetic, personal care, pharmaceutical, plastic, textile, and food products; Lubricants Business Unit and Golden Bear Products, suppliers of branded and private label motor oils and engine lubricants; and Diversified

Products, through the Battery Parts and Concarb Divisions, manufactures rubber and plastic battery containers, covers, and parts, and supplies carbon blacks to tire and rubber manufacturers.

CPC OF VERMONT INC.
P.O. Box 706, Pond Lane, Middlebury VT 05753. 802/388-6381. **Contact:** Personnel. **Description:** Designs and manufactures molds and custom injection molding. **Benefits:** 401(k); Dental Insurance; Disability Coverage; Life Insurance; Medical Insurance; Profit Sharing. **Corporate headquarters location:** This Location.

CADILLAC PRODUCTS INC.
1250 Allen Drive, Troy MI 48083. 248/589-3113. **Contact:** Recruiting. **Description:** Manufactures plastics, thermoformed plastics, paper packaging materials, and films for industrial use. **Common positions include:** Buyer; Chemical Engineer; Computer Programmer; Cost Estimator; Electrical/Electronics Engineer; Electrician; Industrial Engineer; Mechanical Engineer; Purchasing Agent/Manager; Quality Control Supervisor; Sales Representative. **Educational backgrounds include:** Accounting; Business Administration; Engineering; Marketing. **Benefits:** 401(k); Dental Insurance; Disability Coverage; Life Insurance; Medical Insurance; Pension Plan; Profit Sharing; Tuition Assistance. **Special programs:** Internships. **Corporate headquarters location:** This Location. **Other area locations:** Rogers City MI. **Other U.S. locations:** Dallas GA; Paris IL.

CALBIOCHEM-NOVABIOCHEM
10394 Pacific Center Court, San Diego CA 92121. 858/450-9600. **Contact:** Human Resources. **World Wide Web address:** http://www.calbiochem.com. **Description:** Manufactures fine chemicals for the research, biochemical, and pharmaceutical industries. **Common positions include:** Biological Scientist; Chemist. **Educational backgrounds include:** Biology; Chemistry. **Benefits:** 401(k); Dental Insurance; Disability Coverage; Life Insurance; Medical Insurance; Savings Plan. **Corporate headquarters location:** This Location. **Parent company:** CN Biosciences, Inc.

CALGON CARBON CORPORATION
P.O. Box 717, Pittsburgh PA 15230-0717. 412/787-6700. **Fax:** 412/787-6717. **Contact:** Human Resources. **World Wide Web address:** http://www.calgoncarbon.com. **Description:** Offers purification, separation, and concentration products and services to consumers worldwide. **Common positions include:** Accountant; Buyer; Chemical Engineer; Chemist; Civil Engineer; Computer Programmer; Cost Estimator; Credit Manager; Customer Service Rep.; Designer; Draftsperson; Electrical/Electronics Engineer; Human Resources Manager; Purchasing Agent/Manager; Quality Control Supervisor; Systems Analyst; Transportation/Traffic Specialist. **Educational backgrounds include:** Accounting; Business; Chemistry; Communications; Computer Science; Economics; Engineering; Finance; Liberal Arts; Marketing. **Benefits:** 401(k); Dental Insurance; Disability Coverage; Life Insurance; Medical Insurance; Pension Plan; Tuition Assistance. **Corporate headquarters location:** This Location. **Other U.S. locations:** Blue Lake CA; Catlettsburg KY; Pearlington MS; Neville Island PA.

CAMBREX CORPORATION
One Meadowlands Plaza, East Rutherford NJ 07073. 201/804-3000. **Fax:** 201/804-9852. **Contact:** Human Resources. **World Wide Web address:** http://www.cambrex.com. **Description:** Produces and markets products and provides services to the life sciences industries. Cambrex Corporation operates in four segments: Human Health; Biotechnology; Animal Health and Agriculture; and Specialty Products. Founded in 1981. **Corporate headquarters location:** This Location.

CAMBRIDGE INDUSTRIES
203 North Street, Canandaigua NY 14424. 716/394-3680. **World Wide Web address:** http://www.cambrinc.com. **Contact:** John Gebhardt, Human Resources. **Description:** Cambridge Industries manufactures interior trim panels for the automotive industry, as well as blowmolded and injection molded plastic components for cars and trucks. **Company slogan:** Where solutions take shape. **Common positions include:** Accountant; Administrative Assistant; Controller; Draftsperson; General Manager; Human Resources Manager; Industrial Production Manager; Manufacturing Engineer; Project Manager; Quality Assurance Engineer. **Educational backgrounds include:** Accounting; Business Administration; Engineering; Microsoft Office; Microsoft Word; Spreadsheets. **Benefits:** 401(k); Casual Dress - Daily; Dental Insurance; Disability Coverage; Life Insurance; Medical Insurance; Tuition Assistance. **Corporate headquarters location:** Madison Heights MI. **Other U.S. locations:** Nationwide. **International locations:** Worldwide. **Listed on:** Privately held. **Annual sales/revenues:** More than $100 million.

CAPROCK MANUFACTURING, INC.
2303 120th Street, Lubbock TX 79423. 806/745-6454. **Contact:** Human Resources Department. **World Wide Web address:** http://www.caprock-mfg.com. **Description:** A plastic injection molding company that manufactures plastic parts for cellular phones including phone windows and battery cases. **NOTE:** Second and third shifts are offered. **Common positions include:** Advertising Clerk; Buyer; Controller; Customer Service Rep.; Design Engineer; General Manager; Human Resources Manager; Manufacturing Engineer; Production Manager; Purchasing Agent/Manager; Quality Control Supervisor; Secretary. **Educational backgrounds include:** Accounting; Art/Design; Business; Chemistry; Communications; Computer Science; Engineering; Finance; Mathematics; Public Relations. **Benefits:** 401(k); Dental Insurance; Disability Coverage; Life Insurance; Medical Insurance; Savings Plan. **Corporate headquarters location:** This Location. **Listed on:** Privately held. **Annual sales/revenues:** $51 - $100 million.

CARPENTER COMPANY
P.O. Box 27205, Richmond VA 23261. 804/359-0800. **Physical address:** 5016 Monument Avenue, Richmond VA 23230. **Toll-free phone:** 800/288-3834. **Fax:** 804/278-9689. **Contact:** Human Resources. **Description:** Manufactures urethane-related products for use in carpet padding, insulation, packaging, and bedding. **NOTE:** Entry-level positions are offered. **Common positions include:** Account Manager; Account Rep.; Accountant/Auditor; Administrative Assistant; Attorney; Auditor; Blue-Collar Worker Supervisor; Branch Manager; Chemical Engineer; Chemist; Computer Operator; Computer Programmer; Credit Manager; Customer Service Rep.; Electrical/Electronics Engineer; Electrician; Environmental Engineer; Financial Analyst; General Manager; Human Resources Manager; Industrial Engineer; Management Trainee; Manufacturing Engineer; Mechanical Engineer; MIS Specialist; Production Manager; Project Manager; Purchasing Agent/Manager; Sales Executive; Sales Manager; Sales Representative; Secretary; Systems Analyst; Systems Manager; Technical Writer/Editor. **Educational backgrounds include:** Accounting;

Business Administration; Chemistry; Computer Science; Engineering; Marketing. **Benefits:** Disability Coverage; Life Insurance; Medical Insurance; Profit Sharing; Tuition Assistance. **Corporate headquarters location:** This Location. **Other U.S. locations:**
- P.O. Box 2386, Elkhart IN 46515. 219/522-2800.

CARROLL COMPANY
2900 West Kingsley Road, Garland TX 75041. 972/278-1304. **Toll-free phone:** 800/527-5722. **Fax:** 972/840-0678. **Recorded jobline:** 972/278-1304x600. **Contact:** Human Resources. **World Wide Web address:** http://www.carrollco.com. **Description:** A manufacturer of institutional cleaning products. **NOTE:** Entry-level positions and second and third shifts are offered. **Common positions include:** Account Manager; Account Rep.; Accountant; Administrative Assistant; Blue-Collar Worker Supervisor; Buyer; Chemist; Computer Programmer; Controller; Credit Manager; Customer Service Rep.; Database Manager; Electrician; Graphic Artist; Human Resources Manager; Industrial Engineer; Marketing Manager; Production Manager; Purchasing Agent/Manager; Sales Executive; Sales Manager; Secretary; Video Production Coordinator. **Educational backgrounds include:** Accounting; Art/Design; Marketing. **Benefits:** 401(k); Dental Insurance; Disability Coverage; Employee Discounts; Life Insurance; Medical Insurance; Tuition Assistance. **Corporate headquarters location:** This Location. **Other U.S. locations:** Carson CA; Santa Fe Springs CA; Walbridge OH. **Listed on:** Privately held. **President/CEO:** Kyle Ogden.

CHEMFAB CORPORATION
P.O. Box 1137, Merrimack NH 03054. 603/424-9000. **Fax:** 603/424-9012. **Contact:** Human Resources. **Description:** Chemfab Corporation is an international company that develops, manufactures, and markets polymer-based engineered products and materials systems for use in severe service environments. Products typically consist of fiber-reinforced flexible composites coated or laminated with fluoropolymers and specialty fluoropolymer films. **Benefits:** Retirement Plan; Savings Plan; Stock Option. **Corporate headquarters location:** This Location. **Other U.S. locations:** IL; NY; VT. **International locations:** Denmark; England; Ireland; Spain. **Listed on:** NASDAQ.

CHEMICAL LIME COMPANY
P.O. Box 985004, Fort Worth TX 76185. 817/732-8164. **Contact:** Human Resources. **Description:** A manufacturer and distributor of chemical lime products with facilities located in the West, Southwest, and Southeast. The company's principal products are high calcium limestone, dolomite limestone, dolomite glass flux, high calcium quicklime, dolomitic quicklime, calcium hydrated lime, and dolomitic hydrated lime under the trade name Type S Hydrated Lime for use in the construction industry. **Common positions include:** Accountant; Chemist; Civil Engineer; Computer Programmer; Electrical Engineer; Financial Analyst; Geologist/Geophysicist; Industrial Engineer; Mechanical Engineer; Mining Engineer; Operations/Production Manager; Quality Control Supervisor; Systems Analyst. **Educational backgrounds include:** Accounting; Business; Chemistry; Computer Science; Engineering; Geology. **Benefits:** Dental Insurance; Disability Coverage; Life Insurance; Medical Insurance; Profit Sharing; Savings Plan; Tuition Assistance. **Corporate headquarters location:** This Location.

CHEMPRENE INC.
483 Fishkill Avenue, Beacon NY 12508. 914/831-2800. **Fax:** 914/831-5967. **Contact:** Human Resources Administrator. **Description:** Chemprene produces a wide range of specialty industrial diaphragms, belting, and coated fabrics by spread coating, dip coating, and calendering methods. **Common positions include:** Blue-Collar Worker Supervisor; Chemist; Customer Service Rep.; Designer; Draftsperson; Electrician; Industrial Production Manager; Mechanical Engineer. **Educational backgrounds include:** Accounting; Business Administration; Chemistry; Engineering; Marketing. **Benefits:** 401(k); Dental Insurance; Disability Coverage; Life Insurance; Medical Insurance; Pension Plan; Savings Plan; Tuition Assistance. **Corporate headquarters location:** This Location.

COGNIS
5051 Estecreek Drive, Cincinnati OH 45232. 513/482-2100. **Fax:** 513/482-5503. **Contact:** Human Resources. **World Wide Web address:** http://www.cognis-us.com. **Description:** Develops specialty chemicals for cosmetics, detergents, cleaning products, and industrial processes. **Corporate headquarters location:** This Location. **Other U.S. locations:** Tucson AZ; Kankakee IL; La Grange IL; Hoboken NJ; Charlotte NC; Ambler PA; Mauldin SC.

CONDEA VISTA
900 Threadneedle Street, Houston TX 77079. 281/588-3000. **Contact:** Human Resources. **World Wide Web address:** http://www.condeavista.com. **Description:** Manufactures and sells specialty and commodity chemicals for domestic and international markets. **Corporate headquarters location:** This Location. **Parent company:** RWE-DEA (Hamburg, Germany).

CONTICO INTERNATIONAL, INC.
1101 North Warson Road, St. Louis MO 63132. 314/997-2160. **Contact:** Personnel. **Description:** Contico International designs, manufactures, and markets a broad range of molded plastic and liquid dispensing products for consumer and industrial use including sanitary maintenance products, industrial containers, and materials handling products. **Common positions include:** Accountant/Auditor; Administrator; Advertising Clerk; Blue-Collar Worker Supervisor; Branch Manager; Buyer; Chemical Engineer; Chemist; Claim Representative; Computer Programmer; Credit Manager; Customer Service Representative; Department Manager; Draftsperson; Electrical/Electronics Engineer; Financial Analyst; General Manager; Industrial Designer; Industrial Engineer; Management Trainee; Manufacturer's/Wholesaler's Sales Rep.; Mechanical Engineer; Metallurgical Engineer; Operations/Production Manager; Quality Control Supervisor; Statistician; Transportation/Traffic Specialist. **Educational backgrounds include:** Accounting; Business Administration; Chemistry; Communications; Engineering; Finance; Marketing; Mathematics. **Benefits:** Dental Insurance; Disability Coverage; Employee Discounts; Life Insurance; Medical Insurance; Pension Plan; Profit Sharing; Savings Plan. **Corporate headquarters location:** This Location. **Other U.S. locations:** Los Angeles CA; El Paso TX; Houston TX.

CONTINENTAL CARBON COMPANY
333 Cypress Run, Suite 100, Houston TX 77094. 281/647-3700. **World Wide Web address:** http://www.continentalcarbon.com. **Contact:** Human Resources. **Description:** Manufactures carbon black for the tire and rubber industries. **Corporate headquarters location:** This Location.

COOPER TIRE & RUBBER COMPANY
P.O. Box 550, Findlay OH 45839. 419/423-1321.
Fax: 419/424-7320. **Contact:** Personnel. **World Wide Web address:** http://www.coopertire.com. **Description:** Produces a wide variety of carbon black and fabric reinforced parts for the consumer and industrial markets. The company also manufactures and markets automobile and truck tires, inner tubes, reinforced hose, high-technology rubber-to-metal bonded parts, and complex molded and extruded rubber products. **Common positions include:** Chemical Engineer; Chemist; Computer Programmer; Design Engineer; Manufacturer's/Wholesaler's Sales Rep.; Mechanical Engineer; Systems Analyst. **Educational backgrounds include:** Chemistry; Computer Science; Engineering; Marketing. **Benefits:** 401(k); Dental Insurance; Disability Coverage; Life Insurance; Medical Insurance; Pension Plan; Profit Sharing; Tuition Assistance. **Special programs:** Co-ops. **Corporate headquarters location:** This Location.

CPAC, INC.
2364 Leicester Road, P.O. Box 175, Leicester NY 14481. 716/382-3223. **Fax:** 716/382-3031. **Contact:** Human Resources. **World Wide Web address:** http://www.cpac-fuller.com. **Description:** CPAC is a leader in the production of specialty chemicals used in the imaging industry and the cleaning and personal care markets. The Cleaning and Personal Care Division offers hundreds of household and commercial cleaning products sold through a direct sales force, retail outlet stores, and mail order. The Imaging Division serves commercial customers in photo labs, dental offices, X-ray facilities, and printing houses. Founded in 1969. **Corporate headquarters location:** This Location. **International locations:** Belgium; Italy; South Africa; Thailand. **Subsidiaries include:** Comprising the Imaging segment are Allied Diagnostic Imaging Resources, Inc. (Irwindale CA; Norcross GA), a producer of processing chemicals for medical, dental, graphic arts, microfilm, and industrial applications; CPAC Equipment Division (also at this location), a manufacturer of silver recovery/chemical recycling systems and chemical mixers for all imaging markets; Fuller Brush; PRS, Inc. (also at this location), a U.S. marketing and sales organization for CPAC Equipment, Trebla products, and silver refining services; Stanley Home Products; and Trebla Chemical Company (St. Louis MO), a manufacturer of processing formulas for the color photography market. The Cleaning and Personal Care segment consists of The Fuller Brush Company, Inc. and Stanley Home Products. **Listed on:** NASDAQ. **Stock exchange symbol:** CPAK.

CREATIVE FOAM CORPORATION
300 North Alloy Drive, Fenton MI 48430. 810/629-4149. **Contact:** Human Resources. **Description:** A fabricator and manufacturer of OEM foam products and foam packaging. **Common positions include:** Customer Service Rep.; Industrial Engineer; Manufacturer's/Wholesaler's Sales Rep.; Mechanical Engineer; Operations/Production Manager; Quality Control Supervisor. **Educational backgrounds include:** Business Administration; Engineering. **Benefits:** 401(k); Disability Coverage; Employee Discounts; Life Insurance; Medical Insurance; Profit Sharing; Savings Plan; Tuition Assistance. **Corporate headquarters location:** This Location.

CROSSVILLE RUBBER, INC.
65 Highland Street, Crossville TN 38555. 931/484-5187. **Contact:** Human Resources. **World Wide Web address:** http://www.crossvillerubber.com. **Description:** Manufactures rubber floor coverings for automotive equipment, automotive aftermarket, and automotive replacement markets; and industrial mats. **Common positions include:** Accountant; Auditor; Administrator; Blue-Collar Worker Supervisor; Buyer; Chemical Engineer; Chemist; Computer Programmer; Customer Service Representative; Department Manager; Electrical/Electronics Engineer; General Manager; Industrial Engineer; Management Trainee; Manufacturer's/Wholesaler's Sales Rep.; Mechanical Engineer; Operations/Production Manager; Purchasing Agent; Quality Control Supervisor. **Educational backgrounds include:** Business; Chemistry; Computer Science; Engineering. **Benefits:** Dental Insurance; Disability Coverage; Life Insurance; Medical Insurance; Pension Plan; Profit Sharing; Tuition Assistance. **Special programs:** Internships. **Corporate headquarters location:** This Location.

CYTEC FIBERITE INC.
501 West Third Street, Winona MN 55987. 507/452-8038. **Fax:** 507/452-8195. **Contact:** Employee Resources. **World Wide Web address:** http://www.cytec.com. **Description:** Manufactures advanced composite and adhesives for aerospace, industrial, recreational, and othr applications. **NOTE:** Entry-level positions and second and third shifts are offered. **Common positions include:** Account Rep.; Accountant; Buyer; Chemical Engineer; Chemist; Controller; Customer Service Rep.; Design Engineer; Draftsperson; Electrical/Electronics Engineer; Electrician; General Manager; Human Resources Manager; Manufacturing Engineer; Marketing Specialist; MIS Specialist; Occupational Therapist; Sales Rep.; Secretary. **Educational backgrounds include:** Accounting; Business Administration; Chemistry; Engineering. **Benefits:** 401(k); Dental Insurance; Disability Coverage; Flexible Schedule; Life Insurance; Medical Insurance; Pension Plan; Savings Plan; Tuition Assistance. **Special programs:** Internships; Training. **Corporate headquarters location:** This Location. **Parent company:** Cytec Industries. **General Manager:** William Wood.
Other U.S. locations:
- 2055 East Technology Circle, Tempe AZ 85284. 480/730-2000.

DH COMPOUNDING COMPANY
1260 Carden Farm Drive, Clinton TN 37716. 865/457-1200. **Contact:** Personnel. **Description:** Produces customized thermoplastic resins. **NOTE:** Second and third shifts are offered. **Educational backgrounds include:** Accounting; Business Administration; Chemistry; Engineering. **Benefits:** 401(k); Dental Insurance; Disability Coverage; Life Insurance; Medical Insurance; Pension Plan; Tuition Assistance. **Special programs:** Training. **Corporate headquarters location:** This Location. **Listed on:** Privately held.

DSM ENGINEERING PLASTIC PRODUCTS
P.O. Box 14235, Reading PA 19612-4235. 610/320-6600. **Fax:** 610/320-6817. **Contact:** Personnel. Director. **World Wide Web address:** http://www.dsmepp.com. **Description:** Manufactures industrial plastic stock shapes and hose products. **Common positions include:** Accountant/Auditor; Chemical Engineer; Computer Programmer; Customer Service Representative; Manufacturer's/Wholesaler's Sales Rep.; Operations/Production Manager. **Educational backgrounds include:** Business Administration; Chemistry; Engineering; Finance. **Benefits:** Disability Coverage; Life Insurance; Medical Insurance; Pension Plan; Tuition Assistance. **Corporate headquarters location:** This Location.

DAP INC.
875 North Third Street, Tipp City OH 45371. 937/667-4461. **Contact:** Personnel. **World Wide Web address:** http://www.dap.com. **Description:**

Manufactures and markets sealant and adhesive products. **NOTE:** All resumes should be sent to Human Resources, 2400 Boston Street, Baltimore MD 21224. **Corporate headquarters location:** This Location. **Parent company:** Wassall plc is a holding company whose subsidiaries are principally involved in the provision of prepress and packaging services, and the manufacture and distribution of sealants, adhesives, bottle closures, and office furniture.

DAYCO PRODUCTS, INC.
P.O. Box 1004, Dayton OH 45401. 937/226-7000. **Fax:** 937/226-8698. **Contact:** Human Resources. **World Wide Web address:** http://www.dayco.com. **Description:** A worldwide manufacturer and distributor of a wide range of highly-engineered rubber and plastic products, many of which are used for replacement purposes. The company's principal markets include the agricultural, automotive, construction, energy, printing, mining, textile, and transportation industries. **Common positions include:** Accountant; Computer Programmer; Credit Manager; Customer Service Rep.; Manufacturer's/Wholesaler's Sales Rep.; Marketing Specialist; Systems Analyst. **Educational backgrounds include:** Accounting; Business Administration; Computer Science; Marketing. **Benefits:** 401(k); Dental Insurance; Disability Coverage; Employee Discounts; Flexible Schedule; Life Insurance; Medical Insurance; Pension Plan; Tuition Assistance. **Corporate headquarters location:** This Location. **Other U.S. locations:** Nationwide. **International locations:** Worldwide. **Parent company:** Mark IV Industries.

DEGUSSA-HULS AG
220 Davidson Avenue, Somerset NJ 08873. 732/560-6800. **Fax:** 732/560-6706. **Contact:** Human Resources. **Description:** Manufactures specialty chemicals, polymers, colorants, additives, and raw materials for the coatings industry. **Common positions include:** Accountant; Administrative Assistant; AS400 Programmer Analyst; Attorney; Auditor; Biological Scientist; Chemist; Claim Representative; Computer Operator; Computer Programmer; Controller; Credit Manager; Database Manager; Financial Analyst; General Manager; Human Resources Manager; Industrial Production Manager; Internet Services Manager; Marketing Manager; Marketing Specialist; MIS Specialist; Network/Systems Administrator; Sales Manager; Sales Rep.; Secretary; Systems Analyst. **Educational backgrounds include:** Accounting; Business Administration; Chemistry; Computer Science; Engineering; Finance; Liberal Arts; Marketing; Microsoft Word; Spreadsheets; Visual Basic. **Benefits:** 401(k); Casual Dress - Fridays; Dental Insurance; Disability Coverage; Life Insurance; Medical Insurance; Pension Plan; Profit Sharing; Savings Plan; Tuition Assistance. **Special programs:** Internships. **Corporate headquarters location:** This Location. **Other U.S. locations:** Theodore AL; Pleasanton CA; Piscataway NJ; Lockland OH. **Parent company:** Huls Group. **Operations at this facility include:** Divisional Headquarters; Regional Headquarters. **Annual sales/revenues:** More than $100 million.

DIAMOND VOGEL PAINT
4500 East 48th Avenue, Denver CO 80216. 303/333-3117. **Contact:** Personnel. **Description:** Produces a variety of paints, stains, and resins. **Corporate headquarters location:** This Location.

DIVERSIFOAM PRODUCTS
9091 County Road 50, Rockford MN 55373. 763/477-5854. **Contact:** Personnel Director. **World Wide Web address:** http://www.diversifoam.com. **Description:** Manufactures polystyrene insulation and protective packaging. **Corporate headquarters location:** This Location.

DOW AGROSCIENCES LLC
9330 Zionsville Road, Indianapolis IN 46268. 317/337-3000. **Contact:** Human Resources. **World Wide Web address:** http://www.dowagro.com. **Description:** Produces a variety of agricultural products including herbicides and insecticides. Founded in 1989. **NOTE:** Entry-level positions are offered. **Company slogan:** Improving the quality of life around the world. **Common positions include:** Administrative Assistant; Biochemist; Biological Scientist; Chemist; Computer Programmer; Credit Manager; Financial Analyst; MIS Specialist; Paralegal; Secretary; Systems Analyst. **Educational backgrounds include:** Biology; Business Administration; Chemistry; Computer Science; Finance. **Benefits:** 401(k); Dental Insurance; Disability Coverage; Flexible Schedule; Life Insurance; Medical Insurance; Pension Plan; Profit Sharing; Savings Plan; Tuition Assistance. **Special programs:** Internships; Training. **Corporate headquarters location:** This Location. **Other U.S. locations:** Nationwide. **International locations:** Worldwide. **Parent company:** Dow Chemical Company.

THE DOW CHEMICAL COMPANY
P.O. Box 1655, Midland MI 48641-9944. 517/636-1000. **Contact:** Applicant Center. **World Wide Web address:** http://www.dow.com. **Description:** One of the largest chemical companies in the U.S., Dow manufactures industrial and consumer products. Consumer products include Saran Wrap, Spray 'N Wash, Dow bathroom cleaners, prescription drugs, and over-the-counter health care products. Industrial chemicals are used in the food processing, pharmaceuticals, and utilities markets. Plastics are manufactured for the automotive, electronics, packaging, and recreation markets. Other operations include cogeneration and steam power for the utility market and petrochemical production. **Corporate headquarters location:** This Location. **Other U.S. locations:** Nationwide. **International locations:** Worldwide.

E.I. DuPONT DE NEMOURS AND COMPANY
1007 Market Street, Wilmington DE 19898. 302/774-1000. **Contact:** Human Resources. **World Wide Web address:** http://www.dupont.com. **Description:** Involved in the manufacture of biomedical, industrial, and consumer products (such as photographic, data-recording, and video devices); the production of manmade fiber products; polymer products (such as plastic resins, elastomers, and films); and agricultural and industrial chemicals (such as herbicides and insecticides, pigments, fluorochemicals, petroleum additives, and mineral acids); the exploration and production of crude oil and natural gas; the refining, marketing, and downstream transportation of petroleum; and the mining and distribution of steam and metallurgical coals. The company supplies products to the aerospace, agriculture, apparel, transportation, health care, and printing and publishing industries. **Corporate headquarters location:** This Location. **Listed on:** New York Stock Exchange. **CEO:** Charles O. Holliday, Jr.

DURON PAINTS & WALL COVERINGS
10406 Tucker Street, Beltsville MD 20705. 301/937-4600. **Toll-free phone:** 800/723-8766. **Fax:** 301/595-0435. **Contact:** Human Resources. **Description:** One of the East Coast's largest manufacturers and wholesalers of paint and related products. **Common positions include:** Accountant/Auditor; Adjuster; Administrative

Manager; Budget Analyst; Buyer; Chemist; Clerical Supervisor; Clinical Lab Technician; Collector; Computer Programmer; Construction Contractor; Credit Manager; Customer Service Representative; Draftsperson; Editor; Financial Analyst; Human Resources Manager; Investigator; Operations/ Production Manager; Property and Real Estate Manager; Purchasing Agent/Manager; Quality Control Supervisor; Services Sales Representative; Systems Analyst; Transportation/Traffic Specialist. **Educational backgrounds include:** Business Administration; Communications; High School Diploma/GED; Liberal Arts. **Benefits:** 401(k); Dental Insurance; Disability Coverage; Employee Discounts; Life Insurance; Medical Insurance; Pension Plan; Profit Sharing; Tuition Assistance. **Corporate headquarters location:** This Location. **Listed on:** Privately held.

DYNASIL CORPORATION OF AMERICA
385 Cooper Road, West Berlin NJ 08091. 856/767-4600. **Fax:** 856/767-6813. **Contact:** Human Resources. **World Wide Web address:** http://www.dynasil.com. **Description:** Manufactures synthetic fused silica. Founded in 1960. **Benefits:** 401(k); Disability Coverage; Financial Planning Assistance; Life Insurance; Medical Insurance; Profit Sharing. **Corporate headquarters location:** This Location. **Other U.S. locations:** San Luis Obispo CA. **Listed on:** NASDAQ. **Annual sales/revenues:** $5 - $10 million.

ERB INDUSTRIES
P.O. Box 1237, Woodstock GA 30188. 770/926-7944. **Contact:** Human Resources Manager. **World Wide Web address:** http://www.erbind.com. **Description:** Engaged in custom plastic molding and mold building, cutting and sewing, and safety equipment. **Common positions include:** Credit Manager; Department Manager; Manufacturer's/ Wholesaler's Sales Rep.; Operations/Production Manager; Purchasing Agent/Manager; Quality Control Supervisor. **Benefits:** Life Insurance; Medical Insurance; Pension Plan; Profit Sharing. **Corporate headquarters location:** This Location.

EASTMAN CHEMICAL COMPANY
P.O. Box 511, Kingsport TN 37662. 423/229-3884. **Fax:** 423/224-0995. **Contact:** Employment. **World Wide Web address:** http://www.eastman.com. **Description:** An international chemical company offering a broad line of plastic, chemical, and fiber products. Eastman Chemical is among the leading chemical companies in the United States and is a world leader in polyester plastics for packaging applications. The company is also a leading supplier of cellulose acetate filter tow (used in the manufacture of cigarette filters), as well as a leader in the coatings and fine chemicals markets. **NOTE:** Please check the Website for a list of available openings before applying. **Common positions include:** Accountant/Auditor; Chemical Engineer; Chemist; Electrical/Electronics Engineer; Industrial Engineer; Mechanical Engineer; Systems Analyst. **Educational backgrounds include:** Accounting; Chemistry; Computer Science; Engineering. **Benefits:** 401(k); Dental Insurance; Disability Coverage; Employee Discounts; ESOP; Life Insurance; Medical Insurance; Pension Plan; Profit Sharing; Savings Plan; Tuition Assistance. **Special programs:** Internships. **Corporate headquarters location:** This Location. **Other U.S. locations:** Batesville AK; Charlotte NC; Columbia SC; Longview TX.

ECHO ROCK VENTURES
13620 Lincoln Way, Suite 380, Auburn CA 95603. 530/823-9600. **Fax:** 530/823-9650. **Contact:** Human Resources. **Description:** Operates through three business groups: the Quikset Organization designs, manufactures, and distributes underground, precast concrete structures. The group has developed a patented line of pre-cast concrete sectional boxes to house underground transformers, distribution systems, and splicing manholes. The Plastics Segment manufactures products using a fiber-reinforced plastic process and a structural foam process developed for injection molding; Surfer Publications publishes *SURFER Magazine*, *Powder*, *Snowboarder*, *Bike Magazine*, and *Skateboarder*. The group also produces cable television and home video programs. **Corporate headquarters location:** This Location.

ELECTRA FORM, INC.
852 Scholz Drive, Vandalia OH 45377. 937/898-8460. **Contact:** Human Resources Manager. **World Wide Web address:** http://www.electraform.com. **Description:** Manufactures plastic injection molds. **Common positions include:** Accountant/Auditor; Blue-Collar Worker Supervisor; Buyer; Ceramics Engineer; Cost Estimator; Customer Service Representative; Designer; Draftsperson; Electrical/ Electronics Engineer; Financial Analyst; General Manager; Industrial Engineer; Industrial Production Manager; Manufacturer's/Wholesaler's Sales Rep.; Materials Engineer; Mechanical Engineer; Metallurgical Engineer; Operations/Production Manager; Purchasing Agent/Manager; Quality Control Supervisor; Services Sales Rep.; Wholesale and Retail Buyer. **Educational backgrounds include:** Accounting; Business Administration; Computer Science; Engineering; Finance; Liberal Arts; Marketing. **Benefits:** 401(k); Dental Insurance; Disability Coverage; Life Insurance; Medical Insurance; Profit Sharing; Tuition Assistance. **Corporate headquarters location:** This Location.

ELF ATOCHEM NORTH AMERICA INC.
2000 Market Street, Philadelphia PA 19103. 215/419-7000. **Contact:** Human Resources Manager. **World Wide Web address:** http://www.elf-atochem.com. **Description:** Manufactures a variety of chemicals. **Benefits:** 401(k); Dental Insurance; Disability Coverage; Life Insurance; Medical Insurance; Pension Plan; Tuition Assistance. **Corporate headquarters location:** This Location. **Other U.S. locations:** Nationwide. **International locations:** Worldwide. **Parent company:** Elf Atochem S.A. **Listed on:** New York Stock Exchange. **Annual sales/revenues:** More than $100 million.

ENERGETIC SOLUTIONS
9781 South Meridian Boulevard, Englewood CO 76063. 303/268-5000. **Contact:** Human Resources Manager. **World Wide Web address:** http://www.energeticsolutions.com. **Description:** Manufactures commercial explosives, nitrogen products, and chemicals. **Corporate headquarters location:** This Location. **Parent company:** ICI, plc.

ENPLAS U.S.A., INC.
1901 West Oak Circle, Marietta GA 30062. 770/795-1100. **Fax:** 770/795-1190. **Contact:** Jerry Mullis, Manager of Human Resources. **Description:** Manufactures high-precision engineered plastic parts.

ENVIROTEK PUMPSYSTEMS
P.O. Box 209, Salt Lake City UT 84110. 801/359-8731. **Fax:** 801/355-9303. **Contact:** Human Resources Department. **Description:** Manufactures and markets industrial pumps and pump systems. The company also manufactures rubber products for industrial and mining applications and is engaged in bulk injection molding. **Common positions**

include: Accountant/Auditor; Buyer; Computer Programmer; Designer; Draftsperson; General Manager; Human Resources Manager; Industrial Engineer; Manufacturer's/Wholesaler's Sales Rep.; Mechanical Engineer; Metallurgical Engineer; Mining Engineer; Purchasing Agent/Manager; Quality Control Supervisor; Systems Analyst; Transportation/Traffic Specialist. **Educational backgrounds include:** Accounting; Business Administration; Computer Science; Engineering; Finance; Marketing. **Benefits:** 401(k); Daycare Assistance; Dental Insurance; Disability Coverage; Employee Discounts; Life Insurance; Medical Insurance; Tuition Assistance. **Special programs:** Internships. **Corporate headquarters location:** This Location. **Other U.S. locations:** Fresno CA; Sacramento CA; St. Louis MO. **Parent company:** Weir (Scotland).

EVANS INDUSTRIES
200 Renaissance Center, Detroit MI 48243. 313/259-2266. **Contact:** Human Resources. **Description:** Manufactures various industrial products including casters, wheels, glue, and other rubber and plastic parts. **Educational backgrounds include:** Business Administration. **Corporate headquarters location:** This Location.

EXOTIC RUBBER & PLASTICS CORP.
P.O. Box 395, Farmington MI 48332. 248/473-7951. **Fax:** 248/473-7972. **Contact:** Human Resources. **World Wide Web address:** http://www. erpc.com. **Description:** Manufactures and markets plastic and rubber products including rollers, O-rings, and die strippers. Founded in 1962. **Common positions include:** Accountant/Auditor; Computer Programmer; Cost Estimator; Customer Service Rep.; Industrial Production Manager; Management Trainee; Manufacturer's/Wholesaler's Sales Rep.; Operations/Production Manager; Purchasing Agent/Manager. **Educational backgrounds include:** Accounting; Business Administration; Marketing. **Benefits:** 401(k); Bonus Award/Plan; Daycare Assistance; Life Insurance; Medical Insurance; Profit Sharing; Tuition Assistance. **Special programs:** Internships. **Corporate headquarters location:** This Location. **Other U.S. locations:** Indianapolis IN; Freeland MI; Grand Rapids MI; Jackson MI; Trenton MI; Franklin OH. **Listed on:** Privately held. **Annual sales/revenues:** $21 - $50 million.

FMC CORPORATION
200 East Randolph Drive, Chicago IL 60601. 312/861-6000. **Contact:** Human Resources . **World Wide Web address:** http://www.fmc.com. **Description:** FMC is a diversified manufacturer of specialty, industrial, and agricultural chemicals; defense-related systems; and industrial machinery. **Corporate headquarters location:** This Location. **Subsidiaries include:** Fluid Control Systems; FMC Gold. **Listed on:** New York Stock Exchange. **Annual sales/revenues:** More than $100 million. **Other U.S. locations:**
• 1735 Market Street, Philadelphia PA 19103. 215/299-6000.

FARREL CORPORATION
25 Main Street, Ansonia CT 06401. 203/734-3331. **Contact:** Human Resources Manager. **World Wide Web address:** http://www.farrel.com. **Description:** Designs, manufactures, sells, and services machinery and associated equipment used in the processing and conversion of rubber and plastics. Along with sales of capital equipment, Farrel provides process engineering, process design, and related services for rubber and plastics installations. The company's aftermarket services consist of repair, refurbishment and upgrade, spare parts sales,

and field services. **Benefits:** 401(k); Medical Insurance; Pension Plan; Stock Option. **Corporate headquarters location:** This Location. **Other U.S. locations:** NC; OH; TX. **International locations:** Australia; England; Singapore; The Netherlands. **Listed on:** NASDAQ.

FAWN INDUSTRIES, INC.
1920 Green Spring Drive, Suite 140, Timonium MD 21093. 410/308-9200. **Contact:** Human Resources. **World Wide Web address:** http://www.fawn-ind.com. **Description:** Manufactures electronic subassemblies and related injection-molded plastic parts used by the automotive, industrial electronics, and personal computer industries. Founded in 1953. **Corporate headquarters location:** This Location. **Other U.S. locations:** MI; NC; TN.

FEDERAL PACKAGING CORPORATION
P.O. Box 930, St. Paris OH 43072. 937/663-4142. **Contact:** Lawrence J. Subler, Human Resources Manager. **Description:** Manufactures composite cans and tubes, as well as injection-molded plastic parts. **Common positions include:** Accountant/Auditor; Blue-Collar Worker Supervisor; Buyer; Customer Service Rep.; Purchasing Agent/Manager. **Benefits:** Dental Insurance; Disability Coverage; Life Insurance; Medical Insurance; Profit Sharing; Tuition Assistance. **Corporate headquarters location:** This Location.

FERRO CORPORATION
1000 Lakeside Avenue, Cleveland OH 44114. 216/641-8580. **Contact:** Human Resources. **Description:** Produces specialty materials through organic and inorganic chemical processes for the construction, furnishings, appliance, industrial, and transportation markets. Products include coatings, colors, ceramics, refractories, and chemicals. **Corporate headquarters location:** This Location. **Listed on:** New York Stock Exchange.

THE FERTILIZER INSTITUTE
501 Second Street NE, Washington DC 20002. 202/675-8250. **Contact:** Director of Personnel. **World Wide Web address:** http://www.tfi.org. **Description:** A trade association representing companies that make commercial fertilizer available to farmers worldwide. **Benefits:** Dental Insurance; Disability Coverage; Life Insurance; Medical Insurance; Pension Plan; Savings Plan; Tuition Assistance. **Special programs:** Internships. **Corporate headquarters location:** This Location.

FIBERVISIONS, INC.
7101 Alcovy Road NE, Covington GA 30014. 770/786-7011. **Contact:** Human Resources. **Description:** Engaged in the manufacture and sale of a wide variety of chemicals and allied products which are supplied to the plastics, paper, synthetic fiber, agriculture, and food industries. Products are divided into the following business segments: Organics, Plastics, Water Soluble Polymers, Explosives and Aerospace. **NOTE:** Entry-level positions and part-time jobs are offered. **Common positions include:** Account Manager; Accountant; Clinical Lab Technician; Computer Support Technician; Customer Service Representative; Electrician; Finance Director; Financial Analyst; General Manager; Human Resources Manager; Internet Services Manager; Network Administrator; Product Manager; Purchasing Agent/Manager; Quality Assurance Engineer; Quality Control Supervisor; Sales Manager; Sales Representative; Systems Analyst; Systems Manager. **Educational backgrounds include:** Accounting; Engineering; Finance; Microsoft Word; Physics; Software Tech. Support. **Benefits:** 401(k); Casual Dress - Daily; Dental Insurance; Disability Coverage; Life

Insurance; Medical Insurance; Savings Plan; Tuition Assistance. **Special programs:** Co-ops; Summer Jobs. **Corporate headquarters location:** Wilmington DE. **Other U.S. locations:** Athens GA. **International locations:** China; Denmark. **Parent company:** Hercules Inc. **Listed on:** New York Stock Exchange.

FINA OIL & CHEMICAL COMPANY
6000 Legacy Drive, Plano TX 75024. 972/801-2000. **Contact:** Human Resources. **World Wide Web address:** http://www.fina.com. **Description:** Explores for crude oil and natural gas; markets natural gas; refines, supplies, transports, and markets petroleum products; manufactures specialty chemicals, primarily petrochemicals and plastics including polypropylene, polystyrene, styrene monomer, high-density polyethylene, and aromatics; licenses certain chemical processes; and manufactures and markets paints and coatings. **Corporate headquarters location:** This Location.

FLEXIBLE PRODUCTS COMPANY
P.O. Box 3190, Marietta GA 30062. 770/428-2684. **Fax:** 770/428-9431. **Contact:** Human Resources Manager. **World Wide Web address:** http://www.flexibleproducts.com. **Description:** Manufactures polyurethane and vinyl compounds. **Common positions include:** Accountant/Auditor; Chemist; Computer Programmer; Credit Manager; Customer Service Rep.; Electrician; Financial Manager; General Manager; Human Resources Manager; Industrial Engineer; Manufacturer's/Wholesaler's Sales Rep.; Market Research Analyst; Mechanical Engineer; Payroll Clerk; Purchasing Agent/Manager; Quality Control Supervisor; Receptionist; Secretary; Systems Analyst; Truck Driver; Welder. **Educational backgrounds include:** Accounting; Business Administration; Chemistry; Computer Science; Engineering; Finance; Marketing. **Benefits:** Disability Coverage; Life Insurance; Medical Insurance; Pension Plan; Savings Plan; Tuition Assistance. **Corporate headquarters location:** This Location. **Other U.S. locations:** CA; IL.

FOAMEX INTERNATIONAL, INC.
1000 Columbia Avenue, Linwood PA 19061. 610/859-3000. **Contact:** Lois Spencer, Human Resources. **World Wide Web address:** http://www.foamex.com. **Description:** One of the nation's largest manufacturers of flexible polyurethane foam products. Foamex products are classified into four groups: Cushion Foams are used for mattresses, quilting and borders, home and office furniture, computer and electronics packaging, and padding foams for health care. Customers include mattress manufacturers, furniture manufacturers, specialized packaging users, and health care companies; Carpet Cushions include prime, bonded, sponge rubber, felt carpet cushion, synthetic grass turf, and a variety of textured carpeting and wallcoverings; Automotive Foams include foams for cushioning and seating, acoustical foams, headliner foams, trim foams, and foams for door panel parts; Technical Foams include those for filtration, reservoiring, sound absorption and transmission, carburetors, high-speed inkjet printers, speaker grilles, oxygenators, and EKG pads, as well as cosmetic applicators, mop heads, paint brushes, and diapers. **Corporate headquarters location:** This Location. **Other U.S. locations:** Nationwide. **Listed on:** NASDAQ. **Stock exchange symbol:** FMXI. **Annual sales/revenues:** More than $100 million.

H.B. FULLER COMPANY
P.O. Box 64683, St. Paul MN 55164. 651/481-4600. **Fax:** 651/236-5100. **Contact:** Human Resources Manager. **World Wide Web address:** http://www. hbfuller.com. **Description:** Manufactures adhesives, sealants, coatings, and specialty chemicals. **Common positions include:** Accountant/Auditor; Attorney; Chemical Engineer; Chemist; Computer Programmer; Customer Service Representative; Industrial Production Manager; Manufacturer's/Wholesaler's Sales Representative. **Educational backgrounds include:** Accounting; Chemistry; Engineering; Finance. **Benefits:** 401(k); Daycare Assistance; Dental Insurance; Disability Coverage; Life Insurance; Medical Insurance; Pension Plan; Profit Sharing; Tuition Assistance. **Special programs:** Internships. **Corporate headquarters location:** This Location. **Other U.S. locations:** Nationwide. **Annual sales/revenues:** More than $100 million.

THE GATES RUBBER COMPANY
P.O. Box 5887, Denver CO 80217. 303/744-1911. **Physical address:** 990 South Broadway, Denver CO. **Contact:** Human Resources Manager. **World Wide Web address:** http://www.gates.com. **Description:** Develops, manufactures and distributes of a broad range of rubber and plastic products. The company also operates area subsidiaries engaged in the production of automotive and heavy-duty batteries. **Common positions include:** Accountant; Chemical Engineer; Chemist; Computer Programmer; Customer Service Rep.; Draftsperson; Editor; Electrical/Electronics Engineer; Human Resources Manager; Management Trainee; Manufacturer's/Wholesaler's Sales Rep.; Marketing Specialist; Mechanical Engineer; Metallurgical Engineer; Physicist; Purchasing Agent/Manager; Quality Control Supervisor; Reporter; Statistician; Systems Analyst; Technical Writer/Editor; Transportation/Traffic Specialist. **Educational backgrounds include:** Accounting; Business; Chemistry; Communications; Computer Science; Engineering; Finance; Liberal Arts; Marketing; Mathematics; Physics. **Benefits:** 401(k); Dental Insurance; Disability Coverage; Employee Discounts; Life Insurance; Medical Insurance; Pension Plan; Savings Plan; Tuition Assistance. **Corporate headquarters location:** This Location.

GENERAL CHEMICAL CORPORATION
90 East Halsey Road, Parsippany NJ 07054. 973/515-0900. **Contact:** Human Resources. **World Wide Web address:** http://www.genchem.com. **Description:** Manufactures and markets inorganic chemicals and soda ash. **Common positions include:** Accountant; Chemical Engineer; Customer Service Rep.; Financial Analyst; Financial Manager; Human Resources Manager; Manufacturer's/Wholesaler's Sales Rep.; Mining Engineer; Secretary. **Educational backgrounds include:** Accounting; Business Administration; Engineering; Finance; Liberal Arts; Marketing. **Benefits:** 401(k); Dental Insurance; Disability Coverage; Life Insurance; Medical Insurance; Pension Plan; Tuition Assistance. **Corporate headquarters location:** This Location. **Other U.S. locations:** Claymont DE; Syracuse NY; Pittsburgh PA; Green River WY. **Parent company:** The General Chemical Group Inc. (Hampton NH).

GENOVA PRODUCTS
7034 East Court Street, P.O. Box 309, Davison MI 48423. 810/744-4500. **Contact:** Human Resources. **World Wide Web address:** http://www.genovaproducts.com. **Description:** Engaged in the manufacture of PVC. **Corporate headquarters location:** This Location.

THE GEON COMPANY
One Geon Center, Avon Lakes OH 44012. 440/930-1000. **Contact:** Human Resources. **World Wide Web address:** http://www.geon.com. **Description:**

A leading North American producer of vinyl (PVC) resins and compounds marketed under the GEON trademark and applied in building products including piping, siding, and windows. **Corporate headquarters location:** This Location. **Other U.S. locations:** Long Beach CA; Henry IL; Terre Haute IN; Louisville KY; Plaquemine LA; Pedricktown NJ; Deer Park TX; LaPorte TX. **International locations:** Australia; Canada.

GEORGIA DUCK & CORDAGE MILL
P.O. Box 865, Scottdale GA 30079. 404/294-5272. **Contact:** Human Resources Manager. **Description:** Manufactures PVC, rubber, and polyurethane conveyer belting; industrial fabrics; and cordage. **Common positions include:** Blue-Collar Worker Supervisor; Chemical Engineer; Industrial Engineer; Industrial Production Manager. **Educational backgrounds include:** Business Administration; Chemistry; Engineering. **Benefits:** 401(k); Life Insurance; Medical Insurance; Profit Sharing. **Corporate headquarters location:** This Location. **Listed on:** Privately held.

GEORGIA GULF CORPORATION
P.O. Box 105197, Atlanta GA 30348. 770/395-4500. **Fax:** 770/395-4529. **Contact:** Personnel. **Description:** A manufacturer and worldwide marketer of several highly-integrated lines of commodity chemicals and polymers including aromatic, natural gas, and electrochemical products. The company's chemical products have a number of consumer and industrial uses such as water purification, paper production, and production of high-performance plastics, pharmaceuticals, and construction materials. **Corporate headquarters location:** This Location. **Other U.S. locations:** DE; LA; MS; TN; TX. **Listed on:** New York Stock Exchange.

THE GLIDDEN COMPANY
300 Sprowl Road, Huron OH 44839. 419/433-5664. **Contact:** Human Resources Manager. **Description:** Manufactures and markets resin packaging products and decorative oil- and water-based paints. **Common positions include:** Accountant/Auditor; Blue-Collar Worker Supervisor; Chemical Engineer; Chemist; Electrical Engineer; Electronics Engineer; Environmental Engineer; Industrial Engineer; Industrial Production Manager; Operations/ Production Manager; Purchasing Agent/Manager; Quality Control Supervisor; Secretary; Software Engineer; Systems Analyst; Transportation/Traffic Specialist. **Educational backgrounds include:** Accounting; Business Administration; Chemistry; Engineering; Novell. **Benefits:** 401(k); Casual Dress - Daily; Dental Insurance; Disability Coverage; Employee Discounts; Life Insurance; Medical Insurance; Pension Plan; Tuition Assistance. **Corporate headquarters location:** Cleveland OH. **O Parent company:** ICI Inc.

GOODALL RUBBER COMPANY
790 Birney Highway, Suite 100, Aston PA 19014. 610/361-0800. **Contact:** Personnel. **Description:** Manufactures, distributes, and sells rubber through 45 U.S. and Canadian sales and service centers. Products include hoses, belting products, lined pipes, and fittings. **Corporate headquarters location:** This Location.

GOODYEAR TIRE & RUBBER COMPANY
1144 Market Street, Akron OH 44316. 330/796-2596. **Contact:** Human Resources Manager. **World Wide Web address:** http://www.goodyear.com. **Description:** This location manufactures tires and chemicals and houses a technical center, tire proving grounds, and airship operations. Overall, Goodyear Tire & Rubber Company's principal business is the development, manufacture, distribution, and sale of tires for applications worldwide. The company also manufactures and markets a broad spectrum of rubber products and rubber-related chemicals for various industrial and consumer markets, and provides auto repair services. **Corporate headquarters location:** This Location. **Other U.S. locations:** Nationwide. **International locations:** Worldwide. **Subsidiaries include:** Celeron; Goodyear Asia; Goodyear Europe; Goodyear Latin America; Goodyear Racing; Kelly-Springfield; North American Tire. **OListed on:** New York Stock Exchange. **Annual sales/revenues:** More than $100 million.

W.L. GORE & ASSOCIATES, INC.
P.O. Box 9206, Newark DE 19714. 302/738-4880. **Physical address:** 551 Paper Mill Road, Newark DE. **Contact:** Human Resources Manager. **World Wide Web address:** http://www.gore.com. **Description:** Manufactures dental floss, guitar strings, bicycle cable systems, vacuum filters, and water/stain repellent. The company also produces electronic products including copper and optical signal transmission products, digital and analog cable assemblies, circuit chips and related products; chemical products including a chemical polymer used to repair diseased arteries and also as an industrial sealant; and GORE-TEX fabric. **Common positions include:** Attorney; Chemical Engineer; Chemist; Electrical Engineer; Electronics Engineer; Mechanical Engineer; Metallurgical Engineer; Sales Engineer. **Educational backgrounds include:** Chemistry; Engineering. **Benefits:** Dental Insurance; Disability Coverage; Fitness Program; Life Insurance; Medical Insurance; Profit Sharing. **Special programs:** Internships. **Corporate headquarters location:** This Location. **Annual sales/revenues:** More than $100 million.

W.R. GRACE & COMPANY
7500 Grace Drive, Columbia MD 21044. 410/531-4000. **Fax:** 410/531-4367. **Contact:** Employee Relations. **World Wide Web address:** http://www.grace.com. **Description:** One of the leading global suppliers of specialty chemicals and flexible packaging. W.R. Grace operates through four major divisions. Grace Packaging specializes in flexible packaging systems for meat, poultry, cheese, and other perishable food products, as well as shrink packaging materials for consumer and industrial products. Grace Davison catalysts crack crude oil into fuel and related by-products. Davison polyolefin catalysts are involved in polyethylene production, and its silica and zeolite adsorbents are ingredients in industrial and consumer applications. Grace Construction products include concrete and cement additives, fireproofing, and waterproofing systems which strengthen concrete, fight corrosion, stop water damage, and protect structural steel from fire damage. Grace Container includes container sealant systems that keep food and beverages protected from bacteria and other contaminants, extend shelf-life, and preserve flavor. **Common positions include:** Accountant/Auditor; Attorney; Financial Analyst; Human Resources Specialist; Network Support Technician; Systems Analyst. **Educational backgrounds include:** Accounting; Business Administration; Finance. **Benefits:** 401(k); Dental Insurance; Life Insurance; Medical Insurance; Pension Plan; Tuition Assistance. **Corporate headquarters location:** This Location. **Listed on:** New York Stock Exchange. **Annual sales/revenues:** More than $100 million.

GREAT LAKES CHEMICAL CORPORATION
P.O. Box 2200, West Lafayette IN 47996. 765/497-6100. **Recorded jobline:** 765/497-6377. **Contact:** Human Resources. **World Wide Web address:**

http://www.greatlakeschem.com. **Description:** A leading supplier of specialty chemical solutions to customers in the plastics, additives, and life sciences industries. The company also develops performance chemicals for use in fire protection, oil and gas drilling, and recreational water treatment. **NOTE:** Please call the jobline for application procedures and a list of available positions before sending a resume. **Corporate headquarters location:** This Location. **Listed on:** New York Stock Exchange. **Stock exchange symbol:** GLK.

HAMMOND GROUP, INC.
1414 Field Street, Hammond IN 46320. 219/931-9360. **Contact:** Human Resources. **Description:** This location houses administrative offices. Overall, Hammond Group manufactures lead chemicals and products under the name Hammond Lead Products including lead carbonates, silicates, and sulfates for a variety of industries. The company also manufactures a dedusted granular litharge called 400Y. **Corporate headquarters location:** This Location.

HAUSER CHEMICAL RESEARCH, INC.
5555 Airport Boulevard, Boulder CO 80301. 303/443-4662. **Fax:** 303/413-0867. **Recorded jobline:** 303/441-5841x3000. **Contact:** Human Resources. **Description:** Hauser Chemical Research extracts and purifies specialty products from natural resources using its proprietary technologies. **Common positions include:** Chemical Engineer; Chemist; Mechanical Engineer; Metallurgical Engineer. **Educational backgrounds include:** Chemistry; Engineering. **Benefits:** 401(k); Dental Insurance; Disability Coverage; Life Insurance; Medical Insurance. **Corporate headquarters location:** This Location. **Listed on:** NASDAQ.

HERCULES INC.
Hercules Plaza, 1313 North Market Street, Wilmington DE 19894. 302/594-5000. **Contact:** Professional Employment Manager. **World Wide Web address:** http://www.herc.com. **Description:** Manufactures cellulose and natural gum thickeners; flavors and fragrances; natural and hydrocarbon rosins and resins; polypropylene fibers and films; graphite fibers; and aerospace products. **Common positions include:** Chemical Engineer; Chemist; Mechanical Engineer. **Educational backgrounds include:** Chemistry; Engineering. **Benefits:** Dental Insurance; Disability Coverage; Life Insurance; Medical Insurance; Pension Plan; Savings Plan; Tuition Assistance. **Special programs:** Internships. **Corporate headquarters location:** This Location.

HI-PORT INC.
409 East Wallisville Road, Highlands TX 77562. 281/426-3541. **Contact:** Mike Lewis, Vice President of Human Resources. **Description:** This location houses three separate divisions of Hi-Port Inc. SMS Division manufactures canned and bottled fruit drinks, and canned petroleum products; HiOrganite Division produces organic fertilizers; Chemola Division produces consumer and industrial detergents, lubricants, penetrants, and lubrication equipment. Overall, the company provides contract packaging, blending, and distribution services for automotive care, as well as agricultural, chemical, and bulk powder products. **Corporate headquarters location:** This Location.

HI-TECH MOLD AND ENGINEERING SOUTHEAST
466 Baxter Lane, Winchester TN 37398. 931/962-3332. **Fax:** 931/962-4401. **Contact:** Personnel. **Description:** Manufactures plastic injection molds. **Corporate headquarters location:** Rochester Hills MI.

HIGHLAND SUPPLY CORPORATION
1111 Sixth Street, Highland IL 62249. 618/654-2161. **Contact:** Personnel Director. **World Wide Web address:** http://www.highlandsupply.com. **Description:** Manufactures foils, polypropylene film, cellophane, and printed and plain bags. **Common positions include:** Accountant/Auditor; Chemist; Computer Programmer; General Manager; Manufacturer's/Wholesaler's Sales Rep.; Mechanical Engineer; Operations/Production Manager; Quality Control Supervisor. **Educational backgrounds include:** Accounting; Business Administration; Chemistry; Computer Science; Engineering; Marketing. **Benefits:** Life Insurance; Medical Insurance; Tuition Assistance. **Corporate headquarters location:** This Location.

HOFFER'S INC.
310 South Bellis Street, Wausau WI 54403. 715/845-7221. **Contact:** Human Resources. **World Wide Web address:** http://www.hoffers.com. **Description:** Manufactures a wide variety of paints and coatings. Hoffer's also manufactures the Enviro-Prep system which aids in lead paint disposal. **Corporate headquarters location:** This Location. **Number of employees at this location:** 300.

HOLM INDUSTRIES INC.
P.O. Box 450, Scottsburg IN 47170. 812/752-2526. **Fax:** 812/752-3563. **Contact:** Human Resources. **Description:** Involved in the extrusion of plastic, rubber, and vinyl for the appliance and building trade industries. **Common positions include:** Accountant/Auditor; Biological Scientist; Blue-Collar Worker Supervisor; Buyer; Chemical Engineer; Chemist; Claim Rep.; Computer Programmer; Cost Estimator; Customer Service Rep.; General Manager; Human Resources Manager; Industrial Engineer; Industrial Production Manager; Mechanical Engineer; Operations/Production Manager; Purchasing Agent/Manager; Quality Control Supervisor; Transportation/Traffic Specialist. **Educational backgrounds include:** Business; Chemistry; Communications; Finance; Marketing. **Benefits:** 401(k); Dental Insurance; Disability Coverage; Life Insurance; Medical Insurance; Pension Plan; Tuition Assistance. **Corporate headquarters location:** This Location. **Other U.S. locations:** Hartselle AL; San Diego CA; St. Charles IL; New Ulm MN. **Parent company:** The Standard Products Company.

HONEYWELL INTERNATIONAL
P.O. Box 2830, Baton Rouge LA 70821. 225/383-5222. **Recorded jobline:** 225/346-3685. **Contact:** Human Resources. **World Wide Web address:** http://www.honeywell.com. **Description:** This location manufactures environmentally safe refrigerants. Overall, Honeywell is engaged in the research, development, manufacture, and sale of advanced technology products and services in the fields of electronics, automation, and controls. The company's major businesses are home and building automation and control, industrial automation and control, space and aviation systems, and defense and marine systems. **NOTE:** Entry-level positions and part-time jobs are offered. **Common positions include:** Chemist; Controller; Design Engineer; Financial Analyst; Human Resources Manager; Manufacturing Engineer; Quality Assurance Engineer. **Educational backgrounds include:** Chemistry; Engineering; Finance. **Benefits:** 401(k); Casual Dress - Daily; Dental Insurance; Disability Coverage; Employee Discounts; Financial Planning Assistance; Life Insurance; Medical Insurance; Pension Plan; Profit Sharing; Relocation Assistance; Savings Plan; Tuition Assistance. **Special programs:** Co-ops; Internships; Summer Jobs. **Corporate headquarters location:** Morristown NJ.

HUNTSMAN CORPORATION
500 Huntsman Way, Salt Lake City UT 84108.
801/532-5200. **Contact:** Human Resources. **World Wide Web address:** http://www.huntsman.com.
Description: Manufactures and markets chemicals and plastic products including ethylene, propylene, ethanlolamines, alkylalkanolamines, olefins, and a variety of others. **Corporate headquarters location:** This Location. **International locations:** Armenia; Canada; China; Singapore; the Ukraine.
Other U.S. locations:
• Huntsman Polymers Corporation, P.O. Box 3986, Odessa TX 79760. 915/640-7200.

HUTCHINSON SEAL CORPORATION NATIONAL O-RING DIVISION
11634 Patton Road, Downey CA 90241. 562/862-8163. **Fax:** 562/862-4596. **Contact:** Human Resources. **Description:** Engaged in distribution and manufacturing operations. The company includes National O-Ring, which manufactures and distributes a full-range of standard-size, low-cost, synthetic rubber o-ring sealing devices for use in automotive and industrial applications. **Corporate headquarters location:** This Location.

ICI PAINTS
925 Euclid Avenue, Cleveland OH 44115. 216/344-8105. **Contact:** Human Resources **World Wide Web address:** http://www.ici.com. **Description:** Manufactures and sells packaging products, decorative latex, and Glidden oil-based paints and coatings. **Educational backgrounds include:** Accounting; Business Administration; Chemistry; Engineering. **Corporate headquarters location:** This Location.

IMC GLOBAL INC.
2100 Sanders Road, Suite 200, Northbrook IL 60062. 847/272-9200. **Fax:** 847/412-5829. **Contact:** Director of Human Resources. **E-mail address:** hr@imcglobal.com. **World Wide Web address:** http://www.imcglobal.com. **Description:** This location houses administrative offices. Overall, IMC Global mines and manufactures crop nutrients including potash and phosphates; supplies animal feed ingredients necessary for raising livestock; and produces salt for road maintenance. **NOTE:** Entry-level positions are offered. **Common positions include:** Accountant; Administrative Assistant; Blue-Collar Worker Supervisor; Budget Analyst; Chemical Engineer; Database Administrator; Electrical/Electronics Engineer; Financial Analyst; General Manager; Human Resources Manager; Industrial Production Manager; Manufacturing Engineer; Operations Manager; Systems Analyst. **Educational backgrounds include:** Business Administration; Engineering; Finance; Microsoft Word; Spreadsheets; Visual Basic. **Benefits:** 401(k); Dental Insurance; Disability Coverage; Employee Discounts; Flexible Schedule; Life Insurance; Medical Insurance; Profit Sharing; Tuition Assistance; Vacation Days (6 - 10). **Corporate headquarters location:** This Location. **Other U.S. locations:** Tampa FL; Carlsbad NM; Ogden UT. **International locations:** Hong Kong; United Kingdom. **Listed on:** New York Stock Exchange. **Stock exchange symbol:** IGL. **CEO:** Robert E. Fowler. **Annual sales/revenues:** More than $100 million.

INDUSTRIAL MOLDING CORPORATION
616 East Slaton Road, Lubbock TX 79404. 806/474-1000. **Contact:** Personnel Manager. **World Wide Web address:** http://www.indmolding.com. **Description:** Manufactures and markets injection molded plastics. **Corporate headquarters location:** This Location.

INOLEX CHEMICAL COMPANY
Jackson & Swanson Streets, Philadelphia PA 19148. 215/271-0800. **Contact:** Human Resources. **Description:** Manufactures specialty chemicals for the cosmetics industry. **Common positions include:** Accountant; Administrative Manager; Budget Analyst; Chemical Engineer; Clerical Supervisor; Computer Programmer; Credit Manager; Customer Service Representative; Financial Analyst; Operations/Production Manager; Quality Control Supervisor; Services Sales Representative; Systems Analyst. **Educational backgrounds include:** Accounting; Engineering; Marketing. **Benefits:** 401(k); Dental Insurance; Disability Coverage; Life Insurance; Medical Insurance; Pension Plan; Tuition Assistance. **Corporate headquarters location:** This Location.

INTERNATIONAL FLAVORS & FRAGRANCES
521 West 57th Street, New York NY 10019. 212/765-5500x7149. **Contact:** Personnel Director. **Description:** Creates and manufactures flavors and fragrances used by other manufacturers in a wide variety of consumer products. Fragrance products are sold principally to manufacturers of perfumes, cosmetics, personal care items, soaps, detergents, air fresheners, and household products. Flavor products are sold principally to manufacturers of dairy, meat, processed foods, beverages, pharmaceuticals, snacks, baked goods, confectioneries, tobacco products, oral care products, and animal foods. **Common positions include:** Accountant/Auditor; Chemist; Computer Programmer; Customer Service Representative; Human Resources Manager; Marketing Specialist; Secretary; Systems Analyst. **Educational backgrounds include:** Business Administration; Chemistry; Computer Science; Marketing. **Benefits:** 401(k); Bonus Award/Plan; Dental Insurance; Disability Coverage; Life Insurance; Medical Insurance; Pension Plan; Profit Sharing; Tuition Assistance. **Corporate headquarters location:** This Location. **Other U.S. locations:** Hazlet NJ; South Brunswick NJ; Union Beach NJ.

INTERNATIONAL SPECIALTY PRODUCTS
1361 Alps Road, Wayne NJ 07470. 973/628-4000. **Contact:** Director of Human Resources. **World Wide Web address:** http://www.ispcorp.com. **Description:** Manufactures specialty chemicals and building materials. Chemicals include high-pressure acetylene derivatives, industrial organic and inorganic chemicals, GAF filter systems, and GAF mineral products. Building materials include prepared roofing, roll roofing, built-up roofing systems, and single-ply roofing. **Common positions include:** Accountant; Advertising Clerk; Attorney; Biological Scientist; Biomedical Engineer; Budget Analyst; Buyer; Chemical Engineer; Chemist; Computer Programmer; Financial Analyst; General Manager; Paralegal; Pharmacist; Systems Analyst. **Educational backgrounds include:** Chemistry; Engineering. **Benefits:** 401(k); Dental Insurance; Disability Coverage; Life Insurance; Medical Insurance; Savings Plan; Tuition Assistance. **Corporate headquarters location:** This Location. **Listed on:** New York Stock Exchange.

INTERPLASTIC CORPORATION
1225 Willow Lake Boulevard, Vadnais Heights MN 55110. 651/481-6860. **Contact:** Human Resources Manager. **Description:** Produces synthetic resins and companion items, polyethylene containers, and sheet molding compound. **Common positions include:** Accountant/Auditor; Budget Analyst; Buyer; Chemical Engineer; Clinical Lab Technician; Computer Programmer; Credit Manager; Customer Service Rep.; Financial Analyst; Human Resources Manager; Mechanical Engineer; Operations/

Production Manager. **Educational backgrounds include:** Accounting; Chemistry; Engineering; Marketing. **Benefits:** 401(k); Dental Insurance; Disability Coverage; Life Insurance; Medical Insurance; Profit Sharing; Tuition Assistance. **Corporate headquarters location:** This Location. **Listed on:** Privately held.

INTESYS TECHNOLOGIES
265 Briggs Avenue, Costa Mesa CA 92626. 714/546-4460. **Fax:** 714/556-6955. **Contact:** Personnel. **Description:** Develop and manufactures high-performance plastic components for commercial, industrial, and medical uses. The company also custom formulates and compounds reinforced thermoplastic materials. InteSys produces engineered parts and subassemblies that are key components for computer equipment, printers, data cartridges, telecommunication devices, business machines, electronic products, commercial irrigation, automobile, and plumbing systems. **Common positions include:** Accountant/Auditor; Adjuster; Administrative Manager; Advertising Clerk; Blue-Collar Worker Supervisor; Buyer; Chemical Engineer; Clerical Supervisor; Computer Programmer; Cost Estimator; Customer Service Representative; Draftsperson; Electrical/Electronics Engineer; Electrician; General Manager; Industrial Engineer; Industrial Production Manager; Mechanical Engineer; Purchasing Agent/Manager; Quality Control Supervisor; Systems Analyst. **Educational backgrounds include:** Accounting; Business Administration; Computer Science; Engineering. **Benefits:** 401(k); Dental Insurance; Disability Coverage; Life Insurance; Medical Insurance; Profit Sharing; Tuition Assistance. **Corporate headquarters location:** This Location. **Other U.S. locations:** NC; NV.

IVEX PACKAGING CORPORATION
100 Tri-State Drive, Suite 200, Lincolnshire IL 60069. 847/945-9100. **Contact:** Human Resources. **World Wide Web address:** http://www. ivexpackaging.com. **Description:** Manufactures paper and plastic packaging products including dessert trays, containers, and toilet tissue overwraps. **Corporate headquarters location:** This Location.

JONES BLAIR COMPANY
P.O. Box 35286, Dallas TX 75235. 214/353-1661. **Contact:** Personnel. **Description:** A manufacturer of paints, resins, elastomers, and powder coatings. **Common positions include:** Chemical Engineer; Chemist; Industrial Engineer; Industrial Production Manager; Management Trainee; Operations/ Production Manager. **Educational backgrounds include:** Chemistry; Engineering. **Benefits:** 401(k); Disability Coverage; Employee Discounts; Life Insurance; Medical Insurance; Tuition Assistance. **Corporate headquarters location:** This Location. **Other U.S. locations:** Chattanooga TN. **Listed on:** Privately held.

JONES CHEMICALS INC.
P.O. Box 115, Caledonia NY 14423. 716/768-6281. **Contact:** Human Resources. **Description:** Produces chemicals used for water purification applications. **Corporate headquarters location:** This Location.

KAMTECH PLASTICS CO.
P.O. Box 572, Montpelier VT 05601. 802/223-5012. **Fax:** 802/223-6145. **Contact:** Human Resources. **Description:** Manufactures custom injection molds and thermoplastic engineering resins. **NOTE:** Second and third shifts are offered. **Corporate headquarters location:** This Location. **Annual sales/revenues:** Less than $5 million.

KELLY-MOORE PAINT COMPANY
1075 Commercial Street, San Carlos CA 94070. 650/595-1654. **Contact:** Human Resources. **Description:** Manufactures and markets a wide variety of interior and exterior paints. **Corporate headquarters location:** This Location.

KELLY-SPRINGFIELD TIRE COMPANY
12501 Willowbrook Road SE, Cumberland MD 21502-2599. 301/777-6000. **Contact:** Human Resources. **World Wide Web address:** http://www. kelly-springfield.com. **Description:** A manufacturer of automobile tires and inner tubes. **Corporate headquarters location:** This Location. **International locations:** Worldwide. **Parent company:** Goodyear Tire & Rubber Company's principal business is the development, manufacture, distribution, marketing, and sale of tires for markets worldwide. Goodyear also manufactures and sells a broad range of rubber products and rubber-related chemicals for various industrial and consumer markets and also provides auto repair services. **Listed on:** New York Stock Exchange. **Other U.S. locations:**
• 3769 U.S. Route 20 East, Freeport IL 61032-9653. 815/235-4185.

KERR-McGEE CORPORATION
P.O. Box 368, Savannah GA 31402. 912/652-1000. **Contact:** Human Resources. **World Wide Web address:** http://www.kerr-mcgee.com. **Description:** This location manufactures industrial pigments including titanium dioxide, as part of the chemical products segment of the diversified multi-national organization.

KLEEN-BRITE CHEMICAL COMPANY
P.O. Box 20408, Rochester NY 14602. 716/637-0630. **Fax:** 716/637-0960. **Contact:** Human Resources Director. **Description:** A manufacturer of household cleaning products including laundry detergent, dish detergent, bleach, ammonia, and fabric softener. **Common positions include:** Administrative Assistant; Chemical Engineer; Chemist; Computer Operator; Electrician; Graphic Designer; Industrial Production Manager; Manufacturing Engineer; Mechanical Engineer; Sales Representative. **Benefits:** 401(k); Dental Insurance; Disability Coverage; Employee Discounts; Job Sharing; Life Insurance; Medical Insurance; Pension Plan; Profit Sharing; Tuition Assistance. **Corporate headquarters location:** This Location. **Listed on:** Privately held.

KOHL & MADDEN PRINTING INK CORP.
222 Bridge Plaza South, Suite 701, Fort Lee NJ 07024. 201/886-1203. **Contact:** Human Resources. **World Wide Web address:** http://www. kohlmadden.com. **Description:** Produces and markets printing inks, compounds, and varnishes. **Common positions include:** Clinical Lab Technician; Services Sales Rep. **Educational backgrounds include:** Chemistry; Marketing. **Benefits:** 401(k); Dental Insurance; Disability Coverage; Life Insurance; Medical Insurance; Pension Plan; Tuition Assistance. **Corporate headquarters location:** This Location. **Parent company:** Sun Chemical Corporation. **Operations at this facility include:** Administration; Divisional Headquarters; Sales. **Listed on:** Privately held.

KOLENE CORPORATION
12890 Westwood Avenue, Detroit MI 48223. 313/273-9220. **Contact:** Human Resources. **World Wide Web address:** http://www.kolene.com. **Description:** Engaged in the sale of metal cleaning chemicals and related equipment. **Corporate headquarters location:** This Location.

LEARONAL INC.
272 Buffalo Avenue, Freeport NY 11520. 516/868-8800. **Fax:** 516/868-8824. **Contact:** Joan Rappa, Human Resources. **World Wide Web address:** http://www.learonal.com. **Description:** Develops and markets specialty chemicals to the printed circuit, electronics, and metal finishing industries. **Corporate headquarters location:** This Location.

LETICA CORPORATION
P.O. Box 5005, Rochester MI 48308. 248/652-0557. **Contact:** Director of Personnel. **Description:** Manufactures plastic and paper packaging materials. **Common positions include:** Accountant/Auditor; Buyer; Computer Programmer; Customer Service Rep.; Draftsperson; Electrician; Environmental Engineer; Human Resources Manager; Industrial Production Manager; Maintenance Supervisor; Management Trainee; Mechanical Engineer; Plant Manager; Public Relations Specialist; Purchasing Agent/Manager; Quality Control Supervisor; Systems Analyst. **Educational backgrounds include:** Business Administration; Engineering; Marketing. **Benefits:** 401(k); Life Insurance; Medical Insurance; Profit Sharing. **Corporate headquarters location:** This Location. **Other U.S. locations:** Nationwide.

LIQUI-BOX CORPORATION
P.O. Box 494, Worthington OH 43085. 614/888-9280. **Physical address:** 6950 Worthington-Galena Road, Columbus OH. **Contact:** Human Resources. **World Wide Web address:** http://www.liquibox.com. **Description:** Manufactures plastic containers used in the packaging of liquids. **Corporate headquarters location:** This Location.

LOCTITE CORPORATION
1001 Trout Brook Crossing, Rocky Hill CT 06067. 860/571-5100. **Contact:** Human Resources. **World Wide Web address:** http://www.loctite.com. **Description:** Loctite manufactures and markets a broad range of sealants, adhesives, and coatings. **Corporate headquarters location:** This Location. **International locations:** Worldwide. **CEO:** Heinrich Grun.

LUBRICATION ENGINEERS INC.
P.O. Box 7128, Fort Worth TX 76111. 817/834-6321. **Physical address:** 3851 Airport Freeway, Fort Worth TX 76111. **Contact:** Personnel Director. **Description:** Produces a variety of industrial lubricants. **Corporate headquarters location:** This Location.

LUBRIZOL CORPORATION
29400 Lakeland Boulevard, Wickliffe OH 44092. 440/943-4200. **Contact:** Human Resources. **World Wide Web address:** http://www.lubrizol.com. **Description:** A diversified specialty chemical company engaged in chemical, mechanical, and genetic research to develop products for the world markets in transportation, industry, and agriculture. **Common positions include:** Accountant/Auditor; Attorney; Buyer; Chemical Engineer; Chemist; Computer Programmer; Financial Analyst; Mechanical Engineer; Purchasing Agent/Manager; Systems Analyst. **Educational backgrounds include:** Chemistry; Engineering. **Benefits:** Dental Insurance; Disability Coverage; Employee Discounts; Life Insurance; Medical Insurance; Pension Plan; Profit Sharing; Tuition Assistance. **Corporate headquarters location:** This Location.

LYONDELL PETROCHEMICAL COMPANY EQUISTAR CHEMICALS, LP
P.O. Box 3646, Houston TX 77253-3646. 713/652-7200. **Contact:** Human Resources Manager. **World Wide Web address:** http://www.lyondell.com. **Description:** This location is one of the world's leading producers of propylene oxide, propylene glycol, and styrene monomer. Overall, the company specializes in the production of propylene derivatives, olefins, and refining chemicals. Equistar Chemicals, LP (also at this location) produces ethylene, propylene, and polyethelene as well as color compounds, resins, and fine powders. **Corporate headquarters location:** This Location. **Subsidiaries include:** Lyondell Methanol Company, LP; Lyondell-Citgo Refining Company, Ltd. **Listed on:** New York Stock Exchange.

MACDERMID INCORPORATED
245 Freight Street, Waterbury CT 06702. 203/575-5700. **Contact:** Human Resources Manager. **World Wide Web address:** http://www.macdermid.com. **Description:** Manufactures specialty chemicals for metal finishing. Founded in 1922. **Corporate headquarters location:** This Location. **Listed on:** New York Stock Exchange. **Stock exchange symbol:** MRD.

MACK MOLDING COMPANY
Warm Brook Road, P.O. Box 127, Arlington VT 05250. 802/375-2511. **Contact:** Leslie Perra, Manager of Human Resources. **World Wide Web address:** http://www.mack.com. **Description:** Mack Molding Company is a custom molder and manufacturer of injection-molding plastic products and assemblies including components and housing for computers, and packaging for razors and other consumer products. **Common positions include:** Engineer; General Manager; Industrial Production Manager; Operations/Production Manager; Quality Control Supervisor. **Educational backgrounds include:** Business Administration; Engineering. **Benefits:** 401(k); Dental Insurance; Disability Coverage; Life Insurance; Medical Insurance; Pension Plan; Tuition Assistance. **Corporate headquarters location:** This Location. **Other U.S. locations:** Chelmsford MA; Statesville NC; Inman SC; Cavendish VT; Pownal VT. **Listed on:** Privately held.

MASTER BUILDERS TECHNOLOGIES
23700 Chagrin Boulevard, Beachwood OH 44122. 216/831-5500. **Contact:** Human Resources Manager. **World Wide Web address:** http://www.masterbuilders.com. **Description:** Produces and sells concrete chemical additives, grouts, adhesives, curing and joint compounds, and decorative and protective coatings and toppings. **Corporate headquarters location:** This Location. **Parent company:** Sandoz Ltd.

MATTHEWS PAINT COMPANY
8201 100th Street, Pleasant Prairie WI 53158. 262/947-0700. **Contact:** Personnel. **Description:** A manufacturer of paints. This location manufactures base colors with suppliers making up custom colors. **Corporate headquarters location:** This Location.

McKECHNIE PLASTIC COMPONENTS
7309 West 27th Street, St. Louis Park MN 55426. 612/929-3312. **Fax:** 612/929-8404. **Contact:** Human Resources Department. **World Wide Web address:** http://www.mckechnie.com. **Description:** Manufactures injection-molded plastics. **Common positions include:** Accountant/Auditor; Biomedical Engineer; Blue-Collar Worker Supervisor; Buyer; Customer Service Manager; Customer Service Rep. Designer; Human Resources Manager; Industrial Engineer; Mechanical Engineer; Meteorologist; Operations/Production Manager; Quality Control Supervisor; Sales Representative. **Benefits:** 401(k); Dental Insurance; Disability Coverage; Life Insurance; Medical Insurance; Tuition Assistance. **Corporate headquarters location:** This Location.

McNEEL INTERNATIONAL CORPORATION
5401 West Kennedy Boulevard, Tampa FL 33609.
813/286-8680. **Contact:** Personnel. **Description:**
Manufactures rubber and plastic products.
Corporate headquarters location: This Location.
International locations: Worldwide.

METOKOTE CORPORATION
1340 Neubrecht Road, Lima OH 45801. 419/227-
1100. **Fax:** 419/222-0946. **Contact:** Personnel
Director. **World Wide Web address:** http://www.
metokote.com. **Description:** Provides a full line of
coating services including electrocoating, powder
coating, and liquid paint. Metokote supplies coating
solutions to the agriculture, automotive, computer,
industrial equipment, and recreational markets.
Corporate headquarters location: This Location.

MILLENNIUM CHEMICALS, INC.
230 Half Mile Road, Red Bank NJ 07701. 732/933-
5000. **Contact:** Human Resources. **Description:**
Produces a range of chemical products including
detergents and fragrances. **Corporate headquarters
location:** This Location. **Other U.S. locations:**
Hunt Valley MD. **Subsidiaries include:** Millennium
Petrochemicals Inc.

MILLENNIUM INORGANIC CHEMICALS
200 International Circle, Suite 5000, Hunt Valley
MD 21030. 410/229-4400. **Fax:** 410/229-4466.
Contact: Human Resources. **World Wide Web
address:** http://www.mic-global.com. **Description:**
This location produces specialized titanium dioxide
pigments for industrial and related uses. Overall,
Millennium Inorganinc Chemicals manufactures
paints, coatings, resins, and lacquers. **Corporate
headquarters location:** This Location. **Other U.S.
locations:** Baltimore MD; Marsh MD; Ashtabula
OH.

MINNESOTA RUBBER
3630 Wooddale Avenue, St. Louis Park MN 55416.
612/927-1400. **Contact:** John Camp, Director of
Human Resources. **World Wide Web address:**
http://www.mnrubber.com. **Description:** Produces
precision-molded rubber and plastic parts. **Common
positions include:** Accountant/Auditor; Advertising
Clerk; Blue-Collar Worker Supervisor; Chemist;
Computer Programmer; Credit Manager; Customer
Service Representative; Department Manager;
Draftsperson; General Manager; Human Resources
Manager; Industrial Engineer; Manufacturer's/
Wholesaler's Sales Rep.; Mechanical Engineer;
Operations/Production Manager; Purchasing
Agent/Manager; Quality Control Supervisor;
Systems Analyst. **Benefits:** Dental Insurance;
Disability Coverage; Life Insurance; Medical
Insurance; Profit Sharing; Savings Plan; Tuition
Assistance. **Corporate headquarters location:**
This Location. **Parent company:** Quadion
Corporation.

MISSISSIPPI CHEMICAL CORPORATION
P.O. Box 388, Yazoo City MS 39194. 662/746-
4131. **Fax:** 662/751-2926. **Contact:** Jim Golden,
Human Resources. **World Wide Web address:**
http://www.misschem.com. **Description:** This
location houses administrative offices and also
produces nitrogen fertilizer. Overall, Mississippi
Chemical Corporation produces and markets three
primary crop nutrients, which include diammonium
phosphate fertilizer, nitrogen fertilizer, and potash
fertilizer. **Corporate headquarters location:** This
Location. **Subsidiaries include:** Mississippi
Phosphates Corporation (Pascagoula MS) produces
diammonium phosphate fertilizer. Mississippi
Potash, Inc. (Carlsbad NM) produces potash
fertilizer at its mines and refinery. Triad Nitrogen,
Inc. (Donaldsonville LA) produces nitrogen

fertilizer. **Listed on:** New York Stock Exchange.
Stock exchange symbol: GRO. **President/CEO:**
Charles O. Dunn.

MOLDED FIBER GLASS COMPANY
P.O. Box 675, Ashtabula OH 44005-0675. 440/997-
5851. **Physical address:** 4301 Benefit Avenue,
Ashtabula OH. **Contact:** Personnel. **World Wide
Web address:** http://www.moldedfiberglass.com.
Description: Manufactures custom molded
fiberglass and reinforced plastic products. **Common
positions include:** Accountant/Auditor; Blue-Collar
Worker Supervisor; Buyer; Chemical Engineer;
Chemist; Computer Programmer; Department
Manager; Draftsperson; Human Resources Manager;
Industrial Production Manager; Management
Trainee; Manufacturer's/Wholesaler's Sales Rep.;
Mechanical Engineer; Operations/Production
Manager; Purchasing Agent/Manager; Quality
Control Supervisor. **Educational backgrounds
include:** Accounting; Business Administration;
Chemistry; Engineering; Marketing. **Benefits:**
Disability Coverage; Life Insurance; Medical
Insurance; Pension Plan; Profit Sharing; Tuition
Assistance. **Corporate headquarters location:**
This Location.

NCH CORPORATION
2727 Chemsearch Boulevard, Irving TX 75062.
Toll-free phone: 800/527-9919. **Fax:** 972/438-
0707. **Recorded jobline:** 972/721-6116. **Contact:**
Human Resources. **World Wide Web address:**
http://www.nch.com. **Description:** Manufactures
and supplies specialty chemicals, water treatment
products, fasteners, welding supplies, plumbing and
electronic parts, and safety supplies to a worldwide
customer base. **NOTE:** Entry-level positions and
part-time jobs are offered. **Common positions
include:** Account Rep.; Accountant; Administrative
Assistant; Advertising Clerk; Applications
Engineer; Assistant Manager; Attorney; Biochemist;
Blue-Collar Worker Supervisor; Chemist; Clerical
Supervisor; Clinical Lab Technician; Computer
Engineer; Computer Programmer; Computer
Support Credit Manager; Customer Service Rep.;
Database Administrator; Desktop Publishing
Specialist; Draftsperson; Editorial Assistant;
Electrician; Environmental Engineer; General
Manager; Graphic Artist; Graphic Designer; Human
Resources Manager; Industrial Production Manager;
Intellectual Property Lawyer; Internet Services
Manager; Management Trainee; Market Research
Analyst; Marketing Manager; Marketing Specialist;
MIS Specialist; Multimedia Designer; Network/
Systems Administrator; Operations Manager;
Paralegal; Production Manager; Purchasing
Agent/Manager; Quality Control Supervisor; Sales
Manager; Sales Rep.; Secretary; Technical Writer/
Editor; Telecommunications Manager; Typist/Word
Processor; Webmaster. **Educational backgrounds
include:** Accounting; Art/Design; Business
Administration; Chemistry; Communications;
Liberal Arts; Marketing. **Benefits:** 401(k); Adoption
Assistance; Credit Union; Dental Insurance;
Disability Coverage; Employee Discounts; Financial
Planning Assistance; Flexible Schedule; Job
Sharing; Life Insurance; Medical Insurance; Profit
Sharing; Public Transit Available; Telecommuting;
Tuition Assistance; Vacation Days (6 - 10). **Special
programs:** Internships; Training. **Corporate
headquarters location:** This Location. **Other U.S.
locations:** El Segundo CA; Atlanta GA; Chicago IL;
Paramus NJ; Seattle WA. **International locations:**
Asia; Australia; Europe; South America. **Listed on:**
New York Stock Exchange. **Stock exchange
symbol:** NCH. **Chairman/Executive Director:**
Lester Levy, Sr. **Annual sales/revenues:** More than
$100 million.

NEN LIFE SCIENCE PRODUCTS, INC.
549 Albany Street, Boston MA 02118; 617/482-9595. **Fax:** 617/338-9758. **Contact:** Staffing Manager. **World Wide Web address:** http://www. nenlifesci.com. **Description:** Provides radioactive, chemilluminescent and fluorescent labeling and detection products for life science and drug discovery. **Common positions include:** Biochemist; Biological Scientist; Chemist. **Educational backgrounds include:** Biology; Chemistry; Master of Arts; Ph.D. **Benefits:** 401(k); Dental Insurance; Disability Coverage; Flexible Schedule; Life Insurance; Medical Insurance; Pension Plan; Public Transit Available; Tuition Assistance. **Special programs:** Co-ops; Internships. **Corporate headquarters location:** This Location. **Other area locations:** Billerica MA; Westwood MA. **Parent company:** Genstar Capital Partners II. **Listed on:** New York Stock Exchange.

NL INDUSTRIES, INC.
P.O. Box 4272, Houston TX 77210. 281/423-3300. **Physical address:** 16825 Northchase, Suite 1200, Houston TX 77060. **Contact:** Human Resources. **Description:** Manufactures and markets titanium dioxide pigments and other specialty chemicals used in a wide variety of products including paints, plastics, inks, and paper. **Corporate headquarters location:** This Location. **International locations:** Worldwide. **Subsidiaries include:** Kronos, Inc.; Rheox, Inc. **Listed on:** New York Stock Exchange.

NACO INDUSTRIES, INC.
395 West 1400 North, Logan UT 84341. 435/753-8020. **Contact:** Human Resources. **Description:** Manufactures polyvinyl chloride products, primarily pipe fittings and valves. These products are distributed by wholesalers to the irrigation, construction, industrial, and utility industries. **Corporate headquarters location:** This Location. **Other U.S. locations:** Lodi CA; Garden City KS.

NALCO CHEMICAL COMPANY
One Nalco Center, Naperville IL 60563. 630/305-1000. **Contact:** Human Resources Department. **World Wide Web address:** http://www.nalco.com. **Description:** Engaged in the manufacture and sale of highly-specialized service chemicals used in water treatment, pollution control, energy conservation, oil production and refining, steel making, paper making, mining, and other industrial processes. Founded in 1928. **Common positions include:** Accountant/Auditor; Attorney; Ceramics Engineer; Chemical Engineer; Chemist; Computer Programmer; Customer Service Representative; Electrical/Electronics Engineer; Financial Analyst; Financial Manager; Librarian; Manufacturer's/Wholesaler's Sales Rep.; Materials Engineer; Mechanical Engineer; Metallurgical Engineer; Mining Engineer; Petroleum Engineer; Services Sales Representative; Systems Analyst; Technical Writer/Editor. **Educational backgrounds include:** Accounting; Chemistry; Computer Science; Engineering; Finance. **Benefits:** 401(k); Daycare Assistance; Dental Insurance; Disability Coverage; Life Insurance; Medical Insurance; Pension Plan; Profit Sharing; Savings Plan; Tuition Assistance. **Corporate headquarters location:** This Location. **Other U.S. locations:** Sugar Land TX. **Listed on:** New York Stock Exchange.

NAN YA PLASTICS CORPORATION, AMERICA
140 East Beulah Road, Lake City SC 29560-0939. 843/389-7800. **Fax:** 843/389-3559. **Contact:** Human Resources. **Description:** This location manufactures polyester fiber, chip, and filament. Overall, the company's products include PVC rigid film; PET sheet; PVC panel and pipe; electronic-related products (printed circuit boards, copper-clad laminates, copper foil, epoxy, BPA, and glass fiber and cloth); PP synthetic paper (a product similar in quality to wood pulp paper); and polyester fiber. Founded in 1990. **NOTE:** Entry-level positions are offered. **Common positions include:** Account Manager; Administrative Assistant; Chemical Engineer; Civil Engineer; Computer Engineer; Computer Support Technician; Electrical/Electronics Engineer; Electrician; Human Resources Manager; Industrial Engineer; Industrial Production Manager; Manufacturing Engineer; Mechanical Engineer; Operations Manager; Production Manager; Project Manager; Purchasing Agent/Manager; Quality Assurance Engineer; Quality Control Supervisor; Sales Representative; Systems Analyst. **Benefits:** 401(k); Bonus Award/Plan; Dental Insurance; Disability Coverage; Employee Discounts; Life Insurance; Medical Insurance; Pension Plan; Sick Days (1 - 5); Tuition Assistance; Vacation Days (6 - 10). **Corporate headquarters location:** Livingston NJ. **Other U.S. locations:** LA; TX. **International locations:** Worldwide. **Parent company:** Formosa Plastics Group. **Listed on:** Privately held. **CEO:** Y.C. Wang. **Facilities Manager:** J.S. Tseng. **Information Systems Manager:** Wei-Min Lee. **Purchasing Manager:** Alan Lu. **Sales Manager:** David Lin. **Annual sales/revenues:** More than $100 million.

NATIONAL SERVICE INDUSTRIES INC.
NATIONAL LINEN SERVICE
1420 Peachtree Street NE, Atlanta GA 30309. 404/853-1000. **Contact:** Human Resources. **Description:** A diversified manufacturing and service company with operations in five industries. The majority of revenue is made in lighting equipment, textile rental, and specialty chemicals, but the corporation also does business in insulation services and envelope manufacturing. National Linen Service (also at this location, 404/853-6000) is a linen rental supplier, serving the hospitality and health care industries. Products include napkins; table and bed linens; bath, bar, and shop towels; uniforms; specialized garments; sterilized products; restroom products; mats; and mops. **Corporate headquarters location:** This Location. **Subsidiaries include:** Lithonia Lighting manufactures lighting fixtures for the commercial, industrial, institutional, and residential construction and renovation markets. Products include fluorescent lighting fixtures, indoor and outdoor high-intensity discharge fixtures, recessed down lighting fixtures, sports lighting fixtures, architectural outdoor fixtures, emergency lighting fixtures, controls, and wiring systems. Zep Manufacturing Company, Selig Chemical Industries, and National Chemical are manufacturers of specialty chemicals for the automotive, diversified manufacturing, food, hospitality, and institutional markets. Products include specialty chemicals and equipment used in cleaning, sanitizing, polishing, degreasing, and water treatment. North Brothers Company fabricates, distributes, and installs insulation and other building products and related services for the construction, renovation, cold storage, manufactured housing, process manufacturing, power generation, and services sectors. Products and services include insulation products, accessories, and contracting services. Atlantic Envelope Company manufactures custom and standard envelopes and related office products. **Listed on:** New York Stock Exchange.

NATIONAL STARCH AND CHEMICAL COMPANY
10 Finderne Avenue, Bridgewater NJ 08807. 908/685-5000. **Toll-free phone:** 800/366-4031. **Fax:** 908/685-6956. **Contact:** Personnel. **E-mail address:** nstarch.jobs@nstarch.com. **World Wide**

Web address: http://www.nationalstarch.com.
Description: Manufactures industrial chemicals including adhesives, resins, starches, and specialty chemicals for the packaging, textile, paper, food, furniture, electronic materials, and automotive markets. **NOTE:** Entry-level positions are offered. **Common positions include:** Accountant; Biochemist; Chemical Engineer; Chemist; Customer Service Rep.; Food Scientist/Technologist; MIS Specialist. **Educational backgrounds include:** Accounting; Chemistry; Computer Science; Engineering. **Benefits:** 401(k); Dental Insurance; Disability Coverage; Life Insurance; Medical Insurance; Pension Plan; Profit Sharing; Tuition Assistance. **Special programs:** Co-ops; Internships. **Corporate headquarters location:** This Location. **Other U.S. locations:** Nationwide. **International locations:** Worldwide. **Parent company:** The ICI Group. **Listed on:** New York Stock Exchange. **Annual sales/revenues:** More than $100 million. N

NEPHI RUBBER PRODUCTS
255 West 1100 North, Nephi UT 84648. 435/623-1740. **Contact:** Human Resources Department. **Description:** Manufactures a variety of rubber and plastic fabricated products, primarily hoses. **Corporate headquarters location:** This Location.

NEPTCO, INC.
30 Hamlet Street, P.O. Box 2323, Pawtucket RI 02861. 401/722-5500. **Contact:** Human Resources Manager. **World Wide Web address:** http://www.neptco.com. **Description:** Designs, manufactures, and supplies laminated flexible products, composite materials, and outside plant products for use in a variety of applications. These materials include advanced polymeric coatings and laminates for films, foils, fibers, composites, papers, nonwovens, and custom-formulated adhesives. **Corporate headquarters location:** This Location.

NORTON PERFORMANCE PLASTICS CORP.
150 Dey Road, Wayne NJ 07470. 973/696-4700. **Contact:** Human Resources Director. **World Wide Web address:** http://www.nortonplastics.com. **Description:** Manufactures a wide range of plastic products and shapes including pipes, rods, sheet, tape, rectangular stock, insulated wire, and coaxial cable core; finished plastic products such as laboratory wire; and nylon products such as rods, tubes, slabs, and custom castings. **Common positions include:** Chemical Engineer; Customer Service Representative. **Benefits:** Employee Discounts; Life Insurance; Pension Plan; Savings Plan; Tuition Assistance. **Special programs:** Internships. **Corporate headquarters location:** This Location. **Other U.S. locations:** IL; NY; OH. **Parent company:** Norton Company (Worcester MA) produces abrasives, petroleum, mining products and services, engineering materials, and construction products.

OAKITE PRODUCTS, INC.
50 Valley Road, Berkeley Heights NJ 07922. 908/464-6900. **Contact:** Suzanne Watson, Recruiter. **World Wide Web address:** http://www.oakite.com. **Description:** Manufactures and markets specialty chemical products used primarily for industrial cleaning, metal conditioning, and surface preparation. **Common positions include:** Accountant; Chemist; Manufacturer's/Wholesaler's Sales Rep.; Marketing Specialist. **Educational backgrounds include:** Accounting; Business Administration; Chemistry; Marketing. **Benefits:** Dental Insurance; Disability Coverage; Life Insurance; Medical Insurance; Profit Sharing; Tuition Assistance. **Corporate headquarters location:** This Location. **Other U.S. locations:** Nationwide. **International locations:** Canada.

OCCIDENTAL CHEMICAL CORPORATION
P.O. Box 809050, Dallas TX 75380-9050. 972/404-3800. **Contact:** Staffing. **World Wide Web address:** http://www.oxychem.com. **Description:** Manufactures commodity and specialty chemicals. The company has approximately 25 manufacturing facilities nationwide. **NOTE:** The company does most of its hiring through Texas employment agencies and local colleges. **Common positions include:** Accountant; Chemical Engineer; Electrical/Electronics Engineer; Mechanical Engineer. **Educational backgrounds include:** Accounting; Engineering. **Benefits:** 401(k); Dental Insurance; Disability Coverage; Life Insurance; Medical Insurance; Pension Plan; Tuition Assistance. **Corporate headquarters location:** Los Angeles CA. **Other U.S. locations:** Nationwide. **Parent company:** Occidental Petroleum Corporation.

OLIN CORPORATION
501 Merritt Seven, Norwalk CT 06851. 203/750-3000. **Contact:** Human Resources. **World Wide Web address:** http://www.olin.com. **Description:** Manufactures copper alloys, ammunition, and chlorine and caustic soda. **Corporate headquarters location:** This Location. **International locations:** Worldwide. **Listed on:** New York Stock Exchange.

ONEIDA ROSTONE CORPORATION
P.O. Box 7497, Lafayette IN 47903. 765/474-2421. **Fax:** 765/474-8785. **Contact:** Human Resources Manager. **World Wide Web address:** http://www.oneidarostone.com. **Description:** A custom molder of thermoset plastic products for the automotive and electric industries. **Common positions include:** Accountant; Chemical Engineer; Customer Service Representative; Electrical/Electronics Engineer; Electrician; Environmental Engineer; Human Resources Manager; Industrial Production Manager; Operations/Production Manager; Purchasing Agent; Services Sales Rep.; Systems Analyst. **Educational backgrounds include:** Chemistry; Computer Science; Engineering. **Benefits:** 401(k); Dental Insurance; Disability Coverage; Employee Discounts; Life Insurance; Medical Insurance; Relocation Assistance; Savings Plan; Tuition Assistance. **Corporate headquarters location:** This Location. **Other U.S. locations:** Nationwide.

ORSCHELN INDUSTRIES
P.O. Box 280, Moberly MO 65270. 660/263-4377. **Fax:** 660/269-4530. **Contact:** Employment Manager. **World Wide Web address:** http://www.orscheln.com. **Description:** A manufacturer of mechanical and electromechanical automotive and industrial equipment components; sealants; and adhesives for the automotive and construction industries. Orscheln's divisions include manufacturing, retail, and property development. Retail operations include 89 stores in eight midwestern states. **NOTE:** Entry-level positions and second and third shifts are offered. **Common positions include:** Accountant/Auditor; Blue-Collar Worker Supervisor; Buyer; Chemical Engineer; Computer Programmer; Construction Contractor; Customer Service Representative; Design Engineer; Draftsperson; Electrician; Financial Analyst; Human Resources Manager; Industrial Production Manager; Management Trainee; Mechanical Engineer; Operations/Production Manager; Purchasing Agent/Manager; Quality Control Supervisor; Services Sales Representative; Software Engineer; Systems Analyst. **Educational backgrounds include:** Accounting; Business Administration; Computer Science; Engineering; Finance; Marketing. **Benefits:** 401(k); Casual Dress - Daily; Dental Insurance; Disability Coverage; Employee Discounts; Flexible Schedule; Life Insurance; Medical Insurance; Relocation Assistance; Tuition

Assistance. **Special programs:** Training. **Corporate headquarters location:** This Location. **International locations:** England. **Listed on:** Privately held. **Annual sales/revenues:** More than $100 million.

O'SULLIVAN CORPORATION
P.O. Box 3510, Winchester VA 22604. 540/667-6666. **Physical address:** 1944 Valley Avenue, Winchester VA. **Contact:** Human Resources. **Description:** Operates in two business segments: calendered and molded plastic products, which involves the manufacture of calendered plastics for the automotive and specialty plastics manufacturing industries; and lawn and garden consumer products. **Corporate headquarters location:** This Location.

PCS NITROGEN
3175 Lenox Park Boulevard, Suite 400, Memphis TN 38115. 901/758-5200. **Contact:** Human Resources. **Description:** An international producer and marketer of nitrogen fertilizers and chemicals used in agricultural and industrial applications. The company's principal products are ammonia, urea, ammonium nitrate, nitric acid, and nitrogen solutions. **Corporate headquarters location:** This Location. **Listed on:** New York Stock Exchange.

PPG INDUSTRIES, INC.
One PPG Place, Pittsburgh PA 15272. 412/434-3131. **Contact:** Human Resources. **World Wide Web address:** http://www.ppg.com. **Description:** A diversified global manufacturer, PPG Industries is a supplier of products for manufacturing, building, automotive, processing, and numerous other industries. The company also makes decorative and protective coatings, flat glass and fabricated glass **Corporate headquarters location:** This Location. **International locations:** Worldwide. **Listed on:** New York Stock Exchange.

PRC-DeSOTO
P.O. Box 1800, Glendale CA 91209. 818/240-2060. **Contact:** Employment Specialist. **Description:** Produces aerospace sealants and coatings; packaging application systems; and high performance sealants for insulating glass. **Common positions include:** Chemist; Manufacturer's/Wholesaler's Sales Rep. **Educational backgrounds include:** Chemistry. **Benefits:** Dental Insurance; Disability Coverage; Life Insurance; Medical Insurance; Pension Plan; Profit Sharing; Tuition Assistance. **Corporate headquarters location:** This Location. **Other U.S. locations:** Burbank CA.

PACTIV CORPORATION
14505 Proctor Avenue, City of Industry CA 91746. 626/968-3801. **Contact:** Human Resources. **Description:** Manufactures proprietary products made entirely or partially of plastics. Major product lines include food packaging, apparel hangers, internally-illuminated signs, recreational vehicle components, and swimming pool products. **Corporate headquarters location:** This Location.

PARK-OHIO INDUSTRIES, INC.
23000 Euclid Avenue, Cleveland OH 44117. 216/692-7200. **Contact:** Human Resources. **Description:** Manufactures plastic containers, molded plastic leisure products, forged and machined products, aluminum permanent mold castings, induction heating systems, and industrial rubber products. The company's transportation segment includes forged and machined products, induction heating systems, aluminum permanent mold castings, and industrial rubber products. **Corporate headquarters location:** This Location. **Other area locations:** Wellington OH. **Subsidiaries include:** Bennett Industries

manufactures plastic pails for packages of food, paint, and building materials; Castle Rubber Company manufactures rubber products including roll coverings, tank linings, and pump parts; General Aluminum Manufacturing Company manufactures aluminum mold castings for the transportation industry; Kay Home Products manufactures barbecue grills, lawn spreaders, and patio tables; Tocco Inc. manufactures heating systems for heat treating, surface hardening, and forging.

PHILLIPS PLASTICS CORPORATION
7 Longlake Drive, Phillips WI 54555. 715/339-3005. **Contact:** Human Resources. **Description:** Engaged in the custom injection molding of plastics. The company's services include high engineering and tooling. **Common positions include:** Blue-Collar Worker Supervisor; Department Manager; General Manager; Human Resources Manager; Industrial Engineer; Management Analyst/Consultant; Manufacturer's/Wholesaler's Sales Rep.; Mechanical Engineer; Operations/Production Manager; Purchasing Agent/Manager; Quality Control Supervisor; Systems Analyst. **Educational backgrounds include:** Engineering. **Benefits:** 401(k); Bonus Award/Plan; Disability Coverage; Life Insurance; Medical Insurance; Pension Plan; Profit Sharing; Stock Option; Tuition Assistance. **Corporate headquarters location:** This Location. **Other U.S. locations:** Minneapolis MN.

PLASTECH CORPORATION
P.O. Box 7, Rush City MN 55069. 320/358-4771. **Physical address:** 920 Field Avenue South, Rush City MN 55069. **Fax:** 320/407-5612. **Contact:** Personnel Manager. **Description:** A manufacturer of assorted plastic products including injection moldings. **Common positions include:** Blue-Collar Worker Supervisor; Computer Programmer; Industrial Engineer; Mechanical Engineer. **Educational backgrounds include:** Engineering. **Special programs:** Internships. **Corporate headquarters location:** This Location. **Other U.S. locations:** Albuquerque NM.

PLASTIC MOLDINGS CORPORATION
2181 Grand Avenue, Cincinnati OH 45214-1593. 513/921-5040. **Contact:** Personnel. **Description:** Manufactures precision-molded plastic parts used in a wide variety of applications including electrical and automotive parts. **Corporate headquarters location:** This Location.

PLASTOMER CORPORATION
37819 Schoolcraft Road, Livonia MI 48150. 734/464-0700. **Contact:** Human Resources Director. **World Wide Web address:** http://www.plastomer.com. **Description:** Manufactures and markets polyurethane foam. **Benefits:** Dental Insurance; Disability Coverage; Life Insurance; Medical Insurance; Pension Plan; Profit Sharing; Savings Plan; Tuition Assistance; Vision Insurance. **Corporate headquarters location:** This Location.

POLY-SEAL CORPORATION
1810 Portal Street, Baltimore MD 21224. 410/633-1990. **Fax:** 410/633-6311. **Contact:** Human Resources. **World Wide Web address:** http://www.poly-seal.com. **Description:** Manufactures plastic caps for pharmaceutical and personal health care product bottles including lotion and shampoo bottles. **Common positions include:** Accountant/Auditor; Administrator; Chemical Engineer; Computer Programmer; Customer Service Rep.; Department Manager; Draftsperson; Human Resources Manager; Manufacturer's/Wholesaler's Sales Rep.; Mechanical Engineer; Operations/Production Manager; Purchasing Agent/Manager;

Quality Control Supervisor; Systems Analyst. **Educational backgrounds include:** Accounting; Business Administration; Computer Science; Engineering; Marketing. **Benefits:** 401(k); Dental Insurance; Disability Coverage; Life Insurance; Medical Insurance; Pension Plan; Public Transit Available; Tuition Assistance. **Corporate headquarters location:** This Location. O

PRAXAIR TECHNOLOGY, INC.
39 Old Ridgebury Road, Danbury CT 06810. 203/837-2000. **Contact:** Human Resources. **World Wide Web address:** http://www.praxair.com. **Description:** Praxair produces gases and gas production equipment for customers in the aerospace, chemicals, electronics, food processing, health care, glass, metal fabrication, petroleum, primary metals, pulp, and as paper industries. Praxair also coats customer-supplied parts and equipment with metallic and ceramic coatings for the textile, aircraft engine, paper, petrochemical, metals, and printing industries. **Corporate headquarters location:** This Location. **International locations:** Worldwide.

PRINTPACK INC.
P.O. Box 43687, Atlanta GA 30336. 404/691-5830. **Contact:** Human Resources. **Description:** Produces flexible packaging material for the snack, candy, meat, and cookie industries. **Common positions include:** Accountant/Auditor; Chemical Engineer; Computer Programmer; Customer Service Rep.; Electrical/Electronics Engineer; Financial Analyst; Human Resources Manager; Industrial Engineer; Management Trainee; Manufacturer's/Wholesaler's Sales Rep.; Mechanical Engineer; Operations/Production Manager; Quality Control Supervisor; Systems Analyst. **Educational backgrounds include:** Accounting; Business Administration; Chemistry; Computer Science; Engineering; Marketing. **Benefits:** Dental Insurance; Disability Coverage; Life Insurance; Medical Insurance; Pension Plan; Profit Sharing; Savings Plan; Tuition Assistance. **Corporate headquarters location:** This Location.

PURITAN CHURCHILL CHEMICAL COMPANY
1341 East Capital Circle, Marietta GA 30067. 404/875-7331. **Contact:** Human Resources. **Description:** Manufactures industrial specialty chemicals and institutional and commercial sanitary products. Puritan Churchill Chemical Company's products include soaps, disinfectants, floor finishes, insecticides, and industrial cleaners. **Common positions include:** Accountant/Auditor; Blue-Collar Worker Supervisor; Chemist; Manufacturer's/Wholesaler's Sales Rep. **Educational backgrounds include:** Accounting; Business Administration; Chemistry; Engineering. **Benefits:** Dental Insurance; Disability Coverage; Employee Discounts; Life Insurance; Medical Insurance; Pension Plan; Profit Sharing; Savings Plan. **Corporate headquarters location:** This Location. **Parent company:** Gibson Chemicals (Australia).

PUTNAM PRECISION MOLDING, INC.
11 Danco Road, Putnam CT 06260. 860/928-7911. **Contact:** Human Resources Manager. **Description:** Manufactures custom injection-molded plastics. **Common positions include:** Accountant/Auditor; Customer Service Rep.; Industrial Engineer; Operations/Production Manager; Purchasing Agent/Manager; Quality Control Supervisor; Sales Rep.. **Educational backgrounds include:** Accounting; Business Administration; Engineering; Marketing. **Benefits:** 401(k); Disability Coverage; Life Insurance; Medical Insurance. **Corporate headquarters location:** This Location. **Parent company:** Ensinger Industries.

QMR PLASTICS
434 Highland Drive, River Falls WI 54022. 715/426-4700. **Fax:** 715/426-5115. **Contact:** Human Resources. **World Wide Web address:** http://www.qmrplastics.com. **Description:** Engaged in plastic injection molding. **NOTE:** Entry-level positions, part-time jobs, and second and third shifts are offered. **Common positions include:** Accountant; Administrative Assistant; Controller; Customer Service Rep.; Design Engineer; Manufacturing Engineer; Mechanical Engineer; Network/Systems Administrator; Purchasing Agent/Manager; Sales Executive; Sales Manager; Sales Rep. **Educational backgrounds include:** Accounting; Business Administration; Computer Science; Engineering; Finance; Marketing; Mathematics. **Benefits:** 401(k); Casual Dress - Daily; Dental Insurance; Disability Coverage; Financial Planning Assistance; Flexible Schedule; Life Insurance; Medical Insurance; Profit Sharing; Telecommuting; Tuition Assistance. **Special programs:** Internships; Training. **OCorporate headquarters location:** Minneapolis MN. **Listed on:** Privately held. **Annual sales/revenues:** $11 - $20 million.

QUAKER CHEMICAL CORPORATION
Elm & Lee Streets, Conshohocken PA 19428. 610/832-4000. **Fax:** 610/832-8682. **Contact:** Personnel. **World Wide Web address:** http://www.quakerchem.com. **Description:** Manufactures rolling lubricants for steel and nonferrous metals; corrosion preventives; machining, grinding, and drawing compounds; hydraulic fluids; metal finishing compounds; and other products. The company also provides chemical management services to industrial customers. **Common positions include:** Chemical Engineer; Chemist; Customer Service Rep.; Industrial Engineer; Mechanical Engineer; Systems Analyst. **Educational backgrounds include:** Chemistry; Engineering; Marketing. **Benefits:** 401(k); Daycare Assistance; Dental Insurance; Disability Coverage; Fitness Program; Life Insurance; Medical Insurance; Pension Plan; Profit Sharing; Savings Plan; Tuition Assistance. **Corporate headquarters location:** This Location. **Other U.S. locations:** Savannah GA; Detroit MI.

RBP CHEMICAL CORPORATION
150 South 118th Street, P.O. Box 14069, Milwaukee WI 53214-0069. 414/258-0911. **Fax:** 414/258-7908. **Contact:** Human Resources. **Description:** Manufactures chemicals for the graphic arts and for the production of printed circuit boards. **Common positions include:** Accountant/; Blue-Collar Worker Supervisor; Chemist; Customer Service Rep.; Department Manager; Manufacturer's/Wholesaler's Sales Representative; Marketing Specialist; Quality Control Supervisor. **Educational backgrounds include:** Accounting; Business Administration; Chemistry; Liberal Arts; Marketing. **Benefits:** 401(k); Disability Coverage; Life Insurance; Medical Insurance; Stock Option; Tuition Assistance. **Special programs:** Internships. **Corporate headquarters location:** This Location.

RJF INTERNATIONAL CORPORATION
3875 Embassy Parkway, Fairlawn OH 44333. 330/668-7600. **Contact:** Human Resources. **World Wide Web address:** http://www.koroseal.com. **Description:** Manufactures and markets polymer-based products under the Koroseal name. **Common positions include:** Accountant/Auditor; Attorney; Chemical Engineer; Computer Programmer; Credit Clerk and Authorizer; Credit Manager; Customer Service Rep.; Department Manager; Employment Interviewer; Human Resources Manager; Industrial Engineer; Management Trainee; Manufacturer's/

Wholesaler's Sales Rep.; Mechanical Engineer; Order Clerk; Payroll Clerk; Receptionist; Secretary; Systems Analyst; Transportation/Traffic Specialist. **Educational backgrounds include:** Accounting; Business Administration; Chemistry; Computer Science; Engineering; Liberal Arts; Marketing. **Benefits:** Disability Coverage; Life Insurance; Medical Insurance; Pension Plan; Savings Plan. **Special programs:** Internships. **Corporate headquarters location:** This Location. **Other area locations:** Cincinnati OH; Columbus OH; Marietta OH. **Other U.S. locations:** Livonia MI.

RADVA CORPORATION
P.O. Drawer 2900, Radford VA 24143. 540/639-2458. **Contact:** Human Resources Director. **Description:** Manufactures and sells molded and fabricated expanded polystyrene foam products such as packaging materials and containers. Radva Corporation has also developed and patented housing construction panels utilizing expanded polystyrene foam reinforced with steel. In addition, the company builds and sells machinery used to manufacture the panels, and sells the licensing rights to market the panels. **Corporate headquarters location:** This Location. **Other U.S. locations:** Portsmouth VA. **Subsidiaries include:** Radva RU, Inc.; Thermastructure, Ltd.

BRAD RAGAN, INC.
629 Stallings Road, Matthews NC 28104. 704/821-5139. **Contact:** Human Resources. **Description:** A retail and wholesale provider of new and off-road tires. The company also provides on- and off-road truck tire retreading and repairs, as well as related on- and off-site services. **Corporate headquarters location:** This Location. **Listed on:** American Stock Exchange.

RED DEVIL, INC.
2400 Vauxhall Road, Union NJ 07083. 908/688-6900. **Fax:** 908/688-8872. **Contact:** Human Resources. **World Wide Web address:** http://www. reddevil.com. **Description:** Manufactures and distributes paint sundries; hand tools; and a full-line of caulks, sealants, and adhesives for home and professional use. **Corporate headquarters location:** This Location.

RED SPOT PAINT & VARNISH COMPANY
1107 East Louisiana Street, Evansville IN 47703-0418. 812/428-9100. **Contact:** Human Resources. **E-mail address:** redspot@redspot.com. **World Wide Web address:** http://www.redspot.com. **Description:** Manufactures household paints and varnish, automotive plastics, and related coatings. Founded in 1903. **NOTE:** Please send resumes to Human Resources, P.O. Box 418, Evansville IN 47703-0418. **Corporate headquarters location:** This Location. **President/CEO:** Charles D. Storms.

REHAU INC.
P.O. Box 1706, Leesburg VA 20177. 703/777-5255. **Fax:** 703/777-3053. **Contact:** Human Resources. **World Wide Web address:** http://www.rehau-na.com. **Description:** Processes polymers and compounds used in the manufacture of more than 40,000 products. Founded in 1948. **Corporate headquarters location:** This Location.

RHEOX, INC.
P.O. Box 700, Highstown NJ 08520. 609/443-2000. **Contact:** Human Resources Manager. **Description:** Manufactures a variety of chemicals. **Corporate headquarters location:** This Location.

ROGERS CORPORATION
One Technology Drive, P.O. Box 188, Rogers CT 06263. 860/774-9605. **Contact:** Human Resources.

World Wide Web address: http://www.rogers-corp.com. **Description:** Rogers Corporation develops and manufactures specialty polymer composite materials and components for the imaging, communications, computer and peripheral, consumer products, and transportation markets. Rogers Corporation is divided into segments according to the materials produced. The Poron Materials Unit manufactures urethane and silicone foam materials. The Elastomeric Components Unit manufactures foam and solid elastomeric components. The Microwave and Circuit Materials Divisions manufacture high-frequency laminates that are used to make circuits for communications applications and flexible circuit materials used for interconnections in computers and peripherals. The Composite Materials Division (also at this location) manufactures dielectric material for most of these microwave laminates. The Molding Materials Division produces moldable composites using polymer engineering and filler technology. Durel Corporation is a joint venture between Rogers and 3M, whose business focuses on electroluminescent lamps. **Benefits:** 401(k); Incentive Plan; Investment Plan; Life Insurance; Medical Insurance; Pension Plan; Savings Plan; Stock Option. **Corporate headquarters location:** This Location. **Listed on:** American Stock Exchange; Pacific Stock Exchange.

ROHM & HAAS COMPANY
100 Independence Mall West, Philadelphia PA 19106. 215/592-3000. **Contact:** Human Resources. **World Wide Web address:** http://www. rohmhaas.com. **Description:** A specialty chemicals company that produces polymers, resins, and monomers; plastics; industrial chemicals; and agricultural chemicals. Rohm & Haas Company is also engaged in nonchemical industries such as forestry products, carpet production, and biomedical testing. **Corporate headquarters location:** This Location. **Listed on:** New York Stock Exchange. **Stock exchange symbol:** ROH.

ROPAK CORPORATION
660 South State College Boulevard, Fullerton CA 92831. 714/870-9757. **Contact:** Human Resources. **Description:** Manufactures plastic containers for a wide range of uses. **Corporate headquarters location:** This Location.

RUST-OLEUM CORPORATION
11 Hawthorne Parkway, Vernon Hills IL 60061. 847/367-7700. **Contact:** Personnel Director. **World Wide Web address:** http://www.rustoleum.com. **Description:** Manufactures and markets rust-fighting, decorative, and roof repair paints to the commercial and industrial markets. **Corporate headquarters location:** This Location. **Other U.S. locations:** Evanston IL.

RUTGERS ORGANICS CORPORATION
201 Struble Road, State College PA 16801. 814/238-2424. **Fax:** 814/231-9268. **Contact:** Human Resources. **E-mail address:** humanres@ ruetgers-organics-corp.com. **World Wide Web address:** http://www.ruetgers-organics-corp.com. **Description:** A chemical manufacturer specializing in custom and intermediate chemicals such as hydrotapes, surfactants, and specialty sulfuric acids. **Common positions include:** Accountant; Administrative Assistant; Chemical Engineer; Chemist; Customer Service Rep.; Environmental Engineer; Manufacturing Engineer; Operations Manager; Production Manager; Purchasing Agent/ Manager; Secretary. **Educational backgrounds include:** Business Administration; Chemistry; Engineering. **Benefits:** 401(k); Dental Insurance; Disability Coverage; Life Insurance; Medical Insurance; Pension Plan; Public Transit Available;

Tuition Assistance. **Corporate headquarters location:** This Location. **Other U.S. locations:** Augusta GA; Cincinnati OH. **Parent company:** RUTGERS AG. **Listed on:** Privately held. **Annual sales/revenues:** $51 - $100 million.

W.H. SALISBURY & COMPANY
7520 North Long Avenue, Skokie IL 60077. 847/679-6700. **Fax:** 847/679-2401. **Contact:** Rosa Martinez, Human Resources Manager. **Description:** Manufactures a variety of insulating equipment that protects workers from electrical shock. The company also manufactures temporary grounding equipment, plastic covers, and insulated bypass jumpers. **Corporate headquarters location:** This Location.

SCHOLLE CORPORATION
200 West North Avenue, Northlake IL 60164. 708/562-7290. **Contact:** Human Resources. **Description:** A manufacturer and distributor of flexible film packaging for the food and beverage industries; specialty chemical solutions for coating and related industries; and bulk and packaged acid. Scholle also manufactures filling equipment for food and beverage packages. **Common positions include:** Accountant/Auditor; Buyer; Chemical Engineer; Chemist; Credit Clerk and Authorizer; Customer Service Rep.; Department Manager; Draftsperson; Financial Analyst; Human Resources Manager; Industrial Engineer; Management Trainee; Manufacturer's/Wholesaler's Sales Rep.; Mechanical Engineer; Operations Manager; Purchasing Agent/Manager; Quality Control Supervisor; Supervisor; Transportation/Traffic Specialist. **Educational backgrounds include:** Accounting; Business Administration; Chemistry; Engineering; Finance; Marketing. **Benefits:** 401(k); Dental Insurance; Disability Coverage; Employee Discounts; Life Insurance; Medical Insurance; Pension Plan; Tuition Assistance. **Corporate headquarters location:** This Location.

A. SCHULMAN, INC.
3550 West Market Street, Akron OH 44333. 330/666-3751. **Contact:** Human Resources. **World Wide Web address:** http://www.aschulman.com. **Description:** Supplies plastic compounds and resins to clients worldwide. The company's products include custom-engineered plastic compounds, color concentrates and additives, and rubber products for the automotive industry. **Corporate headquarters location:** This Location. **International locations:** Canada; Europe.

SECURITY PLASTICS INC.
14427 NW 60th Avenue, Miami Lakes FL 33014. 305/364-7700. **Contact:** Personnel. **Description:** Security Plastics manufactures plastic components for original equipment manufacturers. **Common positions include:** Accountant; Administrator; Computer Programmer; Credit Manager; Customer Service Rep.; Department Manager; Manufacturer's/Wholesaler's Sales Representative; Marketing Specialist; Mechanical Engineer; Operations/Production Manager; Plastics Engineer; Quality Control Supervisor. **Educational backgrounds include:** Business Administration; Computer Science; Engineering; Marketing; Mathematics. **Benefits:** Dental Insurance; Disability Coverage; Employee Discounts; Life Insurance; Medical Insurance; Pension Plan; Savings Plan; Tuition Assistance. **Corporate headquarters location:** This Location.

SELIG CHEMICAL INDUSTRIES
845 Selig Drive SW, Atlanta GA 30336. 404/691-9220. **Fax:** 404/699-7024. **Contact:** Human Resources. **World Wide Web address:** http://www. seligchem.com. **Description:** Manufactures and markets specialty cleaning, polishing, and sanitation preparations. **Common positions include:** Accountant; Administrative Assistant; Chemist; Customer Service Rep.; Sales Manager; Sales Representative; Secretary. **Benefits:** 401(k); Dental Insurance; Disability Coverage; Life Insurance; Medical Insurance; Profit Sharing. **Other U.S. locations:** Los Angeles CA; Miami FL; Louisville KY; New Orleans LA; Charlotte NC; Dallas TX. **Parent company:** National Service Industries (NSI). **Annual sales/revenues:** $21 - $50 million.

SETON COMPANY
849 Broadway, Newark NJ 07104. 973/485-4800. **Contact:** Human Resources. **Description:** Company operations are conducted primarily through two business segments. The Leather Division's operations include tanning, finishing, and distributing whole-hide cattle leathers for the automotive and furniture upholstery industries, cattle hide side leathers for footwear, handbag, and other markets, and cattle products for collagen, rawhide pet items, and other applications. The Chemicals and Coated Products Division is engaged in the manufacture and distribution of epoxy and urethane chemicals, specialty leather finishes, industrial and medical tapes, foams, films, and laminates. Other manufacturing facilities are located in Wilmington DE (epoxy, urethane chemicals, leather finishes); Toledo OH (cattle hide processing); Malvern PA (industrial coated products); and Saxton PA (cutting of finished leathers). **Corporate headquarters location:** This Location. **Subsidiaries include:** Radel Leather Manufacturing Company; Seton Leather Company.

THE SHERWIN-WILLIAMS COMPANY
101 Prospect Avenue NW, Cleveland OH 44115. 216/566-2000. **Contact:** Human Resources. **World Wide Web address:** http://www.sherwin.com. **Description:** Manufactures, sells, and distributes coatings and related products. Coatings are produced for original equipment manufacturers in various industries, as well as for the automotive aftermarket, the industrial maintenance market, and the traffic paint market. Sherwin-Williams labeled architectural and industrial coatings are sold through approximately 2,000 company-owned specialty paint and wallcovering stores. The Sherwin-Williams Company also manufactures paint under the Dutch Boy, Martin-Senour, Kem-Tone, Lucas, Acme, and Rogers brand names, as well as private labels, and sells it to independent dealers, mass merchandisers, and home improvement centers. **Corporate headquarters location:** This Location. **Other U.S. locations:** Nationwide. **Listed on:** New York Stock Exchange. **Annual sales/revenues:** More than $100 million.

SIGMA CHEMICAL COMPANY
P.O. Box 14508, St. Louis MO 63178. 314/771-5765. **Toll-free phone:** 800/521-8956. **Fax:** 314/535-3550. **Contact:** Human Resources. **World Wide Web address:** http://www.sigma-aldrich.com. **Description:** Manufactures and distributes a broad range of biochemicals, organic and inorganic chemicals, chromatography products, diagnostic reagents, and related products. **Common positions include:** Accountant/Auditor; Biological Scientist; Chemist; Computer Programmer; Credit Manager; Customer Service Rep.; Operations/Production Manager; Purchasing Agent/Manager; Quality Control Supervisor; Science Technologist; Services Sales Rep.; Systems Analyst. **Educational backgrounds include:** Biology; Chemistry; Computer Science. **Benefits:** 401(k); Dental Insurance; Disability Coverage; Life Insurance; Medical Insurance; Pension Plan; Savings Plan;

Tuition Assistance. **Special programs:** Internships. **Corporate headquarters location:** This Location. **Parent company:** Sigma Aldrich Corp.

SIKA CORPORATION
201 Polito Avenue, Lyndhurst NJ 07071. 201/933-8800. **Fax:** 201/933-6166. **Contact:** Human Resources. **Description:** Manufactures specialty chemicals including sealants and adhesives for the construction and transportation industries. Founded in 1937. **NOTE:** Second and third shifts are offered. **Common positions include:** Administrative Assistant; Chemist; Customer Service Rep.; Secretary; Services Sales Rep.; Systems Analyst. **Educational backgrounds include:** Accounting; Business Administration; Chemistry; Engineering; Finance; Marketing. **Benefits:** 401(k); Dental Insurance; Disability Coverage; Life Insurance; Medical Insurance; Tuition Assistance. **Corporate headquarters location:** This Location. **Parent company:** Sika Finanz AG.

THE STANDARD PRODUCTS COMPANY
2130 West 110th Street, Cleveland OH 44102. 216/281-8300. **Contact:** Human Resources. **World Wide Web address:** http://www.stand-prod.com. **Description:** Produces rubber and plastic components for the automotive, construction, and marine industries, as well as tread rubber and magnetic seals used on the doors of appliances. **Corporate headquarters location:** This Location.

STAR-GLO INDUSTRIES, INC.
2 Carlton Avenue, East Rutherford NJ 07073. 201/939-6162. **Contact:** Personnel. **Description:** Manufactures precision-molded rubber and plastic parts, often bonded to metal. Sales are made primarily to original equipment manufacturers in the business machine and computer, welding, food packaging equipment, chemical, and aerospace industries. **Corporate headquarters location:** This Location.

STATE INDUSTRIAL PRODUCTS
3100 Hamilton Avenue, Cleveland OH 44114. 216/861-7114. **Contact:** Human Resources. **E-mail address:** recruit@stateindustrial.com. **World Wide Web address:** http://www.stateindustrial.com. **Description:** Manufactures maintenance chemicals including degreasers and various institutional cleaning supplies. The company also packages and distributes industrial products. **Corporate headquarters location:** This Location.

STEPAN COMPANY
22 West Frontage Road, Northfield IL 60093. 847/446-7500. **Contact:** Director of Human Resources. **World Wide Web address:** http://www.stepan.com. **Description:** Develops, manufactures, and markets a wide range of chemical intermediates sold to producers of shampoos, toothpaste, household detergents, and other personal care items. Products are also used as ingredients in industrial detergents and cleansers, agricultural fertilizers, herbicides, and petroleum-based detergents. Stepan Company is a major producer of phthalic anhydride, an essential ingredient in plastics and polyesters, and also manufactures urethane foam systems and other specialty products. **Common positions include:** Accountant/Auditor; Chemical Engineer; Chemist; Customer Service Representative; Manufacturer's/Wholesaler's Sales Rep.; Systems Analyst. **Educational backgrounds include:** Accounting; Biology; Chemistry; Engineering; Finance; Liberal Arts. **Benefits:** Dental Insurance; Disability Coverage; Life Insurance; Medical Insurance; Pension Plan; Profit Sharing; Savings Plan; Stock Option; Tuition Assistance. **Corporate headquarters location:** This Location.

STERLING CHEMICALS, INC.
1200 Smith Street, Suite 1900, Houston TX 77002. 713/650-3700. **Contact:** Human Resources. **Description:** A chemical manufacturer engaged in the production of sodium chlorate, lactic acid, acetic acid, plasticizers, and sodium cyanide. **Corporate headquarters location:** This Location.

SYBRON CHEMICALS INC.
Birmingham Road, Birmingham NJ 08011. 609/893-1100. **Contact:** Stephen Adler, Director of Human Resources. **Description:** An international specialty chemical company that supplies chemicals and related technology to two markets: environmental products and services, primarily related to water and waste treatment; and textile processing. The company's chemical specialties are used to enhance the aesthetic and physical characteristics of textiles during textile preparation, printing, dyeing, and finishing. Sybron's environmental products soften and demineralize water, purify drinking water for safe consumption, and biologically break down waste matter into harmless components. **Corporate headquarters location:** This Location.

SYMONS CORPORATION
200 East Touhy Avenue, Des Plaines IL 60018. 847/298-3200. **Fax:** 847/635-9287. **Contact:** Human Resources Manager. **E-mail address:** info@symons.com. **World Wide Web address:** http://www.symons.com. **Description:** Develops and manufactures standard, custom, and fiberglass concrete-forming equipment. The company also manufactures chemical systems including acrylic sealers, bonding agents, construction grouts, and curing compounds. **Common positions include:** Accountant/Auditor; Advertising Clerk; Buyer; Civil Engineer; Computer Programmer; Credit Manager; Customer Service Rep.; Draftsperson; Human Resources Manager; Industrial Engineer; Manufacturer's/Wholesaler's Sales Rep.; Purchasing Agent/Manager; Quality Control Supervisor. **Educational backgrounds include:** Business Administration; Computer Science; Engineering; Marketing. **Benefits:** Dental Insurance; Disability Coverage; Employee Discounts; Life Insurance; Medical Insurance; Pension Plan; Savings Plan; Tuition Assistance. **Corporate headquarters location:** This Location.

SYNTHETECH, INC.
P.O. Box 646, Albany OR 97321. 541/967-6575. **Fax:** 541/967-9424. **Contact:** Human Resources. **E-mail address:** synthetech@proaxis.com. **World Wide Web address:** http://www.synthetech.com. **Description:** A manufacturer of fine chemicals. The company's primary products are specialty amino acids used by drug companies as raw materials to make peptide-based drugs. **Common positions include:** Accountant/Auditor; Administrator; Biological Scientist; Chemical Engineer; Chemist; Financial Analyst; General Manager; Operations/Production Manager. **Educational backgrounds include:** Accounting; Business Administration; Chemistry; Engineering; Finance; Marketing. **Benefits:** Dental Insurance; Disability Coverage; Life Insurance; Medical Insurance. **Corporate headquarters location:** This Location.

TECHMER PM, LLC
One Quality Circle, Clinton TN 37716. 865/457-6700. **Fax:** 865/457-3012. **Contact:** Human Resources. **World Wide Web address:** http://www.techmerpm.com. **Description:** A manufacturer of custom colorants and additives for plastics and fibers. **Common positions include:** Accountant; Administrative Assistant; Blue-Collar Worker Supervisor; Buyer; Chemical Engineer; Chemist;

Computer Programmer; Controller; Credit Manager; Customer Service Rep.; Database Manager; Design Engineer; Education Administrator; Electrician; Environmental Engineer; General Manager; Human Resources Manager; Industrial Engineer; Industrial Production Manager; Management Trainee; Manufacturing Engineer; Marketing Manager; Mechanical Engineer; MIS Specialist; Operations Manager; Production Manager; Project Manager; Purchasing Agent/Manager; Quality Control Supervisor; Sales Engineer; Sales Executive; Sales Manager; Sales Rep.; Secretary; Software Engineer. **Educational backgrounds include:** Accounting; Business Administration; Chemistry; Computer Science; Engineering; Finance; Marketing. **Benefits:** 401(k); Dental Insurance; Disability Coverage; Job Sharing; Life Insurance; Medical Insurance; Profit Sharing; Tuition Assistance. **Corporate headquarters location:** This Location. **Other U.S. locations:** Rancho Dominguez CA; Gainesville GA. **Listed on:** Privately held. **Annual sales/revenues:** $51 - $100 million.

TEKNOR APEX COMPANY
505 Central Avenue, Pawtucket RI 02861. 401/725-8000. **Contact:** Human Resources Manager. **World Wide Web address:** http://www.teknorapex.com. **Description:** Manufactures custom-compounded PVC (thermoplastic), color concentrates, pre-cured tread rubber, custom rubber compounds, garden hoses, and rubber mats. **Common positions include:** Accountant; Chemical Engineer; Chemist; Manufacturer's/Wholesaler's Sales Rep.; Mechanical Engineer. **Educational backgrounds include:** Accounting; Chemistry; Engineering; Marketing. **Benefits:** 401(k); Dental Insurance; Disability Coverage; Life Insurance; Medical Insurance; Pension Plan. **Corporate headquarters location:** This Location. **Other U.S. locations:** CA; MA; SC; TN. **Listed on:** Privately held.

TELEDYNE FLUID SYSTEMS
10367 Brecksville Road, Brecksville OH 44141. 440/526-5900. **Fax:** 440/838-7684. **Contact:** Director of Staffing. **E-mail address:** tfsjobs@teledynefluid.com. **World Wide Web address:** http://www.teledynefluid.com. **Description:** Builds nitrogen die systems for metal stamping and pressure relief valves. **Special programs:** Internships.

TERRA INDUSTRIES INC.
600 Fourth Street, Sioux City IA 51101. 712/277-1340. **Contact:** Human Resources. **World Wide Web address:** http://www.terraindustries.com. **Description:** Markets and produces nitrogen fertilizers and crop protection products such as herbicides, insecticides, plant growth regulators, and fungicides. Terra Industries also provides seeds and crop protection services to farmers. **Common positions include:** Accountant/Auditor; Buyer; Claim Representative; Computer Programmer; Credit Manager; Financial Analyst; Human Resources Manager; Public Relations Specialist. **Educational backgrounds include:** Accounting; Computer Science; Finance. **Benefits:** Dental Insurance; Disability Coverage; Life Insurance; Medical Insurance; Pension Plan; Savings Plan; Tuition Assistance. **Corporate headquarters location:** This Location.

TEXAS PETROCHEMICALS CORPORATION
8600 Park Place Boulevard, Houston TX 77017. 713/477-9211. **Contact:** Personnel Department. **Description:** Manufactures petroleum-based compounds and chemicals including ether and butane. **Corporate headquarters location:** This Location.

TORAY PLASTICS AMERICA
50 Belver Avenue, North Kingstown RI 02852. 401/294-4511. **Fax:** 401/294-2154. **Contact:** Human Resources Director. **World Wide Web address:** http://www.toray.com. **Description:** A leading developer of oriented polypropylene and polyester film products and technology. Products are used in food packaging and magnetic tape manufacturing. An affiliate of Toray Industries, Inc., Toray Plastics, is part of a corporate structure that encompasses textiles, biotechnology, medicine, specialty fibers, and office equipment, in addition to plastics and chemicals. More than 15 percent of Toray Industries' total work force is dedicated exclusively to research and development. **Corporate headquarters location:** This Location.

TREMCO INCORPORATED
3735 Green Road, Beachwood OH 44122. 216/292-5009. **Fax:** 216/292-5041. **Contact:** Personnel. **E-mail address:** jobs@tremcoinc.com. **World Wide Web address:** http://www.tremcosealants.com. **Description:** Manufactures specialty chemical products including sealants, coatings, and roofing materials used in new and remedial construction and OEM applications. **NOTE:** Entry-level positions are offered. **Common positions include:** Accountant; Administrative Assistant; Administrative Manager; Attorney; Budget Analyst; Chemist; Clinical Lab Technician; Controller; Credit Manager; Customer Service Rep.; Draftsperson; Financial Analyst; Marketing Manager; Marketing Specialist; Network/Systems Administrator; Operations Manager; Paralegal; Sales Executive; Sales Manager; Sales Rep.; Systems Analyst; Vice President. **Educational backgrounds include:** Accounting; Business Administration; Chemistry; Computer Science; Finance; Marketing; Novell; Software Development; Spreadsheets. **Benefits:** 401(k); Casual Dress - Fridays; Dental Insurance; Disability Coverage; Employee Discounts; Life Insurance; Medical Insurance; Pension Plan; Profit Sharing; Savings Plan; Tuition Assistance. **Special programs:** Internships; Co-ops. **Corporate headquarters location:** This Location. **Parent company:** RPM.

TREMONT CORPORATION
1999 Broadway, Suite 4300, Denver CO 80202. 303/296-5652. **Contact:** Personnel. **Description:** A holding company. **Corporate headquarters location:** This Location. **Subsidiaries include:** Titanium Metals Corporation (also at this location) is one of the world's largest integrated producers of high-quality titanium metal products for aerospace and industrial applications. NL Industries, Inc. is one of the world's largest suppliers of titanium dioxide pigments, which are used to impart whiteness, brightness, and opacity to paint, plastics, paper, fiber, and ceramics. NL is also a supplier of water-based and solvent-based rheological additives which are used to control the flow and leveling characteristics of paints, inks, lubricants, sealants, adhesives, and cosmetics.

TRINTEX CORPORATION
P.O. Box 309, Bowdon GA 30108. 770/258-5551. **Contact:** Personnel. **Description:** Manufactures and distributes a wide range of molded rubber and plastic products. **Common positions include:** Accountant; Blue-Collar Worker Supervisor; Chemist; Computer Programmer; Credit Manager; Department Manager; Electrical/Electronics Engineer; General Manager; Human Resources Manager; Industrial Engineer; Manufacturer's/Wholesaler's Sales Rep.; Mechanical Engineer; Operations/Production Manager; Quality Control Supervisor. **Educational backgrounds include:** Accounting; Business Administration; Chemistry;

Communications; Computer Science; Engineering; Finance; Liberal Arts; Marketing; Mathematics. **Corporate headquarters location:** This Location.

TURTLE WAX, INC.
5655 West 73rd Street, Chicago IL 60638. 708/563-3600. **Contact:** Human Resources Manager. **World Wide Web address:** http://www.turtlewax.com. **Description:** Manufactures Turtle Wax brand polishing products. **Corporate headquarters location:** This Location.

UFE INC.
P.O. Box 7, Stillwater MN 55082-0007. 651/351-4100. **Physical address:** 1850 South Greeley Street, Stillwater MN 55082. **Fax:** 651/351-4287. **Recorded jobline:** 651/351-4397. **Contact:** Human Resources. **Description:** A leader in the design and production of precision-molded plastic components. **NOTE:** Entry-level positions are offered. **Common positions include:** Computer Programmer; Systems Analyst. **Educational backgrounds include:** Business Administration; Computer Science; Engineering. **Benefits:** 401(k); Dental Insurance; Disability Coverage; Employee Discounts; Financial Planning Assistance; Life Insurance; Medical Insurance; Profit Sharing; Tuition Assistance. **Corporate headquarters location:** This Location. **Other U.S. locations:** El Paso TX; Dresser WI; River Falls WI.

U.S. AGRI-CHEMICALS CORPORATION
3225 State Road 630 West, Fort Meade FL 33841. 941/285-8121x231. **Fax:** 941/285-9654. **Contact:** Director of Human Resources. **Description:** Manufacturer and supplier of phosphate fertilizers for domestic and international wholesale markets. **Common positions include:** Accountant; Buyer; Chemist; Civil Engineer; Electrical/Electronics Engineer; Human Resources Manager; Mechanical Engineer; Operations/Production Manager; Public Relations Specialist; Purchasing Agent/Manager; Quality Control Supervisor; Systems Analyst; Transportation/Traffic Specialist. **Educational backgrounds include:** Accounting; Business Administration; Chemistry; Engineering. **Benefits:** 401(k); Dental Insurance; Disability Coverage; Employee Discounts; Life Insurance; Medical Insurance; Pension Plan; Tuition Assistance; Vision Insurance. **Corporate headquarters location:** This Location. **Parent company:** Sinochem.

U.S. PAINT CORPORATION
831 South 21st Street, St. Louis MO 63103. 314/621-0525. **Fax:** 314/621-0722. **Contact:** Personnel. **World Wide Web address:** http://www.uspaint.com. **Description:** Manufactures a wide variety of industrial finishes. **Common positions include:** Accountant/Auditor; Blue-Collar Worker Supervisor; Chemical Engineer; Chemist; Computer Programmer; Customer Service Representative; Economist; Manufacturer's/Wholesaler's Sales Rep. **Educational backgrounds include:** Accounting; Business Administration; Chemistry; Computer Science; Marketing. **Benefits:** 401(k); Dental Insurance; Disability Coverage; Life Insurance; Medical Insurance; Tuition Assistance. **Corporate headquarters location:** This Location.

USA DETERGENTS
1735 Jersey Avenue, North Brunswick NJ 08902. 732/828-1800. **Fax:** 732/828-0596. **Contact:** Human Resources. **Description:** Manufactures laundry detergents, household cleaners, and scented candles.

ULTRA TOOL & PLASTICS INC.
155 Pineview Drive, Amherst NY 14228. 716/691-6223. **Fax:** 716/691-7888. **Contact:** Director of Human Resources. **Description:** Manufactures injection-molded plastic parts. **Benefits:** 401(k); Medical Insurance; Tuition Assistance. **Corporate headquarters location:** This Location.

UNIFLEX, INC.
383 West John Street, Hicksville NY 11802. 516/932-2000. **Contact:** Human Resources. **Description:** Designs, manufactures, and markets a broad line of customized plastic packaging for sales and advertising promotions; clear bags for apparel and soft goods manufacturers; and specialized, recyclable bags and other products for use in hospitals, medical laboratories, and emergency care centers. Medical products include patented, disposable bags for the safe handling of specimens, and general purpose bags for personal belongings. Specialty advertising products include handle bags, drawstring bags, tote bags, and litter bags. The Haran Packaging Division manufactures and markets custom flexible plastic for the health care, food, financial, and other markets. Tamper-evident security bags are sold to banks, retailers, casino operations, stockbrokers, and courier firms which have security concerns for cash and other valuables. **Corporate headquarters location:** This Location. **Other U.S. locations:** Albuquerque NM; Westbury NY. **Subsidiaries include:** The Cycle Plastics produces and markets jumbo flexible loop handle bags, double drawstring bags, and reclosable, resealable, Trac-Loc bags. These products are sold to retailers, cosmetics firms, food packing companies, and medical/health care supply firms.

UNILEVER CORPORATION
390 Park Avenue, New York NY 10022. 212/688-6000. **Contact:** Personnel. **World Wide Web address:** http://www.unilever.com. **Description:** An international consumer products firm manufacturing a wide range of soaps, toiletries, and foods. **Corporate headquarters location:** This Location. **Parent company:** Unilever NV (Netherlands).

UNION CARBIDE CORPORATION
39 Old Ridgebury Road, Danbury CT 06817. **Contact:** Personnel. **World Wide Web address:** http://www.unioncarbide.com. **Description:** Union Carbide Corporation is a worldwide chemicals and polymers company operating through two business segments: Specialties and Intermediates, and Basic Chemicals and Polymers. Union Carbide is a leading North American supplier of specialty chemicals and polymers and services used in the personal care products, pharmaceuticals, automotive, wire and cable, oil and gas, and industrial lubricant industries. Union Carbide is also among the largest manufacturers of polyethylene and polypropylene. The company is one of the world's largest producers of ethylene oxide, and its derivative, ethylene glycol, used for polyester fiber, resin and film, automotive anti-freeze, and other products. **NOTE:** In August 1999, Dow Chemical Company and Union Carbide Corporation announced plans to merge. The merger was expected to be completed by the end of 2000, and the new company will operate under the name Dow Chemical Company. Please contact this location for more information. Only jobseekers applying for upper-level positions should contact the corporate headquarters. **Corporate headquarters location:** This Location. **Other U.S. locations:**
- P.O. Box 8004, South Charleston WV 25303.

VALENITE, INC.
P.O. Box 9636, Madison Heights MI 48071. 248/589-1000. **Contact:** Human Resources Director. **Description:** A manufacturer of pressed and extruded carbide products. **Common positions**

include: Accountant; Attorney; Ceramics Engineer; Computer Programmer; Credit Manager; Examiner; Financial Analyst; General Manager; Human Resources Manager; Industrial Engineer; Industrial Production Manager; Manufacturer's/Wholesaler's Sales Rep.; Mechanical Engineer; Metallurgical Engineer; Purchasing Agent/Manager; Quality Control Supervisor. **Educational backgrounds include:** Business Administration; Computer Science; Finance; Marketing; Science. **Benefits:** Dental Insurance; Disability Coverage; Life Insurance; Medical Insurance; Pension Plan; Savings Plan; Stock Option; Tuition Assistance. **Corporate headquarters location:** This Location. **Parent company:** Milacron Inc.

THE VALSPAR CORPORATION
P.O. Box 1461, Minneapolis MN 55440. 612/375-7740. **Physical address:** 1101 Third Street South, Minneapolis MN 55415. **Contact:** Human Resources. **World Wide Web address:** http://www.valspar.com. **Description:** Manufactures paints, varnishes, lacquers, and related products. **Common positions include:** Accountant; Administrator; Blue-Collar Worker Supervisor; Buyer; Chemical Engineer; Chemist; Computer Programmer; Credit Manager; Customer Service Rep.; Financial Analyst; Human Resources Manager; Industrial Production Manager; Manufacturer's/Wholesaler's Sales Rep.; Mechanical Engineer; Operations/Production Manager; Purchasing Agent/Manager; Systems Analyst. **Educational backgrounds include:** Accounting; Business Administration; Chemistry; Computer Science; Engineering; Finance; Marketing. **Benefits:** 401(k); Daycare Assistance; Dental Insurance; Disability Coverage; Employee Discounts; Life Insurance; Medical Insurance; Pension Plan; Profit Sharing; Savings Plan; Stock Option; Tuition Assistance. **Special programs:** Internships. **Corporate headquarters location:** This Location. **Other U.S. locations:** Nationwide.

VAN LEER CONTAINERS, INC.
4300 West 130th Street, Alsip IL 60803. 708/371-4777. **Fax:** 708/385-9175. **Contact:** Human Resources. **Description:** Manufactures plastic and fiber containers including intermediate bulk containers and closures. The consumer packaging business includes molded fiber products, flexible packaging such as metalized paper, strength films, folding cartons, tubs, and lids. **Common positions include:** Accountant; Administrative Manager; Blue-Collar Worker Supervisor; Budget Analyst; Buyer; Chemical Engineer; Chemist; Clerical Supervisor; Computer Programmer; Cost Estimator; Credit Manager; Customer Service Rep.; Designer; Electrical/Electronics Engineer; Electrician; General Manager; Industrial Engineer; Industrial Production Manager; Management Trainee; Manufacturer's/Wholesaler's Sales Rep.; Mechanical Engineer; Metallurgical Engineer; Operations/Production Manager; Services Sales Rep.; Systems Analyst; Transportation/Traffic Specialist. **Educational backgrounds include:** Accounting; Business Administration; Chemistry; Computer Science; Economics; Engineering; Finance; Liberal Arts; Marketing; Mathematics. **Benefits:** 401(k); Dental Insurance; Disability Coverage; EAP; Employee Discounts; Life Insurance; Medical Insurance; Pension Plan; Profit Sharing; Savings Plan; Tuition Assistance. **Corporate headquarters location:** This Location. **Other U.S. locations:** Atlanta GA; Bradley IL; Chicago IL; Florence KY; Canton MS; Greenville OH; Warminster PA. **Parent company:** Royal Packaging Industries Van Leer B.V. (the Netherlands). **Listed on:** Privately held. **Annual sales/revenues:** More than $100 million.

VIRATEC THIN FILMS, INC.
2150 Airport Drive, Faribault MN 55021. 507/334-0051. **Fax:** 507/334-0059. **Contact:** Human Resources. **World Wide Web address:** http://www.viratec.com. **Description:** Designs, develops, and manufactures high-performance, optical, thin film coatings for both glass and plastic. **Corporate headquarters location:** This Location. **Other U.S. locations:** San Diego CA. **Parent company:** Apogee Enterprises, Inc.

VISKASE CORPORATION
6855 West 65th Street, Chicago IL 60638. 708/496-4200. **Fax:** 708/496-4374. **Contact:** Human Resources. **World Wide Web address:** http://www.viskase.com. **Description:** Manufactures cellulose casings and flexible packaging used primarily in the food industry. **Common positions include:** Accountant/Auditor; Chemical Engineer; Computer Programmer; Credit Manager; Customer Service Representative; Draftsperson; Electrical/Electronics Engineer; Food Scientist/Technologist; Industrial Engineer; Mechanical Engineer; Operations/Production Manager; Quality Control Supervisor; Software Engineer; Systems Analyst. **Educational backgrounds include:** Accounting; Art/Design; Computer Science; Engineering; Marketing. **Benefits:** 401(k); Daycare Assistance; Dental Insurance; Disability Coverage; Life Insurance; Medical Insurance; Pension Plan; Profit Sharing; Savings Plan; Tuition Assistance. **Special programs:** Internships. **Corporate headquarters location:** This Location. **Parent company:** Envirodyne Industries.

VULCAN MATERIALS COMPANY
P.O. Box 385014, Birmingham AL 35238-5014. 205/298-3000. **Fax:** 205/298-2924. **Contact:** Human Resources. **Description:** A producer of construction aggregates and a manufacturer of chemicals. The company operates 129 permanent crushed stone plants, 13 sand and gravel plants, five slag plants, and four plants that produce other aggregates. Vulcan Materials' construction products are used primarily in the construction and maintenance of highways, roads, and other public works. The remainder of the company's products are used in the construction of housing and nonresidential, commercial, and industrial facilities, as well as railroad ballasts; and in nonconstruction uses such as agriculture and various industrial applications. Vulcan Chemicals Division's principal products are the coproducts chlorine and caustic soda. Primary markets for the chemicals include pulp and paper, energy, food, pharmaceuticals, chemicals processing, and fluorocarbons industries. **Common positions include:** Accountant/Auditor; Civil Engineer; Electrical/Electronics Engineer; Geologist/Geophysicist; Mechanical Engineer; Mining Engineer; Statistician; Structural Engineer. **Educational backgrounds include:** Accounting; Business Administration; Computer Science; Economics; Engineering; Geology; Marketing; Mathematics. **Benefits:** 401(k); Dental Insurance; Disability Coverage; Life Insurance; Medical Insurance; Pension Plan; Tuition Assistance. **Corporate headquarters location:** This Location. **Other U.S. locations:** Nationwide.

WD-40 COMPANY
P.O. Box 80607, San Diego CA 92138. 619/275-1400. **Physical address:** 1061 Cudahy Place, San Diego CA 92110. **Fax:** 619/275-5823. **Contact:** Human Resources. **World Wide Web address:** http://www.wd40.com. **Description:** Manufactures and markets WD-40, a petroleum-based industrial lubricant spray. WD-40 is also a rust preventative, a penetrant, and a moisture displacer. **Corporate headquarters location:** This Location.

WACKER SILICONES CORPORATION
3301 Sutton Road, Adrian MI 49221-9397.
517/264-8500. **Fax:** 517/264-8520. **Contact:** Personnel. **World Wide Web address:** http://www. wackersilicones.com. **Description:** A manufacturer of silicone which is used in a variety of applications including car waxes, paper coating, paints, textiles, sealants, and caulking. **Common positions include:** Accountant; Advertising Clerk; Buyer; Chemical Engineer; Chemist; Clinical Lab Technician; Computer Programmer; Customer Service Rep.; Draftsperson; Environmental Engineer; Financial Analyst; Human Resources Manager; Industrial Production Manager; Library Technician; Materials Engineer; Mechanical Engineer; Systems Analyst; Technical Writer/Editor. **Educational backgrounds include:** Accounting; Business Administration; Chemistry; Computer Science; Engineering; Finance; Marketing; Physics. **Benefits:** 401(k); Dental Insurance; Disability Coverage; Employee Discounts; Life Insurance; Medical Insurance; Pension Plan; Prescription Drugs; Profit Sharing; Service Award; Tuition Assistance. **Corporate headquarters location:** Germany. **Other U.S. locations:** CA; IA; SC. **Parent company:** Wacker Chemie.

WARNER-JENKINSON COMPANY
2526 Baldwin Avenue, St. Louis MO 63106. 314/658-7310. **Contact:** Personnel. **Description:** Manufacturers and distributors of colored dyes for the food, drug, and cosmetics industries. **NOTE:** Entry-level positions, part-time jobs, and second and third shifts are offered. **Common positions include:** Account Rep.; Chemical Engineer; Chemist; Customer Service Manager; Food Scientist/Technologist. **Educational backgrounds include:** AS400 Certification; Chemistry; Engineering. **Benefits:** 401(k); Dental Insurance; Disability Coverage; Flexible Schedule; Life Insurance; Medical Insurance; Pension Plan; Public Transit Available; Relocation Assistance; Savings Plan; Sick Days; Tuition Assistance; Vacation Days. **Special programs:** Co-ops; Summer Jobs. **Parent company:** Universal Foods Corporation.

WELLMARK INTERNATIONAL
12200 Denton Drive, Dallas TX 75234. 972/243-2321. **Contact:** Human Resources.**Description:** An international producer of a wide range of insecticide products including strips, flea and tick collars, and agricultural insecticides and dips. **Corporate headquarters location:** Bensonville IL. **Parent company:** Central Garden and Pet.

WINCUP
7980 West Buckeye Road, Phoenix AZ 85043. 623/936-1791. **Contact:** Human Resources. **World Wide Web address:** http://www.wincup.com. **Description:** Produces polystyrene foam cups, containers, lids, and glasses. **Corporate headquarters location:** This Location. **Parent company:** Dart & Kraft Inc. (Glenview IL) is an international food products and food packaging firm.

ZEP MANUFACTURING COMPANY
P.O. Box 2015, Atlanta GA 30301. 404/352-1680. **Physical address:** 1310 Seaboard Industrial Boulevard NW, Atlanta GA 30318. **Fax:** 404/630-7764. **Contact:** Personnel. **World Wide Web address:** http://www.zepmfg.com. **Description:** Manufactures and distributes industrial cleaning products. **NOTE:** Entry-level positions are offered. **Common positions include:** Accountant; Administrative Assistant; Applications Engineer; Branch Manager; Chemical Engineer; Chemist; Clinical Lab Technician; Computer Programmer; Controller; Customer Service Rep.; Environmental Engineer; Financial Analyst; Food Scientist/ Technologist; Graphic Artist; Human Resources Manager; Industrial Engineer; Industrial Production Manager; Management Trainee; Manufacturing Engineer; Marketing Specialist; MIS Specialist; Operations Manager; Quality Control Supervisor; Sales Executive; Sales Manager; Sales Rep.; Secretary; Systems Analyst; Video Production Coordinator. **Educational backgrounds include:** Accounting; Business Administration; Chemistry; Computer Science; Engineering; Finance; Liberal Arts; Marketing. **Benefits:** 401(k); Dental Insurance; Disability Coverage; Employee Discounts; Life Insurance; Medical Insurance; Profit Sharing; Public Transit Available; Tuition Assistance. **Corporate headquarters location:** This Location. **International locations:** Belgium; Canada; France; Italy; Switzerland; the Netherlands. **Parent company:** National Service Industries, Inc. (Atlanta GA).

For more information on career opportunities in the chemicals/rubber and plastics industries:

Associations

AMERICAN ASSOCIATION FOR CLINICAL CHEMISTRY
2101 L Street NW, Suite 202, Washington DC 20037-1526. 202/857-0717. Toll-free phone: 800/892-1400. World Wide Web address: http://www.aacc.org. International scientific/medical society of individuals involved with clinical chemistry and other clinical lab science-related disciplines.

AMERICAN CHEMICAL SOCIETY
Career Services, 1155 16th Street NW, Washington DC 20036. 202/872-4600. World Wide Web address: http://www.acs.org.

AMERICAN INSTITUTE OF CHEMICAL ENGINEERS
3 Park Avenue, New York NY 10016. 212/591-7338. Toll-free phone: 800/242-4363. World Wide Web address: http://www.aiche.org. Provides leadership in advancing the chemical engineering profession as it meets the needs of society.

CHEMICAL MANUFACTURERS ASSOCIATION
1300 Wilson Boulevard, Arlington VA 22209. 703/741-5000. World Wide Web address: http://www.cmahq.com. A trade association that develops and implements programs and services and advocates public policy that benefits the industry and society.

THE ELECTROCHEMICAL SOCIETY
65 South Main Street, Pennington NJ 08534. 609/737-1902. An international educational society dealing with electrochemical issues. Also publishes monthly journals.

SOAP AND DETERGENT ASSOCIATION
475 Park Avenue South, New York NY 10016. 212/725-1262. World Wide Web address: http://www.sdahq.org. A trade association and research center.

SOCIETY OF PLASTICS ENGINEERS
P.O. Box 403, Brookfield CT 06804-0403. 203/775-0471. World Wide Web address: http://www.4spe.org. Dedicated to helping members

attain higher professional status through increased scientific, engineering, and technical knowledge.

THE SOCIETY OF THE PLASTICS INDUSTRY, INC.

1801 K Street NW, Suite 600K, Washington DC 20006. 202/974-5200. Promotes the development of the plastics industry and enhances public understanding of its contributions while meeting the needs of society.

Directories

CHEMICALS DIRECTORY

Cahners Business Information, 275 Washington Street, Newton MA 02458. 617/964-3030. World Wide Web address: http://www.cahners.com.

DIRECTORY OF CHEMICAL PRODUCERS

SRI International, 333 Ravenswood Avenue, Menlo Park CA 94025. 650/326-6200. World Wide Web address: http://www.sri.com.

Magazines

CHEMICAL & ENGINEERING NEWS

American Chemical Society, 1155 16th Street NW, Washington DC 20036. 202/872-4600. World Wide Web address: http://www.acs.org.

CHEMICAL MARKET REPORTER

Schnell Publishing Company, 2 Rector Street, 26th Floor, New York NY 10004. 212/791-4267. Toll-free phone: 877/550-3839.

CHEMICAL WEEK

888 Seventh Avenue, 26th Floor, New York NY 10106. 212/621-4900. World Wide Web address: http://www.chemweek.com.

Communications: Telecommunications and Broadcasting

You can expect to find the following types of companies in this chapter:
*Cable/Pay Television Services • Communications Equipment
Radio and Television Broadcasting Systems • Telephone, Telegraph, and other Message Communications*

Some helpful information: *The average salary range for telecommunications equipment repairers is $20,000 - $25,000. Experienced telephone/cable mechanics and broadcast technicians earn $35,000 on average per year. Experienced electronics engineers earn an average of $50,000 - $60,000.*

ABC7/KGO-TV
900 Front Street, San Francisco CA 94111. 415/954-7222. **Recorded jobline:** 415/954-7958. **Contact:** Heather McCann, Personnel Manager. **World Wide Web address:** http://www.abc7news.com. **Description:** An ABC-affiliated television station. **Benefits:** Dental Insurance; Disability Coverage; Employee Discounts; Life Insurance; Medical Insurance; Pension Plan; Profit Sharing; Savings Plan; Tuition Assistance. **Special programs:** Internships. **Internship information:** Internships are offered to college juniors, seniors, and graduate students. Interns are paid minimum wage and receive college credit for their work. Approximately 16 interns are selected each semester. **Corporate headquarters location:** New York NY.

ACTV INC.
1270 Avenue of the Americas, Rockefeller Center, Suite 2401, New York NY 10020-1700. 212/262-2570. **Fax:** 212/459-9548. **Contact:** Personnel. **E-mail address:** info@actv.com. **World Wide Web address:** http://www.actv.com. **Description:** ACTV is engaged in individual television programming. The company's primary markets are in-home entertainment and education. **Corporate headquarters location:** This Location. **Other U.S. locations:** Los Angeles CA. **Operations at this facility include:** Administration; Research and Development; Sales; Service. **Number of employees nationwide:** 25.

AETN
P.O. Box 1250, Conway AR 72033. 501/682-2386. **Fax:** 501/682-4122. **Contact:** Teresa Fason, Administrative Services Manager. **Description:** A public education television network. **Common positions include:** Accountant; Broadcast Technician; Designer; Editor; Electrical Engineer; Operations Manager; Public Relations Specialist; Radio Announcer; Systems Analyst; Teacher. **Educational backgrounds include:** Accounting; Art; Communications; Liberal Arts; Marketing. **Benefits:** Life Insurance; Medical Insurance; Pension Plan. **Special programs:** Internships. **Corporate headquarters location:** This Location.

AM COMMUNICATIONS
100 Commerce Boulevard, Quakertown PA 18951. 215/536-1354. **Fax:** 215/538-8779. **Contact:** Chuck Wilson, Controller. **World Wide Web address:** http://www.amcomm.com. **Description:** One of the world's leading suppliers of network status and performance monitoring systems for hybrid fiber/coaxial telecommunications networks. Products are sold directly to cable system operators and through original equipment manufacturers. Founded in 1974. **Corporate headquarters location:** This Location.

AT&T CORPORATION
32 Avenue of the Americas, New York NY 10013. 212/387-5400. **Contact:** Employment and Staffing. **World Wide Web address:** http://www.att.com. **Description:** A major long-distance telephone company which provides domestic and international voice and data communications and management services, telecommunications products, and leasing and financial services. The company manufactures data communications products, switching and transmission equipment, and other products and components. **NOTE:** Please send resumes to the resume scanning center, 1200 Peachtree Street, Promenade 1, Atlanta GA 30309. **Corporate headquarters location:** This Location. **Other U.S. locations:**
• AT&T Media Services, 647 Clinic Road, Hannibal MO 63401-3607. 573/221-1203.
• AT&T Wireless, 2002 Pisgah Church Road, Suite 300, Greensboro NC 27455. 336/282-3690.

ACCOM, INC.
1490 O'Brien Drive, Menlo Park CA 94025. 650/328-3818. **Fax:** 415/327-2511. **Contact:** Personnel. **World Wide Web address:** http://www.accom.com. **Description:** Designs, manufactures, and sells digital video production, recording, and editing equipment for television broadcasting and computer video markets worldwide. **Corporate headquarters location:** This Location.

THE ACKERLEY GROUP
1301 Fifth Avenue, Suite 4000, Seattle WA 98101. 206/624-2888. **Contact:** Human Resources. **World Wide Web address:** http://www.ackerley.com. **Description:** Operates a media and entertainment companies. The Ackerley Group includes an outdoor advertising agency, 17 television stations, five radio stations, and a sports/entertainment division that operates the NBA's Seattle SuperSonics and the WNBA's Seattle Storm. **Corporate headquarters location:** This Location. **Subsidiaries include:** AK/Media Airport; AK/Media Florida; AK/Media Massachusetts; AK/Media Northwest; Full House Sports & Entertainment.

ACRODYNE INDUSTRIES, INC.
516 Township Line Road, Blue Bell PA 19422. 215/542-7000. **Contact:** Bob Beers, Human Resources Manager. **World Wide Web address:** http://www.acrodyne.com. **Description:** Designs, manufactures, and markets television broadcast transmitters and translators for domestic and international television stations, broadcasters, government agencies, nonprofit organizations, and educational institutions. **Benefits:** Stock Option. **Corporate headquarters location:** This Location. **Parent company:** Acrodyne Holdings, Inc.

ACTIVE VOICE CORPORATION
2901 Third Avenue, Suite 500, Seattle WA 98121-1049. 206/441-4700. **Fax:** 206/441-4784. **Contact:** Personnel. **World Wide Web address:** http://www.activevoice.com. **Description:** A leading provider of PC-based voice processing systems. The company's software products enable small- to medium-sized businesses and offices to communicate more effectively by integrating their traditional office telephone systems with voicemail, automated attendant, and interactive voice response functions. The company's products are used by the manufacturing, retail, service, health care, government, and institutional fields. **Corporate headquarters location:** This Location. **International locations:** Australia; England; Hong Kong; India; the Netherlands. **Subsidiaries include:** Pronexus, Inc. (Ontario, Canada).

ADAPTIVE BROADBAND
1143 Borregas Avenue, Sunnyvale CA 94089. 408/732-4000. **Contact:** Personnel. **World Wide Web address:** http://www.adaptivebroadband.com. **Description:** Manufactures and markets electronic communications equipment and systems to support Internet access and broadcast TV transport. **Corporate headquarters location:** This Location.

ADELPHIA COMMUNICATIONS CORP.
One Main Street, Coudersport PA 16915. 814/274-9830. **Fax:** 814/274-6692. **Contact:** Mr. Orby Kelley, Vice President of Administration/Labor Relations. **World Wide Web address:** http://www.adelphia.net. **Description:** Provides digital cable television, long distance telephone, paging, and high-speed Internet connection services. **NOTE:** Entry-level positions are offered. **Common positions include:** Accountant; Attorney; Automotive Mechanic; Branch Manager; Broadcast Technician; Budget Analyst; Clerical Supervisor; Computer Programmer; Credit Manager; Customer Service Rep.; Design Engineer; Designer; Draftsperson; Electrical Engineer; Financial Analyst; General Manager; Human Resources Manager; Internet Services Manager; Management Trainee; Market Research Analyst; MIS Specialist; Operations Manager; Paralegal; Public Relations Specialist; Purchasing Agent; Quality Control Supervisor; Radio Announcer; Statistician; Systems Analyst; Technical Writer; Telecommunications Manager; Video Production Coordinator. **Educational backgrounds include:** Accounting; Business Administration; Communications; Computer Science; Engineering; Finance; Liberal Arts; Marketing. **Benefits:** 401(k); Dental Insurance; Disability Coverage; Employee Discounts; Life Insurance; Medical Insurance; Tuition Assistance. **Special programs:** Internships; Training. **Corporate headquarters location:** This Location. **Other U.S. locations:** Nationwide. **Operations at this facility include:** Administration; Sales; Service.

ADTRAN
P.O. Box 140000, Huntsville AL 35814-4000. 256/963-8000. **Contact:** Pete Rich, Director of Personnel. **World Wide Web address:** http://www.adtran.com. **Description:** ADTRAN provides digital transmission products to telephone companies and corporate end users to implement advanced digital data services over existing telephone networks. The company has three primary markets: Telco products for telephone companies; Customer Premises Equipment (CPE) for end users; and OEM products for firms who incorporate ADTRAN technology into their own products. CPE products provide end users access to Telco digital services and often include additional features for specific end user applications. Customized versions of both Telco and CPE products are supplied in OEM versions to suppliers of T1 multiplexers including high-volume end users and private label distributors. **Corporate headquarters location:** This Location.

AEROTRON REPCO SYSTEMS INC.
4602 Parkway Commerce Boulevard, Orlando FL 32808. 407/856-1953. **Fax:** 407/856-1960. **Contact:** Ted McDonald, Personnel Manager. **World Wide Web address:** http://www.aerotron-repco.com. **Description:** A manufacturer of communications equipment including wireless modems and hand-held radios. **Corporate headquarters location:** This Location.

ALCATEL USA INC.
1225 North Alma Road, Richardson TX 75081. 972/996-5000. **Contact:** Human Resources. **World Wide Web address:** http://www.usa.alcatel.com. **Description:** Manufactures telecommunications equipment including fiberoptic transmission systems and optical networks. **Corporate headquarters location:** This Location. **Parent company:** Alcatel Alsthom (Paris, France). **Other U.S. locations:**
- 1000 Coit Road, Mail Stop 210, Plano TX 75075-5813. 972/519-3000.

ALLTEL CORPORATION
P.O. Box 2177, Little Rock AR 72203. 501/661-8000. **Physical address:** One Allied Drive, Little Rock AR. **Contact:** Human Resources. **World Wide Web address:** http://www.alltel.com. **Description:** A leading telecommunications and information services company. Its subsidiaries provide local telephone, cellular telephone, and information services, and communications products. Business segments include Telephone Operations; Cellular Operations; Information Services; and Product Distribution. In addition to its four core businesses, ALLTEL operates companies that provide wide-area paging, directory publishing, long-distance service, and cable television service. **Corporate headquarters location:** This Location. **Subsidiaries include:** ALLTEL Supply is a leading provider of telecommunications and data products; HWC is one of the nation's largest master distributors of specialty wire and cable products; ALLTEL Mobile Communications provides cellular telecommunications services. **Other U.S. locations:**
- ALLTEL Communications, 50 Executive Parkway, Hudson OH 44236. 330/650-1700.

AMERICAN MOBILE SATELLITE CORP.
10802 Parkridge Boulevard, Reston VA 20191. 703/758-6000. **Fax:** 703/758-6111. **Contact:** Susan Byrd Lubert, Vice President of Personnel. **World Wide Web address:** http://www.ammobile.com. **Description:** Provides wireless communications services and solutions nationwide including satellite mobile messaging systems, wireless e-mail services, and two-way wireless data services. **Corporate headquarters location:** This Location. **Number of employees nationwide:** 470.

AMERILINK CORPORATION
RADIOSHACK INSTALLATION SERVICE
1900 East Dublin Granville Road, Suite 100A, Columbus OH 43229. 614/895-1313. **Fax:** 614/895-8942. **Recorded jobline:** 800/669-8765x4775. **Contact:** Personnel. **E-mail address:** resume@alnk.com. **World Wide Web address:** http://www.alnk.com. **Description:** Designs, constructs, installs, and maintains cable systems. Founded in 1971. **Corporate headquarters location:** This Location.

AMERITECH CORPORATION
30 South Wacker Drive, Chicago IL 60606. 312/750-5000. **Contact:** Human Resources. **World Wide Web address:** http://www.ameritech.com. **Description:** A telephone holding company. Ameritech Corporation conducts business through 15 diversified units. Services provided by these units include advertising; communications including pay phone, long-distance telephone, and cellular telephone; information services; new media; capital; and security services. **Common positions include:** Accountant; Financial Analyst; Marketing Specialist; Sales Rep. **Educational backgrounds include:** Business Administration. **Corporate headquarters location:** This Location.

ANDREW CORPORATION
10500 West 153rd Street, Orland Park IL 60462. 708/349-3300. **Fax:** 708/873-3640. **Contact:** Roger Blaylock, Personnel Manager. **World Wide Web address:** http://www.andrew.com. **Description:** A manufacturer of telecommunications equipment including Earth Station Satellite, cellular, and microwave antennas, towers, shelters, cables, and associated equipment. **Common positions include:** Accountant; Administrative Manager; Buyer; Computer Programmer; Customer Service Rep.; Draftsperson; Electrical Engineer; Electrician; Financial Analyst; General Manager; Human Resources Manager; Industrial Engineer; Industrial Production Manager; Mechanical Engineer; Operations Manager; Purchasing Agent; Quality Control Supervisor; Registered Nurse; Services Sales Rep.; Software Engineer; Statistician; Systems Analyst; Technical Writer. **Educational backgrounds include:** Accounting; Art/Design; Communications; Computer Science; Engineering; Finance; Marketing; Mathematics. **Benefits:** 401(k); Dental Insurance; Disability Coverage; Employee Discounts; Life Insurance; Medical Insurance; Profit Sharing; Savings Plan; Stock Option; Tuition Assistance. **Special programs:** Internships. **Corporate headquarters location:** This Location. **Other U.S. locations:** Simi Valley CA; Austin TX; Dallas TX; Denton TX; Garland TX; Richardson TX; Bothell WA. **Operations at this facility include:** Administration; Manufacturing; Research and Development; Sales; Service.

ANIXTER INC.
4711 Golf Road, Skokie IL 60076. 847/677-2600. **Fax:** 847/715-7606. **Contact:** Peggy Baumruck, Personnel Manager. **World Wide Web address:** http://www.anixter.com. **Description:** A value-added provider of industrial wire and cabling solutions that support voice and data applications. Solutions include customized pre- and post-sale services and products. **Common positions include:** Accountant; Computer Programmer; Customer Service Rep.; Electrical Engineer; Marketing Specialist; Network Engineer; Software Engineer; Systems Analyst; Systems Engineer; Transportation Specialist. **Educational backgrounds include:** Accounting; Business Administration; Computer Science; Engineering; Finance; Marketing; Telecommunications. **Benefits:** 401(k); Disability Coverage; EAP; Employee Discounts; Life Insurance; Medical Insurance; Pension Plan; Stock Purchase; Tuition Assistance. **Corporate headquarters location:** This Location. **Other U.S. locations:** Nationwide. **Parent company:** Anixter International. **Operations at this facility include:** Administration; Marketing; Research and Development; Service.

APPLIED INNOVATION INC.
5800 Innovation Drive, Dublin OH 43016. **Toll-free phone:** 800/247-9482. **Fax:** 614/798-1770. **Contact:** Larenda Johnson, Employment Manager. **E-mail address:** larendaj@aiinet.com. **World Wide Web address:** http://www.aiinet.com. **Description:** A provider of data communications equipment used by telecommunications companies including switches, routers, and Internet access devices. **Company slogan:** Bridging the technology gap. **Common positions include:** Account Manager; Account Representative; Administrative Assistant; Applications Engineer; Computer Engineer; Computer Technician; Customer Service Rep.; Market Research Analyst; Network Administrator; Sales Engineer; Software Engineer. **Educational backgrounds include:** C/C++; Cold Fusion; Computer Science; Engineering; Java; Software Development; Software Tech. Support; Visual Basic. **Benefits:** 401(k); Casual Dress - Daily; Dental Insurance; Disability Coverage; Employee Discounts; Life Insurance; Medical Insurance; Profit Sharing; Sick Days (1 - 5); Tuition Assistance; Vacation Days (10 - 20). **Corporate headquarters location:** This Location. **Other U.S. locations:** Denver CO; Atlanta GA; Chicago IL; Dallas TX. **President/CEO:** Gerard Moersdorf.

ARCH COMMUNICATIONS GROUP, INC.
1800 West Park Drive, Suite 250, Westborough MA 01581-3912. 508/898-0962. **Contact:** Personnel. **World Wide Web address:** http://www.arch.com. **Description:** Provides telephone paging services. **Common positions include:** Accountant; Administrator; Sales Rep. **Corporate headquarters location:** This Location.

ASPECT TELECOMMUNICATIONS
1730 Fox Drive, San Jose CA 95131. 408/325-2200. **Fax:** 408/325-2260. **Contact:** Staffing Department. **E-mail address:** staffing@aspect.com. **World Wide Web address:** http://www.aspect.com. **Description:** Provides comprehensive business solutions for mission-critical call centers worldwide. Products include automatic call distributors, computer-telephony integration solutions, call center management and reporting software, automation solutions, and planning and forecasting packages. **NOTE:** Entry-level positions are offered. **Common positions include:** Account Manager; Account Rep.; Accountant; Administrative Assistant; Controller; Customer Service Rep.; Database Manager; Financial Analyst; Human Resources Manager; Marketing Manager; Marketing Specialist; MIS Specialist; Network Administrator; Software Engineer. **Educational backgrounds include:** Accounting; Business Administration; C/C++; Computer Science; Engineering; Finance; Marketing; MCSE; Oracle; Software Development; Software Tech. Support; Visual Basic. **Benefits:** 401(k); Bonus Award/Plan; Casual Dress - Daily; Dental Insurance; Disability Coverage; Flextime Plan; Life Insurance; Medical Insurance; Telecommuting; Tuition Assistance. **Special programs:** Internships. **Corporate headquarters location:** This Location.

BET SERVICES
BLACK ENTERTAINMENT TELEVISION NETWORK
1900 W Place NE, Washington DC 20018. 202/608-2000. **Fax:** 202/608-2589. **Contact:** Curtis Scott,

Vice President of Personnel. **Description:** Operates the Black Entertainment Television Network (BET Network) which is an advertiser-supported basic cable television network. BET Services is also the publisher of *YSB* and *Emerge*, two magazines that are geared toward the African-American community. **Common positions include:** Accountant; Attorney; Broadcast Technician; Editor; Electrical Engineer; Human Resources Manager; Operations Manager; Systems Analyst. **Educational backgrounds include:** Accounting; Communications; Computer Science; Liberal Arts. **Benefits:** 401(k); Dental Insurance; Disability Coverage; Life Insurance; Medical Insurance; Profit Sharing. **Special programs:** Internships. **Corporate headquarters location:** This Location. **Other U.S. locations:** Santa Monica CA; Chicago IL; New York NY. **Operations at this facility include:** Administration; Sales.

BALL CORPORATION
10 Longs Peak Drive, Broomfield CO 80021. 303/469-3131. **Contact:** Personnel. **World Wide Web address:** http://www.ball.com. **Description:** Produces metal and plastic packaging products for foods and beverages, and provides aerospace and communications products and services to government and commercial customers. **Corporate headquarters location:** This Location.

BAY TECHNICAL ASSOCIATES
200 North Second Street, P.O. Box 387, Bay St. Louis MS 39520. 228/467-8231. **Contact:** Personnel Administrator. **World Wide Web address:** http://www.baytechdcd.com. **Description:** Designs, manufactures, and markets data communication components and equipment. **Common positions include:** Computer Programmer; Electrical Engineer; Manufacturer's Sales Rep.; Marketing Specialist; Purchasing Agent; Technical Writer. **Educational backgrounds include:** Computer Science; Engineering; Marketing. **Benefits:** Dental Insurance; Disability Coverage; Life Insurance; Medical Insurance; Pension Plan; Profit Sharing. **Corporate headquarters location:** This Location. **Operations at this facility include:** Administration; Manufacturing; Sales; Service.

BELLSOUTH CORPORATION
1155 Peachtree Street NE, Atlanta GA 30309. 404/249-2000. **Contact:** Human Resources. **World Wide Web address:** http://www.bellsouthcorp.com. **Description:** A communications company offering telecommunications, wireless communications, entertainment, e-commerce, and directory advertising services. **Corporate headquarters location:** This Location.

A.H. BELO CORPORATION
P.O. Box 655237, Dallas TX 75265. 214/977-6600. **Contact:** Mr. Lee Smith, Employment Manager. **World Wide Web address:** http://www.dallasnews.com. **Description:** A.H. Belo Corporation owns and operates newspapers and network-affiliated television stations in seven U.S. metropolitan areas. One of its papers, The Dallas Morning News (also at this location), has a circulation of 550,000 during the week and 800,000 on Sunday. A.H. Belo traces its roots to The Galveston Daily News, which was first published in 1842. **Subsidiaries include:** DFW Printing Company, Inc.; DFW Suburban Newspapers, Inc.

BONNEVILLE INTERNATIONAL CORP.
55 North 300 West, Salt Lake City UT 84110. 801/575-7540. **Fax:** 801/575-7548. **Contact:** Claire Bjelland, Vice President of Employee Relations. **World Wide Web address:** http://www.bonnint.

com. **Description:** Operates a television station, 15 radio stations, an advertising agency, a video production house, a nationwide special service radio network, a news bureau in Washington DC, a signatory and corporate sales company, and a satellite transmission company. **NOTE:** Entry-level positions and part-time jobs are offered. **Common positions include:** Account Rep.; Accountant; Administrative Assistant; Applications Engineer; Attorney; Broadcast Technician; CFO; Computer Engineer; Computer Operator; Computer Programmer; Controller; Editor; Editorial Assistant; General Manager; Graphic Artist; Graphic Designer; Human Resources Manager; Managing Editor; Marketing Manager; Marketing Specialist; MIS Specialist; Network Administrator; Public Relations Specialist; Reporter; Sales Executive; Sales Manager; Sales Rep.; Secretary; Technical Writer; Telecommunications Manager; TV Broadcaster; Typist; Video Production Coordinator. **Educational backgrounds include:** Accounting; Art/Design; Communications; Computer Science; Economics; Engineering; Finance; Marketing; Public Relations. **Benefits:** 401(k); Casual Dress - Fridays; Dental Insurance; Disability Coverage; Employee Discounts; Life Insurance; Medical Insurance; Pension Plan; Profit Sharing; Savings Plan; Tuition Assistance. **Corporate headquarters location:** This Location. **Subsidiaries include:** Bonneville Communications (Salt Lake City UT) is an advertising agency that specializes in public service announcements and direct response; The Bonneville Media Group; Bonneville Worldwide Entertainment provides 24-hour programming for members of The Church of Jesus Christ of Latter-Day Saints; The Bonneville Satellite Company provides uplinking and downlinking services, primarily for The Church of Jesus Christ of Latter-Day Saints. **President/CEO:** Bruce T. Reese. **Information Systems Manager:** Roger Graves.

BROADBEAM CORPORATION
600 Alexander Road, Princeton NJ 08540. 609/734-0300. **Fax:** 609/734-0346. **Contact:** Human Resources. **World Wide Web address:** http://www.broadbeam.com. **Description:** Provides wireless solutions by developing platform and professional services that allow companies to develop, deploy, and manage mobile data solutions. **Corporate headquarters location:** This Location.

CBS INC.
51 West 52nd Street, 19th Floor, New York NY 10019. 212/975-4321. **Contact:** Human Resources. **World Wide Web address:** http://www.cbs.com. **Description:** A broad-based entertainment and communications company which operates one of the country's major commercial television networks and two nationwide radio networks. **Special programs:** Internships. **Internship information:** The company offers unpaid, full-time, summer internship positions for students. **Corporate headquarters location:** This Location. **Parent company:** Viacom.

CFW COMMUNICATIONS COMPANY
P.O. Box 1990, Waynesboro VA 22980. 540/946-3500. **Physical address:** 401 Spring Lane, Suite 300, Waynesboro VA. **Contact:** Cindy Knupp, Director of Personnel/Government Relations. **World Wide Web address:** http://www.cfw.com. **Description:** A holding company providing telecommunications products and services through its operating subsidiaries. **Corporate headquarters location:** This Location. **Subsidiaries include:** CFW Telephone Company provides telephone service to the cities of Waynesboro, Clifton Forge, and Covington VA, and surrounding communities; CFW Network Inc. leases transmission capacity on

an advanced 350 mile fiber-optic network throughout the Shenandoah Valley; CFW Cellular Inc. provides cellular telephone service for Harrisonburg, Staunton, and Waynesboro Virginia; CFW Communications Services Inc. offers regional customers a single point-of-contact for business phone systems, paging, voicemail, network access, long-distance, prepaid calling cards, security systems, and alarm monitoring; CFW Cable Inc. operates wireless cable TV systems in the Charlottesville area and the Shenandoah Valley; CFW Information Services provides long-distance directory assistance services for interexchange and local exchange carriers in a multistate region.

CNN (CABLE NEWS NETWORK)
One CNN Center, Box 105366, Atlanta GA 30348-5366. 404/827-1700. **Contact:** Human Resources. **World Wide Web address:** http://www.cnn.com. **Description:** A cable news network. CNN has 28 bureaus worldwide and provides 24-hour news programming worldwide. Programming includes international, domestic, and business news; sports; weather; and topical programming. **Educational backgrounds include:** Communications; Liberal Arts. **Benefits:** Dental Insurance; Disability Coverage; Life Insurance; Medical Insurance; Profit Sharing; Savings Plan. **Special programs:** Internships. **Corporate headquarters location:** This Location. **Operations at this facility include:** Administration; Sales.
Other U.S. locations:
• 820 First Street NE, Washington DC 20002. 202/515-2916.

CTC COMMUNICATIONS
220 Bear Hill Road, Waltham MA 02451. 781/466-8080. **Contact:** Personnel. **Description:** An independent sales agent for the Regional Bell Operating Companies. The company markets discounted telephone calling plans, 800-number services, Centrex systems, and data transport networks to mid-sized commercial accounts. The company operates 15 branch offices in the Northeast. **Corporate headquarters location:** This Location. **Number of employees nationwide:** 180.

CTI GROUP HOLDINGS INC.
CTI DATA SOLUTIONS/CTI SOFT-COM
2550 Eisenhower Avenue, Norristown PA 19403. 610/666-1700. **Fax:** 610/666-7707. **Contact:** Personnel. **E-mail address:** ctiusa@ctigroup.com. **World Wide Web address:** http://www.ctigroup.com. **Description:** A diversified holding company. **Corporate headquarters location:** This Location. **Subsidiaries include:** CTI Data Solutions Inc. (also at this location) and CTI Data Solutions, Ltd. (United Kingdom) supply PC-based call management products; CTI Soft-Com Inc. (also at this location) offers telecommunications management software; Plymouth Communications Inc.; Regional Communications, Inc.; Telephone Budgeting Systems, Inc.

CXR TELCOM
47233 Fremont Boulevard, Fremont CA 94538-6502. 510/657-8810. **Contact:** Personnel. **World Wide Web address:** http://www.cxr.com. **Description:** Designs and manufactures electronic telecommunications test and data communications equipment. Customers include interconnect carriers, independent telephone operating companies, private communications networks, banks, brokerage firms, and government agencies. **Corporate headquarters location:** Ontario CA.

CABLE & WIRELESS USA
8219 Leesburg Pike, Vienna VA 22182-2625. 703/790-5300. **Fax:** 703/760-1758. **Contact:** Personnel. **World Wide Web address:** http://www.cw-usa.net. **Description:** Offers domestic and international voice and data services to businesses. **Common positions include:** Accountant; Adjuster; Attorney; Budget Analyst; Buyer; Computer Operator; Computer Programmer; Credit Clerk and Authorizer; Customer Service Rep.; Draftsperson; Electrical Engineer; Employment Interviewer; Financial Analyst; Manufacturer's Sales Rep.; Market Research Analyst; Paralegal; Payroll Clerk; Receptionist; Secretary; Software Engineer; Systems Analyst; Technical Writer; Typist. **Educational backgrounds include:** Accounting; Business Administration; Communications; Computer Science; Engineering; Finance; Liberal Arts; Marketing; Mathematics. **Benefits:** Dental Insurance; Disability Coverage; Employee Discounts; Life Insurance; Medical Insurance; Pension Plan; Savings Plan; Stock Option; Tuition Assistance. **Corporate headquarters location:** This Location. **Other U.S. locations:** Nationwide. **Parent company:** Cable & Wireless plc. **Operations at this facility include:** Administration; Manufacturing; Research and Development; Sales; Service.

CABLEVISION SYSTEMS CORPORATION
1111 Stewart Avenue, Bethpage NY 11714. 516/803-2300. **Fax:** 516/803-3065. **Contact:** Diane Sabato, Corporate Director of Personnel. **World Wide Web address:** http://www.cablevision.com. **Description:** Owns and operates cable television systems serving customers in the Boston, Cleveland, and New York markets. **Common positions include:** Accountant; Attorney; Blue-Collar Worker Supervisor; Broadcast Technician; Budget Analyst; Buyer; Cashier; Computer Operator; Computer Programmer; Customer Service Rep.; Department Manager; Employment Interviewer; Financial Analyst; Graphic Artist; Human Resources Manager; Industrial Engineer; Marketing Specialist; Payroll Clerk; Public Relations Specialist; Purchasing Agent; Receptionist; Reporter; Services Sales Rep.; Statistician; Systems Analyst; TV Broadcaster. **Educational backgrounds include:** Accounting; Art/Design; Business Administration; Communications; Finance; Marketing. **Benefits:** 401(k); Daycare Assistance; Dental Insurance; Disability Coverage; Employee Discounts; Life Insurance; Medical Insurance; Pension Plan; Profit Sharing; Savings Plan; Tuition Assistance. **Special programs:** Internships. **Corporate headquarters location:** This Location. **Operations at this facility include:** Administration.

CELLULARONE
8755 Walker Drive, Suite 100, Greenbelt MD 20770. 301/489-3600. **Fax:** 301/489-3298. **Recorded jobline:** 301/489-3939. **Contact:** Recruiter. **World Wide Web address:** http://www.getcellone.com. **Description:** Manufactures and sells mobile phone systems. This location also hires seasonally. **NOTE:** Entry-level positions and second shifts are available. **Common positions include:** Account Manager; Account Rep.; Accountant; Administrative Assistant; Applications Engineer; Assistant Manager; Branch Manager; Computer Technician; Customer Service Rep.; Database Administrator; Electrical Engineer; Financial Analyst; Network Administrator; Sales Executive; Sales Manager; Sales Rep.; Systems Analyst; Telecommunications Manager; Website Developer. **Educational backgrounds include:** Accounting; Business Administration; Cold Fusion; Communications; Computer Science; Economics; Finance; Microsoft Office; SQL. **Benefits:** 401(k); Casual Dress - Daily; Daycare Assistance; Dental Insurance; Disability Coverage; Employee Discounts; Financial Planning Assistance; Life

Insurance; Medical Insurance; Pension Plan; Public Transit Available; Savings Plan; Sick Days (6 - 10); Tuition Assistance; Vacation Days (10 - 20). **Corporate headquarters location:** This Location. **Other U.S. locations:** DC; MD. **Parent company:** SBC Communications. **President:** Robert Gordon. **Number of employees at this location:** 850.

CENTIGRAM COMMUNICATIONS CORP.
91 East Tasman Drive, San Jose CA 95134. 408/944-0250. **Fax:** 408/428-3625. **Contact:** Human Resources. **World Wide Web address:** http://www.centigram.com. **Description:** Designs, manufactures, and markets communications systems that enable users to access and interact with a broad range of information in a variety of formats including voice, text, data, e-mail, and facsimile from a touch-tone telephone. The company's applications, such as voice messaging, facsimile store-and-forward, and interactive voice response, are integrated on the company's Adaptive Information Processing platform, a communication server that is based on industry-standard hardware and software. **Common positions include:** Computer Programmer; Electrical Engineer; Software Engineer; Systems Analyst. **Educational backgrounds include:** Engineering. **Benefits:** 401(k); Dental Insurance; Disability Coverage; Life Insurance; Medical Insurance; Pension Plan; Profit Sharing; Savings Plan; Tuition Assistance. **Corporate headquarters location:** This Location. **Operations at this facility include:** Administration; Manufacturing; Research and Development; Sales.

CIDCO INC.
220 Cochrane Circle, Morgan Hill CA 95037. 408/779-1162. **Fax:** 408/779-3106. **Contact:** Personnel. **World Wide Web address:** http://www.cidco.com. **Description:** Designs and develops subscriber telephone equipment that supports intelligent network services being introduced by telephone operating companies. The company's specialization is Caller ID, a service that allows subscribers to view the name and telephone number of the calling party before the call is answered. **Corporate headquarters location:** This Location.

CINCINNATI BELL, INC.
201 East Fourth Street, Room M30, Cincinnati OH 45202. 513/397-9900. **Contact:** Personnel. **World Wide Web address:** http://www.cinbelltel.com. **Description:** A local telephone company that provides local telephone service in southwestern Ohio and parts of northern Kentucky and Indiana. Other businesses include a cellular mobile telephone service; Cincinnati Bell Long Distance, a reseller of long-distance communication services; and the Yellow Pages Directory services. **Common positions include:** Accountant; Customer Service Rep.; Electrical Engineer; Marketing Specialist; Services Sales Rep.; Statistician; Systems Analyst; Technical Writer. **Educational backgrounds include:** Accounting; Business Administration; Communications; Computer Science; Economics; Engineering; Finance; Liberal Arts; Marketing; Mathematics. **Benefits:** Dental Insurance; Disability Coverage; Life Insurance; Medical Insurance; Pension Plan; Savings Plan; Tuition Assistance. **Special programs:** Internships. **Corporate headquarters location:** This Location. **Subsidiaries include:** Cincinnati Bell Information Systems, Inc. designs and markets information systems, and provides consulting and technical services for telecommunications companies. MATRIXX Marketing, Inc. offers a wide range of inbound and outbound telemarketing and other marketing services to clients in the consumer goods, telecommunications, and financial services fields.

CITADEL COMMUNICATIONS CORP.
500 Fourth Street NW, Albuquerque NM 87102. 505/767-6700. **Fax:** 505/767-6767. **Contact:** Personnel. **Description:** The parent company of local radio broadcasters KOB-AM, KOB-FM, KHTL, KMGA-FM, KTBL-FM, KHFM-FM, KNML-AM, and KRST-FM. **Corporate headquarters location:** Las Vegas NV.

CLEAR CHANNEL COMMUNICATIONS
P.O. Box 659512, San Antonio TX 78265-9512. 210/822-2828. **Fax:** 210/822-2299. **Contact:** Personnel. **World Wide Web address:** http://www.clearchannel.com. **Description:** A nationwide television and radio broadcasting company. The company operates 39 radio stations in 12 different markets and four radio networks, as well as 13 television stations in nine different markets. **Corporate headquarters location:** This Location.

CNET (THE COMPUTER NETWORK)
150 Chestnut Street, San Francisco CA 94111. 415/395-7805. **Fax:** 415/395-7811. **Contact:** Human Resources. **World Wide Web address:** http://www.cnet.com. **Description:** Provides a network of technology-related Internet sites and produces several television shows. **Corporate headquarters location:** This Location.

COASTAL COMMUNICATIONS
P.O. Box 585, Hinesville GA 31310. 912/368-3300. **Contact:** Human Resources. **Description:** Provides telephone service to customers throughout the area. **Corporate headquarters location:** This Location.

COGNITRONICS CORPORATION
3 Corporate Drive, Danbury CT 06810. 203/830-3400. **Contact:** Janet Freund, Director of Personnel. **World Wide Web address:** http://www.cognitronics.com. **Description:** The company designs, manufactures, and markets voice processing systems. Products include passive announcers, which are used by telephone operating companies to inform callers about network conditions or procedures; intelligent announcers, which are primarily used by telephone companies to provide voice announcements in connection with custom calling features, such as selective call forwarding and caller originator trace; interactive voice response; audiotex, a UNIX-based voice processing platform; and call processing, automated attendant, and audiotex systems. **Benefits:** 401(k); Medical Insurance; Pension Plan; Stock Option. **Corporate headquarters location:** This Location. **Subsidiaries include:** Dacon Electronics, plc.

COMCAST CORPORATION
1500 Market Street, East Tower, Philadelphia PA 19102. 215/665-1700. **Contact:** Human Resources. **World Wide Web address:** http://www.comcast.com. **Description:** A cable television system operator, which also distributes Muzak and provides cellular phone services. **Common positions include:** Accountant; Administrator; Customer Service Rep.; Financial Analyst; General Manager; Operations Manager; Purchasing Agent. **Educational backgrounds include:** Accounting; Business Administration; Engineering; Finance; Marketing; Mathematics. **Corporate headquarters location:** This Location. **Operations at this facility include:** Administration. **Other U.S. locations:**
- Comcast Cablevision, 4151 Spruill Avenue, North Charleston SC 29405. 843/747-1403.

COMDIAL CORPORATION
1180 Seminole Trail, Charlottesville VA 22906. 804/978-2200. **Fax:** 804/978-2239. **Contact:** Joe Ford, Vice President of Human Resources. **World**

Wide Web address: http://www.comdial.com. **Description:** Designs, manufactures, and markets small- to medium-sized business telephone systems. The company also offers a broad range of advanced telecommunications products and systems solutions based on computer telephone integration, primarily for the hospitality industry. **Corporate headquarters location:** This Location. **Subsidiaries include:** American Phone Centers; American Telecommunications Corp.; Comdial Business Communications Corp.; Comdial Consumer Communications Corp.; Comdial Enterprise Systems; Comdial Telecommunications International; Comdial Telecommunications; Scott Technologies Corp.

COMSAT CORPORATION
6560 Rock Spring Drive, Bethesda MD 20817-1146. 301/214-3000. **Contact:** Betty Alewine, CEO/President. **World Wide Web address:** http://www.comsat.com. **Description:** A global provider of telecommunications via satellite. **Corporate headquarters location:** This Location. **Subsidiaries include:** COMSAT International operates through three units: COMSAT World Systems provides telecommunications and broadcast services between the U.S. and other countries through INTELSAT; COMSAT Mobile Communications provides maritime, aeronautical, and land-mobile communications services via the global Inmarsat system; and COMSAT International Ventures forms domestic and international telecommunications ventures overseas, providing a range of private-line and public-switched digital communications services. COMSAT Laboratories is a leader in research and development for advanced communications technology. Ascent Entertainment Group, Inc., produces major theatrical films and television entertainment through Beacon Communications, a Los Angeles-based supplier of motion pictures to Columbia/TriStar Pictures.

COMTECH TELECOMMUNICATIONS CORP.
105 Baylis Road, Melville NY 11747-3833. 516/777-8900. **Contact:** Linda Compitello, Personnel Manager. **World Wide Web address:** http://www.comtechtel.com. **Description:** Comtech manufactures and markets high-tech microwave and telecommunications products and systems including antennas, frequency converters, and VSAT transceivers and modems. Products are used worldwide in satellite, tropospheric scatter, and wireless communications systems. The company also manufactures high-power amplifiers which are used to test electronic systems for electromagnetic compatibility and susceptibility; for defense systems; and for high power testing of electronic components and systems. Comtech, through its subsidiaries, offers products to customers including domestic and foreign common carriers and telephone companies, defense contractors, medical and automotive suppliers, oil companies, private and wireless networks, broadcasters, utilities, and government entities. **Educational backgrounds include:** Accounting; Business Administration; Engineering; Marketing. **Benefits:** Dental Insurance; Disability Coverage; Employee Discounts; Life Insurance; Medical Insurance; Tuition Assistance. **Corporate headquarters location:** This Location. **Operations at this facility include:** Administration; Manufacturing.

COMVERSE NETWORK SYSTEMS
100 Quannapowitt Parkway, Wakefield MA 01880. 781/246-9000. **Contact:** Human Resources. **World Wide Web address:** http://www.comversens.com. **Description:** Manufactures and designs networking equipment for the telecommunications industry. **Corporate headquarters location:** This Location.

COMVERSE TECHNOLOGY INC.
170 Crossways Park Drive, Woodbury NY 11797-2048. 516/677-7200. **Contact:** Thelma McFarland, Personnel Manager. **World Wide Web address:** http://www.comverse.com. **Description:** Comverse Technology manufactures, markets, and supports telecommunications systems for multimedia communications and information processing applications. The company's systems are used by fixed and wireless telephone network operators, government agencies, financial institutions, and other public and commercial organizations. Products include AUDIODISK, a multimedia digital monitoring system; and the ULTRA series, a variety of multimedia recording systems. **Subsidiaries include:** Comverse Network Systems; Comverse Infosys; Ulticom; and Startel.

CONESTOGA ENTERPRISES, INC.
202 East First Street, Birdsboro PA 19508. 610/582-8711. **Contact:** Elton Butler, Personnel. **World Wide Web address:** http://www.ceni.com. **Description:** A holding company for three communications firms. **Benefits:** Deferred Compensation; Pension Plan; Retirement Plan; Savings Plan. **Corporate headquarters location:** This Location. **Subsidiaries include:** Conestoga Telephone and Telegraph Company furnishes both regulated and nonregulated telecommunications services to an area in Pennsylvania, which includes parts of Berks, Chester, Lancaster, and Montgomery Counties; Northern Communications, Inc. resells long-distance services; Conestoga Mobile Systems, Inc. provides paging communication services.

CONSOLIDATED SERVICES GROUP
661 Pleasant Street, Norwood MA 02062. 781/769-7716. **Toll-free phone:** 800/780-5080. **Fax:** 781/440-0024. **Contact:** Personnel. **Description:** A telecommunications and voice data firm. **NOTE:** Entry-level positions are offered. **Common positions include:** Design Engineer; Project Manager; Sales Rep. **Educational backgrounds include:** Communications. **Benefits:** 401(k); Dental Insurance; Tuition Assistance. **Special programs:** Apprenticeships; Internships; Training. **Corporate headquarters location:** This Location. **Other U.S. locations:** Anaheim CA; Denver CO; North Stonington CT; Las Vegas NV. **Parent company:** Constar International, Inc.

CONVERGENT NATIONAL ACCOUNTS
400 Inverness Drive South, Suite 400, Englewood CO 80112. 303/749-3000. **Contact:** Manager of Human Resources. **Description:** Convergent National Accounts develops, manufactures, and markets key telecommunications systems for the business and residential markets. The company offers 24-hour customer service support and also provides services to help uncover 800 telephone number fraud. **Common positions include:** Accountant; Advertising Clerk; Attorney; Blue-Collar Worker Supervisor; Buyer; Commercial Artist; Computer Programmer; Customer Service Rep.; Draftsperson; Electrical Engineer; Financial Analyst; Human Resources Manager; Industrial Engineer; Public Relations Specialist; Quality Control Supervisor; Services Sales Rep.; Systems Analyst. **Educational backgrounds include:** Communications; Engineering. **Benefits:** Dental Insurance; Life Insurance; Medical Insurance; Tuition Assistance. **Corporate headquarters location:** This Location. **Subsidiaries include:** Convergent Capital Corporation; Convergent Communications Services, Inc.

COX RADIO, INC.
10 Middle Street, Bridgeport CT 06604-4277. 203/333-4800. **Contact:** Human Resources. **World**

Wide Web address: http://www.coxradio.com. **Description:** Owns and operates more than 15 radio stations. **Corporate headquarters location:** This Location. **Subsidiaries include:** NewCity Communications, Inc.

CYLINK CORPORATION
3131 Jay Street, Santa Clara CA 95054. 408/855-6000. **Fax:** 408/855-6120. **Contact:** Personnel. **E-mail address:** jobs@cylink.com. **World Wide Web address:** http://www.cylink.com. **Description:** Sells satellite dishes to telephone companies for use in underdeveloped countries without existing phone lines. The company also manufactures transcriptions, which are devices that can be attached to a modem to encode data for security purposes. **Common positions include:** Software Engineer. **Educational backgrounds include:** Computer Science; Engineering. **Benefits:** 401(k); Dental Insurance; Employee Discounts; Life Insurance; Medical Insurance; Spending Account; Vision Insurance. **Corporate headquarters location:** This Location. **Other U.S. locations:** DC; IL; NJ. **International locations:** China; Singapore; United Kingdom.

DMC STRATEX NETWORKS
170 Rose Orchard Way, San Jose CA 95134. 408/943-0777. **Fax:** 408/944-1678. **Contact:** Personnel. **World Wide Web address:** http://www. dmcstratexnetworks.com. **Description:** Designs and manufactures wireless products for communications networks. **Corporate headquarters location:** This Location. **International locations:** Asia; Europe; Latin America; Singapore; United Kingdom.

DMX MUSIC LLC
11400 West Olympic Boulevard, Suite 1100, Los Angeles CA 90064. 310/444-1744. **Fax:** 310/444-1717. **Contact:** Personnel. **World Wide Web address:** http://www.dmxmusic.com. **Description:** Programs, distributes, and markets a premium digital music service, Digital Music Express, which provides continuous, commercial-free, CD-quality music programming. DMX is delivered by two methods: for a monthly, per-subscriber license fee, it is sent direct to cable operators by C-Band satellite for distribution to residential and commercial cable subscribers; for a monthly, per-subscriber fee, it is distributed by KuBand direct broadcast satellite (DBS) to small satellite dishes which connect through a specially designed DMX tuner to a commercial subscriber's stereo system. **Corporate headquarters location:** This Location.

DANTEL, INC.
2991 North Argyle Avenue, Fresno CA 93727. 559/292-1111. **Fax:** 559/348-1426. **Contact:** Stephanie Thiessen, Personnel Manager. **World Wide Web address:** http://www.dantel.com. **Description:** Manufactures telecommunications equipment including data transport products. **Common positions include:** Accountant; Blue-Collar Worker Supervisor; Buyer; Computer Programmer; Customer Service Rep.; Draftsperson; Electrical Engineer; Financial Analyst; Manufacturer's Sales Rep.; Mechanical Engineer; Operations Manager; Purchasing Agent; Quality Control Supervisor; Software Engineer; Systems Analyst; Technical Writer; Wholesale Buyer. **Educational backgrounds include:** Accounting; Business Administration; Computer Science; Engineering; Finance; Marketing. **Benefits:** 401(k); Dental Insurance; EAP; Employee Discounts; Life Insurance; Medical Insurance; Tuition Assistance; Vision Insurance. **Corporate headquarters location:** This Location. **Operations at this facility include:** Administration; Manufacturing; Research and Development; Sales; Service.

DAVOX CORPORATION
6 Technology Park Drive, Westford MA 01886. 978/952-0200. **Contact:** Brian Logue, Director of Human Resources. **World Wide Web address:** http://www.davox.com. **Description:** Develops, markets, implements, supports, and services outbound and inbound/outbound management systems for call center operations. These systems consist mainly of predictive dialing products and related autodialing systems responsible for important business applications including credit/collections, customer service, and telephone sales. Davox Corporation provides unified call center solutions to banks, consumer finance organizations, retailers, and utilities. **Common positions include:** Accountant/Auditor; Budget Analyst; Computer Programmer; Software Engineer; Systems Analyst. **Educational backgrounds include:** Business Administration; Computer Science. **Benefits:** 401(k); Dental Insurance; Disability Coverage; Life Insurance; Medical Insurance; Tuition Assistance. **Special programs:** Internships. **Corporate headquarters location:** This Location. **Other U.S. locations:** Santa Clara CA; Norcross GA; Newtown PA; Dallas TX. **Operations at this facility include:** Administration; Manufacturing; Research and Development; Sales; Service.

DENRO INC.
9318 Gaither Road, Gaithersburg MD 20877. 301/840-1597. **Contact:** Joan Nielubowski, Personnel Manager. **World Wide Web address:** http://www.denro.com. **Description:** Designs, manufactures, and services electronic communications equipment for the air traffic control industry. **Common positions include:** Accountant; Buyer; Computer Operator; Customer Service Rep.; Draftsperson; Electrical Engineer; Marketing Manager; Purchasing Agent; Software Engineer. **Educational backgrounds include:** Accounting; Business Administration; Communications; Computer Science; Engineering; Finance; Marketing. **Benefits:** Dental Insurance; Disability Coverage; Life Insurance; Medical Insurance; Savings Plan; Tuition Assistance. **Special programs:** Internships. **Corporate headquarters location:** This Location. **Parent company:** Litton Systems, Inc. **Operations at this facility include:** Research and Development; Sales; Service.

DENVER & EPHRATA TELEPHONE AND TELEGRAPH COMPANY (D & E)
4139 Oregon Pike, Ephrata PA 17522. 717/733-4101. **Contact:** Personnel. **Description:** Furnishes telephone service to an estimated population of 100,000 in parts of Berks, Lancaster, and Lebanon Counties in Pennsylvania. The company also owns and operates 25 remote digital dial tone facilities throughout its service area. Local, national, and international telephone services are furnished through these facilities and interconnections with the facilities of other companies. The company also provides videoconferencing services and one-way tone, display, and wide-area paging services. **Benefits:** 401(k); ESOP; Retirement Plan. **Subsidiaries include:** Red Rose Systems, Inc. sells, installs, and maintains telecommunications equipment, and provides long-distance telephone services; D&E Marketing Corporation provides residential and business telecommunications services in Hungary.

DIALOGIC CORPORATION
1515 Route 10, Parsippany NJ 07054. 973/993-3000. **Contact:** Personnel. **World Wide Web address:** http://www.dialogic.com. **Description:** Offers computer telephony services that provide

telephone network access to computer terminals. **Corporate headquarters location:** This Location.

R.L. DRAKE COMPANY
230 Industrial Drive, Franklin OH 45005. 513/746-4556. **Fax:** 513/743-4507. **Contact:** Steve Morgan, Vice President & General Manager. **E-mail address:** morgan@rldrake.com. **World Wide Web address:** http://www.rldrake.com. **Description:** A major manufacturer of satellite receivers. **Common positions include:** Accountant; AS400 Programmer Analyst; CFO; Communications Engineer; Customer Service Rep.; Design Engineer; Draftsperson; Electrical Engineer; Electrician; General Manager; Industrial Designer; Industrial Production Manager; Manufacturing Engineer; Marketing Manager; Mechanical Engineer; MIS Specialist; Production Manager; Quality Assurance Engineer; Sales Manager; Secretary. **Educational backgrounds include:** Accounting; AS400 Certification; Business Administration; C/C++; Engineering; MBA; Microsoft Office; Microsoft Word; Spreadsheets. **Benefits:** 401(k); Casual Dress - Daily; Employee Discounts; Life Insurance; Medical Insurance; Relocation Assistance; Tuition Assistance. **Corporate headquarters location:** This Location. **President/CEO/Owner:** Ron Wysong.

ELCOTEL, INC.
6428 Parkland Drive, Sarasota FL 34243. 941/758-0389. **Toll-free phone:** 800/352-6835. **Fax:** 941/753-2610. **Contact:** Kathy Fischer, Human Resources Manager. **World Wide Web address:** http://www.elcotel.com. **Description:** Offers telecommunications systems and services. **NOTE:** Entry-level positions are offered. **Common positions include:** Customer Service Rep.; Design Engineer; Electrical Engineer; Software Engineer. **Educational backgrounds include:** Engineering. **Benefits:** 401(k); Dental Insurance; Life Insurance; Medical Insurance; Tuition Assistance. **Corporate headquarters location:** This Location. **Operations at this facility include:** Administration; Research and Development; Sales; Service.

ELECTRONICS TELE-COMMUNICATIONS
1915 MacArthur Road, Waukesha WI 53188. 262/542-5600. **Fax:** 262/542-1524. **Contact:** Personnel. **World Wide Web address:** http://www.etcia.com. **Description:** Develops, manufactures, markets, services, and leases interactive voice systems for the telephone industry. Services include software design, equipment installation, recording services, and technical support. **Corporate headquarters location:** This Location.

EMCEE BROADCAST PRODUCTS, INC.
P.O. Box 68, White Haven PA 18661-0068. 570/443-9575. **Toll-free phone:** 800/233-6193. **Fax:** 570/443-9257. **Contact:** Ms. Nelda Seibel, Personnel Manager. **World Wide Web address:** http://www.emceebrd.com. **Description:** Sells and manufactures Multichannel Multipoint Distribution Service microwave transmitters for the wireless cable industry and low-power television translators and transmitters for the television broadcast industry. The company also provides all services relative to the design, procurement, and installation of television broadcast stations, with the exception of licensing submissions. **Benefits:** Incentive Plan. **Corporate headquarters location:** This Location. **Subsidiaries include:** Pro-Community TV (PA); EMCEE Cellular (DE); EMCEE Export Sales Company (DE); and R.F. Systems (DE).

EMMIS COMMUNICATIONS
40 Monument Circle, Suite 700, Indianapolis IN 46204. 317/266-0100. **Contact:** Carolyn Herald, Personnel Director. **Description:** Owns and operates FM radio stations and publishes a monthly statistical publication for the radio industry. **Corporate headquarters location:** This Location.

ERICSSON INC.
P.O. Box 13969, Research Triangle Park NC 27709. 919/472-7000. **Contact:** Human Resources. **World Wide Web address:** http://www.ericsson.com. **Description:** Provides advanced technology for wireless handset development, and sales and marketing support for North American locations. **Common positions include:** Account Manager; Accountant; Applications Engineer; Budget Analyst; Computer Engineer; Computer Scientist; Financial Analyst; Human Resources Manager; Intellectual Property Lawyer; Market Research Analyst; Marketing Manager; Sales Manager; Software Engineer; Systems Manager. **Educational backgrounds include:** Java. **Special programs:** Co-ops. **Corporate headquarters location:** Richardson TX. **Other U.S. locations:** Lynchburg VA. **International locations:** Worldwide. **Parent company:** L.M. Ericsson.

EXECUTONE INFORMATION SYSTEMS
478 Wheelers Farms Road, Milford CT 06460. 203/876-7600. **Contact:** Human Resources. **World Wide Web address:** http://www.executone.com. **Description:** Designs, manufactures, and supports voice processing and health care communications systems including call center management, telephone and locator systems, videoconferencing, health care communications, and network and data services. Brand names include EXECUTONE, INFOSTAR, and IDS. **Benefits:** 401(k); Stock Option. **Corporate headquarters location:** This Location. **International locations:** Worldwide. **Other U.S. locations:**
- Executone Business Systems, 1700 West Big Beaver Road, Suite 100, Troy MI 48084. 248/649-9100.

FKW INC.
900 NW 63rd, Oklahoma City OK 73116. 405/848-2297. **Fax:** 405/848-2332. **Contact:** Micki Savage, Human Resources Manager. **Description:** Performs telecommunications and information systems maintenance under government contract. **Common positions include:** Blue-Collar Worker Supervisor; Computer Operator; Computer Programmer; Electrical/Electronics Engineer; MIS Specialist; Systems Analyst; Systems Manager; Technical Writer/Editor. **Educational backgrounds include:** Computer Science; Engineering. **Benefits:** 401(k); Dental Insurance; Disability Coverage; Financial Planning Assistance; Life Insurance; Medical Insurance; Profit Sharing. **Corporate headquarters location:** This Location. **Other U.S. locations:** CA; IN; NC; NE; TX; VA. **Listed on:** Privately held.

THE FAIRCHILD CORPORATION
FAIRCHILD COMMUNICATIONS SERVICES
45025 Aviation Drive, Dulles VA 20166. 703/478-5800. **Fax:** 703/478-5767. **Contact:** Personnel. **World Wide Web address:** http://www.fairchildcorp.com. **Description:** Operates in many different divisions: Fairchild Communications Services Company (also at this location) provides comprehensive centralized telecommunications services for commercial office buildings; Fairchild Fasteners U.S. (Torrance CA) manufactures and supplies precision fastening systems, components, and latching devices for aerospace and industrial applications; D-M-E Company (Madison Heights MI) manufactures and supplies tooling and electronic control systems for the plastics injection molding industry; Fairchild Convac U.S. (Fremont CA) manufactures and supplies process equipment

and systems for the semiconductor and related industries; and Fairchild Data Corporation (Scottsdale AZ) manufactures and supplies satellite modems and other high-speed products providing transmission of RF signals. **Common positions include:** Accountant; Administrator; Attorney. **Educational backgrounds include:** Accounting; Business Administration; Liberal Arts. **Benefits:** Dental Insurance; Disability Coverage; Medical Insurance; Pension Plan; Savings Plan; Tuition Assistance. **Corporate headquarters location:** This Location. **Subsidiaries include:** Camloc GmbH (Germany); Fairchild Fasteners (Europe); Fairchild Scandinavian Bellyloading Company AB (Sweden); Fairchild Convac GmbH (Germany); Voi-Shan/Diessel GmbH (Germany). **Number of employees worldwide:** 3,500.

FARMSTEAD TELEPHONE GROUP, INC.
22 Prestige Park Circle, East Hartford CT 06105. 860/282-0010. **Contact:** Human Resources. **World Wide Web address:** http://www.farmstead.com. **Description:** A secondary market reseller of used and/or refurbished AT&T business telephone parts and systems. The company is also a designer, manufacturer, and supplier of proprietary voice processing systems that provide automated call handling, voice and fax messaging, interactive voice response, automated call distribution, and message notification functionality. Farmstead Telephone also provides inventory management, leasing and rental services, disaster recovery services, in-house maintenance training, and other related value-added services to customers worldwide. These products and services are primarily sold to end users, ranging from small companies to large corporations including equipment wholesalers, dealers, distributors, and government agencies and municipalities. **Corporate headquarters location:** This Location.

GAYLORD ENTERTAINMENT COMPANY
One Gaylord Drive, Nashville TN 37214. 615/316-6000. **Contact:** Human Resources Department. **World Wide Web address:** http://www. gaylordentertainment.com. **Description:** diversified entertainment and communications company. Gaylord owns and operates Opryland, the entertainment center and hotel complex. The company also owns the Grand Ole Opry, the General Jackson Showboat, Fiesta Texas, and Opryland Music Group. New operations include the Wildhorse Saloon, Nashville on Stage, the BellSouth Senior Classic at Opryland Golf Tournament, and the Ryman Auditorium renovation. The broadcasting division owns two television stations in Texas and one in Seattle, as well as two radio stations in Tennessee and one in Oklahoma City.

GENERAL COMMUNICATION, INC. (GCI)
2550 Denali Street, Suite 1000, Anchorage AK 99503. 907/265-5600. **Contact:** Human Resources Department. **World Wide Web address:** http://www.gci.com. **Description:** Supplies long-distance and other telecommunications products and services to residential, commercial, and government users. GCI operates in two industry segments: the message and data transmission services industry segment offers message toll, private line, and private network services; and the system sales and the service industry segment offers data communication equipment sales and technical services. **Corporate headquarters location:** This Location. **Subsidiaries include:** GCI Communication Services, Inc. provides private network, point-to-point data, and voice transmission services between Alaska, Hawaii, and the western contiguous United States. GCI Leasing Company,

Inc. owns and leases undersea fiberoptic cable for switched message and private line long-distance services between Alaska and the continental United States.

GENTNER COMMUNICATIONS CORP.
1825 Research Way, Salt Lake City UT 84119. 801/975-7200. **Contact:** Human Resources. **World Wide Web address:** http://www.gentner.com. **Description:** Develops, markets, and distributes audio conferencing products and services for use in the broadcast and teleconferencing markets. Gentner Communications also manufactures listening products which provide amplification at places such as sporting events, museums, and tour buses for those who are hearing impaired. **Corporate headquarters location:** This Location.

GLENAYRE TECHNOLOGIES INC.
5935 Carnegie Boulevard, Charlotte NC 28209. 704/553-0038. **Toll-free phone:** 800/543-2382. **Fax:** 704/553-7878. **Contact:** Personnel. **World Wide Web address:** http://www.glenayre.com. **Description:** Provides paging products and systems including messaging pagers. Other services are for both mobile and fixed telecommunications systems and include voicemail, fax messaging, and debit/prepaid calling card platforms. **Corporate headquarters location:** This Location. **International locations:** Worldwide. **President/CEO:** Eric Doggett.
Other U.S. locations:
- Glenayre Electronics, Inc., One Glenayre Way, Quincy IL 62301. 217/223-3211.

HEARST-ARGYLE TELEVISION, INC.
888 Seventh Avenue, 27th Floor, New York NY 10106. 212/887-6800. **Fax:** 212/887-6835. **Contact:** Personnel. **World Wide Web address:** http://www.hearstargyle.com. **Description:** Owns and manages 26 network affiliated television stations nationwide, and manages seven radio stations. The company's television stations comprise one of the largest non-network owned television station groups. Hearst-Argyle Television, Inc.'s television stations include: WCVB-TV (ABC affiliate in Boston MA); WTAE-TV (ABC affiliate in Pittsburgh PA); WBAL-TV (NBC affiliate in Baltimore MD); WLWT-TV (NBC affiliate in Cincinnati OH); WISN-TV (ABC affiliate in Milwaukee WI); KMBC-TV (ABC affiliate in Kansas City MO); KCCI-TV (CBS affiliate in Des Moines IA); KCRA-TV (NBC affiliate in Sacramento CA); KQCA-TV (WB affiliate in Sacramento/Stockton/Modesto CA); KSBW-TV (NBC affiliate in Monterey/Salinas CA); KOCO-TV (ABC affiliate in Oklahoma City OK); WNAC-TV (Fox affiliate in Providence RI); WDTN-TV (ABC affiliate in Dayton OH); KITV-TV (ABC affiliate in Honolulu HI); WYFF-TV (NBC affiliate in Greenville/Spartanburg SC); WNNE-TV (NBC affiliate in Burlington VT); WAPT-TV (ABC affiliate in Jackson MS); KHBS-TV (ABC affiliate in Fort Smith AR); and KHOG-TV (ABC affiliate in Fayetteville AR). Hearst-Argyle Television also provides management services for WWWB-TV (WB affiliate in Tampa FL); WPBF-TV (ABC affiliate in West Palm Beach FL); KCWB-TV (UPN affiliate in Kansas City MO); WBAL-AM (radio station in Baltimore MD); and WIYY-FM (radio station in Baltimore MD). **NOTE:** In September 1999, Hearst-Argyle Television, Inc. announced a partnership with Internet Broadcasting Systems, Inc. to form a network of "convergence"-based Internet portals. Please contact this location for more information. **Corporate headquarters location:** This Location. **Subsidiaries include:** Hearst-Argyle

Television Productions. **Parent company:** Hearst Publications. **Listed on:** New York Stock Exchange.

HOST COMMUNICATIONS, INC.
546 East Main Street, Lexington KY 40508. 606/226-4678. **Contact:** Personnel. **Description:** Provides media and marketing services to universities, athletic conferences, and the National Collegiate Athletic Association (NCAA). These services primarily include the production, sales, and syndication of Internet, radio, and television broadcasts of football and basketball games; the publishing and printing of athletic and championship programs and magazines; and the management of NCAA Corporate Partner Program. The company's sports services include five national radio broadcasts, one national NCAA magazine, nationally-televised NCAA football and basketball shows, and numerous Internet sites. Host Communications, Inc. also manages the NCAA Corporate Partner Program which features blue chip companies. Included in its products is the Historically Black Collegiate Coalition (HBCC), a collection of more than 20 historically black institutions. The company's Main Street Productions Division operates recording studios that provide live broadcast productions and soundtracks for radio, video, and multirange presentations. The company's publishing division produces 400 annual publications and NCAA basketball championship programs. The printing division of the company offers services including graphic design, computerized typesetting and image assembly, and printing and binding. **Corporate headquarters location:** This Location. **Parent company:** Bull Run Corporation (Atlanta GA) is a diversified holding company with other subsidiaries including Gray Communications Systems (Albany GA) and Datasouth Computer Corporation (Charlotte NC).

INTEGRATED COMMUNICATION SERVICES
44 East Mifflin Street, Suite 501, Madison WI 53703. 608/251-8008. **Fax:** 608/251-7679. **Recorded jobline:** 608/283-3333. **Contact:** Personnel. **Description:** A telecommunications answering service. **Benefits:** Dental Insurance; Medical Insurance. **Corporate headquarters location:** This Location. **Parent company:** Telephone & Data Systems (TDS) is a communications company that provides telecommunications services through local telephone companies, consolidated cellular markets, managed non-consolidated cellular markets, and paging operations centers to telephone, cellular telephone, and radio paging customers across the United States. TDS's business units are TDS Telecommunications Corporation (TDS Telecom), which provides local telephone and access service to rural and suburban areas across the nation and pursues an active program of acquiring operating telephone companies; United States Cellular Corporation, which manages and invests in cellular systems throughout the nation; and American Paging, Inc., which operates paging and voicemail systems, offering a wide variety of service packages including basic local paging service, statewide, regional, and nationwide paging, and voicemail with fax options. TDS's associated service companies include American Communications Consultants, Inc., TDS's engineering and management consulting company, which provides the TDS family of companies and a strong base of non-affiliated clients with solutions for telecommunications technologies; Suttle Press, Inc., TDS's commercial printing subsidiary, which provides high-quality flat-color and full-color printed products to a growing base of commercial customers; and TDS Computing Services, Inc., TDS's information systems subsidiary, which provides systems development,

integration, and operations services to TDS and non-affiliated companies, delivering advanced information system solutions in areas such as billing, network operations, customer contact, financial and human resource management, and office automation.

INTELSAT
3400 International Drive NW, Washington DC 20008. 202/944-7329. **Fax:** 202/295-3279. **Contact:** Human Resources. **World Wide Web address:** http://www.intelsat.int. **Description:** An international telecommunications satellite organization which provides global video, data, and voice communications through 19 satellites. **NOTE:** Part-time jobs and second and third shifts are offered. **Common positions include:** Account Manager; Account Rep.; Accountant; Administrative Assistant; Advertising Executive; Attorney; Auditor; Budget Analyst; Buyer; CFO; Communications Engineer; Computer Programmer; Computer Scientist; Controller; Customer Service Rep.; Database Administrator; Database Manager; Desktop Publishing Specialist; Economist; Electrical Engineer; Event Planner; Graphic Artist; Graphic Designer; Human Resources Manager; Industrial Engineer; Intellectual Property Lawyer; Internet Services Manager; Intranet Developer; Market Research Analyst; Marketing Manager; Marketing Specialist; Mechanical Engineer; Network Engineer; Network Administrator; Paralegal; Public Relations Specialist; Purchasing Agent; Quality Assurance Engineer; Registered Nurse; Sales Rep.; Secretary; Software Engineer; Systems Analyst; Systems Manager; Technical Writer; Vice President of Marketing and Sales; Vice President of Operations; Web Advertising Specialist; Webmaster; Website Developer. **Educational backgrounds include:** Accounting; Art/Design; Business Administration; C/C++; Communications; Computer Science; Engineering; Finance; HTML; Internet Development; Marketing; Mathematics; MBA; MCSE; Microsoft Office; Microsoft Word; Public Relations; Software Development; Spreadsheets. **Benefits:** 401(k); Casual Dress - Daily; Dental Insurance; Disability Coverage; Employee Discounts; Flexible Schedule; Life Insurance; Medical Insurance; On-Site Daycare; Pension Plan; Public Transit Available; Relocation Assistance; Sick Days (6 - 10); Tuition Assistance; Vacation Days (16+). **Special programs:** Internships; Summer Jobs. **Corporate headquarters location:** This Location. **Operations at this facility include:** Administration; Sales; Service.

ITRON, INC.
2818 North Sullivan Road, Spokane WA 99216. 509/924-9900. **Fax:** 800/462-6119. **Contact:** Personnel. **E-mail address:** itron@webhire.com. **World Wide Web address:** http://www.itron.com. **Description:** A leading supplier of data acquisition and wireless communications products for the remote data management needs of electric, gas, and water utilities worldwide. The company also designs, manufactures, markets, installs, and services hardware, software, and integrated systems for automatic meter reading and other related applications. Itron's systems are installed at over 1,200 utilities worldwide to read approximately 220 million meters. **NOTE:** Resumes should be sent to Human Resources, P.O. Box 430, Burlington MA 01803. Entry-level positions are offered. **Company slogan:** Collect data, deliver information, enable innovation. **Common positions include:** Account Rep.; Accountant; Administrative Assistant; AS400 Programmer Analyst; Business Analyst; Buyer; Database Administrator; Electrical Engineer; Financial Analyst; Human Resources Manager;

Marketing Manager; Marketing Specialist; Mechanical Engineer; Network Engineer; Network Administrator; Software Engineer. **Educational backgrounds include:** AS400 Certification; C/C++; Microsoft Office; Novell; Software Development; SQL; Visual Basic. **Benefits:** 401(k); Casual Dress - Fridays; Life Insurance; Medical Insurance; Relocation Assistance; Telecommuting; Tuition Assistance. **Corporate headquarters location:** This Location. **Other U.S. locations:** Waseca MN; Raleigh NC; Pittsburgh PA; Philadelphia PA.

KCTS-TV CHANNEL 9
401 Mercer Street, Seattle WA 98109. 206/728-6463. **Fax:** 206/443-6691. **Contact:** Personnel. **World Wide Web address:** http://www.kcts.org. **Description:** A public television station. **Corporate headquarters location:** This Location. **Other U.S. locations:** Washington DC. **Subsidiaries include:** Pacific Coast Public TV (Vancouver, Canada).

KIRO-TV
2807 Third Avenue, Seattle WA 98121. 206/728-7777. **Fax:** 206/728-8784. **Recorded jobline:** 206/728-5205. **Contact:** Julie Kelsch, Human Resources Manager. **World Wide Web address:** http://www.kirotv.com. **Description:** A television broadcasting company. **NOTE:** Part-time jobs are offered. **Common positions include:** Account Manager; Account Representative; Accountant; Administrative Assistant; Broadcast Technician; Controller; Credit Manager; Customer Service Rep.; Editor; Financial Analyst; General Manager; Graphic Artist; Graphic Designer; Human Resources Manager; Managing Editor; Market Research Analyst; Marketing Manager; Public Relations Specialist; Reporter; Sales Manager; TV Broadcaster. **Educational backgrounds include:** Communications. **Benefits:** 401(k); Casual Dress - Fridays; Dental Insurance; Disability Coverage; Employee Discounts; Life Insurance; Medical Insurance; Pension Plan; Public Transit Available; Savings Plan; Tuition Assistance. **Special programs:** Internships. **Internship information:** Applicants for internships must be in their junior or senior years of college or be in their final year of community college or vocational school. Resumes and letters of interest are required. **Corporate headquarters location:** Atlanta GA. **Parent company:** Cox Broadcasting, Inc.

KNME-TV
1130 University Boulevard NE, Albuquerque NM 87102. 505/277-2121. **Fax:** 505/277-2191. **Recorded jobline:** 505/272-5627. **Contact:** Sue Kurman, Office Manager. **World Wide Web address:** http://www.knmetv.org. **Description:** A public television station providing a comprehensive educational format. KNME-TV programs have been broadcast nationwide and honored with both Emmy and Peabody awards. **NOTE:** KNME-TV is considered a department of the University of New Mexico and all hiring is done through the university's Human Resources office. **Common positions include:** Account Rep.; Accountant; Administrative Assistant; Assistant Manager; Broadcast Technician; CFO; Computer Programmer; General Manager; Human Resources Manager; Marketing Manager; Marketing Specialist; Producer; Production Manager; Production Technician; Sales Manager; Sales Rep.; Secretary; Systems Analyst; Systems Manager; Video Production Coordinator. **Educational backgrounds include:** Business Administration; Communications. **Benefits:** Dental Insurance; Disability Coverage; Employee Discounts; Financial Planning Assistance; Flexible Schedule; Life Insurance; Medical Insurance; Pension Plan; Public Transit Available; Savings Plan; Tuition Assistance.

Special programs: Internships. **Internship information:** Unpaid internships can be used towards UNM credit. **Parent company:** University of New Mexico.

KPHO-TV5
4016 North Black Canyon Highway, Phoenix AZ 85017. 602/264-1000. **Fax:** 602/274-1596. **Recorded jobline:** 602/650-5562. **Contact:** Personnel. **World Wide Web address:** http://www.kphotv.com. **Description:** A CBS-affiliated television station. **NOTE:** Part-time jobs are offered. **Common positions include:** Account Manager; Account Representative; Accountant; Administrative Assistant; Advertising Clerk; Advertising Executive; Controller; Credit Manager; General Manager; Graphic Artist; Human Resources Manager; Market Research Analyst; Marketing Specialist; MIS Specialist; Operations Manager; Reporter; Sales Executive; Sales Manager; Technical Writer; Telecommunications Manager; Video Production Coordinator; Web Advertising Specialist. **Educational backgrounds include:** Communications; Journalism; Microsoft Office; Microsoft Word. **Benefits:** 401(k); Casual Dress - Fridays; Dental Insurance; Disability Coverage; Employee Discounts; Financial Planning Assistance; Flexible Schedule; Life Insurance; Medical Insurance; Pension Plan; Relocation Assistance; Sick Days (11+); Tuition Assistance; Vacation Days (10 - 20). **Corporate headquarters location:** Des Moines IA. **Parent company:** Meredith Corporation. **President:** Pat North.

KVWB
3830 South Jones Boulevard, Las Vegas NV 89103. 702/382-2121. **Contact:** Human Resources. **World Wide Web address:** http://www.sbgi.net. **Description:** A Warner Bros.-affiliated television station. **Common positions include:** Account Manager; Accountant; Administrative Assistant; Computer Support Technician; Controller; Credit Manager; Financial Analyst; General Manager; Marketing Manager; Sales Executive; Webmaster. **Educational backgrounds include:** Accounting; Business Administration; Engineering; Finance; Marketing; Microsoft Office; Microsoft Word; Novell; Spreadsheets. **Benefits:** 401(k); Dental Insurance; Medical Insurance; Tuition Assistance. **Corporate headquarters location:** Hunt Valley MD. **Parent company:** Sinclair Broadcast Group.

THE KENTUCKY NETWORK
KENTUCKY EDUCATIONAL SERVICES
600 Cooper Drive, Lexington KY 40502. 606/258-7112. **Contact:** Human Resources. **Description:** A broadcasting network company. **Common positions include:** Electrical/Electronics Engineer; Human Resources Manager; Production Worker. **Benefits:** Life Insurance; Medical Insurance; Pension Plan; Tuition Assistance. **Corporate headquarters location:** This Location. **Operations at this facility include:** Administration.

KEPTEL, INC.
56 Park Road, Tinton Falls NJ 07724. 732/389-8800. **Fax:** 732/460-5483. **Contact:** Peggy Morrissey, Personnel Manager. **Description:** Designs and manufactures telecommunications network interface systems and connection apparatus. The majority of sales are made directly to the Regional Bell Operating Companies. Keptel also manufactures various interconnect and transmission devices used in fiberoptic networks, concentrating on products for standard telephone lines installed for voice transmission. **Common positions include:** Accountant; Buyer; Designer; Draftsperson; Electrical Engineer; Human Resources Manager; Mechanical Engineer; Purchasing Agent; Software

Engineer. **Educational backgrounds include:** Accounting; Business Administration; Engineering; Finance; Marketing; Physics. **Benefits:** 401(k); Dental Insurance; Disability Coverage; Life Insurance; Medical Insurance; Tuition Assistance. **Corporate headquarters location:** This Location. **Other U.S. locations:** El Paso TX. **Parent company:** ANTEC Corporation. **Operations at this facility include:** Administration; Manufacturing; Research and Development; Sales; Testing.

LXE INC.
EMS TECHNOLOGIES
P.O. Box 7700, Norcross GA 30091. 770/447-4224. **Contact:** Human Resources Manager. **World Wide Web address:** http://www.lxe.com. **Description:** Manufactures wireless radio equipment and data communications systems including scanners for warehouses and narrowband wireless systems. **Corporate headquarters location:** This Location.

LORAL SPACE & COMMUNICATIONS
600 Third Avenue, 38th Floor, New York NY 10016. 212/697-1105. **Contact:** Human Resources. **World Wide Web address:** http://www.loral.com. **Description:** A satellite communications company operating through three subsidiaries. **Corporate headquarters location:** This Location. **Other U.S. locations:** Washington DC. **Subsidiaries include:** Space Systems/Loral (Palo Alto CA) manufactures communications and weather satellites used by companies and NASA; Globalstar enables wireless service providers to offer services in every area of the world through a network of 48 low-Earth-orbit satellites; Skyne operates the Telstar network which provides direct-to-home subscription and pay-per-view television via satellite systems, and leases transponder capacity in order to distribute network programming to local television affiliates. **Number of employees nationwide:** 40,000.

L3 COMMUNICATIONS
SATELLITE TRANSMISSION SYSTEMS DIVISION
125 Kennedy Drive, Hauppauge NY 11788. 631/231-1919. **Contact:** Personnel. **Description:** Manufactures and installs satellite Earth station ground communication equipment and systems. **Corporate headquarters location:** This Location. **Other U.S. locations:** Melbourne FL. **Number of employees nationwide:** 460.

LUCENT TECHNOLOGIES INC.
600-700 Mountain Avenue, Murray Hill NJ 07974. **Contact:** Employment Manager. **World Wide Web address:** http://www.lucent.com. **Description:** Manufactures communications products including switching, transmission, fiberoptic cable, wireless systems, and operations systems to fulfill the needs of telephone companies and other communications services providers. **Corporate headquarters location:** This Location.

MCC PANASONIC
776 Highway 74 South, Peachtree City GA 30269. 770/487-3356. **Fax:** 770/487-3357. **Contact:** Personnel. **Description:** A manufacturer of original equipment car audio parts. The company also manufactures telecommunications products including digital business systems (DBS). **Common positions include:** Electrical Engineer; Mechanical Engineer; Telecommunications Manager. **Educational backgrounds include:** Engineering. **Benefits:** 401(k); Credit Union; Dental Insurance; Disability Coverage; Employee Discounts; Life Insurance; Medical Insurance; Pension Plan; Tuition Assistance. **Corporate headquarters location:** This Location. **Other U.S. locations:** Nationwide. **Operations at this facility include:** Manufacturing.

METRO TEL CORPORATION
250 South Milpitas Boulevard, Milpitas CA 95035. 408/946-4600. **Contact:** Human Resources. **Description:** Manufactures and sells telephone test, station, and customer premise equipment, and related accessories. Metro Tel's products are marketed to independently-operating telephone companies, long-distance resellers, telephone interconnect companies, and large corporations with their own telecommunications systems. **Corporate headquarters location:** This Location.

METROCALL, INC.
6677 Richmond Highway, Alexandria VA 22306. 703/660-6677. **Contact:** Human Resources. **Description:** A leading provider of local and regional paging services in the Northeast, mid-Atlantic, and Southeast regions of the United States, as well as California, Nevada, and Arizona. Metrocall also provides nationwide wireless communications for pagers, data terminals, personal computers, and personal digital assistants. **Corporate headquarters location:** This Location. **Number of employees nationwide:** 2,500.

MONTGOMERY COMMUNITY TELEVISION
7548 Standish Place, Rockville MD 20855. 301/424-1730. **Fax:** 301/294-7476. **Contact:** Human Resources. **Description:** Operates two cable channels, produces original programming, and provides production training and facilities for residents of Montgomery County. **Common positions include:** Broadcast Technician; Production Technician. **Educational backgrounds include:** Communications; Television. **Benefits:** 401(k); Dental Insurance; Disability Coverage; Job Sharing; Life Insurance; Medical Insurance; Pension Plan. **Corporate headquarters location:** This Location. **Number of employees at this location:** 70.

MOTOROLA, INC.
1303 East Algonquin Road, Schaumburg IL 60196. 847/576-5000. **Contact:** Human Resources. **World Wide Web address:** http://www.motorola.com. **Description:** This location manufactures two-way radios. Overall, Motorola manufactures communications equipment and electronic products including car radios, cellular phones, semiconductors, computer systems, cellular infrastructure equipment, pagers, cordless phones, and LANs. **Corporate headquarters location:** This Location. **Other U.S. locations:** Nationwide. **International locations:** Worldwide.

NBC
30 Rockefeller Plaza, New York NY 10112. 212/664-4444. **Contact:** Personnel. **World Wide Web address:** http://www.nbc.com. **Description:** A national television broadcasting communications firm. **Corporate headquarters location:** This Location. **Parent company:** General Electric Corporation.

NBC INTERNET
300 Montgomery Street, 3rd Floor, San Francisco CA 94104. 415/288-2500. **Contact:** Human Resources. **World Wide Web address:** http://www. nbci.com. **Description:** A global integrated media company that uses the Internet, broadcast and cable television, and radio to connect advertisers and partners with users and customers.

NEC AMERICA INC.
14040 Park Center Road, Herndon VA 20171. 703/834-4000. **Contact:** Personnel. **World Wide Web address:** http://www.nec.com. **Description:** Manufactures communications systems and

equipment, computers, industrial electronic systems, electronic devices, and home electronic products.

THE NASHVILLE NETWORK COUNTRY MUSIC TELEVISION (CMT)
2806 Opryland Drive, Nashville TN 37214. 615/889-6840. **Recorded jobline:** 888/866-0352. **Contact:** Personnel. **World Wide Web address:** http://www.cbsnashvillejobs.com. **Description:** A cable network serving national cable viewers with country music and country lifestyle programming. Country Music Television (also at this location) is a 24-hour country music video channel featuring top country hits. **Parent company:** CBS Cable.

NATIONAL PUBLIC RADIO (NPR)
635 Massachusetts Avenue NW, Washington DC 20001-3753. 202/414-2000. **Fax:** 202/414-3047. **Recorded jobline:** 202/414-3030. **Contact:** Donald Washington, Personnel Associate. **E-mail address:** employment@npr.org. **World Wide Web address:** http://www.npr.org. **Description:** Production center of the national public radio network. **NOTE:** Second and third shifts are offered. **Common positions include:** Administrative Assistant; Attorney; Broadcast Technician; Computer Programmer; Editor; Editorial Assistant; Financial Analyst; Graphic Artist; Graphic Designer; Human Resources Manager; Internet Services Manager; Librarian; Production Manager; Radio Announcer; Reporter; Systems Analyst; Technical Writer; Typist; Webmaster. **Educational backgrounds include:** Accounting; Art; Business Administration; Communications; Computer Science; Economics; Engineering; Finance; Liberal Arts; Marketing; Public Relations; Software Development; Software Tech. Support. **Benefits:** 401(k); Dental Insurance; Disability Coverage; Flexible Schedule; Job Sharing; Life Insurance; Medical Insurance; Pension Plan. **Special programs:** Internships; Co-ops; Summer Jobs. **Corporate headquarters location:** This Location. **Other U.S. locations:** Los Angeles CA; Chicago IL; New York NY. **International locations:** Worldwide. **CEO:** Delano Lewis.

NATURAL MICROSYSTEMS CORP.
100 Crossing Boulevard, Framingham MA 01702. 508/620-9300. **Contact:** Personnel. **World Wide Web address:** http://www.nmss.com. **Description:** Designs, manufactures, and markets enabling technology products for the call processing market. These products permit others to efficiently develop and implement high performance, PC-based call processing systems which provide applications in one or a combination of areas such as automated attendant, voicemail, and interactive voice response. Product applications include telephone banking, medical alert services, pay-per-view cable services, and telemarketing. **Corporate headquarters location:** This Location.

NEXTEL COMMUNICATIONS
2001 Edmund Halley Drive, Reston VA 20191. 703/433-4000. **Contact:** Human Resources. **World Wide Web address:** http://www.nextel.com. **Description:** Engaged in the specialized mobile radio (SMR) wireless communications business. These services permit the company's customers to dispatch fleets of vehicles and place calls using their two-way mobile radios to or from any telephone in North America through interconnection with the public switched telephone network. Nextel Communications also sells and rents two-way mobile radio equipment and provides related installation, repair, and maintenance services. **Corporate headquarters location:** This Location. **Other U.S. locations:**
- 6700 North Andrews Avenue, Suite 700, Fort Lauderdale FL 33309. 954/275-2400.

NORTHLAND COMMUNICATIONS CORP.
1201 Third Avenue, Suite 3600, Seattle WA 98101. 206/621-1351. **Toll-free phone:** 800/448-0273. **Fax:** 206/623-9015. **Contact:** Human Resources. **Description:** Provides cable television services, local news production, and local advertising for small market radio and cable systems. **Common positions include:** Accountant; Advertising Clerk; Attorney; Broadcast Technician; Budget Analyst; Clerical Supervisor; Computer Programmer; Customer Service Rep.; Financial Analyst; General Manager; Paralegal; Reporter; Systems Analyst; TV Broadcaster; Video Editor. **Educational backgrounds include:** Accounting; Business Administration; Communications; Computer Science; Economics; Finance; Liberal Arts; Marketing. **Benefits:** 401(k); Dental Insurance; Employee Discounts; Life Insurance; Medical Insurance. **Corporate headquarters location:** This Location. **Other U.S. locations:** Nationwide. **Operations at this facility include:** Administration. **Number of employees nationwide:** 470.

OUTLET COMMUNICATIONS, INC.
23 Kenney Drive, Cranston RI 02920. 401/455-9222. **Contact:** Joanne Schenck, Personnel Administrator. **Description:** A television broadcasting company. Outlet Communications, Inc. owns and operates two NBC network affiliates, one independent UHF television station, and two VHF television stations. The UHF station is based in Clayton NC (WNCN-TCV) and broadcasts to the Raleigh-Durham area. One VHF station is located in Columbus OH (WCMH-TV), and the other is based in Cranston RI (WJAR-TV) and serves the Providence RI and New Bedford MA communities. Another UHF television station (WWHO-TV) operates under a local marketing agreement and broadcasts to the Columbus OH area. **Common positions include:** Accountant; Broadcast Engineer; Editor; Manufacturer's Sales Rep.; Reporter. **Educational backgrounds include:** Accounting; Business Administration; Communications; Liberal Arts. **Benefits:** Dental Insurance; Disability Coverage; Life Insurance; Medical Insurance; Pension Plan; Tuition Assistance. **Corporate headquarters location:** This Location. **Other U.S. locations:** Clayton NC; Chillicothe OH; Columbus OH. **Operations at this facility include:** Administration. **Listed on:** NASDAQ.

PAGENET
14911 Quorum Drive, Dallas TX 75240. 972/801-8000. **Contact:** Personnel. **World Wide Web address:** http://www.pagenet.com. **Description:** Provides paging services. **Corporate headquarters location:** This Location.

PAIRGAIN TECHNOLOGIES, INC.
14402 Franklin Avenue, Tustin CA 92780-7013. 714/832-9922. **Fax:** 714/832-9924. **Contact:** Personnel. **World Wide Web address:** http://www.pairgain.com. **Description:** A major supplier of High-bit-rate Digital Subscriber Line (HDSL)-based and HDSL2-based products and systems. PairGain's CopperOptics allows transmission of fiberoptic quality communications over copper cable. PairGain's Solutions give end users instant access to digital services including LAN internetworking and video conferencing. **Corporate headquarters location:** This Location.

PANDUIT CORPORATION
17301 South Ridgeland Avenue, Tinley Park IL 60477. 708/532-1800. **Toll-free phone:** 800/777-3300. **Fax:** 708/614-8357. **Contact:** Cheryl Lewis, Supervisor of Corporate Recruiting. **World Wide Web address:** http://www.panduit.com. **Description:** Manufactures electrical wiring

components, electrical accessories, and communications products. **NOTE:** Entry-level positions are offered. **Common positions include:** Accountant; Buyer; Computer Programmer; Design Engineer; Draftsperson; Electrical Engineer; Industrial Engineer; Manufacturing Engineer; Mechanical Engineer; Purchasing Agent; Sales Engineer. **Educational backgrounds include:** Business Administration; Computer Science; Engineering; Marketing. **Benefits:** 401(k); Daycare Assistance; Dental Insurance; Disability Coverage; Employee Discounts; Flexible Schedule; Life Insurance; Medical Insurance; Profit Sharing; Tuition Assistance. **Special programs:** Internships. **Corporate headquarters location:** This Location. **Other area locations:** Burr Ridge IL; New Lenox IL; Romeoville IL. **International locations:** Costa Rica; Italy; Singapore. **Listed on:** Privately held.

PEOPLE'S CHOICE-TV CORPORATION
2 Corporate Drive, Suite 249, Shelton CT 06484. 203/929-2800. **Fax:** 203/929-1454. **Contact:** Personnel. **Description:** This location houses administrative offices. Overall, People's Choice-TV Corporation develops and operates wireless cable television in various markets throughout the United States. The company offers approximately 48 different entertainment, information, news, and educational services to customers. In addition to channel rights in its operating markets, the company also owns or has rights to operate a portfolio of 73 channels in 14 other markets. **Corporate headquarters location:** This Location. **Other U.S. locations:** AZ; MO; TX. **Parent company:** Sprint Corporation.

PHOTONETICS
200 Corporate Place, Suite 1A, Peabody MA 01960-3840. 978/535-7333. **Contact:** Human Resources. **Description:** This location houses administrative offices. Overall, Photonetics is an international manufacturer and distributor of fiber optic products. **Corporate headquarters location:** This Location.

PIRELLI CABLE CORPORATION
700 Industrial Drive, Lexington SC 29072. 803/951-4800. **Contact:** Human Resources. **Description:** A manufacturer of a broad range of energy cables, fiberoptic telecommunications cables, optical-electronic devices, systems for the telecommunications market, and associated accessories and services. **Common positions include:** Accountant; Blue-Collar Worker Supervisor; Budget Analyst; Buyer; Chemical Engineer; Computer Programmer; Credit Manager; Customer Service Rep.; Designer; Electrical Engineer; Electrician; Financial Analyst; General Manager; Human Resources Manager; Industrial Engineer; Industrial Production Manager; Manufacturer's Sales Rep.; Materials Engineer; Mechanical Engineer; Operations Manager; Purchasing Agent; Quality Control Supervisor; Systems Analyst; Technical Writer. **Educational backgrounds include:** Accounting; Computer Science; Engineering; Marketing. **Benefits:** 401(k); Dental Insurance; Disability Coverage; Life Insurance; Medical Insurance; Pension Plan; Savings Plan; Tuition Assistance. **Corporate headquarters location:** This Location. **Other area locations:** Abbeville SC. **Other U.S. locations:** Colusa CA. **Operations at this facility include:** Administration; Manufacturing; Research and Development; Sales; Service. **Number of employees nationwide:** 1,250.

POPVISION CABLE COMPANY
2510 Metropolitan Drive, Trevose PA 19053. 215/396-9400. **Contact:** Personnel. **Description:** Provides television programming to subscribers through the utilization of FCC-licensed microwave frequencies. PopVision's wireless cable service is available in the Philadelphia PA, Cleveland OH, and Bakersfield CA areas. Additionally, the company has certain license rights to develop wireless cable service in the Stockton/Modesto CA area. **Corporate headquarters location:** This Location.

PUBLIC BROADCASTING SYSTEM (PBS)
1320 Braddock Place, Alexandria VA 22314. 703/739-5000. **Contact:** Personnel. **World Wide Web address:** http://www.pbs.org. **Description:** A publicly-funded television network. PBS operates 350 noncommercial stations in all 50 states, Puerto Rico, the U.S. Virgin Islands, Guam, and American Samoa. **Corporate headquarters location:** This Location. **President:** Ervin Duggan.

PULSEPOINT COMMUNICATIONS
6307 Carpinteria Avenue, Carpinteria CA 93013. 805/566-2000. **Contact:** Human Resources. **World Wide Web address:** http://www.plpt.com. **Description:** Designs, manufactures, and markets information processing systems which deliver unified messaging. The company's products enable service providers and large corporations to offer a wide variety of services to end users including basic voicemail, automated attendant, fax mail, and fax overflow (guaranteed fax). **Corporate headquarters location:** This Location.

Q COMM INTERNATIONAL, INC.
1145 South 1680 West, Orem UT 84058. 801/226-4222. **Fax:** 801/222-9555. **Contact:** Personnel. **World Wide Web address:** http://www.qcomm.com. **Description:** A telecommunications services provider that mainly sells prepaid calling cards.

QVC NETWORK, INC.
1365 Enterprise Drive, West Chester PA 19380. 610/701-1000. **Fax:** 610/701-1150. **Recorded jobline:** 610/344-7777. **Contact:** Human Resources Manager. **World Wide Web address:** http://www.qvc.com. **Description:** A leader in electronic retailing with shopping available on television 24 hours per day. The retail programming is transmitted to over 55 million U.S. households. **Common positions include:** Accountant; Administrative Assistant; Broadcast Technician; Budget Analyst; Buyer; Computer Programmer; Customer Service Rep.; Financial Analyst; Graphic Designer; Human Resources Manager; Industrial Engineer; Librarian; Market Research Analyst; Marketing Specialist; MIS Specialist; Project Manager; Public Relations Specialist; Purchasing Agent; Quality Control Supervisor; Sales Executive; Secretary; Software Engineer; Systems Analyst; Systems Manager; Telecommunications Manager; Video Production Coordinator. **Educational backgrounds include:** Accounting; Art/Design; Business Administration; Communications; Computer Science; Engineering; Finance; Marketing; Mathematics; Public Relations; Radio. **Benefits:** 401(k); Dental Insurance; Disability Coverage; Employee Discounts; Flexible Schedule; Life Insurance; Medical Insurance; Pension Plan; Tuition Assistance. **Special programs:** Internships. **Internship information:** The company offers internships in broadcasting, merchandising, customer service, distribution, guest relations, information systems and technology, finance, and creative services. Please send a resume and cover letter to the College Relations Department. Applications are accepted on a rolling basis. **Corporate headquarters location:** This Location. **Other U.S. locations:** DE; TX; VA. **International locations:** Germany; United Kingdom. **Parent company:** Comcast Corporation.

QUALCOMM INCORPORATED
P.O. Box 919013, San Diego CA 92191-9013. 858/587-1121. **Recorded jobline:** 858/658-JOBS. **Contact:** Human Resources Staffing. **E-mail address:** resumes@qualcomm.com. **World Wide Web address:** http://www.qualcomm.com. **Description:** This location houses the corporate headquarters as well as CDMA University, the company's training facility. Overall, QUALCOMM Incorporated designs and manufactures CDMA (Code Division Multiple Access) wireless products. These products include digital cellular portable phones that use microprocessors, allowing good voice quality, low power requirements, and a wide coverage area. The company manufactures a wide variety of communications products from desktop phones to the OmniTRACS satellite communications system, all using CDMA technology. QUALCOMM Incorporated also designs and manufactures network planning software to help design wireless networks; and indoor or outdoor base stations for cellular and wireless local loop systems. The company also offers wireless network planning and deployment services. **Company slogan:** We're building the wireless world. **Benefits:** 401(k); Computer Loans; Credit Union; Death/Dismemberment Insurance; Dependent Care Expense; EAP; ESOP; Health Care Reimbursement; Life Insurance; Medical Insurance; STD/LTD Coverage; Tuition Assistance; Workers' Compensation Plan. **Special programs:** Training. **Corporate headquarters location:** This Location. **Other U.S. locations:** Boulder CO. **International locations:** Beijing, China; Buenos Aires, Argentina; New Delhi, India; Ontario, Canada.

QWEST COMMUNICATIONS
555 17th Street, Suite 1000, Denver CO 80202. 303/992-1400. **Contact:** Human Resources. **World Wide Web address:** http://www.qwest.com. **Description:** A long-distance telecommunications carrier that provides a broad array of domestic and international voice and data services to commercial and residential customers. Qwest Communications provides services to customers through its network of digital fiberoptic facilities. **Corporate headquarters location:** This Location.

RCN CORPORATION
105 Carnegie Center, Princeton NJ 08540. 609/734-3700. **Fax:** 609/734-3789. **Contact:** Employment Administrator. **World Wide Web address:** http://www.rcn.com. **Description:** A full-service communications company that provides customers with cable, Internet, long-distance telephone, and local telephone services. **NOTE:** Entry-level positions and second and third shifts are offered. **Common positions include:** Accountant; Administrative Assistant; Computer Programmer; Customer Service Rep.; Financial Analyst; General Manager; Graphic Artist; Human Resources Manager; Internet Services Manager; Market Research Analyst; MIS Specialist; Paralegal; Sales Executive; Sales Rep.; Typist; Webmaster. **Educational backgrounds include:** Accounting; Marketing; Software Tech. Support. **Benefits:** 401(k); Dental Insurance; Disability Coverage; Flexible Schedule; Life Insurance; Medical Insurance; Profit Sharing; Tuition Assistance. **Special programs:** Co-ops. **Corporate headquarters location:** This Location. **Other U.S. locations:** DC; MA; NY; PA; VA. **Subsidiaries include:** Starpower LLC. **Annual sales/revenues:** $51 - $100 million. **Number of employees nationwide:** 1,400.

RF MONOLITHICS, INC.
4347 Sigma Road, Dallas TX 75244. 972/233-2903. **Contact:** Personnel. **World Wide Web address:** http://www.rfm.com. **Description:** Designs, sells, develops, and manufactures a broad range of radio frequency components and modules for the low-power wireless, high-frequency timing, and telecommunications markets. The company's products are based on surface acoustic wave reduced power consumption. The company markets its line of more than 500 resonators, filters, delay lines, and related modules to original equipment manufacturers worldwide. **Corporate headquarters location:** This Location. **Listed on:** NASDAQ.

RADIO FREE EUROPE/RADIO LIBERTY
1201 Connecticut Avenue NW, Suite 400, Washington DC 20036. 202/457-6900. **Contact:** Human Resources. **World Wide Web address:** http://www.rferl.org. **Description:** A radio station. **Special programs:** Internships. **Internship information:** The RFE/RL journalism intern program introduces qualified graduate students to news reporting in Central Europe and the successor states of the former Soviet Union. Interns should be graduate students at schools of journalism, communications, political science, or international relations and should have some relevant on-the-job experience. Applicants are asked to submit two letters of recommendation, samples of broadcast or published material, and a resume and cover letter indicating interest and summarizing qualifications. In addition, applicants are asked to fill out an additional application form. **Corporate headquarters location:** This Location. **International locations:** Prague, Czech Republic.

RESOURCE CONSULTANTS INC. (RCI)
1960 Gallows Road, Vienna VA 22182. 703/893-6120. **Fax:** 703/893-0917. **Contact:** Personnel. **E-mail address:** rcijobs@resourceconsultants.com. **World Wide Web address:** http://www.rcihome.com. **Description:** A diversified defense contractor holding U.S. Navy communications equipment contracts. RCI also provides support for the U.S. Postal Service and job placement counseling for the U.S. Army. **NOTE:** Entry-level positions and part-time jobs are offered. **Common positions include:** Administrative Assistant; Applications Engineer; Counselor; Operations Manager; Software Engineer; Systems Analyst; Technical Writer; Webmaster. **Educational backgrounds include:** C/C++; CGI; Cold Fusion; Computer Science; Engineering; HTML; Internet; Java; Mathematics; MCSE; Microsoft Word; Spreadsheets; Visual Basic. **Benefits:** 401(k); Dental Insurance; Disability Coverage; Flexible Schedule; Job Sharing; Life Insurance; Medical Insurance; Tuition Assistance; Vacation Days (6 - 10). **Special programs:** Training. **Corporate headquarters location:** This Location. **Other U.S. locations:** Nationwide. **Number of employees nationwide:** 1,400.

ROANWELL CORPORATION
180 Varick Street, New York NY 10014. 212/989-1090. **Contact:** Ken Dobbins, President. **World Wide Web address:** http://www.roanwellcorp.com. **Description:** Manufactures terminal voice communication equipment.

SBC COMMUNICATIONS INC.
SOUTHWESTERN BELL
175 East Houston Street, San Antonio TX 78205. 210/821-4105. **Contact:** Personnel. **World Wide Web address:** http://www.sbc.com. **Description:** Provides telecommunications products and services throughout the U.S. and internationally. **Corporate headquarters location:** This Location. **Subsidiaries include:** Ameritech, CellularOne, Nevada Bell, Pacific Bell, SBC Telecom, SNET, and Southwestern Bell (also at this location) provides local telephone and cellular services.

SED INTERNATIONAL
4916 North Royal Atlanta Drive, Tucker GA 30084. 770/491-8962. **Toll-free phone:** 800/444-8962. **Contact:** Human Resources. **World Wide Web address:** http://www.sedonline.com. **Description:** A wholesaler of computer systems and cellular phones. **Corporate headquarters location:** This Location.

SFX ENTERTAINMENT
650 Madison Avenue, 16th Floor, New York NY 10022. 212/980-4455. **Contact:** Human Resources. **Description:** Acquires, owns, and operates radio stations in small- and medium-sized markets in the eastern U.S. SFX Entertainment's stations are WHMP-FM, WHMP-AM, and WPKX-FM, each operating in the Springfield/Northampton MA market; WYAK-FM and WYAK-AM, operating in the Myrtle Beach SC market; and WKBG-FM and WRXR-FM, each operating in the Augusta GA market. The company also sells advertising to WVCO-FM. **Corporate headquarters location:** This Location. **Parent company:** Sillerman Companies.

SCIENTIFIC-ATLANTA, INC.
BROADBAND COMMUNICATIONS SYSTEMS
One Technology Parkway South, Norcross GA 30092. 770/903-5000. **Toll-free phone:** 800/722-2009. **Contact:** Human Resources. **E-mail address:** sa.staffing@sciatl.com. **World Wide Web address:** http://www.sciatl.com. **Description:** This location develops, manufactures, and supports a line of equipment and systems for broadband terrestrial network delivery of cable television, telephony, and electric utility services. Overall, Scientific-Atlanta, Inc. is a provider of communications equipment, electronics, instrumentation products, and satellite-based network systems. Products and systems are used by cable operations in more than 100 countries, as well as in 9,000 local cable sites in the United States. Scientific-Atlanta also designs, manufactures, installs, operates, and services Earth Station systems and networks that provide audio, video, and data communication services to 135 countries. **Corporate headquarters location:** This Location. **Other area locations:** Atlanta GA. **Other U.S. locations:** Chicago IL. **International locations:** Canada; Mexico.

THE E.W. SCRIPPS COMPANY
312 Walnut Street, Suite 2800, Cincinnati OH 45202. 513/977-3000. **Contact:** Human Resources. **World Wide Web address:** http://www.scripps.com. **Description:** Operates 19 daily newspapers, nine large market television stations, cable systems, two television production companies, a 24-hour cable channel, the Home and Garden television network, and United Media, a licenser and syndicator of news features and comics. **Common positions include:** Accountant; Human Resources Manager; Payroll Clerk; Secretary; Systems Analyst. **Benefits:** Dental Insurance; Disability Coverage; Life Insurance; Long-Term Care; Medical Insurance; Pension Plan; Savings Plan. **Corporate headquarters location:** This Location. **Other U.S. locations:** CA; Evansville IN; Knoxville TN; Memphis TN. **Listed on:** New York Stock Exchange. **Number of employees nationwide:** 8,200.

SHARED TECHNOLOGIES INC.
100 Great Meadow Road, Suite 104, Wethersfield CT 06109. 860/258-2400. **Fax:** 860/258-2401. **Contact:** Human Resources. **Description:** Provides communications equipment and services, facilities management, and consulting services to businesses across the United States. Shared Technologies has on-site personnel that provide sales, service, analysis, maintenance, and customized billing. The company categorizes its services into three divisions: Shared Tenant Services, Cellular Business Services, and Long-Distance Services. Shared Tenant Services offers such products as telephone equipment and services, long-distance and local telephone service, 800 service, voicemail, copiers, facsimile machines, cellular rentals, and LANs. Cellular Business Services provides cellular phone services, wireless facsimile machines and pagers, and mobile telephones. Discounted long-distance services, 800 service, international calling plans, and calling cards are part of the Long-Distance Services division. **Benefits:** 401(k). **Corporate headquarters location:** This Location. **Other U.S. locations:** Nationwide. **Number of employees at this location:** 90.

SIEMENS INFORMATION AND COMMUNICATIONS NETWORKS, INC.
2205 Grand Avenue Parkway, Austin TX 78728-3811. 512/990-1000. **Recorded jobline:** 877/287-8647. **Contact:** Employment Department. **World Wide Web address:** http://www.icnsiemens.com. **Description:** A developer of communications equipment for *Fortune* 1000 businesses, mid- to large-sized companies, retailers, small businesses, and the consumer electronics market. Siemens ICN consists of three units: Communication Devices; Information Technology Services; and Computer Systems. **NOTE:** Applications without current job opening numbers will not be considered. Please call the jobline for current openings. **Common positions include:** Accountant; Electrical Engineer; Industrial Engineer; Mechanical Engineer. **Educational backgrounds include:** Engineering; Finance. **Benefits:** 401(k); Dental Insurance; Disability Coverage; Life Insurance; Medical Insurance; Pension Plan; Savings Plan; Tuition Assistance. **Corporate headquarters location:** Boca Raton FL. **Other U.S. locations:** Cherry Hill NJ. **Parent company:** Siemens AG (Berlin, Germany). **Operations at this facility include:** Administration; Manufacturing; Research and Development. **Listed on:** Privately held. **Number of employees worldwide:** 24,000.

SIGNATRON TECHNOLOGY CORP.
29 Domino Drive, Concord MA 01742. 978/371-0550. **Contact:** Personnel. **World Wide Web address:** http://www.signatron.com. **Description:** Engaged in research and development for advanced communication systems and precision radio location systems. **Common positions include:** Electrical Engineer; Software Engineer. **Educational backgrounds include:** Engineering. **Benefits:** 401(k); Casual Dress - Daily; Dental Insurance; Disability Coverage; Life Insurance; Medical Insurance; Sick Days (6 - 10); Vacation Days (6 - 10). **Corporate headquarters location:** This Location.

SKYTEL COMMUNICATIONS
200 South Lamar Street, 10th Floor, Jackson MS 39201. 601/944-1300. **Fax:** 601/944-7106. **Contact:** Human Resources. **Description:** A telecommunications company specializing in global wireless data communications. Products and services include SkyPager, a nationwide numeric paging service; SkyTalk, a full-featured voicemail system with instant notification of messages via the SkyTel System; and SkyWord, a nationwide wireless text messaging service. Integration with services and computer software features SkyNews, a wireless information service which provides Reuters news headlines to SkyWord subscribers. **Corporate headquarters location:** This Location.

SOUTHWESTERN BELL
1610 Des Peres Road, Suite 200, St. Louis MO 63131. 314/957-3900. **Fax:** 314/957-3912. **Contact:** Eric Anthony, Recruiter. **E-mail address:** ea6487@sbc.com. **World Wide Web address:** http://www.sbc.com. **Description:** Provides local telephone and cellular services. **NOTE:** Part-time jobs and second and third shifts are offered. **Common positions include:** Computer Programmer; Customer Service Representative; Database Administrator; Secretary. **Educational backgrounds include:** Microsoft Office; Microsoft Word; Software Tech. Support; Spreadsheets. **Benefits:** 401(k); Casual Dress - Daily; Dental Insurance; Disability Coverage; Employee Discounts; Flexible Schedule; Life Insurance; Medical Insurance; Pension Plan; Profit Sharing; Savings Plan; Tuition Assistance. **Corporate headquarters location:** San Antonio TX. **Parent company:** SBC Communications Inc.
Other U.S. locations:
- 823 Quincy, Room 104, Topeka KS 66612. 785/276-8952.
- 515 West Pershing, North Little Rock AR 72117. 501/371-9700.

SYMETRICS INDUSTRIES
1615 West NASA Boulevard, Melbourne FL 32901. 321/254-1500. **Contact:** Human Resources. **World Wide Web address:** http://www.symetrics.com. **Description:** Manufactures voicemail and telecommunications systems. **Corporate headquarters location:** This Location.

TDS TELECOM
301 South Westfield Road, Madison WI 53705. 608/664-4000. **Toll-free phone:** 877/741-5627. **Fax:** 608/664-4485. **Contact:** National Recruitment and Selection Team. **World Wide Web address:** http://www.tdstelecom.com. **Description:** Provides local telephone and access service to rural and suburban areas across the nation and pursues an active program of acquiring operating telephone companies. **Common positions include:** Account Manager; Account Rep.; Accountant; Adjuster; Administrative Assistant; Administrative Manager; Blue-Collar Worker Supervisor; Branch Manager; Clerical Supervisor; Computer Programmer; Computer Support Technician; Controller; Cost Estimator; Customer Service Rep.; Database Administrator; Database Manager; Finance Director; Financial Analyst; General Manager; Human Resources Manager; Internet Services Manager; Marketing Manager; Marketing Specialist; MIS Specialist; Operations Manager; Project Manager; Public Relations Specialist; Sales Executive; Sales Manager; Sales Representative; Secretary; Telecommunications Manager. **Educational backgrounds include:** Accounting; Business Administration; Communications; Computer Science; Finance; Marketing; MBA; Microsoft Office; Microsoft Word; Public Relations. **Benefits:** 401(k); Dental Insurance; Disability Coverage; Employee Discounts; Flexible Schedule; Life Insurance; Medical Insurance; Pension Plan; Relocation Assistance; Sick Days (11+); Tuition Assistance; Vacation Days (6 - 10). **Corporate headquarters location:** This Location. **Other U.S. locations:** Nationwide. **Parent company:** Telephone & Data Systems, Inc.'s (TDS) business units include United States Cellular Corporation, which manages and invests in cellular systems throughout the nation; and American Paging, Inc., which operates paging and voicemail systems, offering a wide variety of service packages including basic local paging service, statewide, regional, and nationwide paging, and voicemail with fax options. TDS's associated service companies include American Communications Consultants,

Inc., an engineering and management consulting company; Suttle Press, Inc., a commercial printing subsidiary; and TDS Computing Services, Inc., an information systems subsidiary.

TV GUIDE INC.
7140 South Lewis Avenue, Tulsa OK 74136-5422. 918/488-4000. **Contact:** Human Resources. **World Wide Web address:** http://www.tvguideinc.com. **Description:** A satellite communications company providing video, audio, data, and program promotion services to a worldwide network of cable companies, satellite dish owners, and radio stations. **Corporate headquarters location:** This Location. **Subsidiaries include:** Prevue Networks; SpaceCom Systems; SSDS; Superstar Satellite Entertainment; UVTV. **President/COO:** Peter C. Boylan III. **Annual sales/revenues:** More than $100 million.

TEL-COM WIRELESS CABLE TV CORP.
3957 NE 163rd Street, North Miami Beach FL 33160. 305/947-3010. **Contact:** Human Resources. **Description:** Provides television, cable, and a variety of related services. Tel-Com's wireless cable system is transmitted via microwave frequency to a receiving antenna at the subscriber's home. Founded in 1993. **NOTE:** Despite the location of the company's corporate headquarters in Florida, Tel-Com Wireless Cable TV Corporation offers its cable services only in La Crosse WI. **Corporate headquarters location:** This Location. **Other U.S. locations:** La Crosse WI.

TELECOMMUNICATIONS SYSTEMS, INC.
275 West Street, Suite 400, Annapolis MD 21401. 410/263-7616. **Fax:** 410/263-7617. **Contact:** Jennifer English, Human Resources. **World Wide Web address:** http://www.tcsnet.net. **Description:** Develops prepaid wireless and short message service applications. Founded in 1988. **Common positions include:** Applications Engineer; Auditor; Computer Programmer; Database Manager; Electrical Engineer; Financial Analyst; Internet Services Manager; MIS Specialist; Systems Analyst; Technical Writer; Telecommunications Manager; Webmaster. **Educational backgrounds include:** Communications; Computer Science; Engineering; Finance; Software Development; Software Tech. Support. **Benefits:** 401(k); Dental Insurance; Life Insurance; Medical Insurance. **Corporate headquarters location:** This Location. **Other U.S. locations:** Tampa FL; Atlanta GA; Arlington VA; Newington VA. **President:** Maurice B. Tosc. **Number of employees at this location:** 100. **Number of employees nationwide:** 270.

TELECOMMUNICATIONS TECHNIQUES CORP.
20400 Observation Drive, Germantown MD 20876-4023. 301/353-1550. **Fax:** 301/353-8774. **Contact:** Marilyn Herbert, Recruiter. **World Wide Web address:** http://www.ttc.com. **Description:** This location manufactures portable and digital test equipment for the communications industry. Overall, Telecommunications Techniques provides equipment and services that support and build worldwide information infrastructures. **Common positions include:** Accountant; Buyer; Customer Service Rep.; Electrical Engineer; Industrial Production Manager; Software Engineer; Technical Writer. **Educational backgrounds include:** Accounting; Business Administration; Computer Science; Engineering. **Benefits:** 401(k); Dental Insurance; Disability Coverage; Employee Discounts; Life Insurance; Medical Insurance; Profit Sharing; Tuition Assistance. **Corporate headquarters location:** This Location. **Other U.S. locations:** Nationwide. **Parent company:** Dynatech Corporation's business is separated into two groups: Information Support Products consists of the

businesses which support voice, video, and data communications; Diversified Instrumentation represents a group of electronics and software businesses. **Operations at this facility include:** Administration; Manufacturing; Research and Development; Sales; Service. **Number of employees nationwide:** 800.

TELECRAFTER SERVICES CORP.
13131 West Cedar Drive, Lakewood CO 80228. 303/987-3300. **Contact:** Ms. Bobbie Sharp, Human Resources Manager. **Description:** A subcontractor for cable television companies. Telecrafter Services is involved in the installation and marketing of client companies' products. **Common positions include:** Accountant; Blue-Collar Worker Supervisor; Cable TV Installer; Computer Programmer; Human Resources Manager; Operations Manager; Services Sales Representative. **Educational backgrounds include:** Accounting; Computer Science. **Benefits:** Dental Insurance; Disability Coverage; Life Insurance; Medical Insurance; Tuition Assistance. **Corporate headquarters location:** This Location. **Parent company:** Nassau Communications, Inc.

TELECT, INC.
2111 North Molter Road, Liberty Lake WA 99019. 509/926-6000. **Fax:** 509/927-0852. **Recorded jobline:** 509/892-6200. **Contact:** Personnel. **World Wide Web address:** http://www.telect.com. **Description:** An international designer and manufacturer of fiberoptic, digital, analog, professional audio/video, power, and electronic monitoring and control equipment. **NOTE:** Entry-level positions and second and third shifts are offered. **Common positions include:** Account Manager; Account Representative; Accountant; Administrative Assistant; Advertising Clerk; Advertising Executive; Applications Engineer; Budget Analyst; Buyer; Computer Operator; Computer Programmer; Controller; Cost Estimator; Credit Manager; Customer Service Rep.; Database Manager; Design Engineer; Draftsperson; Electrical Engineer; Finance Director; Financial Analyst; General Manager; Graphic Designer; Human Resources Manager; Industrial Engineer; Internet Services Manager; Manufacturing Engineer; Market Research Analyst; Marketing Manager; Marketing Specialist; Mechanical Engineer; MIS Specialist; Operations Manager; Production Manager; Project Manager; Purchasing Agent; Quality Control Supervisor; Sales Engineer; Sales Executive; Sales Manager; Sales Rep.; Secretary; Software Engineer; Systems Analyst; Systems Manager; Technical Writer; Webmaster. **Educational backgrounds include:** Accounting; Art/Design; Business Administration; Computer Science; Economics; Engineering; Finance; Liberal Arts; Marketing. **Benefits:** 401(k); Daycare Assistance; Dental Insurance; Disability Coverage; Life Insurance; Medical Insurance; Profit Sharing; Savings Plan; Telecommuting; Tuition Assistance. **Special programs:** Internships; Training. **Corporate headquarters location:** This Location. **International locations:** Guadalajara, Mexico. **Number of employees nationwide:** 950. **Number of employees worldwide:** 1,150.

TELEPHONE AND DATA SYSTEMS, INC.
30 North LaSalle Street, Suite 4000, Chicago IL 60602. 312/630-1900. **Fax:** 312/630-9408. **Recorded jobline:** 888/837-5627. **Contact:** Personnel. **World Wide Web address:** http://www. teldta.com. **Description:** Provides local telecommunications services including cellular, landline telephone, and paging to customers nationwide. TDS's strategic business units include United States Cellular Corporation, which manages and invests in cellular systems throughout the nation; TDS Telecommunications Corporation, which provides local telephone and access service to rural and suburban areas across the nation and acquires operating telephone companies; American Paging, Inc., which operates paging and voicemail systems; and Aerial Communications, Inc., which is one of the largest licensees of personal communications services in the United States. **Common positions include:** Accountant; Administrative Assistant; Financial Analyst. **Educational backgrounds include:** Accounting; Business Administration; Communications; Economics; Finance. **Benefits:** 401(k); Dental Insurance; Disability Coverage; Life Insurance; Medical Insurance; Pension Plan; Public Transit Available; Savings Plan; Tuition Assistance. **Corporate headquarters location:** This Location. **Other U.S. locations:** Nationwide. **Subsidiaries include:** Suttle Press, Inc. is a commercial printing subsidiary; TDS Computing Services, Inc. is an information systems subsidiary. **Operations at this facility include:** Administration. **Annual sales/revenues:** More than $100 million. **Number of employees nationwide:** 7,000.

TELLABS
1000 Remington Boulevard, Bolingbrook IL 60440. **Fax:** 630/378-5620. **Contact:** Manager of Global College Relations. **E-mail address:** collegegraduates@tellabs.com. **World Wide Web address:** http://www.tellabs.com. **Description:** Designs, manufactures, markets, and services voice and data transport systems and network access systems used worldwide by public telephone companies, long-distance carriers, alternate service providers, cellular and wireless service providers, cable operators, government agencies, and businesses. **NOTE:** Entry-level positions are offered. **Common positions include:** Hardware Engineer; Software Engineer; Technical Writer. **Educational backgrounds include:** Computer Science; Engineering. **Benefits:** 401(k); Daycare Assistance; Dental Insurance; Disability Coverage; Financial Planning Assistance; Flexible Schedule; Life Insurance; Medical Insurance; Profit Sharing; Stock Option; Tuition Assistance. **Special programs:** Internships. **Internship information:** Tellabs hires 130 summer interns each year. Internships are primarily in software development and testing, and in hardware design and testing. Some positions are available in Web development, technical writing, marketing, and human resources. Applications must be completed by February. **Corporate headquarters location:** This Location. **International locations:** Helsinki, Finland; Shannon, Ireland. **Operations at this facility include:** Administration; Manufacturing; Research and Development; Sales; Service. **Number of employees at this location:** 3,000. **Number of employees nationwide:** 5,000. **Number of employees worldwide:** 7,000. **Other U.S. locations:**
- Tellabs, Nets Division, 45085 University Drive, Ashburn VA 20147. 703/729-6400.

TELS CORPORATION
705 East Main Street, American Fork UT 84003. 801/756-9606. **Contact:** Human Resources. **World Wide Web address:** http://www.telscorp.com. **Description:** Manufactures and services call accounting and other telecommunications systems. **Corporate headquarters location:** This Location.

TELTONE CORPORATION
22121 20th Avenue SE, Bothell WA 98021-4408. 425/487-1515. **Contact:** Ms. Marnie Vitt, Human Resources Manager. **World Wide Web address:** http://www.teltone.com. **Description:** Manufactures

telecommunications equipment including testing equipment for the communications industry and telecommuting products. **Common positions include:** Accountant/Auditor; Buyer; Computer Programmer; Credit Manager; Customer Service Rep.; Electrical Engineer; Financial Analyst; Manufacturer's Sales Rep.; Marketing Specialist; Public Relations Specialist; Quality Control Supervisor; Systems Analyst; Technical Writer. **Educational backgrounds include:** Accounting; Business Administration; Communications; Computer Science; Engineering; Finance; Marketing; Mathematics; Physics. **Benefits:** Dental Insurance; Disability Coverage; Employee Discounts; Life Insurance; Medical Insurance; Profit Sharing; Savings Plan; Stock Option; Tuition Assistance. **Special programs:** Internships. **Corporate headquarters location:** This Location. **Operations at this facility include:** Administration; Manufacturing; Research and Development; Sales; Service. **Number of employees at this location:** 75.

TIME WARNER, INC.
75 Rockefeller Plaza, New York NY 10019. 212/484-8000. **Contact:** Human Resources. **World Wide Web address:** http://www.timewarner.com. **Description:** Publishes and distributes books and magazines including the weekly *Time* magazine. Time Warner also produces, distributes, licenses, and publishes recorded music; owns and administers music copyrights; produces, finances, and distributes motion pictures and television programming; distributes videocassettes; produces and distributes pay television and cable programming; and operates and manages cable television systems. **NOTE:** In January 2000, America Online, Inc. and Time Warner, Inc. announced plans to merge. The new company will be named AOL Time Warner Inc. Also in January 2000, EMI Group PLC and Time Warner, Inc. announced plans to merge their music businesses. Companies affected by this merger will be named Warner EMI Music. Please contact this location for more information. **Corporate headquarters location:** This Location. **Number of employees worldwide:** 38,100.
Other U.S. locations:
- Time Warner Cable, Liberty Division, One Cablevision Center, Suite 2, Ferndale NY 12734. 914/295-2650.

TIMEPLEX GROUP
400 Chestnut Ridge Road, Woodcliff Lake NJ 07652. 201/391-1111. **Toll-free phone:** 800/776-2677. **Fax:** 201/391-0961. **Contact:** Human Resources. **World Wide Web address:** http://www.timeplex.com. **Description:** A leader in enterprise networking solutions for voice, data, and video traffic in the telecommunications industry. **Common positions include:** Electrical Engineer; Industrial Engineer; Software Engineer; Systems Analyst. **Educational backgrounds include:** Business Administration; Communications; Computer Science; Engineering; Finance; Marketing. **Benefits:** 401(k); Dental Insurance; Disability Coverage; Employee Discounts; Life Insurance; Medical Insurance; Profit Sharing; Tuition Assistance. **Special programs:** Internships. **Corporate headquarters location:** This Location. **Other U.S. locations:** Nationwide. **International locations:** Worldwide. **Operations at this facility include:** Administration; Manufacturing; Research and Development; Sales; Service.

TONE COMMANDER SYSTEMS INC.
11609 49th Place West, Mukilteo WA 98275-4255. 425/349-1000. **Fax:** 425/349-1010. **Contact:** Personnel. **World Wide Web address:** http://www. tonecommander.com. **Description:** Manufactures telecommunications equipment including Centrex attendant consoles and ISDN equipment. **Common positions include:** Electrical/Electronics Engineer; Software Engineer. **Educational backgrounds include:** Computer Science; Engineering. **Benefits:** 401(k); Dental Insurance; Disability Coverage; Life Insurance; Medical Insurance; Vacation Days. **Corporate headquarters location:** This Location. **Operations at this facility include:** Administration; Manufacturing; Research and Development; Sales. **Number of employees at this location:** 40.

U S WEST COMMUNICATIONS
1801 California Street, Suite 200, Denver CO 80202. **Fax:** 303/896-7788. **Recorded jobline:** 303/896-7683x1. **Contact:** Manager of Human Resources. **World Wide Web address:** http://www. uswest.com. **Description:** A telecommunications company that operates through several divisions. U S WEST Communications provides a full range of connection solutions to more than 25 million business, government, and residential customers in 14 western and midwestern states. U S WEST's Marketing Resources Group connects buyers and sellers through telephone directories, database marketing, and new multimedia services. The Multimedia Group manages U S WEST's entry into domestic broadband markets outside the region served by U S WEST Communications. Working with local partners, U S WEST International and Business Development Group provides advanced communications and entertainment services to more than 1.8 million customers in 15 rapidly expanding markets around the world. **Corporate headquarters location:** This Location. **Other U.S. locations:** Nationwide.

UNITEDGLOBALCOM, INC.
4643 South Ulster Street, Suite 1300, Denver CO 80237. 303/770-4001. **Fax:** 303/770-4207. **Contact:** Human Resources Department. **World Wide Web address:** http://www.unitedglobal.com. **Description:** UnitedGlobalCom provides integrated broadband television, telephone, and Internet access services. **Corporate headquarters location:** This Location. **Chairman and CEO:** Gene W. Schneider.

VERAMARK TECHNOLOGIES INC.
3750 Monroe Avenue, Pittsford NY 14534. 716/381-6000. **Contact:** Renee Peters, Human Resources. **Description:** Designs and manufactures telecommunication management systems and voice processing products. For businesses that own a telephone system, Veramark Technologies produces call accounting systems which provide a variety of reports to help control telecommunications expenses and usage. For telephone operating companies, the company offers the INFO series of products for management of telecommunications data at the carrier's central office. The INFO/MDR products enable telephone companies to capture and organize message detail records carried by the telephone network in reports that can be used internally by the phone company or provided to their customers as a value-added service. INFO Verabill is a rating and billing system for small telephone and cellular companies. The INFO Bill provides telephone, cellular, and cable television companies with complete billing and support systems. In the voice processing market, Veramark produces voice recognition, speaker verification, and voicemail systems. Veramark's Votan Division (Pleasanton CA) develops computer-based products utilizing patented continuous speech voice-recognition technology. **Corporate headquarters location:** This Location.

VERMONT PUBLIC TELEVISION (VPT)
88 Ethan Allen Avenue, Colchester VT 05446.
802/655-2458. **Fax:** 802/655-6593. **Contact:**
Human Resources. **World Wide Web address:**
http://www.vpt.org. **Description:** Vermont Public
Television (VPT) is a member of Public
Broadcasting Service (PBS) and carries a complete
schedule of PBS programming, as well as programs
purchased from other national sources. VPT
produces programming of local interest and has
several weekly series. **NOTE:** Entry-level positions
are offered. **Common positions include:** Account
Manager; Accountant; Administrative Assistant;
Broadcast Technician; CFO; Marketing Manager;
Video Production Coordinator. **Educational
backgrounds include:** Accounting; Business
Administration; Communications; Marketing;
Public Relations. **Benefits:** 403(b); Dental
Insurance; Disability Coverage; Life Insurance;
Medical Insurance; Public Transit Available;
Tuition Assistance. **Office hours:** Monday - Friday,
8:30 a.m. - 5:00 p.m. **Corporate headquarters
location:** This Location. **President:** Hope Green.
Number of employees at this location: 45.

VERTEX COMMUNICATIONS CORP.
2600 Longview Street, Kilgore TX 75662. 903/984-
0555. **Fax:** 903/984-7769. **Contact:** Ann Jerden,
Manager of Personnel. **World Wide Web address:**
http://www.vertexcomm.com. **Description:** Designs
and manufactures satellite Earth station antennas
which use domestic, international, and military
radio frequencies. The company also offers a
complete line of standard antenna products. **NOTE:**
Entry-level positions are offered. **Common
positions include:** Buyer; Civil Engineer; Computer
Programmer; Design Engineer; Draftsperson;
Electrical Engineer; Mechanical Engineer; MIS
Specialist; Operations Manager; Software Engineer;
Structural Engineer; Systems Analyst; Technical
Writer/Editor; Transportation/Traffic Specialist.
Educational backgrounds include: Accounting;
Computer Science; Engineering; Finance;
Marketing. **Benefits:** 401(k); Dental Insurance;
Disability Coverage; Life Insurance; Medical
Insurance; Pension Plan; Profit Sharing; Savings
Plan; Tuition Assistance. **Corporate headquarters
location:** This Location. **Other U.S. locations:**
Torrance CA; State College PA. **Operations at this
facility include:** Administration; Manufacturing;
Research and Development; Sales; Service.
Number of employees at this location: 400.
Number of employees nationwide: 575. **Number
of employees worldwide:** 605.

VIACOM INC.
1515 Broadway, 31st Floor, New York NY 10036.
212/258-6000. **Contact:** Human Resources. **World
Wide Web address:** http://www.viacom.com.
Description: A diversified entertainment and
communications company with operations in four
principal segments: Networks, Entertainment, Cable
Television, and Broadcasting. Viacom Networks
operates three advertiser-supported basic cable
television program services: MTV (Music
Television including MTV Europe and MTV
Latino), VH-1/Video Hits One, and Nickelodeon/
Nick at Nite; and three premium subscription
television services: SHOWTIME, The Movie
Channel, and FLIX. Viacom Entertainment
distributes television series, feature films, made-for-
television movies, miniseries, and movies for prime
time broadcast network television; acquires and
distributes television series for initial exhibition on
a first-run basis; and develops, produces, distributes,
and markets interactive software for multimedia
markets. Viacom Cable Television owns and
operates cable television systems in California, the
Pacific Northwest, and the Midwest. Viacom

Broadcasting owns and operates five network-
affiliated television stations and 14 radio stations.
Corporate headquarters location: This Location.

VTEL
108 Wild Basin Road South, Austin TX 78746.
512/437-2700. **Contact:** Personnel. **World Wide
Web address:** http://www.vtel.com. **Description:** A
leading provider of interactive videoconferencing
systems in the distance learning and health care
markets. VTEL products are distributed primarily
through resellers and co-marketers. **Corporate
headquarters location:** This Location.

WBEB-FM
10 Presidential Boulevard, Bala-Cynwyd PA 19004.
610/667-8400. **Fax:** 610/667-6795. **Contact:**
Human Resources. **World Wide Web address:**
http://www.b101radio.com. **Description:** A radio
station featuring adult contemporary music.

WBNS-TV
DISPATCH BROADCAST GROUP
P.O. Box 1010, Columbus OH 43216. 614/460-
3700. **Physical address:** 770 Twin Rivers Drive,
Columbus OH 43215. **Fax:** 614/460-2809. **Contact:**
Meg Wood, Director of Human Resources. **World
Wide Web address:** http://www.wbns10tv.com.
Description: A local television station. **NOTE:**
Part-time jobs are offered. **Common positions
include:** Accountant; Administrative Assistant;
Advertising Executive; Broadcast Technician; Chief
Financial Officer; Computer Support Technician;
Credit Manager; Editor; Graphic Artist; Graphic
Designer; Market Research Analyst; MIS Specialist;
Operations Manager; Reporter; Sales Executive;
Sales Manager; Webmaster. **Educational
backgrounds include:** Accounting; Art; Business
Administration; Communications; Computer
Science; Engineering; Marketing; Microsoft Word;
Novell; Spreadsheets. **Benefits:** 401(k); Casual
Dress - Fridays; Dental Insurance; Disability
Coverage; Employee Discounts; Life Insurance;
Medical Insurance; Pension Plan; Tuition
Assistance. **Special programs:** Internships.
Corporate headquarters location: This Location.
Other U.S. locations: Indianapolis IN. **Parent
company:** Dispatch Broadcast Group (also at this
location) has several operations in addition to
WBNS-TV: Dispatch Interactive Television offers
wireless interfaces using the television remote
control; Dispatch Productions provides
programming services; Ohio News Network
provides up-to-the-minute news, sports, and weather
across the state; Radio Sound Network is a satellite
delivery system; Radiohio is comprised of WBNS-
AM, an all-sports radio station, and WBNS-FM, an
oldies station; WALV-TV offers a variety of
television programming; and WTHR-TV is an all-
news television station. **Operations at this facility
include:** Administration; Sales. **Listed on:** Privately
held. **President/CEO:** Michael J. Fiorile. **Number
of employees at this location:** 325. **Number of
employees nationwide:** 600.

WDAY-TV-AM
P.O. Box 2466, Fargo ND 58108. 701/237-6500.
Contact: Personnel. **E-mail address:** wday@
forumcomm.com. **World Wide Web address:**
http://www.in-forum.com. **Description:** Operates an
AM radio station and an ABC-affiliated television
station. **Common positions include:** Accountant;
Administrative Assistant; General Manager;
Operations Manager; Production Manager; Radio
Announcer; Reporter; Sales Executive; Sales
Manager; Technical Writer; Typist; Video
Production Coordinator. **Educational backgrounds
include:** Communications; Journalism.

WFXT-TV, CHANNEL 25
dba FOX 25
25 Fox Drive, P.O. Box 9125, Dedham MA 02027-9125. 781/326-8825. **Fax:** 781/467-7212. **Contact:** Director of Human Resources. **Description:** A television station affiliated with the Fox Broadcasting Network. **Common positions include:** Accountant; Advertising Clerk; Broadcast Technician; Credit Manager; Electrical Engineer; TV Broadcaster. **Educational backgrounds include:** Business Administration; Communications. **Benefits:** 401(k); Dental Insurance; Disability Coverage; Life Insurance; Medical Insurance; Savings Plan; Tuition Assistance. **Special programs:** Internships. **Corporate headquarters location:** This Location. **Parent company:** Boston Celtics Broadcasting. **Number of employees at this location:** 60.

WYOU COMMUNITY TV
650 East Main Street, Madison WI 53703-2913. 608/258-9644. **Fax:** 608/258-8803. **Contact:** Human Resources. **Description:** A public access cable television station. **Corporate headquarters location:** This Location.

THE WEATHER CHANNEL, INC.
300 Interstate North Parkway, Atlanta GA 30339. 770/226-0000. **Contact:** Human Resource Manager. **World Wide Web address:** http://www.weather.com. **Description:** A cable television network with 24-hour live weather service. Founded in 1982. **Common positions include:** Accountant/Auditor; Commercial Artist; Marketing Specialist; Meteorologist; Production Coordinator; Systems Analyst. **Educational backgrounds include:** Accounting; Business Administration; Communications; Computer Science; Marketing; Meteorology; Television. **Benefits:** Life Insurance; Medical Insurance; Pension Plan; Savings Plan; Tuition Assistance. **Special programs:** Internships. **Parent company:** Landmark Communications, Inc. **Operations at this facility include:** Administration; Sales; Service.

WEGENER CORPORATION
11350 Technology Circle, Duluth GA 30097. 770/623-0096. **Fax:** 770/623-9648. **Contact:** Elaine Miller, Personnel Manager. **World Wide Web address:** http://www.wegener.com. **Description:** Manufactures electronics including digital compression products for cable television operators, radio and television broadcasters, the business music industry, data communications, and private network systems. **Corporate headquarters location:** This Location. **Subsidiaries include:** Wegener Communications International, Inc. **Number of employees nationwide:** 115.

WESTELL TECHNOLOGIES INC.
750 North Commons Drive, Aurora IL 60504. 630/898-2500. **Fax:** 630/375-4148. **Contact:** Human Resources. **E-mail address:** employment@westell.com. **World Wide Web address:** http://www.westell.com. **Description:** Manufactures telecommunications access products. The company's DSL products enable telephone companies to provide interactive media services through existing telephone lines. These products are used to provide faster Internet access as well as telecommuting opportunities. **Corporate headquarters location:** This Location. **Subsidiaries include:** Westell, Inc.

WINDOW TO THE WORLD COMMUNICATIONS
5400 North St. Louis Avenue, Chicago IL 60625-4698. 773/583-5000. **Fax:** 773/583-3046. **Recorded jobline:** 773/509-5333. **Contact:** Jerry Frank, Director of Human Resources. **World Wide Web address:** http://www.wttw.com. **Description:** Owns and operates WTTW Channel 11, The Chicago Production Center, and WFMT & The Radio Networks. **Educational backgrounds include:** Business Administration; Liberal Arts. **Benefits:** Dental Insurance; Disability Coverage; Life Insurance; Medical Insurance; Pension Plan. **Corporate headquarters location:** This Location. **Number of employees at this location:** 280.

WORLD WRESTLING FEDERATION ENTERTAINMENT, INC.
1241 East Main Street, P.O. Box 3857, Stamford CT 06902. 203/352-8600. **Contact:** Human Resources. **World Wide Web address:** http://www.wwf.com. **Description:** Develops and markets television programming and pay-per-view broadcasting for the World Wrestling Federation. The company also produces and manages live wrestling events. **Corporate headquarters location:** This Location.

WORLDCOM
500 Clinton Center Drive, Clinton MS 39060. 601/460-5600. **Contact:** Personnel. **World Wide Web address:** http://www.wcom.com. **Description:** One of the world's largest suppliers of local, long distance, and international telecommunications services, and a global Internet service provider. **Corporate headquarters location:** This Location. **International locations:** Worldwide. **Listed on:** NASDAQ. **Stock exchange symbol:** WCOM. **Annual sales/revenues:** More than $100 million. **Other U.S. locations:**
- 2330 Shawnee Mission Parkway, Westwood KS 66205. 913/624-6000.
- One Fluor Daniel Drive, Building C, Sugar Land TX 77478. 281/276-4000.

XETRON CORPORATION
460 West Crescentville Road, Cincinnati OH 45246. 513/881-3254. **Fax:** 513/881-3275. **Contact:** Arthur Bush, Manager of Personnel. **World Wide Web address:** http://www.xetron.com. **Description:** Engaged in the research and development of electronic communication systems. Founded in 1973. **Common positions include:** Accountant; Buyer; Electrical Engineer; Financial Analyst; Manufacturing Engineer; Software Engineer. **Educational backgrounds include:** Accounting; Computer Science; Engineering; Finance. **Benefits:** 401(k); Dental Insurance; Disability Coverage; Life Insurance; Medical Insurance; Pension Plan; Tuition Assistance. **Special programs:** Internships. **Corporate headquarters location:** This Location. **Parent company:** Northrop Grumman. **Operations at this facility include:** Administration; Manufacturing; Research and Development; Sales; Service. **Number of employees at this location:** 150.

For more information on career opportunities in the communications industries:

Associations

ACADEMY OF TELEVISION ARTS & SCIENCES
5220 Lankershim Boulevard, North Hollywood CA 91601. 818/754-2800. World Wide Web address: http://www.emmys.org.

AMERICAN DISC JOCKEY ASSOCIATION
10882 Demarr Road, White Plains MD 20695. 301/705-5150. Fax: 301/843-7284. World Wide Web address: http://www.adja.org. A membership organization for professional disc jockeys that publishes a newsletter of current events and new products.

AMERICAN WOMEN IN RADIO AND TELEVISION, INC.
1650 Tysons Boulevard, Suite 200, McLean VA 22102. 703/506-3290. World Wide Web address: http://www.awrt.org. A national, nonprofit professional organization for the advancement of women who work in electronic media and related fields. Services include *News and Views,* a fax newsletter transmitted biweekly to members; *Careerline,* a national listing of job openings available to members only; and the AWRT Foundation, which supports charitable and educational programs and annual awards.

THE COMPETITIVE TELECOMMUNICATIONS ASSOCIATION
1900 M Street NW, Suite 800, Washington DC 20036. 202/296-6650. World Wide Web address: http://www.comptel.org. A national association providing a wide variety of resources including telecommunications trade shows.

INTERNATIONAL TELEVISION ASSOCIATION
9202 North Meridian Street, Suite 200, Annapolis IN 46260. 317/816-6269. World Wide Web address: http://www.itva.org. Membership required.

NATIONAL ASSOCIATION OF BROADCASTERS
1771 N Street NW, Washington DC 20036. 202/429-5300, ext. 5490. Fax: 202/429-5343. World Wide Web address: http://www.nab.org. Provides employment information.

NATIONAL CABLE TELEVISION ASSOCIATION
1724 Massachusetts Avenue NW, Washington DC 20036-1969. 202/775-3669. Fax: 202/775-3695. World Wide Web address: http://www.ncta.com. A trade association. Publications include *Cable Television Developments, Secure Signals,* and *Kids and Cable*.

PROMAX INTERNATIONAL
2029 Century Park East, Suite 555, Los Angeles CA 90067. 310/788-7600. Fax: 310/788-7616. A nonprofit organization for radio, film, television, video, and other broadcasting professionals. Ask for the jobline.

RADIO-TELEVISION NEWS DIRECTORS ASSOCIATION
1000 Connecticut Avenue NW, Suite 615, Washington DC 20036. 202/659-6510. Fax: 202/223-4007. World Wide Web address: http://www.rtnda.org.

U.S. TELEPHONE ASSOCIATION
1401 H Street NW, Suite 600, Washington DC 20005. 202/326-7300. World Wide Web address: http://www.usta.org. A trade association for local telephone companies.

Magazines

ELECTRONIC MEDIA
Crain Communications, 740 North Rush Street, Chicago IL 60611-2590. 312/649-5200.

Online Services

BROADCAST PROFESSIONALS FORUM
Go: BPForum. A CompuServe discussion group for professionals in radio and television.

CPB JOBLINE
World Wide Web address: http://www.cpb.org/jobline/index.html. The Corporation for Public Broadcasting, a nonprofit company, operates this site which provides a list of job openings in the public radio and television industries.

JOURNALISM FORUM
Go: Jforum. A CompuServe discussion group for journalists in print, radio, or television.

ON-LINE DISC JOCKEY ASSOCIATION
World Wide Web address: http://www.odja.com. Provides members with insurance, Internet advertising, a magazine, and networking resources. This site also posts job opportunities.

Computer Hardware, Software, and Services

You can expect to find the following types of companies in this chapter:
Computer Components and Hardware Manufacturers • Consultants and Computer Training Companies • Internet and Online Service Providers • Networking and Systems Services • Repair Services/Rental and Leasing • Resellers, Wholesalers, and Distributors • Software Developers/Programming Services • Web Technologies

Some helpful information: *The average salary for entry-level computer professionals (such as programmers, systems analysts, software developers and engineers) ranges between $25,000 and $40,000, with salary remaining largely dependent upon experience and performance. Experienced computer specialists frequently earn over $50,000 per year, and those in management can receive $75,000 and up.*

ACS TECHNOLOGY SOLUTIONS
4506 South Miami Boulevard, Suite 180, Durham NC 27703. 919/941-0081. **Toll-free phone:** 800/833-2894. **Fax:** 919/941-0082. **Contact:** Recruiter. **World Wide Web address:** http://www.acsts.com. **Description:** Provides information technology and software consulting services. **Common positions include:** AS400 Programmer Analyst; Computer Engineer; Computer Operator; Computer Programmer; Computer Support Technician; Computer Technician; Database Administrator; Database Manager; Network Administrator; Software Engineer; SQL Programmer; Systems Analyst. **Educational backgrounds include:** C/C++; HTML; Internet; Java; MCSE; Microsoft Word; Novell; Software Development; Software Tech. Support; Visual Basic. **Benefits:** 401(k); Dental Insurance; Disability Coverage; Life Insurance; Medical Insurance; Profit Sharing; Sick Days (6 - 10); Vacation Days (6 - 10). **Corporate headquarters location:** Dallas TX. **Other U.S. locations:** San Diego CA; Atlanta GA; Philadelphia PA. **Parent company:** ACS. **President:** Duaine Goulding. **Number of employees nationwide:** 1,200.

ADC APEX
7151 Columbia Gateway Drive, Suite F, Columbia MD 21046. 410/312-2640. **Contact:** Kristen Thames, Manager of Staffing and Planning. **E-mail address:** careers@adcapex.com. **World Wide Web address:** http://www.adcapex.com. **Description:** A full systems integrator with services ranging from network design and integration to telecommunications and OSS consulting services. **NOTE:** Entry-level positions are offered. **Common positions include:** Account Manager; Accountant; Administrative Assistant; Applications Engineer; AS400 Programmer Analyst; Computer Engineer; Computer Operator; Computer Programmer; Computer Scientist; Computer Support Technician; Computer Technician; Consultant; Content Developer; Database Administrator; Database Manager; Marketing Specialist; MIS Specialist; Multimedia Designer; Network Administrator; Project Manager; Software Engineer; SQL Programmer; Systems Analyst; Typist; Webmaster. **Educational backgrounds include:** C/C++; CGI; Cold Fusion; Computer Science; Engineering; HTML; Internet; Java; MCSE; Microsoft Word; Novell; Software Development; Software Tech. Support; Spreadsheets; Visual Basic. **Benefits:** 401(k); Casual Dress - Daily; Dental Insurance; Disability Coverage; Employee Discounts; Financial Planning Assistance; Flexible Schedule; Life Insurance; Medical Insurance; Savings Plan; Sick Days (6 - 10); Tuition Assistance; Vacation Days (6 - 10). **Special programs:** Internships; Training. **Other U.S. locations:** CA; FL; NC. **Parent company:** ADC Telecommunications. **President:** Jay Swearingen. **Annual sales/revenues:** $51 - $100 million. **Number of employees at this location:** 250.

ADI SYSTEMS, INC.
2115 Ringwood Avenue, San Jose CA 95131. 408/944-0100. **Fax:** 408/944-0300. **Contact:** Shelly Venegan, Personnel Manager. **World Wide Web address:** http://www.adiusa.com. **Description:** Manufactures computer monitors. **Corporate headquarters location:** This Location. **Parent company:** ADI Corporation.

AM BEST COMPANY
AM Best Road, Oldwick NJ 08858. 908/439-2200. **Fax:** 908/439-3296. **Contact:** Human Resources. **World Wide Web address:** http://www.ambest.com. **Description:** Manufactures products including software, CD-ROMs, and diskette support products for the insurance industry. **Corporate headquarters location:** This Location.

ASA INTERNATIONAL LTD.
10 Speen Street, Framingham MA 01701. 508/626-2727. **Fax:** 508/626-0645. **Contact:** Human Resources. **World Wide Web address:** http://www.asaint.com. **Description:** Designs, develops, and installs proprietary vertical market software. **Common positions include:** Computer Programmer; Sales Rep.; Software Engineer; Technical Support Rep. **Educational backgrounds include:** Business Administration; Computer Science; Engineering. **Benefits:** 401(k); Credit Union; Dental Insurance; Disability Coverage; Life Insurance; Medical Insurance. **Special programs:** Internships. **Corporate headquarters location:** This Location. **Other U.S. locations:** Nashua NH; Blue Bell PA. **Subsidiaries include:** ASA Italy; ASA Legal Systems; ASA Tire Systems. **Operations at this facility include:** Administration; Research and Development; Sales; Service. **Annual sales/revenues:** $21 - $50 million. **Number of employees at this location:** 85. **Number of employees nationwide:** 190.

ASD SOFTWARE
4650 Arrow Highway, Suite E6, Montclair CA 91763. 909/624-2594. **Contact:** Human Resources. **World Wide Web address:** http://www.asdsoft.com. **Description:** Manufactures and markets utility

program software for Macintosh operating systems. **Corporate headquarters location:** This Location.

AST RESEARCH, INC.
dba ARI SERVICE
16225 Alton Parkway, Irvine CA 92618. 949/727-4141. **Contact:** Staffing Department. **World Wide Web address:** http://www.ari-service.com. **Description:** Manufactures and sells desktop computer systems, printers, scanners, and backup devices. The company also offers network integration services. **Common positions include:** Computer Programmer; Design Engineer; Hardware Engineer; Marketing Specialist; Project Engineer; Sales Representative; Software Engineer. **Corporate headquarters location:** This Location. **Number of employees nationwide:** 4,500.

AVT CORP.
P.O. Box 97025, Kirkland WA 98083. 425/820-6000. **Physical address:** 11410 NE 122nd Way, Kirkland WA 98034. **Contact:** Human Resources. **World Wide Web address:** http://www.avtc.com. **Description:** Develops, manufactures, markets, and supports a broad line of open systems-based, computer technology software products and systems that automate call answering. CallXpress3, the company's multi-application call processing product, enables users to manage their facsimiles, access computer-based information, and develop customized computer-telephony server applications. The company's PhoneXpress and px100 products are designed for basic call answering and voicemail. **Corporate headquarters location:** This Location.

ACCESS CORPORATION
4350 Glendale-Milford Road, Suite 250, Cincinnati OH 45242-3700. 513/786-8350. **Fax:** 513/786-8363. **Contact:** Liz Forg, Personnel Administrator. **Description:** Produces document storage and retrieval systems. **Common positions include:** Computer Programmer; Systems Analyst. **Educational backgrounds include:** Computer Science. **Benefits:** 401(k); Dental Insurance; Disability Coverage; Life Insurance; Medical Insurance. **Corporate headquarters location:** This Location. **Operations at this facility include:** Administration; Sales; Service.

ACER AMERICA CORPORATION
2641 Orchard Parkway, San Jose CA 95134. 408/432-6200. **Toll-free phone:** 800/SEE-ACER. **Fax:** 408/428-0947. **Contact:** Human Resources. **E-mail address:** careers@acer.com. **World Wide Web address:** http://www.acer.com. **Description:** One of the largest microcomputer manufacturers and OEM suppliers. The company also manufactures a variety of computer peripherals and components including monitors, keyboards, expansion cards, and CD-ROM drives. **Common positions include:** Account Manager; Account Representative; Administrative Assistant; Computer Programmer; Software Engineer; Systems Analyst. **Educational backgrounds include:** Business Administration; C/C++; Computer Science; Engineering; HTML; Internet; Microsoft Word; Spreadsheets. **Benefits:** 401(k); Casual Dress - Fridays; Dental Insurance; Disability Coverage; Employee Discounts; Life Insurance; Medical Insurance; Tuition Assistance. **Parent company:** Acer Group, Inc. **Operations at this facility include:** Manufacturing. **Number of employees nationwide:** 1,200. **Number of employees worldwide:** 25,000.

ACTEL CORPORATION
955 East Arques Avenue, Sunnyvale CA 94086-4533. 408/739-1010. **Contact:** Suzanne Kinner, Vice President of Human Resources. **World Wide Web address:** http://www.actel.com. **Description:** Manufactures field programmable gate arrays and develops the software to program them. **Common positions include:** Computer-Aided Designer; Design Engineer; Manufacturing Engineer; Marketing Specialist; Software Engineer; Systems Analyst; Test Engineer. **Corporate headquarters location:** This Location. **Number of employees at this location:** 200.

ADAC LABORATORIES
NUCLEAR MEDICINE DIVISION
540 Alder Drive, Milpitas CA 95035. 408/321-9100. **Contact:** Judy Rowe, Vice President of Personnel. **World Wide Web address:** http://www.adaclabs.com. **Description:** Produces medical diagnostic computer systems and components including state-of-the-art digital radiography image processing, nuclear medicine image processing, and radiation therapy planning systems. **Common positions include:** Accountant; Design Engineer; Electrical/Electronics Engineer; Financial Analyst; Manufacturing Engineer; Marketing Specialist; Mechanical Engineer; Software Engineer. **Corporate headquarters location:** This Location.

ADAM SOFTWARE, INC.
1600 River Edge Parkway, Suite 800, Atlanta GA 30328. 770/980-0888. **Toll-free phone:** 888/833-ADAM. **Fax:** 770/955-3088. **Contact:** Maureen Burke, Office Administrator/Benefits Coordinator. **World Wide Web address:** http://www.adam.com. **Description:** Develops anatomy software for medical schools, educational institutions, and consumer use. **Common positions include:** Accountant; Administrative Assistant; Administrative Manager; Attorney; CFO; Computer Animator; Computer Support Technician; Content Developer; Controller; Customer Service Rep.; Database Administrator; Database Manager; Help-Desk Technician; Human Resources Manager; Internet Services Manager; Intranet Developer; Market Research Analyst; Marketing Manager; MIS Specialist; Network Administrator; Operations Manager; Paralegal; Secretary; Software Engineer; SQL Programmer; Systems Analyst; Systems Manager; Webmaster; Website Developer. **Educational backgrounds include:** Accounting; ASP; Business Administration; C/C++; CGI; Cold Fusion; Communications; Finance; Health Care; HTML; Internet Development; Java; Marketing; MBA; MCSE; Microsoft Office; Novell; QuarkXPress; Software Development; SQL; Visual Basic. **Benefits:** 401(k); Casual Dress - Daily; Dental Insurance; Disability Coverage; Flexible Schedule; Life Insurance; Medical Insurance; Profit Sharing; Public Transit Available; Telecommuting. **Special programs:** Apprenticeships; Internships. **Corporate headquarters location:** This Location. **Other U.S. locations:** San Francisco CA. **CEO:** Robert S. Cramer. **Sales Manager:** Inger Rarick. **Number of employees nationwide:** 110.

THE ADCOMNET
P.O. Box 840, Sherborn MA 01770. 508/651-3932. **Contact:** Carl Shedd, Publisher. **Description:** Provides online services for the advertising, marketing, and public relations industries. **Common positions include:** Editor; Systems Manager. **Educational backgrounds include:** Journalism. **Special programs:** Internships. **Corporate headquarters location:** This Location. **Operations at this facility include:** Administration; Sales.

ADOBE SYSTEMS, INC.
345 Park Avenue, San Jose CA 95110. 408/536-6000. **Contact:** Human Resources. **World Wide Web address:** http://www.adobe.com. **Description:** Develops, markets, and supports computer software

products and technologies that enable users to create, display, and print electronic documents for Macintosh, Windows, and OS/2 compatibles. The company distributes its products through a network of original equipment manufacturers, distributors and dealers, value-added resellers, and systems integrators. **Common positions include:** Electrical Engineer; Graphic Artist; Software Engineer. **Corporate headquarters location:** This Location. **Other U.S. locations:** Nationwide. **International locations:** Worldwide.

ADVANCED DATA CONCEPTS, INC.
827 NE Oregon Street, Suite 210, Portland OR 97232. 503/233-1220. **Fax:** 503/230-2517. **Contact:** Jan Owens, Personnel Specialist. **E-mail address:** adc@adcnet.com. **World Wide Web address:** http://www.adcnet.com. **Description:** Provides outsourcing services for a variety of areas in the field of information technology including computer center operation; electronic commerce; GIS analysis; Internet; intranet; network design, installation, and operation; and help desk support. **CEO:** Frank Rivera.

ADVANCED ENGINEERING & RESEARCH ASSOCIATES, INC. (AERA)
1919 South Eads Street, Suite 400, Arlington VA 22202. 703/486-1993. **Fax:** 703/486-0795. **Contact:** Personnel. **E-mail address:** hr@mail.aera.com. **World Wide Web address:** http://www.aera.com. **Description:** An engineering services firm offering expertise in propulsion systems, satellite systems, advanced logistics, and mechanical systems. AERA also provides networked multimedia such as LAN and WAN; and interactive multimedia such as CD-ROM, 3D and 2D animation, digital video and audio; and hypertext and graphics.

ADVANCED MANAGEMENT TECHNOLOGY
1515 Wilson Boulevard, Suite 1100, Arlington VA 22209. 703/841-2684. **Contact:** Recruiter/Staffing Specialist. **E-mail address:** recruiter@amti.com. **World Wide Web address:** http://www.amti.com. **Description:** Provides MIS and systems engineering consulting services. **NOTE:** Entry-level positions are offered. **Company slogan:** Our employees are integral to our continued success. **Common positions include:** Accountant; Administrative Assistant; Advertising Clerk; Applications Engineer; Budget Analyst; Computer Programmer; Computer Support Technician; Computer Technician; Consultant - Computer; Cost Estimator; Database Administrator; Database Manager; Desktop Publishing Specialist; Graphic Artist; Graphic Designer; Internet Services Manager; MIS Specialist; Multimedia Designer; Network Administrator; Project Manager; Systems Analyst; Technical Writer; Telecommunications Manager; Webmaster. **Educational backgrounds include:** Accounting; ASP; Business Administration; C/C++; CGI; Cold Fusion; Communications; Computer Science; Engineering; Finance; HTML; Internet; Java; MCSE; Novell; Software Development; Software Tech. Support. **Benefits:** 401(k); Casual Dress - Fridays; Dental Insurance; Disability Coverage; Flexible Schedule; Life Insurance; Medical Insurance; Pension Plan; Public Transit Available; Savings Plan; Sick Days (1 - 5); Tuition Assistance; Vacation Days (10 - 20). **Special programs:** Training. **Corporate headquarters location:** This Location. **Other U.S. locations:** Los Angeles CA; Atlanta GA; Jamaica NY; Fort Worth TX. **International locations:** New Delhi, India. **Listed on:** Privately held. **President/CEO:** Anita Talwar. **Number of employees at this location:** 50. **Number of employees nationwide:** 250.

ADVANTAGE COMPUTING SYSTEMS
3850 Ranchero Drive, Ann Arbor MI 48108. 734/327-3600. **Contact:** Personnel Manager. **E-mail address:** jobs@advantagecs.com. **World Wide Web address:** http://www.advantagecs.com. **Description:** Markets Publisher's Advantage Computing System brand software to special interest publishers. The company also resells a wide range of hardware options. **Common positions include:** Account Manager; Accountant/Auditor; Administrative Assistant; Administrator; Computer Programmer; Marketing Manager; Packaging Engineer; Project Manager; Sales Manager; Services Sales Rep.; Software Engineer; Systems Analyst. **Educational backgrounds include:** Business Administration; Computer Science; Engineering; MCSE; Software Development; Software Tech. Support. **Benefits:** 401(k); Bonus Award/Plan; Casual Dress - Fridays; Dental Insurance; Disability Coverage; Life Insurance; Medical Insurance; Tuition Assistance. **Corporate headquarters location:** This Location. **Operations at this facility include:** Administration; Manufacturing; Research and Development; Sales; Service. **Number of employees at this location:** 60.

AEGIS ASSOCIATES, INC.
98 Galen Street, Watertown MA 02472. 617/923-2500. **Contact:** Kerry Keane, Human Resources Coordinator. **E-mail address:** hr@aegis-inc.com. **World Wide Web address:** http://www.aegis-inc.com. **Description:** A computer reseller and network integrator. This location also hires seasonally. **NOTE:** Entry-level positions are offered. **Company slogan:** Your technology experts. **Common positions include:** Account Representative; Computer Engineer; Computer Support Technician; Computer Technician; Help-Desk Technician; MIS Specialist; Network Engineer; Network/Systems Administrator; Sales Executive; Sales Representative. **Benefits:** 401(k); Casual Dress - Fridays; Dental Insurance; Disability Coverage; Life Insurance; Medical Insurance; Sick Days (6 - 10); Tuition Assistance; Vacation Days (6 - 10). **Special programs:** Training. **Corporate headquarters location:** This Location.

AIR GAGE CORPORATION
12170 Globe Road, Livonia MI 48150. 734/591-9220. **Contact:** Human Resources. **Description:** Develops and manufactures air gages and statistical process control software that allow manufacturers to monitor, regulate, or collect data on their manufacturing processes. **Corporate headquarters location:** This Location.

AJILON SERVICES INC.
2222 Chapel Hill, Nelson Highway, Suite 120, Durham NC 27713. 919/572-2750. **Toll-free phone:** 888/296-7575. **Fax:** 919/572-2656. **Contact:** Dick Smith, Manager. **E-mail address:** dsmith@ajilon.com. **World Wide Web address:** http://www.ajilon.com. **Description:** Ajilon offers computer consulting services, project support, and end user services. **Common positions include:** Computer Engineer; Computer Support Technician; Computer Technician; Database Administrator; Help-Desk Technician; Intranet Developer; Network Engineer; Network Administrator; Software Engineer. **Educational backgrounds include:** C/C++; CGI; Internet Development; Java; MCSE; Microsoft Office; Software Development; Software Tech. Support; Visual Basic. **Benefits:** 401(k); Casual Dress - Daily; Dental Insurance; Disability Coverage; Employee Discounts; Life Insurance; Medical Insurance; Relocation Assistance; Sick Days (1 - 5); Tuition Assistance; Vacation Days (6 - 10). **Corporate headquarters location:** Towson MD. **International locations:** Australia; United

Kingdom. **Parent company:** Adecco. **CEO:** Roy Haggerty. **Number of employees nationwide:** 8,000. **Number of employees worldwide:** 8,500. **Other U.S. locations:**
- 400 West Division Street, Suite 102, Syracuse NY 13204. 315/422-2480.

ALLAIRE CORPORATION
One Alewife Center, Cambridge MA 02140. 617/761-2000. **Contact:** Human Resources. **World Wide Web address:** http://www.allaire.com. **Description:** Develops and supports application development and server software that allow businesses to develop e-commerce systems. **Corporate headquarters location:** This Location.

ALLEN COMMUNICATIONS
5 Triad Center, 5th Floor, Salt Lake City UT 84180. 801/537-7800. **Toll-free phone:** 800/325-7850. **Fax:** 801/537-7805. **Contact:** Human Resources. **E-mail address:** info@allencomm.com. **World Wide Web address:** http://www.allencomm.com. **Description:** Provides computer-based training (CBT) and Web-based training solutions to businesses. Founded in 1981. **NOTE:** Entry-level positions and part-time positions are offered. **Common positions include:** Account Manager; Account Rep.; Accountant; Administrative Assistant; CFO; Computer Engineer; Computer Programmer; Computer Support Technician; Computer Technician; Database Administrator; Event Planner; Financial Analyst; Graphic Artist; Graphic Designer; Human Resources Manager; Intranet Developer; Marketing Manager; Marketing Specialist; Multimedia Designer; Network/Systems Administrator; Operations Manager; Public Relations Specialist; Sales Executive; Sales Manager; Sales Representative; Software Engineer; Technical Support Manager; Technical Writer; Vice President of Marketing and Sales; Vice President of Operations; Webmaster. **Educational backgrounds include:** Art/Design; Business Administration; C/C++; Computer Science; Education; Finance; HTML; Internet Development; Java; Marketing; MBA; Microsoft Office; Microsoft Word; Novell; Software Development; Software Tech. Support; Spreadsheets; Visual Basic. **Benefits:** 401(k); Casual Dress - Daily; Dental Insurance; Disability Coverage; Employee Discounts; Flexible Schedule; Life Insurance; Medical Insurance; Public Transit Available; Relocation Assistance; Sick Days; Vacation Days (10 - 20). **Special programs:** Apprenticeships; Internships; Training; Summer Jobs. **Corporate headquarters location:** This Location. **Other U.S. locations:** PA; TX. **International locations:** United Kingdom. **Parent company:** Times Mirror Corporation. **Listed on:** New York Stock Exchange. **Stock exchange symbol:** TIMMR. **CEO:** Timothy Sukle. **Annual sales/revenues:** $11 - $20 million. **Number of employees at this location:** 115. **Number of employees nationwide:** 130. **Number of employees worldwide:** 135.

ALLSTAR SYSTEMS, INC.
6401 Southwest Freeway, Houston TX 77074. 713/795-2000. **Contact:** Kathleen Crain, Human Resources Director. **World Wide Web address:** http://www.allstar.com. **Description:** Provides customers with computer systems and sets up networks. **Common positions include:** Account Rep.; Accountant; Buyer; Computer Programmer; Computer Support Technician; Customer Service Rep.; Purchasing Agent/Manager; Sales Executive; Sales Representative. **Educational backgrounds include:** Accounting; Computer Science. **Benefits:** 401(k); Dental Insurance; Medical Insurance; Profit Sharing. **Corporate headquarters location:** This Location. **Other area locations:** Dallas TX.

Number of employees at this location: 200. **Number of employees nationwide:** 300.

ALPHA MICROSYSTEMS
dba ALPHASERV.COM
2722 South Fairview Street, Santa Ana CA 92704-5947. 714/957-8500. **Fax:** 714/957-8705. **Contact:** Human Resources. **World Wide Web address:** http://www.alphamicro.com. **Description:** Provides consulting, networking, software support, and maintenance services. **Corporate headquarters location:** This Location.

ALPHANET SOLUTIONS, INC.
7 Ridgedale Avenue, Cedar Knolls NJ 07927. 973/267-0088. **Fax:** 973/267-5361. **Contact:** Susan Pfeffer, Vice President of Human Resources. **World Wide Web address:** http://www.alphanetcorp.com. **Description:** A leading systems integrator. The company's services include computer network design; installation and administration; help desk support; technical education; cabling and telecommunications sales and service; computer product sales and services; and Internet services. Clients include many small- and mid-range companies, national and global *Fortune* 1000 companies, and large government agencies. **Common positions include:** Computer Programmer; Internet Services Manager; MIS Specialist; Systems Analyst; Systems Manager; Webmaster. **Corporate headquarters location:** This Location. **Other U.S. locations:** NY; PA. **Annual sales/revenues:** More than $100 million.

ALPHATECH CORPORATION
2300 Clarendon Boulevard, Suite 302, Arlington VA 22201. 703/243-8700. **Fax:** 703/243-8226. **Contact:** Greg Free, Technical Recruiter. **E-mail address:** recruiting@atcnet.com. **World Wide Web address:** http://www.atcnet.com. **Description:** Specializes in systems software integration as well as systems life cycle management. Founded in 1989. **NOTE:** Entry-level positions are offered. **Common positions include:** Accountant; Administrative Assistant; Applications Engineer; Computer Engineer; Computer Operator; Computer Programmer; Computer Support Technician; Computer Technician; Controller; Database Administrator; Database Manager; Human Resources Manager; Internet Services Manager; Marketing Manager; Marketing Specialist; MIS Specialist; Network Administrator; Project Manager; Software Engineer; SQL Programmer; Systems Analyst; Systems Manager; Technical Writer; Webmaster. **Educational backgrounds include:** C/C++; CGI; Cold Fusion; Computer Science; Engineering; HTML; Internet; Java; Mathematics; MCSE; Microsoft Word; Novell; Software Development; Software Tech. Support; Spreadsheets; Visual Basic. **Benefits:** 401(k); Casual Dress - Fridays; Dental Insurance; Disability Coverage; Life Insurance; Medical Insurance; Profit Sharing; Sick Days (1 - 5); Tuition Assistance; Vacation Days (6 - 10). **Corporate headquarters location:** This Location. **President:** Mr. Kwang Kim. **Annual sales/revenues:** $5 - $10 million.

ALTAIRE ENTERPRISES, INC.
144 East Grant, Spearfish SD 57732. 605/578-1400. **Contact:** Human Resources. **Description:** Operates a Website that provides Internet access and e-mail accounts. **Corporate headquarters location:** This Location.

ALTEC LANSING TECHNOLOGIES, INC.
P.O. Box 277, Milford PA 18337. 570/296-4434. **Toll-free phone:** 800/258-3288. **Fax:** 570/296-1528. **Contact:** Personnel. **World Wide Web address:** http://www.altecmm.com. **Description:**

Manufactures computer speakers and surround sound systems. **NOTE:** Entry-level positions are offered. **Common positions include:** Account Manager; Customer Service Representative; Design Engineer; Draftsperson; Electrical/Electronics Engineer; Graphic Artist; Graphic Designer; Internet Services Manager; Marketing Manager; Mechanical Engineer; MIS Specialist; Multimedia Designer; Project Manager; Sales Engineer; Sales Executive; Sales Representative; Secretary; Software Engineer; Webmaster. **Educational backgrounds include:** Business Administration; Computer Science; Engineering; Software Development. **Benefits:** 401(k); Dental Insurance; Disability Coverage; Employee Discounts; Life Insurance; Medical Insurance; Tuition Assistance. **Special programs:** Internships; Co-ops. **Corporate headquarters location:** This Location. **Other U.S. locations:** Nationwide. **International locations:** Worldwide. **Number of employees at this location:** 130.

ALTEON WEBSYSTEMS, INC.
50 Great Oaks Boulevard, San Jose CA 95119. 408/360-5500. **Contact:** Human Resources Department. **E-mail address:** info@alteon.com. **World Wide Web address:** http://www. websystems.com. **Description:** Provides next-generation Internet infrastructure equipment. **Corporate headquarters location:** This Location.

ALTIA INC.
5030 Corporate Plaza Drive, Suite 200, Colorado Springs CO 80919. 719/598-4299. **Fax:** 719/598-4392. **Contact:** Personnel. **E-mail address:** info@altia.com. **World Wide Web address:** http://www.altia.com. **Description:** Manufactures feature prototyping software for engineers and marketing professionals. **Corporate headquarters location:** This Location.

ALTRIS SOFTWARE
9339 Carroll Park Drive, San Diego CA 92021. 858/625-3000. **Fax:** 858/546-7671. **Contact:** Personnel. **World Wide Web address:** http://www. altris.com. **Description:** Designs, develops, integrates, and markets electronic document management software for industrial, utility, commercial, and government applications. **Corporate headquarters location:** This Location.

AMAZON.COM
P.O. Box 80185, Seattle WA 98108-0185. 206/622-2335. **Physical address:** 1516 Second Avenue, Seattle WA 98101. **Contact:** Personnel. **E-mail address:** jobs@amazon.com. **World Wide Web address:** http://www.amazon.com. **Description:** An online store engaged in the sale of books, videos, music, toys, and electronics. Amazon.com also offers online auctions. **NOTE:** If sending a resume via e-mail, please be sure the information is in an ASCII-text format. **Corporate headquarters location:** This Location. **Other U.S. locations:** New Castle DE; McDonough GA; Coffeyville KS; Cambellsville KY; Lexington KY; Fernley NV. **International locations:** Europe. **President/CEO:** Jeffrey Bezos.

AMBASSADOR BUSINESS SOLUTIONS
425 South Martingale Road, Schaumburg IL 60173. 847/706-3480. **Fax:** 847/706-3419. **Contact:** Erica Reiner, Corporate Recruiter. **E-mail address:** ereiner@ambassador.canon.com. **World Wide Web address:** http://www.ambassador.canon.com. **Description:** Offers customized solutions for business offices. Ambassador Business Solutions markets the full line of Canon office equipment including copiers, fax machines, laser printers, and scanners. **NOTE:** Entry-level positions are offered. **Common positions include:** Account Manager; Account Rep.; Marketing Specialist; Sales Executive; Sales Manager; Sales Rep. **Educational backgrounds include:** Internet Development; Microsoft Office; Microsoft Word; Spreadsheets. **Benefits:** 401(k); Dental Insurance; Disability Coverage; Employee Discounts; Life Insurance; Medical Insurance; Profit Sharing; Sick Days (6 - 10); Tuition Assistance; Vacation Days (6 - 10). **Corporate headquarters location:** This Location. **Other U.S. locations:** Downers Grove IL; Chicago IL. **Parent company:** Canon USA. **President:** Emily Reynolds. **Number of employees at this location:** 500.

AMDAHL CORPORATION
1250 East Arques Avenue, Sunnyvale CA 94088. 408/746-6000. **Toll-free phone:** 800/538-8460. **Fax:** 408/992-2389. **Contact:** Gene Plonka, Director of Corporate Staffing. **E-mail address:** jobs@amdahl.com. **World Wide Web address:** http://www.amdahl.com. **Description:** Designs, develops, manufactures, markets, and services large-scale, high-performance, general purpose computer systems. Customers are primarily large corporations, government agencies, and large universities with high-volume data processing requirements. **Common positions include:** Accountant; Computer Programmer; Customer Service Rep.; Financial Analyst; Human Resources Manager; Mechanical Engineer; Software Engineer; Systems Analyst; Technical Writer; Transportation. **Educational backgrounds include:** Accounting; Business Administration; Communications; Computer Science; Engineering; Finance; Liberal Arts; Marketing. **Benefits:** 401(k); Daycare Assistance; Dental Insurance; Disability Coverage; Employee Discounts; Life Insurance; Medical Insurance; Pension Plan; Profit Sharing; Savings Plan; Tuition Assistance. **Special programs:** Internships. **Corporate headquarters location:** This Location. **Other U.S. locations:** Nationwide. **International locations:** Worldwide. **Parent company:** Fujitsu, Ltd. **Operations at this facility include:** Administration; Manufacturing; Research and Development; Sales; Service. **CEO:** David Wright. **Number of employees nationwide:** 6,000. **Number of employees worldwide:** 9,500.

AMERICA ONLINE, INC. (AOL)
22000 AOL Way, Dulles VA 20166. 703/448-8700. **Contact:** Vice President of Personnel. **World Wide Web address:** http://www.aol.com. **Description:** A global leader in the interactive services market. America Online (AOL) offers its members a wide variety of services via personal computer and other devices. Services include e-mail, conferencing, software, computing support, interactive magazines and newspapers, online classes, and Internet access. AOL is also a provider of data network services, new media and interactive marketing services, and multimedia and CD-ROM production services. **NOTE:** In January 2000, America Online, Inc. and Time Warner, Inc. announced plans to merge. The new company will be named AOL Time Warner Inc. Please contact this location for more information. **Benefits:** 401(k); ESOP. **Corporate headquarters location:** This Location. **Subsidiaries include:** Netscape Communications Corporation. **Number of employees nationwide:** 2,500.

AMERICAN MANAGEMENT SYSTEMS
4050 Legato Road, Fairfax VA 22033. 703/267-8000. **Contact:** Human Resources Director. **World Wide Web address:** http://www.amsinc.com. **Description:** A management consulting firm that assists large organizations in solving complex management problems by applying information technology and systems engineering solutions. Customers include financial service institutions;

insurance companies; federal agencies; state and local government; colleges and universities; telecommunications firms; health care providers; and energy companies. **Corporate headquarters location:** This Location.

AMERICAN MEGATRENDS, INC.
6145 Northbelt Parkway, Suite F, Norcross GA 30071. 770/263-8181. **Contact:** Human Resources. **World Wide Web address:** http://www.ami.com. **Description:** Manufactures computer motherboards. **Corporate headquarters location:** This Location.

AMERICAN POWER CONVERSION (APC)
132 Fairgrounds Road, West Kingston RI 02892. 401/789-5735. **Toll-free phone:** 888/289-2722. **Fax:** 401/788-2710. **Contact:** Human Resources. **E-mail address:** apcinfo@apcc.com. **World Wide Web address:** http://www.apcc.com. **Description:** Designs, develops, manufactures, and markets surge suppressers, un-interruptible power supplies (UPS), power conditioning equipment, and related software for computer and computer-related equipment including local area networks (LANs), midrange computers, and engineering workstations. American Power Conversion also publishes a newsletter called *APC Currents* which provides news about the company and the company's products. **Common positions include:** Buyer; Computer Programmer; Credit Manager; Customer Service Rep.; Economist; Electrical Engineer; General Manager; Industrial Engineer; Industrial Production Manager; Materials Engineer; Mechanical Engineer; Operations Manager; Public Relations Specialist; Purchasing Agent; Quality Control Supervisor; Software Engineer; Systems Analyst. **Educational backgrounds include:** Business Administration; Computer Science; Engineering. **Benefits:** Dental Insurance; Disability Coverage; ESOP; Incentive Plan; Life Insurance; Medical Insurance; Tuition Assistance. **Corporate headquarters location:** This Location. **International locations:** China; Galway, Ireland (European headquarters); India; Japan; Korea; North Sydney, NSW/Australia (Asia Pacific headquarters); Singapore.

AMERICAN SOFTWARE, INC.
470 East Paces Ferry Road NE, Atlanta GA 30305. 404/261-4381. **Fax:** 404/264-5232. **Contact:** Chad Veen, Director of Personnel. **World Wide Web address:** http://www.amsoftware.com. **Description:** Develops, markets, and supports integrated supply chain management and financial control systems software. The company's multiplatform enterprise software applications are primarily used for forecasting and inventory management, purchasing and materials control, and order processing and receivables control. The company also provides consulting and outsourcing services. **Common positions include:** Accountant; Computer Programmer; Customer Service Rep.; Software Engineer; Systems Analyst; Technical Writer. **Educational backgrounds include:** Accounting; Business Administration; Computer Science; Finance; Liberal Arts; Marketing; Mathematics. **Benefits:** 401(k); Dental Insurance; Disability Coverage; Life Insurance; Medical Insurance; Profit Sharing. **Corporate headquarters location:** This Location. **Other U.S. locations:** Costa Mesa CA; Chicago IL; Boston MA; Minneapolis MN; Tarrytown NY; Philadelphia PA; Dallas TX. **Operations at this facility include:** Administration; Research and Development; Sales; Service. **Number of employees nationwide:** 600. **Number of employees worldwide:** 660.

ANACOMP, INC.
P.O. Box 509005, San Diego CA 92150. 858/679-9797. **Physical address:** 12365 Crosthwaite Circle,

Poway CA 92064. **Contact:** Human Resources. **World Wide Web address:** http://www.anacomp.com. **Description:** Provides document storage solutions; manufactures computer hardware and software; and develops customized financial software. **Common positions include:** Accountant; Computer Programmer; Customer Service Rep.; Electrical Engineer; Financial Analyst; Human Resources Manager; Industrial Engineer; Manufacturer's Sales Rep.; Mechanical Engineer; Operations Manager; Purchasing Agent; Quality Control Supervisor; Systems Analyst; Technical Writer. **Educational backgrounds include:** Accounting; Business Administration; Computer Science; Economics; Engineering; Finance; Marketing; Mathematics; Physics. **Benefits:** Dental Insurance; Disability Coverage; Employee Discounts; Life Insurance; Medical Insurance; Pension Plan; Profit Sharing; Savings Plan; Tuition Assistance. **Corporate headquarters location:** This Location. **Other U.S. locations:** Nationwide. **International locations:** Worldwide. **Operations at this facility include:** Administration; Engineering and Design; Manufacturing; Marketing; Research and Development; Sales.

ANALYSIS & TECHNOLOGY, INC.
P.O. Box 220, North Stonington CT 06359-9801. 860/599-3910. **Fax:** 860/599-6516. **Contact:** Jennifer Dauster-Bevacqua, Human Resources Administrator. **World Wide Web address:** http://www.aati.com. **Description:** A leading provider of technology-based solutions in the areas of engineering, information technology, and interactive multimedia services. **Common positions include:** Accountant; Administrative Assistant; Auditor; Buyer; CFO; Clerical Supervisor; Computer Operator; Computer Programmer; Consultant; Controller; Draftsperson; Editor; Electrical Engineer; Financial Analyst; General Manager; Graphic Artist; Graphic Designer; Human Resources Manager; Marketing Manager; Mechanical Engineer; MIS Specialist; Multimedia Designer; Project Manager; Purchasing Agent; Secretary; Software Engineer; Systems Analyst; Technical Writer; Telecommunications Manager; Typist. **Educational backgrounds include:** Accounting; Art/Design; Business Administration; Communications; Computer Science; Engineering; Finance; Marketing. **Benefits:** 401(k); Dental Insurance; Disability Coverage; Life Insurance; Medical Insurance; Tuition Assistance. **Corporate headquarters location:** This Location. Nationwide. **International locations:** Worldwide. **Annual sales/revenues:** More than $100 million. **Number of employees nationwide:** 1,500.
Other U.S. locations:
- One Corporate Place, Middletown RI 02842. 401/849-5952.

ANALYSTS INTERNATIONAL CORP. (AiC)
3601 West 76th Street, Minneapolis MN 55435-3000. 952/835-5900. **Toll-free phone:** 800/800-5044. **Contact:** Senior Staffing Assistant. **World Wide Web address:** http://www.analysts.com. **Description:** AiC is an international computer consulting firm. The company assists clients in analyzing, designing, and developing systems using different programming languages and software. **NOTE:** A minimum of one to two years of programming experience is required. **Common positions include:** Computer Programmer; Management Analyst; Software Engineer; Systems Analyst; Technical Writer/Editor. **Educational backgrounds include:** Business Administration; Computer Science; Engineering; Mathematics. **Benefits:** 401(k); Dental Insurance; Disability Coverage; Employee Discounts; Life Insurance; Medical Insurance; Pension Plan; Profit Sharing;

Savings Plan; Tuition Assistance. **Corporate headquarters location:** This Location. **International locations:** Canada; England. **Operations at this facility include:** Administration; Sales; Service.
Other U.S. locations:
- 621 NW 53rd Street, Suite 140, Boca Raton FL 33487-8211. 561/241-5912.
- 5750 Castle Creek Parkway North, Suite 259, Indianapolis IN 46250. 317/842-1100.
- 6450 Rockside Woods Boulevard South, Suite 350, Cleveland OH 44131. 216/524-8990.
- 1415 North Loop West, Suite 300, Houston TX 77008. 713/869-3420.

ANDERSEN CONSULTING
161 North Clark Street, Chicago IL 60601. 312/693-0161. **Contact:** Recruiting Manager. **World Wide Web address:** http://www.andersenconsulting.com. **Description:** Andersen Consulting provides services to help organizations effectively apply technology to their business advantage. By combining general business knowledge with information systems skills, the company develops solutions that help clients in many industries manage technology. **Common positions include:** Computer Programmer; Consultant; Systems Analyst. **Educational backgrounds include:** Business Administration; Computer Science; Economics; Engineering; Finance; Mathematics. **Benefits:** Dental Insurance; Disability Coverage; Employee Discounts; Life Insurance; Medical Insurance; Pension Plan; Profit Sharing; Savings Plan; Tuition Assistance. **Parent company:** Arthur Andersen Worldwide Organization.

ANNUAL STATEMENT AUTOMATION PRODUCTS
6 Heartland Drive, Suite B, Bloomington IL 61704. 309/662-6100. **Fax:** 309/662-6149. **Contact:** Human Resources. **E-mail address:** mail@asap1.com. **World Wide Web address:** http://www.asap1.com. **Description:** Develops computer software for the insurance industry. **NOTE:** Entry-level positions are offered. **Common positions include:** Administrative Manager; Computer Programmer; Network Administrator; Systems Analyst; Website Developer. **Educational backgrounds include:** Accounting; Computer Science; MCSE; Visual Basic. **Benefits:** 401(k); Casual Dress - Daily; Dental Insurance; Disability Coverage; Flexible Schedule; Life Insurance; Medical Insurance; Savings Plan; Tuition Assistance. **Special programs:** Internships. **Corporate headquarters location:** Atlanta GA. **Other U.S. locations:** Denver CO. **Parent company:** SunGard Corporation. **President:** Richard H. Gudeman. **Information Systems Manager:** Roger Miller.

ANSWERTHINK CONSULTING GROUP
3200 Windy Hill Road, Suite 800 West, Atlanta GA 30339. 770/690-9700. **Fax:** 770/690-9710. **Contact:** Personnel. **E-mail address:** careers@answerthink.com. **World Wide Web address:** http://www.answerthink.com. **Description:** Provides computer consulting and IT services to *Fortune* 1000 companies. **Corporate headquarters location:** This Location. **Other U.S. locations:** Fremont CA; Miami FL; Chicago IL; Burlington MA; Iselin NJ; Marlton NJ; New York NY; Hudson OH; Conshohocken PA; Dallas TX.

APCON, INC.
17938 SW Upper Boones Ferry Road, Portland OR 97224. 503/639-6700. **Fax:** 503/639-6740. **Contact:** Personnel. **E-mail address:** hr@apcon.com. **World Wide Web address:** http://www.apcon.com. **Description:** Manufactures and markets a line of products for SCSI bus computer systems.

APCON, Inc. manufactures PowerSwitch/NT, a clustering solution for Windows NT, which protects network servers from downtime. The company also offers PowerLink which provides disaster recovery for RAIDS's and tape backup devices. **Common positions include:** Account Manager; Administrative Assistant; Assembler; Marketing Specialist; Software Engineer. **Benefits:** 401(k); Dental Insurance; Medical Insurance; Public Transit Available; Sick Days (1 - 5); Vacation Days (6 - 10). **Corporate headquarters location:** This Location. **President:** Richard B. Rauch. **Number of employees at this location:** 40.

APNET
650 Avis Drive, Suite 100, Ann Arbor MI 48108. 734/996-3636. **Fax:** 734/669-2330. **Contact:** David J. Cortright, Director of Technical Recruiting. **Description:** A strategic information technology consulting company specializing in client/server applications development, network integration, and staffing and support services. Founded in 1976. **NOTE:** The company offers IT Academy, a program for recent college graduates which allows for hands-on training leading to certification. **Common positions include:** Computer Programmer; Database Manager; Electrical Engineer; Instructor; Internet Services Manager; MIS Specialist; Multimedia Designer; Network Administrator; Network Engineer; Online Content Specialist; Project Manager; Software Engineer; Systems Analyst; Systems Manager; Technical Writer; Webmaster. **Educational backgrounds include:** Business Administration; Computer Science; Engineering; Software Development; Software Tech. Support. **Benefits:** 401(k); Dental Insurance; Disability Coverage; Employee Discounts; Life Insurance; Medical Insurance; Tuition Assistance. **Special programs:** Training. **Corporate headquarters location:** This Location. **Number of employees at this location:** 200.

APPLE COMPUTER, INC.
One Infinite Loop, Cupertino CA 95014. 408/996-1010. **Fax:** 408/974-5691. **Recorded jobline:** 408/974-0529. **Contact:** Employment Department. **E-mail address:** applejobs@apple.com. **World Wide Web address:** http://www.apple.com. **Description:** Develops, manufactures, and markets personal computer systems and peripherals. The company's desktop publishing and communications products are marketed internationally. **Common positions include:** Computer Engineer; Computer Programmer; Marketing Specialist; Software Engineer. **Educational backgrounds include:** Business Administration; Computer Science; Finance. **Special programs:** Internships. **Corporate headquarters location:** This Location. **Other area locations:** Elk Grove CA. **Other U.S. locations:** Phoenix AZ; Fountain CO; Austin TX.

APPLIED STATISTICS, INC.
2055 White Bear Avenue, Maplewood MN 55109. 651/773-7888. **Fax:** 651/773-4930. **Contact:** Personnel Manager. **World Wide Web address:** http://www.appliedstatistics.com. **Description:** The company develops software for the Windows operating system utilizing Microsoft Visual C++. **Common positions include:** Administrative Assistant; Administrative Manager; Computer Programmer; Sales Manager; Software Engineer. **Educational backgrounds include:** Computer Science; Engineering. **Benefits:** 401(k); Dental Insurance; Medical Insurance; Tuition Assistance. **Corporate headquarters location:** This Location.

APPLIX, INC.
112 Turnpike Road, Westborough MA 01581. 508/870-0300. **Contact:** Human Resources. **World**

Wide Web address: http://www.applix.com. **Description:** Develops and markets software applications for the UNIX market. **Corporate headquarters location:** This Location.

AQUIDNECK MANAGEMENT ASSOCIATES
28 Jacome Way, Middletown RI 02842. 401/849-8900. **Contact:** Personnel. **World Wide Web address:** http://www.amaltd.com. **Description:** Develops software for local and state governments. Products are used to automate court systems. **NOTE:** Part-time jobs are offered. **Common positions include:** Accountant; Administrative Assistant; Administrative Manager; Advertising Clerk; Budget Analyst; CFO; Computer Programmer; Database Administrator; Desktop Publishing Specialist; Graphic Artist; Graphic Designer; Marketing Specialist; Multimedia Designer; Network Administrator; Project Manager; Public Relations Specialist; Sales Executive; Software Engineer; SQL Programmer; Technical Writer; Webmaster. **Educational backgrounds include:** Art/Design; Business Administration; C/C++; Computer Science; HTML; Internet; Java; MCSE; Microsoft Word; Software Development; Software Tech. Support; Spreadsheets; Visual Basic. **Benefits:** 401(k); Casual Dress - Fridays; Dental Insurance; Disability Coverage; Flexible Schedule; Life Insurance; Medical Insurance; Telecommuting; Tuition Assistance. **Corporate headquarters location:** This Location. **Other U.S. locations:** Newport RI. **Number of employees nationwide:** 250.

ARC TECHNOLOGIES GROUP, INC.
Center City Tower, Suite 910, 650 Smithfield Avenue, Pittsburgh PA 15222. 412/281-4427. **Toll-free phone:** 888/434-6734. **Fax:** 412/434-6167. **Contact:** Jim Leindecker, Director of Human Resources. **World Wide Web address:** http://www.arctechgroup.com. **Description:** Provides systems management solutions and data processing services. **Common positions include:** Database Manager; Systems Analyst; Systems Manager. **Educational backgrounds include:** Computer Science; Engineering; Software Development; Software Tech. Support. **Benefits:** 401(k); Dental Insurance; Disability Coverage; Flexible Schedule; Life Insurance; Medical Insurance; Telecommuting. **Corporate headquarters location:** This Location. **Number of employees at this location:** 35.

ARDENT SOFTWARE, INC.
50 Washington Street, Westborough MA 01581-1021. 508/366-3888. **Fax:** 508/389-8955. **Contact:** Mary Parker, Human Resources Manager. **World Wide Web address:** http://www.ardentsoftware.com. **Description:** Manufactures a wide range of software products including database systems and warehouse development tools. Ardent serves government and business customers in the manufacturing, health care, telecommunications, aerospace, defense, financial services, and utilities industries. **Common positions include:** Computer Programmer; Financial Analyst; Sales Rep.; Software Engineer. **Educational backgrounds include:** Computer Science; Engineering; Marketing. **Benefits:** 401(k); Dental Insurance; Disability Coverage; Employee Discounts; Life Insurance; Medical Insurance; Tuition Assistance. **Corporate headquarters location:** This Location. **Other U.S. locations:** CA; CO; GA; IL; NC; NJ; TX; WA. **International locations:** Australia; Canada; France; Germany; Japan; Malaysia; South Africa; Spain; United Kingdom. **Operations at this facility include:** Administration; Research and Development; Sales; Service. **Annual sales/revenues:** More than $100 million. **Number of employees worldwide:** 570.

ARISTOTLE INTERNET ACCESS
401 West Capitol, Suite 700, Little Rock AR 72201. 501/374-4638. **Contact:** Human Resources. **E-mail address:** info@aristotle.net. **World Wide Web address:** http://www.aristotle.net. **Description:** Provides Internet access to central Arkansas. The company also offers Website design, Internet applications training, and HTML programming. **Corporate headquarters location:** This Location.

ARKSYS
17500 Chenal Parkway, Little Rock AR 72223. 501/218-7300. **Fax:** 501/218-7302. **Contact:** Human Resources. **E-mail address:** jobs@arksys.com. **World Wide Web address:** http://www.arksys.com. **Description:** Develops payment processing software for the banking industry. **NOTE:** Entry-level positions are offered. **Common positions include:** Account Manager; Account Rep.; Administrative Assistant; Sales Executive; Software Engineer; Systems Analyst; Systems Manager; Technical Writer/Editor. **Educational backgrounds include:** Business Administration; Computer Science; Mathematics; Physics. **Benefits:** 401(k); Dental Insurance; Disability Coverage; Life Insurance; Medical Insurance; Profit Sharing; Tuition Assistance. **Corporate headquarters location:** This Location. **Parent company:** Euronet. **Number of employees at this location:** 140.

ARTISOFT, INC.
5 Cambridge Center, Cambridge MA 02142. 617/354-0600. **Fax:** 617/354-7744. **Contact:** Personnel. **World Wide Web address:** http://www.artisoft.com. **Description:** A provider of networking solutions for businesses. The company offers the LANtastic network operating system as well as network management, backup, and multiplatform connectivity systems. **Corporate headquarters location:** This Location. **Other U.S. locations:** Tucson AZ.

ASPEN SYSTEMS, INC.
3900 Youngfield Street, Wheat Ridge CO 80033-4165. **Fax:** 303/431-7196. **Contact:** Human Resources. **World Wide Web address:** http://www.aspsys.com. **Description:** A manufacturer of high-performance workstations and servers for the OEM, VAR, and retail industries. **Common positions include:** Administrative Assistant; Computer Support Technician; Sales Engineer. **Corporate headquarters location:** This Location.

ASPEN TECHNOLOGY, INC.
10 Canal Park, Cambridge MA 02141-2201. 617/949-1000. **Fax:** 617/949-1030. **Contact:** Human Resources. **World Wide Web address:** http://www.aspentech.com. **Description:** Supplies computer-aided chemical engineering software to the chemicals, petroleum, pharmaceuticals, metals, minerals, food products, consumer products, and utilities industries. **Benefits:** 401(k). **Corporate headquarters location:** This Location. **Other U.S. locations:** Houston TX. **International locations:** Belgium; England; Hong Kong; Japan. **Number of employees nationwide:** 300. **Number of employees worldwide:** 1,200.

ASTEA INTERNATIONAL INC.
455 Business Center Drive, Horsham PA 19044. 215/682-2500. **Contact:** Jack Phillips, Director of Personnel. **World Wide Web address:** http://www.astea.com. **Description:** Develops, markets, and supports a variety of applications for client/server and host-based environments that permit organizations of various sizes across a wide range of industries to automate and integrate field service and customer support functions. Astea also offers a full range of consulting, training, and customer

support services. **NOTE:** Entry-level positions are offered. **Common positions include:** Computer Programmer; Customer Service Rep.; Software Engineer; Technical Writer/Editor. **Educational backgrounds include:** Business Administration; Computer Science; Mathematics. **Benefits:** 401(k); Dental Insurance; Disability Coverage; Life Insurance; Medical Insurance; Pension Plan; Profit Sharing. **Corporate headquarters location:** This Location. **Other U.S. locations:** San Mateo CA; Denver CO; Bedford MA. **International locations:** Australia; France; Germany; Israel; the Netherlands; United Kingdom. **Operations at this facility include:** Administration; Sales; Service. **Listed on:** NASDAQ. **Number of employees at this location:** 200. **Number of employees nationwide:** 450.

ASTRO-MED, INC.
600 East Greenwich Avenue, West Warwick RI 02893. 401/828-4000. **Contact:** Director of Personnel. **World Wide Web address:** http://www.astro-med.com. **Description:** Manufactures and supplies specialty printers that display, monitor, analyze, and print data for aerospace, industrial, and medical applications. Products are sold under the Grass-Telefactor, QuickLabel Systems, and Astro-Med brand names. Customers include leading aircraft manufacturers, automotive product manufacturers, telecommunications companies, electrical utility companies, steel companies, and paper manufacturers. **Corporate headquarters location:** This Location. **President/CEO/Owner:** Everett V. Pizzuti. **Number of employees at this location:** 250.

ATARI GAMES CORPORATION
675 Sycamore Drive, Milpitas CA 95035. 408/434-3700. **Contact:** Personnel. **World Wide Web address:** http://www.atarigames.com. **Description:** This location is a research and development facility. Overall, Atari Games Corporation develops video game software. **Corporate headquarters location:** This Location.

ATEX MEDIA SOLUTIONS
15 Crosby Drive, Bedford MA 01730. 781/275-2323. **Fax:** 781/276-1254. **Contact:** Personnel. **World Wide Web address:** http://www.atex.com. **Description:** Designs, develops, and sells computer software products for the newspaper, magazine, and prepress publishing markets worldwide. **Common positions include:** Accountant; Administrative Manager; Blue-Collar Worker Supervisor; Budget Analyst; Buyer; Computer Programmer; Credit Manager; Customer Service Rep.; Editor; Electrical Engineer; Financial Analyst; General Manager; Human Resources Manager; Public Relations Specialist; Purchasing Agent; Quality Control Supervisor; Services Sales Rep.; Software Engineer; Systems Analyst; Technical Writer. **Educational backgrounds include:** Accounting; Art/Design; Business Administration; Communications; Computer Science; Engineering; Finance; Liberal Arts; Marketing. **Benefits:** 401(k); Daycare Assistance; Dental Insurance; Disability Coverage; Employee Discounts; Life Insurance; Medical Insurance; Pension Plan; Profit Sharing; Savings Plan; Tuition Assistance. **Corporate headquarters location:** This Location. **Other U.S. locations:** Nationwide. **Operations at this facility include:** Administration; Research and Development; Sales; Service. **Number of employees at this location:** 240. **Number of employees nationwide:** 400.

ATLANTIC DATA SERVICES
One Batterymarch Park, Quincy MA 02169. 617/770-3333. **Contact:** Director of Human Resources. **World Wide Web address:** http://www.atlanticdataservices.com. **Description:** Atlantic

Data Services is a professional services firm providing computer consulting and project management services to the banking and financial industries. **Common positions include:** Computer Programmer; Consultant; Management Analyst; Sales Executive; Systems Analyst. **Educational backgrounds include:** Business Administration; Computer Science; Finance; Mathematics. **Benefits:** 401(k); Dental Insurance; Disability Coverage; Life Insurance; Medical Insurance; Tuition Assistance. **Corporate headquarters location:** This Location. **Other U.S. locations:** Nationwide. **Number of employees nationwide:** 200.

ATLAS BUSINESS SOLUTIONS, INC.
3330 Fiechtner Drive SW, Fargo ND 58103. 701/235-5226. **Fax:** 701/280-0842. **Contact:** Personnel. **Description:** Develops software including Visual Staff Scheduler, an employee scheduling system. **Corporate headquarters location:** This Location.

ATTACHMATE CORPORATION
P.O. Box 90026, Bellevue WA 98009-9026. 425/644-4010. **Toll-free phone:** 800/426-6283. **Contact:** Recruiter. **E-mail address:** cooljobs@attachmate.com. **World Wide Web address:** http://www.attachmate.com. **Description:** Designs, manufactures, and markets personal computer to mainframe data communications products worldwide. Products are marketed under the IRMA, Crosstalk, and Quickapp brand names. **NOTE:** Entry-level positions are offered. **Common positions include:** Account Manager; Account Rep.; Accountant; Administrative Assistant; Administrative Manager; Advertising Executive; Applications Engineer; AS400 Programmer Analyst; Assistant Manager; Attorney; Budget Analyst; CFO; Computer Engineer; Computer Operator; Computer Programmer; Computer Support Technician; Computer Technician; Content Developer; Controller; Cost Estimator; Credit Manager; Customer Service Rep.; Database Administrator; Database Manager; Desktop Publishing Specialist; Event Planner; Finance Director; Financial Analyst; Graphic Artist; Graphic Designer; Help-Desk Technician; Human Resources Manager; Internet Services Manager; Intranet Developer; Market Research Analyst; Marketing Manager; Marketing Specialist; Media Planner; MIS Manager; Multimedia Designer; Network/Systems Administrator; Operations Manager; Paralegal; Production Manager; Project Manager; Public Relations Specialist; Purchasing Agent; Sales Executive; Sales Manager; Sales Rep.; Software Engineer; SQL Programmer; Systems Analyst; Systems Manager; Technical Support Manager; Web Advertising Specialist; Webmaster; Website Developer. **Special programs:** Internships. **Corporate headquarters location:** This Location. **Other U.S. locations:** Nationwide. **International locations:** Worldwide. **Listed on:** Privately held. **Number of employees nationwide:** 1,000.

AUSPEX SYSTEMS, INC.
2300 Central Expressway, Santa Clara CA 95050. 408/566-2000. **Contact:** Senior Recruiter. **World Wide Web address:** http://www.auspex.com. **Description:** A leading provider of high-performance network data servers that are optimized to move large amounts of data from central information repositories to users' workstations. **Common positions include:** Budget Analyst; Credit Manager; Manufacturing Engineer; Marketing Specialist; Mechanical Engineer; Sales Representative; Software Engineer. **Educational backgrounds include:** Computer Science. **Corporate headquarters location:** This Location. **International locations:** Worldwide. **Operations at**

this facility include: Manufacturing; Research and Development; Sales; Service. **Annual sales/ revenues:** More than $100 million. **Number of employees worldwide:** 500.

AUTO-GRAPHICS, INC.
3201 Temple Avenue, Pomona CA 91768-3200. 909/595-7204. **Fax:** 909/595-3506. **Contact:** Human Resources. **World Wide Web address:** http://www.auto-graphics.com. **Description:** Offers software and processing services to database and information publishers. Services include the computerized preparation and processing of customer-supplied information to be published in various formats including print, microform, CD-ROM, and/or online computer access. In addition, the company markets CD-ROM hardware and software packages for access to computer generated information. **Corporate headquarters location:** This Location.

AUTO-TROL TECHNOLOGY CORP.
12500 North Washington Street, Denver CO 80241-2400. **Toll-free phone:** 800/233-2882. **Fax:** 303/252-2249. **Recorded jobline:** 303/252-2007. **Contact:** Personnel. **World Wide Web address:** http://www.auto-trol.com. **Description:** Develops and markets software for the CAD/CAM/CAE, technical illustration, network configuration, and technical information management industries. Auto-Trol Technology Corporation integrates computer hardware, operating systems, proprietary graphics software, and applications software into systems for process plant design, civil engineering, discrete manufacturing, facilities layout and design, mechanical design, technical publishing, and network configuration management. **NOTE:** Entry-level positions are offered. **Common positions include:** Computer Programmer; Mathematician; Mechanical Engineer; Software Engineer; Systems Analyst; Technical Writer/Editor. **Educational backgrounds include:** Computer Science; Engineering; Mathematics. **Benefits:** 401(k); Credit Union; Dental Insurance; Disability Coverage; Life Insurance; Medical Insurance; Tuition Assistance; Vacation Days. **Special programs:** Internships. **Corporate headquarters location:** This Location. **Other U.S. locations:** Nationwide. **Number of employees at this location:** 200.

AUTODESK, INC.
111 McInnis Parkway, San Rafael CA 94903. 415/507-5000. **Contact:** Steve McMahon, Vice President of Human Resources. **World Wide Web address:** http://www.autodesk.com. **Description:** Designs, develops, markets, and supports a line of computer-aided design (CAD), engineering, and animation software products for desktop computers and workstations. **Common positions include:** Computer Programmer; Quality Control Supervisor; Systems Analyst. **Educational backgrounds include:** Computer Science. **Benefits:** Dental Insurance; Disability Coverage; Life Insurance; Medical Insurance; Pension Plan; Tuition Assistance. **Corporate headquarters location:** This Location. **Operations at this facility include:** Administration; Manufacturing; Research and Development; Sales; Service. **Number of employees nationwide:** 1,800.

AUTOLOGIC INFORMATION INTERNATIONAL
1050 Rancho Conejo Boulevard, Thousand Oaks CA 91320. 805/498-9611. **Fax:** 805/376-5003. **Recorded jobline:** 805/376-5400. **Contact:** Human Resources. **E-mail address:** personnel@autoiii.com. **World Wide Web address:** http://www.autoiii.com. **Description:** Develops, assembles, and markets computer-based systems that automate the functions of prepress production for the publishing

and printing industries. Products can be separated into three categories: Automated Workflow Solutions includes servers, plateroom management tracking systems, and output file managers; Document Distribution Systems provides electronic document distribution and other communication services; and Integrated Products includes drum and flatbed scanners, and drum and computer-to-plate imagers. **Common positions include:** Administrative Manager; Computer Operator; Electronics Technician; Software Engineer. **Educational backgrounds include:** Computer Science; Engineering. **Benefits:** 401(k); Dental Insurance; Disability Coverage; Employee Discounts; Life Insurance; Medical Insurance; Tuition Assistance. **Special programs:** Internships. **Corporate headquarters location:** This Location. **Other U.S. locations:** Nationwide. **International locations:** Worldwide. **Number of employees worldwide:** 385.

AUTOMATED SYSTEMS, INC.
4827 Pioneers Boulevard, Lincoln NE 68506. 402/489-2717. **Contact:** Human Resources. **World Wide Web address:** http://www.asiweb.com. **Description:** This location houses administrative offices. Overall, Automated Systems is engaged in network design, sales, installation, management, training, and support services. Founded in 1981. **Corporate headquarters location:** This Location.

AVAIL NETWORKS, INC.
305 East Eisenhower Parkway, Suite 200, Ann Arbor MI 48108. 734/761-5005. **Fax:** 734/995-1114. **Contact:** Mary Cutting, Personnel and Site Services Manager. **E-mail address:** careers@availnetworks.com. **World Wide Web address:** http://www.availnetworks.com. **Description:** Avail Networks designs, develops, and markets advanced dial-up and broadband access products for diverse applications. Founded in 1999. **Common positions include:** Account Rep.; Accountant; Administrative Assistant; Administrative Manager; Applications Engineer; CFO; Computer Engineer; Computer Programmer; Computer Support Technician; Computer Technician; Electrical Engineer; Human Resources Manager; Marketing Manager; Network Administrator; Operations Manager; Software Engineer; Technical Support Manager; Technical Writer; Vice President of Operations; Vice President of Sales. **Educational backgrounds include:** C/C++; Computer Science; Engineering; Microsoft Office; Microsoft Word; Software Development; Software Tech. Support; Visual Basic. **Benefits:** 401(k); Casual Dress - Daily; Dental Insurance; Disability Coverage; Flexible Schedule; Life Insurance; Medical Insurance; Sick Days; Stock Option; Tuition Assistance; Vacation Days. **Special programs:** Co-ops. **Corporate headquarters location:** This Location. **Listed on:** Privately held. **President/CEO:** David Hartmann.

AVANT! CORPORATION
1101 Slater Road, Suite 300, Durham NC 27703. 919/941-6600. **Contact:** Director of Human Resources. **World Wide Web address:** http://www.avanticorp.com. **Description:** Develops, markets, and supports software products that assist IC design engineers in performing automated design, layout, physical verification, and analysis of advanced integrated circuits. Products include VeriCheck design verification software and layout products compatible with UNIX or MS-DOS operating systems. **Corporate headquarters location:** This Location.

AVERSTAR, INC.
23 Fourth Avenue, Northwest Park, Burlington MA 01803. 781/221-6990. **Contact:** Human Resources.

World Wide Web address: http://www.averstar. com. **Description:** Provides software systems, services, and products to a broad base of customers around the world. The company specializes in language design and programmer productivity tools; digital signal processing tools and application; hardware and system simulation; computer and network security; guidance, navigation, and control; and information systems integration. **Corporate headquarters location:** This Location.

AVID TECHNOLOGY, INC.

Avid Technology Park, One Park West, Tewksbury MA 01876. 978/640-6789. **Contact:** Director of Employment. **World Wide Web address:** http://www.avid.com. **Description:** A leading provider of digital audio and video tools. Products include digital editing systems and networking and shared storage systems. The company's products are used for various media and entertainment applications. Founded in 1987. **Common positions include:** Computer Programmer; Computer Scientist; Hardware Engineer; Software Engineer; Systems Analyst. **Corporate headquarters location:** This Location.

AVNET, INC.

2211 South 47th Street, Phoenix AZ 85034. 480/643-2000. **Contact:** Personnel. **World Wide Web address:** http://www.avnet.com. **Description:** Distributes electronic components and computer products for industrial and military customers. The company also produces and distributes other electronic, electrical, and video communications products. **Corporate headquarters location:** This Location.

AXIS COMPUTER SYSTEMS

RK Executive Center, 201 Boston Post Road West, Marlborough MA 01752. 508/481-9600. **Contact:** Personnel. **World Wide Web address:** http://www. axiscomp.com. **Description:** Develops software for manufacturing facilities in the metals industry.

AXON TECHNOLOGIES

2000 Commonwealth Avenue, Auburndale MA 02466. 617/332-7200. **Contact:** Human Resources. **Description:** Manages LANs and WANs through the development and manufacture of hardware and software integration products. **Corporate headquarters location:** This Location.

AZTEC TECHNOLOGY PARTNERS

52 Roland Street, Boston MA 02129. 617/623-3100. **Toll-free phone:** 800/831-1114x308. **Fax:** 617/623-4368. **Contact:** Laurie Connors, Staffing Specialist. **World Wide Web address:** http://www.aztectech. com. **Description:** Aztec Technology Partners delivers a full range of integrated e-Solutions for businesses, institutions, and government. Their consultants design, implement, and support web and network-based solutions. **Common positions include:** Account Manager; Administrative Assistant; Communications Engineer; Computer Engineer; Controller; Credit Manager; Customer Service Rep.; Human Resources Manager; Internet Services Manager; Intranet Developer; Network Engineer; Network Administrator; Operations Manager; Production Manager; Project Manager; Purchasing Agent; Sales Executive; Sales Manager; Sales Rep.; Systems Analyst. **Educational backgrounds include:** Accounting; Business Administration; C/C++; Computer Science; Engineering; Finance; Mathematics; MCSE; Novell; Solaris. **Benefits:** 401(k); Casual Dress - Fridays; Dental Insurance; Disability Coverage; Employee Discounts; Life Insurance; Medical Insurance; Public Transit Available; Sick Days (6 - 10); Stock Purchase; Tuition Assistance; Vacation Days (6 -

10). **Corporate headquarters location:** Braintree MA. **Other U.S. locations:** Hackensack NJ; Edison NJ; New York City NY. **Parent company:** U.S. Office Products. **Number of employees at this location:** 250. **Number of employees nationwide:** 1,200.

BAE SYSTEMS

1601 Research Boulevard, Rockville MD 20850. 301/838-6000. **Toll-free phone:** 800/638-8512. **Fax:** 301/838-6303. **Contact:** Kenneth Aubrey, Employment Manager. **World Wide Web address:** http://www.baesystems.com. **Description:** Provides a full spectrum of systems engineering and technical services in the areas of systems development, operation, and maintenance. Technical services include system design, integration, and testing; software development, engineering, and maintenance; and integrated logistics support including safety, reliability, and quality assurance engineering. **NOTE:** Entry-level positions are offered. **Common positions include:** Budget Analyst; Computer Programmer; Database Manager; Design Engineer; Electrical Engineer; Financial Analyst; Mechanical Engineer; Multimedia Designer; Software Engineer; Systems Analyst; Technical Writer; Webmaster. **Educational backgrounds include:** Business Administration; Computer Science; Engineering; Finance; Mathematics; Physics; Software Development; Software Tech. Support. **Benefits:** 401(k); Dental Insurance; Disability Coverage; Flexible Schedule; Life Insurance; Medical Insurance; Public Transit Available; Tuition Assistance. **Special programs:** Internships; Co-ops. **Corporate headquarters location:** This Location. **Other U.S. locations:** Nationwide.

BMC SOFTWARE, INC.

2101 CityWest Boulevard, Houston TX 77042-2827. 713/918-8800. **Contact:** Human Resources. **World Wide Web address:** http://www.bmc.com. **Description:** Develops, markets, and supports standard systems software products to enhance and increase the performance of large-scale (mainframe) computer database management systems and data communications software systems. Founded in 1980. **Common positions include:** Computer Programmer; Sales and Marketing Rep.; Software Engineer; Systems Analyst. **Educational backgrounds include:** Computer Science; Marketing. **Benefits:** 401(k); Dental Insurance; Disability Coverage; Employee Discounts; Life Insurance; Medical Insurance; Profit Sharing; Savings Plan; Tuition Assistance. **Corporate headquarters location:** This Location. **Annual sales/revenues:** More than $100 million. **Number of employees nationwide:** 900. **Number of employees worldwide:** 1,800.

BTG, INC.

3877 Fairfax Ridge Road, Fairfax VA 22030. 703/383-8000. **Fax:** 703/383-8030. **Contact:** Staffing Manager. **World Wide Web address:** http://www.btg.com. **Description:** An information technology company providing networking services, systems integration, and systems engineering to the government and other customers. **Common positions include:** Applications Engineer; Computer Programmer; Cost Estimator; Customer Service Rep.; Internet Services Manager; Multimedia Designer; Online Content Specialist; Webmaster. **Educational backgrounds include:** Computer Science; Engineering. **Benefits:** 401(k); Dental Insurance; Disability Coverage; Employee Discounts; Life Insurance; Medical Insurance. **Corporate headquarters location:** This Location. **Other U.S. locations:** Nationwide.

BANCTEC SYSTEMS, INC.
4851 LBJ Freeway, Dallas TX 75244. 972/341-4000. **Contact:** Personnel. **E-mail address:** jobs@banctec.com. **World Wide Web address:** http://www.banctec.com. **Description:** BancTec is engaged in systems integration and specializes in document management solutions. The company also provides network support services and develops image management software. **Common positions include:** Manufacturing Engineer. **Corporate headquarters location:** This Location. **Number of employees worldwide:** 4,000.

BARRA, INC.
2100 Milvia Street, Berkeley CA 94704. 510/548-5442. **Fax:** 510/548-4374. **Contact:** Personnel. **E-mail address:** careers@barra.com. **World Wide Web address:** http://www.barra.com. **Description:** Develops, markets, and supports application software and information services used to analyze and manage portfolios of equity, fixed income, and other financial instruments. The company serves more than 750 clients in 30 countries including many of the world's largest portfolio managers, fund sponsors, pension and investment consultants, brokers/dealers, and master trustees. **NOTE:** Entry-level positions are offered. **Common positions include:** Administrative Assistant; Computer Programmer; Computer Support Technician; Consultant; Customer Service Rep.; Economist; Help-Desk Technician; Network Administrator; Project Manager; Sales Manager; Software Engineer; SQL Programmer; Systems Analyst; Systems Manager. **Educational backgrounds include:** Business Administration; C/C++; Computer Science; Economics; Engineering; Finance; Mathematics; MBA; MCSE; Software Development; Software Tech. Support; SQL; Visual Basic. **Benefits:** 401(k); Casual Dress - Daily; Dental Insurance; Disability Coverage; Flexible Schedule; Life Insurance; Medical Insurance; Profit Sharing; Tuition Assistance. **Special programs:** Internships; Training; Summer Jobs. **Corporate headquarters location:** This Location. **Other U.S. locations:** New York NY. **International locations:** Frankfurt; Hong Kong; London; Paris; Sydney; Yokohama. **Operations at this facility include:** Administration; Research and Development; Sales; Service. **Annual sales/revenues:** More than $100 million. **Number of employees nationwide:** 450. **Number of employees worldwide:** 750.

BELL MICROPRODUCTS INC.
1941 Ringwood Avenue, San Jose CA 95131. 408/451-9400. **Fax:** 408/451-1600. **Contact:** Personnel. **World Wide Web address:** http://www.bellmicro.com. **Description:** Markets and distributes a select group of computer products to original equipment manufacturers and value-added resellers. Products include logic microprocessors; disk, tape, and optical drives and subsystems; drive controllers; and board-level products. The company also provides a variety of manufacturing and value-added services to its customers including the supply of board-level products to customer specifications on a turnkey basis; certain types of components and subsystem testing services; systems integration and disk drive formatting and testing; and the packaging of electronic component kits to customer specifications. Founded in 1987. **Corporate headquarters location:** This Location.

BERISH & ASSOCIATES, INC.
6 Corporation Center Drive, Broadview Heights OH 44147. 440/526-1454. **Toll-free phone:** 800/784-5253. **Fax:** 440/526-1406. **Contact:** Personnel. **E-mail address:** careers@berish.com. **World Wide Web address:** http://www.berish.com. **Description:** Develops and implements computer systems and

provides network and infrastructure consulting services. Berish & Associates operates in the areas of client/server development, Internet/intranet development, Microsoft Office integration, LAN and WAN services, and installation and implementation. Founded in 1985. **Common positions include:** Account Rep.; Administrative Assistant; Computer Programmer; Database Administrator; Human Resources Manager; Network Administrator; Sales Manager; Sales Rep.; Software Engineer; Webmaster. **Educational backgrounds include:** AS400 Certification; ASP; C/C++; CGI; HTML; Internet; Java; Oracle; Software Development; SQL; Visual Basic. **Benefits:** 401(k); Bonus Award/Plan; Casual Dress - Fridays; Dental Insurance; Disability Coverage; Flexible Schedule; Life Insurance; Medical Insurance; Sick Days (1 - 5); Telecommuting; Tuition Assistance; Vacation Days (6 - 10). **Special programs:** Co-ops; Internships. **Listed on:** Privately held. **President/Owner:** Joseph Berish.

BEST CONSULTING
11255 Kirkland Way, Kirkland WA 98033. 425/814-8104. **Toll-free phone:** 888/878-1888. **Contact:** Recruiting Department. **E-mail address:** recruiting@bestnet.com. **World Wide Web address:** http://www.bestnet.com. **Description:** Offers software consulting services. BEST Consulting provides businesses with support for mainframes, personal computers, systems configurations, information systems, and software testing. **Company slogan:** Knowledge is our #1 resource; Clients are our #1 concern. **Common positions include:** Applications Engineer; AS400 Programmer Analyst; Computer Programmer; Computer Support Technician; Content Developer; Database Administrator; Database Manager; Help-Desk Technician; Internet Services Manager; Intranet Developer; Network Engineer; Network Administrator; Software Engineer; SQL Programmer; Systems Analyst; Systems Manager; Webmaster; Website Developer. **Educational backgrounds include:** AS400 Certification; ASP; C/C++; CGI; Computer Science; HTML; Internet Development; Java; Mathematics; MCSE; Software Development; Software Tech. Support; SQL; Visual Basic. **Benefits:** 401(k); Casual Dress - Fridays; Dental Insurance; Disability Coverage; Employee Discounts; Flexible Schedule; Life Insurance; Medical Insurance; Tuition Assistance. **Corporate headquarters location:** This Location. **Other U.S. locations:** Phoenix AZ; Sacramento CA; Palm Springs CA; Boise ID; Minneapolis MN; Las Vegas NV; Reno NV; Portland OR; Salem OR; Salt Lake City UT; Olympia WA. **Parent company:** Personnel Group of America. **CEO:** Craig Newbold. **Number of employees nationwide:** 1,200.

BEST POWER
P.O. Box 280, Necedah WI 54646. 608/565-7200. **Fax:** 608/565-3114. **Contact:** Human Resources. **World Wide Web address:** http://www.bestpower.com. **Description:** A designer, manufacturer, and marketer of power protection products for PCs, LANs, WANs, and global networks. Best Power also provides support services.

BISPOINT TECHNOLOGIES
465 Main Street, Buffalo NY 14203-1788. 716/845-5010. **Toll-free phone:** 800/442-2472. **Fax:** 716/845-5033. **Contact:** Donna Lonca, Human Resources Manager. **World Wide Web address:** http://www.bispoint.com. **Description:** Distributes systems and software to the legal market. The company also supplies minicomputers, personal computers, local area networks, software, systems integration services, software support, and equipment maintenance to its clients. **NOTE:** Entry-

level positions are offered. **Common positions include:** Account Manager; Accountant/Auditor; Applications Engineer; Buyer; Computer Engineer; Computer Programmer; Computer Scientist; Computer Support Technician; Credit Manager; Customer Service Rep.; Financial Analyst; Marketing Specialist; MIS Specialist; Public Relations Specialist; Purchasing Agent; Sales Executive; Sales Rep.; Services Sales Rep.; Software Engineer; SQL Programmer; Systems Analyst. **Educational backgrounds include:** Accounting; Business Administration; Communications; Computer Science; Engineering; Finance; HTML; Internet Development; Marketing; Mathematics; MBA; MCSE; Microsoft Word; Novell; Software Development; SQL; Visual Basic. **Benefits:** 401(k); Casual Dress - Daily; Disability Coverage; Life Insurance; Medical Insurance; Relocation Assistance; Sick Days (1 - 5); Tuition Assistance; Vacation Days (6 - 10). **Corporate headquarters location:** This Location. **Operations at this facility include:** Administration; Manufacturing; Research and Development; Sales; Service. **President/CEO:** Henry P. Semmelhack. **Facilities Manager:** Thomas Wrinn. **Information Systems Manager:** David Hayes. **Purchasing Manager:** Paul Myers. **Number of employees at this location:** 100. **Number of employees nationwide:** 190.

BLUE MARBLE GEOGRAPHICS
261 Water Street, Gardiner ME 04345. 207/582-6747. **Fax:** 207/582-7001. **Contact:** Human Resources. **World Wide Web address:** http://www. bluemarblegeo.com. **Description:** Develops mapping software. **Common positions include:** Technical Support Rep. **Corporate headquarters location:** This Location.

BLUESTONE INC.
1000 Briggs Road, Mount Laurel NJ 08054. 856/727-4600. **Fax:** 856/727-0124. **Contact:** Shelley Dougherty, Director of Human Resources. **World Wide Web address:** http://www.bluestone. com. **Description:** Develops computer technology programs and provides user training. Bluestone offers Web-based software including dynamic Web applications and GUIs. **NOTE:** Entry-level positions are offered. **Common positions include:** Administrative Assistant; Marketing Specialist; MIS Specialist; Sales Engineer; Sales Representative; Software Engineer. **Educational backgrounds include:** Computer Science; Engineering. **Benefits:** 401(k); Dental Insurance; Disability Coverage; Flexible Schedule; Life Insurance; Medical Insurance. **Special programs:** Training. **Corporate headquarters location:** This Location. **Other U.S. locations:** CA.

BOCA RESEARCH
1601 Clint Moore Road, Boca Raton FL 33487. 561/241-8088. **Contact:** Human Resources. **World Wide Web address:** http://www.bocaresearch.com. **Description:** Manufactures computer components including network cards and video cards. **Corporate headquarters location:** This Location.

BOKLER SOFTWARE CORPORATION
P.O. Box 261, Huntsville AL 35804. 256/539-9901. **Fax:** 256/883-7242. **Contact:** Human Resources. **E-mail address:** info@bokler.com. **World Wide Web address:** http://www.bokler.com. **Description:** Develops cryptographic software that allows businesses to set up information security systems. **Corporate headquarters location:** This Location.

BREECE HILL TECHNOLOGIES
6287 Arapahoe Avenue, Boulder CO 80303. 303/449-2673. **Toll-free phone:** 800/941-0550.

Contact: Human Resources. **World Wide Web address:** http://www.breecehill.com. **Description:** A developer and manufacturer of Digital Linear Tape (DLT) drive systems. **Corporate headquarters location:** This Location. **Number of employees at this location:** 100.

BROADREACH CONSULTING, INC.
676 East Swedesford Road, Suite 200, Wayne PA 19087. 610/687-4000. **Fax:** 610/687-8811. **Contact:** Patty Murray, Senior Recruiter. **World Wide Web address:** http://www. broadreachconsulting.com. **Description:** Offers computer consulting services to a variety of businesses. **Common positions include:** Account Rep.; Administrative Assistant; Applications Engineer; Computer Engineer; Computer Programmer; Computer Support Technician; Database Administrator; Database Manager; Human Resources Manager; Internet Services Manager; Multimedia Designer; Network Administrator; Software Engineer; SQL Programmer; Systems Analyst; Systems Manager; Webmaster. **Educational backgrounds include:** ASP; C/C++; CGI; Cold Fusion; Computer Science; HTML; Internet; Java; MCSE; Microsoft Word; Novell; Software Development; Software Tech. Support; Spreadsheets; Visual Basic. **Benefits:** 401(k); Dental Insurance; Disability Coverage; Financial Planning Assistance; Life Insurance; Medical Insurance; Sick Days (6 - 10); Tuition Assistance; Vacation Days (6 - 10). **Corporate headquarters location:** This Location. **Other U.S. locations:** Phoenix AZ; Jacksonville FL; Raleigh NC. **Number of employees at this location:** 250. **Number of employees nationwide:** 360.

BROOKTROUT TECHNOLOGY, INC.
410 First Avenue, Needham MA 02494-2722. 781/449-4100. **Fax:** 781/449-9009. **Contact:** Human Resources. **World Wide Web address:** http://www.brooktrout.com. **Description:** Designs, manufactures, and markets software, hardware, and systems solutions for electronic messaging applications in telecommunications and networking environments worldwide. These products help integrate voice, fax, and data communications across networks. **Benefits:** Stock Option. **Corporate headquarters location:** This Location. **Subsidiaries include:** Brooktrout Networks Group, Inc. (Texas); Brooktrout Securities Corporation; Brooktrout Technology Europe, Ltd.

BULL HN INFORMATION SYSTEMS INC.
300 Concord Road, Billerica MA 01821-4199. 978/294-6000. **Contact:** Debra Metrano, Personnel Administrator. **World Wide Web address:** http://www.bull.com. **Description:** A major systems and technologies integrator with a comprehensive range of solutions, services, and support capabilities. Bull's strategy, the Distributed Computing Model, which allows users to integrate multivendor systems in a flexible, open environment. **Common positions include:** Accountant; Computer Programmer; Financial Analyst; Marketing Specialist; Sales Executive. **Corporate headquarters location:** This Location. **Parent company:** Groupe Bull (France).

CACI, INC.
1100 North Glebe Road, Arlington VA 22201. 703/841-7800. **Contact:** Personnel. **World Wide Web address:** http://www.caci.com. **Description:** Develops and integrates systems, software, and simulation products for the government and international commercial customers. **Common positions include:** Accountant; Computer Programmer; Department Manager; Electrical Engineer; Financial Analyst; Marketing Specialist;

Purchasing Agent; Quality Control Supervisor; Systems Analyst; Technical Writer/Editor. **Educational backgrounds include:** Accounting; Business Administration; Computer Science; Engineering; Finance; Marketing; Mathematics. **Benefits:** Dental Insurance; Disability Coverage; Life Insurance; Medical Insurance; Pension Plan; Tuition Assistance. **Corporate headquarters location:** This Location. **Other U.S. locations:** Nationwide. **International locations:** Worldwide. **Number of employees nationwide:** 1,500.

CHS ELECTRONICS INC.
2000 NW 84th Avenue, Miami FL 33122. 305/908-7200. **Fax:** 305/908-7040. **Contact:** Personnel. **World Wide Web address:** http://www.chse.com. **Description:** An international distributor of microcomputer products. **Corporate headquarters location:** This Location.

CMGI
100 Brickstone Square, Andover MA 01810. 978/684-3600. **Contact:** Personnel. **World Wide Web address:** http://www.cmgi.com. **Description:** Develops and integrates a variety of advanced Internet and database management technologies. **Corporate headquarters location:** This Location. **Other U.S. locations:** Wilmington MA.

CMS INFORMATION SERVICES
301 Maple Avenue West, White Oak Tower Building, Vienna VA 22180-4300. 703/938-2600. **Contact:** Human Resources. **Description:** Offers a variety of computer consulting services including networking systems integration to the Department of Defense and commercial clients. **Corporate headquarters location:** This Location. **Other U.S. locations:** Santa Barbara CA; Overland Park KS.

CMS/DATA CORPORATION
101 North Monroe Street, Suite 800, Tallahassee FL 32301. 850/224-2200. **Contact:** Pati Rice, Human Resources Manager. **World Wide Web address:** http://www.cmsopen.com. **Description:** Develops financial software. **NOTE:** Entry-level positions and part-time jobs are offered. **Common positions include:** Account Manager; Accountant; Administrative Assistant; Administrative Manager; Applications Engineer; Budget Analyst; Computer Engineer; Computer Programmer; Computer Support Technician; Computer Technician; Controller; Customer Service Rep.; Database Administrator; Human Resources Manager; Marketing Manager; Marketing Specialist; MIS Specialist; Network Administrator; Project Manager; Public Relations Specialist; Purchasing Agent; Sales Manager; Sales Rep.; Software Engineer; SQL Programmer; Systems Analyst; Vice President; Webmaster. **Educational backgrounds include:** Accounting; Business Administration; C/C++; Computer Science; Finance; HTML; Internet; Java; Marketing; MCSE; Microsoft Word; Novell; Software Development; Software Tech. Support; Visual Basic. **Benefits:** 401(k); Casual Dress - Fridays; Dental Insurance; Disability Coverage; Employee Discounts; Flexible Schedule; Life Insurance; Medical Insurance; Sick Days (6 - 10); Telecommuting; Tuition Assistance; Vacation Days (10 - 20). **Special programs:** Training; Co-ops; Summer Jobs. **Corporate headquarters location:** This Location. **Other U.S. locations:** Nationwide. **Parent company:** PC Docs Group International. **Number of employees nationwide:** 300.

CPA SOFTWARE
One Pensacola Plaza, Suite 500, Pensacola FL 32501. 850/434-2685. **Contact:** Administrative Manager. **World Wide Web address:** http://www. cpasoftware.com. **Description:** Develops software for certified public accountants. **Common positions include:** Computer Programmer; Customer Service Representative; Marketing Specialist; Public Relations Specialist; Purchasing Agent/Manager; Services Sales Representative; Systems Analyst; Technical Writer/Editor. **Educational backgrounds include:** Accounting; Business Administration; Communications; Computer Science; Marketing. **Benefits:** Dental Insurance; Disability Coverage; Life Insurance; Medical Insurance; Profit Sharing; Tuition Assistance. **Corporate headquarters location:** This Location. **Parent company:** Fenimore Software Group, Inc.

CSPI
40 Linnell Circle, Billerica MA 01821. 978/663-7598. **Toll-free phone:** 800/325-3110. **Fax:** 978/663-0150. **Contact:** Karen Lacroix, Human Resources Manager. **World Wide Web address:** http://www.cspi.com. **Description:** CSPI designs, manufactures, and markets digital signal processing, high-performance, multiprocessing systems for real-time applications. These low-power, special purpose computers enhance a system's ability to perform high-speed arithmetic and are primarily used for defense, medical, industrial, and real-time applications. **Common positions include:** Applications Engineer; Design Engineer; Field Engineer; Software Engineer. **Educational backgrounds include:** Computer Science; Engineering; Mathematics; Physics. **Benefits:** 401(k); Dental Insurance; Disability Coverage; Life Insurance; Medical Insurance; Stock Purchase; Tuition Assistance. **Special programs:** Co-ops. **Corporate headquarters location:** This Location. **Other U.S. locations:** CA; FL; MD; VA. **Subsidiaries include:** MODCOMP, Inc. sells real-time process control systems and legacy solutions; Scanalytics, Inc. is focused on hardware and software products for scientific imaging. **Number of employees nationwide:** 150.

CTA
301 South 13th Street, Suite 500, Lincoln NE 68508. 402/476-2400. **Contact:** Human Resources. **World Wide Web address:** http://www.cta.com. **Description:** Provides network development and integration, IT systems engineering, data warehousing, and database migrations. **Corporate headquarters location:** Bethesda MD.

CTC PARKER AUTOMATION
50 West TechneCenter Drive, Milford OH 45150. 513/831-2340. **Fax:** 513/831-5042. **Contact:** Personnel. **World Wide Web address:** http://www.ctcusa.com. **Description:** Develops interface software to monitor the operation of industrial machinery. **Corporate headquarters location:** This Location.

CTI GROUP HOLDINGS INC.
CTI DATA SOLUTIONS/CTI SOFT-COM
2550 Eisenhower Avenue, Norristown PA 19403. 610/666-1700. **Fax:** 610/666-7707. **Contact:** Personnel. **E-mail address:** ctiusa@ctigroup.com. **World Wide Web address:** http://www.ctigroup.com. **Description:** A diversified holding company. **Corporate headquarters location:** This Location. **Subsidiaries include:** CTI Data Solutions Inc. (also at this location) and CTI Data Solutions, Ltd. (United Kingdom) supply PC-based call management products; CTI Soft-Com Inc. (also at this location) offers telecommunications management software; Plymouth Communications Inc.; Regional Communications, Inc.; Telephone Budgeting Systems, Inc. **Stock exchange symbol:** CTIG.

CABLES TO GO
1501 Webster Street, Dayton OH 45404. 937/224-8646. **Fax:** 937/496-2646. **Contact:** Cindy Pretekin, Personnel Administrator. **World Wide Web address:** http://www.cablestogo.com. **Description:** Manufactures and distributes computer connection equipment including adapters, cables, connectors, and networking equipment. **Corporate headquarters location:** This Location.

CABLETRON SYSTEMS, INC.
P.O. Box 5005, 35 Industrial Way, Rochester NH 03866. 603/332-9400. **Contact:** Human Resources. **World Wide Web address:** http://www.cabletron. com. **Description:** Develops, manufactures, markets, installs, and supports a wide range of standards-based LAN connectivity products such as network management software, high-speed adapter cards, smart hubs, and other network interconnection equipment. **Common positions include:** Account Manager; Accountant; Customer Service Rep.; Electrical Engineer; Mechanical Engineer; Software Engineer; Technical Writer. **Special programs:** Internships. **Corporate headquarters location:** This Location. **Other U.S. locations:** Nationwide. **Operations at this facility include:** Administration; Sales.

CADENCE DESIGN SYSTEMS, INC.
555 River Oaks Parkway, San Jose CA 95134. 408/943-1234. **Fax:** 408/955-0820. **Contact:** Personnel. **World Wide Web address:** http://www. cadence.com. **Description:** Manufactures electronic design automation software. **Common positions include:** Design Engineer; Electrical/Electronics Engineer. **Benefits:** 401(k); Dental Insurance; Disability Coverage; Life Insurance; Medical Insurance; Tuition Assistance. **Special programs:** Internships. **Corporate headquarters location:** This Location. **Operations at this facility include:** Research and Development; Sales.

CADKEY CORPORATION
33 Boston Post Road West, Suite 420, Marlborough MA 01752. 508/229-2020. **Fax:** 508/229-2121. **Contact:** Personnel. **World Wide Web address:** http://www.cadkey.com. **Description:** Develops 3-D mechanical design software for CAD systems. **Corporate headquarters location:** This Location.

CALDWELL-SPARTIN
1640 Powers Ferry Road, Building 14, Marietta GA 30067. 770/955-1528. **Contact:** Jackie Fitzgerald, Personnel Assistant. **World Wide Web address:** http://www.caldwell-spartin.com. **Description:** Distributes computer hardware and staffing software. **Common positions include:** Account Manager; Account Rep.; Administrative Assistant; Applications Engineer; Computer Programmer; Customer Service Rep.; Management Analyst; MIS Specialist; Sales Executive; Sales Manager; Sales Rep.; Software Engineer; Systems Analyst; Systems Manager. **Educational backgrounds include:** Accounting; Business Administration; Communications; Computer Science; Engineering; Marketing. **Benefits:** 401(k); Cafeteria Plan; Dental Insurance; Disability Coverage; Life Insurance; Medical Insurance; Tuition Assistance. **Corporate headquarters location:** This Location. **Operations at this facility include:** Accounting/Auditing; Customer Service; Marketing; Sales.

CALYPSO SYSTEM SOLUTIONS
213 West Institute Place, Suite 702, Chicago IL 60610. 312/587-7500. **Fax:** 312/587-0689. **Contact:** Joanne Liautaud, Director of Client Services. **E-mail address:** joanne@calsys.com. **World Wide Web address:** http://www.calsys.com. **Description:** An independent software development firm specializing in client/server and Internet/intranet application development. The company focuses on consumer products, financial institutions, health care, and manufacturing industries. **Company slogan:** Your partner for database and Web applications. **Common positions include:** Applications Engineer; Computer Programmer; Database Manager; MIS Specialist; Multimedia Designer; Webmaster. **Educational backgrounds include:** Computer Science; Software Development. **Benefits:** 401(k); Dental Insurance; Profit Sharing. **Special programs:** Internships. **Corporate headquarters location:** This Location. **President:** Alexander Tait.

CAM DATA SYSTEMS, INC.
17520 Newhope Street, Fountain Valley CA 92708. 714/241-9241. **Contact:** Human Resources. **World Wide Web address:** http://www.camdata.com. **Description:** Designs, manufactures, markets, and services inventory management, point-of-sale, order entry, and accounting software systems for small- to medium-sized retailers and wholesalers. CAM provides its products and services on a direct basis only. The company also offers after-sale services including phone support, nationwide hardware and software service, database conversions, and regular program enhancements. Founded in 1983. **Corporate headquarters location:** This Location. **Chairman and CEO:** Geoff Knapp. **Number of employees at this location:** 115.

CAMBEX CORPORATION
360 Second Avenue, Waltham MA 02451. 781/890-6000. **Fax:** 781/890-2899. **Contact:** Human Resources. **World Wide Web address:** http://www. cambex.com. **Description:** Develops, manufactures, and markets a variety of direct access storage products that improve the performance of large- and mid-size IBM computers. These products include central and expanded memory, controller cache memory, disk array systems, disk and tape subsystems, and related software products. **Common positions include:** Branch Manager; Buyer; Computer Programmer; Customer Service Rep.; Electrical Engineer; Human Resources Manager; Manufacturer's Sales Rep.; Marketing Specialist; Operations/Production Manager; Quality Control Supervisor. **Educational backgrounds include:** Accounting; Business Administration; Communications; Computer Science; Engineering; Liberal Arts; Marketing. **Benefits:** Dental Insurance; Disability Coverage; Employee Discounts; Life Insurance; Medical Insurance; Profit Sharing; Savings Plan; Tuition Assistance. **Corporate headquarters location:** This Location. **Other U.S. locations:** Scottsdale AZ; Thousand Oaks CA; Walnut Creek CA; Westport CT; Clearwater FL; Roswell GA; Schaumburg IL; Troy MI; Chesterfield MO; Charlotte NC; Clark NJ; Cincinnati OH; Blue Bell PA; Dallas TX; Reston VA.

CAMBRIDGE TECHNOLOGY PARTNERS
8 Cambridge Center, Cambridge MA 02142. 617/374-9800. **Contact:** Personnel. **World Wide Web address:** http://www.ctp.com. **Description:** Provides information technology consulting and software development services to organizations with large-scale information processing and distribution needs that are utilizing or migrating to open systems computing environments. **Corporate headquarters location:** This Location. **Other U.S. locations:** Los Angeles CA; Atlanta GA; Chicago IL; Detroit MI; Lansing MI; New York NY; Dallas TX.

CANON BUSINESS MACHINES, INC.
3191 Red Hill Avenue, Costa Mesa CA 92626. 714/556-4700. **Fax:** 714/433-8103. **Contact:** Bonnie Robinson, Personnel Manager. **World Wide**

Web address: http://www.cbm.canon.com. **Description:** This location is a research and development facility. Operations at this facility focus on the bubble-jet printer development and image processing technology. Overall, Canon Business Machines manufactures bubble-jet printer consumables, copier toner and drums, and operates a product recycling facility. **Company slogan:** Think again, think Canon. **Common positions include:** Accountant; Buyer; Chemical Engineer; Computer Programmer; Computer Support Technician; Design Engineer; Electrical/Electronics Engineer; Mechanical Engineer; Network/Systems Administrator; Software Engineer. **Educational backgrounds include:** Business Administration; C/C++; Computer Science; Engineering; Software Development. **Benefits:** 401(k); Casual Dress - Daily; Dental Insurance; Disability Coverage; Employee Discounts; Life Insurance; Medical Insurance; Profit Sharing; Section 125 Plan; Sick Days (6 - 10); Tuition Assistance. **Special programs:** Internships. **Corporate headquarters location:** This Location. **Parent company:** Canon, Inc. (Japan). **Operations at this facility include:** Administration; Manufacturing; Research and Development. **Annual sales/revenues:** More than $100 million.

CANTERBURY INFORMATION TECHNOLOGY
1600 Medford Plaza, Medford NJ 08055. 609/953-0044. **Fax:** 609/953-0062. **Contact:** Darcy Teibel, Office Manager. **World Wide Web address:** http://www.canterburyciti.com. **Description:** A corporate training company providing information technology services. Training covers entry-level vocational, managerial, executive, and technical areas. **Corporate headquarters location:** This Location. **Subsidiaries include:** ATM/Canterbury Corp. is a software development and consulting firm. CALC/Canterbury Corp. is a computer software training company. MSI/Canterbury Corp. is a management, sales, and communication training company. ProSoft/Canterbury Corp. is a provider of technical staffing, applications development, and corporate training.

CAPSOFT
2222 South 950 East, Provo UT 84606. 801/354-8000. **Fax:** 801/354-8099. **Contact:** Human Resources. **E-mail address:** jobs@capsoft.com. **World Wide Web address:** http://www.capsoft.com. **Description:** Develops document assembly software. **NOTE:** Entry-level positions are offered. **Common positions include:** Account Rep.; Applications Engineer; Content Developer; Graphic Designer; Human Resources Manager; MIS Specialist; Network Engineer; Sales Manager; Software Engineer; Systems Manager. **Educational backgrounds include:** Business Administration; C/C++; Computer Science; HTML; Mathematics; Microsoft Office; Novell; Spreadsheets; SQL; Visual Basic. **Benefits:** 401(k); Casual Dress - Daily; Dental Insurance; Disability Coverage; Employee Discounts; Flexible Schedule; Life Insurance; Medical Insurance; Pension Plan; Tuition Assistance. **Annual sales/revenues:** More than $100 million.

CELERITY SYSTEMS, INC.
122 Perimeter Park Drive, Knoxville TN 37922. 865/539-5300. **Fax:** 865/539-5390. **Contact:** Human Resources. **World Wide Web address:** http://www.celerity.com. **Description:** A leader in the development and integration of interactive video hardware including video servers and digital set-top boxes. Founded in 1993. **Corporate headquarters location:** This Location. **Listed on:** NASDAQ. **Number of employees at this location:** 80.

CELLULAR TECHNICAL SERVICES CO.
2401 Fourth Avenue, Suite 400, Seattle WA 98121. 206/443-6400. **Contact:** Human Resources. **World Wide Web address:** http://www.cellulartech.com. **Description:** Develops and markets real-time information management software systems used for fraud detection, billing, and customer service. Cellular Technical Services Company serves clients in the wireless communications industry. **Corporate headquarters location:** This Location.

THE CENTECH GROUP, INC.
4600 North Fairfax Drive, 4th Floor, Arlington VA 22203. 703/525-4444. **Toll-free phone:** 800/938-1026. **Fax:** 703/525-2349. **Contact:** Human Resources. **E-mail address:** hrdept@centechgroup.com. **World Wide Web address:** http://www.centechgroup.com. **Description:** Specializes in providing information technology integration services to the federal government. The company is also involved in a variety of software development programs throughout the metropolitan Washington DC area. **NOTE:** Entry-level positions are offered. **Common positions include:** Computer Programmer; Software Engineer. **Educational backgrounds include:** Business Administration; Computer Science. **Benefits:** 401(k); Bonus Award/Plan; Dental Insurance; Disability Coverage; Life Insurance; Medical Insurance; Profit Sharing; Public Transit Available; Tuition Assistance. **Special programs:** Internships; Summer Jobs. **Corporate headquarters location:** This Location. **President:** Fernando V. Galaviz.

CENTENNIAL TECHNOLOGIES, INC.
7 Lopez Road, Wilmington MA 01887. 978/988-8848. **Contact:** Personnel. **World Wide Web address:** http://www.cent-tech.com. **Description:** Designs, manufactures, and sells personal computer cards used in portable computers and industrial applications, and font cartridges used in laser printers. The PC cards enhance the utility of portable computers and electronic equipment by adding memory, data/fax capabilities, and custom applications. The company's laser printer font cartridges broaden the capabilities of laser printers with applications in desktop publishing, word processing, and spreadsheet preparation. **Corporate headquarters location:** This Location.

CENTURA SOFTWARE CORPORATION
975 Island Drive, Redwood Shores CA 94065. 650/596-3400. **Contact:** Human Resources. **World Wide Web address:** http://www.centurasoft.com. **Description:** Develops software for local area networks and database management systems. Services include support, consulting, and training. **Common positions include:** Software Engineer; Technical Support Rep.. **Educational backgrounds include:** Computer Science; Engineering. **Benefits:** 401(k); Dental Insurance; Disability Coverage; Employee Discounts; Flexible Benefits; Life Insurance; Medical Insurance. **Corporate headquarters location:** This Location. **Other U.S. locations:** Los Angeles CA; Washington DC; Atlanta GA; Chicago IL; New York NY; Dallas TX. **Operations at this facility include:** Administration; Research and Development; Sales; Service. **Number of employees nationwide:** 300.

CERNER CORPORATION
2800 Rockcreek Parkway, Kansas City MO 64117. 816/221-1024. **Contact:** Human Resources. **World Wide Web address:** http://www.cerner.com. **Description:** This location develops software. Overall, Cerner designs, installs, and supports software systems for the health care industry including hospitals, HMOs, clinics, physicians' offices, and integrated health organizations. All

Cerner applications are structured around a single architectural design, called Health Network Architecture (HNA), which allows information to be shared among clinical disciplines and across multiple facilities. Products include PathNet, which automates the processes of the clinical laboratory; RadNet, which focuses on automating radiology department operations; PharmNet, which automates the processes of the pharmacy; ProFile, which stores, tracks, and accesses medical records; and SurgiNet, which addresses the information management needs of the operating room team. Repositories include the Open Clinical Foundation, an enterprisewide, relational database that contains information captured by various clinical systems to form the computer-based patient record; and Open Management Foundation, a repository of process-related information to support management analysis and decision making. **Corporate headquarters location:** This Location. **Other U.S. locations:** Nationwide. **Annual sales/revenues:** More than $100 million.

THE CERPLEX GROUP, INC.
111 Pacifica, Suite 300, Irvine CA 92618-7428. 949/754-5300. **Fax:** 949/754-5493. **Contact:** Personnel. **World Wide Web address:** http://www. cerplex.com. **Description:** An independent provider of repair services for computers, peripherals, and printed circuit board assemblies. The company repairs, refurbishes, upgrades, and tests a wide range of electronic equipment for the computer, telecommunications, medical instrumentation, and other industries utilizing electronic equipment. **Corporate headquarters location:** This Location. **Other U.S. locations:** Sacramento CA; San Diego CA; San Jose CA; Memphis TN. **International locations:** The Netherlands.

CHANEY SYSTEMS, INC.
5100 South Calhoun Road, New Berlin WI 53151. 262/679-3908. **Fax:** 262/679-3715. **Contact:** Human Resources. **World Wide Web address:** http://www.chaney.net. **Description:** A systems integration and consulting firm providing information technology solutions, design, implementation, support, and training to *Fortune* 500 companies. **Common positions include:** Applications Engineer; Computer Programmer; Database Manager; Information Systems Consultant; Internet Services Manager; Management Analyst; MIS Specialist; Network Engineer; Project Manager; Software Engineer; Systems Analyst; Systems Manager; Webmaster. **Educational backgrounds include:** Business Administration; Computer Science. **Benefits:** 401(k); Dental Insurance; Disability Coverage; Employee Discounts; Life Insurance; Medical Insurance. **Special programs:** Training. **Corporate headquarters location:** This Location. **Other area locations:** Madison WI; Milwaukee WI. **Number of employees at this location:** 70.

CHECKFREE CORPORATION
4411 East Jones Bridge Road, Norcross GA 30092. 678/375-3387. **Contact:** Human Resources. **World Wide Web address:** http://www.checkfree.com. **Description:** Provides a wide range of services and products that enable consumers, businesses, and financial institutions to conduct business over the Internet. CheckFree operates in three divisions: Electronic Commerce, Investment Services, and Software. **Corporate headquarters location:** This Location. **Other U.S. locations:** Aurora IL; Chicago IL; Downers Grove IL; Baltimore MD; Jersey City NJ; Dublin OH; Austin TX. **Number of employees nationwide:** 1,600.

CHILD & ELDER CARE INSIGHTS, INC.
19111 Detroit Road, Suite 104, Rocky River OH 44116. 440/356-2900. **Fax:** 440/356-2919. **Contact:** Elisabeth A. Bryenton, President. **E-mail address:** info@carereports.com. **World Wide Web address:** http://www.carereports.com. **Description:** A national dependent care resource and referral service that maintains two national databases: CHILDBASE and ELDERBASE. CHILDBASE provides working parents with information about child care services including family day care providers, preschools, adoption resources, in-home care, and schools. ELDERBASE provides information on nursing homes, home health agencies, nutrition services, continuing care/ retirement communities, and transportation services. **Common positions include:** Administrative Assistant; Database Administrator; Database Manager; Librarian; MIS Specialist. **Other U.S. locations:** Nationwide.

CIBER, INC.
5251 DTC Parkway, Suite 1400, Englewood CO 80111. 303/220-0100. **Toll-free phone:** 800/669-0401. **Fax:** 303/220-7100. **Contact:** National Recruiting. **World Wide Web address:** http://www.ciber.com. **Description:** Provides consulting for client/server development, mainframe and legacy systems, industry-specific analysis, application-specific analysis, and network development. **Common positions include:** Computer Operator; Computer Programmer; Sales Rep.; Systems Analyst; Systems Manager; Technical Writer; Telecommunications Manager. **Educational backgrounds include:** Computer Science; Mathematics. **Benefits:** 401(k); Adoption Assistance; Daycare Assistance; Dental Insurance; Disability Coverage; Life Insurance; Medical Insurance; Profit Sharing; Tuition Assistance. **Corporate headquarters location:** This Location. **International locations:** Canada; the Netherlands. **Subsidiaries include:** Business Information Technology; Spectrum Technologies. **Annual sales/ revenues:** More than $100 million. **Number of employees worldwide:** 6,700.
Other U.S. locations:
- One Parklane Boulevard, 1200 East, Dearborn MI 48126. 313/271-1221.
- 8210 University Executive Park Drive, Suite 290, Charlotte NC 28262. 704/535-7150.

CINCOM SYSTEMS, INC.
55 Merchant Street, Cincinnati OH 45246. 513/612-2300. **Fax:** 513/612-2300. **Contact:** Patricia A. Sledge, Manager of Staffing and Placement. **E-mail address:** psledge@cincom.com. **World Wide Web address:** http://www.cincom.com. **Description:** Develops business software for manufacturing companies; solutions for object-oriented and fourth generation language application development; client/server and relational, object-oriented databases; workflow automation; and document solutions. **Common positions include:** Computer Programmer; Sales Executive; Software Engineer. **Educational backgrounds include:** Computer Science. **Benefits:** Dental Insurance; Disability Coverage; Employee Discounts; Flexible Schedule; Life Insurance; Medical Insurance; Profit Sharing; Tuition Assistance. **Corporate headquarters location:** This Location. **Listed on:** Privately held. **Annual sales/revenues:** More than $100 million.

CISCO SYSTEMS, INC.
170 West Tasman Drive, San Jose CA 95134. 408/526-4000. **Contact:** Human Resources. **World Wide Web address:** http://www.cisco.com. **Description:** Develops, manufactures, markets, and supports high-performance internetworking systems that enable customers to build large-scale integrated

computer networks. The company's products connect and manage communications among local and wide area networks that employ a variety of protocols, media interfaces, network topologies, and cable systems. **Corporate headquarters location:** This Location.

CLARIFY INC.
2560 Orchard Parkway, San Jose CA 95131. 408/428-2000. **Contact:** Human Resources. **E-mail address:** hr@clarify.com. **World Wide Web address:** http://www.clarify.com. **Description:** Develops customer support management software. **Corporate headquarters location:** This Location. **Number of employees nationwide:** 150.

CNET (THE COMPUTER NETWORK)
150 Chestnut Street, San Francisco CA 94111. 415/395-7805. **Fax:** 415/395-7811. **Contact:** Personnel. **World Wide Web address:** http://www. cnet.com. **Description:** Provides a network of technology-related Internet sites and produces several television shows. **Corporate headquarters location:** This Location.

COGNEX CORPORATION
One Vision Drive, Natick MA 01760. 508/650-3000. **Fax:** 508/650-3340. **Recorded jobline:** 508/650-3232. **Contact:** Human Resources. **E-mail address:** hr@cognex.com. **World Wide Web address:** http://www.cognex.com. **Description:** Designs, develops, manufactures, and markets machine vision systems used to automate a wide range of manufacturing processes. Cognex machine vision systems are used in the electronics, semiconductor, pharmaceutical, health care, aerospace, automotive, packaging, and graphic arts industries to gauge, guide, inspect, and identify products in manufacturing operations. **NOTE:** Entry-level positions and part-time jobs are offered. **Company slogan:** To preserve and enhance vision. **Common positions include:** Account Manager; Accountant; Administrative Assistant; Applications Engineer; Attorney; CFO; Computer Engineer; Computer Programmer; Computer Support Technician; Computer Technician; Controller; Credit Manager; Database Administrator; Database Manager; Electrical Engineer; Finance Director; Financial Analyst; Human Resources Manager; Manufacturing Engineer; Market Research Analyst; Marketing Manager; Marketing Specialist; MIS Specialist; Network Administrator; Production Manager; Project Manager; Public Relations Specialist; Quality Assurance Engineer; Sales Engineer; Sales Executive; Sales Manager; Software Engineer; Systems Analyst; Technical Writer. **Educational backgrounds include:** Accounting; Business Administration; C/C++; Communications; Computer Science; Economics; Engineering; Finance; HTML; Java; Marketing; MCSE; Microsoft Word; Novell; Public Relations; Software Development; Software Tech. Support; Visual Basic. **Benefits:** 401(k); Dental Insurance; Disability Coverage; Employee Discounts; Financial Planning Assistance; Life Insurance; Medical Insurance; Profit Sharing; Savings Plan; Tuition Assistance. **Special programs:** Co-ops; Internships; Training; Summer Jobs. **Corporate headquarters location:** This Location. **Other U.S. locations:** CA; IL; TX; WI. **International locations:** Worldwide. **President/CEO:** Dr. Bob Shillman. **Annual sales/revenues:** More than $100 million. **Number of employees nationwide:** 450. **Number of employees worldwide:** 600.

COGNOS CORPORATION
67 South Bedford Street, Burlington MA 01803. 781/229-6600. **Fax:** 781/229-9844. **Contact:** Personnel. **World Wide Web address:** http://www. cognos.com. **Description:** Develops a line of business management software. **Corporate headquarters location:** This Location.

COLE-LAYER-TRUMBLE COMPANY
3199 Klepinger Road, Dayton OH 45406. 937/276-5261. **Fax:** 937/278-3711. **Contact:** Personnel. **World Wide Web address:** http://www.cltco.com. **Description:** One of the nation's largest mass appraisal firms offering both manual and computer-assisted appraisals. The company also offers consulting services for appraisals, data processing, training, and systems design. **Common positions include:** Real Estate Appraiser. **Benefits:** Dental Insurance; Disability Coverage; Life Insurance; Medical Insurance; Pension Plan; Savings Plan; Tuition Assistance. **Corporate headquarters location:** This Location. **Operations at this facility include:** Research and Development; Sales; Service. **Listed on:** Privately held. **Number of employees nationwide:** 600.

COLUMBIA SERVICES GROUP, INC.
2751 Prosperity Avenue, Suite 600, Fairfax VA 22031. 703/207-1000. **Fax:** 703/208-1650. **Contact:** Elaine Crocker, Human Resources Specialist. **World Wide Web address:** http://www. columbiaservices.com. **Description:** Provides IT services in the areas of document declassification, document management, and systems integration. Founded in 1984. **Common positions include:** Accountant; Administrative Assistant; AS400 Programmer Analyst; CFO; Computer Engineer; Computer Programmer; Computer Technician; Help-Desk Technician; Human Resources Manager; Internet Services Manager; Marketing Manager; Network Engineer; Network Administrator; Systems Analyst; Technical Writer; Website Developer. **Educational backgrounds include:** ASP; Engineering; MCSE; Microsoft Office; Novell. **Benefits:** 401(k); Dental Insurance; Disability Coverage; Flexible Schedule; Life Insurance; Medical Insurance; Public Transit Available; Sick Days (6 - 10); Tuition Assistance; Vacation Days (10 - 20). **Corporate headquarters location:** This Location. **President/CEO:** Emmett R. Anderson. **Annual sales/revenues:** $11 - $20 million. **Number of employees nationwide:** 250.

COMARK, INC.
444 Scott Drive, Bloomingdale IL 60108-3111. 630/924-6700. **Toll-free phone:** 800/723-2254. **Fax:** 630/924-6684. **Contact:** Matt Flaskamp, Corporate Staffing Associate. **E-mail address:** recruiting@comark.com. **World Wide Web address:** http://www.comark.com. **Description:** Sells and distributes computer hardware, software and peripherals to *Fortune* 500 companies. Comark also offers information technology solutions including network design and installation, leasing and remarketing asset management, and advanced integration Internet and e-commerce services. **Company slogan:** Your technology partner. **Common positions include:** Administrative Assistant; Buyer; Computer Support Technician; Customer Service Rep.; Database Administrator; Financial Analyst; Network Engineer; Network Administrator; Project Manager; Sales Rep.; SQL Programmer; Systems Analyst. **Educational backgrounds include:** MCSE; Microsoft Office; Novell. **Benefits:** 401(k); Casual Dress - Fridays; Dental Insurance; Disability Coverage; Employee Discounts; Life Insurance; Medical Insurance; Sick Days (1 - 5); Tuition Assistance; Vacation Days (6 - 10). **Corporate headquarters location:** This Location. **Other U.S. locations:**
• 1600 Hunter Court, Hanover Park IL 60103. 630/924-6700.

COMDISCO, INC.
6111 North River Road, Rosemont IL 60018. 847/518-5010. **Fax:** 847/518-5008. **Contact:** Personnel. **World Wide Web address:** http://www. comdisco.com. **Description:** Provides computer equipment leasing, remarketing, and refurbishing; business continuity; consulting; strategic and financial planning; asset management software tools; data center moving services; and consolidations. **Common positions include:** Accountant; Attorney; Biomedical Engineer; Clerical Supervisor; Computer Programmer; Customer Service Rep.; Electrical Engineer; Financial Analyst; Human Resources Manager; Mechanical Engineer; Paralegal; Public Relations Specialist; Secretary; Services Sales Rep.; Systems Analyst; Technical Writer/Editor. **Educational backgrounds include:** Accounting; Business Administration; Computer Science. **Benefits:** 401(k); Daycare Assistance; Dental Insurance; Disability Coverage; Employee Discounts; Life Insurance; Medical Insurance; Profit Sharing; Savings Plan; Tuition Assistance; Vision Insurance. **Special programs:** Internships. **Corporate headquarters location:** This Location. **International locations:** Worldwide. **Number of employees nationwide:** 1,600.

COMMAND TECHNOLOGIES, INC.
P.O. Box 670, Warrenton VA 20188. 540/349-8623. **Physical address:** 405 Belle Air Lane, Warrenton VA. **Contact:** Human Resources. **World Wide Web address:** http://www.commtechinc.com. **Description:** A computer systems engineering firm offering a wide variety of services including technical assistance and network engineering. **Corporate headquarters location:** This Location.

COMMUNICATION INTELLIGENCE CORP.
275 Shoreline Drive, Suite 500, Redwood Shores CA 94065. 650/802-7888. **Fax:** 650/802-7777. **Contact:** Personnel. **World Wide Web address:** http://www.cic.com. **Description:** Develops, markets, and licenses handwriting recognition and related technologies for the emerging pen-based computer market. The company has created a natural input recognition system which allows a computer to recognize hand-printed character input. **Corporate headquarters location:** This Location.

COMPAQ COMPUTER CORPORATION
P.O. Box 692000, Houston TX 77269-2000. 281/370-0670. **Contact:** Human Resources. **World Wide Web address:** http://www.compaq.com. **Description:** Designs, manufactures, sells, and services computers, peripheral equipment, and related software and supplies. Applications and programs include scientific research, computation, communications, education, data analysis, industrial control, time sharing, commercial data processing, graphic arts, word processing, health care, instrumentation, engineering, and simulation. **Corporate headquarters location:** This Location. **Other U.S. locations:** Nationwide.

COMPLETE BUSINESS SOLUTIONS, INC.
1600 NW Comptons Drive, Suite 210, Beaverton OR 97006. 503/748-8000. **Fax:** 503/748-8001. **Contact:** Human Resources. **Description:** An international systems integration consulting firm specializing in strategic systems development, systems integration, software application development, projects, contracts, and business process/system re-engineering. **Corporate headquarters location:** This Location.

COMPREHENSIVE COMPUTER CONSULTING
7000 Central Parkway, Suite 1000, Atlanta GA 30328. 770/512-0100. **Contact:** Human Resources

Department. **Description:** Provides businesses with long-term, contract computer consultants. **Corporate headquarters location:** This Location.

COMPRO SYSTEMS, INC.
7798 Jessup Road, Jessup MD 20794-9476. 410/799-9600. **Fax:** 410/799-3390. **Contact:** Human Resources. **E-mail address:** info@compro. com. **World Wide Web address:** http://www. compro.com. **Description:** Fulfills the automation needs of clients through systems integration, LANs, networking, the Internet, customized application software development, database management, document image processing, and business modeling. ComPro's customers include both government and commercial clients. **Common positions include:** Applications Engineer; Computer Animator; Computer Operator; Computer Programmer; Consultant; Customer Service Rep.; Database Manager; Internet Services Manager; Management Analyst; MIS Specialist; Project Manager; Software Engineer; Systems Analyst; Systems Manager; Telecommunications Manager; Webmaster. **Educational backgrounds include:** Business Administration; Communications; Computer Science; Engineering; Mathematics; Physics. **Benefits:** 401(k); Dental Insurance; Disability Coverage; Flexible Schedule; Life Insurance; Medical Insurance; Tuition Assistance. **Corporate headquarters location:** This Location. **Number of employees nationwide:** 225.

COMPUCOM SYSTEMS, INC.
7171 Forest Lane, Dallas TX 75230. 214/265-3600. **Contact:** Human Resources. **World Wide Web address:** http://www.compucom.com. **Description:** A leading PC integration services company providing product procurement, advanced configuration, network integration, and support services. **Common positions include:** Accountant; Buyer; Computer Operator; Computer Programmer; Customer Service Rep.; Software Engineer; Systems Analyst. **Educational backgrounds include:** Business Administration; Computer Science. **Corporate headquarters location:** This Location. **Other U.S. locations:** Nationwide. **Number of employees at this location:** 800. **Number of employees nationwide:** 1,600.

COMPUSERVE INC.
5000 Arlington Center Boulevard, Columbus OH 43220. 614/457-8600. **Fax:** 614/538-1780. **Contact:** Anita Marcus, Human Resources Director. **Description:** An Internet access and online services provider. **NOTE:** In January 2000, America Online, Inc. and Time Warner, Inc. announced plans to merge. The new company will be named AOL Time Warner Inc. Please contact this location for more information. **Common positions include:** Account Manager; Computer Programmer; Customer Service Rep.; Field Engineer; Marketing Specialist. **Educational backgrounds include:** Business Administration; Communications; Computer Science; Marketing. **Benefits:** 401(k); Dental Insurance; Disability Coverage; Employee Discounts; Life Insurance; Medical Insurance; Savings Plan; Tuition Assistance. **Special programs:** Internships. **Corporate headquarters location:** This Location. **Parent company:** America Online, Inc.

COMPUTER ASSOCIATES INTERNATIONAL
One Computer Associates Plaza, Islandia NY 11788. **Toll-free phone:** 800/454-3788. **Fax:** 800/962-9224. **Contact:** Human Resources. **E-mail address:** resumes-usa-r1@cai.com. **World Wide Web address:** http://www.cai.com. **Description:** This location houses the corporate offices. Overall, Computer Associates International is one of the

world's leading developers of client/server and distributed computing software. The company develops, markets, and supports enterprise management, database and applications development, business applications, and consumer software products for a broad range of mainframe, midrange, and desktop computers. Computer Associates International serves major business, government, research, and educational organizations. **Common positions include:** Account Manager; Administrative Assistant; Computer Operator; Computer Programmer; Consultant; Customer Service Rep.; Daycare Worker; Project Manager; Sales Executive; Sales Manager; Sales Rep.; Systems Analyst; Systems Manager; Teacher; Technical Writer. **Educational backgrounds include:** Computer Science. **Benefits:** 401(k); Daycare Assistance; Dental Insurance; Disability Coverage; Life Insurance; Medical Insurance; On-Site Daycare; Profit Sharing; Tuition Assistance. **Special programs:** Internships. **Corporate headquarters location:** This Location. **International locations:** Worldwide. **Operations at this facility include:** Administration; Research and Development; Sales. **CEO:** Charles Wang. **Number of employees at this location:** 2,500.
Other U.S. locations:
- 909 Las Colinas Boulevard East, Irving TX 75039. 972/556-7100.
- 2291 Wood Oak Drive, Herndon VA 20701. 703/709-4500.

COMPUTER CURRICULUM CORP.
1287 Lawrence Station Road, P.O. Box 3711, Sunnyvale CA 94088-3711. 408/541-3308. **Contact:** Human Resources. **Description:** Develops educational software. **Common positions include:** Accountant; Administrative Manager; Attorney; Budget Analyst; Buyer; Claim Rep.; Clerical Supervisor; Computer Programmer; Credit Manager; Electrician; Financial Analyst; Human Resources Manager; Human Service Worker; Librarian; Mathematician; Services Sales Rep.; Software Engineer; Statistician; Systems Analyst; Technical Writer. **Educational backgrounds include:** Accounting; Art; Business Administration; Communications; Computer Science; Engineering; Finance; Liberal Arts; Marketing; Mathematics. **Benefits:** 401(k); Dental Insurance; Disability Coverage; Employee Discounts; Life Insurance; Medical Insurance; Savings Plan; Tuition Assistance. **Special programs:** Internships. **Operations at this facility include:** Administration; Research and Development; Sales; Service. **Number of employees at this location:** 400. **Number of employees nationwide:** 600.

COMPUTER DECISIONS INTERNATIONAL
22260 Haggerty Road, Suite 300, Northville MI 48167. 248/347-4600. **Contact:** Human Resources. **World Wide Web address:** http://www.cdi-usa.com. **Description:** A computer hardware and software reseller. Founded in 1981.

COMPUTER HORIZONS CORPORATION
49 Old Bloomfield Avenue, Mountain Lakes NJ 07046. 973/402-7400. **Contact:** Human Resources. **World Wide Web address:** http://www.computerhorizons.com. **Description:** A full-service technology solutions company offering contract staffing, outsourcing, re-engineering, migration, downsizing support, and network management. **Corporate headquarters location:** This Location. **Subsidiaries include:** Birla Horizons International Ltd.; Horizons Consulting, Inc.; Strategic Outsourcing Services, Inc.; Unified Systems Solutions, Inc. **Listed on:** NASDAQ. **Number of employees nationwide:** 1,500.

Other U.S. locations:
- Computer Horizons Corporation, Recruiting Center, Midwest Region, 6400 Shafer Court, Suite 600, Rosemont IL 60018. 847/698-6800.

COMPUTER MAINTENANCE CENTER
4500 Hawkins Street NE, Albuquerque NM 87109. 505/345-8800. **Contact:** Owner. **Description:** Specializes in repairing a wide variety of computer hardware and software problems.

THE COMPUTER MERCHANT, LTD.
95 Longwater Circle, Norwell MA 02061. 781/878-1070. **Fax:** 781/878-4712. **Contact:** Karen Brosnahan, Personnel Administrator. **World Wide Web address:** http://www.tcml.com. **Description:** Provides software consulting services. **NOTE:** Part-time jobs are offered. **Common positions include:** Account Manager; Accountant; Administrative Assistant; Applications Engineer; AS400 Programmer Analyst; Computer Engineer; Computer Support Technician; Consultant; Credit Manager; Database Administrator; MIS Specialist; Multimedia Designer; Network Administrator; Sales Representative; Secretary; Software Engineer; SQL Programmer; Systems Analyst; Systems Manager; Technical Writer/Editor; Typist/Word Processor; Webmaster. **Benefits:** 401(k); Casual Dress - Fridays; Dental Insurance; Disability Coverage; Life Insurance; Medical Insurance; On-Site Exercise Facility; Profit Sharing; Tuition Assistance. **Special programs:** Internships; Summer Jobs. **Listed on:** Privately held. **CEO:** John Danieli. **Number of employees at this location:** 80.

COMPUTER SCIENCES CORPORATION
2100 East Grand Avenue, El Segundo CA 90245. 310/615-0311. **Contact:** Marv Pulliam, Vice President of Corporate Personnel. **World Wide Web address:** http://www.csc.com. **Description:** This location primarily serves the U.S. government. Overall, Computer Sciences Corporation helps clients in industry and government use information technology to achieve strategic and operational objectives. The company tailors solutions from a broad suite of integrated service and technology offerings including e-business strategies and technologies; management and IT consulting; systems development and integration; application software; and IT and business process outsourcing. **Common positions include:** Business Analyst; Computer Scientist; Economist; Engineer; Geologist; Mathematician; Operations Research Analyst; Physicist; Statistician. **Corporate headquarters location:** This Location. **Number of employees nationwide:** 20,000.
Other U.S. locations:
- 5885 Landerbrook Drive, Suite 300, Cleveland OH 44124-4031. 440/449-3600.

COMPUTONE CORPORATION
1060 Windward Ridge Parkway, Suite 100, Alpharetta GA 30005. 770/475-2725. **Contact:** Keith Daniel, Manager of Human Resources. **World Wide Web address:** http://www.computone.com. **Description:** Designs, manufactures, and markets hardware and software connectivity products for personal computers, servers, and workstations. The company's principal products are software-driven multiport communications adapters that manage the flow of data between serial devices (e.g., terminals, printers, and modems) and the central processing unit of the host computer. The majority of the company's multiport systems are intelligent devices that incorporate on-board processors, memory chips, and related circuitry. These multiport products are available for IBM PCs and a number of industry-standard operating systems including UNIX, Xenix, IBM AIX, IBM OS/2, DOS, and multi-user DOS.

These products are offered under the IntelliPort, ValuePort, and Power RackPort brand names. The company's multiport communications server for Ethernet local area networks is marketed under the brand name IntelliServer. **Common positions include:** Buyer; Credit Manager; Customer Service Rep.; Hardware Engineer; Manufacturer's Sales Rep.; Marketing Specialist; Operations/Production Manager; Quality Control Supervisor; Software Engineer; Systems Analyst; Technical Writer. **Benefits:** Disability Coverage; Life Insurance; Tuition Assistance. **Special programs:** Internships. **Corporate headquarters location:** This Location. **Operations at this facility include:** Administration; Manufacturing; Research and Development; Sales; Service.

COMPUWARE CORPORATION

31440 Northwestern Highway, Farmington Hills MI 48334-2564. 248/737-7300. **Contact:** Recruiting. **World Wide Web address:** http://www.compuware.com. **Description:** Markets, develops, and supports an integrated line of systems software products which improve the productivity of programmers and analysts in application program testing, test data preparation, error analysis, and maintenance. Compuware also provides a broad range of professional data processing services including business systems analysis, design, and programming, and systems planning and consulting. **Corporate headquarters location:** This Location. **Other U.S. locations:**
- 3600 West 80th Street, Bloomington MN 55431. 651/490-5700.

COMSHARE INC.

555 Briarwood Circle, Ann Arbor MI 48108. 734/994-4800. **Contact:** Human Resources. **World Wide Web address:** http://www.comshare.com. **Description:** Develops financial applications software. **Corporate headquarters location:** This Location. **Number of employees nationwide:** 800.

COMSYS

2 Chase Corporate Drive, Suite 105, Birmingham AL 35244. 205/987-8878. **Fax:** 205/987-1014. **Contact:** Human Resources. **Description:** A full-service computer consulting firm. **NOTE:** Entry-level positions are offered. **Common positions include:** Computer Programmer; Systems Analyst. **Educational backgrounds include:** C/C++; COBOL; Computer Science; HTML; Internet; Java; Visual Basic. **Benefits:** 401(k); Dental Insurance; Disability Coverage; Life Insurance; Medical Insurance; Profit Sharing; Tuition Assistance. **Special programs:** Training. **Corporate headquarters location:** Houston TX. **Other U.S. locations:** Nationwide. **International locations:** Worldwide. **Parent company:** Metamor Worldwide. **Number of employees at this location:** 500. **Number of employees nationwide:** 5,000.

COMTREX SYSTEMS CORPORATION

102 Executive Drive, Suite 1, Moorestown NJ 08057. 856/778-0090. **Fax:** 856/778-9322. **Contact:** Human Resources. **World Wide Web address:** http://www.comtrex.com. **Description:** Designs, develops, assembles, and markets computer software electronic terminals which provide retailers with transaction processing, in-store controls, and management information. The company primarily serves the food service and hospitality industries. Founded in 1981. **Corporate headquarters location:** This Location.

CONCENTREX INC.

400 SW Sixth Avenue, Portland OR 97204. 503/274-7280. **Toll-free phone:** 800/274-7280. **Fax:** 503/274-7284. **Contact:** Carina Le,

Employment Manager. **World Wide Web address:** http://www.concentrex.com. **Description:** A leading provider of integrated, financial software. **NOTE:** Entry-level positions and part-time jobs are offered. **Common positions include:** Account Manager; Account Rep.; Accountant; Administrative Assistant; Applications Engineer; Attorney; Budget Analyst; CFO; Computer Engineer; Computer Programmer; Computer Support Technician; Controller; Customer Service Rep.; Database Administrator; Database Manager; Event Planner; Finance Director; Financial Analyst; Help-Desk Technician; Human Resources Manager; Intellectual Property Lawyer; Intranet Developer; Marketing Manager; Media Planner; Multimedia Designer; Network Engineer; Network Administrator; Project Manager; Public Relations Specialist; Purchasing Agent; Quality Control Supervisor; Sales Executive; Sales Manager; Sales Rep.; Software Engineer; SQL Programmer; Systems Analyst; Systems Manager; Technical Support Manager; Technical Support Manager; Technical Writer; Website Developer. **Educational backgrounds include:** Accounting; Business Administration; C/C++; Computer Science; HTML; Internet Development; Java; Marketing; Mathematics; MBA; MCSE; Microsoft Office; Microsoft Word; Novell; Software Development; Software Tech. Support; Spreadsheets; SQL; Visual Basic. **Benefits:** 401(k); Casual Dress - Daily; Dental Insurance; Disability Coverage; Flexible Schedule; Life Insurance; Medical Insurance; Public Transit Available; Relocation Assistance; Sick Days; Tuition Assistance; Vacation Days. **Special programs:** Internships. **Corporate headquarters location:** This Location. **Other U.S. locations:** Pleasanton CA; Denver CO; Trumbull CT; Atlanta GA; Minneapolis MN; Englewood Cliffs NJ; Huntington NY; Dayton OH; Charleston SC; Houston TX. **CEO:** Matt Chapman. **Facilities Manager:** Gary Pete. **Purchasing Manager:** Lisa Jorsensen. **Sales Manager:** Lincoln Baker. **Number of employees at this location:** 400. **Number of employees nationwide:** 1,100.

CONNECTING POINT/4G COMPUTERS

1515 Wyoming Street, Missoula MT 59801. 406/728-5454. **Fax:** 406/721-2744. **Contact:** John Oeteinger, Owner. **World Wide Web address:** http://www.cp4g.com. **Description:** Provides networking services for a variety of systems including Compaq and Hewlett-Packard. **Educational backgrounds include:** Computer Science. **Benefits:** Dental Insurance; Employee Discounts; Medical Insurance. **Corporate headquarters location:** This Location.

CONNECTNET

6370 Lusk Boulevard, Suite F-208, San Diego CA 92121. 858/638-2029. **Fax:** 858/450-3216. **Contact:** Human Resources. **World Wide Web address:** http://www.connectnet.com. **Description:** Provides Internet access for businesses, supports World Wide Web home pages, and offers co-location services. **NOTE:** Entry-level positions are offered. **Common positions include:** Controller; Human Resources Manager; Internet Services Manager; Marketing Manager; Marketing Specialist; MIS Manager; Sales Executive; Sales Manager; Sales Rep.; Systems Manager. **Educational backgrounds include:** Liberal Arts; Marketing; Mathematics; Public Relations; Software Development; Software Tech. Support. **Benefits:** Daycare Assistance; Employee Discounts; Flexible Schedule; Medical Insurance. **Special programs:** Co-ops; Internships; Summer Jobs. **Corporate headquarters location:** This Location. **President/ CEO:** Tim Sears. **Number of employees at this location:** 15.

CONSILIUM, INC.
485 Clyde Avenue, Mountain View CA 94043.
650/691-6100. **Contact:** Human Resources. **World Wide Web address:** http://www.consilium.com. **Description:** One of the world's leading suppliers of integrated manufacturing execution systems software and services. The company's WorkStream and FlowStream product lines allow manufacturers to identify and implement practices in cost, quality, service, and speed. **Corporate headquarters location:** This Location.

CONTINENTAL DESIGN & ENGINEERING
2710 Enterprise Drive, Anderson IN 46013. 765/778-9999. **Toll-free phone:** 800/875-4557. **Fax:** 765/778-8590. **Contact:** Cathy Mellinger, Director of Technical Recruiting. **E-mail address:** cdcin@continental-design.com. **World Wide Web address:** http://www.continental-design.com. **Description:** This location houses administrative offices as well as the engineering and design center. Overall, Continental Design & Engineering provides computer-aided engineering and design services. **Common positions include:** Applications Engineer; AS400 Programmer Analyst; Computer Animator; Computer Engineer; Computer Programmer; Database Administrator; Database Manager; Design Engineer; Draftsperson; Electrical Engineer; Industrial Engineer; Manufacturing Engineer; Mechanical Engineer; Network Administrator; Quality Assurance Engineer; Software Engineer; SQL Programmer; Systems Analyst; Systems Manager. **Benefits:** 401(k); Cafeteria Plan; Dental Insurance; Medical Insurance; Paid Holidays; Vacation Days. **Corporate headquarters location:** This Location. **Other U.S. locations:** Troy MI.

CONTINENTAL RESOURCES, INC.
175 Middlesex Turnpike, P.O. Box 9137, Bedford MA 01730-9137. 781/275-0850. **Toll-free phone:** 800/937-4688. **Fax:** 781/533-0212. **Contact:** Human Resources. **World Wide Web address:** http://www.conres.com. **Description:** Configures, integrates, sells, services, and supports computer systems and electronic test equipment. **NOTE:** Entry-level positions are offered. **Common positions include:** Account Rep.; Administrative Assistant; Buyer; Computer Programmer; Customer Service Rep.; Human Resources Manager; Sales Engineer; Sales Executive; Sales Rep.; Software Engineer; Systems Analyst. **Educational backgrounds include:** Accounting; Business Administration; Computer Science; Marketing. **Benefits:** 401(k); Dental Insurance; Disability Coverage; Employee Discounts; Life Insurance; Medical Insurance; Savings Plan; Tuition Assistance. **Special programs:** Internships. **Corporate headquarters location:** This Location. **Other U.S. locations:** Milpitas CA; Torrance CA; Orlando FL; Bensenville IL; Beltsville MD; Mount Laurel NJ; Somerset NJ; New York NY. **Subsidiaries include:** Wall Industries manufactures AC/DC power sources and DC/DC converters; Continental Leasing is a lease financing company. **Operations at this facility include:** Administration; Manufacturing; Sales; Service. **Number of employees nationwide:** 275.

CONTROL DYNAMICS INTERNATIONAL
211 Highland Cross, Suite 114, Houston TX 77073. 281/209-3900. **Fax:** 281/209-3901. **Contact:** Van Wilson, Human Resources Manager. **E-mail address:** van.wilson@controldynamics.com. **World Wide Web address:** http://www.controldynamics. com. **Description:** Uses hardware and software components to provide open automation system solutions to the industrial manufacturing and process industries. Applications include custom solutions for data acquisition, control, relational database, and network computing needs. Founded in 1991. **Company slogan:** Turning information into knowledge for industry. **Common positions include:** Account Manager; Account Rep.; Administrative Assistant; Chemical Engineer; Computer Programmer; Database Manager; Design Engineer; Electrical/Electronics Engineer; Project Manager; Sales Engineer; Software Engineer. **Educational backgrounds include:** Computer Science; Engineering; Software Development. **Benefits:** 401(k); Dental Insurance; Disability Coverage; Financial Planning Assistance; Flexible Schedule; Life Insurance; Medical Insurance; Profit Sharing; Tuition Assistance. **Special programs:** Internships; Co-ops. **Corporate headquarters location:** This Location. **Listed on:** Privately held. **President:** Anthony George. **Facilities Manager:** Jerry Christian. **Number of employees at this location:** 30.

CONTROL SYSTEMS INTERNATIONAL
8040 Nieman Road, Lenexa KS 66214. 913/599-5010. **Contact:** Human Resources. **World Wide Web address:** http://www.csiks.com. **Description:** Manufactures networking systems that aid in fuel distribution management. Founded in 1968. **NOTE:** Entry-level positions are offered. **Common positions include:** Electrical Engineer; Software Engineer. **Educational backgrounds include:** C/C++; Computer Science; Engineering; Software Development. **Benefits:** 401(k); Casual Dress - Fridays; Dental Insurance; Disability Coverage; Life Insurance; Medical Insurance; Profit Sharing; Tuition Assistance. **Corporate headquarters location:** Kansas City KS. **Other U.S. locations:** Irvine CA. **International locations:** Hong Kong; London. **Annual sales/revenues:** $21 - $50 million. **Number of employees worldwide:** 160.

CORNELL TECHNICAL SERVICES
1921 Gallows Road, Suite 880, Vienna VA 22182. 703/734-8599. **Fax:** 703/734-2949. **Contact:** Amy Becker, Director of Recruiting. **World Wide Web address:** http://www.cornelltech.com. **Description:** Provides computer consulting services. Founded in 1991. **NOTE:** Entry-level positions are offered. **Common positions include:** Computer Programmer; Systems Analyst; Technical Writer. **Educational backgrounds include:** Computer Science; Engineering. **Benefits:** 401(k); Dental Insurance; Disability Coverage; Financial Planning Assistance; Life Insurance; Medical Insurance; Tuition Assistance. **Corporate headquarters location:** This Location. **Other U.S. locations:** Atlanta GA; Richmond VA. **Number of employees nationwide:** 200.

CORNERSTONE PERIPHERALS TECHNOLOGY
225 Hammond Avenue, Fremont CA 94539. 510/580-8900. **Fax:** 510/580-5305. **Contact:** Lauri Walker, Personnel Representative. **E-mail address:** hr@cptmail.com. **World Wide Web address:** http://www.bigmonitors.com. **Description:** A leader in the design of computer displays and graphics controller cards. Founded in 1986. **Common positions include:** Accountant; Computer Support Technician; Marketing Manager; Sales Executive; Sales Manager; Software Engineer. **Educational backgrounds include:** Accounting; Computer Science; Engineering; Finance; Marketing. **Benefits:** 401(k); Casual Dress - Daily; Dental Insurance; Disability Coverage; Life Insurance; Medical Insurance; Profit Sharing; Sick Days (6 - 10); Vacation Days (6 - 10). **Special programs:** Internships. **Corporate headquarters location:** This Location. **President/CEO:** John Noellert. **Number of employees at this location:** 55. **Number of employees worldwide:** 65.

CORNET INTERNATIONAL, LTD.
701 Main Street, Stroudsburg PA 18360. 570/420-0800. **Fax:** 570/420-0818. **Contact:** Patricia Kennedy, Human Resources. **World Wide Web address:** http://www.cornetltd.com. **Description:** Develops sales force automation software. Founded in 1986. **Common positions include:** Account Manager; Computer Programmer; Customer Service Rep.; Database Manager; Sales Executive; Software Engineer; Systems Analyst; Systems Manager; Technical Writer; Telecommunications Manager. **Educational backgrounds include:** Business Administration; Computer Science; Engineering; Mathematics. **Benefits:** 401(k); Dental Insurance; Flexible Schedule; Life Insurance; Medical Insurance; Profit Sharing. **Special programs:** Internships. **Corporate headquarters location:** This Location. **Number of employees at this location:** 190.

COUNTERPOINT SOFTWARE, INC.
800 East Dimond Boulevard, Suite 3-415, Anchorage AK 99515-2028. 907/522-8783. **Toll-free phone:** 800/525-8783. **Fax:** 907/522-1663. **Contact:** Human Resources. **E-mail address:** info@counterpointsoftware.com. **World Wide Web address:** http://www.counterpointsoftware.com. **Description:** Develops self-insurance software to be used by small- and medium-sized companies. **Corporate headquarters location:** This Location.

CREATIVE COMPUTER APPLICATIONS
26115-A Mureau Road, Calabasas CA 91302. 818/880-6700. **Contact:** Human Resources. **World Wide Web address:** http://www.ccainc.com. **Description:** Designs and manufactures computer-based, clinical information systems and products that automate the acquisition and management of clinical data for the health care industry. The company sells its products and systems to hospitals, clinics, reference laboratories, veterinarians, other health care institutions, and original equipment manufacturers. **Corporate headquarters location:** This Location.

CREATIVE LABS, INC.
1901 McCarthy Boulevard, Milpitas CA 95035. 408/428-6600. **Fax:** 408/232-1284. **Recorded jobline:** 408/428-6600x6604. **Contact:** Personnel. **World Wide Web address:** http://www.creative.com. **Description:** Creative Labs manufactures computer game software. **Corporate headquarters location:** This Location. **Other U.S. locations:** Stillwater OK. **International locations:** Canada; Latin America. **Parent company:** Creative Technology, Ltd. **Listed on:** NASDAQ.

CREATIVE SOLUTIONS
7322 Newman Boulevard, Dexter MI 48130. 734/426-5860. **Contact:** Human Resources. **World Wide Web address:** http://www.creativesolutions.com. **Description:** Develops, markets, and supports accounting and tax software.

CRYPTEK SECURE COMMUNICATIONS
14130-C Sullyfield Circle, Chantilly VA 20151. 703/802-9300. **Fax:** 703/818-3706. **Contact:** Human Resources. **World Wide Web address:** http://www.cryptek.com. **Description:** Designs, produces, and markets secure digital facsimile equipment and networks. Founded in 1954. **Corporate headquarters location:** This Location.

CUBIX CORPORATION
2800 Lockheed Way, Carson City NV 89706. 775/888-1000. **Fax:** 775/888-1002. **Contact:** Joanne L. Lanigir, Personnel Manager. **World Wide Web address:** http://www.cubix.com. **Description:** Designs and manufactures computer networking products for use as mission-critical communication, specialty, and file servers. **Common positions include:** Customer Service Representative; Electrical Engineer; Manufacturing Engineer; Mechanical Engineer; MIS Specialist; Sales Engineer; Sales Rep.; Secretary; Software Engineer. **Educational backgrounds include:** Computer Science. **Benefits:** 401(k); Dental Insurance; Disability Coverage; Life Insurance; Medical Insurance; Tuition Assistance. **Corporate headquarters location:** This Location. **Other U.S. locations:** Tampa FL. **Annual sales/revenues:** $51 - $100 million. **Number of employees at this location:** 140.

CYBER DIGITAL, INC.
400 Oser Avenue, Suite 1650, Hauppauge NY 11788-3641. 631/231-1200. **Fax:** 631/231-1446. **Contact:** Personnel. **E-mail address:** cyberdig@ix.netcom.com. **World Wide Web address:** http://www.cyberdigitalinc.com. **Description:** Cyber Digital designs, develops, manufactures, and markets digital switching and networking systems that enable simultaneous communication of voice and data to a large number of users. The company's systems are based on its proprietary software technology which permits the modemless transmission of data between a variety of incompatible and dissimilar end user equipment including computers, printers, workstations, and data terminals over standard telephone lines. **Common positions include:** Design Engineer; Electrical Engineer; Purchasing Agent/Manager; Telecommunications Manager. **Educational backgrounds include:** Business Administration; Communications; Engineering; Marketing. **Benefits:** Disability Coverage; Medical Insurance. **Corporate headquarters location:** This Location. **Operations at this facility include:** Administration; Research and Development; Sales.

CYMA SYSTEMS, INC.
2330 West University, Suite 7, Tempe AZ 85281. 480/303-2962. **Contact:** Nancy Bliss, Human Resources. **World Wide Web address:** http://www.cyma.com. **Description:** Develops and distributes microcomputer-based software focusing on accounting, medical practice management, point-of-sale, and related vertical applications. **Common positions include:** Accountant; Administrator; Computer Programmer; Customer Service Rep.; Manufacturer's Sales Rep.; Marketing Specialist; Operations Manager; Public Relations Specialist; Quality Control Supervisor; Systems Analyst; Technical Writer. **Educational backgrounds include:** Accounting; Computer Science; Marketing. **Benefits:** Dental Insurance; Disability Coverage; Life Insurance; Medical Insurance; Savings Plan; Tuition Assistance. **Corporate headquarters location:** This Location.

CYSIVE
11480 Sunset Hills Road, Suite 200E, Reston VA 20190. 703/742-0865. **Contact:** Personnel. **World Wide Web address:** http://www.cysive.com. **Description:** Develops Internet and e-commerce systems, data systems, and financial workflow systems for Global 2000 companies. **Corporate headquarters location:** This Location.

D-LINK SYSTEMS, INC.
53 Discovery Drive, Irvine CA 92618. 949/788-0805. **Contact:** Personnel. **World Wide Web address:** http://www.dlink.com. **Description:** Manufactures networking, connectivity, and data communications products. The company's products include adapters, routers, and print servers. **Corporate headquarters location:** This Location.

DMR CONSULTING GROUP INC.
333 Thornall Street, Edison NJ 08837-2246. 732/549-4100. **Fax:** 732/549-2375. **Contact:** Recruiting Administrator. **World Wide Web address:** http://www.dmr.com. **Description:** Provides computer consulting services including outsourcing solutions and systems integration. **Common positions include:** Administrative Assistant; Applications Engineer; AS400 Programmer Analyst; Computer Animator; Computer Engineer; Computer Operator; Computer Programmer; Computer Scientist; Computer Support Technician; Computer Technician; Content Developer; Database Administrator; Database Manager; Financial Analyst; Internet Services Manager; MIS Specialist; Multimedia Designer; Network Administrator; Software Engineer; SQL Programmer; Systems Analyst; Systems Manager; Webmaster. **Educational backgrounds include:** AS400 Certification; C/C++; CGI; HTML; Internet; Java; MCSE; Microsoft Word; Novell; QuarkXPress; Software Development; Software Tech. Support; Spreadsheets; Visual Basic. **Benefits:** 401(k); Casual Dress - Fridays; Dental Insurance; Life Insurance; Medical Insurance; Tuition Assistance. **Corporate headquarters location:** This Location. **Number of employees worldwide:** 8,000.

DP SOLUTIONS INC.
4411 West Market Street, Suite 200, Greensboro NC 27407. 336/292-4535x224. **Toll-free phone:** 800/897-7233. **Fax:** 336/854-7715. **Contact:** Personnel. **World Wide Web address:** http://www.dpsi-cmms.com. **Description:** Designs, develops, and supports computerized maintenance management software. **Common positions include:** Computer Programmer; Technical Writer/Editor. **Benefits:** 401(k); Casual Dress - Fridays; Dental Insurance; Medical Insurance; Vacation Days (10 - 20). **Corporate headquarters location:** This Location. **Other U.S. locations:** FL. **Information Systems Manager:** Joe Claxton.

DRS AHEAD TECHNOLOGY
3550 Annapolis Lane, Suite 60, Plymouth MN 55447. 763/519-9129. **Contact:** Human Resources. **World Wide Web address:** http://www.drs.com. **Description:** A producer of magnetic recording heads for the information processing industry. **Common positions include:** Accountant; Actuary; Buyer; Ceramics Engineer; Computer Programmer; Computer-Aided Designer; Credit Manager; Customer Service Rep.; Department Manager; Electrical/Electronics Engineer; General Manager; Industrial Engineer; Industrial Production Manager; Manufacturer's Sales Rep.; Mechanical Engineer; Metallurgical Engineer; Operations Manager; Purchasing Agent; Quality Control Supervisor; Systems Analyst; Technical Writer/Editor. **Educational backgrounds include:** Accounting; Business Administration; Chemistry; Economics; Engineering; Finance; Marketing; Mathematics; Metallurgy; Physics. **Benefits:** 401(k); Dental Insurance; Disability Coverage; Life Insurance; Medical Insurance; Tuition Assistance. **Corporate headquarters location:** This Location. **Operations at this facility include:** Financial Offices; Manufacturing; Research and Development.

DST SYSTEMS, INC.
333 West 11th Street, 3rd Floor, Kansas City MO 64105. 816/435-8614. **Fax:** 816/435-8618. **Contact:** Personnel. **World Wide Web address:** http://www.dstsystems.com. **Description:** DST Systems is a software developer and transfer agent for the financial industry. **NOTE:** Entry-level positions are offered. **Common positions include:** Administrative Assistant; Computer Programmer;

Customer Service Rep.; Systems Analyst. **Educational backgrounds include:** Accounting; Business Administration; Computer Science; Finance; Liberal Arts; Mathematics. **Benefits:** 401(k); Dental Insurance; Employee Discounts; Life Insurance; Medical Insurance; Profit Sharing; Tuition Assistance. **Special programs:** Internships. **Corporate headquarters location:** This Location. **Subsidiaries include:** Argus Health Systems, Inc.; NFDS.

DATA GENERAL CORPORATION
3400 Computer Drive, Westborough MA 01580. 508/898-5000. **Contact:** Vice President. **World Wide Web address:** http://www.dg.com. **Description:** Designs, manufactures, and markets general purpose computer systems and related products and services including peripheral equipment, software services, training, and maintenance. Data General markets directly to end users and OEMs and offers six product families whose applications include industrial manufacturing for controlling discrete assembly line operations, monitoring continuous production processes, testing, production planning, inventory management, and environmental surveillance. The company's products are also used in business data systems. **Corporate headquarters location:** This Location. **Other U.S. locations:** Nationwide. **Parent company:** EMC Corporation.

DATA TECHNOLOGY CORPORATION
1222 Alderwood Avenue, Sunnyvale CA 94089. 408/745-9320. **Contact:** Human Resources. **Description:** Develops and manufactures computer peripherals including printers, disk drives, terminals, controllers, and supplies. Products are marketed to both original equipment manufacturers and distributors. **Common positions include:** Computer Programmer; Editor; Electrical Engineer; Systems Analyst; Technical Writer. **Educational backgrounds include:** Computer Science; Engineering. **Benefits:** Dental Insurance; Disability Coverage; Employee Discounts; Life Insurance; Medical Insurance; Profit Sharing; Savings Plan; Tuition Assistance; Vision Insurance. **Corporate headquarters location:** This Location.

DATACUBE, INC.
300 Rosewood Drive, Danvers MA 01923. 978/777-4200. **Fax:** 978/777-3117. **Contact:** Ms. Pat Wonson, Human Resources Director. **E-mail address:** pat@datacube.com. **World Wide Web address:** http://www.datacube.com. **Description:** A manufacturer of board- and system-level hardware for image processing. **NOTE:** Entry-level positions are offered. **Common positions include:** Applications Engineer; Design Engineer; Sales Engineer; Software Engineer; Technical Writer. **Educational backgrounds include:** Engineering; Mathematics. **Benefits:** 401(k); Dental Insurance; Disability Coverage; Life Insurance; Medical Insurance; Tuition Assistance. **Corporate headquarters location:** This Location. **Annual sales/revenues:** $11 - $20 million. **Number of employees at this location:** 140.

DATALOGICS INC.
101 North Wacker Drive, Chicago IL 60606. 312/853-8200. **Contact:** Human Resources. **World Wide Web address:** http://www.datalogics.com. **Description:** Develops and markets software for publishing companies. **Corporate headquarters location:** This Location.

DATARAM CORPORATION
P.O. Box 7528, Princeton NJ 08543-7528. 609/799-0071. **Toll-free phone:** 800/DATARAM. **Fax:** 609/897-7021. **Contact:** Dawn Craft, Human

Resources Administrator. **E-mail address:** hr@dataram.com. **World Wide Web address:** http://www.dataram.com. **Description:** Designs and manufactures memory products that improve the performance of computer systems. Dataram primarily serves HP, DEC, Sun, and IBM users in the manufacturing, finance, government, telecommunications, utilities, research, and education industries. **Common positions include:** Accountant; Design Engineer; Designer; Sales Rep.; Test Engineer. **Benefits:** 401(k); Dental Insurance; Disability Coverage; Life Insurance; Medical Insurance; Tuition Assistance. **Corporate headquarters location:** This Location. **Number of employees at this location:** 100. **Number of employees nationwide:** 150.

DATASOUTH COMPUTER CORP.
4216 Stuart Andrew Boulevard, Charlotte NC 28217. 704/523-8500. **Fax:** 704/525-6104. **Contact:** Personnel Manager. **World Wide Web address:** http://www.datasouth.com. **Description:** Designs, manufactures, and markets heavy-duty dot matrix and thermal printers used for high-volume print applications. The company's product lines include the XL series for medium-volume dot matrix printing applications and Documax, which has high-speed dot matrix printing capabilities. The company also manufactures a portable thermal printer, Freeliner, which is used primarily for printing one packing or shipping label at a time. **Corporate headquarters location:** This Location. **Parent company:** Bull Run Corporation (Atlanta GA). **Number of employees nationwide:** 125.

DATASTREAM SYSTEMS, INC.
50 Datastream Plaza, Greenville SC 29605. 864/422-5001. **Fax:** 864/422-5000. **Contact:** Human Resources. **World Wide Web address:** http://www.dstm.com. **Description:** Develops maintenance management software. Datastream serves many major industries including government, health care, hospitality, manufacturing, and transportation. **Common positions include:** Client Specialist; Consultant; Software Developer; Technical Writer/Editor. **Corporate headquarters location:** This Location. **Annual sales/revenues:** $21 - $50 million.

DATATREND INFORMATION SYSTEMS
1200 17th Street, Suite 2640, Denver CO 80202. 303/572-6262. **Contact:** Human Resources. **Description:** Offers systems consulting services. **Common positions include:** Applications Engineer; AS400 Programmer Analyst; Computer Engineer; Computer Programmer; Computer Scientist; Database Administrator; Database Manager; Internet Services Manager; MIS Specialist; Multimedia Designer; Network Administrator; Software Engineer; SQL Programmer; Systems Analyst; Systems Manager; Webmaster. **Educational backgrounds include:** AS400 Certification; ASP; C/C++; CGI; Cold Fusion; HTML; Internet; Java; MCSE; Software Development; Software Tech. Support; Spreadsheets; Visual Basic. **Benefits:** 401(k); Disability Coverage; Flexible Schedule; Job Sharing; Life Insurance; Medical Insurance; Profit Sharing; Public Transit Available. **Corporate headquarters location:** This Location. **Other U.S. locations:** Chicago IL. **Number of employees nationwide:** 45.

DATAVIZ, INC.
55 Corporate Drive, Trumbull CT 06611. 203/268-0030. **Contact:** Mr. Chris Stenz, Human Resources. **World Wide Web address:** http://www.dataviz.com. **Description:** Develops file conversion software. **Common positions include:** Software Engineer. **Educational backgrounds include:**

Computer Science; Engineering; Mathematics; Physical Science. **Corporate headquarters location:** This Location.

DATAWARE TECHNOLOGIES INC.
One Canal Park, Cambridge MA 02141. 617/621-0820. **Contact:** Personnel. **Description:** A leading international developer and marketer of high-performance, multiplatform, and multilingual products. Dataware provides database software products including CD-author, CD-answer, and recorded reference books to the CD-ROM market; and provides an extensive range of services to enable CD-ROM publishers to create, distribute, and support their electronic information products. **Corporate headquarters location:** This Location.

DAUGHERTY SYSTEMS
One City Place Drive, Suite 240, St. Louis MO 63141. 314/432-8200. **Fax:** 314/432-8217. **Contact:** Personnel Manager. **World Wide Web address:** http://www.daugherty.com. **Description:** A computer consulting firm. **Common positions include:** Computer Programmer; Database Manager; Information Systems Consultant; MIS Specialist; Software Engineer; Systems Analyst; Systems Manager; Webmaster. **Educational backgrounds include:** Computer Science; Engineering; Mathematics. **Benefits:** 401(k); Dental Insurance; Disability Coverage; Life Insurance; Medical Insurance; Tuition Assistance. **Special programs:** Training. **Corporate headquarters location:** This Location. **Other U.S. locations:** Atlanta GA; Chicago IL; Baltimore MD; Dallas TX. **Annual sales/revenues:** $21 - $50 million. **Number of employees at this location:** 190. **Number of employees nationwide:** 300.

DAY-TIMERS, INC.
One Day-Timer Plaza, Lehigh Valley PA 18195. **Toll-free phone:** 800/225-5005. **Contact:** Human Resources. **World Wide Web address:** http://www.daytimer.com. **Description:** Day-Timers designs and manufactures personal and organizational calendars, accessories, and software. **Corporate headquarters location:** This Location.

DECISIONONE
50 East Swedesford Road, Frazer PA 19355. **Toll-free phone:** 800/860-1647. **Contact:** Human Resources. **World Wide Web address:** http://www.decisionone.com. **Description:** An international supplier of plug-compatible computer equipment and accessories. Products include disk and tape storage devices, terminals, intelligent workstations and systems, controllers, printers, airline reservation systems, and a comprehensive range of computer supplies. **Corporate headquarters location:** This Location. **International locations:** Worldwide.

DELEX SYSTEMS INC.
1953 Gallows Road, Suite 700, Vienna VA 22182. 703/734-8300. **Fax:** 703/893-5338. **Contact:** Personnel Director. **World Wide Web address:** http://www.delex.com. **Description:** Provides a variety of computer-related services including database design and development, systems engineering, technical training, and intelligence support. **Common positions include:** Accountant; Computer Programmer; Economist; Electrical Engineer; Financial Analyst; Human Resources Manager; Purchasing Agent; Software Engineer; Systems Analyst; Technical Writer. **Educational backgrounds include:** Computer Science; Engineering; Mathematics; Physics. **Benefits:** 401(k); Dental Insurance; Disability Coverage; Life Insurance; Medical Insurance; Tuition Assistance. **Corporate headquarters location:** This Location. **Other U.S. locations:** CA; OH. **Operations at this**

facility include: Administration; Sales. **Number of employees at this location:** 140. **Number of employees nationwide:** 250.

DELL COMPUTER CORPORATION
One Dell Way, Round Rock TX 78682. 512/338-4400. **Contact:** Human Resources. **World Wide Web address:** http://www.dell.com. **Description:** Designs, develops, manufactures, markets, services, and supports personal computer systems and related equipment including servers, workstations, notebooks, and desktop systems. The company also offers over 4,000 software packages and peripherals. **Corporate headquarters location:** This Location. **International locations:** Ireland.

DELORME MAPPING
2 DeLorme Drive, Yarmouth ME 04096. 207/846-7000. **Contact:** Human Resources. **E-mail address:** jobs@delorme.com. **World Wide Web address:** http://www.delorme.com. **Description:** Publishes atlases and gazetteers and mapping software. **Common positions include:** Computer Programmer; Graphic Designer; Project Manager; Sales Manager. **Corporate headquarters location:** This Location.

DELPHI FORUMS
141 Portland Street, Cambridge MA 02139. 617/491-3342. **Fax:** 617/441-4902. **Contact:** Recruiting. **World Wide Web address:** http://www.delphi.com. **Description:** Manages a Website which helps people create online forums, and supports thousands of special interest communities including free do-it-yourself message boards, chat rooms, and personal home pages. **Common positions include:** Computer Programmer. **Corporate headquarters location:** This Location.

DELTA COMPUTEC, INC. (DCI)
900 Huyler Street, Teterboro NJ 07608. 201/440-8585. **Toll-free phone:** 800/477-8586. **Fax:** 201/440-6726. **Contact:** Recruiting. **E-mail address:** recruiting@dcis.com. **World Wide Web address:** http://www.amso-online.com/dci. **Description:** Provides businesses with integrated networking solutions. **Common positions include:** Computer Support Technician; Computer Technician; Network Administrator; Systems Analyst; Systems Manager. **Benefits:** 401(k); Casual Dress - Fridays; Dental Insurance; Disability Coverage; Life Insurance; Medical Insurance. **Office hours:** Monday - Friday, 8:00 a.m. - 5:00 p.m. **Parent company:** Alpha Microsystems. **Annual sales/revenues:** $51 - $100 million. **Number of employees nationwide:** 400.

DELTEK SYSTEMS INC.
8280 Greensboro Drive, Suite 300, McLean VA 22102. 703/734-8606. **Toll-free phone:** 800/456-2009. **Fax:** 703/734-0346. **Contact:** Abbie Martin, Recruiter. **World Wide Web address:** http://www.deltek.com. **Description:** Designs, develops, and supports advanced enterprise-level software for project-oriented companies. Services include implementation consulting, training, software maintenance, and telephone support. **NOTE:** Entry-level positions are offered. **Common positions include:** Account Manager; Accountant; Administrative Assistant; Auditor; CFO; Computer Engineer; Computer Programmer; Computer Support Technician; Computer Technician; Controller; Cost Estimator; Database Administrator; Database Manager; Finance Director; Financial Analyst; Marketing Manager; Marketing Specialist; MIS Specialist; Network Administrator; Quality Assurance Engineer; Sales Executive; Sales Rep.; SQL Programmer; Systems Analyst; Webmaster.

Educational backgrounds include: Accounting; C/C++; Computer Science; HTML; MCSE; Microsoft Word; Novell; Software Development; Spreadsheets; Visual Basic. **Benefits:** 401(k); Casual Dress - Daily; Dental Insurance; Disability Coverage; Employee Discounts; Flexible Schedule; Life Insurance; Medical Insurance; Profit Sharing; Sick Days (1 - 5); Telecommuting; Tuition Assistance; Vacation Days (6 - 10). **Special programs:** Internships. **Corporate headquarters location:** This Location. **Other U.S. locations:** San Jose CA; Englewood CO; Cambridge MA; St. Louis MO. **International locations:** United Kingdom. **President/CEO:** Ken DeLaski. **Number of employees at this location:** 575.

DESIGN DATA SYSTEMS
13830 58th Street North, Suite 401, Clearwater FL 33760. 727/539-1077. **Toll-free phone:** 800/655-6598. **Fax:** 727/539-8042. **Contact:** Kathrine Woodling, Human Resources Manager. **E-mail address:** info@designdatasystems.com. **World Wide Web address:** http://www.designdatasystems.com. **Description:** Provides software design, consulting, and related services. Design Data offers client/server applications for all major platforms including Windows, UNIX, Novell, and OS2, and in many areas including accounting, distribution, and project management. **Common positions include:** Account Manager; Accountant; Administrative Assistant; Computer Programmer; Computer Support Technician; Controller; Customer Service Rep.; Database Administrator; Financial Analyst; Marketing Specialist; MIS Specialist; Network Administrator; Sales Executive; Sales Rep.; Software Engineer; SQL Programmer; Systems Analyst; Webmaster. **Educational backgrounds include:** Accounting; Computer Science; Finance; Software Development; Software Tech. Support. **Benefits:** 401(k); Casual Dress - Daily; Dental Insurance; Disability Coverage; Life Insurance; Medical Insurance; Sick Days (6 - 10); Telecommuting; Tuition Assistance; Vacation Days (10 - 20). **Special programs:** Internships. **Corporate headquarters location:** This Location. **Other U.S. locations:** San Francisco CA; Atlanta GA; New York NY. **Listed on:** Privately held. **President/CEO/Owner:** Mike Meli. **Information Systems Manager:** Sean Canady.

DIALOGIC CORPORATION
1515 Route 10, Parsippany NJ 07054. 973/993-3000. **Contact:** Personnel. **World Wide Web address:** http://www.dialogic.com. **Description:** Offers computer telephony services that provide telephone network access to computer terminals. **Corporate headquarters location:** This Location.

DIGI INTERNATIONAL INC.
11001 Bren Road East, Minnetonka MN 55343. 952/912-3444. **Contact:** Personnel. **World Wide Web address:** http://www.dgii.com. **Description:** Provides data communications hardware and software that enable connectivity solutions for multi-user environments, remote access, and LAN connectivity markets. These products support most major microcomputer and workstation architectures and most popular single- and multi-user systems. Digi International also provides cross-platform compatibility and software and technical support services. The company's products are marketed to a broad range of worldwide distributors, system integrators, value-added resellers, and OEMs. **Educational backgrounds include:** Business Administration; C/C++; Computer Science; Engineering; MCSE; Microsoft Word; Novell; Software Development; Spreadsheets. **Benefits:** 401(k); Dental Insurance; Disability Coverage; Life Insurance; Medical Insurance; Tuition Assistance.

Corporate headquarters location: This Location. **International locations:** Worldwide. **President/CEO:** Jerry A. Dusa.

DIGITAL INSTRUMENTATION TECHNOLOGY
127 Eastgate Drive, Suite 20500, Los Alamos NM 87544. 505/662-1459. **Fax:** 505/662-0897. **Contact:** Personnel. **World Wide Web address:** http://www.dit.com. **Description:** Develops file transfer program software. **Corporate headquarters location:** This Location.

DIGITAL SYSTEMS INTERNATIONAL CORP.
4301 North Fairfax Drive, Suite 725, Arlington VA 22203. 703/522-6067. **Fax:** 703/522-6367. **Contact:** Personnel. **Description:** Provides systems integration through database development and data warehousing. **Corporate headquarters location:** This Location.

DRAGON SYSTEMS, INC.
320 Nevada Street, Newton MA 02460. 617/965-5200. **Contact:** Ms. T. Rosker, Vice President of Personnel. **E-mail address:** tamahr@dragonsys.com. **World Wide Web address:** http://www.dragonsys.com. **Description:** Manufactures speech recognition technology for both the PC and Macintosh. Dragon Systems' voice-activated products are offered in American English, British English, French, German, Italian, Spanish, and Swedish. Platforms include MS-DOS, Windows, Mac OS, UNIX, telephony, and portable systems. **Corporate headquarters location:** This Location. **Number of employees worldwide:** 200.

DYNATECH CORPORATION
3 New England Executive Park, Burlington MA 01803-5087. 781/272-6100. **Fax:** 781/272-2304. **Contact:** Vice President of Personnel. **World Wide Web address:** http://www.dynatech.com. **Description:** Manufactures products that support voice, video, and data communications. These products enhance video images, allow real-time interactive visual communications, and test and monitor networks to ensure clear, uninterrupted transmissions. The company focuses on developing, manufacturing, and marketing hardware and software used to support the generation, transmission, and presentation of information. Dynatech's operations are segmented into two groups: Information Support Products and Diversified Instrumentation. **Corporate headquarters location:** This Location. **International locations:** Australia; Canada; Czech Republic; France; Germany; Great Britain; Hong Kong; Ireland; Italy; Japan.

DYNETICS INC.
P.O. Box 5500, Huntsville AL 35814-5500. 256/922-9230. **Physical address:** 1000 Explorer Boulevard, Huntsville AL. **Contact:** Human Resources. **World Wide Web address:** http://www.dynetics.com. **Description:** A research and development firm for the defense, aerospace, and automotive industries. Products and services include software, computer imaging, systems analysis, simulation, computer modeling, and test evaluation. **Common positions include:** Computer Programmer; Electrical Engineer; Systems Analyst. **Educational backgrounds include:** Computer Science; Engineering; Mathematics; Physics. **Benefits:** Disability Coverage; Life Insurance; Medical Insurance; Pension Plan; Tuition Assistance. **Corporate headquarters location:** This Location.

ECCS, INC.
One Sheila Drive, Tinton Falls NJ 07724. 732/747-6995. **Contact:** Sharon Wallace, Director of Human Resources. **World Wide Web address:** http://www.eccs.com. **Description:** Designs and configures computer systems. ECCS's mass storage enhancement products include RAID (Redundant Array of Independent Disks) products and technology; external disk, optical, and tape systems; internal disk and tape storage devices; and RAM. The company also provides technical services. **Corporate headquarters location:** This Location.

ECI COMPUTERS
70 East 3750 South, Salt Lake City UT 84115. 801/265-8500. **Contact:** Human Resources. **World Wide Web address:** http://www.ecicomputers.com. **Description:** Resells computer products including motherboards, hard drives, monitors, and routers.

ECI TELECOM
1201 West Cypress Creek Road, Fort Lauderdale FL 33309. 954/351-4490. **Fax:** 954/351-4404. **Contact:** Personnel. **World Wide Web address:** http://www.ecitele.com. **Description:** Provides wide-area network systems for voice and data systems. **Common positions include:** Electrical Engineer; Systems Analyst. **Educational backgrounds include:** Computer Science; Engineering. **Benefits:** 401(k); Dental Insurance; Disability Coverage; Life Insurance; Medical Insurance; Tuition Assistance. **Corporate headquarters location:** This Location. **Other U.S. locations:** Calabasas CA; Clearwater FL; Orlando FL; Herndon VA.

EDS (ELECTRONIC DATA SYSTEMS CORP.)
5400 Legacy Drive, Mail Slot H4-GB-35, Plano TX 75024. 972/605-2700. **Fax:** 800/562-6241. **Contact:** Personnel. **E-mail address:** staffing@eds.com. **World Wide Web address:** http://www.eds.com. **Description:** Provides consulting, systems development, systems integration, and systems management services for large-scale and industry-specific applications. **NOTE:** Entry-level positions are offered. **Common positions include:** Applications Engineer; Computer Programmer; Database Manager; Financial Analyst; Software Engineer; Systems Analyst; Systems Manager. **Educational backgrounds include:** Accounting; Business Administration; Communications; Computer Science; Engineering; Finance; Marketing. **Benefits:** Dental Insurance; Employee Discounts; Life Insurance; Medical Insurance. **Special programs:** Internships; Training. **Corporate headquarters location:** This Location. **International locations:** Worldwide. **Parent company:** General Motors Corporation. **President/CEO/Owner:** Richard Brown. **Other U.S. locations:**
- 180 Blue Ravine Road, Folsom CA 95630. 916/351-8937.

EIS INTERNATIONAL INC.
555 Herndon Parkway, Herndon VA 20170. 703/326-6509. **Toll-free phone:** 800/274-5676. **Contact:** Personnel. **E-mail address:** info@eisi.com. **World Wide Web address:** http://www.eisi.com. **Description:** Designs, manufactures, markets, sells, leases, and maintains computerized telephone call processing systems and software for the call center industry. EIS International's automated systems integrate voice technology and information management for companies that depend upon efficient telephone contact with customers and prospects. Customers are primarily consumer direct marketing companies, major financial institutions, telecommunications companies, catalogs, cable television providers, and nonprofit organizations. **Corporate headquarters location:** This Location. **Listed on:** NASDAQ. **Stock exchange symbol:** EISI. **President/CEO:** James E. McGowan.

EMC CORPORATION

P.O. Box 9103, Hopkinton MA 01748-9103. 508/435-1000. **Contact:** Human Resources. **World Wide Web address:** http://www.emc.com. **Description:** EMC designs, manufactures, markets, and supports high-performance data storage products. The company also provides related services for selected mainframe and mid-range computer systems primarily manufactured by IBM and Unisys. **Corporate headquarters location:** This Location.

EAGLE POINT SOFTWARE CORP.

4131 Westmark Drive, Dubuque IA 52002-2627. 319/556-8392. **Toll-free phone:** 800/678-6565. **Fax:** 319/556-5321. **Contact:** Teresa Davis, Human Resources. **E-mail address:** hr@eaglepoint.com. **World Wide Web address:** http://www.eaglepoint. com. **Description:** Develops integrated software for the architectural, landscaping, civil engineering, and structural marketplaces. Founded in 1983. **Common positions include:** Administrative Assistant; Architect; Civil Engineer; Computer Programmer; Construction Contractor; Graphic Artist; Human Resources Manager; Landscape Architect; Marketing Manager; Multimedia Designer; Technical Writer/Editor. **Educational backgrounds include:** Business Administration; C/C++; Computer Science; Engineering; Frame Maker; HTML; Marketing; Microsoft Word. **Benefits:** 401(k); Casual Dress - Daily; Disability Coverage; Life Insurance; Medical Insurance; Profit Sharing; Sick Days (1 - 5); Vacation Days (10 - 20). **Office hours:** Monday - Friday, 8:00 a.m. - 5:00 p.m. **Corporate headquarters location:** This Location. **Other U.S. locations:** Church Hill TN.

EARTHLINK NETWORK, INC.

3100 New York Drive, Pasadena CA 91107. 626/296-2400. **Recorded jobline:** 626/296-JOBS. **Contact:** Human Resources. **World Wide Web address:** http://www.earthlink.net. **Description:** One of the nation's largest Internet access providers. The company also offers Web hosting packages, networking services, and personal Websites. **Corporate headquarters location:** This Location. **Number of employees at this location:** 785.

EARTHWEB

3 Park Avenue, 32nd Floor, New York NY 10016. 212/725-6550. **Contact:** Human Resources. **World Wide Web address:** http://www.earthweb.com. **Description:** Provides online technical data, training, and support for the IT industry. **Corporate headquarters location:** This Location.

EDIFY CORPORATION

2840 San Tomas Expressway, Santa Clara CA 95051. 408/982-2000. **Fax:** 408/982-4122. **Contact:** Human Resources. **E-mail address:** hr@ edify.com. **World Wide Web address:** http://www. edify.com. **Description:** Develops software including Electronic Workforce, which provides a company's customers with corporate information through connections using the World Wide Web, telephone, and other interactive media; and SMART Options, which helps companies to develop and deliver marketing strategies. **Corporate headquarters location:** This Location. **Number of employees nationwide:** 200.

EDMARK CORPORATION

P.O. Box 97021, Redmond WA 98073. 425/556-8400. **Physical address:** 18465 NE 68th Street, Redmond WA. **Fax:** 425/556-3776. **Contact:** Human Resources. **World Wide Web address:** http://www.edmark.com. **Description:** Develops, publishes, and markets educational software and other products for the early childhood and special education markets. **Corporate headquarters location:** This Location. **Number of employees at this location:** 150.

J.D. EDWARDS & COMPANY

One Technology Way, Denver CO 80237. 303/488-4000. **Contact:** Human Resources Department. **World Wide Web address:** http://www.jdedwards. com. **Description:** Designs, markets, and supports a wide variety of software applications for businesses. **Corporate headquarters location:** This Location. **Operations at this facility include:** Development.

ELECTRIFIER INC.

2605 Meridian Parkway, Suite 205, Durham NC 27713. 919/806-4000. **Contact:** Human Resources. **World Wide Web address:** http://www.electrifier. com. **Description:** Develops and markets Web authoring products for fast downloading multimedia and graphics. **Common positions include:** Computer Animator; Computer Programmer; Graphic Artist; Graphic Designer; Marketing Manager; Multimedia Designer; Public Relations Specialist; Sales Manager; Software Engineer. **Educational backgrounds include:** Art/Design; Business Administration; Computer Science; Marketing; Public Relations. **Benefits:** 401(k); Dental Insurance; Life Insurance; Medical Insurance; Profit Sharing. **Special programs:** Internships. **Internship information:** Internships are available in the marketing, public relations, and programming fields. **Corporate headquarters location:** This Location. **Listed on:** Privately held.

ELECTRO RENT CORPORATION

6060 Sepulveda Boulevard, Van Nuys CA 91411-2525. 818/787-2100. **Contact:** Human Resources. **World Wide Web address:** http://www.electrorent. com. **Description:** Rents and leases electronic equipment including test and measurement instruments, workstations, personal computers, and data communication products. **Common positions include:** Account Manager; Administrative Assistant; Advertising Clerk; Computer Operator; Customer Service Rep.; Electronics Technician; Secretary. **Corporate headquarters location:** This Location. **Other U.S. locations:** Nationwide. **Number of employees nationwide:** 500.

ENCAD, INC.

6059 Cornerstone Court West, San Diego CA 92121. 858/452-0882. **Fax:** 858/452-0891. **Contact:** Personnel. **World Wide Web address:** http://www.encad.com. **Description:** Designs, develops, manufactures, and markets wide-format, color ink-jet printers and plotters. Typical users are in industries utilizing computer-aided design; architectural, engineering, and construction design; geographic information systems such as surveying and mapping; and graphic arts such as digital photo imaging and editing, sign-making, three-dimensional renderings, and presentation graphics. **Corporate headquarters location:** This Location.

ENCORE REAL TIME COMPUTING, INC.

1700 NW 66th Avenue, Suite 103, Fort Lauderdale FL 33313. 954/377-1100. **Fax:** 954/377-1145. **Contact:** Personnel Director. **World Wide Web address:** http://www.encore.com. **Description:** Encore specializes in the manufacture of minicomputers for aerospace, defense, simulation, energy, and information systems. **Common positions include:** Electrical Engineer; Software Engineer; Systems Analyst; Technical Writer. **Educational backgrounds include:** Computer Science; Engineering. **Benefits:** 401(k); Dental Insurance; Disability Coverage; Life Insurance; Medical Insurance; Savings Plan; Tuition Assistance. **Special programs:** Internships.

Corporate headquarters location: This Location. **Operations at this facility include:** Research and Development; Service. **Listed on:** NASDAQ.

ENSCICON CORPORATION
1775 Sherman Street, Suite 1700, Denver CO 80203. 303/832-8200. **Fax:** 303/832-6700. **Contact:** Staffing. **E-mail address:** info@enscicon.com. **World Wide Web address:** http://www.enscicon.com. **Description:** Provides computer science engineering and high-tech consulting services. **Common positions include:** Applications Engineer; Architect; Biomedical Engineer; Chemical Engineer; Civil Engineer; Computer Operator; Computer Programmer; Consultant; Database Manager; Design Engineer; Electrical Engineer; Environmental Engineer; Geographer; Industrial Engineer; Internet Services Manager; Manufacturing Engineer; Mechanical Engineer; Metallurgical Engineer; Software Engineer; Webmaster. **Educational backgrounds include:** Computer Science; Engineering; Software Development. **Corporate headquarters location:** This Location. **Other U.S. locations:** Portland OR. **President:** William Smith.

THE ENTERPRISE SYSTEMS GROUP
427A Hayden Station Road, Kennedy Business Park, Windsor CT 06095. 860/688-3745. **Fax:** 860/298-7949. **Contact:** Human Resources. **Description:** A computer systems integrator for Novell and Microsoft NT local and wide area networks. The company also provides application and network administration training. **Common positions include:** Systems Analyst. **Educational backgrounds include:** Accounting; Business Administration; Computer Science. **Benefits:** Disability Coverage; Employee Discounts; Flexible Schedule; Life Insurance; Medical Insurance; Profit Sharing; Tuition Assistance. **Special programs:** Internships. **Corporate headquarters location:** This Location.

ENTEX INFORMATION SERVICES
6 International Drive, Suite 6, Rye Brook NY 10573. 914/935-3600. **Fax:** 914/935-3725. **Contact:** Personnel. **World Wide Web address:** http://www.entex.com. **Description:** Provides systems integration, help desk, and PC repair services to *Fortune* 1000 companies and federal clients. ENTEX Information Services also resells hardware and software products. Founded in 1993. **Common positions include:** Account Manager; Accountant; Applications Engineer; Computer Engineer; Computer Support Technician; Computer Technician; Network Administrator; Operations Manager; Sales Engineer; Sales Manager; Systems Manager. **Educational backgrounds include:** Computer Science; MCSE; Novell; Software Tech. Support. **Benefits:** 401(k); Casual Dress - Daily; Dental Insurance; Disability Coverage; Employee Discounts; Life Insurance; Medical Insurance; Profit Sharing; Tuition Assistance; Vacation Days (16+). **Corporate headquarters location:** This Location. **Other U.S. locations:** Nationwide. **Annual sales/revenues:** More than $100 million. **Number of employees nationwide:** 9,000.

EPICOR SOFTWARE CORPORATION
195 Technology Drive, Irvine CA 92618. 949/585-4000. **Fax:** 949/585-4091. **Contact:** Personnel. **E-mail address:** careers@epicor.com. **World Wide Web address:** http://www.epicor.com. **Description:** Develops financial and manufacturing software for use in a client/server environment. Epicor Software focuses exclusively on mid-market companies. **Common positions include:** Account Manager; Account Rep.; Accountant; Administrative Assistant; Applications Engineer; Attorney; Buyer;

CFO; Computer Programmer; Computer Support Technician; Controller; Credit Manager; Customer Service Rep.; Database Administrator; Database Manager; Event Planner; Finance Director; Financial Analyst; Human Resources Manager; Market Research Analyst; Marketing Manager; MIS Specialist; Network Engineer; Network/Systems Administrator; Public Relations Specialist; Purchasing Agent; Sales Executive; Sales Manager; Sales Rep.; Software Engineer; SQL Programmer; Systems Analyst; Webmaster. **Educational backgrounds include:** Accounting; ASP; Business Administration; C/C++; Communications; Computer Science; Economics; Finance; Frame Maker; HTML; Java; Marketing; MBA; MCSE; Microsoft Office; Microsoft Word; Novell; Public Relations; Software Development; Software Tech. Support; Spreadsheets; SQL; Visual Basic. **Benefits:** 401(k); Casual Dress - Fridays; Dental Insurance; Disability Coverage; Life Insurance; Medical Insurance; Relocation Assistance; Tuition Assistance. **Office hours:** Monday - Friday, 8:00 a.m. - 5:00 p.m. **Corporate headquarters location:** This Location. **Other U.S. locations:** Nationwide. **International locations:** Worldwide. **Number of employees worldwide:** 1,700.

ePRESENCE, INC.
120 Flanders Road, P.O. Box 5013, Westboro MA 01581. 508/898-1000. **Contact:** Human Resources. **World Wide Web address:** http://www.epresence.com. **Description:** Provides a variety of e-services through its ePresence Solutions divisions. This division offers Internet-based solutions to companies so that they can develop better customer, business partner, and employee relationships. **Corporate headquarters location:** This Location.

EPSILON
50 Cambridge Street, Burlington MA 01803. 781/273-0250. **Fax:** 781/685-0800. **Contact:** Andrea Curran, Personnel. **E-mail address:** jobs@epsilon.com. **World Wide Web address:** http://www.epsilon.com. **Description:** Designs, implements, and supports database marketing programs in a variety of industries including financial services, retail, health care, technology, telecommunications, and nonprofit. **NOTE:** Entry-level positions and second and third shifts are offered. **Common positions include:** Account Manager; Account Representative; Accountant; Administrative Assistant; Advertising Executive; Applications Engineer; Computer Operator; Computer Programmer; Computer Support Technician; Database Administrator; Database Manager; Financial Analyst; MIS Specialist; Network Administrator; Project Manager; Software Engineer; SQL Programmer; Systems Analyst; Systems Manager. **Educational backgrounds include:** Business Administration; Computer Science; Finance; Marketing; Software Development; Software Tech. Support; Visual Basic. **Benefits:** 401(k); Casual Dress - Daily; Dental Insurance; Disability Coverage; Employee Discounts; Life Insurance; Medical Insurance; Sick Days (1 - 5); Tuition Assistance; Vacation Days (11 - 15). **Special programs:** Internships; Summer Jobs. **Corporate headquarters location:** This Location. **Other U.S. locations:** Newport Beach CA; San Francisco CA; Dallas TX. **Operations at this facility include:** Administration; Research and Development; Sales; Service. **President/CEO/Owner:** Bob Mohr. **Annual sales/revenues:** More than $100 million. **Number of employees nationwide:** 700.

EPSON PORTLAND INC.
3950 NW Aloclek Place, Hillsboro OR 97124-7199. 503/645-1118. **Contact:** Human Resources.

Description: Manufactures computer printers. **Corporate headquarters location:** Torrance CA. **Parent company:** Epson Corporation.

ESSENTIAL COMMUNICATIONS, INC.
1551 Mercantile Avenue NE, Suite A, Albuquerque NM 87107-7001. 505/344-0080. **Toll-free phone:** 800/278-7897. **Fax:** 505/344-0408. **Contact:** Joe Bradley, Vice President of Engineering. **World Wide Web address:** http://www.esscom.com. **Description:** Develops switches and network interface cards that connect computers and supercomputers into networks. **Corporate headquarters location:** This Location.

ETAK, INC.
1605 Adams Drive, Menlo Park CA 94025. 650/328-3825. **Contact:** Human Resources. **E-mail address:** hr@etak.com. **World Wide Web address:** http://www.etak.com. **Description:** Develops digital mapping software for the automotive and transportation industries.

E*TRADE
4500 Bohannon Drive, Menlo Park CA 94025. 650/331-6000. **Contact:** Personnel. **Description:** Operates a Website that provides online investing services. **Corporate headquarters location:** This Location.

EVANS & SUTHERLAND COMPUTER CORP.
600 Komas Drive, Salt Lake City UT 84108. 801/588-1000. **Fax:** 801/588-4517. **Contact:** Bob Morishita, Human Resources Director. **World Wide Web address:** http://www.es.com. **Description:** Designs, manufactures, sells, and services special purpose 3-D computer graphics hardware and software. The products are developed to help people solve complicated problems and to help train people to perform complex tasks. Uses of this equipment include visual simulation systems for pilot training and engineering workstations for molecular modeling or engineering design. The majority of Evans & Sutherland's customers are in the aerospace and defense-related markets. **Common positions include:** Database Manager; Hardware Engineer; Software Engineer; Systems Analyst. **Educational backgrounds include:** Computer Science; Engineering; Mathematics. **Benefits:** Dental Insurance; Disability Coverage; Life Insurance; Medical Insurance; Pension Plan; Savings Plan; Stock Option; Tuition Assistance. **Corporate headquarters location:** This Location. **Operations at this facility include:** Administration; Research and Development; Sales; Service. **Number of employees at this location:** 900.

EVANS SYSTEMS, INC. (ESI)
P.O. Box 2480, Bay City TX 77404-2480. 979/245-2424. **Fax:** 979/244-5070. **Contact:** Personnel. **Description:** A holding company. **Corporate headquarters location:** This Location. **Subsidiaries include:** Way Energy distributes wholesale and retail refined petroleum products and lubricants and owns and operates convenience stores in southern Texas and Louisiana; Chem-Way Systems, Inc. produces, packages, and markets automotive aftermarket chemical products in 23 states; EDCO Environmental Systems, Inc. provides environmental remediation services and installations of underground storage tanks; Distributor Information Systems Corporation provides information systems and software for distributors and convenience store owners and operators.

EVEREX SYSTEMS INC.
5020 Brandin Court, Fremont CA 94538. 510/498-1111. **Fax:** 510/683-2099. **Contact:** Personnel. **World Wide Web address:** http://www.everex. com. **Description:** Manufactures computer peripheral equipment. **Benefits:** 401(k); Dental Insurance; Disability Coverage; Life Insurance; Medical Insurance. **Corporate headquarters location:** This Location. **Operations at this facility include:** Administration; Manufacturing; Sales; Service. **Number of employees nationwide:** 110.

EX-CEL SOLUTIONS, INC.
14618 Grover Street, Suite 200, Omaha NE 68144. 402/333-6541. **Fax:** 402/330-6349. **Contact:** Nancy M. Gaeta, Human Resources Generalist. **World Wide Web address:** http://www.excels.com. **Description:** Provides customized computer sales, service, and maintenance. Ex-Cel Solutions is a systems integrator for Novell Netware and Windows NT networks. Founded in 1974. **NOTE:** Entry-level positions are offered. **Common positions include:** Account Manager; Account Rep.; Administrative Assistant; Applications Engineer; Buyer; Computer Engineer; Computer Programmer; Computer Support Technician; Computer Technician; Customer Service Rep.; Database Administrator; Database Manager; Help-Desk Technician; MIS Specialist; Network Engineer; Network Administrator; Sales Manager; Sales Rep.; Software Engineer; SQL Programmer; Systems Analyst; Systems Manager; Website Developer. **Educational backgrounds include:** Accounting; Business Administration; Computer Science; Marketing. **Benefits:** 401(k); Casual Dress - Fridays; Dental Insurance; Disability Coverage; Employee Discounts; Life Insurance; Medical Insurance; Profit Sharing; Savings Plan; Sick Days (6 - 10); Tuition Assistance; Vacation Days (6 - 10). **Corporate headquarters location:** This Location. **Other U.S. locations:** Livermore CA; Santa Fe Springs CA; Dubuque IA; Chicago IL; Blaine MN; Grandview MO; Park Ridge NJ. **President:** Glenn J. Stenger. **Number of employees nationwide:** 65.

EXCALIBUR TECHNOLOGIES CORP.
1959 Palomar Oaks Way, Carlsbad CA 92009. 760/438-7900. **Contact:** Human Resources. **World Wide Web address:** http://www.excalib.com. **Description:** Designs, develops, markets, and supports computer software products used for the document imaging and multimedia information retrieval marketplaces. The company also offers consulting, training, maintenance, and systems integration services. In addition, the company performs research and development under contract and licenses proprietary software products for use in office, identification, and multimedia information retrieval systems. The company distributes its products through direct sales, distributors, select resellers, and vertical market suppliers. **Corporate headquarters location:** This Location.

EXCITE INC.
555 Broadway, Redwood City CA 94063. 650/568-6000. **Contact:** Human Resources. **E-mail address:** resumes@excite.com. **World Wide Web address:** http://www.excite.com. **Description:** An Internet search engine that offers Web navigation services and features site reviews, editorial columns, news, and regional information. **Common positions include:** Account Manager; Account Rep.; Administrative Assistant; Advertising Manager; Client Specialist; Computer Programmer; Internet Specialist; Public Relations Manager; Sales Manager; Sales Rep.; Systems Engineer; Systems Specialist. **Benefits:** Medical Insurance; Stock Option. **Corporate headquarters location:** This Location. **Annual sales/revenues:** $5 - $10 million.

EXECUTIVE SOFTWARE INTERNATIONAL
701 North Brand Boulevard, 6th Floor, Glendale CA 91203. 818/547-2050. **Fax:** 818/545-9241.

Contact: Director of Personnel. **World Wide Web address:** http://www.execsoft.com. **Description:** Develops and markets systems software and applications for the Windows NT operating system. **Common positions include:** Applications Engineer; Computer Programmer; Systems Manager; Technical Writer. **Benefits:** Dental Insurance; Medical Insurance. **Corporate headquarters location:** This Location. **Number of employees at this location:** 100.

EXEMPLAR LOGIC, INC.
880 Ridder Park Drive, San Jose CA 95131. 408/487-7000. **Contact:** Human Resources. **World Wide Web address:** http://www.exemplar.com. **Description:** A developer and marketer of EDA software tools. **Corporate headquarters location:** This Location.

EXIGENT INTERNATIONAL, INC.
1225 Evans Road, Melbourne FL 32904. 321/952-7550. **Toll-free phone:** 888/952-9468. **Fax:** 321/733-7570. **Contact:** Mark Phillips, Corporate Recruiter. **E-mail address:** recruiter@xgnt.com. **World Wide Web address:** http://www.xgnt.com. **Description:** Develops software solutions for commercial and government applications. **NOTE:** Entry-level positions are offered. **Common positions include:** Administrative Assistant; Computer Programmer. **Educational backgrounds include:** Computer Science; Engineering; Software Development; Software Tech. Support. **Benefits:** 401(k); Dental Insurance; Disability Coverage; Employee Discounts; Flexible Schedule; Life Insurance; Medical Insurance; Pension Plan; Profit Sharing; Savings Plan; Tuition Assistance. **Special programs:** Internships; Co-ops; Summer Jobs. **Corporate headquarters location:** This Location. **Subsidiaries include:** FotoTag; Software Technology Inc. **President/CEO:** Bernie Smedley. **Number of employees nationwide:** 300.

EXODUS COMMUNICATIONS
2350 Mission College Boulevard, Suite 705, Santa Clara CA 95054. 408/346-2200. **Toll-free phone:** 888/239-6387. **Fax:** 408/982-3868. **Contact:** Human Resources. **World Wide Web address:** http://www.exodus.net. **Description:** Offers Internet server hosting, network solutions, and system management and monitoring services. **Corporate headquarters location:** This Location.

EXTENDED SYSTEMS, INC.
P.O. Box 4937, Boise ID 83711. 208/322-7575. **Fax:** 208/327-5011. **Contact:** Debbie Kaylor, Human Resources Manager. **World Wide Web address:** http://www.extendsys.com. **Description:** Designs, manufactures, and markets computer enhancement products, primarily printer sharing products and network print servers. **Common positions include:** Accountant; Computer Programmer; Electrical Engineer; Financial Analyst; Human Resources Manager; Purchasing Agent; Software Engineer; Systems Analyst. **Educational backgrounds include:** Accounting; Business Administration; Computer Science; Engineering; Finance; Marketing. **Benefits:** 401(k); Dental Insurance; Disability Coverage; Life Insurance; Medical Insurance. **Special programs:** Internships. **Corporate headquarters location:** This Location. **Other U.S. locations:** Bozeman MT. **Operations at this facility include:** Manufacturing; Research and Development; Sales; Service.

EYRING CORPORATION
6912 South 185 West, Midvale UT 84047. 801/561-1111. **Fax:** 801/565-4697. **Contact:** Human Resources. **World Wide Web address:** http://www.eyring.com. **Description:** Engaged in computer software development including Assembly Management Systems (AMS) paperless workstations. **NOTE:** Entry-level positions are offered. **Common positions include:** Accountant; Computer Programmer; Department Manager; Electrical Engineer; Human Resources Manager; Operations Manager; Purchasing Agent; Systems Analyst; Technical Writer/Editor. **Educational backgrounds include:** Accounting; Computer Science; Engineering; Finance; Marketing. **Benefits:** Dental Insurance; Disability Coverage; Life Insurance; Medical Insurance; Profit Sharing; Savings Plan; Tuition Assistance; Vision Insurance. **Corporate headquarters location:** This Location. **Other U.S. locations:** IL; MO.

FAIR, ISAAC AND CO., INC.
120 North Redwood Drive, San Rafael CA 94903-1996. 415/472-2211. **Fax:** 415/491-5100. **Contact:** Human Resources. **E-mail address:** resumes@fairisaac.com. **World Wide Web address:** http://www.fairisaac.com. **Description:** Develops and provides data management software and services for the consumer credit, personal lines insurance, and direct marketing industries. **Common positions include:** Account Rep.; Accountant; Actuary; Administrative Assistant; Administrative Manager; Attorney; Bookkeeper; Business Analyst; Clerk; Client Services Representative; Client Specialist; Computer Graphics Specialist; Computer Programmer; Computer Programming Manager; Computer Support Technician; Content Developer; Content Manager; Controller; Credit Manager; Customer Service Rep.; Development Manager; Economist; Educational Specialist; Executive Assistant; Field Engineer; Financial Analyst; Financial Manager; Human Resources Manager; Logistics Manager; Management Analyst; Marketing Manager; Marketing Specialist; Mathematician; Product Specialist; Production Manager; Project Analyst; Project Manager; Quality Control Supervisor; Recruiter; Research and Support Engineer; Secretary; Software Developer; Software Engineer; Statistician; Strategy Consultant; Systems Analyst; Systems Engineer; Systems Specialist; Technical Writer; Training Specialist; UNIX System Administrator. **Educational backgrounds include:** Account Management; Accounting; Advertising; Automotive Lending; Bachelor of Arts; Bachelor of Science; Banking; Basic; BSCS; Budgeting; Business Administration; Business Development; C/C++; CGI; Clerical/Secretarial; Client/Server Systems; COBOL; COBOL II; Collections; Communications; Computer Programming; Computer Science; Computer Tech Support; Consumer Credit; Consumer Lending; Contract Law; CPA; Credit Risk Management; Customer Support; Database Software; Economics; Editing; Education; English; Event Planning/Management; Excel; Finance; Financial Reporting; FORTRAN; Frame Maker; Graphic Design; Health Care; Hospital Administration; HTML; HTTP; Human Resources; IBM Mainframe; Insurance; Intellectual Property Law; Japanese; Java; Journalism; Juris Doctorate; LAN; Macintosh Computer; Mainframe; Management/Planning; Marketing; Master of Arts; Master of Sciences; Mathematics; MBA; Microsoft Access; Microsoft Windows 95; Microsoft Windows NT; Microsoft Word; Operations; Operations Research; Oracle; P&L Experience; Pascal; PC; Ph.D.; Physical Science; Portuguese; PowerBuilder; Product Development; Recruiting; Relational Databases; Retail; Revenue Forecasting; RoboHelp; Sales; SAS Programming; Software Development; Software Tech. Support; Solaris; Spanish; Spreadsheets; SQL; SQLWindows; Statistics; Systems Analysis; Systems Engineering; Teaching; Technical Writing; Telecommunications;

Underwriting; UNIX; Visual Basic; Visual C++; Word Processing; Writing. **Benefits:** 401(k); Dental Insurance; Disability Coverage; Life Insurance; Medical Insurance; Pension Plan; Profit Sharing; Savings Plan; Tuition Assistance. **Corporate headquarters location:** This Location. **Other U.S. locations:** New Castle DE; Wilmington DE; Atlanta GA; Chicago IL. **Subsidiaries include:** Dynamark, Minneapolis MN; European Analytic Products Group(Birmingham, United Kingdom). **Operations at this facility include:** Research and Development; Sales. **Number of employees at this location:** 800. **Number of employees nationwide:** 1,400.

FAIRCOM
2100 Forum Boulevard, Columbia MO 65203-0100. 573/445-6833. **Fax:** 573/445-9698. **Contact:** Human Resources. **E-mail address:** faircom@faircom.com. **World Wide Web address:** http://www.faircom.com. **Description:** Develops database file handler software. **NOTE:** Entry-level positions are offered. **Common positions include:** Computer Programmer. **Educational backgrounds include:** Computer Science; Engineering. **Benefits:** 401(k); Dental Insurance; Life Insurance; Medical Insurance. **Corporate headquarters location:** This Location. **International locations:** Brazil; Italy; Japan. **Number of employees worldwide:** 35.

FEDERAL DATA CORPORATION
4800 Hampden Lane, Suite 1100, Bethesda MD 20814. 301/986-0800. **Contact:** Patricia Fargas, Recruitment Manager. **World Wide Web address:** http://www.feddata.com. **Description:** Provides information technology services and solutions. **Common positions include:** Accountant; Applications Engineer; Database Administrator; MIS Specialist; Network Administrator; Software Engineer; SQL Programmer; Systems Analyst; Systems Manager; Webmaster. **Educational backgrounds include:** Accounting; Business Administration; Computer Science; Engineering; HTML; Internet; Java; MCSE; Oracle; Software Development; Visual Basic. **Benefits:** 401(k); Casual Dress - Fridays; Dental Insurance; Disability Coverage; Financial Planning Assistance; Life Insurance; Medical Insurance; Training; Tuition Assistance. **Special programs:** Internships; Training; Summer Jobs. **Corporate headquarters location:** This Location. **Other U.S. locations:** Nationwide. **Number of employees nationwide:** 2,700.

FILENET CORPORATION
3565 Harbor Boulevard, Costa Mesa CA 92626. 714/966-3400. **Contact:** Kenneth Ross, Employment Manager. **World Wide Web address:** http://www.filenet.com. **Description:** Develops and markets document imaging and workflow management software for companies in various industries. **Common positions include:** Accountant; Computer Programmer; Customer Service Rep.; Financial Analyst; Human Resources Manager; Management Analyst; Software Developer; Systems Analyst; Teacher; Technical Writer/Editor. **Educational backgrounds include:** Business Administration; Computer Science; Engineering; Marketing. **Benefits:** 401(k); Dental Insurance; Disability Coverage; Employee Discounts; ESOP; Life Insurance; Medical Insurance; Profit Sharing; Savings Plan; Tuition Assistance. **Special programs:** Internships. **Corporate headquarters location:** This Location. **Other U.S. locations:** Nationwide.

FILETEK, INC.
9400 Key West Avenue, Rockville MD 20850. 301/251-0600. **Fax:** 301/251-1991. **Contact:** Debbie Mobley, Manager of Human Resources. **E-**mail address: djm@filetek.com. **World Wide Web address:** http://www.filetek.com. **Description:** Uses hierarchical relational database technology to design, develop, and deliver mass data storage software systems for large corporations. Founded in 1984. **Common positions include:** Accountant; Financial Analyst; Sales Rep.; Software Engineer. **Educational backgrounds include:** Computer Science; Engineering; Finance. **Benefits:** 401(k); Dental Insurance; Disability Coverage; Fitness Program; Life Insurance; Medical Insurance; Prescription Drugs; Public Transit Available; Spending Account; Tuition Assistance. **Corporate headquarters location:** This Location. **Number of employees at this location:** 100.

FIRST DATA POS
2155 Barrett Park Drive, Suite 215, Kennesaw GA 30144. 770/218-5000. **Recorded jobline:** 770/218-4989. **Contact:** Human Resources. **Description:** Provides various information services, such as training, technical support, asset management, credit applications, software development, hardware leasing, repair services, and warehousing and development of POS terminals. **Corporate headquarters location:** This Location. **Parent company:** First Data Corporation.

FIRSTLOGIC, INC.
100 Harbor View Plaza, La Crosse WI 54601-4071. 608/782-5000. **Toll-free phone:** 888/215-6442. **Fax:** 608/788-1188. **Contact:** Sarah Heiden, Employment Specialist. **E-mail address:** hr@firstlogic.com. **World Wide Web address:** http://www.firstlogic.com. **Description:** Develops and manufactures software for postal automation, document processing, and database management. **NOTE:** Entry-level positions are offered. **Common positions include:** MIS Specialist; Software Engineer. **Educational backgrounds include:** Computer Science; Engineering; Mathematics; Software Development; Software Tech. Support. **Benefits:** 401(k); Dental Insurance; Disability Coverage; Flexible Schedule; Life Insurance; Medical Insurance; Profit Sharing. **Special programs:** Internships. **Corporate headquarters location:** This Location. **Other U.S. locations:** Nationwide. **Subsidiaries include:** FirstSolutions; i.d.Centric; MailCode; Postalsoft. **President/CEO:** Doug Schmidt. **Number of employees nationwide:** 350.

FIRSTWAVE TECHNOLOGIES, INC.
2859 Paces Ferry Road, Suite 1000, Atlanta GA 30339. 770/431-1200. **Fax:** 770/431-1201. **Contact:** Personnel. **Description:** Develops, markets, and supports software systems that automate the integrated sales, marketing, and customer service functions of business organizations in a wide range of industries. These sales performance solutions provide end users with closed-loop business solutions. Founded in 1984. **Common positions include:** Computer Programmer; MIS Specialist; Software Engineer; Systems Analyst; Technical Writer. **Educational backgrounds include:** Computer Science. **Benefits:** 401(k); Dental Insurance; Disability Coverage; Life Insurance; Medical Insurance; Profit Sharing. **Corporate headquarters location:** This Location. **Operations at this facility include:** Administration; Research and Development; Sales; Service. **Number of employees at this location:** 230.

FORCE COMPUTERS, INC.
5799 Fontanoso Way, San Jose CA 95138. 408/369-6000. **Contact:** Personnel. **E-mail address:** hr@fci.com. **World Wide Web address:** http://www.forcecomputers.com. **Description:** A manufacturer

of embedded systems. The company supplies high-performance computer products to a broad range of worldwide telecommunication, industrial, and government customers. **Common positions include:** Buyer; Customer Service Rep.; Electrical Engineer; Financial Analyst; Hardware Engineer; Human Resources Manager; Manufacturing Engineer; MIS Specialist; Public Relations Specialist; Quality Control Supervisor; Sales Engineer; Software Engineer; Systems Manager; Technical Writer; Webmaster. **Educational backgrounds include:** Computer Science; Engineering; Marketing; Public Relations. **Benefits:** 401(k); Dental Insurance; Disability Coverage; Flexible Schedule; Life Insurance; Medical Insurance; Profit Sharing; Stock Option; Tuition Assistance. **Special programs:** Internships. **Corporate headquarters location:** This Location. **International locations:** Germany. **Number of employees nationwide:** 170. **Number of employees worldwide:** 500.

FORMATION, INC.
121 Whittendale Drive, Moorestown NJ 08057. 856/234-5020. **Fax:** 856/234-8543. **Contact:** Kathy Cava, Manager of Personnel. **World Wide Web address:** http://www.formation.com. **Description:** Designs and manufactures communications products and real-time, high-performance storage and retrieval systems. The company's products are capable of integrating a number of inputs including video, audio, data/text, and radar, and can employ a variety of communications protocols. The company supplies an open systems storage system using Redundant Array of Independent Disks (RAID) technology. Formation also supplies plug compatible data storage systems for IBM AS/400 computers, as well as data storage systems to open systems computer manufacturers and systems integrators. **Common positions include:** Computer Engineer; Electrical Engineer; Mechanical Engineer; Software Engineer. **Educational backgrounds include:** Engineering. **Benefits:** Dental Insurance; Disability Coverage; Flextime Plan; Investment Plan; Life Insurance; Medical Insurance; Profit Sharing; Savings Plan; Tuition Assistance. **Corporate headquarters location:** This Location. **Operations at this facility include:** Administration; Manufacturing; Research and Development; Sales; Service. **Number of employees at this location:** 75.

FOUNTAIN TECHNOLOGIES, INC.
50 Randolph Road, Somerset NJ 08873. 732/563-4800. **Fax:** 732/563-4999. **Contact:** Human Resources. **Description:** Manufactures IBM-compatible computers. **NOTE:** Entry-level positions are offered. **Common positions include:** Account Rep.; Accountant; Computer Operator; Computer Programmer; Customer Service Rep.; Database Manager; Electrical/Electronics Engineer; Graphic Artist; Industrial Engineer; Internet Services Manager; Marketing Specialist; Mechanical Engineer; MIS Specialist; Multimedia Designer; Online Content Specialist; Operations Manager; Production Manager; Public Relations Specialist; Purchasing Agent; Quality Control Supervisor; Sales Executive; Sales Rep.; Software Engineer; Systems Analyst; Technical Writer; Webmaster. **Educational backgrounds include:** Accounting; Art/Design; Business Administration; Communications; Computer Science; Engineering; Finance; Liberal Arts; Marketing; Public Relations. **Benefits:** Dental Insurance; Disability Coverage; Employee Discounts; Life Insurance; Medical Insurance. **Corporate headquarters location:** This Location. **Listed on:** Privately held. **Annual sales/revenues:** More than $100 million. **Number of employees at this location:** 1,000.

FUJITSU COMPUTER PRODUCTS OF AMERICA
2904 Orchard Parkway, San Jose CA 95134. 408/432-6333. **Contact:** Human Resources. **World Wide Web address:** http://www.fcpa.com. **Description:** This location houses administrative offices. Overall, Fujitsu Computer Products of America manufactures hard drives, magneto-optical drives, printers, scanners, and tape drives. **Corporate headquarters location:** This Location. **Other U.S. locations:** Hillsboro CO; Longmont CO. **Parent company:** Fujitsu, Ltd. (Japan).

FUNK SOFTWARE, INC.
222 Third Street, Suite 2163, Cambridge MA 02142. 617/497-6339. **Fax:** 617/547-1031. **Contact:** Personnel. **World Wide Web address:** http://www.funk.com. **Description:** Develops remote access and LAN-based communications software. Products include Steel-Belted Radius for NetWare which provides centralized authentication for dial-in users; WanderLink remote access software for NetWare; Proxy remote control software which allows remote operation of PCs; and AppMeter II software usage metering product. **Corporate headquarters location:** This Location.

GB TECH INC.
2200 Space Park Drive, Suite 400, Houston TX 77058. 281/333-3703. **Contact:** Human Resources. **World Wide Web address:** http://www.gbtech.net. **Description:** Performs aerospace and computer engineering services. GB Tech contracts with several organizations including NASA. **Corporate headquarters location:** This Location.

GCC TECHNOLOGIES
209 Burlington Road, Bedford MA 01730. 781/275-5800. **Contact:** Personnel. **World Wide Web address:** http://www.gcctech.com. **Description:** Manufactures software for personal computers. GCC also does research in the areas of computer graphics, VLSI design, consumer robotics, and digital sound generation. **NOTE:** Applicants must show proven ability in one or more of the following areas: real-time programming for microprocessors; applications software for personal computers; or computer graphics. **Common positions include:** Accountant; Administrator; Blue-Collar Worker Supervisor; Computer Programmer; Credit Manager; Customer Service Rep.; Electrical Engineer; Manufacturer's Sales Rep.; Mechanical Engineer; Technical Writer/Editor. **Educational backgrounds include:** Computer Science; Economics; Engineering; Finance; Liberal Arts; Marketing. **Benefits:** Dental Insurance; Disability Coverage; Life Insurance; Medical Insurance; Savings Plan. **Corporate headquarters location:** This Location. **Operations at this facility include:** Administration; Manufacturing; Research and Development; Sales; Service.

GE CAPITAL IT SOLUTIONS
700 Canal Street, Stamford CT 06902. 203/357-1464. **Contact:** Human Resources Department. **World Wide Web address:** http://www.gecits.ge. com. **Description:** Resells computer products to commercial, governmental, and educational users. The company's products and services include value-added systems, systems integration, networking services, maintenance, facilities management, outsourcing, software and business consulting services, and rental services. **Benefits:** 401(k). **Corporate headquarters location:** This Location. **Other U.S. locations:** Nationwide. **Number of employees nationwide:** 2,100.

GP STRATEGIES CORPORATION
9 West 57th Street, Suite 4170, New York NY 10019. 212/230-9500. **Contact:** Human Resources.

Description: A holding company for computer training and consulting firms. **Corporate headquarters location:** This Location. **Subsidiaries include:** General Physics Corporation is a computer consulting and training firm that evaluates and resolves performance problems. Learning Technologies provides computer training and consulting services. Specialised Technical Services Limited (United Kingdom) provides language and technical training services. The Deltapoint Corporation (Seattle WA) is a management consulting firm specializing in large-scale systems changes. **Number of employees worldwide:** 2,100.

GRC INTERNATIONAL, INC.

1900 Gallows Road, Vienna VA 22182. 703/506-5000. **Fax:** 703/903-9431. **Contact:** Human Resources. **World Wide Web address:** http://www.grci.com. **Description:** Creates large-scale, decision support systems and software engineering environments; applies operations research and mathematical modeling to business and management systems; and implements advanced database technology. GRC International also provides studies and analysis capabilities for policy development and planning; modeling and simulation of hardware and software used in real-time testing of sensor, weapon, and battlefield management command, control, and communication systems; and testing and evaluation. The company's services are offered to government and commercial customers. **Corporate headquarters location:** This Location. **Other U.S. locations:** Nationwide. **Number of employees worldwide:** 1,300.

GALACTIC TECHNOLOGIES, INC.

400 North Loop 1604 East, Suite 210, San Antonio TX 78232. 210/496-7250. **Fax:** 210/490-6790. **Contact:** Cynthia J. Chatelain, Director of Programs. **World Wide Web address:** http://www.galactictech.com. **Description:** Provides computer hardware and software engineering, PC support, and networking services. Galactic Technologies also operates as a value-added reseller. **Common positions include:** Administrative Assistant; Computer Engineer; Computer Programmer; Computer Scientist; Computer Support Technician; Computer Technician; Database Administrator; Database Manager; Electrical Engineer; Internet Services Manager; MIS Specialist; Network Administrator; Software Engineer; SQL Programmer; Systems Analyst; Systems Manager; Webmaster. **Educational backgrounds include:** C/C++; CGI; Cold Fusion; Computer Science; Engineering; HTML; Internet; Java; MCSE; Microsoft Word; Novell; Software Development; Software Tech. Support; Visual Basic. **Benefits:** 401(k); Casual Dress - Fridays; Dental Insurance; Life Insurance; Medical Insurance. **Corporate headquarters location:** This Location.

GALILEO INTERNATIONAL

9700 West Higgins Road, Suite 400, Rosemont IL 60018. 847/518-4000. **Contact:** Human Resources. **World Wide Web address:** http://www.galileo.com. **Description:** Designs and installs software for the travel industry that provides easier access to inventory, scheduling, and pricing information. **Corporate headquarters location:** This Location. **Other U.S. locations:** Englewood CO.

GATEFIELD CORPORATION

47436 Fremont Boulevard, Fremont CA 94538-6503. 510/623-4400. **Fax:** 510/623-4484. **Contact:** Personnel. **Description:** Designs, manufactures, and markets computer chips. **Corporate headquarters location:** This Location. **Listed on:** NASDAQ. **Number of employees nationwide:** 200.

GATES ARROW

39 Pelham Ridge Drive, Greenville SC 29615. 864/234-0736. **Contact:** Human Resources Director. **World Wide Web address:** http://www.gatesarrow.com. **Description:** Gates Arrow distributes microcomputers, networking software, and computer peripheral equipment including monitors, hard-disk drives, and modems. The company also packages computer systems, offers systems integration services, and provides technical support services. **Common positions include:** Buyer; Computer Operator; Computer Programmer; Credit Clerk and Authorizer; Credit Manager; Customer Service Rep.; Human Resources Manager; Marketing Manager; Payroll Clerk; Services Sales Rep. **Educational backgrounds include:** Accounting; Business Administration; Computer Science; Marketing. **Benefits:** 401(k); Credit Union; Dental Insurance; Disability Coverage; Life Insurance; Medical Insurance. **Corporate headquarters location:** This Location. **Number of employees at this location:** 300. **Number of employees nationwide:** 400.

GATEWAY

4545 Towne Centre Court, San Diego CA 92121. 858/799-3401. **Contact:** Human Resources. **World Wide Web address:** http://www.gateway.com. **Description:** A computer manufacturer whose business is generated primarily through mail order. Gateway also offers financing, Internet service, peripherals, software, and service. **Corporate headquarters location:** This Location.

GENERAL AUTOMATION INC.

17731 Mitchell North, Irvine CA 92614. 949/250-4800. **Fax:** 949/752-6772. **Contact:** Personnel. **World Wide Web address:** http://www.genauto.com. **Description:** Engaged in systems and software integration services. **Corporate headquarters location:** This Location.

GENERAL DATACOMM, INC.

Park Road Extension, Middlebury CT 06762-1299. 203/574-1118. **Fax:** 203/598-7944. **Contact:** Manager of Corporate Human Resources. **E-mail address:** hr@gdc.com. **World Wide Web address:** http://www.gdc.com. **Description:** Provides business solutions for enterprise and telecommunications networks based on Asynchronous Transfer Mode (ATM) products and services. General DataComm operates in three areas: ATM products, internetworking products, and network access products. The company designs, assembles, markets, installs, and maintains products and services that enable telecommunications common carriers, corporations, and governments to build, upgrade, and manage their global telecommunications networks. General DataComm's networks transmit information via telephone lines, microwaves, satellites, fiber optic cables, and other media between computers and terminals or information processing systems. Founded in 1969. **Common positions include:** Accountant; Applications Engineer; Computer Programmer; Customer Service Rep.; Human Resources Manager; Marketing Manager; Public Relations Specialist; Registered Nurse; Technical Writer. **Benefits:** Dental Insurance; Disability Coverage; Life Insurance; Medical Insurance; Pension Plan; Profit Sharing; Tuition Assistance. **Corporate headquarters location:** This Location. **Annual sales/revenues:** More than $100 million. **Number of employees nationwide:** 1,800.

GENERAL SCIENCES CORPORATION

4600 Powder Mill Road, Suite 400, Beltsville MD 20705. 301/931-2900. **Contact:** Personnel Manager. **World Wide Web address:** http://www.saicgsc.com. **Description:** Develops software for a variety of scientific applications. **Parent company:** Science Applications International Corporation.

GENICOM CORPORATION
14800 Conference Center Drive, Suite 400, Chantilly VA 20151. 703/802-9200. **Fax:** 703/802-9039. **Contact:** Personnel. **World Wide Web address:** http://www.genicom.com. **Description:** An international supplier of network system, service, and printer solutions. GENICOM Corporation is divided into two different business units: Enterprising Service Solutions provides logo and multivendor product field support and depot repair, express parts, and professional services; and Document Solutions provides supplies, parts, and services for high performance serial matrix and line matrix printers. **Common positions include:** Accountant; Services Sales Rep. **Educational backgrounds include:** Business Administration; Computer Science; Marketing. **Benefits:** 401(k); Dental Insurance; Disability Coverage; Life Insurance; Medical Insurance. **Corporate headquarters location:** This Location. **Other U.S. locations:** Nationwide. **Subsidiaries include:** GENICOM Pty. Ltd. (Australia); GENICOM Canada, Inc. (Canada); GENICOM S.A. (France); GENICOM GmbH (Germany); GENICOM SpA (Italy); GENICOM Limited (UK); Harris Adacom Inc. (Canada). **Operations at this facility include:** Administration; Sales. **Number of employees nationwide:** 2,150.

GENUITY INC.
150 Cambridge Park Drive, Cambridge MA 02140. 617/873-2000. **Toll-free phone:** 800/472-4565. **Contact:** Human Resources. **World Wide Web address:** http://www.genuity.com. **Description:** A diversified high-technology company that develops and markets statistical data analysis software used in a variety of fields including research and development, quality control and manufacturing, and clinical data management. Products include statistical advisor systems for the design of experiments, time series, data analysis and graphics, clinical trials management, and quality control via statistical process control. **NOTE:** As of June 1999, GTE Corporation and Bell Atlantic Corporation were awaiting regulatory approval for a planned merger. Call this location for more information. **Common positions include:** Accountant; Financial Analyst; Hardware Engineer; Software Engineer. **Corporate headquarters location:** This Location. **Parent company:** GTE Corporation.

GEO QUEST
5599 San Felipe, Suite 1700, Houston TX 77056. 713/513-2000. **Contact:** Human Resources. **Description:** Develops and sells advanced scientific and engineering software and digital mapping products to major oil companies and governments. The company helps clients find and produce oil and gas, manage environmental concerns, and plan regional and urban development. **Corporate headquarters location:** This Location. **Other U.S. locations:** Denver CO.

GNOSSOS SOFTWARE INC.
1625 K Street NW, Suite 1250, Washington DC 20006-1604. 202/463-1200. **Fax:** 202/785-9562. **Contact:** President. **E-mail address:** jobs@gnossos.com. **World Wide Web address:** http://www.gnossos.com. **Description:** Develops database applications software for client businesses using Paradox for Windows and Delphi. Products are marketed under the Keep brand name. Founded in 1986. **Common positions include:** Computer Programmer; Marketing Specialist; Systems Analyst; Technical Support Rep. **Educational**

backgrounds include: Art/Design; Biology; Business Administration; Computer Science; Liberal Arts; Marketing; Mathematics. **Benefits:** Life Insurance; Medical Insurance; Profit Sharing; Savings Plan; Stock Option; Tuition Assistance. **Special programs:** Internships; Summer Jobs. **Corporate headquarters location:** This Location.

GOLDEN SOFTWARE, INC.
809 14th Street, Golden CO 80401-1866. **Toll-free phone:** 800/972-1021. **Fax:** 303/279-0909. **Contact:** Personnel. **World Wide Web address:** http://www.golden.com. **Description:** Develops contouring, mapping, and graphing software for Windows and DOS operating systems. **Corporate headquarters location:** This Location.

BILL GOOD MARKETING
406 West South Jordan Parkway, Suite 600, South Jordan UT 84095. 801/572-1480. **Contact:** Susan Kelly, Personnel Manager. **World Wide Web address:** http://www.billgood.com. **Description:** Develops and markets software. Products are primarily sold to stockbrokers. **Common positions include:** Computer Operator; Customer Service Rep.; Database Manager; Editor; Finance Director; Graphic Artist; Human Resources Manager; Managing Editor; Marketing Manager; Marketing Specialist; Project Manager; Quality Control Supervisor; Sales and Marketing Rep.; Sales Manager; Statistician; Technical Writer; Typist. **Educational backgrounds include:** Computer Science; Finance; Marketing. **Benefits:** 401(k); Dental Insurance; Life Insurance; Medical Insurance. **Corporate headquarters location:** This Location.

GOVERNMENT TECHNOLOGY SERVICES
3901 Stonecroft Boulevard, Chantilly VA 20151. 703/631-3333. **Toll-free phone:** 800/999-GTSI. **Fax:** 703/222-5240. **Recorded jobline:** 703/502-2950. **Contact:** Susan Esces, Human Resources Generalist. **World Wide Web address:** http://www.gtsi.com. **Description:** A leading reseller of microcomputer and UNIX workstation hardware, software, and networking products. The company also provides network configuration and installation services to the government. Founded in 1983. **Common positions include:** Accountant; Administrative Assistant; Budget Analyst; Buyer; Computer Programmer; Customer Service Rep.; Financial Analyst; Graphic Designer; Marketing Manager; Marketing Specialist; Sales Manager; Sales Rep.; Software Engineer; Systems Analyst; Systems Manager. **Educational backgrounds include:** Accounting; Business Administration; Computer Science; Engineering; Marketing. **Benefits:** 401(k); Dental Insurance; Disability Coverage; Employee Discounts; Financial Planning Assistance; Life Insurance; Medical Insurance; Tuition Assistance. **Special programs:** Internships. **Corporate headquarters location:** This Location. **Operations at this facility include:** Administration; Sales; Service. **Number of employees at this location:** 400.

GRANITE SYSTEMS RESEARCH
1228 Elm Street, 5th Floor, Manchester NH 03101-1115. 603/625-0100. **Fax:** 603/625-4812. **Contact:** Personnel. **E-mail address:** granite@granite.com. **World Wide Web address:** http://www.granite.com. **Description:** Develops network operations software under the Xpercom brand name. **Common positions include:** Account Manager; Administrative Assistant; CFO; Clerical Supervisor; Computer Programmer; Controller; Human Resources Manager; Marketing Manager; Marketing Specialist. **Educational backgrounds include:** Computer Science; Marketing; Mathematics;

Software Development; Software Tech. Support; Telecommunications. **Benefits:** Dental Insurance; Flexible Schedule; Medical Insurance; Pension Plan; Telecommuting; Tuition Assistance. **Corporate headquarters location:** This Location. **President:** John Borden, Jr.

GREAT PLAINS SOFTWARE, INC.
1701 38th Street SW, Fargo ND 58103. 701/281-0550. **Fax:** 701/281-3752. **Contact:** Human Resources. **World Wide Web address:** http://www.gps.com. **Description:** Develops integrated and modular accounting and financial management software. The company offers solutions for customers ranging from small businesses to mid-range corporations. Great Plains provides solutions for companies that want to take advantage of technologies such as graphical user interfaces, cross-platform interoperability, SQL, and client/server computing. **NOTE:** Entry-level positions are offered. **Common positions include:** Account Manager; Accountant; Administrative Assistant; Consultant; Controller; Customer Service Rep.; Database Manager; Design Engineer; Editor; Education Administrator; Electrical Engineer; Financial Analyst; Graphic Artist; Human Resources Manager; Internet Services Manager; Librarian; Market Research Analyst; Marketing Manager; MIS Specialist; Multimedia Designer; Public Relations Specialist; Purchasing Agent; Quality Control Supervisor; Sales Executive; Sales Manager; Sales Rep.; Systems Analyst; Systems Manager; Technical Writer; Telecommunications Manager; Vice President of Marketing. **Educational backgrounds include:** Accounting; Art/Design; Business Administration; Communications; Computer Science; Economics; Engineering; Finance; Liberal Arts; Marketing; Mathematics; Public Relations. **Benefits:** 401(k); Dental Insurance; Disability Coverage; Employee Discounts; Financial Planning Assistance; Life Insurance; Medical Insurance; Pension Plan; Profit Sharing; Savings Plan; Telecommuting; Tuition Assistance. **Special programs:** Training. **Corporate headquarters location:** This Location. **Number of employees nationwide:** 600.

GRECO SYSTEMS
372 Coogan Way, El Cajon CA 92020. 619/442-0205. **Toll-free phone:** 800/234-7326. **Fax:** 619/447-8982. **Contact:** Director of Human Resources. **E-mail address:** hrweb@grecosystems.com. **World Wide Web address:** http://www.grecosystems.com. **Description:** Manufactures industrial computer software and hardware systems for communication and storage in factory automation facilities. **Common positions include:** Sales Rep.; Software Engineer. **Benefits:** 401(k); Dental Insurance; Disability Coverage; Life Insurance; Medical Insurance; Profit Sharing; Tuition Assistance. **Corporate headquarters location:** This Location. **Number of employees at this location:** 60.

GREENBRIER & RUSSEL, INC.
1450 East American Lane, Suite 1700, Schaumburg IL 60173. 847/706-4000. **Toll-free phone:** 800/453-0347. **Fax:** 847/706-4020. **Contact:** Sherry Harmon, Recruiter. **E-mail address:** recruiting@gr.com. **World Wide Web address:** http://www.gr.com. **Description:** A leader in providing strategic business solutions through technical services and software. The company offers technical and management consulting; information systems training; and a wide range of intranet and client/server software. The consulting division is a national practice that focuses on helping clients meet business goals through the use of technology. The company's training division offers instructor-led intranet, client/server, AS/400, and DB2 classes. **NOTE:** Entry-level positions are offered. **Common positions include:** Computer Programmer; Consultant; Database Manager; Software Engineer; Systems Analyst. **Educational backgrounds include:** Computer Science. **Benefits:** 401(k); Dental Insurance; Disability Coverage; Life Insurance; Medical Insurance; Tuition Assistance. **Corporate headquarters location:** This Location. **Other U.S. locations:** Denver CO; Atlanta GA; Dallas TX. **Number of employees nationwide:** 500.

GROUP 1 SOFTWARE, INC.
4200 Parliament Place, Suite 600, Lanham MD 20706-1844. 301/731-2300. **Contact:** Murray Osbourn, Manager of Personnel. **World Wide Web address:** http://www.g1.com. **Description:** Group 1 develops, acquires, and markets specialized, integrated list management, mail management, and marketing support software systems. Group 1 Software also publishes list and mail management software products. **Common positions include:** Accountant; Administrator; Computer Programmer; Customer Service Rep.; Financial Analyst; Instructor; Marketing Specialist; Operations Manager; Public Relations Specialist; Sales Executive; Software Developer; Software Engineer; Systems Analyst; Technical Writer. **Educational backgrounds include:** Accounting; Business Administration; Communications; Computer Science; Engineering; Finance; Marketing. **Benefits:** 401(k); Dental Insurance; Disability Coverage; Life Insurance; Medical Insurance; Tuition Assistance. **Corporate headquarters location:** This Location. **Other U.S. locations:** CA; GA; IL; MN; NJ; NV; TX; VA. **Parent company:** Comnet Corporation. **Operations at this facility include:** Research and Development; Sales. **Number of employees worldwide:** 365.

HK SYSTEMS
P.O. Box 1512, Milwaukee WI 53201-1512. 262/860-7000. **Physical address:** 2855 South James Drive, New Berlin WI 53151-3662. **Contact:** Personnel. **World Wide Web address:** http://www.hksystems.com. **Description:** This location houses the corporate offices only. Overall, HK Systems designs and manufactures computer-controlled machinery for manufacturing and various warehousing processes. **Corporate headquarters location:** This Location.

HMT TECHNOLOGY
843 Auburn Court, Fremont CA 94538. 510/490-3100. **Recorded jobline:** 510/770-3000. **Contact:** Human Resources. **World Wide Web address:** http://www.hmtt.com. **Description:** Manufactures hard disk drives. **Common positions include:** Accountant; Computer Programmer; Designer; Electrical Engineer; Industrial Engineer; Mechanical Engineer; Science Technologist; Software Engineer; Systems Analyst. **Educational backgrounds include:** Computer Science; Engineering. **Benefits:** 401(k); Dental Insurance; Disability Coverage; Employee Discounts; Life Insurance; Medical Insurance; Tuition Assistance. **Special programs:** Internships. **Corporate headquarters location:** This Location. **Parent company:** Hitachi Metals. **Operations at this facility include:** Manufacturing; Research and Development; Sales; Service.

HNC SOFTWARE INC.
5935 Cornerstone Court West, San Diego CA 92121-3728. 858/546-8877. **Fax:** 800/438-0957. **Contact:** Personnel. **World Wide Web address:** http://www.hnc.com. **Description:** Develops and markets advanced decision software for the financial services, retail, educational publishing, insurance information, Internet commerce, and market

research industries. **NOTE:** Resumes should be sent to the Resume Processing Center, P.O. Box 828, Burlington MA 01803. **Corporate headquarters location:** This Location. **President/CEO:** Robert L. North.

HALIFAX CORPORATION
P.O. Box 11904, Alexandria VA 22312. 703/750-2202. **Physical address:** 5250 Cherokee Avenue, Alexandria VA. **Contact:** Personnel Department. **World Wide Web address:** http://www.hxcorp. com. **Description:** Performs a variety of computer-related services such as systems integration, consulting, computer maintenance and repair, facilities management, and outsourcing. **Common positions include:** Account Manager; Account Rep.; Accountant; Computer Engineer; Computer Programmer; Computer Support Technician; Computer Technician; Database Administrator; Financial Analyst; Internet Services Manager; Network Administrator; Sales Manager; Sales Rep.; Secretary; Software Engineer; Systems Analyst; Systems Manager; Webmaster. **Educational backgrounds include:** Accounting; Business Administration; Communications; Computer Science; Engineering; Marketing; MCSE; Software Tech. Support. **Benefits:** 401(k); Dental Insurance; Disability Coverage; Life Insurance; Medical Insurance; Tuition Assistance. **Corporate headquarters location:** This Location. **Other U.S. locations:** Nationwide. **Operations at this facility include:** Administration; Sales; Service. **Number of employees nationwide:** 680.

HARBINGER CORPORATION
1277 Lenox Park Boulevard, Atlanta GA 30319. 404/841-4334. **Contact:** Human Resources. **E-mail address:** resumes@harbinger.com. **World Wide Web address:** http://www.harbinger.com. **Description:** Develops EDI (electronic data interface) software. **NOTE:** Entry-level positions and second and third shifts are offered. **Common positions include:** Accountant; Administrative Assistant; Computer Operator; Computer Programmer; Customer Service Rep.; Database Manager; MIS Specialist; Online Content Specialist; Sales Executive; Software Engineer; Technical Writer; Webmaster. **Educational backgrounds include:** Accounting; Business Administration; Computer Science. **Benefits:** 401(k); Casual Dress - Daily; Dental Insurance; Disability Coverage; Employee Discounts; Life Insurance; Medical Insurance; Profit Sharing; Public Transit Available; Tuition Assistance. **Corporate headquarters location:** This Location. **Other U.S. locations:** Ann Arbor MI; Dallas TX. **Annual sales/revenues:** $51 - $100 million.

HARDWARE THAT FITS
P.O. Box 3028, Conroe TX 77305. 936/441-2650. **Contact:** Human Resources. **Description:** A reseller of computers. **Corporate headquarters location:** This Location.

HARRIS INFOSOURCE
2057 East Aurora Road, Twinsburg OH 44087-1999. 330/425-9000. **Contact:** Director of Human Resources. **World Wide Web address:** http://www. harrisinfo.com. **Description:** Publishes magazine directories and software containing lists of manufacturers nationwide. **Common positions include:** Account Rep.; Administrative Assistant; Customer Service Rep.; Database Manager; Sales Representative; Secretary; Webmaster. **Educational backgrounds include:** Software Development; Software Tech. Support. **Benefits:** 401(k); Dental Insurance; Disability Coverage; EAP; Employee Discounts; Life Insurance; Medical Insurance. **Corporate headquarters location:** This Location.

HAVAS INTERACTIVE
19840 Pioneer Avenue, Torrance CA 90503. 310/793-0600. **Recorded jobline:** 310/793-0599. **Contact:** Corporate Recruiter. **World Wide Web address:** http://www.havasint.com. **Description:** A publisher and distributor of multimedia educational and entertainment software for both the home and school markets. **Corporate headquarters location:** This Location. **Subsidiaries include:** Blizzard Entertainment develops games; Knowledge Adventure develops, publishes, and distributes multimedia educational software; and Sierra, Inc. develops and publishes interactive software for PCs.

HEWLETT-PACKARD COMPANY
EMPLOYMENT RESPONSE CENTER
Mail Stop 20-APP, 3000 Hanover Street, Palo Alto CA 94304-1181. 650/857-1501. **Fax:** 650/852-8138. **Contact:** Personnel. **World Wide Web address:** http://www.hp.com. **Description:** This location is a resume processing center. Overall, Hewlett-Packard is engaged in the design and manufacture of measurement and computation products and systems used in business, engineering, science, health care, and education. Principal products are integrated instrument and computer systems such as hardware and software, peripheral products, and electronic medical equipment and systems. **Educational backgrounds include:** Accounting; Business Administration; Chemistry; Engineering; Finance; Marketing; Mathematics; Physics. **Benefits:** Dental Insurance; Disability Coverage; Employee Discounts; Life Insurance; Medical Insurance; Pension Plan; Profit Sharing; Savings Plan; Tuition Assistance. **Corporate headquarters location:** This Location.

HIGH MEADOW BUSINESS SOLUTIONS
P.O. Box 1546, Manchester Center VT 05255. 802/362-2296. **Fax:** 802/362-2298. **Contact:** Personnel. **E-mail address:** info@highmeadow. com. **World Wide Web address:** http://www. highmeadow.com. **Description:** Manufactures a line of cash register, retail management, and point-of-sale software under the brand name RetailEdge. **Corporate headquarters location:** This Location.

HITACHI KOKI IMAGING SOLUTIONS
1757 Tapo Canyon Road, Simi Valley CA 93063. 805/578-4000. **Fax:** 805/578-4009. **Contact:** Personnel. **World Wide Web address:** http://www. hitachi-hkis.com. **Description:** Develops, markets, and manufactures data handling and output equipment. The company's products include printers and digital communications equipment. **Common positions include:** Electrical/Electronics Engineer; Mechanical Engineer. **Educational backgrounds include:** Computer Science; Engineering; Marketing. **Benefits:** Dental Insurance; Disability Coverage; Employee Discounts; Medical Insurance; Pension Plan; Tuition Assistance. **Corporate headquarters location:** This Location.

HOWTEK, INC.
21 Park Avenue, Hudson NH 03051. 603/882-5200. **Fax:** 603/880-3843. **Contact:** Connie Webster, Director of Corporate Services. **World Wide Web address:** http://www.howtek.com. **Description:** Designs, engineers, and manufactures flatbed and drum scanners for the graphic arts and desktop publishing industries, densitometers for the life sciences industry, and film digitizers for the medical imaging industry. **Benefits:** Stock Option. **Corporate headquarters location:** This Location.

HOYA CORPORATION USA
MEMORY DIVISION
960 Rincon Circle, San Jose CA 95131. 408/435-1450. **Contact:** Human Resources. **Description:**

Develops, produces, and markets glass, thin-film, rigid disks for use in hard drives for mobile computing applications. **NOTE:** Entry-level positions are offered. Resumes should be sent to Human Resources, Hoya Corporation USA, 3400 Edison Way, Fremont CA 94538. **Common positions include:** Machine Operator. **Benefits:** 401(k); Dental Insurance; Disability Coverage; Employee Discounts; Life Insurance; Medical Insurance; Savings Plan; Tuition Assistance. **Corporate headquarters location:** This Location. **Subsidiaries include:** Continuum; Probe Tech. **Parent company:** Hoya Corporation (Japan). **Number of employees worldwide:** 1,000.

HUTCHINSON TECHNOLOGY INC.

40 West Highland Park, Hutchinson MN 55350. 320/587-1962. **Fax:** 320/587-1290. **Contact:** Personnel. **World Wide Web address:** http://www. htch.com. **Description:** Manufactures suspension assemblies for disk drives. **Common positions include:** Chemical Engineer; Design Engineer; Electrical Engineer; Industrial Engineer; Mechanical Engineer. **Educational backgrounds include:** Engineering. **Benefits:** 401(k); Dental Insurance; Disability Coverage; Life Insurance; Medical Insurance; Profit Sharing; Tuition Assistance. **Special programs:** Internships. **Corporate headquarters location:** This Location. **Operations at this facility include:** Administration; Manufacturing; Research and Development; Sales. **Other U.S. locations:**

- 2301 East 60th Street North, Sioux Falls SD 57104. 605/367-9445.

HYPERION SOLUTIONS

900 Long Ridge Road, Stamford CT 06902. 203/703-3000. **Fax:** 203/595-8500. **Contact:** Personnel. **World Wide Web address:** http://www. hyperion.com. **Description:** Hyperion Solutions develops, markets, and supports a family of network-based business information software products for large multidivision or multilocation companies worldwide. The product line provides executives, managers, and analysts with the capability to collect, process, access, and analyze critical business information in a timely manner, using networked personal computers. **Common positions include:** Accountant/Auditor; Computer Programmer; Software Engineer. **Educational backgrounds include:** Accounting; Business Administration; Computer Science; Engineering; Marketing. **Benefits:** 401(k); Dental Insurance; Disability Coverage; Life Insurance; Medical Insurance; Stock Option; Tuition Assistance. **Special programs:** Internships. **Corporate headquarters location:** This Location. **Other U.S. locations:** Nationwide.

IBM CORPORATION

New Orchard Road, Armonk NY 10504. 914/765-1900. **Recorded jobline:** 800/964-4473. **Contact:** IBM Staffing Services Center. **World Wide Web address:** http://www.ibm.com. **Description:** A developer, manufacturer, and marketer of advanced information processing products including computers and micro-electronics technology, software, networking systems, and information technology-related services. **NOTE:** Jobseekers should send a resume to IBM Staffing Services Center, 1DPA/051, 3808 Six Forks Road, Raleigh, NC 27609. **Corporate headquarters location:** This Location. **International locations:** Worldwide. **Subsidiaries include:** IBM Credit Corp.; IBM Instruments, Inc.; IBM World Trade Corporation.

ICS ADVENT

6260 Sequence Drive, San Diego CA 92121. 858/677-0877. **Fax:** 858/677-0955. **Contact:** Personnel. **Description:** Manufactures ruggedized PC chassis and a reseller of computer hardware. **Corporate headquarters location:** This Location.

IDT CORPORATION

190 Main Street, Hackensack NJ 07601. 201/928-1000. **Toll-free phone:** 800/CALL-IDT. **Fax:** 201/907-5188. **Contact:** Human Resources Manager. **World Wide Web address:** http://www. idt.net. **Description:** An Internet access provider that offers dial-up services, Web hosting, and e-mail by phone. **NOTE:** Entry-level positions, part-time jobs, and second and third shifts are offered. **Common positions include:** Account Manager; Account Rep.; Accountant; Administrative Assistant; Administrative Manager; Applications Engineer; Assistant Manager; Attorney; Blue-Collar Worker Supervisor; Clerical Supervisor; Computer Operator; Computer Programmer; Computer Support Technician; Computer Technician; Customer Service Rep.; Database Administrator; Database Manager; Financial Analyst; General Manager; Help-Desk Technician; Internet Services Manager; Intranet Developer; Management Trainee; Marketing Specialist; MIS Specialist; Multimedia Designer; Network Engineer; Network/Systems Administrator; Online Sales Manager; Operations Manager; Paralegal; Production Manager; Project Manager; Public Relations Specialist; Quality Control Supervisor; Sales Executive; Sales Manager; Sales Rep.; Software Engineer; SQL Programmer; Systems Analyst; Systems Manager; Technical Support Manager; Typist; Web Advertising Specialist; Webmaster; Website Developer. **Educational backgrounds include:** Accounting; Business Administration; C/C++; Computer Science; Economics; Finance; HTML; Java; Liberal Arts; Marketing; MBA; MCSE; Microsoft Office; Microsoft Word; Novell; Public Relations; Software Tech. Support; SQL; Visual Basic. **Benefits:** 401(k); Casual Dress - Daily; Dental Insurance; Disability Coverage; Employee Discounts; Flexible Schedule; Life Insurance; Medical Insurance; Public Transit Available; Sick Days (1 - 5); Telecommuting; Tuition Assistance; Vacation Days (6 - 10). **Special programs:** Internships; Apprenticeships; Summer Jobs. **Corporate headquarters location:** This Location. **Other U.S. locations:** Nationwide. **International locations:** London, England; Mexico City, Mexico. **Subsidiaries include:** Amerimax; Net2Phone; Union Telecard Alliances. **Annual sales/revenues:** More than $100 million. **Number of employees at this location:** 1,000. **Number of employees worldwide:** 1,500.

IDX SYSTEMS CORPORATION

P.O. Box 1070, Burlington VT 05402-1070. 802/862-1022. **Physical address:** 1400 Shelburne Road, South Burlington VT 05403. **Contact:** Administrative Manager. **World Wide Web address:** http://www.idx.com. **Description:** Develops medical software for hospitals. IDX Systems Corporation provides health care information to physician groups and academic medical centers across the country. **Common positions include:** Computer Programmer; Customer Service Rep.; Manufacturer's Sales Rep.; Systems Analyst; Technical Writer. **Educational backgrounds include:** Computer Science; Medical Technology. **Benefits:** Dental Insurance; Disability Coverage; Life Insurance; Medical Insurance; Profit Sharing; Savings Plan. **Corporate headquarters location:** This Location. **Annual sales/revenues:** More than $100 million. **Number of employees nationwide:** 3,600.
Other U.S. locations:
- 116 Huntington Avenue, Boston MA 02116. 617/424-6800.

IPC INFORMATION SYSTEMS

88 Pine Street, New York NY 10005. 212/825-9060. **Contact:** Human Resources. **World Wide Web address:** http://www.ipc.com. **Description:** An international supplier of instant access voice communications systems including communications workstations, switching equipment, technical services, and WAN solutions. Products are used in the trading of stocks, bonds, and other financial instruments. **Corporate headquarters location:** This Location. **International locations:** Asia; Europe. **Number of employees nationwide:** 775.

IPC INFORMATION SYSTEMS

42 Pequot Park Road, Westbrook CT 06498. 860/399-5981. **Contact:** Human Resources. **World Wide Web address:** http://www.ipc.com. **Description:** An international supplier of instant access voice communications systems including communications workstations, switching equipment, technical services, and WAN solutions. Products are used in the trading of stocks, bonds, and other financial instruments. **Common positions include:** Electrical/Electronics Engineer; Software Engineer. **Educational backgrounds include:** Computer Science; Engineering; Mathematics. **Benefits:** 401(k); Dental Insurance; Disability Coverage; Life Insurance; Medical Insurance; Profit Sharing; Tuition Assistance. **Corporate headquarters location:** This Location. **Number of employees nationwide:** 200. **Number of employees worldwide:** 250.

IPC TECHNOLOGIES, INC.

7200 Glen Forest Drive, Richmond VA 23226. 804/285-1496. **Toll-free phone:** 800/296-4472. **Fax:** 804/673-9744. **Contact:** Stormy Hamlin, Personnel Manager. **E-mail address:** stormy@ipctech.com. **World Wide Web address:** http://www.ipctech.com. **Description:** Provides computer consulting services. The company specializes in GUI application and database design. **Common positions include:** Computer Programmer; Financial Analyst; Internet Services Manager; MIS Specialist; Software Engineer; Technical Writer/Editor. **Corporate headquarters location:** This Location.

ITC LEARNING CORPORATION

13515 Dulles Technology Drive, Herndon VA 20171. 703/713-3335. **Toll-free phone:** 800/638-3757. **Contact:** Personnel. **World Wide Web address:** http://www.itclearning.com. **Description:** A full-service training company specializing in the development, production, marketing, and sale of both off-the-shelf and custom-designed multimedia training courseware for commercial, educational, and government organizations. The company also markets, sells, and distributes linear training products (primarily videotape and text-based) through its Training Department. Standard multimedia platforms for ITC products include both laser disc and CD-ROM. Founded in 1977. **Common positions include:** Account Manager; Account Rep.; Accountant; Administrative Assistant; Administrative Manager; CFO; Controller; Customer Service Rep.; Database Manager; Financial Analyst; Human Resources Manager; Marketing Specialist; President; Sales Manager; Sales Rep.; Secretary; Software Engineer; Typist Processor; Vice President of Marketing and Sales; Video Production Coordinator. **Educational backgrounds include:** Accounting; Business Administration; Communications; Computer Science; Marketing; Sales. **Benefits:** 401(k); Dental Insurance; Disability Coverage; ESOP; Life Insurance; Medical Insurance; Stock Purchase. **Corporate headquarters location:** This Location. **Other U.S. locations:** Atlanta GA. **International**

locations: Australia; United Kingdom. **Subsidiaries include:** CI Acquisition Corporation. **Annual sales/revenues:** $21 - $50 million. **Number of employees nationwide:** 100.

ITG INC.

380 Madison Avenue, 4th Floor, New York NY 10017. 212/444-6300. **Contact:** Human Resources. **World Wide Web address:** http://www.itginc.com. **Description:** Provides automated securities trade execution and analysis services to institutional equity investors. ITG's two main services are POSIT, one of the largest automated stock crossing systems operated during trading hours, and QuantEX, a proprietary software to enhance customers' trading efficiencies, access to market liquidity, and portfolio analysis capabilities. **Corporate headquarters location:** This Location. **Other U.S. locations:** Los Angeles CA; Boston MA. **International locations:** London, England. **Parent company:** Investment Technology Group.

ITT INDUSTRIES

4 West Red Oak Lane, White Plains NY 10604. 914/641-2000. **Contact:** Personnel. **World Wide Web address:** http://www.ittind.com. **Description:** Designs and engineers software for satellite communications under government contracts. **Corporate headquarters location:** This Location.

IAMBIC SOFTWARE

12 South First Street, Suite 300, San Jose CA 95113. 408/882-0390. **Fax:** 408/367-1606. **Contact:** Personnel. **E-mail address:** helpwanted@iambic.com. **World Wide Web address:** http://www.iambic.com. **Description:** Develops and manufactures software applications for the handheld computing market. **Common positions include:** Software Engineer. **Corporate headquarters location:** This Location.

IKON OFFICE SOLUTIONS TECHNOLOGY SERVICES

5050 West Lemon Street, Tampa FL 33609. 813/261-2000. **Fax:** 813/289-8088. **Contact:** Personnel. **World Wide Web address:** http://www.ikon.com. **Description:** Provides client/server and workflow consulting, network integration, product fulfillment, and technical training. **Common positions include:** Account Manager; Account Rep.; Computer Programmer; Customer Service Rep.; Marketing Specialist; MIS Specialist; Project Manager; Sales Executive; Systems Analyst; Systems Manager. **Educational backgrounds include:** Computer Science. **Benefits:** 401(k); Dental Insurance; Disability Coverage; Employee Discounts; Life Insurance; Medical Insurance. **Special programs:** Internships; Apprenticeships; Training. **Other U.S. locations:** Fort Lauderdale FL; Jacksonville FL; Orlando FL; Tallahassee FL; Pittsburgh PA. **Annual sales/revenues:** $51 - $100 million. **Number of employees nationwide:** 210.

IKON TECHNOLOGY SERVICES

11425 West Lake Park Drive, Suite 900, Milwaukee WI 53224. 414/577-6600. **Contact:** Susan Sheldon, Director of Human Resources. **Description:** Provides computer networking services.

IKOS SYSTEMS, INC.

19050 Pruneridge Avenue, Cupertino CA 95014. 408/255-4567. **Fax:** 408/366-8699. **Contact:** Personnel. **World Wide Web address:** http://www.ikos.com. **Description:** Designs, manufactures, and supports logic simulation software and compatible hardware accelerators. IKOS's simulators are used in the design of Application Specific Integrated Circuits (ASIC) and ASIC-based systems. **Corporate headquarters location:** This Location.

ILLUMINET
4501 Intelco Loop SE, P.O. Box 2909, Olympia WA 98507. 360/493-6000. **Contact:** Human Resources. **Description:** Develops databases, networking products, software, and information systems for telephone companies. **Common positions include:** Computer Programmer; Customer Service Rep.; Financial Analyst; Systems Analyst. **Educational backgrounds include:** Computer Science; Engineering; Marketing. **Benefits:** Dental Insurance; Disability Coverage; Life Insurance; Medical Insurance; Profit Sharing; Tuition Assistance. **Corporate headquarters location:** This Location. **Operations at this facility include:** Administration; Research and Development; Sales. **Number of employees at this location:** 150.

IMAGE SYSTEMS CORPORATION
6103 Blue Circle Drive, Minnetonka MN 55343. 952/935-1171. **Fax:** 952/935-1386. **Contact:** Laura Sorensen, Manager of Human Resources. **E-mail address:** lauras@imagesystemscorp.com. **World Wide Web address:** http://www.imagesystemscorp. com. **Description:** Designs and manufactures high-resolution computer monitors for medical and document imaging and air traffic control. **NOTE:** Second and third shifts are offered. **Company slogan:** You'll like what you see! **Common positions include:** Design Engineer; Electrical Engineer; Electronics Technician; Industrial Engineer; Manufacturing Engineer; Quality Control Supervisor. **Educational backgrounds include:** Business Administration; Engineering. **Benefits:** 401(k); Disability Coverage; Medical Insurance. **Special programs:** Internships. **Corporate headquarters location:** This Location.

IMATION CORPORATION
One Imation Place, Oakdale MN 55128-3414. 651/704-4000. **Toll-free phone:** 888/466-3456. **Fax:** 651/704-4445. **Contact:** Staffing Specialist. **E-mail address:** info@imation.com. **World Wide Web address:** http://www.imation.com. **Description:** Manufactures data storage products including diskettes, backup tapes, and network optical disks. The company also provides laser videodisk services. **Corporate headquarters location:** This Location. **Annual sales/revenues:** More than $100 million. **Number of employees worldwide:** 10,000.

IMSPACE SYSTEMS CORPORATION
3089C Clairemont Drive, Suite 349, San Diego CA 92117. 858/272-2600. **Contact:** Human Resources. **World Wide Web address:** http://www.imspace. com. **Description:** Develops and publishes image and multimedia cataloging software. The company's product line includes Kudo software for managing and publishing digital images. Imspace's products and services allow digital photographers, desktop publishers, and multimedia producers to work with collections of digital images, video, sound, and documents. The company's software is used on Macintosh and Windows-based computers. **Corporate headquarters location:** This Location.

INACOM CORPORATION
10810 Farnam Drive, Omaha NE 68154. 402/758-3900. **Contact:** Personnel. **World Wide Web address:** http://www.inacom.com. **Description:** A computer consulting firm offering procurement, integration, and support services. **Corporate headquarters location:** This Location. **Listed on:** New York Stock Exchange. **Number of employees worldwide:** 5,600.
Other U.S. locations:
• Inacom Professional Services, 1239 East Newport Center Drive, Suite 101, Deerfield Beach FL 33442. 954/481-6660.

INCYTE, INC.
3160 Porter Drive, Palo Alto CA 94304. 650/855-0555. **Contact:** Human Resources. **World Wide Web address:** http://www.incyte.com. **Description:** Designs and develops genomic software. **Corporate headquarters location:** This Location.

INFODATA SYSTEMS INC.
12150 Monument Drive, Suite 400, Fairfax VA 22033. 703/934-5205. **Fax:** 703/934-7154. **Contact:** Eva Franklin, Human Resources Director. **World Wide Web address:** http://www.infodata. com. **Description:** Provides complete electronic document management systems solutions to address developing client/server technologies, through the sale of products and software integration services. The company also offers product support services including training, a telephone hotline service, product enhancements, and maintenance releases. **Corporate headquarters location:** This Location.

INFOQUEST SYSTEMS, INC.
256 Chapman Road, Suite 203, Newark DE 19702. 302/456-3392. **Fax:** 302/368-7544. **Contact:** Human Resources. **E-mail address:** iquest@iqsi. com. **World Wide Web address:** http://www. iqsi.com. **Description:** Develops software for the health care industry that assists with billing patients and scheduling appointments; attaches dictation to patients' files; and sends appointment reminders. **Corporate headquarters location:** This Location.

INFORMATION ANALYSIS INC.
11240 Waples Mill Road, Suite 400, Fairfax VA 22030. 703/383-3000. **Contact:** Leslie Reed, Personnel Director. **World Wide Web address:** http://www.infoa.com. **Description:** Develops software applications, offers hardware and software consulting services, and provides software sales and support services. These services include systems re-engineering, feasibility and requirements analysis, systems planning analysis and design, database design and management, software development, and project management. **Corporate headquarters location:** This Location. **Subsidiaries include:** Allied Health and Information Systems, Inc.; DHD Systems, Inc. **Number of employees nationwide:** 160.

INFORMATION BUILDERS INC.
2 Penn Plaza, New York NY 10121. 212/736-4433. **Fax:** 212/967-6406. **Contact:** Lila Goldberg, Personnel Manager. **World Wide Web address:** http://www.ibi.com. **Description:** A software development firm. Products include FOCUS, EDA, and SmartMart software for various platforms. **Common positions include:** Accountant; Computer Programmer; Customer Service Rep.; Operations Manager; Systems Analyst; Technical Writer. **Educational backgrounds include:** Accounting; Business Administration; Communications; Computer Science; Marketing. **Benefits:** 401(k); Dental Insurance; Disability Coverage; Medical Insurance; Pension Plan; Tuition Assistance. **Corporate headquarters location:** This Location. **Other U.S. locations:** Nationwide. **Operations at this facility include:** Administration; Research and Development. **Listed on:** Privately held. **Number of employees at this location:** 800. **Number of employees nationwide:** 1,500.

INFORMATION INTEGRATION, INC.
901 Russell Avenue, Gaithersburg MD 20879. 301/840-8977. **Fax:** 301/840-5386. **Contact:** Dorothy Louder, Operations Manager. **World Wide Web address:** http://www.gotoiii.com. **Description:** A computer wholesaler. **Common positions include:** Account Manager; Account Rep.; Accountant; Administrative Assistant; Branch

Manager; Computer Programmer; Controller; Credit Manager; Operations Manager; Project Manager; Sales Manager; Sales Rep.; Secretary; Software Engineer. **Benefits:** 401(k); Dental Insurance; Disability Coverage; Employee Discounts; Life Insurance; Medical Insurance. **Corporate headquarters location:** This Location.

INFORMATION RESOURCES, INC.
150 North Clinton Street, Chicago IL 60661. 312/726-1221. **Fax:** 312/726-5304. **Contact:** Personnel. **World Wide Web address:** http://www. infores.com. **Description:** Develops and maintains computerized proprietary databases, decision support software, and analytical models to assist clients, primarily in the consumer packaged goods industry, in testing and evaluating their marketing plans for new products, media advertising, price, and sales promotions. **Common positions include:** Accountant; Computer Programmer; Human Resources Manager; Market Research Analyst; Marketing Manager; Secretary; Systems Analyst. **Educational backgrounds include:** Business Administration; Computer Science; Economics; Finance; Liberal Arts; Marketing; Mathematics. **Benefits:** 401(k); Daycare Assistance; Dental Insurance; Disability Coverage; Life Insurance; Medical Insurance; Tuition Assistance. **Corporate headquarters location:** This Location. **Other U.S. locations:** Los Angeles CA; San Francisco CA; Darien CT; Waltham MA; Fairfield NJ; Cincinnati OH. **Number of employees nationwide:** 5,800.

INFORMATION SYSTEMS AND SERVICES, INC. (ISSI)
8405 Colesville Road, 6th Floor, Silver Spring MD 20910. 301/588-3800. **Contact:** Human Resources. **World Wide Web address:** http://www.issinet. com. **Description:** Develops enterprise software.

INFORMATION SYSTEMS SUPPORT
4151 Middlefield Road, Suite 101, Palo Alto CA 94303. 650/496-2400. **Contact:** Human Resources. **Description:** Provides computer consulting services including information technology and facility management support. **Corporate headquarters location:** This Location.

INFORMIX SOFTWARE, INC.
4100 Bohannon Drive, Menlo Park CA 94025. 650/926-6300. **Fax:** 650/926-6873. **Contact:** Personnel. **World Wide Web address:** http://www. informix.com. **Description:** Provides database technology to build, deploy, run, and evolve applications. Informix products include distributed database management systems, application development tools, and graphical- and character-based productivity software for delivering information to desktop platforms. **Common positions include:** Product Engineer; Software Engineer; Technical Support Rep. **Educational backgrounds include:** Computer Science; Engineering. **Benefits:** 401(k); Dental Insurance; Disability Coverage; Life Insurance; Medical Insurance; Profit Sharing; Tuition Assistance. **Corporate headquarters location:** This Location. **Other U.S. locations:** Englewood CO; Downers Grove IL; Lenexa KS; Portland OR. **International locations:** England; Singapore. **Number of employees at this location:** 800. **Number of employees nationwide:** 1,300.

INGRAM MICRO
1600 East Saint Andrew Place, Santa Ana CA 92705. 714/566-1000. **Contact:** Human Resources. **World Wide Web address:** http://www. ingrammicro.com. **Description:** Distributes microcomputer products including desktop and notebook PCs, servers, CD-Rom drives, printers, and software. **Corporate headquarters location:** This Location. **CEO:** Jerre L. Stead.

INKTOMI CORPORATION
4100 East Third Avenue, Foster City CA 94404. 650/653-2800. **Contact:** Human Resources. **World Wide Web address:** http://www.inktomi.com. **Description:** Creator and operator of HotBot, a search engine on the World Wide Web.

INNOVEX
530 11th Street South, Hopkins MN 55343. 952/938-4155. **Contact:** Human Resources. **Description:** Manufactures lead wire assemblies for heads of computer hard drives. **Corporate headquarters location:** This Location.

INSIGHT ELECTRONICS, INC.
9980 Huennekens Street, San Diego CA 92121. 858/677-3111. **Contact:** Personnel/Computers. **World Wide Web address:** http://www.insight-electronics.com. **Description:** Distributes computers and semiconductors. **Corporate headquarters location:** This Location.

INSO CORPORATION
31 St. James Avenue, 11th Floor, Boston MA 02116. 617/753-6500. **Contact:** Staffing Manager. **World Wide Web address:** http://www.inso.com. **Description:** A leading provider of electronic publishing and information sharing software products that operate in environments ranging from computer desktops to the Internet. Inso Corporation markets its products worldwide to original equipment manufacturers of computer hardware, software, and consumer electronics products, as well as to major corporations, government agencies, and end users. **Corporate headquarters location:** This Location. **Other U.S. locations:** Chicago IL.

INSPIRATION SOFTWARE, INC.
7412 SW Beaverton Hillsdale Highway, Suite 102, Portland OR 97225-2167. 503/297-3004. **Fax:** 503/297-4676. **Contact:** Personnel. **World Wide Web address:** http://www.inspiration.com. **Description:** Develops visual creative planning and diagramming tool software. **Corporate headquarters location:** This Location.

INSTINCTIVE TECHNOLOGY, INC.
725 Concord Avenue, Cambridge MA 02138. 617/497-6300. **Contact:** Human Resources. **E-mail address:** resumes@instinctive.com. **World Wide Web address:** http://www.instinctive.com. **Description:** Develops eRoom, a leading Web-based project management application. **Corporate headquarters location:** This Location.

INSTITUTE FOR SCIENTIFIC INFORMATION
3501 Market Street, Philadelphia PA 19104. 215/386-0100. **Fax:** 215/387-4231. **Contact:** Brian Richards, Employment Manager. **World Wide Web address:** http://www.isinet.com. **Description:** Supplies researchers and scientists with needed information in electronic formats. Institute for Scientific Information produces indexes and databases that provide information from journals, books, and other significant materials published in the sciences, social sciences, and arts and humanities. The company also offers online services and technical support. **Common positions include:** Accountant; Computer Programmer; Customer Service Rep.; Database Manager; Editor; Financial Analyst; Indexer; Marketing Specialist; Operations Manager; Proofreader; Quality Control Supervisor; Systems Analyst; Technical Writer; Translator. **Educational backgrounds include:** Accounting; Biology; Chemistry; Computer Science; Finance; Liberal Arts; Library Science; Marketing. **Benefits:**

401(k); Dental Insurance; Disability Coverage; Life Insurance; Medical Insurance; Tuition Assistance. **Corporate headquarters location:** This Location. **Other area locations:** Cherry Hill NJ; Mount Laurel NJ. **Parent company:** Thomson Company. **Number of employees nationwide:** 750.

INTEGRATED SYSTEMS, INC.
201 Moffett Park Drive, Sunnyvale CA 94089-1322. 408/542-1500. **Fax:** 408/542-1955. **Contact:** Personnel. **World Wide Web address:** http://www. isi.com. **Description:** Develops embedded systems software for a variety of industrial and consumer uses. **Corporate headquarters location:** This Location. **International locations:** Asia; Europe. **Annual sales/revenues:** $51 - $100 million.

INTEL CORPORATION
2200 Mission College Boulevard, P.O. Box 58119, Santa Clara CA 95052-8119. 408/987-8080. **Contact:** Staffing Department. **World Wide Web address:** http://www.intel.com. **Description:** One of the largest semiconductor manufacturers in the world. Other products include supercomputers; embedded control chips and flash memories; video technology software; multimedia hardware; personal computer enhancement products; and design and marketing of microcomputer components, modules, and systems. Intel sells its products to original equipment manufacturers and other companies that incorporate them into their products. **Corporate headquarters location:** This Location. **Subsidiaries include:** Shiva produces a line of direct-dial products and remote access servers. **Other U.S. locations:**
• 4100 Sara Road, Rio Rancho NM 87124. 505/893-7000.

INTELLICORP
1975 El Camino Real West, Suite 101, Mountain View CA 94040-2216. 650/965-5500. **Fax:** 650/965-5647. **Contact:** Human Resources. **World Wide Web address:** http://www.intellicorp.com. **Description:** Designs, develops, and markets software development tools and provides related training, customer support, and consulting services. IntelliCorp provides its customers with object-oriented software tools for the design, development, and delivery of scalable client/server applications. **Corporate headquarters location:** This Location. **Other U.S. locations:** Nationwide. **International locations:** Europe.

INTERACTIVE SOLUTIONS, INC.
377 Route 17 South, Hasbrouck Heights NJ 07604. 201/288-6699. **Contact:** Personnel. **Description:** Develops custom software applications to meet specific client needs. **Common positions include:** Account Rep.; Applications Engineer; Computer Programmer; Database Manager; MIS Specialist; Multimedia Designer; Sales Rep.; Software Engineer; Systems Analyst; Telecommunications Manager; Typist. **Educational backgrounds include:** Accounting; Art/Design; Computer Science; Mathematics; Physics. **Benefits:** Disability Coverage; Financial Planning Assistance; Life Insurance; Medical Insurance; Tuition Assistance. **Corporate headquarters location:** This Location.

INTEREX INC.
XLR8
8447 East 35th Street North, Wichita KS 67226. 316/636-5544. **Contact:** Human Resources. **World Wide Web address:** http://www.interexinc.com. **Description:** Manufactures computer accessories including cables, surge suppressors, and networking equipment. XLR8 (also at this location) sells computer parts and accessories. **Corporate headquarters location:** This Location.

INTERFACE SYSTEMS, INC.
5855 Interface Drive, Ann Arbor MI 48103. 734/769-5900. **Fax:** 734/769-1047. **Contact:** John Morand, Human Resources Manager. **Description:** Provides software-based tools and solutions to integrate legacy systems with Internet technology, distribute mainframe documents, and provide host connectivity. Interface Systems specializes in Internet bill presentation and payment, as well as electronic delivery of statements and other content via e-mail, fax, or Internet. **NOTE:** Part-time jobs are offered. **Common positions include:** Computer Support Technician; Computer Technician; Sales Executive; Sales Representative; Software Engineer. **Educational backgrounds include:** ASP; C/C++; Communications; Computer Science; Engineering; HTML; Java; Marketing; MCSE; Software Development; Software Tech. Support; Visual Basic. **Benefits:** 401(k); Casual Dress - Fridays; Dental Insurance; Disability Coverage; Life Insurance; Medical Insurance. **Corporate headquarters location:** This Location. **Other U.S. locations:** Loves Park IL. **International locations:** United Kingdom. **CEO:** Robert Nero. **Number of employees at this location:** 100. **Number of employees worldwide:** 150.

INTERLEAF INC.
62 Fourth Avenue, Waltham MA 02451. 781/290-0710. **Contact:** Personnel Department. **Description:** Develops document management systems and solutions software. **Common positions include:** Computer Programmer; Consultant; Software Engineer; Technical Writer/Editor. **Educational backgrounds include:** Computer Science. **Special programs:** Internships. **Corporate headquarters location:** This Location.

INTERLINQ SOFTWARE CORPORATION
11980 NE 24th Street, Bellevue WA 98005. 425/827-1112. **Fax:** 425/827-0927. **Contact:** Personnel. **World Wide Web address:** http://www. interlinq.com. **Description:** A leading provider of PC-based software solutions for the residential mortgage lending industry. The company's MortgageWare Enterprise product line is sold to banks, savings institutions, mortgage banks, mortgage brokers, and credit unions. The MortgageWare Enterprise product line is a complete PC-based software system that automates all aspects of the loan origination and secondary marketing processes, from qualifying a borrower to processing, settling, closing, and selling loans. MortgageWare Enterprise also includes tools to help lenders track and manage loans in their system, as well as a proprietary electronic communications system that enables data to be transferred via modem between headquarters, branch offices, and laptop origination systems. **Corporate headquarters location:** This Location.

INTERNATIONAL ASSEMBLY SPECIALISTS
945 East Ohio Street, Suite 3, Tucson AZ 85714. 520/294-0898. **Contact:** Mr. Dale Marthaler, General Manager. **Description:** Manufactures, repairs, and refurbishes a large variety of computer peripheral equipment and electromechanical subassemblies. **Common positions include:** Buyer; Customer Service Rep.; Database Manager; Design Engineer; Electrical Engineer; General Manager; Internet Services Manager; Production Manager; Purchasing Agent; Quality Control Supervisor; Sales Manager; Software Engineer. **Listed on:** Privately held. **Number of employees nationwide:** 600.

INTERNATIONAL DATA GROUP INC.
140 Whittington Parkway, Louisville KY 40222. **Toll-free phone:** 800/829-4434. **Fax:** 502/394-

9938. Contact: Doresa Smith, Sales Representative. **E-mail address:** dsmith@idgtech.com. **World Wide Web address:** http://www.idgtech.com. **Description:** A computer consulting firm. **NOTE:** Entry-level positions are offered. **Common positions include:** Computer Programmer; Software Engineer; SQL Programmer; Website Developer. **Educational backgrounds include:** ASP; C/C++; Cold Fusion; HTML; Internet Development; Java; SQL; Visual Basic. **Benefits:** 401(k); Casual Dress - Daily; Dental Insurance; Flexible Schedule; Life Insurance; Medical Insurance; Profit Sharing; Relocation Assistance; Tuition Assistance; Vacation Days (10 - 20). **Special programs:** Internships; Training; Co-ops. **Corporate headquarters location:** This Location. **International locations:** Australia; India. **CEO:** David Noronha. **Number of employees at this location:** 75.

INTERNET COMMUNICATIONS CORP.

7100 East Belleview Avenue, Suite 201, Greenwood Village CO 80111. 303/770-7600. **Contact:** Personnel. **World Wide Web address:** http://www.incc.net. **Description:** Specializes in the design, support, and management of local and wide area networks. The company also provides Internet access to corporate customers. The company's diverse client base includes health care and insurance companies, financial and securities firms, educational and government organizations, and retail and manufacturing companies. Founded in 1986. **Common positions include:** Account Manager; Network/Systems Administrator. **Educational backgrounds include:** MCSE; Microsoft Windows NT. **Benefits:** 401(k); Casual Dress - Fridays; Dental Insurance; Disability Coverage; Life Insurance; Medical Insurance; Sick Days (1 - 5); Vacation Days (6 - 10). **Corporate headquarters location:** This Location. **Number of employees at this location:** 100. **Number of employees nationwide:** 150.

INTERPHASE CORPORATION

13800 Senlac, Dallas TX 75234. 214/654-5000. **Toll-free phone:** 800/777-3722. **Fax:** 214/654-5500. **Contact:** Pat Flatbush, Human Resources Manager. **E-mail address:** resumes@iphase.com. **World Wide Web address:** http://www.iphase.com. **Description:** Interphase Corporation is a developer, manufacturer, and marketer of networking and mass storage controllers, as well as stand alone networking devices for computer systems. Many of the networking products are sold to original equipment manufacturers, value-added resellers, systems integrators, and large end users. **Common positions include:** Design Engineer; Electrical/Electronics Engineer; Software Engineer. **Educational backgrounds include:** Computer Science; Engineering. **Benefits:** 401(k); Dental Insurance; Disability Coverage; Life Insurance; Medical Insurance; Pension Plan; Tuition Assistance; Vision Insurance. **Corporate headquarters location:** This Location. **Number of employees at this location:** 200.

INTERVOICE, INC.

17811 Waterview Parkway, Dallas TX 75252. 972/454-8000. **Fax:** 972/454-8408. **Contact:** Personnel. **World Wide Web address:** http://www.intervoice.com. **Description:** InterVoice, Inc. develops, sells, and services interactive voice response systems that allow individuals to access a computer database using a telephone keypad, computer keyboard, or human voice. Applications are functioning in industries including insurance, banking, higher education, government, utilities, health care, retail distribution, transportation, and operator services. **Corporate headquarters location:** This Location.

IOMEGA CORPORATION

1821 West Iomega Way, Roy UT 84067. 801/778-1000. **Contact:** Personnel. **World Wide Web address:** http://www.iomega.com. **Description:** Creates information storage solutions that enhance the usefulness of personal computers and workstations in a variety of applications. Iomega's products help people manage their information storage needs. The company's products include Zip drives which are three drives in one, offering expansion for hard drives, mobile storage with portable convenience, and backup information. **Corporate headquarters location:** This Location. **International locations:** Geneva, Switzerland; Singapore. **President/CEO:** Bruce R. Albertson. **Number of employees worldwide:** 3,750.

IOTECH, INC.

25971 Cannon Road, Cleveland OH 44146. 440/439-4091. **Fax:** 440/439-4093. **Contact:** Personnel. **World Wide Web address:** http://www.iotech.com. **Description:** Develops, manufactures, and markets interfaces and data acquisition instruments. The company's hardware and software products are used primarily to support personal computers and engineering workstations. **Common positions include:** Applications Engineer; Design Engineer; Electrical Engineer; Manufacturing Engineer; Mechanical Engineer; Software Engineer. **Educational backgrounds include:** Engineering. **Benefits:** 401(k); Dental Insurance; Disability Coverage; Life Insurance; Medical Insurance. **Corporate headquarters location:** This Location. **Number of employees at this location:** 90.

IRIS GRAPHICS INC.

3 Federal Street, Billerica MA 01821. 978/313-4747. **Contact:** Human Resources Manager. **World Wide Web address:** http://www.irisgraphics.com. **Description:** Manufactures continuous ink jet printers. The company's product line serves markets such as desktop publishing, digital photography, fine art signage, 3-D design, packaging, and geotechnology. **Common positions include:** Chemist; Electrical Engineer; Mechanical Engineer; Software Engineer; Technical Writer/Editor. **Educational backgrounds include:** Computer Science; Engineering; Marketing. **Benefits:** 401(k); Dental Insurance; Disability Coverage; Employee Discounts; Life Insurance; Medical Insurance; Profit Sharing; Tuition Assistance. **Corporate headquarters location:** This Location. **Other U.S. locations:** Nationwide. **Parent company:** Scitex Corp., Ltd. **Operations at this facility include:** Manufacturing; Research and Development. **Annual sales/revenues:** More than $100 million. **Number of employees at this location:** 280.

ITAC SYSTEMS, INC.

3113 Benton Street, Garland TX 75042. 972/494-3073. **Fax:** 972/494-4159. **Contact:** Personnel. **World Wide Web address:** http://www.mousetrak.com. **Description:** Manufactures the mouse-trak trackball, a computer peripheral product. **NOTE:** Entry-level positions are offered. **Common positions include:** Account Manager; Accountant; Administrative Assistant; Controller; Credit Manager; Customer Service Rep.; Database Manager; Design Engineer; Electrical Engineer; Finance Director; Human Resources Manager; Internet Services Manager; Manufacturing Engineer; Marketing Specialist; Mechanical Engineer; Operations Manager; Production Manager; Purchasing Agent; Sales Executive; Sales Manager; Systems Manager; Vice President of Operations; Webmaster. **Educational backgrounds include:** Accounting; Computer Science; Engineering; Marketing. **Benefits:** 401(k); Dental Insurance; Disability Coverage; Life Insurance;

Medical Insurance; Tuition Assistance. **Corporate headquarters location:** This Location. **Operations at this facility include:** Administration; Manufacturing; Research and Development; Sales; Service.

ITERATED SYSTEMS INC.
7 Piedmont Center, Suite 600, Atlanta GA 30305. 404/264-8000. **Contact:** Human Resources. **World Wide Web address:** http://www.iterated.com. **Description:** Develops digital imaging technologies and software.

JC COMPUTER SERVICES, INC.
4705 Eisenhower Avenue, Alexandria VA 22304. 703/461-0860. **Fax:** 703/370-4017. **Contact:** Harriet Atkinson, Vice President of Government Operations. **World Wide Web address:** http://www.jccs.com. **Description:** Provides computer and network services including maintenance and repair, network design and installation, multivendor hardware and software sales, security and risk analysis, HTML design, Internet services, training, and information technology consulting. **NOTE:** Entry-level positions are offered. **Common positions include:** Administrative Assistant; Applications Engineer; Computer Programmer; Customer Service Rep.; Database Manager; Design Engineer; Electrical Engineer; Internet Services Manager; MIS Specialist; Multimedia Designer; Online Content Specialist; Software Engineer; Systems Analyst; Technical Writer; Telecommunications Manager. **Educational backgrounds include:** Business Administration; Communications; Computer Science; Engineering; Liberal Arts. **Benefits:** Dental Insurance; Employee Discounts; Life Insurance; Medical Insurance; Tuition Assistance. **Corporate headquarters location:** This Location.

JUNO ONLINE SERVICES, INC.
1540 Broadway, 27th Floor, New York NY 10036. 212/597-9000. **Fax:** 212/597-9200. **Contact:** Jennifer Mayer, Vice President/Director of Strategic Growth. **E-mail address:** recruit@juno.com. **World Wide Web address:** http://www.juno.com. **Description:** A leading Internet access provider offering a variety of online services. **Common positions include:** Account Rep.; Administrative Assistant; Advertising Executive; Applications Engineer; Computer Engineer; Computer Programmer; Computer Support Technician; Computer Technician; Content Developer; Customer Service Rep.; Database Administrator; Database Manager; Financial Analyst; Help-Desk Technician; Human Resources Manager; Internet Services Manager; Intranet Developer; Market Research Analyst; Marketing Manager; Marketing Specialist; MIS Specialist; Multimedia Designer; Network Engineer; Network Administrator; Online Sales Manager; Public Relations Specialist; Sales Representative; Secretary; Software Engineer; SQL Programmer; Systems Analyst; Systems Manager; Technical Writer; Web Advertising Specialist; Webmaster; Website Developer. **Educational backgrounds include:** Accounting; C/C++; CGI; Cold Fusion; Computer Science; Engineering; Finance; HTML; Internet Development; Java; Mathematics; MCSE; Microsoft Office; Microsoft Word; Novell; QuarkXPress; Software Development; Software Tech. Support; Spreadsheets; SQL; Visual Basic. **Benefits:** 401(k); Casual Dress - Daily; Dental Insurance; Disability Coverage; Life Insurance; Medical Insurance; Relocation Assistance; Savings Plan. **Special programs:** Internships. **Corporate headquarters location:** This Location. **Other U.S. locations:** San Francisco CA; Washington DC; Boston MA. **International locations:** India. **President:** Charles

Ardai. **Number of employees at this location:** 200. **Number of employees nationwide:** 210. **Number of employees worldwide:** 270.

KYE INTERNATIONAL CORPORATION
2605 East Cedar Street, Ontario CA 91761. 909/923-3510. **Fax:** 909/923-1469. **Contact:** Human Resources. **Description:** A manufacturer of computer hardware peripherals including mice, scanners, CD-ROM drives, and networking products. **Common positions include:** Accountant; Adjuster; Blue-Collar Worker Supervisor; Computer Programmer; Credit Manager; Customer Service Rep.; Electrical Engineer; Financial Analyst; General Manager; Industrial Engineer; Systems Analyst. **Benefits:** Dental Insurance; Disability Coverage; Medical Insurance. **Corporate headquarters location:** This Location. **Operations at this facility include:** Administration; Sales; Service.

KEANE, INC.
10 City Square, Boston MA 02129. 617/241-9200. **Contact:** Human Resources. **World Wide Web address:** http://www.keane.com. **Description:** Designs, develops, and manages software for corporations and health care facilities. Keane, Inc.'s services enable clients to leverage existing information systems and develop and manage new software applications more rapidly and proficiently. **Common positions include:** Accountant; Computer Programmer; Systems Analyst. **Educational backgrounds include:** Computer Science. **Benefits:** 401(k); Daycare Assistance; Dental Insurance; Disability Coverage; Life Insurance; Medical Insurance; Profit Sharing; Savings Plan; Tuition Assistance. **Corporate headquarters location:** This Location. **Operations at this facility include:** Administration. **Annual sales/revenues:** More than $100 million.
Other U.S. locations:
- 11270 West Park Place, Suite 400, Milwaukee WI 53224. 414/410-2000.

KENNSCO INC.
14700 28th Avenue North, Plymouth MN 55447. 763/559-5100. **Toll-free phone:** 800/358-5574. **Contact:** Katy Bentrott, Operations Manager. **Description:** Sells and services PC, LAN, and WAN equipment. **NOTE:** Entry-level positions are offered. **Common positions include:** Account Manager; Account Rep.; Accountant; Adjuster; Administrative Assistant; Administrative Manager; Branch Manager; Buyer; Electrical Engineer; MIS Specialist; Operations Manager; Project Manager; Sales Executive; Sales Manager; Sales Rep. **Benefits:** 401(k); Dental Insurance; Disability Coverage; Flexible Schedule; Life Insurance; Medical Insurance; Profit Sharing; Tuition Assistance. **Corporate headquarters location:** This Location. **Number of employees nationwide:** 200.

KENSINGTON TECHNOLOGY GROUP
2855 Campus Drive, San Mateo CA 94403. **Toll-free phone:** 800/243-2972. **Fax:** 650/372-9463. **Contact:** Personnel. **E-mail address:** jobs@kensington.com. **World Wide Web address:** http://www.kensington.com. **Description:** Designs and markets computer accessories, peripherals, and software for the computer aftermarket. Products include mice and trackballs, joysticks, gamepads, surge suppressor systems, cable and lock security devices, and carrying cases. **NOTE:** Entry-level positions are offered. **Common positions include:** Account Manager; Customer Service Rep.; Desktop Publishing Specialist; Graphic Designer; Marketing Manager; Marketing Specialist; Operations Manager; Product Manager; Web Advertising

Specialist; Webmaster. **Educational backgrounds include:** Art/Design; Computer Science; Marketing; MBA. **Benefits:** 401(k); Casual Dress - Daily; Dental Insurance; Disability Coverage; Employee Discounts; Flexible Schedule; Life Insurance; Medical Insurance; Pension Plan; Profit Sharing; Vacation Days (11 - 15). **Special programs:** Internships. **Corporate headquarters location:** This Location. **Parent company:** ACCO Brands, Inc. **Number of employees nationwide:** 145.

KEY TRONIC CORPORATION
P.O. Box 14687, Spokane WA 99214. 509/928-8000. **Physical address:** 4424 North Sullivan Road, Spokane WA 99216. **Fax:** 509/927-5307. **Contact:** Staffing Specialist. **E-mail address:** jobs@keytronic.com. **World Wide Web address:** http://www.keytronic.com. **Description:** One of the world's largest independent manufacturers of computer keyboards and input devices. Key Tronic designs, develops, and manufactures standard and custom keyboards for integration with personal computers, terminals, and word processors made by original equipment manufacturers. **NOTE:** Entry-level positions and second and third shifts are offered. **Common positions include:** Accountant; Administrative Assistant; Blue-Collar Worker Supervisor; Buyer; CFO; Computer Programmer; Controller; Design Engineer; Electrical Engineer; Electrician; Finance Director; Human Resources Manager; Industrial Production Manager; Manufacturing Engineer; Marketing Manager; Marketing Specialist; Mechanical Engineer; MIS Specialist; Operations Manager; Production Manager; Purchasing Agent; Quality Control Supervisor; Sales Executive; Sales Manager; Transportation/Traffic Specialist. **Educational backgrounds include:** Accounting; Business Administration; Communications; Computer Science; Engineering; Finance; Marketing. **Benefits:** 401(k); Casual Dress - Fridays; Dental Insurance; Profit Sharing. **Special programs:** Internships. **Internship information:** Internships are offered on an as needed basis. The company has year-round internships, but primarily has openings in the summer and recruits through local colleges. Please call this location for more information. **Corporate headquarters location:** This Location. **Other U.S. locations:** Las Cruces NM; El Paso TX. **International locations:** Dundalk, Ireland; Juarez, Mexico. **Operations at this facility include:** Administration; Manufacturing; Research and Development; Sales; Service. **Number of employees at this location:** 550. **Number of employees nationwide:** 650. **Number of employees worldwide:** 3,000.

KINGSTON TECHNOLOGY
17600 Newhope Street, Fountain Valley CA 92708. 714/435-2600. **Fax:** 714/427-3555. **Contact:** Human Resources. **E-mail address:** jobs@kingston.com. **World Wide Web address:** http://www.kingston.com. **Description:** A leading independent manufacturer of more than 2,000 memory, processor, and other peripheral products. Founded in 1987. **NOTE:** Entry-level positions are offered. **Common positions include:** Account Manager; Account Rep.; Accountant; Administrative Assistant; AS400 Programmer Analyst; Buyer; CFO; Computer Engineer; Computer Operator; Computer Programmer; Computer Support Technician; Controller; Credit Manager; Customer Service Rep.; Database Administrator; Database Manager; Electrical Engineer; Financial Analyst; Graphic Designer; Human Resources Manager; Internet Services Manager; Manufacturing Engineer; Market Research Analyst; Marketing Manager; Marketing Specialist; Mechanical Engineer; MIS Specialist; Network Administrator;

Operations Manager; Production Manager; Public Relations Specialist; Purchasing Agent; Quality Assurance Engineer; Quality Control Supervisor; Sales Manager; Sales Rep.; Software Engineer; SQL Programmer; Systems Analyst; Systems Manager; Technical Writer/Editor; Webmaster. **Educational backgrounds include:** Accounting; Art/Design; AS400 Certification; ASP; Business Administration; C/C++; CGI; Communications; Computer Science; Economics; Engineering; Finance; HTML; Internet; Java; Marketing; MCSE; Microsoft Word; Novell; Public Relations; QuarkXPress; Software Development; Software Tech. Support; Spreadsheets; Visual Basic. **Benefits:** 401(k); Casual Dress - Daily; Dental Insurance; Disability Coverage; Employee Discounts; Life Insurance; Medical Insurance; Pension Plan; Sick Days (6 - 10); Tuition Assistance; Vacation Days (6 - 10). **Office hours:** Monday - Friday, 6:00 a.m. - 6:00 p.m. **Corporate headquarters location:** This Location. **International locations:** France; Germany; Ireland; Taiwan; United Kingdom. **Listed on:** Privately held. **President:** John Tu. **Annual sales/revenues:** More than $100 million. **Number of employees worldwide:** 1,200.

KNOZALL SYSTEMS
8912 East Pinnacle Road, Suite 601, Scottsdale AZ 85225. 480/419-3841. **Contact:** Human Resources. **World Wide Web address:** http://www.knozall.com. **Description:** Manufactures networking utilities for local and wide area networks. **Corporate headquarters location:** This Location.

KOMAG, INC.
1704 Automation Parkway, San Jose CA 95131. 408/576-2000. **Fax:** 408/944-9469. **Contact:** Personnel. **World Wide Web address:** http://www.komag.com. **Description:** A leading independent manufacturer of magnetic thin-film disks. **NOTE:** Entry-level positions and second and third shifts are offered. **Company slogan:** Survival through continuous improvement. Success through innovation. **Common positions include:** Accountant; Administrative Assistant; AS400 Programmer Analyst; Chemical Engineer; Computer Programmer; Computer Support Technician; Computer Technician; Controller; Environmental Engineer; Finance Director; Financial Analyst; Internet Services Manager; Manufacturing Engineer; Mechanical Engineer; Metallurgical Engineer; MIS Specialist; Network Administrator; Production Manager; Quality Assurance Engineer; Typist. **Educational backgrounds include:** Accounting; AS400 Certification; Business Administration; Chemistry; Computer Science; Economics; Engineering; Finance; Internet; Marketing; Microsoft Word; Novell; Physics; Software Tech. Support; Spreadsheets; Visual Basic. **Benefits:** 401(k); Casual Dress - Fridays; Dental Insurance; Disability Coverage; Employee Discounts; Life Insurance; Medical Insurance; Profit Sharing; Sick Days (6 - 10); Tuition Assistance; Vacation Days (11 - 15). **Special programs:** Internships. **Corporate headquarters location:** This Location. **Other area locations:** Santa Rosa CA. **International locations:** Japan; Malaysia. **Annual sales/revenues:** More than $100 million. **Number of employees at this location:** 1,300. **Number of employees worldwide:** 4,000.

KRONOS INC.
297 Billerica Road, Chelmsford MA 01824. 978/250-9800. **Contact:** Human Resources. **World Wide Web address:** http://www.kronos.com. **Description:** Designs, develops, and markets labor management software and computerized systems that measure employee attendance and schedules. Founded in 1977. **Common positions include:**

Electrical Engineer; Software Engineer; Technical Writer/Editor. **Educational backgrounds include:** Computer Science; Engineering; Mathematics. **Benefits:** 401(k); Dental Insurance; Disability Coverage; Employee Discounts; Life Insurance; Medical Insurance; Tuition Assistance. **Special programs:** Internships. **Corporate headquarters location:** This Location. **International locations:** Canada; United Kingdom. **Operations at this facility include:** Research and Development; Sales; Service. **Annual sales/revenues:** More than $100 million. **Number of employees at this location:** 900.

L-SOFT INTERNATIONAL, INC.
8100 Corporate Drive, Suite 350, Landover MD 20785. 301/731-0440. **Toll-free phone:** 800/399-5449. **Fax:** 301/731-6302. **Contact:** Personnel. **World Wide Web address:** http://www.lsoft.com. **Description:** Develops mailing list management software. The company's product line includes LISTSERV, an electronic mailing list management product; LSMTP, a program for large quantity delivery of Internet mail; and EASE, which allows users to create mail lists on L-Soft's centrally maintained servers. Founded in 1994. **Common positions include:** Computer Programmer; Engineer; Sales and Marketing Representative. **Corporate headquarters location:** This Location.

LAHEY COMPUTER SYSTEMS, INC.
P.O. Box 6091, Incline Village NV 89450. 775/831-2500. **Fax:** 775/831-8123. **Contact:** Personnel. **World Wide Web address:** http://www.lahey.com. **Description:** Develops scientific and engineering solutions software. **Common positions include:** Computer Programmer. **Corporate headquarters location:** This Location.

LANSHARK SYSTEMS, INC.
1027 Hurley Court, Gahanna OH 43230. 614/751-1111. **Fax:** 614/751-1112. **Contact:** Scott Sharkey, President/CEO. **World Wide Web address:** http://www.lanshark.com. **Description:** Develops LAN-based enterprise messaging software products. Products include mail and mail-enabled applications, network user applications, and network administration tools and utilities. **Common positions include:** Computer Programmer; Customer Service Rep.; Management Trainee; Services Sales Rep.; Software Engineer; Systems Analyst. **Educational backgrounds include:** Business Administration; Computer Science; Engineering; Marketing. **Benefits:** 401(k); Casual Dress - Daily; Dental Insurance; Disability Coverage; Life Insurance; Medical Insurance; Pension Plan; Profit Sharing; Tuition Assistance. **Special programs:** Internships. **Corporate headquarters location:** This Location. **Operations at this facility include:** Administration; Manufacturing; Research and Development; Sales; Service. **Number of employees nationwide:** 20.

LANTRONIX
15353 Barranca Parkway, Irvine CA 92618. 949/453-3990. **Fax:** 949/453-7165. **Contact:** Linda Duffy, Director of Personnel. **World Wide Web address:** http://www.lantronix.com. **Description:** Provides network-enabling technology that allows for configuring and communicating over the Internet and shared networks. **Corporate headquarters location:** This Location.

LAW OFFICE INFORMATION SYSTEMS
105 North 28th Street, Van Buren AR 72956. 501/471-5581. **Contact:** Human Resources. **Description:** An online, full-text database service providing access to state and federal law libraries. The service enables lawyers, business professionals, and government agencies to electronically research thousands of resources from their own computers. The company also publishes the information in CD-ROM format. **Corporate headquarters location:** This Location.

LEARN2.COM, INC.
One American Way, Pryor OK 74361. 918/825-6700. **Fax:** 918/825-6359. **Contact:** Rick Ogg, Human Resources Manager. **Description:** Offers online tutorials on a variety of topics. **Corporate headquarters location:** This Location.

LEGACY COMMUNICATIONS
3868 Carson Street, Suite 205, Torrance CA 90503. 310/792-0844. **Contact:** Personnel. **Description:** Designs, programs, manufactures, markets, and services LAN-to-LAN routers. **Common positions include:** Accountant; Administrator; Buyer; Computer Programmer; Credit Manager; Customer Service Rep.; Department Manager; Draftsperson; Electrical Engineer; Human Resources Manager; Operations Manager; Purchasing Agent; Quality Control Supervisor. **Educational backgrounds include:** Communications; Computer Science. **Benefits:** Dental Insurance; Disability Coverage; Employee Discounts; Life Insurance; Medical Insurance; Tuition Assistance. **Corporate headquarters location:** This Location.

LERNOUG & HAUSPIE SPEECH PRODUCTS
52 Third Avenue, Burlington MA 01803. 781/203-5000. **Contact:** Human Resources. **World Wide Web address:** http://www.lhs.com. **Description:** Develops, markets, and supports automated speech recognition systems used to create documents and interact with computers by voice. **Common positions include:** Software Engineer; Technical Writer. **Corporate headquarters location:** This Location. **Number of employees nationwide:** 100.

LEWIS COMPUTER SERVICES, INC.
9522 Brookline Avenue, Suite 100, Baton Rouge LA 70809. 225/709-2000. **Contact:** Personnel. **World Wide Web address:** http://www.lewis.com. **Description:** Develops software for home health agencies. The company's products include Prompt IPS, PROMPT-LINK, and PROMPT-LITE. **Corporate headquarters location:** This Location. **Other U.S. locations:** Rosemont IL.

LEXMARK INTERNATIONAL, INC.
740 New Circle Road NW, Lexington KY 40550-0001. 606/232-2379. **Contact:** Employment Manager. **World Wide Web address:** http://www. lexmark.com. **Description:** Develops, markets, and manufactures printers, typewriters, computer keyboards, and related supplies. **Common positions include:** Accountant; Chemical Engineer; Chemist; Computer Programmer; Electrical Engineer; Industrial Engineer; Manufacturer's Sales Rep.; Marketing Specialist; Mechanical Engineer; Technical Writer/Editor. **Educational backgrounds include:** Accounting; Chemistry; Computer Science; Engineering; Finance; Marketing. **Benefits:** Dental Insurance; Employee Discounts; Medical Insurance; Savings Plan. **Corporate headquarters location:** This Location. **Other U.S. locations:** Boulder CO. **Operations at this facility include:** Research and Development; Sales. **Number of employees at this location:** 4,000.

LIANT SOFTWARE CORPORATION
354 Waverly Street, Framingham MA 01702. 508/872-8700. **Fax:** 508/626-2221. **Contact:** Human Resources. **E-mail address:** abs@liant.com. **World Wide Web address:** http://www.liant.com. **Description:** A developer of network-based programming and software development tools that

enhance client/server systems and architectures. **Educational backgrounds include:** Business Administration; Computer Science. **Corporate headquarters location:** This Location. **Number of employees at this location:** 100.

LIEBERT CORPORATION
1050 Dearborn Drive, P.O. Box 29186, Columbus OH 43229. 614/888-0246. **Fax:** 614/841-5890. **Contact:** Human Resources. **World Wide Web address:** http://www.liebert.com. **Description:** A leading worldwide manufacturer of computer support equipment and related applications. **NOTE:** Entry-level positions are offered. **Common positions include:** Account Rep.; Administrative Assistant; Applications Engineer; Buyer; Computer Operator; Computer Programmer; Customer Service Rep.; Design Engineer; Electrical Engineer; Financial Analyst; Industrial Engineer; Marketing Specialist; Mechanical Engineer; MIS Specialist; Sales Rep.; Software Engineer; Technical Writer; Telecommunications Manager. **Educational backgrounds include:** Accounting; Business Administration; Computer Science; Engineering; Finance; Marketing; Software Development; Software Tech. Support. **Benefits:** 401(k); Dental Insurance; Employee Discounts; Flexible Schedule; Life Insurance; Medical Insurance; Profit Sharing; Tuition Assistance. **Special programs:** Internships; Training; Co-ops; Summer Jobs. **Corporate headquarters location:** This Location. **Other U.S. locations:** Nationwide. **Parent company:** Emerson Electric. **Number of employees at this location:** 950.

LILLY SOFTWARE ASSOCIATES, INC.
500 Lafayette Road, Hampton NH 03842. 603/926-9696. **Fax:** 603/926-9698. **Contact:** Human Resources. **E-mail address:** info@visualmfg.com. **World Wide Web address:** http://www.visualmfg. com. **Description:** Develops materials requirement planning (MRP) client/server software, called Visual Manufacturing, which allows managers to track all phases of production. **Corporate headquarters location:** This Location. **President:** Richard T. Lilly.

LINK COMPUTER CORPORATION
317 East Pleasant Valley Boulevard, Altoona PA 16602. 814/946-3085. **Fax:** 814/946-1522. **Contact:** Nicole Matusky, Corporate Recruiter. **E-mail address:** resume@linkcorp.com. **World Wide Web address:** http://www.linkcorp.com. **Description:** Provides a wide range of information technology solutions including networking services, consulting, programming, Internet development, and systems analysis. **NOTE:** Entry-level positions are offered. **Common positions include:** Account Rep.; Administrative Assistant; AS400 Programmer Analyst; Computer Programmer; Computer Support Technician; Consultant - Computer; Consultant - Technical; Content Developer; Customer Service Rep.; Database Administrator; Database Manager; Internet Services Manager; MIS Specialist; Multimedia Designer; Network Administrator; Sales Rep.; Software Engineer; SQL Programmer; Systems Analyst; Webmaster. **Educational backgrounds include:** AS400 Certification; C/C++; HTML; Internet; Microsoft Word; Novell; Software Development; Software Tech. Support; Visual Basic. **Benefits:** 401(k); Casual Dress - Daily; Employee Discounts; Life Insurance; Medical Insurance. **Special programs:** Internships; Co-ops; Summer Jobs. **Corporate headquarters location:** This Location. **Other U.S. locations:** Pittsburgh PA. **Listed on:** Privately held. **Annual sales/revenues:** $21 - $50 million. **Number of employees at this location:** 80. **Number of employees nationwide:** 110.

LOGICAL SYSTEM SERVICES, INC.
2800 Woodlawn Drive, Suite 148, Honolulu HI 96822. 808/539-3700. **Fax:** 808/539-3695. **Contact:** Personnel **E-mail address:** info@lss1. com. **Description:** A computer consulting firm specializing in data collection and management applications for distribution companies. **Corporate headquarters location:** This Location. **President:** Brian Ho.

LOGICON, INC.
3701 Skypark Drive, Suite 200, Torrance CA 90505. 310/373-0220. **Contact:** Human Resources. **World Wide Web address:** http://www.logicon. com. **Description:** Develops state-of-the-art software technology for the U.S. military and government. **Corporate headquarters location:** This Location.

LOGITECH, INC.
6505 Kaiser Drive, Fremont CA 94555. 510/795-8500. **Fax:** 510/792-8901. **Contact:** Human Resources Manager. **World Wide Web address:** http://www.logitech.com. **Description:** Designs, manufactures, and markets computer hardware and software products. Logitech is a leading worldwide manufacturer of computer pointing devices including mice, trackballs, and joysticks, and imaging devices such as scanners and cameras for PC, MAC, and other platforms. **Common positions include:** Accountant/Auditor; Buyer; Computer Programmer; Customer Service Rep.; Electrical Engineer; Financial Analyst; Manufacturer's Sales Rep.; Software Engineer; Systems Analyst; Technical Support Rep. **Educational backgrounds include:** Accounting; Computer Science; Engineering; Marketing. **Benefits:** 401(k); Dental Insurance; Disability Coverage; Employee Discounts; Life Insurance; Medical Insurance; Tuition Assistance. **Special programs:** Internships. **Corporate headquarters location:** This Location. **Other U.S. locations:** Framingham MA; Dallas TX. **Parent company:** Logitech International S.A. **Number of employees at this location:** 350.

LOOKING GLASS STUDIOS
100 Cambridge Park Drive, Suite 300, Cambridge MA 02140. 617/441-6333. **Fax:** 617/441-3946. **Contact:** Personnel. **World Wide Web address:** http://www.lglass.com. **Description:** Designs 3-D interactive and virtual reality computer games. **Corporate headquarters location:** This Location.

LOTUS DEVELOPMENT CORPORATION
55 Cambridge Parkway, Cambridge MA 02142. 617/577-8500. **Contact:** Human Resources. **World Wide Web address:** http://www.lotus.com/jobs. **Description:** Lotus develops, manufactures, and markets applications software and services that meet the evolving technology and business application needs for individuals, work groups, and entire organizations. Products include Lotus Notes, a software application that provides groupware links allowing workers to share information. **Corporate headquarters location:** This Location. **Parent company:** IBM. **Number of employees nationwide:** 4,400.

LOWRY COMPUTER PRODUCTS
7100 Whitmore Lake Road, Brighton MI 48116. 810/229-7200. **Toll-free phone:** 800/733-0210. **Fax:** 810/227-8155. **Contact:** Personnel. **World Wide Web address:** http://www.lowrycomputer. com. **Description:** A leading national systems integrator and distributor specializing in bar code printing, automatic data collection, wireless data communications, and time accounting systems. The company serves the manufacturing, distribution, logistics, health care, and government markets with

over 35 offices nationwide. **NOTE:** Part-time jobs are offered. **Common positions include:** Account Manager; Account Representative; Accountant; Administrative Assistant; Applications Engineer; Computer Operator; Computer Programmer; Controller; Credit Manager; Customer Service Rep.; Financial Analyst; General Manager; Human Resources Manager; Marketing Specialist; MIS Specialist; Operations Manager; Purchasing Agent; Sales Engineer; Sales Executive; Sales Manager; Sales Rep.; Secretary; Software Engineer; Systems Analyst; Systems Manager; Technical Writer; Transportation/Traffic Specialist; Typist. **Benefits:** 401(k); Casual Dress - Daily; Dental Insurance; Disability Coverage; Life Insurance; Medical Insurance; Paid Holidays; Sick Days (6 - 10); Vacation Days (10 - 20). **Special programs:** Internships. **Corporate headquarters location:** This Location. **Annual sales/revenues:** $51 - $100 million. **Number of employees nationwide:** 250.

LUCAS ARTS ENTERTAINMENT CO.
P.O. Box 10307, San Rafael CA 94912. **Fax:** 415/444-8438. **Recorded jobline:** 415/444-8495. **Contact:** Human Resources. **World Wide Web address:** http://www.lucasarts.com. **Description:** An international developer and publisher of entertainment software, some of which incorporate a Star Wars theme. **Corporate headquarters location:** This Location.

LUCAS DIGITAL LTD.
P.O. Box 2459, San Rafael CA 94912. 415/258-2200. **Recorded jobline:** 415/448-2100. **Contact:** Recruitment Department. **World Wide Web address:** http://www.ilm.com. **Description:** A digital effects company engaged in motion picture film production. The company is comprised of Industrial Light & Magic (ILM), a visual effects company; and Skywalker Sound, a state-of-the-art audio facility. **Common positions include:** Database Manager; Network Administrator; Software Engineer; Systems Specialist; Technician; Video Maintenance Engineer. **Corporate headquarters location:** This Location.

LUGARU SOFTWARE LTD.
1645 Shady Avenue, Pittsburgh PA 15217. 412/421-5911. **Contact:** Human Resources. **World Wide Web address:** http://www.lugaru.com. **Description:** Manufactures an EMACS-style programmer's text editor for Windows, DOS, and OS/2 called Epsilon Programmer's Editor. **Corporate headquarters location:** This Location.

LUMINANT WORLDWIDE CORP.
13737 Noel Road, Suite 1400, Dallas TX 75240. 972/581-7000. **Contact:** Human Resources. **World Wide Web address:** http://www.luminant.com. **Description:** Provides e-business consulting services and solutions.

LYCOS, INC.
400-2 Totten Pond Road, Waltham MA 02451-2000. 781/370-2700. **Contact:** Human Resources. **World Wide Web address:** http://www.lycos.com. **Description:** An Internet search engine which finds, indexes, and filters information from the World Wide Web. **Corporate headquarters location:** This Location.

MAI SYSTEMS CORPORATION
HOTEL INFORMATION SYSTEMS
9601 Jeronimo Road, Irvine CA 92618. 949/598-6000. **Fax:** 714/598-6391. **Contact:** Human Resources. **World Wide Web address:** http://www. maisystems.com. **Description:** A worldwide provider of total information systems solutions software for the hospitality industry and mid-size

manufacturers and distributors. **Common positions include:** Accountant; Administrative Assistant; Applications Engineer; Attorney; Buyer; CFO; Computer Operator; Computer Programmer; Controller; Customer Service Rep.; Design Engineer; Finance Director; Financial Analyst; Human Resources Manager; Marketing Manager; Marketing Specialist; MIS Specialist; Paralegal; Project Manager; Public Relations Specialist; Purchasing Agent; Quality Control Supervisor; Sales Rep.; Secretary; Software Engineer; Systems Analyst; Systems Manager; Technical Writer. **Educational backgrounds include:** Accounting; Business Administration; Communications; Computer Science; Engineering; Finance; Marketing; Mathematics. **Benefits:** 401(k); Dental Insurance; Disability Coverage; Life Insurance; Medical Insurance; Tuition Assistance. **Corporate headquarters location:** This Location. **Operations at this facility include:** Administration; Manufacturing; Research and Development; Sales; Service. **Number of employees nationwide:** 365. **Number of employees worldwide:** 575.

MRJ TECHNOLOGY SOLUTIONS
10560 Arrowhead Drive, Fairfax VA 22030. 703/277-1807. **Fax:** 703/277-1675. **Contact:** Anne Goins, Administrative Assistant. **E-mail address:** careers@mrj.com. **World Wide Web address:** http://www.mrj.com. **Description:** Provides information systems and engineering analysis. **Common positions include:** Database Manager; Electrical/Electronics Engineer; Geographer; MIS Specialist; Software Engineer; Systems Analyst. **Educational backgrounds include:** Computer Science; Engineering; Geography; Mathematics; Physics. **Benefits:** 401(k); Dental Insurance; Disability Coverage; Flexible Schedule; Life Insurance; Medical Insurance; Profit Sharing; Tuition Assistance. **Number of employees at this location:** 700.

MTI TECHNOLOGIES CORPORATION
SYSTEM INDUSTRIES, INC.
474 Potrero Avenue, Sunnyvale CA 94086. 408/730-1664. **Contact:** Heidi Hegel, Office Manager. **World Wide Web address:** http://www. mti.com. **Description:** MTI designs, manufactures, markets, and services high-performance storage solutions for the DEC, IBM, and open UNIX systems computing environments. These storage solutions integrate MTI's proprietary application and embedded software with its advanced servers and industry standard storage peripherals. Products include NetBacker client/server application software, Infinity Automated Tape Library Series, and other systems and related application software. **Common positions include:** Accountant; Administrator; Attorney; Blue-Collar Worker Supervisor; Buyer; Computer Programmer; Credit Manager; Customer Service Rep.; Department Manager; Draftsperson; Electrical Engineer; Financial Analyst; Human Resources Manager; Industrial Engineer; Marketing Specialist; Mechanical Engineer; Operations Manager; Public Relations Specialist; Quality Control Supervisor; Services Sales Rep.; Systems Analyst; Technical Writer/Editor; Transportation Specialist. **Benefits:** Dental Insurance; Disability Coverage; Life Insurance; Medical Insurance; Pension Plan; Tuition Assistance. **Corporate headquarters location:** This Location. **Operations at this facility include:** Administration; Manufacturing; Research and Development; Service.

MACAULAY-BROWN, INC.
4021 Executive Drive, Dayton OH 45430. 937/426-3421. **Fax:** 937/426-5364. **Contact:** Ken Simon, Senior Human Resources Manager. **E-mail**

address: kensimon@macb.com. **World Wide Web address:** http://www.macb.com. **Description:** A technical firm specializing in intelligence/threat analysis; systems engineering; digital system model development; technique development; test and evaluation of hardware in the loop; software engineering; instrumentation system design and development; computer system/LAN development; facility modification and operation; and management support. **Common positions include:** Electrical Engineer; Physicist; Project Manager; Software Engineer; Systems Analyst. **Educational backgrounds include:** Computer Science; Engineering; Physics. **Benefits:** 401(k); Dental Insurance; Disability Coverage; ESOP; Flexible Schedule; Life Insurance; Medical Insurance; Non-Smoking Environment; Pension Plan; Profit Sharing; Tuition Assistance. **Corporate headquarters location:** This Location. **Other U.S. locations:** CA; FL; GA; IL; MD; NM; TX. **Operations at this facility include:** Analysis; Computer Modeling; Management Support; Testing. **Number of employees at this location:** 95. **Number of employees nationwide:** 140.

MACOLA SOFTWARE

333 East Center Street, Marion OH 43301-1824. **Toll-free phone:** 800/468-0834. **Fax:** 740/382-0239. **Contact:** Recruiting Services Manager. **World Wide Web address:** http://www.macola. com. **Description:** Develops client/server-based accounting, distribution, and manufacturing business software solutions. **NOTE:** Entry-level positions are offered. **Common positions include:** Account Manager; Accountant; Administrative Assistant; Applications Engineer; Computer Programmer; Controller; Customer Service Rep.; Database Manager; Design Engineer; Graphic Artist; Graphic Designer; Human Resources Manager; Internet Services Manager; Market Research Analyst; Marketing Manager; Marketing Specialist; MIS Specialist; Multimedia Designer; Online Content Specialist; Quality Control Supervisor; Sales Engineer; Sales Executive; Sales Manager; Sales Rep.; Software Engineer; Systems Analyst; Systems Manager; Technical Writer; Webmaster. **Educational backgrounds include:** Accounting; Business Administration; Communications; Computer Science; Engineering; Marketing; Software Development; Software Tech. Support. **Benefits:** 401(k); Disability Coverage; Flexible Schedule; Life Insurance; Medical Insurance; Tuition Assistance. **Special programs:** Internships. **Corporate headquarters location:** This Location. **Other U.S. locations:** Nationwide. **International locations:** China; Malaysia; Thailand. **Parent company:** Macola Inc. **Listed on:** Privately held. **President/CEO/Owner:** Bruce Hollinger. **Number of employees worldwide:** 330.

MAGNET INTERACTIVE COMMUNICATIONS

3255 Grace Street NW, Washington DC 20007. 202/471-5867. **Fax:** 202/625-5107. **Contact:** Personnel Manager. **E-mail address:** jobsdc@ magnet.com. **World Wide Web address:** http://www.magnet.com. **Description:** Develops Websites. **Common positions include:** Account Manager; Administrative Assistant; Computer Programmer; Database Manager; Graphic Artist; Graphic Designer; Market Research Analyst; Marketing Specialist; Multimedia Designer; Production Manager; Project Manager; Software Engineer; Webmaster. **Educational backgrounds include:** Art/Design; Communications; Computer Science; Finance; Marketing. **Benefits:** 401(k); Dental Insurance; Disability Coverage; Life Insurance; Medical Insurance. **Special programs:** Internships; Summer Jobs. **Corporate headquarters location:** This Location. **Other U.S.**

locations: Los Angeles CA; Detroit MI. **Parent company:** Magnet Interactive Group. **Number of employees at this location:** 125. **Number of employees nationwide:** 185.

MANAGEMENT SCIENCE ASSOCIATES

6565 Penn Avenue, Pittsburgh PA 15204. 412/362-2000. **Contact:** Recruiting. **World Wide Web address:** http://www.msa.com. **Description:** Develops analytical software and related systems. **NOTE:** Part-time jobs are offered. **Common positions include:** Applications Engineer; AS400 Programmer Analyst; Computer Operator; Computer Programmer; Computer Support Technician; Computer Technician; Database Administrator; Database Manager; Network Administrator; Software Engineer; SQL Programmer; Systems Analyst; Systems Manager; Webmaster. **Educational backgrounds include:** C/C++; HTML; Software Development; Software Tech. Support; Visual Basic. **Benefits:** 401(k); Casual Dress - Daily; Dental Insurance; Disability Coverage; Employee Discounts; Flexible Schedule; Life Insurance; Medical Insurance; Pension Plan; Profit Sharing; Public Transit Available; Savings Plan. **Special programs:** Summer Jobs.

MANUGISTICS, INC.

2115 East Jefferson Street, Rockville MD 20852. 301/984-5000. **Contact:** Carl DiPietro, Personnel Director. **World Wide Web address:** http://www. manugistics.com. **Description:** Develops decision support software and provides support services for *Fortune* 500 manufacturing, transportation, and distribution companies. **Common positions include:** Computer Programmer; Industrial Engineer; Instructor; Mechanical Engineer; Operations Manager; Statistician; Systems Analyst; Technical Writer; Transportation/Traffic Specialist. **Educational backgrounds include:** Business Administration; Computer Science; Engineering; Marketing. **Benefits:** Dental Insurance; Disability Coverage; Life Insurance; Medical Insurance; Savings Plan; Stock Option; Tuition Assistance. **Special programs:** Internships. **Corporate headquarters location:** This Location. **Operations at this facility include:** Sales; Service. **Number of employees at this location:** 300.

MASTECH SYSTEMS CORPORATION

1004 McKee Road, Oakdale PA 15071. 412/787-2100. **Toll-free phone:** 800/311-1970. **Contact:** Personnel. **E-mail address:** exploretheworld@ mastech.com. **World Wide Web address:** http://www.mastech.com. **Description:** Provides high value information technology services including e-business solutions, enterprise solutions implementation, network services, and supply chain management solutions and applications design. **Common positions include:** Account Manager; Account Representative; Administrative Assistant; Applications Engineer; AS400 Programmer Analyst; CFO; Computer Animator; Computer Engineer; Computer Operator; Computer Programmer; Computer Support Technician; Computer Technician; Content Developer; Customer Service Rep.; Database Administrator; Database Manager; Finance Director; Financial Analyst; Fund Manager; Help-Desk Technician; Internet Services Manager; Intranet Developer; MIS Specialist; Network Engineer; Network Administrator; Purchasing Agent; Software Engineer; SQL Programmer; Systems Analyst; Systems Manager; Webmaster; Website Developer. **Educational backgrounds include:** Business Administration; C/C++; Computer Science; Engineering; Finance; HTML; Internet Development; Java; Microsoft Office; Software Development; Software Tech. Support. **Benefits:**

401(k); Casual Dress - Daily; Daycare Assistance; Dental Insurance; Employee Discounts; Life Insurance; Medical Insurance; Tuition Assistance. **Corporate headquarters location:** Pittsburgh PA. **Other U.S. locations:** San Francisco CA; Hartford CT; Atlanta GA; Raleigh NC; New York NY; Philadelphia PA; Dallas TX. **International locations:** Australia; Canada; India; Japan; Malaysia; New Zealand; Singapore; South Africa; Switzerland; the Netherlands; United Kingdom.

MATHSOFT, INC.
101 Main Street, Cambridge MA 02142. 617/577-1017. **Fax:** 617/577-8829. **Contact:** Personnel Representative. **E-mail address:** hrjobs@mathsoft.com. **World Wide Web address:** http://www.mathsoft.com. **Description:** A leading developer of mathematical software and electronic books for desktop computers. Products include Mathcad, a live interactive environment for mathematics work in a wide variety of fields including engineering, science, and education. MathSoft also publishes the Mathcad Library of Electronic Books, Maple V symbolic computation software, and other third-party mathematical software. Founded in 1984. **Common positions include:** Software Engineer. **Educational backgrounds include:** Engineering; Mathematics. **Benefits:** 401(k); Dental Insurance; Disability Coverage; Life Insurance; Medical Insurance; Savings Plan; Tuition Assistance. **Corporate headquarters location:** This Location. **Other U.S. locations:** Seattle WA. **Number of employees nationwide:** 150.

MATTEL INTERACTIVE
One Martha's Way, Hiawatha IA 52233. 319/395-9626. **Contact:** Human Resources. **Description:** Develops more than 80 software programs for a wide range of business applications and provides technical support services. **Corporate headquarters location:** This Location.

MAXTOR CORPORATION
510 Cottonwood Drive, Milpitas CA 95035. 408/432-1700. **Contact:** Human Resources. **World Wide Web address:** http://www.maxtor.com. **Description:** Manufactures hard disk drives and related electronic data storage equipment for computers, as well as related components for original equipment manufacturers. **Corporate headquarters location:** This Location. **International locations:** Hong Kong; Singapore.

MAXVISION CORPORATION
2705 Artie Street, Huntsville AL 35805. 256/533-5800. **Fax:** 256/533-5801. **Contact:** Personnel. **World Wide Web address:** http://www.maxvision.com. **Description:** A designer and manufacturer of Pentium Pro and Alpha-based Windows NT workstations for CAD/CAM/CAE uses. MaxVision is a leading 3-D technology developer. **Corporate headquarters location:** This Location.

MAXWELL SYSTEMS INC.
2860 DeKalb Pike, Norristown PA 19401. 610/277-3515. **Contact:** Human Resources. **Description:** This location is a computer training facility. Overall, Maxwell Systems sells software for construction, service, and related industries. **Corporate headquarters location:** This Location.

MEDITECH
MEDITECH Circle, Westwood MA 02090. 781/821-3000. **Contact:** Employment Specialist. **E-mail address:** jobs@meditech.com. **World Wide Web address:** http://www.meditech.com. **Description:** Develops, sells, installs, and supports computer software designed to help the medical community share critical information. **NOTE:**

Entry-level positions are offered. **Common positions include:** Computer Programmer; Dietician; EMT; Graphic Artist; Licensed Practical Nurse; Marketing Specialist; Medical Assistant; Medical Secretary; Registered Nurse; Sales Rep. **Educational backgrounds include:** Accounting; Biology; Business Administration; C/C++; Chemistry; Computer Science; Economics; Education; Finance; Health Care; Liberal Arts; Marketing; Mathematics; Software Development; Software Tech. Support. **Benefits:** Dental Insurance; Disability Coverage; Life Insurance; Medical Insurance; Profit Sharing; Sick Days (6 - 10); Tuition Assistance; Vacation Days (10 - 20). **Corporate headquarters location:** This Location. **Other U.S. locations:** Canton MA; Framingham MA; Norwood MA. **Operations at this facility include:** Research and Development; Sales; Service. **Number of employees nationwide:** 1,900.

THE MEDSTAT GROUP, INC.
777 East Eisenhower Parkway, Ann Arbor MI 48108. 734/996-1180. **Contact:** Human Resources. **World Wide Web address:** http://www.medstat.com. **Description:** A health care information, software, and consulting firm that designs and builds database systems for use in analyzing health care claims and benefits for large employers, insurance companies, and the research industry. **Common positions include:** Computer Programmer; Consultant; Data Analyst; Database Manager; Services Sales Rep. **Educational backgrounds include:** Business Administration; Communications; Computer Science; Finance; Health Care; Marketing. **Benefits:** Dental Insurance; Disability Coverage; Flexible Benefits; Life Insurance; Medical Insurance; Profit Sharing. **Corporate headquarters location:** This Location. **Other U.S. locations:** San Francisco CA; Atlanta GA; Boston MA; Nashville TN. **Operations at this facility include:** Administration; Research and Development; Sales; Service.

MENTOR GRAPHICS CORPORATION
8005 SW Boeckman Road, Wilsonville OR 97070-7777. 503/685-7000. **Recorded jobline:** 800/554-5259. **Contact:** Staffing. **World Wide Web address:** http://www.mentorg.com. **Description:** Develops electronic design automation (EDA) software used to automate the design, analysis, and documentation of electronic components and systems. The company is one of the world's leading suppliers of EDA software and professional services, and markets its products primarily to companies in the aerospace, computer, consumer electronics, semiconductor, and telecommunications industries. **Common positions include:** Software Engineer; Technical Writer/Editor. **Educational backgrounds include:** Computer Science. **Benefits:** 401(k); Daycare Assistance; Dental Insurance; Life Insurance; Medical Insurance; Tuition Assistance. **Special programs:** Internships. **Corporate headquarters location:** This Location. **Other U.S. locations:** San Jose CA; Warren NJ; Dallas TX. **Number of employees nationwide:** 1,900.

MERCATOR SOFTWARE
45 Danbury Road, Wilton CT 06897-0840. 203/761-8600. **Fax:** 203/761-8578. **Contact:** Ann Curry, Director of Human Resources. **E-mail address:** hr@mercator.com. **World Wide Web address:** http://www.mercator.com. **Description:** Develops electronic data interchange software (EDI) software that helps businesses become e-businesses. **Corporate headquarters location:** This Location.

MERCURY COMPUTER SYSTEMS, INC.
199 Riverneck Road, Chelmsford MA 01824. 978/256-1300. **Contact:** Lisa Weingarten, Human

Resources. **E-mail address:** lweingarten@mc.com. **World Wide Web address:** http://www.mc.com. **Description:** A leading provider of high-performance, real-time, embedded solutions for diverse applications including medical imaging, defense electronics, and shared storage configurations. **NOTE:** Entry-level positions are offered. **Common positions include:** Account Manager; Administrative Assistant; Computer Support Technician; Electrical Engineer; Financial Analyst; Manufacturing Engineer; Marketing Manager; MIS Specialist; Network Administrator; Software Engineer. **Educational backgrounds include:** C/C++; Computer Science; Engineering; Mathematics; Microsoft Word; Software Development; Software Tech. Support. **Benefits:** 401(k); Casual Dress - Daily; Dental Insurance; Disability Coverage; Flexible Schedule; Life Insurance; Medical Insurance; Profit Sharing; Tuition Assistance. **Special programs:** Internships; Co-ops; Summer Jobs. **Annual sales/revenues:** $51 - $100 million. **Number of employees nationwide:** 370.

MERCURY INTERACTIVE CORP.
1325 Borregas Avenue, Sunnyvale CA 94089. 408/822-5200. **Fax:** 408/822-5300. **Contact:** Human Resources. **World Wide Web address:** http://www.merc-int.com. **Description:** Develops automated software quality tools for enterprise applications testing. The company's products are used to isolate software and system errors prior to application deployment. **Corporate headquarters location:** This Location.

MERISEL, INC.
200 Continental Boulevard, El Segundo CA 90245. 310/615-3080. **Toll-free phone:** 800/201-1322. **Fax:** 310/615-6418. **Contact:** Human Resources. **E-mail address:** hr.elsegundo@merisel.com. **World Wide Web address:** http://www.merisel.com. **Description:** A wholesaler of computer hardware and software products. Merisel distributes products to computer resellers throughout the U.S. and Canada. **Common positions include:** Accountant; Claim Representative; Marketing Manager; Sales Representative. **Educational backgrounds include:** Accounting; Business Administration; Computer Science; Finance; Marketing; Public Relations. **Benefits:** 401(k); Casual Dress - Daily; Dental Insurance; Disability Coverage; Employee Discounts; Life Insurance; Medical Insurance; Tuition Assistance. **Office hours:** Monday - Friday, 8:30 a.m. - 5:30 p.m. **Corporate headquarters location:** This Location. **Other U.S. locations:** Marlborough MA; Cary NC. **International locations:** Canada. **Annual sales/revenues:** More than $100 million. **Number of employees at this location:** 800. **Number of employees nationwide:** 1,500. **Number of employees worldwide:** 2,500.

MESQUITE SOFTWARE, INC.
P.O. Box 26306, Austin TX 78755. 512/338-9153. **Contact:** Human Resources. **World Wide Web address:** http://www.mesquite.com. **Description:** Develops software and provides support services for the system simulation market. The company's product line includes CSIM18-The Simulation Engine, a process-oriented, general purpose simulation toolkit. **Corporate headquarters location:** This Location.

META SOFTWARE CORPORATION
125 Cambridge Park Drive, Cambridge MA 02140. 617/576-6920. **Fax:** 617/661-2008. **Contact:** Personnel. **E-mail address:** resumes@metasoft.com. **World Wide Web address:** http://www.metasoftware.com. **Description:** Develops business process re-engineering software and provides

consulting services. Founded in 1985. **Common positions include:** Applications Engineer; Sales Executive. **Benefits:** 401(k); Dental Insurance; Disability Coverage; Education Assistance; Life Insurance; Medical Insurance. **Corporate headquarters location:** This Location.

METAMOR GLOBAL SOLUTIONS
133 Technology Drive, Suite 200, Irvine CA 92618. 949/450-4600. **Toll-free phone:** 800/315-8306. **Fax:** 949/450-4658. **Contact:** Joni Walton, Human Resources Manager. **E-mail address:** joni.walton@metamorgs.com. **World Wide Web address:** http://www.metamor.com. **Description:** A software development and consulting firm providing systems and software applications to the transportation, finance, health care, and insurance industries. **Common positions include:** Account Manager; Accountant; Administrative Assistant; Advertising Executive; CFO; Computer Engineer; Computer Support Technician; Controller; Database Administrator; Database Manager; Desktop Publishing Specialist; Event Planner; Financial Analyst; Graphic Artist; Graphic Designer; Help-Desk Technician; Human Resources Manager; Internet Services Manager; Market Research Analyst; Marketing Manager; Marketing Specialist; MIS Specialist; Network Engineer; Network Administrator; Operations Manager; Project Manager; Public Relations Specialist; Purchasing Agent; Sales Executive; Sales Manager; Sales Rep.; Secretary; Software Engineer; Systems Analyst; Systems Manager; Technical Writer/Editor; Typist; Webmaster. **Educational backgrounds include:** Accounting; AS400 Certification; Business Administration; C/C++; Communications; Computer Science; Finance; HTML; Internet Development; Java; Liberal Arts; Marketing; MBA; MCSE; Microsoft Office; Microsoft Word; Public Relations; QuarkXPress; Software Development; Software Tech. Support; Spreadsheets; Visual Basic. **Benefits:** 401(k); Casual Dress - Fridays; Dental Insurance; Disability Coverage; Employee Discounts; Life Insurance; Medical Insurance; Relocation Assistance; Savings Plan; Vacation Days (11 - 15). **Corporate headquarters location:** This Location. **International locations:** Worldwide. **Parent company:** Metamor Worldwide. **Annual sales/revenues:** $51 - $100 million. **Number of employees at this location:** 50. **Number of employees nationwide:** 320. **Number of employees worldwide:** 1,500.

MICRO DATA BASE SYSTEMS INC.
P.O. Box 2438, West Lafayette IN 47996. 765/463-7200. **Contact:** Human Resources Department. **World Wide Web address:** http://www.mdbs.com. **Description:** Manufactures database management systems software for small computers and artificial intelligence systems. **Educational backgrounds include:** Accounting; Business Administration; Computer Science; Marketing. **Benefits:** Dental Insurance; Life Insurance; Medical Insurance; Profit Sharing. **Corporate headquarters location:** This Location. **Other U.S. locations:** Shaumburg IL. **Operations at this facility include:** Computer Programming; Research and Development; Service.

MICRO 2000, INC.
1100 East Broadway, Suite 301, Glendale CA 91205. 818/547-0125. **Fax:** 818/502-0086. **Contact:** Jacqui Mendelsohn, Vice President of Administration. **World Wide Web address:** http://www.micro2000.com. **Description:** Develops and markets computer diagnostic products for troubleshooting. Founded in 1990. **Common positions include:** Customer Service Rep.; Sales Executive; Software Engineer; Technical Support Representative. **Educational backgrounds include:**

Computer Science; Engineering. **Benefits:** Credit Union; Dental Insurance; Disability Coverage; Medical Insurance. **Corporate headquarters location:** This Location. **International locations:** Australia; Germany; Holland; United Kingdom.

MICRO-INTEGRATION CORPORATION
One Science Park, Frostburg MD 21532. 301/689-2811. **Contact:** Ms. Terry Frost, Human Resources Manager. **Description:** Develops communications software for use in a variety of industries. **Corporate headquarters location:** This Location.

MICROAGE
2400 South MicroAge Way, Tempe AZ 85282. 480/366-2000. **Contact:** Human Resources. **World Wide Web address:** http://www.microage.com. **Description:** Provides information technology products and services to institutions and governmental agencies throughout the country and corporations worldwide. **Corporate headquarters location:** This Location. **Subsidiaries include:** MicroAge Channel Services provides purchasing and marketing services for resellers and vendors. MicroAge Infosystems Services coordinates and services large-account marketing efforts in conjunction with franchised resellers. MicroAge Product Services provides distribution, logistics, technical, and outsourcing services. MicroAge Technologies markets to value-added resellers. **Number of employees nationwide:** 6,100.

MICROELECTRONICS & COMPUTER TECHNOLOGY CORPORATION
3500 West Balcones Center Drive, Austin TX 78759-5398. 512/343-0978. **Fax:** 512/338-3894. **Contact:** Personnel. **World Wide Web address:** http://www.mcc.com. **Description:** Provides research and consulting services for software, information technology, and electronics companies. **Common positions include:** Buyer; Computer Programmer; Controller; Design Engineer; Electrical Engineer; Hardware Engineer; Human Resources Manager; Internet Services Manager; Marketing Manager; MIS Specialist; Project Manager; Software Engineer; Systems Analyst; Webmaster. **Educational backgrounds include:** Business Administration; Computer Science; Engineering; Finance; Marketing; Mathematics; Physics. **Benefits:** Dental Insurance; Disability Coverage; Employee Discounts; Life Insurance; Medical Insurance; Profit Sharing; Savings Plan; Telecommuting; Tuition Assistance. **Corporate headquarters location:** This Location. **Other U.S. locations:** Santa Clara CA. **Number of employees at this location:** 130.

MICROFRONTIER, INC.
P.O. Box 71190, Des Moines IA 50325. 515/225-9800. **Fax:** 515/996-9022. **Contact:** Personnel. **E-mail address:** mfi@microfrontier.com. **World Wide Web address:** http://www.microfrontier.com. **Description:** Develops graphic arts software. **NOTE:** Entry-level positions are offered. **Common positions include:** Computer Programmer; Marketing Manager; Marketing Specialist; Sales Representative; Software Engineer. **Educational backgrounds include:** Computer Science; Marketing. **Benefits:** Dental Insurance; Life Insurance; Medical Insurance. **Corporate headquarters location:** This Location.

MICROGRAFX, INC.
505 Millennium Drive, Allen TX 75013. 972/234-1769. **Fax:** 972/994-6036. **Contact:** Personnel. **World Wide Web address:** http://www.micrografx.com. **Description:** Develops, markets, and supports a line of graphic application software products for IBM PCs and compatibles running under the Microsoft Windows operating environment. Products are designed for both business and professional use and include professional illustration, basic drawing and charting products, data-driven graphics, image editing, and reusable clip-art libraries. Micrografx, Inc. also offers systems software products designed to enhance the Windows and OS/2 operating environments. **Common positions include:** Account Rep.; Applications Engineer; Computer Programmer; Sales Rep.; Software Engineer; Systems Analyst. **Educational backgrounds include:** Business Administration; Computer Science; Engineering; Finance; Marketing. **Benefits:** 401(k); Dental Insurance; Disability Coverage; Employee Discounts; Life Insurance; Medical Insurance; Tuition Assistance. **Corporate headquarters location:** This Location. **International locations:** Australia; Italy; Japan; United Kingdom. **Listed on:** NASDAQ. **Number of employees at this location:** 200. **Number of employees worldwide:** 300.

MICROLOG CORPORATION
20270 Goldenrod Lane, Germantown MD 20876. 301/428-9100. **Fax:** 301/916-2471. **Contact:** Barbara Joltin, Technical Recruiter. **E-mail address:** bjoltin@mlog.com. **World Wide Web address:** http://www.mlog.com. **Description:** Designs, assembles, and supports a line of interactive communications systems and application solutions software for customers worldwide. **Common positions include:** Account Rep.; Sales Executive; Software Engineer. **Educational backgrounds include:** Computer Science; Software Development; Software Tech. Support. **Benefits:** 401(k); Dental Insurance; Disability Coverage; Life Insurance; Medical Insurance; Pension Plan; Profit Sharing; Tuition Assistance. **Corporate headquarters location:** This Location. **International locations:** The Netherlands. **President/CEO:** Richard A. Thompson. **Number of employees at this location:** 105. **Number of employees nationwide:** 300.

MICROMATH SCIENTIFIC SOFTWARE
P.O. Box 71550, Salt Lake City UT 84171-0550. 801/483-2949. **Toll-free phone:** 800/942-6284. **Fax:** 801/483-3025. **Contact:** Human Resources. **World Wide Web address:** http://www.micromath.com. **Description:** Develops scientific software. **Corporate headquarters location:** This Location.

MICRON TECHNOLOGY, INC.
8000 South Federal Way, P.O. Box 6, Boise ID 83707-0006. 208/368-3700. **Fax:** 208/368-4641. **Recorded jobline:** 800/932-4991. **Contact:** Human Resources. **E-mail address:** hrwebmaster@micron.com. **World Wide Web address:** http://www.micron.com. **Description:** Manufactures and markets 16- and 64-megabyte dynamic random access memory (DRAM) components in varying word widths (x4, x8, x16); Graphics DRAMs; Synchronous SRAMs, pipelined and non-pipelined; and Flash Memory. The company also manufactures integrated circuits and small semiconductor dies. Products are used by the computer, consumer electronics, telecommunications, and data processing industries. **Common positions include:** Chemical Engineer; Computer Programmer; Electrical/Electronics Engineer; Software Engineer. **Educational backgrounds include:** Chemistry; Computer Science; Engineering. **Benefits:** 401(k); Dental Insurance; Disability Coverage; Life Insurance; Medical Insurance; Profit Sharing; Tuition Assistance. **Special programs:** Internships. **Corporate headquarters location:** This Location. **Subsidiaries include:** Micron Communications; Micron Display Technology; Micron Europe Limited; Micron Quantum Devices, Inc.; Micron

Semiconductor (Deutschland) GmbH; Micron Semiconductor Asia Pacific Pte. Ltd.; Micron Semiconductor Asia Pacific, Inc.; Micron Semiconductor Products, Inc.; Micron Technology Japan, K.K. **Operations at this facility include:** Administration; Manufacturing; Research and Development; Sales. **President/CEO:** Steve Appleton. **Number of employees at this location:** 7,825. **Number of employees nationwide:** 11,400. **Other U.S. locations:**

- Micron Electronics, Inc., 900 East Karcher Road, Nampa ID 83687. 208/898-3920.

MICROS SYSTEMS, INC.
12000 Baltimore Avenue, Beltsville MD 20705. 301/210-6000. **Fax:** 301/210-3727. **Contact:** Human Resources. **E-mail address:** employment@ micros.com. **World Wide Web address:** http://www.micros.com. **Description:** Engaged in enterprise systems integration for the leisure and entertainment industries. **NOTE:** Entry-level positions are offered. **Common positions include:** Accountant; Computer Programmer; Design Engineer; Electrical Engineer; Network Engineer; Software Engineer; Technical Writer. **Educational backgrounds include:** Accounting; Computer Science; Engineering; Hospital Administration. **Benefits:** 401(k); Dental Insurance; Disability Coverage; Life Insurance; Medical Insurance; Public Transit Available; Tuition Assistance; Vision Plan. **Special programs:** Internships. **Corporate headquarters location:** This Location. **Other U.S. locations:** Nationwide. **International locations:** Worldwide. **Subsidiaries include:** Fidelio Software Corporation; Fidelio Software GmbH. **Operations at this facility include:** Administration; Manufacturing; Research and Development; Sales; Service. **Annual sales/revenues:** More than $100 million. **Number of employees nationwide:** 900. **Number of employees worldwide:** 1,100.

MICROSOFT CORPORATION
One Microsoft Way, Redmond WA 98052-6399. 425/882-8080. **Contact:** Recruiting Department/NJB. **World Wide Web address:** http://www. microsoft.com/jobs. **Description:** Designs, sells, and supports a product line of systems and applications software for business, home, and professional use. Microsoft also produces related books and hardware products. Software products include spreadsheet, desktop publishing, project management, graphics, word processing, and database applications, as well as operating systems and programming languages. **Corporate headquarters location:** This Location. **Annual sales/revenues:** More than $100 million.

MICROTECH COMPUTERS, INC.
4921 Legends Drive, Lawrence KS 66049. 785/841-9513. **Fax:** 785/841-1809. **Contact:** Personnel Manager. **World Wide Web address:** http://www. microtechcomp.com. **Description:** Develops, manufactures, markets, installs, and services personal computers and related equipment. Primary customers are end users, retailers, corporations, and government agencies. **Company slogan:** Your key business partner. **Common positions include:** Account Manager; Account Rep.; Accountant; Administrator; Advertising Clerk; Computer Engineer; Computer Programmer; Computer Support Technician; Computer Technician; Credit Manager; Customer Service Rep.; Department Manager; Electrical Engineer; Financial Analyst; Hardware Engineer; Help-Desk Technician; Manufacturer's Sales Rep.; Marketing Specialist; MIS Specialist; Network Engineer; Network Administrator; Operations Manager; Production Manager; Public Relations Specialist; Quality Control Supervisor; Sales Executive; Sales Manager; Sales Rep.; Secretary; Systems Analyst; Technical Support Manager; Typist; Web Advertising Specialist; Webmaster; Website Developer. **Educational backgrounds include:** Accounting; Business Administration; CGI; Cold Fusion; Communications; Computer Science; Education; Engineering; Finance; HTML; Internet Development; Java; Journalism; Liberal Arts; Marketing; MCSE; Microsoft Office; Microsoft Word; Spreadsheets. **Benefits:** Casual Dress - Daily; Dental Insurance; Disability Coverage; Employee Discounts; Flexible Schedule; Life Insurance; Medical Insurance; Profit Sharing; Sick Days (6 - 10); Tuition Assistance; Vacation Days (6 - 10). **Corporate headquarters location:** This Location. **Other U.S. locations:** Denver CO. **Subsidiaries include:** A-Plus Open; MicroOpen. **Operations at this facility include:** Administration; Manufacturing; Research and Development; Sales; Service. **President:** Mike Zheng. **Facilities Manager:** Darryl Stone. **Information Systems Manager:** Qiwu Liu. **Sales Manager:** Kurt Schaffer. **Number of employees nationwide:** 120.

MICROTOUCH SYSTEMS, INC.
300 Griffin Brook Park, Methuen MA 01844. 978/659-9000. **Fax:** 978/659-9100. **Contact:** Personnel. **E-mail address:** jobs@microtouch.com. **World Wide Web address:** http://www. microtouch.com. **Description:** A manufacturer of touch-screen products. Products are used in a broad range of applications including point-of-sale terminals, self-service kiosks, gaming machines, industrial systems, ATMs, multimedia applications, and many other computer-based systems. MicroTouch also manufactures and markets TouchPen, a touch- and pen-sensitive digitizer used for pen-based and whiteboarding applications; TouchMate, a pressure-sensitive pad that makes any monitor placed on it touch-sensitive; and ThruGlass, a product that can sense a touch through up to two inches of glass, allowing kiosks to be placed behind store windows for 24-hour access. **Corporate headquarters location:** This Location.

MIDWEST CAD SYSTEMS
4119 Brown's Lane, Suite 3, Louisville KY 40220-1500. 502/452-6743. **Fax:** 502/452-1105. **Contact:** Personnel. **World Wide Web address:** http://www. midwest-cad.com. **Description:** A reseller of AUTOCAD systems. **Corporate headquarters location:** This Location.

MILLENNIUM SOFTWARE, INC.
1503 Goodwin Road, Ruston LA 71270. 318/251-2392. **Fax:** 318/255-7397. **Contact:** Personnel. **World Wide Web address:** http://www. millennium-software.com. **Description:** Develops PC-HAP housing management software. **NOTE:** Entry-level positions are offered. **Common positions include:** Accountant; Computer Operator; Computer Programmer; Computer Support Technician; Technical Writer. **Educational backgrounds include:** Microsoft Word; Software Development; Software Tech. Support; Spreadsheets. **Benefits:** Casual Dress - Daily; Dental Insurance; Employee Discounts; Life Insurance; Medical Insurance; Pension Plan; Savings Plan; Sick Days. **Corporate headquarters location:** This Location. **President:** Mark Lewis. **Sales Manager:** Lela Bryan.

MILTOPE CORPORATION
76 Pearl Street, Springfield VT 05156. 802/885-4100. **Contact:** Sandi D'Amore, Office Manager. **World Wide Web address:** http://www.miltope. com. **Description:** Manufactures disk drives. **Parent company:** Miltope Group, Inc.

MINDSPRING ENTERPRISES, INC.
1430 West Peachtree Street NW, Atlanta GA 30309.
404/815-0770. **Toll-free phone:** 800/719-4664.
Contact: Human Resources. **World Wide Web
address:** http://www.mindspring.net. **Description:**
Provides Internet access and Web hosting services
to individuals and small businesses. Founded in
1994. **Corporate headquarters location:** This
Location. **Other area locations:** Columbus GA;
West Point GA.
Other U.S. locations:
• 2 North Second Street, Plaza A, San Jose CA
95113.

MIPS TECHNOLOGIES, INC.
1225 Charleston Road, Mountain View CA 94043.
650/567-5052. **Fax:** 650/567-5150. **Contact:**
Human Resources. **World Wide Web address:**
http://www.mips.com. **Description:** Designs 32-
and 64-bit RISC processors for license to
semiconductor suppliers. MIPS Technologies'
products are then embedded in such items as digital
cameras, handheld computing devices, and video
game systems. **Common positions include:**
Applications Engineer; Computer Engineer;
Computer Scientist; Design Engineer; Software
Engineer. **Benefits:** 401(k); Bonus Award/Plan;
Casual Dress - Daily; Dental Insurance; Disability
Coverage; Flexible Schedule; Life Insurance;
Medical Insurance.

MODIS
One Independent Drive, Jacksonville FL 32202.
Toll-free phone: 877/MODIS-IT. **Fax:** 904/360-
2110. **Contact:** Personnel. **World Wide Web
address:** http://www.modisit.com. **Description:**
Provides a wide range of computer consulting
services. **Corporate headquarters location:** This
Location. **Other U.S. locations:** Nationwide.

**MOORE NORTH AMERICA
PUBLICATIONS GROUP**
2117 West River Road North, Minneapolis MN
55411. 612/588-7200. **Contact:** Human Resources.
Description: Provides commercial printing and
electronic, on-demand, and database publishing to
Fortune 500 companies. **Corporate headquarters
location:** Bannockburn IL. **Other U.S. locations:**
Nationwide. **Parent company:** Moore Corporation.
Number of employees at this location: 100.

MOTOROLA COMPUTER GROUP
2900 South Diablo Way, Tempe AZ 85282.
602/438-3000. **Contact:** Human Resources. **World
Wide Web address:** http://www.mcg.mot.com.
Description: This location manufactures computer
hardware. Overall, Motorola Computer Group
supplies embedded computer technology. The
Embedded Technologies group manufactures
embedded board lines. The Technical Systems
group manufactures electronic products used in
industrial automation, electronic imaging, and
communications applications. The New Ventures
group researches emerging technologies. **Corporate
headquarters location:** This Location.

MPCT SOLUTIONS CORPORATION
180 North Stetson Street, 42nd Floor, Chicago IL
60601. 312/540-0100. **Fax:** 312/540-0118.
Contact: Gerri Floyd, Employee Services Analyst.
E-mail address: gerri.floyd@mpct.com. **World
Wide Web address:** http://www.mpct.com.
Description: Designs and develops solutions for
financial institutions including the ATLAS software
product line, a series of financial transaction
processing systems which allow companies to
increase productivity and reduce operating costs.
Common positions include: Bank Officer;
Computer Programmer; Database Manager;

Financial Analyst; Online Content Specialist;
Software Engineer; Technical Writer; Webmaster.
Educational backgrounds include: Accounting;
Computer Science; Finance; Mathematics; Software
Development; Software Tech. Support. **Benefits:**
401(k); Dental Insurance; Disability Coverage;
Flexible Schedule; Life Insurance; Medical
Insurance; Public Transit Available; Tuition
Assistance. **Office hours:** Monday - Friday, 8:30
a.m. - 5:00 p.m. **Corporate headquarters location:**
This Location. **Number of employees at this
location:** 140. **Number of employees worldwide:**
400.

MULTIMAX, INC.
1441 McCormick Drive, Largo MD 20774.
301/925-8222. **Contact:** Human Resources. **World
Wide Web address:** http://www.multimax.com.
Description: Provides LAN/WAN design and
networking services. **Corporate headquarters
location:** This Location.

MUZE INC.
304 Hudson Street, 8th Floor, New York NY 10013.
212/824-0300. **Contact:** Jeanne Petras, Director of
Human Resources. **World Wide Web address:**
http://www.muze.com. **Description:** Muze is a
multimedia company that develops software for
touch-screen, point-of-sales terminals which allow
users access to a musical database. **Common
positions include:** Accountant; Administrative
Manager; Budget Analyst; Computer Programmer;
Financial Analyst; Human Resources Manager;
Purchasing Agent/Manager; Sales Executive; Sales
Manager; Sales Rep.; Software Engineer; Systems
Analyst. **Educational backgrounds include:**
Art/Design; Communications; Computer Science;
Finance; Liberal Arts; Marketing. **Benefits:** 401(k);
Medical Insurance. **Special programs:** Internships.
Corporate headquarters location: This Location.
Parent company: MetroMedia. **Operations at this
facility include:** Manufacturing; Research and
Development; Sales; Service. **Listed on:** Privately
held. **Number of employees at this location:** 120.

MYLEX CORPORATION
34551 Ardenwood Boulevard, Fremont CA 94555.
510/796-6100. **Contact:** Human Resources. **World
Wide Web address:** http://www.mylex.com.
Description: Designs and manufactures disk array
controllers, system boards, and network interface
cards. The company also supports proprietary
software for a wide range of personal computers,
workstations, and servers. Mylex is a world leader
in RAID (Redundant Array of Independent Disks)
technology. **Corporate headquarters location:**
This Location.

NBC INTERNET
300 Montgomery Street, 3rd Floor, San Francisco
CA 94104. 415/288-2500. **Contact:** Personnel.
World Wide Web address: http://www.nbci.com.
Description: A global integrated media company
that uses the Internet, broadcast and cable
television, and radio to connect advertisers and
partners with users and customers.

NCR CORPORATION
1700 South Patterson Boulevard, WHQ-3, Dayton
OH 45479-0001. 937/445-5000. **Contact:** College
Relations Consultant. **World Wide Web address:**
http://www.ncr.com. **Description:** Provides
computer products and services through five groups.
The company provides computer solutions to three
targeted industries: retail, financial, and
communication. NCR Computer Systems Group
develops, manufactures, and markets computer
systems. NCR Financial Systems Group is an
industry leader in three target areas: financial

delivery systems, relationship banking data warehousing solutions, and payments systems/item processing. NCR Retail Systems Group is a world leader in end-to-end retail solutions serving the food, general merchandise, and hospitality industries. NCR Worldwide Services provides data warehousing services solutions; end-to-end networking services; and designs, implements, and supports complex open systems environments. NCR Systemedia Group develops, produces, and markets a complete line of information technology products including transaction processing media, auto identification media, business form communication products, managing documents and media, and a full line of integrated equipment solutions. **Educational backgrounds include:** Business Administration; Computer Science. **Benefits:** 401(k); Dental Insurance; Disability Coverage; Life Insurance; Medical Insurance; Pension Plan; Profit Sharing; Savings Plan; Tuition Assistance. **Special programs:** Internships. **Corporate headquarters location:** This Location. **Other U.S. locations:** Nationwide. **Annual sales/revenues:** More than $100 million. **Number of employees nationwide:** 19,000. **Number of employees worldwide:** 38,000.

NDC HEALTH INFORMATION SERVICES
6100 South Yale Avenue, Suite 1900, Tulsa OK 74136. 918/496-2451. **Contact:** Personnel. **World Wide Web address:** http://www.ndchealth.com. **Description:** Develops software and Web-base applications used by hospitals and other health care providers for electronic billing and other EDI transactions.

NEC AMERICA INC.
14040 Park Center Road, Herndon VA 20171. 703/834-4000. **Contact:** Personnel. **World Wide Web address:** http://www.nec.com. **Description:** Manufactures communications systems and equipment, computers, industrial electronic systems, electronic devices, and home electronic products.

NEC CORPORATION
P.O. Box 299002, Mail Station 150-14, Sacramento CA 95828-9002. 916/388-0101. **Fax:** 916/388-5459. **Recorded jobline:** 800/382-6444. **Contact:** Human Resources. **Description:** One of the world's largest designers, manufacturers, and marketers of a wide range of PC-compatible desktop and laptop computers. **Common positions include:** Accountant; Applications Engineer; Business Analyst; Computer Programmer; Contract Administrator; Database Manager; Design Engineer; Desktop Publishing Specialist; Editor; Employee Relations Director; Facilities Engineer; Financial Analyst; Graphic Artist; Industrial Engineer; Manufacturing Engineer; MIS Specialist; Process Engineer; Product Engineer; Quality Assurance Engineer; Safety Specialist; Sales Rep.; Software Engineer; Systems Engineer; Technical Support Rep. **Corporate headquarters location:** This Location. **Other U.S. locations:** Westlake CA; Magna UT; Fife WA. **Subsidiaries include:** Zenith Data Systems Corporation, 2150 East Lake Cook Road, Buffalo Grove IL 60089, 847/808-5000. **Annual sales/revenues:** More than $100 million.

NATIONAL COMPUTER SYSTEMS (NCS)
11000 Prairie Lakes Drive, Eden Prairie MN 55344. 952/829-3000. **Toll-free phone:** 800/431-1421. **Contact:** Mark Sullivan, Director of Sourcing and Staffing. **World Wide Web address:** http://www.ncs.com. **Description:** A global information services company providing software, service, and systems for the collection, management, and interpretation of data. **NOTE:** Entry-level positions are offered. **Common positions include:** Account Manager; Applications Engineer; Computer Programmer; Database Manager; Financial Analyst; Internet Services Manager; Project Manager; Systems Analyst; Systems Engineer; Systems Manager; Webmaster. **Educational backgrounds include:** Accounting; Computer Science; Engineering; Mathematics; Software Development; Software Tech. Support. **Benefits:** 401(k); Dental Insurance; Disability Coverage; Flexible Schedule; Life Insurance; Medical Insurance; Tuition Assistance. **Special programs:** Internships. **Corporate headquarters location:** This Location. **Other U.S. locations:** Mesa AZ; Laguna Hills CA; Iowa City IA; Edina MN. **Annual sales/revenues:** More than $100 million. **Number of employees nationwide:** 3,000.

NATIONAL SYSTEMS AND RESEARCH CO.
5385 Mark Dabbling Boulevard, Suite 200, Colorado Springs CO 80918. 719/590-8880. **Contact:** Human Resources Department. **World Wide Web address:** http://www.nsr.com. **Description:** Provides ADP support services including software development and testing for commercial and government clients in the aerospace industry. **Common positions include:** Accountant; Branch Manager; Computer Operator; Computer Programmer; Department Manager; Electrical Engineer; Payroll Clerk; Receptionist; Secretary; Software Engineer; Systems Analyst; Typist. **Educational backgrounds include:** Business Administration; Computer Science; Engineering. **Benefits:** 401(k); Dental Insurance; Disability Coverage; Life Insurance; Medical Insurance; Savings Plan; Tuition Assistance. **Corporate headquarters location:** This Location. **Other area locations:** Boulder CO; Golden CO; Loveland CO. **Other U.S. locations:** Camarillo CA; Tulsa OK; Portland OR; Vancouver WA. **Subsidiaries include:** NSR Information, Inc. **Number of employees nationwide:** 500.

NAVIGATION TECHNOLOGIES
740 East Arques, Sunnyvale CA 94086-3833. 408/737-3200. **Toll-free phone:** 800/888-7222. **Fax:** 408/730-0691. **Contact:** Human Resources. **World Wide Web address:** http://www.navtech.com. **Description:** Develops digital databases for in-vehicle navigation systems. **NOTE:** Entry-level positions are offered. **Common positions include:** Accountant; Geographer; Market Research Analyst; Marketing Manager; Marketing Specialist; Sales Executive; Sales Rep. **Educational backgrounds include:** Geography. **Benefits:** 401(k); Dental Insurance; Disability Coverage; Life Insurance; Medical Insurance. **Corporate headquarters location:** This Location. **Other U.S. locations:** Fargo ND. **International locations:** Canada; Europe; Japan. **Number of employees at this location:** 150. **Number of employees nationwide:** 400. **Number of employees worldwide:** 800.

NET.GENESIS CORPORATION
150 Cambridge Park Drive, Cambridge MA 02140. 617/577-9800. **Contact:** Human Resources. **World Wide Web address:** http://www.netgen.com. **Description:** A provider of solutions for improving Internet service performance and usage. The products of net.Genesis allow users to analyze customers' behavior on the Internet. **Corporate headquarters location:** This Location.

NETMANAGE, INC.
11332 NE 122nd Way, Kirkland WA 98034. 425/814-9255. **Contact:** Human Resources. **World Wide Web address:** http://www.netmanage.com. **Description:** Develops, markets, and supports Windows-based connectivity software and associated applications tools. The company's software products provide PC users easy access to

and use of computer applications and data residing on multiple host mainframes and minicomputers in enterprisewide information systems networks. **Common positions include:** Account Manager; Account Rep.; Accountant; Administrative Assistant; Applications Engineer; AS400 Programmer Analyst; Attorney; Budget Analyst; Buyer; CFO; Computer Programmer; Computer Support Technician; Controller; Database Administrator; Desktop Publishing Specialist; Editor; Financial Analyst; Graphic Artist; Graphic Designer; Help-Desk Technician; Human Resources Manager; Instructional Technologist; Marketing Manager; Marketing Specialist; Multimedia Designer; Operations Manager; Paralegal; Public Relations Specialist; Sales Manager; Software Engineer; SQL Programmer; Systems Analyst; Systems Manager; Technical Support Manager; Technical Writer; Vice President of Marketing and Sales; Vice President of Operations; Web Advertising Specialist; Webmaster; Website Developer. **Educational backgrounds include:** C/C++; Computer Science; HTML; Java; Marketing; MBA; MCSE; Microsoft Office; Microsoft Word; Software Development; Software Tech. Support; Visual Basic. **Benefits:** 401(k); Casual Dress - Fridays; Dental Insurance; Disability Coverage; Life Insurance; Medical Insurance; Profit Sharing. **Corporate headquarters location:** Cupertino CA.

NETPRO COMPUTING, INC.
7150 East Camelback Road, Suite 100, Scottsdale AZ 85251. 480/941-3600. **Contact:** Human Resources. **E-mail address:** tonir@netpro.com. **World Wide Web address:** http://www.netpro.com. **Description:** Designs and sells directory services management software. **Company slogan:** The directory experts. **Common positions include:** Account Manager; Account Rep.; CFO; Computer Support Technician; Sales Engineer; Sales Rep.; Software Engineer; Systems Analyst; Technical Writer; Webmaster. **Educational backgrounds include:** C/C++; Computer Science; Engineering; Java; Mathematics; MCSE; Microsoft Word; Novell; Software Development; Software Tech. Support. **Benefits:** 401(k); Casual Dress - Daily; Dental Insurance; Disability Coverage; Employee Discounts; Flexible Schedule; Life Insurance; Medical Insurance; Public Transit Available; Sick Days (1 - 5); Telecommuting; Tuition Assistance; Vacation Days (11 - 15). **Special programs:** Internships; Summer Jobs. **Corporate headquarters location:** This Location. **Other area locations:** Tucson AZ. **Number of employees nationwide:** 95.

NETRIX CORPORATION
13595 Dulles Technology Drive, Herndon VA 20171. 703/742-6000. **Fax:** 703/793-2082. **Contact:** Sharon Devonshire, Vice President of Human Resources. **E-mail address:** jobs@netrix.com. **World Wide Web address:** http://www.netrix.com. **Description:** Manufactures WAN switching products that incorporate compressed-voice technology. **Corporate headquarters location:** This Location. **Other U.S. locations:** Los Angeles CA; San Francisco CA; Atlanta GA; Chicago IL; Boston MA; New York NY; Pittsburgh PA; Houston TX. **International locations:** United Kingdom. **Subsidiaries include:** Netrix International Corp.; Netrix Telcom Systems Corp. **Number of employees worldwide:** 295.

NETSCAPE COMMUNICATIONS CORP.
501 East Middlefield Road, Mountain View CA 94043. 650/254-1900. **Fax:** 650/937-5451. **Contact:** Personnel. **World Wide Web address:** http://www.home.netscape.com. **Description:** An

Internet service provider. The company also develops software including the brand name Constellation. **NOTE:** In January 2000, America Online, Inc. and Time Warner, Inc. announced plans to merge. The new company will be named AOL Time Warner Inc. Please contact this location for more information. **Common positions include:** Client/Server Specialist; Computer Engineer; Computer Programmer; Sales Representative; Software Engineer; Technical Writer/Editor. **Corporate headquarters location:** This Location. **Other area locations:** Manhattan Beach CA. **Other U.S. locations:** Washington DC; Atlanta GA; Chicago IL; New York NY; Dallas TX. **Parent company:** America Online, Inc. (AOL).

NETWORK COMPUTING DEVICES, INC.
350 North Bernardo Avenue, Mountain View CA 94043. 650/694-0650. **Toll-free phone:** 800/866-4080. **Fax:** 650/961-7711. **Contact:** Human Resources. **E-mail address:** resumes@ncd.com. **World Wide Web address:** http://www.ncd.com. **Description:** Provides desktop information access solutions for network computing environments. The company is a leading worldwide supplier of X Window System terminals and PC-X server software products which integrate Microsoft Windows- and DOS-based PCs into X/UNIX networks. The company also supplies the Z-Mail family of cross-platform electronic mail and messaging software for open systems environments, as well as Mariner, an Internet access and navigation software tool that provides a unified interface to all Internet resources. **Common positions include:** Administrative Assistant; Buyer; Marketing Manager; Sales Rep.; Software Engineer; Systems Engineer; Technical Support Rep.; Webmaster. **Benefits:** 401(k); Credit Union; Dental Insurance; Disability Coverage; EAP; Flexible Benefits; Life Insurance; Long-Term Care; Medical Insurance; Sabbatical Leave; Stock Purchase; Tuition Assistance; Vision Insurance. **Corporate headquarters location:** This Location.

NETWORK SIX INC.
475 Kilvert Street, Warwick RI 02886. 401/732-9000. **Fax:** 401/732-9009. **Contact:** Human Resources. **World Wide Web address:** http://www.networksix.com. **Description:** Provides systems integration and consulting services to state government human services agencies. The company provides project management, systems design, software development, hardware procurement and installation, training, and data conversion services. The company's Network Services Division provides network administration, LAN/WAN support, Internet/Intranet support, Web page development, remote communication, and LAN/Legacy system integration to existing customers. **Common positions include:** Computer Programmer; Database Manager; Network Administrator; Network Engineer; Systems Analyst; Technical Writer; Webmaster. **Educational backgrounds include:** Business Administration; Computer Science; Mathematics. **Benefits:** 401(k); Dental Insurance; Disability Coverage; Life Insurance; Medical Insurance; Profit Sharing. **Corporate headquarters location:** This Location. **Other U.S. locations:** ID; ME; WV. **Number of employees nationwide:** 80.

NETWORK SOLUTIONS, INC. (NSI)
505 Huntmar Park Drive, Herndon VA 20170. 703/742-0400. **Fax:** 703/742-4837. **Contact:** Staffing Manager. **World Wide Web address:** http://www.netsol.com. **Description:** Provides domain registration services for the Internet. **Common positions include:** Computer Programmer; Systems Manager. **Parent company:** Science Applications International Corporation.

NEWBRIDGE NETWORKS, INC.
2400 Camino Ramon, Suite 325, San Ramon CA 94583. 925/824-4200. **Contact:** Human Resources. **World Wide Web address:** http://www.newbridge. com. **Description:** Designs computer networks. **NOTE:** Resumes should be sent to Human Resources, Newbridge Networks, Inc., 593 Herndon Parkway, Herndon VA 20170. **Common positions include:** Accountant; Buyer; Customer Service Rep.; Electrical Engineer; Financial Analyst; Human Resources Manager; Public Relations Specialist; Software Engineer; Systems Analyst; Technical Writer. **Educational backgrounds include:** Computer Science; Engineering; Finance. **Benefits:** 401(k); Daycare Assistance; Dental Insurance; Disability Coverage; Employee Discounts; Life Insurance; Medical Insurance; Tuition Assistance. **Corporate headquarters location:** This Location. **Other U.S. locations:** Andover MA; Cincinnati OH. **Operations at this facility include:** Administration; Divisional Headquarters; Research and Development; Sales; Service. **Number of employees at this location:** 450. **Number of employees nationwide:** 750.

NEWCOME CORPORATION
9005 Antares Avenue, Columbus OH 43240. 614/848-5688. **Fax:** 614/848-9921. **Contact:** Kelly Fox, Director of Personnel. **E-mail address:** kelly.fox@newcome.com. **World Wide Web address:** http://www.newcome.com. **Description:** Designs and installs voice and data distribution systems, primarily to support the communications needs of commercial enterprises in LAN- and WAN-based environments. **NOTE:** Entry-level positions are offered. **Common positions include:** Computer Operator; Computer Programmer; Cost Estimator; Draftsperson; Electrician; General Manager; Human Resources Manager; Marketing Manager; Marketing Specialist; MIS Specialist; Operations Manager; Purchasing Agent; Sales Engineer; Sales Executive; Sales Manager; Sales Representative; Secretary; Systems Analyst; Telecommunications Manager; Typist; Vice President. **Educational backgrounds include:** Accounting; Business Administration; Communications; Computer Science; Engineering; Liberal Arts. **Benefits:** 401(k); Disability Coverage; Employee Discounts; Flexible Schedule; Life Insurance; Profit Sharing. **Special programs:** Internships; Apprenticeships; Training. **Internship information:** Newcome Corporation hires interns interested in the areas of LAN/WAN environments and the design, installation, and marketing of audio/video systems. **Corporate headquarters location:** This Location. **Other U.S. locations:** Somerville NJ. **President:** Tim Newcome.

NEWSEDGE CORPORATION
80 Blanchard Road, Burlington MA 01803. 781/229-3000. **Contact:** Human Resources. **World Wide Web address:** http://www.newsedge.com. **Description:** Provides customized, real-time news and information delivered to knowledge workers over their organizations' local area networks. The company's NewsEDGE service delivers more than 480 news and information sources, in real-time, to users' personal computers; automatically monitors and filters the news according to pre-established personal interest profiles; and alerts users to stories matching their profiles. The NewsEDGE service is used by executives, salespeople, marketers, lawyers, accountants, consultants, bankers, and financial professionals. News and information sources available on NewsEDGE include newswire from AFP/Extel News Limited; The Associated Press; Dow Jones; Knight-Ridder/Tribune Information Services; and the text of stories in *The Financial Post*, *Financial Times*, the *New York Times News Service*, *USA Today*, and *The Wall Street Journal*. Also available on NewsEDGE are the business sections of over 100 North American newspapers; periodicals such as *Forbes*, *Fortune*, *InfoWorld*, *MacWeek*, and *PC Week*; and newsletters such as those distributed by American Banker and Philips Business Information Services, Inc. **Corporate headquarters location:** This Location.

NICHOLS
4090 South Memorial Parkway, Huntsville AL 35802. 256/883-1140. **Fax:** 256/880-0367. **Contact:** Personnel. **E-mail address:** resumes@ nichols.com. **World Wide Web address:** http://www.nichols.com. **Description:** Provides information technology solutions and technical services for the Department of Defense and intelligence agencies, federal civilian agencies and state government clients, health care organizations, and other commercial customers. Founded in 1976. **NOTE:** Entry-level positions are offered. **Common positions include:** Aerospace Engineer; Computer Programmer; Computer Scientist; Database Administrator; Electrical Engineer; Network Administrator; Software Engineer; Systems Analyst. **Educational backgrounds include:** C/C++; Computer Science; Engineering; MCSE; Physics; Visual Basic. **Benefits:** 401(k); Computer Loans; Dental Insurance; Disability Coverage; Employee Discounts; Life Insurance; Medical Insurance; Tuition Assistance. **Corporate headquarters location:** This Location. **Other U.S. locations:** CA; CO; DC; FL; MA; MS; NM; OH; UT. **Operations at this facility include:** Administration; Research and Development. **Number of employees at this location:** 1,000. **Number of employees nationwide:** 3,000.

NISSEI SANGYO AMERICA (NSA), LTD.
200 Lowder Brook Drive, Suite 2200, Westwood MA 02090. 781/461-8300. **Toll-free phone:** 800/441-4832. **Fax:** 781/329-6601. **Contact:** Personnel. **World Wide Web address:** http://www. nissei.com. **Description:** This location is a sales office and imports and distributes computer monitors. Overall, Nissei Sangyo America markets scientific instruments, computers, and electronic equipment. **NOTE:** Entry-level positions are offered. **Common positions include:** Account Manager; Administrative Assistant; Administrative Manager; Database Administrator; Marketing Manager; Marketing Specialist; Operations Manager; Public Relations Specialist; Sales Executive; Sales Manager; Sales Rep.; Systems Analyst; Transportation Specialist. **Educational backgrounds include:** Accounting; Business Administration; Marketing; Microsoft Word; Spreadsheets. **Benefits:** 401(k); Casual Dress - Fridays; Dental Insurance; Life Insurance; Medical Insurance; Pension Plan. **Corporate headquarters location:** Rolling Meadows IL. **Other U.S. locations:** Nationwide. **Parent company:** Nissei Sangyo Company, Ltd. (Tokyo, Japan). **Sales Manager:** Kevin Bowler. **Annual sales/revenues:** $51 - $100 million. **Number of employees nationwide:** 155.

NORTEL NETWORKS
4100 Guardian Way, Simi Valley CA 93063. 805/583-8600. **Contact:** Charlie Dichirico, Director of Personnel. **E-mail address:** cdichirico@ nortelnetworks.com. **World Wide Web address:** http://www.nortelnetworks.com. **Description:** Designs, produces, and supports multimedia access devices for use in building corporate, public, and Internet networks. The primary focus of the company's services is the consolidation of voice, fax, video, and data and multimedia traffic into a single network link. **Company slogan:** How the

world shares ideas. **Common positions include:** Accountant; Administrative Assistant; Customer Service Rep.; Electrical Engineer; Finance Director; Help-Desk Technician; Manufacturing Engineer; Marketing Specialist; Multimedia Designer. **Educational backgrounds include:** Accounting; AS400 Certification; Business Administration; C/C++; Communications; Computer Science; Engineering; HTML; Internet Development; Software Development; Software Tech. Support. **Benefits:** 401(k); Casual Dress - Daily; Dental Insurance; Disability Coverage; Employee Discounts; Flexible Schedule; Life Insurance; Medical Insurance; Pension Plan; Profit Sharing; Public Transit Available; Relocation Assistance; Savings Plan; Telecommuting; Tuition Assistance; Vacation Days (10 - 20). **Office hours:** Monday - Friday, 8:00 a.m. - 5:00 p.m. **Other U.S. locations:** Nationwide. **International locations:** Worldwide. **Parent company:** Nortel. **President/CEO:** John Roth. **Information Systems Manager:** Orville Beach. **Annual sales/revenues:** More than $100 million. **Number of employees worldwide:** 70,000.

NOVELL, INC.
1555 North Technology Way, Orem UT 84097. 801/222-6000. **Contact:** Human Resources. **World Wide Web address:** http://www.novell.com. **Description:** This location provides networking services. Overall, Novell, Inc. develops software tools and systems, works in partnership with other companies, and provides computer network management services. Products include NetWare 5.1, GroupWise 5.5, ManageWise 2.7, and Novell Net Publisher. **Corporate headquarters location:** This Location. **Other U.S. locations:** Nationwide. **International locations:** Worldwide. **Number of employees nationwide:** 7,900.

NxTREND TECHNOLOGY, INC.
5555 Tech Center Drive, Suite 300, Colorado Springs CO 80919. 719/590-8940. **Fax:** 719/528-1465. **Recorded jobline:** 719/264-4660. **Contact:** Human Resources. **World Wide Web address:** http://www.nxtrend.com. **Description:** Develops, sells, and supports software applications for the wholesale distribution industry. **NOTE:** Entry-level positions are offered. **Common positions include:** Account Rep.; Applications Engineer; Computer Operator; Computer Programmer; Customer Service Rep.; Database Manager; Design Engineer; Financial Analyst; Multimedia Designer; Project Manager; Software Engineer; Systems Analyst; Systems Manager; Webmaster. **Educational backgrounds include:** Accounting; Business Administration; Computer Science; Engineering; Finance; Software Development; Software Tech. Support. **Benefits:** 401(k); Dental Insurance; Disability Coverage; Flexible Schedule; Life Insurance; Medical Insurance; On-Site Exercise Facility; Profit Sharing; Savings Plan; Tuition Assistance. **Special programs:** Training. **Corporate headquarters location:** This Location. **Other U.S. locations:** Atlanta GA; Minneapolis MN; Dallas TX. **International locations:** Toronto, Canada. **Number of employees nationwide:** 340.

OCTAGON SYSTEMS
6510 West 91st Avenue, Suite 110, Westminster CO 80030. 303/430-1500. **Contact:** Human Resources. **Description:** Manufactures personal computers for extreme environments. Founded in 1981. **Common positions include:** Applications Engineer; Customer Service Rep.; Design Engineer; Electrical Engineer; Sales Manager; Software Engineer. **Educational backgrounds include:** Engineering; Marketing. **Benefits:** 401(k); Dental Insurance; Disability Coverage; Flexible Schedule; Life Insurance; Medical Insurance; Tuition Assistance. **Corporate**

headquarters location: This Location. **Number of employees at this location:** 70.

OLICOM
450 Donald Lynch Boulevard, Marlborough MA 01752. 508/481-4060. **Fax:** 508/229-5535. **Contact:** Personnel Manager. **World Wide Web address:** http://www.olicom.com. **Description:** Develops, manufactures, markets, and supports advanced internetworking products. **Benefits:** 401(k); Dental Insurance; Disability Coverage; Life Insurance; Medical Insurance. **Corporate headquarters location:** This Location. **Other U.S. locations:** Nationwide. **Operations at this facility include:** Manufacturing; Service. **Number of employees at this location:** 165. **Number of employees nationwide:** 215.

ONTARIO SYSTEMS CORPORATION
1150 West Kilgore Avenue, Muncie IN 47305. 765/751-7000. **Fax:** 765/751-7099. **Contact:** Andrea Weston, Human Resources Specialist. **E-mail address:** andrea@ontario.com. **World Wide Web address:** http://www.ontariosystems.com. **Description:** Develops software for businesses that offer accounts receivable management, collection, and teleservicing services. **NOTE:** Part-time jobs are offered. **Company slogan:** People are our foundation. **Common positions include:** Account Manager; Account Representative; Accountant; Administrative Assistant; Attorney; Computer Programmer; Computer Support Technician; Controller; Desktop Publishing Specialist; Graphic Designer; Human Resources Manager; Managing Editor; Market Research Analyst; Marketing Manager; Marketing Specialist; Network/Systems Administrator; Project Manager; Public Relations Specialist; Purchasing Agent; Quality Assurance Engineer; Quality Control Supervisor; Sales Manager; Sales Rep.; Systems Analyst; Technical Writer; Vice President of Marketing; Webmaster. **Educational backgrounds include:** Accounting; Business Administration; Communications; Computer Science; Marketing; Microsoft Word; Novell; Public Relations; QuarkXPress; Software Development; Software Tech. Support; Spreadsheets; Visual Basic. **Benefits:** 401(k); Casual Dress - Daily; Dental Insurance; Disability Coverage; Employee Discounts; Financial Planning Assistance; Flexible Schedule; Life Insurance; Medical Insurance; Profit Sharing; Sick Days (6 - 10); Tuition Assistance; Vacation Days (10 - 20). **Special programs:** Training. **Corporate headquarters location:** This Location. **Other U.S. locations:** Berlin OH; Cle Elum WA. **Subsidiaries include:** CDS Leopold; Sherry Labs. **Parent company:** Ontario Corporation. **President:** Wil Davis. **Annual sales/revenues:** More than $100 million. **Number of employees nationwide:** 330.

OPTRONICS INTERNATIONAL CORP.
21 Alpha Road, Chelmsford MA 01824. 978/256-4511. **Fax:** 978/250-5400. **Contact:** Lisa Vincent, Personnel Manager. **E-mail address:** lvincent@optronics-intl.com. **World Wide Web address:** http://www.optronics-intl.com. **Description:** Makes high-performance color scanners. Founded in 1968. **Common positions include:** Accountant; Administrative Assistant; Applications Engineer; CFO; Customer Service Rep.; Design Engineer; Draftsperson; Human Resources Manager; Manufacturing Engineer; Marketing Specialist; Operations Manager; Sales Manager; Software Engineer; Technical Writer/Editor. **Educational backgrounds include:** Accounting; Business Administration; Computer Science; Engineering; Finance; Public Relations; Software Development; Software Tech. Support. **Benefits:** 401(k); Disability Coverage; Life Insurance; Medical

Insurance; Tuition Assistance. **Corporate headquarters location:** This Location. **International locations:** The Netherlands. **Number of employees at this location:** 70.

ORACLE CORPORATION
500 Oracle Parkway, Mail Stop MS2OP2, Redwood Shores CA 94065. 650/506-7000. **Contact:** Recruiting. **World Wide Web address:** http://www.oracle.com. **Description:** Provides computer programming services. **Common positions include:** Administrative Manager; Computer Programmer; Economist; Electrical Engineer; Purchasing Agent; Software Engineer; Systems Analyst. **Educational backgrounds include:** Accounting; Business Administration; Computer Science; Engineering. **Benefits:** 401(k); Dental Insurance; Disability Coverage; Employee Discounts; Life Insurance; Medical Insurance; Profit Sharing; Savings Plan; Tuition Assistance. **Corporate headquarters location:** This Location. **Other U.S. locations:** Nationwide. **Operations at this facility include:** Administration; Sales. **Number of employees nationwide:** 12,000.

OUTPUT TECHNOLOGY CORPORATION
2310 North Fancher Road, Spokane WA 99212. 509/533-1257. **Contact:** Personnel Administration. **World Wide Web address:** http://www.output. com. **Description:** Manufactures and distributes printers and related products. **Common positions include:** Account Rep.; Administrative Assistant; Blue-Collar Worker Supervisor; Buyer; CFO; Clerical Supervisor; Controller; Customer Service Rep.; Design Engineer; Draftsperson; Electrical Engineer; Manufacturing Engineer; Market Research Analyst; Marketing Manager; Marketing Specialist; Mechanical Engineer; MIS Specialist; Production Manager; Project Manager; Purchasing Agent; Sales Manager; Sales Rep.; Software Engineer; Technical Writer; Transportation/Traffic Specialist; Vice President of Marketing and Sales; Vice President of Operations. **Educational backgrounds include:** Accounting; Business Administration; Communications; Engineering; Finance; Marketing. **Benefits:** 401(k); Dental Insurance; Disability Coverage; Life Insurance; Medical Insurance; Tuition Assistance. **Corporate headquarters location:** This Location. **Number of employees at this location:** 130.

PDA, INC.
7701 College Boulevard, Overland Park KS 66210. 913/469-8700. **Fax:** 913/469-5814. **Contact:** Personnel Manager. **World Wide Web address:** http://www.pdainc.com. **Description:** Designs computer software for the insurance industry and offers software consulting services. **Educational backgrounds include:** Computer Science. **Benefits:** 401(k); Dental Insurance; Disability Coverage; Employee Discounts; Flexible Schedule; Life Insurance; Medical Insurance; Tuition Assistance. **Corporate headquarters location:** This Location. **Subsidiaries include:** Viking Computing. **Number of employees at this location:** 100.

PNY TECHNOLOGIES, INC.
299 Webro Road, Parsippany NJ 07054. 973/515-9700. **Toll-free phone:** 800/234-4597. **Fax:** 973/560-5283. **Contact:** Jocelyn Rondina, Human Resources Manager. **World Wide Web address:** http://www.pny.com. **Description:** Manufactures and designs computer memory products. Founded in 1985. **NOTE:** Entry-level positions are offered. **Common positions include:** Account Manager; Account Rep.; Design Engineer; Quality Control Supervisor; Sales and Marketing Rep. **Educational backgrounds include:** Accounting; Computer Science; Engineering. **Benefits:** 401(k); Dental

Insurance; Disability Coverage; Life Insurance; Medical Insurance; Tuition Assistance. **Corporate headquarters location:** This Location. **Annual sales/revenues:** More than $100 million. **Number of employees nationwide:** 320. **Number of employees worldwide:** 420.

PRC, INC.
1500 PRC Drive, McLean VA 22102. 703/556-1000. **Fax:** 703/556-2547. **Contact:** Human Resources. **Description:** A global provider of scientific and technology-based systems and services. The company provides computer systems integration, systems engineering, software development, environmental engineering, and consulting services to both government and commercial clients. **Common positions include:** Accountant; Aerospace Engineer; Attorney; Budget Analyst; Chemical Engineer; Computer Operator; Computer Programmer; Electrical Engineer; Employment Interviewer; Financial Analyst; Graphic Artist; Industrial Engineer; Mechanical Engineer; Meteorologist; Nuclear Engineer; Receptionist; Secretary; Software Engineer; Systems Analyst; Technical Support Rep.; Typist. **Educational backgrounds include:** Accounting; Computer Science; Economics; Engineering; Finance; Geology; Liberal Arts. **Benefits:** 401(k); Dental Insurance; Disability Coverage; Employee Discounts; Life Insurance; Medical Insurance; Pension Plan; Savings Plan; Tuition Assistance. **Corporate headquarters location:** This Location. **Parent company:** Black & Decker. **Number of employees at this location:** 3,500. **Number of employees nationwide:** 7,000.

PSI INTERNATIONAL INC.
10306 Eaton Place, Suite 400, Fairfax VA 22030. 703/352-8700. **Contact:** Personnel Representative. **Description:** Offers computer consulting services and develops software. **Common positions include:** Computer Operator; Computer Programmer; Software Engineer; Systems Analyst. **Educational backgrounds include:** Computer Science. **Benefits:** 401(k); Dental Insurance; Disability Coverage; Life Insurance; Medical Insurance; Public Transit Available; Tuition Assistance. **Corporate headquarters location:** This Location. **Number of employees nationwide:** 175.

PSI TECHNOLOGIES CORPORATION
1101 South Capital of Texas Highway, Building K, Suite 200, Austin TX 78746. 512/329-0081. **Contact:** Human Resources. **World Wide Web address:** http://www.psiaustin.com. **Description:** Develops retrieval and conversion software. **Corporate headquarters location:** This Location.

PSINET
510 Huntmar Park Drive, Herndon VA 20170-5100. 703/904-4100. **Toll-free phone:** 800/395-1056. **Fax:** 703/397-5302. **Contact:** Human Resources. **E-mail address:** info@psi.com. **World Wide Web address:** http://www.psinet.com. **Description:** An Internet service provider offering a wide range of Internet access services to organizations and individuals by means of its high-performance computer network. PSINet offers a broad spectrum of Internet access services designed to meet the various needs of its customers, from low-cost network dial-up services, to high-performance continuous access services using dedicated high-speed telephone circuits. Founded in 1989. **Common positions include:** Account Manager; Account Rep.; Accountant; Administrative Assistant; Advertising Executive; Applications Engineer; Attorney; Auditor; Branch Manager; Budget Analyst; Buyer; CFO; Computer Engineer; Computer Operator; Computer Programmer;

Computer Support Technician; Computer Technician; Content Developer; Controller; Cost Estimator; Credit Manager; Customer Service Rep.; Database Administrator; Database Manager; Design Engineer; Editorial Assistant; Electrical Engineer; Event Planner; Finance Director; Financial Analyst; Graphic Artist; Graphic Designer; Help-Desk Technician; Human Resources Manager; Internet Services Manager; Intranet Developer; Market Research Analyst; Marketing Manager; Marketing Specialist; MIS Specialist; Multimedia Designer; Network Engineer; Network Administrator; Online Sales Manager; Paralegal; Project Manager; Public Relations Specialist; Purchasing Agent; Sales Executive; Sales Manager; Sales Rep.; Software Engineer; SQL Programmer; Systems Analyst; Systems Manager; Technical Writer; Web Advertising Specialist; Webmaster; Website Developer. **Educational backgrounds include:** Accounting; Art/Design; Business Administration; C/C++; CGI; Cold Fusion; Communications; Computer Science; Economics; Engineering; Finance; HTML; Internet Development; Java; Liberal Arts; Marketing; MBA; MCSE; Microsoft Office; Microsoft Word; Public Relations; QuarkXPress; Software Development; Software Tech. Support; Spreadsheets; SQL; Visual Basic. **Benefits:** 401(k); Casual Dress - Daily; Dental Insurance; Disability Coverage; Financial Planning Assistance; Flexible Schedule; Life Insurance; Medical Insurance; Profit Sharing; Relocation Assistance; Savings Plan; Sick Days (6 - 10); Telecommuting; Tuition Assistance; Vacation Days (10 - 20). **Corporate headquarters location:** This Location. **Other U.S. locations:** Nationwide. **International locations:** Worldwide. **CEO:** William Schrader. **Annual sales/revenues:** More than $100 million. **Number of employees at this location:** 600. **Number of employees nationwide:** 1,000. **Number of employees worldwide:** 3,300.

PANURGY CORPORATION
857 West South Jordan Parkway, Suite 200, South Jordan UT 84095. 801/364-7007. **Fax:** 801/364-7099. **Contact:** Ray Warner, Director of Operations. **World Wide Web address:** http://www.panurgy.com. **Description:** Sells software and hardware MRP packages to manufacturers. **Common positions include:** Computer Programmer; Management Analyst/Consultant; Systems Analyst. **Educational backgrounds include:** Computer Science. **Benefits:** 401(k); Dental Insurance; Disability Coverage; Life Insurance; Medical Insurance; Pension Plan; Profit Sharing. **Corporate headquarters location:** This Location. **Operations at this facility include:** Sales; Support Services.

PARAMETRIC TECHNOLOGY CORP.
128 Technology Drive, Waltham MA 02453. **Fax:** 781/398-6000. **Contact:** Personnel. **World Wide Web address:** http://www.ptc.com. **Description:** Designs and develops fully-integrated software products for mechanical engineering and automated manufacturing based upon a parametric solids modeling system. **Common positions include:** Applications Engineer; Computer Programmer; Educational Specialist; Mathematician; Sales Rep.; Software Engineer; Systems Analyst. **Educational backgrounds include:** Computer Science; Engineering; Finance; Marketing. **Benefits:** 401(k); Dental Insurance; ESOP; Medical Insurance; Vision Insurance. **Corporate headquarters location:** This Location. **International locations:** Worldwide. **Operations at this facility include:** Administration; Marketing; Research and Development; Sales. **Listed on:** NASDAQ. **Number of employees at this location:** 500. **Number of employees nationwide:** 1,600.

PARASOFT CORPORATION
2031 South Myrtle Avenue, Monrovia CA 91016. 626/305-0041. **Fax:** 626/305-3036. **Contact:** Personnel. **E-mail address:** jobs@parasoft.com. **World Wide Web address:** http://www.parasoft.com. **Description:** Develops software using C and C++. **Corporate headquarters location:** This Location.

PEOPLESOFT, INC.
4305 Hacienda Drive, Pleasanton CA 94588. 925/225-3000. **Fax:** 925/694-2699. **Contact:** Personnel. **E-mail address:** jobs@peoplesoft.com. **World Wide Web address:** http://www.peoplesoft.com. **Description:** Provides client/server applications and software solutions for businesses worldwide. PeopleSoft develops, markets, and supports a variety of enterprise solutions for accounting, materials management, distribution, manufacturing, and human resources, as well as offering industry-specific enterprise solutions to markets including financial services, health care, manufacturing, higher education, the public sector, and the federal government. **NOTE:** Entry-level positions are offered. **Common positions include:** Account Manager; Applications Engineer; Computer Programmer; Consultant; Database Manager; Design Engineer; Education Administrator; Market Research Analyst; Marketing Manager; Marketing Specialist; MIS Specialist; Sales Manager; Software Engineer; Systems Analyst; Systems Manager; Technical Writer/Editor. **Educational backgrounds include:** Business Administration; Computer Science; Marketing. **Benefits:** 401(k); Dental Insurance; Disability Coverage; Employee Discounts; Flexible Schedule; Life Insurance; Medical Insurance; Profit Sharing; Public Transit Available; Telecommuting. **Special programs:** Internships. **Corporate headquarters location:** This Location. **International locations:** Australia; France; Germany; Japan; Latin America; the Netherlands; Singapore; Spain. **Annual sales/revenues:** More than $100 million. **Number of employees at this location:** 1,500. **Number of employees nationwide:** 2,500. **Number of employees worldwide:** 3,000.
Other U.S. locations:
• 2525 Augustine Drive, Santa Clara CA 95054. 408/982-5700.

PERSOFT, INC. - AN ESKER COMPANY
465 Science Drive, Madison WI 53711. 608/273-6000. **Toll-free phone:** 800/368-5283. **Fax:** 608/273-8227. **Contact:** Human Resources Department. **E-mail address:** personnel@persoft.com. **World Wide Web address:** http://www.persoft.com. **Description:** Persoft, Inc. develops communications software. The company's product lines include SmarTerm and Persona. Founded in 1982. **Common positions include:** Account Manager; Account Rep.; Administrative Assistant; Computer Engineer; Computer Scientist; Desktop Publishing Specialist; Event Planner; Graphic Artist; Graphic Designer; Help-Desk Technician; Market Research Analyst; Marketing Manager; Marketing Specialist; MIS Specialist; Multimedia Designer; Network Engineer; Network Administrator; Public Relations Specialist; Sales Executive; Sales Manager; Sales Rep.; Software Engineer; Technical Writer/Editor; Web Advertising Specialist; Webmaster; Website Developer. **Educational backgrounds include:** C/C++; Computer Science; HTML; Internet Development; Java; MCSE. **Benefits:** 401(k); Casual Dress - Daily; Dental Insurance; Disability Coverage; Flexible Schedule; Life Insurance; Medical Insurance; Profit Sharing; Public Transit Available; Sick Days (6 - 10); Vacation Days (10 - 20). **Corporate headquarters location:** This Location.

Other U.S. locations: Stillwater OK. **International locations:** Worldwide. **Parent company:** Esker, Inc. **Number of employees nationwide:** 180. **Number of employees worldwide:** 300.

PERVASIVE SOFTWARE INC.
12365 Riata Trace Parkway, Building Two, Austin TX 78727. 512/231-6000. **Fax:** 512/231-6010. **Contact:** Recruiter. **E-mail address:** greatjobs@pervasive.com. **World Wide Web address:** http://www.pervasive.com. **Description:** Develops embedded database software. **Corporate headquarters location:** This Location. **International locations:** Brussels, Belgium; Dublin, Ireland; Frankfurt, Germany; Hong Kong; London, England; Paris, France; Tokyo, Japan; Toronto, Canada.

PHOENIX TECHNOLOGIES LTD.
135 Technology Drive, Irvine CA 92618. 949/790-2000. **Fax:** 949/790-2001. **Contact:** Personnel. **World Wide Web address:** http://www.phoenix.com. **Description:** This location is a supplier of standards-based system software and semiconductor IP for PCs and information appliances. Overall, Phoenix Technologies designs, develops, and markets systems software and end user software products. The Peripherals Division designs, develops, and supplies printer emulation software, page distribution languages, and controller hardware designs for the printing industry. The PhoenixPage imaging software architecture enables printer manufacturers to offer products that are compatible with the PostScript language, the PCL printer language, and other imaging standards. Phoenix Technologies' PC Division works with leading vendors and standards committees to ensure that Phoenix products enable manufacturers to develop and deploy next-generation PCs quickly and cost-effectively. The company's Package Products Division is a single-source publisher of MS-DOS, Windows, and other software packages. **NOTE:** Entry-level positions are offered. **Common positions include:** Applications Engineer; Software Engineer. **Educational backgrounds include:** Computer Science; Engineering; Software Development. **Benefits:** 401(k); Casual Dress - Daily; Dental Insurance; Disability Coverage; Employee Discounts; Life Insurance; Medical Insurance; Tuition Assistance. **Special programs:** Internships. **Corporate headquarters location:** San Jose CA. **International locations:** Worldwide. **Annual sales/revenues:** More than $100 million. **Number of employees at this location:** 140. **Number of employees worldwide:** 800.

PHYCOM CORPORATION
11241 Slater Avenue NE, Suite 200, Kirkland WA 98033-4603. 425/576-8600. **Fax:** 425/893-8222. **Contact:** Human Resources. **E-mail address:** careers@phycom.com. **World Wide Web address:** http://www.phycom.com. **Description:** Develops software for health care providers. PhyCom's product suite includes case management and utilization management applications integrated with a web-based managed care transaction-processing system. **Common positions include:** Computer Programmer; Computer Support Technician; Database Administrator; Network Administrator; Sales Executive. **Educational backgrounds include:** C/C++; Computer Science; Engineering; Health Care; Software Development; SQL. **Benefits:** 401(k); Casual Dress - Daily; Daycare Assistance; Dental Insurance; Disability Coverage; Employee Discounts; Flexible Schedule; Life Insurance; Medical Insurance; Relocation Assistance; Sick Days (6 - 10); Telecommuting; Tuition Assistance; Vacation Days (10 - 20). **Corporate headquarters location:** This Location.

Other U.S. locations: Westlake OH. **Listed on:** Privately held. **President/CEO:** Julie Klapstein. **Number of employees nationwide:** 80.

PINNACLE MICRO, INC.
30191 Avenida de las Banderas, Suite A, Rancho Santa Margarita CA 92688. 949/635-3000. **Fax:** 949/635-3020. **Contact:** Chuck McGee, Director of Personnel. **World Wide Web address:** http://www.pinnaclemicro.com. **Description:** Manufactures a CD-ROM information storage system for general data storage and data intensive applications with read/write and rewrite capabilities. **Common positions include:** Account Manager; Account Rep.; Administrative Assistant; Applications Engineer; MIS Specialist; Quality Control Supervisor; Sales Executive; Sales Manager; Sales Rep. **Educational backgrounds include:** Business Administration; Computer Science; Engineering. **Benefits:** 401(k); Dental Insurance; Disability Coverage; Life Insurance; Medical Insurance; Tuition Assistance. **Corporate headquarters location:** This Location. **Other U.S. locations:** Colorado Springs CO. **Annual sales/revenues:** $51 - $100 million. **Number of employees at this location:** 100. **Number of employees worldwide:** 165.

PINNACLE SYSTEMS
280 North Bernardo Avenue, Mountain View CA 94043. 650/526-1600. **Contact:** Human Resources. **Description:** Develops digital and video-editing tools for both professional and consumer markets. Products include DVExtreme, a digital special effects system; and Studio 400, a video-editing system for consumers. **Corporate headquarters location:** This Location.

POD ASSOCIATES, INC.
2309 Renard Place SE, Suite 201, Albuquerque NM 87106. 505/243-2287. **Fax:** 505/243-4677. **Contact:** Sheryl Nanco, Personnel. **E-mail address:** pod@podassoc.com. **World Wide Web address:** http://www.podassoc.com. **Description:** Provides solutions for the development, maintenance, and support of information systems. POD specializes in network setup and support, database creation and support, and Web development and support. **Company slogan:** Stay connected. **Common positions include:** Administrative Assistant; Applications Engineer; Computer Animator; Computer Engineer; Computer Programmer; Computer Support Technician; Computer Technician; Content Developer; Database Administrator; Database Manager; Help-Desk Technician; Internet Services Manager; Intranet Developer; Mechanical Engineer; MIS Specialist; Multimedia Designer; Network Engineer; Network Administrator; Software Engineer; SQL Programmer; Systems Analyst; Webmaster; Website Developer. **Educational backgrounds include:** ASP; CGI; Computer Science; HTML; Internet Development; Java; MCSE; Microsoft Office; Microsoft Word; Novell; Software Development; Software Tech. Support; SQL; Visual Basic. **Benefits:** 401(k); Dental Insurance; Disability Coverage; Flexible Schedule; Life Insurance; Medical Insurance; Profit Sharing; Tuition Assistance. **Special programs:** Internships; Apprenticeships. **President/CEO:** Samantha Lapin. **Information Systems Manager:** Bill York.

POLICY MANAGEMENT SYSTEMS CORP.
P.O. Box 10, Columbia SC 29202. 803/735-4000. **Contact:** Recruiting. **World Wide Web address:** http://www.pmsc.com. **Description:** Develops and licenses standardized insurance software systems and provides automation and administrative support and information services to the insurance industry

worldwide. The company also provides professional support services, which include implementation and integration assistance; consulting and education services; and information and outsourcing services. **Corporate headquarters location:** This Location.

POMEROY COMPUTER RESOURCES
1020 Petersburg Road, Hebron KY 41048-9605. 606/586-0600. **Contact:** Human Resources. **Description:** A full-service systems integration company that sells, installs, and services microcomputers and microcomputer equipment primarily for business, professional, educational, and government customers. The company also offers customer support services including network analysis and design, systems configuration, custom installation, training, maintenance, and repair. **Common positions include:** Accountant; Computer Programmer; Purchasing Agent; Services Sales Rep.; Software Engineer; Systems Analyst. **Educational backgrounds include:** Accounting; Business Administration; Computer Science; Marketing. **Benefits:** 401(k); Life Insurance; Medical Insurance; Profit Sharing. **Corporate headquarters location:** This Location. **Other U.S. locations:** Knoxville KY; Lexington KY; Cincinnati OH; Louisville OH; Kingsport TN; Nashville TN. **Subsidiaries include:** Xenas Multimedia. **Operations at this facility include:** Administration; Sales; Service. **Listed on:** NASDAQ. **Number of employees at this location:** 120. **Number of employees nationwide:** 450.

PONY COMPUTER, INC.
10036 Aurora Hudson Road, Streetsboro OH 44241. 330/528-3888. **Toll-free phone:** 800/989-7669. **Fax:** 330/528-3851. **Contact:** Personnel. **World Wide Web address:** http://www.ponycomputer. com. **Description:** Manufactures and customizes PCs for the computer reseller market. **Corporate headquarters location:** This Location.

THE PORTLAND GROUP, INC. (PGI)
9150 SW Pioneer Court, Suite H, Wilsonville OR 97070. 503/682-2806. **Fax:** 503/682-2637. **Contact:** Personnel. **World Wide Web address:** http://www.pgroup.com. **Description:** A developer of scalar and parallel compilers and software development tools. **Corporate headquarters location:** This Location.

POWERQUEST CORPORATION
P.O. Box 1911, Orem UT 84059. 801/226-8977. **Fax:** 801/226-8941. **Contact:** Personnel. **World Wide Web address:** http://www.powerquest.com. **Description:** Develops hard-disk and file system software. Products include ServerMagic, DriveCopy, and PartitionMagic. **Corporate headquarters location:** This Location.

PRESCIENT SYSTEMS, INC.
7111 Valley Green Road, Suite 230, Fort Washington PA 19034. 215/836-5161. **Contact:** Barbara Rufe, Director of Human Resources. **World Wide Web address:** http://www.prescientsystems. com. **Description:** A developer and supplier of forecasting and logistics software solutions. The company's supply chain management software provides a solution for demand forecasting, inventory planning, and continuous replenishment. This software is used by manufacturers, distributors, and retailers worldwide. **Common positions include:** Accountant; Administrative Manager; Computer Programmer; Human Resources Manager; Operations Manager; Purchasing Agent; Quality Control Supervisor; Software Engineer; Systems Analyst; Technical Writer/Editor. **Educational backgrounds include:** Computer Science; Marketing; Mathematics. **Benefits:** 401(k); Dental Insurance; Disability Coverage; Life Insurance; Medical Insurance. **Corporate headquarters location:** This Location. **Operations at this facility include:** Administration; Sales; Service. **Number of employees at this location:** 30. **Number of employees nationwide:** 45.

THE PRESIDIO CORPORATION
5100-J Philadelphia Way, Lanham MD 20706. 301/459-2200. **Contact:** Human Resources. **World Wide Web address:** http://www.presidio.com. **Description:** Provides applications and systems integration which enable electronic mail, file exchanges, shared peripherals, and a wide range of group applications. **Company slogan:** Delivering unified solutions. **Common positions include:** Account Manager; Account Rep.; Accountant; Administrative Assistant; Computer Support Technician; Controller; Customer Service Rep.; Database Administrator; Database Manager; Human Resources Manager; Internet Services Manager; Marketing Manager; MIS Specialist; Network Administrator; Purchasing Agent/Manager; Quality Assurance Engineer; Sales Engineer; Sales Executive; Sales Manager; Sales Representative; Webmaster. **Educational backgrounds include:** Accounting; Business Administration; Computer Science; Finance; Internet; Marketing; MCSE; Microsoft Word; Software Tech. Support; Spreadsheets. **Benefits:** 401(k); Casual Dress - Fridays; Dental Insurance; Disability Coverage; Employee Discounts; Life Insurance; Medical Insurance; Tuition Assistance. **Corporate headquarters location:** This Location. **Other U.S. locations:** CA; FL; GA; VA.

PREVIEW SYSTEMS, INC.
1000 SW Broadway, Suite 1850, Portland OR 97205. 503/220-2300. **Fax:** 503/525-6802. **Contact:** Personnel. **World Wide Web address:** http://www.previewsystems.com. **Description:** Develops e-commerce tools that allow for the electronic distribution and licensing of digital goods including software and music. **Common positions include:** Software Engineer. **Corporate headquarters location:** This Location.

PRIMAVERA SYSTEMS INC.
3 Bala Plaza West, Bala-Cynwyd PA 19004. 610/667-8600. **Fax:** 610/949-6761. **Contact:** Joanne McCool, Vice President of Human Resources. **E-mail address:** jobs@primavera.com. **World Wide Web address:** http://www.primavera. com. **Description:** Develops and supports an array of project management software for assisting clients in risk analysis, large-scale projects, contract management, team communication, and remote real-time updating. **NOTE:** Entry-level positions are offered. **Common positions include:** Administrative Assistant; Computer Programmer; Database Manager; Marketing Manager; Sales Engineer; Sales Rep.; Secretary; Software Engineer. **Educational backgrounds include:** Business Administration; Computer Science; Engineering; Software Development; Software Tech. Support. **Benefits:** 401(k); Adoption Assistance; Dental Insurance; Disability Coverage; Employee Discounts; Flexible Schedule; Life Insurance; Medical Insurance; Pension Plan; Profit Sharing; Public Transit Available; Savings Plan; Stock Option; Tuition Assistance. **Special programs:** Internships; Co-ops. **Corporate headquarters location:** This Location. **Other U.S. locations:** Nationwide. **International locations:** Worldwide. **Listed on:** Privately held. **Annual sales/revenues:** $21 - $50 million. **Number of employees at this location:** 180. **Number of employees nationwide:** 230. **Number of employees worldwide:** 260.

PRINCETON FINANCIAL SYSTEMS INC.
600 College Road East, Princeton NJ 08540.
609/987-2400. **Fax:** 609/514-4798. **Contact:** Cara
Verba, Staffing Manager. **World Wide Web
address:** http://www.pfs.com. **Description:**
Develops and supports investment management
software. **NOTE:** Entry-level positions are offered.
Common positions include: Accountant; Computer
Programmer; Fund Manager; Sales Manager;
Software Engineer; Systems Analyst; Technical
Writer/Editor. **Educational backgrounds include:**
Accounting; Computer Science; Finance. **Benefits:**
401(k); Dental Insurance; Disability Coverage; Life
Insurance; Medical Insurance; Tuition Assistance.
Special programs: Apprenticeships. **Corporate
headquarters location:** This Location.
International locations: London; Toronto. **Parent
company:** State Street Boston Corporation.
Number of employees nationwide: 185. **Number
of employees worldwide:** 200.

PRINCETON SOFTECH
1060 State Road, Princeton NJ 08540-1423.
609/688-5000. **Toll-free phone:** 800/457-7060.
Fax: 609/497-0302. **Contact:** Human Resources. **E-
mail address:** info@princetonsoftech.com. **World
Wide Web address:** http://www.princetonsoftech.
com. **Description:** Provides IT professionals with
software solutions. Develops, researches, sells, and
markets software products which are focused on
intelligent data migration and database
synchronization. The company offers data and
program synchronization tools to solve application
development and database problems. Founded in
1989. **Corporate headquarters location:** This
Location. **International locations:** Worldwide.
Parent company: Computer Horizons Corporation.

PRINTEK, INC.
1517 Townline Road, Benton Harbor MI 49022.
616/925-3200. **Fax:** 616/925-8539. **Contact:**
Shirley Sommers, Personnel Administrator. **E-mail
address:** ssommers@printek.com. **Description:**
Manufactures high-speed, high-performance, dot
matrix printers. Founded in 1980. **Common
positions include:** Accountant; Administrative
Assistant; CFO; Customer Service Rep.; Design
Engineer; Electrical Engineer; Finance Director;
General Manager; Manufacturing Engineer;
Marketing Manager; Mechanical Engineer;
Operations Manager; Production Manager;
Purchasing Agent; Quality Control Supervisor;
Sales Executive; Sales Manager; Sales Rep.;
Software Engineer; Systems Manager. **Educational
backgrounds include:** Business Administration;
Engineering; Marketing. **Benefits:** 401(k); Dental
Insurance; Employee Discounts; Life Insurance;
Medical Insurance; Tuition Assistance. **Corporate
headquarters location:** This Location. **Other U.S.
locations:** Wheaton IL. **President:** Thomas C.
Yeager. **Facilities Manager:** Julie Payovich.
Number of employees at this location: 100.

PRINTRONIX INC.
14600 Myford Road, Irvine CA 92606. 949/863-
1900. **Contact:** Julie Holder, Human Resources.
World Wide Web address: http://www.printronix.
com. **Description:** Designs, manufactures, and
markets impact line printers and laser printers for
use with minicomputers, microcomputers, and other
computer systems. **Common positions include:**
Accountant; Buyer; Computer Programmer;
Customer Service Rep.; Draftsperson; Electrical
Engineer; Financial Analyst; Mechanical Engineer;
Operations Manager; Quality Control Supervisor;
Technical Writer. **Educational backgrounds
include:** Business Administration; Computer
Science; Engineering. **Benefits:** Dental Insurance;
Disability Coverage; Employee Discounts; Life

Insurance; Medical Insurance; Profit Sharing;
Savings Plan; Tuition Assistance. **Corporate
headquarters location:** This Location. **Operations
at this facility include:** Manufacturing; Research
and Development; Sales; Service.

PRODIGY, INC.
44 South Broadway, White Plains NY 10601. **Toll-
free phone:** 800/PRODIGY. **Fax:** 914/448-3467.
Contact: Human Resources. **E-mail address:**
human_resources@prodigy.net. **World Wide Web
address:** http://www.prodigy.com. **Description:** An
online service provider. Services include a Web
browser, chat rooms, e-mail, personal Web pages,
live news, games, and bulletin boards. **NOTE:**
Entry-level positions are offered. **Common
positions include:** Account Manager;
Administrative Assistant; Budget Analyst;
Computer Animator; Computer Operator; Computer
Programmer; Database Manager; Editor; Financial
Analyst; Graphic Artist; Graphic Designer; Internet
Services Manager; Marketing Manager; Multimedia
Designer; Online Content Specialist; Project
Manager; Sales Executive; Secretary; Systems
Analyst; Technical Writer; Webmaster.
Educational backgrounds include: Art/Design;
Business Administration; Computer Science;
Marketing. **Benefits:** 401(k); Dental Insurance;
Disability Coverage; Flexible Schedule; Life
Insurance; Medical Insurance; Tuition Assistance.
Special programs: Internships. **Corporate
headquarters location:** This Location. **Other U.S.
locations:** MA. **International locations:** Africa;
China; Mexico. **Subsidiaries include:** Africa
Online; GES; Prodigy Services Corp.; Prodigy
Ventures, Inc. **Number of employees nationwide:**
700. **Number of employees worldwide:** 1,500.

PROFITKEY INTERNATIONAL, INC.
382 Main Street, Salem NH 03079. 603/898-9800.
Fax: 603/898-7554. **Contact:** Allison Batchelder,
Human Resources. **World Wide Web address:**
http://www.profitkey.com. **Description:** A leader in
the advanced planning and scheduling industry,
providing manufacturers with real-time ERP
systems. ProfitKey International markets Rapid
Response Manufacturing Client/Server, a graphical
32-bit application. **NOTE:** Part-time jobs are
offered. **Common positions include:** Account
Manager; Administrative Assistant; Applications
Engineer; Computer Programmer; Computer
Scientist; Computer Technician; Customer Service
Rep.; Graphic Designer; Internet Services Manager;
MIS Specialist; Network Administrator; Project
Manager; Sales Rep.; Technical Writer/Editor;
Webmaster. **Educational backgrounds include:**
HTML; Internet; Java; MCSE; Microsoft Word;
Novell; Software Development; Software Tech.
Support; Spreadsheets; Visual Basic. **Special
programs:** Co-ops. **Corporate headquarters
location:** This Location. **President/CEO/Owner:**
Joseph DiZazzo. **Sales Manager:** Timothy J.
Conroy. **Number of employees at this location:** 45.

PROJECT SOFTWARE & DEVELOPMENT
100 Crosby Drive, Bedford MA 01730. 781/280-
2000. **Contact:** Human Resources. **World Wide
Web address:** http://www.psdi.com. **Description:**
Develops, markets, and supports enterprisewide
client/server applications software used to assist in
maintaining and developing high-value capital
assets such as facilities, systems, and production
equipment. The company's products enable
customers to reduce downtime, control maintenance
expenses, cut spare parts inventories, improve
purchasing efficiency, shorten product development
cycles, and deploy productive assets and personnel
more effectively. **Benefits:** Deferred Compensation;
Profit Sharing; Stock Option. **Corporate**

headquarters location: This Location. **Other U.S. locations:** Irvine CA; Denver CO; Watertown MA; Rockville MD; Dearborn MI; Rochelle Park NJ; Hauppauge NY; Irving TX; Bellevue WA. **Subsidiaries include:** Project Software Canada (Toronto); PSDI (UK) Ltd. (United Kingdom); PSDI Australia Pty. Ltd. (Sydney); PSDI Benelux NV (The Netherlands); PSDI Deutschland GmbH (Munich); PSDI France SARL (Paris). **Listed on:** NASDAQ. **Number of employees nationwide:** 215. **Number of employees worldwide:** 385.

PROVAR, INC.
2624 Lord Baltimore Drive, Suite D, Baltimore MD 21244. 410/265-8010. **Fax:** 410/265-8077. **Contact:** Personnel. **World Wide Web address:** http://www.pvar.com. **Description:** An information technology solutions provider specializing in implementing open, client/server systems and networks as well as providing applications and application development services. **Common positions include:** Computer Programmer; Project Manager; Sales Executive; Systems Analyst. **Educational backgrounds include:** Business Administration; Computer Science; Engineering. **Benefits:** 401(k); Dental Insurance; Employee Discounts; Life Insurance; Medical Insurance; Profit Sharing; Public Transit Available; Telecommuting; Tuition Assistance. **Corporate headquarters location:** This Location.

PROXIMA CORPORATION
9440 Carroll Park Drive, San Diego CA 92121-2298. 858/457-5500. **Fax:** 858/457-8551. **Contact:** Human Resources. **World Wide Web address:** http://www.proxima.com. **Description:** Markets and distributes computer peripheral desktop projectors. Products are used to project images by accessing video signals through a PC's video port. Founded in 1982. **NOTE:** Entry-level positions are offered. **Common positions include:** Accountant; Administrative Assistant; Buyer; CFO; Computer Programmer; Customer Service Rep.; Database Manager; Design Engineer; Electrical Engineer; Financial Analyst; Graphic Artist; Human Resources Manager; Manufacturing Engineer; Market Research Analyst; Marketing Manager; Marketing Specialist; Mechanical Engineer; Multimedia Designer; Operations Manager; Production Manager; Purchasing Agent; Quality Control Supervisor; Sales Executive; Sales Rep.; Software Engineer; Transportation Specialist. **Educational backgrounds include:** Business Administration; Engineering; Marketing. **Benefits:** 401(k); Dental Insurance; Disability Coverage; Employee Discounts; Flexible Schedule; Life Insurance; Medical Insurance; Tuition Assistance. **Special programs:** Internships. **Corporate headquarters location:** This Location. **Annual sales/revenues:** More than $100 million. **Number of employees worldwide:** 200.

QAD INC.
6450 Via Real, Carpinteria CA 93013. 805/684-6614. **Fax:** 805/566-6091. **Contact:** Human Resources. **World Wide Web address:** http://www.qad.com. **Description:** This location houses administrative offices. Overall, QAD develops software including MFG/PRO, a software package designed to aid in supply and distribution management for large companies. **Corporate headquarters location:** This Location.

QCP WHOLESALE, INC.
1400 Northbrook Parkway, Suite 360, Suwanee GA 30024. 678/377-1700. **Fax:** 678/377-1742. **Contact:** Personnel. **World Wide Web address:** http://www.qcpwholesale.com. **Description:** A full-service distributor of memory and CPU products. **Corporate headquarters location:** This Location.

QDI COMPUTER
41456 Christy Street, Fremont CA 94538. 510/668-4933. **Contact:** Personnel. **World Wide Web address:** http://www.qdius.com. **Description:** A manufacturer of computer components and motherboards. **Corporate headquarters location:** This Location.

QMS, INC.
P.O. Box 81250, Mobile AL 36689-1250. 334/633-4300. **Contact:** Todd St. Mary, Personnel Manager. **World Wide Web address:** http://www.qms.com. **Description:** Manufactures laser printers. **Corporate headquarters location:** This Location. **Other U.S. locations:** Orlando FL.

QUADRAMED
22 Pelican Way, San Rafael CA 94901. 415/482-2100. **Contact:** Personnel. **World Wide Web address:** http://www.quadramed.com. **Description:** Develops and markets specialized decision support software designed to improve the organizational and clinical effectiveness of hospitals, academic medical centers, managed care providers, large physician groups, and other health care providers. **Corporate headquarters location:** This Location.

QUALITY SOFTWARE ENGINEERING
1065 Executive Parkway Drive, Suite 305, St. Louis MO 63141. 314/579-9898. **Fax:** 314/579-9853. **Contact:** Personnel. **E-mail address:** qse@qse.com. **World Wide Web address:** http://www.qse.com. **Description:** An information technology consulting and services firm. The Information Systems Consulting Division provides services to professionals including application system development and maintenance, database administration, system installation and management, network installation and management, technical writing, training, quality assurance, project management, and management consulting. The Information Technologies Division provides services for clients who outsource those functions, including hardware and software evaluation and selection, installation, systems integration, project development services, training, and end user support. **Common positions include:** Applications Engineer; Computer Operator; Computer Programmer; Database Manager; Internet Services Manager; MIS Specialist; Project Manager; Software Engineer; Systems Manager; Technical Writer; Webmaster. **Educational backgrounds include:** Business Administration; Computer Science; Engineering. **Benefits:** 401(k); Dental Insurance; Disability Coverage; Life Insurance; Medical Insurance; Tuition Assistance. **Corporate headquarters location:** This Location.

QUALITY SYSTEMS, INC.
17822 East 17th Street, Center Building 210, Tustin CA 92780. 714/731-7171. **Fax:** 714/731-9494. **Contact:** Samantha Anderson, Manager of Human Resources. **E-mail address:** hr@qsii.com. **World Wide Web address:** http://www.qsii.com. **Description:** Develops and markets computerized information processing systems primarily to group dental and medical practices. The systems provide advanced computer-based automation in various aspects of group practice management including the retention of patient information, treatment planning, appointment scheduling, billing, insurance claims processing, electronic insurance claims submission, allocation of income among group professionals, managed care reporting, word processing, and accounting. **NOTE:** Entry-level positions are offered. **Common positions include:** Account

Manager; Account Rep.; Applications Engineer; Internet Services Manager; Project Manager; Sales Representative; Software Engineer; Technical Writer/Editor. **Educational backgrounds include:** Computer Science; Economics; Marketing. **Benefits:** 401(k); Dental Insurance; Disability Coverage; Life Insurance; Medical Insurance. **Special programs:** Internships. **Corporate headquarters location:** This Location. **Number of employees at this location:** 160.

QUANTUM CORPORATION
500 McCarthy Boulevard, Milpitas CA 95035. 408/894-4000. **Contact:** Human Resources. **World Wide Web address:** http://www.quantum.com. **Description:** Designs, manufactures, and markets small hard disk drives used in desktop PCs, workstations, and notebook computers. The company's primary product line is the ProDrive series of high-performance, 3-1/2 inch hard disk drives. **Corporate headquarters location:** This Location. **Annual sales/revenues:** More than $100 million. **Number of employees nationwide:** 2,455.

QUICK EAGLE NETWORKS
217 Humboldt Court, Sunnyvale CA 94089. 408/745-6200. **Fax:** 408/745-6250. **Contact:** Personnel. **World Wide Web address:** http://www.quickeagle.com. **Description:** Develops, markets, and manufactures high-speed digital access products for the WAN marketplace. **Corporate headquarters location:** This Location.

RJO ENTERPRISES
5200G Philadelphia Way, Lanham MD 20706. 301/731-3600. **Fax:** 301/731-8413. **Contact:** Personnel. **World Wide Web address:** http://www.rjo.com. **Description:** Develops software, provides technology solutions, and installs integrated systems. The company also designs, integrates, and manages complex programs built around computers, telecommunications, electronics, and acquisition systems. The majority of RJO's business is conducted with the U.S. government. **Common positions include:** Accountant; Aerospace Engineer; Budget Analyst; Buyer; Computer Programmer; Electrical Engineer; Electronics Technician; Financial Analyst; Mechanical Engineer; Software Engineer; Systems Analyst. **Educational backgrounds include:** Accounting; Business Administration; Computer Science; Engineering; Marketing. **Benefits:** 401(k); Dental Insurance; Disability Coverage; Life Insurance; Medical Insurance; Profit Sharing; Tuition Assistance. **Corporate headquarters location:** This Location. **Other area locations:** Hunt Valley MD. **Other U.S. locations:** Dayton OH; Middletown RI. **Number of employees nationwide:** 300.

RSA SECURITY
20 Crosby Drive, Bedford MA 01730. 781/687-7000. **Contact:** Personnel. **World Wide Web address:** http://www.rsasecurity.com. **Description:** Develops and markets software for security applications. **Corporate headquarters location:** This Location.

RADISYS CORPORATION
5445 NE Dawson Creek Drive, Hillsboro OR 97124. 503/615-1100. **Fax:** 503/615-1150. **Contact:** Personnel. **World Wide Web address:** http://www.radisys.com. **Description:** Designs and manufactures embedded computer technology used by OEMs in the manufacturing automation, medical devices, transportation, test and measurement, telecommunications, and retail automation industries. RadiSys offers a broad range of embedded computer subsystems, board-level

modules, and chip-level products at varying levels of customization from standard products to full custom solutions. **Corporate headquarters location:** This Location.

RADIX INTERNATIONAL
4855 Wiley Post Way, Salt Lake City UT 84116. 801/537-1717. **Contact:** Ms. Tish Dysart, Personnel Manager. **World Wide Web address:** http://www.radix-intl.com. **Description:** Radix International manufactures hand-held computer systems used in meter readings and other applications. **Corporate headquarters location:** This Location.

RARITAN COMPUTER INC.
400 Cottontail Lane, Somerset NJ 08873. 732/764-8886. **Fax:** 732/764-8887. **Contact:** Susan Chan, Human Resources Manager. **E-mail address:** hr@raritan.com. **World Wide Web address:** http://www.raritan.com. **Description:** Designs and manufactures a line of products for sharing PCs and peripherals. Products include MasterConsole, a keyboard/video/mouse switch; CompuSwitch, a KVM switch allowing central control for up to four PCs; and Guardian, a virtual keyboard and mouse device which emulates keyboard and mouse signals. **Common positions include:** Account Manager; Account Rep.; Accountant/Auditor; Administrative Assistant; Advertising Clerk; Applications Engineer; Buyer; Clerical Supervisor; Computer Programmer; Customer Service Rep.; General Manager; Human Resources Manager; Internet Services Manager; Marketing Manager; MIS Specialist; Operations Manager; Project Manager; Purchasing Agent; Quality Control Supervisor; Sales Manager; Sales Rep.; Secretary; Software Engineer; Systems Analyst; Technical Writer; Telecommunications Manager; Vice President of Marketing. **Educational backgrounds include:** Accounting; Art/Design; Computer Science; Engineering. **Benefits:** 401(k); Dental Insurance; Life Insurance; Medical Insurance; Profit Sharing; Savings Plan; Tuition Assistance. **Corporate headquarters location:** This Location. **International locations:** Japan; Taiwan; the Netherlands. **Number of employees nationwide:** 100. **Number of employees worldwide:** 175.

ROGUE WAVE SOFTWARE
815 NW Ninth Street, Corvallis OR 97330. 541/754-4096. **Fax:** 541/753-1912. **Contact:** Human Resources. **E-mail address:** hr@roguewave.com. **World Wide Web address:** http://www.roguewave.com. **Description:** Develops C++ and Java reusable cross-platform software and tools. **NOTE:** Entry-level positions and part-time jobs are offered. **Common positions include:** Account Manager; Account Representative; Accountant; Administrative Assistant; Applications Engineer; CFO; Computer Engineer; Computer Programmer; Computer Support Technician; Customer Service Rep.; Database Administrator; Database Manager; Graphic Artist; Graphic Designer; Human Resources Manager; Marketing Manager; Marketing Specialist; MIS Specialist; Network Administrator; Sales Representative; Software Engineer; SQL Programmer; Systems Analyst; Systems Manager; Webmaster. **Educational backgrounds include:** AS400 Certification; C/C++; Internet; Java; Microsoft Word; Novell; Software Development; Software Tech. Support; Spreadsheets. **Benefits:** 401(k); Casual Dress - Daily; Dental Insurance; Disability Coverage; Financial Planning Assistance; Flexible Schedule; Life Insurance; Medical Insurance; Profit Sharing; Sick Days (11+); Tuition Assistance; Vacation Days (10 - 20). **Special programs:** Internships; Co-ops; Summer Jobs. **Corporate headquarters location:** Boulder CO.

Other U.S. locations: Nationwide. **International locations:** Worldwide. **President/CEO:** Mike Scally. **Facilities Manager:** Dan Hale.

SAP AMERICA, INC.
3999 West Chester Pike, Newtown Square PA 19073. 610/355-2500. **Contact:** Human Resources. **World Wide Web address:** http://www.sap.com. **Description:** Develops a variety of client/server computer software packages including programs for finance, human resources, and materials management applications. **Corporate headquarters location:** This Location. **Other U.S. locations:** Nationwide. **International locations:** Germany. **Parent company:** SAP AG. **Number of employees nationwide:** 3,000. **Number of employees worldwide:** 13,000.

SCC COMMUNICATIONS CORPORATION
6285 Lookout Road, Boulder CO 80301. 303/581-5600. **Contact:** Personnel. **World Wide Web address:** http://www.scc911.com. **Description:** Develops public safety computer software and systems that implement emergency communication networks with telephone service providers. **Corporate headquarters location:** This Location.

SCH TECHNOLOGIES
3 Centennial Plaza, 895 Central Avenue, Cincinnati OH 45202. 513/579-0455. **Fax:** 513/579-1064. **Contact:** Lisa Sayers, Administrative Assistant. **World Wide Web address:** http://www.sch.com. **Description:** Develops and markets software products for managers of open systems installations worldwide. SCH products address the needs of network management; distributed systems management including systems administration, data center management, and tape management; connectivity; and integrated office automation. The company also provides consulting and support services. **Common positions include:** Computer Programmer; Customer Service Rep.; Marketing Specialist; Technical Rep.; Technical Support Representative. **Educational backgrounds include:** Accounting; Art/Design; Business Administration; Communications; Liberal Arts; Marketing. **Benefits:** Disability Coverage; Life Insurance; Medical Insurance. **Corporate headquarters location:** This Location.

SCT CORPORATION
4 Country View Road, Malvern PA 19355. 610/647-5930. **Fax:** 610/578-7778. **Contact:** Human Resources. **World Wide Web address:** http://www.sctcorp.com. **Description:** Develops software and offers computer-related services to the higher education, local government, utility, and manufacturing communities. The company operates through the following divisions: Information Resource Management (IRM); Software & Technology Services (STS); SCT Public Sector, Inc.; and SCT Utility Systems, Inc. **NOTE:** Entry-level positions are offered. **Common positions include:** Accountant; Budget Analyst; Computer Programmer; Human Resources Specialist; Management Analyst; Management Trainee; MIS Specialist; Systems Analyst; Technical Writer. **Educational backgrounds include:** Accounting; Communications; Computer Science; Economics; Liberal Arts; Marketing. **Benefits:** 401(k); Dental Insurance; Disability Coverage; Job Sharing; Life Insurance; Medical Insurance; Telecommuting; Tuition Assistance. **Corporate headquarters location:** This Location. **Listed on:** NASDAQ. **Annual sales/revenues:** More than $100 million.

SED INTERNATIONAL
4916 North Royal Atlanta Drive, Tucker GA 30084. 770/491-8962. **Toll-free phone:** 800/444-8962.

Contact: Human Resources Department. **World Wide Web address:** http://www.sedonline.com. **Description:** A wholesaler of computer systems and cellular phones. **Corporate headquarters location:** This Location.

SFA, INC.
1401 McCormick Drive, Largo MD 20774. 301/925-9400. **Fax:** 301/925-8568. **Contact:** Tony Collands, Recruiter. **World Wide Web address:** http://www.sfa.com. **Description:** A diversified international supplier of products and services aimed at helping clients capitalize on leading edge systems and technologies. SFA conducts advanced research studies; designs and develops state-of-the-art prototypes; and produces customized hardware and software systems for defense, communications, and other commercial applications. **Common positions include:** Accountant; Aerospace Engineer; Biological Scientist; Biomedical Engineer; Buyer; Chemist; Electrical Engineer; Financial Analyst; Materials Engineer; Mechanical Engineer; Metallurgical Engineer; Physicist; Purchasing Agent; Software Engineer; Systems Analyst; Technical Writer/Editor. **Educational backgrounds include:** Accounting; Biology; Communications; Computer Science; Engineering; Marketing; Mathematics; Physics. **Benefits:** 401(k); Dental Insurance; Disability Coverage; Life Insurance; Medical Insurance; Tuition Assistance. **Corporate headquarters location:** This Location. **Other U.S. locations:** Washington DC; Columbia MD; Frederick MD; Landover MD; Lexington Park MD. **Subsidiaries include:** SFA DataComm, Inc.; SFA SACOM. **Operations at this facility include:** Administration; Manufacturing; Research and Development; Sales; Service.

S.I. TECH, INC.
P.O. Box 609, Geneva IL 60134. 630/761-3640. **Fax:** 630/761-3644. **Contact:** Ramesh Sheth, Personnel Manager. **E-mail address:** admin@sitech-bitdriver.com. **World Wide Web address:** http://www.sitech-bitdriver.com. **Description:** Manufactures and markets fiberoptic products such as modems, multiplexers, F.O. hubs, LAN/WAN products, short haul modems, and cable assemblies for data communications use. **NOTE:** Part-time jobs are offered. **Common positions include:** Account Rep.; Accountant; Administrative Assistant; Applications Engineer; AS400 Programmer Analyst; Buyer; Electrical Engineer; Human Resources Manager; Marketing Manager; Network Administrator; Operations Manager; Sales Manager; Sales Representative. **Educational backgrounds include:** Accounting; AS400 Certification; Business Administration; Engineering; MBA. **Benefits:** 401(k); Casual Dress - Fridays; Disability Coverage; Flexible Schedule; Life Insurance; Medical Insurance; Pension Plan; Profit Sharing; Tuition Assistance; Vacation Days (10 - 20). **Special programs:** Internships. **Corporate headquarters location:** This Location. **President:** Ramesh Sheth. **Facilities Manager:** Sandeep Sheth. **Information Systems Manager:** Norman Tan. **Purchasing Manager:** Richard Metcalf.

SMS TECHNOLOGIES, INC.
9877 Waples Street, San Diego CA 92121. 858/587-6900. **Fax:** 858/450-0218. **Contact:** Deborah L. Reinhard, Personnel Manager. **World Wide Web address:** http://www.smstech.com. **Description:** Provides turnkey electronic manufacturing services to the telecommunications, medical electronics, computer, and industrial equipment industries. **NOTE:** Second and third shift positions are offered. **Common positions include:** Account Manager; Accountant; Administrative Manager; Buyer; Computer Operator; Controller; Cost Estimator;

Draftsperson; Electrical Engineer; Human Resources Manager; Industrial Engineer; Manufacturing Engineer; Mechanical Engineer; MIS Specialist; Operations Manager; Production Manager; Quality Assurance Engineer; Quality Control Supervisor; Sales Rep.; Secretary; Systems Manager; Webmaster. **Educational backgrounds include:** Accounting; Business Administration; Computer Science; Engineering; Finance; Marketing; Microsoft Word; Software Development; Spreadsheets. **Benefits:** 401(k); Casual Dress - Fridays; Dental Insurance; Disability Coverage; Employee Discounts; Financial Planning Assistance; Flexible Schedule; Life Insurance; Medical Insurance; Profit Sharing; Sick Days (6 - 10); Tuition Assistance; Vacation Days (11 - 15). **Special programs:** Training. **Corporate headquarters location:** This Location. **Operations at this facility include:** Administration; Manufacturing; Research and Development. **Listed on:** Privately held. **CEO:** Robert L. Blumberg. **Sales Manager:** Elliot Shev. **Number of employees at this location:** 200.

SOS COMPUTER SYSTEMS, INC.
720 East Timpanagos Parkway, Orem UT 84097. 801/222-0200. **Fax:** 801/222-0250. **Contact:** Personnel. **World Wide Web address:** http://www. soscomputers.com. **Description:** Develops and sells operations software used by credit unions. Founded in 1976. **Common positions include:** Computer Programmer; Software Engineer. **Educational backgrounds include:** Accounting; Business Administration; Computer Science; Finance. **Benefits:** 401(k); Life Insurance; Medical Insurance; Tuition Assistance. **Corporate headquarters location:** This Location. **Number of employees at this location:** 55.

STG, INC.
11250 Waples Mill Road, 4th Floor, South Tower, Fairfax VA 22030. 703/691-2480. **Fax:** 703/691-1810. **Contact:** Technical Recruiter. **E-mail address:** recruiting@stginc.com. **World Wide Web address:** http://www.stginc.com. **Description:** A full-service information management firm. STG provides high-tech consulting services to the government, military, and commercial sector. Core business areas include software and systems engineering; network management and computer operations; technical support and training; and computer and physical security services. Founded in 1986. **NOTE:** Entry-level positions and second and third shifts are offered. **Common positions include:** Accountant; Administrative Manager; Computer Operator; Computer Programmer; Database Manager; Electrical Engineer; MIS Specialist; Secretary; Software Engineer; Systems Analyst; Technical Writer; Typist. **Educational backgrounds include:** Business Administration; Computer Science; Engineering. **Benefits:** 401(k); Daycare Assistance; Dental Insurance; Disability Coverage; Life Insurance; Medical Insurance; Tuition Assistance. **Special programs:** Training. **Corporate headquarters location:** This Location. **Other U.S. locations:** FL; KY; MD; MI; OH; SC. **Number of employees nationwide:** 250.

SACO RIVER TECHNOLOGIES
70 Shadagee Road, Saco ME 04072. 207/282-4380. **Contact:** Hiring Manager. **World Wide Web address:** http://www.sacorivertech.com. **Description:** Provides a variety of computer services including consulting, programming, and web design to help clients understand their technology options. Founded in 1991. **Office hours:** Monday - Friday, 9:00 a.m. - 5:00 p.m. **Corporate headquarters location:** This Location.

SAFEGUARD SCIENTIFICS, INC.
800 Safeguard Building, 435 Devon Park Drive, Wayne PA 19087. 610/293-0600. **Fax:** 610/293-0601. **Contact:** Personnel. **World Wide Web address:** http://www.safeguard.com. **Description:** A strategic information systems holding company. **Corporate headquarters location:** This Location. **Subsidiaries include:** Cambridge Technology Partners; ChromaVision Medical Systems; CompuCom Systems, Inc.; Diamond Technology Partners; DocuCorp International; OAD Technology Solutions; Sanchez Computer Association; Tangram Enterprise Solutions; and USDATA Corporation. **Listed on:** New York Stock Exchange.

SAI SOFTWARE CONSULTANTS, INC.
2313 Timber Shadows Drive, Suite 200, Kingwood TX 77339. 281/358-1858. **Fax:** 281/358-8952. **Contact:** Personnel. **E-mail address:** info@saisoft. com. **World Wide Web address:** http://www. saisoft.com. **Description:** A computer consulting company. Sai Software Consultants offers IT staffing expertise and off-site automated software testing services to *Fortune* 500 firms in a wide range of industries including telecommunications, banking, manufacturing, and transportation.

SANDYBROOK SOFTWARE
456 Boom Road, Saco ME 04072. 207/294-7430. **Contact:** Human Resources. **World Wide Web address:** http://www.sandybrook.com. **Description:** Develops plug-in software for Adobe FrameMaker. Products include Enhance. **Corporate headquarters location:** This Location.

SAPIENT CORPORATION
One Memorial Drive, 3rd Floor, Cambridge MA 02142. 617/621-0200. **Contact:** Director of Hiring. **World Wide Web address:** http://www.sapient. com. **Description:** Provides systems integration, consulting, and software integration services. **Corporate headquarters location:** This Location. **Other U.S. locations:** Los Angeles CA; San Francisco CA; Atlanta GA; Chicago IL; Portland ME; Jersey City NJ; Dallas TX. **International locations:** London, England.

SCANSOFT, INC.
9 Centennial Drive, Peabody MA 01960. 978/977-2000. **Toll-free phone:** 800/248-6550. **Fax:** 978/977-2129. **Contact:** Candace Richter, Employment Manager. **World Wide Web address:** http://www.scansoft.com. **Description:** Scansoft manufactures TextBridge and Pagis scanning software and OCR (Optical Character Recognition) software. **NOTE:** Entry-level positions are offered. **Common positions include:** Account Rep.; Administrative Assistant; Computer Programmer; Database Manager; Financial Analyst; Internet Services Manager; Marketing Specialist; MIS Specialist; Project Manager; Software Engineer; Webmaster. **Educational backgrounds include:** Accounting; Computer Science; Engineering; Marketing; Software Development; Software Tech. Support. **Benefits:** 401(k); Dental Insurance; Disability Coverage; Employee Discounts; Financial Planning Assistance; Flexible Schedule; Job Sharing; Life Insurance; Medical Insurance; Profit Sharing; Tuition Assistance; Vision Insurance. **Special programs:** Internships; Training; Co-ops; Summer Jobs. **Corporate headquarters location:** This Location. **Other U.S. locations:** Nationwide. **President:** Mike Tivnan. **Number of employees worldwide:** 140.

SCIENCE APPLICATIONS INTERNATIONAL CORPORATION
10260 Campus Point Drive, San Diego CA 92121. 858/546-6000. **Contact:** Human Resources. **World

Wide Web address: http://www.saic.com. **Description:** Offers technology development, computer system integration, and technology support services. **Common positions include:** Account Manager; Business Analyst; Systems Manager. **Special programs:** Internships. **Corporate headquarters location:** This Location. **Subsidiaries include:** AMSEC; Carreker-Antinori; Danet; GSC; Global Integrity Corp.; Hicks & Assoc.; INTESA; Leadership 2000; Network Solutions, Inc.; PAI. **Annual sales/revenues:** More than $100 million. **Number of employees worldwide:** 36,000.

SEAGATE TECHNOLOGY

920 Disc Drive, Scotts Valley CA 95067-0360. 831/438-6550. **Contact:** Human Resources. **World Wide Web address:** http://www.seagate.com. **Description:** Designs and manufactures data storage devices and related products including hard disk drives, tape drives, software, and systems for a variety of computer-related applications and operating systems. **NOTE:** Resumes should be sent to Human Resources, 900 Disc Drive, Scotts Valley CA 95067. **Common positions include:** Accountant; Administrator; Buyer; Chemist; Computer Programmer; Credit Manager; Customer Service Rep.; Draftsperson; Electrical Engineer; Financial Analyst; Human Resources Manager; Industrial Engineer; Marketing Specialist; Mechanical Engineer; Quality Control Supervisor; Systems Analyst; Technical Writer. **Educational backgrounds include:** Accounting; Business Administration; Chemistry; Computer Science; Engineering; Finance; Marketing. **Corporate headquarters location:** This Location. **Other U.S. locations:** OK. **Number of employees nationwide:** 87,000.

SEMAPHORE, INC.

3 East 28th Street, 11th Floor, New York NY 10016. 212/545-7300. **Toll-free phone:** 800/545-7484. **Fax:** 212/545-7443. **Contact:** Margie Rodriguez, Human Resources. **World Wide Web address:** http://www.sema4.com. **Description:** Develops accounting and project management software for architects, engineers, and designers. The company also provides training, customization, and systems integration services. **NOTE:** Entry-level positions are offered. **Company slogan:** Providing the true perspective. **Common positions include:** Account Rep.; Administrative Assistant; Computer Engineer; Computer Programmer; Computer Scientist; Computer Support Technician; Database Manager; MIS Specialist; Multimedia Designer; Network Administrator; Sales Rep.; Software Engineer; SQL Programmer; Systems Analyst; Systems Manager; Technical Writer; Webmaster. **Educational backgrounds include:** Accounting; Computer Science; Engineering; HTML; Internet; Software Development; Software Tech. Support. **Benefits:** 401(k); Casual Dress - Daily; Dental Insurance; Disability Coverage; Medical Insurance; Tuition Assistance. **Special programs:** Internships. **Corporate headquarters location:** This Location. **Other U.S. locations:** Walnut CA; Minneapolis MN; Portland OR. **International locations:** Taiwan. **Parent company:** Novax Group. **President:** Raymond King. **Annual sales/revenues:** $11 - $20 million. **Number of employees at this location:** 100. **Number of employees worldwide:** 140.

SHARED MEDICAL SYSTEMS CORP.

51 Valley Stream Parkway, Malvern PA 19355. 610/219-3359. **Fax:** 610/219-8266. **Contact:** Personnel. **E-mail address:** human.resources@smed.com. **World Wide Web address:** http://www.smed.com. **Description:** A leading provider of health information and service solutions to hospitals, multi-entity health care corporations, integrated health networks, physician groups, and other health care providers in North America and Europe. The company also provides a full complement of solutions for the newly-emerging community health information networks, which include payers and employers as well as providers. Shared Medical Systems offers a comprehensive line of health care information systems including clinical, financial, administrative, ambulatory, and decision support systems for both the public and private health care sectors. These systems are offered on computers operating at the customer site, at the SMS Information Services Center, or as part of a distributed network. Shared Medical Systems also provides a portfolio of professional services including systems installation, support, and education. In addition, the company provides specialized consulting services for the design and integration of software and networks, facilities management, information systems planning, and systems-related process reengineering. Founded in 1969. **NOTE:** Entry-level positions are offered. **Common positions include:** Accountant; Computer Programmer; Licensed Practical Nurse; MIS Specialist; Network Engineer; Pharmacist; Project Manager; Radiological Technologist; Registered Nurse; Software Engineer; Systems Analyst; Technical Writer. **Educational backgrounds include:** Accounting; Business Administration; Communications; Computer Science; Health Care; Marketing; Mathematics. **Benefits:** 401(k); Dental Insurance; Disability Coverage; Employee Discounts; Life Insurance; Medical Insurance; Profit Sharing; Savings Plan; Tuition Assistance. **Special programs:** Internships. **Corporate headquarters location:** This Location. **Other U.S. locations:** Nationwide. **Operations at this facility include:** Administration; Research and Development; Sales; Service. **Annual sales/revenues:** More than $100 million. **Number of employees at this location:** 3,200. **Number of employees worldwide:** 5,000.

SIEBEL SYSTEMS, INC.

1855 South Grant Street, San Mateo CA 94402. 650/295-5000. **Toll-free phone:** 800/647-4300. **Contact:** Personnel. **E-mail address:** info@siebel.com. **World Wide Web address:** http://www.siebel.com. **Description:** A leading provider of e-commerce application software. **Corporate headquarters location:** This Location. **Number of employees worldwide:** 4,500.

SIEMENS BUSINESS SYSTEMS

200 Wheeler Road, Burlington MA 01803. 781/273-0480. **Fax:** 781/313-4231. **Contact:** Personnel. **World Wide Web address:** http://www.sbs-usa.siemens.com. **Description:** A manufacturer of computer systems, software, and peripherals. The company also offers consulting, planning, and implementation services. **Common positions include:** Customer Service Representative; Software Engineer; Systems Analyst. **Educational backgrounds include:** Business Administration; Communications; Computer Science; Marketing. **Benefits:** 401(k); Dental Insurance; Disability Coverage; Life Insurance; Medical Insurance; Tuition Assistance. **Corporate headquarters location:** This Location. **Operations at this facility include:** Administration; Sales; Service.

SIERRA, INC.

3380 146th Place SE, Suite 300, Bellevue WA 98007. 425/649-9800. **Fax:** 425/401-4926. **Contact:** Personnel. **E-mail address:** recruit@sierra.com. **World Wide Web address:** http://www.sierra.com. **Description:** Develops and distributes entertainment and educational software. The company's products are designed for IBM compatible and Macintosh systems. Founded in 1979. **Common positions include:** Software Engineer. **Educational backgrounds include:** Computer Science. **Benefits:** 401(k); Dental Insurance; Disability Coverage; Employee Discounts; Flexible Schedule; Life Insurance; Medical Insurance; Tuition Assistance. **Corporate headquarters location:** Oakhurst CA. **Other U.S. locations:** Nationwide. **International locations:** France; Germany. **Number of employees at this location:** 450.

SILICON GRAPHICS INC. (SGI)
1600 Amphitheatre Parkway, Mountain View CA 94043. 650/960-1980. **Contact:** Human Resources. **World Wide Web address:** http://www.sgi.com. **Description:** Manufactures a family of workstation and server systems that are used by engineers, scientists, and other creative professionals to develop, analyze, and simulate complex, three-dimensional objects. **Corporate headquarters location:** This Location.

SILKNET SOFTWARE
50 Phillipe Cote Street, Manchester NH 03101. 603/625-0070. **Contact:** Human Resources. **Description:** Develops and manufactures customer support software. **Corporate headquarters location:** This Location.

SILVERPLATTER INFORMATION
100 River Ridge Drive, Norwood MA 02062. 781/769-2599. **Fax:** 781/769-8763. **Contact:** Marcella Nelson, Director of Personnel. **E-mail address:** staffing@silverplatter.com. **World Wide Web address:** http://www.silverplatter.com. **Description:** Publishes and distributes over 225 authoritative databases. SilverPlatter Information also publishes CD-ROMs and develops software systems for data retrieval and full text linking. Founded in 1985. **NOTE:** Entry-level positions are offered. **Common positions include:** Account Rep.; Accountant; Administrative Assistant; Attorney; Budget Analyst; CFO; Computer Scientist; Computer Support Technician; Controller; Credit Manager; Customer Service Rep.; Financial Analyst; General Manager; Human Resources Manager; Intellectual Property Lawyer; Internet Services Manager; Librarian; Marketing Manager; Marketing Specialist; MIS Specialist; Network Administrator; Production Manager; Project Manager; Public Relations Specialist; Sales Manager; Sales Rep.; Systems Analyst; Systems Manager; Webmaster. **Educational backgrounds include:** Accounting; C/C++; Computer Science; Engineering; Finance; HTML; Internet; Java; Liberal Arts; Library Science; Marketing; Microsoft Word; Public Relations; Software Development; Software Tech. Support; Spreadsheets. **Benefits:** 401(k); Casual Dress - Daily; Dental Insurance; Disability Coverage; Life Insurance; Medical Insurance; Telecommuting; Tuition Assistance. **Corporate headquarters location:** This Location. **Other area locations:** Boston MA. **Other U.S. locations:** Pasadena CA; Newton MA. **International locations:** Berlin, Germany; Bologna, Italy; Hong Kong; London, England; Paris, France; Sydney, Australia. **Number of employees at this location:** 200. **Number of employees nationwide:** 240.

SIMPLE TECHNOLOGY INC.
3001 Daimler Street, Santa Ana CA 92705. 949/260-8372. **Toll-free phone:** 800/367-7330. **Fax:** 949/476-0852. **Contact:** Personnel. **E-mail address:** jobs@simpletech.com. **World Wide Web address:** http://www.simpletech.com. **Description:** Designs and manufactures computer memory

products, portable storage devices, and PC cards. **NOTE:** Second and third shifts are offered. **Common positions include:** Accountant; Applications Engineer; Manufacturing Engineer; Process Engineer; Purchasing Agent; Sales Engineer; Sales Manager; Sales Rep.; Software Engineer; Technical Writer; Test Engineer. **Educational backgrounds include:** Business Administration; Computer Science; Engineering; Software Tech. Support. **Benefits:** 401(k); Dental Insurance; Disability Coverage; Employee Discounts; Financial Planning Assistance; Life Insurance; Medical Insurance. **Corporate headquarters location:** This Location. **International locations:** Canada; Scotland. **Annual sales/revenues:** More than $100 million. **Number of employees nationwide:** 350.

SINBAD NETWORK COMMUNICATIONS
3101 Penland Parkway, Suite K26, Anchorage AK 99508. 907/274-6223. **Contact:** Human Resources. **World Wide Web address:** http://www.sinbad.net. **Description:** Provides online services to subscribers including a Web browser, chat rooms, e-mail, personal Web pages, live news, investment tools, computer training, and bulletin boards. **Corporate headquarters location:** This Location.

SKYWARD, INC.
5233 Coye Drive, Stevens Point WI 54481. **Toll-free phone:** 800/236-7274. **Fax:** 715/341-1370. **Contact:** Human Resources. **World Wide Web address:** http://www.skyward.com. **Description:** Develops school administration software. **NOTE:** Entry-level positions are offered. **Common positions include:** Computer Programmer; Customer Service Rep.; Network Engineer; Sales Rep.; Systems Analyst. **Educational backgrounds include:** Computer Science; Software Development; Software Tech. Support. **Benefits:** 401(k); Dental Insurance; Disability Coverage; Flexible Schedule; Life Insurance; Medical Insurance; Profit Sharing; Section 125 Plan. **Corporate headquarters location:** This Location. **Other U.S. locations:** Bloomington IL; St. Cloud MN. **Number of employees at this location:** 110.

SMITH MICRO SOFTWARE, INC.
51 Columbia, Suite 200, Aliso Viejo CA 92656. 949/362-5800. **Contact:** Human Resources. **World Wide Web address:** http://www.smithmicro.com. **Description:** A computer consulting firm. **Corporate headquarters location:** This Location. **Other U.S. locations:** Boulder CO.

SOFTMART, INC.
450 Acorn Lane, Downingtown PA 19335. 610/518-4000. **Fax:** 610/518-3014. **Recorded jobline:** 800/334-3495. **Contact:** Milissa Ronayne, Recruiting Manager. **E-mail address:** mronayne@softmart.com. **World Wide Web address:** http://www.softmart.com. **Description:** Resells computer software and hardware to government and commercial clients. **NOTE:** Entry-level positions and second and third shifts are offered. **Common positions include:** Account Manager; Account Rep.; Accountant; Administrative Assistant; Advertising Clerk; Advertising Executive; Assistant Manager; Attorney; Budget Analyst; Buyer; Clerical Supervisor; Computer Operator; Computer Programmer; Controller; Credit Manager; Customer Service Rep.; Database Manager; Editor; Financial Analyst; Graphic Artist; Graphic Designer; Human Resources Manager; Marketing Manager; Marketing Specialist; MIS Specialist; Multimedia Designer; Production Manager; Project Manager; Quality Control Supervisor; Sales Executive; Sales Manager; Sales Rep.; Secretary; Software Engineer; Systems Analyst; Systems Manager; Technical

Writer/Editor; Telecommunications Manager; Webmaster. **Educational backgrounds include:** Accounting; Art/Design; Business Administration; Communications; Computer Science; Economics; Finance; Liberal Arts; Marketing; Public Relations; Software Development; Software Tech. Support. **Benefits:** 401(k); Daycare Assistance; Dental Insurance; Disability Coverage; EAP; Employee Discounts; Flexible Schedule; Life Insurance; Medical Insurance; Prescription Drugs; STD/LTD Coverage; Vision Insurance. **Special programs:** Internships; Training; Summer Jobs. **Corporate headquarters location:** This Location. **President:** Elliot Levine. **Annual sales/revenues:** More than $100 million. **Number of employees at this location:** 490.

SOFTWARE SPECTRUM INC.
2140 Merritt Drive, Garland TX 75041. 972/840-6600. **Fax:** 972/864-3219. **Contact:** Personnel. **World Wide Web address:** http://www. softwarespectrum.com. **Description:** Resells microcomputer software and services to businesses and government agencies. Software Spectrum also offers technical support and volume software license services. **Common positions include:** Accountant; Advertising Clerk; Blue-Collar Worker Supervisor; Buyer; Collector; Computer Programmer; Credit Manager; Customer Service Representative; Electrical Engineer; Human Resources Manager; Operations Manager; Public Relations Specialist; Purchasing Agent; Quality Control Supervisor; Services Sales Rep.; Systems Analyst; Technical Writer. **Educational backgrounds include:** Accounting; Art/Design; Business Administration; Communications; Computer Science; Economics; Engineering; Finance; Liberal Arts; Marketing. **Benefits:** 401(k); Dental Insurance; Disability Coverage; Employee Discounts; Life Insurance; Medical Insurance; Profit Sharing. **Corporate headquarters location:** This Location. **Other U.S. locations:** Nationwide. **International locations:** Worldwide. **Subsidiaries include:** Spectrum Integrated Services. **Operations at this facility include:** Administration; Sales; Service. **Listed on:** NASDAQ. **Number of employees at this location:** 500. **Number of employees nationwide:** 575.

SOFTWARE TECHNOLOGIES CORP.
404 East Huntington Drive, Monrovia CA 91016. 626/471-6000. **Fax:** 626/471-6100. **Contact:** Personnel. **World Wide Web address:** http://www. stc.com. **Description:** Develops data interface engines and database software for enterprisewide solutions. Products include e*Gate, an enterprise integration program. **Corporate headquarters location:** This Location.

SOURCE MEDIA, INC.
One Lincoln Center, 5400 LBJ Freeway, Suite 680, Dallas TX 75240. 972/701-5400. **Contact:** Ms. Avis Novak, Human Resources Manager. **World Wide Web address:** http://www.srcm.com. **Description:** Operates the Interactive Channel, an online television browser and programming service. The Interactive Channel is broadcast over cable television networks, and provides on-demand information covering education, news, sports, entertainment, and shopping. **Corporate headquarters location:** This Location.

SPEAR TECHNOLOGIES
One Market Street, Suite 700, San Francisco CA 94105-1018. **Contact:** Personnel. **Description:** Develops, markets, and supports a line of maintenance management software for the transportation industry. **Corporate headquarters location:** This Location. **Other U.S. locations:** Hartford CT. **International locations:** The Netherlands. **Number of employees at this location:** 225.

SPECTRA INC.
P.O. Box 68-C, Hanover NH 03755. 603/643-4390. **Fax:** 603/298-6860. **Contact:** Bonnie Bauer, Human Resources Manager. **E-mail address:** bbauer@spectra-inc.com. **World Wide Web address:** http://www.spectra-inc.com. **Description:** Manufactures computer printer heads and ink. **NOTE:** Entry-level positions and second and third shifts are offered. **Common positions include:** Buyer; Chemical Engineer; Chemist; Design Engineer; Designer; Electrical Engineer; Financial Analyst; Industrial Engineer; Manufacturing Engineer; Mechanical Engineer; MIS Specialist; Project Manager; Quality Control Supervisor; Software Engineer; Systems Analyst. **Educational backgrounds include:** Chemistry; Computer Science; Engineering; Mathematics; Physics. **Benefits:** 401(k); Dental Insurance; Disability Coverage; Job Sharing; Life Insurance; Medical Insurance; Profit Sharing; Tuition Assistance. **Special programs:** Training. **Corporate headquarters location:** This Location. **Parent company:** Markem Corporation. **Number of employees at this location:** 130.

SPECTRA LOGIC
1700 North 55th Street, Boulder CO 80301. 303/449-6400. **Fax:** 303/939-8844. **Contact:** Troy Bettinger, Staffing Director. **E-mail address:** hireme@spectralogic.com. **World Wide Web address:** http://www.spectralogic.com. **Description:** Manufactures backup hardware and automated tape libraries. **NOTE:** Entry-level positions are offered. **Common positions include:** Account Manager; Account Rep.; Accountant; Computer Engineer; Computer Support Technician; Design Engineer; Electrical Engineer; Help-Desk Technician; Manufacturing Engineer; Mechanical Engineer; Network Administrator; Quality Assurance Engineer; Sales Engineer; Sales Manager; Sales Rep.; Software Engineer; Technical Writer/Editor. **Educational backgrounds include:** Computer Science; Engineering; UNIX. **Benefits:** 401(k); Casual Dress - Daily; Computer Loans; Disability Coverage; Employee Discounts; Flexible Schedule; Life Insurance; Medical Insurance; Profit Sharing; Public Transit Available; Tuition Assistance; Vacation Days (10 - 20). **Special programs:** Internships. **Internship information:** For detailed internship information, visit the company's Website. **Corporate headquarters location:** This Location. **International locations:** London, England; Tokyo, Japan. **Listed on:** Privately held. **President:** Michael Sausa. **Number of employees at this location:** 150.

SPECTRAL DYNAMICS INC.
1983 Concourse Drive, San Jose CA 95131. 408/474-1700. **Contact:** Human Resources. **World Wide Web address:** http://www.sd-corp.com. **Description:** Specializes in the design and manufacture of computer-controlled test, measurement, and development systems and software for a wide variety of customers in three high-technology markets: electronic equipment, mechanical equipment, and semiconductor manufacturers. **Corporate headquarters location:** This Location. **Parent company:** Carrier Corp.

SPECTRUM HUMAN RESOURCE SYSTEMS
1625 Broadway, Suite 2600, Denver CO 80202-4720. 303/592-3200. **Toll-free phone:** 800/334-5660. **Fax:** 303/595-9970. **Contact:** Karen S. Dolan, Human Resources Manager. **E-mail address:** spectrum-info@spectrumhr.com. **World Wide Web address:** http://www.spectrumhr.com.

Description: Develops computer software for use in human resources management, benefits administration, and training development administration. **NOTE:** Entry-level positions are offered. **Common positions include:** Accountant; Administrative Assistant; Computer Operator; Computer Programmer; Customer Service Rep.; Marketing Specialist; Quality Assurance Engineer; Sales Manager; Sales Rep.; Secretary; Software Engineer; Technical Writer/Editor. **Educational backgrounds include:** Accounting; Business Administration; Communications; Computer Science; Human Resources; Liberal Arts; Marketing; Public Relations. **Benefits:** 401(k); Dental Insurance; Disability Coverage; Flexible Schedule; Life Insurance; Medical Insurance; Profit Sharing; Public Transit Available; Savings Plan. **Corporate headquarters location:** This Location. **Number of employees at this location:** 100. **Number of employees nationwide:** 115.

SPYGLASS, INC.
1240 East Diehl Road, Suite 400, Naperville IL 60563. 630/245-6575. **Toll-free phone:** 800/647-8901. **Fax:** 630/245-6647. **Contact:** Shelley Hughes, Human Resources Coordinator. **E-mail address:** info@spyglass.com. **World Wide Web address:** http://www.spyglass.com. **Description:** This location houses executive offices and the Technical Support Group and Server Research & Development team. Overall, Spyglass is a leading provider of expertise, software, and services for making devices work with the Internet. Spyglass provides consulting for defining, developing, and delivering complete, end-to-end project solutions. **Common positions include:** Accountant; Administrative Assistant; Applications Engineer; AS400 Programmer Analyst; Attorney; CEO; Computer Engineer; Computer Programmer; Computer Support Technician; Controller; Financial Analyst; General Manager; Human Resources Manager; Marketing Manager; Marketing Specialist; Multimedia Designer; Network Administrator; Public Relations Specialist; Sales Manager; Software Engineer; Webmaster. **Educational backgrounds include:** Accounting; Business Administration; C/C++; Computer Science; Engineering; HTML; Internet; Java; Software Development; Software Tech. Support. **Benefits:** 401(k); Casual Dress - Daily; Dental Insurance; Disability Coverage; Flexible Schedule; Life Insurance; Medical Insurance; Vacation Days (16+). **Corporate headquarters location:** This Location. **President/CEO:** Doug Colbeth. **Number of employees nationwide:** 140.

STANDARD MICROSYSTEMS CORP.
80 Arkay Drive, P.O. Box 18047, Hauppauge NY 11788. 631/435-6000. **Fax:** 631/273-5550. **Contact:** Personnel. **E-mail address:** hr@smsc.com. **World Wide Web address:** http://www.smsc.com. **Description:** This location houses the VLSI circuit design and LAN hub and switch engineering centers, marketing, customer support, and wafer fabrication, as well as operations and administrative staff. The company's Component Products Division supplies MOS/VLSI circuits for personal computers and embedded control systems. These include input/output devices for disk drive control, communications interface, power management and other PC motherboard functions, Ethernet and Fast Ethernet controllers for local area network applications, and ARCNET controllers for embedded networking applications. The System Products Division provides a broad range of networking solutions for scaling, managing, and controlling LANs. Its products include network adapters, hubs, switches, and network management software. This division has an installed base of over 12 million nodes. Standard Microsystems uses internally developed integrated circuits. Founded in 1971. **NOTE:** Entry-level positions and second and third shifts are offered. **Common positions include:** Account Manager; Accountant; Administrative Assistant; Computer Programmer; Customer Service Rep.; Design Engineer; Electrical Engineer; Financial Analyst; Manufacturing Engineer; Market Research Analyst; Marketing Manager; Marketing Specialist; Mechanical Engineer; MIS Specialist; Project Manager; Public Relations Specialist; Purchasing Agent; Quality Control Supervisor; Sales Engineer; Sales Rep.; Secretary; Software Engineer; Systems Analyst; Systems Manager; Technical Writer/Editor. **Educational backgrounds include:** Business Administration; Chemistry; Computer Science; Engineering; Marketing. **Benefits:** 401(k); Daycare Assistance; Dental Insurance; Disability Coverage; Employee Discounts; Life Insurance; Medical Insurance; Tuition Assistance. **Special programs:** Internships. **Corporate headquarters location:** This Location. **Other U.S. locations:** Irvine CA; San Jose CA; Danvers MA; Austin TX. **International locations:** Worldwide. **Annual sales/revenues:** More than $100 million. **Number of employees worldwide:** 800.

STATSOFT, INC.
2300 East 14th Street, Tulsa OK 74104. 918/749-1119. **Fax:** 918/749-2217. **Contact:** Human Resources. **E-mail address:** jobs@statsoft.com. **World Wide Web address:** http://www.statsoft.com. **Description:** A leading manufacturer of statistics software. **NOTE:** Entry-level positions are offered. **Common positions include:** Software Engineer; Statistician; Technical Support Engineer. **Educational backgrounds include:** Biology; Computer Science; Mathematics; Statistics. **Benefits:** Medical Insurance; Retirement Plan. **Corporate headquarters location:** This Location. **International locations:** Worldwide.

STORAGE COMPUTER CORPORATION
11 Riverside Street, Nashua NH 03062-1373. 603/880-3005. **Fax:** 603/880-6459. **Contact:** Human Resources Manager. **World Wide Web address:** http://www.storage.com. **Description:** Designs, manufactures, and sells standards-based, high-performance, fault-tolerant storage solutions for use in client/server, online transaction processing, large database, multimedia, video-on-demand, and high-volume imaging applications. **Common positions include:** Accountant; Buyer; Computer Programmer; Draftsperson; Electrical Engineer; Mechanical Engineer; Quality Control Supervisor. **Educational backgrounds include:** Engineering. **Corporate headquarters location:** This Location. **Operations at this facility include:** Administration; Manufacturing; Research and Development; Sales; Service.

STORAGETEK
One StorageTek Drive, Louisville CO 80028. 719/536-4055. **Contact:** Human Resources. **World Wide Web address:** http://www.stortek.com. **Description:** StorageTek supplies high-performance computer information storage and retrieval systems for mainframe and mid-frame computers and networks. Products include automated cartridge systems, random access subsystems, and fault-tolerant disk arrays. The company also distributes equipment; sells new peripherals, software, and hardware; and offers support services. **Corporate headquarters location:** This Location. **Operations at this facility include:** Administration; Manufacturing; Research and Development. **Listed on:** New York Stock Exchange.

STRANDWARE INC.
P.O. Box 634, Eau Claire WI 54702. 715/833-2331.
Fax: 715/833-1995. **Contact:** Personnel. **E-mail address:** info@strandware.com. **World Wide Web address:** http://www.strandware.com. **Description:** Develops and markets bar code labeling software.

STRATAGEM, INC.
200 Woodland Prime, Menomonee Falls WI 53051. 262/532-2700. **Toll-free phone:** 800/228-4422. **Fax:** 262/532-2702. **Contact:** Sally Spicer, Recruiting Manager. **E-mail address:** careers@stratagemnet.com. **World Wide Web address:** http://www.stratagemconsulting.com. **Description:** Offers comprehensive information technology solutions. Founded in 1986. **Common positions include:** Administrative Assistant; Applications Engineer; Computer Engineer; Computer Programmer; Computer Support Technician; Database Administrator; Internet Services Manager; Intranet Developer; MIS Specialist; Network Engineer; Network Administrator; Software Engineer; SQL Programmer; Systems Analyst; Systems Manager; Webmaster; Website Developer. **Educational backgrounds include:** Internet Development; Java; MCSE; Microsoft Office; Microsoft Word; Novell; Software Development; Software Tech. Support; Visual Basic. **Benefits:** 401(k); Dental Insurance; Disability Coverage; Life Insurance; Medical Insurance; Profit Sharing; Relocation Assistance; Sick Days; Tuition Assistance; Vacation Days. **Corporate headquarters location:** This Location. **Other U.S. locations:** Minnetonka MN; Appleton WI; Madison WI; Wausau WI. **President:** Gary Krieger. **Facilities Manager:** Cornel Rosario. **Information Systems Manager:** Keith Campbell. **Purchasing Manager:** Cornel Rosario. **Sales Manager:** Jerry Tobin. **Number of employees at this location:** 250. **Number of employees nationwide:** 450.

STRATEGIC TECHNOLOGIES
301 Gregson Drive, Cary NC 27511. 919/379-8000. **Contact:** Monica Smith, Recruiter. **World Wide Web address:** http://www.stratech.com. **Description:** Provides network integration services. **Corporate headquarters location:** This Location.

STRATUS COMPUTER, INC.
111 Powdermill Road, Maynard MA 01754. 978/461-7000. **Contact:** Human Resources. **World Wide Web address:** http://www.stratus.com. **Description:** Offers a broad range of computer systems, application solutions, middleware, and professional services for critical online operations. **Corporate headquarters location:** This Location. **Subsidiaries include:** Shared Systems Corporation provides software and professional services to the financial services, retail, and health care industries. SoftCom Systems provides data communications middleware and related professional services that bridge the gap between open distributed systems and legacy mainframe and midrange systems used for online applications. Isis Distributed Systems, Inc. develops advanced messaging middleware products that enable businesses to develop reliable, high-performance distributed computing applications involving networked desktop computers and shared systems.

STRUCTURAL DYNAMICS RESEARCH CORP.
2000 Eastman Drive, Milford OH 45150. 513/576-2400. **Fax:** 513/576-2922. **Contact:** Derek Jackson, Director of Human Resources. **World Wide Web address:** http://www.sdrc.com. **Description:** An international supplier of mechanical computer-aided engineering (MCAE) software and engineering services. **Common positions include:** Aerospace Engineer; Civil Engineer; Computer Programmer;

Mathematician; Mechanical Engineer; Software Engineer; Systems Analyst. **Educational backgrounds include:** Computer Science; Engineering; Mathematics. **Benefits:** 401(k); Dental Insurance; Disability Coverage; Employee Discounts; Life Insurance; Medical Insurance; Tuition Assistance. **Corporate headquarters location:** This Location. **Operations at this facility include:** Research and Development; Sales; Service. **Number of employees at this location:** 1,000. **Number of employees nationwide:** 1,200.

S2 SYSTEMS INC.
1000 Windward Concourse Parkway, Suite 450, Alpharetta GA 30005. 770/551-2551. **Fax:** 770/551-2550. **Contact:** Human Resources. **Description:** A provider of data communications middleware and related professional services that bridge the gap between open distributed systems and legacy mainframe and midrange systems used for online applications. **Corporate headquarters location:** Marlborough MA. **Parent company:** Stratus Computer, Inc. offers a broad range of computer platforms, application solutions, middleware, and professional services for critical online operations. Other Stratus subsidiaries include Shared Systems Corporation, a provider of software and professional services to the financial services, retail, and health care industries; and Isis Distributed Systems, Inc., a developer of advanced messaging middleware products that enable businesses to develop reliable, high performance distributed computing applications involving networked desktop computers and shared systems. **Number of employees nationwide:** 200.

SUN MICROSYSTEMS, INC.
901 San Antonio Road, Palo Alto CA 94303. **Toll-free phone:** 800/555-9786. **Contact:** Personnel. **World Wide Web address:** http://www.sun.com. **Description:** Produces high-performance computer systems, workstations, servers, CPUs, peripherals, and operating systems software. Products are sold to engineering, scientific, technical, and commercial markets worldwide. **Corporate headquarters location:** This Location. **Subsidiaries include:** Forte Software Inc. manufactures enterprise application integration software. **Number of employees nationwide:** 26,300.

SUNBURST COMMUNICATIONS INC.
101 Castleton Street, Pleasantville NY 10570. 914/747-3310. **Fax:** 914/747-4109. **Contact:** Human Resources. **World Wide Web address:** http://www.sunburst.com. **Description:** Develops and markets educational videos and software. **Common positions include:** Computer Animator; Computer Programmer; Customer Service Rep.; Editor; Software Engineer; Technical Writer/Editor. **Educational backgrounds include:** Accounting; Computer Science; Finance; Marketing. **Benefits:** 401(k); Dental Insurance; Disability Coverage; Life Insurance; Medical Insurance; Profit Sharing; Public Transit Available; Telecommuting; Tuition Assistance. **Special programs:** Internships. **Corporate headquarters location:** This Location. **Number of employees at this location:** 150.

SUNGARD ASSET MANAGEMENT SYSTEMS
333 Technology Drive, Malvern PA 19355. 610/251-1813. **Fax:** 610/251-6585. **Contact:** Teresa Urban, Human Resources Coordinator. **World Wide Web address:** http://www.sungard.com. **Description:** Develops, markets, and supports software for the financial industry. **NOTE:** Entry-level positions are offered. **Common positions include:** Software Engineer. **Educational backgrounds include:** Business Administration; Computer Science; Finance; Mathematics. **Benefits:**

401(k); Dental Insurance; Disability Coverage; Employee Discounts; Life Insurance; Medical Insurance; Profit Sharing; Telecommuting; Tuition Assistance. **Special programs:** Internships; Training. **Corporate headquarters location:** This Location. **Other U.S. locations:** Nationwide. **Operations at this facility include:** Administration; Sales; Service.

SUNGARD DATA SYSTEMS INC./SUNGARD RECOVERY SERVICES

1285 Drummers Lane, Suite 300, Wayne PA 19087. 610/341-8700. **Contact:** Karen Bilinski, Human Resources Vice President. **World Wide Web address:** http://www.sungard.com. **Description:** Provides specialized computer services including proprietary investment support systems for the financial services industry and computer disaster planning/recovery services. SunGard Data Systems Inc.'s investment accounting and portfolio systems maintain the books and records of large investment portfolios including those managed by banks and mutual funds. The company's disaster recovery services include alternate-site backup, testing, and recovery services for IBM, Prime, Stratus, Tandem, and Unisys computer installations. The company's computer service unit provides remote-access IBM computer processing, direct marketing, and automated mailing services. SunGard Data Systems Inc. also provides computer software, data processing, programming, and repair services. SunGard Recovery Systems (also at this location) provides business recovery services for both mainframe and mid-range computer platforms. **Corporate headquarters location:** This Location. **Number of employees at this location:** 2,100.

SYBASE, INC.

6475 Christie Avenue, Emeryville CA 94608. 510/922-3500. **Contact:** Human Resources. **World Wide Web address:** http://www.sybase.com. **Description:** Develops, markets, and supports a full line of relational database management software products and services for integrated, enterprisewide information management systems. **Corporate headquarters location:** This Location. **Number of employees at this location:** 2,350.

SYMANTEC CORPORATION

10201 Torre Avenue, Cupertino CA 95014-2132. 408/253-9600. **Contact:** Staffing. **E-mail address:** jobs@symantec.com. **World Wide Web address:** http://www.symantec.com. **Description:** This location houses finance, sales, and marketing operations. Overall, Symantec Corporation is a global organization that develops, manufactures, and markets software products for individuals and businesses. The company is a vendor of utility software for stand-alone and networked personal computers. In addition, the company offers a wide range of project management products, productivity applications, and development languages and tools. The company is organized into several product groups that are devoted to product marketing, engineering, technical support, quality assurance, and documentation. Founded in 1982. **Common positions include:** Software Developer; Software Engineer. **Educational backgrounds include:** Accounting; Computer Science; Engineering; Marketing. **Benefits:** 401(k); Dental Insurance; Disability Coverage; Employee Discounts; Life Insurance; Medical Insurance; Profit Sharing; Tuition Assistance. **Special programs:** Internships. **Corporate headquarters location:** This Location.

SYSTEMAX INC.

22 Harbor Park Drive, Port Washington NY 11050. 516/625-1555. **Fax:** 516/608-7111. **Contact:** Karen Center, Corporate Recruiter. **World Wide Web address:** http://www.systemax.com. **Description:** A direct marketer of brand name and private label computer, office, and industrial products targeting mid-range and major corporate accounts, small office/home customers, and value-added resellers. Founded in 1949. **NOTE:** Entry-level positions are offered. **Common positions include:** Account Rep.; Accountant; Administrative Assistant; Advertising Executive; Applications Engineer; Auditor; Buyer; Computer Operator; Computer Programmer; Computer Support Technician; Computer Technician; Customer Service Rep.; Database Administrator; Database Manager; Desktop Publishing Specialist; Graphic Artist; Industrial Engineer; Internet Services Manager; Market Research Analyst; Marketing Manager; Marketing Specialist; MIS Specialist; Network Administrator; Sales Rep.; Software Engineer; Systems Analyst; Technical Writer; Transportation Specialist; Webmaster. **Educational backgrounds include:** Accounting; Art/Design; Business Administration; Computer Science; HTML; Java; Marketing; MCSE; Microsoft Word; QuarkXPress; Software Development; Software Tech. Support; Spreadsheets. **Benefits:** 401(k); Casual Dress - Fridays; Dental Insurance; Disability Coverage; Employee Discounts; Flexible Schedule; Life Insurance; Medical Insurance. **Special programs:** Internships; Summer Jobs. **Corporate headquarters location:** This Location. **Other U.S. locations:** CA; FL; GA; IL; NC; NJ; OH. **Subsidiaries include:** Global Computer Supplies; Global Equipment Company; Midwest Micro Corp.; Misco America, Inc.; Misco Canada Inc.; TigerDirect Inc. **Annual sales/revenues:** More than $100 million. **Number of employees at this location:** 500. **Number of employees nationwide:** 2,000. **Number of employees worldwide:** 2,500.

SYSTEMS SOLUTIONS INC.

2108 East Thomas Road, Suite 300, Phoenix AZ 85016. 602/955-5566x125. **Toll-free phone:** 800/232-0026. **Fax:** 602/955-0085. **Contact:** Personnel. **World Wide Web address:** http://www.syspac.com. **Description:** Provides Internet services and offers technical services and solutions for Website design, Website hosting, database programming, local- and wide-area networks, computer telephony, and software development. Systems Solutions also offers SYSPAC, a comprehensive library of distribution, inventory control, and accounting software modules. **NOTE:** Entry-level positions are offered. **Company slogan:** Full Service Computer Group Since 1982. **Common positions include:** Account Manager; Account Rep.; Accountant; Administrative Assistant; Administrative Manager; Advertising Clerk; Applications Engineer; Buyer; CFO; Clerical Supervisor; Computer Animator; Computer Operator; Computer Programmer; Controller; Credit Manager; Customer Service Rep.; Database Manager; Financial Analyst; Graphic Designer; Human Resources Manager; Internet Services Manager; Network Support Technician; Purchasing Agent; Quality Control Supervisor; Repair Specialist; Software Engineer; Systems Analyst; Systems Manager; Teacher; Typist; Webmaster. **Educational backgrounds include:** Accounting; Business Administration; Computer Science; Marketing; Software Development; Software Tech. Support. **Benefits:** 401(k); Dental Insurance; Disability Coverage; Employee Discounts; Flexible Schedule; Job Sharing; Life Insurance; Medical Insurance; Profit Sharing; Public Transit Available. **Special programs:** Training; Summer Jobs. **Office hours:** Monday - Friday, 8:00 a.m. - 5:00 p.m. **Corporate headquarters location:** This Location. **Listed on:** Privately held. **President:** Dr. Tony Kakar. **Facilities Manager:** Dan Troxel.

SYSTEMSOFT CORPORATION
2 Apple Hill, Natick MA 01760. 508/651-0088. **Fax:** 508/647-0711. **Contact:** Human Resources. **World Wide Web address:** http://www.systemsoft. com. **Description:** Supplies PCMCIA (Personal Computer Memory Card International Association) and other system-level software to the rapidly growing market of mobile computers, comprised of laptops, notebooks, subnotebooks, and personal computing devices. System-level software provides both a connectivity layer, which facilitates the addition, configuration, and use of peripheral devices; and a hardware adaptation layer including the communication link between a computer operating system and hardware. **Educational backgrounds include:** Computer Science; Engineering. **Benefits:** 401(k); Incentive Plan; Stock Option. **Corporate headquarters location:** This Location. **Parent company:** Rocket Software. **Number of employees nationwide:** 250.

SYSTRAN CORPORATION
4126 Linden Avenue, Dayton OH 45432. 937/252-5601. **Fax:** 937/252-1480. **Contact:** Manager of Human Resources. **E-mail address:** careers@ systran.com. **World Wide Web address:** http://www.systran.com. **Description:** Manufactures I/O boards, memory systems, and network interface cards. **Common positions include:** Electrical Engineer; Software Engineer. **Educational backgrounds include:** Computer Science; Engineering. **Benefits:** 401(k); Dental Insurance; Disability Coverage; Flexible Schedule; Life Insurance; Medical Insurance; Public Transit Available; Tuition Assistance. **Corporate headquarters location:** This Location. **Number of employees at this location:** 135.

SYVOX
2545 Central Avenue, Boulder CO 80301. 303/938-1110. **Fax:** 303/938-1874. **Contact:** Human Resources. **World Wide Web address:** http://www. syvox.com. **Description:** A developer of advanced speech recognition technology, tools, and solutions. **Corporate headquarters location:** This Location.

T-NETIX, INC.
67 Inverness Drive East, Englewood CO 80112. 303/790-9111. **Fax:** 303/790-9540. **Contact:** Human Resources. **World Wide Web address:** http://www.t-netix.com. **Description:** Manufactures software for fraud prevention and advanced call processing. **Corporate headquarters location:** This Location. **Subsidiaries include:** Cell-Tel (Tampa FL). **CFO:** Alvyn A. Schopp. **Annual sales/revenues:** $21 - $50 million.

TDS COMPUTING SERVICES, INC.
8401 Greenway Boulevard, Suite 230, Middleton WI 53562-0980. 608/664-8600. **Contact:** Human Resources Performance Solutions. **E-mail address:** careers@teldta.com. **World Wide Web address:** http://www.tdscs.com. **Description:** Provides information technology and services to assist customers in reaching their business objectives. TDS Computing Services offers system integration, development, support, and processing. The company also provides bill printing and mailing services for customers. **Common positions include:** Administrative Manager; Computer Operator; Computer Programmer; Database Administrator; Help-Desk Technician; Machine Operator; Project Manager; Systems Analyst; Systems Manager. **Educational backgrounds include:** C/C++; Computer Science; Internet Development; M.I.S.; MCSE; Microsoft Windows NT; Oracle; PowerBuilder; UNIX; Visual Basic. **Benefits:** 401(k); Dental Insurance; Disability Coverage; Employee Discounts; Life Insurance; Medical

Insurance; Pension Plan; Public Transit Available; Relocation Assistance; Tuition Assistance. **Corporate headquarters location:** Chicago IL. **Parent company:** Telephone & Data Systems, Inc.'s (TDS) business units include United States Cellular Corporation, which manages and invests in cellular systems throughout the nation; and American Paging, Inc., which operates paging and voicemail systems, offering a wide variety of service packages including basic local paging service, statewide, regional, and nationwide paging, and voicemail with fax options. TDS' associated service companies include American Communications Consultants, Inc., an engineering and management consulting company; and Suttle Press, Inc., a commercial printing subsidiary. **Number of employees at this location:** 320.

TFE (TELOS FIELD ENGINEERING)
6767 Old Madison Pike NW, Suite 300, Huntsville AL 35806. 256/922-8000. **Contact:** Maria Heflin, Human Resources. **Description:** Offers hardware maintenance services to the federal government. **Common positions include:** Account Manager; Account Representative; Administrative Assistant; Buyer; Customer Service Representative; Inventory Control Specialist; Project Manager; Quality Control Supervisor; Systems Manager. **Educational backgrounds include:** Accounting; Business Administration; Computer Science; Engineering; Mathematics. **Benefits:** 401(k); Casual Dress - Fridays; Daycare Assistance; Dental Insurance; Disability Coverage; Life Insurance; Medical Insurance; Tuition Assistance. **Corporate headquarters location:** Ashburn VA. **Other U.S. locations:** Santa Monica CA; Bountiful UT.

TMSSEQUOIA
P.O. Box 1358, Stillwater OK 74076. 405/377-0880. **Contact:** Kristen McCaul, Human Resources Manager. **World Wide Web address:** http://www. tmsinc.com. **Description:** Develops a wide range of business management software products.

TNB, INC.
3155 Hickory Hill, Suite 103, Memphis TN 38115. 901/753-1468. **Fax:** 901/755-2245. **Contact:** Human Resources. **World Wide Web address:** http://www.tnbcorp.com. **Description:** Develops and distributes RealWorld Accounting and Synchronics Counterpoint software. **Corporate headquarters location:** This Location. **Other U.S. locations:** Cordova TN.

TAG-DATAFLOW/ALASKA
P.O. Box 241845, Anchorage AK 99524-1845. 907/276-4472. **Physical address:** 2627 C Street, Anchorage AK. **Fax:** 907/279-2757. **Contact:** Personnel. **E-mail address:** resumes@tagdfa.com. **World Wide Web address:** http://www.tagdfa.com. **Description:** Provides systems analysis, programming services, technical support, and training to federal and state agencies. **Corporate headquarters location:** This Location. **Other area locations:** Juneau AK.

TANGRAM ENTERPRISE SOLUTIONS
11000 Regency Parkway, Suite 401, Cary NC 27511. 919/653-6000. **Contact:** Susan E. Barbee, Manager of Personnel. **E-mail address:** jobs@ tangram.com. **World Wide Web address:** http://www.tangram.com. **Description:** Tangram Enterprise Solutions manufactures asset tracking software. **NOTE:** Entry-level positions are offered. **Common positions include:** Computer Programmer; Marketing Specialist; Sales Engineer; Sales Rep.; Software Engineer; Systems Analyst; Technical Support Rep.; Technical Writer. **Educational backgrounds include:** Computer

Science; Engineering; Marketing. **Benefits:** 401(k); Dental Insurance; Disability Coverage; Life Insurance; Medical Insurance; Telecommuting. **Special programs:** Internships. **Corporate headquarters location:** This Location. **Other U.S. locations:** Malvern PA. **Number of employees nationwide:** 155.

TECH DATA CORPORATION
5350 Tech Data Drive, Clearwater FL 33760. 727/538-7032. **Fax:** 727/538-7054. **Contact:** Director of Human Resources. **World Wide Web address:** http://www.techdata.com. **Description:** Distributes microcomputer-related hardware and software products to value-added resellers and computer retailers throughout the United States, Canada, Europe, Latin America, and the Caribbean. Tech Data Corporation purchases its products in large quantities directly from manufacturers and publishers, maintains an inventory of more than 25,000 products, and sells to an active base of over 50,000 customers. Tech Data Corporation provides its customers with products in networking, mass storage, peripherals, software, and systems from more than 600 manufacturers and publishers. **NOTE:** Entry-level positions and second and third shifts are offered. **Common positions include:** Account Manager; Account Rep.; Accountant; Administrative Assistant; Administrative Manager; Assistant Manager; Attorney; Auditor; Budget Analyst; Buyer; CFO; Clerical Supervisor; Computer Operator; Computer Programmer; Credit Manager; Customer Service Rep.; Database Manager; Finance Director; Financial Analyst; Human Resources Manager; Management Trainee; Marketing Manager; Marketing Specialist; MIS Specialist; Multimedia Designer; Operations Manager; Paralegal; Project Manager; Purchasing Agent; Sales Executive; Sales Manager; Sales Rep.; Secretary; Systems Analyst; Systems Manager; Technical Writer; Telecommunications Manager; Vice President. **Educational backgrounds include:** Accounting; Business Administration; Communications; Computer Science; Economics; Finance; Marketing. **Benefits:** 401(k); Daycare Assistance; Dental Insurance; Disability Coverage; Employee Discounts; Job Sharing; Life Insurance; Medical Insurance; Profit Sharing; Tuition Assistance. **Corporate headquarters location:** This Location. **Other U.S. locations:** CA; GA; IN; NJ; TX. **International locations:** Canada; France. **Subsidiaries include:** Computer 2000 AG (Germany); Tech Data Canada Inc. (Ontario, Canada); Tech Data Education, Inc. (Clearwater FL); Tech Data Finance, Inc. (Walnut Creek CA); Tech Data France, SNC (Bobigny, France); Tech Data Latin America (Miami FL); Tech Data Pacific, Inc. (Clearwater FL); Tech Data Product Management, Inc. (Clearwater FL). **Operations at this facility include:** Administration; Sales; Service. **Chairman and CEO:** Steven A. Raymund. **Number of employees at this location:** 2,300. **Number of employees nationwide:** 3,000. **Number of employees worldwide:** 3,300.

TECHNICAL AND MANAGEMENT SERVICES CORPORATION (TAMSCO)
4041 Powder Mill Road, Suite 500, Calverton MD 20705. 301/595-0710. **Contact:** Human Resources. **World Wide Web address:** http://www.tamsco.com. **Description:** Offers a variety of ADP-oriented and telecommunications system development, manufacturing, and integration services. These products and services include requirements definition; systems engineering; systems and telecommunications network design; software development; electronics and telecommunications equipment; hardware development and manufacturing; and systems integration and

implementation. **Common positions include:** Aerospace Engineer; Aircraft Mechanic; Budget Analyst; Computer Programmer; Designer; Draftsperson; Electrical Engineer; Financial Analyst; Management Analyst; Mechanical Engineer; Software Engineer; Systems Analyst; Technical Writer. **Educational backgrounds include:** Business Administration; Computer Science; Engineering. **Benefits:** 401(k); Dental Insurance; Disability Coverage; Life Insurance; Medical Insurance; Tuition Assistance. **Corporate headquarters location:** This Location. **Operations at this facility include:** Administration. **Number of employees nationwide:** 500.

TECHNICAL COMMUNICATIONS CORP.
100 Domino Drive, Concord MA 01742. 978/287-5100. **Fax:** 978/287-4475. **Contact:** Pam Salo, Director of Human Resources. **World Wide Web address:** http://www.tccsecure.com. **Description:** Technical Communications Corporation designs, manufactures, and sells communications security devices and systems. Products include the Cipher family of encryption devices, which protect computer terminals with an encryption key that needs to be changed on a regular basis; and KEYNET key management system, which is an advanced system that permits geographically dispersed data networks to be managed economically and safely from a single secured site. The KEYNET system provides an electronic courier to distribute the keys automatically, securely, cost-effectively, and invisibly. KEYNET protects and manages the sensitive data traveling between U.S. government agencies on government networks. **Corporate headquarters location:** This Location. **Annual sales/revenues:** $11 - $20 million. **Number of employees at this location:** 65.

TECHNIUM, INC.
8745 West Higgins Road, Suite 350, Chicago IL 60631. 773/380-0555. **Fax:** 773/380-0568. **Contact:** Recruiter. **World Wide Web address:** http://www.technium.com. **Description:** Technium provides computer consulting services focusing on client/server technologies. The company's client base represents a variety of industries, from consumer products and health care to financial services and software. Technium provides a full range of services to deploy client/server applications including architecture planning, application analysis, visualization, and design; graphical user interface development using Visual C++, Visual Basic, PowerBuilder, and Delphi; object-oriented development with C, C++, and Smalltalk; relational database development in SQL Server, Microsoft Access, Oracle, and Sybase; and decision support systems development using OLAP and Data Warehousing technologies. **NOTE:** Entry-level positions are offered. **Common positions include:** Computer Programmer; Internet Services Manager; MIS Specialist; Software Engineer; Systems Analyst. **Educational backgrounds include:** Computer Science; Information Systems; Marketing. **Benefits:** 401(k); Dental Insurance; Disability Coverage; Employee Discounts; Life Insurance; Medical Insurance; Profit Sharing; Public Transit Available; Savings Plan; Tuition Assistance. **Special programs:** Training. **Corporate headquarters location:** This Location. **Other U.S. locations:** Dallas TX; Milwaukee WI. **Operations at this facility include:** Administration; Research and Development; Sales; Service. **Number of employees nationwide:** 75.

TECHSMITH CORPORATION
1780 East Grand River Avenue, East Lansing MI 48823. 517/333-2100. **Toll-free phone:** 800/517-3001. **Fax:** 517/333-1888. **Contact:** Donald J.

Nourse, Human Resources Manager. **E-mail address:** info@techsmith.com. **World Wide Web address:** http://www.techsmith.com. **Description:** Develops SnagIt screen capture software; Camtasia, a desktop camcorder, and DuBit, an audio editing utility. **Common positions include:** Administrative Assistant; Controller; Customer Service Rep.; Database Administrator; Marketing Manager; Software Engineer; Webmaster; Website Developer. **Educational backgrounds include:** C/C++; MCSE; Software Tech. Support. **Benefits:** Casual Dress - Daily; Disability Coverage; Life Insurance; Medical Insurance; Profit Sharing; Savings Plan; Sick Days (6 - 10); Tuition Assistance; Vacation Days (10 - 20). **Corporate headquarters location:** This Location. **President/CEO/Owner:** William D. Hamilton. **Information Systems Manager:** Daniel S. Brown.

TECHWORKS, INC.
4030 West Braker Lane, Suite 350, Austin TX 78759. 512/794-8533. **Contact:** Human Resources. **World Wide Web address:** http://www.techworks. com. **Description:** Manufactures computer memory.

TELCO SYSTEMS INC.
63 Nahatan Street, Norwood MA 02062. 781/551-0300. **Contact:** Human Resources. **World Wide Web address:** http://www.telco.com. **Description:** Develops, manufactures, and markets fiberoptic transmission products, customer premises network access products, and LAN/WAN internetworking products. Applications include voice, data, and video communication networks. Primary customers are independent telephone companies, resellers, competitive access providers, interexchange carriers, and corporate end users. **Corporate headquarters location:** This Location.

TELESCAN, INC.
5959 Corporate Drive, Suite 2000, Houston TX 77036. 281/588-9700. **Fax:** 281/588-9797. **Contact:** Human Resources. **World Wide Web address:** http://www.telescan.com. **Description:** Develops customized Internet and online data networks for the financial and publishing industries. Telescan also provides proprietary analytics and content to investors. **Corporate headquarters location:** This Location. **Other U.S. locations:** Berwyn PA.

TELOS CORPORATION
19886 Ashburn Road, Ashburn VA 20147. 703/724-3800. **Fax:** 703/724-3860. **Contact:** Human Resources. **World Wide Web address:** http://www. telos.com. **Description:** A holding company whose subsidiaries provide information technology solutions to the Business-to-Business and Business-to-Government e-marketplaces in order to build more e-commerce. **Common positions include:** Accountant; Buyer; Draftsperson; Electrical Engineer; Financial Analyst; Industrial Engineer; Mechanical Engineer; Operations Manager; Quality Control Supervisor; Receptionist; Secretary; Software Engineer; Stock Clerk; Systems Analyst; Technical Writer. **Educational backgrounds include:** Accounting; Business Administration; Economics; Finance; Marketing. **Benefits:** Daycare Assistance; Dental Insurance; Disability Coverage; Life Insurance; Medical Insurance; Pension Plan; Tuition Assistance. **Corporate headquarters location:** This Location. **Subsidiaries include:** Enterworks; SecureTrade; and Xacta. **Number of employees nationwide:** 2,100.

TELXON CORPORATION
P.O. Box 5582, Akron OH 44334-0582. 330/867-3700. **Contact:** Meg Pais, Vice President of Employee Services. **World Wide Web address:** http://www.telxon.com. **Description:** Manufactures hand-held microcomputer systems. **Corporate headquarters location:** This Location.

TENEX SYSTEMS INC.
2011 Renaissance Boulevard, King of Prussia PA 19406. 610/687-1160. **Contact:** Human Resources. **World Wide Web address:** http://www.tenexsys. com. **Description:** Provides administrative software development and support services for school districts. **Common positions include:** AS400 Programmer Analyst. **Educational backgrounds include:** Software Tech. Support. **Benefits:** 401(k); Medical Insurance. **President:** Ron Cranford.

TERA COMPUTER COMPANY
Merrill Place, 411 First Avenue South, Suite 600, Seattle WA 98104-2860. 206/701-2000. **Contact:** Marney Reed, Corporate Recruiter. **E-mail address:** resume@tera.com. **World Wide Web address:** http://www.tera.com. **Description:** Tera Computer Company develops supercomputers. **Corporate headquarters location:** This Location.

3COM CORPORATION
5400 Bayfront Plaza, Santa Clara CA 95052. 408/326-5000. **Contact:** Human Resources. **World Wide Web address:** http://www.3com.com. **Description:** 3Com is a *Fortune* 500 company delivering global data networking solutions to organizations around the world. 3Com designs, manufactures, markets, and supports a broad range of ISO 9000-compliant global data networking solutions including routers, hubs, remote access servers, switches, and adapters for Ethernet, Token Ring, and high-speed networks. These products enable computers to communicate at high speeds and share resources including printers, disk drives, modems, and minicomputers. **Corporate headquarters location:** This Location.

3X CORPORATION
760 Lakeview Plaza Boulevard, Worthington OH 43085. 614/433-9406. **Toll-free phone:** 800/860-9406. **Fax:** 614/433-9430. **Contact:** Recruiter. **World Wide Web address:** http://www.3x.com. **Description:** A computer consulting firm. **Common positions include:** AS400 Programmer Analyst; Computer Programmer; Computer Scientist; Content Developer; Database Administrator; Database Manager; Internet Services Manager; Intranet Developer; Network Engineer; Network Administrator; Software Engineer; Systems Analyst; Website Developer. **Number of employees nationwide:** 350.

TIAC
175 Great Road, Suite 2, Bedford MA 01730. 781/276-7200. **Contact:** Human Resources Director. **World Wide Web address:** http://www. tiac.net. **Description:** Provides access to the Internet for customers across the Northeast. The company's software enables users to browse the World Wide Web and send and receive e-mail. **Corporate headquarters location:** This Location.

TIDESTONE TECHNOLOGIES, INC.
12980 Metcalf Avenue, Suite 300, Overland Park KS 66213. 913/851-2200. **Contact:** Human Resources. **World Wide Web address:** http://www. tidestone.com. **Description:** Designs spreadsheet technology for Web-based computing. **Corporate headquarters location:** This Location.

TIMBERLINE SOFTWARE CORP.
15195 NW Greenbriar Parkway, Beaverton OR 97006. 503/626-6775. **Fax:** 503/641-7498. **Contact:** Executive Secretary. **World Wide Web address:** http://www.timberline.com. **Description:**

Develops and markets computer software programs, primarily for the construction and property management industries. **Corporate headquarters location:** This Location.

TRANSITION NETWORKS
6475 City West Parkway, Eden Prairie MN 55344. 952/941-7600. **Fax:** 952/941-2322. **Contact:** Personnel. **E-mail address:** info@transition.com. **World Wide Web address:** http://www.transition. com. **Description:** Provides network connectivity solutions that allow for the conversion of different media types. **Corporate headquarters location:** This Location.

TRAVELING SOFTWARE, INC.
18702 North Creek Parkway, Suite 102, Bothell WA 98011. 425/483-8088. **Fax:** 425/487-5677. **Recorded jobline:** 425/487-5499. **Contact:** Human Resources Generalist. **E-mail address:** hotjobs@laplink.com. **World Wide Web address:** http://www.laplink.com. **Description:** Manufactures Laplink, a remote access software product. **Common positions include:** Product Manager; Sales Manager; Software Engineer. **Educational backgrounds include:** Business Administration; C/C++; Computer Science; Marketing; Software Development. **Benefits:** 401(k); Casual Dress - Daily; Dental Insurance; Disability Coverage; Employee Discounts; Flexible Schedule; Life Insurance; Medical Insurance; Profit Sharing; Public Transit Available; Sick Days (6 - 10); Telecommuting; Tuition Assistance; Vacation Days (6 - 10). **Corporate headquarters location:** This Location. **Number of employees worldwide:** 90.

TRI-COR INDUSTRIES, INC.
2900 Eisenhower Avenue, 5th Floor, Alexandria VA 22314. 703/682-2000. **Fax:** 703/682-2001. **Contact:** Human Resources. **World Wide Web address:** http://www.tricorind.com. **Description:** This location houses administrative offices. Overall, Tri-Cor Industries provides contractual computer services to the federal government. Services include networking, software development, operations, and security. **Common positions include:** Account Manager; Accountant; Administrative Assistant; Administrative Manager; CFO; Computer Operator; Computer Programmer; Controller; Cost Estimator; Database Manager; Financial Analyst; General Manager; Human Resources Manager; Internet Services Manager; Marketing Manager; Marketing Specialist; Operations Manager; Project Manager; Secretary; Software Engineer; Systems Analyst; Systems Manager; Technical Writer/Editor; Telecommunications Manager; Typist; Vice President. **Educational backgrounds include:** Business Administration; Communications; Computer Science; Finance; Marketing; Software Development; Software Tech. Support. **Benefits:** 401(k); Dental Insurance; Disability Coverage; Life Insurance; Medical Insurance; Tuition Assistance. **Corporate headquarters location:** This Location.

TRIDIA CORPORATION
1000 Cobb Place Boulevard NW, Building 200, Suite 210, Kennesaw GA 30144. 770/428-5000. **Fax:** 770/428-5009. **Contact:** Human Resources. **World Wide Web address:** http://www.tridia.com. **Description:** A provider of SCO UNIX-based solutions and a software developer and reseller. The company's product line includes DOUBLEVISION remote control software which allows a user to connect to another user's screen. **Corporate headquarters location:** This Location.

TRIVERSITY INC.
311 Sinclair Street, Bristol PA 19007. 215/785-4321. **Contact:** Personnel. **World Wide Web address:** http://www.triversity.com. **Description:** Provides transaction processing and customer relationship management solutions for physical, catalog, and online retailers. **Corporate headquarters location:** Toronto, Canada.

TYBRIN CORPORATION
1030 Titan Court, Fort Walton Beach FL 32547. 850/337-2500. **Toll-free phone:** 800/989-2746. **Contact:** Personnel. **E-mail address:** jobs@tybrin.com. **World Wide Web address:** http://www.tybrin.com. **Description:** Tybrin Corporation provides engineering and computer support services to government and commercial customers. **Common positions include:** Administrative Assistant; Advertising Clerk; Budget Analyst; CFO; Computer Operator; Computer Programmer; Controller; Cost Estimator; Database Manager; Design Engineer; Financial Analyst; General Manager; Graphic Artist; Human Resources Manager; Marketing Manager; MIS Specialist; Online Content Specialist; Project Manager; Secretary; Software Engineer; Systems Analyst; Technical Writer. **Educational backgrounds include:** Accounting; Business Administration; Communications; Computer Science; Engineering; Finance; Marketing. **Benefits:** 401(k); Dental Insurance; Disability Coverage; Life Insurance; Medical Insurance; Pension Plan; Tuition Assistance. **Corporate headquarters location:** This Location. **Other U.S. locations:** Huntsville AL; Edwards Air Force Base CA. **Number of employees at this location:** 320. **Number of employees nationwide:** 425.

UUNET
22001 Loudoun County Parkway, Ashburn VA 20147. 703/857-0000. **Toll-free phone:** 800/488-6383. **Fax:** 703/886-0524. **Contact:** Personnel. **World Wide Web address:** http://www.uu.net. **Description:** A commercial Internet access provider. UUNET also provides a variety of Internet access options, applications, and consulting services. **Corporate headquarters location:** This Location.

ULTIMUS
15200 Weston Parkway, Suite 106, Cary NC 27513. 919/678-0900. **Fax:** 919/678-0901. **Contact:** Human Resources. **E-mail address:** info@ultimus1.com. **World Wide Web address:** http://www.ultimus1.com. **Description:** Offers workflow automation software through client/server Windows applications, allowing users to design, simulate, implement, monitor, and measure workflow for various administrative business processes. **Company slogan:** Workflow on the Web. **Common positions include:** Computer Engineer; Computer Programmer; Sales Engineer. **Educational backgrounds include:** C/C++; HTML; Internet; Java; MCSE; Software Development; Software Tech. Support. **Benefits:** Casual Dress - Daily; Dental Insurance; Disability Coverage; Medical Insurance; Sick Days (6 - 10); Vacation Days (6 - 10). **Corporate headquarters location:** This Location.

UNILINK INC.
P.O. Box 1630, Jackson WY 83001. 307/733-1666. **Fax:** 307/733-5934. **Contact:** Personnel. **World Wide Web address:** http://www.unilink-inc.com. **Description:** Develops software for the accounting industry. **Common positions include:** Computer Programmer; Computer Support Technician; Network/Systems Administrator; SQL Programmer; Webmaster. **Educational backgrounds include:** C/C++; Microsoft Access; Visual Basic.

UNION PACIFIC CORPORATION
1416 Dodge Street, Omaha NE 68179. 402/271-5777. **Contact:** Human Resources. **World Wide Web address:** http://www.up.com. **Description:** Provides transportation, computer technology, and logistics services. Union Pacific Corporation operates in three divisions: Union Pacific Railroad; Overnite Transportation; and Union Pacific Technologies. **Corporate headquarters location:** This Location. **Number of employees nationwide:** 65,000.

UNISYS CORPORATION
Unisys Way - E2114, Blue Bell PA 19424. 215/986-3501. **Fax:** 215/986-6732. **Contact:** Terry Laudal, Vice President of Recruiting and Staffing. **E-mail address:** jobs@unisys.com. **World Wide Web address:** http://www.unisys.com. **Description:** Provides information services, technology, and software. Unisys specializes in developing critical business solutions based on open information networks. The company's Enabling Software Team creates a variety of software projects which facilitate the building of user applications and the management of distributed systems. The company's Platforms Group is responsible for UNIX Operating Systems running across a wide range of multiple processor server platforms including all peripheral and communication drivers. The Unisys Commercial Parallel Processing Team develops microkernel-based operating systems, I/O device drivers, ATM hardware, diagnostics, and system architectures. The System Management Group is in charge of the overall management of development programs for UNIX desktop and entry-server products. **NOTE:** Entry-level positions and part-time jobs are offered. **Company slogan:** Unisys -- we eat, sleep, and drink this stuff. **Common positions include:** Account Manager; Account Rep.; Administrative Assistant; Applications Engineer; AS400 Programmer Analyst; Computer Engineer; Computer Programmer; Computer Scientist; Computer Support Technician; Computer Technician; Content Developer; Customer Service Rep.; Database Administrator; Database Manager; Finance Director; Financial Analyst; General Manager; Help-Desk Technician; Human Resources Manager; Internet Services Manager; Intranet Developer; Market Research Analyst; Marketing Specialist; MIS Specialist; Network Engineer; Network Manager; Network Administrator; Online Sales Manager; Project Manager; Purchasing Agent/Manager; Sales Executive; Sales Manager; Sales Rep.; Software Engineer; SQL Programmer; Systems Analyst; Systems Manager; Technical Support Manager; Webmaster; Website Developer. **Educational backgrounds include:** Accounting; AS400 Certification; ASP; C/C++; CGI; Communications; Computer Science; Engineering; Finance; HTML; Internet Development; Java; Marketing; MCSE; Microsoft Office; Microsoft Word; Software Development; Software Tech. Support; Spreadsheets; SQL; Visual Basic. **Benefits:** 401(k); Casual Dress - Daily; Dental Insurance; Disability Coverage; Employee Discounts; Flexible Schedule; Life Insurance; Medical Insurance; Pension Plan; Relocation Assistance; Savings Plan; Sick Days; Stock Purchase; Telecommuting; Tuition Assistance; Vacation Days. **Special programs:** Internships; Training; Co-ops; Summer Jobs. **Corporate headquarters location:** This Location. **Other U.S. locations:** Nationwide. **International locations:** Worldwide. **CEO:** Larry Weinbach. **Annual sales/revenues:** More than $100 million. **Number of employees nationwide:** 37,000. **Number of employees worldwide:** 49,000. **Number of projected hires for 2000 - 2001 at this location:** 2,000.

UNITED INTERNET SERVICES, INC.
1287 East Newport Center Drive, Suite 207, Deerfield Beach FL 33442. **Toll-free phone:** 800/657-5786. **Fax:** 800/214-8499. **Contact:** Personnel. **World Wide Web address:** http://www.unitedinternetservices.com. **Description:** Provides Website design and hosting services. **Corporate headquarters location:** This Location.

UNITED STATES DATA CORPORATION
2435 North Central Expressway, Suite 100, Richardson TX 75080-2722. 972/680-9700. **Fax:** 972/680-9324. **Contact:** Personnel Administrator. **World Wide Web address:** http://www.usdata.com. **Description:** Develops, markets, and supports application-enabler software products that customers configure to implement a wide range of real-time monitoring, analysis, information management, and control solutions in worldwide industrial automation markets. USData also develops, markets, and supports integrated hardware, software, and systems solutions for automated identification and data collection applications that are sold to a broad base of customers throughout North America. The company also acts as a full-service distributor and value-added remarketer for manufacturers of bar code equipment. **Common positions include:** Computer Programmer; Designer; Electrical Engineer; Industrial Engineer; Manufacturer's Sales Rep.; Mathematician; Mechanical Engineer; Petroleum Engineer; Software Engineer; Systems Analyst; Technical Writer. **Educational backgrounds include:** Business Administration; Computer Science; Engineering; Marketing. **Benefits:** 401(k); Dental Insurance; Life Insurance; Medical Insurance; Tuition Assistance. **Special programs:** Internships. **Corporate headquarters location:** This Location. **Other U.S. locations:** Atlanta GA; Chicago IL; Boston MA; Seattle WA. **Operations at this facility include:** Administration; Research and Development; Sales; Service. **Number of employees at this location:** 200. **Number of employees nationwide:** 300.

UNIVERSAL COMPUTER SYSTEMS (UCS) DEALER COMPUTER SYSTEMS (DCS)
6700 Hollister, Houston TX 77040. 713/718-1800. **Toll-free phone:** 800/883-3031. **Contact:** Recruiting Department. **World Wide Web address:** http://www.universalcomputersys.com. **Description:** Supplies computer software and hardware systems specifically designed for the business of automobile dealerships. **NOTE:** Entry-level positions, part-time jobs, and second and third shifts are offered. **Common positions include:** Account Manager; Accountant; Administrative Assistant; Auditor; Computer Operator; Computer Programmer; Computer Support Technician; Computer Technician; Consultant; Customer Service Rep.; Help-Desk Technician; Network Administrator; Sales Rep.; Teacher; Technical Writer/Editor. **Educational backgrounds include:** Accounting; Business Administration; C/C++; Computer Science; Economics; Education; Finance; Liberal Arts; Marketing; Mathematics; MCSE; Microsoft Office; Microsoft Word; Visual Basic. **Benefits:** 401(k); Dental Insurance; Disability Coverage; Life Insurance; Medical Insurance; Sick Days; Vacation Days. **Special programs:** Internships; Co-ops. **Corporate headquarters location:** This Location. **Other U.S. locations:** Southfield MI; College Station TX. **International locations:** Worldwide. **Operations at this facility include:** Administration; Manufacturing; Research and Development; Sales; Service. **Number of employees nationwide:** 1,600.

UNIVERSAL SYSTEMS & TECHNOLOGY
12450 Fair Lakes Circle, Suite 625, Fairfax VA 22033. 703/502-9600. **Contact:** Recruiting/Staffing. **Description:** Provides computer information technology systems and services including network management, network design, and LAN/WAN implementation. **NOTE:** Entry-level positions are offered. **Common positions include:** Administrative Assistant; Computer Operator; Computer Programmer; Design Engineer; Electrical Engineer; Financial Analyst; Graphic Artist; Graphic Designer; Multimedia Designer; Sales Executive; Technical Writer; Telecommunications Manager. **Educational backgrounds include:** Business Administration; Computer Science; Engineering; Finance; Liberal Arts; Marketing. **Benefits:** 401(k); Dental Insurance; Disability Coverage; Life Insurance; Medical Insurance; Public Transit Available; Tuition Assistance. **Special programs:** Internships; Training. **Corporate headquarters location:** This Location. **Other U.S. locations:** Orlando FL; Albuquerque NM. **Number of employees nationwide:** 170.

UNIVERSAL SYSTEMS INC. (USI)
14585 Avion Parkway, Chantilly VA 20151. 703/222-2840. **Fax:** 703/222-7222. **Contact:** Charles Virtue, Human Resources Manager. **Description:** Develops workflow and document management software and provides systems integration services. The company provides turnkey solutions to *Fortune* 500 and government clients utilizing the latest in client/server platforms and SQL compliant databases. **Common positions include:** Applications Engineer; Computer Programmer; Database Manager; Environmental Engineer; MIS Specialist; Multimedia Designer; Project Engineer; Software Engineer; Systems Analyst; Systems Manager; Technical Writer; Video Production Coordinator. **Educational backgrounds include:** Computer Science; Engineering. **Benefits:** 401(k); Dental Insurance; Disability Coverage; Employee Discounts; Flexible Schedule; Life Insurance; Medical Insurance; Public Transit Available; Tuition Assistance; Vision Insurance. **Corporate headquarters location:** This Location. **Other U.S. locations:** CA; FL; MA; NJ; NY; OH; UT. **Annual sales/revenues:** $51 - $100 million.

USER TECHNOLOGY ASSOCIATES (UTA)
950 North Glebe Road, Suite 100, Arlington VA 22203. **Contact:** Human Resources. **Description:** Provides information management technology and systems integration services. **Corporate headquarters location:** This Location.

VSI ENTERPRISES, INC.
5801 Goshen Springs Road, Norcross GA 30071. 770/242-7566. **Contact:** Drew Jacobs, Human Resources Manager. **Description:** Designs, produces, and markets tailored software for interactive group video conferencing systems. Using standard telecommunication transmissions, VSI Enterprises's products allow many people at different geographic locations to see and hear one another on live television. **Corporate headquarters location:** This Location. **Subsidiaries include:** VSI; VSI Europe. **Listed on:** Boston Stock Exchange.

VAIL RESEARCH AND TECHNOLOGY CORP.
5904 Richmond Highway, Alexandria VA 22303. 703/329-9403. **Contact:** Human Resources Manager. **Description:** Provides engineering, computer science, and program management support to government and commercial clients. **Corporate headquarters location:** This Location. **Other area locations:** Arlington VA. **Other U.S. locations:** Fort Walton Beach FL.

VERIDIAN, INC.
2001 North Beauregard Street, Suite 1200, Alexandria VA 22311. 703/575-3100. **Contact:** Personnel. **World Wide Web address:** http://www.veridian.com. **Description:** Provides engineering systems integration and technical services to government agencies. **Corporate headquarters location:** This Location.

VERITAS SOFTWARE CORPORATION
900 Alta Avenue, Mountain View CA 94043. 650/335-8000. **Fax:** 650/335-8050. **Contact:** Human Resources. **World Wide Web address:** http://www.veritas.com. **Description:** Designs, develops, and markets enterprise data and storage management software including Volume Manager. The company's products are designed to improve system performance and to reduce administration costs. **Corporate headquarters location:** This Location. **Annual sales/revenues:** $21 - $50 million. **Number of employees nationwide:** 90.

VERITY INC.
894 Ross Drive, Sunnyvale CA 94089. 408/541-1500. **Contact:** Human Resources. **World Wide Web address:** http://www.verity.com. **Description:** Develops and markets software tools and applications for searching, retrieving, and filtering information on the Internet. **Corporate headquarters location:** This Location.

VIASOFT INC.
4343 East Camelback Road, Suite 205, Phoenix AZ 85018. 602/952-0050. **Contact:** Human Resources. **World Wide Web address:** http://www.viasoft.com. **Description:** Viasoft develops management and enterprise applications software. **Corporate headquarters location:** This Location.

VIEWLOGIC SYSTEMS, INC.
293 Boston Post Road West, Marlborough MA 01752. 508/480-0881. **Contact:** Human Resources. **World Wide Web address:** http://www.viewlogic.com. **Description:** Develops, markets, and supports software products that aid engineers in the design of advanced electronic products. Viewlogic provides electronics firms with a portfolio of state-of-the-art software products, available as stand-alone or fully-integrated, and featuring open standards-based architectures which operate on every major computer platform. **Common positions include:** Accountant; Electrical Engineer; Software Engineer. **Educational backgrounds include:** Computer Science; Engineering. **Benefits:** Dental Insurance; Disability Coverage; Employee Discounts; Life Insurance; Medical Insurance; Pension Plan; Savings Plan; Tuition Assistance. **Special programs:** Internships. **Corporate headquarters location:** This Location. **Other U.S. locations:** Camarillo CA; Fremont CA. **Operations at this facility include:** Research and Development. **Number of employees at this location:** 200. **Number of employees nationwide:** 500.

VIGNETTE CORPORATION
901 South MoPac Expressway, Building 3, Austin TX 78746-5776. 512/306-4300. **Contact:** Human Resources. **World Wide Web address:** http://www.vignette.com. **Description:** Supplies e-business applications to online business clients. **Corporate headquarters location:** This Location.

VISICOM
10052 Mesa Ridge Court, San Diego CA 92121. 858/457-2111. **Fax:** 858/457-0888. **Contact:** Brenda Koistinen, Per Manager. **E-mail address:** resumes@visicom.com. **World Wide Web address:** http://www.visicom.com. **Description:** Develops real-time video and image processing

boards targeting medical, machine vision, security, and surveillance applications. Founded in 1988. **NOTE:** Entry-level positions are offered. **Common positions include:** Computer Engineer; Computer Programmer; Computer Scientist; Electrical Engineer. **Educational backgrounds include:** C/C++; Computer Science; Engineering; Java; Microsoft Office; Software Development. **Benefits:** 401(k); Casual Dress - Daily; Employee Discounts; Flexible Schedule; Life Insurance; Medical Insurance; Profit Sharing; Relocation Assistance; Tuition Assistance; Vacation Days (11 - 15). **Corporate headquarters location:** This Location. **Parent company:** The Titan Corporation. **Number of employees at this location:** 200. **Number of employees nationwide:** 330.

VIZACOM
Glenpoint Center East, 300 Frank W. Burr Boulevard, Teaneck NJ 07666. 201/928-1001. **Fax:** 201/929-1003. **Contact:** Personnel. **Description:** A developer of IBM- and World Wide Web-compatible visual communications software. **Common positions include:** Software Engineer. **Benefits:** 401(k); Stock Purchase. **Corporate headquarters location:** This Location.

WPI GROUP, INC.
1155 Elm Street, Manchester NH 03101. 603/627-3500. **Fax:** 603/627-3150. **Contact:** Catherine Lisk, Human Resources Director. **Description:** A holding company. **Corporate headquarters location:** This Location. **Subsidiaries include:** WPI Electronics, Inc.; WPI Magnetic, Inc.; WPI Micro Palm, Inc.; WPI Power Systems, Inc.; WPI Termiflex, Inc. Each subsidiary operates through two groups: Magnetics and Electronics. The Magnetics groups design and manufacture large magnetic power systems, electromechanical devices, and systems that power and control high-temperature industrial furnaces. The Electronics groups design and produce hand-held computer terminals and DOS-based computers used to collect data; related software; and arc lamp electronic ballasts for overhead and video projectors, medical endoscopes, and lighting applications. **Listed on:** NASDAQ.

WALKER INTERACTIVE SYSTEMS
303 Second Street, Suite 3N, San Francisco CA 94107. 415/495-8811. **Fax:** 415/957-1711. **Contact:** Recruiter. **World Wide Web address:** http://www.walker.com. **Description:** A developer of high-end financial applications software, primarily for *Fortune* 100 companies and government agencies. **Common positions include:** Computer Programmer; Consultant; Marketing Specialist; Sales Executive; Sales Manager; Software Engineer; Systems Analyst. **Educational backgrounds include:** Accounting; Engineering; Mathematics; Physics. **Benefits:** 401(k); Dental Insurance; Life Insurance; Medical Insurance; Pension Plan; Tuition Assistance. **Corporate headquarters location:** This Location. **Other U.S. locations:** Atlanta GA; Chicago IL; Boston MA. **International locations:** Australia; Singapore; United Kingdom.

WEBHIRE, INC.
91 Hartwell Avenue, Lexington MA 02421. 781/869-5000. **Contact:** Human Resources. **World Wide Web address:** http://www.webhire.com. **Description:** Manufactures and sells software that sorts and ranks resumes by criteria selected by the resume screener. **Corporate headquarters location:** This Location.

WELCOM SOFTWARE TECHNOLOGY
15995 North Barkers Landing, Suite 275, Houston TX 77079. 281/558-0514. **Toll-free phone:** 800/274-4WST. **Fax:** 281/584-7828. **Contact:** Human Resources. **E-mail address:** personnel@welcom.com. **World Wide Web address:** http://www.welcom.com. **Description:** Designs, develops, and markets project- and cost-management software. **NOTE:** Entry-level positions are offered. **Common positions include:** Computer Programmer; Design Engineer; Management Analyst; Project Manager; Quality Control Supervisor; Software Engineer; Systems Analyst; Systems Manager; Technical Writer/Editor; Telecommunications Manager; Webmaster. **Educational backgrounds include:** Computer Science; Software Development; Software Tech. Support. **Benefits:** 401(k); Disability Coverage; Life Insurance; Medical Insurance; Pension Plan; Profit Sharing. **Special programs:** Internships; Training; Summer Jobs. **Corporate headquarters location:** This Location. **President:** Tony Welsh. **Number of employees worldwide:** 60.

WEN TECHNOLOGY CORPORATION
999 Central Park Avenue, Yonkers NY 10704. 914/376-5435. **Fax:** 914/376-7092. **Contact:** Human Resources Department. **World Wide Web address:** http://www.wentech.com. **Description:** Manufactures computer monitors and displays. **NOTE:** Entry-level positions are offered. **Common positions include:** Account Manager; Account Rep.; Administrative Assistant; Applications Engineer; Buyer; CFO; Credit Manager; Customer Service Representative; Design Engineer; Designer; Electrical Engineer; Industrial Engineer; Manufacturing Engineer; Mechanical Engineer; Multimedia Designer; Project Manager; Purchasing Agent; Quality Control Supervisor; Sales Engineer; Sales Executive; Sales Manager; Sales Rep.; Secretary; Systems Manager. **Educational backgrounds include:** Accounting; Computer Science; Engineering; Finance; Marketing; Physics. **Benefits:** Medical Insurance. **Corporate headquarters location:** This Location.

WHITE PINE SOFTWARE
542 Amherst Street, Nashua NH 03063. 603/886-9050. **Fax:** 603/886-9051. **Contact:** Human Resources. **E-mail address:** hr@wpine.com. **World Wide Web address:** http://www.wpine.com. **Description:** A developer of computer-based information access and communications software. The company offers cross-platform desktop videoconferencing, desktop-to-host connectivity, network access, and file transfer. **Corporate headquarters location:** This Location.

WHOLEPEOPLE.COM
1500 East 128th Avenue, Thornton CO 80241. 303/474-2300. **Fax:** 303/474-2715. **Recorded jobline:** 303/474-3094. **Contact:** Personnel. **World Wide Web address:** http://www.wholepeople.com. **Description:** Markets and sells vitamins, nutritional supplements, and personal health care products. **NOTE:** In the first half of 2000, WholePeople.com and Gaiam.com announced plans to merge. The new company will operate as Gaiam.com. Please contact this location for more information. **Common positions include:** Account Manager; Account Rep.; Accountant; Administrative Assistant; Administrative Manager; Buyer; Computer Programmer; Content Developer; Customer Service Rep.; Database Administrator; Financial Analyst; General Manager; Graphic Artist; Graphic Designer; Help-Desk Technician; Internet Services Manager; Market Research Analyst; Marketing Manager; Marketing Specialist; MIS Manager; Online Sales Manager; Operations Manager; Production Manager; Project Manager; Sales Rep.; Systems Analyst; Systems Manager; Web Advertising Specialist; Webmaster; Website Developer.

Educational backgrounds include: HTML; Internet Development; Java; MCSE; Oracle; SQL. **Benefits:** 401(k); Casual Dress - Daily; Daycare Assistance; Dental Insurance; Disability Coverage; Employee Discounts; Financial Planning Assistance; Flexible Schedule; Life Insurance; Medical Insurance; Public Transit Available; Savings Plan; Sick Days (6 - 10); Vacation Days (6 - 10).

WIN LABORATORIES
11090 Industrial Road, Manassas VA 20109. 703/330-1426. **Contact:** Personnel. **Description:** Manufactures IBM-compatible computers. **Corporate headquarters location:** This Location.

WORLDCOM
500 Clinton Center Drive, Clinton MS 39060. 601/460-5600. **Contact:** Human Resources. **World Wide Web address:** http://www.wcom.com. **Description:** One of the world's largest suppliers of local, long distance, and international telecommunications services, and a global Internet service provider. **Corporate headquarters location:** This Location. **International locations:** Worldwide.
Other U.S. locations:
• One Fluor Daniel Drive, Building C, Sugar Land TX 77478. 281/276-4000.

XVT SOFTWARE, INC.
4888 Pearl East Circle, Suite 110, Boulder CO 80301. 303/443-4223. **Toll-free phone:** 800/678-7988. **Fax:** 303/443-0969. **Contact:** Michelle Cremers, Manager of Human Resources. **World Wide Web address:** http://www.xvt.com. **Description:** XVT Software, Inc. is a leading provider of cross-platform graphical user interface (GUI) solutions for C and C++ developers. XVT Software, Inc. offers C and C++ development solutions that allow programmers to build a single application and port to every major GUI without rewriting code. The company also offers consulting and training. **Common positions include:** Computer Programmer; Customer Service Representative; Human Resources Manager; Public Relations Specialist; Quality Control Supervisor; Services Sales Representative; Software Engineer; Technical Writer/Editor. **Educational backgrounds include:** Accounting; Computer Science; Engineering; Finance; Marketing. **Benefits:** 401(k); Dental Insurance; Disability Coverage; Life Insurance; Medical Insurance; Tuition Assistance. **Corporate headquarters location:** This Location. **CEO:** Robert Sanders. **Facilities Manager:** Jonathan Auerbach. **Number of employees at this location:** 125.

XANTE CORPORATION
2800 Dauphin Street, Suite 100, Mobile AL 36606. 334/473-6502. **Contact:** Kathleen Parker, Personnel Manager. **World Wide Web address:** http://www. xante.com. **Description:** Designs, develops, manufactures, and markets laser printers and peripheral equipment. **Common positions include:** Computer Programmer; Database Administrator; MIS Specialist; Network Administrator; Software Engineer. **Educational backgrounds include:** Novell; Software Development; Solaris. **Benefits:** 401(k); Casual Dress - Daily; Dental Insurance; Disability Coverage; Employee Discounts; Life Insurance; Medical Insurance; Savings Plan; Sick Days (6 - 10); Tuition Assistance; Vacation Days (6 - 10). **Corporate headquarters location:** This Location.

XATA CORPORATION
151 East Cliff Road, Suite 10, Burnsville MN 55337. 952/894-3680. **Fax:** 952/894-2463.

Contact: Human Resources. **E-mail address:** info@xata.com. **World Wide Web address:** http://www.xata.com. **Description:** Manufactures onboard computers and software for the transportation and logistics segments of the fleet trucking industry. **Educational backgrounds include:** Engineering; Software Development; Transportation/Logistics. **Benefits:** 401(k); Dental Insurance; Disability Coverage; Life Insurance; Medical Insurance; Pension Plan; Profit Sharing. **Office hours:** Monday - Friday, 7:30 a.m. - 5:30 p.m. **Corporate headquarters location:** This Location. **Other U.S. locations:** Peoria IL. **President/CEO:** Dennis Johnson. **Number of employees nationwide:** 90.

XILINX, INC.
2100 Logic Drive, San Jose CA 95124. 408/559-7778. **Contact:** Ms. Chris Taylor, Vice President of Human Resources. **Description:** A leading supplier of field programmable gate arrays and related development system software used by electronic systems manufacturers. **Common positions include:** Accountant; Computer Programmer; Customer Service Rep.; Electrical Engineer; Financial Analyst; Industrial Engineer; Software Engineer; Systems Analyst; Technical Writer. **Educational backgrounds include:** Accounting; Computer Science; Engineering. **Benefits:** 401(k); Dental Insurance; Disability Coverage; Life Insurance; Medical Insurance; Profit Sharing; Tuition Assistance. **Special programs:** Internships. **Corporate headquarters location:** This Location. **Operations at this facility include:** Administration; Manufacturing; Research and Development; Sales; Service. **Number of employees nationwide:** 900.

XYQUAD INC.
2921 South Brentwood Boulevard, St. Louis MO 63144. 314/961-5995. **Contact:** Human Resources. **World Wide Web address:** http://www.xyquad. com. **Description:** Sells, installs, and maintains computer networks. **Corporate headquarters location:** This Location.

XYVISION ENTERPRISE SOLUTIONS
30 New Crossing Road, Reading MA 01867. 781/756-4400. **Fax:** 781/756-4330. **Contact:** Michael Borin, Vice President of Human Resources. **World Wide Web address:** http://www.xyvision. com. **Description:** Develops and supports software for document management, publishing, and prepress applications worldwide. The company combines its software with standard computer hardware, selected third-party software, and support services to create integrated systems that improve productivity and strategic position. Xyvision's color electronic prepress applications are marketed to commercial trade shops, printers, prepress service organizations, consumer goods companies, advanced design firms, and packaging manufacturers. **Corporate headquarters location:** This Location.

YAHOO! INC.
3420 Central Expressway, Santa Clara CA 95051. **Fax:** 800/284-9195. **Contact:** Nancy Larocca, Staffing Manager. **World Wide Web address:** http://www.yahoo.com. **Description:** A global Internet communications, commerce, and media company that offers a comprehensive branded network of services to millions of users each month. **NOTE:** The company does not accept phone calls regarding employment. Entry-level positions are offered. **Common positions include:** Account Manager; Administrative Assistant; Broadcast Technician; Computer Programmer; Content Developer; Desktop Publishing Specialist; Editor; Financial Analyst; Graphic Artist; Graphic

Designer; Help-Desk Technician; Intranet Developer; Market Research Analyst; Marketing Manager; Marketing Specialist; MIS Specialist; Multimedia Designer; Network Administrator; Project Manager; Public Relations Specialist; Radio Announcer; Sales Executive; Sales Manager; Sales Rep.; Software Engineer; Systems Analyst; Technical Writer; Web Advertising Specialist; Webmaster; Website Developer. **Educational backgrounds include:** C/C++; HTML; Internet Development; Java; Software Development; SQL. **Benefits:** 401(k); Casual Dress - Daily; Daycare Assistance; Dental Insurance; Disability Coverage; Employee Discounts; Financial Planning Assistance; Flexible Schedule; Life Insurance; Medical Insurance; Relocation Assistance; Sick Days; Tuition Assistance; Vacation Days (10 - 20). **Special programs:** Internships. **Corporate headquarters location:** This Location. **Other U.S. locations:** Nationwide. **International locations:** Asia; Central America; Europe; South America.

ZH COMPUTER, INC.
7600 France Avenue South, Suite 550, Minneapolis MN 55435-5939. 952/844-0915. **Fax:** 952/844-9025. **Contact:** Personnel. **World Wide Web address:** http://www.zhcomputer.com. **Description:** Develops software and products for the application of advanced science and mathematics. **President/CEO/Owner:** Margaret Loftus.

ZOOM TELEPHONICS INC.
207 South Street, Boston MA 02111. 617/423-1072. **Fax:** 617/423-2836. **Contact:** Karen Player, Director of Human Resources. **World Wide Web address:** http://www.zoomtel.com. **Description:** Designs, produces, and markets internal, external, and PCMCIA modems and fax modems. **Common positions include:** Accountant; Design Engineer; Industrial Engineer; Mechanical Engineer; MIS Specialist; Software Engineer; Technical Writer. **Educational backgrounds include:** Business Administration; Engineering; Marketing. **Benefits:** 401(k); Dental Insurance; Life Insurance; Medical Insurance; Public Transit Available; Tuition Assistance. **Corporate headquarters location:** This Location. **Annual sales/revenues:** $51 - $100 million.

ZYPCOM, INC.
2301 Industrial Parkway West, Hayward CA 94545-5029. 510/783-2501. **Fax:** 510/783-2414. **Contact:** Heidi Zorzi, Personnel Manager. **World Wide Web address:** http://www.zypcom.com. **Description:** Develops, manufactures, and markets software and hardware products for data communications applications. **Common positions include:** Applications Engineer; Design Engineer; Electrical Engineer; Sales Engineer; Sales Executive; Sales Manager; Software Engineer. **Educational backgrounds include:** Computer Science; Engineering; Marketing. **Benefits:** Dental Insurance; Disability Coverage; Employee Discounts; Life Insurance; Medical Insurance. **Special programs:** Internships; Apprenticeships. **Corporate headquarters location:** This Location.

For more information on career opportunities in the computer industry:

Associations

AMERICAN SOCIETY FOR INFORMATION SCIENCE
8720 Georgia Avenue, Suite 501, Silver Spring MD 20910-3602. 301/495-0900. Fax: 301/495-0810. World Wide Web address: http://www.asis.org. Offers *Challenging Careers in Information: Join the Information Age*, which covers education and job opportunities.

ASSOCIATION FOR COMPUTING MACHINERY
1515 Broadway, 17th Floor, New York NY 10036. 212/869-7440. World Wide Web address: http://www.acm.org. Membership required.

ASSOCIATION FOR MULTIMEDIA COMMUNICATIONS
P.O. Box 10645, Chicago IL 60610. 312/409-1032. E-mail address: amc@amcomm.org. World Wide Web address: http://www.amcomm.org. A multimedia and Internet association.

ASSOCIATION FOR WOMEN IN COMPUTING
41 Sutter Street, Suite 1006, San Francisco CA 94104. 415/905-4663. E-mail address: awc@awc-hq.org. World Wide Web address: http://www.awc-hq.org. A nonprofit organization promoting women in computing professions.

BLACK DATA PROCESSING ASSOCIATES
8401 Corporate Drive, Suite 405, Lanham MD 20785. Toll-free phone: 800/727-BDPA. E-mail address: nbdpa@ix.netcom.com. World Wide Web address: http://www.bdpa.org. An organization of information technology professionals.

THE CENTER FOR SOFTWARE DEVELOPMENT
111 West St. John, Suite 200, San Jose CA 95113. 408/494-8378. E-mail address: info@center.org. World Wide Web address: http://www.center.org. A nonprofit organization providing technical and business resources for software developers.

COMMERCIAL INTERNET EXCHANGE ASSOCIATION (CIX)
P.O. Box 1726, Herndon VA 20172-1726. 703/709-8200. E-mail address: helpdesk@cix.org. World Wide Web address: http://www.cix.org. A nonprofit trade association of data internetworking service providers.

ELECTRONIC PUBLISHING ASSOCIATION
One Rodney Square, 10th Floor, 10th & King Streets, Wilmington DE 19801. World Wide Web address: http://www.epaonline.com. An international association of companies that publish electronically using such formats as CD-ROM, DVD-ROM, and the Internet.

HTML WRITERS GUILD
World Wide Web address: http://www.hwg.org. An international organization of Web page writers and Internet professionals.

INFORMATION TECHNOLOGY ASSOCIATION OF AMERICA
1616 North Fort Myer Drive, Suite 1300, Arlington VA 22209. 703/522-5055. World Wide Web address: http://www.itaa.org.

INTERNET ALLIANCE
1825 Eye Street, Suite 400, P.O. Box 65782, Washington DC 20006. 202/955-8091. World Wide Web address: http://www.isa.net.

MULTIMEDIA DEVELOPMENT GROUP
520 Third Street, Suite 257, San Francisco CA 94107. 415/512-3556. Fax: 415/512-3569. E-mail address: geninfo@mdg.org. A nonprofit trade

association dedicated to the business and market development of multimedia companies.

THE OPEN GROUP
29-B Montvale Avenue, Woburn MA 01801. 781/376-8200. World Wide Web address: http://www.opengroup.org. A consortium concerned with open systems technology in the information systems industry. Membership required.

SOCIETY FOR INFORMATION MANAGEMENT
401 North Michigan Avenue, Chicago IL 60611-4267. 312/644-6610. E-mail address: info@simnet.org. World Wide Web address: http://www.simnet.org. A forum for information technology professionals.

SOFTWARE & INDUSTRY INFORMATION ASSOCIATION (SIIA)
1730 M Street NW, Suite 700, Washington DC 20036. 202/452-1600. World Wide Web address: http://www.siaa.net.

SOFTWARE DEVELOPMENT FORUM
953 Industrial Avenue, Suite 117, Palo Alto CA 94303. 650/856-3706. E-mail address: info@sdforum.org. World Wide Web address: http://www.sdforum.org. An independent, nonprofit organization for software industry professionals.

SOFTWARE SUPPORT PROFESSIONALS ASSOCIATION
11858 Bernardo Plaza Court, Suite 101C, San Diego CA 92128. Toll-free phone: 877/ASK-SSPA. World Wide Web address: http://www.supportgate.com. A forum for service and support professionals in the software industry.

USENIX ASSOCIATION
2560 Ninth Street, Suite 215, Berkeley CA 94710. 510/528-8649. World Wide Web address: http://www.usenix.org. An advanced computing systems professional association.

WORLD WIDE WEB TRADE ASSOCIATION
World Wide Web address: http://www.web-star.com/wwwta.html. An association promoting responsible use of the World Wide Web.

Career Fairs

EXPO INTERNATIONAL, INC.
101 West 23rd Street, Suite 2390, New York NY 10011. 212/655-4505. Fax: 212/655-4501. World Wide Web address: http://www.tech-expo.com. One of the nation's leading technical career fairs.

Magazines

COMPUTER-AIDED ENGINEERING
Penton Media, Inc., 1100 Superior Avenue, Cleveland OH 44114. 216/696-7000. World Wide Web address: http://www.penton.com/cae.

DATAMATION
Earthweb Inc., 10 Post Office Square, Suite 600 South, Boston MA 02109. World Wide Web address: http://www.datamation.com.

IDC REPORT
International Data Corporation, 5 Speen Street, Framingham MA 01701. 508/872-8200.

Online Services

COMPUTER CONSULTANTS
Go: Consult. A CompuServe discussion group for computer professionals interested in networking and business development.

COMPUTER JOBS STORE
World Wide Web address: http://www.computerjobs.com. Over 5,000 job listings are available on this site which also offers salary information and links to other sites.

COMPUTERWORLD
World Wide Web address: http://www.computerworld.com. A weekly online newspaper for information sciences professionals. *Computerworld* conducts a job search by skills, job level (entry-level or experienced), job title, company, and your choice of three cities and three states. One feature of this site is "Career Central," a service which e-mails you when a job matches the skills you have submitted online. This site also has corporate profiles, an events calendar, *Computerworld*'s publications, an index of graduate schools, and other informative and educational resources.

DICE.COM
World Wide Web address: http://www.dice.com. Offers listings for jobs in the high-tech field.

IDEAS JOB NETWORK
World Wide Web address: http://www.ideasjn.com. Offers job listings for computer engineers.

INFOWORKS USA
World Wide Web address: http://www.infoworksusa.com. Provides job listings, profiles of member companies, and a skills quiz.

IT JOBS
World Wide Web address: http://www.internet-solutions.com/itjobs/us/usselect.htm. This Website provides links to companies that have job openings in the information technology industry.

JOBSERVE
World Wide Web address: http://www.jobserve.com. Provides information on job openings in the field of information technology for companies throughout Europe. The site also offers resume posting services and a directory of recruiters.

MACTALENT
World Wide Web address: http://www.mactalent.com. Updated daily with job postings for computer professionals with specialized Mac skills.

SELECTJOBS
World Wide Web address: http://www.selectjobs.com. Post a resume and search the job database by region, discipline, special requirements, and skills on *SelectJOBS*. Once your search criteria has been entered, this site will automatically e-mail you when a job opportunity matches your requests.

THE SOFTWARE JOBS HOMEPAGE
World Wide Web address: http://www.softwarejobs.com. This Website offers a searchable database of openings for jobseekers looking in the software and information technology industries. The site is run by Allen Davis & Associates.

‫&‬ 19 ‫&‬

Educational Services

You can expect to find the following types of facilities in this chapter:
Business/Secretarial/Data Processing Schools • Colleges/Universities/Professional Schools • Community Colleges/Technical Schools/Vocational Schools • Elementary and Secondary Schools • Preschool and Child Daycare Services

Some helpful information: *The average salary range for teachers (grades K-12) is $30,000 - $40,000 annually, though salaries vary significantly between states. Instructors at colleges typically earn approximately $30,000 annually. Educational administrators earn approximately $50,000 - $70,000 per year. Assistant and associate college professors earn between $35,000 and $55,000 on average, and full professors can receive considerably more. Deans normally receive salaries commensurate with that of full professors in the same discipline.*

ADELPHI UNIVERSITY
One South Avenue, Garden City NY 11530. 516/877-3222. **Toll-free phone:** 800/ADELPHI. **Fax:** 516/877-4970. **Contact:** Jane Fisher, Employment Manager. **World Wide Web address:** http://www.adelphi.edu. **Description:** A private university with approximately 7,000 undergraduate and graduate students enrolled. Founded in 1896. **NOTE:** Entry-level positions are offered. **Common positions include:** Administrative Assistant; Computer Programmer; Professor; Secretary. **Educational backgrounds include:** Accounting; Business Administration; Computer Science. **Benefits:** 403(b); Disability Coverage; Employee Discounts; Life Insurance; Medical Insurance; On-Site Daycare; Tuition Assistance.

AMERICAN INTERCONTINENTAL UNIVERSITY
3330 Peachtree Road NE, Atlanta GA 30326. 404/231-9000. **Fax:** 404/965-5701. **Contact:** Dr. Derrek Moore, Dean of Academic Affairs. **World Wide Web address:** http://www.aiuniv.edu. **Description:** A college offering associate's and bachelor's degrees in international business, interior and fashion design, information technology, and multimedia communication. **Common positions include:** Counselor; Video Production Coordinator. **Benefits:** 401(k); Life Insurance; Medical Insurance; Tuition Assistance. **Corporate headquarters location:** This Location. **Other U.S. locations:** Los Angeles CA.

ANDERSON COUNTY SCHOOL DISTRICT 1
P.O. Box 99, Williamston SC 29697. 864/847-7344. **Contact:** Personnel. **Description:** Administrative offices for the public school district.

ANDOVER COLLEGE
901 Washington Avenue, Portland ME 04103. 207/774-6126. **Toll-free phone:** 800/639-3110. **Fax:** 207/774-1715. **Contact:** Human Resources. **World Wide Web address:** http://www. andovercollege.com. **Description:** A two-year college offering associate's degrees and certificate programs in the fields of business administration, computer sciences, travel tourism, medical, and more. **NOTE:** Entry-level positions and part-time jobs are offered. **Company slogan:** Skills for success in a changing work place. **Common positions include:** Accountant; Administrative Assistant; Administrative Manager; Clerical Supervisor; Computer Support Technician; Computer Technician; Controller; Database Administrator; Database Manager; Marketing Specialist; MIS Specialist; Public Relations Specialist; Purchasing Agent; Secretary;

Webmaster. **Educational backgrounds include:** Accounting; Business Administration; Communications; Computer Science; Finance; Health Care; Liberal Arts; Marketing; Microsoft Office; Microsoft Word; Spreadsheets. **Benefits:** 401(k); Dental Insurance; Disability Coverage; Financial Planning Assistance; Life Insurance; Medical Insurance; Profit Sharing; Sick Days (6 - 10); Tuition Assistance; Vacation Days (6 - 10). **Special programs:** Internships; Co-ops. **Corporate headquarters location:** This Location. **President/CEO:** Brenda Berry. **Facilities Manager:** Mark Jenkins. **Number of employees at this location:** 60.

ANNA MARIA COLLEGE
50 Sunset Lane, Paxton MA 01612. 508/849-3300. **Contact:** Joyce Danielson, Personnel Department. **World Wide Web address:** http://www.annamaria.edu. **Description:** A nonprofit, private, liberal arts college for women. The college offers both undergraduate and graduate degrees. **NOTE:** Entry-level positions and part-time jobs are offered. **Common positions include:** Accountant; Administrative Assistant; CFO; Counselor; Database Administrator; ESL Teacher; Finance Director; Graphic Artist; Help-Desk Technician; Human Resources Manager; Instructional Technologist; Librarian; Marketing Manager; Nurse Practitioner; Psychologist; Public Relations Specialist; Purchasing Agent; Secretary; Teacher; Technical Support Manager; Webmaster. **Educational backgrounds include:** Accounting; AS400 Certification; Business Administration; Education; Finance; Marketing; Mathematics; MBA; Microsoft Office; Spreadsheets. **Benefits:** 403(b); Dental Insurance; Disability Coverage; Employee Discounts; Life Insurance; Medical Insurance; Pension Plan; Sick Days (11+); Tuition Assistance; Vacation Days (10 - 20). **Special programs:** Internships; Summer Jobs. **President:** William McGarry. **Purchasing Manager:** Susan Lynch. **Number of employees at this location:** 165.

AQUINAS COLLEGE
303 Adams Street, Milton MA 02186. 617/696-3100. **Contact:** Sarah Barrett, Academic Dean. **Description:** A two-year college offering full-time and part-time programs in business including accounting, business management, medical office management, legal secretarial, paralegal, executive assistant, and liberal studies/business. **Corporate headquarters location:** This Location. **Other area locations:** Newton MA. **Number of employees at this location:** 50.

ARAMARK EDUCATIONAL RESOURCES
573 Park Point Drive, Golden CO 80401. 303/526-3400. **Fax:** 303/526-3393. **Recorded jobline:** 800/818-6819. **Contact:** Human Resources. **World Wide Web address:** http://www.aramarkeducation. com. **Description:** A leading educational service provider, serving more than 100,000 children in 28 states. AER is the umbrella organization for four divisions: Children's World Learning Centers (early care and education), Meritor Academy (private education), Medallion School Partnerships (before and after school educational programs), and ARAMARK Work/Life Partnerships (consulting services). This location also hires seasonally. **NOTE:** Entry-level positions and part-time jobs are offered. **Common positions include:** Accountant; Administrative Assistant; Child Care Center Director; Computer Programmer; Database Administrator; Human Resources Manager; Marketing Manager; Network Administrator; Preschool Worker; Public Relations Specialist; Sales Manager; Sales Rep.; Secretary; Teacher; Vice President. **Educational backgrounds include:** Education; MBA; Microsoft Office; Microsoft Word. **Benefits:** 401(k); Daycare Assistance; Dental Insurance; Disability Coverage; Employee Discounts; Flexible Schedule; Life Insurance; Medical Insurance; On-Site Daycare; Relocation Assistance; Tuition Assistance. **Special programs:** Internships; Training; Summer Jobs. **Other U.S. locations:** Nationwide. **Parent company:** ARAMARK provides a broad range of services to businesses of all sizes. ARAMARK's major businesses include Food, Leisure & Support Services including Campus Dining Services, School Nutrition Services, Leisure Services, Business Dining Services, International Services, Healthcare Support Services, Conference Center Management, and Refreshment Services; Facility Services, Correctional Services, and Industrial Services; Uniform Services, which includes Wearguard, a direct marketer of work clothing; and Health & Education Services, which includes Spectrum Healthcare Services and Educational Resources. **President:** Duane Larson. **Number of employees nationwide:** 15,000.

ASHEBORO CITY SCHOOLS
P.O. Box 1103, Asheboro NC 27204-1103. 336/625-5104. **Fax:** 336/625-9238. **Contact:** Director of Personnel. **Description:** Operates the public school system in Asheboro for students in kindergarten through grade 12. The curriculum includes both a vocational and college preparatory program. **NOTE:** Entry-level positions are offered. **Common positions include:** Counselor; Daycare Worker; ESL Teacher; Librarian; Preschool Worker; Registered Nurse; Secretary; Social Worker; Speech-Language Pathologist; Teacher/Professor. **Educational backgrounds include:** Biology; Chemistry; Education. **Benefits:** 401(k); Dental Insurance; Disability Coverage; Employee Discounts; Life Insurance; Medical Insurance; Pension Plan; Savings Plan. **Corporate headquarters location:** This Location. **Number of employees at this location:** 485.

ASSUMPTION COLLEGE
P.O. Box 15005, Worcester MA 01615-0005. 508/767-7000. **Fax:** 508/756-1780. **Contact:** Personnel. **World Wide Web address:** http://www. assumption.edu. **Description:** A Catholic college with an undergraduate enrollment of approximately 1,600 students. Approximately 1,200 students are enrolled in graduate and continuing education programs. The college also offers a Center for Continuing and Professional Education, which grants associate's and bachelor's degrees on a part-time basis; The French Institute, an academic research facility and a center for French cultural activities; and the Institute for Social and Rehabilitation Services. Founded in 1904. **Corporate headquarters location:** This Location.

AUGUSTA SCHOOL DEPARTMENT
Rural Route 7, Box 2525, Augusta ME 04330. 207/626-2468. **Contact:** Personnel. **Description:** Manages and staffs all public schools in Augusta. These schools include one high school (Cony High School), two middle schools, four elementary schools, and one secondary technical school (Capital Area Technical Center). **Common positions include:** Education Administrator; ESL Teacher; Instructional Technologist; Librarian; Special Education Teacher; Teacher/Professor. **Benefits:** 403(b); Dental Insurance; Job Sharing; Medical Insurance; Sick Days (11+); Tuition Assistance.

AZTEC PUBLIC SCHOOLS
1118 West Aztec Boulevard, Aztec NM 87410. 505/334-9474. **Fax:** 505/334-9861. **Contact:** Dr. Linda Paul, Associate Superintendent. **World Wide Web address:** http://www.aztecschools.com. **Description:** Administrative office of the Aztec public school system. **NOTE:** Entry-level positions are offered. **Common positions include:** Education Administrator; ESL Teacher; Special Education Teacher; Teacher/Professor. **Benefits:** Dental Insurance; Disability Coverage; Life Insurance; Medical Insurance; Pension Plan; Savings Plan. **Superintendent:** James W. Magee. **Number of employees at this location:** 460.

BAKER COLLEGE
1903 Marquette Avenue, Muskegon MI 49442. 231/777-8800. **Contact:** Human Resources. **World Wide Web address:** http://www.baker.edu. **Description:** A business college offering both undergraduate and graduate programs of study.

BALDWIN-WALLACE COLLEGE
275 Eastland Road, Berea OH 44017-2088. 440/826-2900. **Contact:** Human Resources. **World Wide Web address:** http://www.baldwinw.edu. **Description:** A liberal arts college offering undergraduate, graduate, and preprofessional programs. Baldwin-Wallace College has an enrollment of 2,750 undergraduates, 600 graduate students, and 1,300 evening and weekend students. **Corporate headquarters location:** This Location.

BATES COLLEGE
215 College Street, Lewiston ME 04240. 207/786-6255. **Contact:** Human Resources. **World Wide Web address:** http://www.bates.edu. **Description:** A four-year, liberal arts college offering bachelor's degree programs. Approximately 1,500 students attend Bates College.

BERKLEE COLLEGE OF MUSIC
1140 Boylston Street, Boston MA 02215. 617/266-1400. **Fax:** 617/247-0166. **Contact:** Employee Relations Manager. **World Wide Web address:** http://www.berklee.edu. **Description:** A music college offering four-year programs of study in composition, film scoring, music business/management, music education, music production and engineering, music synthesis, music therapy, and performance. The college enrolls 3,000 students. **Common positions include:** Accountant; Management Trainee; Secretary; Teacher; Typist. **Educational backgrounds include:** Accounting; Liberal Arts; Music. **Benefits:** Dental Insurance; Disability Coverage; Employee Discounts; Life Insurance; Medical Insurance; Pension Plan; Savings Plan; Tuition Assistance. **Corporate headquarters location:** This Location.

BERLITZ INTERNATIONAL, INC.
400 Alexander Park, Princeton NJ 08540. 609/514-9650. **Contact:** Donna Russomano, Director of Human Resources. **World Wide Web address:** http://www.berlitz.com. **Description:** A language services firm providing instruction and translation services through 298 language centers in 28 countries around the world. The company also publishes travel guides, foreign language phrase books, and home study materials. **Common positions include:** Accountant; Director; Instructor; Services Sales Rep. **Educational backgrounds include:** Accounting; Business Administration; Finance; Foreign Languages; Liberal Arts. **Corporate headquarters location:** This Location. **Operations at this facility include:** Administration. **Number of employees nationwide:** 3,500.

BIOSIS
2 Commerce Square, 2001 Market Street, Suite 700, Philadelphia PA 19103-7095. 215/587-4800. **Fax:** 215/587-2041. **Contact:** Dana Felt, Senior Human Resources Generalist. **World Wide Web address:** http://www.biosis.org. **Description:** A nonprofit educational organization whose mission is to foster the growth, communication, and use of biological knowledge. BIOSIS offers one of the world's largest collections of abstracts and bibliographical references of biological and medical literature available for public use. BIOSIS abstracts and organizes information for users. **NOTE:** Entry-level positions are offered. **Common positions include:** Biological Scientist; Computer Programmer; Marketing Specialist; MIS Specialist; Systems Analyst; Technical Writer/Editor. **Educational backgrounds include:** Biology; Chemistry; Communications; Computer Science; Geology; Health Care; Marketing. **Benefits:** 403(b); Dental Insurance; Disability Coverage; Flextime Plan; Life Insurance; Medical Insurance; Public Transit Available; Tuition Assistance. **Special programs:** Training. **Corporate headquarters location:** This Location. **International locations:** Worldwide. **Subsidiaries include:** BIOSIS, UK. **Operations at this facility include:** Administration; Marketing; Production; Sales. **President:** John E. Anderson. **Number of employees at this location:** 250.

BLACK HILLS STATE UNIVERSITY
1200 University Street, Unit 9568, Spearfish SD 57799-9568. 605/642-6545. **Fax:** 605/642-6055. **Contact:** Anita Haeder, Personnel Director. **World Wide Web address:** http://www.bhsu.edu. **Description:** A university offering associate's, bachelor's, and master's degrees. The university is composed of the College of Arts and Sciences; the College of Business and Technology; and the College of Education. Black Hills State also offers the following special programs and specialized educational divisions: the Center for Business and Tourism; the Center for American Indian Studies; the Division of Military Science; the Junior College; and extension/summer session services. **NOTE:** Entry-level positions are offered. **Common positions include:** Accountant; Biochemist; Blue-Collar Worker Supervisor; Buyer; Chemist; CFO; Clerical Supervisor; Computer Operator; Computer Programmer; Controller; Daycare Worker; Economist; Education Administrator; Electrician; ESL Teacher; Finance Director; Geologist; Graphic Artist; Graphic Designer; Human Resources Manager; Librarian; Licensed Practical Nurse; Multimedia Designer; Preschool Worker; Psychologist; Public Relations Specialist; Purchasing Agent; Registered Nurse; Secretary; Systems Analyst; Teacher; Typist. **Educational backgrounds include:** Accounting; Art/Design; Biology; Business Administration; Chemistry; Communications; Computer Science; Economics;

Geology; Liberal Arts; Marketing; Mathematics; Physics. **Benefits:** 403(b); Dental Insurance; Disability Coverage; Life Insurance; Medical Insurance; On-Site Daycare; Pension Plan. **Corporate headquarters location:** This Location. **Parent company:** South Dakota Board of Regents.

BLUEFIELD STATE COLLEGE
219 Rock Street, Bluefield WV 24701. 304/327-4000. **Fax:** 304/325-7747. **Contact:** Elizabeth M. Belcher, Director of Human Resources. **E-mail address:** ebelcher@bscvax.wvnet.edu. **World Wide Web address:** http://www.bluefield.wvnet.edu. **Description:** A state-supported commuter college with a primary focus on career and technical two- and four-year programs. The college offers associate's and bachelor's degrees and certificate programs. **Common positions include:** Accountant; Administrative Assistant; CFO; Computer Operator; Computer Programmer; Controller; Counselor; Database Manager; Education Administrator; ESL Teacher; Human Resources Manager; Librarian; Public Relations Specialist; Purchasing Agent; Secretary; Teacher; Typist. **Educational backgrounds include:** Accounting; Art/Design; Biology; Business Administration; Chemistry; Computer Science; Economics; Engineering; Finance; Health Care; Liberal Arts; Marketing; Mathematics; Physics. **Benefits:** 403(b); Dental Insurance; Disability Coverage; Life Insurance; Medical Insurance; Tuition Assistance. **Corporate headquarters location:** This Location. **Number of employees at this location:** 200.

BOISE STATE UNIVERSITY
Human Resources Services, A218, 1910 University Drive, Boise ID 83725. 208/426-1616. **Fax:** 208/426-3100. **Contact:** Viola Boman, Employment Manager. **World Wide Web address:** http://www.idbsu.edu. **Description:** Boise State University has one of the largest student enrollments in Idaho with approximately 15,000 students. The university offers courses in seven colleges: Arts and Sciences, Business, Education, Health Science, Social Sciences and Public Affairs, Technology, and Graduate Studies. The university is fully accredited by the Northwest Association of Schools and Colleges and is a member of the College Entrance Examination Board and the College Scholarship Service Assembly. **Common positions include:** Buyer; Counselor; Electrician; Human Resources Manager; Librarian; Preschool Worker; Public Relations Specialist; Purchasing Agent; Radio Announcer; Teacher; Technical Writer/Editor; Telecommunications Manager; Typist. **Benefits:** Dental Insurance; Disability Coverage; Employee Discounts; Job Sharing; Life Insurance; Medical Insurance; Pension Plan; Profit Sharing; Public Transit Available; Savings Plan; Tuition Assistance. **Corporate headquarters location:** This Location. **Number of employees at this location:** 1,500.

BOSTON UNIVERSITY
25 Buick Street, Boston MA 02215. 617/353-2380. **Contact:** Personnel. **World Wide Web address:** http://www.bu.edu/personnel. **Description:** A private, four-year university offering both undergraduate and graduate degrees. **Corporate headquarters location:** This Location. **Other U.S. locations:** Foxboro MA; Tyngsboro MA.

BOWDOIN COLLEGE
3500 College Station, Brunswick ME 04011-8426. 207/725-3491. **Fax:** 207/725-3976. **Recorded jobline:** 207/725-3923. **Contact:** Kimberly Bonsey, Manager of Employment. **E-mail address:** kbonsey@bowdoin.edu. **World Wide Web address:** http://www.bowdoin.edu. **Description:** A private, four-year, liberal arts college with

approximately 1,500 students. **NOTE:** This firm does not accept unsolicited resumes. Please call the jobline for a listing of available positions. Entry-level positions, part-time jobs, and second and third shifts are offered. **Common positions include:** Accountant; Administrative Manager; Applications Engineer; Architect; CFO; Clinical Lab Technician; Computer Programmer; Computer Support Technician; Computer Technician; Construction Contractor; Controller; Database Administrator; Database Manager; Education Administrator; Instructional Technologist; Internet Services Manager; Librarian; Licensed Practical Nurse; Project Manager; Secretary; SQL Programmer; Systems Analyst; Systems Manager; Telecommunications Manager; Typist; Video Production Coordinator; Webmaster. **Educational backgrounds include:** AS400 Certification; HTML; Internet; Java; Microsoft Word; Novell; Software Tech. Support; Spreadsheets. **Benefits:** 403(b); Dental Insurance; Disability Coverage; Flexible Schedule; Job Sharing; Life Insurance; Medical Insurance; On-Site Daycare. **Special programs:** Internships; Summer Jobs. **Number of employees at this location:** 1,000.

BRADLEY UNIVERSITY
1501 West Bradley Avenue, Peoria IL 61625. 309/676-7611. **Fax:** 309/677-3313. **Contact:** Personnel. **World Wide Web address:** http://www.bradley.edu. **Description:** A private, four-year university offering both undergraduate and graduate degrees. Programs are offered through the Slane College of Communications and Fine Arts; Engineering and Technology; Education and Health Sciences; Liberal Arts and Sciences; and the Foster College of Business Administration. **Common positions include:** Cashier; Civil Engineer; Computer Operator; Computer Programmer; Counselor; Education Administrator; Electrical Engineer; Electrician; Financial Manager; Geologist; Health Services Manager; Heating Technician; Human Resources Manager; Human Service Worker; Industrial Engineer; Librarian; Mathematician; Mechanical Engineer; Psychologist; Purchasing Agent; Receptionist; Secretary; Sociologist; Software Engineer; Statistician; Stock Clerk; Structural Engineer; Systems Analyst; Typist. **Benefits:** Dental Insurance; Disability Coverage; Employee Discounts; Life Insurance; Medical Insurance; Pension Plan; Tuition Assistance. **Corporate headquarters location:** This Location.

BRANDEIS UNIVERSITY
Mail Stop 118, P.O. Box 9110, Waltham MA 02454-9110. 781/736-4473. **Contact:** Employment Administrator. **World Wide Web address:** http://www.brandeis.edu. **Description:** A four-year university offering both undergraduate and graduate programs of study. **Common positions include:** Accountant/Auditor; Administrator; Assistant Manager; Biological Scientist; Blue-Collar Worker Supervisor; Chemist; Computer Programmer; Counselor; Editor; Librarian; Library Technician; Registered Nurse; Systems Analyst. **Educational backgrounds include:** Accounting; Biology; Business Administration; Chemistry; Computer Science; Finance; Liberal Arts; Physics. **Benefits:** Dental Insurance; Disability Coverage; Employee Discounts; Life Insurance; Medical Insurance; Pension Plan; Tuition Assistance. **Corporate headquarters location:** This Location. **Number of employees at this location:** 1,300.

BROOKHAVEN COLLEGE
3939 Valley View Lane, Farmers Branch TX 75244. 972/860-4813. **Contact:** Human Resources. **World Wide Web address:** http://www.dcccd.edu. **Description:** A two-year community college offering a full range of transferable, freshman- and sophomore-level college courses. The college serves the northern portion of Dallas County, including North Dallas, Carrollton, Farmers Branch, Addison, Lewisville, Flower Mound, and The Colony. Brookhaven College serves 2,400 international students representing more than 100 countries and 65 languages. Founded in 1978. **Corporate headquarters location:** This Location.

BROWN UNIVERSITY
P.O. Box 1879, Providence RI 02912. 401/863-3174. **Contact:** Personnel. **World Wide Web address:** http://www.brown.edu. **Description:** An Ivy League university with 7,700 students. **Corporate headquarters location:** This Location.

CALIFORNIA CULINARY ACADEMY, INC.
625 Polk Street, San Francisco CA 94102. 415/771-3536. **Contact:** Personnel. **World Wide Web address:** http://www.baychef.com. **Description:** One of the largest accredited schools for professional chef training in the United States. The academy offers instruction in classic and modern methods of food preparation in its core degree program; specialized baking and pastry certificate programs; and a full range of classes for cooking and wine enthusiasts. Founded in 1977. **Corporate headquarters location:** This Location.

CALIFORNIA SCHOOL OF PROFESSIONAL PSYCHOLOGY
2728 Hyde Street, Suite 100, San Francisco CA 94109. 415/346-4500. **Contact:** Denise A. Hanson, Chief Human Resources Officer. **World Wide Web address:** http://www.cspp.edu. **Description:** A nonprofit institution offering post-graduate programs leading to a doctorate in psychology. **Common positions include:** Accountant; Administrative Manager; Administrative Worker; Admissions Officer; Computer Programmer; Contract Administrator; Department Manager; Financial Aid Officer; Human Resources Manager; Marketing Specialist; Public Relations Specialist; Systems Analyst. **Educational backgrounds include:** Accounting; Business Administration; Communications; Computer Science; Finance; Liberal Arts. **Benefits:** Cafeteria; Dental Insurance; Disability Coverage; Life Insurance; Medical Insurance; Pension Plan; Tuition Assistance. **Corporate headquarters location:** This Location. **Number of employees nationwide:** 1,100.

CATHOLIC UNIVERSITY OF AMERICA
620 Michigan Avenue NE, Room 170, Leahy Hall, Washington DC 20064. 202/319-5050. **Contact:** Personnel. **World Wide Web address:** http://www.cua.edu. **Description:** A four-year, Catholic university offering bachelor's, master's, first professional, and doctoral degrees. Approximately 2,800 undergraduate and 3,700 graduate students attend the university. **Common positions include:** Accountant; Administrator; Architect; Biological Scientist; Biomedical Engineer; Blue-Collar Worker Supervisor; Chemical Engineer; Civil Engineer; Claim Representative; Computer Programmer; Counselor; Customer Service Rep.; Draftsperson; Editor; Electrical Engineer; General Manager; Human Resources Manager; Marketing Specialist; Mechanical Engineer; Metallurgical Engineer; Public Relations Specialist; Purchasing Agent; Quality Control Supervisor; Reporter; Secretary; Systems Analyst; Technical Writer. **Benefits:** Daycare Assistance; Dental Insurance; Disability Coverage; Employee Discounts; Life Insurance; Medical Insurance; Pension Plan; Tuition Assistance. **Corporate headquarters location:** This Location.

CENTRAL ARIZONA COLLEGE
8470 North Overfield Road, Coolidge AZ 85228. 520/723-4141. **Contact:** Human Resources. **World Wide Web address:** http://www.cac.cc.az.us. **Description:** A public, two-year community college offering a variety of programs. **Common positions include:** Accountant; Administrator; Buyer; Computer Programmer; Counselor; Customer Service Rep.; Human Resources Manager; Public Relations Specialist; Purchasing Agent; Systems Analyst; Teacher. **Educational backgrounds include:** Education. **Benefits:** Daycare Assistance; Dental Insurance; Disability Coverage; Life Insurance; Medical Insurance; Pension Plan; Tuition Assistance. **Special programs:** Internships. **Corporate headquarters location:** This Location.

CENTRAL INSTITUTE FOR THE DEAF
818 South Euclid Avenue, St. Louis MO 63110. 314/977-0000. **Fax:** 314/977-0025. **Contact:** Personnel Services Manager. **Description:** A specialized educational agency that operates speech and hearing clinics, professional education programs, research facilities, and an elementary school for deaf children. **Common positions include:** Accountant; Administrative Manager; Biological Scientist; Clinical Lab Technician; Computer Programmer; Construction Contractor; Dietician; Editor; Education Administrator; Electrician; Financial Analyst; Food Scientist; Health Services Manager; Human Resources Manager; Human Service Worker; Librarian; Library Technician; Medical Records Technician; Preschool Worker; Property and Real Estate Manager; Public Relations Specialist; Recreational Therapist; Registered Nurse; Restaurant/Food Service Manager; Science Technologist; Social Worker; Sociologist; Speech-Language Pathologist; Systems Analyst; Teacher; Technical Writer/Editor; Veterinarian. **Educational backgrounds include:** Accounting; Biology; Business Administration; Computer Science; Education; Finance; Health Care. **Benefits:** Dental Insurance; Disability Coverage; Life Insurance; Medical Insurance; Pension Plan; Savings Plan. **Corporate headquarters location:** This Location. **Operations at this facility include:** Administration; Research and Development. **Number of employees at this location:** 180.

CENTRAL KITSAP SCHOOL DISTRICT
P.O. Box 8, Silverdale WA 98383-3078. 360/692-3118. **Physical address:** 9210 Silverdale Way NW, Silverdale WA. **Fax:** 360/698-5499. **Contact:** Personnel. **Description:** Administrative offices for the school district. **Common positions include:** Accountant; Blue-Collar Worker Supervisor; Budget Analyst; Clerical Supervisor; Construction Contractor; Counselor; Human Resources Manager; Librarian; Occupational Therapist; Purchasing Agent; Social Worker; Systems Analyst; Teacher. **Benefits:** Dental Insurance; Disability Coverage; Life Insurance; Medical Insurance. **Corporate headquarters location:** This Location. **Number of employees at this location:** 1,500.

CENTRAL MICHIGAN UNIVERSITY
109 Rowe Hall, Mount Pleasant MI 48859. 517/774-3753. **Contact:** Human Resources. **World Wide Web address:** http://www.cmich.edu. **Description:** A four-year university with an enrollment of approximately 16,000 undergraduate and graduate students. **Common positions include:** Accountant; Blue-Collar Worker Supervisor; Broadcast Technician; Budget Analyst; Buyer; Cashier; Chef Worker; Clerical Supervisor; Computer Operator; Computer Programmer; Counselor; Department Manager; Dispatcher; Editor; Electrician; Graphic Artist; Heating Technician; Human Resources Manager; Librarian; Library Technician; Licensed Practical Nurse; Paralegal; Payroll Clerk; Photographer Operator; Physician; Physician Assistant; Printing Press Operator; Receptionist; Registered Nurse; Secretary; Stenographer; Stock Clerk; Systems Analyst; Typist; Welder; Wholesale and Retail Buyer. **Educational backgrounds include:** Accounting; Biology; Business Administration; Chemistry; Finance; Management/Planning. **Benefits:** Dental Insurance; Disability Coverage; Life Insurance; Medical Insurance; Pension Plan; Savings Plan; Tuition Assistance. **Corporate headquarters location:** This Location. **Number of employees nationwide:** 2,000.

CHARLOTTE-MECKLENBURG SCHOOL SYSTEM
P.O. Box 30035, Charlotte NC 28230. 704/343-6220. **Fax:** 704/343-6645. **Recorded jobline:** 704/343-5384. **Contact:** Human Resources. **E-mail address:** hr@cms.k12.nc.us. **World Wide Web address:** http://www.cms.k12.nc.us. **Description:** Administrative offices of the public school system. **Common positions include:** Administrative Assistant; Computer Programmer; ESL Teacher; Preschool Worker; Secretary; Special Education Teacher; Teacher. **Benefits:** 401(k); Dental Insurance; Life Insurance; Medical Insurance. **Corporate headquarters location:** This Location.

CHILD & ELDER CARE INSIGHTS, INC.
19111 Detroit Road, Suite 104, Rocky River OH 44116. 440/356-2900. **Fax:** 440/356-2919. **Contact:** Elisabeth A. Bryenton, President. **E-mail address:** info@carereports.com. **World Wide Web address:** http://www.carereports.com. **Description:** A national dependent care resource and referral service that maintains two national databases: CHILDBASE and ELDERBASE. CHILDBASE provides working parents with information about child care services including family day care providers, preschools, adoption resources, in-home care, and schools. ELDERBASE provides information on nursing homes, home health agencies, nutrition services, continuing care/retirement communities, and transportation services. **Common positions include:** Administrative Assistant; Database Administrator; Database Manager; Librarian; MIS Specialist. **Other U.S. locations:** Nationwide.

CLARK UNIVERSITY
950 Main Street, Worcester MA 01610. 508/793-7294. **Fax:** 508/793-8809. **Contact:** Anne Fredette, Human Resources Assistant. **E-mail address:** resumes@clarku.edu. **World Wide Web address:** http://www.clarku.edu. **Description:** A four-year research university offering bachelor's, master's, and doctoral degrees. The student body consists of approximately 2,200 graduate and undergraduate students. During the summer the College of Professional and Continuing Education (C.O.P.A.C.E.) program offers select classes for credit or personal enrichment. **NOTE:** Entry-level positions and part-time jobs are offered. **Common positions include:** Accountant; Administrative Assistant; Chemist; Clerical Supervisor; Computer Support Technician; Customer Service Rep.; Database Manager; Education Administrator; General Manager; Librarian; Secretary; SQL Programmer; Systems Manager; Webmaster. **Educational backgrounds include:** HTML; Microsoft Word; Spreadsheets. **Benefits:** 403(b); Casual Dress - Daily; Dental Insurance; Disability Coverage; Employee Discounts; Financial Planning Assistance; Life Insurance; Medical Insurance; Pension Plan; Tuition Assistance. **Other area locations:** Framingham MA.

CLOVIS MUNICIPAL SCHOOLS

1009 North Main, P.O. Box 19000, Clovis NM 88101-9000. 505/769-4300. **Fax:** 505/769-4333. **Contact:** Jim McDaniel, Assistant Superintendent for Personnel. **E-mail address:** jmcdaniel@cms. k12.nm.us. **World Wide Web address:** http://www. cms.k12.nm.us. **Description:** Houses the administrative offices for the Clovis public school system. The office is responsible for staffing all public schools in the community. **NOTE:** Part-time jobs are offered. **Common positions include:** Accountant; Administrative Assistant; AS400 Programmer Analyst; Blue-Collar Worker Supervisor; Certified Occupational Therapy Assistant; Computer Programmer; Computer Support Technician; Computer Technician; Counselor; Education Administrator; Electrician; ESL Teacher; Finance Director; Instructional Technologist; Librarian; Occupational Therapist; Physical Therapist; Physical Therapy Assistant; Preschool Worker; Psychologist; Purchasing Agent; Registered Nurse; Secretary; Social Worker; Special Education Teacher; Speech-Language Pathologist; Teacher; Typist. **Educational backgrounds include:** AS400 Certification; Biology; Liberal Arts; Mathematics; Software Tech. Support. **Benefits:** Casual Dress - Daily; Dental Insurance; Disability Coverage; Life Insurance; Medical Insurance; Pension Plan; Savings Plan. **Corporate headquarters location:** This Location. **Number of employees at this location:** 1,100.

COLLEGE FOR LIFELONG LEARNING

125 North State Street, Concord NH 03301. 603/228-3000. **Contact:** Human Resources. **World Wide Web address:** http://www.usnh.unh.edu/cll. **Description:** A part of the University System of New Hampshire, The College For Lifelong Learning offers a bachelor's of professional studies in management, behavioral science, criminal justice, and early childhood education; bachelor's of general studies; associate's degrees in general studies, microcomputer applications, business studies, early childhood education, and behavioral sciences; certificate programs in child care, library techniques, computer applications, adult learning and development, leadership in the workplace, and paralegal studies; and professional continuing education with teacher education courses, management development training, real estate recertification, real estate appraisal, certified nurses assistant, administrative assistant programs, and computer training workshops. **Corporate headquarters location:** This Location. **Other U.S. locations:**

- 325 Mount Support Road, Suite 2, Lebanon NH 03766. 603/448-6797.

COLLEGE OF THE SOUTHWEST

6610 North Lovington Highway, Hobbs NM 88240. 505/392-6561. **Fax:** 505/392-6006. **Contact:** Dr. James Kashner, Vice President. **World Wide Web address:** http://www.csw.edu. **Description:** An independent, five-year, liberal arts college that also offers master's programs in education and education administration. Approximately 700 students attend College of the Southwest. **President:** Joan Tucker.

COLLIN COUNTY COMMUNITY COLLEGE DISTRICT

P.O. Box 8001, McKinney TX 75070-8001. 972/881-5660. **Physical address:** 2200 West University Drive, McKinney TX 75070-8001. **Fax:** 972/985-3778. **Recorded jobline:** 972/881-5627. **Contact:** Brenda McNeacon, Director of Human Resources. **World Wide Web address:** http://www. ccccd.edu. **Description:** A community college offering courses in computer science, humanities, international studies, fine arts, mathematics/natural science, health sciences, education, and engineering. **Common positions include:** Clerical Supervisor; Computer Programmer; Customer Service Rep.; Education Administrator; Human Resources Manager; Librarian; Library Technician; Purchasing Agent; Systems Analyst; Teacher. **Educational backgrounds include:** Business Administration; Computer Science. **Benefits:** Dental Insurance; Disability Coverage; Life Insurance; Medical Insurance; Pension Plan; Tuition Assistance. **Special programs:** Internships. **Corporate headquarters location:** This Location.

COLUMBIA COLLEGE OF MISSOURI

1001 Rogers Street, Columbia MO 65216. 573/875-8700. **Contact:** Director of Personnel. **World Wide Web address:** http://www.ccis.edu. **Description:** A post-secondary educational institution offering undergraduate and graduate programs of study. **Common positions include:** Clerk; Support Personnel; Professor. **Benefits:** 403(b); Disability Coverage; Employee Discounts; Life Insurance; Medical Insurance; Tuition Assistance. **Corporate headquarters location:** This Location.

COLUMBIA UNIVERSITY

475 Riverside Drive, Room 1901, New York NY 10115. 212/870-2403. **Contact:** Employment Manager. **World Wide Web address:** http://www. cc.columbia.edu. **Description:** A private university comprised of 15 schools and 71 academic departments and divisions. The university is affiliated with Barnard College, Teachers College, and Union Theological Seminary. There are approximately 20,000 students enrolled at the university including 11,800 graduate and professional, 5,600 undergraduate, and 2,500 nondegree students. **Common positions include:** Administrative Assistant; Administrative Manager; Budget Analyst; Computer Programmer; Editor; Education Administrator; Librarian; Library Technician; Systems Analyst; Typist. **Educational backgrounds include:** Bachelor of Arts; Business Administration; Liberal Arts. **Benefits:** Dental Insurance; Disability Coverage; Life Insurance; Medical Insurance; Pension Plan; Tuition Assistance. **Corporate headquarters location:** This Location.

CONTRA COSTA COMMUNITY COLLEGE DISTRICT

500 Court Street, Martinez CA 94553. 925/229-1000. **Fax:** 925/229-2490. **Contact:** Teresa Gula, District Human Resources Technician. **World Wide Web address:** http://www.collegesofcc.cc.ca.us. **Description:** Administers to Contra Costa College (San Pablo CA); Diablo Valley College (Pleasant Hill CA); Los Medanos College (Pittsburg CA); San Ramon Valley Center (San Ramon CA); and Brentwood Center (Brentwood CA). Contra Costa Community College District is the eighth largest school district in California. **Common positions include:** Education Administrator; Human Service Worker; Professor. **Educational backgrounds include:** Master of Arts; Teaching. **Corporate headquarters location:** This Location.

COPPIN STATE COLLEGE

2500 West North Avenue, Baltimore MD 21216. 410/383-5757. **Contact:** Valerie A. Bell, Director of Human Resources. **World Wide Web address:** http://www.coppin.umd.edu. **Description:** A four-year, liberal arts college offering both bachelor's and master's degrees. Approximately 2,500 undergraduate and 275 graduate students attend the college. **Common positions include:** Accountant; Budget Analyst; Buyer; Counselor; Electrician; Human Resources Manager; Librarian; Library Technician; Licensed Practical Nurse; Mechanical

Engineer; Purchasing Agent; Stationary Engineer. **Educational backgrounds include:** Accounting; Art/Design; Biology; Business Administration; Chemistry; Communications; Computer Science; Economics; Engineering; Finance; Health Care; Liberal Arts; Marketing; Mathematics; Physics. **Benefits:** 401(k); Dental Insurance; Life Insurance; Medical Insurance; Pension Plan; Savings Plan; Tuition Assistance. **Special programs:** Internships. **Corporate headquarters location:** This Location. **Number of employees at this location:** 530.

DAKOTA STATE UNIVERSITY
820 North Washington Avenue, Madison SD 57042. 605/256-5111. **Contact:** Nancy Grassel, Director of Human Resources. **World Wide Web address:** http://www.dsu.com. **Description:** A four-year, nonprofit university consisting of the College of Liberal Arts, the College of Natural Sciences, the College of Business and Information Systems, and the College of Education. **Common positions include:** Accountant; Administrative Assistant; Administrative Manager; CFO; Computer Programmer; Computer Support Technician; Controller; Education Administrator; ESL Teacher; Human Resources Manager; Instructional Technologist; Librarian; Network Administrator; Public Relations Specialist; Secretary; Teacher; Vice President; Website Developer. **Benefits:** Sick Days (11+); Vacation Days (10 - 20). **President:** Jerald Tunheim.

DALLAS COUNTY COMMUNITY COLLEGE DISTRICT
701 Elm Street, Dallas TX 75202. 214/860-2135. **Contact:** Human Resources. **World Wide Web address:** http://www.dcccd.edu. **Description:** A community college district. **Common positions include:** Accountant/Auditor; Administrator; Buyer; Education Administrator; Instructor; Systems Manager. **Educational backgrounds include:** Accounting; Art/Design; Biology; Business Administration; Chemistry; Communications; Computer Science; Economics; Education; Engineering; Finance; Geology; Liberal Arts; Marketing; Mathematics; Physics. **Benefits:** Dental Insurance; Disability Coverage; Life Insurance; Medical Insurance; Pension Plan. **Corporate headquarters location:** This Location. **Operations at this facility include:** Research and Development.

DAVIS COUNTY SCHOOL DISTRICT
P.O. Box 588, Farmington UT 84025-0588. 801/444-5122. **Fax:** 801/444-5354. **Contact:** Human Resources. **World Wide Web address:** http://www.davis.k12.ut.us. **Description:** Operates the public schools in Davis County. **NOTE:** Entry-level positions are offered. **Common positions include:** Accountant; Architect; Blue-Collar Worker Supervisor; Buyer; CFO; Computer Operator; Computer Programmer; Counselor; Database Manager; Daycare Worker; Education Administrator; Electrician; ESL Teacher; Finance Director; Human Resources Manager; Librarian; Occupational Therapist; Physical Therapist; Preschool Worker; Psychologist; Public Relations Specialist; Purchasing Agent; Secretary; Speech-Language Pathologist; Systems Analyst; Systems Manager; Teacher; Telecommunications Manager; Typist. **Educational backgrounds include:** Biology; Chemistry; Education; Education Administration; Liberal Arts; Mathematics; Physics; Software Development; Software Tech. Support. **Special programs:** Training. **Corporate headquarters location:** This Location.

DETROIT COLLEGE OF BUSINESS
4801 Oakman Boulevard, Dearborn MI 48126. 313/581-4400. **Contact:** Pamela L. Hodge, Director of Human Resources. **World Wide Web address:** http://www.dcb.edu. **Description:** A business college offering associate's, bachelor's, and master's degrees in business administration. **Common positions include:** Accountant; Counselor; Librarian; Receptionist; Teacher. **Educational backgrounds include:** Business Administration. **Benefits:** Dental Insurance; Disability Coverage; Employee Discounts; Life Insurance; Medical Insurance; Pension Plan; Tuition Assistance. **Corporate headquarters location:** This Location. **Other U.S. locations:** Flint MI; Warren MI. **President:** James Mendola. **Number of employees at this location:** 275.

DOWLING COLLEGE
150 Idle Hour Boulevard, Oakdale NY 11769-1999. 631/244-3020. **Fax:** 631/589-6123. **Contact:** Barbara Nolan, Employment Specialist. **World Wide Web address:** http://www.dowling.edu. **Description:** Dowling College is an independent, comprehensive, coeducational college. The college serves approximately 6,000 full- and part-time students, offering undergraduate programs leading to Bachelor of Arts, Bachelor of Science, and Bachelor of Business Administration degrees. Graduate program degrees include Master of Science in Reading and Special Education, Master of Business Administration, and Master of Education with the following concentrations: Elementary Education, Secondary Education, Special Education, Life-Span Special Services, and Reading. **Common positions include:** Accountant; Administrative Assistant; Budget Analyst; Controller; Counselor; Editor; ESL Teacher; Financial Analyst; Graphic Artist; Librarian; Purchasing Agent; Secretary; Teacher; Typist. **Educational backgrounds include:** Accounting; Business Administration; Communications; Finance; Liberal Arts; Marketing; Public Relations. **Benefits:** Dental Insurance; Life Insurance; Medical Insurance; Pension Plan; Tuition Assistance. **Corporate headquarters location:** This Location. **Number of employees at this location:** 900.

EAST CAROLINA UNIVERSITY
210 East First Street, Greenville NC 27858. 252/328-6352. **Fax:** 252/328-4191. **Contact:** Human Resources. **World Wide Web address:** http://www.ecu.edu. **Description:** A university offering undergraduate, graduate, and medical programs. **Common positions include:** Accountant; Administrative Manager; Bindery Worker; Cashier; Clerical Supervisor; Computer Operator; Computer Programmer; Construction Contractor; Customer Service Rep.; Dietician; Electrician; Employment Interviewer; General Manager; Graphic Artist; Health Services Worker; Heating Technician; Human Resources Manager; Librarian; Library Technician; Licensed Practical Nurse; Line Installer; Medical Records Technician; Occupational Therapist; Payroll Clerk; Pharmacist; Physical Therapist; Physician Assistant; Printing Press Operator; Receptionist; Recreation Worker; Registered Nurse; Social Worker; Speech-Language Pathologist; Stenographer; Stock Clerk; Surgical Technician; Systems Analyst; Typist. **Educational backgrounds include:** Accounting; Biology; Business Administration; Computer Science; Engineering; Finance; Marketing. **Benefits:** Disability Coverage; Life Insurance; Medical Insurance; Pension Plan; Tuition Assistance. **Corporate headquarters location:** This Location.

EASTERN WASHINGTON UNIVERSITY
526 Fifth Street, Mail Stop 114, Cheney WA 99004-2431. 509/359-2381. **Fax:** 509/359-2874. **Recorded jobline:** 509/359-4390. **Contact:** Division of Human Resources. **World Wide Web address:**

http://www.ewu.edu. **Description:** A four-year university offering undergraduate and graduate degrees to approximately 8,500 students. **Common positions include:** Accountant; Administrative Manager; Architect; Automotive Mechanic; Broadcast Technician; Budget Analyst; Buyer; Clerical Supervisor; Computer Programmer; Construction and Building Inspector; Construction Contractor; Counselor; Designer; Editor; Education Administrator; Electrician; Financial Analyst; Human Resources Manager; Librarian; MIS Specialist; Psychologist; Public Relations Specialist; Purchasing Agent; Restaurant Manager; Stationary Engineer; Systems Analyst; Teacher; Telecommunications Manager; Typist. **Educational backgrounds include:** Accounting; Business Administration; Computer Science; Finance; Liberal Arts. **Benefits:** Dental Insurance; Disability Coverage; Life Insurance; Medical Insurance; Pension Plan; Tuition Assistance. **Corporate headquarters location:** This Location. **Number of employees at this location:** 1,100.

EDISON COMMUNITY COLLEGE
P.O. Box 60210, Fort Myers FL 33906-6210. 941/489-9280. **Fax:** 941/489-9041. **Recorded jobline:** 941/489-9120. **Contact:** Wanda Gebhardt, Human Resources Specialist. **E-mail address:** wgebhardt@edison.edu. **World Wide Web address:** http://www.edison.edu. **Description:** A two-year college offering associate's degrees as well as certification in two programs and non-credit continuing education courses. **NOTE:** Part-time jobs are offered. **Common positions include:** Accountant; Administrative Assistant; CFO; Computer Programmer; Computer Technician; Counselor; Education Administrator; Finance Director; Human Resources Manager; Librarian; Library Technician; Purchasing Agent; Secretary; Systems Analyst; Teacher; Vice President of Finance; Vice President of Operations. **Educational backgrounds include:** Accounting; Art/Design; Biology; Business Administration; Chemistry; Computer Science; Economics; Engineering; Finance; Geology; Mathematics; Microsoft Office; Microsoft Word; Physics; Spreadsheets. **Benefits:** 403(b); Dental Insurance; Disability Coverage; Life Insurance; Medical Insurance; Pension Plan; Sick Days (11+); Tuition Assistance; Vacation Days (10 - 20). **Corporate headquarters location:** This Location. **Other area locations:** Naples FL; Port Charlotte FL. **President:** Kenneth P. Walker. **Facilities Manager:** Ronald White. **Purchasing Manager:** Jay Collier. **Number of employees at this location:** 300.

EMERSON COLLEGE
100 Beacon Street, Boston MA 02116. 617/824-8500. **Contact:** Personnel. **World Wide Web address:** http://www.emerson.edu. **Description:** A four-year communications college offering both undergraduate and graduate degrees to approximately 2,000 students. **Common positions include:** Accountant; Administrator; Computer Programmer; Counselor; Department Manager; General Manager; Instructor; Public Relations Specialist; Purchasing Agent; Systems Analyst; Teacher/Professor. **Educational backgrounds include:** Accounting; Business Administration; Communications; Computer Science; Liberal Arts; Marketing. **Benefits:** Dental Insurance; Disability Coverage; Life Insurance; Medical Insurance; Pension Plan; Tuition Assistance. **Special programs:** Internships. **Corporate headquarters location:** This Location.

FAIRFIELD UNIVERSITY
1073 North Benson Road, Fairfield CT 06430. 203/254-4080. **Fax:** 203/254-4295. **Contact:**

Manager of Employment and Compensation. **Description:** A four-year university providing both undergraduate and graduate programs. **NOTE:** Entry-level positions, part-time jobs, and second and third shifts are offered. **Common positions include:** Accountant; Administrative Manager; Architect; Biochemist; Computer Support Technician; Controller; Counselor; Database Administrator; Draftsperson; Education Administrator; Electrician; Graphic Artist; Human Resources Manager; Internet Services Manager; Librarian; Psychologist; Public Relations Specialist; Purchasing Agent; Secretary; Social Worker; SQL Programmer; Telecommunications Manager; Webmaster. **Educational backgrounds include:** HTML; Java; MCSE; Microsoft Word; Software Tech. Support. **Benefits:** 403(b); Casual Dress - Fridays; Dental Insurance; Disability Coverage; Employee Discounts; Flexible Schedule; Job Sharing; Life Insurance; Medical Insurance; Telecommuting; Tuition Assistance. **Special programs:** Internships. **Corporate headquarters location:** This Location. **Number of employees at this location:** 800.

FLORIDA COMMUNITY COLLEGE AT JACKSONVILLE
501 West State Street, Jacksonville FL 32202. 904/632-3210. **Recorded jobline:** 904/632-3161. **Contact:** Employment Officer. **World Wide Web address:** http://www.fccj.org. **Description:** An accredited institution offering associate's degrees, corporate and technical training, and special and continuing education programs. Total enrollment is approximately 28,000. **NOTE:** Entry-level positions and part-time jobs are offered. **Common positions include:** Advisor; Computer Support Technician; Network Administrator; Secretary; Systems Analyst; Typist. **Benefits:** Casual Dress - Daily; Dental Insurance; Employee Discounts; Flexible Schedule; Life Insurance; Medical Insurance; Pension Plan; Tuition Assistance. **President:** Dr. Steven Wallace.

FOOTHILL - DE ANZA COMMUNITY COLLEGE DISTRICT
12345 El Monte Road, Los Altos Hills CA 94022. 650/949-6217. **Recorded jobline:** 650/949-6218. **Contact:** Employment Services. **E-mail address:** employment@fhda.edu. **World Wide Web address:** http://www.fhda.edu. **Description:** A nonprofit community college district comprised of Foothill College (also at this location) and De Anza College (Cupertino CA). **NOTE:** Entry-level positions and part-time jobs are offered. **Common positions include:** Accountant; Administrative Assistant; Administrative Manager; Assistant Manager; Budget Analyst; Buyer; Clerical Supervisor; Computer Operator; Computer Programmer; Computer Support Technician; Computer Technician; Database Administrator; Database Manager; Education Administrator; Electrician; ESL Teacher; Librarian; MIS Specialist; Network Administrator; Preschool Worker; Secretary; Special Education Teacher; Systems Analyst; Systems Manager; Teacher; Typist. **Educational backgrounds include:** Microsoft Word; Spreadsheets. **Benefits:** 403(b); Casual Dress - Daily; Dental Insurance; Disability Coverage; Life Insurance; Medical Insurance; Pension Plan; Tuition Assistance. **Corporate headquarters location:** This Location. **Annual sales/revenues:** More than $100 million. **Number of employees at this location:** 2,500.

FORSYTH TECHNICAL COMMUNITY COLLEGE
2100 Silas Creek Parkway, Winston-Salem NC 27103. 336/723-0371. **Fax:** 336/761-2351. **Contact:** Larry V. Weaver, Dean of Human

Resources. **World Wide Web address:** http://www.forsyth.tec.nc.us. **Description:** A community college. **Common positions include:** Administrative Assistant; Counselor; Electrician; Emergency Medical Technician; ESL Teacher; Human Resources Manager; Purchasing Agent/Manager; Secretary; Teacher. **Educational backgrounds include:** Accounting; Art/Design; Biology; Business Administration; Chemistry; Computer Science; Economics; Engineering; Finance; Health Care; Liberal Arts; Marketing; Mathematics; Physics. **Benefits:** 401(k); Dental Insurance; Disability Coverage; Life Insurance; Medical Insurance; Tuition Assistance. **Corporate headquarters location:** This Location. **Operations at this facility include:** Research and Development. **Number of employees at this location:** 310.

GALLUP-McKINLEY COUNTY PUBLIC SCHOOLS
P.O. Box 1318, Gallup NM 87305-1318. 505/722-7711. **Toll-free phone:** 800/842-5587. **Fax:** 505/722-9630. **Contact:** Richard Johnson, Director of Personnel. **World Wide Web address:** http://www.gmcs.k12.nm.us. **Description:** A public school district serving 14,500 students in grades K-12 in northwestern New Mexico. **Common positions include:** CFO; Controller; Counselor; Education Administrator; ESL Teacher; Instructional Technologist; Librarian; Preschool Worker; Psychologist; Purchasing Agent/Manager; Registered Nurse; Respiratory Therapist; Secretary; Social Worker; Special Education Teacher; Speech-Language Pathologist. **Educational backgrounds include:** Chemistry; Communications; Computer Science; Mathematics; Physics. **Benefits:** Dental Insurance; Life Insurance; Medical Insurance; Pension Plan; Sick Days (11+); Vacation Days (16+). **Number of employees at this location:** 2,000.

GUIDANCE INVESTORS, INC.
dba AMERICAN GRADE SCHOOLS/ AMERICAN CHILD CARE CENTERS
17223 North 19th Avenue, Phoenix AZ 85023. 602/993-6070. **Contact:** Employment. **Description:** Operates 25 child care centers in Arizona, Oklahoma, and California that provide daycare and preschool services. **Common positions include:** Preschool Worker; Teacher/Professor. **Educational backgrounds include:** Child Development. **Benefits:** Daycare Assistance; Dental Insurance; Life Insurance; Medical Insurance. **Special programs:** Internships. **Corporate headquarters location:** This Location.

HARDIN-SIMMONS UNIVERSITY
HSU Box 16030, Abilene TX 79698. 915/670-1507. **Physical address:** 2200 South Hickory Street, Abilene TX. **Fax:** 915/670-5874. **Contact:** Earl T. Garrett, Director of Human Resources. **World Wide Web address:** http://www.hsutx.edu. **Description:** A Southern Baptist university offering both graduate and undergraduate degrees. **Common positions include:** Accountant; Administrative Manager; Blue-Collar Worker Supervisor; Budget Analyst; Clerical Supervisor; Computer Programmer; Counselor; Education Administrator; Fundraising Specialist; Human Resources Manager; Librarian; Library Technician; Licensed Practical Nurse; Public Relations Specialist; Registered Nurse; Reporter; Systems Analyst; Teacher. **Educational backgrounds include:** Accounting; Art/Design; Biology; Business Administration; Chemistry; Communications; Computer Science; Economics; Finance; Geology; Liberal Arts; Marketing; Mathematics; Physical Therapy; Physics; Religion. **Benefits:** 403(b); Cafeteria; Dental Insurance; Disability Coverage; Employee Discounts; Life Insurance; Medical Insurance;

Pension Plan; Tuition Assistance. **Corporate headquarters location:** This Location. **Number of employees at this location:** 300.

HILLSBOROUGH COMMUNITY COLLEGE
4001 Tampa Bay Boulevard, Tampa FL 33614. 813/253-7000. **Physical address:** 4001 Tampa Bay Boulevard, Tampa FL 33614. **Fax:** 813/253-7034. **Contact:** Human Resources. **World Wide Web address:** http://www.hcc.cc.fl.us. **Description:** A multicampus, state-run community college, accredited by the Southern Association of Colleges and Schools. **Common positions include:** Accountant; Administrative Worker; Administrator; Buyer; Cashier; Clinical Lab Technician; Computer Programmer; Education Administrator; Human Resources Manager; Instructor; Library Technician; Security Officer; Teacher/Professor. **Educational backgrounds include:** Accounting; Biology; Business Administration; Chemistry; Computer Science; Education; Mathematics; Radiologic Technology; Sonography. **Benefits:** Dental Insurance; Disability Coverage; Employee Discounts; Life Insurance; Medical Insurance; Retirement Plan; Tuition Assistance. **Corporate headquarters location:** This Location. **Number of employees at this location:** 1,500.

ITT EDUCATIONAL SERVICES, INC. (ESI)
P.O. Box 50466, Indianapolis IN 46250-0466. **Toll-free phone:** 800/388-3368. **Fax:** 317/594-4327. **Contact:** Lisa Cardona, Personnel Manager. **World Wide Web address:** http://www.itttech.edu. **Description:** A leading private college system providing associate's and bachelor's degrees in technology-based disciplines. ESI operates 67 ITT Technical Institutes in 27 states. **Company slogan:** We teach technology. **Common positions include:** Account Representative; Education Administrator; Finance Director; General Manager; Sales Manager; Secretary; Teacher. **Educational backgrounds include:** MCSE; Novell. **Benefits:** 401(k); Dental Insurance; Disability Coverage; Employee Discounts; Life Insurance; Medical Insurance; Pension Plan; Sick Days (1 - 5); Tuition Assistance; Vacation Days (6 - 10). **Corporate headquarters location:** This Location. **Annual sales/revenues:** More than $100 million. **Number of employees nationwide:** 3,500.

INDIANA UNIVERSITY/ PURDUE UNIVERSITY AT INDIANAPOLIS
620 Union Drive, Student Union Building, Room 342, Indianapolis IN 46202-5168. 317/274-7617. **Fax:** 317/274-5481. **Contact:** Marcia Combs, Employment Coordinator. **E-mail address:** hra@iupui.edu. **World Wide Web address:** http://www.iupui.edu. **Description:** A four-year state university with professional schools, teaching hospitals, and schools of medicine and dentistry. IUPUI offers degrees from both Indiana University and Purdur University. **Common positions include:** Accountant; Architect; Biological Scientist; Biomedical Engineer; Broadcast Technician; Buyer; Chemist; Claim Rep.; Clerical Supervisor; Computer Programmer; Counselor; Customer Service Representative; Dental Assistant; Draftsperson; Editor; Education Administrator; EEG Technologist; Electrician; Financial Analyst; Landscape Architect; Librarian; Library Technician; Millwright; Plumber; Psychologist; Public Relations Specialist; Purchasing Agent; Social Worker; Speech-Language Pathologist; Statistician; Systems Analyst; Veterinarian. **Educational backgrounds include:** Accounting; Biology; Business Administration; Chemistry; Computer Science; Health Care. **Benefits:** 403(b); Dental Insurance; Disability Coverage; Life Insurance; Medical Insurance; Pension Plan; Tuition Assistance.

INTERDENOMINATIONAL THEOLOGY CENTER
700 Martin Luther King Jr. Drive, Atlanta GA 30314. 404/527-7711. **Contact:** Roseanna Brannon, Manager of Human Resources. **Description:** A graduate school of theology. **Common positions include:** Accountant; Computer Programmer; Human Resources Manager; Human Service Worker; Librarian; Teacher; Technical Writer. **Educational backgrounds include:** Business Administration; Communications; Liberal Arts. **Benefits:** 401(k); Dental Insurance; Disability Coverage; Life Insurance; Medical Insurance; Pension Plan; Tuition Assistance. **Corporate headquarters location:** This Location. **Number of employees at this location:** 90.

JACKSON STATE UNIVERSITY
1400 John R. Lynch Street, P.O. Box 17028, Jackson MS 39217. 601/968-2015. **Fax:** 601/974-5856. **Contact:** Ester W. Stokes, Director of Human Resources. **World Wide Web address:** http://www.jsums.edu. **Description:** A state university. **Common positions include:** Accountant; Administrative Assistant; Architect; Automotive Mechanic; Biochemist; Biological Scientist; Blue-Collar Worker Supervisor; Broadcast Technician; Budget Analyst; Buyer; Chemist; CFO; Child Care Center Director; Clerical Supervisor; Computer Operator; Computer Programmer; Computer Technician; Construction and Building Inspector; Controller; Cost Estimator; Counselor; Database Administrator; Dietician; Draftsperson; Editor; Electrician; Finance Director; General Manager; Graphic Designer; Human Resources Manager; Instructional Technologist; Internet Services Manager; Landscape Architect; Librarian; Library Technician; Licensed Practical Nurse; Mathematician; MIS Specialist; Network Administrator; Physician; Preschool Worker; Production Manager; Project Manager; Psychologist; Public Relations Specialist; Purchasing Agent; Radio Announcer; Registered Nurse; Restaurant Manager; Secretary; Social Worker; Sociologist; Special Education Teacher; Speech-Language Pathologist; Statistician; Systems Analyst; Teacher; Technical Writer/Editor; Telecommunications Manager; Transportation Specialist; Typist; Vice President of Finance; Webmaster. **Educational backgrounds include:** Accounting; Art; Biology; Business Administration; Chemistry; Communications; Computer Science; Economics; Education; Engineering; Finance; Health Care; HTML; Internet Development; Java; Liberal Arts; Marketing; Mathematics; MBA; Microsoft Office; Microsoft Word; Novell; Physics; Software Development; Software Tech. Support; Spreadsheets; Visual Basic. **Benefits:** Casual Dress - Fridays; Daycare Assistance; Dental Insurance; Disability Coverage; Employee Discounts; Job Sharing; Life Insurance; Medical Insurance; On-Site Daycare; Pension Plan; Public Transit Available; Savings Plan; Sick Days (11+); Tuition Assistance; Vacation Days (10 - 20). **Special programs:** Internships. **Corporate headquarters location:** This Location. **Annual sales/revenues:** $51 - $100 million. **Number of employees at this location:** 1,165.

JAMES MADISON UNIVERSITY
MSC 7009, Harrisonburg VA 22807. 540/568-6144. **Fax:** 540/568-7916. **Contact:** Human Resources. **World Wide Web address:** http://www.jmu.edu/humanresources. **Description:** A four-year university offering bachelor's and master's degrees. Approximately 10,000 undergraduate and 700 graduate students attend James Madison University. **Common positions include:** Accountant; Administrator; Blue-Collar Worker Supervisor; Buyer; Computer Programmer; Editor; Human Resources Manager; Public Relations Specialist; Purchasing Agent; Reporter; Systems Analyst; Teacher. **Benefits:** Dental Insurance; Disability Coverage; Employee Discounts; Life Insurance; Medical Insurance; Pension Plan; Tuition Assistance. **Corporate headquarters location:** This Location.

JEFFERSON COLLEGE
1000 Viking Drive, Hillsboro MO 63050. 636/789-3951x157. **Contact:** Beth Ferguson, Director of Human Resources. **World Wide Web address:** http://www.jeffco.edu. **Description:** A two-year community college. **Common positions include:** Education Administrator; Secretary; Teacher. **Educational backgrounds include:** Accounting. **Benefits:** 403(b); Dental Insurance; Life Insurance; Medical Insurance; On-Site Daycare; Tuition Assistance. **Corporate headquarters location:** This Location. **Number of employees at this location:** 220.

JORDAN SCHOOL DISTRICT
9361 South 300 East, Sandy UT 84070. 801/567-8150. **Fax:** 801/567-8056. **Contact:** George Welch, Assistant Superintendent/Personnel. **Description:** Operates the public schools in southern Salt Lake County, servicing more than 73,000 students. **Common positions include:** Account Manager; Accountant; Administrative Assistant; Architect; Assistant Superintendent; Buyer; Computer Animator; Computer Operator; Computer Programmer; Counselor; Editor; Education Administrator; Electrician; ESL Teacher; Human Resources Manager; Occupational Therapist; Physical Therapist; Preschool Worker; Psychologist; Public Relations Specialist; Secretary; Social Worker; Software Engineer; Speech-Language Pathologist; Teacher; Transportation Specialist; Webmaster. **Educational backgrounds include:** Accounting; Art; Biology; Business Administration; Chemistry; Communications; Computer Science; Economics; Engineering; Finance; Geology; Health Care; Liberal Arts; Marketing; Mathematics; Nutrition; Physics; Public Relations; Software Development; Software Tech. Support. **Benefits:** 401(k); Disability Coverage; Job Sharing; Life Insurance; Medical Insurance; Pension Plan. **Superintendent:** Barry L. Newbold. **Number of employees at this location:** 630.

KNOWLEDGE LEARNING CORP.
4340 Redwood Highway, Building B, San Rafael CA 94903. 415/444-1600. **Fax:** 415/444-1664. **Contact:** Human Resources Department. **World Wide Web address:** http://www.knowledgelc.com. **Description:** Operates one of the largest chains of child care centers in the United States with more than 150 child care centers in 15 states. KLC's community schools operate under the names Children's Discovery Centers, Magic Years, Learning Universe, and Hildebrandt Learning Centers. **Corporate headquarters location:** This Location. **Parent company:** Knowledge Universe.

LAMAR UNIVERSITY
P.O. Box 11127, Beaumont TX 77710. 409/880-8375. **Contact:** Human Resources. **World Wide Web address:** http://www.lamar.edu. **Description:** A university offering associate's, bachelor's, master's, and doctoral degrees. Both two- and four-year programs are available. Approximately 7,300 undergraduate and 700 graduate students attend Lamar University. **Common positions include:** Teacher/Professor. **Educational backgrounds include:** Education. **Benefits:** Disability Coverage; Life Insurance; Medical Insurance; Pension Plan; Savings Plan; Tuition Assistance. **Corporate headquarters location:** This Location.

LAREDO COMMUNITY COLLEGE
West End Washington Street, Laredo TX 78040.
956/722-0521. **Contact:** Human Resources. **World Wide Web address:** http://www.laredo.cc.tx.us. **Description:** Offers a variety of associate's degrees in programs including business, computers, electronics, and nursing. Approximately 6,900 students attend the college. Founded in 1947.

LAWRENCE TECHNOLOGICAL UNIVERSITY
21000 West Ten Mile Road, Southfield MI 48075-1058. 248/204-4000. **Contact:** Personnel. **World Wide Web address:** http://www.ltu.edu. **Description:** An independent university specializing in technology and management. Approximately 5,000 students are enrolled in the university. **Common positions include:** Civil Engineer; Clerical Supervisor; Department Manager; Education Administrator; Electrical Engineer; Librarian; Mechanical Engineer. **Benefits:** Dental Insurance; Life Insurance; Medical Insurance; Pension Plan. **Corporate headquarters location:** This Location.

LEHIGH UNIVERSITY
428 Brodhead Avenue, Bethlehem PA 18015. 610/758-3900. **Contact:** Human Resources. **World Wide Web address:** http://www.lehigh.edu. **Description:** A four-year university offering bachelor's, master's (including MBAs), and doctoral degrees. Approximately 4,400 undergraduate and 2,000 graduate students attend Lehigh University. **Common positions include:** Accountant; Administrator; Biological Scientist; Buyer; Civil Engineer; Computer Programmer; Draftsperson; Electrical Engineer; Geologist; Human Resources Manager; Industrial Engineer; Mechanical Engineer; Metallurgical Engineer; Reporter; Systems Analyst; Technical Writer; Transportation Specialist. **Educational backgrounds include:** Accounting; Biology; Business Administration; Chemistry; Computer Science; Economics; Engineering; Finance; Geology; Liberal Arts; Marketing; Mathematics; Physics. **Benefits:** Daycare Assistance; Disability Coverage; Employee Discounts; Life Insurance; Medical Insurance; Pension Plan; Savings Plan; Tuition Assistance. **Corporate headquarters location:** This Location.

LINDENWOOD UNIVERSITY
209 Southkings Highway, St. Charles MO 63301. 636/949-2000. **Contact:** Personnel Director. **World Wide Web address:** http://www.lindenwood.edu. **Description:** A four-year university. **Common positions include:** Accountant; Administrator; Blue-Collar Worker Supervisor; Computer Programmer; Purchasing Agent/Manager; Student Services Specialist. **Educational backgrounds include:** Accounting; Business Administration; Communications. **Benefits:** Dental Insurance; Disability Coverage; Employee Discounts; Life Insurance; Medical Insurance; Pension Plan; Savings Plan; Tuition Assistance. **Corporate headquarters location:** This Location.

LIPSCOMB UNIVERSITY
3901 Granny White Pike, Nashville TN 37204-3951. 615/269-1000. **Toll-free phone:** 800/333-4358. **Contact:** Personnel. **World Wide Web address:** http://www.lipscomb.edu. **Description:** A private university offering more than 100 bachelor's and master's degree programs. Lipscomb University is affiliated with the churches of Christ. **Company slogan:** Lighting the way. **Common positions include:** Accountant; Administrative Assistant; Advertising Clerk; Attorney; Auditor; Budget Analyst; CFO; Computer Operator; Computer Programmer; Computer Support Technician; Computer Technician; Controller; Cost Estimator;

Customer Service Rep.; Database Administrator; Database Manager; Desktop Publishing Specialist; Editor; Editorial Assistant; Education Administrator; Finance Director; Fund Manager; Graphic Artist; Graphic Designer; Instructional Technologist; Internet Services Manager; Librarian; Managing Editor; Marketing Specialist; MIS Specialist; Network Administrator; Preschool Worker; Public Relations Specialist; Purchasing Agent; Radio Announcer; Reporter; Secretary; Software Engineer; Systems Analyst; Systems Manager; Teacher; Technical Writer. **Educational backgrounds include:** Accounting; Art/Design; Biology; Business Administration; Chemistry; Communications; Computer Science; Economics; Engineering; Finance; Geology; Health Care; Liberal Arts; Marketing; Mathematics; MCSE; Nutrition; Physics; Public Relations; QuarkXPress; Software Tech. Support; Spreadsheets. **President:** Dr. Stephen F. Flatt.

LONG ISLAND UNIVERSITY
C.W. Post Campus, 720 Northern Boulevard, Brookville NY 11548. 516/299-2504. **Contact:** Human Resources. **World Wide Web address:** http://www.liunet.edu. **Description:** A university offering undergraduate and graduate programs of study. The university's programs of study are offered through its six schools: College of Liberal Arts & Sciences; School of Education; College of Management; School of Health Professions; School of Visual & Performing Arts; and the Palmer School of Library & Information Sciences. **Common positions include:** Accountant; Attorney; Biological Scientist; Blue-Collar Worker Supervisor; Chemist; Claim Rep.; Department Manager; Draftsperson; Economist; Financial Analyst; Geographer; Geologist; Human Resources Manager; Industrial Production Manager; Marketing Specialist; Public Relations Specialist; Systems Analyst; Technical Writer/Editor. **Educational backgrounds include:** Accounting; Biology; Chemistry; Computer Science; Economics; Finance; Geology; Liberal Arts; Marketing; Mathematics; Physics. **Benefits:** Disability Coverage; Life Insurance; Medical Insurance; Pension Plan; Tuition Assistance. **Special programs:** Internships. **Corporate headquarters location:** This Location. **Other U.S. locations:** Brentwood NY; Brooklyn NY; Greenvale NY; Southampton NY. **Number of employees nationwide:** 2,000.

LOUISIANA TECH UNIVERSITY
P.O. Box 3173 T.S., Ruston LA 71272. 318/257-2235. **Fax:** 318/257-2482. **Contact:** Donald M. Dyson, Director. **E-mail address:** dysond@latech.edu. **World Wide Web address:** http://www.latech.edu. **Description:** A technical university offering a range of fully accredited undergraduate degrees, master's degrees in a variety of areas, and doctoral programs in business administration and engineering. Approximately 10,000 students are enrolled. **President:** Dr. Daniel D. Reneau.

LOYOLA UNIVERSITY OF CHICAGO
6525 North Sheridan Road, Chicago IL 60626. 773/274-3000. **Contact:** Human Resources. **World Wide Web address:** http://www.luc.edu. **Description:** A private university and medical center. Loyola University operates four additional campuses in the greater Chicago area including Loyola University Medical Center in Maywood, Lake Shore and Water Tower campuses in Chicago, and Mallinckrodt campus in Wilmette. **Corporate headquarters location:** This Location.

MACALESTER COLLEGE
1600 Grand Avenue, St. Paul MN 55105. 651/696-6000. **Fax:** 651/696-6612. **Contact:** Ms. Terry

Bailey, Human Resources Representative. **World Wide Web address:** http://www.macalester.edu. **Description:** A private, four-year, liberal arts college. **Common positions include:** Accountant; Administrative Assistant; Advertising Clerk; Advertising Executive; Auditor; Biochemist; Biological Scientist; Budget Analyst; Chemist; CFO; Clinical Lab Technician; Computer Programmer; Computer Technician; Controller; Counselor; Database Administrator; Database Manager; Editor; Education Administrator; Electrician; Event Planner; Finance Director; Fund Manager; Geologist; Help-Desk Technician; Human Resources Manager; Librarian; Licensed Practical Nurse; Managing Editor; Market Research Analyst; Network Administrator; Nurse Practitioner; Psychologist; Public Relations Specialist; Purchasing Agent; Registered Nurse; Secretary; Systems Analyst; Systems Manager; Web Advertising Specialist; Webmaster; Website Developer. **Educational backgrounds include:** Accounting; Biology; Business Administration; Chemistry; Communications; Computer Science; Economics; Education; Finance; HTML; Liberal Arts; Marketing; Mathematics; MBA; Microsoft Office; Microsoft Word; Novell; Public Relations; Software Tech. Support; Spreadsheets. **Benefits:** 403(b); Casual Dress - Daily; Dental Insurance; Disability Coverage; Employee Discounts; Financial Planning Assistance; Flexible Schedule; Job Sharing; Life Insurance; Medical Insurance; Pension Plan; Public Transit Available; Relocation Assistance; Sick Days (11+); Telecommuting; Tuition Assistance; Vacation Days (16+). **Corporate headquarters location:** This Location.

MARIN COMMUNITY COLLEGE
835 College Avenue, Kentfield CA 94904. 415/485-9340. **Fax:** 415/485-0135. **Recorded jobline:** 415/485-9693. **Contact:** Connie Lehua, Personnel Technician. **E-mail address:** hrjobs@marin.cc.ca. us. **World Wide Web address:** http://www.marin. cc.ca.us. **Description:** A community college. **Superintendent/President:** James Middleton. **President of Business Services:** Scott Miller.

MASSACHUSETTS COLLEGE OF ART
621 Huntington Avenue, Boston MA 02115. 617/232-1555. **Fax:** 617/264-4540. **Contact:** Todd Swartz, Director of Personnel. **World Wide Web address:** http://www.massart.edu. **Description:** An art school offering multimedia courses in a variety of disciplines including photography and painting.

McKENDREE COLLEGE
701 College Road, Lebanon IL 62254. 618/537-6524. **Fax:** 618/537-6960. **Contact:** Hubert Place, Human Resources Director. **World Wide Web address:** http://www.mckendree.edu. **Description:** A four-year college offering 28 academic majors to an enrollment of over 1,000. **NOTE:** Entry-level positions are offered. **Common positions include:** Accountant; Administrative Manager; Budget Analyst; CFO; Computer Programmer; Computer Support Technician; Computer Technician; Controller; Database Administrator; Database Manager; Emergency Medical Technician; ESL Teacher; Instructional Technologist; Internet Services Manager; Librarian; Marketing Manager; Operations Manager; Psychologist; Public Relations Specialist; Registered Nurse; Secretary; Special Education Teacher; Systems Analyst; Systems Manager; Teacher; Typist; Vice President; Webmaster. **Educational backgrounds include:** Accounting; Biology; Business Administration; Communications; Computer Science; Economics; Finance; Geology; Health Care; Liberal Arts; Marketing; Mathematics; Microsoft Word; Novell; Nursing; Physics; Software Development; Software

Tech. Support; Spreadsheets. **Benefits:** 403(b); Dental Insurance; Disability Coverage; Financial Planning Assistance; Life Insurance; Medical Insurance; Pension Plan; Public Transit Available; Savings Plan; Sick Days (11+); Tuition Assistance. **Corporate headquarters location:** This Location. **Other U.S. locations:** Louisville KY; Radcliff KY. **Number of employees at this location:** 185.

MIAMI-DADE COMMUNITY COLLEGE
11011 SW 104th Street, Miami FL 33176. 305/237-2051. **Toll-free phone:** 800/955-8771. **Fax:** 305/237-0961. **Recorded jobline:** 305/237-2050. **Contact:** Human Resources. **World Wide Web address:** http://www.mdcc.edu. **Description:** A two-year state college. **NOTE:** Entry-level positions as well as second and third shifts are offered. **Common positions include:** Account Rep.; Administrative Assistant; Blue-Collar Worker Supervisor; Buyer; Clerical Supervisor; Computer Operator; Computer Programmer; Counselor; Electrical Engineer; Electrician; Emergency Medical Technician; ESL Teacher; Licensed Practical Nurse; Physical Therapist; Registered Nurse; Secretary; Systems Analyst; Telecommunications Manager; Typist. **Educational backgrounds include:** Biology; Business Administration; Computer Science; Engineering; Health Care; Mathematics. **Benefits:** 401(k); Dental Insurance; Disability Coverage; Employee Discounts; Financial Planning Assistance; Life Insurance; Matching Gift; Medical Insurance; Pension Plan; Public Transit Available; Savings Plan; Tuition Assistance. **Corporate headquarters location:** This Location. **Number of employees at this location:** 2,300.

MIDWESTERN STATE UNIVERSITY
3410 Taft Boulevard, Wichita Falls TX 76308. 940/397-4221. **Fax:** 940/397-4780. **Contact:** Steve Holland, Director of Personnel. **E-mail address:** steve.holland@nexus.mwsu.edu. **World Wide Web address:** http://www.mwsu.edu. **Description:** A state university with approximately 6,000 students enrolled in its undergraduate and graduate degree programs. **Common positions include:** Accountant; Buyer; Computer Programmer; Counselor; Education Administrator; Electrician; Human Resources Manager; Librarian; Library Technician; Property and Real Estate Manager; Public Relations Specialist; Radiological Technologist; Registered Nurse; Systems Analyst; Teacher. **Educational backgrounds include:** Accounting; Art/Design; Biology; Business Administration; Chemistry; Communications; Computer Science; Economics; Engineering; Finance; Geology; Marketing; Mathematics; Ph.D.; Physics. **Benefits:** 401(k); Dental Insurance; Disability Coverage; Employee Discounts; Life Insurance; Medical Insurance; Pension Plan; Savings Plan; Tuition Assistance. **Corporate headquarters location:** This Location. **President:** Dr. Louis J. Rodriguez. **Facilities Manager:** Al Hooten. **Number of employees at this location:** 900.

MILLIKIN UNIVERSITY
1184 West Main Street, Decatur IL 62522-2084. 217/362-6416. **Fax:** 217/424-5070. **Contact:** Human Resources. **World Wide Web address:** http://www.millikin.edu. **Description:** A liberal arts university affiliated with the Presbyterian Church. Approximately 2,000 students are enrolled at Millikin University. **Common positions include:** Accountant; Blue-Collar Worker Supervisor; Chief Financial Officer; Clerical Supervisor; Computer Programmer; Controller; Counselor; Electrician; Graphic Designer; Human Resources Manager; Librarian; Licensed Practical Nurse; MIS Specialist; Secretary; Systems Analyst; Teacher/Professor. **Educational backgrounds include:** Accounting;

Business Administration; Communications; Computer Science. **Benefits:** 403(b); Disability Coverage; Employee Discounts; Life Insurance; Medical Insurance; Pension Plan; Tuition Assistance. **Special programs:** Internships. **Corporate headquarters location:** This Location. **Number of employees at this location:** 500.

MILWAUKEE PUBLIC SCHOOLS
P.O. Box 2181, Milwaukee WI 53201-2182. 414/475-8220. **Fax:** 414/475-8722. **Contact:** Doctor K. Gomez, Manager of Staff Services. **World Wide Web address:** http://www.milwaukee. k12.wi.us. **Description:** A nonprofit group overseeing the public school system for the city of Milwaukee. The Milwaukee Public Schools also offers alternative certification programs for teachers. **NOTE:** Entry-level positions and part-time jobs are offered. **Company slogan:** High standards start here. **Common positions include:** Administrative Assistant; Administrative Manager; Attorney; Bank Officer; Budget Analyst; CFO; Child Care Center Director; Controller; Counselor; Education Administrator; Electrician; Human Resources Manager; Instructional Technologist; Librarian; Psychologist; Public Relations Specialist; Secretary; Social Worker; Special Education Teacher; Speech-Language Pathologist; Teacher; Typist/Word Processor. **Educational backgrounds include:** Accounting; Art/Design; Biology; Chemistry; Communications; Computer Science; Economics; Education; Finance; Mathematics; Novell; Public Relations; Software Tech. Support; Spreadsheets; Teaching. **Benefits:** 403(b); Casual Dress - Fridays; Disability Coverage; Life Insurance; Medical Insurance; Pension Plan; Public Transit Available. **Special programs:** Internships; Training; Co-ops; Summer Jobs. **Corporate headquarters location:** This Location. **Facilities Manager:** Larry Lenox. **Purchasing Manager:** Michael Torza. **Number of employees at this location:** 15,760.

MILWAUKEE SCHOOL OF ENGINEERING
1025 North Broadway Street, Milwaukee WI 53202. 414/277-7132. **Fax:** 414/277-7450. **Contact:** Kevin Morin, Director of Human Resources. **World Wide Web address:** http://www.msoe.edu. **Description:** A technical university that offers associate's, bachelor's, and master's degrees in the areas of engineering, engineering technology, technical communication, and business. **Common positions include:** Teacher. **Educational backgrounds include:** Engineering. **Benefits:** 403(b); Dental Insurance; Disability Coverage; Life Insurance; Medical Insurance; Tuition Assistance. **Corporate headquarters location:** This Location. **Operations at this facility include:** Administration; Service.

MISSISSIPPI STATE UNIVERSITY
P.O. Box 9603, Mississippi State MS 39762-9603. 662/325-3713. **Contact:** Employment Section/ Personnel Department. **World Wide Web address:** http://www.msstate.edu. **Description:** One of Mississippi's largest universities, with over 13,800 students and 840 faculty members. The university offers a wide range of bachelor's degrees and pre-professional programs, as well as master's and doctoral degree programs. **Common positions include:** Accountant; Administrative Manager; Agricultural Scientist; Aircraft Mechanic; Architect; Attorney; Automotive Mechanic; Biological Scientist; Broadcast Technician; Budget Analyst; Buyer; Chemist; Claim Rep.; Clerical Supervisor; Clinical Lab Technician; Computer Programmer; Construction Contractor; Cost Estimator; Counselor; Designer; Draftsperson; Economist; Editor; Education Administrator; EKG Technician; Electrician; EMT; Engineer; Financial Analyst; Geologist; Health Services Manager; Librarian;

Library Technician; Licensed Practical Nurse; Mathematician; Physician; Physicist; Psychologist; Scientist; Sociologist; Speech-Language Pathologist; Statistician; Systems Analyst; Teacher. **Educational backgrounds include:** Accounting; Art/Design; Biology; Business Administration; Chemistry; Communications; Computer Science; Economics; Engineering; Finance; Geology; Liberal Arts; Marketing; Mathematics; Physics. **Benefits:** Dental Insurance; Disability Coverage; Employee Discounts; Life Insurance; Medical Insurance; Savings Plan; Tuition Assistance. **Corporate headquarters location:** This Location. **Number of employees at this location:** 4,240.

MOBILE COUNTY PUBLIC SCHOOLS
P.O. Box 1327, Mobile AL 36633. 334/690-8260. **Fax:** 334/690-7290. **Recorded jobline:** 334/690-8394. **Contact:** Louise Smith, Executive Director. **E-mail address:** humanresources@mcpss.com. **World Wide Web address:** http://www.mcpss.com. **Description:** Provides public education through city and county schools. **NOTE:** Entry-level positions are offered. **Common positions include:** Accountant; Administrative Manager; Assistant Superintendent; Auditor; Blue-Collar Worker Supervisor; Budget Analyst; Computer Operator; Computer Programmer; Computer Technician; Controller; Counselor; Dietician; Draftsperson; Education Administrator; Electrician; ESL Teacher; Finance Director; Human Resources Manager; Librarian; Licensed Practical Nurse; Media Specialist; MIS Specialist; Network Administrator; Occupational Therapist; Psychologist; Public Relations Specialist; Registered Nurse; Secretary; Special Education Teacher; Speech-Language Pathologist; Systems Analyst; Teacher/Professor. **Educational backgrounds include:** Accounting; Biology; Business Administration; Chemistry; Education; Mathematics. **Benefits:** Dental Insurance; Disability Coverage; Life Insurance; Medical Insurance; Pension Plan; Sick Days (6 - 10); Vacation Days (10 - 20). **Corporate headquarters location:** This Location. **Operations at this facility include:** Research and Development. **Number of employees at this location:** 7,800.

MOHAVE COMMUNITY COLLEGE (MCC)
1971 Jagerson Avenue, Kingman AZ 86401. 520/757-0877. **Fax:** 520/757-0875. **Contact:** Linda Yarbrough, Director of Human Resources. **World Wide Web address:** http://www.mohave.cc.az.us. **Description:** One location of the multicampus community college. Mohave Community College (MCC) uses a microwave communications system to link the three campus sites in Bullhead, Kingman, and Lake Havasu City. MCC offers three associate's degrees and more than 45 certificates including an Associate of Arts degree for students planning to transfer to a four-year institution; an Associate of Applied Science degree designed to prepare students for employment; and an Associate of Science degree for students pursuing a career in the life sciences, nursing, and paramedic fields. Founded in 1971. **NOTE:** Part-time jobs are offered. **Common positions include:** Accountant; Administrative Assistant; AS400 Programmer Analyst; Computer Operator; Computer Programmer; Computer Support Technician; Computer Technician; Controller; Counselor; Education Administrator; Human Resources Manager; Internet Services Manager; Librarian; Multimedia Designer; Network Administrator; Systems Analyst; Teacher/Professor; Webmaster. **Educational backgrounds include:** AS400 Certification; ASP; C/C++; HTML; Internet; Microsoft Word; Novell; Software Tech. Support. **Benefits:** 401(k); Casual Dress - Fridays; Dental Insurance; Disability Coverage; Life Insurance; Medical Insurance; Pension Plan; Tuition

Assistance. **Corporate headquarters location:** This Location. **Operations at this facility include:** Regional Headquarters. **President:** Michael Tacha. **Facilities Manager:** Russell "Butch" Henson. **Number of employees at this location:** 575.

MOHAWK VALLEY COMMUNITY COLLEGE
1101 Sherman Drive, Utica NY 13501-5394. 315/792-5636. **Contact:** Jerome Brown, Human Resources. **Description:** A two-year community college with an enrollment of approximately 6,500 full- and part-time students. The college was the first of five state-operated institutes of applied arts and sciences. Mohawk Valley Community College offers Developmental and Remedial programming. Certificates and degrees offered include accounting, banking and insurance, chef training, chemical technology, criminal justice, drafting technology, engineering drawing, food service, graphic arts, human services, international studies, media marketing and management, photography, and respiratory care. Founded in 1946.

MONTANA STATE UNIVERSITY - NORTHERN
P.O. Box 7751, Havre MT 59501. 406/265-3700. **Toll-free phone:** 800/662-6132. **Fax:** 406/265-3777. **Contact:** Employee Relations Specialist. **E-mail address:** emprel@msun.edu. **World Wide Web address:** http://www.msun.edu. **Description:** Montana State University - Northern is a university with an enrollment of approximately 1,750 students. The university offers certificate programs, as well as associate's, bachelor's, and master's degrees. **Chancellor:** Mike Rao.

MOREHEAD STATE UNIVERSITY
HM Room 101, Morehead KY 40351. 606/783-2097. **Fax:** 606/783-5028. **Contact:** Office of Human Resources. **World Wide Web address:** http://www.morehead-st.edu. **Description:** A state university with approximately 8,200 undergraduate and graduate students enrolled. **Common positions include:** Accountant; Budget Analyst; Buyer; Clerical Supervisor; Computer Programmer; Construction Contractor; Counselor; Editor; Education Administrator; Electrician; Human Resources Manager; Librarian; Library Technician; Operations Manager; Psychologist; Radio Announcer; Registered Nurse; Systems Analyst; Teacher; Technical Writer/Editor. **Educational backgrounds include:** Accounting; Art/Design; Biology; Business Administration; Chemistry; Communications; Computer Science; Economics; Engineering; Finance; Geology; Liberal Arts; Marketing; Mathematics; Physics. **Benefits:** Dental Insurance; Employee Discounts; Life Insurance; Medical Insurance; Pension Plan; Tuition Assistance. **Corporate headquarters location:** This Location. **Number of employees at this location:** 920.

MOTT ADULT HIGH SCHOOL
2421 Corunna Road, Flint MI 48503. 810/760-7763. **Contact:** Human Resources. **Description:** Provides educational opportunities for adults including high school completion, GED, and/or vocational training. **Common positions include:** Clerical Supervisor; Education Administrator; Teacher. **Educational backgrounds include:** Education. **Benefits:** Employee Discounts; Medical Insurance. **Corporate headquarters location:** This Location. **Number of employees at this location:** 400.

MOUNT MARY COLLEGE
2900 North Menomonee River Parkway, Milwaukee WI 53222. 414/258-4810. **Fax:** 414/256-0195. **Contact:** Madeline Smith, Director of Human Resources. **World Wide Web address:** http://www.mtmary.edu. **Description:** A four-year, Catholic, women's, liberal arts institution with approximately 12,000 undergraduate and 1,000 graduate students. **Common positions include:** Counselor; Librarian; Library Technician; Public Relations Specialist; Teacher. **Educational backgrounds include:** Communications; Computer Science. **Benefits:** Dental Insurance; Disability Coverage; Employee Discounts; Medical Insurance; Pension Plan; Tuition Assistance. **Corporate headquarters location:** This Location. **Operations at this facility include:** Administration; Service. **Number of employees at this location:** 300.

MUHLENBERG COLLEGE
2400 Chew Street, Allentown PA 18104-5586. 610/821-3165. **Fax:** 484/664-3680. **Contact:** Ann Hochella, Personnel Director. **World Wide Web address:** http://www.muhlenberg.edu. **Description:** A four-year, undergraduate, liberal arts college. Founded in 1848. **Common positions include:** Secretary; Teacher/Professor. **Benefits:** 403(b); Dental Insurance; Disability Coverage; Employee Discounts; Life Insurance; Medical Insurance; Pension Plan; Tuition Assistance. **President:** Arthur R. Taylor. **Facilities Manager:** Mike Brewer. **Number of employees at this location:** 500.

NASHVILLE STATE TECHNICAL INSTITUTE
120 White Bridge Road, Nashville TN 37209. 615/353-3304. **Contact:** Human Resources. **World Wide Web address:** http://www.nsti.tec.tn.us. **Description:** A two-year technical institute offering certificate and associate's degree programs.

NATIONAL EDUCATION ASSOCIATION
1201 16th Street NW, Washington DC 20036-3290. 202/822-7600. **Fax:** 202/822-7619. **Recorded jobline:** 202/822-7642. **Contact:** Employment Manager. **World Wide Web address:** http://www.nea.org/jobs. **Description:** A national, nonprofit membership organization that represents teachers, the teaching profession, and education support personnel. Major programs and functions include organizing and membership, education policy, government relations, communications, publishing, research, human and civil rights, negotiations, and administration. **Common positions include:** Accountant; Administrative Manager; Attorney; Electrician; Human Resources Manager; Licensed Practical Nurse; Public Relations Specialist; Technical Writer; Typist; Video Production Coordinator. **Educational backgrounds include:** Business Administration. **Benefits:** 401(k); Dental Insurance; Disability Coverage; Life Insurance; Medical Insurance; Pension Plan; Tuition Assistance. **Corporate headquarters location:** This Location. **Other U.S. locations:** Nationwide. **Number of employees at this location:** 500.

NATIONAL EDUCATION TRAINING GROUP
1751 West Diehl Road, Suite 200, Naperville IL 60563. 630/369-3000. **Fax:** 630/983-4800. **Contact:** Personnel. **World Wide Web address:** http://www.netg.com. **Description:** A source of products and services for training and education in the areas of advanced technologies. **Common positions include:** Accountant; Computer Programmer; Customer Service Rep.; Education Administrator; Marketing Manager; Services Sales Rep.; Software Engineer; Systems Analyst. **Educational backgrounds include:** Accounting; Computer Science; Marketing; Technology. **Benefits:** Dental Insurance; Disability Coverage; Employee Discounts; Life Insurance; Medical Insurance; Pension Plan; Savings Plan; Tuition Assistance. **Corporate headquarters location:** This Location. **Parent company:** Harcourt, Inc. **Number of employees at this location:** 275. **Number of employees nationwide:** 380.

NATIONAL EVALUATION SYSTEMS

30 Gatehouse Road, Amherst MA 01002. 413/256-0444. **Contact:** Betsy Rider, Personnel Director. **Description:** A contract-based company providing educational products and services in a variety of areas including professional licensing and certification testing programs, large-scale pupil assessment, and print-based educational materials. Clients include state departments of education and professional licensing boards. **Common positions include:** Computer Programmer; Customer Service Rep.; Department Manager; Editor; Operations Manager; Project Manager. **Educational backgrounds include:** Computer Science; English; Journalism; Liberal Arts; Psychology; Sociology. **Benefits:** 401(k); Disability Coverage; Life Insurance; Medical Insurance; Profit Sharing; Tuition Assistance. **Corporate headquarters location:** This Location. **Operations at this facility include:** Research and Development; Service.

NATIONAL-LOUIS UNIVERSITY

1000 Capitol Drive, Wheeling IL 60090. 847/465-0575. **Fax:** 847/465-5610. **Recorded jobline:** 847/465-5400. **Contact:** Sue Mueller, Assistant Human Resources Manager. **World Wide Web address:** http://www.nl.edu. **Description:** A university offering undergraduate and graduate programs to approximately 1,600 students. **NOTE:** Entry-level positions, part-time jobs, and second and third shifts are offered. **Common positions include:** Account Rep.; Administrative Assistant; Certified Nurses Aide; Computer Support Technician; Counselor; Education Administrator; ESL Teacher; Librarian; Multimedia Designer; Network Administrator; Sales Rep.; Secretary; Teacher; Typist. **Educational backgrounds include:** Business Administration; Clerical; Computer Science; Liberal Arts; Marketing; Microsoft Word; Public Relations; Spreadsheets. **Benefits:** 403(b); Casual Dress - Fridays; Dental Insurance; Disability Coverage; Employee Discounts; Financial Planning Assistance; Life Insurance; Medical Insurance; Pension Plan; Savings Plan; Sick Days (6 - 10); Tuition Assistance; Vacation Days (6 - 10). **Corporate headquarters location:** This Location. **Other area locations:** Chicago IL; Evanston IL. **Other U.S. locations:** Washington DC; Orlando FL; Tampa FL; Atlanta GA; St. Louis MO; Milwaukee WI. **Operations at this facility include:** Administration; Education. **Number of employees at this location:** 150.

NAZARETH COLLEGE OF ROCHESTER

4245 East Avenue, Rochester NY 14618-3790. 716/389-2060. **Fax:** 716/389-2063. **Contact:** Carol O'Neill, Director of Personnel. **World Wide Web address:** http://www.nazarethcollege.edu. **Description:** A four-year college that offers undergraduate and graduate programs in a wide variety of disciplines. **NOTE:** Entry-level positions and part-time jobs are offered. **Common positions include:** Administrative Assistant; Computer Operator; Computer Programmer; Controller; Counselor; Daycare Worker; Human Resources Manager; Librarian; Public Relations Specialist; Registered Nurse; Secretary; Speech-Language Pathologist; Teacher; Typist; Video Production Coordinator. **Educational backgrounds include:** Accounting; Business Administration; Computer Science; Liberal Arts. **Benefits:** 403(b); Dental Insurance; Disability Coverage; Employee Discounts; Life Insurance; Medical Insurance; On-Site Daycare; Public Transit Available; Tuition Assistance; Vision Insurance. **Special programs:** Internships. **Corporate headquarters location:** This Location. **Number of employees at this location:** 300.

NEW ENGLAND CONSERVATORY OF MUSIC

290 Huntington Avenue, Boston MA 02115. 617/585-1230. **Contact:** Personnel. **World Wide Web address:** http://www.newenglandconservatory. edu. **Description:** A music school that also operates a preparatory school and offers continuing education classes for students of all levels.

NEW HAMPSHIRE COLLEGE

2500 North River Road, Manchester NH 03106. 603/668-2211. **Fax:** 603/645-9661. **Contact:** Human Resources. **World Wide Web address:** http://www.nhc.edu. **Description:** New Hampshire College (NHC) is a private, independent college offering undergraduate, graduate, and doctoral academic programs. NHC has a day college enrollment of over 1,000 students, 1,500 in the graduate school of business, and nearly 4,000 in the division of continuing education. NHC offers associate's degrees in culinary arts and several business-related fields; Bachelor of Science degrees in 20 areas of business and liberal arts; master's degrees in business administration, accounting, business education, computer information systems, community economic development, and international business; and Doctoral programs in international business and community economic development. **NOTE:** Part-time positions are offered. **Company slogan:** Where the world comes to mind. **Common positions include:** Accountant; Administrative Assistant; Administrative Manager; Assistant Manager; Blue-Collar Worker Supervisor; Budget Analyst; CFO; Clerical Supervisor; Computer Programmer; Computer Support Technician; Computer Technician; Controller; Counselor; Credit Manager; Customer Service Representative; Database Administrator; Database Manager; Education Administrator; ESL Teacher; Graphic Designer; Human Resources Manager; Internet Services Manager; Librarian; Marketing Manager; MIS Specialist; Network Administrator; Nurse Practitioner; Public Relations Specialist; Purchasing Agent; Sales Rep.; Secretary; Systems Analyst; Systems Manager; Teacher/Professor; Telecommunications Manager; Typist/Word Processor; Vice President of Finance; Video Production Coordinator; Webmaster. **Educational backgrounds include:** Accounting; Business Administration; Communications; Computer Science; HTML; Internet; Liberal Arts; Microsoft Word; Novell; Public Relations; Software Tech. Support; Spreadsheets. **Benefits:** Daycare Assistance; Dental Insurance; Disability Coverage; Employee Discounts; Financial Planning Assistance; Life Insurance; Meal Discounts; Medical Insurance; Pension Plan; Sick Days (11+); Tuition Assistance; Vacation Days (10 - 20). **Special programs:** Internships; Summer Jobs. **Other U.S. locations:** Maine. **International locations:** Greece; Puerto Rico.

NEW JERSEY CITY UNIVERSITY

2039 Kennedy Boulevard, Hepburn Hall 105, Jersey City NJ 07305. 201/200-2335. **Fax:** 201/200-2219. **Contact:** Robert Piaskowsky, Director of Human Resources. **World Wide Web address:** http://www. njcu.edu. **Description:** A state university with approximately 10,000 students enrolled in undergraduate, graduate, and continuing education programs. **Common positions include:** Education Administrator; Teacher/Professor. **Benefits:** 403(b); Dental Insurance; Disability Coverage; Flexible Schedule; Life Insurance; Medical Insurance; Pension Plan; Tuition Assistance.

NEW YORK INSTITUTE OF TECHNOLOGY

P.O. Box 8000, Old Westbury NY 11568-8000. 516/686-7667. **Physical address:** Old Westbury Campus, Old Westbury NY 11568. **Fax:** 516/686-

7929. **Contact:** Employment Manager. **World Wide Web address:** http://www.nyit.edu. **Description:** A technical university offering associate, bachelor's, and master's degree programs in health and life sciences, architecture, arts/ sciences, education, technology, and management.

NORTHERN VIRGINIA COMMUNITY COLLEGE
4001 Wakefield Chapel Road, Annandale VA 22003. 703/323-3124. **Fax:** 703/323-3155. **Recorded jobline:** 703/323-3444. **Contact:** Diane Kownacki, Director of Human Resources. **World Wide Web address:** http://www.nv.cc.va.us/hr. **Description:** A two-year, nonprofit college offering transfer and occupational/technical programs. Northern Virginia Community College has five campuses and an Extended Learning Institute. **NOTE:** Second and third shifts are offered. **Common positions include:** Accountant; Advertising Executive; Applications Engineer; Architect; Buyer; Clerical Supervisor; Computer Programmer; Counselor; Education Administrator; Electrician; ESL Teacher; Graphic Artist; Human Resources Manager; Librarian; Public Relations Specialist; Secretary; Systems Analyst; Teacher. **Educational backgrounds include:** Accounting; Business Administration; Computer Science. **Benefits:** 403(b); Dental Insurance; Disability Coverage; Flexible Schedule; Life Insurance; Medical Insurance; Pension Plan; Savings Plan; Tuition Assistance. **Special programs:** Training. **Corporate headquarters location:** This Location. **Number of employees nationwide:** 600.

NORTHWEST NAZARENE UNIVERSITY
623 Holly Street, Nampa ID 83686. 208/467-8011. **Toll-free phone:** 800/NNU-4YOU. **Fax:** 208/467-8597. **Contact:** Human Resources. **World Wide Web address:** http://www.nnu.edu. **Description:** A liberal arts college affiliated with the Church of the Nazarene. Founded in 1913. **President:** Dr. Richard A. Hagood.

OKLAHOMA STATE UNIVERSITY
405 Whitehurst Hall, Stillwater OK 74078-1037. 405/744-5646. **Fax:** 405/744-8345. **Recorded jobline:** 405/744-7692. **Contact:** Donna J. Anders, Assistant Director of Personnel Services. **World Wide Web address:** http://www.okstate.edu. **Description:** A state university. **Common positions include:** Accountant; Administrative Manager; Aerospace Engineer; Agricultural Engineer; Agricultural Scientist; Biological Scientist; Blue-Collar Worker Supervisor; Broadcast Technician; Budget Analyst; Chemical Engineer; Civil Engineer; Clerical Supervisor; Clinical Lab Technician; Computer Programmer; Construction and Building Inspector; Counselor; Customer Service Rep.; Dietician; Draftsperson; Economist; Editor; Education Administrator; Electrical Engineer; Electrician; Emergency Medical Technician; Environmental Engineer; Financial Analyst; Health Services Manager; Hotel Manager; Human Resources Manager; Landscape Architect; Librarian; Library Technician; Licensed Practical Nurse; Management Analyst; Management Trainee; Mathematician; Mechanical Engineer; Medical Records Technician; Operations Manager; Physical Therapist; Physician; Preschool Worker; Psychologist; Public Relations Specialist; Purchasing Agent; Radio Announcer; Registered Nurse; Restaurant Manager; Science Technologist; Software Engineer; Speech-Language Pathologist; Statistician; Structural Engineer; Surgical Technician; Surveyor; Systems Analyst; Teacher; Veterinarian. **Educational backgrounds include:** Accounting; Biology; Business Administration; Chemistry; Communications; Computer Science; Economics; Engineering; Finance; Marketing. **Benefits:** Dental Insurance; Disability Coverage; Employee Discounts; Life Insurance; Medical Insurance; Pension Plan; Tuition Assistance. **Operations at this facility include:** Research and Development; Service. **Number of employees at this location:** 6,000.

OLYMPIC COLLEGE
1600 Chester Avenue, Bremerton WA 98337-1699. 360/792-6050. **Contact:** Human Resources. **World Wide Web address:** http://www.oc.otc.edu. **Description:** A two-year community college which offers associate degrees in arts and science, transfer programs, and various technical degrees. **Common positions include:** Accountant; Administrative Manager; Clerical Supervisor; Counselor; Education Administrator; General Manager; Human Resources Manager; Human Service Worker; Librarian; Library Technician; Preschool Worker; Public Relations Specialist; Recreational Therapist; Restaurant Manager; Systems Analyst; Teacher. **Educational backgrounds include:** Accounting; Biology; Business Administration; Chemistry; Communications; Computer Science; Economics; Geology; Mathematics; Physics. **Benefits:** Daycare Assistance; Dental Insurance; Disability Coverage; Life Insurance; Medical Insurance; Pension Plan. **Corporate headquarters location:** This Location.

PACIFIC UNIVERSITY
2043 College Way, Forest Grove OR 97116-1797. 503/357-6151. **Recorded jobline:** 503/359-2838. **Contact:** Human Resources. **World Wide Web address:** http://www.pacificu.edu. **Description:** A university offering undergraduate and graduate programs of study in liberal arts, education, and health care. **NOTE:** The faculty is hired through the Dean's Office, while administration is hired through Human Resources. **Corporate headquarters location:** This Location. **Number of employees at this location:** 475.

POMONA COLLEGE
550 North College Avenue, Claremont CA 91711-6318. 909/621-8175. **Contact:** Human Resources. **World Wide Web address:** http://www.pomona.edu. **Description:** A private, four-year, liberal arts college.

PROFESSIONAL TUTORS FOR ALL AGES
P.O. Box 22224, Denver CO 80222. 303/329-3900. **Contact:** Director. **Description:** Provides tutors for a wide variety of subjects. at all grade levels. Professional Tutors For All Ages tutors students with learning disabilities, as well as those preparing for special exams including advanced placement and college preparation tests. Founded in 1985. **NOTE:** Tutors are only hired on a per-student basis, on a contract ranging from 20 to 40 hours of work. Applicants are encouraged to send a resume and cover letter prior to contacting the Professional Tutors by phone. All tutors must have proven teaching experience and a degree in the subject they are to teach. Applicants will be screened and investigated, and all hires are trained and observed. **Common positions include:** Teacher/Professor; Tutor (part-time). **Educational backgrounds include:** Accounting; Algebra; Bachelor of Arts; Bachelor of Science; Biology; Calculus; Chemistry; E.S.L.; Education; Engineering; Foreign Languages; Geometry; Mathematics; Physics; Science; Statistics; Teaching; Trigonometry; Writing. **Special programs:** Internships. **Number of employees at this location:** 45.

THE PSYCHOLOGICAL CORPORATION
555 Academic Court, San Antonio TX 78204. 210/299-3616. **Fax:** 210/299-3662. **Recorded**

jobline: 210/299-2700. **Contact:** Lori Bowman, Recruiter. **World Wide Web address:** http://www. hbtpc.com. **Description:** One of the oldest and largest commercial test publishers in the nation. The company provides tests (e.g. the Stanford Achievement Test Series, the Metropolitan Achievement Tests, and Wechsler Intelligence Scales for Children and Adults) and related services to schools and colleges, clinicians and professional organizations, businesses, and public entities. The company's services include test research and development, printing, marketing, distribution, administration, and scoring. Psychological Corporation has three divisions: an educational measurement division; a psychological measurement and communications division; and a division that awards licenses and credentials. **NOTE:** Entry-level positions and second and third shifts are offered. **Common positions include:** Accountant; Administrative Assistant; Computer Operator; Computer Programmer; Customer Service Rep.; Database Manager; Desktop Publishing Specialist; Editor; Financial Analyst; Graphic Designer; Human Resources Manager; Managing Editor; Market Research Analyst; Marketing Specialist; Occupational Therapist; Psychologist; Purchasing Agent; Research Assistant; Sales Representative; Speech-Language Pathologist; Statistician; Systems Analyst; Teacher; Warehouse Manager. **Educational backgrounds include:** Business Administration; Computer Science; Psychology. **Benefits:** 401(k); Dental Insurance; Disability Coverage; Employee Discounts; Financial Planning Assistance; Flexible Schedule; Life Insurance; Medical Insurance; Pension Plan; Public Transit Available; Savings Plan; Tuition Assistance. **Corporate headquarters location:** Orlando FL. **Parent company:** Harcourt Brace & Company. **Number of employees at this location:** 1,000.

PURDUE UNIVERSITY
1126 Freehafer Hall, West Lafayette IN 47907. 765/494-9687. **Fax:** 765/494-6138. **Contact:** Personnel. **World Wide Web address:** http://www. purdue.edu. **Description:** Purdue has an enrollment of approximately 64,000 students across five campuses with numerous teaching and research sites statewide. Degrees are offered in agriculture, consumer and family sciences, education, engineering, health sciences, liberal arts, management, nursing, pharmacy and pharmaceutical sciences, science, technology, and veterinary medicine. **Common positions include:** Accountant; Administrative Manager; Agricultural Engineer; Agricultural Scientist; Architect; Biological Scientist; Blue-Collar Worker Supervisor; Budget Analyst; Buyer; Chemical Engineer; Chemist; Civil Engineer; Clerical Supervisor; Clinical Lab Technician; Computer Programmer; Construction and Building Inspector; Construction Contractor; Cost Estimator; Counselor; Draftsperson; Editor; Electrical Engineer; Electrician; Financial Analyst; Hotel Manager; Human Resources Manager; Industrial Engineer; Librarian; Library Technician; Management Trainee; Mechanical Engineer; Nuclear Engineer; Public Relations Specialist; Purchasing Agent; Radiological Technologist; Restaurant Manager; Science Technologist; Structural Engineer; Systems Analyst; Technical Writer; Veterinarian. **Educational backgrounds include:** Accounting; Biology; Business Administration; Chemistry; Communications; Computer Science; Engineering; Finance; Liberal Arts. **Benefits:** Life Insurance; Medical Insurance; Pension Plan; Tuition Assistance. **Special programs:** Internships. **Corporate headquarters location:** This Location. **Operations at this facility include:** Research and Development; Service. **Number of employees at this location:** 10,000.

Other U.S. locations:
- 2200 169th Street, Hammond IN 46323-2094. 219/989-2251.

J. SERGEANT REYNOLDS COMMUNITY COLLEGE
P.O. Box 85622, Richmond VA 23285-5622. 804/371-3249. **Contact:** Human Resources. **World Wide Web address:** http://www.jsr.cc.va.us. **Description:** A community college offering one- and two-year programs of study in business, liberal arts, community service, education, and science. **Common positions include:** Blue-Collar Worker Supervisor; Counselor; Education Administrator; Librarian; Library Technician; Teacher/Professor. **Educational backgrounds include:** Business Administration; Finance; Liberal Arts; Teaching. **Benefits:** 401(k); Dental Insurance; Employee Discounts; Life Insurance; Medical Insurance; Pension Plan; Savings Plan; Tuition Assistance. **Corporate headquarters location:** This Location. **Number of employees at this location:** 1,000.

RHODES COLLEGE
2000 North Parkway, Memphis TN 38112. 901/843-3750. **Recorded jobline:** 901/843-3759. **Contact:** Human Resources. **World Wide Web address:** http://www.rhodes.edu. **Description:** A four-year liberal arts college. Founded in 1848.

RICE UNIVERSITY
Mail Stop 56, P.O. Box 1892, Houston TX 77252-1892. 713/527-4074. **Fax:** 713/285-5496. **Recorded jobline:** 713/348-6080. **Contact:** Employment Coordinator. **World Wide Web address:** http://employment.rice.edu. **Description:** An independent, co-educational, private university for undergraduate and graduate studies, research, and professional training in selected disciplines. Rice University has an undergraduate student enrollment of approximately 2,700; a graduate and professional student enrollment of approximately 1,400. **Common positions include:** Accountant; Administrative Assistant; Budget Analyst; ESL Teacher; Systems Analyst. **Benefits:** 403(b); Dental Insurance; Disability Coverage; Life Insurance; Medical Insurance; Pension Plan; Public Transit Available; Tuition Assistance. **President:** Malcolm Gillis. **Number of employees at this location:** 2,000.

ST. EDWARD'S UNIVERSITY
3001 South Congress Avenue, Austin TX 78704-6489. 512/448-8587. **Fax:** 512/448-8492. **Recorded jobline:** 512/448-8541. **Contact:** Human Resources. **World Wide Web address:** http://www. stedwards.edu/humr/jobs.htm. **Description:** A private university affiliated with the Catholic Church. St. Edward's University offers a liberal arts program to undergraduate and graduate students interested in business or human services. **Common positions include:** Computer Programmer; Counselor; Customer Service Rep.; Education Administrator; Electrician; Human Resources Manager; Psychologist; Public Relations Specialist; Systems Analyst; Technical Writer. **Educational backgrounds include:** Accounting; Business Administration; Computer Science; Liberal Arts. **Benefits:** 403(b); Disability Coverage; Life Insurance; Medical Insurance; Pension Plan; Section 125 Plan; Tuition Assistance. **Corporate headquarters location:** This Location. **Number of employees at this location:** 500.

ST. MARY'S UNIVERSITY
One Camino Santa Maria, San Antonio TX 78228-8565. 210/436-3725. **Fax:** 210/431-2223. **Contact:** Director of Human Resources. **World Wide Web address:** http://www.stmarytx.edu. **Description:** A

liberal arts university affiliated with the Catholic church. St. Mary's University has three undergraduate programs and two graduate programs including a law school. The school is one of the oldest and largest Catholic universities in the Southwest. Founded in 1852. **Common positions include:** Accountant; Biological Scientist; Biomedical Engineer; Chemical Engineer; Civil Engineer; Clerical Supervisor; Computer Support Technician; Counselor; Economist; Education Administrator; Electrical Engineer; Electrician; Geologist; Human Resources Manager; Librarian; Library Technician; Mathematician; Mechanical Engineer; Psychologist; Public Relations Specialist; Registered Nurse; Reporter; Secretary; Sociologist; Statistician; Systems Analyst; Teacher; Technical Writer/Editor. **Educational backgrounds include:** Accounting; Art/Design; Biology; Business Administration; Chemistry; Communications; Computer Science; Economics; Engineering; Finance; Geology; Law/Pre-Law; Liberal Arts; Marketing; Mathematics; Physics. **Benefits:** Dental Insurance; Disability Coverage; Life Insurance; Medical Insurance; Pension Plan; Tuition Assistance. **Special programs:** Internships. **Corporate headquarters location:** This Location. **Operations at this facility include:** Research and Development; Service. **Number of employees at this location:** 540.

SALEM COLLEGE
SALEM ACADEMY
P.O. Box 10548, Winston-Salem NC 27108-0548. 336/721-2600. **Fax:** 336/721-2832. **Contact:** Human Resources. **World Wide Web address:** http://www.salem.edu. **Description:** A women's liberal arts college offering both undergraduate and graduate programs of study. Salem Academy (also at this location) is a private, college preparatory boarding and day school for girls in grades nine through 12. **Common positions include:** General Manager; Librarian; Technician. **Educational backgrounds include:** Art/Design; Business Administration; Liberal Arts; Music; Theater. **Benefits:** Dental Insurance; Life Insurance; Medical Insurance; Pension Plan; Tuition Assistance. **Corporate headquarters location:** This Location. **Operations at this facility include:** Administration; Service.

SAN JUAN COLLEGE
4601 College Boulevard, Farmington NM 87402. 505/599-0215. **Recorded jobline:** 505/599-0448. **Contact:** Personnel Department. **World Wide Web address:** http://www.sjc.cc.nm.us. **Description:** A comprehensive community college offering vocational, industrial, and academic transfer programs. Enrollment at San Juan College is approximately 5,200. **Number of employees at this location:** 320.

SEATTLE PACIFIC UNIVERSITY
3307 Third Avenue West, Seattle WA 98119. 206/281-2809. **Fax:** 206/281-2846. **Recorded jobline:** 206/281-2065. **Contact:** Human Resources. **World Wide Web address:** http://www. spu.edu. **Description:** A Christian university of arts and sciences with an enrollment of approximately 3,400.

SETON HALL UNIVERSITY
400 South Orange Avenue, Stafford Hall, South Orange NJ 07079. 973/761-9138. **Fax:** 973/761-9007. **Contact:** Deborah Raikes-Colbert, Assistant Vice President of Human Resources. **E-mail address:** raikesde@shu.edu. **World Wide Web address:** http://www.shu.edu. **Description:** A Catholic university offering a wide range of undergraduate and graduate programs.

SILVER CITY SCHOOLS
2810 North Swan Street, Silver City NM 88061. 505/388-1527. **Fax:** 505/538-5885. **Contact:** Dick Pool, Superintendent. **Description:** The administrative offices of the Silver City school system, responsible for staffing municipal schools. **Common positions include:** Education Administrator; ESL Teacher; Instructional Technologist; Librarian; Secretary; Special Education Teacher; Teacher/Professor. **Educational backgrounds include:** Computer Science; Education; Mathematics. **Number of employees at this location:** 470.

SKAGIT VALLEY COLLEGE
2405 East College Way, Mount Vernon WA 98273. 360/416-7600. **Fax:** 360/416-7878. **Recorded jobline:** 360/416-7800. **Contact:** Melinda Crawford, Director of Human Resources. **World Wide Web address:** http://www.svc.ctc.edu. **Description:** A community college offering degrees in more than 20 disciplines.

SOUTH DAKOTA STATE UNIVERSITY
Box 2201, Brookings SD 57007. 605/688-4128. **Fax:** 605/688-5822. **Contact:** Kellie Peters, Personnel Specialist. **World Wide Web address:** http://web.sdstate.edu. **Description:** A state university offering bachelor's, master's, and doctoral degrees in Agriculture and Biological Sciences; Arts and Sciences; Education and Counseling; Engineering; Family and Consumer Sciences; General Registration; Nursing; Pharmacy; and Graduate School Studies. Founded in 1881. **Common positions include:** Accountant; Administrative Assistant; Architect; Biological Scientist; Blue-Collar Worker Supervisor; Broadcast Technician; Budget Analyst; Buyer; Chemist; Clerical Supervisor; Computer Operator; Computer Programmer; Counselor; Database Manager; Economist; Education Administrator; Electrical Engineer; Electrician; Food Scientist; Graphic Designer; Human Resources Manager; Librarian; Mechanical Engineer; Nurse Practitioner; Radio Announcer; Secretary; Software Engineer; Systems Analyst; Systems Manager; Teacher; Technical Writer; Typist; Video Production Coordinator; Webmaster. **Educational backgrounds include:** Accounting; Biology; Business Administration; Chemistry; Computer Science; Economics; Engineering; Finance; Health Care; Mathematics. **Benefits:** Daycare Assistance; Dental Insurance; Disability Coverage; Life Insurance; Medical Insurance; Pension Plan; Tuition Assistance. **Special programs:** Internships; Summer Jobs. **Corporate headquarters location:** This Location. **Operations at this facility include:** Administration; Service. **President:** Dr. Peggy Gordon Elliot.

SOUTH TEXAS COLLEGE OF LAW
1303 San Jacinto Street, Houston TX 77002-7000. 713/646-1812. **Fax:** 713/646-1833. **Contact:** Margaret Kautc, Director of Human Resources. **World Wide Web address:** http://www.stcl.edu. **Description:** A private law school with an enrollment of approximately 1,250 students. **Common positions include:** Accountant; Customer Service Rep.; Human Resources Manager; Librarian; Library Technician; Public Relations Specialist; Purchasing Agent. **Educational backgrounds include:** Accounting; Business Administration; Communications; Computer Science; Finance. **Benefits:** Dental Insurance; Disability Coverage; Life Insurance; Medical Insurance; Pension Plan. **Corporate headquarters location:** This Location. **Number of employees at this location:** 200.

SOUTHEASTERN LOUISIANA UNIVERSITY
SLU 10799, Hammond LA 70402. 504/549-2001.
Fax: 504/549-2308. **Contact:** Ms. Jessie R.
Roberts, Human Resources Director. **World Wide
Web address:** http://www.selu.edu. **Description:** A
state university offering a variety of academic
programs. Founded in 1925. **Common positions
include:** Accountant; Biological Scientist; Buyer;
Commercial Artist; Computer Programmer;
Department Manager; Draftsperson; Human
Resources Manager; Public Relations Specialist;
Purchasing Agent. **Educational backgrounds
include:** Accounting; Biology; Business
Administration; Chemistry; Communications;
Computer Science; Economics; Finance; Liberal
Arts; Marketing; Mathematics; Physics. **Benefits:**
Dental Insurance; Life Insurance; Medical
Insurance; Pension Plan; Tuition Assistance.
Corporate headquarters location: This Location.
Operations at this facility include: Service.
Number of employees at this location: 1,500.

SOUTHERN METHODIST UNIVERSITY
P.O. Box 750232, Dallas TX 75275-0232. 214/768-
1111. **Contact:** Employment Office. **World Wide
Web address:** http://www.smu.edu. **Description:** A
university offering bachelor's, master's,
professional, and doctoral degrees to approximately
9,700 students. **Common positions include:**
Accountant; Administrator; Attorney; Biological
Scientist; Blue-Collar Worker Supervisor; Buyer;
Chemist. **Benefits:** Dental Insurance; Disability
Coverage; Employee Discounts; Life Insurance;
Medical Insurance; Pension Plan; Tuition
Assistance. **Special programs:** Internships.
Corporate headquarters location: This Location.
Number of employees at this location: 1,820.

SOUTHERN UTAH UNIVERSITY
351 West Center Street, Cedar City UT 84720.
435/586-7754. **Fax:** 435/865-8420. **Contact:**
Human Resources Department. **World Wide Web
address:** http://www.suu.edu. **Description:** A
public, state-assisted university. The university
offers programs in over 80 fields including arts,
letters, and humanities; business, technology, and
communication; and education. The college offers
master's, bachelor's, and associate's degrees as well
as certification programs. The university has
approximately 6,000 students enrolled. The campus
includes a land observatory, mountain range, and
archeology site. **Common positions include:**
Accountant; Administrative Manager; Agricultural
Scientist; Biological Scientist; Blue-Collar Worker
Supervisor; Broadcast Technician; Budget Analyst;
Chemical Engineer; Chemist; Civil Engineer;
Clerical Supervisor; Counselor; Education
Administrator; Electrical Engineer; Financial
Analyst; Geographer; Geological Engineer;
Geologist; Health Services Manager; Human
Resources Manager; Librarian; Library Technician;
Mathematician; Mechanical Engineer; Preschool
Worker; Psychologist; Public Relations Specialist;
Purchasing Agent; Restaurant Manager; Sociologist;
Statistician; Systems Analyst. **Benefits:** 401(k);
Dental Insurance; Disability Coverage; Employee
Discounts; Life Insurance; Medical Insurance;
Pension Plan; Tuition Assistance. **Corporate
headquarters location:** Salt Lake City UT.
Operations at this facility include: Research and
Development; Service. **Number of employees at
this location:** 600.

SOUTHWESTERN ILLINOIS COLLEGE
2500 Carlyle Avenue, Belleville IL 62221. 618/235-
2700. **Contact:** Human Resources. **World Wide
Web address:** http://www.southwestern.cc.il.us.
Description: A public, two-year community
college. **Benefits:** Daycare Assistance; Disability

Coverage; Employee Discounts; Life Insurance;
Medical Insurance; Pension Plan; Savings Plan;
Tuition Assistance.

**STATE UNIVERSITY OF NEW YORK AT
STONY BROOK**
390 Administration, Stony Brook NY 11794-0751.
Fax: 631/632-6168. **Recorded jobline:** 631/632-
9222. **Contact:** Lynn Johnson, Assistant Director.
World Wide Web address: http://www.sunysb.
edu/hr. **Description:** A state university which offers
bachelor's, master's, and doctoral degrees. The
university has over 17,000 students enrolled.

STATE UNIVERSITY OF WEST GEORGIA
1600 Maple Street, Carrollton GA 30118. 770/836-
6500. **Recorded jobline:** 770/830-2280. **Contact:**
Human Resources Department. **World Wide Web
address:** http://www.westga.edu. **Description:** A
four-year college offering associate's, bachelor's,
and master's degrees including MBAs. **Common
positions include:** Accountant; Administrative
Assistant; Architect; Auditor; Budget Analyst;
Buyer; CFO; Civil Engineer; Computer Operator;
Controller; Counselor; Design Engineer; Desktop
Publishing Specialist; Draftsperson; Electrical
Engineer; Electrician; Environmental Engineer;
Financial Analyst; Help-Desk Technician; Human
Resources Manager; Landscape Architect;
Librarian; Licensed Practical Nurse; Managing
Editor; Marketing Manager; Mechanical Engineer;
Network Administrator; Nurse Practitioner;
Pharmacist; Physician; Production Manager; Project
Manager; Public Relations Specialist; Purchasing
Agent; Registered Nurse; Secretary; Teacher;
Telecommunications Manager; Typist. **Educational
backgrounds include:** Accounting; Business
Administration; Communications; Education;
Engineering; Finance; Liberal Arts; Marketing;
Mathematics; MBA; Public Relations; Publishing.
Number of employees at this location: 900.

STEPHEN F. AUSTIN STATE UNIVERSITY
P.O. Box 13039, Nacogdoches TX 75962. 936/468-
2304. **Contact:** Personnel Department. **World
Wide Web address:** http://www.sfasu.edu.
Description: A four-year college offering bachelor's
and master's degrees.

TAOS MUNICIPAL SCHOOLS
213 Paseo del Canon, Taos NM 87571. 505/758-
5200. **Fax:** 505/758-5298. **Contact:** Liz Maes,
Administrative Assistant. **Description:** The
administrative offices of the Taos school system that
are responsible for staffing municipal schools.
NOTE: Part-time jobs are offered. **Common
positions include:** Administrative Assistant;
Certified Nurses Aide; Certified Occupational
Therapy Assistant; Computer Programmer;
Computer Support Technician; Computer
Technician; Counselor; ESL Teacher; Finance
Director; Librarian; Licensed Practical Nurse;
Medical Assistant; Nurse Practitioner; Occupational
Therapist; Physical Therapist; Preschool Worker;
Psychologist; Registered Nurse; Secretary; Social
Worker; Special Education Teacher; Speech-
Language Pathologist; Teacher; Transportation
Specialist. **Benefits:** Dental Insurance; Disability
Coverage; Employee Discounts; Life Insurance.
Special programs: Internships; Summer Jobs.
Superintendent: Andres Gallegos. **Purchasing
Manager:** Arlene Martinez. **Number of employees
at this location:** 500.

TARRANT COUNTY JUNIOR COLLEGE
1500 Houston Street, Fort Worth TX 76102.
817/515-5100. **Contact:** Human Resources. **World
Wide Web address:** http://www.tcjc.cc.tx.us.
Description: A two-year college offering associate's

degrees and certificates. **Common positions include:** Accountant; Clerical Supervisor; Teacher. **Benefits:** Dental Insurance; Life Insurance; Medical Insurance; Pension Plan; Tuition Assistance. **Corporate headquarters location:** This Location. **Operations at this facility include:** Administration.

TASA
P.O. Box 382, 4 Hardscrabble Heights, Brewster NY 10509. 914/277-4900. **Fax:** 914/277-3548. **Contact:** Personnel. **World Wide Web address:** http://www.tasa.com. **Description:** TASA designs, develops, publishes, and distributes educational tests, instructional materials, and microcomputer software to elementary and secondary schools, colleges, and universities. The educational tests, known as Primary, Standard, and Advanced Degrees of Reading Power tests and Degrees of Word Meaning tests, are components on the company's Degrees of Literacy Power program. **Corporate headquarters location:** This Location.

TEMPLE UNIVERSITY
University Services Building, 1601 North Broad Street, Room 203, Philadelphia PA 19122. 215/204-7174. **Contact:** Personnel Department. **World Wide Web address:** http://www.temple.edu. **Description:** A four-year university offering bachelor's, master's (including MBAs), first professional, and doctoral degrees. Approximately 22,000 undergraduate and 9,400 graduate students attend Temple University. **Common positions include:** Clinical Lab Technician; Computer Programmer; Counselor; Dental Assistant; Education Administrator; Health Services Manager; Librarian; Library Technician; Licensed Practical Nurse; Nuclear Medicine Technologist; Occupational Therapist; Physical Therapist; Registered Nurse; Secretary; Typist. **Educational backgrounds include:** Biology; Chemistry; Computer Science. **Benefits:** Dental Insurance; Disability Coverage; Employee Discounts; Life Insurance; Medical Insurance; Pension Plan; Savings Plan; Tuition Assistance. **Corporate headquarters location:** This Location. **Operations at this facility include:** Administration; Research and Development. **Number of employees at this location:** 9,000.

TESSERACT GROUP
9977 North 90th Street, Suite 180, Scottsdale AZ 85258. 480/767-2300. **Toll-free phone:** 800/326-3354. **Fax:** 480/767-2361. **Contact:** Darien Fuller, Recruiter. **E-mail address:** dfuller@corp. tesseractgroup.org. **World Wide Web address:** http://www.tesseractgroup.org. **Description:** An integrated education management company, serving preschool through college levels. Founded in 1986. **NOTE:** Entry-level positions and part-time jobs are offered. **Common positions include:** Child Care Center Director; Education Administrator; ESL Teacher; Instructional Technologist; Preschool Worker; Special Education Teacher; Teacher. **Educational backgrounds include:** Communications; Computer Science; Education; Teaching. **Benefits:** 401(k); Dental Insurance; Disability Coverage; Employee Discounts; Life Insurance; Medical Insurance. **Special programs:** Internships. **Office hours:** Monday - Friday, 8:00 a.m. - 5:00 p.m. **Corporate headquarters location:** This Location. **Other U.S. locations:** CO; DC; MN; TX. **Number of employees at this location:** 50.

TEXAS A&M UNIVERSITY
809 East University Drive, Suite 101A, College Station TX 77843-1475. 979/845-5154. **Contact:** Employment Office. **World Wide Web address:** http://www.tamu.edu/hrd/employment. **Description:** A university that offers a wide range of bachelor's, master's, doctoral and professional programs. Texas A&M also provides continuing education programs that serve the needs of area businesses and professionals. **Common positions include:** Accountant; Administrator; Attorney; Biological Scientist; Blue-Collar Worker Supervisor; Buyer; Chemist; Civil Engineer; Computer Programmer; Draftsperson; Editor; Electrical Engineer; Food Scientist; Geologist; Human Resources Manager; Mechanical Engineer; Physicist; Reporter; Systems Analyst; Transportation/Traffic Specialist. **Educational backgrounds include:** Accounting; Art/Design; Biology; Business Administration; Chemistry; Communications; Computer Science; Engineering; Geology; Liberal Arts; Physics. **Benefits:** Dental Insurance; Disability Coverage; Life Insurance; Medical Insurance; Pension Plan. **Corporate headquarters location:** This Location.

TEXAS CHRISTIAN UNIVERSITY
P.O. Box 298200, Fort Worth TX 76129. 817/257-7790. **Contact:** John Weif, Director of Employee Relations. **World Wide Web address:** http://www. tcu.edu. **Description:** A university offering undergraduate and graduate programs to approximately 7,000 students. **Common positions include:** Blue-Collar Worker Supervisor; Cashier; Construction Trade Worker; Dispatcher; Heating Technician; Library Technician; Payroll Clerk; Postal Clerk/Mail Carrier; Printing Press Operator; Secretary; Teacher; Typist. **Educational backgrounds include:** Accounting; Art/Design; Biology; Business Administration; Chemistry; Communications; Computer Science; Economics; Engineering; Finance; Geology; Liberal Arts; Marketing; Mathematics; Physics. **Benefits:** Dental Insurance; Disability Coverage; Employee Discounts; Life Insurance; Medical Insurance; Pension Plan; Tuition Assistance. **Corporate headquarters location:** This Location. **Number of employees at this location:** 1,300.

TEXAS TECH UNIVERSITY
P.O. Box 41097, Lubbock TX 79409-1097. 806/742-2011. **Contact:** Jim Brown, Personnel Director. **World Wide Web address:** http://www. ttu.edu. **Description:** A state university. The university offers undergraduate and graduate degrees in liberal arts, law, applied health, and medicine. **Benefits:** Dental Insurance; Disability Coverage; Life Insurance; Medical Insurance; Pension Plan; Savings Plan. **Corporate headquarters location:** This Location.

TEXAS WESLEYAN UNIVERSITY
1201 Wesleyan Street, Fort Worth TX 76105. 817/531-4403. **Fax:** 817/531-4402. **Contact:** Human Resources. **World Wide Web address:** http://www.txwesleyan.edu. **Description:** A small, private university affiliated with the United Methodist Church. Texas Wesleyan University offers a variety of undergraduate and graduate degrees to approximately 3,000 students. **Common positions include:** Accountant; Administrative Manager; Administrator; Biological Scientist; Blue-Collar Worker Supervisor; Chemist; Clerical Supervisor; Computer Programmer; Construction Contractor; Counselor; Dietician; Economist; Education Administrator; Financial Analyst; Food Scientist; Librarian; Library Technician; Mathematician; Paralegal; Psychologist; Public Relations Specialist; Registered Nurse; Systems Analyst; Teacher. **Educational backgrounds include:** Accounting; Art; Biology; Business Administration; Chemistry; Communications; Computer Science; Economics; Finance; Liberal Arts; Marketing; Mathematics; Physics. **Benefits:** Dental Insurance; Disability Coverage; Employee

Discounts; Life Insurance; Medical Insurance; Pension Plan; Tuition Assistance. **Corporate headquarters location:** This Location. **Number of employees at this location:** 285.

TEXAS WOMAN'S UNIVERSITY (TWU)
P.O. Box 425739, Denton TX 76204-3739. 940/898-3555. **Fax:** 940/898-3566. **Contact:** Lois Morris, Assistant Manager of Employment. **World Wide Web address:** http://www.twu.edu. **Description:** A university offering bachelor's, master's, and doctoral degrees. Founded in 1903. **Common positions include:** Accountant; Computer Programmer; Counselor; Dispatcher; Electrician; Financial Analyst; Human Resources Manager; Librarian; Purchasing Agent; Receptionist; Registered Nurse; Secretary; Systems Analyst; Typist. **Educational backgrounds include:** Accounting; Business Administration; Computer Science; Finance; Marketing; Mathematics. **Benefits:** Dental Insurance; Disability Coverage; Life Insurance; Medical Insurance; Pension Plan. **Special programs:** Internships. **Corporate headquarters location:** This Location. **Other U.S. locations:** Dallas TX; Houston TX. **Number of employees at this location:** 1,000.

THOMAS EDISON STATE COLLEGE
101 West State Street, Trenton NJ 08608. 609/984-1114. **Contact:** Human Resources. **World Wide Web address:** http://www.tesc.edu. **Description:** A state college operating as part of the state's senior public higher education system. **Benefits:** Dental Insurance; Disability Coverage; Life Insurance; Medical Insurance; Pension Plan; Tuition Assistance. **Corporate headquarters location:** This Location.

THE TRAVEL TRADE SCHOOL, INC.
7921 South Park Plaza, Suite 105, Littleton CO 80120. 303/795-1825. **Fax:** 303/795-2615. **Contact:** Carolyn Patton, President. **Description:** A vocational trade school that provides career services and specializes in travel industry training. **Common positions include:** Travel Agent. **Other area locations:** Boulder CO; Fort Collins CO.

UNIVERSITY OF ALABAMA
P.O. Box 870126, Tuscaloosa AL 35487-0126. 205/348-6690. **Contact:** Personnel. **World Wide Web address:** http://www.ua.edu. **Description:** A university offering bachelor's, master's, and doctoral degrees. **Common positions include:** Accountant; Blue-Collar Worker Supervisor; Buyer; Computer Programmer; Human Resources Manager; Licensed Practical Nurse; Systems Analyst. **Benefits:** 401(k); Dental Insurance; Disability Coverage; Life Insurance; Medical Insurance; Pension Plan; Tuition Assistance. **Corporate headquarters location:** This Location. **Number of employees at this location:** 3,700.

UNIVERSITY OF BRIDGEPORT
380 University Avenue, Bridgeport CT 06601. 203/576-4000. **Contact:** Human Resources. **World Wide Web address:** http://www.bridgeport.edu. **Description:** A four-year, liberal arts university offering over 30 undergraduate and 14 graduate degree programs. **Corporate headquarters location:** This Location.

UNIVERSITY OF CALIFORNIA, IRVINE
Berkeley Place, Suite 2500, Irvine CA 92697. **Recorded jobline:** 949/UCI-JOBS. **Contact:** Human Resources. **World Wide Web address:** http://www.uci.edu. **Description:** A research university which is part of the University of California system. University of California, Irvine offers bachelor's, master's, and doctoral degrees.

NOTE: Part-time positions are offered. **Common positions include:** Accountant; Administrative Assistant; Administrative Manager; Architect; AS400 Programmer Analyst; Assistant Manager; Auditor; Biochemist; Biological Scientist; Budget Analyst; Buyer; Certified Occupational Therapy Assistant; Civil Engineer; Claim Rep.; Clinical Lab Technician; Computer Operator; Computer Programmer; Computer Support Technician; Computer Technician; Construction Contractor; Counselor; Database Administrator; Database Manager; Desktop Publishing Specialist; Dietician; Editor; EEG Technologist; EKG Technician; Electrician; Finance Director; Financial Analyst; Industrial Engineer; Internet Services Manager; Librarian; Medical Assistant; Medical Records Technician; MIS Specialist; Network Administrator; Nurse Practitioner; Occupational Therapist; Pharmacist; Physical Therapist; Physical Therapy Assistant; Physician; Preschool Worker; Project Manager; Public Relations Specialist; Purchasing Agent; Radiological Technologist; Registered Nurse; Respiratory Therapist; Secretary; Social Worker; Speech-Language Pathologist; SQL Programmer; Systems Analyst; Systems Manager; Technical Writer; Telecommunications Manager; Webmaster. **Educational backgrounds include:** Accounting; Biology; Business Administration; C/C++; Chemistry; Computer Science; Finance; Health Care; HTML; Internet; Java; Microsoft Word; Novell; Public Relations; QuarkXPress; Software Tech. Support; Spreadsheets. **Benefits:** 401(k); Dental Insurance; Disability Coverage; Employee Discounts; Financial Planning Assistance; Life Insurance; Medical Insurance; On-Site Daycare; Pension Plan; Public Transit Available; Sick Days (11+); Tuition Assistance; Vacation Days (11 - 15). **Special programs:** Summer Jobs. **Operations at this facility include:** Research and Development; Service. **Number of employees at this location:** 5,000.

UNIVERSITY OF CALIFORNIA, LOS ANGELES
10920 Wilshire Boulevard, Suite 205, Los Angeles CA 90024. 310/794-0890. **Fax:** 310/794-0895. **Recorded jobline:** 310/825-9151. **Contact:** Virginia Oaxaca, Staff Employment Division. **World Wide Web address:** http://www.chr.ucla.edu. **Description:** A campus of the state university system offering undergraduate and graduate degree programs. **NOTE:** Part-time positions are offered. **Company slogan:** UCLA - The University of Big Ideas. **Common positions include:** Account Manager; Accountant; Administrative Assistant; Administrative Manager; Applications Engineer; Architect; AS400 Programmer Analyst; Auditor; Biochemist; Budget Analyst; Buyer; Chemist; CFO; Clerical Supervisor; Clinical Lab Technician; Computer Engineer; Computer Programmer; Computer Support Technician; Computer Technician; Construction Contractor; Controller; Database Administrator; Database Manager; Design Engineer; Desktop Publishing Specialist; Editor; EEG Technologist; EKG Technician; Electrician; Emergency Medical Technician; Environmental Engineer; Financial Analyst; Fund Manager; Graphic Artist; Home Health Aide; Internet Services Manager; Librarian; Licensed Practical Nurse; Market Research Analyst; Medical Assistant; MIS Specialist; Multimedia Designer; Network Administrator; Nurse Practitioner; Paralegal; Pharmacist; Physical Therapist; Quality Assurance Engineer; Registered Nurse; Secretary; Social Worker; Software Engineer; SQL Programmer; Statistician; Systems Analyst; Systems Manager; Technical Writer; Underwriter; Webmaster. **Educational backgrounds include:** AS400 Certification; C/C++; CGI; Finance; Health Care; HTML; Internet; Java; MCSE; Microsoft Word;

Novell; Software Development; Software Tech. Support; Spreadsheets; Visual Basic. **Benefits:** 403(b); Casual Dress - Fridays; Dental Insurance; Disability Coverage; Employee Discounts; Life Insurance; Medical Insurance; Pension Plan; Public Transit Available; Savings Plan; Tuition Assistance. **Special programs:** Internships. **Corporate headquarters location:** This Location. **Number of employees at this location:** 18,000.

UNIVERSITY OF CHARLESTON

2300 MacCorkle Avenue SE, Charleston WV 25304. 304/357-4736. **Fax:** 304/357-4715. **Contact:** Angela Hall, Director of Personnel. **World Wide Web address:** http://www.uchaswv.edu. **Description:** A private, undergraduate university with an enrollment of 1,500 students. **Common positions include:** Blue-Collar Worker Supervisor; Computer Programmer; Education Administrator; Electrician; Human Resources Manager; Librarian; Library Technician; Purchasing Agent; Restaurant Manager; Systems Analyst; Teacher. **Educational backgrounds include:** Accounting; Art; Biology; Business Administration; Chemistry; Communications; Computer Science; Economics; Engineering; Finance; Geology; Liberal Arts; Marketing; Mathematics; Physics. **Benefits:** 403(b); Dental Insurance; Disability Coverage; Employee Discounts; Life Insurance; Medical Insurance; Tuition Assistance. **Corporate headquarters location:** This Location. **Operations at this facility include:** Administration; Service.

UNIVERSITY OF CINCINNATI

P.O. Box 210117, Cincinnati OH 45221-0117. 513/556-1246. **Contact:** Employment Services. **World Wide Web address:** http://www.uc.edu. **Description:** A university offering over 200 undergraduate and 125 graduate programs. The university is comprised of 16 colleges, a medical center, and a library with 1.8 million volumes. **NOTE:** Entry-level positions and second and third shifts are offered. **Common positions include:** Account Manager; Accountant; Administrative Assistant; Administrator; Architect; Architectural Engineer; Attorney; Auditor; Budget Analyst; Computer Operator; Computer Programmer; Construction Contractor; Controller; Counselor; Database Manager; Education Administrator; Electrician; Financial Analyst; Fund Manager; Graphic Designer; Health Services Worker; Human Resources Manager; Instructor; Librarian; Mechanical Engineer; MIS Specialist; Purchasing Agent; Secretary; Social Worker; Software Engineer; Systems Analyst; Teacher/Professor; Telecommunications Manager; Typist/Word Processor; Vice President. **Educational backgrounds include:** Accounting; Biology; Business Administration; Chemistry; Computer Science; Finance. **Benefits:** 403(b); Dental Insurance; Disability Coverage; Employee Discounts; Life Insurance; Medical Insurance; Pension Plan. **Special programs:** Internships. **Corporate headquarters location:** This Location. **Annual sales/revenues:** More than $100 million.

UNIVERSITY OF DELAWARE

51 East Main Street, Newark DE 19716. 302/831-2171. **Recorded jobline:** 302/831-6122. **Contact:** Joyce D. Henderson, Human Resources Manager. **World Wide Web address:** http://www.udel.edu. **Description:** A four-year, state university offering bachelor's, master's (including MBAs), and doctoral degrees. Approximately 15,000 undergraduate and 2,600 graduate students attend the University of Delaware. **Educational backgrounds include:** Accounting; Art/Design; Biology; Business Administration; Chemistry; Communications; Computer Science; Economics; Engineering;

Finance; Geology; Liberal Arts; Marketing; Mathematics; Physics. **Benefits:** Dental Insurance; Disability Coverage; Life Insurance; Medical Insurance; Pension Plan; Tuition Assistance. **Corporate headquarters location:** This Location. **President:** David P. Roselle. **Number of employees at this location:** 4,500.

UNIVERSITY OF DENVER

2020 East Evans Avenue, Room 101, Denver CO 80208. 303/871-2000. **Recorded jobline:** 303/871-3460. **Contact:** Human Resources. **World Wide Web address:** http://www.du.edu. **Description:** A four-year university offering undergraduate, graduate, and continuing education programs to more than 8,500 students. **Common positions include:** Accountant; Blue-Collar Worker Supervisor; Department Manager; Financial Analyst; Management Trainee; Public Relations Specialist. **Educational backgrounds include:** Accounting; Business Administration; Communications; Finance; Liberal Arts; Marketing. **Benefits:** Dental Insurance; Disability Coverage; Employee Discounts; Life Insurance; Medical Insurance; Pension Plan; Savings Plan; Tuition Assistance. **Special programs:** Internships. **Corporate headquarters location:** This Location. **Operations at this facility include:** Research and Development; Service.

UNIVERSITY OF EVANSVILLE

1800 Lincoln Avenue, Evansville IN 47722. 812/479-2943. **Fax:** 812/479-2320. **Contact:** Gregory R. Bordfeld, Director of Personnel. **E-mail address:** gb5@evansville.edu. **World Wide Web address:** http://www.evansville.edu. **Description:** A nonprofit, four-year university offering bachelor's and master's degrees. Approximately 2,600 undergraduate and 500 graduate students attend the University of Evansville. **NOTE:** Entry-level positions and second and third shifts are offered. **Common positions include:** Accountant/Auditor; Administrative Manager; Biochemist; Biological Scientist; Budget Analyst; Chemical Engineer; Chemist; CFO; Civil Engineer; Computer Programmer; Controller; Counselor; Database Manager; Economist; Editor; Editorial Assistant; Education Administrator; Electrician; ESL Teacher; Finance Director; Fund Manager; Geographer; Graphic Artist; Graphic Designer; Human Resources Manager; Internet Services Manager; Librarian; Paralegal; Physician; Psychologist; Public Relations Manager; Purchasing Agent; Radio Announcer; Registered Nurse; Secretary; Systems Analyst; Teacher; Technical Writer; Vice President. **Educational backgrounds include:** Accounting; Biology; Business Administration; Chemistry; Communications; Computer Science; Economics; Engineering; Finance; Liberal Arts; Marketing; Mathematics. **Benefits:** 403(b); Dental Insurance; Disability Coverage; Flexible Benefits; Life Insurance; Medical Insurance; Pension Plan; Tuition Assistance. **Corporate headquarters location:** This Location.

UNIVERSITY OF FINDLAY

1000 North Main Street, Findlay OH 45840-3695. 419/424-6964. **Toll-free phone:** 800/548-0932. **Contact:** Human Resources. **World Wide Web address:** http://www.findlay.edu. **Description:** A private, coeducational university. Programs include Bilingual Business Education, Criminal Justice, Environmental and Hazardous Materials Management, Equestrian Studies, Japanese, Nuclear Medicine Technology, and Theatre Production.

UNIVERSITY OF FLORIDA

P.O. Box 115002, Gainesville FL 32611. 352/392-4621. **Fax:** 352/392-7094. **Recorded jobline:**

352/392-4631. **Contact:** Greg Marwede, Assistant Director of Personnel Services. **World Wide Web address:** http://www.ufl.edu. **Description:** A state university. **NOTE:** Entry-level positions are offered. **Common positions include:** Accountant; Administrative Assistant; Applications Engineer; Architect; AS400 Programmer Analyst; Auditor; Biological Scientist; Budget Analyst; Certified Occupational Therapy Assistant; Chemist; Computer Engineer; Computer Operator; Computer Programmer; Computer Support Technician; Computer Technician; Counselor; Database Administrator; Database Manager; Desktop Publishing Specialist; Dietician; Editor; Editorial Assistant; Education Administrator; Electrical Engineer; Electrician; Graphic Artist; Industrial Engineer; Instructional Technologist; Internet Services Manager; Librarian; Licensed Practical Nurse; MIS Specialist; Multimedia Designer; Network Administrator; Purchasing Agent; Registered Nurse; Secretary; Software Engineer; Special Education Teacher; SQL Programmer; Systems Analyst; Systems Manager; Teacher; Typist; Webmaster. **Educational backgrounds include:** Accounting; Biology; C/C++; Chemistry; Computer Science; HTML; Internet; Java; Microsoft Word; Software Tech. Support; Spreadsheets. **Benefits:** 403(b); Casual Dress - Fridays; Dental Insurance; Disability Coverage; Employee Discounts; Financial Planning Assistance; Medical Insurance; Pension Plan; Tuition Assistance. **Corporate headquarters location:** This Location.

UNIVERSITY OF HOUSTON/DOWNTOWN
One Main Street, Suite 925 South, Houston TX 77002. 713/221-8060. **Contact:** Human Resources. **E-mail address:** uhdinfo@dt.uh.edu. **World Wide Web address:** http://www.dt.uh.edu. **Description:** One of four campuses within the University of Houston system.

UNIVERSITY OF IDAHO
415 West Sixth Street, Moscow ID 83844-4332. 208/885-3609. **Contact:** Human Resources. **World Wide Web address:** http://www.uidaho.edu/hrs. **Description:** A state university.

UNIVERSITY OF IOWA
120 USB, Iowa City IA 52242-1411. 319/335-2656. **Fax:** 319/335-0202. **Recorded jobline:** 319/335-2682. **Contact:** Peter Sheets, Employment Representative. **E-mail address:** psheets@blue. weeg.uiowa.edu. **World Wide Web address:** http://www.uiowa.edu. **Description:** A university with 27,900 students enrolled in over 150 areas of study. **NOTE:** Entry-level positions, part-time jobs, and second and third shifts are offered. **Common positions include:** Accountant; Administrative Assistant; Administrative Manager; Architect; Blue-Collar Worker Supervisor; Budget Analyst; Certified Nurses Aide; Certified Occupational Therapy Assistant; Clerical Supervisor; Clinical Lab Technician; Computer Programmer; Computer Technician; Customer Service Rep.; Database Manager; Editorial Assistant; EEG Technologist; EKG Technician; Electrical Engineer; Electrician; Financial Analyst; Graphic Designer; Help-Desk Technician; Human Resources Manager; Librarian; Licensed Practical Nurse; Medical Assistant; Medical Records Technician; Medical Secretary; MIS Specialist; Nuclear Medicine Technologist; Nurse; Occupational Therapist; Physical Therapist; Physical Therapy Assistant; Project Manager; Purchasing Agent; Radiological Technologist; Registered Nurse; Respiratory Therapist; Secretary; Social Worker; Surgical Technician; Systems Analyst; Systems Manager; Technical Writer; Typist; Web Advertising Specialist; Webmaster; Website Developer. **Educational backgrounds include:** Accounting; Biology; Business Administration; Chemistry; Communications; Computer Science; Education; Engineering; Finance; Health Care; HTML; Internet Development; Liberal Arts; Marketing; Mathematics; MBA; Microsoft Word; Public Relations; Software Tech. Support; Spreadsheets. **Benefits:** 403(b); Daycare Assistance; Dental Insurance; Disability Coverage; Life Insurance; Medical Insurance; Pension Plan; Public Transit Available; Savings Plan. **Number of employees at this location:** 21,000.

UNIVERSITY OF MAINE AT FARMINGTON
86 Main Street, Farmington ME 04938. 207/778-7246. **Fax:** 207/778-7247. **Contact:** Director of Personnel. **World Wide Web address:** http://www. umf.maine.edu. **Description:** One location of the state university. University of Maine is a four-year, undergraduate, public university with an emphasis on education and liberal arts. **Common positions include:** Accountant; Blue-Collar Worker Supervisor; Budget Analyst; Chemist; Clerical Supervisor; Computer Programmer; Counselor; Education Administrator; Financial Analyst; General Manager; Health Services Manager; Human Resources Manager; Human Service Worker; Librarian; Library Technician; Licensed Practical Nurse; Mathematician; Medical Records Technician; Physician; Public Relations Specialist; Purchasing Agent; Sociologist; Speech-Language Pathologist; Systems Analyst; Teacher/Professor. **Educational backgrounds include:** Accounting; Art/Design; Biology; Business Administration; Chemistry; Computer Science; Economics; Finance; Geology; Liberal Arts; Mathematics; Physics. **Benefits:** 401(k); Daycare Assistance; Disability Coverage; Life Insurance; Medical Insurance; Pension Plan; Tuition Assistance. **Operations at this facility include:** Administration; Service. **Number of employees at this location:** 330.

UNIVERSITY OF MARYLAND AT BALTIMORE COUNTY
1000 Hilltop Circle, 5th Floor, Administration Building, Baltimore MD 21250. 410/455-2337. **Fax:** 410/455-1064. **Contact:** Human Resources. **World Wide Web address:** http://www.umbc.edu. **Description:** A research university serving the Baltimore metropolitan region. The university places special emphasis on its undergraduate programs, offering 30 majors. The facility's graduate and research emphasis is on sciences, engineering, and public policy. The university has an enrollment of more than 10,500 students. **Common positions include:** Accountant; Administrative Assistant; Administrative Manager; Computer Programmer; Counselor; Education Administrator; Human Service Worker; Librarian; Marketing Specialist; Public Relations Specialist; Social Worker. **Benefits:** Medical Insurance; Tuition Assistance. **Parent company:** University System of Maryland. **Operations at this facility include:** Administration; Research and Development; Service. **Number of employees at this location:** 1,800.

UNIVERSITY OF MINNESOTA TWIN CITIES
319 15th Avenue SE, Room 200, Donhowe Building, Minneapolis MN 55455. 612/625-3861. **Fax:** 612/624-6037. **Contact:** Nan Wilhemson, Director of Staffing and Employment. **World Wide Web address:** http://www.umn.edu/ohr/jobs. **Description:** A branch of the four-year, state university offering 161 bachelor's degrees, 218 master's degrees, 114 doctoral degrees, and five professional degrees. **Common positions include:** Accountant; Administrative Manager; Agricultural Scientist; Attorney; Biological Scientist; Chemist;

Clerical Supervisor; Computer Programmer; Counselor; Customer Service Rep.; Dental Assistant Hygienist; Editor; Human Resources Manager; Library Technician; Medical Records Technician; Pharmacist; Physical Therapist; Physician; Physicist; Public Relations Specialist; Purchasing Agent; Radiological Technologist; Real Estate Agent; Registered Nurse; Restaurant Manager; Science Technologist; Systems Analyst; Teacher; Transportation/Traffic Specialist; Veterinarian. **Educational backgrounds include:** Accounting; Art/Design; Business Administration; Chemistry; Communications; Computer Science; Health Care. **Benefits:** Dental Insurance; Disability Coverage; Life Insurance; Medical Insurance; Pension Plan; Tuition Assistance. **Corporate headquarters location:** This Location. **Operations at this facility include:** Research and Development; Service.

UNIVERSITY OF MISSOURI/COLUMBIA
201 South Seventh Street, 130 Heinkel Building, Columbia MO 65211. 573/882-2121. **Contact:** Personnel. **World Wide Web address:** http://www.missouri.edu. **Description:** A university. **Common positions include:** Accountant; Architectural Engineer; Biological Scientist; Computer Programmer; Department Manager; Human Resources Manager; Public Relations Specialist; Systems Analyst; Technical Writer. **Educational backgrounds include:** Accounting; Biology; Chemistry; Computer Science; Finance; Marketing. **Benefits:** Dental Insurance; Disability Coverage; Employee Discounts; Life Insurance; Medical Insurance; Pension Plan; Tuition Assistance. **Special programs:** Internships. **Corporate headquarters location:** This Location. **Operations at this facility include:** Administration; Research and Development; Service.

UNIVERSITY OF NEW ENGLAND
11 Hills Beach Road, Biddeford ME 04005. 207/797-7261. **Contact:** Human Resources. **World Wide Web address:** http://www.une.edu. **Description:** A four-year college offering associate's, bachelor's, and master's degree programs, with a total student enrollment of 2,800. **NOTE:** Entry-level positions and part-time jobs are offered. **Common positions include:** Accountant; Administrative Assistant; Administrative Manager; CFO; Child Care Center Director; Counselor; Electrician; Event Planner; Help-Desk Technician; Human Resources Manager; Internet Services Manager; Librarian; Medical Assistant; Medical Secretary; MIS Specialist; Network Administrator; Nurse Practitioner; Physician; Preschool Worker; Registered Nurse; Secretary; Teacher; Typist; Webmaster. **Educational backgrounds include:** Computer Science; Education; Health Care; HTML; Liberal Arts; Microsoft Word; Novell; Spreadsheets. **Benefits:** 403(b); Dental Insurance; Disability Coverage; Employee Discounts; Life Insurance; Medical Insurance; On-Site Daycare; Relocation Assistance; Sick Days (11+); Tuition Assistance; Vacation Days (10 - 20).

UNIVERSITY OF NEW HAVEN
300 Orange Avenue, West Haven CT 06516. 203/932-7240. **Contact:** Personnel Administrator. **World Wide Web address:** http://www.newhaven.edu. **Description:** An independent, four-year university. Founded in 1920. **NOTE:** Resumes sent via e-mail or fax will not be accepted. **Benefits:** Disability Coverage; Life Insurance; Medical Insurance; Pension Plan; Tuition Assistance. **Corporate headquarters location:** This Location.

UNIVERSITY OF NEW MEXICO
1717 Roma NE, Albuquerque NM 87131. 505/277-2454. **Contact:** Human Resources. **World Wide Web address:** http://www.unm.edu. **Description:** One of the largest of New Mexico's four-year collegiate institutions. University of New Mexico offers programs in Latin American studies, anthropology, photography, biology, nuclear pharmacy, laser optics, and environmental studies. **Common positions include:** Accountant/Auditor; Automotive Mechanic; Biological Scientist; Broadcast Technician; Chemical Engineer; Civil Engineer; Clerical Supervisor; Clinical Lab Technician; Computer Programmer; Education Administrator; Health Services Manager; Librarian; Licensed Practical Nurse; Medical Records Technician; Occupational Therapist; Physical Therapist; Physician; Radiological Technologist; Registered Nurse; Science Technologist; Social Worker; Software Engineer; Systems Analyst; Technical Writer/Editor. **Educational backgrounds include:** Accounting; Biology; Business Administration; Criminal Justice; Engineering; Physics. **Benefits:** 403(b); Daycare Assistance; Dental Insurance; Disability Coverage; Employee Discounts; Life Insurance; Medical Insurance; Pension Plan; Tuition Assistance. **Corporate headquarters location:** This Location. **Number of employees at this location:** 10,000.

UNIVERSITY OF NORTH TEXAS HEALTH SCIENCE AT FORT WORTH
3500 Camp Bowie Boulevard, Suite 735, Fort Worth TX 76107-2699. 817/735-2690. **Contact:** Human Resources Services. **World Wide Web address:** http://www.hsc.unt.edu. **Description:** A health science education center. **Common positions include:** Accountant/Auditor; Biological Scientist; Biomedical Engineer; Buyer; Chemist; Claim Rep.; Clinical Lab Technician; Computer Programmer; Graphic Artist; Library Technician; Licensed Practical Nurse; Receptionist; Registered Nurse; Science Technologist; Secretary; Systems Analyst; Typist. **Educational backgrounds include:** Accounting; Biology; Business Administration; Computer Science; Education; Mathematics. **Benefits:** Dental Insurance; Disability Coverage; Employee Discounts; Life Insurance; Medical Insurance; Pension Plan. **Corporate headquarters location:** This Location. **Operations at this facility include:** Education; Research and Development. **Number of employees at this location:** 1,000.

UNIVERSITY OF NORTHERN COLORADO
501 20th Street, Carter Hall, Room 2002, Greeley CO 80639. 970/351-2718. **Contact:** Judith Zewe, Director of Personnel. **World Wide Web address:** http://www.unco.edu. **Description:** A four-year university offering undergraduate and graduate degree programs to more than 12,000 students.

UNIVERSITY OF PENNSYLVANIA
3401 Walnut Street, Suite 521A, Philadelphia PA 19104-6228. 215/898-7284. **Contact:** Alicia Brill, Manager, Recruitment and Staffing. **World Wide Web address:** http://www.hr.upenn.edu/jobs. **Description:** An Ivy League university offering undergraduate and graduate degrees. **NOTE:** Resumes must be submitted online. Please check the Website for more information. Entry-level positions are offered. **Common positions include:** Account Manager; Accountant; Administrative Assistant; Administrative Manager; Advertising Clerk; Advertising Executive; Architect; Assistant Manager; Auditor; Biomedical Engineer; Broadcast Technician; Budget Analyst; Buyer; Certified Nurses Aide; Clerical Supervisor; Computer Operator; Computer Programmer; Counselor; Customer Service Representative; Database Manager; Editor; Editorial Assistant; Financial Analyst; Graphic Designer; Human Resources Manager; Internet Services Manager; Librarian;

Licensed Practical Nurse; Managing Editor; Market Research Analyst; Marketing Manager; Marketing Specialist; Mechanical Engineer; MIS Specialist; Operations Manager; Production Manager; Project Manager; Purchasing Agent; Registered Nurse; Secretary; Systems Analyst; Systems Manager; Technical Writer; Telecommunications Manager; Typist; Veterinarian. **Educational backgrounds include:** Accounting; Biology; Business Administration; Chemistry; Communications; Computer Science; Engineering; Finance; Health Care; Liberal Arts; Marketing; Mathematics; Physics. **Benefits:** Daycare Assistance; Dental Insurance; Financial Planning Assistance; Flexible Schedule; Life Insurance; Medical Insurance; Pension Plan; Public Transit Available; Savings Plan; Tuition Assistance. **Special programs:** Internships; Training.

UNIVERSITY OF PITTSBURGH
200 South Craig Street, 100 Craig Hall, Pittsburgh PA 15260. 412/624-8150. **Contact:** Ronald Frisch, Associate Vice Chancellor for Human Resources. **World Wide Web address:** http://www.pitt.edu. **Description:** A university. **Common positions include:** Accountant; Administrator; Biological Scientist; Biomedical Engineer; Buyer; Chemical Engineer; Chemist; Computer Programmer; Counselor; Editor; Electrical Engineer; Financial Analyst; Mechanical Engineer; Public Relations Specialist; Purchasing Agent; Reporter; Systems Analyst; Technical Writer. **Educational backgrounds include:** Accounting; Biology; Business Administration; Chemistry; Computer Science; Engineering; Liberal Arts; Mathematics. **Benefits:** Disability Coverage; Employee Discounts; Life Insurance; Medical Insurance; Pension Plan; Tuition Assistance. **Corporate headquarters location:** This Location. **Operations at this facility include:** Administration; Research and Development; Service.

UNIVERSITY OF PORTLAND
5000 North Willamette Boulevard, Portland OR 97203. 503/943-7911. **Fax:** 503/943-7399. **Recorded jobline:** 503/943-7536. **Contact:** Jim Kuffner, Human Resources Director. **World Wide Web address:** http://www.up.edu. **Description:** A Catholic university. **NOTE:** The university also hires through the Oregon State Employment Office.

UNIVERSITY OF ST. THOMAS
3800 Montrose Boulevard, Houston TX 77006. 713/522-7911. **Fax:** 713/525-2125. **Contact:** Employment Department. **World Wide Web address:** http://www.stthom.edu. **Description:** A liberal arts university affiliated with the Catholic Church. The university has an enrollment of 2,700 students. **NOTE:** Entry-level positions and part-time jobs are offered. **Common positions include:** Accountant; Administrative Assistant; Computer Programmer; Education Administrator; Instructor; Librarian; Secretary; SQL Programmer; Systems Analyst; Teacher. **Educational backgrounds include:** Accounting; Business Administration; Liberal Arts; Microsoft Word; Spreadsheets; SQL. **Benefits:** 403(b); Casual Dress - Fridays; Dental Insurance; Disability Coverage; Employee Discounts; Life Insurance; Medical Insurance; Savings Plan; Sick Days (6 - 10); Tuition Assistance; Vacation Days (6 - 10). **Corporate headquarters location:** This Location. **Number of employees at this location:** 250.

UNIVERSITY OF SAN FRANCISCO
2130 Fulton Street, San Francisco CA 94117-1080. 415/422-6707. **Fax:** 415/386-1074. **Recorded jobline:** 415/422-5600. **Contact:** Nora Lee, Personnel Analyst. **E-mail address:** resumes@ usfca.edu. **World Wide Web address:** http://www. usfca.edu. **Description:** Established as one of San Francisco's first universities, the University of San Francisco serves 8,000 students in the schools of arts and sciences, business, education, nursing, law, and professional studies. The university is a nonprofit, private, Catholic and Jesuit institution. **Common positions include:** Administrative Assistant; Administrative Manager; Computer Support Technician; Librarian; Network Engineer; Network Administrator; Psychologist; Secretary; Webmaster. **Educational backgrounds include:** Accounting; Business Administration; C/C++; Communications; Computer Science; Education; HTML; Liberal Arts; MCSE; Microsoft Office; Microsoft Word; QuarkXPress; Software Tech. Support; Spreadsheets. **Benefits:** Daycare Assistance; Dental Insurance; Disability Coverage; Financial Planning Assistance; Life Insurance; Medical Insurance; Public Transit Available; Sick Days (11+); Tuition Assistance; Vacation Days (6 - 10). **Corporate headquarters location:** This Location. **Other area locations:** Cupertino CA; Sacramento CA; San Ramon CA; Santa Rosa CA. **President:** Father Schlegel, S.J. **Number of employees at this location:** 1,100.

UNIVERSITY OF SOUTH CAROLINA
508 Assembly Street, Columbia SC 29208. 803/777-3821. **Contact:** Ms. Barbara Clark, Employment Manager. **World Wide Web address:** http://www.hr.sc.edu. **Description:** A four-year, state university. The university awards bachelor's, master's, and doctoral degrees and enrolls over 25,000 students per year. The University of South Carolina also has campuses in Spartanburg and Aiken. Founded in 1801. **Common positions include:** Accountant; Administrator; Biological Scientist; Blue-Collar Worker Supervisor; Buyer; Chemist; Commercial Artist; Computer Programmer; Department Manager; Economist; General Manager; Geographer; Geologist; Management Trainee; Physicist; Systems Analyst; Technical Writer. **Educational backgrounds include:** Accounting; Art; Biology; Business Administration; Chemistry; Communications; Computer Science; Economics; Engineering; Finance; Geology; Liberal Arts; Marketing; Mathematics; Physics. **Benefits:** Dental Insurance; Disability Coverage; Life Insurance; Medical Insurance; Pension Plan. **Corporate headquarters location:** This Location. **Operations at this facility include:** Research and Development; Service. **Number of employees at this location:** 1,400.

UNIVERSITY OF SOUTHERN CALIFORNIA
3535 South Figueroa Street, Los Angeles CA 90089-1260. 213/740-7252. **Contact:** Employment Manager. **World Wide Web address:** http://www. usc.edu. **Description:** A private university offering bachelor's, master's, doctoral, and professional degrees to approximately 28,000 students. **Common positions include:** Accountant; Administrative Worker; Administrator; Attorney; Buyer; Civil Engineer; Computer Programmer; Electrical Engineer; Financial Analyst; Human Resources Manager; Mechanical Engineer; Project Planner; Purchasing Agent; Secretary; Student Services Specialist; Technical Writer/Editor. **Educational backgrounds include:** Accounting; Art/Design; Biology; Business Administration; Chemistry; Communications; Computer Science; Engineering; Finance; Liberal Arts. **Benefits:** Dental Insurance; Disability Coverage; Employee Discounts; Life Insurance; Medical Insurance; Pension Plan; Savings Plan; Tuition Assistance. **Corporate headquarters location:** This Location. **Operations at this facility include:** Administration; Research and Development; Service.

UNIVERSITY OF SOUTHERN MAINE

96 Falmouth Street, P.O. Box 9300, Portland ME 04104-9300. 207/780-4141. **Contact:** Employment Manager. **World Wide Web address:** http://www. usm.maine.edu. **Description:** University of Southern Maine has an enrollment of approximately 10,500. The university is a comprehensive public institution comprised of eight academic units including applied science, arts and sciences, business, education and human development, law, Lewiston-Auburn College, Muskie School of Public Service, and nursing and health professions. **NOTE:** Part-time jobs and second and third shifts are offered. **Common positions include:** Administrative Assistant; Administrative Manager; Blue-Collar Worker Supervisor; Clerical Supervisor; Computer Support Technician; Database Administrator; Desktop Publishing Specialist; Librarian; Preschool Worker; Teacher. **Benefits:** 403(b); Disability Coverage; Life Insurance; Medical Insurance; On-Site Daycare; Pension Plan; Tuition Assistance. **Number of employees at this location:** 1,200.

UNIVERSITY OF TEXAS AT DALLAS

2601 North Floyd Street, Richardson TX 75080-0688. 972/883-2221. **Contact:** Dorothy Miller, Human Resources Specialist. **World Wide Web address:** http://www.utdallas.edu. **Description:** A state university offering programs at the undergraduate, graduate, and doctoral levels. Enrollment at the university is approximately 10,000. **NOTE:** Part-time jobs are offered. **Common positions include:** Accountant; Administrative Assistant; Auditor; Biochemist; Biological Scientist; Budget Analyst; Computer Engineer; Computer Operator; Computer Programmer; Computer Support Technician; Counselor; Customer Service Rep.; Database Administrator; Database Manager; Dietician; Electrician; Finance Director; Financial Analyst; Graphic Artist; Graphic Designer; Help-Desk Technician; Human Resources Manager; Librarian; MIS Specialist; Molecular Biologist; Multimedia Designer; Psychologist; Purchasing Agent/Manager; Secretary; Software Engineer; Systems Analyst; Technical Writer; Typist. **Educational backgrounds include:** Accounting; Biology; C/C++; Education; Finance; HTML; MBA; Microsoft Office; Microsoft Word. **Benefits:** 401(k); Casual Dress - Fridays; Dental Insurance; Life Insurance; Medical Insurance. **Number of employees at this location:** 2,075.

UNIVERSITY OF TEXAS-PAN AMERICAN

1201 West University Drive, Edinburg TX 78539. 956/381-2011. **Fax:** 956/381-2340. **Recorded jobline:** 956/381-2551. **Contact:** Maribel Ramirez, Employment Representative. **E-mail address:** ramirezm5@panam.edu. **World Wide Web address:** http://www.panam.edu. **Description:** One location of the state university. **Common positions include:** Accountant; Auditor; Buyer; Computer Programmer; Computer Technician; Editor; Graphic Designer; Librarian; Network Administrator; Public Relations Specialist; Purchasing Agent/Manager; Secretary; Systems Analyst. **Educational backgrounds include:** Business Administration; Communications; Computer Science; Education; Microsoft Word; Public Relations; Spreadsheets. **Benefits:** Dental Insurance; Disability Coverage; Life Insurance; Medical Insurance; Pension Plan. **Corporate headquarters location:** Austin TX.

UNIVERSITY OF THE INCARNATE WORD

4301 Broadway Street, Box 320, San Antonio TX 78209. 210/829-6019. **Contact:** Human Resources. **World Wide Web address:** http://www.uiw.edu. **Description:** A Catholic, co-educational, four-year university offering liberal arts and professional studies. The university offers such majors as fine arts, nursing, pre-professional studies, business, and education. The enrollment for the college is approximately 3,000 undergraduate and graduate students. Founded in 1881.

UNIVERSITY OF VIRGINIA

914 Emmett Street, Charlottesville VA 22906. 804/924-4598. **Fax:** 804/924-6911. **Recorded jobline:** 804/924-4400. **Contact:** Human Resources. **World Wide Web address:** http://www. hrs.virginia.edu. **Description:** A state university with 18,000 undergraduate and graduate students enrolled. **NOTE:** Entry-level positions are offered. **Common positions include:** Account Manager; Accountant; Applications Engineer; Architect; Auditor; Budget Analyst; Buyer; Certified Nurses Aide; Civil Engineer; Computer Operator; Computer Programmer; Draftsperson; Editor; Education Administrator; EEG Technologist; Electrician; Financial Analyst; Licensed Practical Nurse; MIS Specialist; Multimedia Designer; Nuclear Medicine Technologist; Nurse Practitioner; Occupational Therapist; Pharmacist; Physical Therapist; Radiological Technologist; Registered Nurse; Respiratory Therapist; Secretary; Software Engineer; Speech-Language Pathologist; Statistician; Surgical Technician; Systems Analyst; Systems Manager; Technical Writer/Editor; Telecommunications Manager; Video Production Coordinator; Webmaster. **Educational backgrounds include:** Biology; Business Administration; Chemistry; Communications; Computer Science; Finance; Health Care. **Benefits:** 401(k); Daycare Assistance; Dental Insurance; Disability Coverage; Job Sharing; Life Insurance; Medical Insurance; Pension Plan; Savings Plan; Tuition Assistance. **Special programs:** Internships. **Corporate headquarters location:** This Location.

UNIVERSITY OF WYOMING

P.O. Box 3422, Laramie WY 82071. 307/766-2215. **Fax:** 307/766-5607. **Recorded jobline:** 307/766-5602. **Contact:** Human Resources. **E-mail address:** jobapps@uwyo.edu. **World Wide Web address:** http://www.uwyo.edu/hr. **Description:** A state university offering bachelor's, master's, and doctoral degree programs. **NOTE:** Part-time jobs are offered. **Common positions include:** Accountant; Administrator; Advertising Clerk; Agricultural Engineer; Architect; Attorney; Automotive Mechanic; Biological Scientist; Blue-Collar Worker Supervisor; Buyer; Chemical Engineer; Chemist; Civil Engineer; Clerical Supervisor; Computer Programmer; Counselor; Department Manager; Draftsperson; Economist; Editor; Education Administrator; Electrician; Financial Analyst; Forester; General Manager; Geographer; Geologist; Human Resources Manager; Human Service Worker; Librarian; Library Technician; Licensed Practical Nurse; Mechanical Engineer; Petroleum Engineer; Physicist; Psychologist; Public Relations Specialist; Purchasing Agent; Radio Announcer; Radiological Technologist; Registered Nurse; Reporter; Restaurant/Food Service Manager; Software Engineer; Speech-Language Pathologist; Systems Analyst; Teacher; Technical Writer/Editor; Wholesale and Retail Buyer. **Educational backgrounds include:** Accounting; Art/Design; Biology; Business Administration; Chemistry; Communications; Computer Science; Economics; Engineering; Finance; Geology; Liberal Arts; Marketing; Mathematics; Physics. **Benefits:** 403(b); Dental Insurance; Disability Coverage; Employee Discounts; Flexible Schedule; Life Insurance; Medical Insurance; Pension Plan; Public Transit Available; Sick Days; TSAs; Tuition Assistance; Vacation Days. **Special programs:** Internships;

Summer Jobs. **Corporate headquarters location:** This Location. **Operations at this facility include:** Administration; Education; Regional Headquarters. **Number of employees at this location:** 2,600.

UTAH STATE UNIVERSITY

9510 Old Main Hill, Logan UT 84322-9510. 435/797-1805. **Contact:** Clark M. England, Director of Personnel Services. **World Wide Web address:** http://www.usu.edu. **Description:** A four-year state university with an enrollment of approximately 20,000 students. **Common positions include:** Accountant; Administrator; Advertising Clerk; Aerospace Engineer; Agricultural Scientist; Architect; Biological Scientist; Biomedical Engineer; Blue-Collar Worker Supervisor; Buyer; Ceramics Engineer; Chemist; Civil Engineer; Computer Programmer; Dietician; Draftsperson; Economist; Editor; Electrical Engineer; Financial Analyst; Food Scientist; Forester; Geographer; Geologist; Human Resources Manager; Industrial Engineer; Marketing Specialist; Mechanical Engineer; Metallurgical Engineer; Physicist; Public Relations Specialist; Purchasing Agent; Quality Control Supervisor; Reporter; Statistician; Systems Analyst; Technical Writer. **Educational backgrounds include:** Accounting; Agricultural Science; Art; Biology; Business Administration; Chemistry; Communications; Computer Science; Economics; Engineering; Finance; Geology; Liberal Arts; Marketing; Mathematics; Physics. **Benefits:** Dental Insurance; Disability Coverage; Employee Discounts; Life Insurance; Medical Insurance; Pension Plan; Tuition Assistance. **Special programs:** Internships. **Corporate headquarters location:** This Location.

VALDOSTA STATE UNIVERSITY

1500 North Patterson Street, Valdosta GA 31698. 912/293-6100. **Contact:** Laurie Fontaine, Employment Manager. **World Wide Web address:** http://www.valdosta.edu. **Description:** A state university with 9,700 students enrolled. **Common positions include:** Accountant; Assistant Manager; Budget Analyst; Buyer; Cashier; Chef Worker; Clerical Supervisor; Computer Operator; Computer Programmer; Construction Contractor; Department Manager; Dietician/Nutritionist; Electrician; Employment Interviewer; Financial Manager; Graphic Artist; Human Resources Manager; Landscape Architect; Librarian; Library Technician; Payroll Clerk; Postal Clerk; Preschool Worker; Printing Press Operator; Psychologist; Purchasing Agent/Manager; Registered Nurse; Restaurant Manager; Secretary; Systems Analyst; Teacher/Professor; Truck Driver; Typist; Welder. **Educational backgrounds include:** Accounting; Art/Design; Biology; Business Administration; Chemistry; Communications; Computer Science; Economics; Engineering; Finance; Geology; Liberal Arts; Marketing; Mathematics; Physics. **Benefits:** Daycare Assistance; Dental Insurance; Disability Coverage; Life Insurance; Medical Insurance; Pension Plan.

VASSAR COLLEGE

124 Raymond Avenue, Poughkeepsie NY 12604. 914/437-7000. **Fax:** 914/437-7298. **Contact:** G.H. Chasen, Director. **World Wide Web address:** http://www.vassar.edu. **Description:** Vassar College is a four-year undergraduate college focusing on the liberal arts. Approximately 2,250 students are enrolled at Vassar. Founded in 1860. **Common positions include:** Administrative Assistant; Clerical Supervisor; Computer Programmer; Licensed Practical Nurse; Secretary; Typist. **Benefits:** Life Insurance; Medical Insurance; Pension Plan.

VILLANOVA UNIVERSITY

800 Lancaster Avenue, Villanova PA 19085-1699. 610/519-7900. **Fax:** 610/519-6667. **Contact:** Barbara Kearns, Employment Coordinator. **World Wide Web address:** http://www.vill.edu. **Description:** A Catholic university serving approximately 6,000 full-time undergraduates and 4,000 graduate and part-time students in the Colleges of Arts & Sciences, Engineering, Commerce & Finance, Nursing, and Law, as well as an MBA program. Founded in 1842. **Common positions include:** Accountant; Administrative Assistant; Blue-Collar Worker Supervisor; Budget Analyst; Buyer; Chemist; CFO; Clerical Supervisor; Computer Animator; Computer Operator; Computer Programmer; Controller; Cost Estimator; Counselor; Database Manager; Electrician; Financial Analyst; Graphic Artist; Graphic Designer; Human Resources Manager; Librarian; MIS Specialist; Psychologist; Public Relations Specialist; Purchasing Agent; Registered Nurse; Secretary; Systems Analyst; Systems Manager; Teacher; Telecommunications Manager; Typist. **Educational backgrounds include:** Accounting; Business Administration; Computer Science; Engineering; Finance; Liberal Arts. **Benefits:** 403(b); Dental Insurance; Disability Coverage; Employee Discounts; Life Insurance; Medical Insurance; Pension Plan; Public Transit Available; Savings Plan; Tuition Assistance. **Corporate headquarters location:** This Location. **President:** Reverend Edmund J. Dobbin.

VIRGINIA POLYTECHNICAL INSTITUTE

Southgate Center, 1st Floor, Blacksburg VA 24061-0318. 540/231-5301. **Fax:** 540/231-3830. **Contact:** Personnel Services. **World Wide Web address:** http://www.ps.vt.edu. **Description:** A land grant university that provides advanced instruction, research, and outreach programs. Continuing education is also offered at Roanoke Graduate Center, Northern Virginia Graduate Center, and Tidewater Graduate Center. **Common positions include:** Accountant; Administrative Manager; Agricultural Engineer; Agricultural Scientist; Architect; Budget Analyst; Clerical Supervisor; Computer Programmer; Counselor; Education Administrator; Electrician; Food Scientist; Forester; Human Resources Manager; Landscape Architect; Librarian; Library Technician; Mechanical Engineer; Pharmacist; Physicist; Property and Real Estate Manager; Public Relations Specialist; Purchasing Agent; Radio Announcer; Registered Nurse; Restaurant Manager; Science Technologist; Sociologist; Software Engineer; Systems Analyst. **Educational backgrounds include:** Accounting; Art/Design; Biology; Business Administration; Chemistry; Communications; Computer Science; Economics; Engineering; Finance; Geology; Health Care; Liberal Arts; M.D./Medicine; Marketing; Mathematics; Physics. **Benefits:** Dental Insurance; Leave Time; Life Insurance; Medical Insurance; Pension Plan; Sabbatical Leave; Savings Plan. **Corporate headquarters location:** This Location.

WALSH COLLEGE

P.O. Box 7006, Troy MI 48007-7006. 248/689-8282. **Fax:** 248/689-3306. **Contact:** Personnel Coordinator. **Description:** A business college with approximately 4,000 undergraduate and graduate students. **Common positions include:** Accountant; Admissions Rep.; Buyer; Computer Programmer; Counselor; Customer Service Representative; Education Administrator; Marketing Specialist; Public Relations Specialist; Systems Analyst; Teacher/Professor. **Educational backgrounds include:** Accounting; Business Administration; Computer Science; Marketing. **Benefits:** 401(k); Daycare Assistance; Dental Insurance; Disability

Coverage; Employee Discounts; Life Insurance; Medical Insurance; Pension Plan; Savings Plan; Tuition Assistance. **Corporate headquarters location:** This Location. **Operations at this facility include:** Administration; Sales; Service. **Listed on:** Privately held. **Number of employees at this location:** 200.

WELDON CITY SCHOOL DISTRICT
301 Mulberry Street, Weldon NC 27890. 252/536-4821. **Fax:** 252/536-3062. **Contact:** Personnel Director. **Description:** A public school district. **Common positions include:** Counselor; Education Administrator; Librarian; Preschool Worker; Speech-Language Pathologist; Teacher; Typist. **Educational backgrounds include:** Biology; Chemistry; Mathematics. **Benefits:** 401(k); Dental Insurance; Life Insurance; Medical Insurance; Tuition Assistance. **Special programs:** Training. **Corporate headquarters location:** This Location.

WENTWORTH INSTITUTE OF TECHNOLOGY
550 Huntington Avenue, Boston MA 02115-5998. 617/442-9010. **Fax:** 617/989-4196. **Contact:** Anne Gill, Associate Vice President of Human Resources. **World Wide Web address:** http://www.wit.edu. **Description:** A technical university noted for its strengths in engineering, science, architecture, and design. Total student enrollment is approximately 3,300. **Common positions include:** Accountant; Dispatcher; Education Administrator; Instructor; Library Technician; Receptionist; Secretary; Teacher; Typist. **Educational backgrounds include:** Art/Design; Business Administration; Engineering; Liberal Arts. **Benefits:** Daycare Assistance; Dental Insurance; Disability Coverage; Employee Discounts; Life Insurance; Medical Insurance; Pension Plan; Savings Plan; Tuition Assistance. **Special programs:** Internships. **Corporate headquarters location:** This Location.

WESTED
730 Harrison Street, San Francisco CA 94107. 415/565-3000. **Contact:** Personnel Manager. **E-mail address:** jobs@wested.org. **World Wide Web address:** http://www.wested.org. **Description:** WestEd is a nonprofit educational agency focused on improving the quality of education by helping policy makers and practitioners apply knowledge from research, development, and practice. Founded in 1966. **NOTE:** Jobseekers should send resumes to Ann Williams, Personnel Manager, 4665 Lampson Avenue, Los Alamitos CA 90720. **Common positions include:** Education Administrator; Mathematician; Secretary; Systems Analyst. **Educational backgrounds include:** Accounting; Computer Science; Education; Liberal Arts; Mathematics. **Benefits:** Dental Insurance; Disability Coverage; Life Insurance; Medical Insurance; Pension Plan; Savings Plan. **Corporate headquarters location:** This Location. **Other U.S. locations:** Tucson AZ. **Operations at this facility include:** Research and Development.

WESTERN MICHIGAN UNIVERSITY
1300 Seibert Administration Building, Kalamazoo MI 49008. 616/387-3626. **Contact:** Don Keith, Director of Employment. **Description:** A four-year university offering undergraduate and graduate programs of study. **Common positions include:** Accountant; Administrator; Architect; Attorney; Biological Scientist; Buyer; Chemist; Civil Engineer; Computer Programmer; Department Manager; Dietician; Draftsperson; Editor; Electrical Engineer; Financial Analyst; General Manager; Human Resources Manager; Instructor; Marketing Specialist; Operations Manager; Physicist; Public Relations Specialist; Purchasing Agent; Reporter; Systems Analyst; Technical Writer; Transportation

Specialist. **Educational backgrounds include:** Accounting; Art; Biology; Business Administration; Chemistry; Communications; Computer Science; Economics; Engineering; Finance; Geology; Liberal Arts; Marketing; Mathematics; Physics. **Benefits:** Dental Insurance; Disability Coverage; Employee Discounts; Life Insurance; Medical Insurance; Pension Plan; Tuition Assistance. **Corporate headquarters location:** This Location.

WHITWORTH COLLEGE
300 West Hawthorne Road, Spokane WA 99251. 509/777-1000. **Fax:** 509/777-3773. **Recorded jobline:** 509/777-3202. **Contact:** Human Resources. **World Wide Web address:** http://www. whitworth.edu. **Description:** A private, liberal arts college affiliated with the Presbyterian Church. Academic programs include majors in 17 departments, interdisciplinary areas of concentration, off-campus internships and foreign studies, graduate learning opportunities, and career preparation programs. **President:** Bill Robinson. **Facilities Manager:** Keith Sullivan.

WICHITA AREA TECHNICAL COLLEGE
201 North Water, Wichita KS 67211. 316/973-9282. **Contact:** Human Resources. **World Wide Web address:** http://www.watc.tec.ks.us. **Description:** A nonprofit technical college. **NOTE:** Entry-level positions are offered. **Common positions include:** Administrative Assistant; Computer Programmer; Computer Support Technician; Computer Technician; Controller; Counselor; Education Administrator; Graphic Artist; Network Administrator; Preschool Worker; Public Relations Specialist; Secretary; Teacher. **Educational backgrounds include:** Computer Science; Education; Finance; HTML; MCSE; Microsoft Office; Microsoft Word; Public Relations; Spreadsheets. **Benefits:** Dental Insurance; Disability Coverage; Flexible Schedule; Life Insurance; Medical Insurance; Pension Plan. **President:** Dr. Rosemary A. Kirby.

WICHITA STATE UNIVERSITY
1845 North Fairmount Street, Box 15, Wichita KS 67260-0015. 316/978-3065. **Fax:** 316/978-3201. **Recorded jobline:** 316/978-3344. **Contact:** Frankie Brown, Human Resources. **World Wide Web address:** http://www.wichita.edu. **Description:** A state university with an enrollment of approximately 13,000 part-time students who are predominantly beyond the traditional college age. The university offers undergraduate, graduate, and continuing education courses. **NOTE:** Entry-level positions as well as second and third shifts are offered. **Common positions include:** Account Rep.; Accountant; Administrative Assistant; Administrative Manager; Architect; Auditor; Blue-Collar Worker Supervisor; Broadcast Technician; Budget Analyst; Buyer; Civil Engineer; Clerical Supervisor; Computer Operator; Computer Programmer; Controller; Counselor; Customer Service Representative; Daycare Worker; Editor; Editorial Assistant; Education Administrator; Electrician; General Manager; Graphic Artist; Graphic Designer; Human Resources Manager; Internet Services Manager; Librarian; Licensed Practical Nurse; Management Analyst; Marketing Specialist; Multimedia Designer; Psychologist; Public Relations Specialist; Purchasing Agent; Radio Announcer; Registered Nurse; Reporter; Secretary; Systems Analyst; Systems Manager; Teacher; Technical Writer; Telecommunications Manager; Typist; Video Production Coordinator; Webmaster. **Educational backgrounds include:** Accounting; Art/Design; Business Administration; Communications; Computer Science; Public Relations. **Benefits:** Dental Insurance; Disability Coverage; Employee

Discounts; Financial Planning Assistance; Life Insurance; Medical Insurance; On-Site Daycare; Pension Plan; Public Transit Available; Savings Plan; Tuition Assistance. **Corporate headquarters location:** This Location. **Operations at this facility include:** Administration; Research and Development; Service. **President:** Dr. Donald L. Beggs.

WILLIAM PATERSON UNIVERSITY OF NEW JERSEY
300 Pompton Road, Wayne NJ 07470. 973/720-2603. **Contact:** Director of Human Resources. **World Wide Web address:** http://www.willpaterson.edu. **Description:** A public university with approximately 9,000 students. Programs include liberal arts, nursing, sciences, English, history, and music.

WILLIAMSBURG COUNTY SCHOOL DISTRICT
423 School Street, Kingstree SC 29556. 843/354-5571. **Fax:** 843/354-9515. **Contact:** Mr. Francis Burrows, Director of Human Resources. **Description:** A public school district. **Common positions include:** Accountant; Clerical Supervisor; Computer Operator; Computer Programmer; Education Administrator; Human Resources

Manager; Librarian; Payroll Clerk; Preschool Worker; Psychologist; Public Relations Specialist; Purchasing Agent; Receptionist; Registered Nurse; Restaurant Manager; Secretary; Social Worker; Speech-Language Pathologist; Systems Analyst; Teacher Aide; Teacher; Transportation Specialist; Typist. **Educational backgrounds include:** Accounting; Art; Biology; Business Administration; Chemistry; Communications; Computer Science; Economics; Finance; Mathematics; Physics; Special Education. **Benefits:** Credit Union; Dental Insurance; Disability Coverage; Life Insurance; Medical Insurance; Pension Plan; Tuition Assistance. **Corporate headquarters location:** This Location.

XAVIER UNIVERSITY
3800 Victory Parkway, Cincinnati OH 45207-4641. 513/745-3638. **Fax:** 513/745-3644. **Contact:** Kathleen Riga, Assistant Vice President of Human Resources. **World Wide Web address:** http://www.xu.edu. **Description:** A private, coeducational, liberal arts, Jesuit university. **Benefits:** 403(b); Dental Insurance; Disability Coverage; Employee Discounts; Life Insurance; Medical Insurance; Tuition Assistance.

For more information on career opportunities in educational services:

<u>Associations</u>

AMERICAN ASSOCIATION FOR HIGHER EDUCATION
One DuPont Circle, Suite 360, Washington DC 20036. 202/293-6440. World Wide Web address: http://www.aahe.org.

AMERICAN ASSOCIATION OF SCHOOL ADMINISTRATORS
1801 North Moore Street, Arlington VA 22209. 703/528-0700. Fax: 703/841-1543. World Wide Web address: http://www.aasa.org. An organization of school system leaders. The $244.00 membership includes a national conference on education; programs and seminars; *The School Administrator,* a monthly magazine; *Leadership News,* a monthly newspaper; *Leaders' Edge, Back Fence,* and *Edge City,* quarterly publications; and a catalog of other publications and audiovisuals.

AMERICAN FEDERATION OF TEACHERS
555 New Jersey Avenue NW, Washington DC 20001. 202/879-4400. World Wide Web address: http://www.aft.org.

COLLEGE AND UNIVERSITY PERSONNEL ASSOCIATION
1233 20th Street NW, Suite 301, Washington DC 20036. 202/429-0311. World Wide Web address: http://www.cupa.org. An organization of higher education human resource professionals. Membership is required and is available for students.

NATIONAL ASSOCIATION FOR COLLEGE ADMISSION COUNSELING
1631 Prince Street, Alexandria VA 22314. 703/836-2222. World Wide Web address: http://www.nacac.com. An education association of school counselors and admissions officers who assist students in making the transition from high school to post-secondary education.

NATIONAL ASSOCIATION OF BIOLOGY TEACHERS
11250 Roger Bacon Drive, Suite 19, Reston VA 20190. 703/471-1134. Toll-free phone: 800/406-0775. Fax: 703/435-5582. E-mail address:

nabter@aol.com. World Wide Web address: http://www.nabt.org. A professional organization for biology and life science educators.

NATIONAL ASSOCIATION OF COLLEGE AND UNIVERSITY BUSINESS OFFICERS
2501 M Street NW, Suite 400, Washington DC 20037. 202/861-2500. World Wide Web address: http://www.nacubo.org. Association for those involved in the financial administration and management of higher education. Membership required.

NATIONAL COMMISSION FOR COOPERATIVE EDUCATION (NCCE)
360 Huntington Avenue, 384 CP, Boston MA 02115. 617/373-3770. E-mail address: ncce@lynx.neu.edu. Offers free information to students interested in learning more about cooperative education programs.

NATIONAL COUNCIL FOR THE SOCIAL STUDIES
3501 Newark Street NW, Washington DC 20016. 202/966-7840. Fax: 202/966-2061. World Wide Web address: http://www.ncss.org. Offers publications, conferences, Internet resources, and information on awards and grants to 20,000 educators nationwide.

NATIONAL COUNCIL OF TEACHERS OF ENGLISH
1111 West Kenyon Road, Urbana IL 61801. 217/328-3870. Toll-free phone: 800/369-6283. Fax: 217/328-9645. World Wide Web address: http://ncte.org. Fosters professional growth for English teachers. The organization has 80,000 members worldwide and publishes a newspaper and related journals.

NATIONAL SCIENCE TEACHERS ASSOCIATION
1840 Wilson Boulevard, Arlington VA 22201-3000. 703/243-7100. World Wide Web address: http://www.nsta.org. Organization committed to the improvement of science education at all levels, preschool through college. Publishes five journals, a newspaper, and a number of special publications. Also conducts national and regional conventions.

NATIONAL SOCIETY FOR EXPERIENTIAL EDUCATION (NSEE)
1703 North Beauregard Street, 4th Floor, Alexandria VA 22311-1714. 703/575-5475. E-mail address: info@nsee.org. World Wide Web address: http://www.nsee.org. A membership organization offering publications, conferences, and a resource center. Among the society's publications is *The Experienced Hand: A Student Manual for Making the Most of an Internship*.

TEACHERS OF ENGLISH TO SPEAKERS OF OTHER LANGUAGES, INC. (TESOL)
700 South Washington Street, Suite 200, Alexandria VA 22314. 703/836-0774. Fax: 703/836-7864. E-mail address: tesol@tesol.edu. World Wide Web address: http://www.tesol.edu. An advocacy group that develops programs, services, and products which promote the professional development of both students and teachers of English as a second or foreign language.

Directories

NON-PROFITS & EDUCATION JOB FINDER
Planning/Communications, 7215 Oak Avenue, River Forest IL 60305. 708/366-5200. World Wide Web address: http://www.jobfindersonline.com. Provides Websites, BBS listings, job and resume databases, newspapers, magazines, and salary surveys.

WASHINGTON EDUCATION ASSOCIATION DIRECTORY
Council for Advancement and Support of Education, 1307 New York Avenue, Suite 1000, Washington DC 20005-4701. 202/328-5900. World Wide Web address: http://www.case.org.

Magazines

AMERICAN LANGUAGE REVIEW
6363 Wilshire Boulevard, Suite 214, Los Angeles CA 90048. 323/658-7620. Fax: 323/658-7530. World Wide Web address: http://www.alr.org. Subscription: $19.95 per year for six issues.

THE ENGLISH TEACHER: AN INTERNATIONAL JOURNAL
Assumption University, Huamark, Bangkapi, Bangkok 10240 Thailand. Contact: John Joseph Courtney, Managing Editor. World Wide Web address: http://elt.au.edu/info.html. Subscription: $35.00 per year for three issues.

TRANSITIONS ABROAD
Transitions Abroad Publishing Inc., P.O. Box 1300, Amherst MA 01004-1300. 413/256-3414. Fax: 413/256-0373. E-mail address: info@transabroad.com. World Wide Web address: http://www.transabroad.com. Discusses international teaching programs and opportunities.

Online Services

ACADEMIC EMPLOYMENT NETWORK
World Wide Web address: http://www.academploy. com. This site offers information for the educational professional, and allows you to search for positions nationwide. It also has information on other sites of interest, educational products, certification requirements by state, and relocation services.

ACADEMIC POSITION NETWORK
World Wide Web address: http://www.apnjobs.com. Updated daily with employment listings for national and international positions.

THE CHRONICLE OF HIGHER EDUCATION
World Wide Web address: http://chronicle.com/jobs. This Website provides job listings from the weekly published newspaper *The Chronicle of Higher Education*. Besides featuring articles from the paper, this site also offers employment opportunities. You can search for information by geographic location, type of position, and teaching fields.

DAVE'S ESL CAFE
World Wide Web address: http://www.eslcafe.com. A site for English as a Second Language (ESL) and English as a Foreign Language (EFL) students and teachers. Services include an ESL bookstore, a job center, and many other links.

EDUCATION FORUM
Go: Edforum. This CompuServe discussion group is open to educators of all levels.

HIGHEREDJOBS ONLINE
World Wide Web address: http://www.higheredjobs. com. This site is searchable by type of position, state, or a specific institution.

JOBWEB SCHOOL DISTRICTS SEARCH
World Wide Web address: http://www.jobweb. org/search/schools. Provides a search engine for school districts across the country. The site is run by the National Association of Colleges and Employers and it also provides information on colleges and career fairs.

LIBRARY & INFORMATION SCIENCE JOBSEARCH
World Wide Web address: http://carousel.lis.uiuc. edu/~jobs.

THE PRIVATE SCHOOL EMPLOYMENT NETWORK
World Wide Web address: http://www. privateschooljobs.com. Offers private school openings. There is a $25.00 fee to post a resume on the site.

THE TEACHER'S LOUNGE
Keyword: teacher's lounge. An America Online discussion group for teachers of kindergarten through the twelfth grade.

VISUAL NATION ARTS JOBS LINKS
World Wide Web address: http://www.visualarts. com. Provides links to other sites that post academic and arts job openings and information.

Electronic/Industrial Electrical Equipment

You can expect to find the following types of companies in this chapter:
Electronic Machines and Systems • Semiconductor Manufacturers

Some helpful information: *The average annual salary of electricians is approximately $25,000 - $30,000. Precision assemblers of electronic products generally earn between $15,000 and $22,000. Electrical and electronics engineers can earn upwards of $50,000 annually.*

ADE CORPORATION
80 Wilson Way, Westwood MA 02090. 781/467-3500. **Contact:** Human Resources. **World Wide Web address:** http://www.ade.com. **Description:** Develops and manufactures measurement and automation equipment for the instrumentation, electronics, and semiconductor markets. **NOTE:** Entry-level positions are offered. **Common positions include:** Accountant/Auditor; Buyer; Electrical/Electronics Engineer; Human Resources Manager; Materials Engineer; Mechanical Engineer; MIS Specialist; Physicist; Purchasing Agent/Manager; Quality Control Supervisor; Software Engineer; Technical Writer/Editor. **Educational backgrounds include:** Accounting; Computer Science; Engineering; Finance; Physics. **Benefits:** 401(k); Dental Insurance; Disability Coverage; Life Insurance; Medical Insurance; Tuition Assistance. **Special programs:** Internships. **Corporate headquarters location:** This Location. **Other U.S. locations:** San Jose CA; Charlotte NC; Dallas TX; Vancouver WA. **Number of employees at this location:** 200.

AER ENERGY RESOURCES, INC.
4600 Highland Parkway, Suite G, Smyrna GA 30082. 770/433-2127. **Contact:** Diana Lampkin, Human Resources Manager. **World Wide Web address:** http://www.aern.com. **Description:** Develops high-energy density, zinc-air batteries that provide long, continuous run-time for portable electronic equipment. **Corporate headquarters location:** This Location. **Number of employees at this location:** 40.

AFC CABLE SYSTEMS, INC.
50 Kennedy Plaza, Suite 1250, Providence RI 02903. 401/453-2000. **Contact:** Human Resources. **World Wide Web address:** http://www.afcweb.com. **Description:** Designs, manufactures, and supplies electrical transmission products, which are typically used in office buildings, institutional facilities, computer centers, office equipment, and other nonresidential constructions. Products include flexible wiring systems, prewired armored cable, flexible conduit, and steel fittings used in the installation of telephone, fax, and data systems. Primary customers are electrical supply wholesalers and distributors, and do-it-yourself retail outlets nationwide. **NOTE:** Interested jobseekers should address inquiries to Human Resources, AFC Cable Systems, 272 Duchaine Boulevard, New Bedford MA 02745. **Benefits:** 401(k); Medical Insurance; Retirement Plan. **Corporate headquarters location:** This Location. **Other U.S. locations:** Brea CA; Burlington NJ; Linden NJ; Byesville OH; Bensalem PA; Garland TX. **Subsidiaries include:** TNK, Inc. **Parent company:** Tyco International Ltd. **Listed on:** NASDAQ. **Number of employees nationwide:** 495.

AVX CORPORATION
P.O. Box 867, Myrtle Beach SC 29578-0867. 843/448-9411. **Contact:** Kathryn Byrd, Human Resources Manager. **World Wide Web address:** http://www.avxcorp.com. **Description:** A worldwide manufacturer and supplier of a broad line of passive electronic components and related products. Passive electronic components include ceramic and tantalum capacitors, both in leaded and surface-mount versions. AVX Corporation's customers include original equipment manufacturers in industries such as telecommunications, computers, automotive electronics, medical devices and instrumentation, industrial instrumentation, military and aerospace electronic systems, and consumer electronics. The company also manufactures and sells electronic connectors and distributes and sells certain passive components and connectors manufactured by its parent company. **Corporate headquarters location:** This Location. **Parent company:** Kyocera Corporation, a public Japanese company, is principally engaged in the worldwide manufacture and distribution of ceramic and related products including fine ceramic parts, semiconductor parts, electronic components, and consumer-related products; electronic equipment; and optical instruments. **Listed on:** New York Stock Exchange. **Stock exchange symbol:** AVX. **Other U.S. locations:**
• 5701 East Fourth Plain Boulevard, Vancouver WA 98661. 360/696-2840.

ACCU-SORT SYSTEMS, INC.
511 School House Road, Telford PA 18969. 215/723-0981. **Toll-free phone:** 800/BAR-CODE. **Fax:** 215/721-5551. **Contact:** Roxanne Detweiler, Human Resources. **E-mail address:** jobs@accusort.com. **World Wide Web address:** http://www.accusort.com. **Description:** A leading manufacturer of bar code scanners and other material handling systems. **NOTE:** Entry-level positions and part-time jobs are offered. **Common positions include:** Account Manager; Accountant; Administrative Assistant; Customer Service Rep.; Design Engineer; Draftsperson; Electrical/Electronics Engineer; Human Resources Manager; Manufacturing Engineer; Marketing Specialist; Mechanical Engineer; MIS Specialist; Quality Assurance Engineer; Sales Representative; Software Engineer. **Educational backgrounds include:** Accounting; Business Administration; C/C++; Engineering; MBA; Microsoft Office; Microsoft Word; Software Development; Spreadsheets; Visual Basic. **Benefits:** 401(k); Casual Dress - Daily; Dental Insurance; Disability Coverage; Employee Discounts; Flexible Schedule; Life Insurance; Medical Insurance; Profit Sharing; Relocation Assistance; Sick Days (1 - 5); Telecommuting; Tuition Assistance; Vacation Days (10 - 20). **Special programs:** Internships; Training; Co-ops;

Summer Jobs. **Office hours:** Monday - Friday, 8:00 a.m. - 5:30 p.m. **Corporate headquarters location:** This Location. **Other U.S. locations:** Nationwide. **International locations:** Worldwide. **Chairman/ CEO:** Al Wurz. **Number of employees nationwide:** 500.

ACME ELECTRIC CORPORATION
9962 Route 446, Cuba NY 14727. 716/968-2400. **Fax:** 716/968-3948. **Contact:** Sandra Sleggs, Human Resources Manager. **World Wide Web address:** http://www.acmeelec.com. **Description:** Provides program management to develop sophisticated electronics products. Products encompass all disciplines associated with the design and manufacture of electronic products including hardware (analog, RF, power supply, and digital interface); mechanical (structural specifications, electronic packaging, wiring, cable, and thermal); prototyping (renderings, models, and fast turnaround); and validation testing (design compliance, safety, and regulatory). Capabilities include 3-D modeling, CAD/CAE/CAM systems, HALT/HASS test equipment, and EMI. Acme Electric Corporation serves the telecommunications, computer, medical diagnostics, and industrial markets. **Common positions include:** Accountant/ Auditor; Computer Programmer; Customer Service Rep.; Electrical/Electronics Engineer; Human Resources Manager; Industrial Engineer; Mechanical Engineer; Operations/Production Manager; Purchasing Agent/Manager; Quality Control Supervisor. **Educational backgrounds include:** Accounting; Business Administration; Computer Science; Engineering. **Benefits:** 401(k); Dental Insurance; Disability Coverage; Life Insurance; Medical Insurance; Pension Plan; Profit Sharing; Savings Plan; Tuition Assistance. **Corporate headquarters location:** East Aurora NY. **Other U.S. locations:** Tempe AZ; Lumberton NC. **Listed on:** New York Stock Exchange. **Number of employees at this location:** 340.

ACTION MANUFACTURING COMPANY
100 East Erie Avenue, Philadelphia PA 19134. 215/739-6400. **Contact:** Personnel. **Description:** A manufacturer of precision electromechanical instruments and ordnance products. **Common positions include:** Accountant; Administrator; Chemist; Computer Programmer; Financial Analyst; Geologist/Geophysicist; Mechanical Engineer. **Educational backgrounds include:** Accounting; Chemistry; Engineering; Finance; Geology. **Benefits:** Dental Insurance; Disability Coverage; Life Insurance; Medical Insurance; Savings Plan; Tuition Assistance. **Corporate headquarters location:** This Location.

ADVACOM, INC.
5620 West Road, McKean PA 16426. 814/476-7774. **Toll-free phone:** 800/678-0512. **Fax:** 814/476-7724. **Contact:** Human Resources. **World Wide Web address:** http://www.advacom.com. **Description:** Distributes electronic components. Founded in 1971. **NOTE:** Entry-level positions and second and third shifts are offered. **Common positions include:** Account Manager; Account Rep.; Administrative Assistant; Branch Manager; Buyer; Chief Financial Officer; Computer Programmer; Credit Manager; Customer Service Rep.; Human Resources Manager; Marketing Manager; Marketing Specialist; Operations Manager; Purchasing Agent/Manager; Quality Control Supervisor; Sales Executive; Sales Manager; Sales Representative; Systems Analyst. **Benefits:** 401(k); Disability Coverage; Life Insurance; Medical Insurance; Profit Sharing. **Special programs:** Summer Jobs. **Corporate headquarters location:** This Location. **President:**

Tom Calicchio. **Number of employees at this location:** 120.

ADVANCED INPUT DEVICES
600 West Wilbur Avenue, Coeur d'Alene ID 83815. 208/765-8000. **Fax:** 208/772-7807. **Contact:** Mrs. Frances Brastrup, Personnel Manager. **World Wide Web address:** http://www.advanced-input.com. **Description:** A leading manufacturer of custom keyboards for electronic instruments and systems. **Common positions include:** Accountant; Buyer; Computer Programmer; Customer Service Rep.; Draftsperson; Electrical/Electronics Engineer; Mechanical Engineer; Operations/Production Manager; Project Engineer; Purchasing Agent/ Manager. **Benefits:** 401(k); Dental Insurance; Disability Coverage; Life Insurance; Medical Insurance; Sick Days; Tuition Assistance; Vacation Days. **Special programs:** Internships. **Corporate headquarters location:** This Location. **Number of employees at this location:** 280.

ADVANCED INTERCONNECTIONS CORP.
5 Energy Way, West Warwick RI 02893. 401/823-5200. **Fax:** 401/823-8723. **Contact:** Dana C. DaCosta, Personnel. **World Wide Web address:** http://www.advintcorp.com. **Description:** Designs, develops, and manufactures interconnect products for the electronics industry. **NOTE:** Entry-level positions are offered. **Common positions include:** Applications Engineer; Design Engineer; Electrical/ Electronics Engineer; Manufacturing Engineer; Mechanical Engineer; Quality Control Supervisor. **Educational backgrounds include:** Engineering. **Benefits:** 401(k); Dental Insurance; Disability Coverage; Life Insurance; Medical Insurance; Tuition Assistance. **Corporate headquarters location:** This Location. **Listed on:** Privately held. **Number of employees at this location:** 140.

ADVANCED MICRO DEVICES, INC. (AMD)
One AMD Place, P.O. Box 3453, Sunnyvale CA 94088-3453. 408/732-2400. **Contact:** Human Resources. **World Wide Web address:** http://www. amd.com. **Description:** Designs, develops, manufactures, and markets complex monolithic integrated circuits for use by electronic equipment and systems manufacturers, primarily for instrument applications and products involved in computation and communications. **Common positions include:** Computer Engineer; Electrical/Electronics Engineer; Materials Engineer. **Corporate headquarters location:** This Location.

ADVANCED PHOTONIX, INC.
1240 Avenida Acaso, Camarillo CA 93012. 805/987-0146. **Contact:** Human Resources Manager. **Description:** Advanced Photonix, Inc., with its subsidiary, Silicon Detector Corporation, develops, markets, and manufactures proprietary, advanced, solid-state silicon photodetection devices which utilize Avalanche Photodetection (APD) technology. These devices are designed to detect and amplify signals from light and radiant energy sources and convert them into electrical impulses or signals. Products are used for measurement, control, monitoring, and other functions in industrial, medical, military, scientific, and other commercial applications. Such applications include medical diagnostic imaging, airport security detection, fiberoptic communications, and nuclear radiation monitoring and detection systems. **Corporate headquarters location:** This Location. **Number of employees at this location:** 95.

ADVANCED TECHNOLOGY MATERIALS, INC. (ATMI)
7 Commerce Drive, Danbury CT 06810. 203/794-1100. **Fax:** 203/792-8040. **Contact:** Phyllis

Banucci, Human Resources Manager. **World Wide Web address:** http://www.atmi.com. **Description:** A leading developer of semiconductor materials and devices. ATMI specializes in chemical vapor deposition and thin-film technology, synthesis of organometallic reagents, wide bandgap semiconductor substrates and devices, and both adsorption- and combustion-based air pollution abatement equipment. **Common positions include:** Chemical Engineer; Chemist; Electrical/Electronics Engineer; Mechanical Engineer; Metallurgical Engineer. **Educational backgrounds include:** Chemistry; Engineering; Physics. **Benefits:** 401(k); Dental Insurance; Life Insurance; Medical Insurance; Tuition Assistance. **Special programs:** Internships. **Corporate headquarters location:** This Location. **Other U.S. locations:** Phoenix AZ; San Jose CA. **Subsidiaries include:** EcoSys manufactures environmental equipment for the semiconductor industry. **Listed on:** NASDAQ. **Stock exchange symbol:** ATMI. **Annual sales/revenues:** $21 - $50 million. **Number of employees at this location:** 120. **Number of employees nationwide:** 225.

ALIGN-RITE
2428 North Ontario Street, Burbank CA 91504. 818/843-7220. **Contact:** Human Resources. **World Wide Web address:** http://www.alignrite.com. **Description:** A manufacturer of photomasks for the semiconductor industry. **Corporate headquarters location:** This Location.

ALPHA INDUSTRIES, INC.
20 Sylvan Road, P.O. Box 1044, Woburn MA 01801. 781/935-5150. **Contact:** Employment Supervisor. **World Wide Web address:** http://www.alphaind.com. **Description:** A manufacturer of integrated circuits and microwave semiconductor devices including gallium arsenide microwave monolithic integrated circuits; microwave ferrite and other microwave ceramic materials; microwave solid state switches, oscillators, gallium arsenide field effect transistor amplifiers; and millimeter wave components, subsystems, and antennas. **Common positions include:** Electrical/Electronics Engineer; Microwave Engineer. **Educational backgrounds include:** Engineering; Physics. **Benefits:** Dental Insurance; Disability Coverage; Employee Discounts; Life Insurance; Medical Insurance; Savings Plan; Stock Option; Tuition Assistance. **Corporate headquarters location:** This Location. **Subsidiaries include:** Trans-Tech, Inc. Is a manufacturer of advanced technical ceramics. **Listed on:** NASDAQ.

ALPHA WIRE COMPANY
711 Lidgerwood Avenue, Elizabeth NJ 07207. 908/925-8000. **Toll-free phone:** 800/52-ALPHA. **Fax:** 908/925-3346. **Contact:** Human Resources. **World Wide Web address:** http://www. alphawire.com. **Description:** An international distributor of high-technology and high-reliability wire, cable, tubing, and connector products including communications and control cables, shrinkable and nonshrinkable tubing and insulation, instrumentation cables, flat cable and connectors, coaxial and data cables, plenum cable, and hook-up wire used for electrical and electronic equipment. Products are sold to a network of distributors and OEMs. Founded in 1922. **NOTE:** Entry-level positions and part-time jobs are offered. **Common positions include:** Account Rep.; Accountant; Administrative Assistant; AS400 Programmer Analyst; Chief Financial Officer; Computer Programmer; Controller; Credit Manager; Customer Service Rep.; Design Engineer; Financial Analyst; General Manager; Human Resources Manager;

Industrial Engineer; Intranet Developer; Marketing Manager; Marketing Specialist; Purchasing Agent/ Manager; Sales Executive; Sales Manager; Secretary; Vice President of Marketing and Sales. **Educational backgrounds include:** Accounting; AS400 Certification; Business Administration; Education; Engineering; Finance; Marketing; Mathematics; Microsoft Office; Microsoft Word; Novell. **Benefits:** 401(k); Casual Dress - Daily; Dental Insurance; Disability Coverage; Employee Discounts; Life Insurance; Medical Insurance; Pension Plan; Relocation Assistance; Vacation Days. **Special programs:** Internships. **Office hours:** Monday - Friday, 8:00 a.m. - 8:00 p.m. **Corporate headquarters location:** St. Louis MO. **Other U.S. locations:** Nationwide. **International locations:** Worldwide. **Director:** Mayur Gohil. **General Manager:** Brian O'Connell. **Purchasing Manager:** Ben Ochinegro. **Vice President of Sales:** Allan Marconi. **Annual sales/revenues:** $51 - $100 million. **Number of employees at this location:** 120. **Number of employees nationwide:** 180.

ALTERA CORPORATION
101 Innovation Drive, San Jose CA 95134-1941. 408/544-7000. **Fax:** 408/544-6409. **Contact:** Staffing. **E-mail address:** hr@altera.com. **World Wide Web address:** http://www.altera.com. **Description:** Designs and develops high-performance, high-density programmable logic devices and associated computer-aided engineering (CAE) logic development tools. These products are used in a variety of areas including telecommunications, data communications, computers, and industrial applications. **Common positions include:** Design Engineer; Electrical/ Electronics Engineer; Software Engineer. **Educational backgrounds include:** Computer Science; Engineering. **Benefits:** 401(k); Dental Insurance; Disability Coverage; Employee Discounts; Life Insurance; Medical Insurance; Profit Sharing; Public Transit Available; Tuition Assistance. **Special programs:** Internships. **Corporate headquarters location:** This Location. **Listed on:** NASDAQ. **Stock exchange symbol:** ALTR. **CEO/President:** Rodney Smith. **Annual sales/revenues:** More than $100 million. **Number of employees at this location:** 700. **Number of employees worldwide:** 1,100.

AMERICAN GAS & CHEMICAL COMPANY
220 Pegasus Avenue, Northvale NJ 07647. 201/767-7300. **Toll-free phone:** 800/288-3647. **Fax:** 201/767-1741. **Contact:** Human Resources. **E-mail address:** hr@amgas.com. **World Wide Web address:** http://www.amgas.com. **Description:** Manufactures electronic chemical and gas leak detectors. **Common positions include:** Accountant/ Auditor; Applications Engineer; Buyer; Chemist; Chief Financial Officer; Clerical Supervisor; Computer Programmer; Customer Service Rep.; Design Engineer; Draftsperson; Electrical/ Electronics Engineer; Industrial Production Manager; Marketing Manager; Purchasing Agent/Manager; Quality Control Supervisor; Sales Engineer; Sales Manager. **Educational backgrounds include:** Chemistry; Engineering. **Benefits:** 401(k); Dental Insurance; Life Insurance; Medical Insurance. **Corporate headquarters location:** This Location. **Listed on:** Privately held. **Number of employees at this location:** 125.

AMERICAN MEDICAL ALERT CORP.
3265 Lawson Boulevard, Oceanside NY 11572. 516/536-5850. **Toll-free phone:** 800/645-3244. **Fax:** 516/561-1478. **Contact:** Human Resources Director. **World Wide Web address:** http://www. amacalert.com. **Description:** A manufacturer and distributor of the Personal Emergency Response

System for the home health industry. The Personal Emergency Response System is an in-home safety device used by the chronically ill or physically impaired allowing them to communicate with emergency care providers using digital-wireless technology. **Common positions include:** Administrative Assistant; Electrical/Electronics Engineer; Marketing Specialist; Sales Rep.; Telecommunications Manager. **Educational backgrounds include:** Liberal Arts. **Benefits:** Disability Coverage; Employee Discounts; ESOP. **Corporate headquarters location:** This Location. **Listed on:** NASDAQ. **Stock exchange symbol:** AMAC. **Annual sales/revenues:** $5 - $10 million. **Number of employees at this location:** 70. **Number of employees nationwide:** 80.

AMERICAN SUPERCONDUCTOR CORP.
2 Technology Drive, Westborough MA 01581. 508/836-4200. **Contact:** Human Resources. **E-mail address:** resumes@amsuper.com. **World Wide Web address:** http://www.amsuper.com. **Description:** Manufactures flexible high-temperature superconductor wires, wire products, and systems. Products are incorporated in compact, cost-effective electric power and magnet systems such as power transmission cables, motors, generators, transformers, energy storage devices, and magnetic resonance imaging systems. **Benefits:** 401(k); Incentive Plan; Stock Option. **Corporate headquarters location:** This Location. **Subsidiaries include:** American Superconductor Europe, GmbH (Germany). **Listed on:** NASDAQ.

AMERICAN TECHNICAL CERAMICS CORP. (ATC)
15 Stepar Place, Huntington Station NY 11746. 631/622-4774. **Contact:** Sue Vignali, Human Resources Manager. **World Wide Web address:** http://www.atceramics.com. **Description:** A high-technology firm engaged in the design, development, and manufacture of ceramic and porcelain capacitors. ATC's processing technology creates high-performance capacitors for critical applications in both the commercial and military markets including missile systems, satellite broadcasting equipment, mobile telephones, medical electronics, and aircraft radar and navigation systems. **Corporate headquarters location:** This Location. **Other U.S. locations:** Jacksonville FL. **Subsidiaries include:** Phase Components Ltd. (Sussex, England).

AMETEK DREXELBROOK
205 Keith Valley Road, Horsham PA 19044-1499. 215/674-1234. **Fax:** 215/674-2731. **Contact:** Janet Formeilo, Personnel Manager. **World Wide Web address:** http://www.drexelbrook.com. **Description:** Manufactures level control and level measurement instrumentation for the process control industry.

AMISTAR CORPORATION
237 Via Vera Cruz, San Marcos CA 92069. 760/471-1700. **Contact:** Human Resources. **World Wide Web address:** http://www.amistar.com. **Description:** Designs, develops, manufactures, markets, and services a broad variety of automatic and semi-automatic equipment for assembling electronic components to be placed in printed circuit boards. The company is also a contract assembler of printed circuit boards. **Corporate headquarters location:** This Location. **Number of employees at this location:** 170.

AMPEX CORPORATION
500 Broadway, Redwood City CA 94063. 650/367-2011. **Contact:** Human Resources. **World Wide Web address:** http://www.ampex.com. **Description:** A manufacturer of equipment for professional television, mass data storage, and instrumentation. Products include recorders, editors, switchers, special effects, robotic libraries, tapes, and interconnect equipment. **Common positions include:** Accountant/Auditor; Budget Analyst; Buyer; Electrical/Electronics Engineer; Financial Analyst; Human Resources Manager; Mechanical Engineer; Software Engineer. **Educational backgrounds include:** Accounting; Business Administration; Computer Science; Engineering; Finance; Marketing. **Benefits:** 401(k); Dental Insurance; Disability Coverage; Life Insurance; Medical Insurance; Savings Plan. **Corporate headquarters location:** This Location. **Subsidiaries include:** Ampex Data Systems; MicroNet Technologies; NEXTV.

AMPHENOL CORPORATION
358 Hall Avenue, Wallingford CT 06492. 203/265-8900. **Contact:** Human Resources. **World Wide Web address:** http://www.amphenol.com. **Description:** Manufactures electronic connectors and cables. **Common positions include:** Accountant; Electrical/Electronics Engineer; Marketing Specialist; Sales Rep. **Benefits:** 401(k); Dental Insurance; Disability Coverage; Life Insurance; Medical Insurance; Pension Plan; Tuition Assistance. **Corporate headquarters location:** This Location. **Other U.S. locations:** Danbury CT; Hamden CT. **Listed on:** New York Stock Exchange. **Number of employees at this location:** 100.

AMTOTE INTERNATIONAL, INC.
11200 Pepper Road, Hunt Valley MD 21031. 410/771-8700. **Contact:** Human Resources. **Description:** Manufactures Totalisator machines for the pari-mutuel wagering industry. **Corporate headquarters location:** This Location.

ANALOG DEVICES, INC.
One Technology Way, P.O. Box 9106, Norwood MA 02062-9106. 781/329-4700. **Contact:** Personnel. **World Wide Web address:** http://www. analog.com. **Description:** Designs, manufactures, and markets a broad line of high-performance analog, mixed-signal, and digital integrated circuits (ICs) that address a wide range of real-world signal processing applications. The company's principal products include system-level ICs and general purpose, standard linear ICs. Other products include devices manufactured using assembled product technology such as hybrids, which combine unpackaged IC chips and other chip-level components in a single package. Analog Devices' system-level ICs are used predominately in communications and computer applications. The company's largest communications application is the pan-European GSM (Global System for Mobile Communications) digital cellular telephone system. **Common positions include:** Accountant/Auditor; Buyer; Computer Programmer; Customer Service Rep.; Draftsperson; Electrical/Electronics Engineer; Financial Analyst; Human Resources Manager; Purchasing Agent/Manager; Quality Control Supervisor. **Educational backgrounds include:** Accounting; Business Administration; Computer Science; Engineering; Finance. **Benefits:** Dental Insurance; Disability Coverage; Employee Discounts; Life Insurance; Medical Insurance; Pension Plan; Profit Sharing; Savings Plan; Tuition Assistance. **Corporate headquarters location:** This Location. **Other U.S. locations:** Nationwide. **International locations:** Worldwide.

ANALOGIC CORPORATION
8 Centennial Drive, Peabody MA 01960. 978/977-3000. **Fax:** 978/977-6810. **Contact:** Human Resources. **World Wide Web address:** http://www.

analogic.com. **Description:** Designs, manufactures, and sells a broad line of high-precision data-conversion and signal-processing equipment. Principal customers are original equipment manufacturers who incorporate products into systems for medical, industrial, and telecommunications applications. The company's products include measurement, display, and control instruments, consisting of digital panel instruments, digital test instruments, and industrial digitizing systems; data acquisition and conversion products, consisting of A/D and D/A converters, supporting modules, data acquisition systems, and subsystems; and computer-based products, consisting of medical imaging equipment and array processors. **Common positions include:** Accountant; Administrative Assistant; Applications Engineer; Biomedical Engineer; Computer Engineer; Computer Operator; Computer Programmer; Computer Support Technician; Computer Technician; Controller; Customer Service Rep.; Database Administrator; Design Engineer; Draftsperson; Electrical/Electronics Engineer; Manufacturing Engineer; Mechanical Engineer; Network/Systems Administrator; Operations Manager; Production Manager; Purchasing Agent/Manager; Quality Assurance Engineer; Quality Control Supervisor; Secretary; Software Engineer. **Educational backgrounds include:** Engineering; Physics. **Benefits:** 401(k); Dental Insurance; Disability Coverage; Employee Discounts; Life Insurance; Medical Insurance; Profit Sharing; Savings Plan; Sick Days (1 - 5); Tuition Assistance; Vacation Days (11 - 15). **Special programs:** Co-ops. **Corporate headquarters location:** This Location. **Other U.S. locations:** WI. **Listed on:** NASDAQ. **Annual sales/revenues:** More than $100 million. **Number of employees at this location:** 1,150.

ANAREN MICROWAVE, INC.
6635 Kirkville Road, East Syracuse NY 13057. 315/432-8909. **Contact:** Stan Slingerland, Vice President of Human Resources. **World Wide Web address:** http://www.anaren.com. **Description:** A government contracting defense facility. The company designs and manufactures microwave components, subsystems, and receiver systems for use in the electronic defense of ships, airplanes, and tactical land vehicles. **Corporate headquarters location:** This Location.

ANICOM, INC.
6133 North River Road, Suite 1000, Rosemont IL 60018. 847/518-8700. **Fax:** 847/518-8791. **Contact:** Human Resources. **World Wide Web address:** http://www.anicommm.com. **Description:** Sells and distributes multimedia wiring products used to relay voice, video, and data information. Products include wire, cable, fiber optics, and other connectivity products. **Corporate headquarters location:** This Location. **Listed on:** NASDAQ. **Stock exchange symbol:** ANIC.

ANTON/BAUER INC.
14 Progress Drive, Shelton CT 06484. 203/929-1100. **Fax:** 203/929-9935. **Contact:** Human Resources. **World Wide Web address:** http://www.antonbauer.com. **Description:** Manufactures electronic products including battery packs and chargers for video cameras. **Corporate headquarters location:** This Location. **International locations:** England; Scotland.

ANZA, INC.
P.O. Box 1445, Watertown SD 57201. 605/886-3889. **Fax:** 605/886-0112. **Contact:** Corporate Recruiter. **Description:** A holding company. **Common positions include:** Accountant/Auditor; Blue-Collar Worker Supervisor; Buyer; Computer Programmer; Customer Service Rep.; Design Engineer; Electrical/Electronics Engineer; Human Resources Manager; Industrial Engineer; Industrial Production Manager; Internet Services Manager; Management Trainee; Manufacturer's/Wholesaler's Sales Rep.; Mechanical Engineer; Occupational Therapist; Operations/Production Manager; Physical Therapist; Purchasing Agent/Manager; Quality Control Supervisor; Software Engineer; Systems Analyst; Teacher/Professor; Technical Writer/Editor; Telecommunications Manager. **Educational backgrounds include:** Accounting; Business Administration; Communications; Computer Science; Engineering; Finance; Liberal Arts; Marketing. **Benefits:** 401(k); Dental Insurance; Disability Coverage; Life Insurance; Medical Insurance; Savings Plan; Tuition Assistance. **Special programs:** Internships. **Corporate headquarters location:** This Location. **Other U.S. locations:** Waverly IA; Aberdeen SD; Huron SD; Madison SD. **Subsidiaries include:** PERSONA, Inc. is one of the nation's largest sign manufacturers, shipping signs to all 50 states, Canada, and Mexico. MIDCOM, Inc. is the largest of the ANZA group serving its customers in the design and manufacturing of analog, digital, and switchboard power transformers for the telecommunications industry. OEM Worldwide, Inc. is a full-service electronics manufacturing service providing design/development, consulting, and state-of-the-art manufacturing to its customers in an environmentally-controlled facility. ICONtrol, Inc. develops business management software. **Listed on:** Privately held. **Number of employees at this location:** 1,500. **Number of employees nationwide:** 2,000.

APPLIED MATERIALS, INC.
3050 Bowers Avenue, Mail Stop 1826, Santa Clara CA 95054. 408/727-5555. **Contact:** Corporate Employment. **World Wide Web address:** http://www.appliedmaterials.com. **Description:** A *Fortune* 500 company that is a leading producer of wafer fabrication systems for the semiconductor industry. The company also sells related spare parts and services. Applied Materials's products include dry etch systems for the creation of circuit paths in semiconductors and implementation products for silicon wafers. **Common positions include:** Electrical/Electronics Engineer; Financial Analyst; Human Resources Manager; Marketing Specialist; Mechanical Engineer; Process Engineer; Sales Rep.; Software Engineer. **Corporate headquarters location:** This Location. **Listed on:** NASDAQ. **Number of employees nationwide:** 16,200.

ARK-LES CORPORATION
95 Mill Street, Stoughton MA 02072. 781/297-6000. **Contact:** Personnel. **Description:** ARK-LES manufactures electrical components and switches. **Corporate headquarters location:** This Location. **Other U.S. locations:** South Portland ME; El Paso TX. **International locations:** Juarez, Mexico.

ARROW ELECTRONICS, INC.
25 Hub Drive, Melville NY 11747. 516/391-1300. **Contact:** Human Resources. **World Wide Web address:** http://www.arrow.com. **Description:** A distributor of electronics components, systems, and related items through a network in North America, Europe, and Asia. The company supplies components to approximately 175,000 original equipment manufacturers and commercial customers. **Corporate headquarters location:** This Location.
Other U.S. locations:
• Arrow/Zeus Electronics, 2900 Westchester Avenue, Suite 401, Purchase NY 10577. 914/701-7400.

ASTEX (APPLIED SCIENCE AND TECHNOLOGY, INC.)
90 Industrial Way, Wilmington MA 01887. 978/284-4000. **Contact:** Human Resources. **World Wide Web address:** http://www.astex.com. **Description:** A manufacturer of systems and components used in the production of advanced semiconductors and chemical vapor deposition (CVD) diamond. ASTeX components are used in a number of semiconductor fabrication steps such as stripping, etching, CVD, and physical vapor deposition. The company's CVD diamond production systems are used to develop and manufacture tool coatings, optics and optical coatings, thermal management substrates for high performance electronics, and bearing seals and wear parts for a variety of applications. ASTeX markets its systems to producers of CVD diamond while its microwave power generators, plasma sources, and ozone generators and subsystems are marketed to semiconductor capital equipment manufacturers. **Corporate headquarters location:** This Location.

ASTREX, INC.
205 Express Street, Plainview NY 11803. 516/433-1700. **Toll-free phone:** 800/633-6360. **Fax:** 516/433-5709. **Contact:** Human Resources. **Description:** Distributes electronic components used to connect, control, regulate, or store electricity in equipment. Products assembled and sold by Astrex include connectors, relays, switches, and LEDs. Founded in 1961. **Common positions include:** Administrative Assistant; Assistant Manager; Blue-Collar Worker Supervisor; Credit Manager; Customer Service Rep.; Purchasing Agent/Manager; Sales Executive; Sales Manager; Sales Rep. **Benefits:** 401(k); Life Insurance; Medical Insurance. **Corporate headquarters location:** This Location. **Other U.S. locations:** Woburn MA; Endwell NY; Willow Grove PA. **Stock exchange symbol:** ASXI. **Annual sales/revenues:** $11 - $20 million. **Number of employees at this location:** 40. **Number of employees nationwide:** 60.

AULT INC.
7105 Northland Terrace, Minneapolis MN 55428. 763/592-1900. **Fax:** 763/592-1911. **Contact:** Judy Sand, Benefits and Compensation Administrator. **World Wide Web address:** http://www.aultinc.com. **Description:** A designer, manufacturer, and marketer of power conversion products for the OEM market. **NOTE:** Entry-level positions are offered. **Common positions include:** Accountant/Auditor; Buyer; Computer Programmer; Customer Service Rep.; Design Engineer; Draftsperson; Electrical/Electronics Engineer; Human Resources Manager; Industrial Engineer; Mechanical Engineer; Operations/Production Manager; Systems Analyst; Typist/Word Processor. **Educational backgrounds include:** Accounting; Business Administration; Computer Science; Engineering; Finance; Marketing. **Benefits:** 401(k); Dental Insurance; Disability Coverage; Life Insurance; Medical Insurance; Profit Sharing; Savings Plan; Stock Option; Tuition Assistance. **Corporate headquarters location:** This Location. **Listed on:** NASDAQ. **Stock exchange symbol:** AULT. **Annual sales/revenues:** $21 - $50 million. **Number of employees at this location:** 145.

AUREAL, INC.
45757 Northport Loop West, Fremont CA 94538. 510/252-4245. **Fax:** 510/252-4400. **Contact:** Human Resources. **World Wide Web address:** http://www.aureal.com. **Description:** Designs, develops, and markets semiconductor and audio solutions for the electronic consumer market. Products include interactive 3-D audio, virtual surround sound, digital mixing, and wave guide synthesis. **NOTE:** Entry-level positions are offered. **Common positions include:** Applications Engineer; Design Engineer; Software Engineer. **Educational backgrounds include:** Computer Science; Engineering. **Benefits:** 401(k); Dental Insurance; Disability Coverage; Employee Discounts; Life Insurance; Medical Insurance; Tuition Assistance. **Corporate headquarters location:** This Location. **Number of employees at this location:** 115.

AUTOMATA INTERNATIONAL
1200 Severn Way, Sterling VA 20166. 703/450-2600. **Contact:** Human Resources. **World Wide Web address:** http://www.automata.com. **Description:** Manufactures printed circuit boards. **Common positions include:** Account Manager; Account Rep.; Accountant/Auditor; Blue-Collar Worker Supervisor; Buyer; Chemical Engineer; Chemist; Computer Programmer; Customer Service Representative; Database Manager; Designer; Electrical/Electronics Engineer; Human Resources Manager; Industrial Engineer; Manufacturer's/Wholesaler's Sales Rep.; Manufacturing Engineer; Mechanical Engineer; MIS Specialist; Operations/Production Manager; Production Manager; Purchasing Agent/Manager; Quality Control Supervisor. **Educational backgrounds include:** Accounting; Chemistry; Engineering; Marketing. **Benefits:** 401(k); Dental Insurance; Disability Coverage; Life Insurance; Medical Insurance; Profit Sharing; Tuition Assistance. **Special programs:** Training. **Corporate headquarters location:** This Location. **Listed on:** Privately held. **Annual sales/revenues:** $51 - $100 million. **Number of employees at this location:** 420.

AUTOMATIC SWITCH COMPANY (ASCO)
50-60 Hanover Road, Florham Park NJ 07932. 973/966-2000. **Fax:** 973/966-2628. **Contact:** Manager of Personnel. **World Wide Web address:** http://www.asco.com. **Description:** An international manufacturer of a line of electrical equipment used for the automation of machinery, equipment, and industrial processes and for the control of electric power. **Common positions include:** Accountant/Auditor; Electrical/Electronics Engineer; Industrial Engineer; Management Trainee; Mechanical Engineer; Operations/Production Manager. **Educational backgrounds include:** Accounting; Engineering; Finance; Liberal Arts; Marketing. **Benefits:** Dental Insurance; Disability Coverage; Employee Discounts; Life Insurance; Medical Insurance; Pension Plan; Profit Sharing; Savings Plan; Tuition Assistance. **Corporate headquarters location:** This Location. **Other U.S. locations:** CA; IL; SC. **Subsidiaries include:** A&M Ludwig Corporation (Parsippany NJ) manufactures screw machine parts; ASCO Electrical Products Company (Parsippany NJ) manufactures metal enclosures and electrical distribution equipment; Auger Scientific (Cedar Knolls NJ) manufactures miniature and microminiature solenoid valves and controls for medical, analytical, and pharmaceutical uses; ASCO Sisc Inc. (Dover DE); ASCO Investment Corporation; ASCO Services Inc. (also at this location). **Parent company:** Emerson Electric.

AVNET, INC.
390 Rabro Drive, Hauppauge NY 11788. 631/434-7470. **Contact:** Human Resources. **World Wide Web address:** http://www.avnet.com. **Description:** One of the nation's largest distributors of electronic components and computer products for industrial and military customers. The company also manufactures and distributes other electronic, electrical, and video communications products. **NOTE:** Resumes must be sent to Avnet, Inc., Human Resources, 2211 South 47th Street, Phoenix

AZ 85034. Resumes can be faxed to 602/643-4670. **Corporate headquarters location:** Phoenix AZ. **Other U.S. locations:**
• 9320 Telstar Avenue, El Monte CA 91731. 626/307-6065.

AVO INTERNATIONAL
4271 Bronze Way, Dallas TX 75237. 214/333-3201. **Contact:** Manager of Human Resources. **World Wide Web address:** http://www.avointl.com. **Description:** Manufactures test equipment and measurement instruments for electric power applications. **Corporate headquarters location:** This Location.

BAE SYSTEMS
6500 Tracor Lane, Austin TX 78725. 512/926-2800. **Contact:** Recruiting. **World Wide Web address:** http://www.baesystems.com. **Description:** Provides a full spectrum of systems engineering and technical services in the areas of systems development, operation, and maintenance. Technical services include system design, integration, and testing; software development, engineering, and maintenance; and integrated logistics support including safety, reliability, and quality assurance engineering.

BI INCORPORATED
6400 Lookout Road, Boulder CO 80301. **Toll-free phone:** 800/241-2911. **Fax:** 303/218-1189. **Contact:** Human Resources. **World Wide Web address:** http://www.bi.com. **Description:** A leading provider of electronic home arrest and jail management systems to corrections agencies worldwide. The company also offers a computerized interactive telephone service and monitoring service for its electronic monitoring systems. **Office hours:** Monday - Friday, 8:00 a.m. - 5:30 p.m. **Corporate headquarters location:** This Location. **Other U.S. locations:** GA; IL; IN; OH; OR; TX. **International locations:** Puerto Rico. **Number of employees worldwide:** 800.

BKC SEMICONDUCTORS INC.
MICROSEMI CORPORATION
6 Lake Street, Lawrence MA 01841-3011. 978/681-0392. **Fax:** 978/681-9135. **Contact:** Sandie Victor, Human Resources. **World Wide Web address:** http://www.bkcs.com. **Description:** Manufactures a wide range of semiconductor diodes for signal switching, voltage conversion, rectification, and surge suppression of electrical units. BKC Semiconductors sells its products primarily to the military and the commercial/industrial markets. **Parent company:** MicroSemi Corporation (also at this location).

BLH ELECTRONICS, INC.
75 Shawmut Road, Canton MA 02021. 781/821-2000. **Contact:** Personnel. **World Wide Web address:** http://www.blh.com. **Description:** An electronics manufacturer that produces strain gauges, transducers, and instrumentation controls. **Common positions include:** Accountant; Assembly Worker; Buyer; Industrial Designer; Industrial Engineer. **Educational backgrounds include:** Accounting; Art/Design; Business Administration; Engineering. **Benefits:** 401(k); Dental Insurance; Disability Coverage; Life Insurance; Medical Insurance; Pension Plan; Sick Days; Tuition Assistance. **Corporate headquarters location:** This Location.

BABCOCK, INC.
14930 East Alondra Boulevard, La Mirada CA 90638-5752. 714/994-6500. **Fax:** 714/994-0967. **Contact:** Human Resources. **World Wide Web address:** http://www.babcockinc.com. **Description:**

Designs and manufactures electronic components including switch mode power supplies for satellites and military and aerospace applications, gas plasma and vacuum fluorescent displays, and electromagnetic relays for high-reliability aerospace applications. **Common positions include:** Accountant; Administrative Assistant; Chemist; Chief Financial Officer; Computer Programmer; Computer Support Technician; Controller; Customer Service Rep.; Database Administrator; General Manager; Human Resources Manager; Marketing Manager; Production Manager; Purchasing Agent/Manager; Quality Control Supervisor; Sales Manager; Secretary. **Educational backgrounds include:** Engineering; Microsoft Word; Spreadsheets. **Benefits:** 401(k); Casual Dress - Daily; Dental Insurance; Disability Coverage; Life Insurance; Medical Insurance. **Corporate headquarters location:** This Location. **Parent company:** Electro-Module. **Listed on:** Privately held. **President:** Richard S. Dixon. **Annual sales/revenues:** $21 - $50 million. **Number of employees at this location:** 250.

BALDOR ELECTRIC COMPANY
P.O. Box 2400, Fort Smith AR 72902. 501/646-4711. **Contact:** Charles Kramer, Vice President of Personnel. **World Wide Web address:** http://www.baldor.com. **Description:** Manufactures industrial electrical components such as grinders and motors. **Corporate headquarters location:** This Location.

BANNER ENGINEERING CORPORATION
9714 10th Avenue North, Minneapolis MN 55441-5019. 612/544-3164. **Fax:** 612/544-0383. **Contact:** Human Resources. **E-mail address:** resume@baneng.com. **World Wide Web address:** http://www.baneng.com. **Description:** Designs and manufactures photo-electric control systems. **Common positions include:** Accountant; Administrative Assistant; Computer Programmer; Computer Support Technician; Controller; Customer Service Manager; Database Manager; Design Engineer; Draftsperson; Electrical/Electronics Engineer; Graphic Artist; Graphic Designer; Human Resources Manager; Industrial Engineer; Manufacturing Engineer; Marketing Manager; Mechanical Engineer; Media Planner; MIS Manager; Multimedia Designer; Network/Systems Administrator; Operations Manager; Production Manager; Purchasing Agent/Manager; Sales Rep.; Software Engineer; Systems Analyst; Technical Writer/Editor; Webmaster. **Educational backgrounds include:** Engineering. **Corporate headquarters location:** This Location. **Number of employees at this location:** 200.

BASE TEN SYSTEMS, INC.
P.O. Box 3151, Trenton NJ 08619. 609/586-7010. **Contact:** Human Resources. **Description:** Designs, manufactures, and markets electronic systems employing safety critical software for the defense industry. The company also manufactures defense products to meet specifications set by prime government contractors, and designs and builds proprietary electronic systems for use in secure communications applications by various U.S. government agencies. Base Ten Systems is also involved in medical screening, image processing, and pharmaceutical manufacturing software programs. **Corporate headquarters location:** This Location.

BASIC ELECTRIC SUPPLY
P.O. Box 12326, Columbus OH 43212. 614/481-8801. **Fax:** 614/488-0453. **Contact:** Personnel. **World Wide Web address:** http://www.basicelectric.com. **Description:** Distributes

electrical equipment. **Benefits:** 401(k); Dental Insurance; Disability Coverage; Employee Discounts; Life Insurance; Medical Insurance; Profit Sharing; Savings Plan. **Office hours:** Monday - Friday, 7:30 a.m. - 5:00 p.m., Saturday, 8:00 a.m. - 12:00 p.m. **Corporate headquarters location:** This Location. **Listed on:** Privately held. **Number of employees at this location:** 40.

BELDEN INC.
7701 Forsyth Boulevard, Suite 800, St. Louis MO 63105. 314/854-8000. **Contact:** Human Resources. **World Wide Web address:** http://www.belden.com. **Description:** A holding company. **NOTE:** Resumes should be sent to Belden Wire and Cable Company, Human Resources, 2200 U.S. Highway 27 South, Richmond IN 47374. **Corporate headquarters location:** This Location. **Subsidiaries include:** Belden Wire and Cable Company (Richmond IN) is a leader in the design and manufacture of wire, cable, and cord products. The company serves the computer market with a broad range of multiconductor, coaxial, flat, and fiberoptic cables. Belden Wire also serves the industrial market by providing a broad spectrum of industrial products, ranging from general purpose control cables to highly-sophisticated cables for process control. The company's electrical products include power supply cords, electrical motor lead wire, and Canadian building wire. The Cord Products Division (Indianapolis IN) focuses on the electrical cord market. **Number of employees at this location:** 10.

BENCHMARK ELECTRONICS INC.
3000 Technology Drive, Angleton TX 77515. 979/849-6550. **Contact:** Human Resources. **World Wide Web address:** http://www.bench.com. **Description:** Assembles printed circuit boards for original equipment manufacturers. **Corporate headquarters location:** This Location.

BENTLY NEVADA CORPORATION
1631 Bently Parkway South, Minden NV 89423. 775/782-3611. **Contact:** Personnel. **World Wide Web address:** http://www.bently.com. **Description:** Produces monitoring and diagnostic systems for rotating machinery. The company's product line includes vibration transducers, monitors, and systems for predictive maintenance, as well as test equipment for the diagnostics of rotating machines. The company's services include technical training, design and installation services, product service, and machinery diagnostics services. **Common positions include:** Accountant; Computer Programmer; Data Processor; Design Engineer; Electrical/Electronics Engineer; Financial Analyst; Manufacturing Engineer; Mechanical Engineer. **Corporate headquarters location:** This Location. **Other U.S. locations:** Naitonwide.

BEST ACCESS SYSTEMS
P.O. Box 50444, Indianapolis IN 46250. 317/849-2250. **Physical address:** 6161 East 75th Street, Indianapolis IN. **Fax:** 317/845-7651. **Contact:** Human Resources Department. **E-mail address:** employment@bestlock.com. **World Wide Web address:** http://www.bestaccess.com. **Description:** Manufactures and distributes access control and security systems for corporations and institutions worldwide. **Common positions include:** Accountant; Computer Programmer; Manufacturer's/Wholesaler's Sales Rep.; Mechanical Engineer; Systems Analyst. **Educational backgrounds include:** Accounting; Business Administration; Communications; Engineering; Marketing. **Benefits:** 401(k); Dental Insurance; Disability Coverage; Life Insurance; Medical Insurance; Tuition Assistance. **Corporate**

headquarters location: This Location. **Other U.S. locations:** Nationwide. **Number of employees at this location:** 700.

BLONDER TONGUE LABORATORIES
One Jake Brown Road, Old Bridge NJ 08857. 732/679-4000. **Fax:** 732/679-4353. **Contact:** Daniel J. Altiere, Senior Vice President. **World Wide Web address:** http://www.blondertongue.com. **Description:** Designs and manufactures signal processing equipment for the television industry. Products are used for satellite communications, master antennae systems (MATV), and other systems using RF technology. **Common positions include:** Accountant/Auditor; Buyer; Customer Service Rep.; Draftsperson; Electrical/Electronics Engineer; General Manager; Industrial Engineer; Mechanical Engineer. **Educational backgrounds include:** Engineering. **Benefits:** 401(k); Dental Insurance; Disability Coverage; Life Insurance; Medical Insurance; Pension Plan; Tuition Assistance. **Corporate headquarters location:** This Location. **Listed on:** American Stock Exchange. **Stock exchange symbol:** BDR. **Annual sales/revenues:** $51 - $100 million. **Number of employees at this location:** 500.

BOURNS, INC.
1200 Columbia Avenue, Riverside CA 92507. 909/781-5690. **Contact:** Charles McBeth, Personnel. **World Wide Web address:** http://www.bourns.com. **Description:** A manufacturer of electronic components and high-technology equipment. Products include semiconductor devices, aerial reconnaissance cameras, and potentiometers. **Corporate headquarters location:** This Location. **Other U.S. locations:**
- Sensors/Controls Division, 2533 North 1500 West, Ogden UT 84404. 801/786-6200.

BRANOM INSTRUMENT COMPANY
P.O. Box 80307, Seattle WA 98108-0307. 206/762-6050. **Toll-free phone:** 800/767-6051. **Fax:** 206/767-5669. **Contact:** Personnel. **World Wide Web address:** http://www.branom.com. **Description:** A wholesaler of electronic parts and equipment including timing and counting, temperature, pressure, flow, level, and AC/DC instruments. Founded in 1947. **Common positions include:** Accountant; Administrative Assistant; Administrative Manager; Assistant Manager; Branch Manager; Controller; Electrical/Electronics Engineer; Electrician; General Manager; Industrial Engineer; Marketing Specialist; Mechanical Engineer; Sales Manager; Sales Rep.; Web Advertising Specialist. **Educational backgrounds include:** HTML; Microsoft Office; Microsoft Word; Spreadsheets. **Benefits:** 401(k); Casual Dress - Daily; Dental Insurance; Employee Discounts; Life Insurance; Medical Insurance; Profit Sharing; Relocation Assistance; Sick Days (1 - 5); Tuition Assistance; Vacation Days (10 - 20). **Office hours:** Monday - Friday, 8:00 a.m. - 5:00 p.m. **Corporate headquarters location:** This Location. **CEO:** William W. Branom. **Sales Manager:** Joanne Nunn. **Number of employees at this location:** 40.

BROOKS AUTOMATION, INC.
15 Elizabeth Drive, Chelmsford MA 01824. 978/262-2400. **Contact:** Human Resources. **World Wide Web address:** http://www.brooks.com. **Description:** Manufactures robotic arms, wafer disks, vacuum cassette elevators, and other electronic devices. **Corporate headquarters location:** This Location.

BURR-BROWN CORPORATION
P.O. Box 11400, Tucson AZ 85734. 520/746-1111. **Fax:** 520/746-7211. **Contact:** Employment. **World**

Wide Web address: http://www.burr-brown.com. **Description:** Manufactures high-precision, high-reliability micro-electronic devices and microcomputer systems for use in data acquisition, signal conditioning, and industrial control. Burr-Brown Corporation operates in three market segments: instrumentation (including electronic test, analytical, and medical); industrial (including process control, factory data collection, LANs, test, and measurement); and communications (including data communications, telecommunications, and audio/visual signal processing). Operating divisions include Data Conversion, Analog, Linear, Microtechnology, and LANpoint. **Common positions include:** Accountant/Auditor; Budget Analyst; Buyer; Computer Programmer; Customer Service Rep.; Electrical/Electronics Engineer; Operations/Production Manager; Precision Assembler; Purchasing Agent/Manager; Systems Analyst. **Educational backgrounds include:** Accounting; Engineering; Physics. **Benefits:** 401(k); Dental Insurance; Disability Coverage; Employee Discounts; Life Insurance; Medical Insurance; Pension Plan; Profit Sharing; Savings Plan; Tuition Assistance. **Corporate headquarters location:** This Location. **International locations:** England; France; Italy; Japan; Scotland. **Listed on:** NASDAQ. **Number of employees at this location:** 1,000. **Number of employees nationwide:** 1,400.

C-CUBE MICROSYSTEMS INC.
1778 McCarthy Boulevard, Milpitas CA 95035. 408/944-6300. **Fax:** 408/490-8700. **Contact:** Human Resources. **World Wide Web address:** http://www.c-cube.com. **Description:** Designs and markets integrated circuits that implement the compression, decompression, and transmission of digital full-motion video and still images for consumer electronics, communications, and computer applications such as video CD players, direct broadcast of television programming by satellites, and multimedia computing. **Corporate headquarters location:** This Location. **Number of employees at this location:** 600.

CEM CORPORATION
P.O. Box 200, Matthews NC 28106. 704/821-7015. **Fax:** 704/821-7894. **Contact:** Human Resources. **World Wide Web address:** http://www.cemx.com. **Description:** Develops, manufactures, markets, and services microwave-based instrumentation for testing and analysis in the industrial and analytical laboratory markets. The company's products include microwave digestion systems, moisture/solids analyzers, fat analyzer systems, microwave extraction systems, microwave ashing systems, and SpectroPrep systems. **Corporate headquarters location:** This Location. **Subsidiaries include:** CEM GmbH (Kamp-Linfort, Germany); CEM (France); CEM Ltd. (Buckingham, UK); CEM S.r.l. (Cologno al Serio, Italy). **Listed on:** NASDAQ. **Number of employees nationwide:** 175.

CII TECHNOLOGIES
CORCOM DIVISION
844 East Rockland Road, Libertyville IL 60048-3375. 847/680-7400. **Fax:** 847/680-8169. **Contact:** Human Resources. **World Wide Web address:** http://www.cor.com. **Description:** One of the world's largest suppliers of radio frequency interference (RFI) filters. Products are used to control noise pollution in a wide variety of digital electronic devices. Founded in 1955. **Corporate headquarters location:** This Location.

CTS CORPORATION
905 West Boulevard North, Elkhart IN 46514. 219/293-7511. **Contact:** Human Resources. **World Wide Web address:** http://www.ctscorp.com. **Description:** This location houses administrative offices. Overall, CTS Corporation designs, manufactures, and sells electronic components. **Corporate headquarters location:** This Location. **Parent company:** Dynamics Corporation of America. **Listed on:** New York Stock Exchange.

CABLE DESIGN TECHNOLOGIES (CDT)
Foster Plaza 7, 661 Andersen Drive, Pittsburgh PA 15220. 412/937-2300. **Fax:** 412/937-9690. **Contact:** Personnel. **World Wide Web address:** http://www.cdtc.com. **Description:** Manufactures electronic data transmission cables for a variety of industrial applications including voice and data wiring and fiberoptic connective solutions. **Corporate headquarters location:** This Location. **Other U.S. locations:** Nationwide. **International locations:** Australia; Canada; China; Denmark; Germany; Italy; Malaysia; Mexico; Poland; Spain; Sweden; United Kingdom. **Listed on:** New York Stock Exchange. **Stock exchange symbol:** CDT. **President/CEO:** Paul M. Olson.

CALIFORNIA MICRO DEVICES CORP.
215 Topaz Street, Milpitas CA 95035-5430. 408/263-3214. **Toll-free phone:** 800/325-4966. **Fax:** 408/263-7846. **Contact:** Human Resources. **World Wide Web address:** http://www.calmicro.com. **Description:** Manufactures integrated thin film, silicon-based termination and filtering components. The company specializes in combining thin film, passive electronic components and semiconductor devices into single chip solutions for various electronic applications. **Corporate headquarters location:** This Location. **Other U.S. locations:** Tempe AZ. **Listed on:** NASDAQ. **Stock exchange symbol:** CAMD. **President/CEO:** Jeffrey C. Kalb. **Number of employees at this location:** 150.

CASINO DATA SYSTEMS (CDS)
3300 Bircher Drive, Las Vegas NV 89118. 702/269-5000. **Contact:** Ms. Peppy Caccavale, Human Resources Director. **Description:** Designs, manufactures, and distributes products including a slot machine accounting system, a player tracking system known as OASIS System II, and products that link slot machines in various locations. Founded in 1990.

CATALYST SEMICONDUCTOR, INC.
1250 Borregas Avenue, Sunnyvale CA 94089. 408/542-1000. **Fax:** 408/542-1200. **Contact:** Human Resources. **World Wide Web address:** http://www.catsemi.com. **Description:** Supplies nonvolatile semiconductors that provide design solutions for a broad range of applications including computers, wireless communications, networks, instrumentation, and automotive systems. The company's devices include FLASH, mixed signal devices, Serial and Parallel EEPROMs (electrically erasable programmable, read-only memory), and NVRAMs. **Corporate headquarters location:** This Location.

CHASE CORPORATION
26 Summer Street, Bridgewater MA 02324. 508/279-1789. **Contact:** Human Resources. **World Wide Web address:** http://www.chasecorp.com. **Description:** Manufactures insulating products. The company's divisions produce and market products worldwide to insulated electric, electronic, and telecommunications cable manufacturers, producers of electronic parts, and to contractors involved in the construction of underground gas and oil pipelines and highway and bridge construction and repairs. **Benefits:** 401(k); Pension Plan; Stock Option. **Corporate headquarters location:** This Location. **Subsidiaries include:** Chase & Sons

produces shielding and binding tapes for electronic and telecommunication cables; Chase Canada manufactures tapes for electronic, telecommunication, and fiber optic cables as well as specialty tapes and laminates for packaging and industrial applications; Fluid Polymers (Pittsburgh PA) provides sealants, adhesives coating, and dielectric materials for fluid purification and other processes; Sunburst EMS (West Bridgewater MA) manufactures electronics; HumiSeal (Woodside NY) provides insulating conformal coatings, potting compounds, and ancillary products for electronic applications; and Royston (Pittsburgh PA) offers insulating and protective mastics, coatings, and tapes for pipelines, highways, and bridges as well as waterproofing membranes for commercial and residential construction.

CHECKPOINT SYSTEMS, INC.
101 Wolf Drive, Thorofare NJ 08086. 856/848-1800. **Contact:** Theresa McHale, Manager of Human Resources. **World Wide Web address:** http://www.checkpointsystems.com. **Description:** Develops, manufactures, and markets Electronic Article Surveillance systems to control shoplifting in retail stores and protect books and materials in libraries and universities; electronic access control systems to secure buildings and areas within buildings; and closed circuit television systems and solutions to control shoplifting and internal theft. **Corporate headquarters location:** This Location.

CHEROKEE NATION INDUSTRIES, INC.
Highway 51 West, Stilwell OK 74960. 918/696-3151. **Fax:** 918/696-5510. **Contact:** Personnel. **World Wide Web address:** http://www.cnicnd.com. **Description:** Builds products such as cable assemblies, wire harnesses, electrical control units, and printed circuit assemblies for a variety of defense contractors. **Common positions include:** Accountant/Auditor; Buyer; Computer Programmer; Cost Estimator; Customer Service Rep.; Electrical/Electronics Engineer; Human Resources Manager; Industrial Engineer; Licensed Practical Nurse; Mechanical Engineer; Quality Control Supervisor; Systems Analyst. **Educational backgrounds include:** Accounting; Business Administration; Engineering; Marketing. **Benefits:** Dental Insurance; Disability Coverage; Life Insurance; Medical Insurance; Savings Plan; Tuition Assistance. **Special programs:** Internships. **Corporate headquarters location:** This Location. **Number of employees at this location:** 325.

THE CHERRY CORPORATION
3600 Sunset Avenue, P.O. Box 718, Waukegan IL 60087. 847/662-9200. **Contact:** Human Resources. **World Wide Web address:** http://www.cherrycorp.com. **Description:** Manufactures and distributes a wide range of electrical components for the computer, automotive, consumer, and commercial markets worldwide. The principal segments are electromechanical devices including snap-action, selector, and special-use switches principally for use in automobiles, home appliances, office and industrial equipment, and vending machines; and electronic assemblies including keyboards, keyboard switches, gas discharge displays, and automotive electronics for use in data entry terminals, automobiles, industrial and commercial control devices, business machines, and amusement products. **Corporate headquarters location:** This Location.

CHROMALOX
WIEGAND INDUSTRIAL DIVISION
701 Alpha Drive, 3rd Floor, Pittsburgh PA 15238. 412/967-3800. **Fax:** 412/967-3898. **Contact:** Barbara Richmond, Human Resources. **World Wide**

Web address: http://www.chromaloxheating.com. **Description:** Engaged in the manufacture of electrical heating elements, systems, and controls. **Common positions include:** Accountant; Administrative Assistant; Computer Programmer; Credit Manager; Electrical/Electronics Engineer; Finance Director; Financial Analyst; Human Resources Manager; Market Research Analyst; Marketing Specialist; Mechanical Engineer; Secretary; Systems Analyst; Technical Writer/Editor; Vice President. **Educational backgrounds include:** Accounting; Business Administration; Engineering; Marketing; Microsoft Office; Microsoft Word. **Benefits:** 401(k); Dental Insurance; Disability Coverage; Employee Discounts; Life Insurance; Medical Insurance; Pension Plan; Tuition Assistance. **Office hours:** Monday - Friday, 8:30 a.m. - 5:15 p.m. **Corporate headquarters location:** This Location. **Other U.S. locations:** Lavergne TN; Ogden UT. **Parent company:** Emerson Electric Company. **Annual sales/revenues:** More than $100 million. **Number of employees at this location:** 65.

CHYRON CORPORATION
5 Hub Drive, Melville NY 11747. 631/845-2069. **Fax:** 631/845-2090. **Contact:** Melody Dillier, Employment Manager. **E-mail address:** careers@chyron.com. **World Wide Web address:** http://www.chyron.com. **Description:** Designs, manufactures, and markets worldwide digital equipment, software, systems, and solutions which facilitate the production and enhance the presentation of live and programmed television content. Chyron also provides comprehensive solutions that address the management and routing of video and data signals prior to transmission. **NOTE:** Entry-level positions are offered. **Common positions include:** Administrative Assistant; Computer Programmer; Computer Support Technician; Customer Service Rep.; Electrical/Electronics Engineer; Help-Desk Technician; Software Engineer; Website Developer. **Educational backgrounds include:** Computer Science; Engineering; Java; Software Development; Software Tech. Support. **Benefits:** 401(k); Casual Dress - Fridays; Dental Insurance; Disability Coverage; Employee Discounts; Life Insurance; Medical Insurance; Pension Plan; Sick Days (6 - 10); Tuition Assistance; Vacation Days (11 - 15). **Special programs:** Internships. **Corporate headquarters location:** This Location. **Other U.S. locations:** Santa Clara CA. **Listed on:** New York Stock Exchange. **Stock exchange symbol:** CHY. **President/CEO:** Roger Henderson. **Facilities Manager:** Nancy Erickson. **Information Systems Manager:** Mary Sanders. **Number of employees at this location:** 120.

CINCINNATI ELECTRONICS CORP.
7500 Innovation Way, Mason OH 45040. 513/573-6100. **Fax:** 513/573-6741. **Contact:** Danny Fisher, Personnel Director. **World Wide Web address:** http://www.cinele.com. **Description:** A leader in the design, development, production, and field support of sophisticated high-technology military electronic equipment. The company's business areas include contract production, communications systems and equipment, electronic warfare systems, and space electronics. **Common positions include:** Electrical/Electronics Engineer; Mechanical Engineer; Software Engineer. **Educational backgrounds include:** Computer Science; Engineering. **Benefits:** 401(k); Disability Coverage; Life Insurance; Medical Insurance; Tuition Assistance. **Corporate headquarters location:** This Location. **Parent company:** BA Systems (also at this location). **Listed on:** Privately held. **Number of employees at this location:** 340.

CIPRICO, INC.
2800 Campus Drive, Suite 60, Plymouth MN 55441. 763/551-4000. **Contact:** Jeanne Vincill, Director of Human Resources. **World Wide Web address:** http://www.ciprico.com. **Description:** A designer and manufacturer of intelligent disk and tape controller boards.

CIRRUS LOGIC, INC.
3100 West Warren Avenue, Fremont CA 94538. 510/623-8300. **Contact:** Employment Manager. **World Wide Web address:** http://www.cirrus.com. **Description:** Develops innovative architectures for analog and digital systems functions and implements these architectures in very large scale integrated (VLSI) circuits for applications that include mass storage, user interface (graphics, audio, and video), communications, and data acquisition. **Common positions include:** Accountant/Auditor; Buyer; Design Engineer; Electrical/Electronics Engineer; Software Engineer. **Educational backgrounds include:** Business Administration; Engineering; Finance. **Benefits:** 401(k); Dental Insurance; Disability Coverage; Life Insurance; Medical Insurance; Tuition Assistance. **Corporate headquarters location:** Austin TX. **Other U.S. locations:** CO; FL; IN; NH. **Number of employees at this location:** 1,400.

COHU, INC.
3912 Calle Fortunada, San Diego CA 92123. 858/277-6700. **Contact:** Personnel. **E-mail address:** info@cohu.com. **World Wide Web address:** http://www.cohu.com/cctv. **Description:** Supplies television camera equipment for use in such fields as area surveillance, teleconferencing, and industrial process control. **Corporate headquarters location:** This Location. **Listed on:** NASDAQ.

COLORADO CRYSTAL CORPORATION
2303 West Eighth Street, Loveland CO 80537. 970/667-9248. **Contact:** Personnel. **Description:** Manufactures quartz crystals for a variety of OEMs. **Corporate headquarters location:** This Location.

COMPEQ INTERNATIONAL CORPORATION
620 North John Glenn Road, Salt Lake City UT 84116. 801/990-2000. **Contact:** Human Resources Manager. **World Wide Web address:** http://www.compeq.com. **Description:** Manufactures printed circuit boards. **NOTE:** Entry-level positions are offered. **Common positions include:** Administrative Manager; Chemical Engineer; Controller; Draftsperson; Electrical/Electronics Engineer; Emergency Medical Technician; Environmental Engineer; Finance Director; Marketing Manager; Mechanical Engineer; Production Manager; Purchasing Agent/Manager; Quality Assurance Engineer. **Educational backgrounds include:** Engineering. **Benefits:** 401(k); Dental Insurance; Disability Coverage; Life Insurance; Medical Insurance; Profit Sharing; Tuition Assistance. **Corporate headquarters location:** This Location. **Annual sales/revenues:** $51 - $100 million. **Number of employees at this location:** 750.

COMPUTATIONAL SYSTEMS, INC. (CSI)
835 Innovation Drive, Knoxville TN 37932. 865/675-2110. **Fax:** 865/675-3100. **Contact:** Human Resources. **World Wide Web address:** http://www.compsys.com. **Description:** One of the world's largest manufacturers of Reliability-Based Maintenance (RBM) products and allied services. CSI is a technical leader in vibration analysis, with products in four major categories: batteries, adapters, vibration software modules, and advanced machinery analyzers. CSI's tribology products and services include the Tribology Minilab, the Tribology Total Solution system, and its Fluid Analysis Lab. CSI's infrared thermography systems include a focal-plane array camera, and Infranalysis data/image management system which provide a systematic route-based approach to IR that saves time and simplifies diagnoses. CSI's alignment and balancing services include both electromechanical and laser alignment systems. **Common positions include:** Electrical/Electronics Engineer; Manufacturer's/Wholesaler's Sales Rep.; Mechanical Engineer; Nuclear Engineer; Software Engineer; Technical Writer/Editor. **Benefits:** 401(k); Dental Insurance; Life Insurance; Medical Insurance; Profit Sharing; Tuition Assistance. **Corporate headquarters location:** This Location. **Other U.S. locations:** San Diego CA; Eddystone PA; Houston TX. **International locations:** Belgium; Germany; Italy; United Kingdom. **Parent company:** Emerson Electric Company. **Listed on:** Privately held.

COMTREX SYSTEMS CORPORATION
102 Executive Drive, Suite 1, Moorestown NJ 08057. 856/778-0090. **Fax:** 856/778-9322. **Contact:** Human Resources. **World Wide Web address:** http://www.comtrex.com. **Description:** Designs, develops, assembles, and markets computer software electronic terminals which provide retailers with transaction processing, in-store controls, and management information. The company primarily serves the food service and hospitality industries. Founded in 1981. **Corporate headquarters location:** This Location. **Listed on:** NASDAQ. **Stock exchange symbol:** COMX.

CONAX FLORIDA CORPORATION
2801 75th Street North, St. Petersburg FL 33710. 727/345-8000. **Fax:** 727/345-4217. **Contact:** Sandy Nitz, Personnel Administrator. **World Wide Web address:** http://www.conaxfl.com. **Description:** Manufactures temperature sensing devices, explosive actuated devices, and electrical penetrators. **Common positions include:** Electrical/Electronics Engineer; Mechanical Engineer. **Educational backgrounds include:** Engineering. **Benefits:** 401(k); Dental Insurance; Disability Coverage; Life Insurance; Medical Insurance; Tuition Assistance. **Corporate headquarters location:** This Location. **Listed on:** Privately held. **Number of employees at this location:** 125.

CONDUCTUS, INC.
969 West Maude Avenue, Sunnyvale CA 94086. 408/523-9950. **Fax:** 408/523-9973. **Contact:** Human Resources. **World Wide Web address:** http://www.conductus.com. **Description:** Develops, manufactures, and markets electronic systems and components based on superconductors. Conductus has developed high-temperature, thin-film superconducting materials and devices for wireless communications and magnetic resonance instruments. Research and development efforts at the company focus on developing superconductive technology for high speed communications. **Corporate headquarters location:** This Location. **Listed on:** NASDAQ. **Stock exchange symbol:** CDTS.

CONTROLS/INC. (CI)
One Technology Way, Caller Box 7011, Logansport IN 46947. 219/722-1167. **Fax:** 219/722-3100. **Contact:** Human Resources. **Description:** Designs and manufactures electronic controls. **Common positions include:** Accountant/Auditor; Blue-Collar Worker Supervisor; Buyer; Customer Service Representative; Designer; Electrical/Electronics Engineer; Human Resources Manager; Purchasing Agent/Manager; Quality Control Supervisor; Systems Analyst. **Educational backgrounds**

include: Engineering; Finance; Marketing. **Benefits:** 401(k); Disability Coverage; Life Insurance; Medical Insurance; Profit Sharing; Savings Plan; Tuition Assistance. **Corporate headquarters location:** This Location. **Number of employees at this location:** 200.

COOPER INDUSTRIES INC.
600 Travis Street, Suite 5800, Houston TX 77002. 713/209-8400. **Contact:** Brad Davison, Manager of Training and Development. **World Wide Web address:** http://www.cooperindustries.com. **Description:** This location houses administrative offices. Overall, Cooper Industries is a *Fortune* 500 company engaged in three areas of manufacturing: tools and hardware, electrical and electronic products, and automotive products. **Common positions include:** Accountant/Auditor; Attorney; Blue-Collar Worker Supervisor; Ceramics Engineer; Computer Programmer; Electrical/Electronics Engineer; Financial Analyst; Human Resources Manager; Industrial Engineer; Industrial Production Manager; Materials Engineer; Mechanical Engineer; Metallurgical Engineer; Operations/Production Manager; Quality Control Supervisor. **Educational backgrounds include:** Accounting; Business Administration; Computer Science; Engineering; Finance. **Benefits:** 401(k); Dental Insurance; Disability Coverage; Employee Discounts; Life Insurance; Medical Insurance; Pension Plan; Tuition Assistance. **Corporate headquarters location:** This Location. **Number of employees at this location:** 325.

COORSTEK
16000 Table Mountain Parkway, Golden CO 80403. 303/271-7000. **Contact:** Human Resources. **World Wide Web address:** http://www.coorstek.com. **Description:** Manufactures advanced technical ceramics, precision-machined metals, and engineered plastic products. **Corporate headquarters location:** This Location.

CREDENCE SYSTEMS CORPORATION
215 Fourier Avenue, Fremont CA 94539. 510/657-7400. **Contact:** Human Resources. **World Wide Web address:** http://www.credence.com. **Description:** Manufactures automatic testing equipment for digital and mixed-signal integrated circuits. **Corporate headquarters location:** This Location.

CREE INC.
4600 Silicon Drive, Durham NC 27703. 919/313-5300. **Fax:** 919/313-5452. **Contact:** Human Resources. **World Wide Web address:** http://www.cree.com. **Description:** Develops, manufactures, and markets electronic devices made from silicon carbide (SiC), a semiconductor material. The company manufactures a commercialized super bright blue light-emitting diode based on a combination of SiC and gallium nitride. Cree Research, Inc. markets its SiC wafers to corporate, government, and university research laboratories. Other devices developed by the company SiC radio frequency and microwave power devices, and high-temperature semiconductors. **Corporate headquarters location:** This Location. **Listed on:** NASDAQ. **Stock exchange symbol:** CREE.

CRESCENT ELECTRIC SUPPLY COMPANY
5333 Fairbank Street, Anchorage AK 99518. 907/562-2800. **Contact:** Human Resources. **World Wide Web address:** http://www.cesco.com. **Description:** A wholesaler of electrical supplies. **Common positions include:** Accountant/Auditor; Branch Manager; Buyer; Computer Programmer; General Manager. **Educational backgrounds include:** Accounting; Business Administration.

Benefits: 401(k); Dental Insurance; Employee Discounts; Medical Insurance; Pension Plan; Tuition Assistance. **Corporate headquarters location:** East Dubuque IL.

CROWN INTERNATIONAL
P.O. Box 1000, Elkhart IN 46515. 219/294-8000. **Physical address:** 1718 West Mishawaka Road, Elkhart IN 46517. **Fax:** 219/294-8083. **Contact:** Employment. **World Wide Web address:** http://www.crownintl.com. **Description:** Manufactures a wide variety of amplification equipment for the professional audio and industrial markets. The company also manufactures microphones, amplifiers, and transmitters for the broadcast market; and amplifiersand imaging products for the medical industry. **NOTE:** Second and third shifts are offered. **Common positions include:** Accountant; Computer Programmer; Designer; Draftsperson; Electrical/Electronics Engineer; Industrial Engineer; Internet Services Manager; Marketing Manager; Mechanical Engineer; Purchasing Agent/Manager; Sales Manager; Secretary; Software Engineer; Systems Analyst; Webmaster. **Educational backgrounds include:** Accounting; Business Administration; Communications; Computer Science; Economics; Engineering; Finance; Liberal Arts; Marketing. **Benefits:** 401(k); Casual Dress - Daily; Dental Insurance; Disability Coverage; Employee Discounts; Life Insurance; Medical Insurance; Tuition Assistance. **Special programs:** Summer Jobs. **Corporate headquarters location:** This Location. **Listed on:** Privately held. **Annual sales/revenues:** $51 - $100 million. **Number of employees at this location:** 700.

CRYPTEK SECURE COMMUNICATIONS
14130-C Sullyfield Circle, Chantilly VA 20151. 703/802-9300. **Fax:** 703/818-3706. **Contact:** Human Resources. **World Wide Web address:** http://www.cryptek.com. **Description:** Designs, produces, and markets secure digital facsimile equipment and networks. Founded in 1986. **Corporate headquarters location:** This Location. **Number of employees nationwide:** 40.

CUBIC CORPORATION
MS 10-23, P.O. Box 85587, San Diego CA 92186. 858/277-6780. **Fax:** 858/505-1524. **Contact:** Human Resources. **E-mail address:** jobs@cubic.com. **World Wide Web address:** http://www.cubic.com. **Description:** Cubic Corporation operates through two major segments: the Cubic Transportation Systems Group and the Cubic Defense Group. The Cubic Transportation Systems Group designs and manufactures automatic revenue collection systems throughout the world for public mass transit including railroads, buses, bridges, tunnels, toll roads, and parking lots. The Cubic Defense Group provides instrument training systems for the U.S. Army, Air Force, and Navy, as well as avionics, data links, aerospace systems, and logistical product support. The Defense Group also provides battle command training, radio communication systems, and field service operation and maintenance. Founded in 1951. **Corporate headquarters location:** This Location.

CURTIS INDUSTRIES, INC.
P.O. Box 343925, Milwaukee WI 53234-3925. 414/649-4200. **Contact:** James Livingston, Controller. **World Wide Web address:** http://www.curtisind.com. **Description:** An electronic components company that builds, designs, and manufactures a variety of electronic equipment including terminal blocks, RFI filters, and relay sockets. **Common positions include:** Accountant/Auditor; Blue-Collar Worker Supervisor; Buyer;

Computer Programmer; Credit Manager; Customer Service Rep.; Department Manager; Draftsperson; Electrical/Electronics Engineer; General Manager; Manufacturer's/Wholesaler's Sales Rep.; Marketing Specialist; Mechanical Engineer; Operations/Production Manager; Purchasing Agent/Manager; Quality Control Supervisor. **Educational backgrounds include:** Accounting; Business Administration; Computer Science; Engineering; Marketing. **Benefits:** Disability Coverage; Life Insurance; Medical Insurance; Savings Plan; Tuition Assistance. **Corporate headquarters location:** This Location.

CUSTOM CONTROL SENSORS, INC.
21111 Plummer Street, Chatsworth CA 91311. 818/341-4610. **Contact:** Personnel. **World Wide Web address:** http://www.ccsdualsnap.com. **Description:** Manufactures pressure, flow, and temperature gauges/switches for industrial and airborne applications. **Corporate headquarters location:** This Location.

CYBERNET SYSTEMS CORPORATION
727 Airport Boulevard, Ann Arbor MI 48108. 734/668-2567. **Fax:** 734/668-8780. **Contact:** Human Resources. **World Wide Web address:** http://www.cybernet.com. **Description:** A developer of virtual reality, force feedback, robotics, human/computer interactions, electromechanical systems, computer vision, and real-time systems. Cybernet Systems Corporation also provides integrated network client/server services. **Common positions include:** Administrative Assistant; Electrical/Electronics Engineer; Graphic Designer; Mechanical Engineer. **Educational backgrounds include:** Engineering; Finance. **Corporate headquarters location:** This Location.

CYBEROPTICS CORPORATION
5900 Golden Hills Drive, Minneapolis MN 55416. 612/542-5000. **Contact:** Human Resources. **World Wide Web address:** http://www.cyberoptics.com. **Description:** Designs, develops, and manufactures intelligent, laser-based sensor systems that are used for optical process control sensors and electronics inspections and related applications. **Corporate headquarters location:** This Location.

DBA SYSTEMS, INC.
P.O. Box 550, Melbourne FL 32902-0550. 321/727-0660. **Contact:** Paul Carney, Director of Human Resources. **World Wide Web address:** http://www.dba-sys.com. **Description:** Develops and manufactures advanced analytical software for use in remote sensing and orbital mechanics; and electronic systems for video tracking and precision film scanning digitizer applications. The company also develops specialized electronic systems for the U.S. Defense Department. **Common positions include:** Computer Programmer; Electrical/Electronics Engineer; Systems Analyst. **Educational backgrounds include:** Computer Science; Engineering. **Benefits:** 401(k); Dental Insurance; Disability Coverage; Employee Discounts; Life Insurance; Medical Insurance; Profit Sharing; Tuition Assistance. **Corporate headquarters location:** This Location. **Other U.S. locations:** Fairfax VA. **Parent company:** The Titan Corporation. **Listed on:** NASDAQ. **Number of employees at this location:** 130.

DCS CORPORATION
1330 Braddock Place, Alexandria VA 22314. 703/683-8430. **Fax:** 703/684-0930. **Contact:** Tina Venables, President of Human Resources. **World Wide Web address:** http://www.dcscorp.com. **Description:** A research and development firm providing services and products for the government

and private industry in areas such as electro-optics, virtual reality, fiber optics, and defense weapons and tactics. The company also provides services in the areas of simulation and training, satellite navigation, program management, and test evaluation. **Common positions include:** Administrative Assistant; Applications Engineer; Computer Engineer; Computer Programmer; Computer Scientist; Electrical/Electronics Engineer; Instructional Technologist; Software Engineer; Systems Analyst; Systems Manager. **Educational backgrounds include:** Computer Science; Engineering. **Benefits:** 401(k); Casual Dress - Fridays; Dental Insurance; Disability Coverage; Flexible Schedule; Life Insurance; Medical Insurance; Pension Plan; Sick Days (1 - 5); Tuition Assistance; Vacation Days (10 - 20). **Office hours:** Monday - Friday, 8:00 a.m. - 5:00 p.m. **Corporate headquarters location:** This Location. **Other U.S. locations:** AL; CA; FL; MD. **Listed on:** Privately held. **CEO:** Carl du Bac. **Number of employees at this location:** 195.

DSP GROUP, INC.
3120 Scott Boulevard, Santa Clara CA 95054. 408/986-4300. **Fax:** 408/986-4323. **Contact:** Human Resources. **World Wide Web address:** http://www.dspg.com. **Description:** Develops, licenses, and markets digital signal processing software and digital signal processor technologies for use in digital speech products. DSP Group offers a wide range of products and licensed technologies to major original equipment manufacturers in the personal computer, telecommunications, and consumer electronics markets. Products include digital speech processors for telephone answering machines. **Corporate headquarters location:** This Location.

DAKTRONICS INC.
331 32nd Avenue, P.O. Box 5128, Brookings SD 57006. 605/697-4000. **Fax:** 605/697-4700. **Contact:** Nancy Bohlen, Personnel Coordinator. **World Wide Web address:** http://www.daktronics.com. **Description:** Designs, manufactures, sells, and services computer programmable display systems such as stadium and arena scoring systems. Founded in 1968. **NOTE:** Entry-level positions and second and third shifts are offered. **Common positions include:** Accountant; Computer Engineer; Computer Programmer; Design Engineer; Electrical/Electronics Engineer; Graphic Artist; Manufacturing Engineer; Mechanical Engineer. **Educational backgrounds include:** Accounting; C/C++; Computer Science; Engineering; Novell; Software Development; Software Tech. Support; Visual Basic. **Benefits:** 401(k); Casual Dress - Daily; Dental Insurance; Disability Coverage; Medical Insurance; Tuition Assistance; Vacation Days (20+). **Special programs:** Internships; Summer Jobs. **Corporate headquarters location:** This Location. **Other U.S. locations:** Nationwide. **Listed on:** NASDAQ. **Stock exchange symbol:** DAKT. **Number of employees at this location:** 870. **Number of employees nationwide:** 900.

DALLAS SEMICONDUCTOR CORPORATION
4401 South Beltwood Parkway, Dallas TX 75244. 972/371-4000. **Contact:** Human Resources. **World Wide Web address:** http://www.dalsemi.com. **Description:** Manufactures semiconductors. **NOTE:** Entry-level positions are offered. **Common positions include:** Administrative Assistant; Applications Engineer; Customer Service Rep.; Database Administrator; Design Engineer; Electrical/Electronics Engineer; Internet Services Manager; Marketing Manager; Marketing Specialist; Mechanical Engineer; MIS Specialist;

Software Engineer; Systems Manager; Webmaster. **Educational backgrounds include:** Computer Science; Engineering; Physics. **Benefits:** 401(k); Dental Insurance; Disability Coverage; Life Insurance; Medical Insurance; Profit Sharing. **Corporate headquarters location:** This Location. **Listed on:** New York Stock Exchange. **Number of employees at this location:** 1,500.

DATA DEVICE CORPORATION
105 Wilbur Place, Bohemia NY 11716. 631/567-5600. **Fax:** 631/567-6357. **Contact:** Christine Ortize, Human Resources. **World Wide Web address:** http://www.ddc-web.com. **Description:** A manufacturer of high-performance microelectronic components for military, aerospace, and industrial applications. **Common positions include:** Accountant/Auditor; Design Engineer; Designer; Draftsperson; Electrical/Electronics Engineer; Human Resources Manager; Operations/Production Manager. **Educational backgrounds include:** Accounting; Business Administration; Engineering. **Benefits:** 401(k); Daycare Assistance; Dental Insurance; Disability Coverage; Life Insurance; Medical Insurance; Tuition Assistance; Vision Insurance. **Special programs:** Internships. **Corporate headquarters location:** This Location. **Subsidiaries include:** Beta Transformer Technology Corp. **Annual sales/revenues:** $5 - $10 million. **Number of employees at this location:** 500. **Number of employees nationwide:** 800.

DATA I/O CORPORATION
10525 Willows Road NE, P.O. Box 97046, Redmond WA 98073. 425/881-6444. **Recorded jobline:** 425/867-6963. **Contact:** Employment Department. **World Wide Web address:** http://www.data-io.com. **Description:** Manufactures programmable integrated circuit chips. **NOTE:** Entry-level positions are offered. **Common positions include:** Buyer; Computer Operator; Computer Programmer; Design Engineer; Electrical/Electronics Engineer; Manufacturing Engineer; Mechanical Engineer; Software Engineer. **Educational backgrounds include:** Engineering. **Benefits:** 401(k); Dental Insurance; Disability Coverage; Life Insurance; Medical Insurance; Paid Holidays; Profit Sharing; Tuition Assistance; Vacation Days. **Special programs:** Internships. **Corporate headquarters location:** This Location. **Other U.S. locations:** Nationwide. **Listed on:** NASDAQ. **Number of employees at this location:** 285. **Number of employees nationwide:** 320.

DATACOM TEXTRON
11001 31st Place West, Everett WA 98204. 425/355-0590. **Contact:** Personnel. **World Wide Web address:** http://www.datacom.textron.com. **Description:** Manufactures high-technology support equipment, digital test equipment, and related products. **Common positions include:** Accountant/Auditor; Administrator; Advertising Clerk; Blue-Collar Worker Supervisor; Buyer; Computer Programmer; Credit Manager; Customer Service Rep.; Department Manager; Draftsperson; Electrical/Electronics Engineer; Financial Analyst; Human Resources Manager; Manufacturer's/Wholesaler's Sales Rep.; Marketing Specialist; Mechanical Engineer; Operations/Production Manager; Purchasing Agent/Manager; Quality Control Supervisor; Systems Analyst. **Educational backgrounds include:** Accounting; Business Administration; Communications; Computer Science; Engineering; Finance; Marketing. **Benefits:** Dental Insurance; Disability Coverage; Life Insurance; Medical Insurance; Pension Plan; Profit Sharing; Tuition Assistance. **Corporate headquarters location:** This Location. **Parent company:** Greenlee Textron.

DATAMATIC.COM
P.O. Box 850461, Richardson TX 75085-0461. 972/234-5000. **Physical address:** 715 North Glenville Drive, Suite 450, Richardson TX 75081. **Toll-free phone:** 800/880-2878. **Fax:** 972/234-1134. **Contact:** Human Resources. **E-mail address:** hr@datamatic.com. **World Wide Web address:** http://www.datamatic.com. **Description:** Supplies test and measurement systems to investor-owned utilities and municipalities. Founded in 1977. **Office hours:** Monday - Friday, 8:00 a.m. - 5:00 p.m.

DATUM INC.
6781 Via del Oro, San Jose CA 95119. 408/578-4161. **Contact:** Human Resources. **World Wide Web address:** http://www.datum.com. **Description:** Designs, develops, manufactures, and markets precision frequency and timing instrumentation products. Datum's principal products are cesium and quartz crystal frequency standards that produce or stabilize frequencies. Datum's timing instrumentation products use a stable frequency standard to generate, encode, translate, and distribute precise time information. These products are used in a broad range of applications including accurate synchronization of telecommunications networks, synchronization of computers in local area networks, generation of precise time information, and control of global navigation satellite systems. **Corporate headquarters location:** Irvine CA.

DENSE-PAC MICROSYSTEMS, INC.
7321 Lincoln Way, Garden Grove CA 92841. 714/898-0007. **Fax:** 714/896-0748. **Contact:** Human Resources. **World Wide Web address:** http://www.dense-pac.com. **Description:** Designs, develops, manufactures, and markets a broad line of standard and custom monolithic memories and memory/logic/analog modules and subsystems. The company's products are used in a variety of military, industrial, and commercial applications where high-density, high-performance, and high-reliability standards are required. Typical product applications are in the areas of communications, medical instrumentation, missiles, avionics, and space satellites. **Corporate headquarters location:** This Location. **Listed on:** NASDAQ. **Stock exchange symbol:** DPAC.

DETECTOR ELECTRONICS CORPORATION
6901 West 110th Street, Minneapolis MN 55438. 952/941-5665. **Toll-free phone:** 800/765-FIRE. **Fax:** 952/829-8745. **Contact:** Dee Possin, Human Resources Manager. **World Wide Web address:** http://www.detronics.com. **Description:** An international leader in manufacturing electronic flame and gas detection equipment and systems. **NOTE:** Entry-level positions and second and third shifts are offered. **Common positions include:** Account Manager; Accountant; Administrative Assistant; AS400 Programmer Analyst; Buyer; Chemical Engineer; Chief Financial Officer; Computer Programmer; Controller; Credit Manager; Customer Service Rep.; Design Engineer; Electrical/Electronics Engineer; Graphic Designer; Human Resources Manager; Manufacturing Engineer; Marketing Manager; Marketing Specialist; Mechanical Engineer; Network/Systems Administrator; Operations Manager; Production Manager; Project Manager; Purchasing Agent/Manager; Quality Control Supervisor; Sales Manager; Sales Representative; Secretary; Systems Analyst; Systems Manager; Technical Support Manager; Technical Writer/Editor; Transportation/Traffic Specialist; Vice President of Marketing and Sales. **Educational backgrounds include:** Accounting; AS400 Certification; Business Administration; C/C++; Engineering; Marketing;

Microsoft Office; Microsoft Word; Novell; Software Development; Software Tech. Support; Spreadsheets; SQL; Visual Basic. **Benefits:** 401(k); Dental Insurance; Disability Coverage; Employee Discounts; Life Insurance; Medical Insurance; Pension Plan; Profit Sharing; Public Transit Available; Sick Days (6 - 10); Tuition Assistance; Vacation Days (10 - 20). **Office hours:** Monday - Friday, 7:30 a.m. - 5:30 p.m. **Corporate headquarters location:** This Location. **International locations:** Worldwide. **Parent company:** Williams Holdings PLC. **Listed on:** Privately held. **President:** Jerry Slocum. **Number of employees at this location:** 200. **Number of employees worldwide:** 260.

DEUTSCH RELAYS INC.
65 Daly Road, East Northport NY 11731. 631/499-6000. **Contact:** Diane Goerz, Human Resources Manager. **Description:** Manufactures miniature electronic relays. **Corporate headquarters location:** This Location.

DEWEY ELECTRONICS CORPORATION
27 Muller Road, Oakland NJ 07436. 201/337-4700. **Contact:** Carol Grofsik, Director of Administration. **Description:** Develops, designs, engineers, and manufactures electronics systems for military and civilian customers. **Common positions include:** Buyer; Draftsperson; Electrical/Electronics Engineer; Industrial Engineer; Mechanical Engineer; Quality Control Supervisor. **Educational backgrounds include:** Business Administration; Computer Science; Engineering. **Benefits:** Disability Coverage; Life Insurance; Medical Insurance; Pension Plan; Tuition Assistance. **Corporate headquarters location:** This Location.

DICKEY-JOHN CORPORATION
P.O. Box 10, Auburn IL 62615. 217/438-2243. **Fax:** 217/438-3623. **Contact:** Director of Human Resources. **World Wide Web address:** http://www. dickey-john.com. **Description:** DICKEY-john Corporation is an electronic design and manufacturing company. Products include application control systems, grain moisture monitoring equipment, ice control systems, and hand-held analytical viscometers. The company's primary markets are the agriculture, public works, and construction industries. **Common positions include:** Accountant/Auditor; Blue-Collar Worker Supervisor; Chemical Engineer; Chemist; Computer Programmer; Draftsperson; Electrical/Electronics Engineer; Human Resources Manager; Industrial Engineer; Mechanical Engineer; Quality Control Supervisor; Software Engineer; Systems Analyst. **Educational backgrounds include:** Computer Science; Engineering; Marketing. **Benefits:** 401(k); Dental Insurance; Disability Coverage; Life Insurance; Medical Insurance; Profit Sharing. **Special programs:** Internships. **Corporate headquarters location:** This Location. **Parent company:** Churchill Companies. **Number of employees at this location:** 450.

DIEBOLD, INC.
5995 Mayfair Road, P.O. Box 3077, Department 9-58, North Canton OH 44720-8077. 330/489-4000. **Fax:** 330/490-4549. **Contact:** Human Resources. **World Wide Web address:** http://www. diebold.com. **Description:** Engaged in the sale, manufacture, installation, and service of automated teller machines, physical and electronic security systems, and software for the financial and commercial industries. Other products include vaults, vault doors, lockers, safes, alarms, video surveillance systems, and data line security systems. Founded in 1859. **Common positions include:** Accountant/Auditor; Buyer; Computer Programmer;

Electrical/Electronics Engineer; Marketing Specialist; Systems Analyst; Technical Writer/ Editor. **Educational backgrounds include:** Accounting; Computer Science; Engineering; Marketing. **Benefits:** Dental Insurance; Disability Coverage; Employee Discounts; Life Insurance; Medical Insurance; Pension Plan; Tuition Assistance. **Corporate headquarters location:** This Location. **Listed on:** New York Stock Exchange.

DIGITAL SYSTEMS CORPORATION
P.O. Box 158, Walkersville MD 21793-0158. 301/845-4141. **Fax:** 301/898-3331. **Contact:** Human Resources. **Description:** Manufactures access control systems and security systems. The company also provides software support for the U.S. Navy. **Common positions include:** Administrative Assistant; Buyer; Computer Programmer; Design Engineer; Electrical/Electronics Engineer; General Manager; Internet Services Manager; Marketing Manager; MIS Specialist; Sales Engineer; Software Engineer; Systems Analyst; Systems Manager. **Educational backgrounds include:** Engineering; Marketing. **Benefits:** 401(k); Life Insurance; Medical Insurance. **Corporate headquarters location:** This Location. **Other U.S. locations:** Lexington Park MD. **Listed on:** Privately held. **Number of employees at this location:** 30.

DYNACIRCUITS MANUFACTURING CO.
11230 Addison Street, Franklin Park IL 60131. 847/451-1700. **Fax:** 847/451-9266. **Contact:** Ivanne Alcate, Human Resources Manager. **Description:** A manufacturer of printed circuit boards. **Common positions include:** Computer Programmer; Cost Estimator; Customer Service Representative; Electrical/Electronics Engineer; Human Resources Manager; Industrial Engineer; Mechanical Engineer; Quality Control Supervisor; Systems Analyst. **Educational backgrounds include:** Engineering. **Benefits:** Dental Insurance; Life Insurance; Medical Insurance; Pension Plan; Profit Sharing; Tuition Assistance. **Corporate headquarters location:** This Location. **Listed on:** Privately held. **Number of employees at this location:** 215.

EFI ELECTRONICS CORPORATION
1751 South 4800 West, Salt Lake City UT 84104. 801/977-9009. **Toll-free phone:** 800/877-1174. **Fax:** 801/977-0200. **Contact:** Human Resources. **World Wide Web address:** http://www.efinet.com. **Description:** Manufactures and markets TVSS and UPS products. The company's TVSS products protect electronic equipment from electrical disturbances such as lightning, grid switching, and electrical accidents which can lead to hardware failure, data communication disruptions, equipment damage. **Corporate headquarters location:** This Location. **Other U.S. locations:** DE.

EGS ELECTRICAL GROUP
7770 Frontage Road, Skokie IL 60077. 847/679-7800. **Fax:** 847/763-6032. **Contact:** Human Resources. **World Wide Web address:** http://www. egseg.com. **Description:** Manufactures electronic components such as conduit bodies and boxes, plugs and receptacles, industrial lighting fixtures, cord reels, and junction bodies. **Common positions include:** Accountant/Auditor; Designer; Mechanical Engineer; Secretary. **Educational backgrounds include:** Accounting; Engineering. **Corporate headquarters location:** This Location. **Parent company:** Emerson Electric Company.

EHV-WEIDMANN INDUSTRIES, INC.
P.O. Box 903, St. Johnsbury VT 05819. 802/748-8106. **Contact:** Mark Bechtold, Human Resources

Manager. **Description:** Manufactures electrical insulation products primarily for transformers. The company also produces electrical systems. **Common positions include:** Accountant/Auditor; Chemical Engineer; Chemist; Civil Engineer; Computer Programmer; Customer Service Rep.; Education Administrator; Electrical/Electronics Engineer; Industrial Engineer; Mechanical Engineer; Operations/Production Manager; Systems Analyst. **Educational backgrounds include:** Engineering. **Benefits:** 401(k); Dental Insurance; Disability Coverage; Life Insurance; Medical Insurance; Pension Plan; Savings Plan; Tuition Assistance. **Corporate headquarters location:** This Location. **Listed on:** Privately held. **Number of employees at this location:** 310.

EMC TEST SYSTEMS, L.P.
P.O. Box 80589, Austin TX 78708. 512/835-4684. **Fax:** 512/835-4729. **Contact:** Kristen Kobierowski, Human Resources Manager. **E-mail address:** human.resources@emctest.com. **World Wide Web address:** http://www.emctest.com. **Description:** Designs, manufactures, and maintains products that measure, contain, and suppress electromagnetic, RF, and microwave energy. The company markets its products under the names Rantec, EMCO, Rayproof, and Enroshield. **NOTE:** Second and third shifts are offered. **Common positions include:** Account Rep.; Accountant; Administrative Assistant; Blue-Collar Worker Supervisor; Cost Estimator; Draftsperson; Electrical/Electronics Engineer; Manufacturing Engineer; Marketing Specialist; Sales Manager; Sales Representative. **Educational backgrounds include:** Accounting; Business Administration; Engineering; Liberal Arts. **Benefits:** 401(k); Casual Dress - Daily; Dental Insurance; Disability Coverage; Employee Discounts; Life Insurance; Medical Insurance; Pension Plan; Stock Purchase; Tuition Assistance. **Special programs:** Internships. **Other U.S. locations:** Durant OK. **International locations:** Enra, Finland. **Parent company:** ESCO Electronics Corporation is a diversified producer of commercial products. ESCO's products include electronic equipment, valves and filters, filtration and fluid flow components, automatic test equipment, utility load management equipment, and anechoic/shielding systems. ESCO's other operating subsidiaries include PTI Technologies, Inc.; VACCO Industries; Distribution Control Systems, Inc.; Rantec Microwave & Electronics; Lindgren RF Enclosures; Comtrak Technologies, Inc.; and Filtertek Inc. **Listed on:** New York Stock Exchange. **Stock exchange symbol:** ESE. **Number of employees at this location:** 100. **Number of employees nationwide:** 150. **Number of employees worldwide:** 200.

EMR SCHLUMBERGER PHOTOELECTRIC
20 Wallace Road, Princeton Junction NJ 08550. 609/799-1000. **Contact:** Personnel. **World Wide Web address:** http://www.schlumberger.com. **Description:** This location is engaged in the engineering and manufacturing of critical, high-reliability transducers and transducer systems; nuclear sources and detectors for oil field services; and sensors/transducers for high-value measurement and control. Overall, EMR Schlumberger Photoelectric is a research, development, and manufacturing division for Schlumberger Ltd. **Common positions include:** Chemical Engineer; Electrical/Electronics Engineer; Mechanical Engineer; Physicist. **Educational backgrounds include:** Engineering; Physics. **Benefits:** Dental Insurance; Disability Coverage; Life Insurance; Medical Insurance; Pension Plan; Profit Sharing; Savings Plan; Stock Option; Tuition Assistance. **Corporate headquarters location:** This Location.

Parent company: Schlumberger Ltd. **Listed on:** New York Stock Exchange. **Number of employees at this location:** 60.

ESE, INC.
P.O. Box 1107, Marshfield WI 54449. 715/387-4778. **Physical address:** 3600 Downwind Drive, Marshfield WI. **Fax:** 715/387-0125. **Contact:** Human Resources. **E-mail address:** ese1@ese1.com. **World Wide Web address:** http://www.ese1.com. **Description:** Designs and engineers process control systems for the food, dairy, brewery, and pharmaceutical industries. Founded in 1981. **Common positions include:** Cost Estimator; Sales Manager; Software Engineer. **Educational backgrounds include:** Engineering. **Benefits:** 401(k); Disability Coverage; Life Insurance; Medical Insurance; Profit Sharing. **Office hours:** Monday - Friday, 8:00 a.m. - 5:00 p.m. **Corporate headquarters location:** This Location. **Number of employees at this location:** 30.

EAGLE ELECTRIC MANUFACTURING CO.
45-31 Court Square, Long Island City NY 11101. 718/937-8000. **Contact:** Human Resources. **World Wide Web address:** http://www.eagle-electric.com. **Description:** Manufactures electrical wiring devices. **Common positions include:** Administrator; Advertising Clerk; Blue-Collar Worker Supervisor; Commercial Artist; Computer Programmer; Credit Manager; Customer Service Rep.; Draftsperson; Electrical/Electronics Engineer; Human Resources Manager; Industrial Engineer; Manufacturer's/Wholesaler's Sales Rep.; Mechanical Engineer; Purchasing Agent/Manager; Quality Control Supervisor; Transportation/Traffic Specialist. **Educational backgrounds include:** Art/Design; Computer Science; Engineering. **Benefits:** Dental Insurance; Disability Coverage; Employee Discounts; Life Insurance; Medical Insurance; Pension Plan; Savings Plan; Tuition Assistance. **Corporate headquarters location:** This Location.

EESCO, INC.
3939 South Karlov Avenue, Chicago IL 60632-3813. 773/376-8750. **Fax:** 773/376-8288. **Contact:** Denise Allen, Human Resources Representative. **Description:** A wholesale distributor of electrical, electronic, and communication systems products. **NOTE:** Human Resources can be reached at 412/454-2384. **Common positions include:** Branch Manager; Customer Service Rep.; Electrical/Electronics Engineer; Management Trainee; Manufacturer's/Wholesaler's Sales Rep.; Operations/Production Manager. **Educational backgrounds include:** Communications; Marketing. **Benefits:** 401(k); Dental Insurance; Disability Coverage; Employee Discounts; Life Insurance; Medical Insurance; Profit Sharing; Tuition Assistance. **Special programs:** Internships. **Corporate headquarters location:** This Location. **Other U.S. locations:** FL; GA; IN; MI; MN; SC; WI. **Number of employees at this location:** 125. **Number of employees nationwide:** 800.

ELECTRO CORPORATION
1845 57th Street, Sarasota FL 34243. 941/355-8411. **Contact:** Beverly Morrell, Human Resources Manager. **World Wide Web address:** http://www.electrocorp.com. **Description:** A manufacturer of magnetic sensing devices, tachometers, proximity switches, and circuit and control systems. **Common positions include:** Accountant/Auditor; Blue-Collar Worker Supervisor; Buyer; Computer Programmer; Customer Service Rep.; Draftsperson; Electrical/Electronics Engineer; Human Resources Manager; Industrial Engineer; Marketing Specialist; Mechanical Engineer; Operations/Production Manager; Purchasing Agent/Manager; Quality

Control Supervisor; Services Sales Rep.; Systems Analyst. **Educational backgrounds include:** Accounting; Computer Science; Engineering; Finance; Marketing. **Benefits:** Disability Coverage; Life Insurance; Medical Insurance; Profit Sharing; Savings Plan; Tuition Assistance. **Corporate headquarters location:** This Location. **Parent company:** Invensys Sensor Systems.

ELECTRO SCIENTIFIC INDUSTRIES, INC.
13900 NW Science Park Drive, Portland OR 97229. 503/641-4141. **Contact:** Human Resources. **World Wide Web address:** http://www.elcsci.com. **Description:** Designs and builds advanced production equipment used throughout the world in electronics manufacturing. The principal end markets for products made using ESI equipment include the computer, telecommunications, and automotive industries. ESI's principal product lines include precision, high-speed production, and test equipment for ceramic capacitor manufacturing; industry leading laser processing systems for semiconductor memory yield improvement; and advanced laser trimming systems for the precise tuning of electronic circuits. Founded in 1949. **Common positions include:** Electrical/Electronics Engineer; Mechanical Engineer; Software Engineer. **Educational backgrounds include:** Engineering; Physics. **Benefits:** 401(k); Dental Insurance; Disability Coverage; Life Insurance; Medical Insurance; Profit Sharing; Tuition Assistance. **Corporate headquarters location:** This Location.

ELECTROGLAS, INC.
6024 Silver Creek Valley Road, San Jose CA 95138. 408/528-3000. **Contact:** Human Resources Department. **World Wide Web address:** http://www.electroglas.com. **Description:** Develops, manufactures, markets, and services automatic wafer probing equipment for use in the fabrication of semiconductor devices. The company's primary products are its Horizon 4000 Series wafer probers. **Corporate headquarters location:** This Location.

ELECTROTEK CORPORATION
7745 South 10th Street, Oak Creek WI 53154. 414/762-1390. **Contact:** Katie Rowland, Human Resources Manager. **Description:** Manufactures printed circuit boards. Founded in 1968. **NOTE:** Entry-level positions and second and third shifts are offered. **Common positions include:** Account Manager; Accountant; Administrative Assistant; Computer Operator; Computer Programmer; Controller; Cost Estimator; Credit Manager; Human Resources Manager; Manufacturing Engineer; Operations/Production Manager; Purchasing Agent/Manager; Quality Control Supervisor; Sales Manager; Systems Analyst. **Educational backgrounds include:** Accounting; Business Administration; Chemistry; Computer Science; Mathematics. **Benefits:** 401(k); Dental Insurance; Disability Coverage; Life Insurance; Medical Insurance; Profit Sharing; Tuition Assistance. **Special programs:** Training. **Corporate headquarters location:** This Location. **Annual sales/revenues:** $11 - $20 million. **Number of employees at this location:** 160.

ELGAR ELECTRONICS CORPORATION
9250 Brown Deer Road, San Diego CA 92121-2294. 858/458-0201. **Fax:** 858/458-0257. **Contact:** Tom Erickson, Vice President of Human Resources. **World Wide Web address:** http://www.elgar.com. **Description:** Manufactures power electronics equipment including AC/DC programmable power supplies for test and measurement purposes and power conditioning/back-up systems for special applications such as harsh environments. **Common positions include:** Accountant/Auditor; Buyer;

Computer Programmer; Customer Service Rep.; Designer; Draftsperson; Electrical/Electronics Engineer; Financial Analyst; General Manager; Mechanical Engineer; Purchasing Agent/Manager; Quality Control Supervisor; Software Engineer; Systems Analyst. **Educational backgrounds include:** Accounting; Business Administration; Computer Science; Engineering; Marketing. **Benefits:** 401(k); Dental Insurance; Disability Coverage; Employee Discounts; Life Insurance; Medical Insurance; Savings Plan; Tuition Assistance. **Corporate headquarters location:** This Location. **Listed on:** London Stock Exchange. **Number of employees at this location:** 400.

ELMO SEMICONDUCTOR CORPORATION
7590 North Glenoaks Boulevard, Burbank CA 91504. 818/252-3566. **Fax:** 818/252-3522. **Contact:** Human Resources. **World Wide Web address:** http://www.elmosemiconductor.com. **Description:** Processes, screens, and tests semiconductor die; manufactures packaging products; and offers testing services. **Common positions include:** Accountant; Administrator; Aerospace Engineer; Blue-Collar Worker Supervisor; Buyer; Computer Programmer; Customer Service Rep.; Department Manager; Electrical/Electronics Engineer; Human Resources Manager; Manufacturer's/Wholesaler's Sales Rep.; Marketing Specialist; Metallurgical Engineer; Operations/Production Manager; Purchasing Agent/Manager; Quality Control Supervisor; Systems Analyst; Technical Writer/Editor. **Educational backgrounds include:** Business Administration; Communications; Engineering; Liberal Arts; Marketing. **Benefits:** Credit Union; Dental Insurance; Disability Coverage; Life Insurance; Medical Insurance; Profit Sharing; Tuition Assistance. **Corporate headquarters location:** This Location. **Parent company:** Kimball Electronics Group.

ELPAC ELECTRONICS INC.
1562 Reynolds Avenue, Irvine CA 92614. 949/476-6070. **Fax:** 949/476-6080. **Contact:** Human Resources. **World Wide Web address:** http://www.elpac.com. **Description:** Manufactures power supplies, capacitors, and filters. **Common positions include:** Accountant/Auditor; Blue-Collar Worker Supervisor; Buyer; Credit Manager; Customer Service Rep.; Designer; Draftsperson; Electrical/Electronics Engineer; Industrial Engineer; Manufacturer's/Wholesaler's Sales Rep.; Operations/Production Manager; Purchasing Agent/Manager; Quality Control Supervisor; Systems Analyst; Technician. **Educational backgrounds include:** Accounting; Business Administration; Economics; Engineering; Finance; Marketing; Mathematics; Physics. **Benefits:** Commuter Bonus Plan; Dental Insurance; Disability Coverage; Life Insurance; Medical Insurance; Safety Bonus Plan; Savings Plan; Tuition Assistance. **Corporate headquarters location:** This Location.

ELTEC INSTRUMENTS INC.
P.O. Box 9610, Daytona Beach FL 32120. 904/252-0411. **Contact:** Samuel D. Mollenkof, Director of Personnel. **Description:** Develops, manufactures, and markets infrared sensors, industrial control systems, and ohm resistors. Primary customers include alarm manufacturers; building automation systems, heating, air conditioning, and lighting control marketers; and process control systems developers. **Common positions include:** Accountant; Administrator; Buyer; Draftsperson; Electrical/Electronics Engineer; Human Resources Manager; Operations/Production Manager; Purchasing Agent/Manager; Sensors Engineer; Systems Engineer. **Educational backgrounds**

include: Accounting; Business Administration; Engineering; Marketing. Benefits: Dental Insurance; Life Insurance; Medical Insurance; Tuition Assistance. Corporate headquarters location: This Location.

EMCORE CORPORATION

394 Elizabeth Avenue, Somerset NJ 08873. 732/271-9090. Contact: Joan Thomas, Manager of Technical Staffing. World Wide Web address: http://www.emcore.com. Description: Manufactures semiconductors through the metal organic chemical vapor deposition production system. NOTE: Entry-level positions and second and third shifts are offered. Common positions include: Chemical Engineer; Customer Service Manager; Design Engineer; Electrical/Electronics Engineer; Manufacturing Engineer; Mechanical Engineer; Software Engineer. Educational backgrounds include: Engineering. Benefits: 401(k); Casual Dress - Daily; Dental Insurance; Disability Coverage; Flexible Schedule; Life Insurance; Medical Insurance; Pension Plan; Relocation Assistance; Sick Days (1 - 5); Tuition Assistance; Vacation Days (10 - 20). Special programs: Training; Co-ops. Office hours: Monday - Friday, 8:00 a.m. - 5:00 p.m. Listed on: NASDAQ. Stock exchange symbol: EMKR. President/CEO: Reuben F. Richards, Jr. Annual sales/revenues: $21 - $50 million. Number of employees at this location: 250.

EMERSON ELECTRIC COMPANY

8000 West Florissant Avenue, St. Louis MO 63136. 314/553-2000. Contact: Human Resources. World Wide Web address: http://www.emersonelectric.com. Description: This location operates as part of the Electronics and Space division. Overall, Emerson Electric Company produces process control instrumentation and systems, industrial motors and drives; industrial machinery and components; computer support products; fractional horsepower motors; and components for air conditioners, heaters, and hand tools. Common positions include: Accountant/Auditor; Computer Programmer; Electrical/Electronics Engineer; Systems Analyst; Technical Writer/Editor. Educational backgrounds include: Engineering. Benefits: Dental Insurance; Disability Coverage; Employee Discounts; Medical Insurance; Savings Plan; Tuition Assistance. Corporate headquarters location: This Location. Number of employees nationwide: 117,000.

ENDEVCO CORPORATION

30700 Rancho Viejo Road, San Juan Capistrano CA 92675. 949/493-8181. Contact: Susan Duberg, Human Resources Administrator. World Wide Web address: http://www.endevco.com. Description: Manufactures electronic instrumentation systems which measure vibration, shock, motion, and pressure. Common positions include: Computer Programmer; Electrical/Electronics Engineer; Mechanical Engineer; Metallurgical Engineer. Educational backgrounds include: Computer Science; Engineering. Benefits: Dental Insurance; Disability Coverage; Employee Discounts; Life Insurance; Medical Insurance; Savings Plan; Tuition Assistance. Corporate headquarters location: This Location. Parent company: Meggitt PLC.

ENSCO, INC.

5400 Port Royal Road, Springfield VA 22151-2312. 703/321-9000. Contact: Professional Staffing. World Wide Web address: http://www.ensco.com. Description: A research and development, applied systems engineering, and professional services firm providing sensor- and computer-based systems in

the areas of defense, environmental sciences, transportation, and business applications. Common positions include: Computer Programmer; Department Manager; Electrical/Electronics Engineer; Mechanical Engineer; Systems Analyst; Technical Writer/Editor. Educational backgrounds include: Computer Science; Engineering; Mathematics; Physics. Benefits: Dental Insurance; Disability Coverage; Employee Discounts; Life Insurance; Medical Insurance; Pension Plan; Tuition Assistance. Corporate headquarters location: This Location. Other U.S. locations: AL; CA; FL; IN; MI; NY. Listed on: Privately held. Number of employees at this location: 140.

ERIM (ENVIRONMENTAL RESEARCH INSTITUTE OF MICHIGAN)

P.O. Box 134008, Ann Arbor MI 48113-4008. 734/994-1200. Contact: Technical Recruiting Manager. World Wide Web address: http://www.erim.org. Description: A private, nonprofit research and development organization engaged in the design and development of radar and electro-optical sensors and imaging systems. Common positions include: Accountant/Auditor; Buyer; Computer Programmer; Editor; Electrical/Electronics Engineer; Geographer; Geologist/Geophysicist; Mechanical Engineer; Metallurgical Engineer; Physicist; Technical Writer/Editor; Writer. Educational backgrounds include: Accounting; Art/Design; Business Administration; Communications; Computer Science; Engineering; Geology; Mathematics; Physics. Benefits: Dental Insurance; Disability Coverage; Life Insurance; Medical Insurance; Pension Plan; Tuition Assistance. Special programs: Internships. Corporate headquarters location: This Location. Other U.S. locations: Orange Park FL; Arlington VA. Number of employees at this location: 850.

ESTERLINE TECHNOLOGIES

10800 NE Eighth Street, Suite 600, Bellevue WA 98004. 425/453-9400. Fax: 425/519-1895. Contact: Personnel. World Wide Web address: http://www.esterline.com. Description: A manufacturing company serving several market areas including commercial aerospace, the defense industry, and various manufacturing industries. The company is divided into three business groups: Instrumentation, Aerospace/Defense, and Automation. Each business group has two main subsidiaries which focus on the development and manufacture of products within the relevant area. Corporate headquarters location: This Location. Listed on: New York Stock Exchange. Stock exchange symbol: ESL. CEO: Wendell P. Hurlbut.

EXAR CORPORATION

48720 Kato Road, Fremont CA 94538. 510/668-7000. Contact: Human Resources. World Wide Web address: http://www.exar.com. Description: Engaged in the design, manufacture, and marketing of analog and mixed signal integrated circuits and subsystems, primarily for use in telecommunications, data communications, microperipherals, and consumer electronics products. Common positions include: Accountant; Administrator; Buyer; Customer Service Rep.; Department Manager; Electrical/Electronics Engineer; General Manager; Human Resources Manager; Manufacturer's/Wholesaler's Sales Rep.; Marketing Specialist; Operations/Production Manager; Quality Control Supervisor. Educational backgrounds include: Accounting; Business Administration; Communications; Computer Science; Engineering; Marketing; Physics. Benefits: Dental Insurance; Disability Coverage; Employee Discounts; Life Insurance; Medical Insurance; Savings Plan; Stock Option; Tuition Assistance.

Corporate headquarters location: This Location. **Listed on:** NASDAQ. **Number of employees at this location:** 500.

FAS TECHNOLOGIES
10480 Markison Road, Dallas TX 75230. 214/553-9991. **Fax:** 214/553-9919. **Contact:** Human Resources. **E-mail address:** personnel@fas.com. **World Wide Web address:** http://www.fas.com. **Description:** Manufactures semiconductor processing equipment. Founded in 1988. **Common positions include:** Administrative Assistant; Buyer; Customer Service Rep.; Electrical/Electronics Engineer; Mechanical Engineer; Software Engineer; Technical Writer/Editor. **Educational backgrounds include:** Engineering. **Benefits:** Dental Insurance; Employee Discounts; Life Insurance; Medical Insurance; Tuition Assistance. **Corporate headquarters location:** This Location. **International locations:** Japan. **Subsidiaries include:** FAS-Asia, Ltd. **Listed on:** Privately held.

FSI INTERNATIONAL, INC.
322 Lake Hazeltine Drive, Chaska MN 55318. 952/448-5440. **Contact:** Mark Almond, Human Resources Representative. **World Wide Web address:** http://www.fsi-intl.com. **Description:** A worldwide leader in producing automated silicon wafer processing equipment used by semiconductor manufacturers. The company offers three types of products: microlithography clusters, surface conditioning products, and chemical management systems. Microlithography clusters apply and develop photosensitive materials on the surface of silicon wafers. Surface conditioning products are used for preparing silicon wafers for the processing of integrated circuits. Chemical management systems are used by semiconductor manufacturers for purposes such as the controlled distribution and conditioning of chemicals throughout a semiconductor manufacturing facility and the blending of concentrated chemicals with deionized water. **Common positions include:** Customer Service Representative; Electrical/Electronics Engineer; Mechanical Engineer; Process Engineer. **Educational backgrounds include:** Chemistry; Engineering. **Benefits:** Disability Coverage; Life Insurance; Medical Insurance; Pension Plan; Profit Sharing; Tuition Assistance. **Corporate headquarters location:** This Location.

FANUC ROBOTICS NORTH AMERICA, INC.
3900 West Hamlin Road, Rochester Hills MI 48309. 248/377-7000. **Fax:** 248/377-7362. **Recorded jobline:** 248/377-7677. **Contact:** Human Resources. **E-mail address:** resume@fanucrobotics.com. **World Wide Web address:** http://www.fanucrobotics.com. **Description:** Engaged in the business of automation intelligence and solutions for assembling, cutting, dispensing, laser processing, material handling and removing, painting, palletizing, and welding processes. **Common positions include:** Electrical/Electronics Engineer; Mechanical Engineer; Software Engineer. **Educational backgrounds include:** Engineering. **Benefits:** 401(k); Disability Coverage; Life Insurance; Medical Insurance; Pension Plan; Profit Sharing; Tuition Assistance. **Corporate headquarters location:** This Location. **Other U.S. locations:** Los Angeles CA; Chicago IL; Cincinnati OH. **Parent company:** Fanuc Ltd. **Number of employees at this location:** 500. **Number of employees nationwide:** 600.

FARGO ASSEMBLY COMPANY
P.O. Box 2340, Fargo ND 58108-2340. 701/281-0331. **Contact:** Human Resources. **Description:** Manufactures electronic wire harnesses for heavy equipment including tractors and combines.

Common positions include: Blue-Collar Worker Supervisor; Buyer; General Manager; Industrial Engineer; Management Trainee; Production Manager. **Benefits:** Medical Insurance; Pension Plan; Profit Sharing. **Corporate headquarters location:** This Location. **Other U.S. locations:** NE; PA. **Listed on:** Privately held. **Number of employees at this location:** 250. **Number of employees nationwide:** 700.

FAST (FOOD AUTOMATION-SERVICE TECHNIQUES)
905 Honeyspot Road, Stratford CT 06615. 203/377-4414. **Contact:** Personnel. **E-mail address:** employment@fastinc.com. **World Wide Web address:** http://www.fastinc.com. **Description:** A developer and manufacturer of electronic control systems and timers for the food service industry. **Common positions include:** Accountant/Auditor; Administrator; Computer Programmer; Credit Manager; Customer Service Rep.; Department Manager; Draftsperson; Electrical/Electronics Engineer; Food Scientist/Technologist; Human Resources Manager; Management Trainee; Marketing Specialist; Operations/Production Manager; Purchasing Agent/Manager. **Educational backgrounds include:** Accounting; Business Administration; Engineering; Marketing. **Benefits:** Disability Coverage; Life Insurance; Medical Insurance; Tuition Assistance. **Corporate headquarters location:** This Location.

FAWN INDUSTRIES, INC.
1920 Green Spring Drive, Suite 140, Timonium MD 21093. 410/308-9200. **Contact:** Human Resources. **World Wide Web address:** http://www.fawn-ind.com. **Description:** Manufactures electronic subassemblies and related injection-molded plastic parts used by the automotive, medical instrumentation, office/business, industrial electronics, and personal computer industries. **Corporate headquarters location:** This Location. **Other U.S. locations:** MI; NC; TN.

FIRECOM, INC.
39-27 59th Street, Woodside NY 11377. 718/899-6100. **Fax:** 718/899-1932. **Contact:** Human Resources. **Description:** Designs, manufactures, and distributes fire alarm and communications systems used for safety in large commercial buildings, primarily in the metropolitan New York area. **Corporate headquarters location:** This Location. **Subsidiaries include:** Commercial Radio-Sound Corporation; Fire Controls, Inc. **Number of employees at this location:** 120.

FIRST CLASS SECURITY SYSTEMS
3835 West 10th Street, Suite 100C, Greeley CO 80634-1551. 970/339-2449. **Fax:** 970/336-3119. **Contact:** Richard Newman, Office Manager. **E-mail address:** firstclass@westgs.com. **World Wide Web address:** http://go.to/fcss. **Description:** Installs and services burglar and fire alarm, video surveillance, and access control systems. Founded in 1983. **Company slogan:** The best service in the business. **Common positions include:** Administrative Assistant; Installer. **Benefits:** Dental Insurance; Medical Insurance. **Office hours:** Monday - Friday, 8:00 a.m. - 5:00 p.m. **Corporate headquarters location:** This Location. **Owner:** Bob Stewart. **Annual sales/revenues:** Less than $5 million.

FLEXTRONICS INTERNATIONAL
2090 Fortune Drive, San Jose CA 95131. 408/428-1300. **Contact:** Human Resources. **World Wide Web address:** http://www.flextronics.com. **Description:** Provides electronic design, engineering, and manufacturing services to OEMs in various industries.

FLIR SYSTEMS, INC.
16505 SW 72nd Avenue, Portland OR 97224. 503/684-3731. **Contact:** Ms. Marti Bunyard, Human Resources Director. **World Wide Web address:** http://www.flir.com. **Description:** Designs, manufactures, and markets thermal imaging systems for law enforcement and drug interdiction agencies, search and rescue units, border and maritime patrols, and environmental protection. **Corporate headquarters location:** This Location.

FLUKE CORPORATION
P.O. Box 9090, Everett WA 98206-9090. 425/347-6100. **Physical address:** 6920 Seaway Boulevard, Everett WA. **Contact:** Personnel. **World Wide Web address:** http://www.fluke.com. **Description:** A manufacturer of electronic instrumentation for test measurement and calibration. **Corporate headquarters location:** This Location. **Parent company:** Danaher Corporation.

FORTREND ENGINEERING COMPANY
1273 Hammerwood Avenue, Sunnyvale CA 94089. 408/734-9311. **Fax:** 408/734-4299. **Contact:** Human Resources. **World Wide Web address:** http://www.fortrend.com. **Description:** Designs and manufactures automated equipment for wafer and disk handling in the semiconductor industry. **Common positions include:** Administrative Assistant; Applications Engineer; Design Engineer; Electrical/Electronics Engineer; Mechanical Engineer; Software Engineer. **Educational backgrounds include:** Computer Science; Engineering; Mathematics. **Benefits:** 401(k); Dental Insurance; Life Insurance; Medical Insurance; Pension Plan; Profit Sharing; Tuition Assistance. **Corporate headquarters location:** This Location. **Annual sales/revenues:** $5 - $10 million. **Number of employees at this location:** 50.

FUELLGRAF ELECTRIC COMPANY
600 South Washington Street, Butler PA 16001. 724/282-4800. **Fax:** 724/282-1926. **Contact:** Claudia Fischer, Human Resources. **E-mail address:** feco@fuellgraf.com. **World Wide Web address:** http://www.fuellgraf.com. **Description:** An electrical/teledata construction and engineering firm. Founded in 1946. **NOTE:** Entry-level positions are offered. **Common positions include:** Administrative Assistant; Administrative Manager; Construction Contractor; Electrical/Electronics Engineer; Electrician; Secretary. **Benefits:** 401(k); Casual Dress - Daily; Disability Coverage; Life Insurance; Medical Insurance; Sick Days (1 - 5); Vacation Days (10 - 20). **Office hours:** Monday - Friday, 7:00 a.m. - 5:00 p.m. **Corporate headquarters location:** This Location. **Other U.S. locations:** Williamsport PA. **Number of employees at this location:** 100.

G&W ELECTRIC COMPANY
3500 West 127th Street, Blue Island IL 60406. 708/388-5010. **Contact:** Personnel. **Description:** Manufactures power cable terminals, switches, and splices. **Common positions include:** Accountant/Auditor; Blue-Collar Worker Supervisor; Buyer; Computer Programmer; Credit Manager; Designer; Draftsperson; Electrical/Electronics Engineer; Mechanical Engineer; Systems Analyst; Technical Writer/Editor. **Educational backgrounds include:** Business Administration; Engineering; Marketing. **Benefits:** 401(k); Dental Insurance; Disability Coverage; Life Insurance; Medical Insurance; Profit Sharing; Tuition Assistance. **Corporate headquarters location:** This Location. **Listed on:** Privately held. **Number of employees at this location:** 250.

GE AUTOMATION SERVICES
P.O. Box 7126, Pensacola FL 32534. 850/968-2191. **Contact:** Human Resources. **World Wide Web address:** http://www.ge.com. **Description:** A manufacturer of industrial control instruments.

GSI LUMONICS INC.
500 Arsenal Street, Watertown MA 02472. 617/924-1010. **Fax:** 617/923-1877. **Contact:** Human Resources. **World Wide Web address:** http://www.gsilumonics.com. **Description:** Produces laser-based, automated manufacturing systems, instrumentation, and components for a wide range of industries. **Corporate headquarters location:** This Location.

GASONICS INTERNATIONAL CORP.
2730 Junction Avenue, San Jose CA 95134. 408/570-7400. **Contact:** Human Resources. **E-mail address:** hr@gasonics.com. **World Wide Web address:** http://www.gasonics.com. **Description:** GaSonics International is a leading supplier of process systems used in the fabrication of advanced integrated circuits. The company is one of the world's largest suppliers of equipment for dry removal of photoresist and other mask layer materials applied to semiconductor wafers during fabrication. GaSonics International also offers systems for related phases of semiconductor manufacturing including thermal growth of oxide layers and selective cleaning applications. The company's products feature proprietary technologies that help semiconductor manufacturers increase fabrication throughput and reduce wafer damage, which in turn raise production yields. **Corporate headquarters location:** This Location.

GENERAL DYNAMICS ELECTRONIC SYSTEMS
100, Ferguson Drive, P.O. Box 7188, Mountain View CA 94039. 650/966-2995. **Contact:** Employment Office. **World Wide Web address:** http://www.gd-es.com. **Description:** Engaged in the advancement of information systems and command, control, communications, computer, and intelligence technology. General Dynamics Electronic Systems designs and produces customized systems for defense, government, and industry. **Common positions include:** Electrical/Electronics Engineer; Software Engineer. **Benefits:** 401(k); Dental Insurance; Disability Coverage; Employee Discounts; Life Insurance; Medical Insurance; Pension Plan; Savings Plan; Tuition Assistance. **Corporate headquarters location:** This Location. **Parent company:** General Dynamics Corporation (Falls Church VA). **Number of employees at this location:** 1,200.

GENERAL KINETICS INC.
14130-A Sullyfield Circle, Chantilly VA 20151. 703/802-4848. **Contact:** Manager. **World Wide Web address:** http://www.gki.com. **Description:** Custom designs and manufactures electronic enclosures and systems for severe environments. General Kinetics's customers include computer, government, military, telecommunications, and industrial clients. Founded in 1954. **Corporate headquarters location:** This Location. **Other U.S. locations:** Johnstown PA. **Number of employees nationwide:** 120.

GENRAD INC.
7 Technology Park Drive, Westford MA 01886. 978/589-7000. **Fax:** 978/589-7007. **Contact:** Nina Rock, Manager of Human Resources. **World Wide Web address:** http://www.genrad.com. **Description:** A supplier of integrated test and diagnostic systems for the manufacture and maintenance of electronic products. The company offers products and services in three core business

areas: Electronic Manufacturing Solutions, GR Software, and Automotive Diagnostic Systems. **Common positions include:** Buyer; Computer Programmer; Customer Service Representative; Electrical/Electronics Engineer; Financial Analyst; Human Resources Manager; Management Trainee; Market Research Analyst; Purchasing Agent/Manager; Quality Control Supervisor; Software Engineer; Systems Analyst; Technical Writer/Editor. **Educational backgrounds include:** Accounting; Business Administration; Communications; Computer Science; Engineering; Finance; Marketing. **Benefits:** 401(k); Dental Insurance; Disability Coverage; Employee Discounts; Life Insurance; Medical Insurance; Profit Sharing; Public Transit Available; Savings Plan; Tuition Assistance. **Corporate headquarters location:** This Location. **Number of employees at this location:** 600.

GENUS, INC.
1139 Karlstad Drive, Sunnyvale CA 94089. 408/747-7120. **Contact:** Human Resources. **World Wide Web address:** http://www.genus.com. **Description:** Designs, manufactures, markets, and services advanced thin film deposition used in the fabrication of complex ultra-large scale integration semiconductor devices. Genus's products are used for several critical process steps required to produce integrated circuits for the computer, aerospace, communications, medical, military, aeronautical, automotive, and consumer electronics industries. The company's customer base consists of semiconductor manufacturers worldwide. **Corporate headquarters location:** This Location.

GERBER SCIENTIFIC, INC.
83 Gerber Road West, South Windsor CT 06074. 860/644-1551. **Contact:** Anthony Pagliuco, Director of Human Resources. **World Wide Web address:** http://www.gerberscientific.com. **Description:** Designs and manufactures high-technology imaging systems for the electronics industry, graphic arts industry, and a variety of other industries. **NOTE:** Entry-level positions are offered. **Common positions include:** Accountant/Auditor; Administrative Assistant; Applications Engineer; Buyer; Chief Financial Officer; Controller; Draftsperson; Electrical/Electronics Engineer; General Manager; Human Resources Manager; Internet Services Manager; Manufacturing Engineer; Market Research Analyst; Marketing Specialist; Mechanical Engineer; Operations/Production Manager; Production Manager; Purchasing Agent/Manager; Quality Control Supervisor; Sales Engineer; Sales Manager; Secretary; Software Engineer; Technical Writer/Editor. **Educational backgrounds include:** Business Administration; Computer Science; Engineering; Marketing. **Benefits:** 401(k); Dental Insurance; Disability Coverage; Employee Discounts; Life Insurance; Medical Insurance; Pension Plan; Tuition Assistance. **Special programs:** Internships. **Corporate headquarters location:** This Location. **Other U.S. locations:** Nationwide. **Listed on:** New York Stock Exchange.

CHARLES E. GILMAN COMPANY
907 East Frontage Road, Rio Rico AZ 85648. 520/281-1141. **Contact:** Ms. Reyna Armenta, Personnel Director. **Description:** Manufactures wiring harnesses and cable assemblies for sale to electronics OEMs. **Corporate headquarters location:** This Location.

GLENAIR INC.
1211 Air Way, Glendale CA 91201. 818/247-6000. **Contact:** Orlando Bernal, Personnel Director. **World Wide Web address:** http://www. glenair.com. **Description:** Manufactures electrical connector accessories and other electrical products. **Corporate headquarters location:** This Location.

W.L. GORE & ASSOCIATES, INC.
P.O. Box 9206, Newark DE 19714-9206. 302/738-4880. **Physical address:** 551 Paper Mill Road, Newark DE. **Contact:** Barbara Pizzala, Recruiter. **World Wide Web address:** http://www.gore.com. **Description:** Manufactures dental floss, guitar strings, vacuum filters, and water/stain repellent. The company also produces electronic products including copper and optical signal transmission products, digital and analog cable assemblies, chemical products including a chemical polymer used to repair diseased arteries and also as an industrial sealant; and GORE-TEX fabric. **Common positions include:** Attorney; Chemical Engineer; Chemist; Electrical/Electronics Engineer; Mechanical Engineer; Metallurgical Engineer; Sales Engineer. **Educational backgrounds include:** Chemistry; Engineering. **Benefits:** Dental Insurance; Disability Coverage; Employee Discounts; Fitness Program; Life Insurance; Medical Insurance; Profit Sharing. **Special programs:** Internships. **Corporate headquarters location:** This Location. **Annual sales/revenues:** More than $100 million. **Number of employees nationwide:** 6,000.

GOULD ELECTRONICS INC.
34929 Curtis Boulevard, Eastlake OH 44095. 440/953-5000. **Contact:** Human Resources. **World Wide Web address:** http://www. gouldelectronics.com. **Description:** Designs and manufactures materials, components, and related technologies for the electronics marketplace and a range of original equipment manufacturers. Gould Electronics is divided into six major individual businesses: Gould Foil Division develops electro-deposited copper foil for electronic interconnection applications; Gould Copper Aluminum Copper manufactures two sheets of copper separated by aluminum; Gould Electronic Materials produces adhesiveless flexible copper laminate and other metal foils; Gould ElectroCopper Products manufactures low-cost electrolytic copper powder and extruded copper shapes; Gould Powerdex produces primary and secondary lithium batteries; and Gould Fiber Optics provides standard and customized passive coupler components and wavelength division multiplexers to the telecommunications, cable television, instrumentation, and optical sensor markets. **Common positions include:** Accountant/Auditor; Administrator; Attorney; Chemist; Computer Programmer; Electrical/Electronics Engineer; Financial Analyst; Human Resources Manager; Mechanical Engineer; Metallurgical Engineer; Operations/Production Manager; Physicist; Quality Control Supervisor. **Educational backgrounds include:** Accounting; Business Administration; Chemistry; Engineering; Finance; Physics. **Benefits:** Dental Insurance; Disability Coverage; Employee Discounts; Life Insurance; Medical Insurance; Pension Plan; Savings Plan; Tuition Assistance. **Corporate headquarters location:** This Location. **International locations:** Asia; Europe. **Parent company:** Japan Energy Corporation.

GRAYBAR ELECTRIC COMPANY
P.O. Box 7231, St. Louis MO 63177. 314/727-3900. **Physical address:** 34 North Meramec Avenue, Clayton MO 63105. **Contact:** Martha Bloodsaw, Manager of Personnel. **World Wide Web address:** http://www.graybar.com. **Description:** Distributes electrical and telecommunications equipment including wire, transformers, lighting fixtures,

power transmission equipment, telephone station apparatuses, and other hardware, primarily to independent telephone companies and public power utilities. Founded in 1869. **Common positions include:** Accountant/Auditor; Buyer; Computer Operator; Computer Programmer; Customer Service Rep.; Order Clerk; Payroll Clerk; Sales Rep.; Secretary; Stock Clerk; Systems Analyst; Truck Driver; Typist/Word Processor. **Educational backgrounds include:** Accounting; Business Administration; Computer Science; Liberal Arts; Sales. **Benefits:** Dental Insurance; Disability Coverage; Employee Discounts; Life Insurance; Medical Insurance; Pension Plan; Profit Sharing; Savings Plan; Tuition Assistance. **Corporate headquarters location:** This Location. **Number of employees at this location:** 180. **Number of employees nationwide:** 9,300.

GRAYHILL, INC.
561 Hillgrove Avenue, LaGrange IL 60525. 708/354-1040. **Contact:** Human Resources. **World Wide Web address:** http://www.grayhill.com. **Description:** Manufactures rotary, push-button, and DIP switches, keyboards and keypads, encoders, wireless products, I/O modules, and industrial control systems. **Common positions include:** Electrical/Electronics Engineer; Mechanical Engineer. **Educational backgrounds include:** Engineering. **Benefits:** 401(k); Disability Coverage; Life Insurance; Medical Insurance; Prescription Drugs; Tuition Assistance. **Corporate headquarters location:** This Location. **Other U.S. locations:** Carpentersville IL; Fox River Grove IL; Iola WI. **Listed on:** Privately held. **Number of employees at this location:** 475.

GROUP TECHNOLOGIES CORPORATION
10901 Malcolm McKinley Drive, Tampa FL 33612. 813/972-6000. **Fax:** 813/972-6168. **Contact:** Janice Beal, Personnel Director. **Description:** Custom designs and manufactures electronics systems, subsystems, and circuit card assemblies for the U.S. government and the avionics, communications, and medical industries. **Corporate headquarters location:** This Location. **Listed on:** NASDAQ.

HRL LABORATORIES, LLC
3011 Malibu Canyon Road, Malibu CA 90265. 310/317-5000. **Contact:** Lynn W. Ross, Human Resources. **World Wide Web address:** http://www.hrl.com. **Description:** Researches and develops lasers, fiber optic devices and systems, computational electromagnetics, optoelectronics, and radar. **Parent company:** HRL Laboratories is jointly owned by Hughes Electronics Corporation and Raytheon Company.

HARBOUR INDUSTRIES, INC.
P.O. Box 188, Shelburne VT 05482. 802/985-3311. **Fax:** 802/985-3447. **Contact:** Human Resources. **World Wide Web address:** http://www. harbourind.com. **Description:** Manufactures high-performance wire and cable. **NOTE:** Entry-level positions and second and third shifts are offered. **Common positions include:** Account Representative; Administrative Assistant; Blue-Collar Worker Supervisor; Buyer; Controller; Human Resources Manager; Industrial Engineer; Industrial Production Manager; Mechanical Engineer; Quality Control Supervisor; Sales Executive; Sales Manager; Systems Manager; Vice President of Sales. **Educational backgrounds include:** Accounting; Business Administration; Computer Science; Engineering; Finance; Marketing. **Benefits:** 401(k); Dental Insurance; Disability Coverage; Life Insurance; Medical Insurance; Tuition Assistance; Vision Insurance. **Corporate headquarters location:** This Location.

Other U.S. locations: Irvine CA. **Parent company:** The Marmon Group. **Listed on:** Privately held. **Number of employees at this location:** 125. **Number of employees nationwide:** 155.

HARRIS CORPORATION
1025 West NASA Boulevard, Mail Stop 19, Melbourne FL 32919. 321/727-9207. **Toll-free phone:** 800/4-HARRIS. **Contact:** Human Resources. **World Wide Web address:** http://www. harris.com. **Description:** Operates through two sectors: The Communications Sector offers a broad range of communications products including digital telephone switching platforms, microwave radios, multiband and secure wireless radios, and analog and digital television and radio broadcasting systems; The Electronic Systems Sector develops communication and information processing systems including data processing systems, aircraft and missile communications, and electronic warfare. **Common positions include:** Accountant/Auditor; Administrator; Attorney; Blue-Collar Worker Supervisor; Computer Programmer; Customer Service Rep.; Department Manager; Editor; Electrical/Electronics Engineer; Financial Analyst; General Manager; Human Resources Manager; Industrial Engineer; Manufacturer's/Wholesaler's Sales Rep.; Marketing Specialist; Mechanical Engineer; Metallurgical Engineer; Operations/Production Manager; Public Relations Specialist; Purchasing Agent/Manager; Quality Control Supervisor; Reporter; Systems Analyst. **Educational backgrounds include:** Accounting; Business Administration; Communications; Computer Science; Economics; Engineering; Finance; Marketing; Physics. **Benefits:** Dental Insurance; Disability Coverage; Employee Discounts; Life Insurance; Medical Insurance; Pension Plan; Profit Sharing; Savings Plan; Tuition Assistance. **Corporate headquarters location:** This Location. **Listed on:** New York Stock Exchange.

HARVARD CUSTOM MANUFACTURING
600 Glen Avenue, Salisbury MD 21804. 410/548-7800. **Fax:** 410/548-7839. **Contact:** Steve Robertson, Director of Human Resources. **E-mail address:** hr@harvardcm.com. **World Wide Web address:** http://www.harvardcm.com. **Description:** Provides electronic assembly cables and harnesses for the military and commercial telecommunications industries. **Common positions include:** Accountant; Administrative Assistant; Budget Analyst; Computer Programmer; Controller; Cost Estimator; Industrial Engineer; Manufacturing Engineer; Mechanical Engineer; Purchasing Agent/Manager; Quality Control Supervisor; Systems Analyst. **Educational backgrounds include:** Accounting; Business Administration; Computer Science; Engineering; Finance. **Benefits:** 401(k); Dental Insurance; Disability Coverage; Life Insurance; Medical Insurance. **Corporate headquarters location:** This Location. **Number of employees at this location:** 220.

HELIX TECHNOLOGY CORPORATION
Mansfield Corporate Center, 9 Hampshire Street, Mansfield MA 02048. 508/337-5500. **Contact:** Human Resources. **Description:** Manufactures vacuum technology products for the semiconductor industry. **Common positions include:** Account Manager; Accountant; Auditor; Budget Analyst; Chemical Engineer; Chief Financial Officer; Computer Engineer; Computer Support Technician; Controller; Customer Service Rep.; Database Administrator; Electrical/Electronics Engineer; Financial Analyst; Help-Desk Technician; Human Resources Manager; Manufacturing Engineer; Market Research Analyst; Marketing Manager;

Mechanical Engineer; Network Engineer; Network/ Systems Administrator; Operations Manager; Production Manager; Purchasing Agent/Manager; Quality Assurance Engineer; Sales Executive; Software Engineer; Systems Analyst; Systems Manager; Technical Support Manager. **Educational backgrounds include:** HTML; Internet; Java; Microsoft Office; Microsoft Word; Software Development; Software Tech. Support; SQL. **Benefits:** 401(k); Casual Dress - Fridays; Dental Insurance; Disability Coverage; Flexible Schedule; Life Insurance; Medical Insurance; Pension Plan; Relocation Assistance; Savings Plan; Tuition Assistance; Vacation Days (10 - 20). **Special programs:** Internships; Training; Co-ops. **Corporate headquarters location:** This Location. **Other U.S. locations:** AZ; CA; CO; TX. **International locations:** Japan. **Subsidiaries include:** GPC. **Listed on:** NASDAQ. **Stock exchange symbol:** HELX. **Annual sales/revenues:** More than $100 million. **Number of employees at this location:** 300.

HERAEUS AMERSIL INC.
3473 Satellite Boulevard, Suite 300, Duluth GA 30096. 770/623-6000. **Contact:** Human Resources. **Description:** Manufactures silica glass and quartz electronic components. **Corporate headquarters location:** This Location.

HI-TECH ELECTRONIC DISPLAYS
13900 U.S. Highway 19 North, Clearwater FL 33764. 727/531-4800. **Toll-free phone:** 800/723-9402. **Fax:** 727/524-6655. **Contact:** Laurie Danielson, Personnel. **World Wide Web address:** http://www.hitechled.com. **Description:** Manufactures electronic, computer-operated signs. **NOTE:** Entry-level positions are offered. **Common positions include:** Advertising Clerk; Computer Programmer; Electrical/Electronics Engineer; Graphic Artist; Production Manager; Project Manager; Quality Control Supervisor; Sales Representative; Software Engineer. **Educational backgrounds include:** Business Administration; Computer Science; Engineering; Marketing. **Benefits:** Medical Insurance. **Corporate headquarters location:** This Location. **Number of employees at this location:** 95.

HOFFMAN ENGINEERING
900 Ehlen Drive, Anoka MN 55303. 763/421-2240. **Contact:** Vice President. **World Wide Web address:** http://www.hoffmanonline.com. **Description:** Manufactures and distributes electrical and electronic enclosures. **Common positions include:** Accountant; Attorney; Buyer; Computer Programmer; Draftsperson; General Manager; Human Resources Manager; Marketing Specialist; Mechanical Engineer; Metallurgical Engineer; Systems Analyst; Technical Writer/Editor; Transportation/Traffic Specialist. **Educational backgrounds include:** Accounting; Business Administration; Communications; Computer Science; Engineering. **Benefits:** Dental Insurance; Disability Coverage; Employee Discounts; Life Insurance; Medical Insurance; Pension Plan; Profit Sharing; Savings Plan; Tuition Assistance. **Corporate headquarters location:** This Location. **Parent company:** Pentair, Inc. (Minneapolis MN).

HONEYWELL-MEASUREX CORPORATION
One Results Way, Mail Stop 8109, Cupertino CA 95014-5991. 408/255-1500. **Fax:** 408/864-7570. **Contact:** Professional Staffing. **Description:** Honeywell-Measurex is a leading supplier of measurement, control, and information systems and services for continuous and batch manufacturing processes. Industries served by the company include pulp and paper, plastics, nonwovens, aluminum, and rubber. **Corporate headquarters location:** This Location. **International locations:** Worldwide. **Number of employees worldwide:** 2,000.

HOWELL INSTRUMENTS, INC.
P.O. Box 985001, Fort Worth TX 76185. 817/336-7411. **Physical address:** 3479 West Vickery Boulevard, Fort Worth TX 76107. **Fax:** 817/336-7874. **Contact:** Nell Whaylen, Personnel Manager. **E-mail address:** nmwhaylen@howellinst.com. **World Wide Web address:** http://www.howellinst.com. **Description:** Manufactures turbine engine instrumentation and test equipment for military and commercial applications. **NOTE:** Entry-level positions are offered. **Common positions include:** Computer Programmer; Sales Engineer; Software Engineer. **Educational backgrounds include:** Computer Science; Engineering. **Benefits:** Dental Insurance; Disability Coverage; Life Insurance; Medical Insurance; Pension Plan; Profit Sharing; Public Transit Available. **Corporate headquarters location:** This Location. **President/CEO:** John Howell. **Annual sales/revenues:** $11 - $20 million.

HUBBELL INC.
584 Derby Milford Road, Orange CT 06477. 203/799-4255. **Contact:** George D. Zurman, Vice President of Human Resources. **World Wide Web address:** http://www.hubbell.com. **Description:** Manufactures electrical and electronic products, power systems, industrial lighting, and wiring systems. **Common positions include:** Accountant; Computer Programmer; Electrical/Electronics Engineer; Industrial Engineer; Manufacturer's/ Wholesaler's Sales Rep.; Mechanical Engineer; Metallurgical Engineer; Systems Analyst. **Educational backgrounds include:** Accounting; Business Administration; Computer Science; Engineering; Finance; Marketing. **Benefits:** Daycare Assistance; Dental Insurance; Disability Coverage; Life Insurance; Medical Insurance; Pension Plan; Savings Plan; Tuition Assistance. **Corporate headquarters location:** This Location. **International locations:** Canada; United Kingdom. **Listed on:** New York Stock Exchange.

HYTEK MICROSYSTEMS, INC.
400 Hot Springs Road, Carson City NV 89706. 775/883-0820. **Fax:** 775/883-0827. **Contact:** Human Resources. **World Wide Web address:** http://www.hytek.com. **Description:** Designs, manufactures, and markets hybrid microcircuits for medical, military, and space applications. Products are sold to original equipment manufacturers in various industries including telecommunications and industrial electronics. Founded in 1974. **NOTE:** Entry-level positions are offered. **Common positions include:** Applications Engineer; Assembler; Electrical/Electronics Engineer; Electronics Technician. **Educational backgrounds include:** Engineering. **Benefits:** Dental Insurance; Disability Coverage; Life Insurance; Medical Insurance; Profit Sharing; Tuition Assistance. **Corporate headquarters location:** This Location. **Number of employees at this location:** 100.

IFR
10200 West York Street, Wichita KS 67215. 316/522-4981. **Contact:** Bob Browning, Human Resources Director. **World Wide Web address:** http://www.ifrinternational.com. **Description:** Designs and manufactures electronic testing equipment especially for the communications and avionics industries. Founded in 1968. **Common positions include:** Accountant/Auditor; Buyer; Computer Programmer; Department Manager; Draftsperson; Electrical/Electronics Engineer; Electronics Technician; Industrial Engineer;

Marketing Specialist; Mechanical Engineer; Operations/Production Manager; Purchasing Agent/ Manager; Systems Analyst; Technical Writer/Editor. **Educational backgrounds include:** Business Administration; Computer Science; Engineering; Liberal Arts. **Benefits:** Dental Insurance; Disability Coverage; Life Insurance; Medical Insurance; Pension Plan; Profit Sharing; Savings Plan. **Corporate headquarters location:** This Location. **Listed on:** NASDAQ. **Number of employees at this location:** 550.

IMP, INC.
2830 North First Street, San Jose CA 95134. 408/432-9100. **Fax:** 408/434-0335. **Contact:** Human Resources. **World Wide Web address:** http://www.impweb.com. **Description:** Develops and manufactures application-specific standard integrated circuits for mass storage and power management applications. **Corporate headquarters location:** This Location. **Listed on:** NASDAQ.

ISE LABS, INC.
2095 Ringwood Avenue, San Jose CA 95131. 408/954-8378. **Fax:** 408/954-1676. **Contact:** Joanna Koo, Manager of Administrative Operations. **E-mail address:** info@iselabs.com. **World Wide Web address:** http://www.iselabs.com. **Description:** Provides electrical and environmental testing services for integrated circuits. Founded in 1983. **Common positions include:** Designer; Sales Engineer; Test Engineer. **Educational backgrounds include:** Computer Science; Engineering. **Benefits:** Casual Dress - Fridays; Dental Insurance; Disability Coverage; Life Insurance; Medical Insurance; Sick Days (1 - 5); Vacation Days (6 - 10). **Corporate headquarters location:** This Location. **Other U.S. locations:** Manteca CA; Santa Clara CA. **International locations:** Hong Kong; Singapore. **Annual sales/revenues:** $51 - $100 million. **Number of employees at this location:** 140.

ITT INDUSTRIES
P.O. Box 15012, Colorado Springs CO 80935. 719/591-3600. **Contact:** Rebecca Simoneaux, Employment Specialist. **Description:** Serves the defense, energy, and communications markets with research and development services in weapons effects, computer systems, space systems, C3I, SDI, range testing, and instrumentation. **Common positions include:** Aerospace Engineer; Electrical/ Electronics Engineer. **Educational backgrounds include:** Computer Science; Engineering; Mathematics; Physics. **Benefits:** Dental Insurance; Disability Coverage; Life Insurance; Medical Insurance; Pension Plan; Savings Plan; Tuition Assistance. **Corporate headquarters location:** This Location.

IVI CHECKMATE
1003 Mansell Road, Roswell GA 30076. 770/594-6000. **Fax:** 770/594-6020. **Contact:** Human Resources. **World Wide Web address:** http://www. ivicm.com. **Description:** Develops, manufactures, and markets point-of-sale payment automation systems and terminals including check readers, payment authorization systems, signature capture devices, and MICR analyzers. **Common positions include:** Accountant; Customer Service Rep.; Design Engineer; Electrical/Electronics Engineer; Sales Executive; Software Engineer. **Benefits:** 401(k); Dental Insurance; Disability Coverage; Life Insurance; Medical Insurance; Tuition Assistance. **Corporate headquarters location:** This Location. **Other U.S. locations:** Tampa FL; Baltimore MD. **Listed on:** NASDAQ. **Stock exchange symbol:** IVI. **Annual sales/revenues:** $21 - $50 million. **Number of employees at this location:** 190.

IDEAL ELECTRIC COMPANY
330 East First Street, Mansfield OH 44902. 419/522-3611. **Fax:** 419/524-9524. **Contact:** Barb Raudabaugh, Personnel Director. **Description:** A producer of electric power generation equipment and machinery. **Common positions include:** Accountant; Blue-Collar Worker Supervisor; Buyer; Computer Programmer; Draftsperson; Electrician; Human Resources Manager; Industrial Engineer; Mechanical Engineer; Purchasing Agent/Manager; Quality Control Supervisor. **Educational backgrounds include:** Accounting; Business Administration; Engineering; Finance; Marketing. **Benefits:** 401(k); Dental Insurance; Disability Coverage; Life Insurance; Medical Insurance; Pension Plan; Profit Sharing; Tuition Assistance. **Corporate headquarters location:** This Location. **Listed on:** Privately held. **Number of employees at this location:** 300.

INFOCUS SYSTEMS, INC.
27700B SW Parkway Avenue, Wilsonville OR 97070-9215. 503/685-8888. **Toll-free phone:** 800/294-6400. **Fax:** 503/685-8887. **Recorded jobline:** 503/685-8777. **Contact:** Human Resources. **E-mail address:** jobs@infocus.com. **World Wide Web address:** http://www. infocus.com. **Description:** A leader in developing, manufacturing, and marketing projection products and services to present video, audio, and data from personal computers and other electronic devices. The company's products include LCD projection panels and portable projection systems with integrated full-motion video, data, and audio. LCD panels are used with overhead projectors to display data and video from personal computers, or from LiteShow presentation software onto a screen for meetings and presentations. **Corporate headquarters location:** This Location. **Number of employees nationwide:** 645.

INFORMATION STORAGE DEVICES (ISD)
2727 North First Street, San Jose CA 95134. 408/943-6666. **Fax:** 408/544-1784. **Contact:** Human Resources. **World Wide Web address:** http://www.isd.com. **Description:** Designs, develops, and markets integrated circuit products for voice recording and playback using the company's proprietary ChipCorder high-density storage technology and mixed signal expertise. The company's products offer voice reproduction, low-power consumption, and battery-less storage in a single-chip solution. **Corporate headquarters location:** This Location.

INPUT/OUTPUT, INC.
11104 West Airport Boulevard, Stafford TX 77477. 281/933-3339. **Contact:** Human Resources. **E-mail address:** careers@i-o.com. **World Wide Web address:** http://www.i-o.com. **Description:** Designs, manufactures, and markets seismic data acquisition systems and related equipment as well as marine positioning systems. Founded in 1968. **Corporate headquarters location:** This Location. **Subsidiaries include:** Output Exploration Company conducts geophysical operations and acquires oil and gas leases. **Listed on:** New York Stock Exchange. **President/CEO:** W.J. Zeringue. **Annual sales/revenues:** More than $100 million.

INTEGRATED SILICON SOLUTION, INC.
2231 Lawson Lane, Santa Clara CA 95054. 408/588-0800. **Contact:** Human Resources. **World Wide Web address:** http://www.issiusa.com. **Description:** Designs, develops, and markets high-performance SRAM and nonvolatile memory semiconductors used in personal computers, data communications, telecommunications, and instrumentation. **Corporate headquarters**

location: This Location. **International locations:** China; Hong Kong. **Number of employees nationwide:** 220.

INTEL CORPORATION

2200 Mission College Boulevard, P.O. Box 58119, Santa Clara CA 95052-8119. 408/987-8080. **Contact:** Staffing Department. **World Wide Web address:** http://www.intel.com. **Description:** One of the largest semiconductor manufacturers in the world. Other products include supercomputers; embedded control chips and flash memories; motherboards; multimedia hardware; personal computer enhancement products; and design and marketing of microcomputer components, modules, and systems. Intel sells its products to original equipment manufacturers and other companies that incorporate them into their products. **Corporate headquarters location:** This Location. **Subsidiaries include:** Shiva produces a line of direct-dial products and remote access servers. **Listed on:** NASDAQ.

INTERLINK ELECTRONICS

546 Flynn Road, Camarillo CA 93012. 805/484-8855. **Fax:** 805/484-8989. **Contact:** Human Resources. **Description:** Interlink's force-sensing technology transforms physical pressure applied to a sensor into a corresponding electronic response. Products incorporating a sensor using the company's force-sensing resistor (FSR) devices can react to pressure when applied by any means such as through human touch, a mechanical device, a fluid, or a gas. With supporting electronics, an FSR sensor can start, stop, intensify, select, direct, detect, or measure a desired response. **Corporate headquarters location:** This Location.

INTERMAGNETICS GENERAL CORP.

P.O. Box 461, Latham NY 12110. 518/782-1122. **Physical address:** 450 Old Niskayuna Road, Latham NY. **Fax:** 518/783-2601. **Contact:** Human Resources. **World Wide Web address:** http://www. igc.com. **Description:** Intermagnetics General Corporation, through its Electromagenetics Division and Superconducting Materials Division, is principally involved in the development and sale of commercial superconductive products including those used for medical diagnostic magnetic resonance imaging (MRI) applications. The company primarily operates in three industry segments: the design, development, and manufacture of superconductive magnets and materials, permanent magnets, and other magnetic products; the design of LTS materials; and the design, development, and manufacture of cryogenic refrigeration equipment. **Common positions include:** Accountant/Auditor; Blue-Collar Worker Supervisor; Buyer; Computer Programmer; Financial Analyst; Industrial Engineer; Mechanical Engineer; Quality Control Supervisor; Systems Analyst. **Educational backgrounds include:** Accounting; Business Administration; Computer Science; Engineering; Marketing. **Benefits:** 401(k); Dental Insurance; Disability Coverage; Life Insurance; Medical Insurance; Pension Plan; Profit Sharing; Savings Plan; Tuition Assistance. **Corporate headquarters location:** This Location. **Other U.S. locations:** Waterbury CT; Allentown PA. **Subsidiaries include:** APD Cryogenics Inc. is a supplier of specialty cryogenic refrigeration equipment for use in medical diagnostics, laboratory research, military guidance, and semiconductor manufacturing. **Listed on:** NASDAQ. **Number of employees at this location:** 250.

INTERMEC TECHNOLOGIES CORP.

550 Second Street SE, Cedar Rapids IA 52401. 319/369-3100. **Fax:** 319/369-3791. **Contact:** Human Resources Department. **World Wide Web address:** http://www.intermec.com. **Description:** Manufactures and markets portable, computerized data collection systems and hand-held radio frequency terminals used in a wide range of applications including route accounting, inventory management, and warehouse data management. These systems are used by companies to improve accountability, productivity, and management control. **Common positions include:** Accountant/Auditor; Administrative Manager; Buyer; Computer Operator; Computer Programmer; Department Manager; Electrical/Electronics Engineer; Financial Analyst; General Manager; Human Resources Manager; Market Research Analyst; Mechanical Engineer; Software Engineer; Systems Analyst. **Educational backgrounds include:** Business Administration; Computer Science; Engineering; Finance; Marketing. **Benefits:** Dental Insurance; Disability Coverage; Life Insurance; Medical Insurance; Profit Sharing; Savings Plan; Stock Option; Tuition Assistance. **Corporate headquarters location:** Everett WA. **Listed on:** NASDAQ. **Number of employees at this location:** 750. **Number of employees nationwide:** 835. **Other U.S. locations:**
* Amtech Systems Division, 19111 Dallas Parkway, Suite 300, Dallas TX 75287. 972/733-6600.

INTERNATIONAL GAME TECHNOLOGY

P.O. Box 10580, Reno NV 89510. 775/688-0100. **Physical address:** 9295 Prototype Drive, Reno NV. **Fax:** 775/686-1600. **Contact:** Human Resources. **World Wide Web address:** http://www. igtonline.com. **Description:** One of the world's leading designers and manufacturers of video gaming equipment, slot machines, and proprietary software for computerized wide-area game monitoring systems. The company offers an extensive product line including the S-Plus spinning reel slot; Player's Edge-Plus series; Game King video gaming machines; wide-area progressive products including Megabucks; and a variety of specialty casino devices such as carousel displays. Founded in 1975. **NOTE:** Entry-level positions, part-time jobs, and second and third shifts are offered. **Common positions include:** Account Manager; Account Rep.; Administrative Assistant; AS400 Programmer Analyst; Attorney; Buyer; Computer Animator; Computer Engineer; Computer Operator; Computer Programmer; Computer Support Technician; Customer Service Rep.; Database Administrator; Graphic Artist; Graphic Designer; Human Resources Manager; Market Research Analyst; Marketing Manager; MIS Specialist; Network/Systems Administrator; Paralegal; Public Relations Specialist; Secretary; Systems Analyst; Systems Manager; Technical Writer/Editor; Transportation/Traffic Specialist; Video Production Coordinator. **Educational backgrounds include:** AS400 Certification; C/C++; MCSE; Microsoft Word; Novell. **Benefits:** 401(k); Casual Dress - Fridays; Daycare Assistance; Dental Insurance; Disability Coverage; Employee Discounts; Financial Planning Assistance; Life Insurance; Medical Insurance; Pension Plan; Profit Sharing; Tuition Assistance; Vacation Days (11 - 15). **Special programs:** Internships; Training. **Corporate headquarters location:** This Location. **Other U.S. locations:** Nationwide. **Subsidiaries include:** Barcrest Ltd. (England); Olympic Gaming (Australia).

INTERNATIONAL MICROWAVE CORP.

25 Van Zant Street, Norwalk CT 06855. 203/857-4222. **Contact:** Personnel. **Description:** Engaged in the manufacture and repair of microwave radios. **Common positions include:** Design Engineer;

Draftsperson; Electrical/Electronics Engineer; Sales Executive. **Educational backgrounds include:** Engineering. **Benefits:** 401(k); Dental Insurance; Medical Insurance. **Corporate headquarters location:** This Location. **Listed on:** Privately held. **Number of employees at this location:** 35.

INTEGRAL VISION INC.
38700 Grand River Avenue, Farmington Hills MI 48335. 248/471-2660. **Contact:** Human Resources. **Description:** Manufactures machine vision-based inspection systems and resistance welding controls. Integral's machine vision-based inspection systems are designed for the automatic inspection of compact discs, glass containers, and other manufacturing processes. The company's resistance welding controls provide important data about the welding process in order to assure quality. **Corporate headquarters location:** This Location. **Listed on:** NASDAQ. **Chairman/CEO:** Charles J. Drake. **Annual sales/revenues:** $21 - $50 million.

ION CORPORATION
1507 South Sixth Street, Hopkins MN 55343. 952/936-9490. **Fax:** 952/936-7527. **Contact:** Human Resources. **Description:** Manufactures electronic products including circuitboards, cables, and harnesses. **Educational backgrounds include:** Engineering. **Benefits:** Dental Insurance; Life Insurance; Medical Insurance; Section 125 Plan. **Corporate headquarters location:** This Location. **Number of employees at this location:** 100.

ISOMET CORPORATION
5263 Port Royal Road, Springfield VA 22151. 703/321-8301. **Fax:** 703/321-8546. **Contact:** Human Resources. **World Wide Web address:** http://www.isomet.com. **Description:** Designs and manufactures acousto-optic laser control components and electronics for information handling. Isomet also produces digital color scanners, laser film recorders, and specialized interface software and electronics packages for color image reproduction markets. **Corporate headquarters location:** This Location. **Subsidiaries include:** Isomet, Ltd. (Wales UK) markets and services graphic arts equipment in Europe. **Listed on:** NASDAQ.

JDS UNIPHASE CORPORATION
210 Baypointe Parkway, San Jose CA 95134. 408/434-1800. **Fax:** 408/954-0760. **Contact:** Human Resources. **World Wide Web address:** http://www.jdsunph.com. **Description:** Develops, manufactures, and distributes fiberoptic products including cable assemblies, fusion splicers, couplers, and lasers. Products are primarily sold to companies in the cable television and telecommunications fields. **Corporate headquarters location:** This Location. **Listed on:** NASDAQ. **Stock exchange symbol:** JDSU.

JABIL CIRCUIT COMPANY
1700 Atlantic Boulevard, Auburn Hills MI 48326. 248/391-5300. **Contact:** Human Resources. **World Wide Web address:** http://www.jabil.com. **Description:** Manufacturers circuit boards. **Number of employees at this location:** 1,000.

JACKPOT ENTERPRISES, INC.
1110 Palms Airport Drive, Las Vegas NV 89119. 702/263-5555. **Contact:** Marge Chervinski, Director of Human Resources. **Description:** Owns, installs, operates, and services gaming machines primarily in large retail stores, bars, and restaurants. Jackpot Enterprises, Inc. operates nearly 4,200 video poker machines in various retail locations. The company also operates approximately 500 additional machines in four Nevada casinos in Las Vegas, Reno, Battle Mountain, and Jackpot. **Corporate headquarters location:** This Location. **Listed on:** New York Stock Exchange.

JACO ELECTRONICS, INC.
145 Oser Avenue, Hauppauge NY 11788. 631/273-5500. **Contact:** Diane Ecknoff-Stiekle, Human Resources Director. **World Wide Web address:** http://www.jacoelectronics.com. **Description:** Distributes computer systems, computer subsystems, electronic components, and electromechanical devices produced by other companies. Active products include computer subsystems and semiconductors, and passive products include capacitors, electro mechanical devices, and motors and resistors. **Corporate headquarters location:** This Location. **Subsidiaries include:** Nexus Custom Electronics, Inc. is a contract manufacturer of printed circuit board assemblies and complete systems from print to final product. Nexus offers surface-mount, thru-hole, and mixed PCB technologies; global test resources; and total systems integration.

JETRONIC INDUSTRIES, INC.
4200 Mitchell Street, Philadelphia PA 19128. 215/482-7660. **Contact:** Mr. L.W. Pietrzak, Vice President of Finance. **Description:** Engaged in the manufacture of power supplies and switchgears. **Corporate headquarters location:** This Location.

JOSLYN ELECTRONIC SYSTEMS COMPANY
6868 Cortona Drive, Santa Barbara Research Park, Goleta CA 93117. 805/968-3551. **Fax:** 805/968-5218. **Contact:** Judy Cable, Senior Human Resources Representative. **World Wide Web address:** http://www.jesc.com. **Description:** Manufactures communications and transportation surge protection devices. **NOTE:** Part-time jobs and second and third shifts are offered. **Common positions include:** Blue-Collar Worker Supervisor; Customer Service Rep.; Draftsperson; Electrical/Electronics Engineer; Manufacturing Engineer. **Educational backgrounds include:** Engineering; Microsoft Office. **Benefits:** 401(k); Dental Insurance; Disability Coverage; Employee Discounts; Financial Planning Assistance; Life Insurance; Medical Insurance; Pension Plan; Savings Plan; Sick Days (6 - 10); Tuition Assistance; Vacation Days (1 - 5). **Special programs:** Summer Jobs. **Office hours:** Monday - Friday, 8:00 a.m. - 5:00 p.m. **Corporate headquarters location:** Washington DC. **Number of employees at this location:** 220.

KEARFOTT GUIDANCE & NAVIGATION CORPORATION
150 Totowa Road, Wayne NJ 07474. 973/785-5908. **Fax:** 973/785-6255. **Contact:** Human Resources. **World Wide Web address:** http://www.kearfott.com. **Description:** Manufactures precision electromechanical and electronic components used to generate, sense, control, and display motion such as synchros, cant angle sensors, and servo motors. **Common positions include:** Buyer; Electrical/Electronics Engineer; Mechanical Engineer; Software Engineer. **Benefits:** 401(k); Dental Insurance; Disability Coverage; Life Insurance; Medical Insurance; Profit Sharing; Tuition Assistance. **Corporate headquarters location:** This Location. **Parent company:** Astronautics Corporation of America.
Other U.S. locations:
- Route 70, Black Mountain NC 28711. 828/686-3811.

KEITHLEY INSTRUMENTS INC.
28775 Aurora Road, Solon OH 44139-1891. 440/248-0400. **Contact:** Human Resources. **World

Wide Web address: http://www.keithley.com. **Description:** Provides instrumentation to semiconductor manufacturers, medical equipment manufacturers, and growth segments of the electronics industry. The company's Test Instrumentation Group supplies instruments for benchtop and systems applications and automatic parametric test systems. Keithley also supplies sensitive instruments that measure a wide range of electrical properties such as voltage, resistance, current, capacitance, and charge. The products produced by the Keithley MetraByte Division include a wide range of data acquisition and analysis hardware and software products designed for use with personal computers. The Radiation Measurements Division designs, develops, manufactures, and markets products and systems that accurately measure the radiation emission levels of X-ray machines and nuclear radiation sources. **Corporate headquarters location:** This Location.

KENT ELECTRONICS CORPORATION

1111 Gillingham Lane, Sugar Land TX 77478. 281/243-5000. **Fax:** 281/243-5107. **Contact:** Human Resources. **Description:** A multiregional distributor of a wide variety of electronic products including wire and cable, connectors, and other passive and electromechanical products and interconnect assemblies used by customers in assembling and manufacturing electronic equipment. **Common positions include:** Buyer; Cost Estimator; Customer Service Rep.; Purchasing Agent/Manager; Sales Representative. **Educational backgrounds include:** Accounting; Computer Science; Engineering; Finance; Marketing. **Benefits:** 401(k); Dental Insurance; Disability Coverage; Life Insurance; Medical Insurance; Tuition Assistance. **Corporate headquarters location:** This Location. **Other U.S. locations:** San Jose CA; Redmond WA. **International locations:** Scotland. **Subsidiaries include:** Futronix Systems; K&TEC Electronics; Kent Components; Kent Datacomm. **Listed on:** New York Stock Exchange. **Stock exchange symbol:** KNT. **Number of employees at this location:** 665.

KINGS ELECTRONICS COMPANY INC.

1685 Overview Drive, Rock Hill SC 29730. 803/909-5000. **Fax:** 803/909-5044. **Contact:** Charles Robinson, Director of Human Resources. **World Wide Web address:** http://www.kingselectronics.com. **Description:** Manufactures, sells, and distributes a large line of specialized RF coaxial connectors for various electronics and aerospace industry applications.

KOEHLER-BRIGHT STAR, INC.

380 Stewart Road, Wilkes-Barre PA 18706-1459. 570/825-1900. **Contact:** Patti Leonard, Human Resources Manager. **World Wide Web address:** http://www.flashlight.com. **Description:** Manufactures and distributes industrial batteries, dry cell batteries, and other related lighting products. **Corporate headquarters location:** This Location. **Other U.S. locations:** Passaic NJ; Paterson NJ.

KOLLMORGEN CORPORATION
ELECTRO-OPTICAL DIVISION

347 King Street, Northampton MA 01060. 413/586-2330. **Fax:** 413/585-1088. **Contact:** Kelly Feudo, Human Resources Manager. **World Wide Web address:** http://www.kollmorgen.com. **Description:** This location designs and supplies advanced submarine periscopes, weapon directors, and military optics for the armed forces of the U.S. and its allies. Products allow the operator to search, detect, and identify targets anytime during the day or night using thermal imaging, high-resolution TV, lasers, direct-viewing channels, and video tracking and processing technologies. Overall, Kollmorgen operates in three business segments: Electronic Interconnections, Motors and Controls, and Electro-Optical Instruments. Founded in 1916. **NOTE:** Entry-level positions are offered. **Common positions include:** Electrical/Electronics Engineer; Electronics Technician; Mechanical Engineer; Software Engineer. **Educational backgrounds include:** Engineering. **Benefits:** 401(k); Daycare Assistance; Dental Insurance; Disability Coverage; Employee Discounts; Flexible Schedule; Life Insurance; Medical Insurance; Pension Plan; Profit Sharing; Public Transit Available; Tuition Assistance. **Corporate headquarters location:** Waltham MA. **Number of employees at this location:** 230.

KOLLSMAN, INC.

220 Daniel Webster Highway, Merrimack NH 03054. 603/889-2500. **Contact:** Human Resources. **E-mail address:** careers@kollsman.com. **World Wide Web address:** http://www.kollsman.com. **Description:** Designs and manufactures avionic flight instruments, high-tech weapon systems and subsystems, and diagnostic medical equipment. Founded in 1996. **Common positions include:** Design Engineer; Electrical/Electronics Engineer; Mechanical Engineer; Quality Assurance Engineer; Software Engineer; Systems Analyst. **Educational backgrounds include:** C/C++; Computer Science; Engineering; Software Development. **Benefits:** 401(k); Casual Dress - Daily; Dental Insurance; Disability Coverage; Life Insurance; Medical Insurance; Pension Plan; Sick Days (6 - 10); Tuition Assistance; Vacation Days (6 - 10). **Corporate headquarters location:** This Location. **Subsidiaries include:** KMC Systems, Inc. **Listed on:** Privately held. **President/CEO:** John S. Dehne. **Annual sales/revenues:** More than $100 million. **Number of employees nationwide:** 600.

KOPIN CORPORATION

695 Myles Standish Boulevard, Taunton MA 02780. 508/824-6696. **Fax:** 508/822-1381. **Contact:** Human Resources. **World Wide Web address:** http://www.kopin.com. **Description:** Kopin Corporation is a developer of advanced, flat panel display products. The company's products include compact projectors and head-mounted display systems featuring higher resolution, lighter weight, and greater portability; as well as large-screen monitors offering higher definition and streamlined dimensions. Kopin's proprietary wafer engineering has a broad range of computer, entertainment, business product, medical imaging, avionics, and industrial applications. **Corporate headquarters location:** This Location. **Other U.S. locations:** Westborough MA.

KRONOS INC.

297 Billerica Road, Chelmsford MA 01824. 978/250-9800. **Contact:** Human Resources. **World Wide Web address:** http://www.kronos.com. **Description:** Designs, develops, and markets labor management software and computerized systems that measure employee attendance and schedules. Founded in 1977. **Common positions include:** Electrical/Electronics Engineer; Software Engineer; Technical Writer/Editor. **Educational backgrounds include:** Computer Science; Engineering; Mathematics. **Benefits:** 401(k); Dental Insurance; Disability Coverage; Employee Discounts; Life Insurance; Medical Insurance; Tuition Assistance. **Special programs:** Internships. **Corporate headquarters location:** This Location. **International locations:** Canada; United Kingdom. **Listed on:** NASDAQ. **Stock exchange symbol:**

KRON. Annual sales/revenues: More than $100 million. **Number of employees at this location:** 900.

KULICKE & SOFFA INDUSTRIES, INC.
2101 Blair Mill Road, Willow Grove PA 19090. 215/784-6253. **Toll-free phone:** 800/523-1321. **Fax:** 215/784-6628. **Contact:** Human Resources. **E-mail address:** hr@kns.com. **World Wide Web address:** http://www.kns.com. **Description:** A leader in semiconductor assembly systems and services. The company designs, manufactures, markets, and supports equipment for IC semiconductor manufacturers worldwide. Kulicke & Soffa Industries, Inc.'s product lines include wafer and hard materials dicing, die bonding and wire bonding equipment, service and spare parts, and the Micro-Swiss line of bonding and dicing tools and production accessories. Founded in 1951. **Common positions include:** Account Manager; Accountant; Applications Engineer; Assembler; Blue-Collar Worker Supervisor; Buyer; Clerical Supervisor; Computer Programmer; Credit Manager; Customer Service Rep.; Electrical/Electronics Engineer; Financial Analyst; Human Resources Manager; Manufacturing Engineer; Marketing Manager; Marketing Specialist; Mechanical Engineer; MIS Specialist; Production Manager; Purchasing Agent/Manager; Quality Control Supervisor; Sales Engineer; Secretary; Software Engineer; Systems Analyst; Systems Manager; Technical Writer/Editor; Typist/Word Processor. **Educational backgrounds include:** Accounting; Business Administration; Computer Science; Engineering; Finance; Marketing; Mathematics. **Benefits:** 401(k); Daycare Assistance; Dental Insurance; Disability Coverage; Employee Discounts; Flexible Schedule; Life Insurance; Medical Insurance; Tuition Assistance. **Corporate headquarters location:** This Location. **Other U.S. locations:** Santa Clara CA. **International locations:** Worldwide. **Listed on:** NASDAQ. **Stock exchange symbol:** KLIC. **Annual sales/revenues:** More than $100 million. **Number of employees at this location:** 900.

KYOCERA AMERICA, INC.
8611 Balboa Avenue, San Diego CA 92123. 858/576-2600. **Fax:** 858/268-3035. **Contact:** Human Resources. **World Wide Web address:** http://www.kyocera.com/KAI. **Description:** Manufactures a broad line of products for the electronics industry including integrated circuit packages, chip capacitors, industrial ceramics, and insulator parts. Other operations include the manufacturing of such consumer and office products as cameras, jewelry, copiers, and portable and personal computers. **NOTE:** Entry-level positions are offered. **Common positions include:** Accountant/Auditor; Computer Programmer; Credit Manager; Industrial Engineer; Manufacturing Engineer; Operations/Production Manager; Sales Engineer; Systems Analyst. **Educational backgrounds include:** Accounting; Business Administration; Engineering. **Benefits:** 401(k); Dental Insurance; Disability Coverage; Employee Discounts; Life Insurance; Medical Insurance; Pension Plan. **Special programs:** Internships; Training. **Corporate headquarters location:** This Location. **Parent company:** Kyocera International, Inc. **Listed on:** New York Stock Exchange. **Annual sales/revenues:** More than $100 million. **Number of employees at this location:** 1,000.

LSI SPECIALTY ELECTRICAL PRODUCTS
1231 Shadowdale, Houston TX 77043. 713/464-1393. **Fax:** 713/464-7731. **Contact:** Vice President/General Manager. **Description:** Distributes electrical products used in hazardous areas and harsh environments. **Common positions include:**

Administrative Manager; Buyer; Clerical Supervisor; Computer Operator; Credit Manager; Customer Service Representative; Management Trainee; Manufacturer's/Wholesaler's Sales Rep.; Receptionist; Secretary; Warehouse/Distribution Worker; Wholesale and Retail Buyer. **Educational backgrounds include:** Accounting; Engineering; Liberal Arts; Marketing. **Benefits:** Bonus Award/Plan; Life Insurance; Medical Insurance. **Corporate headquarters location:** This Location. **Other U.S. locations:** Lafayette LA; Oklahoma City OK.

LTX CORPORATION
LTX Park at University Avenue, Westwood MA 02090. 781/461-1000. **Contact:** Human Resources. **World Wide Web address:** http://www.ltx.com. **Description:** Manufactures and markets testing equipment for testing semiconductors and electronic assemblies. The company's semiconductor test systems include digital test systems, which test digital ICs such as microprocessors and microcontrollers; linear/mixed signal test systems, which test a wide range of linear and mixed signal ICs; and discrete component test systems. The company also provides applications support for its test systems. Founded in 1976. **Corporate headquarters location:** This Location.

LAM RESEARCH CORPORATION
4650 Cushing Parkway, Fremont CA 94538. 510/659-0200. **Contact:** Human Resources. **World Wide Web address:** http://www.lamrc.com. **Description:** Develops, manufactures, and markets single-wafer plasma etch systems used primarily in the fabrication of very large scale integrated (VLSI) circuits. The company's products are used to deposit specific film on a silicon wafer and selectively etch away portions of various films to create a circuit design. Depositions and etch processes, which are repeated numerous times during the fabrication cycle, are required to manufacture virtually every semiconductor device produced today. **Common positions include:** Accountant/Auditor; Blue-Collar Worker Supervisor; Budget Analyst; Buyer; Chemical Engineer; Clerical Supervisor; Computer Programmer; Credit Manager; Designer; Draftsperson; Electrical/Electronics Engineer; Financial Analyst; Human Resources Manager; Industrial Engineer; Mechanical Engineer; Metallurgical Engineer; Software Developer; Systems Analyst; Technical Writer/Editor. **Educational backgrounds include:** Business Administration; Chemistry; Engineering; Finance. **Benefits:** 401(k); Dental Insurance; Disability Coverage; Employee Discounts; Life Insurance; Medical Insurance; Profit Sharing; Savings Plan; Tuition Assistance. **Corporate headquarters location:** This Location. **Other U.S. locations:** Nationwide. **Number of employees at this location:** 1,600.

LANSDALE SEMICONDUCTOR INC.
2502 West Huntington Drive, Tempe AZ 85282. 602/438-0123. **Fax:** 602/438-0138. **Contact:** Cheryl Warianka, Human Resources. **E-mail address:** cheryl@lansdale.com. **World Wide Web address:** http://www.lansdale.com. **Description:** Manufactures semiconductors. Lansdale Semiconductor manufactures products discontinued by such major manufacturers as Intel, Motorola, National/Fairchild, and Harris, and supports spare parts requirements by purchasing lines from the original manufacturer. **Corporate headquarters location:** This Location.

LASER POWER OPTICS
12777 High Bluff Drive, San Diego CA 92130. 858/755-0700. **Contact:** Ofelia Flores, Human

Resources Manager. **World Wide Web address:** http://www.laserpower.com. **Description:** A manufacturer of optics for high-power lasers. **Common positions include:** Accountant/Auditor; Administrator; Assistant Manager; Blue-Collar Worker Supervisor; Customer Service Rep.; Manufacturer's/Wholesaler's Sales Rep.; Mechanical Engineer; Operations/Production Manager; Optical Engineer. **Benefits:** Dental Insurance; Disability Coverage; Employee Discounts; Life Insurance; Medical Insurance. **Special programs:** Internships. **Corporate headquarters location:** This Location. **Number of employees at this location:** 100.

LASER TECHNOLOGY, INC. (LTI)
7070 South Tucson Way, Englewood CO 80112. 303/649-1000. **Fax:** 303/649-9710. **Contact:** Annette Spencer, Human Resources Director. **World Wide Web address:** http://www. lasertech.com. **Description:** Provides laser-based measurement systems to a wide variety of markets worldwide. Products include the Marksman, a laser speed detection system. Founded in 1985. **NOTE:** Part-time jobs are offered. **Common positions include:** Accountant; Administrative Assistant; Chief Financial Officer; Computer Programmer; Computer Technician; Controller; Customer Service Rep.; Design Engineer; Electrical/Electronics Engineer; Human Resources Manager; Internet Services Manager; Manufacturing Engineer; Marketing Manager; Operations Manager; Production Manager; Sales Manager; Sales Rep.; Webmaster. **Educational backgrounds include:** Accounting; Engineering; Finance; Marketing. **Benefits:** 401(k); Casual Dress - Daily; Dental Insurance; Employee Discounts; Life Insurance; Medical Insurance; Tuition Assistance. **Special programs:** Apprenticeships. **Listed on:** American Stock Exchange. **President:** David Williams. **Annual sales/revenues:** $11 - $20 million. **Number of employees at this location:** 85. **Number of employees nationwide:** 95.

LASERTECHNICS MARKING CORP.
5500 Wilshire Avenue NE, Albuquerque NM 87113-1960. 505/822-1123. **Fax:** 505/821-2213. **Contact:** Human Resources. **Description:** A designer, developer, manufacturer, and marketer of laser systems for use in marking a variety of products and containers, continuous tone printers that create high-resolution hard copy images, and other laser-related equipment.

LATTICE SEMICONDUCTOR CORP.
5555 NE Moore Court, Hillsboro OR 97124. 503/681-0118. **Contact:** Mr. Terry Dols, Human Resources. **World Wide Web address:** http://www.latticesemi.com. **Description:** A leader in the design, development, and marketing of high-speed Programmable Logic Devices (PLDs) in both low-density and high-density ranges. Lattice products are sold primarily to original equipment manufacturers of microcomputers, graphic systems, workstations, peripherals, telecommunications, military, and industrial controls. CMOS PLDs are assembled in 20 to 207 PIN standard packages and offered with various speed, power, and packaging options in commercial, industrial, and military temperature versions. **Corporate headquarters location:** This Location. **Number of employees at this location:** 395.

THE LeCROY CORPORATION
700 Chestnut Ridge Road, Chestnut Ridge NY 10977. 914/425-2000. **Toll-free phone:** 800/553-2769. **Fax:** 914/578-4461. **Contact:** Corporate Staffing. **E-mail address:** humanresources@ lecroy.com. **World Wide Web address:** http://www.lecroy.com. **Description:** A leading manufacturer of digital oscilloscopes and related products for the electronics, computer, and communications markets. Founded in 1964. **NOTE:** Entry-level positions are offered. **Common positions include:** Applications Engineer; Customer Service Rep.; Design Engineer; Electrical/ Electronics Engineer; Hardware Engineer; Manufacturing Engineer; Marketing Specialist; Sales Engineer; Software Engineer; Technical Writer/Editor. **Educational backgrounds include:** Computer Science; Engineering; Marketing; Physics. **Benefits:** 401(k); Dental Insurance; Disability Coverage; Life Insurance; Medical Insurance; Public Transit Available; Tuition Assistance. **Corporate headquarters location:** This Location. **International division location:** Geneva, Switzerland. **Listed on:** NASDAQ. **Annual sales/revenues:** More than $100 million. **Number of employees at this location:** 200. **Number of employees worldwide:** 500.

LEPCO
5204 North Expressway, Brownsville TX 78521. 956/350-5650. **Contact:** Office Manager. **World Wide Web address:** http://www.ies.net/lepco. **Description:** A manufacturer of transformers and conductors. **Corporate headquarters location:** This Location.

LEVEL ONE COMMUNICATIONS, INC.
9750 Goethe Road, Sacramento CA 95827. 916/855-5000. **Contact:** Human Resources. **World Wide Web address:** http://www.level1.com. **Description:** Produces silicon connectivity solutions for high growth communications markets. The company uses its proprietary design and testing methodologies, combined with its extensive proprietary library of cells and blocks, to accelerate the development of new, application specific semiconductors. **Parent company:** Intel Corporation. **Listed on:** NASDAQ. **Annual sales/revenues:** More than $100 million.

LEVITON MANUFACTURING COMPANY
59-25 Little Neck Parkway, Little Neck NY 11362. 718/281-4400. **Fax:** 718/281-6549. **Contact:** Janet Perens Howitt, Human Resources Manager. **World Wide Web address:** http://www.leviton.com. **Description:** Manufactures electrical wiring devices. Leviton produces more than 80,000 variations of light switches, sockets, and plugs for both consumers and industry. Products are used in small appliances, lamps, and similar products. **NOTE:** Entry-level positions are offered. **Common positions include:** Account Manager; Account Rep.; Accountant; Administrative Assistant; Applications Engineer; Budget Analyst; Computer Operator; Computer Programmer; Cost Estimator; Credit Manager; Electrical/Electronics Engineer; Finance Director; Financial Analyst; Human Resources Manager; Industrial Engineer; Industrial Production Manager; Manufacturing Engineer; Marketing Manager; Marketing Specialist; Mechanical Engineer; MIS Specialist; Software Engineer; Systems Analyst; Systems Manager. **Educational backgrounds include:** Accounting; Business Administration; Communications; Computer Science; Economics; Engineering; Finance; Marketing; Software Development; Software Tech. Support. **Benefits:** 401(k); Dental Insurance; Medical Insurance; Pension Plan; Tuition Assistance. **Corporate headquarters location:** This Location. **Other U.S. locations:** Atlanta GA; Chicago IL; Coffeyville KS; Sparks NV; Pawtucket RI; Bothell WA.

LIGHTING COMPONENTS & DESIGN
692 South Military Trail, Deerfield Beach FL 33442. 954/425-0123. **Contact:** Human Resources.

World Wide Web address: http://www. lightingcomponents.com. **Description:** A manufacturer of prewired electrical devices, indicator lights, and lamp holders. **Corporate headquarters location:** This Location.

LITHONIA LIGHTING COMPANY
P.O. Box A, 1400 Lester Road, Conyers GA 30012. 770/922-9000. **Fax:** 770/860-9403. **Contact:** Joyce Cobb, Human Resources Specialist. **E-mail address:** recruiter@lithonia.com. **World Wide Web address:** http://www.lithonia.com. **Description:** Manufactures commercial and industrial lighting equipment and related wiring, controls, and emergency systems. **Common positions include:** Accountant; Computer Programmer; Credit Manager; Customer Service Rep.; Electrical/Electronics Engineer; Financial Analyst; Human Resources Manager; Management Trainee; Marketing Analyst; MIS Specialist; Systems Analyst; Transportation/Traffic Specialist; Typist/Word Processor. **Educational backgrounds include:** Accounting; Art/Design; Business Administration; Computer Science; Engineering; Finance; Marketing. **Benefits:** 401(k); Dental Insurance; Disability Coverage; Employee Discounts; Life Insurance; Medical Insurance; Tuition Assistance. **Special programs:** Training. **Corporate headquarters location:** This Location. **Parent company:** National Service Industries, Inc. **Number of employees nationwide:** 4,800.

LITTELFUSE, INC.
800 East Northwest Highway, Des Plaines IL 60016. 847/824-1188. **Fax:** 847/391-0434. **Contact:** Human Resources. **World Wide Web address:** http://www.littelfuse.com. **Description:** Manufactures a wide variety of fuses. **Common positions include:** Accountant/Auditor; Buyer; Ceramics Engineer; Computer Programmer; Designer; Draftsperson; Electrical/Electronics Engineer; Electrician; Financial Analyst; Human Resources Manager; Industrial Engineer; Industrial Production Manager; Licensed Practical Nurse; Management Trainee; Materials Engineer; Mechanical Engineer; Metallurgical Engineer; Operations/Production Manager; Purchasing Agent/Manager; Registered Nurse; Software Engineer; Systems Analyst. **Educational backgrounds include:** Accounting; Business Administration; Computer Science; Engineering; Finance; Marketing; Physics. **Benefits:** 401(k); Dental Insurance; Disability Coverage; Life Insurance; Medical Insurance; Pension Plan; Tuition Assistance. **Special programs:** Internships. **Corporate headquarters location:** This Location. **Other U.S. locations:** Arcola IL; Centralia IL. **Listed on:** NASDAQ. **Number of employees nationwide:** 1,500.

LITTON INDUSTRIES, INC.
21240 Burbank Boulevard, Woodland Hills CA 91367. 818/598-5000. **Contact:** Human Resources. **World Wide Web address:** http://www. littoncorp.com. **Description:** A leader in defense and commercial electronics, shipbuilding, and information technology. Litton is involved in the electronic warfare and command, navigation, and guidance and control markets. Litton also designs, repairs, and modernizes ships. Founded in 1953. **Corporate headquarters location:** This Location. **International locations:** Canada; Germany; Italy. **Other U.S. locations:**
- Litton Advanced Systems, Inc. 4747 Hellyer Avenue, San Jose CA 95138. 408/365-4747.
- Litton Clifton Precision, P.O. Box 160, Murphy NC 28906. 828/837-5115.
- Litton Electro-Optical Systems, 1215 South 52nd Street, Tempe AZ 85281. 480/968-4471.

LOCKHEED MARTIN CORPORATION
P.O. Box 85, Mail Stop 1013, Litchfield Park AZ 85340-0085. 623/925-7067. **Fax:** 623/925-7568. **Contact:** Barbara Seyfried, Recruiter/Human Resources Specialist. **E-mail address:** barbara.i.seyfried@lmco.com. **World Wide Web address:** http://www.lmco.com. **Description:** This location produces Synthetic-Aperture Radar (SAR) and is expanding this technology into weapon delivery applications. Overall, Lockheed Martin also produces ground-based sensor support equipment; command, control, communications, and intelligence (C3I) systems; and computer-based training systems. **Common positions include:** Computer Programmer; Electrical/Electronics Engineer; Software Engineer. **Educational backgrounds include:** Computer Science; Engineering; Mathematics; Physics; Software Development. **Benefits:** 401(k); Dental Insurance; Disability Coverage; Flexible Schedule; Life Insurance; Medical Insurance; Paid Sick Child Care; Pension Plan; Tuition Assistance. **Corporate headquarters location:** Bethesda MD. **Other U.S. locations:** Nationwide.

LOGIMETRICS INC.
50 Orville Drive, Bohemia NY 11716. 631/784-4110. **Contact:** Human Resources. **Description:** LogiMetrics manufactures and sells traveling wave tube amplifiers and complete electronic test systems for the measurement and control of electronic pollution in the field of electromagnetic susceptibility and for microwave communications including Earth satellite stations and wireless cable. Traveling wave amplifiers are used as communication devices, as radar and mapping devices, for radiated susceptibility testing, for microwave studies, and for general high-power component testing. They are also sold to the federal government for both military and non-military purposes. Complete turnkey systems are used in various activities from automatic electromagnetic susceptibility testing systems to complicated electronic ground-based airborne electronic warfare. **Corporate headquarters location:** This Location.

M&G ELECTRONICS
P.O. Box 8187, Virginia Beach VA 23450. 757/468-6000. **Fax:** 757/468-5442. **Contact:** Audra Diggs, Human Resources Manager. **Description:** Assembles wiring harnesses and installs gauges for boat dashboards. Founded in 1975. **NOTE:** Entry-level positions and second and third shifts are offered. **Common positions include:** Assembler; Buyer; Controller; Customer Service Rep.; Design Engineer; Electrical/Electronics Engineer; General Manager; Human Resources Manager; Industrial Engineer; Machine Operator; MIS Specialist; Operations Manager; Production Manager; Purchasing Agent/Manager; Quality Control Supervisor; Sales Manager; Sales Representative. **Educational backgrounds include:** Business Administration; Computer Science; Engineering; Marketing. **Benefits:** 401(k); Dental Insurance; Life Insurance; Medical Insurance. **Corporate headquarters location:** This Location. **Other U.S. locations:** NC; SC. **Listed on:** Privately held. **Annual sales/revenues:** $21 - $50 million. **Number of employees at this location:** 500. **Number of employees nationwide:** 530.

MEMC ELECTRONIC MATERIALS, INC.
501 Pearl Drive, P.O. Box 8, St. Peters MO 63376-0008. 636/474-5000. **Contact:** Brad Eldredge, Director of Human Resources. **World Wide Web address:** http://www.memc.com. **Description:** One of the largest silicon wafer suppliers in North America and Europe, as well as one of the largest Western suppliers to Japan. Products include

Czochralaski-grown silicon wafers, sold as polished or with an epitaxial layer in diameter ranges from four to eight inches. Application uses range from discrete diodes to complex microprocessors and DRAM memories. Another affiliate of MEMC is SiBond, LLC, which manufactures silicon-on-insulator wafers (SOI) used for high-speed microprocessors, high-density memory, and low-power applications. Silicon wafers form the base substrate for integrated circuits serving the electronic industry's semiconductor market. **Common positions include:** Accountant/Auditor; Applications Engineer; Chemical Engineer; Computer Programmer; Database Manager; Electrical/Electronics Engineer; Manufacturing Engineer; Mechanical Engineer; Metallurgical Engineer; Operations/Production Manager; Systems Analyst. **Corporate headquarters location:** This Location. **Parent company:** Huls AG (Marl, Germany). **Listed on:** New York Stock Exchange. **Stock exchange symbol:** MEMC.

MTS, INC.
9944 Antelope Road, White City OR 97503. 541/826-7655. **Fax:** 541/826-1713. **Contact:** Michelle Julian, Human Resources. **E-mail address:** mjulian@mts-smt.com. **World Wide Web address:** http://www.mts-smt.com. **Description:** Assembles electro-mechanical products on a contract basis. **Common positions include:** Account Manager; Administrative Assistant; Blue-Collar Worker Supervisor; Buyer; Chief Financial Officer; Electrical/Electronics Engineer; Human Resources Manager; Industrial Engineer; Manufacturing Engineer; MIS Specialist; Production Manager; Project Manager; Purchasing Agent/Manager; Quality Control Supervisor; Sales Rep.; Typist/Word Processor. **Educational backgrounds include:** Accounting; Business Administration; Engineering; Finance. **Benefits:** Dental Insurance; Medical Insurance. **Office hours:** Monday - Friday, 8:00 a.m. - 5:00 p.m. **Corporate headquarters location:** This Location. **Listed on:** Privately held. **Facilities Manager:** Dan Fox. **Annual sales/revenues:** $5 - $10 million. **Number of employees at this location:** 90.

MACAULAY-BROWN, INC.
4021 Executive Drive, Dayton OH 45430. 937/426-3421. **Fax:** 937/426-5364. **Contact:** Ken Simon, Senior Human Resources Manager. **E-mail address:** kensimon@macb.com. **World Wide Web address:** http://www.macb.com. **Description:** A technical firm specializing in intelligence/threat analysis; systems engineering; digital system model development; technique development; test and evaluation of hardware in the loop; software engineering; instrumentation system design and development; computer system/LAN development; and management support. Founded in 1978. **Common positions include:** Electrical/Electronics Engineer; Physicist; Project Manager; Software Engineer; Systems Analyst. **Educational backgrounds include:** Computer Science; Engineering; Physics. **Benefits:** 401(k); Dental Insurance; Disability Coverage; ESOP; Flexible Schedule; Life Insurance; Medical Insurance; Non-Smoking Environment; Pension Plan; Profit Sharing; Tuition Assistance. **Corporate headquarters location:** This Location. **Other U.S. locations:** AL; CA; FL; GA; IL; MD; NM; TX. **Listed on:** Privately held. **Annual sales/revenues:** $11 - $20 million. **Number of employees at this location:** 95.

MAGNETEK, INC.
26 Century Boulevard, Suite 600, Nashville TN 37214. 615/316-5100. **Contact:** Personnel. **World Wide Web address:** http://www.magnetek.com.

Description: A designer, producer, and marketer of electrical, electronic, and industrial components and products. The company also offers services and repair support for its products. MagneTek's principal products include ballasts and transformers for lighting; motors; and control components for motors and generators, systems, and controls. The company's service group rebuilds and repairs large motors, generators, and transformers primarily for utility companies and industrial manufacturers. **Corporate headquarters location:** This Location. **Listed on:** New York Stock Exchange.

MATERIALS RESEARCH CORPORATION
542 Route 303, Orangeburg NY 10962. 914/398-8307. **Contact:** Human Resources Director. **Description:** Designs and manufactures thin film coating and etching systems which are utilized in the manufacture of integrated circuits, for sale principally to the semiconductor, computer, and telecommunications industries. The company also processes and fabricates ultra-high purity metals and metal alloys, principally for thin-film purposes. Materials Research Corporation's thin-film technology products are also used in nonelectronic applications such as protective coatings for corrosion and wear resistance in razor blades and various automotive products. The company operates in three segments: Sputtering Equipment, Associated Target Materials, and Other High-Purity Materials. **Common positions include:** Buyer; Computer Programmer; Customer Service Rep.; Designer; Electrical/Electronics Engineer; Financial Analyst; General Manager; Human Resources Manager; Industrial Engineer; Industrial Production Manager; Materials Engineer; Mechanical Engineer; Metallurgical Engineer; Operations/Production Manager; Physicist; Purchasing Agent/Manager; Science Technologist; Software Engineer; Systems Analyst; Technical Writer/Editor. **Educational backgrounds include:** Accounting; Business Administration; Computer Science; Engineering; Finance; Marketing; Physics. **Benefits:** 401(k); Dental Insurance; Disability Coverage; Employee Discounts; Life Insurance; Medical Insurance; Pension Plan; Tuition Assistance. **Special programs:** Internships. **Corporate headquarters location:** This Location. **Other U.S. locations:** Phoenix AZ. **Parent company:** Sony Corporation of America.

MERIX CORPORATION
P.O. Box 3000, Forest Grove OR 97116. 503/359-9300. **Fax:** 503/357-1504. **Contact:** Ms. Terri Timberman, Vice President of Human Resources. **Description:** A leading manufacturer of electronic interconnect solutions including printed circuit boards, backplanes, flexible circuits, and subassemblies for use in sophisticated electronic equipment. The company provides these complex electronic interconnect products to a diversified base of manufacturers in the industrial and medical instrumentation, computer, and communications segments of the electronics industry. The company's broad offering of interconnect products employs a variety of technologies including rigid and high-performance substrates and flexible circuitry. **Corporate headquarters location:** This Location.

MERRIMAC INDUSTRIES INC.
41 Fairfield Place, West Caldwell NJ 07006. 973/575-1300. **Contact:** Personnel. **World Wide Web address:** http://www.merrimacind.com. **Description:** An international manufacturer of high-reliability signal-processing components. Products include IF-baseband components (used by electronics and military electronics OEMs); RF-microwave components (for military electronics and fiber-optics users); high-reliability space and missile

products (electronic components used in military satellite and missile programs); integrated microwave products (for the military and commercial communications markets); and satellite reception products (products for the CATV and satellite master antenna systems). **Common positions include:** Accountant; Buyer; Computer Programmer; Customer Service Rep.; Draftsperson; Electrical/Electronics Engineer; Industrial Designer; Mechanical Engineer; Operations/Production Manager; Purchasing Agent/Manager; Quality Control Supervisor; Sales Executive; Technical Writer/Editor. **Educational backgrounds include:** Business Administration; Engineering; Marketing. **Benefits:** 401(k); Dental Insurance; Disability Coverage; Life Insurance; Medical Insurance; Profit Sharing; Tuition Assistance. **Corporate headquarters location:** This Location.

MESA LABORATORIES, INC.
12100 West Sixth Avenue, Lakewood CO 80228. 303/987-8000. **Fax:** 303/987-8989. **Contact:** Steve Peterson, Vice President of Finance. **World Wide Web address:** http://www.mesalabs.com. **Description:** Develops, manufactures, and markets computer-based, electronic measurement instruments used across a wide range of industries. Mesa's products include DATARACE patented instruments for measuring and recording temperature, humidity, and pressure; NUSONICS flow meters and sonic concentration analyzers; and Western Meters and the ECHO Dialyzer Reprocessor are two product lines used in kidney dialysis. **Common positions include:** Accountant/Auditor; Buyer; Chemist; Designer; Electrical/Electronics Engineer; Operations/Production Manager; Quality Control Supervisor. **Educational backgrounds include:** Business Administration; Engineering; Marketing. **Benefits:** Life Insurance; Medical Insurance; Profit Sharing; Stock Option. **Corporate headquarters location:** This Location. **Listed on:** NASDAQ. **Stock exchange symbol:** MLAB. **Number of employees at this location:** 50.

METHODE ELECTRONICS, INC.
7401 West Wilson Avenue, Harwood Heights IL 60706. 708/867-9600. **Contact:** Personnel Director. **Description:** Manufactures component devices for sale to equipment manufacturers of electronic data processing equipment, instruments, voice and data communications, and the automotive industry. These products include electronic connectors for discrete wire, flat wire, and printed circuits; microcircuit sockets; interconnect devices, fiber-optic connectors and cable assemblies; and cable distribution products. Methode Electronics supplies the transportation and off-road vehicle industries with a variety of automotive controls, air bag transducers, and wiring harnesses. Facilities on the East and West Coasts manufacture high-reliability, multilayer, flexible, metal core and plated-through-hole printed circuit boards. Heavy current power distribution systems serving the data processing, telecommunications, motor control, and electric vehicle marketplaces are also produced. The company has environmental laboratories for qualification testing and certification of printed circuit boards, connection devices, and other components used in aerospace and transportation applications. Methode Electronics also produces electronic chemicals, rectifier leads, emulator interface adapters, battery cables, and all-molded harnesses. **Corporate headquarters location:** This Location. **Other area locations:** Carthage IL; Rolling Meadows IL; Warsaw IL.

METRON, INC.
1505 West Third Avenue, Denver CO 80223. 303/592-1903. **Fax:** 303/592-1969. **Contact:** Bob Warren, Personnel Manager. **Description:** A manufacturer of fire pump controllers and custom electrical products including switch gear and switchboard equipment. **Common positions include:** Accountant/Auditor; Buyer; Customer Service Rep.; Department Manager; Draftsperson; Electrical/Electronics Engineer; Financial Manager; Machinist; Manufacturer's/Wholesaler's Sales Rep.; Mechanical Engineer; Precision Assembler; Receptionist; Sheet-Metal Worker; Welder. **Benefits:** Disability Coverage; Life Insurance; Medical Insurance; Pension Plan; Savings Plan; Tuition Assistance. **Corporate headquarters location:** This Location. **Number of employees at this location:** 85.

MICRO NETWORKS CORPORATION
ANDERSEN LABORATORIES
324 Clark Street, Worcester MA 01606. 508/852-5400. **Contact:** Mr. T.D. Vangel, Director of Human Resources. **World Wide Web address:** http://www.mnc.com. **Description:** Micro Networks supplies microelectronic circuits to OEMs. These circuits are used for frequency control and data conversion in the information technology field. **Common positions include:** Electrical/Electronics Engineer; Marketing Manager; Marketing Specialist; Mechanical Engineer; Sales Engineer; Sales Manager; Sales Representative. **Educational backgrounds include:** Accounting; Engineering; Marketing; Physics. **Benefits:** 401(k); Dental Insurance; Disability Coverage; Life Insurance; Medical Insurance; Pension Plan; Profit Sharing; Public Transit Available; Tuition Assistance. **Corporate headquarters location:** This Location. **Subsidiaries include:** Andersen Laboratories (also at this location) manufactures acoustic signal processing products and other related products for use in the commercial communications market. **Listed on:** Privately held. **Number of employees at this location:** 95.

MICRO SYSTEMS, INC.
35 Hill Avenue, Fort Walton Beach FL 32548. 850/244-2332. **Fax:** 850/243-1378. **Contact:** Tami L. Manard, Director of Human Resources. **Description:** Designs and manufactures real-time, microprocessor-based control systems which create interfaces between targets and their controlling ground stations. The company's equipment is built under contract for Department of Defense agencies. **NOTE:** Entry-level positions are offered. **Common positions include:** Design Engineer; Draftsperson; Electrical/Electronics Engineer; Production Manager; Software Engineer. **Educational backgrounds include:** Engineering; Mathematics; Physics. **Benefits:** 401(k); Dental Insurance; Disability Coverage; Employee Discounts; Life Insurance; Medical Insurance; Profit Sharing; Savings Plan; Tuition Assistance. **Special programs:** Internships. **Corporate headquarters location:** This Location. **Listed on:** Privately held. **Annual sales/revenues:** $5 - $10 million. **Number of employees at this location:** 100.

MICROCHIP TECHNOLOGY INC.
2355 West Chandler Boulevard, Chandler AZ 85224. 480/786-7200. **Fax:** 480/786-7790. **Recorded jobline:** 480/786-7777. **Contact:** Human Resources. **E-mail address:** resumes@ microchip.com. **World Wide Web address:** http://www.microchip.com. **Description:** A semiconductor manufacturer. Microchip Technology specializes in 8-bit microcontrollers, eeproms, and other nonvolatile memory products. **Common positions include:** Accountant/Auditor; Applications Engineer; Budget Analyst; Buyer; Clerical Supervisor; Computer Programmer; Customer Service Representative; Designer;

Electrical/Electronics Engineer; Financial Analyst; Human Resources Manager; Systems Analyst. **Educational backgrounds include:** Accounting; Business Administration; Chemistry; Engineering; Marketing. **Benefits:** 401(k); Dental Insurance; Disability Coverage; Life Insurance; Medical Insurance; Profit Sharing; Savings Plan; Tuition Assistance. **Special programs:** Internships. **Corporate headquarters location:** This Location. **Other U.S. locations:** Tempe AZ. **Listed on:** NASDAQ.

MICROWAVE DISTRIBUTORS COMPANY
1707-32 Veterans Memorial Highway, Islandia NY 11722. 631/234-3434. **Contact:** Human Resources. **Description:** Distributes microwave and RF components. **Common positions include:** Accountant; Customer Service Rep.; Design Engineer. **Corporate headquarters location:** This Location.

MIDWEST ELECTRIC PRODUCTS, INC.
P.O. Box 910, Mankato MN 56002-0910. 507/625-4414. **Contact:** Human Resources. **World Wide Web address:** http://www.midwestelectric.com. **Description:** A manufacturer of outdoor waterproof and weatherproof electrical equipment including junction boxes, meter sockets, power outlets, RV products, and transfer switches. **Corporate headquarters location:** This Location.

MIKOHN GAMING CORPORATION
1045 Palms Airport Drive, Las Vegas NV 89119. 702/896-3890. **Contact:** Human Resources. **World Wide Web address:** http://www.mikohn.com. **Description:** Develops, manufactures, and distributes progressive jackpot systems for use with gaming machines. The company also designs, manufactures, and distributes custom electrical signs for both internal and external use. The company's jackpot systems and interior casino sign products are marketed and sold both separately and together as integrated, value-added casino marketing and promotional packages through a broad domestic and international distribution network. **Common positions include:** Account Manager; Account Representative; Accountant; Administrative Assistant; Administrative Manager; Buyer; Chief Financial Officer; Computer Animator; Computer Operator; Controller; Customer Service Rep.; Financial Analyst; Graphic Artist; Graphic Designer; Industrial Production Manager; Sales Representative; Secretary; Software Engineer; Systems Analyst; Systems Manager; Technical Writer/Editor. **Educational backgrounds include:** Accounting; Art/Design; Business Administration; Computer Science; Engineering. **Benefits:** 401(k); Dental Insurance; Disability Coverage; Employee Discounts; Flexible Schedule; Life Insurance; Medical Insurance; Pension Plan; Profit Sharing; Tuition Assistance. **Special programs:** Training. **Corporate headquarters location:** This Location. **Other U.S. locations:** MS; SD. **International locations:** Australia; Holland; South Africa. **Listed on:** NASDAQ. **Number of employees at this location:** 650.

MITRE CORPORATION
202 Burlington Road, Bedford MA 01730. 781/271-2000. **Contact:** David Gentes, Human Resources. **World Wide Web address:** http://www.mitre.org. **Description:** An international, high-technology electronics and communications firm that produces large-scale command, control, and communications (C3) systems for the U.S. Air Force. **Common positions include:** Computer Programmer; Electrical/Electronics Engineer; Physicist. **Educational backgrounds include:** Computer Science; Engineering; Mathematics; Physics.

Benefits: Dental Insurance; Disability Coverage; Life Insurance; Medical Insurance; Pension Plan; Tuition Assistance. **Corporate headquarters location:** This Location.

MITSUBISHI SILICON AMERICA
P.O. Box 7748, Salem OR 97303. 503/371-0041. **Contact:** Human Resources. **World Wide Web address:** http://www.mmc-sil.com. **Description:** Supplies electronic grade silicon wafers to the semiconductor industry. **Common positions include:** Chemical Engineer; Computer Programmer; Electrical/Electronics Engineer; Manufacturing Engineer; Mechanical Engineer; Operations/Production Manager; Production Manager; Quality Control Supervisor; Systems Analyst. **Educational backgrounds include:** Computer Science; Engineering. **Benefits:** 401(k); Dental Insurance; Disability Coverage; Employee Discounts; Life Insurance; Medical Insurance; Tuition Assistance. **Corporate headquarters location:** This Location. **Listed on:** Privately held. **Number of employees at this location:** 1,400.

MOLEX INC.
2222 Wellington Court, Lisle IL 60532. 630/969-4550. **Contact:** Human Resources. **World Wide Web address:** http://www.molex.com. **Description:** Designs, manufactures, and distributes electrical and electronic devices such as terminals, connectors, switches, and related application tooling. Products are used by television, stereo, home computer, electronic game, audio, video, and other consumer manufacturing firms, as well as by the automotive, and farm equipment industries. **Corporate headquarters location:** This Location. **Other U.S. locations:**
- 641 North Poplar Street, Orange CA 92868. 714/937-9388.

S.D. MYERS, INC.
180 South Avenue, Tallmadge OH 44278. 330/630-7000. **Fax:** 330/633-4786. **Contact:** Human Resources. **World Wide Web address:** http://www.sdmyers.com. **Description:** Engaged in transformer maintenance services, testing, rewinding, and maintenance seminars. **NOTE:** Entry-level positions, part-time jobs, and second and third shifts are offered. **Common positions include:** Account Manager; Account Representative; Accountant; Administrative Assistant; Administrative Manager; AS400 Programmer Analyst; Blue-Collar Worker Supervisor; Budget Analyst; Buyer; Chemist; Chief Financial Officer; Computer Technician; Controller; Customer Service Rep.; Design Engineer; Draftsperson; Electrical/Electronics Engineer; Electrician; Finance Director; Financial Analyst; Help-Desk Technician; Human Resources Manager; Industrial Production Manager; Mechanical Engineer; Production Manager; Purchasing Agent/Manager; Sales Executive; Sales Manager; Sales Rep.; Secretary; Web Advertising Specialist; Website Developer. **Educational backgrounds include:** Accounting; AS400 Certification; Chemistry; Engineering; Finance; Marketing; MBA; Microsoft Office; Microsoft Word; Spreadsheets. **Benefits:** 401(k); Dental Insurance; Disability Coverage; Life Insurance; Medical Insurance; Sick Days (1 - 5); Vacation Days (10 - 20). **Office hours:** Monday - Friday, 8:00 a.m. - 5:00 p.m. **Corporate headquarters location:** This Location. **Other U.S. locations:** Bessemer AL; Phoenix AZ; Fremont CA; Colorado Springs CO; Bedford NH; Fort Mill SC; Seabrook TX; Seattle WA. **Listed on:** Privately held. **Number of employees at this location:** 285.

NEC AMERICA INC.
14040 Park Center Road, Herndon VA 20171. 703/834-4000. **Contact:** Human Resources. **World

Wide Web address: http://www.nec.com. **Description:** Manufactures communications systems and equipment, computers, industrial electronic systems, electronic devices, and home electronic products.

NAPCO SECURITY GROUP
333 Bayview Avenue, Amityville NY 11701. 631/842-9400. **Contact:** Human Resources. **World Wide Web address:** http://www.napcosecurity.com. **Description:** Manufactures electronic security equipment. The company's products are used in residential, commercial, institutional, and industrial installations. **Corporate headquarters location:** This Location. **Subsidiaries include:** Alarm Lock; Excalibur Access Systems.

NATIONAL INSTRUMENT CORPORATION
6504 Bridge Point Parkway, Austin TX 78730-5039. 512/794-0100. **Contact:** Human Resources. **World Wide Web address:** http://www.ni.com. **Description:** Manufactures interface boards for the test measurement industry. **Corporate headquarters location:** This Location.

NATIONAL OIL WELL
1530 West Sam Houston Parkway North, Houston TX 77043. 713/467-9888. **Contact:** Human Resources. **Description:** Designs and develops electronic control systems for industrial applications. The company is a world leader in the field of power conversion equipment. It is one of the largest suppliers of variable speed drives to the oil industry and one of the world's largest users of large thyristor devices. **Corporate headquarters location:** This Location.

NATIONAL SEMICONDUCTOR CORP.
P.O. Box 58090, Santa Clara CA 95052-8090. 408/721-5000. **Contact:** Staffing. **World Wide Web address:** http://www.nsc.com. **Description:** Designs, develops, and manufactures microprocessors, consumer products, integrated circuits, memory systems, computer products, telecommunication systems, and high-speed bipolar circuits. **Common positions include:** Computer Programmer; Department Manager; Electrical/Electronics Engineer; Financial Analyst; Human Resources Manager; Industrial Engineer; Mechanical Engineer; Physicist; Technical Writer/Editor. **Educational backgrounds include:** Business Administration; Computer Science; Engineering; Finance; Marketing; Mathematics; Physics. **Benefits:** Dental Insurance; Disability Coverage; Employee Discounts; Life Insurance; Medical Insurance; Pension Plan; Profit Sharing; Savings Plan; Tuition Assistance. **Special programs:** Internships. **Corporate headquarters location:** This Location. **International locations:** Scotland. **Listed on:** New York Stock Exchange.

THE J.M. NEY COMPANY
2 Douglas Street, Ney Industrial Park, Bloomfield CT 06002. 860/242-2281. **Fax:** 860/286-6113. **Contact:** Karen Ruhlemann, Recruiter. **Description:** A manufacturer of electronic components. Founded in 1812. **NOTE:** Second and third shifts are offered. **Common positions include:** Accountant; Administrative Assistant; Applications Engineer; AS400 Programmer Analyst; Blue-Collar Worker Supervisor; Chemist; Chief Financial Officer; Clinical Lab Technician; Computer Programmer; Computer Support Technician; Controller; Customer Service Rep.; Database Administrator; Design Engineer; Draftsperson; Human Resources Manager; Industrial Production Manager; Manufacturing Engineer; Marketing Manager; Marketing Specialist; Mechanical

Engineer; Metallurgical Engineer; Network/Systems Administrator; Operations Manager; Purchasing Agent/Manager; Quality Assurance Engineer; Quality Control Supervisor; Systems Analyst; Vice President of Operations. **Educational backgrounds include:** Accounting; AS400 Certification; Business Administration; C/C++; Computer Science; Engineering; Finance; Marketing; Microsoft Word; Novell; Software Development; Software Tech. Support; Spreadsheets. **Benefits:** 401(k); Casual Dress - Fridays; Dental Insurance; Disability Coverage; Life Insurance; Medical Insurance; Pension Plan; Tuition Assistance. **Special programs:** Apprenticeships. **Office hours:** Monday - Friday, 7:00 a.m. - 5:00 p.m. **Corporate headquarters location:** This Location. **Parent company:** Andersen Group, Inc. **Listed on:** NASDAQ. **President:** Ronald N. Cerny. **Annual sales/revenues:** $21 - $50 million. **Number of employees at this location:** 165.

NORTHROP GRUMMAN ELECTRONIC SENSORS & SYSTEMS SECTOR
Mail Stop 1162, P.O. Box 1897, Baltimore MD 21203-1897. 410/765-1000. **Fax:** 410/993-7800. **Contact:** Steven S. Kawakami, Manager of Employment. **E-mail address:** jobs_ESSS@md.northgrum.com. **World Wide Web address:** http://sensor.northgrum.com. **Description:** This location is engaged in the research and development, design, integration, and manufacture of advanced electronic sensors and systems for the U.S. government, its allies, and other industrial and commercial customers. Major products include airborne and ground-based radars; electronic countermeasures; air traffic control and air defense systems; electro-optical systems; solid state devices; sonar and anti-submarine/mine warfare systems; and advanced imaging systems. Overall, Northrop Grumman manufactures military aircraft, commercial aircraft, and electronic systems. Northrop Grumman has developed the B-2 Stealth Bomber and parts for the F/A-18 and the 747. Other operations include computer systems developed for management and scientific applications. **NOTE:** Entry-level positions and part-time jobs are offered. **Common positions include:** Accountant; Administrative Assistant; Administrative Manager; Applications Engineer; Attorney; Auditor; Blue-Collar Worker Supervisor; Budget Analyst; Buyer; Chief Financial Officer; Computer Engineer; Computer Programmer; Computer Scientist; Computer Support Technician; Content Developer; Controller; Cost Estimator; Database Administrator; Database Manager; Design Engineer; Desktop Publishing Specialist; Draftsperson; Editor; Electrical/Electronics Engineer; Financial Analyst; General Manager; Graphic Artist; Graphic Designer; Human Resources Manager; Industrial Engineer; Industrial Production Manager; Intellectual Property Lawyer; Internet Services Manager; Manufacturing Engineer; Market Research Analyst; Marketing Manager; Marketing Specialist; Mechanical Engineer; MIS Specialist; Network/Systems Administrator; Operations Manager; Production Manager; Project Manager; Public Relations Specialist; Purchasing Agent/Manager; Quality Assurance Engineer; Quality Control Supervisor; Secretary; Software Engineer; Systems Analyst; Systems Manager; Technical Writer/Editor; Typist/Word Processor; Webmaster. **Educational backgrounds include:** Accounting; Business Administration; C/C++; Computer Science; Engineering; Finance; HTML; Java; Liberal Arts; Marketing; Mathematics; Microsoft Word; Physics; Software Development; Software Tech. Support; Spreadsheets; Visual Basic. **Benefits:** 401(k); Casual Dress - Fridays; Dental Insurance; Disability Coverage; Flexible Schedule; Life Insurance;

Medical Insurance; Pension Plan; Public Transit Available; Savings Plan; Tuition Assistance. **Special programs:** Internships; Training; Summer Jobs. **Internship information:** Summer internship opportunities are offered for college juniors and seniors in electrical engineering, computer science, mechanical engineering, and industrial engineering. An overall GPA of 3.5/4.0 is required. Resumes and transcripts must be received by March 1. **Corporate headquarters location:** Los Angeles CA. **Other U.S. locations:** Nationwide. **International locations:** Worldwide. **Subsidiaries include:** Norden Systems (Norwalk CT); Xetron Corporation (Cincinnati OH). **Parent company:** Northrop Grumman Corporation. **Listed on:** New York Stock Exchange. **Stock exchange symbol:** NOC. **President:** Dr. James G. Roche. **Number of employees at this location:** 6,000. **Number of employees nationwide:** 14,000.

NOVELLUS SYSTEMS, INC.
3970 North First Street, San Jose CA 95134. 408/943-9700. **Fax:** 408/943-3422. **Contact:** Matt Moscovich, Professional Staffing. **E-mail address:** info@novellus.com. **World Wide Web address:** http://www.novellus.com. **Description:** Manufactures semiconductor capital equipment. **NOTE:** Entry-level positions are offered. **Common positions include:** Draftsperson; Electrical/ Electronics Engineer; Financial Analyst; Manufacturing Engineer; Mechanical Engineer; MIS Specialist; Sales Engineer; Software Engineer; Systems Analyst; Technical Writer/Editor. **Educational backgrounds include:** Chemistry; Engineering. **Benefits:** 401(k); Dental Insurance; Disability Coverage; Life Insurance; Medical Insurance; Profit Sharing; Stock Option; Tuition Assistance. **Corporate headquarters location:** This Location. **Other U.S. locations:** Nationwide. **International locations:** Worldwide. **Annual sales/revenues:** More than $100 million. **Number of employees at this location:** 650.

nVIEW CORPORATION
860 Omni Boulevard, Newport News VA 23606. 757/873-1354. **Fax:** 757/873-2153. **Contact:** Human Resources. **World Wide Web address:** http://www.nview.com. **Description:** Manufactures and markets devices designed to project high-quality images from personal computers, VCRs, laser disc players, television receivers, and video cameras on standard overhead projectors and in proprietary self-contained projectors. nVIEW's products allow audiences to view computer generated and multimedia images interactively and in real time for business, educational, entertainment, and other purposes. **Corporate headquarters location:** This Location. **Listed on:** NASDAQ.

OECO CORPORATION
4607 SE International Way, Milwaukie OR 97222-4619. 503/659-5999. **Contact:** Human Resources. **Description:** A manufacturer of power supplies, dimmers, and circuit boards. **Corporate headquarters location:** This Location. **Number of employees at this location:** 260.

OKONITE COMPANY
102 Hilltop Road, Ramsey NJ 07470. 201/825-0300. **Fax:** 201/825-3524. **Contact:** Kathy Cuomo, Administrator of Personnel. **World Wide Web address:** http://www.okonite.com. **Description:** Manufactures power cable for large-scale users. **Corporate headquarters location:** This Location. **Other area locations:** Passaic NJ; Paterson NJ.

OMNISHORE
1700 Forrest Way, Carson City NV 89706. 775/687-2800. **Contact:** Doris Bauman, Director of Personnel. **Description:** A contract manufacturer of printed circuit assemblies, computers, subsystems, and other electronic equipment. **Common positions include:** Accountant/Auditor; Administrator; Blue-Collar Worker Supervisor; Buyer; Controller; Credit Manager; Customer Service Rep.; General Manager; Human Resources Manager; Manufacturer's/ Wholesaler's Sales Rep.; Operations/Production Manager; Quality Control Supervisor; Transportation/Traffic Specialist. **Educational backgrounds include:** Accounting; Business Administration; Communications; Engineering; Finance; Marketing. **Benefits:** Dental Insurance; Life Insurance; Medical Insurance; Tuition Assistance. **Corporate headquarters location:** This Location.

OPTICAL CABLE CORPORATION
P.O. Box 11967, Roanoke VA 24019. 540/265-0690. **Contact:** Personnel. **World Wide Web address:** http://www.occfiber.com. **Description:** Manufactures tight-buffered fiber optic cables. **Corporate headquarters location:** This Location.

ORBIT INTERNATIONAL CORPORATION
80 Cabot Court, Hauppauge NY 11788. 631/435-8300. **Contact:** Lynn Cooper, Human Resources Manager. **World Wide Web address:** http://www.orbitintl.com. **Description:** Manufactures electronic devices for the aerospace industry. Founded in 1957. **Common positions include:** Accountant; Administrative Assistant; Design Engineer; Draftsperson; Electrical/ Electronics Engineer; Mechanical Engineer; Production Manager; Quality Control Supervisor; Sales Engineer; Secretary. **Educational backgrounds include:** Accounting; AS400 Certification; Computer Science; Engineering; Microsoft Word; Spreadsheets. **Benefits:** 401(k); Casual Dress - Daily; Dental Insurance; Disability Coverage; Life Insurance; Medical Insurance; Profit Sharing; Tuition Assistance. **Special programs:** Summer Jobs. **Corporate headquarters location:** This Location. **Subsidiaries include:** Behlman Electronics, Inc. through its military division, designs and manufactures power conversion devices and electronic products for measurement and display. The commercial products division of Behlman produces distortion-free commercial power units and low-noise, uninterruptable power sources. **Listed on:** NASDAQ. **Stock exchange symbol:** ORBIT. **President:** Dennis Sunshine. **Annual sales/revenues:** $11 - $20 million. **Number of employees at this location:** 120.

ORECK MANUFACTURING
21180 Oreck Avenue, Long Beach MS 39560. 228/867-8253. **Contact:** Diane Necaise, Director of Human Resources. **Description:** Manufactures electronic machinery such as vacuum cleaners. **NOTE:** Entry-level positions and second and third shifts are offered. **Common positions include:** Accountant; Administrative Assistant; AS400 Programmer Analyst; Chief Financial Officer; Computer Programmer; Computer Support Technician; Customer Service Rep.; Design Engineer; Desktop Publishing Specialist; Draftsperson; Electrical/Electronics Engineer; Financial Analyst; Graphic Designer; Human Resources Manager; Industrial Designer; Manufacturing Engineer; MIS Specialist; Operations Manager; Production Manager; Project Manager; Transportation/Traffic Specialist. **Educational backgrounds include:** AS400 Certification. **Benefits:** 401(k); Casual Dress - Daily; Dental Insurance; Disability Coverage; Employee Discounts; Life Insurance; Medical Insurance; Relocation Assistance. **Special programs:** Apprenticeships; Training; Co-ops.

President: James McCain. **Purchasing Manager:** Candi Mauffray. **Number of employees at this location:** 465.

ORINCON INDUSTRIES
9363 Towne Centre Drive, San Diego CA 92121. 858/455-5530. **Fax:** 858/453-9274. **Contact:** Beth Mitchell, Human Resources Administrator. **E-mail address:** blmitchell@orincon.com. **World Wide Web address:** http://www.orincon.com. **Description:** Engaged in the design, development, and evaluation of signal processing communications, navigation, artificial intelligence, and tracking systems for U.S. Department of Defense applications as well as for the transportation, biotechnology, and financial markets. **NOTE:** Entry-level positions are offered. **Common positions include:** Software Engineer. **Educational backgrounds include:** Engineering. **Benefits:** 401(k); Daycare Assistance; Dental Insurance; Disability Coverage; Life Insurance; Medical Insurance; Profit Sharing. **Corporate headquarters location:** This Location. **Annual sales/revenues:** $11 - $20 million. **Number of employees at this location:** 100.

PSC, INC.
959 Terry Street, Eugene OR 97402. 541/683-5700. **Toll-free phone:** 800/547-2507. **Fax:** 541/687-7982. **Contact:** Oshara D. Helton, Technical Recruiter. **World Wide Web address:** http://www.pscnet.com. **Description:** Manufactures high-performance laser bar code scanners for the retail automation and the automatic data collection industries. **NOTE:** Entry-level positions, part-time jobs, and second and third shifts are offered. **Common positions include:** Account Manager; Accountant; Administrative Assistant; Chief Financial Officer; Computer Support Technician; Computer Technician; Controller; Cost Estimator; Customer Service Rep.; Database Administrator; Electrical/Electronics Engineer; Financial Analyst; Human Resources Manager; Human Resources Rep.; Intellectual Property Lawyer; Manufacturing Engineer; Marketing Manager; Marketing Specialist; Mechanical Engineer; Operations Manager; Production Manager; Purchasing Agent/Manager; Sales Executive; Software Engineer; Vice President of Marketing; Vice President of Sales. **Educational backgrounds include:** Accounting; Business Administration; Computer Science; Engineering; Marketing; Mathematics; Physics. **Benefits:** 401(k); Casual Dress - Fridays; Dental Insurance; Disability Coverage; Employee Discounts; Flexible Schedule; Life Insurance; Medical Insurance; Profit Sharing; Savings Plan; Tuition Assistance; Vacation Days (6 - 10). **Special programs:** Internships; Training; Summer Jobs. **Corporate headquarters location:** Webster NY.

PANDUIT CORPORATION
17301 South Ridgeland Avenue, Tinley Park IL 60477. 708/532-1800. **Toll-free phone:** 800/777-3300. **Fax:** 708/614-8357. **Contact:** Cheryl Lewis, Supervisor of Corporate Recruiting. **World Wide Web address:** http://www.panduit.com. **Description:** Manufactures electrical wiring components, electrical accessories, and communications products. **NOTE:** Entry-level positions are offered. **Common positions include:** Accountant; Buyer; Computer Programmer; Design Engineer; Draftsperson; Electrical/Electronics Engineer; Industrial Engineer; Manufacturing Engineer; Mechanical Engineer; Purchasing Agent/Manager; Sales Engineer. **Educational backgrounds include:** Business Administration; Computer Science; Engineering; Marketing. **Benefits:** 401(k); Daycare Assistance; Dental Insurance; Disability Coverage; Employee

Discounts; Flexible Schedule; Life Insurance; Medical Insurance; Profit Sharing; Tuition Assistance. **Special programs:** Internships. **Corporate headquarters location:** This Location. **Other area locations:** Burr Ridge IL; New Lenox IL; Romeoville IL. **International locations:** Worldwide. **Listed on:** Privately held.

PARLEX CORPORATION
One Parlex Place, Methuen MA 01844. 978/685-4341. **Contact:** Ms. Fran Spechts, Director of Human Resources. **World Wide Web address:** http://www.parlex.com. **Description:** Manufactures flexible and rigid printed circuits, multilayer boards, flat cable products, and other electronic components. **Common positions include:** Accountant/Auditor; Administrator; Blue-Collar Worker Supervisor; Buyer; Chemical Engineer; Chemist; Computer Programmer; Credit Manager; Customer Service Representative; Department Manager; Draftsperson; Financial Analyst; General Manager; Human Resources Manager; Industrial Engineer; Manufacturer's/Wholesaler's Sales Rep.; Mechanical Engineer; Operations/Production Manager; Purchasing Agent/Manager; Quality Control Supervisor; Systems Analyst. **Educational backgrounds include:** Accounting; Business Administration; Chemistry; Computer Science; Engineering; Finance; Marketing. **Benefits:** Disability Coverage; Employee Discounts; Life Insurance; Medical Insurance; Profit Sharing; Retirement Plan; Savings Plan; Tuition Assistance. **Corporate headquarters location:** This Location.

PASS & SEYMOUR/LEGRAND
P.O. Box 4822, Syracuse NY 13221-4822. 315/468-6211. **Contact:** Personnel Department. **Description:** Manufactures and sells wiring devices for use primarily in residential, institutional, industrial, and commercial buildings. Products include switches, electrical outlets, connectors, wallplates, weather-resistant boxes and covers, plastic outlet boxes, wire mesh cable grips, group fault interrupter receptacles, and various lighting products. **Corporate headquarters location:** This Location.

PEAVEY ELECTRONICS CORPORATION
P.O. Box 2898, Meridian MS 39302. 601/486-1443. **Fax:** 601/486-1198. **Contact:** Human Resources. **World Wide Web address:** http://www.peavey.com. **Description:** Manufactures sound equipment including power amplifiers, mixing consiles, speakers, and microphones. Peavey's products under the Audio Media Research (AMR) name are designed specifically for the recording studio environment. Products under the Architectural Acoustics (AA) name are found in a wide range of places including supermarkets and theme parks. **Common positions include:** Accountant/Auditor; Buyer; Chemical Engineer; Chemist; Clerical Supervisor; Commercial Artist; Computer Operator; Computer Programmer; Construction Contractor; Cost Estimator; Customer Service Rep.; Designer; Draftsperson; Electrical/Electronics Engineer; Electrician; Employment Interviewer; Graphic Artist; Human Resources Manager; Industrial Engineer; Industrial Production Manager; Interviewing Clerk; Landscape Architect; Machinist; Market Research Analyst; Marketing Manager; Mechanical Engineer; Millwright; New Accounts Clerk; Payroll Clerk; Prepress Worker; Printing Press Operator; Purchasing Agent/Manager; Quality Control Supervisor; Receptionist; Secretary; Sheet-Metal Worker; Stenographer; Systems Analyst; Tool and Die Maker; Typist/Word Processor; Welder. **Educational backgrounds include:** Accounting; Art/Design; Business Administration; Chemistry; Computer Science; Engineering; Marketing; Mathematics; Physics.

Benefits: Dental Insurance; Disability Coverage; Employee Discounts; Life Insurance; Medical Insurance; Pension Plan; Profit Sharing; Tuition Assistance. **Corporate headquarters location:** This Location. **Listed on:** Privately held. **Number of employees at this location:** 2,000.

PERKINELMER OPTOELECTRONICS
345 Potrero Avenue, Sunnyvale CA 94086-4197. 408/738-4266. **Contact:** Professional Employment Department. **World Wide Web address:** http://www.perkinelmer.com. **Description:** This location manufactures solid-state image sensors for electronics applications. Overall, PerkinElmer designs and manufactures a variety of image sensors, multiplexors, and camera systems for use in medical, scientific, and document scanning applications. **Corporate headquarters location:** Santa Clara CA.

PHILIPS ELECTRONICS NORTH AMERICA CORPORATION
1251 Avenue of the Americas, New York NY 10020. 212/536-0500. **Contact:** Denise Townsen, Supervisor, Human Resources. **World Wide Web address:** http://www.philips.com. **Description:** This location provides service including intellectual property, legal, tax, customs, employee benefits, communications and processing, government affairs, manufacturing technology, purchasing, travel, environmental affairs, audit, compensation, training, and development to Philips companies in many areas. Overall, Philips Electronics North America is a multimarket manufacturing organization with nationwide locations and various subsidiaries, concentrating its efforts primarily in the fields of consumer electronics, consumer products, electrical and electronics components, and professional equipment. **Common positions include:** Accountant/Auditor; Attorney; Computer Programmer; Financial Analyst; Human Resources Manager; Systems Analyst. **Educational backgrounds include:** Accounting; Communications; Computer Science; Liberal Arts. **Benefits:** 401(k); Dental Insurance; Disability Coverage; Employee Discounts; Life Insurance; Medical Insurance; Pension Plan; Tuition Assistance. **Corporate headquarters location:** This Location. **Number of employees at this location:** 230.

PHILLIPS SEMICONDUCTORS
1109 McKay Drive, San Jose CA 95131. 408/434-3000. **Contact:** Human Resources. **Description:** Designs and manufactures application-specific and application-standard integrated circuits for computer, telecommunications, consumer, and industrial uses. **Common positions include:** Electrical/Electronics Engineer; Financial Analyst; Software Engineer; Systems Analyst; Technician. **Educational backgrounds include:** Engineering. **Benefits:** 401(k); Dental Insurance; Disability Coverage; Life Insurance; Medical Insurance; Profit Sharing; Savings Plan; Tuition Assistance. **Special programs:** Internships. **Corporate headquarters location:** This Location. **Other U.S. locations:** Tempe AZ; San Antonio TX. **Listed on:** NASDAQ. **Number of employees at this location:** 1,500.

PHOTOBIT CORPORATION
135 North Los Robles Avenue, 7th Floor, Pasadena CA 91101. 626/683-2200. **Fax:** 626/683-2220. **Contact:** Human Resources. **World Wide Web address:** http://www.photobit.com. **Description:** Manufactures electronic imaging sensors, cameras, and systems. The company is a leader in CMOS Imaging Technology. Founded in 1995. **Corporate headquarters location:** This Location.

PHOTOCIRCUITS CORPORATION
31 Sea Cliff Avenue, Glen Cove NY 11542. 516/609-1000. **Fax:** 516/609-1080. **Recorded jobline:** 516/609-1088. **Contact:** Judy Conord, Manager of Human Resources. **World Wide Web address:** http://www.photocircuits.com. **Description:** A manufacturer of printed circuit boards. **Common positions include:** Buyer; Chemical Engineer; Customer Service Rep.; Electrical/Electronics Engineer; Electrician; Industrial Engineer; Industrial Production Manager; Mechanical Engineer; Operations/Production Manager; Purchasing Agent/Manager; Quality Control Supervisor; Software Engineer. **Educational backgrounds include:** Business Administration; Computer Science; Engineering. **Benefits:** 401(k); Dental Insurance; Disability Coverage; Employee Discounts; Life Insurance; Medical Insurance; Pension Plan; Savings Plan; Tuition Assistance. **Special programs:** Internships. **Corporate headquarters location:** This Location. **Other U.S. locations:** Peachtree City GA. **Listed on:** Privately held. **Number of employees at this location:** 2,400.

PHOTRONICS INC.
15 Secor Road, Brookfield CT 06804-3972. 203/775-9000. **Contact:** Human Resources. **Description:** A leading manufacturer of photomasks used for the manufacture of semiconductors and integrated circuits. **Corporate headquarters location:** This Location. **Other U.S. locations:** Milpitas CA; Sunnyvale CA; Dallas TX.

PHYSICAL ELECTRONICS, INC.
6509 Flying Cloud Drive, Eden Prairie MN 55344. 952/828-6100. **Contact:** Human Resources. **World Wide Web address:** http://www.phi.com. **Description:** Manufacturers of electronic instruments including surface analysis equipment. **Common positions include:** Accountant/Auditor; Buyer; Customer Service Rep.; Designer; Electrical/Electronics Engineer; Human Resources Manager; Mechanical Engineer; Physicist; Science Technologist; Software Engineer; Technical Writer/Editor. **Educational backgrounds include:** Accounting; Business Administration; Chemistry; Computer Science; Engineering; Physics. **Benefits:** 401(k); Daycare Assistance; Dental Insurance; Disability Coverage; Employee Discounts; Life Insurance; Medical Insurance; Pension Plan; Profit Sharing; Savings Plan; Tuition Assistance. **Corporate headquarters location:** This Location. **Listed on:** Privately held. **Number of employees at this location:** 300.

PITTWAY CORPORATION
200 South Wacker Drive, Suite 700, Chicago IL 60606. 312/831-1070. **Contact:** Administrative Assistant. **World Wide Web address:** http://www.pittway.com. **Description:** A diverse international corporation that manufactures security systems and fire alarms. **Corporate headquarters location:** This Location. **Other U.S. locations:** St. Charles IL. **Listed on:** American Stock Exchange.

PLEXUS CORP.
P.O. Box 529, Neenah WI 54957. 920/722-3451. **Fax:** 920/751-5673. **Contact:** Geoff Rulland, Human Resources Coordinator. **World Wide Web address:** http://www.plexus.com. **Description:** Designs, develops, manufactures, and tests electronic products for major corporations in a variety of industries including computer, medical, communications, industrial, and transportation. Founded in 1980. **NOTE:** Entry-level positions and second and third shifts are offered. **Common positions include:** AS400 Programmer Analyst; Buyer; Electrical/Electronics Engineer; Financial

Analyst; Industrial Engineer; Manufacturing Engineer; Marketing Specialist; Mechanical Engineer; Network/Systems Administrator; Purchasing Agent/Manager; Quality Assurance Engineer; Software Engineer; Webmaster. **Educational backgrounds include:** Accounting; AS400 Certification; Business Administration; C/C++; Computer Science; Engineering; Finance; HTML; Marketing; Microsoft Word; Novell; Spreadsheets. **Benefits:** 401(k); Casual Dress - Daily; Dental Insurance; Disability Coverage; Employee Discounts; Life Insurance; Medical Insurance; Public Transit Available; Sick Days (6 - 10); Tuition Assistance; Vacation Days (6 - 10). **Special programs:** Internships. **Corporate headquarters location:** This Location. **Other U.S. locations:** Richmond KY; Minneapolis MN. **Subsidiaries include:** Plexus Technology Group; Plexus Electronic Assembly. **Listed on:** NASDAQ. **Stock exchange symbol:** PLXS. **Annual sales/revenues:** More than $100 million. **Number of employees at this location:** 2,100.

POLHEMUS, INC.
P.O. Box 560, Colchester VT 05446. 802/655-3159. **Fax:** 802/655-1439. **Contact:** Human Resources. **World Wide Web address:** http://www. polhemus.com. **Description:** Develops electromagnetic measuring systems which measure the position and orientation of objects in three-dimensional space. The company also provides motion capture and digitizing technology solutions. **Corporate headquarters location:** This Location.

POLY-PLANAR, INC.
1927 Stout Drive, Unit 4, Warminster PA 18974. 215/675-7805. **Contact:** Barbara Lange, Personnel Director. **World Wide Web address:** http://www. polyplanar.com. **Description:** Produces and distributes portable electronics products including all-weather loudspeakers for communications systems. Poly Planar also manufactures consumer audio products, primarily speakers. **Corporate headquarters location:** This Location.

POWELL INDUSTRIES, INC.
P.O. Box 12818, Houston TX 77217-2818. 713/944-6900. **Contact:** Human Resources. **World Wide Web address:** http://www.powellind.com. **Description:** Manufactures a wide variety of power distribution equipment including switchgear and power breakers, switchboards, instrument panels, and portable control houses. **Common positions include:** Accountant/Auditor; Blue-Collar Worker Supervisor; Draftsperson; Electrical/Electronics Engineer; Electronics Technician; Mechanical Engineer. **Educational backgrounds include:** Engineering. **Benefits:** Dental Insurance; Disability Coverage; Life Insurance; Medical Insurance; Profit Sharing; Savings Plan; Tuition Assistance. **Corporate headquarters location:** This Location. **Listed on:** American Stock Exchange.

POWER-ONE, INC.
740 Calle Plano, Camarillo CA 93012. 805/987-8741. **Toll-free phone:** 800/678-9445. **Fax:** 805/389-8911. **Contact:** Melissa Dugan, Human Resources Director. **E-mail address:** melissadugan@power-one.com. **World Wide Web address:** http://www.power-one.com. **Description:** Engaged in the manufacturing of DC power supplies. The company's product line includes linears, switchers, and hi-power to three kilowatts. Founded in 1973. **Common positions include:** Buyer; Computer Programmer; Customer Service Rep.; Design Engineer; Draftsperson; Electrical/ Electronics Engineer; Purchasing Agent/Manager; Quality Control Supervisor; Software Engineer. **Educational backgrounds include:** Business

Administration; Engineering. **Benefits:** 401(k); Bonus Award/Plan; Dental Insurance; Disability Coverage; Employee Discounts; Life Insurance; Medical Insurance; Tuition Assistance. **Corporate headquarters location:** This Location. **Listed on:** Privately held. **Annual sales/revenues:** $51 - $100 million. **Number of employees at this location:** 250. **Number of employees worldwide:** 1,800.

POWEREX, INC.
200 Hillis Street, Youngwood PA 15697. 724/925-7272. **Contact:** Andy Varga, Human Resources Director. **World Wide Web address:** http://www.pwrx.com. **Description:** Manufactures semiconductors. **Corporate headquarters location:** This Location. **President/CEO:** Stan Hunt. **Number of employees at this location:** 325.

POWERWARE CORPORATION
8380 Capital Boulevard, Raleigh NC 27604. 919/872-3020. **Contact:** Paul Rousseau, Human Resources Manager. **Description:** Manufactures and markets uninterruptible power supplies. **NOTE:** Entry-level positions are offered. **Common positions include:** Accountant/Auditor; Advertising Clerk; Computer Programmer; Customer Service Rep.; Designer; Electrical/Electronics Engineer; Financial Analyst; Human Resources Manager; Manufacturer's/Wholesaler's Sales Rep.; Marketing Specialist; Mechanical Engineer; Public Relations Specialist; Purchasing Agent/Manager; Quality Control Supervisor; Services Sales Representative; Software Engineer; Systems Analyst; Technical Writer/Editor; Transportation/Traffic Specialist. **Educational backgrounds include:** Accounting; Business Administration; Computer Science; Engineering; Finance; Marketing; Mathematics. **Benefits:** 401(k); Dental Insurance; Disability Coverage; Employee Discounts; Life Insurance; Medical Insurance; Profit Sharing; Savings Plan; Stock Option; Tuition Assistance. **Special programs:** Internships. **Corporate headquarters location:** This Location. **Listed on:** NASDAQ. **Annual sales/revenues:** More than $100 million. **Number of employees at this location:** 300.

PRECISION INTERCONNECT
16640 SW 72nd Avenue, Portland OR 97224-7756. 503/620-9400. **Contact:** Human Resources. **World Wide Web address:** http://www.precisionint.com. **Description:** An electric cable manufacturer for electronic OEMs. **Common positions include:** Assembly Worker; Electronics Technician; Engineer; Machine Operator. **Number of employees at this location:** 910.

PRIME SOURCE CORPORATION
4425 Sheila Street, Los Angeles CA 90023. 323/268-9500. **Contact:** Human Resources. **Description:** A wholesaler of electronic components. **Common positions include:** Accountant/Auditor; Computer Programmer; Credit Manager; Electrical/Electronics Engineer; Human Resources Manager; Manufacturer's/Wholesaler's Sales Rep.; MIS Specialist; Purchasing Agent/Manager; Systems Analyst. **Educational backgrounds include:** Accounting; Business Administration; Computer Science; Engineering. **Benefits:** Dental Insurance; Disability Coverage; Life Insurance; Medical Insurance; Profit Sharing; Savings Plan; Tuition Assistance. **Corporate headquarters location:** This Location. **Other U.S. locations:** Nationwide. **Operations at this facility include:** Administration; Regional Headquarters; Sales. **Listed on:** New York Stock Exchange. **Annual sales/revenues:** More than $100 million. **Number of employees at this location:** 200. **Number of employees nationwide:** 1,500.

PROGRESS LIGHTING, INC.
P.O. Box 989, Cowpens SC 29330. 864/463-3274. **Contact:** Human Resources. **World Wide Web address:** http://www.progresslighting.com. **Description:** A manufacturer of home and commercial lighting systems and fixtures. **Common positions include:** Accountant/Auditor; Blue-Collar Worker Supervisor; Buyer; Claim Rep.; Computer Programmer; Credit Manager; Customer Service Representative; Department Manager; Draftsperson; Electrical/Electronics Engineer; General Manager; Human Resources Manager; Industrial Designer; Industrial Engineer; Management Trainee; Manufacturer's/Wholesaler's Sales Rep.; Marketing Specialist; Mechanical Engineer; Operations/Production Manager; Purchasing Agent/Manager; Quality Control Supervisor; Systems Analyst; Transportation/Traffic Specialist. **Educational backgrounds include:** Accounting; Art/Design; Business Administration; Computer Science; Engineering; Finance; Liberal Arts; Marketing. **Benefits:** Dental Insurance; Employee Discounts; Life Insurance; Medical Insurance; Pension Plan; Savings Plan. **Corporate headquarters location:** This Location.

PULSE ENGINEERING INC.
12220 World Trade Drive, San Diego CA 92128. 858/674-8100. **Fax:** 858/674-8292. **Contact:** Sheila Ricks, Human Resources Director. **World Wide Web address:** http://www.pulseeng.com. **Description:** Designs, manufactures, and markets a variety of electronic components and modules for original equipment manufacturers in data processing, telecommunications networking, and power supply environments. **Common positions include:** Accountant/Auditor; Customer Service Rep.; Designer; Electrical/Electronics Engineer; Financial Analyst; Manufacturer's/Wholesaler's Sales Rep.; Mechanical Engineer. **Educational backgrounds include:** Accounting; Engineering; Finance. **Benefits:** 401(k); Dental Insurance; Disability Coverage; Life Insurance; Medical Insurance; Pension Plan; Tuition Assistance. **Special programs:** Internships. **Corporate headquarters location:** This Location. **Other U.S. locations:** Wesson MI. **Number of employees at this location:** 170. **Number of employees nationwide:** 4,000.

PYXIS CORPORATION
3750 Torrey View Court, San Diego CA 92130. 858/625-3300. **Contact:** Human Resources. **World Wide Web address:** http://www.pyxiscorp.com. **Description:** A manufacturer of automated point-of-use systems. Products are used in hospitals for the distribution management and control of supplies and medicines. **Corporate headquarters location:** This Location. **Parent company:** Cardinal Health, Inc. **Annual sales/revenues:** More than $100 million.

QUAD SYSTEMS CORPORATION
2405 Maryland Road, Willow Grove PA 19090. 215/657-6202. **Fax:** 215/784-4514. **Contact:** Therese Mantell, Human Resources Director. **E-mail address:** recruiter@quad-sys.com. **World Wide Web address:** http://www.quad-sys.com. **Description:** A multinational company that designs, manufactures, and supports surface mount equipment and related peripherals and services used in the manufacture of printed circuit boards. The company also manufactures placement systems and reflow ovens and provides screen printers used in the surface mount process. Founded in 1980. **NOTE:** Entry-level positions are offered. **Common positions include:** Account Manager; Accountant; Administrative Assistant; Advertising Executive; Applications Engineer; Assistant Manager; Attorney; Controller; Electrical/Electronics Engineer; Finance Director; Human Resources Manager; Management Analyst/Consultant; Marketing Manager; Mechanical Engineer; MIS Specialist; Project Manager; Quality Control Supervisor; Secretary; Software Engineer. **Educational backgrounds include:** Accounting; Art/Design; Business Administration; Communications; Computer Science; Engineering; Finance; Liberal Arts; Marketing; Mathematics; Public Relations; Software Development; Software Tech. Support. **Benefits:** 401(k); Daycare Assistance; Dental Insurance; Disability Coverage; Life Insurance; Medical Insurance; Profit Sharing; Savings Plan; Tuition Assistance. **Special programs:** Summer Jobs. **Corporate headquarters location:** This Location. **Other U.S. locations:** Nationwide. **International locations:** Worldwide. **Listed on:** NASDAQ. **Stock exchange symbol:** QSYS. **Facilities Manager:** Jack Stollenwerk. **Annual sales/revenues:** $51 - $100 million. **Number of employees at this location:** 280.

RFI ENTERPRISES, INC.
360 Turtle Creek Court, San Jose CA 95125. 408/298-5400. **Fax:** 408/882-4405. **Contact:** Human Resources. **World Wide Web address:** http://www.rfi-ent.com. **Description:** A multisystem integrator for low voltage systems including alarm systems, public announcement systems, and communications applications. Founded in 1979. **NOTE:** Entry-level positions are offered. **Common positions include:** Account Rep.; Accountant/Auditor; Administrative Assistant; Applications Engineer; Buyer; Draftsperson; Electrical/Electronics Engineer; Electrician; MIS Specialist; Operations/Production Manager; Project Manager; Sales Rep.; Secretary. **Educational backgrounds include:** Accounting; Engineering. **Benefits:** 401(k); Dental Insurance; Disability Coverage; Employee Discounts; Life Insurance; Medical Insurance; Tuition Assistance. **Special programs:** Internships; Apprenticeships. **Corporate headquarters location:** This Location. **Other U.S. locations:** Sacramento CA; Reno NV; Beaverton OR; Seattle WA. **Listed on:** Privately held. **Number of employees at this location:** 250.

RS ELECTRONICS
34443 Schoolcraft Road, Livonia MI 48150. 734/525-1155. **Toll-free phone:** 800/366-7750. **Fax:** 734/525-1184. **Contact:** Human Resources. **World Wide Web address:** http://www.rselectronics.com. **Description:** A wholesale distributor of electrical parts and measurement equipment. Founded in 1929. **Common positions include:** Accountant; Administrative Assistant; AS400 Programmer Analyst; Branch Manager; Buyer; Computer Support Technician; Controller; Credit Manager; Customer Service Rep.; Human Resources Manager; Marketing Manager; MIS Specialist; Operations Manager; Purchasing Agent/Manager; Sales Manager; Sales Rep.; Secretary. **Educational backgrounds include:** Accounting; AS400 Certification; Business Administration; Computer Science; Marketing; Microsoft Office; Microsoft Word. **Benefits:** 401(k); Casual Dress - Daily; Dental Insurance; Disability Coverage; Life Insurance; Medical Insurance; Tuition Assistance. **Special programs:** Internships; Summer Jobs. **Office hours:** Monday - Friday, 8:00 a.m. - 5:00 p.m. **CEO:** Winston Stalcup. **President:** Howard Taxe. **Number of employees at this location:** 100. **Number of employees nationwide:** 180.

RVSI ACUITY CIMATRIX
5 Shawmut Road, Canton MA 02021. 781/821-0830. **Fax:** 781/828-8942. **Contact:** Ms. Pat Green, Personnel Manager. **Description:** A leader in the development of bar code and symbology solutions

that automatically capture, analyze, and communicate identification information in industrial, material handling, and manufacturing environments. The company also manufactures machine vision systems, industrial controllers, and LANs. **Corporate headquarters location:** This Location. **Parent company:** Robotic Vision Systems, Inc. **Listed on:** NASDAQ.
Other U.S. locations:
• 9 Townsend West, Suite 4, Nashua NH 03063. 603/598-8400.

RACO & HUBBELL ELECTRICAL PRODUCTS
3902 West Sample Street, South Bend IN 46634. 219/234-7151. **Fax:** 219/283-4244. **Contact:** Human Resources. **World Wide Web address:** http://www.racoinc.com. **Description:** Manufactures non-current carrying electronic wiring devices. **Corporate headquarters location:** This Location.

RAMTRON INTERNATIONAL CORP.
1850 Ramtron Drive, Colorado Springs CO 80921. 719/481-7000. **Contact:** Diane Ratliff, Human Resources Manager. **World Wide Web address:** http://www.ramtron.com. **Description:** Manufactures semiconductors. **Corporate headquarters location:** This Location.

RAULAND-BORG CORPORATION
3450 West Oakton Street, Skokie IL 60076. 847/679-0900. **Contact:** Debbie Summers, Personnel Manager. **World Wide Web address:** http://www.rauland.com. **Description:** Manufactures electronic communications and sound equipment. **Common positions include:** Electrical/Electronics Engineer. **Educational backgrounds include:** Communications; Computer Science; Engineering; Marketing. **Benefits:** Dental Insurance; Disability Coverage; Life Insurance; Medical Insurance; Tuition Assistance. **Corporate headquarters location:** This Location. **Number of employees at this location:** 250.

RAYCHEM CORPORATION
300 Constitution Drive, Menlo Park CA 94025. 650/361-3333. **Contact:** Staffing Department. **World Wide Web address:** http://www.raychem.com. **Description:** Raychem develops, manufactures, and markets a wide range of high-performance polymer and metal products and systems for the electronics, industrial, and telecommunications markets. Electronics products include insulation, wire, cable, fiber optics, circuit protection devices, and heating products. **NOTE:** Interested jobseekers can send resumes to the Raychem Resume Processing Center, P.O. Box 92016, Los Angeles CA 90009. **Common positions include:** Electrical/Electronics Engineer; Financial Analyst; Manufacturer's/Wholesaler's Sales Rep.; Mechanical Engineer; Metallurgical Engineer. **Educational backgrounds include:** Chemistry; Engineering. **Benefits:** Dental Insurance; Employee Discounts; Life Insurance; Medical Insurance; Pension Plan; Profit Sharing; Savings Plan; Tuition Assistance. **Special programs:** Internships. **Corporate headquarters location:** This Location. **Subsidiaries include:** Raynet designs, manufactures, and markets fiber-optic loop carrier systems for television and CATV systems. **Listed on:** New York Stock Exchange.

RAYTHEON COMPANY
141 Spring Street, Lexington MA 02421. 781/862-6600. **Contact:** Human Resources. **World Wide Web address:** http://www.raytheon.com. **Description:** A diversified, international, multi-industry technology-based company ranked among the 100 largest U.S. industrial corporations.

Raytheon has 110 facilities in 28 states and the District of Columbia. Overseas facilities and representative offices are located in 26 countries, principally in Europe, the Middle East, and the Pacific Rim. The company's four business segments include Electronics, Major Appliances, Aircraft Products, and Energy and Environmental. **Corporate headquarters location:** This Location. **International locations:** Worldwide.
Other U.S. locations:
• P.O. Box 831359, Richardson TX 75083- 1359. 972/470-2000.

RELIABILITY INC.
P.O. Box 218370, Houston TX 77218. 281/492-0550. **Physical address:** 16400 Park Road, Houston TX. **Fax:** 281/492-0615. **Contact:** Manager of Human Resources. **World Wide Web address:** http://www.relinc.com. **Description:** Engaged in the testing of electronic components. **Common positions include:** Accountant/Auditor; Computer Programmer; Draftsperson; Electrical/Electronics Engineer; Human Resources Manager; Purchasing Agent/Manager; Quality Control Supervisor; Technical Writer/Editor. **Educational backgrounds include:** Accounting; Engineering; Finance. **Benefits:** Dental Insurance; Disability Coverage; Employee Discounts; Life Insurance; Medical Insurance; Savings Plan; Stock Option; Tuition Assistance. **Office hours:** Monday - Thursday, 7:00 a.m. - 5:00 p.m.; Friday, 7:00 a.m. - 11:00 a.m. **Corporate headquarters location:** This Location. **Listed on:** American Stock Exchange.

REMEC, INC.
9404 Chesapeake Drive, San Diego CA 92123. 858/560-1301. **Fax:** 858/569-7111. **Contact:** Lillian Turman, Human Resources Manager. **World Wide Web address:** http://www.remec.com. **Description:** An electronics company engaged in the design, development, and manufacture of custom RF, filters, transmitters, and microwave products. **Common positions include:** Accountant/Auditor; Draftsperson; Electrical/Electronics Engineer; Human Resources Manager; Mechanical Engineer; Software Engineer. **Educational backgrounds include:** Business Administration; Engineering. **Corporate headquarters location:** This Location. **Subsidiaries include:** Humphrey, Inc. manufactures motion sensor devices. **Listed on:** NASDAQ. **Number of employees at this location:** 525.

REXEL INC.
P.O. Box 9085, Addison TX 75001. 972/387-3600. **Contact:** Human Resources. **World Wide Web address:** http://www.rexel.com. **Description:** One of the world's largest distributors of electronic parts and supplies. **NOTE:** Resumes should be addressed to Human Resources, Rexel Inc., 6700 LBJ Freeway, Suite 3200, Dallas TX 75240. **Common positions include:** Accountant; Administrator; Credit Manager; Department Manager; Financial Analyst; Human Resources Manager; Management Trainee; Marketing Specialist; Operations/Production Manager. **Educational backgrounds include:** Accounting; Business Administration; Communications; Liberal Arts; Marketing. **Benefits:** Dental Insurance; Disability Coverage; Employee Discounts; Life Insurance; Medical Insurance; Pension Plan; Profit Sharing; Savings Plan; Tuition Assistance. **Corporate headquarters location:** This Location. **Parent company:** Pinault-Printemps-Redoute.

RICHARDSON ELECTRONICS, LTD.
P.O. Box 393, LaFox IL 60147-0393. 630/208-2200. **Fax:** 630/208-2550. **Contact:** Human Resources Director. **World Wide Web address:** http://www.rell.com. **Description:** An international

distributor of electronic components such as electron tubes, RF and microwave components, semiconductors, and security equipment. **Common positions include:** Accountant/Auditor; Buyer; Computer Programmer; Credit Manager; Customer Service Rep.; Electrical/Electronics Engineer; Financial Analyst; Marketing Specialist; Purchasing Agent/Manager; Systems Analyst. **Educational backgrounds include:** Accounting; Business Administration; Communications; Computer Science; Engineering; Finance; Marketing. **Benefits:** 401(k); Dental Insurance; Disability Coverage; Life Insurance; Medical Insurance; Pension Plan; Profit Sharing; Savings Plan; Tuition Assistance. **Corporate headquarters location:** This Location. **International locations:** Worldwide. **Listed on:** NASDAQ.

ROBERTSHAW CONTROLS COMPANY GRAYSON CONTROL DIVISION

100 West Victoria Street, Long Beach CA 90805. 310/638-6111. **Contact:** Personnel. **Description:** A manufacturer of control instrumentation. Products include automatic controls used in homes, commercial buildings, and industrial applications to conserve energy and to enable machinery to work efficiently and automatically; level controls such as RF/microprocessor-based level controls and precision level controls; vibration detectors including monitor and control; recorders and controllers; accessories; diaphragm-actuated control valves; self-actuated temperature regulators; and control systems including system components. The company also produces Sylphon-formed bellows and assemblies, automobile thermostats, caps, water outlet housings, and heater control valves. **Corporate headquarters location:** This Location.

ROBINSON NUGENT, INC.

800 East Eighth Street, New Albany IN 47150. 812/945-0211. **Toll-free phone:** 800/457-2412. **Fax:** 812/941-3568. **Contact:** Michael W. Schreiweis, Director of Human Resources. **E-mail address:** mikes@robinsonnugent.com. **World Wide Web address:** http://www.robinsonnugent.com. **Description:** Manufactures electronic connectors and integrated circuit sockets for the electronics industry. **Common positions include:** Accountant; Administrative Assistant; Advertising Executive; Chief Financial Officer; Controller; Customer Service Rep.; Design Engineer; Draftsperson; Electrical/Electronics Engineer; Financial Analyst; Human Resources Manager; Manufacturing Engineer; Market Research Analyst; Marketing Manager; Marketing Specialist; Network/Systems Administrator; Quality Assurance Engineer; Secretary. **Educational backgrounds include:** Accounting; Business Administration; Engineering; Finance; MBA; Microsoft Office; Microsoft Word; Spreadsheets; SQL; Visual Basic. **Benefits:** 401(k); Casual Dress - Daily; Dental Insurance; Life Insurance; Medical Insurance; Pension Plan; Relocation Assistance; Tuition Assistance; Vacation Days (10 - 20). **Special programs:** Internships; Co-ops. **Office hours:** Monday - Friday, 8:00 a.m. - 5:00 p.m. **Corporate headquarters location:** This Location. **Subsidiaries include:** Cablelink, Inc. **Listed on:** NASDAQ. **Stock exchange symbol:** RNIC. **President/CEO:** Larry Burke. **Information Systems Manager:** Timothy Rice. **Sales Manager:** Raymond Wandell. **Annual sales/revenues:** $51 - $100 million. **Number of employees at this location:** 100. **Number of employees nationwide:** 450. **Number of employees worldwide:** 760. **Other U.S. locations:**
- 2640 Tarna Drive, Dallas TX 75229. 972/241-1738.

ROCHESTER GAUGES, INC.

P.O. Box 29242, Dallas TX 75229. 972/241-2161. **Contact:** Barbara Nitishin, Corporate Human Resources Generalist. **Description:** A manufacturer of gauges, thermometers, and measuring devices. **NOTE:** Entry-level positions are offered. **Common positions include:** Blue-Collar Worker Supervisor; Customer Service Rep.; Manufacturer's/Wholesaler's Sales Rep.; Mechanical Engineer; MIS Specialist. **Educational backgrounds include:** Engineering. **Benefits:** 401(k); Dental Insurance; Disability Coverage; Life Insurance; Medical Insurance; Pension Plan; Public Transit Available; Savings Plan; Tuition Assistance. **Corporate headquarters location:** This Location. **Number of employees at this location:** 300. **Number of employees nationwide:** 500.

ROCHESTER INSTRUMENT SYSTEMS

255 North Union Street, Rochester NY 14605. 716/238-4983. **Fax:** 716/238-4980. **Contact:** Human Resources. **Description:** Manufactures electrical monitoring equipment used in power plants and manufacturing facilities. Products include alarms and enunciators to monitor system malfunctions. **Common positions include:** Accountant; Blue-Collar Worker Supervisor; Budget Analyst; Buyer; Customer Service Rep.; Electrical/Electronics Engineer; Financial Analyst; Human Resources Manager; Manufacturer's/Wholesaler's Sales Rep.; Mechanical Engineer; Operations/Production Manager; Quality Control Supervisor; Securities Sales Representative; Software Engineer; Technical Writer/Editor. **Educational backgrounds include:** Business Administration; Computer Science; Engineering; Mathematics. **Benefits:** 401(k); Dental Insurance; Disability Coverage; Employee Discounts; Life Insurance; Pension Plan; Profit Sharing; Tuition Assistance. **Corporate headquarters location:** This Location. **International locations:** Scotland. **Parent company:** Marmon. **Number of employees at this location:** 200.

ROCKBESTOS-SURPRENANT CABLE CORP.

172 Sterling Street, Clinton MA 01510. 978/365-6331. **Toll-free phone:** 800/444-3792. **Fax:** 978/365-3287. **Contact:** Peter Stephan, Human Resources Manager. **World Wide Web address:** http://r-scc.com. **Description:** Manufactures quality-assured, specialty purpose insulated wire and cable products. **Common positions include:** Accountant; Blue-Collar Worker Supervisor; Chemist; Customer Service Rep.; Design Engineer; Electrical/Electronics Engineer; Human Resources Manager; Industrial Engineer; Industrial Production Manager; MIS Specialist; Operations/Production Manager; Process Engineer; Purchasing Agent/Manager; Quality Control Supervisor; Typist/Word Processor. **Educational backgrounds include:** Accounting; Business Administration; Communications; Computer Science; Engineering; Finance; Marketing. **Benefits:** 401(k); Dental Insurance; Disability Coverage; Life Insurance; Medical Insurance; Tuition Assistance. **Special programs:** Internships. **Office hours:** Monday - Friday, 8:00 a.m. - 5:00 p.m. **Corporate headquarters location:** This Location. **Other U.S. locations:** CT. **Listed on:** Privately held. **President:** Fred Schwelm.

ROYALITE COMPANY

101 Burton Street, Flint MI 48503. 810/238-4641. **Contact:** Bob Workman, Marketing Manager. **Description:** A wholesale distributor of electrical apparatus and equipment including service panels. **Common positions include:** Branch Manager; Buyer; Computer Programmer; Electrical/Electronics Engineer; Manufacturer's/Wholesaler's

Sales Rep.; Sales Executive; Systems Analyst. **Educational backgrounds include:** Business Administration; Engineering. **Benefits:** 401(k); Disability Coverage; Employee Discounts; Life Insurance; Medical Insurance; Pension Plan; Profit Sharing. **Corporate headquarters location:** This Location. **Listed on:** Privately held. **Number of employees at this location:** 50.

SCI SYSTEMS, INC.

P.O. Box 1000, Huntsville AL 35807. 256/882-4800. **Contact:** Mr. Francis Henry, Human Resources Manager. **World Wide Web address:** http://www.sci.com. **Description:** Designs, develops, manufactures, markets, distributes, and services electronic products for the computer, aerospace, defense, telecommunications, medical, and consumer industries, as well as for the United States government. SCI is one of the world's largest electronics contract manufacturers and operates one of the largest surface mount technology (SMT) production facilities in the merchant market. Operations are conducted through a Commercial Division and a Government Division. The Commercial Division operates in six geographically-organized business units: Eastern, Central, and Western Regions of North America; and European and Asian Regions. Each unit operates multiple plants that manufacture components, subassemblies, and finished products for original equipment manufacturers. Design, engineering, purchasing, manufacturing, distribution, and support services are also offered. The Government Division provides data management, instrumentation, and communications services, and computer subsystems to the U.S. government and its prime contractors, as well as to several foreign governments. **Common positions include:** Computer Programmer; Electrical/Electronics Engineer; Industrial Engineer; Manufacturing Engineer; Production Coordinator; Software Engineer. **Educational backgrounds include:** Computer Science; Engineering. **Benefits:** Dental Insurance; Disability Coverage; Life Insurance; Medical Insurance; Pension Plan; Savings Plan; Tuition Assistance. **Corporate headquarters location:** This Location. **International locations:** Canada; France; Ireland; Scotland; Singapore; Thailand. **Other U.S. locations:**
- 300 Technology Drive, Hooksett NH 03106-2520. 603/628-4800.

SI HANDLING SYSTEMS INC.

600 Kubler Road, P.O. Box 70, Easton PA 18044-0070. 610/252-7321. **Contact:** Human Resources. **World Wide Web address:** http://www.sihs.com. **Description:** Designs, manufactures, sells, and installs computer-directed, automated material-handling and automated order selection systems and equipment worldwide. **Common positions include:** Accountant; Draftsperson; Electrical/Electronics Engineer; Industrial Engineer; Mechanical Engineer; Software Engineer. **Educational backgrounds include:** Accounting; Business Administration; Computer Science; Engineering; Finance; Liberal Arts; Marketing. **Benefits:** Disability Coverage; Employee Discounts; Life Insurance; Medical Insurance; Pension Plan; Profit Sharing; Savings Plan; Tuition Assistance. **Corporate headquarters location:** This Location. **Parent company:** Paragon Technologies Company (also at this location). **Number of employees at this location:** 175.

SPD TECHNOLOGIES

13500 Roosevelt Boulevard, Philadelphia PA 19116. 215/677-4900. **Contact:** Lawrence V. Wasnock, Manager of Employee and Labor Relations. **Description:** A world leader in the design, development, and manufacture of circuit breakers, switchgear, and related electrical protection systems for shipboard applications in the United States and around the world. **Common positions include:** Account Rep.; Accountant; Administrative Assistant; Administrative Manager; Applications Engineer; Assistant Manager; Blue-Collar Worker Supervisor; Buyer; Chief Financial Officer; Clerical Supervisor; Computer Operator; Computer Programmer; Controller; Customer Service Rep.; Database Manager; Design Engineer; Draftsperson; Electrical/Electronics Engineer; Electrician; Finance Director; Financial Analyst; Human Resources Manager; Industrial Engineer; Industrial Production Manager; Manufacturing Engineer; Marketing Manager; Marketing Specialist; Mechanical Engineer; MIS Specialist; Operations Manager; Production Manager; Project Manager; Purchasing Agent/Manager; Quality Control Supervisor; Sales Engineer; Sales Executive; Sales Manager; Sales Rep.; Secretary; Software Engineer; Systems Manager; Technical Writer/Editor; Transportation/Traffic Specialist. **Educational backgrounds include:** Business Administration; Engineering. **Benefits:** 401(k); Dental Insurance; Disability Coverage; Life Insurance; Medical Insurance; Profit Sharing; Tuition Assistance. **Corporate headquarters location:** This Location. **Subsidiaries include:** Henschel (Newburyport MA); Pac Ord (San Diego CA); SPD Switchgear (Montgomeryville PA). **Number of employees at this location:** 450.

SAFETRAN TRAFFIC SYSTEMS INC.

P.O. Box 7009, Colorado Springs CO 80933. 719/599-5600. **Contact:** Georgine Fries, Human Resources Manager. **World Wide Web address:** http://www.safetran-traffic.com. **Description:** Manufactures traffic control products and systems. **Corporate headquarters location:** This Location. **Number of employees at this location:** 100.

SANMINA CORPORATION

355 East Trimboe Road, San Jose CA 95131. 408/435-8444. **Fax:** 408/964-3799. **Contact:** Human Resources. **World Wide Web address:** http://www.sanmina.com. **Description:** Manufactures custom-designed backplane assemblies and subassemblies; multilayer, high-density printed circuit boards; testing equipment; and surface mount technology assemblies used in sophisticated electronics equipment with primary customers in the telecommunications, data communications, industrial/medical, computer systems, and contract assembly business sectors. **Common positions include:** Accountant; Budget Analyst; Buyer; Chemist; Customer Service Rep.; Electrical/Electronics Engineer; Financial Analyst; Manufacturer's/Wholesaler's Sales Rep.; Manufacturing Engineer; Operations Research Analyst; Quality Control Supervisor. **Educational backgrounds include:** Accounting; Business Administration; Engineering; Finance; Marketing. **Benefits:** 401(k); Dental Insurance; Disability Coverage; Life Insurance; Medical Insurance; Tuition Assistance. **Corporate headquarters location:** This Location. **Listed on:** NASDAQ. **Number of employees at this location:** 100. **Other U.S. locations:**
- 12-A Manor Parkway, Salem NH 03079. 603/898-8000.

SCANTRON CORPORATION

1361 Valencia Avenue, Tustin CA 92780. 714/247-2700. **Fax:** 714/247-0010. **Contact:** Sherre Cox, Director of Human Resources. **World Wide Web address:** http://www.scantron.com. **Description:** Manufactures and markets optical mark reader, test scoring, and data entry equipment. **Common positions include:** Electrical/Electronics Engineer; Human Service Worker; Mechanical Engineer; Services Sales Rep. **Benefits:** 401(k); Dental Insurance; Disability Coverage; Employee Discounts; Life Insurance; Medical Insurance; Tuition Assistance. **Corporate headquarters location:** This Location. **Other U.S. locations:** Nationwide. **Parent company:** J.H. Harland. **Listed on:** New York Stock Exchange. **Number of employees at this location:** 600.

SCIENTIFIC TECHNOLOGIES INC. (STI)
6550 Dumbarton Circle, Fremont CA 94555-3611. 510/608-3400. **Fax:** 510/744-1309. **Contact:** Human Resources. **E-mail address:** employment@sti.com. **World Wide Web address:** http://www.sti.com. **Description:** Designs, manufactures, and distributes electrical and electronic controls for the industrial market. **Corporate headquarters location:** This Location. **Listed on:** NASDAQ. **President/CEO:** Joseph J. Lazzara.

SEMICOA SEMICONDUCTORS, INC.
333 McCormick Avenue, Costa Mesa CA 92626. 714/979-1900. **Fax:** 714/557-4541. **Contact:** Ticia Luna, Human Resources Manager. **World Wide Web address:** http://www.semicoa.com. **Description:** A custom manufacturer of discrete, bi-polar transistors and photo diodes. Founded in 1968. **NOTE:** Entry-level positions and second and third shifts are offered. **Common positions include:** Accountant; Administrative Assistant; Applications Engineer; Assistant Manager; Blue-Collar Worker Supervisor; Buyer; Chemical Engineer; Clerical Supervisor; Computer Programmer; Customer Service Rep.; Database Manager; Electrical/Electronics Engineer; Manufacturing Engineer; Marketing Manager; Mechanical Engineer; Metallurgical Engineer; MIS Specialist; Production Manager; Purchasing Agent/Manager; Quality Control Supervisor; Sales Engineer; Sales Executive; Sales Manager; Sales Rep.; Secretary; Systems Analyst. **Educational backgrounds include:** Accounting; Business Administration; Chemistry; Computer Science; Engineering; Finance; Marketing; Physics. **Benefits:** 401(k); Dental Insurance; Disability Coverage; Employee Discounts; Financial Planning Assistance; Life Insurance; Medical Insurance; Profit Sharing; Tuition Assistance. **Special programs:** Training. **Corporate headquarters location:** This Location. **Number of employees at this location:** 90.

SENCORE ELECTRONICS INC.
3200 Sencore Drive, Sioux Falls SD 57107. 605/339-0100. **Contact:** Jacky Jockheck, Director of Corporate Relations. **World Wide Web address:** http://www.sencore.com. **Description:** Designs, manufactures, and markets electronic test equipment. **Common positions include:** Electrical/Electronics Engineer. **Educational backgrounds include:** Electronics; Engineering. **Benefits:** Disability Coverage; Employee Discounts; Life Insurance; Medical Insurance; Pension Plan; Profit Sharing; Savings Plan; Tuition Assistance. **Corporate headquarters location:** This Location.

SENTROL, INC.
12345 SW Leveton Drive, Tualatin OR 97062. 503/692-4052. **Fax:** 503/691-7569. **Contact:** Human Resources. **World Wide Web address:** http://www.sentrol.com. **Description:** Manufactures security devices. **Common positions include:** Buyer; Customer Service Rep.; Electrical/Electronics Engineer; General Manager; Human Resources Manager; Industrial Engineer; Manufacturer's/Wholesaler's Sales Rep.; Mechanical Engineer; Purchasing Agent/Manager; Services

Sales Rep. **Educational backgrounds include:** Accounting; Art/Design; Business Administration; Communications; Engineering; Finance; Marketing; Mathematics; Physics. **Benefits:** 401(k); Dental Insurance; Disability Coverage; Employee Discounts; Life Insurance; Medical Insurance; Profit Sharing; Tuition Assistance. **Special programs:** Internships. **Corporate headquarters location:** This Location. **Other U.S. locations:** Hickory NC. **Parent company:** Berwind Corporation. **Number of employees at this location:** 400.

SHURE INC.
222 Hartrey Avenue, Evanston IL 60202-3696. 847/866-2237. **Fax:** 847/866-2608. **Contact:** Marcie Austen, Human Resources Manager. **E-mail address:** hr@shure.com. **World Wide Web address:** http://www.shure.com. **Description:** Manufactures a wide range of electronic equipment including microphones, mixers, audio processors, and wireless systems. **Common positions include:** Electrical/Electronics Engineer; Mechanical Engineer; Software Engineer. **Educational backgrounds include:** Engineering; Marketing. **Benefits:** 401(k); Dental Insurance; Disability Coverage; Employee Discounts; Life Insurance; Medical Insurance; Pension Plan; Savings Plan; Tuition Assistance. **Corporate headquarters location:** This Location. **Other U.S. locations:** Douglas AZ; Wheeling IL; El Paso TX.

SIEMENS ELECTROCOM L.P.
2910 Avenue F, Arlington TX 76011. 817/640-5690. **Contact:** Human Resources. **World Wide Web address:** http://www.siemenselectrocom.com. **Description:** Designs, manufactures, integrates, and services high-speed automated document processing, materials handling, mobile data, and voice communications systems. Primary customers are the U.S. Postal Service and other government agencies. **Parent company:** Siemens Corporation.

SIEMENS ENERGY & AUTOMATION, INC.
3333 Old Milton Parkway, Alpharetta GA 30005. 770/751-2000. **Contact:** Human Resources. **Description:** Manufactures and markets a broad range of primarily large-scale electrical products including a variety of circuit protection devices that are sold to electronics OEMs throughout the country. The company also produces circuit-breaker load centers, metering panels, and related accessories. These products are sold to users such as electric utilities and industrial manufacturers. **Common positions include:** Accountant/Auditor; Advertising Clerk; Attorney; Computer Programmer; Customer Service Rep.; Department Manager; Draftsperson; Electrical/Electronics Engineer; Financial Analyst; General Manager; Human Resources Manager; Industrial Engineer; Management Trainee; Marketing Specialist; Mechanical Engineer; Sales Executive; Systems Analyst; Transportation/Traffic Specialist. **Educational backgrounds include:** Accounting; Business Administration; Computer Graphics; Engineering; Finance; Marketing. **Benefits:** 401(k); Dental Insurance; Disability Coverage; Life Insurance; Medical Insurance; Pension Plan; Savings Plan; Tuition Assistance. **Corporate headquarters location:** This Location. **Other U.S. locations:**
• 6427 NE 59th Place, Portland OR 97218. 503/288-0101.

SIGMA GAME, INC.
7160 South Amigo Street, Las Vegas NV 89119. 702/260-3193. **Fax:** 702/260-0675. **Contact:** Human Resources Specialist. **World Wide Web address:** http://www.sigmagame.com. **Description:** A manufacturer of electronic video and slot gaming

devices. Founded in 1984. **Common positions include:** Account Rep.; Accountant; Administrative Assistant; Advertising Executive; Blue-Collar Worker Supervisor; Branch Manager; Buyer; Chief Financial Officer; Computer Animator; Computer Engineer; Computer Programmer; Controller; Credit Manager; Customer Service Rep.; Design Engineer; Electrical/Electronics Engineer; Graphic Artist; Human Resources Manager; Manufacturing Engineer; Marketing Manager; Mechanical Engineer; MIS Specialist; Operations Manager; Production Manager; Purchasing Agent/Manager; Sales Executive; Sales Manager; Secretary; Software Engineer; Statistician; Technical Writer/Editor. **Educational backgrounds include:** Accounting; Art/Design; Business Administration; Computer Science; Engineering; Finance; Marketing; Mathematics; Public Relations. **Benefits:** 401(k); Casual Dress - Daily; Dental Insurance; Disability Coverage; Employee Discounts; Life Insurance; Medical Insurance; Profit Sharing; Tuition Assistance. **Office hours:** Monday - Friday, 8:00 a.m. - 5:00 p.m. **Corporate headquarters location:** This Location.

SIGNAL TECHNOLOGY CORPORATION
975 Benecia Avenue, Sunnyvale CA 94086. 408/730-6300. **Contact:** Gloria L. Duran, Human Resources Manager. **World Wide Web address:** http://www.sigtech.com. **Description:** Manufactures a wide variety of microwave and electronics components in four product areas: solid state devices including test equipment and microwave assemblies and subsystems; microwave components including isofilters and multiplexers; semiconductor products including solid state RF switches and double-balanced mixers; and YIG Products including harmonic generators and tracking filter-oscillator sets. **Common positions include:** Department Manager; Draftsperson; Electrical/Electronics Engineer; Financial Analyst. **Educational backgrounds include:** Engineering; Marketing. **Benefits:** Dental Insurance; Disability Coverage; Employee Discounts; Life Insurance; Medical Insurance; Savings Plan; Tuition Assistance. **Corporate headquarters location:** This Location.

SILICON HILLS DESIGN INC.
9101 Burnet Road, Suite 107, Austin TX 78758. 512/836-1088. **Contact:** Harold Tantaze, President. **World Wide Web address:** http://www.siliconhills.com. **Description:** Designs printed circuit boards for computers as well as for the space and satellite markets.

SIMCO ELECTRONICS
1178 Bordeaux Drive, Sunnyvale CA 94089. 408/734-9750. **Contact:** Jan Smith, Manager of Human Resources. **World Wide Web address:** http://www.simco.com. **Description:** Engaged in the calibration and repair of electronic test and measuring equipment; electrical and physical standards; physical, dimensional, mechanical gauges and tools; and the calibration and validation of biomedical process equipment. **Common positions include:** Repair Specialist; Services Sales Rep.; Technician. **Benefits:** 401(k); Credit Union; Dental Insurance; Disability Coverage; Life Insurance; Medical Insurance; Tuition Assistance. **Corporate headquarters location:** This Location. **Other area locations:** Anaheim CA; Burbank CA; San Diego CA; Santa Fe Springs CA. **Other U.S. locations:** Huntsville AL; Naperville IL; St. Louis MO; Greensboro NC; Springsboro OH; Allentown PA; Austin TX; Dallas TX; Sterling VA. **Listed on:** Privately held. **CEO:** Lee McKenna. **Number of employees at this location:** 70. **Number of employees nationwide:** 300.

SIMKAR CORPORATION
700 Ramona Avenue, Philadelphia PA 19120. 215/831-7700. **Contact:** Ken McArthur, Vice President of Human Resources. **World Wide Web address:** http://www.simkar.com. **Description:** Manufactures fluorescent lighting fixtures. **Common positions include:** Accountant; Customer Service Rep.; Management Trainee; Manufacturer's/Wholesaler's Sales Rep.; Manufacturing Engineer. **Educational backgrounds include:** Engineering; Marketing. **Benefits:** Disability Coverage; Life Insurance; Medical Insurance; Savings Plan. **Corporate headquarters location:** This Location.

SIMPLEX TIME RECORDER COMPANY
One Simplex Plaza, Gardner MA 01441. 978/632-2500. **Contact:** Human Resources. **World Wide Web address:** http://www.simplexnet.com. **Description:** Markets, designs, and manufactures state-of-the-art commercial safety, security, energy management, and data communications products. **Corporate headquarters location:** This Location.

SOLECTRON CORPORATION
847 Gibraltar Drive, Milpitas CA 95035. 408/957-8500. **Contact:** Human Resources. **World Wide Web address:** http://www.solectron.com. **Description:** Manufactures complex printed circuit boards using surface mount technology and pin-through hole interconnection technology. The company also provides electronic subsystem testing and assembly services for OEMs in the electronics industry. **Corporate headquarters location:** This Location.

SOLITRON DEVICES, INC.
3301 Electronics Way, West Palm Beach FL 33407. 561/848-4311. **Fax:** 561/881-5652. **Contact:** Human Resources. **World Wide Web address:** http://www.solitrondevices.com. **Description:** Designs and manufactures high-density power components and circuitry. The company's semiconductor and hybrid circuit products are sold to national and international aerospace and defense programs. **Common positions include:** Accountant; Advertising Clerk; Budget Analyst; Buyer; Chemical Engineer; Clerical Supervisor; Cost Estimator; Credit Clerk and Authorizer; Credit Manager; Customer Service Rep.; Department Manager; Designer; Draftsperson; Electrical/Electronics Engineer; Electrician; Financial Manager; General Manager; Human Resources Manager; Industrial Engineer; Machinist; Manufacturer's/Wholesaler's Sales Rep.; Marketing Manager; Mechanical Engineer; Order Clerk; Payroll Clerk; Precision Assembler; Purchasing Agent/Manager; Quality Control Supervisor; Receptionist; Secretary; Stock Clerk; Systems Analyst; Tool and Die Maker. **Educational backgrounds include:** Accounting; Business Administration; Chemistry; Engineering; Finance; Marketing; Physics. **Benefits:** 401(k); Dental Insurance; Disability Coverage; Life Insurance; Medical Insurance; Pension Plan; Profit Sharing; Tuition Assistance. **Corporate headquarters location:** This Location. **Other U.S. locations:** Nationwide. **Listed on:** NASDAQ. **Number of employees at this location:** 120.

SONALYSTS INC.
215 Parkway North, Waterford CT 06385. 860/442-4355. **Fax:** 860/447-8883. **Contact:** Recruiting Officer. **E-mail address:** recruiting@sonalysts.com. **World Wide Web address:** http://www.sonalysts.com. **Description:** A diversified business offering operations research and systems analysis; acoustical system design, testing, and development; tactical development and evaluation for surface, submarine, and air platforms; training and trainer

development; and technical services for nuclear, gas, and electric companies. Sonalysts also provides audio and visual production in full production facilities, film studios, and recording studios. **NOTE:** Entry-level positions are offered. **Common positions include:** Accountant; Administrative Manager; Animator; Attorney; Broadcast Technician; Buyer; Chemical Engineer; Clerical Supervisor; Computer Programmer; Cost Estimator; Designer; Editor; Education Administrator; Electrical/Electronics Engineer; Environmental Engineer; Financial Analyst; General Manager; Geologist/Geophysicist; Human Resources Manager; Industrial Engineer; Internet Services Manager; Mathematician; Mechanical Engineer; MIS Specialist; Multimedia Designer; Musician/ Musical Arranger; Nuclear Engineer; Operations/ Production Manager; Paralegal; Pharmacist; Physicist; Psychologist; Public Relations Specialist; Purchasing Agent/Manager; Radio/TV Announcer/ Broadcaster; Software Engineer; Structural Engineer; Systems Analyst; Teacher/Professor; Technical Writer/Editor; Telecommunications Manager; Transportation/Traffic Specialist; Typist/ Word Processor; Video Production Coordinator. **Educational backgrounds include:** Accounting; Art/Design; Business Administration; Chemistry; Communications; Computer Science; Engineering; Finance; Geology; Liberal Arts; Marketing; Mathematics; Physics; Psychology. **Benefits:** 401(k); Daycare Assistance; Disability Coverage; Life Insurance; Medical Insurance; Pension Plan; Profit Sharing; Savings Plan; Tuition Assistance. **Special programs:** Internships; Apprenticeships; Training. **Corporate headquarters location:** This Location. **Other U.S. locations:** Nationwide.

SONY SEMICONDUCTOR COMPANY OF AMERICA
One Sony Place, San Antonio TX 78245. 210/681-9000. **Fax:** 210/647-6492. **Recorded jobline:** 210/647-6255. **Contact:** Senior Staff Recruiter. **E-mail address:** resumes@ssa-sa.sel.sony.com. **World Wide Web address:** http://www. sel.sony.com/semi. **Description:** Manufactures semiconductor devices in CMOS and bipolar technology. **Common positions include:** Accountant; Computer Operator; Controller; Database Administrator; Equipment Service Engineer; Manufacturing Engineer; Network/ Systems Administrator; Software Engineer; Systems Analyst; Systems Engineer; Systems Specialist; Test Engineer. **Educational backgrounds include:** C/C++; Computer Science; Engineering; FORTRAN; Java; Microelectronics; Novell. **Benefits:** 401(k); Casual Dress - Daily; Dental Insurance; Disability Coverage; Employee Discounts; Life Insurance; Medical Insurance; Pension Plan; Profit Sharing; Savings Plan; Tuition Assistance. **Corporate headquarters location:** Park Ridge NJ.

SOUTHERN STATES, INC.
30 Georgia Avenue, Hampton GA 30228. 770/946-4562. **Contact:** Mr. Marlin Gilbert, Manager of Employee Relations. **World Wide Web address:** http://www.southernstatesinc.com. **Description:** Manufactures high-voltage switchgear, cut-outs, power fuses, and protective devices for the transmission and distribution of electricity. **Corporate headquarters location:** This Location.

SPECTRA-MAT, INC.
100 Westgate Drive, Watsonville CA 95076. 831/722-4116. **Fax:** 831/722-4172. **Contact:** Kathy Pybrum, Human Resources Director. **World Wide Web address:** http://www.spectramat.com. **Description:** Manufactures electronic components such as electron emitters. Spectra-Mat also produces materials and parts for use in thermal management and semiconductor equipment. Founded in 1963. **NOTE:** Entry-level positions and second and third shifts are offered. **Common positions include:** Accountant; Blue-Collar Worker Supervisor; Buyer; Customer Service Representative; Design Engineer; Finance Director; Human Resources Manager; Manufacturing Engineer; Mechanical Engineer; MIS Specialist; Operations Manager; Quality Assurance Engineer; Sales Engineer; Salon Manager. **Educational backgrounds include:** Accounting; Business Administration; Engineering; Physics. **Benefits:** 401(k); Casual Dress - Fridays; Daycare Assistance; Dental Insurance; Disability Coverage; Employee Discounts; Flexible Schedule; Life Insurance; Medical Insurance; Pension Plan; Sick Days (6 - 10); Tuition Assistance; Vacation Days (6 - 10). **Corporate headquarters location:** This Location. **Listed on:** Privately held. **President:** Jim Abendschan. **Annual sales/revenues:** $5 - $10 million. **Number of employees at this location:** 60.

SPECTRAL DYNAMICS INC.
1983 Concourse Drive, San Jose CA 95131. 408/474-1700. **Contact:** Personnel. **World Wide Web address:** http://www.sd-corp.com. **Description:** Specializes in the design and manufacture of computer-controlled test, measurement, and development systems and software for a wide variety of customers in three high-technology markets: electronic equipment manufacturers, mechanical equipment manufacturers, and semiconductor manufacturers and users. **Corporate headquarters location:** This Location. **Parent company:** Carrier Corporation.

SPECTRUM CONTROL, INC.
8061 Avonia Road, Fairview PA 16415. 814/474-1571. **Contact:** Human Resources. **World Wide Web address:** http://www.spectrumcontrol.com. **Description:** This location manufactures filtered connectors. Overall, Spectrum Control, Inc. designs, manufactures, and markets a broad line of electromagnetic compatibility (EMC) products designed to protect electronic equipment against interference from random electromagnetic waves. The company's product offerings include discrete electromagnetic interference (EMI) and radio frequency interference (RFI) filters, filtered connectors, multiline EMI and RFI filters, and specialty ceramic capacitors. Spectrum Control also offers customers consulting, diagnostic testing, and manufacturing services. These services include testing for EMC problems, analyzing test results, proposing design solutions, producing the required components, and supplying these components on a continuing basis. Spectrum Control sells its EMC testing services and components to a broad base of customers for use in communication systems, data processing, telecommunications, process control, and other equipment. **Corporate headquarters location:** This Location. **Listed on:** NASDAQ.

SPECTRUM CONTROLS, INC.
P.O. Box 5533, Bellevue WA 98006. 425/746-9481. **Fax:** 425/641-9473. **Contact:** Lynn Robbins, Human Resources Manager. **World Wide Web address:** http://www.spectrumcontrols.com. **Description:** Designs and manufactures electronic industrial control products for the industrial automation market. Founded in 1983. **Company slogan:** We are a product leadership company. **Common positions include:** Applications Engineer; Buyer; Customer Service Rep.; Design Engineer; Electrical/Electronics Engineer; Finance Director; Financial Analyst; Manufacturing Engineer; Marketing Manager; MIS Specialist; Production Manager; Software Engineer; Systems Analyst. **Educational backgrounds include:** Accounting;

Computer Science; Engineering; Finance; Software Development. **Benefits:** 401(k); Cafeteria; Dental Insurance; Disability Coverage; Flexible Schedule; Life Insurance; Medical Insurance; Profit Sharing; Tuition Assistance. **Corporate headquarters location:** This Location. **Other U.S. locations:** GA; MI; TX. **President:** Bruce Wanta. **Annual sales/revenues:** $5 - $10 million. **Number of employees at this location:** 40.

SPIRE CORPORATION
One Patriots Park, Bedford MA 01730-2396. 781/275-6000. **Fax:** 781/275-7470. **Contact:** Human Resources. **E-mail address:** hr@spirecorp.com. **World Wide Web address:** http://www.spirecorp.com. **Description:** Provides products and services to customers in photovoltaics, optoelectronics, and biomedical markets. The company's products include compound semiconductor wafers and devices, photovoltaic manufacturing equipment and production lines, and ion beam-based processing services for medical components. **Corporate headquarters location:** This Location. **Number of employees at this location:** 150.

SQUARE D COMPANY
1601 Mercer Road, Lexington KY 40511. 606/243-8000. **Contact:** Human Resources. **World Wide Web address:** http://www.squared.com. **Description:** Manufactures electrical distribution products for the construction industry. Products are used in commercial and residential construction, industrial facilities, and machinery, as well as original equipment manufacturers' products. Residential building products feature circuit breakers with an exclusive quick-open mechanism that isolates potential dangers quickly. Square D also equips public buildings such as schools, stadiums, museums, hospitals, prisons, military bases, and wastewater treatment plants with electrical distribution systems. **Corporate headquarters location:** Palatine IL. **Parent company:** Groupe Schneider possesses global expertise in electrical contracting, industrial engineering, and construction. The company has four major operating divisions: Modicon, Merlin Gerin, Square D, and Telemecanique.

I I STANLEY CO., INC.
1500 Hill Brady Road, Battle Creek MI 49015. 616/660-7777. **Contact:** Human Resources. **Description:** Manufactures automotive lighting and electronic office automation products. **Common positions include:** Accountant; Buyer; Computer Programmer; Cost Estimator; Environmental Engineer; Human Resources Manager; Manufacturer's/Wholesaler's Sales Rep.; Mechanical Engineer; Operations/Production Manager; Purchasing Agent/Manager; Quality Control Supervisor; Systems Analyst. **Educational backgrounds include:** Accounting; Business Administration; Computer Science; Engineering. **Benefits:** 401(k); Dental Insurance; Disability Coverage; Life Insurance; Medical Insurance. **Other U.S. locations:** London OH. **Parent company:** Stanley Electric. **Listed on:** Privately held.

STEAG RTP SYSTEMS INC.
4425 Fortran Drive, San Jose CA 95134. 408/935-2000. **Toll-free phone:** 800/635-2250. **Contact:** Mary Jade Chiang, Human Resources. **World Wide Web address:** http://www.steag.com. **Description:** Manufactures rapid thermal processing systems for the semiconductor industry. **NOTE:** Entry-level positions and part-time jobs are offered. **Common positions include:** Accountant; Administrative Assistant; Buyer; Chief Financial Officer; Computer Support Technician; Controller; Customer Service Rep.; Financial Analyst; Human Resources Manager; Network/Systems Administrator; Operations Manager; Production Manager; Project Manager; Purchasing Agent/Manager; Quality Control Supervisor; Sales Manager; Sales Rep.; Software Engineer; Systems Manager. **Educational backgrounds include:** Accounting; Business Administration; C/C++; Computer Science; Engineering; Finance; Marketing; MCSE; Microsoft Office; Microsoft Word; Software Development. **Benefits:** 401(k); Dental Insurance; Disability Coverage; Flexible Schedule; Life Insurance; Medical Insurance; Relocation Assistance; Tuition Assistance. **Special programs:** Internships. **Office hours:** Monday - Friday, 8:00 a.m. - 5:00 p.m. **Corporate headquarters location:** This Location. **International locations:** Worldwide. **Subsidiaries include:** AG Israel. **Parent company:** Steag Electronic Systems AG.

SUPERIOR ELECTRIC
383 Middle Street, Bristol CT 06010. 860/582-9561. **Contact:** Human Resources. **Description:** Manufactures electronic and electrical control equipment, incremental motion devices (including voltage regulators and voltage conditioning equipment), and synchronous/stepping motors.

SUPERTEX INC.
1235 Bordeaux Drive, Sunnyvale CA 94089. 408/744-0100. **Contact:** Melba L. Stathis, Personnel Manager. **Description:** Produces integrated silicon circuits and other microelectronic products for computer and electronics original equipment manufacturers. **Common positions include:** Accountant/Auditor; Buyer; Computer Programmer; Customer Service Representative; Electrical/Electronics Engineer; Systems Analyst. **Educational backgrounds include:** Accounting; Business Administration; Chemistry; Computer Science; Engineering; Marketing. **Benefits:** Dental Insurance; Disability Coverage; Life Insurance; Medical Insurance; Profit Sharing; Savings Plan; Tuition Assistance. **Corporate headquarters location:** This Location.

KARL SUSS AMERICA, INC.
P.O. Box 157, Waterbury Center VT 05677. 802/244-5181. **Physical address:** 228 Suss Drive, Waterbury Center VT. **Contact:** Human Resources. **Description:** Manufactures electronics equipment including mask aligners, spinners, and coating equipment for use in the semiconductor industry. **Number of employees at this location:** 110.

SWITCHCRAFT, INC.
5555 North Elston Avenue, Chicago IL 60630. 773/792-2700. **Contact:** Sheila Sanders, Director of Human Resources. **World Wide Web address:** http://www.switchcraft.com. **Description:** Manufactures electronic components including switches, connectors, jacks, plugs, cable assemblies and cards. **Corporate headquarters location:** This Location.

SYSTEM SENSOR
3825 Ohio Avenue, St. Charles IL 60174. 630/377-6580. **Fax:** 630/377-6593. **Contact:** Richard Braun, Manager of Human Resources. **World Wide Web address:** http://www.systemsensor.com. **Description:** Manufactures commercial smoke and heat detection devices. **Common positions include:** Automation Engineer; Electrical/Electronics Engineer; Human Resources Manager; Industrial Engineer; Mechanical Engineer; Quality Control Supervisor; Technical Writer/Editor. **Educational backgrounds include:** Business Administration; Communications; Engineering; Liberal Arts; Marketing. **Benefits:** 401(k); Dental Insurance;

Disability Coverage; Life Insurance; Medical Insurance; Pension Plan; Savings Plan; Tuition Assistance. **Corporate headquarters location:** This Location. **Parent company:** Pittway Corporation. **Listed on:** American Stock Exchange. **Number of employees at this location:** 950.

TECCOR ELECTRONICS INC.
1801 Hurd Drive, Irving TX 75038. 972/580-1515. **Contact:** Human Resources. **Description:** Manufactures electronic power controls and related equipment. A second plant (also at this location) manufactures semiconductor power devices, solid state relays, and a variety of silicon chips and rectifiers. **Common positions include:** Accountant; Administrator; Blue-Collar Worker Supervisor; Buyer; Ceramics Engineer; Chemical Engineer; Chemist; Computer Programmer; Customer Service Representative; Department Manager; Draftsperson; Electrical/Electronics Engineer; Industrial Engineer; Purchasing Agent/Manager; Quality Control Supervisor; Sales Executive; Systems Analyst. **Educational backgrounds include:** Accounting; Business Administration; Chemistry; Engineering; Marketing. **Benefits:** Dental Insurance; Disability Coverage; Employee Discounts; Life Insurance; Medical Insurance; Pension Plan; Profit Sharing; Savings Plan; Tuition Assistance. **Corporate headquarters location:** This Location.

TECH/OPS SEVCON, INC.
40 North Avenue, Burlington MA 01803-3300. 781/229-7896. **Contact:** Human Resources. **Description:** A world leader in the design, manufacture, and marketing of microcomputer-based solid-state controls for electric vehicles. These controllers vary the speed of vehicles, improve performance, and prolong the shift life of batteries. The company's customers include manufacturers of fork lift trucks, mining vehicles, airport tractors, aerial lifts, sweepers, and other battery-powered vehicles.

TELEDYNE ELECTRONIC TECHNOLOGIES
110 Lowell Road, Hudson NH 03051. 603/889-6191. **Contact:** Marc Filipowicz, Manager of Human Resources. **World Wide Web address:** http://www.tet.com. **Description:** Manufactures electronic components including electronic relays, multichip modules, microwave filters, aviation data management systems, and circuit boards. **Common positions include:** Applications Engineer; Design Engineer; Electrical/Electronics Engineer. **Educational backgrounds include:** Engineering. **Benefits:** 401(k); Dental Insurance; Disability Coverage; Life Insurance; Medical Insurance; Pension Plan; Tuition Assistance. **Special programs:** Internships; Co-ops. **Corporate headquarters location:** Los Angeles CA. **Other U.S. locations:** Nationwide. **Parent company:** Teledyne Technologies, Inc.

TELEX COMMUNICATIONS INC.
9600 Aldrich Avenue South, Minneapolis MN 55420. 952/884-4051. **Contact:** Kathy Curran, Vice President of Human Resources. **World Wide Web address:** http://www.telex.com. **Description:** Manufactures electronic components for intercom systems and related communications products. **Corporate headquarters location:** This Location. **Other U.S. locations:**
- 1720 East 14th Street, Glencoe MN 55336. 320/864-3177.

TEXAS INSTRUMENTS, INC. (TI)
P.O. Box 660199, Dallas TX 75243. **Fax:** 972/917-1335. **Contact:** Human Resources. **E-mail address:** epsjobs@ti.com. **World Wide Web address:** http://www.ti.com. **Description:** One of the world's foremost high-technology companies, with sales and manufacturing operations in more than 30 countries. Texas Instruments (TI) is one of the world's largest suppliers of semiconductor products. TI's defense electronics business is a leading supplier of avionics, infrared, and weapons guidance systems to the U.S. Department of Defense and U.S. allies. The company is also a technology leader in high-performance notebook computers and model-based software development tools. TI sensors monitor and regulate pressure and temperature in products ranging from automobiles to air conditioning systems. **Common positions include:** Computer Programmer; Electrical/Electronics Engineer; Industrial Engineer; Mechanical Engineer; Systems Analyst. **Educational backgrounds include:** Computer Science; Engineering. **Benefits:** Dental Insurance; Disability Coverage; Life Insurance; Medical Insurance; Pension Plan; Profit Sharing; Savings Plan; Tuition Assistance. **Corporate headquarters location:** This Location. **Other U.S. locations:**
- 300 North Main Street, Versailles KY 40383. 606/873-2600.

THERMA-WAVE INC.
1250 Reliance Way, Fremont CA 94539. 510/490-3663. **Fax:** 510/656-3863. **Contact:** Julie Venierakis, Human Resources Manager. **World Wide Web address:** http://www.thermawave.com. **Description:** Manufactures semiconductor testing equipment. **Common positions include:** Applications Engineer; Design Engineer; Electrical/Electronics Engineer; Manufacturing Engineer; Marketing Specialist; Mechanical Engineer; Project Manager; Sales Engineer; Software Engineer. **Educational backgrounds include:** Engineering; Physics. **Benefits:** 401(k); Dental Insurance; Disability Coverage; Employee Discounts; Life Insurance; Medical Insurance; Profit Sharing; Tuition Assistance. **Corporate headquarters location:** This Location. **Other U.S. locations:** AZ; CO; FL; MA; OR; TX. **International locations:** Worldwide.

THERMALLOY INC.
P.O. Box 810839, Dallas TX 75381-0839. 972/243-4321. **Contact:** Personnel. **World Wide Web address:** http://www.thermalloy.com. **Description:** Produces a variety of electronics components and systems, and machined products including ceramic electrical products, electronic semiconductor equipment, semiconductor insulating covers, screw machine products, plastic injected molding products for electronics use, and printed circuit board guides. **Corporate headquarters location:** This Location.

THERMO ELECTRIC COMPANY, INC.
109 North Fifth Street, Saddle Brook NJ 07663. 201/843-5800. **Contact:** Human Resources. **Description:** An international leader in industrial temperature instrumentation. Thermo Electric Company, Inc. is a resource for solutions to temperature control needs worldwide. Products include temperature sensors, instrumentation, and specialty wire and cable. **Common positions include:** Accountant/Auditor; Electrical/Electronics Engineer; Manufacturer's/Wholesaler's Sales Rep.; Mechanical Engineer. **Educational backgrounds include:** Accounting; Engineering; Marketing. **Benefits:** 401(k); Dental Insurance; Disability Coverage; Life Insurance; Medical Insurance; Profit Sharing; Tuition Assistance. **Corporate headquarters location:** This Location.

THOMAS & BETTS CORPORATION
8155 T & B Boulevard, Memphis TN 38125. **Toll-free phone:** 800/888-0211. **Contact:** Human Resources Manager. **Description:** This location

manufactures street lighting equipment. Overall, Thomas & Betts Corporation is engaged in the design, manufacture, and marketing of electrical and electronic components and systems for connecting, fastening, protecting, and identifying wires, components, and conduits. The company's products include fittings and accessories for electrical raceways; solderless terminals for small wires and heavy power cables; wire fastening devices and markers; insulation products, flat cable, connectors, and IC sockets for electronic applications; ceramic chip capacitors for electronic circuitry; fiber-optic connectors and accessories; wire management systems; and customer specific products for major original equipment manufacturers. **Common positions include:** Accountant; Draftsperson; Electrical/Electronics Engineer; Human Resources Manager; Industrial Engineer; Mechanical Engineer; Purchasing Agent/Manager; Registered Nurse. **Educational backgrounds include:** Engineering. **Benefits:** 401(k); Dental Insurance; Disability Coverage; Life Insurance; Medical Insurance; Pension Plan; Tuition Assistance. **Corporate headquarters location:** This Location.

THOMAS ELECTRONICS, INC.
100 Riverview Drive, Wayne NJ 07470. 973/696-5200. **Contact:** Personnel. **World Wide Web address:** http://www.thomaselectronics.com. **Description:** Manufactures cathode ray tubes and liquid crystal displays for use by military and industrial OEMs. **Corporate headquarters location:** This Location.

TOOH DINEH INDUSTRIES, INC.
HC 61, P.O. Box E, Winslow AZ 86047. 520/686-6477. **Fax:** 520/686-6516. **Contact:** Mary R. Begay, Human Resources. **E-mail address:** toohdineh-industries@worldnet.att.net. **Description:** A contract electronics manufacturer for the communications, transportation, and computer industries. Founded in 1987. **NOTE:** Entry-level positions and second and third shifts are offered. **Common positions include:** Accountant; Computer Technician; Customer Service Rep.; Electrical/Electronics Engineer; General Manager; Human Resources Manager; Industrial Engineer; Manufacturing Engineer; Mechanical Engineer; Network/Systems Administrator; Operations Manager; Production Manager; Purchasing Agent/Manager; Quality Assurance Engineer; Quality Control Supervisor. **Educational backgrounds include:** Accounting; Business Administration; Computer Science; Engineering; MCSE; Software Tech. Support. **Benefits:** 401(k); Casual Dress - Daily; Dental Insurance; Disability Coverage; Employee Discounts; Life Insurance; Medical Insurance; Sick Days (1 - 5); Tuition Assistance; Vacation Days (10 - 20). **Special programs:** Training. **Office hours:** Monday - Friday, 7:00 a.m. - 3:30 p.m. **Corporate headquarters location:** Chinle AZ. **Parent company:** Dineh Cooperatives Inc. **Number of employees at this location:** 105.

TRANS-LUX CORPORATION
110 Richards Avenue, Norwalk CT 06854. 203/853-4321. **Contact:** Human Resources Department. **World Wide Web address:** http://www.trans-lux.com. **Description:** Designs, produces, leases, sells, and services large-scale, multicolor, real-time electronic information displays for both indoor and outdoor use. These displays are used primarily in applications for the financial, banking, gaming, corporate, transportation, and sports markets. The company also owns an expanding chain of movie theaters in the southwestern region of the United States and owns real estate in the U.S. and Canada. **Corporate headquarters location:** This Location.

TRANSWITCH CORPORATION
3 Enterprise Drive, Shelton CT 06484. 203/929-8810. **Fax:** 203/926-9453. **Contact:** Human Resources. **Description:** Designs high-speed semiconductor solutions for broadband network telecommunications and data communications applications. Products include very large scale integration (VLSI) devices for original equipment manufacturers in four markets: telephone networks, local area networks (LANs), wide area networks (WANs), and cable TV (CATV) systems. **Corporate headquarters location:** This Location.

TRION, INC.
P.O. Box 760, Sanford NC 27331-0760. 919/775-2201. **Contact:** Gary Waters, Director of Human Resources. **World Wide Web address:** http://www.trioninc.com. **Description:** Manufactures electronic indoor air cleaners for home, office, and industrial use. Founded in 1947. **Common positions include:** Advertising Clerk; Buyer; Computer Programmer; Credit Manager; Customer Service Rep.; Designer; Draftsperson; Electrical/Electronics Engineer; Electrician; Mechanical Engineer; Quality Control Supervisor. **Educational backgrounds include:** Business Administration; Engineering; Marketing. **Benefits:** 401(k); Disability Coverage; Life Insurance; Medical Insurance; Pension Plan; Savings Plan; Tuition Assistance. **Corporate headquarters location:** This Location. **Number of employees at this location:** 300.

TRIQUINT SEMICONDUCTOR, INC.
2300 NE Brookwood Parkway, Hillsboro OR 97124. 503/615-9000. **Contact:** Human Resources. **World Wide Web address:** http://www.tqs.com. **Description:** This location houses administrative offices. Overall, TriQuint Semiconductor designs, develops, manufactures, and markets a broad range of high-performance analog and mixed signal integrated circuits for the wireless communications, telecommunications, and computing markets. **Common positions include:** Designer; Electrical/Electronics Engineer; Financial Analyst; Product Engineer; Test Engineer; Test Operator. **Educational backgrounds include:** Business Administration; Engineering. **Benefits:** 401(k); Daycare Assistance; Dental Insurance; Disability Coverage; Life Insurance; Medical Insurance; Profit Sharing; Stock Option; Tuition Assistance. **Corporate headquarters location:** This Location. **Number of employees at this location:** 260.

TUSONIX, INC.
P.O. Box 37144, Tucson AZ 85740-7144. 520/744-0400. **Contact:** Rita M. O'Flaherty, Personnel Manager. **World Wide Web address:** http://www.tusonix.com. **Description:** Develops, manufactures, and markets electronic ceramic capacitors and EMI/RFI filters. The company also has a maquiladora plant (a plant that manufactures its products in Mexico and then ships them to a sister or parent plant over the border that distributes the products) in Nogales, Mexico. **Common positions include:** Accountant; Buyer; Ceramics Engineer; Computer Programmer; Customer Service Rep.; Electrical/Electronics Engineer; Materials Engineer; Metallurgical Engineer; Quality Control Supervisor. **Educational backgrounds include:** Engineering; Marketing. **Benefits:** 401(k); Dental Insurance; Disability Coverage; Life Insurance; Medical Insurance; Tuition Assistance. **Corporate headquarters location:** This Location.

II-VI INC.
375 Saxonburg Boulevard, Saxonburg PA 16056. 724/352-4455. **Contact:** Human Resources. **World Wide Web address:** http://www.ii-vi.com. **Description:** Designs, manufactures, and markets

optical and electro-optical components, devices, and materials for precision use in infrared, near-infrared, visible, and X-ray/gamma-ray instruments and applications. II-VI Inc.'s infrared products are used in high-power carbon dioxide lasers for industrial processing and for commercial and military sensing systems. The company's near-infrared and visible products (Virgo Optics) are used in industrial, scientific, and medical instruments, and in solid-state yttrium aluminum garnet lasers. II-VI Inc. also develops and markets X-ray and gamma-ray products (eV PRODUCTS) for the nuclear radiation detection industry. **Corporate headquarters location:** This Location. **Listed on:** NASDAQ.

UCAR INTERNATIONAL, INC.
39 Old Ridgebury Road, Danbury CT 06817. 203/207-7700. **Contact:** Human Resources. **World Wide Web address:** http://www.ucar.com. **Description:** Manufactures graphite and carbon electrodes. **Corporate headquarters location:** This Location.

UNICO INC.
3725 Nicholson Road, Franksville WI 53126-0505. 262/886-5678. **Fax:** 262/504-7396. **Contact:** Jim Kudulis, Personnel Manager. **Description:** Produces microprocessor-based control systems and products. **Common positions include:** Accountant; Buyer; Computer Programmer; Credit Manager; Customer Service Rep.; Designer; Draftsperson; Electrical/Electronics Engineer; General Manager; Human Resources Manager; Industrial Engineer; Mechanical Engineer; Operations/Production Manager; Purchasing Agent/Manager; Quality Control Supervisor; Software Engineer; Technical Writer/Editor. **Educational backgrounds include:** Computer Science; Engineering. **Benefits:** 401(k); Daycare Assistance; Dental Insurance; Disability Coverage; Life Insurance; Medical Insurance; Pension Plan; Profit Sharing; Savings Plan; Tuition Assistance. **Corporate headquarters location:** This Location. **Other U.S. locations:** Nationwide. **Number of employees at this location:** 185.

UNIVERSAL ELECTRONICS INC.
6101 Gateway Drive, Cypress CA 90630-4841. 714/820-1000. **Fax:** 714/820-1010. **Contact:** Marie Reece, Human Resources Manager. **E-mail address:** mreece@ueic.com. **World Wide Web address:** http://www.universalelectronicsus.com. **Description:** Develops, designs, engineers, and markets preprogrammed universal remote controls for use with home video and audio entertainment equipment. Universal Electronics also produces home safety and automation equipment. **Office hours:** Monday - Friday, 7:00 a.m. - 5:00 p.m. **Number of employees at this location:** 90.

UNIVERSAL INSTRUMENTS CORPORATION
P.O. Box 825, Binghamton NY 13902. 607/779-7522. **Fax:** 607/779-5125. **Contact:** Human Resources. **E-mail address:** employment@uic.com. **World Wide Web address:** http://www.uic.com. **Description:** A leader in the automation of electronic circuit assembly. Universal Instruments Corporation manufactures automated factory equipment for the electronics industry including machines that assemble PC boards used in VCRs and televisions. **Common positions include:** Applications Engineer; Chemical Engineer; Computer Programmer; Computer Scientist; Computer Support Technician; Design Engineer; Electrical/Electronics Engineer; Manufacturing Engineer; Mechanical Engineer; Network/Systems Administrator; Quality Assurance Engineer; Sales Engineer. **Educational backgrounds include:** C/C++; Chemistry; Computer Science; Engineering; HTML; Java; Mathematics; Physics; Software

Development. **Benefits:** 401(k); Casual Dress - Fridays; Dental Insurance; Disability Coverage; Medical Insurance; Pension Plan; Profit Sharing; Tuition Assistance. **Special programs:** Internships; Apprenticeships; Co-ops. **President:** Gerhard Meese.

VICOR CORPORATION
25 Frontage Road, Andover MA 01810. 978/470-2900. **Fax:** 978/749-7700. **Contact:** Tracy Rosenthal, Manager of Human Resources. **Description:** Develops, manufactures, and markets components for modular power systems and complete power systems using a patented, high-frequency, electronic power conversion technology called zero current switching. Components are used in electronic products to convert power from a primary power source into the direct current required by most contemporary electronic circuits. **Common positions include:** Buyer; Customer Service Rep.; Designer; Draftsperson; Electrical/Electronics Engineer; Industrial Production Manager; Manufacturer's/Wholesaler's Sales Rep.; Mechanical Engineer; Metallurgical Engineer; Operations/Production Manager; Purchasing Agent/Manager; Services Sales Rep.; Software Engineer; Systems Analyst. **Educational backgrounds include:** Computer Science; Engineering; Finance; Liberal Arts; Marketing; Physics. **Benefits:** 401(k); Dental Insurance; Disability Coverage; Employee Discounts; Life Insurance; Medical Insurance; Profit Sharing; Tuition Assistance. **Corporate headquarters location:** This Location. **Number of employees at this location:** 700.

VIDEO DISPLAY CORPORATION
1868 Tucker Industrial Drive, Tucker GA 30084. 770/938-2080. **Contact:** Personnel. **Description:** One of the leading international manufacturers of new and recycled cathode ray tubes (CRTs) and component parts. Video Display Corporation is also one of the largest domestic distributors of consumer electronic parts and accessories. Founded in 1975. **Corporate headquarters location:** This Location. **Subsidiaries include:** Fox International and Vanco are two of the largest domestic distributors of warranty and non-warranty consumer electronic parts and accessories.

VISHAY DALE ELECTRONICS
P.O. Box 609, Columbus NE 68602-0609. 402/564-3131. **Physical address:** 1122 23rd Street, Columbus NE 68601. **Fax:** 402/563-6418. **Contact:** Human Resources. **Description:** This location manufactures wirewound resistors and plasma displays. Overall, Vishay Dale Electronics is one of the largest manufacturers of fixed resistors and inductors in the U.S. and a producer of other passive electronic components including transformers, specialty connectors, and plasma displays. **Common positions include:** Accountant/Auditor; Advertising Clerk; Buyer; Computer Programmer; Customer Service Rep.; Designer; Draftsperson; Electrical/Electronics Engineer; General Manager; Human Resources Manager; Industrial Engineer; Mechanical Engineer; Purchasing Agent/Manager; Quality Control Supervisor; Systems Analyst. **Benefits:** 401(k); Disability Coverage; Life Insurance; Medical Insurance; Pension Plan; Tuition Assistance. **Corporate headquarters location:** This Location. **Other U.S. locations:** Norfolk NE; Yankton SD. **Parent company:** Vishay Intertechnology (Malvern PA) is a leader in passive electronic component manufacturing. Other Vishay subsidiaries include Draloric Electronic GmbH, one of the largest manufacturers of resistors in Germany and also a producer of specialty ceramic capacitors; Sfernice, S.A., one of the largest manufacturers of fixed and variable resistors (potentiometers) and

printed circuit boards in France; Sprague, a leading supplier of tantalum capacitors to the commercial, industrial, military, and aerospace electronics markets, and also a manufacturer of thick film resistor networks; and Roederstein, a leading European and U.S. film capacitor manufacturer and also a producer of tantalum, aluminum, and ceramic disk capacitors, hybrids, and other passive electronic components. **Number of employees at this location:** 700.

VITRONICS SOLTEC
2 Marin Way, Stratham NH 03885. 603/772-7778. **Contact:** Human Resources Director. **Description:** Designs, engineers, manufactures, and markets thermal process and associated systems for production soldering, cleaning, and repair of surface-mounted devices to printed circuit boards. The primary market for these products is the electronics industry, although other markets include computers and peripheral office equipment; military, consumer, mechanical, and automotive electronics; telecommunications equipment; test and measurement equipment; and contract assembly. **Benefits:** 401(k); Stock Option. **Corporate headquarters location:** This Location. **International locations:** Vitronics Europe Limited (England). **Listed on:** American Stock Exchange. **Number of employees at this location:** 90.

WPI GROUP, INC.
1155 Elm Street, Manchester NH 03101. 603/627-3500. **Fax:** 603/627-3150. **Contact:** Catherine Lisk, Human Resources Director. **Description:** A holding company. **Corporate headquarters location:** This Location. **Subsidiaries include:** WPI Electronics, Inc.; WPI Magnetic, Inc.; WPI Micro Palm, Inc.; WPI Power Systems, Inc.; WPI Termiflex, Inc. Each subsidiary operates through two groups: Magnetics and Electronics. The Magnetics group designs and manufactures large magnetic power systems, electromechanical devices, and systems that power and control high-temperature industrial furnaces. The Electronics group designs and produces hand-held computer terminals and DOS-based computers used to collect data; related software; and arc lamp electronic ballasts for overhead and video projectors, medical endoscopes, and lighting applications. **Listed on:** NASDAQ.

WACKER SILTRONIC CORPORATION
P.O. Box 83180, Portland OR 97283. 503/243-7264. **Fax:** 503/219-4606. **Recorded jobline:** 503/241-7547. **Contact:** Corporate Recruiter. **E-mail address:** employment@siltronic.com. **World Wide Web address:** http://www.siltronic.com. **Description:** Manufactures polish and epitaxially coat silicon wafers for the semiconductor industry. **Common positions include:** Accountant; Applications Engineer; Budget Analyst; Chemical Engineer; Chemist; Computer Programmer; Computer Scientist; Database Administrator; Environmental Engineer; Financial Analyst; Industrial Engineer; Manufacturing Engineer; Mechanical Engineer; Network/Systems Administrator; Process Engineer; Purchasing Agent/ Manager; Quality Assurance Engineer; Software Engineer; SQL Programmer; Systems Analyst. **Educational backgrounds include:** Accounting; Business Administration; Chemistry; Computer Science; Engineering; Finance; Mathematics; Microsoft Word; Novell; Physics. **Benefits:** 401(k); Casual Dress - Daily; Daycare Assistance; Dental Insurance; Disability Coverage; Employee Discounts; Life Insurance; Medical Insurance; Pension Plan; Profit Sharing; Public Transit Available; Savings Plan; Tuition Assistance; Vacation Days (11 - 15). **Corporate headquarters location:** Munich, Germany. **Parent company:**

Wacker Siltronic A.G. **Listed on:** Privately held. **Annual sales/revenues:** More than $100 million. **Number of employees at this location:** 1,500.

WELLS-GARDNER ELECTRONICS CORP.
2701 North Kildare Avenue, Chicago IL 60639. 773/252-8220. **Fax:** 773/252-8072. **Contact:** Gene Ahner, Human Resources Director. **World Wide Web address:** http://www.wgec.com. **Description:** Designs and manufactures CRT video monitors for arcade games, and for the leisure and fitness, automotive, intranet, and video wall markets. **Common positions include:** Accountant; Draftsperson; Electrical/Electronics Engineer; Electronics Technician. **Educational backgrounds include:** Engineering. **Benefits:** 401(k); Dental Insurance; Disability Coverage; Life Insurance; Medical Insurance; Public Transit Available; Tuition Assistance; Vision Plan. **Corporate headquarters location:** This Location. **Listed on:** American Stock Exchange. **Annual sales/revenues:** $21 - $50 million. **Number of employees at this location:** 180.

WEMS ELECTRONICS INC.
4650 West Rosecrans Avenue, Hawthorne CA 90250. 310/644-0251. **Fax:** 310/644-5334. **Contact:** Theresa Sunbury, Human Resources Manager. **World Wide Web address:** http://www.wems.com. **Description:** Specializes in box build turnkey manufacturing. Current programs include products that incorporate electrical, electro-mechanical, pneumatic, hydraulic, and mechanical components as well as high level electronics. **Common positions include:** Accountant; Administrative Assistant; Buyer; Controller; Customer Service Representative; Design Engineer; Draftsperson; Electrical/Electronics Engineer; Human Resources Manager; Mechanical Engineer; Network/Systems Administrator; Operations Manager; Production Manager; Quality Control Supervisor; Sales Executive. **Educational backgrounds include:** Accounting; Business Administration; Engineering; Marketing; Microsoft Office; Microsoft Word; Spreadsheets. **Benefits:** 401(k); Casual Dress - Fridays; Disability Coverage; Life Insurance; Medical Insurance; Profit Sharing; Tuition Assistance; Vacation Days (6 - 10). **Office hours:** Monday - Friday, 8:00 a.m. - 5:00 p.m. **Corporate headquarters location:** This Location. **Other U.S. locations:** Danvers MA. **Listed on:** Privately held. **President:** Ronald Hood. **Number of employees at this location:** 120.

WESCO DISTRIBUTION, INC.
Commerce Court, Suite 700, 4 Station Square, Pittsburgh PA 15219. 412/454-2200. **Contact:** Human Resources. **World Wide Web address:** http://www.wescodist.com. **Description:** Distributors of electrical supplies, data communications products, industrial automation equipment, and industrial supplies. **Corporate headquarters location:** This Location. **Listed on:** New York Stock Exchange. **Stock exchange symbol:** WCC.

WESTERN ELECTRONICS CORPORATION
560 Commercial Street, Eugene OR 97402. 541/683-8118. **Contact:** Kristee Megown, Human Resources Manager. **Description:** A manufacturer of wire cable. **Corporate headquarters location:** This Location. **Number of employees at this location:** 200.

WESTRONICS
GAME MASTERS
2575 South Highland Drive, Las Vegas NV 89109. 702/732-1414. **Contact:** Claudia Wichinsky, President. **Description:** Manufactures, distributes,

sells, and leases coin-operated gaming machines. **Common positions include:** Accountant/Auditor; Buyer; Draftsperson; Purchasing Agent/Manager. **Benefits:** Dental Insurance; Life Insurance; Medical Insurance. **Corporate headquarters location:** This Location.

WILCOXON RESEARCH, INC.
21 Firstfield Road, Gaithersburg MD 20878. 301/330-8811. **Toll-free phone:** 800/WILCOXON. **Fax:** 301/527-9761. **Recorded jobline:** 301/216-3000. **Contact:** Catherine Galasso, Director of Human Resources. **E-mail address:** wrjobs@wilcoxon.com. **World Wide Web address:** http://www.wilcoxon.com. **Description:** A designer and producer of a variety of electromechanical devices for use in machinery maintenance, predictive maintenance programs, and laboratory research. Products include electromagnetic vibration generators and underwater accelerometers. **Common positions include:** Account Manager; Accountant; Administrative Assistant; Buyer; Computer Technician; Customer Service Rep.; Draftsperson; Electrical/Electronics Engineer; Finance Director; Financial Analyst; Graphic Designer; Manufacturing Engineer; Mechanical Engineer; Network/Systems Administrator; Production Manager; Purchasing Agent/Manager; Quality Assurance Engineer. **Educational backgrounds include:** Engineering; Finance; Marketing; Microsoft Word; Novell; Spreadsheets. **Benefits:** 401(k); Dental Insurance; Disability Coverage; Employee Discounts; Flexible Schedule; Life Insurance; Medical Insurance; Profit Sharing; Tuition Assistance. **Office hours:** Monday - Friday, 8:00 a.m. - 4:30 p.m. **Corporate headquarters location:** This Location. **Listed on:** Privately held. **President/CEO:** Fred Wilcoxon. **Number of employees at this location:** 110.

WYLE ELECTRONICS
15370 Barranca Parkway, Irvine CA 92718. 949/753-9953. **Contact:** Human Resources. **World Wide Web address:** http://www.wyle.com. **Description:** Engaged in the distribution of selected lines of electronic supplies and components to the electronics, computer, military, and aerospace industries. Principal products include semiconductors, capacitors, resistors, and various computer products such as printers, video display terminals, and other products supplied by major computer manufacturing firms. **Corporate headquarters location:** This Location. **Other U.S. locations:** Nationwide. **Listed on:** Privately held.

XETEL
2105 Gracy Farms Lane, Austin TX 78758. 512/834-2266. **Contact:** Human Resources. **World Wide Web address:** http://www.xetel.com. **Description:** XeTel's broad range of services includes product development engineering; printed circuit board layout and design; program management; materials management and procurement; quick-turn prototyping; board-level mixed, fine-pitch, and advanced technology assembly; PCMCIA card assembly; in-circuit, functional, and environmental stress screening (ESS) testing; complete unit assembly and final packaging; and depot repair. **Common positions include:** Accountant/Auditor; Blue-Collar Worker Supervisor; Buyer; Clerical Supervisor; Computer Programmer; Credit Manager; Designer; Financial Analyst; Human Resources Manager; Operations/Production Manager; Public Relations Specialist; Systems Analyst. **Educational backgrounds include:** Accounting; Business Administration; Engineering; Finance; Marketing. **Benefits:** 401(k); Dental Insurance; Disability Coverage; Life Insurance; Medical Insurance; Profit Sharing;

Tuition Assistance. **Special programs:** Internships. **Corporate headquarters location:** This Location. **Listed on:** NASDAQ. **Number of employees at this location:** 440.

XONTECH, INC.
6862 Hayvenhurst Avenue, Van Nuys CA 91406. 818/787-7380. **Fax:** 818/904-9440. **Contact:** Human Resources. **World Wide Web address:** http://www.xontech.com. **Description:** A research and development firm specializing in the development of advanced concepts, technologies, and systems to support defense programs. Xontech is engaged in the fields of radar and communications, missile and sensor phenomenology, flight test data analysis, and applied physics. The company also deals in state-of-the-art software applications and algorithm development. **Common positions include:** Computer Programmer; Mathematician; Software Engineer. **Educational backgrounds include:** Computer Science; Engineering; Mathematics; Physics. **Benefits:** 401(k); Dental Insurance; Disability Coverage; Life Insurance; Medical Insurance; Profit Sharing; Tuition Assistance. **Corporate headquarters location:** This Location. **Other U.S. locations:** AL; CA; CO; DC.

YORK CAPACITOR CORPORATION
P.O. Box 278, Winooski VT 05404. 802/655-2550. **Contact:** Personnel. **Description:** Manufactures electrical motors and capacitors. **Corporate headquarters location:** This Location.

ZILOG, INC.
910 East Hamilton Avenue, Campbell CA 95008. 408/558-8500. **Fax:** 408/558-8380. **Contact:** Tony S. Perez, Principal Human Resources Representative. **World Wide Web address:** http://www.zilog.com. **Description:** Designs, develops, manufactures, and markets application-specific standard integrated circuit products (ASSPs) for the data communications, intelligent peripheral controller, consumer product controller, and memory markets. **Common positions include:** Chemical Engineer; Electrical/Electronics Engineer; Software Engineer. **Educational backgrounds include:** Engineering. **Benefits:** 401(k); Dental Insurance; Disability Coverage; Employee Discounts; Life Insurance; Medical Insurance; Profit Sharing; Savings Plan; Tuition Assistance. **Corporate headquarters location:** This Location. **Other U.S. locations:** Nampa ID. **Listed on:** NASDAQ. **Number of employees at this location:** 250. **Number of employees nationwide:** 1,500.

ZIMMERMAN SIGN COMPANY
9846 Highway 31 East, Tyler TX 75705. 903/535-7400. **Contact:** Human Resources. **Description:** An electric sign manufacturer. **Common positions include:** Accountant/Auditor; Blue-Collar Worker Supervisor; Budget Analyst; Buyer; Cost Estimator; Customer Service Rep.; Designer; Draftsperson; Human Resources Manager; Purchasing Agent/Manager; Quality Control Supervisor; Systems Analyst. **Educational backgrounds include:** Accounting; Art/Design; Business Administration; Computer Science; Engineering; Marketing. **Benefits:** Disability Coverage; Life Insurance; Medical Insurance. **Corporate headquarters location:** This Location. **Other U.S. locations:** Jacksonville TX; Longview TX. **Number of employees at this location:** 50.

ZYGO CORPORATION
Laurel Brook Road, P.O. Box 448, Middlefield CT 06455-0448. 860/347-8506. **Fax:** 860/347-8372. **Contact:** Human Resources. **World Wide Web address:** http://www.zygo.com. **Description:**

Develops and manufactures high-precision noncontact measuring instruments and precision optical components. Zygo developed one of the first easy-to-use laser interferometer systems, one of the first microprocessor-based interferometer analysis systems, and one of the first commercially successful phase-measuring interferometer systems. These interferometers are used throughout the world to measure the surface shape and optical performance of glass or plastic optic components such as flats, lenses, and prisms; precision metal components such as hard disks and bearing and sealing surfaces; polished ceramics; and contact lens molds. **Benefits:** Profit Sharing; Stock Option. **Corporate headquarters location:** This Location. **Other U.S. locations:** CA; CO. **International locations:** Germany. **Listed on:** NASDAQ.

ZYMARK CORPORATION
Zymark Center, 68 Elm Street, Hopkinton MA 01748. 508/435-9500. **Fax:** 508/497-2685. **Contact:** Human Resources. **E-mail address:** human.resources@zymark.com. **World Wide Web address:** http://www.zymark.com. **Description:** Designs and manufactures robots and robotic systems for use in laboratories to speed the discovery process in the biotechnological and pharmaceutical industries. **NOTE:** Entry-level positions are offered. **Common positions include:** Account Rep.; Accountant; Administrative Assistant; Applications Engineer; Auditor; Budget Analyst; Chemist; Chief Financial Officer; Clerical Supervisor; Computer Programmer; Controller; Draftsperson; Electrical/Electronics Engineer; Human Resources Manager; Marketing Manager; Marketing Specialist; Mechanical Engineer; MIS Specialist; Multimedia Designer; Product Manager; Project Manager; Public Relations Specialist; Quality Control Supervisor; Sales Executive; Sales Manager; Sales Rep.; Secretary; Software Engineer; Technical Writer/Editor; Typist/Word Processor; Validation Scientist; Vice President of Sales; Video Editor. **Educational backgrounds include:** Chemistry; Computer Science; Engineering; Marketing; Software Development; Software Tech. Support. **Benefits:** 401(k); Adoption Assistance; Dental Insurance; Disability Coverage; Employee Discounts; Flexible Schedule; Job Sharing; Life Insurance; Medical Insurance; Profit Sharing; Savings Plan; Telecommuting; Tuition Assistance. **Special programs:** Internships; Co-ops; Summer Jobs. **Office hours:** Monday - Friday, 8:00 a.m. - 5:00 p.m. **Corporate headquarters location:** This Location. **Other U.S. locations:** Nationwide. **International locations:** Canada; England; France; Germany; Japan; Switzerland. **Parent company:** Berwind Corporation. **Listed on:** Privately held. **President/CEO:** Kevin Hrusousky.

For more information on career opportunities in the electronic/industrial electrical equipment industry:

Associations

AMERICAN CERAMIC SOCIETY
P.O. Box 6136, Westerville OH 43086-6136. 614/890-4700. World Wide Web address: http://www.acers.org. Provides ceramics industry information. Membership required.

ELECTROCHEMICAL SOCIETY
65 South Main Street, Pennington NJ 08534. 609/737-1902. World Wide Web address: http://www.electrochem.org. An international society which holds bi-annual meetings internationally and periodic meetings through local sections.

ELECTRONIC INDUSTRIES ASSOCIATION
2500 Wilson Boulevard, Arlington VA 22201. 703/907-7500. World Wide Web address: http://www.eia.org.

ELECTRONICS TECHNICIANS ASSOCIATION
602 North Jackson Street, Greencastle IN 46135. 765/653-4301. World Wide Web address: http://www.eta-sda.com. Offers published job-hunting advice from the organization's officers and members. Also offers educational material and certification programs.

FABLESS SEMICONDUCTOR ASSOCIATION
Three Lincoln Centre, 5430 LBJ Freeway, Suite 280, Dallas TX 75240-6636. 972/866-7579. Fax: 972/239-2292. World Wide Web address: http://www.fsa.org. A semiconductor industry association.

INSTITUTE OF ELECTRICAL AND ELECTRONICS ENGINEERS, INC. (IEEE)
305 East 47th Street, 9th Floor, New York NY 10017. 212/705-8900. Toll-free customer service line: 800/678-4333. World Wide Web address: http://www.ieee.org.

INTERNATIONAL SOCIETY OF CERTIFIED ELECTRONICS TECHNICIANS
2708 West Berry Street, Fort Worth TX 76109. 817/921-9101. World Wide Web address: http://www.iscet.org.

NATIONAL ELECTRONICS SERVICE DEALERS ASSOCIATION
2708 West Berry Street, Fort Worth TX 76109. 817/921-9061. World Wide Web address: http://www.nesda.com. Provides newsletters and directories to members.

SEMICONDUCTOR EQUIPMENT AND MATERIALS INTERNATIONAL
805 East Middlefield Road, Mountain View CA 94043-4080. 650/964-5111. E-mail address: semihq@semi.org. World Wide Web address: http://www.semi.org. An international trade association concerned with the semiconductor and flat-panel display industries. Membership required.

Career Fairs

JOB EXPO INTERNATIONAL, INC.
175 Fifth Avenue, Suite 2390, New York NY 10010. 212/655-4505. Fax: 212/655-4501. World Wide Web address: http://www.tech-expo.com. One of the nation's leading technical career fairs.

Online Services

SEMICONDUCTOR JOBS
World Wide Web address: http://www. semiconductorjobs.com. Provides links to job postings related to the semiconductor industry.

Environmental and Waste Management Services

You can expect to find the following types of companies in this chapter:
Environmental Engineering Firms • Sanitary Services

Some helpful information: *The average salary for entry-level sanitation workers is approximately $20,000 - $25,000 annually, with experienced workers earning an average of $30,000 per year. Environmental engineers can earn upwards of $40,000 annually.*

ATC ASSOCIATES
1117 Lone Palm Avenue, Suite B, Modesto CA 95351. 209/579-2221. **Contact:** Human Resources. **World Wide Web address:** http://www.atc-enviro.com. **Description:** Performs comprehensive environmental consulting, engineering, and on-site remediation services throughout the United States for a variety of clients including federal, state, and local government agencies.

AIR PRODUCTS AND CHEMICALS, INC.
7201 Hamilton Boulevard, Allentown PA 18195-1501. 610/481-7050. **Contact:** Human Resources. **World Wide Web address:** http://www.airproducts.com. **Description:** Manufactures industrial gases, process equipment, and chemicals. Products include cryogenic equipment, air separation systems, hydrogen purification devices, and nitrogen rejection equipment. In addition, the company is a provider of engineering services, and is involved in landfill gas recovery, waste management, waste-to-energy ventures, flue gas desulfurization, and cogeneration operations. **Common positions include:** Chemical Engineer; Financial Analyst; Mechanical Engineer. **Educational backgrounds include:** Engineering; Finance; Marketing; MBA. **Benefits:** Dental Insurance; Disability Coverage; Life Insurance; Pension Plan; Savings Plan; Stock Option; Tuition Assistance. **Special programs:** Internships. **Corporate headquarters location:** This Location.

ALLIED WASTE INDUSTRIES
15880 North Greenway-Hayden Loop, Scottsdale AZ 85260. 480/627-2700. **Contact:** Human Resources. **World Wide Web address:** http://www.awin.com. **Description:** One of the world's largest waste services company. Allied Waste provides collection, disposal, and recycling services to residential, commercial, and industrial customers. **Corporate headquarters location:** This Location.

AMERICAN ENVIRONMENTAL & INDUSTRIAL SERVICES INC.
P.O. Box 83, Galena IL 61036. 815/777-2616. **Toll-free phone:** 800/377-2616. **Fax:** 815/777-1574. **Contact:** Human Resources. **Description:** Provides tank removals, soil remediation, industrial pumping, tank cleaning and cutting, industrial cleaning, and emergency spill response. **Common positions include:** Environmental Engineer; Human Resources Manager; Project Manager; Secretary. **Educational backgrounds include:** Business Administration; Communications; Engineering; Geology; Marketing. **Benefits:** Dental Insurance; Medical Insurance. **Corporate headquarters location:** This Location.

ARCADIS GERAGHTY & MILLER, INC.
88 Duryea Road, Melville NY 11747. 516/249-7600. **Fax:** 516/249-7610. **Contact:** Human Resources. **World Wide Web address:** http://www.arcadis-us.com. **Description:** An international consulting, engineering, and contracting company, specializing in the fields of the environment and infrastructure. Founded in 1888. **NOTE:** Please send resumes to Human Resources, 1099 18th Street, Denver CO 80202. **Corporate headquarters location:** This Location. **Subsidiaries include:** JSA Environmental Inc. (Long Beach CA) provides environmental assessment and analysis services. **Listed on:** Amsterdam Stock Exchange; NASDAQ. **Other U.S. locations:**
• 35 East Wacker Drive, Suite 1000, Chicago IL 60601. 312/263-6703.

ASHLAND NATURE CENTER
P.O. Box 700, Hockessin DE 19707. 302/239-2334. **Contact:** Helen Fischel, Associate Director, Education. **World Wide Web address:** http://www.delawarenaturesociety.org/ashland.htm. **Description:** A private, nonprofit, membership organization dedicated to environmental education and the preservation of natural areas. **Parent company:** Delaware Nature Society operates Ashland Nature Center and Abbott's Mill, offering year-round programming for all age groups.

THE BSC GROUP, INC.
425 Summer Street, Boston MA 02210. 617/330-5300. **Toll-free phone:** 800/288-8123. **Fax:** 617/345-8008. **Contact:** Alison Hunt, Human Resources. **E-mail address:** hrdept@bscgroup.com. **Description:** A land resource and engineering firm providing a variety of consulting services in the fields of land surveying and mapping, geographic information systems, civil engineering, environmental engineering, planning, and landscape architecture. The BSC Group focuses on coastal, land development, and transportation projects. Founded in 1965. **Common positions include:** Biological Scientist; Civil Engineer; Draftsperson; Environmental Engineer; Software Engineer; Surveyor; Transportation/Traffic Specialist. **Educational backgrounds include:** Biology; Computer Science; Engineering; Surveying/Mapping. **Benefits:** 401(k); Dental Insurance; Disability Coverage; Life Insurance; Medical Insurance; Profit Sharing; Tuition Assistance. **Corporate headquarters location:** This Location.

BLACK & VEATCH
230 Congress Street, Suite 802, Boston MA 02110. 617/451-6900. **Contact:** Personnel. **World Wide Web address:** http://www.bv.com. **Description:** An environmental/civil engineering and construction firm serving utilities, commerce, and government agencies worldwide. Black & Veatch provides a broad range of study, design, construction management, and turnkey capabilities to clients in the water and wastewater fields. The firm is one of the leading authorities on drinking water treatment

through the use of activated carbon, ozone, and other state-of-the-art processes. Black & Veatch is also engaged in wastewater treatment work including reclamation and reuse projects and the beneficial use of wastewater residuals. Other services are provided for solid waste recycling and disposal, transportation, and storm water management. In the energy field, Black & Veatch is a leader in providing engineering procurement and construction for electric power plants. The firm's areas of expertise include coal-fueled plants, simple and combined-cycle combustion turbines, fluidized bed combustion, waste-to-energy facilities, hydroelectric plants, and cogeneration facilities. Black & Veatch's capabilities also include nuclear power projects, advanced technology, air quality control, performance monitoring, plant life management, and facilities modification. In addition, Black & Veatch operates in the transmission and distribution field. In the industrial sector, Black & Veatch focuses on projects involving cleanrooms, industrial processes and planning, utility systems, and cogeneration. In addition to engineering, procurement, and construction, Black & Veatch offers a variety of management and financial services including institutional strengthening, privatization, strategic financial planning, and information management. **Common positions include:** Accountant; Administrative Assistant; Applications Engineer; Architect; Attorney; Auditor; Civil Engineer; Computer Programmer; Computer Support Technician; Database Administrator; Database Manager; Draftsperson; Electrical/Electronics Engineer; Environmental Engineer; Human Resources Manager; Librarian; Marketing Manager; Marketing Specialist; Mechanical Engineer; Network/Systems Administrator; Paralegal; Secretary; Software Engineer; Systems Analyst; Typist/Word Processor; Webmaster. **Educational backgrounds include:** Accounting; Computer Science; Engineering; Finance; Marketing. **Benefits:** 401(k); Dental Insurance; Disability Coverage; Flexible Schedule; Life Insurance; Medical Insurance. **Special programs:** Co-ops. **Corporate headquarters location:** Kansas City MO. **Other U.S. locations:** Nationwide. **International locations:** Worldwide.

BROWN & CALDWELL

P.O. Box 8045, Walnut Creek CA 94596-1220. 925/937-9010. **Physical address:** 3480 Buskirk Avenue, Suite 150, Pleasant Hill CA 94523-4342. **Toll-free phone:** 800/727-2224. **Fax:** 925/937-9026. **Contact:** Professional Staffing. **World Wide Web address:** http://www.brownandcaldwell.com. **Description:** An employee-owned environmental engineering and consulting firm. Brown & Caldwell specializes in the planning, engineering, and design of waste management systems. The company is also engaged in construction management and environmental analytical testing. **Common positions include:** Air Quality Scientist; Chemist; Environmental Engineer; Environmental Scientist; Hydrogeologist. **Educational backgrounds include:** Chemistry; Engineering; Environmental Science. **Benefits:** Daycare Assistance; Dental Insurance; Disability Coverage; Life Insurance; Medical Insurance; Pension Plan; Tuition Assistance. **Corporate headquarters location:** This Location.

CAMP DRESSER & McKEE, INC. (CDM)

660 Reynolds Arcade, 16 East Main Street, Rochester NY 14614. 716/262-6070. **Contact:** Human Resources. **World Wide Web address:** http://www.cdm.com. **Description:** Camp Dresser & McKee is a worldwide provider of environmental engineering, scientific, planning, and management

services. The company focuses on professional activities for the management of water resources, hazardous and solid wastes, wastewater, infrastructure, and environmental systems for industry and government. **Corporate headquarters location:** Cambridge MA. **Other U.S. locations:**
- P.O. Box 3885, Bellevue WA 98009. 425/453-8383.

CATALYTICA, INC.

430 Ferguson Drive, Building 3, Mountain View CA 94043. 650/960-3000. **Contact:** Human Resources. **Description:** Develops catalytic technologies for the prevention of pollution in combustion systems, advanced process technologies, and chemical products. The company also develops an ultralow emission-combustion system for natural gas turbines. Catalytica provides contract research, development, and consulting services to the petroleum refining and chemical industries. Additional programs include the development of a process for manufacturing gasoline alkylate to eliminate the use of liquid acid catalysts, the conversion of methane to transportation fuels, and the application of nanotechnology for new catalysts and materials. The company also manufactures fine chemical products. **Corporate headquarters location:** This Location. **Subsidiaries include:** Advanced Sensor Devices develops environmental monitoring devices including a continuous emissions monitor.

CEIMIC CORPORATION

16935 West Bernardo Drive, Suite 239-D, San Diego CA 92127. 858/674-7400. **Contact:** Human Resources. **World Wide Web address:** http://www.ceimic.com. **Description:** A laboratory that conducts a variety of environmental tests. Subjects include inorganic substances, metals, pollutants, soil, and water. **Common positions include:** Chemist; Laboratory Technician. **Educational backgrounds include:** Biology; Chemistry. **Corporate headquarters location:** This Location. **Other U.S. locations:** Anchorage AK; Phoenix AZ; Pensacola FL; Albuquerque NM; Portland OR. **Parent company:** Ogden Environmental & Energy Services.

CLEAN HARBORS, INC.

1501 Washington Street, Braintree MA 02184. 781/849-1800. **Fax:** 781/356-1363. **Contact:** Human Resources Department. **World Wide Web address:** http://www.cleanharbors.com. **Description:** Through its subsidiaries, Clean Harbors, Inc. provides comprehensive environmental services in 35 states in the Northeast, Midwest, Central, and Mid-Atlantic regions. Clean Harbors provides a wide range of hazardous waste management and environmental support services. The company's hazardous waste management services include treatment, storage, recycling, transportation, risk analysis, site assessment, laboratory analysis, site closure, and disposal of hazardous materials through environmentally-sound methods. Environmental remediation services include emergency response, surface remediation, groundwater restoration, industrial maintenance, and facility decontamination. Customers include regional utilities; oil, pharmaceutical, and chemical companies; small businesses; and the high-tech and biotech industries. **Corporate headquarters location:** This Location. **Other U.S. locations:** Nationwide.

COMMODORE APPLIED TECHNOLOGIES

150 East 58th Street, Suite 3400, New York NY 10155. 212/308-5800. **Contact:** Human Resources. **World Wide Web address:** http://www.

commodore.com. **Description:** Develops technologies to destroy PCBs, chemical weapons, dioxins, and pesticides. Commodore Applied Technologies also salvages and resells cross-contaminated CFCs, and acquires and cleans up environmentally distressed properties. **Corporate headquarters location:** This Location. **Subsidiaries include:** Commodore Advanced Sciences, Inc.; Commodore Separation Technologies, Inc.; Commodore Solution Technologies, Inc.; Teledyne-Commodore LLC.

ETS INTERNATIONAL, INC.
1401 Municipal Road NW, Roanoke VA 24012-1309. 540/265-0004. **Fax:** 540/265-0082. **Contact:** Cathy Wray, Human Resources Coordinator. **World Wide Web address:** http://www.etsi-inc.com. **Description:** Provides environmental and infrastructure products and services. ETS International specializes in toxic emission measurement and control as well as infrastructure design, construction, and maintenance. **Corporate headquarters location:** This Location. **Subsidiaries include:** ETS, Inc. (Roanoke VA, Philadelphia PA, and Taiwan) offers training, contract research and development, engineering, consulting, regulatory assistance, and field testing. ETS Analytical Services, Inc. (Roanoke and Richmond VA) is an environmentally-oriented analytical lab serving both government and industry. ETS Water and Waste Management, Inc. (Richmond and Fairfax VA) is a construction and maintenance service firm providing storm and sewer line, water system and gas line construction, and the design and installation of septic and irrigation systems. **Listed on:** American Stock Exchange. **Number of employees nationwide:** 70.

ECO SYSTEMS, INC.
439 Katherine Drive, Suite 2A, Jackson MS 39208. 601/936-4440. **Contact:** Operations Manager. **Description:** An environmental consulting company providing consulting services to large and small companies seeking assistance with complex environmental problems. These services include contamination assessments, remedial planning and design, disposal site engineering, groundwater plans, air quality, water quality, ecological assessments, environmental audits, regulatory compliance assistance, facility permitting, health and safety training, and OSHA compliance. Founded in 1993. **Common positions include:** Biological Scientist; Chemical Engineer; Chemist; Civil Engineer; Draftsperson; Environmental Engineer; Geologist/Geophysicist; Mechanical Engineer. **Educational backgrounds include:** Biology; Chemistry; Computer Science; Economics; Engineering; Geology. **Benefits:** 401(k); Dental Insurance; Disability Coverage; Medical Insurance. **Corporate headquarters location:** This Location. **Other U.S. locations:** Little Rock AR; Houston TX.

ENVIROMETRICS INC.
9229 University Boulevard, Charleston SC 29406. 843/553-9456. **Contact:** Human Resources Manager. **World Wide Web address:** http://www.envirometrics.com. **Description:** An engineering firm that specializes in air pollution control, environmental solutions, and technical services. Envirometrics markets a number of products including pilot control systems, the HVS3 (High Volume Small Surface Sampler), and air quality monitoring and source testing equipment. **Corporate headquarters location:** This Location.

ENVIRONMENTAL MATERIALS CORP.
550 James Street, Lakewood NJ 08701. 732/370-3400. **Contact:** Human Resources. **Description:** Engaged in the marketing and sale of refrigerants and refrigerant reclaiming services. The company has also developed and commercialized a line of equipment designed to recycle and recover refrigerants contained in air conditioning and refrigeration systems. **Corporate headquarters location:** This Location. **Parent company:** Environmental Technologies Corporation.

EVANS SYSTEMS, INC. (ESI)
P.O. Box 2480, Bay City TX 77404-2480. 979/245-2424. **Fax:** 979/244-5070. **Contact:** Human Resources. **Description:** A holding company. **Corporate headquarters location:** This Location. **Subsidiaries include:** Way Energy distributes wholesale and retail refined petroleum products and lubricants and owns and operates convenience stores in southern Texas and Louisiana; Chem-Way Systems, Inc. produces, packages, and markets automotive aftermarket chemical products in 23 states; EDCO Environmental Systems, Inc. provides environmental remediation services and installations of underground storage tanks; Distributor Information Systems Corporation provides information systems and software for distributors and convenience store owners and operators. **Annual sales/revenues:** More than $100 million.

FAY, SPOFFORD & THORNDIKE, INC.
5 Burlington Woods, Burlington MA 01803. 781/221-1000. **Fax:** 781/229-1115. **Contact:** Human Resources Department. **World Wide Web address:** http://www.fstinc.com. **Description:** A civil engineering and consulting firm that specializes in airports, bridges and viaducts, environmental permits, wastewater systems, and waterworks. **Common positions include:** Civil Engineer; Structural Engineer. **Corporate headquarters location:** This Location. **Number of employees at this location:** 175.

GZA GEOENVIRONMENTAL TECHNOLOGIES
320 Needham Street, Newton Upper Falls MA 02464. 617/969-0700. **Contact:** Human Resources. **World Wide Web address:** http://www.gza.com. **Description:** Provides consulting, remediation, and geotechnical services, principally in the Northeast and the Midwest. The company also maintains its own drilling, laboratory, and instrumentation facilities to support environmental and geotechnical activities. Environmental services range from initial assessment and evaluation of contaminated sites to design, construction, and operation of remediation systems. **Corporate headquarters location:** This Location. **Subsidiaries include:** GZA Drilling, Inc. provides drilling services; and GZA GeoEnvironmental, Inc. provides environmental consulting and geotechnical services. **Number of employees nationwide:** 450.

GABRIEL ENVIRONMENTAL SERVICES
1421 North Elston Avenue, Chicago IL 60622. 773/486-2123. **Contact:** Human Resources. **Description:** Provides environmental consulting, fieldwork, and laboratory services. **Common positions include:** Chemist; Clinical Lab Technician; Environmental Engineer; General Manager; Geographer; Science Technologist; Services Sales Representative; Software Engineer. **Educational backgrounds include:** Chemistry; Engineering; Environmental Science; Geology. **Benefits:** 401(k); Dental Insurance; Medical Insurance. **Special programs:** Internships. **Corporate headquarters location:** This Location.

GENERAL ENGINEERING LABORATORIES
P.O. Box 30712, Charleston SC 29417. 843/553-8171. **Fax:** 843/766-1178. **Recorded jobline:** 843/769-7376x4798. **Contact:** Daisy Hamrick, Human Resources Director. **E-mail address:** dch@

gel.com. **World Wide Web address:** http://www.
gel.net. **Description:** Provides environmental
testing on soil, air, water, and sludge for private
industry and the government. This location also
hires seasonally. Founded in 1981. **NOTE:** Entry-
level positions, part-time jobs, and second and third
shifts are offered. **Common positions include:**
Accountant; Administrative Assistant;
Administrative Manager; Biochemist; Chemical
Engineer; Chemist; Civil Engineer; Computer
Programmer; Computer Support Technician;
Consultant; Controller; Customer Service Rep.;
Database Administrator; Draftsperson;
Environmental Engineer; Geologist/Geophysicist;
Human Resources Manager; Industrial Engineer;
MIS Specialist; Network/Systems Administrator;
Project Manager; Public Relations Specialist;
Quality Control Supervisor; SQL Programmer;
Systems Manager; Typist/Word Processor; Website
Developer. **Educational backgrounds include:**
Biology; C/C++; Chemistry; Engineering; Microsoft
Access; Microsoft Office; SQL. **Benefits:** 401(k);
Casual Dress - Daily; Dental Insurance; Disability
Coverage; Employee Discounts; Flexible Schedule;
Life Insurance; Medical Insurance; Paid Holidays;
Profit Sharing; Relocation Assistance; Sick Days (6
- 10); Vacation Days (10 - 20). **Special programs:**
Internships. **Corporate headquarters location:**
This Location. **Other U.S. locations:** Durham NC.
Listed on: Privately held. **President:** Molly F.
Greene.

GEO-MARINE, INC.
550 East 15th Street, Plano TX 75074. 972/423-
5480. **Contact:** Human Resources. **World
Wide Web address:** http://www.geo-marine.com.
Description: An environmental engineering and
consulting firm.

GEOLABS, INC.
10 Plain Street, Braintree MA 02184. 781/848-7844.
Fax: 781/848-7811. **Contact:** Human Resources. **E-
mail address:** geolabs@mediaone.net. **World
Wide Web address:** http://www.geolabs.com.
Description: Provides analytical environmental
testing of soil, ground water, wastewater, and air.
Founded in 1995. **NOTE:** Entry-level positions are
offered. **Company slogan:** Quick service without
sacrificing. **Common positions include:** Chemist.
Educational backgrounds include: Chemistry.
Benefits: 401(k); Disability Coverage; Life
Insurance; Medical Insurance; Public Transit
Available; Savings Plan; Tuition Assistance.
Special programs: Internships; Training; Co-ops;
Summer Jobs. **Office hours:** Monday - Friday, 8:00
a.m. - 5:00 p.m. **Corporate headquarters location:**
This Location. **Listed on:** Privately held.
President/Owner: David J. Kahler. **Number of
employees at this location:** 20.

GRAEF, ANHALT, SCHLOEMER & ASSOCIATES, INC.
125 South 84th Street, Suite 401, Milwaukee WI
53214-1470. 414/259-1500. **Fax:** 414/259-0037.
Contact: Carrie Warner, Human Resources
Assistant. **World Wide Web address:** http://www.
gasai.com. **Description:** A full-service civil
engineering and consulting firm. Founded in 1961.
NOTE: Entry-level positions are offered. **Common
positions include:** Architect; Civil Engineer;
Design Engineer; Draftsperson; Environmental
Engineer; Industrial Engineer; Landscape Architect.
Educational backgrounds include: Engineering.
Benefits: 401(k); Dental Insurance; Disability
Coverage; Flexible Schedule; Life Insurance;
Medical Insurance; Profit Sharing; Public Transit
Available; Relocation Assistance; Savings Plan;
Tuition Assistance. **Special programs:** Co-ops.
Office hours: Monday - Friday, 8:00 a.m. - 5:00

p.m. **Corporate headquarters location:** This
Location. **Other area locations:** Green Bay WI;
Madison WI. **Other U.S. locations:** Chicago IL.
Number of employees at this location: 175.
Number of employees nationwide: 230.

GREAT LAKES ANALYTICAL
1380 Busch Parkway, Buffalo Grove IL 60089.
847/808-7766. **Fax:** 847/808-7772. **Contact:**
Tanger Dunn, Accounting Manager. **World
Wide Web address:** http://www.glalabs.com.
Description: An analytical laboratory that provides
a full spectrum of environmental analyses on soil,
water, and waste samples. Founded in 1990. **NOTE:**
Entry-level positions, part-time jobs, and
second and third shifts are offered. **Common
positions include:** Account Manager; Account
Representative; Accountant; Administrative
Assistant; Administrative Manager; Buyer; Chemist;
Computer Operator; Credit Manager; Customer
Service Rep.; Department Manager; Laboratory
Technician; Project Manager; Receptionist; Sales
Representative. **Educational backgrounds include:**
Biochemistry; Biology; Chemistry; Geology.
Benefits: 401(k); Dental Insurance; Flexible
Schedule; Medical Insurance. **Special programs:**
Co-ops; Summer Jobs. **Corporate headquarters
location:** This Location. **Other U.S. locations:** AZ;
CA; CO; HI; NV; OR; PA; TX; WA. **Listed on:**
Privately held. **President:** Kevin W. Keeley.

HARDING ESE
8901 North Industrial Road, Peoria IL 61615. **Toll-
free phone:** 800/373-1999. **Fax:** 309/693-5594.
Contact: Karin Hyler, Human Resources Manager.
E-mail address: klhyler@esemail.com. **World
Wide Web address:** http://www.eseworld.com.
Description: An engineering and consulting
company providing environmental and
infrastructure services to commercial and municipal
clients, as well as to state and federal government
agencies. **NOTE:** Entry-level positions and part-
time jobs are offered. **Common positions include:**
Accountant; Administrative Assistant; Architect;
Chemical Engineer; Chemist; Chief Financial
Officer; Civil Engineer; Computer Programmer;
Computer Support Technician; Computer
Technician; Controller; Design Engineer; Desktop
Publishing Specialist; Draftsperson; Environmental
Engineer; Financial Analyst; General Manager;
Geographer; Geologist/Geophysicist; Graphic
Artist; Graphic Designer; Human Resources
Manager; Industrial Engineer; Librarian; Marketing
Manager; Marketing Specialist; Mechanical
Engineer; Network/Systems Administrator; Public
Relations Specialist; Purchasing Agent/Manager;
Statistician; Systems Manager; Technical Writer/
Editor; Typist/Word Processor; Vice President of
Operations; Video Production Coordinator;
Webmaster. **Educational backgrounds include:**
Accounting; Biology; Chemistry; Communications;
Computer Science; Engineering; Marketing;
Mathematics; MBA; MCSE; Microsoft Office;
Microsoft Word; Novell; Public Relations;
QuarkXPress; Software Development; Spreadsheets;
Visual Basic. **Benefits:** 401(k); Adoption
Assistance; Casual Dress - Fridays; Dental
Insurance; Disability Coverage; Employee
Discounts; Flexible Schedule; Life Insurance;
Medical Insurance; Relocation Assistance; Sick
Days; Telecommuting; Tuition Assistance; Vacation
Days. **Special programs:** Internships; Co-ops.
Office hours: Monday - Friday, 8:00 a.m. - 5:00
p.m. **Parent company:** MACTEC, Inc.
President/COO: Karen Jensen.

HART CROWSER
1910 Fairview Avenue East, Seattle WA 98102.
206/324-9530. **Contact:** Human Resources. **World**

Wide Web address: http://www.hartcrowser.com. **Description:** An environmental consulting firm offering site development, remediation, and waste management services. Founded in 1974. **Corporate headquarters location:** This Location. **Other U.S. locations:** AK; CA; CO; IL; NJ; OR.

IT CORPORATION
100 River Ridge Drive, Norwood MA 02062. 781/769-7600. **Contact:** Human Resources. **World Wide Web address:** http://www.itcorporation.com. **Description:** One of the largest environmental consulting, engineering, and remediation firms in the world. IT Corporation develops advanced technologies for the environmental restoration of contaminated sites.

INTERNATIONAL TECHNOLOGY GROUP
2790 Mosside Boulevard, Monroeville PA 15146. 412/372-7701. **Contact:** Ann Harris, Vice President of Human Resources. **Description:** International Technology Group delivers a full range of environmental management services through an integrated approach for total turnkey solutions. The company applies engineering, analytical, remediation, and pollution control expertise to meet the environmental needs of its clients, from site assessment to remediation. **Corporate headquarters location:** This Location.

KTI, INC.
7000 Boulevard East, Guttenberg NJ 07093. 201/854-7777. **Contact:** Office Manager. **Description:** Develops and owns waste-to-energy facilities which provide a means of disposal of nonhazardous municipal solid waste. **Corporate headquarters location:** This Location.

KAISER ENGINEERS
9300 Lee Highway, Fairfax VA 22031. 703/934-3600. **Contact:** Employment Manager. **World Wide Web address:** http://www.icfkaiser.com. **Description:** One of the nation's largest engineering, construction, and program management services companies. Kaiser Engineers provides fully-integrated capabilities to clients worldwide in six related market areas: transportation; alumina/aluminum; mining and minerals; facilities and wastewater; iron and steel; and microelectronics and clean technology. **Corporate headquarters location:** This Location.
Other U.S. locations:
• 2101 Webster Street, Oakland CA 94612. 510/419-6000.

THE KILLAM GROUP, INC.
27 Bleeker Street, Millburn NJ 07041. 973/379-3400. **Toll-free phone:** 800/832-3272. **Fax:** 973/912-3354. **Contact:** Human Resources. **E-mail address:** personnel@killam.com. **World Wide Web address:** http://www.killam.com. **Description:** An infrastructure engineering, environmental, and industrial process consulting firm that services both public and private sectors. The company operates within a wide range of areas providing architectural, environmental, outsourcing, transportation engineering, and water resource management services. **NOTE:** Entry-level positions are offered. **Common positions include:** Account Manager; Account Representative; Accountant; Administrative Assistant; Administrative Manager; Advertising Clerk; Advertising Executive; Architect; Assistant Manager; Attorney; Auditor; Branch Manager; Budget Analyst; Chemical Engineer; Chief Financial Officer; Civil Engineer; Clerical Supervisor; Computer Operator; Computer Programmer; Controller; Database Manager; Design Engineer; Draftsperson; Editorial Assistant; Electrical/Electronics Engineer; Environmental Engineer; Finance Director; Financial Analyst; General Manager; Geologist/Geophysicist; Graphic Artist; Graphic Designer; Human Resources Manager; Industrial Engineer; Internet Services Manager; Librarian; Management Trainee; Marketing Manager; Marketing Specialist; Mechanical Engineer; MIS Specialist; Paralegal; Project Manager; Purchasing Agent/Manager; Quality Control Supervisor; Sales Engineer; Sales Executive; Sales Manager; Sales Representative; Secretary; Software Engineer; Systems Analyst; Systems Manager; Technical Writer/Editor; Transportation/Traffic Specialist; Typist/Word Processor; Vice President; Webmaster. **Educational backgrounds include:** Accounting; Business Administration; Communications; Computer Science; Engineering; Environmental Science; Finance; Geology; Liberal Arts; Marketing; Mathematics; Physics. **Benefits:** 401(k); Dental Insurance; Disability Coverage; Employee Discounts; ESOP; Life Insurance; Medical Insurance; Tuition Assistance. **Special programs:** Internships. **Internship information:** Internships are offered May through September, as well as during December and January. **Corporate headquarters location:** This Location. **Other area locations:** Cape May Court House NJ; Freehold NJ; Hackensack NJ; Randolph NJ; Toms River NJ; Whitehouse NJ. **Other U.S. locations:** Nationwide. **Subsidiaries include:** BAC Killam, Inc.; Carlan Killam Consulting Group, Inc.; E3-Killam, Inc.; Killam Associates - New England; Killam Management & Operational Services, Inc. **Parent company:** Thermo Electron Corporation.

LOCUS TECHNOLOGIES
1333 North California Boulevard, Suite 540, Walnut Creek CA 94596. **Fax:** 925/906-8101. **Contact:** Human Resources. **World Wide Web address:** http://www.locustec.com. **Description:** Performs environmental consulting, engineering, and remediation services. **NOTE:** Candidates should send a resume with salary requirements and references. **Corporate headquarters location:** This Location. **Other U.S. locations:** El Segundo CA; Mountain View CA; Newark CA. **Listed on:** Privately held.

MSE, INC.
220 North Alaska, P.O. Box 4078, Butte MT 59702. 406/723-8213. **Fax:** 406/723-8328. **Contact:** Human Resources. **Description:** Provides technology development, demonstration, and fabrication services to government agencies. The company operates within a variety of areas including plasma-based systems for the treatment of hazardous materials and waste; civil engineering design and project management; biological treatment; thermal spraying technologies; and specialized technology development and research services. **Common positions include:** Accountant; Administrative Manager; Aerospace Engineer; Biological Scientist; Blue-Collar Worker Supervisor; Branch Manager; Buyer; Chemical Engineer; Chemist; Civil Engineer; Clerical Supervisor; Computer Programmer; Designer; Draftsperson; Electrical/Electronics Engineer; Electrician; Environmental Engineer; Financial Analyst; General Manager; Geologist/Geophysicist; Human Resources Manager; Librarian; Marketing Specialist; Materials Engineer; Mathematician; Mechanical Engineer; Metallurgical Engineer; Mining Engineer; Petroleum Engineer; Process Engineer; Purchasing Agent/Manager; Quality Control Supervisor; Registered Nurse; Safety Engineer; Safety Specialist; Systems Analyst; Technical Writer/Editor. **Educational backgrounds include:** Accounting; Biology; Business Administration; Chemistry; Communications;

Computer Science; Engineering; Finance; Geology; Mathematics; Science. **Benefits:** 401(k); Dental Insurance; Disability Coverage; Life Insurance; Medical Insurance; Pension Plan; Savings Plan; Spending Account; Tuition Assistance. **Special programs:** Internships. **Corporate headquarters location:** This Location. **Other U.S. locations:** Grand Junction CO; Boise ID; Idaho Falls ID; Billings MT; Bozeman MT; Helena MT; Miles City MT; Albany NY; Sheridan WY.

META ENVIRONMENTAL, INC.
49 Clarendon Street, Watertown MA 02472. 617/923-4662. **Fax:** 617/923-4610. **Contact:** Personnel. **Description:** An environmental engineering firm. This location also houses a research laboratory. **NOTE:** Entry-level positions are offered. **Common positions include:** Chemical Engineer; Chemist; Controller; Environmental Engineer; Geologist/Geophysicist; Marketing Manager. **Educational backgrounds include:** Chemistry; Engineering; Geology. **Benefits:** 401(k); Dental Insurance; Life Insurance; Medical Insurance; Tuition Assistance. **Special programs:** Co-ops. **Corporate headquarters location:** This Location.

METCALF & EDDY, INC.
30 Harvard Mill Square, P.O. Box 4071, Wakefield MA 01880. 781/246-5200. **Contact:** Human Resources. **World Wide Web address:** http://www. m-e.com. **Description:** An environmental engineering firm offering professional consulting services for water, wastewater, hazardous waste, and landfills. Metcalf & Eddy, Inc. specializes in design engineering. The firm's projects include wastewater treatment facilities, waterworks projects, industrial and hazardous waste treatment, environmental modeling, and solid waste treatment. **Common positions include:** Chemical Engineer; Civil Engineer; Environmental Engineer; Geologist/ Geophysicist. **Educational backgrounds include:** Chemistry; Engineering; Geology. **Benefits:** 401(k); Dental Insurance; Disability Coverage; Life Insurance; Medical Insurance; Profit Sharing; Tuition Assistance. **Corporate headquarters location:** This Location. **Other U.S. locations:** Itasca IL; Holbrook MA. **Parent company:** CGE (France). **Listed on:** NASDAQ.

METRO WASTEWATER RECLAMATION DISTRICT
6450 York Street, Denver CO 80229. 303/286-3000. **Fax:** 303/286-3034. **Contact:** Beverly Bishop, Human Resources Analyst. **World Wide Web address:** http://www.metrowastewater.com. **Description:** A wastewater treatment facility.

MONTGOMERY WATSON
300 North Lake Avenue, Suite 1200, Pasadena CA 91101. 626/796-9141. **Contact:** Corporate Human Resources. **Description:** Offers engineering consulting services for water, wastewater, and hazardous waste facilities. **Common positions include:** Accountant; Architect; Chemist; Civil Engineer; Computer Programmer; Draftsperson; Electrical/Electronics Engineer; Environmental Engineer; Hydrogeologist; Mechanical Engineer; Microbiologist; Sanitary Engineer; Software Engineer; Structural Engineer. **Educational backgrounds include:** Accounting; Business Administration; Chemistry; Computer Science; Engineering; Geology. **Benefits:** 401(k); Credit Union; Dental Insurance; Disability Coverage; Life Insurance; Medical Insurance; Pension Plan; Profit Sharing; Tuition Assistance; Vision Insurance. **Special programs:** Internships. **Corporate headquarters location:** This Location. **Other U.S. locations:** Nationwide. **Listed on:** Privately held.

MORETRENCH AMERICAN CORP.
P.O. Box 316, 100 Stickle Avenue, Rockaway NJ 07866. 973/627-2100. **Fax:** 973/624-3950. **Contact:** Personnel. **World Wide Web address:** http://www.moretrench.com. **Description:** An engineering and contracting firm specializing in groundwater control and hazardous waste removal. **Common positions include:** Accountant; Civil Engineer; Draftsperson; Geologist/Geophysicist; Human Resources Manager; Purchasing Agent/ Manager; Sales Executive. **Educational backgrounds include:** Engineering. **Benefits:** Disability Coverage; Life Insurance; Medical Insurance; Pension Plan; Profit Sharing; Tuition Assistance. **Corporate headquarters location:** This Location.

MORRISON KNUDSEN CORPORATION
P.O. Box 73, Boise ID 83729. 208/386-5000. **Fax:** 208/386-6425. **Recorded jobline:** 208/386-6966. **Contact:** Stacie L. Farnham, Human Resources Specialist/Recruiter. **E-mail address:** stacie-farnham@mk.com. **World Wide Web address:** http://www.mk.com. **Description:** Provides construction, engineering, environmental, and mining services. The company works through four major divisions: Engineering & Construction Group, Environmental/Government Group, Heavy Civil Construction Group, and the Mining Group. Founded in 1912. **NOTE:** Entry-level positions are offered. **Common positions include:** Accountant; Architect; Biological Scientist; Chemical Engineer; Civil Engineer; Electrical/Electronics Engineer; Environmental Engineer; Financial Analyst; Geologist/Geophysicist; Human Resources Manager; Industrial Engineer; Mechanical Engineer; Operations Manager; Project Manager; Quality Control Supervisor. **Educational backgrounds include:** Accounting; Economics; Engineering. **Benefits:** 401(k); Dental Insurance; Disability Coverage; Life Insurance; Medical Insurance; Tuition Assistance. **Special programs:** Internships; Co-ops; Summer Jobs. **Corporate headquarters location:** This Location. **Other U.S. locations:** San Francisco CA; Denver CO; Cleveland OH; San Antonio TX. **International locations:** Worldwide.

NSC CORPORATION
40 Lydecker Street, Nyack NY 10960. 914/727-8300. **Contact:** Human Resources. **World Wide Web address:** http://www.nsc-corp.com. **Description:** An environmental services firm that specializes in asbestos and lead abatement. The company also provides removal services for other hazardous materials and low-level radiation materials. **Corporate headquarters location:** This Location. **Subsidiaries include:** National Surface Cleaning.

NORCAL WASTE SYSTEMS INC.
160 Pacific Avenue, Suite 200, San Francisco CA 94111. 415/875-1000. **Fax:** 415/875-1217. **Contact:** Human Resources. **World Wide Web address:** http://www.norcalwaste.com. **Description:** Engaged in waste management and recycling services. **Corporate headquarters location:** This Location.

NUCLEAR FUEL SERVICE
1205 Banner Hill Road, Erwin TN 37650. 423/743-9141. **Contact:** Human Resources. **World Wide Web address:** http://www.atnfs.com. **Description:** Provides advanced nuclear technology and manufacturing services to both government and commercial clients. Founded in 1961. **Common positions include:** Accountant; Chemical Engineer; Chemist; Computer Programmer; Environmental Engineer; Geologist/Geophysicist; Industrial Engineer; Mechanical Engineer; Metallurgical

Engineer; Process Engineer; Quality Assurance Engineer; Statistician. **Educational backgrounds include:** Chemistry; Engineering. **Benefits:** 401(k); Casual Dress - Daily; Dental Insurance; Flexible Schedule; Life Insurance; Medical Insurance; Pension Plan; Relocation Assistance; Tuition Assistance. **Office hours:** Monday - Friday, 8:00 a.m. - 5:00 p.m. **Listed on:** Privately held. **Number of employees at this location:** 500.

OGDEN CORPORATION
2 Pennsylvania Plaza, New York NY 10121. **Contact:** Human Resources. **World Wide Web address:** http://www.ogdencorp.com. **Description:** A diversified company with interests in management, waste disposal and wastewater services, food services, and entertainment. The company offers engineering, consultation, catering, promotion, management, and asbestos abatement services for clients in the airline, government, and finance. Ogden Corporation also operates waste-to-energy plants nationwide. **Corporate headquarters location:** This Location.

PAI CORPORATION
116 Milan Way, Oak Ridge TN 37830. 865/483-0666. **Fax:** 865/481-0003. **Contact:** Office Manager. **Description:** This location provides technical and environmental support services to the Department of Energy; engineering, environmental, research, and development services to Lockheed Martin Energy Systems, Inc.; and environmental restoration and management support to DOE/OR through Jacobs Engineering Group. Overall, PAI Corporation provides services to commercial and government programs that require expertise in science, technology, and regulations. **Corporate headquarters location:** This Location. **Other U.S. locations:** Livermore CA; Paducah KY; St. Charles MO; Albuquerque NM; Las Vegas NV; Aiken SC; Richland WA.

PARSONS CORPORATION
100 West Walnut Street, Pasadena CA 91124. 626/440-2000. **Fax:** 626/440-2630. **Contact:** Staffing Department. **World Wide Web address:** http://www.parsons.com. **Description:** This location is an environmental engineering firm that provides consulting, design, construction, and program management services. Overall, Parsons Corporation provides engineering, planning, design, project management, and related services for a variety of projects including rail systems, highways, bridges, hazardous waste management, aviation facilities, environmental engineering, resorts, power generation and delivery systems, natural resources development, defense systems, industrial and institutional facilities, and community planning and development. **NOTE:** All jobseekers should express a geographic preference when applying for a position. **Common positions include:** Biological Scientist; Chemical Engineer; Civil Engineer; Environmental Engineer; Geologist/Geophysicist. **Educational backgrounds include:** Biology; Chemistry; Engineering; Geology. **Benefits:** 401(k); Dental Insurance; Disability Coverage; Employee Discounts; Life Insurance; Medical Insurance; Tuition Assistance. **Corporate headquarters location:** This Location. **Other U.S. locations:** Nationwide.

RADIAN INTERNATIONAL
P.O. Box 201088, Austin TX 78720-1088. 512/454-4797. **Contact:** Human Resources. **World Wide Web address:** http://www.radian.com. **Description:** This location is involved in scientific research and development. Overall, Radian International offers a full range of services including regulatory compliance support, site investigation and remediation, air pollution control, VOC and air toxins control, biotreatment, waste management, ambient and source monitoring, risk management, information management, project chemistry, specialty chemicals, remote sensing services, materials and machinery analysis, and electronic services. Founded in 1969. **Corporate headquarters location:** This Location. **Parent company:** Dames & Moore Group.

RADIAN INTERNATIONAL
1979 Lakeside Parkway, Suite 800, Tucker GA 30084. 770/414-4522. **Contact:** Human Resources. **World Wide Web address:** http://www.radian.com. **Description:** Provides regulatory compliance support, site investigation and remediation, air pollution controls, VOC and air toxins control, biotreatment, waste management, ambient and source monitoring, risk management, information management, project chemistry, specialty chemicals, remote sensing services, materials and machinery analysis, and electronic services. **Corporate headquarters location:** Austin TX. **Parent company:** Dames & Moore Group.

RANSOM ENVIRONMENTAL CONSULTANTS
Brown's Wharf, Newburyport MA 01950. 978/465-1822. **Fax:** 978/465-2986. **Contact:** Human Resources. **World Wide Web address:** http://www.ransomenv.com. **Description:** An environmental consulting firm specializing in remediation design and environmental risk assessment. **Corporate headquarters location:** This Location. **Other U.S. locations:** Bristol RI.

REPUBLIC INDUSTRIES
2343 Alexandria Drive, Suite 400, Lexington KY 40504. 606/223-3824. **Contact:** Human Resources. **Description:** Engaged in waste collection, recycling, and disposal, as well as mining. **Common positions include:** Accountant/Auditor; Chemist; Construction Contractor; Operations/Production Manager. **Educational backgrounds include:** Accounting; Business Administration; Chemistry; Engineering. **Benefits:** 401(k); Life Insurance; Medical Insurance. **Corporate headquarters location:** This Location.

RIZZO ASSOCIATES, INC.
235 West Central Street, Natick MA 01760. 508/903-2401. **Fax:** 508/903-2001. **Contact:** Human Resources. **E-mail address:** hr@rizzo.com. **World Wide Web address:** http://www.rizzo.com. **Description:** An engineering and environmental consulting firm. **NOTE:** Entry-level positions and part-time jobs are offered. **Common positions include:** Chemical Engineer; Civil Engineer; Design Engineer; Draftsperson; Environmental Engineer; Mechanical Engineer; Technical Writer/Editor. **Educational backgrounds include:** Biology; Engineering; Geology. **Benefits:** 401(k); Casual Dress - Fridays; Dental Insurance; Disability Coverage; ESOP; Flexible Schedule; Life Insurance; Medical Insurance; On-Site Daycare; Sick Days (6 - 10); Tuition Assistance. **Special programs:** Internships; Co-ops. **Office hours:** Monday - Friday, 9:00 a.m. - 5:30 p.m. **Listed on:** Privately held. **Annual sales/revenues:** $21 - $50 million.

RUST CONSTRUCTORS, INC.
RAYTHEON ENGINEERS & CONSTRUCTORS
100 Corporate Parkway, Birmingham AL 35242-2928. 205/995-3540. **Fax:** 205/995-6691. **Contact:** Edward Wick, Human Resources Manager. **E-mail address:** edward_wick@rec.raytheon.com. **World Wide Web address:** http://www.rayjobs.com. **Description:** Sells and manages industrial maintenance contracts. Raytheon Engineers & Constructors (also at this location, 205/995-7878) is

an environmental and industrial consulting engineering firm offering scientific services in the areas of solid waste, hazardous waste, wastewater, and water resources. The company's construction projects include industrial plants, pulp and paper mills, steel mills, chemical plants, and other energy-related construction projects. Founded in 1905. **NOTE:** Entry-level positions are offered. **Common positions include:** Accountant; Administrative Assistant; Administrative Manager; Assistant Manager; Blue-Collar Worker Supervisor; Buyer; Civil Engineer; Claim Rep.; Computer Operator; Computer Programmer; Computer Support Technician; Computer Technician; Construction Contractor; Controller; Cost Estimator; Customer Service Rep.; Design Engineer; Electrical/ Electronics Engineer; Electrician; Environmental Engineer; General Manager; Human Resources Manager; Mechanical Engineer; Operations Manager; Project Manager; Quality Assurance Engineer; Quality Control Supervisor; Sales Executive; Sales Manager; Sales Rep.; Secretary; Typist/Word Processor. **Educational backgrounds include:** Accounting; Business Administration; Chemistry; Computer Science; Engineering; Finance; Marketing; Mathematics; MBA; Microsoft Office; Physics. **Benefits:** 401(k); Casual Dress - Daily; Dental Insurance; Employee Discounts; Life Insurance; Medical Insurance; Pension Plan; Relocation Assistance; Tuition Assistance. **Special programs:** Apprenticeships; Training; Co-ops. **Office hours:** Monday - Friday, 7:30 a.m. - 4:30 p.m. **Corporate headquarters location:** Lexington MA. **Other U.S. locations:** Nationwide. **International locations:** Worldwide. **Parent company:** Raytheon Company.

SEVENSON ENVIRONMENTAL SERVICES
2749 Lockport Road, Niagara Falls NY 14305-0396. 716/284-0431. **Contact:** Paul Hitcho, Human Resources. **World Wide Web address:** http://www. sevenson.com. **Description:** Provides a range of services for the remediation of sites and facilities contaminated by hazardous materials. **Corporate headquarters location:** This Location. **Other U.S. locations:** Munster IN; Livingston LA; Chadds Ford PA; Delmont PA. **Subsidiaries include:** Sevenson Environmental, Ltd. (also at this location); Sevenson Industrial Services, Inc. (also at this location); Waste Stream Technology Inc.

SHANNON & WILSON
P.O. Box 300303, Seattle WA 98103. 206/632-8020. **Physical address:** 400 North 34th Street, Suite 100, Seattle WA. **Contact:** Human Resources. **World Wide Web address:** http://www. shannonwilson.com. **Description:** Provides geotechnical consulting services to a variety of industrial and government clients. Services include foundation engineering studies, waste management, and construction monitoring. **Corporate headquarters location:** This Location.

TEAM INDUSTRIAL SERVICES, INC.
P.O. Box 123, Alvin TX 77512. 281/331-6154. **Contact:** Human Resources. **World Wide Web address:** http://www.teamindustrialservices.com. **Description:** Provides a wide variety of environmental services for industrial corporations including consulting, engineering, monitoring, and leak repair. **Common positions include:** Account Rep.; Administrative Assistant; AS400 Programmer Analyst; Computer Programmer; Design Engineer; Draftsperson; Industrial Engineer; Secretary. **Educational backgrounds include:** Industrial Design. **Benefits:** 401(k); Casual Dress - Fridays; Dental Insurance; Disability Coverage; Life Insurance; Medical Insurance; Vacation Pay. **Corporate headquarters location:** This Location.

TELLUS INSTITUTE
11 Arlington Street, Boston MA 02116. **Contact:** Human Resources. **World Wide Web address:** http://www.tellus.org. **Description:** An environmental research and consulting agency. Much of the Tellus Institute's work is under government contract in the fields of energy, gas, and solid waste. **Corporate headquarters location:** This Location.

TEST AMERICA
850 West Bartlett Road, Bartlett IL 60103. 630/289-7333. **Contact:** Human Resources Manager. **Description:** Performs testing of wastewater, hazardous waste, and food. **Corporate headquarters location:** This Location.

TETRA TECH, INC.
670 North Rosemead Boulevard, Pasadena CA 91107-2101. 626/351-4664. **Fax:** 626/351-8808. **Contact:** Rachel Breitbach, Human Resources Manager. **E-mail address:** jobs@tetratech.com. **World Wide Web address:** http://www. tetratech.com. **Description:** Provides specialized management consulting and technical services in resource management, infrastructure, and communications. **NOTE:** Entry-level positions and part-time jobs are offered. **Common positions include:** Accountant; Administrative Assistant; Architect; Chemical Engineer; Chief Financial Officer; Civil Engineer; Computer Programmer; Controller; Design Engineer; Environmental Engineer; Financial Analyst; Geologist/ Geophysicist; Human Resources Manager; Landscape Architect; Marketing Specialist; Network/Systems Administrator; Project Manager; Secretary; Systems Analyst; Systems Manager; Website Developer. **Educational backgrounds include:** Accounting; C/C++; Engineering; Java; MCSE; Microsoft Office; Microsoft Word; Science; SQL; Visual Basic. **Benefits:** 401(k); Dental Insurance; Disability Coverage; Flexible Schedule; Life Insurance; Medical Insurance; Savings Plan; Tuition Assistance. **Office hours:** Monday - Friday, 8:00 a.m. - 5:00 p.m. **Corporate headquarters location:** This Location. **Other U.S. locations:** Nationwide. **Subsidiaries include:** Environmental Management, Inc.; FLO Engineering; HSI GeoTrans; IWA Engineers; KCM Inc.; Simons, Li & Associates.

THERMO INSTRUMENT SYSTEMS
P.O. Box 2108, Santa Fe NM 87504-2108. 505/438-3171. **Fax:** 505/473-9221. **Contact:** Human Resources. **Description:** Designs, manufactures, and markets advanced analytical and monitoring instruments used to detect and measure radioactivity, air pollution, toxic metals, chemical compounds, and other substances. The company also provides specialized environmental and radiochemical analysis and environmental science/ engineering services. **Corporate headquarters location:** This Location.

URS CORPORATION
911 Wilshire Boulevard, Suite 800, Los Angeles CA 90017. 213/683-0471. **Fax:** 213/996-2458. **Contact:** Personnel. **World Wide Web address:** http://www.urscorp.com. **Description:** An architectural, engineering, and environmental consulting firm that specializes in air transportation, environmental solutions, surface transportation, and industrial environmental and engineering concerns. **Corporate headquarters location:** San Francisco CA.
Other U.S. locations:
• 4582 South Ulster Street, Stanford Place Three, Suite 600, Denver CO 80237. 303/740-2600.

USA BIOMASS CORPORATION
7314 Scout Avenue, Bell Gardens CA 90201. 562/928-9900. **Contact:** Human Resources. **World Wide Web address:** http://www.usabiomass.com. **Description:** This location houses administrative offices. Overall, USA Biomass provides waste removal services primarily for greenery and shrubbery. **Common positions include:** Accountant/Auditor; Administrative Manager; Clerical Supervisor; Typist/Word Processor. **Educational backgrounds include:** Accounting; Agricultural Science; Business Administration. **Benefits:** Dental Insurance; Medical Insurance. **Corporate headquarters location:** This Location. **Operations at this facility include:** Administration. **Annual sales/revenues:** $11 - $20 million. **Number of employees at this location:** 10.

UXB INTERNATIONAL, INC.
21641 Beaumeade Circle, Suite 301, Ashburn VA 20147. 703/724-9600. **Contact:** Human Resources. **World Wide Web address:** http://www.uxb.com. **Description:** Provides ordnance and explosive waste services for the United States Army. The company specializes in chemical warfare identification, recovery, and disposal; extraction and transportation of reactive materials; geophysical studies; metal detection; seismic refraction; and humanitarian remining. **Corporate headquarters location:** This Location.

UNITED WASTE SERVICE CENTER
1300A Bay Area Boulevard, Houston TX 77058. 281/282-6000. **Contact:** Human Resources. **Description:** United Waste Service Center provides integrated solid waste management services to commercial, industrial, and residential customers. These services include nonhazardous landfill operations, waste collection services, waste reuse and reduction programs (such as composting and recycling), and related environmental services. Fourteen nonhazardous landfill locations are currently in operation, as well as 11 waste collection companies serving over 215,000 customers and operating 16 waste transfer stations. United Waste Service Center also owns and operates several facilities with waste reuse and reduction programs including four composting facilities. **Benefits:** Medical Insurance; Pension Plan; Profit Sharing. **Corporate headquarters location:** This Location. **Other U.S. locations:** KY; MA; MI; MS; PA. **Number of employees nationwide:** 825.

WTE CORPORATION
7 Alfred Circle, Bedford MA 01730. 781/275-6400. **Contact:** Human Resources. **World Wide Web address:** http://www.wte.com. **Description:** Recycles plastics and metals. **Corporate headquarters location:** This Location.

WAID AND ASSOCIATES
14205 Burnet Road, Suite 500, Austin TX 78728. 512/255-9999. **Fax:** 512/255-8780. **Contact:** Personnel. **E-mail address:** waid@waid.com. **World Wide Web address:** http://www.waid.com. **Description:** An engineering and environmental services company. Services include air quality consulting, waste management, and wastewater management. **Corporate headquarters location:** This Location. **Number of employees at this location:** 35.

WASTE MANAGEMENT, INC.
1001 Fannin Street, Suite 4000, Houston TX 77002. 713/512-6200. **Contact:** Human Resources. **World Wide Web address:** http://www.wm.com. **Description:** An international provider of comprehensive waste management services as well as engineering, construction, industrial, and related services. **Corporate headquarters location:** This Location.
Other U.S. locations:
- 720 East Butterfield Road, Lombard IL 60148. 630/572-8800.

WESTERN TECHNOLOGIES, INC.
P.O. Box 21387, Phoenix AZ 85036. 602/437-3737. **Fax:** 602/437-8897. **Contact:** Susan Allanson, Director of Human Resources. **Description:** Provides engineering, consulting, and testing of environmental, geotechnical, and construction materials. Environmental services include site assessments, investigations, feasibility studies, problem solving, and remedial services. Geotechnical services are provided with use of a wide variety of exploration equipment including highly-mobile drilling rigs. Materials Engineering and Testing provides analysis and quality assurance of materials and methods for clients. Materials Research develops methods of improving the strength and durability of conventional construction materials through research into the feasibility of using waste and less expensive or more available materials. Construction Quality Control provides interpretation of geotechnical reports, observation and testing of reinforced steel and concrete, visual and nondestructive evaluation of bolted and welded structural steel components, preparing concrete and asphalt mix designs, as well as sampling and testing many other architectural and structural components. Founded in 1955. **Company slogan:** The quality people. **Common positions include:** Civil Engineer; Environmental Engineer; Geologist/ Geophysicist; Project Manager. **Educational backgrounds include:** Engineering; Geology. **Benefits:** 401(k); Dental Insurance; Disability Coverage; Life Insurance; Medical Insurance; Tuition Assistance. **Corporate headquarters location:** This Location. **Listed on:** Privately held.

For more information on career opportunities in environmental and waste management services:

Associations

AIR & WASTE MANAGEMENT ASSOCIATION
One Gateway Center, 3rd Floor, Pittsburgh PA 15222. 412/232-3444. E-mail address: info@awma.org. World Wide Web address: http://www.awma.org. A nonprofit, technical and educational organization providing a neutral forum where all points of view regarding environmental management issues can be addressed.

AMERICAN ACADEMY OF ENVIRONMENTAL ENGINEERS
130 Holiday Court, Suite 100, Annapolis MD 21401. 410/266-3311. World Wide Web address:

http://www.aaee.net. Publishes *Environmental Engineer*, a quarterly magazine addressing policies and technical issues.

ENVIRONMENTAL INDUSTRY ASSOCIATIONS
4301 Connecticut Avenue NW, Suite 300, Washington DC 20008. 202/244-4700. World Wide Web address: http://www.envasns.org.

INSTITUTE OF CLEAN AIR COMPANIES
1660 L Street NW, Suite 1100, Washington DC 20036. 202/457-0911. World Wide Web address: http://www.icac.com. A national association of companies involved in stationary source air pollution control.

WATER ENVIRONMENT FEDERATION
601 Wythe Street, Alexandria VA 22314. 703/684-
2452. World Wide Web address: http://www.
wef.org.

Magazines

**JOURNAL OF THE AIR & WASTE
MANAGEMENT ASSOCIATION**
One Gateway Center, 3rd Floor, Pittsburgh PA
15222. 412/232-3444. Toll-free phone: 800/275-
5851. World Wide Web address: http://www.
awma.org.

Newsletters

**SOLID WASTE DIGEST
SOLID WASTE MARKET: REVIEW, TRENDS,
& FORECAST**
Chartwell Information Publishers, 805 Cameron
Street, Alexandria VA 22314. 703/519-3630. Fax:
703/519-7881. World Wide Web address:
http://www.wasteinfo.com.

Online Services

ECOLOGIC
World Wide Web address: http://www.eng.rpi.
edu/dept/union/pugwash/ecojobs.htm. This Website
provides links to a variety of environmental job
resources. This site is run by the Rensselaer Student
Pugwash.

**ENVIRONMENTAL JOBS SEARCH
PAGE/UBIQUITY**
World Wide Web address: http://ourworld.
compuserve.com/homepages/ubikk/env4.htm. This
Website includes internships, tips, and links to other
databases of environmental job openings.

**INTERNATIONAL & ENVIRONMENTAL JOB
BULLETINS**
World Wide Web address: http://www.sas.
upenn.edu/African_Studies/Publications/Internation
al_Environmental_16621.html. Provides a wealth of
information on bulletins, magazines, and resources
for jobseekers who are looking to get into the
environmental field. Most of these resources are on
a subscription basis and provide job openings and
other information. This information was compiled
by Dennis F. Desmond.

**LINKS TO SOURCES OF INFORMATION ON
ENVIRONMENTAL JOBS**
World Wide Web address: http://www.utexas.
edu/ftp/student/scb/joblinks.html. Provides links to
numerous sites that offer job openings and
information in the environmental field. The site is
run by the University of Texas at Austin.

WATER ENVIRONMENT WEB
World Wide Web address: http://www.wef.org. A
service of the Water Environment Federation.

Financial Services

You can expect to find the following types of companies in this chapter:
*Consumer Finance and Credit Agencies • Investment Specialists • Mortgage Bankers and
Loan Brokers • Security and Commodity Brokers, Dealers, and Exchanges*

Some helpful information: *Salary depends heavily on a broker's production and
experience in the field. Average compensation for experienced brokers and financial
managers ranges between $40,000 and $100,000, depending on the size of the firm. Many
successful brokers earn considerably more. The average salary for junior stock and
research analysts can be as high as $70,000 if the candidate has an M.B.A. and a bit of
experience, and senior analysts and managing directors can earn over $150,000 annually.*

AAMES FINANCIAL CORPORATION
3731 Wilshire Boulevard, Suite 630, Los Angeles
CA 90010. 213/388-9044. **Toll-free phone:**
800/851-8538. **Contact:** Human Resources. **World
Wide Web address:** http://www.
aamesfinancial.com. **Description:** Offers mortgage
loans to homeowners. Aames Financial Corporation
also functions as an insurance agent and mortgage
trustee through some of its subsidiaries. Services
include originating (brokering and funding),
purchasing, selling, and servicing first and junior
trust deed loans primarily for single-family
residences in the western United States. **NOTE:**
Please send resumes to Human Resources, 350
South Grand Avenue, 51st Floor, Los Angeles CA
90071. 323/210-5300. **Corporate headquarters
location:** This Location. **Other U.S. locations:** CO;
NV.

THE ACACIA GROUP
7315 Wisconsin Avenue, Bethesda MD 20814.
301/280-1000. **Contact:** Karen Mayo, Manager of
Recruitment. **World Wide Web address:**
http://www.acaciagroup.com. **Description:** Provides
diversified financial services through its operating
companies. **Common positions include:**
Accountant; Actuary; Attorney; Bank Officer/
Manager; Branch Manager; Brokerage Clerk; Claim
Rep.; Customer Service Rep.; Financial Analyst;
Human Resources Manager; Insurance Agent/
Broker; Paralegal; Securities Sales Rep.; Systems
Analyst. **Educational backgrounds include:**
Accounting; Business Administration; Finance;
Liberal Arts; Marketing. **Benefits:** 401(k); Daycare
Assistance; Dental Insurance; Disability Coverage;
Employee Discounts; Job Sharing; Life Insurance;
Medical Insurance; Profit Sharing; Public Transit
Available; Telecommuting; Tuition Assistance.
Corporate headquarters location: This Location.
Subsidiaries include: Acacia Life and Acacia
National Life offer life insurance policies. The
Advisors Group provides investment management
services. The Calvert Group, Ltd. offers mutual fund
management services. Acacia Federal Savings Bank
provides traditional savings and loan services.
Parent company: Ameritas Acacia Mutual Holding
Company.

THE ADVEST GROUP, INC.
90 State House Square, Hartford CT 06103.
860/509-1000. **Contact:** Human Resources. **World
Wide Web address:** http://www.advest.com.
Description: Provides diversified financial services
including securities brokerage, trading, investment
banking, commercial and consumer lending, and
asset management. **Benefits:** 401(k); Incentive Plan;
Retirement Plan; Savings Plan; Stock Option; Thrift
Plan. **Corporate headquarters location:** This
Location. **Subsidiaries include:** Advest, Inc. is a

regional broker/dealer providing investment
services to a primarily retail client base, with offices
in 17 states and the District of Columbia. Advest
Bank is a Connecticut-chartered savings bank
offering lending, deposit, and trust services to
individuals, businesses, and institutions. Boston
Security Counselors is an investment management
company that serves private clients and handles the
proprietary mutual funds of The Advest Group, Inc.
Billings & Company specializes in private
placement offerings, primarily in real estate.
Financial Institutions Group is a financial
consulting firm that specializes in the banking and
thrift industry. **Listed on:** New York Stock
Exchange.

AFCO CREDIT CORPORATION
525 Washington Boulevard, Jersey City NJ 07310.
201/876-6600. **Contact:** Human Resources.
Description: Finances insurance premiums,
primarily for commercial policies. **Common
positions include:** Branch Manager; Clerical
Supervisor; Computer Programmer; Credit
Manager; Financial Analyst; Systems Analyst;
Underwriter/Assistant Underwriter. **Educational
backgrounds include:** Business Administration;
Liberal Arts; Marketing. **Benefits:** 401(k);
Disability Coverage; Life Insurance; Medical
Insurance; Pension Plan; Public Transit Available;
Tuition Assistance. **Corporate headquarters
location:** This Location. **Other U.S. locations:**
Nationwide. **Parent company:** Mellon Financial
Corporation. **Listed on:** New York Stock Exchange.

ALLIANCE MORTGAGE COMPANY
8100 Nations Way, Jacksonville FL 32256.
904/281-6000. **Fax:** 904/281-6165. **Contact:**
Staffing Specialist, Human Resources Department.
Description: Engaged in the origination, purchase,
sale, and servicing of residential first mortgages.
Common positions include: Accountant/Auditor;
Clerical Supervisor; Customer Service Rep.; Loan
Officer; Loan Processor. **Educational backgrounds
include:** Business Administration; Finance; Liberal
Arts. **Benefits:** 401(k); Dental Insurance; Disability
Coverage; Life Insurance; Medical Insurance; Profit
Sharing; Tuition Assistance. **Corporate
headquarters location:** This Location.

AMERICAN APPRAISAL ASSOCIATION
411 East Wisconsin Avenue, Suite 1900, Milwaukee
WI 53202. 414/271-7240. **Contact:** Nannette
Wellstein, Human Resources Manager.
Description: An international valuation consulting
organization specializing in tangible and intangible
assets; closely held securities; insurance services;
and merger, acquisition, and investment services.
Common positions include: Financial Analyst;
Real Estate Appraiser. **Educational backgrounds**

include: Accounting; Business Administration; Economics; Engineering; Finance. **Benefits:** 401(k); Dental Insurance; Disability Coverage; Life Insurance; Medical Insurance; Savings Plan; Tuition Assistance. **Corporate headquarters location:** This Location.

AMERICAN CENTURION LIFE ASSURANCE
P.O. Box 5550, Albany NY 12205. **Toll-free phone:** 800/633-3565. **Fax:** 518/452-3857. **Contact:** Human Resources. **Description:** Administers annuity products. **Office hours:** Monday - Friday, 8:00 a.m. - 4:30 p.m. **COO:** Maureen Buckley.

AMERICAN EXPRESS COMPANY
American Express Tower C, 3 World Financial Center, 200 Vesey Street, New York NY 10285. 212/640-2000. **Contact:** Staffing Department. **World Wide Web address:** http://www. americanexpress.com. **Description:** A diversified travel and financial services company. Founded in 1850. **Common positions include:** Administrative Assistant; Administrative Manager; Assistant Manager; Computer Programmer; Database Manager; Economist; Financial Analyst; Graphic Artist; Human Resources Manager; Industrial Engineer; Market Research Analyst; Marketing Manager; Marketing Specialist; MIS Specialist; Multimedia Designer; Online Content Specialist; Operations Manager; Public Relations Specialist; Purchasing Agent/Manager; Quality Control Supervisor; Software Engineer; Statistician; Typist/ Word Processor. **Educational backgrounds include:** Economics; Engineering; Finance; Liberal Arts; Marketing; Mathematics. **Benefits:** 401(k); Dental Insurance; Disability Coverage; Life Insurance; Medical Insurance; Tuition Assistance. **Corporate headquarters location:** This Location. **Other U.S. locations:** Nationwide. **International locations:** Worldwide. **Subsidiaries include:** American Express Travel Related Services offers consumers the Personal, Gold, and Platinum Cards, as well as revolving credit products such as Optima Cards, which allow customers to extend payments. Other products include the American Express Corporate Card, which helps businesses manage their travel and entertainment expenditures; and the Corporate Purchasing Card, which helps businesses manage their expenditures on supplies, equipment, and services. American Express Travel Related Services also offers American Express Traveler's Cheques and travel services including trip planning, reservations, ticketing, and management information. American Express Financial Advisors provides a variety of financial products and services to help individuals, businesses, and institutions meet their financial goals. American Express Financial Advisors has a staff of more than 8,000 in the United States and offers products and services that include financial planning; annuities; mutual funds; insurance; investment certificates; and institutional investment advisory trust, tax preparation, and retail securities brokerage services.

AMERICAN EXPRESS FINANCIAL ADVISORS
200 Bellevue Parkway, Suite 250, Wilmington DE 19809. 302/798-3199. **Contact:** Human Resources. **World Wide Web address:** http://www. americanexpress.com. **Description:** Provides a variety of financial products and services to help individuals, businesses, and institutions establish and achieve their financial goals. American Express Financial Advisors has a field of more than 8,000 financial advisors in the United States and offers financial planning, annuities, mutual funds, insurance, investment certificates. Other services include institutional investment advisory trust, tax preparation, and retail securities brokerage.

AMERICAN GENERAL FINANCE
601 NW Second Street, Evansville IN 47701. 812/468-5677. **Fax:** 812/468-5119. **Recorded jobline:** 812/468-5600. **Contact:** Employment. **Description:** A consumer lending and finance company. Founded in 1920. **Common positions include:** Accountant; Actuary; Attorney; Budget Analyst; Computer Programmer; Credit Manager; Economist; Electrical/Electronics Engineer; Financial Analyst; Human Resources Manager; Industrial Engineer; Management Analyst/ Consultant; Management Trainee; Market Research Analyst; Mathematician; Mechanical Engineer; MIS Specialist; Statistician; Systems Analyst. **Educational backgrounds include:** Accounting; Business Administration; Computer Science; Economics; Engineering; Finance; Liberal Arts; Marketing; Mathematics. **Benefits:** 401(k); Dental Insurance; Disability Coverage; Life Insurance; Medical Insurance; Pension Plan; Profit Sharing; Savings Plan; Tuition Assistance. **Corporate headquarters location:** This Location. **Other U.S. locations:** Nationwide. **Subsidiaries include:** MorEquity. **Parent company:** American General Corporation. **Number of employees at this location:** 1,300. **Number of employees nationwide:** 10,000.

AMERICAN PHYSICIANS SERVICE GROUP
1301 Capital of Texas Highway, Suite C-300, Austin TX 78746. 512/328-0888. **Fax:** 512/314-4398. **Contact:** Bill Hayes, Senior Vice President of Finance. **World Wide Web address:** http://www. amph.com. **Description:** A management and financial services firm with subsidiaries and affiliates that provide medical malpractice insurance services for doctors; brokerage and investment services to institutions and individuals; lithotripsy services in 34 states; refractive vision surgery; and dedicated care facilities for Alzheimer's patients. **Corporate headquarters location:** This Location. **Other area locations:** Dallas TX; Houston TX. **Subsidiaries include:** APS Asset Management, Inc.; APS Consulting, Inc.; APS Facilities Management, Inc.; APS Financial Corporation; APS Insurance Services, Inc.; APS Investment Services, Inc.; APS Realty, Inc.; APSC, Inc.; APSFM, Inc.; American Physicians Insurance Agency, Inc. **Number of employees nationwide:** 130.

AMERICAN STOCK EXCHANGE
86 Trinity Place, New York NY 10006. 212/306-1215. **Fax:** 212/306-1218. **Contact:** Human Resources. **E-mail address:** hrdept@amex.com. **World Wide Web address:** http://www.amex.com. **Description:** One of the nation's largest stock exchanges, the American Stock Exchange is one of the only primary marketplaces for both stocks and derivative securities. The American Stock Exchange also handles surveillance, legal, and regulatory functions that are related to the stock exchange. **Common positions include:** Compliance Analyst; Financial Analyst; Public Relations Specialist; Research Assistant; Sales Rep.; Systems Analyst. **Educational backgrounds include:** Business Administration; Communications; Economics; Finance; Liberal Arts; Marketing. **Benefits:** 401(k); Bonus Award/Plan; Dental Insurance; Employee Discounts; Life Insurance; Medical Insurance; Tuition Assistance. **Special programs:** Internships. **Corporate headquarters location:** This Location. **Number of employees at this location:** 700.

AMERITRADE HOLDING CORPORATION
4211 South 102nd Street, Omaha NE 68127. **Toll-free phone:** 800/237-8692. **Contact:** Human Resources. **World Wide Web address:** http://www. ameritradeholding.com. **Description:** Provides discount brokerage and financial services including

electronic trading, market data, and research services. **Corporate headquarters location:** This Location.

AMPLICON FINANCIAL, INC.
5 Hutton Centre Drive, Suite 500, Santa Ana CA 92707. 714/751-7551. **Contact:** Lavon Jackson, Human Resources. **World Wide Web address:** http://www.amplicon.com. **Description:** A lessor of capital assets including high-technology equipment and systems. Founded in 1977. **Corporate headquarters location:** This Location.

THE ASSOCIATES
P.O. Box 660237, Dallas TX 75266. 972/652-4000. **Fax:** 972/652-7420. **Contact:** Human Resources. **World Wide Web address:** http://www.theassociates.com. **Description:** The Associates is comprised of two groups. The Finance Group offers secured and unsecured consumer loans, loans secured by real property, and also purchases installment contracts through retail dealers, such as appliance and furniture stores, through 1,198 branch offices in seven countries. This group also has special business unites, which include leasing, revolving credit, military loans, and the national dealer center. The Insurance Group, Avco Insurance Services, primarily sells credit life, credit disability, and involuntary unemployment insurance to customers of the Financial Group and to independent financial institutions, such as banks, credit unions, and savings and loans. Avco Insurance also offers collateral protection, personal lines auto and renters insurance, and other life insurance products and services to many of these same customers. **Other U.S. locations:** Nationwide.

ROBERT W. BAIRD & COMPANY
777 East Wisconsin Avenue, Milwaukee WI 53202. 414/765-3500. **Toll-free phone:** 800/792-2473. **Fax:** 414/765-7303. **Recorded jobline:** 414/298-7700. **Contact:** Human Resources. **World Wide Web address:** http://www.rwbaird.com. **Description:** A full-service investment firm. Founded in 1919. **NOTE:** Entry-level positions and part-time jobs are offered. **Common positions include:** Accountant; Administrative Assistant; Advertising Clerk; AS400 Programmer Analyst; Assistant Manager; Attorney; Auditor; Branch Manager; Chief Financial Officer; Clerical Supervisor; Computer Operator; Computer Programmer; Computer Support Technician; Controller; Customer Service Representative; Database Administrator; Desktop Publishing Specialist; Economist; Event Planner; Finance Director; Financial Analyst; Graphic Designer; Help-Desk Technician; Human Resources Manager; Intranet Developer; Marketing Specialist; Network/Systems Administrator; Operations Manager; Paralegal; Project Manager; Public Relations Specialist; Purchasing Agent/Manager; Secretary; SQL Programmer; Systems Analyst; Technical Support Manager; Technical Writer/Editor; Telecommunications Manager; Typist/Word Processor; Vice President; Website Developer. **Educational backgrounds include:** Accounting; AS400 Certification; Business Administration; Economics; Finance; HTML; Internet Development; Java; Marketing; Mathematics; MBA; MCSE; Microsoft Office; Microsoft Word; Software Development; Software Tech. Support; Spreadsheets; SQL; Visual Basic. **Benefits:** 401(k); Casual Dress - Daily; Dental Insurance; Disability Coverage; Employee Discounts; Financial Planning Assistance; Flexible Schedule; Job Sharing; Life Insurance; Medical Insurance; Pension Plan; Profit Sharing; Public Transit Available; Savings Plan; Sick Days; Telecommuting; Tuition Assistance; Vacation Days.

Office hours: Monday - Friday, 8:00 a.m. - 5:00 p.m. **Corporate headquarters location:** This Location. **Listed on:** Privately held. **Number of employees at this location:** 1,200. **Number of employees nationwide:** 2,300.

THE BEAR STEARNS COMPANIES INC.
245 Park Avenue, New York NY 10167. 212/272-2000. **Contact:** Human Resources. **World Wide Web address:** http://www.bearstearns.com. **Description:** A leading worldwide investment banking, securities trading, and brokerage firm. **Corporate headquarters location:** This Location. **Other U.S. locations:** Nationwide. **International locations:** Worldwide. **Subsidiaries include:** Bear, Stearns & Company, Inc. is an investment banking and brokerage firm; Bear, Stearns Securities Corporation provides professional and correspondent clearing services including securities lending; Custodial Trust Company provides master trust, custody, and government securities services. **Listed on:** New York Stock Exchange. **Annual sales/revenues:** More than $100 million. **Number of employees nationwide:** 9,200.

J.C. BRADFORD & COMPANY
330 Commerce Street, Nashville TN 37201. 615/748-9000. **Contact:** Human Resources. **World Wide Web address:** http://www.jcbradford.com. **Description:** A regional investment firm with offices in over 60 cities in the Southeast and Ohio. The company specializes in services to individual investors such as retirement, college education, parental care, capital preservation, and cash flow. Investment solutions range from managed accounts and retirement plans to options, commodities, and stock portfolios. Tax-free bonds, government backed securities, mutual funds, annuities, and limited partnerships are offered. J.C. Bradford provides underwriting corporate securities, trading equity, and debt securities in the secondary markets; mergers and acquisitions; and financing of public debt for state and local governments. Founded in 1927. **Corporate headquarters location:** This Location. **Listed on:** Privately held.
Other U.S. locations:
* 1717 West Massey Road, Memphis TN 38120. 901/761-3010.

CANTOR FITZGERALD SECURITIES CORP.
One World Trade Center, New York NY 10048. 212/938-5000. **Fax:** 212/938-2120. **Contact:** Human Resources. **World Wide Web address:** http://www.cantor.com. **Description:** An institutional brokerage firm dealing in fixed income securities, equities, derivatives, options, eurobonds, and emerging markets. **Common positions include:** Broker. **Special programs:** Internships; Training. **Corporate headquarters location:** This Location. **Other U.S. locations:** Los Angeles CA; Chicago IL; Boston MA; Dallas TX. **International locations:** Worldwide. **Listed on:** Privately held. **Number of employees at this location:** 1,300. **Number of employees nationwide:** 1,500. **Number of employees worldwide:** 2,000.

THE CAPITAL GROUP COMPANIES
AMERICAN FUNDS DISTRIBUTORS
11100 Santa Monica Boulevard, Los Angeles CA 90025. 310/996-6000. **Contact:** Recruiting. **World Wide Web address:** http://www.capgroup.com. **Description:** An investment management company with 15 mutual funds and 10 companies. American Funds Distributors (also at this location: 800/421-9900; http://www.americanfunds.com) provides financial advisement services including 28 mutual funds, variable annuities, and retirement planning. **Common positions include:** Accountant/Auditor; Administrative Manager; Attorney; Computer

Programmer; Customer Service Representative; Economist; Financial Analyst; Statistician; Systems Analyst. **Educational backgrounds include:** Accounting; Business Administration; Economics; Finance. **Benefits:** Dental Insurance; Disability Coverage; Life Insurance; Medical Insurance; Profit Sharing; Tuition Assistance. **Corporate headquarters location:** This Location.

CAPITAL ONE FINANCIAL CORP.
2980 Fairview Park Drive, Suite 1300, Falls Church VA 22042. 703/205-1000. **Contact:** Management Recruiter. **World Wide Web address:** http://www. capitalone.com. **Description:** A holding company whose subsidiaries are some of the largest credit card issuers in the United States. Capital One markets a customized array of secured cards, college student cards, joint account cards, and affinity offers. **Benefits:** Pension Plan; Stock Option. **Corporate headquarters location:** This Location. **Other U.S. locations:** Fredericksburg VA; Richmond VA. **Subsidiaries include:** Capital One Bank; Capital One, FSB. **Number of employees nationwide:** 2,600.

CAPITAL RESOURCE ADVISORS
233 South Wacker Road, Suite 4450, Chicago IL 60606. 312/575-1816. **Toll-free phone:** 888/677-4272. **Fax:** 312/575-1960. **Contact:** Brenda Wiggins, Human Resources Manager. **World Wide Web address:** http://www.cradv.com. **Description:** One of the leading asset consulting firms in the country advising corporate, private, and public clients. Founded in 1968. **NOTE:** Entry-level positions are offered. **Common positions include:** Financial Analyst; Financial Consultant; Sales Rep.; Secretary. **Educational backgrounds include:** Business Administration; Finance; Microsoft Word; Spreadsheets. **Benefits:** 401(k); Casual Dress - Daily; Dental Insurance; Disability Coverage; Life Insurance; Medical Insurance; Public Transit Available; Sick Days (6 - 10); Tuition Assistance; Vacation Days (10 - 20). **Special programs:** Internships. **Office hours:** Monday - Friday, 8:30 a.m. - 5:00 p.m. **Corporate headquarters location:** This Location. **Other U.S. locations:** San Francisco CA; Atlanta GA; King of Prussia PA.

CENTEX CORPORATION
P.O. Box 199000, Dallas TX 75219. 214/981-5000. **Contact:** Human Resources. **World Wide Web address:** http://www.centex.com. **Description:** Provides home building, mortgage banking, contracting, and construction products and services. **Corporate headquarters location:** This Location. **Subsidiaries include:** Centex Homes is one of America's largest home builders. CTX Mortgage Company is among the top retail originators of single-family home mortgages. Centex Construction Company, Inc. is one of the largest general building contractors in the U.S., as well as one of the largest constructors of health care facilities. Centex Construction Products, Inc., which manufactures and distributes cement, ready-mix concrete, aggregates, and gypsum wallboard, is one of the largest U.S.-owned cement producers. Centex Development Company, LP conducts real estate development activities. **Listed on:** New York Stock Exchange. **Annual sales/revenues:** More than $100 million.

CHARLES SCHWAB & CO., INC.
101 Montgomery Street, San Francisco CA 94104. 415/627-7000. **Fax:** 415/627-7316. **Recorded jobline:** 415/627-7227. **Contact:** Human Resources. **World Wide Web address:** http://www. schwab.com. **Description:** One of the largest discount brokerage companies in the U.S. The firm has more than 2.5 million active customer accounts.

NOTE: All resumes received will be scanned into a recruiting database. Resumes should be sent on white or light-colored paper without any bullets, boldface print, italics, or underlines. **Common positions include:** Accountant; Administrative Manager; Advertising Clerk; Attorney; Branch Manager; Brokerage Clerk; Computer Programmer; Customer Service Rep.; Financial Analyst; Financial Services Sales Representative; Human Resources Manager; Management Analyst/Consultant; Management Trainee; Securities Sales Rep.; Systems Analyst. **Educational backgrounds include:** Accounting; Business Administration; Communications; Computer Science; Economics; Finance; Liberal Arts; Marketing; Mathematics. **Benefits:** 401(k); Dental Insurance; Disability Coverage; Employee Discounts; Life Insurance; Medical Insurance; Pension Plan; Profit Sharing; Tuition Assistance. **Special programs:** Internships. **Corporate headquarters location:** This Location. **Parent company:** Charles Schwab Corporation. **Listed on:** New York Stock Exchange. **Number of employees at this location:** 2,200.

CHASE CAPITAL PARTNERS
1221 Avenue of the Americas, New York NY 10020-1080. 212/899-3400. **Fax:** 212/899-3401. **Contact:** Human Resources. **World Wide Web address:** http://www.chasecapital.com. **Description:** Provides equity and other financial services.

THE CHICAGO BOARD OF TRADE
141 West Jackson Boulevard, Suite 2080, Chicago IL 60604. 312/435-3494. **Fax:** 312/435-7150. **Contact:** Employment Office. **World Wide Web address:** http://www.cbot.com. **Description:** A commodities, futures, and options exchange. **Common positions include:** Accountant/Auditor; Computer Programmer; Economist; Financial Analyst; Investigator. **Educational backgrounds include:** Accounting; Computer Science; Economics; Finance. **Benefits:** 401(k); Dental Insurance; Disability Coverage; Medical Insurance; Tuition Assistance. **Corporate headquarters location:** This Location.

THE CHICAGO BOARD OPTIONS EXCHANGE
400 South LaSalle Street, Chicago IL 60605. 312/786-7800. **Toll-free phone:** 800/OPTIONS. **Fax:** 312/786-7808. **Contact:** Joe Morice, Human Resources. **World Wide Web address:** http://www.cboe.com. **Description:** A nonprofit financial institution engaged in options trading. **NOTE:** Entry-level positions are offered. **Common positions include:** Administrative Assistant; Computer Operator; Computer Programmer; Database Manager; MIS Specialist; Software Engineer; Systems Analyst; Systems Manager. **Educational backgrounds include:** Accounting; Business Administration; Communications; Computer Science; Economics; Engineering; Finance; Marketing. **Benefits:** 401(k); Dental Insurance; Disability Coverage; Flexible Schedule; Job Sharing; Life Insurance; Medical Insurance; Tuition Assistance. **Corporate headquarters location:** This Location. **Number of employees at this location:** 880.

CHICAGO MERCANTILE EXCHANGE
30 South Wacker Drive, Chicago IL 60606. 312/930-8240. **Fax:** 312/930-2036. **Contact:** Human Resources. **World Wide Web address:** http://www.cme.com. **Description:** One of the world's largest commodities, futures, and options exchanges. **Common positions include:** Accountant; Attorney; Computer Operator; Computer Programmer; Financial Analyst; Librarian; Mathematician; Paralegal; Systems

Analyst. **Educational backgrounds include:** Accounting; Computer Science; Finance; Marketing; Mathematics. **Benefits:** 401(k); Dental Insurance; Medical Insurance; Pension Plan; Tuition Assistance. **Corporate headquarters location:** This Location. **Other U.S. locations:** Washington DC; New York NY. **Number of employees at this location:** 1,000.

CHICAGO STOCK EXCHANGE INC.
440 South LaSalle Street, Chicago IL 60605. 312/663-2526. **Contact:** Human Resources. **World Wide Web address:** http://www.chicagostockex.com. **Description:** A stock exchange offering securities trading and depository services. **Common positions include:** Administrator; Computer Programmer; Systems Analyst. **Educational backgrounds include:** Accounting; Computer Science; Economics; Finance; Liberal Arts; Marketing; Mathematics. **Benefits:** Dental Insurance; Disability Coverage; Life Insurance; Medical Insurance; Pension Plan; Savings Plan; Tuition Assistance. **Corporate headquarters location:** This Location. **Other U.S. locations:** New York NY. **Number of employees at this location:** 660.

CHRYSLER FINANCIAL COMPANY LLC
27777 Franklin Road, Southfield MI 48034. **Toll-free phone:** 800/700-3750. **Contact:** Human Resources. **World Wide Web address:** http://www.chryslerfinancial.com. **Description:** Provides automotive and dealer leasing and other related financial services. **Common positions include:** Accountant; Actuary; Attorney; Claim Rep.; Computer Programmer; Customer Service Rep.; Financial Analyst; Human Resources Manager; Marketing Specialist; Operations/Production Manager; Systems Analyst; Underwriter/Assistant Underwriter. **Educational backgrounds include:** Accounting; Business Administration; Computer Science; Finance. **Special programs:** Internships. **Corporate headquarters location:** This Location. **Parent company:** DaimlerChrysler Corporation.

CITICORP MORTGAGE, INC.
15851 Clayton Road, Mail Stop 398, Ballwin MO 63011. 636/256-5000. **Contact:** Employment Department. **Description:** Operates a nationwide network of mortgage lending offices. The company specializes in mortgage products, policies, processes, systems, and standards. **Common positions include:** Computer Programmer; Credit Manager; Customer Service Rep.; Financial Analyst; Management Trainee; Marketing Specialist; Operations/Production Manager; Quality Control Supervisor; Services Sales Rep.; Systems Analyst; Underwriter/Assistant Underwriter. **Educational backgrounds include:** Accounting; Business Administration; Computer Science; Finance; Marketing; MBA. **Benefits:** Daycare Assistance; Dental Insurance; Disability Coverage; Employee Discounts; Life Insurance; Medical Insurance; Pension Plan; Profit Sharing; Savings Plan; Tuition Assistance. **Special programs:** Internships. **Corporate headquarters location:** This Location. **Listed on:** New York Stock Exchange.

CITIGROUP INC.
153 East 53rd Street, New York NY 10043. 212/559-1000. **Contact:** Human Resources. **World Wide Web address:** http://www.citigroup.com. **Description:** A holding company offering a wide range of financial services through its subsidiaries. **NOTE:** Please send resumes to Citigroup, North America Recruiting, 575 Lexington Avenue, 12th Floor, New York NY 10043. **Corporate headquarters location:** This Location. **Subsidiaries include:** Citibank; CitiFinancial; Global Corporate & Investment Banking; Primerica Financial Services; Salomon Smith Barney; SSB Citi Asset Management Group; Travelers Life & Annuity; Travelers Property Casualty Corp. **Listed on:** New York Stock Exchange.

CITY FINANCIAL
300 St. Paul Place, Baltimore MD 21202. 410/332-3000. **Contact:** Human Resources. **Description:** Provides small personal loans. The company operates through 830 branch offices. **Common positions include:** Accountant/Auditor; Branch Manager; Budget Analyst; Clerical Supervisor; Computer Programmer; Credit Manager; Customer Service Representative; Financial Analyst; Human Resources Manager; Management Trainee; Systems Analyst. **Educational backgrounds include:** Accounting; Business Administration; Computer Science; Finance; Liberal Arts; Marketing. **Benefits:** 401(k); Dental Insurance; Disability Coverage; Life Insurance; Medical Insurance; Pension Plan; Tuition Assistance. **Corporate headquarters location:** This Location. **Other U.S. locations:** Nationwide. **Parent company:** The Travelers Group. **Listed on:** New York Stock Exchange. **Number of employees at this location:** 450. **Number of employees nationwide:** 4,000.

COLLEGE CREDIT CARD CORPORATION
One Penn Center, 12th Floor, 1617 JFK Boulevard, Philadelphia PA 19103. 215/568-1700. **Fax:** 215/568-1701. **Contact:** Carrie Carmany, Recruitment Manager. **Description:** Markets credit cards and other financial services to college students on-campus and to the general public at special events and venues. **Special programs:** Internships. **Corporate headquarters location:** This Location. **Other U.S. locations:** Monroeville PA. **Parent company:** Campus Dimensions Inc. **Listed on:** Privately held. **Number of employees at this location:** 60. **Number of employees nationwide:** 115.

COMMONWEALTH FINANCIAL CORP.
524 Escondido Avenue, Vista CA 92084. 760/945-9891. **Fax:** 760/945-4991. **Contact:** Human Resources. **World Wide Web address:** http://www.cfchomeloan.com. **Description:** Provides a wide range of mortgages, home loans, and debt consolidation services. **Corporate headquarters location:** This Location.

CONSECO FINANCIAL CORPORATION
600 Landmark Towers, 345 St. Peter Street, St. Paul MN 55102-1639. 651/293-4887. **Fax:** 651/293-3622. **Recorded jobline:** 651/293-5825. **Contact:** Human Resources. **World Wide Web address:** http://www.conseco.com. **Description:** Aggregates and secures conventional manufactured home, motorcycle, and home improvement contracts and sells securities through public offerings and private placements. Conseco's FHA-insured and VA-guaranteed manufactured home contracts are converted into GNMA certificates and are sold in the secondary market. The company also markets homeowners and life insurance. Founded in 1976. **Special programs:** Internships. **Corporate headquarters location:** This Location. **Parent company:** Conseco, Inc. (Carmel IN) is a leading provider of insurance and financial products. **Number of employees at this location:** 1,200.

CONSUMER PORTFOLIO SERVICES, INC.
P.O. Box 57071, Irvine CA 92619-7071. 949/753-6800. **Contact:** Human Resources. **World Wide Web address:** http://www.consumerportfolio.com. **Description:** Consumer Portfolio Services, Inc. and

its subsidiaries purchase, sell, and service retail automobile installment sales contracts originated by dealers located primarily in California. The company purchases contracts to resell them to institutional investors either as bulk sales or in the form of securities backed by the contracts. **Corporate headquarters location:** This Location.

CORUM GROUP LTD.
10500 NE Eighth Street, Suite 1500, Bellevue WA 98004. 425/455-8281. **Fax:** 425/451-8951. **Contact:** Human Resources. **World Wide Web address:** http://www.corumgroup.com. **Description:** Assists software companies to successfully execute company mergers and alliances. **Corporate headquarters location:** This Location.

COUNTRYWIDE CREDIT INDUSTRIES
4500 Park Granada, Calabasas CA 91302. 818/225-3000. **Contact:** Human Resources. **World Wide Web address:** http://www.countrywide.com. **Description:** A holding company. **Corporate headquarters location:** This Location. **Subsidiaries include:** Countrywide Funding Corporation originates, purchases, sells, and services mortgage loans. The company's mortgage loans are principally first-lien loans secured by single-family residences.

CUNA MUTUAL LIFE INSURANCE CO.
2000 Heritage Way, Waverly IA 50677. 319/352-1000. **Fax:** 319/352-1272. **Contact:** Kathryn Olson, Manager of Human Resources. **World Wide Web address:** http://www.cunamutual.com. **Description:** A financial services company designing, marketing, and administrating individual investments, life insurance plans, and annuity products. **Number of employees nationwide:** 1,100.

DVI, INC.
4041 MacArthur Boulevard, Suite 401, Newport Beach CA 92660. 949/474-5800. **Contact:** Human Resources. **World Wide Web address:** http://www. dvifs.com. **Description:** Provides equipment financing and related services for the users of diagnostic imaging, radiation therapy, and other medical technologies. The company's customer base consists principally of outpatient health care providers, physician groups, and hospitals. **Corporate headquarters location:** This Location. **Number of employees at this location:** 90.

DAIN RAUSCHER
INTER-REGIONAL FINANCIAL GROUP
60 South Sixth Street, Minneapolis MN 55402. 612/371-2711. **Contact:** Human Resources. **World Wide Web address:** http://www.dainrauscher.com. **Description:** A financial consulting and securities firm. The company also provides real estate syndication and property investment services, as well as data processing services. **Common positions include:** Broker; Financial Analyst; Operations/Production Manager. **Educational backgrounds include:** Accounting; Business Administration; Economics; Finance. **Benefits:** Dental Insurance; Disability Coverage; Employee Discounts; Life Insurance; Medical Insurance; Pension Plan; Profit Sharing; Tuition Assistance. **Corporate headquarters location:** This Location. **Parent company:** Inter-Regional Financial Group, Inc. (also at this location) is a holding company whose subsidiaries provide securities brokerage and investment banking services.

DEUTSCHE BANK
130 Liberty Street, New York NY 10006. 212/250-2500. **Contact:** Human Resources. **Description:** A merchant investment bank. Deutsche Bank also manages index funds. **Corporate headquarters location:** This Location.

DONALDSON, LUFKIN & JENRETTE INC.
280 Park Avenue, 5th Floor, New York NY 10017. 212/892-3900. **Contact:** Irene Rosendale, Vice President. **World Wide Web address:** http://www. dlj.com. **Description:** An independent investment banking and securities firm. Services are directed primarily toward professional markets including corporations, institutions, other securities firms, and substantial individual investors. Donaldson, Lufkin & Jenrette provides a full range of capital-raising, merger and acquisition, and related financial advisory services.

DRAKE COMPANY
7 Hanover Square, 2nd Floor, New York NY 10004. 212/742-1500. **Contact:** Human Resources. **Description:** A full-service securities brokerage firm offering a diverse range of financial products and services. **NOTE:** Resumes should be sent to Human Resources, 1250 East Hallandale Beach Boulevard, Suite 300, Hallandale FL 33009. 954/458-5800. **Common positions include:** Broker. **Educational backgrounds include:** Accounting; Business Administration; Communications; Economics; Finance; Liberal Arts; Mathematics. **Benefits:** 401(k); Disability Coverage; Medical Insurance. **Corporate headquarters location:** This Location. **Other U.S. locations:** Nationwide. **Listed on:** Privately held. **Annual sales/revenues:** $11 - $20 million. **Number of employees at this location:** 100.

DREYFUS CORPORATION
200 Park Avenue, 7th Floor, New York NY 10166. 212/922-6000. **Contact:** Linda Vanwart, Human Resources. **World Wide Web address:** http://www. dreyfus.com. **Description:** A nationwide investment corporation managing over 150 mutual funds. **NOTE:** Entry-level positions are offered. **Common positions include:** Accountant; Administrative Assistant; Customer Service Representative; Secretary. **Educational backgrounds include:** Accounting; Computer Science; Finance; Liberal Arts. **Benefits:** 401(k); Dental Insurance; Disability Coverage; Life Insurance; Medical Insurance; Pension Plan; Tuition Assistance. **Corporate headquarters location:** This Location. **Parent company:** Mellon Financial Corporation.

EDWARD JONES
201 Progress Parkway, Maryland Heights MO 63043. 314/515-2000. **Contact:** Human Resources. **World Wide Web address:** http://www. edwardjones.com. **Description:** A securities brokerage firm. **Corporate headquarters location:** This Location. **Listed on:** Privately held. **Other U.S. locations:**
- 212 East Main Street, Sun Prairie WI 53590. 608/837-2700.

GEORGE ELKINS MORTGAGE BANKING CO.
12100 Wilshire Boulevard, Suite 300, Los Angeles CA 90025. 310/207-3456. **Contact:** Personnel Department. **Description:** Provides mortgage and loan services to individuals and commercial clients. **Common positions include:** Accountant/Auditor; Computer Programmer; Department Manager; Insurance Agent/Broker; Property and Real Estate Manager; Underwriter/Assistant Underwriter. **Benefits:** 401(k); Dental Insurance; Disability Coverage; Life Insurance; Medical Insurance. **Corporate headquarters location:** This Location.

EQUIFAX, INC.
P.O. Box 4081, Atlanta GA 30302. 404/885-8000. **Contact:** Human Resources. **World Wide Web**

address: http://www.equifax.com. **Description:** Provides a range of financial and information management services, enabling global commerce between buyers and sellers. Equifax operates through Equifax Europe, Equifax Latin America, Knowledge Engineering, North American Information Services, and Payment Services. Operations include consumer credit reporting, collection services, credit card authorization, insurance underwriting, and hospital bill audits. Founded in 1899. **Common positions include:** Branch Manager; Computer Programmer; Credit Manager; Customer Service Rep.; Department Manager; Financial Analyst; General Manager; Management Trainee; Marketing Specialist; Operations/Production Manager; Public Relations Specialist; Quality Control Supervisor; Services Sales Rep.; Statistician; Systems Analyst; Technical Writer/Editor. **Educational backgrounds include:** Accounting; Business Administration; Computer Science; Economics; Finance; Liberal Arts; Marketing; Mathematics. **Benefits:** Daycare Assistance; Dental Insurance; Disability Coverage; Employee Discounts; Life Insurance; Medical Insurance; Pension Plan; Profit Sharing; Savings Plan; Tuition Assistance. **Corporate headquarters location:** This Location. **Listed on:** New York Stock Exchange.

E*TRADE
4500 Bohannon Drive, Menlo Park CA 94025. 650/331-6000. **Contact:** Human Resources. **Description:** Operates a website that provides online investing services. **Corporate headquarters location:** This Location.

FEDERAL NATIONAL MORTGAGE ASSOCIATION (FANNIE MAE)
3900 Wisconsin Avenue NW, Washington DC 20016. 202/752-7000. **Contact:** Ms. Frances Jordan, Director of Human Resources. **World Wide Web address:** http://www.fanniemae.com. **Description:** A stockholder-owned corporation chartered by Congress for the purpose of helping to finance housing by supplementing the supply of mortgage funds. Fannie Mae purchases a variety of mortgage plans including adjustable rate mortgages, conventional fixed rate home mortgages, and second mortgages. The company also participates in pools of conventional first and second mortgages and guarantees conventional mortgage-based securities. **Common positions include:** Attorney; Computer Programmer; Economist; Financial Analyst; Systems Analyst. **Educational backgrounds include:** Accounting; Business Administration; Computer Science; Economics; Finance; Mathematics. **Benefits:** 401(k); Daycare Assistance; Dental Insurance; Disability Coverage; Employee Discounts; Life Insurance; Medical Insurance; Pension Plan; Profit Sharing; Savings Plan; Tuition Assistance. **Special programs:** Internships. **Corporate headquarters location:** This Location. **Other U.S. locations:** Atlanta GA; Chicago IL; Philadelphia PA; Dallas TX. **Listed on:** New York Stock Exchange. **Number of employees at this location:** 3,800.

FIDELITY INVESTMENTS
82 Devonshire Street, Boston MA 02109. 617/563-7000. **Fax:** 617/476-4262. **Contact:** Human Resources. **World Wide Web address:** http://www.fidelity.com/employment. **Description:** One of the nation's leading investment counseling and mutual fund/discount brokerage firms. **Common positions include:** Branch Manager; Brokerage Clerk; Budget Analyst; Computer Programmer; Customer Service Rep.; Financial Analyst; Financial Services Sales Rep.; Human Resources Manager; Securities Sales Rep.; Systems Analyst; Technical Writer/Editor. **Educational backgrounds include:** Accounting; Communications; Computer Science; Finance; Marketing. **Benefits:** 401(k); Dental Insurance; Disability Coverage; Employee Discounts; Life Insurance; Medical Insurance; Pension Plan; Tuition Assistance. **Special programs:** Internships. **Corporate headquarters location:** This Location. **Other U.S. locations:** Braintree MA; Burlington MA; Marlborough MA; Worcester MA; New York NY; Cincinnati OH; Dallas TX; Salt Lake City UT.

FIDUCIARY TRUST COMPANY INTERNATIONAL
2 World Trade Center, New York NY 10048. 212/466-4100. **Fax:** 212/313-2646. **Contact:** Allison Katz, Employment Manager. **E-mail address:** akatz@ftci.com. **World Wide Web address:** http://www.ftci.com. **Description:** Provides global investment management and custody services for institutional and individual clients. **Common positions include:** Administrative Assistant; Financial Analyst; Investment Manager; Systems Analyst. **Educational backgrounds include:** Business Administration; Economics; Liberal Arts; Microsoft Office. **Benefits:** 401(k); Dental Insurance; Life Insurance; Medical Insurance; Pension Plan; Tuition Assistance. **Corporate headquarters location:** This Location. **Other U.S. locations:** Los Angeles CA; Washington DC; Wilmington DE; Miami FL. **International locations:** Geneva; Hong Kong; London; Melbourne; Tokyo. **Number of employees at this location:** 600.

THE FINANCE COMPANY
P.O. Box 10306, Norfolk VA 23513-0306. 757/858-1400. **Physical address:** 5425 Robin Hood Road, Suite 101A, Norfolk VA. **Fax:** 757/858-6939. **Contact:** Human Resources Manager. **Description:** This location is the mid-Atlantic regional service center. Overall, The Finance Company buys and services installment contracts originated by used-car dealers. The company also receives revenue from commissions on ancillary products such as credit insurance, limited physical damage insurance, and product warranties offered by the company and underwritten by third-party vendors. **Corporate headquarters location:** This Location. **Parent company:** TFC Enterprises.

FINANCIAL FEDERAL CORPORATION
733 Third Avenue, 7th Floor, New York NY 10017. 212/599-8000. **Fax:** 212/286-5885. **Contact:** Human Resources. **World Wide Web address:** http://www.financialfederal.com. **Description:** Provides financing of leases and capital loans on industrial, commercial, and professional equipment to middle market customers in a variety of industries. Founded in 1989. **Corporate headquarters location:** This Location. **Other U.S. locations:** Mesa AZ; Westmont IL; Charlotte NC; Teaneck NJ; Houston TX. **Listed on:** New York Stock Exchange. **Stock exchange symbol:** FIF. **Annual sales/revenues:** $51 - $100 million.

FIRST COMMONWEALTH TRUST CO.
614 Philadelphia Street, Indiana PA 15701. 724/465-3282. **Fax:** 724/463-5719. **Contact:** Rose Cogley, Personnel Manager. **Description:** A state-chartered trust company specializing in estate planning, living trusts, pension plans, and investment management. **Common positions include:** Attorney; Financial Analyst; Paralegal. **Benefits:** 401(k); Disability Coverage; Employee Discounts; Life Insurance; Medical Insurance; Pension Plan. **Corporate headquarters location:** This Location. **Other U.S. locations:** Bridgeville PA; Chambersburg PA; DuBois PA; Hollidaysburg PA; Huntingdon PA; Johnstown PA; New Castle

PA. Parent company: First Commonwealth Financial Corporation. **Listed on:** New York Stock Exchange. **Number of employees at this location:** 20. **Number of employees nationwide:** 35.

FIRST INVESTORS CORPORATION
95 Wall Street, 23rd Floor, New York NY 10005. 212/858-8000. **Contact:** Personnel. **Description:** Specializes in the distribution and management of investment programs for individuals and corporations, as well as retirement plans. First Investors operates through several area locations in Westchester County, New Jersey, and Long Island. **Common positions include:** Accountant/Auditor; Attorney; Computer Programmer; Customer Service Rep.; Financial Analyst; Management Trainee; Securities Sales Rep. **Educational backgrounds include:** Accounting; Computer Science; Finance; Mathematics. **Benefits:** Disability Coverage; Life Insurance; Medical Insurance; Profit Sharing; Tuition Assistance. **Corporate headquarters location:** This Location.

FIRST MORTGAGE CORPORATION
3230 Fallow Field Drive, Diamond Bar CA 91765. 909/595-1996. **Contact:** Human Resources. **Description:** Originates, purchases, sells, and services first deed of trust loans (mortgage loans) for the purchase or refinance of owner-occupied one- to four-family residences. Founded in 1975. **Corporate headquarters location:** This Location. **Other U.S. locations:** NV; OR; WA. **Listed on:** NASDAQ. **Stock exchange symbol:** FMOR.

FIRST OF MICHIGAN INC.
300 River Place, Suite 4000, Detroit MI 48207. 313/259-2600. **Contact:** Human Resources Director. **World Wide Web address:** http://www.firstofmichigan.com. **Description:** An investment banking corporation and one of Michigan's leading brokerage firms. Founded in 1933. **Common positions include:** Branch Manager; Brokerage Clerk. **Educational backgrounds include:** Accounting; Business Administration; Finance; Marketing. **Benefits:** 401(k); Disability Coverage; Medical Insurance; Profit Sharing. **Corporate headquarters location:** This Location. **Parent company:** Fahnestock Viner Holdings Inc. **Listed on:** New York Stock Exchange. **Number of employees nationwide:** 600.

FIRST USA BANK
201 North Walnut Street, Wilmington DE 19801. 302/594-4000. **Recorded jobline:** 302/594-8050. **Contact:** Human Resources. **World Wide Web address:** http://www.firstusa.com. **Description:** One of the nation's largest issuers of Visa and MasterCard credit cards, serving more than 56 million customers. **Common positions include:** Budget Analyst; Computer Programmer; Financial Analyst; Human Resources Manager; Industrial Engineer; Management Trainee; Mathematician; Statistician; Systems Analyst. **Educational backgrounds include:** Accounting; Business Administration; Computer Science; Economics; Engineering; Finance. **Benefits:** 401(k); Daycare Assistance; Dental Insurance; Disability Coverage; Employee Discounts; Health Benefits; Life Insurance; Medical Insurance; Pension Plan; Savings Plan; Tuition Assistance; Vacation Days. **Special programs:** Internships. **Corporate headquarters location:** This Location. **Other U.S. locations:** Tempe AZ; Lake Mary FL; Baton Rouge LA; Dayton OH; Westerville OH; Youngstown OH; Austin TX; Dallas TX. **Parent company:** Bank One. **Operations at this facility include:** Administration; Sales; Service. **Listed on:** New York Stock Exchange. **Number of employees nationwide:** 13,000.

FIRST UNION HOME EQUITY BANK, N.A.
1000 Louis Rose Place, Charlotte NC 28262-8546. 704/593-9300. **Contact:** Human Resources. **World Wide Web address:** http://www.firstunion.com. **Description:** Offers home equity loans through 184 offices in 42 states. **Corporate headquarters location:** This Location. **Parent company:** First Union Corporation (Charlotte NC) is one of the nation's largest bank holding companies with subsidiaries which operate over 1,330 full-service bank branches in the south Atlantic states. These subsidiaries provide retail banking, retail investment, and commercial banking services. The corporation provides other financial services including mortgage banking, home equity lending, leasing, insurance, and securities brokerage services from branch locations. The corporation also operates one of the nation's largest ATM networks. **Listed on:** New York Stock Exchange.

FIRST UNION SECURITIES, INC.
77 West Wacker Drive, 25th Floor, Chicago IL 60601. 312/574-6000. **Contact:** Human Resources Department. **World Wide Web address:** http://www.firstunionsec.com. **Description:** A full-service brokerage firm with more than 300 offices serving 1.5 million clients. **Office hours:** Monday - Friday, 8:00 a.m. - 5:00 p.m. **Corporate headquarters location:** This Location. **Other U.S. locations:** Nationwide.

FIRSTMARK CAPITAL CORPORATION
P.O. Box 599, Waterville ME 04903. 207/873-0691. **Toll-free phone:** 800/274-3476. **Fax:** 207/873-5999. **Contact:** Ivy Gilbert, Senior Vice President. **Description:** Engaged in financial services, real estate, and timber operations. Financial services are offered in the areas of insurance consulting and marketing, registered investment advisory services, personal and corporate financial planning, management consulting, and venture capital services. Real estate operations consist of commercial and investment real estate brokerage, real estate investment and development, timber harvesting, and residential and commercial construction. **Corporate headquarters location:** This Location. **Subsidiaries include:** Firstmark Capital Corporation; Firstmark Construction, Inc.; Firstmark Investment Corporation; QFAN Marketing Services, Inc.; Southern Capital Corporation. **Listed on:** NASDAQ. **Stock exchange symbol:** FIRM.

FLEET CREDIT CARD SERVICES
300 North Wakefield Drive, Newark DE 19702. 302/266-5600. **Fax:** 302/266-5468. **Recorded jobline:** 302/266-JOBS. **Contact:** Human Resources. **World Wide Web address:** http://www.fleet.com. **Description:** Provides consumer credit card services. **Company slogan:** Ready when you are. **Common positions include:** Customer Service Rep.; Human Resources Manager; MIS Specialist. **Educational backgrounds include:** Spreadsheets. **Benefits:** 401(k); Bonus Award/Plan; Dental Insurance; Disability Coverage; Financial Planning Assistance; Life Insurance; Medical Insurance; Paid Holidays; Pension Plan; Stock Option; Tuition Assistance; Wellness Program. **Corporate headquarters location:** Horsham PA. **Other U.S. locations:** Colorado Springs CO. **Parent company:** FleetBoston Financial. **CEO:** Joe Saunders. **Number of employees at this location:** 700.

FLEET MORTGAGE GROUP INC.
1333 Main Street, Columbia SC 29201. 803/929-7900. **Contact:** Human Resources. **Description:** A servicer of single-family residential mortgages and one of the nation's largest originators of home loans. Founded in 1971. **Corporate headquarters**

location: This Location. **Parent company:** FleetBoston Financial. **Listed on:** New York Stock Exchange.

THE FOOTHILL GROUP, INC.
11111 Santa Monica Boulevard, Suite 1500, Los Angeles CA 90025. 310/996-7000. **Contact:** Human Resources. **Description:** The Foothill Group is one of the largest publicly-owned commercial lenders in the nation. The company operates two businesses: commercial lending and money management. **Corporate headquarters location:** This Location. **Subsidiaries include:** Foothill Capital Corporation provides asset-based financing to businesses throughout the United States and engages in money management for institutional investors through two limited partnerships.

FORETHOUGHT FINANCIAL SERVICES
Forethought Center, Highway 46 East, Batesville IN 47006. 812/934-8148. **Contact:** Human Resources. **Description:** Provides financial services for the planning of funeral arrangements. **Corporate headquarters location:** This Location.

FOUNDERS ASSET MANAGEMENT, INC.
2930 East Third Avenue, Denver CO 80206. 303/394-4404. **Fax:** 303/394-7840. **Contact:** Human Resources. **World Wide Web address:** http://www.founders.com. **Description:** Offers mutual funds including small-stock, international funds and conservative bond funds. The company services approximately 125,000 account holders worldwide and manages assets of approximately $2 billion. Founded in 1938. **Common positions include:** Accountant; Customer Service Rep.; Financial Analyst; Financial Services Sales Rep. **Educational backgrounds include:** Accounting; Business Administration; Economics; Finance. **Benefits:** 401(k); Dental Insurance; Disability Coverage; Life Insurance; Medical Insurance; Savings Plan; Tuition Assistance. **Corporate headquarters location:** This Location.

FOUR CORNERS FINANCIAL CORP.
370 East Avenue, Rochester NY 14604. 716/454-2263. **Contact:** Human Resources. **Description:** Four Corners Financial Corporation and its subsidiaries provide services and products including real estate title searching, preparation of abstracts of title, issuance of title insurance as an agent for certain national underwriting companies, and real estate appraisals, primarily in western and central New York state. **Corporate headquarters location:** This Location. **Other U.S. locations:** Albany NY; Binghamton NY; Buffalo NY; Goshen NY; Lockport NY; Syracuse NY; Utica NY. **Subsidiaries include:** Four Corners Abstract Corporation; Proper Appraisal Specialists, Inc.

FRANKLIN RESOURCES, INC.
777 Mariners Island Boulevard, San Mateo CA 94404. 650/312-2578. **Contact:** Human Resources. **World Wide Web address:** http://www.franklintempleton.com/public/corporate. **Description:** Provides mutual fund and money market services. **Common positions include:** Accountant; Administrative Worker/Clerk; Business Analyst; Computer Programmer; Customer Service Rep.; Systems Analyst. **Educational backgrounds include:** Accounting; Business Administration; Computer Science; Liberal Arts; Marketing. **Benefits:** 401(k); Dental Insurance; Disability Coverage; Employee Discounts; Life Insurance; Medical Insurance; Profit Sharing; Tuition Assistance. **Corporate headquarters location:** This Location. **Subsidiaries include:** Franklin Templeton Group. **Listed on:** New York Stock Exchange.

FREDDIE MAC
8200 Jones Branch Drive, McLean VA 22102. 703/903-2000. **Contact:** Director of Employment. **World Wide Web address:** http://www. freddiemac.com. **Description:** Provides mortgage credit services and secondary mortgages. Founded in 1970. **NOTE:** Second and third shifts are offered. **Company slogan:** We open doors. **Common positions include:** Account Manager; Accountant; Administrative Assistant; AS400 Programmer Analyst; Attorney; Budget Analyst; Computer Animator; Computer Engineer; Computer Operator; Computer Programmer; Computer Scientist; Computer Support Technician; Computer Technician; Content Developer; Database Administrator; Database Manager; Economist; Finance Director; Financial Analyst; Help-Desk Technician; Human Resources Manager; Internet Services Manager; Intranet Developer; MIS Specialist; Network Engineer; Network/Systems Administrator; Paralegal; Software Engineer; SQL Programmer; Systems Analyst; Systems Manager; Underwriter/Assistant Underwriter; Webmaster; Website Developer. **Educational backgrounds include:** Accounting; Business Administration; C/C++; Communications; Computer Science; Economics; Engineering; Finance; HTML; Internet Development; Java; Marketing; Mathematics; MBA; MCSE; Microsoft Office; Microsoft Word; Public Relations; Software Development; Software Tech. Support; SQL; Visual Basic. **Benefits:** 401(k); Dental Insurance; Disability Coverage; Flexible Schedule; Life Insurance; Medical Insurance; Pension Plan; Relocation Assistance; Tuition Assistance. **Special programs:** Internships; Co-ops. **Corporate headquarters location:** This Location. **Other U.S. locations:** Woodland Hills CA; Washington DC; Atlanta GA; Chicago IL; New York NY; Dallas TX. **Listed on:** New York Stock Exchange.

GATX CAPITAL CORPORATION
4 Embarcadero Center, Suite 2200, San Francisco CA 94111. 415/955-3200. **Fax:** 415/403-3517. **Contact:** Human Resources. **World Wide Web address:** http://www.gatxcap.com. **Description:** A diversified, international financial services company providing asset-based financing for transportation and industrial equipment. The company arranges full payout financing leases, secured loans, operating leases, and other structured financing both as an investing principal and with institutional partners. **Common positions include:** Accountant; Attorney; Computer Programmer; Credit Manager; Financial Analyst; Human Resources Manager; Paralegal; Systems Analyst. **Educational backgrounds include:** Accounting; Business Administration; Computer Science; Finance; Liberal Arts; Marketing; Mathematics; MBA. **Benefits:** 401(k); Adoption Assistance; Dental Insurance; Disability Coverage; Life Insurance; Medical Insurance; Pension Plan; Tuition Assistance. **Corporate headquarters location:** This Location. **Subsidiaries include:** GATX Rail acquires, leases, and sells railcars and locomotives for GATX Capital's own portfolio and for managed portfolios. **Parent company:** GATX Corporation. **Listed on:** New York Stock Exchange. **Number of employees at this location:** 190.

GE CAPITAL CORPORATION
260 Long Ridge Road, Stamford CT 06927. 203/357-4000. **Contact:** Mr. Saperstein, Manager of Human Resources. **Description:** One of the largest leasing companies in the U.S. and Canada, providing financing and related management services to corporate clients through 27 divisions. **Corporate headquarters location:** This Location. **Parent company:** General Electric Company

operates in the following areas: aircraft engines (jet engines, replacement parts, and repair services for commercial, military, executive, and commuter aircraft); appliances; broadcasting (NBC); industrial (lighting products, electrical distribution and control equipment, transportation systems products, electric motors and related products, a broad range of electrical and electronic industrial automation products, and a network of electrical supply houses); materials (plastics, ABS resins, silicones, superabrasives, and laminates); power systems (products for the generation, transmission, and distribution of electricity); technical products and systems (medical systems and equipment, as well as a full range of computer-based information and data interchange services for both internal use and external commercial and industrial customers); and capital services (consumer services, financing, and specialty insurance).

GMAC-RFC
8400 Normandale Lake Boulevard, Suite 250, Minneapolis MN 55437. 952/832-7000. **Contact:** Human Resources. **World Wide Web address:** http://www.rfc.com. **Description:** A secondary mortgage provider. **Common positions include:** Accountant; Computer Programmer; Customer Service Rep.; Department Manager; Financial Analyst; Human Resources Manager; Systems Analyst; Underwriter/Assistant Underwriter. **Educational backgrounds include:** Accounting; Banking; Business Administration; Computer Science; Economics; Finance. **Benefits:** 401(k); Dental Insurance; Disability Coverage; Employee Discounts; Life Insurance; Medical Insurance; Pension Plan; Profit Sharing; Savings Plan; Tuition Assistance. **Special programs:** Internships. **Corporate headquarters location:** This Location. **Parent company:** GMAC Mortgage Corporation.

GENAMERICA FINANCIAL
700 Market Street, St. Louis MO 63101. 314/231-1700. **Contact:** Human Resources. **World Wide Web address:** http://www.genamerica.com. **Description:** Offers life insurance, securities, and other related financial services to corporate and individual clients. **Corporate headquarters location:** This Location.

JW GENESIS FINANCIAL CORPORATION
980 North Federal Highway, Boca Raton FL 33432. 561/338-2600. **Contact:** Human Resources. **Description:** Provides a wide range of financial services including research. **Corporate headquarters location:** This Location.

GOLDMAN SACHS & COMPANY
85 Broad Street, New York NY 10004. 212/902-1000. **Contact:** Recruiting Department. **World Wide Web address:** http://www.gs.com. **Description:** An investment banking firm. **Corporate headquarters location:** This Location.

GREAT LAKES HIGHER EDUCATION CORP.
2401 International Lane, Madison WI 53704. 608/246-1800. **Toll-free phone:** 800/274-4611. **Fax:** 608/246-1600. **Recorded jobline:** 608/240-1150. **Contact:** Human Resources Department. **E-mail address:** hresource@glhec.org. **World Wide Web address:** http://www.glhec.org. **Description:** A leading servicer and guarantor of student loans. **NOTE:** Entry-level positions are offered. **Common positions include:** Computer Operator; Computer Programmer; Customer Service Representative; Systems Analyst. **Educational backgrounds include:** Business Administration; C/C++; COBOL; Computer Science; Software Development; UNIX. **Benefits:** 403(b); Dental Insurance; Disability Coverage; Life Insurance; Medical Insurance;

Pension Plan; Tuition Assistance; Vision Insurance. **Special programs:** Internships. **Corporate headquarters location:** This Location. **Other U.S. locations:** Oak Brook IL; St. Paul MN; Columbus OH; Eau Claire WI. **Number of employees at this location:** 550.

GRUNTAL & CO., L.L.C.
One Liberty Plaza, New York NY 10006. 212/820-8200. **Fax:** 212/820-8988. **Contact:** Robert Getzewich, Director of Human Resources. **Description:** A financial services firm offering retail clients investment banking, trading, insurance, retirement plans, investment advisory services, fixed income research, and brokerage accounts. Gruntal & Company is one of the nation's largest full-service brokerage firms. **Common positions include:** Accountant; Attorney; Brokerage Clerk; Budget Analyst; Financial Analyst; Paralegal; Research Analyst; Telecommunications Manager; Typist/Word Processor. **Educational backgrounds include:** Accounting; Business Administration; Communications; Computer Science; Finance; Marketing. **Benefits:** 401(k); Disability Coverage; Life Insurance; Medical Insurance; Profit Sharing; Savings Plan. **Corporate headquarters location:** This Location. **Other U.S. locations:** Nationwide. **Listed on:** Privately held. **Number of employees at this location:** 600. **Number of employees nationwide:** 1,500.

J.B. HANAUER & COMPANY
4 Gatehall Drive, Parsippany NJ 07054. **Toll-free phone:** 888/524-8181. **Fax:** 973/829-0565. **Contact:** Human Resources. **Description:** A full-service brokerage firm specializing in fixed-income investments. J.B. Hanauer & Company provides a broad range of financial products and services. **NOTE:** Entry-level positions are offered. **Educational backgrounds include:** Accounting; Business Administration; Communications; Finance; Marketing; Mathematics. **Benefits:** 401(k); Dental Insurance; Disability Coverage; Employee Discounts; Financial Planning Assistance; Life Insurance; Medical Insurance. **Special programs:** Internships; Training. **Corporate headquarters location:** This Location. **Other U.S. locations:** North Miami FL; Tampa FL; West Palm Beach FL; Princeton NJ; Rye Brook NY; Philadelphia PA. **Listed on:** Privately held. **Number of employees at this location:** 250.

HAWTHORNE CORPORATION
P.O. Box 61000, Charleston SC 29419. 803/797-8484. **Contact:** Sue Johnson, Vice President. **World Wide Web address:** http://www.hawthornecorp.com. **Description:** A holding company whose companies are engaged in a wide variety of industries including aviation (operating airports); real estate operations that develop land for fixed base operations; and financial services (investor services). **Corporate headquarters location:** This Location.

HILLENBRAND INDUSTRIES, INC.
112 North Main Street, Batesville IN 47006. 812/934-7000. **Contact:** Tim Dietz, Human Resources. **World Wide Web address:** http://www.hillenbrand.com. **Description:** A holding company. **Corporate headquarters location:** This Location. **Subsidiaries include:** Batesville Casket Company, Inc. (Batesville IN) manufactures funeral-related products including caskets and urns. Forethought Financial Services (Batesville IN) provides financial services for the purpose of planning funeral arrangements. Hill-Rom Company, Inc. (Batesville IN) manufactures and rents a variety of health care products including birthing beds, hospital beds, and stretchers. **Listed on:** New York Stock Exchange.

HOME GOLD
3901 Pelham Road, Greenville SC 29615. 864/289-5319. **Contact:** Human Resources. **Description:** A mortgage lending company. **Corporate headquarters location:** This Location. **Subsidiaries include:** Carolina Investors, Inc. **CEO:** Jack Sterling. **Number of employees nationwide:**

HOMEBANC MORTGAGE CORP.
5555 Glenridge Connector NE, Suite 800, Atlanta GA 30328. 404/303-4113. **Fax:** 404/303-4116. **Contact:** Human Resources. **Description:** A full-service mortgage lender. **Common positions include:** Accountant; Computer Programmer; Customer Service Rep.; Financial Analyst; Human Resources Manager; Management Trainee; MIS Specialist; Purchasing Agent/Manager; Systems Analyst; Underwriter/Assistant Underwriter. **Educational backgrounds include:** Accounting; Business Administration; Finance; Liberal Arts; Marketing. **Benefits:** Dental Insurance; Disability Coverage; Employee Discounts; Life Insurance; Medical Insurance; Savings Plan; Tuition Assistance. **Corporate headquarters location:** This Location.

HOUSEHOLD INTERNATIONAL
2700 Sanders Road, Prospect Heights IL 60070. 847/564-6463. **Fax:** 847/205-7401. **Contact:** Sue Keenan, Human Resources Manager. **World Wide Web address:** http://www.household.com. **Description:** Household International is a provider of consumer finance and banking services, insurance, and investment products. **Common positions include:** Accountant; Administrator; Attorney; Bank Officer/Manager; Credit Manager; Financial Analyst; Human Resources Manager; Management Trainee; Marketing Specialist; Public Relations Specialist; Purchasing Agent/Manager; Systems Analyst. **Educational backgrounds include:** Accounting; Business Administration; Communications; Computer Science; Economics; Finance; Liberal Arts; Marketing; Mathematics. **Benefits:** Daycare Assistance; Dental Insurance; Disability Coverage; Employee Discounts; Life Insurance; Medical Insurance; Pension Plan; Profit Sharing; Savings Plan. **Special programs:** Internships. **Corporate headquarters location:** This Location. **Subsidiaries include:** Beneficial is a financial services company. Household Finance Corporation is one of the oldest and largest independent consumer finance companies in the U.S. and provides secured and unsecured loans for home improvement, education, bill consolidation, and leisure activities. Household Credit Services is one of the largest Visa/MasterCard providers in the U.S. Household Retail Services is a private credit card issuer. Household Bank, N.A. is a full-service banking institution. Household Automotive Finance Corporation provides financing services. **Listed on:** New York Stock Exchange.

K. HOVNANIAN COMPANIES
10 Highway 35, Red Bank NJ 07701. 732/747-7800. **Contact:** Human Resources. **World Wide Web address:** http://www.khov.com. **Description:** Designs, constructs, and sells condominium apartments, townhouses, and single-family residences in planned residential communities. The company is also engaged in mortgage banking. Founded in 1959. **NOTE:** Entry-level positions are offered. **Common positions include:** Accountant; Administrative Assistant; Architect; Attorney; Auditor; Civil Engineer; Computer Operator; Computer Programmer; Controller; Financial Analyst; Human Resources Manager; Market Research Analyst; Marketing Manager; Marketing Specialist; MIS Specialist; Online Content Specialist; Real Estate Agent; Sales Manager; Secretary; Systems Analyst; Systems Manager; Technical Writer/Editor; Webmaster. **Educational backgrounds include:** Accounting; Business Administration; Computer Science; Engineering; Marketing. **Benefits:** 401(k); Dental Insurance; Disability Coverage; Life Insurance; Medical Insurance; Profit Sharing; Tuition Assistance. **Corporate headquarters location:** This Location. **Other U.S. locations:** CA; FL; NC; NY; PA; VA. **Subsidiaries include:** New Fortis Homes. **Listed on:** American Stock Exchange. **Annual sales/revenues:** More than $100 million. **Number of employees at this location:** 90.

IMPERIAL CREDIT INDUSTRIES, INC.
23550 Hawthorne Boulevard, Building One, Suite 230, Torrance CA 90505. 310/791-8080. **Contact:** Human Resources. **World Wide Web address:** http://www.icii.com. **Description:** Offers business and consumer financing through five divisions: Business Finance Lending, Consumer Lending, Commercial Mortgage Lending, Franchise Lending, and Investment/Asset Management Services. **Corporate headquarters location:** This Location. **Subsidiaries include:** Auto Marketing Network, Inc. (Boca Raton FL); Franchise Mortgage Acceptance Company, LLC (Greenwich CT); Imperial Business Credit, Inc. (San Diego CA); Imperial Credit Advisors, Inc. (Santa Ana Heights CA); Southern Pacific Thrift and Loan Association (Los Angeles CA). **Listed on:** NASDAQ. **Stock exchange symbol:** ICII.

INTERPACIFIC INVESTORS SERVICES
2623 Second Avenue, Seattle WA 98121-1294. 206/269-5050. **Fax:** 206/269-5055. **Contact:** Human Resources. **E-mail address:** iistrading@aol.com. **World Wide Web address:** http://www.iisbonds.com. **Description:** A regional securities broker/dealer specializing in conservative investments such as corporate and municipal bonds, mutual funds, stocks, and life insurance. **Common positions include:** Branch Manager; Customer Service Rep.; Financial Services Sales Rep.; Securities Sales Rep. **Benefits:** Dental Insurance; Medical Insurance. **President/CEO/Owner:** Gary Lundgren. **Sales Manager:** Bill Shultheis.

ITEX CORPORATION
One Lincoln Center, 10300 SW Greenburg Road, Suite 370, Portland OR 97223. 503/244-4673. **Fax:** 503/244-2342. **Contact:** Human Resources. **World Wide Web address:** http://www.itex.com. **Description:** Operates one of the nation's largest barter exchanges with over 130 offices nationwide. ITEX operates an internationally accessible electronic trading and communications system known as BarterWire, which allows ITEX members coast-to-coast to market and purchase goods and services. The company publishes alt.finance, which focuses on the barter industry. All goods and services advertised within its pages are sold for ITEX trade dollars.

J.P. MORGAN & COMPANY, INC.
60 Wall Street, New York NY 10260-0060. 212/483-2323. **Contact:** Human Resources. **World Wide Web address:** http://www.jpmorgan.com. **Description:** One of the largest financial services firms in the United States. J.P. Morgan & Company, Inc. operates in five business sectors: Asset Management and Servicing, focusing on meeting the financial objectives of clients by structuring investment strategies and providing administrative, brokerage, and operational services; Finance and Advisory, providing advisory and financing services to a broad range of U.S. and international clients; Sales and Trading, which includes making markets

and taking positions in swap, fixed income securities, foreign exchange, and commodities; Equity Investments, managing J.P. Morgan's portfolio of equity investment securities; and Asset and Liability Management, which manages the firm's liquidity risk profile. Founded in 1838. **Educational backgrounds include:** Liberal Arts; Macintosh Computer; Mainframe; PC. **Special programs:** Internships; Co-ops. **Corporate headquarters location:** This Location. **Listed on:** New York Stock Exchange.

JANNEY MONTGOMERY SCOTT (JMS)
1801 Market Street, Philadelphia PA 19103-1675. 215/665-6000. **Toll-free phone:** 800/JAN-NEYS. **Contact:** Maryanne Melchiorre, Personnel Director. **World Wide Web address:** http://www. janneys.com. **Description:** A full-service brokerage firm with over 60 branch offices. **Common positions include:** Accountant; Financial Services Sales Rep.; Securities Sales Rep. **Educational backgrounds include:** Accounting. **Benefits:** Disability Coverage; Employee Discounts; Life Insurance; Medical Insurance; Profit Sharing; Savings Plan. **Corporate headquarters location:** This Location. **Parent company:** Penn Mutual Life Insurance Company. **Listed on:** American Stock Exchange; New York Stock Exchange.

JANUS CAPITAL
100 Fillmore Street, Denver CO 80206. 303/333-3863. **Contact:** Recruiting Manager. **World Wide Web address:** http://www.janus.com. **Description:** Manages mutual funds and offers a wide variety of account options and investment services. **Common positions include:** Clerical Supervisor; Computer Programmer; Customer Service Representative; Systems Analyst. **Educational backgrounds include:** Accounting; Computer Science; Liberal Arts. **Benefits:** Dental Insurance; Disability Coverage; Life Insurance; Medical Insurance; Pension Plan; Profit Sharing; Tuition Assistance. **Corporate headquarters location:** This Location. **Parent company:** KCSI. **Listed on:** Privately held. **Number of employees at this location:** 700.

JEFFERIES & COMPANY, INC.
11100 Santa Monica Boulevard, Los Angeles CA 90025. 310/445-1199. **Contact:** Human Resources. **World Wide Web address:** http://www.jefco.com. **Description:** Jefferies & Company is engaged in equity, convertible debt and taxable fixed income securities brokerage and trading, and corporate finance. Jefferies & Company is one of the leading national firms engaged in the distribution and trading of blocks of equity securities primarily in the third market. Founded in 1962. **Corporate headquarters location:** This Location. **Parent company:** Jefferies Group, Inc. is a holding company which, through Investment Technology Group, Inc., Jefferies & Company, Inc., Jefferies International Limited, and Jefferies Pacific Limited, is engaged in securities brokerage and trading, corporate finance, and other financial services.

JOHN HANCOCK FINANCIAL SERVICES
John Hancock Place, Box 111, Boston MA 02117. 617/572-4500. **Fax:** 617/572-4539. **Contact:** Employment Office. **E-mail address:** employment@jhancock.com. **World Wide Web address:** http://www.jhancock.com. **Description:** An insurance and financial services firm operating through two divisions: The Retail Sector offers protection and investment products to middle- and upper-income markets; The Investment & Pension Group is involved in bond and corporate finance services as well as in real estate and mortgage loans. Founded in 1862. **NOTE:** Entry-level positions are offered. **Common positions include:** Accountant;

Administrative Assistant; Computer Programmer; Consultant; Customer Service Representative; Database Manager; Daycare Worker; Financial Analyst; Management Trainee; Registered Nurse; Secretary; Systems Analyst; Systems Manager; Telecommunications Manager; Underwriter. **Educational backgrounds include:** Business Administration; Communications; Computer Science; Finance; Marketing; Mathematics. **Benefits:** 401(k); Daycare Assistance; Dental Insurance; Disability Coverage; Employee Discounts; Life Insurance; Medical Insurance; Pension Plan; Public Transit Available; Savings Plan; Telecommuting; Tuition Assistance. **Special programs:** Internships; Training. **Corporate headquarters location:** This Location. **International locations:** Belgium; Canada; England; Ireland; Malaysia; Singapore; Thailand. **Annual sales/revenues:** More than $100 million.

JOHNSTON, LEMON & COMPANY INC.
1101 Vermont Avenue NW, Suite 800, Washington DC 20005. 202/842-5500. **Contact:** Patty Maddox, Personnel Director. **Description:** Underwrites, distributes, and deals in corporate and municipal securities, revenue bonds, and mutual funds, and provides business management services. **Corporate headquarters location:** This Location.

JORDAN AMERICAN HOLDINGS, INC.
dba EQUITY ASSETS MANAGEMENT
2155 Resort Drive, Suite 108, Steamboat Springs CO 80487. **Toll-free phone:** 800/879-1189. **Fax:** 970/879-1272. **Contact:** Human Resources. **E-mail address:** info@jahi.com. **World Wide Web address:** http://www.jahi.com. **Description:** An investment advisory firm which manages equity portfolios. **Corporate headquarters location:** This Location. **Other U.S. locations:** Richardson TX.

KEYCORP
127 Public Square, Cleveland OH 44114. 216/689-3000. **Contact:** Human Resources. **World Wide Web address:** http://www.key.com. **Description:** A diverse financial services company offering commercial and retail banking, financial management, brokerage services, mortgage banking, and trust services. **Common positions include:** Accountant/Auditor; Bank Officer/Manager; Branch Manager; Computer Programmer; Credit Manager; Customer Service Rep.; Department Manager; Financial Analyst; Human Resources Manager; Management Trainee; Marketing Specialist; Operations/Production Manager; Public Relations Specialist; Quality Control Supervisor; Services Sales Rep.; Systems Analyst. **Educational backgrounds include:** Accounting; Business Administration; Economics; Finance; Marketing. **Benefits:** Dental Insurance; Disability Coverage; Employee Discounts; Life Insurance; Medical Insurance; Pension Plan; Profit Sharing; Savings Plan; Tuition Assistance. **Corporate headquarters location:** This Location.

J.I. KISLAK MORTGAGE CORPORATION
7900 Miami Lakes Drive West, Miami Lakes FL 33016. 305/364-4116. **Contact:** Human Resources. **Description:** A mortgage banking and real estate firm. **Common positions include:** Accountant; Bank Officer/Manager; Branch Manager; Claim Rep.; Computer Programmer; Customer Service Rep.; Department Manager; Financial Analyst; Human Resources Manager; Industrial Agent/Broker; Loan Officer; Marketing Specialist; Systems Analyst; Underwriter. **Educational backgrounds include:** Accounting; Business Administration; Computer Science; Finance; Marketing. **Benefits:** Dental Insurance; Disability Coverage; Employee Discounts; Life Insurance;

Medical Insurance; Pension Plan; Profit Sharing; Tuition Assistance. **Corporate headquarters location:** This Location.

KOMATSU FINANCIAL
P.O. Box 7049, Downers Grove IL 60515-7049. 630/434-3500. **Fax:** 630/434-3940. **Contact:** Denise Cat, Human Resources Administrator. **World Wide Web address:** http://www. komatsuamerica.com. **Description:** Provides finance and leasing services to distributors and customers of Komatsu Construction and Mining Equipment. **NOTE:** Entry-level positions are offered. **Common positions include:** Accountant; Computer Programmer; Financial Analyst; Network/Systems Administrator; Secretary. **Educational backgrounds include:** Accounting; Finance; Microsoft Word; Spreadsheets. **Benefits:** 401(k); Casual Dress - Fridays; Dental Insurance; Disability Coverage; Employee Discounts; Life Insurance; Medical Insurance; Pension Plan; Tuition Assistance; Vacation Days (6 - 10). **Special programs:** Training. **Office hours:** Monday - Friday, 8:00 a.m. - 5:00 p.m. **Corporate headquarters location:** Vernon Hills IL. **Parent company:** Komatsu America.

LEGG MASON WOOD WALKER, INC.
100 Light Street, Baltimore MD 21202. 410/539-3400. **Contact:** Human Resources. **World Wide Web address:** http://www.leggmason.com. **Description:** A full-service broker-dealer that also offers investment banking services. **Parent company:** Legg Mason, Inc. (Baltimore MD) is a holding company with subsidiaries engaged in securities brokerage and trading; investment management of mutual funds and individual and institutional accounts; underwriting of corporate and municipal securities and other investment banking activities; sales of annuities and banking services; and the provision of other financial services. The company serves its brokerage clients through 128 offices and manages $82 billion in assets for individual and institutional accounts and mutual funds. The company's mortgage banking subsidiaries have direct and master servicing responsibilities for $12 billion of commercial mortgages.

LEHMAN BROTHERS HOLDINGS
3 World Financial Center, New York NY 10285. 212/526-7000. **Contact:** Human Resources. **World Wide Web address:** http://www.lehman.com. **Description:** A stock brokerage and investment banking firm. **Corporate headquarters location:** This Location. **Annual sales/revenues:** More than $100 million.

LIBERTY FUNDS SERVICES, INC.
12100 East Iliff Avenue, Suite 300, Aurora CO 80014. 303/337-6555. **Toll-free phone:** 800/627-2472. **Fax:** 303/743-6341. **Recorded jobline:** 800/225-2365x3230. **Contact:** Human Resources. **World Wide Web address:** http://www. libertyfunds.com. **Description:** Provides transfer agency services for the shareholders of funds managed by the parent company's other subsidiaries including Colonial Management Associates, Inc., Stein Roe and Farnham Inc., The Crabbe Huson Group, Inc., and Newport Fund Management. Founded in 1931. **NOTE:** Entry-level positions are offered. **Common positions include:** Customer Service Representative. **Educational backgrounds include:** Business Administration; Economics; Finance. **Benefits:** 401(k); Casual Dress - Daily; Dental Insurance; Disability Coverage; Employee Discounts; Flexible Schedule; Life Insurance; Medical Insurance; Profit Sharing; Tuition Assistance; Vacation Days (6 - 10). **Special**

programs: Training. **Office hours:** Monday - Friday, 6:00 a.m. - 6:00 p.m. **Corporate headquarters location:** Boston MA. **Number of employees at this location:** 100.

LINCOLN FINANCIAL ADVISORS
8755 West Higgins Road, Suite 550, Chicago IL 60631. 773/380-8518. **Fax:** 773/693-2531. **Contact:** Helen S. Rancich, Director of Recruiting. **E-mail address:** hsrancich@lnc.com. **World Wide Web address:** http://www.lfaonline.com. **Description:** Markets financial planning, permanent and term life insurance, annuities, disability coverage, and investment products to business owners and professionals. The company also provides complex estate planning and business planning advice. Founded in 1905. **Common positions include:** Insurance Agent/Broker; Sales Executive; Sales Rep. **Educational backgrounds include:** Accounting; Business Administration; Communications; Economics; Finance; Liberal Arts; Marketing. **Benefits:** 401(k); Dental Insurance; Medical Insurance; Tuition Assistance. **Special programs:** Training. **Office hours:** Monday - Friday, 9:00 a.m. - 5:00 p.m. **Other U.S. locations:** Nationwide. **International locations:** Argentina; China; United Kingdom. **Parent company:** Lincoln Financial Group. **Listed on:** New York Stock Exchange. **Stock exchange symbol:** LNC. **CEO:** James Morris.

LUTHERAN BROTHERHOOD COMPANY
625 Fourth Avenue South, Minneapolis MN 55415. 612/340-7054. **Contact:** Gwen Martin, Manager of Staffing and Employee Relations. **World Wide Web address:** http://www.luthbro.com. **Description:** A financial institution providing life, health, and disability insurance, in addition to annuities and mutual funds. **Common positions include:** Actuary; Computer Programmer. **Educational backgrounds include:** Computer Science; Mathematics. **Benefits:** Dental Insurance; Disability Coverage; Life Insurance; Medical Insurance; Pension Plan; Tuition Assistance. **Corporate headquarters location:** This Location.

MBNA AMERICA
1100 North King Street, Wilmington DE 19884. **Toll-free phone:** 800/441-7048. **Contact:** Personnel. **World Wide Web address:** http://www. mbna.com. **Description:** This location oversees satellite telesales centers in Dover DE, State College PA, and Towson MD. MBNA America is a leader in issuing MasterCard Gold cards and affinity credit cards. The company also offers home equity and personal loans. **Common positions include:** Bank Officer/Manager; Collections Agent; Customer Service Representative; Financial Analyst. **Educational backgrounds include:** Business Administration; Liberal Arts. **Benefits:** 401(k); Daycare Assistance; Dental Insurance; Disability Coverage; Employee Discounts; Life Insurance; Medical Insurance; Pension Plan; Savings Plan; Tuition Assistance. **Special programs:** Internships. **Corporate headquarters location:** This Location. **Subsidiaries include:** MBNA America Bank, N.A.

MFS INVESTMENT MANAGEMENT
500 Boylston Street, Boston MA 02116. 617/954-5000. **Fax:** 617/236-7540. **Contact:** Joyce Schroeder, Senior Human Resources Generalist. **E-mail address:** resume@mfs.com. **World Wide Web address:** http://www.mfs.com. **Description:** A full-service investment management firm. **NOTE:** Entry-level positions are offered. **Common positions include:** Accountant; Administrative Assistant; Computer Operator; Computer Programmer; Customer Service Rep.; Database Manager; Financial Analyst; Market Research

Analyst; MIS Specialist; Paralegal; Project Manager; Software Engineer; Systems Analyst; Systems Manager; Technical Writer/Editor. **Educational backgrounds include:** Accounting; Business Administration; Computer Science; Economics; Finance; Liberal Arts; Marketing. **Benefits:** 401(k); Daycare Assistance; Dental Insurance; Disability Coverage; EAP; Employee Discounts; Life Insurance; Medical Insurance; Pension Plan; Public Transit Available; Tuition Assistance. **Corporate headquarters location:** This Location. **Parent company:** Sun Life Assurance.

MS DIVERSIFIED CORPORATION

P.O. Box 6005, Ridgeland MS 39158. 601/978-6732. **Contact:** Human Resources. **Description:** Provides a wide range of products and services to automotive dealers and financial institutions. Products and services include credit life insurance; accident and health insurance; vehicle extended service contracts; administrative services; automobile financing; and financial services. **Common positions include:** Accountant; Computer Programmer; Customer Service Representative; MIS Specialist; Paralegal; Systems Analyst. **Educational backgrounds include:** Accounting; Business Administration; Computer Science; Finance; Marketing. **Benefits:** 401(k); Disability Coverage; Flexible Schedule; Life Insurance; Medical Insurance; Tuition Assistance. **Corporate headquarters location:** This Location. **Subsidiaries include:** CMS Insurance Agency, Inc.; Gulf Atlantic Insurance Agency; MRS Insurance Company; MS Byrider Sales, Inc.; MS Casualty Insurance Company; MS Dealer Services, Inc.; MS Life Insurance Company; MS Loan Center, Inc.; MS Services, Inc. **Number of employees at this location:** 100.

MARSHALL & ILSLEY TRUST COMPANY OF FLORIDA

800 Laurel Oak Drive, Suite 101, Naples FL 34108. 941/597-2933. **Contact:** William A. Wade, President. **World Wide Web address:** http://www. mitrust.com. **Description:** Provides trust and custodial services for corporate, institutional, and individual clients in the Southeast. **Parent company:** Marshall & Ilsley Corporation (Milwaukee WI) is a diversified, interstate bank holding company. Other subsidiaries of Marshall & Ilsley include M&I Data Services, Inc. (supplies data processing services and software for financial institutions throughout the United States and in foreign countries); M&I Investment Management Corp. (manages investment portfolios for corporations, nonprofit organizations, and individuals throughout the United States and acts as an investment advisor to the Marshall Funds); M&I Marshall & Ilsley Trust Company of Arizona (provides trust and custodial services to clients in the Southwest); M&I First National Leasing Corp. (leases equipment and machinery to businesses throughout the United States, primarily to middle-market corporations); M&I Capital Markets Group, Inc. (invests in small- and medium-sized companies to help establish new businesses or recapitalize existing companies); M&I Brokerage Services, Inc. (a brokerage company providing a full range of investment products including stocks, bonds, and mutual funds for individual investors and small businesses); M&I Mortgage Corp. (originates and services a wide variety of home mortgages for M&I banks and other financial institutions); Richter-Schroeder Company, Inc. (provides construction loans and arranges permanent financing on income properties); and M&I Insurance Services, Inc. (acts as an independent insurance agency providing a full range of insurance products including annuities).

MELLON FINANCIAL CORPORATION

500 Grant Street, One Mellon Bank Center, Room 705, Pittsburgh PA 15258. 412/234-5000. **Contact:** Human Resources Department. **E-mail address:** recruiting@mellon.com. **World Wide Web address:** http://www.mellon.com. **Description:** A holding company for national commercial banks with assets of $30 billion. Through its subsidiaries, the company offers consumer investment services (private asset management services and retail mutual funds); consumer banking services (consumer lending, branch banking, credit cards, mortgage loan origination and servicing, and jumbo residential mortgage lending); corporate/institutional investment services (institutional trust and custody, institutional asset and institutional mutual fund management and administration, securities lending, foreign exchange, cash management, and stock transfer); corporate/institutional banking services (large corporate and middle market lending, asset-based lending, certain capital market and leasing activities, commercial real estate lending, and insurance premium financing); and real estate workout (commercial real estate and mortgage banking recovery operations). **Corporate headquarters location:** This Location. **Subsidiaries include:** Mellon Mortgage Company.

MERRILL LYNCH

World Financial Center, North Tower, 250 Vesey, New York NY 10281. 212/449-1000. **Contact:** Human Resources. **World Wide Web address:** http://www.ml.com. **Description:** One of the largest securities brokerage firms in the United States, Merrill Lynch provides financial services in the following areas: securities, extensive insurance, and real estate and related services. The company also brokers commodity futures, commodity options, and corporate and municipal securities. In addition, Merrill Lynch is engaged in investment banking activities. **NOTE:** Jobseekers are asked to call for specific information on where to mail resumes. **Corporate headquarters location:** This Location. **Other U.S. locations:** Nationwide. **International locations:** Worldwide. **Listed on:** New York Stock Exchange. **Annual sales/revenues:** More than $100 million. **Number of employees worldwide:** 63,800.

M.H. MEYERSON & COMPANY, INC.

525 Washington Boulevard, Jersey City NJ 07303. 201/459-9515. **Toll-free phone:** 800/888-8118. **Contact:** Human Resources. **World Wide Web address:** http://www.mhmeyerson.com. **Description:** Markets and trades approximately 2,000 securities. The company is also an active underwriter of small and mid-sized capitalization debt and equity services. M.H. Meyerson is licensed in 38 states and Washington DC and services approximately 8,500 retail accounts through its retail clearing agent, Bear, Stearns Securities Corporation. The company is also engaged in a variety of investment banking, underwriting, and venture capital activities. M.H. Meyerson provides comprehensive planning services to its corporate clients including public offerings and private placements of securities. Founded in 1960. **Corporate headquarters location:** This Location. **Other U.S. locations:** North Miami Beach FL. **CEO:** Martin H. Meyerson.

THE MONY GROUP

1740 Broadway, New York NY 10019. 212/708-2000. **Contact:** Personnel Department. **Description:** A mutual life insurer offering life insurance, disability income, and annuities. The company also operates investment subsidiaries engaged in the management of mutual funds and the distribution of securities. **Educational backgrounds include:** Accounting; Mathematics. **Benefits:** 401(k); Dental

Insurance; Disability Coverage; Life Insurance; Medical Insurance; Pension Plan; Savings Plan; Tuition Assistance. **Special programs:** Internships. **Corporate headquarters location:** This Location.

MORGAN STANLEY DEAN WITTER & CO.
1585 Broadway, New York NY 10036. 212/761-4000. **Contact:** Human Resources. **World Wide Web address:** http://www.msdw.com. **Description:** One of the largest investment banking firms in the United States. Services include financing; financial advisory services; real estate services; corporate bond services; equity services; government and money market services; merger and acquisition services; investment research services; investment management services; and individual investor services. **Corporate headquarters location:** This Location.

NVR, INC.
7601 Lewinsville Road, Suite 300, McLean VA 22102. 703/761-2000. **Fax:** 703/761-2259. **Contact:** Human Resources. **World Wide Web address:** http://www.nvrinc.com. **Description:** A national home builder and mortgage company. Founded in 1948. **NOTE:** Entry-level positions and part-time jobs are offered. **Common positions include:** Accountant; Architect; Auditor; Civil Engineer; Construction Contractor; Draftsperson; Financial Analyst; Management Trainee; Production Manager; Project Manager; Sales Executive; Sales Manager; Sales Rep. **Educational backgrounds include:** Accounting; Business Administration; Computer Science; Engineering; Finance; Marketing; MBA; Microsoft Office; Microsoft Word; Spreadsheets. **Benefits:** 401(k); Casual Dress - Daily; Dental Insurance; Disability Coverage; Employee Discounts; Life Insurance; Medical Insurance; Pension Plan; Profit Sharing; Relocation Assistance; Savings Plan; Sick Days; Tuition Assistance; Vacation Days (10 - 20). **Special programs:** Internships; Training; Co-ops; Summer Jobs. **Office hours:** Monday - Friday, 8:00 a.m. - 5:00 p.m. **Corporate headquarters location:** This Location. **Other U.S. locations:** DE; MD; NC; NJ; NY; OH; PA; SC; TN.

NVR MORTGAGE FINANCE INC.
100 Ryan Court, Pittsburgh PA 15205. 412/276-4225. **Fax:** 412/429-4542. **Contact:** Lawrence M. Gorney, Manager of Human Resources. **Description:** Provides financial and mortgage services. **Common positions include:** Accountant; Customer Service Rep.; Loan Officer; Quality Control Supervisor; Underwriter. **Educational backgrounds include:** Accounting; Business Administration; Economics; Finance; Marketing. **Benefits:** 401(k); Dental Insurance; Life Insurance; Medical Insurance; Profit Sharing. **Corporate headquarters location:** This Location. **Other U.S. locations:** Nationwide. **Parent company:** NVR.

NATIONAL ASSOCIATION OF SECURITIES DEALERS, INC.
1735 K Street NW, Washington DC 20006. 202/728-8470. **Contact:** Human Resources. **Description:** A self-regulatory organization of the securities industry responsible for the regulation of NASDAQ and the over-the-counter securities markets. **Common positions include:** Attorney; Customer Service Rep.; Human Resources Manager; Marketing Specialist; Statistician; Systems Analyst. **Educational backgrounds include:** Accounting; Business Administration; Finance; Marketing. **Benefits:** Dental Insurance; Disability Coverage; Life Insurance; Medical Insurance; Pension Plan; Savings Plan; Tuition Assistance. **Special programs:** Internships. **Corporate headquarters location:** This Location.

NATIONAL RURAL UTILITIES COOPERATIVE FINANCE CORPORATION
2201 Cooperative Way, Herndon VA 20171. 703/709-6700. **Contact:** Human Resources. **World Wide Web address:** http://www.nrucfc.org. **Description:** A nonprofit financial institution owned by more than 1,000 rural electric systems and related organizations. National Rural Utilities Cooperative Finance Corporation offers its members/owners a variety of loan, investment, service, and specialized financing options to supplement the loan programs of the Rural Utilities Service of the United States Department of Agriculture. The company operates through 13 regional representatives located throughout the United States. The company also has two controlled affiliates, Rural Telephone Finance Cooperative and Guaranty Funding Cooperative. **Corporate headquarters location:** This Location.

NATIONAL SECURITIES CORPORATION
1001 Fourth Avenue, Suite 2200, Seattle WA 98154. 206/622-7200. **Contact:** Human Resources. **World Wide Web address:** http://www. nationalsecurities.com. **Description:** A securities brokerage. **Corporate headquarters location:** This Location.

NEW YORK STOCK EXCHANGE
11 Wall Street, New York NY 10005. 212/656-2266. **Contact:** Martin Bressler, Managing Director of Staffing and Training. **World Wide Web address:** http://www.nyse.com. **Description:** The principal securities trading marketplace in the United States, serving a broad range of industries within and outside of the securities industry. More than 2,500 corporations, accounting for approximately 40 percent of American corporate revenues, are listed on the exchange. The New York Stock Exchange is engaged in a wide range of public affairs and economic research programs. **Common positions include:** Accountant/Auditor; Administrative Manager; Assistant Manager; Attorney; Blue-Collar Worker Supervisor; Branch Manager; Broadcast Technician; Budget Analyst; Cashier; Claim Representative; Computer Operator; Computer Programmer; Customer Service Rep.; Department Manager; Economist; Editor; Education Administrator; Electrician; Financial Manager; General Manager; Human Resources Manager; Inspector/Tester/Grader; Library Technician; Management Trainee; Market Research Analyst; Marketing Manager; Operations Research Analyst; Paralegal; Payroll Clerk; Photographer/Camera Operator; Postal Clerk/Mail Carrier; Property and Real Estate Manager; Public Relations Specialist; Purchasing Agent/Manager; Radio/TV Announcer/Broadcaster; Receptionist; Secretary; Software Engineer; Stenographer; Systems Analyst; Technical Writer/Editor; Typist/Word Processor. **Educational backgrounds include:** Accounting; Business Administration; Communications; Computer Science; Economics; Finance; Liberal Arts; Marketing. **Benefits:** Dental Insurance; Disability Coverage; Employee Discounts; Life Insurance; Medical Insurance; Pension Plan; Savings Plan; Tuition Assistance; Vision Insurance. **Corporate headquarters location:** This Location.

NISSAN MOTOR ACCEPTANCE CORP.
P.O. Box 2870, Torrance CA 90509-2870. 310/719-8000. **Contact:** Human Resources. **Description:** An automotive finance company whose primary services are dealership and retail customer financing. **Common positions include:** Accountant; Administrative Manager; Attorney; Budget Analyst; Customer Service Rep.; Financial Analyst; Financial Services Sales Rep.; Human Resources Manager; Paralegal; Securities Sales Rep. **Educational**

backgrounds include: Accounting; Business Administration; Finance; Marketing. **Benefits:** 401(k); Dental Insurance; Disability Coverage; Employee Discounts; Life Insurance; Medical Insurance; Pension Plan; Tuition Assistance. **Corporate headquarters location:** This Location. **Other U.S. locations:** Dallas TX. **Number of employees at this location:** 175.

NORTHERN LIFE INSURANCE
P.O. Box 12530, Seattle WA 98111-4530. **Toll-free phone:** 800/426-7050. **Fax:** 800/531-5026. **Recorded jobline:** 206/676-2737. **Contact:** Suzanne Crosby, Staffing Specialist. **World Wide Web address:** http://www.northernlifetsa.com. **Description:** A leading provider of financial products including tax sheltered annuities to the educational market. **NOTE:** Entry-level positions and part-time jobs are offered. **Common positions include:** Accountant; Administrative Assistant; Applications Engineer; Computer Operator; Computer Programmer; Computer Support Technician; Computer Technician; Customer Service Rep.; Database Administrator; Desktop Publishing Specialist; Financial Analyst; Human Resources Manager; MIS Specialist; Network/Systems Administrator; Paralegal; Sales Rep.; Secretary; Software Engineer; SQL Programmer; Systems Analyst; Technical Writer/Editor; Telecommunications Manager; Typist/Word Processor. **Educational backgrounds include:** Accounting; Business Administration; C/C++; Communications; Computer Science; Economics; Finance; HTML; Internet; Java; Marketing; Mathematics; MCSE; Microsoft Word; Novell; QuarkXPress; Software Development; Software Tech. Support; Spreadsheets. **Benefits:** 401(k); Casual Dress - Daily; Daycare Assistance; Dental Insurance; Disability Coverage; Employee Discounts; Financial Planning Assistance; Flexible Schedule; Health Club Discount; Job Sharing; Life Insurance; Medical Insurance; Profit Sharing; Public Transit Available; Savings Plan; Sick Days (6 - 10); Telecommuting; Tuition Assistance; Vacation Days (6 - 10). **Special programs:** Internships; Summer Jobs. **Corporate headquarters location:** Minneapolis MN. **Other U.S. locations:** CT; ND; NY; TX; VA. **Parent company:** Reliastar. **Sales Manager:** Brad Corbin. **Annual sales/revenues:** More than $100 million.

OLD KENT FINANCIAL CORPORATION
1830 East Paris SE, Grand Rapids MI 49546. 616/771-5812. **Fax:** 616/771-6992. **Recorded jobline:** 800/552-4350. **Contact:** Human Resources. **E-mail address:** careers@oldkent.com. **World Wide Web address:** http://www.oldkent.com. **Description:** A financial services institution which, through its subsidiaries, provides mortgage loans and traditional banking services. **NOTE:** Entry-level positions, part-time jobs, and second and third shifts are offered. **Common positions include:** Administrative Assistant; Assistant Manager; Bank Officer/Manager; Branch Manager; Computer Programmer; Credit Manager; Customer Service Rep.; Database Administrator; Database Manager; Financial Analyst; Help-Desk Technician; Intranet Developer; Management Trainee; Marketing Specialist; Sales Manager; Sales Rep.; Secretary; Underwriter/Assistant Underwriter; Webmaster; Website Developer. **Educational backgrounds include:** Accounting; Business Administration; Communications; Computer Science; Economics; Finance; Marketing; MBA; Microsoft Office; Microsoft Word; Spreadsheets. **Benefits:** 401(k); Dental Insurance; Disability Coverage; Employee Discounts; Financial Planning Assistance; Life Insurance; Medical Insurance; Pension Plan; Profit Sharing; Relocation Assistance;

Sick Days (6 - 10); Tuition Assistance; Vacation Days. **Special programs:** Internships; Training. **Corporate headquarters location:** This Location. **Other area locations:** Southfield MI. **Other U.S. locations:** Elmhurst IL. **Subsidiaries include:** Old Kent Bank; Old Kent Mortgage. **Listed on:** New York Stock Exchange. **Stock exchange symbol:** OK. **CEO:** David Wagner. **Number of employees at this location:** 4,500.

OPPENHEIMER CAPITAL, L.P.
1345 Avenue of the Americas, New York NY 10105. 212/739-3000. **Contact:** Personnel. **Description:** Engaged in nationwide management, finance, investment banking, and securities brokering. **Corporate headquarters location:** This Location.

PNC FINANCIAL SERVICES GROUP
2 PNC Plaza, 620 Liberty Avenue, 2nd Floor, Pittsburgh PA 15222-2719. **Fax:** 800/267-3755. **Recorded jobline:** 800/PNC-JOBS. **Contact:** Human Resources. **World Wide Web address:** http://www.pnc.com. **Description:** One of the nation's largest financial services companies. Major businesses include corporate banking, consumer banking, PNC Mortgage, and PNC Asset Management Group. **NOTE:** Entry-level positions, part-time jobs, and second and third shifts are offered. **Common positions include:** Accountant; Adjuster; Administrative Assistant; Administrative Manager; Assistant Manager; Attorney; Auditor; Bank Officer/Manager; Bank Teller; Budget Analyst; Clerical Supervisor; Computer Operator; Computer Programmer; Computer Support Technician; Computer Technician; Credit Manager; Customer Service Rep.; Database Administrator; Database Manager; Finance Director; Financial Analyst; Fund Manager; Human Resources Manager; Management Trainee; MIS Specialist; Network/Systems Administrator; Operations Manager; Paralegal; Purchasing Agent/Manager; Secretary; Securities Sales Rep.; Services Sales Representative; SQL Programmer; Systems Analyst; Systems Manager; Typist/Word Processor; Webmaster. **Educational backgrounds include:** Accounting; Business Administration; COBOL; Communications; Computer Science; Economics; Finance; Internet; Java; Liberal Arts; Marketing; MCSE; Microsoft Word; Novell; Software Development; Software Tech. Support; Spreadsheets; SQL. **Benefits:** 401(k); Adoption Assistance; Casual Dress - Fridays; Dental Insurance; Disability Coverage; EAP; Employee Discounts; Financial Planning Assistance; Flexible Schedule; Job Sharing; Life Insurance; Medical Insurance; Pension Plan; Sick Days (6 - 10); Telecommuting; Tuition Assistance; Vacation Days (6 - 10). **Special programs:** Training; Co-ops; Summer Jobs. **Corporate headquarters location:** This Location. **Other area locations:** Philadelphia PA. **Other U.S. locations:** Chicago IL; Louisville KY; Cincinnati OH. **Subsidiaries include:** Blackrock Financial Management; PNC Mortgage. **President/CEO:** James E. Rohr. **Number of employees at this location:** 5,000.

PNC MORTGAGE
75 North Fairway Drive, Vernon Hills IL 60061. 847/549-6500. **Fax:** 847/549-2568. **Contact:** Human Resources. **World Wide Web address:** http://www.pncmortgage.com. **Description:** A full-service mortgage banking company that originates, acquires, and services residential mortgage loans. **Common positions include:** Accountant/Auditor; Administrative Manager; Attorney; Brokerage Clerk; Claim Rep.; Computer Programmer; Credit Manager; Customer Service Rep.; Financial Analyst; General Manager; Human Resources

Manager; MIS Specialist; Paralegal; Services Sales Rep.; Software Engineer; Systems Analyst; Underwriter/Assistant Underwriter. **Educational backgrounds include:** Accounting; Business Administration; Communications; Computer Science; Finance; Liberal Arts; Marketing; Mathematics. **Benefits:** 401(k); Daycare Assistance; Dental Insurance; Disability Coverage; Employee Discounts; Life Insurance; Medical Insurance; Profit Sharing; Savings Plan; Stock Option; Tuition Assistance. **Special programs:** Internships. **Corporate headquarters location:** This Location. **Other U.S. locations:** Nationwide. **Parent company:** PNC Financial Services Group.

PACIFIC LIFE INSURANCE
700 Newport Center Drive, Newport Beach CA 92660. 949/640-3011. **Contact:** Human Resources. **World Wide Web address:** http://www. pacificlife.com. **Description:** Provides insurance services including group health, life, and pensions. Pacific Life Insurance also provides financial services including annuities, mutual funds, and investments. **Corporate headquarters location:** This Location.

PAINEWEBBER INC.
1285 Avenue of the Americas, 3rd Floor, New York NY 10019. 212/713-2000. **Contact:** Human Resources. **World Wide Web address:** http://www. painewebber.com. **Description:** An investment banking firm assisting corporations, governments, and individuals in meeting their long-term financial needs. PaineWebber also has operations in equity and fixed-income securities. **Common positions include:** Accountant/Auditor; Brokerage Clerk; Computer Programmer; Payroll Clerk; Secretary; Systems Analyst. **Educational backgrounds include:** Accounting; Computer Science; Finance. **Benefits:** Disability Coverage; Employee Discounts; Life Insurance; Medical Insurance; Pension Plan; Savings Plan; Tuition Assistance. **Corporate headquarters location:** This Location. **Other U.S. locations:** Nationwide.

PAULSON INVESTMENT COMPANY
811 SW Naito Parkway, Suite 200, Portland OR 97204. 503/243-6000. **Contact:** Human Resources. **Description:** Paulson Investment Company is a full-service brokerage firm engaged in the purchase and sale of securities, trading, market-making, and other investment banking activities. The company has independent branch offices in cities throughout the West, Midwest, and on the East Coast, with more than 141 brokers dedicated to providing services to professional investors and corporations, as well as to individual investors. **Corporate headquarters location:** This Location. **Parent company:** Paulson Capital Corporation. **Number of employees at this location:** 100.

PEACHTREE PLANNING CORPORATION
3131 Maple Drive NE, Atlanta GA 30305. 404/231-0839. **Contact:** Robert E. Mathis, President/CEO. **Description:** Specializes in estate planning (wealth creation and wealth conservation). Product lines include stocks, bonds, mutual funds, life insurance, disability insurance, and annuities. **Common positions include:** Administrative Worker/Clerk; Insurance Agent/Broker; Sales Rep.; Securities Sales Rep. **Educational backgrounds include:** Accounting; Business Administration; College Degree; Communications; Economics; Finance; Marketing; Mathematics; Sales. **Benefits:** Dental Insurance; Disability Coverage; Employee Discounts; Life Insurance; Medical Insurance; Pension Plan; Tuition Assistance. **Corporate headquarters location:** This Location. **Number of employees at this location:** 45.

PHILLIPS & COMPANY SECURITIES
220 NW Second Avenue, Suite 950, Portland OR 97209. 503/228-2723. **Toll-free phone:** 888/667-4114. **Fax:** 503/224-8207. **Contact:** Executive Recruiter. **Description:** A brokerage firm specializing in private client sales which are directed to CEOs and institutional accounts. **NOTE:** Entry-level positions are offered. **Common positions include:** Broker. **Educational backgrounds include:** Accounting; Business Administration; Economics; Finance; Marketing; Mathematics; Public Relations. **Benefits:** 401(k); Dental Insurance; Medical Insurance. **Special programs:** Training. **Corporate headquarters location:** This Location.

THE PIONEER GROUP, INC.
60 State Street, Mail Code MA02109, Boston MA 02109. 617/742-7825. **Contact:** Human Resources. **World Wide Web address:** http://www. pioneerfunds.com. **Description:** Offers individual investment, institutional investment management, real estate advisory, venture capital, and emerging market services. **Corporate headquarters location:** This Location.

PRINCIPAL FINANCIAL GROUP
711 High Street, Des Moines IA 50392. 515/247-5224. **Contact:** Human Resources. **World Wide Web address:** http://www.principal.com. **Description:** Provides financial services including annuities, home mortgages, mutual funds, and retirement plans. The Principal Financial Group also offers dental, disability, health, life, and vision insurance policies. **Corporate headquarters location:** This Location. **Subsidiaries include:** Principal Life Insurance Company; Principal Residential Mortgage, Inc.

PROVIDIAN FINANCIAL
201 Mission Street, San Francisco CA 94105. 415/543-0404. **Contact:** Human Resources. **World Wide Web address:** http://www.providian.com. **Description:** Provides lending, deposit, bank card issuing, and other related financial services. **Corporate headquarters location:** This Location.

PRUDENTIAL PREFERRED FINANCIAL SERVICES
3495 Piedmont Road, Building 12, Suite 300, Atlanta GA 30305. 404/262-2600. **Fax:** 404/262-1835. **Contact:** Pat Churchill, Human Resources Director. **World Wide Web address:** http://www. prudential.com. **Description:** Markets a complete portfolio of insurance (group life and health) and financial services products to business owners, professionals, and upper-income individuals. Founded in 1875. **Common positions include:** Attorney; Bank Officer/Manager; Financial Consultant; Insurance Agent/Broker; Management Trainee; Sales Representative; Teacher/Professor. **Educational backgrounds include:** Accounting; Business Administration; Finance; Liberal Arts; Management/Planning; Marketing. **Benefits:** 401(k); Dental Insurance; Disability Coverage; Life Insurance; Medical Insurance; Pension Plan; Savings Plan; Tuition Assistance. **Special programs:** Training. **Office hours:** Monday - Friday, 8:00 a.m. - 5:00 p.m. **Corporate headquarters location:** Newark NJ. **Other U.S. locations:** Nationwide. **International locations:** Worldwide. **Parent company:** Prudential Insurance Company of America.

PRUDENTIAL SECURITIES INC.
One New York Plaza, New York NY 10292. 212/778-1000. **Contact:** Director of Personnel. **World Wide Web address:** http://www. prusec.com. **Description:** An international

securities brokerage and investment firm. The company offers clients more than 70 investment products including stocks, options, bonds, commodities, tax-favored investments, and insurance, as well as several specialized financial services. **Corporate headquarters location:** This Location. **Parent company:** Prudential Insurance Company of America.
Other U.S. locations:
• 2300 Kettering Tower, Dayton OH 45423. 937/228-2828.

PUBLIC FINANCIAL MANAGEMENT, INC.
2 Logan Square, Suite 1600, Philadelphia PA 19103. 215/567-6100. **Fax:** 215/567-4180. **Contact:** Chris Hinke, Human Resources Associate. **E-mail address:** recruit@publicfm.com. **World Wide Web address:** http://www.pfm.com. **Description:** A leading financial advisory firm serving the public sector. Public Financial Management oversees $7.5 billion in public sector funds. **Common positions include:** Financial Analyst. **Educational backgrounds include:** Economics; Finance; Liberal Arts; Mathematics. **Benefits:** 401(k); Casual Dress - Fridays; Dental Insurance; Disability Coverage; Employee Discounts; Life Insurance; Medical Insurance; Profit Sharing; Tuition Assistance. **Corporate headquarters location:** This Location. **Other area locations:** Harrisburg PA. **Other U.S. locations:** Newport Beach CA; San Francisco CA; Washington DC; Miami FL; Fort Myers FL; Orlando FL; Sarasota FL; Atlanta GA; Des Moines IA; Boston MA; Trenton NJ; New York NY; Harrisburg PA; Pittsburgh PA; Memphis TN; Dallas TX; Austin TX; Houston TX. **Parent company:** Marine Midland Bank. **CEO:** F. John White.

PUTNAM INVESTMENTS
One Post Office Square, Mail Code A4D, Boston MA 02109. 617/292-1000. **Contact:** Robert Burke, Senior Managing Director of Personnel. **World Wide Web address:** http://www.putnaminv.com. **Description:** A money management firm. **Corporate headquarters location:** This Location. **Other U.S. locations:** Franklin MA; Quincy MA.

RAYMOND & JAMES
One Griswold Street, Detroit MI 48226. 313/963-6700. **Fax:** 313/963-9546. **Contact:** Director of Human Resources. **Description:** A regional, full-service investment banking and securities brokerage firm. Products and services include mutual funds, insurance, corporate bonds, investment management services, and retirement planning. **Common positions include:** Brokerage Clerk; Financial Services Sales Rep.; Securities Sales Rep. **Benefits:** 401(k); Accident/Emergency Insurance; Dental Insurance; Disability Coverage; Life Insurance; Medical Insurance; Spending Account; Travel Insurance. **Corporate headquarters location:** This Location. **Other U.S. locations:** IN; OH.

THE ROBINSON-HUMPHREY COMPANY
Atlanta Financial Center, 3333 Peachtree Road NE, Atlanta GA 30326. 404/266-6000. **Contact:** Human Resources. **Description:** Provides a complete range of stocks, bonds, and dealer/brokerage services. **Corporate headquarters location:** This Location.

FRANK RUSSELL COMPANY
909 A Street, Tacoma WA 98402. 253/596-3056. **Fax:** 253/594-1727. **Recorded jobline:** 253/596-5454. **Contact:** Human Resources. **E-mail address:** empsvc@russell.com. **World Wide Web address:** http://www.russell.com. **Description:** Provides a variety of financial services such as investment management, mutual funds, and investment consulting. **Educational backgrounds include:**

Accounting; Business Administration; Computer Science; Finance. **Corporate headquarters location:** This Location. **Other U.S. locations:** Boston MA; New York NY. **International locations:** Auckland; London; Paris; Sydney; Tokyo; Toronto; Zurich. **Listed on:** Privately held.

SEI INVESTMENTS COMPANY
One Freedom Valley Drive, Oaks PA 19456. 610/676-1000. **Toll-free phone:** 800/610-1114. **Contact:** Human Resources. **World Wide Web address:** http://www.seic.com. **Description:** SEI operates primarily in two business markets: Trust and Banking, and Fund Sponsor/Investment Advisory. The company invests for clients worldwide in both public and private markets, and also provides investment and business solutions to those in the investment business who in turn serve their own investor clients. SEI provides direct investment solutions for $50 billion of investable capital and delivers systems and business solutions to organizations investing nearly $1 trillion. SEI is one of the largest providers of trust systems in the world. **NOTE:** Entry-level positions are offered. **Common positions include:** Accountant; Applications Engineer; Attorney; Computer Engineer; Computer Programmer; Computer Technician; Content Developer; Database Administrator; Database Manager; Economist; Finance Director; Financial Analyst; Internet Services Manager; Intranet Developer; Marketing Manager; Marketing Specialist; MIS Specialist; Multimedia Designer; Network Engineer; Network/ Systems Administrator; Paralegal; Public Relations Specialist; Sales Executive; Sales Rep.; Software Engineer; Systems Analyst; Web Advertising Specialist; Webmaster; Website Developer. **Educational backgrounds include:** Business Administration; Computer Science; Economics; Engineering; Marketing; MBA. **Benefits:** 401(k); Casual Dress - Daily; Daycare Assistance; Dental Insurance; Disability Coverage; Employee Discounts; Financial Planning Assistance; Flexible Schedule; Life Insurance; Medical Insurance; On-Site Daycare; Relocation Assistance; Sick Days (1 - 5); Tuition Assistance; Vacation Days (10 - 20). **Office hours:** Monday - Friday, 8:30 a.m. - 5:30 p.m. **Corporate headquarters location:** This Location. **CEO:** Alfred West.

SG COWEN SECURITIES CORPORATION
1221 Avenue of the Americas, 9th Floor, New York NY 10020. 212/278-6000. **Contact:** Human Resources. **World Wide Web address:** http://www. sgcowen.com. **Description:** An investment banking firm. **Common positions include:** Financial Analyst; Investment Manager; Researcher; Sales Executive; Systems Analyst. **Educational backgrounds include:** Accounting; Business Administration; Computer Science; Finance; Liberal Arts. **Benefits:** 401(k); Disability Coverage; Life Insurance; Medical Insurance; Spending Account; Tuition Assistance. **Corporate headquarters location:** This Location. **Other U.S. locations:** Phoenix AZ; San Francisco CA; Chicago IL; Boston MA; Albany NY; Cleveland OH; Dayton OH; Philadelphia PA; Houston TX. **Parent company:** Societe Generale Group (Paris, France). **Number of employees at this location:** 1,000.

SAFECO INSURANCE CORPORATION
Safeco Plaza, Seattle WA 98185. 206/545-5000. **Contact:** Personnel. **World Wide Web address:** http://www.safeco.com. **Description:** A diversified financial services company with operations including property and liability, life and health insurance, pension plans, mutual funds, commercial credit, and real estate development. **Common positions include:** Accountant/Auditor; Actuary;

Administrator; Advertising Clerk; Attorney; Buyer; Claim Rep.; Computer Programmer; Customer Service Rep.; Purchasing Agent/Manager; Systems Analyst; Technical Writer/Editor; Underwriter/ Assistant Underwriter. **Educational backgrounds include:** Accounting; Business Administration; Computer Science; Economics; Finance; Liberal Arts; Marketing; Mathematics. **Benefits:** Daycare Assistance; Disability Coverage; Life Insurance; Medical Insurance; Pension Plan; Tuition Assistance. **Special programs:** Internships. **Corporate headquarters location:** This Location. **Subsidiaries include:** Safeco Insurance Companies.

SAGEMARK CONSULTING
303 Second Street, Suite 660, San Francisco CA 94107. 415/546-9424. **Contact:** Tricia Thomas, Director of Recruiting. **Description:** Markets financial services and products to high net worth individuals and business owners. **Common positions include:** Financial Services Sales Representative; Securities Sales Representative. **Educational backgrounds include:** Accounting; Business Administration; Economics; Finance; Marketing. **Benefits:** 401(k); Dental Insurance; Disability Coverage; Life Insurance; Medical Insurance; Pension Plan. **Corporate headquarters location:** Bloomfield CT.

SALOMON SMITH BARNEY
7 World Trade Center, 34th Floor, New York NY 10048. 212/783-7000. **Contact:** Human Resources. **World Wide Web address:** http://www. salomonsmithbarney.com. **Description:** An international investment banking, market making, and research firm serving corporations, state, local, and foreign governments, central banks, and other financial institutions. **NOTE:** Resumes should be sent to Human Resources, 388 Greenwich Street, New York NY 10013. **Office hours:** Monday - Friday, 7:30 a.m. - 7:00 p.m. **Corporate headquarters location:** This Location.

SCOTT & STRINGFELLOW INC.
909 East Main Street, Richmond VA 23219. 804/643-1811. **Contact:** Jordan Ball, Manager. **World Wide Web address:** http://www. scottstringfellow.com. **Description:** A full-service regional brokerage and investment banking firm. Services of Scott & Stringfellow include investment advice and brokerage for individual and institutional clients, investment banking and securities underwriting for corporations and municipalities, and a wide array of other investment-related financial services including investment advisory services. Scott & Stringfellow provides services in Virginia, North Carolina, South Carolina, and West Virginia. **Corporate headquarters location:** This Location. **Parent company:** BB&T Corporation.

SECURITY CAPITAL GROUP INC.
7777 Market Center Avenue, El Paso TX 79912. 915/877-1781. **Fax:** 915/877-5192. **Recorded jobline:** 800/554-9011. **Contact:** Sandy Chappel, Manager of Recruiting. **Description:** Provides accounting, finance, MIS, internal audit, tax, cash management, human resources, and risk management. **NOTE:** Entry-level positions are offered. **Common positions include:** Accountant; Administrative Assistant; Applications Engineer; Auditor; Computer Programmer; Controller; Financial Analyst; Project Manager; Systems Analyst; Technical Writer/Editor; Telecommunications Manager; Webmaster. **Educational backgrounds include:** Accounting; Business Administration; Computer Science; Finance. **Benefits:** 401(k); Dental Insurance; Disability Coverage; Employee Discounts; Life Insurance; Medical Insurance; Tuition Assistance.

Special programs: Internships. **Corporate headquarters location:** This Location. **Subsidiaries include:** SCGRS; SCI; Security Capital Atlantic; Security Capital Pacific.

SOUTHWEST SECURITIES GROUP, INC.
1201 Elm Street, Suite 3500, Dallas TX 75270-2180. 214/651-1800. **Contact:** Human Resources. **World Wide Web address:** http://www. southwestsecurities.com. **Description:** A holding company with subsidiaries engaged in providing securities brokerage, investment banking, and investment advisory services. Founded in 1972. **Corporate headquarters location:** This Location. **Other area locations:** 701 Brazos Street, Suite 400, Austin TX 78701, 512/320-5859; 908 Town & Country Boulevard, Houston TX 77024, 713/984-7631; 415 North Center, Suite One, Longview TX 75601, 903/758-0111; 711 Navarro, Suite 490, San Antonio TX 78205, 210/226-8677. **Other U.S. locations:** Chicago IL; Albuquerque NM; Santa Fe NM. **Subsidiaries include:** Brokers Transaction Services, Inc., 7001 Preston Road, Dallas TX 75205-1187; NorAm Investment Services, Inc., (also at this location); Southwest Securities, Inc., (also at this location); Sovereign Securities, Inc., (also at this location); SW Capital Corporation, (also at this location); SWST Computer Corporation, (also at this location); Westwood Management Corporation, 300 Crescent Court, Dallas TX 75201. **Listed on:** New York Stock Exchange. **Stock exchange symbol:** SWS. **President/CEO:** David Glatstein.

STATE STREET CORPORATION
225 Franklin Street, Boston MA 02110. 617/786-3000. **Contact:** Employment Manager. **World Wide Web address:** http://www.statestreet.com. **Description:** Provides securities and recordkeeping services to nearly 2,000 mutual funds and manages a large number of tax-exempt assets. State Street is a major manager of international index assets and provides corporate banking services, specialized lending, and international banking services. **Corporate headquarters location:** This Location. **Parent company:** State Street Boston Corporation.

STATE TEACHERS RETIREMENT SYSTEM OF OHIO
275 East Broad Street, Columbus OH 43215-3771. 614/227-2908. **Fax:** 614/227-2952. **Contact:** Marilyn A. Thomas, Staffing Coordinator. **World Wide Web address:** http://www. strsoh.org/jobs.htm. **Description:** One of the largest pension funds in the United States, serving Ohio's teachers and managing assets totaling $50 billion. The nonprofit fund serves over 375,000 members and retirees. Founded in 1920. **Common positions include:** Accountant; Administrative Assistant; Auditor; Clerical Supervisor; Computer Operator; Counselor; Customer Service Rep.; Database Manager; Economist; Editorial Assistant; Finance Director; Financial Analyst; Fund Manager; General Manager; Graphic Designer; Human Resources Manager; MIS Specialist; Operations/Production Manager; Preschool Worker; Quality Control Supervisor; Secretary; Software Engineer; Statistician; Systems Analyst; Systems Manager; Telecommunications Manager; Typist/Word Processor. **Educational backgrounds include:** Accounting; Business Administration; Computer Science; Economics; Finance; Public Relations. **Benefits:** Dental Insurance; Disability Coverage; Flexible Schedule; Life Insurance; Medical Insurance; On-Site Daycare; Pension Plan; Tuition Assistance. **Special programs:** Training. **Office hours:** Monday - Friday, 8:00 a.m. - 4:30 p.m. **Corporate headquarters location:** This Location. **Number of employees at this location:** 550.

STEIN ROE & FARNHAM
One South Wacker Drive, Chicago IL 60606.
312/368-7700. **Fax:** 312/368-8129. **Contact:**
Human Resources. **World Wide Web address:**
http://www.steinroe.com. **Description:** An
investment counseling firm offering professional
advice and services to individuals, institutions, and
other organizations. Stein Roe & Farnham also
manages no-load mutual funds. **Common positions
include:** Accountant; Customer Service Rep.; Fund
Manager; SQL Programmer; Systems Analyst.
Educational backgrounds include: Accounting;
Computer Science; Economics; Finance. **Benefits:**
401(k); Disability Coverage; Medical Insurance;
Profit Sharing; Tuition Assistance. **Corporate
headquarters location:** This Location. **Other U.S.
locations:** San Francisco CA; New York NY;
Cleveland OH. **Number of employees at this
location:** 400.

STEPHENS, INC.
111 Center Street, Little Rock AR 72201. 501/377-
2001. **Fax:** 501/377-2111. **Contact:** Ellen Gray,
Senior Vice President of Human Resources. **E-mail
address:** egray@stephens.com. **World Wide Web
address:** http://www.stephens.com. **Description:**
An investment banking firm. **Common positions
include:** Accountant; Administrative Worker/Clerk;
Brokerage Clerk; Computer Programmer; Financial
Analyst; Systems Analyst; Underwriter/Assistant
Underwriter. **Benefits:** 401(k); Dental Insurance;
Disability Coverage; Life Insurance; Medical
Insurance; Profit Sharing; Tuition Assistance.
Corporate headquarters location: This Location.
Number of employees at this location: 650.

STIFEL, NICOLAUS & COMPANY
501 North Broadway, St. Louis MO 63102.
314/342-2000. **Fax:** 314/342-2051. **Recorded
jobline:** 314/342-2900. **Contact:** Carrie Kramer,
Assistant Vice President of Human Resources.
World Wide Web address: http://www.stifel.com.
Description: A full-service regional investment
firm. Services include fixed income securities,
corporate finance, public finance, syndicate
participation, trading, broker-dealer services,
options, research, mutual funds, asset management,
and estate planning. Founded in 1890. **Common
positions include:** Accountant/Auditor; Brokerage
Clerk; Customer Service Rep. **Educational
backgrounds include:** Accounting; Business
Administration; Economics; Finance; Marketing.
Benefits: Dental Insurance; Disability Coverage;
Employee Discounts; Life Insurance; Medical
Insurance; Profit Sharing; Stock Option; Tuition
Assistance. **Corporate headquarters location:**
This Location. **Other U.S. locations:** Chicago IL;
Louisville KY; OK. **Parent company:** Stifel
Financial Corporation.

STIFEL, NICOLAUS, HANIFEN & IMHOFF
1125 17th Street, Suite 1600, Denver CO 80202-
2032. 303/296-1200. **Contact:** Human Resources.
Description: A securities brokerage firm.
Corporate headquarters location: This Location.

STRONG CAPITAL MANAGEMENT
100 Heritage Reserve, Menomonee Falls WI 53051.
414/359-3400. **Contact:** Human Resources. **World
Wide Web address:** http://www.strong-funds.com.
Description: A mutual fund retailer and investment
firm. **Corporate headquarters location:** This
Location.

**STUDENT   LOAN   MARKETING
ASSOCIATION (SALLIE MAE)**
11600 Sallie Mae Drive, Reston VA 20193.
703/810-3000. **Contact:** Employment. **World Wide**

Web address: http://www.salliemae.com.
Description: A major financial intermediary to the
educational financing market in the U.S. The
company provides student loan services, as well as
other financial and management services to loan
originators. The association also provides financing
for academic equipment. **Common positions
include:** Accountant; Computer Programmer;
Financial Analyst; Marketing Specialist; Systems
Analyst. **Corporate headquarters location:** This
Location. **Parent company:** SLM Holding
Corporation (also at this location).

SUNAMERICA INC.
One SunAmerica Center, Century City, Los Angeles
CA 90067. 310/772-6000. **Fax:** 310/772-6361.
Contact: Human Resources. **World Wide Web
address:** http://www.sunamerica.com. **Description:**
SunAmerica Inc. is a large financial services
company specializing in long-term, tax-deferred,
investment-oriented savings products. **Common
positions include:** Accountant; Actuary; Attorney;
Computer Programmer; Customer Service Rep.;
Financial Analyst; Human Resources Manager;
Manufacturer's/Wholesaler's Sales Rep.; Paralegal;
Public Relations Specialist; Securities Sales Rep.;
Systems Analyst. **Educational backgrounds
include:** Accounting; Business Administration;
Computer Science; Economics; Finance. **Benefits:**
401(k); Dental Insurance; Disability Coverage; Life
Insurance; Medical Insurance; Tuition Assistance.
Corporate headquarters location: This Location.

SUNAMERICA SECURITIES
2800 North Central Avenue, Suite 2100, Phoenix
AZ 85004. 602/744-3000. **Contact:** Human
Resources. **World Wide Web address:** http://www.
sunamerica-securities.com. **Description:** A financial
services company specializing in retirement
planning. **Corporate headquarters location:** This
Location. **Parent company:** SunAmerica Inc. (Los
Angeles CA).

SUTRO & COMPANY INC.
201 California Street, San Francisco CA 94111.
415/445-8500. **Fax:** 415/421-7632. **Contact:**
Human Resources. **World Wide Web address:**
http://www.sutro.com. **Description:** A full-service,
regional investment brokerage firm. **Common
positions include:** Accountant; Branch Manager;
Brokerage Clerk; Budget Analyst; Computer
Programmer; Credit Manager; Editor; Financial
Analyst; Human Resources Manager; Insurance
Agent/Broker; Operations/Production Manager;
Purchasing Agent/Manager; Securities Sales Rep.;
Systems Analyst; Technical Writer/Editor.
Educational backgrounds include: Accounting;
Business Administration; Communications;
Economics; Finance; Liberal Arts; Marketing.
Benefits: 401(k); Dental Insurance; Disability
Coverage; Health Club Discount; Life Insurance;
Medical Insurance; Profit Sharing; Savings Plan;
Tuition Assistance. **Corporate headquarters
location:** This Location. **Parent company:** Tucker
Anthony Sutro.

SYNOVUS FINANCIAL CORPORATION
P.O. Box 120, Columbus GA 31902. 706/649-4545.
Fax: 706/649-5797. **Recorded jobline:** 706/649-
4758. **Contact:** Mrs. Danni Harris, Director of
Employment Services. **E-mail address:** careers@
synovus.com. **World Wide Web address:**
http://www.synovus.com. **Description:** A
multiservice financial company. Synovus Financial
owns 80 percent of Total Systems Services, Inc.
(also at this location, 706/649-2310,
http://www.totalsystem.com), one of the largest
credit, debit, commercial, and private label
processing companies in the world. Synovus

Financial Corporation also operates 34 banks in the Southeast. Affiliate banks operate under a decentralized management structure. Founded in 1888. **NOTE:** All applicants should contact the jobline for available positions. Entry-level positions and second and third shifts are offered. **Common positions include:** Administrative Assistant; Assistant Manager; Auditor; Bank Officer/Manager; Blue-Collar Worker Supervisor; Branch Manager; Computer Operator; Computer Programmer; Customer Service Rep.; Editor; Financial Analyst; Management Trainee; Marketing Specialist; Project Manager; Sales Rep.; Software Engineer; Systems Analyst; Technical Writer/Editor. **Educational backgrounds include:** Accounting; Business Administration; Communications; Computer Science; Finance; M.I.S.; Marketing; Software Development. **Benefits:** 401(k); Dental Insurance; Disability Coverage; Employee Discounts; Fitness Program; Life Insurance; Medical Insurance; Pension Plan; Profit Sharing; Tuition Assistance. **Special programs:** Internships; Training; Summer Jobs. **Corporate headquarters location:** This Location. **Other U.S. locations:** AL; FL; SC. **Subsidiaries include:** Synovus Securities, Inc. is a full-service brokerage firm; Synovus Trust Company is one of the Southeast's largest providers of trust services; Synovus Mortgage Corporation offers mortgage servicing throughout the Southeast; Synovus Leasing Company offers equipment leasing; Synovus Insurance Services offers insurance services.

TRANSAMERICA CORPORATION
600 Montgomery Street, 23rd Floor, San Francisco CA 94111. 415/983-4000. **Contact:** Human Resources. **World Wide Web address:** http://www.transamerica.com. **Description:** Operates diversified financial services and insurance companies. **NOTE:** The corporation's personnel functions are decentralized and each company handles its own recruiting needs. **Common positions include:** Accountant; Administrator; Financial Analyst; Human Resources Manager; Secretary. **Educational backgrounds include:** Accounting; Business Administration; Economics; Finance. **Benefits:** 401(k); Dental Insurance; Disability Coverage; Life Insurance; Medical Insurance; Pension Plan; Tuition Assistance. **Corporate headquarters location:** This Location.

UNITED ASSET MANAGEMENT CORP.
One International Place, 44th Floor, Boston MA 02110. 617/330-8900. **Contact:** Pamela Woodnick, Director of Human Resources. **World Wide Web address:** http://www.uam.com. **Description:** Provides investment management services primarily to institutional investors through 42 operating firms. **Corporate headquarters location:** This Location. **Subsidiaries include:** Acadian Asset Management; Analytic Investment Management; Barrow, Hanley, Mewhinney & Strauss; C.S. McKee & Company; Cambiar Investors; Chicago Asset Management Company; Cooke & Bieler; Dewey Square Investors Corporation; Dwight Asset Management Company; Fiduciary Management Associates; First Pacific Advisors; GSB Investment Management; Hagler, Mastrovita & Hewitt; Hamilton, Allen & Associates; Hanson Investment Management Company; Heitman Financial; Hellman, Jordan Management Company; Investment Counselors of Maryland; Investment Research Company; Murray Johnstone Limited; Nelson, Benson & Zellmer; Newbold's Asset Management; Northern Capital Management; NWQ Investment Management Company; Olympic Capital Management; Pell, Rudman & Co.; Provident Investment Counsel; Regis Retirement Plan Services; Rice, Hall, James & Associates; Rothschild/Pell, Rudman & Co.;

Sirach Capital Management; Spectrum Asset Management; Sterling Capital Management Company; Suffolk Capital Management; The Campbell Group; The L&B Group; Thompson, Siegel & Walmsley; Tom Johnson Investment Management; UAM Investment Services.

UNITED SERVICES AUTOMOBILE ASSOCIATION (USAA)
9800 Fredericksburg Road, San Antonio TX 78288. 210/498-2211. **Fax:** 210/498-1489. **Recorded jobline:** 210/498-1289. **Contact:** Employment. **World Wide Web address:** http://www.usaa.com. **Description:** An integrated family of companies providing insurance and financial products and services to officers of the United States Armed Forces and their families. Products and services include automobile, life, health, property, and rental insurance; a family of mutual funds; credit cards; calling cards; and a federal savings bank (USAA Federal Savings Bank). Members also receive discounts from certain companies. **NOTE:** USAA only accepts resumes and cover letters for jobs listed on the USAA jobline. The USAA Jobline is updated Monday through Friday at 5:00 p.m. The company prefers jobseekers to fax their resumes if possible. **Common positions include:** Accountant; Actuary; Adjuster; Administrative Manager; Aircraft Mechanic/Engine Specialist; Attorney; Blue-Collar Worker Supervisor; Broadcast Technician; Budget Analyst; Buyer; Civil Engineer; Claim Rep.; Clerical Supervisor; Computer Programmer; Construction and Building Inspector; Construction Contractor; Cost Estimator; Counselor; Customer Service Rep.; Designer; Dietician/Nutritionist; Draftsperson; Economist; Editor; Education Administrator; Electrical/Electronics Engineer; Electrician; Financial Analyst; General Manager; Health Services Manager; Human Resources Manager; Insurance Agent/Broker; Librarian; Library Technician; Licensed Practical Nurse; Management Analyst/Consultant; Management Trainee; Mechanical Engineer; Medical Records Technician; Operations/Production Manager; Property and Real Estate Manager; Public Relations Specialist; Purchasing Agent/Manager; Quality Control Supervisor; Radio/TV Announcer/Broadcaster; Real Estate Agent; Registered Nurse; Reporter; Services Sales Rep.; Statistician; Systems Analyst; Teacher/Professor; Technical Writer/Editor; Transportation/Traffic Specialist; Travel Agent; Underwriter/Assistant Underwriter; Wholesale and Retail Buyer. **Educational backgrounds include:** Accounting; Bachelor of Arts; Business Administration; Communications; Computer Science; Finance; Liberal Arts. **Benefits:** Dental Insurance; Disability Coverage; Employee Discounts; Life Insurance; Medical Insurance; Pension Plan; Smoke-free; Tuition Assistance. **Special programs:** Internships. **Corporate headquarters location:** This Location. **Other U.S. locations:** CA; CO; FL; VA; WA.

UNITED STATES TRUST COMPANY OF NEW YORK
114 West 47th Street, New York NY 10036. 212/852-1000. **Contact:** Carolyn C. Connolly, Vice President, Employment Manager. **World Wide Web address:** http://www.ustrust.com. **Description:** An investment management, private banking, and securities services firm. Service categories include investment management; estate and trust administration; financial planning; and corporate trust. **Common positions include:** Accountant; Administrator; Computer Programmer; Department Manager; Financial Analyst; Operations/Production Manager; Systems Analyst. **Educational backgrounds include:** Accounting; Communications; Computer Science; Economics;

Finance; Liberal Arts; Marketing. **Benefits:** 401(k); Bonus Award/Plan; Dental Insurance; Disability Coverage; Employee Discounts; Life Insurance; Medical Insurance; Savings Plan; Tuition Assistance. **Corporate headquarters location:** This Location. **Listed on:** NASDAQ.

UNITRIN, INC.
One East Wacker Drive, Chicago IL 60601. 312/661-4600. **Toll-free phone:** 800/999-0546. **Contact:** Human Resources. **World Wide Web address:** http://www.unitrin.com. **Description:** A financial services company with subsidiaries engaged in three business areas: life and health insurance, property and casualty insurance, and consumer finance. **NOTE:** Part-time jobs are offered. **Common positions include:** Accountant; Attorney; Auditor; Paralegal. **Educational backgrounds include:** Accounting; Finance. **Benefits:** 401(k); Casual Dress - Daily; Dental Insurance; Disability Coverage; Flexible Schedule; Life Insurance; Medical Insurance; Pension Plan; Profit Sharing; Sick Days (6 - 10); Tuition Assistance. **Special programs:** Internships; Summer Jobs. **Corporate headquarters location:** This Location.

VALUE LINE
220 East 42nd Street, 6th Floor, New York NY 10017. 212/907-1500. **Contact:** Human Resources. **Description:** An investment advisory firm. **Corporate headquarters location:** This Location.

THE VANGUARD GROUP, INC.
P.O. Box 2600, Valley Forge PA 19482-2600. 610/669-6000. **Contact:** Human Resources. **World Wide Web address:** http://www.vanguard.com. **Description:** A mutual funds company that also offers assistance in educational financing, retirement planning, and trust services. **Corporate headquarters location:** This Location.

WADDELL & REED INC.
P.O. Box 29217, Shawnee Mission KS 66201. 913/236-2000. **Contact:** Employment Specialist. **World Wide Web address:** http://www.waddell.com. **Description:** Offers a variety of financial services. **Common positions include:** Accountant; Auditor; Computer Operator; Computer Programmer; Computer Support Technician; Customer Service Rep.; Financial Analyst; Fund Manager; Sales Rep.; Secretary; Systems Analyst. **Educational backgrounds include:** Accounting; Business Administration; COBOL; Computer Science; Finance. **Benefits:** 401(k); Casual Dress - Fridays; Dental Insurance; Financial Planning Assistance; Life Insurance; Medical Insurance; Pension Plan; Savings Plan; Tuition Assistance.

WATERHOUSE SECURITIES, INC.
100 Wall Street, New York NY 10005. 212/806-3500. **Contact:** Human Resources. **Description:** Provides brokerage and banking services for individuals that manage their own investments and financial affairs. **Common positions include:** Accountant; Brokerage Clerk; Computer Programmer; Computer Support Technician; Customer Service Rep.; Financial Services Sales Rep.; Human Resources Manager; Securities Sales Representative; Software Engineer. **Educational backgrounds include:** Accounting; Business Administration; Computer Science; Economics; Finance. **Benefits:** 401(k); Dental Insurance; Disability Coverage; Life Insurance; Medical Insurance; Profit Sharing. **Corporate headquarters location:** This Location. **Other U.S. locations:** Nationwide. **Parent company:** Waterhouse Investor Services.

WEDBUSH MORGAN SECURITIES
1000 Wilshire Boulevard, 10th Floor, Los Angeles CA 90017. 213/688-8000. **Contact:** Karen Ames, Recruiter. **World Wide Web address:** http://www. wedbush.com. **Description:** An investment banking securities brokerage. **Common positions include:** Accountant; Branch Manager; Brokerage Clerk; Computer Programmer; Credit Manager; Customer Service Rep.; Human Resources Manager; Marketing Manager; Purchasing Agent/Manager; Services Sales Rep. **Educational backgrounds include:** Accounting; Business Administration; Computer Science; Economics; Finance. **Benefits:** 401(k); Dental Insurance; Disability Coverage; Employee Discounts; Life Insurance; Medical Insurance; Pension Plan; Profit Sharing; Stock Option; Tuition Assistance. **Special programs:** Internships. **Corporate headquarters location:** This Location.

WERTHEIM SCHRODER & COMPANY
787 Seventh Avenue, New York NY 10019. 212/492-6290. **Fax:** 212/492-7188. **Contact:** Human Resources. **Description:** An international investment banking, asset management, and securities firm. **Common positions include:** Accountant; Brokerage Clerk; Budget Analyst; Computer Operator; Computer Programmer; Credit Manager; Department Manager; Employment Interviewer; Librarian; Library Technician; Payroll Clerk; Postal Clerk/Mail Carrier; Public Relations Specialist; Receptionist; Secretary; Statistician; Systems Analyst; Typist/Word Processor. **Educational backgrounds include:** Accounting; Business Administration; Communications; Computer Science; Economics; Finance; Marketing; Mathematics. **Benefits:** Disability Coverage; Employee Discounts; Life Insurance; Medical Insurance; Pension Plan; Savings Plan; Tuition Assistance. **Corporate headquarters location:** This Location. **Other U.S. locations:** Beverly Hills CA; Los Angeles CA; Chicago IL; Boston MA; Philadelphia PA. **International locations:** Amsterdam; Geneva; London; Paris.

WESTERN SURETY COMPANY
P.O. Box 5077, Sioux Falls SD 57117. 605/336-0850. **Contact:** Human Resources. **World Wide Web address:** http://www.westernsurety.com. **Description:** Writes fidelity and surety bonds. **Common positions include:** Accountant Customer Service Rep.; Marketing Specialist; Underwriter/ Assistant Underwriter. **Educational backgrounds include:** Accounting; Business Administration; Communications; Computer Science; Economics; Marketing. **Benefits:** Dental Insurance; Life Insurance; Medical Insurance; Pension Plan; Tuition Assistance. **Special programs:** Internships. **Corporate headquarters location:** This Location.

WHITE MOUNTAINS INSURANCE GROUP
80 South Main Street, Hanover NH 03755. 603/643-1567. **Contact:** Human Resources. **Description:** A major financial services holding company specializing in mortgage banking operations. **Corporate headquarters location:** This Location. **Subsidiaries include:** Source One Mortgage Services Corporation conducts business through 195 retail branches in 27 states. Sales representatives originate loans with real estate brokers, developers, and consumer home buyers.

WUKASCH COMPANY
2340 Guadalupe Street, Austin TX 78705-5218. **Contact:** Don C. Wukasch, President. **Description:** A diversified real estate and securities investment company providing real estate property management and securities portfolio management. The company is a member of the Commercial Investment Real

Estate Institute (CIREI), NAR, NASD, NFA, and SPIC. **Common positions include:** Accountant/ Auditor; Administrative Manager; Budget Analyst; Construction Contractor; Economist; Financial Analyst; General Manager; Real Estate Agent; Statistician; Systems Analyst; Typist/Word Processor. **Educational backgrounds include:** Accounting; Business Administration; Computer Science; Economics; Finance. **Benefits:** Medical Insurance. **Special programs:** Internships. **Corporate headquarters location:** This Location. **Listed on:** Privately held. **Annual sales/revenues:** Less than $5 million. **Number of employees at this location:** 5. **Number of employees nationwide:** 10.

For more information on career opportunities in financial services:

Associations

ASSOCIATION FOR FINANCIAL PROFESSIONALS (AFP)
7315 Wisconsin Avenue, Suite 600-W, Bethesda MD 20814. 301/907-2862. World Wide Web address: http://www.AFPonline.org.

THE BOND MARKET ASSOCIATION
40 Broad Street, 12th Floor, New York NY 10004. 212/809-7000. Publishes an annual report and several newsletters.

FINANCIAL EXECUTIVES INSTITUTE
P.O. Box 1938, Morristown NJ 07962-1938. 973/898-4600. World Wide Web address: http://www.fei.org. Fee and membership required. Publishes biennial member directory. Provides member referral service.

INSTITUTE OF FINANCIAL EDUCATION
55 West Monroe Street, Suite 2800, Chicago IL 60603-5014. Toll-free phone: 800/946-0488. World Wide Web address: http://www.theinstitute.com. Offers career development programs.

NATIONAL ASSOCIATION OF BUSINESS ECONOMISTS
1233 20th Street NW, Suite 505, Washington DC 20036. 202/463-6223. World Wide Web address: http://www.nabe.com. Offers a newsletter and Website that provide a list of job openings.

NATIONAL ASSOCIATION OF CREDIT MANAGEMENT
8840 Columbia 100 Parkway, Columbia MD 21045. 410/740-5560. World Wide Web address: http://www.nacm.org. Publishes a business credit magazine.

NATIONAL ASSOCIATION OF TAX PRACTITIONERS
720 Association Drive, Appleton WI 54914-1483. E-mail address: natp@natptax.com. World Wide Web address: http://www.natptax.com. A membership organization that offers newsletters and nationwide workshops.

Career Fairs

CAREER FAIRS INTERNATIONAL
World Wide Web address: http://www.career-fairs.com. Organizes career fairs in the fields of accounting, banking, finance, and insurance.

Directories

DIRECTORY OF AMERICAN FINANCIAL INSTITUTIONS
Thomson Business Publications, 4709 West Golf Road, 6th Floor, Skokie IL 66076-1253. Sales: 800/321-3373.

MOODY'S BANK AND FINANCE MANUAL
Financial Information Services, 60 Madison Avenue, 6th Floor, New York NY 10010. Toll-free phone: 800/342-5647. World Wide Web address: http://www.moodys.com.

Magazines

BARRON'S: NATIONAL BUSINESS AND FINANCIAL WEEKLY
Barron's, 200 Liberty Street, New York NY 10281. 212/416-2700.

FINANCIAL PLANNING
Securities Data Publishing, 1290 Avenue of the Americas, 36th Floor, New York NY 10104. 212/765-5311.

FUTURES: THE MAGAZINE OF COMMODITIES AND OPTIONS
250 South Wacker Drive, Suite 1150, Chicago IL 60606. Toll-free phone: 888/898-5514. World Wide Web address: http://www.futuresmag.com.

Online Services

ACCOUNTING & FINANCE JOBS
World Wide Web address: http://www.accountingjobs.com. Provides national and international job listings and offers links to related sites.

BLOOMBERG.COM
World Wide Web address: http://www. bloomberg.com. Provides national and some international job postings.

FINANCIAL, ACCOUNTING, AND INSURANCE JOBS PAGE
World Wide Web address: http://www.nationjob. com/financial. This Website provides a list of financial, accounting, and insurance job openings.

FINCAREER.COM
World Wide Web address: http://www. fincareer.com. A searchable database of financial jobs worldwide.

JOBS IN CORPORATE FINANCE
World Wide Web address: http://www.cob.ohio-state.edu/dept/fin/jobs/corpfin.htm. Provides information and resources for jobseekers looking to work in the field of corporate finance.

NATIONAL BANKING NETWORK: RECRUITING FOR BANKING AND FINANCE
World Wide Web address: http://www.banking-financejobs.com. Offers a searchable database of job openings in financial services and banking. The database is searchable by region, keyword, and job specialty.

Food and Beverages/Agriculture

You can expect to find the following types of companies in this chapter:
Crop Services and Farm Supplies • Dairy Farms • Food Manufacturers/Processors and Agricultural Producers • Tobacco Products

Some helpful information: *Farmers and agricultural workers earn, on average, $20,000 - $25,000 annually (though employees of large commercial farms may earn more). Earnings tend to fluctuate according to the season and government subsidy. Food inspectors earn approximately $30,000 - $35,000 annually, while general manufacturing salaries tend to be lower ($25,000 per year is average).*

AGP
P.O. Box 2047, Omaha NE 68103-2047. 402/496-7809. **Fax:** 402/498-5548. **Contact:** Personnel Manager. **Description:** Processes soybean and soy flour. AGP is also engaged in vegetable oil refinement; grain merchandising and storage; the development, manufacture, and sale of pet foods; and livestock feed production, sales, and research and development. **Common positions include:** Accountant; Advertising Clerk; Agricultural Engineer; Agricultural Scientist; Attorney; Blue-Collar Worker Supervisor; Brokerage Clerk; Chemical Engineer; Chemist; Civil Engineer; Claim Rep.; Clerical Supervisor; Clinical Lab Technician; Computer Programmer; Credit Manager; Customer Service Rep.; Electrician; Financial Analyst; Food Scientist/Technologist; Human Resources Manager; Management Trainee; Mechanical Engineer; Paralegal; Purchasing Agent/Manager; Quality Control Supervisor; Systems Analyst. **Educational backgrounds include:** Accounting; Business Administration; Chemistry; Computer Science; Economics; Engineering; Finance. **Benefits:** 401(k); Dental Insurance; Disability Coverage; Life Insurance; Medical Insurance; Pension Plan; Tuition Assistance. **Corporate headquarters location:** This Location. **Other U.S. locations:** Nationwide. **International locations:** Canada.

ADAMS & BROOKS INC.
P.O. Box 7303, Los Angeles CA 90007. 213/749-3226. **Fax:** 213/746-7614. **Contact:** Personnel Director. **World Wide Web address:** http://www.adams-brooks.com. **Description:** Manufactures candy including P-Nuttles toffee coated peanuts, Coffee Rio caramel candy, Cup-O-Gold chocolate cups, specialty lollipops, and Fairtime Taffy. Founded in 1932.. **Common positions include:** Food Scientist/Technologist; Industrial Engineer; Science Technologist; Services Sales Rep.. **Benefits:** Dental Insurance; Life Insurance; Medical Insurance. **Corporate headquarters location:** This Location.

AG SERVICES OF AMERICA, INC.
P.O. Box 668, Cedar Falls IA 50613. 319/277-0261. **Fax:** 319/277-0144. **Contact:** Human Resources Director. **World Wide Web address:** http://www.agservices.com. **Description:** Supplies farm inputs including seed; fertilizer; agricultural chemicals; crop insurance; and cash advances for rent, fuel, and irrigation, to farmers primarily in the central United States. Ag Services extends credit and provides farmers with the convenience of purchasing and financing a wide variety of farm inputs from a single source at competitive prices. **Corporate headquarters location:** This Location.

AGRIBIOTECH, INC. (ABT)
120 Corporate Park Drive, Henderson NV 89104. 702/566-2440. **Contact:** Human Resources. **World Wide Web address:** http://www.agribiotech.com. **Description:** A specialized distributor of forage (hay crops) and turf grass seed to the forage and turf cash crop sectors. The company distributes the following non-seed products: Bloatenz Plus, a liquid bloat preventative administered to the drinking water of cattle permitting them to graze on alfalfa without bloating and dying; and PDS-1000, marketed in conjunction with Bloatenz Plus, a microprocessor-controlled precision dispensing system designed to dispense solutions into the drinking water of livestock at a preset dosage rate. **Corporate headquarters location:** This Location. **Subsidiaries include:** Halsey Seed Company; Hobart Seed Company; Scott Seed Company; Seed Resource, Inc.; Sphar & Company. **Listed on:** NASDAQ. **Stock exchange symbol:** ABTX.

AGRILINK FOODS
90 Linden Oaks, Rochester NY 14625. 716/383-1850. **Fax:** 716/383-9153. **Contact:** Staffing Manager. **World Wide Web address:** http://www.agrilinkfoods.com. **Description:** Processes and markets a variety of food product lines of regional branded, private label, and food service products through facilities located throughout the United States. Products include pie fillings, pretzels, cookies, and salad dressings.

ALEXANDER & BALDWIN, INC.
P.O. Box 3440, Honolulu HI 96801-3440. 808/525-6611. **Contact:** John Gasher, Vice President of Human Resources. **World Wide Web address:** http://www.alexanderbaldwin.com. **Description:** Alexander & Baldwin, through its subsidiaries, is involved in ocean transportation, property development and management, trucking and storage, and sugar production and refinement. **Corporate headquarters location:** This Location. **Other U.S. locations:** Crockett CA; San Francisco CA; Kauai HI; Maui HI. **Subsidiaries include:** Matson Navigation, which offers a shuttle service across the Pacific serving ports in the continental U.S. and Canada, the Marshall Islands, and Johnston Island; Matson Terminals; Matson Services; Matson Leasing, one of the world's largest leasing companies involved in marine containers with 145,000 units; Matson Intermodal System; Hawaiian Commercial & Sugar; McBryde Sugar; A&B Hawaii; Kahului Trucking & Storage; East Maui Irrigation Company; Kauai Commercial Company; California & Hawaiian Sugar Company (C&H).

ALTA DENA CERTIFIED DAIRY
P.O. Box 388, City of Industry CA 91747-0388. 626/964-6401. **Contact:** Personnel Director. **World Wide Web address:** http://www.altadenadairy.com. **Description:** Specializes in the production of a full line of dairy products. **Corporate headquarters location:** This Location.

THE AMALGAMATED SUGAR COMPANY
P.O. Box 1520, Ogden UT 84402. 801/399-3431.
Contact: Personnel Department. **Description:** One of the nation's largest producers of sugar. The company's White Satin brand sugar is sold primarily to industrial users in pacific, intermountain, and midwestern states. **Corporate headquarters location:** This Location.

AMERICAN CRYSTAL SUGAR COMPANY
101 North Third Street, Moorhead MN 56560. 218/236-4400. **Contact:** Human Resources. **Description:** American Crystal Sugar Company, an agricultural cooperative, processes and markets sugar, sugar beet pulp, molasses, and seed. Customers are primarily American companies in the food processing industry. American Crystal is a partner in Midwest Agri-Commodities with Minn-Dak Farmers Cooperative and Southern Minnesota Beet Sugar Cooperative. **Corporate headquarters location:** This Location. **Other U.S. locations:** Crookston MN; East Grand Forks MN; Drayton ND; Hillsboro ND.

AMERICAN PRIDE
P.O. Box 98, Henderson CO 80640. 303/659-3640. **Contact:** Office Manager. **Description:** Markets bulk and bagged fertilizer, agricultural chemicals, seeds, feed, and veterinary supplies. **Common positions include:** Agricultural Scientist. **Educational backgrounds include:** Business Administration; Marketing. **Benefits:** Dental Insurance; Disability Coverage; Life Insurance; Medical Insurance; Pension Plan; Savings Plan; Tuition Assistance. **Corporate headquarters location:** This Location.

AMERICAN RICE, INC. (ARI)
411 North Sam Houston Parkway East, Suite 500, Houston TX 77060. 281/272-0330. **Contact:** Personnel. **World Wide Web address:** http://www. amrice.com. **Description:** An international agribusiness company active in all phases of rice milling, processing, and marketing. ARI markets parboiled rice, white rice, instant rice, brown rice, and rice mixes, primarily under proprietary, trademarked brand names throughout the world. ARI operates rice processing facilities in the U.S., Jamaica, and Haiti. Founded in 1987. **Corporate headquarters location:** This Location.

ANHEUSER-BUSCH COMPANIES
One Busch Place, St. Louis MO 63118. 314/577-0701. **Contact:** Employment Services. **World Wide Web address:** http://www.anheuser-busch.com. **Description:** Anheuser-Busch is a diverse company which is involved in the entertainment, brewing, baking, and manufacturing industries. The company operates 13 breweries throughout the U.S. and distributes through over 900 independent wholesalers. Beer brands include Budweiser, Michelob, Busch, and King Cobra, as well as O'Doul's (non-alcoholic). Related businesses include can manufacturing, paper printing, and barley malting. Anheuser-Busch is also one of the largest operators of amusement parks in the U.S., with locations in Florida, Virginia, Texas, Ohio, and California. **Corporate headquarters location:** This Location. **Subsidiaries include:** Campbell Taggart Inc. is one of the largest commercial baking companies in the United States, producing foods under the Colonial brand name, among others.

ARCHER DANIELS MIDLAND COMPANY
P.O. Box 1470, Decatur IL 62525. 217/424-5230. **Toll-free phone:** 800/637-5843. **Fax:** 217/424-4383. **Contact:** Personnel. **World Wide Web address:** http://www.admworld.com. **Description:** A worldwide firm engaged in the procuring, transporting, storing, processing, and merchandising of agricultural commodities. The company processes agricultural products such as corn, soybeans, wheat, rice, cottonseed, and canola; and produces a variety of products including vegetable oils, cooking oil, margarine, vitamin E, soy flour, soy isolates, soy protein, soy milk, TVP, high fructose corn syrup, sorbitol, starch, ethanol, xanthan gum, tryptophan, vitamin C, fermentation products, pasta, and cottonseed flour products. **NOTE:** Entry-level positions are offered. **Common positions include:** Auditor; Chemical Engineer; Chemist; Computer Programmer. **Educational backgrounds include:** Accounting; Business Administration; Chemistry; Engineering; Finance; M.I.S.; Marketing. **Benefits:** 401(k); Dental Insurance; Disability Coverage; Life Insurance; Medical Insurance; Pension Plan; Tuition Assistance. **Corporate headquarters location:** This Location. **Other U.S. locations:** Nationwide. **International locations:** Worldwide.

ARCHWAY MOTHER'S COOKIES
810 81st Avenue, Oakland CA 94621. 510/569-2323. **Contact:** Human Resources. **Description:** Develops, manufactures, imports, and markets cookies in the western United States. Primary customers are wholesale food distributors and retail food markets. **Corporate headquarters location:** This Location.

ASSOCIATED FOOD STORES, INC.
1850 West 2100 South, Salt Lake City UT 84119. 801/973-4400. **Fax:** 801/973-2158. **Contact:** Paul Jones, Human Resources Manager. **Description:** A wholesale food company. **Common positions include:** Accountant/Auditor; Blue-Collar Worker Supervisor; Buyer; Clerical Supervisor; Computer Programmer; Human Resources Manager; Human Service Worker; Systems Analyst; Warehouse/ Distribution Worker. **Educational backgrounds include:** Communications; Computer Science; Finance. **Benefits:** 401(k); Dental Insurance; Disability Coverage; Employee Discounts; Life Insurance; Medical Insurance; Pension Plan; Profit Sharing; Tuition Assistance. **Corporate headquarters location:** This Location.

ASSOCIATED GROCERS, INC.
P.O. Box 3763, Seattle WA 98124. **Fax:** 206/767-8785. **Recorded jobline:** 206/767-8788. **Contact:** Human Resources Department. **E-mail address:** jobs@agsea.com. **World Wide Web address:** http://www.agsea.com. **Description:** Provides general merchandise and grocery products to over 300 independently-owned retail markets in several western states. The company also offers a variety of related services including retail promotion, human resources, accounting, procurement, warehousing, and transportation. Founded in 1934. **NOTE:** Jobseekers interested in driver or warehouse positions must call the Human Resources Department to set up an application appointment. All driver and warehouse positions are part-time, on-call positions, and applicants must be at least 18 years old. **Company slogan:** The food people. **Common positions include:** Accountant; Accounting Clerk; Administrative Assistant; Buyer; Computer Operator; Computer Programmer; Customer Service Representative; Graphic Artist; Nurse Practitioner; Secretary. **Educational backgrounds include:** Accounting; Business Administration; Computer Science; Finance; Liberal Arts. **Benefits:** 401(k); Daycare Assistance; Dental Insurance; Disability Coverage; Employee Discounts; Life Insurance; Medical Insurance; On-Site Exercise Facility; Pension Plan; Public Transit Available; Savings Plan; Tuition Assistance. **Corporate headquarters location:** This Location.

Listed on: Privately held. **Annual sales/revenues:** More than $100 million.
Other U.S. locations:
- Associated Grocers of the South, 3600 Vanderbilt Road, Birmingham AL 35217. 205/841-6781.

ASSOCIATED WHOLESALE GROCERS
P.O. Box 2932, Kansas City KS 66110-2932. 913/288-1000. **Contact:** Human Resources Manager. **World Wide Web address:** http://www. awginc.com. **Description:** Operates wholesale grocery distribution centers supplying products to 859 stores in 10 states. Founded in 1926. **NOTE:** Entry-level positions, as well as second and third shifts are offered. **Common positions include:** Administrative Manager; Auditor; Blue-Collar Worker Supervisor; Buyer; Computer Operator; Computer Programmer; Financial Analyst; Graphic Artist; Sales Representative; Systems Analyst. **Educational backgrounds include:** Accounting; Art/Design; Business Administration; Computer Science; Finance; Liberal Arts; Marketing. **Benefits:** 401(k); Dental Insurance; Disability Coverage; Employee Discounts; Financial Planning Assistance; Flexible Schedule; Life Insurance; Medical Insurance; Pension Plan; Tuition Assistance; Vision Insurance. **Special programs:** Training. **Corporate headquarters location:** This Location. **Other U.S. locations:** Springfield MO; Oklahoma City OK. **Subsidiaries include:** Supermarket Insurance Group. **Listed on:** Privately held. **Annual sales/revenues:** More than $100 million.

ATLANTIC BEVERAGE COMPANY
8106 Stayton Drive, Jessup MD 20794. 410/792-7055. **Contact:** Human Resources. **Description:** A leading, independent, wholesale distributor of specialty non-alcoholic beverages for retail trade in the greater Baltimore and metropolitan Washington DC area. Products include teas, natural sodas, sparkling waters with juice, fruit juices, and juice drinks. Atlantic Beverage Company distributes its specialty beverage products to independent grocery stores, delicatessens, restaurants, and convenience store chains. **Corporate headquarters location:** This Location. **Listed on:** NASDAQ.

BAILEY NURSERIES, INC.
1325 Bailey Road, St. Paul MN 55119. 651/459-9744. **Contact:** Personnel Manager. **World Wide Web address:** http://www.baileynursery.com. **Description:** A large wholesale grower of nursery products including evergreens, trees, shrubs, bedding plants, annuals, and perennials. **Common positions include:** Agricultural Scientist; Horticulturist. **Educational backgrounds include:** Agricultural Science; Horticulture. **Benefits:** 401(k); Dental Insurance; Disability Coverage; Employee Discounts; Life Insurance; Medical Insurance; Pension Plan; Profit Sharing; Savings Plan; Tuition Assistance. **Special programs:** Internships. **Corporate headquarters location:** This Location. **Listed on:** Privately held.

BAKE-LINE PRODUCTS, INC.
One Bake-Line Plaza, Des Plaines IL 60016. 847/699-1000. **Toll-free phone:** 800/323-5944. **Fax:** 847/795-2066. **Contact:** Human Resources. **Description:** A leading private label cookie manufacturer. **NOTE:** Entry-level positions and second and third shifts are offered. **Company slogan:** Eat more cookies. **Common positions include:** Accountant; Administrative Assistant; Auditor; Budget Analyst; Computer Operator; Computer Programmer; Controller; Customer Service Rep.; Database Administrator; Financial Analyst; Human Resources Manager; Market Research Analyst; Purchasing Agent/Manager; Sales Rep.; Transportation/Traffic Specialist; Typist/Word Processor. **Educational backgrounds include:** Accounting; Business Administration; Finance; Marketing; Mathematics; Microsoft Word; Spreadsheets. **Benefits:** 401(k); Casual Dress - Daily; Dental Insurance; Disability Coverage; Financial Planning Assistance; Life Insurance; Medical Insurance; Pension Plan; Sick Days; Tuition Assistance; Vacation Days (6 - 10); Vision Insurance. **Special programs:** Internships; Summer Jobs. **Corporate headquarters location:** Elmhurst IL. **Parent company:** Keebler Company. **President:** Dave Shanholtz.

BALCHEM CORPORATION
P.O. Box 175, Slate Hill NY 10973. 914/355-5300. **Contact:** Director of Human Resources. **World Wide Web address:** http://www.balchem.net. **Description:** A leader in the manufacturing and marketing of encapsulated food ingredients for a variety of industries. The company is also a leading supplier of ethylene oxide, a packaging sterilant. Founded in 1967. **Corporate headquarters location:** This Location. **Listed on:** American Stock Exchange. **Stock exchange symbol:** BCP.

BALL HORTICULTURAL COMPANY
622 Town Road, West Chicago IL 60185-2698. 630/231-3600. **Fax:** 630/231-3605. **Contact:** Human Resources Manager. **World Wide Web address:** http://www.ballhort.com. **Description:** An international horticulture producer and distributor. **NOTE:** Entry-level positions are offered. **Educational backgrounds include:** Biology; Horticulture. **Benefits:** 401(k); Daycare Assistance; Dental Insurance; Disability Coverage; Employee Discounts; Life Insurance; Medical Insurance; Pension Plan; Profit Sharing; Savings Plan; Tuition Assistance. **Special programs:** Internships; Training. **Corporate headquarters location:** This Location. **Subsidiaries include:** Ball FloraPlant; Ball Seed Company; Ball Superior Ltd.; ColorLink; PanAmerican Seed Company; Vegmo Plant, BV.

BAR-S FOODS COMPANY
P.O. Box 29049, Phoenix AZ 85038. 602/264-7272. **Contact:** Personnel. **World Wide Web address:** http://www.bar-s.com. **Description:** Engaged in the production and distribution of cheese and smoked meat products including ham, bacon, franks, sausage, and luncheon meat. **Common positions include:** Accountant/Auditor; Blue-Collar Worker Supervisor; Food Scientist/Technologist; General Manager; Mechanical Engineer; Purchasing Agent/Manager; Quality Control Supervisor; Systems Analyst. **Educational backgrounds include:** Accounting; Business Administration; Chemistry; Computer Science; Finance; Liberal Arts. **Benefits:** 401(k); Dental Insurance; Disability Coverage; Life Insurance; Medical Insurance; Profit Sharing; Savings Plan. **Corporate headquarters location:** This Location.

BARBER DAIRIES INC.
36 Barber Court, Birmingham AL 35209. 205/942-2351. **Contact:** Personnel. **Description:** Processes and distributes dairy products and juices. **Common positions include:** Accountant/Auditor; Automotive Mechanic; Blue-Collar Worker Supervisor; Branch Manager; Buyer; Computer Programmer; Customer Service Rep.; Food Scientist/Technologist; General Manager; Human Resources Manager; Industrial Production Manager; MIS Specialist; Operations/Production Manager; Purchasing Agent/Manager. **Benefits:** 401(k); Dental Insurance; Disability Coverage; Life Insurance; Medical Insurance; Pension Plan. **Corporate headquarters location:** This Location.

BASKIN-ROBBINS, INC.
31 Baskin-Robbins Place, Glendale CA 91201-2738. 818/956-0031. **Contact:** Human Resources. **Description:** An ice cream manufacturer that also operates retail locations. **Corporate headquarters location:** This Location.

BAY STATE MILLING COMPANY
100 Congress Street, Quincy MA 02169. 617/328-4400. **Toll-free phone:** 800/553-5687. **Fax:** 617/479-8910. **Contact:** Human Resources Manager. **World Wide Web address:** http://www.baystatemilling.com. **Description:** A flour milling company with nationwide manufacturing facilities. **Corporate headquarters location:** This Location.

BEN & JERRY'S INC.
30 Community Drive, South Burlington VT 05403. 802/651-9600. **Contact:** Human Resources. **World Wide Web address:** http://www.benjerry.com. **Description:** Ben & Jerry's manufactures and distributes traditional as well as original flavors of ice cream and low-fat frozen yogurt. Franchised stores are located in Vermont and surrounding states. **Corporate headquarters location:** This Location.

BERINGER VINEYARDS
P.O. Box 111, St. Helena CA 94574. 707/963-7115. **Contact:** Personnel Coordinator. **Description:** Operates vineyards and wineries. **Corporate headquarters location:** This Location.

BESTFOODS BAKING COMPANY
700 Sylvan Avenue, Englewood Cliffs NJ 07632. 201/894-4000. **Contact:** Corporate Personnel Services. **World Wide Web address:** http://www.bestfoods.com. **Description:** This location houses the administrative and marketing offices and is also the world headquarters. Overall, Bestfoods produces and distributes a variety of food products including soups, sauces, and bouillons; dressings including Hellmann's mayonnaise; starches and syrups; bread spreads including Skippy peanut butter; desserts and baking aids; and pasta. **Corporate headquarters location:** This Location.

BEVERAGE DISTRIBUTORS CORPORATION
14200 East Moncrieff Place, Suite G, Aurora CO 80011. 303/371-3421. **Contact:** Human Resources. **Description:** Provides beverage distribution services. **Common positions include:** Computer Operator; Computer Programmer; Credit Manager; Human Resources Manager; Sales Manager; Sales Representative. **Benefits:** 401(k); Casual Dress - Fridays; Dental Insurance; Disability Coverage; Life Insurance; Medical Insurance; Profit Sharing; Sick Days; Tuition Assistance; Vacation Days.

BORDEN, INC.
180 East Broad Street, Columbus OH 43215. 614/225-4000. **Fax:** 614/225-7263. **Contact:** Human Resources. **Description:** Operates two major industry segments (foods and chemicals), through three major operating divisions. The North American Foods division consists of pasta and sauce, niche grocery, and U.S. dairy products. The International Foods segment includes European bakery products, international milk powder, Latin American dairy, and European grocery and pasta products. Borden's Packaging and Industrial Products/Domestic and International sector is comprised of resins, plastic film and packaging, decorative products, consumer adhesives, and pasta in Brazil. Name brands include Borden dairy products, Cracker Jack snacks, Elmer's glue, Creamette pasta, and Classico pasta sauces. **Common positions include:** Accountant/Auditor; Chemical Engineer; Financial Analyst; Marketing Specialist; Sales Representative. **Corporate headquarters location:** This Location. **Other U.S. locations:**
- Borden Foods Corporation, 2301 Shermer Road, Northbrook IL 60062. 847/291-3900.

BORDER FOODS INC.
P.O. Box 751, Deming NM 88031. 505/546-8863. **Fax:** 505/546-8676. **Contact:** Human Resources Manager. **World Wide Web address:** http://www.borderfoodsinc.com. **Description:** Manufactures and processes green chile and jalapeno peppers. This location also hires seasonally. Founded in 1974. **NOTE:** Second and third shifts are offered. **Common positions include:** Accountant; Computer Support Technician; Controller; Electrician; Industrial Production Manager; MIS Specialist; Production Manager; Purchasing Agent/Manager; Quality Control Supervisor; Sales Rep. **Educational backgrounds include:** Accounting; Engineering; Microsoft Office; Microsoft Word; Spreadsheets. **Benefits:** 401(k); Casual Dress - Fridays; Disability Coverage; Employee Discounts; Life Insurance; Medical Insurance; Relocation Assistance; Sick Days; Tuition Assistance; Vacation Days (10 - 20). **Corporate headquarters location:** This Location. **Other area locations:** Las Cruces NM.

BOUYEA-FASSETTS
1805 Shelburne Road, South Burlington VT 05403-7719. 802/862-2222. **Contact:** Human Resources Manager. **Description:** A commercial bakery. **Parent company:** Bestfoods Baking Company.

BOYDS COFFEE COMPANY
P.O. Box 20547, Portland OR 97294. 503/666-4545. **Contact:** Human Resources Manager. **World Wide Web address:** http://www.boyds.com. **Description:** Roasts, packages, and distributes coffee and food products.

BRACH & BROCK CONFECTIONS, INC.
4120 Jersey Pike, Chattanooga TN 37422. 423/899-1100. **Contact:** Human Resources. **Description:** A candy and snack food manufacturer and marketer. **Common positions include:** Accountant/Auditor; Budget Analyst; Computer Programmer; Customer Service Rep.; Electrician; Financial Analyst; General Manager; Systems Analyst. **Educational backgrounds include:** Accounting; Computer Science; Engineering; Finance. **Benefits:** 401(k); Disability Coverage; Employee Discounts; Life Insurance; Medical Insurance; Pension Plan; Savings Plan; Tuition Assistance. **Corporate headquarters location:** This Location.

BROWN & WILLIAMSON TOBACCO CORP.
200 B&W Tower, 401 South Fourth Avenue, Louisville KY 40202. 502/568-7000. **Contact:** Human Resources. **World Wide Web address:** http://www.bw.com. **Description:** Brown & Williamson researches, develops, manufactures, and markets tobacco products including cigarettes. **Common positions include:** Auditor; Chemical Engineer; Computer Programmer; Electrical/Electronics Engineer; Financial Analyst; Food Scientist/Technologist; Industrial Engineer; Manufacturing Engineer; Market Research Analyst; Marketing Specialist; MIS Specialist; Sales Rep.; Software Engineer; Systems Analyst. **Educational backgrounds include:** Business Administration; Chemistry; Computer Science; Engineering; Finance; Marketing; Software Tech. Support. **Benefits:** 401(k); Dental Insurance; Disability Coverage; Life Insurance; Medical Insurance; Pension Plan; Profit Sharing; Stock Purchase; Tuition Assistance. **Corporate headquarters location:** This Location. **Parent company:** BAT Industries (London, England).

BROWN-FORMAN CORPORATION

P.O. Box 1080, Louisville KY 40201-1080. 502/585-1100. **Physical address:** 850 Dixie Highway, Louisville KY 40210. **Contact:** Human Resources. **World Wide Web address:** http://www. brown-forman.com. **Description:** Brown-Forman is a distiller, marketer, and importer of alcoholic beverages such as hard liquors, wines, and champagnes. Brands include Jack Daniels, Southern Comfort, Korbel, Bolla, and Canadian Mist. The company also produces durable goods such as china, crystal, and giftware which are sold through retail stores and company-affiliated outlets. These brands include Hartman Luggage and Lenox china. Other businesses include an aquaculture operation. **Corporate headquarters location:** This Location.

BUENO FOODS

P.O. Box 293, Albuquerque NM 87103-0293. 505/243-2722. **Contact:** Human Resources. **World Wide Web address:** http://www.buenofoods.com. **Description:** A producer, wholesaler, and retailer of frozen Mexican foods.

BUNGE CORPORATION
BUNGE COMMODITIES GROUP

11720 Borman Drive, St. Louis MO 63146-1000. 314/872-3030. **Contact:** Director of Human Resources. **Description:** This location houses the Grain and Soybean Divisions. Overall, Bunge Corporation handles and processes grains and oilseeds. The company also manufactures and markets food ingredients. The company does business through the Bunge Commodities Group and the Bunge Foods Group. The Bunge Commodities Group, the company's largest component, is formed around the company's original agricultural commodity businesses and includes the Grain, Soybean Processing, and Lauhoff Milling Divisions. The Soybean Processing Division produces soybean meal and soybean oil for both export and domestic customers. The meal is sold as a feed ingredient for poultry, hogs, cattle, and fish. The oil is sold to refineries, including the company's own, to make shortenings and cooking oils. With numerous plants located throughout the Midwest and South, Bunge is one of the largest soybean processors in the U.S. The Grain Division operates in the United States and Canada, and markets bulk sorghum, oats, and barley. **Corporate headquarters location:** This Location.

W. ATLEE BURPEE & COMPANY

300 Park Avenue, Warminster PA 18974. 215/674-4900. **Contact:** Human Resources Manager. **World Wide Web address:** http://www.burpee.com. **Description:** Produces seeds. **Common positions include:** Accountant/Auditor; Blue-Collar Worker Supervisor; Computer Programmer; Customer Service Rep.; Graphic Artist; Horticulturist; Manufacturer's/Wholesaler's Sales Rep.; Operations/Production Manager; Purchasing Agent/Manager; Systems Analyst; Technical Writer/Editor. **Educational backgrounds include:** Accounting; Art/Design; Business Administration; Computer Science; Finance; Marketing. **Benefits:** 401(k); Dental Insurance; Disability Coverage; Employee Discounts; Life Insurance; Medical Insurance; Profit Sharing; Tuition Assistance. **Corporate headquarters location:** This Location.

C&S WHOLESALE GROCERS, INC.

Old Ferry Road, P.O. Box 821, Brattleboro VT 05302. 802/257-4371. **Contact:** Human Resources. **Description:** One of the largest grocery wholesalers in New England. **Common positions include:** Warehouse/Distribution Worker. **Corporate headquarters location:** This Location.

CABOT COOPERATIVE CREAMERY

P.O. Box 128, Main Street, Cabot VT 05647. 802/563-2231. **Contact:** Human Resources. **Description:** Produces and distributes a variety of cheese and dairy products including Cabot cheeses, cottage cheese, sour cream, and yogurt.

CAGLE'S INC.

2000 Hills Avenue NW, Atlanta GA 30318. 404/355-2820. **Contact:** Human Resources. **Description:** Produces, markets, and distributes a variety of fresh and frozen poultry products. Its operations consist of the breeding, hatching, and raising of chickens, feed milling, processing, and marketing. **Corporate headquarters location:** This Location. **Other area locations:** Dalton GA; Forsyth GA; Lovejoy GA; Macon GA; Pine Mountain Valley GA. **Other U.S. locations:** Birmingham AL; Collinsville AL. **Subsidiaries include:** Cagle's Farms, Inc.

CALGENE, INC.

1920 Fifth Street, Davis CA 95616. 530/753-6313. **Fax:** 530/792-2453. **Contact:** Human Resources. **Description:** Develops genetically-engineered plants and plant products for the food and seed industries. The company's research and business efforts are focused in three main crop areas: fresh market tomato, edible and industrial plant oils, and cotton. **Corporate headquarters location:** This Location.

CAMPBELL SOUP COMPANY

One Campbell Place, Camden NJ 08103-1799. 856/342-4800. **Contact:** Human Resources Manager. **World Wide Web address:** http://www. campbellsoups.com. **Description:** This location houses administrative offices. Overall, Campbell Soup Company is a producer of commercial soups, juices, pickles, frozen foods, canned beans, canned pasta products, spaghetti sauces, and baked goods. The company's products are distributed worldwide. U.S. brand names include Campbell's, Vlasic, V8, Chunky, Home Cookin', Prego, Pepperidge Farm, Inc., LeMenu, Mrs. Paul's, and Swanson. European foods are sold under brand names such as Pleybin, Biscuits Delacre, Freshbake, Groko, Godiva, and Betis. Campbell Soup Company also owns Arnotts Biscuits of Australia. **Corporate headquarters location:** This Location.

CANANDAIGUA BRANDS, INC.

300 Willowbrook Office Park, Fairport NY 14450. 716/218-2169. **Contact:** Human Resources. **World Wide Web address:** http://www.cbrands.com. **Description:** A leading producer and distributor of wine, beer, spirits, cider, and bottled water. The company services 17,000 customers worldwide. **Corporate headquarters location:** This Location. **Subsidiaries include:** Barton Incorporated; Canandaigua Wine Company; Matthew Clark plc (Bristol England) produces and distributes cider, table wines, British wines, light wines, and bottled water.

CANTEEN CORPORATION

216 West Diversey Avenue, Elmhurst IL 60126. 630/833-3666. **Contact:** Human Resources. **World Wide Web address:** http://www.canteen.com. **Description:** One of the world's largest food and beverage vending companies. Canteen Corporation has over 150,000 vending machines in service. **Corporate headquarters location:** This Location. **Parent company:** Compass Group plc (London, England).

CARGILL INC.

P.O. Box 9300, Mail Stop 10, Minneapolis MN 55440. 612/742-7200. **Physical address:** 15407

McGinty Road West, Wayzata MN. **Toll-free phone:** 800/741-7431. **Contact:** Human Resources Manager. **World Wide Web address:** http://www. cargill.com. **Description:** Cargill, with its subsidiaries and its affiliates, is involved in nearly 50 individual lines of business. The company deals in commodity trading, handling, transporting, processing, and risk management. Cargill is a major trader of grains and oilseeds, as well as a marketer of other agricultural and non-agricultural commodities. As a transporter, the company moves bulk commodities using a network of rail and road systems, inland waterways, and ocean-going routes combining its own fleet and transportation services purchased from outside sources. Agricultural products include a wide variety of feed, seed, fertilizers, and other goods and services for producers worldwide. Cargill is also a leader in producing and marketing seed varieties and hybrids. Cargill Central Research (also at this location) aims to develop new agricultural products to address the needs of customers around the world. Cargill's Financial Markets Division supports Cargill and its subsidiaries through financial instrument trading, emerging markets instrument trading, value investing, and money management. Cargill's worldwide food processing businesses supply products ranging from basic ingredients used in food production to name brands. The company also operates a number of industrial businesses including the production of steel, industrial-grade starches, ethanol, and salt products. **NOTE:** Entry-level positions and second and third shifts are offered. **Common positions include:** Account Manager; Account Rep.; Accountant; Attorney; Auditor; Biochemist; Buyer; Chemical Engineer; Chemist; Computer Operator; Computer Programmer; Database Manager; Electrical Engineer; Electronics Engineer; Environmental Engineer; Food Scientist/ Technologist; Management Trainee; Marketing Specialist; Mechanical Engineer; Metallurgical Engineer; MIS Specialist; Operations Manager; Production Manager; Project Manager; Quality Control Supervisor; Sales Manager; Software Engineer. **Educational backgrounds include:** Accounting; Business Administration; Chemistry; Computer Science; Economics; Engineering; Finance; Liberal Arts; Software Tech. Support. **Benefits:** 401(k); Dental Insurance; Disability Coverage; Financial Planning Assistance; Life Insurance; Medical Insurance; Pension Plan; Profit Sharing; Public Transit Available; Telecommuting; Tuition Assistance. **Special programs:** Internships; Training; Co-ops; Summer Jobs. **Corporate headquarters location:** This Location. **International locations:** Worldwide.

CARVEL CORPORATION
20 Batterson Park Road, Farmington CT 06032. 860/677-6811. **Contact:** Human Resources Manager. **Description:** Engaged in the manufacture of ice cream products and franchising operations for the chain of Carvel Ice Cream stores. **Corporate headquarters location:** This Location.

CASS-CLAY CREAMERY
P.O. Box 2947, Fargo ND 58108. 701/232-1566. **Contact:** Manager. **Description:** Produces butter, ice cream, and milk. **Corporate headquarters location:** This Location.

CELESTIAL SEASONINGS, INC.
4600 Sleepytime Drive, Boulder CO 80301. 303/530-5300. **Contact:** Human Resources Manager. **World Wide Web address:** http://www. celestialseasonings.com. **Description:** Produces herbal teas and beverages. **Corporate headquarters location:** This Location. **Founder/Chairman:** Mo Siegel.

CENEX HARVEST STATES COOPERATIVES
P.O. Box 64089, St. Paul MN 55164. **Physical address:** 5600 Cenex Drive, Inver Grove Heights MN 55077. **Toll-free phone:** 800/328-6539. **Contact:** Human Resources Manager. **World Wide Web address:** http://www.cenexharveststates.com. **Description:** A grain marketing company. **Common positions include:** Accountant/Auditor; Procurement Specialist. **Educational backgrounds include:** Accounting; Business Administration; Finance; Marketing. **Benefits:** 401(k); Dental Insurance; Disability Coverage; Employee Discounts; Life Insurance; Medical Insurance; Pension Plan; Savings Plan; Tuition Assistance. **Corporate headquarters location:** This Location.

CERTIFIED GROCERS MIDWEST, INC.
One Certified Drive, Hodgkins IL 60525. 708/579-2100. **Contact:** Human Resources. **Description:** A food wholesaler. **Corporate headquarters location:** This Location.

CHALONE WINE GROUP, LTD.
621 Airpark Road, Napa CA 94558-6272. 707/254-4200. **Fax:** 707/254-4207. **Contact:** Human Resources. **World Wide Web address:** http://www. chalonewinegroup.com. **Description:** Chalone Wine Group, Ltd. produces, markets, and sells premium white and red varietal table wines, primarily Chardonnay, Pinot Noir, Cabernet Sauvignon, and Sauvignon Blanc. **Corporate headquarters location:** This Location.

CHIQUITA BRANDS INTERNATIONAL
250 East Fifth Street, Cincinnati OH 45202. 513/784-8000. **Fax:** 513/784-8030. **Contact:** Human Resources. **World Wide Web address:** http://www.chiquita.com. **Description:** Produces, processes, and distributes fresh and prepared foods which are sold under the Chiquita and other brand names. Products include fresh fruits and vegetables from the U.S. and South and Central American countries, as well as juices, purees, salads, margarine, and shortening products. **Corporate headquarters location:** This Location.

CHOCTAW MAID FARMS, INC.
P.O. Box 577, Carthage MS 39051. 601/298-5300. **Contact:** Human Resources Director. **Description:** A poultry processing company. **NOTE:** Entry-level positions and second and third shifts are offered. **Common positions include:** Accountant; Administrative Assistant; AS400 Programmer Analyst; Blue-Collar Worker Supervisor; Chief Financial Officer; Computer Support Technician; Industrial Production Manager; Licensed Practical Nurse; Purchasing Agent/Manager; Secretary. **Educational backgrounds include:** Business Administration; Liberal Arts. **Benefits:** 401(k); Dental Insurance; Disability Coverage; Life Insurance; Medical Insurance; Profit Sharing; Tuition Assistance. **Special programs:** Internships. **Corporate headquarters location:** This Location.

CLIFFSTAR CORPORATION
One Cliffstar Avenue, Dunkirk NY 14048. 716/366-6100x296. **Fax:** 716/366-1678. **Contact:** Human Resources. **Description:** Produces and distributes private label juices and juice products. Customers include grocery stores, mass merchandisers, and drug stores. **Common positions include:** Accountant/Auditor; Chemical Engineer; Chemist; Computer Programmer; Credit Manager; Customer Service Rep.; Food Scientist/Technologist; Human Resources Manager; Industrial Engineer; Mechanical Engineer; Quality Control Supervisor; Systems Analyst. **Educational backgrounds include:** Accounting; Chemistry; Computer Science; Engineering; Finance; Marketing.

Benefits: 401(k); Disability Coverage; Employee Discounts; Life Insurance; Medical Insurance; Profit Sharing; Tuition Assistance. **Corporate headquarters location:** This Location. **Other U.S. locations:** Joplin MO.

CLOVERDALE FOODS
P.O. Box 667, Mandan ND 58554. 701/663-9511. **Physical address:** 3015 34th Street NW, Mandan ND. **Toll-free phone:** 800/669-9511. **Fax:** 701/663-0690. **Contact:** Human Resources. **Description:** A major processor of specialty hams, bacon, and other pork products. **NOTE:** Entry-level positions are offered. **Common positions include:** Accountant/Auditor; Administrative Manager; Advertising Clerk; Blue-Collar Worker Supervisor; Buyer; Computer Programmer; Credit Manager; Customer Service Rep.; Electrician; Food Scientist/Technologist; General Manager; Human Resources Manager; Manufacturer's/Wholesaler's Sales Rep.; Market Research Analyst; Operations/Production Manager; Quality Control Supervisor; Systems Analyst. **Educational backgrounds include:** Accounting; Computer Science; Marketing; Sales. **Benefits:** 401(k); Dental Insurance; Disability Coverage; Life Insurance; Medical Insurance; Pension Plan; Tuition Assistance; Vision Plan. **Corporate headquarters location:** This Location. **Other U.S. locations:** Minot ND.

CLOVERLAND GREEN SPRING DAIRY
2701 Loch Raven Road, Baltimore MD 21218. 410/235-4477. **Contact:** Debra Webster, Personnel Manager. **Description:** Produces and distributes milk, ice cream, bakery products, and citrus juices. **Corporate headquarters location:** This Location.

COCA-COLA BOTTLING COMPANY
P.O. Box 9140, Austin TX 78766. 512/836-7272. **Contact:** Human Resources. **World Wide Web address:** http://www.coca-cola.com. **Description:** A distribution plant which bottles and ships Coca-Cola products to the surrounding area. **Parent company:** Coca-Cola Company is one of the world's largest marketers, distributors, and producers of bottle and can products. Coca-Cola Enterprises, part of The Coca-Cola Company, is in the liquid non-alcoholic refreshment business, which includes traditional carbonated soft drinks, still and sparkling waters, juices, isotonics, and teas.

THE COCA-COLA COMPANY
P.O. Drawer 1734, Atlanta GA 30301. 404/676-2121. **Physical address:** One Coca-Cola Plaza NW, Atlanta GA 30310. **Contact:** Human Resources. **World Wide Web address:** http://www.coca-cola.com. **Description:** One of the world's largest soft drink makers. The Coca-Cola Company manufactures concentrates and syrups which are sold to bottlers and wholesalers. Brand names include Coca-Cola, Diet Coke, Coca-Cola light (international); Sprite, Diet Sprite, Mr. PiBB, Mello Yello, Fanta, TAB, Fresca, Fruitopia, Powerade, and Minute Maid. The Coca-Cola Company owns 100 supporting brands around the world including PowerAde, Aquarius, Hi-C, Georgia (canned coffee, sold in Japan), Thums Up & Limca (India), Sparletta Brands (South Africa), Nestea (distributed by Coca-Cola Enterprises Inc.), and Seiryusabo (Japan). **Corporate headquarters location:** This Location. **Subsidiaries include:** Coca-Cola Enterprises Inc. is one of the world's largest sellers of juice and juice-related products under brands such as FiveAlive, Hi-C, Bright & Early, Bacardi, and Coca-Cola Foods.

COCA-COLA ENTERPRISES INC.
P.O. Box 723040, Atlanta GA 31139. 770/989-3000. **Physical address:** 2500 Windy Ridge Parkway, Atlanta GA 30334. **Contact:** Human Resources. **World Wide Web address:** http://www.cokecce.com. **Description:** One of the world's largest marketers, distributors, and producers of bottled and canned, non-alcoholic beverages. The company operates approximately 400 facilities, over 40,000 vehicles and more than 1.5 million vending machines, beverage dispensers, and coolers. The product line includes traditional carbonated soft drinks, still and sparkling waters, juices, isotonics, and teas. **Corporate headquarters location:** This Location. **Other U.S. locations:** Nationwide.

COLUMBIA FARMS
P.O. Box 3628, Leesville SC 29070. 803/532-4488. **Contact:** Human Resources. **Description:** A fully-integrated poultry processing and food distribution company. **Common positions include:** Accountant/Auditor; Food Scientist/Technologist; Human Resources Manager; Management Trainee; Quality Control Supervisor. **Educational backgrounds include:** Business Administration. **Benefits:** Life Insurance; Medical Insurance. **Corporate headquarters location:** This Location. **Other area locations:** Columbia SC; Greenville SC.

CONAGRA BEEF COMPANY
P.O. Box 1470, Nampa ID 83653. 208/466-4627x123. **Toll-free phone:** 800/550-0176. **Contact:** Human Resources. **World Wide Web address:** http://www.conagra.com. **Description:** A slaughtering and processing plant for a major food processing company. **Common positions include:** Accountant; Administrative Assistant; Blue-Collar Worker Supervisor; Computer Support Technician; Controller; Electrician; Environmental Engineer; General Manager; Human Resources Manager; Industrial Engineer; Mechanical Engineer; MIS Specialist; Purchasing Agent/Manager; Registered Nurse. **Educational backgrounds include:** Accounting; Business Administration; Computer Science; Engineering; Microsoft Word; Spreadsheets. **Benefits:** 401(k); Dental Insurance; Disability Coverage; Life Insurance; Medical Insurance; Pension Plan; Relocation Assistance; Stock Purchase; Tuition Assistance. **Corporate headquarters location:** Greeley CO.

CONAGRA, INC.
One ConAgra Drive, Omaha NE 68102. 402/595-4000. **Contact:** Human Resources Manager. **World Wide Web address:** http://www.conagra.com. **Description:** A diversified, international food company. Products range from convenient prepared foods to farming supplies. ConAgra has major businesses in branded grocery products including shelf-stable and frozen foods, processed meats, chicken and turkey products, and cheeses. The company also has major businesses in potato products, private label grocery products, beef, pork, seafood, grain and pulse (edible beans) merchandising, grain processing, specialty trailing, crop protection chemicals, fertilizers, and animal feed. ConAgra is a family of independent operating companies operating in three industry segments: prepared foods, trading and processing, and agri-products. **Corporate headquarters location:** This Location.
Other U.S. locations:
• ConAgra Poultry Company, P.O. Box 1389, Duluth GA 30096. 770/232-4200.
• ConAgra Refrigerated Prepared Foods, 2001 Butterfield Road, Downers Grove IL 60515-1049. 630/512-1000.

CREAMLAND DAIRIES INC.
P.O. Box 25067, Albuquerque NM 87125. 505/247-0721. **Contact:** Linda Shores, Human Resources

Director. **Description:** A regional dairy that produces milk, cream, and ice cream. **Corporate headquarters location:** This Location.

CRIDER'S POULTRY
P.O. Box 398, Stillmore GA 30464. 912/562-4435. **Contact:** Human Resources. **Description:** Engaged in poultry dressing operations. **Common positions include:** Accountant/Auditor; Industrial Production Manager; Management Trainee; Operations/ Production Manager; Purchasing Agent/Manager. **Benefits:** Dental Insurance; Disability Coverage; Life Insurance; Medical Insurance; Tuition Assistance. **Corporate headquarters location:** This Location.

CRYSTAL FARMS, INC.
CRYSTAL FARM MILLS, INC.
P.O. Box 7101, Chestnut Mountain GA 30502. 770/967-6152. **Contact:** Human Resources M. **Description:** One of the largest egg producers in the state of Georgia, operating a layer complex, a hatchery, two feed mills, and two processing plants. **Common positions include:** Accountant; Blue-Collar Worker Supervisor; Computer Programmer; Credit Manager; Department Manager; General Manager; Management Trainee; Manufacturer's/ Wholesaler's Sales Representative; Operations/ Production Manager; Quality Control Supervisor; Transportation/Traffic Specialist. **Educational backgrounds include:** Accounting; Business Administration; Computer Science; Food Science. **Benefits:** Employee Discounts; Life Insurance; Medical Insurance; Pension Plan; Tuition Assistance. **Corporate headquarters location:** This Location.

CUISINE SOLUTIONS INC.
85 South Bragg Street, Suite 600, Alexandria VA 22312. 703/750-9600. **Contact:** Personnel Manager. **World Wide Web address:** http://www. cuisinesolutions.com. **Description:** A producer of prepared foods using a sous vide cooking process. **Common positions include:** Accountant; Chef/ Cook/Kitchen Worker; Computer Programmer; Electrical/Electronics Engineer; Food Scientist/ Technologist; Industrial Production Manager; Manufacturer's/Wholesaler's Sales Rep.; Operations/ Production Manager. **Educational backgrounds include:** Accounting; Computer Science; Culinary Arts/Cooking; Marketing. **Benefits:** 401(k); Dental Insurance; Disability Coverage; Employee Discounts; Life Insurance; Medical Insurance. **Corporate headquarters location:** This Location. **International locations:** Norway.

CUTLER DAIRY PRODUCTS, INC.
612-30 West Sedgley Avenue, Philadelphia PA 19140. 215/229-5400. **Fax:** 215/229-5637. **Contact:** Human Resources. **Description:** Processes and supplies eggs to the food industry. **Common positions include:** Administrative Manager; Biological Scientist; Blue-Collar Worker Supervisor; Food Scientist/Technologist; General Manager; Heating/AC/Refrigeration Technician; Inspector/Tester/Grader; Production Manager; Truck Driver. **Educational backgrounds include:** Biology; Business Administration; Liberal Arts. **Benefits:** Dental Insurance; Life Insurance; Medical Insurance; Pension Plan; Profit Sharing. **Corporate headquarters location:** This Location. **Other U.S. locations:** Abbeyville AL.

DNA PLANT TECHNOLOGY CORPORATION
6701 San Pablo Avenue, Oakland CA 94608. 510/547-2395. **Contact:** Human Resources. **Description:** A leading agribusiness biotechnology company focused on developing and marketing premium, fresh, and processed fruits and vegetables, using advanced breeding, genetic engineering, and other biotechniques. **Corporate headquarters location:** This Location. **Subsidiaries include:** FreshWorld Farms markets a line of premium vegetables under the FreshWorld Farms brand name including tomatoes, carrot bites, sweet red mini-peppers, and carrot sticks.

DAIRY FRESH FOODS INC.
15004 Third Avenue, Highland Park MI 48203. 313/868-5511. **Contact:** Human Resources. **Description:** A wholesale distributor of dairy and deli products. **Benefits:** 401(k); Dental Insurance; Life Insurance; Medical Insurance; Profit Sharing. **Special programs:** Training. **Corporate headquarters location:** This Location. **Listed on:** Privately held. **Annual sales/revenues:** $51 - $100 million.

DANKWORTH PACKAGING
P.O. Box 584, Ballinger TX 76821. 915/365-3553. **Fax:** 915/365-2367. **Contact:** Plant Manager. **Description:** A meat packaging plant. **Corporate headquarters location:** This Location.

DARIGOLD INC.
P.O. Box 79007, Seattle WA 98119. 206/284-7220. **Toll-free phone:** 800/283-6450. **Contact:** Human Resources. **World Wide Web address:** http://www. darigold.com. **Description:** Manufactures, sells, and distributes dairy products. **Common positions include:** Accountant; Administrative Worker/Clerk; Blue-Collar Worker Supervisor; Branch Manager; Computer Programmer; Customer Service Rep.; Department Manager; Financial Analyst; Food Scientist/Technologist; Manufacturer's/Wholesaler's Sales Rep.; Operations/Production Manager; Production Worker; Quality Control Supervisor; Systems Analyst; Truck Driver. **Educational backgrounds include:** Accounting; Biology; Computer Science; Finance; High School Diploma/GED; Liberal Arts; Marketing. **Benefits:** 401(k); Dental Insurance; Disability Coverage; Life Insurance; Medical Insurance; Pension Plan; Savings Plan; Tuition Assistance. **Corporate headquarters location:** This Location. **Other area locations:** Chehalis WA; Issaquah WA; Lynden WA; Spokane WA; Sunnyside WA; Yakima WA. **Other U.S. locations:** Los Angeles CA; San Jose CA; Boise ID; Caldwell ID; Eugene OR; Medford OR; Portland OR.

DARLING INTERNATIONAL INC.
251 O'Connor Ridge Boulevard, Suite 300, Irving TX 75038. 972/717-0300. **World Wide Web address:** http://www.darlingii.com. **Contact:** Human Resources. **Description:** Darling International Recycles animal by-products including fats and proteins into tallow protein meals, and yellow grease. **Common positions include:** Accountant; Agricultural Engineer; Computer Programmer; Management Trainee; Systems Analyst. **Educational backgrounds include:** Accounting; Business Administration; Computer Science; Marketing. **Benefits:** 401(k); Dental Insurance; Disability Coverage; Medical Insurance; Pension Plan; Tuition Assistance. **Corporate headquarters location:** This Location.

DEAN FOODS COMPANY
3600 North River Road, Franklin Park IL 60131. 847/678-1680. **Contact:** Human Resources. **World Wide Web address:** http://www.deanfoods.com. **Description:** A producer and distributor of dairy and specialty food items. Products include milk, cheese, yogurt, sour cream, eggnog, ice cream, vegetables, pickles, salad dressings, pudding, dips, and other condiments. The company also sells and distributes canned meat products to the federal

government. **Common positions include:** Accountant/Auditor; Attorney; Buyer; Computer Programmer; Credit Manager; Customer Service Rep.; Human Resources Manager; Paralegal; Systems Analyst. **Educational backgrounds include:** Accounting; Business Administration; Communications; Computer Science; Economics; Finance; Liberal Arts; Marketing. **Benefits:** 401(k); Dental Insurance; Disability Coverage; Employee Discounts; Life Insurance; Medical Insurance; Pension Plan; Profit Sharing; Savings Plan; Tuition Assistance. **Special programs:** Internships. **Corporate headquarters location:** This Location. **Other U.S. locations:** Nationwide. **Listed on:** New York Stock Exchange.

DELTA BEVERAGE GROUP, INC.
2221 Democrat Road, Memphis TN 38132. 901/344-7100. **Contact:** Raymond R. Stitle, Vice President of Human Resources. **Description:** Engaged in the bottling and sale of Pepsi-Cola and 7-Up. **Common positions include:** Accountant/Auditor; Computer Programmer; Financial Analyst; Human Resources Manager. **Educational backgrounds include:** Business Administration; Marketing. **Benefits:** 401(k); Dental Insurance; Disability Coverage; Life Insurance; Medical Insurance; Tuition Assistance. **Corporate headquarters location:** This Location. **Other U.S. locations:** AK; LA; MI.

DIAMOND FRUIT GROWERS INC.
P.O. Box 180, Hood River OR 97031. 541/354-5300. **Contact:** Dave Simons, Human Resources. **Description:** Processes fruits to be distributed both in the United States and internationally. **Corporate headquarters location:** This Location.

DOLE FOOD COMPANY, INC.
One Dole Drive, Westlake Village CA 91362. 818/879-6600. **Contact:** Human Resources. **World Wide Web address:** http://www.dole.com. **Description:** Processes canned fruits. Founded in 1851. **Corporate headquarters location:** This Location.

EAGLE MILLING COMPANY
P.O. Box 15007, Casa Grande AZ 85230-5007. 520/836-2131. **Contact:** Human Resources. **Description:** Produces a complete range of animal feed products for dealers and commercial customers. The company also markets animal health products statewide. **Common positions include:** Accountant/Auditor; Branch Manager; Buyer; Computer Programmer; Department Manager; Manufacturer's/Wholesaler's Sales Rep.; Operations/Production Manager. **Educational backgrounds include:** Accounting; Computer Science; Marketing. **Benefits:** Disability Coverage; Employee Discounts; Life Insurance; Medical Insurance. **Corporate headquarters location:** This Location.

EDWARDS BAKING COMPANY
One Lemon Lane NE, Atlanta GA 30307. 404/377-0511. **Toll-free phone:** 800/241-0559. **Contact:** Recruiter. **Description:** Produces frozen bakery items. **NOTE:** Jobseekers should send resumes to Human Resources, 6875 Jimmy Carter Boulevard, Suite 3200, Norcross GA 30071. **Common positions include:** Accountant; Administrator; Blue-Collar Worker Supervisor; Buyer; Computer Programmer; Customer Service Representative; Department Manager; Dietician/Nutritionist; Electrical/Electronics Engineer; Food Scientist/Technologist; Industrial Engineer; Management Trainee; Mechanical Engineer; Mixer; Operations/Production Manager; Packaging/Processing Worker; Production Worker; Purchasing Agent/Manager; Quality Control Supervisor; Transportation/Traffic

Specialist. **Educational backgrounds include:** Accounting; Business Administration; Computer Science; Engineering; Finance; Food Science; Home Economics; Marketing. **Benefits:** 401(k); Disability Coverage; Employee Discounts; Life Insurance; Medical Insurance; Pension Plan; Profit Sharing; Savings Plan; Tuition Assistance. **Corporate headquarters location:** This Location.

ESKIMO PIE CORPORATION
P.O. Box 26906, Richmond VA 23261. 804/560-8400. **Physical address:** 901 Moorefield Park Drive, Richmond VA 23236. **Contact:** Director of Personnel. **World Wide Web address:** http://www. eskimopie.com. **Description:** Eskimo Pie Corporation markets a broad range of frozen novelty, frozen yogurt, and frozen dairy dessert products under the brand names Eskimo Pie, Sugar Creek, Welch's, Weight Watchers, and 7-Up. Eskimo Pie Corporation also manufactures and markets Sugar Creek and Eskimo Pie brand soft-serve frozen yogurt mix, and various ingredients and packaging for the dairy industry. **Benefits:** Retirement Plan; Stock Option. **Corporate headquarters location:** This Location. **Other U.S. locations:** Los Angeles CA; Bloomfield NJ; New Berlin WI.

EXCEL CORPORATION
P.O. Box 2519, Wichita KS 67201. 316/291-2500. **Physical address:** 151 North Main, Wichita KS 67202. **Contact:** Corporate Recruiter. **World Wide Web address:** http://www.excelmeats.com. **Description:** A leading beef and pork packing company. **NOTE:** Entry-level positions and part-time jobs are offered. **Common positions include:** Account Manager; Account Rep.; Accountant; Administrative Assistant; Applications Engineer; Assistant Manager; Auditor; Biological Scientist; Budget Analyst; Buyer; Chief Financial Officer; Computer Engineer; Computer Operator; Computer Programmer; Computer Scientist; Computer Support Technician; Computer Technician; Content Developer; Controller; Cost Estimator; Credit Manager; Customer Service Rep.; Database Administrator; Database Manager; Editor; Electrical Electronics Engineer; Electrician; Environmental Engineer; Finance Director; Financial Analyst; Food Scientist/Technologist; General Manager; Graphic Designer; Human Resources Manager; Industrial Engineer; Industrial Production Manager; Internet Services Manager; Licensed Practical Nurse; Management Trainee; Manufacturing Engineer; Marketing Manager; Mechanical Engineer; Metallurgical Engineer; MIS Specialist; Multimedia Network/Systems Administrator; Occupational Therapist; Operations Manager; Paralegal; Production Manager; Project Manager; Quality Assurance Engineer; Quality Control Supervisor; Registered Nurse; Sales Executive; Sales Manager; Sales Rep.; Software Engineer; SQL Programmer; Systems Analyst; Systems Manager; Transportation/Traffic Specialist; Vice President; Webmaster. **Educational backgrounds include:** Accounting; AS400 Certification; Biology; Business Administration; C/C++; Computer Science; Economics; Engineering; Finance; Health Care; HTML; Internet; Java; Marketing; Mathematics; MCSE; Microsoft Word; Novell; Software Development; Software Tech. Support; Spreadsheets; Visual Basic. **Benefits:** 401(k); Casual Dress - Fridays; Daycare Assistance; Dental Insurance; Disability Coverage; Employee Discounts; Financial Planning Assistance; Flexible Schedule; Life Insurance; Medical Insurance; Pension Plan; Savings Plan; Tuition Assistance. **Special programs:** Internships. **Corporate headquarters location:** This Location. **Parent company:** Cargill, Inc.

F&F FOODS, INC.
3501 West 48th Place, Chicago IL 60632. 773/927-3737. **Contact:** Human Resources Manager. **World Wide Web address:** http://www.fffoods.com. **Description:** Manufactures cough drops, dietary supplements, candy, crackers, and a variety of other items under the product names Fast Dry Zinc, F&F Dietary Supplements, Daily C, Smith Brothers Cough Drops, and Foxes.

FARBEST FOODS INC.
P.O. Box 480, Huntingburg IN 47542. 812/683-4200. **Fax:** 812/683-4226. **Contact:** Human. Resources Manager. **World Wide Web address:** http://www.farbestfoods.com. **Description:** A turkey processing plant. **Common positions include:** Agricultural Engineer; Blue-Collar Worker Supervisor; Clerical Supervisor; Electrical/Electronics Engineer; Food Scientist/Technologist; Human Resources Manager; Industrial Engineer; Manufacturer's/Wholesaler's Sales Rep.; Operations/Production Manager; Wholesale and Retail Buyer. **Educational backgrounds include:** Agricultural Science; Engineering. **Benefits:** 401(k); Dental Insurance; Disability Coverage; Employee Discounts; Life Insurance; Medical Insurance. **Corporate headquarters location:** This Location.

LEON FARMER & COMPANY
P.O. Box 1352, Athens GA 30603. 706/353-1166. **Contact:** General Manager. **Description:** A wholesale beverage distributor. **Common positions include:** Accountant/Auditor; Branch Manager; Computer Programmer; Department Manager; General Manager; Operations/Production Manager. **Benefits:** Disability Coverage; Life Insurance; Medical Insurance; Pension Plan. **Corporate headquarters location:** This Location.

FARMER JOHN MEATS COMPANY
3049 East Vernon Avenue, Los Angeles CA 90058. 323/583-4621. **Contact:** Personnel Director. **World Wide Web address:** http://www.farmerjohn.com. **Description:** Processes and packs meat products. **Corporate headquarters location:** This Location.

FARMLAND INDUSTRIES, INC.
P.O. Box 7305, Kansas City MO 64116. 816/459-6000. **Physical address:** 3315 North Oak Trafficway, Kansas City MO 64116. **Fax:** 816/459-5954. **Contact:** Human Resources Department. **World Wide Web address:** http://www.farmland.com. **Description:** One of the largest farmer-owned agricultural food marketing and manufacturing cooperative associations in the U.S. The company is engaged in grain marketing, pork and beef processing, and manufacturing of fertilizers, livestock feeds, and petroleum products. Membership includes farmers from Iowa, Kansas, Oklahoma, South Dakota, Illinois, Nebraska, and Mexico. **Common positions include:** Accountant; Administrative Manager; Advertising Clerk; Attorney; Biological Scientist; Chemical Engineer; Chemist; Clerical Supervisor; Computer Programmer; Credit Manager; General Manager; Human Resources Manager; Industrial Engineer; Paralegal; Systems Analyst. **Educational backgrounds include:** Accounting; Business Administration; Chemistry; Communications; Finance. **Benefits:** 401(k); Daycare Assistance; Dental Insurance; Disability Coverage; Employee Discounts; Life Insurance; Medical Insurance; Pension Plan; Savings Plan; Tuition Assistance. **Special programs:** Internships. **Corporate headquarters location:** This Location. **Other U.S. locations:** Nationwide.

FAYGO BEVERAGES, INC.
3579 Gratiot Avenue, Detroit MI 48207. 313/925-1600. **Contact:** Human Resources Manager. **Description:** A bottler and canner of soft drinks.

FEDERAL BEEF PROCESSORS
P.O. Box 2130, Rapid City SD 57709. 605/343-1414. **Contact:** Personnel Director. **Description:** Packages meat and meat products. **Corporate headquarters location:** This Location.
Other U.S. locations:
• 2815 Blaisdell Avenue, Minneapolis MN 55408. 612/870-8078.

FIELD PACKING COMPANY INC.
P.O. Box 20003, Owensboro KY 42304. 270/926-2324. **Contact:** Personnel Manager. **World Wide Web address:** http://www.kentuckianham.com. **Description:** Field Packing Company Inc. is engaged in the processing of fresh and cured pork products. Products include ham, bacon, bologna, and hot dogs. **Common positions include:** Accountant/Auditor; Biological Scientist; Blue-Collar Worker Supervisor; Chemist; Computer Programmer; Customer Service Representative; Dietician/Nutritionist; Food Scientist/Technologist; Industrial Engineer; Manufacturer's/Wholesaler's Sales Rep.; Quality Control Supervisor. **Educational backgrounds include:** Accounting; Biology; Business Administration; Chemistry; Liberal Arts. **Benefits:** Disability Coverage; Employee Discounts; Life Insurance; Medical Insurance; Pension Plan; Tuition Assistance. **Corporate headquarters location:** This Location.

FIELDALE FARMS CORPORATION
P.O. Box 558, Baldwin GA 30511. 706/778-5100. **Contact:** Personnel. **Description:** Engaged in poultry processing and marketing nationwide. **Corporate headquarters location:** This Location. **Other U.S. locations:** Cornelia GA; Gainesville GA; Murraysville GA.

FINK BAKING CORPORATION
5-35 54th Avenue, Long Island City NY 11101. 718/392-8300. **Contact:** Chief Financial Officer. **Description:** Produces a full-line of bakery products. Fink also supplies bread and rolls to airlines, restaurants, steamship operators, hotels, and other institutional customers. **Corporate headquarters location:** This Location.

FLEMING COMPANIES, INC.
P.O. Box 26647, Oklahoma City OK 73126. 405/840-7200. **Physical address:** 6301 Waterford Boulevard, Oklahoma City OK 73118. **Contact:** Human Resources. **World Wide Web address:** http://www.fleming.com. **Description:** Fleming Companies distributes a wide variety of meats, dairy and delicatessen products, frozen foods, fresh produce, and a variety of general merchandise and related items; provides a full range of support services including collateralized long-term financing, merchandising, marketing, and computerized order entry and shelf management systems; operates a dairy facility; owns and operates supermarkets and a bakery; and operates a truck fleet. **NOTE:** Entry-level positions are offered. **Corporate headquarters location:** This Location. **Listed on:** New York Stock Exchange. **Annual sales/revenues:** More than $100 million.
Other U.S. locations:
• 3501 Marshall Street NE, Minneapolis MN 55418. 612/782-4419.

FLORIDA GLOBAL CITRUS LIMITED
P.O. Box 37, Auburndale FL 33823. 941/967-4431. **Fax:** 941/965-2480. **Contact:** Human Resources. **Description:** Processes citrus fruits and citrus fruit

by-products for bulk concentrate sales. The company is also engaged in warehousing. **Common positions include:** Accountant/Auditor; Blue-Collar Worker Supervisor; Clerical Supervisor; Computer Programmer; Human Resources Manager; Payroll Clerk; Production Manager; Purchasing Agent/ Manager; Quality Control Supervisor; Receptionist; Secretary; Truck Driver; Typist/Word Processor; Welder. **Educational backgrounds include:** Accounting; Business Administration; Computer Science; Engineering; Finance; Marketing. **Benefits:** 401(k); Dental Insurance; Disability Coverage; Life Insurance; Medical Insurance; Pension Plan; Scholarship Program. **Corporate headquarters location:** This Location.

FLORIDA JUICE, INC.
P.O. Box 3628, Lakeland FL 33802-2004. 941/686-1173. **Contact:** Sandy Sexton, Personnel Manager. **Description:** Processes a wide variety of juices. **Corporate headquarters location:** This Location.

FLORIDA'S NATURAL GROWERS
P.O. Box 1111, Lake Wales FL 33859-1111. 941/676-1411. **Physical address:** 650 Highway 27 North, Lake Wales FL. **Recorded jobline:** 941/679-4111. **Contact:** Human Resources. **Description:** Processes and packages citrus juice. Brand names of Citrus World include Florida Natural, Donald Duck, Bluebird, Texsun, and Vintage. **Common positions include:** Accountant/Auditor; Blue-Collar Worker Supervisor; Buyer; Chemical Engineer; Chemist; Clerical Supervisor; Computer Programmer; Customer Service Representative; Draftsperson; Electrical/Electronics Engineer; Electrician; Food Scientist/Technologist; General Manager; Industrial Production Manager; Mechanical Engineer; Operations/Production Manager; Purchasing Agent/Manager; Quality Control Supervisor; Systems Analyst; Typist/Word Processor. **Educational backgrounds include:** Accounting; Biology; Business Administration; Chemistry; Computer Science; Engineering; Finance; Marketing. **Benefits:** 401(k); Dental Insurance; Disability Coverage; Employee Discounts; Life Insurance; Medical Insurance; Tuition Assistance. **Corporate headquarters location:** This Location.

FLOWERS INDUSTRIES, INC.
1919 Flowers Circle, Thomasville GA 31757. 912/226-9110. **Contact:** Human Resources Manager. **World Wide Web address:** http://www. flowersindustries.com. **Description:** Serves regional and national markets with a variety of branded food products including fresh and frozen baked goods and frozen specialty vegetables, fruits, and desserts. Name brands include Beebo, Blue-Bird, Broad Street Bakery, Cobblestone Mill, Dan-Co, Danish Kitchens, European Bakers, Jubilee, Nature's Own, Our Special Touch, and Pies, Inc. The company operates 34 food production facilities and conducts distribution operations through 2,300 agents to grocery, food service, restaurant, and fast food markets. Flowers Industries also owns outlet stores where surplus merchandise is sold. Founded in 1919. **Corporate headquarters location:** This Location. **Listed on:** New York Stock Exchange.

FOODBRANDS AMERICA INC.
P.O. Box 26724, Oklahoma City OK 73126-0724. 405/879-4100. **Contact:** Human Resources. **World Wide Web address:** http://www.foodbrands.com. **Description:** Manufactures and markets processed meat products including ham, sausage, bacon, pepperoni, delicatessen meats, sauces, and meat toppings for the supermarket, warehouse, food service, restaurant, institutional, and fast food industries. **Corporate headquarters location:** This Location.

FREEDMAN DISTRIBUTORS
621 Waverly, Houston TX 77007. 713/864-7741. **Contact:** Personnel. **Description:** Distributes boxed meat products to retail outlets. **Common positions include:** Blue-Collar Worker Supervisor; Transportation/Traffic Specialist. **Benefits:** Disability Coverage; Employee Discounts; Life Insurance; Medical Insurance; Profit Sharing. **Corporate headquarters location:** This Location.

FRESH MARK, INC.
1600 Harmont Avenue NE, Canton OH 44705. 330/455-5253. **Contact:** Human Resources. **E-mail address:** info@freshmark.com. **World Wide Web address:** http://www.freshmark.com. **Description:** Processes, packages and distributes meats including ham, deli meats, smoked sausage and related products. **Corporate headquarters location:** This Location. **Other area locations:** Massillon OH.

FRITO-LAY, INC.
P.O. Box 660634, Dallas TX 75266-0634. 972/334-7000. **Physical address:** 7701 Legacy Drive, Plano TX 75024-4099. **Fax:** 972/334-2019. **Contact:** Staffing. **World Wide Web address:** http://www. fritolay.com. **Description:** A manufacturer and wholesaler of a wide range of snack products including Fritos Corn Chips, Lays Potato Chips, Doritos Tortilla Chips, Ruffles Potato Chips, Chee-tos, and Smartfood Popcorn. **Special programs:** Internships. **Corporate headquarters location:** This Location. **Other U.S. locations:** Nationwide. **Parent company:** PepsiCo, Inc. (Purchase NY) consists of Frito-Lay Company, Pepsi-Cola Company, and Tropicana Products, Inc. **Listed on:** New York Stock Exchange.

GFI PREMIUM FOODS, INC.
2815 Blaisdell Avenue South, Minneapolis MN 55408. 612/872-6262. **Fax:** 612/870-4955. **Contact:** Human Resources Manager. **E-mail address:** jayo@gfiamerica.com. **World Wide Web address:** http://www.gfiamerica.com. **Description:** A premium meat products company that processes, packages, and distributes wholesale and retail beef, pork, and veal products. GFI Premium Foods distributes to large national and local markets. **NOTE:** Second and third shifts are offered. **Common positions include:** Assistant Manager; Blue-Collar Worker Supervisor; Industrial Engineer; Mechanical Engineer; Secretary. **Educational backgrounds include:** Accounting; Engineering; Finance. **Benefits:** 401(k); Casual Dress - Daily; Disability Coverage; Employee Discounts; Life Insurance; Medical Insurance; Profit Sharing. **Special programs:** Training. **Listed on:** Privately held. **President:** Robert Goldberger.

GAI'S NORTHWEST BAKERIES
P.O. Box 24327, Seattle WA 98124. 206/322-0931. **Contact:** Human Resources. **Description:** A regional wholesale baking company. **Common positions include:** Accountant; Blue-Collar Worker Supervisor; Controller; Customer Service Rep.; Sales Manager; Sales Rep.; Secretary; Systems Analyst. **Benefits:** 401(k); Dental Insurance; Medical Insurance. **Listed on:** Privately held.

GALLO SALAMI
2411 Baumann Avenue, San Lorenzo CA 94580. 510/276-1300. **Contact:** Personnel. **Description:** Manufactures and distributes sausage and related products. **Corporate headquarters location:** This Location.

GALLO WINE COMPANY
2700 South Eastern Avenue, Commerce CA 90040. 323/869-6435. **Toll-free phone:** 800/499-1761. **Fax:** 323/869-6460. **Contact:** Manager of

Recruiting. **E-mail address:** gallola@earthlink.net. **Description:** Produces, markets, and distributes premium wines and brandy. Founded in 1933. **Common positions include:** Sales Representative. **Educational backgrounds include:** Business Administration; Liberal Arts; Marketing. **Benefits:** 401(k); Company Car; Dental Insurance; Medical Insurance. **Corporate headquarters location:** Modesto CA. **Other U.S. locations:** Nationwide. **International locations:** Worldwide. **Parent company:** E&J Gallo Winery.

GARDENBURGER, INC.
1411 SW Morrison Street, Suite 400, Portland OR 97205. 503/205-1500. **Contact:** Human Resources. **World Wide Web address:** http://www.gardenburger.com. **Description:** Makes and sells a variety of meatless, soy-based food items including the Gardenburger. **NOTE:** Entry-level positions are offered. **Common positions include:** Accountant/Auditor; Advertising Clerk; Computer Programmer; Customer Service Representative; Electrician; Financial Analyst; Food Scientist/Technologist; General Manager; Human Resources Manager; Human Service Worker; Industrial Production Manager; MIS Specialist; Operations/Production Manager; Public Relations Specialist; Purchasing Agent/Manager; Quality Control Supervisor; Systems Analyst; Typist/Word Processor. **Educational backgrounds include:** Accounting; Art/Design; Business Administration; Chemistry; Computer Science; Finance; Marketing. **Benefits:** 401(k); Dental Insurance; Disability Coverage; Employee Discounts; Job Sharing; Life Insurance; Medical Insurance; Pension Plan; Profit Sharing; Tuition Assistance. **Corporate headquarters location:** This Location.

GEARY BREWING
38 Evergreen Drive, Portland ME 04103. 207/878-2337. **Contact:** Personnel. **Description:** A beer brewing facility. **Corporate headquarters location:** This Location.

GENERAL DISTRIBUTING COMPANY
P.O. Box 16070, Salt Lake City UT 84116. 801/531-7895. **Contact:** Evelyn Purdie, Office Manager. **Description:** Engaged in the wholesale distribution of beverages. **Corporate headquarters location:** This Location.

GENERAL MILLS, INC.
P.O. Box 1113, Minneapolis MN 55440-1113. 612/540-2311. **Contact:** Human Resources. **World Wide Web address:** http://www.generalmills.com. **Description:** Produces and markets consumer foods. Food products include Cheerios, Wheaties, and Total cereals; Betty Crocker desserts, frostings, and baking mixes; Pop Secret microwave popcorn; Gorton's frozen seafood; Yoplait yogurt; Bisquik pancake mix; and Gold Medal flour. General Mills is also engaged in the full-service dinnerhouse restaurant business, operating over 1,000 company-owned Red Lobster and Olive Garden restaurants in North America. Founded in 1928. **Common positions include:** Chemical Engineer; Food Scientist/Technologist; Mechanical Engineer. **Educational backgrounds include:** Accounting; Chemistry; Computer Science; Engineering; Finance; Food Science; Marketing; MBA. **Corporate headquarters location:** This Location.

GENESEE CORPORATION
445 Saint Paul Street, Rochester NY 14605-1726. 716/546-1030. **Fax:** 716/546-5011. **Contact:** Personnel Department. **Description:** Brews beer under the name Genesee, Genny, Michael Shea's, and JW Dundee. **Corporate headquarters location:** This Location.

GILROY FOODS
P.O. Box 1088, Gilroy CA 95021. 408/846-3457. **Fax:** 408/846-3529. **Contact:** Human Resources Manager. **Description:** A dehydrator of vegetable products. Founded in 1959. **NOTE:** Second and third shifts are offered. **Common positions include:** Account Manager; Account Rep.; Accountant; Administrative Assistant; AS400 Programmer Analyst; Chemist; Chief Financial Officer; Computer Operator; Computer Programmer; Computer Technician; Controller; Credit Manager; Customer Service Rep.; Design Engineer; Electrical/Electronics Engineer; Electrician; Financial Analyst; Food Scientist/Technologist; Human Resources Manager; Network/Systems Administrator; Operations Manager; Production Manager; Purchasing Agent/Manager; Quality Control Supervisor; Registered Nurse; Sales Representative; Secretary; Statistician; Systems Analyst; Transportation/Traffic Specialist. **Educational backgrounds include:** Accounting; AS400 Certification; Business Administration; Chemistry; Computer Science; Engineering; Finance; Marketing; Microsoft Word; Novell; Software Tech. Support; Spreadsheets. **Benefits:** 401(k); Casual Dress - Fridays; Dental Insurance; Disability Coverage; Employee Discounts; Life Insurance; Medical Insurance; Pension Plan; Profit Sharing; Sick Days (1 - 5); Tuition Assistance. **Special programs:** Internships; Summer Jobs. **Corporate headquarters location:** Omaha NE. **Parent company:** Conagra, Inc. **Listed on:** NASDAQ. **Stock exchange symbol:** CAG. **President:** Randy Tognazzini.

GLACIER WATER SERVICES, INC.
2261 Cosmos Court, Carlsbad CA 92009. 760/930-2420. **Fax:** 760/930-0156. **Contact:** Human Resources. **World Wide Web address:** http://www.glacierwater.com. **Description:** A leading provider of drinking water dispensed to consumers through coin-operated, self-service vending machines. **Corporate headquarters location:** This Location. **President:** Jerry A. Gordon.

GOLD KIST, INC.
P.O. Box 2210, Atlanta GA 30301. 770/393-5000. **Fax:** 770/393-5262. **Contact:** Employment. **E-mail address:** jobs@goldkist.com. **World Wide Web address:** http://www.goldkist.com. **Description:** A diversified agricultural cooperative with approximately 25,000 active member farms located primarily in Georgia, Alabama, Florida, North Carolina, and South Carolina. Gold Kist is one of the largest poultry processors in the country. The company also operates pork production facilities, and aquaculture research and peanut genetics research facilities. Retail poultry products are marketed under the Gold Kist Farms label or under customer's private labels. Founded in 1933. **Common positions include:** Account Manager; Accountant; Administrative Manager; AS400 Programmer Analyst; Attorney; Auditor; Blue-Collar Worker Supervisor; Buyer; Chief Financial Officer; Civil Engineer; Clerical Supervisor; Clinical Lab Technician; Computer Operator; Computer Programmer; Computer Support Technician; Computer Technician; Controller; Credit Manager; Customer Service Representative; Database Administrator; Draftsperson; Economist; Electrical/Electronics Engineer; Environmental Engineer; Financial Analyst; Food Scientist/Technologist; General Manager; Help-Desk Technician; Human Resources Manager; Industrial Production Manager; Internet Services Manager; Management Trainee; Manufacturing Engineer; Marketing Manager; Marketing Specialist; MIS Specialist; Network/Systems Administrator; Operations Manager; Public Relations Specialist;

Purchasing Agent/Manager; Real Estate Agent; Sales Executive; Sales Manager; Sales Rep.; Secretary; SQL Programmer; Systems Analyst; Telecommunications Manager; Transportation/ Traffic Specialist; Typist/Word Processor; Vice President of Operations; Webmaster. **Educational backgrounds include:** Agricultural Science; AS400 Certification; Biology; Business Administration; MCSE; Microsoft Office; Microsoft Word; Novell; Software Development; Software Tech. Support. **Benefits:** 401(k); Casual Dress - Daily; Dental Insurance; Disability Coverage; Employee Discounts; Flexible Schedule; Life Insurance; Medical Insurance; Pension Plan; Profit Sharing; Relocation Assistance; Tuition Assistance. **Special programs:** Internships. **Corporate headquarters location:** This Location. **CEO:** G.O. Coan. **Annual sales/revenues:** More than $100 million.

GOLDEN GEM GROWERS, INC.
P.O. Drawer 9, Umatilla FL 32784-0009. 352/669-2101. **Contact:** Personnel Manager. **Description:** Processors of fresh and frozen citrus fruits. **Benefits:** Disability Coverage; Employee Discounts; Life Insurance; Medical Insurance; Savings Plan; Tuition Assistance. **Corporate headquarters location:** This Location.

GOLDEN PEANUT COMPANY
100 North Point Center East, Suite 400, Alpharetta GA 30022. 770/752-8160. **Contact:** Human Resources. **Description:** Handles and shells raw peanuts. Golden Peanut Company is one of the largest peanut procurement, processing, and marketing companies in the United States. **Educational backgrounds include:** Accounting; Business Administration; Engineering; Liberal Arts. **Benefits:** Dental Insurance; Disability Coverage; Life Insurance; Medical Insurance; Pension Plan; Savings Plan. **Corporate headquarters location:** This Location.

GONNELLA BAKING CO.
2006 West Erie Street, Chicago IL 60612. 312/733-2020. **Toll-free phone:** 800/262-3442. **Fax:** 312/733-7670. **Contact:** Human Resources. **E-mail address:** lpasquesi@gonnella.com. **Description:** Makers of bread, rolls, frozen dough, garlic bread, and other bakery products. Founded in 1886. **NOTE:** Entry-level positions, part-time jobs, and second and third shifts are offered. **Common positions include:** Accountant; Blue-Collar Worker Supervisor; Clerical Supervisor; Computer Technician; Customer Service Representative; Electrician; Food Scientist/Technologist; Typist/ Word Processor. **Educational backgrounds include:** Accounting; Business Administration; Computer Science; Marketing; Microsoft Office; Microsoft Word; Spreadsheets. **Benefits:** Dental Insurance; Disability Coverage; Employee Discounts; Life Insurance; Medical Insurance; Pension Plan; Public Transit Available; Relocation Assistance. **Special programs:** Internships; Apprenticeships; Training; Summer Jobs. **Corporate headquarters location:** This Location. **Listed on:** Privately held. **President:** Louis M. Gonnella.

GOODMARK FOODS, INC.
P.O. Box 18300, Raleigh NC 27619. 919/790-9940. **Physical address:** 6131 Falls of Neuse Road, Raleigh NC 27609. **Contact:** Director of Human Resources. **World Wide Web address:** http://www. slimjim.com. **Description:** A producer and marketer of meat snacks. GoodMark Foods' principal meat snack brands include Slim Jim, Penrose, Pemmican, and Smokey Mountain. The company also produces an extruded grain snack under the Andy Capp's brand name, and produces and sells packaged meats

under the Jesse Jones brand name. **Corporate headquarters location:** This Location. **Other area locations:** Garner NC. **Subsidiaries include:** Acme Foods Company, MD; GFI Holdings, Inc., CA; Specialty Snacks, Inc., PA. **Listed on:** NASDAQ. **Stock exchange symbol:** GDMK.

GORDON FOOD SERVICE
P.O. Box 1787, Grand Rapids MI 49501. 616/530-7000. **Contact:** Employment Coordinator. **World Wide Web address:** http://www.gfs.com. **Description:** One of the largest family-owned food distributors in the nation. **Common positions include:** Accountant/Auditor; Buyer; Computer Programmer; Customer Service Representative; Dietician/Nutritionist; Education Administrator; Financial Analyst; Management Trainee; Purchasing Agent/Manager; Sales Representative; Systems Analyst. **Educational backgrounds include:** Accounting; Computer Science; Marketing. **Benefits:** Daycare Assistance; Dental Insurance; Disability Coverage; Employee Discounts; Life Insurance; Medical Insurance; Prescription Drugs; Profit Sharing; Savings Plan; Tuition Assistance; Vision Insurance. **Corporate headquarters location:** This Location. **Other U.S. locations:** IL; IN; OH.

GORTON'S, INC.
128 Rogers Street, Gloucester MA 01930. 978/283-3000. **Contact:** Personnel Department. **World Wide Web address:** http://www.gortons.com. **Description:** Processes frozen and canned seafood products. Founded in 1849. **Common positions include:** Accountant/Auditor; Blue-Collar Worker Supervisor; Computer Programmer; Customer Service Rep.; Food Scientist/Technologist; Industrial Engineer; Manufacturer's/Wholesaler's Sales Rep.; Mechanical Engineer; Operations/ Production Manager; Purchasing Agent/ Manager; Quality Control Supervisor. **Educational backgrounds include:** Accounting; Business Administration; Chemistry; Engineering; Finance; Marketing. **Benefits:** Dental Insurance; Disability Coverage; Employee Discounts; Life Insurance; Medical Insurance; Pension Plan; Profit Sharing; Savings Plan; Stock Option; Tuition Assistance. **Special programs:** Internships. **Corporate headquarters location:** This Location. **Parent company:** General Mills, Inc. (Minneapolis MN)

GOSSNER FOODS
1051 North 10 West, Logan UT 84321. 435/752-9365. **Contact:** Personnel. **World Wide Web address:** http://www.gossner.com. **Description:** Processes and distributes a variety of cheese products. **Corporate headquarters location:** This Location.

GRANNY GOOSE FOODS INC.
930 98th Avenue, Oakland CA 94603. 510/635-5400. **Contact:** Human Resources. **Description:** Manufactures and distributes potato chips and other specialty snack foods. **Corporate headquarters location:** This Location.

GREENWICH MILLS
520 Secaucus Road, Secaucus NJ 07096. 201/865-0200. **Contact:** Lorraine Sadowski, Office Manager. **Description:** Produces and distributes coffee used in institutions, restaurants, and food service companies. **Corporate headquarters location:** This Location.

GROCERS SUPPLY COMPANY, INC.
3131 East Holcombe Boulevard, Houston TX 77021. 713/747-5000. **Contact:** Human Resources. **Description:** A wholesaler of a variety of goods including hardware and groceries. **Common**

positions include: Blue-Collar Worker Supervisor; Buyer; Claim Rep.; Clerical Supervisor; Computer Programmer; Credit Manager; Customer Service Rep.; Management Trainee; Operations/Production Manager; Quality Control Supervisor; Services Sales Rep. Systems Analyst; Wholesale and Retail Buyer. **Educational backgrounds include:** Business Administration; Computer Science. **Benefits:** 401(k); Dental Insurance; Life Insurance; Medical Insurance; Tuition Assistance. **Corporate headquarters location:** This Location.

H.J. HEINZ
P.O. Box 57, Pittsburgh PA 15230. 412/456-5700. **Contact:** Human Resources. **World Wide Web address:** http://www.heinz.com. **Description:** A worldwide producer of food products including ketchup, sauces, condiments, baby food, seafood, pet food, frozen potato products, frozen meats, beverages, and a wide selection of other processed consumables. These foods are marketed under brand names including Heinz, Steak-Umm, and Ore-Ida. The company also operates and sells franchise licenses for Weight Watchers International weight control classes and related programs. **Corporate headquarters location:** This Location. **Subsidiaries include:** Starkist Foods; Weight Watchers. **Listed on:** New York Stock Exchange.

HI-PORT INC.
409 East Wallisville Road, Highlands TX 77562. 281/426-3541. **Contact:** Human Resources. **Description:** This location houses three separate divisions of Hi-Port Inc. SMS Division manufactures canned and bottled fruit drinks, and canned petroleum products; HiOrganite Division produces organic fertilizers; Chemola Division produces consumer and industrial detergents, lubricants, penetrants, and lubrication equipment. Overall, the company provides contract packaging, blending, and distribution services for automotive care, as well as agricultural, chemical, and bulk powder products. **Corporate headquarters location:** This Location.

HILLSHIRE FARM AND KAHN'S
3241 Spring Grove Avenue, Cincinnati OH 45225. 513/541-4000. **Fax:** 513/853-1386. **Contact:** Personnel. **World Wide Web address:** http://www. hillshirefarm.com. **Description:** Manufacturers of packaged meats including sausages, luncheon meats, hot dogs, and breakfast sandwiches. **Common positions include:** Accountant/Auditor; Blue-Collar Worker Supervisor; Computer Operator; Computer Programmer; Credit Manager; Customer Service Rep.; Employment Interviewer; Human Resources Manager; Industrial Engineer; Management Trainee; Manufacturer's/Wholesaler's Sales Rep.; Marketing Manager; Mechanical Engineer; Order Clerk; Payroll Clerk; Quality Control Supervisor; Receptionist; Registered Nurse; Secretary; Systems Analyst. **Educational backgrounds include:** Accounting; Business Administration; Engineering; Finance; Liberal Arts; Marketing. **Benefits:** Dental Insurance; Disability Coverage; Life Insurance; Medical Insurance; Pension Plan; Tuition Assistance. **Special programs:** Internships. **Corporate headquarters location:** This Location. **Parent company:** Sara Lee Corporation is a global manufacturer and marketer of consumer products with brand names including Hanes, Leggs, Hillshire Farms, and Playtex.
• P.O. Box 227, New London WI 54961.
  920/982-2611.

HINCKLEY & SCHMITT
6055 South Harlem Avenue, Chicago IL 60638. 773/586-8600. **Fax:** 773/586-6542. **Recorded jobline:** 800/329-0835. **Contact:** Personnel.

Description: Hinkley & Schmitt processes and distributes bottled water. Founded in 1888. **NOTE:** Entry-level positions and second and third shifts are offered. **Common positions include:** Administrative Assistant; Blue-Collar Worker Supervisor; Branch Manager; Clerical Supervisor; Customer Service Rep.; Food Scientist/ Technologist; Industrial Production Manager; Production Manager; Sales Manager; Sales Rep. **Benefits:** 401(k); Casual Dress - Daily; Dental Insurance; Disability Coverage; Employee Discounts; Life Insurance; Medical Insurance; Profit Sharing; Sick Days (1 - 5); Tuition Assistance; Vacation Days (6 - 10). **Office hours:** Monday - Friday, 8:15 a.m. - 5:00 p.m. **Corporate headquarters location:** Atlanta GA. **Other U.S. locations:** Indianapolis IN; Kansas City MO. **Parent company:** Suntory Water Group.

HOBAN FOODS, INC.
1599 East Warren Avenue, Detroit MI 48207. 313/833-1500. **Fax:** 313/833-0629. **Contact:** Human Resources. **Description:** Distributes frozen foods to restaurants and nursing homes. **Benefits:** 401(k); Employee Discounts; Medical Insurance. **Corporate headquarters location:** This Location.

HOLSUM INC.
P.O. Box 2527, Roswell NM 88202-2527. 505/622-7163. **Contact:** Human Resources Department. **Description:** Holsum produces wholesale baked goods. **Corporate headquarters location:** This Location.

H.P. HOOD INC.
90 Everett Avenue, Chelsea MA 02150. 617/887-3000. **Contact:** Employment Manager. **World Wide Web address:** http://www.hphood.com. **Description:** One of New England's largest food products firms, engaged in the processing and distribution of dairy products. **Corporate headquarters location:** This Location.

HORMEL FOODS CORPORATION
One Hormel Place, Austin MN 55912. **Toll-free phone:** 800/533-2000. **Fax:** 507/437-5171. **Contact:** Supervisor of Professional Recruitment. **E-mail address:** careers@hormel.com. **World Wide Web address:** http://www.hormel.com. **Description:** A *Fortune* 500 company, Hormel Foods is one of the leading processors and marketers of branded, value-added meat and food products. Principal products of the company are processed meat and food entrees which are sold fresh, frozen, cured, smoked, and cooked; and canned foods including sausages, hams, franks, bacon, luncheon meats, shelf-stable microwaveable entrees, stews, chili, hash, meat spreads, and frozen processed products. The majority of the company's products are sold under the Hormel brand name. Other trademarks include Farm Fresh, Little Sizzlers, Quick Meal, Kid's Kitchen, Chi-Chi's, House of Tsang, Mary Kitchen, Dinty Moore, Light & Lean, Chicken by George, Black Label, and SPAM. Founded in 1891. **NOTE:** Second and third shifts are offered. **Common positions include:** Account Manager; Account Rep.; Accountant; Administrative Assistant; Administrative Manager; Applications Engineer; Assistant Manager; Attorney; Budget Analyst; Buyer; Chemist; Clerical Supervisor; Clinical Lab Technician; Computer Operator; Computer Programmer; Financial Analyst; Food Scientist/Technologist; General Manager; Human Resources Manager; Industrial Engineer; Librarian; Manufacturing Engineer; Market Research Analyst; Mechanical Engineer; MIS Specialist; Operations Manager; Paralegal; Production Manager; Sales Executive; Sales Manager; Secretary; Systems Analyst; Systems

Manager; Webmaster. **Educational backgrounds include:** Accounting; Business Administration; Chemistry; Communications; Computer Science; Engineering; Marketing. **Benefits:** 401(k); Dental Insurance; Employee Discounts; Flexible Schedule; Life Insurance; Medical Insurance; Pension Plan; Profit Sharing. **Special programs:** Internships. **Office hours:** Monday - Friday, 7:00 a.m. - 4:00 p.m. **Corporate headquarters location:** This Location. **Other U.S. locations:** Nationwide. **International locations:** Worldwide. **Subsidiaries include:** Dan's Prize, Inc.; Dubuque Foods; Jennie-O Foods. **Listed on:** New York Stock Exchange. **Stock exchange symbol:** HRL.

HUMPTY DUMPTY
P.O. Box 2247, South Portland ME 04116. 207/883-8422. **Physical address:** 51 U.S. Route 1, Scarborough ME 04074. **Fax:** 207/885-0773. **Contact:** Human Resources Manager. **World Wide Web address:** http://www.humptydumpty.com. **Description:** Manufactures potato chips. **NOTE:** Entry-level positions are offered. **Company slogan:** A taste worth falling for. **Common positions include:** Account Manager; Account Rep.; Accountant; Administrative Assistant; Controller; Credit Manager; MIS Specialist; Purchasing Agent/Manager; Quality Control Supervisor; Sales Manager; Sales Rep.; Secretary. **Educational backgrounds include:** Accounting; Business Administration; Finance; Marketing. **Benefits:** 401(k); Employee Discounts; Medical Insurance. **Corporate headquarters location:** This Location.

IBP INC.
800 Stevens Port Drive, Dakota Dunes SD 57049. 605/235-2061. **Contact:** Staffing. **World Wide Web address:** http://www.ibpinc.com. **Description:** Processes beef and pork for grocery chains, meat distributors, and restaurants; and meat by-products used for leather and pharmaceutical products. The company's production and processing facilities are at 19 locations in nine states. **NOTE:** Entry-level positions are offered. **Common positions include:** Accountant/; Aerospace Engineer; Agricultural Engineer; Aircraft Mechanic/Engine Specialist; Architect; Attorney; Biological Scientist; Blue-Collar Worker Supervisor; Budget Analyst; Buyer; Chemical Engineer; Chemist; Claim Representative; Computer Programmer; Draftsperson; Economist; Electrical/Electronics Engineer; Financial Analyst; Human Resources Manager; Industrial Engineer; Management Trainee; Mechanical Engineer; MIS Specialist; Quality Control Supervisor; Systems Analyst. **Educational backgrounds include:** Accounting; Agricultural Science; Business Administration; Chemistry; Communications; Computer Science; Economics; Liberal Arts; Marketing; Mathematics. **Benefits:** 401(k); Dental Insurance; Disability Coverage; Employee Discounts; Life Insurance; Medical Insurance; Pension Plan; Profit Sharing; Savings Plan; Tuition Assistance. **Special programs:** Internships; Training. **Corporate headquarters location:** This Location.
Other U.S. locations:
• 26999 Central Park Boulevard, Suite 300, Southfield MI 48076. 248/213-1000.

IMC GLOBAL INC.
2100 Sanders Road, Suite 200, Northbrook IL 60062. 847/272-9200. **Fax:** 847/412-5829. **Contact:** Director of Human Resources. **E-mail address:** hr@imcglobal.com. **World Wide Web address:** http://www.imcglobal.com. **Description:** This location houses administrative offices. Overall, IMC Global mines and manufactures crop nutrients including potash and phosphates; supplies animal feed ingredients necessary for raising livestock; and produces salt for road maintenance. **NOTE:** Entry-level positions are offered. **Common positions include:** Accountant; Administrative Assistant; Blue-Collar Worker Supervisor; Budget Analyst; Chemical Engineer; Database Administrator; Electrical/Electronics Engineer; Financial Analyst; General Manager; Human Resources Manager; Industrial Production Manager; Manufacturing Engineer; Operations Manager; Systems Analyst. **Educational backgrounds include:** Business Administration; Engineering; Finance; Microsoft Word; Spreadsheets; Visual Basic. **Benefits:** 401(k); Dental Insurance; Disability Coverage; Employee Discounts; Flexible Schedule; Life Insurance; Medical Insurance; Profit Sharing; Tuition Assistance; Vacation Days (6 - 10). **Corporate headquarters location:** This Location. **Other U.S. locations:** Tampa FL; Carlsbad NM; Ogden UT. **International locations:** Hong Kong; United Kingdom. **Listed on:** New York Stock Exchange. **Stock exchange symbol:** IGL. **CEO:** Robert E. Fowler. **Annual sales/revenues:** More than $100 million.

IDAHOAN FOODS
P.O. Box 130, Lewisville ID 83431. 208/754-4686. **Fax:** 208/754-0094. **Contact:** Personnel. **World Wide Web address:** http://www.idahoan.com. **Description:** A producer of dehydrated potato products. **Corporate headquarters location:** This Location.

INTERNATIONAL MULTIFOODS
200 East Lake Street, Wayzata MN 55391. 612/340-3300. **Contact:** Human Resources. **Web address:** http://www.multifoods.com. **Description:** An international processor and distributor of food products. Segments of International Multifoods include U.S. Food Services, which prepares food products for a variety of industries; Canadian Foods, which produces consumer, institutional, and industrial flour, mixes, cereals, and condiments; and Venezuelan Foods, which provides foods and animal feeds. **Common positions include:** Accountant/Auditor; Computer Programmer; Department Manager; General Manager; Human Resources Manager; Operations/Production Manager; Systems Analyst. **Educational backgrounds include:** Accounting; Business Administration; Computer Science; Finance. **Benefits:** Dental Insurance; Disability Coverage; Employee Discounts; Life Insurance; Medical Insurance; Pension Plan; Profit Sharing; Savings Plan; Tuition Assistance. **Corporate headquarters location:** This Location.

INTERSTATE BAKERIES CORPORATION
INTERSTATE BRANDS CORPORATION
12 East Armour Boulevard, Kansas City MO 64111. 816/502-4000. **Contact:** Director of Human Resources. **World Wide Web address:** http://www. irin.com/ibc. **Description:** A major baker and distributor of fresh baked products for 29 bakeries throughout the U.S. The company markets its products through over 100,000 food outlets on its 4,200 direct delivery routes and operates 780 thrift stores. Products include breads, rolls, buns, and English muffins under the brand names Eddy's, Merita, Mrs. Karl's, Sweetheart, Weber's, Butternut, Cotton Holsum, and Millbrook. Other products include sweet rolls, cakes, donuts, pies, and pastries primarily for the convenience store industry. **Corporate headquarters location:** This Location. **Parent company:** Interstate Brands Corporation (also at this location).

INTERSTATE BRANDS CORPORATION
5130 Winnetka Avenue North, New Hope MN 55428. 763/533-2221. **Contact:** Personnel Manager.

World Wide Web address: http://www.
irin.com/ibc. **Description:** Manufactures and
distributes a line of bread and cake products.
Common positions include: Retail Sales Worker;
Route Sales Rep. **Educational backgrounds
include:** Business Administration; Computer
Science; Marketing. **Benefits:** 401(k); Dental
Insurance; Disability Coverage; Life Insurance;
Medical Insurance; Pension Plan. **Corporate
headquarters location:** Kansas City MO.

JAC PAC FOODS, LTD.
163 Hancock Street, Manchester NH 03101.
603/669-3300. **Fax:** 603/669-9886. **Contact:**
Human Resources. **World Wide Web address:**
http://www.jacpac.com. **Description:** Engaged in
meat processing. Founded in 1929. **Common
positions include:** Account Manager; Account
Rep.; Accountant; Administrative Assistant;
Administrative Manager; Biochemist; Biological
Scientist; Blue-Collar Worker Supervisor; Buyer;
Chief Financial Officer; Clerical Supervisor;
Clinical Lab Technician; Computer Operator;
Computer Programmer; Controller; Credit Manager;
Customer Service Manager; Dietician/Nutritionist;
Electrician; Finance Director; Financial Analyst;
Food Scientist/Technologist; General Manager;
Human Resources Manager; Industrial Engineer;
Management Trainee; Market Research Analyst;
Marketing Specialist; MIS Specialist; Operations
Manager; Production Manager; Purchasing
Agent/Manager; Quality Control Supervisor; Sales
Executive; Sales Manager; Sales Rep.; Secretary;
Software Engineer; Systems Analyst; Systems
Manager; Transportation/Traffic Specialist; Typist/
Word Processor. **Educational backgrounds
include:** Accounting; Biology; Business
Administration; Computer Science; Finance;
Nutrition; Software Development; Software Tech.
Support. **Benefits:** 401(k); Casual Dress - Fridays;
Dental Insurance; Disability Coverage; Employee
Discounts; Financial Planning Assistance; Flexible
Schedule; Life Insurance; Medical Insurance;
Pension Plan; Performance Bonus; Profit Sharing;
Public Transit Available; Savings Plan; Tuition
Assistance. **Special programs:** Training; Co-ops;
Summer Jobs. **Corporate headquarters location:**
This Location. **Listed on:** Privately held. **CEO:**
Irwin Muskat. **Annual sales/revenues:** More than
$100 million.

JENNIE-O FOODS, INC.
P.O. Box 778, Willmar MN 56201. 320/235-2622.
Fax: 320/231-7785. **Contact:** Director of Human
Resources. **World Wide Web address:** http://www.
jennie-o.com. **Description:** One of the nation's
largest turkey processors. Jennie-O Foods grows,
processes, and markets turkey products nationally
and internationally. Founded in 1949. **NOTE:**
Entry-level positions are offered. **Common
positions include:** Accountant; Administrative
Assistant; Blue-Collar Worker Supervisor; Claim
Rep.; Computer Operator; Computer Programmer;
Customer Service Representative; Food Scientist/
Technologist; Human Resources Manager;
Industrial Engineer; Industrial Production Manager;
Marketing Manager; Mechanical Engineer; Quality
Assurance Engineer; Quality Control Supervisor;
Sales Manager; Secretary; Transportation/Traffic
Specialist. **Educational backgrounds include:**
Accounting; Business Administration; Computer
Science; Engineering. **Benefits:** 401(k); Dental
Insurance; Disability Coverage; Employee
Discounts; Life Insurance; Medical Insurance;
Pension Plan; Profit Sharing; Tuition Assistance.
Special programs: Internships. **Corporate
headquarters location:** This Location.
Subsidiaries include: Heartland Foods; West
Central Turkeys. **Parent company:** Hormel Foods.

KAL KAN FOODS INC.
P.O. Box 58853, Vernon CA 90058. 323/587-2727.
Physical address: 3250 East 44th Street, Vernon
CA. **Contact:** Personnel Director. **Description:**
Manufactures pet foods. Founded in 1936.
Corporate headquarters location: This Location.

KARLER PACKING COMPANY
P.O. Box 1005, Albuquerque NM 87103. 505/877-
3550. **Contact:** Human Resources. **Description:**
Engaged in meat packing operations. **Corporate
headquarters location:** This Location.

KEEBLER COMPANY
5000 Osage Street, Denver CO 80221. 303/433-
6221. **Recorded jobline:** 303/226-6861. **Contact:**
Human Resources. **Description:** A national
manufacturer and marketer of cookies and crackers.
Common positions include: Administrative
Assistant; Blue-Collar Worker Supervisor; Buyer;
Controller; General Manager; Operations Manager;
Production Manager; Purchasing Agent/Manager;
Quality Control Supervisor. **Educational
backgrounds include:** Accounting; Business
Administration; Chemistry; Computer Science;
Engineering; Finance; Food Science; Marketing.
Benefits: 401(k); Dental Insurance; Disability
Coverage; Life Insurance; Medical Insurance;
Pension Plan; Savings Plan; Tuition Assistance.
Corporate headquarters location: Elmhurst IL.
Other U.S. locations: Macon GA; Grand Rapids
MI; Cincinnati OH.

KEEBLER COMPANY
One Hollow Tree Lane, Elmhurst IL 60126.
630/833-2900. **Contact:** Personnel. **Description:** A
national manufacturer and marketer of cookies,
crackers, and other snack foods. **NOTE:** Positions
at this location require specific functional and/or
industry experience. Other positions are handled at
individual locations throughout the U.S. **Common
positions include:** Account Representative;
Accountant/Auditor; Computer Programmer; Food
Scientist/Technologist; Maintenance Technician;
Market Research Analyst; Marketing Specialist;
Product Manager; Production Coordinator;
Production Worker; Project Engineer; Retail
Merchandiser; Truck Driver; Warehouse/
Distribution Worker. **Educational backgrounds
include:** Accounting; Business Administration;
Computer Science; Engineering; Food Science;
Marketing. **Benefits:** Dental Insurance; Disability
Coverage; Employee Discounts; Life Insurance;
Medical Insurance; Pension Plan; Savings Plan;
Tuition Assistance. **Corporate headquarters
location:** This Location. **Other U.S. locations:**
Denver CO; Macon GA; Grand Rapids MI;
Cincinnati OH. **Parent company:** United Biscuits
(Holdings) plc. 0.

KELLOGG COMPANY
One Kellogg Square, Battle Creek MI 49016-3599.
616/961-2000. **Toll-free phone:** 800/KEL-LOGG.
Fax: 616/961-9047. **Contact:** Human Resources.
World Wide Web address: http://www.
kelloggs.com. **Description:** Kellogg Company is
the world's leading producer of ready-to-eat cereal
products and a leading producer of other grain-
based convenience foods including toaster pastries,
frozen waffles, and cereal bars. The company's
products are manufactured on six continents and
sold in more than 160 countries around the world.
Founded in 1906. **Company slogan:** A healthy life
is within your reach. **Common positions include:**
Account Representative; Accountant; Attorney;
Auditor; Chemist; Customer Service Representative;
Database Administrator; Dietician/Nutritionist;
Financial Analyst; Food Scientist/Technologist;
Human Resources Manager; Manufacturing

Engineer; Marketing Manager; Media Planner; Network/Systems Administrator; Project Manager; Public Relations Specialist; Purchasing Agent/Manager; Quality Assurance Engineer; Sales Manager; Sales Representative; Systems Analyst; Systems Manager. **Educational backgrounds include:** Accounting; Business Administration; Chemistry; Computer Science; Engineering; Finance; HTML; Human Resources; Internet Development; Marketing; MBA; MCSE; Microsoft Office; Microsoft Word; Nutrition; Public Relations. **Benefits:** 401(k); Dental Insurance; Disability Coverage; Flexible Schedule; Life Insurance; Medical Insurance; Pension Plan; Relocation Assistance; Savings Plan; Sick Days (6 - 10); Telecommuting; Tuition Assistance; Vacation Days (10 - 20). **Special programs:** Training. **Office hours:** Monday - Friday, 8:00 a.m. - 4:45 p.m. **Corporate headquarters location:** This Location. **Other U.S. locations:** San Jose CA; Atlanta GA; Omaha NE; Blue Anchor NJ; Lancaster PA; Muncy PA; Memphis TN; Rossville TN. **International locations:** Worldwide. **President/CEO:** Carlos Gutierrez.

KENDALL FOODS CORPORATION
P.O. Box 8, Goulds FL 33170. 305/258-1631. **Contact:** Human Resources. **Description:** Grows, markets, and processes tropical fruits including avocados, limes, mangos, and papayas. **Common positions include:** Accountant; Administrator; Agricultural Engineer; Blue-Collar Worker Supervisor; Buyer; Chemist; Credit Manager; Food Scientist; Industrial Engineer; Marketing Specialist; Operations/Production Manager; Purchasing Agent/Manager; Quality Control Supervisor; Sales Executive. **Educational backgrounds include:** Accounting; Business Administration; Marketing. **Benefits:** Dental Insurance; Disability Coverage; Employee Discounts; Medical Insurance; Tuition Assistance. **Corporate headquarters location:** This Location.

KENOSHA BEEF
P.O. Box 639, Kenosha WI 53141. 262/859-2816. **Fax:** 262/859-2594. **Contact:** Director of Personnel. **Description:** A beef packer whose product line includes boxed beef for large quantity sales both nationwide and internationally. Kenosha Beef also produces hamburger patties for Burger King, Dairy Queen, A&W, Hardee's, and under the company's own label. The company also supplies mixed and cooked ground beef to Taco Bell. Founded in 1936. **NOTE:** Entry-level positions and second and third shifts are offered. **Common positions include:** Accountant; Administrative Assistant; Blue-Collar Worker Supervisor; Computer Operator; Computer Programmer; Licensed Practical Nurse; MIS Specialist; Sales Rep.; Secretary; Systems Analyst. **Benefits:** 401(k); Dental Insurance; Disability Coverage; Employee Discounts; Life Insurance; Medical Insurance; Pension Plan; Profit Sharing. **Corporate headquarters location:** This Location. **Other U.S. locations:** Atlanta GA; Columbus OH. **Subsidiaries include:** Birchwood Meats and Provision; Birchwood Transport.

ORVAL KENT FOOD COMPANY, INC.
120 West Palatine Road, Wheeling IL 60090. 847/459-9000. **Fax:** 847/459-0634. **Contact:** Human Resources. **World Wide Web address:** http://www.orvalkent.com. **Description:** Markets a variety of chilled, freshly prepared foods for restaurants, wholesalers, and consumers. **NOTE:** Entry-level positions and second and third shifts are offered. **Common positions include:** Account Manager; Administrative Assistant; Administrative Manager; Biochemist; Biological Scientist; Blue-Collar Worker Supervisor; Chief Financial Officer;

Controller; Credit Manager; Customer Service Rep.; Dietician/Nutritionist; Food Scientist/Technologist; Manufacturing Engineer; Marketing Manager; Operations Manager; Production Manager; Purchasing Agent/Manager; Quality Control Supervisor; Sales Executive; Sales Manager; Sales Rep.; Secretary; Systems Analyst; Systems Manager; Typist/Word Processor. **Educational backgrounds include:** Biology; Business Administration; Chemistry; Computer Science; Finance; Marketing; Nutrition. **Benefits:** 401(k); Dental Insurance; Disability Coverage; Employee Discounts; Life Insurance; Medical Insurance; Public Transit Available; Tuition Assistance. **Special programs:** Internships. **Corporate headquarters location:** This Location. **Other U.S. locations:** Vernon CA; Fort Worth TX. **International locations:** Mexico. **Parent company:** OKF Holding Company.

KING AND PRINCE SEAFOOD CORP.
GOLDEN SHORE SEAFOODS
100 Lanier Boulevard, Brunswick GA 31520. 912/265-5155. **Fax:** 912/264-4812. **Contact:** Director of Human Resources. **Description:** A seafood processor offering a wide range of frozen and prepared products. **Common positions include:** Accountant/Auditor; Administrator; Advertising Clerk; Biological Scientist; Blue-Collar Worker Supervisor; Buyer; Clerical Supervisor; Computer Programmer; Department Manager; Food Scientist/Technologist; Human Resources Manager; Industrial Engineer; Marketing Specialist; Mechanical Engineer; Operations/Production Manager; Purchasing Agent/Manager; Quality Control Supervisor; Registered Nurse; Services Sales Rep.; Systems Analyst. **Educational backgrounds include:** Accounting; Business Administration; Chemistry; Computer Science; Engineering; Finance; Liberal Arts; Marketing. **Benefits:** Dental Insurance; Disability Coverage; Employee Discounts; Life Insurance; Medical Insurance; Pension Plan; Profit Sharing; Tuition Assistance. **Corporate headquarters location:** This Location.

KING RANCH, INC.
1415 Louisiana Street, Suite 2300, Houston TX 77002. 713/752-5700. **Contact:** Human Resources. **World Wide Web address:** http://www.king-ranch.com. **Description:** One of the largest private agribusinesses in the world. The company also operates ranches and farms in Arizona, Kentucky, Florida, and Brazil. Founded in 1850. **Common positions include:** Accountant; Administrative Assistant; AS400 Programmer Analyst; Attorney; Auditor; Chief Financial Officer; Controller; Paralegal; Secretary. **Educational backgrounds include:** Agricultural Science; AS400 Certification; Business Administration; Microsoft Office; Microsoft Word. **Benefits:** 401(k); Casual Dress - Fridays; Dental Insurance; Disability Coverage; Employee Discounts; Flexible Schedule; Life Insurance; Medical Insurance; Pension Plan; Public Transit Available; Relocation Assistance; Sick Days (6 - 10); Tuition Assistance; Vacation Days (10 - 20). **Special programs:** Co-ops. **Office hours:** Monday - Friday, 8:00 a.m. - 5:00 p.m.

KRAFT FOODS, INC.
3 Lakes Drive, Northfield IL 60093. 847/646-2000. **Fax:** 847/646-4333. **Contact:** Corporate Staffing. **Description:** One of the largest producers of packaged food in North America. Major brands include Jell-O, Post, Kool-Aid, Crystal Light, Entenmann's, Miracle Whip, Stove Top, and Shake 'n Bake. Kraft Foods markets a number of products under the Kraft brand name including natural and processed cheeses and dry packaged dinners. The

Oscar Mayer unit markets processed meats, poultry, lunch combinations, and pickles under the Oscar Mayer, Louis Rich, Lunchables, and Claussen brand names. Kraft is also one of the largest coffee companies with principal brands including Maxwell House, Sanka, Brim, and General Foods International Coffees. **Corporate headquarters location:** This Location. **Parent company:** Philip Morris Companies (New York) is a holding company whose principal wholly-owned subsidiaries are Philip Morris Inc. (Philip Morris U.S.A.), Philip Morris International Inc., Kraft Foods, Inc., Miller Brewing Company, and Philip Morris Capital Corporation. In the tobacco industry, Philip Morris U.S.A. and Philip Morris International together form one of the largest international cigarette operations in the world. U.S. brand names include Marlboro, Parliament, Virginia Slims, Benson & Hedges, and Merit. Miller Brewing Company brews beer under brand names including Molson Ice, Miller Genuine Draft, Miller High Life, Sharp's non-alcoholic, Red Dog, Miller Lite, Icehouse, Foster's Lager, and Lowenbrau. Philip Morris Capital Corporation is engaged in financial services and real estate.

KRASDALE FOODS INC.
65 West Red Oak Lane, White Plains NY 10604. 718/378-1100. **Contact:** Personnel. **Description:** Engaged in the wholesale distribution of canned goods and other processed food products. **Corporate headquarters location:** This Location.

LAMB WESTON, INC.
P.O. Box 1900, Tri-Cities WA 99302. 509/735-4651. **Contact:** Personnel Administrator. **World Wide Web address:** http://www.lamb-weston.com. **Description:** Processes a broad line of nationally distributed frozen potato products including French fries and potato wedges. **Common positions include:** Accountant/Auditor; Biological Scientist; Chemical Engineer; Computer Programmer; Credit Manager; Customer Service Representative; Department Manager; Food Scientist/Technologist; Industrial Engineer; Manufacturer's/Wholesaler's Sales Rep.; Marketing Specialist; Mechanical Engineer; Operations/Production Manager; Quality Control Supervisor; Transportation/Traffic Specialist. **Educational backgrounds include:** Accounting; Business Administration; Chemistry; Economics; Engineering; Finance; Marketing. **Benefits:** Dental Insurance; Disability Coverage; Employee Discounts; Life Insurance; Medical Insurance; Pension Plan; Profit Sharing; Relocation Assistance; Savings Plan; Tuition Assistance. **Corporate headquarters location:** This Location. **Parent company:** ConAgra, Inc. is a diversified, international food company. Products range from prepared foods to supplies farmers need to grow their crops. ConAgra has major businesses in branded grocery products including shelf-stable and frozen foods, processed meats, chicken and turkey products, and cheeses, as well as major businesses in potato products, private-label grocery products, beef, pork, seafood, grain and pulse merchandising, grain processing, specialty trailing, crop protection chemicals, fertilizers, and animal feed. ConAgra is a family of independent operating companies.

LANCE, INC.
P.O. Box 32368, Charlotte NC 28232. 704/554-1421. **Contact:** Human Resources Director. **Description:** Produces snack products under the Home-pak, Club-pak, Snack-Right, and Vista brand names. The company also operates Midwest Biscuit (Burlington IA) and Caronuts (Boykins VA). Founded in 1913. **Corporate headquarters location:** This Location. **Listed on:** NASDAQ.

LAND O'LAKES, INC.
P.O. Box 64101, St. Paul MN 55164. 651/481-2222. **Contact:** Human Resources. **World Wide Web address:** http://www.landolakes.com. **Description:** A large agricultural cooperative of farmers and ranchers involved in the processing and distribution of dairy-related food products including deli cheeses, butter, milk, sour cream, yogurt, ice cream, dips, sauces, and butter blends. The company provides management, research, advisory, lobbying, and other farm-related services for its more than 300,000 members. Founded in 1921. **Common positions include:** Account Manager; Account Rep.; Accountant; Administrative Assistant; Assistant Manager; Attorney; Auditor; Biochemist; Budget Analyst; Buyer; Chemical Engineer; Chemist; Chief Financial Officer; Computer Operator; Computer Programmer; Controller; Credit Manager; Customer Service Rep.; Database Manager; Dietician/Nutritionist; Editor; Editorial Assistant; Environmental Engineer; Finance Director; Financial Analyst; Food Scientist/Technologist; Human Resources Manager; Internet Services Manager; Librarian; Managing Editor; Manufacturing Engineer; Marketing Manager; Marketing Specialist; MIS Specialist; Operations Manager; Paralegal; Project Manager; Public Relations Specialist; Purchasing Agent/Manager; Quality Control Supervisor; Sales Executive; Sales Manager; Sales Rep.; Secretary; Software Engineer; Systems Analyst; Systems Manager; Telecommunications Manager; Transportation/Traffic Specialist; Typist/Word Processor; Vice President. **Educational backgrounds include:** Accounting; Biology; Chemistry; Computer Science; Engineering; Finance; Liberal Arts; Marketing; Software Development; Software Tech. Support. **Benefits:** 401(k); Dental Insurance; Disability Coverage; Employee Discounts; Financial Planning Assistance; Flexible Schedule; Job Sharing; Life Insurance; Medical Insurance; Pension Plan; Savings Plan; Telecommuting; Tuition Assistance. **Special programs:** Internships. **Corporate headquarters location:** This Location. **Other U.S. locations:** Nationwide. **President/CEO:** John E. Gherty.

LEON'S TEXAS CUISINE
P.O. Box 1850, McKinney TX 75070. 972/529-5050. **Fax:** 972/529-2244. **Contact:** Human Resources. **E-mail address:** cindy@texascuisine.com. **World Wide Web address:** http://www.texascuisine.com. **Description:** Produces corn dogs and other southwestern-style items which are sold and distributed to retail grocery stores nationwide. **NOTE:** Entry-level positions are offered. **Common positions include:** Administrative Assistant; Controller; Customer Service Rep.; Electrician; Human Resources Manager; Marketing Manager; Mechanical Engineer; Purchasing Agent/Manager; Quality Control Supervisor; Sales Manager; Sales Rep.; Secretary; Transportation/Traffic Specialist. **Benefits:** 401(k); Casual Dress - Fridays; Dental Insurance; Employee Discounts; Life Insurance; Medical Insurance; Sick Days (6 - 10); Vacation Days (1 - 5). **Corporate headquarters location:** This Location. **Subsidiaries include:** Shoreline Restaurant Corporation.

LEVEL VALLEY
807 Pleasant Valley Road, West Bend WI 53095-9761. 262/675-6533. **Fax:** 262/675-2827. **Contact:** Human Resources. **Description:** A producer of butter, cream cheese, and a variety of evaporated and dried milk products. **Common positions include:** Food Scientist/Technologist; Production Manager. **Educational backgrounds include:** Food Science. **Benefits:** 401(k); Dental Insurance;

Disability Coverage; Life Insurance; Medical Insurance; Pension Plan. **Corporate headquarters location:** This Location. **Other U.S. locations:** Antioch TN. **Annual sales/revenues:** More than $100 million.

LINCOLN SNACKS COMPANY
4 High Ridge Park, Stamford CT 06905. 203/329-4545. **Contact:** Human Resources. **World Wide Web address:** http://www.lincolnsnacks.com. **Description:** Lincoln Snacks Company manufactures and markets caramelized popcorn and glazed popcorn and nut mixes. Brand names include Poppycock, Fiddle Faddle, Screaming Yellow Zonkers, and Golden Gourmet Nuts. **Benefits:** 401(k). **Corporate headquarters location:** This Location. **Parent company:** Noel Group, Inc. **Listed on:** NASDAQ. **Stock exchange symbol:** SNAX.

LIPTON
800 Sylvan Avenue, Englewood Cliffs NJ 07632. 201/567-8000. **Contact:** Personnel Administrator. **World Wide Web address:** http://www.lipton.com. **Description:** Manufactures food and beverage products. The Beverage Division produces and distributes tea bags, herbal teas, flavored teas, iced tea mixes, and instant tea. The Food Division produces soup mixes and Cup-a-Soup products. **Corporate headquarters location:** This Location. **Other U.S. locations:** Flemington NJ.

LONGMONT FOODS
P.O. Box 1479, Longmont CO 80502-1479. 303/776-6611. **Physical address:** 150 Main Street, Longmont CO. **Contact:** Personnel Director. **Description:** Engaged in poultry dressing operations. **Corporate headquarters location:** This Location.

M&M/MARS INC.
800 High Street, Hackettstown NJ 07840. 908/852-1000. **Contact:** Human Resources. **Description:** This location houses administrative offices. Overall, M&M/Mars produces a variety of candy and snack foods. **Corporate headquarters location:** This Location. **Other U.S. locations:** Albany GA; Burr Ridge IL.

MCT DAIRIES, INC.
15 Bleeker Street, Millburn NJ 07041. 973/258-9600. **Fax:** 973/258-9222. **Contact:** Human Resources. **Description:** Buys and sells cheeses and other industrial dairy products including bulk domestic and imported cheeses, whey powders, dairy flavorings, and buttermilk. **Corporate headquarters location:** This Location.

MFA INCORPORATED
201 Ray Young Drive, Columbia MO 65201. 573/876-5206. **Contact:** Personnel. **World Wide Web address:** http://www.mfaincorporated.com. **Description:** An agricultural cooperative supplying feed, seed, plant foods, farm supplies, agricultural chemicals, and associated services. **Common positions include:** Accountant/Auditor; Administrator; Agricultural Engineer; Branch Manager; Buyer; Commercial Artist; Computer Programmer; Credit Manager; Department Manager; Editor; Financial Analyst; General Manager; Human Resources Manager; Management Trainee; Marketing Specialist; Operations/Production Manager; Purchasing Agent/Manager; Services Sales Rep.; Systems Analyst; Transportation/Traffic Specialist. **Educational backgrounds include:** Accounting; Agronomy; Animal Science; Art/Design; Business Administration; Communications; Computer Science; Economics; Finance; Marketing. **Benefits:** Dental Insurance; Disability Coverage;

Life Insurance; Medical Insurance; Pension Plan; Savings Plan. **Corporate headquarters location:** This Location.

MAR-JAC INC.
P.O. Box 1017, Gainesville GA 30503. 770/536-0561. **Contact:** Human Resources. **Description:** Engaged in poultry processing. **Corporate headquarters location:** This Location.

MARATHON ENTERPRISES INC.
66 East Union Avenue, East Rutherford NJ 07073. 201/935-3330. **Contact:** Personnel Manager. **Description:** Manufactures Sabrett brand hot dogs. **Corporate headquarters location:** This Location.

MARIGOLD FOODS
2929 University Avenue SE, Minneapolis MN 55414. 612/331-3775. **Contact:** Human Resources Director. **Description:** A producer of ice cream and related products. **Common positions include:** Accountant/Auditor; Computer Programmer; Human Resources Manager; Operations/Production Manager. **Educational backgrounds include:** Accounting; Business Administration; Computer Science; Liberal Arts; Marketing. **Benefits:** Dental Insurance; Disability Coverage; Life Insurance; Medical Insurance; Pension Plan; Tuition Assistance. **Corporate headquarters location:** This Location. **Parent company:** Wessanen, Inc.

THE MARTIN-BROWER COMPANY
333 East Butterfield Road, Suite 500, Lombard IL 60148. 630/271-8300. **Contact:** Human Resources. **Description:** An international company that provides food distribution services to the restaurant industry. **Common positions include:** Buyer; Computer Programmer; Customer Service Rep.; Human Resources Manager; Human Service Worker; Systems Analyst; Transportation Specialist. **Educational backgrounds include:** Accounting; Business Administration; Communications; Computer Science; Finance. **Benefits:** 401(k); Dental Insurance; Disability Coverage; Life Insurance; Medical Insurance; Tuition Assistance. **Corporate headquarters location:** This Location. **Parent company:** Dalgety, plc.

McCORMICK & COMPANY
P.O. Box 6000, Sparks MD 21152-6000. 410/771-7301. **Physical address:** 18 Loveton Circle, Sparks MD 21152. **Contact:** Vice President of Human Relations. **World Wide Web address:** http://www.mccormick.com. **Description:** A diversified, specialty food company engaged in the manufacturing and marketing of seasonings and flavoring products to the food industry. Products are sold in 84 countries and processed at more than 40 facilities throughout the world. Principal products include spices, herbs, seeds, vegetable products, seasoning blends, seasoning mixes, and specialty frozen foods. Trademarks of McCormick & Company include McCormick and Schilling. The company also manufactures plastic bottles and tubes used in the pharmaceutical, cosmetic, and food packaging and preparation industries. McCormick & Company also operates a cogeneration facility which supplies energy to a subsidiary and is sold to utility companies. **Corporate headquarters location:** Hunt Valley MD. **Listed on:** New York Stock Exchange.

McDONALD WHOLESALE
P.O. Box 2340, Eugene OR 97402. 541/345-8421. **Contact:** Personnel Department. **Description:** A food and candy wholesaler. **Corporate headquarters location:** This Location. **Number of employees at this location:** 200.

McGLYNN BAKERIES, INC.
7350 Commerce Lane NE, Minneapolis MN 55432. 763/574-2222. **Toll-free phone:** 800/624-5966. **Fax:** 763/574-2210. **Contact:** Human Resources. **World Wide Web address:** http://www. mcglynn.com. **Description:** A producer of cookies and other baked goods that operates in three divisions: McGlynn's Retail Bakeries, which operates over 200 locations; Concept 2 Bakers, which produces and markets frozen bakery foods; and DecoPac, which markets cake decorating sets and supplies in the United States and Canada. **Corporate headquarters location:** This Location. **Parent company:** Pillsbury Company manufactures and markets food products for consumer, industrial, and international markets.

MEADOW GOLD DAIRIES
55 South Wakea Avenue, Kahului HI 96732-1395. 808/877-5541. **Fax:** 808/877-6224. **Contact:** Human Resources Manager. **World Wide Web address:** http://www.meadowgolddairies.com. **Description:** A manufacturer and wholesale distributor of dairy cultured products; juices and fruit drinks; ice cream; purified drinking water; and other foodstuffs. Founded in 1896. **NOTE:** Entry-level positions are offered. **Common positions include:** Account Manager; Account Representative; Accountant; Controller; Customer Service Rep.; Purchasing Agent/Manager; Sales Representative; Secretary; Typist/Word Processor. **Educational backgrounds include:** Accounting; Business Administration; Finance; Marketing; Public Relations. **Benefits:** 401(k); Dental Insurance; Disability Coverage; Employee Discounts; Flexible Schedule; Job Sharing; Life Insurance; Medical Insurance; Pension Plan; Savings Plan. **Special programs:** Training. **Corporate headquarters location:** This Location. **Other U.S. locations:**
- P.O. Box 1880, Honolulu HI 96805. 808/944-5949.

MERCHANTS DISTRIBUTORS INC. (MDI)
5005 Alex Lee Boulevard, Hickory NC 28601. 828/323-4016. **Fax:** 828/323-4120. **Contact:** Human Resources. **Description:** A wholesaler of groceries. **Common positions include:** Accountant /Auditor; Buyer; Computer Programmer; Customer Service Representative; Manufacturer's/Wholesaler's Sales Rep.; Operations/Production Manager; Systems Analyst; Transportation/Traffic Specialist; Wholesale and Retail Buyer. **Educational backgrounds include:** Accounting; Business Administration; Computer Science; Finance; Marketing. **Benefits:** 401(k); Credit Union; Dental Insurance; Disability Coverage; Life Insurance; Medical Insurance; Pension Plan; Tuition Assistance. **Special programs:** Internships. **Corporate headquarters location:** This Location. eld.

MERRICK'S, INC.
P.O. Box 99, 654 Bridge Street, Union Center WI 53962. 608/462-8201. **Contact:** Human Resources Manager. **World Wide Web address:** http://www. merricks.com. **Description:** Manufactures animal feed ingredients for the agricultural industry such as milk replacers for baby animals. The milk replacers are derived from a variety of sources including milk protein, animal plasma, and plant protein. **Common positions include:** Sales Manager. **Benefits:** 401(k); Casual Dress - Daily; Disability Coverage; Life Insurance; Medical Insurance; Tuition Assistance. **International locations:** Worldwide. **Parent company:** Merrick Management Group LLC. **Listed on:** Privately held. **Annual sales/revenues:** $51 - $100 million.

METZ BAKING COMPANY
P.O. Box 448, Sioux City IA 51102. 712/255-7611. **Contact:** Human Resources. **Description:** Produces bread and a variety of other wholesale bakery products. **NOTE:** Please send resumes to Deborah Tate, Director of Human Resources, 520 Lake Cook Road, Suite 520, Deerfield IL 60015. 847/267-3000. **Corporate headquarters location:** This Location. **Other U.S. locations:**
- P.O. Box 838, Sioux Falls SD 57101. 605/336-2035.

MICHAEL FOODS, INC.
5353 Wayzata Boulevard, Suite 324, Minneapolis MN 55416. 612/546-1500. **Toll-free phone:** 800/EGG-LINE. **Fax:** 612/595-4710. **Recorded jobline:** 888/2MF-IJOB. **Contact:** Human Resources. **World Wide Web address:** http://www. michaelfoods.com. **Description:** Processes and distributes food products including dairy, egg, and refrigerated grocery and potato products. **NOTE:** Entry-level positions are offered. **Company slogan:** Fresher thinking. **Common positions include:** Accountant; Administrative Assistant; Customer Service Representative; Financial Analyst; Human Resources Manager; MIS Specialist; Network/ Systems Administrator. **Educational backgrounds include:** Accounting; Business Administration; Computer Science; Finance. **Benefits:** 401(k); Dental Insurance; Disability Coverage; Life Insurance; Medical Insurance; Tuition Assistance. **Special programs:** Internships; Summer Jobs. **Corporate headquarters location:** This Location. **Annual sales/revenues:** More than $100 million.

MIDWEST GRAIN PRODUCTS, INC.
P.O. Box 130, Atchison KS 66002. 913/367-1480. **Fax:** 913/367-0192. **Contact:** Corporate Director of Human Resources. **Description:** A producer of food additives, alcohol, and flour. **Common positions include:** Accountant/Auditor; Advertising Clerk; Blue-Collar Worker Supervisor; Buyer; Chemical Engineer; Chemist; Clerical Supervisor; Computer Operator; Customer Service Representative; Department Manager; Dispatcher; Electrician; Financial Manager; Food Scientist/Technologist; General Manager; Health Services Worker; Human Resources Manager; Industrial Engineer; Industrial Production Manager; Machinist; Management Trainee; Marketing Manager; Mechanical Engineer; Payroll Clerk; Purchasing Agent/Manager; Quality Control Supervisor; Receptionist; Secretary; Services Sales Rep.; Stock Clerk; Systems Analyst; Transportation/Traffic Specialist; Typist/Word Processor; Welder. **Educational backgrounds include:** Accounting; Biology; Business Administration; Chemistry; Communications; Computer Science; Economics; Engineering; Finance; Marketing; Mathematics. **Special programs:** Internships. **Corporate headquarters location:** This Location. **Other U.S. locations:** Pekin IL.

MILLER BREWING COMPANY
P.O. Box 482, Milwaukee WI 53201-0482. 414/931-2000. **Physical address:** 3939 West Highland Boulevard, Milwaukee WI 53208-2866. **Contact:** Human Resources Manager. **World Wide Web address:** http://www.millerbrewing.com. **Description:** Produces and distributes beer and other malt beverages. Principal beer brands include Miller Lite, Lite Ice, Miller Genuine Draft, Miller Genuine Draft Light, Miller High Life, Miller Reserve, Lowenbrau, Milwaukee's Best, Meister Brau, Red Dog, and Icehouse. Miller also produces Sharp's, a non-alcoholic brew. **Corporate headquarters location:** This Location. **Other U.S. locations:** Irwindale CA; Albany GA; Eden NC; Trenton OH; Fort Worth TX. **Subsidiaries include:**

The Jacob Leinenkugel Brewing Company (Chippewa Falls WI) brews Leinenkugel's Original Premium, Leinenkugel's Light, Leinie's Ice, Leinenkugel's Limited, Leinenkugel's Red Lager, and four seasonal beers: Leinenkugel's Genuine Bock, Leinenkugel's Honey Weiss, Leinenkugel's Autumn Gold, and Leinenkugel's Winter Lager. Miller owns and operates one of the largest beer importers in the United States, Molson Breweries U.S.A., Inc., based in Reston VA, which imports Molson beers from Canada, as well as Foster's Lager and many other brands. **Parent company:** Philip Morris Companies Inc. (New York).

MORONI FEED PROCESSING
P.O. Box 308, Moroni UT 84646. 435/436-8211. **Contact:** Personnel Director. **Description:** A poultry processing plant. **Common positions include:** Blue-Collar Worker Supervisor; Branch Manager; Clinical Lab Technician; Human Resources Manager; Quality Control Supervisor; Restaurant/Food Service Manager; Systems Analyst; Veterinarian. **Educational backgrounds include:** Accounting; Marketing. **Benefits:** 401(k); Life Insurance; Medical Insurance. **Corporate headquarters location:** This Location.

JOHN MORRELL & COMPANY
1400 North Weber Avenue, Sioux Falls SD 57103. 605/330-3126. **Fax:** 605/330-3162. **Contact:** Manager of Human Resources. **E-mail address:** banderson@johnmorrell.com. **World Wide Web address:** http://www.johnmorrell.com. **Description:** A full-line meat packing and processing plant. The company sells approximately one billion pounds of meat per year. Founded in 1857. **Common positions include:** Accountant; Administrator; Blue-Collar Worker Supervisor; Branch Manager; Buyer; Chemist; Civil Engineer; Computer Programmer; Credit Manager; Draftsperson; Electrical/Electronics Engineer; Electrician; Food Scientist/Technologist; General Manager; Human Resources Manager; Industrial Engineer; Industrial Production Manager; Licensed Practical Nurse; Management Trainee; Manufacturer's/Wholesaler's Sales Rep.; Marketing Specialist; Mechanical Engineer; Operations/Production Manager; Purchasing Agent/Manager; Quality Control Supervisor; Registered Nurse; Statistician; Systems Analyst. **Educational backgrounds include:** Accounting; Biology; Business Administration. **Benefits:** 401(k); Dental Insurance; Disability Coverage; Employee Discounts; Life Insurance; Medical Insurance; Pension Plan; Savings Plan; Tuition Assistance. **Special programs:** Internships. **Corporate headquarters location:** Cincinnati OH. **Parent company:** Smithfield Foods, Inc.

MOUNT ARBOR NURSERIES
201 East Ferguson, P.O. Box 129, Shenandoah IA 51601. 712/246-4250. **Contact:** Craig Holmes, Director of Human Resources. **Description:** A grower and wholesaler of nursery stock. **Common positions include:** Accountant/Auditor; Automotive Mechanic; Blue-Collar Worker Supervisor; Customer Service Representative; Human Resources Manager; Purchasing Agent/Manager; Quality Control Supervisor; Statistician; Wholesale and Retail Buyer. **Educational backgrounds include:** Accounting; Business Administration; Marketing. **Benefits:** 401(k); Dental Insurance; Employee Discounts; Life Insurance; Medical Insurance. **Corporate headquarters location:** This Location.

MOUNTAIRE OF DELMARVA INC.
P.O. Box 710, Selbyville DE 19975. 302/436-8241. **Contact:** Human Resources Manager. **Description:** A poultry processing plant. **Corporate headquarters location:** This Location.

MRS. BAIRD'S BAKERIES
P.O. Box 417, Dallas TX 75221. 214/526-7201. **Contact:** Personnel Director. **Description:** Bakes bread and other goods. The company operates 11 facilities located throughout Texas. **Corporate headquarters location:** This Location.

MRS. FIELD'S ORIGINAL COOKIES, INC.
2855 East Cottonwood Parkway, Suite 400, Salt Lake City UT 84121-7050. 801/736-5600. **Contact:** Vice President of Administration. **Description:** Produces cookies. Founded in 1978. **Common positions include:** Accountant; Administrative Assistant; Assistant Manager; Clerical Supervisor; Customer Service Rep.; General Manager; Human Resources Manager; Marketing Specialist; MIS Specialist; Operations Manager. **Educational backgrounds include:** Accounting; Business Administration; Communications; Computer Science; Finance; Marketing. **Benefits:** 401(k); Dental Insurance; Employee Discounts; Life Insurance; Medical Insurance. **Special programs:** Apprenticeships; Internships; Summer Jobs. **Corporate headquarters location:** This Location. **Listed on:** Privately held. **Annual sales/revenues:** More than $100 million.

MURRY'S INC.
8300 Pennsylvania Avenue, Upper Marlboro MD 20772.. 301/420-6400. **Contact:** Human Resources. **Description:** Engaged in the manufacture, distribution, retail, and wholesale of frozen meats and specialty food items. **Corporate headquarters location:** This Location. **Other U.S. locations:** Washington DC; Baltimore MD.

NABISCO GROUP HOLDINGS
7 Campus Drive, P.O. Box 311, Parsippany NJ 07054. 973/682-5000. **Contact:** Human Resources. **World Wide Web address:** http://www. nabisco.com. **Description:** This location houses administrative offices. Overall, Nabisco is one of the largest consumer foods operations in the country. The company markets a broad line of cookie and cracker products including brand names such as Oreo, Ritz, Premium, Teddy Grahams, Chips Ahoy!, and Wheat Thins. The company operates 10 cake and cookie bakeries, a flour mill, and a cheese plant. The bakeries produce over 1 billion pounds of finished products each year. Over 150 biscuit brands reach the consumer via one of the industry's largest distribution networks. **NOTE:** In June 2000, Philip Morris Companies Inc. announced plans to acquire Nabisco Group Holdings. The acquisition is expected to be completed by the end of 2000. Please contact this location for more information. **Corporate headquarters location:** This Location.
Other U.S. locations:
• 1301 Sixth Avenue, New York NY 10019. 212/258-5600.

NABISCO INC.
100 DeForest Avenue, East Hanover NJ 07936. 973/503-2000. **Contact:** Staffing Center. **World Wide Web address:** http://www.nabiscocareers. com. **Description:** One of the largest consumer foods operations in the country. The company markets a broad line of cookie and cracker products including brand names such as Oreo, Ritz, Premium, Teddy Grahams, Chips Ahoy!, and Wheat Thins. The company operates 10 cake and cookie bakeries, a flour mill, and a cheese plant. The bakeries produce over 1 billion pounds of finished products each year. Over 150 biscuit brands reach the consumer via one of the industry's largest distribution networks. **NOTE:** In June 2000, Philip Morris Companies Inc. announced plans to acquire Nabisco Group Holdings. The acquisition is

expected to be completed by the end of 2000. Please contact this location for more information. **Common positions include:** Logistics Manager; Marketing Manager; Systems Analyst. **Educational backgrounds include:** Accounting; Computer Science; Marketing. **Benefits:** 401(k); Dental Insurance; Employee Discounts; Life Insurance; Medical Insurance; Pension Plan; Savings Plan; Tuition Assistance. **Special programs:** Internships. **Corporate headquarters location:** Parsippany NJ. **Other U.S. locations:** Buena Park CA; Atlanta GA; Chicago IL; Fair Lawn NJ; Toledo OH; Portland OR; Philadelphia PA; Richmond VA; Wrightstown WI.

NASH FINCH COMPANY
P.O. Box 355, Minneapolis MN 55440. 952/832-0534. **Physical address:** 7600 France Avenue South, Minneapolis MN 55435. **Contact:** Personnel Administration. **E-mail address:** careers@nashfinch.com. **World Wide Web address:** http://www.nashfinch.com. **Description:** Engaged in wholesale distribution, retail distribution, and produce marketing. The wholesale distribution segment supplies products to supermarkets, military bases, convenience stores, and other customers in 31 states. The retail distribution segment consists of approximately 120 company-owned retail stores in 16 states. Nash Finch's corporate stores operate under names such as Econofoods, Sun Mart, Family Thrift Center, Food Folks, and Easter's. Nash DeCamp markets fresh fruits and vegetables to wholesalers and retailers worldwide. **Corporate headquarters location:** This Location.

NATIONAL DISTRIBUTING COMPANY
P.O. Box 44127, Atlanta GA 30336. 404/696-9440. **Physical address:** One National Drive SW, Atlanta GA 30336. **Contact:** Vice President and Director of Operations. **World Wide Web address:** http://www.natdistco.com. **Description:** Engaged in wholesale beverage (beer, wine, and spirits) distribution and the linen supply business. **Corporate headquarters location:** This Location.

NATIONAL FRUIT PRODUCT COMPANY
P.O. Box 2040, Winchester VA 22604. 540/662-3401. **Physical address:** 5050 Fairmont Avenue, Winchester VA 22601. **Contact:** Corporate Human Resources Manager. **Description:** A food processor. National Fruit primarily produces apple juice, apple sauce, vinegar, apple butter, apple slices, and pie fillings. **Common positions include:** Accountant; Blue-Collar Worker Supervisor; Buyer; Computer Programmer; Electrical/Electronics Engineer; Food Scientist/Technologist; General Manager; Human Resources Manager; Industrial Production Manager; Mechanical Engineer; Operations/Production Manager; Purchasing Agent/Manager; Systems Analyst. **Educational backgrounds include:** Accounting; Business Administration; Chemistry; Computer Science; Engineering. **Benefits:** Disability Coverage; Employee Discounts; Life Insurance; Medical Insurance; Pension Plan; Profit Sharing; Tuition Assistance. **Corporate headquarters location:** This Location.

NESTLE USA, INC.
800 North Brand Boulevard, Glendale CA 91203. 818/549-6000. **Contact:** Human Resources. **World Wide Web address:** http://www.nestle.com. **Description:** One of the largest food and beverage companies in the nation. Brand names include Nestle Crunch, Baby Ruth, and Butterfinger candy bars; Taster's Choice and Nescafe coffee; Contadina tomato and refrigerated pastas and sauces; Friskies and Fancy Feast cat food; and Beringer wines. **Common positions include:** Accountant/Auditor; Agricultural Scientist; Chemical Engineer;

Computer Programmer; Electrical Engineer; F Industrial Engineer; Management Trainee; Manufacturer's/Wholesaler's Sales Rep.; Marketing Specialist; Mechanical Engineer; Operations/Production Manager; Purchasing Agent/Manager; Quality Control Supervisor; Systems Analyst; Transportation/Traffic Specialist. **Educational backgrounds include:** Accounting; Business Administration; Communications; Computer Science; Economics; Engineering; Finance; Marketing. **Benefits:** Dental Insurance; Disability Coverage; Life Insurance; Medical Insurance; Pension Plan; Profit Sharing; Tuition Assistance. **Corporate headquarters location:** This Location. **Parent company:** Nestle S.A.

NEW GLARUS FOODS, INC.
Industrial Drive, New Glarus WI 53574. 608/527-2131. **Fax:** 608/527-2931. **Contact:** Human Resources Manager. **Description:** A specialty foods manufacturer of meat snacks, sausages, and processed meats. **NOTE:** Entry-level positions are offered. **Common positions include:** Food Scientist/Technologist; Industrial Engineer; Industrial Production Manager; Management Trainee. **Educational backgrounds include:** Biology; Business Administration; Chemistry; Engineering; Finance; Marketing. **Benefits:** 401(k); Disability Coverage; Employee Discounts; Life Insurance; Medical Insurance; Tuition Assistance. **Special programs:** Apprenticeships; Training. **Corporate headquarters location:** This Location.

NEW ORLEANS COLD STORAGE & WAREHOUSE COMPANY
3401 Alvar Street, New Orleans LA 70126. 504/944-4400. **Contact:** Human Resources. **Description:** Services include public refrigerated warehouses, custom house brokerage services, and USDA meat inspection facilities. **Common positions include:** Blue-Collar Worker Supervisor; Refrigeration Engineer. **Benefits:** Dental Insurance; Life Insurance; Medical Insurance; Pension Plan. **Corporate headquarters location:** This Location.

NORPAC FOODS, INC.
4755 Brooklake Road NE, Salem OR 97305. 503/393-4221. **Contact:** Personnel Manager. **Description:** Processes and packages fruits and vegetables for retail stores and restaurants.

NOVARTIS SEED COMPANY
5300 Katrine Avenue, Downers Grove IL 60515. 630/969-6300. **Fax:** 630/969-9456. **Contact:** Human Resources Department. **World Wide Web address:** http://www.novartis.com. **Description:** A horticulture broker. **Common positions include:** Agricultural Scientist; Customer Service Rep.. **Educational backgrounds include:** Horticulture. **Benefits:** 401(k); Dental Insurance; Disability Coverage; EAP; Life Insurance; Medical Insurance; Profit Sharing; Savings Plan; Tuition Assistance. **Special programs:** Internships. **Corporate headquarters location:** This Location. **Other U.S. locations:** Ridgefield NJ; Akron OH. **Subsidiaries include:** Sluis & Groot Seeds. **Parent company:** Sandoz Ltd.

OCEAN SPRAY CRANBERRIES, INC.
One Ocean Spray Drive, Lakeville MA 02349. 508/946-1000. **Contact:** Employment Manager. **World Wide Web address:** http://www.oceanspray.com. **Description:** A food processor engaged in the packaging, processing, and marketing of fresh cranberries, cranberry sauces, and fruit juices. **Common positions include:** Accountant/Auditor; Agricultural Scientist; Customer Service Representative; Industrial Engineer; Software Engineer; Systems Analyst.

Benefits: Dental Insurance; Disability Coverage; Life Insurance; Medical Insurance; Pension Plan; Savings Plan; Tuition Assistance. **Corporate headquarters location:** This Location. **Other area locations:** Middleborough MA. **Other U.S. locations:** Vero Beach FL; Bordenton NJ; Sulphur Springs TX; Markham WA; Kenosha WI.

OPTA FOOD INGREDIENTS, INC.
25 Wiggins Avenue, Bedford MA 01730. 781/276-5100. **Toll-free phone:** 800/353-OPTA. **Contact:** Human Resources. **World Wide Web address:** http://www.opta-food.com. **Description:** Develops food ingredients including fiber-based texturizers, starch-based texturizers, and protein-based coatings. These products improve the nutrition, texture, and taste of food products and are targeted at the baking, dairy, and meat industries. Founded in 1991. **Common positions include:** Accountant; Administrative Assistant; Biochemist; Chemist; Food Scientist/Technologist; Marketing Manager; Sales Rep. **Educational backgrounds include:** Chemistry; Finance; Marketing; Nutrition. **Benefits:** 401(k); Casual Dress - Daily; Dental Insurance; Disability Coverage. **Corporate headquarters location:** This Location. **Other U.S. locations:** Galesburg IL; Louisville KY. **President/CEO:** Lewis C. Paine.

ORE-IDA FOODS, INC.
P.O. Box 10, Boise ID 83706. 208/383-6206. **Physical address:** 220 West Parkcenter Boulevard, Boise ID. **Fax:** 208/383-6902. **Recorded jobline:** 208/383-6167. **Contact:** Human Resources. **E-mail address:** employment@oreida.com. **World Wide Web address:** http://www.oreida.com. **Description:** One of the largest diversified frozen food manufacturers in the nation. In addition to a wide variety of frozen potato products, Ore-Ida manufactures Bagel Bites and Rosetto frozen stuffed pasta. Founded in 1961. **Common positions include:** Accountant; Administrative Assistant; Administrative Manager; Clerical Supervisor; Computer Operator; Computer Programmer; Controller; Credit Manager; Customer Service Representative; Environmental Engineer; Financial Analyst; Food Scientist/Technologist; General Manager; Graphic Artist; Graphic Designer; Human Resources Manager; Industrial Engineer; Industrial Production Manager; Manufacturing Engineer; Market Research Analyst; Marketing Manager; Mechanical Engineer; MIS Specialist; Operations Manager; Production Manager; Project Manager; Public Relations Specialist; Purchasing Agent/Manager; Sales Manager; Secretary; Statistician; Systems Analyst; Systems Manager; Transportation/Traffic Specialist; Typist/Word Processor. **Educational backgrounds include:** Accounting; Business Administration; Communications; Computer Science; Engineering; Finance; Marketing; Public Relations. **Benefits:** 401(k); Dental Insurance; Disability Coverage; Employee Discounts; Financial Planning Assistance; Flexible Schedule; Job Sharing; Life Insurance; Medical Insurance; Pension Plan; Public Transit Available; Savings Plan; Telecommuting; Tuition Assistance. **Special programs:** Internships. **Corporate headquarters location:** This Location. **Other U.S. locations:** Clarksville AR; Torrance CA; Fort Meyers FL; Ontario OR; Bloomsburg PA; West Chester PA. **Parent company:** H.J. Heinz.

OREGON FREEZE DRY INC.
P.O. Box 1048, Albany OR 97321. 541/926-6001. **Contact:** Human Resources Manager. **World Wide Web address:** http://www.ofd.com. **Description:** A processor of frozen fruits, vegetables, and poultry. **Corporate headquarters location:** This Location.

OSCAR MAYER FOODS CORPORATION
P.O. Box 7188, Madison WI 53707. 608/241-3311. **Physical address:** 910 Mayer Avenue, Madison WI 53704. **Contact:** Human Resources Department. **World Wide Web address:** http://www.oscar-mayer.com. **Description:** A nationwide meat and poultry processor. **Corporate headquarters location:** This Location. **Other U.S. locations:** Englewood CO; Chicago IL.

OWENS COUNTRY SAUSAGE INC.
P.O. Box 830249, Richardson TX 75083. 972/235-7181. **Contact:** Human Resources Manager. **World Wide Web address:** http://www.owensinc.com. **Description:** Produces sausage and other pork products. **Corporate headquarters location:** This Location.

PYA MONARCH INC.
P.O. Box 1328, Greenville SC 29602. 864/676-8600. **Contact:** Human Resources. **World Wide Web address:** http://www.pyamonarch.com. **Description:** This location houses the administrative offices. Overall, PYA Monarch distributes food to restaurants. **Corporate headquarters location:** This Location. **Parent company:** Sara Lee Corporation is a diversified consumer products company.

PACIFIC SHRIMP COMPANY
P.O. Box 1230, Newport OR 97365. 541/265-4215. **Contact:** Personnel. **Description:** A crab and shrimp fishing and processing company. **NOTE:** Jobs are largely seasonal and available only through the Oregon State Employment Office. **Corporate headquarters location:** This Location.

PANCHO'S MEXICAN FOODS
PANCHO'S MANAGEMENT INC.
2855 Lamb Place, Memphis TN 38118. 901/744-3900. **Contact:** Human Resources. **Description:** Operates a chain of Mexican restaurants. Pancho's Management Inc. (also at this location) is a wholesaler of food products to other restaurants. **Common positions include:** Industrial Production Manager; Operations/Production Manager; Services Sales Representative. **Benefits:** Dental Insurance; Employee Discounts; Life Insurance; Medical Insurance. **Corporate headquarters location:** This Location.

PENFORD CORPORATION
P.O. Box 1688, Bellevue WA 98009-1688. 425/462-6000. **Physical address:** 777 108th Avenue NE, Suite 2390, Bellevue WA 98004. **Toll-free phone:** 800/204-PENX. **Contact:** Personnel Department. **World Wide Web address:** http://www.penx.com. **Description:** A holding company. **Corporate headquarters location:** This Location. **Other U.S. locations:** Englewood CO; Cedar Rapids IA; Idaho Falls ID; Richland WA; Plover WI. **Subsidiaries include:** Penford Food Ingredients Co.; Penford Products Co.

PEPPERIDGE FARM INC.
595 Westport Avenue, Norwalk CT 06851. 203/846-7000. **Fax:** 203/846-7033. **Contact:** Human Resources. **Description:** Manufactures and distributes a range of fresh and frozen baked goods and confections including bread, cookies, cakes, pastries, and crackers. **Common positions include:** Accountant/Auditor; Computer Programmer; Credit Manager; Customer Service Rep.; Financial Analyst; Industrial Engineer; Manufacturing Engineer; Market Research Analyst; Marketing Manager; Purchasing Agent/Manager; Systems Analyst. **Educational backgrounds include:** Accounting; Business; Communications; Computer Science; Economics; Engineering; Finance; Liberal

Arts; Marketing; Mathematics. **Benefits:** 401(k); Dental Insurance; Disability Coverage; Employee Discounts; Life Insurance; Medical Insurance; Pension Plan; Savings Plan; Spending Account; Tuition Assistance. **Special programs:** Internships. **Corporate headquarters location:** This Location. **Parent company:** Campbell Soup Company (Camden NJ).

PEPSICO, INC.
700 Anderson Hill Road, Purchase NY 10577. 914/253-2000. **Contact:** Staffing Director. **World Wide Web address:** http://www.pepsico.com. **Description:** Operates on a worldwide basis within three companies which include Frito-Lay Company, Pepsi-Cola Company, and Tropicana Products, Inc. Pepsi-Cola Company primarily markets its brands worldwide and manufactures concentrates for its brands for sale to franchised bottlers worldwide. The segment also operates bottling plants and distribution facilities located in the U.S. and key international markets. Frito-Lay manufactures, distributes, and markets chips and other snacks worldwide. **Common positions include:** Accountant/Auditor; Attorney; Computer Programmer; Department Manager; Financial Analyst; General Manager; Human Resources Manager; Public Relations Specialist. **Educational backgrounds include:** Accounting; Business Administration; Communications; Economics; Finance. **Benefits:** Dental Insurance; Disability Coverage; Employee Discounts; Life Insurance; Medical Insurance; Pension Plan; Profit Sharing; Savings Plan; Tuition Assistance. **Corporate headquarters location:** This Location. **International locations:** Canada; Mexico; United Kingdom.

PERDUE FARMS, INC.
P.O. Box 1537, Salisbury MD 21802. 410/543-3000. **Fax:** 410/543-3292. **Contact:** Human Resources. **Description:** One of the largest suppliers of fresh and processed poultry products in the United States. The company's products are sold in supermarkets, small grocery stores, warehouse clubs, and butcher shops. The company is a fully-integrated operation, from overseeing breeding and hatching to delivering packaged goods to market. **Common positions include:** Accountant; Agricultural Engineer; Computer Programmer; Customer Service Rep.; Field Engineer; Financial Analyst; Food Scientist/Technologist; Human Resources Manager; Human Resources Specialist; Industrial Engineer; Marketing Manager; Operations/Production Manager; Purchasing Agent/Manager; Quality Control Supervisor; Registered Nurse; Systems Analyst; Transportation/Traffic Specialist. **Educational backgrounds include:** Agricultural Science; Animal Science; Biology; Business Administration; Chemistry; Computer Science; Engineering; Finance; Food Services; Marketing; Mathematics. **Benefits:** 401(k); Disability Coverage; Employee Discounts; Life Insurance; Medical Insurance; Pension Plan; Tuition Assistance. **Special programs:** Internships. **Corporate headquarters location:** This Location.

PETERSON FARMS
P.O. Box 248, Decatur AR 72722. 501/752-5295. **Fax:** 501/752-5678. **Contact:** Human Resources Manager. **World Wide Web address:** http://www. petersonfarms.com. **Description:** Engaged in poultry research and development and poultry processing. Peterson Farms also operates a cattle feedlot. **NOTE:** Entry-level positions are offered. **Common positions include:** Blue-Collar Worker Supervisor; Buyer; Clerical Supervisor; Computer Programmer; Electrician; Human Resources Manager; Operations/Production Manager;

Pharmacist; Quality Control Supervisor; Restaurant/Food Service Manager; Systems Analyst; Typist/Word Processor; Veterinarian. **Educational backgrounds include:** Accounting; Business Administration; Computer Science; Marketing. **Benefits:** 401(k); Dental Insurance; Disability Coverage; Employee Discounts; Life Insurance; Medical Insurance; Pension Plan. **Special programs:** Internships; Training. **Corporate headquarters location:** This Location. **Other U.S. locations:** Cullman AL; Trion GA; Luane MO; Olten TX.

PHILIP MORRIS COMPANIES INC.
PHILIP MORRIS INC.
120 Park Avenue, New York NY 10017. 212/880-5000. **Contact:** Human Resources Department. **Description:** Philip Morris Companies is a holding company whose principal wholly-owned subsidiaries are Philip Morris Inc. (also at this location), Philip Morris U.S.A., Philip Morris International Inc., Kraft Foods, Inc., Miller Brewing Company, and Philip Morris Capital Corporation. In the tobacco industry, Philip Morris U.S.A. and Philip Morris International together form one of the largest international cigarette operations in the world. U.S. brand names include Marlboro, Parliament, Virginia Slims, Benson & Hedges, and Merit. In the food industry, Kraft Foods, Inc. is one of the largest producers of packaged grocery products in North America. Major brands include Jell-O, Post, Kool-Aid, Crystal Light, Entenmann's, Miracle Whip, Stove Top, and Shake 'n Bake. Kraft markets a number of products under the Kraft brand including natural and process cheeses and dry packaged dinners. The Oscar Mayer unit markets processed meats, poultry, lunch combinations, and pickles under the Oscar Mayer, Louis Rich, Lunchables, and Claussen brand names. Kraft is also one of the largest coffee companies with principal brands including Maxwell House, Sanka, Brim, and General Foods International Coffees. Kraft Foods Ingredients Corporation manufactures private-label and industrial food products for sale to other food processing companies. Miller Brewing Company brews beer under the labels Molson Ice, Miller Genuine Draft, Miller High Life, Sharp's non-alcoholic, Red Dog, Miller Lite, Icehouse, Foster's Lager, and Lowenbrau. Philip Morris Capital Corporation is engaged in financial services and real estate. **NOTE:** In June 2000, Philip Morris Companies Inc announced plans to acquire Nabisco Group Holdings. The acquisition is expected to be completed by the end of 2000. Please contact this location for more information. **Corporate headquarters location:** This Location. **Other U.S. locations:** Stamford CT; Rye Brook NY; Richmond VA. **International locations:** Australia; Brazil; Hong Kong; Japan; Switzerland. **Listed on:** Amsterdam Stock Exchange; Antwerp Stock Exchange; Australian Stock Exchange; Brussels Stock Exchange; Frankfurt Stock Exchange; London Stock Exchange; Luxembourg Stock Exchange; New York Stock Exchange; Paris Stock Exchange; Swiss Stock Exchange; Tokyo Stock Exchange; Vienna Stock Exchange.

PIERCE FOODS
104 South Main Street, Moorefield WV 26836. 304/538-2381. **Contact:** Human Resources. **Description:** Produces precooked and frozen chicken products. **Corporate headquarters location:** This Location.

PILGRIM'S PRIDE CORPORATION
P.O. Box 93, Pittsburg TX 75686-0093. 903/855-1000. **Contact:** Human Resources. **Description:** Produces chicken products and eggs for the restaurant, institutional, food service, grocery, and

wholesale markets. The company's operations include breeding, hatching, growing, processing, packaging, and preparing poultry. Pilgrim's Pride Corporation also produces animal feeds and ingredients. The company is one of the largest producers of chicken products in the United States and Mexico. The company's primary domestic distribution is handled through restaurants and retailers in central, southwestern, and western United States, and through the food service industry throughout the country. **Common positions include:** Accountant/Auditor; Blue-Collar Worker Supervisor; Computer Programmer; Credit Manager; Customer Service Representative; Food Scientist/Technologist; Human Resources Manager; Management Trainee; Manufacturer's/Wholesaler's Sales Rep. **Benefits:** 401(k); Daycare Assistance; Disability Coverage; ESOP; Life Insurance; Medical Insurance; Tuition Assistance. **Corporate headquarters location:** This Location. **Other U.S. locations:** AR; AZ; OK.

THE PILLSBURY COMPANY
200 South Sixth Street, Mail Stop 37A4, Minneapolis MN 55402. 612/330-4966. **Contact:** Human Resources Manager. **World Wide Web address:** http://www.pillsbury.com. **Description:** Manufactures and markets food products for consumers and industrial customers worldwide. **Common positions include:** Accountant/Auditor; Computer Programmer; Financial Analyst; Human Resources Manager; Marketing Specialist; Science Technologist. **Educational backgrounds include:** Accounting; Engineering; Finance; Marketing. **Benefits:** 401(k); Dental Insurance; Disability Coverage; Medical Insurance; Pension Plan; Profit Sharing; Savings Plan; Tuition Assistance. **Special programs:** Internships. **Corporate headquarters location:** This Location. **Parent company:** Grand Metropolitan.

PINE STATE TOBACCO & CANDY COMPANY
8 Ellis Avenue, Augusta ME 04330. 207/622-3741. **Contact:** Personnel. **Description:** A wholesaler of a wide variety of foods and other products for retail stores. **Corporate headquarters location:** This Location.

PIONEER FLOUR MILLS
P.O. Box 118, San Antonio TX 78291. 210/227-1401. **Contact:** Human Resources Manager. **World Wide Web address:** http://www.pioneermills.com. **Description:** A flour mill. **Corporate headquarters location:** This Location.

POLLY-O DAIRY PRODUCTS CORP.
120 Mineola Boulevard, Mineola NY 11501. 516/741-8000. **Contact:** Human Resources. **Description:** Engaged in the manufacturing and distribution of Italian-style soft cheeses and food products. **Common positions include:** Accountant/Auditor; Computer Programmer; Credit Manager; Financial Analyst; Manufacturer's/Wholesaler's Sales Rep.; Marketing Specialist. **Educational backgrounds include:** Accounting; Business Administration; Computer Science; Finance; Liberal Arts; Marketing; Mathematics. **Benefits:** Dental Insurance; Disability Coverage; Employee Discounts; Life Insurance; Medical Insurance; Pension Plan; Profit Sharing; Savings Plan; Tuition Assistance. **Corporate headquarters location:** This Location.

PORTIS MERCANTILE COMPANY
P.O. Box 710, Leponto AR 72354. 870/475-2200. **Contact:** Manager. **Description:** Engaged in farmland management, cotton ginning, the sale of farm supplies, and the operation of grain elevators.

Products include cotton, cotton seed, soybeans, wheat, fertilizer, rice, grain sorghum, and soybeans. **Common positions include:** Accountant/Auditor; Agricultural Engineer; Blue-Collar Worker Supervisor; General Manager; Management Trainee; Operations/Production Manager; Property and Real Estate Manager. **Educational backgrounds include:** Business; Computer Science; Liberal Arts. **Benefits:** Employee Discounts; Medical Insurance. **Corporate headquarters location:** This Location.

PROCTER & GAMBLE
One Procter & Gamble Plaza, Cincinnati OH 45202. 513/983-1100. **Contact:** Personnel. **World Wide Web address:** http://www.pg.com. **Description:** This location houses administrative offices. Overall, Procter & Gamble manufactures over 300 laundry, cleaning, paper, beauty care, health care, food, and beverage products in more than 140 countries. Laundry and household cleaning products include Mr. Clean, and Bounce and Downy brand fabric softeners. Paper products include Pampers and Luvs diapers, Charmin bath tissue, and Bounty paper towels. Beauty products include Pantene Pro-V and Vidal Sassoon hair care, Cover Girl cosmetics, and Giorgio Beverly Hills fragrances. Health care products include Vicks brand cold remedies; Aleve, a nonprescription version of Naprosyn; Didro-Kit therapy for osteoporosis; and Asacol, a treatment for ulcerative colitis. Food and beverage products include brand names such as Sunny Delight juices and Pringles potato chips. Other Procter & Gamble brands include Tide, Ariel, Crest, Crisco, and Max Factor. **Common positions include:** Chemical Engineer; Electrical/Electronics Engineer; Financial Analyst; Industrial Engineer; Manufacturer's/Wholesaler's Sales Rep.; Mechanical Engineer; Operations/Production Manager; Purchasing Agent/Manager. **Educational backgrounds include:** Business Administration; Computer Science; Engineering; Finance; Liberal Arts; Marketing. **Corporate headquarters location:** This Location. **International locations:** Asia; Canada; Europe; Latin America.

THE QUAKER OATS COMPANY
P.O. Box 049001, Chicago IL 60604. 312/222-7111. **Contact:** Placement Office. **World Wide Web address:** http://www.quakeroats.com. **Description:** A producer of grain-based foods and sports beverages. Products include Gatorade; Golden Grain pasta and rice; and Quaker Oats hot and ready-to-eat cereals, granola bars, and rice cakes. Founded in 1877. **Corporate headquarters location:** This Location. **Other U.S. locations:** Nationwide. **International locations:** Worldwide. **Listed on:** New York Stock Exchange.

R&R MARKETING
10 Patton Drive, West Caldwell NJ 07006. 973/228-5100. **Contact:** Human Resources. **Description:** Engaged in the wholesale importation and distribution of liquors and wines. **Corporate headquarters location:** This Location.

R.J. REYNOLDS TOBACCO HOLDINGS
P.O. Box 2866, Winston-Salem NC 27102. 336/741-5500. **Physical address:** 401 North Main Street, Winston-Salem NC 27101. **Contact:** Human Resources. **World Wide Web address:** http://www.rjrt.com. **Description:** A holding company. **Corporate headquarters location:** This Location. **Subsidiaries include:** R.J. Reynolds Tobacco Company manufactures tobacco products.

RALSTON PURINA COMPANY
Checkerboard Square, St. Louis MO 63164. 314/982-1000. **Contact:** Director of Human Resources. **World Wide Web address:**

http://www.ralston.com. **Description:** This location manufactures pet food. Overall, Ralston Purina Company is one of the world's largest producers of dry dog and soft-moist cat foods, which are marketed under the Purina brand name; one of the largest wholesale bakers of fresh delivered bakery products in the United States with such brands as Wonderbread and Hostess sweet baked goods; one of the world's largest manufacturers of dry cell battery products including Eveready and Energizer brand products; and a major producer of dietary soy protein, fiber food ingredients, polymer products, and, outside the U.S., feeds for livestock and poultry. Founded in 1894. **Corporate headquarters location:** This Location.

REFINED SUGARS INC.
One Federal Street, Yonkers NY 10702. 914/963-2400. **Contact:** Human Resources Manager. **Description:** Refines raw sugar and distributes it to major national clients in the soft drink, confectionary, and baking industries. **Common positions include:** Accountant; Biological Scientist; Blue-Collar Worker Supervisor; Buyer; Chemical Engineer; Chemist; Clinical Lab Technician; Computer Programmer; Credit Manager; Customer Service Rep.; Department Manager; Electrical/Electronics Engineer; Financial Analyst; Food Scientist/Technologist; Human Resources Manager; Industrial Engineer; Manufacturer's/Wholesaler's Sales Rep.; Marketing Specialist; Mechanical Engineer; Operations/Production Manager; Purchasing Agent/Manager; Systems Analyst. **Educational backgrounds include:** Accounting; Business Administration; Chemistry; Computer Science; Engineering; Finance; Marketing. **Benefits:** 401(k); Dental Insurance; Disability Coverage; Life Insurance; Medical Insurance; Savings Plan; Tuition Assistance. **Corporate headquarters location:** This Location.

REQUEST FOODS, INC.
P.O. Box 2577, Holland MI 49422. 616/786-0900. **Fax:** 616/786-9180. **Contact:** Director of Training/Development. **Description:** A producer of frozen food entrees. **Common positions include:** Accountant/Auditor; Buyer; Customer Service Rep.; Dietician/Nutritionist; Electrician; Financial Analyst; General Manager; Human Resources Manager; Industrial Engineer; Industrial Production Manager; Management Trainee; Operations/Production Manager; Purchasing Agent/Manager; Quality Control Supervisor; Systems Analyst. **Educational backgrounds include:** Accounting; Business Administration; Finance; Food Science; Liberal Arts. **Benefits:** 401(k); Dental Insurance; Disability Coverage; Employee Discounts; Life Insurance; Medical Insurance; Profit Sharing; Tuition Assistance. **Corporate headquarters location:** This Location. **Other U.S. locations:** Chicago IL.

RESERS FINE FOODS, INC.
P.O. Box 8, Beaverton OR 97075-0008. 503/643-6431. **Fax:** 503/526-8378. **Recorded jobline:** 503/526-8399. **Contact:** Human Resources. **Description:** A food processor specializing in salads, desserts, dips, meat, and Mexican foods. **Common positions include:** Accountant/Auditor; Advertising Clerk; Buyer; Clerical Supervisor; Credit Manager; Dietician/Nutritionist; Electrician; Food Scientist/Technologist; Manufacturer's/Wholesaler's Sales Rep.; Operations/Production Manager. **Educational backgrounds include:** Business Administration; Food Science. **Benefits:** 401(k); Dental Insurance; Disability Coverage; Employee Discounts; Life Insurance; Medical Insurance; Pension Plan; Profit Sharing; Savings Plan; Tuition Assistance. **Special programs:** Internships. **Corporate headquarters location:** This Location. **Other U.S. locations:** Nationwide.

RICH PRODUCTS CORPORATION
P.O. Box 245, Buffalo NY 14240. 716/878-8000. **Physical address:** 1150 Niagara Street, Buffalo NY 14213. **Contact:** Human Resources. **World Wide Web address:** http://www.richs.com. **Description:** Rich Products is a family-owned, frozen foods manufacturer. The company operates manufacturing sites and field offices throughout North America and abroad. Rich's also operates more than 30 production facilities involved in producing a wide spectrum of premium quality products, including non-dairy creamers, toppings and icings, frozen dough, baked goods, sweet goods, pastas, and specialty meats. Founded in 1945. **Corporate headquarters location:** This Location.

RICH SEAPAK CORPORATION
P.O. Box 20670, St. Simons Island GA 31522. 912/638-5000. **Physical address:** McKinnon Airport Road, St. Simons Island GA. **Toll-free phone:** 800/654-9731. **Fax:** 912/634-3104. **Contact:** Human Resources. **World Wide Web address:** http://www.seapak.com. **Description:** Processes and distributes frozen seafood and vegetable products. **NOTE:** Entry-level positions and part-time jobs are offered. **Common positions include:** Account Manager; Accountant; Administrative Assistant; Computer Programmer; Computer Support Technician; Controller; Credit Manager; Customer Service Representative; Finance Director; Financial Analyst; Food Scientist/Technologist; Graphic Artist; Human Resources Manager; Industrial Engineer; Marketing Manager; Network/Systems Administrator; Purchasing Agent/Manager; Sales Executive; Sales Manager. **Educational backgrounds include:** Accounting; Biology; Business Administration; Computer Science; Engineering; Finance; Marketing; MBA; MCSE; Novell; Software Tech. **Benefits:** 401(k); Casual Dress - Fridays; Disability Coverage; Employee Discounts; Life Insurance; Medical Insurance; Relocation Assistance; Sick Days (6 - 10); Tuition Assistance; Vacation Days (10 - 20). **Corporate headquarters location:** This Location. **Parent company:** Rich Products Corporation (Buffalo NY) is a family-owned, frozen foods manufacturer. The company operates manufacturing sites and field offices throughout North America and abroad. Rich Products also operates more than 30 production facilities involved in producing a wide spectrum of products including non-dairy creamers, toppings, and icings; frozen dough; baked goods; sweet goods; pastas; and specialty meats.

RICHFOOD INC.
P.O. Box 26967, Richmond VA 23261. 804/746-6000. **Contact:** Human Resources Department. **World Wide Web address:** http://www.richfood.com. **Description:** One of the largest wholesale food distributors in the mid-Atlantic. **Corporate headquarters location:** This Location. **Parent company:** SUPERVALU.

ROBINSON DAIRY INC.
P.O. Box 5774, Denver CO 80217. 303/825-2990. **Contact:** Scott Darkey, Human Resources Manager. **Description:** Produces a complete range of dairy products including milk and ice cream. Robinson Dairy also produces a variety of fruit-flavored drinks. **Corporate headquarters location:** This Location.

ROCCO, INC.
P.O. Box 549, Harrisonburg VA 22801. 540/568-1542. **Fax:** 540/568-1401. **Contact:** Human Resources. **World Wide Web address:**

http://www.rocco.com. **Description:** A producer and marketer of poultry food products. **NOTE:** Jobseekers should fax a resume with salary requirements. Entry-level positions are offered. **Common positions include:** Accountant; Administrative Manager; Auditor; Chief Financial Officer; Computer Operator; Computer Support Technician; Controller; Credit Manager; Database Administrator; Food Scientist/Technologist; Graphic Artist; Marketing Manager; Network/Systems Administrator; Public Relations Specialist; Purchasing Agent/Manager; Quality Assurance Engineer; Sales Manager; Sales Rep. **Educational backgrounds include:** Accounting; Biology; Business Administration; Chemistry; Computer Science; Economics; Engineering; Finance; Marketing; Mathematics; Public Relations. **Benefits:** 401(k); Dental Insurance; Disability Coverage; Employee Discounts; Life Insurance; Medical Insurance; Tuition Assistance. **Corporate headquarters location:** This Location.

B.C. ROGERS POULTRY INC.
4688 Highway 80 East, Morton MS 39117. 601/732-8911. **Fax:** 601/732-2642. **Contact:** Human Resources Coordinator. **E-mail address:** kwebb@bcrogers.com. **World Wide Web address:** http://www.bcrogers.com. **Description:** A poultry processor. **Common positions include:** Accountant; AS400 Programmer Analyst; Blue-Collar Worker Supervisor; Electrical Engineer; Management Trainee; Mechanical Engineer; Operations Manager; Production Manager; Project Manager; Quality Control Supervisor. **Other U.S. locations:** Forest MS; McComb MS; Morton MS.

ROUNDY'S
23000 Roundy Drive, Pewaukee WI 53072. 262/547-7999. **Recorded jobline:** 262/524-5700. **Contact:** Human Resources. **World Wide Web address:** http://www.roundys.com. **Description:** Manufactures and distributes food products to warehouses and supermarkets throughout the midwestern U.S. Founded in 1875. **NOTE:** Entry level positions and second and third shifts are offered. **Common positions include:** Accountant; Administrative Assistant; Budget Analyst; Buyer; Clerical Supervisor; Computer Operator; Computer Programmer; Controller; Database Manager; Finance Director; Human Resources Manager; Market Research Analyst; Online Content Specialist; Paralegal; Sales Manager; Systems Analyst; Systems Manager; Vice President. **Educational backgrounds include:** Accounting; Business Administration; Communications; Computer Science; Finance; Software Tech. Support. **Benefits:** 401(k); Daycare Assistance; Dental Insurance; Disability Coverage; Employee Discounts; Financial Planning Assistance; Flexible Schedule; Job Sharing; Life Insurance; Medical Insurance; Pension Plan; Public Transit Available; Tuition Assistance. **Corporate headquarters location:** This Location.

ROYAL CROWN BOTTLING COMPANY
2429 Victory Drive, Columbus GA 31901. 706/689-8203. **Contact:** Controller. **Description:** A primary bottler of the soft drink concentrates and syrups manufactured by the Royal Crown Company. The company's principal product of its carbonated beverage line is RC Cola. **Corporate headquarters location:** This Location. **Other U.S. locations:** La Mirada CA; Cincinnati OH; Columbus OH. **Parent company:** Royal Crown Company (Fort Lauderdale FL).

RUIZ FOOD PRODUCTS, INC.
P.O. Box 37, Dinuba CA 93618. 559/591-5510. **Contact:** Human Resources Manager. **Description:** Produces Mexican-style frozen foods that are distributed throughout the U.S., Mexico, and Canada. **Common positions include:** Accountant/Auditor; Blue-Collar Worker Supervisor; Budget Analyst; Buyer; Claim Representative; Clerical Supervisor; Computer Programmer; Education Administrator; Financial Analyst; Food Scientist/Technologist; Human Resources Manager; Industrial Engineer; Industrial Production Manager; Public Relations Specialist; Purchasing Agent/Manager; Quality Control Supervisor; Systems Analyst; Teacher/Professor; Transportation/Traffic Specialist. **Educational backgrounds include:** Accounting; Business Administration; Computer Science; Finance; Marketing. **Benefits:** Dental Insurance; Life Insurance; Medical Insurance; Pension Plan. **Corporate headquarters location:** This Location.

ST. ALBANS COOPERATIVE CREAMERY
140 Federal Street, St. Albans VT 05478. 802/524-6581. **Contact:** Controller. **Description:** This location is a milk and cream processing facility. Overall, St. Albans Cooperative Creamery, Inc. is a dairy plant that manufactures products including powdered milk, ice cream, and skim milk. **Common positions include:** Accountant/Auditor; Blue-Collar Worker Supervisor; General Manager; Industrial Production Manager; Operations/Production Manager; Quality Control Supervisor. **Educational backgrounds include:** Accounting; Business Administration; Chemistry; Computer Science; Finance. **Benefits:** Dental Insurance; Disability Coverage; Life Insurance; Medical Insurance; Pension Plan. **Corporate headquarters location:** This Location.

SARA LEE CORPORATION
3 First National Plaza, Chicago IL 60602. 312/726-2600. **Contact:** Human Resources Manager. **World Wide Web address:** http://www.saralee.com. **Description:** This location houses the administrative offices of the international food and consumer products company. **NOTE:** For employment opportunities, please contact each division directly. **Common positions include:** Accountant; Attorney; Computer Programmer; Public Relations Specialist; Systems Analyst. **Educational backgrounds include:** Accounting; Business Administration; Finance. **Benefits:** 401(k); Dental Insurance; Disability Coverage; Employee Discounts; Life Insurance; Medical Insurance; Pension Plan; Savings Plan; Tuition Assistance. **Corporate headquarters location:** This Location.

SARATOGA BEVERAGE GROUP, INC.
11 Geyser Road, Saratoga Springs NY 12866. 518/584-6363. **Contact:** Human Resources Manager. **World Wide Web address:** http://www.saratogabeverage.com. **Description:** Bottles, markets, and distributes natural spring water. The product line includes six water products, a sparkling water product with bi-carbonates added, and non-carbonated spring water. Distributors are primarily located in New York state, the mid-Atlantic region, and Florida. **Corporate headquarters location:** This Location.

SAVANNAH FOODS & INDUSTRIES
P.O. Box 339, Savannah GA 31402. 912/234-1261. **Contact:** Human Resources. **Description:** This facility produces sugar, sugar-derived products, and liquid animal feeds. Savannah Foods & Industries is one of the nation's largest refined cane and beet sugar producers, marketing products primarily in the eastern U.S. under the names Dixie Crystals, Evercane, Colonial, and Pioneer. Cane sugar refineries are located in Georgia, Florida, and Louisiana, and there are four sugar beet processing

plants in Michigan, one in Ohio, and a raw sugar mill in Louisiana. The company also produces individual portions of salt, pepper, sugar, and sugar substitutes for the food service trade. **Corporate headquarters location:** This Location.

SCENIC FRUIT COMPANY
7510 SE Altman Road, Gresham OR 97080. 503/663-3434. **Contact:** Personnel. **Description:** A berry processing plant. **NOTE:** Work is largely seasonal with staffing reduced to approximately 15 during the winter. **Corporate headquarters location:** This Location.

SCHIEFFELIN & SOMERSET COMPANY
2 Park Avenue, 17th Floor, New York NY 10016. 212/251-8355. **Fax:** 212/251-8384. **Contact:** Human Resources. **Description:** Sells and markets premium alcoholic beverages. **Common positions include:** Accountant/Auditor; Administrative Manager; Attorney; Budget Analyst; Computer Programmer; Human Resources Manager; Public Relations Specialist; Sales Representative; Systems Analyst. **Educational backgrounds include:** Marketing. **Benefits:** 401(k); Disability Coverage; Employee Discounts; Life Insurance; Medical Insurance; Pension Plan; Savings Plan; Tuition Assistance. **Corporate headquarters location:** This Location. **Other U.S. locations:** San Francisco CA; Coral Gables FL; Chicago IL. **Parent company:** United Distillers.

SCHREIBER FOODS INC.
425 Pine Street, Green Bay WI 54301. 920/437-7601. **Contact:** Human Resources Manager. **Description:** A food processing company. **Corporate headquarters location:** This Location.

SCHULTZ SAV-O STORES, INC.
P.O. Box 419, Sheboygan WI 53082-0419. 920/457-4433. **Physical address:** 2215 Union Avenue, Sheboygan WI. **Contact:** Human Resources. **World Wide Web address:** http://www.shopthepig.com. **Description:** Distributes food and related products for wholesale and retail sale. This location also houses the Springtime bottling plant, which bottles soft drinks, drinking water, and distilled water. The company also owns the right to grant Piggly Wiggly franchises in its market area under a Submaster Franchise Agreement with Piggly Wiggly Corporation. The company is the primary supplier to its franchise and corporate stores, as well as to other smaller independent retail stores in its market area. The company also provides its stores and other customers with fresh, frozen, and processed meat products from a third-party distribution facility on a contract basis. **Corporate headquarters location:** This Location.

SCHWEBEL BAKING COMPANY
P.O. Box 6018, Youngstown OH 44501. 330/783-2860. **Physical address:** 965 East Midlothian Boulevard, Youngstown OH 44502. **Contact:** Human Resources. **Description:** Produces bakery products and related goods. **Common positions include:** Accountant/Auditor; Administrator; Buyer; Computer Programmer; Human Resources Manager; Purchasing Agent/Manager. **Benefits:** Dental Insurance; Disability Coverage; Employee Discounts; Life Insurance; Medical Insurance; Profit Sharing; Savings Plan. **Corporate headquarters location:** This Location.

THE SCOTTS COMPANY
14111 Scottslawn Road, Marysville OH 43041. 937/644-0011. **Fax:** 937/644-7244. **Contact:** Personnel. **E-mail address:** human.resources@scottsco.com. **World Wide Web address:** http://www.scottscompany.com. **Description:** Manufactures and markets lawn and garden products serving the do-it-yourself consumer and professional users. Brands include Scotts Turf Builder seed and spreaders; Miracle Gro lawn and garden products; and Hyponex organic products. Founded in 1870. **NOTE:** Entry-level positions and second and third shifts are offered. **Common positions include:** Accountant; Administrative Assistant; Administrative Manager; Applications Engineer; Assistant Manager; Attorney; Auditor; Blue-Collar Worker Supervisor; Budget Analyst; Buyer; Chemical Engineer; Chemist; Chief Financial Officer; Clerical Supervisor; Computer Operator; Computer Programmer; Controller; Credit Manager; Customer Service Rep.; Database Manager; Environmental Engineer; Finance Director; Financial Analyst; Human Resources Manager; Industrial Engineer; Marketing Manager; Marketing Specialist; MIS Specialist; Operations Manager; Production Manager; Project Manager; Public Relations Specialist; Purchasing Agent/Manager; Quality Control Supervisor; Sales Executive; Sales Manager; Sales Representative; Software Engineer; Systems Analyst; Systems Manager; Transportation/Traffic Specialist; Vice President; Webmaster. **Educational backgrounds include:** Accounting; Business Administration; Chemistry; Communications; Computer Science; Engineering; Finance; Human Resources; Marketing; Public Relations. **Benefits:** 401(k); Dental Insurance; Disability Coverage; Employee Discounts; Life Insurance; Medical Insurance; Pension Plan; Profit Sharing; Savings Plan; Tuition Assistance. **Special programs:** Internships. **Internship information:** The Scotts Company offers various internships including landscape services, human resources, and marketing. **Corporate headquarters location:** This Location. **International locations:** Herleens, Netherlands. **Subsidiaries include:** Hyponex; Miracle-Gro; Republic Tool; Sierra.

THE SCOULAR COMPANY
2027 Dodge Street, Omaha NE 68102. 402/342-3500. **Contact:** Human Resources Manager. **World Wide Web address:** http://www.scoular.com. **Description:** A privately-owned grain and feed ingredient trading company. **Common positions include:** Accountant/Auditor; Buyer; Credit Manager; Merchandiser. **Educational backgrounds include:** Agricultural Science; Economics. **Benefits:** 401(k); Dental Insurance; Disability Coverage; Life Insurance; Medical Insurance; Pension Plan; Profit Sharing; Tuition Assistance. **Corporate headquarters location:** This Location. **Other U.S. locations:** FL; IA; IL; KS; MN; MO; MT; NY.

SEABOARD CORPORATION
9000 West 67th Street, Shawnee Mission KS 66202. 913/676-8800. **Contact:** Human Resources. **World Wide Web address:** http://www.seaboardcorp.com. **Description:** Seaboard Corporation is a diversified international company with interests in food processing and transportation. Food operations include poultry and pork processing, primarily in the eastern U.S., with hog farrowing plants in Colorado and Oklahoma; flour milling and baked goods production in Puerto Rico; and fruit, vegetables, shrimp, flour, pen-raised salmon, and animal feed processing and production. Seaboard Corporation operates an oceanliner service for cargo, with routes running between Florida and Latin America; and operates bulk carriers in the Atlantic Basin. The company also trades bulk grain and oil seed commodities. **Corporate headquarters location:** This Location. **Listed on:** American Stock Exchange.

SEE'S CANDIES
210 El Camino Real, South San Francisco CA 94080. 650/583-7307. **Contact:** Human Resources. **Description:** This location houses administrative offices. Overall, See's Candies manufactures candy. **Corporate headquarters location:** This Location.

SENECA FOODS CORPORATION
1162 Pittsford-Victor Road, Pittsford NY 14534. 716/385-9500. **Contact:** Human Resources. **World Wide Web address:** http://www.senecafoods.com. **Description:** Seneca Foods produces a number of juice products; various vegetables; and other foods and sells them to supermarkets and other retail businesses. Products are sold under a variety of brand names including Libby's and Blue Boy. **Corporate headquarters location:** This Location. **Subsidiaries include:** Seneca Flight Operations provides air charter service primarily to industries located in upstate New York.

SHASTA BEVERAGES INC.
BEVPAK MANUFACTURING
P.O. Box 4617, Hayward CA 94540. 510/783-3200. **Physical address:** 26901 Industrial Boulevard, Hayward CA 94545. **Contact:** Human Resources Director. **Description:** A producer of a variety of regular and diet soft drinks. Bevpak Manufacturing (also at this location) bottles beverages produced by Shasta. **Common positions include:** Accountant/Auditor; Blue-Collar Worker Supervisor; Computer Programmer; Customer Service Representative; Financial Analyst; Manufacturer's/Wholesaler's Sales Rep.; Secretary; Systems Analyst. **Educational backgrounds include:** Business Administration; Finance. **Special programs:** Internships. **Corporate headquarters location:** This Location. **Parent company:** National Beverage.

SIMMONS FOODS
P.O. Box 430, Siloam Springs AR 72761. 501/524-8151. **Contact:** Roger Brune, Vice President of Human Resources. **World Wide Web address:** http://www.simmonsfoods.com. **Description:** A poultry processing company and producer of pet food. The company's service base includes fast food restaurants, retailers, school programs, and other food processing companies. **Common positions include:** Accountant; Agricultural Engineer; Automotive Mechanic; Blue-Collar Worker Supervisor; Clinical Lab Technician; Computer Programmer; Credit Manager; Department Manager; Dispatcher; Draftsperson; Electrician; Employment Interviewer; Financial Manager; Food Scientist/Technologist; General Manager; Heating/AC/Refrigeration Technician; Human Resources Manager; Industrial Engineer; Industrial Production Manager; Inspector/Tester/Grader; Management Trainee; Manufacturer's/Wholesaler's Sales Rep.; Market Research Analyst; Marketing Manager; Mechanical Engineer; Operations/Production Manager; Payroll Clerk; Postal Clerk/Mail Carrier; Purchasing Agent/Manager; Quality Control Supervisor; Receptionist; Secretary; Services Sales Rep.; Systems Analyst; Transportation/Traffic Specialist; Truck Driver; Typist/Word Processor; Veterinarian. **Educational backgrounds include:** Accounting; Agricultural Science; Business Administration; Communications; Computer Science; Engineering; Finance; Human Services; Marketing. **Benefits:** 401(k); Dental Insurance; Disability Coverage; Employee Discounts; Life Insurance; Medical Insurance; Profit Sharing; Savings Plan; Tuition Assistance. **Special programs:** Internships. **Corporate headquarters location:** This Location. **Other U.S. locations:** MO; OK.

SINTON DAIRY FOODS COMPANY, INC.
3801 North Sinton Road, Colorado Springs CO 80907. 719/633-3821. **Contact:** Personnel. **Description:** Processes dairy products.

SMITHFIELD FOODS INC.
200 Commerce Street, Smithfield VA 23430. 757/365-3000. **Contact:** Human Resources Manager. **Description:** Processes and packages pork. **Corporate headquarters location:** This Location. **Annual sales/revenues:** More than $100 million.
Other U.S. locations:
• Smithfield Packaging Company, 5801 Columbia Park Road, Landover MD 20785. 301/773-3322.

SNOWBALL FOODS, INC.
1051 Sykes Lane, Williamstown NJ 08094. 856/629-4081. **Contact:** Human Resources. **Description:** Engaged in poultry processing. **Common positions include:** Accountant/Auditor; Blue-Collar Worker Supervisor; Buyer; Customer Service Rep.; Food Scientist/Technologist; Human Resources Manager; Management Trainee; Manufacturer's/Wholesaler's Sales Rep.; Operations/Production Manager; Quality Control Supervisor; Transportation/Traffic Specialist. **Educational backgrounds include:** Accounting; Business Administration; Marketing. **Benefits:** 401(k); Dental Insurance; Life Insurance; Medical Insurance; Tuition Assistance. **Special programs:** Internships. **Corporate headquarters location:** This Location.

SOUTHERN PRIDE CATFISH COMPANY
P.O. Box 436, Greensboro AL 36744. 334/624-4021. **Fax:** 334/624-8224. **Contact:** Human Resources. **World Wide Web address:** http://www.southernpride.net. **Description:** A processor and distributor of processed catfish products. **Common positions include:** Accountant/Auditor; Agricultural Scientist; Clerical Supervisor; Credit Manager; Customer Service Rep.; General Manager; Human Resources Manager; Purchasing Agent/Manager; Quality Control Supervisor; Services Sales Rep. **Educational backgrounds include:** Accounting; Business Administration; Marketing. **Benefits:** Disability Coverage; Life Insurance; Medical Insurance; Savings Plan. **Corporate headquarters location:** This Location. **O**

STANDARD COMMERCIAL CORPORATION
P.O. Box 450, Wilson NC 27894. 252/291-5507. **Contact:** Human Resources Director. **Description:** Buys and processes a variety of tobaccos for sale to domestic and international makers of cigarettes, cigars, and pipe tobaccos in 85 countries. Standard Commercial Corporation also purchases, processes, and markets wool to international customers. The company operates three tobacco processing plants in the United States and 17 other plants throughout the world; and eight wool manufacturing and storage plants in eight countries. The company is also involved in importing-exporting in Eastern Europe and operates a building supply company. **Corporate headquarters location:** This Location.

STINSON SEAFOOD COMPANY
One Edward Street, Bath ME 04530. 207/963-7331. **Contact:** Human Resources Manager. **World Wide Web address:** http://www.ibgm.com/stinson. **Description:** Catches, processes, cans, packages, and ships sardines and sardine products. Plants also manufacture the aluminum cans used in packaging. The company's plants are located in Bath (not this location), Belfast, and Prospect Harbor. **Note:** Employment information is available at this location. **Corporate headquarters location:** This Location.

SUIZA FOODS
2515 McKinney Avenue, Suite 1200, Dallas TX 75201. 214/303-3400. **Fax:** 214/303-3499. **Contact:** Human Resources. **World Wide Web address:** http://www.suizafoods.com. **Description:** Manufactures and distributes fresh milk and related dairy products, shelf-stable and refrigerated food and beverage products, frozen food products, coffee, and plastic containers. **Corporate headquarters location:** This Location.

SUNDAY HOUSE FOODS INC.
P.O. Box 818, Fredericksburg TX 78624. 830/997-2136. **Contact:** Personnel Department. **Description:** Processes and sells turkey and ham. **Corporate headquarters location:** This Location.

SUNKIST GROWERS, INC.
P.O. Box 7888, Van Nuys CA 91409. 818/986-4800. **Contact:** Human Resources Manager. **World Wide Web address:** http://www.sunkist.com. **Description:** A citrus growing and processing firm, with additional operations in confections and soft drinks. **Corporate headquarters location:** This Location. **Other area locations:** Los Angeles CA. **International locations:** Ontario, Canada. **Subsidiaries include:** Fruit Growers Supply Company (also at this location).

SUNNYLAND, INC.
603 Cassidy Road, Thomasville GA 31792. 912/226-1611. **Contact:** Human Resources. **Description:** A food processor and distributor whose products include beef and pork. **Common positions include:** Accountant/Auditor; Blue-Collar Worker Supervisor; Computer Programmer; Credit Manager; Electrical/Electronics Engineer; Food Scientist/Technologist; General Manager; Human Resources Manager; Industrial Engineer; Management Trainee; Manufacturer's/Wholesaler's Sales Rep.; Marketing Specialist; Operations/ Production Manager; Purchasing Agent/Manager; Statistician; Transportation/Traffic Specialist. **Educational backgrounds include:** Accounting; Agricultural Science; Computer Science; Engineering; Finance; Food Science; Marketing. **Benefits:** Disability Coverage; Employee Discounts; Life Insurance; Medical Insurance; Pension Plan; Profit Sharing; Savings Plan; Tuition Assistance. **Corporate headquarters location:** This Location.

SUPERIOR COFFEE COMPANY
990 Supreme Drive, Bensenville IL 60106. 630/860-1400. **Contact:** Human Resources. **World Wide Web address:** http://www.superiorcoffee.com. **Description:** Produces and sells coffee, tea, salad dressings, syrups, and vending products. **Corporate headquarters location:** This Location. **Other U.S. locations:** Chicago IL; Elk Grove Village IL.

SUPREMA SPECIALTIES INC.
P.O. Box 280, Paterson NJ 07543. 973/684-2900. **Contact:** Employment Office. **Description:** Manufactures and markets a variety of premium gourmet natural cheese products from the U.S., Europe, and South America. Suprema Specialties' product line encompasses grated and shredded parmesan and pecorino romano cheeses, mozzarella and ricotta cheese products, low-fat versions of these products, and a provolone cheese. **Corporate headquarters location:** This Location.

SYLVEST FARMS OF GEORGIA
P.O. Box 489, Union City GA 30291. 404/766-0921. **Contact:** Director of Human Resources. **Description:** Engaged in poultry processing. **Corporate headquarters location:** This Location.

SYSCO CORPORATION
1390 Enclave Parkway, Houston TX 77077-2099. 281/584-1390. **Contact:** Personnel. **World Wide Web address:** http://www.sysco.com. **Description:** Engaged principally in the wholesale distribution of food and related products and services to the food service industry. Products include a full line of frozen foods. **Corporate headquarters location:** This Location.

SYSCO FOOD SERVICES
250 Wieboldt Drive, Des Plaines IL 60016. 847/699-5400. **Toll-free phone:** 800/767-8899. **Fax:** 847/699-6734. **Contact:** Human Resources Manager. **E-mail address:** rybicki.suzi.r024@ sysco.com. **World Wide Web address:** http://www. sysco.com. **Description:** Sells and distributes food service products through more than 65 locations nationwide. **NOTE:** Entry-level positions and second and third shifts are offered. **Common positions include:** Administrative Assistant; AS400 Programmer Analyst; Blue-Collar Worker Supervisor; Computer Operator; Computer Support Technician; Customer Service Representative; Help-Desk Technician; Network/Systems Administrator; Sales Representative. **Educational backgrounds include:** Accounting; Business Administration; Computer Science; Finance; Health Care; Marketing; Microsoft Office. **Benefits:** 401(k); Casual Dress - Fridays; Dental Insurance; Disability Coverage; Employee Discounts; Life Insurance; Medical Insurance; Pension Plan; Public Transit Available; Savings Plan; Sick Days; Vacation Days. **Corporate headquarters location:** Houston TX. **Other U.S. locations:** Nationwide.

TASTY BAKING COMPANY
2801 Hunting Park Avenue, Philadelphia PA 19129. 215/221-8500. **Contact:** Human Resources. **World Wide Web address:** http://www.tastykake.com. **Description:** Engaged in the manufacture and sale of a variety of small, single-portion cakes, pies, and cookies under the brand name Tastykake. The company offers approximately 45 different products. **Corporate headquarters location:** This Location.

TAYLOR PACKING COMPANY INC.
P.O. Box 188, Wyalusing PA 18853. 570/746-3000. **Fax:** 570/746-3888. **Contact:** Human Resources Manager. **E-mail address:** humanresources@ taylorpacking.com. **World Wide Web address:** http://www.taylorpacking.com. **Description:** This location is a beef processing plant. Overall, Taylor Packing Company is a multimillion-dollar operation capable of processing 1,800 cattle daily. Taylor Packing produces a complete line of vacuum-packaged, boxed beef cuts; custom-blended coarse ground beef; and fresh, vacuum-packed, and frozen variety meats for sale to supermarket chains, wholesalers, food-service distributors, institutions, and processed beef manufacturers. **NOTE:** Entry-level positions, part-time jobs and second and third shifts are offered. This location also hires seasonally. **Common positions include:** Accountant/Auditor; Biological Scientist; Blue-Collar Worker Supervisor; Claim Rep.; Computer Programmer; Credit Manager; Draftsperson; Electrical/Electronics Engineer; Electrician; Financial Analyst; General Manager; Industrial Engineer; Industrial Production Manager; Licensed Practical Nurse; Management Trainee; Operations/ Production Manager; Purchasing Agent/Manager; Quality Control Supervisor; Registered Nurse. **Educational backgrounds include:** Accounting; AS400 Certification; Biology; Computer Science; Engineering; Finance; Marketing; Novell; Software Tech. Support. **Benefits:** 401(k); Dental Insurance; Disability Coverage; Employee Discounts; Life

Insurance; Medical Insurance; Profit Sharing; Tuition Assistance. **Special programs:** Internships; Training; Summer Jobs. **Corporate headquarters location:** This Location. **Subsidiaries include:** Taylor By-Products, Inc. (also at this location) operates a modern rendering plant that produces tallow and protein meals for sale to feed companies, pet food manufacturers, and chemical processors.

TETLEY U.S.A., INC.
100 Commerce Drive, P.O. Box 856, Shelton CT 06484. 203/929-9200. **Contact:** Human Resources. **Description:** Manufactures and distributes beverage and food products under the Tetley, Martinson, Bustelo, Savarin, and Medaglia D'Oro labels. **Corporate headquarters location:** This Location.

TEUFEL NURSERIES INC.
12345 NW Barnes Road, Portland OR 97229. 503/646-1111. **Fax:** 503/646-1112. **Recorded jobline:** 503/643-8706. **Contact:** Human Resources Representative. **E-mail address:** tylers@teufel.com. **World Wide Web address:** http://www.teufel.com. **Description:** Engaged in nursery production, wholesale horticultural supplies, wholesale plant sales, and landscape construction. Founded in 1890. **NOTE:** Entry-level positions are offered. **Common positions include:** Account Manager; Account Rep.; Administrative Assistant; Blue-Collar Worker Supervisor; Buyer; Computer Operator; Computer Programmer; Construction Contractor; Controller; Database Manager; Finance Director; Human Resources Manager; Production Manager; Project Manager; Sales Rep.; Secretary; Systems Manager; Typist/Word Processor. **Educational backgrounds include:** Accounting; Business Administration. **Benefits:** 401(k); Daycare Assistance; Dental Insurance; Employee Discounts; Medical Insurance; Public Transit Available; Vision Insurance. **Special programs:** Internships; Training. **Corporate headquarters location:** This Location. **Other U.S. locations:** Seattle WA. L

TILAMOOK COUNTY CREAMERY ASSOC.
P.O. Box 313, Tilamook OR 97141. 503/842-4481. **Fax:** 503/842-6039. **Contact:** Human Resources Manager. **E-mail address:** tcca@oregonconst.com. **Description:** An area processor of a wide range of dairy and creamery products including butter, cheese, and milk. **Common positions include:** Accountant; Administrative Manager; Assistant Manager; Biological Scientist; Blue-Collar Worker Supervisor; Chief Financial Officer; Clerical Supervisor; Clinical Lab Technician; Computer Animator; Computer Programmer; Design Engineer; Draftsperson; Electrician; Emergency Medical Technician; Food Scientist/Technologist; General Manager; Manufacturing Engineer; Marketing Manager; MIS Specialist; Purchasing Agent/ Manager; Quality Control Supervisor; Sales Manager; Sales Rep.; Secretary; Systems Manager. **Educational backgrounds include:** Biology; Business Administration; Chemistry; Computer Science; Economics; Engineering. **Benefits:** 401(k); Dental Insurance; Disability Coverage; Life Insurance; Medical Insurance; Pension Plan; Tuition Assistance. **Corporate headquarters location:** This Location.

TIP TOP POULTRY INC.
P.O. Box 6338, Marietta GA 30065. 770/973-8070. **Contact:** Personnel. **Description:** Engaged in poultry processing and distributing. **Corporate headquarters location:** This Location.

TOM THUMB FOOD MARKETS, INC.
POLKA DOT DAIRY, INC.
110 East 17th Street, Hastings MN 55033. 651/437-9023. **Fax:** 651/438-2638. **Contact:** Human Resources. **Description:** Tom Thumb Food Markets operates an area grocery and convenience store chain. Polka Dot Dairy (also at this location) is a distributor of bottled milk. **Common positions include:** Management Trainee. **Educational backgrounds include:** Accounting; Business Administration; Economics; Finance; Marketing. **Benefits:** Dental Insurance; Disability Coverage; Life Insurance; Medical Insurance; Profit Sharing. **Corporate headquarters location:** This Location.

TOM'S FOODS
P.O. Box 60, Columbus GA 31902. 706/323-2721. **Contact:** Human Resources. **Description:** A nationwide manufacturer and distributor of a wide range of snack food products including potato chips, peanuts, candy, crackers, and bakery items. **Common positions include:** Computer Programmer; Financial Analyst; Food Scientist/ Technologist; Systems Analyst. **Educational backgrounds include:** Accounting; Business Administration. **Benefits:** 401(k); Dental Insurance; Disability Coverage; Employee Discounts; Life Insurance; Medical Insurance; Pension Plan; Profit Sharing; Savings Plan; Tuition Assistance. **Corporate headquarters location:** This Location. **Other U.S. locations:** CA; FL; TN; TX.

TOOTSIE ROLL INDUSTRIES, INC.
7401 South Cicero Avenue, Chicago IL 60629. 773/838-3400. **Contact:** Human Resources. **Description:** Manufactures and distributes candy, sold primarily under the Tootsie Roll brand name. The company also produces Cella's and Mason candies. Tootsie Roll Industries is one of the largest U.S. confectioners of lollipops sold mainly under the Charms and Blow-Pop brand names. **Corporate headquarters location:** This Location.

TOPPS COMPANY
One Whitehall Street, New York NY 10004. 212/376-0300. **Contact:** Personnel Department. **Description:** Internationally manufactures and markets a variety of chewing gum, candy, and other similar products. Topps also licenses its technology and trademarks and sells its chewing gum base and flavors to other overseas manufacturers. The company is best known for its internationally registered trademark Bazooka and its perennial Topps Baseball Bubble Gum picture cards. Topps is a leading marketer, under exclusive licenses, of collectible picture cards, albums, and stickers for baseball, football, and hockey. The company is also a leading producer and distributor of cards and stickers featuring pictures of popular motion picture, television, and cartoon characters, also under exclusive licenses. **Corporate headquarters location:** This Location. **Other U.S. locations:** Duryea PA. **International locations:** Ireland.

TRIARC BEVERAGE GROUP INTERNATIONAL
1000 Corporate Drive, 4th Floor, Fort Lauderdale FL 33334. 954/351-5621. **Contact:** Human Resources Department. **World Wide Web address:** http://www.triarc.com. **Description:** Manufactures soft drink concentrates and syrups. **Common positions include:** Accountant/Auditor; Administrative Manager; Attorney; Budget Analyst; Computer Programmer; Human Resources Manager; Systems Analyst. **Educational backgrounds include:** Accounting; Finance; Marketing. **Benefits:** 401(k); Dental Insurance; Disability Coverage; Life Insurance; Medical Insurance; Tuition Assistance. **Other U.S. locations:** La Mirada CA; White Plains NY; Cincinnati OH; Columbus OH. **Parent company:** Triarc Companies, Inc.

TRINIDAD/BENHAM CORPORATION
P.O. Box 22139, Denver CO 80222. 303/220-1400. **Contact:** Human Resources Manager. **Description:** Engaged in the warehousing, packaging, and wholesaling of dry beans and aluminum foil. **Common positions include:** Accountant; Accounting Clerk; Bookkeeper; Clerk; Computer Programmer; Customer Service Rep.; Human Resources Rep.; Operations/Production Manager; Sales Manager; Systems Analyst; Transportation/ Traffic Specialist. **Educational backgrounds include:** Accounting; Business Administration; Computer Science; Liberal Arts; Marketing. **Benefits:** 401(k); Disability Coverage; ESOP; Life Insurance; Medical Insurance; Tuition Assistance. **Corporate headquarters location:** This Location. **Other U.S. locations:** Chino CA; Murfreesboro TN; Mineola TX.

TROPICANA NORTH AMERICA
P.O. Box 338, Bradenton FL 34206. 941/747-4461. **Contact:** Professional Staffing. **World Wide Web address:** http://www.tropicana.com. **Description:** A leading producer and marketer of orange juice. **Common positions include:** Accountant/Auditor; Biological Scientist; Blue-Collar Worker Supervisor; Buyer; Chemical Engineer; Chemist; Computer Programmer; Draftsperson. **Educational backgrounds include:** Accounting; Biology; Business Administration; Chemistry; Computer Science; Engineering; Marketing. **Benefits:** Dental Insurance; Disability Coverage; Employee Discounts; Life Insurance; Medical Insurance; Pension Plan; Profit Sharing; Tuition Assistance. **Corporate headquarters location:** This Location. **Parent company:** The Seagram Company Ltd.

TUR-PAK FOODS, INC.
P.O. Box 116, Sioux City IA 51102. 712/277-8484. **Contact:** Human Resources. **Description:** A custom meat processing company. **Common positions include:** Blue-Collar Worker Supervisor; Chemist; Electrical/Electronics Engineer; Electrician; Food Scientist/Technologist; General Manager; Human Resources Manager; Mechanical Engineer; Operations/Production Manager; Quality Control Supervisor; Registered Nurse; Science Technologist; Stationary Engineer. **Educational backgrounds include:** Chemistry; Computer Science; Engineering. **Benefits:** Employee Discounts; Life Insurance; Medical Insurance; Tuition Assistance. **Corporate headquarters location:** This Location.

TUSCAN DAIRY FARM
750 Union Avenue, Union NJ 07083. 908/686-1500. **Contact:** Human Resources. **Description:** Produces and distributes milk and related products throughout northern New Jersey and adjacent areas. **Corporate headquarters location:** This Location.

TUSCAN/LEHIGH VALLEY DAIRIES, L.P.
880 Allentown Road, Lansdale PA 19446. 215/855-8205. **Toll-free phone:** 800/937-3233. **Fax:** 215/855-7858. **Contact:** Human Resources. **Description:** Engaged in the production of dairy products. **Common positions include:** Accountant/ Auditor; Branch Manager; Clerical Supervisor; Computer Programmer; Credit Manager; Electrician; Environmental Engineer; Financial Analyst; General Manager; Human Resources Manager; Industrial Production Manager; Manufacturer's/Wholesaler's Sales Rep.; Operations/ Production Manager; Purchasing Agent/Manager; Quality Control Supervisor; Systems Analyst. **Educational backgrounds include:** Accounting; Business Administration; Finance; Marketing. **Benefits:** 401(k); Dental Insurance; Disability Coverage; Life Insurance; Medical Insurance;

Pension Plan; Tuition Assistance. **Corporate headquarters location:** This Location. **Other U.S. locations:** Schuylkill Haven PA.

TYSON FOODS, INC.
P.O. Box 2020, Springdale AR 72765. 501/290-4000. **Physical address:** 2210 West Oaklawn Drive, Springdale AR 72762. **Contact:** Human Resources Director. **World Wide Web address:** http://www.tyson.com. **Description:** One of the world's largest fully-integrated producers, processors, and marketers of poultry products. The company also markets other food items including meats, seafood, and pork products. Tyson is involved in all stages of poultry production including genetic research, feeding mills, and veterinary services. Products are sold to hospitals, schools, airlines, retail stores, and wholesaling markets under the brand names Weaver, Tyson Holly Farms, Healthy Portion, Premium Pies, Complete Kits, Louis Kemp Crab, and Lobster Delights. **Corporate headquarters location:** This Location.

U.S. FOODSERVICE
9755 Patuxent Woods Drive, Columbia MD 21046. 410/712-7111. **Contact:** Human Resources Manager. **World Wide Web address:** http://www.usfoodservice.com. **Description:** Distributes food products, fresh meats, dairy products, and cleaning supplies to restaurants and other institutional food service establishments. **Corporate headquarters location:** This Location.
Other U.S. locations:
- 15155 Northam Street, La Mirada CA 90638. 714/670-3500.
- Contract and Design Division, 140 Morgan Drive, Norwood MA 02062. 781/551-3145.

UST
100 West Putnam Avenue, Greenwich CT 06830. 203/661-1100. **Fax:** 203/622-3626. **Contact:** Manager of Employee Relations. **Description:** A holding company whose subsidiaries produce and market moist, smokeless tobacco products. **Common positions include:** Accountant/Auditor; Budget Analyst; Buyer; Computer Programmer; Credit Manager; Customer Service Representative; Financial Analyst; Human Resources Manager; Paralegal; Purchasing Agent/Manager; Systems Analyst. **Educational backgrounds include:** Accounting; Business Administration; Finance; Marketing. **Benefits:** 401(k); Dental Insurance; Disability Coverage; Life Insurance; Medical Insurance; Pension Plan; Savings Plan; Tuition Assistance. **Special programs:** Internships. **Corporate headquarters location:** This Location. **Subsidiaries include:** International Wine & Spirits Ltd.; United States Tobacco Company; UST Enterprises Inc.; UST International Inc.

UNCLE BEN'S INC.
P.O. Box 1752, Houston TX 77251-1752. 713/674-9484. **Contact:** Human Resources Department. **Description:** A rice packager and distributor. **Corporate headquarters location:** This Location.

UNITED LIQUORS LTD.
One United Drive, West Bridgewater MA 02379. 617/323-0500. **Contact:** Personnel. **Description:** A beverage wholesaler. **Common positions include:** Accountant; Computer Programmer; Credit Clerk and Authorizer; Credit Manager; Customer Service Rep.; Data Entry Clerk; Payroll Clerk; Purchasing Agent/Manager; Systems Analyst. **Benefits:** 401(k); Credit Union; Dental Insurance; EAP; Employee Discounts; Medical Insurance; Pension Plan; Tuition Assistance; Vision Insurance. **Corporate headquarters location:** This Location.

UNITED STATES BAKERY

P.O. Box 14769, Portland OR 97293. 503/232-2191. **Contact:** Personnel. **Description:** A producer of baked goods including bread. **NOTE:** This company hires through the State of Oregon Employment Department, 30 North Webster, Suite E, Portland OR 97217. 503/280-6046. **Corporate headquarters location:** This Location.

UNITED STATES SUGAR CORPORATION

111 Ponce de Leon Avenue, Clewiston FL 33440. 941/983-8121. **Contact:** Personnel Officer. **World Wide Web address:** http://www.ussugar.com. **Description:** One of the nation's largest agricultural cooperatives, with primary interests in sugar and citrus. Founded in 1931. **Common positions include:** Accountant; Agricultural Engineer; Biological Scientist; Blue-Collar Worker Supervisor; Buyer; Chemical Engineer; Chemist; Claim Rep.; Computer Programmer; Department Manager; Electrical/Electronics Engineer; General Manager; Human Resources Manager; Industrial Engineer; Mechanical Engineer; Operations/Production Manager; Systems Analyst. **Educational backgrounds include:** Accounting; Biology; Business; Chemistry; Communications; Computer Science; Economics; Engineering; Finance. **Benefits:** Dental Insurance; Life Insurance; Medical Insurance; Pension Plan; Stock Option; Tuition Assistance. **Corporate headquarters location:** This Location.

UNIVERSAL CORPORATION

P.O. Box 25099, Richmond VA 23260. 804/359-9311. **Contact:** Human Resources. **World Wide Web address:** http://www.universalcorp.com. **Description:** An agricultural products holding company with interests primarily in tobacco through its subsidiary, Universal Leaf Company. Other subsidiaries are involved in coffee, tea, rubber, sunflower seeds, lumber, and building materials. The company's tobacco operations consist of selecting, buying, shipping, processing, packing, storing, and financing tobacco for manufacture and distribution. **Corporate headquarters location:** This Location.

UNIVERSAL FOODS CORPORATION

433 East Michigan Street, Milwaukee WI 53202. 414/271-6755. **Fax:** 414/347-4733. **Contact:** Manager of Employment and Development. **World Wide Web address:** http://www.ufoods.com. **Description:** A producer of food, dairy, and beverage flavors; food, drug, and cosmetic colors; dehydrated vegetables; and a line of yeast products and specialty by-products. **Common positions include:** Accountant/Auditor; Attorney; Chemical Engineer; Computer Programmer; Customer Service Representative; Employment Interviewer; Financial Manager; Food Scientist/Technologist; Heating/AC/Refrigeration Technician; Order Clerk; Payroll Clerk; Secretary; Systems Analyst. **Educational backgrounds include:** Accounting; Business Administration; Engineering; Finance; Food Science; Marketing. **Benefits:** 401(k); Dental Insurance; Disability Coverage; Life Insurance; Medical Insurance; Retirement Plan; Tuition Assistance. **Corporate headquarters location:** This Location. **Other U.S. locations:** Turlock CA; Indianapolis IN; St. Louis MO. **International locations:** Worldwide.

VERMONT PURE SPRINGS

P.O. Box C, Randolph VT 05060. 802/728-3600. **Contact:** Human Resources. **Description:** Bottles, markets, and distributes a full line of natural spring water products under the Vermont Pure and Vermont Hidden Spring brands. The company's product lines include seven bottle sizes and are sold primarily in the East and Midwest. **Corporate headquarters location:** This Location.

VIENNA BEEF LTD.

2501 North Damen Avenue, Chicago IL 60647. 773/278-7800. **Contact:** Mr. Jamie Eisenberg, Vice President of Personnel. **Description:** This location houses the corporate headquarters as well as a meat cutting plant. Overall, Vienna Beef Ltd. is an international distributor and processor of meat and sausage. **Common positions include:** Accountant/Auditor; Computer Programmer; Customer Service Rep.; Food Scientist/Technologist; Manufacturer's/Wholesaler's Sales Rep. **Educational backgrounds include:** Accounting; Business Administration; Computer Science. **Benefits:** Dental Insurance; Disability Coverage; Employee Discounts; Life Insurance; Medical Insurance; Pension Plan; Profit Sharing. **Corporate headquarters location:** This Location.

WLR FOODS

P.O. Box 7000, Broadway VA 22815. 540/896-7001. **Fax:** 540/896-0498. **Contact:** Human Resources. **World Wide Web address:** http://www.wlrfoods.com. **Description:** A fully-integrated poultry and turkey processor, marketer, and distributor. WLR Foods offers over 250 poultry and related products and operates processing plants and packaging facilities. **Corporate headquarters location:** This Location. **Subsidiaries include:** Rockingham Poultry, Inc. is an export company; Wampler Foods is a domestic poultry company.

WARDS COVE PACKING COMPANY INC.

88 East Hamlin Street, Seattle WA 98102. 206/323-3200. **Fax:** 206/323-9165. **Recorded jobline:** 206/325-4621. **Contact:** Personnel Department. **Description:** Operates seasonal salmon canneries in Alaska. Founded in 1912. **Corporate headquarters location:** This Location. **Other U.S. locations:** AK. **Parent company:** Wards Cove Packing. **Listed on:** Privately held.

THE WEETABIX COMPANY, INC.

20 Cameron Street, Clinton MA 01510. 978/368-0991. **Contact:** Human Resources. **Description:** A cereal manufacturer. **Common positions include:** Accountant; Blue-Collar Worker Supervisor; Buyer; Chemical Engineer; Credit Manager; Customer Service Rep.; Food Scientist/Technologist; Human Resources Manager; Manufacturer's/Wholesaler's Sales Rep.; Mechanical Engineer; Operations/Production Manager; Purchasing Agent/Manager; Quality Control Supervisor. **Educational backgrounds include:** Accounting; Biology; Business Administration; Chemistry; Engineering; Marketing. **Benefits:** Disability Coverage; Employee Discounts; Life Insurance; Medical Insurance; Pension Plan; Tuition Assistance. **Corporate headquarters location:** This Location.

WESTERN GROWERS ASSOCIATION

P.O. Box 2130, Newport Beach CA 92658. 949/863-1000. **Fax:** 949/863-9028. **Contact:** Human Resources. **Description:** An agricultural trade association providing services such as medical insurance, workers' compensation insurance, legal advice, and marketing services. Founded in 1926. **Common positions include:** Accountant/Auditor; Attorney; Claims Investigator; Clerical Supervisor; Computer Programmer; Customer Service Rep.; Medical Records Technician; Public Relations Specialist; Restaurant/Food Service Manager; Sales Executive; Systems Analyst; Technical Writer/Editor; Transportation/Traffic Specialist; Typist/Word Processor; Underwriter/Assistant Underwriter. **Educational backgrounds include:** Accounting. **Benefits:** 401(k); Daycare Assistance; Dental

Insurance; Disability Coverage; Employee Discounts; Life Insurance; Medical Insurance; Pension Plan. **Corporate headquarters location:** This Location.

WHITMAN GENERAL BOTTLERS

3501 Algonquin Road, Rolling Meadows IL 60008. 847/818-5000. **Contact:** Human Resources. **World Wide Web address:** http://www.whitmancorp.com. **Description:** This location houses administrative offices. Overall, Whitman Corporation is a holding company for diverse industrial interests including automotive and food and beverages. **Corporate headquarters location:** This Location. **Subsidiaries include:** Pepsi-Cola General Bottlers (also at this location) is a producer and distributor of soft drinks and nonalcoholic beverages in 12 states; Midas International provides automobile suspension systems, exhaust systems, and brake services through 2,525 outlets across the U.S.; and Hussmann Corporation manufactures refrigeration systems and related components for the food industry. **Listed on:** New York Stock Exchange.

WINDER DAIRY

P.O. Box 70009, West Valley City UT 84170. 801/969-3401. **Contact:** Personnel. **Description:** Produces a full range of dairy products for area distribution. **Corporate headquarters location:** This Location.

M.L. WISMER DISTRIBUTING CO. BUDWEISER

600 South Main Street, Baytown TX 77520. 281/427-7345. **Fax:** 281/422-6322. **Contact:** Human Resources Manager. **Description:** A Budweiser distribution center. **NOTE:** Entry-level positions and part-time jobs are offered. **Common positions include:** Attorney; Blue-Collar Worker Supervisor; Computer Operator; Controller; Customer Service Rep.e; General Manager; Human Resources Manager; Management Trainee; Sales Manager; Typist/Word Processor. **Benefits:** 401(k); Casual Dress - Daily; Dental Insurance; Life Insurance; Medical Insurance; Pension Plan; Vacation Days. **Special programs:** Summer Jobs. **Parent company:** Anheuser-Busch Companies is involved in the entertainment, brewing, baking, and manufacturing industries. The company is one of the largest domestic brewers, operating 13 breweries throughout the U.S. and distributing through over 900 independent wholesalers. Beer brands include Budweiser, Michelob, Busch, King Cobra, and O'Doul's. Related businesses include can manufacturing, paper printing, and barley malting. Anheuser-Busch Companies is also one of the largest operators of theme parks in the U.S., with locations in Florida, Virginia, Texas, Ohio, and California. Through subsidiary Campbell Taggart Inc., Anheuser-Busch is one of the largest commercial baking companies in the United States, producing foods under the Colonial brand name, among others. Anheuser-Busch Companies also has various real estate interests. **Listed on:** Privately held. **Annual sales/revenues:** $21 - $50 million.

WONDERBREAD/HOSTESS CAKES

80 East 62nd Avenue, Denver CO 80216. 303/428-7431. **Contact:** Human Resources. **Description:** A wholesale bakery which produces Wonderbread and Hostess snack cakes. **Corporate headquarters location:** Kansas City MO.

WONDERBREAD/HOSTESS CAKES

6301 North Broadway, St. Louis MO 63147. 314/385-1600. **Contact:** Personnel Department. **Description:** Manufactures bread, cake, and other bakery products. **Corporate headquarters location:** This Location.

WOODSTOCK BREWING INC.

P.O. Box 5021, Kingston NY 12402-5021. 914/331-2810. **Physical address:** 20 Saint James Street, Kingston NY 12401. **Contact:** Personnel. **Description:** A local beer brewing company.

WORLD'S FINEST CHOCOLATE

4801 South Lawndale Avenue, Chicago IL 60632. 773/847-4600. **Contact:** Human Resources. **World Wide Web address:** http://www.wfchocolate.com. **Description:** An international manufacturer of chocolate and cocoa products. **Corporate headquarters location:** This Location.

WM. WRIGLEY JR. COMPANY

410 North Michigan Avenue, Chicago IL 60611. 312/644-2121. **Fax:** 312/644-0353. **Contact:** Personnel Manager. **World Wide Web address:** http://www.wrigley.com. **Description:** One of the largest producers of chewing gum in the world. Brand name gums include Wrigley's Spearmint, Juicy Fruit, Big Red, Extra, and Freedent. **Common positions include:** Accountant/Auditor; Attorney; Chemist; Computer Programmer; Financial Analyst; Human Resources Manager; Mechanical Engineer; Systems Analyst. **Educational backgrounds include:** Accounting; Business; Chemistry; Computer Science; Engineering; Finance. **Benefits:** 401(k); Dental Insurance; Disability Coverage; Life Insurance; Medical Insurance; Pension Plan; Tuition Assistance. **Corporate headquarters location:** This Location. **Other U.S. locations:** GA; NJ. **International locations:** Worldwide. **Subsidiaries include:** Amurol Products Company manufactures and markets novelty chewing gum products; Northwestern Flavors, Inc. produces flavors and mint oil for Wrigley's gums and other food-related products; WRICO Packaging converts raw paper and carton stock into printed packaging materials used by the company; and L.A. Dreyfus manufactures chewing gum base.

YOUNG'S MARKET COMPANY, LLC

2164 North Batavia Street, Orange CA 92865. 714/283-4933. **Contact:** Director of Human Resources. **World Wide Web address:** http://www.youngsmarket.com. **Description:** A beer, wine, and spirits distributor. Founded in 1888. **Corporate headquarters location:** This Location. **Other U.S. locations:** AZ; CT; DC; FL; HI; MD; NY; PA; SC.

For more information on career opportunities in the food, beverage, and agriculture industries:

Associations

AMERICAN ASSOCIATION OF CEREAL CHEMISTS (AACC)

3340 Pilot Knob Road, St. Paul MN 55121. 651/454-7250. E-mail address: aacc@scisoc.org. World Wide Web address: http://www.scisoc.org/aacc. Dedicated to the dissemination of technical information and continuing education in cereal science.

AMERICAN CROP PROTECTION ASSOCIATION

1156 15th Street NW, Suite 400, Washington DC 20005. 202/296-1585. World Wide Web address: http://www.acpa.org.

AMERICAN FROZEN FOOD INSTITUTE

2000 Corporate Ridge, Suite 1000, McLean VA 22102. 703/821-0770. Fax: 703/821-1350. World

Wide Web address: http://www.affi.com. A national trade association representing the interests of the frozen food industry.

AMERICAN SOCIETY OF AGRICULTURAL ENGINEERS
2950 Niles Road, St. Joseph MI 49085-9659. 616/429-0300. World Wide Web address: http://www.asae.org.

AMERICAN SOCIETY OF BREWING CHEMISTS
3340 Pilot Knob Road, St. Paul MN 55121-2097. 651/454-7250. World Wide Web address: http://www.scisoc.org/asbc. Founded in 1934 to improve and bring uniformity to the brewing industry on a technical level.

CIES - THE FOOD BUSINESS FORUM
5549 Lee Highway, Arlington VA 22207. 703/534-8880. World Wide Web address: http://www.ciesnet.com. A global food business network. Membership is on a company basis. Members learn how to manage their businesses more effectively and gain access to information and contacts.

DAIRY MANAGEMENT, INC.
10255 West Higgins Road, Suite 900, Rosemont IL 60018. 847/803-2000. World Wide Web address: http://www.dairyinfo.com. A federation of state and regional dairy promotion organizations that develop and execute effective programs to increase consumer demand for U.S.-produced milk and dairy products.

INTERNATIONAL ASSOCIATION OF FOOD INDUSTRY SUPPLIERS
1451 Dolley Madison Boulevard, McLean VA 22101. 703/761-2600. Fax: 703/761-4334. Contact: Dorothy Brady. E-mail address: info@iafis.org. World Wide Web address: http://www.iafis.org. A trade association whose members are suppliers to the food, dairy, liquid processing, and related industries.

MASTER BREWERS ASSOCIATION OF THE AMERICAS (MBAA)
2421 North Mayfair Road, Suite 310, Wauwatosa WI 53226. 414/774-8558. World Wide Web address: http://www.mbaa.com. Promotes, advances, improves, and protects the professional interests of brew and malt house production and technical personnel. Disseminates technical and practical information.

NATIONAL BEER WHOLESALERS' ASSOCIATION
1100 South Washington Street, Alexandria VA 22314-4494. 703/683-4300. Fax: 703/683-8965. Contact: Karen Craig.

NATIONAL CATTLEMEN'S BEEF ASSOCIATION
P.O. Box 3469, Englewood CO 80155. 303/694-0305. World Wide Web address: http://www.beef.org. Operates to improve the economic, political, and social interests of the U.S. cattle industry.

NATIONAL FOOD PROCESSORS ASSOCIATION
1350 I Street NW, Suite 300, Washington DC 20005. 202/639-5900. World Wide Web address: http://www.nfpa-food.org.

NATIONAL SOFT DRINK ASSOCIATION
1101 16th Street NW, Washington DC 20036. 202/463-6732. World Wide Web address: http://www.nsda.org.

USA POULTRY AND EGG EXPORT COUNCIL
2300 West Park Place Boulevard, Suite 100, Stone Mountain GA 30087. 770/413-0006. Fax: 770/413-0007. E-mail address: info@usapeec.org. World Wide Web address: http://www.usapeec.org.

Directories

THOMAS FOOD INDUSTRY REGISTER
Thomas Publishing Company, Five Penn Plaza, New York NY 10001. 212/290-7341. World Wide Web address: http://www.tfir.com.

Magazines

FROZEN FOOD AGE
Bill Communications, 355 Park Avenue South, New York NY 10010-1789. 212/592-6200.

Online Servies

CHEFJOBSNETWORK
World Wide Web address: http://www.chefjobsnetwork.com. Posts job openings for chefs, pastry chefs, bakers, sous chefs, restaurant managers, and other foodservice positions. Members can register, free of charge, for a job search agent.

Health Care:
Services, Equipment, and Products

You can expect to find the following types of companies in this chapter:
Dental Labs and Equipment • Home Health Care Agencies • Hospitals and Medical Centers • Medical Equipment Manufacturers and Wholesalers • Offices and Clinics of Health Practitioners • Residential Treatment Centers/Nursing Homes Veterinary Services

Some helpful information: *Doctors earn an average of $150,000 annually, with large variations depending on specialty (general practitioners may earn less than $100,000, while some surgeons earn as much as $250,000 or more). Dentists' salaries average about $120,000. Entry-level workers in residential care and home health care generally earn approximately $22,000 - $25,000, with more experienced workers and managerial staff earning $30,000 - $40,000. Experienced veterinarians in private practice earn an average of $50,000 per year. Jobs in hospital administration generally begin at $50,000 for qualified candidates. Nurses' starting salaries range from $25,000 - $35,000, and experienced practitioners can earn as much as $60,000 annually (the average range, however, is $30,000 -$45,000).*

AFP IMAGING CORPORATION
250 Clearbrook Road, Elmsford NY 10523. 914/592-6100. **Fax:** 914/592-6148. **Contact:** Human Resources Manager. **World Wide Web address:** http://www.afpimaging.com. **Description:** AFP Imaging provides equipment utilized by radiologists, cardiologists, and other medical professionals for generating, recording, processing, and viewing hard copy diagnostic images. The company's products are applied in medical diagnostics X-ray inspection. Dental X-ray film processors and consumables are marketed internationally under the DENT-X brand name. **Corporate headquarters location:** This Location. **Subsidiaries include:** Regam Medical Systems International AB, Sundsvall, Sweden. **Listed on:** NASDAQ. **Stock exchange symbol:** AFPC.

ATL ULTRASOUND
P.O. Box 3003, Bothell WA 98041-3003. 425/487-7000. **Physical address:** 22100 Bothell Everett Highway, Bothell WA 98021. **Recorded jobline:** 425/487-7799. **Contact:** Human Resources. **E-mail address:** atljobs@atl.com. **World Wide Web address:** http://www.atl.com. **Description:** Engaged in the development and manufacture of medical diagnostic ultrasound systems. These systems serve a variety of uses in radiology, cardiology, obstetrics/gynecology, vascular, musculoskeletal, and intraoperative applications. Founded in 1969. **NOTE:** Second and third shifts are offered. Please call the jobline to obtain the specific job number before applying. **Common positions include:** Account Rep.; Accountant; Administrative Assistant; Buyer; Computer Operator; Computer Programmer; Customer Service Rep.; Electrical/ Electronics Engineer; Financial Analyst. **Educational backgrounds include:** Accounting; Business Administration; Computer Science; Engineering; Finance; Marketing. **Benefits:** 401(k); Dental Insurance; Disability Coverage; Life Insurance; Medical Insurance; Profit Sharing; Tuition Assistance. **Special programs:** Internships; Training. **Corporate headquarters location:** This Location. **Other U.S. locations:** Reedsville PA. **International locations:** Munich, Germany. **Subsidiaries include:** Echo; Interspec; NMS. **Listed on:** NASDAQ. **Stock exchange symbol:** ATLI. **Annual sales/revenues:** More than $100

million. **Number of employees at this location:** 1,750. **Number of employees nationwide:** 2,650.

ATS MEDICAL, INC.
3905 Annapolis Lane, Suite 105, Plymouth MN 55447. 763/553-7736. **Contact:** Human Resources. **World Wide Web address:** http://www. atsmedical.com. **Description:** Develops, manufactures, and markets medical devices including aortic valve graft prostheses, mechanical heart valves, and related cardiovascular devices. **Corporate headquarters location:** This Location. **Subsidiaries include:** ATS Medical, Ltd. (Glasgow, Scotland). **Listed on:** NASDAQ.

ABIOMED, INC.
22 Cherry Hill Drive, Danvers MA 01923. 978/777-5410. **Contact:** Human Resources. **World Wide Web address:** http://www.abiomed.com. **Description:** Develops, manufactures, and markets cardiovascular, medical, and dental products. The company is also engaged in the research and development of heart support systems. **Common positions include:** Account Manager; Biomedical Engineer; Buyer; Customer Service Representative; Electrical/Electronics Engineer; Industrial Engineer; Manufacturer's/Wholesaler's Sales Rep.; Mechanical Engineer. **Educational backgrounds include:** Business Administration; Engineering; Marketing. **Benefits:** Daycare Assistance; Dental Insurance; Disability Coverage; Life Insurance; Medical Insurance; Pension Plan; Profit Sharing; Stock Option; Tuition Assistance. **Corporate headquarters location:** This Location. **Subsidiaries include:** Abiodent; Abiomed Cardiovascular; Abiomed R&D. **Listed on:** NASDAQ. **Number of employees at this location:** 140. **Number of employees nationwide:** 170.

ACCESS HEALTH GROUP OF McKESSONHBOC
11020 White Rock Road, Rancho Cordova CA 95670. 916/576-4000. **Fax:** 916/852-3680. **Contact:** Human Resources. **World Wide Web address:** http://www.access-health.com. **Description:** Provides personal health management services to members and consumers through broadcast, telephone, and computer-based programs. Programs include health counseling and prevention

services. **Common positions include:** Account Manager; Administrative Assistant; Applications Engineer; Computer Operator; Computer Programmer; Database Manager; Market Research Analyst; Marketing Manager; Marketing Specialist; MIS Specialist; Public Relations Specialist; Registered Nurse; Secretary; Software Engineer; Systems Analyst; Systems Manager. **Educational backgrounds include:** Business Administration; Computer Science; Health Care; Liberal Arts; Marketing. **Benefits:** 401(k); Dental Insurance; Disability Coverage; Life Insurance; Medical Insurance; Tuition Assistance.

ACME UNITED CORPORATION
75 Kings Highway Cutoff, Fairfield CT 06430. 203/332-7330. **Fax:** 203/576-0007. **Contact:** Human Resources. **World Wide Web address:** http://www.acmeunited.com. **Description:** A holding company. **NOTE:** Please send resumes to Human Resources, P.O. Box 458, Fremont NC 27830. **Benefits:** Pension Plan; Profit Sharing. **Corporate headquarters location:** This Location. **Subsidiaries include:** Acme United Ltd. (England) manufactures medical scissors, household scissors and shears, nail files, and other manicure items. Acme United Limited (Canada) markets scissors, rulers, and yardsticks. Emil Schlemper GmbH (Germany) and Peter Altenbach and Son (Germany) both manufacture knives, scissors, shears, and manicure products. **Listed on:** American Stock Exchange. **Number of employees nationwide:** 570.

ACUSON
1220 Charleston Road, Mountain View CA 94043. 650/969-9112. **Toll-free phone:** 800/4AC-USON. **Fax:** 650/943-7006. **Recorded jobline:** 800/3AC-USON. **Contact:** Suzanne Suzuki, Employment Programs Specialist. **World Wide Web address:** http://www.acuson.com. **Description:** A manufacturer, marketer, and service provider of medical diagnostic ultrasound systems and image management products for hospitals, clinics, and private practice physicians throughout the world. Founded in 1979. **NOTE:** Entry-level positions are offered. **Common positions include:** Administrative Assistant; Applications Engineer; Computer Engineer; Customer Service Rep.; Database Administrator; Design Engineer; Electrical/Electronics Engineer; Financial Analyst; Human Resources Manager; Manufacturing Engineer; Mechanical Engineer; Sales Manager; Sales Rep.; Software Engineer; Systems Analyst; Systems Manager. **Educational backgrounds include:** C/C++; Computer Science; Engineering; HTML; Microsoft Word. **Benefits:** 401(k); Casual Dress - Daily; Dental Insurance; Disability Coverage; Employee Discounts; Financial Planning Assistance; Flexible Schedule; Life Insurance; Medical Insurance; Profit Sharing; Sabbatical Leave; Tuition Assistance. **Special programs:** Internships; Summer Jobs. **Corporate headquarters location:** This Location. **Listed on:** New York Stock Exchange. **Stock exchange symbol:** ACN. **CEO:** Samuel H. Maslak. **Facilities Manager:** Richard Sage. **Annual sales/revenues:** More than $100 million.

AFFILIATED HEALTH SERVICES
1415 East Kincaid Street, Mount Vernon WA 98273-1376. 360/428-2174. **Fax:** 360/428-2482. **Recorded jobline:** 360/416-8345. **Contact:** Human Resources. **World Wide Web address:** http://www.affiliatedhealth.org. **Description:** A nonprofit, regional health system offering a full line of medical services. Affiliated Health Services is comprised of Skagit Home Health, Skagit Valley Hospital, Skagit Valley Kidney Center, Stanwood Camano Medical Center, United General Hospital, Whatcom Hospice,

and Whatcom Visiting Nurses Home Health. **NOTE:** Part-time jobs and second and third shifts are offered. **Common positions include:** Accountant; Certified Nurses Aide; Certified Occupational Therapy Assistant; Claim Rep.; Customer Service Rep.; Dietician/Nutritionist; Electrical/Electronics Engineer; Emergency Medical Technician; Help-Desk Technician; Human Resources Manager; Industrial Engineer; Librarian; Licensed Practical Nurse; Medical Records Technician; Medical Secretary; Nuclear Medicine Technologist; Occupational Therapist; Pharmacist; Physical Therapist; Physical Therapy Assistant; Radiological Technologist; Recreational Therapist; Registered Nurse; Respiratory Therapist; Secretary; Social Worker; Speech-Language Pathologist; Structural Engineer; Surgical Technician; Webmaster. **Educational backgrounds include:** Accounting; Business Administration; Commercial Art; Engineering; Health Care; MBA. **Benefits:** Dental Insurance; Employee Discounts; Financial Planning Assistance; Life Insurance; Medical Insurance; Pension Plan; Tuition Assistance. **Corporate headquarters location:** This Location.

ALBUQUERQUE MANOR
500 Louisiana Boulevard NE, Albuquerque NM 87108. 505/255-1717. **Contact:** Carole Cambron, Human Resources Director. **World Wide Web address:** http://www.abqmanor.com. **Description:** One of New Mexico's largest and most progressive long-term nursing care facilities. Albuquerque Manor has an on-site medical clinic, pharmacy, and rehabilitative care center for physical, occupational, speech, and respiratory therapy. A child development center, which is open to the general public, offers an Intergenerational Program. Founded in 1986. **Common positions include:** Certified Nurses Aide; Licensed Practical Nurse; Registered Nurse. **Educational backgrounds include:** Health Care. **Benefits:** 401(k); Casual Dress - Fridays; Dental Insurance; Disability Coverage; Life Insurance; Medical Insurance; Tuition Assistance. **Internship information:** GN, GPN, and Social Services internships are available on a limited basis. **Listed on:** Privately held. **Number of employees at this location:** 350.

ALEXANDRIA ANIMAL HOSPITAL
2660 Duke Street, Alexandria VA 22314. 703/751-2022. **Fax:** 703/370-8049. **Contact:** Practice Manager. **Description:** An animal hospital for pets providing medical, dental, and surgical services. **Common positions include:** Receptionist; Veterinarian. **Benefits:** 401(k); Dental Insurance; Disability Coverage; Employee Discounts; Flexible Schedule; Life Insurance; Medical Insurance; Profit Sharing; Public Transit Available. **Number of employees at this location:** 100.

ALL CARE VISITING NURSE ASSOCIATION
16 City Hall Square, Lynn MA 01901. 781/598-2454x548. **Toll-free phone:** 800/287-2454. **Fax:** 781/586-1636. **Contact:** Nancy Glidden, Human Resources Representative. **World Wide Web address:** http://www.allcarevna.org. **Description:** A nonprofit, offers HIV/AIDS, mental health, pediatric, oncology, rehabilitation nursing, home nursing, and paraprofessional health care services. **NOTE:** Entry-level positions and second and third shifts are offered. **Common positions include:** Accountant; Administrative Assistant; Certified Nurses Aide; Home Health Aide; Licensed Practical Nurse; Occupational Therapist; Physical Therapist; Registered Nurse. **Educational backgrounds include:** Health Care. **Benefits:** 403(b); Dental Insurance; Disability Coverage; Employee Discounts; Life Insurance; Medical Insurance; Pension Plan; Public Transit Available; Tuition

Assistance; Wellness Program. **Special programs:** Training; Summer Jobs. **Office hours:** Monday - Friday, 8:00 a.m. - 5:00 p.m. **Corporate headquarters location:** This Location. **Subsidiaries include:** All Care Resources provides private-duty nurses and companion care to the elderly. **President/CEO:** Adele Hoffman. **Number of employees nationwide:** 650.

ALL METRO HEALTH CARE

50 Broadway, Lynbrook NY 11563. 516/887-1200. **Toll-free phone:** 800/225-1200. **Fax:** 516/593-2848. **Contact:** Phyllis Siliznol, Personnel Department. **E-mail address:** all-metro@aol.com. **Description:** A home health care provider. Plaza Domestic Agency and Caregivers on Call also operate out of this facility. Founded in 1955. **Common positions include:** Accountant; Branch Manager; Certified Nurses Aide; Chief Financial Officer; Clerical Supervisor; Computer Programmer; Computer Support Technician; Computer Technician; Controller; Customer Service Representative; Home Health Aide; Human Resources Manager; Licensed Practical Nurse; Marketing Manager; MIS Specialist; Nanny; Occupational Therapist; Physical Therapist; Purchasing Agent/Manager; Registered Nurse; Sales Manager; Sales Representative; Secretary. **Educational backgrounds include:** Accounting; Business Administration; Computer Science; Health Care. **Benefits:** 401(k); Casual Dress - Fridays; Disability Coverage; Flexible Schedule; Medical Insurance; Public Transit Available. **Office hours:** Sunday - Saturday, 8:30 a.m. - 8:30 p.m. **Corporate headquarters location:** This Location. **Other area locations:** Mount Vernon NY; New York NY. **Other U.S. locations:** FL; Saint Louis MO; NJ. **Listed on:** Privately held. **President:** Glenn Edwards. **Annual sales/revenues:** $21 - $50 million. **Number of employees at this location:** 2,000. **Number of employees nationwide:** 3,000.

ALLEGHENY VALLEY SCHOOL

1996 Ewings Mill Road, Coraopolis PA 15108. 412/299-7777. **Fax:** 412/299-6701. **Contact:** Richard R. Rizzutto, Director of Human Resources. **World Wide Web address:** http://trfn. clpgh.org/avs. **Description:** A nonprofit company that operates residential facilities for individuals with mental disabilities. Founded in 1960. **NOTE:** Entry-level positions, part-time jobs, and second and third shifts are offered. **Common positions include:** Administrative Assistant; Blue-Collar Worker Supervisor; Certified Nurses Aide; Licensed Practical Nurse; Medical Records Technician; Psychologist; Registered Nurse; Social Worker; Special Education Teacher; Speech-Language Pathologist; Typist/Word Processor. **Educational backgrounds include:** Education; Health Care; Microsoft Office; Microsoft Word; Spreadsheets. **Benefits:** 403(b); Casual Dress - Daily; Dental Insurance; Flexible Schedule; Job Sharing; Life Insurance; Medical Insurance; Pension Plan; Sick Days (11+); Vacation Days (10 - 20). **Corporate headquarters location:** This Location. **Executive Director:** Regis G. Champ. **Annual sales/revenues:** $51 - $100 million.

ALLEGIANCE HEALTHCARE CORP.

1430 Waukegan Road, McGaw Park IL 60085. 847/689-8410. **Contact:** Human Resources. **World Wide Web address:** http://www.allegiance.net. **Description:** A producer, developer, and distributor of medical products and technologies for use in hospitals and other health care settings. The company operates through two industry segments: medical specialties, and medical/laboratory products and distribution. **Corporate headquarters location:** This Location.

ALLIANCE IMAGING, INC.

1065 PacifiCenter Drive, Suite 200, Anaheim CA 92806. 714/688-7100. **Fax:** 714/688-3481. **Contact:** Christi Braun, Director of Human Resources. **World Wide Web address:** http://www. allianceimaging.com. **Description:** Provides medical diagnostic imaging services to hospitals, physicians, and patients. Services include MRI, Open-MRI, computed tomography (CT), ultrasound, and position emission tomography (PET). **Corporate headquarters location:** This Location. **Other U.S. locations:**
• 10521 Perry Highway, Suite 200, Wexford PA 15090. 724/933-3300.

ALLIED HEALTHCARE PRODUCTS, INC.

1720 Sublette Avenue, St. Louis MO 63110-1968. 314/771-2400. **Contact:** Human Resources. **World Wide Web address:** http://www.alliedhpi.com. **Description:** Manufactures respiratory products for both home health care and hospital use. Product lines include respiratory therapy equipment (respiratory care/anesthesia products and home respiratory care products); emergency medical products (respiratory/resuscitation products); and medical gas equipment (medical gas system construction products, medical gas system regulation devices, disposable oxygen and specialty gas cylinders, and portable suction equipment). **Common positions include:** Accountant/Auditor; Computer Programmer; Financial Analyst; Mechanical Engineer. **Corporate headquarters location:** This Location. **Number of employees at this location:** 830.

ALWAYS-CARE HOME HEALTH SERVICES

9312 Olive Boulevard, St. Louis MO 63130. 314/993-2274. **Fax:** 314/993-1196. **Contact:** Tracy Frischkorn, Director of Administration. **Description:** A home health care agency offering private duty nursing services, supplemental staffing, live-in companions, short-term respite, therapy services, social work, and in-home support services. Founded in 1976. **NOTE:** Entry-level positions and second and third shifts are offered. **Common positions include:** Certified Nurses Aide; Licensed Practical Nurse; Program Manager; Registered Nurse. **Educational backgrounds include:** Health Care. **Benefits:** Disability Coverage; Flexible Schedule; Life Insurance; Medical Insurance. **Special programs:** Summer Jobs. **Office hours:** Monday - Friday, 8:00 a.m. - 5:30 p.m. **Corporate headquarters location:** This Location. **Other area locations:** Hillsboro MO; St. Charles MO.

AMERICAN DENTAL ASSOCIATION

211 East Chicago Avenue, Chicago IL 60611. 312/440-2500. **Contact:** Danica Weyer, Manager of Recruiting. **World Wide Web address:** http://www.ada.org. **Description:** A professional association serving the dental community. **Common positions include:** Accountant; Attorney; Computer Programmer; Customer Service Rep.; Department Manager; Human Resources Manager; Purchasing Agent/Manager; Systems Analyst; Technical Writer/Editor. **Educational backgrounds include:** Accounting; Chemistry; Communications; Computer Science; Finance; Marketing. **Benefits:** Dental Insurance; Disability Coverage; Life Insurance; Medical Insurance; Pension Plan; Savings Plan; Tuition Assistance. **Corporate headquarters location:** This Location.

AMERICAN HEALTHCORP DIABETES TREATMENT CENTERS OF AMERICA

3841 Green Hills Village Drive, Nashville TN 37215. 615/665-1122. **Contact:** Rita Sailer, Senior Vice President of Human Resources. **Description:**

American Healthcorp, through its wholly-owned subsidiary, Diabetes Treatment Centers of America (also at this location), is one of the nation's leading providers of diabetes treatment services to physicians and hospitals. American Healthcorp created the business of hospital-based diabetes treatment centers in 1984 and has 63 centers in operation. Founded in 1981. **Common positions include:** Administrative Assistant; Database Administrator; Dietician/Nutritionist; Finance Director; Marketing Manager; Registered Nurse; SQL Programmer. **Educational backgrounds include:** Microsoft Word; Novell; Oracle; Visual Basic. **Benefits:** 401(k); Casual Dress - Daily; Dental Insurance; Life Insurance; Medical Insurance; Sick Days (11+); Tuition Assistance; Vacation Days (10 - 20). **Corporate headquarters location:** This Location. **Subsidiaries include:** ArthritisCare Centers of America operates two comprehensive treatment centers for individuals with arthritis. **Listed on:** NASDAQ. **Stock exchange symbol:** AMHC. **CEO:** Tom Cigarran. **Number of employees at this location:** 80. **Number of employees nationwide:** 650.

AMERICAN MEDICAL RESPONSE (AMR)
4 Tech Circle, Natick MA 01760. 508/650-5600. **Toll-free phone:** 800/950-9266. **Fax:** 508/650-5656. **Contact:** Stephani Gramaglia, Human Resources Department. **Description:** Provides emergency medical transportation. **Common positions include:** EKG Technician; Emergency Medical Technician. **Benefits:** 401(k); Dental Insurance; Life Insurance; Medical Insurance; Tuition Assistance. **Other U.S. locations:** Nationwide. **Listed on:** New York Stock Exchange.

AMERICAN MEDICAL SYSTEMS
10700 Bren Road West, Minnetonka MN 55343. 952/933-4666. **Contact:** Human Resources. **World Wide Web address:** http://www.visitams.com. **Description:** Manufactures and distributes medical devices for the diagnosis and treatment of a variety of illnesses including prostate disease, severe fecal incontinence, and urethral strictures, and urinary incontinence. **Common positions include:** Administrator; Biomedical Engineer; Buyer; Customer Service Rep.; Mechanical Engineer.

AMERICAN PSYCHOLOGICAL ASSOCIATION (APA)
750 First Street NE, Washington DC 20002. 202/336-5500. **Contact:** Human Resources. **World Wide Web address:** http://www.apa.org. **Description:** Works to advance psychology as a science, a profession, and a means of promoting human welfare. The association has divisions in 49 subfields of psychology and affiliations with 57 state and Canadian provincial associations. Membership includes more than 159,000 researchers, educators, clinicians, and students. **Common positions include:** Accountant; Administrative Assistant; Computer Programmer; Customer Service Rep.; Lobbyist; Marketing Specialist; Receptionist; Secretary; Typist/Word Processor. **Educational backgrounds include:** Accounting; Business Administration; Communications; Computer Science; Finance; Liberal Arts; Marketing; Psychology. **Benefits:** Dental Insurance; Disability Coverage; Life Insurance; Medical Insurance; Reimbursement Accounts; Retirement Plan. **Corporate headquarters location:** This Location. **Number of employees at this location:** 500.

AMERICAN STANDARD COMPANIES INC.
One Centennial Avenue, Piscataway NJ 08855. 732/980-6000. **Contact:** Human Resources. **World Wide Web address:** http://www. americanstandard.com. **Description:** A global, diversified manufacturer. The company's operations are comprised of four segments: air conditioning products, plumbing products, automotive products, and medical systems. The air conditioning products segment (through subsidiary The Trane Company) develops and manufactures Trane and American Standard air conditioning equipment for use in central air conditioning systems for commercial, institutional, and residential buildings. The plumbing products segment develops and manufactures American Standard, Ideal Standard, Porcher, Armitage Shanks, Dolomite, and Standard bathroom and kitchen fixtures and fittings. The automotive products segment develops and manufactures truck, bus, and utility vehicle braking and control systems under the WABCO and Perrot brands. The medical systems segment manufactures Copalis, DiaSorin, and Pylori-Chek medical diagnostic products and systems for a variety of diseases including HIV, osteoporosis, and renal disease. **Corporate headquarters location:** This Location. **International locations:** Worldwide. **Listed on:** New York Stock Exchange. **Stock exchange symbol:** ASD. **Chairman/CEO:** Frederic M. Poses.

ANCILLA SYSTEMS, INC.
1000 South Lake Park Avenue, Hobart IN 46342. 219/947-8500. **Contact:** Ms. Toni Mola, Vice President of Human Resources. **Description:** A multi-institutional, nonprofit health care corporation. Ancilla Systems is sponsored by the Poor Handmaids of Jesus Christ. The company operates seven hospitals in Illinois and Indiana, a home health care affiliate, and a community hospital. Founded in 1857. **Common positions include:** Accountant; Administrative Assistant; Chief Financial Officer; Computer Operator; Computer Programmer; Controller; EEG Technologist; EKG Technician; Finance Director; Financial Analyst; Human Resources Manager; Pharmacist; Physical Therapist; Physician; Public Relations Specialist; Radiological Technologist; Registered Nurse; Respiratory Therapist; Secretary; Social Worker; Surgical Technician; Systems Analyst. **Educational backgrounds include:** Accounting; Business Administration; Computer Science; Finance; Health Care. **Benefits:** 401(k); 403(b); Dental Insurance; Disability Coverage; Employee Discounts; Life Insurance; Medical Insurance; Pension Plan; Tuition Assistance. **Corporate headquarters location:** This Location. **Subsidiaries include:** Harbor Health Services, Inc.; Lakeshore Health Systems Incorporated; Michiana Community Hospital, Inc.; St. Elizabeth's Hospital of Chicago, Inc.; St. Joseph Medical Center of Fort Wayne; St. Joseph Mishawaka Health Services, Inc.; St. Mary's Hospital of East St. Louis, Inc. **Listed on:** Privately held. **Number of employees at this location:** 135.

M.D. ANDERSON CANCER CENTER
1100 Holcombe Boulevard, Houston TX 77030. 713/792-8002. **Fax:** 713/794-5951. **Recorded jobline:** 713/792-8010. **Contact:** Human Resources. **World Wide Web address:** http://www. mdacc.tmc.edu. **Description:** Works to eliminate cancer and allied diseases by developing and maintaining integrated quality programs in patient care, research, education, and prevention. **NOTE:** Entry-level positions are offered. **Common positions include:** Accountant/Auditor; Biological Scientist; Budget Analyst; Chemist; Claim Representative; Computer Programmer; Customer Service Representative; Dietician/Nutritionist; Editor; Education Administrator; Financial Analyst; General Manager; Health Services Manager; Human Resources Manager; Licensed Practical Nurse;

Management Analyst/Consultant; Medical Records Technician; Occupational Therapist; Pharmacist; Physical Therapist; Preschool Worker; Quality Control Supervisor; Registered Nurse; Respiratory Therapist; Social Worker; Software Engineer; Systems Analyst; Typist/Word Processor. **Educational backgrounds include:** Business Administration; Computer Science; Finance; Health Care; Nursing. **Benefits:** Dental Insurance; Disability Coverage; Employee Discounts; Life Insurance; Medical Insurance; On-Site Daycare; Pension Plan; Public Transit Available; Tuition Assistance. **Special programs:** Training. **Corporate headquarters location:** This Location. **Parent company:** The University of Texas System. **Number of employees at this location:** 7,500.

APRIA HEALTHCARE GROUP INC.
3560 Hyland Avenue, Costa Mesa CA 92626. 714/427-2000. **Contact:** Human Resources. **Description:** Provides a broad range of respiratory therapy services, home medical equipment, and infusion therapy services. Apria Healthcare Group's home health care services are provided to patients who have been discharged from hospitals, skilled nursing facilities, or convalescent homes and are being treated at home. In conjunction with medical professionals, Apria personnel deliver, install, and service medical equipment, as well as provide appropriate therapies and coordinate plans of care for their patients. Apria personnel also instruct patients and care-givers in the correct use of equipment and monitor the equipment's effectiveness. Patients and their families receive training from registered nurses and respiratory therapy professionals concerning the therapy administered including instruction in proper infusion technique and the care and use of equipment and supplies. **Common positions include:** Accountant/Auditor; Attorney; Branch Manager; Buyer; Computer Programmer; Financial Analyst; Human Resources Manager; MIS Specialist; Paralegal; Pharmacist; Registered Nurse; Respiratory Therapist; Systems Analyst; Telecommunications Manager. **Educational backgrounds include:** Accounting; Computer Science; Finance; Health Care; Marketing. **Benefits:** 401(k); Dental Insurance; Disability Coverage; Employee Discounts; Life Insurance; Medical Insurance; Savings Plan; Tuition Assistance. **Corporate headquarters location:** This Location. **Other U.S. locations:** Nationwide. **International locations:** United Kingdom.

ARBOUR SENIOR CARE & COUNSELING SERVICES
100 Ledgewood Place, Suite 202, Rockland MA 02370. 781/871-6550. **Contact:** Human Resources. **Description:** Provides behavioral health services delivered by mobile multidisciplinary teams of clinicians at outpatient service sites. The company offers therapeutic, psychiatric, neurologic, and diagnostic imaging services. **Corporate headquarters location:** This Location. **Number of employees at this location:** 100.

JOHN D. ARCHBOLD MEMORIAL HOSPITAL
915 Gordon Avenue, Thomasville GA 31792. 912/228-2000. **Contact:** Employment Manager. **Description:** A 265-bed, regional trauma center serving the southwest region of Georgia. **Common positions include:** Accountant/Auditor; Biomedical Engineer; Clinical Lab Technician; Computer Programmer; Counselor; Dietician/Nutritionist; EEG Technologist; EKG Technician; Emergency Medical Technician; Health Services Manager; Human Resources Manager; Human Service Worker; Licensed Practical Nurse; Medical Records Technician; Nuclear Medicine Technologist;

Occupational Therapist; Pharmacist; Physical Therapist; Physician; Physicist; Systems Analyst. **Educational backgrounds include:** Health Care. **Benefits:** 401(k); Dental Insurance; Disability Coverage; Employee Discounts; Life Insurance; Medical Insurance; Pension Plan; Recruiting Incentive; Relocation Assistance; Savings Plan; Tuition Assistance. **Special programs:** Internships. **Corporate headquarters location:** This Location. **Subsidiaries include:** Brooks County Hospital; Grady General Hospital; Mitchell County Hospital. **Listed on:** Privately held. **Number of employees at this location:** 1,400. **Number of employees nationwide:** 2,200.

ARKANSAS CHILDREN'S HOSPITAL
1821 West Maryland, Little Rock AR 72202-3591. 501/320-1100. **Toll-free phone:** 800/844-1891. **Fax:** 501/320-3499. **Contact:** Human Resources. **World Wide Web address:** http://www. archildrens.org. **Description:** One of the largest pediatric medical centers in the United States. The hospital also supports the Arkansas Children's Hospital Research Institute, a nutrition research center. Through a partnership with the University of Arkansas for Medical Sciences, the hospital is the site of pediatric training for medical and nursing students, post-doctoral residents, and paramedical professionals. Service areas include emergency care including a Level I Trauma Center, the Cecil and Alice Peason Emergency Department, and Angel One, a state-of-the-art intensive care transport system; acute care including intensive care, dialysis, and treatment of pediatric cancer; life care including asthma care, an epilepsy clinic, and a lung center; and community care including the KIDS FIRST program and the Home Instruction for Preschool Youngsters program. **Common positions include:** Accountant; Certified Nurses Aide; Claim Rep.; Computer Operator; Database Administrator; EEG Technologist; Electrician; Medical Assistant; Medical Records Technician; Medical Secretary; Pharmacist; Preschool Worker; Radiological Technologist; Registered Nurse; Respiratory Therapist; Secretary; Social Worker; Special Education Teacher; Surgical Technician; Systems Analyst; Typist/Word Processor. **Educational backgrounds include:** Accounting; Computer Science; Education; Health Care. **Benefits:** 403(b); Dental Insurance; Disability Coverage; Employee Discounts; Life Insurance; Medical Insurance; On-Site Daycare; Tuition Assistance.

ARLINGTON HOSPITAL
1701 North George Mason Drive, Arlington VA 22205. 703/558-5000. **Contact:** Ms. Lori Wallace, Employment Coordinator. **World Wide Web address:** http://www.arlingtonhospital.com. **Description:** A full-service, nonprofit, tertiary care facility. Arlington Hospital operates outpatient clinics, a cancer center, and a cardiac unit.

THE AROOSTOOK MEDICAL CENTER
P.O. Box 151, Presque Isle ME 04769. 207/768-4000. **Fax:** 207/768-4252. **Contact:** Debbie Kierstead, Employment Coordinator. **World Wide Web address:** http://www.tamc.org. **Description:** A 212-bed, tri-campus facility located in northern Maine. The center is a nonprofit organization and offers a wide range of services. Founded in 1912. **NOTE:** Entry-level positions, part-time jobs, and second and third shifts are offered. **Common positions include:** Accountant; Administrative Assistant; AS400 Programmer Analyst; Budget Analyst; Certified Nurses Aide; Certified Occupational Therapy Assistant; Chief Financial Officer; Claim Representative; Clerical Supervisor; Computer Operator; Computer Programmer; Controller; Customer Service Representative;

Dietician/Nutritionist; EEG Technologist; EKG Technician; Emergency Medical Technician; General Manager; Human Resources Manager; Librarian; Licensed Practical Nurse; Medical Records Technician; MIS Specialist; Network Administrator; Nuclear Medicine Technologist; Nurse Practitioner; Occupational Therapist; Pharmacist; Physical Therapist; Physical Therapy Assistant; Physician; Project Manager; Public Relations Specialist; Purchasing Agent/Manager; Quality Control Supervisor; Radiological Technologist; Registered Nurse; Respiratory Therapist; Secretary; Social Worker; Surgical Technician; Systems Analyst. **Educational backgrounds include:** Accounting; AS400 Certification; Business Administration; Communications; Computer Science; Finance; Health Care; Nutrition; Public Relations. **Benefits:** 403(b); Dental Insurance; Disability Coverage; Employee Discounts; Flexible Schedule; Life Insurance; Medical Insurance; Pension Plan; Tuition Assistance.

ARRHYTHMIA RESEARCH TECHNOLOGY
1101 South Capital of Texas Highway, Building G, Suite 200, Austin TX 78746. 512/347-9640. **Fax:** 512/347-9649. **Contact:** Human Resources. **World Wide Web address:** http://www.arthrt.com. **Description:** Engaged in the marketing and manufacturing of computerized medical instruments which acquire data and analyze the electrical impulses of the heart in order to detect and aid in the treatment of potentially lethal arrhythmias. Arrhythmia Research Technology, Inc. markets a variety of products including the 1200 EPX, a specialized high-resolution electrocardiographic (ECG) system; the LP-Pac Q, a less expensive high-resolution ECG system which acquires, digitizes, and averages cardiac signals; the PREDICTOR I, a personal computer-based signal averaging system; CardioMapp, a computerized cardiac mapping system used during open heart surgery to assist surgeons in locating and treating electrical malfunctions of the heart; and CardioLab, a computerized recording and analysis system. **Corporate headquarters location:** This Location.

ARROW INTERNATIONAL INC.
P.O. Box 12888, Reading PA 19612. 610/378-0131. **Fax:** 610/478-3194. **Contact:** Steve Bell, Staffing Manager. **World Wide Web address:** http://www.arrowintl.com. **Description:** Develops, manufactures, and markets central vascular access catheterization products. Arrow International's products are also used for patient monitoring, diagnosis, pain management, and treating patients with heart and vascular disease. **Common positions include:** Mechanical Engineer. **Educational backgrounds include:** Engineering. **Benefits:** 401(k); Dental Insurance; Disability Coverage; Life Insurance; Medical Insurance; Pension Plan; Profit Sharing; Tuition Assistance. **Corporate headquarters location:** This Location. **Other U.S. locations:** NC; NJ. **Listed on:** NASDAQ. **Number of employees nationwide:** 1,540.

ASK...FOR HOME CARE
P.O. Box 886, 11 Union Street, Rockland ME 04864. 207/594-8418. **Fax:** 207/594-9090. **Contact:** Joanne Miller, Administrator. **Description:** A home health care agency. **Common positions include:** Certified Nurses Aide.

ASO CORPORATION
300 Sarasota Center Boulevard, Sarasota FL 34240. 941/379-0300. **Fax:** 941/378-9040. **Contact:** Human Resources. **E-mail address:** asocorp@ aol.com. **World Wide Web address:** http://www. asocorp.com. **Description:** A manufacturer and distributor of wound care products. **NOTE:** Second and third shifts are offered. **Common positions include:** Account Manager; Accountant; Administrative Assistant; Blue-Collar Worker Supervisor; Buyer; Chief Financial Officer; Computer Programmer; Controller; Credit Manager; Customer Service Representative; Human Resources Manager; Marketing Manager; MIS Specialist; Purchasing Agent/Manager; Quality Control Supervisor; Sales Executive; Sales Manager; Secretary; Systems Analyst; Technical Writer/Editor; Typist/Word Processor. **Educational backgrounds include:** Business Administration. **Benefits:** 401(k); Dental Insurance; Disability Coverage; Employee Discounts; Life Insurance; Medical Insurance; Public Transit Available. **Corporate headquarters location:** This Location. **Subsidiaries include:** Aso Pharmaceutical Co., Ltd., Kumamoto, Japan; Aso Seiyaku Philippines, Inc., Cebu, Philippines; Texas Aso Corporation, El Paso TX. **Parent company:** Aso International. **Listed on:** Privately held. **Number of employees at this location:** 100.

ASPEN COMMUNITY SERVICES
17100 Pioneer Boulevard, Suite 300, Cerritos CA 90701-2709. 562/467-5536. **Fax:** 562/468-4407. **Contact:** Human Resources. **Description:** Provides outpatient mental health services for children and adolescents.

ASSISTED LIVING CONCEPTS, INC.
11835 NE Glen Widing Drive, Building E, Portland OR 97220. 503/252-6233. **Fax:** 503/252-6597. **Contact:** Human Resources. **Description:** Owns, operates, and develops assisted living facilities for elderly persons. The company also provides personal care and support services. **Common positions include:** Construction Contractor; Operations/Production Manager; Typist/Word Processor. **Educational backgrounds include:** Accounting; Business Administration; Health Care. **Benefits:** Dental Insurance; Disability Coverage; Life Insurance; Medical Insurance. **Corporate headquarters location:** This Location. **Other U.S. locations:** Nationwide. **Operations at this facility include:** Administration; Regional Headquarters; Service. **Listed on:** American Stock Exchange.

AURORA HEALTH CARE
3307 West Flores Home Avenue, Milwaukee WI 53234. 414/647-3000. **Contact:** Employment Office. **World Wide Web address:** http://www. aurorahealthcare.org. **Description:** Owns and operates several hospitals, medical groups, and walk-in clinics. Aurora Health Care is one of the largest health care corporations in Wisconsin. **Corporate headquarters location:** This Location.

AURORA HEALTHCARE, INC.
3737 Lawton, Detroit MI 48208. 313/361-7600. **Fax:** 313/361-7960. **Contact:** Twanda Booker, Director of Human Resources. **E-mail address:** tbooker@psy-med.com. **World Wide Web address:** http://www.aurorahealthcare.org. **Description:** An adult, nonprofit, outpatient, community clinic offering 24-hour crisis intervention; family, group, and individual therapy; and psychiatric assessments and referrals. **NOTE:** Part-time jobs and second and third shifts are offered. **Common positions include:** Administrative Assistant; Certified Occupational Therapy Assistant; Dietician/Nutritionist; Librarian; Medical Records Technician; Occupational Therapist; Registered Nurse; Secretary; Social Worker; Teacher/Professor. **Benefits:** 403(b); Dental Insurance; Disability Coverage; Life Insurance; Medical Insurance; Tuition Assistance. **Corporate headquarters location:** Redford MI.

CEO: Ervin Johnson, Jr. **Annual sales/revenues:** $5 - $10 million. **Number of employees at this location:** 430.

AXELGAARD MANUFACTURING CO.
329 West Aviation Road, Fallbrook CA 92028. 760/728-3424. **Fax:** 760/728-3467. **Contact:** Human Resources Manager. **World Wide Web address:** http://www.axelgaard.com. **Description:** Manufactures electrodes for neurosimulation. **Common positions include:** Accountant; Administrative Assistant; Applications Engineer; Blue-Collar Worker Supervisor; Chemist; Chief Financial Officer; Controller; Customer Service Rep.; Database Manager; Design Engineer; Electrical/Electronics Engineer; Financial Analyst; Human Resources Manager; Manufacturing Engineer; Marketing Manager; Mechanical Engineer; MIS Specialist; Production Manager; Purchasing Agent/Manager; Sales Manager; Secretary; Transportation/Traffic Specialist. **Educational backgrounds include:** Engineering. **Benefits:** 401(k); Dental Insurance; Disability Coverage; Life Insurance; Medical Insurance; Profit Sharing; Tuition Assistance.

BALLARD MEDICAL PRODUCTS
12050 Lone Peak Parkway, Draper UT 84020. 801/572-6800. **Contact:** Joe Reker, Human Resources. **World Wide Web address:** http://www.bmed.com. **Description:** Manufactures a wide variety of medical products used in intensive care units, emergency rooms, gastrointestinal and radiology procedure rooms, main operating rooms, burn units, and outpatient/satellite surgical centers. **Corporate headquarters location:** This Location. **Subsidiaries include:** Medical Innovations Corp. **Number of employees nationwide:** 700.

BANNER HEALTH SYSTEMS
4310 17th Avenue SW, Fargo ND 58103. 701/277-7500. **Contact:** Human Resources. **World Wide Web address:** http://www.bannerhealth.com **Description:** This location provides facilities with direct support in the areas of accounting, audit services, finance, operations management (aging services, hospitals, home care, clinics), marketing/planning, risk and quality management, physician recruitment, service bureau, computer information systems, payroll, field innovation, human resources (employee relations, benefits, compensation, communications), materials management, and legal services. Overall, Banner Health Systems is a nonprofit health care system which operates hospitals, nursing homes, and clinics, and provides home care and other services in primarily rural communities across 14 states. **Corporate headquarters location:** This Location. **Number of employees at this location:** 180. **Number of employees nationwide:** 11,000.

BAPTIST HEALTH SYSTEM
P.O. Box 1788, Knoxville TN 37901. 865/632-5936. **Fax:** 865/632-5223. **Recorded jobline:** 865/632-5977. **Contact:** Human Resources. **World Wide Web address:** http://www.bhset.org. **Description:** Operates Baptist Hospital, Baptist Eye Institute, and the Baptist Regional Cancer Center. Baptist Hospital is a 438-bed, acute care hospital offering services in a variety of specialties including cardiac care, eye care, cancer care, neurosciences, and medical/surgical care. The hospital provides a comprehensive cardiac program which includes angioplasty, open heart surgery, and cardiac rehabilitation. The Baptist Eye Institute is one of the region's first facilities devoted exclusively to eye care. The Baptist Regional Cancer Center is accredited by the American College of Surgeons as a Comprehensive Community Cancer Center

offering both inpatient and outpatient facilities. Founded in 1948. **Common positions include:** Accountant; Computer Programmer; Dietician/ Nutritionist; Emergency Medical Technician; Financial Analyst; Licensed Practical Nurse; Medical Records Technician; MIS Specialist; Nuclear Medicine Technologist; Occupational Therapist; Pharmacist; Physical Therapist; Physician; Purchasing Agent/Manager; Registered Nurse; Respiratory Therapist; Social Worker; Speech-Language Pathologist; Surgical Technician; Systems Analyst; Telecommunications Manager. **Educational backgrounds include:** Accounting; Computer Science; Health Care. **Benefits:** 401(k); 403(b); Daycare Assistance; Dental Insurance; Disability Coverage; Employee Discounts; Life Insurance; Medical Insurance; Pension Plan; Savings Plan; Tuition Assistance; Vision Plan. **Corporate headquarters location:** This Location. **Subsidiaries include:** Home Care East. **Annual sales/revenues:** $5 - $10 million. **Number of employees at this location:** 2,200.

BAPTIST HEALTHCARE SYSTEM
4007 Kresge Way, Louisville KY 40207. 502/896-5000. **Fax:** 502/896-5097. **Contact:** Rob Gamage, Human Resources. **E-mail address:** recruiter@ bhsi.com. **World Wide Web address:** http://www. bhsi.com. **Description:** Baptist Healthcare System is one of the largest, nonprofit health care systems in Kentucky, with acute care hospitals in Louisville, Paducah, Lexington, Corbin, and La Grange. The system has over 1,500 licensed beds. Baptist Healthcare System is comprised of Baptist Hospital East, Western Baptist Hospital, Central Baptist Hospital, Baptist Regional Medical Center, and Tri-County Baptist Hospital. **Corporate headquarters location:** This Location. **Number of employees nationwide:** 6,700.

BARBERTON CITIZENS HOSPITAL
155 Fifth Street NE, Barberton OH 44203. 330/745-1611. **Fax:** 330/848-7833. **Recorded jobline:** 330/848-7777. **Contact:** Human Resources. **World Wide Web address:** http://www.barbhosp.com. **Description:** A 347-bed, acute care hospital. The hospital provides intensive care, coronary, extended care, pediatric, psychiatry, and surgery services. Outpatient services and community outreach programs are also available. **NOTE:** Entry-level positions, part-time jobs, and second and third shifts are offered. **Common positions include:** Certified Nurses Aide; Home Health Aide; Licensed Practical Nurse; Network/Systems Administrator; Nuclear Medicine Technologist; Pharmacist; Public Relations Specialist; Radiological Technologist; Registered Nurse; Respiratory Therapist; Surgical Technician. **Educational backgrounds include:** Health Care; Microsoft Word; Novell. **Benefits:** 401(k); Casual Dress - Daily; Dental Insurance; Disability Coverage; Employee Discounts; Life Insurance; Medical Insurance; Pension Plan; Tuition Assistance. **Special programs:** Internships. **Corporate headquarters location:** Brentwood TN. **Parent company:** Quorum Health Group. **Listed on:** NASDAQ.

C.R. BARD ACCESS SYSTEMS
5425 West Amelia Earhart Drive, Salt Lake City UT 84116. 801/595-0700. **Toll-free phone:** 800/443-5505. **Fax:** 801/595-4947. **Contact:** Human Resources. **World Wide Web address:** http://www. crbard.com. **Description:** Develops, manufactures, and markets medical devices that focus on oncology, urology, and vascular diseases. C.R. Bard Access Systems also offers specialty products that focus on hemostasis, hernia repair, and performance irrigation. **NOTE:** Entry level positions and second and third shifts are offered. **Common positions**

include: Accountant; Biomedical Engineer; Blue-Collar Worker Supervisor; Budget Analyst; Clinical Lab Technician; Computer Programmer; Computer Support Technician; Controller; Cost Estimator; Finance Director; Financial Analyst; General Manager; Graphic Designer; Help-Desk Technician; Human Resources Manager; Manufacturing Engineer; Market Research Analyst; Marketing Manager; Marketing Specialist; Production Manager; Project Manager; Purchasing Agent/Manager; Quality Assurance Engineer; Quality Control Supervisor; Sales Executive; Sales Manager; Sales Representative; Systems Manager; Technical Support Manager; Vice President. **Educational backgrounds include:** Accounting; Business Administration; Engineering; Finance; Marketing; MBA. **Benefits:** 401(k); Casual Dress - Daily; Dental Insurance; Disability Coverage; Employee Discounts; Flexible Schedule; Life Insurance; Medical Insurance; Pension Plan; Relocation Assistance; Savings Plan; Tuition Assistance; Vacation Days (10 - 20). **Special programs:** Internships; Training. **Office hours:** Monday - Friday, 8:00 a.m. - 5:00 p.m. **Corporate headquarters location:** Murray Hill NJ. **Other U.S. locations:** Phoenix AZ; Atlanta GA; Boston MA. **International locations:** Mexico.

C.R. BARD, INC.
730 Central Avenue, Murray Hill NJ 07974. 908/277-8000. **Fax:** 908/277-8412. **Contact:** Human Resources. **World Wide Web address:** http://www.crbard.com. **Description:** Manufactures and distributes disposable medical, surgical, diagnostic, and patient care products. Cardiovascular products include angioplastic recanalization devices such as balloon angioplasty catheters, inflation devices, and developmental atherectomy and laser devices; electrophysiology products such as temporary pacing catheters, diagnostic and therapeutic electrodes, and cardiac mapping systems; a cardiopulmonary system; and blood oxygenators, cardiotomy reservoirs, and other products used in open heart surgery. Urological products include Foley catheters, trays, and related urine contract collection systems used extensively in postoperative bladder drainage. Surgical products include wound and chest drainage systems and implantable blood vessel replacements. **Corporate headquarters location:** This Location.

BARNES-JEWISH ST. PETERS HOSPITAL
10 Hospital Drive, St. Peters MO 63376. 636/447-6600. **Fax:** 636/916-9405. **Recorded jobline:** 636/916-9734. **Contact:** Recruiter. **World Wide Web address:** http://www.bjc.org/bjshp.html. **Description:** An acute care community hospital. The hospital offers general care, intensive care, obstetric, and pediatric services. **Common positions include:** Administrative Assistant; Certified Nurses Aide; Certified Occupational Therapy Assistant; Dietician/Nutritionist; EEG Technologist; EKG Technician; Emergency Medical Technician; Licensed Practical Nurse; Medical Assistant; Medical Records Technician; Medical Secretary; Nuclear Medicine Technologist; Nurse Practitioner; Occupational Therapist; Pharmacist; Physical Therapist; Physician; Physician Assistant; Radiological Technologist; Registered Nurse; Respiratory Therapist; Secretary; Social Worker; Speech-Language Pathologist; Surgical Technician. **Educational backgrounds include:** Health Care. **Benefits:** 403(b); Dental Insurance; Disability Coverage; Flexible Schedule; Job Sharing; Life Insurance; Medical Insurance; Pension Plan; Tuition Assistance. **Corporate headquarters location:** St. Louis MO. **Parent company:** BJC Health System. **Number of employees at this location:** 700.

BARNES-JEWISH WEST COUNTY HOSPITAL
12634 Olive Boulevard, St. Louis MO 63141. 314/434-0600. **Contact:** Human Resources. **World Wide Web address:** http://www.bjc.org/bjwch.html. **Description:** A general hospital. The hospital specializes in cosmetic surgery, dermatology, sports medicine, and urology. **Corporate headquarters location:** This Location. **Number of employees at this location:** 200.

BAUSCH & LOMB, INC.
World Headquarters, One Bausch & Lomb Place, Rochester NY 14604. 716/338-6000. **Toll-free phone:** 800/344-8815. **Contact:** Human Resources. **World Wide Web address:** http://www.bausch.com. **Description:** Bausch & Lomb participates in selected segments of global health care and optical markets. The health care segment consists of three sectors: Personal Health, Medical, and Biomedical. The Personal Health sector is comprised of branded products purchased directly by consumers in health and beauty aid sections of pharmacies, food stores, and mass merchandise outlets. Products include lens care solutions; oral care, eye care, and skin care products; and nonprescription medications. The Medical sector manufactures contact lenses, ophthalmic pharmaceuticals, hearing aids, dental implants, and other products sold to health care professionals or obtained by consumers through a prescription. The Biomedical sector includes products and services supplied to customers engaged in the research and development of pharmaceuticals and the production of genetically engineered materials. These include purpose-bred research animals, bioprocessing services, and products derived from pathogen-free eggs. The optics segment consists primarily of premium-priced sunglasses sold under brand names such as Ray-Ban and Revo. **Corporate headquarters location:** This Location.

BAXTER ALTHIN MEDICAL
14620 NW 60th Avenue, Miami Lakes FL 33014-2811. 305/823-5240. **Contact:** Human Resources. **World Wide Web address:** http://www.althin.com. **Description:** An international company that manufactures and markets critical therapies for conditions involving the blood and circulatory system. The company operates through three main areas: the BioScience division manufactures products that collect, separate, and store blood; the Renal products are designed to cleanse the blood; and the Intravenous products are designed to help infuse drugs and other solutions into the bloodstream. **Common positions include:** Accountant/Auditor; Biomedical Engineer; Blue-Collar Worker Supervisor; Buyer; Chemical Engineer; Chemist; Computer Programmer; Credit Manager; Customer Service Representative; Human Resources Manager; Marketing Specialist; Mechanical Engineer; Operations/Production Manager; Purchasing Agent/Manager; Quality Control Supervisor; Systems Analyst. **Educational backgrounds include:** Accounting; Biology; Business Administration; Chemistry; Computer Science; Engineering; Marketing. **Benefits:** Dental Insurance; Disability Coverage; Employee Discounts; Life Insurance; Medical Insurance; Profit Sharing; Savings Plan; Tuition Assistance.

BAXTER INTERNATIONAL, INC.
One Baxter Parkway, Deerfield IL 60015. 847/948-2000. **Fax:** 847/948-2964. **Contact:** Human Resources. **World Wide Web address:** http://www.baxter.com. **Description:** A global medical products and services company that is a leader in technologies related to blood and the circulatory system. The company operates four global businesses: Biotechnology develops therapies and

products in transfusion medicine; Cardiovascular Medicine develops products and provides services to treat late-stage cardiovascular disease; Renal Therapy develops products and provides services to improve therapies to fight kidney disease; and Intravenous Systems/Medical Products develops technologies and systems to improve intravenous medication delivery and distributes disposable medical products. **Common positions include:** Accountant; Auditor; Chemical Engineer; Computer Programmer; Electrical/Electronics Engineer; Human Resources Manager; Mechanical Engineer. **Educational backgrounds include:** Accounting; Chemistry; Computer Science; Engineering; Finance. **Benefits:** 401(k); Daycare Assistance; Dental Insurance; Disability Coverage; Employee Discounts; Life Insurance; Medical Insurance; Pension Plan; Savings Plan; Tuition Assistance. **Special programs:** Internships. **Corporate headquarters location:** This Location. **Annual sales/revenues:** More than $100 million.

BAYER DIAGNOSTICS
511 Benedict Avenue, Tarrytown NY 10591-5097. 914/631-8000. **Fax:** 914/524-2372. **Contact:** Wayne Bedenbaug, Human Resources. **World Wide Web address:** http://www.bayerdiag.com. **Description:** Develops, manufactures, and sells clinical dagnostic systems. Bayer diagnostics specializes in critical care, laboratory, and point-of-care testing. **Common positions include:** Accountant/Auditor; Attorney; Biological Scientist; Biomedical Engineer; Budget Analyst; Buyer; Chemist; Clinical Lab Technician; Computer Programmer; Customer Service Representative; Designer; Draftsperson; Electrical/Electronics Engineer; Electrician; Financial Analyst; Human Resources Manager; Librarian; Mathematician; Mechanical Engineer; Medical Records Technician; Public Relations Specialist; Purchasing Agent/ Manager; Science Technologist; Services Sales Representative; Software Engineer; Statistician; Systems Analyst; Technical Writer/Editor. **Educational backgrounds include:** Biology; Chemistry; Computer Science; Engineering; Finance; Marketing. **Benefits:** 401(k); Dental Insurance; Disability Coverage; Employee Discounts; Life Insurance; Medical Insurance; Pension Plan; Savings Plan; Tuition Assistance. **Corporate headquarters location:** Pittsburgh PA. **Other U.S. locations:** CA; IN; MA; NC. **Number of employees at this location:** 800.

BECTON DICKINSON & COMPANY
One Becton Drive, Franklin Lakes NJ 07417. 201/847-6800. **Contact:** Human Resources. **World Wide Web address:** http://www.bd.com. **Description:** A medical company engaged in the manufacture of health care products, medical instrumentation, diagnostic products, and industrial safety equipment. Major medical equipment product lines include hypodermics, intravenous equipment, operating room products, thermometers, gloves, and specialty needles. The company also offers contract packaging services. Founded in 1896. **Corporate headquarters location:** This Location. **Listed on:** New York Stock Exchange. **Stock exchange symbol:** BDX. **Number of employees worldwide:** 18,000.

BEECH HILL HOSPITAL
P.O. Box 254, Dublin NH 03444. 603/563-8511x403. **Toll-free phone:** 800/843-4455. **Fax:** 603/563-8771. **Contact:** Karen Ball, Human Resources Director. **Description:** A medical facility specializing in chemical dependency and dual diagnosis treatments. Founded in 1948. **NOTE:** Entry-level positions, part-time jobs, and second and third shifts are offered. This location also hires

seasonally. **Common positions include:** Administrative Assistant; Blue-Collar Worker Supervisor; Certified Nurses Aide; Clerical Supervisor; Controller; Counselor; Credit Manager; Customer Service Rep.; Dietician/Nutritionist; Education Administrator; Human Resources Manager; Licensed Practical Nurse; Marketing Manager; Marketing Specialist; Medical Records Technician; Medical Secretary; MIS Specialist; Nurse Practitioner; Operations Manager; Pharmacist; Physician; Psychologist; Registered Nurse; Sales Rep.; Secretary; Social Worker; Special Education Teacher; Teacher/Professor; Transportation/Traffic Specialist; Typist/Word Processor. **Educational backgrounds include:** Accounting; Business Administration; Education; Finance; Health Care; Liberal Arts; Marketing; MBA; Microsoft Office; Nursing; Spreadsheets. **Benefits:** 401(k); Casual Dress - Fridays; Dental Insurance; Disability Coverage; Life Insurance; Medical Insurance; Sick Days; Tuition Assistance; Vacation Days. **Special programs:** Internships; Training; Summer Jobs. **Office hours:** Monday - Friday, 9:00 a.m. - 5:00 p.m. **Corporate headquarters location:** Austin TX. **Listed on:** Privately held. **CEO:** Matthew Feeheny. **Facilities Manager:** John Cressy. **Annual sales/revenues:** Less than $5 million. **Number of employees at this location:** 150.

BEHAVIORAL HEALTH CARE OF CAPE FEAR VALLEY HEALTH SYSTEM MELROSE CENTER
3425 Melrose Road, Fayetteville NC 28304. 910/609-3000. **Toll-free phone:** 800/659-5546. **Fax:** 910/609-3088. **Recorded jobline:** 910/609-3888. **Contact:** Polly Collins, Personnel Manager. **E-mail address:** vpcollins@capefearvalley.com. **World Wide Web address:** http://www.capefearvalley.com. **Description:** A nonprofit, psychiatric hospital offering inpatient treatment and residential programs for all ages. **NOTE:** Entry-level positions, part-time jobs, and second and third shifts are offered. Associate administrator: James P. Sprouse. **Common positions include:** Administrative Assistant; Advertising Executive; Claim Rep.; Controller; Counselor; Customer Service Rep.; Environmental Engineer; Human Resources Manager; Marketing Specialist; Mechanical Engineer; Media Planner; Medical Assistant; Medical Records Technician; Pharmacist; Physician; Physician Assistant; Psychiatrist; Purchasing Agent/Manager; Quality Control Supervisor; Registered Nurse; Secretary; Social Worker; Teacher/Professor. **Educational backgrounds include:** Accounting; Business Administration; Education; Health Care; Marketing; Microsoft Office; Microsoft Word; Public Relations; Spreadsheets. **Benefits:** 403(b); Dental Insurance; Disability Coverage; Life Insurance; Medical Insurance; On-Site Daycare; Pension Plan; Sick Days; Tuition Assistance; Vacation Days. **Special programs:** Internships. **Office hours:** Monday - Friday, 8:00 a.m. - 5:00 p.m. **Corporate headquarters location:** This Location. **Facilities Manager:** Ernest Bonnett. **Purchasing Manager:** Toni Blackmon.

BEL-AIR NURSING HOME
29 Center Street, Goffstown NH 03045-2936. 603/497-4871. **Contact:** Robert Lenox, Administrator. **Description:** An intermediate care nursing home. Founded in 1970. **NOTE:** Part-time jobs and second and third shifts are offered. **Common positions include:** Administrative Assistant; Certified Nurses Aide; Certified Occupational Therapy Assistant; General Manager; Human Resources Manager; Licensed Practical Nurse; Medical Assistant; Occupational Therapist;

Pharmacist; Physical Therapist; Public Relations Specialist; Registered Nurse; Secretary; Social Worker. **Educational backgrounds include:** Health Care. **Benefits:** Casual Dress - Daily; Dental Insurance; Employee Discounts; Flexible Schedule; Job Sharing; Medical Insurance; Relocation Assistance. **Special programs:** Internships. **Office hours:** Monday - Friday, 9:00 a.m. - 5:00 p.m. **Annual sales/revenues:** Less than $5 million. **Number of employees at this location:** 60.

BERGEN BRUNSWIG CORPORATION
4000 Metropolitan Drive, Orange CA 92868. 714/385-4000. **Fax:** 714/385-8877. **Recorded jobline:** 714/385-HIRE. **Contact:** Human Resources Recruiting. **E-mail address:** bbcjobs@ deltanet.com. **World Wide Web address:** http://www.bergenbrunswig.com. **Description:** One of the nation's leading distributors of pharmaceuticals and medical-surgical supplies. The company also offers consulting and information management services. Bergen Brunswig Corporation is a *Fortune* 500 company. Founded in 1888. **Common positions include:** Accountant; Administrative Assistant; Budget Analyst; Buyer; Computer Programmer; Consultant; Data Entry Clerk; Financial Analyst; Marketing Specialist; Project Manager; Secretary; Systems Analyst; Technical Writer/Editor; Telecommunications Manager; Typist/Word Processor. **Educational backgrounds include:** Accounting; Business Administration; Communications; Computer Science; Finance; Marketing. **Benefits:** 401(k); Daycare Assistance; Dental Insurance; Disability Coverage; Financial Planning Assistance; Life Insurance; Medical Insurance; On-Site Exercise Facility; Public Transit Available; Savings Plan; Tuition Assistance. **Office hours:** Monday - Friday, 7:30 a.m. - 4:30 p.m. **Corporate headquarters location:** This Location. **Other U.S. locations:** Nationwide. **Subsidiaries include:** Bergen Brunswig Drug Company; Bergen Brunswig Medical Corporation; Bergen Brunswig Specialty Company. **Listed on:** New York Stock Exchange. **Stock exchange symbol:** BBC. **CEO:** Donald R. Roden. **Annual sales/revenues:** More than $100 million. **Number of employees nationwide:** 5,400.

BERNAFON-MAICO INC.
9675 West 76th Street, Eden Prairie MN 55344. 952/941-4200. **Toll-free phone:** 888/941-4203. **Fax:** 952/903-4200. **Contact:** Human Resources. **World Wide Web address:** http://www.bernafon-maico.com. **Description:** Produces and sells hearing aides and audiometer equipment. The company also provides a variety of valuable resources and information for the hearing impaired. Founded in 1936. **Common positions include:** Account Manager; Account Rep.; Accountant; Blue-Collar Worker Supervisor; Buyer; Credit Manager; Customer Service Rep.; Electrical/Electronics Engineer; General Manager; Manufacturer's/ Wholesaler's Sales Rep.; Marketing Specialist; Mechanical Engineer; Operations/Production Manager; Purchasing Agent/Manager; Quality Control Supervisor; Systems Analyst; Technical Writer/Editor. **Educational backgrounds include:** Accounting; Business Administration; Communications; Health Care; Marketing. **Benefits:** 401(k); Casual Dress - Daily; Dental Insurance; Disability Coverage; Flexible Schedule; Life Insurance; Medical Insurance; Paid Holidays; Public Transit Available; Sick Days; Tuition Assistance. **Office hours:** Monday - Friday, 8:00 a.m. - 5:00 p.m. **Corporate headquarters location:** This Location. **Parent company:** William Demant Holding. **President:** Peter Van Nest. **Annual sales/revenues:** $5 - $10 million.

BETH ISRAEL HEALTH CARE SYSTEM
First Avenue at 16th Street, New York NY 10003. 212/420-2000. **Contact:** Human Resources. **World Wide Web address:** http://www.bethisraelny.org. **Description:** An integrated health care system providing a full continuum of primary, acute, tertiary, and long-term care. The system also operates New York HealthCare/Doctors' Walk In, the Japanese Medical Practice, Schnurmacher Nursing Home of Beth Israel Medical Center, Robert Mapplethorpe Residential Treatment Facility, Phillips Beth Israel School of Nursing, Karpas Health Information Center, and D-O-C-S, a multisite, private group medical practice in the suburbs. **NOTE:** Resumes should be sent to Human Resources, 555 West 57th Street, New York NY 10003. **Corporate headquarters location:** This Location.

BETHANY HOMES, INC.
201 South University Drive, Fargo ND 58103. 701/239-3000. **Fax:** 701/239-3237. **Contact:** Christie Rossow, Employment Coordinator. **World Wide Web address:** http://www.bethanyhomes.org. **Description:** A 192-bed nursing home and retirement living center. Overall, Bethany Homes is a nonprofit corporation affiliated with the Evangelical Lutheran Church of America and is sponsored by 45 corporate congregation members. **NOTE:** Entry-level positions and second and third shifts are offered. **Common positions include:** Account Manager; Accountant; Administrative Assistant; Buyer; Certified Nurses Aide; Dietician/Nutritionist; Environmental Engineer; Finance Director; Human Resources Manager; Licensed Practical Nurse; Medical Records Technician; Occupational Therapist; Physical Therapist; Purchasing Agent/Manager; Registered Nurse; Secretary; Social Worker. **Educational backgrounds include:** Health Care. **Benefits:** 401(k); Dental Insurance; Employee Discounts; Life Insurance; Medical Insurance; Pension Plan; Public Transit Available; Savings Plan; Tuition Assistance. **Special programs:** Training. **Number of employees at this location:** 420.

BEVERLY ENTERPRISES, INC.
1000 Beverly Way, Fort Smith AR 72919. 501/452-6712. **Toll-free phone:** 800/360-7633. **Fax:** 501/478-3996. **Contact:** Human Resources. **E-mail address:** recruit@beverlycorp.com. **World Wide Web address:** http://www.beverlynet.com. **Description:** A post-acute health care provider that operates a variety of acute care hospitals, assisted living centers, hospice and home health centers, institutional and mail-service pharmacies, and nursing and rehabilitation facilities nationwide. **Common positions include:** Accountant/Auditor; Administrative Worker/Clerk; Attorney; Budget Analyst; Claim Rep.; Construction Contractor; Dietician/Nutritionist; Financial Analyst; Licensed Practical Nurse; Paralegal; Physical Therapist; Registered Nurse; Respiratory Therapist; Systems Analyst. **Educational backgrounds include:** Accounting; Computer Science; MCSE; Nursing. **Benefits:** 401(k); Credit Union; Daycare Assistance; Dental Insurance; Disability Coverage; Employee Discounts; Life Insurance; Medical Insurance; Stock Option. **Corporate headquarters location:** This Location. **Listed on:** New York Stock Exchange. **Number of employees at this location:** 650. **Number of employees nationwide:** 90,000.

BIG SPRING STATE HOSPITAL
1901 North Highway 87, Big Spring TX 79721. 915/268-7256. **Fax:** 915/268-7285. **Contact:** Lisa Wiggins, Human Resources Clerk. **World Wide Web address:** http://www.mhmr.state.tx.us. **Description:** A nonprofit, state-governed facility

that specializes in the treatment of patients with mental illness. **NOTE:** Entry-level positions and second and third shifts are offered. **Common positions include:** Certified Nurses Aide; Registered Nurse; Secretary; Typist/Word Processor. **Educational backgrounds include:** Business Administration; Computer Science; Health Care. **Benefits:** 401(k); Life Insurance; Medical Insurance; Pension Plan. **Special programs:** Internships. **Corporate headquarters location:** Austin TX. **Parent company:** Texas Department of Mental Health and Mental Retardation.

BIOMET, INC.
P.O. Box 587, Warsaw IN 46581-0587. 219/267-6639. **Physical address:** Airport Industrial Park, Warsaw IN 46580. **Fax:** 219/267-8137. **Contact:** Darlene Whaley, Vice President of Human Resources. **World Wide Web address:** http://www. biomet.com. **Description:** Designs, manufactures, and markets products used by orthopedic medical specialists in both surgical and non-surgical therapy. Products include reconstructive and trauma devices, electrical bone growth stimulators, orthopedic support devices, operating room supplies, powered surgical instruments, general surgical instruments, arthroscopy products, and oral-maxillofacial implants and instruments. **Common positions include:** AS400 Programmer Analyst; Biomedical Engineer; Manufacturing Engineer; Marketing Manager; Quality Assurance Engineer; Systems Analyst. **Corporate headquarters location:** This Location. **International locations:** Worldwide. **Listed on:** NASDAQ. **Annual sales/revenues:** More than $100 million. **Number of employees nationwide:** 1,360.

BIOSPHERICS INC.
12051 Indian Creek Court, Beltsville MD 20705. 301/419-3900. **Fax:** 301/210-4908. **Recorded jobline:** 800/799-4186. **Contact:** Human Resources. **E-mail address:** hrdept@ biospherics.com. **World Wide Web address:** http://www.biospherics.com. **Description:** Develops and maintains hotlines for public and professional inquiries about the health care and government industries. Biospherics also provides information technology services and develops biotech products. **Common positions include:** Accountant/Auditor; Biological Scientist; Computer Programmer; Counselor; Customer Service Rep.; Editor; Licensed Practical Nurse; Pharmacist; Registered Nurse; Reporter; Systems Analyst; Teacher/Professor; Technical Writer/Editor. **Educational backgrounds include:** Biology; Chemistry; Computer Science; Health Care; Nursing. **Benefits:** 401(k); Dental Insurance; Disability Coverage; Life Insurance; Medical Insurance. **Office hours:** Monday - Friday, 8:00 a.m. - 5:30 p.m. **Corporate headquarters location:** This Location. **Other U.S. locations:** Cumberland MD. **Listed on:** NASDAQ. **Number of employees at this location:** 300. **Number of employees nationwide:** 500.

BLOCK DRUG COMPANY INC.
257 Cornelison Avenue, Jersey City NJ 07302. 201/434-3000. **Contact:** Human Resources. **World Wide Web address:** http://www.blockdrug.com. **Description:** Develops, manufactures, and sells products in four general categories: denture, dental care, oral hygiene, and professional dental products; proprietary products; ethical pharmaceutical products; and household products. Dental-related products include Polident denture cleansers. **Corporate headquarters location:** This Location.

BLOUNT MEMORIAL HOSPITAL
907 East Lamar Alexander Parkway, Maryville TN 37804-5193. 865/977-5659. **Contact:** Joe B. Hill,

Director of Human Resources. **World Wide Web address:** http://www.bmnet.com. **Description:** A fully-accredited, 334-bed, acute care facility. The hospital provides care and education in hospital, outpatient, worksite, and community settings. Blount Memorial Hospital offers a 24-hour physician-staffed emergency department (a designated Level III Trauma Center); comprehensive therapeutic and diagnostic facilities; a state-of-the-art surgery center, same-day surgery, and an intensive care unit; industrial medicine, occupational health, and employee assistance programs for business and industry; a primary care and occupational health clinic network; a family birthing center; and alcohol, drug, and eating disorders treatment. **NOTE:** Entry-level positions are offered. **Company slogan:** Close to home. **Common positions include:** Licensed Practical Nurse; Medical Records Technician; Occupational Therapist; Physical Therapist; Physician; Registered Nurse. **Educational backgrounds include:** Health Care. **Benefits:** Dental Insurance; Disability Coverage; Employee Discounts; Financial Planning Assistance; Flexible Schedule; Job Sharing; Life Insurance; Medical Insurance; Tuition Assistance. **Special programs:** Training. **Annual sales/revenues:** $51 - $100 million. **Number of employees at this location:** 1,300.

BOSTON PUBLIC HEALTH COMMISSION
1010 Massachusetts Avenue, Boston MA 02118. 617/547-5657. **Fax:** 617/547-2418. **Contact:** Patty Hall, Staffing Specialist. **E-mail address:** patty_hall@bphc.org. **World Wide Web address:** http://www.tiac.net/users/bdph. **Description:** A nonprofit agency whose mission is to protect, preserve, and promote the well-being of all Boston residents. Boston Public Health Commission provides community-based public health programs including tobacco control, domestic violence prevention, environmental health, communicable disease awareness, maternal/child health, addictions services, homeless services, and AIDS services. **NOTE:** All positions with Boston Public Health Commission require residency in the city of Boston or a willingness to move to Boston if hired. Entry-level positions and second and third shifts are offered. **Common positions include:** Administrative Assistant; Administrative Manager; Budget Analyst; Computer Programmer; Counselor; Data Entry Clerk; Database Manager; Daycare Worker; Dietician/Nutritionist; Emergency Medical Technician; Finance Director; Financial Analyst; Health Care Administrator; Human Resources Manager; Licensed Practical Nurse; MIS Specialist; Nurse Practitioner; Operations Manager; Program Manager; Project Manager; Receptionist; Registered Nurse; Secretary; Statistician; Systems Analyst; Typist/Word Processor. **Educational backgrounds include:** Computer Science; Counseling; Health Care; Human Services; Liberal Arts; Psychology; Public Health. **Benefits:** 403(b); Disability Coverage; EAP; Life Insurance; Medical Insurance; Pension Plan; Public Transit Available; Savings Plan. **Annual sales/revenues:** $51 - $100 million. **Number of employees at this location:** 1,100.

BOSTON SCIENTIFIC CORPORATION
One Boston Scientific Place, Natick MA 01760-1537. 508/650-8000. **Contact:** Human Resources. **World Wide Web address:** http://www.bsci.com. **Description:** A worldwide developer, manufacturer, and marketer of medical devices used in a broad range of interventional procedures including cardiology, gastroenterology, pulmonary medicine, and vascular surgery. **Corporate headquarters location:** This Location. **Other U.S. locations:** San Jose CA; Miami FL; Spencer IN; Maple Grove MN; Oakland NJ; Redmond WA. **International**

locations: Buenos Aires, Argentina; Freeport, Bahamas; Galway, Ireland; Jaunay, France; Paris, France; Singapore; Stenlose, Denmark; Tel-Aviv, Israel; Tokyo, Japan. **Listed on:** New York Stock Exchange. **Stock exchange symbol:** BSX.

BRONSON HEALTHCARE GROUP
BRONSON METHODIST HOSPITAL
252 East Lovell Street, Box G, Kalamazoo MI 49007. 616/341-6310. **Fax:** 616/341-8696. **Recorded jobline:** 616/341-6800. **Contact:** Christine Martin, Employment Specialist. **World Wide Web address:** http://www. bronsonhealth.com. **Description:** Bronson Healthcare Group is a community-owned, nonprofit health care provider. The group operates Bronson Methodist Hospital, a 414-bed medical center that provides both inpatient and outpatient services. The hospital specializes in trauma, burn care, women's and children's health, prenatal care, and pediatrics. Comprehensive care is also offered in a number of areas including cardiology, critical care, and neurosciences, home health care, and rehabilitation. **NOTE:** Entry-level positions and second and third shifts are offered. **Common positions include:** Certified Nurses Aide; Clinical Lab Technician; Dietician/Nutritionist; EEG Technologist; EKG Technician; Emergency Medical Technician; Licensed Practical Nurse; Nuclear Medicine Technologist; Occupational Therapist; Pharmacist; Physical Therapist; Physician; Radiological Technologist; Registered Nurse; Respiratory Therapist; Social Worker; Speech-Language Pathologist; Surgical Technician; Typist/Word Processor. **Educational backgrounds include:** Health Care. **Benefits:** 401(k); 403(b); Daycare Assistance; Dental Insurance; Disability Coverage; Employee Discounts; Flexible Schedule; Life Insurance; Medical Insurance; On-Site Daycare; Pension Plan; Tuition Assistance. **Special programs:** Internships. **Office hours:** Monday - Friday, 7:30 a.m. - 4:30 p.m. **Corporate headquarters location:** This Location. **Subsidiaries include:** Bronson Health Foundation; Bronson Home Health Care; Bronson Medical Group; Bronson Outpatient Surgery; Bronson Vicksburg Hospital; IBA Health and Life Assurance Company; Physicians Health Plan of Southwest Michigan. **Number of employees at this location:** 2,750.

BROOKS MEMORIAL HOSPITAL
529 Central Avenue, Dunkirk NY 14048. 716/366-1111x4210. **Fax:** 716/366-6919. **Contact:** Desiree Coon, Human Resources Administrator/Trainer. **E-mail address:** bmhhr@netsync.net. **World Wide Web address:** http://www.brookshospital.org. **Description:** A nonprofit, primary acute care hospital. The hospital is JCAHO accredited. Founded in 1898. **NOTE:** Entry-level positions, part-time jobs, and second and third shifts are offered. **Common positions include:** Computer Operator; Dietician/Nutritionist; EEG Technologist; EKG Technician; Licensed Practical Nurse; Medical Assistant; Medical Records Technician; Nuclear Medicine Technologist; Pharmacist; Physical Therapist; Physical Therapy Assistant; Radiological Technologist; Registered Nurse; Respiratory Therapist; Social Worker; Surgical Technician; Typist/Word Processor. **Educational backgrounds include:** Health Care; Novell; Nutrition. **Benefits:** 403(b); Disability Coverage; Employee Discounts; Flexible Schedule; Life Insurance; Pension Plan; Sick Days (11+); Tuition Assistance; Vacation Days (6 - 10). **Special programs:** Internships. **Corporate headquarters location:** This Location. **President:** Richard Ketcham. **Information Systems Manager:** Kathy Kucharski. **Number of employees at this location:** 475.

THE BROWN SCHOOLS
1407 West Stassney Lane, Austin TX 78745. 512/464-0200. **Contact:** Human Resources. **World Wide Web address:** http://www. brownschools.com. **Description:** Provides specialty services including psychiatric and behavioral services, rehabilitation, education, in-home services, outpatient care, residential treatment and adoption and foster care. The Brown Schools operat more than 15 facilities in six states. **Corporate headquarters location:** This Location.

BURDETTE TOMLIN MEMORIAL HOSPITAL
2 Stone Harbor Boulevard, Cape May Court House NJ 08210. 609/463-2000. **Fax:** 609/463-2379. **Contact:** Human Resources. **World Wide Web address:** http://www.btmh.com. **Description:** A 242-bed, acute care, community hospital. **Common positions include:** Chef/Cook/Kitchen Worker; Construction Trade Worker; Dietician/Nutritionist; EEG Technologist; EKG Technician; Electrician; Emergency Medical Technician; Medical Records Technician; Nuclear Medicine Technologist; Occupational Therapist; Physical Therapist; Radiological Technologist; Registered Nurse; Respiratory Therapist; Social Worker; Speech-Language Pathologist; Stationary Engineer; Systems Analyst. **Benefits:** Dental Insurance; Disability Coverage; Life Insurance; Medical Insurance; Pension Plan; Tuition Assistance.

BURLINGTON HEALTH & REHABILITATION CENTER
300 Pearl Street, Burlington VT 05401. 802/658-4200. **Contact:** Human Resources. **Description:** A for-profit nursing home that provides therapy, social services, and respite care. **NOTE:** Part-time jobs and second and third shifts are offered. **Common positions include:** Certified Nurses Aide; Licensed Practical Nurse; Occupational Therapist; Physical Therapist; Registered Nurse; Social Worker; Speech-Language Pathologist. **Educational backgrounds include:** Health Care. **Benefits:** 401(k); Flexible Schedule; Life Insurance; Medical Insurance; On-Site Daycare; Sick Days (11+); Vacation Days (6 - 10). **Special programs:** Training.

CMP INDUSTRIES INC.
413 North Pearl Street, Albany NY 12207. 518/434-3147. **Fax:** 518/434-1288. **Contact:** Robert J. Briggs, Director of Administration. **World Wide Web address:** http://www.cmpindustry.com. **Description:** A manufacturer of dental materials, dental equipment, and other dental supplies. Product lines include DEMCO, NIRANIUM, NOBILIUM, and TICONIUM. **Common positions include:** Accountant/Auditor; Administrator; Blue-Collar Worker Supervisor; Credit Manager; Customer Service Rep.; Electrical/Electronics Engineer; General Manager; Human Resources Manager; Manufacturer's/Wholesaler's Sales Rep.; Marketing Specialist; Operations/Production Manager; Purchasing Agent/Manager. **Educational backgrounds include:** Accounting; Business Administration; Engineering; Finance; Marketing. **Benefits:** Dental Insurance; Disability Coverage; Employee Discounts; Life Insurance; Medical Insurance; Pension Plan; Tuition Assistance. **Corporate headquarters location:** This Location.

CTI PET SYSTEMS, INC.
810 Innovation Drive, Knoxville TN 37932. 865/966-7539. **Fax:** 865/218-3000. **Contact:** Human Resources. **World Wide Web address:** http://www.cti-pet.com. **Description:** CTI PET Systems, Inc. operates as a joint venture with Siemens Medical Systems, Inc., developing and manufacturing equipment used in Positron Emission

Tomography (PET), a non-invasive medical imaging technique that is able to detect abnormal functions of the body in the early stages by imaging biochemical and metabolic changes. **Common positions include:** Accountant/Auditor; Biomedical Engineer; Buyer; Chemical Engineer; Designer; Electrical/Electronics Engineer; Human Resources Manager; Mechanical Engineer; Software Engineer; Systems Analyst. **Benefits:** 401(k); Dental Insurance; Disability Coverage; Life Insurance; Medical Insurance; Pension Plan; Savings Plan; Tuition Assistance. **Corporate headquarters location:** This Location. **Number of employees at this location:** 150.

CALIFORNIA DENTAL ASSOCIATION
P.O. Box 13749, Sacramento CA 95853. 916/443-0505. **Fax:** 916/444-0718. **Recorded jobline:** 916/443-4526. **Contact:** Brenda Dilchrist, Human Resources Director. **World Wide Web address:** http://www.cda.org. **Description:** A nonprofit dental association providing membership programs and services for California dentists. **Common positions include:** Accountant/Auditor; Adjuster; Administrative Manager; Attorney; Claim Rep.; Clerical Supervisor; Computer Programmer; Customer Service Representative; Financial Analyst; Human Resources Manager; Insurance Agent/Broker; Public Relations Specialist; Reporter; Systems Analyst; Technical Writer/Editor; Travel Agent; Underwriter/Assistant Underwriter. **Educational backgrounds include:** Accounting; Business Administration; Communications; Finance; Marketing. **Benefits:** Dental Insurance; Disability Coverage; Employee Discounts; Life Insurance; Medical Insurance; Tuition Assistance. **Corporate headquarters location:** This Location.

CAMTRONICS MEDICAL SYSTEMS
P.O. Box 950, Hartland WI 53029. 262/367-0700. **Contact:** Human Resources. **World Wide Web address:** http://www.camtronics.com. **Description:** This location is the main office and manufacturing facility. Overall, Camtronics Medical Systems manufactures diagnostic imaging equipment and products for cardiology and radiology. Founded in 1986. **Corporate headquarters location:** This Location.

CANDELA CORPORATION
530 Boston Post Road, Wayland MA 01778. 508/358-7400. **Contact:** Human Resources. **World Wide Web address:** http://www.clzr.com. **Description:** Designs, manufactures, markets, and services lasers for a variety of medical applications. The company also licenses medical products and sells them through its worldwide distribution network. Products include Vbeam, which treats vascular lesions; AlexLAZR, which removes tattoos; and GentleLASE Plus, which removes unwanted hairs and also treats vascular lesions. **Corporate headquarters location:** This Location. **Number of employees at this location:** 200.

CARDIOVASCULAR CONSULTANTS, PC
4330 Wornall Road, Suite 2000, Kansas City MO 64111. 816/931-1883. **Fax:** 816/931-7714. **Contact:** Human Resources. **Description:** A 20-physician cardiology practice providing patient care and research services in the fields of nuclear cardiology, preventive cardiology, and EP/rhythm. **Common positions include:** Claim Representative; Clinical Lab Technician; EKG Technician; Nuclear Medicine Technologist; Physician; Registered Nurse; Secretary; Transcriptionist. **Educational backgrounds include:** Health Care. **Benefits:** 401(k); Dental Insurance; Flexible Schedule; Life Insurance; Medical Insurance; Profit Sharing; Tuition Assistance; Vision Insurance. **Office hours:** Monday - Friday, 8:00 a.m. - 5:00 p.m. **Corporate headquarters location:** This Location. **Number of employees at this location:** 125.

CARE MATRIX
197 First Avenue, Needham MA 02194. 781/433-1000. **Contact:** Human Resources. **World Wide Web address:** http://www.carematrix.com. **Description:** A health care services company which provides assisted living and related specialized services to senior citizens. Three of the company's business activities include acquiring and managing existing assisted living and related senior living communities; developing assisted living communities; and managing and marketing communities owned by third parties. **Corporate headquarters location:** This Location.

CAREMARK RX
3000 Galleria Tower, Suite 1000, Birmingham AL 35244. 205/733-8996. **Contact:** Human Resources. **World Wide Web address:** http://www. caremark.com. **Description:** A pharmaceutical company that provides pharmacy benefit management and therapeutic pharmaceutical services. The company also offers pharmaceutical services that target chronic or genetic disorders, and biotechnology. **Corporate headquarters location:** This Location.

CARONDELET HEALTH NETWORK
1601 West St. Mary's Road, Tucson AZ 85745. **Toll-free phone:** 800/669-5745. **Fax:** 520/740-6067. **Contact:** Human Resources. **World Wide Web address:** http://www.carondelet.org. **Description:** Operates a nonprofit hospital and medical center. Founded in 1880. **NOTE:** Entry-level positions and second and third shifts are offered. **Common positions include:** Administrative Assistant; Biomedical Engineer; Certified Nurses Aide; Claim Representative; Clinical Lab Technician; Computer Operator; Counselor; Customer Service Representative; Daycare Worker; EEG Technologist; EKG Technician; Financial Analyst; Licensed Practical Nurse; Nuclear Medicine Technologist; Nurse Practitioner; Occupational Therapist; Pharmacist; Physical Therapist; Purchasing Agent/Manager; Radiological Technologist; Registered Nurse; Respiratory Therapist; Secretary; Social Worker; Surgical Technician; Systems Analyst. **Educational backgrounds include:** Accounting; Biology; Business Administration; Chemistry; Computer Science; Finance; Health Care; Nutrition; Software Development. **Benefits:** 403(b); Daycare Assistance; Dental Insurance; Disability Coverage; Employee Discounts; Flexible Schedule; Life Insurance; Medical Insurance; On-Site Daycare; Pension Plan; Savings Plan; Tuition Assistance. **Special programs:** Internships; Training. **Corporate headquarters location:** This Location.

CEDARS-SINAI HEALTH SYSTEM
8723 Alden Drive, Room 110, Los Angeles CA 90048. 310/855-5523. **Recorded jobline:** 310/967-8230. **Contact:** Employee Relations. **World Wide Web address:** http://www.csmc.edu. **Description:** A nonprofit health care delivery system that operates through Cedars-Sinai Medial Center, as well as a network of primary care physicians. Cedars-Sinai specializes in acute, sub-acute, and home patient care; biomedical research; community service; and continuing medical education. **Common positions include:** Biological Scientist; Claim Rep.; Clerical Supervisor; Clinical Lab Technician; Computer Programmer; Dietician/Nutritionist; EEG Technologist; Health Services Manager; Licensed Practical Nurse; Nuclear Medicine Technologist; Occupational Therapist;

Pharmacist; Physical Therapist; Physician; Psychologist; Radiological Technologist; Registered Nurse; Respiratory Therapist; Speech-Language Pathologist; Surgical Technician; Systems Analyst. **Educational backgrounds include:** Biology; Chemistry. **Benefits:** Daycare Assistance; Dental Insurance; Employee Discounts; Life Insurance; Medical Insurance; Pension Plan; Savings Plan. **Corporate headquarters location:** This Location.

CENTRA HEALTH INC.
1920 Atherholt Road, Lynchburg VA 24501. 804/947-4738. **Fax:** 804/947-4892. **Contact:** Meralyn Autry, Employment Coordinator. **World Wide Web address:** http://www.centrahealth.com. **Description:** A regional, nonprofit health care system that operates through two hospitals in central Virginia. Lynchburg General Hospital offers cardiology, critical care, emergency and trauma care, orthopedics, neurology, and neurosurgery. Virginia Baptist Hospital is a regional care facility that provides ambulatory surgery, chemical dependency treatment, physical rehabilitation, home health care, oncology, and women's and children's services. **NOTE:** Entry-level positions and second and third shifts are offered. **Common positions include:** Accountant/Auditor; Administrative Assistant; Biomedical Engineer; Buyer; Certified Nurses Aide; Chemist; Chief Financial Officer; Clinical Lab Technician; Computer Operator; Computer Programmer; Controller; Counselor; Customer Service Representative; Database Manager; Daycare Worker; Dietician/Nutritionist; EEG Technologist; EKG Technician; Electrician; Emergency Medical Technician; Financial Analyst; Human Resources Manager; Industrial Engineer; Licensed Practical Nurse; Marketing Specialist; Medical Records Technician; MIS Specialist; Nuclear Medicine Technologist; Occupational Therapist; Pharmacist; Physical Therapist; Physician; Project Manager; Public Relations Specialist; Radiological Technologist; Registered Nurse; Respiratory Therapist; Secretary; Social Worker; Speech-Language Pathologist; Systems Analyst; Teacher/Professor; Telecommunications Manager. **Educational backgrounds include:** Accounting; Biology; Business Administration; Chemistry; Communications; Computer Science; Finance; Health Care; Marketing; Nutrition. **Benefits:** 403(b); Dental Insurance; Disability Coverage; Employee Discounts; Flexible Schedule; Life Insurance; Medical Insurance; On-Site Daycare; Pension Plan; Savings Plan; Tuition Assistance. **Corporate headquarters location:** This Location. **Number of employees at this location:** 3,300.

CENTRAL IOWA HEALTH SYSTEM
1313 High Street, Suite 111, Des Moines IA 50309. 515/241-6313. **Fax:** 515/241-8515. **Contact:** Human Resources. **World Wide Web address:** http://www.ihs.org/central.html. **Description:** Iowa Methodist Medical Center, Iowa Lutheran Hospital, and St. Luke's are affiliated hospitals under the Central Iowa Health System. They form one of Iowa's largest nonprofit medical facilities with a combined total of 1,175 beds. Iowa Methodist is central Iowa's only designated trauma center and is also a teaching, regional referral center. Iowa Lutheran is a community hospital which focuses on family medicine and behavioral health sciences. St. Luke's is a general hospital located in Cedar Rapids. **Common positions include:** Accountant/Auditor; Administrative Manager; Advertising Clerk; Attorney; Biomedical Engineer; Blue-Collar Worker Supervisor; Cashier; Chef/Cook/Kitchen Worker; Chemist; Claim Representative; Clerical Supervisor; Clinical Lab Technician; Computer Operator; Computer Programmer; Counselor; Credit Clerk and Authorizer; Credit Manager; Customer Service Representative; Dietician/Nutritionist; Dispatcher; Economist; Education Administrator; EEG Technologist; EKG Technician; Electrician; Emergency Medical Technician; Employment Interviewer; Environmental Engineer; Financial Analyst; Food and Beverage Service Worker; Food Scientist/Technologist; Graphic Artist; Health Services Worker; Heating/AC/Refrigeration Technician; Human Resources Manager; Librarian; Library Technician; Licensed Practical Nurse; Management Analyst/Consultant; Management Trainee; Market Research Analyst; Marketing Manager; Mechanical Engineer; Medical Records Technician; Nuclear Medicine Technologist; Nursing Psychiatric Aide; Occupational Therapist; Paralegal; Payroll Clerk; Pharmacist; Physical Therapist; Physician; Printing Press Operator; Public Relations Specialist; Purchasing Agent/Manager; Quality Control Supervisor; Radiological Technologist; Receptionist; Recreational Therapist; Registered Nurse; Respiratory Therapist; Science Technologist; Secretary; Social Worker; Speech-Language Pathologist; Stock Clerk; Surgical Technician; Systems Analyst; Teacher Aide; Teacher/Professor; Truck Driver; Typist/Word Processor. **Educational backgrounds include:** Accounting; Biology; Business Administration; Chemistry; Communications; Computer Science; Finance; Health Care; Marketing. **Benefits:** 401(k); Daycare Assistance; Dental Insurance; Disability Coverage; Employee Discounts; Life Insurance; Medical Insurance; Pension Plan; Profit Sharing; Savings Plan; Tuition Assistance; Wellness Program. **Special programs:** Internships. **Corporate headquarters location:** This Location. **Listed on:** Privately held. **Number of employees at this location:** 5,200. **Number of employees nationwide:** 7,000.

CENTRAL VIRGINIA TRAINING CENTER
P.O. Box 1098, Lynchburg VA 24505. 804/947-6000. **Recorded jobline:** 804/947-6332. **Contact:** Human Resources. **Description:** A state residential facility for individuals with mental retardation.

CERAMCO INC.
6 Terri Lane, Suite 100, Burlington NJ 08016. 609/386-8900. **Toll-free phone:** 800/487-0100. **Fax:** 609/386-5266. **Contact:** Ms. Pat McDade, Office Administrator. **E-mail address:** directhr@ aol.com. **World Wide Web address:** http://www. ceramco.com. **Description:** A leading manufacturer of dental porcelain, raw materials, and equipment. Ceramco distributes these products to dental laboratories for use in preparing crowns, bridges, and restorations. Founded in 1959. **Common positions include:** Materials Engineer; Sales Representative. **Educational backgrounds include:** Business Administration; Engineering. **Benefits:** 401(k); Dental Insurance; Disability Coverage; Life Insurance; Medical Insurance; Pension Plan; Tuition Assistance. **Office hours:** Monday - Friday, 8:00 a.m. - 5:00 p.m. **Corporate headquarters location:** This Location. **International locations:** England; Puerto Rico. **Parent company:** Dentsply International, Inc. **Number of employees at this location:** 65.

CHAD THERAPEUTICS, INC.
21622 Plummer Street, Chatsworth CA 91311. 818/882-0363. **Contact:** Human Resources. **World Wide Web address:** http://www. chadtherapeutics.com. **Description:** Designs, manufactures, and markets home oxygen systems. Product names include OXYLITE, OXYMATIC, and OXYMIZER. **Corporate headquarters location:** This Location.

CHARTER BEHAVIORAL HEALTH SYSTEMS OF NEW JERSEY
19 Prospect Street, Summit NJ 07902. 908/277-9094. **Fax:** 908/522-7098. **Contact:** Keith Andreotta, Human Resources Director. **Description:** A psychiatric hospital that provides a full range of services and a wide variety of treatment options for adults, adolescents, and children. Charter offers care for depression, drug and alcohol problems, anxiety, compulsive behaviors, and other emotional illnesses. Treatment options include an intensive outpatient program, partial hospitalization, and inpatient treatment. **NOTE:** Entry-level positions and second and third shifts are offered. **Common positions include:** Registered Nurse; Social Worker. **Educational backgrounds include:** Psychiatry; Social Work. **Benefits:** 401(k); Dental Insurance; Disability Coverage; Employee Discounts; Life Insurance; Medical Insurance; Public Transit Available; Tuition Assistance. **Special programs:** Internships. **Corporate headquarters location:** Atlanta GA. **Other U.S. locations:** Nationwide. **Listed on:** American Stock Exchange. **CEO:** Lori Ann Rizzuto. **Annual sales/revenues:** Less than $5 million. **Number of employees at this location:** 200.

CHARTER BEHAVIORAL HEALTH SYSTEMS OF NORTHWEST INDIANA
101 West 61st Avenue, Hobart IN 46342. 219/947-4464. **Contact:** Human Resources. **Description:** A psychiatric hospital that provides a full range of services and a wide variety of treatment options for adults, adolescents, and children. Charter offers care for depression, drug and alcohol problems, anxiety, compulsive behaviors, and other emotional illnesses. Treatment options include an intensive outpatient program, partial hospitalization, and inpatient treatment. **NOTE:** Part-time jobs are offered. **Common positions include:** Account Manager; Administrative Assistant; Counselor; Psychologist; Registered Nurse; Social Worker. **Educational backgrounds include:** Health Care; Liberal Arts; Microsoft Word. **Benefits:** 401(k); Casual Dress - Fridays; Dental Insurance; Disability Coverage; Life Insurance; Medical Insurance; Tuition Assistance; Vacation Days (16+). **Corporate headquarters location:** Atlanta GA. **Other U.S. locations:** Nationwide. **CEO:** James Gallagher. **Annual sales/revenues:** Less than $5 million. **Number of employees at this location:** 75.

CHILD & ELDER CARE INSIGHTS, INC.
19111 Detroit Road, Suite 104, Rocky River OH 44116. 440/356-2900. **Fax:** 440/356-2919. **Contact:** Elisabeth A. Bryenton, President. **E-mail address:** info@carereports.com. **World Wide Web address:** http://www.carereports.com. **Description:** A national dependent care resource and referral service that maintains two national databases: CHILDBASE and ELDERBASE. CHILDBASE provides working parents with information about child care services including family day care providers, preschools, adoption resources, in-home care, and schools. ELDERBASE provides information on nursing homes, home health agencies, nutrition services, continuing care/retirement communities, and transportation services. **Common positions include:** Administrative Assistant; Database Administrator; Database Manager; Librarian; MIS Specialist. **Other U.S. locations:** Nationwide.

CHILDREN'S HOSPITAL
SCOTTISH RITE CENTER FOR CHILDHOOD LANGUAGE DISORDERS
1630 Columbia Road NW, Washington DC 20009. 202/939-4703. **Contact:** Human Resources. **Description:** A medical center for children with language disorders. **Corporate headquarters location:** This Location.

CHRISTIAN CITY
7290 Lester Road, Union City GA 30219. 770/964-3301. **Fax:** 770/964-7041. **Contact:** Charlotte Miceli, Human Resources Assistant. **World Wide Web address:** http://www.christiancity.org. **Description:** A nonprofit company operating a home for children, a retirement center, a convalescent center, an Alzheimer's care center, and residential health care services. Founded in 1964. **NOTE:** Entry-level positions and second and third shifts are offered. **Common positions include:** Accountant; Administrative Assistant; Certified Nurses Aide; Controller; Daycare Worker; Dietician/Nutritionist; Electrician; Emergency Medical Technician; Human Resources Manager; Licensed Practical Nurse; Medical Records Technician; Pharmacist; Public Relations Specialist; Registered Nurse; Secretary; Social Worker. **Educational backgrounds include:** Business Administration; Health Care; Nutrition; Public Relations. **Benefits:** 403(b); Daycare Assistance; Dental Insurance; Disability Coverage; Employee Discounts; Life Insurance; Medical Insurance; On-Site Daycare. **Special programs:** Summer Jobs. **Corporate headquarters location:** This Location. **Listed on:** Privately held. **President/CEO:** Robert Crutchfield.

CHRISTIANA CARE
WILMINGTON HOSPITAL
501 West 14th Street, Wilmington DE 19899. 302/733-1000. **Toll-free phone:** 800/999-9169. **Fax:** 302/428-5770. **Contact:** Director of Employment. **World Wide Web address:** http://www.christianacare.com. **Description:** An integrated health care system comprised of acute care hospitals, outpatient services, rehabilitative medicine, a primary care network, transitional/long-term care facilities, and home health care agencies. **Common positions include:** Accountant; Applications Engineer; Certified Nurses Aide; Certified Occupational Therapy Assistant; Computer Operator; Computer Programmer; Computer Support Technician; Customer Service Rep.; Database Administrator; Dietician/Nutritionist; EEG Technologist; EKG Technician; Emergency Medical Technician; Home Health Aide; Human Resources Manager; Licensed Practical Nurse; Medical Assistant; Medical Records Technician; Network Administrator; Nuclear Medicine Technologist; Nurse Practitioner; Occupational Therapist; Pharmacist; Physical Therapist; Physical Therapy Assistant; Physician; Radiological Technologist; Registered Nurse; Respiratory Therapist; Secretary; Social Worker; Speech-Language Pathologist; Surgical Technician. **Educational backgrounds include:** Accounting; Business Administration; Computer Science; Finance; Health Care. **Benefits:** 403(b); Casual Dress - Fridays; Daycare Assistance; Dental Insurance; Disability Coverage; Life Insurance; Medical Insurance; On-Site Daycare; Pension Plan; Tuition Assistance.

CHRISTUS ST. PATRICK HOSPITAL
P.O. Box 3401, Lake Charles LA 70602. 337/491-7572. **Physical address:** 1607 Foster Street, Lake Charles LA. **Fax:** 337/491-7769. **Recorded jobline:** 337/491-7519. **Contact:** Jo Anderson, Recruiter. **E-mail address:** jo_anderson@sph.christushealth.org. **World Wide Web address:** http://www.stpatrickhospital.org. **Description:** A nonprofit hospital that offers a variety of services including cardiovascular care, inpatient and outpatient services, cancer treatments, rehabilitation, physical therapy, and behavioral health services. Founded in

1908. **NOTE:** Entry-level positions are offered. **Common positions include:** Certified Nurses Aide; Dietician/Nutritionist; EEG Technologist; EKG Technician; Licensed Practical Nurse; Medical Records Technician; Nuclear Medicine Technologist; Occupational Therapist; Pharmacist; Physical Therapist; Physician; Registered Nurse; Respiratory Therapist; Secretary; Social Worker; Speech-Language Pathologist; Surgical Technician. **Educational backgrounds include:** Health Care; Nursing; Nutrition. **Benefits:** 403(b); Dental Insurance; Disability Coverage; Employee Discounts; Financial Planning Assistance; Flexible Schedule; Life Insurance; Medical Insurance; Pension Plan; Savings Plan; Scholarship Program; Tuition Assistance. **Office hours:** Monday - Friday, 8:00 a.m. - 4:30 p.m. **Parent company:** Christus Health. **CEO:** Jim Garoner.

CIVISTA MEDICAL CENTER
701 East Charles Street, P.O. Box 1070, La Plata MD 20646. 301/609-4444. **Fax:** 301/609-4417. **Recorded jobline:** 301/638-1805. **Contact:** Karen Savoy, Employment Coordinator. **World Wide Web address:** http://www. civista.org. **Description:** A 131-bed, full-service, community hospital. Founded in 1939. **Common positions include:** Accountant/Auditor; Administrative Assistant; Administrative Manager; Biomedical Engineer; Certified Nurses Aide; Chief Financial Officer; Claim Representative; Clerical Supervisor; Clinical Lab Technician; Collector; Computer Operator; Computer Programmer; Customer Service Representative; Dietician/Nutritionist; Education Administrator; EEG Technologist; EKG Technician; Electrician; Emergency Medical Technician; Finance Director; Health Services Manager; Human Resources Manager; Human Service Worker; Market Research Analyst; Marketing Specialist; Mechanical Engineer; Medical Records Technician; Nuclear Medicine Technologist; Occupational Therapist; Pharmacist; Physical Therapist; Psychologist; Public Relations Specialist; Radiological Technologist; Recreational Therapist; Registered Nurse; Respiratory Therapist; Secretary; Social Worker; Speech-Language Pathologist; Surgical Technician; Typist/Word Processor. **Educational backgrounds include:** Accounting; Biology; Business Administration; Chemistry; Communications; Computer Science; Engineering; Finance; Health Care; Marketing; Nutrition; Public Relations. **Benefits:** 403(b); Dental Insurance; Disability Coverage; Employee Discounts; Life Insurance; Medical Insurance; Pension Plan; Savings Plan; Tuition Assistance. **Special programs:** Internships. **Corporate headquarters location:** Waldorf MD. **President/CEO:** Susan Hunsaker.

CLEVELAND CLINIC FOUNDATION
9500 Euclid Avenue, Cleveland OH 44195. 216/444-2380. **Contact:** Human Resources. **World Wide Web address:** http://www. clevelandclinic.org. **Description:** A national referral center and international health resource center specializing in tertiary care, medical research, and medical education. **Common positions include:** Accountant; Administrator; Advertising Clerk; Architect; Attorney; Computer Programmer; Counselor; Credit Manager; Customer Service Rep.; Department Manager; Dietician/Nutritionist; Draftsperson; Human Resources Manager; Instructor/Trainer; Licensed Practical Nurse; Paralegal; Purchasing Agent/Manager; Sales Executive; Systems Analyst. **Educational backgrounds include:** Accounting; Business Administration; Communications; Computer Science; Finance; Health Care; Marketing. **Benefits:** Dental Insurance; Disability Coverage; Employee

Discounts; Life Insurance; Medical Insurance; Pension Plan; Savings Plan; Tuition Assistance. **Corporate headquarters location:** This Location. **Other U.S. locations:** Fort Lauderdale FL. **Number of employees nationwide:** 10,000.

COHERENT MEDICAL GROUP
2400 Condensa Street, Santa Clara CA 95051. 408/764-3000. **Fax:** 408/764-3948. **Contact:** Human Resources. **World Wide Web address:** http://www.coherentmedical.com. **Description:** Manufactures medical lasers for use in hair removal, skin resurfacing, removal of lesions and tattoos, lithotripsy, arthroscopy, and retinal surgery. Founded in 1966. **Common positions include:** Customer Service Rep.; Design Engineer; Electrical/Electronics Engineer; Industrial Engineer; Manufacturing Engineer; Marketing Manager; Mechanical Engineer; Quality Assurance Engineer; Sales Representative. **Corporate headquarters location:** This Location. **Parent company:** Coherent Inc.

COLLEGIATE HEALTH CARE
800 Connecticut Avenue, Norwalk CT 06854. 203/851-2400. **Contact:** Human Resources. **World Wide Web address:** http://www.collegiate.com. **Description:** Provides consulting, financial management, and technical services to educational institutions nationwide. **Common positions include:** Accountant; Administrative Assistant; Chief Financial Officer; Computer Support Technician; Controller; Dietician/Nutritionist; Human Resources Manager; Licensed Practical Nurse; Medical Assistant; Medical Records Technician; MIS Specialist; Nurse Practitioner; Occupational Therapist; Pharmacist; Physical Therapist; Physical Therapy Assistant; Physician; Radiological Technologist; Registered Nurse; Sales Executive; Secretary.

COLORADO MEDTECH, INC.
6175 Longbow Drive, Boulder CO 80301. 303/530-2660. **Fax:** 303/581-1010. **Contact:** Human Resources. **E-mail address:** cmedinfo@cmed.com. **World Wide Web address:** http://www.cmed.com. **Description:** Manufactures electro-mechanical medical devices, catheters, respiratory diagnostic instruments, MRI (Magnetic Resonance Imaging) systems, and similar medical devices. **Corporate headquarters location:** This Location. **Subsidiaries include:** Erbtec Engineering, Boulder CO; Novel Biomedical, Inc., Plymouth MN; RELA, Inc., Longmont CO. **Listed on:** NASDAQ. **Stock exchange symbol:** CMED.

COLUMBIA NEW PORT RICHEY HOSPITAL
5637 Marine Parkway, New Port Richey FL 34656. 727/845-9117. **Fax:** 727/845-9167. **Recorded jobline:** 727/845-4379. **Contact:** Mark Cohen, Director of Human Resources. **Description:** A 415-bed, JCAHO-accredited hospital. Services offered to the community include medical/surgical nursing, telemetry, psychiatry, ambulatory surgery, a catheterization lab, an in-house pool, critical care nursing, emergency rooms, and OR/RR. Columbia New Port Richey Hospital also has laboratory, radiology, nuclear medicine, pharmacy, and surgical suites. **NOTE:** Second and third shifts are offered. **Common positions include:** Accountant; Certified Nurses Aide; Clinical Lab Technician; Dietician/Nutritionist; EEG Technologist; EKG Technician; Electrician; Emergency Medical Technician; Licensed Practical Nurse; Medical Records Technician; Nuclear Medicine Technologist; Pharmacist; Radiological Technologist; Registered Nurse; Respiratory Therapist; Social Worker; Surgical Technician; Systems Analyst. **Educational backgrounds include:** Accounting; Business

Administration; Computer Science; Health Care. **Benefits:** 401(k); Daycare Assistance; Dental Insurance; Disability Coverage; Employee Discounts; Flexible Schedule; Life Insurance; Medical Insurance; Pension Plan; Tuition Assistance. **Office hours:** Monday - Friday, 8:00 a.m. - 4:30 p.m. **Corporate headquarters location:** Nashville TN. **CEO:** Andrew Oravec, Jr. **Number of employees at this location:** 1,150.

COMMUNITY HEALTH SYSTEM
FRESNO COMMUNITY MEDICAL CENTER
P.O. Box 1232, Fresno CA 93715. 559/442-6000. **Toll-free phone:** 800/442-3944. **Contact:** Human Resources. **World Wide Web address:** http://www. chsnet.com. **Description:** A comprehensive medical system with three acute care hospitals, three long-term care facilities, and home care services. Specialties include cancer, cardiology, emergency services, rehabilitation, and family birthing centers. **Common positions include:** Accountant/Auditor; Assistant Manager; Budget Analyst; Cashier; Chef/Cook/Kitchen Worker; Clerical Supervisor; Clinical Lab Technician; Computer Operator; Computer Programmer; Construction Trade Worker; Department Manager; Dietician/Nutritionist; EEG Technologist; EKG Technician; Electrician; Employment Interviewer; Financial Manager; Health Services Manager; Human Resources Manager; Interviewing Clerk; Librarian; Licensed Practical Nurse; Medical Records Technician; Nuclear Medicine Technologist; Occupational Therapist; Payroll Clerk; Pharmacist; Physical Therapist; Physician; Psychologist; Radiological Technologist; Receptionist; Recreation Worker; Recreational Therapist; Registered Nurse; Respiratory Therapist; Secretary; Social Worker; Sociologist; Speech-Language Pathologist; Stock Clerk; Surgical Technician; Systems Analyst; Typist/Word Processor. **Educational backgrounds include:** Accounting; Business Administration. **Benefits:** 403(b); Daycare Assistance; Dental Insurance; Disability Coverage; Employee Discounts; Life Insurance; Medical Insurance; Pension Plan; Tuition Assistance. **Corporate headquarters location:** This Location. **Number of employees at this location:** 4,200.

COMMUNITY HOSPITALS OF WILLIAMS COUNTY INC.
433 West High Street, Bryan OH 43506. 419/636-1131. **Fax:** 419/636-3100. **Contact:** Marianne Potts, Personnel Director. **Description:** Operates a 120-bed acute care hospital. **Common positions include:** Clerical Supervisor; Clinical Lab Technician; Computer Programmer; Counselor; Credit Manager; Customer Service Rep.; Dietician/Nutritionist; EKG Technician; Health Services Manager; Human Resources Manager; Human Service Worker; Licensed Practical Nurse; Medical Records Technician; Nuclear Medicine Technologist; Occupational Therapist; Pharmacist; Physical Therapist; Psychologist; Purchasing Agent/Manager; Radiological Technologist; Recreational Therapist; Registered Nurse; Respiratory Therapist; Social Worker; Surgical Technician. **Educational backgrounds include:** Health Care. **Benefits:** Dental Insurance; Employee Discounts; Life Insurance; Medical Insurance; Pension Plan; Tuition Assistance. **Corporate headquarters location:** This Location. **Number of employees at this location:** 600.

COMPUTERIZED MEDICAL SYSTEMS
1145 Corporate Lakes Drive, Suite 100, St. Louis MO 63132. 314/993-0003. **Contact:** Human Resources. **World Wide Web address:** http://www.cms-stl.com. **Description:** A developer of computerized radiation treatment systems.

CONCORD HOSPITAL
250 Pleasant Street, Concord NH 03301. 603/224-2759x3700. **Fax:** 603/228-7346. **Contact:** Suzanne McKendry, Director of Human Resources. **World Wide Web address:** http://www. concordhospital.org. **Description:** A full-service, nonprofit hospital offering both inpatient and outpatient services. **NOTE:** Second and third shifts are offered. **Common positions include:** Accountant; Administrative Assistant; Biomedical Engineer; Certified Nurses Aide; Computer Operator; Computer Programmer; Daycare Worker; EEG Technologist; EKG Technician; Librarian; Occupational Therapist; Pharmacist; Physical Therapist; Radiological Technologist; Registered Nurse; Respiratory Therapist; Secretary; Speech-Language Pathologist; Surgical Technician; Systems Analyst; Video Production Coordinator; Webmaster. **Educational backgrounds include:** Accounting; Biology; Computer Science; Health Care; Nutrition. **Benefits:** 403(b); Daycare Assistance; Dental Insurance; Disability Coverage; Employee Discounts; Flexible Schedule; Job Sharing; Life Insurance; Medical Insurance; On-Site Daycare; Pension Plan; Public Transit Available; Telecommuting; Tuition Assistance. **Special programs:** Internships. **Number of employees at this location:** 1,800.

MOSES CONE HEALTH SYSTEM
1200 North Elm Street, Greensboro NC 27401-1020. **Toll-free phone:** 800/476-6737. **Fax:** 336/832-2999. **Contact:** Diane Everhart, Director of Corporate Recruitment. **World Wide Web address:** http://www.mosescone.com. **Description:** A nonprofit hospital system operating The Moses H. Cone Memorial Hospital (547 beds), The Women's Hospital of Greensboro (115 beds), and Wesley Long Community Hospital. Moses Cone Memorial Hospital is a Level II trauma center as well as a teaching hospital and referral center. The hospital operates five centers specializing in neuroscience, cardiology, cancer, rehabilitation, and trauma. **Common positions include:** Accountant/Auditor; Blue-Collar Worker Supervisor; Claim Rep.; Clerical Supervisor; Clinical Lab Technician; Computer Programmer; Dental Assistant/Dental Hygienist; Dietician/Nutritionist; EEG Technologist; EKG Technician; Electrician; Emergency Medical Technician; Financial Analyst; Library Technician; Mechanical Engineer; Medical Records Technician; Nuclear Medicine Technologist; Occupational Therapist; Pharmacist; Physical Therapist; Physician; Preschool Worker; Psychologist; Public Relations Specialist; Purchasing Agent/Manager; Radiological Technologist; Recreational Therapist; Registered Nurse; Respiratory Therapist; Restaurant/Food Service Manager; Social Worker; Speech-Language Pathologist; Surgical Technician; Systems Analyst; Teacher/Professor. **Educational backgrounds include:** Accounting; Biology; Computer Science; Finance; Marketing. **Benefits:** 403(b); Daycare Assistance; Dental Insurance; Disability Coverage; Employee Discounts; Life Insurance; Medical Insurance; Pension Plan; Tuition Assistance. **Office hours:** Monday - Friday, 8:30 a.m. - 5:00 p.m. **Corporate headquarters location:** This Location. **Number of employees at this location:** 5,500.

CONMED CORPORATION
310 Broad Street, Utica NY 13501. 315/797-8375. **Fax:** 315/735-1523. **Contact:** Personnel. **World Wide Web address:** http://www.conmed.com. **Description:** Develops, manufactures, and markets advanced electrosurgical and single-use medical products for surgeons and other critical care providers located throughout the world. The company offers complete electrosurgical systems

which include generators and disposable electrosurgical pencils, instruments, and ground pads. Patient care products include disposable electrocardiogram electrodes to monitor the heart, a disposable stabilization device for intravenous therapy, electrodes for neuromuscular stimulation, and various cable and wire products used in medical telemetry. **Common positions include:** Accountant; Biological Scientist; Biomedical Engineer; Buyer; Chemical Engineer; Computer Programmer; Customer Service Rep.; Draftsperson; EEG Technologist; Financial Analyst; General Manager; Human Resources Manager; Industrial Engineer; Industrial Production Manager; Materials Engineer; Mechanical Engineer; Operations/Production Manager; Systems Analyst. **Educational backgrounds include:** Accounting; Business Administration; Chemistry; Computer Science; Engineering; Finance; Health Care; Liberal Arts; Marketing. **Benefits:** 401(k); Dental Insurance; Disability Coverage; Life Insurance; Medical Insurance; Tuition Assistance. **Corporate headquarters location:** This Location.

CONTINUUM
10920 Via Frontera, San Diego CA 92127-1704. 858/485-0933. **Contact:** Field Recruiting. **Description:** A nationwide mobile health testing service. Continuum provides health screening for unions, major corporations, public utilities, and other public and private organizations. **NOTE:** Entry-level positions are offered. **Common positions include:** Licensed Practical Nurse; Medical Assistant; Radiological Technologist; Registered Nurse. **Benefits:** 401(k); Dental Insurance; Disability Coverage; Financial Planning Assistance; Life Insurance; Medical Insurance; Profit Sharing; Tuition Assistance. **Corporate headquarters location:** This Location. **Other U.S. locations:** Nationwide. **Listed on:** Privately held.

CORAM HEALTHCARE CORPORATION
1125 17th Street, Suite 2100, Denver CO 80202. 303/292-4973. **Fax:** 303/298-0043. **Contact:** Human Resources. **World Wide Web address:** http://www.coram-healthcare.com. **Description:** One of the largest home health infusion therapy companies in the United States. The company provides a wide range of alternate site delivery services including ambulatory and home infusion therapies, lithotripsy, and institutional pharmacy services. **Corporate headquarters location:** This Location. **Other U.S. locations:** Nationwide. **Subsidiaries include:** Coraflex Health Services; HealthInfusion Inc.; Medisys Inc.; T2 Medical. **Listed on:** New York Stock Exchange. **Stock exchange symbol:** CRH. **Annual sales/revenues:** More than $100 million.

CORPORATE JETS, INC.
57 Allegheny County Airport, West Mifflin PA 15122. 412/466-2500. **Toll-free phone:** 800/245-0230. **Fax:** 412/469-1556. **Contact:** Dawn Chambers, Director of Human Resources. **World Wide Web address:** http://www.corpjet.com. **Description:** This location houses the company's aircraft maintenance facility. Overall, Corporate Jets, Inc. is a general aviation company, primarily engaged in providing both charter and air medical services (AMS) including patient and organ transport. Founded in 1969. **Common positions include:** Accountant; Aircraft Mechanic/Engine Specialist; Human Resources Specialist; Safety Specialist. **Corporate headquarters location:** This Location. **Other U.S. locations:** Scottsdale AZ. **International locations:** Naples; Singapore. **Number of employees at this location:** 320. **Number of employees nationwide:** 520.

COVENANT HEALTHCARE
1020 Almira Street, Saginaw MI 48602. 517/583-4080. **Fax:** 517/583-4816. **Contact:** Human Resources. **E-mail address:** resume@chs-mi.com. **World Wide Web address:** http://www. covenanthealthcare.com. **Description:** A comprehensive health care facility that operates a main medical facility, numerous outpatient facilities, and two acute care medical centers. Covenant Healthcare offers a broad range of services including acute care, cardiology, oncology, obstetrics, and neonatal and pediatric care.

COX HEALTH SYSTEM
3801 South National Avenue, Springfield MO 65807. 417/269-6162. **Fax:** 417/269-6595. **Recorded jobline:** 417/269-5525. **Contact:** Human Resources. **Description:** Operates a multifacility hospital. **Common positions include:** Computer Programmer; Dietician/Nutritionist; EEG Technologist; Electrician; Licensed Practical Nurse; Medical Records Technician; Nuclear Medicine Technologist; Occupational Therapist; Pharmacist; Physical Therapist; Registered Nurse; Respiratory Therapist; Social Worker; Surgical Technician; Systems Analyst. **Educational backgrounds include:** Health Care. **Benefits:** Dental Insurance; Disability Coverage; Life Insurance; Medical Insurance; Pension Plan; Savings Plan; Tuition Assistance. **Corporate headquarters location:** This Location. **Subsidiaries include:** Burrell; Cox Monett; Oxford Health Care. **Number of employees at this location:** 4,500.

CRITICARE SYSTEMS, INC.
20925 Crossroads Circle, Waukesha WI 53186. 262/798-8282. **Contact:** Human Resources. **World Wide Web address:** http://www.csiusa.com. **Description:** Designs, manufactures, and markets products using proprietary technologies that improve patient management and reduce health care costs. The company also develops and markets patient monitors for respiratory care, anesthesia, and outpatient ambulatory care. Founded in 1984. **Corporate headquarters location:** This Location. **International locations:** Barcelona, Spain; Copenhagen, Denmark; Melbourne, Australia; Osaka, Japan; Singapore. **Listed on:** NASDAQ.

THE CUTTING EDGE
395 Park Avenue, Worcester MA 01610. 508/363-3000. **Contact:** Human Resources. **World Wide Web address:** http://www.tcedge.com. **Description:** Distributes used medical equipment including stretchers, oxygen tents, blood pressure monitors, and portable ventilators. **Corporate headquarters location:** This Location.

CYPRESS FAIRBANKS MEDICAL CENTER HOSPITAL
10655 Steepletop Drive, Houston TX 77065-4222. 281/897-3500. **Fax:** 281/890-0236. **Recorded jobline:** 281/897-3530. **Contact:** Melanie Webb, Recruiter. **E-mail address:** cfmch.jobs@ tenethealth.com. **World Wide Web address:** http://www.cyfairhospital.com. **Description:** A 149-bed acute care hospital offering diagnostic services on both outpatient and inpatient bases. Founded in 1983. **NOTE:** Entry-level positions, part-time jobs, and second and third shifts are offered. **Common positions include:** Certified Nurses Aide; Certified Occupational Therapy Assistant; Customer Service Rep.; Dietician/Nutritionist; EEG Technologist; EKG Technician; Emergency Medical Technician; Home Health Aide; Medical Records Technician; Medical Secretary; Nuclear Medicine Technologist; Pharmacist; Physical Therapist; Radiological Technologist; Registered Nurse; Respiratory Therapist; Secretary; Speech-Language Pathologist;

Surgical Technician. **Educational backgrounds include:** Health Care. **Benefits:** 401(k); Dental Insurance; Life Insurance; Medical Insurance; Sick Days; Tuition Assistance; Vacation Days. **Parent company:** Tenet Houston HealthSystem. **CEO:** Elizabeth Primeaux.

DOC OPTICS CORPORATION
19800 West Eight Mile Road, Southfield MI 48075. 248/354-7100. **Contact:** Bridget Gauthier, Director of Personnel. **World Wide Web address:** http://www.docoptics.com. **Description:** A full-service retail optical chain that provides eye examinations, laser surger, and eyeglass repair. **Corporate headquarters location:** This Location. **Number of employees at this location:** 800.

D.R.E., INC.
1800 Williamson Court, Louisville KY 40223. 502/244-4444. **Toll-free phone:** 800/477-2006. **Fax:** 502/244-0369. **Contact:** Human Resources. **E-mail address:** dre-inc@worldnet.att.net. **World Wide Web address:** http://www.dremedical.com. **Description:** A distributor of new and used medical equipment. The Domestic Medical Equipment Division sells anesthesia equipment, surgical equipment, and operating room tables. The company also has a Veterinary Medical Equipment Division. **Corporate headquarters location:** This Location.

DAVIS BEHAVIORAL HEALTH
P.O. Box 689, Farmington UT 84025. 801/451-7799. **Fax:** 801/451-6331. **Contact:** Dawn MacKinnon, Personnel Director. **Description:** Provides mental health and alcohol and drug services for adults and children. Services include inpatient, outpatient, residential, prevention, day treatment, 24-hour emergency response, evaluation, and therapeutic foster care. **NOTE:** Entry-level positions are offered. **Common positions include:** Counselor; Licensed Practical Nurse; Physician; Psychologist; Registered Nurse; Secretary; Social Worker. **Educational backgrounds include:** Health Care; Social Science. **Benefits:** 401(k); Dental Insurance; Disability Coverage; Flexible Schedule; Life Insurance; Medical Insurance; Pension Plan; Sick Days (11+); Vacation Days (10 - 20). **Number of employees at this location:** 250.

DAVIS DENTAL LABORATORY
3680 Hagen Drive SE, Grand Rapids MI 49548. 616/243-3311. **Fax:** 616/243-4710. **Contact:** Human Resources. **World Wide Web address:** http://www.dentalservices.net. **Description:** A full-service dental laboratory that manufactures and supplies various restorative dental products. **NOTE:** Entry-level positions are offered. **Benefits:** 401(k); Dental Insurance; Disability Coverage; Employee Discounts; Life Insurance; Medical Insurance; Sick Days (1 - 5); Vacation Days (6 - 10). **Special programs:** Internships; Co-ops. **Number of employees at this location:** 130.

DAVOL INC.
100 Sockanossett Crossroad, Cranston RI 02920. 401/463-7000. **Fax:** 401/464-9446. **Contact:** Human Resources. **World Wide Web address:** http://www.davol.com. **Description:** Designs, develops, and manufactures surgical products. The company specializes in hernia repair, laparoscopy, and orthopeadics products. **Common positions include:** Accountant; Biomedical Engineer; Buyer; Clinical Lab Technician; Computer Programmer; Customer Service Representative; Design Engineer; Financial Analyst; Graphic Artist; Graphic Designer; Manufacturing Engineer; Marketing Manager; Mechanical Engineer; MIS Specialist; Purchasing Agent/Manager; Sales Representative; Secretary. **Educational backgrounds include:** Accounting; Biology; Business Administration; Chemistry; Computer Science; Engineering; Finance; Marketing; Software Development; Software Tech. Support. **Benefits:** 401(k); Dental Insurance; Disability Coverage; Life Insurance; Medical Insurance; Pension Plan; Tuition Assistance. **Corporate headquarters location:** This Location. **Other U.S. locations:** Lawrence KS; Woburn MA. **Parent company:** C.R. Bard Inc. **Listed on:** New York Stock Exchange.

DEACONESS HOSPITAL
P.O. Box 37000, Billings MT 59107. 406/657-4000. **Physical address:** 2800 10th Avenue North, Billings MT 59101. **Contact:** Recruitment Office. **World Wide Web address:** http://www.billingsclinic.org. **Description:** A full-service, nonprofit, 272-bed, regional medical center. Affiliates include Billings Clinic, a 140-physician multispecialty medical clinic with six locations; Deaconess Research Institute; Deaconess Foundation; and Deaconess Psychiatric Billings Clinic Services, which includes the Psychiatric Center and Behavioral Health Clinic, providing adults and youth with a continuum of comprehensive mental health care. Long-term care is provided through Aspen Meadows, a skilled nursing facility, and Deaconess Hospital's Transitional Care Unit. Cardiology services are provided at the Deaconess Medical Center and the Billings Clinic. Deaconess also provides a series of educational programs and a women's resource center.

DEAN MEDICAL CENTER
1313 Fish Hatchery Road, Madison WI 53715. 608/252-8000. **Recorded jobline:** 608/252-5354. **Contact:** Human Resources. **Description:** A multispecialty group practice with over 30 locations in southwestern Wisconsin. **Common positions include:** Health Care Administrator; Health Services Manager; Licensed Practical Nurse; Registered Nurse. **Corporate headquarters location:** This Location.

DEL MAR MEDICAL SYSTEMS, LLC
1621 Alton Parkway, Irvine CA 92606. 949/250-3200. **Fax:** 949/261-0529. **Contact:** Mr. E.L. Phillips, Personnel Manager. **World Wide Web address:** http://www.delmarmedical.com. **Description:** Develops, manufactures, and markets a wide range of medical monitoring and testing equipment. Products include stress tests, ambulatory blood pressure monitors, ambulatory transesophagael testing devics, and the Adiovisual Superimposed Electrocardiographic Presentation (AVSEP). **Corporate headquarters location:** This Location.

DENCOR/WILLAMETTE DENTAL GROUP OREGON DENTAL SPECIALISTS
14025 SW Farmington Road, Suite 300, Beaverton OR 97005. 503/644-6444. **Recorded jobline:** 503/671-9486. **Contact:** Human Resources. **Description:** This location houses administrative offices. Overall, Dencor/Willamette Dental Group operates dentist's offices in Oregon and Washington. The company also provides dental insurance plans. **Corporate headquarters location:** This Location.

DENTSPLY INTERNATIONAL INC.
570 West College Avenue, P.O. Box 872, York PA 17405-0872. 717/845-7511. **Fax:** 717/849-4752. **Contact:** Human Resources. **World Wide Web address:** http://www.dentsply.com. **Description:** A leading manufacturer of X-ray equipment and other products for the dental field including artificial teeth, prophylaxis paste, ultrasonic sealers, and bone substitute/grafting

materials. **Corporate headquarters location:** This Location. **Other U.S. locations:** Carlsbad CA; Encino CA; Los Angeles CA; Lakewood CO; Milford DE; Des Plaines IL; Elgin IL; Burlington NJ; Maumee OH; Tulsa OK; Johnson City TN. **International locations:** Argentina; Australia; Brazil; Canada; China; England; France; Germany; Hong Kong; India; Italy; Japan; Mexico; Philippines; Puerto Rico; Russia; Switzerland; Thailand; Vietnam. **Listed on:** NASDAQ. **Stock exchange symbol:** XRAY.

DEPUY INC.
P.O. Box 988, Warsaw IN 46581-0988. 219/267-8143. **Contact:** Human Resources. **World Wide Web address:** http://www.depuy.com. **Description:** A medical device manufacturing company specializing in orthopedic products including total joint replacement and fracture management devices. **Common positions include:** Accountant/Auditor; Biological Scientist; Biomedical Engineer; Blue-Collar Worker Supervisor; Buyer; Computer Programmer; Credit Manager; Customer Service Representative; Draftsperson; Financial Analyst; Human Resources Manager; Industrial Engineer; Marketing Specialist; Mechanical Engineer; Metallurgical Engineer; Operations/Production Manager; Purchasing Agent/Manager; Quality Control Supervisor; Systems Analyst; Technical Writer/Editor. **Educational backgrounds include:** Accounting; Biology; Business Administration; Computer Science; Engineering; Finance; Marketing. **Benefits:** Dental Insurance; Disability Coverage; Employee Discounts; Life Insurance; Medical Insurance; Pension Plan; Tuition Assistance. **Special programs:** Internships. **Corporate headquarters location:** This Location. **Other U.S. locations:** Jackson MI; Albuquerque NM. **Number of employees nationwide:** 785.

DES MOINES GENERAL HOSPITAL
603 East 12th Street, Des Moines IA 50309. 515/263-4200. **Contact:** Human Resources. **World Wide Web address:** http://www.dmgeneral.com. **Description:** A nonprofit hospital offering a complete range of health care services including inpatient and outpatient surgical services, rehabilitation services, Gateway (centers for both inpatient and outpatient treatment of addictions), Connections (mental health care for adults 55 and older), obstetrical services, One Call Information Services, Des Moines General Family Practice Clinics, skilled nursing services, home health services, neurological services, inpatient and outpatient cardiac diagnostic and rehabilitation services, diagnostic imaging services, critical care services, and emergency services.

DIELECTRICS INDUSTRIES, INC.
DMC
300 Burnett Road, Chicopee MA 01020. 413/594-4320. **Contact:** Human Resources. **World Wide Web address:** http://www.dielectrics.com. **Description:** As the medical division of Dielectrics Industries, DMC designs and fabricates a variety of sophisticated medical devices for the laparoscopic, orthopedic, and blood fluid delivery markets. Overall, Dielectrics Industries is a leading designer, developer, fabricator, and supplier of air cell and other bladder technologies. Markets served include medical, aerospace, automotive, recreational, and industrial. Products include laparoscopic surgical devices, inflatable vests, in-line skate inserts, and lumbar support systems. **Corporate headquarters location:** This Location.

DIOCESAN HEALTH FACILITIES
368 North Main Street, Fall River MA 02720. 508/679-8154. **Contact:** Human Resources. **World Wide Web address:** http://www.dhfo.org. **Description:** Operates nonprofit nursing homes including Catholic Memorial Home (Fall River MA), Our Lady's Haven (Fairhaven MA), Marian Manor (Taunton MA), Madonna Manor (North Attleboro MA), and Sacred Heart (New Bedford MA). **Corporate headquarters location:** This Location.

DOCTORS HOSPITAL NORTH
1087 Dennison Avenue, Columbus OH 43201. 614/297-4000. **Fax:** 614/297-4992. **Recorded jobline:** 614/297-4367. **Contact:** Beth West, Human Resources Specialist. **World Wide Web address:** http://www.doctors-10tv.com. **Description:** A 450-bed, nonprofit, acute care, osteopathic hospital. Founded in 1940. **NOTE:** Entry-level positions and second and third shifts are offered. **Common positions include:** Account Rep.; Administrative Assistant; Biomedical Engineer; Clinical Lab Technician; Customer Service Rep.; EKG Technician; Electrical/Electronics Engineer; Electrician; Emergency Medical Technician; Environmental Engineer; Medical Records Technician; MIS Specialist; Nuclear Medicine Technologist; Occupational Therapist; Pharmacist; Physical Therapist; Physician; Public Relations Specialist; Radiological Technologist; Registered Nurse; Respiratory Therapist; Secretary; Social Worker; Speech-Language Pathologist; Surgical Technician; Systems Analyst. **Educational backgrounds include:** Business Administration; Chemistry; Health Care; Nutrition. **Benefits:** 403(b); Dental Insurance; Disability Coverage; Employee Discounts; Flexible Schedule; Job Sharing; Life Insurance; Medical Insurance; Pension Plan; Public Transit Available; Savings Plan; Tuition Assistance. **Special programs:** Internships. **Internship information:** Doctors Hospital North has an RN internship program. **Parent company:** D.H. Corporation. **Listed on:** Privately held. **Annual sales/revenues:** $21 - $50 million. **Number of employees at this location:** 2,100.

DODD DENTAL LABORATORIES, INC.
24 Lukens Drive, P.O. Box 1005, New Castle DE 19720-7005. 302/661-6000. **Fax:** 302/661-6016. **Contact:** Human Resources. **Description:** A dental laboratory providing dental prosthetic devices. **Benefits:** 401(k); Incentive Plan; Stock Option. **Other U.S. locations:** Nationwide. **Parent company:** National Dentex Corporation is one of the largest operators of dental laboratories in the United States. These dental laboratories provide a full range of custom-made dental prosthetic appliances divided into three main groups: restorative products (crowns and bridges); reconstructive products (partial and full dentures); and cosmetic products (porcelain veneers and ceramic crowns). Each lab is operated as a stand-alone facility under the direction of a local manager. All sales and marketing is done through each lab's own direct sales force. **Listed on:** NASDAQ.

DURHAM REGIONAL HOSPITAL
WATTS NURSING SCHOOL
3643 North Roxboro Street, Durham NC 27704. 919/470-4000. **Contact:** Human Resources. **World Wide Web address:** http://www.drh.duhs.duke.edu. **Description:** A full-service hospital. Watts Nursing School (also at this location) can be contacted at 919/470-7346. **Parent company:** Duke University Health System.

EBI MEDICAL SYSTEMS, INC.
100 Interpace Parkway, Parsippany NJ 07054. 973/299-9300. **Fax:** 973/402-1396. **Contact:** Human Resources. **World Wide Web address:** http://www.ebimedical.com. **Description:** Designs,

develops, manufactures, and markets products used primarily by orthopedic medical specialists in both surgical and nonsurgical therapies. Products include electrical bone growth stimulators, orthopedic support devices, spinal fixation devices for spinal fusion, external fixation devices, and cold temperature therapy. Founded in 1977. **NOTE:** Entry-level positions and part-time jobs are offered. **Common positions include:** Accountant; Computer Operator; Computer Programmer; Customer Service Rep.; Design Engineer; Electrical/Electronics Engineer; Marketing Manager; Mechanical Engineer; Sales Rep.; Secretary. **Educational backgrounds include:** AS400 Certification; Biology; Business Administration; Computer Science; Engineering; Health Care; Marketing; Microsoft Office. **Benefits:** 401(k); Dental Insurance; Life Insurance; Medical Insurance; Tuition Assistance. **Special programs:** Internships; Training; Summer Jobs. **Corporate headquarters location:** This Location. **Other U.S. locations:** OK. **International locations:** Puerto Rico. **Parent company:** Biomet, Inc. **Listed on:** NASDAQ. **Stock exchange symbol:** BMET. **Number of employees at this location:** 360.

EDWARDS LIFESCIENCES
One Edwards Way, Irvine CA 92614. 949/250-2500. **Contact:** Human Resources. **World Wide Web address:** http://www.edwards.com. **Description:** Designs, develops, manufactures, and markets disposable medical devices used in the handling, processing, and purifying of blood during surgical and medical procedures. **Corporate headquarters location:** This Location. **International locations:** Worldwide. **Listed on:** New York Stock Exchange. **Stock exchange symbol:** EW. **Annual sales/revenues:** More than $100 million.

EMPI, INC.
599 Cardigan Road, St. Paul MN 55126-4099. 651/415-9000. **Fax:** 651/415-8406. **Contact:** Human Resources. **World Wide Web address:** http://www.empi.com. **Description:** Manufactures and markets products for incontinence, physical rehabilitation, and orthopedics. Major products include neuromuscular stimulators, braces and splints, drug administering devices, and cervical traction devices. **Corporate headquarters location:** This Location. **Listed on:** NASDAQ. **Stock exchange symbol:** EMPI.

ENDOSONICS CORPORATION
2870 Kilgore Road, Rancho Cordova CA 95670. 916/638-8008. **Contact:** Human Resources. **World Wide Web address:** http://www.endosonics.com. **Description:** Develops, manufactures, and markets interventional catheter products such as balloon angioplasty catheters, ultrasound imaging, and site-specific drug delivery catheters. These products target coronary angioplasty, peripheral vascular, neurointerventional, and drug delivery procedures. **Corporate headquarters location:** This Location.

EPISCOPAL MINISTRIES TO THE AGING
7200 Third Avenue, Sykesville MD 21784. 410/795-8800. **Fax:** 410/549-6788. **Contact:** Susan Summers, Vice President of Human Resources. **World Wide Web address:** http://www.emaseniorcare.org. **Description:** A nonprofit company that provides a variety of prgrams and services to the elderly. Facilities include: Brightwood is a retirement community; Buckingham's Choice is a continuing care retirement community; Copper Ridge conducts care, education, and research for the memory impaired; and Fairhaven is a continuing care retirment community that provide assisted living, independent living, and health care. **NOTE:** Entry-level positions and second and third shifts are offered. **Common positions include:** Certified Nurses Aide; Licensed Practical Nurse; Registered Nurse. **Educational backgrounds include:** Health Care. **Benefits:** 403(b); Dental Insurance; Disability Coverage; Flexible Schedule; Job Sharing; Medical Insurance; Pension Plan; Savings Plan; Tuition Assistance. **Special programs:** Training. **Office hours:** Monday - Friday, 9:00 a.m. - 5:00 p.m. **Corporate headquarters location:** This Location. **Subsidiaries include:** Fairhaven Inc. is a continuing care retirement community with 420 residents in independent living, assisted living, and comprehensive care units. Copper Ridge, Inc. is a nursing facility specializing in care for the memory-impaired, with accommodations for 126 residents in its assisted living and comprehensive care units. Buckingham's Choice is a continuing care retirement community. **Annual sales/revenues:** $11 - $20 million.

EPIX MEDICAL INC.
71 Rogers Street, Cambridge MA 02142. 617/250-6000. **Contact:** Human Resources. **World Wide Web address:** http://www.epixmed.com. **Description:** Engaged in the development of advanced imaging agents. The company's initial products in development are for magnetic resonance imaging. **Common positions include:** Chemist. **Educational backgrounds include:** Chemistry. **Benefits:** 401(k); Dental Insurance; Disability Coverage; Life Insurance; Medical Insurance; Tuition Assistance. **Corporate headquarters location:** This Location.

ETHICON, INC.
U.S. Route 22, P.O. Box 151, Somerville NJ 08876. 908/218-0707. **Contact:** Human Resources. **Description:** Manufactures products for precise wound closure including sutures, ligatures, mechanical wound closure instruments, and related products. The company also makes its own surgical needles and provides needle-suture combinations to surgeons. **Corporate headquarters location:** This Location. **Parent company:** Johnson & Johnson (New Brunswick NJ).

EVANSTON HOSPITAL CORPORATION
2650 Ridge Avenue, Evanston IL 60201. 847/570-2600. **Fax:** 847/570-1903. **Contact:** Employment Office. **Description:** Operates Evanston Hospital (also at this location), as well as Glenbrook Hospital (Glenview IL). **Common positions include:** Buyer; Dental Assistant/Dental Hygienist; EKG Technician; Medical Records Technician; Pharmacist; Surgical Technician. **Educational backgrounds include:** Accounting; Biology; Business Administration; Chemistry; Liberal Arts. **Benefits:** Dental Insurance; Disability Coverage; Employee Discounts; Life Insurance; Medical Insurance; Pension Plan; Profit Sharing. **Corporate headquarters location:** This Location. **Number of employees at this location:** 3,000. **Number of employees nationwide:** 4,000.

EVEREST & JENNINGS
3601 Rider Trail South, Earth City MO 63045. 314/512-7000. **Contact:** Human Resource Director. **Description:** Everest & Jennings is a holding company whose subsidiaries design, manufacture, and market wheelchairs, home care beds, nursing home and hospital beds and furniture, and oxygen therapy products. **Common positions include:** Accountant; Computer Programmer; Draftsperson; Electrical/Electronics Engineer; Mechanical Engineer; Quality Control Supervisor. **Educational backgrounds include:** Accounting; Business Administration; Computer Science; Marketing;

Mathematics. **Benefits:** Dental Insurance; Disability Coverage; Employee Discounts; Life Insurance; Medical Insurance; Pension Plan; Tuition Assistance. **Corporate headquarters location:** This Location. **Parent company:** Graham Field. **Listed on:** American Stock Exchange.

EVEREST MEDICAL CORPORATION
13755 First Avenue North, Suite 500, Plymouth MN 55441-5454. 612/473-6262. **Fax:** 612/473-6465. **Contact:** Human Resources. **World Wide Web address:** http://www.everestmedical.com. **Description:** Manufactures bipolar laparoscopy, cardiac surgery, and gastrointestinal products used during surgery. **Corporate headquarters location:** This Location. **Listed on:** NASDAQ. **Stock exchange symbol:** EVMD. **Annual sales/revenues:** $5 - $10 million.

EXETER HOSPITAL
11 Court Street, Exeter NH 03833. 603/778-7311. **Fax:** 603/778-6713. **Recorded jobline:** 603/778-6660. **Contact:** Danielle Hughes, Human Resources Department. **E-mail address:** ehrjobs@ehr.org. **Description:** An acute care, 100-bed hospital. Founded in 1892. **NOTE:** Entry-level positions and second and third shifts are offered. **Common positions include:** Account Manager; Account Representative; Administrative Assistant; Certified Nurses Aide; Clerical Supervisor; Clinical Lab Technician; Customer Service Representative; EEG Technologist; EKG Technician; Emergency Medical Technician; Licensed Practical Nurse; Medical Records Technician; Nurse Practitioner; Occupational Therapist; Physical Therapist; Physician; Radiological Technologist; Registered Nurse; Respiratory Therapist; Secretary; Speech-Language Pathologist; Surgical Technician; Systems Analyst; Typist/Word Processor. **Educational backgrounds include:** Accounting; Business Administration; Finance; Health Care; Software Development; Software Tech. Support. **Benefits:** 401(k); 403(b); Dental Insurance; Disability Coverage; Employee Discounts; Flexible Schedule; Job Sharing; Life Insurance; Medical Insurance; Pension Plan; Savings Plan; Tuition Assistance. **Special programs:** Internships; Summer Jobs. **Corporate headquarters location:** This Location. **Parent company:** Exeter Health Resources is a nonprofit company comprised of Exeter Hospital, an acute care, 100-bed hospital; Exeter Healthcare, a long term care, subacute, rehabilitative hospital with 125 beds; Rockingham Visiting Nurse Association and Hospice; Synergy Health and Fitness; and CORE Physician Health Services, which offers primary care physicians and family medical services. **President/CEO:** Kevin Callahan. **Number of employees at this location:** 1,200.

FAIRVIEW HEALTH SERVICES
2450 Riverside Avenue, Minneapolis MN 55454. 612/672-4545. **Fax:** 612/672-6337. **Contact:** Human Resources. **World Wide Web address:** http://www.fairview.org. **Description:** A nonprofit, regionally integrated health care network that provides primary, specialty, acute, long-term, and home care services. Fairview Health Services offers hospitals, primary and specialty care clinics, retail pharmacies, and long-term care facilities. **NOTE:** Entry-level positions are offered. **Common positions include:** Accountant; Administrative Assistant; Biomedical Engineer; Blue-Collar Worker Supervisor; Buyer; Certified Nurses Aide; Clerical Supervisor; Clinical Lab Technician; Computer Operator; Computer Programmer; Counselor; Customer Service Representative; Database Manager; Dietician/Nutritionist; EEG Technologist; EKG Technician; Electrician; Emergency Medical Technician; Finance Director; Financial Analyst; Human Resources Manager; Librarian; Licensed Practical Nurse; Medical Records Technician; MIS Specialist; Nuclear Medicine Technologist; Nurse Practitioner; Occupational Therapist; Pharmacist; Physical Therapist; Physician; Psychologist; Public Relations Specialist; Purchasing Agent/Manager; Radiological Technologist; Registered Nurse; Respiratory Therapist; Secretary; Social Worker; Speech-Language Pathologist; Surgical Technician; Typist/Word Processor. **Educational backgrounds include:** Accounting; Biology; Business Administration; Computer Science; Health Care; Nursing; Nutrition. **Benefits:** 403(b); Dental Insurance; Disability Coverage; Employee Discounts; Life Insurance; Medical Insurance; Pension Plan. **Special programs:** Internships. **Corporate headquarters location:** This Location. **Parent company:** Fairview Health Services. **Listed on:** Privately held. **President/CEO:** David R. Page. **Number of employees nationwide:** 15,000.

FIDELITY HEALTHCARE INC.
3832 Kettering Boulevard, Dayton OH 45439. 937/208-6400. **Fax:** 937/208-6482. **Contact:** Sherri Pekar, Human Resources Secretary. **Description:** A home health care agency that provides nurses and home health aides to clients. **Common positions include:** Certified Nurses Aide; Claim Rep.; Home Health Aide; Human Resources Manager; Licensed Practical Nurse; Medical Records Technician; Occupational Therapist; Physical Therapist; Physical Therapy Assistant; Registered Nurse; Respiratory Therapist; Secretary; Social Worker; Systems Analyst. **Educational backgrounds include:** Computer Science; Health Care. **Benefits:** 403(b); Casual Dress - Fridays; Daycare Assistance; Dental Insurance; Disability Coverage; Flexible Schedule; Life Insurance; Medical Insurance; Pension Plan. **Office hours:** Monday - Friday, 8:00 a.m. - 5:00 p.m.

FISCHER IMAGING CORPORATION
12300 North Grant Street, Denver CO 80241-3120. 303/452-6800. **Fax:** 303/450-4335. **Contact:** Human Resources. **World Wide Web address:** http://www.fischerimaging.com. **Description:** Develops, manufactures, and markets medical imaging systems. The company provides medical systems for the electrophysiology, fluoroscopic, mammography, and radiographic markets. **Common positions include:** Accountant/Auditor; Buyer; Computer Programmer; Credit Manager; Customer Service Representative; Designer; Draftsperson; Electrical/Electronics Engineer; Electrician; Mechanical Engineer; Purchasing Agent/Manager; Quality Control Supervisor; Software Engineer. **Educational backgrounds include:** Accounting; Engineering. **Benefits:** 401(k); Daycare Assistance; Dental Insurance; Disability Coverage; Life Insurance; Medical Insurance; Tuition Assistance. **Corporate headquarters location:** This Location. **Listed on:** New York Stock Exchange. **Number of employees at this location:** 350. **Number of employees nationwide:** 540.

FISHKILL HEALTH CENTER
130 North Road, Beacon NY 12508. 914/831-8704. **Fax:** 914/831-1124. **Contact:** Human Resources. **Description:** A 160-bed, skilled care nursing home. **NOTE:** Entry-level positions and second and third shifts are offered. **Common positions include:** Activity Director; Certified Nurses Aide; Dietician/Nutritionist; Licensed Practical Nurse; Occupational Therapist; Physical Therapist; Registered Nurse; Social Worker. **Educational backgrounds include:** Health Care. **Benefits:** 401(k); Dental Insurance; Employee Discounts; Flexible Schedule; Life Insurance; Medical

Insurance; Public Transit Available; Tuition Assistance. **Special programs:** Internships; Training; Summer Jobs. **Office hours:** Monday - Friday, 8:30 a.m. - 8:00 p.m. **Corporate headquarters location:** This Location. **Other U.S. locations:** Wappingers Falls NY. **Listed on:** Privately held. **Owner:** Lynn Kasin. **Number of employees at this location:** 300. **Number of employees nationwide:** 400.

FLAGSTAFF MEDICAL CENTER
1200 North Beaver, Flagstaff AZ 86001. 520/773-2067. **Toll-free phone:** 800/446-2324. **Fax:** 520/773-2579. **Contact:** Diane Ross, Recruiter. **World Wide Web address:** http://www. nahealth.com/fmc.html. **Description:** A medical center. Flagstaff Medical Center offers a variety of services including audiology, critical care, endoscopy, imaging, pediatrics, pharmacy, cancer research and care, and cardiology. Founded in 1936. **Common positions include:** Accountant/Auditor; Administrative Manager; Biomedical Engineer; Budget Analyst; Buyer; Certified Nurses Aide; Claim Representative; Clinical Lab Technician; Computer Programmer; Customer Service Representative; Dietician/Nutritionist; Education Administrator; Emergency Medical Technician; Financial Analyst; Human Resources Manager; Human Service Worker; MIS Specialist; Nuclear Medicine Technologist; Occupational Therapist; Pharmacist; Physical Therapist; Public Relations Specialist; Registered Nurse; Respiratory Therapist; Social Worker; Stationary Engineer; Surgical Technician; Systems Analyst; Telecommunications Manager; Typist/Word Processor. **Educational backgrounds include:** Accounting; Biology; Business Administration; Chemistry; Communications; Computer Science; Engineering; Finance; Marketing. **Benefits:** 403(b); Dental Insurance; Disability Coverage; Employee Discounts; Financial Planning Assistance; Flexible Schedule; Life Insurance; Medical Insurance; Pension Plan; Profit Sharing; Savings Plan; Tuition Assistance. **Corporate headquarters location:** This Location. **Parent company:** Northern Arizona Health Care.

FONAR CORPORATION
110 Marcus Drive, Melville NY 11747. 516/694-2929x220. **Fax:** 516/694-5434. **Contact:** Fred Peipman, Director of Personnel. **World Wide Web address:** http://www.fonar.com. **Description:** Researches, manufactures, sells, and services MRI medical diagnostic scanners. **Common positions include:** Computer Programmer; Engineer; Purchasing Agent/Manager. **Educational backgrounds include:** Engineering. **Benefits:** 401(k); Disability Coverage; Medical Insurance. **Corporate headquarters location:** This Location. **Listed on:** NASDAQ. **Number of employees at this location:** 250.

FORT SANDERS HEALTH SYSTEM
FORT SANDERS REGIONAL MEDICAL CENTER
1901 Clinch Avenue, Knoxville TN 37916. 865/541-1111. **Contact:** Human Resources. **Description:** A nonprofit health care system that includes hospitals, physicians, clinics, and specialized health services throughout eastern Tennessee. The system's specialty areas include cardiology, neuroscience, orthopedics, physical rehabilitation, oncology, and women's services (including perinatology). Fort Sanders Health System also offers managed care and home health services through joint ownership with Methodist Medical Center of Oak Ridge and MedCenters HomeCare, a comprehensive home health company providing home infusion therapy, durable medical equipment, respiratory therapy, and home health nursing. **Corporate headquarters location:** This Location. **Subsidiaries include:** Fort Sanders Louden Medical Center; Fort Sanders Parkwest Medical Center; Fort Sanders Regional Medical Center (also at this location); Fort Sanders Sevier Medical Center; Fort Sanders West; Maternity Center of East Tennessee; Patricia Neal Rehabilitation Center; Thompson Cancer Survival Center.

4-D NEUROIMAGING
9727 Pacific Heights Boulevard, San Diego CA 92121. 858/453-6300. **Contact:** Human Resources. **World Wide Web address:** http://www.4dni.com. **Description:** Manufactures specialized instruments for ultra-sensitive magnetic field and low-temperature measurements. The company incorporates its core magnetic sensing technologies into its magnetic source imaging (MSI) system, an instrument designed to assist in the noninvasive diagnosis of a broad range of medical disorders. The MSI system developed by the company uses advanced superconducting technology to measure and locate the source of magnetic fields generated by the human body. The company is focusing the development of its technology on market applications such as brain surgery and the diagnosis and surgical planning for treatment of epilepsy and life-threatening cardiac arrhythmias. **Corporate headquarters location:** This Location.

FOX CHASE CANCER CENTER
7701 Burholme Avenue, Philadelphia PA 19111. 215/728-6900. **Contact:** Human Resources. **World Wide Web address:** http://www.fccc.edu. **Description:** A comprehensive cancer center that serves as a national resource for converting research findings into medical applications. These applications are designed to improve cancer detection, treatment, and prevention. **Corporate headquarters location:** This Location. **Number of employees at this location:** 1,700.

FRANCISCAN HEALTH SYSTEMS OF NEW JERSEY
25 McWilliams Place, Jersey City NJ 07302. 201/418-2065. **Fax:** 201/418-2063. **Contact:** Linda Halleran, Employment Manager. **Description:** Operates two community hospitals: St. Mary Hospital (Hoboken NJ) and St. Francis Hospital (Jersey City NJ). **NOTE:** Entry-level positions are offered. **Common positions include:** Accountant; Administrative Assistant; Certified Nurses Aide; Clinical Lab Technician; Computer Operator; Credit Manager; Customer Service Representative; Dietician/Nutritionist; Emergency Medical Technician; Food Scientist/Technologist; Human Resources Manager; Licensed Practical Nurse; MIS Specialist; Nuclear Medicine Technologist; Occupational Therapist; Pharmacist; Physical Therapist; Physician; Psychologist; Registered Nurse; Respiratory Therapist; Social Worker; Speech-Language Pathologist. **Educational backgrounds include:** Health Care; Nutrition. **Benefits:** 403(b); Dental Insurance; Disability Coverage; Employee Discounts; Life Insurance; Medical Insurance; On-Site Daycare; Pension Plan; Tuition Assistance. **Special programs:** Internships. **Corporate headquarters location:** This Location.

FRANCISCAN SERVICES CORPORATION
6832 Convent Boulevard, Sylvania OH 43560. 419/882-8373. **Contact:** John W. O'Connell, President. **Description:** This location's facilities include Providence Corporation, which offers long-term care services; Providence Hospital; Franciscan Center, a performing arts and conference center; and Franciscan Properties, which manages Convert Park

Apartments, an independent living complex for senior adults. Overall, Franciscan Services Corporation is a nonprofit health care provider. Other facilities include Bethany House (Toledo OH), which serves women and children; St. John Medical Center (Steubenville OH); Trinity Medical Center (Brenham TX); Holy Cross Hospital (Detroit MI); and St. Francis Services Corporation (Bryan TX), a free clinic. **Corporate headquarters location:** This Location.

FRANCISCAN SKEMP MEDICAL CENTER
700 West Avenue South, La Crosse WI 54601. 608/791-9756. **Toll-free phone:** 800/246-6499. **Fax:** 608/791-9504. **Recorded jobline:** 608/791-9850. **Contact:** Human Resources Department. **Description:** A Mayo Health System affiliate providing health services to the tri-state communities of Iowa, Minnesota, and Wisconsin. The system includes hospitals, clinics, elderly care services, behavioral health, and services for women. **NOTE:** Entry-level positions are offered. **Common positions include:** Clinical Lab Technician; Computer Programmer; Counselor; Customer Service Representative; Dietician/Nutritionist; Human Service Worker; Licensed Practical Nurse; Occupational Therapist; Pharmacist; Physical Therapist; Physician; Psychologist; Radiological Technologist; Recreational Therapist; Registered Nurse; Respiratory Therapist; Social Worker; Speech-Language Pathologist; Surgical Technician; Systems Analyst; Typist/Word Processor. **Educational backgrounds include:** Computer Science; Health Care. **Benefits:** Dental Insurance; Disability Coverage; Employee Discounts; Life Insurance; Medical Insurance; Pension Plan; Savings Plan; Tuition Assistance. **Corporate headquarters location:** This Location. **Number of employees at this location:** 2,900.

FREEDOM VILLAGE
6501 17th Avenue West, Bradenton FL 34209. 941/798-8200. **Contact:** Sharon Peters, Human Resources Director. **World Wide Web address:** http://www.freedomvillage.com. **Description:** A continuing care retirement center offering skilled nursing, assisted living, and independent living options. **Common positions include:** Accountant; Administrative Assistant; Certified Nurses Aide; Certified Occupational Therapy Assistant; Dietician/Nutritionist; Home Health Aide; Human Resources Manager; Licensed Practical Nurse; Marketing Specialist; Medical Records Technician; Occupational Therapist; Physical Therapist; Physical Therapy Assistant; Registered Nurse; Respiratory Therapist; Sales Representative; Social Worker; Speech-Language Pathologist. **Educational backgrounds include:** Accounting; Health Care; Marketing; Microsoft Office; Microsoft Word; Spreadsheets. **Benefits:** 401(k); Dental Insurance; Disability Coverage; Employee Discounts; Flexible Schedule; Life Insurance; Medical Insurance; Sick Days; Tuition Assistance; Vacation Days. **Office hours:** Monday - Friday, 8:30 a.m. - 5:00 p.m. **Corporate headquarters location:** This Location. **Number of employees at this location:** 550.

DANIEL FREEMAN MEMORIAL HOSPITAL
333 North Prairie Avenue, Inglewood CA 90301. 310/674-7050. **Contact:** Recruitment Coordinator. **World Wide Web address:** http://www.danielfreeman.org. **Description:** A nonprofit hospital that offers a variety of services including behavioral health, heart care, women's and children's services, and rehabilitation. The hospital also offers a varity of specialty programs such as the Center for Heart and Health, complementary medicine, and emergency services. **Common**

positions include: Environmental Engineer; Food Scientist/Technologist; Licensed Practical Nurse; Occupational Therapist; Pharmacist; Physical Therapist; Recreational Therapist; Registered Nurse; Respiratory Therapist; Speech-Language Pathologist; Systems Analyst. **Benefits:** Daycare Assistance; Dental Insurance; Disability Coverage; Employee Discounts; Life Insurance; Medical Insurance; Pension Plan; Savings Plan; Tuition Assistance. **Corporate headquarters location:** This Location. **Listed on:** Privately held. **Number of employees nationwide:** 1,500.

FRESENIUS MEDICAL CARE NORTH AMERICA
2 Ledgemont Center, 95 Hayden Avenue, Lexington MA 02173. 781/402-9000. **Toll-free phone:** 800/662-1237. **Fax:** 781/402-9005. **Contact:** John Lenotte, Employment Manager. **E-mail address:** corphr@fmc-na.com. **World Wide Web address:** http://www.fmcna.com. **Description:** One of the nation's leading manufacturers and distributors of renal dialysis products and services. The company also provides dialysis treatment, diagnostic testing, blood testing, and home health programs. Fresenius Medical Care's dialysis services include outpatient hemodialysis, peritoneal dialysis, and support for home dialysis patients. **Common positions include:** Accountant; Administrative Assistant; Architect; Attorney; Auditor; Computer Programmer; Controller; Customer Service Representative; Database Administrator; Dietician/Nutritionist; Finance Director; Network/Systems Administrator; Paralegal; Registered Nurse; Secretary; SQL Programmer; Systems Analyst. **Educational backgrounds include:** Accounting; Business Administration; Computer Science; Finance; Health Care; Java; Marketing; MBA; Microsoft Office; Microsoft Word; Physics; Software Development; Software Tech. Support; Spreadsheets; SQL. **Benefits:** 401(k); Casual Dress - Daily; Dental Insurance; Disability Coverage; Employee Discounts; Life Insurance; Medical Insurance; Pension Plan; Tuition Assistance. **Special programs:** Co-ops. **Corporate headquarters location:** This Location. **Parent company:** Fresenius Medical Care AG (Germany). **Annual sales/revenues:** More than $100 million.

FRIENDSHIP HAVEN, INC.
420 South Kenyon Road, Fort Dodge IA 50501. 515/573-6096. **Fax:** 515/573-6013. **Contact:** Amy Porter, Human Resources Director. **World Wide Web address:** http://www.friendshiphaven.net. **Description:** A nonprofit retirement community offering continuing care ranging from independent living to 24-hour nursing care. Founded in 1950. **NOTE:** Entry-level positions and second and third shifts are offered. Administrator: Diane Rollins. **Common positions include:** Certified Nurses Aide; Licensed Practical Nurse; Registered Nurse. **Educational backgrounds include:** Health Care. **Benefits:** 403(b); Dental Insurance; Disability Coverage; Employee Discounts; Life Insurance; Medical Insurance; Sick Days; Tuition Assistance; Vacation Days. **Special programs:** Training. **Office hours:** Monday - Friday, 8:00 a.m. - 4:30 p.m. **Corporate headquarters location:** This Location. **President/CEO:** Craig Johnsen. **Annual sales/revenues:** Less than $5 million. **Number of employees at this location:** 385.

FULTON STATE HOSPITAL
600 East Fifth Street, Fulton MO 65251. 573/592-3450. **Fax:** 573/592-3032. **Contact:** Personnel. **World Wide Web address:** http://modmh.state.mo.us/fulton/fshhtml.htm. **Description:** A maximum-security psychiatric hospital that provides long-term residential care to mentally ill patients.

Common positions include: Certified Nurses Aide; Clerical Supervisor; Dietician/Nutritionist; Electrician; Licensed Practical Nurse; MIS Specialist; Occupational Therapist; Physician; Psychologist; Registered Nurse; Secretary; Social Worker; Systems Analyst; Typist/Word Processor. **Educational backgrounds include:** Health Care. **Benefits:** Life Insurance; Medical Insurance; Pension Plan; Savings Plan; Tuition Assistance. **Special programs:** Internships. **Office hours:** Monday - Friday, 8:00 a.m. - 4:30 p.m. **Corporate headquarters location:** Jefferson City MO. **CEO:** Felix Vincenz. **Number of employees at this location:** 1,400.

GN RESOUND CORPORATION
220 Saginaw Drive, Redwood City CA 94063. 650/780-7800. **Toll-free phone:** 800/582-4327. **Contact:** Human Resources. **E-mail address:** hr@gnresound.com. **World Wide Web address:** http://www.gnresound.com. **Description:** Develops, manufactures, and markets hearing aids. Brand names include ReSound, Danavox, and Viennatone. **Company slogan:** Partners in hearing innovation. **Common positions include:** Accountant; Administrative Assistant; Attorney; Controller; Finance Director; Financial Analyst; General Manager; Human Resources Manager; Marketing Manager; Marketing Specialist; Operations Manager; Paralegal; Production Manager; Purchasing Agent/Manager; Quality Control Supervisor; Sales Manager; Sales Representative; Technical Support Manager. **Educational backgrounds include:** Accounting; Business Administration; Engineering; Finance; Health Care; Liberal Arts; Marketing; MBA; Microsoft Office; Microsoft Word; Software Development; Software Tech. Support; Spreadsheets; Visual Basic. **Benefits:** 401(k); Casual Dress - Fridays; Dental Insurance; Disability Coverage; Employee Discounts; Life Insurance; Medical Insurance; Relocation Assistance; Savings Plan; Sick Days (6 - 10); Tuition Assistance; Vacation Days (6 - 10). **Corporate headquarters location:** This Location. **Other U.S. locations:** Minneapolis MN. **International locations:** Worldwide. **Listed on:** London Stock Exchange.

GALENA-STRAUSS HOSPITAL & NURSING CARE FACILITY
215 Summit Street, Galena IL 61036. 815/777-1340. **Contact:** Mary Doyle, Human Resources Representative. **Description:** A 25-bed, nonprofit, acute care hospital and 60-bed nursing home. Founded in 1962. **NOTE:** Entry-level positions and second and third shifts are offered. **Common positions include:** Certified Nurses Aide; Daycare Worker; Licensed Practical Nurse; Physical Therapist; Registered Nurse. **Educational backgrounds include:** Health Care. **Benefits:** 401(k); Life Insurance; Medical Insurance; Pension Plan; Savings Plan; Tuition Assistance. **Special programs:** Summer Jobs. **Office hours:** Monday - Friday, 8:00 a.m. - 4:00 p.m. **Corporate headquarters location:** This Location. **Administrator:** Roger Hervey. **Annual sales/revenues:** Less than $5 million. **Number of employees at this location:** 115.

GENESIS HEALTH VENTURES, INC.
101 East State Street, Kennett Square PA 19348. 610/444-6350. **Fax:** 610/925-4352. **Contact:** Recruitment Manager. **World Wide Web address:** http://www.ghv.com. **Description:** Provides services, centers, and programs for the elderly. Genesis Health Ventures operates its skilled nursing and assisted living centers under the Genesis ElderCare name. Founded in 1985. **Common positions include:** Accountant; Administrative

Assistant; Auditor; Certified Nurses Aide; Computer Operator; Computer Programmer; Database Manager; Licensed Practical Nurse; MIS Specialist; Secretary; Systems Analyst. **Educational backgrounds include:** Accounting; Business Administration; Computer Science; Finance; Health Care; Liberal Arts; Marketing; Nutrition. **Benefits:** 401(k). **Corporate headquarters location:** This Location. **Listed on:** New York Stock Exchange. **Number of employees at this location:** 270. **Number of employees nationwide:** 30,000.

GISH BIOMEDICAL, INC.
2681 Kelvin Avenue, Irvine CA 92614-5821. 949/756-5485. **Toll-free phone:** 800/938-0531. **Fax:** 949/553-7390. **Contact:** Human Resources. **World Wide Web address:** http://www.gishbiomedical.com. **Description:** Designs, produces, and markets innovative specialty surgical devices. Gish Biomedical specializes in blood handling and fluid delivery as well as blood management systems for cardiovascular surgery, oncology, and orthopedics. Founded in 1976. **Corporate headquarters location:** This Location. **Listed on:** NASDAQ. **Stock exchange symbol:** GISH. **President:** Jack W. Brown.

GRAHAM-FIELD
81 Spence Street, Bay Shore NY 11706. 631/273-2200. **Contact:** Human Resources. **World Wide Web address:** http://www.grahamfield.com. **Description:** Manufactures and distributes a broad line of medical products, including ace bandages, crutches, stethoscopes, and wheelchairs. **Corporate headquarters location:** This Location.

GREENVILLE HOSPITAL SYSTEM
701 Grove Road, Greenville SC 29605. 864/455-8976. **Fax:** 864/455-5959. **Recorded jobline:** 864/455-8799. **Contact:** Human Resources. **World Wide Web address:** http://www.ghs.org. **Description:** A multihospital system that provides health care services to several communities and major tertiary referral services for the upstate area. **Common positions include:** Administrative Worker/Clerk; EEG Technologist; EKG Technician; Licensed Practical Nurse; Management; Nuclear Medicine Technologist; Occupational Therapist; Pharmacist; Physical Therapist; Physician; Registered Nurse; Respiratory Therapist; Speech-Language Pathologist; Surgical Technician. **Educational backgrounds include:** Health Care. **Benefits:** 403(b); Dental Insurance; Disability Coverage; Life Insurance; Medical Insurance; Pension Plan; Savings Plan; Tuition Assistance. **Corporate headquarters location:** This Location. **Number of employees at this location:** 5,000.

GUIDANT CORPORATION
P.O. Box 44906, Indianapolis IN 46244-0906. 317/971-2000. **Physical address:** 111 Monument Circle, 29th Floor, Indianapolis IN 46204. **Fax:** 317/971-2040. **Contact:** Human Resources. **World Wide Web address:** http://www.guidant.com. **Description:** Designs, develops, manufactures, and markets a broad range of products for use in cardiac rhythm management, coronary artery disease intervention, and other forms of minimally invasive surgery. **Corporate headquarters location:** This Location.

HCA THE HEALTHCARE COMPANY
One Park Plaza, Nashville TN 37203. 615/344-9551. **Contact:** Human Resources. **World Wide Web address:** http://www.hcahealthcare.com. **Description:** Operates a chain of hospitals and medical centers. **Other U.S. locations:** Nationwide. **International locations:** England; Switzerland. **Annual sales/revenues:** More than $100 million.

HAEMONETICS CORPORATION
400 Wood Road, Braintree MA 02184. 781/848-7100. **Toll-free phone:** 800/225-5242. **Fax:** 781/848-9959. **Contact:** Human Resources. **World Wide Web address:** http://www.haemonetics.com. **Description:** Designs, manufactures, markets, and services blood processing systems and related sterile, disposable items used for the processing of human blood for transfusion and other therapeutic medical purposes. The company sells its products to blood banks, hospitals, and commercial plasma centers. **Common positions include:** Accountant; Administrative Worker/Clerk; Biomedical Engineer; Blue-Collar Worker Supervisor; Computer Programmer; Customer Service Rep.; Electrical/Electronics Engineer; Financial Analyst; Industrial Engineer; Industrial Production Manager; Licensed Practical Nurse; Machinist; Materials Engineer; Mechanical Engineer; Operations/Production Manager; Paralegal; Precision Assembler; Quality Control Supervisor; Registered Nurse; Software Engineer; Systems Analyst. **Educational backgrounds include:** Accounting; Biology; Business Administration; Chemistry; Computer Science; Engineering; Finance; Liberal Arts; Mathematics; Nursing. **Benefits:** 401(k); Daycare Assistance; Dental Insurance; Disability Coverage; Life Insurance; Medical Insurance; Profit Sharing; Savings Plan; Tuition Assistance. **Corporate headquarters location:** This Location. **Other U.S. locations:** Tucson AZ; Pittsburgh PA. **Listed on:** New York Stock Exchange. **Number of employees at this location:** 700.

HAMILTON MEDICAL CENTER
P.O. Box 1168, Dalton GA 30722. 706/272-6145. **Recorded jobline:** 706/217-2020. **Contact:** Human Resources. **World Wide Web address:** http://www.hhcs.org. **Description:** A 282-bed, acute care medical center. The hospital provides a variety of services including cancer care, diabetes treatment, substance abuse, and psychiatry services. **Common positions include:** EKG Technician; Emergency Medical Technician; Librarian; Licensed Practical Nurse; Medical Records Technician; Occupational Therapist; Pharmacist; Psychologist; Registered Nurse; Respiratory Therapist; Social Worker; Surgical Technician; Systems Analyst. **Educational backgrounds include:** Business Administration; Computer Science; Nursing; Occupational Therapy; Physical Therapy. **Benefits:** 401(k); Dental Insurance; Disability Coverage; Employee Discounts; Life Insurance; Medical Insurance; Pension Plan; Savings Plan; Tuition Assistance. **Number of employees at this location:** 1,300.

HARRIS METHODIST FORT WORTH HOSPITAL
1301 Pennsylvania Avenue, Fort Worth TX 76104. 817/882-2882. **Fax:** 817/882-2865. **Recorded jobline:** 800/477-7876. **Contact:** Human Resources. **World Wide Web address:** http://www.texashealth.org. **Description:** A 606-bed, tertiary care facility that also houses a multidisciplinary cancer center. **NOTE:** Entry-level positions, and part-time jobs, and second and third shifts are offered. **Common positions include:** Biomedical Engineer; Clinical Lab Technician; Nuclear Medicine Technologist; Occupational Therapist; Pharmacist; Physical Therapist; Radiological Technologist; Registered Nurse; Respiratory Therapist; Social Worker; Speech-Language Pathologist; Surgical Technician. **Educational backgrounds include:** Health Care. **Benefits:** 401(k); Dental Insurance; Disability Coverage; Financial Planning Assistance; Life Insurance; Medical Insurance; On-Site Daycare; Pension Plan; Public Transit Available; Tuition Assistance. **Special programs:** Internships.

HAUSMANN INDUSTRIES
130 Union Street, Northvale NJ 07647. 201/767-0255. **Contact:** Human Resources. **World Wide Web address:** http://www.hausmann.com. **Description:** Manufactures medical examination tables and physical therapy equipment. **Corporate headquarters location:** This Location.

HEALTHALLIANCE/LEOMINSTER HOSPITAL
60 Hospital Road, Leominster MA 01453. 978/466-2000. **Fax:** 978/466-2189. **Contact:** Employment Coordinator. **World Wide Web address:** http://www.healthalliance.com. **Description:** An acute care medical facility. The hospital provides inpatient and outpatient services including medical, surgical, and subspecialty care, as well as same-day surgery and 24-hour emergency coverage. The hospital also offers the Center for Cancer Care and Blood Disorders, diagnostic services including mobile MRIs, cardiac catheterization labs, and a diagnostic lab for the study of sleep disorders. **NOTE:** Entry-level positions are offered. **Common positions include:** Certified Nurses Aide; Certified Occupational Therapy Assistant; Clinical Lab Technician; Computer Operator; Computer Programmer; EEG Technologist; EKG Technician; Home Health Aide; Licensed Practical Nurse; Medical Records Technician; Network/Systems Administrator; Nuclear Medicine Technologist; Occupational Therapist; Physical Therapist; Physical Therapy Assistant; Radiological Technologist; Recreational Therapist; Registered Nurse; Respiratory Therapist; Social Worker; Speech-Language Pathologist. **Educational backgrounds include:** Business Administration; Health Care. **Benefits:** 403(b); Daycare Assistance; Dental Insurance; Disability Coverage; Employee Discounts; Flexible Schedule; Life Insurance; Medical Insurance; Tuition Assistance. **Annual sales/revenues:** More than $100 million. **Number of employees at this location:** 750. **Number of employees nationwide:** 2,000.

HEALTHCARE IMAGING SERVICES, INC.
One Harding Road, Red Bank NJ 07701. 732/544-8200. **Contact:** Human Resources. **Description:** Operates five fixed-site MRI centers and one fixed-site multimodality imaging center consisting of MRI, ultrasonography, and mammography facilities. **Corporate headquarters location:** This Location.

HEALTHSOUTH
3340 Plaza 10 Boulevard, Beaumont TX 77707. 409/835-0835. **Fax:** 409/835-1401. **Contact:** Ellen Zimmerman, Director of Human Resources. **World Wide Web address:** http://www.healthsouth.com. **Description:** A physical rehabilitation hospital that also offers outpatient and home care services. **NOTE:** Part-time jobs and second and third shifts are offered. **Common positions include:** Administrative Assistant; Certified Nurses Aide; Certified Occupational Therapy Assistant; Clerical Supervisor; Counselor; Dietician/Nutritionist; Human Resources Manager; Licensed Practical Nurse; Marketing Manager; Medical Records Technician; Occupational Therapist; Pharmacist; Physical Therapist; Physical Therapy Assistant; Psychologist; Registered Nurse; Respiratory Therapist; Secretary; Social Worker; Speech-Language Pathologist. **Educational backgrounds include:** Accounting; Health Care; Marketing; Microsoft Office; Microsoft Word; Spreadsheets. **Benefits:** 401(k); Dental Insurance; Disability Coverage; Life Insurance; Medical Insurance; Profit Sharing. **Special programs:** Internships. **Other U.S. locations:** Nationwide. **International locations:** Worldwide. **Listed on:** New York Stock Exchange. **CEO:** Mike Hagan. **Number of employees at this location:** 250.

HEALTHSOUTH CORPORATION
One HealthSouth Parkway, Birmingham AL 35243. 205/967-7116. **Contact:** Human Resources. **World Wide Web address:** http://www.healthsouth.com. **Description:** Provides rehabilitative health care services through approximately 250 outpatient and 40 inpatient rehabilitation facilities, as well as through several medical centers. Services offered include rehabilitation, occupational therapy, physical therapy, head injury therapy, respiratory therapy, speech-language pathology, surgery, laser treatment of tumors, and rehabilitation nursing. **Corporate headquarters location:** This Location. **Other U.S. locations:** Nationwide. **International locations:** Canada.

HEART INSTITUTE OF NEVADA
1090 East Desert Inn Road, Suite 100, Las Vegas NV 89109-2803. 702/765-5712. **Toll-free phone:** 800/782-0088. **Fax:** 702/765-5826. **Contact:** Kori Rowsell, Operations Manager. **Description:** A medical practice specializing in cardiology. **NOTE:** Entry-level positions are offered. **Common positions include:** Administrative Assistant; Administrative Manager; Chief Financial Officer; Controller; EKG Technician; Medical Assistant; Medical Records Technician; Medical Secretary; Network/Systems Administrator; Nuclear Medicine Technologist; Public Relations Specialist; Purchasing Agent/Manager; Radiological Technologist; Registered Nurse. **Educational backgrounds include:** Business Administration; Computer Science; Finance; Health Care; Marketing; Microsoft Office; Microsoft Word; Novell; Public Relations; QuarkXPress; Spreadsheets; SQL. **Benefits:** 401(k); Daycare Assistance; Dental Insurance; Disability Coverage; Life Insurance; Medical Insurance; Sick Days (6 - 10); Tuition Assistance; Vacation Days (10 - 20). **Special programs:** Internships. **Office hours:** Monday - Friday, 8:00 a.m. - 5:00 p.m. **Parent company:** Cardiology Associates of Nevada. **Number of employees at this location:** 65.

HELP AT HOME INC.
223 West Jackson Boulevard, Suite 500, Chicago IL 60606. 312/663-4244. **Fax:** 312/663-1290. **Contact:** Human Resources. **Description:** Provides homemaker and nurses aide services for the elderly. **Corporate headquarters location:** This Location. **Other area locations:** Belleville IL; Danville IL; East Alton IL; Mount Vernon IL; Oak Forest IL; Ottawa IL; Rock Island IL; Rockford IL; Skokie IL; Springfield IL; St. Charles IL; Waukegan IL. **Other U.S. locations:** Munster IN; Brentwood MO; Fenton MO. **Subsidiaries include:** Lakeside Health Care; Oxford Health Care; Rosewood Health Care. **Listed on:** NASDAQ. **Stock exchange symbol:** HAHI.

HENDERSON MEMORIAL HOSPITAL
300 Wilson Street, Henderson TX 75652. 903/655-6533. **Toll-free phone:** 800/329-7541. **Fax:** 903/655-3661. **Recorded jobline:** 903/655-3773. **Contact:** Human Resources. **World Wide Web address:** http://www.hmhmychoice.com. **Description:** A private, nonprofit, acute care hospital. **NOTE:** Entry-level positions and second and third shifts are offered. **Common positions include:** Account Representative; Accountant; Adjuster; Administrative Assistant; Biomedical Engineer; Certified Nurses Aide; Claim Representative; Clerical Supervisor; Clinical Lab Technician; Computer Operator; Counselor; Customer Service Rep.; Dietician/Nutritionist; Education Administrator; EEG Technologist; EKG Technician; Emergency Medical Technician; Environmental Engineer; Financial Analyst; Food Scientist/Technologist; Licensed Practical Nurse; Licensed Vocational Nurse; Medical Records

Technician; Operations Manager; Pharmacist; Physical Therapist; Physician; Purchasing Agent/ Manager; Quality Control Supervisor; Radiological Technologist; Recreational Therapist; Registered Nurse; Respiratory Therapist; Restaurant/Food Service Manager; Secretary; Social Worker; Surgical Technician; Systems Analyst; Systems Manager; Typist/Word Processor. **Educational backgrounds include:** Accounting; Biology; Business Administration; Chemistry; Health Care; Nursing. **Benefits:** 403(b); Dental Insurance; Disability Coverage; Employee Discounts; Flexible Schedule; Life Insurance; Medical Insurance; Pension Plan; Tuition Assistance. **Special programs:** Apprenticeships; Internships. **Office hours:** Monday - Friday, 7:30 a.m. - 5:00 p.m. **Corporate headquarters location:** This Location.

THE HERITAGE CENTER
P.O. Box 105, Provo UT 84603. 801/225-5552. **Physical address:** 5800 North Heritage School Drive, Provo UT 84604. **Toll-free phone:** 800/433-9413. **Fax:** 801/226-4696. **Recorded jobline:** 801/226-4640. **Contact:** Anneta Foote, Human Resources Director. **E-mail address:** htgschool@ aol.com. **Description:** A nonprofit, 100-bed, long-term residential treatment center for adolescents ages 12 - 18. The Heritage Center offers psychotherapy, family therapy, milieu therapy, and therapeutic recreation. Specialty groups deal with the issues of adoption, eating disorders, attention deficit disorder, sexual abuse, and parent/child conflict. The center also provides an on-campus education program, as well as services for the treatment of substance abuse. Founded in 1984. **Common positions include:** Accountant; Administrative Assistant; Buyer; Certified Nurses Aide; Chief Financial Officer; Claim Rep.; Clerical Supervisor; Computer Operator; Computer Programmer; Controller; Counselor; Database Manager; Dietician/Nutritionist; Emergency Medical Technician; ESL Teacher; Human Resources Manager; Internet Services Manager; Librarian; Licensed Practical Nurse; Marketing Manager; Marketing Specialist; Medical Records Technician; MIS Specialist; Pharmacist; Physician; Psychologist; Purchasing Agent/Manager; Quality Control Supervisor; Registered Nurse; Secretary; Social Worker; Speech-Language Pathologist; Teacher/Professor; Telecommunications Manager; Typist/Word Processor. **Educational backgrounds include:** Accounting; Computer Science; Health Care; Marketing. **Benefits:** 401(k); Dental Insurance; Disability Coverage; Employee Discounts; Job Sharing; Life Insurance; Medical Insurance. **Office hours:** Monday - Friday, 8:00 a.m. - 6:00 p.m. **Corporate headquarters location:** This Location. **President/CEO:** Jerry Spanos. **Annual sales/revenues:** $5 - $10 million. **Number of employees at this location:** 240.

HILL-ROM COMPANY, INC.
1069 State Route 46 East, Batesville IN 47006. 812/934-7777. **Contact:** Human Resources. **World Wide Web address:** http://www.hill-rom.com. **Description:** Manufactures and rents a variety of health care products including birthing beds, hospital beds, and stretchers. **Corporate headquarters location:** This Location. **Parent company:** Hillenbrand Industries, Inc.

HILLENBRAND INDUSTRIES, INC.
112 North Main Street, Batesville IN 47006. 812/934-7000. **Contact:** Tim Dietz, Human Resources. **World Wide Web address:** http://www.hillenbrand.com. **Description:** A holding company. **Corporate headquarters location:** This Location. **Subsidiaries include:** Batesville Casket Company, Inc. (Batesville IN)

manufactures funeral-related products including caskets and urns. Forethought Financial Services (Batesville IN) provides financial services for the purpose of planning funeral arrangements. Hill-Rom Company, Inc. (Batesville IN) manufactures and rents a variety of health care products including birthing beds, hospital beds, and stretchers. **Listed on:** New York Stock Exchange.

HILLVIEW MENTAL HEALTH CENTER

11500 Eldridge Avenue, Suite 206, Lake View Terrace CA 91342. 818/896-1161. **Contact:** Human Resources. **Description:** An outpatient and residential mental health services facility for individuals with persistent mental disabilities. Founded in 1985. **NOTE:** Entry-level positions and second and third shifts are offered. **Common positions include:** Accountant; Administrative Assistant; Computer Operator; Counselor; Physician; Psychologist; Social Worker; Typist/Word Processor. **Educational backgrounds include:** Accounting. **Benefits:** Dental Insurance; Medical Insurance; Pension Plan. **Corporate headquarters location:** This Location. **Annual sales/revenues:** Less than $5 million. **Number of employees at this location:** 80.

HOLY SPIRIT HEALTH SYSTEM

503 North 21st Street, Camp Hill PA 17011-2288. 717/763-2100. **Fax:** 717/763-2351. **Recorded jobline:** 717/972-4121. **Contact:** Ann Moyer, Employment Manager. **E-mail address:** resume@hsh.org. **World Wide Web address:** http://www.hsh.org. **Description:** A nonprofit health system that operates a 349-bed hospital as well as several home health, hospice, and family care centers. Holy Spirit Health System also provides ambulance and emergency care services. Founded in 1963. **NOTE:** Entry-level positions, part-time jobs, and second and third shifts are offered. Public Relations Manager: J. Scott Dugan. Vice President: G. Randall Newhouse. CIO: Marc Gibbs. Director: Carol Powley. **Company slogan:** Spirit of Caring. **Common positions include:** Administrative Assistant; Certified Nurses Aide; Claim Rep.; EEG Technologist; EKG Technician; Emergency Medical Technician; Help-Desk Technician; Home Health Aide; Licensed Practical Nurse; Medical Assistant; Medical Records Technician; Medical Secretary; Network/Systems Administrator; Nuclear Medicine Technologist; Occupational Therapist; Pharmacist; Physical Therapist; Radiological Technologist; Registered Nurse; Respiratory Therapist; Secretary; Social Worker; Speech-Language Pathologist; Surgical Technician. **Educational backgrounds include:** Health Care; Microsoft Office; Microsoft Word; Spreadsheets. **Benefits:** 401(k); Daycare Assistance; Dental Insurance; Disability Coverage; Employee Discounts; Life Insurance; Medical Insurance; Public Transit Available; Sick Days (6 - 10); Tuition Assistance; Vacation Days (10 - 20). **Special programs:** Internships. **Office hours:** Monday - Friday, 7:30 a.m. - 4:00 p.m. **Corporate headquarters location:** This Location. **Parent company:** Holy Spirit Health System. **Listed on:** Privately held..

HOOPER HOLMES, INC.
dba PORTAMEDIC

170 Mount Airy Road, Basking Ridge NJ 07920. 908/766-5000. **Contact:** Human Resources. **E-mail address:** hres@hooperholmes.com. **World Wide Web address:** http://www.hooperholmes.com. **Description:** Performs health exams for insurance companies. Founded in 1899. **Common positions include:** Account Manager; Accountant/Auditor; Administrative Assistant; Administrative Manager; Assistant Manager; Attorney; Chief Financial Officer; Clerical Supervisor; Computer Operator; Computer Programmer; Controller; Credit Manager; Customer Service Rep.; Financial Analyst; General Manager; Help-Desk Technician; Human Resources Manager; Licensed Practical Nurse; Marketing Manager; Marketing Specialist; Multimedia Designer; Network/Systems Administrator; Nurse Practitioner; Operations Manager; Paralegal; Purchasing Agent/Manager; Quality Control Supervisor; Registered Nurse; Sales Executive; Sales Manager; Sales Representative; Systems Analyst; Systems Manager; Vice President. **Educational backgrounds include:** Accounting; Business Administration; Communications; Computer Science; Finance; Marketing; Microsoft Office; Microsoft Word; Spreadsheets. **Benefits:** 401(k); Casual Dress - Daily; Dental Insurance; Disability Coverage; Life Insurance; Medical Insurance; Tuition Assistance. **Office hours:** Monday - Friday, 8:30 a.m. - 5:00 p.m. **Corporate headquarters location:** This Location. **Other U.S. locations:** Nationwide. **Listed on:** American Stock Exchange. **Stock exchange symbol:** HH. **Annual sales/revenues:** More than $100 million. **Number of employees at this location:** 120. **Number of employees nationwide:** 2,500.

HOPE COMMUNITY RESOURCES, INC.

540 West International Airport Road, Anchorage AK 99518. 907/561-5335. **Toll-free phone:** 800/478-0078. **Fax:** 907/564-7429. **Recorded jobline:** 907/562-6226. **Contact:** Char Taranto, Hiring Specialist. **World Wide Web address:** http://www.hopealaska.org. **Description:** A private, nonprofit organization providing support to people with developmental disabilities. Services focus on adults and children, community building, mental health, family support, consumer rights, employment, and cultural relevance. This location also hires seasonally. Founded in 1968. **NOTE:** Entry-level positions, part-time jobs, and second and third shifts are offered. **Common positions include:** Administrative Assistant; Administrative Manager; Case Manager; Event Planner; Human Resources Manager; Licensed Practical Nurse; MIS Specialist; Public Relations Manager; Public Relations Specialist; Registered Nurse; Secretary; Social Worker. **Educational backgrounds include:** Health Care; Human Services; Social Work. **Benefits:** 403(b); Casual Dress - Fridays; Dental Insurance; Disability Coverage; Life Insurance; Medical Insurance. **Special programs:** Internships; Training; Summer Jobs. **Internship information:** Summer practicums are offered for students from New York, Oregon, and Ireland. **Office hours:** Monday - Friday, 8:00 a.m. - 5:00 p.m. **Corporate headquarters location:** This Location. **Other U.S. locations:** Dillingham AK; Juneau AK; Kodiak AK; Seward AK; Wasilla AK. **Listed on:** Privately held. **Annual sales/revenues:** $11 - $20 million.

IHS HOSPITAL AT DALLAS

7955 Harry Heinz Boulevard, Dallas TX 75235. 214/637-0000. **Fax:** 214/905-0566. **Contact:** Ruby Williams, Human Resources Manager. **World Wide Web address:** http://www.ihs-inc.com. **Description:** A long-term, acute care hospital. **NOTE:** Entry-level positions and part-time jobs are offered. **Common positions include:** Accountant; Administrative Assistant; Certified Nurses Aide; Certified Occupational Therapy Assistant; Controller; Dietician/Nutritionist; Medical Records Technician; Occupational Therapist; Pharmacist; Physical Therapist; Registered Nurse; Respiratory Therapist; Secretary; Social Worker; Speech-Language Pathologist. **Educational backgrounds include:** Business Administration; Finance; Health Care; Marketing; Microsoft Word; Nutrition.

IMATRON INC.
389 Oyster Point Boulevard, South San Francisco CA 94080. 650/583-9964. **Fax:** 650/871-0418. **Contact:** Joseph Bavaresco, Human Resources Administrator. **World Wide Web address:** http://www.imatron-web.com. **Description:** Designs, develops, manufactures, and markets a high performance EBT (Electron Beam Tomography) scanner. The EBT is used for high volume imaging applications used in cardiology, gastro-enterology, and pulmonology. **Common positions include:** Designer; Draftsperson; Electrical/Electronics Engineer; Field Engineer; Mechanical Engineer; Physicist; Purchasing Agent/Manager; Quality Control Supervisor; Radiological Technologist; Software Engineer. **Educational backgrounds include:** Business Administration; Computer Science; Engineering; Mathematics; Physics. **Benefits:** 401(k); Bonus Award/Plan; Dental Insurance; Disability Coverage; EAP; Employee Discounts; Life Insurance; Medical Insurance; Pension Plan; Savings Plan; Stock Option; Tuition Assistance. **Corporate headquarters location:** This Location. **Listed on:** NASDAQ. **Number of employees at this location:** 130. **Number of employees nationwide:** 160.

IN HOME HEALTH, INC.
601 Carlson Parkway, Suite 500, Minnetonka MN 55305. 612/449-7500. **Toll-free phone:** 800/666-7919x537. **Fax:** 612/449-7664. **Contact:** Sue Beasley, Recruitment Manager. **E-mail address:** sue.beasley@ihhi.com. **World Wide Web address:** http://www.ihhi.com. **Description:** In Home Health, Inc. provides comprehensive health care and home-making services to clients in their residences. Services are provided through a network of over 40 offices and two infusion pharmacies in more than 20 geographic markets. **Common positions include:** Account Representative; Administrative Assistant; Branch Manager; Certified Nurses Aide; Certified Occupational Therapy Assistant; Home Health Aide; Licensed Practical Nurse; Nurse Practitioner; Occupational Therapist; Pharmacist; Physical Therapist; Physical Therapy Assistant; Registered Nurse; Social Worker; Speech-Language Pathologist; Typist/Word Processor. **Educational backgrounds include:** Business Administration; Health Care; MBA. **Benefits:** 401(k); Dental Insurance; Disability Coverage; Flexible Schedule; Life Insurance; Medical Insurance; Tuition Assistance; Vacation Days (11 - 15). **Corporate headquarters location:** Minneapolis MN. **Listed on:** NASDAQ. **Stock exchange symbol:** IHHI. **Annual sales/revenues:** $51 - $100 million. **Number of employees at this location:** 50. **Number of employees nationwide:** 2,000.

INAMED CORPORATION
5540 Ekwil Street, Suite D, Santa Barbara CA 93111. 805/692-5400. **Contact:** Corporate Manager. **Description:** Develops, manufactures, and markets implantable products including mammary prostheses, tissue expanders, and facial implants; develops, produces, and distributes premium products for dermatology, wound care, and burn treatment; and packages and sterilizes medical grade components for other medical device companies. **Corporate headquarters location:** This Location. **Subsidiaries include:** Bioenterics Corporation, Carpinteria CA; McGhan Medical Corporation, Santa Barbara CA; McGhan, Ltd., Arklow, Ireland. **Listed on:** NASDAQ.

INLAND HOSPITAL
200 Kennedy Memorial Drive, Waterville ME 04901. 207/861-3028. **Fax:** 207/861-3025. **Contact:** Doris Lyons, Assistant Director of Human Resources. **Description:** A 78-bed, nonprofit, acute care hospital, which uses both osteopathic and allopathic physicians. **NOTE:** Second and third shifts are offered. **Common positions include:** Certified Nurses Aide; Chief Financial Officer; Laboratory Technician; Nuclear Medicine Technologist; Occupational Therapist; Physical Therapist; Physician; Radiological Technologist; Registered Nurse; Respiratory Therapist; Surgical Technician. **Educational backgrounds include:** Health Care. **Benefits:** 403(b); Dental Insurance; Disability Coverage; Life Insurance; Medical Insurance; Pension Plan; Tuition Assistance. **Corporate headquarters location:** This Location. **Parent company:** Eastern Maine Healthcare. **Number of employees at this location:** 315.

INNERDYNE, INC.
1244 Reamwood Avenue, Sunnyvale CA 94089. 408/745-6010. **Fax:** 408/745-7490. **Contact:** Human Resources. **World Wide Web address:** http://www.innerdyne.com. **Description:** Manufactures minimally invasive surgery products incorporating radial dilation technology. **Corporate headquarters location:** This Location. **Other U.S. locations:** Salt Lake City UT. **Listed on:** NASDAQ. **Stock exchange symbol:** IDYN.

INSIGHT HEALTH SERVICES CORP.
4400 MacArthur Boulevard, Suite 800, Newport Beach CA 92660. 949/476-0733. **Fax:** 949/476-1013. **Contact:** Human Resources. **World Wide Web address:** http://www.insighthealthcorp.com. **Description:** Engaged in the establishment and operation of outpatient diagnostic and treatment centers utilizing magnetic resonance imaging systems (MRI), computerized tomography systems (CT), multimodality radiologic imaging systems, cardiovascular diagnostic imaging systems, medical linear accelerators, and Leksell Stereotactic Gamma Units (Gamma Knife). **Common positions include:** Accountant; Administrative Assistant; Assistant Manager; Attorney; Chief Financial Officer; Finance Director; Financial Analyst; Human Resources Manager; Marketing Manager; Medical Records Technician; MIS Specialist; Nuclear Medicine Technologist; Operations Manager; Project Manager; Quality Control Supervisor; Radiological Technologist; Transportation/Traffic Specialist. **Educational backgrounds include:** Accounting. **Benefits:** 401(k); Dental Insurance; Disability Coverage; Life Insurance; Medical Insurance. **Office hours:** Monday - Friday, 8:00 a.m. - 5:00 p.m. **Corporate headquarters location:** This Location. **Other U.S. locations:** Nationwide. **Listed on:** NASDAQ. **Stock exchange symbol:** IHSC. **Number of employees at this location:** 60.

INTEGRAMED AMERICA, INC.
One Manhattanville Road, Purchase NY 10577. 914/253-8000. **Contact:** Rita Gruber, Human Resources Director. **World Wide Web address:** http://www.integramed.com. **Description:** Manages and provides services to clinical facilities and physician practices that provide assisted reproductive technology (ART) and/or infertility services to infertile couples. ART services consist of medical, psychological, and financial consultations and administration of the appropriate ART services and techniques. Infertility services provided include diagnostic testing, fertility drug therapy, tubal surgery, and intra-uterine insemination. **Corporate headquarters location:** This Location. **Other U.S. locations:** Boston MA; Hackensack NJ; Livingston NJ; Long Island NY; North Tarrytown NY; Port Chester NY.

INTERNATIONAL BIOMEDICAL, INC.
P.O. Box 143449, Austin TX 78714. 512/873-0033. **Contact:** Human Resources. **World Wide Web**

address: http://www.int-bio.com. **Description:** A manufacturer of high-technology medical instruments including infant incubators and radiation gloves. The company also manufactures and markets electronic equipment used in research, testing, and education. **Common positions include:** Accountant; Customer Service Rep.; Draftsperson; Electrical/Electronics Engineer; Manufacturer's/ Wholesaler's Sales Rep.; Operations/Production Manager; Production Worker; Purchasing Agent/Manager. **Educational backgrounds include:** Accounting; Business Administration; Engineering. **Benefits:** Dental Insurance; Disability Coverage; Life Insurance; Medical Insurance; Profit Sharing. **Corporate headquarters location:** Cleburne TX.

INVACARE CORPORATION

One Invacare Way, Elyria OH 44035. 440/329-6000. **Fax:** 440/365-7480. **Contact:** Human Resources. **World Wide Web address:** http://www.invacare.com. **Description:** Designs, manufactures, and distributes an extensive line of durable medical equipment for the home health care and extended care markets. Products include standard manual wheelchairs, motorized and lightweight prescription wheelchairs, motorized scooters, patient aids, home care beds, home respiratory products, and seating and positioning products. Invacare is one of the leading home medical equipment manufacturers in the country. **NOTE:** Entry-level positions and second and third shifts are offered. **Common positions include:** Account Manager; Account Rep.; Accountant; Administrative Assistant; Attorney; Blue-Collar Worker Supervisor; Buyer; Chemical Engineer; Computer Operator; Computer Programmer; Computer Support Technician; Computer Technician; Content Developer; Controller; Credit Manager; Customer Service Rep.; Database Administrator; Database Manager; Design Engineer; Draftsperson; Electrical/Electronics Engineer; Electrician; Financial Analyst; Help-Desk Technician; Human Resources Manager; Industrial Designer; Industrial Engineer; Industrial Production Manager; Internet Services Manager; Manufacturing Engineer; Market Research Analyst; Marketing Manager; Mechanical Engineer; MIS Specialist; Network/Systems Administrator; Occupational Therapist; Operations Manager; Paralegal; Physical Therapist; Production Manager; Project Manager; Public Relations Specialist; Purchasing Agent/ Manager; Quality Assurance Engineer; Quality Control Supervisor; Sales Executive; Sales Representative; Systems Analyst; Systems Manager; Technical Support Manager; Telecommunications Manager; Transportation/Traffic Specialist; Webmaster; Website Developer. **Educational backgrounds include:** Accounting; Business Administration; Communications; Computer Science; Engineering; Finance; Health Care; Internet Development; Liberal Arts; Marketing; MBA; Microsoft Office; Microsoft Word; Public Relations; Software Development; Software Tech. Support. **Benefits:** 401(k); Casual Dress - Daily; Dental Insurance; Disability Coverage; Employee Discounts; Life Insurance; Medical Insurance; Profit Sharing; Relocation Assistance; Tuition Assistance. **Special programs:** Internships; Co-ops; Summer Jobs. **Corporate headquarters location:** This Location. **Other U.S. locations:** CA; FL; NY; TX.

JACKSON COUNTY HEALTHCARE AUTHORITY

P.O. Box 1050, Scottsboro AL 35768. 256/259-4444. **Fax:** 256/259-0985. **Contact:** Human Resources. **Description:** Operates Jackson County Hospital and North Jackson Hospital. **Common positions include:** Accountant; Claim Rep.; Clinical Lab Technician; Computer Programmer; Dietician/ Nutritionist; Education Administrator; EEG Technologist; EKG Technician; Emergency Medical Technician; Human Resources Manager; Licensed Practical Nurse; Medical Records Technician; Pharmacist; Physical Therapist; Physician; Public Relations Specialist; Purchasing Agent/Manager; Quality Control Supervisor; Registered Nurse; Respiratory Therapist; Social Worker; Surgical Technician; Systems Analyst. **Educational backgrounds include:** Accounting; Business Administration. **Benefits:** Disability Coverage; Employee Discounts; Life Insurance; Medical Insurance; Pension Plan. **Corporate headquarters location:** This Location.

JENNY CRAIG INTERNATIONAL

11355 North Torrey Pines Road, La Jolla CA 92037. 858/812-7000. **Contact:** Human Resources. **World Wide Web address:** http://www.jennycraig.com. **Description:** Provides a comprehensive weight loss program. Jenny Craig International sells protein- and calorie-controlled food items to program participants throughout the U.S. and in four other countries. **Corporate headquarters location:** This Location. **Number of employees nationwide:** 5,370.

JOHN KNOX VILLAGE

400 NW Murray Road, Lees Summit MO 64081. 816/246-4343. **Fax:** 816/246-9154. **Contact:** Linda Duncan, Employment Specialist. **World Wide Web address:** http://www.johnknoxvillage.com. **Description:** One of the nation's largest continuing care retirement communities that offers various living options and services including support groups, social, nursing, nutritional, rehabilitation, and ambulance services. Founded in 1970. **NOTE:** Entry-level positions and second and third shifts are offered. **Common positions include:** Certified Nurses Aide; Emergency Medical Technician; Licensed Practical Nurse; Occupational Therapist; Physical Therapist; Registered Nurse; Speech-Language Pathologist. **Educational backgrounds include:** Health Care. **Benefits:** 403(b); Daycare Assistance; Dental Insurance; Employee Discounts; Flexible Schedule; Life Insurance; Medical Insurance; On-Site Daycare; Pension Plan; Tuition Assistance. **Special programs:** Training. **Office hours:** Monday - Friday, 8:00 a.m. - 4:30 p.m. **Corporate headquarters location:** This Location.

JOHNSON & JOHNSON MEDICAL, INC.

2500 East Arbrook Boulevard, Arlington TX 76014. 817/262-3900. **Contact:** Human Resources. **World Wide Web address:** http://www.jnj.com. **Description:** Manufactures and markets an extensive line of disposable packs and gowns, surgical products, decontamination and disposal systems, latex gloves, and surgical antiseptics. **Common positions include:** Accountant; Biological Scientist; Buyer; Chemical Engineer; Chemist; Clinical Lab Technician; Computer Programmer; Human Resources Manager; Industrial Production Manager; Operations/Production Manager; Purchasing Agent/Manager; Quality Control Supervisor; Software Engineer; Systems Analyst. **Educational backgrounds include:** Accounting; Biology; Business Administration; Chemistry; Computer Science; Engineering; Finance; Marketing. **Benefits:** 401(k); Dental Insurance; Disability Coverage; Employee Discounts; Life Insurance; Medical Insurance; Pension Plan; Tuition Assistance. **Special programs:** Internships. **Corporate headquarters location:** This Location. **Other U.S. locations:** Irvine CA; Southington CT; Tampa FL; El Paso TX; Jacksonville TX; Sherman TX. **Parent company:** Johnson & Johnson (New Brunswick NJ).

JORDAN HEALTH SERVICES
P.O. Box 889, Mount Vernon TX 75457. 903/537-2376. **Contact:** John McAuley, Human Resources Manager. **Description:** A diversified home health care agency. **Common positions include:** Licensed Practical Nurse; Occupational Therapist; Physical Therapist; Registered Nurse; Respiratory Therapist; Social Worker; Speech-Language Pathologist. **Educational backgrounds include:** Health Care. **Benefits:** 401(k); Disability Coverage; Life Insurance; Medical Insurance. **Corporate headquarters location:** This Location. **Listed on:** Privately held. **Annual sales/revenues:** $21 - $50 million. **Number of employees at this location:** 500.

JUST LIKE HOME
1604 71st Street NW, Bradenton FL 34209. 941/756-2555. **Contact:** Human Resources. **World Wide Web address:** http://www.justlikehome.com. **Description:** Provides residential housing and assisted living services for the elderly. Founded in 1987. **Corporate headquarters location:** This Location. **Listed on:** NASDAQ. **Stock exchange symbol:** JLHC.

KCI (KINECTIC CONCEPTS, INC.)
P.O. Box 659508, San Antonio TX 78265-9508. 210/524-9000. **Contact:** Human Resources. **World Wide Web address:** http://www.kci1.com. **Description:** Manufactures, sells, services, and rents hospital beds for the critically ill. **Corporate headquarters location:** This Location.

THE KENDALL COMPANY
15 Hampshire Street, Mansfield MA 02048. 508/261-8000. **Fax:** 508/261-8105. **Contact:** Employment Manager. **E-mail address:** jobs@kendallhq.com. **World Wide Web address:** http://www.kendallhq.com. **Description:** Manufactures and markets disposable medical supplies and adhesives for general medical and industrial uses. The company sells its products to hospitals and to alternative health care facilities worldwide, and also markets products to pharmacies and retail outlets. Products include wound care; vascular therapy, urological care, incontinence care, anesthetic care, and adhesives and tapes. Founded in 1903. **NOTE:** Entry-level positions are offered. **Common positions include:** Accountant; Administrative Assistant; Attorney; Biomedical Engineer; Buyer; Chemist; Clinical Lab Technician; Computer Operator; Computer Programmer; Controller; Credit Manager; Customer Service Representative; Database Manager; Finance Director; Financial Analyst; General Manager; Graphic Artist; Human Resources Manager; Librarian; Management Trainee; Managing Editor; Marketing Manager; Marketing Specialist; Mechanical Engineer; MIS Specialist; Operations Manager; Project Manager; Public Relations Specialist; Quality Control Supervisor; Registered Nurse; Sales Manager; Secretary; Statistician; Systems Analyst; Technical Writer/Editor; Typist/Word Processor; Webmaster. **Educational backgrounds include:** Accounting; Biology; Business Administration; Chemistry; Communications; Computer Science; Economics; Engineering; Finance; Health Care; Liberal Arts; Marketing. **Benefits:** 401(k); Dental Insurance; Disability Coverage; Employee Discounts; ESOP; Financial Planning Assistance; Flexible Schedule; Job Sharing; Life Insurance; Medical Insurance; Tuition Assistance. **Special programs:** Internships; Co-ops. **Corporate headquarters location:** This Location. **Other U.S. locations:** Nationwide. **International locations:** Worldwide. **Parent company:** Tyco International Inc. **Listed on:** New York Stock Exchange. **Stock exchange symbol:** TYC. **CEO:** Richard Meelia. **Annual sales/revenues:** More than $100 million.

KESWICK MULTI-CARE CENTER
700 West 40th Street, Baltimore MD 21211. 410/662-4260. **Fax:** 410/662-4263. **Recorded jobline:** 410/662-4350. **Contact:** Charlene Woolery, Human Resources Specialist. **E-mail address:** hr@keswick-multicare.org. **Description:** A nursing home that provides adult daycare and assisted living services. Founded in 1883. **NOTE:** Entry-level positions and second and third shifts are offered. **Company slogan:** We can make it happen. **Common positions include:** Accountant; Administrative Assistant; Applications Engineer; Certified Nurses Aide; Chief Financial Officer; Computer Programmer; Controller; Dietician/Nutritionist; Human Resources Manager; Marketing Manager; Marketing Specialist; MIS Specialist; Purchasing Agent/Manager; Registered Nurse; Social Worker; Systems Analyst. **Educational backgrounds include:** Accounting; Communications; Computer Science; Health Care; Nutrition. **Benefits:** 401(k); 403(b); Dental Insurance; Disability Coverage; Financial Planning Assistance; Life Insurance; Medical Insurance; Pension Plan; Public Transit Available; Savings Plan; Telecommuting; Tuition Assistance. **Special programs:** Summer Jobs. **Corporate headquarters location:** This Location. **Listed on:** Privately held. **CEO:** Andrea Braid. **Annual sales/revenues:** $21 - $50 million. **Number of employees at this location:** 435.

KING SYSTEMS
15011 Herriman Boulevard, Noblesville IN 46060. 317/776-6823. **Fax:** 317/776-6827. **Contact:** Diana Russell, Human Resources Director. **World Wide Web address:** http://www.kingsystems.com. **Description:** Manufactures plastic disposable breathing circuits used for the delivery of anesthesia in the operating room. **NOTE:** Entry-level positions and second and third shifts are offered. **Common positions include:** Administrative Assistant; Assembler; Blue-Collar Worker Supervisor; Customer Service Rep.; Manufacturing Engineer; Production Manager; Quality Assurance Engineer; Quality Control Supervisor; Warehouse/Distribution Worker. **Benefits:** 401(k); Dental Insurance; Life Insurance; Medical Insurance; Tuition Assistance. **Special programs:** Summer Jobs. **Office hours:** Monday - Friday, 8:00 a.m. - 5:00 p.m. **Corporate headquarters location:** This Location. **Listed on:** Privately held. **President/Owner:** Flois Burrow.

KUALA HEALTHCARE
910 Sylvan Avenue, Englewood Cliffs NJ 07632. 201/567-4600. **Contact:** Human Resources. **Description:** Provides parenteral and enteral nutrition, hydration, chemotherapy, antibiotic and chronic pain management therapies, and related products and services to patients in nursing homes. The company also offers intravenous therapy to patients recovering at home. **Corporate headquarters location:** This Location.

LASERSCOPE
3052 Orchard Drive, San Jose CA 95134-2011. 408/943-0636. **Fax:** 408/944-9401. **Contact:** Human Resources. **World Wide Web address:** http://www.laserscope.com. **Description:** Designs and markets an advanced line of medical laser systems and related energy delivery products. The company markets its products to hospitals, outpatient surgical centers, and physicians offices in the U.S., the U.K., and France through its direct sales force and through exclusive distributor arrangements in Europe, Asia, the Middle East, and the Pacific Rim. **Common positions include:**

Accountant/Auditor; Design Engineer; Mechanical Engineer; MIS Specialist; Operations/Production Manager; Software Engineer. **Educational backgrounds include:** Engineering. **Benefits:** 401(k); Dental Insurance; Disability Coverage; Domestic Partner Benefits; Employee Discounts; Job Sharing; Life Insurance; Medical Insurance; Profit Sharing; Tuition Assistance. **Corporate headquarters location:** This Location. **Listed on:** NASDAQ. **Stock exchange symbol:** LSCP. **President/CEO:** Robert V. McCormick. **Annual sales/revenues:** $21 - $50 million. **Number of employees at this location:** 170. **Number of employees nationwide:** 220.

LE BONHEUR CHILDREN'S MEDICAL CENTER
850 Poplar Avenue, Memphis TN 38105. 901/572-3000. **Contact:** Stephanie Pastona, Human Resources Director. **World Wide Web address:** http://www.lebonheur.org. **Description:** A fully-accredited,nonprofit, 225-bed medical center. Le Bonheur Children's Medical Center is a pediatric specialty and subspecialty referral center. The center serves more than 105,000 children and adolescents each year through inpatient care, specialty clinics, and a fully-staffed emergency department. Facilities include the Crippled Children's Foundation Research Center, a same-day surgery unit, an emergency department, an 18-bed intensive care unit, and a 12-bed transitional care unit. Le Bonheur also serves as the pediatric teaching facility of the University of Tennessee, Memphis.

LEE MEMORIAL HEALTH SYSTEM
P.O. Box 2218, Fort Myers FL 33902. 941/332-1111. **Physical address:** 2776 Cleveland Avenue, Fort Myers FL. **Toll-free phone:** 800/642-5267. **Fax:** 941/332-4199. **Recorded jobline:** 941/433-4636. **Contact:** Human Resources. **Description:** A leading provider of health care in southwest Florida. The nonprofit hospital is comprised of three acute care hospitals, a skilled nursing facility, home health services, and physician offices. Founded in 1916. **NOTE:** Entry-level positions and second and third shifts are offered. **Common positions include:** Attorney; Biomedical Engineer; Buyer; Certified Nurses Aide; Chief Financial Officer; Clinical Lab Technician; Computer Operator; Computer Programmer; Daycare Worker; Dietician/Nutritionist; EEG Technologist; EKG Technician; Emergency Medical Technician; Financial Analyst; Human Resources Manager; Licensed Practical Nurse; Marketing Specialist; Medical Records Technician; MIS Specialist; Nuclear Medicine Technologist; Nurse Practitioner; Occupational Therapist; Pharmacist; Physical Therapist; Physician; Public Relations Specialist; Radiological Technologist; Registered Nurse; Respiratory Therapist; Secretary; Social Worker; Speech-Language Pathologist; Surgical Technician; Telecommunications Manager. **Educational backgrounds include:** Accounting; Business Administration; Computer Science; Health Care; Nutrition. **Benefits:** 403(b); Daycare Assistance; Dental Insurance; Disability Coverage; Employee Discounts; Financial Planning Assistance; Flexible Schedule; Job Sharing; Life Insurance; Medical Insurance; On-Site Daycare; Tuition Assistance. **Corporate headquarters location:** This Location. **Number of employees at this location:** 4,500.

LEGACY HEALTH SYSTEM
1919 NW Lovejoy Street, Portland OR 97209. 503/225-8600. **Recorded jobline:** 503/833-3236. **Contact:** Human Resources. **World Wide Web address:** http://www.legacyhealth.org. **Description:** Operates four Portland area hospitals and offers visiting nurse services. **Common positions include:**

Administrative Worker/Clerk. **Corporate headquarters location:** This Location. **Number of employees at this location:** 275.

LIFECARE ALLIANCE
1699 West Mound Street, Columbus OH 43223. 614/278-3130. **Fax:** 614/278-3143. **Contact:** Celia Jarvis, Senior Personnel Associate. **Description:** A nonprofit home health care agency. LifeCare Alliance also provides Meals on Wheels. Founded in 1898. **NOTE:** Entry-level positions and part-time jobs are offered. **Common positions include:** Administrative Assistant; Certified Nurses Aide; Certified Occupational Therapy Assistant; Computer Programmer; Customer Service Rep.; Dietician/Nutritionist; Event Planner; Home Health Aide; Human Resources Manager; Network/Systems Administrator; Occupational Therapist; Physical Therapist; Registered Nurse; Speech-Language Pathologist; Transportation/Traffic Specialist. **Educational backgrounds include:** Accounting; Business Administration; Computer Science; Health Care; Human Resources; Marketing; MBA; Public Relations. **Benefits:** 403(b); Casual Dress - Daily; Dental Insurance; Disability Coverage; Employee Discounts; Flexible Schedule; Life Insurance; Medical Insurance; Pension Plan; Public Transit Available; Savings Plan; Sick Days; Tuition Assistance; Vacation Days. **Special programs:** Internships. **Office hours:** Monday - Friday, 8:00 a.m. - 5:00 p.m. **Corporate headquarters location:** This Location.

LIFECARE HOSPITALS, INC.
1128 Louisiana Avenue, Shreveport LA 71101. 318/459-3603. **Toll-free phone:** 800/280-5433. **Fax:** 318/429-8341. **Contact:** Rob Lindsey, Human Resources Director. **Description:** A long-term, acute care hospital with 40 beds specializing in individualized, therapy-driven treatment for trauma/extremely ill patients. LifeCare services include respiratory, physical, occupational, speech, and recreational therapy. **NOTE:** Entry-level positions and second and third shifts are offered. **Common positions include:** Administrative Assistant; Certified Nurses Aide; Human Resources Manager; Licensed Practical Nurse; Marketing Manager; Medical Records Technician; Occupational Therapist; Pharmacist; Physical Therapist; Physician; Registered Nurse; Respiratory Therapist; Secretary; Social Worker. **Educational backgrounds include:** Business Administration; Health Care; Marketing. **Benefits:** 401(k); Dental Insurance; Disability Coverage; Employee Discounts; Flexible Schedule; Life Insurance; Medical Insurance. **Office hours:** Monday - Friday, 8:00 a.m. - 5:00 p.m. **Corporate headquarters location:** This Location. **Other U.S. locations:** New Orleans LA; Reno NV. **Listed on:** Privately held. **President:** David LeBlanc. **Number of employees at this location:** 160.

LIFECARE MEDICAL TRANSPORTS, INC.
1170 International Parkway, Fredericksburg VA 22406. 540/752-5883. **Contact:** Human Resources. **World Wide Web address:** http://www.monumental.com/lifecare. **Description:** An ambulance service.

LIFECORE BIOMEDICAL INC.
3515 Lyman Boulevard, Chaska MN 55318. 952/368-4300. **Contact:** Human Resources. **Description:** Manufactures and markets implantable biomaterials and medical and surgical devices. Lifecore Biomedical's products are generally used in the fields of dentistry, drug delivery, general surgery, opthamology, and wound care management. **Corporate headquarters location:** This Location.

LIFELINE SYSTEMS, INC.
111 Lawrence Street, Framingham MA 01702-8156.
508/988-1000. **Fax:** 508/988-1384. **Contact:**
Human Resources. **World Wide Web address:**
http://www.lifelinesys.com. **Description:**
Manufactures personal emergency response systems
and provides monitoring and related services. The
company's services consist of 24-hour, at-home
assistance and personalized support for elderly and
physically challenged individuals. The company's
principal product is LIFELINE, which consists of
equipment manufactured by the company combined
with a monitoring service. **Common positions
include:** Blue-Collar Worker Supervisor; Budget
Analyst; Buyer; Computer Programmer; Customer
Service Rep.; Economist; Electrical/Electronics
Engineer; Financial Analyst; General Manager;
Manufacturer's/Wholesaler's Sales Rep.; Mechanical
Engineer; Operations/Production Manager;
Purchasing Agent/Manager; Quality Control
Supervisor; Services Sales Representative; Software
Engineer; Systems Analyst. **Educational
backgrounds include:** Business Administration;
Communications; Engineering; Finance; Liberal
Arts; Marketing. **Benefits:** 401(k); Dental
Insurance; Disability Coverage; Life Insurance;
Medical Insurance; Profit Sharing; Savings Plan.
Corporate headquarters location: This Location.

LITTLE COMPANY OF MARY HOSPITAL
2800 West 95th Street, Evergreen Park IL 60805.
708/422-6200. **Fax:** 708/229-5878. **Recorded
jobline:** 708/229-5050. **Contact:** Human
Resources. **World Wide Web address:** http://www.
lcmh.org. **Description:** A nonprofit hospital
offering a variety of services including oncology,
orthopedics, pediatrics, mother/baby care, home
care, senior services, and a full-service emergency
room. NOTE: Entry-level positions, part-time jobs,
and second and third shifts are offered. **Company
slogan:** A healing presence. **Common positions
include:** Accountant; Administrative Assistant;
Attorney; Budget Analyst; Buyer; Certified Nurses
Aide; Certified Occupational Therapy Assistant;
Chief Financial Officer; Claim Representative;
Computer Programmer; Computer Support
Technician; Counselor; Customer Service Rep.;
Dietician/Nutritionist; EEG Technologist; EKG
Technician; Electrical/Electronics Engineer;
Electrician; Emergency Medical Technician;
Finance Director; Financial Analyst; Graphic
Designer; Home Health Aide; Librarian; Marketing
Manager; Mechanical Engineer; Medical Assistant;
Medical Records Technician; Medical Secretary;
MIS Specialist; Network Engineer; Network/
Systems Administrator; Nuclear Medicine
Technologist; Occupational Therapist; Paralegal;
Pharmacist; Physical Therapist; Physician;
Psychologist; Public Relations Specialist;
Radiological Technologist; Registered Nurse;
Respiratory Therapist; Secretary; Social Worker;
Speech-Language Pathologist; Surgical Technician;
Systems Analyst; Telecommunications Manager;
Website Developer. **Educational backgrounds
include:** Accounting; Business Administration;
Computer Science; Health Care; Novell; Public
Relations; Spreadsheets. **Benefits:** 403(b); Dental
Insurance; Disability Coverage; Flexible Schedule;
Life Insurance; Medical Insurance; Pension Plan;
Public Transit Available; Tuition Assistance.
Special programs: Internships; Summer Jobs.

LONGMONT UNITED HOSPITAL
1950 Mountain View Avenue, Longmont CO
80501. 303/485-4136. **Fax:** 303/485-4137.
Recorded jobline: 303/651-5241. **Contact:** Human
Resources. **World Wide Web address:** http://www.
luhonline.org. **Description:** A 143-bed general,
acute care, nonprofit, community hospital. The

hospital offers a cancer care center, cardiac lab,
cardiopulmonary services, sports rehabilitation
center, complimentary medicine, cardiovascular
rehabilitation, trauma/emergency center, and
inpatient/outpatient behavioral health services.
NOTE: Second and third shifts are offered.
Common positions include: Certified Nurses Aide;
Clinical Lab Technician; Counselor; Dietician/
Nutritionist; EKG Technician; Licensed Practical
Nurse; Medical Records Technician; Nuclear
Medicine Technologist; Occupational Therapist;
Pharmacist; Physical Therapist; Radiological
Technologist; Registered Nurse; Respiratory
Therapist; Social Worker; Speech-Language
Pathologist; Surgical Technician. **Educational
backgrounds include:** Health Care. **Benefits:**
403(b); Daycare Assistance; Dental Insurance;
Disability Coverage; Employee Discounts; Flexible
Schedule; Job Sharing; Life Insurance; Medical
Insurance; Public Transit Available; Tuition
Assistance. **Special programs:** Training.
Corporate headquarters location: This Location.
Annual sales/revenues: $51 - $100 million.
Number of employees at this location: 930.

LONGVIEW REGIONAL MEDICAL CENTER
P.O. Box 14000, Longview TX 75607. 903/758-
1818. **Fax:** 903/232-3888. **Recorded jobline:**
903/232-3726. **Contact:** Human Resources. **World
Wide Web address:** http://www.
longviewregional.com. **Description:** A 164-bed,
acute care, medical center providing cardiovascular,
pediatric, dialysis, intensive care, intermediate care,
outpatient care, and laboratory services. Founded in
1980. NOTE: Entry-level positions, part-time jobs,
and second and third shifts are offered. **Common
positions include:** Administrative Assistant;
Certified Nurses Aide; Clerical Supervisor; Clinical
Lab Technician; Computer Technician; Dietician/
Nutritionist; EKG Technician; Emergency Medical
Technician; Licensed Practical Nurse; Medical
Records Technician; Medical Secretary; Nuclear
Medicine Technologist; Nurse Practitioner;
Pharmacist; Physician Assistant; Radiological
Technologist; Registered Nurse; Respiratory
Therapist; Secretary; Social Worker; Speech-
Language Pathologist; Surgical Technician;
Typist/Word Processor. **Educational backgrounds
include:** Health Care; Microsoft Office; Microsoft
Word; Spreadsheets. **Benefits:** 401(k); Dental
Insurance; Disability Coverage; Life Insurance;
Medical Insurance; Pension Plan; Profit Sharing;
Tuition Assistance. **Corporate headquarters
location:** Dallas TX. **Other U.S. locations:**
Nationwide. **CEO:** Vicki Romero. **Number of
employees at this location:** 730.

LUXTEC CORPORATION
326 Clark Street, Worcester MA 01606. 508/856-
9454. **Contact:** Human Resources. **World Wide
Web address:** http://www.luxtec.com. **Description:**
Designs, develops, manufactures, and markets
illumination and vision products utilizing fiberoptic
technology for the medical and dental industries.
These products are designed to produce high-quality
light delivered directly to the operative site.
Products include fiberoptic headlights and headlight
television camera systems for audio/video
recordings of surgical procedures; light sources;
cables; retractors; loupes; surgical telescopes; and
other custom-made surgical specialty instruments.
Benefits: Stock Option. **Corporate headquarters
location:** This Location. **Subsidiaries include:**
Cathtec, Inc.; Fiber Imaging Technologies, Inc.;
Luxtec Fiber Optics B.V.

LUZERNE OPTICAL LABORATORIES
180 North Wilkes-Barre Boulevard, P.O. Box 998,
Wilkes-Barre PA 18703-0998. 570/822-3183. **Toll-**

free phone: 800/233-9637. **Fax:** 570/823-4299. **Contact:** Lorraine Dougherty, Human Resources Representative. **Description:** Manufactures optical products including eyeglasses and contact lenses. Founded in 1973. **NOTE:** Entry-level positions and second and third shifts are offered. **Common positions include:** Clerical Supervisor; Computer Operator; Computer Programmer; Controller; Credit Manager; Customer Service Representative; Database Manager; General Manager; Marketing Manager; Production Manager; Purchasing Agent/Manager; Quality Control Supervisor; Sales Executive; Sales Manager; Sales Representative. **Educational backgrounds include:** Accounting; Business Administration; Finance; Marketing; Software Development. **Benefits:** Disability Coverage; Employee Discounts; Life Insurance; Medical Insurance; Pension Plan; Profit Sharing. **Office hours:** Monday - Friday, 7:00 a.m. - 6:30 p.m. **Corporate headquarters location:** This Location.

MHM SERVICES
8605 Westwood Center Drive, Suite 400, Vienna VA 22182. 703/749-4600. **Fax:** 703/749-4604. **Contact:** Human Resources. **Description:** Provides behavioral health services through its seven psychiatric and substance abuse facilities. MHM Services provides inpatient care and alternative care such as partial hospitalization and outpatient treatment. The company's Extended Care Services Division provides specialized medical and behavioral health services to more than 800 nursing homes and assisted living centers. **Corporate headquarters location:** This Location. **Listed on:** American Stock Exchange. **Number of employees nationwide:** 510.

MALLINCKRODT, INC.
2800 Northwest Boulevard, Plymouth MN 55441. 763/694-3500. **Toll-free phone:** 800/497-4979. **Fax:** 763/694-3600. **Contact:** Kathy Henderson, Human Resources Coordinator. **World Wide Web address:** http://www.mallinckrodt.com. **Description:** Manufactures and markets health care products through three main specialty groups. The Imaging Group provides magnetic resonance, nuclear medicine, and X-ray products. The Pharmaceutical Group provides pharmaceutical products for addiciton therapy and pain relief. The Respiratory Group manufactures airway management systems and respiratory devices. **NOTE:** Entry-level positions are offered. **Common positions include:** Accountant; Administrative Assistant; AS400 Programmer Analyst; Auditor; Blue-Collar Worker Supervisor; Budget Analyst; Computer Support Technician; Controller; Customer Service Representative; Design Engineer; Draftsperson; Electrical/Electronics Engineer; Financial Analyst; General Manager; Human Resources Manager; Industrial Production Manager; Manufacturing Engineer; Marketing Manager; Mechanical Engineer; MIS Specialist; Network/Systems Administrator; Operations Manager; Production Manager; Project Manager; Purchasing Agent/Manager; Quality Assurance Engineer; Software Engineer; Systems Analyst; Systems Manager; Technical Writer/Editor. **Educational backgrounds include:** AS400 Certification; C/C++; Computer Science; Engineering; Finance; Marketing; Microsoft Word; Novell; Software Development; Software Tech. Support. **Benefits:** 401(k); Casual Dress - Daily; Dental Insurance; Disability Coverage; Employee Discounts; Life Insurance; Medical Insurance; Profit Sharing; Sick Days; Tuition Assistance. **Special programs:** Internships; Co-ops. **Corporate headquarters location:** St. Louis MO. **Other U.S. locations:** Nationwide. **International locations:** Worldwide.

MANOR CARE HEALTH SERVICES
800 Court Street, Sunbury PA 17801. 570/286-7121. **Contact:** Joyce Little, Administrative Assistant. **World Wide Web address:** http://www.manorcare.com. **Description:** An inpatient and outpatient rehabilitation center providing physical, occupational, and speech therapies. **NOTE:** Part-time jobs and second and third shifts are offered. **Common positions include:** Certified Nurses Aide; Human Resources Manager; Licensed Practical Nurse; Medical Records Technician; Occupational Therapist; Physical Therapist; Physical Therapy Assistant; Registered Nurse; Social Worker; Speech-Language Pathologist. **Educational backgrounds include:** Health Care. **Benefits:** 401(k); Dental Insurance; Employee Discounts; Tuition Assistance. **Office hours:** Monday - Friday, 7:30 a.m. - 5:30 p.m. **Corporate headquarters location:** Gaithersburg MD. **Listed on:** New York Stock Exchange. **Number of employees at this location:** 130.
Other U.S. locations:
- 640 Bethlehem Pike, Montgomeryville PA 18936. 215/368-4350.

MARCONI MEDICAL SYSTEMS
595 Miner Road, Cleveland OH 44143. 440/473-3000. **Fax:** 440/473-2624. **Contact:** Human Resource Coordinator. **World Wide Web address:** http://www.picker.com. **Description:** Specializes in the research, design, development, and manufacture of X-ray equipment for the worldwide medical community. **Common positions include:** Electrical/Electronics Engineer; Mechanical Engineer; Software Engineer. **Educational backgrounds include:** Accounting; Business Administration; Communications; Computer Science; Finance; Marketing. **Corporate headquarters location:** This Location.

MARIETTA MEMORIAL HOSPITAL
401 Matthew Street, Marietta OH 45750-1635. 740/374-1400. **Toll-free phone:** 800/523-3977. **Fax:** 740/376-5045. **Recorded jobline:** 740/374-4997. **Contact:** James Offenberger, Employment Manager. **World Wide Web address:** http://www.mmhospital.org. **Description:** A community-based, acute care hospital. Marietta Memorial offers a variety of services including behavioral health, cardiac rehabilitation, community outreach, home nursing, mammography, radiology, outpatient surgery, and the Strecker Cancer Center. Founded in 1929. **Common positions include:** Certified Occupational Therapy Assistant; Home Health Aide; Nuclear Medicine Technologist; Nurse Practitioner; Occupational Therapist; Pharmacist; Physical Therapist; Physical Therapy Assistant; Physician; Radiological Technologist; Registered Nurse; Respiratory Therapist; Social Worker; Speech-Language Pathologist; Surgical Technician. **Benefits:** 403(b); Dental Insurance; Disability Coverage; Employee Discounts; Life Insurance; Medical Insurance; Pension Plan; Sick Days (6 - 10); Tuition Assistance; Vacation Days (6 - 10). **Special programs:** Internships. **Annual sales/revenues:** $51 - $100 million. **Number of employees at this location:** 900.

MARINER POST-ACUTE NETWORK
15415 Katy Freeway, Suite 800, Houston TX 77094. 281/578-4600. **Fax:** 281/578-4506. **Contact:** Human Resources. **Description:** Mariner Post-Acute Network provides a wide variety of health care services including long-term care, rehabilitation services, and pharmaceutical services. Mariner Post-Acute Network operates more than 290 centers with more than 26,000 beds. **Corporate headquarters location:** This Location. **Other U.S. locations:** Nationwide. **Subsidiaries include:**

Rehability Corporation operates over 160 outpatient centers and provides contract rehabilitation services to over 50 acute care hospitals and roughly 600 nursing homes. Therapy Management Innovations provides consulting, program enhancement, and general oversight of the rehabilitation services provided at nursing facilities. American Pharmaceutical Services, Inc. operates 31 pharmacies and, through its various product segments, provides services to more than 100,000 beds in more than 1,000 facilities nationwide.

MARKESAN RESIDENT HOME, INC.
1130 North Margaret Street, P.O. Box 130, Markesan WI 53946. 920/398-2751. **Fax:** 920/398-3937. **Contact:** Business Office Manager. **Description:** A nonprofit nursing home with residential assisted living and Alzheimer's units. **NOTE:** Second and third shifts are offered. **Common positions include:** Licensed Practical Nurse. **Educational backgrounds include:** Health Care. **Benefits:** 403(b); Flexible Schedule; Medical Insurance; Tuition Assistance. **Special programs:** Internships; Training. **Corporate headquarters location:** This Location. **Listed on:** Privately held. **Number of employees at this location:** 90.

MARSHALLTOWN MEDICAL & SURGICAL CENTER
3 South Fourth Avenue, Marshalltown IA 50158. 515/754-5113. **Fax:** 515/753-2570. **Contact:** Personnel Department. **Description:** A 176-bed, acute care medical center with a rehabilitation and sports medicine facility. **Common positions include:** Certified Occupational Therapy Assistant; Certified Physical Therapy Assistant; Clerical Supervisor; Dietician/Nutritionist; Licensed Practical Nurse; Occupational Therapist; Pharmacist; Physical Therapist; Physician; Physician Assistant; Radiological Technologist; Registered Nurse; Respiratory Therapist; Social Worker. **Benefits:** Dental Insurance; Disability Coverage; Employee Discounts; Life Insurance; Medical Insurance; Pension Plan; Tuition Assistance. **Corporate headquarters location:** This Location. **Number of employees at this location:** 700.

MARTIN MEMORIAL HEALTH SYSTEMS
P.O. Box 9010, Stuart FL 34995. 561/287-5200. **Physical address:** 200 SE Hospital Avenue, Stuart FL. **Contact:** Jennifer T. Slaugh, Employment Coordinator. **Description:** A nonprofit, 336-bed, multifacility health care organization. Martin Memorial Health Systems is comprised of Martin Memorial Medical Center and Martin Memorial Hospital South, both accredited facilities. The medical center is a 236-bed, acute care facility providing a range of inpatient and outpatient services including cancer and cardiac care, a 24-hour emergency department, maternity and pediatrics, and a wide variety of laser surgeries. Martin Memorial Hospital South is a 100-bed community hospital providing inpatient and outpatient services with 92 private rooms, an 8-bed intensive care unit, and a 24-hour emergency department. **Common positions include:** EEG Technologist; EKG Technician; Emergency Medical Technician; Medical Technologist; MIS Specialist; Occupational Therapist; Pharmacist; Physical Therapist; Physician; Radiological Technologist; Registered Nurse; Respiratory Therapist; Speech-Language Pathologist; Surgical Technician; Telecommunications Manager. **Educational backgrounds include:** Health Care. **Benefits:** 401(k); Daycare Assistance; Dental Insurance; Disability Coverage; Employee Discounts; Life Insurance; Medical Insurance; Pension Plan; Savings Plan; Tuition Assistance. **Corporate**

headquarters location: This Location. **Annual sales/revenues:** More than $100 million. **Number of employees at this location:** 2,000.

MARYVALE HOSPITAL MEDICAL CENTER
5102 West Campbell Avenue, Phoenix AZ 85031. 623/848-5050. **Toll-free phone:** 800/581-9393. **Fax:** 623/848-5959. **Recorded jobline:** 623/848-5675. **Contact:** Robert Bodine, Director of Human Resources. **Description:** Maryvale Hospital Medical Center is a 239-bed medical facility staffed by over 400 physicians. The medical facility's services include an emergency department; women and children's services which offers each patient a private labor, delivery, recovery, and postpartum room; special and intermediate care units; surgery; cardiology services including EKGs, echocardiograms, cardiac dopplers, and treadmill tests; magnetic resonance imaging; oncology; radiation therapy, and other types of treatments and consultations; and rehabilitation services including physical therapy, occupational therapy, and speech-language pathology. **NOTE:** Entry-level positions, part-time jobs, and second and third shifts are offered. **Common positions include:** Account Manager; Accountant; Administrative Assistant; Administrative Manager; Assistant Manager; Auditor; Blue-Collar Worker Supervisor; Certified Nurses Aide; Certified Occupational Therapy Assistant; Chief Financial Officer; Clerical Supervisor; Computer Operator; Controller; Credit Manager; Customer Service Representative; Database Administrator; Dietician/Nutritionist; EEG Technologist; EKG Technician; Emergency Medical Technician; Home Health Aide; Human Resources Manager; Licensed Practical Nurse; Medical Assistant; Medical Records Technician; MIS Specialist; Nuclear Medicine Technologist; Nurse Practitioner; Occupational Therapist; Pharmacist; Physical Therapist; Physical Therapy Assistant; Physician; Public Relations Specialist; Purchasing Agent/Manager; Radiological Technologist; Registered Nurse; Respiratory Therapist; Secretary; Social Worker; Speech-Language Pathologist; Surgical Technician; Technical Writer/Editor; Typist/Word Processor. **Educational backgrounds include:** Accounting; AS400 Certification; Biology; Business Administration; Chemistry; Communications; Computer Science; Finance; Health Care; HTML; Liberal Arts; Marketing; Mathematics; MCSE; Nutrition; Physics; Public Relations; Software Tech. Support. **Benefits:** 401(k); Dental Insurance; Disability Coverage; Employee Discounts; Flexible Schedule; Job Sharing; Life Insurance; Medical Insurance; Pension Plan; Profit Sharing; Public Transit Available; Savings Plan; Sick Days (11+); Telecommuting; Tuition Assistance; Vacation Days (6 - 10). **Special programs:** Internships; Training; Co-ops; Summer Jobs. **Corporate headquarters location:** Nashville TN. **Parent company:** Vanguard Health. **Listed on:** Privately held. **CEO:** Art Layne. **Annual sales/revenues:** $51 - $100 million. **Number of employees at this location:** 1,100.

MASSACHUSETTS GENERAL HOSPITAL
55 Fruit Street, Boston MA 02114. 617/726-2000. **Fax:** 617/724-2266. **Contact:** Human Resources. **World Wide Web address:** http://www.mgh.harvard.edu. **Description:** An 820-bed medical center that is the oldest and largest teaching hospital of Harvard Medical School. The hospital offers diagnostic and therapeutic care in virtually every specialty and subspecialty of medicine and surgery. **NOTE:** Please direct resumes to Partners HealthCare System Inc., Human Resources, 101 Merrimac Street, 5th Floor, Boston MA 02114. 617/726-2210. Entry-level positions are offered. **Common positions include:** Accountant;

Administrative Assistant; Administrative Manager; Applications Engineer; Architect; Attorney; Auditor; Biochemist; Biological Scientist; Biomedical Engineer; Blue-Collar Worker Supervisor; Budget Analyst; Certified Nurses Aide; Certified Occupational Therapy Assistant; Chef/ Cook/Kitchen Worker; Chemist; Chief Financial Officer; Child Care Center Director; Clinical Lab Technician; Computer Support Technician; Construction Contractor; Controller; Customer Service Rep.; Database Administrator; Database Manager; Dietician/Nutritionist; Editor; Editorial Assistant; EEG Technologist; EKG Technician; Electrician; Emergency Medical Technician; Finance Director; Financial Analyst; Help-Desk Technician; Human Resources Manager; Librarian; Licensed Practical Nurse; Medical Assistant; Medical Records Technician; Medical Secretary; MIS Specialist; Molecular Biologist; Network Engineer; Network/Systems Administrator; Nuclear Medicine Technologist; Nurse Practitioner; Occupational Therapist; Operations Manager; Paralegal; Pediatric Anesthesiologist; Pharmacist; Physical Therapist; Physical Therapy Assistant; Physician; Physician Assistant; Preschool Worker; Project Manager; Psychologist; Purchasing Agent/ Manager; Radiological Technologist; Registered Nurse; Respiratory Therapist; Secretary; Social Worker; Software Engineer; Speech-Language Pathologist; Surgical Technician; Systems Analyst; Technical Support Manager; Technical Writer/ Editor; Veterinarian; Webmaster. **Educational backgrounds include:** Accounting; Biology; Business Administration; Chemistry; Computer Science; Engineering; Finance; Health Care; Liberal Arts; Marketing; MBA; Microsoft Office; Microsoft Word; Novell; Public Relations; QuarkXPress; Spreadsheets; SQL; Visual Basic. **Benefits:** 403(b); Casual Dress - Fridays; Daycare Assistance; Dental Insurance; Disability Coverage; Employee Discounts; Financial Planning Assistance; Job Sharing; Life Insurance; Medical Insurance; On-Site Daycare; Pension Plan; Public Transit Available. **Special programs:** Internships; Training; Co-ops; Summer Jobs. **Office hours:** Monday - Friday, 8:30 a.m. - 4:30 p.m. **Parent company:** Partners HealthCare System Inc. **Number of employees at this location:** 10,000.

McCREADY HEALTH SERVICES FOUNDATION
201 Hall Highway, Crisfield MD 21817. 410/968-1200. **Fax:** 410/968-3005. **Contact:** Human Resources. **Description:** Operates The Edward W. McCready Memorial Hospital, The Alice Byrd Tawes Nursing Home, and The Peyton Center. Combined, these facilities offer emergency services; inpatient accommodations including acute medical and surgical beds, skilled nursing beds, and a comprehensive care unit; surgical services including inpatient and outpatient general, gynecological, plastic, and dental surgeries; diagnostic services; rehabilitation and extended recovery services; and social services. **NOTE:** Entry-level positions and second and third shifts are offered. **Common positions include:** Administrative Assistant; Assistant Manager; Blue-Collar Worker Supervisor; Certified Nurses Aide; Chief Financial Officer; Clerical Supervisor; Clinical Lab Technician; Computer Animator; Computer Operator; Computer Programmer; Controller; Counselor; Credit Manager; Customer Service Rep.; Dietician/ Nutritionist; EEG Technologist; EKG Technician; Electrical/Electronics Engineer; Electrician; Emergency Medical Technician; Environmental Engineer; Finance Director; Food Scientist/ Technologist; Human Resources Manager; Industrial Engineer; Licensed Practical Nurse; Marketing Manager; Medical Records Technician;

MIS Specialist; Nuclear Medicine Technologist; Occupational Therapist; Operations Manager; Pharmacist; Physical Therapist; Physician; Psychologist; Public Relations Specialist; Purchasing Agent/Manager; Quality Control Supervisor; Radiological Technologist; Registered Nurse; Respiratory Therapist; Secretary; Social Worker; Speech-Language Pathologist; Statistician; Surgical Technician; Typist/Word Processor. **Educational backgrounds include:** Accounting; Business Administration; Communications; Computer Science; Finance; Health Care; Marketing; Nutrition; Public Relations. **Benefits:** 401(k); Disability Coverage; Flexible Schedule; Life Insurance; Medical Insurance; Pension Plan; Tuition Assistance. **Special programs:** Training; Co-ops; Summer Jobs. **Corporate headquarters location:** This Location. **CEO:** J. Allan Bickling. **Number of employees at this location:** 300.

McKESSONHBOC
One Post Street, 31st Floor, San Francisco CA 94104. 415/983-9087. **Fax:** 415/983-8900. **Contact:** Human Resources. **World Wide Web address:** http://www.mckhboc.com. **Description:** Provides information systems and technology to health care enterprises including hospitals, integrated delivery networks, and managed care organizations. McKessonHBOC's primary products are Pathways 2000, a family of client/server-based applications that allow the integration and uniting of health care providers; STAR, Series, and HealthQuest transaction systems; TRENDSTAR decision support system; and QUANTUM enterprise information system. The company also offers outsourcing services that include strategic information systems planning, data center operations, receivables management, business office administration, and major system conversions. **Common positions include:** Accountant/Auditor; Attorney; Computer Programmer; Human Resources Manager; Operations/Production Manager; Paralegal; Pharmacist; Systems Analyst; Wholesale and Retail Buyer. **Educational backgrounds include:** Accounting; Computer Science; Finance; Liberal Arts; Marketing; Mathematics. **Benefits:** 401(k); Dental Insurance; Disability Coverage; Life Insurance; Medical Insurance; Pension Plan; Profit Sharing; Savings Plan; Tuition Assistance. **Corporate headquarters location:** This Location. **Other U.S. locations:** Nationwide. **Subsidiaries include:** Automated Healthcare Inc.; Healthcare Delivery Systems, Inc.; McKesson BioServices Corporation; McKesson Pharmacy Systems; Medis Health and Pharmaceutical Services, Inc.; MedPath; U.S. Healthcare; Zee Medical, Inc. **Listed on:** New York Stock Exchange; Pacific Stock Exchange. **Stock exchange symbol:** MCK.

MEDA-CARE AMBULANCE SERVICE
2515 West Vliet Street, Milwaukee WI 53205. 414/342-1148x12. **Fax:** 414/342-0888. **Contact:** Linda Wiedmann, Director of Operations. **Description:** Provides both emergency and non-emergency transportation via ambulance. **NOTE:** Second and third shifts are offered. **Common positions include:** Emergency Medical Technician; Registered Nurse. **Educational backgrounds include:** Emergency Medical Svcs. **Benefits:** Medical Insurance; Public Transit Available; Tuition Assistance. **Special programs:** Training. **Corporate headquarters location:** This Location. **Annual sales/revenues:** $5 - $10 million. **Number of employees at this location:** 140.

MEDCENTRAL HEALTH SYSTEM
335 Glessner Avenue, Mansfield OH 44903. 419/526-8000. **Fax:** 419/526-8848. **Contact:** Recruiter. **World Wide Web address:** http://www.

medcentral.org. **Description:** MedCentral Health System is a leading health care delivery system that operates three acute care hospitals: Crestline Hospital, Mansfield Hospital, and Shelby Hospital. The system also operates a cardiac care center, substance abuse programs, a walk-in medical center, and industrial health and safety services. **Common positions include:** Accountant; Administrative Assistant; Certified Nurses Aide; Certified Occupational Therapy Assistant; Clinical Lab Technician; Computer Operator; Computer Programmer; Counselor; Dietician/Nutritionist; EEG Technologist; EKG Technician; Electrician; Emergency Medical Technician; Home Health Aide; Licensed Practical Nurse; Medical Records Technician; Network/Systems Administrator; Nuclear Medicine Technologist; Nurse Practitioner; Occupational Therapist; Pharmacist; Physical Therapist; Physical Therapy Assistant; Physician; Psychologist; Radiological Technologist; Registered Nurse; Respiratory Therapist; Secretary; Social Worker; Speech-Language Pathologist; Surgical Technician; Typist/Word Processor. **Benefits:** Dental Insurance; Financial Planning Assistance; Life Insurance; Medical Insurance; Pension Plan; Savings Plan; Tuition Assistance. **Other area locations:** Crestline OH; Shelby OH. **Number of employees at this location:** 2,000.

MEDEX INC.
6250 Shier Rings Road, Dublin OH 43016. 614/876-2413. **Contact:** Human Resources. **Description:** An international manufacturer and supplier of critical care products and infusion systems for medical and surgical applications. These products are sold to hospitals, alternative health care facilities, home health care providers, and original equipment manufacturers. **Common positions include:** Accountant/Auditor; Biological Scientist; Blue-Collar Worker Supervisor; Budget Analyst; Chemical Engineer; Computer Programmer; Customer Service Rep.; Draftsperson; Electrician; Environmental Engineer; Human Resources Manager; Industrial Engineer; Industrial Production Manager; Materials Engineer; Mechanical Engineer; Operations/Production Manager; Quality Control Supervisor; Registered Nurse; Software Engineer; Systems Analyst; Wholesale and Retail Buyer. **Educational backgrounds include:** Accounting; Biology; Business Administration; Chemistry; Communications; Computer Science; Engineering; Finance; Marketing. **Benefits:** 401(k); Dental Insurance; Disability Coverage; Employee Discounts; Life Insurance; Medical Insurance; Pension Plan; Profit Sharing; Savings Plan; Tuition Assistance. **Special programs:** Internships. **Corporate headquarters location:** This Location. **Other U.S. locations:** Atlanta GA. **Listed on:** NASDAQ.

MEDICAL CITY DALLAS HOSPITAL
7777 Forest Lane, Building B, Suite 250, Dallas TX 75230. 972/566-7070. **Toll-free phone:** 800/224-4733. **Recorded jobline:** 888/344-5627. **Contact:** Recruiting. **World Wide Web address:** http://www.medicalcityhospital.com. **Description:** A full-service hospital. **NOTE:** Entry-level positions, part-time jobs, and second and third shifts are offered. **Common positions include:** Accountant; Administrative Assistant; Certified Nurses Aide; Chief Financial Officer; Computer Operator; Computer Technician; Controller; Customer Service Rep.; Dietician/Nutritionist; EEG Technologist; EKG Technician; Librarian; Licensed Practical Nurse; Marketing Manager; Medical Records Technician; Network/Systems Administrator; Nuclear Medicine Technologist; Occupational Therapist; Pharmacist; Physical Therapist; Physical Therapy Assistant; Purchasing

Agent/Manager; Radiological Technologist; Registered Nurse; Respiratory Therapist; Secretary; Social Worker; Speech-Language Pathologist; Statistician; Surgical Technician; Vice President; Vice President of Finance. **Educational backgrounds include:** Accounting; Biology; Business Administration; Computer Science; Finance; Health Care; Microsoft Word; Nursing; Nutrition; Spreadsheets. **Benefits:** 401(k); Daycare Assistance; Dental Insurance; Disability Coverage; Employee Discounts; Flexible Schedule; Life Insurance; Medical Insurance; Retirement Plan; Sick Days (6 - 10); Tuition Assistance; Vacation Days (16+). **Special programs:** Internships; Training; Summer Jobs. **CEO:** Steve Corbeil.

MEDICAL RESOURCES, INC.
125 State Street, Suite 200, Hackensack NJ 07601. 201/488-6230. **Fax:** 201/488-8455. **Contact:** Personnel. **World Wide Web address:** http://www.mrii.com. **Description:** Owns and manages outpatient medical diagnostic imaging centers nationwide. The centers offer Magnetic Resonance Imaging (MRI), Computerized Tomography (CT), nuclear medicine, mammography, ultrasound, and X-ray. **Common positions include:** Accountant; Administrative Assistant; Architect; Attorney; Construction Contractor; Human Resources Manager; Nuclear Medicine Technologist; Public Relations Specialist; Radiological Technologist; Sales Representative. **Benefits:** 401(k); Casual Dress - Fridays; Dental Insurance; Disability Coverage; Life Insurance; Medical Insurance; Tuition Assistance; Vacation Days (6 - 10). **Listed on:** NASDAQ. **Stock exchange symbol:** MRII. **Annual sales/revenues:** More than $100 million.

MEDICALODGES, INC.
P.O. Box 509, Coffeyville KS 67337. 316/251-6700. **Physical address:** 201 West Eighth, Coffeyville KS. **Fax:** 316/251-6756. **Contact:** Human Resources. **Description:** Medicalodges operates 25 long-term care facilities. Founded in 1961. **Common positions include:** Accountant; Administrator; Assistant Manager; Blue-Collar Worker Supervisor; Certified Nurses Aide; Computer Programmer; Customer Service Rep.; Food Scientist/Technologist; Home Health Aide; Licensed Practical Nurse; Maintenance Technician; Marketing Specialist; Public Relations Specialist; Registered Nurse; Social Worker. **Educational backgrounds include:** Accounting; Business Administration; Health Care; Marketing. **Benefits:** 401(k); Dental Insurance; Disability Coverage; ESOP; Life Insurance; Medical Insurance; Sick Days (1 - 5); Vacation Days (10 - 20). **Special programs:** Internships. **Corporate headquarters location:** This Location. **Other U.S. locations:** AR; MO; OK. **Parent company:** Medicalodges, Inc.

MEDIQ INC.
One Mediq Plaza, Pennsauken NJ 08110. 856/665-9300. **Fax:** 856/661-0223. **Contact:** Human Resources. **World Wide Web address:** http://www.mediqprn.com. **Description:** Rents life support equipment such as ventilators, monitors, and incubators to hospitals and nursing homes. **Corporate headquarters location:** This Location.

MEDLINE INDUSTRIES, INC.
One Medline Place, Mundelein IL 60060. 847/949-3009. **Toll-free phone:** 800/MED-LINE. **Fax:** 847/949-2109. **Contact:** Siggy Letheby, Recruitment Manager. **World Wide Web address:** http://www.medline.net. **Description:** One of the largest privately held manufacturers and distributors of health care products including beds, cots, gowns, and wheelchairs. Founded in 1910. **NOTE:** Entry-level positions and second and third shifts are

offered. **Common positions include:** Account Rep.; Accountant; Buyer; Customer Service Rep.; Management Trainee; Manufacturing Engineer; Marketing Manager; Marketing Specialist; Mechanical Engineer; Production Manager; Project Manager; Sales Executive; Sales Representative; Secretary; Software Engineer; Systems Analyst; Systems Manager; Typist/Word Processor. **Educational backgrounds include:** Accounting; Business Administration; Engineering; Finance; Liberal Arts; Marketing; Software Development. **Benefits:** 401(k); Dental Insurance; Life Insurance; Medical Insurance; Tuition Assistance. **Special programs:** Co-ops; Internships; Summer Jobs. **Office hours:** Monday - Friday, 8:00 a.m. - 5:00 p.m. **Corporate headquarters location:** This Location. **Other U.S. locations:** AL; CA; FL; GA; MO; NC; NV; NY; PA; TX; WA. **Listed on:** Privately held. **CEO:** Charlie Mills. **Number of employees at this location:** 900. **Number of employees nationwide:** 2,500.

MEDRAD, INC.

One Medrad Drive, Indianola PA 15051. 412/767-2400. **Contact:** Keith Young, Human Resources Director. **World Wide Web address:** http://www.medrad.com. **Description:** Designs, manufactures, and markets high-tech equipment and disposable products such as CT and angiography injectors, syringes, magnetic resonance coils, and other imaging equipment. **Common positions include:** Accountant/Auditor; Buyer; Clerical Supervisor; Computer Programmer; Credit Manager; Customer Service Representative; Designer; Draftsperson; Electrical/Electronics Engineer; Financial Analyst; General Manager; Industrial Engineer; Industrial Production Manager; Manufacturer's/Wholesaler's Sales Rep.; Mechanical Engineer; Purchasing Agent/Manager; Quality Control Supervisor; Radiological Technologist; Services Sales Rep.; Software Engineer; Systems Analyst; Technical Writer/Editor. **Educational backgrounds include:** Accounting; Business Administration; Computer Science; Engineering; Finance; Marketing; Mathematics. **Benefits:** 401(k); Dental Insurance; Disability Coverage; Life Insurance; Medical Insurance; Profit Sharing; Tuition Assistance. **Corporate headquarters location:** This Location. **International locations:** Brazil; Canada; France; Germany; Italy; Japan; Singapore; the Netherlands; United Kingdom. **Parent company:** Schering AG (Berlin, Germany). **Listed on:** NASDAQ. **Annual sales/revenues:** More than $100 million. **Number of employees at this location:** 670. **Number of employees nationwide:** 780. **Number of employees worldwide:** 870.

MEDSTAR HEALTH

5565 Sterrett Place, 5th Floor, Columbia MD 21044. 410/772-6500. **Contact:** Human Resources. **World Wide Web address:** http://www.medstarhealth.org. **Description:** MedStar Health operates Franklin Square Hospital; Harbor Hospital Center; National Rehabilitation Hospital; Washington Hospital Center; Union Memorial Hospital; Good Samaritan Hospital; nursing centers; Ask-A-Nurse health information and physician referral; home health care services; and rehabilitation services. **Corporate headquarters location:** This Location.

MEDTRONIC, INC.

Medtronic Employment Center, P.O. Box 976, Minneapolis MN 55440-0976. 763/574-4000. **Recorded jobline:** 763/514-7724. **Contact:** Human Resources. **E-mail address:** employment@medtronic.com. **World Wide Web address:** http://www.medtronic.com. **Description:** Engaged in the application of biomedical engineering in the research, design, manufacture, and sale of medical equipment that alleviates pain, restores health, and extends life. Medtronic's products include pacemakers and related support systems, artificial heart valves, and neurological devices. Pacemaker brands include Elite, Activitrax, Minix, Minvet, and Legend. Founded in 1949. **Company slogan:** When life depends on medical technology. **Common positions include:** Accountant; Administrative Assistant; Applications Engineer; AS400 Programmer Analyst; Attorney; Auditor; Biochemist; Biological Scientist; Biomedical Engineer; Chemical Engineer; Chemist; Clinical Lab Technician; Computer Programmer; Computer Scientist; Computer Support Technician; Computer Technician; Database Administrator; Design Engineer; Electrical/Electronics Engineer; Financial Analyst; Help-Desk Technician; Intellectual Property Lawyer; Manufacturing Engineer; Market Research Analyst; Marketing Manager; Mechanical Engineer; Metallurgical Engineer; Network Engineer; Network/Systems Administrator; Project Manager; Quality Assurance Engineer; Sales Representative; Secretary; Software Engineer; SQL Programmer; Statistician; Systems Analyst; Systems Manager; Technical Writer/Editor. **Educational backgrounds include:** Accounting; AS400 Certification; Biology; C/C++; Computer Science; Engineering; Finance; Java; Marketing; MBA; MCSE; Microsoft Office; Microsoft Word; Novell; Software Development; Software Tech. Support; Spreadsheets; SQL; Visual Basic. **Benefits:** 401(k); Adoption Assistance; Casual Dress - Fridays; Daycare Assistance; Dental Insurance; Disability Coverage; Employee Discounts; Flexible Schedule; Job Sharing; Life Insurance; Medical Insurance; Pension Plan; Profit Sharing; Sick Days; Tuition Assistance; Vacation Days. **Office hours:** Monday - Friday, 8:00 a.m. - 5:00 p.m. **Corporate headquarters location:** This Location. **Other U.S. locations:** Nationwide. **International locations:** Worldwide. **Listed on:** New York Stock Exchange. **President:** Bill George. **Annual sales/revenues:** More than $100 million.

MEDTRONIC PHYSIO-CONTROL INC.

P.O. Box 97006, Redmond WA 98073-9706. 425/867-4000. **Physical address:** 11811 Willows Road NE, Redmond WA. **Contact:** Human Resources. **World Wide Web address:** http://www.physiocontrol.com. **Description:** Manufactures, sells, and services defibrillators, monitors, and pacemakers. **Common positions include:** Accountant; Biomedical Engineer; Budget Analyst; Buyer; Computer Operator; Computer Programmer; Credit Clerk and Authorizer; Customer Service Rep.; Department Manager; Draftsperson; Electrical/Electronics Engineer; Employment Interviewer; Financial Manager; Human Resources Manager; Industrial Engineer; Inspector/Tester/Grader; Librarian; Manufacturer's/Wholesaler's Sales Rep.; Market Research Analyst; Marketing Manager; Mechanical Engineer; Paralegal; Payroll Clerk; Precision Assembler; Purchasing Agent/Manager; Quality Assurance Engineer; Quality Control Supervisor; Receptionist; Secretary; Software Engineer; Systems Analyst; Technical Writer/Editor; Test Engineer. **Educational backgrounds include:** Accounting; Business Administration; Chemistry; Computer Science; Engineering; Finance; Marketing. **Benefits:** Dental Insurance; Disability Coverage; Life Insurance; Medical Insurance; Pension Plan; Profit Sharing; Savings Plan; Tuition Assistance. **Parent company:** Medtronic, Inc.

MEMORIAL HOSPITAL

111 Brewster Street, Pawtucket RI 02860. 401/729-2000. **Fax:** 401/729-3054. **Recorded jobline:** 401/729-2562. **Contact:** Personnel. **World Wide**

Web address: http://www.mhri.org. **Description:** A nonprofit hospital that offers a variety of services including adult day care, a birthing center, cardiology, home care, pediatrics, primary care, neurology, radiology, and rehabilitation. **NOTE:** Entry-level positions, part-time jobs, and second and third shifts are offered. **Common positions include:** Accountant; Administrative Assistant; Certified Nurses Aide; Certified Occupational Therapy Assistant; Computer Operator; Computer Programmer; Controller; Dietician/Nutritionist; EEG Technologist; EKG Technician; Electrician; Help-Desk Technician; Home Health Aide; Human Resources Manager; Librarian; Licensed Practical Nurse; Medical Assistant; Medical Records Technician; Medical Secretary; Nuclear Medicine Technologist; Nurse Practitioner; Pediatric Anesthesiologist; Pharmacist; Physical Therapist; Physical Therapy Assistant; Physician; Physician Assistant; Public Relations Specialist; Radiological Technologist; Registered Nurse; Respiratory Therapist; Secretary; Social Worker; Speech-Language Pathologist. **Educational backgrounds include:** Business Administration; Health Care; Liberal Arts; MBA; Microsoft Office; Microsoft Word. **Benefits:** 403(b); Dental Insurance; Disability Coverage; Employee Discounts; Medical Insurance; Pension Plan; Tuition Assistance. **Special programs:** Internships; Training. **Corporate headquarters location:** This Location.

MEMORIAL HOSPITAL OF BURLINGTON
252 McHenry Street, Burlington WI 53105-1828. 262/741-2247. **Fax:** 262/767-6308. **Recorded jobline:** 262/767-6307. **Contact:** Dana Crowell, Recruiter. **Description:** An acute care, nonprofit, community hospital. **NOTE:** Entry-level positions and second and third shifts are offered. **Common positions include:** Administrative Assistant; Biomedical Engineer; Blue-Collar Worker Supervisor; Budget Analyst; Certified Nurses Aide; Chief Financial Officer; Clerical Supervisor; Clinical Lab Technician; Computer Operator; Computer Programmer; Customer Service Representative; Dietician/Nutritionist; Education Administrator; EEG Technologist; EKG Technician; Emergency Medical Technician; Environmental Engineer; Financial Analyst; Human Resources Manager; Licensed Practical Nurse; Marketing Manager; Marketing Specialist; Medical Records Technician; MIS Specialist; Multimedia Designer; Nuclear Medicine Technologist; Nurse Practitioner; Occupational Therapist; Pharmacist; Physical Therapist; Physician; Public Relations Specialist; Purchasing Agent/Manager; Quality Control Supervisor; Radiological Technologist; Registered Nurse; Respiratory Therapist; Secretary; Social Worker; Speech-Language Pathologist; Surgical Technician; Typist/Word Processor; Vice President of Finance. **Educational backgrounds include:** Business Administration; Communications; Finance; Health Care; Marketing; Nutrition; Public Relations. **Benefits:** 403(b); Dental Insurance; Disability Coverage; Employee Discounts; Life Insurance; Medical Insurance; Pension Plan; Tuition Assistance. **Corporate headquarters location:** Milwaukee WI. **Parent company:** Aurora Health Care. **Number of employees at this location:** 500.

MEMORIAL HOSPITAL OF CONVERSE COUNTY
P.O. Box 1450, Douglas WY 82633. 307/358-2122. **Physical address:** 111 South Fifth Street, Douglas WY. **Fax:** 307/358-9216. **Contact:** Linda York, Human Resources Officer. **Description:** A nonprofit, 44-bed county hospital. **NOTE:** Entry-level positions and part-time jobs are offered. **Common positions include:** Account Rep.; Administrative Assistant; Certified Nurses Aide;

Chief Financial Officer; Clerical Supervisor; Clinical Lab Technician; Computer Technician; EKG Technician; Home Health Aide; Human Resources Manager; Marketing Specialist; Medical Records Technician; Physician; Physician Assistant; Purchasing Agent/Manager; Radiological Technologist; Registered Nurse; Respiratory Therapist; Secretary; Surgical Technician; Typist/Word Processor. **Educational backgrounds include:** Health Care; Novell. **Benefits:** Dental Insurance; Employee Discounts; Life Insurance; Medical Insurance; Sick Days (6 - 10); Vacation Days (10 - 20). **Office hours:** Monday - Friday, 8:30 a.m. - 5:00 p.m. **Corporate headquarters location:** This Location.

MEMORIAL HOSPITAL OF SWEETWATER COUNTY
P.O. Box 1359, Rock Springs WY 82902. 307/362-3711. **Fax:** 307/362-8391. **Contact:** Bob Walters, Director of Human Resources. **World Wide Web address:** http://www.minershospital.com. **Description:** A full-service, acute care hospital that offers a variety of services including anesthesiology, emergency medicine, general surgery, internal medicine, obstetrics, opthamology, plastic surgery, radiology, and urology. **Common positions include:** Biomedical Engineer; Clinical Lab Technician; Computer Programmer; Dietician/Nutritionist; EEG Technologist; EKG Technician; Environmental Engineer; Licensed Practical Nurse; Medical Records Technician; Nuclear Medicine Technologist; Purchasing Agent/Manager; Quality Control Supervisor; Radiological Technologist; Registered Nurse; Respiratory Therapist; Social Worker; Surgical Technician; Systems Analyst. **Educational backgrounds include:** Health Care. **Benefits:** Dental Insurance; Disability Coverage; Life Insurance; Medical Insurance; Pension Plan; Tuition Assistance. **Number of employees at this location:** 365.

MENTOR CORPORATION
201 Mentor Drive, Santa Barbara CA 93111. 805/681-6000. **Contact:** Human Resources. **World Wide Web address:** http://www.mentorcorp.com. **Description:** Develops, manufactures, and markets a broad range of products for plastic and reconstructive surgery, urology, and ophthalmology. Mentor Corporation's products include surgically implantable devices, diagnostic and surgical instruments, disposable instruments, and disposable products for hospitals and home health care. **Corporate headquarters location:** This Location.

MERCY FITZGERALD HOSPITAL
1500 Lansdowne Avenue, Darby PA 19023. 610/237-4000. **Contact:** Ellie Albright, Director, Employee Relations. **World Wide Web address:** http://www.mercyhealth.org. **Description:** An acute care community hospital that serves Delaware County and Southwest Philadelphia. **Parent company:** Mercy Health System.

MERCY HEALTH SYSTEM
1000 Mineral Point Avenue, P.O. Box 5003, Janesville WI 53547. 608/756-6721. **Fax:** 608/755-5378. **Recorded jobline:** 608/741-6979. **Contact:** Human Resources. **World Wide Web address:** http://www.mercyhealthsystem.org. **Description:** A fully integrated health care system that includes four acute care hospitals; skilled nursing facilities; home health care services; an independent living facility; and several ambulatory care centers. Mercy Health System also offrs full residency training for diagnostic radiology, general surgery, and internal medicine. **NOTE:** Entry-level positions and second and third shifts are offered. **Common positions include:** Accountant; Administrative Assistant;

Buyer; Certified Nurses Aide; Chief Financial Officer; Clerical Supervisor; Clinical Lab Technician; Computer Operator; Computer Programmer; Counselor; Customer Service Rep.; Database Manager; Dietician/Nutritionist; Education Administrator; EEG Technologist; EKG Technician; Electrician; Finance Director; Financial Analyst; Graphic Artist; Graphic Designer; Licensed Practical Nurse; Management Trainee; Marketing Manager; Marketing Specialist; Medical Records Technician; Occupational Therapist; Pharmacist; Physical Therapist; Physician; Psychologist; Purchasing Agent/Manager; Quality Control Supervisor; Radiological Technologist; Registered Nurse; Respiratory Therapist; Secretary; Social Worker; Software Engineer; Speech-Language Pathologist; Surgical Technician; Systems Analyst; Transportation/Traffic Specialist; Typist/Word Processor. **Educational backgrounds include:** Business Administration; Nursing. **Benefits:** 403(b); Dental Insurance; Employee Discounts; Flexible Schedule; Life Insurance; Pension Plan; Savings Plan; Tuition Assistance. **Special programs:** Internships; Summer Jobs; Training. **Office hours:** Monday - Friday, 8:00 a.m. - 5:00 p.m. **Corporate headquarters location:** This Location. **Other U.S. locations:** IL. **CEO:** Javon Bea. **Number of employees at this location:** 2,300.

MERCY MEDICAL CENTER
301 St. Paul Place, Baltimore MD 21202. 410/332-9743. **Fax:** 410/783-5863. **Recorded jobline:** 410/332-9414. **Contact:** Human Resources. **World Wide Web address:** http://www.mdmercy.com. **Description:** An acute care general hospital. Specialties at Mercy Medical Center include eating disorder treatment programs, women's services, detoxification facilities, and a sexual assault and crisis center. **Common positions include:** Certified Nurses Aide; Dietician/Nutritionist; EEG Technologist; Emergency Medical Technician; Medical Secretary; Occupational Therapist; Pharmacist; Physical Therapist; Radiological Technologist; Registered Nurse; Respiratory Therapist; Surgical Technician. **Benefits:** Dental Insurance; Disability Coverage; Life Insurance; Medical Insurance; Pension Plan; Tuition Assistance.

MERCY MEDICAL CENTER
1301 15th Avenue West, Williston ND 58801. 701/774-7400. **Fax:** 701/774-7670. **Contact:** Ildiko A. Kiss, Human Resources Supervisor. **Description:** A 134-bed acute care hospital. Mercy Medical Center is a member of Catholic Health Initiatives (CHI). **Common positions include:** Accountant; Biomedical Engineer; Certified Nurses Aide; Computer Programmer; Computer Support Technician; Credit Manager; Desktop Publishing Specialist; Dietician/Nutritionist; Education Administrator; Electrician; Environmental Engineer; Help-Desk Technician; Home Health Aide; Human Resources Manager; Marketing Specialist; Medical Records Technician; Medical Secretary; Network/Systems Administrator; Nuclear Medicine Technologist; Physician; Psychologist; Public Relations Specialist; Purchasing Agent/Manager; Quality Assurance Engineer; Radiological Technologist; Registered Nurse; Respiratory Therapist; Social Worker; Systems Analyst. **Educational backgrounds include:** Business Administration; Health Care; Microsoft Word; Novell; Spreadsheets. **Benefits:** 403(b); Casual Dress - Fridays; Dental Insurance; Disability Coverage; Employee Discounts; Flexible Schedule; Life Insurance; Medical Insurance; Pension Plan; Relocation Assistance; Tuition Assistance. **Number of employees at this location:** 460.

MERIT MEDICAL SYSTEMS, INC.
1600 West Merit Parkway, South Jordan UT 84095. 801/253-1600. **Fax:** 801/253-1687. **Recorded jobline:** 801/263-4020. **Contact:** Human Resources. **World Wide Web address:** http://www.merit.com. **Description:** Develops, manufactures, and distributes disposable proprietary medical products used in interventional diagnostic procedures. The products primarily serve the cardiology and radiology markets. The company serves client hospitals worldwide. Founded in 1987. **Corporate headquarters location:** This Location. **Listed on:** NASDAQ. **Stock exchange symbol:** MMSI. **Annual sales/revenues:** $21 - $50 million.

MERITER HEALTH SERVICES INC.
202 South Park Street, Madison WI 53715. 608/267-6134. **Fax:** 608/267-6568. **Recorded jobline:** 608/267-6055. **Contact:** Jenna Linmann, Employment Coordinator. **World Wide Web address:** http://www.meriter.com. **Description:** A full-service health care provider that includes Meriter Hospital, a nonprofit, acute care hospital; Meriter Retirement Services; Meriter Home Health; General Medical Laboratories; and the Meriter Foundation. **Common positions include:** Accountant/Auditor; Computer Programmer; Counselor; Dental Assistant/Dental Hygienist; Dietician/Nutritionist; EEG Technologist; EKG Technician; Human Resources Manager; Licensed Practical Nurse; Medical Records Technician; Nuclear Medicine Technologist; Occupational Therapist; Pharmacist; Physical Therapist; Preschool Worker; Recreational Therapist; Registered Nurse; Respiratory Therapist; Restaurant/Food Service Manager; Social Worker; Speech-Language Pathologist; Surgical Technician. **Educational backgrounds include:** Accounting; Business Administration; Computer Science. **Benefits:** 401(k); Daycare Assistance; Dental Insurance; Disability Coverage; Employee Discounts; Life Insurance; Medical Insurance; Tuition Assistance. **Special programs:** Internships. **Corporate headquarters location:** This Location. **Subsidiaries include:** Meriter Health Enterprises; Meriter Retirement Services. **Number of employees at this location:** 3,200.

METHODIST HEALTHCARE, INC.
1265 Union Avenue, Memphis TN 38104. 901/726-2300. **Contact:** Kathy Sullivant, Vice President of Human Resources. **World Wide Web address:** http://www.methodisthealth.org. **Description:** Operates a regional network of health care facilities. Methodist Healthcare is affiliated with Methodist Hospitals of Memphis (MHM), one of the largest private hospital systems in the United States. MHM is made up of five separate facilities located throughout the city: Methodist Central, Methodist North, Methodist South, Methodist Germantown, and Le Bonheur Children's Medical Center. **Corporate headquarters location:** 1211 Union Avenue, Suite 700, Memphis TN 38104. **Special programs:** Summer Jobs.

THE METHODIST HOSPITAL
6565 Fannin, MT 1425, Houston TX 77030. 713/394-6614. **Fax:** 713/793-7128. **Recorded jobline:** 713/394-6613. **Contact:** Patti Stone, Supervisor. **E-mail address:** pstone@tmh.tmc.edu. **World Wide Web address:** http://www.methodisthealth.com. **Description:** A non-profit, full-service hospital. The Methodist Hospital is also the primary teaching hospital for the Baylor College of Medicine. **Common positions include:** Accountant; Administrative Assistant; Applications Engineer; AS400 Programmer Analyst; Auditor; Certified Nurses Aide; Certified Occupational Therapy Assistant; Claim Representative; Computer

Animator; Computer Engineer; Computer Operator; Computer Programmer; Computer Scientist; Computer Support Technician; Computer Technician; Content Developer; Customer Service Representative; Database Administrator; Database Manager; Dietician/Nutritionist; EEG Technologist; EKG Technician; Financial Analyst; Internet Services Manager; Market Research Analyst; Marketing Specialist; MIS Specialist; Multimedia Designer; Network/Systems Administrator; Public Relations Specialist; Secretary; Software Engineer; SQL Programmer; Systems Analyst; Systems Manager; Typist/Word Processor; Webmaster. **Corporate headquarters location:** This Location. **Parent company:** Methodist Health Care System.

THE METROHEALTH SYSTEM
2500 MetroHealth Drive, Cleveland OH 44109. 216/778-7800. **Fax:** 216/778-8905. **Contact:** Human Resources. **E-mail address:** humres@ metrohealth.org. **World Wide Web address:** http://www.metrohealth.org. **Description:** Provides comprehensive health care services through its member facilities and affiliation with Case Western University School of Medicine. The MetroHealth System is comprised of several facilities: MetroHealth Medical Center (also at this location) is one of the nation's most successful publicly-owned hospitals. The 690-bed hospital provides a variety of medical services including dentistry, dermatology, ambulatory care, medical aircraft services, obstetrics, gynecology, psychiatry, family practice, substance abuse, and surgery; MetroHealth's Outpatient Plaza houses separate centers for rehabilitation, women and children, specialty services including cardiology and neurology, and cancer care; The Charles H. Rammelkamp, Jr., M.D. Center for Research and Education; MetroHealth Center for Rehabilitation; MetroHealth Clement Center for Family Care; and MetroHealth Center for Skilled Nursing Care. **Common positions include:** Administrative Assistant; Certified Nurses Aide; Certified Occupational Therapy Assistant; Claim Rep.; Customer Service Rep.; Home Health Aide; Licensed Practical Nurse; Medical Secretary; Nuclear Medicine Technologist; Pharmacist; Physical Therapy Assistant; Radiological Technologist; Registered Nurse; Respiratory Therapist; Secretary. **Office hours:** Monday - Friday, 8:00 a.m. - 5:00 p.m.

MIDWEST DENTAL MANAGEMENT
P.O. Box 69, Mondovi WI 54755. 715/926-5050. **Toll-free phone:** 800/782-7186. **Fax:** 715/926-5405. **Contact:** Terry L. Vajgrt, Director of Human Resources. **E-mail address:** mdmgnt@ win.bright.net. **Description:** This location houses administrative offices. Overall, Midwest Dental Management is a statewide dental management company. Founded in 1968. **NOTE:** Entry-level positions are offered. **Common positions include:** Clinical Lab Technician; Customer Service Representative; Dental Assistant/Dental Hygienist; Dental Lab Technician. **Educational backgrounds include -** Health Care. **Benefits:** 401(k); Casual Dress - Fridays; Dental Insurance; Employee Discounts; Flexible Schedule; Job Sharing; Life Insurance; Medical Insurance; Profit Sharing; Sick Days (1 - 5); Tuition Assistance; Vacation Days (10 - 20). **Special programs:** Internships. **Corporate headquarters location:** This Location. **CEO:** Yvonne Mayberry. **Annual sales/revenues:** $11 - $20 million.

MIMBRES MEMORIAL HOSPITAL & NURSING HOME
P.O. Box 710, Deming NM 88031. 505/546-2761. **Physical address:** 900 West Ash, Deming NM.

Fax: 505/546-9734. **Contact:** Lynn Duffey, Human Resources Director. **Description:** A full-service hospital and nursing home. **NOTE:** Entry-level positions and part-time jobs are offered. **Common positions include:** Administrative Assistant; Certified Nurses Aide; Chief Financial Officer; Clerical Supervisor; Clinical Lab Technician; Emergency Medical Technician; Home Health Aide; Human Resources Manager; Licensed Practical Nurse; Medical Records Technician; Network/ Systems Administrator; Nurse Practitioner; Pharmacist; Physical Therapist; Physical Therapy Assistant; Physician; Radiological Technologist; Registered Nurse; Respiratory Therapist; Social Worker; Surgical Technician. **Educational backgrounds include:** AS400 Certification; Health Care; Novell. **Benefits:** 401(k); Dental Insurance; Disability Coverage; Employee Discounts; Life Insurance; Medical Insurance; Profit Sharing. **Special programs:** Internships; Training. **Corporate headquarters location:** Brentwood TN. **Parent company:** Community Health System. **CEO:** Timothy Schmidt. **Annual sales/revenues:** Less than $5 million.

MISSION ST. JOSEPH'S HOSPITAL
509 Biltmore Avenue, Asheville NC 28801. 828/213-4410. **Contact:** Personnel. **Description:** A hospital. **Common positions include:** Clinical Lab Technician; Dietician/Nutritionist; EEG Technologist; EKG Technician; Electrician; Medical Records Technician; Nuclear Medicine Technologist; Occupational Therapist; Pharmacist; Physical Therapist; Radiological Technologist; Registered Nurse; Respiratory Therapist; Social Worker; Speech-Language Pathologist; Surgical Technician. **Benefits:** Dental Insurance; Disability Coverage; Employee Discounts; Life Insurance; Medical Insurance; Pension Plan; Tuition Assistance. **Corporate headquarters location:** This Location. **Number of employees at this location:** 1,400.

MISSOURI SLOPE LUTHERAN CARE CENTER
2425 Hillview Avenue, Bismarck ND 58501. 701/223-9407x110. **Contact:** Patty Tangen, Director of Human Resources. **Description:** A nonprofit, residential nursing home. Founded in 1967. **NOTE:** Second and third shifts are offered. **Common positions include:** Accountant; Administrative Assistant; Blue-Collar Worker Supervisor; Certified Nurses Aide; Clerical Supervisor; Computer Operator; Consultant; Dietician/Nutritionist; Finance Director; Human Resources Manager; Licensed Practical Nurse; Occupational Therapist; Pharmacist; Physical Therapist; Registered Nurse; Secretary; Social Worker; Speech-Language Pathologist; Typist/Word Processor. **Educational backgrounds include:** Accounting; Business Administration; Health Care; Liberal Arts; Nutrition. **Benefits:** Dental Insurance; Employee Discounts; Life Insurance; Medical Insurance; Retirement Plan; Scholarship Program; Tax-Deferred Annuity; Tuition Assistance. **Special programs:** Co-ops; Internships; Summer Jobs; Training. **Corporate headquarters location:** This Location. **President:** Robert Thompson. **Annual sales/revenues:** $5 - $10 million.

MITEK PRODUCTS
60 Glacier Drive, Westwood MA 02090. 781/251-2700. **Toll-free phone:** 800/35M-ITEK. **Fax:** 781/278-9578. **Contact:** Human Resources. **World Wide Web address:** http://www.mitek.com. **Description:** Develops, manufactures, and markets minimally invasive proprietary surgical implants which facilitate the reattachment of damaged tendons, ligaments, and other soft tissue to bones.

These devices reduce tissue trauma, speed patient recovery, and shorten operating time. Primary products consist of a line of suture anchors utilizing nitinol, a highly elastic nickel titanium alloy, as well as related surgical instruments such as drill guides and inserters. **NOTE:** Second and third shifts are offered. **Common positions include:** Administrative Assistant; Customer Service Rep.; Design Engineer; Financial Analyst; Manufacturing Engineer; Mechanical Engineer; Sales Manager; Sales Representative; Secretary. **Benefits:** 401(k); Casual Dress - Daily; Dental Insurance; Disability Coverage; Employee Discounts; Life Insurance; Medical Insurance; Pension Plan; Profit Sharing; Savings Plan; Tuition Assistance. **Corporate headquarters location:** This Location. **Parent company:** Ethicon, Inc. **Number of employees at this location:** 275.

MODERN MEDICAL MODALITIES CORP.
1719 Route 10, Suite 119, Parsippany NJ 07054. 973/538-9955. **Contact:** Human Resources. **Description:** Provides high-tech, diagnostic imaging services to physicians, hospitals, and other health care facilities. The company's primary focus is on Magnetic Resonance Imaging (MRI) and Computer Axial Tomography (CT scan) technologies. Modern Medical Modalities also offers a range of services including full, partial, or joint venture financing; site selection, design, and construction; equipment supply, maintenance, and operation; personnel placement and training; and facility marketing, management, billing, and collections. **Corporate headquarters location:** This Location.

THE MONROE CLINIC
515 22nd Avenue, Monroe WI 53566. 608/324-1458. **Fax:** 608/324-1114. **Contact:** Human Resources. **World Wide Web address:** http://www. themonroeclinic.org. **Description:** A nonprofit, multispecialty, general hospital with outpatient facilities. Founded in 1939. **NOTE:** Second and third shifts are offered. **Common positions include:** Biomedical Engineer; Certified Nurses Aide; Claim Rep.; Computer Programmer; Dietician/Nutritionist; EEG Technologist; EKG Technician; Human Resources Manager; Licensed Practical Nurse; Medical Records Technician; Nuclear Medicine Technologist; Occupational Therapist; Pharmacist; Physical Therapist; Physician; Radiological Technologist; Registered Nurse; Secretary; Social Worker. **Educational backgrounds include:** Computer Science; Health Care. **Benefits:** 403(b); Dental Insurance; Disability Coverage; Employee Discounts; Financial Planning Assistance; Life Insurance; Medical Insurance; Pension Plan; Savings Plan; Tuition Assistance. **Special programs:** Internships. **Office hours:** Monday - Friday, 8:00 a.m. - 5:00 p.m. **Corporate headquarters location:** This Location. **President/CEO:** Kenneth Blount. **Facilities Manager:** Jim Johnson. **Annual sales/revenues:** $21 - $50 million.

MORROW MEMORIAL HOME FOR THE AGED, INC.
331 South Water Street, Sparta WI 54656. 608/269-3168. **Fax:** 608/269-7642. **Contact:** Carla Newquist, NHA/Human Resources Director. **World Wide Web address:** http://www.morrowhome.org. **Description:** A nonprofit nursing home offering long-term care. Founded in 1917. **NOTE:** Entry-level positions, part-time jobs, and second and third shifts are offered. **Common positions include:** Administrative Assistant; Administrative Manager; Certified Nurses Aide; Chief Financial Officer; Dietician/Nutritionist; Education Administrator; Fund Manager; Home Health Aide; Human

Resources Manager; Licensed Practical Nurse; Medical Records Technician; Medical Secretary; Purchasing Agent/Manager; Registered Nurse; Secretary; Social Worker; Transportation/Traffic Specialist. **Educational backgrounds include:** Accounting; Microsoft Office. **Benefits:** 401(k); Casual Dress - Fridays; Disability Coverage; Employee Discounts; Financial Planning Assistance; Flexible Schedule; Job Sharing; Life Insurance; Medical Insurance; Pension Plan; Profit Sharing; Savings Plan; Sick Days (6 - 10); Tuition Assistance; Vacation Days. **Special programs:** Apprenticeships; Co-ops; Internships; Summer Jobs; Training. **Corporate headquarters location:** This Location. **Annual sales/revenues:** Less than $5 million.

MORTON PLANT MEASE HEALTH CARE
734 Virginia Street, Dunedin FL 34698. 727/734-6435. **Fax:** 727/734-6119. **Recorded jobline:** 727/734-6937. **Contact:** Human Resources. **World Wide Web address:** http://www.mpmhealth.com. **Description:** A nonprofit, full-service hospital. The hospital specializes in cancer treatment, cardiovascular medicine, neurosciences, orthopedics, rehabilitation, and surgery services. **Common positions include:** Accountant; Certified Nurses Aide; Claim Representative; Clinical Lab Technician; Computer Operator; Computer Programmer; Customer Service Representative; Dietician/Nutritionist; EEG Technologist; EKG Technician; Electrician; Emergency Medical Technician; Financial Analyst; Librarian; Licensed Practical Nurse; Medical Records Technician; Nuclear Medicine Technologist; Occupational Therapist; Pharmacist; Physical Therapist; Physician; Registered Nurse; Respiratory Therapist; Secretary; Social Worker; Software Engineer; Speech-Language Pathologist; Surgical Technician; Systems Analyst. **Benefits:** Dental Insurance; Employee Discounts; Financial Planning Assistance; Life Insurance; Medical Insurance; Pension Plan; Tuition Assistance. **Corporate headquarters location:** This Location. **Number of employees at this location:** 6,000.

MUNSON MEDICAL CENTER
1105 Sixth Street, Traverse City MI 49684-2386. 231/935-5000. **Toll-free phone:** 800/713-3206. **Fax:** 231/935-7191. **Contact:** Gina Stein, Recruiter. **World Wide Web address:** http://www.mhc.net. **Description:** A 368-bed, acute care, regional referral center. Founded in 1915. **NOTE:** Second and third shifts are offered. **Company slogan:** Expertise, when and where you need it most. **Common positions include:** Certified Nurses Aide; Computer Operator; EEG Technologist; EKG Technician; Emergency Medical Technician; Licensed Practical Nurse; Medical Records Technician; Occupational Therapist; Pharmacist; Physical Therapist; Radiological Technologist; Registered Nurse; Respiratory Therapist; Speech-Language Pathologist; Surgical Technician; Systems Analyst. **Educational backgrounds include:** Health Care. **Benefits:** 403(b); Dental Insurance; Employee Discounts; Life Insurance; Medical Insurance; On-Site Daycare; Pension Plan; Savings Plan; Tuition Assistance. **Office hours:** Monday - Friday, 7:00 a.m. - 4:30 p.m. **Corporate headquarters location:** This Location. **Parent company:** Munson Healthcare System. **CEO:** Ralph Cerney. **Number of employees at this location:** 3,000.

NAPLES MEDICAL CENTER
400 Eighth Street North, Naples FL 34102. 941/649-3355. **Fax:** 941/649-3301. **Contact:** Kathleen Phelps, Human Resources Director. **World Wide Web address:** http://www.

naplesmedicalcenter.com. **Description:** A multispecialty medical center with diagnostic and administrative departments. Founded in 1958. **NOTE:** Entry-level positions are offered. **Common positions include:** Account Manager; Accountant; Administrative Assistant; Administrative Manager; Certified Nurses Aide; Chief Financial Officer; Controller; Database Manager; EKG Technician; Human Resources Manager; Licensed Practical Nurse; Medical Records Technician; Physician; Registered Nurse; Secretary; Speech-Language Pathologist. **Educational backgrounds include:** Accounting; Health Care; Microsoft Office; Microsoft Word; Spreadsheets. **Benefits:** 401(k); Dental Insurance; Disability Coverage; Employee Discounts; Life Insurance; Medical Insurance; Sick Days (11+); Vacation Days (10 - 20). **Office hours:** Monday - Friday, 8:30 a.m. - 5:30 p.m. **Parent company:** ProMedCo Management Corporation. **Listed on:** Privately held. **President:** Daniel Cundiff.

NATIONAL DENTEX CORPORATION
526 Boston Post Road, Suite 207, Wayland MA 01778. 508/820-4800. **Contact:** Human Resources. **World Wide Web address:** http://www.nadx.com. **Description:** National Dentex Corporation is one of the largest operators of dental laboratories in the United States. These dental laboratories provide a full range of custom-made dental prosthetic appliances, divided into three main groups: restorative products including crowns and bridges; reconstructive products including partial and full dentures; and cosmetic products including porcelain veneers and ceramic crowns. **Benefits:** 401(k); Incentive Plan; Stock Option. **Corporate headquarters location:** This Location. **Subsidiaries include:** Dodd Dental Laboratories; H&O Associated Dental Laboratories; H&O Eliason; Lakeland Dental; Massachusetts Dental Associates. **Listed on:** NASDAQ.

NATIONAL HOME HEALTH CARE CORP.
700 White Plains Road, Suite 275, Scarsdale NY 10583. 914/722-9000. **Contact:** Human Resources. **World Wide Web address:** http://www.nhhc.net. **Description:** A regional provider of a variety of health related services including health care, home care, nurses, and therapists. The company operates through its wholly owned subsidiaries. **Corporate headquarters location:** This Location. **Subsidiaries include:** Health Acquisition Corporation provides home health care services, primarily through certified home health aides and personal care aides in the New York metropolitan area; Brevard Medical Center, Inc. provides both primary and specialty outpatient medical services in Brevard County FL; First Health, Inc. provides primary care outpatient medical services in Volusia County FL.

NAVAJO AREA INDIAN HEALTH SERVICE
P.O. Box 9020, Window Rock AZ 86515-9020. 520/871-5880. **Physical address:** IHS Building, Highway 264 & St. Michael's, Window Rock AZ. **Contact:** Division Director, Professional Services. **Description:** Provides direct clinical care to 230,000 Native Americans at six hospitals and seven 24-hour health centers in the Four Corners area. **NOTE:** Clerkships and residency rotations for medical students and engineers are offered. **Common positions include:** Civil Engineer; Clinical Lab Technician; Dietician/Nutritionist; Mechanical Engineer; Medical Technologist; Midwife; Occupational Therapist; Pharmacist; Physical Therapist; Physician; Psychologist; Radiological Technologist; Registered Nurse; Respiratory Therapist. **Educational backgrounds include:** Engineering; Health Care. **Benefits:**

Flexible Schedule; Life Insurance; Medical Insurance; Pension Plan; Savings Plan. **Special programs:** Internships. **Corporate headquarters location:** This Location. **Parent company:** U.S. Public Health Service. **Annual sales/revenues:** More than $100 million.

NELLCOR PURITAN BENNETT CORP.
4280 Hacienda Drive, Pleasanton CA 94588. 925/463-4000. **Fax:** 925/463-4718. **Contact:** Professional Employment. **Description:** Designs, manufactures, and markets high-performance monitoring equipment, sensors, and accessories for patient safety and management in hospitals, emergency care units, and in the home. Nellcor is a leading producer of pulse oximeters used in hospitals for the measurement of patient oxygen status. Nellcor's line of oximetry sensors includes both adhesive and reusable sensors as well as a sensor recycling program. Founded in 1981. **Common positions include:** Accountant/Auditor; Biomedical Engineer; Clinical Lab Technician; Computer Operator; Computer Programmer; Customer Service Rep.; Electrical/Electronics Engineer; Financial Analyst; Human Resources Manager; Mechanical Engineer; Paralegal; Purchasing Agent/Manager; Registered Nurse; Respiratory Therapist; Software Engineer; Systems Analyst; Technical Writer/Editor. **Educational backgrounds include:** Business Administration; Computer Science; Engineering; Marketing; Physics. **Benefits:** Dental Insurance; Disability Coverage; Life Insurance; Medical Insurance; Profit Sharing; Savings Plan; Tuition Assistance. **Corporate headquarters location:** This Location. **Other U.S. locations:** Chula Vista CA; Lenexa KS; Eden Prairie MN. **International locations:** Tijuana, Mexico. **Subsidiaries include:** EdenTec, Eden Prairie MN. **Listed on:** NASDAQ.

NEW MEXICO VETERANS' CENTER
P.O. Box 927, Truth or Consequences NM 87901. 505/894-4200. **Toll-free phone:** 800/964-3976. **Fax:** 505/894-4229. **Contact:** Beth Woolf, Director of Human Resources. **Description:** A nonprofit long term/nursing facility for veterans, spouses of veterans, and Gold Star parents. Founded in 1985. **NOTE:** Entry-level positions and second and third shifts are offered. **Common positions include:** Administrative Assistant; Advertising Clerk; Assistant Manager; Certified Nurses Aide; Chief Financial Officer; Dietician/Nutritionist; Human Resources Manager; Licensed Practical Nurse; Medical Records Technician; Medical Secretary; Network Engineer; Network/Systems Administrator; Nurse Practitioner; Occupational Therapist; Pharmacist; Physical Therapist; Physical Therapy Assistant; Physician; Physician Assistant; Purchasing Agent/Manager; Registered Nurse; Respiratory Therapist; Secretary; Social Worker; Speech-Language Pathologist. **Educational backgrounds include:** Business Administration; Computer Science; Finance; Health Care; Microsoft Office; Microsoft Word; Spreadsheets. **Benefits:** Casual Dress - Fridays; Dental Insurance; Disability Coverage; Flexible Schedule; Job Sharing; Life Insurance; Medical Insurance; Pension Plan; Savings Plan; Sick Days (11+); Tuition Assistance; Vacation Days (10 - 20). **Special programs:** Internships. **Office hours:** Monday - Friday, 8:00 a.m. - 5:00 p.m. **Corporate headquarters location:** Santa Fe NM. **Parent company:** State of New Mexico Department of Health.

NEW YORK UNIVERSITY MEDICAL CENTER
550 First Avenue, New York NY 10016. 212/263-6660. **Fax:** 212/263-0340. **Contact:** Employment Recruitment Services Department. **E-mail address:** resume@med.nyu.edu. **World Wide Web address:**

http://www.med.nyu.edu. **Description:** A nonprofit medical center engaged in patient care, research, and education. The central component of New York University Medical Center is Tisch Hospital, a 726-bed acute care facility and a major center for specialized procedures in cardiovascular services, neurosurgery, AIDS, cancer treatment, reconstructive surgery, and transplantation. The medical center also includes the Rusk Institute of Rehabilitation Medicine, the Hospital of Joint Diseases, and several medical schools. The Rusk Institute of Rehabilitation Medicine, a 152-bed unit, is one of the world's largest university-affiliated centers for the treatment and training of physically disabled adults and children, as well as for research in rehabilitation medicine. The Hospital of Joint Diseases, with 226 beds, is dedicated solely to neuromusculoskeletal diseases. The School of Medicine, the Post-Graduate Medical School, and the Skirball Institute of Biomolecular Medicine are also part of the medical center. **NOTE:** Entry-level positions are offered. **Common positions include:** Account Rep.; Accountant; Administrative Assistant; Administrative Manager; Biological Scientist; Budget Analyst; Buyer; Certified Nurses Aide; Claim Rep.; Clerical Supervisor; Clinical Lab Technician; Computer Operator; Customer Service Rep.; Database Manager; Dietician/Nutritionist; Financial Analyst; General Manager; Human Resources Manager; MIS Specialist; Network/Systems Administrator; Occupational Therapist; Pharmacist; Physical Therapist; Project Manager; Psychologist; Purchasing Agent/Manager; Registered Nurse; Respiratory Therapist; Secretary; Social Worker; Speech-Language Pathologist; Systems Analyst; Systems Manager; Typist/Word Processor; Website Developer. **Educational backgrounds include:** Accounting; Biology; Business Administration; Chemistry; Computer Science; Finance; Health Care; Liberal Arts; Public Relations. **Benefits:** Dental Insurance; Disability Coverage; Employee Discounts; Life Insurance; Medical Insurance; Pension Plan; Tuition Assistance. **Special programs:** Internships; Summer Jobs. **Corporate headquarters location:** This Location.

NEWPORT HOSPITAL
11 Friendship Street, Newport RI 02840. 401/845-1304. **Contact:** Diane Carruba, Employment Coordinator. **Description:** A private, nonprofit, general hospital with 200 beds. Newport Hospital participates in cooperative programs with colleges and universities for the education of nurses, X-ray technicians, physical therapists, and other allied health care personnel. Founded in 1873. **NOTE:** Second and third shifts are offered. **Common positions include:** Certified Nurses Aide; Clinical Lab Technician; EEG Technologist; EKG Technician; Licensed Practical Nurse; Nuclear Medicine Technologist; Occupational Therapist; Pharmacist; Physical Therapist; Radiological Technologist; Registered Nurse; Respiratory Therapist; Surgical Technician; Typist/Word Processor. **Educational backgrounds include:** Health Care. **Benefits:** 403(b); Dental Insurance; Disability Coverage; Employee Discounts; Life Insurance; Medical Insurance; Pension Plan; Tuition Assistance. **Special programs:** Internships. **Corporate headquarters location:** This Location. **Parent company:** NHCC.

NORTH CENTRAL HEALTH CARE FACILITIES
1100 Lake View Drive, Wausau WI 54403. 715/848-4600. **Fax:** 715/845-5398. **Contact:** Mike Jelen, Director of Human Resources. **Description:** A psychiatric hospital that provides diagnostic treatment of mental health disorders, alcohol and drug abuse, and developmental disabilities. The hospital also provides a variety of geriatric services. **Common positions include:** Dietician/Nutritionist; Licensed Practical Nurse; Medical Records Technician; Occupational Therapist; Pharmacist; Physical Therapist; Psychologist; Recreational Therapist; Registered Nurse; Social Worker; Speech-Language Pathologist. **Benefits:** Dental Insurance; Disability Coverage; Life Insurance; Medical Insurance; Pension Plan; Savings Plan. **Corporate headquarters location:** This Location. **Number of employees at this location:** 850.

NORTHEAST HEALTH
2212 Burdett Avenue, Troy NY 12180. **Recorded jobline:** 518/271-3340. **Contact:** Human Resources. **World Wide Web address:** http://www.nehealth.com. **Description:** A comprehensive network of health care and community services that operates through three full-service hospitals: Albany Memorial Hospital, The Eddy, and Samaratin Hospital. **Common positions include:** Certified Nurses Aide; Dietician/Nutritionist; EEG Technologist; EKG Technician; Home Health Aide; Licensed Practical Nurse; Medical Records Technician; Nuclear Medicine Technologist; Nurse Practitioner; Occupational Therapist; Physical Therapist; Physical Therapy Assistant; Radiological Technologist; Registered Nurse; Respiratory Therapist; Surgical Technician. **CEO:** Craig Duncan.

NORTHERN HOME CARE
933 Old Rockford Street, Suite 6, Mount Airy NC 27030. 336/719-7434. **Fax:** 336/719-7435. **Contact:** Human Resources. **Description:** Offers home health care services. **Common positions include:** Occupational Therapist; Physical Therapist; Registered Nurse; Social Worker; Speech-Language Pathologist. **Educational backgrounds include:** Health Care. **Benefits:** Dental Insurance; Disability Coverage; Employee Discounts; Life Insurance; Medical Insurance; Pension Plan; Savings Plan; Tuition Assistance. **Corporate headquarters location:** This Location. **Other U.S. locations:** Cana VA. **Number of employees at this location:** 200.

NORTHERN ITASCA HEALTH CARE CENTER
P.O. Box 258, Bigfork MN 56628. 218/743-4116. **Fax:** 218/743-3559. **Contact:** Faye Reigel, Human Resources Manager. **World Wide Web address:** http://www.nihcc.com. **Description:** A nonprofit medical facility consisting of a 20-bed hospital, a 40-bed long-term care unit, and 30 apartments attached to an outpatient clinic. The center also offers adult daycare and pharmacy services. **NOTE:** Entry-level positions and second and third shifts are offered. **Common positions include:** Administrative Assistant; Certified Nurses Aide; Chief Financial Officer; Clinical Lab Technician; Environmental Engineer; Human Resources Manager; Licensed Practical Nurse; Medical Records Technician; Occupational Therapist; Pharmacist; Physical Therapist; Purchasing Agent/Manager; Radiological Technologist; Registered Nurse; Social Worker. **Educational backgrounds include:** Health Care. **Benefits:** 403(b); Employee Discounts; Life Insurance; Medical Insurance; Savings Plan. **Special programs:** Training. **Corporate headquarters location:** This Location.

NORTHSTAR HEALTH SERVICES, INC.
665 Philadelphia Street, Indiana PA 15701. 724/349-7500. **Contact:** Human Resources. **World Wide Web address:** http://www.northstarhealth.com. **Description:** A leading

provider of rehabilitation therapy in western Pennsylvania, offering services at outpatient rehabilitation clinics to patients with physical disabilities. **Corporate headquarters location:** This Location. **Subsidiaries include:** Keystone Rehabilitation Systems. **Listed on:** NASDAQ. **Number of employees nationwide:** 200.

NOVACARE, INC.
1016 West Ninth Avenue, King of Prussia PA 19406. 610/992-7200. **Toll-free phone:** 800/331-8840. **Contact:** Human Resources. **World Wide Web address:** http://www.novacare.com. **Description:** Provides comprehensive medical rehabilitation services to patients with physical disabilities. NovaCare's services include speech-language pathology, occupational therapy, and physical therapy. Services are provided on a contract basis primarily to long-term health care institutions, through inpatient rehabilitation hospitals and community integrated programs, and through a national network of patient care centers providing orthotic and prosthetic rehabilitation services. **Corporate headquarters location:** This Location. **Listed on:** New York Stock Exchange. **Stock exchange symbol:** NOV.

NOVAMETRIX MEDICAL SYSTEMS INC.
5 Technology Drive, Wallingford CT 06492. 203/265-7701. **Fax:** 203/284-0753. **Contact:** Human Resources. **World Wide Web address:** http://www.novametrix.com. **Description:** Develops, manufactures, and markets noninvasive, critical care blood gas monitors, respiratory monitors, and disposable products. Distributed worldwide, these electronic medical instruments provide continuous patient monitoring capabilities in hospital and non-hospital environments. The company's product line is comprised of capnographs, pulse oximeters, transcutaneous blood gas monitors, respiratory mechanics monitors, and reusable and disposable sensors, adapters, related accessories, and replacement parts. **Corporate headquarters location:** This Location. **Listed on:** NASDAQ. **Number of employees nationwide:** 165.

NUMED HOME HEALTH CARE, INC.
5770 Roosevelt Boulevard, Suite 700, Clearwater FL 33760. 727/524-3227. **Fax:** 727/524-3349. **Contact:** Human Resources. **World Wide Web address:** http://www.numed.com. **Description:** A holding company for home health care organizations. **Corporate headquarters location:** This Location. **Listed on:** NASDAQ.

NURSES TODAY INCORPORATED
4230 LBJ Freeway, Suite 110, Dallas TX 75244. 972/233-9966. **Toll-free phone:** 800/830-7616. **Fax:** 972/233-5354. **Contact:** Beth Goucher, Human Resources Manager. **World Wide Web address:** http://www.nursestoday.com. **Description:** A service organization that provides nursing care. Businesses that have utilized these services include assisted living facilities, clinics, doctors offices, hospitals, nursing homes, and independent living facilities. **NOTE:** Part-time jobs are offered. **Common positions include:** Administrative Assistant; Certified Nurses Aide; Home Health Aide; Licensed Practical Nurse; Medical Assistant; Physical Therapist; Registered Nurse. **Educational backgrounds include:** Health Care. **Benefits:** Casual Dress - Fridays; Credit Union; Flexible Schedule; Job Sharing; Public Transit Available; Sick Days (1 - 5); Telecommuting; Vacation Days (10 - 20). **Office hours:** Monday - Friday, 8:00 a.m. - 5:00 p.m. **Corporate headquarters location:** This Location. **Listed on:** Privately held. **CEO:** Anita Porco. **Annual sales/revenues:** Less than $5 million.

NUTRI/SYSTEM L.P.
202 Welsh Road, Horsham PA 19044. 215/706-5300. **Fax:** 215/706-5388. **Contact:** Denise Bergner, Director of Human Resources. **Description:** A chain of weight loss/weight maintenance centers providing professionally supervised services through a network of 700 company-owned and franchised centers. **Common positions include:** Accountant; Advertising Clerk; Attorney; Computer Programmer; Customer Service Rep.; Dietician/Nutritionist; Financial Analyst; Food Scientist/Technologist; Health Services Manager; Marketing Specialist; Operations/Production Manager; Public Relations Specialist; Purchasing Agent/Manager; Quality Control Supervisor; Systems Analyst; Technical Writer/Editor. **Educational backgrounds include:** Accounting; Computer Science; Finance; Marketing. **Benefits:** 401(k); Dental Insurance; Life Insurance; Medical Insurance. **Corporate headquarters location:** This Location. **Other U.S. locations:** Nationwide.

OCHSNER CLINIC
1514 Jefferson Highway, New Orleans LA 70121. 504/842-4000. **Contact:** Human Resources. **World Wide Web address:** http://www.ochsner.org. **Description:** Operates satellite clinics throughout Louisiana. Each clinic provides family medical services and offers laboratory and X-ray services for routine care. Founded in 1942. **Corporate headquarters location:** This Location.

OHIO VALLEY GENERAL HOSPITAL
25 Heckel Road, McKees Rocks PA 15136. 412/777-6218. **Fax:** 412/777-6804. **Contact:** Human Resources. **World Wide Web address:** http://www.ohiovalleyhospital.org. **Description:** A 118-bed, nonprofit community hospital serving Pittsburgh's western suburbs and the Pittsburgh International Airport area. **NOTE:** Resumes are accepted in person in the Human Resources office Monday through Friday, from 9:00 a.m. - 4:00 p.m. Entry-level positions, part-time jobs, and second and third shifts are offered. **Common positions include:** Accountant; Administrative Assistant; Auditor; Certified Nurses Aide; Chief Financial Officer; Computer Operator; Controller; Counselor; Database Administrator; EKG Technician; Licensed Practical Nurse; Medical Records Technician; Network/Systems Administrator; Nuclear Medicine Technologist; Pharmacist; Physical Therapy Assistant; Radiological Technologist; Registered Nurse; Respiratory Therapist; Secretary; Social Worker; Surgical Technician; Systems Analyst; Teacher/Professor. **Educational backgrounds include:** Accounting; Business Administration; Computer Science; Health Care; MBA; Public Relations. **Benefits:** 403(b); Dental Insurance; Disability Coverage; Employee Discounts; Life Insurance; Medical Insurance; Pension Plan; Public Transit Available; Savings Plan; Sick Days (11+); Tuition Assistance; Vacation Days (10 - 20).

OLYMPUS AMERICA INC.
2 Corporate Center Drive, Melville NY 11747. 516/844-5000. **Contact:** Human Resources. **World Wide Web address:** http://www.olympus.com. **Description:** This location houses administrative offices only. Overall, Olympus America manufactures and markets cameras and imaging equipment as well as a variety of surgical and medical instruments. **Corporate headquarters location:** This Location.

OMEGA OPTICAL COMPANY, INC.
13515 North Stemmons Freeway, Dallas TX 75234. 972/241-4141. **Contact:** Personnel Manager. **Description:** A manufacturer of prescription optical

lenses and ophthalmic products. **Common positions include:** Accountant/Auditor; Blue-Collar Worker Supervisor; Clerical Supervisor; Computer Programmer; Credit Manager; Customer Service Representative; Electrician; General Manager; Human Resources Manager; Operations/Production Manager; Quality Control Supervisor; Systems Analyst. **Educational backgrounds include:** Accounting; Business Administration. **Benefits:** 401(k); Dental Insurance; Disability Coverage; Employee Discounts; Life Insurance; Medical Insurance. **Corporate headquarters location:** This Location. **Parent company:** Benson Eyecare.

ONEIDA CITY HOSPITALS
321 Genesee Street, Oneida NY 13421. 315/361-2040. **Contact:** John G. Margo, Director of Human Resources. **Description:** A 101-bed acute care hospital and 160-bed extended care facility adjoining three outpatient clinics serving the health care needs of Madison County. **Common positions include:** Clinical Lab Technician; Licensed Practical Nurse; Nuclear Medicine Technologist; Physical Therapist; Preschool Worker; Radiological Technologist; Registered Nurse; Respiratory Therapist. **Benefits:** Daycare Assistance; Dental Insurance; Disability Coverage; Employee Discounts; Life Insurance; Medical Insurance; Pension Plan; Savings Plan; Tuition Assistance. **Corporate headquarters location:** This Location.

OPHTHALMIC IMAGING SYSTEMS
221 Lathrop Way, Suite I, Sacramento CA 95815. 916/646-2020. **Contact:** Human Resources. **World Wide Web address:** http://www.oisi.com. **Description:** Designs, manufactures, and markets ophthalmic digital imaging systems and other diagnostic imaging equipment used by eye care professionals. Ophthalmic Imaging Systems also develops image enhancement and analysis software. **Corporate headquarters location:** This Location. **Listed on:** NASDAQ. **Stock exchange symbol:** OISI. **Number of employees at this location:** 25.

OPTICAL ENTERPRISE
21 Academy Avenue, Middletown NY 10940. 914/343-2111. **Contact:** Personnel Director. **Description:** Produces optical supplies including lenses and frames. **Corporate headquarters location:** This Location.

ORLANDO REGIONAL HEALTHCARE
1414 South Kuhl Avenue, Orlando FL 32806-2008. 407/841-5111. **Fax:** 407/841-5186. **Contact:** Christy Pearson, Assistant Director of Staffing. **World Wide Web address:** http://www.orhs.org. **Description:** A comprehensive medical system that operates several health care facilities throughout central Florida. **NOTE:** Entry-level positions, part-time jobs, and second and third shifts are offered. **Common positions include:** Accountant; Administrative Assistant; Assistant Manager; Budget Analyst; Certified Nurses Aide; Certified Occupational Therapy Assistant; Computer Programmer; Computer Technician; Customer Service Representative; Dietician/Nutritionist; EEG Technologist; EKG Technician; Electrical/Electronics Engineer; Electrician; Emergency Medical Technician; Financial Analyst; Geneticist; Help-Desk Technician; Home Health Aide; Human Resources Manager; Librarian; Licensed Practical Nurse; Market Research Analyst; Marketing Specialist; Medical Assistant; Medical Records Technician; Medical Secretary; Network/Systems Administrator; Nuclear Medicine Technologist; Nurse Practitioner; Occupational Therapist; Pharmacist; Physical Therapist; Physical Therapy Assistant; Physician Assistant; Radiological Technologist; Registered Nurse; Respiratory

Therapist; Secretary; Social Worker; Speech-Language Pathologist; Surgical Technician; Systems Analyst; Webmaster. **Benefits:** 403(b); Dental Insurance; Employee Discounts; Flexible Schedule; Job Sharing; Life Insurance; Medical Insurance; Public Transit Available; Savings Plan; Telecommuting; Tuition Assistance. **Special programs:** Internships; Summer Jobs.

ORMCO/A COMPANY
9900 Old Grove Road, San Diego CA 92131. 858/577-3573. **Fax:** 858/577-3568. **Contact:** Christine A. Comer, Human Resources Manager. **World Wide Web address:** http://www.ormco.com. **Description:** Manufactures and markets orthodontic appliances and supplies. **Common positions include:** Accountant; Administrative Assistant; Computer Support Technician; Controller; Design Engineer; Draftsperson; Human Resources Manager; Manufacturing Engineer; Operations Manager; Production Manager; Purchasing Agent/Manager; Quality Control Supervisor. **Educational backgrounds include:** Accounting; Business Administration; Engineering; Finance; Microsoft Word; Spreadsheets. **Benefits:** 401(k); Casual Dress - Fridays; Dental Insurance; Disability Coverage; Life Insurance; Medical Insurance; Tuition Assistance. **Office hours:** Monday - Friday, 8:00 a.m. - 5:00 p.m. **Corporate headquarters location:** Orange CA. **Parent company:** Sybron Dental Specialties. **Operations at this facility include:** Manufacturing. **Annual sales/revenues:** More than $100 million. **Number of employees at this location:** 110.

ORTHODONTIC CENTERS OF AMERICA
13000 Sawgrass Village Circle, Suite 41, Ponte Vedra Beach FL 32082. 904/273-0004. **Fax:** 904/285-7406. **Contact:** Human Resources. **World Wide Web address:** http://www.ocai.com. **Description:** Develops and manages orthodontic centers. The company handles the business and marketing aspects of the centers. **Corporate headquarters location:** This Location. **Listed on:** New York Stock Exchange. **Stock exchange symbol:** OCA.

ORTHOLOGIC
1275 West Washington Street, Tempe AZ 85281-1210. 602/286-5520. **Contact:** Human Resources. **World Wide Web address:** http://www.orthologic.com. **Description:** OrthoLogic develops, manufactures, and markets advanced orthopedic devices. **Corporate headquarters location:** This Location.

OVERLAKE HOSPITAL MEDICAL CENTER
1035 116th Avenue NE, Bellevue WA 98004. 425/688-5000. **Fax:** 425/688-5758. **Recorded jobline:** 425/688-5150. **Contact:** Nella Cochran, Human Resource Specialist. **World Wide Web address:** http://www.overlakehospital.org. **Description:** A 227-bed, nonprofit, acute care medical center. Overlake Hospital specializes in open heart surgery and offers a comprehensive cardiac program. **NOTE:** Entry-level positions, part-time jobs, and second and third shifts are offered. **Common positions include:** Administrative Assistant; Certified Nurses Aide; Computer Operator; Controller; Dietician/Nutritionist; EKG Technician; Graphic Designer; Human Resources Manager; Licensed Practical Nurse; Marketing Manager; Medical Assistant; Medical Records Technician; Occupational Therapist; Pharmacist; Physical Therapist; Radiological Technologist; Registered Nurse; Respiratory Therapist; Secretary; Social Worker; Speech-Language Pathologist; Surgical Technician; Systems Analyst; Webmaster. **Educational**

backgrounds include: Communications; Computer Science; Health Care; HTML; Internet; Liberal Arts; Marketing; Microsoft Word; Nutrition; Public Relations; Spreadsheets. **Benefits:** 403(b); Dental Insurance; Disability Coverage; Employee Discounts; Flexible Schedule; Life Insurance; Medical Insurance; Pension Plan. **Special programs:** Internships.

OWENS & MINOR
4800 Cox Road, Glen Allen VA 23060. 804/747-9794. **Fax:** 804/270-7281. **Contact:** Erika Davis, Manager of Human Resources. **World Wide Web address:** http://www.owens-minor.com. **Description:** One of the nation's largest wholesale distributors of national branded medical, surgical, and nontraditional supplies. The distribution centers of Owens & Minor serve hospitals, integrated health care systems, primary care facilities, and group purchasing organizations throughout the United States. The company also helps customers control health care costs and improve inventory management through services in asset management, logistics, and electronic data interchange. **Common positions include:** Accountant; Administrative Manager; Computer Programmer; Sales Manager. **Educational backgrounds include:** Accounting; Business Administration; Communications; Computer Science; Finance; Marketing. **Benefits:** 401(k); Dental Insurance; Disability Coverage; Life Insurance; Medical Insurance; Stock Purchase; Tuition Assistance. **Special programs:** Internships. **Corporate headquarters location:** This Location. **Other U.S. locations:** Nationwide. **Annual sales/revenues:** More than $100 million. **Number of employees at this location:** 3,000.

OWENSBORO MERCY HEALTH SYSTEM
811 East Parrish Avenue, Owensboro KY 42304. 270/688-2786. **Fax:** 270/688-1610. **Recorded jobline:** 270/688-2790. **Contact:** Donna Sympson, Employment Specialist. **E-mail address:** dsympson@omhs.org. **World Wide Web address:** http://www.omhs.org. **Description:** A comprehensive health system that operates health care facilities in Kentucky and Indiana. **NOTE:** Entry-level positions as well as second and third shifts are offered. **Common positions include:** Accountant; Administrative Assistant; Certified Nurses Aide; Certified Occupational Therapy Assistant; Computer Operator; Dietician/Nutritionist; Home Health Aide; Licensed Practical Nurse; Nuclear Medicine Technologist; Occupational Therapist; Pharmacist; Physical Therapist; Physical Therapy Assistant; Radiological Technologist; Registered Nurse; Respiratory Therapist; Secretary; Social Worker; Surgical Technician; Systems Analyst. **Educational backgrounds include:** Accounting; Business Administration; Computer Science; Nursing. **Benefits:** 403(b); Dental Insurance; Disability Coverage; Employee Discounts; Financial Planning Assistance; Life Insurance; Medical Insurance; Pension Plan; Tuition Assistance. **Number of employees at this location:** 2,400.

OZARKS MEDICAL CENTER
P.O. Box 1100, West Plains MO 65775. 417/257-6747. **Fax:** 417/257-6754. **Contact:** Joann Blackburn, Human Resources Manager. **Description:** A medical center. **Common positions include:** EEG Technologist; EKG Technician; Emergency Medical Technician; Licensed Practical Nurse; Medical Records Technician; Nuclear Medicine Technologist; Occupational Therapist; Physical Therapist; Physician; Psychologist; Social Worker; Speech-Language Pathologist; Surgical Technician. **Educational backgrounds include:** Health Care. **Benefits:** 403(b); Dental Insurance;

Life Insurance; Medical Insurance; Tuition Assistance. **Number of employees at this location:** 1,200.

PLC MEDICAL SYSTEMS, INC.
10 Forge Park, Franklin MA 02038. 508/541-8800. **Fax:** 508/541-7990. **Contact:** Human Resources. **World Wide Web address:** http://www.plcmed.com. **Description:** Develops cardiovascular products used to perform transmyocardia revascularization (TMR). **Corporate headquarters location:** This Location. **Parent company:** PLC Systems Inc. **Listed on:** American Stock Exchange. **Stock exchange symbol:** PLC.

PALO PINTO GENERAL HOSPITAL
400 SW 25th Avenue, Mineral Wells TX 76067. 940/328-6390. **Fax:** 940/328-6389. **Contact:** Barbara Stagner, Director of Human Resources. **Description:** A nonprofit, acute care hospital. **NOTE:** Entry-level positions, part-time jobs, and second and third shifts are offered. **Common positions include:** Administrative Assistant; Certified Nurses Aide; Chief Financial Officer; Computer Support Technician; Dietician/Nutritionist; Home Health Aide; Human Resources Manager; Licensed Practical Nurse; Marketing Specialist; Medical Assistant; Medical Records Technician; MIS Specialist; Nuclear Medicine Technologist; Nurse Practitioner; Occupational Therapist; Pharmacist; Physical Therapist; Physical Therapy Assistant; Physician; Public Relations Specialist; Purchasing Agent/Manager; Radiological Technologist; Registered Nurse; Respiratory Therapist; Secretary; Social Worker; Speech-Language Pathologist; Surgical Technician. **Educational backgrounds include:** Business Administration; Chemistry; Finance; Health Care; Marketing; Nutrition. **Benefits:** 403(b); Dental Insurance; Disability Coverage; Employee Discounts; Life Insurance; Medical Insurance; Savings Plan; Tuition Assistance. **Annual sales/revenues:** $21 - $50 million. **Number of employees at this location:** 420.

PALOMAR MEDICAL TECHNOLOGIES
82 Cambridge Street, Burlington MA 01803-4107. 781/993-2300. **Fax:** 781/993-2330. **Contact:** Human Resources. **World Wide Web address:** http://www.palmed.com. **Description:** Palomar Medical Technologies designs, manufactures, and markets lasers, delivery systems, and related disposable products for use in medical and surgical procedures. The company operates in two business segments. The Medical Product segment develops and manufactures pulsed dye and diode medical lasers for use in clinical trials and is engaged in the research and development of additional medical and surgical products. The Electronic Products segment manufactures high-density, flexible, electronic circuitry for use in industrial, military, and medical devices. **Corporate headquarters location:** This Location. **Subsidiaries include:** Dynaco Corp., Tempe AZ; Nexar Technologies, Inc., Westborough MA; Spectrum Medical Technologies, Inc., Lexington MA; Star Medical Technologies, Inc., Pleasanton CA; Tissue Technologies, Inc., Albuquerque NM. **Listed on:** NASDAQ. **Stock exchange symbol:** PMTI.

PALOS COMMUNITY HOSPITAL
12251 South 80th Avenue, Palos Heights IL 60463. 708/923-4880. **Fax:** 708/923-4888. **Recorded jobline:** 708/923-8088. **Contact:** Employment. **Description:** A community hospital. **NOTE:** Part-time jobs and second and third shifts are offered. **Common positions include:** Certified Nurses Aide; Certified Occupational Therapy Assistant; Dietician/Nutritionist; EEG Technologist; EKG Technician;

Emergency Medical Technician; Home Health Aide; Medical Records Technician; Nuclear Medicine Technologist; Occupational Therapist; Pharmacist; Physical Therapist; Physician; Radiological Technologist; Registered Nurse; Respiratory Therapist; Social Worker; Speech-Language Pathologist. **Benefits:** 403(b); Dental Insurance; Disability Coverage; Life Insurance; Medical Insurance; Pension Plan; Tuition Assistance. **Number of employees at this location:** 2,100.

PAPERPACK PRODUCTS
100 Readington Road, Somerville NJ 08876. 908/707-1800. **Contact:** Lisa Stewart, Human Resources Coordinator. **Description:** Manufactures disposable underpads, cloths, and wipes for the health care, industrial, food service, and janitorial markets.

PARK EAST ANIMAL HOSPITAL
52 East 64th Street, New York NY 10021. 212/832-8417. **Fax:** 212/355-3620. **Contact:** Vicki Ungar, Office Manager. **E-mail address:** info@parkeastanimalhospital.com. **World Wide Web address:** http://www.parkeastanimalhospital.com. **Description:** A 24-hour small animal hospital offering medical, nursing, and surgical services for pets. **NOTE:** Entry-level positions and second and third shifts are offered. **Common positions include:** Administrative Assistant; Administrative Manager; EEG Technologist; Medical Assistant; Medical Records Technician; Medical Secretary; Radiological Technologist; Surgical Technician; Veterinarian. **Educational backgrounds include:** Accounting; Biology; Business Administration; Chemistry; Communications; Computer Science; Health Care; Public Relations. **Benefits:** Employee Discounts; Medical Insurance; Paid Holidays; Sick Days (6 - 10); Vacation Days (11 - 15). **Special programs:** Internships; Training; Summer Jobs. **Corporate headquarters location:** This Location. **President:** Dr. Lewis Berman. **Annual sales/revenues:** Less than $5 million. **Number of employees at this location:** 25.

PARK VIEW HOSPITAL
P.O. Box 129, El Reno OK 73036. 405/262-2640x3023. **Physical address:** 2115 Park View Drive, El Reno OK 73036. **Fax:** 405/422-2521. **Contact:** Personnel Assistant. **Description:** A nonprofit hospital that provides inpatient care, inpatient/outpatient surgical care, and outpatient services. **NOTE:** Entry-level positions, part-time jobs, and second and third shifts are offered. **Common positions include:** Accountant/Auditor; Clinical Lab Technician; Dietician/Nutritionist; EEG Technologist; EKG Technician; Electrician; Emergency Medical Technician; Food Scientist/Technologist; Licensed Practical Nurse; Medical Records Technician; Occupational Therapist; Pharmacist; Physical Therapist; Purchasing Agent/Manager; Quality Control Supervisor; Radiological Technologist; Registered Nurse; Respiratory Therapist; Social Worker; Surgical Technician. **Educational backgrounds include:** Accounting; Business Administration; Chemistry. **Benefits:** Dental Insurance; Disability Coverage; Employee Discounts; Life Insurance; Medical Insurance; Pension Plan; Savings Plan; Tuition Assistance.

PARKSIDE, INC.
1620 East 12th Street, Tulsa OK 74120. 918/586-4215. **Fax:** 918/588-8813. **Recorded jobline:** 918/586-4213. **Contact:** Martha Albin, Director of Human Resources. **Description:** A private, nonprofit, psychiatric facility. Parkside provides inpatient, outpatient, crisis, day treatment, partial hospitalization, and residential services to individuals of all ages. **NOTE:** Entry-level

positions, part-time jobs, and second and third shifts are offered. **Common positions include:** Accountant; Administrative Assistant; Advertising Executive; Applications Engineer; Chief Financial Officer; Claim Representative; Computer Programmer; Computer Support Technician; Database Administrator; Help-Desk Technician; Human Resources Manager; Licensed Practical Nurse; Marketing Manager; Medical Records Technician; Network/Systems Administrator; Pharmacist; Physician; Registered Nurse; Secretary; Systems Analyst. **Educational backgrounds include:** Accounting; Computer Science; Education; Health Care; Microsoft Office; Microsoft Word; Spreadsheets. **Benefits:** 401(k); Casual Dress - Fridays; Dental Insurance; Disability Coverage; Employee Discounts; Flexible Schedule; Medical Insurance; Savings Plan; Tuition Assistance; Vacation Days (10 - 20). **Special programs:** Apprenticeships; Internships; Training. **Office hours:** Monday - Friday, 8:00 a.m. - 5:00 p.m. **Corporate headquarters location:** This Location. **CEO:** Paul Greever. **Annual sales/revenues:** $11 - $20 million. **Number of employees at this location:** 300.

PARMA COMMUNITY GENERAL HOSPITAL
7007 Powers Boulevard, Parma OH 44129. 440/743-3000. **Fax:** 440/843-4092. **Recorded jobline:** 440/843-4005. **Contact:** Human Resources. **Description:** A 321-bed, acute care hospital. **Common positions include:** Accountant; Biomedical Engineer; Buyer; Clinical Lab Technician; Computer Programmer; Dietician/Nutritionist; Financial Analyst; Human Resources Manager; Licensed Practical Nurse; Medical Records Technician; MIS Specialist; Nuclear Medicine Technologist; Occupational Therapist; Pharmacist; Physical Therapist; Physician; Preschool Worker; Public Relations Specialist; Radiological Technologist; Secretary; Speech-Language Pathologist; Stationary Engineer; Surgical Technician; Systems Analyst; Telecommunications Manager; Typist/Word Processor. **Educational backgrounds include:** Health Care. **Benefits:** 401(k); Daycare Assistance; Dental Insurance; Disability Coverage; Employee Discounts; Fitness Program; Job Sharing; Life Insurance; Medical Insurance; Pension Plan; Public Transit Available; Tuition Assistance. **Corporate headquarters location:** This Location. **President/CEO:** Thomas A. Selden. **Number of employees at this location:** 2,000. 0.

PEARLE VISION, INC.
2534 Royal Lane, Dallas TX 75229. 972/277-5000. **Fax:** 972/277-5944. **Contact:** Human Resources. **World Wide Web address:** http://www.colenational.com. **Description:** Manufactures and retails prescription eyewear. **Common positions include:** Accountant/Auditor; Advertising Clerk; Attorney; Computer Programmer; Customer Service Representative; Department Manager; Financial Analyst; Human Resources Manager; Management Trainee; Manufacturer's/Wholesaler's Sales Rep.; Marketing Specialist; Purchasing Agent/Manager; Systems Analyst. **Educational backgrounds include:** Accounting; Business Administration; Computer Science; Finance; Marketing; Merchandising. **Benefits:** Dental Insurance; Disability Coverage; Employee Discounts; Life Insurance; Medical Insurance; Profit Sharing; Savings Plan; Tuition Assistance. **Corporate headquarters location:** This Location.

PERFECSEAL
9800 Bustleton Avenue, Philadelphia PA 19115. 215/673-4500. **Fax:** 215/856-6393. **Contact:** Mr. Reno Bianco, Human Resources Manager. **World**

Wide Web address: http://www.perfecseal.com. **Description:** Manufactures sterilizable medical packaging for the medical device industry. The company is a world leader in thermoplastic flexible packaging, heat-sealed coated Tyvek, and paper. Products include Perfecseal adhesive coating on Tyvek and paper, film and foil lamination; Breather Bag and linear tear packaging; easy-open and chevron peel pouches; oriented films; custom thermoformed trays and die-cut lids; pharmaceutical labels, cold seal technology, extrusion and saran coating, flexographic and rotogravure printing; and vacuum metallizing. Founded in 1905. **NOTE:** Entry-level positions and second and third shifts are offered. **Common positions include:** Accountant; Administrative Assistant; Blue-Collar Worker Supervisor; Buyer; Chemical Engineer; Chemist; Computer Programmer; Controller; Customer Service Representative; Electrician; Graphic Designer; Human Resources Manager; Marketing Manager; Mechanical Engineer; Operations Manager; Production Manager; Purchasing Agent/ Manager; Quality Control Supervisor; Sales Executive; Sales Manager; Sales Representative; Secretary; Systems Manager. **Educational backgrounds include:** Accounting; Business Administration; Chemistry; Computer Science; Engineering; Marketing. **Benefits:** 401(k); Daycare Assistance; Dental Insurance; Disability Coverage; Employee Discounts; Life Insurance; Medical Insurance; Pension Plan; Public Transit Available; Tuition Assistance. **Special programs:** Internships. **Corporate headquarters location:** This Location. **Other U.S. locations:** Mankato MN; New London WI; Oshkosh WI. **International locations:** Londonderry, Northern Ireland; Carolina, Puerto Rico. **Parent company:** Bemis, Inc. **Annual sales/revenues:** More than $100 million. **Number of employees at this location:** 200.

PETSMART, INC.
19601 North 27th Avenue, Phoenix AZ 85027. 623/580-6100. **Fax:** 623/580-6502. **Contact:** Human Resources. **World Wide Web address:** http://www.petsmart.com. **Description:** A national retail chain which sells pet supplies and animals. PETSMART also offers veterinary services, animal adoption centers, grooming services, and obedience classes. **Corporate headquarters location:** This Location. **Other U.S. locations:** Nationwide.

PFIZER
235 East 42nd Street, New York NY 10017. 212/573-2323. **Recorded jobline:** 212/733-4150. **Contact:** Employee Resources. **E-mail address:** resumes@pfizer.com. **World Wide Web address:** http://www.pfizer.com. **Description:** A leading pharmaceutical company that distributes products concerning cardiovascular health, central nervous system disorders, infectious diseases, and womens health worldwide. The company's brand-name products include Benadryl, Ben Gay, Cortizone, Desitin, Halls, Listerine, Sudafed, and Zantac 75. **Corporate headquarters location:** This Location. **International locations:** Worldwide. **Listed on:** London Stock Exchange; New York Stock Exchange; Swiss Stock Exchange. **Stock exchange symbol:** PFE.

PHILHAVEN BEHAVIORAL HEALTH SERVICES
283 South Butler Road, Mount Gretna PA 17064. 717/273-8871. **Fax:** 717/270-2455. **Contact:** Human Resources. **Description:** A psychiatric treatment center offering inpatient, outpatient, residential, and community-based services. **NOTE:** Entry-level positions and second and third shifts are offered. **Common positions include:** Account Representative; Licensed Practical Nurse; Medical Records Technician; Physician; Psychologist; Registered Nurse; Secretary; Social Worker. **Educational backgrounds include:** Health Care. **Benefits:** 401(k); 403(b); Dental Insurance; Disability Coverage; Life Insurance; Medical Insurance; Tuition Assistance. **Special programs:** Internships. **Corporate headquarters location:** This Location. **CEO:** LaVern J. Yutzy. **Annual sales/revenues:** $21 - $50 million. **Number of employees at this location:** 600.

PHOENIX MEDICAL TECHNOLOGY, INC.
P.O. Box 346, Andrews SC 29510. 843/221-5100. **Fax:** 843/221-5174. **Contact:** Deonna Alford, Personnel Assistant. **World Wide Web address:** http://www.cleanroomgloves.com. **Description:** Manufactures and markets vinyl and latex examination gloves. The company also manufactures and markets gloves for electronics manufacturers, clean room applications, food handlers, and meat processors. **Common positions include:** Accountant; Administrator; Biological Scientist; Blue-Collar Worker Supervisor; Buyer; Chemist; Computer Programmer; Customer Service Representative; General Manager; Industrial Production Manager; Management Trainee; Marketing Specialist; Operations/Production Manager; Quality Control Supervisor. **Educational backgrounds include:** Accounting; Business Administration; Chemistry; Marketing. **Benefits:** Disability Coverage; Life Insurance; Medical Insurance; Pension Plan; Profit Sharing; Tuition Assistance. **Corporate headquarters location:** This Location.

PHOENIX MEMORIAL HEALTH SYSTEM
1201 South Seventh Avenue, Phoenix AZ 85007. 602/824-3285. **Fax:** 602/824-3420. **Recorded jobline:** 602/824-3285x1. **Contact:** Human Resources. **World Wide Web address:** http://www. phxmemorialhospital.com. **Description:** A general acute care hospital and health services network. Phoenix Memorial's specialties include total joint replacement and cardiovascular services. **Common positions include:** Accountant/Auditor; Claim Representative; Clinical Lab Technician; Computer Programmer; Dietician/Nutritionist; Emergency Medical Technician; Food Scientist/Technologist; Health Services Manager; Licensed Practical Nurse; Medical Records Technician; Nuclear Medicine Technologist; Pharmacist; Physician; Preschool Worker; Registered Nurse; Respiratory Therapist; Social Worker; Surgical Technician; Systems Analyst. **Educational backgrounds include:** Health Care. **Benefits:** 401(k); Daycare Assistance; Dental Insurance; Disability Coverage; Employee Discounts; Life Insurance; Medical Insurance; Pension Plan; Tuition Assistance. **Corporate headquarters location:** This Location. **Listed on:** New York Stock Exchange. **Number of employees at this location:** 1,100.

PHYCOR, INC.
30 Burton Hills Boulevard, Suite 400, Nashville TN 37215. 615/665-9066. **Contact:** Brandon Dyson, Vice President of Human Resources. **World Wide Web address:** http://www.phycor.com. **Description:** Operates multispecialty medical clinics. PhyCor owns and operates 18 clinics in 11 states and manages the operations of two additional clinics. **Corporate headquarters location:** This Location.

PIONEER BEHAVIORAL HEALTH
200 Lake Street, Suite 102, Peabody MA 01960. 978/536-2777. **Toll-free phone:** 800/543-2447. **Fax:** 978/536-2677. **Contact:** Human Resources. **World Wide Web address:** http://www.phc-inc.com. **Description:** Operates a variety of mental

health, chemical dependency, and dual diagnosis programs throughout the country which provide inpatient and outpatient services, partial hospitalization, residential care, aftercare, and employee assistance programs. Founded in 1976. **Subsidiaries include:** Behavioral Stress Center (Elmhurst NY); Harbor Oaks Hospital (New Baltimore MI); Harmony Healthcare (Las Vegas NV); Highland Ridge Hospital (Salt Lake City UT); Mount Regis Center (Salem VA); Pioneer Counseling Centers of Michigan (Farmington Hills MI); Pioneer Counseling of Virginia (Salem VA); Pioneer Development & Support Services (Salt Lake City UT). **President/CEO:** Bruce A. Shear. **Number of employees at this location:** 300.

PITTSBURGH MERCY HEALTH SYSTEM
1400 Locust Street, Pittsburgh PA 15219. 412/232-7970. **Recorded jobline:** 412/232-7225. **Contact:** Central Employment Office. **World Wide Web address:** http://www.mercylink.com. **Description:** A nonprofit health care system operating several hospitals in the Pittsburgh area. **Common positions include:** Biological Scientist; Clinical Lab Technician; Dietician/Nutritionist; Human Service Worker; Medical Records Technician; Occupational Therapist; Pharmacist; Physical Therapist; Registered Nurse; Speech-Language Pathologist; Surgical Technician. **Educational backgrounds include:** Health Care; M.D./Medicine. **Benefits:** Daycare Assistance; Dental Insurance; Disability Coverage; Employee Discounts; Life Insurance; Medical Insurance; Pension Plan; Savings Plan; Tuition Assistance. **Corporate headquarters location:** This Location. **Subsidiaries include:** Mercy Hospital of Pittsburgh; Mercy Providence Hospital; Mercy Psychiatric Institute; St. Joseph Nursing and Health Care Center.

PLAZA MEDICAL GROUP
3433 NW 56th Street, Suite 400, Oklahoma City OK 73112. 405/945-3172. **Fax:** 405/941-4359. **Contact:** Human Resources. **Description:** Multispecialty physicians' offices. **Common positions include:** Certified Nurses Aide; EKG Technician; Licensed Practical Nurse; Medical Records Technician; Nuclear Medicine Technologist; Physician; Registered Nurse; Typist/Word Processor. **Educational backgrounds include:** Health Care. **Benefits:** 401(k); Dental Insurance; Disability Coverage; Life Insurance; Medical Insurance; Profit Sharing. **Corporate headquarters location:** This Location. **Number of employees at this location:** 140.

POLYMEDICA CORPORATION
11 State Street, Woburn MA 01801. 781/933-2020. **Fax:** 781/933-7992. **Contact:** Human Resources. **World Wide Web address:** http://www.polymedica.com. **Description:** A leading provider of targeted medical products and services focusing primarily on the diabetes and consumer health care markets. Founded in 1988. **Common positions include:** Accountant; Administrative Assistant; Buyer; Chief Financial Officer; Operations Manager; Production Manager; Purchasing Agent/Manager. **Educational backgrounds include:** Accounting. **Benefits:** 401(k); Dental Insurance; Disability Coverage; Life Insurance; Medical Insurance. **Special programs:** Co-ops. **Corporate headquarters location:** This Location. **Other U.S. locations:** Golden CO; Palm City FL. **Subsidiaries include:** Liberty Medical Supply is one of the largest direct-mail distributors of diabetes supplies covered by Medicare. Liberty distributes more than 200,000 diabetes products to over 70,000 customers. PolyMedica Healthcare, Inc. holds leading positions in the urinary health and over-the-counter medical device markets by distributing a broad range of products to food, drug, and mass retailers nationwide. PolyMedica Pharmaceuticals (USA), Inc. manufactures, distributes, and markets prescription urological and suppository products. **Listed on:** American Stock Exchange. **Stock exchange symbol:** PM. **CEO:** Steven J. Lee. **Number of employees at this location:** 30. **Number of employees nationwide:** 345.

POMONA VALLEY HOSPITAL MEDICAL CENTER
1798 North Garey Avenue, Pomona CA 91767. **Fax:** 909/623-3253. **Recorded jobline:** 909/865-9840. **Contact:** Rolanda Bradshaw, Employment Specialist. **World Wide Web address:** http://www.pvhmc.com. **Description:** A 449-bed, nonprofit, acute care, teaching hospital. The hospital offers medical services through the Robert and Beverly Lewis Cancer Care Center; the Stead Heart Center; and the Women's Center. Founded in 1903. **Common positions include:** Clinical Lab Technician; Dietician/Nutritionist; EEG Technologist; EKG Technician; Emergency Medical Technician; Food Scientist/Technologist; Health Services Manager; Licensed Practical Nurse; Medical Records Technician; Nuclear Medicine Technologist; Occupational Therapist; Pharmacist; Physical Therapist; Physician; Radiological Technologist; Registered Nurse; Respiratory Therapist; Social Worker; Surgical Technician; Systems Analyst. **Educational backgrounds include:** Biology; Business Administration; Computer Science; Finance; Health Care. **Benefits:** 403(b); Daycare Assistance; Dental Insurance; Disability Coverage; Employee Discounts; Life Insurance; Medical Insurance. **Number of employees at this location:** 2,300.

POTTSTOWN MEMORIAL MEDICAL CENTER
1600 East High Street, Pottstown PA 19464. 610/327-7000. **Fax:** 610/327-7690. **Contact:** Debra Zlomek, Employment Manager. **World Wide Web address:** http://www.pmmctr.org. **Description:** A nonprofit,full-service hospital. **NOTE:** Entry-level positions and second and third shifts are offered. **Common positions include:** Accountant; Administrative Assistant; Certified Nurses Aide; Clerical Supervisor; Computer Operator; Controller; Credit Manager; Dietician/Nutritionist; EEG Technologist; EKG Technician; Financial Analyst; Human Resources Manager; Librarian; Licensed Practical Nurse; Medical Records Technician; MIS Specialist; Nuclear Medicine Technologist; Occupational Therapist; Pharmacist; Physical Therapist; Physician; Radiological Technologist; Registered Nurse; Respiratory Therapist; Secretary; Social Worker; Speech-Language Pathologist; Surgical Technician; Telecommunications Manager; Typist/Word Processor; Vice President. **Benefits:** 403(b); Dental Insurance; Disability Coverage; Employee Discounts; Flexible Schedule; Life Insurance; Medical Insurance; Pension Plan; Public Transit Available; Savings Plan; Tuition Assistance. **Corporate headquarters location:** This Location. **Number of employees at this location:** 1,100.

PRAIRIE VIEW INC.
P.O. Box 467, Newton KS 67114. 316/284-6311. **Fax:** 316/284-6491. **Contact:** Human Resources. **World Wide Web address:** http://www.prairieview.com. **Description:** Established by the Mennonite churches, Prairie View is a private, nonprofit psychiatric hospital and mental health center. Prairie View provides a complete range of psychiatric services including individual, marriage, and family therapy, aging services, pastoral counseling, treatment for severe and persistent mental illness, chemical dependency treatment,

child and adolescent services, trauma treatment, sex offender treatment, and employee assistance programs. A 60-bed psychiatric hospital and partial hospitalization program are at this location. Outpatient services are available. **Common positions include:** Accountant/Auditor; Clerical Supervisor; Computer Programmer; Counselor; Financial Analyst; Human Resources Manager; Human Service Worker; Licensed Practical Nurse; Medical Records Technician; Physician; Psychologist; Registered Nurse; Restaurant/Food Service Manager; Social Worker; Systems Analyst; Teacher/Professor; Technical Writer/Editor. **Educational backgrounds include:** Accounting; Business Administration; Communications; Finance; Health Care; Liberal Arts; M.D./Medicine; Marketing. **Benefits:** Disability Coverage; Employee Discounts; Life Insurance; Medical Insurance; Pension Plan. **Corporate headquarters location:** This Location. **Other area locations:** Marion KS; McPherson KS; Newton KS; Wichita KS. **Number of employees at this location:** 250. **Number of employees nationwide:** 375.

PRECISION OPTICS CORPORATION
22 East Broadway, Gardner MA 01440. 978/630-1800. **Fax:** 978/630-1487. **Contact:** Human Resources. **World Wide Web address:** http://www.poci.com. **Description:** Designs, develops, manufactures, and sells specialized optical systems and components and optical thin film coatings. The products and services are used in the medical and advanced optical systems industries. Medical products include endoscopes and image couplers, beamsplitters, and adapters which are used as accessories to endoscopes. Advanced optical design and developmental services provide advanced lens design, image analysis, optical system design, structural design and analysis, prototype production and evaluation, optics testing, and optical system assembly. **Corporate headquarters location:** This Location.

PRESBYTERIAN HOMES OF MINNESOTA
3220 Lake Johanna Boulevard, Arden Hills MN 55112. 651/631-6126. **Fax:** 651/631-6108. **Contact:** Human Resources. **Description:** Offers a broad range of residential and support services to the elderly. Services include apartment living, long-term nursing care, and home health respite programs. **NOTE:** Entry-level positions and second and third shifts are offered. **Common positions include:** Certified Nurses Aide; Dietician/Nutritionist; Environmental Engineer; Licensed Practical Nurse; Registered Nurse; Secretary; Social Worker. **Educational backgrounds include:** Health Care. **Benefits:** 403(b); Dental Insurance; Employee Discounts; Life Insurance; Medical Insurance; Pension Plan; Tuition Assistance. **Special programs:** Summer Jobs. **Corporate headquarters location:** This Location. **CEO:** Daniel Lindh. **Number of employees at this location:** 1,500.

PRESTERA CENTER
P.O. Box 8069, Huntington WV 25705. 304/525-7851. **Physical address:** 3375 U.S. Route 60 East, Huntington WV. **Fax:** 304/525-1504. **Contact:** Linda Persun, Director of Human Resources. **World Wide Web address:** http://www.prestera.org. **Description:** A nonprofit, community, mental health center that offers outpatient and residential treatment for children, adolescents, and adults with behavioral problems, mental illness, or substance addictions. Founded in 1967. **NOTE:** Entry-level positions are offered. **Company slogan:** Serving everyday people with everyday problems - every day. **Common positions include:** Account Manager; Account Representative; Accountant; Administrative Assistant; Administrative Manager;

Chief Financial Officer; Clerical Supervisor; Computer Operator; Counselor; Database Manager; Finance Director; Human Resources Manager; Marketing Manager; Marketing Specialist; Medical Records Technician; Physician; Psychologist; Registered Nurse; Secretary; Social Worker; Teacher/Professor; Typist/Word Processor. **Educational backgrounds include:** Accounting; Business Administration; Counseling; Health Care; Human Services; Psychology; Social Work. **Benefits:** 401(k); Dental Insurance; Disability Coverage; Flexible Schedule; Life Insurance; Medical Insurance. **Special programs:** Internships; Summer Jobs. **Corporate headquarters location:** This Location. **Executive Director:** Robert Hansen. **Annual sales/revenues:** $5 - $10 million. **Number of employees at this location:** 400.

PRIME CARE HEALTH AGENCY INC.
3900 NW 79th Avenue, Suite 334, Miami FL 33166. 305/591-7774. **Toll-free phone:** 800/591-7747. **Fax:** 305/594-8951. **Recorded jobline:** 305/591-7774x815. **Contact:** Josie Melero, Human Resources Director. **Description:** Provides in-home nursing services. Founded in 1985. **Common positions include:** Certified Nurses Aide; Home Health Aide; Licensed Practical Nurse; Registered Nurse; Respiratory Therapist. **Office hours:** Monday - Friday, 8:00 a.m. - 5:00 p.m. **President:** Barry G. Shoor. **Number of employees at this location:** 250.

PRINCE WILLIAM HOSPITAL
8700 Sudley Road, Manassas VA 20110. 703/369-8000. **Contact:** Susan Barrett, Employment Coordinator. **World Wide Web address:** http://www.pwhs.org. **Description:** A nonprofit community hospital. Founded in 1964. **Number of employees at this location:** 1,000.

PRO-DEX INC.
1401 Walnut Street, Suite 540, Boulder CO 80302. 303/443-6136. **Fax:** 303/443-2770. **Contact:** Human Resources. **World Wide Web address:** http://www.pdex.com. **Description:** A holding company. **Corporate headquarters location:** This Location. **Subsidiaries include:** Biotrol International, Inc. (Louisville CO) manufactures products for the dental industry; Challenge Products, Inc. (Osage Beach MO) manufactures fluoride; Micro Motors, Inc. (Santa Ana CA) manufactures miniature pneumatic motors and dental instruments; Oregon Micro Systems, Inc. (Beaverton OR). **Listed on:** NASDAQ. **Stock exchange symbol:** PDEX. **CEO:** Kent Searl.

PROCYTE CORPORATION
8511 154th Avenue NE, Building A, Redmond WA 98052. 425/869-1239. **Contact:** Human Resources. **World Wide Web address:** http://www.procyte.com. **Description:** A health care company that specializes in cosmetic surgery, hair care, and skin health. **Corporate headquarters location:** This Location.

PROFESSIONAL DENTAL TECHNOLOGIES
P.O. Box 3889, Batesville AR 72503. 870/698-2300. **Physical address:** 633 Lawrence Street, Batesville AR 72501. **Contact:** Human Resources. **World Wide Web address:** http://www.prodentec.com. **Description:** Designs and manufactures products that assist dental professionals in diagnosing, treating, and preventing periodontal and other dental diseases. Products include the Rota-dent plaque removal instrument, the Prism intra-oral camera, the Periocheck in-office enzyme test, and the PerfectByte Practice Management Software System. **Corporate headquarters location:** This Location.

PROFESSIONAL POSITIONERS, INC.
2525 Three Mile Road, Racine WI 53404. 262/639-8617. **Toll-free phone:** 800/742-6640. **Fax:** 262/639-0190. **Contact:** Sandra Ivanoski, Vice President of Operations. **E-mail address:** prolab@execpc.com. **World Wide Web address:** http://www.proorthodonticlab.com. **Description:** Manufactures custom orthodontic appliances and products. Founded in 1968. **NOTE:** Entry-level positions are offered. **Common positions include:** Buyer; Customer Service Representative; Sales Manager. **Educational backgrounds include:** Marketing. **Benefits:** 401(k); Dental Insurance; Disability Coverage; Life Insurance; Medical Insurance; Public Transit Available. **Special programs:** Training. **Office hours:** Monday - Friday, 7:30 a.m. - 5:30 p.m. **Corporate headquarters location:** This Location. **Other U.S. locations:** Enfield CT; Vancouver WA. **Listed on:** Privately held. **President:** Joseph Toussaint. **Annual sales/revenues:** $5 - $10 million. **Number of employees at this location:** 100.

PROTOCOL SYSTEMS, INC.
8500 SW Creekside Place, Beaverton OR 97008. 503/526-8500. **Fax:** 503/526-4200. **Contact:** Allen Oyler, Human Resources Representative. **World Wide Web address:** http://www.protocol.com. **Description:** A manufacturer of vital sign monitoring systems. **Common positions include:** Accountant/Auditor; Buyer; Computer Programmer; Customer Service Rep.; Human Resources Manager; Mechanical Engineer; Production Manager; Purchasing Agent/Manager; Quality Control Supervisor; Registered Nurse; Software Engineer; Technical Writer/Editor. **Educational backgrounds include:** Accounting; Business Administration; Computer Science; Engineering; Health Care; Marketing. **Benefits:** 401(k); Dental Insurance; Disability Coverage; ESOP; Life Insurance; Medical Insurance; Tuition Assistance. **Corporate headquarters location:** This Location. **Listed on:** NASDAQ. **Number of employees at this location:** 200. **Number of employees nationwide:** 250.

THE QUEEN'S MEDICAL CENTER
1301 Punchbowl Street, Honolulu HI 96813. 808/547-4355. **Contact:** Human Resources. **World Wide Web address:** http://www.queens.org. **Description:** A private, nonprofit, acute care medical facility. It is one of the largest private hospitals in Hawaii and the Pacific Basin, licensed to operate 530 acute care beds, 30 subacute beds, and 30 trauma/ER beds. As a leading medical referral center in Hawaii and the Pacific Basin, The Queen's Medical Center offers a comprehensive range of primary and specialized care services. The hospital's departments include oncology, orthopedics, cardiology, obstetrics, and trauma and critical care. The hospital also offers a broad spectrum of adult mental health services. **Common positions include:** Accountant; Attorney; Biomedical Engineer; Budget Analyst; Certified Nurses Aide; Certified Occupational Therapy Assistant; Claim Representative; Computer Operator; Computer Programmer; Computer Support Technician; Database Administrator; Dietician/Nutritionist; EEG Technologist; EKG Technician; Electrician; Financial Analyst; Geneticist; Help-Desk Technician; Licensed Practical Nurse; Medical Assistant; Medical Records Technician; Medical Secretary; Network Engineer; Network/Systems Administrator; Nuclear Medicine Technologist; Nurse Practitioner; Occupational Therapist; Pharmacist; Physical Therapist; Physical Therapy Assistant; Psychologist; Public Relations Specialist; Purchasing Agent/Manager; Radiological Technologist; Registered Nurse; Respiratory

Therapist; Secretary; Social Worker; Special Education Teacher; Speech-Language Pathologist; Statistician; Surgical Technician; Systems Analyst. **Educational backgrounds include:** Accounting; Business Administration; Computer Science; Economics; Finance; Health Care; MBA; Novell. **Benefits:** 401(k); Dental Insurance; Disability Coverage; Employee Discounts; Life Insurance; Medical Insurance; Pension Plan; Public Transit Available; Tuition Assistance. **Corporate headquarters location:** This Location. **Parent company:** The Queen's Health Systems. **Operations at this facility include:** Administration. **Number of employees nationwide:** 3,500.

QUEST MEDICAL, INC.
ATRION CORPORATION
One Allentown Parkway, Allen TX 75002-4211. 972/390-9800. **Contact:** Human Resources. **World Wide Web address:** http://www.atrioncorp.com. **Description:** Develops, manufactures, markets, sells, and distributes proprietary products for the health care industry. **Corporate headquarters location:** This Location. **Parent company:** Atrion Corporation (also at this location) is a holding company that designs, develops, manufactures, markets, sells, and distributes proprietary products and components for the health care industry. Other subsidiaries of Atrion Corporation include Atrion Medical Products and Halkey-Roberts. **Listed on:** NASDAQ. **Stock exchange symbol:** QMED. **Number of employees at this location:** 250.

QUORUM HEALTH GROUP, INC.
105 Continental Place, Brentwood TN 37027. 615/371-7979. **Contact:** Recruitment. **World Wide Web address:** http://www.quorumhealth.com. **Description:** Operates acute care hospitals and health care systems nationwide. **Corporate headquarters location:** This Location. **Other U.S. locations:** Dothan AL; Enterprise AL; Gadsen AL; Jacksonville AL; Macon GA; Fort Wayne IN; Frankfort IN; Hattiesburg MS; Vicksburg MS; Las Vegas NV; Barberton OH; Massillon OH; Florence SC; Kingstree SC; Lake City SC; Spartanburg SC; Abilene TX. **Subsidiaries include:** Quorum Health Resources, Inc. manages over 240 acute care hospitals and provides consulting services to hospitals throughout the country. **Number of employees nationwide:** 8,500.

RAMSEY CLINIC
640 Jackson Street, St. Paul MN 55101. 651/221-3152. **Toll-free phone:** 800/332-5720. **Fax:** 651/221-1249. **Recorded jobline:** 651/221-1227. **Contact:** Ruth Bremer, Human Resources Representative. **E-mail address:** ruth.n.bremer@healthpartners.com. **Description:** A nonprofit, multispecialty, outpatient clinic with emphasis on quality patient care, teaching, and research. **NOTE:** Part-time jobs are offered. **Common positions include:** Administrative Assistant; Administrative Manager; Clerical Supervisor; Clinical Lab Technician; Customer Service Representative; Licensed Practical Nurse; Medical Assistant; Medical Records Technician; Medical Secretary; Nurse Practitioner; Physician Assistant; Registered Nurse; Secretary; Typist/Word Processor. **Educational backgrounds include:** Biology; Business Administration; Chemistry; Health Care; MBA; Microsoft Office; Microsoft Word; Spreadsheets. **Benefits:** 401(k); Dental Insurance; Disability Coverage; Employee Discounts; Life Insurance; Medical Insurance; Pension Plan; Public Transit Available; Tuition Assistance; Vacation Days (16+). **Special programs:** Internships. **Office hours:** Monday - Friday, 8:00 a.m. - 4:30 p.m. **Corporate headquarters location:** This Location. **Number of employees at this location:** 500.

RAVENSWOOD HOSPITAL MEDICAL CENTER (RHMC)
4550 North Winchester, Chicago IL 60640. 773/878-4300. **Contact:** Human Resources. **Description:** A 462-bed medical facility offering acute care and rehabilitative services to the Chicago area. RHMC also operates eight satellite locations. **Common positions include:** Accountant/Auditor; Adjuster; Biomedical Engineer; Claim Rep.; Clinical Lab Technician; Computer Programmer; Counselor; Customer Service Rep.; Dietician/ Nutritionist; Emergency Medical Technician; Environmental Engineer; Food Scientist/ Technologist; Licensed Practical Nurse; Medical Records Technician; Occupational Therapist; Pharmacist; Physical Therapist; Preschool Worker; Radiological Technologist; Recreational Therapist; Registered Nurse; Respiratory Therapist; Social Worker; Speech-Language Pathologist; Stationary Engineer; Systems Analyst; Teacher/Professor. **Educational backgrounds include:** Accounting; Biology; Business Administration; Finance; Health Care. **Benefits:** 403(b); Daycare Assistance; Dental Insurance; Disability Coverage; Employee Discounts; Life Insurance; Medical Insurance; Pension Plan; Tuition Assistance. **Corporate headquarters location:** This Location. **Number of employees at this location:** 1,400.

REDINGTON-FAIRVIEW GENERAL HOSPITAL
P.O. Box 468, Skowhegan ME 04976. 207/474-5121. **Fax:** 207/474-7004. **Contact:** Mabel Larsen, Human Resources Director. **Description:** A nonprofit, acute care hospital. Founded in 1969. **NOTE:** Entry-level positions, part-time jobs, and second and third shifts are offered. **Common positions include:** Account Representative; Administrative Assistant; Certified Nurses Aide; Certified Occupational Therapy Assistant; Chief Financial Officer; Clinical Lab Technician; Computer Operator; Computer Programmer; Dietician/Nutritionist; EEG Technologist; Electrician; Emergency Medical Technician; Financial Analyst; Human Resources Manager; Librarian; Licensed Practical Nurse; Medical Records Technician; Nuclear Medicine Technologist; Occupational Therapist; Pharmacist; Physical Therapist; Physical Therapy Assistant; Physician; Physician Assistant; Purchasing Agent/Manager; Radiological Technologist; Registered Nurse; Respiratory Therapist; Secretary; Social Worker. **Educational backgrounds include:** Health Care. **Benefits:** 403(b); Dental Insurance; Disability Coverage; Employee Discounts; Flexible Schedule; Life Insurance; Medical Insurance; Pension Plan; Savings Plan; Tuition Assistance. **Special programs:** Summer Jobs. **Number of employees at this location:** 495.

REHABILITATION HOSPITAL OF THE PACIFIC
226 North Kuakini Street, Honolulu HI 96817. **Toll-free phone:** 800/973-4226. **Fax:** 808/544-3337. **Contact:** Human Resources. **World Wide Web address:** http://www.rehabhospital.org. **Description:** A comprehensive, physical rehabilitation hospital offering both inpatient and outpatient services to individuals with physical disabilities. The hospital is licensed for 100 acute beds. The outpatient network consists of clinics located at various sites on the islands of Hawaii (Hilo and Kona), Kauai, Maui, and Oahu. **Common positions include:** Occupational Therapist; Physical Therapist; Registered Nurse; Speech-Language Pathologist. **Benefits:** Dental Insurance; Disability Coverage; Employee Discounts; Life Insurance; Medical Insurance; Pension Plan; Vision Insurance. **Corporate headquarters location:** This Location. **Number of employees at this location:** 400.

THE REHABILITATION INSTITUTE OF CHICAGO
345 East Superior Street, Chicago IL 60011. 312/238-6290. **Toll-free phone:** 800/782-7342. **Fax:** 312/238-1263. **Recorded jobline:** 312/238-5600. **Contact:** Human Resources. **World Wide Web address:** http://www.rehabchicago.org. **Description:** A comprehensive rehabilitation facility offering inpatient, outpatient, subacute, and day treatment rehabilitation. The Institute also offers home care rehabilitation. **NOTE:** Second and third shifts are offered. **Common positions include:** Account Rep.; Accountant; Administrative Assistant; Applications Engineer; Biomedical Engineer; Certified Nurses Aide; Computer Programmer; Controller; Database Manager; Human Resources Manager; Licensed Practical Nurse; Medical Records Technician; Occupational Therapist; Physical Therapist; Registered Nurse; Secretary; Speech-Language Pathologist; Systems Analyst; Typist/Word Processor. **Educational backgrounds include:** Health Care. **Benefits:** Dental Insurance; Disability Coverage; Employee Discounts; Life Insurance; Medical Insurance; Pension Plan; Public Transit Available; Savings Plan; Tuition Assistance. **Corporate headquarters location:** This Location. **CEO:** Dr. Wayne Lerner. **Number of employees at this location:** 1,200.

REM-HEALTH, INC.
3101 West 69th Street, Suite 121, Edina MN 55435. 612/926-9808. **Toll-free phone:** 800/896-8814. **Fax:** 612/926-4002. **Contact:** Erin McNeely, Human Resources Manager. **Description:** A home health care agency offering private duty nursing care, live-in companions, respiratory therapy, physical therapy, occupational therapy, psychological services, and applied behavior analysis. Founded in 1989. **NOTE:** Entry-level positions and second and third shifts are offered. **Common positions include:** Administrative Assistant; Certified Nurses Aide; Computer Operator; Licensed Practical Nurse; Occupational Therapist; Physical Therapist; Psychologist; Registered Nurse; Respiratory Therapist; Secretary; Speech-Language Pathologist; Typist/Word Processor. **Educational backgrounds include:** Accounting; Health Care; Liberal Arts. **Benefits:** 401(k); Dental Insurance; Disability Coverage; Flexible Schedule; Life Insurance; Medical Insurance; Profit Sharing. **Special programs:** Training; Summer Jobs. **Corporate headquarters location:** This Location. **Other U.S. locations:** Woodbine IA; Annandale MN; Cokato MN; Maple Lake MN; New Prague MN; St. Paul MN; Madison WI. **Parent company:** REM, Inc. **Listed on:** Privately held. **Administrator:** Pat Shafer. **Annual sales/revenues:** $11 - $20 million. **Number of employees at this location:** 1,000.

REMUDA RANCH CENTER
One East Apache Street, Suite A, Wickenburg AZ 85390. 520/684-4244. **Fax:** 520/684-4247. **Recorded jobline:** 520/684-4530. **Contact:** Linda Hughes, Recruiter. **E-mail address:** remuda@ goodnet.com. **World Wide Web address:** http://www.emuda-ranch.com. **Description:** A treatment center for women and adolescent girls suffering from anorexia, bulimia, and related disorders. The center offers individualized inpatient, partial, residential, and outpatient treatments. Founded in 1990. **Common positions include:** Counselor; Dietician/Nutritionist; Licensed Practical Nurse; Physician; Registered Nurse; Social Worker. **Educational backgrounds include:** Health Care. **Benefits:** 401(k); Dental Insurance; Disability Coverage; Life Insurance; Medical Insurance; Tuition Assistance. **Special programs:** Internships. **Internship information:** Internships are offered for

psychologists, master level therapists, RNs, LPNs, and dietitians. **Office hours:** Monday - Friday, 8:00 a.m. - 5:00 p.m. **Corporate headquarters location:** This Location. **Listed on:** Privately held. **CEO:** Ward Keller. **Facilities Manager:** Cindy Logan. **Annual sales/revenues:** $21 - $50 million. **Number of employees at this location:** 270.

RESISTANCE TECHNOLOGY, INC.
1260 Red Fox Road, Arden Hills MN 55112. 651/636-9770. **Fax:** 651/636-8944. **Contact:** Cari Sather, Human Resources Coordinator. **World Wide Web address:** http://www.rtihearing.com. **Description:** A worldwide producer of medical hearing products including ultra-miniature volume controls, CIC faceplates, and programmable hearing systems. **NOTE:** Entry-level positions and second and third shifts are offered. **Common positions include:** Account Manager; Accountant/Auditor; Administrative Assistant; Applications Engineer; Buyer; Controller; Credit Manager; Design Engineer; Designer; Electrical/Electronics Engineer; Human Resources Manager; Industrial Engineer; Manufacturing Engineer; Marketing Manager; Mechanical Engineer; MIS Specialist; Operations/Production Manager; Project Manager; Purchasing Agent/Manager; Sales Engineer; Sales Manager; Systems Analyst. **Educational backgrounds include:** Accounting; Business Administration; Computer Science; Engineering; Marketing. **Benefits:** 401(k); Cafeteria Plan; Daycare Assistance; Dental Insurance; Disability Coverage; Employee Discounts; Life Insurance; Medical Insurance; Pension Plan; Tuition Assistance. **Corporate headquarters location:** This Location. **Parent company:** Selas. **Annual sales/revenues:** $21 - $50 million. **Number of employees at this location:** 260.

RESPIRONICS INC.
1001 Murry Ridge Lane, Murrysville PA 15668-8550. 724/733-0200. **Fax:** 724/387-4299. **Contact:** Human Resources. **World Wide Web address:** http://www.respironics.com. **Description:** Manufactures respiratory medical products. **NOTE:** Entry-level positions are offered. **Common positions include:** Biomedical Engineer; Blue-Collar Worker Supervisor; Computer Programmer; Customer Service Rep.; Design Engineer; Designer; Draftsperson; Electrical/Electronics Engineer; Internet Services Manager; Manufacturer's/Wholesaler's Sales Rep.; Market Research Analyst; Mechanical Engineer; MIS Specialist; Regulatory Affairs Director; Respiratory Therapist; Systems Analyst; Technical Writer/Editor. **Educational backgrounds include:** Engineering; Health Care. **Benefits:** 401(k); Dental Insurance; Disability Coverage; Life Insurance; Medical Insurance; Profit Sharing; Tuition Assistance. **Special programs:** Internships. **Corporate headquarters location:** This Location. **Listed on:** NASDAQ. **Annual sales/revenues:** More than $100 million. **Number of employees at this location:** 480.

RESPONSE ONCOLOGY
1805 Moriah Woods Boulevard, Memphis TN 38117. 901/763-7020. **Contact:** Nicole Roleson, Director of Human Resources. **World Wide Web address:** http://www.responseoncology.com. **Description:** Provides advanced cancer treatments and related services, principally on an outpatient basis, through treatment centers owned and operated by the company. The centers, known as IMPACT Centers, are staffed by oncology nurses, pharmacists, laboratory technologists, and other support personnel to deliver outpatient services under the direction of practicing oncologists. The centers provide chemotherapy; home pharmacy services, such as pain medications, antibiotics, and nutritional support; outpatient infusion services; blood banking services; and specialized nursing and laboratory services. **Corporate headquarters location:** This Location. **Other area locations:** Nashville TN.

RICHLAND MEMORIAL HOSPITAL
5 Richland Medical Park, Columbia SC 29203. 803/434-6271. **Contact:** Employment Services. **World Wide Web address:** http://www.rmh.edu. **Description:** A 626-bed, regional, community teaching hospital. Richland Memorial Hospital's facilities include a Children's Hospital; the Center for Cancer Treatment and Research; the Heart Center; the Midlands Trauma Center; and Richland Springs, a free-standing psychiatric hospital. Specialty services include a partially-matched bone marrow transplantation program, high-risk obstetrics, orthopedics, psychiatry, cardiology, oncology, nephrology, neonatology, neurology, neurosurgery, and medical and surgical services. The hospital is affiliated with the University of South Carolina and other universities. **Common positions include:** Accountant/Auditor; Budget Analyst; Buyer; Clinical Lab Technician; Computer Programmer; Construction Contractor; Customer Service Rep.; Dental Assistant/Dental Hygienist; Dental Lab Technician; Dentist; Dietician/Nutritionist; Draftsperson; EEG Technologist; EKG Technician; Electrician; Human Resources Manager; Librarian; Library Technician; Licensed Practical Nurse; Medical Records Technician; Nuclear Medicine Technologist; Occupational Therapist; Pharmacist; Physical Therapist; Physician; Public Relations Specialist; Purchasing Agent/Manager; Radiological Technologist; Recreational Therapist; Registered Nurse; Respiratory Therapist; Social Worker; Speech-Language Pathologist; Statistician; Surgical Technician; Systems Analyst. **Educational backgrounds include:** Accounting; Biology; Business Administration; Computer Science; Finance; Health Care; Marketing; Mathematics. **Benefits:** 401(k); Dental Insurance; Disability Coverage; Employee Discounts; Life Insurance; Medical Insurance; On-Site Daycare; Tuition Assistance. **Special programs:** Internships. **Corporate headquarters location:** This Location.

ROCKINGHAM MEMORIAL HOSPITAL
235 Cantrell Avenue, Harrisonburg VA 22801. 540/433-4100. **Fax:** 540/564-5446. **Contact:** Diane Ray, Recruitment/Employment Manager. **Description:** A 330-bed, nonprofit, community hospital. **Common positions include:** Accountant/Auditor; Clerical Supervisor; Computer Programmer; Customer Service Rep.; Dentist; EEG Technologist; EKG Technician; Electrician; Financial Analyst; Human Resources Manager; Librarian; Licensed Practical Nurse; Mechanical Engineer; Medical Records Technician; Nuclear Medicine Technologist; Occupational Therapist; Pharmacist; Physical Therapist; Physician; Purchasing Agent/Manager; Recreational Therapist; Registered Nurse; Respiratory Therapist; Restaurant/Food Service Manager; Social Worker; Surgical Technician; Systems Analyst. **Educational backgrounds include:** Accounting; Business Administration; Engineering; Finance; Marketing. **Benefits:** Dental Insurance; Disability Coverage; Employee Discounts; Life Insurance; Medical Insurance; Pension Plan; Savings Plan; Tuition Assistance.

ROGER WILLIAMS MEDICAL CENTER
825 Chalkstone Avenue, Providence RI 02908-4735. 401/456-2000. **Contact:** Human Resources. **World Wide Web address:** http://www.rwmc.com. **Description:** A major medical complex which

provides advanced diagnostic, treatment, education, and support services. The hospital provides treatment for a wide range of medical and surgical conditions as well as advanced cancer care, including the state's only bone marrow transplant unit. The facility also offers diagnostic and imaging services and houses an alcohol and substance abuse treatment center. The center's Elmhurst Extended Care offers rehabilitative, respite, and long-term nursing care, and the Home Care Department serves hundreds of patients across the state each day. Roger Williams Medical Center is also a major teaching and research facility affiliated with Boston University School of Medicine.

ROSE MEDICAL CENTER
4567 East Ninth Avenue, Denver CO 80220. 303/320-2121. **Contact:** Human Resources. **World Wide Web address:** http://www.rosemed.com. **Description:** A 420-bed medical center that provides inpatient and outpatient services. Off-site services include 11 primary care centers, four physical therapy sites, and an outpatient surgery center. Rose Women's Center offers programs for parent education, infertility, and high-risk pregnancies. Women's services also include a mammography service and breast diagnostic center. Additionally, a program for middle-aged women addresses the concerns surrounding menopause and healthy aging. Comprehensive services for children include a pediatric emergency service; a 14-bed, inpatient unit; and a multispecialty outpatient service supported by general and specialty pediatricians. Other areas of specialized expertise include the treatment of diabetes, comprehensive surgical services, a regional cleft lip and palate reconstructive surgery clinic, and an institute for joint replacement surgery. Founded in 1949. **Common positions include:** Accountant/Auditor; Buyer; Clinical Lab Technician; Computer Programmer; EEG Technologist; EKG Technician; Financial Analyst; Medical Records Technician; Nuclear Medicine Technologist; Occupational Therapist; Pharmacist; Physical Therapist; Radiological Technologist; Registered Nurse; Respiratory Therapist; Social Worker; Speech-Language Pathologist; Surgical Technician. **Benefits:** Dental Insurance; Disability Coverage; Employee Discounts; Life Insurance; Medical Insurance; Pension Plan; Savings Plan; Tuition Assistance. **Corporate headquarters location:** This Location. **Listed on:** Privately held. **Number of employees at this location:** 1,600.

POLLY RYON MEMORIAL HOSPITAL
1705 Jackson Street, Richmond TX 77469. 281/341-4831. **Fax:** 281/341-2883. **Recorded jobline:** 281/341-2852. **Contact:** Jane Hardesty, Human Resources Director. **World Wide Web address:** http://www.pollyryon.org. **Description:** A nonprofit, acute care medical facility with 185 beds. In addition to general medical and surgical procedures, Polly Ryon offers a wide range of services including active health education in the community; PROMISE, the birthing center; imaging services such as CT scanning, mammography, and MRIs; hospice care; and STAR, the Sports Therapy and Rehabilitation service. Founded in 1949. **NOTE:** Second and third shifts are offered. **Common positions include:** Certified Nurses Aide; EKG Technician; Licensed Practical Nurse; Medical Records Technician; Radiological Technologist; Registered Nurse; Respiratory Therapist; Secretary; Social Worker; Surgical Technician; Systems Analyst. **Educational backgrounds include:** Health Care. **Benefits:** 403(b); Dental Insurance; Disability Coverage; Life Insurance; Medical Insurance; Tuition Assistance. **Corporate**

headquarters location: This Location. **Number of employees at this location:** 450.

S.H. MEDICAL CORPORATION
2699 Collins Avenue, Suite 103, Miami Beach FL 33140. 305/672-6202. **Fax:** 305/672-9837. **Contact:** Hiring Manager. **World Wide Web address;** http://www.shmedical.com. **Description:** A medical equipment distribution and export company that sells new, refurbished, and pre-owned medical equipment. The company specializes in diagnostic equipment, endoscopy equipment and instruments, fetal monitors, medical parts, pulse oximeters, surgical instruments, and ultrasounds. **Corporate headquarters location:** This Location.

SJ NURSES
850 Hamilton Avenue, Trenton NJ 08629. 609/396-7100. **Toll-free phone:** 800/727-2476. **Fax:** 609/396-7559. **Contact:** Sally Jane Poblete, Vice President. **E-mail address:** sjpoblete@aol.com. **Description:** Provides home health care placements. **Corporate headquarters location:** This Location.

SAFESKIN CORPORATION
12671 High Bluff Drive, San Diego CA 92130. 858/794-8111. **Fax:** 858/350-2365. **Contact:** Human Resources. **World Wide Web address:** http://www.safeskin.com. **Description:** Manufactures hypo-allergenic, powder-free, latex gloves used primarily in the medical and dental industries. **Corporate headquarters location:** This Location. **International locations:** Breda, the Netherlands; Glasgow, Scotland; Hat Yai, Thailand; Ipoh, Malaysia; Munich, Germany. **Subsidiaries include:** Tactyl Technologies, Inc. (Vista CA). **Listed on:** NASDAQ. **Stock exchange symbol:** SFSK.

ST. ANTHONY REGIONAL HOSPITAL
311 South Clark Street, P.O. Box 628, Carroll IA 51401. 712/792-8232. **Fax:** 712/792-2124. **Contact:** Gina Ramaekers, Human Resources Representative. **World Wide Web address:** http://www.stanthonyhospital.org. **Description:** A nonprofit, full-service community hospital. **NOTE:** Entry-level positions and second and third shifts are offered. **Company slogan:** People caring for people. **Common positions include:** Licensed Practical Nurse; Occupational Therapist; Registered Nurse. **Educational backgrounds include:** Health Care. **Benefits:** 403(b); Dental Insurance; Disability Coverage; Employee Discounts; Flexible Schedule; Life Insurance; Medical Insurance; Savings Plan. **Corporate headquarters location:** This Location. **Listed on:** Privately held. **President/CEO:** Gary Riedmann. **Annual sales/revenues:** $11 - $20 million.

ST. BENEDICT'S SENIOR COMMUNITY
1810 Minnesota Boulevard SE, St. Cloud MN 56304-2416. 320/252-0010. **Fax:** 320/252-8611. **Contact:** Andrea Schroetke, Recruitment Coordinator. **E-mail address:** schroetkea@centracare.com. **Description:** Offers nonprofit health care and housing for older adults. St. Benedict's Senior Community also offers the Subacute Care Unit, the Special Care Unit, Hospice Care, and Respite Care. The center also operates a retirement community, an assisted living facility, income-based senior housing, a residential center for those in the early stages of Alzheimer's disease or memory loss, home care services, and a senior dining program for the residents of southeast St. Cloud. Founded in 1978. **NOTE:** Entry-level positions, part-time jobs, and second and third shifts are offered. **Company slogan:** All shall be treated as Christ. **Common positions include:** Certified Nurses Aide; Dietician/Nutritionist; Home Health

Aide; Licensed Practical Nurse; Registered Nurse; Social Worker. **Educational backgrounds include:** Health Care; Nutrition. **Benefits:** 403(b); Dental Insurance; Disability Coverage; Flexible Schedule; Life Insurance; Medical Insurance; Public Transit Available; Savings Plan; Tuition Assistance. **Special programs:** Internships; Summer Jobs. **Internship information:** Unpaid internships are offered during the fall and spring. Opportunities are available in Human Resources, working with people suffering from cognitive disorders, and social services. For more information or to volunteer, call the Volunteer Coordinator at 320/252-0010. **Office hours:** Monday - Friday, 8:00 a.m. - 4:30 p.m. **Parent company:** CentraCare Health Systems. **Number of employees at this location:** 525.

ST. CAMILLUS CAMPUS
10101 West Wisconsin Avenue, Milwaukee WI 53226. 414/258-1814. **Fax:** 414/259-7767. **Recorded jobline:** 414/259-3792. **Contact:** Pam Loveless, Human Resources Director. **Description:** A nonprofit health care center offering home health care services, supportive living, adult day services, and a subacute unit. **NOTE:** Entry-level positions and second and third shifts are offered. **Common positions include:** Certified Nurses Aide; Dietician/Nutritionist; Licensed Practical Nurse; Occupational Therapist; Physical Therapist; Registered Nurse; Speech-Language Pathologist. **Educational backgrounds include:** Health Care. **Benefits:** 403(b); Daycare Assistance; Dental Insurance; Flexible Schedule; Life Insurance; Medical Insurance; Public Transit Available; Tuition Assistance. **Special programs:** Training. **Office hours:** Monday - Friday, 8:00 a.m. - 5:00 p.m. **Corporate headquarters location:** This Location. **COO:** Rick Johnson. **Number of employees at this location:** 625.

ST. CLARE'S HOSPITAL
600 McClellan Street, Schenectady NY 12304. 518/382-2000. **Toll-free phone:** 800/462-1713. **Fax:** 518/347-5522. **Recorded jobline:** 518/382-2207. **Contact:** Peter Jones, Employment Coordinator. **E-mail address:** pjones@albanynet.com. **World Wide Web address:** http://www.stclares.org. **Description:** A 200-bed acute care hospital. St. Clare's specializes in diagnostic, medical, surgical, and therapeutic services. Founded in 1949. **NOTE:** Entry-level positions and second and third shifts are offered. **Common positions include:** Account Rep.; Blue-Collar Worker Supervisor; Buyer; Chief Financial Officer; Computer Operator; Computer Programmer; Daycare Worker; Dietician/Nutritionist; EEG Technologist; EKG Technician; Electrician; Human Resources Manager; Licensed Practical Nurse; Medical Records Technician; Nuclear Medicine Technologist; Nursing Aide; Pharmacist; Physical Therapist; Preschool Worker; Public Relations Specialist; Purchasing Agent/Manager; Radiological Technologist; Registered Nurse; Respiratory Therapist; Secretary; Social Worker; Surgical Technician; Systems Analyst; Systems Manager; Teacher/Professor. **Educational backgrounds include:** Accounting; Biology; Computer Science; Engineering; Health Care; Public Relations. **Benefits:** 403(b); Daycare Assistance; Dental Insurance; Disability Coverage; Employee Discounts; Financial Planning Assistance; Life Insurance; Medical Insurance; On-Site Daycare; Pension Plan; Public Transit Available; Savings Plan; Tuition Assistance. **Office hours:** Monday - Friday, 10:00 a.m. - 2:00 p.m. **Corporate headquarters location:** This Location. **Annual sales/revenues:** $11 - $20 million. **Number of employees at this location:** 1,150.

ST. ELIZABETH HOSPITAL
707A North 11th Street, Beaumont TX 77702. 409/899-7165. **Fax:** 409/899-7697. **Recorded jobline:** 409/899-7666. **Contact:** Human Resources. **Description:** A nonprofit, 474-bed, general acute care hospital. Founded in 1962. **NOTE:** Entry-level positions, part-time jobs, and second and third shifts are offered. **Common positions include:** Biomedical Engineer; Certified Nurses Aide; Certified Occupational Therapy Assistant; Clinical Lab Technician; Dietician/Nutritionist; EEG Technologist; EKG Technician; Electrician; Emergency Medical Technician; Health Services Manager; Home Health Aide; Human Resources Manager; Licensed Practical Nurse; Medical Records Technician; Nuclear Medicine Technologist; Nurse Practitioner; Occupational Therapist; Pharmacist; Physical Therapist; Physical Therapy Assistant; Public Relations Specialist; Radiological Technologist; Recreational Therapist; Registered Nurse; Respiratory Therapist; Secretary; Social Worker; Speech-Language Pathologist; Stationary Engineer; Surgical Technician; Typist/Word Processor. **Educational backgrounds include:** Business Administration; Computer Science; Nursing. **Benefits:** 403(b); Dental Insurance; Disability Coverage; Employee Discounts; Financial Planning Assistance; Life Insurance; Medical Insurance; Pension Plan; Savings Plan; Sick Days (11+); Tuition Assistance. **Corporate headquarters location:** Houston TX. **Listed on:** Privately held. **Number of employees at this location:** 2,600.

ST. JOHN'S HOSPITAL
800 East Carpenter Street, Springfield IL 62769. 217/525-5644. **Toll-free phone:** 800/419-2296. **Fax:** 217/525-5601. **Recorded jobline:** 217/525-5600. **Contact:** Joan Stannard, Human Resources Representative. **World Wide Web address:** http://www.st-johns.org. **Description:** A 750-bed, nonprofit, tertiary care, teaching facility affiliated with Southern Illinois University School of Medicine. **NOTE:** Entry-level positions and second and third shifts are offered. **Common positions include:** Certified Nurses Aide; Dietician/Nutritionist; Licensed Practical Nurse; Medical Records Technician; MIS Specialist; Nuclear Medicine Technologist; Occupational Therapist; Pharmacist; Physical Therapist; Radiological Technologist; Registered Nurse; Respiratory Therapist; Social Worker; Surgical Technician; Systems Analyst. **Educational backgrounds include:** Computer Science; Health Care; Nutrition. **Benefits:** 403(b); Dental Insurance; Disability Coverage; Employee Discounts; Flexible Schedule; Life Insurance; Medical Insurance; On-Site Daycare; Pension Plan; Public Transit Available; Tuition Assistance. **Corporate headquarters location:** This Location. **Other U.S. locations:** WI. **Parent company:** Hospital Sisters Health System. **CEO:** Al Laabs. **Number of employees at this location:** 3,500.

ST. JOSEPH HEALTHCARE
ST. JOSEPH MEDICAL CENTER
P.O. Box 25555, Albuquerque NM 87125. 505/727-8000. **Contact:** Cathy Haymaker, Hiring Coordinator. **World Wide Web address:** http://www.sjhs.org. **Description:** A fully integrated health care system that operates five acute care hospitals, a physical rehabilitation hospital, and several physician's facilities throughout Alburquerque. St Joseph Medical Center (also at this location) specializes in cardiology/cardiovascular, neurology, oncology, opthamology, and orthopedics. **Corporate headquarters location:** This Location.

ST. JOSEPH HOSPITAL
1404 Saint Joseph's Parkway, Houston TX 77002. 713/756-5669. **Recorded jobline:** 713/757-7433. **Contact:** Human Resources. **Description:** A 834-bed, nonprofit medical center. Founded in 1887. **NOTE:** Entry-level positions and second and third shifts are offered. **Common positions include:** Administrative Assistant; Advertising Executive; Certified Nurses Aide; Clinical Lab Technician; Computer Operator; Computer Programmer; Counselor; Daycare Worker; Editor; EEG Technologist; EKG Technician; Electrician; Emergency Medical Technician; Librarian; Licensed Practical Nurse; Medical Records Technician; Nuclear Medicine Technologist; Nurse Practitioner; Occupational Therapist; Pharmacist; Physical Therapist; Physician; Preschool Worker; Psychologist; Quality Control Supervisor; Radiological Technologist; Registered Nurse; Secretary; Social Worker; Speech-Language Pathologist; Surgical Technician; Systems Analyst; Systems Manager; Teacher/Professor. **Educational backgrounds include:** Biology; Business Administration; Chemistry; Communications; Computer Science; Economics; Engineering; Geology; Health Care; Liberal Arts; Marketing; Mathematics; Nursing; Occupational Therapy; Physical Therapy; Public Relations; Software Tech. Support. **Benefits:** 403(b); Daycare Assistance; Dental Insurance; Disability Coverage; Employee Discounts; Life Insurance; Medical Insurance; On-Site Daycare; Pension Plan; Public Transit Available; Savings Plan; Tuition Assistance. **Special programs:** Internships; Training; Co-ops. **Corporate headquarters location:** This Location. **Other U.S. locations:** AR; LA; UT.

ST. JOSEPH HOSPITAL & HEALTH CENTER
1907 West Sycamore Street, Kokomo IN 46901. 765/456-5403. **Fax:** 765/456-5823. **Contact:** Human Resources. **World Wide Web address:** http://www.stjhhc.org. **Description:** A nonprofit, acute care medical facility that offers diagnostic and therapeutic services. **NOTE:** Entry-level positions, part-time jobs, and second and third shifts are offered. **Common positions include:** Account Manager; Biomedical Engineer; Buyer; Certified Nurses Aide; Computer Operator; Emergency Medical Technician; Home Health Aide; Librarian; Licensed Practical Nurse; Medical Records Technician; Network/Systems Administrator; Nuclear Medicine Technologist; Pharmacist; Psychologist; Purchasing Agent/Manager; Radiological Technologist; Registered Nurse; Respiratory Therapist; Secretary; Social Worker; Surgical Technician; Systems Analyst. **Educational backgrounds include:** AS400 Certification; Business Administration; Computer Science; Finance; Health Care; Microsoft Office; Microsoft Word; Software Tech. Support; Spreadsheets. **Benefits:** 401(k); Casual Dress - Fridays; Dental Insurance; Disability Coverage; Employee Discounts; Financial Planning Assistance; Life Insurance; Medical Insurance; On-Site Daycare; Pension Plan; Sick Days; Tuition Assistance; Vacation Days. **Special programs:** Training. **Number of employees at this location:** 875.

ST. JUDE MEDICAL, INC.
One Lillehei Plaza, St. Paul MN 55117-9983. 651/483-2000. **Fax:** 651/482-8318. **Contact:** Human Resources. **World Wide Web address:** http://www.sjm.com. **Description:** A world leader in the development of cardiovascular medical devices. The company operates through three divisions: the Heart Valve Division, which manufactures products for the management of heart valve disease; the Cardiac Rhythm Management Division, which manufactures cardiac rhythm products; and Daig, which specializes in the manufacture of catheters. **Common positions include:** Accountant; Administrative Assistant; Attorney; Biochemist; Biological Scientist; Biomedical Engineer; Chemical Engineer; Chemist; Chief Financial Officer; Controller; Customer Service Representative; Draftsperson; Event Planner; Finance Director; Financial Analyst; Human Resources Manager; Intellectual Property Lawyer; Librarian; Manufacturing Engineer; Market Research Analyst; Marketing Manager; Mechanical Engineer; Metallurgical Engineer; Operations Manager; Quality Assurance Engineer; Sales Executive; Sales Manager; Sales Representative; Secretary; Statistician. **Benefits:** 401(k); Casual Dress - Daily; Dental Insurance; Disability Coverage; Employee Discounts; Financial Planning Assistance; Flexible Schedule; Life Insurance; Medical Insurance; Profit Sharing. **Corporate headquarters location:** This Location. **International locations:** Worldwide. **Annual sales/revenues:** More than $100 million.

ST. LOUIS CHILDREN'S HOSPITAL
4444 Forest Park Boulevard, Suite 200, St. Louis MO 63110-4871. 314/286-0910. **Fax:** 314/454-4775. **Recorded jobline:** 314/863-JOBS. **Contact:** Human Resources. **Description:** A hospital that specializes in pediatrics. **Common positions include:** Accountant/Auditor; Administrative Manager; Biomedical Engineer; Blue-Collar Worker Supervisor; Budget Analyst; Buyer; Collector; Dental Assistant/Dental Hygienist; Designer; Dietician/Nutritionist; Draftsperson; Economist; Editor; EEG Technologist; EKG Technician; Electrical/Electronics Engineer; Electrician; Emergency Medical Technician; Financial Analyst; Food Scientist/Technologist; Health Services Manager; Human Resources Manager; Industrial Engineer; Landscape Architect; Librarian; Library Technician; Medical Records Technician; Occupational Therapist; Pharmacist; Physical Therapist; Physician; Preschool Worker; Psychologist; Public Relations Specialist; Purchasing Agent/Manager; Radiological Technologist; Recreational Therapist; Registered Nurse; Respiratory Therapist; Social Worker; Speech-Language Pathologist; Stationary Engineer; Surgical Technician; Technical Writer/Editor. **Educational backgrounds include:** Accounting; Biology; Business Administration; Chemistry; Communications; Computer Science; Engineering; Finance; Marketing. **Benefits:** Dental Insurance; Disability Coverage; Employee Discounts; Life Insurance; Medical Insurance; Pension Plan; Tuition Assistance. **Parent company:** BJC Health Systems. **Number of employees at this location:** 2,300. **Number of employees nationwide:** 22,000.

ST. LOUIS REHABILITATION CENTER
5300 Arsenal Street, St. Louis MO 63139. 314/644-8000. **Contact:** Director of Human Resources. **Description:** A long-term, psychosocial rehabilitation hospital. The facility provides treatment and rehabilitation services to forensic patients committed to the Department of Mental Health as the result of a criminal offense and the diagnosis of a serious mental disorder. Specific rehabilitation programs are available for individuals with severe and persistent mental illnesses, individuals with personality disorders, and individuals requiring restoration of competence to stand trial. **Common positions include:** Certified Nurses Aide; Computer Programmer; Dietician/Nutritionist; Licensed Practical Nurse; MIS Specialist; Occupational Therapist; Psychiatrist; Psychologist; Recreational Therapist; Registered Nurse; Secretary; Social Worker; Therapist; Typist/Word Processor. **Educational backgrounds**

include: Nursing; Psychiatry; Psychology; Social Work. **Benefits:** Disability Coverage; Life Insurance; Medical Insurance; Pension Plan; Savings Plan; Vacation Days. **Corporate headquarters location:** Jefferson City MO. **Parent company:** Missouri Department of Mental Health.

ST. LUKE'S HEALTH CARE SYSTEM
2720 Stone Park Boulevard, Sioux City IA 51104. 712/279-3160. **Contact:** Human Resources. **World Wide Web address:** http://www.siouxlan.com/stlukes. **Description:** A regional health care system that operates outpatient rehabilitation centers, physician clinics, a senior living community, and a charitable foundation. The system is also affiliated with serveral area hospital. **Common positions include:** Accountant/Auditor; Administrator; Computer Programmer; Dietician/Nutritionist; Electrical/Electronics Engineer; Financial Analyst; Food Scientist/Technologist; Human Resources Manager; Instructor/Trainer; Purchasing Agent/Manager; Systems Analyst; Teacher/Professor. **Educational backgrounds include:** Accounting; Biology; Business Administration; Chemistry; Computer Science; Engineering; Finance. **Benefits:** Dental Insurance; Employee Discounts; Life Insurance; Medical Insurance; Pension Plan; Savings Plan; Stock Option; Tuition Assistance. **Special programs:** Internships. **Corporate headquarters location:** This Location.

ST. LUKE'S HOSPITAL
4500 San Pueblo Road, Jacksonville FL 32224. 904/953-2000. **Toll-free phone:** 800/336-2838. **Fax:** 904/296-3710. **Recorded jobline:** 904/296-5588. **Contact:** Human Resources. **E-mail address:** mcjhr@mayo.edu. **World Wide Web address:** http://www.mayo.edu. **Description:** Operates St. Luke's Hospital, a 289-bed, nonprofit hospital offering general acute services and specializing in medical/surgical procedures. Founded in 1873. **President/CEO:** Robert M. Walters.

ST. MARY'S HOSPITAL
56 Franklin Street, Waterbury CT 06706. 203/574-6224. **Fax:** 203/575-7753. **Contact:** Dee Anderson, Recruiter. **E-mail address:** danderson@stmh.org. **World Wide Web address:** http://www.stmh.org. **Description:** A nonprofit, full-service hospital offering behavioral health care, a famiy health center, a children's health center, a women's center, a Level II trauma center, and pediatric care. **NOTE:** Part-time jobs and second and third shifts are offered. **Common positions include:** Clinical Lab Technician; Counselor; EEG Technologist; EKG Technician; Nurse Practitioner; Pharmacist; Physician; Physician Assistant; Radiological Technologist; Registered Nurse; Respiratory Therapist; Social Worker; Surgical Technician. **Educational backgrounds include:** Health Care. **Benefits:** 401(k); Daycare Assistance; Dental Insurance; Disability Coverage; Employee Discounts; Life Insurance; Medical Insurance; On-Site Daycare; Pension Plan; Savings Plan; Tuition Assistance. **CEO:** Sister Marguerite Waite.

ST. MARY'S HOSPITAL OZAUKEE INC.
13111 North Port Washington Road, Mequon WI 53097. 262/243-7498. **Fax:** 262/243-7532. **Recorded jobline:** 414/291-1040. **Contact:** Beth Burston, Employment Coordinator. **Description:** A nonprofit, acute care hospital with affiliated clinics. **NOTE:** Entry-level positions, part-time jobs, and second and third shifts are offered. **Common positions include:** Dietician/Nutritionist; EKG Technician; Health Services Manager; Licensed Practical Nurse; Medical Records Technician; Nuclear Medicine Technologist; Occupational

Therapist; Pharmacist; Physical Therapist; Physician; Psychologist; Public Relations Specialist; Radiological Technologist; Registered Nurse; Respiratory Therapist; Social Worker; Speech-Language Pathologist; Surgical Technician. **Benefits:** 403(b); Disability Coverage; On-Site Daycare; Pension Plan; Public Transit Available. **Corporate headquarters location:** St. Louis MO. **Other U.S. locations:** Nationwide. **Parent company:** DCNHS. **Listed on:** Privately held. **Number of employees at this location:** 850.

ST. PETER'S HOSPITAL
315 South Manning Boulevard, Albany NY 12208. 518/525-1108. **Toll-free phone:** 800/451-6616. **Fax:** 518/525-1907. **Recorded jobline:** 518/525-6669. **Contact:** Christine McCarthy, Human Resources Coordinator. **Description:** A nonprofit general hospital. **NOTE:** Entry-level positions and second and third shifts are offered. **Common positions include:** Administrative Assistant; Certified Nurses Aide; Clerical Supervisor; Computer Operator; Computer Programmer; Database Manager; Dietician/Nutritionist; MIS Specialist; Occupational Therapist; Physical Therapist; Registered Nurse; Respiratory Therapist; Systems Manager. **Educational backgrounds include:** Computer Science; Health Care; Nutrition. **Benefits:** Daycare Assistance; Dental Insurance; Disability Coverage; Employee Discounts; Flexible Schedule; Job Sharing; Life Insurance; Medical Insurance; On-Site Daycare; Pension Plan; Public Transit Available; Savings Plan; Tuition Assistance. **Special programs:** Internships. **Corporate headquarters location:** This Location. **Parent company:** MercyCare.

ST. THERESE HOME
8000 Bass Lake Road, New Hope MN 55428. 763/531-5000. **Fax:** 763/531-5004. **Contact:** Jeff Mutz, Director of Human Resources. **Description:** A religious-sponsored nonprofit organization that provides long-term health care to the elderly. The company consists of a 302-bed care center, 220 units of senior housing, home care services, and a rehabilitation agency. **NOTE:** Entry-level positions and second and third shifts are offered. **Common positions include:** Certified Nurses Aide; Dietician/Nutritionist; Licensed Practical Nurse; Medical Records Technician; Occupational Therapist; Pharmacist; Physical Therapist; Registered Nurse; Social Worker; Speech-Language Pathologist; Typist/Word Processor. **Educational backgrounds include:** Health Care; Nutrition. **Benefits:** 403(b); Dental Insurance; Life Insurance; Medical Insurance; Public Transit Available; Savings Plan; Tuition Assistance. **Special programs:** Internships; Summer Jobs. **Corporate headquarters location:** This Location. **Annual sales/revenues:** $11 - $20 million. **Number of employees at this location:** 600.

ST. VINCENT HOSPITAL
455 St. Michael's Drive, Santa Fe NM 87505. 505/983-3361. **Recorded jobline:** 800/475-4578. **Contact:** Human Resources. **World Wide Web address:** http://www.stvin.org. **Description:** A 268-bed, non-affiliated, nonprofit acute care facility. Founded in 1865. **NOTE:** Entry-level positions, part-time jobs, and second and third shifts are offered. **Common positions include:** Certified Nurses Aide; Counselor; Customer Service Rep.; EEG Technologist; EKG Technician; Nuclear Medicine Technologist; Occupational Therapist; Pharmacist; Physical Therapist; Radiological Technologist; Registered Nurse; Respiratory Therapist; Secretary; Speech-Language Pathologist; Surgical Technician. **Educational backgrounds include:** Health Care; Microsoft Office. **Benefits:**

Dental Insurance; Employee Discounts; Life Insurance; Medical Insurance; Pension Plan; Sick Days; Tuition Assistance; Vacation Days. **Office hours:** Monday - Friday, 8:00 a.m. - 4:30 p.m. **Number of employees at this location:** 1,200.

SANNES SKOGDALEN
P.O. Box 177, Soldiers Grove WI 54655. 608/624-5244. **Fax:** 608/624-3478. **Contact:** Donald A. Sannes, Administrator. **Description:** A nursing home. **Common positions include:** Certified Nurses Aide; Registered Nurse. **Educational backgrounds include:** Health Care. **Benefits:** Dental Insurance; Disability Coverage; Medical Insurance; Profit Sharing. **Corporate headquarters location:** This Location. **Parent company:** Milarn Inc. **Listed on:** Privately held. **Number of employees at this location:** 90.

HENRY SCHEIN, INC.
135 Duryea Road, Melville NY 11747. 516/843-5500. **Fax:** 516/843-5658. **Contact:** Human Resources. **World Wide Web address:** http://www.henryschein.com. **Description:** Manufactures and markets health care products to office-based physicians. Henry Schein serves the dental, medical and veterinary markets. **Common positions include:** Accountant/Auditor; Advertising Clerk; Buyer; Computer Programmer; Customer Service Rep.; Dental Assistant/Dental Hygienist; Sales Representative; Systems Analyst; Telemarketer. **Benefits:** 401(k); Daycare Assistance; Dental Insurance; Disability Coverage; Employee Discounts; Life Insurance; Medical Insurance; Pension Plan. **Corporate headquarters location:** This Location. **Other U.S. locations:** Nationwide.

SCIMED LIFE SYSTEMS, INC.
2 SciMed Place, Maple Grove MN 55311. 763/494-1700. **Fax:** 763/494-2290. **Contact:** Human Resources. **World Wide Web address:** http://www.bsci.com/scimed/. **Description:** SciMed Life Systems, Inc. develops, manufactures, and markets disposable medical devices principally for the non-surgical diagnosis and treatment of coronary, peripheral, and neurovascular disease. **Common positions include:** Accountant/Auditor; Manufacturing Manager; Mechanical Engineer; Product Manager. **Educational backgrounds include:** Accounting; Engineering; Marketing. **Benefits:** 401(k); Dental Insurance; Disability Coverage; Life Insurance; Medical Insurance; Tuition Assistance. **Corporate headquarters location:** This Location.

SCOTTSDALE HEALTH CARE CORP.
3621 Wells Fargo Avenue, Scottsdale AZ 85251. 480/481-4327. **Contact:** Human Resources. **World Wide Web address:** http://www.shc.org. **Description:** A nonprofit health care organization that operates two hospitals, home health services, outpatient centers, a primary health care network, and community outreach programs. **Corporate headquarters location:** This Location. **Subsidiaries include:** Scottsdale Memorial Hospital-Osborn is a 250-bed, full-service hospital. Scottsdale Memorial Hospital-North is a 240-bed hospital.

SETON HEALTH SYSTEM
ST. MARY'S HOSPITAL OF TROY
1300 Massachusetts Avenue, Troy NY 12180. 518/268-5000. **Fax:** 518/268-5733. **Contact:** Human Resources. **World Wide Web address:** http://www.setonhealth.org. **Description:** A comprehensive health care system providing health care services to the tri-county area. St. Mary's Hospital (also at this location) is the anchor hospital for Seton Health System. **NOTE:** Entry-level

positions, part-time jobs, and second and third shifts are offered. **Common positions include:** Account Rep.; Accountant; Administrative Assistant; Administrative Manager; Blue-Collar Worker Supervisor; Budget Analyst; Buyer; Certified Nurses Aide; Chief Financial Officer; Civil Engineer; Claim Rep.; Clerical Supervisor; Computer Operator; Computer Programmer; Controller; Customer Service Rep.; Desktop Publishing Specialist; Dietician/Nutritionist; EEG Technologist; EKG Technician; Electrician; Finance Director; General Manager; Home Health Aide; Human Resources Manager; Librarian; Licensed Practical Nurse; Medical Records Technician; MIS Specialist; Network/Systems Administrator; Nuclear Medicine Technologist; Nurse Practitioner; Occupational Therapist; Pharmacist; Physical Therapist; Physical Therapy Assistant; Physician; Public Relations Specialist; Purchasing Agent/ Manager; Radiological Technologist; Registered Nurse; Respiratory Therapist; Secretary; Systems Analyst; Systems Manager; Typist/Word Processor. **Educational backgrounds include:** Accounting; Business Administration; Computer Science; Finance; Health Care; Liberal Arts; Nutrition; Public Relations. **Benefits:** 403(b); Daycare Assistance; Dental Insurance; Disability Coverage; Employee Discounts; Financial Planning Assistance; Flexible Schedule; Job Sharing; Life Insurance; Medical Insurance; Pension Plan; Public Transit Available; Savings Plan; Tuition Assistance. **Corporate headquarters location:** This Location.

SHAMOKIN AREA COMMUNITY HOSPITAL
4200 Hospital Road, Coal Township PA 17866. 570/644-4200. **Fax:** 570/644-4338. **Contact:** Mrs. Kirby Wilson, Vice President of Human Resources. **E-mail address:** kwilson@shamokinhospital.org. **World Wide Web address:** http://www.shamokinhospital.org. **Description:** A 61-bed nonprofit, community hospital offering acute care, general surgery, subacute and outpatient rehabilitation, inpatient and partial hospitalization care for geriatric-psychiatric patients, 24-hour emergency services, occupational health, specialty clinics and community health programs. Founded in 1912. **NOTE:** Entry-level positions, part-time jobs, and second and third shifts are offered. **Company slogan:** Quality care close to home. **Common positions include:** Accountant; Certified Nurses Aide; Certified Occupational Therapy Assistant; Chief Financial Officer; Clinical Lab Technician; Dietician/Nutritionist; Education Administrator; Emergency Medical Technician; Licensed Practical Nurse; Medical Assistant; Medical Records Technician; Nuclear Medicine Technologist; Pharmacist; Physical Therapist; Physical Therapy Assistant; Physician; Physician Assistant; Radiological Technologist; Registered Nurse; Respiratory Therapist; Secretary; Social Worker; Surgical Technician; Systems Manager. **Educational backgrounds include:** Accounting; Health Care; Microsoft Office. **Benefits:** 403(b); Disability Coverage; Employee Discounts; Life Insurance; Medical Insurance; Savings Plan; Sick Days (1 - 5); Tuition Assistance; Vacation Days (1 - 5). **Special programs:** Summer Jobs. **Office hours:** Monday - Friday, 8:00 a.m. - 5:00 p.m. **Corporate headquarters location:** This Location. **Other U.S. locations:** Elysburg PA. **Subsidiaries include:** Northumberland Health Services. **President/CEO:** John P. Wiercinski. **Annual sales/revenues:** $21 - $50 million. **Number of employees at this location:** 285.

SHANNON MEDICAL CENTER
MEMORIAL CAMPUS
120 East Harris Avenue, San Angelo TX 76903. 915/657-5243. **Fax:** 915/481-8521. **Recorded**

jobline: 915/657-5298. **Contact:** Joyce Duncan, Employment Manager. **E-mail address:** joyceduncan@shannonhealth.com. **World Wide Web address:** http://www.shannonhealth.com. **Description:** A 274-bed, nonprofit hospital offering surgery, intensive care, orthopedic, oncology, telemetry, skilled nursing, and cardiac services. Shannon Medical Center also cooperates a Level II trauma and sleep disorder center. Founded in 1932. **NOTE:** Entry-level positions and second and third shifts are offered. **Common positions include:** Accountant; Buyer; Certified Nurses Aide; Clerical Supervisor; Clinical Lab Technician; Computer Operator; Computer Programmer; Dietician/ Nutritionist; Emergency Medical Technician; Human Resources Manager; Licensed Practical Nurse; Marketing Specialist; Medical Records Technician; Nuclear Medicine Technologist; Occupational Therapist; Pharmacist; Physical Therapist; Physician; Public Relations Specialist; Radiological Technologist; Registered Nurse; Respiratory Therapist; Secretary; Social Worker; Speech-Language Pathologist; Surgical Technician. **Educational backgrounds include:** Health Care. **Benefits:** 401(k); Casual Dress - Fridays; Dental Insurance; Disability Coverage; Employee Discounts; Life Insurance; Medical Insurance; Pension Plan; Tuition Assistance. **Special programs:** Training. **Office hours:** Monday - Friday, 8:00 a.m. - 5:00 p.m. **Corporate headquarters location:** This Location. **Annual sales/revenues:** $51 - $100 million. **Number of employees at this location:** 1,500.

SHARON HOSPITAL, INC.
50 Hospital Hill Road, P.O. Box 789, Sharon CT 06069-0789. 860/364-4080. **Contact:** Human Resources. **World Wide Web address:** http://www. sharon.org. **Description:** A full-service hospital. **NOTE:** Entry-level positions and second and third shifts are offered. **Company slogan:** Quality health care for our community. **Common positions include:** Accountant; Administrative Assistant; Budget Analyst; Certified Nurses Aide; Chief Financial Officer; Clinical Lab Technician; Computer Operator; Controller; Customer Service Representative; Dietician/Nutritionist; EEG Technologist; EKG Technician; Emergency Medical Technician; Human Resources Manager; Marketing Manager; Medical Records Technician; MIS Specialist; Nuclear Medicine Technologist; Occupational Therapist; Physical Therapist; Physician; Radiological Technologist; Registered Nurse; Respiratory Therapist; Secretary; Social Worker; Speech-Language Pathologist; Surgical Technician. **Benefits:** 403(b); Daycare Assistance; Dental Insurance; Disability Coverage; Employee Discounts; Financial Planning Assistance; Life Insurance; Medical Insurance; On-Site Daycare; Pension Plan; Savings Plan; Tuition Assistance. **Special programs:** Internships; Summer Jobs. **Office hours:** Monday - Friday, 8:00 a.m. - 4:30 p.m. **Corporate headquarters location:** This Location. **President:** James E. Sok.

SHARON REGIONAL HEALTH SYSTEM
740 East State Street, Sharon PA 16146. 724/983-3911. **Contact:** Human Resources. **World Wide Web address:** http://www.sharonregional.com. **Description:** A comprehensive health care system that offers a variety of clinical programs and services. **Common positions include:** Certified Nurses Aide; Certified Occupational Therapy Assistant; Dietician/Nutritionist; Licensed Practical Nurse; Medical Records Technician; Nuclear Medicine Technologist; Nurse Practitioner; Occupational Therapist; Pharmacist; Physical Therapist; Physical Therapy Assistant; Radiological Technologist; Registered Nurse; Respiratory

Therapist; Speech-Language Pathologist; Surgical Technician.

SHARP HEALTHCARE
8695 Spectrum Center Court, San Diego CA 92123. 858/499-4000. **Fax:** 858/499-5938. **Contact:** Human Resources. **E-mail address:** sharpjob@ sharp.com. **World Wide Web address:** http://www. sharp.com. **Description:** A nonprofit organization consisting of six acute care hospitals, one specialty women's hospital, three medical groups, medical clinics, urgent care centers, skilled nursing facilities, and a variety of other community health education programs and related services. Founded in 1954. **NOTE:** Second and third shifts are offered. **Common positions include:** Account Rep.; Accountant; Auditor; Budget Analyst; Certified Nurses Aide; Chief Financial Officer; Claim Representative; Clerical Supervisor; Clinical Lab Technician; Computer Operator; Computer Programmer; Controller; Customer Service Rep.; Dietician/Nutritionist; EEG Technologist; EKG Technician; Financial Analyst; Human Resources Manager; Licensed Practical Nurse; Medical Records Technician; Nuclear Medicine Technologist; Occupational Therapist; Pharmacist; Physical Therapist; Physician; Public Relations Specialist; Registered Nurse; Respiratory Therapist; Secretary; Social Worker; Speech-Language Pathologist; Surgical Technician; Systems Analyst; Systems Manager; Typist/Word Processor. **Educational backgrounds include:** Accounting; Computer Science; Finance; Health Care. **Benefits:** Dental Insurance; Disability Coverage; Employee Discounts; Flexible Schedule; Life Insurance; Medical Insurance; Pension Plan; Tuition Assistance. **Office hours:** Monday - Friday, 7:00 a.m. - 7:00 p.m. **Corporate headquarters location:** This Location.

SHELTERING ARMS REHABILITATION HOSPITAL
1311 Palmyra Avenue, Richmond VA 23227. 804/342-4350. **Fax:** 804/342-4316. **Contact:** Pam Thornton, Director of Personnel. **World Wide Web address:** http://www.shelteringarms.com. **Description:** A nonprofit hospital providing comprehensive services to individuals with physical and cognitive disabilities. **Common positions include:** Certified Nurses Aide; Computer Programmer; Controller; Dietician/Nutritionist; Education Administrator; EEG Technologist; EKG Technician; Human Resources Manager; MIS Specialist; Nuclear Medicine Technologist; Physical Therapist; Physician; Psychologist; Public Relations Specialist; Quality Control Supervisor; Registered Nurse; Respiratory Therapist; Secretary; Social Worker; Speech-Language Pathologist. **Educational backgrounds include:** Business Administration; Health Care. **Benefits:** 403(b); Dental Insurance; Employee Discounts; Financial Planning Assistance; Flexible Schedule; Life Insurance; Medical Insurance; Pension Plan. **Office hours:** Monday - Friday, 8:00 a.m. - 4:30 p.m. **Corporate headquarters location:** This Location.

SHENANDOAH MEMORIAL HOSPITAL
300 Pershing Avenue, Shenandoah IA 51601. 712/246-1230. **Fax:** 712/246-7357. **Contact:** Human Resource Director. **World Wide Web address:** http://www.shenandoahmedcenter.com. **Description:** A nonprofit hospital offering acute care, outpatient services, skilled nursing, long-term care, and home health services. **NOTE:** Entry-level positions and second and third shifts are offered. **Common positions include:** Accountant; Administrative Assistant; Blue-Collar Worker Supervisor; Certified Nurses Aide; Chief Financial Officer; Clinical Lab Technician; Computer

Operator; Controller; Customer Service Rep.; Dietician/Nutritionist; Emergency Medical Technician; Finance Director; Human Resources Manager; Licensed Practical Nurse; Mechanical Engineer; Medical Records Technician; Physician; Public Relations Specialist; Purchasing Agent/Manager; Registered Nurse; Secretary; Social Worker; Surgical Technician; Typist/Word Processor. **Educational backgrounds include:** Accounting; Business Administration; Finance; Health Care. **Benefits:** 403(b); Dental Insurance; Disability Coverage; Employee Discounts; Flexible Schedule; Medical Insurance; Pension Plan; Savings Plan; Tuition Assistance. **Special programs:** Summer Jobs. **Office hours:** Monday - Friday, 8:00 a.m. - 4:30 p.m. **Corporate headquarters location:** This Location. **CEO:** Chuck Millburg. **Annual sales/revenues:** $5 - $10 million.

SHOSHONE MEDICAL CENTER
Three Jacobs Gulch, Kellogg ID 83837. 208/784-1221. **Fax:** 208/784-0961. **Contact:** Sheryl Bewick, Employee Services Coordinator. **Description:** A nonprofit, 36-bed, acute care facility. Shoshone Medical Center has an obstetrics unit, 24-hour emergency services, a walk-in immediate care center open 365 days per year, primary and specialty care physicians clinics, North Idaho Addiction Recovery Center, and Healthworks Fitness Center. Founded in 1958. **Common positions include:** Accountant; Administrative Assistant; Applications Engineer; AS400 Programmer Analyst; Certified Nurses Aide; Chief Financial Officer; Clinical Lab Technician; Counselor; Environmental Engineer; Home Health Aide; Human Resources Manager; Licensed Practical Nurse; Medical Assistant; Medical Records Technician; Medical Secretary; Occupational Therapist; Pharmacist; Physical Therapist; Physical Therapy Assistant; Physician; Physician Assistant; Purchasing Agent/Manager; Quality Assurance Engineer; Radiological Technologist; Registered Nurse; Respiratory Therapist; Secretary; Social Worker; Speech-Language Pathologist; Typist/Word Processor. **Educational backgrounds include:** Health Care. **Benefits:** 401(k); Dental Insurance; Disability Coverage; Financial Planning Assistance; Life Insurance; Medical Insurance; Paid Holidays; Relocation Assistance; Sick Days; Vacation Days. **Corporate headquarters location:** This Location. **CEO:** Gary Moore. **Number of employees at this location:** 165.

SHRINER'S HOSPITAL FOR CHILDREN
2001 South Lindbergh Boulevard, St. Louis MO 63131. 314/432-3600. **Fax:** 314/872-7873. **Recorded jobline:** 314/872-7852. **Contact:** Louis Pounds, Employment & Benefits Manager. **E-mail address:** lpounds@shrinenet.org. **World Wide Web address:** http://www.shriners.com. **Description:** A nonprofit hospital providing free care, inpatient services, and outpatient services for orthopedically handicapped children. **NOTE:** Entry-level positions, part-time jobs, and second and third shifts are offered. **Common positions include:** Accountant; Administrative Assistant; Buyer; Certified Nurses Aide; Clinical Lab Technician; Computer Technician; Counselor; Dietician/Nutritionist; Finance Director; Graphic Artist; Human Resources Manager; Licensed Practical Nurse; Medical Assistant; Medical Records Technician; Medical Secretary; Nurse Practitioner; Occupational Therapist; Pharmacist; Physical Therapist; Physician; Physician Assistant; Psychologist; Public Relations Specialist; Quality Control Supervisor; Radiological Technologist; Registered Nurse; Respiratory Therapist; Secretary; Social Worker; Surgical Technician; Transportation/

Traffic Specialist; Typist/Word Processor. **Educational backgrounds include:** Accounting; Business Administration; Computer Science; Health Care; Nursing. **Benefits:** 403(b); Casual Dress - Daily; Daycare Assistance; Dental Insurance; Disability Coverage; Job Sharing; Life Insurance; Medical Insurance; Pension Plan; Sick Days; Vacation Days. **Corporate headquarters location:** Tampa FL. **Listed on:** Privately held.

SIBLEY MEMORIAL HOSPITAL
5255 Loughboro Road NW, Washington DC 20016. 202/537-4750. **Fax:** 202/363-2677. **Recorded jobline:** 202/364-8665. **Contact:** Andrea Fricke, Employment Manager. **World Wide Web address:** http://www.sibley.org. **Description:** A nonprofit, full-service community hospital. Founded in 1890. **NOTE:** Second and third shifts are offered. **Common positions include:** Biomedical Engineer; Clinical Lab Technician; Licensed Practical Nurse; Medical Records Technician; Nuclear Medicine Technologist; Occupational Therapist; Pharmacist; Physical Therapist; Physician; Radiological Technologist; Registered Nurse; Respiratory Therapist; Systems Analyst. **Educational backgrounds include:** Health Care. **Benefits:** 403(b); Dental Insurance; Disability Coverage; Employee Discounts; Life Insurance; Medical Insurance; Pension Plan; Tuition Assistance. **Special programs:** Summer Jobs. **Corporate headquarters location:** This Location. **Number of employees at this location:** 1,200.

SIEMENS MEDICAL
186 Wood Avenue South, Iselin NJ 08830. 732/321-4500. **Contact:** Personnel Office. **World Wide Web address:** http://www.sms.siemens.com. **Description:** Develops, manufactures, and sells medical systems including digital X-rays and 3-D ultrasound equipment. Products are used in a variety of areas including cardiology, audiology, surgery, critical care, and oncology. **Corporate headquarters location:** This Location.

SIEMENS MEDICAL SYSTEMS
4040 Nelson Avenue, Concord CA 94520. 925/246-8200. **Contact:** Employment Representative. **World Wide Web address:** http://www.siemens.com. **Description:** Engaged in the design and manufacture of medical linear accelerators for use in radiation therapy. **Common positions include:** Electrical/Electronics Engineer; Mechanical Engineer; Physicist; Software Engineer; Technical Writer/Editor. **Educational backgrounds include:** Computer Science; Engineering; Physics. **Corporate headquarters location:** This Location. **Parent company:** Siemens A.G. (Berlin, Germany).

SIMS DELTEC, INC.
1265 Grey Fox Road, St. Paul MN 55112-6967. 651/633-2556. **Contact:** Human Resources. **World Wide Web address:** http://www.deltec.com. **Description:** Manufactures and markets ambulatory infustion systems, large volume infusion pumps, and vascular access systems. **Corporate headquarters location:** This Location.

SOUTHERN CHESTER COUNTY MEDICAL CENTER
1015 West Baltimore Pike, West Grove PA 19390. 610/869-1000. **Fax:** 610/869-1246. **Recorded jobline:** 610/869-1200. **Contact:** Employment Coordinator. **World Wide Web address:** http://www.sccmc.com. **Description:** A 75-bed, nonprofit acute care medical center that offers a surgery/ER center, an intensive care unit, and maternity and outpatient services. The hospital also operates Jenner's Pond, an independent and assisted living retirement community. Founded in 1920.

NOTE: Entry-level positions, part-time jobs, and second and third shifts are offered. **Common positions include:** Certified Nurses Aide; Dietician/Nutritionist; EKG Technician; Emergency Medical Technician; Home Health Aide; Human Resources Manager; Medical Records Technician; Occupational Therapist; Pharmacist; Physical Therapist; Physical Therapy Assistant; Physician; Psychologist; Radiological Technologist; Registered Nurse; Respiratory Therapist; Social Worker; Surgical Technician. **Educational backgrounds include:** Accounting; Business Administration; Finance; Health Care; Marketing. **Benefits:** 403(b); Dental Insurance; Disability Coverage; Employee Discounts; Flexible Schedule; Life Insurance; Medical Insurance; Pension Plan; Sick Days; Tuition Assistance; Vacation Days. **Special programs:** Summer Jobs. **Number of employees at this location:** 600.

SOUTHERN ILLINOIS HEALTHCARE
405 West Jackson Street, Carbondale IL 62902. 618/457-5200. **Contact:** Human Resources. **World Wide Web address:** http://www.sih.net. **Description:** A nonprofit, multihospital health care corporation that operates six hospitals, rural clinics, home health care services, and community outreach programs. **Common positions include:** Accountant/Auditor; Biomedical Engineer; Clinical Lab Technician; Computer Programmer; EEG Technologist; EKG Technician; Health Services Manager; Licensed Practical Nurse; Medical Records Technician; Nuclear Medicine Technologist; Occupational Therapist; Pharmacist; Physical Therapist; Radiological Technologist; Registered Nurse; Respiratory Therapist; Speech-Language Pathologist; Surgical Technician. **Benefits:** Daycare Assistance; Dental Insurance; Disability Coverage; Employee Discounts; Life Insurance; Medical Insurance; Pension Plan; Savings Plan; Tuition Assistance. **Corporate headquarters location:** This Location. **Number of employees at this location:** 1,400.

SOUTHPOINTE HOSPITAL
2639 Miami Street, St. Louis MO 63118. 314/268-6000. **Fax:** 314/577-5808. **Contact:** Human Resources. **World Wide Web address:** http://www.southpointehospital.com. **Description:** A general, acute care medical center. **Common positions include:** Dietician/Nutritionist; Medical Technologist; Occupational Therapist; Physical Therapist; Registered Nurse. **Educational backgrounds include:** Nursing; Physical Therapy. **Benefits:** Dental Insurance; Disability Coverage; Employee Discounts; Life Insurance; Medical Insurance; Pension Plan; Profit Sharing; Tuition Assistance. **Corporate headquarters location:** Los Angeles CA. **Listed on:** New York Stock Exchange.

SOUTHWOOD PSYCHIATRIC HOSPITAL
2575 Boyce Plaza Road, Pittsburgh PA 15241. 412/257-2290. **Contact:** Dorothy Scanlon, Human Resources Manager. **World Wide Web address:** http://www.southwoodhospital.com. **Description:** A psychiatric hospital that offers inpatient and outpatient care to adolescents suffering from psychiatric disorders. **NOTE:** Entry-level positions are offered. **Common positions include:** Registered Nurse; Social Worker; Teacher/Professor. **Educational backgrounds include:** Health Care. **Benefits:** 401(k); Dental Insurance; Life Insurance; Medical Insurance. **Corporate headquarters location:** This Location. **Parent company:** Lakewood Psychiatric Hospital.

SPACELABS MEDICAL, INC.
P.O. Box 97013, Redmond WA 98073-9713. 425/882-3700. **Physical address:** 15220 NE 40th Street, Redmond WA. **Contact:** Human Resources. **E-mail address:** resumes@slmd.com. **World Wide Web address:** http://www.spacelabs.com. **Description:** Manufactures patient monitoring equipment, clinical information systems, ambulatory monitoring products, and monitoring supplies. **Common positions include:** Account Rep.; Accountant/Auditor; Accounting Supervisor; Administrative Manager; Assembler; Assembly Worker; Biomedical Engineer; Bookkeeper; Business Development Manager; Buyer; Clerk; Clinical Applications Specialist; Computer Operator; Computer Programmer; Contract/Grant Administrator; Controller; Customer Service Representative; Design Engineer; Dispatcher; EKG Technician; Electrical/Electronics Engineer; Executive Assistant; Factory Repair Manager; Field Engineer; Financial Analyst; Financial Manager; Hardware Engineer; Human Resources Manager; Inspector/Tester/Grader; Machine Operator; Manufacturing Engineer; Market Research Analyst; Mechanical Engineer; MIS Manager; Order Clerk; Payroll Clerk; Precision Assembler; Product Manager; Project Manager; Purchasing Agent/Manager; Receptionist; Research Manager; Safety Engineer; Sales Executive; Sales Representative; Secretary; Software Developer; Software Engineer; Stock Clerk; Systems Analyst; Systems Specialist; Technical Support Engineer; Technical Writer/Editor; Technician; Telecommunications Analyst; Telemarketer. **Educational backgrounds include:** Accounting; Bachelor of Arts; BSEE; Business Administration; Computer Science; CPA; Engineering; Excel; Finance; Marketing; MBA; Nursing; Oracle. **Benefits:** Dental Insurance; Disability Coverage; Life Insurance; Medical Insurance; Pension Plan; Savings Plan; Tuition Assistance. **Corporate headquarters location:** This Location. **Other U.S. locations:** AZ; CA; CO; FL; NC; NY; OR. **Number of employees at this location:** 1,200. **Number of employees nationwide:** 1,700.

SPAN-AMERICA MEDICAL SYSTEMS
P.O. Box 5231, Greenville SC 29606. 864/288-8877. **Toll-free phone:** 800/888-6752. **Fax:** 864/288-8692. **Contact:** Marie Sitter, Vice President of Human Resources. **World Wide Web address:** http://www.spanamerica.com. **Description:** Manufactures and distributes a variety of polyurethane foam products for the health care, consumer, and industrial markets. The company's principal health care products consist of polyurethane foam mattress overlays including its Geo-Matt overlay, therapeutic replacement mattresses, patient positioners, and single-use flexible packaging products. These products are marketed primarily to hospitals but are also marketed to long-term care facilities in the United States. Span-America's specialty products are sold under the trademark Span-Aids, which consists of over 300 different foam items that relieve the basic patient positioning problems of elevation, immobilization, muscle contraction, foot drop, and foot or leg rotation. Founded in 1970. **Corporate headquarters location:** This Location.

SPARROW HEALTH SYSTEM
1215 East Michigan Avenue, Lansing MI 48912. 517/364-5858. **Fax:** 517/364-5818. **Contact:** Human Resources. **World Wide Web address:** http://www.sparrow.com. **Description:** A nonprofit, community health care system. **Corporate headquarters location:** This Location.

THE SPECTRANETICS CORPORATION
96 Talamine Court, Colorado Springs CO 80907. 719/633-8333. **Toll-free phone:** 800/633-0960. **Fax:** 719/633-2248. **Contact:** Human Resources.

World Wide Web address: http://www. spectranetics.com. **Description:** Researches, develops, manufactures, services, supports, and sells medical lasers and attendant catheters used in heart surgery. **Common positions include:** Account Manager; Accountant; Administrative Assistant; Biomedical Engineer; Buyer; Chief Financial Officer; Controller; Customer Service Rep.; Human Resources Manager; Manufacturing Engineer; Marketing Manager; Mechanical Engineer; MIS Specialist; Sales Executive. **Educational backgrounds include:** Engineering. **Benefits:** 401(k); Dental Insurance; Disability Coverage; Flexible Schedule; Life Insurance; Medical Insurance. **Corporate headquarters location:** This Location. **Other U.S. locations:** Nationwide. **International locations:** Worldwide. **Listed on:** NASDAQ. **Number of employees at this location:** 75. **Number of employees nationwide:** 140.

SPECTRUM HEALTHCARE SERVICES
12647 Olive Boulevard, St. Louis MO 63141. 314/919-9500. **Toll-free phone:** 800/325-3982. **Fax:** 314/919-8903. **Recorded jobline:** 314/919-9547. **Contact:** Human Resources. **World Wide Web address:** http://www.spectrumhealth.com. **Description:** A leading clinical management company that provides outpatient services in emergency care. Spectrum offers health care and administrative management services to hospitals, physicians, clinics, managed care programs, insurers, businesses, and government entities. **NOTE:** Entry-level positions are offered. **Common positions include:** Accountant; Chief Financial Officer; Claim Rep.; Computer Programmer; Controller; Database Manager; Financial Analyst; Human Resources Manager; Marketing Manager; Marketing Specialist; MIS Specialist; Paralegal; Public Relations Specialist; Purchasing Agent/Manager; Sales Executive; Sales Rep.; Software Engineer; Systems Analyst; Telecommunications Manager. **Educational backgrounds include:** Accounting; Business Administration; Computer Science; Finance; Health Care. **Benefits:** 401(k); Daycare Assistance; Dental Insurance; Disability Coverage; Employee Discounts; Life Insurance; Medical Insurance; Tuition Assistance. **Special programs:** Internships; Training. **Corporate headquarters location:** This Location. **Other U.S. locations:** Nationwide.

SPRINGFIELD HOSPITAL
P.O. Box 2003, 25 Ridgewood Road, Springfield VT 05156. 802/885-2999. **Fax:** 802/885-3959. **Contact:** Susan Pare, Human Resources Assistant. **World Wide Web address:** http://www. springfieldhospital.org. **Description:** A full-service, nonprofit, voluntary hospital. **NOTE:** Entry-level positions and second and third shifts are offered. **Common positions include:** Account Manager; Account Rep.; Accountant; Administrative Assistant; Biomedical Engineer; Budget Analyst; Certified Nurses Aide; Clinical Lab Technician; Computer Operator; Controller; Daycare Worker; Dietician/Nutritionist; Electrician; Finance Director; Human Resources Manager; Medical Records Technician; MIS Specialist; Nuclear Medicine Technologist; Occupational Therapist; Pharmacist; Physical Therapist; Physician; Preschool Worker; Public Relations Specialist; Purchasing Agent/ Manager; Radiological Technologist; Registered Nurse; Respiratory Therapist; Secretary; Social Worker. **Benefits:** 403(b); Dental Insurance; Disability Coverage; Employee Discounts; Financial Planning Assistance; Flexible Schedule; Job Sharing; Life Insurance; Medical Insurance; On-Site Daycare; Pension Plan; Tuition Assistance. **Special programs:** Apprenticeships; Summer Jobs. **Corporate headquarters location:** This Location.

STAAR SURGICAL COMPANY
1911 Walker Avenue, Monrovia CA 91016. 626/303-7902. **Contact:** Human Resources. **World Wide Web address:** http://www.staar.com. **Description:** Develops, manufactures, and markets ophthalmic medical devices. The company's main product is a foldable lens used in the treatment of cataracts. Founded in 1982. **Corporate headquarters location:** This Location. **Listed on:** NASDAQ. **Stock exchange symbol:** STAA. **President:** John Wolf.

STAFF BUILDERS HOME HEALTH
1983 Marcus Avenue, Suite 200, Lake Success NY 11042. 516/358-1000. **Fax:** 516/358-2465. **Contact:** Recruiter. **World Wide Web address:** http://www.staffbuilders.com. **Description:** A home health care agency. **Common positions include:** Accountant; Budget Analyst; Claim Representative; Clerical Supervisor; Computer Programmer; Credit Manager; Dietician/Nutritionist; Financial Analyst; Licensed Practical Nurse; Medical Records Technician; Purchasing Agent/Manager; Registered Nurse; Systems Analyst. **Educational backgrounds include:** Accounting; Biology; Business Administration; Communications; Computer Science; Finance; Liberal Arts. **Benefits:** 401(k); Dental Insurance; Disability Coverage; Employee Discounts; Life Insurance; Medical Insurance; Profit Sharing. **Corporate headquarters location:** This Location. **Other U.S. locations:** Nationwide.

STERIS CORPORATION
5960 Heisley Road, Mentor OH 44060-1834. 440/354-2600. **Toll-free phone:** 800/548-4873. **Fax:** 440/354-7043. **Contact:** Human Resources. **World Wide Web address:** http://www.steris.com. **Description:** A leading provider of infection prevention products, contamination control, and surgical support systems and products to health care, scientific, research, and industrial customers worldwide. Founded in 1987. **NOTE:** Entry-level positions and second and third shifts are offered. **Common positions include:** Account Manager; Accountant; Buyer; Chemist; Customer Service Representative; Draftsperson; Electrical/Electronics Engineer; Human Resources Manager; Manufacturing Engineer; Mechanical Engineer; Sales Rep.; Secretary; Software Engineer; Systems Analyst. **Educational backgrounds include:** Accounting; Biology; Business Administration; Chemistry; Computer Science; Engineering; Finance; Marketing; Software Tech. Support. **Benefits:** 401(k); Dental Insurance; Disability Coverage; Life Insurance; Medical Insurance; Savings Plan; Tuition Assistance. **Office hours:** Monday - Friday, 8:00 a.m. - 5:00 p.m. **Corporate headquarters location:** This Location. **Other U.S. locations:** Nationwide. **International locations:** Worldwide. **Subsidiaries include:** Amsco International, Inc.; Iosmedix, Inc. **Listed on:** New York Stock Exchange. **Stock exchange symbol:** STE. **Annual sales/revenues:** $51 - $100 million. **Number of employees at this location:** 585. **Number of employees worldwide:** 4,000.

STEVENS COMMUNITY MEDICAL CENTER
400 East First Street, Box 660, Morris MN 56267. 320/589-1313. **Fax:** 320/589-3533. **Contact:** Karla Larson, Personnel Director. **Description:** A nonprofit, multispecialty clinic and hospital serving the west central Minnesota region. Founded in 1951. **Company slogan:** Caring is our reason for being. **Common positions include:** Certified Nurses Aide; Clinical Lab Technician; Counselor; Customer Service Representative; Home Health Aide; Licensed Practical Nurse; Medical Secretary; Physician; Psychologist; Radiological Technologist; Registered Nurse; Respiratory Therapist; Secretary;

Social Worker; Surgical Technician. **Educational backgrounds include:** Health Care. **Benefits:** 403(b); Dental Insurance; Disability Coverage; Life Insurance; Medical Insurance; Pension Plan. **Corporate headquarters location:** This Location. **President/CEO:** John Rau.

STRAUB CLINIC & HOSPITAL, INC.
888 South King Street, Honolulu HI 96813. 808/522-4000. **Fax:** 808/522-4425. **Recorded jobline:** 808/592-9675x5000. **Contact:** Diane Wataoka, Human Resources. **E-mail address:** dwataoka@straub.net. **Description:** A private, nonprofit hospital and clinic. Straub Clinic & Hospital is one of the oldest and largest private medical practices in Hawaii, with approximately 150 physicians and a 159-bed hospital. The main clinic and seven satellite clinics are located on Oahu. The hospital offers several specialty programs including anesthesiology/pain relief, a burn unit, cardiovascular imaging and intervention, a coronary care unit, emergency services, a home health agency, an intensive care unit, medical/surgical care, rehabilitation therapy, and respiratory care. The clinic services most medical fields including cardiology/cardiovascular surgery; family practice; geriatric medicine; ear, nose, and throat; obstetrics/gynecology; oncology/hematology; sports medicine and rehabilitation; and radiology. Straub offers its own managed care plan. Founded in 1921. **Common positions include:** Claim Representative; Clinical Lab Technician; Computer Programmer; Customer Service Representative; Licensed Practical Nurse; Physical Therapist; Physician; Radiological Technologist; Registered Nurse; Respiratory Therapist; Social Worker; Surgical Technician; Systems Analyst. **Educational backgrounds include:** Accounting; Business Administration; Finance; Health Care. **Benefits:** 401(k); Credit Union; Daycare Assistance; Dental Insurance; Disability Coverage; Employee Discounts; Life Insurance; Medical Insurance; Tuition Assistance. **Office hours:** Tuesday and Thursday, 8:00 a.m. - 4:30 p.m. **Corporate headquarters location:** This Location. **Listed on:** Privately held. **CEO:** Dr. Blake Waterhouse. **Number of employees at this location:** 2,000.

STRYKER CORPORATION
P.O. Box 4085, Kalamazoo MI 49003-4085. 616/385-2600. **Toll-free phone:** 800/726-2725. **Fax:** 616/385-1062. **Contact:** Human Resources. **World Wide Web address:** http://www.strykercorp.com. **Description:** Develops, manufactures, and markets specialty surgical and medical products including endoscopic systems, orthopedic implants, powered surgical instruments, and patient care and handling equipment for the global market. Stryker also provides outpatient physical therapy services in the United States. **Common positions include:** Accountant; Administrative Assistant; Administrative Manager; Attorney; Chief Financial Officer; Controller; Database Administrator; Finance Director; Financial Analyst; Human Resources Manager; Network/ Systems Administrator; Paralegal; Vice President of Finance. **Educational backgrounds include:** Accounting; AS400 Certification; C/C++; CGI; Cold Fusion; Finance; Frame Maker; HTML; Internet Development; Java; MBA; Microsoft Office; Microsoft Word; Novell; Software Development; Software Tech. Support; Spreadsheets. **Benefits:** 401(k); Casual Dress - Daily; Dental Insurance; Disability Coverage; Job Sharing; Life Insurance; Medical Insurance; Pension Plan; Profit Sharing; Public Transit Available; Relocation Assistance; Tuition Assistance. **Special programs:** Internships. **Office hours:** Monday -

Friday, 8:00 a.m. - 5:00 p.m. **Corporate headquarters location:** This Location. **Other U.S. locations:** Santa Clara CA; Allendale NJ; Rutherford NJ. **International locations:** Worldwide. **Subsidiaries include:** Howmedica Osteonics. **Listed on:** New York Stock Exchange. **Stock exchange symbol:** SYK. **President/CEO:** John W. Brown. **Annual sales/revenues:** More than $100 million.

SUBURBAN OSTOMY
75 October Hill Road, Holliston MA 01746. 508/429-1000. **Fax:** 508/429-6669. **Contact:** Amy Francer, Human Resources Assistant. **Description:** A wholesale distributor of medical supplies including ostomy dressings, wound care products, respiratory products, and enteral feeding products. **NOTE:** Entry-level positions and part-time jobs are offered. **Common positions include:** Account Manager; Account Representative; Accountant; Advertising Executive; Applications Engineer; Budget Analyst; Buyer; Chief Financial Officer; Computer Operator; Computer Programmer; Controller; Customer Service Representative; Database Administrator; Desktop Publishing Specialist; Graphic Artist; Graphic Designer; Human Resources Manager; Marketing Manager; MIS Specialist; Network Administrator; Operations Manager; Public Relations Specialist; Sales Manager; Sales Representative; Systems Manager. **Educational backgrounds include:** Accounting; Business Administration; Communications; Computer Science; Finance; Health Care; HTML; Internet; Marketing; Microsoft Word; Public Relations; QuarkXPress; Spreadsheets; Visual Basic. **Benefits:** 401(k); Casual Dress - Fridays; Dental Insurance; Disability Coverage; Employee Discounts; Life Insurance; Medical Insurance; Profit Sharing; Tuition Assistance. **Special programs:** Training; Summer Jobs. **Office hours:** Monday - Friday, 8:00 a.m. - 5:30 p.m. **Corporate headquarters location:** Elyria OH. **Parent company:** Invacare Corporation. **Listed on:** NASDAQ; New York Stock Exchange. **Number of employees at this location:** 100.

SUN HEALTHCARE GROUP, INC.
101 Sun Avenue NE, Albuquerque NM 87109. 505/821-3355. **Contact:** Human Resources. **World Wide Web address:** http://www.sunh.com. **Description:** A comprehensive health care system that operates hospitals, clinics, ambulatory services, and in home and long term patient care services. **Corporate headquarters location:** This Location. **Subsidiaries include:** Sunrise Health Care Corporation and The Mediplex Group, Inc., operators of long-term and subacute care facilities; Sundance Rehabilitation Corporation, a provider of physical, occupational, and speech therapy services; Sunscript Pharmacy Corporation, an institutional pharmacy company; Sun Healthcare Group International, an owner and operator of long-term care facilities in the United Kingdom; and SunSurgery Corporation, a provider of ambulatory surgery services.

SURGICAL LASER TECHNOLOGIES, INC.
147 Keystone Drive, Montgomeryville PA 18936. 215/619-3600. **Contact:** Michael Stewart, Personnel Director. **World Wide Web address:** http://www.slti.com. **Description:** Develops, manufactures, and sells proprietary laser systems for contact surgery. The company's Contact Laser System allows the surgeon to use a laser in direct contact with the tissue being treated, thereby making laser surgery both more precise and easier to perform. Surgical Laser Technologies also provides free-beam, non-contact laser delivery systems. Its product line includes six portable Contact Laser units of various

power levels; a family of disposable optical fibers and handpieces; and more than 80 probes, scalpels, fibers, and hand pieces that provide different wavelength conversion effect properties, power densities, and configurations appropriate for cutting, coagulation, or vaporization. As a result of the system's design, a single contact laser system can be used within most surgical specialties to perform a broad range of minimally-invasive and open surgical procedures. **Corporate headquarters location:** This Location. **Number of employees at this location:** 160.

SURGIDYNE, INC.
9909 South Shore Drive, Minneapolis MN 55441. 612/595-0665. **Fax:** 612/595-0667. **Contact:** Larry Hanson, Financial Administrator. **Description:** Assembles medical devices and manufactures closed-suction wound drainage products. **Common positions include:** Accountant; Controller; Marketing Manager; Operations Manager; Production Manager; Quality Control Supervisor; Vice President. **Educational backgrounds include:** Accounting; Business Administration; Engineering; Finance; Marketing. **Benefits:** Medical Insurance. **Corporate headquarters location:** This Location. **President:** Vance Fiegel. **Number of employees at this location:** 10.

SYNBIOTICS CORPORATION
11011 Via Frontera, San Diego CA 92127. 858/451-3771. **Contact:** Human Resources. **World Wide Web address:** http://www.synbiotics.com. **Description:** Develops, manufactures, and markets products and services to veterinary specialty markets. Synbiotics provides canine reproduction products and services to purebred dog breeders and their veterinarians. In addition, the company markets a line of life-stage nutritional supplements; and PennHip, a new method for the early diagnosis and evaluation of canine hip dysplasia. **Corporate headquarters location:** This Location. **Listed on:** NASDAQ. **Stock exchange symbol:** SBIO.

TNCO, INC.
P.O. Box 231, Whitman MA 02382. 781/447-6661. **Fax:** 781/447-2132. **Contact:** Human Resources. **World Wide Web address:** http://www.tnco-inc.com. **Description:** Manufactures surgical instruments. Founded in 1964. **NOTE:** Part-time jobs are offered. **Common positions include:** Controller; Customer Service Representative; Design Engineer; Human Resources Manager; Manufacturing Engineer; Marketing Manager; Network/Systems Administrator; Production Manager; Sales Manager. **Educational backgrounds include:** Microsoft Office; Microsoft Word; Spreadsheets. **Benefits:** 401(k); Casual Dress - Daily; Dental Insurance; Disability Coverage; Employee Discounts; Life Insurance; Medical Insurance; Public Transit Available; Sick Days (6 - 10); Tuition Assistance; Vacation Days. **Special programs:** Co-ops. **Office hours:** Monday - Friday, 7:00 a.m. - 3:30 p.m. **Corporate headquarters location:** This Location. **Listed on:** Privately held. **Annual sales/revenues:** $5 - $10 million. **Number of employees at this location:** 65.

TENET HEALTHCARE CORPORATION
3820 State Street, Santa Barbara CA 93105. 805/563-7000. **Contact:** Human Resources. **World Wide Web address:** http://www.tenethealth.com. **Description:** A multibillion-dollar, multihospital corporation that, in conjunction with its subsidiaries, owns or operates approximately 130 acute care facilities nationwide. **Corporate headquarters location:** This Location. **Listed on:** New York Stock Exchange; Pacific Stock Exchange. **Number of employees nationwide:** 130,000.

TENNESSEE REHABILITATION CENTER
460 Ninth Avenue, Smyrna TN 37167. 615/741-4921x215. **Fax:** 615/355-1373. **Contact:** Human Resources. **Description:** A comprehensive rehabilitation center offering vocational training and physical rehabilitation services to disabled individuals. Founded in 1977. **NOTE:** Second and third shifts are offered. **Company slogan:** Caring for the present. Preparing for the future. **Common positions include:** Administrative Assistant; Certified Nurses Aide; Certified Occupational Therapy Assistant; Counselor; Dietician/Nutritionist; Licensed Practical Nurse; Network/Systems Administrator; Occupational Therapist; Pharmacist; Physical Therapist; Physical Therapy Assistant; Physician; Psychologist; Public Relations Specialist; Purchasing Agent/Manager; Registered Nurse; Secretary. **Educational backgrounds include:** Counseling; Microsoft Word; Social Science. **Benefits:** Casual Dress - Fridays; Daycare Assistance; Dental Insurance; Disability Coverage; Life Insurance; Medical Insurance; On-Site Daycare; Pension Plan; Sick Days (11+); Vacation Days (11 - 15). **Special programs:** Internships. **Corporate headquarters location:** Nashville TN. **Number of employees at this location:** 125.

TERESIAN HOUSE NURSING HOME
200 Washington Avenue Extension, Albany NY 12203. 518/456-2000x215. **Fax:** 518/456-1142. **Recorded jobline:** 518/456-2000x311. **Contact:** Jodie Scott, PHR/Director of Human Resources. **Description:** A nonprofit, 300-bed skilled and health-related nursing home. Teresian House has a dementia care and an Alzheimer's care unit, which provides private rooms for all residents. Founded in 1974. **NOTE:** Entry-level positions and second and third shifts are offered. **Common positions include:** Administrative Assistant; Assistant Manager; Certified Nurses Aide; Chief Financial Officer; Controller; Dietician/Nutritionist; Human Resources Manager; Licensed Practical Nurse; MIS Manager; Occupational Therapist; Physical Therapist; Physician; Purchasing Agent/Manager; Quality Control Supervisor; Registered Nurse; Secretary; Social Worker; Typist/Word Processor. **Educational backgrounds include:** Accounting; Health Care. **Benefits:** 403(b); Dental Insurance; Disability Coverage; Employee Discounts; Life Insurance; Medical Insurance; Public Transit Available; Savings Plan; Tuition Assistance. **Special programs:** Internships; Summer Jobs. **Number of employees at this location:** 385.

TEXAS CENTER FOR INFECTIOUS DISEASE
TEXAS DEPARTMENT OF HEALTH
2303 SE Military Drive, San Antonio TX 78223. 210/534-8857x2255. **Fax:** 210/531-4504. **Contact:** Human Resources. **World Wide Web address:** http://www.tdh.state.tx.us/tcid. **Description:** A hospital that provides acute and chronic care to all patients referred for evaluation. The Center specializes in the research and medical care of patients with chronic respiratory/pulmonary disease, tuberculosis, and other infectious diseases. **Common positions include:** Accountant/Auditor; Administrative Manager; Biomedical Engineer; Buyer; Claim Representative; Clerical Supervisor; Clinical Lab Technician; Computer Programmer; Cost Estimator; Counselor; Customer Service Representative; Dental Assistant/Dental Hygienist; Dental Lab Technician; Dentist; Dietician/Nutritionist; Education Administrator; EEG Technologist; EKG Technician; Electrician; Emergency Medical Technician; Environmental Engineer; Financial Analyst; Food Scientist/Technologist; General Manager; Health Services Manager; Human Resources Manager; Human Service Worker; Industrial Engineer; Librarian;

Licensed Practical Nurse; Management Analyst/ Consultant; Management Trainee; Medical Records Technician; Nuclear Medicine Technologist; Occupational Therapist; Operations/Production Manager; Pharmacist; Physical Therapist; Physician; Psychologist; Public Relations Specialist; Purchasing Agent/Manager; Quality Control Supervisor; Recreational Therapist; Registered Nurse; Respiratory Therapist; Social Worker; Surgical Technician; Systems Analyst. **Educational backgrounds include:** Accounting; Biology; Business Administration; Chemistry; Communications; Computer Science; Economics; Finance; Health Care; Hospital Administration; M.D./Medicine; Management/Planning; Marketing; Mathematics; Nursing; Public Administration. **Benefits:** 401(k); Dental Insurance; Disability Coverage; Life Insurance; Medical Insurance; Pension Plan; Savings Plan; Tuition Assistance. **Special programs:** Internships. **Corporate headquarters location:** Austin TX.

TEXAS HEALTH RESOURCES
8440 Walnut Hill Lane, Dallas TX 75231. 214/345-4251. **Toll-free phone:** 800/749-6877. **Fax:** 214/345-4003. **Recorded jobline:** 214/345-7863. **Contact:** Linda Ochoa, Employment Manager. **World Wide Web address:** http://www.texashealth.org. **Description:** One of the largest nonprofit health care systems in Texas including a nursing home, 11 acute care hospitals, clinics, and home health services. **NOTE:** Part-time jobs and second and third shifts are offered. **Common positions include:** Accountant; Administrative Assistant; Administrative Manager; AS400 Programmer Analyst; Assistant Manager; Attorney; Auditor; Blue-Collar Worker Supervisor; Certified Nurses Aide; Certified Occupational Therapy Assistant; Claim Rep.; Clerical Supervisor; Computer Operator; Computer Programmer; Computer Support Technician; Computer Technician; Customer Service Rep.; Database Administrator; Database Manager; Dietician/Nutritionist; EEG Technologist; EKG Technician; Emergency Medical Technician; Finance Director; Financial Analyst; Home Health Aide; Human Resources Manager; Licensed Practical Nurse; Medical Assistant; Medical Records Technician; MIS Specialist; Network/Systems Administrator; Nuclear Medicine Technologist; Nurse Practitioner; Occupational Therapist; Paralegal; Pharmacist; Physical Therapist; Physical Therapy Assistant; Physician; Project Manager; Radiological Technologist; Registered Nurse; Respiratory Therapist; Secretary; Social Worker; Speech-Language Pathologist; Surgical Technician; Systems Analyst; Systems Manager. **Educational backgrounds include:** Health Care; Microsoft Word; Novell; Spreadsheets. **Benefits:** 401(k); Dental Insurance; Disability Coverage; Life Insurance; Medical Insurance; On-Site Daycare. **Corporate headquarters location:** This Location. **Other area locations:** Greenville TX; Kaufman TX; Plano TX; Winnsboro TX.

TEXAS MEDICAL AND SURGICAL ASSOCIATES
8440 Walnut Hill Lane, Dallas TX 75231. 214/345-5740. **Contact:** Personnel. **Description:** A private clinic. **Office hours:** Monday - Friday, 8:30 a.m. - 5:00 p.m.

TEXOMA MEDICAL CENTER (TMC)
P.O. Box 890, Denison TX 75021. 903/416-4050. **Fax:** 903/415-4087. **Recorded jobline:** 800/566-1211. **Contact:** Joni Horn, Employment Coordinator. **World Wide Web address:** http://www.thcs.org. **Description:** An acute care hospital with 300 beds. TMC offers general medical and surgical services, intensive care, and pediatric care. Founded in 1965. **NOTE:** Second and third shifts are offered. **Common positions include:** Accountant; Administrative Assistant; Buyer; Certified Nurses Aide; Clerical Supervisor; Clinical Lab Technician; Computer Operator; Controller; Customer Service Representative; Database Manager; Dietician/Nutritionist; EEG Technologist; EKG Technician; Electrician; Human Resources Manager; Licensed Practical Nurse; Marketing Specialist; Medical Records Technician; Nuclear Medicine Technologist; Occupational Therapist; Pharmacist; Physical Therapist; Radiological Technologist; Registered Nurse; Respiratory Therapist; Secretary; Speech-Language Pathologist; Surgical Technician; Systems Analyst; Systems Manager. **Educational backgrounds include:** Computer Science; Health Care. **Benefits:** 403(b); Dental Insurance; Disability Coverage; Job Sharing; Life Insurance; Medical Insurance; Pension Plan; Profit Sharing; Tuition Assistance. **Special programs:** Co-ops; Summer Jobs. **Corporate headquarters location:** This Location. **Other U.S. locations:** Durant OK; Bonham TX; Sherman TX; Trenton TX; Whitewright TX. **Subsidiaries include:** Times Medical Equipment. **Parent company:** Texoma Healthcare Systems, Inc. (also at this location).

THERAGENICS CORPORATION
5203 Bristol Industrial Way, Buford GA 30518. 770/271-0233. **Toll-free phone:** 800/998-8479. **Fax:** 770/381-8447. **Contact:** Human Resources. **World Wide Web address:** http://www.theragenics.com. **Description:** Develops and manufactures implantable radiation devices for the treatment of prostate cancer. Founded in 1981. **Corporate headquarters location:** This Location. **Listed on:** NASDAQ. **Stock exchange symbol:** THRX.

FF THOMPSON HEALTH SYSTEM
350 Parrish Street, Canandaigua NY 14424. 716/396-6000. **Fax:** 716/396-6480. **Contact:** Chuck Waters, Director. **World Wide Web address:** http://www.ffth.com. **Description:** A locally-owned, nonprofit, community-based health care facility comprised of a 113-bed hospital, a 188-bed nursing home, and a planned senior living community. Founded in 1904. **NOTE:** Entry-level positions, part-time jobs, and second and third shifts are offered. **Common positions include:** Administrative Assistant; Administrative Manager; Assistant Manager; Certified Nurses Aide; Clinical Lab Technician; Computer Programmer; Computer Support Technician; Customer Service Rep.; Database Manager; Dietician/Nutritionist; EKG Technician; Electrician; Emergency Medical Technician; Licensed Practical Nurse; Medical Assistant; Medical Records Technician; Medical Secretary; Nuclear Medicine Technologist; Nurse Practitioner; Occupational Therapist; Operations Manager; Pharmacist; Physical Therapist; Physical Therapy Assistant; Physician; Physician Assistant; Public Relations Specialist; Radiological Technologist; Registered Nurse; Respiratory Therapist; Sales Representative; Secretary; Social Worker. **Educational backgrounds include:** Health Care; Microsoft Office; Microsoft Word. **Benefits:** 401(k); 403(b); Dental Insurance; Disability Coverage; Employee Discounts; Financial Planning Assistance; Flexible Schedule; Job Sharing; Life Insurance; Medical Insurance; Pension Plan; Relocation Assistance; Sick Days (6 - 10); Tuition Assistance; Vacation Days. **Special programs:** Summer Jobs; Training. **Office hours:** Monday - Friday, 8:00 a.m. - 4:30 p.m. **CEO:** Linda Janczak. **Annual sales/revenues:** $51 - $100 million. **Number of employees at this location:** 1,100.

TIPTON COUNTY MEMORIAL HOSPITAL
1000 South Main Street, Tipton IN 46072. 765/675-8500. **Contact:** J. Neal Shockney, Human Resources. **World Wide Web address:** http://www.tiptonhospital.org. **Description:** A nonprofit acute care community hospital. The hospital also offers primary and specialty care throughout Tipton and the surrounding area. **NOTE:** Entry-level positions and second and third shifts are offered. **Common positions include:** Account Manager; Account Representative; Administrative Assistant; Certified Nurses Aide; Chief Financial Officer; Claim Representative; Clinical Lab Technician; Dietician/Nutritionist; EEG Technologist; EKG Technician; Electrician; Human Resources Manager; Licensed Practical Nurse; Medical Records Technician; Occupational Therapist; Pharmacist; Physical Therapist; Physician; Purchasing Agent/Manager; Radiological Technologist; Registered Nurse; Secretary; Speech-Language Pathologist; Surgical Technician; Typist/Word Processor. **Educational backgrounds include:** Business Administration; Liberal Arts; Public Relations. **Benefits:** 403(b); Dental Insurance; Disability Coverage; Employee Discounts; Flexible Schedule; Life Insurance; Medical Insurance; Pension Plan; Tuition Assistance. **Corporate headquarters location:** This Location. **CEO:** Al Gajmaitan. **Annual sales/revenues:** $21 - $50 million. **Number of employees at this location:** 350.

TOMAH MEMORIAL HOSPITAL
321 Butts Avenue, Tomah WI 54660. 608/372-2181. **Fax:** 608/374-0289. **Contact:** Brenda Simonson, Human Resources Director. **Description:** A nonprofit, 49-bed general hospital. **NOTE:** Part-time jobs and second and third shifts are offered. Administrator: Philip Stuart. **Common positions include:** Accountant; Administrative Assistant; Certified Nurses Aide; Certified Occupational Therapy Assistant; Chief Financial Officer; Customer Service Rep.; Licensed Practical Nurse; Medical Secretary; Network/Systems Administrator; Occupational Therapist; Pharmacist; Physical Therapist; Physical Therapy Assistant; Radiological Technologist; Registered Nurse; Respiratory Therapist; Secretary; Social Worker; Surgical Technician. **Educational backgrounds include:** Business Administration; Finance; Health Care; Microsoft Office; Microsoft Word. **Benefits:** 403(b); Dental Insurance; Disability Coverage; Employee Discounts; Life Insurance; Medical Insurance; Pension Plan; Tuition Assistance. **Information Systems Manager:** LaVonne Smith. **Number of employees at this location:** 200.

TOMBIGBEE HEALTHCARE AUTHORITY dba BRYAN W. WHITFIELD MEMORIAL HOSPITAL
P.O. Box 890, Demopolis AL 36732. 334/289-4000x2635. **Fax:** 334/287-2681. **Contact:** Danny Smith, Director of Human Resources and Special Projects. **Description:** A nonprofit, government-funded, 99-bed, acute care hospital organized under the Health Care Authority Act. The organization is comprised of the Obstetrical Medicaid Waiver program, an ambulance service, and a home health agency. Bryan W. Whitfield Memorial Hospital is a secondary health care provider for inpatient, outpatient, and acute care. Any major medical emergencies including surgical and clinical, are treated at this location, except for major trauma cases, which are stabilized and then transferred to tertiary hospitals in the hospital's network. The hospital has extensive preferred provider relationships with major tertiary hospitals in the state and is affiliated with all state medical and professional schools. **Common positions include:** Claim Representative; Clinical Lab Technician;

Credit Manager; Customer Service Rep.; Dietician/Nutritionist; Emergency Medical Technician; Licensed Practical Nurse; Medical Records Technician; Nuclear Medicine Technologist; Pharmacist; Physical Therapist; Physician; Purchasing Agent/Manager; Radiological Technologist; Registered Nurse; Respiratory Therapist; Restaurant/Food Service Manager; Surgical Technician. **Educational backgrounds include:** Health Care. **Benefits:** Dental Insurance; Employee Discounts; Life Insurance; Medical Insurance; Pension Plan; Savings Plan. **Corporate headquarters location:** This Location.

TY COBB HEALTHCARE SYSTEM, INC.
P.O. Box 589, Royston GA 30662. 706/245-1846. **Fax:** 706/245-1831. **Contact:** Carolyn Taylor, Director of Human Resources. **E-mail address:** carolynt@tycobbhealthcare.org. **World Wide Web address:** http://www.tycobbhealthcare.org. **Description:** A private, nonprofit health care system that operates two hospitals, two health care centers, a convalescent center, and occupational health services. **NOTE:** Entry-level positions and second and third shifts are offered. **Common positions include:** Account Representative; Accountant; Administrative Assistant; Certified Nurses Aide; Chief Financial Officer; Claim Representative; EKG Technician; Electrician; Environmental Engineer; Finance Director; Human Resources Manager; Licensed Practical Nurse; Marketing Manager; Medical Records Technician; MIS Specialist; Pharmacist; Physical Therapist; Physician; Purchasing Agent/Manager; Radiological Technologist; Registered Nurse; Respiratory Therapist; Secretary; Social Worker; Speech-Language Pathologist; Surgical Technician. **Benefits:** 403(b); Dental Insurance; Employee Discounts; Life Insurance; Medical Insurance; Scholarship Program. **Special programs:** Training.

TYCO/HEALTHCARE/KENDALL
P.O. Box 2078, DeLand FL 32721. 904/734-3685. **Contact:** J. Ralph Mills, Human Resources Manager. **E-mail address:** mills@kendallhq.com. **World Wide Web address:** http://www.kendallhq.com. **Description:** Manufactures disposable hypodermic needles and syringes. Founded in 1903. **NOTE:** Second and third shifts are offered. **Common positions include:** Accountant; Administrative Assistant; AS400 Programmer Analyst; Biological Scientist; Chemist; Computer Programmer; Computer Technician; Controller; Database Administrator; Draftsperson; Electrical/Electronics Engineer; General Manager; Help-Desk Technician; Human Resources Manager; Industrial Engineer; Industrial Production Manager; Manufacturing Engineer; Mechanical Engineer; MIS Specialist; Operations Manager; Purchasing Agent/Manager; Quality Assurance Engineer; Quality Control Supervisor; Secretary; Technical Writer/Editor; Typist/Word Processor. **Educational backgrounds include:** Accounting; AS400 Certification; Biology; Business Administration; Chemistry; Computer Science; Engineering; Finance; Microsoft Office; Microsoft Word; Spreadsheets. **Benefits:** 401(k); Casual Dress - Daily; Dental Insurance; Disability Coverage; Employee Discounts; Life Insurance; Medical Insurance; Relocation Assistance; Savings Plan; Tuition Assistance; Vacation Days (10 - 20). **Special programs:** Apprenticeships; Co-ops. **Office hours:** Monday - Friday, 8:00 a.m. - 5:00 p.m. **Corporate headquarters location:** Mansfield MA. **Other U.S. locations:** Nationwide. **International locations:** Worldwide. **Parent company:** Tyco International. **Listed on:** New York Stock Exchange. **Stock exchange symbol:** TYC. **Annual sales/revenues:** More than $100 million.

UPMC BEAVER VALLEY
2500 Hospital Drive, Aliquippa PA 15001-2191. 724/857-1212. **Fax:** 724/857-1298. **Contact:** Human Resources. **World Wide Web address:** http://www.upmc.edu/beavervalley. **Description:** A nonprofit hospital. **NOTE:** Entry-level positions, part-time jobs, and second and third shifts are offered. **Common positions include:** Accountant; Administrative Assistant; Administrative Manager; Certified Nurses Aide; Certified Occupational Therapy Assistant; Counselor; Dietician/ Nutritionist; EEG Technologist; EKG Technician; Emergency Medical Technician; Finance Director; Home Health Aide; Human Resources Manager; Licensed Practical Nurse; Medical Assistant; Medical Records Technician; Nuclear Medicine Technologist; Nurse Practitioner; Occupational Therapist; Pharmacist; Physical Therapist; Physical Therapy Assistant; Physician; Psychologist; Radiological Technologist; Registered Nurse; Respiratory Therapist; Social Worker; Speech-Language Pathologist; Surgical Technician. **Benefits:** 403(b); Dental Insurance; Disability Coverage; Employee Discounts; Life Insurance; Medical Insurance; Pension Plan; Public Transit Available; Savings Plan; Sick Days (11+); Tuition Assistance; Vacation Days (11 - 15).

U.S. HOMECARE
141 South Central Avenue, Hartsdale NY 10530. 914/946-9601. **Fax:** 914/946-0916. **Contact:** Human Resources. **Description:** Provides comprehensive home health care services including infusion and other specialized therapies, nursing care, and personal care. **NOTE:** Interested applicants should send resumes to 2 Hartford Square West, Suite 300, Hartford CT 06106. **Common positions include:** Accountant/Auditor; Financial Analyst; Licensed Practical Nurse; Registered Nurse. **Educational backgrounds include:** Accounting; Business Administration; Computer Science; Marketing. **Benefits:** 401(k); Dental Insurance; Life Insurance; Medical Insurance; Tuition Assistance. **Special programs:** Internships. **Corporate headquarters location:** This Location. **Other U.S. locations:** Hartford CT; New Haven CT; Fort Lauderdale FL; Miami FL; West Palm Beach FL; Allendale NJ; Scottsdale NJ; Hicksville NY; Latham NY; New York NY; Philadelphia PA; Pittsburgh PA.

UNION HOSPITAL HEALTH GROUP
1606 North Seventh Street, Terre Haute IN 47804. 812/238-7000. **Recorded jobline:** 812/238-7200. **Contact:** Mary Halsted, Employment Manager. **World Wide Web address:** http://www.uhhg.org. **Description:** Owns and operates two hospitals, a physicians/surgeons clinic, and physician office sites. Union Hospital Health Group is a nonprofit, regional referral center. **NOTE:** Entry-level positions, part-time jobs, and second and third shifts are offered. **Common positions include:** Certified Nurses Aide; Computer Operator; Computer Support Technician; EKG Technician; Home Health Aide; Licensed Practical Nurse; Pharmacist; Radiological Technologist; Registered Nurse; Respiratory Therapist; Secretary; Speech-Language Pathologist; Surgical Technician. **Benefits:** 403(b); Daycare Assistance; Dental Insurance; Disability Coverage; Employee Discounts; Flexible Schedule; Life Insurance; Medical Insurance; On-Site Daycare; Pension Plan; Public Transit Available; Tuition Assistance; Vacation Days (6 - 10). **Special programs:** Internships. **Office hours:** Monday - Friday, 8:00 a.m. - 4:30 p.m. **Corporate headquarters location:** This Location. **Other area locations:** Clinton IN. **Number of employees at this location:** 2,900.

THE UNIONTOWN HOSPITAL
500 West Berkeley Street, Uniontown PA 15401. 724/430-5000. **Fax:** 724/430-5646. **Recorded jobline:** 724/430-5290. **Contact:** Joann Kaminsky, Employment Manager. **Description:** An acute care hospital. **Common positions include:** Accountant; Administrative Assistant; Certified Nurses Aide; Certified Occupational Therapy Assistant; Computer Support Technician; Computer Technician; Dietician/Nutritionist; EEG Technologist; EKG Technician; Finance Director; Help-Desk Technician; Human Resources Manager; Licensed Practical Nurse; Medical Records Technician; Medical Secretary; Nurse Practitioner; Occupational Therapist; Pharmacist; Physical Therapist; Physical Therapy Assistant; Physician Assistant; Purchasing Agent/Manager; Radiological Technologist; Registered Nurse; Respiratory Therapist; Secretary; Speech-Language Pathologist; Surgical Technician; Systems Analyst. **Benefits:** Daycare Assistance; Dental Insurance; Disability Coverage; Life Insurance; Medical Insurance; Pension Plan; Tuition Assistance. **Special programs:** Internships. **Corporate headquarters location:** This Location. **Parent company:** UHRI.

UNIVERSAL HEALTH SERVICES, INC.
367 South Gulph Road, P.O. Box 61558, King of Prussia PA 19406-0958. 610/768-3300. **Contact:** Coleen Johnson, Personnel Assistant. **World Wide Web address:** http://www.uhsinc.com. **Description:** Owns and operates acute care hospitals, behavioral health centers, ambulatory surgery centers, and radiation/oncology centers. The company operates 29 hospitals with approximately 3,600 licensed beds. Of these facilities, 15 are general acute care hospitals and 14 are psychiatric care facilities (two of which are substance abuse facilities). The company, as a part of its Ambulatory Treatment Centers Division, owns, operates, or manages surgery and radiation therapy centers located in various states. Universal Health Services has also entered into other specialized medical service arrangements including laboratory services, mobile computerized tomography and magnetic imaging services, preferred provider organization agreements, health maintenance organization contracts, medical office building leasing, construction management services, and real estate management and administrative services. **Common positions include:** Accountant/Auditor; Computer Programmer; Paralegal; Systems Analyst. **Educational backgrounds include:** Accounting; Business Administration; Computer Science. **Benefits:** 401(k); Dental Insurance; Life Insurance; Medical Insurance; Tuition Assistance. **Corporate headquarters location:** This Location.

UNIVERSITY HEALTH CARE SYSTEM UNIVERSITY HOSPITAL
1350 Walton Way, Augusta GA 30901-2629. 706/774-8982. **Toll-free phone:** 800/338-9599. **Fax:** 706/774-8782. **Recorded jobline:** 706/774-8933. **Contact:** Employment Office. **World Wide Web address:** http://www.universityhealth.org. **Description:** A nonprofit, comprehensive health care system. University Hospital (also at this location) is a full-service, 612-bed hospital. Founded in 1818. **NOTE:** Entry-level positions and second and third shifts are offered. **Common positions include:** Certified Nurses Aide; Computer Programmer; Daycare Worker; EEG Technologist; EKG Technician; Graphic Designer; Licensed Practical Nurse; Medical Records Technician; MIS Specialist; Nuclear Medicine Technologist; Occupational Therapist; Pharmacist; Physical Therapist; Radiological Technologist; Registered Nurse; Respiratory Therapist; Secretary; Social Worker; Speech-Language Pathologist; Surgical

Technician; Systems Analyst. **Educational backgrounds include:** Business Administration; Computer Science; Health Care; Information Systems. **Benefits:** 403(b); Dental Insurance; Disability Coverage; Employee Discounts; Financial Planning Assistance; Flexible Schedule; Job Sharing; Life Insurance; Medical Insurance; On-Site Daycare; Pension Plan; Public Transit Available; Savings Plan; Tuition Assistance; Wellness Program. **Special programs:** Internships. **Corporate headquarters location:** This Location. **Listed on:** Privately held. **Number of employees at this location:** 3,500.

UNIVERSITY HOSPITALS & CLINICS
421 Wakara Way, Suite 140, Salt Lake City UT 84108. 801/581-2300. **Fax:** 801/581-4579. **Recorded jobline:** 801/581-2310. **Contact:** Human Resources. **Description:** University Hospitals & Clinics is comprised of University of Utah Hospital, a 392-bed tertiary and acute care facility. University Hospitals serves as the clinical arm for the medical school and the college of health, nursing, and pharmacy. Special research centers include the Institute for Human Genetics, which houses the Howard Hughes Medical Institute, a world-class genetics research program. Other centers include the Center for Human Toxicology; the Cardiovascular Research and Training Institute; the Institute for Biomedical Engineering/Division of Artificial Organs; and the Center for Diagnostic Imaging Research in the radiology department. As a major referral facility, University Hospitals has numerous specialties including burns and trauma; heart, kidney, and bone marrow transplants; newborn intensive care; shock wave lithotripsy; and cancer care. University Hospitals has expanded to include the University Neuropsychiatric Institute. **NOTE:** Entry-level positions are offered. **Common positions include:** Accountant; Administrative Manager; Budget Analyst; Claim Representative; Clerical Supervisor; Computer Programmer; Counselor; Customer Service Rep.; Dental Assistant/Dental Hygienist; Dietician/Nutritionist; EEG Technologist; EKG Technician; Financial Analyst; Health Services Manager; Licensed Practical Nurse; Medical Records Technician; Nuclear Medicine Technologist; Occupational Therapist; Physical Therapist; Radiological Technologist; Recreational Therapist; Registered Nurse; Respiratory Therapist; Speech-Language Pathologist; Surgical Technician; Systems Analyst; Typist/Word Processor. **Educational backgrounds include:** Accounting; Business Administration; Computer Science; Health Care. **Benefits:** 401(k); Dental Insurance; Disability Coverage; Employee Discounts; Life Insurance; Medical Insurance; Pension Plan; Spending Account; Tuition Assistance. **Corporate headquarters location:** This Location. **Other U.S. locations:** Park City UT; Sugarhouse UT; Wendover UT. **Number of employees at this location:** 3,200.

UNIVERSITY OF TEXAS SOUTHWESTERN MEDICAL CENTER AT DALLAS
5323 Harry Hines Boulevard, Dallas TX 75390. 214/648-3111. **Fax:** 214/648-9874. **Contact:** Human Resources. **World Wide Web address:** http://www.swmed.edu. **Description:** An academic medical center affiliated with Southwestern Medical School, Southwestern Graduate School of Biomedical Sciences, and Southwestern Allied Health Sciences School. **NOTE:** Entry-level positions are offered. **Common positions include:** Accountant; Administrative Assistant; Administrative Manager; AS400 Programmer Analyst; Attorney; Auditor; Biochemist; Biological Scientist; Biomedical Engineer; Budget Analyst; Computer Operator; Computer Programmer;

Computer Support Technician; Counselor; Database Administrator; Database Manager; Electrician; Emergency Medical Technician; Financial Analyst; Intellectual Property Lawyer; Librarian; Medical Assistant; Network/Systems Administrator; Nurse Practitioner; Psychologist; Purchasing Agent/ Manager; Radiological Technologist; Registered Nurse; Secretary; Systems Analyst; Systems Manager. **Educational backgrounds include:** Accounting; AS400 Certification; Biology; Business Administration; C/C++; Chemistry; Computer Science; Finance; Health Care; HTML; Internet; MCSE; Novell; PowerBuilder; Software Tech. Support; Visual Basic. **Benefits:** 403(b); Dental Insurance; Disability Coverage; Financial Planning Assistance; Life Insurance; Medical Insurance; Pension Plan; Public Transit Available; Savings Plan; Sick Days (11+); Vacation Days (11 - 15). **Special programs:** Internships.

UTAH MEDICAL PRODUCTS, INC.
7043 South 300 West, Midvale UT 84047. 801/566-1200. **Fax:** 801/566-2062. **Contact:** Human Resources/Corporate Recruiter. **World Wide Web address:** http://www.utahmed.com. **Description:** Develops, manufactures, assembles, and markets a broad range of products serving the critical care and obstetrics/gynecology markets. Products include a line of transducers and catheters used in monitoring blood pressure and uterine contraction pressure, an electrosurgery generator and disposable electrodes used in a new treatment to remove precancerous cervical tissue, a line of disposable infant oxygen therapy products, and female incontinence therapy products. The company's markets include specialties where new treatment techniques are being performed in hospitals, outpatient surgery centers, and doctors' offices. Founded in 1978. **NOTE:** Entry-level positions and second and third shifts are offered. **Common positions include:** Accountant; Administrative Assistant; Biological Scientist; Biomedical Engineer; Blue-Collar Worker Supervisor; Buyer; Chemical Engineer; Chief Financial Officer; Clerical Supervisor; Computer Programmer; Controller; Customer Service Representative; Design Engineer; Draftsperson; Electrical/Electronics Engineer; Human Resources Manager; Industrial Engineer; Industrial Production Manager; Manufacturing Engineer; Market Research Analyst; Marketing Manager; Mechanical Engineer; MIS Specialist; Network/Systems Administrator; Production Manager; Purchasing Agent/Manager; Quality Assurance Engineer; Quality Control Supervisor; Registered Nurse; Sales Manager; Sales Representative; Secretary; Software Engineer; Webmaster. **Educational backgrounds include:** Accounting; Business Administration; Engineering; Marketing; Software Development; Spreadsheets. **Benefits:** 401(k); Casual Dress - Daily; Daycare Assistance; Dental Insurance; Disability Coverage; Flexible Schedule; Life Insurance; Medical Insurance; Tuition Assistance. **Special programs:** Internships. **Corporate headquarters location:** This Location. **Other U.S. locations:** Redmond OR. **International locations:** Athlone, Ireland. **Operations at this facility include:** Administration; Divisional Headquarters; Manufacturing; Regional Headquarters; Research and Development; Sales; Service.

VALLEY BAPTIST MEDICAL CENTER
P.O. Box 2588, Harlingen TX 78550. 956/389-1100. **Contact:** Personnel Manager. **World Wide Web address:** http://www.vbmc.com. **Description:** A 588-bed, nonprofit, acute care medical center. **NOTE:** Second and third shifts are offered. **Common positions include:** Account Manager; Account Representative; Accountant; Budget Analyst; Buyer; Certified Nurses Aide; Chief

Financial Officer; Clerical Supervisor; Clinical Lab Technician; Computer Operator; Computer Programmer; Controller; Counselor; Customer Service Rep.; Dietician/Nutritionist; Education Administrator; EEG Technologist; EKG Technician; Electrical/Electronics Engineer; Electrician; Emergency Medical Technician; Environmental Engineer; Finance Director; Financial Analyst; Graphic Artist; Human Resources Manager; Librarian; Licensed Practical Nurse; Medical Records Technician; MIS Specialist; Nurse Practitioner; Occupational Therapist; Paralegal; Pharmacist; Physical Therapist; Physician; Psychologist; Public Relations Specialist; Purchasing Agent/Manager; Quality Control Supervisor; Radiological Technologist; Registered Nurse; Respiratory Therapist; Secretary; Social Worker; Speech-Language Pathologist; Surgical Technician; Systems Analyst. **Educational backgrounds include:** Accounting; Biology; Business Administration; Communications; Computer Science; Finance; Health Care; Nursing. **Benefits:** 401(k); 403(b); Employee Discounts; Life Insurance; Medical Insurance; Tuition Assistance. **Special programs:** Co-ops; Internships; Summer Jobs. **Corporate headquarters location:** This Location.

VANDERBILT UNIVERSITY MEDICAL CENTER

Box 7700, Station B, Nashville TN 37235. 615/322-8300. **Fax:** 615/343-6692. **Contact:** Recruitment. **World Wide Web address:** http://www. vanderbilt.edu. **Description:** A comprehensive health care facility that combines the education of health professionals, patient care, and biomedical research. Through its programs, Vanderbilt University Medical Center has become a major referral center for the Southeast and the nation. The medical center is comprised of The School of Medicine, The School of Nursing, The Vanderbilt Clinic, Children's Hospital, Vanderbilt Psychiatric Hospital, and Vanderbilt Stallworth Rehabilitation Hospital. **Common positions include:** Accountant; Architect; Attorney; Biological Scientist; Blue-Collar Worker Supervisor; Budget Analyst; Clerical Supervisor; Clinical Lab Technician; Computer Programmer; Counselor; Dental Assistant/Dental Hygienist; Dental Lab Technician; Dietician/ Nutritionist; Draftsperson; Editor; Education Administrator; EEG Technologist; EKG Technician; Electrical/Electronics Engineer; Financial Analyst; Health Services Manager; Human Resources Manager; Librarian; Library Technician; Medical Records Technician; Medical Technologist; Nuclear Medicine Technologist; Occupational Therapist; Pharmacist; Physical Therapist; Preschool Worker; Psychologist; Public Relations Specialist; Purchasing Agent/Manager; Radiological Technologist; Registered Nurse; Reporter; Research Assistant; Respiratory Therapist; Science Technologist; Social Worker; Speech-Language Pathologist; Statistician; Structural Engineer; Surgical Technician; Systems Analyst; Teacher/ Professor; Technical Writer/Editor. **Educational backgrounds include:** Accounting; Art/Design; Biology; Business Administration; Chemistry; Computer Science; Liberal Arts. **Benefits:** 401(k); Daycare Assistance; Dental Insurance; Disability Coverage; Employee Discounts; Life Insurance; Medical Insurance; Pension Plan; Tuition Assistance; Wellness Program. **Corporate headquarters location:** This Location.

VENCOR HOSPITAL LAS VEGAS

5110 West Sahara Avenue, Las Vegas NV 89146. 702/871-1418. **Contact:** Human Resources. **Description:** Specializes in providing long-term, acute care. **Corporate headquarters location:** This

Location. **Listed on:** Boston Stock Exchange; Chicago Stock Exchange; New York Stock Exchange; Pacific Stock Exchange. **Stock exchange symbol:** THY.

VENCOR, INC.

680 South Fourth Street, Louisville KY 40202. 502/596-7300. **Contact:** Human Resources. **World Wide Web address:** http://www.vencor.com. **Description:** Provides long-term hospital care for patients with cardiopulmonary and other medically complex needs. **Corporate headquarters location:** This Location. **Listed on:** New York Stock Exchange. **Stock exchange symbol:** VC. **Number of employees nationwide:** 3,680.

VERMONT MEDICAL, INC.
ANGIOLAZ

P.O. Box 556, Bellows Falls VT 05101. 802/463-9976. **Fax:** 802/463-9228. **Contact:** Russel Farral, Manager of Human Resources. **Description:** Manufactures disposable medical monitoring electrodes and other special purpose medical electrodes. Vermont Medical also distributes medical monitoring accessories. Angiolaz (also at this location) manufactures scopes for various medical uses including exploratory surgical procedures. **NOTE:** Entry-level positions are offered. **Common positions include:** Blue-Collar Worker Supervisor; General Manager; Industrial Production Manager; Mechanical Engineer; Purchasing Agent/Manager; Typist/Word Processor. **Benefits:** 401(k); Life Insurance; Medical Insurance. **Corporate headquarters location:** This Location.

VERNON MANOR

E7404A, County BB, Viroqua WI 54665. 608/637-8311. **Fax:** 608/637-8386. **Contact:** Administrator. **Description:** A nursing home. Founded in 1981. **NOTE:** Entry-level positions are offered. **Common positions include:** Dietician/Nutritionist; Licensed Practical Nurse; Medical Records Technician; Nurse Practitioner; Registered Nurse; Social Worker. **Educational backgrounds include:** Health Care; Nutrition. **Benefits:** Disability Coverage; Life Insurance; Medical Insurance; Pension Plan; Savings Plan. **Special programs:** Internships. **Office hours:** Monday - Friday, 8:30 a.m. - 4:30 p.m. **Corporate headquarters location:** This Location. **Parent company:** Vernon County.

VERNON WICHITA FALLS STATE HOSPITAL

P.O. Box 300, Wichita Falls TX 76307. 940/689-5878. **Recorded jobline:** 940/552-9901x4030. **Contact:** Staffing. **Description:** A nonprofit, forensic and mental health hospital. **Common positions include:** Certified Nurses Aide; Dietician/ Nutritionist; Electrician; Human Resources Manager; Licensed Practical Nurse; Occupational Therapist; Pharmacist; Psychiatrist; Psychologist; Registered Nurse; Secretary; Social Worker; Typist/Word Processor. **Educational backgrounds include:** Health Care. **Benefits:** Disability Coverage; Medical Insurance; Pension Plan; Sick Days (11+); Vacation Days (6 - 10). **Special programs:** Internships. **Corporate headquarters location:** Austin TX. **Parent company:** Texas Department of Mental Health.

VILLA TERESA

1051 Avila Road, Harrisburg PA 17109. 717/652-5900. **Fax:** 717/652-5941. **Contact:** Personnel Director. **Description:** Provides skilled nursing care for the elderly. Founded in 1973. **Common positions include:** Accountant; Administrative Assistant; Certified Nurses Aide; Controller; Dietician/Nutritionist; Human Resources Manager;

Licensed Practical Nurse; Medical Records Technician; Occupational Therapist; Physical Therapist; Purchasing Agent/Manager; Quality Control Supervisor; Registered Nurse; Secretary; Social Worker; Speech-Language Pathologist; Typist/Word Processor. **Educational backgrounds include:** Accounting; Business Administration; Computer Science; Finance; Health Care; Liberal Arts; Nutrition; Public Relations. **Benefits:** 403(b); Dental Insurance; Disability Coverage; Employee Discounts; Flexible Schedule; Life Insurance; Medical Insurance; Pension Plan; Public Transit Available; Savings Plan; Tuition Assistance. **Office hours:** Monday - Friday, 8:00 a.m. - 4:00 p.m. **Corporate headquarters location:** This Location. **Number of employees at this location:** 230.

VILLAVIEW COMMUNITY HOSPITAL
5550 University Avenue, San Diego CA 92105. 619/582-3516. **Contact:** Human Resources. **Description:** An acute care hospital. **Common positions include:** EEG Technologist; EKG Technician; Emergency Medical Technician; Financial Analyst; Licensed Practical Nurse; Radiological Technologist; Registered Nurse; Respiratory Therapist; Social Worker. **Educational backgrounds include:** Health Care. **Benefits:** Dental Insurance; Disability Coverage; Employee Discounts; Life Insurance; Medical Insurance; TSAs.

VISION-EASE LENS, INC.
7000 Sunwood Drive, Ramsey MN 55303. 763/576-3930. **Fax:** 763/576-5152. **Contact:** Diane Wilson, Human Resources Manager. **World Wide Web address:** http://www.highperformancelenses.com. **Description:** Manufactures polycarbonate lenses for eyeglasses. **NOTE:** Entry-level positions and second and third shifts are offered. **Common positions include:** Accountant; Administrative Assistant; Auditor; Blue-Collar Worker Supervisor; Chemical Engineer; Controller; Human Resources Manager; Manufacturing Engineer; Mechanical Engineer; Production Manager; Quality Control Supervisor; Secretary; Vice President of Operations. **Educational backgrounds include:** Engineering. **Benefits:** 401(k); Dental Insurance; Disability Coverage; Life Insurance; Medical Insurance; Profit Sharing; Savings Plan; Tuition Assistance. **Special programs:** Internships; Summer Jobs; Training. **Corporate headquarters location:** This Location. **Other U.S. locations:** St. Cloud MN. **Parent company:** BMC Industries. **Listed on:** New York Stock Exchange. **Stock exchange symbol:** BMC. **CEO:** Paul Burke.

VISION-SCIENCES INC.
9 Strathmore Road, Natick MA 01760. 508/650-9971. **Fax:** 508/650-9976. **Contact:** James A. Tracy, Personnel. **World Wide Web address:** http://www.visionsciences.com. **Description:** Manufactures a flexible endoscopy system that utilizes single-use protective sheaths designed to reduce reprocessing time and infection concerns. Founded in 1990. **NOTE:** Entry-level positions are offered. **Educational backgrounds include:** Spreadsheets. **Benefits:** 401(k); Casual Dress - Fridays; Dental Insurance; Disability Coverage; Life Insurance; Medical Insurance; Vacation Days (6 - 10). **Office hours:** Monday - Friday, 8:00 a.m. - 5:00 p.m. **Corporate headquarters location:** This Location. **Other U.S. locations:** Orangeburg NY. **International locations:** Israel. **Listed on:** NASDAQ.

VITAL SIGNS, INC.
20 Campus Road, Totowa NJ 07512. 973/790-1330. **Fax:** 973/790-4475. **Contact:** Liz Greenberg, Director of Human Resources. **World Wide Web address:** http://www.vital-signs.com. **Description:** Manufactures disposable medical products such as face masks, manual resuscitators, anesthesia kits, and other respiratory-related critical care products. **Common positions include:** Computer Programmer; Customer Service Rep.; Electrical/Electronics Engineer; Materials Engineer; Operations/Production Manager; Systems Analyst. **Educational backgrounds include:** Business Administration; Computer Science; Engineering; Finance; Marketing. **Benefits:** 401(k); Dental Insurance; Disability Coverage; Life Insurance; Pension Plan; Savings Plan. **Corporate headquarters location:** This Location. **Number of employees at this location:** 350.

WAKE FOREST UNIVERSITY-BAPTIST MEDICAL CENTER
Medical Center Boulevard, Winston-Salem NC 27157. 336/716-2011. **Contact:** Human Resources. **World Wide Web address:** http://www.wfubmc.edu. **Description:** A full-service medical center that operates through two institutions: Wake Forest University School of Medicine, and the North Carolina Baptist Hospitals. **Corporate headquarters location:** This Location. **Number of employees at this location:** 5,500.

WALGREEN HEALTH INITIATIVE
3724 West Wisconsin Avenue, Milwaukee WI 53208. 414/342-9292. **Toll-free phone:** 800/334-4572. **Fax:** 414/342-6877. **Contact:** Human Resources. **Description:** Sells medical supplies and equipment to nursing homes, operates institutional pharmacies for long-term care facilities, and provides home health care services. Founded in 1986. **Common positions include:** Accountant; Administrative Assistant; Billing Analyst; Branch Manager; Budget Analyst; Buyer; Certified Nurses Aide; Computer Operator; Customer Service Rep.; Financial Analyst; General Manager; Marketing Manager; Marketing Specialist; Medical Records Technician; Occupational Therapist; Pharmacist; Physical Therapist; Psychologist; Purchasing Agent/Manager; Registered Nurse; Respiratory Therapist; Sales Manager; Sales Representative; Secretary; Social Worker; Systems Analyst; Typist/Word Processor. **Educational backgrounds include:** Accounting; Business Administration; Computer Science; Health Care; Liberal Arts; Marketing; Pharmacology; Respiratory Therapy. **Benefits:** 401(k); Daycare Assistance; Dental Insurance; Disability Coverage; Life Insurance; Medical Insurance; Public Transit Available; Tuition Assistance. **Corporate headquarters location:** This Location. **Other U.S. locations:** Nationwide. **Parent company:** Extendicare Health Services, Inc. **Listed on:** Canadian Stock Exchange; New York Stock Exchange. **Annual sales/revenues:** More than $100 million. **Number of employees at this location:** 300.

CLEO WALLACE CENTERS
8405 West Church Ranch Boulevard, Westminster CO 80021. **Fax:** 303/466-0904. **Contact:** Gayle Collins, Human Resources Administrator. **Description:** A nonprofit, psychiatric treatment center offering both inpatient and outpatient treatments for children and adolescents. **NOTE:** Entry-level positions and second and third shifts are offered. **Common positions include:** Account Rep.; Administrative Assistant; Chief Financial Officer; Controller; Counselor; Licensed Practical Nurse; Medical Records Technician; Psychologist; Registered Nurse; Social Worker; Speech-Language Pathologist; Systems Analyst; Teacher/Professor. **Educational backgrounds include:** Accounting; Health Care. **Benefits:** 403(b); Daycare Assistance; Dental Insurance; Disability Coverage; Life

Insurance; Medical Insurance; Tuition Assistance. **Special programs:** Internships. **Corporate headquarters location:** This Location. **Other area locations:** Colorado Springs CO; Westminster CO. **CEO:** James Cole. **Number of employees at this location:** 100.

WAR MEMORIAL HOSPITAL
500 Osborn Boulevard, Sault Ste. Marie MI 49783. 906/635-4421. **Fax:** 906/635-4423. **Contact:** Julie Coneset, Human Resources Associate. **World Wide Web address:** http://www.warmem.org. **Description:** A full-service 82-bed facility. The hospital also offers a long term care center. **Common positions include:** Administrative Assistant; Certified Nurses Aide; EEG Technologist; EKG Technician; Electrician; Emergency Medical Technician; Licensed Practical Nurse; Occupational Therapist; Pharmacist; Physical Therapist; Radiological Technologist; Registered Nurse; Respiratory Therapist; Secretary; Speech-Language Pathologist. **Educational backgrounds include:** Business Administration; Health Care. **Benefits:** Dental Insurance; Employee Discounts; Life Insurance; Medical Insurance; Pension Plan; Tuition Assistance. **Corporate headquarters location:** This Location.

WASHINGTON COUNTY HOSPITAL
400 East Polk Street, Washington IA 52353. 319/653-5481x246. **Physical address:** 400 East Polk Street, Washington IA. **Fax:** 319/653-4271. **Contact:** Julie Lenz, Director of Human Resources. **E-mail address:** jobs@wchc.org. **World Wide Web address:** http://www.wchc.org. **Description:** A nonprofit, rural health care facility with 24-hour emergency care, a family birthing center, medical/surgical care, an intensive care unit, skilled care, long-term care, home health services, and broad diagnostic capabilities. Founded in 1912. **NOTE:** Entry-level positions, part-time jobs, and second and third shifts are offered. **Common positions include:** Account Manager; Account Rep.; Accountant; Administrative Assistant; Blue-Collar Worker Supervisor; Certified Nurses Aide; Chief Financial Officer; Clinical Lab Technician; Computer Support Technician; Credit Manager; Customer Service Rep.; Dietician/Nutritionist; EEG Technologist; EKG Technician; Emergency Medical Technician; Help-Desk Technician; Home Health Aide; Human Resources Manager; Licensed Practical Nurse; Marketing Specialist; Medical Assistant; Medical Records Technician; Medical Secretary; MIS Specialist; Nurse Practitioner; Pharmacist; Physical Therapist; Physician; Physician Assistant; Public Relations Specialist; Purchasing Agent/Manager; Radiological Technologist; Registered Nurse; Respiratory Therapist; Secretary; Social Worker; Surgical Technician; Systems Manager. **Educational backgrounds include:** Business Administration; Communications; Computer Science; Education; Finance; Health Care; Lab Technology; Liberal Arts; Marketing; Microsoft Office; Nursing; Public Relations. **Benefits:** 403(b); Dental Insurance; Employee Discounts; Life Insurance; Medical Insurance; Sick Days (1 - 5); Tuition Assistance; Vacation Days. **Special programs:** Apprenticeships; Internships; Summer Jobs; Training. **Annual sales/revenues:** $5 - $10 million. **Number of employees at this location:** 230.

WAUSAU MEDICAL CENTER
2727 Plaza Drive, Wausau WI 54401. 715/847-3000. **Contact:** Human Resources. **Description:** A medical clinic with roughly 70 doctors practicing a wide range of medicine. **Number of employees at this location:** 450.

WEIGHT WATCHERS INTERNATIONAL
175 Crossways Park West, Woodbury NY 11797. 516/390-1400. **Contact:** Brian Powers, General Manager of Human Resources. **Description:** Conducts and supervises franchised weight-control classes in 21 countries, markets packaged products through its food licensees, and publishes the *Weight Watchers* magazine in three countries. **Corporate headquarters location:** This Location.

WESLEY WOODS CENTER OF EMORY UNIVERSITY
1817 Clifton Road, Atlanta GA 30329. 404/728-6226. **Recorded jobline:** 404/728-6280. **Contact:** Employment Coordinator. **Description:** A 100-bed geriatric hospital specializing in rehabilitation, psychiatry, and neurology. Wesley Woods is a residential facility providing intermediate health care. **Common positions include:** Administrative Assistant; Certified Nurses Aide; Dietician/Nutritionist; Licensed Practical Nurse; Occupational Therapist; Pharmacist; Physical Therapist; Registered Nurse; Respiratory Therapist; Secretary; Social Worker. **Educational backgrounds include:** Business Administration; Health Care; Liberal Arts. **Benefits:** Dental Insurance; Disability Coverage; Employee Discounts; Life Insurance; Medical Insurance; Public Transit Available; Tuition Assistance. **Special programs:** Internships.

WEST HILLS HOSPITAL
1240 East Ninth Street, Reno NV 89520. 775/323-0478. **Recorded jobline:** 775/789-4286. **Contact:** Peggy L. Hindes, Director of Human Resources. **E-mail address:** bhchr@aol.com. **Description:** A medical facility that specializes in the treatment of alcohol and chemical dependency. The hospital also offers psychiatric and mental health services. **NOTE:** Entry-level positions, part-time jobs, and second and third shifts are offered. **Common positions include:** Accountant; Certified Nurses Aide; Claim Representative; Counselor; Licensed Practical Nurse; Marketing Specialist; Pharmacist; Psychologist; Registered Nurse; Social Worker; Teacher/Professor. **Educational backgrounds include:** Health Care; Microsoft Office. **Benefits:** 401(k); Casual Dress - Fridays; Dental Insurance; Disability Coverage; Flexible Schedule; Life Insurance; Medical Insurance; Savings Plan; Sick Days (6 - 10); Tuition Assistance; Vacation Days (10 - 20); Vision Insurance. **Special programs:** Internships; Apprenticeships. **CEO:** Alan Chapman.

WILCOX MEMORIAL HOSPITAL
3420 Kuhio Highway, Lihue HI 96766. 808/245-1140. **Fax:** 808/245-1211. **Contact:** Human Resources. **Description:** A 185-bed, acute and long-term care hospital. The hospital specializes in arthroscopic surgery, dermatology, emergency medicine, internal medicine, laser surger, neurology, pathology, pediatrics, radiology, obstetrics, orthopedics, and urology. **Common positions include:** Accountant; Buyer; Claim Representative; Clinical Lab Technician; Computer Programmer; Dietician/Nutritionist; EKG Technician; Human Resources Manager; Licensed Practical Nurse; Medical Records Technician; Nuclear Medicine Technologist; Occupational Therapist; Pharmacist; Physical Therapist; Physician; Public Relations Specialist; Purchasing Agent/Manager; Radiological Technologist; Registered Nurse; Respiratory Therapist; Social Worker; Surgical Technician. **Educational backgrounds include:** Accounting; Business Administration; Computer Science; Finance; Health Care; Marketing. **Benefits:** 401(k); Dental Insurance; Disability Coverage; Life Insurance; Medical Insurance; Pension Plan; Tuition Assistance; Vision Insurance. **Corporate headquarters location:** This Location.

WILLAMETTE VALLEY MEDICAL CENTER
2700 Three Mile Lane, McMinnville OR 97128.
503/435-6131. **Fax:** 503/435-6374. **Recorded
jobline:** 503/435-6372. **Contact:** Ernie Pressman,
Human Resources Director. **World Wide Web
address:** http://www.wvmcweb.com. **Description:**
An acute care inpatient and outpatient medical
center. Founded in 1904. **NOTE:** Part-time jobs and
second and third shifts are offered. **Common
positions include:** Certified Nurses Aide; Licensed
Practical Nurse; Medical Records Technician;
Nuclear Medicine Technologist; Nurse Practitioner;
Occupational Therapist; Pharmacist; Physical
Therapist; Physical Therapy Assistant; Radiological
Technologist; Registered Nurse; Respiratory
Therapist; Social Worker; Surgical Technician.
Educational backgrounds include: Health Care.
Benefits: 401(k); Dental Insurance; Disability
Coverage; Life Insurance; Medical Insurance;
Pension Plan. **Office hours:** Monday - Friday, 8:00
a.m. - 5:00 p.m. **Corporate headquarters location:**
Dallas TX. **Other U.S. locations:** Nationwide.
Parent company: Triad Hospital, Inc.

WILSON CENTER
P.O. Box 917, Faribault MN 55021. 507/334-5561.
Fax: 507/334-9208. **Contact:** Cindy Oestreich,
Human Resources Director. **World Wide
Web address:** http://www.wilsoncenter.com.
Description: A residential psychiatric facility for
children, adolescents, and adults. Founded in 1971.
NOTE: Entry-level positions and second and third
shifts are offered. **Common positions include:**
Accountant; Administrative Assistant; Chief
Financial Officer; Counselor; Electrician; Human
Resources Manager; Licensed Practical Nurse;
Medical Records Technician; Occupational
Therapist; Physician; Psychologist; Registered
Nurse; Secretary; Social Worker; Teacher/Professor;
Typist/Word Processor. **Educational backgrounds
include:** Health Care; Human Services; Liberal
Arts. **Benefits:** 401(k); Dental Insurance; Disability
Coverage; Life Insurance; Medical Insurance; Profit
Sharing; Savings Plan. **Special programs:**
Internships; Summer Jobs; Training. **Corporate
headquarters location:** This Location.

**WOMEN'S CHRISTIAN ASSOCIATION
HOSPITAL**
207 Foote Avenue, Jamestown NY 14701. 716/664-
8227. **Fax:** 716/664-8307. **Contact:** Karen Bohall,
Employment Coordinator. **Description:** A 342-bed,
nonsectarian, nonprofit, regional medical center.
NOTE: Entry-level positions, part-time jobs, and
second and third shifts are offered. **Common
positions include:** Accountant; Certified Nurses
Aide; Certified Occupational Therapy Assistant;
Computer Programmer; Computer Support
Technician; Counselor; Credit Manager; Dietician/
Nutritionist; EEG Technologist; EKG Technician;
Electrician; Help-Desk Technician; Licensed
Practical Nurse; Medical Secretary; Network/
Systems Administrator; Nuclear Medicine
Technologist; Nurse Practitioner; Occupational
Therapist; Pharmacist; Physical Therapist; Physical
Therapy Assistant; Physician Assistant;
Psychologist; Public Relations Specialist;
Purchasing Agent/Manager; Recreational Therapist;
Registered Nurse; Respiratory Therapist; Secretary;

Social Worker; Speech-Language Pathologist;
Surgical Technician; Systems Analyst. **Educational
backgrounds include:** Accounting; Business
Administration; Liberal Arts; Mathematics;
Microsoft Office; Microsoft Word; Nursing.
Benefits: 403(b); Dental Insurance; Disability
Coverage; Life Insurance; Medical Insurance;
Pension Plan; Relocation Assistance; Savings Plan;
Sick Days (11+); Tuition Assistance; Vacation Days
(10 - 20). **Office hours:** Monday - Friday, 7:00 a.m.
- 5:00 p.m.

XOMED SURGICAL PRODUCTS
6743 Southpoint Drive North, Jacksonville FL
32216. 904/296-9600. **Contact:** Human Resources.
World Wide Web address: http://www.
xomed.com. **Description:** Manufactures medical
devices and products for ear, nose, and throat
surgery. **Common positions include:** Accountant;
Biomedical Engineer; Buyer; Customer Service
Rep.; Draftsperson; Electrical/Electronics Engineer;
Electrician; Financial Manager; Machinist;
Manufacturer's/Wholesaler's Sales Rep.; Market
Research Analyst; Mechanical Engineer; Purchasing
Agent/Manager; Quality Control Supervisor;
Software Engineer; Tool and Die Maker;
Typist/Word Processor. **Educational backgrounds
include:** Accounting; Business Administration;
Communications; Computer Science; Engineering;
Finance; Marketing. **Benefits:** Dental Insurance;
Disability Coverage; Life Insurance; Medical
Insurance; Pension Plan; Profit Sharing; Savings
Plan; Tuition Assistance. **Corporate headquarters
location:** This Location.

YOUVILLE LIFECARE, INC.
1575 Cambridge Street, Cambridge MA 02138-
4398. 617/876-4344. **Fax:** 617/234-7996. **Contact:**
Susan Ditto, Manager of Employment and
Employee Relations. **Description:** A nonprofit
hospital and nursing home offering rehabilitation
and medical care. **Common positions include:**
Occupational Therapist; Pharmacist; Physical
Therapist; Recreational Therapist; Registered Nurse;
Respiratory Therapist. **Educational backgrounds
include:** Health Care; M.D./Medicine. **Benefits:**
401(k); Dental Insurance; Disability Coverage;
Employee Discounts; Life Insurance; Medical
Insurance; Pension Plan; Savings Plan; Tuition
Assistance. **Special programs:** Internships.
Corporate headquarters location: This Location.

ZIMMER INC.
P.O. Box 708, Warsaw IN 46581. 219/267-6131.
Contact: Employment Office. **Description:**
Develops, manufactures, and markets orthopedic
products for human implant and patient care.
Zimmer's primary customers are hospitals.
Common positions include: Accountant/Auditor;
Buyer; Computer Programmer; Financial Analyst;
Human Resources Manager; Mechanical Engineer;
Product Manager. **Educational backgrounds
include:** Business Administration; Engineering;
Finance. **Benefits:** Dental Insurance; Disability
Coverage; Employee Discounts; Life Insurance;
Medical Insurance; Pension Plan; Prescription
Drugs; Savings Plan; Tuition Assistance. **Corporate
headquarters location:** This Location.

For more information on career opportunities in the health care industry:

Associations

**ACCREDITING COMMISSION ON
EDUCATION FOR HEALTH SERVICES
ADMINISTRATION**
730 11th Street NW, 4th Floor, Washington DC
20001. 202/638-5131.

**AMBULATORY INFORMATION
MANAGEMENT ASSOCIATION
BAY VALLEY MEDICAL GROUP**
27212 Calaroga Avenue, Hayward CA 94545.
510/293-5688. Contact: Martha Feinberg,
Membership Coordinator. E-mail address: info@

aim4.org. World Wide Web address: http://www.aim4.org.

AMERICAN ACADEMY OF ALLERGY, ASTHMA, & IMMUNOLOGY
611 East Wells Street, Milwaukee WI 53202. 414/272-6071. World Wide Web address: http://www.aaaai.org.

AMERICAN ACADEMY OF FAMILY PHYSICIANS
11400 Tomahawk Creek Parkway, Leawood KS 66211. 913/906-6000. World Wide Web address: http://www.aafp.org. Promotes continuing education for family physicians.

AMERICAN ACADEMY OF NURSE PRACTITIONERS
P.O. Box 12846, Austin TX 78711. 512/442-4262. Fax: 512/442-6469. World Wide Web address: http://www.aanp.org.

AMERICAN ACADEMY OF OPHTHALMOLOGY
655 Beech Street, San Francisco CA 94109. 415/561-8500. World Wide Web address: http://www.eyenet.org.

AMERICAN ACADEMY OF PEDIATRIC DENTISTRY
211 East Chicago Avenue, Suite 700, Chicago IL 60611-2616. 312/337-2169. World Wide Web address: http://www.aapd.org.

AMERICAN ACADEMY OF PERIODONTOLOGY
737 North Michigan Avenue, Suite 800, Chicago IL 60611-2690. 312/573-3218. World Wide Web address: http://www.perio.org.

AMERICAN ACADEMY OF PHYSICAL MEDICINE AND REHABILITATION
One IBM Plaza, Suite 2500, Chicago IL 60611. 312/464-9700. Fax: 312/464-0227. World Wide Web address: http://www.aapmr.org.

AMERICAN ACADEMY OF PHYSICIAN ASSISTANTS
950 North Washington Street, Alexandria VA 22314-1552. 703/836-2272. World Wide Web address: http://www.aapa.org.

AMERICAN ASSOCIATION FOR CLINICAL CHEMISTRY
2101 L Street NW, Suite 202, Washington DC 20037. 202/857-0717. World Wide Web address: http://www.aacc.org.

AMERICAN ASSOCIATION FOR HEALTH EDUCATION
1900 Association Drive, Reston VA 20191-1599. 703/476-3437. Fax: 703/476-6638. World Wide Web address: http://www.aahperd.org/aahe/aahe-main.html.

AMERICAN ASSOCIATION FOR RESPIRATORY CARE
11030 Ables Lane, Dallas TX 75229. 972/243-2272. World Wide Web address: http://www.aarc.org. Promotes the art and science of respiratory care, while focusing on the needs of the patients.

AMERICAN ASSOCIATION OF COLLEGES OF OSTEOPATHIC MEDICINE
5550 Friendship Boulevard, Suite 310, Chevy Chase MD 20815. 301/968-4100. World Wide Web address: http://www.aacom.org.

AMERICAN ASSOCIATION OF COLLEGES OF PODIATRIC MEDICINE
1350 Piccard Drive, Suite 322, Rockville MD 20850-4307. 301/990-7400. Fax: 301/990-2807. World Wide Web address: http://www.aacpm.org. Provides applications processing services for colleges of podiatric medicine.

AMERICAN ASSOCIATION OF DENTAL SCHOOLS
1625 Massachusetts Avenue NW, Suite 600, Washington DC 20036-2212. 202/667-9433. Fax: 202/667-0642. E-mail address: aads@aads.jhu.edu. World Wide Web address: http://www.aads.jhu.edu.

AMERICAN ASSOCIATION OF HEALTHCARE CONSULTANTS
11208 Waples Mill Road, Suite 109, Fairfax VA 22030. 703/691-2242. World Wide Web address: http://www.aahc.net.

AMERICAN ASSOCIATION OF HOMES AND SERVICES FOR THE AGING
901 E Street NW, Suite 500, Washington DC 20004. 202/783-2242. World Wide Web address: http://www.aahsa.org.

AMERICAN ASSOCIATION OF MEDICAL ASSISTANTS
20 North Wacker Drive, Suite 1575, Chicago IL 60606. 312/899-1500. World Wide Web address: http://www.aama-ntl.org.

AMERICAN ASSOCIATION OF NURSE ANESTHETISTS
222 South Prospect Avenue, Park Ridge IL 60068-4001. 847/692-7050. World Wide Web address: http://www.aana.com

AMERICAN ASSOCIATION OF ORAL AND MAXILLOFACIAL SURGEONS
9700 West Bryn Mawr Avenue, Rosemont IL 60018-5701. 847/678-6200. World Wide Web address: http://www.aaoms.org.

AMERICAN CHIROPRACTIC ASSOCIATION
1701 Clarendon Boulevard, Arlington VA 22209. 703/276-8800. World Wide Web address: http://www.amerchiro.org. A national, nonprofit professional membership organization offering educational services (through films, booklets, texts, and kits), regional seminars and workshops, and major health and education activities that provide information on public health, safety, physical fitness, and disease prevention.

AMERICAN COLLEGE OF HEALTH CARE ADMINISTRATORS
1800 Diagonal Road, Suite 355, Alexandria VA 22314. 703/739-7900. World Wide Web address: http://www.achca.org. A professional membership society for individual long-term care professionals. Sponsors educational programs, supports research, and produces a number of publications.

AMERICAN COLLEGE OF HEALTHCARE EXECUTIVES
One North Franklin Street, Suite 1700, Chicago IL 60606-3491. 312/424-2800. World Wide Web address: http://www.ache.org. Offers credentialing and educational programs. Publishes *Hospital & Health Services Administration* (a journal), and *Healthcare Executive* (a magazine).

AMERICAN COLLEGE OF MEDICAL PRACTICE EXECUTIVES
104 Inverness Terrace East, Englewood CO 80112-5306. 303/799-1111. World Wide Web address: http://www.mgma.com/acmpe.

AMERICAN COLLEGE OF OBSTETRICIANS AND GYNECOLOGISTS
409 12th Street SW, P.O. Box 96920, Washington DC 20090-6920. World Wide Web address: http://www.acog.org.

AMERICAN COLLEGE OF PHYSICIAN EXECUTIVES
4890 West Kennedy Boulevard, Suite 200, Tampa FL 33609-2575. 813/287-2000. Fax: 813/287-8993. World Wide Web address: http://www.acpe.org.

AMERICAN DENTAL HYGIENISTS' ASSOCIATION
444 North Michigan Avenue, Suite 3400, Chicago IL 60611. 312/440-8900. World Wide Web address: http://www.adha.org.

AMERICAN DIABETES ASSOCIATION
1701 North Beauregard Street, Alexandria VA 22311. Toll-free phone: 800/232-3472. World Wide Web address: http://www.diabetes.org. A nonprofit health organization dedicated to researching, preventing, and finding a cure for diabetes.

AMERICAN DIETETIC ASSOCIATION
216 West Jackson Boulevard, Suite 800, Chicago IL 60606. 312/899-0040. Toll-free phone: 800/877-1600. World Wide Web address: http://www.eatright.org. Promotes optimal nutrition to improve public health and well-being.

AMERICAN HEALTH INFORMATION MANAGEMENT ASSOCIATION
233 North Michigan Avenue, Suite 2150, Chicago IL 60601. 312/787-2672. World Wide Web address: http://www.ahima.org.

AMERICAN HEALTHCARE RADIOLOGY ADMINISTRATORS
111 Boston Post Road, Suite 105, Sudbury MA 01776. Toll-free phone: 800/334-2472. Fax: 978/443-8046. World Wide Web address: http://www.ahraonline.org.

AMERICAN HOSPITAL ASSOCIATION
One North Franklin Avenue, Chicago IL 60606. 312/422-3000. World Wide Web address: http://www.aha.org.

AMERICAN LUNG ASSOCIATION
1740 Broadway, New York NY 10019. Toll-free phone: 800/586-4872. World Wide Web address: http://www.lungusa.org. Focused on preventing and curing lung disease through research, education, and fundraising.

AMERICAN MEDICAL ASSOCIATION
515 North State Street, Chicago IL 60610. 312/464-5000. World Wide Web address: http://www.ama-assn.org. An organization for medical doctors.

AMERICAN MEDICAL INFORMATICS ASSOCIATION
4915 St. Elmo Avenue, Suite 401, Bethesda MD 20814. 301/657-1291. World Wide Web address: http://www.amia.org.

AMERICAN MEDICAL TECHNOLOGISTS
710 Higgins Road, Park Ridge IL 60068. 847/823-5169. World Wide Web address: http://www. amt1.com.

AMERICAN MEDICAL WOMEN'S ASSOCIATION
801 North Fairfax Street, Suite 400, Alexandria VA 22314. 703/838-0500. Fax: 703/549-3864. E-mail address: info@amwa-doc.org. World Wide Web

address: http://www.amwa-doc.org. Supports the advancement of women in medicine.

AMERICAN NURSES ASSOCIATION
600 Maryland Avenue SW, Suite 100W, Washington DC 20024. 202/554-4444. World Wide Web address: http://www.nursingworld.org.

AMERICAN OCCUPATIONAL THERAPY ASSOCIATION, INC.
4720 Montgomery Lane, Bethesda MD 20824-1220. 301/652-2682. Toll-free phone: 800/377-8555. Fax: 301/652-7711. World Wide Web address: http://www.aota.org.

AMERICAN ORGANIZATION OF NURSE EXECUTIVES
One North Franklin Street, 34th Floor, Chicago IL 60606. 312/422-2800. World Wide Web address: http://www.aone.org.

AMERICAN ORTHOPAEDIC ASSOCIATION
6300 North River Road, Suite 505, Rosemont IL 60018. 847/318-7330. World Wide Web address: http://www.aoassn.org.

AMERICAN PHYSICAL THERAPY ASSOCIATION
1111 North Fairfax Street, Alexandria VA 22314. 703/684-2782. World Wide Web address: http://www.apta.org. Small fee required for information.

AMERICAN PODIATRIC MEDICAL ASSOCIATION
9312 Old Georgetown Road, Bethesda MD 20814-1698. 301/571-9200. World Wide Web address: http://www.apma.org.

AMERICAN PSYCHIATRIC ASSOCIATION
World Wide Web address: http://www.psych.org. Professional association for mental health professionals.

AMERICAN PUBLIC HEALTH ASSOCIATION
1015 15th Street NW, Suite 300, Washington DC 20005. 202/789-5600. World Wide Web address: http://www.apha.org.

AMERICAN SOCIETY OF ANESTHESIOLOGISTS
520 North NW Highway, Park Ridge IL 60068. 847/825-5586. World Wide Web address: http://www.asahq.org.

AMERICAN SPEECH LANGUAGE HEARING ASSOCIATION
10801 Rockville Pike, Rockville MD 20852. Toll-free phone: 800/498-2071. World Wide Web address: http://www.asha.org. Professional, scientific, and credentialing association for audiologists; speech-language pathologists; and speech, language, and hearing scientists.

AMERICAN VETERINARY MEDICAL ASSOCIATION
1931 North Meacham Road, Suite 100, Schaumburg IL 60173. 847/925-8070. World Wide Web address: http://www.avma.org. Provides a forum for the discussion of issues in the veterinary profession.

ASSOCIATION OF AMERICAN MEDICAL COLLEGES
2450 N Street NW, Washington DC 20037-1126. 202/828-0400. World Wide Web address: http://www.aamc.org.

ASSOCIATION OF UNIVERSITY PROGRAMS IN HEALTH ADMINISTRATION
730 11th Street NW, Washington DC 20001. 202/638-1448.

ASTHMA & ALLERGY FOUNDATION OF AMERICA
1233 20th Street NW,Suite 402, Washington DC 20036. Toll-free phone: 800/727-8462. World Wide Web address: http://www.aafa.org. A nonprofit health organization focused on assisting those suffering from asthma and/or allergies. The organization publishes *BreathingEasier*, a newsletter that provides allergy and asthma sufferers with current information about their diseases.

HEALTHCARE FINANCIAL MANAGEMENT ASSOCIATION
2 Westbrook Corporate Center, Suite 700, Westchester IL 60154-5700. 708/531-9600. World Wide Web address: http://www.hfma.org.

HEALTHCARE INFORMATION AND MANAGEMENT SYSTEMS SOCIETY
230 East Ohio Street, Suite 500, Chicago IL 60611. 312/664-4467. World Wide Web address: http://www.himss.org.

NATIONAL ASSOCIATION FOR CHIROPRACTIC MEDICINE
15427 Baybrook Drive, Houston TX 77062. 281/280-8262. World Wide Web address: http://www.chiromed.org.

NATIONAL COALITION OF HISPANIC HEALTH AND HUMAN SERVICES ORGANIZATIONS
1501 16th Street NW, Washington DC 20036. 202/387-5000. World Wide Web address: http://www.cossmho.org. Strives to improve the health and well-being of Hispanic communities throughout the United States.

NATIONAL HOSPICE ORGANIZATION
1700 Diagonal Road, Suite 300, Alexandria VA 22314. 703/243-5900. World Wide Web address: http://www.nho.org. Educates and advocates for the principles of hospice care to meet the needs of the terminally ill.

NATIONAL MEDICAL ASSOCIATION
1012 10th Street NW, Washington DC 20001. 202/347-1895. World Wide Web address: http://www.nmanet.org.

NATIONAL MENTAL HEALTH ASSOCIATION
1021 Prince Street, Alexandria VA 22314-2971. Toll-free phone: 800/969-6642. World Wide Web address: http://www.nmha.org. Focuses on preventing mental illness, improving mental health services, and educating the public on symptoms of and treatments for mental illnesses.

Magazines

HEALTHCARE EXECUTIVE
American College of Health Care Executives, One North Franklin Street, Suite 1700, Chicago IL 60606-3491. 312/424-2800.

MODERN HEALTHCARE
Crain Communications, 740 North Rush Street, Chicago IL 60611. 312/649-5350. World Wide Web address: http://www.modernhealthcare.com.

NURSEFAX
Springhouse Corporation, 1111 Bethlehem Pike, Springhouse PA 19477. 215/646-8700. World Wide Web address: http://www.springnet.com. This is a jobline service designed to be used in conjunction with *Nursing* magazine. Please call to obtain a copy of a magazine or the *Nursing* directory.

Online Services

AMIA/MEDSIG
Go: MedSIG. A CompuServe forum for health care professionals to discuss and exchange information about topics in medicine.

ACADEMIC PHYSICIAN AND SCIENTIST
World Wide Web address: http://www. acphysci.com.A great resource for jobseekers interested in administrative or clinical positions at teaching hospitals.

AMERICA'S HEALTH CARE SOURCE
World Wide Web address: http://www. healthcaresource.com.

HEALTH CARE JOB STORE
World Wide Web address: http://www. healthcarejobstore.com.

HEALTH CAREER WEB
World Wide Web address: http://www. healthcareerweb.com. Offers career advice, an e-mail service for jobseekers, and links to career books.

MEDSEARCH AMERICA
World Wide Web address: http://www. medsearch.com. Offers national and international job searches, career forums, a resume builder, resume posting, recruiters' sites, listings of professional associations, and employer profiles.

MEDZILLA
E-mail address: info@medzilla.com. World Wide Web address: http://www.medzilla.com. Lists job openings for professionals in the fields of health care, medicine, and science related industries.

NURSING SPECTRUM CAREER FITNESS ONLINE
World Wide Web address: http://www. nursingspectrum.com. Provides a schedule of nationwide nursing events, a chat area, health care policy information, and educational resources.

PHYSICIAN'S EMPLOYMENT
World Wide Web address: http://www.physemp.com. Lists over 2,000 job openings for physicians, nurses, and allied health professionals.

SALUDOS WEB CAREER GUIDE: HEALTH CARE
World Wide Web address: http://www. saludos.com/cguide/hcguide.html. Provides information for jobseekers looking in the health care field. The site includes links to several health care associations and other sites that are sources of job openings in health care.

Hotels and Restaurants

You can expect to find the following types of companies in this chapter:
Casinos • Dinner Theaters • Hotel/Motel Operators • Resorts • Restaurants

Some helpful information: *Hotel workers, such as clerks, food service workers, and housekeepers, generally earn approximately $20,000 or less per year. Excluding tips, restaurant waitstaff and bartenders normally earn between $10,000 and $20,000 per year. Entry-level management candidates with degrees from hotel or restaurant management schools earn an average of $20,000 - $25,000 on their first job, and experienced management personnel at first class hotels or large restaurant chains can earn as much as $100,000 or more annually.*

ACW CORPORATION
110 South Poplar Street, Suite 102, Wilmington DE 19801. 302/427-1776. **Fax:** 302/427-1775. **Contact:** Personnel. **Description:** A franchisee of Arby's restaurants. **Common positions include:** Management Trainee; Restaurant/Food Service Manager. **Educational backgrounds include:** Business Administration; Hospitality; Liberal Arts. **Benefits:** 401(k); Dental Insurance; Disability Coverage; Employee Discounts; Life Insurance; Medical Insurance. **Special programs:** Internships. **Corporate headquarters location:** This Location.

ACAPULCO RESTAURANTS
4001 Via Oro Avenue, Suite 200, Long Beach CA 90810. 310/513-7500. **Contact:** Human Resources. **Description:** Operates a chain of over 40 Mexican restaurants, primarily in Southern California. **Common positions include:** General Manager; Management Trainee. **Benefits:** Dental Insurance; Disability Coverage; Employee Discounts; Life Insurance; Medical Insurance; Savings Plan. **Corporate headquarters location:** This Location. **Parent company:** Restaurant Associates.

ALAMO CAFE
10431 Gulfdale, San Antonio TX 78216. 210/341-1336. **Fax:** 210/341-3036. **Contact:** Personnel. **Description:** A family-style restaurant that serves both American and Mexican foods. **Corporate headquarters location:** This Location. **Other U.S. locations:** Dallas TX. **Parent company:** Alamo Restaurants Inc.

AMBASSADOR FOOD SERVICES CORP.
3269 Roanoke Road, Kansas City MO 64111. 816/561-6474. **Contact:** Human Resources. **Description:** Ambassador Food Services Corporation provides beverages, candy, snacks, and other vending machine items and cafeteria services. The company also provides janitorial and maintenance services. **Corporate headquarters location:** This Location.

AMERICAN RESTAURANT PARTNERS RESTAURANT MANAGEMENT CO.
555 North Woodlawn, Suite 3102, Wichita KS 67208. 316/684-5119. **Fax:** 316/684-9780. **Contact:** Human Resources. **Description:** A limited partnership operating more than 90 Pizza Hut restaurants and delivery/carry-out facilities, located primarily in Texas, Montana, Oklahoma, Georgia, Louisiana, and Wyoming. **NOTE:** Entry-level positions are offered. **Common positions include:** Accountant/Auditor; Property and Real Estate Manager; Public Relations Specialist; Restaurant/ Food Service Manager. **Educational backgrounds include:** Accounting; Business Administration; Marketing. **Benefits:** 401(k); Dental Insurance; Disability Coverage; Life Insurance; Medical Insurance; Profit Sharing; Tuition Assistance. **Special programs:** Training. **Corporate headquarters location:** This Location.

AMERISTAR CASINOS, INC.
3773 Howard Hughes Parkway, Suite 490S, Las Vegas NV 89109. 702/567-7000. **Fax:** 702/369-8860. **Contact:** Human Resources Manager. **World Wide Web address:** http://www.ameristars.com. **Description:** A casino holding company. **Corporate headquarters location:** This Location. **Subsidiaries include:** Ameristar Casino Council Bluffs (Council Bluffs IA); Ameristar Casino Vicksburg (Vicksburg MS); Cactus Petes Resort Casino (Jackpot NV); The Horeshu Hotel and Casino (Jackpot NV).

ANTHONY'S FISH GROTTO
5232 Lovelock Street, San Diego CA 92110. 619/291-7254. **Contact:** Personnel. **World Wide Web address:** http://www.gofishanthonys.com. **Description:** A family-owned restaurant chain specializing in seafood. Anthony's Fish Grotto also sells seafood to the public. **Common positions include:** General Manager; Management Trainee. **Educational backgrounds include:** Business Administration. **Benefits:** Dental Insurance; Life Insurance; Medical Insurance; Pension Plan. **Corporate headquarters location:** This Location.

ARAMARK/LAKE POWELL RESORTS AND MARINAS
P.O. Box 1597, Page AZ 86040. 520/645-1081. **Fax:** 520/645-1016. **Contact:** Staffing & Placement. **Description:** Operates five marinas on Lake Powell and owns resorts located throughout the Glen Canyon recreation area. **Common positions include:** Hotel Manager; Restaurant/Food Service Manager; Water Transportation Specialist. **Benefits:** 401(k); Dental Insurance; Disability Coverage; Employee Discounts; Life Insurance; Medical Insurance; Profit Sharing; Tuition Assistance. **Special programs:** Internships. **Other U.S. locations:** Nationwide. **Parent company:** ARAMARK is one of the world's leading providers of managed services. The company operates in all 50 states and 10 foreign countries, offering a broad range of services to businesses of all sizes, including most *Fortune* 500 companies and thousands of universities, hospitals, and municipal, state, and federal government facilities. ARAMARK's businesses include Food, Leisure and Support Services including Campus Dining Services, School Nutrition Services, Business Dining Services, International Services, Healthcare Support Services, Conference Center Management, and Refreshment Services; Facility Services; Correctional Services; Industrial Services; Uniform

Services, which includes Uniform Services and Wearguard, a direct marketer of work clothing; Health and Education Services, including Spectrum Healthcare Services and Children's World Learning Centers; and Book and Magazine Services.

ARBY'S/FRANCHISE ASSOCIATES INC.
5354 Parkdale Drive, Suite 100, Minneapolis MN 55416. 612/593-4243. **Fax:** 612/546-8342. **Recorded jobline:** 612/593-4298. **Contact:** Staffing Manager. **E-mail address:** fai.tasch@minn.net. **Description:** Operates a franchise of several national restaurant chains including Arby's and Sbarro. **Common positions include:** Assistant Manager; District Manager; General Manager; Management Trainee. **Educational backgrounds include:** Business; Communications; Education; Hospitality; Liberal Arts; Marketing; Psychology. **Benefits:** 401(k); Dental Insurance; Disability Coverage; Employee Discounts; Life Insurance; Medical Insurance; Profit Sharing; Savings Plan; Tuition Assistance. **Corporate headquarters location:** This Location.

ARCTIC CIRCLE RESTAURANTS
P.O. Box 339, Midvale UT 84047. 801/561-3620. **Contact:** Human Resources. **Description:** Owns and operates the Arctic Circle restaurant chain. **Corporate headquarters location:** This Location.

ARGOSY CASINO
219 Piasa Street, Alton IL 62002. 618/474-7500. **Contact:** Human Resources Manager. **World Wide Web address:** http://www.argosycasinos.com. **Description:** A gaming company which operates riverboat casinos. Founded in 1991. **NOTE:** This office only hires for this location. Please contact other locations individually. **Common positions include:** Accountant; Administrative Assistant; Auditor; Emergency Medical Technician; Human Resources Manager; Market Research Analyst; MIS Specialist; Purchasing Agent/Manager; Sales Manager. **Educational backgrounds include:** Accounting; Business; Communications; Computer Science; Finance; Marketing. **Benefits:** 401(k); Dental Insurance; Disability Coverage; Employee Discounts; Flexible Dependent Care; Life Insurance; Medical Insurance; Sick Days. **Corporate headquarters location:** This Location. **Other U.S. locations:** Sioux City IA; Lawrenceburg IN; Baton Rouge LA; Kansas City MO. **International locations:** Worldwide. **Listed on:** New York Stock Exchange. **Stock exchange symbol:** AGY. **President/CEO:** James B. Perry. **Annual sales/revenues:** More than $100 million. **Number of employees at this location:** 25. **Number of employees nationwide:** 5,000.

ARIZONA CHARLIE'S, INC.
740 South Decatur Boulevard, Las Vegas NV 89107. 702/258-5200. **Contact:** Human Resources. **World Wide Web address:** http://www.azcharlies.com. **Description:** Operates a casino hotel which offers a variety of table and coin-operated games. Arizona Charlie's also has a variety of restaurants offering everything from deli sandwiches to fine dining. **Parent company:** Becker Gaming is a holding company with subsidiaries which operate a gaming machine route and own and operate the Charlie's restaurant chain.

ARIZONA FAST FOODS, L.L.C.
dba WHATABURGER
2001 North Third Street, Suite 202, Phoenix AZ 85004. 602/252-0055. **Toll-free phone:** 800/914-9729. **Fax:** 602/495-9942. **Contact:** Human Resources. **World Wide Web address:** http://www.whataburgeraz.com. **Description:** A franchise location of Whataburger, a fast-food restaurant chain. Founded in 1950. **NOTE:** Entry-level positions, second and third shifts, and part-time jobs are offered. **Common positions include:** Assistant Manager; General Manager; Management Trainee; Operations Manager. **Educational backgrounds include:** Business Administration; Finance; Marketing. **Benefits:** 401(k); Daycare Assistance; Dental Insurance; Disability Coverage; Flexible Schedule; Life Insurance; Medical Insurance; Pension Plan; Vacation Days (6 - 10). **Special programs:** Training; Summer Jobs. **Corporate headquarters location:** Corpus Christi TX.

AU BON PAIN CORPORATION
19 Fid Kennedy Avenue, Boston MA 02210. 617/423-2100. **Contact:** Human Resources. **E-mail address:** hr@aubonpain.com. **World Wide Web address:** http://www.aubonpain.com. **Description:** Au Bon Pain Corporation owns and operates a chain of 280 French bakery cafes worldwide. **NOTE:** Entry-level positions are offered. **Common positions include:** Administrative Assistant; Customer Service Rep.. **Educational backgrounds include:** Restaurant Management. **Benefits:** 401(k); Dental Insurance; Disability Coverage; Employee Discounts; Life Insurance; Medical Insurance; Public Transit Available. **Special programs:** Internships. **Corporate headquarters location:** This Location. **Other U.S. locations:** Nationwide. **Listed on:** Privately held.

AZTECA RESTAURANTS
133 SW 158th Street, Seattle WA 98166. 206/243-7021. **Contact:** Human Resources. **Description:** Owns and operates a chain of Mexican restaurants. **Common positions include:** Assistant Manager; Blue-Collar Worker Supervisor; Cashier; Chef/Cook/Kitchen Worker; Department Manager; General Manager; Human Resources Manager; Payroll Clerk. **Educational backgrounds include:** Business Administration. **Benefits:** Dental Insurance; Employee Discounts; Medical Insurance. **Corporate headquarters location:** This Location.

BABBITT BROTHERS TRADING CO.
P.O. Box 1328, Flagstaff AZ 86002. 520/774-8711. **Contact:** Human Resources. **Description:** A holding company involved in a variety of activities including commercial real estate rentals, the operation of hotels and restaurants, and concession services for the Grand Canyon. **Corporate headquarters location:** This Location.

BACK BAY RESTAURANT GROUP, INC.
284 Newbury Street, Boston MA 02115. 617/536-2800. **Contact:** Human Resources. **World Wide Web address:** http://www.great-food.com. **Description:** Owns several Boston-based restaurant chains including Joe's American Bar & Grill, PapaRazzi, Atlantic Fish Company, and Charlie's Saloon. The company also owns a race track in New Hampshire. **Common positions include:** General Manager; Restaurant/Food Service Manager. **Educational backgrounds include:** Business Administration; Communications; Liberal Arts. **Benefits:** 401(k); Dental Insurance; Disability Coverage; Employee Discounts; Life Insurance; Medical Insurance; Profit Sharing. **Corporate headquarters location:** This Location. **Parent company:** Westwood Group.

BACK YARD BURGERS, INC.
1657 North Shelby Oaks Drive, Memphis TN 38134. 901/367-0888. **Contact:** Human Resources. **Description:** Operates and franchises a chain of fast-food restaurants, specializing in charbroiled food. **Corporate headquarters location:** This Location. **Chairman/CEO:** Lattimore M. Michael.

BAYMONT INN & SUITES
250 East Wisconsin Avenue, Suite 1500, Milwaukee WI 53202. 414/905-1000. **Contact:** Corporate Recruiter. **E-mail address:** recruiter@baymontinns.com. **World Wide Web address:** http://www.baymontinns.com. **Description:** A hospitality company operating a wide variety of hotels, theaters, entertainment centers, and restaurants. Lodging operations are partly comprised of 170 limited-service hotels located in 30 states. Founded in 1973. **Common positions include:** Accountant; Administrative Assistant; Administrative Manager; Advertising Clerk; Advertising Executive; Attorney; Claim Rep.; Computer Engineer; Computer Technician; Construction Contractor; Controller; Design Engineer; Finance Director; Financial Analyst; Help-Desk Technician; Human Resources Manager; Marketing Manager; Marketing Specialist; Real Estate Lawyer; Sales Manager; Secretary; Typist/ Word Processor. **Benefits:** 401(k); Casual Dress - Fridays; Dental Insurance; Disability Coverage; Employee Discounts; Life Insurance; Medical Insurance; Pension Plan. **Special programs:** Internships. **Corporate headquarters location:** This Location. **Parent company:** The Marcus Corporation.

BENIHANA INC.
8685 NW 53rd Terrace, Suite 201, Miami FL 33166. 305/593-0770. **Fax:** 305/592-6371. **Contact:** Human Resources. **E-mail address:** contact@benihana.com. **Description:** Owns and operates more than 60 Japanese steakhouses. Additional restaurants are operated by licensees. **Common positions include:** Accountant/Auditor; Data Entry Clerk; Purchasing Agent/Manager; Restaurant/Food Service Manager. **Educational backgrounds include:** Accounting; Business Administration; Liberal Arts. **Benefits:** Dental Insurance; Life Insurance; Medical Insurance. **Corporate headquarters location:** This Location. **Other U.S. locations:** CA; CO; GA; IL; NJ; NY; OH; OR; TX. **Subsidiaries include:** Rudy's Restaurant Group, Inc.

BENNETT ENTERPRISES, INC.
P.O. Box 670, Perrysburg OH 43552. 419/874-1933. **Fax:** 419/874-2615. **Contact:** Human Resources. **World Wide Web address:** http://www.bennett-enterprises.com. **Description:** Operates several restaurants and hotels including three Holiday Inns, one Hampton Inn, six Ralphie's Sports Bars, and 19 Big Boy Family Restaurants. **NOTE:** Entry-level positions and second and third shifts are offered. **Common positions include:** Assistant Manager; General Manager; Hotel Manager; Management Trainee; Restaurant/Food Service Manager. **Educational backgrounds include:** Hospitality; Hotel Administration. **Benefits:** 401(k); Disability Coverage; Employee Discounts; Life Insurance; Medical Insurance; Vacation Days. **Special programs:** Internships. **Corporate headquarters location:** This Location.

BEST WESTERN INTERNATIONAL, INC.
P.O. Box 10203, Phoenix AZ 85064-0203. 602/957-4200. **Contact:** Human Resources Manager. **World Wide Web address:** http://www.bestwestern.com. **Description:** Operates a mid-priced hotel chain with over 3,400 hotels in 60 countries including over 1,000 in Europe. Best Western has over 1,900 meeting facilities worldwide including 900 in the United States. **Corporate headquarters location:** This Location.

BICKFORD'S FAMILY RESTAURANTS
1330 Soldiers Field Road, Boston MA 02135. 617/782-4010. **Contact:** Personnel. **Description:**
Operates the Bickford's Family Restaurants chain in the New England area. **Common positions include:** Assistant Manager; Management Trainee; Restaurant/Food Service Manager. **Educational backgrounds include:** Food Services; High School Diploma/GED. **Benefits:** Life Insurance; Medical Insurance. **Corporate headquarters location:** This Location. **Other area locations:** Kingston, MA; Braintree MA; Brockton MA; Easton MA; Fall River MA; Quincy MA; Seekonk MA.

THE BIG MOUNTAIN SKI & SUMMER RESORT
WINTER SPORTS, INC. (WSI)
P.O. Box 1400, Whitefish MT 59937. 406/862-1936. **Fax:** 406/862-2955. **Contact:** Director of Human Resources. **E-mail address:** jobs@bigmtn.com. **World Wide Web address:** http://www.bigmtn.com. **Description:** The Big Mountain Ski & Summer Resort operates nine ski lifts serving nearly 4,000 acres of land. The Summit House is a mountaintop cafeteria, restaurant, and lounge located on U.S. Forest Service land. Base facilities including lodging, a cafeteria, restaurants and lounges, a daycare center, a ski school, a rental shop, and other related services are located on land owned by WSI. **NOTE:** Entry-level positions are offered. **Common positions include:** Account Manager; Accountant; Administrative Assistant; Advertising Clerk; Advertising Executive; Blue-Collar Worker Supervisor; General Manager; Human Resources Manager; Marketing Manager; Marketing Specialist; MIS Specialist; Public Relations Manager; Public Relations Specialist; Real Estate Agent; Sales Representative; Secretary; Transportation/Traffic Specialist; Vice President of Marketing. **Educational backgrounds include:** Accounting; Computer Science; Marketing; Public Relations. **Benefits:** 401(k); Dental Insurance; Employee Discounts; Life Insurance; Medical Insurance; Tuition Assistance. **Special programs:** Internships. **Corporate headquarters location:** This Location. **Subsidiaries include:** Big Mountain Water Company furnishes the domestic water supply to the resort and adjacent properties. Big Mountain Development Corporation oversees and coordinates the planning and development of certain parcels owned by Winter Sports, Inc.

BILL JOHNSON'S RESTAURANTS INC.
2906 West Fairmount Avenue, Phoenix AZ 85017. 602/264-5565. **Contact:** Personnel Director. **World Wide Web address:** http://www.billjohnsons.com. **Description:** Operates the Bill Johnson's chain of family-style BBQ restaurants. **Corporate headquarters location:** This Location.

BLACK-EYED PEA RESTAURANT U.S.A.
2212 Arlington Downs Road, Suite 204, Arlington TX 76011. 817/633-6992. **Contact:** Human Resources. **Description:** A full-service restaurant chain specializing in homestyle cooking. Black-Eyed Pea operates over 130 locations nationwide. **Common positions include:** Restaurant/Food Service Manager. **Benefits:** Dental Insurance; Disability Coverage; Life Insurance; Medical Insurance; Profit Sharing; Savings Plan; Stock Option; Tuition Assistance. **Corporate headquarters location:** This Location. **Other U.S. locations:** AR; DC; GA; IN; KS; MD; NC; NM; OK; SC; TN; VA. **Parent company:** Phoenix Restaurant Group, Inc. (Scottsdale, AZ).

BOB EVANS FARMS, INC.
3776 South High Street, Columbus OH 43207. 614/491-2225. **Fax:** 614/497-4318. **Contact:** Personnel. **E-mail address:** employment@bobevans.com. **World Wide Web address:** http://www.bobevans.com. **Description:** Owns and

operates over 400 family restaurants in 19 states including Bob Evans Restaurants and Owens Family Restaurants. The company also produces sausage products and deli-style salads, which are distributed primarily to grocery stores in the Midwest, Southwest, and Southeast. **NOTE:** Part-time jobs are offered. **Common positions include:** Account Manager; Accountant; Administrative Assistant; Advertising Clerk; Advertising Executive; Applications Engineer; AS400 Programmer Analyst; Claim Rep.; Computer Programmer; Computer Support Technician; Computer Technician; Construction Contractor; Controller; Customer Service Representative; Food Scientist/ Technologist; General Manager; Management Trainee; Market Research Analyst; Marketing Manager; Marketing Specialist; MIS Specialist; Network/Systems Administrator; Public Relations Specialist; Sales Manager; Sales Re.; Secretary; Systems Analyst; Transportation/Traffic Specialist; Typist/Word Processor. **Educational backgrounds include:** Accounting; AS400 Certification; Business Administration; Communications; Marketing; Microsoft Word; Nutrition; Public Relations; Software Tech. Support. **Benefits:** 401(k); Casual Dress - Fridays; Dental Insurance; Disability Coverage; Life Insurance; Medical Insurance; Public Transit Available; Tuition Assistance. **Corporate headquarters location:** This Location.

BOSTAR FOODS, INC.
dba BOJANGLES
6300 Poplar Tree Court, Suite D, Louisville KY 40228. 502/969-2001. **Contact:** Human Resources. **Description:** A restaurant specializing in fried chicken and related products, catering, and consulting. **Common positions include:** Management Trainee; Restaurant/Food Service Manager. **Benefits:** Dental Insurance; Disability Coverage; Employee Discounts; Life Insurance; Medical Insurance; Profit Sharing. **Corporate headquarters location:** This Location.

BOSTON CONCESSIONS GROUP INC.
111 Sixth Street, Cambridge MA 02141. 617/499-2700. **Fax:** 617/661-3023. **Contact:** Human Resources. **Description:** Provides food services and related products to a wide range of customers. Boston Concessions operates in 15 states. **Corporate headquarters location:** This Location.

BOSTON MARKET, INC.
14103 Denver West Parkway, Golden CO 80401. 303/278-9500. **Contact:** Human Resources. **World Wide Web address:** http://www.boston-market.com. **Description:** Operates and franchises food service stores that specialize in fresh, convenient meals. Boston Market's menu features home-style entrees, fresh vegetables, salads, and other side dishes. **Corporate headquarters location:** This Location.

THE BOULDERS RESORT
P.O. Box 2090, Carefree AZ 85377. 480/488-9009. **Recorded jobline:** 480/488-7314. **Contact:** Human Resources. **Description:** A 160-casita, luxury resort and spa that offers a variety of activities including 36 holes of golf and six tennis courts. **NOTE:** Entry-level positions, second and third shifts, and part-time jobs are offered. **Common positions include:** Administrative Assistant; Auditor; Chef/ Cook/Kitchen Worker; Food and Beverage Service Worker; Guest Services Agent; Housekeeper; Landscape/Grounds Maintenance; Restaurant/Food Service Manager. **Educational backgrounds include:** Accounting; Business Administration; Communications; Hospitality; Liberal Arts; Marketing. **Benefits:** 401(k); Dental Insurance; Disability Coverage; Employee Discounts; Job

Sharing; Life Insurance; Medical Insurance; Sick Days; Tuition Assistance; Vacation Days. **Special programs:** Apprenticeships; Internships; Training. **Corporate headquarters location:** Phoenix AZ. **Parent company:** Patriot American Hospitality.

BOYD GAMING CORPORATION
2950 South Industrial Road, Las Vegas NV 89109-1100. 702/792-7200. **Fax:** 702/792-7354. **Contact:** Human Resources. **Description:** An owner and operator of casino entertainment properties. Boyd Gaming Corporation owns and operates eight properties in Las Vegas: California Hotel & Casino; Eldorado Casino; Fremont Hotel & Casino; Jokers Wild Casino; Main Street Hotel, Casino & Brewery; Sam's Town Las Vegas; and Stardust Resort & Casino. In addition, the company owns and operates Par-A-Dice Hotel & Casino (East Peoria IL), and Treasure Chest Casino (Kenner LA), a riverboat casino; and manages the Silver Star Resort & Casino (Philadelphia MS). **Corporate headquarters location:** This Location. **Other U.S. locations:** IL; LA; MO; MS.

BOYKIN MANAGEMENT COMPANY
45 West Prospect Avenue, Suite 1500, Guildhall Building, Cleveland OH 44115. 216/241-6375. **Fax:** 216/241-1329. **Contact:** Human Resources. **Description:** A Marriott franchisee engaged in the development and management of upscale, full-service hotels. **Common positions include:** Accountant/Auditor; Chef/Cook/Kitchen Worker; Department Manager; General Manager; Hotel Manager; Human Resources Manager; Management Trainee; Marketing Specialist; Operations/ Production Manager; Services Sales Rep. **Educational backgrounds include:** Hotel Administration; Human Resources. **Benefits:** Dental Insurance; Disability Coverage; Employee Discounts; Life Insurance; Medical Insurance; Savings Plan; Tuition Assistance. **Special programs:** Internships. **Corporate headquarters location:** This Location.

BRIGHAM'S INC.
30 Mill Street, Arlington MA 02476. 781/648-9000. **Contact:** Personnel Director. **World Wide Web address:** http://www.brighams.com. **Description:** Operates a chain of more than 60 restaurants and ice cream parlors throughout New England, New York, and New Jersey. **Common positions include:** Management Trainee; Store Manager. **Educational backgrounds include:** Business Administration; Liberal Arts; Marketing. **Benefits:** 401(k); Dental Insurance; Disability Coverage; Employee Discounts; Life Insurance; Medical Insurance; Pension Plan; Savings Plan; Tuition Assistance. **Corporate headquarters location:** This Location.

BRINKER INTERNATIONAL INC.
6820 LBJ Freeway, Dallas TX 75240. 972/980-9917. **Fax:** 972/770-9593. **Contact:** Human Resources. **World Wide Web address:** http://www. brinker.com. **Description:** Operates full-service, casual dining restaurants including Chili's Grill & Bar, Cozymel's, On the Border, Romano's Macaroni Grill, and Spageddie's Italian Foods. In total, Brinker International operates 150 restaurants. **Common positions include:** Accountant/Auditor; Architect; Attorney; Buyer; Computer Programmer; Construction Contractor; Designer; General Manager; Management Trainee; Property and Real Estate Manager; Systems Analyst. **Educational backgrounds include:** Accounting; Computer Science; Finance; Hotel Administration. **Benefits:** 401(k); Daycare Assistance; Dental Insurance; Disability Coverage; Employee Discounts; Life Insurance; Medical Insurance; Profit Sharing; Public Transit Available; Stock Option; Tuition Assistance.

Corporate headquarters location: This Location. **Other U.S. locations:** Nationwide.

THE BROADMOOR HOTEL
P.O. Box 1439, Colorado Springs CO 80901. 719/634-7711. **Fax:** 719/577-5721. **Recorded jobline:** 719/577-5858. **Contact:** Employment. **World Wide Web address:** http://www. broadmoor.com. **Description:** A 700-room, five star, five diamond resort. Facilities include three championship golf courses, 15 retail outlets, nine restaurants, 12 tennis courts, and conference rooms. Founded in 1918. **NOTE:** Entry-level positions, part-time jobs, and second and third shifts are offered. This location also hires seasonally. **Common positions include:** Accountant; Administrative Assistant; Blue-Collar Worker Supervisor; Computer Operator; Customer Service Rep.; Event Planner; Sales Manager; Sales Rep. **Educational backgrounds include:** Accounting; Business Administration; Hospitality; Microsoft Word; Spreadsheets. **Benefits:** 401(k); Dental Insurance; Disability Coverage; Employee Discounts; Medical Insurance; Sick Days; Tuition Assistance; Vacation Days. **Special programs:** Internships; Apprenticeships; Training. **Corporate headquarters location:** This Location. **Parent company:** Oklahoma Publishing Company. **Listed on:** New York Stock Exchange. **President:** Steve Bartolin.

BROCK AND COMPANY, INC.
77 Great Valley Parkway, Malvern PA 19355. 610/647-5656. **Fax:** 610/647-0867. **Contact:** Human Resources Manager. **World Wide Web address:** http://www.brockco.com. **Description:** A contract food service company offering corporate dining, vending, and office coffee services. **Company slogan:** We strive for excellence. **Common positions include:** Account Rep.; Accountant; Administrative Assistant; Computer Operator; Computer Technician; General Manager; Graphic Designer; Marketing Manager; MIS Specialist; Operations Manager; Purchasing Agent/Manager; Secretary. **Benefits:** 401(k); Casual Dress - Fridays; Dental Insurance; Disability Coverage; Employee Discounts; Life Insurance; Medical Insurance. **Special programs:** Apprenticeships; Co-ops. **Corporate headquarters location:** This Location.

BROWN PALACE HOTEL
321 17th Street, Denver CO 80202. 303/297-3111. **Fax:** 303/312-5940. **Contact:** Human Resources. **World Wide Web address:** http://www. brownpalace.com. **Description:** A full-service hotel. **NOTE:** All positions require experience in four- or five-star properties. **Common positions include:** Accountant/Auditor; Cashier; Chef/Cook/Kitchen Worker; Food and Beverage Service Worker; Hotel Manager; Hotel/Motel Clerk; Machine Operator; Maitre d'Hotel; Services Sales Representative. **Educational backgrounds include:** Hospitality. **Benefits:** Dental Insurance; Disability Coverage; Employee Discounts; Free Meals; Life Insurance; Medical Insurance; Pension Plan; Tuition Assistance. **Special programs:** Internships. **Corporate headquarters location:** Dallas TX. **Parent company:** Quorum Hotels and Resorts.

BUCKHEAD AMERICA CORPORATION
7000 Central Parkway, Suite 850, Atlanta GA 30328. 770/393-2662. **Contact:** Human Resources. **World Wide Web address:** http://www. buckheadamerica.com. **Description:** Engaged in hotel franchising, hotel management, settlement, and mortgage services. **Corporate headquarters location:** This Location. **Subsidiaries include:** Country Hearth Inn is a mid-priced hotel chain.

BUFFETS, INC.
dba OLD COUNTRY BUFFET
10260 Viking Drive, Eden Prairie MN 55344. 952/942-9760. **Fax:** 952/903-1356. **Recorded jobline:** 800/388-6506. **Contact:** Human Resources. **World Wide Web address:** http://www. buffet.com. **Description:** Operates a chain of high-volume, buffet-style restaurants. **Common positions include:** Cashier; Chef/Cook/Kitchen Worker; Computer Operator; Computer Programmer; Construction Trade Worker; Draftsperson; Food and Beverage Service Worker; Management Trainee; Payroll Clerk; Restaurant/Food Service Manager; Secretary; Systems Analyst. **Benefits:** Disability Coverage; Employee Discounts; Life Insurance; Medical Insurance; Profit Sharing; Tuition Assistance. **Corporate headquarters location:** This Location. **Other U.S. locations:** Nationwide.

CEC ENTERTAINMENT INC.
dba CHUCK E. CHEESE
4441 West Airport Freeway, Irving TX 75062. 972/258-8507. **Contact:** Human Resources. **Description:** Operates over 350 Chuck E. Cheese's pizza and amusement franchises throughout the United States and Canada. **Common positions include:** Account Rep.; Attorney; Claim Rep.; Computer Programmer; Construction Contractor; General Manager; Human Resources Manager; Operations/Production Manager; Paralegal; Property and Real Estate Manager; Purchasing Agent/Manager; Restaurant/Food Service Manager; Systems Analyst. **Educational backgrounds include:** Accounting; Business Administration; Computer Science; Finance; Marketing. **Benefits:** 401(k); Daycare Assistance; Dental Insurance; Disability Coverage; Employee Discounts; Life Insurance; Medical Insurance. **Corporate headquarters location:** This Location.

CMP (CENTRAL MISSOURI PIZZA, INC.)
dba DOMINO'S PIZZA
1350 Elbridge Payne Road, Suite 208, Chesterfield MO 63017. 636/537-1120. **Fax:** 636/537-1265. **Contact:** Human Resources. **World Wide Web address:** http://www.dominos.com. **Description:** CMP is one of the largest franchisees of Domino's Pizza, with locations in Missouri and Kentucky. **Common positions include:** Management Trainee; Restaurant/Food Service Manager. **Educational backgrounds include:** Business Administration; Communications; Hospitality; Marketing; Restaurant Management. **Benefits:** Employee Discounts; Medical Insurance. **Corporate headquarters location:** This Location.

CALIFORNIA BEACH RESTAURANTS
17383 Sunset Boulevard, Suite 140, Pacific Palisades CA 90272. 310/459-9676. **Contact:** Human Resources. **Description:** Owns and operates Gladstone's 4 Fish, and RJ's - The Rib Joint. **Corporate headquarters location:** This Location.

CARLSON COMPANIES, INC.
CARLSON MARKETING GROUP
P.O. Box 59159, Minneapolis MN 55459. 612/540-5000. **Contact:** Human Resources Manager. **World Wide Web address:** http://www.carlson.com. **Description:** A highly diversified corporation doing business through a variety of subsidiaries. Business areas include hotels, restaurant operations, and retail and wholesale travel. Carlson Marketing Group (also at this location) provides a variety of marketing services for sporting events and airlines; incentive programs for employees of other companies; and strategic consulting to help client companies create customer/brand loyalty. **Corporate headquarters location:** This Location.

CARLSON RESTAURANTS WORLDWIDE
7540 LBJ Freeway, Dallas TX 75251. 972/450-5400. **Fax:** 972/776-5468. **Contact:** Employee Relations. **World Wide Web address:** http://www.tgifridays.com. **Description:** Operates the TGI Friday's chain of casual-dining restaurants, which has over 500 locations. **Corporate headquarters location:** This Location. **Parent company:** Carlson Companies, Inc. (Minneapolis MN).

CARLYLE HOTEL
35 East 76th Street, New York NY 10021. 212/744-1600. **Contact:** Personnel Manager. **Description:** A luxury hotel offering 180-rooms, three restaurants, and banquet/meeting facilities. **Corporate headquarters location:** This Location.

CARROLS CORPORATION
P.O. Box 6969, Syracuse NY 13217. 315/424-0513x318. **Physical address:** 968 James Street, Syracuse NY. **Fax:** 315/425-8874. **Contact:** Human Resources. **Description:** One of the world's largest operators of Burger King restaurants. **Common positions include:** Assistant Manager. **Educational backgrounds include:** Accounting; Business Administration; Liberal Arts. **Benefits:** Dental Insurance; Disability Coverage; Life Insurance; Medical Insurance; Savings Plan; Tuition Assistance. **Corporate headquarters location:** This Location. **Other U.S. locations:** Charlotte NC; Albany NY; Uniontown OH.

CARROLS CORPORATION
1531 Boller Road, Unit F, Uniontown OH 44685. 330/896-3838x12. **Contact:** Human Resources. **Description:** One of the world's largest operators of Burger King restaurants. **Common positions include:** Assistant Manager; Management Trainee; Operations Manager. **Educational backgrounds include:** Business Administration; Hospitality. **Benefits:** Dental Insurance; Disability Coverage; Employee Discounts; Life Insurance; Medical Insurance; Pension Plan; Profit Sharing; Savings Plan; Tuition Assistance. **Corporate headquarters location:** Syracuse NY.

CHECKERS DRIVE-IN RESTAURANTS
14255 49th Street North, Building 1, Clearwater FL 33762. 727/519-2000. **Fax:** 727/519-2237. **Contact:** Human Resources. **Description:** Develops, owns, operates, and franchises quick-service, drive-thru restaurants under the Checkers name. **Common positions include:** Restaurant/Food Service Manager. **Benefits:** 401(k); Bonus Award/Plan; Dental Insurance; Disability Coverage; Employee Discounts; Life Insurance; Medical Insurance; Stock Option. **Special programs:** Training. **Corporate headquarters location:** This Location.

THE CHEESECAKE FACTORY INC.
26950 Agoura Road, Calabasas Hills CA 91301. 818/880-9323. **Contact:** Recruiting. **Description:** The Cheesecake Factory operates a group of restaurants featuring an extensive menu and moderate prices. The company also operates a production facility that manufactures over 50 varieties of its signature cheesecakes and other baked goods for sale both in its restaurants and through wholesale accounts. The company operates restaurants in California, Florida, Georgia, Illinois, Maryland, Massachusetts, Rhode Island, and Washington DC. **Corporate headquarters location:** This Location.

CHEFS INTERNATIONAL, INC.
62 Broadway, P.O. Box 1332, Point Pleasant Beach NJ 08742. 732/295-0350. **Contact:** Human Resources. **World Wide Web address:** http://www.sunet.net/lobstershanty. **Description:** Operates eight Lobster Shanty restaurants in New Jersey and Florida. **Corporate headquarters location:** This Location.

CHESAPEAKE RESTAURANT GROUP
8027 Leesburg Pike, Suite 506, Vienna VA 22182. 703/827-0320. **Contact:** Recruiter. **World Wide Web address:** http://www.chilis.net. **Description:** Operates eight Chesapeake Bay Seafood Houses, 16 Chili's, and four Easby's restaurants. **Common positions include:** Assistant Manager; Management Trainee; Restaurant/Food Service Manager. **Educational backgrounds include:** Business Administration; Hospitality; Hotel Administration; Restaurant Management. **Benefits:** Dental Insurance; Disability Coverage; Employee Discounts; Life Insurance; Medical Insurance; Profit Sharing. **Special programs:** Internships. **Corporate headquarters location:** This Location.

CHI-CHI'S
10200 Linn Station Road, Louisville KY 40223. 502/426-3900. **Contact:** Human Resources. **Description:** A Mexican restaurant chain. **Corporate headquarters location:** This Location.

CHOICE HOTELS INTERNATIONAL
10750 Columbia Pike, Silver Spring MD 20901. 301/592-5000. **Contact:** Human Resources. **World Wide Web address:** http://www.choicehotels.com. **Description:** An internationally franchised hotel company. **Common positions include:** Administrative Manager; Advertising Clerk; Buyer; Computer Operator; Computer Programmer; Customer Service Rep.; Financial Manager; Graphic Artist; Hotel/Motel Clerk; Marketing Manager; Property and Real Estate Manager; Public Relations Specialist; Purchasing Agent/Manager; Quality Control Supervisor; Receptionist; Secretary; Services Sales Representative; Systems Analyst; Travel Agent; Typist/Word Processor. **Educational backgrounds include:** Hospitality; Marketing. **Benefits:** Dental Insurance; Disability Coverage; Employee Discounts; Life Insurance; Medical Insurance; Pension Plan; Profit Sharing; Savings Plan; Tuition Assistance. **Corporate headquarters location:** This Location. **Subsidiaries include:** Clarion Hotels; Comfort Inns; Econo Lodge; Main Stay Suites; Quality Inns; Rodeway; Sleep Inns. **Parent company:** Manor Care, Inc.

THE CLUB GROUP, LTD.
P.O. Drawer 6989, Hilton Head SC 29938. 843/363-5699. **Contact:** Human Resources Manager. **Description:** Operates a resort. **Common positions include:** Accountant/Auditor; Chef/Cook/Kitchen Worker; Food and Beverage Service Worker; Hotel Manager; Human Resources Manager; Restaurant/Food Service Manager.

COLOMEX, INC.
dba TACO BELL
717 North Tejon, Colorado Springs CO 80903. 719/633-2500. **Fax:** 719/633-9610. **Contact:** Human Resources. **Description:** Colomex, Inc. owns the largest Taco Bell franchise in Colorado, operating over 30 restaurants. Taco Bell is a leader in the Mexican, fast-food restaurant industry. **Common positions include:** Restaurant/Food Service Manager. **Educational backgrounds include:** Business Administration; Hospitality. **Benefits:** 401(k); Bonus Award/Plan; Disability Coverage; Employee Discounts; Life Insurance; Medical Insurance; Tuition Assistance. **Corporate headquarters location:** This Location. **Listed on:** Privately held.

COOKER RESTAURANT CORPORATION
5500 Village Boulevard, West Palm Beach FL
33407. 561/615-6000. **Contact:** Management
Recruiter. **World Wide Web address:**
http://www.cookers.com. **Description:** Owns and
operates 35 full-service restaurants. **Common
positions include:** Assistant Kitchen Manager;
Assistant Manager; Restaurant/Food Service
Manager. **Educational backgrounds include:**
Business Administration. **Benefits:** Dental
Insurance; Disability Coverage; Life Insurance;
Medical Insurance; Profit Sharing. **Corporate
headquarters location:** This Location. **Other U.S.
locations:** GA; IN; KY; MD; MI; NC; TN.

AL COPELAND INVESTMENTS
1405 Airline Drive, Metairie LA 70001. 504/830-
1000. **Contact:** Human Resources. **Description:**
Operates Popeye's Famous Fried Chicken
restaurants. **Corporate headquarters location:**
This Location.

COPPER MOUNTAIN RESORTS, INC.
P.O. Box 3001, Copper Mountain CO 80443.
970/968-2318. **Fax:** 970/968-2196. **Contact:**
Human Resources. **E-mail address:** cmr-hr@ski-
copper.com. **World Wide Web address:**
http://www.ski-copper.com. **Description:** Operates
a resort with ski facilities and a wide range of warm-
weather activities. Founded in 1972. **Common
positions include:** Accountant/Auditor; Automotive
Mechanic; Chef/Cook/Kitchen Worker; Computer
Programmer; Electrician; Hotel/Motel Clerk;
Landscape/Grounds Maintenance; Maintenance
Technician; Preschool Worker; Property and Real
Estate Manager; Transportation/Traffic Specialist;
Waitstaff; Warehouse/Distribution Worker.
Benefits: 401(k); Daycare Assistance; Disability
Coverage; Employee Discounts; Life Insurance;
Medical Insurance; Tuition Assistance. **Office
hours:** Sunday - Saturday, 8:00 a.m. - 5:00 p.m.
Corporate headquarters location: This Location.

CRESTLINE CAPITAL CORPORATION
6600 Rockledge Drive, Bethesda MD 20817.
240/694-2000. **Contact:** Human Resources
Manager. **World Wide Web address:** http://www.
crestlinecapital.com. **Description:** A holding
company. **Corporate headquarters location:** This
Location. **Subsidiaries include:** Crestline Hotels &
Resorts, Inc., manages hotels, resorts, conference
rooms, and convention centers.

CROWNE PLAZA RESORT
130 Shipyard Drive, Hilton Head Island SC 29928.
843/842-2400. **Fax:** 843/785-4879. **Contact:**
Personnel Department. **World Wide Web address:**
http://www.crowneplazaresort.com. **Description:** A
340-room hotel located in Shipyard Plantation.
NOTE: Entry-level positions, part-time jobs, and
second and third shifts are offered. This location
also hires seasonally. **Common positions include:**
Administrative Assistant; Event Planner;
Mechanical Engineer; Sales Manager. **Educational
backgrounds include:** Business Administration;
Hotel Administration; Internet Development;
Microsoft Office; Microsoft Word; Restaurant
Management; Spreadsheets. **Benefits:** 401(k);
Casual Dress - Daily; Dental Insurance; Disability
Coverage; Employee Discounts; Flexible Schedule;
Life Insurance; Medical Insurance; Relocation
Assistance; Savings Plan. **Special programs:**
Internships; Training; Summer Jobs. **International
locations:** Worldwide. **Parent company:** Bass
Hotels & Resorts.

CUCOS INC.
110 Veterans Memorial Boulevard, Suite 222,
Metairie LA 70005. 504/835-0306. **Fax:** 504/835-
0336. **Contact:** Human Resources. **Description:**
Owns, operates, and franchises moderately-priced
Sonoran-style Mexican restaurants. **Common
positions include:** Restaurant/Food Service
Manager. **Benefits:** 401(k); Disability Coverage;
Employee Discounts; Life Insurance; Medical
Insurance. **Corporate headquarters location:** This
Location.

DARDEN RESTAURANTS, INC.
P.O. Box 593330, Orlando FL 32859. 407/245-
4000. **Contact:** Human Resources Manager. **World
Wide Web address:** http://www.darden.com.
Description: Operates the Red Lobster, Olive
Garden, and Bahama Breeze restaurant chains.
Corporate headquarters location: This Location.

DAVE & BUSTER'S, INC.
2481 Manana Drive, Dallas TX 75220. 214/357-
9588. **Contact:** Human Resources. **World Wide
Web address:** http://www.daveandbusters.com.
Description: Operates restaurant and entertainment
complexes. Each location houses eating venues and
amusement facilities including billiards, video
games, and virtual reality games. Founded in 1982.
Corporate headquarters location: This Location.
Other U.S. locations: Ontario CA; Denver CO;
Hollywood FL; Atlanta GA; Chicago IL; North
Bethesda MD; Detroit MI; Cincinnati OH;
Philadelphia PA; Houston TX. **International
locations:** Birmingham, England.

DENVER MARRIOTT TECH CENTER
4900 South Syracuse Street, Denver CO 80237.
303/779-1100. **Recorded jobline:** 303/782-3214.
Contact: Human Resources. **World Wide Web
address:** http://www.marriott.com. **Description:** A
625-room hotel. **NOTE:** Entry-level positions, part-
time jobs, and second and third shifts are offered.
This location also hires seasonally. **Common
positions include:** Accountant; Administrative
Assistant; Assistant Manager; Customer Service
Representative; Event Planner; General Manager;
Human Resources Manager; Management Trainee;
Mechanical Engineer; Operations Manager; Sales
Manager; Secretary. **Educational backgrounds
include:** Accounting; Business Administration;
Food Services; Hospitality. **Benefits:** 401(k);
Daycare Assistance; Dental Insurance; Disability
Coverage; Employee Discounts; Flexible Schedule;
Job Sharing; Life Insurance; Medical Insurance;
Profit Sharing; Public Transit Available; Savings
Plan; Tuition Assistance; Vacation Days (10 - 20).
Special programs: Internships; Training; Summer
Jobs. **Corporate headquarters location:**
Washington DC. **Other U.S. locations:** Nationwide.
International locations: Worldwide. **Parent
company:** Marriot International.

DOMINO'S PIZZA, INC.
P.O. Box 997, Ann Arbor MI 48106. 734/930-3030.
Contact: Human Resources. **World Wide Web
address:** http://www.dominos.com. **Description:**
This location houses administrative offices. Overall,
Domino's Pizza is a home-delivery pizza chain.
Corporate headquarters location: This Location.

**DOUBLETREE HOTEL
HAYDEN ISLAND COMPLEX**
1401 North Hayden Island Drive, Portland OR
97217. 503/283-2111. **Fax:** 503/283-4699.
Recorded jobline: 503/296-3386. **Contact:** Human
Resources. **World Wide Web address:**
http://www.doubletree.com. **Description:** A two-
hotel complex with 672 rooms and 70,000 square
feet of banquet/meeting space. **Common positions
include:** Accountant; Administrative Assistant;
General Manager; Human Resources Manager;
Operations Manager; Sales Executive. **Educational**

backgrounds include: Accounting; Business Administration; Communications; Finance; Liberal Arts; Marketing. **Benefits:** 401(k); Dental Insurance; Disability Coverage; Employee Discounts; Flexible Schedule; Life Insurance; Medical Insurance; Relocation Assistance; Tuition Assistance. **Corporate headquarters location:** Beverly Hills CA. **Other U.S. locations:** Nationwide. **International locations:** Worldwide. **Parent company:** Hilton Hotels Corporation.

DUNKIN' DONUTS OF AMERICA INC.
P.O. Box 317, Randolph MA 02368. 781/961-4000. **Physical address:** 14 Pacella Park Drive, Randolph MA 02368. **Contact:** Personnel Manager. **World Wide Web address:** http://www.dunkindonuts.com. **Description:** Develops and franchises Dunkin' Donuts shops that sell coffee, donuts, and baked goods. **Corporate headquarters location:** This Location. **Parent company:** Allied Domecq PLC.

EL CHICO RESTAURANTS, INC.
12200 Stemmons Freeway, Suite 100, Dallas TX 75234. 972/241-5500. **Fax:** 972/888-8150. **Contact:** Personnel. **World Wide Web address:** http://www.elchico.com. **Description:** Operates a chain of full-service restaurants. **Common positions include:** Management Trainee; Restaurant/Food Service Manager. **Educational backgrounds include:** Business Administration; Chemistry; Marketing; Restaurant Management. **Corporate headquarters location:** This Location. **Parent company:** Consolidated Restaurants Inc. (also at this location).

EL TORITO RESTAURANTS INC.
379 Gellert Boulevard, Daly City CA 94015. 650/994-3210. **Contact:** General Manager. **Description:** Operates a chain of Mexican-style and continental dinnerhouses. **Corporate headquarters location:** This Location.

ELDORADO HOTEL
309 West San Francisco Street, Santa Fe NM 87501. 505/988-4455. **Fax:** 505/995-4517. **Contact:** Human Resources. **E-mail address:** david@eldoradohotel.com. **World Wide Web address:** http://www.eldoradohotel.com. **Description:** A four-star/four-diamond, 219-room hotel. Founded in 1986. **NOTE:** Entry-level positions, part-time jobs, and second and third shifts are offered. This location also hires seasonally. **Common positions include:** Administrative Assistant. **Benefits:** 401(k); Dental Insurance; Disability Coverage; Employee Discounts; Life Insurance; Medical Insurance; Tuition Assistance; Vacation Days (6 - 10). **Special programs:** Summer Jobs.

ELMER'S RESTAURANTS, INC.
P.O. Box 16938, Portland OR 97292. 503/252-1485. **Contact:** Human Resources. **Description:** Owns and operates 11 Elmer's Pancake & Steak House restaurants and sells franchises. Franchises and company-owned stores are located throughout the western United States. **Corporate headquarters location:** This Location.

ELSINORE CORPORATION
FOUR QUEENS HOTEL & CASINO
202 Fremont, Las Vegas NV 89101. 702/385-4011. **Fax:** 702/387-5125. **Contact:** Human Resources. **Description:** A publicly-held casino management company that develops and operates gaming facilities throughout the country. In addition to its Las Vegas-based Four Queens Hotel & Casino, Elsinore Corporation is working with Native American tribes to develop, construct, and manage casinos on tribal lands. **Common positions include:** Accountant; Customer Service Representative;

Electrical/Electronics Engineer; Financial Analyst; Hotel Manager; Human Resources Manager; Purchasing Agent/Manager; Restaurant/Food Service Manager. **Educational backgrounds include:** Accounting; Business Administration; Communications; Economics; Finance; Hotel Administration; Liberal Arts; Marketing. **Benefits:** 401(k); Dental Insurance; Disability Coverage; Employee Discounts; Life Insurance; Medical Insurance; Vacation Days; Vision Insurance. **Special programs:** Internships. **Corporate headquarters location:** This Location. **Subsidiaries include:** Pinnacle Gaming.

EMBASSY SUITES AIRPORT WEST
2333 East Thomas Road, Phoenix AZ 85031. 602/957-1910. **Fax:** 602/955-2861. **Contact:** Personnel Department. **World Wide Web address:** http://www.embassysuites.com. **Description:** An all-suites hotel and conference facility operating as one of three Promus hotel chains. **Company slogan:** Satisfying every guest, every time, guaranteed! **Benefits:** 401(k); Dental Insurance; Employee Discounts; Flexible Schedule; Life Insurance; Medical Insurance; Profit Sharing; Public Transit Available; Sick Days; Tuition Assistance; Vacation Days (10 - 20). **Corporate headquarters location:** Memphis TN. **Parent company:** Promus Hotel Corporation.

EXECUSTAY, INC.
3630 Park Central Boulevard North, Pompano Beach FL 33064. 954/975-0900. **Toll-free phone:** 800/780-7829. **Fax:** 954/975-0411. **Contact:** Human Resources. **World Wide Web address:** http://www.execustay.com. **Description:** Provides corporations and executives with interim housing throughout south Florida. **Corporate headquarters location:** This Location.

EXEL INNS OF AMERICA, INC.
4706 East Washington Avenue, Madison WI 53704. 608/241-5271x112. **Fax:** 608/241-3224. **Contact:** Personnel. **World Wide Web address:** http://www.exelinns.com. **Description:** A limited-service motel chain with 35 locations, primarily in the Midwest. Founded in 1973. **NOTE:** The company is always accepting applications for general manager and assistant manager positions. Entry-level positions are also offered. **Common positions include:** Motel Manager. **Educational backgrounds include:** Business Administration; Hospitality. **Benefits:** Employee Discounts; Life Insurance; Medical Insurance. **Corporate headquarters location:** This Location.

FAIRMONT HOTEL
950 Mason Street, San Francisco CA 94108. 415/772-5312. **Fax:** 415/772-5049. **Contact:** Employment Manager. **World Wide Web address:** http://www.fairmont.com. **Description:** A 600-room hotel. Founded in 1907. **NOTE:** Entry-level positions are offered. **Common positions include:** Accountant; Administrative Assistant; Controller; Credit Manager; Customer Service Representative; General Manager; Human Resources Manager; Sales Executive; Sales Manager; Secretary; Systems Manager. **Educational backgrounds include:** Liberal Arts. **Benefits:** 401(k); Dental Insurance; Employee Discounts; Life Insurance; Medical Insurance. **Corporate headquarters location:** This Location. **Other U.S. locations:** San Jose CA; Chicago IL; New Orleans LA; Boston MA; New York NY; Dallas TX.

FAMILY INNS OF AMERICA
P.O. Box 10, Pigeon Forge TN 37868. 865/453-4988. **Contact:** Personnel. **World Wide Web address:** http://www.familyinnsofamerica.com.

Description: Operates a nationwide motel chain. **Common positions include:** Accountant/Auditor; Hotel Manager; Management Trainee. **Educational backgrounds include:** Accounting; Business Administration; Finance; Marketing. **Benefits:** Bonus Award/Plan; Medical Insurance. **Special programs:** Internships. **Corporate headquarters location:** This Location. **Parent company:** KMS Enterprises.

FAMOUS AMOS RESTAURANTS, INC.
2765 Clydo Road, Jacksonville FL 32207. 904/731-3396. **Contact:** Human Resources. **Description:** Operates a chain of 10 area restaurants. **Corporate headquarters location:** This Location.

FARRELL'S ICE CREAM PARLOURS
10606 Camino Ruiz, San Diego CA 92126. 858/578-9895. **Contact:** Store Supervisor. **Description:** A restaurant franchise specializing in ice cream and ice cream products. The restaurants also sell novelties and candy. **Corporate headquarters location:** This Location.

FEDERATED-NATIONAL INC.
358 Toftrees Avenue, State College PA 16803. 814/238-0534. **Contact:** Gloria Jackson, Human Resources. **Description:** Owns and manages hotels. **Corporate headquarters location:** This Location.

FLORIDA RESTAURANTS BUSINESS VENTURE
P.O. Box 2066, Winter Park FL 32790. 407/647-4300. **Fax:** 407/647-5306. **Contact:** Human Resources Manager. **Description:** A restaurant management company. **Common positions include:** Management Trainee. **Educational backgrounds include:** Accounting; Business Administration; Communications; Liberal Arts. **Benefits:** 401(k); Dental Insurance; Disability Coverage; Life Insurance; Medical Insurance; Tuition Assistance. **Corporate headquarters location:** This Location.

FOOD MANAGEMENT CORPORATION
P.O. Box 98807, Seattle WA 98198. 206/824-0887. **Contact:** Human Resources Manager. **World Wide Web address:** http://www.foodmanagement.com. **Description:** Provides contract food services to community colleges and corporations. **Common positions include:** Cashier; Chef/Cook/Kitchen Worker; Dietician/Nutritionist; Food and Beverage Service Worker; Restaurant/Food Service Worker. **Benefits:** Life Insurance; Meal Plan; Medical Insurance; Profit Sharing; Vacation Days. **Corporate headquarters location:** This Location. **Other U.S. locations:** AL; ID; OR; UT.

FOUR SEASONS RESORT AND CLUB
4150 North MacArthur Boulevard, Irving TX 75038. 972/717-0700. **Fax:** 972/717-2578. **Recorded jobline:** 972/717-2544. **Contact:** Human Resources. **World Wide Web address:** http://www.fourseasons.com. **Description:** A 357-room resort offering two championship golf courses, 12 tennis courts, a spa, and a conference center. The 18-hole TPC championship golf course is the site of the annual GTE Byron Nelson Classic on the PGA Tour. The 176,000 square-foot sports club and spa has a racquet sports center, indoor and outdoor pools and tracks, and complete personal training facilities. The 20,000 square-foot conference center includes 26 multipurpose meeting and function rooms. **NOTE:** Entry-level positions, part-time jobs, and second and third shifts are offered. **Educational backgrounds include:** Hotel Administration. **Benefits:** 401(k); Dental Insurance; Disability Coverage; Flexible Schedule; Free Meals; Life Insurance; Medical Insurance; Profit Sharing; Sick Days; Vacation Days. **Special programs:** Training;

Summer Jobs. **Corporate headquarters location:** Toronto, Canada. **Other U.S. locations:** Nationwide. **International locations:** Worldwide.

FOXWOODS RESORT CASINO
99 Mechanic Street, Mashantucket CT 06339. 860/312-4170. **Contact:** Human Resources. **World Wide Web address:** http://www.foxwoods.com. **Description:** A casino. Foxwoods also offers concerts and entertainment, as well as lodging facilities. The casino is operated by the Mashantucket Pequot Indians.

FRESH CHOICE, INC.
2901 Tasman Drive, Suite 109, Santa Clara CA 95054. 408/986-8661. **Fax:** 408/450-0198. **Contact:** Department of Human Resources. **World Wide Web address:** http://www.freshchoiceinc.com. **Description:** Operates 58 casual, self-service restaurants in Northern California, Washington, Texas, and Washington DC under the Fresh Choice name. **Common positions include:** Restaurant/Food Service Manager. **Benefits:** Dental Insurance; ESOP; Life Insurance; Medical Insurance. **Special programs:** Internships. **Corporate headquarters location:** This Location.

FRIENDLY'S ICE CREAM CORPORATION
1855 Boston Road, Wilbraham MA 01095. 413/543-2400. **Contact:** Human Resources. **World Wide Web address:** http://www.friendlys.com. **Description:** Operates approximately 750 Friendly's restaurants serving hamburgers, sandwiches, salads, and ice cream. **Corporate headquarters location:** This Location.

FRISCH'S RESTAURANTS, INC.
2800 Gilbert Avenue, Cincinnati OH 45206. 513/961-2660. **Contact:** Human Resources. **Description:** Operates and licenses family restaurants with drive-through service under the names Frisch's Big Boy, Kip's Big Boy, and Hardee's. The company also operates two hotels with restaurants in metropolitan Cincinnati. **Corporate headquarters location:** This Location. **Other U.S. locations:** FL; IN; KY; OK; TX.

FRONTIER ENTERPRISES
8520 Crownhill Boulevard, San Antonio TX 78209. 210/828-1493. **Contact:** Personnel. **Description:** Owns and operates Magic Time Machine Restaurants and Towers of America Restaurants. Magic Time Machine Restaurants are seafood and steak dining establishments and the Towers of America Restaurants are family-style restaurants set approximately 6,000 feet in the air. **Corporate headquarters location:** This Location.

GENERAL MILLS, INC.
P.O. Box 1113, Minneapolis MN 55440. 612/540-2311. **Contact:** Recruitment Department. **World Wide Web address:** http://www.generalmills.com. **Description:** Produces and markets consumer foods. Food products include Cheerios, Wheaties, and Total cereals; Betty Crocker desserts, frostings, and baking mixes; Pop Secret microwave popcorn; Gorton's frozen seafood; Yoplait yogurt; Bisquick pancake mix; and Gold Medal flour. General Mills is also engaged in the full-service dinnerhouse restaurant business, operating over 1,000 company-owned Red Lobster and Olive Garden restaurants in North America. Founded in 1928. **Common positions include:** Chemical Engineer; Food Scientist/Technologist; Mechanical Engineer. **Educational backgrounds include:** Accounting; Chemistry; Computer Science; Engineering; Finance; Food Science; Marketing; MBA. **Corporate headquarters location:** This Location.

GIVEN ENTERPRISES
3640 Win Place Road, Memphis TN 38118.
901/363-0500. **Contact:** Human Resources.
Description: Owns and operates four restaurants in
Mississippi under the names Shoney's and Captain
D's. Shoney's restaurants offer breakfast, lunch, and
dinner. Captain D's restaurants specialize in seafood
and offer drive-through, take-out service.
Corporate headquarters location: This Location.

GOLDEN CORRAL CORPORATION
5151 Glenwood Avenue, Raleigh NC 27612. **Toll-
free phone:** 800/284-5673. **Fax:** 919/881-4577.
Contact: Human Resources Manager. **World Wide
Web address:** http://www.goldencorralrest.com.
Description: One location of a chain of family
steakhouses. Founded in 1973. **NOTE:** Entry-level
positions are offered. **Company slogan:** Making
pleasurable dining affordable. **Common positions
include:** Accountant; Adjuster; Administrative
Assistant; Budget Analyst; Buyer; Computer
Operator; Computer Programmer; Construction
Contractor; Economist; Financial Analyst; Human
Resources Manager; Market Research Analyst;
Paralegal; Purchasing Agent/Manager; Receptionist;
Restaurant/Food Service Manager; Secretary;
Systems Analyst; Technical Writer/Editor;
Typist/Word Processor. **Educational backgrounds
include:** Accounting; Business Administration;
Communications; Computer Science; Finance;
Marketing; Public Relations; Software Tech.
Support. **Benefits:** 401(k); Adoption Assistance;
Dental Insurance; Disability Coverage; Employee
Discounts; Life Insurance; Medical Insurance;
Tuition Assistance. **Corporate headquarters
location:** This Location. **Other U.S. locations:**
Nationwide.

GOLDEN NUGGET HOTEL AND CASINO
P.O. Box 610, Las Vegas NV 89125. 702/386-8245.
Fax: 702/386-8222. **Recorded jobline:** 702/386-
8181. **Contact:** Employment Manager. **World
Wide Web address:** http://www.goldennugget.com.
Description: A four star, four diamond hotel and
casino. **NOTE:** Entry-level positions, part-time
jobs, and second and third shifts are offered. This
location also hires seasonally. **Common positions
include:** Account Manager; Account Rep.;
Accountant; Administrative Manager; Advertising
Executive; Assistant Manager; Auditor; Blue-Collar
Worker Supervisor; Budget Analyst; Buyer; Chief
Financial Officer; Clerical Supervisor; Controller;
Credit Manager; Customer Service Representative;
Event Planner; Finance Director; Financial Analyst;
Graphic Artist; Human Resources Manager; Market
Research Analyst; Marketing Manager; Marketing
Specialist; Purchasing Agent/Manager; Sales
Executive; Sales Manager; Sales Representative;
Secretary; Technical Support Engineer; Technical
Writer/Editor; Telecommunications Manager;
Typist/Word Processor; Video Production
Coordinator. **Educational backgrounds include:**
Accounting; Business Administration; Engineering;
Finance; Marketing; Microsoft Word; Spreadsheets.
Benefits: 401(k); Casual Dress - Daily; Dental
Insurance; Disability Coverage; Employee
Discounts; Life Insurance; Medical Insurance;
Tuition Assistance. **Special programs:** Internships;
Training; Summer Jobs. **Internship information:**
Internships are available to University of Las Vegas
Nevada students only. **Corporate headquarters
location:** This Location. **Other U.S. locations:**
Biloxi MS; Laughlin NV. **Parent company:** Mirage
Resorts, Inc.

GUEST SERVICES
3055 Prosperity Avenue, Fairfax VA 22031.
703/849-9300. **Contact:** Personnel. **World Wide
Web address:** http://www.guestservices.com.
Description: Manages a variety of contract food
and hospitality services. **Common positions
include:** Accountant/Auditor; Administrator; Claim
Representative; Computer Programmer; Customer
Service Representative; Dietician/Nutritionist;
Electrical/Electronics Engineer; Hotel Manager;
Human Resources Manager; Industrial Engineer;
Management Trainee; Manufacturer's/Wholesaler's
Sales Rep.; Marketing Specialist; Mechanical
Engineer; Operations/Production Manager; Public
Relations Specialist. **Benefits:** Dental Insurance;
Disability Coverage; Employee Discounts; Life
Insurance; Medical Insurance; Pension Plan;
Savings Plan; Tuition Assistance. **Corporate
headquarters location:** This Location.

GURNEY'S INN
P.O. Box 5073, Montauk NY 11954. 631/668-2345.
Physical address: 290 Old Montauk Highway,
Montauk NY 11954. **Fax:** 631/668-3576. **Contact:**
Director of Human Resources. **E-mail address:**
gurneysinn@aol.com. **World Wide Web address:**
http://www.gurneysweb.com. **Description:** A 109-
room hotel featuring fine dining and rooms with an
ocean view. **NOTE:** Entry-level positions are
offered. **Common positions include:** Accountant;
Administrative Assistant; Blue-Collar Worker
Supervisor; Controller; Finance Director; Registered
Nurse; Restaurant/Food Service Manager; Typist/
Word Processor. **Educational backgrounds
include:** Accounting; Business Administration;
Liberal Arts. **Benefits:** Employee Discounts;
Flexible Schedule; Public Transit Available. **Special
programs:** Internships; Apprenticeships; Summer
Jobs. **Corporate headquarters location:** This
Location.

H.I. DEVELOPMENT, INC.
111 West Fortune Street, Tampa FL 33602.
813/229-6686. **Contact:** Human Resources.
Description: A hotel management and consulting
firm. **Common positions include:** Accountant/
Auditor; Administrative Worker/Clerk; Advertising
Clerk; General Manager; Hotel Manager; Human
Resources Manager; Marketing Specialist.
Educational backgrounds include: Accounting.
Benefits: Employee Discounts; Life Insurance;
Medical Insurance. **Corporate headquarters
location:** This Location. **Operations at this facility
include:** Regional Headquarters.

HMSHOST CORPORATION
One Marriott Drive, Washington DC 20058.
301/380-9000. **Contact:** Human Resources. **World
Wide Web address:** http://www.hmscorp.com.
Description: A diversified food service and
hospitality company that does business in more than
25 United States airports and operates restaurants
under various names. **Corporate headquarters
location:** Bethesda MD. **Annual sales/revenues:**
More than $100 million.
Other U.S. locations:
• JFK Airport, Building 51, Jamaica NY 11430.
  718/995-7796.
• 2000 East Plumb Lane, Reno NV 89502-
  3250. 775/785-2587.

HAPPY JOE'S PIZZA AND ICE CREAM
2705 Happy Joe Drive, Bettendorf IA 52722.
319/332-8811. **Contact:** Human Resources
Manager. **World Wide Web address:** http://www.
happyjoes.com. **Description:** A restaurant which
serves pizza, pasta, and ice cream. **Common
positions include:** Accountant/Auditor; Advertising
Clerk; Architect; Budget Analyst; Computer
Programmer; Construction Contractor; General
Manager; Human Resources Manager; Landscape
Architect; Management Analyst/Consultant;
Management Trainee; Public Relations Specialist;

Systems Analyst. **Educational backgrounds include:** Accounting; Art/Design; Computer Science; Marketing. **Benefits:** 401(k); Dental Insurance; Employee Discounts; Life Insurance; Medical Insurance. **Corporate headquarters location:** This Location.

HARRAH'S ENTERTAINMENT

1023 Cherry Road, Memphis TN 38117. 901/762-8600. **Contact:** Human Resources. **Description:** Owns and operates 12 land-based, riverboat, and dockside casinos, 11 of which operate under the Harrah's name. **NOTE:** Resumes should be directed to Marilynn Winn, Vice President of Human Resources, 5100 West Sahara, Suite 200, Las Vegas Nevada 89146. **Corporate headquarters location:** This Location. **Other U.S. locations:** IL; LA; MO; MS; NJ; NV.

HARVEY HOTEL/DFW AIRPORT

4545 West John Carpenter Freeway, Irving TX 75063. 972/929-4500. **Fax:** 972/929-0733. **Contact:** Human Resources. **Description:** A 500-room hotel. Harvey Hotel's business center offers typing, copying, fax, car rental information, travel agency information, and word processing services. **NOTE:** Entry-level positions and second and third shifts are offered. **Common positions include:** Accountant/Auditor; Administrative Assistant; Auditor; General Manager; Human Resources Manager; Management Trainee; Marketing Manager; Sales Manager; Systems Manager. **Educational backgrounds include:** Accounting; Business Administration; Communications; Marketing; Public Relations. **Benefits:** 401(k); Dental Insurance; Disability Coverage; Employee Discounts; Flexible Schedule; Life Insurance; Medical Insurance; Savings Plan. **Corporate headquarters location:** Addison TX. **Parent company:** Bristol Hotel Company.

HELMSLEY PARK LANE HOTEL

36 Central Park South, New York NY 10019. 212/371-4000. **Fax:** 212/521-6666. **Contact:** Human Resources. **Description:** Operates a 650-room, luxury hotel with a wide range of lodging, lounge, dining, and meeting rooms. **Common positions include:** Accountant/Auditor; Blue-Collar Worker Supervisor; Customer Service Rep.; Food Service Manager; General Manager; Hotel Manager; Human Resources Manager; Purchasing Agent/Manager. **Educational backgrounds include:** Accounting; Business; Communications; Finance; Food Services; Hotel Administration; Marketing. **Benefits:** Dental Insurance; Disability Coverage; Life Insurance; Medical Insurance; Pension Plan. **Corporate headquarters location:** This Location. **Parent company:** Helmsley Hotels Group.

HIGH INDUSTRIES, INC.

P.O. Box 10008, Lancaster PA 17605-0008. 717/293-4486. **Contact:** Human Resources. **World Wide Web address:** http://www.high.net. **Description:** Products and services include design and construction, food services, hotel management, prestress/precast concrete products, real estate development and management, and steel fabrication. **Common positions include:** Accountant/Auditor; Architect; Civil Engineer; Computer Programmer; Customer Service Rep.; Draftsperson; Hotel Manager; Human Resources Manager; Services Sales Rep.; Systems Analyst. **Educational backgrounds include:** Accounting; Business Administration; Computer Science; Engineering; Finance; Marketing. **Benefits:** Credit Union; Dental Insurance; Disability Coverage; Life Insurance; Medical Insurance; Pension Plan; Profit Sharing; Savings Plan; Tuition Assistance. **Corporate headquarters location:** This Location.

HILTON HAWAIIAN VILLAGE

2005 Kalia Road, Honolulu HI 96815. 808/949-4321. **Fax:** 808/947-7904. **Recorded jobline:** 808/948-7742. **Contact:** Personnel. **World Wide Web address:** http://www.hilton.com. **Description:** Operates hotels and restaurants. **NOTE:** Entry-level positions are offered. **Common positions include:** Administrative Assistant; Assistant Manager; Customer Service Manager; Restaurant/Food Service Manager; Sales Manager; Secretary. **Educational backgrounds include:** Business Administration; Microsoft Word; Spreadsheets; Visual Basic. **Benefits:** 401(k); Dental Insurance; Disability Coverage; Employee Discounts; Life Insurance; Medical Insurance. **Special programs:** Internships. **Corporate headquarters location:** Beverly Hills CA. **Other U.S. locations:** Nationwide. **International locations:** Worldwide. L

HILTONS OF WESTCHESTER

699 Westchester Avenue, Rye Brook NY 10573. 914/934-2519. **Fax:** 914/939-7374. **Recorded jobline:** 914/524-6445. **Contact:** Human Resources. **World Wide Web address:** http://www.hilton.com. **Description:** Hiltons of Westchester is comprised of two separate Hilton hotels: a 444-room facility in Rye Brook and a 252-room facility in Tarrytown. Founded in 1919. **NOTE:** Entry-level positions, part-time jobs, and second and third shifts are offered. **Common positions include:** Accountant; Administrative Assistant; Assistant Manager; Electrician; Human Resources Manager; Purchasing Agent/Manager; Sales Manager; Sales Representative. **Educational backgrounds include:** Accounting; Engineering; Marketing; Microsoft Word; Public Relations; Visual Basic. **Benefits:** Dental Insurance; Disability Coverage; Employee Discounts; Life Insurance; Medical Insurance; Sick Days (6 - 10); Thrift Plan; Vacation Days (6 - 10). **Special programs:** Internships; Training. **Corporate headquarters location:** Beverly Hills CA. **Other U.S. locations:** Nationwide. **International locations:** Worldwide. **Parent company:** Hilton Hotels Corp.

HOLIDAY INN HOTEL & SUITES

200 West First Street, Duluth MN 55802. 218/722-1202. **Fax:** 218/722-0233. **Contact:** Human Resources **World Wide Web address:** http://www.duluth.com/holidayinn. **Description:** A 353-room, full-service hotel with three restaurants, conference facilities, and meeting space. **NOTE:** Entry-level positions, part-time jobs, and second and third shifts are offered. **Common positions include:** Account Representative; Advertising Executive; Auditor; General Manager; Human Resources Manager; Marketing Specialist; Operations Manager; Sales Executive; Sales Manager; Sales Representative. **Educational backgrounds include:** Accounting; Marketing. **Benefits:** 401(k); Employee Discounts; Flexible Schedule; Job Sharing; Life Insurance; Medical Insurance; Pension Plan; Sick Days (6 - 10). **Special programs:** Internships; Summer Jobs.

HOMESTEAD VILLAGE INC.

2100 RiverEdge Parkway, Suite 900, Atlanta GA 30328. 770/303-2200. **Toll-free phone:** 888/782-9473. **Fax:** 770/303-0015. **Recorded jobline:** 770/303-2229. **Contact:** Human Resources Manager. **World Wide Web address:** http://www.homesteadvillage.com. **Description:** An extended-stay hotel chain. Guests are typically business travelers who are on extended-stay assignments, attending seminars, or in the process of relocating to a new city. The company owns and operates 136 properties. Founded in 1992. **Common positions include:** Administrative Assistant; Assistant Manager; Budget Analyst; Construction Contractor; Customer Service Representative; Facilities

Engineer; Financial Analyst; Front Desk Sales Agent; General Manager; Housekeeper; Marketing Manager; Operations Manager; Purchasing Agent/Manager; Sales Manager; Sales Representative. **Benefits:** 401(k); Dental Insurance; Disability Coverage; Employee Discounts; Life Insurance; Medical Insurance. **Corporate headquarters location:** This Location. **Other U.S. locations:** Nationwide.

THE HOTEL CAPTAIN COOK
P.O. Box 102280, Anchorage AK 99510. 907/343-2278. **Fax:** 907/343-2441. **Contact:** Elizabeth Hill, Human Resources. **World Wide Web address:** http://www.captaincook.com. **Description:** A 565-room, luxury hotel. Founded in 1966. **Educational backgrounds include:** Marketing; Public Relations. **Benefits:** 401(k); Dental Insurance; Disability Coverage; Employee Discounts; Life Insurance; Medical Insurance; Tuition Assistance; Vacation Pay. **Special programs:** Summer Jobs. **Corporate headquarters location:** This Location. **Listed on:** Privately held. **President:** Walter Hickel, Jr.

HOTEL DEL CORONADO
1500 Orange Avenue, Coronado CA 92118. 619/435-6611. **Fax:** 619/522-8160. **Contact:** Human Resources Department. **World Wide Web address:** http://www.hoteldel.com. **Description:** An oceanside resort with nine restaurants and lounges. **Common positions include:** Accountant/Auditor; Attorney; Buyer; Claim Rep.; Clerical Supervisor; Computer Programmer; Construction Contractor; Credit Manager; Customer Service Representative; Designer; Electrician; Financial Analyst; General Manager; Hotel Manager; Human Resources Manager; Management Trainee; Public Relations Specialist; Purchasing Agent/Manager; Restaurant/Food Service Manager; Systems Analyst; Travel Agent; Wholesale and Retail Buyer. **Educational backgrounds include:** Accounting; Business Administration; Communications; Finance; Marketing. **Benefits:** 401(k); Dental Insurance; Disability Coverage; Employee Discounts; Life Insurance; Medical Insurance; Pension Plan; Savings Plan; Tuition Assistance. **Special programs:** Internships. **Corporate headquarters location:** This Location.

HOULIHAN'S RESTAURANT GROUP, INC.
2 Brush Creek Boulevard, Kansas City MO 64112. 816/756-2200. **Contact:** Human Resources. **Description:** Houlihan's Restaurant Group owns, operates, and franchises full-service, casual dining restaurants. **Common positions include:** Accountant; Computer Programmer; Restaurant/Food Service Manager. **Benefits:** 401(k); Dental Insurance; Disability Coverage; Employee Discounts; Life Insurance; Medical Insurance; Savings Plan. **Corporate headquarters location:** This Location. **Other U.S. locations:** Nationwide.

HUDSON HOTEL CORPORATION
300 Bausch and Lomb Place, Rochester NY 14604. 716/454-3400. **Contact:** Recruiter. **Description:** Hudson Hotel Corporation develops and franchises a national chain of economy limited service lodging facilities. **Corporate headquarters location:** This Location.

HUNTINGTON TOWN HOUSE INC.
124 East Jericho Turnpike, Huntington Station NY 11746. 631/427-8485. **Contact:** Vice President. **Description:** A general service catering company specializing in weddings, organizational functions, bar mitzvahs, anniversaries, and special parties through over 25 area locations including the New York City area. **Corporate headquarters location:** This Location.

HYATT REGENCY AT SAN FRANCISCO AIRPORT
1333 Bayshore Highway, Burlingame CA 94010. 650/347-1234. **Fax:** 650/348-2541. **Recorded jobline:** 650/696-2625. **Contact:** Department of Human Resources. **E-mail address:** ccole@ sfobupo.hyatt.com. **World Wide Web address:** http://www.hyatt.com. **Description:** Operates a full-service four-star hotel complex housing restaurants, banquet rooms, and recreational and convention facilities. **Common positions include:** Accountant/Auditor; Administrative Assistant; Assistant Manager; Food and Beverage Service Worker; Hotel Manager; Operations Manager; Services Sales Representative. **Educational backgrounds include:** Accounting; Business Administration; Hospitality. **Benefits:** 401(k); Casual Dress - Fridays; Dental Insurance; Employee Discounts; Life Insurance; Medical Insurance; Tuition Assistance. **Special programs:** Training. **Corporate headquarters location:** Chicago IL. **Other U.S. locations:** Nationwide.

HYATT REGENCY PHOENIX
122 North Second Street, Phoenix AZ 85004. 602/252-3153. **Toll-free phone:** 800/223-1234. **Fax:** 602/440-3124. **Recorded jobline:** 602/440-3154. **Contact:** Employment Manager. **World Wide Web address:** http://www.hyatt.com. **Description:** A full-service hotel with 712 guest rooms including 45 suites. The Hyatt Regency Phoenix also features 42,000 square feet of meeting space as well as several restaurants and lounges. **NOTE:** Entry-level positions, part-time jobs, and second and third shifts are offered. This location also hires seasonally. **Company slogan:** Feel the Hyatt Touch. **Common positions include:** Accountant; Administrative Assistant; Controller; Electrician; General Manager; Human Resources Manager; Management Trainee; MIS Specialist; Purchasing Agent/Manager; Sales Manager. **Educational backgrounds include:** Accounting; Communications; Computer Science; Hotel Administration; Marketing. **Benefits:** 401(k); Daycare Assistance; Dental Insurance; Disability Coverage; Employee Discounts; Flexible Schedule; Life Insurance; Medical Insurance; Relocation Assistance; Savings Plan; Sick Days (6 - 10); Tuition Assistance; Vacation Days (10 - 20). **Corporate headquarters location:** Chicago IL. **Other U.S. locations:** Nationwide. **International locations:** Worldwide.

HYATT REGENCY WASHINGTON DC ON CAPITOL HILL
400 New Jersey Avenue NW, Washington DC 20001. 202/737-1234. **Fax:** 202/942-1552. **Recorded jobline:** 202/942-1586. **Contact:** Employment Manager. **World Wide Web address:** http://www.hyatt.com. **Description:** An 834-room, full-service hotel. **NOTE:** Entry-level positions, part-time jobs, and second and third shifts are offered. **Common positions include:** Accountant; Administrative Assistant; Auditor; Controller; Credit Manager; Customer Service Representative; Electrician; Human Resources Manager; Management Trainee; MIS Specialist; Public Relations Specialist; Purchasing Agent/Manager; Sales Executive; Sales Manager. **Educational backgrounds include:** Accounting; Business Administration; Communications; Engineering; Excel; Finance; Hospitality; Hotel Administration; Marketing; Microsoft Word; Public Relations; Spreadsheets. **Benefits:** 401(k); Dental Insurance; Disability Coverage; Employee Discounts; Free Meals; Life Insurance; Medical Insurance; Savings Plan; Tuition Assistance. **Corporate headquarters location:** Chicago IL. **Other U.S. locations:** Nationwide. **International locations:** Worldwide.

Parent company: Hyatt Hotels Corporation. **Listed on:** Privately held.

IHOP CORPORATION
525 North Brand Boulevard, 3rd Floor, Glendale CA 91203. 818/240-6055. **Contact:** Human Resources. **Description:** Operates the International House of Pancakes restaurant chain. **Corporate headquarters location:** This Location.

IMPERIAL PALACE, INC.
3535 Las Vegas Boulevard South, Las Vegas NV 89109. 702/731-3311. **Toll-free phone:** 800/634-6441. **Fax:** 702/794-3356. **Recorded jobline:** 702/794-3191. **Contact:** Human Resources Manager. **World Wide Web address:** http://www.imperialpalace.com. **Description:** A hotel and casino. **NOTE:** Part-time jobs and second and third shifts are offered. **Common positions include:** Account Manager; Accountant; Administrative Assistant; Administrative Manager; Assistant Manager; Auditor; Budget Analyst; Controller; Database Administrator; Electrician; Finance Director; General Manager; Graphic Artist; Graphic Designer; Human Resources Manager; MIS Specialist; Radio/TV Announcer/Broadcaster; Sales Manager; Sales Representative; Secretary; Systems Analyst; Typist/Word Processor. **Educational backgrounds include:** Accounting. **Benefits:** 401(k); Dental Insurance; Disability Coverage; Employee Discounts; Life Insurance; Medical Insurance; Savings Plan. **Listed on:** Privately held.

INTERNATIONAL DAIRY QUEEN INC.
P.O. Box 39286, 7505 Metro Boulevard, Minneapolis MN 55439-0286. 952/830-0200. **Contact:** Human Resources. **World Wide Web address:** http://www.dairyqueen.com. **Description:** A restaurant chain specializing in burgers and ice cream. International Dairy Queen operates 11 regional offices. **Benefits:** 401(k); Dental Insurance; Disability Coverage; Life Insurance; Medical Insurance. **Corporate headquarters location:** This Location. **Subsidiaries include:** Karmelkorn Shoppes, Inc.; Orange Julius of America. **Listed on:** NASDAQ.

JACK IN THE BOX INC.
9330 Balboa Avenue, San Diego CA 92123-1516. 858/571-2121. **Contact:** Human Resources. **World Wide Web address:** http://www.jackinthebox.com. **Description:** Operates and franchises Jack in the Box restaurants, one of the nation's largest quick-serve hamburger chains. Jack in the Box restaurants are primarily located in the western and southwestern United States. International operations currently include restaurants in Hong Kong and Mexico. **Corporate headquarters location:** This Location.

CARL KARCHER ENTERPRISES INC.
P.O. Box 4349, Anaheim CA 92803-4349. 714/774-5796. **Physical address:** 1200 North Harbor Boulevard, Anaheim CA 92803. **Contact:** Human Resources. **Description:** Operates Carl's Jr. restaurants. **Corporate headquarters location:** This Location.

KETTLE RESTAURANTS INC.
2855 Mangum, Suite 485, Houston TX 77092. 713/263-1237. **Contact:** Human Resources. **Description:** Operates a chain of family restaurants. **Common positions include:** Accountant/Auditor; Administrator; Attorney; Computer Programmer; Management Trainee; Purchasing Agent/Manager; Restaurant/Food Service Manager. **Educational backgrounds include:** Accounting; Business Administration; Computer Science; Finance. **Benefits:** Dental Insurance; Disability Coverage;

Life Insurance; Medical Insurance; Pension Plan; Tuition Assistance. **Corporate headquarters location:** This Location.

LDB CORPORATION
444 Sidney Baker Street South, Kerrville TX 78028. 830/257-2000. **Contact:** Human Resources. **Description:** Operates the Mr. Gatti's national pizza chain. **Corporate headquarters location:** This Location.

LA QUINTA INNS, INC.
112 East Pecan Street, Suite 200, San Antonio TX 78205. 210/302-6000. **Fax:** 210/302-6191. **Recorded jobline:** 210/616-7645. **Contact:** Human Resources. **World Wide Web address:** http://www.laquinta.com. **Description:** Develops, owns, and operates a nationwide chain of lodging inns. La Quinta Inns has more than 280 locations in 28 states. Founded in 1964. **Common positions include:** Accountant; Administrative Assistant; Architect; Attorney; Budget Analyst; Chief Financial Officer; Claim Representative; Computer Programmer; Controller; Database Administrator; Database Manager; Design Engineer; Draftsperson; Financial Analyst; General Manager; Management Trainee; Marketing Manager; Marketing Specialist; Paralegal; Purchasing Agent/Manager; Sales Manager; Secretary; SQL Programmer; Systems Analyst; Systems Manager; Telecommunications Manager. **Educational backgrounds include:** Accounting; C/C++; Engineering; Finance; MCSE; Microsoft Word. **Benefits:** 401(k); Casual Dress - Fridays; Dental Insurance; Disability Coverage; Employee Discounts; Life Insurance; Medical Insurance; Pension Plan; Tuition Assistance. **Corporate headquarters location:** This Location. **Parent company:** Meditrust.

LANDRY'S SEAFOOD RESTAURANTS
1400 Post Oak Boulevard, Suite 310, Houston TX 77056. 713/850-1010. **Contact:** Human Resources Manager. **World Wide Web address:** http://www.landrysseafood.com. **Description:** Operates a chain of seafood restaurants. **Corporate headquarters location:** This Location.

LEE'S INNS OF AMERICA
P.O. Box 86, North Vernon IN 47265. 812/346-5072. **Physical address:** 130 North State Street, North Vernon IN. **Fax:** 812/346-7521. **Contact:** Human Resources. **Description:** Owns and operates 21 limited-service hotels throughout Indiana, Illinois, Michigan, and Ohio. **NOTE:** Entry-level positions are offered. **Educational backgrounds include:** Business Administration; Hotel Administration. **Benefits:** Disability Coverage; Employee Discounts; Incentive Plan; Life Insurance; Medical Insurance. **Special programs:** Internships; Training. **Corporate headquarters location:** This Location.

LEGAL SEAFOODS, INC.
33 Everett Street, Allston MA 02134. 617/783-8084. **Contact:** Human Resources. **World Wide Web address:** http://www.lsf.com. **Description:** Operates a chain of seafood restaurants. **Common positions include:** Restaurant/Food Service Manager. **Educational backgrounds include:** Restaurant Management. **Benefits:** Dental Insurance; Disability Coverage; Employee Discounts; Life Insurance; Medical Insurance; Profit Sharing. **Special programs:** Internships. **Corporate headquarters location:** This Location.

LION'S CHOICE
12015 Manchester Road, Suite 180, St. Louis MO 63131. 314/821-8665. **Contact:** Personnel Manager. **Description:** Owns and operates a chain of fast-

food restaurants. **Corporate headquarters location:** This Location.

LITTLE CAESAR'S
2211 Woodward Avenue, Detroit MI 48201. 313/983-6000. **Contact:** Human Resources. **Description:** This location houses administrative offices. Overall, Little Caesar's is a pizza restaurant chain. **Corporate headquarters location:** This Location.

LODGIAN, INC.
3445 Peachtree Road NE, Suite 700, Atlanta GA 30326. 404/364-9400. **Fax:** 404/364-0088. **Contact:** Personnel. **World Wide Web address:** http://www.lodgian.com. **Description:** Owns or manages more than 140 hotels located in North America and Europe. These hotels are primarily full-service, providing food and beverage service as well as lodging and meeting facilities. Most of the company's hotels are affiliated with nationally recognized hospitality franchises including Holiday Inn, Best Western, Hilton, Doubletree Club Hotel, Radisson, Crowne Plaza, Comfort Inn, and Westin. Lodgian, Inc. was created through a merger between Servico, Inc. and Impac Hotel Group. **Corporate headquarters location:** This Location.

LOEWS CORPORATION
655 Madison Avenue, 7th Floor, New York NY 10021. 212/521-2000. **Contact:** Employment Manager. **World Wide Web address:** http://www.loews.com. **Description:** A holding company. **Corporate headquarters location:** This Location. **Subsidiaries include:** CNA Financial Corporation, which provides insurance services; Lorillard, Inc., which produces tobacco products; Loews Hotels, which owns and operates a nationwide chain of hotels; Diamond Offshore Drilling, Inc., an offshore drilling company; and Bulova Corporation, which distributes watches and clocks.

LOGAN'S ROADHOUSE, INC.
P.O. Box 291047, Nashville TN 37229. 615/885-9056. **Fax:** 615/884-5482. **Contact:** Human Resources. **Description:** Operates 18 company-owned Logan's Roadhouse restaurants. Founded in 1991. **Common positions include:** Assistant Manager; Management Trainee. **Benefits:** Dental Insurance; Disability Coverage; Employee Discounts; Life Insurance; Medical Insurance. **Corporate headquarters location:** This Location. **Other U.S. locations:** Nationwide.

LONE STAR STEAKHOUSE AND SALOON
P.O. Box 12726, Wichita KS 67277. 316/264-8899. **Contact:** Human Resources. **Description:** Lone Star Steakhouse and Saloon owns and operates a chain of 84 mid-priced, full-service, casual dining restaurants. **Common positions include:** General Manager; Management Trainee; Restaurant/Food Service Manager. **Educational backgrounds include:** Business Administration; Restaurant Management. **Benefits:** Employee Discounts; Life Insurance; Medical Insurance; Stock Option. **Special programs:** Internships. **Corporate headquarters location:** This Location.

LONG JOHN SILVER'S
P.O. Box 11988, Lexington KY 40579. 606/388-6000. **Contact:** Director of Human Resources. **Description:** A leading quick-service seafood restaurant chain with 1,423 company-owned and franchised locations. **Corporate headquarters location:** This Location. **Other U.S. locations:** Atlanta GA; Kansas City MO; Dallas TX. **International locations:** Canada; Mexico; Saudi Arabia; Singapore.

LUBY'S CAFETERIAS
P.O. Box 33069, San Antonio TX 78265. 210/654-9000. **Physical address:** 2211 NE Loop 410, San Antonio TX 78217. **Contact:** Human Resources. **Description:** A national chain restaurant that serves cafeteria-style food. **Corporate headquarters location:** This Location.

MGM GRAND HOTEL
3799 Las Vegas Boulevard South, Las Vegas NV 89109. 702/701-1111. **Contact:** Human Resources. **World Wide Web address:** http://www.mgmgrand.com. **Description:** A hotel that includes over 5,000 guest rooms and suites, one of the world's largest casinos divided into areas with different themes, eight restaurants, a fast-food court, three entertainment lounges, and two showrooms. The complex also includes a youth center for younger guests and the Oz Midway & Arcade. The complex's theme park, MGM Grand Adventures, is set on 33 acres and features seven major rides and five shows in four theaters. **NOTE:** Resumes should be sent to the Casting Center, 3155 West Harmon Street, Las Vegas NV 89177. **Common positions include:** Food and Beverage Service Worker; Hotel/Motel Clerk; Retail Sales Worker. **Corporate headquarters location:** This Location. **Parent company:** MGM Grand, Inc.

MACHEEZMO MOUSE RESTAURANTS
1020 SW Taylor Street, Suite 685, Portland OR 97205. 503/274-0001. **Fax:** 503/274-4369. **Contact:** Human Resources. **Description:** Operates a chain of 15 quick-service restaurants that offer Mexican-style food. Macheezmo Mouse restaurants offer dine-in and take-out lunch and dinner service in the Portland OR and Seattle WA metropolitan areas. **Corporate headquarters location:** This Location.

MARIETTA CORPORATION
P.O. Box 5250, Cortland NY 13045. 607/753-6746. **Physical address:** 37 Huntington Street, Cortland NY 13045. **Contact:** Human Resources. **World Wide Web address:** http://www.mariettacorp.com. **Description:** Marietta designs, manufactures, packages, markets, and distributes guest amenity programs to the travel and lodging industries. The company's guest amenity programs feature a wide variety of nationally branded toiletries, personal care products, and accessories which travel and lodging establishments provide for the comfort and convenience of their guests. Marietta is also a provider of customized sample-size and unit-of-use packaging products and services to companies in the toiletries, cosmetics, pharmaceuticals, and household products industries for purposes such as marketing promotions and retail sales. **Corporate headquarters location:** This Location.

MARRIOTT INTERNATIONAL, INC.
10400 Fernwood Road, Bethesda MD 20817. 301/380-9000. **Fax:** 301/380-4202. **Recorded jobline:** 888/462-7746. **Contact:** Director of Staffing and Placement. **E-mail address:** staffing@marriott.com. **World Wide Web address:** http://www.marriott.com. **Description:** One of the world's leading hospitality companies operating lodging facilities. Founded in 1927. **NOTE:** Entry-level positions are offered. **Common positions include:** Accountant/Auditor; Administrative Assistant; Auditor; Budget Analyst; Computer Operator; Computer Programmer; Database Manager; Finance Director; Financial Analyst; Human Resources Manager; Internet Services Manager; Market Research Analyst; Marketing Manager; Marketing Specialist; MIS Specialist; Systems Analyst; Systems Manager; Typist/Word Processor. **Educational backgrounds include:**

Accounting; Business Administration; Computer Science; Economics; Finance; Health Care; Marketing; Nutrition. **Benefits:** 401(k); Daycare Assistance; Dental Insurance; Disability Coverage; Employee Discounts; Flexible Schedule; Life Insurance; Medical Insurance; On-Site Daycare; Pension Plan; Profit Sharing; Public Transit Available; Savings Plan; Telecommuting; Tuition Assistance. **Special programs:** Internships. **Internship information:** Undergraduate candidates should mail resumes to Marriott International, One Marriott Drive, Department 931.15, Washington DC 20058. Graduate candidates should mail resumes to Marriott International, One Marriott Drive, Department 935.51, Washington DC 20058. **Other U.S. locations:** Nationwide. **International locations:** Worldwide.

MARTIN'S INC.
6821 Dogwood Road, Baltimore MD 21244. 410/265-1300. **Contact:** Human Resources Manager. **Description:** A catering company serving the Baltimore area. **Corporate headquarters location:** This Location.

MAX & ERMA'S RESTAURANTS INC.
4849 Evanswood Drive, Columbus OH 43229-6206. 614/431-5800. **Contact:** Human Resources. **World Wide Web address:** http://www.max-ermas.com. **Description:** Operates a chain of approximately 30 restaurants. Founded in 1972. **Corporate headquarters location:** This Location. **Other U.S. locations:** IL; IN; KY; MI; PA.

McCORMICK & SCHMICK MANAGEMENT GROUP
720 SW Washington Street, Suite 550, Portland OR 97205. 503/226-3440. **Fax:** 503/228-7729. **Contact:** Personnel Coordinator. **Description:** A management company which operates a chain of upscale seafood restaurants. **Common positions include:** Accountant; Administrative Assistant. **Educational backgrounds include:** Accounting; Business Administration; Finance; Spreadsheets. **Benefits:** 401(k); Dental Insurance; Disability Coverage; Employee Discounts; Life Insurance; Medical Insurance; Sick Days; Vacation Days. **Corporate headquarters location:** This Location. **Other U.S. locations:** Nationwide. **CEO:** Doug Schmick.

McDONALD'S CORPORATION
One McDonald's Plaza, Oak Brook IL 60523. 630/623-3000. **Contact:** Human Resources. **World Wide Web address:** http://www.mcdonalds.com. **Description:** McDonald's is one of the largest restaurant chains and food service organizations in the world, operating more than 26,000 restaurants in 119 countries. **Corporate headquarters location:** This Location. **Other U.S. locations:** Nationwide. **International locations:** Worldwide.

MERISTAR HOTELS & RESORTS, INC.
1010 Wisconsin Avenue NW, Suite 650, Washington DC 20007. 202/965-4455. **Contact:** Human Resources. **World Wide Web address:** http://www.meristar.com. **Description:** This location houses administrative offices. Overall, MeriStar Hotels & Resorts manages over 200 hotels in the Caribbean, Canada, and the United States. **Corporate headquarters location:** This Location. **Parent company:** MeriStar.

MESA PAVILION HILTON
1011 West Holmes Avenue, Mesa AZ 85210. 480/833-5555. **Fax:** 480/649-1886. **Recorded jobline:** 480/844-6044. **Contact:** Human Resources Representative. **Description:** An independent franchise, Mesa Pavilion Hilton is a 263-room hotel.

NOTE: Entry-level positions and second and third shifts are offered. **Common positions include:** Accountant; Administrative Assistant; General Manager; Human Resources Manager; Purchasing Agent/Manager; Sales Manager. **Educational backgrounds include:** Accounting; Hospitality; Liberal Arts. **Benefits:** Daycare Assistance; Dental Insurance; Disability Coverage; Employee Discounts; Life Insurance; Medical Insurance; Public Transit Available; Sick Days (11+); Sick Days; Tuition Assistance. **Special programs:** Internships. **Parent company:** Quorum Hotels & Resorts Management Company (Dallas TX).

METROMEDIA RESTAURANT GROUP
6500 International Parkway, Suite 1000, Plano TX 75093. 972/588-5000. **Fax:** 972/588-5467. **Contact:** Corporate Recruiter. **Description:** One of the largest, full-service, restaurant chain operators in the nation. The company operates 1,200 restaurants in 45 states and two countries including Bennigan's, Bonanza, and Ponderosa. **NOTE:** Entry-level positions and second and third shifts are offered. **Common positions include:** Accountant; Administrative Assistant; Attorney; Auditor; Budget Analyst; Buyer; Chief Financial Officer; Claim Representative; Computer Programmer; Controller; Customer Service Representative; Database Manager; Financial Analyst; Food Scientist/Technologist; Human Resources Manager; MIS Specialist; Paralegal; Purchasing Agent/Manager; Quality Control Supervisor; Secretary; Systems Analyst; Typist/Word Processor; Video Production Coordinator. **Educational backgrounds include:** Accounting; Business Administration; Finance; Liberal Arts. **Benefits:** 401(k); Dental Insurance; Disability Coverage; Employee Discounts; Fitness Program; Flexible Schedule; Life Insurance; Medical Insurance; Profit Sharing; Savings Plan; Tuition Assistance. **Corporate headquarters location:** This Location.

MOTEL 6
14651 Dallas Parkway, Suite 500, Dallas TX 75240. 972/386-6161. **Contact:** Human Resources. **World Wide Web address:** http://www.motel6.com. **Description:** This location houses the administrative offices. Overall, Motel 6 operates a chain of motels. **Common positions include:** Administrative Assistant; Auditor; Customer Service Representative; General Manager; Human Resources Generalist; Instructor/Trainer; IT Specialist; Management Trainee; Marketing Specialist. **Educational backgrounds include:** Accounting; Business Administration; Computer Science; Liberal Arts. **Benefits:** 401(k); Disability Coverage; Life Insurance; Medical Insurance; Pension Plan; Tuition Assistance. **Corporate headquarters location:** This Location. **Parent company:** Accor (Paris, France).

NE RESTAURANT COMPANY
5 Clock Tower Place, Suite 200, Maynard MA 01754-2530. 978/897-1400. **Contact:** Human Resources Department. **Description:** Operates full-service, casual dining, Italian restaurants. **Common positions include:** Restaurant/Food Service Manager. **Educational backgrounds include:** Restaurant Management. **Benefits:** Bonus Award/Plan; Dental Insurance; Employee Discounts; Medical Insurance; Stock Option; Tuition Assistance. **Corporate headquarters location:** This Location. **Listed on:** NASDAQ.

NPC INTERNATIONAL
720 West 20th Street, Pittsburg KS 66762. 316/231-3390. **Contact:** Human Resources. **Description:** Owns and operates 540 Pizza Hut restaurants and is a franchiser of Tony Roma's, owning 42 of the 185

systemwide units. **Common positions include:** Accountant; Computer Programmer; Financial Analyst; Marketing Specialist. **Educational backgrounds include:** Accounting; Business Administration; Finance; Marketing. **Benefits:** Disability Coverage; Life Insurance; Medical Insurance; Profit Sharing. **Special programs:** Internships. **Corporate headquarters location:** This Location.

NUTRITION MANAGEMENT SERVICES CO.

P.O. Box 725, Kimberton Road, Kimberton PA 19442. 610/935-2050. **Contact:** Personnel. **World Wide Web address:** http://www.nmsc.com. **Description:** A food service management company specializing in food service programs for health care, retirement, and acute care facilities. **Common positions include:** Dietician/Nutritionist; Food Production Worker; Food Scientist/Technologist; Food Service Manager. **Educational backgrounds include:** Food Services. **Benefits:** Disability Coverage; Life Insurance; Medical Insurance. **Corporate headquarters location:** This Location.

OAKLAND MARRIOTT CITY CENTER

1001 Broadway, Oakland CA 94607. 510/451-4000. **Fax:** 510/832-1730. **Recorded jobline:** 510/466-6440. **Contact:** Human Resources Manager. **World Wide Web address:** http://www.marriott.com. **Description:** A full-service hotel and restaurant with over 400 rooms. Oakland Marriott City Center also has conference rooms and meeting space. **NOTE:** Entry-level positions and part-time jobs are offered. This location also hires seasonally. **Common positions include:** Accountant; Administrative Assistant; Assistant Manager; Auditor; Controller; Credit Manager; Customer Service Representative; Event Planner; General Manager; Hotel Manager; Human Resources Manager; Operations Manager; Purchasing Agent/Manager; Restaurant/Food Service Manager; Sales Manager; Systems Manager; Typist/Word Processor. **Educational backgrounds include:** Business Administration; Hotel Administration; Microsoft Office; Microsoft Word. **Benefits:** 401(k); Dental Insurance; Disability Coverage; Employee Discounts; Life Insurance; Medical Insurance; Sick Days (6 - 10); Tuition Assistance; Vacation Days (6 - 10). **Special programs:** Internships. **Office hours:** Monday - Friday, 9:00 a.m. - 5:00 p.m. **Corporate headquarters location:** San Francisco CA. **Parent company:** Park Lane Hotels International.

O'CHARLEY'S INC.

P.O. Box 291809, Nashville TN 37229. 615/256-8500. **Contact:** Human Resources. **World Wide Web address:** http://www.ocharleys.com. **Description:** Operates and franchises 60 full-service restaurants in 10 states in the Southeast and Midwest. **Common positions include:** Restaurant/Food Service Manager. **Educational backgrounds include:** Business Administration. **Benefits:** 401(k); Dental Insurance; Disability Coverage; Employee Discounts; Life Insurance; Medical Insurance. **Corporate headquarters location:** This Location.

OMNI HOTELS

420 Decker Drive, Suite 200, Irving TX 75062-3952. 972/730-6664. **Fax:** 972/871-5669. **Contact:** Recruiting Manager. **World Wide Web address:** http://www.omnihotels.com. **Description:** Operates an international chain of hotels, motels, and resorts. **NOTE:** Entry-level positions are offered. **Common positions include:** Accountant/Auditor; Computer Programmer; Credit Manager; Electrician; Financial Analyst; General Manager; Hotel Manager; Human Resources Manager; Management Trainee; MIS Specialist; Public Relations Specialist; Purchasing Agent/Manager; Quality Control Supervisor; Restaurant/Food Service Manager; Systems Analyst; Technical Writer/Editor; Typist/Word Processor. **Educational backgrounds include:** Accounting; Finance; Hospitality; Liberal Arts; Marketing; Mathematics. **Benefits:** 401(k); Dental Insurance; Disability Coverage; Employee Discounts; Job Sharing; Life Insurance; Medical Insurance; Pension Plan; Profit Sharing; Savings Plan; Tuition Assistance. **Special programs:** Internships; Training. **Corporate headquarters location:** This Location. **Other U.S. locations:** Nationwide. **Parent company:** TRT Holdings, Inc.

OMNI PARKER HOUSE HOTEL

60 School Street, Boston MA 02108. 617/725-1627. **Fax:** 617/725-1645. **Contact:** Personnel. **World Wide Web address:** http://www.omnihotels.com. **Description:** A four-star hotel with 550 rooms. **NOTE:** Entry-level positions are offered. **Common positions include:** Administrative Assistant; Assistant Manager; Auditor; Controller; Credit Manager; Front Desk Sales Agent; General Manager; Hotel Manager; Human Resources Manager; Purchasing Agent/Manager; Restaurant/Food Service Manager; Sales Executive; Sales Manager; Sales Representative; Secretary; Typist/Word Processor. **Educational backgrounds include:** Accounting; Business Administration; Communications; Health Care; Hospitality; Liberal Arts; Public Relations. **Benefits:** 401(k); Dental Insurance; Disability Coverage; Employee Discounts; Life Insurance; Medical Insurance; Pension Plan; Tuition Assistance. **Special programs:** Internships; Summer Jobs. **Corporate headquarters location:** Irving TX. **Other U.S. locations:** Nationwide. **International locations:** Cancun, Mexico. **Parent company:** TRT Holdings, Inc.

1 POTATO 2, INC.

P.O. Box 29325, Brooklyn Center MN 55429. 763/537-3833. **Contact:** Human Resources. **World Wide Web address:** http://www.1potato2.com. **Description:** This location houses administrative offices. Overall, 1 Potato 2 operates a chain of restaurants located in shopping mall food courts. **NOTE:** Opportunities include assistance programs for qualified corporate personnel. **Common positions include:** Chef/Cook/Kitchen Worker; Department Manager; District Manager; Restaurant/Food Service Manager. **Benefits:** Franchise Program; Life Insurance; Medical Insurance; Tuition Assistance. **Corporate headquarters location:** This Location.

OPRYLAND HOTEL CONVENTION CENTER

2802 Opryland Drive, Nashville TN 37214. 615/871-6621. **Fax:** 615/871-7638. **Recorded jobline:** 800/899-6779. **Contact:** Employment Manager. **Description:** Operates entertainment attractions including Opryland Hotel, a 3,000-room convention center; General Jackson Showboat; Springhouse Golf Club; Opryland River Taxis; Grand Ole Opry Tours; and the Opryland USA/KOA Campground. **Common positions include:** Accountant; Engineer; Food and Beverage Service Worker; Guest Services Agent; Horticulturist; Housekeeper; Purchasing Agent/Manager; Secretary; Telephone Service Representative. **Educational backgrounds include:** Accounting; Business Administration; Liberal Arts; Marketing. **Benefits:** 401(k); Daycare Assistance; Dental Insurance; Disability Coverage; Life Insurance; Medical Insurance; Pension Plan; Savings Plan; Tuition Assistance. **Corporate headquarters location:** This Location. **Parent company:** Gaylord Entertainment Company is a diversified entertainment and communications company operating principally in three industry divisions: entertainment, cable networks, and broadcasting. The broadcasting division owns two television stations in Texas and one in Seattle WA, as well as two radio stations in Tennessee and one in Oklahoma City OK.

PANCHO'S MEXICAN BUFFET, INC.
P.O. Box 7407, Fort Worth TX 76111. 817/831-0081. **Physical address:** 3500 Noble Street, Fort Worth TX. **Contact:** Human Resources. **Description:** This location houses administrative offices. Overall, Pancho's Mexican Buffet operates a chain of Mexican restaurants with a buffet-style format. Pancho's Mexican Buffet operates 72 restaurants in Texas, Arizona, Louisiana, New Mexico, and Oklahoma. Founded in 1966. **Corporate headquarters location:** This Location.

PANCHO'S MEXICAN FOODS
PANCHO'S MANAGEMENT INC.
2855 Lamb Place, Memphis TN 38118. 901/744-3900. **Contact:** Human Resources. **Description:** Operates a chain of Mexican restaurants. Pancho's Management Inc. (also at this location) is a wholesaler of food products to other restaurants. **Common positions include:** Industrial Production Manager; Operations/Production Manager; Services Sales Representative. **Benefits:** Dental Insurance; Employee Discounts; Life Insurance; Medical Insurance. **Corporate headquarters location:** This Location.

PAPPAN'S FAMILY RESTAURANTS
1198 Mulberry Street, Bridgewater PA 15009-3032. 724/774-7711. **Contact:** Human Resources. **Description:** Operates a chain of family-style and casual dining restaurants. **Common positions include:** Restaurant/Food Service Manager. **Educational backgrounds include:** Business Administration; Marketing. **Benefits:** Dental Insurance; Employee Discounts; Life Insurance; Medical Insurance; Savings Plan. **Corporate headquarters location:** This Location.

PARK PLACE ENTERTAINMENT CORP.
3930 Howard Hughes Parkway, Las Vegas NV 89109. 702/699-5000. **Contact:** Human Resources. **World Wide Web address:** http://www. parkplace.com. **Description:** Operates 28 casinos including Grand Casinos, Flamingo Casinos, Bally's, and Hilton Gaming Resorts & Casinos. **Corporate headquarters location:** This Location.

PEASANT RESTAURANTS, INC.
489 Peachtree Street NE, Atlanta GA 30308. 404/872-1400. **Contact:** Management Recruiter. **Description:** Operates a chain of casual restaurants. **Common positions include:** Restaurant/Food Service Manager. **Benefits:** 401(k); Dental Insurance; Disability Coverage; Employee Discounts; Life Insurance; Medical Insurance; Profit Sharing. **Special programs:** Internships. **Corporate headquarters location:** This Location. **Other U.S. locations:** Washington DC; Aventura FL; Minneapolis MN; Philadelphia PA; Memphis TN; Nashville TN. **Parent company:** Quantum Restaurant Group. **L**

PERKINS FAMILY RESTAURANTS, L.P.
6075 Poplar Avenue, Suite 800, Memphis TN 38119. 901/766-6400. **Contact:** Human Resources Manager. **World Wide Web address:** http://www. perkinsrestaurants.com. **Description:** Operates a restaurant chain with over 400 locations throughout the United States and Canada. Most of the restaurant locations also include a retail bakery. **Corporate headquarters location:** This Location.

PETER PIPER, INC.
6263 North Scottsdale Road, Suite 100, Scottsdale AZ 85250. 480/609-6400. **Toll-free phone:** 800/899-3425. **Contact:** Human Resources Manager. **World Wide Web address:** http://www. peterpiperpizza.com. **Description:** Operates a chain of family-style pizza restaurants with 120 locations. Founded in 1973. **NOTE:** Entry-level positions and second and third shifts are offered. **Company slogan:** The pizza people pick. **Common positions include:** Management Trainee. **Educational backgrounds include:** Business Administration; Hospitality. **Benefits:** 401(k); Dental Insurance; Disability Coverage; Life Insurance; Medical Insurance; Tuition Assistance. **Special programs:** Training; Summer Jobs. **Corporate headquarters location:** This Location. **Other U.S. locations:** CA; NV; TX; UT.

PHEASANT RUN RESORT & CONVENTION CENTER
4051 East Main Street, St. Charles IL 60174-5200. 630/584-6300. **Contact:** Employee Services Manager. **World Wide Web address:** http://www. pheasantrun.com. **Description:** A hotel and convention center. **Common positions include:** Accountant/Auditor; Chef/Cook/Kitchen Worker; Customer Service Representative; Hotel Manager; Mechanical Engineer; Purchasing Agent/Manager; Sales Executive. **Benefits:** Employee Discounts; Life Insurance; Medical Insurance. **Corporate headquarters location:** This Location.

THE PHOENICIAN
6000 East Camelback Road, Scottsdale AZ 85251. 480/941-8200. **Fax:** 480/423-2543. **Recorded jobline:** 480/423-2555. **Contact:** Human Resources. **World Wide Web address:** http://www. thephoenician.com. **Description:** Operates a chain of hotels and resorts. **NOTE:** Entry-level positions, part-time jobs, and second and third shifts are offered. **Common positions include:** Account Manager; Accountant; Administrative Assistant; AS400 Programmer Analyst; Assistant Manager; Auditor; Computer Support Technician; Controller; Electrician; Event Planner; General Manager; Human Resources Manager; Management Trainee; Marketing Manager; Mechanical Engineer; Operations Manager; Project Manager; Public Relations Specialist; Sales Manager; Secretary; Telecommunications Manager. **Educational backgrounds include:** Accounting; AS400 Certification; Business Administration; Engineering; Finance; Marketing; Microsoft Word. **Benefits:** 401(k); Dental Insurance; Employee Discounts; Life Insurance; Medical Insurance; Tuition Assistance. **Special programs:** Internships. **Parent company:** The Starwood Corporation.

PORT OF SUBS, INC.
5365 May Anne Avenue, Suite A29, Reno NV 89523. 775/747-0555. **Fax:** 775/747-1510. **Contact:** Human Resources. **World Wide Web address:** http://www.portofsubs.com. **Description:** Operates a local chain of sandwich shops. **Corporate headquarters location:** This Location.

PRANDIUM, INC.
P.O. Box 19561, Irvine CA 92623-9561. 949/863-6300. **Fax:** 949/757-7904. **Contact:** Human Resources. **World Wide Web address:** http://www. prandium.com. **Description:** Manages and operates several full-service Mexican restaurant chains including Casa Gallardo, Chi-Chi's, El Torito, Las Brisas, and Keystone Grill. **Common positions include:** Accountant/Auditor; Administrative Assistant; Attorney; Auditor; Market Research Analyst; Marketing Manager; Marketing Specialist. **Educational backgrounds include:** Accounting;

Business Administration; Marketing. **Benefits:** 401(k); Dental Insurance; Disability Coverage; Employee Discounts; Life Insurance; Medical Insurance; Tuition Assistance. **Corporate headquarters location:** This Location.

PRIME HOSPITALITY CORPORATION

700 Route 46 East, Fairfield NJ 07007. 973/882-1010. Contact: Human Resources. **Description:** An independent hotel operating company with ownership and management of 86 full- and limited-service hotels in 19 states and one resort hotel in the U.S. Virgin Islands. Hotels typically contain 100 to 200 guest rooms or suites and operate under franchise agreements with national hotel chains or under the company's Wellesley Inns or AmeriSuites trade names. **Common positions include:** Accountant; Administrative Manager; Advertising Executive; Architect; Attorney; Auditor; Budget Analyst; Buyer; Chief Financial Officer; Computer Operator; Construction Contractor; Controller; Credit Manager; Database Manager; General Manager; Human Resources Manager; Marketing Manager; Quality Control Supervisor; Secretary; Systems Analyst; Systems Manager; Typist/Word Processor. **Educational backgrounds include:** Accounting; Business Administration; Hotel Administration; Liberal Arts. **Benefits:** 401(k); Dental Insurance; Disability Coverage; Employee Discounts; Life Insurance; Medical Insurance. **Corporate headquarters location:** This Location. **Other U.S. locations:** Nationwide.

THE PROMUS HOTEL CORPORATION

755 Crossover Lane, Memphis TN 38117. 901/374-5000. Contact: Human Resources Manager. **World Wide Web address:** http://www.promus.com. **Description:** Operates and franchises several hotel chains including Doubletree, Embassy Suites, Hampton Inns, and Homewood Suites. **Corporate headquarters location:** This Location.

QUALITY DINING, INC.

4220 Edison Lakes Parkway, Mishawaka IN 46545. 219/271-4600. **Fax:** 219/271-4612. **Contact:** Human Resources. **Description:** A franchiser of restaurants. The company operates 71 quick-service Burger King Restaurants, 29 restaurants under the name Chili's Bar & Grill, five casual dining restaurants under the name Papa Vino's, three casual dining restaurants under the name Spageddie's, and 36 casual dining restaurants under the name Grady's American Grill. **NOTE:** Part-time jobs are offered. **Common positions include:** Accountant; Administrative Assistant; Assistant Manager; Attorney; Chief Financial Officer; Computer Programmer; Computer Support Technician; Computer Technician; Controller; Database Administrator; Database Manager; Finance Director; Financial Analyst; Food Service Manager; General Manager; Help-Desk Technician; Human Resources Manager; Intellectual Property Lawyer; Market Research Analyst; Marketing Manager; Network Administrator; Network Engineer; Operations Manager; Paralegal; Purchasing Agent/Manager; Real Estate Broker; Real Estate Lawyer; Software Engineer; Systems Analyst; Systems Manager; Technical Support Manager. **Educational backgrounds include:** Accounting; Business Administration; Computer Science; Finance; Marketing; MCSE; Microsoft Office; Microsoft Word; Software Development; Software Tech. Support; Spreadsheets; Visual Basic. **Benefits:** 401(k); Casual Dress - Daily; Dental Insurance; Disability Coverage; Employee Discounts; Life Insurance; Medical Insurance; Savings Plan; Sick Days (1 - 5); Tuition Assistance; Vacation Days (10 - 20). **Special programs:** Internships; Summer Jobs. **Corporate headquarters location:** This Location.

RTM RESTAURANT GROUP

5995 Barfield Road, Atlanta GA 30328. 404/256-4900. **Contact:** Human Resources Department. **World Wide Web address:** http://www. rtminc.com. **Description:** Operates and franchises national restaurant chains including Arby's, Lee's Famous Recipe Chicken, Mrs. Winner's Chicken & Biscuits, Del Taco Mexican Restaurants, and T.J. Cinnamons. **Common positions include:** Accountant/Auditor; Advertising Clerk; Chef/Cook/Kitchen Worker; Computer Programmer; Financial Manager; Food and Beverage Service Worker; Food Scientist/Technologist; Human Resources Manager; Management Trainee; Payroll Clerk; Receptionist; Restaurant/Food Service Manager; Secretary. **Educational backgrounds include:** Accounting; Business Administration. **Benefits:** Dental Insurance; Disability Coverage; Employee Discounts; Life Insurance; Medical Insurance; Profit Sharing; Savings Plan; Tuition Assistance. **Corporate headquarters location:** This Location. **Other U.S. locations:** San Diego CA; Indianapolis IN; Memphis TN; Nashville TN; San Antonio TX.

RWS ENTERPRISES
dba COUNTRY COOKING

4335 Brambleton Avenue, Roanoke VA 24018. 540/774-0613. **Contact:** Human Resources. **Description:** Operates the Country Cooking restaurant chain with locations throughout Virginia. **Corporate headquarters location:** This Location.

RADISSON HOTEL DENVER

3333 Quebec Street, Denver CO 80207. 303/321-3500. **Fax:** 303/322-7343. **Contact:** Human Resources. **Description:** A 300-room hotel whose facilities include a fitness center and a restaurant. **NOTE:** Entry-level positions, part-time jobs, and second and third shifts are offered. **Common positions include:** Administrative Assistant; Administrative Manager; Assistant Manager; Controller; Customer Service Representative; General Manager; Human Resources Manager; Sales Manager; Secretary.

RADISSON WILSHIRE PLAZA HOTEL

3515 Wilshire Boulevard, Los Angeles CA 90010. 213/368-3065. **Toll-free phone:** 800/333-3333. **Fax:** 213/368-3015. **Contact:** Lisa M. Sanchez, Human Resources Director. **World Wide Web address:** http://www.radisson.com. **Description:** A 393-room hotel, restaurant, and entertainment facility. **NOTE:** Entry-level positions, part-time jobs, and second and third shifts are offered. **Company slogan:** The difference is genuine. **Common positions include:** Account Manager; Account Rep.; Accountant; Administrative Assistant; Administrative Manager; Assistant Manager; Auditor; Clerical Supervisor; Controller; Credit Manager; Customer Service Representative; General Manager; Human Resources Manager; Marketing Manager; Purchasing Agent/Manager; Sales Executive; Sales Manager; Sales Rep.; Secretary; Systems Manager. **Educational backgrounds include:** Accounting; Art/Design; Business; Communications; Economics; Finance; Hotel Administration; Liberal Arts; Marketing; Microsoft Word; Public Relations; Spreadsheets. **Benefits:** 401(k); Dental Insurance; Disability Coverage; Employee Discounts; Life Insurance; Medical Insurance. **Special programs:** Internships; Training; Summer Jobs. **Internship information:** Unpaid internships are available in the fields of rooms; sales and marketing; food and beverage; accounting; and human resources. **Corporate headquarters location:** Minneapolis MN. **President:** Young Sun Kim.

RAMADA HENRY VIII HOTEL & CONFERENCE CENTER
4690 North Lindbergh Boulevard, St. Louis MO 63044. 314/731-3040. **Fax:** 314/731-4210. **Contact:** Personnel Director. **Description:** A full-service hotel. **Common positions include:** Accountant; Hotel Manager; Operations/Production Manager; Purchasing Agent/Manager; Restaurant/Food Service Manager; Services Sales Representative. **Educational backgrounds include:** Accounting; Business Administration; Finance; Marketing. **Benefits:** Dental Insurance; Disability Coverage; Employee Discounts; Life Insurance. **Corporate headquarters location:** This Location.

RARE HOSPITALITY INTERNATIONAL
8215 Roswell Road, Building 600, Atlanta GA 30350. 770/399-9595. **Contact:** Human Resources Manager. **World Wide Web address:** http://www.rarehospitality.com. **Description:** Franchises 147 restaurants and operates over 116 LongHorn Steakhouses (located in the southeastern and midwestern United States), 18 Bugaboo Creek Steak Houses, 11 Capital Grille Restaurants (nationwide), and The Old Grist Mill Tavern. Founded in 1981. **Corporate headquarters location:** This Location.

REGAL BILTMORE HOTEL
506 South Grand Avenue, Los Angeles CA 90071. 213/624-1011. **Contact:** Human Resources. **World Wide Web address:** http://www.thebiltmore.com. **Description:** A luxury hotel. **Common positions include:** Accountant/Auditor; Customer Service Rep.; Hotel Manager; Restaurant/Food Service Manager; Services Sales Rep. **Benefits:** 401(k); Dental Insurance; Disability Coverage; Employee Discounts; Life Insurance; Medical Insurance; Tuition Assistance. **Corporate headquarters location:** This Location. **Other U.S. locations:** Maui HI.

RESORTS CASINO HOTEL
1133 Boardwalk, Atlantic City NJ 08401. 609/344-6000. **Fax:** 609/340-7751. **Contact:** Employment Office. **World Wide Web address:** http://www.resortsac.com. **Description:** Atlantic City's first casino hotel, with more than 800 deluxe rooms and suites. The hotel also houses a fine dining restaurant, a full-service beauty salon, and several shops and boutiques.

RESTAURANT ADMINISTRATION SERVICES
2699 Lee Road, Suite 200, Winter Park FL 32789. 407/645-4811. **Fax:** 407/629-0641. **Contact:** Dale Lucas, Director of Personnel and Training. **Description:** Operates quick-service restaurants. **Common positions include:** Management Trainee; Restaurant/Food Service Manager. **Educational backgrounds include:** Business Administration. **Benefits:** Dental Insurance; Disability Coverage; Employee Discounts; IRA; Life Insurance; Medical Insurance; Tuition Assistance. **Corporate headquarters location:** This Location.

RESTAURANT ASSOCIATES CORP.
36 West 44th Street, 5th Floor, New York NY 10036. 212/789-7900. **Fax:** 212/789-8196. **Contact:** Manager of Recruitment. **Description:** A broad-based company which operates 60 restaurants in major cities, cultural centers, and leisure attractions along the East Coast. Private food service facilities are also offered to corporations, institutions, and clubs. **Common positions include:** Chef/Cook/Kitchen Worker; Restaurant/Food Service Manager. **Educational backgrounds include:** Food Services; Restaurant Management. **Benefits:** 401(k); Dental Insurance; Disability Coverage; Employee Discounts; Life Insurance; Medical Insurance; Tuition Assistance. **Special**

programs: Internships. **Corporate headquarters location:** This Location.

RESTAURANT MANAGEMENT SERVICES
4848 Mercer University Drive, Macon GA 31210. 912/474-5633. **Contact:** Human Resources. **Description:** A restaurant holding company. **Corporate headquarters location:** This Location. **Other U.S. locations:** Orlando FL. **Subsidiaries include:** Popeye's is a chain of fast-food dining facilities located throughout the Southeast.

RESTAURANTS UNLIMITED INC.
1818 North Northlake Way, Seattle WA 98103. 206/634-0550. **Fax:** 206/632-3533. **Contact:** Director of Staffing. **Description:** Owns and operates a chain of full-service dinner houses and Cinnabon quick-service bakeries. **Common positions include:** Chef/Cook/Kitchen Worker; Restaurant/Food Service Manager. **Educational backgrounds include:** Business; Communications; Economics; Hotel Administration; Liberal Arts; Restaurant Management. **Benefits:** 401(k); Dental Insurance; Disability Coverage; Employee Discounts; Life Insurance; Medical Insurance. **Corporate headquarters location:** This Location.

RICHFIELD HOSPITALITY SERVICES
5775 DTC Parkway, Suite 300, Englewood CO 80111. 303/220-2000. **Fax:** 303/220-2039. **Recorded jobline:** 888/887-5627. **Contact:** Leonardo Ranieri, Corporate Director of Human Resources. **E-mail address:** lranieri@richfield.com. **World Wide Web address:** http://richfield.com. **Description:** A company involved in hotel management and ownership. **Common positions include:** Administrative Assistant. **Benefits:** 401(k); Casual Dress - Daily; Dental Insurance; Employee Discounts; Life Insurance; Medical Insurance; Relocation Assistance. **Special programs:** Co-ops; Internships. **Purchasing Manager:** Karen Kratowicz. **Annual sales/revenues:** More than $100 million.

ROCK BOTTOM RESTAURANTS, INC.
248 Centennial Parkway, Suite 100, Louisville CO 80027. 303/664-4000. **Fax:** 303/664-4199. **Contact:** Human Resources. **World Wide Web address:** http://www.rockbottom.com. **Description:** Owns and operates 64 restaurants and breweries under the names Rock Bottom Brew Pub, Old Chicago Pizza, Walnut Brewery, Chop House, and Sing Sing. Restaurants range from casual to upscale dining. Founded in 1993. **NOTE:** Entry-level positions and part-time jobs are offered. **Company slogan:** To run great restaurants with great people. **Common positions include:** Accountant; Administrative Assistant; Chief Financial Officer; Computer Support Technician; Controller; Database Administrator; Financial Analyst; Graphic Artist; Marketing Manager; Operations Manager; Paralegal; Production Manager; Project Manager; Real Estate Agent. **Educational backgrounds include:** Accounting; Business Administration; Computer Science; Finance; Liberal Arts; Marketing; Microsoft Word; Novell; QuarkXPress; Software Tech. Support; Spreadsheets; Visual Basic. **Benefits:** Casual Dress - Daily; Dental Insurance; Life Insurance; Medical Insurance; Sick Days (1 - 5); Vacation Pay. **Special programs:** Internships; Training; Summer Jobs. **Corporate headquarters location:** This Location. **Other U.S. locations:** Nationwide.

RYAN'S FAMILY STEAK HOUSES, INC.
P.O. Box 100, Greer SC 29652. 864/879-1000. **Fax:** 864/877-0974. **Contact:** Human Resources. **World Wide Web address:** http://www.ryansinc.com. **Description:** Owns and franchises over 250

restaurants in 21 states. **Common positions include:** Restaurant/Food Service Manager. **Benefits:** 401(k); Dental Insurance; Disability Coverage; Employee Discounts; Life Insurance; Medical Insurance; Savings Plan; Vision Insurance. **Corporate headquarters location:** This Location.

S&W/CENTERFOODS MANAGEMENT CO.
20300 19th Avenue NE, Seattle WA 98155. 206/362-2255. **Fax:** 206/362-8850. **Contact:** Human Resources. **E-mail address:** Bstewart@ centerfoods.com. **World Wide Web address:** http://www.centerfoods.com. **Description:** Owns and operates several fast-food restaurants located in malls, which are part of the national chains Orange Julius, A&W, Dairy Queen, and Auntie Anne's. Founded in 1971. **NOTE:** Entry-level positions are offered. **Common positions include:** Customer Service Representative; General Manager; Management Trainee. **Educational backgrounds include:** Business Administration; Hospitality; Hotel Administration; Liberal Arts. **Benefits:** 401(k); Daycare Assistance; Dental Insurance; Employee Discounts; Flexible Schedule; Medical Insurance; Profit Sharing; Public Transit Available; Tuition Assistance. **Special programs:** Internships; Training. **Internship information:** The company has a paid internship program for hotel/restaurant or business management students. To apply, submit a letter of application and include goals, schedule, and time frame. Call for more information. **Corporate headquarters location:** This Location.

SANDS RESORTS
201 75th Avenue North, Myrtle Beach SC 29572. 843/445-2623. **Fax:** 843/445-2737. **Contact:** Human Resources. **World Wide Web address:** http://www.sandsresorts.com. **Description:** Owns and manages five resorts in Myrtle Beach and one resort in North Carolina. **Common positions include:** Accountant; Administrative Assistant; Auditor; Clerical Supervisor; Customer Service Rep.; Human Resources Manager; Purchasing Agent/Manager. **Educational backgrounds include:** Accounting; Business Administration; Liberal Arts; Marketing. **Benefits:** 401(k); Dental Insurance; Life Insurance; Medical Insurance; Savings Plan; Tuition Assistance. **Corporate headquarters location:** This Location.

SEA PINES ASSOCIATES, INC.
P.O. Box 7000, Hilton Head Island SC 29938. 843/785-3333. **Fax:** 843/842-1412. **Contact:** Director of Human Resources. **World Wide Web address:** http://www.seapines.com. **Description:** A holding company. **Corporate headquarters location:** This Location. **Subsidiaries include:** Sea Pines Company, Inc. (also at this address) operates resort assets including three golf courses, a 28-court racquet club, a home and villa rental management business, retail sales outlets, food services operations, and other resort recreational facilities. Sea Pines Real Estate Company, Inc. is an independent real estate brokerage firm with 11 offices. Sea Pines Country Club, Inc. owns and operates a full-service private country club providing golf, tennis, and clubhouse facilities for approximately 1,500 club members.

SHERATON FISHERMAN'S WHARF
2500 Mason Street, San Francisco CA 94133. 415/362-5500. **Fax:** 415/627-6529. **Recorded jobline:** 415/627-6567. **Contact:** Human Resources Director. **World Wide Web address:** http://www. sheraton.com. **Description:** A 525-room hotel operating as part of Meristar Hotels and Resorts, Inc. Founded in 1998. **NOTE:** Part-time jobs are offered. **Common positions include:** Account Manager; Administrative Assistant; Administrative Manager; Assistant Manager; Auditor; Controller; Credit Manager; Customer Service Representative; Electrical/Electronics Engineer; General Manager; Human Resources Manager; Sales Manager; Systems Manager. **Benefits:** 401(k); Dental Insurance; Employee Discounts; Life Insurance; Savings Plan; Tuition Assistance. **Corporate headquarters location:** Washington DC. **Listed on:** New York Stock Exchange. **Stock exchange symbol:** MMH. **Chairman/CEO:** Paul Whetsell.

SHOLODGE, INC.
130 Maple Drive North, Hendersonville TN 37075. 615/264-8000. **Contact:** Jim Grout, Executive Vice President of Human Resources. **World Wide Web address:** http://www.sholodge.com. **Description:** SholLodge is the exclusive franchiser of Shoney's Inns, a chain of 63 motels located throughout the Southeast. The company owns and operates 22 of these locations and manages four of the others. The company is also a developer and manager of AmeriSuites hotels. **Corporate headquarters location:** This Location. **Other U.S. locations:** Nationwide.

SIGNATURE DINING
6300 Penn Avenue South, Richfield MN 55423. 612/866-0041. **Contact:** Human Resources. **Description:** This location houses administrative offices. Overall, Signature Dining provides vending machine and cafeteria services. **Educational backgrounds include:** Food Services. **Benefits:** Medical Insurance; Savings Plan. **Corporate headquarters location:** This Location.

SIGNATURE INNS, INC.
250 East 96th Street, Suite 450, Indianapolis IN 46240. 317/581-1111. **Contact:** Human Resources. **World Wide Web address:** http://www.signature-inns.com. **Description:** Manages and operates franchised Signature Inn hotels. **Corporate headquarters location:** This Location.

SIZZLER INTERNATIONAL INC.
6101 West Centinela Avenue, Suite 200, Culver City CA 90230. 310/568-0135. **Contact:** Personnel. **Description:** One of the largest franchises of the KFC Corporation and the majority stockholder for the Sizzler restaurant chain. **Common positions include:** Accountant; Computer Programmer; Management Trainee. **Educational backgrounds include:** Accounting; Business Administration; Computer Science; Restaurant Management. **Corporate headquarters location:** This Location.

SODEXHO MARRIOTT SERVICES
9801 Washingtonian Boulevard, Gaithersburg MD 20878. 301/987-4760. **Toll-free phone:** 800/763-3946. **Contact:** Human Resources. **World Wide Web address:** http://www.sodexhomarriott.com. **Description:** Sodexho Marriott Services is a contract service management company which provides food services to health care facilities, schools, and corporate dining areas. **Corporate headquarters location:** This Location.

SOFITEL HOTEL
5601 West 78th Street, Bloomington MN 55439. 952/835-1900. **Recorded jobline:** 952/835-1900x5959. **Contact:** Personnel Director. **World Wide Web address:** http://www.sofitel.com. **Description:** The first North American location of the French hotel chain, offering 282 rooms. **General Manager:** Feryal Abdulkader.

SONESTA INTERNATIONAL HOTELS CORP.
John Hancock Tower, 200 Clarendon Street, Boston MA 02116. 617/421-5400. **Fax:** 617/421-5402. **Contact:** Human Resources. **World Wide Web**

address: http://www.sonesta.com. **Description:** Operates hotels including the Royal Sonesta Hotels in Cambridge MA and New Orleans LA. **Corporate headquarters location:** This Location.

STARBUCKS COFFEE CORPORATION
P.O. Box 34067, Seattle WA 98124. 206/447-1575. **Physical address:** 2401 Utah Avenue South, Seattle WA 98134. **Contact:** Human Resources. **Description:** Sells whole-bean coffees, along with hot coffees and Italian-style espresso beverages through more than 1,000 retail stores and licensed airport stores. The company purchases green coffee beans for its coffee varieties from coffee-producing regions throughout the world and custom roasts them. In addition to coffee beans and beverages, the company's stores offer a selection of coffee-making equipment, accessories, pastries, and confections. Also, the company sells whole-bean coffees through a specialty sales group and a national mail-order operation. **Corporate headquarters location:** This Location. **Other U.S. locations:** CA; CO; CT; DC; GA; IL; MA; MD; MN; NJ; NY; OR; VA. **International locations:** British Columbia, Canada; United Kingdom. **Subsidiaries include:** The Coffee Connection, Inc.

STARWOOD HOTELS & RESORTS WORLDWIDE, INC.
777 Westchester Avenue, White Plains NY 10604. 914/640-8100. **Fax:** 914/640-8310. **Contact:** Human Resources. **World Wide Web address:** http://www.starwoodhotels.com. **Description:** Manages and operates hotels under the names Westin, Sheraton, Four Points, St. Regis, and others. **Corporate headquarters location:** This Location.

STARWOOD HOTELS & RESORTS WORLDWIDE, INC.
WESTIN WALTHAM-BOSTON
70 Third Avenue, Waltham MA 02451. 781/290-5600. **Fax:** 781/290-5646. **Contact:** Human Resources. **World Wide Web address:** http://www.starwoodlodging.com. **Description:** A Four Star/Four Diamond, 346-room hotel. **NOTE:** Entry-level positions, part-time jobs, and second and third shifts are offered. **Common positions include:** Accountant; Administrative Assistant; Controller; Credit Manager; Customer Service Representative; Electrician; Event Planner; General Manager; Human Resources Manager; Management Trainee; Mechanical Engineer; Purchasing Agent/Manager; Sales Manager. **Educational backgrounds include:** Business Administration; Engineering; Hotel Administration; Microsoft Office; Microsoft Word. **Benefits:** 401(k); Dental Insurance; Disability Coverage; Employee Discounts; Life Insurance; Medical Insurance; Public Transit Available; Relocation Assistance; Tuition Assistance. **Special programs:** Internships. **Corporate headquarters location:** White Plains NY. **Listed on:** New York Stock Exchange. **Stock exchange symbol:** HOT. **CEO:** Barry Sternlicht.

STRANG CORPORATION
8905 Lake Avenue, Cleveland OH 44102. 216/961-6767. **Contact:** Human Resources Manager. **World Wide Web address:** http://www.strangcorp.com. **Description:** A restaurant and hotel management company. **Corporate headquarters location:** This Location.

SUGAR LOAF RESORT CORPORATION
4500 Sugar Loaf Mountain Road, Cedar MI 49621. 231/228-5461. **Contact:** Personnel Director. **World Wide Web address:** http://www.theloaf.com. **Description:** A large hotel and resort providing facilities for golf, tennis, basketball, swimming, and mountain bike rentals. **Common positions include:**

Department Manager; Services Sales Rep. **Educational backgrounds include:** Business Administration; Hospitality; Hotel Administration. **Benefits:** Employee Discounts; Life Insurance; Medical Insurance. **Special programs:** Internships. **Corporate headquarters location:** This Location.

SULLINS & ASSOCIATES, INC.
McDONALD'S CORPORATION
122 South 12th Street, Suite 105, Corsicana TX 75110. 903/872-5611. **Fax:** 903/872-5613. **Contact:** Human Resources. **World Wide Web address:** http://www.sullinsandassociates.com. **Description:** A leader in the fast-food industry, McDonald's offers quick-service meals, specializing in hamburgers. **Common positions include:** Branch Manager; General Manager; Management Trainee; Restaurant/Food Service Manager. **Educational backgrounds include:** Business Administration; Communications. **Benefits:** Dental Insurance; Employee Discounts; Life Insurance; Medical Insurance. **Special programs:** Internships. **Other area locations:** Ennis TX; Greenville TX; Palestine TX; Terrell TX; Waxahachie TX.

SUN INTERNATIONAL, INC.
1415 East Sunrise Boulevard, Suite 800, Fort Lauderdale FL 33304. 954/713-2500. **Contact:** Human Resources. **World Wide Web address:** http://www.sunint.com. **Description:** Owns and operates casinos, resorts, and hotel facilities. **Common positions include:** Accountant/Auditor; Administrative Manager; Computer Programmer; Customer Service Representative; Hotel Manager; Human Service Worker; Management Trainee; Systems Analyst. **Benefits:** 401(k); Dental Insurance; Disability Coverage; Employee Discounts; Medical Insurance; Pension Plan; Tuition Assistance. **Corporate headquarters location:** This Location.

SUN VALLEY COMPANY
One Sun Valley Road, P.O. Box 10, Sun Valley ID 83353. 208/622-4111. **Contact:** Human Resources. **World Wide Web address:** http://www.sunvalley.com. **Description:** Operates a hotel and ski resort. **Corporate headquarters location:** This Location.

SUPER 8 MOTELS, INC.
P.O. Box 4090, Aberdeen SD 57402. 605/225-2272. **Contact:** Director of Human Resources. **Description:** Provides office support for the Super 8 Motels lodging chain. **Common positions include:** Computer Programmer; Customer Service Rep.; Manufacturer's/Wholesaler's Sales Rep.; Purchasing Agent/Manager; Systems Analyst. **Educational backgrounds include:** Business Administration; Communications; Computer Science; Finance; Liberal Arts; Marketing. **Benefits:** Disability Coverage; Life Insurance; Medical Insurance; Pension Plan; Tuition Assistance. **Special programs:** Internships. **Corporate headquarters location:** This Location.

TACO CABANA, INC.
8918 Tesoro Drive, Suite 200, San Antonio TX 78217. 210/804-0990. **Fax:** 210/804-2425. **Contact:** Human Resources. **Description:** Taco Cabana operates a chain of over 100 Mexican restaurants. Founded in 1978. **Corporate headquarters location:** This Location.

TARRYTOWN HOUSE
East Sunnyside Lane, Tarrytown NY 10591. 914/591-8200. **Recorded jobline:** 914/591-8200x1024. **Contact:** Human Resources Director. **Description:** A historic hotel and conference center with 148 guest rooms, 30 meeting rooms, and eight

private dining areas. Founded in 1981. **Common positions include:** Account Manager; Account Representative; Accountant/Auditor; Administrative Assistant; Assistant Manager; Chief Financial Officer; Computer Operator; Controller; Customer Service Rep.; Finance Director; Financial Analyst; General Manager; Management Trainee; Marketing Manager; Marketing Specialist; Mechanical Engineer; Operations/Production Manager; Purchasing Agent/Manager; Sales Executive; Sales Manager; Sales Rep.; Typist/Word Processor. **Educational backgrounds include:** Accounting; Business Administration; Communications; Computer Science; Engineering; Finance; Liberal Arts; Marketing; Public Relations. **Benefits:** 401(k); Dental Insurance; Disability Coverage; Employee Discounts; Flexible Schedule; Life Insurance; Medical Insurance; Savings Plan; Tuition Assistance. **Special programs:** Internships; Training. **Internship information:** Internships are available year round in sales/marketing, accounting, human resources, operations, and the culinary arts. **Corporate headquarters location:** This Location. **Other U.S. locations:** CT; NJ; OR; TX; WA. **International locations:** Canada; France. **Parent company:** Dolce International.

TORTILLA, INC.
dba GARDUNO'S OF MEXICO/YESTERDAVE'S
10555 Montgomery NE, Suite 90, Albuquerque NM 87111. 505/298-5514. **Fax:** 505/298-5549. **Contact:** Personnel Director. **Description:** Operates two restaurant chains. Garduno's are Mexican restaurants with entertainment and YesterDaves is a '50s-style diner. **Common positions include:** Restaurant/Food Service Manager. **Educational backgrounds include:** Accounting; Business Administration. **Benefits:** 401(k); Dental Insurance; Employee Discounts; Life Insurance; Medical Insurance. **Special programs:** Internships. **Corporate headquarters location:** This Location.

TRAVEL CENTERS OF AMERICA, INC.
24601 Center Ridge Road, Suite 200, Westlake OH 44145. 440/808-9100. **Contact:** Human Resources. **Description:** Operates refueling and refreshment stops for motorists. **Benefits:** 401(k); Disability Coverage; Employee Discounts; Life Insurance; Medical Insurance. **Corporate headquarters location:** This Location. **Other U.S. locations:** Nationwide.

TRAVEL SYSTEMS, INC.
P.O. Box 12309, Zephyr Cove NV 89448-4309. 775/588-5678. **Physical address:** 625 Highway 50, Zephyr Cove NV. **Fax:** 775/588-1792. **Contact:** Human Resources. **Description:** Owns and operates Zephyr Cove Resort and Zephyr Cove Snowmobile Center. **Corporate headquarters location:** This Location.

TRICON GLOBAL RESTAURANTS
KFC
1441 Gardiner Lane, Louisville KY 40213. 502/874-8300. **Contact:** Human Resources. **World Wide Web address:** http://www.triconglobal.com. **Description:** Operates fast food restaurant chains including KFC, Pizza Hut, and Taco Bell. KFC (also at this location) is a worldwide fast-food chain specializing in chicken. **Corporate headquarters location:** This Location.

UNO RESTAURANT CORPORATION
100 Charles Park Road, West Roxbury MA 02132. 617/323-9200. **Fax:** 617/469-3949. **Contact:** Human Resources. **Description:** Uno Restaurant Corporation operates and franchises a chain of casual dining, full-service restaurants under the name Pizzeria Uno. **NOTE:** Entry-level positions

are offered. **Common positions include:** Restaurant/Food Service Manager. **Educational backgrounds include:** Business Administration; Hospitality. **Benefits:** 401(k); Dental Insurance; Disability Coverage; Incentive Plan; Life Insurance; Medical Insurance; Profit Sharing; Tuition Assistance. **Special programs:** Training. **Corporate headquarters location:** This Location. **Other U.S. locations:** Nationwide.

VAGABOND INNS CORPORATION
2361 Rosecrans Avenue, Suite 375, El Segundo CA 90245. 310/297-9600. **Fax:** 310/297-9610. **Contact:** Human Resources Manager. **World Wide Web address:** http://www.vagabondinns.com. **Description:** Owns and operates hotels. **Common positions include:** Accountant/Auditor; Buyer; Hotel Manager; Management Trainee. **Educational backgrounds include:** Business Administration. **Benefits:** Dental Insurance; Disability Coverage; Employee Discounts; Medical Insurance; Tuition Assistance. **Corporate headquarters location:** This Location.

VAIL RESORTS MANAGEMENT CO.
P.O. Box 7, Vail CO 81658. 970/845-2460. **Fax:** 970/845-2465. **Recorded jobline:** 888/SKI-JOB1. **Contact:** Human Resources Manager. **World Wide Web address:** http://www.snow.com. **Description:** Operates the Vail, Breckenridge, Beaver Creek, and Keystone resorts. Founded in 1962. **NOTE:** Entry-level positions and second and third shifts are offered. **Common positions include:** Accountant; Advertising Clerk; Assistant Manager; Auditor; Budget Analyst; Buyer; Computer Operator; Computer Programmer; Computer Technician; Controller; Customer Service Representative; Daycare Worker; Electrician; Financial Analyst; Management Trainee; Market Research Analyst; Mechanical Engineer; MIS Specialist; Paralegal; Preschool Worker; Sales Manager; Sales Rep.; Secretary. **Educational backgrounds include:** Accounting; Business; Communications; Computer Science; Finance; Marketing; Microsoft Word; Public Relations; Spreadsheets. **Benefits:** 401(k); Casual Dress - Daily; Daycare Assistance; Dental Insurance; Disability Coverage; Employee Discounts; Flexible Schedule; Life Insurance; Medical Insurance; On-Site Daycare; Public Transit Available; Season Pass; Tuition Assistance. **Special programs:** Internships; Training; Summer Jobs. **Corporate headquarters location:** This Location.

VICORP RESTAURANTS INC.
400 West 48th Avenue, Denver CO 80216. 303/296-2121. **Contact:** Human Resources. **Description:** Operates Village Inn, a national restaurant chain. **Corporate headquarters location:** This Location.

WAFFLE HOUSE, INC.
P.O. Box 6450, Norcross GA 30091. 770/729-5700. **Fax:** 770/729-5758. **Contact:** Human Resources Manager. **World Wide Web address:** http://www.wafflehouse.com. **Description:** One of the largest 24-hour restaurant chains in the country, with more than 1,200 restaurants in 20 states. Founded in 1955. **Common positions include:** General Manager; Management Recruiter; Management Trainee; Restaurant/Food Service Manager. **Benefits:** Dental Insurance; Life Insurance; Medical Insurance; Savings Plan; Stock Option. **Corporate headquarters location:** This Location.

WALL STREET DELI, INC.
One Independence Plaza, Suite 100, Birmingham AL 35209. 205/870-0020. **Contact:** Human Resources. **Description:** Operates a chain of delicatessen-style restaurants in a number of office

buildings, business centers, and high-volume retail districts. The company also franchises in airports, shopping malls, and roadside service areas. **Corporate headquarters location:** This Location.

WENDY'S INTERNATIONAL, INC.
4288 West Dublin Granville Road, Dublin OH 43017. 614/764-3100. **Contact:** Corporate Human Resources. **World Wide Web address:** http://www.wendys.com. **Description:** Operates a fast-food restaurant chain. **Corporate headquarters location:** This Location. **Other U.S. locations:** Nationwide.

WHATABURGER, INC.
P.O. Box 6220, Corpus Christi TX 78466. 361/878-0650. **Contact:** Human Resources Manager. **World Wide Web address:** http://www.whataburger.com. **Description:** Operates 500 restaurants in the Sunbelt area. Founded in 1950. **Corporate headquarters location:** This Location.

WINSTON HOTELS, INC.
2626 Glenwood Avenue, Suite 200, Raleigh NC 27608. 919/510-6010. **Contact:** Human Resources. **World Wide Web address:** http://www.winstonhotels.com. **Description:** Owns 16 hotels, including 11 Hampton Inns in Georgia, North Carolina, South Carolina, and Virginia, and five Comfort Inns in North Carolina and Virginia. **Corporate headquarters location:** This Location.

WYATT'S CAFETERIAS INC.
16970 Dallas Parkway, Suite 701, Dallas TX 75248. 972/248-4145. **Fax:** 972/248-8116. **Contact:** Human Resources Director. **Description:** A cafeteria chain with 68 locations in five states. **Common positions include:** Accountant/Auditor; Claim Representative; Food Scientist/Technologist; General Manager; Management Trainee; Restaurant/Food Service Manager. **Educational backgrounds include:** Business Administration. **Benefits:** Dental Insurance; Employee Discounts; ESOP; Life Insurance; Medical Insurance; Pension Plan. **Corporate headquarters location:** This Location.

WYNDHAM ANATOLE HOTEL
2201 Stemmons Freeway, Dallas TX 75207. 214/748-1200. **Contact:** Employment Manager. **Description:** A luxury convention hotel with over 1,600 rooms. **Common positions include:** Accountant/Auditor; Chef/Cook/Kitchen Worker; Department Manager; Hotel Manager; Operations/Production Manager; Restaurant/Food Service Manager; Services Sales Representative. **Educational backgrounds include:** Business Administration; Liberal Arts; Marketing. **Benefits:** 401(k); Dental Insurance; Employee Discounts; Life Insurance; Medical Insurance; Tuition Assistance. **Corporate headquarters location:** 1950 Stemmons Freeway, Suite 6001, Dallas TX.

For more information on career opportunities in hotels and restaurants:

Associations

AMERICAN HOTEL AND MOTEL ASSOCIATION
1201 New York Avenue NW, Suite 600, Washington DC 20005-3931. 202/289-3100. World Wide Web address: http://www.ahma.com.

THE EDUCATIONAL FOUNDATION OF THE NATIONAL RESTAURANT ASSOCIATION
250 South Wacker Drive, Suite 1400, Chicago IL 60606. 312/715-1010. World Wide Web address: http://www.edfound.org.

NATIONAL RESTAURANT ASSOCIATION
1200 17th Street NW, Washington DC 20036. 202/331-5900. World Wide Web address: http://www.restaurant.org.

Directories

DIRECTORY OF CHAIN RESTAURANT OPERATORS
Lebhar-Friedman, Inc., 425 Park Avenue, New York NY 10022. 212/756-5000. World Wide Web address: http://www.lf.com.

DIRECTORY OF HIGH-VOLUME INDEPENDENT RESTAURANTS
Lebhar-Friedman, Inc., 425 Park Avenue, New York NY 10022. 212/756-5000. World Wide Web address: http://www.lf.com.

Magazines

CORNELL HOTEL AND RESTAURANT ADMINISTRATION QUARTERLY
Elsevier Science, Inc., P.O. Box 945, New York NY 10159-0945. 212/633-3730. World Wide Web address: http://www.sha.cornell.edu/publications/hraq/.

NATION'S RESTAURANT NEWS
Lebhar-Friedman, Inc., 425 Park Avenue, New York NY 10022. 212/756-5000. World Wide Web address: http://www.lf.com.

Online Services

COOLWORKS
World Wide Web address: http://www.coolworks.com. This Website provides links to 22,000 job openings at resorts, summer camps, ski areas, river areas, ranches, fishing areas, and cruise ships. This site also includes information on volunteer openings.

ESCOFFIER ONLINE
World Wide Web address: http://www.escoffier.com/nonscape/employ.shtml.

HOSPITALITY NET VIRTUAL JOB EXCHANGE
World Wide Web address: http://www.hospitalitynet.nl/job. This site allows jobseekers to search for job opportunities worldwide in the hospitality industry including accounting, food and beverage, marketing and sales, and conference and banqueting positions. Jobseekers can also post resume information and a description of the job they want.

JOBNET: HOSPITALITY INDUSTRY
World Wide Web address: http://www.westga.edu:80/~coop/joblinks/subject/hospitality.html. This Website provides links to job openings and information for hotels.

Insurance

You can expect to find the following types of companies in this chapter:
Commercial and Industrial Property/Casualty Insurers • Health Maintenance Organizations (HMOs) • Medical/Life Insurance Companies

Some helpful information: *The average salary of an entry-level actuary ranges between $22,000 and $30,000 (higher salaries are awarded to those who have completed their actuary exams), and experienced actuaries earn an average of $50,000 - $60,000 annually. Insurance agents and brokers can expect approximately $22,000 - $28,000 during training, and after several years the average salary range is $40,000 - $70,000. Experienced agents with a strong sales record can earn over $100,000 annually. Insurance underwriters earn approximately $30,000 - $55,000 per year.*

THE ACACIA GROUP
7315 Wisconsin Avenue, Bethesda MD 20814. 301/280-1000. **Contact:** Manager of Recruitment. **World Wide Web address:** http://www. acaciagroup.com. **Description:** Provides diversified financial and insurance services through its operating companies. **Common positions include:** Accountant/Auditor; Actuary; Attorney; Bank Officer/Manager; Branch Manager; Brokerage Clerk; Claim Rep.; Customer Service Rep.; Financial Analyst; Human Resources Manager; Insurance Agent/Broker; Paralegal; Securities Sales Representative; Systems Analyst. **Educational backgrounds include:** Accounting; Business Administration; Finance; Liberal Arts; Marketing. **Benefits:** 401(k); Daycare Assistance; Dental Insurance; Disability Coverage; Employee Discounts; Job Sharing; Life Insurance; Medical Insurance; Profit Sharing; Public Transit Available; Telecommuting; Tuition Assistance. **Corporate headquarters location:** This Location. **Subsidiaries include:** Acacia Life and Acacia National Life offer life insurance policies. The Advisors Group provides investment management services. The Calvert Group, Ltd. offers mutual fund management services. Acacia Federal Savings Bank provides traditional savings and loan services. **Parent company:** Ameritas Acacia Mutual Holding Company.

ACAP GROUP
P.O. Box 42814, Houston TX 77242. 713/974-2242. **Toll-free phone:** 800/527-2567. **Fax:** 713/953-7920. **Contact:** Personnel Director. **Description:** A holding company for life insurance subsidiaries. **NOTE:** Entry-level positions are offered. **Common positions include:** Claim Rep.; Computer Operator; Computer Programmer; Customer Service Rep. **Educational backgrounds include:** Business Administration; Computer Science; Insurance. **Benefits:** Dental Insurance; Disability Coverage; Life Insurance; Medical Insurance. **Corporate headquarters location:** This Location. **Subsidiaries include:** American Capitol Insurance Company; Imperial Plan; Statesman National Life Insurance Company; Texas Imperial Life Insurance Company.

ACCIDENT FUND COMPANY
232 South Capitol Avenue, Lansing MI 48933. 517/342-4200. **Contact:** Human Resources. **World Wide Web address:** http://www.accidentfund.com. **Description:** A workers' compensation insurance company. **Common positions include:** Accountant; Actuary; Claim Rep.; Computer Programmer; Marketing Analyst; Systems Analyst; Underwriter/Assistant Underwriter. **Educational**

backgrounds include: Business Administration; Computer Science; Insurance; Liberal Arts; Marketing. **Benefits:** 401(k); Dental Insurance; Disability Coverage; Life Insurance; Medical Insurance; Pension Plan; Tuition Assistance. **Special programs:** Internships. **Corporate headquarters location:** This Location.

ADMAR CORPORATION
1551 North Tustin Avenue, Suite 300, Santa Ana CA 92705. 714/953-9600. **Fax:** 714/953-9060. **Contact:** Human Resources. **World Wide Web address:** http://www.admarinc.com. **Description:** Admar Corporation is a leader in the field of managed health care services. Admar works closely with insurance companies, businesses, health care professionals, and consumers nationwide to help manage medical costs. Admar offers comprehensive managed health care services including a hospital network, hospital and physician networks, exclusive provider networks, an HMO alternative program, utilization management programs, and managed care administration. Founded in 1973. **Corporate headquarters location:** This Location.

AEGON USA, INC.
MONUMENTAL LIFE INSURANCE CO.
1111 North Charles Street, Baltimore MD 21202. 410/576-4571. **Contact:** Human Resources. **World Wide Web address:** http://www.aegon.com. **Description:** AEGON USA operates through four groups encompassing 11 insurance divisions. The four groups are Agency, Asset Accumulation, Health, and Home Services. The Individual Division, Western Reserve Life, and Monumental Life Insurance (also at this location) sell life and health insurance products, mutual funds, and annuities. The Insurance Center administers group hospital expense insurance programs that are sold exclusively to the more than 300,000 members of the National Association for the Self-Employed. The NOL Division markets traditional and interest-sensitive life insurance and disability income products. Servicing the financial planning needs of high-income, high-net-worth clients, the Advanced Products Division offers estate planning, deferred compensation, capital transfer, and key-man programs. Offering plan design, participant communication programs, recordkeeping services, and technical guidance, the Diversified Investment Advisors services the retirement plan markets. The Financial Markets Division provides fixed and variable annuity products through national and state banks, savings and loans, and regional brokerage firms. Monumental General has seven business units, each with district objectives including credit, Medicare Supplement, and accidental death

insurance. The Long Term Care Division markets long-term care/nursing home products including nursing home, home health, assisted living, and adult daycare services, while the Supplemental Insurance Division markets intensive care, long-term care, and accident insurance products. **Corporate headquarters location:** This Location. **Other U.S. locations:** Cedar Rapids IA. **Parent company:** AEGON Insurance Group.

AETNA, INC.
151 Farmington Avenue, Hartford CT 06156. 860/273-0123. **Contact:** Recruiting. **World Wide Web address:** http://www.aetna.com. **Description:** Provides health and retirement benefit plans as well as financial services. **Corporate headquarters location:** This Location. **Other U.S. locations:** Nationwide.

AID ASSOCIATION FOR LUTHERANS
4321 North Ballard Road, Appleton WI 54919-0001. 920/734-5721. **Contact:** Human Resources. **World Wide Web address:** http://www.aal.org. **Description:** Provides life and health insurance, as well as investment capital management and annuities. **Corporate headquarters location:** This Location.

ALLIANCE BLUE CROSS & BLUE SHIELD
1831 Chestnut Street, St. Louis MO 63103. 314/923-4444. **Contact:** Human Resources Manager. **World Wide Web address:** http://www. abcbs.com. **Description:** A prepaid health care benefits company. Alliance Blue Cross & Blue Shield provides hospitalization and medical coverage to individuals and groups. **Common positions include:** Actuary; Attorney; Claim Representative; Computer Programmer; Customer Service Representative; Electrical/Electronics Engineer; Financial Analyst; Marketing Specialist; Mechanical Engineer; Technical Writer/Editor; Underwriter/Assistant Underwriter. **Educational backgrounds include:** Accounting; Business Administration; Computer Science; Engineering; Finance; Marketing; Mathematics. **Benefits:** Dental Insurance; Disability Coverage; Life Insurance; Medical Insurance; Pension Plan; Savings Plan; Tuition Assistance. **Corporate headquarters location:** This Location.

ALLIANZ INSURANCE COMPANY
3400 Riverside Drive, Suite 200, Burbank CA 91510-7780. 818/972-8000. **Fax:** 818/972-8533. **Contact:** Human Resources Manager. **Description:** An insurance company specializing in commercial insurance including workers' compensation, specialty property, and casualty. **Common positions include:** Accountant; Actuary; Claim Representative; Clerical Supervisor; Human Resources Manager; Underwriter/Assistant Underwriter. **Educational backgrounds include:** Accounting; Business Administration; Computer Science; Engineering; Liberal Arts. **Benefits:** 401(k); Dental Insurance; Disability Coverage; Life Insurance; Medical Insurance; Pension Plan; Profit Sharing; Savings Plan; Tuition Assistance. **Corporate headquarters location:** This Location. **Other area locations:** Orange CA; Sacramento CA; San Francisco CA. **Parent company:** Allianz (Germany).

ALLIED GROUP INSURANCE
3820 109th Street, Des Moines IA 50391. 515/280-4211. **Contact:** Employment Representative. **World Wide Web address:** http://www.alliedgroup.com. **Description:** A mid-sized regional property, casualty, and life insurance company. Allied Group's other businesses include home mortgages and information systems. **Common positions**

include: Actuary; Adjuster; Applications Engineer; Computer Programmer; Customer Service Rep.; Database Manager; Software Engineer; Systems Analyst; Underwriter/Assistant Underwriter. **Educational backgrounds include:** Business Administration; Computer Science; Finance. **Benefits:** 401(k); Dental Insurance; Disability Coverage; Employee Discounts; ESOP; Life Insurance; Medical Insurance; Tuition Assistance. **Corporate headquarters location:** This Location. **Other U.S. locations:** Santa Rosa CA; Denver CO; Lincoln NE.

ALLMERICA FINANCIAL
440 Lincoln Street, Worcester MA 01653. 508/855-1000. **Fax:** 508/853-5351. **Contact:** Employment Manager. **World Wide Web address:** http://www. allmerica.com. **Description:** A major provider of insurance and financial services and products. Allmerica Financial operates through two business groups, asset accumulation and risk management. The asset accumulation group is comprised of Allmerica Financial Services, which provides insurance and retirement plans to individuals and businesses, and Allmerica Asset Management Inc., which provides investment management services to businesses. As part of the risk management group, Hanover Insurance and Citizens Insurance provide property and casualty insurance to individuals and businesses. The other subsidiaries that operate as part of the risk management group are Sterling Risk Management Services and Citizens Management, both of which offer claims services and benefits administration services. Founded in 1844. **NOTE:** Entry-level positions are offered. **Common positions include:** Account Manager; Account Representative; Accountant; Administrative Assistant; Attorney; Auditor; Budget Analyst; Claim Rep.; Computer Programmer; Customer Service Representative; Database Manager; Financial Analyst; Marketing Specialist; MIS Specialist; Paralegal; Project Manager; Systems Analyst; Systems Manager; Underwriter/Assistant Underwriter. **Educational backgrounds include:** Accounting; Business Administration; Computer Science; Liberal Arts; Marketing; Mathematics. **Benefits:** 401(k); Daycare Assistance; Dental Insurance; Disability Coverage; Employee Discounts; Life Insurance; Medical Insurance; Pension Plan; Profit Sharing; Public Transit Available; Tuition Assistance. **Special programs:** Internships; Training; Summer Jobs. **Corporate headquarters location:** This Location. **Other U.S. locations:** Nationwide.

ALLSTATE INSURANCE COMPANY
2775 Sanders Road, Building A, Northbrook IL 60062. 847/402-5000. **Contact:** Employment Manager. **World Wide Web address:** http://www. allstatecareers.com. **Description:** Provides property, liability, life, reinsurance, and commercial lines of insurance. **Company slogan:** You're in good hands. **Common positions include:** Accountant/Auditor; Actuary; Claim Representative; Computer Programmer; Financial Analyst; Human Resources Manager; Instructor/Trainer; Paralegal; Systems Analyst; Underwriter/Assistant Underwriter. **Educational backgrounds include:** Accounting; Business Administration; Communications; Computer Science; Economics; Finance; Liberal Arts; Marketing; Mathematics. **Benefits:** Daycare Assistance; Dental Insurance; Disability Coverage; Employee Discounts; Life Insurance; Medical Insurance; Pension Plan; Profit Sharing; Savings Plan; Spending Account; Stock Option; Tuition Assistance; Vision Plan. **Special programs:** Internships. **Corporate headquarters location:** This Location. **Parent company:** Sears, Roebuck & Co.

AMALGAMATED LIFE INSURANCE CO.
730 Broadway, New York NY 10003. 212/473-5700. **Contact:** Human Resources. **Description:** A nonprofit insurance firm handling claims service and group medical, life, and health maintenance policies for the national textile workers union. **Common positions include:** Accountant/Auditor; Computer Programmer; Technical Writer/Editor. **Benefits:** Dental Insurance; Disability Coverage; Life Insurance; Medical Insurance; Pension Plan; Savings Plan; Tuition Assistance. **Corporate headquarters location:** This Location.

AMERICA SERVICE GROUP
PRISON HEALTH SERVICES INC.
105 Westpark Drive, Suite 300, Brentwood TN 37027. 615/373-3100. **Contact:** Human Resources. **World Wide Web address:** http://www.asgr.com. **Description:** Provides managed health care and related services to state and local government agencies throughout the United States. America Service Group's core business, Prison Health Services Inc. (also at this location), provides comprehensive managed health care services to correctional systems. **Benefits:** 401(k); Stock Option. **Corporate headquarters location:** This Location. **Subsidiaries include:** UniSource Inc. provides mail-order pharmaceuticals, medical supplies, and institutional pharmacy services to its contract sites and private sector customers.

AMERICAN COUNCIL OF LIFE INSURANCE
1001 Pennsylvania Avenue NW, Suite 500, Washington DC 20004. 202/624-2361. **Contact:** Human Resources. **Description:** A nonprofit trade association representing the life insurance industry. **Common positions include:** Actuary; Attorney; Financial Analyst; Legal Writer/Editor; Public Relations Specialist. **Educational backgrounds include:** Accounting; Business Administration; Communications; Computer Science; Economics; Finance; Journalism; Law/Pre-Law; Mathematics. **Benefits:** 401(k); Adoption Assistance; Dental Insurance; Disability Coverage; Flextime Plan; Life Insurance; Medical Insurance; Pension Plan; Reimbursement Accounts; Tuition Assistance. **Special programs:** Internships. **Corporate headquarters location:** This Location.

AMERICAN FAMILY INSURANCE GROUP
6000 American Parkway, Madison WI 53783-0001. 608/249-2111. **Contact:** Personnel Manager. **World Wide Web address:** http://www.amfam.com. **Description:** A multiline mutual insurance company. **Common positions include:** Accountant; Actuary; Attorney; Brokerage Clerk; Budget Analyst; Claim Rep.; Computer Programmer; Customer Service Rep.; Education Administrator; Financial Analyst; Human Resources Manager; Librarian; Property and Real Estate Manager; Public Relations Specialist; Purchasing Agent/Manager; Software Engineer; Systems Analyst; Technical Writer/Editor. **Educational backgrounds include:** Accounting; Business; Communications; Computer Science; Finance; Liberal Arts; Marketing. **Benefits:** 401(k); Dental Insurance; Disability Coverage; Employee Discounts; Life Insurance; Medical Insurance; Pension Plan; Profit Sharing; Tuition Assistance. **Special programs:** Internships. **Corporate headquarters location:** This Location. **Other U.S. locations:** AZ; CO; IA; IL; IN; KS; MN; MO; ND; NE; OH; SD.

AMERICAN FAMILY LIFE ASSURANCE COMPANY OF COLUMBUS (AFLAC)
AFLAC Worldwide Headquarters, 1932 Wynnton Road, Columbus GA 31999. 706/596-3789. **Contact:** Employment Services. **World Wide Web address:** http://www.aflac.com. **Description:** This location houses administrative offices. Overall, American Family Life Assurance Company of Columbus (AFLAC) is a world leader in guaranteed-renewable supplemental insurance and is a *Fortune* 500 company. **Common positions include:** Accountant/Auditor; Actuary; Claim Rep.; Computer Programmer; Systems Analyst; Technical Writer/Editor; Underwriter/Assistant Underwriter. **Educational backgrounds include:** Accounting; Business Administration; Computer Science; English; Finance; Marketing. **Benefits:** 401(k); Daycare Assistance; Dental Insurance; Disability Coverage; Employee Discounts; Life Insurance; Medical Insurance; On-Site Daycare; Pension Plan. **Corporate headquarters location:** This Location. **International locations:** Japan.

AMERICAN FINANCIAL GROUP (AFG)
One East Fourth Street, Cincinnati OH 45202. 513/579-2121. **Contact:** Human Resources Manager. **World Wide Web address:** http://www.amfnl.com. **Description:** Offers automobile, specialty property, and casualty insurance. AFG specializes in selling tax-deferred annuities, and life and health insurance products. **NOTE:** Hiring for American Financial Group is done through its subsidiary, Great American Insurance Company. Resumes should be sent to Great American Insurance Company, 580 Walnut Street, Cincinnati OH 45202, 513/369-5000. **Corporate headquarters location:** This Location.

AMERICAN GENERAL CORPORATION
2929 Allen Parkway, Houston TX 77019. 713/522-1111. **Contact:** Human Resources Manager. **World Wide Web address:** http://www.agc.com. **Description:** One of the largest public insurance companies in the United States. Other services include mortgage loans, real estate investment and development, investment counseling, and management and distribution of mutual funds. **Corporate headquarters location:** This Location. **Subsidiaries include:** American General Annuities; American General Life Company.

AMERICAN HARDWARE INSURANCE GROUP
P.O. Box 435, Minneapolis MN 55440. 952/939-4615. **Physical address:** 5995 Opus Parkway, Minnetonka MN. **Toll-free phone:** 800/227-4663. **Fax:** 952/930-7348. **Recorded jobline:** 952/939-4545. **Contact:** Human Resources Manager. **World Wide Web address:** http://www.youknowus.com. **Description:** A property and casualty insurance company. **Common positions include:** Insurance Agent/Broker; Underwriter/Assistant Underwriter. **Educational backgrounds include:** Business Administration; Marketing. **Benefits:** 401(k); Dental Insurance; Disability Coverage; Life Insurance; Medical Insurance; Pension Plan; Tuition Assistance. **Corporate headquarters location:** This Location. **Other U.S. locations:** Nationwide.

AMERICAN INTERNATIONAL GROUP
70 Pine Street, New York NY 10270. 212/770-7000. **Contact:** Human Resources Manager. **World Wide Web address:** http://www.aig.com. **Description:** A leading U.S.-based international insurance organization and one of the nation's largest underwriters of commercial and industrial coverage. Member companies write property, casualty, marine, life, and financial services insurance in approximately 130 countries and jurisdictions. The company is also engaged in a broad range of financial businesses. AIG's General Insurance operations group is composed of Domestic General-Brokerage, which markets property and casualty insurance products through brokers to large corporate buyers and other commercial customers; Domestic Personal Lines, which is in the business of

U.S. personal lines, principally personal auto; and Foreign General, which comprises AIG's overseas property and casualty operations. **Corporate headquarters location:** This Location.

AMERICAN MEDICAL SECURITY

P.O. Box 19032, Green Bay WI 54307-9032. 920/661-1111. **Fax:** 920/661-2059. **Contact:** Human Resources. **World Wide Web address:** http://www.amschoices.com. **Description:** An insurance carrier specializing in health and life insurance plans. Founded in 1988. **NOTE:** Entry-level positions and second and third shifts are offered. **Common positions include:** Accountant/ Auditor; Actuary; Administrative Assistant; Attorney; Chief Financial Officer; Claim Rep.; Clerical Supervisor; Computer Operator; Computer Programmer; Controller; Customer Service Rep.; Database Manager; Financial Analyst; Graphic Artist; Human Resources Manager; Insurance Agent/Broker; Insurance Services Manager; Licensed Practical Nurse; Market Research Analyst; Marketing Manager; Marketing Specialist; Medical Records Technician; MIS Specialist; Paralegal; Public Relations Specialist; Registered Nurse; Sales Executive; Sales Manager; Sales Representative; Secretary; Systems Analyst; Systems Manager; Telecommunications Manager; Typist/Word Processor; Underwriter/Assistant Underwriter. **Educational backgrounds include:** Accounting; Art/Design; Business; Communications; Computer Science; Finance; Health Care; Liberal Arts; Marketing; Mathematics. **Benefits:** 401(k); Dental Insurance; Disability Coverage; Employee Discounts; Financial Planning Assistance; Job Sharing; Life Insurance; Medical Insurance; Profit Sharing; Savings Plan; Tuition Assistance. **Special programs:** Internships; Training. **Corporate headquarters location:** This Location. **Other U.S. locations:** Indianapolis IN. **Parent company:** United Wisconsin Services.

AMERICAN RE-INSURANCE COMPANY

555 College Road East, Princeton NJ 08543. 609/243-4649. **Contact:** Employment Manager. **Description:** Underwrites property and casualty reinsurance in both the domestic and international markets. **Common positions include:** Accountant/ Auditor; Actuary; Attorney; Claim Representative; Financial Analyst; Human Resources Manager; Paralegal; Software Engineer; Underwriter/Assistant Underwriter. **Educational backgrounds include:** Accounting; Business; Communications; Computer Science; Finance; Marketing. **Benefits:** 401(k); Dental Insurance; Disability Coverage; Life Insurance; Medical Insurance; Pension Plan; Savings Plan; Tuition Assistance. **Corporate headquarters location:** This Location. **Parent company:** American Re Corporation, through its wholly-owned subsidiaries, is one of the largest providers of property and casualty reinsurance in the United States.

AMERICAN SKANDIA LIFE ASSURANCE CORPORATION (ASLAC)

P.O. Box 883, One Corporate Drive, Shelton CT 06484. 203/926-1888. **Toll-free phone:** 800/752-6342. **Contact:** Human Resources. **World Wide Web address:** http://www.americanskandia.com. **Description:** Provides long-term savings products including variable, fixed, market-value adjusted, and immediate annuities, as well as mutual funds, qualified funds products, and variable life insurance. American Skandia Life Assurance also offers investment management and administrative services through a series trust that provides mutual fund options. **NOTE:** Entry-level positions are offered. **Benefits:** 401(k); Medical Insurance; Tuition Assistance. **Special programs:** Internships.

AMERICAN UNITED LIFE INSURANCE CO.

One American Square, P.O. Box 368, Indianapolis IN 46206-0368. 317/263-1444. **Fax:** 317/285-1931. **Recorded jobline:** 317/263-4444. **Contact:** Human Resources. **E-mail address:** aul_employment@ aul.com. **World Wide Web address:** http://www. aul.com. **Description:** Provides insurance, annuities, reinsurance, and investment services. **Common positions include:** Accountant/Auditor; Actuary; Adjuster; Claim Representative; Computer Programmer; Customer Service Representative; Financial Analyst; Insurance Agent/Broker; Management Analyst/Consultant; Property and Real Estate Manager; Systems Analyst; Underwriter/ Assistant Underwriter. **Educational backgrounds include:** Computer Science; Mathematics. **Benefits:** 401(k); Dental Insurance; Disability Coverage; Employee Discounts; Life Insurance; Medical Insurance; Pension Plan; Profit Sharing; Savings Plan; Tuition Assistance. **Corporate headquarters location:** This Location. **Subsidiaries include:** State Life Insurance.

AMERITAS LIFE INSURANCE CORP.

P.O. Box 81889, Lincoln NE 68510. 402/467-7377. **Physical address:** 5900 O Street, Lincoln NE. **Fax:** 402/467-7935. **Recorded jobline:** 402/467-7199. **Contact:** Human Resources. **World Wide Web address:** http://www.ameritas.com. **Description:** A mutual life insurance company chartered by the state of Nebraska. The company offers life and health insurance and annuity and pension contracts. **Common positions include:** Accountant/Auditor; Actuary; Administrator; Attorney; Claim Rep.; Commercial Artist; Computer Programmer; Customer Service Rep.; Department Manager; Editor; Instructor/Trainer; Insurance Agent/Broker; Management Trainee; Marketing Specialist; Paralegal; Public Relations Specialist; Purchasing Agent/Manager; Reporter; Services Sales Rep.; Systems Analyst; Technical Writer/Editor; Underwriter/Assistant Underwriter. **Educational backgrounds include:** Accounting; Art/Design; Business; Communications; Computer Science; Economics; Finance; Liberal Arts; Marketing. **Benefits:** Dental Insurance; Disability Coverage; Employee Discounts; Life Insurance; Medical Insurance; Pension Plan; Profit Sharing; Savings Plan; Tuition Assistance. **Special programs:** Internships. **Corporate headquarters location:** This Location. **Subsidiaries include:** Ameritas Investment Advisors, Inc., an advisor providing investment management services to the parent company and other insurance companies; Ameritas Managed Dental Plan, Inc., a prepaid dental organization; Ameritas Variable Life Insurance Company, BLN Financial Services, Inc., which owns Ameritas Investment Corp. (a broker/dealer); Bankers Life Nebraska Company, a holding company that owns Ameritas Bankers Assurance Company; FMA Realty Inc., a real estate management firm; First Ameritas Life Insurance Corp. of New York; Pathmark Assurance Company; Veritas Corp., a marketing organization for low-load insurance products.

AMERUS LIFE

611 Fifth Avenue, Des Moines IA 50309. 515/283-2371. **Contact:** Human Resources Manager. **World Wide Web address:** http://www.ameruslife.com. **Description:** Provides individual life insurance policies and annuities. **NOTE:** Entry-level positions are offered. **Common positions include:** Accountant; Actuary; Administrative Worker/Clerk; Administrator; Claim Rep.; Clerical Supervisor; Compliance Analyst; Computer Operator; Computer Programmer; Customer Service Representative; Department Manager; Financial Analyst; General Manager; Human Resources Manager; Marketing

Specialist; Underwriter/Assistant Underwriter. **Educational backgrounds include:** Accounting; Business; Communications; Finance; Liberal Arts; Marketing. **Benefits:** 401(k); Dental Insurance; Disability Coverage; Employee Discounts; Life Insurance; Medical Insurance; Savings Plan; Tuition Assistance. **Corporate headquarters location:** This Location.

AMICA MUTUAL INSURANCE COMPANY
P.O. Box 6008, Providence RI 02940. 401/334-6000. **Physical address:** 100 Amica Way, Lincoln RI 02865. **Fax:** 401/334-1491. **Contact:** Personnel. **World Wide Web address:** http://www.amica.com. **Description:** A personal lines, property, and casualty insurance company. **Educational backgrounds include:** Liberal Arts. **Benefits:** Dental Insurance; Disability Coverage; Life Insurance; Medical Insurance; Pension Plan; Savings Plan. **Corporate headquarters location:** This Location.

AMWEST INSURANCE GROUP, INC.
P.O. Box 4500, Woodland Hills CA 91365-4500. 818/871-2000. **Physical address:** 5230 Las Virgenes Road, Calabasas CA 91302. **Fax:** 818/871-2019. **Contact:** Human Resources. **E-mail address:** info@amwest.com. **World Wide Web address:** http://www.amwest.com. **Description:** A holding company that underwrites property and casualty insurance products. Founded in 1970. **Corporate headquarters location:** This Location. **Other U.S. locations:** Nationwide. **Subsidiaries include:** Amwest Surety Insurance Company; Condor Insurance Company (also at this location); Far West Bond Services; Far West Insurance Company (also at this location); Horizon Business Resources, Inc.; Raven Claims Services, Inc.; SCBS Bonding and Insurance Services, Inc.; Western States Bond Agency, Inc.

ANTHEM BLUE CROSS BLUE SHIELD HMO COLORADO
700 Broadway, Denver CO 80273. 303/831-2028. **Contact:** Human Resources Department. **World Wide Web address:** http://www.anthem-inc.com. **Description:** A nonprofit health care insurance organization. Anthem Blue Cross Blue Shield provides hospitalization insurance coverage to individuals and groups. The company also provides group and individual insurance coverage performed by professional medical services from doctors, dentists, psychiatrists, and other medical professionals. **Corporate headquarters location:** Indianapolis IN. **Other area locations:** Colorado Springs CO; Grand Junction CO; Greeley CO. **Parent company:** Anthem, Inc.

ANTHEM, INC.
6740 North High Street, WN1-428, Worthington OH 43085. 614/438-3591. **Recorded jobline:** 614/438-3538. **Contact:** Human Resources. **World Wide Web address:** http://www.anthem-inc.com. **Description:** An insurance carrier. **NOTE:** Interested jobseekers should fax resumes to 614/438-3707, attention JL. **Common positions include:** Claim Rep.; Computer Programmer; Customer Service Rep.; Insurance Agent/Broker; Systems Analyst. **Educational backgrounds include:** Business Administration; Finance; Marketing. **Benefits:** 401(k); Dental Insurance; Disability Coverage; Life Insurance; Medical Insurance; Pension Plan; Profit Sharing; Savings Plan; Tuition Assistance. **Corporate headquarters location:** Indianapolis IN.
Other U.S. locations:
• 220 Virginia Avenue, Indianapolis IN 46204. 317/287-8892.

AON CORPORATION
123 North Wacker Drive, 14th Floor, Chicago IL 60606. 312/701-3200. **Fax:** 312/701-3290. **Contact:** Human Resources. **World Wide Web address:** http://www.aon.com. **Description:** An insurance holding company. **Common positions include:** Accountant; Actuary; Administrator; Attorney; Branch Manager; Claim Rep.; Computer Programmer; Customer Service Rep.; Department Manager; Financial Analyst; Human Resources Manager; Insurance Agent/Broker; Paralegal; Systems Analyst. **Educational backgrounds include:** Accounting; Business Administration; Computer Science; Finance; Liberal Arts. **Benefits:** 401(k); Dental Insurance; Disability Coverage; Life Insurance; Medical Insurance; Pension Plan; Savings Plan; Tuition Assistance. **Corporate headquarters location:** This Location. **Subsidiaries include:** Aon Risk Services; Aon Consulting Worldwide; Aon Services Group; Aon Re Worldwide; Aon Warranty Group; Combined Insurance Company; Virginia Surety Company.

ARGONAUT GROUP, INC.
250 Middlefield Road, Menlo Park CA 94025. 650/326-0900. **Toll-free phone:** 800/222-7811. **Fax:** 650/858-6677. **Contact:** Human Resources Manager. **World Wide Web address:** http://www.argonautgroup.com. **Description:** Argonaut Group, Inc. is a holding company whose subsidiaries are mainly involved in the selling, underwriting, and servicing of workers' compensation and other lines of property and casualty insurance. **Subsidiaries include:** Argonaut Insurance Company. **Listed on:** NASDAQ. **CEO:** Charles E. Rinsch. **President:** Mark E. Watson III.

ARKWRIGHT MUTUAL INSURANCE CO.
P.O. Box 9198, Waltham MA 02254-9198. 781/890-9300. **Contact:** Manager of Human Resources. **World Wide Web address:** http://www.arkwright.com. **Description:** A commercial and industrial property and casualty insurer. **Common positions include:** Accountant/Auditor; Computer Programmer; Editor; Financial Analyst; Marketing Specialist; Sales Executive; Underwriter/Assistant Underwriter; Writer. **Educational backgrounds include:** Accounting; Business Administration; Computer Science; Finance; Liberal Arts; Marketing. **Benefits:** 401(k); Dental Insurance; Disability Coverage; Life Insurance; Medical Insurance; Pension Plan; Tuition Assistance. **Special programs:** Co-ops; Internships. **Corporate headquarters location:** This Location.

ASSURANT GROUP
11222 Quail Roost Drive, Miami FL 33157. 305/253-2244. **Contact:** Human Resources Manager. **Description:** A holding company. Through its major subsidiaries, the company sells unemployment, accident, health, and homeowners insurance through credit, loans, and mortgages. **Corporate headquarters location:** This Location.

ATLANTA LIFE INSURANCE COMPANY
100 Auburn Avenue, Atlanta GA 30303. 404/659-2100. **Toll-free phone:** 800/235-5422. **Fax:** 404/654-8858. **Contact:** Human Resources Director **E-mail address:** srobinson@atlantalife.net. **World Wide Web address:** http://www.atlantalife.net. **Description:** A life insurance company. This location also hires seasonally. **Common positions include:** Accountant; Administrative Assistant; Auditor; Branch Manager; Budget Analyst; Chief Financial Officer; Claim Representative; Computer Programmer; Computer Support Technician; Controller; Customer Service Representative; Finance Director; Financial Analyst; General Manager; Help-Desk Technician; Human Resources

Manager; Insurance Agent/Broker; Market Research Analyst; Marketing Specialist; Paralegal; Public Relations Specialist; Sales Manager; Sales Representative; SQL Programmer; Underwriter/Assistant Underwriter; Web Advertising Specialist. **Educational backgrounds include:** Accounting; Business Administration; Computer Science. **Benefits:** 401(k); Casual Dress - Fridays; Dental Insurance; Disability Coverage; Life Insurance; Medical Insurance; Pension Plan; Sick Days; Vacation Days. **Special programs:** Internships; Summer Jobs. **Corporate headquarters location:** This Location.

ATLANTIC AMERICAN CORPORATION
P.O. Box 190720, Atlanta GA 31119. 404/266-5500. **Physical address:** 4370 Peachtree Road NE, Atlanta GA. **Toll-free phone:** 800/241-1439. **Fax:** 404/266-5596. **Contact:** Human Resources. **E-mail address:** basnyder@atlam.com. **World Wide Web address:** http://www.atlam.com. **Description:** A holding company. **Common positions include:** Accountant/Auditor; Actuary; Adjuster; Claim Rep. Clerical Supervisor; Computer Programmer; Customer Service Rep. Insurance Agent/Broker; Licensed Practical Nurse; MIS Specialist; Systems Analyst. **Educational backgrounds include:** Accounting; Business; Computer Science; Finance; Insurance; Mathematics. **Benefits:** 401(k); Dental Insurance; Disability Coverage; Life Insurance; Medical Insurance. **Corporate headquarters location:** This Location. **Subsidiaries include:** Bankers Fidelity Life Insurance Company (also at this location) provides life, accident, and health insurance; Georgia Casualty and Surety Company (also at this location) provides workers' compensation insurance.

ATLANTIC MUTUAL COMPANIES
195 Broadway, New York NY 10007. 212/227-3500. **Contact:** Personnel Manager. **World Wide Web address:** http://www.atlanticmutual.com. **Description:** Operates two multiple-line insurance companies that write property, liability, and marine insurance. **Subsidiaries include:** Atlantic Mutual Insurance Company and its wholly-owned subsidiary, Centennial Insurance Company, share the same offices and staff. Services are sold primarily through independent insurance agents and brokers. Another subsidiary is Atlantic Lloyd's Insurance Company of Texas.

AVESIS INC.
3724 North Third Street, Suite 300, Phoenix AZ 85012. 602/241-3400. **Contact:** Human Resources. **Description:** Avesis is a third-party administrator and preferred provider organization that markets and administers vision, hearing, and dental benefit plans. **Common positions include:** Accountant/Auditor; Administrator; Claim Rep.; Customer Service Rep.; Department Manager; Marketing Specialist; Services Sales Rep.. **Educational backgrounds include:** Accounting; Business Administration; Finance; Marketing. **Benefits:** Dental Insurance; Disability Coverage; Employee Discounts; Life Insurance; Medical Insurance; Tuition Assistance. **Corporate headquarters location:** This Location.

THE BALTIMORE LIFE INSURANCE CO.
10075 Red Run Boulevard, Owings Mills MD 21117. 410/581-6629. **Contact:** Human Resources Manager. **World Wide Web address:** http://www.baltimorelife.com. **Description:** A mutual life insurance company. Baltimore Life Insurance Company's product line includes individual life insurance products and annuities. **Common positions include:** Accountant/Auditor; Actuary; Administrator; Attorney; Claim Rep.; Computer Programmer; Customer Service Rep.; Insurance Agent/Broker; Systems Analyst; Underwriter/Assistant Underwriter. **Educational backgrounds include:** Accounting; Computer Science; Mathematics. **Benefits:** Dental Insurance; Disability Coverage; Life Insurance; Medical Insurance; Pension Plan; Tuition Assistance. **Special programs:** Internships. **Corporate headquarters location:** This Location.

BANCINSURANCE CORPORATION
OHIO INDEMNITY CORPORATION
20 East Broad Street, 4th Floor, P.O. Box 182138, Columbus OH 43215. 614/228-2800. **Toll-free phone:** 800/628-8581. **Fax:** 614/228-5552. **Contact:** Human Resources Manager. **Description:** A specialty insurance holding company engaged in underwriting niche insurance. **Corporate headquarters location:** This Location. **Subsidiaries include:** Ohio Indemnity Corporation (also at this location) underwrites property/casualty insurance. Among the company's products are Ultimate Loss Insurance, which protects banks and other lenders against risk arising from theft or damage to certain loan collateral where the borrower has failed to secure and maintain adequate insurance coverage; a surety bond program for a national administrative firm that performs certain services for nonprofit entities; a third party administrator service specializing in workers' compensation programs; and nonstandard private passenger automobile collision and comprehensive policies. Ohio Indemnity is licensed in 44 states and the District of Columbia, and is licensed for surplus lines in Texas. **Chairman and CEO:** Si Sokol.

BANKERS LIFE AND CASUALTY CO.
222 Merchandise Mart Plaza, 19th Floor, Chicago IL 60654. 312/396-7170. **Fax:** 312/396-5969. **Contact:** Human Resources. **Description:** Offers a variety of health plans including Medicare supplements, long-term care, and managed care, as well as life, annuity, and disability product lines. **Common positions include:** Accountant/Auditor; Brokerage Clerk; Computer Programmer; Customer Service Rep.; Market Research Analyst; Technical Writer/Editor; Typist/Word Processor; Underwriter/Assistant Underwriter; Video Production Coordinator. **Educational backgrounds include:** Accounting; Business; Communications; Computer Science; Economics; Finance; Marketing. **Benefits:** 401(k); Dental Insurance; Disability Coverage; Life Insurance; Medical Insurance; Public Transit Available; Tuition Assistance. **Corporate headquarters location:** This Location. **Parent company:** The Conseco Companies.

BANNER LIFE INSURANCE COMPANY
1701 Research Boulevard, Rockville MD 20850. 301/279-4128. **Contact:** Human Resources. **World Wide Web address:** http://www.lgamerica.com. **Description:** An insurance company that specializes in individual life insurance products and annuities. **Common positions include:** Accountant/Auditor; Actuary; Attorney; Budget Analyst; Buyer; Claim Rep.; Computer Programmer; Customer Service Rep.; Department Manager; General Manager; Human Resources Manager; Marketing Specialist; Operations/Production Manager; Paralegal; Payroll Clerk; Public Relations Specialist; Purchasing Agent/Manager; Receptionist; Systems Analyst; Typist/Word Processor; Underwriter/Assistant Underwriter. **Educational backgrounds include:** Accounting; Business; Communications; Computer Science; Finance; Liberal Arts; Marketing; Mathematics. **Benefits:** Dental Insurance; Disability Coverage; Life Insurance; Medical Insurance; Pension Plan; Profit Sharing; Savings Plan; Tuition Assistance. **Special programs:** Internships.

Programmer; Customer Service Rep.; Insurance Agent/Broker; Systems Analyst; Underwriter/Assistant Underwriter. **Educational backgrounds include:** Accounting; Computer Science; Mathematics. **Benefits:** Dental Insurance; Disability Coverage; Life Insurance; Medical Insurance; Pension Plan; Tuition Assistance. **Special programs:** Internships. **Corporate headquarters location:** This Location.

Corporate headquarters location: This Location.
Parent company: The Legal and General America Companies.

BERKSHIRE HATHAWAY INC.
1440 Kiewit Plaza, Omaha NE 68131. 402/346-1400. **Contact:** Human Resources. **World Wide Web address:** http://www.berkshirehathaway.com. **Description:** Berkshire Hathaway is a diverse company involved in insurance, manufacturing, and publishing. The manufacturing units include producing and distributing footwear, candy, home cleaning products, pressure and fluid control devices, uniforms, and electrical components. The insurance division, which conducts business through the National Indemnity Company of Omaha has 14 offices. Services include property and casualty insurance. The company also has a savings and loan association. Berkshire Hathaway's publishing interests include a daily newspaper in Buffalo NY, an encyclopedia, and other educational materials. **Corporate headquarters location:** This Location. **Subsidiaries include:** Dexter Shoe Company; Fechheimer Brothers Co.; H.H. Brown Shoe Co.; Scott & Fetzer Co.; The Buffalo News.

BLUE CROSS BLUE SHIELD OF LOUISIANA
P.O. Box 98029, Baton Rouge LA 70898-9029. 225/295-3307. **Contact:** Human Resources. **World Wide Web address:** http://www.lablue.com. **Description:** Providers of health and life insurance. **Common positions include:** Accountant/Auditor; Actuary; Computer Programmer; Services Sales Representative; Underwriter/Assistant Underwriter. **Educational backgrounds include:** Business Administration; Computer Science; Mathematics. **Benefits:** Dental Insurance; Disability Coverage; Life Insurance; Medical Insurance; Pension Plan; Savings Plan; Tuition Assistance. **Corporate headquarters location:** This Location.

BLUE CROSS BLUE SHIELD
100 Summer Street, Boston MA 02110. 617/832-5000. **Contact:** Human Resources Manager. **World Wide Web address:** http://www.bcbsma.com. **Description:** A health insurance provider. **Common positions include:** Accountant/Auditor; Actuary; Administrator; Attorney; Branch Manager; Claim Rep.; Computer Programmer; Customer Service Representative; Department Manager; General Manager; Human Resources Manager; Instructor/Trainer; Marketing Specialist; Operations/Production Manager; Services Sales Rep.; Systems Analyst; Underwriter/Assistant Underwriter. **Educational backgrounds include:** Business Administration; Communications; Computer Science; Economics; Finance; Marketing. **Benefits:** Dental Insurance; Disability Coverage; Life Insurance; Medical Insurance; Pension Plan; Savings Plan; Tuition Assistance. **Corporate headquarters location:** This Location. **Other U.S. locations:** Nationwide.

BLUE CROSS BLUE SHIELD OF TEXAS
P.O. Box 655730, Dallas TX 75265. 972/766-6336. **Physical address:** 901 South Central Expressway, Richardson TX 75080. **Fax:** 972/766-6102. **Recorded jobline:** 972/766-5364. **Contact:** Human Resources Manager. **World Wide Web address:** http://www.bcbstx.com. **Description:** A health and life insurance company. **Common positions include:** Accountant; Actuary; Attorney; Budget Analyst; Buyer; Claim Rep.; Claims Investigator; Clerical Supervisor; Computer Programmer; Credit Manager; Customer Service Rep.; Financial Analyst; Health Services Manager; Instructor/Trainer; Licensed Practical Nurse; Mathematician; Paralegal; Physician; Public Relations Specialist; Purchasing Agent/Manager; Registered Nurse;

Software Engineer; Supervisor; Systems Analyst; Technical Writer/Editor; Underwriter/Assistant Underwriter. **Educational backgrounds include:** Accounting; Computer Science; Liberal Arts; Mathematics. **Benefits:** 401(k); Dental Insurance; Disability Coverage; EAP; Employee Discounts; Life Insurance; Medical Insurance; Pension Plan; Savings Plan; Tuition Assistance. **Corporate headquarters location:** This Location.

BLUE SHIELD OF CALIFORNIA
P.O. Box 7168, San Francisco CA 94120. 415/229-5000. **Contact:** Human Resources Manager. **World Wide Web address:** http://www.blueshieldca.com. **Description:** A health maintenance organization that provides a variety of group and individual health plan coverage and professional medical services from doctors, dentists, psychiatrists, and other medical professionals. **Common positions include:** Accountant; Actuary; Administrator; Department Manager; Financial Analyst; General Manager; Human Resources Manager; Marketing Specialist; Mathematician; Public Relations Specialist; Services Sales Representative; Systems Analyst; Technical Writer/Editor; Underwriter/Assistant Underwriter. **Educational backgrounds include:** Accounting; Business Administration; Communications; Economics; Liberal Arts; Marketing; Mathematics; Nursing. **Benefits:** Dental Insurance; Disability Coverage; Life Insurance; Medical Insurance; Pension Plan; Savings Plan. **Corporate headquarters location:** This Location.

BOSTON MUTUAL LIFE INSURANCE CO.
120 Royall Street, Canton MA 02021. 781/828-7000. **Fax:** 781/821-4976. **Contact:** Human Resources Manager. **Description:** Provides life insurance. **Common positions include:** Accountant/Auditor; Actuary; Attorney; Claim Rep.; Clerical Supervisor; Computer Operator; Computer Programmer; Customer Service Representative; Department Manager; Human Resources Manager; Insurance Agent/Broker; Payroll Clerk; Services Sales Rep.; Systems Analyst; Underwriter/Assistant Underwriter. **Educational backgrounds include:** Accounting; Business Administration; Computer Science. **Benefits:** Dental Insurance; Disability Coverage; Life Insurance; Medical Insurance; Pension Plan; Savings Plan; Tuition Assistance. **Corporate headquarters location:** This Location.

BREWER & LORD LLP
600 Longwater Drive, P.O. Box 9146, Norwell MA 02061-9146. 781/792-3200. **Fax:** 781/792-3434. **Contact:** Human Resources. **Description:** One of the largest insurance agencies in New England, providing commercial and personal lines of insurance. **Other area locations:** Abington MA; Acton MA; Cambridge MA; Danvers MA; Falmouth MA; Framingham MA; Lexington MA; Marshfield MA.

BROWN & BROWN, INC.
401 East Jackson Street, Suite 1700, Tampa FL 33602. 813/222-4100. **Contact:** Personnel. **World Wide Web address:** http://www.poebrown.com. **Description:** An independent insurance agency that provides a variety of insurance products and services to corporate, institutional, professional, and individual clients. Products and services fall into four major categories: National Programs specializes in liability and property insurance programs; Retail Operations provides property, casualty, life, and health insurance; Brokerage Operations provides property and casualty products; and Service Operations provides claims administration. **Common positions include:** Accountant; Administrative Assistant; Attorney; Chief Financial Officer; Computer Operator;

Computer Programmer; Customer Service Rep.; Marketing Manager; Marketing Specialist; Network/Systems Administrator; Systems Analyst; Typist/Word Processor; Underwriter/Assistant Underwriter. **Educational backgrounds include:** Accounting; Business Administration; Computer Science; Marketing; Microsoft Word; Spreadsheets. **Benefits:** 401(k); Casual Dress - Fridays; Dental Insurance; Disability Coverage; Employee Discounts; Flexible Schedule; Life Insurance; Medical Insurance; Profit Sharing; Tuition Assistance. **Corporate headquarters location:** Daytona FL. **Other U.S. locations:** AZ; CA; CO; CT; GA; NC; NJ; TX.

CGU INSURANCE COMPANIES
One Beacon Street, Boston MA 02108. 617/725-6000. **Contact:** Human Resources. **World Wide Web address:** http://www.cgu-insurance.net. **Description:** A carrier of property, casualty, and life insurance. CGU is licensed in all 50 states. **Corporate headquarters location:** This Location.

CNA COMMERCIAL INSURANCE
CNA Home Office, CNA Plaza, 31S Floor, Chicago IL 60685. 312/822-5000. **Contact:** Human Resources. **World Wide Web address:** http://www.cna.com. **Description:** A property and casualty insurance writer offering commercial and personal policies. **Corporate headquarters location:** This Location.

CALIFORNIA CASUALTY MANAGEMENT COMPANY
P.O. Box M, San Mateo CA 94402. 650/574-4000. **Contact:** Human Resources. **World Wide Web address:** http://www.calcas.com. **Description:** A business and personal insurance firm. **Common positions include:** Accountant/Auditor; Actuary; Administrator; Attorney; Claim Rep.; Commercial Artist; Computer Programmer; Customer Service Rep.; Financial Analyst; Human Resources Manager; Insurance Agent/Broker; Marketing Specialist; Systems Analyst; Underwriter/Assistant Underwriter. **Educational backgrounds include:** Accounting; Business Administration; Computer Science; Finance; Mathematics. **Benefits:** Credit Union; Dental Insurance; Disability Coverage; Employee Discounts; Life Insurance; Medical Insurance; Pension Plan; Savings Plan; Tuition Assistance. **Corporate headquarters location:** This Location.

CALIFORNIA STATE AUTOMOBILE ASSOCIATION
150 Van Ness Avenue, 5th Floor, San Francisco CA 94102. 415/565-4185. **Fax:** 415/565-4582. **Recorded jobline:** 415/565-2194. **Contact:** Human Resources. **World Wide Web address:** http://www.csaa.com. **Description:** Provides automobile and homeowners insurance in California, Nevada, and Utah. The association also provides road and travel services. **Common positions include:** Accountant/Auditor; Actuary; Attorney; Claim Representative; Commercial Artist; Computer Programmer; Customer Service Rep.; Draftsperson; Financial Analyst; Human Resources Manager; Public Relations Specialist; Services Sales Representative; Systems Analyst; Technical Writer/Editor; Transportation/Traffic Specialist; Underwriter/Assistant Underwriter. **Educational backgrounds include:** Accounting; Art/Design; Business; Communications; Computer Science; Economics; Finance. **Benefits:** 401(k); Dental Insurance; Disability Coverage; Employee Discounts; Life Insurance; Medical Insurance; Pension Plan; Tuition Assistance. **Corporate headquarters location:** This Location. **Parent company:** AAA National.

CHICAGO TITLE & TRUST COMPANY
171 North Clark Street, Chicago IL 60601. 312/223-2000. **Contact:** Human Resources. **World Wide Web address:** http://www.ctt.com. **Description:** Provides a variety of insurance related services including credit services, marketing information, flood insurance, field services, and consolidated reconveyance. **Common positions include:** Accountant/Auditor; Attorney; Examiner; Financial Analyst; Human Resources Manager; Services Sales Representative; Systems Analyst. **Educational backgrounds include:** Accounting; Business Administration; Computer Science; Finance; Insurance; Law/Pre-Law. **Benefits:** 401(k); Dental Insurance; Disability Coverage; Employee Discounts; Life Insurance; Medical Insurance; Pension Plan; Profit Sharing; Savings Plan; Tuition Assistance. **Corporate headquarters location:** This Location.

CHICAGO TITLE INSURANCE COMPANY
909 Fannon, Suite 200, Houston TX 77010. 713/659-1411. **Fax:** 713/653-6190. **Contact:** Human Resources. **Description:** Provides title insurance. **Common positions include:** Accountant/Auditor; Attorney; Branch Manager; Clerical Supervisor; Customer Service Rep.; Secretary. **Educational backgrounds include:** Accounting; Business Administration; Finance; Marketing. **Benefits:** 401(k); Dental Insurance; Disability Coverage; Life Insurance; Medical Insurance; Profit Sharing; Tuition Assistance. **Corporate headquarters location:** Chicago IL. **Other U.S. locations:** Nationwide. **Subsidiaries include:** Ticor Title Security Union.

CHUBB EXECUTIVE RISK INC.
P.O. Box 2002, 82 Hopmeadow Street, Simsbury CT 06070. 860/408-2000. **Contact:** Human Resources Manager. **Description:** Chubb Executive Risk is an insurance organization that markets and underwrites insurance coverage for executive and professional liability risks. **Corporate headquarters location:** This Location.

THE CHUBB GROUP OF INSURANCE COMPANIES
15 Mountain View Road, Warren NJ 07059. 908/903-2000. **Contact:** Personnel. **World Wide Web address:** http://www.chubb.com. **Description:** A property and casualty insurer with more than 115 offices in 30 countries worldwide. The Chubb Group of Insurance Companies offers a broad range of specialty insurance products and services designed for individuals and businesses, serving industries including high-technology, financial institutions, and general manufacturers. Founded in 1882. **NOTE:** Entry-level positions are offered. **Common positions include:** Accountant; Administrative Assistant; Attorney; Auditor; Claim Representative; Computer Programmer; Computer Support Technician; Customer Service Rep.; Database Administrator; Database Manager; Financial Analyst; Human Resources Manager; Internet Services Manager; MIS Specialist; Paralegal; Secretary; Systems Analyst; Underwriter/Assistant Underwriter; Webmaster. **Educational backgrounds include:** Accounting; Business Administration; Computer Science; Finance; Liberal Arts; Marketing. **Benefits:** 401(k); Casual Dress - Fridays; Daycare Assistance; Dental Insurance; Disability Coverage; Financial Planning Assistance; Flexible Schedule; Job Sharing; Life Insurance; Medical Insurance; Pension Plan; Profit Sharing; Public Transit Available; Savings Plan; Tuition Assistance. **Special programs:** Internships. **Corporate headquarters location:** This Location.

CIGNA COMPANIES

2 Liberty Place, 1601 Chestnut Street, Philadelphia PA 19192. 215/761-1000. **Contact:** Human Resources. **World Wide Web address:** http://www. cigna.com. **Description:** Provides insurance and financial services to individuals and corporations worldwide. CIGNA ranks among the largest investor-owned insurance organizations in the United States. It is one of the largest U.S.-based insurers active in international markets. CIGNA's operating subsidiaries create and maintain the following products: managed health and dental care products; group health, prepaid health, and integrated health coverage and related services; group life, accident, and disability insurance; property and casualty insurance for businesses and individuals; pension and retirement products and services; individual life and health insurance products; life, accident, and health reinsurance products and services; and investment management for selected segments of capital markets. **NOTE:** Entry-level positions are offered. **Common positions include:** Accountant; Administrative Assistant; Budget Analyst; Claim Rep.; Computer Operator; Computer Programmer; Customer Service Rep.; Database Manager; Financial Analyst; General Manager; Human Resources Manager; Insurance Agent/Broker; Licensed Practical Nurse; Management Trainee; Project Manager; Sales Manager; Sales Representative; Systems Analyst; Systems Manager; Telecommunications Manager; Underwriter/Assistant Underwriter. **Educational backgrounds include:** Accounting; Business Administration; Computer Science; Health Care; Marketing; Mathematics. **Benefits:** 401(k); Daycare Assistance; Dental Insurance; Disability Coverage; Employee Discounts; Financial Planning Assistance; Flexible Schedule; Job Sharing; Life Insurance; Medical Insurance; On-Site Daycare; Pension Plan; Profit Sharing; Public Transit Available; Telecommuting; Tuition Assistance. **Special programs:** Internships; Training. **Corporate headquarters location:** This Location. **Other U.S. locations:** Nationwide. **International locations:** Worldwide. **Subsidiaries include:** Intracorp.

CIGNA HEALTHCARE

2 College Park Drive, Hooksett NH 03106. 603/268-7000. **Contact:** Human Resources. **World Wide Web address:** http://www.cigna.com. **Description:** Provides health insurance. **Corporate headquarters location:** This Location.

CITIZENS, INC.

P.O. Box 149151, Austin TX 78714. 512/837-7100. **Fax:** 512/836-9785. **Contact:** Human Resources. **World Wide Web address:** http://www. citizensinc.com. **Description:** A life insurance holding company. **Common positions include:** Accountant; Administrative Assistant; Computer Programmer; Controller; Customer Service Rep.; Human Resources Manager; Secretary; Underwriter/Assistant Underwriter. **Educational backgrounds include:** Accounting; Business Administration; Computer Science; Health Care. **Benefits:** Dental Insurance; Life Insurance; Medical Insurance; Profit Sharing. **Corporate headquarters location:** This Location. **Subsidiaries include:** American Investment Network, Inc. (Jackson MS); Citizens Insurance Company of America (CICA) is a Colorado life insurance company that provides ordinary whole-life products on an international basis; United Security Life Insurance Company.

COLONIAL LIFE & ACCIDENT INSURANCE COMPANY

P.O. Box 1365, Columbia SC 29202. 803/798-7000. **Fax:** 803/731-2618. **Recorded jobline:** 803/750-0088. **Contact:** Human Resources. **Description:** An accident and health insurance company. **Common positions include:** Accountant; Administrative Manager; Advertising Clerk; Attorney; Budget Analyst; Claim Rep.; Computer Programmer; Custodian; Customer Service Rep.; Designer; Insurance Agent/Broker; Operations/Production Manager; Public Relations Specialist; Systems Analyst; Technical Writer/Editor; Underwriter/Assistant Underwriter. **Educational backgrounds include:** Accounting; Art/Design; Business; Communications; Computer Science; Economics; Finance; Liberal Arts; Marketing. **Benefits:** 401(k); Daycare Assistance; Dental Insurance; Disability Coverage; Employee Discounts; Life Insurance; Pension Plan; Profit Sharing; Savings Plan; Tuition Assistance. **Corporate headquarters location:** This Location. **Parent company:** Unum Provident Corporation (Portland ME) is an insurance company providing income protection to small- and medium-sized employers through a broad range of life, health, disability, and retirement products.

COMMERCE INSURANCE COMPANY

211 Main Street, Webster MA 01570. 508/943-9000. **Fax:** 508/949-4921. **Contact:** Human Resources. **Description:** Underwrites personal and commercial property and casualty insurance such as motor vehicle insurance covering personal automobiles; offers homeowners inland/marine, fire, general liability, and commercial multiperil insurance; and provides residential and commercial mortgage loans. Founded in 1972. **NOTE:** Entry-level positions are offered. **Common positions include:** Administrative Assistant; Claim Rep.; Clerical Supervisor; Computer Operator; Computer Programmer; Customer Service Rep.; Daycare Worker; MIS Specialist; Paralegal; Secretary; Statistician; Systems Analyst; Typist/Word Processor; Underwriter/Assistant Underwriter. **Educational backgrounds include:** Business Administration; Communications; Computer Science. **Benefits:** Daycare Assistance; Dental Insurance; Disability Coverage; Employee Discounts; ESOP; Life Insurance; Medical Insurance; Tuition Assistance. **Special programs:** Training. **Corporate headquarters location:** This Location. **Subsidiaries include:** Western Pioneer Insurance Company (Pleasanton CA).

THE CONSECO COMPANIES

11825 North Pennsylvania Street, Carmel IN 46032. 317/817-6100. **Contact:** Human Resources. **World Wide Web address:** http://www.conseco.com. **Description:** Offers life and health insurance, investment, and lending products. **Corporate headquarters location:** This Location.

CORVEL CORPORATION

2010 Main Street, Suite 1020, Irvine CA 92614. 949/851-1473. **Contact:** Human Resources. **World Wide Web address:** http://www.corvel.com. **Description:** CorVel Corporation manages health care delivery and provider reimbursement. Many customers contract with CorVel as an outsource vendor, while others are served by its 165 branch offices located throughout the United States. CorVel maintains over 1,000 customers and its CorCare PPO network now includes over 70,000 providers located in 26 states. **Common positions include:** Registered Nurse. **Educational backgrounds include:** Health Care. **Benefits:** 401(k); Daycare Assistance; Dental Insurance; Disability Coverage; Life Insurance; Medical Insurance; Stock Option. **Corporate headquarters location:** This Location.

COTTON STATES INSURANCE GROUP

P.O. Box 105303, Atlanta GA 30348. 770/391-8600. **Contact:** Human Resources Department.

World Wide Web address: http://www. cottonstatesinsurance.com. **Description:** A group of insurance providers whose main services are individual life products. Members of the group include Cotton States Life Insurance Company, Cotton States Mutual Insurance Company, Shield Insurance Company, and Cotton States Investment Company. **Common positions include:** Adjuster; MIS Specialist; Technician. **Educational backgrounds include:** Business; Computer Science; Insurance. **Benefits:** 401(k); Dental Insurance; Disability Coverage; Life Insurance; Medical Insurance; Pension Plan; Savings Plan; Tuition Assistance. **Corporate headquarters location:** This Location. **Subsidiaries include:** CS Marketing Resources Inc.; CSI Brokerage Services, Inc.

COUNTRY COMPANIES INSURANCE GROUP
P.O. Box 2020, Bloomington IL 61702. 309/821-3000. **Contact:** Human Resources. **World Wide Web address:** http://www.countrycompanies.com. **Description:** Offers a full line of insurance products including auto, home, life, health, disability income, long term care, farm, ranch, and commercial insurance, as well as annuities, mutual funds, and financial and estate planning. Country Companies include Country Life, Country Mutual, Country Casualty Insurance Companies, and Country Investors Life Assurance Company. Country Companies serves customers in Alaska, Arizona, Colorado, Illinois, Kansas, Missouri, Nevada, Oklahoma, Oregon, and Washington. Founded in 1925. **NOTE:** Entry-level positions and second and third shifts are offered. **Common positions include:** Accountant; Adjuster; Attorney; Auditor; Claim Rep.; Computer Operator; Computer Programmer; Controller; Database Manager; Financial Analyst; Graphic Artist; Insurance Agent/Broker; Market Research Analyst; Secretary; Systems Analyst; Systems Manager; Telecommunications Manager; Typist/Word Processor; Underwriter/Assistant Underwriter. **Educational backgrounds include:** Accounting; Business Administration; Computer Science; Economics; Liberal Arts; Marketing; Mathematics; Software Development; Software Tech. Support. **Benefits:** 401(k); Disability Coverage; Employee Discounts; Financial Planning Assistance; Flexible Schedule; Life Insurance; Medical Insurance; Pension Plan; Tuition Assistance. **Special programs:** Internships; Training. **Corporate headquarters location:** This Location. **Other U.S. locations:** AK; AZ; CO; KS; MO; NV; OK; OR; WA.

CHARLES L. CRANE AGENCY
100 South Fourth Street, Suite 800, St. Louis MO 63102. 314/241-8700. **Contact:** General Manager. **Description:** A full-service insurance agency. **Common positions include:** Accountant/Auditor; Claim Rep.; Computer Programmer; Customer Service Rep.; Department Manager; Financial Analyst; Industrial Engineer; Insurance Agent/Broker; Marketing Specialist; Systems Analyst; Underwriter/Assistant Underwriter. **Benefits:** Dental Insurance; Life Insurance; Medical Insurance; Profit Sharing; Savings Plan; Tuition Assistance. **Corporate headquarters location:** This Location.

CRAWFORD & COMPANY
P.O. Box 5047, Atlanta GA 30302. 404/847-4080. **Physical address:** 5620 Glenridge Drive NE, Atlanta GA 30342. **Contact:** Human Resources Manager. **World Wide Web address:** http://www. rawfordandcompany.com. **Description:** A diversified services firm providing claims, risk management, health care management, and risk control services to insurance companies, self-insured corporations, and governmental entities.

Founded in 1941. **NOTE:** All hiring for adjusters is done at the local branch office level. Staffing for home office support personnel is done at the above address. **Common positions include:** Accountant/Auditor; Administrator; Computer Programmer; Department Manager; Financial Analyst; Graphic Artist; Human Resources Manager; Marketing Specialist; Operations/Production Manager; Systems Analyst; Technical Writer/Editor. **Educational backgrounds include:** Accounting; Business; Communications; Computer Science; Finance; Marketing. **Benefits:** Dental Insurance; Disability Coverage; Life Insurance; Medical Insurance; Pension Plan; Savings Plan. **Corporate headquarters location:** This Location. **International locations:** Worldwide.

THE DANIEL AND HENRY COMPANY
2350 Market Street, Suite 400, St. Louis MO 63103. 314/421-1525. **Fax:** 314/444-1774. **Contact:** Human Resources. **Description:** Provides all types of commercial and personal insurance, as well as brokerage services. Founded in 1921. **Common positions include:** Administrative Assistant; Insurance Agent/Broker; Secretary. **Benefits:** 401(k); Dental Insurance; Flexible Schedule; Life Insurance; Medical Insurance; Pension Plan. **Corporate headquarters location:** This Location.

DEAN HEALTH PLAN, INC.
1277 Deming Way, Madison WI 53717. 608/836-1400. **Fax:** 608/836-6516. **Contact:** Human Resources. **Description:** A managed health care company. Founded in 1983. **Common positions include:** Administrative Assistant; Claim Rep.; Customer Service Rep.; Financial Analyst; Sales Rep.; Secretary; Systems Analyst; Underwriter/Assistant Underwriter. **Educational backgrounds include:** Accounting; Business Administration; Communications; Computer Science; Economics; Finance; Health Care; Liberal Arts; Marketing; Mathematics. **Benefits:** 401(k); Daycare Assistance; Dental Insurance; Disability Coverage; Employee Discounts; Financial Planning Assistance; Flexible Schedule; Life Insurance; Medical Insurance; Pension Plan; Profit Sharing. **Corporate headquarters location:** This Location. **President/CEO:** John Turcott.

DELPHI FINANCIAL GROUP, INC.
1105 North Market Street, Suite 1300, Wilmington DE 19801. 302/478-5142. **Contact:** Personnel. **Description:** An insurance holding company which, through its subsidiaries, offers a diverse portfolio of life, long-term disability, and personal accident insurance products principally to the group employee benefits market nationwide. Delphi Financial Group also offers asset accumulation products to individuals and groups. **Benefits:** ESOP; Pension Plan; Retirement Plan. **Corporate headquarters location:** This Location. **Subsidiaries include:** Reliance Standard Life Insurance Company; Safety National Casualty Corporation.

DELTA DENTAL PLAN OF CALIFORNIA
P.O. Box 7736, San Francisco CA 94120. 415/972-8300. **Physical address:** Delta Tower, 100 First Street, San Francisco CA. **Contact:** Human Resources. **World Wide Web address:** http://www. deltadentalca.org. **Description:** A prepaid, dental insurance firm. **NOTE:** Entry-level positions are offered. **Common positions include:** Accountant; Actuary; Customer Service Rep.; Financial Analyst; Secretary; Underwriter/Assistant Underwriter. **Educational backgrounds include:** Accounting; Business Administration; Economics; Finance. **Benefits:** 401(k); Dental Insurance; Disability Coverage; EAP; Employee Discounts; Life

Insurance; Medical Insurance; Pension Plan; Prescription Drugs; Tuition Assistance. **Corporate headquarters location:** This Location. **Other U.S. locations:** Cerritos CA; Sacramento CA. **Subsidiaries include:** Delta Dental Insurance Company (DDIC); Private Medical Care, Inc. (PMI).

DELTA LIFE INSURANCE COMPANY
4370 Peachtree Road NE, Atlanta GA 30319. 404/231-2111. **Contact:** Human Resources. **Description:** A life, accident, and health insurance company. **Benefits:** Disability Coverage; Life Insurance; Medical Insurance; Profit Sharing; Savings Plan. **Corporate headquarters location:** This Location.

DENCOR/WILLAMETTE DENTAL GROUP OREGON DENTAL SPECIALISTS
14025 SW Farmington Road, Suite 300, Beaverton OR 97005. 503/644-6444. **Recorded jobline:** 503/671-9486. **Contact:** Human Resources. **Description:** This location houses administrative offices. Overall, Dencor/Willamette Dental Group operates dentist's offices in Oregon and Washington and provides dental insurance plans. **Corporate headquarters location:** This Location.

ROBERT F. DRIVER COMPANY, INC.
1620 Fifth Avenue, San Diego CA 92101. 619/238-1828. **Contact:** Human Resources. **Description:** Provides commercial and personal insurance including automobile, business, and homeowners. **Common positions include:** Administrative Worker/Clerk; Bond Specialist; Customer Service Representative; Employee Benefits Administrator; Insurance Agent/Broker; Marketing Specialist. **Educational backgrounds include:** Insurance; Liberal Arts. **Benefits:** Dental Insurance; Employee Discounts; Life Insurance; Medical Insurance; Profit Sharing. **Corporate headquarters location:** This Location.

EMC INSURANCE COMPANIES
P.O. Box 712, Des Moines IA 50303. 515/280-2511. **Fax:** 515/280-2961. **Recorded jobline:** 515/237-2151. **Contact:** Human Resources. **Description:** Provides complete commercial and personal lines of insurance. **Common positions include:** Accountant; Actuary; Attorney; Claim Representative; Computer Programmer; Human Resources Manager; Industrial Engineer; Medical Records Technician; Paralegal; Property and Real Estate Manager; Structural Engineer; Systems Analyst; Technical Writer/Editor; Underwriter/ Assistant Underwriter. **Educational backgrounds include:** Accounting; Business Administration; Communications; Computer Science; Engineering; Finance; Liberal Arts; Mathematics. **Benefits:** 401(k); Dental Insurance; Disability Coverage; Employee Discounts; Life Insurance; Medical Insurance; Pension Plan; Savings Plan; Stock Option; Tuition Assistance. **Corporate headquarters location:** This Location. **Other U.S. locations:** Birmingham AL; Little Rock AR; Phoenix AZ; Irvine CA; Denver CO; Chicago IL; Wichita KS; Davenport LA; Lansing MI; Minneapolis MN; Kansas City MO; St. Louis MO; Jackson MS; Charlotte NC; Bismarck ND; Omaha NE; Valley Forge PA; Providence RI; Dallas TX; Milwaukee WI.

EMPIRE BLUE CROSS AND BLUE SHIELD
One World Trade Center, 29th Floor, New York NY 10048. 212/476-1000. **Contact:** Human Resources. **World Wide Web address:** http://www. empirehealthcare.com. **Description:** A nonprofit health insurance company offering coverage that includes comprehensive hospital, medical,

prescription drug, and dental plans, as well as programs supplemental to Medicare. **Corporate headquarters location:** This Location.

EQUITABLE LIFE & CASUALTY INSURANCE
P.O. Box 2460, Salt Lake City UT 84110. 801/579-3400. **Contact:** Human Resources. **Description:** Provides health, medical, and life insurance policies. **Corporate headquarters location:** This Location.

FIC INSURANCE GROUP
P.O. Box 149138, Austin TX 78714-9138. 512/404-5000. **Contact:** Human Resources Department. **World Wide Web address:** http://www. ficgroup.com. **Description:** An insurance company that specializes in life insurance. **Corporate headquarters location:** This Location. **Other U.S. locations:** Seattle WA.

FARM BUREAU FINANCIAL SERVICES
5400 University Avenue, West Des Moines IA 50266. 515/225-5400. **Fax:** 515/226-6053. **Recorded jobline:** 515/225-5627. **Contact:** JHuman Resources. **World Wide Web address:** http://www.fbfs.com. **Description:** Provides life, disability, and property and casualty insurance; annuities; and mutual funds. **Common positions include:** Accountant/Auditor; Actuary; Adjuster; Claim Representative; Clerical Supervisor; Computer Programmer; Economist; Editor; Human Resources Manager; Insurance Agent/Broker; Mathematician; Systems Analyst; Underwriter/ Assistant Underwriter. **Educational backgrounds include:** Accounting; Business Administration; Computer Science; Mathematics. **Benefits:** 401(k); Dental Insurance; Disability Coverage; Employee Discounts; Flexible Schedule; Life Insurance; Medical Insurance; On-Site Daycare; On-Site Exercise Facility; Pension Plan; Tuition Assistance. **Corporate headquarters location:** This Location.

FARMERS INSURANCE GROUP
4680 Wilshire Boulevard, Los Angeles CA 90010. 323/932-3200. **Contact:** Human Resource Services. **World Wide Web address:** http://www. farmersinsurance.com. **Description:** An insurance organization offering life, automobile, fire, and other forms of coverage to over 9 million property and casualty policyholders. **Common positions include:** Accountant/Auditor; Actuary; Attorney; Claim Representative. **Educational backgrounds include:** Accounting; Business Administration; Mathematics. **Benefits:** Disability Coverage; Life Insurance; Medical Insurance; Pension Plan; Profit Sharing; Tuition Assistance. **Corporate headquarters location:** This Location. **Other U.S. locations:** Phoenix AZ; Pleasanton CA; Simi Valley CA; Colorado Springs CO; Pocatello ID; Aurora IL; Columbus OH; Oklahoma City OK; Portland OR; Austin TX.

FEDERATED INSURANCE
P.O. Box 328, Owatonna MN 55060. 507/455-5200. **Fax:** 507/455-5452. **Contact:** Employment Manager. **World Wide Web address:** http://www. federatedinsurance.com. **Description:** A multi-line insurance company specializing in commercial business insurance for small and medium-sized companies. **Common positions include:** Actuary; Claim Representative; Computer Programmer; Underwriter/Assistant Underwriter. **Educational backgrounds include:** Business Administration; Computer Science; Finance; Liberal Arts; Marketing. **Benefits:** Dental Insurance; Disability Coverage; Life Insurance; Medical Insurance; Pension Plan; Savings Plan. **Corporate headquarters location:** This Location. **Other U.S. locations:** Phoenix AZ; Atlanta GA.

FIDELITY MUTUAL LIFE INSURANCE CO.
250 King of Prussia Road, Radnor PA 19087. 610/964-7000. **Contact:** Human Resources. **Description:** A life insurance company. **Corporate headquarters location:** This Location.

FIDELITY NATIONAL TITLE INSURANCE CO.
3916 State Street, Suite 1B, Santa Barbara CA 93105. 805/563-8560. **Toll-free phone:** 800/815-3969. **Fax:** 805/563-8561. **Contact:** Human Resources. **World Wide Web address:** http://www.fntic.com. **Description:** Writes title insurance policies and performs other title-related services such as escrow, collection, and trust activities in connection with real estate transactions. Founded in 1848. **Common positions include:** Accountant; Administrative Assistant; Advertising Executive; Attorney; Branch Manager; Chief Financial Officer; Clerical Supervisor; Computer Operator; Credit Manager; Finance Director; Financial Analyst; Human Resources Generalist. **Educational backgrounds include:** Accounting; Business Administration; Communications; Finance. **Benefits:** 401(k); Dental Insurance; Disability Coverage; Employee Discounts; Life Insurance; Medical Insurance; Public Transit Available; Spending Account; Stock Option; Tuition Assistance. **Other U.S. locations:** Nationwide. **Parent company:** Fidelity National Financial, Inc.

THE FIRST AMERICAN CORPORATION
One First American Way, Santa Ana CA 92707-5913. 714/558-3211. **Contact:** Personnel. **World Wide Web address:** http://www.firstam.com. **Description:** Offers insurance services through a nationwide network of offices and agents. **Corporate headquarters location:** This Location. **Other area locations:** Bakersfield CA; Los Angeles CA; Santa Barbara CA.

FIRST AMERICAN TITLE COMPANY OF NEVADA
3760 Pecos McLeod, Suite 7, Las Vegas NV 89121-4200. 702/731-4131. **Fax:** 702/458-5144. **Contact:** Human Resources. **World Wide Web address:** http://www.firstam.com. **Description:** Provides title insurance, escrow and loan servicing, home warranties, and lender and national escrow processing services. **NOTE:** Entry-level positions and part-time jobs are offered. **Common positions include:** Administrative Assistant; Administrative Manager; Branch Manager; Clerical Supervisor; Customer Service Rep.; Desktop Publishing Specialist; Marketing Specialist; Network/Systems Administrator; Operations Manager; Public Relations Specialist; Sales Rep.; Secretary; Typist/Word Processor. **Educational backgrounds include:** Accounting; AS400 Certification; Business Administration; Communications; Liberal Arts; Marketing; Microsoft Word; Spreadsheets. **Benefits:** 401(k); Dental Insurance; Disability Coverage; Employee Discounts; Financial Planning Assistance; Life Insurance; Medical Insurance; Pension Plan; Profit Sharing; Savings Plan; Sick Days (6 - 10); Tuition Assistance; Vacation Days (6 - 10). **Special programs:** Internships; Training; Summer Jobs. **Office hours:** Monday - Friday, 8:00 a.m. - 5:00 p.m. **Corporate headquarters location:** Santa Ana CA. **Parent company:** The First American Corporation.

FORT DEARBORN LIFE INSURANCE CO.
300 East Randolph, Chicago IL 60601. 312/938-6500. **Contact:** Personnel Director. **World Wide Web address:** http://www.fdlic.com. **Description:** Provides group life and disability insurance, as well as other financial services. **Common positions include:** Accountant/Auditor; Actuary; Attorney; Branch Manager; Claim Representative; Customer Service Representative; General Manager; Insurance Agent/Broker; Marketing Specialist; Services Sales Representative; Underwriter/Assistant Underwriter. **Educational backgrounds include:** Accounting; Business Administration; Finance; Marketing. **Benefits:** 401(k); Dental Insurance; Disability Coverage; Life Insurance; Medical Insurance; Pension Plan; Tuition Assistance. **Corporate headquarters location:** This Location.

FOUNDATION HEALTH SYSTEMS INC.
21650 Oxnard Street, Woodland Hills CA 91367. 818/676-6000. **Contact:** Human Resources. **World Wide Web address:** http://www.fhs.com. **Description:** Administers the delivery of managed care services to approximately 3.4 million individuals through its HMOs, government contracting, and specialty services managed care facilities. **Corporate headquarters location:** This Location.

FRONTIER INSURANCE GROUP
195 Lake Louise Marie Road, Rock Hill NY 12775-8000. 914/796-2100. **Fax:** 914/796-1925. **Contact:** Stacy Heins, Human Resources. **World Wide Web address:** http://www.frontierins.com. **Description:** Frontier Insurance Group is an underwriter and creator of specialty insurance products. Founded in 1934. **NOTE:** Entry-level positions are offered. **Common positions include:** Accountant/Auditor; Adjuster; Administrative Assistant; Administrative Manager; Attorney; Budget Analyst; Claim Rep.; Clerical Supervisor; Computer Operator; Computer Programmer; Controller; Customer Service Representative; Database Manager; Education Administrator; Finance Director; Financial Analyst; Human Resources Manager; Librarian; MIS Specialist; Paralegal; Secretary; Software Engineer; Statistician; Systems Analyst; Typist/Word Processor; Underwriter/Assistant Underwriter. **Benefits:** 401(k); Dental Insurance; Disability Coverage; Flexible Schedule; Life Insurance; Medical Insurance; Profit Sharing; Telecommuting; Tuition Assistance. **Special programs:** Internships. **Corporate headquarters location:** This Location. **Other U.S. locations:** La Jolla CA; Orlando FL; Atlanta GA; Louisville KY; Charlotte NC; Bedford Hills NY.

GAB ROBINS NORTH AMERICA INC.
9 Campus Drive, Parsippany NJ 07054. 973/993-3400. **Contact:** Human Resources. **World Wide Web address:** http://www.gab.com. **Description:** Provides adjustment, inspection, appraisal, and claims management services to 15,000 insurance industry customers. Specific services include the settlement of claims following major disasters; appraisal, investigation, and adjustment of auto insurance claims; casualty claims; and fire, marine, life, accident, health, and disability claims. **Common positions include:** Accountant; Claim Representative; Computer Programmer; Customer Service Representative; Human Resources Manager. **Educational backgrounds include:** Accounting; Business Administration; Liberal Arts. **Benefits:** Dental Insurance; Disability Coverage; Life Insurance; Medical Insurance; Pension Plan; Savings Plan; Tuition Assistance. **Corporate headquarters location:** This Location. **Parent company:** SGS North America.

GMAC INTEGON
P.O. Box 3199, Winston-Salem NC 27102. 336/770-2000. **Contact:** Human Resources. **Description:** An insurance company operating in 22 states through more than 11,000 independent agents. The company's East Division primarily underwrites nonstandard auto insurance in Alabama, Florida, Georgia, North Carolina, Ohio, and Virginia. The

division also underwrites preferred auto, homeowners, and mobile home insurance in North Carolina. The North Division underwrites nonstandard auto insurance in Connecticut, Illinois, Indiana, Maine, Maryland, New Hampshire, New York, Pennsylvania, Rhode Island, and Vermont. The South Division underwrites nonstandard auto insurance in Kentucky, Louisiana, Mississippi, Tennessee, and Texas. The Specialty Auto division underwrites insurance for business autos and motorcycles. **Corporate headquarters location:** This Location.

ARTHUR J. GALLAGHER & CO.
2 Pierce Place, Itasca IL 60143-3141. 630/773-3800. **Contact:** Human Resources.**World Wide Web address:** http://www.ajg.com. **Description:** An insurance brokerage offering property, casualty, and employee benefit plans. Founded in 1927. **Common positions include:** Account Manager; Account Rep.; Accountant; Administrative Assistant; Auditor; Budget Analyst; Computer Operator; Computer Programmer; Computer Support Technician; Computer Technician; Content Developer; Customer Service Representative; Database Administrator; Database Manager; Help-Desk Technician; Insurance Agent/Broker; Intranet Developer; Typist/Word Processor; Webmaster. **Educational backgrounds include:** Accounting; Business Administration; Finance; Liberal Arts. **Benefits:** 401(k); Casual Dress - Fridays; Disability Coverage; Life Insurance; Medical Insurance; Pension Plan; Tuition Assistance. **Corporate headquarters location:** This Location.

GEICO CORPORATION
One GEICO Boulevard, Fredericksburg VA 22412. 540/286-4499. **Contact:** Human Resources. **World Wide Web address:** http://www.geico.com. **Description:** GEICO Corporation is an insurance organization whose affiliates are personal lines property and casualty insurers. The company is engaged in writing preferred-risk, private passenger automobile insurance for government employees, military personnel, and homeowners; as well as other lines of insurance for all qualified applicants. **Corporate headquarters location:** Washington DC. **Subsidiaries include:** GEICO General Insurance Company (GGIC) writes private passenger automobile insurance for preferred-risk applicants who are not government employees or military personnel. Criterion Life Insurance Company writes structured settlement annuities for its property and casualty affiliates. Government Employees Financial Corporation (GEFCO) is engaged in secured consumer and business lending and loan servicing.

GENERAL REINSURANCE CORP.
Financial Centre, P.O. Box 10351, Stamford CT 06901. 203/328-5000. **Contact:** Human Resources. **World Wide Web address:** http://www.genre.com. **Description:** Provides property and casualty reinsurance to primary insurers on a direct basis. The company markets reinsurance directly to these insurers through its own sales team. Reinsurance is marketed and underwritten on both a treaty and facultative basis. Treaty marketing efforts are focused on small- to medium-sized regional and specialty property and casualty insurers. General Reinsurance Group does not underwrite businesses which involve aviation, ocean marine, and professional liability. **Corporate headquarters location:** This Location. **Subsidiaries include:** Ardent Risk Services, Inc.; Herbert Clough; Cologne Re; Genesis; General Re Europe Limited; General Re Financial Products; General Star; United States Aircraft Insurance Group.

GRANGE INSURANCE GROUP
ROCKY MOUNTAIN FIRE & CASUALTY
200 Cedar Street, Seattle WA 98121. 206/448-4911. **Contact:** Personnel Department. **Description:** A property and casualty insurance firm. **Common positions include:** Accountant/Auditor; Branch Manager; Claim Rep.; Computer Programmer; Customer Service Rep.; Department Manager; Marketing Specialist; Systems Analyst; Underwriter/Assistant Underwriter. **Educational backgrounds include:** Accounting; Business Administration; Computer Science; Finance; Marketing. **Benefits:** Dental Insurance; Disability Coverage; Employee Discounts; Life Insurance; Medical Insurance; Pension Plan; Savings Plan; Tuition Assistance; Vision Insurance. **Corporate headquarters location:** This Location.

GRANGE INSURANCE COMPANIES
650 South Front Street, Columbus OH 43206. 614/445-2900. **Fax:** 614/445-2695. **Recorded jobline:** 614/445-2468. **Contact:** Personnel Manager. **World Wide Web address:** http://www.grangeinsurance.com. **Description:** A holding company for a group of property, casualty, and life insurance companies. **Common positions include:** Actuary; Adjuster; Claim Representative; Computer Programmer; Underwriter/Assistant Underwriter. **Educational backgrounds include:** Business Administration; Computer Science. **Benefits:** 401(k); Daycare Assistance; Dental Insurance; Disability Coverage; Life Insurance; Medical Insurance; Pension Plan; Tuition Assistance. **Corporate headquarters location:** This Location. **Subsidiaries include:** Amerimutual; Trustgard.

GROUP HEALTH INCORPORATED (GHI)
441 Ninth Avenue, New York NY 10001. 212/615-0105. **Contact:** Employment Manager. **World Wide Web address:** http://www.ghi.com. **Description:** One of the largest, nonprofit health services corporations operating throughout New York. The company provides insurance benefits to and third-party administrative services. Founded in 1937. **Common positions include:** Account Representative; Accountant; Case Manager; Claim Representative; Customer Service Representative; MIS Specialist; Network/Systems Administrator; Quality Control Supervisor; Systems Manager. **Educational backgrounds include:** Accounting; Business Administration; Computer Science; Finance; Liberal Arts; Marketing; Mathematics. **Benefits:** Dental Insurance; Disability Coverage; Life Insurance; Medical Insurance; Pension Plan; Prescription Drugs; Savings Plan; Tuition Assistance; Vision Plan. **Corporate headquarters location:** This Location. **Other U.S. locations:** Albany NY; Buffalo NY; Garden City NY; Long Island NY; Rochester NY; Syracuse NY; Tarrytown NY.

GUARANTEE LIFE COMPANY
8801 Indian Hills Drive, Omaha NE 68114. 402/361-7300. **Fax:** 402/361-2755. **Contact:** Human Resources Manager. **E-mail address:** jobs@guar.com. **World Wide Web address:** http://www.guar.com. **Description:** Guarantee Life Company has over $1 billion in assets and markets its group insurance products, individual life insurance, and annuities nationwide. Founded in 1901. **Common positions include:** Accountant/Auditor; Actuary; Attorney; Budget Analyst; Claim Rep.; Customer Service Rep.; Financial Analyst; Human Resources Manager; Paralegal; Systems Analyst; Underwriter/Assistant Underwriter. **Educational backgrounds include:** Accounting; Business Administration; Finance; Marketing; Mathematics. **Benefits:** 401(k); Disability Coverage; Employee Discounts; Life

Insurance; Medical Insurance; Pension Plan; Tuition Assistance. **Special programs:** Internships. **Corporate headquarters location:** This Location. **Other U.S. locations:** Nationwide.

THE GUARDIAN LIFE INSURANCE COMPANY OF AMERICA
7 Hanover Square, New York NY 10004. 212/598-8000. **Contact:** Human Resources. **World Wide Web address:** http://www.glic.com. **Description:** Provides health and life insurance, as well as some financial services. **Corporate headquarters location:** This Location.

HARLEYSVILLE INSURANCE COMPANIES
355 Maple Avenue, Harleysville PA 19438. 215/256-5045. **Contact:** Human Resources Department. **World Wide Web address:** http://www.harleysvillegroup.com. **Description:** A multi-line property/casualty and life insurance carrier with offices located throughout the mid-Atlantic states. Products are marketed through an independent agency system. **Common positions include:** Accountant/Auditor; Actuary; Attorney; Branch Manager; Claim Rep.; Commercial Artist; Computer Programmer; Customer Service Representative; Financial Analyst; Financial Services Sales Rep.; Human Resources Manager; Technical Writer/Editor; Underwriter/Assistant Underwriter. **Educational backgrounds include:** Business Administration; Computer Science; Economics; Finance; Liberal Arts. **Benefits:** Dental Insurance; Disability Coverage; Employee Discounts; Life Insurance; Medical Insurance; Pension Plan; Profit Sharing; Savings Plan; Tuition Assistance. **Corporate headquarters location:** This Location.

THE HARTFORD
The Hartford Plaza, Hartford CT 06115. 860/547-5000. **Contact:** Human Resources Manager. **World Wide Web address:** http://www.thehartford.com. **Description:** One of the largest insurance companies in the United States. The Hartford is a *Fortune* 500 company and offers business, farm, home, life, automobile, marine, and health insurance coverage as well as fidelity and surety bonds and reinsurance. Founded in 1810. **Corporate headquarters location:** This Location.

HASTINGS MUTUAL INSURANCE CO.
404 East Woodlawn Avenue, Hastings MI 49058. 616/945-3405. **Contact:** Personnel. **Description:** Sells property and casualty insurance (home, automotive, and business) through independent agents to policyholders in Michigan, Indiana, Illinois, Ohio, and Wisconsin. **Common positions include:** Accountant/Auditor; Adjuster; Attorney; Claim Rep. Computer Operator; Computer Programmer; Investigator; Operations/Production Manager; Registered Nurse; Systems Analyst; Underwriter/Assistant Underwriter. **Educational backgrounds include:** Accounting; Business Administration; Computer Science; Economics; Finance; Insurance; Liberal Arts; Marketing; Mathematics. **Benefits:** 401(k); Cafeteria; Credit Union; Dental Insurance; Disability Coverage; Employee Discounts; Free Parking; Life Insurance; Medical Insurance; Pension Plan; Profit Sharing; Tuition Assistance. **Special programs:** Internships; Training. **Corporate headquarters location:** This Location.

HAULERS INSURANCE COMPANY, INC.
P.O. Box 270, Columbia TN 38402. 931/381-5406. **Contact:** Human Resources. **Description:** Writes policies covering both personal auto and professional auto insurance.

HEALTH NET
P.O. Box 4353, Woodland Hills CA 91365. **Fax:** 818/676-8544. **Recorded jobline:** 818/676-7236. **Contact:** Human Resources Manager. **Description:** One of California's largest health maintenance organizations. Health Net also organizes wellness programs. **Corporate headquarters location:** This Location. **Parent company:** Foundation Health Systems, Inc.

HEALTH RISK MANAGEMENT INC.
10900 Hampshire Avenue South, Bloomington MN 55438. 952/829-3500. **Fax:** 952/829-3664. **Recorded jobline:** 952/829-3695. **Contact:** Karen Davis, Staffing Specialist. **Description:** A medical review company whose operations include managing benefits and health care services for other companies. Founded in 1977. **NOTE:** Entry-level positions are offered. **Common positions include:** Claim Rep.; Computer Operator; Computer Programmer; Customer Service Rep.; Nurse Practitioner; Secretary; Software Engineer. **Educational backgrounds include:** Business Administration; Health Care; Liberal Arts. **Benefits:** 401(k); Dental Insurance; Employee Discounts; Flexible Schedule; Medical Insurance; Tuition Assistance. **Corporate headquarters location:** This Location. **Other U.S. locations:** Kalamazoo MI; Philadelphia PA; Milwaukee WI. **Subsidiaries include:** Institute for Healthcare Quality.

HILB, ROGAL AND HAMILTON CO.
P.O. Box 1220, Glen Allen VA 23060-1220. 804/747-6500. **Physical address:** 4235 Innslake Drive, Glen Allen VA 23060. **Fax:** 804/747-6046. **Contact:** Human Resources Director. **World Wide Web address:** http://www.hrh.com. **Description:** Performs retail insurance services. Hilb, Rogal and Hamilton Company serves as an intermediary between its clients, traditionally mid-size businesses, and insurance companies that underwrite clients' risks. Hilb, Rogal and Hamilton assists clients in transferring risks in areas such as property, casualty, life, and health insurance, and employee benefits. **Benefits:** 401(k); Dental Insurance; Medical Insurance; Profit Sharing; Retirement Plan. **Corporate headquarters location:** This Location.

HIP HEALTH PLAN OF GREATER NEW YORK
7 West 34th Street, New York NY 10001. 212/630-5000. **Fax:** 212/630-0060. **Recorded jobline:** 212/630-8300. **Contact:** Human Resources. **World Wide Web address:** http://www.hipusa.com. **Description:** A health maintenance organization marketing a comprehensive prepaid health plan with care delivered by independent medical groups and coverage provided for hospitalization. **Common positions include:** Accountant/Auditor; Buyer; Claim Rep.; Computer Programmer; Customer Service Rep.; Department Manager; Financial Analyst; Health Services Manager; Marketing Specialist; Secretary; Services Sales Rep.; Systems Analyst. **Educational backgrounds include:** Accounting; Business Administration; Computer Science; Finance; Marketing; Nursing. **Benefits:** Dental Insurance; Disability Coverage; Life Insurance; Medical Insurance; Pension Plan; Tuition Assistance. **Corporate headquarters location:** This Location.

HOLY CROSS HEALTH SYSTEM
3575 Moreau Court, South Bend IN 46628. 219/233-8558. **Contact:** Human Resources Manager. **World Wide Web address:** http://www.hchs.org. **Description:** A health maintenance organization. **Corporate headquarters location:** This Location.

HOME STATE INSURANCE COMPANY
HOME STATE HOLDINGS
3 South Revmont Drive, Shrewsbury NJ 07702. 732/935-2600. **Contact:** Human Resources. **Description:** Provides personal and commercial automobile insurance throughout New Jersey. **Corporate headquarters location:** This Location. **Parent company:** Home State Holdings (also at this location) is a property and casualty holding company engaged primarily in providing personal and commercial auto insurance through its operating subsidiaries. Home State writes standard and preferred personal auto lines. The company's commercial auto lines focus on public transportation including school buses, charter buses, limousines, and similar transportation risks. Other subsidiaries of Home State Holdings include personal auto and homeowners insurance provided through the company's Home Mutual Insurance Company (Binghamton NY); commercial automobile and commercial multiperil insurance offered through New York Merchant Bankers Insurance Company (NY). The Pinnacle Insurance Company (Carrollton GA) serves as the company's southeastern operations center and offers personal and commercial auto insurance. Quaker City Insurance Company (operating in DC, DE, MD, PA, VA, and WV) and The Westbrook Insurance Company (CT) also provide personal and commercial auto insurance.

HUMANA, INC.
500 West Main Street, Louisville KY 40202. 502/580-1000. **Contact:** Human Resources. **World Wide Web address:** http://www.humana.com. **Description:** Humana is a managed care company operating in 17 markets in 11 states throughout the Southeast and Midwest. The company's health plans serve over 1.6 million people through three product lines: commercial, Medicare risk, and Medicare supplement plans. Commercial health care products are delivered through health maintenance organizations (HMOs) and preferred provider organizations (PPOs), which share the financial risks of delivering cost-effective services. The Medicare risk product is an HMO for Medicare recipients, and the Medicare supplement program covers medical costs for which the Medicare beneficiary is usually responsible. **Corporate headquarters location:** This Location.

INSURANCE COMPANY OF THE WEST
P.O. Box 85563, San Diego CA 92186-5563. 858/350-2400. **Contact:** Human Resources Department. **Description:** A commercial insurance carrier offering multi-rate property/casualty, workers' compensation, specialty auto, and surety lines of coverage. Founded in 1972. **Common positions include:** Adjuster; Claim Representative. **Educational backgrounds include:** Business Administration. **Benefits:** 401(k); Dental Insurance; Disability Coverage; Employee Discounts; Life Insurance; Medical Insurance; Pension Plan; Profit Sharing; Tuition Assistance. **Corporate headquarters location:** This Location. **Other U.S. locations:** AZ; CO; NM; NV; OR; TX; WA.

INSURANCE SERVICES OFFICE, INC.
7 World Trade Center, New York NY 10048. 212/898-6084. **Fax:** 212/898-6167. **Contact:** Recruiting. **E-mail address:** nmerritt@iso.com. **World Wide Web address:** http://www.iso.com. **Description:** Provides services to the property and casualty insurance industry. The company gathers and analyzes data to develop advisory loss costs; conducts research to predict future economic and social trends; and develops model programs for the company's insurer clients. **Common positions include:** Actuary. **Educational backgrounds include:** Economics; Mathematics. **Benefits:** Dental Insurance; Disability Coverage; Employee Discounts; ESOP; Flextime Plan; Life Insurance; Medical Insurance; Pension Plan; Savings Plan; Tuition Assistance. **Corporate headquarters location:** This Location.

INVESTORS TITLE COMPANY
121 North Columbia Street, Chapel Hill NC 27515. 919/968-2200. **Fax:** 919/968-2235. **Contact:** Human Resources Manager. **Description:** Investors Title Company, through its two title insurance subsidiaries, Investors Title Insurance Company and Northeast Investors Title Insurance Company, writes title insurance in Florida, Georgia, Illinois, Indiana, Kentucky, Maryland, Michigan, Minnesota, Mississippi, Nebraska, New York, North Carolina, Pennsylvania, South Carolina, Tennessee, and Virginia. A third subsidiary, Investors Title Exchange Corporation, serves as a qualified intermediary in tax-deferred exchanges of real property. Founded in 1972. **Common positions include:** Paralegal; Typist/Word Processor; Underwriter/Assistant Underwriter. **Benefits:** Disability Coverage; Life Insurance; Medical Insurance; Pension Plan. **Corporate headquarters location:** This Location.

JACKSON NATIONAL LIFE INSURANCE CO.
5901 Executive Drive, Lansing MI 48911. 517/394-3400. **Contact:** Staffing Specialist. **World Wide Web address:** http://www.jacksonnational.com. **Description:** Involved in the underwriting of life insurance and annuity policies. **Common positions include:** Accountant/Auditor; Actuary; Advertising Clerk; Brokerage Clerk; Buyer; Claim Rep.; Clerical Supervisor; Computer Programmer; Customer Service Rep.; Financial Analyst; Insurance Agent/Broker; Public Relations Specialist; Systems Analyst; Technical Writer/Editor; Underwriter/Assistant Underwriter. **Educational backgrounds include:** Accounting; Business Administration; Communications; Economics; Finance; Marketing; Mathematics. **Benefits:** 401(k); Dental Insurance; Disability Coverage; Employee Discounts; Life Insurance; Medical Insurance; Pension Plan; Savings Plan; Tuition Assistance. **Corporate headquarters location:** This Location. **Parent company:** Prudential Place of England.

JEFFERSON INSURANCE GROUP
Newport Tower, 525 Washington Boulevard, Jersey City NJ 07310. 201/222-8666. **Fax:** 201/222-9161. **Contact:** Human Resources. **World Wide Web address:** http://www.jeffgroup.com. **Description:** A property and casualty insurance company. Member companies include Jefferson Insurance Company of New York, Monticello Insurance Company, and Jeffco Management Company, Inc. **Common positions include:** Accountant/Auditor; Actuary; Administrative Manager; Attorney; Claim Rep.; Clerical Supervisor; Computer Programmer; Human Resources Manager; Human Service Worker; Quality Control Supervisor; Systems Analyst; Underwriter/Assistant Underwriter. **Educational backgrounds include:** Accounting; Finance; Marketing. **Benefits:** 401(k); Dental Insurance; Disability Coverage; Employee Discounts; Life Insurance; Medical Insurance; Pension Plan; Profit Sharing; Tuition Assistance. **Corporate headquarters location:** This Location. **Parent company:** Allianz (Germany).

JOHN HANCOCK FINANCIAL SERVICES
John Hancock Place, Box 111, Boston MA 02117. 617/572-4500. **Fax:** 617/572-4539. **Contact:** Human Resources Manager. **E-mail address:** employment@jhancock.com. **World Wide Web address:** http://www.jhancock.com. **Description:**

An insurance and financial services firm operating through two divisions: The Retail Sector offers protection and investment products to middle- and upper-income markets; The Investment & Pension Group is involved in bond and corporate finance services as well as in real estate and mortgage loans. Founded in 1862. **NOTE:** Entry-level positions are offered. **Common positions include:** Accountant; Administrative Assistant; Computer Programmer; Consultant; Customer Service Rep.; Database Manager; Daycare Worker; Financial Analyst; Management Trainee; Registered Nurse; Secretary; Systems Analyst; Telecommunications Manager; Underwriter/Assistant Underwriter. **Educational backgrounds include:** Business; Communications; Computer Science; Finance; Marketing; Mathematics. **Benefits:** 401(k); Daycare Assistance; Dental Insurance; Disability Coverage; Employee Discounts; Life Insurance; Medical Insurance; Pension Plan; Public Transit Available; Savings Plan; Telecommuting; Tuition Assistance. **Special programs:** Internships; Training. **Corporate headquarters location:** This Location. **International locations:** Belgium; Canada; England; Ireland; Malaysia; Singapore; Thailand.

JUNIPER GROUP, INC.
111 Great Neck Road, Suite 604, Great Neck NY 11021. 516/829-4670. **Fax:** 516/829-4691. **Contact:** Human Resources. **Description:** Operates in two segments: health care and entertainment. The company's principal revenues are generated from health care, which consists of management for hospitals and health care cost containment for health care payers. The entertainment segment acquires and distributes film rights to various media including home video, pay-per-view, pay television, cable television, networks, ad-hoc networks, and independent syndicated television stations. **Corporate headquarters location:** This Location. **Subsidiaries include:** Juniper Medical Systems, Inc. whose subsidiaries include Diversified Health Affiliates, Inc. and Juniper Healthcare Containment Systems, Inc. Diversified Health Affiliates operates Juniper Group's management business while Juniper Healthcare Containment Systems conducts health care cost containment service operations.

KAISER PERMANENTE
1441 Kapioalani Boulevard, 17th Floor, Honolulu HI 96814. 808/983-4900. **Fax:** 808/983-4983. **Contact:** Human Resources Manager. **World Wide Web address:** http://www.kaiserpermanente.org. **Description:** A nonprofit, public benefit and charitable health care corporation that enrolls members and arranges for their medical, hospital, and related services nationwide. **Common positions include:** Accountant; Adjuster; Administrator; Attorney; Biomedical Engineer; Blue-Collar Worker Supervisor; Budget Analyst; Buyer; Claim Rep.; Clerical Supervisor; Clinical Lab Technician; Computer Programmer; Construction Contractor; Consultant; Counselor; Credit Manager; Customer Service Rep.; Department Manager; Dietician/Nutritionist; Draftsperson; Economist; Education Administrator; EEG Technologist; EKG Technician; Electrician; Emergency Medical Technician; Environmental Engineer; Financial Analyst; Food and Beverage Service Worker; General Manager; Health Services Manager; Health Services Worker; Human Resources Manager; Human Service Worker; Librarian; Licensed Practical Nurse; Medical Records Technician; Medical Technologist; Nuclear Medicine Technologist; Occupational Therapist; Operating Room Technician; Operations/Production Manager; Paralegal; Pharmacist; Physical Therapist; Physician; Property and Real Estate Manager; Psychologist; Public Relations Specialist; Purchasing Agent/Manager; Quality Control Supervisor; Radiological Technologist; Recreational Therapist; Registered Nurse; Respiratory Therapist; Restaurant/Food Service Manager; Services Sales Rep.; Social Worker; Speech-Language Pathologist; Surgical Technician; Systems Analyst; Teacher/Professor; Technical Writer/Editor; Training Specialist. **Educational backgrounds include:** Accounting; Biology; Business Administration; Chemistry; Computer Science; Finance; Health Care; Liberal Arts; Marketing. **Benefits:** 403(b); Accident/Emergency Insurance; Dental Insurance; Disability Coverage; EAP; Employee Discounts; Home Loan Assistance; Life Insurance; Medical Insurance; Pension Plan; Reimbursement Accounts; Savings Plan; Tuition Assistance; Wellness Program. **Corporate headquarters location:** Oakland CA.

KAISER PERMANENTE
PEOPLE SOLUTIONS
P.O. Box 2074, Oakland CA 94604. 916/973-6848. **Contact:** Human Resources Manager. **World Wide Web address:** http://www.kaiserpermanente.org. **Description:** This location houses administrative offices. Overall, Kaiser Permanente is a nonprofit, public benefit and charitable health care corporation that enrolls members and arranges for their medical, hospital, and related services nationwide. **Common positions include:** Accountant; Chiropractor; Claim Representative; Computer Programmer; Customer Service Representative; Dietician/Nutritionist; Education Administrator; EEG Technologist; EKG Technician; Electrical/Electronics Engineer; Human Resources Manager; Human Service Worker; Librarian; Licensed Practical Nurse; Mechanical Engineer; Medical Records Technician; Nuclear Medicine Technologist; Occupational Therapist; Operations/Production Manager; Pharmacist; Physician; Physician Assistant; Psychologist; Quality Control Supervisor; Radiological Technologist; Registered Nurse; Respiratory Therapist; Social Worker; Speech-Language Pathologist; Stationary Engineer; Surgical Technician. **Educational backgrounds include:** Business Administration; Engineering; Health Care. **Corporate headquarters location:** This Location. **Other U.S. locations:** Nationwide.

KEMPER INSURANCE COMPANIES
One Kemper Drive, Suite D-8, Long Grove IL 60049. 847/320-2000. **Fax:** 847/320-5624. **Contact:** Human Resources Manager. **World Wide Web address:** http://www.kemperinsurance.com. **Description:** Provides property, casualty, and life insurance, reinsurance, and a wide range of diversified financial services operations. Founded in 1912. **NOTE:** Entry-level positions and second and third shifts are offered. **Common positions include:** Applications Engineer; Computer Operator; Computer Programmer; Database Manager; MIS Specialist; Software Engineer; Systems Analyst; Systems Manager. **Educational backgrounds include:** Computer Science; Software Development; Software Tech. Support. **Benefits:** 401(k); Daycare Assistance; Dental Insurance; Disability Coverage; Flexible Schedule; Life Insurance; Medical Insurance; On-Site Exercise Facility; Pension Plan; Profit Sharing; Public Transit Available; Savings Plan; Telecommuting; Tuition Assistance. **Corporate headquarters location:** This Location. **Other U.S. locations:**
- P.O. Box 7993, San Francisco CA 94120. 415/421-2400.

KENTUCKY FARM BUREAU MUTUAL INSURANCE COMPANY
9201 Bunsen Parkway, Louisville KY 40220. 502/495-5000. **Contact:** Human Resources. **Description:** A property and casualty insurance

company that serves all 120 Kentucky counties. A wide range of personal and commercial insurance lines are offered, principally auto, homeowner, farmowner, general liability, and worker's compensation. The company also writes life and health insurance and individual retirement accounts. Founded in 1944. **Common positions include:** Accountant/Auditor; Actuary; Branch Manager; Claim Representative; Computer Programmer; Department Manager; Insurance Agent/Broker; Underwriter/Assistant Underwriter. **Educational backgrounds include:** Accounting; Business; Computer Science; Finance; Marketing; Mathematics. **Benefits:** Disability Coverage; Life Insurance; Medical Insurance; Pension Plan; Tuition Assistance. **Corporate headquarters location:** This Location.

LAWYERS TITLE INSURANCE CORP.
101 Gateway Centre Parkway, Gateway One, Richmond VA 23235. 804/267-8000. **Contact:** Personnel Manager. **World Wide Web address:** http://www.ltic.com. **Description:** Provides title insurance and real estate-related services on commercial and residential transactions in the United States, Canada, the Bahamas, Puerto Rico, and the U.S. Virgin Islands. Lawyers Title Insurance Corporation also provides search and examination services and closing services for a broad-based customer group that includes lenders, developers, real estate brokers, attorneys, and home buyers. **Corporate headquarters location:** This Location. **Other U.S. locations:** Pasadena CA; Tampa FL; Chicago IL; Boston MA; Troy MI; White Plains NY; Westerville OH; Memphis TN; Dallas TX. **Subsidiaries include:** Datatrace Information Services Company, Inc. (Richmond VA), which markets automated public record information for public and private use; Genesis Data Systems, Inc. (Englewood CO), which develops and markets computer software tailored specifically to the title industry; Lawyers Title Exchange Company functions as an intermediary for individual and corporate investors interested in pursuing tax-free property exchanges. **Parent company:** Lawyers Title Corporation.

LEUCADIA NATIONAL CORPORATION
315 Park Avenue South, New York NY 10010. 212/460-1900. **Contact:** Human Resources. **Description:** Leucadia National is a diversified company with subsidiaries involved in the insurance, manufacturing, banking, investment, and incentive service industries. The insurance business offers property, casualty, and life insurance nationwide. **Corporate headquarters location:** This Location. **Subsidiaries include:** Charter, CPL; Empire Group; Intramerica. **Listed on:** New York Stock Exchange; Pacific Stock Exchange.

LIBERTY INSURANCE SERVICES
P.O. Box 789, Greenville SC 29602. 864/609-8334. **Contact:** Human Resources. **Description:** Provides a broad range of insurance services. **NOTE:** Those interested in clerical positions should direct resumes to Ann Vaughn, Human Resources. **Common positions include:** Accountant/Auditor; Actuary; Attorney; Computer Programmer; Customer Service Rep.; Department Manager; Human Resources Manager; Insurance Agent/Broker; Marketing Specialist; Systems Analyst; Underwriter/Assistant Underwriter. **Educational backgrounds include:** Accounting; Business; Communications; Computer Science; Finance; Liberal Arts; Marketing; Mathematics. **Benefits:** Dental Insurance; Disability Coverage; Life Insurance; Medical Insurance; Profit Sharing; Savings Plan; Tuition Assistance. **Corporate headquarters location:** This Location. **Parent company:** The Liberty Corporation is a holding company with subsidiaries engaged in life, accident, and health insurance and television broadcasting.

LIBERTY MUTUAL INSURANCE GROUP
175 Berkeley Street, Boston MA 02117. 617/357-9500. **Fax:** 617/574-5616. **Contact:** Employment Office. **World Wide Web address:** http://www.libertymutual.com. **Description:** A full-line insurance firm offering life, medical, and business insurance, as well as investment and retirement plans. **Common positions include:** Accountant; Actuary; Adjuster; Administrative Manager; Advertising Clerk; Attorney; Blue-Collar Worker Supervisor; Branch Manager; Budget Analyst; Buyer; Civil Engineer; Claim Rep.; Clerical Supervisor; Computer Programmer; Construction and Building Inspector; Cost Estimator; Counselor; Credit Manager; Customer Service Rep.; Editor; Environmental Engineer; General Manager; Human Resources Manager; Industrial Engineer; Industrial Production Manager; Licensed Practical Nurse; Management Analyst/Consultant; Management Trainee; Mathematician; Mechanical Engineer; Medical Records Technician; MIS Specialist; Multimedia Designer; Occupational Therapist; Operations/Production Manager; Paralegal; Property and Real Estate Manager; Psychologist; Public Relations Specialist; Purchasing Agent/Manager; Real Estate Agent; Registered Nurse; Reporter; Securities Sales Representative; Services Sales Representative; Software Engineer; Statistician; Structural Engineer; Surveyor; Systems Analyst; Technical Writer/Editor; Telecommunications Manager. **Educational backgrounds include:** Accounting; Business; Communications; Computer Science; Economics; Engineering; Finance; Liberal Arts; Mathematics. **Benefits:** 401(k); Dental Insurance; Disability Coverage; Life Insurance; Medical Insurance; Pension Plan. **Special programs:** Internships; Training. **Corporate headquarters location:** This Location. **Other U.S. locations:** Des Plaines IL; Itasca IL; Lisle IL; Matteson IL. **Subsidiaries include:** Wausau Insurance Company.

LIFE INSURANCE COMPANY OF GEORGIA
5780 Powers Ferry Road, Atlanta GA 30377. 770/980-5710. **Contact:** Human Resources. **Description:** Provides life and health insurance. **Common positions include:** Accountant; Actuary; Administrator; Claim Rep.; Computer Programmer; Customer Service Rep.; Department Manager; Financial Analyst; Management Trainee; Public Relations Specialist; Systems Analyst; Underwriter/Assistant Underwriter. **Educational backgrounds include:** Accounting; Business Administration; Finance; Liberal Arts; Marketing; Mathematics. **Benefits:** Dental Insurance; Disability Coverage; Employee Discounts; Life Insurance; Medical Insurance; Pension Plan; Profit Sharing; Savings Plan. **Corporate headquarters location:** This Location.

LIFEUSA HOLDING, INC.
LIFEUSA INSURANCE COMPANY
P.O. Box 59060, Minneapolis MN 55459-0060. 612/546-7386. **Physical address:** 300 South Highway 169, Suite 95, Minneapolis MN. **Contact:** Human Resources **Description:** A holding company engaged in a variety of industries. **Corporate headquarters location:** This Location. **Subsidiaries include:** LifeUSA Insurance Company (also at this location) sells life insurance; LifeUSA Marketing, Inc. provides a variety of marketing services for its parent company; LifeUSA Securities, Inc. is a securities broker; LTCAmerica Holding, Inc. **CFO:** Mark A. Zesbaugh.

LINCOLN FINANCIAL ADVISORS
8755 West Higgins Road, Suite 550, Chicago IL 60631. 773/380-8518. **Fax:** 773/693-2531. **Contact:** Recruiting. **E-mail address:** hsrancich@ lnc.com. **World Wide Web address:** http://www. lfaonline.com. **Description:** Lincoln Financial Advisors markets financial planning, permanent and term life insurance, annuities, disability coverage, and investment products to business owners and professionals. The company also provides complex estate planning and business planning advice. Founded in 1905. **Common positions include:** Insurance Agent/Broker; Sales Executive; Sales Representative. **Educational backgrounds include:** Accounting; Business; Economics; Finance; Liberal Arts; Marketing. **Benefits:** 401(k); Dental Insurance; Medical Insurance; Tuition Assistance. **Corporate headquarters location:** Fort Wayne IN. **Other U.S. locations:** Nationwide. **International locations:** Argentina; China; United Kingdom. **Parent company:** Lincoln Financial Group.

LINCOLN NATIONAL CORPORATION (LNC) dba LINCOLN FINANCIAL GROUP
Center Square, West Tower, 1500 Market Street, Suite 3900, Philadelphia PA 19102. 215/448-1400. **Contact:** Human Resources. **World Wide Web address:** http://www.lfg.com. **Description:** An insurance holding company whose businesses sell insurance and investment products. **Corporate headquarters location:** This Location. **Subsidiaries include:** Delaware Investments (investment management services); First Penn-Pacific Life Insurance Company (life insurance); Lincoln National Life Insurance Company (individual life, annuities, and pensions); Lincoln Re (life and health reinsurance); Vantage Investment Advisors (investment management services).

LUMBER INSURANCE COMPANIES
One Speen Street, P.O. Box 9165, Framingham MA 01701. 508/872-8111. **Fax:** 508/872-9711. **Contact:** Human Resources. **Description:** Provides commercial property and casualty insurance. **Corporate headquarters location:** This Location.

LUTHERAN BROTHERHOOD COMPANY
625 Fourth Avenue South, Minneapolis MN 55415. 612/340-7054. **Contact:** Staffing and Employee Relations. **World Wide Web address:** http://www. luthbro.com. **Description:** A financial institution providing life, health, and disability insurance, in addition to annuities and mutual funds. **Common positions include:** Actuary; Computer Programmer. **Educational backgrounds include:** Computer Science; Mathematics. **Benefits:** Dental Insurance; Disability Coverage; Life Insurance; Medical Insurance; Pension Plan; Tuition Assistance. **Corporate headquarters location:** This Location.

MBIA INSURANCE CORPORATION
113 King Street, Armonk NY 10504. 914/273-4545. **Contact:** Human Resources. **World Wide Web address:** http://www.mbia.com. **Description:** A leading insurer of municipal bonds including new issues and bonds traded in the secondary market. The company also guarantees asset-backed transactions offered by financial institutions and provides investment management services for school districts and municipalities. **Common positions include:** Accountant; Administrator; Computer Programmer; Financial Analyst; Marketing Specialist; Public Relations Specialist; Underwriter/Assistant Underwriter. **Educational backgrounds include:** Accounting; Business Administration; Economics; Finance; Marketing. **Corporate headquarters location:** This Location.

MS DIVERSIFIED CORPORATION
P.O. Box 6005, Ridgeland MS 39158. 601/978-6732. **Contact:** Human Resources. **Description:** Provides a wide range of products and services to automotive dealers and financial institutions. Products and services include credit life insurance; accident and health insurance; vehicle extended service contracts; administrative services; automobile financing; and financial services. MS Diversified serves a strong base of auto dealers with approximately 400 dealership agreements throughout the South, and provides products and services to more than 700 financial institutions. **Common positions include:** Accountant; Computer Programmer; Customer Service Representative; MIS Specialist; Paralegal; Systems Analyst. **Educational backgrounds include:** Accounting; Business; Computer Science; Finance; Marketing. **Benefits:** 401(k); Disability Coverage; Flexible Schedule; Life Insurance; Medical Insurance; Tuition Assistance. **Corporate headquarters location:** This Location. **Subsidiaries include:** CMS Insurance Agency, Inc.; Gulf Atlantic Insurance Agency; MRS Insurance Company; MS Byrider Sales, Inc.; MS Casualty Insurance Company; MS Dealer Services, Inc.; MS Life Insurance Company; MS Loan Center, Inc.; MS Services, Inc.

MARKEL CORPORATION
4521 Highwoods Parkway, Glen Allen VA 23060. 804/747-0136. **Toll-free phone:** 800/446-6071. **Fax:** 804/527-3845. **Contact:** Human Resources Manager. **World Wide Web address:** http://www. markelcorp.com. **Description:** Markets and underwrites specialty insurance products and programs for a variety of niche markets. Markel Corporation provides underwriting for professional and product liability, excess and surplus lines, specialty programs, and specialty personal lines. Professional liability coverage is offered to physicians and health care professionals, insurance companies, directors and officers, attorneys, architects, and engineers. Product liability is provided to manufacturers and distributors. Property/casualty insurance for nonstandard and hard-to-place risks is underwritten on an excess and surplus line basis. Specialty program insurance includes coverages for camps, youth and recreation, health and fitness, and agribusiness organizations, as well as accident and health insurance for colleges. The company also underwrites personal lines insurance for watercraft and motorcycles, and maintains wholesale and retail brokerage operations that produce business primarily for its insurance subsidiaries. **Common positions include:** Accountant; Actuary; Computer Programmer; Insurance Agent/Broker; Systems Analyst. **Educational backgrounds include:** Accounting; Business Administration; Finance; Liberal Arts. **Benefits:** 401(k); Daycare Assistance; Dental Insurance; Disability Coverage; Life Insurance; Medical Insurance; Profit Sharing; Tuition Assistance. **Special programs:** Internships. **Corporate headquarters location:** This Location. **Other U.S. locations:** Evanston IL. **Subsidiaries include:** American Underwriting Managers (Glen Allen VA); Essex Insurance Company (Glen Allen VA); Markel Service, Inc. (Glen Allen VA); Markel Underwriters & Brokers (Glen Allen VA); Shade/Evanston Group (Evanston IL).

MARSH & McLENNAN COMPANIES, INC.
1166 Avenue of the Americas, New York NY 10036. 212/345-6000. **Contact:** Human Resources Department. **World Wide Web address:** http://www.mmc.com. **Description:** Provides consulting services worldwide through an insurance brokerage and risk management firm, reinsurance intermediary facilities, and a consulting and financial services group, to clients concerned with

the management of assets and risks. Specific services include insurance and risk management services, reinsurance, consulting and financial services, merchandising, and investment management. Founded in 1871. **Corporate headquarters location:** This Location. **Other U.S. locations:** Nationwide. **International locations:** Worldwide.

MARSH USA, INC.
6 PPG Place, Suite 300, Pittsburgh PA 15222-5499. 412/552-5000. **Fax:** 412/552-5999. **Contact:** Human Resources. **World Wide Web address:** http://www.jhmarshmc.com. **Description:** Provides advice and services worldwide through an insurance brokerage and risk management firm, reinsurance intermediary facilities, and a consulting and financial services group, to clients concerned with the management of assets and risks. Specific services include insurance and risk management services, reinsurance, consulting and financial services, merchandising, and investment management. The company has subsidiaries and affiliates in 57 countries, with correspondents in 20 other countries. Founded in 1871. **Corporate headquarters location:** New York NY. **Other U.S. locations:** Nationwide. **International locations:** Worldwide.

MASSACHUSETTS MUTUAL LIFE INSURANCE COMPANY (MASSMUTUAL)
1295 State Street, Springfield MA 01111. 413/788-8411. **Contact:** Human Resources Manager. **World Wide Web address:** http://www.massmutual.com. **Description:** One of the largest insurers in the United States, with over 500 offices nationwide. MassMutual Life Insurance Company provides both individual and group insurance coverage. **NOTE:** The company actively recruits nationwide for experienced career agents, career agent trainees, and field sales managers. A list of available positions may be viewed on the company's Website. **Common positions include:** Accountant; Actuary; Administrator; Assistant Manager; Attorney; Branch Manager; Claim Rep.; Computer Programmer; Customer Service Rep.; Department Manager; Financial Analyst; Instructor/Trainer; Insurance Agent/Broker; Management Trainee; Market Research Analyst; Operations/Production Manager; Public Relations Specialist; Services Sales Rep.; Statistician; Systems Analyst; Underwriter/Assistant Underwriter. **Educational backgrounds include:** Accounting; Business Administration; Computer Science; Finance; Liberal Arts; Mathematics. **Benefits:** Daycare Assistance; Dental Insurance; Disability Coverage; Domestic Partner Benefits; Employee Discounts; Life Insurance; Medical Insurance; Pension Plan; Profit Sharing; Savings Plan; Tuition Assistance. **Special programs:** Internships. **Corporate headquarters location:** This Location.

MAXICARE HEALTH PLANS
1149 South Broadway Street, 8th Floor, Los Angeles CA 90015. 213/765-2000. **Contact:** Human Resources Deaprtment. **World Wide Web address:** http://www.maxicare.com. **Description:** A health maintenance organization. **Corporate headquarters location:** This Location.

MAYFLOWER TRANSIT, INC.
P.O. Box 26150, Fenton MO 63026. 636/305-4000. **Contact:** Human Resources. **World Wide Web address:** http://www.mayflower.com. **Description:** A diversified holding company whose subsidiaries provide a variety of transportation-related services including household moving services; services for goods that require special handling; and storage and distribution, freight forwarding, and flatbed hauling of containerized shipments. Mayflower Transit also owns and operates moving and storage agencies; provides school bus service to school districts; provides on-demand transportation services for local communities; operates a school bus dealership; sells tractor trailers; operates a road equipment maintenance facility; and sells moving supplies, equipment, and uniforms to agents and owner operators. Mayflower also provides a variety of insurance services including property and casualty coverage. **Corporate headquarters location:** This Location.

McGOWAN & COMPANY, INC.
20575 Center Ridge Road, Suite 300, Rocky River OH 44116. 440/333-6300. **Fax:** 440/333-3214. **Contact:** Human Resources. **Description:** Engaged in insurance underwriting. Founded in 1949. **NOTE:** Entry-level positions are offered. **Common positions include:** Accountant; Administrative Assistant; Auditor; Claim Representative; Clerical Supervisor; Insurance Agent/Broker; Operations Manager; Sales Manager; Sales Representative; Typist/Word Processor. **Educational backgrounds include:** Business Administration; Finance; Liberal Arts; Mathematics. **Benefits:** 401(k); Disability Coverage; Life Insurance; Medical Insurance; Pension Plan; Profit Sharing. **Special programs:** Summer Jobs. **Corporate headquarters location:** This Location.

MERCURY INSURANCE GROUP
555 West Imperial Highway, Brea CA 92821. 714/671-7305. **Recorded jobline:** 714/671-7393. **Contact:** Human Resources Manager. **World Wide Web address:** http://www.mercuryinsurance.com. **Description:** A property and casualty insurance firm. Founded in 1962. **NOTE:** Entry-level positions are offered. **Common positions include:** Adjuster; Claim Rep.; Underwriter/Assistant Underwriter. **Educational backgrounds include:** Business; Communications; Economics; Finance; Liberal Arts. **Benefits:** 401(k); Casual Dress - Fridays; Daycare Assistance; Dental Insurance; Disability Coverage; Employee Discounts; Life Insurance; Medical Insurance; Profit Sharing; Tuition Assistance; Vacation Days (6 - 10). **Special programs:** Internships; Training; Summer Jobs. **Corporate headquarters location:** This Location. **Other U.S. locations:** FL; GA; IL.

MERIDIAN MUTUAL INSURANCE CO.
P.O. Box 1980, Indianapolis IN 46206-1980. 317/931-7173. **Fax:** 317/931-7263. **Recorded jobline:** 317/931-7180. **Contact:** Human Resources. **World Wide Web address:** http://www.meridianins.com. **Description:** A regional property and casualty insurance company. **Common positions include:** Accountant/Auditor; Adjuster; Administrative Manager; Attorney; Budget Analyst; Claim Representative; Clerical Supervisor; Computer Programmer; Financial Analyst; Human Resources Manager; Insurance Agent/Broker; Underwriter/Assistant Underwriter. **Educational backgrounds include:** Accounting; Business Administration; Communications; Computer Science; Finance; Liberal Arts; Marketing. **Benefits:** 401(k); Bonus Award/Plan; Dental Insurance; Disability Coverage; Life Insurance; Medical Insurance; Pension Plan; Tuition Assistance. **Corporate headquarters location:** This Location. **Other U.S. locations:** Louisville KY; Lansing MI.

METROPOLITAN LIFE INSURANCE COMPANY
One Madison Avenue, Corporate Staffing Area 1-F, New York NY 10010-3690. 212/578-2211. **Contact:** Corporate Staffing. **World Wide Web address:** http://www.metlife.com. **Description:** A national insurance and financial services company

that offers a wide range of individual and group insurance including life, annuity, disability, and mutual finds. **Corporate headquarters location:** This Location. **Other U.S. locations:** Nationwide.

MID-ATLANTIC MEDICAL SERVICES, INC. (MAMSI)
4 Taft Court, Rockville MD 20850. 301/294-5140. **Contact:** Human Resources. **World Wide Web address:** http://www.mamsi.com. **Description:** A holding company whose subsidiaries are active in managed health care. MAMSI operates two health maintenance organizations: Maryland Individual Practice Association, Inc.; and Optimum Choice, Inc., a non-federally qualified HMO that serves commercial and other specialized markets such as Medicare and Medicaid. Other MAMSI subsidiaries include Alliance PPO, Inc., a preferred provider organization marketing its provider network products to self-insured employers, indemnity carriers, and other health care purchasing groups; Mid-Atlantic Psychiatric Services, Inc., which provides specialized non-risk mental health services; and FirstCall and HomeCall, which provide nursing and care to patients who are confined to their homes. **Corporate headquarters location:** This Location.

MID-SOUTH INSURANCE COMPANY
P.O. Box 2069, Fayetteville NC 28302. 910/822-1020. **Contact:** Human Resources. **Description:** Engaged primarily in the marketing, underwriting, and servicing of health, accident, and life insurance policies. **Corporate headquarters location:** This Location. **Listed on:** NASDAQ.

MIDDLESEX MUTUAL ASSURANCE CO.
213 Court Street, P.O. Box 891, Middletown CT 06457. 860/347-4621. **Contact:** Human Resources. **Description:** Provides automobile insurance to customers in Connecticut, Vermont, Maine, and Iowa.

MIDWEST EMPLOYERS CASUALTY CO.
13801 Riverport Drive, Suite 200, Maryland Heights MO 63043. 314/298-7332. **Contact:** Personnel. **World Wide Web address:** http://www.mwecc.com. **Description:** Midwest Employers Casualty Company markets and underwrites excess workers' compensation insurance. Founded in 1986. **NOTE:** Entry-level positions and part-time jobs are offered. **Benefits:** 401(k); Casual Dress - Daily; Dental Insurance; Disability Coverage; Flexible Schedule; Life Insurance; Medical Insurance; Relocation Assistance; Tuition Assistance. **Special programs:** Internships; Training; Co-ops; Summer Jobs.

THE MONY GROUP
1740 Broadway, New York NY 10019. 212/708-2000. **Contact:** Personnel Department. **Description:** A mutual life insurer. The Mony Group offers life insurance, disability income, and annuities. The company also operates investment subsidiaries engaged in the management of mutual funds and the distribution of securities. **Educational backgrounds include:** Accounting; Mathematics. **Benefits:** 401(k); Dental Insurance; Disability Coverage; Life Insurance; Medical Insurance; Pension Plan; Savings Plan; Tuition Assistance. **Special programs:** Internships. **Corporate headquarters location:** This Location.

MORTGAGE GUARANTY INSURANCE CORP.
250 East Kilbourn Avenue, Milwaukee WI 53202. 414/347-6575. **Toll-free phone:** 800/558-9900. **Fax:** 414/347-4866. **Contact:** Human Resources. **World Wide Web address:** http://www.mgic.com. **Description:** Provides private mortgage insurance.

MOTOR CLUB OF AMERICA
MOTOR CLUB OF AMERICA INSURANCE COMPANY
95 Route 17 South, Paramus NJ 07653-0931. 201/291-2000. **Contact:** Human Resources Manager. **World Wide Web address:** http://www.motr.com. **Description:** Provides automobile, homeowner, and commercial insurance. Founded in 1926. **Common positions include:** Accountant/Auditor; Adjuster; Claim Rep.; Clerical Supervisor; Computer Programmer; Human Resources Manager; Insurance Agent/Broker; Systems Analyst; Underwriter/Assistant Underwriter. **Benefits:** 401(k); Dental Insurance; Disability Coverage; Life Insurance; Medical Insurance. **Corporate headquarters location:** This Location. **Subsidiaries include:** American Colonial Insurance Company; Motor Club of America Insurance Company; North East Insurance Company; Preserver Insurance Company.

MOTORISTS INSURANCE COMPANIES
471 East Broad Street, Columbus OH 43215. 614/225-8211. **Fax:** 614/225-8693. **Recorded jobline:** 614/225-8313. **Contact:** Human Resources. **World Wide Web address:** http://www.youknowus.com. **Description:** Handles a wide range of property and casualty insurance lines. **Common positions include:** Accountant/Auditor; Actuary; Adjuster; Attorney; Claim Rep.; Clerical Supervisor; Collector; Computer Programmer; Customer Service Rep.; Human Resources Manager; Insurance Agent/Broker; Investigator; Systems Analyst. **Educational backgrounds include:** Business Administration; Computer Science. **Benefits:** 401(k); Dental Insurance; Disability Coverage; Employee Discounts; Life Insurance; Medical Insurance; Pension Plan; Profit Sharing; Tuition Assistance; Vision Insurance. **Corporate headquarters location:** This Location.

MUTUAL OF AMERICA
320 Park Avenue, New York NY 10022. 212/224-1045. **Fax:** 212/224-2501. **Contact:** Human Resources. **Description:** A life insurance company that offers pension plans, tax-deferred annuities, IRAs, deferred compensation plans, individual life insurance and thrift plans, funding agreements, guaranteed interest contracts, group life insurance, and group long-term disability income insurance to nonprofit, tax-exempt employers. Mutual of America also sells 401(k) products nationally. Services include actuarial (annual valuations, cost proposals, and reports to auditors); administrative (preparation of documents, monthly billings, maintenance of employee records, benefit payment services, development of administrative manuals, calculation of benefit estimates, and annual participant benefit statements); assistance with government filings (preparation and release of ERISA Information Bulletins and distribution of employer kits for qualifying pension plans); communications (Mutual of America Report, audio/visual presentations, and annual reports); investments (17 investment funds); and field consulting. **Common positions include:** Accountant/Auditor; Actuary; Claim Rep.; Computer Support Technician; Computer Technician; Customer Service Representative; Financial Analyst; Human Resources Manager; Intranet Developer; Management Trainee; Network Engineer; Network/Systems Administrator; Sales Rep.; Systems Analyst; Underwriter/Assistant Underwriter. **Educational backgrounds include:** Accounting; Business; Communications; Liberal Arts; Marketing; Mathematics. **Benefits:** 401(k); Dental Insurance; Disability Coverage; Flexible Schedule; Life Insurance; Medical Insurance; Pension Plan. **Corporate headquarters location:**

This Location. **Other U.S. locations:** Nationwide. **Subsidiaries include:** Capital Management Corporation.

MUTUAL OF OMAHA INSURANCE CO.
Mutual of Omaha Plaza, Omaha NE 68175. 402/351-5990. **Fax:** 402/351-3026. **Contact:** Personnel. **World Wide Web address:** http://www. mutualofomaha.com. **Description:** Mutual of Omaha offers a full portfolio of insurance coverages and services with $25.4 billion paid in benefits to policy holders. **Common positions include:** Accountant/Auditor; Actuary; Adjuster; Claim Rep.; Computer Programmer; Customer Service Rep.; Financial Analyst; Marketing Specialist; Mathematician; Paralegal; Systems Analyst; Underwriter/Assistant Underwriter. **Educational backgrounds include:** Accounting; Business Administration; Computer Science; Finance; Liberal Arts; Marketing; Mathematics. **Benefits:** 401(k); Dental Insurance; Disability Coverage; Employee Discounts; Life Insurance; Medical Insurance; Pension Plan; Tuition Assistance. **Corporate headquarters location:** This Location.

NAC RE CORPORATION
One Greenwich Plaza, Greenwich CT 06836-2568. 203/622-5200. **Contact:** Human Resources. **Description:** A holding company. Founded in 1985. **Corporate headquarters location:** This Location. **Subsidiaries include:** NAC Reinsurance International Limited is an international reinsurance operation licensed in the United Kingdom. Based in London, NAC Reinsurance International writes property treaty business primarily in Europe, Japan, and Australia; and casualty business primarily in the United Kingdom. NAC Reinsurance Corporation offers treaty and facultative reinsurance protection to property and casualty insurers. Treaty reinsurance is generally marketed to primary insurers through intermediaries. Facultative reinsurance is offered directly to insurers through five regional offices.

NATIONAL ASSOCIATION OF INSURANCE & FINANCIAL ADVISORS (NAIFA)
1922 F Street NW, Washington DC 20006. 202/331-6000. **Fax:** 202/835-9616. **Contact:** Human Resources Manager. **World Wide Web address:** http://www.naifa.org. **Description:** A trade organization representing insurance and financial professionals throughout the United States. **Common positions include:** Accountant/Auditor; Advertising Clerk; Computer Operator; Computer Programmer; Payroll Clerk; Secretary; Systems Analyst. **Educational backgrounds include:** Accounting; Art/Design; Business Administration; Communications; Finance. **Benefits:** Dental Insurance; Disability Coverage; Employee Discounts; Life Insurance; Medical Insurance; Pension Plan; Profit Sharing; Savings Plan; Tuition Assistance. **Corporate headquarters location:** This Location.

NATIONAL BENEFIT LIFE INSURANCE CO.
333 West 34th Street, New York NY 10001. 212/615-7500. **Contact:** Human Resources. **Description:** A nationally licensed insurance firm dealing primarily in health and life insurance. **Corporate headquarters location:** This Location. **Listed on:** New York Stock Exchange.

NATIONAL CHIROPRACTIC MUTUAL INSurance company
P.O. Box 9118, Des Moines IA 50306. 515/222-2941. **Fax:** 515/222-2192. **Contact:** Human Resources Manager. **Description:** A direct writer of chiropractic malpractice insurance. **Common positions include:** Accountant; Adjuster; Claim Rep.; Customer Service Rep.; Systems Analyst;

Underwriter/Assistant Underwriter. **Educational backgrounds include:** Accounting; Business Administration. **Benefits:** 401(k); Dental Insurance; Disability Coverage; Life Insurance; Medical Insurance; Pension Plan; Tuition Assistance. **Corporate headquarters location:** This Location.

NATIONAL FARMER'S UNION INSURANCE
11900 East Cornell Avenue, Aurora CO 80014-3194. 303/337-5500. **Contact:** Human Resources. **Description:** A national insurance company specializing in coverage for farmers. **Corporate headquarters location:** This Location.

NATIONAL FOUNDATION LIFE INSURANCE COMPANY
110 West Seventh Street, Suite 300, Fort Worth TX 76102. 817/878-3300. **Contact:** Human Resources. **Description:** A life insurance company. **Common positions include:** Accountant; Actuary; Attorney; Claim Rep.; Clerical Supervisor; Computer Programmer; Human Resources Manager; Paralegal; Purchasing Agent/Manager; Systems Analyst; Underwriter/Assistant Underwriter. **Educational backgrounds include:** Accounting; Business Administration; Computer Science. **Benefits:** 401(k); Dental Insurance; Disability Coverage; Life Insurance; Medical Insurance. **Corporate headquarters location:** This Location.

NATIONAL GENERAL INSURANCE CO.
One National General Plaza, Earth City MO 63045-1305. 314/493-8000. **Fax:** 314/298-1632. **Contact:** Human Resources. **Description:** Engaged in the direct response marketing of personal lines insurance (homeowners, automobile, and motorcycle) and data management services to sponsoring associations in 48 states. **Common positions include:** Accountant/Auditor; Actuary; Administrator; Claim Rep.; Computer Operator; Computer Programmer; Customer Service Rep.; Department Manager; Human Resources Manager; Technical Writer/Editor; Typist/Word Processor; Underwriter/Assistant Underwriter. **Educational backgrounds include:** Accounting; Business Administration; Communications; Computer Science; Finance; Marketing. **Benefits:** 401(k); Dental Insurance; Disability Coverage; Life Insurance; Medical Insurance; Pension Plan; Profit Sharing; Tuition Assistance. **Corporate headquarters location:** This Location. **Parent company:** General Motors Insurance Company.

NATIONAL GRANGE MUTUAL INSURANCE COMPANY
55 West Street, Keene NH 03431. 603/352-4000. **Contact:** Personnel. **Description:** A full-service property and casualty company which writes all personal lines of insurance including homeowner and automotive, as well as a wide range of commercial products for the small business owner. National Grange Mutual Insurance Company markets these products over a 14 state area in the Northeast through 700 independent insurance agents. **Common positions include:** Accountant/Auditor; Actuary; Claim Rep.; Computer Programmer; Marketing Specialist; Statistician; Systems Analyst; Underwriter/Assistant Underwriter. **Educational backgrounds include:** Accounting; Biology; Computer Science; Mathematics. **Benefits:** Dental Insurance; Disability Coverage; Life Insurance; Medical Insurance; Pension Plan; Profit Sharing. **Corporate headquarters location:** This Location. **Subsidiaries include:** MSA Group.

NATIONWIDE INSURANCE ENTERPRISE
One Nationwide Plaza, Columbus OH 43215. 614/249-7111. **Contact:** Human Resources. **World**

Wide Web address: http://www.nationwide.com. **Description:** Engaged in the sale of automobile, life, group, and business insurance. **Common positions include:** Accountant/Auditor; Actuary; Computer Programmer; Customer Service Rep.; Financial Analyst; Human Resources Manager; Insurance Agent/Broker; Management Trainee; Services Sales Rep.; Systems Analyst; Technical Writer/Editor; Underwriter/Assistant Underwriter. **Educational backgrounds include:** Accounting; Business; Finance; Liberal Arts; Marketing; Mathematics. **Benefits:** Dental Insurance; Disability Coverage; Employee Discounts; Life Insurance; Medical Insurance; Pension Plan; Profit Sharing; Savings Plan; Tuition Assistance. **Corporate headquarters location:** This Location.

THE NAVIGATORS GROUP, INC.
123 William Street, New York NY 10038. 212/349-1600. **Contact:** Human Resources. **Description:** The Navigators Group is a holding company. **Corporate headquarters location:** This Location. **Subsidiaries include:** Navigators Insurance Company and NIC Insurance Company. Both companies underwrite marine insurance including hull, energy, liability, and cargo; aviation insurance including hull and liability on commercial and general aircraft; property insurance including large commercial and industrial all risk coverages; and certain lines of specialty reinsurance including excess of loss and quota share property, surety, and other specialty reinsurance lines.

NEIGHBORHOOD HEALTH PLAN
253 Summer Street, Boston MA 02210. 617/772-5500. **Fax:** 617/478-7198. **Contact:** Human Resources. **World Wide Web address:** http://www.nhp.org. **Description:** A nonprofit HMO serving approximately 46,000 members through 116 community health centers and medical groups across Massachusetts. Founded in 1986. **Common positions include:** Accountant; Computer Programmer; Customer Service Rep.; Database Manager; Registered Nurse; Sales Rep. **Educational backgrounds include:** Accounting; Business; Communications; Computer Science; Finance; Health Care; Liberal Arts; Marketing; Software Development. **Benefits:** 401(k); Disability Coverage; Life Insurance; Medical Insurance; Profit Sharing. **Corporate headquarters location:** This Location.

NEW YORK LIFE INSURANCE COMPANY
51 Madison Avenue, Room 151, New York NY 10010. 212/576-7000. **Fax:** 212/447-4292. **Contact:** Human Resources Department. **World Wide Web address:** http://www.newyorklife.com. **Description:** New York Life Insurance Company, its subsidiaries, and affiliates offer a wide variety of products and services. Services include life, health, and disability insurance, annuities, mutual funds, health care management services, and commercial mortgage financing. The company's Asset Management operation (including pensions, mutual funds, and NYLIFE Securities) is located in Parsippany NJ. Founded in 1845. **NOTE:** In addition to job opportunities offered at the home office and in Parsippany, the company also recruits for sales positions through local offices. **Common positions include:** Accountant/Auditor; Computer Programmer; Customer Service Representative; Financial Analyst. **Educational backgrounds include:** Accounting; Business Administration; Communications; Computer Science; Finance; Liberal Arts; Marketing. **Benefits:** 401(k); Daycare Assistance; Dental Insurance; Disability Coverage; Employee Discounts; Life Insurance; Medical Insurance; Pension Plan; Profit Sharing; Savings Plan; Tuition Assistance. **Corporate headquarters location:** This Location. **Other U.S. locations:** Nationwide.

NORCAL MUTUAL INSURANCE CO.
560 Davis Street, 2nd Floor, San Francisco CA 94111. 415/397-9700. **Fax:** 415/835-9817. **Contact:** Human Resources Department. **World Wide Web address:** http://www.norcalmutual.com. **Description:** Provides physicians with professional liability insurance. **Common positions include:** Attorney; Budget Analyst; Buyer; Claim Rep.; Computer Programmer; Economist; Editor; Financial Analyst; Human Resources Manager; Paralegal; Services Sales Representative; Systems Analyst; Technical Writer/Editor; Underwriter/Assistant Underwriter. **Educational backgrounds include:** Business; Communications; Finance; Liberal Arts. **Benefits:** Dental Insurance; Disability Coverage; Life Insurance; Medical Insurance; Pension Plan; Profit Sharing; Savings Plan; Tuition Assistance; Vision Insurance. **Special programs:** Internships. **Corporate headquarters location:** This Location. **Other U.S. locations:** Anchorage AK; Pasadena CA.

NORMAN-SPENCER McKERNAN AGENCY
P.O. Box 41298, Dayton OH 45441. 937/885-5053. **Physical address:** 10501 Success Lane, Dayton OH 45458. **Contact:** Human Resources. **Description:** An insurance brokerage house. **Common positions include:** Customer Service Rep.; Insurance Agent/Broker; Manufacturer's/Wholesaler's Sales Representative; Marketing Specialist. **Educational backgrounds include:** Business Administration; Communications; Marketing. **Benefits:** 401(k); Dental Insurance; Disability Coverage; Life Insurance; Medical Insurance; Tuition Assistance. **Corporate headquarters location:** This Location. **Parent company:** Norman-Spencer, Inc.

NORTH AMERICAN COMPANY FOR LIFE AND HEALTH INSURANCE
222 South Riverside Plaza, Chicago IL 60606. 312/648-7600. **Fax:** 312/648-7799. **Contact:** Human Resources. **E-mail address:** mhaley@nacolah.com. **World Wide Web address:** http://www.nacolah.com. **Description:** Provides a variety of annuities and individual life insurance policies. **Common positions include:** Accountant/Auditor; Actuary; Attorney; Claim Rep.; Computer Programmer; Customer Service Representative; Underwriter/Assistant Underwriter. **Educational backgrounds include:** Accounting; Business Administration; Computer Science; Finance; Liberal Arts; Marketing; Mathematics. **Benefits:** Dental Insurance; Disability Coverage; Employee Discounts; ESOP; Life Insurance; Medical Insurance; Pension Plan; Tuition Assistance. **Corporate headquarters location:** This Location. **Other U.S. locations:** Woodland Hills CA; Garden City NY.

NORTH CAROLINA MUTUAL LIFE INSURANCE COMPANY
411 West Chapel Hill Street, Durham NC 27701. 919/682-9201. **Fax:** 919/683-1694. **Contact:** Human Resources. **World Wide Web address:** http://www.ncmutuallife.com. **Description:** A life insurance company. **Common positions include:** Accountant/Auditor; Administrative Manager; Assistant Manager; Attorney; Budget Analyst; Cashier; Claim Rep.; Clerical Supervisor; Computer Operator; Computer Programmer; Customer Service Representative; Department Manager; Employment Interviewer; Financial Services Sales Rep.; General Manager; Human Resources Manager; Insurance Agent/Broker; Marketing Manager; Payroll Clerk; Printing Press Operator; Public Relations Specialist;

Purchasing Agent/Manager; Real Estate Agent; Receptionist; Secretary; Securities Sales Rep.; Services Sales Representative; Systems Analyst; Typist/Word Processor; Underwriter/Assistant Underwriter. **Educational backgrounds include:** Accounting; Business; Communications; Computer Science; Finance; Liberal Arts; Marketing; Mathematics. **Benefits:** Dental Insurance; Disability Coverage; Employee Discounts; Legal Services; Medical Insurance; Pension Plan; Profit Sharing; Tuition Assistance. **Corporate headquarters location:** This Location.

THE NORTHWESTERN MUTUAL LIFE INSURANCE COMPANY
THE KERRIGAN AGENCY
888 West Sixth Street, Los Angeles CA 90017. 213/243-7027. **Fax:** 213/243-7001. **Contact:** Human Resources. **World Wide Web address:** http://www.nml-la.com. **Description:** An insurance and investment planning company. The Northwestern Mutual Life insurance Company specializes in individual life insurance coverage. The company's product portfolio includes permanent and term insurance, CompLife, disability income insurance, and annuity plans for the personal, business, estate, and pension planning markets. **Common positions include:** Insurance Agent/Broker. **Educational backgrounds include:** Business; Communications; Finance; Liberal Arts; Marketing. **Special programs:** Internships; Training. **Internship information:** The Kerrigan Agency offers college agent internships. These internships offer professional experience and the flexibility required for full-time students. College agents receive extensive training allowing for hands-on learning. College agents are responsible for the development of a professional practice revolving around the sale of insurance products, annuities, mutual funds, and investments, as well as estate, retirement, education, and pension planning. Successful applicants will be independent, with strong ethics, and have a proven track record for success. **Corporate headquarters location:** Milwaukee WI. **Other U.S. locations:** Nationwide.

THE NORTHWESTERN MUTUAL LIFE INSURANCE COMPANY
720 East Wisconsin Avenue, Milwaukee WI 53202. 414/271-1444. **Recorded jobline:** 414/299-7070. **Contact:** Human Resources Manager. **World Wide Web address:** http://www.northwesternmutual.com. **Description:** Specializes in individual life insurance coverage. The company's product portfolio includes permanent and term insurance, CompLife, disability income insurance, and annuity plans for the personal, business, estate, and pension planning markets. **Common positions include:** Accountant/Auditor; Attorney; Auditor; Claim Rep.; Computer Programmer; Customer Service Rep.; Marketing Specialist; Systems Analyst; Underwriter/Assistant Underwriter. **Educational backgrounds include:** Accounting; Business; Communications; Computer Science; Economics; Finance; Mathematics. **Benefits:** 401(k); Disability Coverage; Life Insurance; Medical Insurance; Pension Plan; Tuition Assistance. **Special programs:** Internships. **Corporate headquarters location:** This Location. **Other U.S. locations:** Los Angeles CA; Woodland Hills CA; Garden City NY; Philadelphia PA.

ODS HEALTH PLANS
601 SW Second Avenue, Portland OR 97204. 503/228-6554. **Fax:** 503/243-3895. **Contact:** Human Resources. **World Wide Web address:** http://www.odshp.com. **Description:** A dental and medical insurance organization. **Common positions include:** Accountant/Auditor; Claim Representative; Computer Programmer; Customer Service Rep.;

Underwriter/Assistant Underwriter. **Educational backgrounds include:** Accounting; Business Administration; Computer Science; Marketing; Mathematics. **Benefits:** 401(k); Cafeteria Plan; Dental Insurance; Disability Coverage; EAP; Life Insurance; Medical Insurance; Pension Plan; Section 125 Plan; Tuition Assistance; Vision Insurance. **Corporate headquarters location:** This Location. **Subsidiaries include:** Best Choice Administrators; Dentist Benefit Insurance Corporation; Dentist Management Corporation.

THE OHIO CASUALTY GROUP
136 North Third Street, Hamilton OH 45025. 513/867-3000. **Contact:** Human Resources Manager. **World Wide Web address:** http://www.ocas.com. **Description:** An insurance holding company. **Corporate headquarters location:** This Location. **Subsidiaries include:** Casualty Group is licensed to do business nationwide, though it is concentrated mainly in New Jersey, Pennsylvania, Ohio, and Kentucky; Ohio Life Insurance Company is an underwriter of universal and personal life insurance, business life insurance, pension and profit sharing plans, and retirement annuities; and Ocasco Budget, Inc. is an insurance premium financier.

OHIO MUTUAL INSURANCE GROUP
UNITED OHIO INSURANCE COMPANY
1725 Hopley Avenue, P.O. Box 111, Bucyrus OH 44820. 419/562-3011. **Contact:** Personnel Director. **Description:** Specializes in providing fire and related insurance coverage to a wide variety of clients. **Common positions include:** Accountant/Auditor; Claim Rep.; Computer Programmer; Data Entry Clerk; Typist/Word Processor; Underwriter/Assistant Underwriter. **Benefits:** Disability Coverage; Life Insurance; Medical Insurance; Pension Plan; Savings Plan; Tuition Assistance. **Corporate headquarters location:** This Location.

OLD REPUBLIC INTERNATIONAL CORP.
307 North Michigan Avenue, Chicago IL 60601. 312/346-8100. **Contact:** Human Resources. **World Wide Web address:** http://www.oldrepublic.com. **Description:** An insurance holding company. **Corporate headquarters location:** This Location. **International locations:** Canada; Hong Kong; Puerto Rico.

OLD REPUBLIC NATIONAL TITLE INSURANCE COMPANY
400 Second Avenue South, Minneapolis MN 55401. 612/371-1111. **Fax:** 612/371-1133. **Contact:** Personnel. **World Wide Web address:** http://www.oldpublictitle.com. **Description:** Provides title insurance. **Common positions include:** Accountant/Auditor; Attorney; Branch Manager; Computer Operator; Computer Programmer; Customer Service Rep.; Department Manager; Employment Interviewer; General Manager; Human Resources Manager; Management Trainee; Order Clerk; Payroll Clerk; Property and Real Estate Manager; Receptionist; Services Sales Rep.; Systems Analyst; Typist/Word Processor. **Educational backgrounds include:** Accounting; Business; Communications; Finance; Marketing. **Benefits:** Daycare Assistance; Dental Insurance; Disability Coverage; Employee Discounts; Life Insurance; Medical Insurance; Pension Plan; Savings Plan; Tuition Assistance. **Corporate headquarters location:** This Location. **Parent company:** Old Republic Title Insurance Group.

OXFORD HEALTH PLANS
P.O. Box 7081, Bridgeport CT 06601. **Toll-free phone:** 800/444-6222. **Contact:** Human Resources. **World Wide Web address:** http://www.oxhp.com.

Description: A managed care company providing health benefit plans in New York, New Jersey, and Connecticut. The company's product lines include traditional health maintenance organizations, a point-of-service Freedom Plan, third-party administration of employer-funded benefit plans, Medicare and Medicaid supplemental plans, and dental plans. Oxford Health Plans markets its health plans to employers and individuals through its direct sales force, as well as through independent insurance agents and brokers. **Corporate headquarters location:** This Location.

P/C WISCONSIN
1002 Deming Way, Madison WI 53717. 608/831-8331. **Fax:** 608/831-0084. **Contact:** Human Resources Manager. **Description:** A carrier of medical liability insurance. The company serves the insurance needs of physicians, hospitals, and clinics. **Common positions include:** Accountant; Administrative Assistant; Claim Rep.; Controller; Database Manager; Market Research Analyst; Marketing Manager; Paralegal; Project Manager; Secretary; Software Developer; Underwriter/Assistant Underwriter. **Educational backgrounds include:** Accounting; Business Administration; Computer Science; Health Care; Marketing. **Benefits:** 401(k); Dental Insurance; Disability Coverage; Life Insurance; Medical Insurance; Tuition Assistance. **Corporate headquarters location:** This Location.

THE PMA GROUP
380 Sentry Parkway, Blue Bell PA 19422. 610/397-5000. **Contact:** Human Resources. **Description:** Provides workers' compensation insurance. **Common positions include:** Actuary; Claim Rep.; Customer Service Rep.; Underwriter/Assistant Underwriter. **Educational backgrounds include:** Business Administration; Computer Science; Liberal Arts. **Benefits:** 401(k); Dental Insurance; Disability Coverage; Fitness Program; Life Insurance; Medical Insurance; Pension Plan; Tuition Assistance. **Special programs:** Internships. **Corporate headquarters location:** This Location. **Other area locations:** Allentown PA; Harrisburg PA; Pittsburgh PA; Ridgeway PA; Valley Forge PA; Williamsport PA. **Other U.S. locations:** Hunt Valley MD; Charlotte NC; Raleigh NC; Mount Laurel NJ; Richmond VA; Roanoke VA.

PACIFIC LIFE INSURANCE
700 Newport Center Drive, Newport Beach CA 92660. 949/640-3011. **Contact:** Human Resources Manager. **World Wide Web address:** http://www.pacificlife.com. **Description:** Provides insurance services including group health, life, and pensions. Pacific Life Insurance also provides financial services including annuities, mutual funds, and investments. **Corporate headquarters location:** This Location.

PACIFICARE HEALTH SYSTEMS, INC.
3120 West Lake Center Drive, Santa Ana CA 92704. 714/825-5200. **Contact:** Human Resources Manager. **World Wide Web address:** http://www.pacificare.com. **Description:** A regionally focused health care company with six HMOs operating in California, Oklahoma, Oregon, Texas, Florida, and Washington. Services include PPOs, life and health insurance, Medicare risk management programs, dental care services, and pharmacy services. The company has a contract to provide health services to military personnel and their dependents in 19 states. **Subsidiaries include:** COMPREMIER, Inc. provides workers' compensation care; Execu-Fit Health Programs, Inc.; LifeLink, Inc., is a mental health services provider; Prescription Solutions.

PARKER, SMITH & FEEK
2233 112th Avenue NE, Bellevue WA 98004. **Contact:** Human Resources. **Description:** Provides a variety of insurance services including commercial property/casualty, health, life, and personal lines. Founded in 1937. **Common positions include:** Insurance Agent/Broker. **Corporate headquarters location:** This Location. **Other U.S. locations:** Anchorage AK.

PEMCO FINANCIAL SERVICES
P.O. Box 778, Seattle WA 98111. 206/628-4090. **Toll-free phone:** 800/552-7430. **Fax:** 206/628-6072. **Recorded jobline:** 206/628-8740. **Contact:** Human Resources Manager. **E-mail address:** jobs@pemco.com. **World Wide Web address:** http://www.pemco.com. **Description:** Provides insurance, banking, and credit union services through its subsidiaries. Founded in 1936. **NOTE:** Entry-level positions and second and third shifts are offered. **Common positions include:** Adjuster; Claim Rep.; Customer Service Rep.; Sales Rep. **Benefits:** 401(k); Dental Insurance; Disability Coverage; Employee Discounts; Life Insurance; Medical Insurance. **Special programs:** Training. **Corporate headquarters location:** This Location.

PENN MUTUAL LIFE INSURANCE CO.
600 Dresher Road, Horsham PA 19044. 215/956-8000. **Contact:** Human Resources. **Description:** Offers life insurance and annuities. **Corporate headquarters location:** This Location. **Subsidiaries include:** Independence Financial Group.

PERMANENT GENERAL AND TENNESSEE INSURANCE COMPANY
P.O. Box 305054, Nashville TN 37217. 615/242-1961. **Fax:** 615/367-2144. **Contact:** Human Resources. **Description:** A non-standard automobile insurance company. Founded in 1963. **NOTE:** Entry-level positions are offered. **Common positions include:** Adjuster; Claim Rep.; Computer Operator; Computer Programmer; Customer Service Rep.; Systems Analyst; Typist/Word Processor; Underwriter/Assistant Underwriter. **Educational backgrounds include:** Business Administration; Computer Science; Software Tech. Support. **Benefits:** 401(k); Dental Insurance; Disability Coverage; Employee Discounts; Life Insurance; Medical Insurance; Tuition Assistance. **Corporate headquarters location:** This Location. **Other area locations:** Knoxville TN; Memphis TN. **Other U.S. locations:** Mission Viejo CA; Marietta GA; New Orleans LA; Cleveland OH. **Parent company:** Ingram Industries, Inc.

PHOENIX HOME LIFE MUTUAL INSURANCE COMPANY
One American Row, P.O. Box 5056, Hartford CT 06102-5056. 860/403-5000. **Contact:** Human Resources. **World Wide Web address:** http://www.phl.com. **Description:** One of the largest mutual life insurance companies in the United States. **Corporate headquarters location:** This Location.

PHYSICIAN CORPORATION OF AMERICA (PCA)
6101 Blue Lagoon Drive, Miami FL 33126. 305/267-6633. **Fax:** 305/265-5341. **Contact:** Human Resources. **Description:** A managed health care company that provides comprehensive services through its health maintenance organizations, and administrative services through its workers' compensation third-party administration companies. **Corporate headquarters location:** This Location. **Parent company:** Humana, Inc.

PHYSICIANS HEALTH SERVICES OF CONNECTICUT, INC. (PHS)
One Far Mill Crossing, Shelton CT 06484. **Toll-free phone:** 800/848-4747. **Contact:** Department of Human Resources. **Description:** Provides managed care throughout the state of Connecticut. **Corporate headquarters location:** This Location. **Subsidiaries include:** Physicians Health Insurance Services; and Total Employee Care. **Parent company:** Physicians Health Services, Inc. (PHS) also operates in New York's Hudson River Valley through its subsidiary Physicians Health Services of New York.

PRINCIPAL FINANCIAL GROUP
711 High Street, Des Moines IA 50392. 515/247-5224. **Contact:** Human Resources Manager. **World Wide Web address:** http://www.principal.com. **Description:** Provides financial services including annuities, home mortgages, mutual funds, and retirement plans. The Principal Financial Group also offers dental, disability, health, life, and vision insurance policies. **Corporate headquarters location:** This Location. **Subsidiaries include:** Principal Life Insurance Company; Principal Residential Mortgage, Inc.

PROGRESSIVE CORPORATION
6300 Wilson Mills Road, Mayfield Village OH 44143. 440/461-5000. **Contact:** Human Resources Manager. **World Wide Web address:** http://www.progressive.com. **Description:** An insurance holding company. **Corporate headquarters location:** This Location. **Subsidiaries include:** Progressive Insurance writes auto insurance in 48 states, the District of Columbia, and Canada.

PROTECTIVE LIFE CORPORATION
P.O. Box 2606, Birmingham AL 35202-2606. 205/879-9230. **Contact:** Human Resources. **World Wide Web address:** http://www.protective.com. **Description:** A provider of life and health insurance. **Corporate headquarters location:** This Location.

PRUDENTIAL INSURANCE COMPANY OF AMERICA
751 Broad Street, Newark NJ 07102. 973/802-8348. **Fax:** 973/802-7763. **Contact:** Human Resources Director. **World Wide Web address:** http://www.prudential.com. **Description:** One of the largest insurance companies in North America and one of the largest diversified financial services organizations in the world. The company offers a full range of products and services in three areas: insurance, investment, and home ownership for individuals and families; health care management and other benefit programs for employees of companies and members of groups; and asset management for institutional clients and their associates. The company insures or provides financial services to more than 50 million people worldwide. **Common positions include:** Accountant/Auditor; Actuary; Administrator; Computer Programmer; Human Resources Manager; Purchasing Agent/Manager; Underwriter/Assistant Underwriter. **Educational backgrounds include:** Accounting; Business; Communications; Computer Science; Economics; Finance; Liberal Arts; Mathematics. **Benefits:** Daycare Assistance; Dental Insurance; Disability Coverage; Life Insurance; Medical Insurance; Pension Plan; Savings Plan; Tuition Assistance. **Special programs:** Internships. **Corporate headquarters location:** This Location. **Other U.S. locations:** Woodland Hills CA; Jacksonville FL; Minneapolis MN; Holmdel NJ; Roseland NJ; Philadelphia PA; Houston TX.

PRUDENTIAL PREFERRED FINANCIAL SERVICES
3495 Piedmont Road, Building 12, Suite 300, Atlanta GA 30305. 404/262-2600. **Fax:** 404/262-1835. **Contact:** Human Resources Director. **World Wide Web address:** http://www.prudential.com. **Description:** Markets a complete portfolio of insurance (group life and health) and financial services products to business owners, professionals, and upper-income individuals. Founded in 1875. **Common positions include:** Attorney; Bank Officer/Manager; Financial Consultant; Insurance Agent/Broker; Management Trainee; Sales Rep.; Teacher/Professor. **Educational backgrounds include:** Accounting; Business Administration; Finance; Liberal Arts; Management/Planning; Marketing. **Benefits:** 401(k); Dental Insurance; Disability Coverage; Life Insurance; Medical Insurance; Pension Plan; Savings Plan; Tuition Assistance. **Special programs:** Training. **Corporate headquarters location:** Newark NJ. **Other U.S. locations:** Nationwide. **International locations:** Worldwide. **Parent company:** Prudential Insurance Company of America.

PRUDENTIAL PROPERTY & CASUALTY INSURANCE
814 Commerce Drive, Oak Brook IL 60523. 630/572-2722. **Fax:** 630/572-8416. **Contact:** Human Resources Manager. **World Wide Web address:** http://www.prudential.com. **Description:** As a regional service office, this location provides underwriting risk analysis and selection services for 18 midwestern and northeastern states; provides claims services for policyholders in several midwestern states; and provides nonclaims services to policyholders nationwide. Overall, Prudential Property & Casualty Insurance underwrites family automobile and homeowner policies. Founded in 1969. **Common positions include:** Claim Representative; Underwriter/Assistant Underwriter. **Educational backgrounds include:** Business Administration; Economics; Finance; Liberal Arts; Mathematics. **Benefits:** 401(k); Dental Insurance; Disability Coverage; Life Insurance; Medical Insurance; Pension Plan; Public Transit Available; Savings Plan; Tuition Assistance. **Parent company:** Prudential Insurance Company of America.

RADIAN GUARANTY INC.
1601 Market Street, Philadelphia PA 19103. 215/564-6600. **Contact:** Personnel **Description:** A national insurance company providing private mortgage insurance and risk management services to mortgage lending institutions. **Corporate headquarters location:** This Location. **Other U.S. locations:** Nationwide. **Parent company:** Radian Group Inc. (also at this location).

RANGER INSURANCE COMPANY
P.O. Box 2807, Houston TX 77252.. 713/954-8100. **Contact:** Human Resources Director. **World Wide Web address:** http://www.rangerinsurance.com. **Description:** Markets specialty lines of commercial property and casualty insurance as well as non-standard automobile insurance. **Common positions include:** Accountant/Auditor; Actuary; Claim Rep.; Industrial Engineer; Systems Analyst; Underwriter/Assistant Underwriter. **Educational backgrounds include:** Business Administration; Insurance. **Benefits:** Dental Insurance; Disability Coverage; Life Insurance; Medical Insurance; Pension Plan; Profit Sharing; Tuition Assistance. **Corporate headquarters location:** This Location.

REGIONS BLUE CROSS & BLUE SHIELD OF UTAH, INC.
2890 East Cottonwood Parkway, P.O. Box 30270, Salt Lake City UT 84130-0270. 801/333-2000.

Recorded jobline: 801/333-2060. **Contact:** Employment Coordinator. **Description:** A health insurance provider. **NOTE:** This firm does not accept unsolicited resumes. Please call the jobline for a list of available positions. **Common positions include:** Accountant/Auditor; Attorney; Blue-Collar Worker Supervisor; Budget Analyst; Claim Rep.; Customer Service Rep.; Licensed Practical Nurse; Public Relations Specialist; Purchasing Agent/Manager; Registered Nurse; Securities Sales Rep.; Statistician; Systems Analyst; Underwriter/Assistant Underwriter. **Educational backgrounds include:** Accounting; Computer Science; Marketing. **Benefits:** 401(k); Dental Insurance; Disability Coverage; Employee Discounts; Life Insurance; Medical Insurance; Pension Plan; Tuition Assistance. **Special programs:** Internships. **Corporate headquarters location:** This Location.

RELIANCE GROUP HOLDINGS, INC.
Park Avenue Plaza, 55 East 52nd Street, New York NY 10055. 212/909-1100. **Contact:** Human Resources. **World Wide Web address:** http://www rgh.com. **Description:** A holding company whose subsidiaries operate primarily in the areas of property and casualty insurance. **Common positions include:** Accountant/Auditor; Attorney; Financial Analyst. **Educational backgrounds include:** Accounting; Business Administration; Economics; Finance. **Benefits:** Dental Insurance; Disability Coverage; Life Insurance; Medical Insurance; Pension Plan; Savings Plan; Tuition Assistance. **Corporate headquarters location:** This Location. **Subsidiaries include:** Reliance Insurance; Reliance National; Reliance Reinsurance; Reliance Surety; RelianceDirect.

RELIASTAR FINANCIAL CORPORATION
20 Washington Avenue South, Minneapolis MN 55401. 612/372-1178. **Fax:** 612/342-3066. **Contact:** Human Resources. **World Wide Web address:** http://www.reliastar.com. **Description:** An insurance and financial services company specializing in both group and individual lines of insurance. Founded in 1884. **NOTE:** Second and third shifts are offered. **Common positions include:** Accountant; Administrative Assistant; Auditor; Computer Operator; Computer Programmer; MIS Specialist; Sales Rep.; Software Engineer; Systems Analyst; Underwriter/Assistant Underwriter. **Educational backgrounds include:** Accounting; Business Administration; Communications; Computer Science; Economics; Finance; Marketing; Software Development; Software Tech. Support. **Benefits:** 401(k); Daycare Assistance; Dental Insurance; Disability Coverage; Employee Discounts; Financial Planning Assistance; Flexible Schedule; Life Insurance; Medical Insurance; Pension Plan; Profit Sharing; Public Transit Available; Tuition Assistance. **Special programs:** Internships. **Corporate headquarters location:** This Location. **Other U.S. locations:** Nationwide.

RISK ENTERPRISE MANAGEMENT, LTD.
59 Maiden Lane, New York NY 10038. 212/530-7000. **Contact:** Human Resources. **Description:** Risk Enterprise Management, Ltd. is an underwriter of commercial insurance. **Corporate headquarters location:** This Location.

ROYAL & SUNALLIANCE USA
P.O. Box 1000, Charlotte NC 28201. 704/522-2000. **Contact:** Personnel. **World Wide Web address:** http://www.royalsunalliance-usa.com. **Description:** Provides commercial property and casualty insurance as well as personal and specialty insurance. **Corporate headquarters location:** This Location. **Parent company:** Royal & SunAlliance Insurance Group plc (London, England).

SAFECO INSURANCE COMPANIES
2800 West Higgins Road, Suite 1100, Hoffman Estates IL 60195. 847/490-2203. **Fax:** 847/490-2452. **Recorded jobline:** 800/753-5330. **Contact:** Human Resources Manager. **World Wide Web address:** http://www.safeco.com. **Description:** An insurance company offering personal, homeowner's, auto, commercial, property, casualty, life, and health insurance products and services. **NOTE:** Entry-level positions are offered. **Common positions include:** Adjuster; Administrative Assistant; Attorney; Claim Rep.; Customer Service Rep.; Financial Analyst; Underwriter/Assistant Underwriter. **Educational backgrounds include:** Accounting; Business; Communications; Computer Science; Economics; Finance; Liberal Arts; Marketing; Mathematics. **Benefits:** Dental Insurance; Disability Coverage; Employee Discounts; Life Insurance; Medical Insurance; Pension Plan; Profit Sharing; Savings Plan; Tuition Assistance. **Special programs:** Internships; Training. **Corporate headquarters location:** Seattle WA. **Parent company:** Safeco Insurance Corporation. DAQ.

SAFECO INSURANCE CORPORATION
Safeco Plaza, Seattle WA 98185. 206/545-5000. **Contact:** Personnel Director. **World Wide Web address:** http://www.safeco.com. **Description:** A diversified financial services company with operations including property and liability, life and health insurance, pension plans, mutual funds, commercial credit, and real estate development. **Common positions include:** Accountant; Actuary; Administrator; Advertising Clerk; Attorney; Buyer; Claim Rep.; Computer Programmer; Customer Service Rep.e; Purchasing Agent/Manager; Systems Analyst; Technical Writer/Editor; Underwriter/Assistant Underwriter. **Educational backgrounds include:** Accounting; Business Administration; Computer Science; Economics; Finance; Liberal Arts; Marketing; Mathematics. **Benefits:** Daycare Assistance; Disability Coverage; Life Insurance; Medical Insurance; Pension Plan; Tuition Assistance. **Special programs:** Internships. **Corporate headquarters location:** This Location. **Subsidiaries include:** Safeco Insurance Companies.

ST. PAUL COMPANIES
385 Washington Street, St. Paul MN 55102. 651/310-7911. **Contact:** Personnel. **World Wide Web address:** http://www.stpaul.com. **Description:** Provides property-liability and life insurance services. **Corporate headquarters location:** This Location.

THE SEIBELS BRUCE GROUP, INC.
P.O. Box 1, Columbia SC 29201. 803/748-2000. **Physical address:** 1501 Lady Street, Columbia SC. **Contact:** Human Resources. **Description:** A property and casualty insurance company. Founded in 1869. **Corporate headquarters location:** This Location. **Subsidiaries include:** Agency Specialty of Kentucky, Inc.; Agency Specialty, Inc.; Catawba Insurance Company; Consolidated American Insurance Company; FLT Plus, Inc.; Forest Lake Travel Service, Inc.; Investors National Life Insurance Company of South Carolina; Kentucky Insurance Company; Policy Finance Company; Seibels Bruce Service Corporation; Seibels, Bruce & Company; South Carolina Insurance Company. **L**

SOUTHERN TRUST INSURANCE CO.
P.O. Box 250, Macon GA 31202-0250. 912/743-7442. **Contact:** Human Resources. **Description:** Operates a multi-line property/casualty insurance company. **Common positions include:** Accountant/Auditor; Claim Rep.; Computer Programmer; Data Entry Clerk; Marketing Specialist; Systems Analyst; Underwriter/Assistant Underwriter. **Educational**

backgrounds include: Accounting; Business Administration; Computer Science; Finance. Benefits: Bonus Award/Plan; Dental Insurance; Disability Coverage; Life Insurance; Medical Insurance; Tuition Assistance. Corporate headquarters location: This Location.

THE STANDARD
1100 SW Sixth Avenue, Mail Code P2C, Portland OR 97204. 503/321-7000. Recorded jobline: 503/321-6736. Contact: Human Resources. World Wide Web address: http://www.standard.com. Description: Provides individual and group insurance and retirement plan services nationwide. NOTE: Jobseekers should apply in person. Benefits: Daycare Assistance; Dental Insurance; Disability Coverage; Life Insurance; Medical Insurance; Pension Plan; Savings Plan; Tuition Assistance; Vision Insurance. Corporate headquarters location: This Location.

STATE FARM INSURANCE
One State Farm Plaza, Bloomington IL 61710. 309/766-2311. Contact: Human Resources. World Wide Web address: http://www.statefarm.com. Description: Provides homeowner's, health, auto, and life insurance. Common positions include: Accountant/Auditor; Actuary; Architect; Attorney; Civil Engineer; Computer Programmer; Electrical/Electronics Engineer; Industrial Engineer; Mechanical Engineer; Structural Engineer; Systems Analyst. Educational backgrounds include: Accounting; Computer Science; Engineering. Benefits: 401(k); Dental Insurance; Disability Coverage; Life Insurance; Medical Insurance; Pension Plan; Tuition Assistance. Special programs: Internships. Corporate headquarters location: This Location.

TIAA-CREF
730 Third Avenue, New York NY 10017. 212/490-9000. Contact: Personnel. World Wide Web address: http://www.tiaa-cref.org. Description: TIAA-CREF provides insurance and investment options for current and retired teachers. Corporate headquarters location: This Location.

TALBERT MEDICAL GROUP
9930 Talbert Avenue, Fountain Valley CA 92708. 714/964-6229. Contact: Personnel. Description: An HMO that offers a full range of health care products and services to over 900,000 people in California, Nevada, Utah, Arizona, Colorado, New Mexico, and Guam. Services include third-party administrative plans, and indemnity medical, group life, and workers' compensation insurance. Corporate headquarters location: This Location.

TORCHMARK CORPORATION
P.O. Box 2612, Birmingham AL 35202. 205/325-4200. Contact: Human Resources. World Wide Web address: http://www.torchmarkcorp.com. Description: A holding company. Corporate headquarters location: This Location. Subsidiaries include: American Income Holdings, Inc., through subsidiary American Income Life Insurance Company, offers individual supplemental life and fixed-benefit accident and health insurance through sponsored marketing programs with labor union locals, credit unions, and other associations; Family Service Life Insurance markets life insurance and annuities to fund prearranged funerals; Globe Life and Accident Insurance Company offers individual life and health insurance through direct response and independent agents; Liberty National offers individual life and health insurance and annuities through a home service sales force; United American Insurance Company offers Medicare supplement and other individual health, life, and annuity products through independent agents; United Investors Life Insurance Company offers individual life and annuity products; Waddell & Reed, Inc. is engaged in institutional investment management services and offers individual financial planning and products including life insurance, annuities, and mutual funds; Torch Energy provides management services with respect to oil and gas production and development, and engages in energy property acquisitions and dispositions, oil and gas product marketing, and well operations.

TRANSATLANTIC HOLDINGS, INC.
80 Pine Street, 7th Floor, New York NY 10005. 212/770-2000. Contact: Human Resources . World Wide Web address: http://www.transre.com. Description: An insurance holding company providing property and casualty reinsurance through its subsidiaries. Corporate headquarters location: This Location. Subsidiaries include: Transatlantic Reinsurance Company and Putnam Reinsurance Company provide general liability, fire, inland marine, workers' compensation, automobile liability, and medical malpractice insurance.

THE TRAVELERS PROPERTY AND CASUALTY COMPANY
P.O. Box 8112, Walnut Creek CA 94596. 925/945-4000. Contact: Human Resources. E-mail address: careers@travelers.com. World Wide Web address: http://www.travelers.com. Description: Provides property and casualty insurance. NOTE: Part-time jobs are offered. Common positions include: Administrative Assistant; Licensed Practical Nurse; Medical Assistant; Registered Nurse. Educational backgrounds include: Health Care. Benefits: 401(k); Dental Insurance; Disability Coverage; Employee Discounts; Job Sharing; Life Insurance; Medical Insurance; Tuition Assistance. Corporate headquarters location: Hartford CT.

TRENWICK GROUP INC.
One Canterbury Green, Stamford CT 06901. 203/353-5500. Contact: Human Resources. Description: A holding company. Corporate headquarters location: This Location. Subsidiaries include: Trenwick America Reinsurance Corporation reinsures property and casualty risks primarily written by U.S. insurance companies. Virtually all of Trenwick America's business is produced by reinsurance brokers. Trenwick America divides its business into three distinct categories: facultative, treaty, and special programs. The company is authorized to write reinsurance nationwide.

TRIGON BLUE CROSS BLUE SHIELD
2221 Edward Holland Drive, Mail Drop 41A, Richmond VA 23230. Recorded jobline: 804/354-2800. Contact: Recruitment & Staffing. World Wide Web address: http://www.trigon.com. Description: A health insurance provider. NOTE: Interested jobseekers should call the jobline to obtain the job code number. A separate resume must be submitted for each position to which you are applying. Please make sure that all resumes are in a scannable form. Common positions include: Actuary; Claim Representative; Systems Analyst; Underwriter/Assistant Underwriter. Educational backgrounds include: Business Administration; Health Care. Benefits: 401(k); Daycare Assistance; Dental Insurance; Disability Coverage; Employee Discounts; Life Insurance; Medical Insurance; Pension Plan; Savings Plan; Tuition Assistance. Corporate headquarters location: This Location. Other U.S. locations: Roanoke VA.

TRUSTMARK INSURANCE COMPANY
400 Field Drive, Lake Forest IL 60045. 847/615-1500. **Contact:** Human Resources. **World Wide Web address:** http://www.trustmarkinsurance.com. **Description:** A legal reserve life insurance company. Trustmark Insurance Company issues a wide variety of individual and group life, disability, annuity, hospital, and medical policies, as well as administrative service-only arrangements for larger groups. **Common positions include:** Accountant/Auditor; Actuary; Claim Rep.; Customer Service Rep.; Marketing Specialist; Systems Analyst; Technical Writer/Editor; Underwriter/Assistant Underwriter. **Educational backgrounds include:** Accounting; Business Administration; Computer Science; Liberal Arts; Mathematics. **Benefits:** Dental Insurance; Disability Coverage; Life Insurance; Medical Insurance; Pension Plan; Savings Plan. **Corporate headquarters location:** This Location. **Other U.S. locations:** Nationwide.

TUFTS HEALTH PLAN
333 Wyman Street, Waltham MA 02154. 781/466-9400. **Contact:** Human Resources. **World Wide Web address:** http://www.tufts-healthplan.com. **Description:** A health maintenance organization offering hospital coverage, doctors in private practice, emergency coverage, and coverage for student dependents. Tufts Health Plan also offers a range of fitness benefits. **Corporate headquarters location:** This Location. **Other U.S. locations:** NH.

21ST CENTURY INSURANCE GROUP
P.O. Box 2000, Woodland Hills CA 91365. 818/704-3700. **Fax:** 818/704-3485. **Contact:** Human Resources. **World Wide Web address:** http://www.21stcenturyinsurance.com. **Description:** Provides automobile insurance. **Common positions include:** Accountant/Auditor; Adjuster; Claim Representative; Computer Programmer; Systems Analyst. **Educational backgrounds include:** Business Administration; Liberal Arts. **Benefits:** 401(k); Dental Insurance; Life Insurance; Medical Insurance; Pension Plan. **Special programs:** Training. **Corporate headquarters location:** This Location.

UNION FIDELITY LIFE INSURANCE CO.
4850 Street Road, Trevose PA 19049. 215/953-3000. **Contact:** Human Resources. **Description:** An insurance company specializing in accident policies and life insurance. **Corporate headquarters location:** This Location.

UNITED HERITAGE MUTUAL LIFE INSURANCE COMPANY
P.O. Box 48, Nampa ID 83653-0048. 208/466-7856. **Contact:** Human Resources Director. **World Wide Web address:** http://www.unitedheritage.com. **Description:** Provides life insurance. **Corporate headquarters location:** This Location.

UNITED INSURANCE COMPANIES INC.
4001 McEwen, Suite 200, Dallas TX 75244. 972/392-6700. **Fax:** 972/392-6737. **Contact:** Human Resources. **Description:** Offers health and life insurance. **NOTE:** Entry-level positions are offered. **Common positions include:** Accountant/Auditor; Actuary; Claim Rep.; Clerical Supervisor; Computer Programmer; Customer Service Rep.; MIS Specialist; Systems Analyst; Typist/Word Processor; Underwriter/Assistant Underwriter. **Educational backgrounds include:** Accounting; Computer Science; Health Care. **Benefits:** 401(k); Daycare Assistance; Dental Insurance; Disability Coverage; Employee Discounts; Life Insurance; Medical Insurance; Profit Sharing; Tuition Assistance. **Special programs:** Training. **Corporate headquarters location:** This Location.

Other U.S. locations: Glendale AZ; Lakewood CO; St. Petersburg FL; Norcross GA; Oklahoma City OK; Sioux Falls SD.

UNITED SERVICES AUTOMOBILE ASSOC.
9800 Fredericksburg Road, San Antonio TX 78288. 210/498-2211. **Fax:** 210/498-1489. **Recorded jobline:** 210/498-1289. **Contact:** Employment. **World Wide Web address:** http://www.usaa.com. **Description:** An integrated family of companies providing insurance and financial products and services to officers of the United States Armed Forces and their families. Products and services include automobile, life, health, property, and rental insurance; a family of mutual funds; credit cards; calling cards; and a federal savings bank (USAA Federal Savings Bank). Members also receive discounts from certain companies. **NOTE:** USAA only accepts resumes and cover letters for jobs listed on the USAA jobline. The USAA jobline is updated Monday through Friday at 5:00 p.m. The company prefers jobseekers to fax their resumes if possible. **Common positions include:** Accountant; Actuary; Adjuster; Administrative Manager; Aircraft Mechanic/Engine Specialist; Attorney; Blue-Collar Worker Supervisor; Broadcast Technician; Budget Analyst; Civil Engineer; Claim Rep.; Clerical Supervisor; Computer Programmer; Construction and Building Inspector; Construction Contractor; Cost Estimator; Counselor; Customer Service Rep.; Designer; Dietician/Nutritionist; Draftsperson; Economist; Editor; Education Administrator; Electrical/Electronics Engineer; Electrician; Financial Analyst; General Manager; Health Services Manager; Human Resources Manager; Insurance Agent/Broker; Librarian; Library Technician; Licensed Practical Nurse; Management Analyst/Consultant; Management Trainee; Medical Records Technician; Operations/Production Manager; Property and Real Estate Manager; Public Relations Specialist; Purchasing Agent/Manager; Quality Control Supervisor; Radio/TV Announcer/Broadcaster; Real Estate Agent; Registered Nurse; Reporter; Services Sales Rep.; Statistician; Systems Analyst; Teacher/Professor; Technical Writer/Editor; Transportation/Traffic Specialist; Underwriter/Assistant Underwriter; Wholesale and Retail Buyer. **Educational backgrounds include:** Accounting; Bachelor of Arts; Business Administration; Communications; Computer Science; Finance; Liberal Arts. **Benefits:** Dental Insurance; Disability Coverage; Employee Discounts; Life Insurance; Medical Insurance; Pension Plan; Smoke-free; Tuition Assistance. **Special programs:** Internships. **Corporate headquarters location:** This Location. **Other U.S. locations:** Sacramento CA; Colorado Springs CO; Tampa FL; Norfolk VA; Reston VA; Seattle WA.

UNITED WISCONSIN SERVICES, INC.
401 West Michigan Street, Milwaukee WI 53203. 414/226-6900. **Contact:** Employment. **World Wide Web address:** http://www.uwz.com. **Description:** A leading provider of managed health care products and services. The company's three primary product lines are health maintenance organization products including Compcare Health Services Insurance Corporation, Valley Health Plan, Inc., HMO of Wisconsin Insurance Corporation, and certain point-of-service products managed by Compcare and Valley; small group preferred provider organization products sold through American Medical Security, the company's joint venture partner in the marketing and administration of low-cost health insurance primarily to groups of 100 or fewer on behalf of the company; and specialty managed care and other products including dental, life, disability, and workers' compensation products, managed care

consulting, electronic claim submission, pharmaceutical management, and managed mental health services. **Corporate headquarters location:** This Location.

UNITEDHEALTH GROUP
P.O. Box 1459, Mail Routing 008-T143, Minneapolis MN 55440. 952/936-1300. **Contact:** Human Resources. **World Wide Web address:** http://www.unitedhealthgroup.com. **Description:** A managed health care company with a nationwide network of owned/managed health plans and integrated specialty companies (pharmaceutical, mental health/substance abuse, and workers' compensation). **Benefits:** Dental Insurance; Disability Coverage; Life Insurance; Tuition Assistance. **Corporate headquarters location:** This Location.

UNITRIN, INC.
One East Wacker Drive, Chicago IL 60601. 312/661-4600. **Toll-free phone:** 800/999-0546. **Contact:** Human Resources. **World Wide Web address:** http://www.unitrin.com. **Description:** A financial services company with subsidiaries engaged in three business areas: life and health insurance, property and casualty insurance, and consumer finance. **Common positions include:** Accountant; Attorney; Auditor; Paralegal. **Educational backgrounds include:** Accounting; Finance. **Benefits:** 401(k); Casual Dress - Daily; Dental Insurance; Disability Coverage; Flexible Schedule; Life Insurance; Medical Insurance; Pension Plan; Profit Sharing; Sick Days (6 - 10); Tuition Assistance. **Special programs:** Internships; Summer Jobs. **Corporate headquarters location:** This Location. **President/CEO:** Richard Vie.

UNUMPROVIDENT CORPORATION
2211 Congress Street, Portland ME 04122. 207/770-2211. **Contact:** Human Resources Consultant. **World Wide Web address:** http://www.unum.com. **Description:** An insurance company providing income protection to small and medium-sized employers through a broad range of life, health, disability, and retirement products. **Corporate headquarters location:** This Location.
Other U.S. locations:
- One Fountain Square, Chattanooga TN 37401-7109. 423/755-1011.

UTICA NATIONAL INSURANCE GROUP
180 Genessee Street, P.O. Box 530, New Hartford NY 13413. 315/734-2292. **Fax:** 315/734-2495. **Contact:** Human Resources Department. **World Wide Web address:** http://www.uticanational.com. **Description:** Provides property and casualty insurance. **Common positions include:** Accountant/Auditor; Actuary; Adjuster; Claim Rep.; Computer Programmer; Customer Service Rep.; Economist; Human Resources Manager; Systems Analyst; Underwriter/Assistant Underwriter. **Educational backgrounds include:** Accounting; Business; Communications; Computer Science; Economics; Finance; Liberal Arts. **Benefits:** 401(k); Dental Insurance; Disability Coverage; Employee Discounts; Life Insurance; Medical Insurance; Pension Plan; Profit Sharing; Tuition Assistance. **Corporate headquarters location:** This Location.

VERMONT MUTUAL INSURANCE CO.
P.O. Box 188, Montpelier VT 05601. 802/229-7623. **Physical address:** 89 State Street, Montpelier VT 05602. **Contact:** Human Resources. **Description:** A property and casualty insurance company. **Common positions include:** Accountant; Adjuster; Claim Rep.; Clerical Supervisor; Computer Programmer; Support Personnel; Systems Analyst; Underwriter. **Benefits:** Dental Insurance; Disability Coverage;

Life Insurance; Medical Insurance; Pension Plan; Profit Sharing; Savings Plan. **Corporate headquarters location:** This Location. **Subsidiaries include:** Granite Mutual Insurance Company; Northern Security Insurance Company.

VISION SERVICE PLAN
3333 Quality Drive, Rancho Cordova CA 95670. 916/851-5000. **Fax:** 916/851-4858. **Recorded jobline:** 916/851-4700. **Contact:** Corporate Recruiter. **World Wide Web address:** http://www.vsp.com. **Description:** Sells and administers a prepaid vision care plan as an employee benefit. **Common positions include:** Accountant; Computer Programmer; Customer Service Rep.; Economist; Financial Analyst; Human Resources Manager; Public Relations Specialist; Purchasing Agent; Systems Analyst; Technical Writer. **Educational backgrounds include:** Accounting; Business Administration; Computer Science; Finance; Health Care; Marketing. **Benefits:** Dental Insurance; Disability Coverage; Employee Discounts; Life Insurance; Medical Insurance; Tuition Assistance. **Special programs:** Internships. **Corporate headquarters location:** This Location. **Subsidiaries include:** Altair Eyewear.

WATTSHEALTH FOUNDATION, INC.
3405 West Imperial Highway, Inglewood CA 90303. 310/412-3521. **Fax:** 310/412-7129. **Recorded jobline:** 310/680-3188. **Contact:** Human Resources Manager. **World Wide Web address:** http://www.wattshealth.com. **Description:** A health maintenance organization. **Company slogan:** A commitment to caring. **Common positions include:** Administrative Assistant; Claim Rep.; Controller; Human Resources Manager; Nurse Practitioner; Physician; Radiological Technologist; Registered Nurse; Social Worker. **Educational backgrounds include:** Business Administration; Health Care. **Benefits:** 403(b); Dental Insurance; Disability Coverage; Employee Discounts; Life Insurance; Medical Insurance; Pension Plan; Sick Days (6 - 10); Tuition Assistance; Vacation Days (6 - 10). **Corporate headquarters location:** This Location. **Subsidiaries include:** UHP Healthcare (also at this location). **Parent company:** WATTSHealth Systems, Inc.

WAUSAU INSURANCE COMPANIES
P.O. Box 8017, Wausau WI 54402. 715/842-0747. **Contact:** Human Resources. **World Wide Web address:** http://www.wausau.com. **Description:** A business insurance company selling casualty, property, and other commercial insurance products to medium- and large-sized companies through roughly 100 service offices located throughout the United States. **Corporate headquarters location:** This Location.

WELLPOINT HEALTH NETWORKS INC.
One WellPoint Way, Thousand Oaks CA 91362. 818/703-4000. **Physical address:** 4553 La Tienda Drive, Thousand Oaks CA. **Contact:** Human Resources Manager. **World Wide Web address:** http://www.wellpoint.com. **Description:** Wllp[oint Health Networks provides health and life insurance through Blue Cross of California and UNICARE. **Corporate headquarters location:** This Location.

WEST COAST LIFE INSURANCE CO.
P.O. Box 193892, San Francisco CA 94119. 415/591-8383. **Toll-free phone:** 800/366-9378. **Fax:** 415/591-7504. **Contact:** Human Resources. **E-mail address:** wcl@wclife.com. **World Wide Web address:** http://www.wclife.com. **Description:** Offers a complete range of life insurance services. **Common positions include:** Administrative Assistant; Claim Rep.; Customer Service Rep.;

Human Resources Manager; Insurance Agent/Broker; Management Trainee; Operations/ Production Manager; Statistician; Systems Analyst; Underwriter/Assistant Underwriter. **Educational backgrounds include:** Accounting; Business; Communications; Computer Science; Economics; Finance; Liberal Arts; Marketing; MBA; Microsoft Office; Public Relations; Software Tech. Support; Spreadsheets. **Benefits:** 401(k); Casual Dress - Daily; Dental Insurance; Disability Coverage; Employee Discounts; Life Insurance; Medical Insurance; Pension Plan; Profit Sharing; Public Transit Available; Tuition Assistance. **Corporate headquarters location:** This Location. **Parent company:** Protective Life Insurance.

WILLIS CORROON CORPORATION
26 Century Boulevard, Nashville TN 37214. 615/872-3000. **Recorded jobline:** 615/872-6343. **Contact:** Employment Services. **World Wide Web address:** http://www.willis.com. **Description:** An insurance company that provides program design, risk assessment, risk control services, risk strategy, and risk transfer transactions. Founded in 1905. **Common positions include:** Account Manager; Account Rep.; Adjuster; Administrative Assistant; Claim Representative; Controller; Financial Analyst; Insurance Agent/Broker; Systems Analyst. **Educational backgrounds include:** Accounting; Business Administration; Finance; Mathematics. **Benefits:** 401(k); Dental Insurance; Disability

Coverage; Employee Discounts; Life Insurance; Medical Insurance; Pension Plan; Savings Plan; Tuition Assistance. **Corporate headquarters location:** This Location.

ZENITH INSURANCE COMPANY
P.O. Box 9055, Van Nuys CA 91409. 818/713-1000. **Fax:** 818/592-0265. **Contact:** Personnel. **World Wide Web address:** http://www.zic.com. **Description:** Provides workers' compensation insurance. **Common positions include:** Accountant; Attorney; Claim Rep.; Computer Programmer; Registered Nurse; Underwriter. **Educational backgrounds include:** Accounting; Business Administration; Communications; Computer Science; Health Care. **Benefits:** 401(k); Dental Insurance; Disability Coverage; Life Insurance; Medical Insurance; Tuition Assistance. **Corporate headquarters location:** This Location. **Other U.S. locations:** IL; PA; TX; UT. **Parent company:** Zenith National Insurance Corp.

ZURICH DIRECT
1400 American Lane, Schaumburg IL 60173. 847/969-3500. **Contact:** Human Resources. **World Wide Web address:** http://www.zurichdirect.com. **Description:** A life insurance company with worldwide operations. **Corporate headquarters location:** This Location. **Parent company:** Zurich Kemper Life.

For more information on career opportunities in insurance:

Associations

ALLIANCE OF AMERICAN INSURERS
3025 Highland Parkway, Suite 800, Downers Grove IL 60515. 630/724-2100. World Wide Web address: http://www.allianceai.org.

HEALTH INSURANCE ASSOCIATION OF AMERICA
555 13th Street NW, Suite 600E, Washington DC 20004. 202/824-1600. World Wide Web address: http://www.hiaa.org.

INSURANCE INFORMATION INSTITUTE
110 William Street, New York NY 10038. 212/669-9200. World Wide Web address: http://www.iii.org.

NATIONAL ASSOCIATION OF PROFESSIONAL INSURANCE AGENTS
400 North Washington Street, Alexandria VA 22314. 703/836-9340. World Wide Web address: http://www.pianet.com.

SOCIETY OF ACTUARIES
475 North Martingale Road, Suite 800, Schaumburg IL 60173. 847/706-3500. World Wide Web address: http://www.soa.org.

Directories

INSURANCE ALMANAC
Underwriter Printing and Publishing Company, 50 East Palisade Avenue, Englewood NJ 07631. 201/569-8808. Available at libraries.

INSURANCE PHONE BOOK
Douglas Publications, 2807 North Parham Road, Suite 200, Richmond VA 23294. Toll-free phone: 800/521-8110. World Wide Web address: http://www.douglaspublications.com.

NATIONAL DIRECTORY OF HEALTH PLANS
American Association of Health Plans, 1129 20th Street NW, Suite 600, Washington DC 20036. 202/778-3200. World Wide Web address: http://www.aahp.org.

Magazines

BEST'S REVIEW
A.M. Best Company, Ambest Road, Oldwick NJ 08858. 908/439-2200. World Wide Web address: http://www.ambest.com. Monthly.

INSURANCE JOURNAL
Wells Publishing, 9191 Towne Centre Drive, Suite 550, San Diego, CA 92122-1231. 858/455-7717. World Wide Web address: http://www.insurancejrnl.com.

Online Services

FINANCIAL, ACCOUNTING, AND INSURANCE JOBS PAGE
World Wide Web address: http://www.nationjob.com/financial. This Website provides a list of financial, accounting, and insurance job openings.

THE INSURANCE CAREER CENTER
World Wide Web address: http://connectyou.com/talent. Offers job openings, career resources, and a resume database for jobseekers.

INSURANCE NATIONAL SEARCH
World Wide Web address: http://www.insurancerecruiters.com/insjobs/jobs.htm. Provides a searchable database of job openings in the insurance industry. The site is run by Insurance National Search, Inc.

Manufacturing:
Miscellaneous Consumer

You can expect to find the following types of companies in this chapter:
*Art Supplies • Batteries • Cosmetics and Related Products • Household Appliances and
Audio/Video Equipment • Jewelry, Silverware, and Plated Ware
Miscellaneous Household Furniture and Fixtures • Musical Instruments
Tools • Toys and Sporting Goods*

Some helpful information: *The average salary of machinery operators is approximately
$20,000 - $25,000, while machine repairers earn approximately $20,000 - $28,000
annually. Inspectors, testers, and graders earn between $25,000 and $40,000.
Manufacturing supervisors earn $30,000 per year on average, though many earn more.*

ACE HARDWARE CORPORATION
2200 Kensington Court, Oak Brook IL 60523.
630/990-6600. **Contact:** Director of Human
Resources. **World Wide Web address:**
http://www.acehardware.com. **Description:** A
worldwide dealer-owned cooperative operating
through 5,100 hardware retailers in 62 countries.
Ace Hardware Corporation also produces a line of
hand and power tools, plumbing products, lawn and
garden products, cleaning supplies, and
manufactures a line of paint. **Corporate
headquarters location:** This Location. **Number of
employees nationwide:** 3,000.

ACME UNITED CORPORATION
75 Kings Highway Cutoff, Fairfield CT 06430.
203/332-7330. **Fax:** 203/576-0007. **Contact:**
Human Resources. **World Wide Web address:**
http://www.acmeunited.com. **Description:** A
holding company. **NOTE:** Please send resumes to
Human Resources, P.O. Box 458, Fremont NC
27830. **Benefits:** Pension Plan; Profit Sharing.
Corporate headquarters location: This Location.
Subsidiaries include: Acme United Ltd. (England)
manufactures medical scissors, household scissors
and shears, nail files, and other manicure items.
Acme United Limited (Canada) markets scissors,
rulers, and yardsticks. Emil Schlemper GmbH
(Germany) and Peter Altenbach and Son (Germany)
both manufacture knives, scissors, shears, and
manicure products. **Listed on:** American Stock
Exchange. **Number of employees nationwide:** 570.

ACTION PERFORMANCE COMPANIES
4707 East Baseline Road, Phoenix AZ 85040.
602/337-3700. **Fax:** 602/337-3910. **Contact:**
Human Resources. **World Wide Web address:**
http://www.action-performance.com. **Description:**
Designs, markets, and distributes a line of licensed
motorsports collectibles and consumer merchandise.
Common positions include: Account
Representative; Accountant; AS400 Programmer
Analyst; Customer Service Representative;
Marketing Manager. **Educational backgrounds
include:** Art/Design; AS400 Certification; ASP;
Business Administration; CGI; Computer Science;
HTML; Internet; Microsoft Word. **Benefits:** 401(k);
Dental Insurance; Disability Coverage; Life
Insurance; Medical Insurance. **Corporate
headquarters location:** This Location. **Other U.S.
locations:** Atlanta GA; Boston MA; Charlotte NC.
Listed on: NASDAQ. **Stock exchange symbol:**
ACTN. **Number of employees nationwide:** 600.

ACUSHNET COMPANY
2819 Loker Avenue East, Carlsbad CA 92008.
760/929-0377. **Contact:** Human Resources.

Description: Designs, manufactures, and markets
golf clubs. The company also offers a line of men's
and women's golf and resort clothing, imported
from Italy under the name Como Sport. **Corporate
headquarters location:** This Location.

ADVANCE INTERNATIONAL INC.
1200 Zerega Avenue, Bronx NY 10462. 718/892-
3460. **Contact:** Human Resources. **Description:**
Produces, imports, and exports holiday lighting sets,
craft items, and other plastic products. **Common
positions include:** Collections Agent; Customer
Service Representative; Data Entry Clerk.
Educational backgrounds include: Business
Administration. **Benefits:** Disability Coverage; Life
Insurance; Medical Insurance. **Corporate
headquarters location:** This Location.

AJAY SPORTS, INC.
7001 Orchard Lake Road, Suite 424, West
Bloomfield MI 48322. 248/851-5651. **Contact:**
Human Resources. **Description:** Designs,
manufactures, and markets golf and billiard
accessories through its wholly-owned subsidiary,
Ajay Leisure Products, Inc. Ajay's products are sold
nationwide to discount stores, department stores,
catalog showrooms, and other mass merchandise
outlets. The products manufactured by the company
are sold primarily under the Ajay, Pro Classic,
Private Pro, and Spalding brand names. **Corporate
headquarters location:** This Location.
Subsidiaries include: Leisure Life, Inc.
manufactures and markets outdoor and indoor
casual living furniture. Leisure Life's products are
sold through independent retailers and larger chains
of home and garden stores.

ALADDIN INDUSTRIES, INC.
703 Murfreesboro Road, Nashville TN 37210.
615/748-3000. **Contact:** Lillian Jenkins, Vice
President of Human Resources. **World Wide Web
address:** http://www.aladdin-inc.com. **Description:**
Manufactures hot and cold insulated products,
lamps, and lunch boxes. Founded in 1908. **Common
positions include:** Account Manager; Accountant;
Administrative Assistant; Administrative Manager;
Blue-Collar Worker Supervisor; Budget Analyst;
Buyer; Computer Operator; Computer Programmer;
Controller; Credit Manager; Customer Service
Representative; Dietician; Environmental Engineer;
Finance Director; Financial Analyst; General
Manager; Human Resources Manager; Industrial
Engineer; Industrial Production Manager; Licensed
Practical Nurse; Manufacturing Engineer;
Marketing Manager; Mechanical Engineer;
Operations Manager; Production Manager; Project
Manager; Public Relations Specialist; Quality

Control Supervisor; Registered Nurse; Sales Executive; Sales Manager; Sales Representative; Secretary; Statistician; Systems Analyst; Systems Manager; Vice President. **Educational backgrounds include:** Accounting; Business Administration; Computer Science; Finance; Health Care; Marketing. **Benefits:** 401(k); Dental Insurance; Disability Coverage; Life Insurance; Medical Insurance; Pension Plan; Profit Sharing; Tuition Assistance. **Corporate headquarters location:** This Location. **International locations:** Worldwide. **Listed on:** Privately held. **Annual sales/revenues:** More than $100 million. **Number of employees at this location:** 1,350. **Number of employees worldwide:** 1,600.

ALL-LUMINUM PRODUCTS, INC.
10981 Decatur Road, Philadelphia PA 19154. 215/632-2800. **Contact:** Valerie L. Holmes, Human Resources Manager. **Description:** A manufacturer of casual outdoor and indoor furniture. **Common positions include:** Accountant/Auditor; Blue-Collar Worker Supervisor; Customer Service Representative; Purchasing Agent/Manager; Quality Control Supervisor. **Educational backgrounds include:** Accounting; Business Administration; Marketing. **Benefits:** Dental Insurance; Disability Coverage; Life Insurance; Medical Insurance; Profit Sharing; Savings Plan. **Corporate headquarters location:** This Location.

ALLEN ORGAN COMPANY
150 Locust Street, Macungie PA 18062. 610/966-2200. **Contact:** Harold Bloch, Personnel Manager. **World Wide Web address:** http://www.allenorgan.com. **Description:** A manufacturer of electronic keyboard musical instruments including digital computer organs and related accessories. **Corporate headquarters location:** This Location.

ALPINE HEALTH INDUSTRIES
1525 West Business Park Drive, Orem UT 84058. 801/225-5525x123. **Toll-free phone:** 800/572-5076. **Fax:** 801/225-0956. **Contact:** Gary Dastrup, Director. **Description:** Manufactures vitamins, over-the-counter drugs, shampoos, and conditioners. Alpine Health Industries manufactures its products under private and custom labeling. **NOTE:** Part-time jobs and second and third shifts are offered. **Common positions include:** Account Manager; Accountant; Administrative Assistant; Chemist; Controller; Customer Service Representative; Graphic Designer; Human Resources Manager; Marketing Manager; Marketing Specialist; Production Manager; Purchasing Agent/Manager; Quality Control Supervisor; Sales Executive; Sales Representative; Systems Manager; Vice President of Operations. **Educational backgrounds include:** Accounting; Marketing; Microsoft Word. **Benefits:** 401(k); Casual Dress - Fridays; Dental Insurance; Disability Coverage; Employee Discounts; Life Insurance; Medical Insurance; Sick Days (1 - 5); Tuition Assistance; Vacation Days (1 - 5). **Special programs:** Summer Jobs. **Corporate headquarters location:** Texarkana TX. **Parent company:** Humco Holding Group, International. **Listed on:** Privately held. **President:** Derek Hall. **Annual sales/revenues:** $11 - $20 million. **Number of employees at this location:** 100. **Number of employees nationwide:** 225.

AMANA APPLIANCES
2800 220th Trail, Amana IA 52204. 319/622-2208. **Fax:** 319/622-8286. **Contact:** Human Resources. **Description:** Designs, develops, manufactures, and sells heating, ventilation, and air conditioning products. Amana also manufactures appliances including dishwashers, refrigerators, and microwaves. **Common positions include:**

Accountant/Auditor; Mechanical Engineer. **Educational backgrounds include:** Accounting; Engineering. **Benefits:** Dental Insurance; Disability Coverage; Employee Discounts; Life Insurance; Medical Insurance; Pension Plan; Profit Sharing; Savings Plan; Tuition Assistance. **Corporate headquarters location:** This Location. **Other U.S. locations:** Nationwide. **Parent company:** Raytheon. **Number of employees nationwide:** 8,100.

AMERICAN HOME PRODUCTS CORPORATION
5 Giralda Farms, Madison NJ 07940. 973/660-5000. **Contact:** Human Resources. **World Wide Web address:** http://www.ahp.com. **Description:** Manufactures and markets prescription drugs and medical supplies, packaged medicines, food products, household products, and housewares. Each division operates through one or more of American Home Products Corporation's subsidiaries. Prescription Drugs and Medical Supplies operates through: Wyeth-Ayerst Laboratories (produces ethical pharmaceuticals, biologicals, nutritional products, over-the-counter antacids, vitamins, and sunburn remedies); Fort Dodge Animal Health (veterinary pharmaceuticals and biologicals); Sherwood Medical (medical devices, diagnostic instruments, test kits, and bacteria identification systems); and Corometrics Medical Systems (medical electronic instrumentation for obstetrics and neonatology). The Packaged Medicines segment operates through Whitehall-Robins Healthcare (produces analgesics, cold remedies, and other packaged medicines). The Food Products segment operates through American Home Foods (canned pasta, canned vegetables, specialty foods, mustard, and popcorn). The Household Products and Housewares segment operates through: Boyle-Midway (cleaners, insecticides, air fresheners, waxes, polishes, and other items for home, appliance, and apparel care); Dupli-Color Products (touch-up, refinishing, and other car care and shop-use products); Ekco Products (food containers, commercial baking pans, industrial coatings, food-handling systems, foilware, and plasticware); Ekco Housewares (cookware, cutlery, kitchen tools, tableware and accessories, and padlocks); and Prestige Group (cookware, cutlery, kitchen tools, carpet sweepers, and pressure cookers). **Corporate headquarters location:** This Location. **Number of employees worldwide:** 53,000.

AMERICAN PLASTIC TOYS INC.
799 Ladd Road, Box 100, Walled Lake MI 48390. 248/624-4881. **Contact:** Human Resources. **Description:** Engaged in the manufacture of plastic-injection molded toys. **Common positions include:** Blue-Collar Worker Supervisor; Industrial Engineer; Management Trainee; Operations/Production Manager; Quality Control Supervisor. **Benefits:** Dental Insurance; Disability Coverage; Employee Discounts; Life Insurance; Medical Insurance; Profit Sharing; Tuition Assistance. **Corporate headquarters location:** This Location. **Number of employees nationwide:** 500.

AMERICAN SAFETY RAZOR COMPANY
One Razor Blade Lane, Verona VA 24482. 540/248-8000. **Fax:** 540/248-9773. **Contact:** Reginald Ryals, Personnel Administrator. **Description:** Designs, manufactures, and markets razors and blades, custom bar soap, and cotton products. **Common positions include:** Accountant/Auditor; Design Engineer; Manufacturing Engineer; Plastics Engineer; Sales Representative. **Benefits:** Life Insurance; Pension Plan; Retirement Plan. **Corporate headquarters location:** This Location. **Other U.S. locations:** Maplewood NJ; Union NJ;

Cleveland OH; Dayton OH. **International locations:** Canada; England; Mexico; Puerto Rico. **Operations at this facility include:** Distribution; Manufacturing; Sales. **Listed on:** NASDAQ. **Number of employees nationwide:** 1,630.

AMERICAN SAW & MANUFACTURING
301 Chestnut Street, East Longmeadow MA 01028. 413/525-3961. **Contact:** Director of Employee Relations. **Description:** A manufacturer of cutting tools and related products. **Common positions include:** Accountant/Auditor; Computer Programmer; Customer Service Representative; Designer; Electrical/Electronics Engineer; Human Resources Manager; Mechanical Engineer; Services Sales Representative; Systems Analyst. **Educational backgrounds include:** Accounting; Engineering. **Benefits:** 401(k); Dental Insurance; Disability Coverage; Employee Discounts; Life Insurance; Medical Insurance; Pension Plan; Profit Sharing; Tuition Assistance. **Corporate headquarters location:** This Location. **Listed on:** Privately held. **Number of employees at this location:** 600.

AMERICAN TACK & HARDWARE
25 Robert Pitt Drive, Monsey NY 10952. 914/352-2400. **Fax:** 914/425-3554. **Contact:** Human Resources. **Description:** Manufactures a broad range of decorative hardware items. **Common positions include:** Accountant/Auditor; Administrative Manager; Budget Analyst; Buyer; Computer Operator; Computer Programmer; Credit Manager; Customer Service Representative; Designer; Electrician; Financial Manager; Industrial Engineer; Inspector/Tester/Grader; Machinist; Manufacturer's/Wholesaler's Sales Rep.; Market Research Analyst; Marketing Manager; Mechanical Engineer; Payroll Clerk; Postal Clerk/Mail Carrier; Purchasing Agent/Manager; Quality Control Supervisor; Receptionist; Secretary; Services Sales Representative; Stock Clerk; Systems Analyst; Tool and Die Maker; Truck Driver. **Educational backgrounds include:** Accounting; Business Administration; Computer Science; Liberal Arts; Marketing. **Benefits:** Disability Coverage; Employee Discounts; Life Insurance; Medical Insurance; Tuition Assistance. **Corporate headquarters location:** This Location. **Number of employees at this location:** 225.

AMES COMPANY
P.O. Box 1774, Parkersburg WV 26101. 304/424-3000. **Fax:** 304/424-3337. **Contact:** Tom Davies, Director of Human Resources. **World Wide Web address:** http://www.ames.com. **Description:** Manufactures hand tools. **Common positions include:** Design Engineer; Industrial Engineer; Mechanical Engineer; MIS Specialist. **Educational backgrounds include:** Engineering. **Benefits:** 401(k); Dental Insurance; Disability Coverage; Employee Discounts; Life Insurance; Medical Insurance; Pension Plan; Profit Sharing; Savings Plan; Tuition Assistance. **Corporate headquarters location:** This Location. **Other U.S. locations:** Nationwide. **International locations:** Canada. **Parent company:** US Industries. **Listed on:** New York Stock Exchange. **Stock exchange symbol:** USI. **Annual sales/revenues:** More than $100 million. **Number of employees at this location:** 1,000.

ARMATRON INTERNATIONAL INC.
2 Main Street, Melrose MA 02176. 781/321-2300. **Contact:** Cindie McCue, Human Resources Director. **Description:** Operates through two segments: The Consumer Products segment manufactures and distributes bug killers, chipper/shredders, and leaf-eaters; and The Industrial Products segment imports and sells radios to a large automobile manufacturer. **Common positions include:** Accountant/Auditor; Administrator; Blue-Collar Worker Supervisor; Buyer; Computer Programmer; Credit Manager; Customer Service Representative; Department Manager; Draftsperson; Human Resources Manager; Industrial Engineer; Mechanical Engineer; Public Relations Specialist; Purchasing Agent/Manager; Quality Control Supervisor. **Educational backgrounds include:** Accounting; Business Administration; Computer Science; Engineering; Finance; Liberal Arts; Marketing; Mathematics. **Benefits:** 401(k); Dental Insurance; Disability Coverage; Employee Discounts; Life Insurance; Medical Insurance; Savings Plan; Tuition Assistance. **Corporate headquarters location:** This Location. **Operations at this facility include:** Administration; Manufacturing; Research and Development; Sales; Service.

ARROW INDUSTRIES
2625 Beltline Road, Carrollton TX 75006. 972/416-6500x238. **Contact:** Kyle Marlin, Vice President of Human Resources. **Description:** A manufacturer, processor, and packager of polyethylene bags, household aluminum foil, paper plates, charcoal, lighter fluid, beans, rice, popcorn, and spices. **Common positions include:** Accountant/Auditor; Blue-Collar Worker Supervisor; Computer Programmer; Department Manager; Human Resources Manager; Manufacturer's/Wholesaler's Sales Rep.; Mechanical Engineer; Operations/Production Manager; Purchasing Agent/Manager; Quality Control Supervisor; Transportation/Traffic Specialist. **Educational backgrounds include:** Accounting; Business Administration; Computer Science; Engineering; Marketing. **Benefits:** Dental Insurance; Life Insurance; Medical Insurance; Profit Sharing. **Corporate headquarters location:** This Location.

ART LEATHER
GROSS NATIONAL PRODUCT
45-10 94th Street, Elmhurst NY 11373. 718/699-9696. **Fax:** 718/699-9621. **Contact:** Julio C. Barreneche, Human Resources Director. **World Wide Web address:** http://www.artleather.com. **Description:** A manufacturer of photo albums and folios. Partnered with Art Leather, Gross National Product manufactures photo image box display cases. **Common positions include:** Advertising Clerk; Buyer; Civil Engineer; Clerical Supervisor; Computer Programmer; Credit Manager; Customer Service Representative; General Manager; Human Resources Manager; Purchasing Agent/Manager. **Educational backgrounds include:** Business Administration; Computer Science; Engineering. **Benefits:** Disability Coverage; Employee Discounts; Life Insurance; Medical Insurance; Profit Sharing. **Corporate headquarters location:** This Location. **Number of employees at this location:** 540.

AUTOMATED PACKAGING SYSTEMS
10175 Philipp Parkway, Streetsboro OH 44241. 330/342-2000. **Fax:** 330/342-2485. **Contact:** Cheryl Evans, Employment Manager. **Description:** Manufactures plastic bags. **Common positions include:** Accountant; Buyer; Customer Service Rep.; Draftsperson; Field Engineer; Human Resources Manager; Manufacturer's/ Wholesaler's Sales Rep.; Marketing Specialist; Mechanical Engineer; Purchasing Agent; Quality Control Supervisor. **Educational backgrounds include:** Accounting; Engineering; Marketing. **Benefits:** 401(k); Dental Insurance; Disability Coverage; Life Insurance; Medical Insurance; Tuition Assistance. **Corporate headquarters location:** This Location.

AVEDA CORPORATION
4000 Pheasant Ridge Drive, Blaine MN 55449. 763/783-4000. **Fax:** 763/783-6850. **Recorded jobline:** 763/783-4282. **Contact:** Human Resources. **E-mail address:** jobs@aveda.com. **World Wide Web address:** http://www.aveda.com. **Description:** Manufactures perfume, makeup, and other beauty products. Aveda Corporation also operates salons and retail stores. **Special programs:** Internships. **Internship information:** Candidates should check the company's Website for application procedures. **Corporate headquarters location:** This Location. **Other U.S. locations:** New York NY. **International locations:** Worldwide.

BALDWIN HARDWARE CORPORATION
P.O. Box 15048, Reading PA 19612. 610/777-7811. **Contact:** Human Resources. **World Wide Web address:** http://www.baldwinbrass.com. **Description:** Manufacturer of decorative hardware including handlesets, door knobs, and hinges. The company also manufactures a variety of home decor products including bath accessories, candlesticks, sconces, and both interior and exterior lighting products. **NOTE:** Entry-level positions and second and third shifts are offered. **Common positions include:** Account Manager; Accountant; AS400 Programmer Analyst; Blue-Collar Worker Supervisor; Buyer; Chief Financial Officer; Computer Operator; Computer Support Technician; Customer Service Representative; Design Engineer; Financial Analyst; General Manager; Industrial Engineer; Internet Services Manager; Manufacturing Engineer; Marketing Manager; Marketing Specialist; Mechanical Engineer; Network/Systems Administrator; Operations Manager; Production Manager; Purchasing Agent/Manager; Sales Manager; Sales Representative; Vice President. **Educational backgrounds include:** Accounting; AS400 Certification; Business Administration; Chemistry; Computer Science; Engineering; Finance; Internet Development; Marketing; MBA. **Benefits:** 401(k); Casual Dress - Daily; Dental Insurance; Disability Coverage; Employee Discounts; Life Insurance; Medical Insurance; Pension Plan; Public Transit Available; Relocation Assistance; Sick Days; Tuition Assistance. **Special programs:** Training; Summer Jobs. **Corporate headquarters location:** This Location. **Parent company:** MASCO Corporation.

BALDWIN PIANO & ORGAN COMPANY
4680 Parkway Drive, Suite 200, Mason OH 45040-5301. 513/754-4500. **Fax:** 513/754-4611. **Contact:** Personnel Manager. **World Wide Web address:** http://www.baldwinpiano.com. **Description:** A manufacturer of musical instruments including pianos and other keyboard instruments. **Common positions include:** Accountant/Auditor; Administrator; Advertising Clerk; Computer Programmer; Credit Manager; Customer Service Representative; Electrical/Electronics Engineer; Human Resources Manager; Manufacturer's/Wholesaler's Sales Rep.; Marketing Specialist; Transportation/Traffic Specialist. **Educational backgrounds include:** Accounting; Business Administration; Computer Science; Engineering; Liberal Arts; Marketing. **Benefits:** Dental Insurance; Disability Coverage; Employee Discounts; Life Insurance; Medical Insurance; Pension Plan; Savings Plan; Tuition Assistance. **Corporate headquarters location:** This Location.

BARNHART INDUSTRIES INC.
P.O. Box 278, Barnhart MO 63012. 636/942-3133. **Contact:** Human Resources. **Description:** Manufacturers of feminine hygiene products, garters, elastic notions, sewing accessories, surgical garments, hospital accessories, advertising novelties, and orthodontic appliances. **Common positions include:** Computer Programmer; Cost Estimator; Customer Service Representative; Purchasing Agent/Manager. **Educational backgrounds include:** Business Administration; Computer Science; Marketing. **Benefits:** Medical Insurance. **Corporate headquarters location:** This Location. **Number of employees at this location:** 50.

BASSETT INDUSTRIES, INC.
P.O. Box 626, Bassett VA 24055. 540/629-6000. **Contact:** Director of Human Resources. **Description:** Manufactures and sells a full-line of furniture for the home such as bedroom and dining suites, accent pieces, tables, wall and entertainment units, upholstered sofas, chairs and love seats, recliners, and mattresses and box springs. **Corporate headquarters location:** This Location. **Other U.S. locations:** Nationwide. **Number of employees nationwide:** 7,800.

BATESVILLE CASKET COMPANY, INC.
One Batesville Boulevard, Batesville IN 47006. 812/934-7444. **Contact:** Human Resources. **World Wide Web address:** http://www.batesville.com. **Description:** Manufactures funeral-related products including caskets and urns. **Corporate headquarters location:** This Location. **Parent company:** Hillenbrand Industries, Inc.

BEMIS MANUFACTURING COMPANY
P.O. Box 901, 300 Mill Street, Sheboygan Falls WI 53085-0901. 920/467-4621. **Fax:** 920/467-8573. **Contact:** Ed Collins, Vice President of Human Resources. **E-mail address:** corp@bemismfg.com. **World Wide Web address:** http://www.bemismfg.com. **Description:** Manufactures toilet seats, cutting boards, deck furniture, air purifiers, planters, gutters, and disposable medical products. **Common positions include:** Mechanical Engineer; Sales Representative. **Corporate headquarters location:** This Location.

BIC CORPORATION
500 Bic Drive, Milford CT 06460. 203/783-2000. **Fax:** 203/783-2660. **Contact:** Paul Moyher, Manager, Human Resources Administration. **Description:** Manufactures consumer items including pens, lighters, shavers, and correction fluids. **Common positions include:** Accountant/Auditor; Attorney; Chemist; Computer Programmer; Credit Manager; Customer Service Representative; Designer; Draftsperson; Electrical/Electronics Engineer; Electrician; Financial Analyst; Graphic Artist; Heating/AC/Refrigeration Technician; Human Resources Manager; Industrial Production Manager; Machinist; Management Trainee; Manufacturer's/Wholesaler's Sales Rep.; Marketing Manager; Mechanical Engineer; Operations/Production Manager; Paralegal; Payroll Clerk; Public Relations Specialist; Quality Control Supervisor; Registered Nurse; Secretary; Software Engineer; Stationary Engineer; Systems Analyst; Tool and Die Maker; Transportation/Traffic Specialist. **Educational backgrounds include:** Accounting; Art/Design; Chemistry; Computer Science; Engineering; Marketing. **Benefits:** 401(k); Bonus Award/Plan; Dental Insurance; Disability Coverage; Employee Discounts; Life Insurance; Medical Insurance; Pension Plan; Profit Sharing; Tuition Assistance. **Corporate headquarters location:** This Location. **Number of employees at this location:** 900.

BINNEY & SMITH, INC.
P.O. Box 431, Easton PA 18044-0431. 610/253-6271. **Contact:** David Burford, Director of Human

Resources. **World Wide Web address:** http://www.crayola.com. **Description:** Produces a line of crayons, markers, writing instruments, chalk, clay, artist kits, oils, acrylics, watercolors, and brushes. Brand names include Crayola, Magic Marker, Liquitex, and Artista. **Common positions include:** Accountant/Auditor; Administrative Manager; Blue-Collar Worker Supervisor; Clerical Supervisor; Computer Programmer; Credit Manager; Customer Service Representative; Financial Analyst; General Manager; Human Resources Manager; Management Analyst/ Consultant; Management Trainee; Mechanical Engineer; Public Relations Specialist; Systems Analyst; Technical Writer/Editor; Travel Agent. **Educational backgrounds include:** Accounting; Art/Design; Business Administration; Chemistry; Communications; Computer Science; Economics; Engineering; Finance; Health Care; Liberal Arts; M.D./Medicine; Marketing; Mathematics; Physics. **Benefits:** 401(k); Dental Insurance; Disability Coverage; Employee Discounts; Life Insurance; Medical Insurance; Pension Plan; Profit Sharing; Savings Plan; Tuition Assistance. **Special programs:** Internships. **Corporate headquarters location:** This Location. **Other U.S. locations:** Winfield KS. **Parent company:** Hallmark Corporation. **Number of employees at this location:** 900. **Number of employees nationwide:** 1,200.

BISSELL INC.
2345 Walker Street NW, Grand Rapids MI 49544. 616/453-4451. **Contact:** Human Resources. **World Wide Web address:** http://www.bissell.com. **Description:** Manufactures vacuums, steam cleaners, sweepers, and related parts, accessories, and cleaning formulas. **Common positions include:** Accountant/Auditor; CADD Operator; Computer Programmer; Industrial Engineer; Mechanical Engineer; Sales Manager. **Educational backgrounds include:** Accounting; Business Administration; Engineering; Marketing. **Benefits:** 401(k); Dental Insurance; Disability Coverage; Employee Discounts; Life Insurance; Medical Insurance; Pension Plan; Tuition Assistance. **Special programs:** Internships. **Corporate headquarters location:** This Location. **Other U.S. locations:** Butler PA. **Subsidiaries include:** Bissell Graphics; Bissell Healthcare. **Listed on:** Privately held. **Number of employees at this location:** 800. **Number of employees nationwide:** 2,700.

BLACK & DECKER CORPORATION
701 East Joppa Road, Towson MD 21286. 410/716-3900. **Contact:** Human Resources. **World Wide Web address:** http://www.blackanddecker.com. **Description:** This location houses administrative offices. Overall, Black & Decker is a global marketer and manufacturer of products used in and around the home and for commercial applications. The company is also a major supplier of information technology and services to government and commercial clients worldwide. The company is one of the world's largest producers of power tools, power tool accessories, security hardware, and electric lawn and garden tools. **Common positions include:** Computer-Aided Designer; Electrical/ Electronics Engineer; Mechanical Engineer. **Corporate headquarters location:** This Location.

BLISTEX, INC.
1800 Swift Drive, Oak Brook IL 60523. 630/571-2870. **Contact:** Human Resources. **World Wide Web address:** http://www.blistex.com. **Description:** Manufactures a line of lip care products under the Blistex and DCT brand names. **Corporate headquarters location:** This Location.

BLYTH INDUSTRIES, INC.
100 Field Point Road, Greenwich CT 06830. 203/661-1926. **Contact:** Jane Casey, Vice President/Organizational Development. **World Wide Web address:** http://www.blythindustries. com. **Description:** Designs, manufactures, markets, and distributes an extensive line of home fragrance products including scented candles, outdoor citronella candles, potpourri, and environmental fragrance products. The company also markets a broad range of candle accessories and decorative gift bags. Its products are sold under various brand names including Colonial Candle of Cape Cod, PartyLite Gifts, Carolina Designs, Ambria, Canterbury, Florasense, and FilterMate. The company is also a leading producer of portable heating fuel products sold under the brand names Sterno and Handy Fuel. **Corporate headquarters location:** This Location. **Listed on:** New York Stock Exchange. **Stock exchange symbol:** BTH.

BOSE CORPORATION
The Mountain, Framingham MA 01701-9168. 508/766-6000. **Contact:** Human Resources. **World Wide Web address:** http://www.bose.com. **Description:** Designs and manufactures audio-related consumer electronics products including speakers, stereos, and related stereo components. **Common positions include:** Accountant/Auditor; Buyer; Chemical Engineer; Civil Engineer; Computer Operator; Electrical/Electronics Engineer; Industrial Engineer; Mechanical Engineer. **Educational backgrounds include:** Engineering. **Benefits:** Dental Insurance; Disability Coverage; Employee Discounts; Life Insurance; Medical Insurance; Pension Plan; Savings Plan; Tuition Assistance. **Corporate headquarters location:** This Location. **Other U.S. locations:** OH. **International locations:** Ireland; Mexico.

BRITE STAR MANUFACTURING COMPANY
2900 South 20th Street, Philadelphia PA 19145. 215/271-7600. **Contact:** Mr. Sandy Kinderman, Vice President. **Description:** Manufactures and imports a wide variety of Christmas decorations, trees, and other holiday items. **Common positions include:** Industrial Engineer; Purchasing Agent/Manager. **Educational backgrounds include:** Business Administration; Engineering; Finance; Marketing. **Benefits:** Disability Coverage; Life Insurance; Medical Insurance; Profit Sharing. **Corporate headquarters location:** This Location.

BROTHER INTERNATIONAL CORPORATION
100 Somerset Corporate Boulevard, Bridgewater NJ 08807. 908/704-1700. **Contact:** Human Resources. **World Wide Web address:** http://www. brother.com. **Description:** One of America's largest manufacturers and distributors of personal word processors and portable electronic typewriters. Brother also markets many industrial products, home appliances, and business machines manufactured by its parent company. Founded in 1954. **Corporate headquarters location:** This Location. **Parent company:** Brother Industries, Ltd. **Number of employees nationwide:** 1,300.

BROWNING COMPANY
One Browning Place, Morgan UT 84050. 801/876-2711. **Fax:** 801/876-3331. **Contact:** David W. Rich, Vice President of Human Resources. **Description:** Manufactures sporting goods, rifles, shotguns, boots, safes, and archery products. **Common positions include:** Accountant/Auditor; Administrator; Advertising Clerk; Computer Programmer; Credit Manager; Customer Service Representative; Human Resources Manager; Public Relations Specialist; Purchasing Agent/Manager; Quality Control Supervisor; Systems Analyst;

Technical Writer/Editor. **Educational backgrounds include:** Accounting; Art/Design; Business Administration; Communications; Computer Science; Engineering; Finance; Marketing. **Benefits:** 401(k); Daycare Assistance; Disability Coverage; Employee Discounts; Life Insurance; Medical Insurance; Pension Plan; Tuition Assistance. **Corporate headquarters location:** This Location. **Parent company:** GIAT International (Paris, France). **Listed on:** Privately held. **Annual sales/revenues:** More than $100 million. **Number of employees at this location:** 360.

THE BUCILLA CORPORATION
One Oak Ridge Road, Hazleton PA 18201-9764. 570/384-2525. **Contact:** Kathy Kalce, Director of Human Resources. **World Wide Web address:** http://www.bucilla.com. **Description:** Manufactures needle-craft kits. Founded in 1867. **Common positions include:** Accountant/Auditor; Blue-Collar Worker Supervisor; Customer Service Representative; Manufacturer's/Wholesaler's Sales Rep.; Purchasing Agent/Manager; Systems Analyst. **Educational backgrounds include:** Accounting; Art/Design; Business Administration; Computer Science; Marketing. **Benefits:** Disability Coverage; Employee Discounts; Life Insurance; Medical Insurance; Pension Plan. **Corporate headquarters location:** This Location.

BULOVA CORPORATION
One Bulova Avenue, Woodside NY 11377. 718/204-3384. **Contact:** Mrs. Eleanor Smith, Vice President of Personnel. **Description:** Manufactures and sells a wide variety of watches, clocks, and jewelry for the consumer market. **Common positions include:** Accountant/Auditor; Computer Programmer; Systems Analyst. **Educational backgrounds include:** Business Administration; Computer Science; Marketing. **Benefits:** 401(k); Dental Insurance; Disability Coverage; Employee Discounts; Life Insurance; Medical Insurance; Pension Plan; Savings Plan; Tuition Assistance. **Corporate headquarters location:** This Location. **Number of employees at this location:** 350. **Number of employees nationwide:** 410.

BUSH INDUSTRIES, INC.
One Mason Drive, P.O. Box 460, Jamestown NY 14702-0460. 716/665-2000. **Contact:** Human Resources. **World Wide Web address:** http://www.bushfurniture.com. **Description:** Bush Industries is one of America's leading designers and manufacturers of ready-to-assemble and assembled furniture products. Entertainment furniture, home theater furniture, home and commercial office products and ensembles, bedroom furniture, storage armoires, and other utility pieces are included in the product line sold through multiple distribution channels under the Bush, Eric Morgan by Bush, and Case Casrad by Bush brand names. Founded in 1959. **Corporate headquarters location:** This Location. **Listed on:** New York Stock Exchange. **Number of employees nationwide:** 1,700.

BUTTERICK COMPANY, INC.
161 Avenue of the Americas, New York NY 10013. 212/620-2500. **Contact:** Roslyn Gardner, Personnel Manager. **Description:** Manufactures two lines of clothing patterns for the home sewing market and produces related fashion publications including *Weddings*, *Butterick Home Catalog*, *Vogue Patterns Magazine*, and *Vogue Knitting Magazine*. **Common positions include:** Apparel Worker; Editorial Assistant; Fashion Designer; Human Resources Manager; Public Relations Specialist; Technical Writer/Editor. **Educational backgrounds include:** Art/Design; Business Administration;

Communications; Fashion; Liberal Arts; Marketing; Merchandising. **Benefits:** Dental Insurance; Disability Coverage; EAP; Employee Discounts; Life Insurance; Medical Insurance; Pension Plan; Savings Plan; Tuition Assistance. **Special programs:** Internships. **Corporate headquarters location:** This Location.

CAREFREE OF COLORADO
2145 West Sixth Avenue, Broomfield CO 80020. 303/469-3324. **Contact:** Venita Fortune, Human Resources. **Description:** Manufactures a large line of products for recreational vehicles. Carefree of Colorado's product line includes awnings, add-a-rooms, and lawn furniture. **Corporate headquarters location:** This Location. **Parent company:** Scott Fetzer Company.

CAROLINA MIRROR COMPANY
P.O. Box 548, North Wilkesboro NC 28659-0548. 336/838-2151. **Contact:** Human Resources Department. **Description:** Manufactures mirrors. **Benefits:** Disability Coverage; Employee Discounts; Life Insurance; Medical Insurance; Pension Plan; Savings Plan. **Corporate headquarters location:** This Location. **Other U.S. locations:** Houston TX. **Listed on:** Privately held. **Number of employees at this location:** 575. **Number of employees nationwide:** 600.

THE CARROWAY COMPANY
P.O. Box 459, Sophia NC 27350. 336/861-4169. **Contact:** Personnel. **Description:** A manufacturer of upholstered household furniture. Products include couches and love seats. **Subsidiaries include:** Buckhorn Carriers, Inc. is a trucking company; National Furniture Manufacturing Company, Inc.; Washington Furniture Company, Inc.

CARSONS INC.
P.O. Box 150, High Point NC 27261. 336/887-3544. **Contact:** Kathy Proctor, Human Resources Manager. **Description:** Carsons Inc. manufactures upholstered furniture. The company wholesales its furniture to retail stores. **Corporate headquarters location:** This Location.

CASIO INC.
570 Mount Pleasant Avenue, Dover NJ 07801. 973/361-5400. **Fax:** 973/537-8910. **Contact:** Ken Sterzer, Human Resources Manager. **E-mail address:** ksterzer@casio.com. **World Wide Web address:** http://www.casio.com. **Description:** Manufactures consumer electronics and computer-based products. **NOTE:** Entry-level positions are offered. **Company slogan:** The unexpected extra. **Common positions include:** Account Manager; Account Representative; Accountant; Administrative Assistant; Administrative Manager; AS400 Programmer Analyst; Assistant Manager; Budget Analyst; Computer Operator; Computer Programmer; Computer Technician; Credit Manager; Customer Service Manager; Database Administrator; General Manager; Internet Services Manager; Intranet Developer; Marketing Manager; Marketing Specialist; Network/Systems Administrator; Purchasing Agent/Manager; Sales Manager; Sales Representative; Secretary; Systems Analyst; Transportation/Traffic Specialist; Web Advertising Specialist; Webmaster; Website Developer. **Educational backgrounds include:** Accounting; AS400 Certification; Business Administration; Communications; Finance; Internet Development; Marketing; MBA; Microsoft Office; Microsoft Word; Spreadsheets. **Benefits:** 401(k); Casual Dress - Fridays; Dental Insurance; Disability Coverage; Employee Discounts; Life Insurance; Medical Insurance; Pension Plan; Sick Days (6 - 10); Spending Account; Vacation Days (10 - 20).

Corporate headquarters location: This Location. **Other U.S. locations:** Glendale Heights IL; Little Ferry NJ. **International locations:** Worldwide. **Parent company:** Casio Computer Company, Ltd. (Tokyo, Japan). **Listed on:** Privately held. **Annual sales/revenues:** More than $100 million. **Number of employees at this location:** 150. **Number of employees nationwide:** 325.

CERTRON CORPORATION
1545 Sawtelle Boulevard, Suite 12, Los Angeles CA 90025. 310/914-0300. **Contact:** Jesse Lopez, Employee Relations. **Description:** Certron designs, develops, manufactures, and distributes blank audiocassettes and blank videocassettes. The company is also active in the contract assembly and manufacturing of products for other firms. Its magnetic media products are sold primarily in the U.S. to wholesale distributors, original equipment manufacturers, mail-order companies, and major retail outlets. **Corporate headquarters location:** This Location.

THE CHINET COMPANY
275 Ferris Avenue, East Providence RI 02916. 401/438-3410. **Contact:** Manager of Human Resources. **World Wide Web address:** http://www. chinetco.com. **Description:** Manufactures paper and plastic dinnerware including paper plates and plastic utensils. **Corporate headquarters location:** This Location.

CLAIROL INC.
One Blachley Road, Stamford CT 06922. 203/357-5000. **Contact:** Director of Human Resources. **Description:** A worldwide marketer and manufacturer of hair care products for home and salon use. The company also manufactures beauty and personal care appliances. **Common positions include:** Accountant/Auditor; Chemical Engineer; Chemist; Computer Programmer; Draftsperson; Electrical/Electronics Engineer; Industrial Engineer; Mechanical Engineer; Operations/Production Manager; Purchasing Agent/Manager. **Educational backgrounds include:** Accounting; Biology; Chemistry; Computer Science; Engineering; Finance; Mathematics. **Benefits:** Daycare Assistance; Dental Insurance; Disability Coverage; Employee Discounts; Life Insurance; Medical Insurance; Pension Plan; Savings Plan; Stock Option; Tuition Assistance. **Special programs:** Internships. **Corporate headquarters location:** This Location. **Other U.S. locations:** CA. **Parent company:** Bristol-Myers Squibb Company (New York NY). **Listed on:** New York Stock Exchange. **Number of employees nationwide:** 1,000.

THE CLOROX COMPANY
P.O. Box 24305, Oakland CA 94623-1305. 510/271-7000. **Contact:** Corporate Staffing. **World Wide Web address:** http://www.clorox.com. **Description:** This location houses the executive offices. Overall, Clorox, a *Fortune* 500 company, is an international manufacturer and marketer of consumer food and cleaning products. Brand names include Clorox, 409, Hidden Valley Ranch, and KC Masterpiece. **Common positions include:** Accountant/Auditor; Buyer; Chemical Engineer; Chemist; Civil Engineer; Computer Programmer; Financial Analyst; Food Scientist/Technologist; Human Resources Manager; Industrial Engineer; Manufacturer's/Wholesaler's Sales Rep.; Marketing Specialist; Mechanical Engineer; Operations/Production Manager; Systems Analyst; Technical Writer/Editor; Transportation/Traffic Specialist. **Educational backgrounds include:** Accounting; Business Administration; Chemistry; Computer Science; Engineering; Finance; Liberal Arts; Marketing. **Benefits:** Dental Insurance; Disability Coverage; Life Insurance; Medical Insurance; Pension Plan; Profit Sharing; Savings Plan; Tuition Assistance. **Corporate headquarters location:** This Location. **Listed on:** New York Stock Exchange.

COBRA ELECTRONICS CORPORATION
6500 West Cortland Street, Chicago IL 60707. 773/889-8870. **Fax:** 773/889-4453. **Contact:** Human Resources. **World Wide Web address:** http://www.cobraelec.com. **Description:** Manufactures telephones and consumer electronics products. **Common positions include:** Customer Service Rep.; Electrical/Electronics Engineer; Operations/Production Manager. **Educational backgrounds include:** Accounting; Business Administration; Communications; Computer Science; Engineering; Finance; Liberal Arts; Marketing. **Benefits:** 401(k); Dental Insurance; Disability Coverage; Employee Discounts; Life Insurance; Medical Insurance; Profit Sharing; Tuition Assistance. **Corporate headquarters location:** This Location. **Listed on:** NASDAQ. **Number of employees at this location:** 225.

COLGATE-PALMOLIVE COMPANY
300 Park Avenue, New York NY 10022. 212/310-2000. **Contact:** Human Resources. **World Wide Web address:** http://www.colgate.com. **Description:** Manufactures and markets a wide variety of products in the U.S. and around the world in two distinct business segments: Oral, Personal, and Household Care; and Specialty Marketing. Oral, Personal, and Household Care products include toothpastes, oral rinses, toothbrushes, bar and liquid soaps, shampoos, conditioners, deodorants and antiperspirants, baby products, shaving products, laundry and dishwashing detergents, fabric softeners, cleansers and cleaners, and bleach. Specialty Marketing products include pet dietary care products, crystal tableware, and portable fuel for warming food. Principal global trademarks and tradenames include Colgate, Palmolive, Mennen, Ajax, Fab, and Science Diet. **Corporate headquarters location:** This Location. **Other U.S. locations:** Kansas City KS; Cambridge MA.

COLOREL BLINDS
13802 East 33rd Place, Aurora CO 80011. 303/744-1863. **Fax:** 303/574-9182. **Contact:** Human Resources. **Description:** A leading national fabricator and retailer of custom-made window coverings for residential and commercial customers. **NOTE:** Entry-level positions are offered. **Common positions include:** Accountant; Administrative Assistant; Assembler; Blue-Collar Worker Supervisor; Controller; Customer Service Representative; Installer; Marketing Specialist; MIS Specialist; Operations Manager; Production Manager; Purchasing Agent/Manager; Sales Manager; Sales Representative; Typist/Word Processor. **Educational backgrounds include:** Accounting; Art/Design; Business Administration; Finance. **Benefits:** Employee Discounts; Medical Insurance. **Special programs:** Training. **Corporate headquarters location:** This Location. **Other U.S. locations:** TX; WA. **Parent company:** Colorel Corporation. **Listed on:** Privately held. **Number of employees nationwide:** 180.

CONAIR CORPORATION
One Cummings Point Road, Stamford CT 06904. 203/351-9000. **Fax:** 203/351-9134. **Contact:** Director of Human Resources. **World Wide Web address:** http://www.conair.com. **Description:** Manufactures and distributes a wide range of personal and health care appliances. **Common positions include:** Buyer; Chemist; Electrical/Electronics Engineer; Marketing

Specialist; Mechanical Engineer; Operations/Production Manager; Purchasing Agent/Manager. **Educational backgrounds include:** Business Administration; Chemistry; Engineering; Marketing. **Benefits:** 401(k); Dental Insurance; Disability Coverage; Employee Discounts; Life Insurance; Medical Insurance; Profit Sharing; Tuition Assistance. **Corporate headquarters location:** This Location. **Listed on:** Privately held. **Number of employees at this location:** 270. **Number of employees nationwide:** 1,100.

CORONET MANUFACTURING COMPANY
P.O. Box 2065, Gardena CA 90247. 310/327-6700. **Contact:** Ms. Pat Peterson, Office Manager. **Description:** Produces lamps and lighting fixtures. **Corporate headquarters location:** This Location.

COSMETIC GROUP U.S.A., INC.
11312 Penrose Street, Sun Valley CA 91352. 818/767-2889. **Fax:** 818/767-4062. **Contact:** Human Resources. **Description:** Develops, formulates, and manufactures a wide range of color cosmetics and other personal care products for customers that market the products under their own brand names. **Corporate headquarters location:** This Location. **Subsidiaries include:** Arnold Zegarelli Products, Inc. manufactures and distributes a line of hair care products.

CULLIGAN INTERNATIONAL COMPANY
One Culligan Parkway, Northbrook IL 60062. 847/205-5902. **Contact:** Manager of Human Resources. **World Wide Web address:** http://www.culligan.com. **Description:** A manufacturer of water filtration equipment and systems. **Common positions include:** Accountant/Auditor; Chemist; Customer Service Representative; Draftsperson; Electrical/Electronics Engineer; Mechanical Engineer; Paralegal. **Educational backgrounds include:** Accounting; Engineering; Liberal Arts. **Corporate headquarters location:** This Location. **Parent company:** Astrum, International.

DALLOZ SAFETY
P.O. Box 622, Reading PA 19603. 610/376-6161. **Contact:** Rodney M. Fogelman, Director of Human Resources. **World Wide Web address:** http://www.cdalloz.com. **Description:** Manufactures respiratory protection and personal safety protection products for the head, ears, and eyes. **Corporate headquarters location:** This Location. **Parent company:** Christian Dalloz (also at this location).

DANAHER CORPORATION
1250 24th Street NW, Suite 800, Washington DC 20037. 202/828-0850. **Contact:** Human Resources. **World Wide Web address:** http://www.danaher.com. **Description:** Designs and manufactures industrial and consumer products in two divisions: Tools and Components, and Process/Environmental Controls. **Corporate headquarters location:** This Location. **Annual sales/revenues:** More than $100 million.

DAVID-EDWARD LTD.
1407 Parker Road, Baltimore MD 21227. 410/242-2222. **Contact:** Human Resources. **Description:** Manufactures custom-made upholstered chairs and sofas. **Corporate headquarters location:** This Location.

DEL LABORATORIES, INC.
178 EAB Plaza, West Tower, 8th Floor, Uniondale NY 11556. 516/844-2020. **Fax:** 516/577-1035. **Contact:** Human Resources. **E-mail address:** resume@dellabs.com. **World Wide Web address:** http://www.dellabs.com. **Description:** A fully-integrated manufacturer and marketer of packaged consumer products including cosmetics, toiletries, beauty aids, and proprietary pharmaceuticals. Products are distributed to chain and independent drug stores, mass merchandisers, and supermarkets. Divisions include Commerce Drug Company, Del International, Natural Glow, La Cross, La Salle Laboratories, Nutri-Tonic, Naturistics, Rejuvia, and Sally Hansen. **NOTE:** Entry-level positions and second and third shifts are offered. **Common positions include:** Account Manager; Account Representative; Accountant; Administrative Assistant; Advertising Clerk; AS400 Programmer Analyst; Blue-Collar Worker Supervisor; Budget Analyst; Buyer; Chemist; Clerical Supervisor; Computer Operator; Customer Service Representative; Database Administrator; Electrician; Environmental Engineer; Event Planner; Financial Analyst; Graphic Artist; Help-Desk Technician; Industrial Engineer; Internet Services Manager; Intranet Developer; Manufacturing Engineer; Marketing Manager; Media Planner; MIS Specialist; Network/Systems Administrator; Production Manager; Public Relations Specialist; Quality Control Supervisor; Sales Manager; Sales Representative; Secretary; Systems Analyst; Systems Manager; Webmaster; Website Developer. **Educational backgrounds include:** Accounting; Art/Design; AS400 Certification; Business Administration; Chemistry; Communications; Computer Science; Engineering; Finance; Marketing; MBA; Microsoft Office; Microsoft Word; Public Relations; Spreadsheets. **Benefits:** 401(k); Casual Dress - Fridays; Dental Insurance; Disability Coverage; ESOP; Life Insurance; Medical Insurance; Pension Plan; Sick Days (6 - 10); Tuition Assistance; Vacation Days (6 - 10). **Corporate headquarters location:** This Location. **Other area locations:** Farmingdale NY. **Other U.S. locations:** Rocky Point NC. **Listed on:** American Stock Exchange. **Stock exchange symbol:** DLI. **Annual sales/revenues:** More than $100 million.

DOUGLAS FURNITURE OF CALIFORNIA
4000 Redondo Beach Avenue, Redondo Beach CA 90278. 310/643-7200. **Contact:** Steve Wilk, Personnel Director. **Description:** Manufactures a line of household cabinets for electronics and appliances. **Corporate headquarters location:** This Location.

DRYPERS CORPORATION
5300 Memorial Drive, Suite 900, Houston TX 77007. 713/869-8693. **Fax:** 713/803-5556. **Contact:** Human Resources. **Description:** Manufactures diapers. **Common positions include:** Accountant/Auditor; Blue-Collar Worker Supervisor; Clerical Supervisor; Computer Programmer; Electrical/Electronics Engineer; Financial Analyst; General Manager; Human Resources Manager; Industrial Engineer; Industrial Hygienist; Manufacturer's/Wholesaler's Sales Rep.; Mechanical Engineer; Operations/Production Manager; Purchasing Agent/Manager; Quality Control Supervisor; Structural Engineer; Systems Analyst. **Educational backgrounds include:** Accounting; Business Administration; Computer Science; Engineering; Manufacturing Management. **Benefits:** 401(k); Dental Insurance; Disability Coverage; Employee Discounts; Life Insurance; Medical Insurance; Savings Plan. **Corporate headquarters location:** This Location. **Number of employees at this location:** 100.

DURACELL NORTH ATLANTIC GROUP
8 Research Drive, Bethel CT 06801. 203/796-4000. **Contact:** Senior Vice President of Human Resources. **Description:** Manufactures a line of

batteries sold worldwide under the Duracell trademark. Battery types include alkaline, zinc, rechargeable, and lithium. The company also manufactures batteries used in hearing aids and photographic and communications equipment. A subsidiary conducts marketing operations for a line of lighting products under the Durabeam name. **Corporate headquarters location:** This Location. **International locations:** Belgium; Canada; Mexico; United Kingdom. **Listed on:** New York Stock Exchange. **Number of employees worldwide:** 7,700.

EASTMAN KODAK COMPANY
343 State Street, Rochester NY 14650-1139. 716/724-4609. **Contact:** Staffing Organization. **World Wide Web address:** http://www.kodak.com. **Description:** Manufactures photographic equipment and supplies; medical products; information storage and retrieval systems; and copiers/duplicators. Consumer brand names include Kodak film, Bayer aspirin, d-Con pest control, Minwax wood finishes, and Resolve carpet cleaner. The company also produces cameras, photo CDs and players, software, printers, and batteries. **Common positions include:** Chemical Engineer; Electrical/Electronics Engineer; Financial Analyst; Mechanical Engineer; Services Sales Representative; Software Engineer; Systems Analyst. **Educational backgrounds include:** Computer Science; Engineering; Finance; Marketing. **Benefits:** 401(k); Dental Insurance; Disability Coverage; Employee Discounts; Life Insurance; Medical Insurance; Pension Plan; Tuition Assistance. **Special programs:** Internships. **Corporate headquarters location:** This Location. **Other U.S. locations:** Nationwide. **Listed on:** New York Stock Exchange. **Number of employees at this location:** 30,000. **Number of employees nationwide:** 45,000.

ECOLOGY KIDS
25 Kay Fries Drive, Stony Point NY 10980. 914/786-5552. **Contact:** Human Resources. **Description:** Ecology Kids manufactures, markets, and distributes infantwear and care products, nursery accessories, and other products for infant and toddler comfort and care. The company's products include infant clothing, cloth diapers, diaper covers, bedding, furniture covers, layettes, infant and child travel products, and other accessories. **Corporate headquarters location:** This Location.

EDEN LLC
812 Jersey Avenue, Jersey City NJ 07310. 201/656-3331. **Fax:** 201/656-3070. **Contact:** Human Resources. **Description:** Manufactures and distributes children's toys and gifts. **Common positions include:** Accountant; Administrative Assistant; Budget Analyst; Buyer; Claim Representative; Computer Programmer; Cost Estimator; Credit Manager; Customer Service Representative; Designer; Graphic Designer; Human Resources Manager; Marketing Manager; Mechanical Engineer; Purchasing Agent/Manager; Quality Control Supervisor; Systems Analyst. **Educational backgrounds include:** Accounting; Art/Design; Business Administration; Communications; Computer Science; Engineering; Finance; Liberal Arts; Marketing. **Benefits:** 401(k); Dental Insurance; Disability Coverage; Employee Discounts; Life Insurance; Medical Insurance; Pension Plan; Tuition Assistance. **Special programs:** Internships. **Corporate headquarters location:** This Location. **Other U.S. locations:** Los Angeles CA; San Francisco CA; Atlanta GA; Chicago IL; Boston MA; Dallas TX. **Parent company:** Penguin Books. **Number of employees at this location:** 170. **Number of employees nationwide:** 200.

EFFANBEE DOLL COMPANY
19 Lexington Avenue, East Brunswick NJ 08816. 732/613-3852. **Contact:** Personnel Director. **World Wide Web address:** http://www.effnbeedolls.com. **Description:** Manufactures dolls. Founded in 1910. **Corporate headquarters location:** This Location.

ELIZABETH ARDEN COMPANY
1345 Avenue of the Americas, 36th Floor, New York NY 10105. 212/261-1000. **Contact:** Human Resources. **World Wide Web address:** http://www.elizabetharden.com. **Description:** An international manufacturer and distributor of a wide range of cosmetics and toiletries. **Common positions include:** Administrative Assistant; Financial Analyst; Marketing Manager. **Educational backgrounds include:** Accounting; Finance; Marketing. **Corporate headquarters location:** This Location. **Parent company:** Unilever.

ELLETT BROTHERS
267 Columbia Avenue, Chapin SC 29036. 803/345-3751. **Contact:** Human Resources. **World Wide Web address:** http://www.ellettbrothers.com. **Description:** This location houses distribution, product sourcing, and teleservicing operations. Overall, Ellett Brothers is a manufacturer of leisure products focusing on outdoor recreational sports such as hunting and shooting, marine activities, camping, and archery. **Corporate headquarters location:** This Location. **Listed on:** NASDAQ. **Number of employees nationwide:** 355.

EMPIRE SCIENTIFIC CORPORATION
P.O. Box 817, Deer Park NY 11729. 631/595-9206. **Fax:** 516/343-5733. **Contact:** Human Resources. **World Wide Web address:** http://www.empirebat.com. **Description:** Manufactures camcorder batteries and related video accessories. **Common positions include:** Welder. **Benefits:** Medical Insurance. **Corporate headquarters location:** This Location.

THE ERTL COMPANY INC.
P.O. Box 500, Highways 136 and 20, Dyersville IA 52040. 319/875-2000. **Contact:** Human Resources. **World Wide Web address:** http://www.ertltoys.com. **Description:** An international toy manufacturer. **Common positions include:** Accountant/Auditor; Blue-Collar Worker Supervisor; Buyer; Ceramics Engineer; Computer Programmer; Customer Service Representative; Designer; Draftsperson; Financial Analyst; Human Resources Manager; Industrial Engineer; Industrial Production Manager; Manufacturer's/Wholesaler's Sales Rep.; Materials Engineer; Mechanical Engineer; Metallurgical Engineer; Operations/Production Manager; Paralegal; Purchasing Agent/Manager; Quality Control Supervisor; Software Engineer; Systems Analyst. **Educational backgrounds include:** Bachelor of Arts. **Benefits:** 401(k); Dental Insurance; Disability Coverage; Employee Discounts; Life Insurance; Medical Insurance; Pension Plan; Relocation Assistance; Savings Plan; Tuition Assistance. **Corporate headquarters location:** This Location. **Parent company:** Hanson Industries. **Listed on:** Privately held. **Number of employees at this location:** 1,100. **Number of employees worldwide:** 2,500.

ESSELTE CORPORATION
71 Clinton Road, Garden City NY 11530. 516/741-3200. **Fax:** 516/873-3456. **Contact:** Human Resources. **Description:** Manufactures and distributes filing and marking systems, storage

systems, and other office materials. Primary products are paper-based filing products, mainly suspension filing systems. The company operates production and sales facilities in the United States and Canada. **Common positions include:** Accountant/Auditor; Blue-Collar Worker Supervisor; Buyer; Claim Representative; Computer Programmer; Draftsperson; Human Resources Manager; Industrial Designer; Industrial Engineer; Manufacturer's/Wholesaler's Sales Rep.; Marketing Specialist; Mechanical Engineer; Operations/ Production Manager. **Educational backgrounds include:** Accounting; Business Administration; Engineering; Finance; Liberal Arts; Marketing. **Benefits:** Dental Insurance; Disability Coverage; Employee Discounts; Life Insurance; Medical Insurance; Pension Plan; Savings Plan; Tuition Assistance. **Special programs:** Internships. **Corporate headquarters location:** This Location. **Other U.S. locations:** Moonachie NJ; New York NY. **Parent company:** Esselte AB (Sweden) is engaged in industrial production, trade, and services, primarily in the fields of office equipment, stationery and price marking, custom printing and binding, consumer and transport packaging, textbooks and instructional materials, cartography, publishing, and bookstores. **Listed on:** New York Stock Exchange. **Number of employees worldwide:** 15,000.

THE ESTEE LAUDER COMPANIES INC.
767 Fifth Avenue, New York NY 10153. 212/572-4200. **Contact:** Human Resources. **World Wide Web address:** http://www.elcompanies.com. **Description:** Manufactures, markets, and distributes cosmetics and skin and hair care products. Founded in 1946. **Corporate headquarters location:** This Location.

THE EUREKA COMPANY
1201 East Bell Street, Bloomington IL 61701. 309/828-2367. **Fax:** 309/823-5203. **Contact:** Cala Laible, Employment & EEO Manager. **E-mail address:** eureka.hrdept@eureka.com **World Wide Web address:** http://www.eureka.com. **Description:** A manufacturer of vacuum cleaners. **NOTE:** Please send resumes to the Human Resources Department, 807 North Main Street, Bloomington IL 61701. **Common positions include:** Blue-Collar Worker Supervisor; Buyer; Computer Operator; Computer Programmer; Credit Manager; Draftsperson; Electrician; Industrial Engineer; Industrial Production Manager; Mechanical Engineer; Network Engineer; Order Clerk; Payroll Clerk; Printing Press Operator; Software Engineer; Systems Analyst; Tool and Die Maker; Transportation/Traffic Specialist. **Educational backgrounds include:** Accounting; Business Administration; Computer Science; Engineering. **Corporate headquarters location:** This Location. **Other U.S. locations:** El Paso TX. **Parent company:** WCI, Inc. **Number of employees nationwide:** 2,100.

EX-CELL HOME FASHIONS INC.
295 Fifth Avenue, Suite 612, New York NY 10016. 212/213-8000. **Contact:** Human Resources. **Description:** Manufactures and distributes home furnishing products including shower curtains, pillows, table cloths, and bathroom accessories. **NOTE:** Resumes should be sent to Ex-Cell Industries, Human Resources, 1605 North George Street, Goldsboro NC 27530. **Corporate headquarters location:** This Location.

FARBERWARE HOME PRODUCTS, INC.
175 McClellan Highway, East Boston MA 02128. 617/561-2200. **Contact:** Human Resources. **Description:** This location houses administrative offices. Overall, Farberware manufactures and sells silverware, flatware, crystal, and water filtration systems. **Corporate headquarters location:** This Location.

FEDDERS CORPORATION
505 Martinsville Road, P.O. Box 813, Liberty Corner NJ 07938. 908/604-8686. **Contact:** Human Resources. **World Wide Web address:** http://www.fedders.com. **Description:** Manufactures room air conditioners. Brand names of the corporation include AIRTEMP, EMERSON QUIET KOOL, and FEDDERS. **Corporate headquarters location:** This Location.

FENDER MUSICAL INSTRUMENTS
7975 North Hayden Road, Suite C-100, Scottsdale AZ 85258. 480/596-9690. **Contact:** Personnel. **World Wide Web address:** http://www. fender.com. **Description:** Manufactures and distributes electric and acoustic guitars, strings, accessories, amplifiers, and professional sound equipment under such brand names as Fender, Squier, and Sunn. **Common positions include:** Accountant/Auditor; Blue-Collar Worker Supervisor; Buyer; Computer Programmer; Credit Manager; Customer Service Representative; Industrial Engineer; Operations/Production Manager. **Educational backgrounds include:** Accounting; Business Administration; Liberal Arts; Marketing. **Benefits:** 401(k); Dental Insurance; Disability Coverage; Employee Discounts; Life Insurance; Medical Insurance. **Corporate headquarters location:** This Location.

FIRST ALERT
BRK BRANDS, INC.
3901 Liberty Street Road, Aurora IL 60504. 630/851-7330. **Contact:** Bob Kwiatkowlski, Human Resources. **World Wide Web address:** http://www.firstalert.com. **Description:** This location houses administrative offices. Overall, First Alert operates through its subsidiaries to manufacture smoke alarms, fire alarms, carbon monoxide detectors, fire extinguishers, fire escape ladders, rechargeable flashlights, and related home safety products. **Corporate headquarters location:** This Location. **Subsidiaries include:** BRK Brands Canada (Ontario, Canada); BRK Brands Europe, Ltd. (Berkshire, England); BRK Brands, Inc. (also at this location); BRK Brands Pty Ltd. (Parramatta, Australia); Electronica RBK de Mexico S.A. de C.V. (Chihuahua, Mexico). **Listed on:** NASDAQ.

FIRST TEAM SPORTS, INC.
1201 Lund Boulevard, Anoka MN 55303. 763/576-3500. **Contact:** Human Resources. **World Wide Web address:** http://www.ultrawheels.com. **Description:** Manufactures in-line skates, skateboards, wheels, backpacks, ice hockey products, apparel, and accessories. Brand names include B!G, Crossover, Heavy, Hespeler, Skate Attack, Subcon, 3rd World, Ultra-Ice, and UltraWheels. **Corporate headquarters location:** This Location.

FISHER-PRICE
636 Girard Avenue, East Aurora NY 14052. 716/687-3000. **Contact:** Employment Coordinator. **World Wide Web address:** http://www.fisher-price.com. **Description:** A manufacturer of toys and children's products. Among Fisher-Price's products are hair accessories, infant bedding, footwear, puzzles, bibs, bikes, sunglasses, headwear, kidswear, home safety products, children's books, and arts and crafts. **Corporate headquarters location:** This Location. **Number of employees at this location:** 1,000.

FISKARS, INC.
7811 West Stewart Avenue, Wausau WI 54401. 715/842-2091. **Contact:** Human Resources. **World Wide Web address:** http://www.fiskars.com. **Description:** Manufactures scissors and shears of all types. **Corporate headquarters location:** This Location.

FLEXSTEEL INDUSTRIES, INC.
P.O. Box 877, Dubuque IA 52004-0877. 319/556-7730. **Fax:** 319/556-8345. **Contact:** Human Resources. **World Wide Web address:** http://www.flexsteel.com. **Description:** Manufactures and markets upholstered furniture for the retail furniture market and the recreational vehicle field. Products of Flexsteel Industries include a variety of wood and upholstered chairs, rockers, sofas, sofabeds, loveseats, buckets seats, and convertible bedding units for use in offices, homes, vans, and recreational vehicles. **Common positions include:** Accountant; Administrative Assistant; Applications Engineer; AS400 Programmer Analyst; Auditor; Buyer; Chief Financial Officer; Computer Operator; Computer Programmer; Controller; Cost Estimator; Credit Manager; Customer Service Representative; Design Engineer; Draftsperson; General Manager; Human Resources Manager; Industrial Engineer; Manufacturing Engineer; Marketing Manager; Mechanical Engineer; MIS Specialist; Operations Manager; Production Manager; Purchasing Agent/Manager; Quality Control Supervisor; Registered Nurse; Sales Manager; Sales Representative; Secretary. **Educational backgrounds include:** Accounting; Art/Design; AS400 Certification; Business Administration; C/C++; Computer Science; Engineering; Finance; Marketing; Microsoft Word; Public Relations; Spreadsheets; Visual Basic. **Benefits:** 401(k); Casual Dress - Fridays; Dental Insurance; Disability Coverage; Employee Discounts; Flexible Schedule; Life Insurance; Medical Insurance; Pension Plan; Sick Days (1 - 5); Tuition Assistance; Vacation Days (10 - 20). **Special programs:** Summer Jobs. **Corporate headquarters location:** This Location. **Other U.S. locations:** Harrison AR; Riverside CA; Dublin GA; Elkhart IN; New Paris IN; Starkville MS; Lancaster PA. **Listed on:** NASDAQ. **Stock exchange symbol:** FLEX. **President:** K. Bruce Lauritsen. **Information Systems Manager:** Jerry Coble. **Sales Manager:** Lee Fautsch. **Annual sales/revenues:** More than $100 million. **Number of employees at this location:** 850. **Number of employees nationwide:** 2,600.

FORSTER, INC.
P.O. Box 657, Wilton ME 04294. 207/645-2574. **Fax:** 207/645-5405. **Contact:** Human Resources. **Description:** A manufacturer and distributor of wood and plastic household products and sporting goods. **Common positions include:** Accountant; Customer Service Representative; Human Resources Manager; Industrial Production Manager. **Educational backgrounds include:** Accounting; Business Administration; Engineering. **Benefits:** 401(k); Dental Insurance; Disability Coverage; Employee Discounts; Life Insurance; Medical Insurance; Profit Sharing; Tuition Assistance. **Corporate headquarters location:** This Location. **Other area locations:** Dryden ME; Strong ME. **Parent company:** Diamond Brands, Inc. (Cloquet MN). **Listed on:** Privately held.

FOUNTAIN POWERBOAT INDUSTRIES
P.O. Drawer 457, Washington NC 27889. 252/975-2000. **Contact:** Manager of Human Resources. **Description:** Designs, manufactures, and sells sport boats, sport cruisers, and sport fishing boats. **Corporate headquarters location:** This Location. **Number of employees at this location:** 280.

GBC/CCTV CORP.
280 Huyler Street, South Hackensack NJ 07606. 201/489-9595. **Contact:** Gary Perlin, Sales Manager. **Description:** Produces a wide variety of video equipment including cameras and monitors. **Corporate headquarters location:** This Location.

GARY PLASTIC PACKAGING
1340 Viele Avenue, Bronx NY 10474-7124. 718/893-2200. **Contact:** Mark Varella, Personnel Director. **World Wide Web address:** http://www.plasticboxes.com. **Description:** Manufactures plastic display and storage boxes for collectibles. Founded in 1963. **Corporate headquarters location:** This Location.

GEM ELECTRIC MANUFACTURING CO.
20 Commerce Drive, Hauppauge NY 11788-0936. 631/273-2230. **Contact:** Personnel Department. **Description:** Manufactures electrical wiring devices, fuses, extension cords, and consumer electric products such as Christmas tree lights. **Corporate headquarters location:** This Location.

GENERAL FIRE EXTINGUISHER CORP.
1685 Shermer Road, Northbrook IL 60062. 847/272-7500. **Fax:** 847/272-7286. **Contact:** Personnel Supervisor. **E-mail address:** info@genfire.com. **World Wide Web address:** http://www.genfire.com. **Description:** Manufactures a complete line of fire extinguishers. Founded in 1903. **Common positions include:** Accountant; Blue-Collar Worker Supervisor; Credit Manager; Customer Service Representative; Industrial Engineer; Industrial Production Manager; Purchasing Agent/Manager. **Educational backgrounds include:** Accounting; Business Administration; Engineering; Marketing. **Benefits:** Life Insurance; Medical Insurance. **Corporate headquarters location:** This Location. **Listed on:** Privately held. **Number of employees at this location:** 160.

GENERAL HOUSEWARES CORPORATION
P.O. Box 4066, Terre Haute IN 47804. 812/232-1000. **Physical address:** 1536 Beech Street, Terre Haute IN. **Toll-free phone:** 800/457-2665. **Fax:** 800/330-9263. **Contact:** Linda Harris, Human Resources Manager. **World Wide Web address:** http://www.ghc.com. **Description:** Engaged in the manufacture and marketing of cookware, cutlery, kitchen tools, commercial knives, and garden tools. **Common positions include:** Accountant/Auditor; Blue-Collar Worker Supervisor; Ceramics Engineer; Computer Programmer; Credit Manager; Customer Service Representative; Department Manager; Draftsperson; Human Resources Manager; Industrial Engineer; Manufacturer's/Wholesaler's Sales Rep.; Marketing Specialist; Mechanical Engineer; Operations/Production Manager; Purchasing Agent/Manager; Quality Control Supervisor; Systems Analyst; Transportation/Traffic Specialist. **Educational backgrounds include:** Accounting; Business Administration; Communications; Computer Science; Economics; Engineering; Finance; Liberal Arts; Marketing. **Benefits:** Dental Insurance; Disability Coverage; Employee Discounts; Life Insurance; Medical Insurance; Pension Plan; Savings Plan; Stock Option; Tuition Assistance. **Special programs:** Internships. **Corporate headquarters location:** This Location.

GIBSON USA
1818 Elm Hill Pike, Nashville TN 37210. 615/871-4500. **Contact:** Diane McGregor, Human Resources Director. **World Wide Web address:** http://www.gibson.com. **Description:** Manufactures and distributes electric and acoustic guitars, as well

as other musical instruments and related accessories. **Common positions include:** Accountant/Auditor; Blue-Collar Worker Supervisor; Buyer; Computer Programmer; Credit Manager; Customer Service Representative; Electrical/Electronics Engineer; Financial Analyst; General Manager; Mechanical Engineer; Operations/Production Manager; Quality Control Supervisor. **Educational backgrounds include:** Accounting; Business Administration; Communications; Computer Science; Engineering; Finance; Marketing. **Benefits:** 401(k); Dental Insurance; Employee Discounts; Life Insurance; Medical Insurance; Profit Sharing; Savings Plan; Tuition Assistance. **Corporate headquarters location:** This Location. **Other U.S. locations:** Huntington Beach CA; Oakland CA; Elgin IL; Bozeman MT. **Listed on:** Privately held.

THE GILLETTE COMPANY
Prudential Tower Building, 40th Floor, Boston MA 02199. 617/421-7000. **Contact:** Personnel Director. **World Wide Web address:** http://www. gillette.com. **Description:** Manufactures consumer products for the personal care and stationery markets. Products include razors and blades including Trac II, Atra, Sensor, Mach 3, MicroTrac, Daisy, and Platinum Plus; toiletries, cosmetics, and deodorants such as Right Guard, and Dry Idea; hair care products including White Rain and Silkience; skin care and shaving cream products; dental accessories including toothbrushes, toothpaste, rinses, and related items; alkaline batteries; and stationery products including Parker Pen, Flair, PaperMate, Waterman, and correction fluids. **Corporate headquarters location:** This Location. **Subsidiaries include:** Braun AG (Germany) manufactures household appliances. **Listed on:** New York Stock Exchange. **Stock exchange symbol:** G.

GOLFSMITH INTERNATIONAL INC.
11000 North Interstate Highway 35, Austin TX 78753. 512/837-8810. **Fax:** 512/821-4191. **Contact:** Human Resources Manager. **World Wide Web address:** http://www.golfsmith.com. **Description:** Designs, assembles, and distributes golf equipment. **Common positions include:** Accountant/Auditor; Buyer; Human Resources Manager; Operations/Production Manager; Purchasing Agent/Manager. **Educational backgrounds include:** Marketing. **Benefits:** Disability Coverage; Employee Discounts; Life Insurance; Medical Insurance; Profit Sharing; Vacation Days. **Corporate headquarters location:** This Location. **Listed on:** Privately held. **Number of employees at this location:** 400.

W.L. GORE & ASSOCIATES, INC.
P.O. Box 9206, Newark DE 19714-9206. 302/738-4880. **Physical address:** 551 Paper Mill Road, Newark DE. **Contact:** Barbara Pizzala, Recruiter. **World Wide Web address:** http://www.gore.com. **Description:** Manufactures dental floss, guitar strings, bicycle cable systems, vacuum filters, and water/stain repellent. The company also produces electronic products including copper and optical signal transmission products, digital and analog cable assemblies, circuit chips and related products; chemical products including a chemical polymer used to repair diseased arteries and also as an industrial sealant; and GORE-TEX fabric. **Common positions include:** Attorney; Chemical Engineer; Chemist; Electrical/Electronics Engineer; Mechanical Engineer; Metallurgical Engineer; Sales Engineer. **Educational backgrounds include:** Chemistry; Engineering. **Benefits:** Dental Insurance; Disability Coverage; Employee Discounts; Fitness Program; Life Insurance; Medical Insurance; Profit Sharing. **Special**

programs: Internships. **Corporate headquarters location:** This Location. **Annual sales/revenues:** More than $100 million. **Number of employees nationwide:** 5,800.

GREAT NECK SAW MANUFACTURERS
165 East Second Street, Mineola NY 11501. 516/746-5352. **Contact:** Mr. Sydney Jacuff, President. **Description:** Manufactures a wide range of consumer and shop-quality hand tools. **Corporate headquarters location:** This Location.

GUEST SUPPLY INC.
4301 U.S. Highway One, P.O. Box 902, Monmouth Junction NJ 08852-0902. 609/514-9696. **Fax:** 609/514-7379. **Contact:** Joan Constanza, Human Resources Manager. **Description:** Manufactures, packages, and distributes travel-size personal care products, housekeeping supplies, room accessories, and textiles to the lodging industry. The company also manufactures and packages products for major consumer products and retail companies. Founded in 1979. **NOTE:** Entry-level positions and second and third shifts are offered. **Common positions include:** Account Manager; Account Representative; Accountant; Blue-Collar Worker Supervisor; Branch Manager; Buyer; Chemist; Chief Financial Officer; Computer Operator; Controller; Credit Manager; Customer Service Representative; Database Manager; Design Engineer; Finance Director; Financial Analyst; Graphic Artist; Graphic Designer; Human Resources Manager; Industrial Engineer; Industrial Production Manager; Manufacturing Engineer; Marketing Manager; Marketing Specialist; MIS Specialist; Operations Manager; Production Manager; Purchasing Agent/Manager; Quality Control Supervisor; Sales Executive; Sales Manager; Sales Representative; Secretary; Systems Analyst; Systems Manager; Telecommunications Manager; Transportation/Traffic Specialist; Typist/Word Processor. **Benefits:** 401(k); Dental Insurance; Disability Coverage; Life Insurance; Medical Insurance; Savings Plan. **Corporate headquarters location:** This Location. **Other U.S. locations:** Nationwide. **Subsidiaries include:** Brecken-Ridge-Remy; Guest Distribution; Guest Packaging. **Listed on:** New York Stock Exchange. **Stock exchange symbol:** GSY. **Annual sales/revenues:** More than $100 million. **Number of employees at this location:** 1,000.

HAMILTON BEACH/PROCTOR-SILEX
4421 Waterfront Drive, Glen Allen VA 23060. 804/273-9777. **Contact:** Human Resources. **World Wide Web address:** http://www.hambeach.com. **Description:** Manufactures small appliances including blenders, can openers, coffee makers, food processors, irons, mixers, and toasters. **Corporate headquarters location:** This Location.

HARLYN PRODUCTS, INC.
2615 South Hill Street, Los Angeles CA 90007. 213/746-0745. **Fax:** 800/346-8966. **Contact:** Human Resources. **Description:** An international manufacturer and supplier of fine jewelry. The company has become a leading manufacturer and marketer of family jewelry, primarily gold rings with birthstones of family members. Harlyn also specializes in the manufacture and worldwide distribution of fine gold diamond and gemstone jewelry. The company's other products include a wide selection of rings, earrings, pendants, bracelets, necklaces, pins, and wedding bands. **Corporate headquarters location:** This Location.

HARRIS MARCUS GROUP
3757 South Ashland Avenue, Chicago IL 60609. 773/247-7500. **Contact:** Human Resources.

Description: Engaged in the manufacture of lamps, furniture, and accessories for the home. **Common positions include:** Accountant/Auditor; Architect; Ceramics Engineer; Credit Manager; Designer; Electrician; Industrial Engineer; Materials Engineer; Metallurgical Engineer. **Educational backgrounds include:** Accounting; Art/Design. **Benefits:** 401(k); Employee Discounts; Life Insurance; Medical Insurance; Savings Plan. **Corporate headquarters location:** This Location. **Operations at this facility include:** Administration; Manufacturing. **Listed on:** Privately held. **Number of employees at this location:** 550.

HARTZ MOUNTAIN INDUSTRIES
400 Plaza Drive, Secaucus NJ 07094. 201/271-4800. **Contact:** Human Resources. **Description:** Engaged in the manufacture, packaging, and distribution of consumer products including pet foods, pet accessories, livestock feed and products; chemical products; home carpet-cleaning products; and equipment rentals. **Corporate headquarters location:** This Location. **Other area locations:** Bloomfield NJ. **Subsidiaries include:** Cooper Pet Supply; Permaline Manufacturing Corporation; Sternco-Dominion Real Estate Corporation; The Pet Library Ltd. **Listed on:** American Stock Exchange.

HASBRO, INC.
P.O. Box 1059, Pawtucket RI 02862-1059. 401/431-8697. **Physical address:** 1027 Newport Avenue, Pawtucket RI. **Contact:** Human Resources. **World Wide Web address:** http://www.hasbro.com. **Description:** A major producer and marketer of toys including brand names GI Joe, My Little Pony, Tonka Trucks, Cabbage Patch Kids, Play-Doh, and Nerf. The company also has a large stake in the board game market. The Hasbro Playskool affiliate manufactures preschool toys, child-care products, play sets, and children's apparel. **Corporate headquarters location:** This Location. **Annual sales/revenues:** More than $100 million.

HELEN OF TROY LTD.
One Helen of Troy Plaza, El Paso TX 79912. 915/225-8000. **Fax:** 915/225-8002. **Contact:** Human Resources. **Description:** This division serves as one of the primary development arenas for all corporate product lines. Overall, Helen of Troy markets hair care appliances through major retail outlets worldwide. The company manufactures products under brand names including Vidal Sassoon, Revlon, Sable, and Helen of Troy. The company also services the professional retail market with an extensive collection of professional hair care appliances for salon use. **Corporate headquarters location:** This Location. **Listed on:** NASDAQ. **Stock exchange symbol:** HELE. **Annual sales/revenues:** More than $100 million.

HILLENBRAND INDUSTRIES, INC.
112 North Main Street, Batesville IN 47006. 812/934-7000. **Contact:** Tim Dietz, Human Resources. **World Wide Web address:** http://www.hillenbrand.com. **Description:** A holding company. **Corporate headquarters location:** This Location. **Subsidiaries include:** Batesville Casket Company, Inc. (Batesville IN) manufactures funeral-related products including caskets and urns. Forethought Financial Services (Batesville IN) provides financial services for the purpose of planning funeral arrangements. Hill-Rom Company, Inc. (Batesville IN) manufactures and rents a variety of health care products including birthing beds, hospital beds, and stretchers.

THE HOLSON BURNES COMPANY
582 Great Road, North Smithfield RI 02896. 401/769-8000. **Contact:** Human Resources.

Description: Manufactures, assembles, markets, and distributes picture frames, photo albums, and other photo storage devices. The current product line includes Holson, Terragrafics, Showbox, and Burnes brand names. **Benefits:** 401(k); Incentive Plan; Profit Sharing; Retirement Plan; Stock Option. **Corporate headquarters location:** This Location. **Parent company:** The Holson Burnes Group, Inc. **Listed on:** NASDAQ. **Number of employees nationwide:** 500.

HOME-STYLE INDUSTRIES INC.
P.O. Box 1500, Nampa ID 83653. 208/466-8481. **Contact:** Human Resources. **Description:** Manufactures furniture. **Corporate headquarters location:** This Location.

HOMER LAUGHLIN CHINA COMPANY
Sixth & Harrison Streets, Newell WV 26050. 304/387-1300. **Fax:** 304/387-9576. **Contact:** E. Furbee, Human Resources Manager. **E-mail address:** hlc@hlchina.com. **World Wide Web address:** http://www.hlchina.com. **Description:** Manufactures ceramic dinnerware sold to restaurants and retailers for consumer use. Founded in 1871. **Common positions include:** Blue-Collar Worker Supervisor; Ceramics Engineer; Industrial Engineer. **Benefits:** Disability Coverage; Employee Discounts; Life Insurance; Medical Insurance; Pension Plan; Profit Sharing; Savings Plan. **Corporate headquarters location:** This Location. **President:** Marcus Aaron II. **Annual sales/revenues:** $51 - $100 million. **Number of employees at this location:** 1,150.

HUFFY CORPORATION
225 Byers Road, Miamisburg OH 45342. 937/866-6251. **Contact:** Don Scheick, Human Resources Director. **World Wide Web address:** http://www.huffy.com. **Description:** Designs, manufactures, and markets recreational, leisure, and juvenile products including bicycles. The company also operates a national in-store assembly and warranty service business and provides inventory services to retailers. Founded in 1955. **Corporate headquarters location:** This Location. **Other area locations:** Celina OH. **Number of employees nationwide:** 6,340.

HUNT CORPORATION
One Commerce Square, 2005 Market Street, Philadelphia PA 19103. 215/656-0300. **Fax:** 215/656-3705. **Contact:** Ms. Fran Lillo, Human Resources Generalist. **Description:** Manufactures art supplies, office supplies, and office furniture. **Common positions include:** Accountant/Auditor; Budget Analyst; Computer Operator; Computer Programmer; Credit Manager; Department Manager; General Manager; Graphic Artist; Human Resources Manager; Manufacturer's/Wholesaler's Sales Rep.; Market Research Analyst; Marketing Manager; Public Relations Specialist; Receptionist; Secretary; Systems Analyst. **Educational backgrounds include:** Accounting; Art/Design; Business Administration; Finance; Marketing. **Benefits:** Dental Insurance; Disability Coverage; Employee Discounts; Life Insurance; Medical Insurance; Pension Plan; Profit Sharing; Savings Plan; Tuition Assistance. **Corporate headquarters location:** This Location. **Other U.S. locations:** AL; CT; KY; NC; TX; WI. **Listed on:** New York Stock Exchange. **Number of employees at this location:** 1,000.

ICON HEALTH & FITNESS, INC.
1500 South 1000 West, Logan UT 84321. 435/750-5000. **Contact:** Human Resources. **World Wide Web address:** http://www.iconfitness.com. **Description:** One of the largest manufacturers of

home fitness equipment in the world. Brand names include Image, Jumpking, ProForm, Weider, NordicTrack, and Weslo products. **Corporate headquarters location:** This Location. **Other U.S. locations:** Denver CO; Garland TX; Clearfield UT; Smithfield UT.

IMPERIAL SCHRADE
7 Schrade Court, P.O. Box 7000, Ellenville NY 12428. 914/647-7600. **Contact:** D. Bruce Kerr, Director. **World Wide Web address:** http://www.schradeknives.com. **Description:** Produces a large line of sporting knives and cutlery. **NOTE:** Entry-level positions and second and third shifts are offered. **Common positions include:** Account Manager; Account Representative; Accountant; Advertising Executive; Applications Engineer; Blue-Collar Worker Supervisor; Buyer; Chief Financial Officer; Clerical Supervisor; Computer Programmer; Controller; Cost Estimator; Credit Manager; Database Manager; Design Engineer; Draftsperson; General Manager; Graphic Designer; Human Resources Manager; Industrial Engineer; Industrial Production Manager; Manufacturing Engineer; Marketing Manager; Marketing Specialist; Mechanical Engineer; MIS Specialist; Operations Manager; Production Manager; Project Manager; Purchasing Agent/Manager; Quality Control Supervisor; Registered Nurse; Sales Executive; Sales Manager; Sales Representative; Secretary; Systems Analyst. **Educational backgrounds include:** Accounting; Business Administration; Engineering; Finance; Marketing. **Benefits:** 401(k); Dental Insurance; Disability Coverage; Employee Discounts; Flexible Schedule; Life Insurance; Medical Insurance; Pension Plan; Profit Sharing; Savings Plan. **Special programs:** Apprenticeships; Co-ops; Summer Jobs. **Corporate headquarters location:** This Location. **Listed on:** Privately held. **Annual sales/revenues:** $51 - $100 million. **Number of employees at this location:** 650.

INDEPENDENT CAN COMPANY
P.O. Box 370, Belcamp MD 21017. 410/272-0090. **Physical address:** 1300 Brass Mill Road, Belcamp MD. **Contact:** Human Resources. **World Wide Web address:** http://www.independentcan.com. **Description:** Manufactures decorative metal tins. **Corporate headquarters location:** This Location. **Other U.S. locations:** City of Industry CA; Fort Madison IA.

INTERTAPE POLYMER GROUP
2000 South Beltline Boulevard, Columbia SC 29201. 803/799-8800. **Contact:** Personnel Manager. **E-mail address:** info@intertapeipg.com. **World Wide Web address:** http://www.intertapepolymer.com. **Description:** Manufactures a variety of pressure-sensitive tape products and polyolefin plastic products. The company's products include duct tape and masking tape. **Common positions include:** Accountant/Auditor; Blue-Collar Worker Supervisor; Chemist; Computer Programmer; Controls Engineer; Customer Service Representative; Electrical/Electronics Engineer; Electrician; Human Resources Manager; Industrial Engineer; Industrial Production Manager; Mechanical Engineer; Operations/Production Manager; Process Engineer; Purchasing Agent/Manager; Quality Control Supervisor; Sales Representative. **Educational backgrounds include:** Accounting; Business Administration; Chemistry; Engineering; Manufacturing Management; Marketing. **Benefits:** 401(k); Dental Insurance; Disability Coverage; Employee Discounts; Life Insurance; Medical Insurance; Tuition Assistance. **Corporate headquarters location:** This Location. **Other U.S. locations:** Covington OH; Kingsport

TN. **Subsidiaries include:** Holliston Mills; Three Sigma. **Listed on:** Privately held. **Number of employees at this location:** 750. **Number of employees nationwide:** 1,400.

JOHNSON & JOHNSON
One Johnson & Johnson Plaza, New Brunswick NJ 08933. **Contact:** Human Resources. **World Wide Web address:** http://www.jnj.com. **Description:** A health care products company. Products include pain relievers, contact lenses, pharmaceuticals, bandages, toothbrushes, and surgical instruments under brand names including Reach, Band-Aid, and Acuvue. **NOTE:** Resumes should be sent to Johnson & Johnson Recruiting Services, Employment Management Center, Room JH-215, 501 George Street, New Brunswick NJ 08906-6597. **Corporate headquarters location:** This Location. **International locations:** Worldwide.

JOSTENS, INC.
5501 Norman Center Drive, Minneapolis MN 55437. 952/830-3300. **Fax:** 952/897-4126. **Contact:** Staffing. **World Wide Web address:** http://www.jostens.com. **Description:** Jostens, Inc.'s primary business segments are School Products, Recognition, and Jostens Learning. The School Products segment is comprised of five businesses: Printing and Publishing, Jewelry, Graduation Products, U.S. Photography, and Jostens Canada. School Products include yearbooks, commercial printing, desktop publishing curriculum kits, class rings, graduation accessories, diplomas, trophies, plaques and other awards, school pictures, group photographs for youth camps and organizations, and senior graduation portraits. This segment serves schools, colleges, and alumni associations in the United States and Canada through 1,100 independent sales representatives. The Recognition segment provides products and services that reflect achievements in service, sales, quality, productivity, attendance, safety, and retirements. This segment also produces awards for championship team accomplishments and affinity products for associations. The Recognition segment serves companies, professional and amateur sports teams, and special interest associations through an independent sales force. Jostens Learning produces educational software for kindergarten through grade 12, offering software-based curriculum in reading, mathematics, language arts, science programs, and early childhood instruction, as well as programs for at-risk learning and home learning. As one of the nation's largest providers of curriculum software, Jostens Learning serves more than 4 million students in 10,000 schools nationwide. **Common positions include:** Accountant/Auditor; Administrative Manager; Advertising Clerk; Attorney; Computer Programmer; Customer Service Representative; Editor; Education Administrator; Human Resources Manager; Management Analyst/Consultant; Operations/Production Manager; Paralegal; Property and Real Estate Manager; Public Relations Specialist; Purchasing Agent/Manager; Quality Control Supervisor; Software Engineer; Systems Analyst. **Educational backgrounds include:** Accounting; Art/Design; Business Administration; Communications; Economics; Finance; Marketing. **Benefits:** 401(k); Daycare Assistance; Dental Insurance; Disability Coverage; Life Insurance; Medical Insurance; Pension Plan; Profit Sharing; Savings Plan. **Corporate headquarters location:** This Location. **Other U.S. locations:** Nationwide. **International locations:** Worldwide. **Listed on:** American Stock Exchange; NASDAQ; New York Stock Exchange. **Number of employees at this location:** 330. **Number of employees nationwide:** 10,000.

KENNEY MANUFACTURING COMPANY
1000 Jefferson Boulevard, Warwick RI 02886. 401/739-2200. **Contact:** Bill Glen, Vice President of Human Resources. **Description:** Manufactures window dressings and accessories including venetian blinds and a variety of drapery items. **Common positions include:** Administrator; Blue-Collar Worker Supervisor; Branch Manager; Buyer; Computer Programmer; Customer Service Representative; Draftsperson; Human Resources Manager; Industrial Engineer; Mechanical Engineer; Operations/Production Manager; Purchasing Agent/Manager. **Educational backgrounds include:** Business Administration; Computer Science; Engineering; Liberal Arts; Marketing. **Benefits:** Dental Insurance; Disability Coverage; Employee Discounts; Life Insurance; Medical Insurance; Pension Plan; Savings Plan; Tuition Assistance. **Corporate headquarters location:** This Location.

KIMBERLY-CLARK CORPORATION
P.O. Box 619100, Dallas TX 75261. 972/281-1200. **Contact:** Human Resources. **E-mail address:** opportunities@kc-careers.com. **World Wide Web address:** http://www.kimberly-clark.com. **Description:** Manufactures and markets products for personal, business, and industrial uses throughout the world. The name brands of Kimberly-Clark Corporation include Kleenex facial and bathroom tissue, Huggies diapers and baby wipes, Pull-Ups training pants, Kotex and New Freedom feminine care products, Depend and Poise incontinence care products, Hi-Dri household towels, Kimguard sterile wrap, Kimwipes industrial wipers, and Classic business and correspondence papers. Most of the company's products are made using advanced technologies in absorbency, fibers, and nonwovens. Kimberly-Clark Corporation has extensive overseas operations in Europe and Asia. **Corporate headquarters location:** This Location. **Annual sales/revenues:** More than $100 million. **Other U.S. locations:**
• 2100 Winchester Road, Neenah WI 54956. 920/721-2631.

KOSS CORPORATION
4129 North Port Washington Road, Milwaukee WI 53212-1052. 414/964-5000. **Fax:** 414/964-8615. **Contact:** Cheryl Mike, Director of Human Resources. **World Wide Web address:** http://www.koss.com. **Description:** Designs, manufactures, and sells stereo headphones, audio/video loudspeakers, and related accessory products. The company's products are sold through audio specialty stores, catalog showrooms, regional department store chains, military exchanges, and national retailers under the Koss name and dual label. The company has more than 1,600 domestic dealers, and its products are carried in more than 11,000 domestic retail outlets. **Corporate headquarters location:** This Location. **International locations:** Canada; Switzerland. **Stock exchange symbol:** KOSS.

LA-Z-BOY INC.
1284 North Telegraph Road, Monroe MI 48162. 734/242-1444. **Contact:** Human Resources. **World Wide Web address:** http://www.la-z-boy.com. **Description:** A leading manufacturer of upholstered seating and residential furniture. La-Z-Boy operates 24 plants in the United States and Canada and sells its products through over 10,000 retail locations. The company operates in five divisions. La-Z-Boy Residential produces stationary chairs, sofas, loveseats, recliners, reclining sofas, sleeper sofas, and modular seating groups, which it sells in a national network of La-Z-Boy proprietary stores, and in department stores, furniture stores, and regional furniture chains. La-Z-Boy Canada manufactures residential seating and markets La-Z-Boy residential products in Canada, and is also initiating a Canadian network of La-Z-Boy proprietary retail stores. Hammary produces high-tables, living room cabinets, wall entertainment units, and upholstered furniture sold in furniture and department stores, as well as CompaTables occasional tables, which are featured in La-Z-Boy proprietary stores. Kincaid makes solid-wood bedroom, dining room, and occasional furniture sold through in-store Kincaid Galleries, select La-Z-Boy Furniture Galleries stores, and better-quality furniture stores nationally. La-Z-Boy Contract Furniture Group includes La-Z-Boy Business Furniture, La-Z-Boy Healthcare Furniture (hospital chairs, recliners, and special mobile recliners marketed through contract dealers and medical sales companies), and La-Z-Boy Hospitality Furniture (specially engineered La-Z-Boy recliners that are sold directly to hotel and motel chains and through hospitality sales companies). **NOTE:** Entry-level positions are offered. **Common positions include:** Accountant/Auditor; Industrial Engineer; Mechanical Engineer. **Educational backgrounds include:** Accounting; Engineering. **Benefits:** Dental Insurance; Employee Discounts; Life Insurance; Medical Insurance; Profit Sharing; Tuition Assistance; Wellness Program. **Special programs:** Internships. **Corporate headquarters location:** This Location. **Other U.S. locations:** Nationwide. **Listed on:** New York Stock Exchange. **Stock exchange symbol:** LZB. **Number of employees nationwide:** 10,000.

LABELON CORPORATION
10 Chapin Street, Canandaigua NY 14424. 716/394-6220. **Toll-free phone:** 800/428-5566. **Fax:** 716/394-3154. **Contact:** Human Resources. **Description:** Manufactures thermal and ink jet imaging supplies and office products. Founded in 1946. **NOTE:** Second and third shifts are offered. **Common positions include:** Administrative Assistant; Advertising Clerk; Assistant Manager; Blue-Collar Worker Supervisor; Budget Analyst; Chemical Engineer; Chemist; Chief Financial Officer; Clerical Supervisor; Computer Operator; Computer Programmer; Controller; Customer Service Representative; Electrician; Finance Director; General Manager; Human Resources Manager; Industrial Engineer; Industrial Production Manager; Manufacturing Engineer; Market Research Analyst; Marketing Manager; Marketing Specialist; Mechanical Engineer; Operations Manager; Production Manager; Quality Control Supervisor; Sales Manager; Sales Representative; Vice President of Finance; Vice President of Sales. **Educational backgrounds include:** Accounting; Business Administration; Chemistry; Engineering; Marketing. **Benefits:** 401(k); Dental Insurance; Disability Coverage; Employee Discounts; Life Insurance; Medical Insurance; Tuition Assistance. **Corporate headquarters location:** This Location. **Listed on:** Privately held. **Annual sales/revenues:** $21 - $50 million. **Number of employees at this location:** 190.

LADD FURNITURE INC.
4620 Grandover Parkway, Greensboro NC 27407. 336/294-5233. **Contact:** Human Resources. **World Wide Web address:** http://www.laddfurniture.com. **Description:** A residential wood, metal, and upholstered furniture designer, manufacturer, and seller, with 26 manufacturing facilities in 10 states and Mexico. LADD markets its broad line of residential and contract furniture under the major brand names American Drew, American of Martinsville, Barclay, Brown Jordan, Clayton Marcus, Daystrom, Design Horizons, Fournier, LADD Home Theatre, Lea, Pennsylvania House,

and Pilliod. The company distributes these products both domestically and, through LADD International, worldwide. **Corporate headquarters location:** This Location. **Subsidiaries include:** LADD Transportation; LADD Upholstery; Lea Lumber & Plywood. **Listed on:** NASDAQ.

LANCASTER COLONY CORPORATION
37 West Broad Street, Suite 500, Columbus OH 43215. 614/224-7141. **Contact:** Personnel Director. **Description:** Manufactures and markets products through three divisions: the Candles Group's glassware and candles are produced and distributed through discount stores, supermarkets, mass merchandisers, gift shops, department stores, and the company's own home party plan. The Candles Group also produces and markets glass containers for the florist industry and imports table and giftware; the Specialty Foods Group includes brand names Marzetti, Pfeiffer, Gizard, Mountain Top, New York, Reames, Inn Maid, and Romanoff; the Automotive group manufactures rubber, vinyl, and carpet-on-rubber car mats. The company also manufactures pickup truck bed mats and liners, truck and trailer splash guards, and aluminum and plastic accessories for light trucks and vans. **Corporate headquarters location:** This Location. **Other area locations:** Cincinnati OH.

LASERCRAFT, INC.
P.O. Box 696, Santa Rosa CA 95402. 707/528-1060. **Contact:** Controller. **World Wide Web address:** http://www.lasercraft.com. **Description:** A manufacturer of laser-engraved wood and paper giftware including stationery and special occasion note cards. **Common positions include:** Accountant; Blue-Collar Worker Supervisor; Buyer; Commercial Artist; Customer Service Rep.; Draftsperson; Operations/Production Manager. **Educational backgrounds include:** Accounting; Art/Design; Business Administration; Marketing. **Benefits:** Dental Insurance; Disability Coverage; Employee Discounts; Life Insurance; Medical Insurance; Pension Plan; Savings Plan; Tuition Assistance. **Corporate headquarters location:** This Location. **Other U.S. locations:** Healdsburg CA.

LEGGETT & PLATT, INC.
P.O. Box 757, Carthage MO 64836. 417/358-8131. **Contact:** Employment Coordinator. **World Wide Web address:** http://www.leggett.com. **Description:** Manufactures and distributes furniture components used in bedding and finished furniture; manufactures and sells finished furniture including adjustable electric beds, bed frames, bunk beds, and wooden headboards; and produces and sells products for industrial and commercial uses, such as custom aluminum die-cast products, metal and wire shelving, display racks, nonwoven textile fiber products, and steel tubing and steel posts for fencing and roadway signs. **Common positions include:** Accountant; Administrator; Advertising Clerk; Attorney; Commercial Artist; Computer Programmer; Credit Manager; Department Manager; Human Resources Manager; Manufacturer's/Wholesaler's Sales Rep.; Operations/Production Manager; Public Relations Specialist; Purchasing Agent/Manager; Systems Analyst; Transportation/Traffic Specialist. **Educational backgrounds include:** Accounting; Business Administration; Computer Science; Finance; Marketing. **Benefits:** Disability Coverage; Medical Insurance; Pension Plan; Stock Option; Tuition Assistance. **Corporate headquarters location:** This Location. **Other U.S. locations:** Nationwide. **Listed on:** New York Stock Exchange; Pacific Stock Exchange. **Number of employees nationwide:** 11,000.

LENOX INC.
100 Lenox Drive, Lawrenceville NJ 08648. 609/896-2800. **Fax:** 609/844-1554. **Contact:** Director of Organization Effectiveness & Staffing. **E-mail address:** lenox-hr@b-f.com. **World Wide Web address:** http://www.lenox.com. **Description:** This location houses administrative offices, staff functions, product management, and logistics. Overall, Lenox is a manufacturer, wholesaler, and retailer of china, crystal dinnerware, and tableware. **Common positions include:** Accountant; Administrative Assistant; AS400 Programmer Analyst; Attorney; Auditor; Chief Financial Officer; Computer Programmer; Computer Support Technician; Controller; Database Administrator; Database Manager; Finance Director; General Manager; Graphic Artist; Graphic Designer; Human Resources Manager; Internet Services Manager; Market Research Analyst; MIS Specialist; Multimedia Designer; Network/Systems Administrator; Operations Manager; Public Relations Specialist; Purchasing Agent/Manager; Sales Executive; Sales Manager; Sales Representative; SQL Programmer; Systems Analyst; Systems Manager; Typist/Word Processor; Webmaster. **Educational backgrounds include:** Accounting; Art/Design; AS400 Certification; Business Administration; C/C++; Computer Science; Finance; HTML; Liberal Arts; Marketing; Microsoft Word; Novell; Software Development; Spreadsheets; Visual Basic. **Benefits:** 401(k); Casual Dress - Daily; Dental Insurance; Disability Coverage; Employee Discounts; Life Insurance; Medical Insurance; Pension Plan; Tuition Assistance; Vacation Days (6 - 10). **Special programs:** Internships; Summer Jobs. **Corporate headquarters location:** This Location. **Other U.S. locations:** Oxford CA; Hagerstown MD; Cranbury NJ; Pomona NJ; Mt. Pleasant PA; Smithfield RI. **Parent company:** Brown-Forman Corp. **President:** Stan Krangel. **Sales Manager:** Moira Gavin. **Annual sales/revenues:** More than $100 million. **Number of employees at this location:** 205. **Number of employees nationwide:** 3,500.

LEUPOLD & STEVENS INC.
P.O. Box 688, Beaverton OR 97075-0688. 503/646-9171. **Contact:** Human Resources. **World Wide Web address:** http://www.leupold.com. **Description:** A manufacturer of sports optical equipment such as scopes and binoculars. **Corporate headquarters location:** This Location. **Listed on:** Privately held.

LIGHTOLIER
631 Airport Road, Fall River MA 02720. 508/679-8131. **Fax:** 508/646-3357. **Contact:** Human Resources. **World Wide Web address:** http://www.lightolier.com. **Description:** Manufactures lighting fixtures. **Company slogan:** Yes We Can! **Common positions include:** Customer Service Representative; Design Engineer; Draftsperson; Financial Analyst; Manufacturing Engineer; Sales Representative; Systems Analyst. **Educational backgrounds include:** Business Administration; Computer Science; Engineering; Finance; Microsoft Word; Novell; Oracle; Spreadsheets. **Benefits:** 401(k); Casual Dress - Fridays; Dental Insurance; Disability Coverage; Employee Discounts; Life Insurance; Medical Insurance; Pension Plan; Tuition Assistance. **Special programs:** Training; Co-ops; Summer Jobs. **Corporate headquarters location:** This Location. **Other U.S. locations:** Nationwide. **Parent company:** GenlyteThomas Group. **Listed on:** NASDAQ. **Annual sales/revenues:** More than $100 million. **Number of employees at this location:** 500. **Number of employees nationwide:** 5,000.

THE LITTLE TIKES COMPANY
2180 Barlow Road, Hudson OH 44236. 330/650-3000. **Contact:** Vice President of Human Resources. **World Wide Web address:** http://www.littletikes.com. **Description:** Manufactures a variety of plastic toys for children. **Parent company:** Newell Rubbermaid. **Listed on:** New York Stock Exchange. **Stock exchange symbol:** NWL.

MACE SECURITY INTERNATIONAL, INC.
160 Benmont Avenue, Bennington VT 05201. 802/447-1503. **Fax:** 802/442-3823. **Contact:** Human Resources. **World Wide Web address:** http://www.mace.com. **Description:** A leading producer of Mace brand defense sprays for the consumer market. **Common positions include:** Account Manager; Accountant; Administrative Assistant; Advertising Executive; Buyer; Chief Financial Officer; Computer Engineer; Controller; Customer Service Representative; General Manager; Graphic Designer; Human Resources Manager; Internet Services Manager; Marketing Manager; Operations Manager; Paralegal; Production Manager; Public Relations Specialist; Sales Executive; Sales Manager; Secretary; Transportation/Traffic Specialist; Vice President of Finance; Vice President of Operations. **Corporate headquarters location:** This Location. **Listed on:** NASDAQ. **Stock exchange symbol:** MACE.

MAGLA PRODUCTS INC.
P.O. Box 1934, Morristown NJ 07962-1934. 973/377-0500. **Contact:** Human Resources. **Description:** Manufactures kitchen and domestic household products including ironing-board covers, dish towels, oven mitts, rubber gloves, disposable wipe cloths, and cling sheets. **Corporate headquarters location:** This Location.

MARCAL PAPER MILLS, INC.
One Market Street, Elmwood Park NJ 07407. 201/796-4000. **Contact:** James H. Nelson, Director of Human Resources. **World Wide Web address:** http://www.marcalpaper.com. **Description:** Manufactures and distributes a broad range of nationally advertised paper products including paper towels, toilet tissue, and napkins. **Common positions include:** Accountant/Auditor; Chemical Engineer; Computer Programmer; Customer Service Representative; Manufacturer's/Wholesaler's Sales Rep.; Mechanical Engineer; Operations/Production Manager. **Educational backgrounds include:** Accounting; Business Administration; Engineering. **Benefits:** 401(k); Dental Insurance; Disability Coverage; Employee Discounts; Life Insurance; Medical Insurance; Savings Plan; Tuition Assistance. **Corporate headquarters location:** This Location.

MASCO CORPORATION
21001 Van Born Road, Taylor MI 48180. 313/274-7400. **Contact:** Personnel Department. **World Wide Web address:** http://www.masco.com. **Description:** Manufactures faucets, plumbing supplies, kitchen and bathroom cabinets, bathroom and spa equipment, locks, and hardware. The company also manufactures home furnishing products including furniture, upholstery and fabrics, mirrors, lamps, and decorative treatments and accessories. **Corporate headquarters location:** This Location. **Subsidiaries include:** Baldwin Hardware Corporation; The Berkline Corporation. **Listed on:** New York Stock Exchange. **Number of employees at this location:** 800.

MATSUSHITA KOTOBUKI ELECTRONICS INDUSTRIES OF AMERICA, INC.
2001 Kotobuki Way, Vancouver WA 98660. 360/695-1338. **Fax:** 360/695-3155. **Contact:**
Human Resources. **Description:** Manufactures combination TV/VCR units. **President:** Kenzo Hayashi.

MATTEL INC.
333 Continental Boulevard, El Segundo CA 90245. 310/252-2000. **Contact:** Corporate Staffing. **World Wide Web address:** http://www.mattel.com. **Description:** Produces and distributes toys, electronic products, games, books, hobby products, and family entertainment products. **Corporate headquarters location:** This Location. **Other U.S. locations:** Fort Wayne IN; Mount Laurel NJ. **Listed on:** New York Stock Exchange. **Number of employees at this location:** 29,000.

MAYTAG CORPORATION
403 West Fourth Street North, P.O. Box 39, Newton IA 50208. 515/792-7000. **Fax:** 515/787-8244. **Contact:** Human Resources. **World Wide Web address:** http://www.maytagcorp.com. **Description:** Manufactures and repairs major home and commercial appliances. **Common positions include:** Accountant; Buyer; Computer Programmer; Design Engineer; Electrical/Electronics Engineer; Industrial Engineer; Mechanical Engineer; Sales Representative; Systems Analyst. **Educational backgrounds include:** Accounting; Business Administration; Communications; Computer Science; Engineering; Liberal Arts; Marketing. **Benefits:** 401(k); Dental Insurance; Disability Coverage; Employee Discounts; Job Sharing; Life Insurance; Medical Insurance; Pension Plan; Profit Sharing; Savings Plan; Stock Option; Tuition Assistance. **Special programs:** Internships. **Corporate headquarters location:** This Location. **Subsidiaries include:** Dixie-Narco, Inc.; G.S. Blodgett Corp.; Maytag Appliances; Maytag International; The Hoover Company. **Listed on:** New York Stock Exchange. **Annual sales/revenues:** More than $100 million. **Number of employees at this location:** 3,800. **Number of employees nationwide:** 24,050.

MEGAS BEAUTY CARE INC.
15501 Industrial Parkway, Cleveland OH 44135. 216/676-6400. **Contact:** Human Resources. **Description:** Manufactures cosmetic puffs, pocket tissue packs, and cotton swabs. **Common positions include:** Accountant/Auditor; Blue-Collar Worker Supervisor; Computer Programmer; Customer Service Representative; Marketing Specialist; Operations/Production Manager; Systems Analyst. **Educational backgrounds include:** Accounting; Computer Science; Marketing. **Benefits:** Life Insurance; Medical Insurance; Pension Plan; Tuition Assistance. **Corporate headquarters location:** This Location.

MELALEUCA
3910 South Yellowstone Highway, Idaho Falls ID 83402. 208/522-0700. **Fax:** 208/528-2090. **Contact:** Human Resources. **E-mail address:** info@melaleuca.com. **World Wide Web address:** http://www.melaleuca.com. **Description:** A consumer-direct marketing company. Melaleuca produces and distributes personal care, home hygiene, nutritional, and pharmaceutical products. **Common positions include:** Accountant/Auditor; Computer Programmer; Customer Service Representative; Human Resources Manager; Management Trainee; Systems Analyst. **Educational backgrounds include:** Accounting; Art/Design; Business Administration; Computer Science; Finance; Liberal Arts; Marketing; Mathematics. **Benefits:** 401(k); Dental Insurance; Employee Discounts; Life Insurance; Medical Insurance; Profit Sharing; Savings Plan; Tuition Assistance. **Corporate headquarters location:**

This Location. **Other U.S. locations:** Nationwide. **Listed on:** Privately held. **Number of employees at this location:** 850. **Number of employees nationwide:** 1,300.

MERLE NORMAN COSMETICS
9130 Bellanca Avenue, Los Angeles CA 90045. 310/337-2200. **Toll-free phone:** 800/421-2060. **Fax:** 310/337-2364. **Recorded jobline:** 310/337-2412. **Contact:** Monica Daigle, Corporate Recruiter. **Description:** Manufactures a complete line of over 500 skin care and cosmetic products sold exclusively through independently-owned studios. **Common positions include:** Administrative Assistant; Chemist; Electrician; Graphic Designer; MIS Specialist; Operations Manager; Production Manager; Secretary. **Educational backgrounds include:** Accounting; Art/Design; Chemistry; Computer Science; Marketing. **Benefits:** 401(k); Dental Insurance; Disability Coverage; Employee Discounts; Life Insurance; Medical Insurance; Pension Plan. **Corporate headquarters location:** This Location. **Listed on:** Privately held. **Annual sales/revenues:** $51 - $100 million. **Number of employees at this location:** 450.

METRUM DATATAPE, INC.
605 East Huntington Drive, Monrovia CA 91016. 626/358-9500. **Contact:** Personnel. **World Wide Web address:** http://www.metrum-datatape.com. **Description:** Manufacturers of analog and digital tape recorders. **Number of employees at this location:** 120.

MICHAEL ANTHONY JEWELERS, INC.
115 South MacQuesten Parkway, Mount Vernon NY 10550. 914/699-0000. **Contact:** Human Resources. **World Wide Web address:** http://www.michaelanthony.com. **Description:** A designer, manufacturer, and distributor of gold jewelry. Michael Anthony Jewelers' largest product line is an extensive selection of gold charms and pendants which include religious symbols; popular sayings (talking charms); sport themes and team logos; animal motifs; nautical, seashore, western, musical, zodiac, and other thematic figures; initials; and abstract artistic creations. The manufacturing division manufactures gold rope chain and designs gold tubing and bangle blanks used in the production of gold bracelets. The Jardinay product line consists of gold chains, earrings, and watches. **Corporate headquarters location:** This Location.

MIDWAY GAMES INC.
3401 North California Avenue, Chicago IL 60618. 773/961-1800. **Contact:** Human Resources. **World Wide Web address:** http://www.midwaygames.com. **Description:** Develops a wide variety of coin-operated arcade and home video game entertainment products. **Common positions include:** Accountant; Administrative Assistant; AS400 Programmer Analyst; Attorney; Auditor; Buyer; Computer Animator; Computer Engineer; Computer Programmer; Computer Support Technician; Computer Technician; Controller; Credit Manager; Customer Service Representative; Database Administrator; Database Manager; Design Engineer; Electrical/Electronics Engineer; Graphic Artist; Graphic Designer; Human Resources Manager; Intellectual Property Lawyer; Market Research Analyst; Marketing Manager; Network/Systems Administrator; Paralegal; Quality Assurance Engineer; Sales Manager; Secretary; Software Engineer; Systems Analyst; Technical Writer/Editor; Webmaster. **Educational backgrounds include:** Accounting; Art/Design; AS400 Certification; Business Administration; C/C++; Computer Science; Engineering; Finance; HTML; Internet; Marketing; Microsoft Word; Software

Development; Spreadsheets; Visual Basic. **Benefits:** 401(k); Casual Dress - Fridays; Dental Insurance; Disability Coverage; Employee Discounts; Life Insurance; Medical Insurance; Public Transit Available; Tuition Assistance. **Corporate headquarters location:** This Location. **Other U.S. locations:** CA; TX. **Subsidiaries include:** Atari Games Corporation (Milpitas CA); Midway Home Entertainment Inc. (Corsicana TX) **Listed on:** New York Stock Exchange. **Stock exchange symbol:** MWY. **CFO:** Harold H. Bach, Jr. **Annual sales/revenues:** More than $100 million. **Number of employees at this location:** 250. **Number of employees nationwide:** 500.

MILWAUKEE ELECTRIC TOOL CORP.
13135 West Lisbon Road, Brookfield WI 53005. 262/783-8333. **Contact:** Human Resources. **World Wide Web address:** http://www.mil-electric-tool.com. **Description:** Engaged in the design, manufacture, sale, and service of portable power tools. **NOTE:** Entry-level positions are offered. **Common positions include:** Electrical/Electronics Engineer; Sales Representative. **Educational backgrounds include:** Business Administration; Engineering; Marketing. **Benefits:** 401(k); Dental Insurance; Disability Coverage; Employee Discounts; Life Insurance; Medical Insurance; Pension Plan; Profit Sharing; Tuition Assistance. **Corporate headquarters location:** This Location. **Other U.S. locations:** AR; MS. **Parent company:** Atlas-Copco. **Number of employees at this location:** 900. **Number of employees nationwide:** 2,000.

MITY-LITE, INC.
1301 West 400 North, Orem UT 84057. 801/224-0589. **Toll-free phone:** 800/327-1692. **Fax:** 801/224-6191. **Contact:** Human Resources. **World Wide Web address:** http://www.mitylite.com. **Description:** Manufactures light weight, durable, plastic folding leg tables and upholstered stacking chairs. Founded in 1987. **NOTE:** Entry-level positions and part-time jobs are offered. **Common positions include:** Accountant; Administrative Assistant; Administrative Manager; Blue-Collar Worker Supervisor; Chief Financial Officer; Clerical Supervisor; Controller; Database Administrator; Design Engineer; Draftsperson; Electrician; General Manager; Human Resources Manager; Industrial Production Manager; Manufacturing Engineer; Market Research Analyst; Marketing Manager; Network/Systems Administrator; Production Manager; Purchasing Agent/Manager; Sales Manager; Sales Representative; Secretary; Vice President. **Educational backgrounds include:** Accounting; Business Administration; Computer Science; Engineering; Finance; Marketing; Microsoft Word; Novell; Spreadsheets. **Benefits:** 401(k); Casual Dress - Daily; Employee Discounts; Life Insurance; Medical Insurance; Profit Sharing. **Corporate headquarters location:** This Location. **Listed on:** NASDAQ. **Stock exchange symbol:** MITY. **Annual sales/revenues:** $21 - $50 million. **Number of employees at this location:** 200.

MOLTECH POWER SYSTEMS
P.O. Box 147114, Gainesville FL 32614-7114. 904/462-4719. **Contact:** Ms. Gerry Bryant, Human Resources. **Description:** A manufacturer of rechargeable batteries. **Common positions include:** Chemical Engineer; Electrical/Electronics Engineer; Mechanical Engineer; Metallurgical Engineer. **Educational backgrounds include:** Chemistry; Engineering. **Benefits:** 401(k); Dental Insurance; Disability Coverage; Life Insurance; Medical Insurance; Tuition Assistance. **Special programs:** Internships. **Corporate headquarters location:**

This Location. **Number of employees at this location:** 1,300.

MONARCH LUGGAGE COMPANY INC.
475 Fifth Avenue, 3rd Floor, New York NY 10017. 212/686-6900. **Contact:** Personnel Department. **Description:** Manufactures and distributes a wide range of luggage products including briefcases, tote bags, athletic bags, attache cases, and related accessories. **Corporate headquarters location:** This Location.

MYRON MANUFACTURING CORPORATION
205 Maywood Avenue, Maywood NJ 07607. 201/843-6464. **Fax:** 201/843-8390. **Contact:** Human Resources. **World Wide Web address:** http://www.myrononline.com. **Description:** Manufactures a line of custom-made vinyl products including pocket calendars for the office and business markets. This location also hires seasonally. Founded in 1949. **NOTE:** Entry-level positions and second and third shifts are offered. **Common positions include:** Account Representative; Accountant; Administrative Assistant; Administrative Manager; Advertising Clerk; Advertising Executive; AS400 Programmer Analyst; Assistant Manager; Blue-Collar Worker Supervisor; Chief Financial Officer; Clerical Supervisor; Computer Operator; Computer Programmer; Controller; Customer Service Representative; Design Engineer; Editor; Financial Analyst; Graphic Artist; Industrial Engineer; Industrial Production Manager; Internet Services Manager; Manufacturing Engineer; Market Research Analyst; Marketing Manager; MIS Specialist; Production Manager; Purchasing Agent/Manager; Quality Assurance Engineer; Quality Control Supervisor; Sales Executive; Sales Manager; Sales Representative; Transportation/Traffic Specialist; Website Developer. **Educational backgrounds include:** Accounting; Art/Design; AS400 Certification; Business Administration; Cold Fusion; Communications; Computer Science; Engineering; Finance; HTML; Java; Marketing; MBA; Microsoft Office; Microsoft Word; QuarkXPress; Spreadsheets. **Benefits:** 401(k); Casual Dress - Daily; Dental Insurance; Disability Coverage; Employee Discounts; Life Insurance; Medical Insurance; On-Site Exercise Facility; Pension Plan; Savings Plan; Tuition Assistance; Vacation Days (10 - 20). **Special programs:** Internships; Training. **Corporate headquarters location:** This Location. **President:** Marie Adler-Kravecas. **Facilities Manager:** Dan Hurtubise. **Information Systems Manager:** Bruce Kalten. **Purchasing Manager:** Jim Ragucci. **Sales Manager:** Terrence Flynn. **Annual sales/revenues:** More than $100 million. **Number of employees at this location:** 600.

NACCO INDUSTRIES, INC.
5875 Landerbrook Drive, Suite 300, Mayfield Heights OH 44124. 440/449-9600. **Contact:** Human Resources. **Description:** Manufactures forklift trucks and produces coal from four surface mines in North Dakota, Texas, and Louisiana. NACCO also makes household appliances including blenders, food processors, electric knives, toasters, coffeemakers, and irons under the brand names Hamilton Beach and Proctor-Silex. The company operates more than 100 Kitchen Collection factory outlets nationwide that sell kitchenware and appliances. **Corporate headquarters location:** This Location. **Listed on:** New York Stock Exchange.

NANIK GROUP
7200 Stewart Avenue, Wausau WI 54401. 715/843-4653. **Contact:** Human Resources. **Description:** Manufactures wooden interior blinds of all styles.

Corporate headquarters location: This Location. **Parent company:** Springs Window Fashions. **Number of employees at this location:** 450.

NATIONAL ASSN. OF MANUFACTURERS
1331 Pennsylvania Avenue NW, Suite 600, Washington DC 20004-1790. 202/637-3016. **Contact:** Director of Human Resources. **World Wide Web address:** http://www.nam.org. **Description:** Involved in lobbying for the interests of manufacturers. **Common positions include:** Attorney; Editor; Lobbyist; Reporter; Services Sales Representative. **Educational backgrounds include:** Communications; Liberal Arts; Political Science. **Benefits:** Dental Insurance; Disability Coverage; Life Insurance; Medical Insurance; Pension Plan; Savings Plan; Tuition Assistance. **Corporate headquarters location:** This Location.

NATIONAL PICTURE AND FRAME
P.O. Box 1910, Greenwood MS 38930. 662/451-4800. **Contact:** Human Resources. **World Wide Web address:** http://www.nationalpicture.com. **Description:** A manufacturer and marketer of picture frames, framed art, and framed mirrors. Primary customers are mass merchants. Founded in 1964. **Corporate headquarters location:** This Location. **Listed on:** NASDAQ. **Stock exchange symbol:** NPAF.

NEFF COMPANY
645 Pine Street, Greenville OH 45331. 937/548-3194. **Contact:** Joseph P. Andros, Vice President of Human Resources. **World Wide Web address:** http://www.neffco.com. **Description:** A manufacturer of sports awards. The company also carries a line of recognition products such as banners, plaques, jackets, T-shirts, and fleecewear. **Common positions include:** Accountant/Auditor; Blue-Collar Worker Supervisor; Buyer; Commercial Artist; Computer Programmer; Customer Service Representative; Department Manager; Financial Analyst; Human Resources Manager; Industrial Engineer; Industrial Production Manager; Management Trainee; Manufacturer's/Wholesaler's Sales Rep.; Marketing Specialist; Operations/Production Manager; Purchasing Agent/Manager; Quality Control Supervisor. **Educational backgrounds include:** Accounting; Art/Design; Business Administration; Communications; Liberal Arts; Marketing. **Benefits:** Disability Coverage; Employee Discounts; Life Insurance; Medical Insurance; Profit Sharing; Retirement Plan; Tuition Assistance. **Corporate headquarters location:** This Location.

NEUTROGENA CORPORATION
5760 West 96th Street, Los Angeles CA 90045. 310/642-1150. **Fax:** 310/337-5537. **Recorded jobline:** 800/265-8648. **Contact:** Human Resources. **World Wide Web address:** http://www.neutrogena.com. **Description:** Manufactures a variety of personal care products focusing on hair, skin, and cosmetics. **Parent company:** Johnson & Johnson (New Brunswick NJ).

NEWELL RUBBERMAID
29 East Stephenson Street, Freeport IL 61032. 815/235-4171. **Contact:** Human Resources. **World Wide Web address:** http://www.newellco.com. **Description:** A manufacturer of housewares, hardware, home furnishings, office products, hair accessories, beauty organizers, picture frames, specialty glass products, and industrial plastics. **Common positions include:** Accountant/Auditor; Administrator; Credit Manager; Financial Analyst; General Manager; Human Resources Manager; Systems Analyst; Technical Writer/Editor. **Educational backgrounds include:** Accounting;

Business Administration; Computer Science; Finance; Mathematics. **Benefits:** Credit Union; Dental Insurance; Disability Coverage; Employee Discounts; Life Insurance; Medical Insurance; Pension Plan; Profit Sharing; Tuition Assistance. **Corporate headquarters location:** This Location. **Listed on:** New York Stock Exchange. **Number of employees worldwide:** 32,000.

NORDIC WARE
5005 Highway 7, St. Louis Park MN 55416. 612/924-8587. **Toll-free phone:** 800/328-4310x587. **Fax:** 612/924-9655. **Contact:** Diane M. Zeller, Human Resources Manager. **E-mail address:** dianezeller@nordicware.com. **World Wide Web address:** http://www.nordicware.com. **Description:** Produces aluminum cookware and related products. Founded in 1946. **NOTE:** Second and third shifts are offered. **Common positions include:** Accountant; Administrative Assistant; Blue-Collar Worker Supervisor; Buyer; Chief Financial Officer; Credit Manager; Customer Service Representative; Electrical Engineer; Graphic Designer; Human Resources Manager; Operations Manager; Production Manager; Sales Manager; Secretary; Systems Analyst; Systems Manager. **Educational backgrounds include:** Accounting; Business Administration; Engineering. **Benefits:** 401(k); Dental Insurance; Disability Coverage; Employee Discounts; Life Insurance; Medical Insurance; Public Transit Available; Tuition Assistance. **Office hours:** Monday - Friday, 8:00 a.m. - 5:00 p.m. **Corporate headquarters location:** This Location. **Parent company:** Northland Aluminum Products, Inc. **Listed on:** Privately held. **Number of employees at this location:** 140.

THE NORTH FACE
2013 Farallon Drive, San Leandro CA 94577. 510/618-3500. **Contact:** Human Resources. **World Wide Web address:** http://www.thenorthface.com. **Description:** A manufacturer, wholesaler, and retailer of outdoor equipment and apparel including tents, backpacks, sleeping bags, outerwear, skiwear, and sportswear. **Common positions include:** Accountant; Blue-Collar Worker Supervisor; Computer Programmer; Credit Manager; Customer Service Representative; Human Resources Manager; Industrial Engineer; Manufacturer's/Wholesaler's Sales Rep.; Marketing Specialist; Operations/Production Manager; Purchasing Agent/Manager; Quality Control Supervisor. **Educational backgrounds include:** Accounting; Business Administration; Computer Science; Finance; Marketing. **Benefits:** Dental Insurance; Disability Coverage; Employee Discounts; Life Insurance; Medical Insurance; Pension Plan; Savings Plan; Tuition Assistance. **Corporate headquarters location:** This Location.

NORTHRIDGE MANUFACTURING GROUP
8500 Balboa Boulevard, Northridge CA 91329. 818/893-8411. **Contact:** Carolina Bowers, Supervisor of Human Resources. **Description:** Designs, manufactures, and distributes audio loudspeaker systems for professional, automotive, and home entertainment use, both domestically and internationally. **Common positions include:** Accountant; Buyer; Chemical Engineer; Draftsperson; Human Resources Manager; Industrial Engineer; Manufacturer's Sales Rep.; Manufacturing Engineer; Purchasing Agent; Services Sales Rep.; Software Engineer; Wholesale and Retail Buyer. **Educational backgrounds include:** Art/Design; Communications; Computer Science; Engineering; Finance; Liberal Arts; Marketing. **Benefits:** 401(k); Life Insurance; Medical Insurance; Tuition Assistance. **Special programs:** Internships. **Corporate headquarters**

location: This Location. **Number of employees at this location:** 2,500.

NU SKIN INTERNATIONAL, INC.
One Nu Skin Plaza, 75 West Center Street, Provo UT 84601-4483. 801/345-1000. **Contact:** Human Resources Department. **Description:** Manufactures and markets personal care and nutritional products. The personal care products division includes hair care, skin care, nail care, sun protection, and oral health care products. The Interior Design Nutritional division operates a weight management lifestyle program. The program consists of nutritional products, weight management supplements, instructional materials, and an interactive health and fitness assessment and counseling program. **Corporate headquarters location:** This Location. **International locations:** Australia; Canada; Hong Kong; Japan; Mexico; New Zealand; Taiwan.

OLSONITE CORPORATION
25 Dart Road, Newnan GA 30265. 770/253-3930. **Contact:** Larry Thompson, Human Resources Manager. **Description:** Manufactures plastic and vinyl toilet seats. **Common positions include:** Accountant/Auditor; Blue-Collar Worker Supervisor; Electrician; General Manager; Human Resources Manager; Industrial Engineer; Industrial Production Manager; Mechanical Engineer; Operations/Production Manager; Purchasing Agent/Manager; Quality Control Supervisor; Transportation/Traffic Specialist. **Educational backgrounds include:** Accounting; Business Administration; Engineering. **Benefits:** 401(k); Disability Coverage; Employee Discounts; Life Insurance; Medical Insurance; Pension Plan; Savings Plan; Tuition Assistance. **Special programs:** Internships. **Corporate headquarters location:** This Location. **Other U.S. locations:** CA; WA. **International locations:** Canada. **Listed on:** Privately held. **Number of employees at this location:** 135.

OLYMPUS AMERICA INC.
2 Corporate Center Drive, Melville NY 11747. 516/844-5000. **Contact:** Human Resources. **World Wide Web address:** http://www.olympus.com. **Description:** This location houses administrative offices only. Overall, Olympus America manufactures and markets cameras and imaging equipment as well as a variety of surgical and medical instruments. **Corporate headquarters location:** This Location.

ONEIDA LTD.
163-181 Kenwood Avenue, Oneida NY 13421. 315/361-3000. **Contact:** Bob Houle, Vice President of Human Resources. **World Wide Web address:** http://www.oneida.com. **Description:** Manufactures and markets tableware and industrial wire products. Through its Consumer Operations, Oneida is one of the world's largest manufacturers of stainless steel flatware (knives, forks, and spoons). Other products include flatware in silverplate, gold electroplate, and sterling silver; silverplated holloware (trays and coffee sets); and crystal stemware and giftware. Through its Foodservice Operations, Oneida offers the industry complete selections of dinnerware, flatware, and holloware under the trademarks of Oneida, Buffalo, D.J., Santa Andrea, and Northland. **Corporate headquarters location:** This Location.

O'SULLIVAN CORPORATION
P.O. Box 3510, Winchester VA 22604. 540/667-6666. **Physical address:** 1944 Valley Avenue, Winchester VA. **Contact:** Human Resources. **Description:** Operates in two business segments: calendered and molded plastic products, which involves the manufacture of calendered plastics for

the automotive and specialty plastics manufacturing industries; and lawn and garden consumer products. **Corporate headquarters location:** This Location.

R.S. OWENS AND COMPANY INC.
5535 North Lynch Avenue, Chicago IL 60630. 773/282-6000. **Contact:** Director of Personnel. **Description:** Manufactures trophies, plaques, and awards. **Common positions include:** Blue-Collar Worker Supervisor; Credit Manager; Department Manager; Human Resources Manager; Manufacturer's/Wholesaler's Sales Rep.; Mechanical Engineer; Purchasing Agent/Manager; Quality Control Supervisor. **Educational backgrounds include:** Business Administration; Computer Science; Finance; Liberal Arts; Marketing. **Benefits:** Disability Coverage; Employee Discounts; Life Insurance; Medical Insurance; Profit Sharing; Savings Plan. **Corporate headquarters location:** This Location.

PARLUX FRAGRANCES
3725 SW 30th Avenue, Fort Lauderdale FL 33312. 954/316-9008x103. **Fax:** 954/316-8155. **Contact:** Tania Espinosa, Personnel Administrator. **Description:** A manufacturer and international distributor of fragrances and cosmetics. The company's product line includes Perry Ellis Cosmetics, Fred Hayman Beverly Hills, Animale Parfums, and Phantom of the Opera. **Corporate headquarters location:** This Location. **International locations:** Paris, France.

PEN-TAB INDUSTRIES, INC.
167 Kelley Drive, Front Royal VA 22630. 540/622-2000. **Contact:** Glenn Wood, Director of Human Resources. **Description:** Manufactures art and school supplies including notebooks, legal pads, and envelopes. **Common positions include:** Accountant; Blue-Collar Worker Supervisor; Buyer; Customer Service Representative; Electrician; General Manager; Human Resources Manager; Industrial Production Manager; Management Trainee; Manufacturer's/Wholesaler's Sales Rep.; Operations/Production Manager; Purchasing Agent/Manager. **Benefits:** 401(k); Disability Coverage; Employee Discounts; Life Insurance; Medical Insurance. **Corporate headquarters location:** This Location. **Other U.S. locations:** Los Angeles CA; Chicago IL. **Listed on:** Privately held. **Number of employees at this location:** 250. **Number of employees nationwide:** 700.

PENN RACQUET SPORTS, INC.
306 South 45th Avenue, Phoenix AZ 85043. 602/269-1492. **Fax:** 602/484-7580. **Contact:** Vicky Moore, Human Resources Manager. **E-mail address:** vmoore@pennracquet.com. **World Wide Web address:** http://www.pennracquet.com. **Description:** Manufactures tennis and racquet balls for domestic and international markets. Founded in 1922. **NOTE:** Entry-level positions and second and third shifts are offered. **Common positions include:** Accountant; Administrative Assistant; Blue-Collar Worker Supervisor; Buyer; Chief Financial Officer; Computer Operator; Computer Programmer; Controller; Credit Manager; Customer Service Representative; Human Resources Manager; Marketing Manager; MIS Specialist; Network Engineer; Production Manager; Purchasing Agent/Manager; Quality Control Supervisor; Sales Representative; Secretary; Systems Analyst; Systems Manager. **Educational backgrounds include:** Accounting; AS400 Certification; Business Administration; Computer Science; Engineering; Finance; Marketing; MBA; Microsoft Office; Novell; SQL. **Benefits:** 401(k); Casual Dress - Daily; Dental Insurance; Disability Coverage; Life Insurance; Medical Insurance; Public Transit Available; Tuition Assistance. **Corporate headquarters location:** This Location. **International locations:** Mullingar, Ireland. **Parent company:** HEAD, USA. **Listed on:** Privately held. **President/CEO:** Gregg Weida. **Facilities Manager:** John Hunter. **Information Systems Manager:** Rich Gliha. **Purchasing Manager:** Larry Gladden. **Sales Manager:** Dave Haggarty. **Annual sales/revenues:** More than $100 million. **Number of employees at this location:** 400.

PENTAX CORPORATION
35 Inverness Drive East, Englewood CO 80112. 303/799-8000. **Contact:** Ann Welsch, Human Resources Manager. **World Wide Web address:** http://www.pentax.com. **Description:** Manufactures cameras, camera supplies, and related photographic products. **Corporate headquarters location:** This Location.

PENTECH INTERNATIONAL INC.
195 Carter Drive, Edison NJ 08817. 732/287-6640. **Contact:** Fay Liff, Human Resources. **Description:** Designs, manufactures, and markets pencils, pens, markers, activity sets, and accessories. **Corporate headquarters location:** This Location.

THE PFALTZGRAFF COMPANY
140 East Market Street, York PA 17405. 717/848-5500. **Contact:** Mr. William Scott, Vice President of Corporate Human Resources. **World Wide Web address:** http://www.pfaltzgraff.com. **Description:** A stoneware and dinnerware manufacturer. The Pfaltzgraff Company also produces a line of table top accessories. **Corporate headquarters location:** This Location.

PHOENIX GOLD INTERNATIONAL, INC.
9300 North Decatur, Portland OR 97203. 503/286-9300. **Fax:** 503/978-3346. **Contact:** Human Resources. **World Wide Web address:** http://www.phoenixgold.com. **Description:** Designs, manufactures, and markets consumer electronics, accessories, and speakers for the car audio aftermarket, and for professional sound and custom audio/video home theater applications. The company also manufactures commercial/professional sound amplifiers. **NOTE:** Entry-level positions are offered. **Common positions include:** Account Representative; Accountant; Chief Financial Officer; Credit Manager; Customer Service Representative; Draftsperson; Electrical/Electronics Engineer; Finance Director; Graphic Artist; Graphic Designer; Human Resources Manager; Manufacturing Engineer; Marketing Manager; Marketing Specialist; MIS Specialist; Network/Systems Administrator; Operations Manager; Production Manager; Purchasing Agent/Manager; Sales Executive; Sales Manager; Vice President of Operations. **Educational backgrounds include:** Accounting; Business Administration; Engineering; Finance; Microsoft Office; Microsoft Word; QuarkXPress; Spreadsheets. **Benefits:** 401(k); Casual Dress - Daily; Dental Insurance; Disability Coverage; Employee Discounts; Life Insurance; Medical Insurance; Profit Sharing; Tuition Assistance; Vacation Days. **Corporate headquarters location:** This Location. **Subsidiaries include:** Carver Professional (also at this location) manufactures stereo amplifiers. **Listed on:** NASDAQ. **Stock exchange symbol:** PGLD. **Annual sales/revenues:** $21 - $50 million. **Number of employees at this location:** 220.

PILOT PEN
60 Commerce Drive, Trumbull CT 06611. 203/377-8800. **Contact:** Human Resources. **World Wide Web address:** http://www.pilotpen.com.

Description: This location houses executive offices only. Overall, Pilot Pen manufactures writing instruments. **Corporate headquarters location:** This Location. **Other U.S. locations:** Fremont CA; Jacksonville FL.

POLK AUDIO
5601 Metro Drive, Baltimore MD 21215. 410/358-3600. **Fax:** 410/764-5266. **Contact:** Human Resources. **World Wide Web address:** http://www.polkaudio.com. **Description:** Designs, manufactures, and markets audio speaker systems under the brand names Polk Audio and Eosone for use in homes and automobiles. Founded in 1972. **Corporate headquarters location:** This Location. **Listed on:** American Stock Exchange. **Stock exchange symbol:** PKA.

PRECOR, INC.
P.O. Box 3004, Bothell WA 98041. 425/486-9292. **Recorded jobline:** 425/482-5444. **Contact:** Human Resources. **World Wide Web address:** http://www.precor.com. **Description:** One of the world's leading designers, manufacturers, and marketers of fitness equipment for home and commercial use. Products include treadmills, stairclimbers, cyclers, and elliptical crosstrainers. **Corporate headquarters location:** This Location. **International locations:** England; Germany; Singapore. **Subsidiaries include:** Pacific Fitness. **Parent company:** Premark International (Deerfield IL). **President:** Bill Potts.

PRESTO PRODUCTS MANUFACTURING
1301 Lavelle Road, Alamogordo NM 88310. 505/437-7660. **Contact:** Plant Manager. **Description:** Manufactures electric appliances and housewares. **Corporate headquarters location:** This Location.

PRINCE SPORTS GROUP
One Sportsystem Plaza, Bordentown NJ 08505-9630. 609/291-5800. **Toll-free phone:** 800/283-6647. **Fax:** 609/291-5791. **Contact:** Mike Soroker, Vice President of Human Resources. **World Wide Web address:** http://www.prince.com. **Description:** Manufactures sports equipment and related accessories. **Common positions include:** Accountant; Adjuster; Administrative Manager; Attorney; Blue-Collar Worker Supervisor; Collector; Computer Programmer; Credit Manager; Customer Service Representative; Draftsperson; Human Resources Manager; Human Service Worker; Investigator; Purchasing Agent/Manager; Systems Analyst; Transportation/Traffic Specialist; Travel Agent. **Educational backgrounds include:** Accounting; Art/Design; Business Administration; Communications; Computer Science; Finance; Marketing. **Benefits:** 401(k); Dental Insurance; Disability Coverage; Employee Discounts; Life Insurance; Medical Insurance; Pension Plan; Profit Sharing; Savings Plan; Tuition Assistance. **Corporate headquarters location:** This Location. **Parent company:** Bennetton. Subsidiaries of the parent company include BSS Active; Eketelon; and Nordica. **Listed on:** NASDAQ. **Number of employees at this location:** 250.

PRO-LINE CORPORATION
2121 Panoramic Circle, Dallas TX 75212. 214/631-4247. **Contact:** Human Resources. **Description:** Manufactures hair care products including relaxers, botanicals, and perm repair products. **Corporate headquarters location:** This Location.

PULASKI FURNITURE CORPORATION
One Pulaski Square, Pulaski VA 24301. 540/980-7330. **Contact:** Diane Hall, Human Resources Director. **Description:** Manufactures bedroom and dining room furniture. **Corporate headquarters location:** This Location. **Listed on:** NASDAQ. **Number of employees nationwide:** 2,285.

PURDY CORPORATION
13201 North Lumbard Street, Portland OR 97203. 503/286-8217. **Contact:** Human Resources. **World Wide Web address:** http://www.purdycorp.com. **Description:** Manufactures hand-crafted painting tools. **Common positions include:** Production Worker. **Benefits:** 401(k); Dental Insurance; Disability Coverage; Medical Insurance; Public Transit Available; Tuition Assistance. **Corporate headquarters location:** This Location. **Listed on:** Privately held. **Number of employees at this location:** 280.

QUEST INTERNATIONAL FRAGRANCES
400 International Drive, Mount Olive NJ 07828. 973/691-7100. **Contact:** Human Resources. **Description:** Develops cosmetic fragrances. **Corporate headquarters location:** This Location.

RANIR DCP
P.O. Box 8547, Grand Rapids MI 49518. 616/698-8880. **Contact:** Human Resources. **World Wide Web address:** http://www.ranirdcp.com. **Description:** Manufactures private label oral health care products including toothbrushes and dental floss. **Common positions include:** Accountant; Blue-Collar Worker Supervisor; Computer Programmer; Customer Service Rep.; Operations Manager; Purchasing Agent/Manager; Quality Control Supervisor. **Educational backgrounds include:** Accounting; Business Administration; Management/Planning. **Benefits:** Dental Insurance; Disability Coverage; Life Insurance; Medical Insurance; Retirement Plan. **Corporate headquarters location:** This Location. **Other U.S. locations:** NJ. **Listed on:** Privately held. **Number of employees at this location:** 350.

RAUCH INDUSTRIES, INC.
P.O. Box 609, Gastonia NC 28053-0609. 704/867-5333. **Fax:** 704/864-2081. **Contact:** Karol Dewitt, Personnel Manager. **Description:** Manufactures and imports Christmas and holiday decorations. **Common positions include:** Blue-Collar Worker Supervisor; Buyer; Customer Service Representative; Electrical/Electronics Engineer. **Educational backgrounds include:** Accounting; Business Administration; Engineering. **Benefits:** 401(k); Dental Insurance; Disability Coverage; Life Insurance; Medical Insurance; Profit Sharing; Savings Plan. **Corporate headquarters location:** This Location. **Listed on:** American Stock Exchange; NASDAQ; New York Stock Exchange. **Number of employees at this location:** 850. **Number of employees nationwide:** 1,000.

RAWLINGS SPORTING GOODS COMPANY
P.O. Box 22000, St. Louis MO 63126. 636/349-3500. **Contact:** Human Resources. **Description:** A leading manufacturer and supplier of team sports equipment in North America and, through its licensee, of baseball equipment and uniforms in Japan. It offers a wide range of quality products for baseball and softball (gloves, baseballs, bats, helmets, protective gear, team uniforms, and accessories); basketball (balls, team uniforms, warm-ups, and accessories); football (balls, shoulder pads, protective gear, and team uniforms); and other sports. The company operates five manufacturing facilities in the United States and Latin America. **Corporate headquarters location:** This Location.

REED & BARTON
144 West Britannia Street, Taunton MA 02780. 508/824-6611. **Contact:** Director of Personnel.

Description: A manufacturer of sterling, silver plate, pewter, and stainless steel silverware. Reed & Barton also produces a line of jewelry products. **Corporate headquarters location:** This Location.

REMINGTON PRODUCTS COMPANY LLC

60 Main Street, Bridgeport CT 06604. 203/367-4400. **Contact:** Human Resources. **World Wide Web address:** http://www.remington-products.com. **Description:** A manufacturer, distributor, and retailer of personal care appliances including electric shavers, hair dryers, beard trimmers, and spa therapy products. Founded in 1937. **Common positions include:** Accountant/Auditor; Blue-Collar Worker Supervisor; Branch Manager; Buyer; Clerical Supervisor; Computer Programmer; Credit Manager; Customer Service Representative; Design Engineer; Designer; Draftsperson; Electrical/Electronics Engineer; Electrician; Financial Analyst; Human Resources Manager; Industrial Engineer; Industrial Production Manager; Management Trainee; Manufacturer's/Wholesaler's Sales Rep.; Market Research Analyst; Mechanical Engineer; Purchasing Agent/Manager; Quality Control Supervisor; Systems Analyst; Typist/Word Processor. **Educational backgrounds include:** Accounting; Business Administration; Engineering; Finance; Marketing. **Benefits:** 401(k); Disability Coverage; Employee Discounts; Life Insurance; Medical Insurance; Savings Plan; Tuition Assistance. **Corporate headquarters location:** This Location. **Listed on:** Privately held. **Annual sales/revenues:** More than $100 million. **Number of employees at this location:** 800. **Number of employees nationwide:** 1,100.

REVLON, INC.

625 Madison Avenue, 8th Floor, New York NY 10022. 212/527-4000. **Contact:** Personnel Department. **World Wide Web address:** http://www.revlon.com. **Description:** Manufactures and distributes a line of skin care products, fragrances, and other cosmetics internationally. **Corporate headquarters location:** This Location. **Listed on:** New York Stock Exchange.

RIDE SNOWBOARD COMPANY

8160 304th Avenue SE, Preston WA 98050. 425/222-8268. **Toll-free phone:** 800/757-5806. **Fax:** 425/222-6499. **Contact:** Human Resources. **World Wide Web address:** http://www.ridesnowboards.com. **Description:** A leading designer, manufacturer, and marketer of snowboards, clothing, and related products under the Ride, Liquid, Preston, Cappel, and SMP brand names. **Common positions include:** Account Manager; Account Representative; Accountant; Administrative Assistant; Administrative Manager; Advertising Executive; Applications Engineer; Assistant Manager; Attorney; Computer Operator; Computer Programmer; Controller; Credit Manager; Customer Service Representative; Financial Analyst; Graphic Artist; Graphic Designer; Human Resources Manager; Internet Services Manager; Marketing Manager; Marketing Specialist; Sales Executive; Sales Manager; Technical Writer/Editor; Telecommunications Manager; Transportation/Traffic Specialist. **Educational backgrounds include:** Accounting; Art/Design; Business Administration; Computer Science; Engineering; Finance; Marketing. **Benefits:** 401(k); Dental Insurance; Disability Coverage; Employee Discounts; Flexible Schedule; Life Insurance; Medical Insurance; Profit Sharing; Public Transit Available; Savings Plan; Stock Purchase; Tuition Assistance. **Special programs:** Internships. **Corporate headquarters location:** This Location. **Subsidiaries include:** Ride - Canada (Toronto, Canada); Ride Manufacturing (Corona CA); SMP

(Chula Vista CA). **Parent company:** Ride Inc. **Listed on:** NASDAQ. **Stock exchange symbol:** RIDE. **Annual sales/revenues:** $51 - $100 million. **Number of employees at this location:** 90. **Number of employees nationwide:** 250.

THE RIVAL COMPANY

800 East 101st Terrace, Suite 100, Kansas City MO 64131. 816/943-4100. **Contact:** Manager. **World Wide Web address:** http://www.rivco.com. **Description:** A leading designer, manufacturer, and marketer of small household appliances, personal care appliances, and sump, well, and utility pumps. The company's product lines are sold to major retail outlets in the United States and Canada, hardware stores, home centers, department stores, catalog showrooms, and warehouse clubs. **Corporate headquarters location:** This Location.

ROLAND CORPORATION U.S.

P.O. Box 910921, Los Angeles CA 90091. 323/890-3700. **Physical address:** 5100 South Eastern Avenue, Los Angeles CA 90040. **Contact:** Debbie Parmenter, Human Resources Director. **World Wide Web address:** http://www.rolandus.com. **Description:** A distributor of electronic musical equipment including keyboards, sound modules, digital samplers, and guitar synthesizers. **Common positions include:** Administrative Assistant; Customer Service Representative. **Educational backgrounds include:** Business Administration; Liberal Arts. **Benefits:** 401(k); Dental Insurance; Disability Coverage; Life Insurance; Medical Insurance. **Corporate headquarters location:** This Location. **Subsidiaries include:** Rodgers Instrument; Roland Audio Development. **Listed on:** Privately held. **Annual sales/revenues:** $51 - $100 million. **Number of employees at this location:** 130. **Number of employees nationwide:** 160.

ROSS BICYCLE

51 Executive Boulevard, Farmingdale NY 11735. 516/249-6000. **Contact:** Eileen Singer, Personnel Director. **Description:** Manufactures a complete line of bicycles, from tricycles to racing bikes, for international distribution. **Corporate headquarters location:** This Location.

ROYAL APPLIANCE MANUFACTURING COMPANY

650 Alpha Drive, Cleveland OH 44143. 440/449-6150. **Contact:** Vice President of Human Resources. **World Wide Web address:** http://www.dirtdevil.com. **Description:** Manufactures and markets the Dirt Devil and Royal brand vacuum cleaners for home and commercial use. **Common positions include:** Customer Service Representative; Designer; Draftsperson; Industrial Engineer; Manufacturer's/Wholesaler's Sales Rep.; Mechanical Engineer; Systems Analyst. **Educational backgrounds include:** Business Administration; Computer Science; Engineering; Marketing. **Benefits:** 401(k); Dental Insurance; Disability Coverage; Employee Discounts; Life Insurance; Medical Insurance; Tuition Assistance. **Special programs:** Internships. **Corporate headquarters location:** This Location. **Listed on:** New York Stock Exchange. **Number of employees at this location:** 150. **Number of employees nationwide:** 700.

RUBBERMAID, INC.

7121 Shelby Avenue, Greenville TX 75401. 903/455-0011. **Contact:** Human Resources. **World Wide Web address:** http://www.rubbermaid.com. **Description:** This location manufactures household products such as plastic food storage containers. Overall, Rubbermaid manufactures and sells rubber and plastic products for the consumer and commercial markets. Products include over 2,500 items for home organization, kitchen and bath, household repairs/do-it-yourself, and agricultural, industrial, and institutional use. **Corporate headquarters location:** Wooster OH.

RUSS BERRIE & COMPANY, INC.

111 Bauer Drive, Oakland NJ 07436. 201/337-9000. **Contact:** Personnel Manager. **World Wide Web address:** http://www.russberrie.com. **Description:** Designs and markets a line of more than 10,000 gift items in the U.S. and abroad. Products include toys, stuffed animals, novelties, and cards. A diverse customer base includes florists, pharmacies, party shops, and stationery stores, as well as hotel, airport, and hospital gift shops. **Common positions include:** Accountant/Auditor; Commercial Artist; Customer Service Representative; Financial Analyst; Manufacturer's/Wholesaler's Sales Rep.; Marketing Specialist. **Educational backgrounds include:** Accounting; Art/Design; Business Administration; Finance; Liberal Arts; Marketing. **Benefits:** Dental Insurance; Employee Discounts; Life Insurance; Medical Insurance; Profit Sharing; Tuition Assistance. **Corporate headquarters location:** This Location. **Listed on:** New York Stock Exchange. **Number of employees nationwide:** 2,000.

S-B POWER TOOL COMPANY

4300 West Peterson Avenue, Chicago IL 60646. 773/286-7330. **Contact:** George Pike, Manager of Human Resources. **Description:** Manufactures hand and power tools. S-B Power Tool is a joint venture between Emerson Electric Company and Robert Bosch GmbH (Germany). **Common positions include:** Buyer; Computer Programmer; Credit Clerk and Authorizer; Customer Service Representative; Draftsperson; Electrical/Electronics Engineer; Financial Analyst; Marketing Specialist; Mechanical Engineer; Purchasing Agent/Manager; Quality Control Supervisor; Systems Analyst. **Educational backgrounds include:** Accounting; Business Administration; Computer Science; Engineering; Finance; Marketing. **Benefits:** Dental Insurance; Disability Coverage; Employee Discounts; Life Insurance; Medical Insurance; Pension Plan; Savings Plan; Tuition Assistance. **Special programs:** Internships. **Corporate headquarters location:** This Location. **Other U.S. locations:** Heber Springs AK; Walnut Ridge AK; Elk Grove IL; New Bern NC. **Number of employees nationwide:** 2,300.

SAMSONITE CORPORATION

11200 East 45th Avenue, Denver CO 80239. 303/373-2000. **Contact:** Human Resources. **Description:** Manufactures and markets luggage and business cases. **Common positions include:** Accountant/Auditor; Blue-Collar Worker Supervisor; Buyer; Computer Programmer; Credit Manager; Customer Service Representative; Draftsperson; Financial Analyst; Industrial Engineer; Manufacturer's/Wholesaler's Sales Rep.; Mechanical Engineer. **Educational backgrounds include:** Accounting; Art/Design; Business Administration; Computer Science; Engineering; Marketing. **Benefits:** Dental Insurance; Disability Coverage; Employee Discounts; Life Insurance; Medical Insurance; Pension Plan; Savings Plan. **Corporate headquarters location:** This Location.

SANFORD CORPORATION

2711 Washington Boulevard, Bellwood IL 60104. 708/547-6650. **Fax:** 708/649-3440. **Contact:** Human Resources. **World Wide Web address:** http://www.sanfordcorp.com. **Description:** Manufactures felt-tip pens. **NOTE:** Entry-level positions, part-time jobs, and second and third shifts

are offered. **Common positions include:** Accountant; Blue-Collar Worker Supervisor; Customer Service Rep.; Industrial Engineer; Management Trainee; Mechanical Engineer; Sales Representative. **Benefits:** 401(k); Casual Dress - Daily; Dental Insurance; Disability Coverage; Employee Discounts; Life Insurance; Medical Insurance; Pension Plan; Public Transit Available; Tuition Assistance; Vacation Days (6 - 10). **Special programs:** Internships; Apprenticeships; Training; Co-ops; Summer Jobs. **Corporate headquarters location:** This Location. **Other U.S. locations:** TN. **International locations:** Worldwide. **Parent company:** Newell Inc. **Listed on:** New York Stock Exchange. **Stock exchange symbol:** NWL. **Annual sales/revenues:** More than $100 million. **Number of employees at this location:** 600. **Number of employees nationwide:** 2,000. **Number of employees worldwide:** 6,000.

T. SARDELLI & SONS, INC.

195 Dupont Drive, Providence RI 02907-3105. 401/944-8510. **Fax:** 401/249-2170. **Contact:** Sandy Morse, Assistant Human Resources Director. **World Wide Web address:** http://www.sarde.com. **Description:** Manufactures precious metal earrings. **Common positions include:** Systems Analyst. **Special programs:** Internships. **Corporate headquarters location:** This Location. **Listed on:** Privately held. **Number of employees at this location:** 250.

SAUCONY, INC.

13 Centennial Drive, P.O. Box 6046, Peabody MA 01961. 978/532-9000. **Contact:** Kerry Smith, Director of Human Resources. **World Wide Web address:** http://www.saucony.com. **Description:** Engaged in the design, manufacture, import, export, development, and marketing of a wide range of athletic footwear and recreational products. In-line, roller, ice skates, and other licensed products are marketed under the Brookfield brand name. **Common positions include:** Accountant; Credit Clerk and Authorizer; Credit Manager; Customer Service Representative; Designer; Draftsperson; Employment Interviewer; Graphic Artist; Human Resources Manager; Industrial Engineer; Industrial Production Manager; Inspector/Tester/Grader; Manufacturer's/Wholesaler's Sales Rep.; Market Research Analyst; Marketing Manager; Mechanical Engineer; Order Clerk; Payroll Clerk; Public Relations Specialist; Receptionist; Retail Sales Worker; Secretary; Stock Clerk; Systems Analyst; Typist/Word Processor. **Educational backgrounds include:** Accounting; Business Administration; Communications; Computer Science; Engineering; Finance; Liberal Arts; Marketing. **Benefits:** 401(k); Dental Insurance; Disability Coverage; Employee Discounts; Life Insurance; Medical Insurance; Tuition Assistance. **Special programs:** Internships. **Corporate headquarters location:** This Location. **Other area locations:** Cambridge MA; East Brookfield MA; Fall River MA. **Other U.S. locations:** Bangor ME. **Listed on:** NASDAQ. **Number of employees at this location:** 140. **Number of employees nationwide:** 415.

SAUDER WOODWORKING CO.

P.O. Box 264, Archbold OH 43502. 419/446-2711. **Fax:** 419/446-3483. **Contact:** Human Resources. **World Wide Web address:** http://www.sauder.com. **Description:** Manufactures furniture and fixtures. This location also hires seasonally. **NOTE:** Entry-level positions, part-time jobs, and second and third shifts are offered. **Common positions include:** Accountant; Administrative Assistant; Applications Engineer; AS400 Programmer Analyst; Blue-Collar Worker Supervisor; Claim Representative; Computer Engineer; Computer

Programmer; Computer Support Technician; Computer Technician; Customer Service Representative; Database Administrator; Database Manager; Design Engineer; Desktop Publishing Specialist; Draftsperson; Electrical/Electronics Engineer; Electrician; Graphic Designer; Help-Desk Technician; Human Resources Manager; Industrial Engineer; Industrial Production Manager; Internet Services Manager; Intranet Developer; Manufacturing Engineer; Mechanical Engineer; MIS Specialist; Multimedia Designer; Network Engineer; Network/Systems Administrator; Production Manager; Project Manager; Purchasing Agent/Manager; Quality Control Supervisor; Software Engineer; SQL Programmer; Systems Analyst; Systems Manager; Transportation/Traffic Specialist; Typist/Word Processor; Webmaster; Website Developer. **Educational backgrounds include:** AS400 Certification; ASP; Business Administration; Communications; Computer Science; Engineering; HTML; Internet Development; Java; MCSE; Microsoft Office; Microsoft Word; Software Development; Software Tech. Support; SQL; Visual Basic. **Benefits:** 401(k); Casual Dress - Fridays; Dental Insurance; Disability Coverage; Employee Discounts; Financial Planning Assistance; Flexible Schedule; Job Sharing; Medical Insurance; Profit Sharing; Relocation Assistance; Tuition Assistance. **Special programs:** Internships; Apprenticeships; Training; Co-ops; Summer Jobs. **Corporate headquarters location:** This Location. **Other U.S. locations:** Salt Lake City UT. **Listed on:** Privately held. **Annual sales/revenues:** More than $100 million. **Number of employees at this location:** 3,200.

SCHWARZKOPF & DEP, INC.
2101 East Via Arado, Rancho Dominguez CA 90220-6189. 310/604-0777. **Contact:** Human Resources Manager. **World Wide Web address:** http://www.dep.com. **Description:** A leading developer, manufacturer, and distributor of diversified personal care products. Products include Dep Styling Gel, Lavoris, Cuticura, Porcelana, Nature's Family, L.A. Looks, Agree, Halsa, Topol, and Lilt. **NOTE:** Part-time jobs are offered. **Common positions include:** Accountant; Administrative Assistant; AS400 Programmer Analyst; Auditor; Budget Analyst; Chief Financial Officer; Computer Operator; Computer Programmer; Computer Support Technician; Computer Technician; Controller; Credit Manager; Customer Service Representative; Financial Analyst; Human Resources Manager; Manufacturing Engineer; Market Research Analyst; Marketing Manager; Production Manager; Purchasing Agent; Quality Assurance Engineer; Quality Control Supervisor; Sales Manager; Secretary; Transportation/Traffic Specialist; Typist/Word Processor; Vice President of Finance; Vice President of Marketing; Vice President of Operations. **Benefits:** 401(k); Casual Dress - Fridays; Dental Insurance; Disability Coverage; Employee Discounts; Life Insurance; Medical Insurance; Pension Plan; Profit Sharing; Sick Days (1 - 5); Tuition Assistance; Vacation Days (6 - 10). **Corporate headquarters location:** This Location. **Parent company:** Henkel. **Listed on:** NASDAQ. **President:** Robert Berglass. **Facilities Manager:** Robert Scheinholtz. **Information Systems Manager:** Oleg Debode. **Purchasing Manager:** Linda Moffat. **Sales Manager:** Dennis Gurka. **Annual sales/revenues:** More than $100 million. **Number of employees at this location:** 285.

SCHWINN CYCLING & FITNESS
1690 38th Street, Boulder CO 80301. 303/939-0100. **Fax:** 303/939-8200. **Contact:** Human Resources. **Description:** Manufactures and distributes bicycles and exercise equipment. **Common positions include:** Accountant/Auditor; Buyer; Computer Programmer; Credit Manager; Department Manager; Draftsperson; Financial Analyst; Human Resources Manager; Industrial Engineer; Industrial Production Manager; Management Trainee; Marketing Specialist; Mechanical Engineer; Purchasing Agent/Manager; Systems Analyst. **Educational backgrounds include:** Accounting; Art/Design; Business Administration; Computer Science; Engineering; Finance; Marketing. **Benefits:** Disability Coverage; Employee Discounts; Life Insurance; Medical Insurance; Pension Plan; Profit Sharing; Tuition Assistance. **Special programs:** Internships. **Corporate headquarters location:** This Location.

SCOTT'S LIQUID GOLD INC.
NEOTERIC COSMETICS
4880 Havana Street, Denver CO 80239. 303/373-4860. **Contact:** Connie Miller, Director of Personnel. **World Wide Web address:** http://www.scottsliquidgold.com. **Description:** Engaged in the manufacture and distribution of household chemical products as well as disposable cigarette filters. Principal products include Scott's Liquid Gold Wood Cleaner and Preservative, Scott's Liquid Gold Glass Cleaner, and Touch of Scent Air Freshener. Neoteric Cosmetics (also at this location) manufactures a skin care line of alpha-hydroxy products. **Common positions include:** Accountant; Chemist; Computer Programmer; Credit Manager; Customer Service Representative; Department Manager; Electrical/Electronics Engineer; Food Scientist/Technologist; Manufacturer's/Wholesaler's Sales Rep.; Marketing Specialist; Mechanical Engineer; Operations/Production Manager; Quality Control Supervisor. **Educational backgrounds include:** Accounting; Business Administration; Chemistry; Computer Science; Engineering; Liberal Arts; Marketing. **Benefits:** Dental Insurance; Employee Discounts; Life Insurance; Medical Insurance; Pension Plan; Profit Sharing; Savings Plan. **Corporate headquarters location:** This Location.

SEALY, INC.
One Office Parkway, Trinity NC 27370. 336/861-3500. **Fax:** 336/861-3501. **Contact:** Human Resources. **World Wide Web address:** http://www.sealy.com. **Description:** A mattress and furniture manufacturer. **Common positions include:** Accountant/Auditor; Attorney; Budget Analyst; Buyer; Clerical Supervisor; Computer Programmer; Electrical/Electronics Engineer; Financial Analyst; General Manager; Human Resources Manager; Industrial Engineer; Industrial Production Manager; Mechanical Engineer; Purchasing Agent/Manager; Systems Analyst; Transportation/Traffic Specialist. **Educational backgrounds include:** Accounting; Business Administration; Communications; Computer Science; Economics; Engineering; Finance; Marketing. **Benefits:** 401(k); Dental Insurance; Disability Coverage; Life Insurance; Medical Insurance; Pension Plan; Profit Sharing; Tuition Assistance. **Corporate headquarters location:** This Location. **Other U.S. locations:** Nationwide. **Listed on:** Privately held. **Number of employees at this location:** 150. **Number of employees nationwide:** 4,800.

SERTA MATTRESS/AW INDUSTRIES
8415 Ardmore Road, Landover MD 20785. 301/322-1000. **Toll-free phone:** 800/638-0520. **Fax:** 301/341-4639. **Contact:** Human Resources. **Description:** Manufactures Serta and private-label mattresses and box springs. Serta Mattress/AW Inc. also distributes bedding related items such as bunk

beds, bed frames, head boards, electric beds, and futons. **Common positions include:** Account Manager; Account Representative; Credit Manager; Customer Service Representative; Production Manager; Quality Control Supervisor; Sales Representative; Transportation/Traffic Specialist. **Benefits:** 401(k); Disability Coverage; Employee Discounts; Life Insurance; Medical Insurance; Profit Sharing. **Corporate headquarters location:** This Location. **President:** Stuart Bannet. **Facilities Manager:** J. Swindell. **Information Systems Manager:** A. Rogers. **Annual sales/revenues:** $21 - $50 million. **Number of employees at this location:** 250.

SHAPE INC.
7 Shape Drive, Kennebunk ME 04043. 207/985-4972. **Fax:** 207/985-4958. **Contact:** Technical/Professional Recruitment. **E-mail address:** careers@shapeglobal.com. **World Wide Web address:** http://www.shapenet.com. **Description:** A manufacturing company specializing in audio- and videocassettes and other magnetic media. **Common positions include:** Accountant; Administrator; Buyer; Computer Programmer; Credit Manager; Customer Service Representative; Department Manager; Electrical/Electronics Engineer; Mechanical Engineer; Operations/Production Manager; Purchasing Agent/Manager; Quality Control Supervisor; Services Sales Representative. **Educational backgrounds include:** Accounting; Business Administration; Engineering; Marketing. **Benefits:** Dental Insurance; Disability Coverage; Employee Discounts; Life Insurance; Medical Insurance; Savings Plan; Tuition Assistance. **Corporate headquarters location:** This Location. **Subsidiaries include:** Shape Audio Product Division, an independent manufacturer of audiocassettes; Shape Video Products, which provides a complete range of manufacturing services from the production of VHS cassettes to the loading, packaging, and distribution of private label cassettes; Shape Segoma, which manufactures high-quality computer printer ribbons for OEM manufacturers and storage media; and Shape South, Inc., which designs and manufactures precision products for the computer, video, and other magnetic media industries.

SHOP VAC CORPORATION
2323 Reach Road, P.O. Box 3307, Williamsport PA 17701. 570/326-0502. **Fax:** 570/321-7089. **Contact:** Employee Relations. **World Wide Web address:** http://www.shopvac.com. **Description:** Manufactures and wholesales vacuum cleaners. **Corporate headquarters location:** This Location. **Listed on:** Privately held.

SIMMONS COMPANY
One Concourse Parkway, Suite 600, Atlanta GA 30328. 770/512-7700. **Contact:** Vice President of Personnel. **World Wide Web address:** http://www. simmonsco.com. **Description:** Manufactures and distributes mattresses and boxsprings. **Common positions include:** Accountant/Auditor; Computer Programmer; Credit Manager; Customer Service Representative; Human Resources Manager; Manufacturer's/Wholesaler's Sales Rep.; Operations/Production Manager; Public Relations Specialist; Purchasing Agent/Manager; Systems Analyst; Transportation/Traffic Specialist. **Educational backgrounds include:** Accounting; Business Administration; Communications; Computer Science; Marketing; Mathematics. **Benefits:** Dental Insurance; Life Insurance; Medical Insurance; Pension Plan; Tuition Assistance. **Corporate headquarters location:** This Location. **Other U.S. locations:** Nationwide. **Number of employees nationwide:** 2,200.

SIMPLICITY PATTERN COMPANY INC.
2 Park Avenue, 12th Floor, New York NY 10016. 212/372-0500. **Contact:** Personnel Manager. **Description:** A manufacturer of clothing patterns. **Common positions include:** Apparel Worker; Technical Writer/Editor. **Educational backgrounds include:** Art/Design. **Benefits:** Dental Insurance; Life Insurance; Medical Insurance; Pension Plan; Tuition Assistance. **Special programs:** Internships. **Corporate headquarters location:** This Location.

SNAP-ON INC.
2801 80th Street, Kenosha WI 53141-1410. 262/656-5200. **Contact:** Human Resources. **Description:** Manufactures and distributes tools, storage units, and diagnostic equipment for professional repair, maintenance, and industrial use. Snap-On's line includes over 14,000 tools, tool chests, custom tools, and diagnostic equipment. Products are supplied through over 5,000 independent dealers and franchises and more than 500 sales representatives. **Common positions include:** Accountant/Auditor; Attorney; Buyer; Ceramics Engineer; Computer Programmer; Credit Clerk and Authorizer; Designer; Draftsperson; Electrical/Electronics Engineer; Financial Analyst; Human Resources Manager; Industrial Engineer; Materials Engineer; Mechanical Engineer; Metallurgical Engineer; Order Clerk; Paralegal; Payroll Clerk; Purchasing Agent/Manager; Receptionist; Sales Representative; Secretary; Systems Analyst; Technical Writer/Editor; Typist/Word Processor. **Educational backgrounds include:** Accounting; Business Administration; Computer Science; Economics; Engineering; Finance; Liberal Arts; Marketing. **Benefits:** 401(k); Dental Insurance; Disability Coverage; Employee Discounts; Life Insurance; Medical Insurance; Pension Plan; Savings Plan; Tuition Assistance. **Corporate headquarters location:** This Location. **Listed on:** New York Stock Exchange. **Number of employees at this location:** 1,000. **Number of employees nationwide:** 9,000.

SNAPPER, INC.
535 Macon Highway, McDonough GA 30253. 770/954-2532. **Toll-free phone:** 800/935-2967. **Fax:** 770/954-2583. **Contact:** Emily James-Lesser, Vice President of Human Resources. **World Wide Web address:** http://www.snapper.com. **Description:** Manufactures Snapper brand power lawnmowers, lawn tractors, garden tillers, snowthrowers, and related parts and accessories. Lawnmowers include rear engine riding mowers, front engine riding mowers, and self-propelled and push-type mowers. Snapper also manufactures a line of commercial lawn and turf equipment. Founded in 1950. **Common positions include:** Account Representative; Accountant; Administrative Assistant; Administrative Manager; Advertising Clerk; Advertising Executive; Applications Engineer; AS400 Programmer Analyst; Assistant Manager; Attorney; Auditor; Budget Analyst; Buyer; Chief Financial Officer; Clerical Supervisor; Computer Operator; Computer Programmer; Computer Support Technician; Controller; Cost Estimator; Database Administrator; Database Manager; Design Engineer; Draftsperson; Electrical/Electronics Engineer; Electrician; Environmental Engineer; Financial Analyst; General Manager; Human Resources Manager; Industrial Engineer; Industrial Production Manager; Manufacturing Engineer; Marketing Manager; Mechanical Engineer; MIS Specialist; Network Administrator; Production Manager; Project Manager; Quality Assurance Engineer; Quality Control Supervisor; Sales Manager; Sales Representative; Secretary; Systems Analyst; Systems Manager; Technical Writer/Editor;

Telecommunications Manager; Typist/Word Processor. **Educational backgrounds include:** Accounting; AS400 Certification; Business Administration; Communications; Computer Science; Engineering; Finance; Marketing. **Benefits:** 401(k); Casual Dress - Daily; Dental Insurance; Disability Coverage; Employee Discounts; Life Insurance; Medical Insurance; Pension Plan; Savings Plan; Tuition Assistance. **Office hours:** Monday - Friday, 8:00 a.m. - 5:00 p.m. **Corporate headquarters location:** This Location. **Parent company:** Metromedia International Group, Inc. **Listed on:** New York Stock Exchange. **President:** Robin G. Chamberlain. **Information Systems Manager:** Howard E. Jones. **Purchasing Manager:** Bruce Broadrick. **Sales Manager:** Mark Chamberlain. **Annual sales/revenues:** More than $100 million. **Number of employees at this location:** 900.

SOUTHERN BINDERS
P.O. Box 1103, Dalton GA 30722. 706/277-2227. **Contact:** Personnel Director. **Description:** Produces ring binders for use in a wide range of consumer products, and specialized binders for display purposes. **Corporate headquarters location:** This Location. **Parent company:** National Service Industries.

SOUTHERN FURNITURE COMPANY
P.O. Box 307, Conover NC 28613. 828/464-0311. **Contact:** Mr. Gail Hall, Personnel & Human Resources Director. **Description:** A manufacturer of upholstery goods and case goods. The company has plants located throughout North Carolina. **Corporate headquarters location:** This Location.

SOUVENIR GROUP
202 F Avenue NW, Cedar Rapids IA 52405. 319/366-7831. **Contact:** Human Resources. **Description:** Manufactures specialty items for advertising, such as ballpoint pens, mechanical pencils, and plastic specialties. **Corporate headquarters location:** This Location. **Parent company:** Bemrose USA.

SPRINGFIELD PRECISION INSTRUMENTS
76 Passaic Street, Wood-Ridge NJ 07075. 973/777-2900. **Contact:** Josie Giovinazzo, Personnel Manager. **Description:** Manufactures thermometers and barometers for consumer use. **Corporate headquarters location:** This Location.

SPRINGS INDUSTRIES, INC.
P.O. Box 70, Fort Mill SC 29716. 803/547-1500. **Physical address:** 205 North White Street, Fort Mill SC 29715. **Contact:** Human Resources. **World Wide Web address:** http://www.springs.com. **Description:** A producer of home furnishings, finished fabrics, and other fabrics for industrial uses. Products include bedroom accessories, bath products, novelties, window treatments, and specialty fabrics for the apparel, home furnishing, home sewing, and sporting good industries. Brand names include Wamsutta, Springmaid, Nanik, Graber, Bali, Springs Baby, Daisy Kingdom, and Regal Rugs. **Corporate headquarters location:** This Location. **Listed on:** New York Stock Exchange. **Stock exchange symbol:** SMI.

SQUARE TWO GOLF, INC.
18 Gloria Lane, Fairfield NJ 07004. 973/227-7783. **Contact:** Human Resources. **World Wide Web address:** http://www.squaretwo.com. **Description:** Manufactures and markets a proprietary line of golf equipment including golf clubs, golf bags, golf balls, and accessories. The company markets these products under the trademarks Square Two, S2, PCX, XGR, ZCX, ONYX, Totally Matched, and Posiflow. Square Two Golf is also the exclusive golf club licensee of the LPGA. **Corporate headquarters location:** This Location.

THE STANLEY WORKS
1000 Stanley Drive, New Britain CT 06053. 860/225-5111. **Contact:** Personnel Department. **World Wide Web address:** http://www.stanleyworks.com. **Description:** A worldwide marketer and manufacturer of quality tools and hardware for do-it-yourselfers and professionals. The company's business is comprised of three segments: Consumer Products including hand tools, fasteners, home hardware, garage door openers, and residential entry doors for the do-it-yourself market; Builders' Products, providing products to the professional construction industry, including architectural and residential hardware, pedestrian power-operated doors, insulated steel entry doors, garage doors and openers, automatic parking gates, and commercial doors; and Industrial Products including products sold to industrial and automotive customers, such as professional hand tools. **Corporate headquarters location:** This Location.

STEARNS INC.
1100 Stearns Drive, Sauk Rapids MN 56379. 320/252-1642. **Toll-free phone:** 800/333-1179. **Fax:** 320/252-4425. **Contact:** Loretta Trulson, Director of Human Resources. **E-mail address:** stearns@stearnsnet.com. **World Wide Web address:** http://www.stearnsinc.com. **Description:** Manufactures life jackets, wet suits, swim products, and other flotation devices. **Common positions include:** Buyer; Computer Programmer; Credit Manager; Customer Service Representative; Designer; Financial Analyst; Human Resources Manager; Industrial Engineer; Industrial Production Manager; Systems Analyst. **Educational backgrounds include:** Accounting; Art/Design; Business Administration; Engineering; Finance; Liberal Arts; Marketing; Mathematics. **Benefits:** 401(k); Disability Coverage; Employee Discounts; Life Insurance; Pension Plan; Profit Sharing; Tuition Assistance. **Special programs:** Internships. **Corporate headquarters location:** This Location.

STONEVILLE FURNITURE COMPANY
P.O. Box 15, Stoneville NC 27048. 336/573-3751. **Fax:** 336/573-9856. **Contact:** Personnel Manager. **Description:** A manufacturer of casual dining furniture, primarily metal-framed chairs and laminate tables. **Common positions include:** Accountant/Auditor; Blue-Collar Worker Supervisor; Buyer; Clerical Supervisor; Computer Programmer; Credit Manager; Customer Service Representative; Designer; Draftsperson; Electrician; General Manager; Human Resources Manager; Industrial Engineer; Industrial Production Manager; Management Trainee; Mechanical Engineer; MIS Specialist; Operations/Production Manager; Purchasing Agent/Manager; Transportation/Traffic Specialist. **Educational backgrounds include:** Accounting; Computer Science; Engineering; Marketing. **Benefits:** 401(k); Dental Insurance; Disability Coverage; Life Insurance; Medical Insurance; Tuition Assistance. **Corporate headquarters location:** This Location. **Parent company:** Stoneville Acquisition Corporation. **Listed on:** Privately held. **Annual sales/revenues:** $21 - $50 million. **Number of employees at this location:** 350.

STROMBECKER CORPORATION
600 North Pulaski Road, Chicago IL 60624. 773/638-1000. **Fax:** 773/638-3679. **Contact:** Robert Knorrek, Director of Human Resources. **E-mail address:** rknorrek@compuserve.com. **World Wide Web address:** http://www.tootsietoy.com.

Description: Manufactures toys under the Tootsie Toy logo. **NOTE:** Entry-level positions are offered. **Company slogan:** Tootsie Toy -- fun, pure, and simple. **Common positions include:** Account Manager; Account Representative; Accountant; Administrative Assistant; Advertising Clerk; AS400 Programmer Analyst; Blue-Collar Worker Supervisor; Branch Manager; Chief Financial Officer; Computer Programmer; Controller; Credit Manager; Customer Service Representative; Database Administrator; Design Engineer; Draftsperson; Graphic Artist; Graphic Designer; Human Resources Manager; Market Research Analyst; Marketing Manager; Marketing Specialist; MIS Specialist; Sales Executive; Sales Representative; Software Engineer. **Educational backgrounds include:** Accounting; Art/Design; Business Administration; Computer Science; Finance; Marketing; Microsoft Word; QuarkXPress; Software Development; Software Tech. Support; Spreadsheets. **Benefits:** 401(k); Casual Dress - Daily; Disability Coverage; Employee Discounts; Life Insurance; Medical Insurance; Profit Sharing; Savings Plan; Tuition Assistance; Vacation Days (6 - 10). **Other U.S. locations:** Nationwide. **International locations:** Worldwide. **President:** Daniel B. Shure. **Annual sales/revenues:** $51 - $100 million. **Number of employees at this location:** 250. **Number of employees nationwide:** 600.

STURM, RUGER & COMPANY INC.
Lacey Place, Southport CT 06490. 203/259-7843. **Contact:** Human Resources Department. **Description:** Designs, manufactures, and sells pistols, revolvers, rifles, and shotguns for a variety of sporting purposes. The company also manufactures and markets various models of police revolvers, pistols, rifles, and selective firearms for law enforcement agencies and military establishments. **Corporate headquarters location:** This Location. **Subsidiaries include:** Pine Tree Castings (Newport NH) produces both chrome and stainless ferrous investment castings; Ruger Investment Casting (Prescott AZ) produces aluminum, ferrous, and titanium commercial investment castings as well as components for the company's firearm production; Uni-Cast (Manchester NH) produces a wide variety of complex parts primarily for defense-related products.

SUNBEAM CORPORATION
2381 Executive Center Drive, Boca Raton FL 33431. 561/912-4100. **Contact:** Human Resources. **Description:** A designer, manufacturer, and marketer of consumer products. The company is divided into several business groups. Outdoor Products includes propane, natural gas, electric, and charcoal barbecue grills; aluminum lawn and patio furniture and related accessories; and wrought iron and wood furniture. Household Products includes electric and conventional blankets, comforters, heated throws, heating pads, bath scales, health monitoring systems, vaporizers, humidifiers, irons, steamers, and dental and hair care products. Small Kitchen Appliances includes hand mixers, blenders, food processors, juice extractors, toasters, can openers, waffle makers, and other culinary accessories. Sunbeam also produces barber and beauty products, personal care products, and animal products, as well as clocks, timers, thermometers, and weather instruments. **Corporate headquarters location:** This Location. **International locations:** Worldwide. **Listed on:** New York Stock Exchange.

SWANK INC.
90 Park Avenue, 13th Floor, New York NY 10016. 212/867-2600. **Contact:** Office Manager.

Description: This location houses the executive, national, and international sales offices. Overall, Swank is a manufacturer and distributor of men's and women's jewelry. **Corporate headquarters location:** This Location.

SWEETHEART CUP COMPANY, INC.
7575 South Kostner Avenue, Chicago IL 60652. 773/767-3300. **Contact:** Human Resources Manager. **Description:** Manufactures and distributes a variety of dinnerware including plates, cups, bowls, drinking straws, and ice cream cones, as well as containers for use in packaging food and dairy products. **Corporate headquarters location:** Owings Mills MD. **Number of employees nationwide:** 7,300.

SWING-N-SLIDE CORPORATION
1212 Barberry Drive, Janesville WI 53545. 608/755-4777. **Contact:** Human Resources. **World Wide Web address:** http://www.swing-n-slide.com. **Description:** A leading designer, manufacturer, and marketer of do-it-yourself, wooden home playground equipment. Swing-N-Slide's kits are specifically designed to be assembled by the consumer, and most kits can be combined with each other and the company's Cool Wave Slides. Swing-N-Slide also manufactures and markets the Tuff Kids line of commercial playground equipment and the Clubhouse, a wooden and plastic outdoor playhouse. **Corporate headquarters location:** This Location. **Number of employees at this location:** 230.

SYRATECH CORPORATION
175 McClellan Highway, East Boston MA 02128. 617/561-2200. **Fax:** 617/568-1528. **Contact:** Katie Ventura, Human Resources Director. **Description:** Manufactures housewares, cookware, and gift items. **NOTE:** Entry-level positions are offered. **Common positions include:** Accountant/Auditor; Advertising Clerk; Attorney; Buyer; Claim Representative; Customer Service Representative; Designer; Paralegal; Public Relations Specialist; Purchasing Agent/Manager; Typist/Word Processor. **Educational backgrounds include:** Accounting; Business Administration; Finance; Liberal Arts; Marketing. **Benefits:** 401(k); Dental Insurance; Disability Coverage; Employee Discounts; Life Insurance; Medical Insurance; Public Transit Available; Tuition Assistance. **Special programs:** Internships. **Corporate headquarters location:** This Location. **Listed on:** New York Stock Exchange. **Stock exchange symbol:** SYR. **Annual sales/revenues:** More than $100 million. **Number of employees at this location:** 350. **Number of employees nationwide:** 1,800.

T&D METAL PRODUCTS INC.
601 East Walnut Street, Watseka IL 60970. 815/432-4938. **Contact:** Human Resources. **Description:** Manufactures tool boxes, table bases, and go-carts. **Common positions include:** Accountant; Blue-Collar Worker Supervisor; Ceramics Engineer; Materials Engineer; Metallurgical Engineer; Quality Control Supervisor. **Educational backgrounds include:** Accounting; Engineering. **Benefits:** 401(k); Dental Insurance; Disability Coverage; Employee Discounts; Life Insurance; Medical Insurance; Profit Sharing; Tuition Assistance. **Special programs:** Internships. **Corporate headquarters location:** This Location. **Other U.S. locations:** Paris IL; Yorkville IL. **Listed on:** Privately held. **Number of employees at this location:** 450.

TDK ELECTRONICS CORPORATION
611 Highway 74 South, Peachtree City GA 30269. 770/487-5200. **Fax:** 770/487-5880. **Contact:** Mr.

Marion Crooke, General Administration Director. **World Wide Web address:** http://www.tdk.com. **Description:** This location manufactures video recording tapes. Overall, TDK Electronics Corporation is one of the world's largest manufacturers of magnetic recording tapes, ferrite products, and CD-ROMs. **Common positions include:** Buyer; Computer Programmer; Electrical Engineer; Human Resources Manager; Industrial Production Manager; Management Trainee; Mechanical Engineer; Purchasing Agent/Manager. **Educational backgrounds include:** Business Administration; Engineering. **Benefits:** 401(k); Dental Insurance; Disability Coverage; Employee Discounts; Life Insurance; Medical Insurance; Pension Plan; Tuition Assistance. **Corporate headquarters location:** Port Washington NY. **Listed on:** New York Stock Exchange. **Number of employees at this location:** 300.

TAMBRANDS INC.
2879 Hotel Road, P.O. Box 1778, Auburn ME 04210-1778. 207/753-5229. **Contact:** John Conde, Human Resource Director. **World Wide Web address:** http://www.tampax.com. **Description:** Tambrands is a manufacturer and marketer of feminine hygiene products. Its primary product, the Tampax tampon, is marketed in over 150 countries worldwide. **Corporate headquarters location:** This Location. **Other U.S. locations:** Rutland VT.

O.C. TANNER
1930 South State Street, Salt Lake City UT 84115. 801/486-2430. **Contact:** Kaye T. Jorgensen, Senior Vice President, Human Resources. **World Wide Web address:** http://www.octanner.com. **Description:** A full-service provider and manufacturer of corporate recognition awards and programs. **Common positions include:** Accountant; Blue-Collar Worker Supervisor; Computer Programmer; Customer Service Representative; Designer; Economist; Electrician; Human Resources Manager; Industrial Engineer; Operations/Production Manager; Production Manager; Public Relations Specialist; Purchasing Agent/Manager; Quality Control Supervisor; Services Sales Rep.; Software Engineer; Systems Analyst. **Educational backgrounds include:** Art/Design; Business Administration; Communications; Engineering; Marketing. **Benefits:** 401(k); Dental Insurance; Employee Discounts; Medical Insurance; Profit Sharing; Savings Plan. **Corporate headquarters location:** This Location. **Listed on:** Privately held. **Number of employees at this location:** 1,700. **Number of employees nationwide:** 2,100.

TARA MATERIALS, INC.
P.O. Box 646, Lawrenceville GA 30046. 770/963-5256. **Contact:** Charlie Miller, Human Resources Director. **Description:** Produces and distributes canvases used by professional artists. **Common positions include:** Blue-Collar Worker Supervisor. **Benefits:** Dental Insurance; Life Insurance; Medical Insurance; Profit Sharing. **Corporate headquarters location:** This Location.

TEMTEX INDUSTRIES INC.
5400 LBJ Freeway, Suite 1375, Dallas TX 75240. 972/726-7175. **Contact:** Human Resources. **Description:** Manufactures ceramic logs for fireplaces. **Corporate headquarters location:** This Location.

TITLEIST AND FOOTJOY WORLDWIDE
P.O. Box 965, Fairhaven MA 02719. 508/979-2000. **Contact:** Human Resources Department. **World Wide Web address:** http://www.titleist.com. **Description:** Manufactures a wide range of golf equipment including golf balls, clubs, and shoes.

Products are sold under the Titleist and Foot-Joy brand names. **Corporate headquarters location:** This Location. **Parent company:** Acushnet Company.

TOASTMASTER, INC.
1801 North Stadium Boulevard, Columbia MO 65202. 573/445-8666. **Contact:** Human Resources. **World Wide Web address:** http://www.toastmaster.com. **Description:** Toastmaster designs, manufactures, markets, and services a wide array of electrical consumer appliances and time pieces including kitchen counter-top appliances, electric fans, heaters, and clocks. **Corporate headquarters location:** This Location.

TOM'S OF MAINE
P.O. Box 710, Kennebunk ME 04043. 207/985-2944. **Contact:** Manager of Benefits and Insurance. **World Wide Web address:** http://www.toms-of-maine.com. **Description:** Manufactures oral and body care products using only natural ingredients. Products include fluoride and nonfluoride toothpaste; children's toothpaste (made with fruit extracts); flossing ribbon made with vegetable waxes; alcohol-free mouthwash; moisturizing, deodorant, and mild children's soaps; shampoo; deodorant and anti-perspirant; and shaving cream. **Corporate headquarters location:** This Location.

THE TORO COMPANY
8111 Lyndale Avenue South, Bloomington MN 55420. 952/888-8801. **Contact:** Dave Tourville, Corporate Human Resources Manager. **World Wide Web address:** http://www.toro.com. **Description:** Engaged in the manufacture and marketing of outdoor power products for consumer, irrigation, and commercial industries. Products include lawn mowers, snowblowers, tractors, trimmers, irrigation systems and components, and appliances marketed under the brand names Toro, Wheel Horse, and Lawn-Boy. The company distributes its products through 10,800 independent retailers worldwide. **Common positions include:** Accountant/Auditor; Attorney; Blue-Collar Worker Supervisor; Buyer; Computer Programmer; Credit Manager; Customer Service Representative; Draftsperson; Industrial Engineer; Marketing Specialist; Purchasing Agent/Manager; Quality Control Supervisor; Systems Analyst; Technical Writer/Editor; Transportation/Traffic Specialist. **Educational backgrounds include:** Accounting; Business Administration; Computer Science; Engineering; Finance; Marketing. **Benefits:** Dental Insurance; Disability Coverage; Employee Discounts; Life Insurance; Medical Insurance; Pension Plan; Savings Plan; Tuition Assistance; Vacation Days. **Corporate headquarters location:** This Location. **Listed on:** New York Stock Exchange.

TOWN & COUNTRY FINE JEWELRY GROUP, INC.
60 State Street, Suite 700, Boston MA 02109-1803. 617/854-7477. **Contact:** Human Resources Representative. **Description:** One of the largest manufacturers of fine jewelry in the nation. **Common positions include:** Accountant; Budget Analyst; Computer Programmer; Customer Service Representative; Purchasing Agent; Systems Analyst. **Educational backgrounds include:** Accounting; Business Administration; Computer Science. **Benefits:** 401(k); Dental Insurance; Disability Coverage; Employee Discounts; ESOP; Life Insurance; Medical Insurance; Tuition Assistance. **Special programs:** Internships. **Corporate headquarters location:** This Location. **Other area locations:** Attleboro MA. **Other U.S. locations:** Dallas TX. **Listed on:** American Stock Exchange. **Number of employees at this location:** 650.

TRINIDAD/BENHAM CORPORATION
P.O. Box 22139, Denver CO 80222. 303/220-1400.
Contact: Becky Kohlbecker, Human Resources
Manager. **Description:** Engaged in the
warehousing, packaging, and wholesaling of dry
beans and aluminum foil. **Common positions
include:** Accountant; Accounting Clerk;
Bookkeeper; Clerk; Computer Programmer;
Customer Service Rep.; Human Resources Rep.;
Operations/Production Manager; Sales Manager;
Systems Analyst; Transportation/Traffic Specialist.
Educational backgrounds include: Accounting;
Business Administration; Computer Science;
Liberal Arts; Marketing. **Benefits:** 401(k);
Disability Coverage; ESOP; Life Insurance; Medical
Insurance; Tuition Assistance. **Corporate
headquarters location:** This Location. **Other U.S.
locations:** Chino CA; Murfreesboro TN; Mineola
TX. **Listed on:** Privately held. **Number of
employees at this location:** 50. **Number of
employees nationwide:** 475.

TUPPERWARE WORLD HEADQUARTERS
P.O. Box 2353, Orlando FL 32802-2353. 407/826-
5050. **Fax:** 407/826-8829. **Recorded jobline:**
407/826-4496. **Contact:** Human Resources. **World
Wide Web address:** http://www.tupperware.com.
Description: Manufactures plastic food storage and
service containers. **Common positions include:**
Accountant/Auditor; Adjuster; Administrative
Assistant; Attorney; Budget Analyst; Buyer;
Customer Service Representative; Designer;
Draftsperson; Economist; Editor; Electrician;
Environmental Engineer; Financial Analyst; Human
Resources Manager; Purchasing Agent/Manager;
Travel Agent; Underwriter/Assistant Underwriter.
Educational backgrounds include: Accounting;
Art/Design; Business Administration;
Communications; Computer Science; Finance;
Marketing; Mathematics. **Benefits:** 401(k); Dental
Insurance; Disability Coverage; Employee
Discounts; Life Insurance; Medical Insurance;
Pension Plan; Savings Plan; Tuition Assistance.
Corporate headquarters location: This Location.
Parent company: Premark. **Number of employees
at this location:** 450.

U.S. INDUSTRIES
101 Wood Avenue, Iselin NJ 08830. 732/767-0700.
Contact: Human Resources. **Description:** A
holding company for four categories of
manufacturing companies: bath and plumbing
products, hardware and non-electric tools,
commercial and residential lighting, and a variety of
consumer products ranging from vacuum cleaners to
toys. **Corporate headquarters location:** This
Location. **Subsidiaries include:** Jacuzzi; Lighting
Corporation of America; Selkirk; Spaulding.

UNILEVER CORPORATION
390 Park Avenue, New York NY 10022. 212/688-
6000. **Contact:** Personnel Department. **World
Wide Web address:** http://www.unilever.com.
Description: An international consumer products
firm manufacturing a wide range of soaps, toiletries,
and foods. **Corporate headquarters location:** This
Location. **Parent company:** Unilever NV
(Netherlands).

VERMONT CASTINGS
MAJESTIC PRODUCTS COMPANY
1000 East Market Street, Huntington IN 46750.
219/356-8000. **Fax:** 219/358-9265. **Contact:**
Human Resources. **World Wide Web address:**
http://www.majesticproducts.com. **Description:**
Manufactures gas and wood fireplaces. **Common
positions include:** Accountant/Auditor; Blue-Collar
Worker Supervisor; Buyer; Credit Manager;
Customer Service Representative; Designer;

Draftsperson; General Manager; Human Resources
Manager; Industrial Production Manager;
Purchasing Agent/Manager; Quality Control
Supervisor; Systems Analyst. **Educational
backgrounds include:** Business Administration.
Benefits: 401(k); Dental Insurance; Disability
Coverage; Employee Discounts; Life Insurance;
Medical Insurance. **Corporate headquarters
location:** This Location. **Other U.S. locations:**
Austin TX. **Number of employees at this location:**
350. **Number of employees nationwide:** 580.

VICTORIA CREATIONS
385 Fifth Avenue, 4th Floor, New York NY 10016.
212/725-0600. **Contact:** Office Manager. **World
Wide Web address:** http://www.victoriacreations.
com. **Description:** Manufactures costume jewelry.
Corporate headquarters location: This Location.

VINYL PRODUCTS MANUFACTURING
P.O. Box 649, Carson City NV 89702. 775/882-
4472. **Contact:** Personnel. **Description:** A producer
of accessories and components for water beds.
Corporate headquarters location: This Location.

WALTHERS TRAINS
5601 West Florist Avenue, Milwaukee WI 53218.
414/527-0770. **Fax:** 414/527-4423. **Contact:** Lisa
Buth, Human Resources Manager. **World Wide
Web address:** http://www.walthers.com.
Description: Develops, markets, and manufactures
model railroad products and provides information
on model railroading. **NOTE:** Entry-level positions
are offered. **Common positions include:**
Warehouse/Distribution Worker. **Benefits:** 401(k);
Dental Insurance; Disability Coverage; Employee
Discounts; Life Insurance; Medical Insurance; Profit
Sharing; Tuition Assistance. **Corporate
headquarters location:** This Location. **Listed on:**
Privately held. **Annual sales/revenues:** $21 - $50
million. **Number of employees at this location:**
150.

THE WELLA CORPORATION
12 Mercedes Drive, Montvale NJ 07645. 201/930-
1020. **Fax:** 201/505-8156. **Contact:** Marybeth
Bubert, Human Resources Director. **Description:**
Manufactures a complete line of hair cosmetics
including hair colors, permanent waves, hair
conditioners, and shampoos. Founded in 1935.
Common positions include: Accountant;
Administrative Assistant; Clerical Supervisor;
Customer Service Representative; Market Research
Analyst; Marketing Manager; Public Relations
Specialist; Purchasing Agent/Manager; Sales
Manager; Sales Representative; Secretary.
Educational backgrounds include: Accounting;
Business Administration; Communications;
Finance; Liberal Arts; Marketing. **Benefits:** 401(k);
Dental Insurance; Disability Coverage; Employee
Discounts; Life Insurance; Medical Insurance;
Pension Plan; Savings Plan; Tuition Assistance.
Corporate headquarters location: This Location.
Subsidiaries include: Wella Manufacturing of
Virginia, Inc., Richmond VA. **Parent company:**
Wella AG. **Listed on:** Privately held. **Annual
sales/revenues:** $51 - $100 million. **Number of
employees at this location:** 90. **Number of
employees nationwide:** 230.

WEN PRODUCTS, INC.
1088 West Thorndale, Bensenville IL 60106.
630/787-0900. **Contact:** Controller. **Description:**
Manufactures a complete line of power tools
including electrical soldering guns, sanders, and
electric saws. **Common positions include:**
Computer Programmer; Electrical/Electronics
Engineer; Mechanical Engineer; Purchasing
Agent/Manager; Systems Analyst. **Benefits:** 401(k);

Dental Insurance; Life Insurance; Medical Insurance. **Corporate headquarters location:** This Location. **Other U.S. locations:** Akron IN; Fowler IN. **Number of employees at this location:** 50. **Number of employees nationwide:** 200.

WHIRLPOOL CORPORATION
2000 North M-63, Benton Harbor MI 49022. 616/923-5000. **Contact:** Greg Lee, Senior Vice President of Human Resources. **World Wide Web address:** http://www.whirlpool.com. **Description:** This location manufactures and markets home appliances. Overall, Whirlpool Corporation has manufacturing locations in 11 countries. Products are marketed in more than 120 countries under the brand names Whirlpool, KitchenAid, Roper, Estate, Bauknecht, Ignis, Laden, and Inglis. Whirlpool is also a principal supplier of major home appliances to Sears Roebuck & Co., marketed under the Kenmore brand name. **Common positions include:** Accountant; Customer Service Representative; Department Manager; Electrical/Electronics Engineer; Financial Manager; General Manager; Market Research Analyst; Mechanical Engineer; Systems Analyst. **Educational backgrounds include:** Accounting; Computer Science; Engineering; Finance; Marketing. **Special programs:** Internships. **Corporate headquarters location:** This Location. **Other U.S. locations:** Fort Smith AR; Clyde OH; Evansville OH; Findlay OH; Marion OH; La Vergne TN. **Listed on:** London Stock Exchange; New York Stock Exchange. **Number of employees at this location:** 2,000.

WHITE CONSOLIDATED INDUSTRIES
18013 Cleveland Parkway, Suite 100, P.O. Box 35920, Cleveland OH 44135-0920. 216/898-1800. **Contact:** Human Resources. **Description:** A diversified manufacturer of products for both consumer and industrial markets worldwide. Products include refrigerators, freezers, ranges, dishwashers, washers, and dryers. **Corporate headquarters location:** This Location. **Listed on:** New York Stock Exchange.

WHITE'S ELECTRONICS
1011 Pleasant Valley Road, Sweet Home OR 97386. 541/367-6121. **Contact:** Human Resources. **World Wide Web address:** http://www.treasurenet.com/whites. **Description:** Manufactures, develops, and markets metal detectors for consumer use. **Common positions include:** Accountant; Administrator; Advertising Clerk; Customer Service Rep.; Department Manager; Draftsperson; Electrical/Electronics Engineer; General Manager; Human Resources Manager; Marketing Specialist; Mechanical Engineer; Operations/Production Manager; Purchasing Agent/Manager; Quality Control Supervisor. **Educational backgrounds include:** Accounting; Business Administration; Engineering; Finance; Marketing. **Benefits:** Dental Insurance; Disability Coverage; Employee Discounts; Life Insurance; Medical Insurance; Profit Sharing; Tuition Assistance; Vision Insurance. **Corporate headquarters location:** This Location.

WHITTIER WOOD PRODUCTS
P.O. Box 2827, Eugene OR 97402. 541/687-0213. **Contact:** Human Resources. **Description:** A manufacturer of ready to assemble wood furniture. **Corporate headquarters location:** This Location. **Number of employees at this location:** 400.

WILLERT HOME PRODUCTS INC.
4044 Park Avenue, St. Louis MO 63110. 314/772-2822. **Fax:** 314/772-3506. **Contact:** Phil Wells, Personnel Director. **Description:** A consumer products manufacturer specializing in the production of such items as household deodorants, moth preventatives, plastic ash trays, and potpourri products. **Common positions include:** Accountant/Auditor; Administrative Manager; Blue-Collar Worker Supervisor; Buyer; Chemist; Computer Programmer; Customer Service Representative; Human Resources Manager; Human Service Worker; Machinist; Payroll Clerk; Public Relations Specialist; Receptionist; Stock Clerk; Truck Driver; Welder. **Educational backgrounds include:** Accounting; Marketing. **Benefits:** Disability Coverage; Employee Discounts; Life Insurance; Medical Insurance; Profit Sharing. **Corporate headquarters location:** This Location. **Number of employees at this location:** 300.

WILSON SPORTING GOODS COMPANY
8700 West Bryn Mawr Avenue, Chicago IL 60631. 773/714-6400. **Contact:** Human Resources. **World Wide Web address:** http://www.wilsonsports.com. **Description:** Manufactures sporting goods for golf, tennis, and team sports. Wilson has been affiliated with the NFL since 1941, has produced the official baseball of the NCAA championships since 1986, and has produced the official ball of many of professional baseball's minor league teams. Wilson also manufactures and supplies uniforms to the NFL, MLB, NBA, and many colleges, universities, and high schools throughout the United States. **Common positions include:** Accountant/Auditor; Administrator; Aerospace Engineer; Architect; Buyer; Chemical Engineer; Chemist; Commercial Artist; Computer Programmer; Credit Manager; Customer Service Representative; Draftsperson; Electrical/Electronics Engineer; Financial Analyst; Industrial Engineer; Manufacturer's/Wholesaler's Sales Rep.; Marketing Specialist; Mechanical Engineer; Operations/Production Manager; Public Relations Specialist; Quality Control Supervisor; Statistician; Technical Writer/Editor. **Educational backgrounds include:** Accounting; Art/Design; Business Administration; Chemistry; Communications; Computer Science; Economics; Engineering; Finance; Liberal Arts; Marketing; Mathematics; Physics. **Benefits:** Dental Insurance; Disability Coverage; Employee Discounts; Life Insurance; Medical Insurance; Pension Plan; Savings Plan; Tuition Assistance. **Corporate headquarters location:** This Location. **Parent company:** Amer Group, plc (Helsinki, Finland) is engaged in the marketing of motor vehicles, paper, communications services, and tobacco. **Number of employees at this location:** 350. **Number of employees worldwide:** 3,000.

WILTON ARMETALE
Plumb & Square Streets, P.O. Box 600, Mount Joy PA 17552. 717/653-4444. **Contact:** Kathleen Adams, Human Resources Director. **World Wide Web address:** http://www.armetale.com. **Description:** Produces Armetale (10-metal composite) giftware products. **Benefits:** 401(k); Dental Insurance; Disability Coverage; Employee Discounts; Life Insurance; Medical Insurance; Tuition Assistance. **Corporate headquarters location:** This Location. **Listed on:** Privately held. **Number of employees at this location:** 180.

WISCONSIN PHARMACAL
WPC HOLDINGS, INC.
One Repel Road, P.O. Box 198, Jackson WI 53037. 262/677-4121. **Contact:** Donna Hueppchen, Office Manager. **Description:** Wisconsin Pharmacal Company, Inc. is comprised of two separate operating entities. **Corporate headquarters location:** This Location. **Other U.S. locations:** Chicago IL. **Subsidiaries include:** WPC Holdings manufactures and distributes specialty chemical and branded consumer products in the leisure time market (insect repellents; sunscreens; lip balms;

chemical fish attractants; biodegradable fishing lures; scent cleansing, masking, and luring products for hunters; water purification tablets; a lotion used to relieve the itching effects of insect bites; citronella candles; scented candles; and a hand cleaner and odor eliminator); the household market (Disposer Care, a product to clean and deodorize garbage disposals); and the institutional care market (Chlorazene antiseptic powder, which is used in hydrotherapy tanks in hospitals, nursing homes, and rehabilitation centers to treat open wounds). The Female Health Company markets and distributes the Reality female condom.

WRIGHT & McGILL
4245 East 46th Avenue, Denver CO 80216. 303/321-1481. **Contact:** Personnel Manager. **Description:** Manufactures a line of fishing rods and tackle. Founded in 1925. **Corporate headquarters location:** This Location.

ZENITH ELECTRONICS CORPORATION
1000 Milwaukee Avenue, Glenview IL 60025. 847/391-7000. **Contact:** Personnel. **World Wide Web address:** http://www.zenith.com. **Description:** Designs, manufactures, and markets consumer electronics products including televisions, videocassette recorders, and cable television and network systems. **Common positions include:** Computer Programmer; Electrical/Electronics Engineer; Financial Analyst. **Educational**

backgrounds include: Computer Science; Engineering; Finance. **Benefits:** Dental Insurance; Disability Coverage; Employee Discounts; Life Insurance; Medical Insurance; Profit Sharing; Savings Plan; Tuition Assistance. **Special programs:** Internships. **Corporate headquarters location:** This Location. **Listed on:** New York Stock Exchange.

ZOTOS INTERNATIONAL, INC.
P.O. Box 71, Geneva NY 14456. 315/789-8001. **Physical address:** 300 Forge Avenue, Geneva NY 14456. **Fax:** 315/789-0744. **Contact:** Dick Jobe, Human Resources Manager. **World Wide Web address:** http://www.zotos.com. **Description:** A manufacturer of hair care products for professional salons. Product lines include Quantum, Naturelle, Zotos, and Lamaur. **Common positions include:** Accountant/Auditor; Blue-Collar Worker Supervisor; Chemist; Industrial Engineer; Management Trainee; Mechanical Engineer. **Educational backgrounds include:** Business Administration; Engineering. **Benefits:** 401(k); Dental Insurance; Disability Coverage; Employee Discounts; Life Insurance; Medical Insurance; Pension Plan. **Corporate headquarters location:** This Location. **Parent company:** Shiseido. **Listed on:** Privately held. **Number of employees at this location:** 320. **Number of employees nationwide:** 500.

For more information on career opportunities in consumer manufacturing:

Associations

ASSOCIATION FOR MANUFACTURING EXCELLENCE
380 West Palatine Road, Wheeling IL 60090. 847/520-3282. World Wide Web address: http://www.ame.org.

ASSOCIATION FOR MANUFACTURING TECHNOLOGY
7901 Westpark Drive, McLean VA 22102. 703/893-2900. World Wide Web address: http://www.mfgtech.org. Offers research services.

ASSOCIATION OF HOME APPLIANCE MANUFACTURERS
1111 19th Street NW, Suite 402, Washington DC 20036. 202/872-5955. World Wide Web address: http://www.aham.org.

NATIONAL HOUSEWARES MANUFACTURERS ASSOCIATION
6400 Schafer Court, Suite 650, Rosemont IL 60018. 847/292-4200. World Wide Web address: http://www.housewares.org. Offers shipping discounts and other services.

SOCIETY OF MANUFACTURING ENGINEERS
P.O. Box 930, One SME Drive, Dearborn MI 48121. 313/271-1500. World Wide Web address: http://www.sme.org. Offers educational events and educational materials on manufacturing.

Directories

AMERICAN MANUFACTURER'S DIRECTORY
InfoUSA, 5711 South 86th Circle, Omaha NE

68127. Toll-free phone: 800/555-5211. World Wide Web address: http://www.infousa.com. Made by the same company that created *American Big Business Directory*, *American Manufacturer's Directory* lists over 531,000 manufacturing companies of all sizes and industries. The directory contains product and sales information, company size, and a key contact name for each company.

APPLIANCE MANUFACTURER ANNUAL DIRECTORY
Appliance Manufacturer, 5900 Harper Road, Suite 105, Solon OH 44139. 440/349-3060. $25.00.

HOUSEHOLD & PERSONAL PRODUCTS INDUSTRY BUYERS GUIDE
Rodman Publishing Group, 17 South Franklin Turnpike, Ramsey NJ 07446. 201/825-2552. World Wide Web address: http://www.happi.com.

Magazines

COSMETICS INSIDERS REPORT
Advanstar Communications, 131 West First Street, Duluth MN 55802-2065. Toll-free phone: 800/346-0085. World Wide Web address: http://www.advanstar.com. $189.00 for a one year subscription; 24 issues annually. Features timely articles on cosmetics marketing and research.

Online Services

CAREER PARK - MANUFACTURING JOBS
World Wide Web address: http://www.careerpark.com/jobs/manulist.html. This Website provides a list of current job openings in the manufacturing industry. The site is run by Parker Advertising Service, Inc.

Manufacturing: Miscellaneous Industrial

You can expect to find the following types of companies in this chapter:
Art Supplies • Batteries • Cosmetics and Related Products • Household Appliances and Audio/Video Equipment • Jewelry, Silverware, and Plated Ware Miscellaneous Household Furniture and Fixtures • Musical Instruments Tools • Toys and Sporting Goods

Some helpful information: *The average salary of machinery operators is approximately $20,000 - $25,000, while machine repairers earn approximately $20,000 - $28,000 annually. Inspectors, testers, and graders earn between $25,000 and $40,000. Manufacturing supervisors earn $30,000 per year on average, though many earn more.*

A-DEC, INC.
P.O. Box 111, Newberg OR 97132. 503/538-9471. **Physical address:** 2601 Crestview Drive, Newberg OR 97132. **Contact:** Tom Eder, Personnel Director. **Description:** Manufactures dental equipment and furniture such as hand pieces, chairs, stools, and cabinets. **Common positions include:** Design Engineer; Industrial Engineer; Materials Engineer; Mechanical Engineer; Systems Analyst; Technical Writer/Editor. **Educational backgrounds include:** Engineering. **Benefits:** Dental Insurance; Disability Coverage; Life Insurance; Medical Insurance; Pension Plan; Profit Sharing; Savings Plan; Tuition Assistance. **Special programs:** Internships. **Corporate headquarters location:** This Location. **Other U.S. locations:** Nationwide. **Listed on:** Privately held. **Number of employees at this location:** 700.

AAR
One AAR Place, 1100 North Wood Dale Road, Wood Dale IL 60191. 630/227-2000. **Contact:** Human Resources Department. **Description:** Provides trading, overhaul, and manufacturing services, primarily to aviation-related customers including commercial airlines, the government, original equipment manufacturers, and aviation service companies. In trading, AAR buys, sells, and leases aircraft, engines, and airframe components and distributes factory-new airframe and engine hardware. The company also customizes programs for airlines seeking inventory management. Overhaul includes the maintenance of aircraft and components including instruments; hydraulic, pneumatic, and electrical systems; landing gear; and engine parts. AAR also designs and manufactures many aviation products with an emphasis on air cargo transport systems and related materials. **Corporate headquarters location:** This Location.

AMF REECE
P.O. Box 15778, Richmond VA 23227. 804/559-5000. **Contact:** Barbara Melton, Personnel Director. **Description:** A manufacturer of industrial sewing machinery. **Common positions include:** Accountant; Department Manager; Financial Analyst. **Educational backgrounds include:** Accounting; Business Administration; Finance; Marketing. **Benefits:** Dental Insurance; Disability Coverage; Life Insurance; Medical Insurance; Salary Continuation; Tuition Assistance. **Corporate headquarters location:** This Location.

API MOTION
110 Westtown Road, West Chester PA 19382. 610/692-2700. **Fax:** 610/696-4598. **Contact:** Mary

L. Powell, Personnel Administrator. **Description:** Manufactures resolvers, brushless DC motors, and geared assemblies. **Common positions include:** Accountant; Administrative Assistant; Blue-Collar Worker Supervisor; Buyer; Computer Programmer; Controller; Customer Service Rep.; Design Engineer; Draftsperson; Electrical/Electronics Engineer; General Manager; Human Service Worker; Industrial Production Manager; Manufacturing Engineer; Mechanical Engineer; MIS Specialist; Operations/Production Manager; Purchasing Agent/Manager; Quality Assurance Engineer; Quality Control Supervisor; Typist/Word Processor. **Educational backgrounds include:** Accounting; Business Administration; Engineering; Finance; Marketing. **Benefits:** 401(k); Casual Dress - Daily; Dental Insurance; Disability Coverage; Employee Discounts; Life Insurance; Medical Insurance; Pension Plan; Profit Sharing; Public Transit Available; Savings Plan; Tuition Assistance; Vacation Days. **Corporate headquarters location:** This Location. **Parent company:** American Precision Industries. **President:** Patrick J. Dulin. **Number of employees at this location:** 105.

APV CREPACO, INC.
9525 West Bryn Mawr Avenue, Rosemont IL 60018. 847/678-4300. **Fax:** 847/678-4407. **Contact:** Human Resources. **World Wide Web address:** http://www.apv.com. **Description:** Designs, engineers, and installs food and beverage processing equipment. Offices in the Americas that report to this location are APV de Brazil (Sao Paolo, Brazil); APV de Mexico (Mexico City, Mexico); APV Sanitary Heat Transfer (Tonawanda NY); and APV Canada (Montreal and Ontario). APV Crepaco, Inc. has a Systems Engineering Group comprised of approximately 70 mechanical, chemical, electrical, and food engineers. APV Crepaco, Inc. has four regional sales offices, each responsible for selling processing systems and parts for existing systems. Once a system has been sold, the sales force submits the engineering work to the Systems Engineering Group at this location. These engineers design dairy and food processing systems for APV's customers. After the design phase is complete, the engineers travel to job sites to supervise the installation of the processing equipment. They remain on-site until the processing systems are installed and running and the customer has been fully trained to operate the systems. **Common positions include:** Accountant; Chemical Engineer; Electrical/Electronics Engineer; Mechanical Engineer. **Educational backgrounds include:** Accounting; Engineering; Physics. **Benefits:** 401(k); Dental Insurance; Disability Coverage; Life Insurance; Medical Insurance;

Pension Plan; Tuition Assistance. **Special programs:** Internships. **Corporate headquarters location:** This Location. **Other U.S. locations:** Cerritos CA; Montvale NJ; Dallas TX. **Parent company:** APV plc (London, England). **Listed on:** London Stock Exchange. **Number of employees at this location:** 100.

ACCO USA, INC.
300 Tower Parkway, Lincolnshire IL 60069. 847/541-9500. **Contact:** Human Resources. **World Wide Web address:** http://www.acco.com. **Description:** Manufactures a wide variety of office supplies and equipment. **Corporate headquarters location:** This Location. **Parent company:** American Brands, Inc. (New York NY).

R.P. ADAMS COMPANY INC.
P.O. Box 963, Buffalo NY 14240-0963. 716/877-2608. **Contact:** David R. Henning, Vice President/Personnel Management. **Description:** A manufacturer of heat exchange and strainer/filtration equipment. **Common positions include:** Blue-Collar Worker Supervisor; Chemical Engineer; Industrial Engineer; Mechanical Engineer; Quality Control Supervisor; Sales Engineer. **Educational backgrounds include:** Business Administration; Engineering. **Benefits:** 401(k); Dental Insurance; Disability Coverage; Life Insurance; Medical Insurance; Pension Plan; Profit Sharing; Tuition Assistance. **Special programs:** Internships. **Corporate headquarters location:** This Location. **Number of employees at this location:** 100.

AG-BAG INTERNATIONAL LIMITED
2320 SE Ag-Bag Lane, Warrenton OR 97146. 503/861-1644. **Fax:** 503/861-2527. **Contact:** Human Resources. **World Wide Web address:** http://www.ag-bag.com. **Description:** Ag-Bag International Limited has developed an alternate method of storing feed for livestock in plastic bags. The company sells ancillary products which complement its main line of products. The grain bagging division assembles and sells grain bagging machines that enable farmers to store whole grains and other products in the company's recyclable plastic bags. In addition, the company has adapted its bagging machines to permit the bagging of compostable organic matter and developed plastic bag bailers that enable the company to bail and pick up the recyclable plastic bags from its customers. **Corporate headquarters location:** This Location.

AG-CHEM EQUIPMENT COMPANY, INC.
5720 Smetana Drive, Suite 300, Minnetonka MN 55343. 952/933-9006. **Contact:** Personnel. **World Wide Web address:** http://www.agchem.com. **Description:** Manufactures equipment for the agricultural and industrial markets. **Corporate headquarters location:** This Location. **Number of employees nationwide:** 1,200.

AGCO
4205 River Green Parkway, Duluth GA 30096. 770/813-9200. **Contact:** Human Resources. **World Wide Web address:** http://www.agcocorp.com. **Description:** Manufactures agricultural equipment including tractors, combines, planters, and replacement parts. **Corporate headquarters location:** This Location.

AGFA
200 Ballardvale Street, Wilmington MA 01887. 978/658-5600. **Contact:** Human Resources. **World Wide Web address:** http://www.agfahome.com. **Description:** This location manufactures phototypesetting equipment including fonts, parts, supplies, and output devices. Overall, AGFA operates through several divisions: the Photographic Division produces films, printing papers, cameras, film projectors, lenses, and other related products used in X-ray and non-destructive testing applications; the Office Systems Division produces office duplicators and printers, a wide range of microfiche and microfilm products, and related supplies; and the Magnetic Tape Division produces professional audio products and amateur videocassette products. **Corporate headquarters location:** This Location. **Other U.S. locations:** West Caldwell NJ; Shoreham NY.

AIR-MAZE CORPORATION
P.O. Box 1459, Stow OH 44224. 330/928-4100. **Fax:** 330/928-0122. **Contact:** Personnel. **Description:** A manufacturer of air and fluid filtration systems. **Common positions include:** Accountant/Auditor; Budget Analyst; Computer Programmer; Cost Estimator; Customer Service Rep.; Electrical/Electronics Engineer; Financial Analyst; Human Resources Manager; Industrial Engineer; Mechanical Engineer; Systems Analyst. **Educational backgrounds include:** Accounting; Business Administration; Engineering; Finance; Marketing. **Benefits:** 401(k); Dental Insurance; Disability Coverage; Life Insurance; Medical Insurance; Savings Plan; Tuition Assistance. **Corporate headquarters location:** This Location. **Other U.S. locations:** Carpinteria CA; Greeneville TN. **Subsidiaries include:** ALFCO. **Listed on:** Privately held. **Number of employees at this location:** 100.

ALAMO GROUP, INC.
1502 East Walnut Street, Seguin TX 78155. 830/379-1480. **Fax:** 830/372-9616. **Contact:** Gabrielle Garcia, Personnel Manager. **Description:** A manufacturer of agricultural and industrial machinery. **Corporate headquarters location:** This Location. **Number of employees at this location:** 350.

ALFA LAVAL SEPARATION INC.
955 Mearns Road, Warminster PA 18974-0556. 215/443-4262. **Fax:** 215/443-4253. **Contact:** Robert Rogala, Director of Human Resources. **World Wide Web address:** http://www.alfalaval.com. **Description:** Alfa Laval Separation is divided into five market sectors: Industrial Separation supplies separation equipment for the chemical, pharmaceutical, and other process industries; Marine and Power specializes in cleaning and conditioning systems for fuel oils and lubricant oils in marine and power station diesel engines, as well as fuel cleaning and forwarding systems for gas-turbine power stations; Desalination supplies desalination plants for producing freshwater for ships, power stations, and offshore platforms; Pulp and Paper's products include equipment for pulp cleaning, filters and presses for dewatering, and new technology for processing recycled fibers; and Oil Field products include high-capacity separation systems for use in onshore and offshore oil and gas production, and in the storage and refining of crude oil. **Common positions include:** Accountant; Administrative Manager; Blue-Collar Worker Supervisor; Buyer; Chemical Engineer; Credit Manager; Customer Service Rep.; Draftsperson; Electrical/Electronics Engineer; Financial Analyst; General Manager; Human Resources Manager; Industrial Engineer; Industrial Production Manager; Management Trainee; Manufacturer's/Wholesaler's Sales Rep.; Materials Engineer; Mechanical Engineer; Metallurgical Engineer; Operations/Production Manager; Purchasing Agent/Manager; Software Engineer; Systems Analyst; Technical Writer/Editor. **Educational backgrounds include:** Accounting; Business Administration; Communications; Computer Science; Economics;

Engineering; Finance; Liberal Arts; Marketing; Physics. **Benefits:** 401(k); Daycare Assistance; Dental Insurance; Disability Coverage; Employee Discounts; Life Insurance; Medical Insurance; Tuition Assistance. **Special programs:** Internships. **Corporate headquarters location:** This Location. **Parent company:** Alfa Laval, one of Sweden's oldest companies, was formed in 1883 to market the continuous separator. Operations include environmental protection, optimal utilization of energy, and food supply. The group develops and markets products such as separators, heat exchangers, flow equipment, and computerized control systems. Alfa Laval has production facilities, marketing companies, and representatives throughout the world. **Listed on:** Privately held. **Number of employees at this location:** 450. **Number of employees nationwide:** 600.

ALLIANCE MACHINE COMPANY
1049 South Mahoning Avenue, Alliance OH 44601. 330/823-6120. **Fax:** 330/823-9249. **Contact:** Margaret Swisher, Personnel Director. **Description:** Produces heavy-duty crane systems, transport equipment, and other industrial machinery.

ALLIED CONSTRUCTION PRODUCTS
3900 Kelley Avenue, Cleveland OH 44114. 216/431-2600. **Fax:** 216/431-2601. **Contact:** Personnel. **Description:** Manufactures construction equipment attachments. **Common positions include:** Accountant; Buyer; Customer Service Rep.; Designer; Draftsperson; Industrial Production Manager; Mechanical Engineer; Operations/ Production Manager; Purchasing Agent/Manager; Quality Control Supervisor. **Educational backgrounds include:** Business Administration; Engineering; Marketing. **Benefits:** 401(k); Dental Insurance; Disability Coverage; Life Insurance; Medical Insurance; Tuition Assistance. **Corporate headquarters location:** This Location. **Parent company:** Chicago Pneumatic Tool Company. **Number of employees at this location:** 75.

ALLIED RESEARCH CORPORATION
8000 Towers Crescent Drive, Suite 260, Vienna VA 22182. 703/847-5268. **Fax:** 703/847-5334. **Contact:** Human Resources. **World Wide Web address:** http://www.cfonews.com/alr. **Description:** A holding company that provides defense and commercial electronic security services through its subsidiaries. **Corporate headquarters location:** This Location. **Subsidiaries include:** MECAR S.A. (Belgium) develops, designs, manufactures, and sells ammunition and weapons systems; Barnes & Reinecke, Inc. is an engineering and manufacturing firm that specializes in design, prototype fabrication, production, test, and inspection documentation for the government and industry; Allied Research Corporation Limited (United Kingdom); and ARC Services, Inc. (also at this location). **Listed on:** American Stock Exchange.

AMERICAN FELT & FILTER COMPANY
361 Watch Avenue, New Windsor NY 12553. 914/561-3560. **Fax:** 914/561-0967. **Contact:** Jack Gibbons, Director of Personnel. **World Wide Web address:** http://www.affco.com. **Description:** Manufactures a line of filter products including bags, cartridges, pressure filters, molded filter media, and nonwoven filter media for air, gas, and liquid filtration. **Common positions include:** Accountant; Credit Manager; Customer Service Rep.; Electrician; Industrial Engineer; Machinist; Manufacturer's/Wholesaler's Sales Rep.; Market Research Analyst; Marketing Manager; Mechanical Engineer. **Educational backgrounds include:** Accounting; Business Administration; Communications; Computer Science; Engineering; Finance; Marketing. **Benefits:** Disability Coverage; Life Insurance; Medical Insurance; Pension Plan; Tuition Assistance. **Corporate headquarters location:** This Location. **Other U.S. locations:** Westerly RI.

AMERICAN LAUNDRY MACHINERY INC.
5050 Section Avenue, Cincinnati OH 45212. 513/731-5500. **Fax:** 513/731-5513. **Contact:** Theodore J. Hyle, Vice President of Human Resources. **World Wide Web address:** http://www. almi.com. **Description:** Manufactures commercial laundry and dry cleaning equipment. **Common positions include:** Accountant; Administrator; Advertising Clerk; Blue-Collar Worker Supervisor; Buyer; Computer Programmer; Credit Manager; Customer Service Rep.; Department Manager; Draftsperson; Electrical/Electronics Engineer; Human Resources Manager; Industrial Engineer; Manufacturer's/Wholesaler's Sales Rep.; Mechanical Engineer; Operations/Production Manager; Public Relations Specialist; Purchasing Agent/Manager; Quality Control Supervisor; Systems Analyst; Technical Writer/Editor; Transportation/Traffic Specialist. **Educational backgrounds include:** Accounting; Business Administration; Computer Science; Economics; Engineering; Finance; Marketing. **Benefits:** Dental Insurance; Disability Coverage; Life Insurance; Medical Insurance; Profit Sharing. **Corporate headquarters location:** This Location. **Operations at this facility include:** Manufacturing. **Listed on:** Privately held.

AMERICAN NTN BEARING MANUFACTURING CORPORATION
1500 Holmes Road, Elgin IL 60123. 847/741-4545. **Contact:** Stuart Moir, Human Resources Director. **Description:** Manufactures bearings. **Common positions include:** Accountant; Blue-Collar Worker Supervisor; Buyer; Computer Programmer; Electrician; Human Resources Specialist; Industrial Engineer; Industrial Production Manager; Mechanical Engineer; Systems Analyst. **Educational backgrounds include:** Accounting; Business Administration; Engineering; Liberal Arts. **Benefits:** 401(k); Dental Insurance; Disability Coverage; Life Insurance; Medical Insurance; Pension Plan; Savings Plan; Tuition Assistance. **Corporate headquarters location:** This Location. **Other U.S. locations:** Schiller Park IL. **Parent company:** NTN.

AMERICAN PRECISION INDUSTRIES INC.
2777 Walden Avenue, Buffalo NY 14225. 716/684-9700. **Contact:** Human Resources Director. **Description:** This location manufactures heat exchangers. Overall, American Precision Industries is a diversified manufacturing company. The company's Heat Transfer Group is comprised of the Basco and Air Technologies Divisions. The Motion Technology Group is comprised of the Controls Division, offering a complete line of drives, controls, power supplies, and applications support for motion control systems; Deltran Division, which manufactures high-quality, electro-magnetic clutches and brakes used in rotary control applications; Harowe, which produces precision motors and feedback devices; and Rapidsyn, offering a full-line of step motors. The Electronic Components Group is comprised of the Delevan and Surface Mounted Devices Divisions which design, manufacture, and market a line of inductors, chokes, and coils for various electrical filtering requirements. **Corporate headquarters location:** This Location.

AMERICAN SCIENCE & ENGINEERING
829 Middlesex Turnpike, Billerica MA 01821. 978/262-8700. **Contact:** Personnel. **Description:**

Researches, develops, produces, and sells instrumentation for X-ray research for use in government space science programs and other scientific applications. The company also manufactures and sells a load management and automatic remote meter-reading system for public utilities; and develops, manufactures, and markets X-ray equipment. **Common positions include:** Accountant; Administrator; Aerospace Engineer; Blue-Collar Worker Supervisor; Buyer; Draftsperson; Electrical/Electronics Engineer; Financial Analyst; Human Resources Manager; Industrial Production Manager; Manufacturer's/ Wholesaler's Sales Rep.; Marketing Specialist; Mechanical Engineer; Physicist; Systems Analyst. **Educational backgrounds include:** Accounting; Business Administration; Computer Science; Engineering; Finance; Liberal Arts; Physics. **Benefits:** Dental Insurance; Disability Coverage; Employee Discounts; Life Insurance; Medical Insurance; Pension Plan; Savings Plan; Stock Option; Tuition Assistance. **Corporate headquarters location:** This Location. **Listed on:** American Stock Exchange. **Number of employees at this location:** 140.

AMERICAN STANDARD COMPANIES INC.
One Centennial Avenue, Piscataway NJ 08855. 732/980-6000. **Contact:** Human Resources. **World Wide Web address:** http://www. americanstandard.com. **Description:** A global, diversified manufacturer. The company's operations are comprised of four segments: air conditioning products, plumbing products, automotive products, and medical systems. The air conditioning products segment (through subsidiary The Trane Company) develops and manufactures Trane and American Standard air conditioning equipment for use in central air conditioning systems for commercial, institutional, and residential buildings. The plumbing products segment develops and manufactures American Standard, Ideal Standard, Porcher, Armitage Shanks, Dolomite, and Standard bathroom and kitchen fixtures and fittings. The automotive products segment develops and manufactures truck, bus, and utility vehicle braking and control systems under the WABCO and Perrot brands. The medical systems segment manufactures Copalis, DiaSorin, and Pylori-Chek medical diagnostic products and systems for a variety of diseases including HIV, osteoporosis, and renal disease. **Corporate headquarters location:** This Location. **International locations:** Worldwide. **Chairman/CEO:** Frederic M. Poses.

AMERON INTERNATIONAL
245 South Los Robles Avenue, Pasadena CA 91101. 626/683-4000. **Fax:** 626/683-4023. **Contact:** Human Resources. **Description:** Manufactures and supplies goods and services to the industrial, utility, marine, and construction markets. The business is divided into four groups. The Protective Coatings Group develops, manufactures, and markets high-performance coatings and surface systems on a worldwide basis. These products are utilized for the preservation of major structures such as metallic and concrete facilities and equipment to prevent their decomposition by corrosion, abrasion, marine fouling, and other forms of chemical and physical attack. The Fiberglass Pipe Group develops, manufactures, and markets filament-wound and molded fiberglass pipe fittings. The Concrete and Steel Pipe Group offers products and services used in the construction of pipeline facilities for various utilities. Eight plants manufacture concrete cylinder pipe, prestressed concrete cylinder pipe, steel pipe, and reinforced concrete pipe for water transmission, and storm and industrial wastewater and sewage collection. The Construction & Allied Products

Group includes the HC&D Division, which supplies ready-mix concrete, crushed and sized basaltic aggregates, dune sand, concrete pipe and box culverts, primarily to the construction industry in Hawaii. **Corporate headquarters location:** This Location. **Listed on:** New York Stock Exchange.

AMETEK, INC.
Station Square, Paoli PA 19301. 610/647-2121. **Fax:** 610/647-0211. **Contact:** Human Resources. **World Wide Web address:** http://www. ametek.com. **Description:** AMETEK is a global manufacturing company which serves a variety of industrial and commercial markets through its Electromechanical, Precision Instruments, and Industrial Materials Groups. **Common positions include:** Accountant; Financial Analyst; Human Resources Manager; Management Trainee; Public Relations Specialist; Purchasing Agent/Manager; Travel Agent. **Educational backgrounds include:** Accounting; Business Administration; Communications; Computer Science; Finance; Marketing. **Benefits:** 401(k); Dental Insurance; Disability Coverage; Life Insurance; Medical Insurance; Pension Plan; Profit Sharing; Savings Plan; Tuition Assistance. **Corporate headquarters location:** This Location. **International locations:** Denmark; England; Italy; Mexico. **Listed on:** New York Stock Exchange; Pacific Stock Exchange. **Number of employees at this location:** 90. **Number of employees worldwide:** 6,200.

AMISTAR CORPORATION
237 Via Vera Cruz, San Marcos CA 92069. 760/471-1700. **Contact:** Human Resources. **World Wide Web address:** http://www.amistar.com. **Description:** Amistar designs, develops, manufactures, markets, and services a broad variety of automatic and semi-automatic equipment for assembling electronic components to be placed in printed circuit boards. The company is also a contract assembler of printed circuit boards. **Corporate headquarters location:** This Location. **Number of employees at this location:** 170.

ANDERSON, GREENWOOD & COMPANY
3950 Greenbriar, Stafford TX 77477. 281/274-4400. **Contact:** Beverly Martinez, Administrative Manager. **Description:** Engaged in the designing, engineering, manufacturing, and marketing of special purpose and conventional precision valves for use in the petroleum, chemical, natural gas transmission, and power generation industries. Product lines include safety relief valves used for over-pressure protection; hand valves and instrument manifolds used in conjunction with pressure and flow measuring devices; and a variety of other valve and valve-related products. **Common positions include:** Accountant; Attorney; Blue-Collar Worker Supervisor; Buyer; Claim Rep.; Commercial Artist; Computer Programmer; Customer Service Rep.; Department Manager; Draftsperson; Electrical/Electronics Engineer; Financial Analyst; General Manager; Human Resources Manager; Industrial Engineer; Marketing Specialist; Mechanical Engineer; Metallurgical Engineer; Operations/Production Manager; Purchasing Agent/Manager; Quality Control Supervisor; Systems Analyst. **Educational backgrounds include:** Accounting; Business Administration; Computer Science; Engineering; Finance. **Benefits:** Dental Insurance; Disability Coverage; Life Insurance; Medical Insurance; Profit Sharing; Tuition Assistance. **Corporate headquarters location:** This Location.

ANDRITZ, INC.
35 Sherman Street, Muncy PA 17756. 570/546-8211. **Fax:** 570/546-1306. **Contact:** Dennis M.

Shulick, Director of Human Resources. **World Wide Web address:** http://www.andritz.com. **Description:** Engineers and manufactures capital equipment for the pulp, paper, feed, and grain industries. Founded in 1866. **Common positions include:** Accountant; Accountant; Administrative Assistant; Agricultural Engineer; Applications Engineer; Attorney; Blue-Collar Worker Supervisor; Buyer; Chemical Engineer; Chief Financial Officer; Computer Engineer; Computer Programmer; Computer Technician; Controller; Credit Manager; Customer Service Rep.; Design Engineer; Designer; Draftsperson; Electrical/Electronics Engineer; Electrician; Environmental Engineer; Financial Analyst; Help-Desk Technician; Human Resources Manager; Industrial Engineer; Manufacturing Engineer; Materials Engineer; Mechanical Engineer; Metallurgical Engineer; Network Engineer; Production Manager; Project Manager; Purchasing Agent/Manager; Quality Assurance Engineer; Secretary; Systems Analyst; Systems Manager. **Educational backgrounds include:** Accounting; Computer Science; Engineering; MCSE; Microsoft Office; Microsoft Word; Spreadsheets. **Benefits:** 401(k); Casual Dress - Daily; Dental Insurance; Disability Coverage; Life Insurance; Medical Insurance; Pension Plan; Profit Sharing; Relocation Assistance; Savings Plan; Sick Days (1 - 5); Tuition Assistance; Vacation Days (10 - 20). **Special programs:** Co-ops. **Office hours:** Monday - Friday, 8:00 a.m. - 5:00 p.m. **Corporate headquarters location:** This Location. **Other U.S. locations:** Atlanta GA; Springfield OH. **Parent company:** Andritz A.G. **Listed on:** Privately held. **Annual sales/revenues:** More than $100 million. **Number of employees at this location:** 450. **Number of employees nationwide:** 500. **Number of employees worldwide:** 3,000.

ANDROS INC.
2332 Fourth Street, Berkeley CA 94710-2402. 510/849-5700. **Fax:** 510/849-5849. **Contact:** Human Resources. **World Wide Web address:** http://www.andros.com. **Description:** A supplier of instrumentation and a leading worldwide designer and supplier to original equipment manufacturers of nondispersive infrared gas analyzers. These devices measure concentrations of carbon dioxide, carbon monoxide, and hydrocarbons. Andros also manufactures medical products that measure gases in human breath including carbon dioxide, halogenated hydrocarbon gases, and nitrous oxide. **Corporate headquarters location:** This Location.

ANGELUS SANITARY CAN MACHINE CO.
4900 Pacific Boulevard, Los Angeles CA 90058. 323/583-2171. **Contact:** Mr. Wiley Fain, Director of Personnel. **Description:** A manufacturer and worldwide distributor of can-closing equipment. **Corporate headquarters location:** This Location.

APPLIED POWER INC.
P.O. Box 3241, Milwaukee WI 53201. 414/781-6600. **Physical address:** 6100 North Baker Road, Milwaukee WI 53209. **Contact:** Human Resources. **Description:** Manufactures and distributes industrial hydraulic power equipment. **NOTE:** Entry-level positions are offered. **Common positions include:** Applications Engineer; Buyer; Controller; Database Manager; Electrical/Electronics Engineer; Graphic Designer; Human Resources Manager; Industrial Engineer; Marketing Manager; MIS Specialist; Purchasing Agent/Manager; Sales Engineer; Sales Manager; Sales Rep.; Technical Writer/Editor. **Educational backgrounds include:** Business Administration; Engineering; Marketing; Mathematics. **Benefits:** 401(k); Dental Insurance; Disability Coverage; Employee Discounts; Flexible Schedule; Life

Insurance; Medical Insurance; Pension Plan; Profit Sharing; Savings Plan; Tuition Assistance. **Special programs:** Internships; Training. **Corporate headquarters location:** This Location. **International locations:** Worldwide.

ARKWIN INDUSTRIES, INC.
686 Main Street, Westbury NY 11590. 516/333-2640. **Contact:** L. Henry, Personnel Manager. **World Wide Web address:** http://www.arkwin.com. **Description:** Designs and manufactures fluid power control components including hydraulics, for a wide range of industries. **Common positions include:** Aerospace Engineer; Blue-Collar Worker Supervisor; Buyer; Computer Programmer; Department Manager; Draftsperson; Human Resources Manager; Industrial Engineer; Management Trainee; Manufacturer's/Wholesaler's Sales Rep.; Marketing Specialist; Mechanical Engineer; Operations/Production Manager; Purchasing Agent/Manager; Statistician; Systems Analyst; Technical Writer/Editor. **Educational backgrounds include:** Business Administration; Computer Science; Engineering; Liberal Arts. **Benefits:** Dental Insurance; Disability Coverage; Life Insurance; Medical Insurance; Profit Sharing; Tuition Assistance. **Corporate headquarters location:** This Location.

ARMSTRONG WORLD INDUSTRIES, INC.
P.O. Box 3001, Lancaster PA 17604. 717/397-0611. **Contact:** Robyn Haegel-Hill, Director of Staffing. **World Wide Web address:** http://www.armstrong.com. **Description:** Manufactures flooring, ceiling systems, furniture, and industrial specialty products through 85 plants worldwide. **Common positions include:** Accountant; Chemical Engineer; Chemist; Electrical/Electronics Engineer; Industrial Engineer; Manufacturer's/Wholesaler's Sales Rep.; Mechanical Engineer; Systems Analyst. **Educational backgrounds include:** Accounting; Business Administration; Communications; Computer Science; Engineering; Liberal Arts; Marketing. **Benefits:** Dental Insurance; Disability Coverage; Employee Discounts; Life Insurance; Medical Insurance; Pension Plan; Profit Sharing; Savings Plan; Tuition Assistance. **Corporate headquarters location:** This Location. **Listed on:** New York Stock Exchange.

ART'S-WAY MANUFACTURING COMPANY
P.O. Box 288, Armstrong IA 50514. 712/864-3131. **Contact:** Esther Meyer, Personnel Manager. **Description:** A manufacturer and distributor of animal feed processing products, sugar beet harvesting equipment, minimum/no-till seed bed preparation equipment, and other agricultural products. **Common positions include:** Accountant; Buyer; Draftsperson; Electrician; Industrial Engineer; Mechanical Engineer; Operations/Production Manager; Quality Control Supervisor. **Educational backgrounds include:** Accounting; Business Administration; Communications; Engineering; Marketing. **Benefits:** 401(k); Disability Coverage; Life Insurance; Medical Insurance; Profit Sharing; Tuition Assistance. **Corporate headquarters location:** This Location. **Listed on:** NASDAQ. **Number of employees at this location:** 200.

ARVIN INDUSTRIES, INC.
One Noblitt Plaza, Box 3000, Columbus IN 47202. 812/379-3603. **Contact:** Raymond P. Mack, Vice President of Human Resources. **World Wide Web address:** http://www.arvin.com. **Description:** Engaged in the manufacture of exhaust systems (OEM and aftermarket) and ride control products that serve the automotive, consumer, and industrial markets. **Common positions include:** Accountant;

Administrator; Computer Programmer; Department Manager; Electrical/Electronics Engineer; Financial Analyst; General Manager; Human Resources Manager; Industrial Engineer; Industrial Production Manager; Management Trainee; Manufacturer's/ Wholesaler's Sales Rep.; Mechanical Engineer; Metallurgical Engineer; Operations/Production Manager; Purchasing Agent/Manager; Quality Control Supervisor; Systems Analyst. **Educational backgrounds include:** Accounting; Business Administration; Computer Science; Economics; Engineering; Finance; Liberal Arts; Marketing. **Benefits:** Dental Insurance; Disability Coverage; Life Insurance; Medical Insurance; Pension Plan; Savings Plan; Stock Option; Tuition Assistance. **Corporate headquarters location:** This Location. **Listed on:** New York Stock Exchange.

ATHEY PRODUCTS CORPORATION
1839 South Main Street, Wake Forest NC 27587. 919/556-5171. **Fax:** 919/556-7950. **Contact:** Human Resources. **Description:** A manufacturer and wholesaler of heavy duty equipment including twin engine and natural gas powered street sweepers, conveyors, force-feed loaders, and refuse collection products. **Corporate headquarters location:** This Location. **Listed on:** NASDAQ. **Number of employees nationwide:** 325.

ATLANTIC RESEARCH CORPORATION
5945 Wellington Road, Gainesville VA 20155. 703/754-5000. **Contact:** Susan Imperatore, Personnel. **World Wide Web address:** http://www. arcmaterials.com. **Description:** Manufactures three-dimensional, braided fiber composites for the aerospace, infrastructure, and marine industries. **Common positions include:** Accountant/Auditor; Aerospace Engineer; Chemical Engineer; Chemist; Computer Programmer; Department Engineer; Electrical/Electronics Engineer; General Manager; Industrial Engineer; Mechanical Engineer; Metallurgical Engineer; Operations/Production Manager; Purchasing Agent/Manager; Quality Control Supervisor; Systems Analyst; Technical Writer/Editor. **Educational backgrounds include:** Accounting; Business Administration; Chemistry; Computer Science; Engineering. **Benefits:** Dental Insurance; Disability Coverage; Life Insurance; Medical Insurance; Pension Plan; Savings Plan; Tuition Assistance. **Corporate headquarters location:** This Location.

ATLAS INDUSTRIES, INC.
1750 East State Street, Fremont OH 43420. 419/355-1000. **Fax:** 419/355-9000. **Contact:** Human Resources. **Description:** Manufactures parts for the air conditioning, refrigeration, and air compression industries. The company also manufactures crankshafts, manifolds, connecting rods, and hubs for diesel engines. **Common positions include:** Accountant; Buyer; Computer Programmer; Draftsperson; Industrial Engineer; Mechanical Engineer; Operations/Production Manager; Purchasing Agent/Manager. **Benefits:** Disability Coverage; Life Insurance; Medical Insurance; Pension Plan; Savings Plan; Tuition Assistance. **Corporate headquarters location:** This Location.

AUTOTOTE SYSTEMS, INC.
100 Bellevue Road, P.O. Box 6009, Newark DE 19714. 302/737-4300. **Contact:** Pam Cummings, Human Resources Director. **E-mail address:** jobs@autotote.com. **World Wide Web address:** http://www.autotote.com. **Description:** Manufactures and leases totalisator equipment for the pari-mutuel wagering industry. **Common positions include:** Accountant/Auditor; Computer Programmer; Electrical/Electronics Engineer; Operations/Production Manager; Software Engineer. **Educational backgrounds include:** Accounting; Computer Science; Engineering. **Benefits:** 401(k); Life Insurance; Medical Insurance; Pension Plan; Tuition Assistance. **Corporate headquarters location:** This Location. **Other U.S. locations:** Nationwide. **Parent company:** Autotote Corporation.

AVERY DENNISON CORPORATION
150 North Orange Grove Boulevard, Pasadena CA 91103. 626/304-2000. **Contact:** Corporate Human Resources. **World Wide Web address:** http://www. averydennison.com. **Description:** A worldwide manufacturer of self-adhesive products, pressure-sensitive base materials, label components, labeling systems, office products, and related products. The company services a broad range of industries with products that are used in applications for marking, identifying, labeling, decorating, fastening, filing, and indexing. **Common positions include:** Accountant; Administrator; Attorney; Chemical Engineer; Chemist; Computer Programmer; Financial Analyst; Mechanical Engineer; Secretary; Systems Analyst. **Educational backgrounds include:** Accounting; Business Administration; Chemistry; Computer Science; Finance; Mathematics; Physics. **Benefits:** Dental Insurance; Disability Coverage; Life Insurance; Medical Insurance; Pension Plan; Savings Plan; Tuition Assistance. **Corporate headquarters location:** This Location.

AVIS INDUSTRIAL CORPORATION
P.O. Box 548, Upland IN 46989. 765/998-8100. **Fax:** 765/998-8111. **Contact:** Judith E. Owen, Human Resources Director. **Description:** This location houses administrative offices. Overall, Avis Industrial Corporation and its subsidiaries manufacture industrial and construction equipment, steel tubing, forgings, and metal fasteners. Founded in 1959. **Common positions include:** Accountant; Administrative Assistant; Chief Financial Officer; Human Resources Manager; Industrial Engineer; Manufacturing Engineer; MIS Specialist; Secretary. **Educational backgrounds include:** Accounting; Business Administration; Computer Science; Engineering; Finance. **Benefits:** 401(k); Dental Insurance; Disability Coverage; Life Insurance; Medical Insurance; Profit Sharing; Tuition Assistance. **Corporate headquarters location:** This Location. **Other U.S. locations:** Nationwide. **Subsidiaries include:** Badger Equipment Company, Airport Industrial Park, P.O. Box 798, Winona MN 55987, 507/454-1563; Burro Crane, Airport Industrial Park, P.O. Box 798, Winona MN 55987, 507/454-8549; Crankshaft Machine Company, 314 North Jackson Street, P.O. Box 1127, Jackson MI 49201, 517/787-3791; Edgerton Forge, Inc., 257 East Morrison, Edgerton OH 43517, 419/298-2333; Fostermation, Inc., 200 Valley View Drive, Meadville PA 16335, 814/336-6211; Hurd Corporation, 503 Bohannon Avenue, P.O. Box 1450, Greeneville TN 37743, 423/787-8800; James Steel & Tube Company, 29774 Stephenson Highway, Madison Heights MI 48071, 248/547-4200; Little Giant Corporation, 1601 NE 66th Avenue, Des Moines IA 50313, 515/289-2112; Melling Forging Company, 1709 Thompson Street, Lansing MI 48906, 517/482-0791; Pacific Forge, Inc., 10641 Etiwanda Avenue, Fontana CA 92337, 909/390-0701; Sellick Equipment, Ltd., P.O. Box 2547, Detroit MI 48231, 519/738-2255; The American Baler Company, 800 East Center Street, P.O. Box 29, Bellevue OH 44811, 419/483-5790; The Pierce Company, Inc., 35 North Eighth Street, P.O. Box 2000, Upland IN 46989, 765/998-2712; U.S. Broach, Inc., 378 East By-Pass, P.O. Box 1649, Sumter SC 29151, 803/775-2357.

AXIOHM TRANSACTION SOLUTIONS

15070 Avenue of Science, San Diego CA 92128. 858/451-3485. **Fax:** 858/451-3573. **Contact:** Human Resources. **World Wide Web address:** http://www.axhiom.com. **Description:** One of the world's largest designers, manufacturers, and marketers of transaction printers. Axiohm Transaction Solutions also designs and manufactures bar code printers, magstripe and smartcard readers and writers, card printers, dot matrix impact printheads, magnetic heads, print and apply labeling systems, and consumables. Founded in 1988. **Corporate headquarters location:** This Location. **International locations:** Australia; England; Mexico.

Other U.S. locations:
- 950 Danby Road, Ithaca NY 14850. 607/274-2450.

B&H LABELING SYSTEMS

P.O. Box 247, Ceres CA 95307. 209/537-5785. **Contact:** Dolores Brooks, Personnel Manager. **World Wide Web address:** http://www.bhlabelingsystems.com. **Description:** Manufactures labeling machines for various industries including beverage and tobacco. **Corporate headquarters location:** This Location.

BHA GROUP

Route 2, Box 1840, Folkston GA 31537. 912/496-2583. **Contact:** Human Resources. **World Wide Web address:** http://www.bhagroup.com. **Description:** Designs, manufactures, and sells replacement parts and accessories for electrostatic precipitators and baghouses, and provides rehabilitation and conversion services for the types of industrial air pollution control equipment it produces. As a fully-integrated company, BHA Group manufactures mechanical and electrical products and has a full range of engineering and service capabilities.

Other U.S. locations:
- 8800 East 63rd Street, Kansas City MO 64133-4864. 816/356-8400.

BOC EDWARDS

301 Ballardvale Street, Wilmington MA 01887. 978/658-5410x3376. **Toll-free phone:** 800/848-9800. **Fax:** 978/988-9360. **Contact:** Michelle Tabor, Human Resources Generalist. **World Wide Web address:** http://www.bocedwards.com. **Description:** Supplies high vacuum manufacturing and process control equipment, industrial freeze dryers, and thin-film coating systems used in a variety of applications including pharmaceutical processing, microchip manufacturing, and vacuum packaging. Founded in 1919. **NOTE:** Entry-level positions are offered. **Common positions include:** Accountant; AS400 Programmer Analyst; Customer Service Rep.; Engineer; Manufacturing Engineer; Sales Engineer; Systems Analyst. **Educational backgrounds include:** AS400 Certification; Business Administration; Chemistry; Engineering; Spreadsheets; Visual Basic. **Benefits:** 401(k); Casual Dress - Daily; Dental Insurance; Disability Coverage; Employee Discounts; Life Insurance; Medical Insurance; Pension Plan; Savings Plan; Sick Days (1 - 5); Tuition Assistance; Vacation Days (11 - 15). **Office hours:** Monday - Friday, 8:30 a.m. - 5:00 p.m. **Corporate headquarters location:** This Location. **Other U.S. locations:** Tempe AZ; Santa Clara CA; Austin TX. **International locations:** Worldwide. **Parent company:** BOC Group. **President:** Mark Rosenzweig.

BTU INTERNATIONAL

23 Esquire Road, North Billerica MA 01862. 978/667-4111. **Contact:** Human Resources. **Description:** A manufacturer of thermal processing systems used in electronics packaging, metals and ceramics sintering, nuclear fuel sintering, and various nonelectronics applications. **Common positions include:** Accountant; Blue-Collar Worker Supervisor; Buyer; Chemical Engineer; Customer Service Rep.; Draftsperson; Electrical/Electronics Engineer; Industrial Designer; Industrial Engineer; Mechanical Engineer; Technical Writer/Editor. **Educational backgrounds include:** Accounting; Chemistry; Computer Science; Engineering. **Benefits:** 401(k); Dental Insurance; Disability Coverage; Life Insurance; Medical Insurance; Profit Sharing; Tuition Assistance. **Corporate headquarters location:** This Location. **Listed on:** NASDAQ.

BADGER METER, INC.

P.O. Box 245036, Milwaukee WI 53223-0099. 414/355-0400. **Contact:** Jeff Byers, Employment Manager. **Description:** Manufactures and markets flow measurement and control products. The company serves industrial and utility markets worldwide. Its products are used to measure and control the flow of liquids and gases in a variety of applications. The company's Industrial Division provides flow meter and control products for markets including energy and petroleum, food and beverage, pharmaceutical, chemical, water and wastewater, process waters, and concrete. The Utilities Division manufactures and markets a complete line of flow measurement products and associated systems for public and private water utilities and selected meter reading products for public and private natural gas utilities. **Corporate headquarters location:** This Location.

BAIRNCO CORPORATION

300 Premier Boulevard, Suite 432, Lake Mary FL 32746. 407/875-2222. **Contact:** Human Resources. **World Wide Web address:** http://www.bairnco.com. **Description:** A holding company. **NOTE:** Hiring is done primarily through individual operating divisions. **Common positions include:** Accountant; Chemist; Computer Programmer; Electrical/Electronics Engineer; Financial Analyst; General Manager; Human Resources Manager; Industrial Engineer; Mechanical Engineer; Operations/Production Manager; Supervisor. **Educational backgrounds include:** Accounting; Business Administration; Chemistry; Computer Science; Engineering; Finance; Marketing. **Benefits:** 401(k); Life Insurance; Medical Insurance; Pension Plan; Tuition Assistance. **Corporate headquarters location:** This Location. **Subsidiaries include:** Kasco Corporation manufactures and services equipment for the supermarket industry; Arlon Inc. manufactures coated and laminated materials for industrial and commercial use. Markets include civilian and military communications, radar and computer systems, electronic testing, and other industrial, scientific, automotive, and military applications. **Number of employees at this location:** 15.

BAKER COMPANY

P.O. Drawer E, Sanford ME 04073. 207/324-8773. **Fax:** 207/324-3869. **Contact:** Joel Plourde, Human Resources Manager. **World Wide Web address:** http://www.bakerco.com. **Description:** An ISO 9001 certified company and a world leader in airflow technology, specializing in the design and manufacture of laminar flow laboratory equipment. **Corporate headquarters location:** This Location. **Other U.S. locations:** Nationwide.

BALDWIN TECHNOLOGY COMPANY

One Norwalk West, 40 Richards Avenue, Norwalk CT 06854. 203/838-7470. **Contact:** Human

Resources. **World Wide Web address:** http://www. baldwintech.com. **Description:** Manufactures material handling and control equipment for the printing industry. Products include cleaning systems and Web control systems. **NOTE:** Interested jobseekers should address inquiries to Human Resources, Baldwin Graphics Products, 12 Commerce Drive, P.O. Box 901, Shelton CT 06484-0941. **Common positions include:** Customer Service Rep.; Financial Analyst; Marketing Specialist; Sales Rep.; Technician. **Corporate headquarters location:** This Location.

BANKHEAD ENTERPRISES, INC.
1080 Bankhead Avenue NW, Atlanta GA 30318. 404/894-7900. **Contact:** Bill Maxwell, Payroll. **Description:** A manufacturer and national distributor of auto-carrier trailers, as well as a fabricator of other metal products including hydraulic cylinders. The company also produces asphalt and provides machine job-shopping and paving services. **Common positions include:** Accountant; Administrator; Blue-Collar Worker Supervisor; Computer Programmer; Credit Manager; Customer Service Rep.; Financial Analyst; Human Resources Manager; Industrial Engineer; Operations/Production Manager; Systems Analyst. **Educational backgrounds include:** Accounting; Business Administration; Engineering; Marketing. **Benefits:** Disability Coverage; Life Insurance; Medical Insurance; Savings Plan; Tuition Assistance. **Corporate headquarters location:** This Location. **Other U.S. locations:** Cartersville GA.

BARNES & REINECKE, INC.
425 East Algonquin Road, Arlington Heights IL 60005. 847/640-7200. **Contact:** Human Resources. **World Wide Web address:** http://www. briwebsite.com. **Description:** Engaged in engineering development and limited manufacturing of rubber-tired and rubber-tracked vehicles, related systems, and components. Primary customers include the construction equipment and agricultural industries and the U.S. military. **Common positions include:** Accountant; Draftsperson; Electrical/Electronics Engineer; Mechanical Engineer; Metallurgical Engineer; Purchasing Agent/Manager; Technical Writer/Editor. **Educational backgrounds include:** Accounting; Business Administration; Engineering. **Benefits:** 401(k); Dental Insurance; Disability Coverage; Life Insurance; Medical Insurance; Tuition Assistance. **Corporate headquarters location:** This Location. **Other U.S. locations:** East Moline IL; Troy MI. **Parent company:** Allied Research Corporation. **Listed on:** American Stock Exchange. **Number of employees at this location:** 100. **Number of employees nationwide:** 130.

BARNSTEAD-THERMOLYNE CORP.
P.O. Box 797, Dubuque IA 52204-0797. 319/556-2241. **Physical address:** 2555 Kerper Boulevard, Dubuque IA 52001. **Contact:** Human Resources. **Description:** Develops, manufactures, and markets precision heating, stirring, and temperature control apparatuses; water purification systems; liquid handling equipment; and replacement parts for such products. Heating, stirring, and temperature control apparatuses include hot plates, stirrers, heating tapes, muffle furnaces, incubators, dribaths, and cryogenic storage apparatus. Barnstead-Thermolyne offers a full range of systems to produce ultra pure water which incorporate distillation, deionization, reverse osmosis, ultraviolet oxidation, and absorption or filtration technologies. Barnstead-Thermolyne products are marketed primarily to industrial, clinical, academic, governmental, and biotechnological laboratories in the United States

and abroad through independent distributors. **Corporate headquarters location:** This Location. **Parent company:** Sybron International Corporation has four operating subsidiaries which hold leadership product positions in laboratory and professional orthodontic and dental markets in the United States and abroad. Sybron International companies have become market leaders by developing, manufacturing, and marketing an expanding array of products which meet demanding customer requirements. Other Sybron International subsidiaries are Nalge Company, Erie Scientific Company, and Sybron Dental Specialties, Inc.

E.J. BARTELLS COMPANY
P.O. Box 4160, Renton WA 98057. 425/228-4111. **Physical address:** 700 Powell Avenue SW, Renton WA. **Fax:** 425/228-8807. **Contact:** Human Resources. **World Wide Web address:** http://www. ejbartells.com. **Description:** A wholesale distributor, fabricator, and manufacturer of insulation and refractory products. **Common positions include:** Accountant; Administrative Manager; Blue-Collar Worker Supervisor; Branch Manager; Construction Contractor; Cost Estimator; Credit Manager; General Manager; Human Resources Manager; Manufacturer's/Wholesaler's Sales Rep.; Purchasing Agent/Manager. **Benefits:** 401(k); Dental Insurance; Disability Coverage; Employee Discounts; Life Insurance; Medical Insurance; Pension Plan; Tuition Assistance. **Corporate headquarters location:** This Location. **Other area locations:** Kennewick WA; Spokane WA. **Other U.S. locations:** Anchorage AK; Denver CO; Billings MT; Eugene OR; Medford OR; Portland OR; Salt Lake City UT. **Subsidiaries include:** Bartells Materials Management, Inc.

BARTON INSTRUMENT SYSTEMS, LLC
900 South Turnbull Canyon Road, City of Industry CA 91749. 626/961-2547. **Contact:** Personnel Services Supervisor. **World Wide Web address:** http://www.barton-instruments.com. **Description:** Develops and manufactures measurement information systems products which provide inventory management, flow measurement, and process monitoring control for the oil, gas, and process industries. **Corporate headquarters location:** This Location. **Parent company:** American Commercial Holdings (Lexington KY).

BAYLOR COMPANY
500 Industrial Boulevard, Sugar Land TX 77478. 281/240-6111. **Contact:** Joan Kettler, Personnel Administrator. **World Wide Web address:** http://www.baylor.com. **Description:** Manufactures electromechanical equipment such as brakes systems and generators. Founded in 1954. **Common positions include:** Accountant; Design Engineer; Draftsperson; Electrical/Electronics Engineer; Industrial Engineer; Mechanical Engineer. **Educational backgrounds include:** Accounting; Business Administration; Engineering; Marketing. **Benefits:** 401(k); Dental Insurance; Disability Coverage; Life Insurance; Medical Insurance; Sick Days; Vacation Days. **Corporate headquarters location:** Houston TX. **Number of employees at this location:** 180.

BELCO TECHNOLOGIES, INC.
7 Entin Road, Parsippany NJ 07054. 973/884-4700. **Contact:** Personnel. **World Wide Web address:** http://www.belcotech.com. **Description:** A worldwide manufacturer of processes and equipment for the removal of air and water pollutants. Pollution control equipment includes electrostatic precipitators and related components. **Common positions include:** Accountant/Auditor; Administrator; Blue-Collar Worker Supervisor;

Chemical Engineer; Department Manager; Draftsperson; Electrical/Electronics Engineer; General Manager; Human Resources Manager; Manufacturer's/Wholesaler's Sales Rep.; Mechanical Engineer; Operations/Production Manager; Purchasing Agent/Manager; Quality Control Supervisor. **Educational backgrounds include:** Accounting; Engineering. **Benefits:** Credit Union; Disability Coverage; Leave Time; Life Insurance; Tuition Assistance. **Corporate headquarters location:** This Location.

BELL & HOWELL COMPANY
5215 Old Orchard Road, Skokie IL 60077. 847/470-7100. **Contact:** Human Resources. **World Wide Web address:** http://www.bellhowell.com. **Description:** This location manufactures mail processing equipment. Overall, Bell & Howell is a diversified corporation doing business in three major areas: Specialized Business Equipment, which produces items such as microfilm recorders, readers, jackets, and services, as well as micropublishing, office collation, and mailing machines; Learning Systems and Materials, which operates technical training schools in electronics and computer science, publishes textbooks, and produces a variety of instructional materials at all levels; and Instrumentation, which produces measuring and recording equipment, magnetic tape instrumentation, and a variety of semiconductor compounds, optics equipment, and photoplates for integrated circuits. **Common positions include:** Accountant; Administrator; Computer Programmer; Credit Manager; Financial Analyst; Human Resources Manager; Services Sales Rep.; Systems Analyst. **Educational backgrounds include:** Accounting; Business Administration; Computer Science; Finance. **Benefits:** Dental Insurance; Disability Coverage; Employee Discounts; Life Insurance; Medical Insurance; Profit Sharing; Savings Plan; Tuition Assistance. **Corporate headquarters location:** This Location.

BELOIT CORPORATION
One St. Lawrence Avenue, Beloit WI 53511. 608/365-3311. **Contact:** Human Resources. **Description:** Designs, manufactures, and markets paper-making machinery and related equipment. Primary customers are producers of pulp and paper products including tissue, newsprint, fine paper, and multi-ply board. **Common positions include:** Accountant; Computer Programmer; Draftsperson; Electrical/Electronics Engineer; Financial Analyst; Industrial Engineer; Manufacturer's/Wholesaler's Sales Rep.; Mechanical Engineer; Software Engineer; Systems Analyst. **Educational backgrounds include:** Accounting; Business Administration; Computer Science; Engineering. **Benefits:** Dental Insurance; Disability Coverage; Life Insurance; Medical Insurance; Pension Plan; Savings Plan; Tuition Assistance. **Corporate headquarters location:** This Location.

BEMIS COMPANY INC.
222 South Ninth Street, Suite 2300, Minneapolis MN 55402. 612/376-3000. **Contact:** Lawrence E. Schwanke, Vice President of Human Resources. **World Wide Web address:** http://www.bemis.com. **Description:** A diversified producer of consumer and industrial packaging materials, film products, and business products. Packaging products include tapes and paper bags for pharmaceuticals, candy, toilet paper, and detergents. The company also produces sheetprint stock, roll labels, laminates, and adhesive products. **Common positions include:** Accountant. **Educational backgrounds include:** Accounting. **Benefits:** 401(k); Dental Insurance; Disability Coverage; Employee Discounts; Life Insurance; Medical Insurance; Pension Plan;

Savings Plan; Tuition Assistance. **Corporate headquarters location:** This Location.

BFGOODRICH
FAIRBANKS MORSE ENGINE DIVISION
701 White Avenue, Beloit WI 53511. 608/364-4411. **Toll-free phone:** 800/356-6955. **Fax:** 608/364-8039. **Contact:** Mary Griffith, Employee Relations Manager. **E-mail address:** fmhr@fairbanksmorse.com. **World Wide Web address:** http://www.fairbanksmorse.com. **Description:** Manufactures large diesel and dual fuel engines used for power generation, marine propulsion, and locomotives. **NOTE:** Second and third shifts are offered. **Common positions include:** Accountant; Administrative Assistant; Applications Engineer; Blue-Collar Worker Supervisor; Budget Analyst; Buyer; Chief Financial Officer; Computer Operator; Computer Programmer; Controller; Customer Service Rep.; Design Engineer; Draftsperson; Electrical/Electronics Engineer; Electrician; Finance Director; General Manager; Human Resources Manager; Industrial Engineer; Industrial Production Manager; Management Trainee; Manufacturing Engineer; MIS Specialist; Operations Manager; Production Manager; Project Manager; Purchasing Agent/Manager; Quality Control Supervisor; Sales Engineer; Sales Executive; Sales Manager; Sales Representative; Secretary; Systems Analyst; Systems Manager; Technical Writer/Editor; Transportation/Traffic Specialist; Typist/Word Processor. **Educational backgrounds include:** Accounting; Business Administration; Computer Science; Engineering; Finance; Marketing; Software Tech. Support. **Benefits:** 401(k); Dental Insurance; Disability Coverage; Life Insurance; Medical Insurance; Pension Plan; Tuition Assistance. **Special programs:** Internships. **Corporate headquarters location:** Charlotte NC. **Listed on:** New York Stock Exchange. **Stock exchange symbol:** GR. **Annual sales/revenues:** More than $100 million. **Number of employees at this location:** 500.

BIJUR LUBRICATING CORPORATION
50 Kocher Drive, Bennington VT 05201. 802/447-2174. **Contact:** Human Resources. **World Wide Web address:** http://www.bijur.com. **Description:** Manufactures automatic lubricating pumps. **Common positions include:** Administrative Assistant; Customer Service Representative; Design Engineer; Draftsperson; Manufacturing Engineer. **Educational backgrounds include:** Accounting; Business Administration; Engineering; Marketing. **Benefits:** 401(k); Dental Insurance; Life Insurance; Medical Insurance; Pension Plan. **Corporate headquarters location:** This Location. **Annual sales/revenues:** $21 - $50 million.

BLACKBOURN MEDIA PACKAGING
5270 West 84th Street, Suite 200, Bloomington MN 55437. 952/835-9040. **Contact:** Human Resources. **Description:** Manufactures vinyl packaging systems. **NOTE:** All hiring is conducted through the parent company. Interested jobseekers should direct resumes to Human Resources, Fey Industries, Inc., 200 Fourth Avenue North, Edgertown MN 56128. 507/442-4311. **Common positions include:** Accountant; Blue-Collar Worker Supervisor; Industrial Engineer; Manufacturer's/Wholesaler's Sales Rep.; Operations/Production Manager. **Educational backgrounds include:** Accounting; Business Administration; Communications; Engineering. **Benefits:** Dental Insurance; Disability Coverage; Life Insurance; Medical Insurance; Profit Sharing; Savings Plan; Tuition Assistance. **Corporate headquarters location:** This Location. **Parent company:** Fey Industries, Inc.

G.S. BLODGETT CORPORATION
50 Lakeside Avenue, Burlington VT 05401.
802/658-6600. **Contact:** Parker Brown, Director of
Human Resources. **World Wide Web address:**
http://www.blodgettovens.com. **Description:**
Manufactures commercial baking and roasting
ovens, charbroilers, and fryers. **Common positions
include:** Accountant; Buyer; Credit Manager;
Customer Service Rep.; Draftsperson; Food
Scientist/Technologist; Industrial Engineer;
Industrial Production Manager; Mechanical
Engineer; Operations/Production Manager;
Purchasing Agent/Manager; Quality Control
Supervisor; Radio/TV Announcer/Broadcaster;
Technical Writer/Editor. **Educational backgrounds
include:** Accounting; Engineering; Finance;
Marketing. **Benefits:** 401(k); Dental Insurance;
Disability Coverage; Life Insurance; Medical
Insurance; Pension Plan; Profit Sharing; Public
Transit Available; Tuition Assistance. **Corporate
headquarters location:** This Location.

BRANDT TECHNOLOGIES, INC.
P.O. Box 350, Windsor NY 13865. 607/655-5000.
Fax: 607/655-5001. **Contact:** Human Resources.
Description: Designs, manufactures, services, and
sells conveying, handling, inspection, and
processing equipment; control systems; and process
controls to the glass container industry. The
company has also developed the ColorCoat process
to allow the production of only clear glass, colored
as desired, eliminating the need for sorting green
and brown glass during recycling; and the
LabelCoat process for the application of full color,
organic, ink-only labels directly on containers.
Corporate headquarters location: This Location.

BRANSON ULTRASONICS CORP.
41 Eagle Road, Danbury CT 06810. 203/796-0400.
Contact: Human Resources. **Description:** A
manufacturer of ultrasonic welders and cleaning
equipment. **Common positions include:** Controls
Engineer; Financial Analyst; Mechanical Engineer;
Software Engineer. **Corporate headquarters
location:** This Location. **Parent company:**
Emerson Electric Company. **Number of employees
at this location:** 500.

BRIDGEPORT MACHINES INC.
500 Lindley Street, Bridgeport CT 06606. 203/367-
3651. **Contact:** David Goldstein, Director of Human
Resources. **World Wide Web address:** http://www.
bpt.com. **Description:** Manufactures and distributes
metal cutting machine tools and accessories. The
company's products include manual milling
machines; computer-controlled, automatic, and
manual tool change milling machines and related
software; surface grinders; lathes; and machine
control software. The company markets its products
under the Bridgeport, Harig, and EZ-CAM brand
names. **Corporate headquarters location:** This
Location. **Other U.S. locations:** Elgin IL.
International locations: England.

BRIGGS & STRATTON
P.O. Box 702, Milwaukee WI 53201-0702.
414/259-5333. **Contact:** Salaried Personnel
Manager. **Description:** Manufactures air-cooled
gasoline engines used in outdoor power equipment.
The company also produces car and truck locking
mechanisms. **Corporate headquarters location:**
This Location. **Listed on:** New York Stock
Exchange.

THE BRINKMANN CORPORATION
4215 McEwen Road, Dallas TX 75244. 972/387-
4939. **Contact:** Milly S. Hall, Executive Vice
President. **World Wide Web address:** http://www.
thebrinkmanncorp.com. **Description:** A diversified

manufacturer producing items such as meat
smokers, spotlights, and metal detectors. **Common
positions include:** Accountant; Advertising Clerk;
Blue-Collar Worker Supervisor; Computer
Programmer; Credit Manager; Customer Service
Rep.; Financial Analyst; Human Resources
Manager; Manufacturer's/Wholesaler's Sales Rep.;
Mechanical Engineer; Operations/Production
Manager; Purchasing Agent/Manager; Systems
Analyst; Transportation/Traffic Specialist.
Educational backgrounds include: Accounting;
Business Administration; Engineering; Finance;
Marketing. **Benefits:** Employee Discounts; Life
Insurance; Medical Insurance. **Corporate
headquarters location:** This Location.

BUCKEYE BUSINESS PRODUCTS
3830 Kelley Avenue, Cleveland OH 44114.
216/391-6300. **Contact:** Recruiting. **Description:**
Manufactures parts for computer printers and
construction equipment. **Common positions
include:** Accountant/Auditor. **Benefits:** Disability
Coverage; Life Insurance; Medical Insurance.
Corporate headquarters location: This Location.
Parent company: Pubco Corporation. **Listed on:**
NASDAQ.

BURNHAM CORPORATION
P.O. Box 3079, Lancaster PA 17604. 717/397-4701.
Fax: 717/390-7808. **Contact:** Robert Beecher,
Human Resources Manager. **World Wide Web
address:** http://www.burnham.com. **Description:**
Manufactures boilers and related heating equipment
for residential, commercial, and industrial
applications. The company operates through two
groups: The Distributor Products Group offers a
broad range of residential boilers, radiators, and
light commercial boilers to plumbing and heating
wholesale distributors through America's Boiler
Company, New Yorker Boiler, and Governale, Inc.
The Commercial Group provides boilers, burners,
and boiler room accessories for large commercial
and industrial applications through Burnham
Commercial Boilers and Kewanee Boiler. The
company's operations are supported by the Burnham
Foundry Division which produces castings for
commercial sales. **NOTE:** Entry-level positions and
second and third shifts are offered. **Common
positions include:** Account Manager; Accountant;
Administrative Assistant; Advertising Clerk;
Applications Engineer; Assistant Manager; Auditor;
Blue-Collar Worker Supervisor; Buyer; Chief
Financial Officer; Computer Operator; Computer
Programmer; Controller; Cost Estimator;
Draftsperson; Electrician; Finance Director; Human
Resources Manager; Industrial Engineer; Marketing
Manager; Marketing Specialist; Public Relations
Specialist; Purchasing Agent/Manager; Quality
Control Supervisor; Sales Manager; Sales Rep.;
Secretary. **Educational backgrounds include:**
Accounting; Business Administration; Engineering;
Marketing; Software Development; Software Tech.
Support. **Benefits:** 401(k); Dental Insurance;
Disability Coverage; Employee Discounts; Life
Insurance; Medical Insurance; Pension Plan;
Savings Plan; Tuition Assistance. **Corporate
headquarters location:** This Location. **Annual
sales/revenues:** More than $100 million. **Number
of employees at this location:** 460.

THE BUSCHMAN COMPANY
10045 International Boulevard, Cincinnati OH
45246. 513/874-0788. **Fax:** 513/881-5383.
Contact: Human Resources. **World Wide Web
address:** http://www.buschman.com. **Description:**
Manufactures conveying equipment for a variety of
applications. **Common positions include:**
Accountant; Blue-Collar Worker Supervisor; Buyer;
Computer Programmer; Draftsperson; Electrical/

Electronics Engineer; Human Resources Manager; Industrial Engineer; Manufacturer's/Wholesaler's Sales Rep.; Mechanical Engineer; Operations/ Production Manager; Purchasing Agent/Manager; Software Engineer. **Educational backgrounds include:** Accounting; Computer Science; Engineering. **Corporate headquarters location:** This Location. **Parent company:** Pinnacle Automation, Inc.

C&D TECHNOLOGIES
1400 Union Meeting Road, Blue Bell PA 19422. 215/619-2700. **Contact:** Human Resources. **World Wide Web address:** http://www.cdpowercom.com. **Description:** Manufactures and supplies industrial and reserve power systems and batteries for the telecommunications and utility switchgear markets. **Corporate headquarters location:** This Location.

CMI CORPORATION
P.O. Box 1985, Oklahoma City OK 73101. 405/787-6020. **Contact:** Human Resources. **World Wide Web address:** http://www.cmicorp.com. **Description:** Manufactures a line of heavy equipment for use in road construction. **Common positions include:** Accountant; Buyer; Computer Programmer; Draftsperson; Electrical/Electronics Engineer; Industrial Designer; Industrial Engineer; Mechanical Engineer; Purchasing Agent/Manager; Systems Analyst. **Educational backgrounds include:** Accounting; Computer Science; Engineering. **Benefits:** 401(k); Dental Insurance; Life Insurance; Medical Insurance; Profit Sharing; Savings Plan; Tuition Assistance. **Corporate headquarters location:** This Location. **Listed on:** New York Stock Exchange. **Annual sales/revenues:** More than $100 million. **Number of employees at this location:** 1,000.

CANON U.S.A., INC.
One Canon Plaza, Lake Success NY 11042. 516/328-5050. **Fax:** 516/328-4669. **Contact:** Jennifer Monahan, Human Resources Administrator. **World Wide Web address:** http://www.usa.canon.com. **Description:** A manufacturer of consumer and business imaging systems products including copy machines, facsimiles, printers, computers, cameras, camcorders, broadcasting lenses, and medical equipment. **Common positions include:** Account Rep.; Accountant; Administrative Assistant; AS400 Programmer Analyst; Auditor; Computer Operator; Customer Service Rep.; Database Manager; Electrical/Electronics Engineer; Event Planner; Human Resources Manager; Market Research Analyst; Marketing Manager; Marketing Specialist; Network/Systems Administrator; Public Relations Specialist; Sales Representative; Secretary; Systems Analyst; Technical Writer/Editor; Transportation/ Traffic Specialist. **Educational backgrounds include:** Accounting; Business Administration; C/C++; Computer Science; Engineering; Finance; HTML; Internet Development; Marketing; MCSE; Microsoft Office; Microsoft Word; Spreadsheets. **Benefits:** 401(k); Casual Dress - Fridays; Dental Insurance; Employee Discounts; Life Insurance; Medical Insurance; Profit Sharing; Tuition Assistance. **Special programs:** Internships. **Corporate headquarters location:** This Location. **Other U.S. locations:** Nationwide. **International locations:** Worldwide. **Parent company:** Canon Inc. **Listed on:** Privately held. **Number of employees at this location:** 800. **Number of employees nationwide:** 12,000.

CARBOLOY, INC.
P.O. Box 330237, Detroit MI 48232-6237. 810/497-5000. **Contact:** Angela Aufdemberge, Director/ Human Resources. **Description:** Engaged in the manufacture of carbide cutting tools. **Common positions include:** Manufacturer's/Wholesaler's Sales Rep.; Marketing Specialist; Mechanical Engineer; Metallurgical Engineer; Quality Control Supervisor. **Educational backgrounds include:** Business Administration; Engineering; Marketing. **Benefits:** Dental Insurance; Disability Coverage; Life Insurance; Medical Insurance; Pension Plan; Savings Plan; Tuition Assistance. **Corporate headquarters location:** This Location. **Number of employees at this location:** 500.

CARLISLE COMPANIES INC.
250 South Clinton Street, Suite 201, Syracuse NY 13202. 315/474-2500. **Contact:** Human Resources. **World Wide Web address:** http://www.carlisle.com. **Description:** Carlisle operates in three business segments. The Construction Materials segment serves the commercial and non-residential roofing; heating, ventilating, and air conditioning; and recreational vehicles markets. Primary products include single-ply roofing systems, adhesives, tapes and sealants, metal roofing components, and waterproofing systems. The Transportation Products segment serves the automotive, heavy-duty vehicles, marine, and aircraft industries. Products include plastic and rubber products, braking systems, refrigerated containers, and inflight entertainment system cable. The General Industry segment includes specialty tires and wheels; and food service. Primary products include bumpers, grass chutes and trailing shields for lawnmowers, molded dispensers, serving trays, acrylic and metal gift and table accessories, and specialized brushes and cleaning tools. **Corporate headquarters location:** This Location.

CASCADE CORPORATION
2201 NE 201st Avenue, Fairview OR 97024-9718. 503/669-6300. **Contact:** Greg Anderson, Human Resources. **World Wide Web address:** http://www.cascorp.com. **Description:** Manufactures industrial equipment and materials handling machinery including hydraulic lift equipment. **Corporate headquarters location:** This Location. **Number of employees at this location:** 300.

CASE CORPORATION
700 State Street, Racine WI 53404. 262/636-6011. **Contact:** Marc Castor, Vice President of Human Resources. **World Wide Web address:** http://www.casecorp.com. **Description:** Engaged in the manufacture and distribution of agricultural and construction equipment and accessories. **Corporate headquarters location:** This Location. **Parent company:** Tenneco Inc.

CATERPILLAR INC.
100 NE Adams Street, Peoria IL 61629-8300. 309/675-5923. **Fax:** 309/675-6476. **Contact:** Matt Cunningham, Corporate Employment Manager. **World Wide Web address:** http://www.cat.com. **Description:** Caterpillar is one of the world's largest manufacturers of construction and mining equipment, natural gas engines, and industrial gas turbines; and a leading global supplier of diesel engines. Products range from track-type tractors to hydraulic excavators, backhoe loaders, motor graders, and off-highway trucks used in the construction, road building, mining, forestry, energy, transportation, and material-handling industries. Caterpillar products and components are manufactured in more than 70 plants worldwide. **NOTE:** Entry-level positions are offered. **Common positions include:** Accountant; Administrative Assistant; Applications Engineer; Attorney; Auditor; Budget Analyst; Buyer; Chemical Engineer; Chief Financial Officer; Claim Rep.; Computer Operator; Computer Programmer;

Customer Service Rep.; Database Manager; Design Engineer; Economist; Finance Director; General Manager; Graphic Artist; Graphic Designer; Human Resources Manager; Industrial Engineer; Internet Services Manager; Librarian; Management Trainee; Marketing Manager; Marketing Specialist; Mechanical Engineer; Metallurgical Engineer; MIS Specialist; Multimedia Designer; Physician; Purchasing Agent/Manager; Sales Engineer; Sales Rep.; Secretary; Software Engineer; Systems Analyst; Systems Manager; Technical Writer/Editor; Telecommunications Manager. **Educational backgrounds include:** Accounting; Computer Science; Engineering; Marketing. **Benefits:** 401(k); Daycare Assistance; Dental Insurance; Disability Coverage; Flexible Schedule; Life Insurance; Medical Insurance; Pension Plan; Profit Sharing; Public Transit Available; Savings Plan; Tuition Assistance. **Special programs:** Internships. **Corporate headquarters location:** This Location. **Listed on:** New York Stock Exchange. **Annual sales/revenues:** More than $100 million. **Number of employees at this location:** 2,000.

CHICAGO RAWHIDE
900 North State Street, Elgin IL 60123. 847/742-7840. **Contact:** Personnel. **World Wide Web address:** http://www.chicago-rawhide.com. **Description:** Manufactures oil seals, filters, gaskets, and other custom-molded products. **Common positions include:** Chemist; Computer Programmer; Industrial Engineer; Mechanical Engineer; Operations/Production Manager. **Educational backgrounds include:** Chemistry; Computer Science; Engineering. **Benefits:** Dental Insurance; Life Insurance; Medical Insurance; Pension Plan; Savings Plan; Tuition Assistance. **Corporate headquarters location:** This Location. **Parent company:** SKF.

CHRONOS RICHARDSON INC.
15 Gardner Road, Fairfield NJ 07004. 973/227-3522. **Contact:** Human Resources. **Description:** Manufactures bagging equipment and batching systems for the food, chemical, rubber, and minerals market. **Office hours:** Monday - Friday, 8:30 a.m. - 5:00 p.m.

J.L. CLARK
P.O. Box 7000, Rockford IL 61125. 815/962-8861. **Contact:** Human Resources. **World Wide Web address:** http://www.jlclark.com. **Description:** Manufactures a variety of packaging products including decorative tins; metal stampings for wire and cable spools; and plastic closures and caps. **Corporate headquarters location:** This Location. **Parent company:** Clarcor.

DAVID CLARK COMPANY, INC.
360 Franklin Street, Box 15054, Worcester MA 01615. 508/751-5800. **Fax:** 508/751-5878. **Recorded jobline:** 508/751-5861. **Contact:** Pete Kasparson, Assistant Human Resources Manager. **E-mail address:** humanresc@davidclark.com. **World Wide Web address:** http://www. davidclark.com. **Description:** Manufacturers of air crew protective clothing, communication headsets, hearing protectors, and antishock trousers. Founded in 1935. **NOTE:** Entry-level positions are offered. **Common positions include:** Accountant; Administrative Assistant; Applications Engineer; Assistant Manager; Blue-Collar Worker Supervisor; Buyer; Chemical Engineer; Chemist; Chief Financial Officer; Computer Operator; Computer Programmer; Controller; Credit Manager; Customer Service Rep.; Design Engineer; Draftsperson; Electrical/Electronics Engineer; Electrician; Graphic Artist; Graphic Designer; Human Resources Manager; Industrial Engineer; Manufacturing

Engineer; Marketing Specialist; Mechanical Engineer; MIS Specialist; Production Manager; Project Manager; Purchasing Agent/Manager; Quality Control Supervisor; Sales Manager; Secretary; Software Engineer; Technical Writer/Editor; Transportation/Traffic Specialist; Webmaster. **Educational backgrounds include:** Accounting; Business Development; Chemistry; Computer Science; Engineering; Software Development; Software Tech. Support. **Benefits:** 401(k); Disability Coverage; Employee Discounts; Life Insurance; Medical Insurance; Profit Sharing; Public Transit Available; Tuition Assistance. **Special programs:** Summer Jobs. **Office hours:** Monday - Friday, 8:00 a.m. - 4:30 p.m. **Corporate headquarters location:** This Location. **Listed on:** Privately held. **President:** Robert Vincent. **Number of employees at this location:** 350.

CLAYTON INDUSTRIES
P.O. Box 5530, El Monte CA 91734. 626/443-9381. **Physical address:** 4213 North Temple City Boulevard, El Monte CA 91731. **Fax:** 626/442-3787. **Contact:** Human Resources. **Description:** Manufactures a broad range of industrial and automotive equipment for a variety of commercial and government customers. Products include steam generators, dynamometers, and a number of automotive diagnostic components. **Common positions include:** Accountant; Administrative Manager; Advertising Clerk; Blue-Collar Worker Supervisor; Buyer; Chemical Engineer; Computer Programmer; Customer Service Rep.; Designer; Electrical/Electronics Engineer; Financial Analyst; General Manager; Industrial Engineer; Industrial Production Manager; Mechanical Engineer; Operations/Production Manager; Purchasing Agent/Manager; Quality Control Supervisor; Services Sales Rep.; Software Engineer; Systems Analyst; Technical Writer/Editor; Transportation/Traffic Specialist. **Educational backgrounds include:** Accounting; Business Administration; Computer Science; Engineering; Marketing. **Benefits:** 401(k); Dental Insurance; Life Insurance; Medical Insurance; Pension Plan; Profit Sharing; Savings Plan; Tuition Assistance. **Special programs:** Internships. **Corporate headquarters location:** This Location. **Other U.S. locations:** Nationwide. **International locations:** Belgium; Mexico.

COLORSPAN CORPORATION
7156 Shady Oak Road, Eden Prairie MN 55344. 952/944-9330. **Fax:** 952/944-0377. **Recorded jobline:** 952/943-3457. **Contact:** Corporate Staffing. **E-mail address:** staffing@colorspan.com. **World Wide Web address:** http://www. colorspan.com. **Description:** A designer and manufacturer of big color, personal filmsetting, plain-paper typesetting systems for graphic arts, prepress, and desktop publishing applications. Founded in 1985. **Common positions include:** Account Manager; Accountant; Administrative Assistant; Buyer; Computer Operator; Computer Programmer; Controller; Credit Manager; Customer Service Rep.; Database Manager; Design Engineer; Electrical/Electronics Engineer; Graphic Artist; Graphic Designer; Human Resources Manager; Intellectual Property Lawyer; Internet Services Manager; Manufacturing Engineer; Marketing Manager; MIS Specialist; Operations Manager; Paralegal; Production Manager; Purchasing Agent/Manager; Quality Control Supervisor; Sales Executive; Sales Manager; Sales Rep.; Software Engineer; Telecommunications Manager; Video Production Coordinator; Webmaster. **Educational backgrounds include:** Engineering; Software Development; Software Tech. Support. **Benefits:** 401(k); Dental Insurance; Disability Coverage; Employee Discounts; Life Insurance; Medical

Insurance. **Special programs:** Internships. **Corporate headquarters location:** This Location. **Other U.S. locations:** San Jose CA; Miami FL. **International locations:** The Netherlands. **Parent company:** Laser Master Technologies. **Annual sales/revenues:** More than $100 million.

COLTEC INDUSTRIES
3 Coliseum Center, 2550 West Tyvola Road, Suite 600, Charlotte NC 28217. 704/423-7000. **Contact:** Lawrence Polsky, Executive Vice President of Administration. **World Wide Web address:** http://www.coltecindustries.com. **Description:** Manufactures aircraft landing gear and engine fuel systems, electric power plant engines, marine and power diesel engines, automotive products, and spray nozzles for agricultural, home heating, and industrial uses. **Corporate headquarters location:** This Location.

COMMERCIAL INTERTECH CORP.
P.O. Box 239, Youngstown OH 44501-0239. 330/746-8011. **Fax:** 330/746-1148. **Contact:** Director of Employee Relations. **Description:** A manufacturer of hydraulic components, metal stampings, and separation and filtration devices. **Common positions include:** Accountant/Auditor; Electrical/Electronics Engineer; Manufacturer's/Wholesaler's Sales Rep.; Mechanical Engineer. **Educational backgrounds include:** Accounting; Engineering; Liberal Arts; Marketing. **Benefits:** 401(k); Dental Insurance; Disability Coverage; Life Insurance; Medical Insurance; Tuition Assistance. **Corporate headquarters location:** This Location.

COMPAIR LEROI
211 East Russell Road, P.O. Box 927, Sidney OH 45365-0927. 937/498-2580. **Fax:** 937/498-2270. **Contact:** Human Resources. **Description:** A manufacturer of portable and stationary air compressors. **Common positions include:** Accountant; Blue-Collar Worker Supervisor; Buyer; Computer Programmer; Credit Manager; Customer Service Rep.; Designer; Draftsperson; Industrial Engineer; Industrial Production Manager; Manufacturer's/Wholesaler's Sales Rep.; Mechanical Engineer; Quality Control Supervisor; Systems Analyst. **Educational backgrounds include:** Accounting; Business Administration; Computer Science; Engineering; Marketing. **Benefits:** 401(k); Dental Insurance; Disability Coverage; Life Insurance; Medical Insurance; Profit Sharing; Savings Plan; Tuition Assistance. **Corporate headquarters location:** This Location. **Listed on:** Privately held. **Number of employees at this location:** 300.

CONE-BLANCHARD CORPORATION
P.O. Box 757, Windsor VT 05089. 802/674-2161. **Contact:** Elizabeth Ryan, Personnel Director. **Description:** Manufactures multiple spindle, automatic bar and chucking machines, and vertical rotary surface grinders. **Corporate headquarters location:** This Location. **Number of employees at this location:** 150.

CONSARC CORPORATION
P.O. Box 156, Rancocas NJ 08073-0156. 609/267-8000. **Physical address:** 100 Indel Avenue, Rancocas NJ. **Contact:** Ms. Pat Vogel, Executive Secretary. **Description:** Designs, manufactures, and sells industrial melting furnaces. **Common positions include:** Buyer; Computer Programmer; Draftsperson; Electrical/Electronics Engineer; Mechanical Engineer; Operations/Production Manager. **Educational backgrounds include:** Computer Science; Engineering. **Benefits:** Disability Coverage; Life Insurance; Medical Insurance; Profit Sharing; Tuition Assistance.

Corporate headquarters location: This Location. **Parent company:** Inducto Therm Industries. **Operations at this facility include:** Administration.

CONTINENTAL EAGLE CORPORATION
P.O. Box 1000, Prattville AL 36067. 334/365-8811. **Fax:** 334/361-7627. **Contact:** Human Resources. **World Wide Web address:** http://www.coneagle.com. **Description:** A designer, manufacturer, and marketer of cotton processing and handling equipment. **NOTE:** Entry-level positions are offered. **Common positions include:** Accountant; Agricultural Engineer; Blue-Collar Worker Supervisor; Branch Manager; Buyer; Computer Programmer; Design Engineer; Designer; Draftsperson; Electrician; General Manager; Industrial Engineer; Industrial Production Manager; Manufacturer's/Wholesaler's Sales Rep.; Mechanical Engineer; Operations/Production Manager; Purchasing Agent/Manager; Quality Control Supervisor; Registered Nurse; Services Sales Rep.; Technical Writer/Editor. **Educational backgrounds include:** Accounting; Business Administration; Computer Science; Engineering; Finance. **Benefits:** 401(k); Dental Insurance; Disability Coverage; Employee Discounts; Life Insurance; Medical Insurance. **Special programs:** Internships. **Corporate headquarters location:** This Location. **Other U.S. locations:** Phoenix AZ; Visalia CA; Augusta GA; Rayville LA; Memphis TN; Harlingen TX; Lubbock TX. **Listed on:** Privately held. **Annual sales/revenues:** $21 - $50 million. **Number of employees at this location:** 320. **Number of employees nationwide:** 395.

CONTROL SPECIALTIES, INC.
P.O. Box 266724, Houston TX 77207-6724. 713/644-5353. **Contact:** Personnel Department. **Description:** Manufactures control valves. **Common positions include:** Accountant/Auditor; Blue-Collar Worker Supervisor; Machinist; Services Sales Rep. **Educational backgrounds include:** Accounting; Business Administration. **Benefits:** Medical Insurance; Pension Plan. **Corporate headquarters location:** This Location.

COOPER CAMERON BELL
16500 South Main Street, Missouri City TX 77489-1300. 281/499-8511. **Contact:** Personnel. **Description:** Manufactures valves, well heads, actuators, and safety systems for oil field markets worldwide, as well as valves for use in chemical, plastics, food processing, and paper-making plants, and conventional and geothermal steam power-producing facilities. **Common positions include:** Accountant; Administrator; Blue-Collar Worker Supervisor; Buyer; Computer Programmer; Credit Manager; Customer Service Rep.; Department Manager; Draftsperson; Electrical/Electronics Engineer; Financial Analyst; General Manager; Human Resources Manager; Industrial Engineer; Industrial Production Manager; Management Trainee; Manufacturer's/Wholesaler's Sales Rep.; Marketing Specialist; Mechanical Engineer; Metallurgical Engineer; Operations Research Analyst; Purchasing Agent/Manager; Quality Control Supervisor; Systems Analyst. **Educational backgrounds include:** Accounting; Business Administration; Computer Science; Economics; Engineering; Finance; Marketing. **Benefits:** Dental Insurance; Disability Coverage; Employee Discounts; Life Insurance; Medical Insurance; Pension Plan; Savings Plan; Tuition Assistance. **Corporate headquarters location:** This Location. **Parent company:** Cooper Industries Inc. **Operations at this facility include:** Administration; Divisional Headquarters; Manufacturing; Research and Development; Sales; Service. **Listed on:** New York Stock Exchange.

COOPER INDUSTRIES INC.
600 Travis Street, Suite 5800, Houston TX 77002. 713/209-8400. **Contact:** Brad Davison, Manager of Training and Development. **World Wide Web address:** http://www.cooperindustries.com. **Description:** Engaged in three areas of manufacturing: tools and hardware, electrical and electronic products, and automotive products. **Common positions include:** Accountant; Attorney; Blue-Collar Worker Supervisor; Ceramics Engineer; Computer Programmer; Electrical/Electronics Engineer; Financial Analyst; Human Resources Manager; Industrial Engineer; Industrial Production Manager; Materials Engineer; Mechanical Engineer; Metallurgical Engineer; Operations/Production Manager; Quality Control Supervisor. **Educational backgrounds include:** Accounting; Business Administration; Computer Science; Engineering; Finance. **Benefits:** 401(k); Dental Insurance; Disability Coverage; Employee Discounts; Life Insurance; Medical Insurance; Pension Plan; Tuition Assistance. **Corporate headquarters location:** This Location.

COPELAND CORPORATION
P.O. Box 669, 1675 West Campbell Road, Sidney OH 45365-0669. 937/498-3981. **Contact:** Mary E. Cleveland, Corporate Manager of Human Resources. **World Wide Web address:** http://www.copeland-corp.com. **Description:** Manufactures compressors and condensing units for the commercial, industrial, and residential air conditioning and refrigeration industries. **Common positions include:** Accountant; Industrial Engineer; Mechanical Engineer. **Educational backgrounds include:** Accounting; Business Administration; Engineering. **Benefits:** Dental Insurance; Disability Coverage; Life Insurance; Medical Insurance; Pension Plan; Profit Sharing; Savings Plan; Tuition Assistance. **Special programs:** Internships. **Corporate headquarters location:** This Location. **Parent company:** Emerson Electric.

COTTRELL INC.
P.O. Box 2455, Gainesville GA 30503. 770/532-7251. **Contact:** Les Jones, Personnel Director. **World Wide Web address:** http://www.cottrell-inc.com. **Description:** Manufactures and sells car haul trailers and materials handling docks. **Corporate headquarters location:** This Location.

COX & COMPANY INC.
200 Varick Street, New York NY 10014. 212/366-0200. **Contact:** John Matuzsa, Personnel Director. **World Wide Web address:** http://www.coxandco.com. **Description:** Manufactures heating and cooling temperature control systems. **Corporate headquarters location:** This Location.

JOHN CRANE INC.
6400 West Oakton Street, Morton Grove IL 60053. 847/967-2400. **Fax:** 847/967-3815. **Contact:** Employee Relations Department. **Description:** Manufactures and markets mechanical seals, packaging, and Teflon products for the industrial, automotive, and marine aftermarkets. John Crane operates over 40 branches throughout the United States including sales, service, and engineering operations. **Common positions include:** Accountant; Administrative Assistant; Blue-Collar Worker Supervisor; Computer Operator; Computer Programmer; Customer Service Rep.; Designer; Financial Analyst; Human Resources Specialist; Industrial Engineer; Mechanical Engineer; Purchasing Agent/Manager; Systems Analyst; Technical Writer/Editor. **Educational backgrounds include:** Accounting; Business Administration; Computer Science; Engineering; Finance. **Benefits:** 401(k); Dental Insurance; Disability Coverage; Life

Insurance; Medical Insurance; Pension Plan; Public Transit Available; Savings Plan; Tuition Assistance. **Corporate headquarters location:** This Location. **Parent company:** TI Group.

CRANE NATIONAL VENDORS
12955 Enterprise Way, Bridgeton MO 63044. 314/298-3500. **Contact:** Human Resources. **Description:** Manufactures vending machines and currency products. **Common positions include:** Accountant; Buyer; Credit Manager; Draftsperson; Electrical/Electronics Engineer; Human Resources Manager; Industrial Engineer; Mechanical Engineer; Operations/Production Manager; Purchasing Agent/Manager; Quality Control Supervisor; Systems Analyst; Technical Writer/Editor. **Educational backgrounds include:** Accounting; Business Administration; Computer Science; Engineering; Liberal Arts. **Benefits:** Dental Insurance; Disability Coverage; Life Insurance; Medical Insurance; Pension Plan; Savings Plan; Tuition Assistance. **Corporate headquarters location:** Stamford CT. **Parent company:** Crane Company.

CROWN CORK & SEAL COMPANY, INC.
One Crown Way, Philadelphia PA 19154. 215/698-5100. **Fax:** 215/676-7245. **Contact:** Personnel. **World Wide Web address:** http://www.crowncork.com. **Description:** Manufactures cans, plastic bottles, and metal and plastic closures, as well as machinery for the packaging industry and disposable medical devices and closures. Founded in 1892. **NOTE:** Entry-level positions are offered. **Common positions include:** Accountant; Administrative Assistant; Applications Engineer; Chemical Engineer; Chief Financial Officer; Clerical Supervisor; Database Manager; Graphic Artist; Graphic Designer; Human Resources Manager; Industrial Engineer; Manufacturing Engineer; Metallurgical Engineer; MIS Specialist; Secretary; Systems Analyst; Systems Manager; Typist/Word Processor. **Educational backgrounds include:** Accounting; Business Administration; Engineering; Software Development; Software Tech. Support. **Benefits:** 401(k); Dental Insurance; Disability Coverage; Life Insurance; Medical Insurance; Pension Plan; Profit Sharing; Savings Plan; Tuition Assistance. **Special programs:** Internships; Co-ops; Summer Jobs. **Corporate headquarters location:** This Location. **International locations:** Worldwide. **Listed on:** New York Stock Exchange. **Annual sales/revenues:** More than $100 million. **Number of employees at this location:** 600.

CROWN EQUIPMENT CORPORATION
44 South Washington Street, New Bremen OH 45869. 419/629-2311. **Fax:** 419/629-2145. **Contact:** Personnel. **World Wide Web address:** http://www.crown.com. **Description:** An industrial and commercial machinery manufacturer. **NOTE:** Entry-level positions are offered. **Common positions include:** Account Rep.; Design Engineer; Electrical/Electronics Engineer; Graphic Artist; Operations Manager; Sales Manager; Technical Writer/Editor. **Educational backgrounds include:** Business Administration; Computer Science; Engineering. **Benefits:** 401(k); Dental Insurance; Disability Coverage; Employee Discounts; Life Insurance; Medical Insurance; Pension Plan; Tuition Assistance. **Corporate headquarters location:** This Location. **Other U.S. locations:** Nationwide. **IListed on:** Privately held. **Number of employees at this location:** 2,500.

CUMBERLAND ENGINEERING LLC
BROWN PLASTIC MACHINERY LLC
100 Roddy Avenue, South Attleboro MA 02703. 508/399-6400. **Fax:** 508/399-6059. **Contact:** Donna

Welch, Director of Human Resources. **World Wide Web address:** http://www.cumberland-plastics.com. **Description:** Manufactures industrial and commercial machinery. **Corporate headquarters location:** This Location. **Number of employees at this location:** 200. **Number of employees nationwide:** 1,250.

CURTISS-WRIGHT CORPORATION
1200 Wall Street West, Lyndhurst NJ 07071. 201/896-8400. **Contact:** Joyce Quinlan, Corporate Executive Director of Human Resources. **World Wide Web address:** http://www.curtisswright.com. **Description:** A multinational manufacturing and service company that designs, manufactures, and overhauls precision components and systems and provides highly engineered services to the aerospace, automotive, shipbuilding, oil, petrochemical, agricultural equipment, power generation, metal working, and fire and rescue industries. Curtiss-Wright's principal operations include five North American manufacturing facilities, more than 35 metal improvement service facilities located in North America and Europe, and four component overhaul facilities located in Florida, North Carolina, Singapore, and Denmark. **Common positions include:** Accountant/Auditor; Administrator; Aerospace Engineer; Attorney; Computer Programmer; Draftsperson; Electrical/Electronics Engineer; Financial Analyst; Human Resources Manager; Industrial Engineer; Mechanical Engineer; Metallurgical Engineer; Operations/Production Manager; Quality Control Supervisor; Systems Analyst. **Educational backgrounds include:** Accounting; Business Administration; Engineering; Finance. **Benefits:** 401(k); Dental Insurance; Disability Coverage; Life Insurance; Medical Insurance; Pension Plan; Tuition Assistance. **Corporate headquarters location:** This Location. **Subsidiaries include:** Curtiss-Wright Flight Systems, Inc.; Curtiss-Wright Flow Control Corporation; Metal Improvement Company, Inc. **Listed on:** New York Stock Exchange. **Number of employees worldwide:** 2,350.

CUSTOM ENGINEERING COMPANY
2800 McClelland Avenue, Erie PA 16510. 814/898-2800. **Fax:** 814/899-2729. **Contact:** Sean W. Osterberg, Human Resource Manager. **E-mail address:** sean@customeng.com. **World Wide Web address:** http://www.customeng.com. **Description:** Manufactures press platens for the paper, rubber, and wood industries. **NOTE:** Entry-level positions and second and third shifts are offered. **Benefits:** 401(k); Dental Insurance; Disability Coverage; Life Insurance; Medical Insurance; Pension Plan; Profit Sharing. **Annual sales/revenues:** $11 - $20 million. **Number of employees at this location:** 150.

CUSTOM PRODUCTS CORPORATION
P.O. Box 300, Menomonee Falls WI 53052-0300. 262/781-8210. **Fax:** 262/781-9481. **Contact:** Richard Clancy, Director of Human Resources. **World Wide Web address:** http://www.customproducts.com. **Description:** A high-volume, long-run, contract machining organization serving the automotive, construction equipment, and computer industries. **NOTE:** Entry-level positions and second and third shifts are offered. **Common positions include:** Accountant; Administrative Assistant; Blue-Collar Worker Supervisor; Buyer; Computer Programmer; Design Engineer; Electrical/Electronics Engineer; Electrician; Industrial Engineer; Manufacturing Engineer; Purchasing Agent/Manager; Quality Control Supervisor; Sales Engineer; Secretary; Systems Analyst. **Educational backgrounds include:** Accounting; Business Administration; Computer Science; Engineering. **Benefits:** 401(k); Dental Insurance; Disability

Coverage; Life Insurance; Medical Insurance; Profit Sharing; Public Transit Available; Tuition Assistance. **Special programs:** Training. **Corporate headquarters location:** This Location. **Other area locations:** Oconomowoc WI. **Listed on:** Privately held. **Annual sales/revenues:** $51 - $100 million.

DANA CORPORATION
P.O. Box 1000, Toledo OH 43697. 419/535-4500. **Physical address:** 4500 Dorr Street, Toledo OH 43615. **Fax:** 419/535-4758. **Contact:** Human Resources. **World Wide Web address:** http://www.dana.com. **Description:** A global leader in the engineering, manufacturing, and marketing of products and systems for the vehicular, industrial, and mobile off-highway original equipment markets and is a major supplier to the related aftermarkets. Dana is also a leading provider of lease financing services in selected markets. The company's products include drivetrain components such as axles, driveshafts, clutches, and transmissions; engine parts such as gaskets, piston rings, seals, pistons, and filters; chassis products such as vehicular frames and cradles and heavy-duty side rails; fluid power components such as pumps, motors, and control valves; and industrial products such as electrical and mechanical brakes and clutches, drives, motion control devices, and mobile off-highway and stationary equipment applications. Dana's vehicular components and parts are used on automobiles, pickup trucks, vans, minivans, sport utility vehicles, medium and heavy trucks, and off-highway vehicles. The company operates approximately 700 facilities worldwide. **Corporate headquarters location:** This Location. **Annual sales/revenues:** More than $100 million.

DANIEL INDUSTRIES, INC.
9720 Oldkaty Road, Houston TX 77055. 713/467-6000. **Contact:** Personnel Department. **World Wide Web address:** http://www.danielind.com. **Description:** A manufacturer of fluid measurement products, primarily for the oil and natural gas industries. **Corporate headquarters location:** This Location.

DATACARD CORPORATION
11111 Bren Road West, Minnetonka MN 55343. 952/933-1223. **Contact:** Human Resources. **World Wide Web address:** http://www.datacard.com. **Description:** A world leader in the development and manufacture of plastic card personalization equipment. Products meet industry needs for conducting transactions, exchanging information, and identification. Customers include financial institutions, health care providers, retailers, oil companies, government agencies, and other industries. **Common positions include:** Accountant; Computer Programmer; Draftsperson; Electrical/Electronics Engineer; Manufacturer's/Wholesaler's Sales Rep.; Mechanical Engineer; Software Engineer; Systems Analyst; Technical Writer/Editor. **Educational backgrounds include:** Accounting; Business Administration; Computer Science; Engineering; Marketing. **Benefits:** 401(k); Dental Insurance; Disability Coverage; Life Insurance; Medical Insurance; Pension Plan; Profit Sharing; Tuition Assistance. **Special programs:** Internships. **Corporate headquarters location:** This Location. **Other U.S. locations:** Nationwide.

DAYTON PROGRESS CORPORATION
500 Progress Road, Dayton OH 45449. 937/859-5111. **Fax:** 937/859-5353. **Contact:** Rich Blue, Director of Employment and Benefits. **Description:** A tool and die manufacturer for the metal stamping industry. **Common positions include:** Accountant; Advertising Clerk; Blue-Collar Worker Supervisor;

Buyer; Claim Rep.; Commercial Artist; Computer Programmer; Cost Estimator; Customer Service Representative; Department Manager; Draftsperson; Electrician; Financial Analyst; Human Resources Manager; Industrial Engineer; Management Trainee; Manufacturer's/Wholesaler's Sales Rep.; Mechanical Engineer; Operations/Production Manager; Purchasing Agent/Manager; Quality Control Supervisor; Technical Writer/Editor. **Educational backgrounds include:** Business Administration; Computer Science. **Benefits:** 401(k); Dental Insurance; Disability Coverage; Employee Discounts; Life Insurance; Medical Insurance; Profit Sharing; Tuition Assistance. **Corporate headquarters location:** This Location. **Other U.S. locations:** IN. **Parent company:** Federal Signal Corporation.

DAYTON RICHMOND CONCRETE ACCESSORIES
721 Richard Street, Miamisburg OH 45342. 937/866-0711. Contact: Human Resources. **World Wide Web address:** http://www. daytonrichmond.com. **Description:** This location houses the administrative offices, the sales and service center, and plant and technical services offices. Overall, Dayton Richmond manufactures concrete accessories including anchors and inserts, screw anchors, taper ties, form hangers, overhand brackets, and other related products. **Common positions include:** Chemist; Civil Engineer; General Manager; Systems Analyst. **Educational backgrounds include:** Chemistry; Engineering. **Benefits:** Dental Insurance; Disability Coverage; Life Insurance; Medical Insurance; Pension Plan; Savings Plan; Tuition Assistance. **Corporate headquarters location:** This Location. **Parent company:** Dayton Superior Corporation.

DE ZURIK
250 Riverside Avenue North, Sartell MN 56377. 320/259-2000. **Fax:** 320/259-2227. **Contact:** Human Resources. **Description:** An international manufacturer, seller, and servicer of industrial valves and flow control products for process industries such as municipal, HVAC, pulp and paper, chemical, power, and mining. **Common positions include:** Accountant; Budget Analyst; Buyer; Chemical Engineer; Computer Programmer; Customer Service Rep.; Designer; Draftsperson; Electrician; Environmental Engineer; Financial Analyst; Human Resources Manager; Industrial Engineer; Industrial Production Manager; Materials Engineer; Mechanical Engineer; Metallurgical Engineer; Operations/Production Manager; Public Relations Specialist; Purchasing Agent/Manager; Quality Control Supervisor; Software Engineer; Systems Analyst; Technical Writer/Editor; Transportation/Traffic Specialist. **Educational backgrounds include:** Accounting; Business Administration; Chemistry; Communications; Computer Science; Engineering; Finance; Marketing. **Benefits:** 401(k); Dental Insurance; Disability Coverage; Life Insurance; Medical Insurance; Pension Plan; Savings Plan; Tuition Assistance. **Special programs:** Internships. **Corporate headquarters location:** This Location. **Other U.S. locations:** Nationwide. **Parent company:** General Signal.

DEARBORN MID-WEST CONVEYOR CO.
2601 Mid-West Drive, Kansas City MO 66111. 913/441-8590. **Fax:** 913/441-8348. **Contact:** Tom Joslin, Human Resources Manager. **E-mail address:** tomj@dmwcc.com. **World Wide Web address:** http://www.dmwcc.com. **Description:** Provides integrated material handling systems for automotive and industrial assembly operations, postal facilities, and bulk handling. **Common**

positions include: Buyer; Design Engineer; Designer; Draftsperson; Electrician; Mechanical Engineer; Project Manager; Structural Engineer. **Educational backgrounds include:** Engineering. **Benefits:** 401(k); Dental Insurance; Disability Coverage; Employee Discounts; Life Insurance; Medical Insurance; Pension Plan; Tuition Assistance. **Corporate headquarters location:** Dayton OH. **Other U.S. locations:** Detroit MI; Howell MI. **Parent company:** Tomkins Industries, Inc. **Listed on:** New York Stock Exchange. **Annual sales/revenues:** More than $100 million. **Number of employees at this location:** 210.

DEERE & COMPANY
One John Deere Place, Moline IL 61265. 309/765-8000. **Contact:** Director of Human Resources. **World Wide Web address:** http://www.deere.com. **Description:** Manufactures, distributes, and finances the sale of heavy equipment and machinery for use in the agricultural and industrial equipment industries. The Agricultural Equipment Sector manufactures tractors, soil, seeding, and harvesting equipment. The Industrial Equipment Segment manufactures a variety of earth moving equipment, tractors, loaders, and excavators. The Consumer Products Division manufactures tractors and products for the homeowner. **Common positions include:** Accountant. **Educational backgrounds include:** Accounting. **Benefits:** Dental Insurance; Disability Coverage; Employee Discounts; Life Insurance; Medical Insurance; Pension Plan; Profit Sharing; Savings Plan; Tuition Assistance. **Corporate headquarters location:** This Location.

DEL MAR AVIONICS
1621 Alton Parkway, Irvine CA 92606. 949/250-3200. **Contact:** Mr. E.L. Phillips, Personnel Manager. **Description:** Manufactures, services, and markets a wide range of precision instruments for medical and industrial applications. Products include stress test, ambulatory blood pressure, and precision loading systems. Del Mar Avionics maintains over 50 dealer/service centers worldwide. **Corporate headquarters location:** This Location. **Number of employees at this location:** 180.

DELATECH INC.
617 River Oaks Parkway, San Jose CA 95134. 408/262-1631. **Toll-free phone:** 800/886-1968. **Fax:** 408/526-1651. **Contact:** Tammy Polanco, Human Resources Manager. **Description:** Manufactures gas exhaust conditioning systems used in the semiconductor industry. **Common positions include:** Accountant; Administrative Assistant; Blue-Collar Worker Supervisor; Chemical Engineer; Chemist; Customer Service Rep.; Database Manager; Design Engineer; Draftsperson; Electrical/Electronics Engineer; Electrician; Human Resources Manager; Production Manager; Purchasing Agent/Manager; Quality Control Supervisor; Sales Engineer; Sales Executive; Technical Writer/Editor; Transportation/Traffic Specialist. **Educational backgrounds include:** Engineering. **Benefits:** Dental Insurance; Life Insurance; Medical Insurance; Profit Sharing; Tuition Assistance. **Corporate headquarters location:** Napa CA. **Other U.S. locations:** Tempe AZ; Brookfield CT; Austin TX.

DELTAK
P.O. Box 9496, Minneapolis MN 55440. 612/544-3371. **Physical address:** 13330 12th Avenue North, Plymouth MN. **Fax:** 612/543-5303. **Contact:** Human Resources. **World Wide Web address:** http://www.deltak.com. **Description:** Custom designs, manufactures, and constructs heat recovery systems worldwide. **Common positions include:** Account Manager; Accountant; Applications

Engineer; Buyer; Computer Programmer; Controls Engineer; Designer; Draftsperson; Estimator; Field Engineer; Marketing Manager; Mechanical Engineer; Product Engineer; Project Engineer; Project Manager; Quality Assurance Engineer; Service Engineer; Structural Engineer; Supervisor; Welder. **Benefits:** 401(k); Dental Insurance; Disability Coverage; Life Insurance; Medical Insurance; Profit Sharing; Tuition Assistance. **Corporate headquarters location:** This Location. **Parent company:** Jason Inc. **Listed on:** NASDAQ.

DESPATCH INDUSTRIES
63 St. Anthony Parkway, Minneapolis MN 55418. 612/781-5363. **Fax:** 612/781-5353. **Contact:** Personnel. **World Wide Web address:** http://www. despatch.com. **Description:** A designer and manufacturer of standard and custom industrial heat processing and environmental test equipment including industrial ovens, environmental simulation chambers, and custom-engineered turnkey systems. **Common positions include:** Accountant; Buyer; Computer Programmer; Cost Estimator; Customer Service Rep.; Designer; Draftsperson; Electrical/Electronics Engineer; Electrician; General Manager; Human Resources Manager; Industrial Engineer; Industrial Production Manager; Manufacturer's/Wholesaler's Sales Rep.; Mechanical Engineer; Purchasing Agent/Manager; Quality Control Supervisor; Software Engineer; Systems Analyst; Technical Writer/Editor. **Educational backgrounds include:** Accounting; Engineering. **Benefits:** 401(k); Casual Dress - Daily; Dental Insurance; Disability Coverage; Employee Discounts; Flexible Schedule; Life Insurance; Medical Insurance; Pension Plan; Tuition Assistance. **Corporate headquarters location:** This Location. **Other area locations:** Lakeville MN. **Number of employees at this location:** 100.

DETROIT DIESEL CORPORATION
13400 West Outer Drive, Detroit MI 48239-4001. 313/592-7155. **Contact:** Personnel. **World Wide Web address:** http://www.detroitdiesel.com. **Description:** Designs, manufactures, and sells heavy-duty diesel engines. Founded in 1988. **Common positions include:** Administrative Assistant; Applications Engineer; Blue-Collar Worker Supervisor; Customer Service Rep.; Electrical/Electronics Engineer; Industrial Engineer; Mechanical Engineer; Sales Rep. **Educational backgrounds include:** Accounting; Business Administration; Engineering; Marketing. **Benefits:** 401(k); Dental Insurance; Disability Coverage; Employee Discounts; Life Insurance; Medical Insurance; Pension Plan; Profit Sharing; Savings Plan; Tuition Assistance. **Special programs:** Internships. **Internship information:** Summer internships are offered. Interested students should send a resume, transcript, and cover letter. **Corporate headquarters location:** This Location. **Listed on:** New York Stock Exchange. **Stock exchange symbol:** DDC. **Annual sales/revenues:** More than $100 million. **Number of employees at this location:** 3,500.

DETROIT TOOL & ENGINEERING
P.O. Box 232, Lebanon MO 65536. 417/532-2141. **Physical address:** 441 West Elm Street, Lebanon MO. **Fax:** 417/532-1039. **Contact:** Human Resources. **E-mail address:** rbailey@ detroittool.com. **World Wide Web address:** http://www.detroittool.com. **Description:** Designs and manufactures special machines, automated assembly systems, tooling, fixturing, and a complete line of thermoforming machines under exclusive license from Rigo. **Common positions include:** Controller; Database Administrator; Design Engineer; Draftsperson; Electrical/Electronics

Engineer; General Manager; Human Resources Manager; Mechanical Engineer; Network/Systems Administrator; Operations Manager; Project Manager; Purchasing Agent/Manager; Quality Assurance Engineer; Quality Control Supervisor; Sales Engineer; Secretary; Systems Manager; Vice President of Operations. **Educational backgrounds include:** Accounting; Business Administration; Computer Science; Engineering; Microsoft Word; Novell; Spreadsheets; Visual Basic. **Benefits:** 401(k); Casual Dress - Fridays; Disability Coverage; Life Insurance; Medical Insurance; Tuition Assistance; Vacation Days (6 - 10). **Special programs:** Apprenticeships; Co-ops. **Office hours:** Monday - Friday, 8:00 a.m. - 5:00 p.m. **Parent company:** DT Industries (Springfield MO). **Annual sales/revenues:** $51 - $100 million.

DIETERICH STANDARD OF BOULDER
P.O. Box 9000, Boulder CO 80301. 303/530-9600. **Physical address:** 5601 North 71st Street, Boulder CO. **Contact:** Personnel Department. **Description:** Produces a wide range of flow and process equipment. **Corporate headquarters location:** This Location. **Parent company:** Dover Industries.

DIONEX CORPORATION
501 Mercury Drive, Sunnyvale CA 94088. 408/481-4125. **Fax:** 408/739-8015. **Contact:** Human Resources. **World Wide Web address:** http://www. dionex.com. **Description:** Develops, manufactures, sells, and services systems and related products that isolate and identify the components of chemical mixtures. The company's products are used extensively for environmental analysis by the pharmaceutical, life science, biotechnology, chemical, petrochemical, power generation, and electronics industries. Customers include industrial companies, government agencies, research institutions, and universities. The company's research and development teams explore new technologies in order to enhance the performance of ion technology, high-performance liquid chromatography, capillary electrophoresis, and supercritical fluid extraction and chromatography technologies. **Common positions include:** Accountant; Biological Scientist; Chemist; Computer Programmer; Customer Service Rep.; Services Sales Representative; Software Engineer. **Educational backgrounds include:** Chemistry; Engineering; Marketing. **Benefits:** 401(k); Dental Insurance; Disability Coverage; Employee Discounts; Life Insurance; Medical Insurance; Profit Sharing; Tuition Assistance. **Special programs:** Internships. **Corporate headquarters location:** This Location. **Other U.S. locations:** Atlanta GA; OH; Salt Lake City UT. **Listed on:** NASDAQ. **Number of employees nationwide:** 565.

DONALDSON COMPANY INC.
P.O. Box 1299, Minneapolis MN 55440. 952/887-3131. **Contact:** Human Resources. **World Wide Web address:** http://www.donaldson.com. **Description:** A manufacturer of filtration systems and noise abatement products. **Common positions include:** Accountant; Buyer; Chemist; Computer Programmer; Draftsperson; Electrical/Electronics Engineer; Financial Analyst; Industrial Engineer; Manufacturer's/Wholesaler's Sales Rep.; Marketing Specialist; Mechanical Engineer; Systems Analyst. **Educational backgrounds include:** Accounting; Business Administration; Chemistry; Computer Science; Engineering; Marketing. **Benefits:** Dental Insurance; Disability Coverage; Life Insurance; Medical Insurance; Pension Plan; Savings Plan; Tuition Assistance. **Corporate headquarters location:** This Location. **Listed on:** New York Stock Exchange.

DORR-OLIVER INC.
612 Wheelers Farms Road, Milford CT 06460. 203/876-5400. **Contact:** Susan Norton, Director of Personnel. **Description:** An international manufacturer of heavy process equipment for handling liquid, solid, and fluid bed technology, as well as machinery for CPI and environmental industries, minerals, and food processing. **Corporate headquarters location:** This Location. **Listed on:** New York Stock Exchange.

DOUGLAS BATTERY MANUFACTURING CO.
P.O. Box 12159, Winston-Salem NC 27117. 336/650-7000. **Fax:** 336/650-7057. **Contact:** Linda Niblock, Manager of Employment. **World Wide Web address:** http://www.douglasbattery.com. **Description:** A manufacturer of lead-acid batteries for industrial, automotive, lawn and garden, marine, and specialty applications. **Common positions include:** Automotive Mechanic; Buyer; Chemical Engineer; Computer Programmer; Customer Service Rep.; Electrical/Electronics Engineer; Electrician; General Manager; Human Resources Manager; Industrial Engineer; Management Trainee; Mechanical Engineer; Operations/Production Manager; Purchasing Agent/Manager; Quality Control Supervisor; Registered Nurse; Systems Analyst. **Educational backgrounds include:** Business Administration; Engineering; Finance; Liberal Arts. **Benefits:** 401(k); Dental Insurance; Disability Coverage; Employee Discounts; Life Insurance; Medical Insurance; Profit Sharing; Savings Plan; Tuition Assistance. **Corporate headquarters location:** This Location. **Other U.S. locations:** Nationwide. **Listed on:** Privately held. **Number of employees at this location:** 550.

DOVER CORPORATION
280 Park Avenue, Suite 34-W, New York NY 10017. 212/922-1640. **Contact:** Human Resources. **World Wide Web address:** http://www.dovercorporation.com. **Description:** Dover is a diversified producer of specialized industrial equipment and components for the petroleum, aerospace, construction, and electronics markets. Divisions include Dover Technologies, which manufactures electronic circuitry assembly equipment, radio frequency filters, microwave filters, and other equipment; and Dover Resources, which makes pumps, compressors, rods, valves, fittings, liquid filtration systems, and gas nozzles. Dover Industries and Dover Diversified manufacture products such as auto lifts, food preparation equipment, solid waste compaction systems, and electromechanical actuators. **Corporate headquarters location:** This Location. **Listed on:** New York Stock Exchange. **Stock exchange symbol:** DOV.

DRESSER INDUSTRIES INSTRUMENT DIVISION
250 East Main Street, Stratford CT 06614. 203/378-8281. **Contact:** Bill Ridolfi, Manager, Industrial Relations. **World Wide Web address:** http://www.dresserinstruments.com. **Description:** Manufactures pressure and temperature instruments and controls for a variety of customers. Dresser Industries supplies engineered products and technical services throughout the world. Operations are divided into several industry segments including petroleum operations; energy processing and conversion equipment; and industrial specialty products.

JOHN DUSENBERY COMPANY INC.
220 Franklin Road, Randolph NJ 07869-1605. 973/366-7500. **Contact:** Alfred Guber, Controller. **Description:** Manufactures machinery for the paper, film, and foil industries. **Corporate headquarters location:** This Location.

ECM MOTOR COMPANY
1061 Proctor Drive, Elkhorn WI 53121. 262/723-6400. **Contact:** Human Resources. **Description:** A manufacturer of sub-fractional horsepower motors and gearmotors. **NOTE:** Entry-level positions are offered. **Common positions include:** General Manager; Human Resources Manager; Operations Manager; Production Manager; Sales Engineer. **Educational backgrounds include:** Engineering. **Benefits:** 401(k); Casual Dress - Daily; Daycare Assistance; Dental Insurance; Disability Coverage; Flexible Schedule; Job Sharing; Life Insurance; Medical Insurance; Pension Plan; Savings Plan; Tuition Assistance. **Special programs:** Internships. **Corporate headquarters location:** This Location. **Parent company:** BTR/FASCO. **Number of employees at this location:** 600.

EAST PENN MANUFACTURING CO.
P.O. Box 147, Lyon Station PA 19536. 610/682-6361. **Contact:** Alan Hohl, Vice President of Personnel. **Description:** Produces automotive and industrial batteries. **Common positions include:** Accountant; Administrator; Advertising Clerk; Blue-Collar Worker Supervisor; Buyer; Chemical Engineer; Chemist; Computer Programmer; Draftsperson; Electrical/Electronics Engineer; Industrial Designer; Industrial Engineer; Marketing Specialist; Mechanical Engineer; Operations/Production Manager; Purchasing Agent/Manager; Quality Control Supervisor; Sales Executive; Transportation/Traffic Specialist. **Educational backgrounds include:** Accounting; Business Administration; Chemistry; Computer Science; Engineering; Marketing. **Benefits:** Dental Insurance; Disability Coverage; Employee Discounts; Life Insurance; Medical Insurance; Pension Plan; Profit Sharing; Savings Plan; Tuition Assistance. **Corporate headquarters location:** This Location.

THE EASTERN COMPANY
112 Bridge Street, Naugatuck CT 06770-2903. 203/729-2255. **Contact:** Human Resources. **Description:** Manufactures locks and security hardware engineered for use in industry, underground mining, and commercial construction. **Benefits:** 401(k); Life Insurance; Medical Insurance; Stock Option. **Corporate headquarters location:** This Location. **Subsidiaries include:** CCL Security Products Division (New Britain CT), The Illinois Lock Company Division (Wheeling IL), and World Lock Company Ltd. (Taipei, Taiwan) manufacture custom locks. Eberhard Manufacturing (Cleveland OH) and Eberhard Hardware Manufacturing, Ltd. (Ontario, Canada) produce transportation and industrial hardware. Frazer & Jones (Syracuse NY) manufactures mine roof fasteners and contract castings.

EATON CORPORATION
1111 Superior Avenue, Cleveland OH 44114. 216/523-5000. **Toll-free phone:** 800/386-1911. **Fax:** 216/479-7014. **Contact:** Human Resources. **World Wide Web address:** http://www.eaton.com. **Description:** A worldwide manufacturer of hydraulic products, fluid connectors, electrical power distribution equipment, engine components, and truck drivetrain systems. The company serves a variety of industries including automotive, aerospace, industrial, and semiconductor. **Corporate headquarters location:** This Location.

EDWARDS ENGINEERING CORP.
101 Alexander Avenue, P.O. Box 487, Pompton Plains NJ 07444. 973/835-2800. **Fax:** 973/835-2805. **Contact:** Rich Lewin, Personnel and Material Manager. **World Wide Web address:** http://www.edwards-eng.com. **Description:**

Manufactures coaxial condensers, coaxial evaporators, and vapor recovery systems using refrigeration and liquid nitrogen, baseboard heat, valance heating/cooling, liquid chillers, and hydronic control valves. **Common positions include:** Accountant; Buyer; Chemical Engineer; Chemist; Computer Programmer; Credit Manager; Draftsperson; Electrical/Electronics Engineer; Electrician; Financial Analyst; Machinist; Manufacturer's/Wholesaler's Sales Rep.; Mechanical Engineer; Payroll Clerk; Purchasing Agent/Manager; Receptionist; Sheet-Metal Worker; Software Engineer; Stock Clerk; Systems Analyst; Tool and Die Maker; Typist/Word Processor; Welder. **Benefits:** 401(k); Dental Insurance; Disability Coverage; Employee Discounts; Life Insurance; Medical Insurance. **Corporate headquarters location:** This Location. **Number of employees at this location:** 150.

ELECTRA-GEAR
1110 North Lemon Street, Anaheim CA 92801. 714/535-6061. **Fax:** 714/535-2489. **Contact:** Rochelle Pittock, Human Resources Administrator. **World Wide Web address:** http://www. electragear.com. **Description:** Manufactures a wide variety of motors, gear boxes, and speed reducers. **Common positions include:** Accountant; Adjuster; Blue-Collar Worker Supervisor; Computer Operator; Customer Service Rep.; Department Manager; Electrical/Electronics Engineer; Human Resources Manager; Industrial Engineer; Inspector/Tester/Grader; Machinist; Manufacturer's/Wholesaler's Sales Rep.; Mechanical Engineer; Receptionist; Secretary. **Educational backgrounds include:** Accounting; Business Administration; Engineering. **Benefits:** Dental Insurance; Disability Coverage; Employee Discounts; Life Insurance; Medical Insurance; Pension Plan; Profit Sharing; Savings Plan; Tuition Assistance. **Corporate headquarters location:** Beloit WI. **Parent company:** Regal-Beloit Corporation. **Listed on:** New York Stock Exchange. **Number of employees at this location:** 130.

ELECTRIC MACHINERY
800 Central Avenue NE, Minneapolis MN 55413. 612/378-8000. **Fax:** 612/378-8050. **Contact:** Human Resources. **World Wide Web address:** http://www.electricmachinery.com. **Description:** Custom manufacturers of heavy industrial electric motors and generators and related equipment. **Common positions include:** Accountant; Administrative Assistant; Blue-Collar Worker Supervisor; Buyer; Computer Programmer; Controller; Draftsperson; Electrical/Electronics Engineer; Electrician; Environmental Engineer; Manufacturing Engineer; Marketing Specialist; Mechanical Engineer; Purchasing Agent/Manager; Quality Control Supervisor; Sales Engineer; Secretary. **Educational backgrounds include:** Engineering. **Benefits:** 401(k); Casual Dress - Daily; Dental Insurance; Disability Coverage; Life Insurance; Medical Insurance; Public Transit Available; Tuition Assistance. **Number of employees at this location:** 240.

ELLICOTT INTERNATIONAL
1611 Bush Street, Baltimore MD 21230. 410/837-7900. **Contact:** Sandra Crawford, Vice President of Human Resources. **World Wide Web address:** http://www.dredge.com. **Description:** Produces dredges, dredging machinery, and related equipment. **Common positions include:** Accountant; Blue-Collar Worker Supervisor; Buyer; Computer Programmer; Customer Service Rep.; Draftsperson; Human Resources Manager; Manufacturer's/Wholesaler's Sales Rep.; Mechanical Engineer; Operations/Production Manager;

Purchasing Agent/Manager; Quality Control Supervisor; Systems Analyst; Transportation/Traffic Specialist. **Educational backgrounds include:** Accounting; Business Administration; Computer Science; Engineering; Finance. **Benefits:** 401(k); Dental Insurance; Disability Coverage; Life Insurance; Medical Insurance; Tuition Assistance. **Corporate headquarters location:** This Location.

ELLIOTT COMPANY
901 North Fourth Street, Jeannette PA 15644. 724/600-8387. **Fax:** 724/527-7151. **Contact:** Robert E. Caughey, Manager of Employee Relations. **World Wide Web address:** http://www. elliott-turbo.com. **Description:** Manufactures heavy turbomachinery. **Common positions include:** Applications Engineer; Mechanical Engineer; Sales Engineer. **Educational backgrounds include:** Business Administration; Engineering. **Corporate headquarters location:** This Location. **Other U.S. locations:** Nationwide. **International locations:** Worldwide.

EMBASSY INDUSTRIES, INC.
P&F INDUSTRIES, INC.
300 Smith Street, Farmingdale NY 11735. 516/694-1800. **Contact:** Human Resources. **World Wide Web address:** http://www.embassyind.com. **Description:** A manufacturing firm specializing in the production of portable pneumatic tools, baseboard heating equipment, hardware, and sheet metal contracting. **Corporate headquarters location:** This Location. **Other U.S. locations:** Boynton Beach FL; New Hyde Park NY. **Parent company:** P&F Industries, Inc. (also at this location).

ENERQUIP INC.
P.O. Box 467, Medford WI 54451. 715/748-5888. **Contact:** Personnel. **Description:** Manufactures heat exchangers, pressure vessels, and tanks for the food, dairy, nuclear, shipbuilding, and power industries. Enerquip custom designs to ASME and other codes. **Common positions include:** Accountant; Blue-Collar Worker Supervisor; Buyer; Chemical Engineer; Customer Service Rep.; Draftsperson; Mechanical Engineer; Operations/Production Manager; Quality Control Supervisor. **Educational backgrounds include:** Accounting; Business Administration; Engineering. **Benefits:** Disability Coverage; Life Insurance; Medical Insurance; Profit Sharing; Savings Plan. **Corporate headquarters location:** This Location.

ENGINEERED AIR SYSTEMS INC.
1270 North Price Road, St. Louis MO 63132. 314/993-5885. **Contact:** Mrs. LaDonna Reno, Manager of Human Resources. **Description:** Manufactures ground support equipment for portable military air conditioning and heating units, environmental control systems, and containers. **Common positions include:** Accountant; Attorney; Blue-Collar Worker Supervisor; Computer Programmer; Draftsperson; Electrical/Electronics Engineer; Financial Analyst; Human Resources Manager; Industrial Engineer; Mechanical Engineer; Metallurgical Engineer; Purchasing Agent/Manager; Quality Control Supervisor; Systems Analyst; Technical Writer/Editor. **Educational backgrounds include:** Accounting; Business Administration; Computer Science; Engineering; Finance; Liberal Arts; Marketing. **Benefits:** Dental Insurance; Disability Coverage; Life Insurance; Medical Insurance; Pension Plan; Tuition Assistance. **Corporate headquarters location:** This Location.

ENVIRONMENTAL ELEMENTS CORP.
3700 Koppers Street, Baltimore MD 21227. 410/368-7397. **Toll-free phone:** 800/333-4331.

Fax: 410/368-7344. **Contact:** Human Resources. **E-mail address:** eec.mail@eec1.com. **World Wide Web address:** http://www.eec1.com. **Description:** Designs and engineers air pollution control systems. Founded in 1946. **NOTE:** Entry-level positions and part-time jobs are offered. **Company slogan:** A breath of fresh air. **Common positions include:** Accountant; Administrative Assistant; Applications Engineer; Attorney; Budget Analyst; Buyer; Chemical Engineer; Chemist; Chief Financial Officer; Civil Engineer; Computer Operator; Computer Programmer; Computer Technician; Construction Contractor; Controller; Cost Estimator; Customer Service Rep.; Database Administrator; Database Manager; Design Engineer; Draftsperson; Electrical/Electronics Engineer; Financial Analyst; Human Resources Manager; Intranet Developer; Marketing Manager; Mechanical Engineer; Network/Systems Administrator; Operations Manager; Paralegal; Project Manager; Public Relations Specialist; Purchasing Agent/Manager; Quality Assurance Engineer; Quality Control Supervisor; Sales Manager; Sales Rep.; Secretary; Systems Analyst. **Educational backgrounds include:** Accounting; AS400 Certification; Business Administration; Chemistry; Engineering; Finance; HTML; Internet Development; Marketing; MBA; MCSE; Microsoft Office; Microsoft Word; Novell; Software Tech. Support; Spreadsheets; Visual Basic. **Benefits:** 401(k); Dental Insurance; Disability Coverage; Flexible Schedule; Life Insurance; Medical Insurance; Pension Plan; Savings Plan; Sick Days (6 - 10); Tuition Assistance; Vacation Days (10 - 20); Vision Plan. **Special programs:** Internships; Co-ops; Summer Jobs. **Office hours:** Monday - Friday, 8:00 a.m. - 5:00 p.m. **Corporate headquarters location:** This Location. **Listed on:** American Stock Exchange. **Stock exchange symbol:** EEC.

ENVIRONMENTAL TECTONICS CO.
125 James Way, County Line Industrial Park, Southampton PA 18966. 215/355-9100. **Fax:** 215/357-4000. **Contact:** Human Resources. **World Wide Web address:** http://www.etcusa.com. **Description:** Designs and manufactures sterilization systems, hyperbaric systems, air crew training systems, and environmental testing equipment. **Common positions include:** Aerospace Engineer; Agricultural Engineer; Electrical/Electronics Engineer; Electrician; Mechanical Engineer; Software Engineer; Structural Engineer. **Corporate headquarters location:** This Location. **Other U.S. locations:** Orlando FL.

ENVIROTEK PUMPSYSTEMS
P.O. Box 209, Salt Lake City UT 84110. 801/359-8731. **Fax:** 801/355-9303. **Contact:** Human Resources. **Description:** Manufactures industrial pumps and pump systems. The company also manufactures rubber products for industrial and mining applications and is engaged in bulk injection molding. **Common positions include:** Accountant; Buyer; Computer Programmer; Designer; Draftsperson; General Manager; Human Resources Manager; Industrial Engineer; Manufacturer's/Wholesaler's Sales Rep.; Mechanical Engineer; Metallurgical Engineer; Mining Engineer; Purchasing Agent/Manager; Quality Control Supervisor; Systems Analyst; Transportation/Traffic Specialist. **Educational backgrounds include:** Accounting; Business Administration; Computer Science; Engineering; Finance; Marketing. **Benefits:** 401(k); Daycare Assistance; Dental Insurance; Disability Coverage; Employee Discounts; Life Insurance; Medical Insurance; Tuition Assistance. **Special programs:** Internships. **Corporate headquarters location:** This Location. **Other U.S. locations:** Fresno CA; Sacramento CA;

St. Louis MO. **Parent company:** Weir (Scotland). **Listed on:** London Stock Exchange. **Annual sales/revenues:** $51 - $100 million. **Number of employees at this location:** 600.

ESCO CORPORATION
P.O. Box 10123, Portland OR 97296-0123. 503/228-2141. **Contact:** Human Resources. **World Wide Web address:** http://www.escocorp.com. **Description:** Manufactures steel products including brackets, dredge cutters, tractor and dozer equipment, chain conveying systems, and custom castings for the mining, food processing, construction, and logging industries. **Common positions include:** Accountant/Auditor; Buyer; Mechanical Engineer. **Educational backgrounds include:** Accounting; Business Administration; Engineering. **Benefits:** Dental Insurance; Disability Coverage; Employee Discounts; Life Insurance; Medical Insurance; Pension Plan; Savings Plan; Tuition Assistance. **Corporate headquarters location:** This Location.

EUTECTIC CORPORATION
9600H Southern Pines Boulevard, Charlotte NC 28273. 704/527-9800. **Contact:** Human Resources. **Description:** A worldwide organization engaged in the development, manufacture, distribution, and sale of special products, processes, and services for maintenance and repair welding. The company's products are designed to increase industrial productivity and prevent production stoppages by making critical machine parts and tools last longer. Overall, Eutectic Corporation is one of the world's largest manufacturers of special alloys for protective maintenance and repair. The company also offers support and consulting services for company products. **Corporate headquarters location:** This Location. **Subsidiaries include:** Eutectic & Castolin Institute provides extensive instructional programs in company technology.

EVA-TONE
P.O. Box 7020, Clearwater FL 33758. 727/572-7000. **Fax:** 727/571-3124. **Contact:** Human Resources. **World Wide Web address:** http://www.evatone.com. **Description:** Manufactures audio materials, CDs, CD-ROMs, cassettes, and soundsheets. The company also provides commercial printing, mailing, and packaging services. **Common positions include:** Factory Worker; Production Worker. **Educational backgrounds include:** Manufacturing Management. **Benefits:** 401(k); Dental Insurance; Disability Coverage; Life Insurance; Medical Insurance; Profit Sharing; Tuition Assistance. **Corporate headquarters location:** This Location. **Number of employees at this location:** 360.

EXIDE CORPORATION
P.O. Box 14205, Reading PA 19612. 610/378-0500. **Contact:** Jack Sosiak, Executive Director, Human Resources. **World Wide Web address:** http://www.exideworld.com. **Description:** Produces lead acid storage batteries for a wide variety of uses including consumer, industrial, and automotive. **Common positions include:** Accountant/Auditor; Computer Programmer; Credit Manager; Customer Service Rep.; Designer; Environmental Engineer; Financial Analyst; Human Resources Manager; Industrial Engineer; Mechanical Engineer; Metallurgical Engineer; Operations/Production Manager; Production Manager; Quality Control Supervisor; Systems Analyst. **Educational backgrounds include:** Accounting; Business Administration; Communications; Computer Science; Engineering; Liberal Arts. **Benefits:** 401(k); Dental Insurance; Disability Coverage; Life Insurance; Medical Insurance; Pension Plan; Tuition

Assistance. **Corporate headquarters location:** This Location. **Other U.S. locations:** Nationwide. **Number of employees at this location:** 300. **Number of employees nationwide:** 6,500.

FMC CORPORATION
200 East Randolph Drive, Chicago IL 60601. 312/861-6000. **Contact:** Troy Dickerson, Human Resources. **World Wide Web address:** http://www.fmc.com. **Description:** A diversified manufacturer of specialty, industrial, and agricultural chemicals; defense-related systems; and industrial machinery. **Corporate headquarters location:** This Location. **Subsidiaries include:** Fluid Control Systems; FMC Gold. **Listed on:** New York Stock Exchange.

THE FAIRCHILD CORPORATION FAIRCHILD COMMUNICATIONS SERVICES COMPANY
45025 Aviation Drive, Dulles VA 20166. 703/478-5800. **Fax:** 703/478-5767. **Contact:** Personnel. **World Wide Web address:** http://www.fairchildcorp.com. **Description:** The Fairchild Corporation operates through several divisions: Fairchild Communications Services Company (also at this location) provides comprehensive centralized telecommunications services for commercial office buildings; Fairchild Fasteners U.S. (Torrance CA) manufactures and supplies precision fastening systems, components, and latching devices for aerospace and industrial applications; D-M-E Company (Madison Heights MI) manufactures and supplies tooling and electronic control systems for the plastics injection molding industry; Fairchild Convac U.S. (Fremont CA) manufactures and supplies process equipment and systems for the semiconductor and related industries; and Fairchild Data Corporation (Scottsdale AZ) manufactures and supplies satellite modems and other high-speed products providing transmission of RF signals. Foreign subsidiaries include: Camloc GmbH (Germany); Fairchild Fasteners (Europe); Fairchild Scandinavian Bellyloading Company AB (Sweden); Fairchild Convac GmbH (Germany); Voi-Shan/Diessel GmbH (Germany). **Common positions include:** Accountant; Administrator; Attorney. **Educational backgrounds include:** Accounting; Business Administration; Liberal Arts. **Benefits:** Dental Insurance; Disability Coverage; Medical Insurance; Pension Plan; Savings Plan; Tuition Assistance. **Corporate headquarters location:** This Location. **Listed on:** New York Stock Exchange.

THE FALK CORPORATION
P.O. Box 492, Milwaukee WI 53201. 414/342-3131. **Contact:** Human Resources. **Description:** Manufactures gears, power transmission parts, and various other parts used in industrial machinery. **Corporate headquarters location:** This Location.

FARGO ELECTRONICS, INC.
6533 Flying Cloud Drive, Eden Prairie MN 55344. 952/941-9470. **Fax:** 952/941-7836. **Contact:** Human Resources. **World Wide Web address:** http://www.fargo.com. **Description:** Manufactures plastic card printers. **Corporate headquarters location:** This Location.

FARR COMPANY
2201 Park Place, El Segundo CA 90245. 310/727-6490. **Fax:** 310/727-6313. **Contact:** Human Resources. **World Wide Web address:** http://www.farrco.com. **Description:** Primarily engaged in the design, manufacture, and sale of filtration systems for use in a wide variety of industrial applications. These include heating, ventilating, and air conditioning systems, as well as gas turbines and construction equipment. Other products include noise-abatement systems and engine protection equipment. **Common positions include:** Accountant; Administrative Manager; Buyer; Computer Programmer; Customer Service Representative; Design Engineer; Draftsperson; Mechanical Engineer; Purchasing Agent/Manager. **Educational backgrounds include:** Accounting; Business Administration; Computer Science; Engineering; Marketing. **Benefits:** 401(k); Dental Insurance; Disability Coverage; Employee Discounts; Life Insurance; Medical Insurance; Tuition Assistance. **Corporate headquarters location:** This Location.

FERRY CAP & SET SCREW COMPANY
2151 Scranton Road, Cleveland OH 44113. 216/771-2533. **Contact:** Robb Reinker, Director of Industrial Relations. **Description:** Manufactures fasteners. **Number of employees at this location:** 330.

FILTERTEK, INC.
P.O. Box 310, Hebron IL 60034-0310. 815/648-2416. **Fax:** 815/648-2929. **Contact:** Mary Ellen Nilles, Director of Human Resources. **World Wide Web address:** http://www.filtertek.com. **Description:** This location manufactures custom-molded filters. Overall, Filtertek, Inc. manufactures filtration elements used in the automotive, health care, and various other industrial and consumer markets. The company sells its automotive filters directly to automotive manufacturers, automotive suppliers, and companies reselling filters in the automotive aftermarket. Filtertek produces filter products ranging from highly sophisticated disposable medical filters that filter contamination from blood, to a simple air filter used to protect machinery from dust contamination. **Common positions include:** Designer; Industrial Engineer; Mechanical Engineer. **Educational backgrounds include:** Engineering. **Benefits:** 401(k); Dental Insurance; Disability Coverage; Life Insurance; Medical Insurance; Savings Plan; Stock Option. **Corporate headquarters location:** This Location. **Parent company:** ESCO Electronics Corporation is a diversified producer of commercial products that are sold to a variety of customers worldwide. ESCO's products include electronic equipment, valves and filters, filtration and fluid flow components, automatic test equipment, utility load management equipment, and anechoic/shielding systems. ESCO's other operating subsidiaries include PTI Technologies, Inc.; VACCO Industries; Distribution Control Systems, Inc.; Rantec Microwave & Electronics; Lindgren RF Enclosures; Comtrak Technologies, Inc.; and EMC Test Systems, L.P. **Listed on:** New York Stock Exchange. **Number of employees at this location:** 350. **Number of employees nationwide:** 650.

FLOW INTERNATIONAL CORPORATION
23500 64th Avenue South, Kent WA 98032. 253/850-3500. **Toll-free phone:** 800/446-3569. **Fax:** 253/813-3285. **Contact:** Cindy McCormick, Human Resources Assistant. **World Wide Web address:** http://www.flowcorp.com. **Description:** One of the world's leading manufacturers of ultrahigh-pressure (UHP) waterjet cutting and cleaning systems, and factory automated equipment. Flow International has three main product categories: UHP cutting and cleaning, HydroMilling and HydroCleaning services, and powered access systems equipment. The company provides environmentally-sound solutions for the manufacturing, industrial cleaning, and factory automation markets. Flow International offers a wide range of robotics articulation capabilities, automated assembly systems, and other specialized manufacturing components. The company sells

original equipment and spare parts. **Common positions include:** Administrative Assistant; Design Engineer; Electrical/Electronics Engineer; Financial Analyst; Manufacturing Engineer; Mechanical Engineer; Quality Assurance Engineer; Sales Manager. **Benefits:** 401(k); Casual Dress - Fridays; Dental Insurance; Disability Coverage; Flexible Schedule; Job Sharing; Life Insurance; Medical Insurance; Profit Sharing; Public Transit Available; Savings Plan; Telecommuting; Tuition Assistance. **Corporate headquarters location:** This Location. **International locations:** Worldwide. **Listed on:** NASDAQ. **CEO:** Ronald Tarrant. **Number of employees at this location:** 320.

FLOW PRODUCTS INCORPORATED
800 Koomey Road, Brookshire TX 77423. 281/934-6014. **Fax:** 281/934-6052. **Contact:** Personnel. **World Wide Web address:** http://www.paco-pumps.com. **Description:** Manufactures industrial pumps and valves through its subsidiaries. **Corporate headquarters location:** This Location. **Other U.S. locations:** AL; CA; OR; TN; UT; VA; WA. **Subsidiaries include:** Johnston Pump; PACO Pumps; General Valve. All three companies are also at this location. **Number of employees at this location:** 350.

FLOWSERVE CORPORATION
222 West Las Colinas Boulevard, Suite 1500, Irving TX 75039. 972/443-6500. **Contact:** Human Resources. **World Wide Web address:** http://www.flowserve.com. **Description:** Manufactures valves for the chemical and petroleum industries. **Corporate headquarters location:** This Location.

FOILMARK MANUFACTURING CORP.
FOILMARK HOLOGRAPHICS
5 Malcolm Hoyt Drive, Newburyport MA 01950. 978/462-7300. **Contact:** Human Resources. **World Wide Web address:** http://www.foilmark.com. **Description:** Manufactures metallized, pigmented, and diffraction foils; and packaging films. Foilmark Holographics (also at this location) manufactures holographic films which are used for hot stamping purposes including the placement of emblems on credit cards. **Common positions include:** Accountant; Chemist; Customer Service Rep.; Sales Rep.; Secretary. **Educational backgrounds include:** Accounting; Business Administration; Chemistry; Engineering; Microsoft Word; Spreadsheets. **Benefits:** 401(k); Casual Dress - Fridays; Dental Insurance; Disability Coverage; Life Insurance; Medical Insurance; Profit Sharing. **Office hours:** Monday - Friday, 8:00 a.m. - 5:00 p.m. **Corporate headquarters location:** This Location. **Parent company:** Foilmark, Inc. also owns Imtran Foilmark, which manufactures pad printing equipment and supplies. **Listed on:** NASDAQ.

FORD METER BOX COMPANY
P.O. Box 443, Wabash IN 46992-0443. 219/563-3171. **Contact:** Human Resources. **World Wide Web address:** http://www.fordmeterbox.com. **Description:** Manufactures brass valves and fittings for the water works industry.

FOSTER WHEELER CORPORATION
Perryville Corporate Park, Clinton NJ 08809-4000. 908/730-4000. **Contact:** Bob Austin, Manager of Recruiting. **World Wide Web address:** http://www.fwc.com. **Description:** Foster Wheeler has three business segments: the process plants segment designs, engineers, and constructs process plants and fired heaters for oil refiners and chemical producers; the utility and engine segment designs and fabricates steam generators, condensers, feedwater heaters, electrostatic precipitators, and other pollution abatement equipment; and the industrial segment supplies pressure vessels and internals, electrical copper products, industrial insulation, welding wire, and electrodes. **Common positions include:** Accountant/Auditor; Chemical Engineer; Civil Engineer; Computer Programmer; Draftsperson; Electrical/Electronics Engineer; Financial Analyst; Industrial Designer; Mechanical Engineer. **Educational backgrounds include:** Accounting; Engineering; Finance. **Benefits:** Disability Coverage; Employee Discounts; Life Insurance; Medical Insurance; Pension Plan; Profit Sharing; Tuition Assistance. **Corporate headquarters location:** This Location.

FREQUENCY ENGINEERING LABORATORIES
Central Avenue, Farmingdale NJ 07727. 732/919-2420. **Fax:** 732/919-2455. **Contact:** David Fursman, Director of Human Resources. **Description:** Engaged in prime and subcontract manufacturing of weapons, missile systems, test equipment, airborne systems, communication systems, and EW and ASW systems. **Common positions include:** Accountant; Administrative Assistant; Buyer; Clerical Supervisor; Computer Operator; Controller; Design Engineer; Draftsperson; Finance Director; Financial Analyst; Industrial Engineer; Manufacturing Engineer; Mechanical Engineer; Project Manager; Purchasing Agent/Manager; Secretary; Software Engineer; Typist/Word Processor. **Educational backgrounds include:** Accounting; Computer Science; Engineering; Finance. **Benefits:** 401(k); Dental Insurance; Disability Coverage; Life Insurance; Medical Insurance; Tuition Assistance. **Corporate headquarters location:** This Location. **Listed on:** Privately held. **Number of employees at this location:** 250.

FULLER COMPANY
2040 Avenue C, Bethlehem PA 18017-2188. 610/264-6011. **Fax:** 610/264-6170. **Contact:** Joseph M. Mangan, Manager of Employee Relations. **Description:** An international producer of equipment for the cement and minerals processing industry. Fuller designs, engineers, manufactures, and installs these products for customers worldwide. **Common positions include:** Accountant; Buyer; Ceramics Engineer; Chemical Engineer; Civil Engineer; Computer Programmer; Customer Service Rep.; Designer; Draftsperson; Electrical/Electronics Engineer; Materials Engineer; Mechanical Engineer; Metallurgical Engineer; Mining Engineer; Purchasing Agent/Manager; Quality Control Supervisor; Structural Engineer; Systems Analyst. **Educational backgrounds include:** Engineering. **Benefits:** 401(k); Dental Insurance; Disability Coverage; Life Insurance; Medical Insurance; Pension Plan; Tuition Assistance. **Corporate headquarters location:** This Location. **Parent company:** FLS Industries. **Number of employees at this location:** 800. **Number of employees nationwide:** 1,200.

GANTON TECHNOLOGIES, INC.
8213 Durand Avenue, Sturtevant WI 53177. 262/504-3366. **Contact:** Human Resources. **World Wide Web address:** http://www.gantontechnologies.com. **Description:** A high-tech manufacturer of non-ferrous castings, machining, assemblies, and other tools. Ganton Technologies supplies products to major automotive and blue chip companies. **Common positions include:** Accountant; Blue-Collar Worker Supervisor; Buyer; Computer Programmer; Designer; Draftsperson; Environmental Engineer; Human Resources Manager; Industrial Engineer; Industrial Production Manager; Materials Engineer; Mechanical Engineer; Metallurgical Engineer; Operations/Production Manager; Quality Control Supervisor; Systems

Analyst; Transportation/Traffic Specialist. **Educational backgrounds include:** Accounting; Business Administration; Computer Science; Engineering. **Benefits:** 401(k); Dental Insurance; Disability Coverage; Life Insurance; Medical Insurance; Pension Plan. **Corporate headquarters location:** This Location. **Other U.S. locations:** Pulaski TN. **Listed on:** Privately held. **Number of employees at this location:** 700. **Number of employees nationwide:** 900.

GASBOY INTERNATIONAL, INC.
P.O. Box 309, Lansdale PA 19446. 215/855-4631. **Physical address:** 707 North Valley Forge Road, Lansdale PA. **Fax:** 215/361-5404. **Contact:** Eleanor Harding, Human Resources Manager. **World Wide Web address:** http://www.gasboy.com. **Description:** Develops, manufactures, and markets petroleum dispensing pumps, computer-controlled management systems, and related components. Founded in 1819. **NOTE:** Entry-level positions and part-time jobs are offered. **Common positions include:** Accountant; Administrative Assistant; AS400 Programmer Analyst; Computer Support Technician; Computer Technician; Customer Service Rep.; Help-Desk Technician; Network Engineer; Purchasing Agent/Manager; Software Engineer; Systems Analyst. **Educational backgrounds include:** AS400 Certification; Microsoft Office; Microsoft Word; Novell; Software Development; Spreadsheets. **Benefits:** 401(k); Casual Dress - Daily; Dental Insurance; Disability Coverage; Employee Discounts; Flexible Schedule; Life Insurance; Medical Insurance; Telecommuting; Tuition Assistance. **Special programs:** Training; Co-ops; Summer Jobs. **Corporate headquarters location:** This Location. **Parent company:** Tokheim Company. **Listed on:** New York Stock Exchange. **Stock exchange symbol:** TOK. **Annual sales/revenues:** $51 - $100 million. **Number of employees at this location:** 310.

GEHL COMPANY
143 Water Street, West Bend WI 53095. 262/334-9461. **Contact:** Ken Feucht, Manager of Human Resources. **World Wide Web address:** http://www.gehl.com. **Description:** Manufactures agricultural and construction equipment. The company is a leading manufacturer of agricultural implements in North America offering a comprehensive product line of equipment for haymaking, forage harvesting, feed-making, manure-handling, and materials-handling. Gehl Company's mobile construction equipment line includes a diversified offering of skid steer loaders; rough-terrain, telescoping-boom forklifts; and paving equipment. **Common positions include:** Accountant; Agricultural Engineer; Blue-Collar Worker Supervisor; Buyer; Computer Programmer; Customer Service Rep.; Department Manager; Draftsperson; Environmental Engineer; Health Services Manager; Human Resources Manager; Industrial Engineer; Mechanical Engineer; Operations/Production Manager; Quality Control Supervisor. **Educational backgrounds include:** Accounting; Business Administration; Engineering; Marketing. **Benefits:** 401(k); Dental Insurance; Disability Coverage; Life Insurance; Medical Insurance; Pension Plan; Savings Plan; Tuition Assistance. **Corporate headquarters location:** This Location. **Other U.S. locations:** Lebanon PA; Madison SD; Yankton SD. **Listed on:** NASDAQ. **Number of employees at this location:** 850.

GENERAL BEARING CORPORATION
44 High Street, West Nyack NY 10994. 914/358-6000. **Fax:** 914/358-6277. **Contact:** Ms. Fran Garner, Personnel Manager. **World Wide Web address:** http://www.generalbearing.com. **Description:** A manufacturer of ball bearings.

Common positions include: Accountant/Auditor; Administrator; Advertising Clerk; Computer Programmer; Credit Manager; Customer Service Rep.; Draftsperson; General Manager; Industrial Engineer; Management Trainee; Mechanical Engineer; Quality Control Supervisor. **Benefits:** Dental Insurance; Disability Coverage; Life Insurance; Medical Insurance; Pension Plan; Profit Sharing; Savings Plan; Tuition Assistance. **Corporate headquarters location:** This Location.

GENERAL DYNAMICS ARMAMENT SYSTEMS
128 Lakeside Avenue, Burlington VT 05401. 802/657-7000. **Fax:** 802/657-6292. **Contact:** Staffing Specialist. **Description:** Designs, develops, and produces complete armament systems used for the U.S. Armed Forces and for more than 20 other allied nations. **NOTE:** Entry-level positions are offered. **Common positions include:** Administrative Assistant; Attorney; Cost Estimator; Draftsperson; Electrical/Electronics Engineer; Environmental Engineer; Financial Analyst; Human Resources Manager; Manufacturing Engineer; Mechanical Engineer; Metallurgical Engineer; Purchasing Agent/Manager; Quality Assurance Engineer; Software Engineer. **Educational backgrounds include:** Engineering; Finance; Marketing; Microsoft Word; Software Development. **Benefits:** 401(k); Dental Insurance; Disability Coverage; Life Insurance; Medical Insurance; Pension Plan; Tuition Assistance. **Corporate headquarters location:** Falls Church VA. **Number of employees at this location:** 720.

GENERAL ELECTRIC COMPANY
3135 Easton Turnpike, Fairfield CT 06431. 203/373-2211. **Contact:** Human Resources. **World Wide Web address:** http://www.ge.com. **Description:** Operates in the following areas: aircraft engines (jet engines, replacement parts, and repair services for commercial, military, executive, and commuter aircraft); appliances; broadcasting (NBC); industrial (lighting products, electrical distribution and control equipment, transportation systems products, electric motors and related products, a broad range of electrical and electronic industrial automation products, and a network of electrical supply houses); materials (plastics, ABS resins, silicones, superabrasives, and laminates); power systems (products for the generation, transmission, and distribution of electricity); technical products and systems (medical systems and equipment, as well as a full range of computer-based information and data interchange services for both internal use and external commercial and industrial customers); and capital services (consumer services, financing, and specialty insurance). **Corporate headquarters location:** This Location.

GENTEX CORPORATION
600 North Centennial Street, Zeeland MI 49464. 616/772-1800. **Fax:** 616/772-7348. **Contact:** Manager of Human Resources. **World Wide Web address:** http://www.gentex.com. **Description:** Designs, develops, manufactures, and markets proprietary products employing electro-optical technology. The company has two primary product lines: automatic rearview mirrors for automobiles and fire protection products for commercial applications. **Common positions include:** Chemical Engineer; Chemist; Designer; Electrical/Electronics Engineer; Human Resources Manager; Industrial Engineer; Mechanical Engineer. **Educational backgrounds include:** Chemistry; Engineering. **Benefits:** 401(k); Dental Insurance; Disability Coverage; Employee Discounts; Life Insurance; Medical Insurance; Profit Sharing; Savings Plan; Tuition Assistance. **Special programs:** Internships.

Corporate headquarters location: This Location. **Listed on:** NASDAQ. **Number of employees at this location:** 750.

THE GLEASON WORKS
1000 University Avenue, P.O. Box 22970, Rochester NY 14692-2970. 716/473-1000. **Contact:** Human Resources. **World Wide Web address:** http://www.gleason.com. **Description:** The Gleason Works designs, manufactures, and sells machinery and equipment for the production of gears. The company manufactures a complete line of machines and tooling for bevel gears and manufactures machines for producing parallel axis gears. The Gleason Works' major customers are in the automotive, truck, aerospace, construction, farm, and marine industries. **Corporate headquarters location:** This Location.

GODDARD VALVE
705 Plantation Street, P.O. Box 765, Worcester MA 01605-0765. 508/852-2435. **Contact:** Human Resources. **World Wide Web address:** http://www.goddardvalve.com. **Description:** Designs and manufactures cryogenic gate, globe, and check valves and control devices required for the handling of liquefied natural gas, liquid oxygen, and other liquefied gases. **Corporate headquarters location:** This Location. **Parent company:** Goddard Industries, Inc.

STEPHEN GOULD CORPORATION
35 South Jefferson Road, Whippany NJ 07981. 973/428-1500. **Contact:** Debbie Habbart, Executive Assistant. **Description:** Designs, produces, and supplies packaging materials including plastic, paper, and metal for a variety of industries. **Corporate headquarters location:** This Location.

GRACO INC.
P.O. Box 1441, Minneapolis MN 55440-1441. 612/623-6000. **Physical address:** 4050 Olson Memorial Highway, Golden Valley MN 55422-2322. **Contact:** Human Resources. **World Wide Web address:** http://www.graco.com. **Description:** Designs, manufactures, and markets fluid handling systems and equipment for both industrial and commercial applications. Graco's products are used by companies in the manufacturing, processing, construction, and maintenance industries. Founded in 1926. **Common positions include:** Accountant; Administrative Assistant; Advertising Clerk; Auditor; Buyer; Computer Operator; Computer Programmer; Computer Technician; Customer Service Rep.; Database Administrator; Design Engineer; Draftsperson; Electrical/Electronics Engineer; Graphic Artist; Human Resources Manager; Manufacturing Engineer; Marketing Manager; Mechanical Engineer; Network/Systems Administrator; Purchasing Agent/Manager; Sales Engineer; Sales Manager; Sales Representative; SQL Programmer; Systems Analyst; Technical Writer/Editor; Transportation/Traffic Specialist. **Educational backgrounds include:** C/C++; Computer Science; Engineering; Internet; Java; Marketing. **Benefits:** 401(k); Casual Dress - Daily; Dental Insurance; Disability Coverage; Life Insurance; Medical Insurance; Tuition Assistance. **Corporate headquarters location:** This Location. **Other U.S. locations:** Los Angeles CA; Plymouth MI; Rogers MN; Sioux Falls SD. **International locations:** Argentina; Australia; Belgium; Brazil; Canada; China; France; Germany; Hong Kong; India; Indonesia; Italy; Japan; Korea; Malaysia; Mexico; New Zealand; Philippines; Spain; Taiwan; United Kingdom. **Listed on:** New York Stock Exchange. **Stock exchange symbol:** GGG. **President/CEO:** James Earnshaw. **Number of employees nationwide:** 2,080.

GRAND RAPIDS CONTROLS, INC.
825 Northland Drive NE, Rockford MI 49341. 616/866-9551. **Fax:** 616/866-0490. **Contact:** Personnel. **World Wide Web address:** http://www.grcontrols.com. **Description:** Manufactures cable assembly products for automotive and furniture manufacturers. **Educational backgrounds include:** Business Administration; Engineering. **Benefits:** 401(k); Daycare Assistance; Dental Insurance; Disability Coverage; Life Insurance; Medical Insurance; Pension Plan; Tuition Assistance. **Corporate headquarters location:** This Location. **Number of employees at this location:** 420.

GREENFIELD INDUSTRIES, INC.
GEOMETRIC TOOL
P.O. Box 2587, Augusta GA 30903. 706/863-7708. **Fax:** 706/860-8559. **Contact:** Wayne Thompson, Manager, Human Resources and Professional Staffing. **World Wide Web address:** http://www.gfii.com. **Description:** Manufactures expendable cutting tools and related products used in four specific markets: Industrial, Electronics, Oil Field Equipment, and Consumer. The company primarily distributes its products to manufacturers, the federal government, electronic OEMs, electronic subcontractors, oil field pump manufacturers, do-it-yourself customers, and contractors. Greenfield Industries is one of North America's leading producers of rotary cutting tools and suppliers of circuit board drills to the Far East. **Common positions include:** Buyer; Computer Programmer; Customer Service Representative; Industrial Production Manager; Marketing Specialist; Mechanical Engineer; Sales Executive. **Educational backgrounds include:** Business Administration; Computer Science; Engineering; Finance; Marketing. **Benefits:** 401(k); Dental Insurance; Disability Coverage; Employee Discounts; Life Insurance; Medical Insurance; Profit Sharing; Public Transit Available; Savings Plan; Tuition Assistance. **Corporate headquarters location:** This Location. **Other U.S. locations:** Nationwide. **Subsidiaries include:** Geometric Tool (also at this location). **Parent company:** Kennametal, Inc. **Annual sales/revenues:** More than $100 million. **Number of employees at this location:** 500.

GREENWALD INDUSTRIES
212 Middlesex Avenue, Chester CT 06412. 860/526-0800. **Fax:** 860/526-4205. **Contact:** Tracey Foreman, Human Resources Manager. **Description:** A designer and manufacturer of coin meter systems including the SmartCard. **Common positions include:** Accountant; Administrative Assistant; Blue-Collar Worker Supervisor; Chief Financial Officer; Controller; Credit Manager; Customer Service Rep.; Human Resources Manager; Industrial Production Manager; Manufacturing Engineer; Network Engineer; Network/Systems Administrator; Operations Manager; Production Manager; Quality Control Supervisor; Sales Manager; Sales Representative; Software Engineer; Systems Analyst. **Educational backgrounds include:** Engineering; MBA. **Benefits:** 401(k); Casual Dress - Daily; Dental Insurance; Disability Coverage; Life Insurance; Medical Insurance; Sick Days (1 - 5); Tuition Assistance; Vacation Days (10 - 20). **Office hours:** Monday - Friday, 8:00 a.m. - 5:00 p.m. **Corporate headquarters location:** This Location. **Parent company:** PubliCard, Inc. **Number of employees at this location:** 95.

GRENEKER
1500 South Evergreen Avenue, Los Angeles CA 90023. 323/263-9000. **Fax:** 323/263-9543. **Contact:** Personnel Director. **World Wide Web address:** http://www.greneker.com. **Description:** Manufactures mannequins. **Common positions**

include: Accountant/Auditor; Buyer; Computer Programmer; Cost Estimator; Credit Manager; Customer Service Rep.; Designer; General Manager; Human Resources Manager; Manufacturer's/ Wholesaler's Sales Rep.; Purchasing Agent/ Manager; Services Sales Rep.; Systems Analyst; Wholesale and Retail Buyer. **Educational backgrounds include:** Accounting; Art/Design; Business Administration; Economics; Engineering; Finance; Marketing; Mathematics. **Benefits:** Dental Insurance; Life Insurance; Medical Insurance; Profit Sharing. **Corporate headquarters location:** This Location. **Other U.S. locations:** NY; TX. **Number of employees at this location:** 285.

GRIFFIN CORPORATION
100 Jericho Quadrangle, Jericho NY 11753. 516/938-5544. **Contact:** Personnel. **Description:** Operates through four business segments: Home Furnishings and Furniture-Related Products (production and sale of bedding products, drapery hardware, and synthetic products); Specialty Hardware (production and sale of industrial hardware and related components); Electronic Communications Equipment (production and sale of communication, control, service, and entertainment systems for the aerospace industry); and Other Products (production and sale of commercial lighting, truck bodies, postal lock boxes, torque converters, and special purpose clutches). **Corporate headquarters location:** This Location. **Subsidiaries include:** Buildex Inc.; Lightron Corporation; Telephonics Corporation. **Listed on:** American Stock Exchange.

GROTH CORPORATION
1202 Hahlo, Houston TX 77020. 713/675-6151. **Contact:** Human Resources. **World Wide Web address:** http://www.grothcorp.com. **Description:** Engaged in the manufacture, sale, and service of valves and related instrumentation products. The company's customer base includes petrochemical and paper/pulp plants, and municipalities. **Benefits:** Dental Insurance; Medical Insurance. **Corporate headquarters location:** This Location. **Number of employees at this location:** 240.

GROVE WORLDWIDE
P.O. Box 21, Shady Grove PA 17256. 717/597-8121. **Fax:** 717/593-5039. **Contact:** Human Resources. **World Wide Web address:** http://www.groveworldwide.com. **Description:** A manufacturer of mobile lifting and access equipment. **Common positions include:** Accountant; Buyer; Ceramics Engineer; Civil Engineer; Computer Programmer; Designer; Electrical/Electronics Engineer; Financial Analyst; Industrial Engineer; Industrial Production Manager; Materials Engineer; Mechanical Engineer; Metallurgical Engineer; Operations/Production Manager; Quality Control Supervisor; Structural Engineer; Systems Analyst. **Educational backgrounds include:** Accounting; Engineering. **Benefits:** 401(k); Dental Insurance; Disability Coverage; Life Insurance; Medical Insurance; Pension Plan; Tuition Assistance. **Corporate headquarters location:** This Location. **Parent company:** Hanson Industries. **Listed on:** New York Stock Exchange. **Number of employees at this location:** 2,000.

GUNTHER INTERNATIONAL, LTD.
One Winnenden Road, Norwich CT 06360. 860/823-1427. **Contact:** Human Resources. **World Wide Web address:** http://www.guntherintl.com. **Description:** Gunther International, Ltd. designs, develops, assembles, markets, services, and maintains high-speed systems that automatically assemble printed documents; fold, staple, or bind the documents; insert completed documents into the

appropriate envelopes for mailing or other distribution; and stamp the correct postage by weight. The systems are computer-driven, with scanning devices used to read bar codes printed on the documents. **Common positions include:** Computer Programmer; Electrical/Electronics Engineer; Mechanical Engineer. **Educational backgrounds include:** Computer Science; Engineering. **Benefits:** 401(k); Dental Insurance; Disability Coverage; Life Insurance; Medical Insurance. **Corporate headquarters location:** This Location. **Listed on:** NASDAQ. **Annual sales/revenues:** $11 - $20 million. **Number of employees at this location:** 75.

HPM CORPORATION
820 Marion Road, Mount Gilead OH 43338. 419/946-0222. **Contact:** Personnel Director. **World Wide Web address:** http://www.hpmcorp.com. **Description:** Produces plastic injection molding machinery, extrusion equipment, and metal die-casting equipment. **Common positions include:** Accountant; Administrator; Buyer; Electrical/ Electronics Engineer; Mechanical Engineer. **Educational backgrounds include:** Accounting; Business Administration; Engineering; Finance. **Benefits:** Dental Insurance; Disability Coverage; Employee Discounts; Life Insurance; Medical Insurance; Pension Plan; Savings Plan; Tuition Assistance. **Corporate headquarters location:** This Location.

HADER SEITZ MANUFACTURING, INC.
P.O. Box 51060, Berlin WI 53151. 262/641-6000. **Contact:** Personnel. **Description:** Engaged in the manufacture of hydraulic cylinders, accumulators, swivels, telescopic cylinders, and circuit components. **Common positions include:** Accountant; Blue-Collar Worker Supervisor; Buyer; Computer Programmer; Draftsperson; Industrial Designer; Industrial Engineer; Manufacturer's/ Wholesaler's Sales Rep.; Purchasing Agent/ Manager; Systems Analyst. **Corporate headquarters location:** This Location.

HAMILTON FIXTURE
3550 Symmes Road, Hamilton OH 45015. 513/870-8700x1248. **Toll-free phone:** 800/889-2165. **Fax:** 513/870-8741. **Contact:** Human Resources. **Description:** A manufacturer of fixtures and displays for retail establishments. Products are made of metal, acrylic, wood, or a combination of materials. **Common positions include:** Account Manager; Account Rep.; Accountant; Adjuster; Blue-Collar Worker Supervisor; Buyer; Computer Programmer; Controller; Cost Estimator; Customer Service Representative; Draftsperson; Human Resources Manager; Industrial Engineer; Manufacturing Engineer; MIS Specialist; Operations Manager; Production Manager; Project Manager; Purchasing Agent/Manager; Sales Executive; Secretary; Typist/Word Processor. **Educational backgrounds include:** Business Administration; Engineering; Finance; Liberal Arts; Marketing. **Benefits:** 401(k); Dental Insurance; Disability Coverage; Employee Discounts; Life Insurance; Medical Insurance; Tuition Assistance. **Corporate headquarters location:** This Location. **Other U.S. locations:** Nationwide. **Listed on:** Privately held. **Annual sales/revenues:** $51 - $100 million. **Number of employees nationwide:** 800.

HANOVIA/COLITE, INC.
825 Lehigh Avenue, Union NJ 07083. 908/688-0050. **Contact:** Rosemary McCann, Director of Human Resources. **Description:** Designs, develops, produces, and markets plasma arc lamps and related equipment including commercial and industrial ultraviolet products and accessories; produces

various phosphorescent pigments, compounds, and films; and designs, develops, manufactures, assembles, and markets high-intensity lighting equipment. **Common positions include:** Ceramics Engineer; Chemist; Electrical/Electronics Engineer; Mechanical Engineer; Metallurgical Engineer. **Educational backgrounds include:** Chemistry; Engineering; Physics. **Benefits:** Dental Insurance; Disability Coverage; Life Insurance; Medical Insurance; Pension Plan; Profit Sharing; Savings Plan; Tuition Assistance. **Corporate headquarters location:** This Location.

HARDINGE INC.
One Hardinge Drive, P.O. Box 1507, Elmira NY 14902-1507. 607/734-2281. **Fax:** 607/732-4925. **Contact:** Thomas Mitchell, Director of Personnel. **Description:** Manufactures machine tools and accessories. Founded in 1890. **Common positions include:** Accountant; Automotive Mechanic; Computer Programmer; Customer Service Rep.; Designer; Draftsperson; Electrical/Electronics Engineer; Financial Analyst; Human Resources Manager; Industrial Engineer; Mechanical Engineer; Software Engineer; Systems Analyst. **Educational backgrounds include:** Computer Science; Engineering. **Benefits:** 401(k); Dental Insurance; Disability Coverage; Life Insurance; Medical Insurance; Pension Plan; Tuition Assistance. **Corporate headquarters location:** This Location. **Number of employees at this location:** 900.

HART SCIENTIFIC
799 East Utah Valley Drive, American Fork UT 84003. 801/763-1600. **Contact:** Human Resources. **World Wide Web address:** http://www. hartscientific.com. **Description:** Manufactures temperature calibration equipment. **Corporate headquarters location:** This Location.

HASKEL INTERNATIONAL, INC.
100 East Graham Place, Burbank CA 91502. 818/843-4000. **Fax:** 818/556-2526. **Contact:** Human Resources. **World Wide Web address:** http://www.haskel.com. **Description:** Manufactures pneumatically driven, high-pressure liquid pumps and gas boosters for industrial, commercial, aerospace, and military applications. The company sells and distributes its own pneumatically driven pumps, gas boosters, air amplifiers, and high-pressure valves, as well as third-party valves, cylinders and actuators, and other hydraulic and pneumatic devices. The company's high-pressure pumps and systems are used worldwide in manufacturing processes for industrial pressure testing and controls, fluid storage and containment, and a wide variety of other applications. Haskel International also specializes in the trading of electronic components. Founded in 1946. **Corporate headquarters location:** This Location.

HASKELL SENATOR INTERNATIONAL
231 Haskell Drive, Verona PA 15147. 412/828-6000. **Fax:** 412/828-6262. **Contact:** Christine A. Thurston, Manager of Human Resources. **Description:** Manufactures steel office furniture. This location also hires seasonally. **NOTE:** Entry-level positions are offered. **Common positions include:** Accountant; Administrative Assistant; Administrative Manager; Chief Financial Officer; Computer Operator; Computer Programmer; Controller; Credit Manager; Customer Service Rep.; Database Administrator; Draftsperson; General Manager; Human Resources Manager; Industrial Designer; Industrial Engineer; Manufacturing Engineer; Marketing Manager; Mechanical Engineer; Production Manager; Project Manager; Purchasing Agent/Manager; Sales Executive; Sales Manager; Sales Rep.; Secretary; Systems Analyst;

Vice President of Finance; Vice President of Operations; Vice President of Sales. **Educational backgrounds include:** Accounting; Computer Science; Engineering; Finance; Liberal Arts. **Benefits:** 401(k); Disability Coverage; Life Insurance; Medical Insurance; Savings Plan. **Corporate headquarters location:** This Location. **Annual sales/revenues:** $21 - $50 million. **Number of employees at this location:** 350.

HAWORTH INC.
One Haworth Center, Holland MI 49423. 616/393-3000. **Fax:** 616/393-1550. **Contact:** Human Resources. **Description:** Manufactures office furniture. **NOTE:** Entry-level positions and second and third shifts are offered. **Common positions include:** Account Manager; Accountant; Auditor; Buyer; Computer Programmer; Customer Service Rep.; Design Engineer; Draftsperson; Electrical/Electronics Engineer; Electrician; Financial Analyst; Human Resources Manager; Industrial Engineer; Industrial Production Manager; Manufacturing Engineer; Marketing Specialist; MIS Specialist; Systems Analyst; Systems Manager. **Educational backgrounds include:** Accounting; Computer Science; Engineering; Finance; Marketing; Software Development; Software Tech. Support. **Benefits:** 401(k); Daycare Assistance; Dental Insurance; Disability Coverage; Job Sharing; Life Insurance; Medical Insurance; Pension Plan; Tuition Assistance. **Special programs:** Internships; Apprenticeships; Training; Summer Jobs. **Corporate headquarters location:** Greenwich CT. **International locations:** Worldwide. **Listed on:** Privately held. **Annual sales/revenues:** More than $100 million. **Number of employees at this location:** 3,600.

HAYWARD INDUSTRIES
620 Division Street, Elizabeth NJ 07207. 908/351-5400. **Contact:** Human Resources. **World Wide Web address:** http://www.haywardnet.com. **Description:** Manufactures swimming pool equipment. The company is engaged in all aspects of production including design and sales. Clients use equipment in the construction, repair, and maintenance of private and commercial swimming pools. The company also manufactures and distributes a standard line of industrial pipeline strainers and valves. **Educational backgrounds include:** Accounting; Business Administration; Communications; Economics; Engineering; Finance; Liberal Arts; Marketing. **Benefits:** 401(k); Dental Insurance; Disability Coverage; Employee Discounts; Life Insurance; Medical Insurance; Pension Plan; Savings Plan; Tuition Assistance. **Corporate headquarters location:** This Location. **International locations:** Belgium.

HAZLETON PUMPS, INC.
225 North Cedar Street, Hazleton PA 18201. 570/455-7711. **Contact:** Ernest M. Stauffer, Personnel Manager. **World Wide Web address:** http://www.hazletonpumps.com. **Description:** Manufactures a wide range of centrifugal pumps. **Common positions include:** Draftsperson; Mechanical Engineer. **Educational backgrounds include:** Engineering. **Benefits:** 401(k); Dental Insurance; Disability Coverage; Life Insurance; Medical Insurance. **Corporate headquarters location:** This Location. **Parent company:** Warman International Group (Australia). **Number of employees at this location:** 200.

HEATCRAFT INC.
REFRIGERATION PRODUCTS DIVISION
2175 West Park Place Boulevard, Stone Mountain GA 30087. 770/465-5600. **Contact:** Human Resources. **World Wide Web address:** http://www.

heatcraftrpd.com. **Description:** Manufactures commercial refrigeration products. **NOTE:** Entry-level positions are offered. **Common positions include:** Accountant; Administrative Assistant; Computer Support Technician; Credit Manager; Customer Service Rep.; Marketing Specialist; Mechanical Engineer; Public Relations Specialist; Purchasing Agent/Manager; Sales Engineer; Sales Manager; Secretary; Systems Analyst. **Educational backgrounds include:** Microsoft Word; Software Tech. Support; Spreadsheets. **Benefits:** 401(k); Casual Dress - Fridays; Dental Insurance; Disability Coverage; Life Insurance; Medical Insurance; Pension Plan; Profit Sharing; Savings Plan; Tuition Assistance. **Special programs:** Co-ops. **Corporate headquarters location:** This Location. **Parent company:** Lennox International. **Number of employees at this location:** 190.

HEDWIN CORPORATION
1600 Roland Heights Avenue, Baltimore MD 21211. 410/467-8209. **Contact:** Human Resources. **World Wide Web address:** http://www. hedwin.com. **Description:** Manufactures industrial-size plastic containers. **Common positions include:** Accountant; Chemical Engineer; Mechanical Engineer; Project Engineer. **Educational backgrounds include:** Engineering. **Benefits:** 401(k); Dental Insurance; Disability Coverage; Life Insurance; Medical Insurance; Pension Plan; Tuition Assistance. **Corporate headquarters location:** This Location. **Other U.S. locations:** La Porte IN. **Parent company:** Solvay America.

HEIDELBERG WEB SYSTEMS
121 Broadway, Dover NH 03820-3290. 603/749-6600. **Fax:** 603/743-5353. **Contact:** Mr. Galen Hoffman, Director of Human Resources. **World Wide Web address:** http://www.heidelberg.com. **Description:** Designs, manufactures, markets, installs, and services printing equipment worldwide for the printing and publishing industries. **Common positions include:** Blue-Collar Worker Supervisor; Buyer; Chemical Engineer; Designer; Draftsperson; Electrical/Electronics Engineer; Industrial Engineer; Mechanical Engineer; Purchasing Agent/Manager; Quality Control Supervisor; Software Engineer; Systems Analyst; Technical Writer/Editor. **Educational backgrounds include:** Computer Science; Engineering. **Benefits:** 401(k); Dental Insurance; Disability Coverage; Employee Discounts; Life Insurance; Medical Insurance; Profit Sharing; Tuition Assistance. **Special programs:** Internships. **Corporate headquarters location:** This Location. **Other U.S. locations:** Nashville TN; Fort Worth TX. **Parent company:** Heidelberg. **Listed on:** Privately held. **Number of employees at this location:** 850. **Number of employees nationwide:** 1,150.

HEIN-WERNER
2120 Peewaukee Road, Waukesha WI 53188. 262/542-6611. **Contact:** Personnel. **Description:** A manufacturer and marketer of collision repair equipment. **Parent company:** Snap-on Inc.

HEKIMIAN LABORATORIES INC.
15200 Omega Drive, Rockville MD 20850-3240. 301/590-3600. **Contact:** Director of Human Resources. **World Wide Web address:** http://www. hekimian.com. **Description:** Designs, manufactures, and markets equipment that provides testing, access, and performance monitoring services for telecommunications networks. **Common positions include:** Accountant; Buyer; Customer Service Rep.; Draftsperson; Electrical/Electronics Engineer; Operations/Production Manager; Sales Executive; Software Engineer; Technical Writer/Editor. **Educational backgrounds include:** Business

Administration; Communications; Computer Science; Engineering; Mathematics. **Benefits:** 401(k); Dental Insurance; Disability Coverage; Life Insurance; Medical Insurance; Pension Plan; Tuition Assistance. **Corporate headquarters location:** This Location. **Parent company:** Axel Johnson, Inc. **Listed on:** Privately held.

HEXCEL CORPORATION
5794 West Las Positas Boulevard, Pleasanton CA 94588. 925/847-9500. **Contact:** Corporate Staffing. **World Wide Web address:** http://www. hexcel.com. **Description:** A manufacturing firm engaged in two primary business segments: structural materials including aerospace products, nonaerospace honeycomb, resin-impregnated industrial fabrics, and nonimpregnated fabrics; and specialty chemicals including bulk pharmaceuticals, custom and special-purpose chemicals, specialty resins, and industrial maintenance chemicals. **Common positions include:** Ceramics Engineer; Chemical Engineer; Computer Programmer; Materials Engineer; Systems Analyst. **Educational backgrounds include:** Accounting; Chemistry; Computer Science; Engineering; Finance. **Benefits:** 401(k); Dental Insurance; Disability Coverage; Employee Discounts; Life Insurance; Medical Insurance; Tuition Assistance. **Corporate headquarters location:** This Location. **Other U.S. locations:** Nationwide. **Listed on:** New York Stock Exchange. **Number of employees at this location:** 250. **Number of employees nationwide:** 5,000.

HI-RISE RECYCLING SYSTEMS, INC.
8505 NW 74th Street, Miami FL 33166. 305/624-9222. **Fax:** 305/594-4228. **Contact:** Human Resources. **World Wide Web address:** http://www. hiri.com. **Description:** Sells, installs, and services the patented Hi-Rise Recycling System for use in residential buildings. Founded in 1990. **Corporate headquarters location:** This Location. **Subsidiaries include:** Wilkinson Company Inc. (Stow OH) manufactures recycling, trash, and linen chutes for high-rise apartment buildings, condominiums, and hotels. **Listed on:** NASDAQ. **Stock exchange symbol:** HIRI.

HIGH VOLTAGE ENGINEERING CORP.
401 Edgewater Place, Suite 680, Wakefield MA 01880. 781/224-1001. **Fax:** 781/224-1011. **Contact:** Human Resources. **Description:** Owns and operates a diversified group of technology-based, middle market, industrial manufacturing businesses.

HILL PHOENIX
709 Sigman Road, Conyers GA 30013. 770/388-0706. **Contact:** Personnel. **World Wide Web address:** http://www.hillphoenix.com. **Description:** Manufactures refrigerator equipment for supermarkets and convenience stores. **Common positions include:** Electrical/Electronics Engineer; Manufacturer's/Wholesaler's Sales Rep.; Mechanical Engineer. **Educational backgrounds include:** Engineering. **Benefits:** 401(k); Dental Insurance; Medical Insurance; Savings Plan. **Corporate headquarters location:** This Location. **Listed on:** American Stock Exchange. **Number of employees at this location:** 115.

HOLLYMATIC CORPORATION
600 East Plainfield Road, Countryside IL 60525. 708/579-3700. **Contact:** Marilyn Krische, General Manager/Operations. **World Wide Web address:** http://www.hollymatic.com. **Description:** Manufactures food processing machines and parts, and paper products. **Corporate headquarters location:** This Location. **Number of employees at this location:** 50.

HOLOPAK TECHNOLOGIES, INC.

15 Cotters Lane, East Brunswick NJ 08816. 732/238-1800. **Fax:** 732/238-3018. **Contact:** Bonnie Eichel, Personnel Manager. **Description:** HoloPak, through its subsidiaries Transfer Print Foils, Inc. and Alubec Industries Inc., is a producer and distributor of hot stamping foils, holographic foils, metallized paper, and technical coatings. Hot stamping foils are elements of the graphics and packaging industries, and are used to decorate a wide variety of products. Holographic foils are high-precision images embossed into specialized coatings, which are used to discourage counterfeiting and provide specialty decorative effects. **Corporate headquarters location:** This Location. **Other U.S. locations:** Nationwide. **International locations:** Canada.

THE HON COMPANY

200 Oak Street, Muscatine IA 52761. 319/264-7400. **Contact:** Member and Community Relations Manager. **World Wide Web address:** http://www.honcompany.com. **Description:** A manufacturer of office furniture and related equipment. **Common positions include:** Account Manager; Accountant; Administrative Assistant; Computer Programmer; Credit Manager; Customer Service Representative; Database Administrator; Human Resources Manager; Industrial Engineer; Mechanical Engineer; MIS Specialist; Production Manager; Sales Manager; Sales Rep.; Secretary; Systems Analyst; Website Developer. **Educational backgrounds include:** Accounting; Business Administration; CGI; COBOL; Computer Science; Engineering; Finance; HTML; Internet Development; Java; Marketing; MBA; Microsoft Office; Microsoft Word; Software Development; Spreadsheets; SQL; Visual Basic. **Benefits:** Dental Insurance; Disability Coverage; Employee Discounts; Life Insurance; Medical Insurance; Profit Sharing; Retirement Plan; Savings Plan; Tuition Assistance. **Special programs:** Internships. **Corporate headquarters location:** This Location. **Other U.S. locations:** Nationwide. **Parent company:** Hon Industries, Inc. is a diversified manufacturer and marketer of office furniture, work space accessories, and home building products, and is comprised of nine operating companies with offices, showrooms, distribution centers, and manufacturing plants nationwide. Five other operating companies, marketing under various brand names (Gunlocke Company, BPI, and Holga) participate in the office furniture industry. Heatilator, Inc. manufactures and markets factory-built fireplaces, fireplace inserts, heating stoves, and accessories. HON Export Limited markets the corporation's products worldwide. **Listed on:** NASDAQ. **Number of employees at this location:** 200. **Number of employees nationwide:** 6,200.

HONEYWELL

101 Columbia Road, Morristown NJ 07962-1057. 973/455-2000. **Contact:** Human Resources. **World Wide Web address:** http://www.honeywell.com. **Description:** An advanced technology and manufacturing company providing customers worldwide with aerospace and automotive products, chemicals, fibers, plastics, and advanced materials. The company primarily manufactures products used by other manufacturers in the production or processing of finished industrial and consumer items. **Corporate headquarters location:** This Location.

HOPPMANN CORPORATION

15395 John Marshall Highway, Haymarket VA 20169. 703/753-3929. **Contact:** Barbara O. Egnor, Director of Human Resources. **World Wide Web address:** http://www.hoppmann.com. **Description:**

Produces automated parts handling systems. **Common positions include:** Administrator; Customer Service Rep.; Designer; Draftsperson; Electrical/Electronics Engineer; Electrician; Mechanical Engineer; Purchasing Agent/Manager; Technical Writer/Editor. **Educational backgrounds include:** Business Administration; Drafting; Engineering; Liberal Arts. **Benefits:** 401(k); Daycare Assistance; Dental Insurance; Disability Coverage; Leave Time; Life Insurance; Medical Insurance; Profit Sharing; Tuition Assistance. **Corporate headquarters location:** This Location. **Other U.S. locations:** Madison Heights VA. **Number of employees at this location:** 150.

HOSHIZAKI AMERICA, INC.

618 Highway 74 South, Peachtree City GA 30269. 770/487-2331. **Contact:** John Gronner, Human Resources Manager. **Description:** Manufactures commercial ice machines, storage bins, dispensers, and refrigerators. **Common positions include:** Accountant; Buyer; Customer Service Rep.; Designer; Draftsperson; Electrical/Electronics Engineer; Electrician; Human Resources Manager; Industrial Engineer; Mechanical Engineer; Purchasing Agent/Manager; Quality Control Supervisor; Systems Analyst; Technical Writer/Editor. **Educational backgrounds include:** Accounting; Engineering; Marketing. **Benefits:** 401(k); Dental Insurance; Disability Coverage; Life Insurance; Medical Insurance; Profit Sharing; Tuition Assistance. **Corporate headquarters location:** This Location. **Parent company:** Hoshizaki Electric, Ltd. **Listed on:** Privately held. **Number of employees at this location:** 250. **Number of employees nationwide:** 290.

HOSOKAWA MANUFACTURING

P.O. Box 880, Santa Rosa CA 95402. 707/585-2373. **Contact:** Personnel. **Description:** Manufactures food and chemical processing machinery. **Common positions include:** Accountant; Department Manager; Draftsperson; General Manager; Manufacturer's/Wholesaler's Sales Rep.; Mechanical Engineer; Operations/Production Manager; Purchasing Agent/Manager. **Educational backgrounds include:** Accounting; Business Administration; Engineering; Marketing. **Benefits:** 401(k); Dental Insurance; Disability Coverage; Life Insurance; Medical Insurance; Pension Plan; Tuition Assistance. **Corporate headquarters location:** This Location. **Parent company:** Berwind Corporation.

HUDSON PRODUCTS CORPORATION

6464 Savoy Drive, Suite 800, Houston TX 77036. 713/785-4000. **Contact:** Human Resources Department. **World Wide Web address:** http://www.hudsonproducts.com. **Description:** Manufactures heat exchangers, axial flow fans, vacuum steam condensers, and air pre-heaters. **Corporate headquarters location:** This Location. **Parent company:** McDermott International, Inc.

HURCO INDUSTRIES

P.O. Box 9119, Ogden UT 84409. 801/394-9471. **Contact:** Personnel. **Description:** Produces wooden partitions and various fixtures. **Corporate headquarters location:** This Location.

HUSCO INTERNATIONAL

P.O. Box 257, Waukesha WI 53187-0257. 262/547-0261. **Fax:** 262/547-5978. **Contact:** Jim Tarkowski, Vice President of Human Resources. **World Wide Web address:** http://www.huscointl.com. **Description:** Designs and manufactures electrohydraulic and hydraulic controls for mobile equipment markets worldwide. **NOTE:** Entry-level positions are offered. **Common positions include:**

Agricultural Engineer; Design Engineer; Designer; Draftsperson; Industrial Production Manager; Mechanical Engineer. **Educational backgrounds include:** Business Administration; Engineering. **Benefits:** 401(k); Dental Insurance; Disability Coverage; Life Insurance; Medical Insurance; Savings Plan; Stock Option; Tuition Assistance. **Special programs:** Internships. **Corporate headquarters location:** This Location. **Parent company:** HUSCO International Limited (England). **Annual sales/revenues:** More than $100 million. **Number of employees at this location:** 475.

HUSSMANN CORPORATION
12999 St. Charles Rock Road, Bridgeton MO 63044. 314/298-6589. **Fax:** 314/298-6456. **Contact:** Personnel. **Description:** Manufacturers of refrigerated display fixtures and cases, walk-in coolers, condensing units, shelving, and refrigeration systems. **Benefits:** Dental Insurance; Disability Coverage; Life Insurance; Medical Insurance; Pension Plan; Savings Plan; Tuition Assistance. **Special programs:** Internships. **Corporate headquarters location:** This Location. **Parent company:** Whitman Corporation.

HUTCHINSON SEAL CORPORATION
NATIONAL O-RING DIVISION
11634 Patton Road, Downey CA 90241-5295. 562/862-8163. **Fax:** 562/862-4596. **Contact:** Human Resources. **Description:** Engaged in distribution and manufacturing operations. The company includes National O-Ring, which manufactures and distributes a full-range of standard-size, low-cost, synthetic rubber o-ring sealing devices for use in automotive and industrial applications. **Corporate headquarters location:** This Location.

IMO INDUSTRIES, INC.
11811 North Freeway, Suite 190, Houston TX 77060. 281/448-1337. **Contact:** Office Manager. **Description:** Manufactures engine components, power supplies, temperature switches, valves, pneumatic controls, and other control products. **Corporate headquarters location:** This Location. **Parent company:** Transamerica Corporation. **Listed on:** New York Stock Exchange.

ITM CORPORATION
MACHINING DIVISION
533 West Godfrey, Lowell MI 49331. 616/897-9205. **Fax:** 616/897-5040. **Contact:** Human Resources. **Description:** Operates precision machining, manufacturing, and die-casting facilities serving the automotive, appliance, and furniture industries. **Common positions include:** Accountant; Computer Programmer; Designer; Draftsperson; General Manager; Manufacturing Engineer; Mechanical Engineer; Operations/Production Manager; Purchasing Agent/Manager; Quality Control Supervisor. **Educational backgrounds include:** Business Administration; Engineering; Manufacturing Management. **Benefits:** 401(k); Dental Insurance; Disability Coverage; Life Insurance; Medical Insurance; Tuition Assistance. **Corporate headquarters location:** This Location. **Other area locations:** Grand Rapids MI. **Listed on:** Privately held. **Number of employees at this location:** 475.

ITT A-C PUMP
240 Fall Street, Seneca Falls NY 13148. 315/568-2811. **Contact:** Manager of Employee Relations. **Description:** Produces pumps for the chemical process industry, water and wastewater facilities, and HVAC applications. **Corporate headquarters location:** This Location. **Parent company:** ITT Corporation is a diversified, global enterprise engaged in three major business areas: Financial and Business Services, which includes ITT Hartford, ITT Financial Corporation, and ITT Communications and Information Services, Inc.; Manufactured Products, which includes ITT Automotive, ITT Defense and Electronics, Inc., and ITT Fluid Technology Corporation; and Sheraton Hotels (ITT Sheraton Corporation).

ITT INDUSTRIES
CANNON RF DIVISION
100 Sebethe Drive, Cromwell CT 06416. 860/635-1500. **Toll-free phone:** 800/683-7666. **Fax:** 860/635-2010. **Contact:** Human Resources. **Description:** Engaged in the manufacturing of cable assemblies and coaxial connectors. **Common positions include:** Chemical Engineer; Customer Service Rep.; Department Manager; Designer; Electrical/Electronics Engineer; Industrial Engineer; Machinist; Manufacturer's/Wholesaler's Sales Rep.; Mechanical Engineer; Tool and Die Maker. **Educational backgrounds include:** Engineering. **Benefits:** Dental Insurance; Disability Coverage; Life Insurance; Medical Insurance; Profit Sharing; Savings Plan; Tuition Assistance. **Corporate headquarters location:** New York NY. **Parent company:** ITT Corporation is a diversified, global enterprise engaged in three major business areas: Financial and Business Services, which includes ITT Hartford, ITT Financial Corporation, and ITT Communications and Information Services, Inc.; Manufactured Products, which includes ITT Automotive, ITT Defense and Electronics, Inc., and ITT Fluid Technology Corporation; and Sheraton Hotels (ITT Sheraton Corporation).

ILLINOIS TOOL WORKS INC. (ITW)
3600 West Lake Avenue, Glenview IL 60025. 847/724-7500. **Contact:** Robyn McCarthy, Manager of Human Resources. **World Wide Web address:** http://www.itwinc.com. **Description:** Develops, produces, and markets various components, fasteners, assemblies, and packaging systems for clients in the industrial and construction markets. Products include metal components, construction products and polymers, consumer packaging products and systems, industrial packaging systems, and finishing systems. **Corporate headquarters location:** This Location. **Listed on:** New York Stock Exchange.

IMTRAN FOILMARK
25 Hale Street, Newburyport MA 01950. 978/462-2722. **Contact:** Human Resources. **World Wide Web address:** http://www.foilmark.com. **Description:** Manufactures pad printing equipment and supplies, dies, tooling, and silicone rubber products. **Corporate headquarters location:** This Location. **Parent company:** Foilmark, Inc. **Listed on:** NASDAQ. **Stock exchange symbol:** FLMK.

INDUSTRIAL TECHNOLOGIES, INC.
70 Cascade Boulevard, Milford CT 06460. 203/876-1800. **Contact:** Norma Gold, Human Resources Director. **World Wide Web address:** http://www.web-inspect.com. **Description:** Designs, develops, and markets sensor, monitoring, processing, and inspection technologies that operate under demanding factory floor conditions found in a wide range of industries. Customers include aerospace, communications, and industrial equipment suppliers as well as a wide range of web process manufacturers of paper, plastic sheet, film, photosensitive materials, nonwovens, steel, aluminum, other nonferrous metals, glass, and rubber. The company's primary line is a family of standard inspection systems used in web process industries for final inspection of finished materials and for control of intermediate processes. The

second product line is a full line of industrial strength computer processors, displays, and peripherals. These products operate under harsh temperatures, humidity, and shock conditions. In addition, the company maintains a contract development service providing customized design and production of automated inspection and measurement systems for industrial customers. **Corporate headquarters location:** This Location.

INDUSTRIAL TECTONICS INC.
7222 West Huron River Drive, Dexter MI 48130. 734/426-4681. **Contact:** Aurora Dickson, Personnel Director. **Description:** Engaged in the manufacture of high precision ball products. **Number of employees at this location:** 55.

INGERSOLL-DRESSER PUMP COMPANY
5715 Bickett Street, Huntington Park CA 90255-2634. 323/588-2201. **Contact:** Jualene Tapp, Human Resources. **Description:** Manufactures centrifugal pumps for several process services. A joint venture company of Ingersoll-Rand and Dresser Industries, Inc., the company is one of the world's leading suppliers of technology products and services to worldwide energy, natural resource, and industrial markets. Operations include petroleum, energy processing and conversion, mining and construction, and general industry. **Common positions include:** Applications Engineer; Buyer; Computer Programmer; Design Engineer; Draftsperson; Industrial Engineer; Mechanical Engineer; Secretary. **Educational backgrounds include:** Computer Science; Engineering. **Benefits:** 401(k); Dental Insurance; Disability Coverage; Life Insurance; Medical Insurance; Pension Plan; Tuition Assistance. **Special programs:** Co-ops. **Number of employees at this location:** 260.

INGERSOLL-RAND COMPANY
200 Chestnut Ridge Road, Woodcliff Lake NJ 07675. 201/573-0123. **Contact:** Human Resources. **World Wide Web address:** http://www.ingersoll-rand.com. **Description:** Manufactures compressors, pumps, and other nonelectrical industrial equipment and machinery. Ingersoll-Rand Company's products include air compression systems, antifriction systems, construction equipment, air tools, bearings, locks, tools, and pumps. **Corporate headquarters location:** This Location. **Other U.S. locations:** Nationwide. **Subsidiaries include:** The Torrington Company. **Listed on:** New York Stock Exchange.

INSTRON CORPORATION
100 Royall Street, Canton MA 02021. 781/828-2500. **Toll-free phone:** 800/877-6674. **Fax:** 781/575-5776. **Contact:** Human Resources. **World Wide Web address:** http://www.instron.com. **Description:** Manufactures, markets, and services materials testing instruments, systems, software, and accessories used to evaluate the mechanical properties and performance of metals, plastics, composites, textiles, ceramics, rubber, adhesives, and other materials. Instron's applications technology is used by research scientists, design engineers, and quality control managers in industry, academia, and government. The systems include electromechanical and servohydraulic instruments, structural components, computer software, temperature chambers, and hardness testers. **Common positions include:** Account Manager; Computer Programmer; Customer Service Rep.; Electrical/Electronics Engineer; Financial Analyst; Manufacturing Engineer; Mechanical Engineer; Purchasing Agent/Manager; Software Engineer; Systems Analyst; Technical Writer/Editor. **Educational backgrounds include:** Engineering. **Benefits:** 401(k); Dental Insurance; Disability Coverage; Employee Discounts; Life Insurance;

Medical Insurance; Pension Plan; Profit Sharing; Tuition Assistance. **Corporate headquarters location:** This Location. **Other U.S. locations:** Nationwide. **Subsidiaries include:** Laboratory Microsystems (Troy NY). **Listed on:** American Stock Exchange. **Number of employees at this location:** 400.

INTERLAKE MATERIAL HANDLING, INC.
1240 East Diehl Road, Suite 200, Naperville IL 60563. 630/245-8800. **Contact:** Human Resources. **World Wide Web address:** http://www.interlake.com. **Description:** Operates through two divisions. The company's Engineered Materials Division manufactures ferrous powders used in aircraft parts. The Handling Division produces warehouse storage equipment, conveyor systems, and inventory control systems. **Corporate headquarters location:** This Location. **Chairman/CEO:** W. Robert Reum.

INVENSYS APPLIANCE CONTROLS
703 West South Street, North Manchester IN 46962. 219/982-2161. **Contact:** Human Resources. **Description:** Manufactures electro-mechanical control units and small appliance motors. **Common positions include:** Accountant; Administrative Assistant; Budget Analyst; Cost Estimator; Design Engineer; Electrical/Electronics Engineer; Environmental Engineer; Human Resources Manager; Industrial Engineer; Manufacturing Engineer; Mechanical Engineer; Production Manager; Quality Assurance Engineer; Quality Control Supervisor; Secretary. **Educational backgrounds include:** AS400 Certification; Business Administration; Microsoft Word; Spreadsheets. **Benefits:** 401(k); Casual Dress - Daily; Dental Insurance; Disability Coverage; Life Insurance; Medical Insurance; Pension Plan; Tuition Assistance; Vacation Days (11 - 15). **Corporate headquarters location:** Richmond VA. **Parent company:** RobertShaw. **Number of employees at this location:** 350.

INVENSYS POWER SYSTEMS
8609 Six Forks Road, Raleigh NC 27615. 919/872-3020. **Fax:** 919/870-3119. **Contact:** Al Williams, Human Resources Director. **E-mail address:** jobs@powerware.com. **World Wide Web address:** http://www.invensys-power.com. **Description:** Manufactures power control and energy storage products. The company operates four product groups: Secure Power, Energy Storage, Power Conversion, and Energy Systems. These groups provide customers with every element of their power systems including remote monitoring and comprehensive support systems. **Parent company:** Invensys plc (London, England). **Number of employees at this location:** 45.

IONICS INC.
P.O. Box 9131, Watertown MA 02471. 617/926-2500. **Physical address:** 65 Grove Street, Watertown MA 02472. **Contact:** Marianne Manzon Winsser, Director of Human Resources. **World Wide Web address:** http://www.ionics.com. **Description:** Designs, manufactures, and sells four groups of products: Water Processing Systems are used for water desalination, food processing, chemical manufacturing, and biological separations that include ion-exchange membranes and electrochemical cells. Membrane Cell Products include products used in food processing, the manufacture of chlorination chemicals, and products used by the food, pharmaceutical, and chemical industries for special process problems; Energy Related & Other Fabricated Products include products used in nuclear or fossil fuel power plants and heat recuperating systems; and Instruments &

Medical Products include laboratory and process control instruments and medical products. **Common positions include:** Accountant/Auditor; Buyer; Chemical Engineer; Chemist; Draftsperson; Electrical/Electronics Engineer; Operations/ Production Manager; Quality Control Supervisor. **Educational backgrounds include:** Accounting; Chemistry; Computer Science; Engineering; Finance. **Benefits:** 401(k); Dental Insurance; Disability Coverage; Life Insurance; Medical Insurance; Pension Plan; Tuition Assistance. **Corporate headquarters location:** This Location. **International locations:** Worldwide. **Listed on:** New York Stock Exchange.

IOWA INDUSTRIAL HYDRAULICS, INC.
21201 510th Street, Pocahontas IA 50574. 712/335-3311. **Fax:** 712/335-4778. **Contact:** Human Resources. **Description:** Manufactures hydraulic cylinders for agriculture, construction, mining, and other industries. Iowa Industrial Hydraulics also designs cylinders and manufactures prototypes. **Common positions include:** Accountant/Auditor; Design Engineer; Mechanical Engineer; Securities Sales Rep.; Systems Analyst. **Educational backgrounds include:** Computer Science; Engineering; Marketing; Mathematics. **Benefits:** 401(k); Dental Insurance; Disability Coverage; Employee Discounts; Life Insurance; Medical Insurance; Tuition Assistance. **Corporate headquarters location:** This Location. **Parent company:** Hydraulic Technologies Inc. **Annual sales/revenues:** $21 - $50 million. **Number of employees at this location:** 275.

ISCO, INC.
P.O. Box 82531, Lincoln NE 68501-2531. 402/464-0231. **Fax:** 402/465-3944. **Contact:** Human Resources. **World Wide Web address:** http://www.isco.com. **Description:** A designer, manufacturer, and worldwide marketer of instruments used by scientists and engineers addressing concerns such as water pollution, biological research, environmental testing, and industrial quality control. The company's products include wastewater samplers, open channel flow meters, parameter monitoring products, liquid chromatography products, supercritical fluid extraction products, and syringe pumps. Markets served include enforcement agencies, dischargers, environmental consulting engineers, environmental analysis labs, bioseparators, food processors, plastics manufacturers, and petroleum manufacturers. Isco also collaborates with commercial and academic scientists and technicians concerned with separating and analyzing the components of a wide variety of materials. These components and materials include the fat content of food, pollutants in environmental samples, and additives in plastics. The company's separation instruments are also used by customers involved in biotechnology, pharmaceutical, life science, and medical research. **Common positions include:** Accountant; Administrative Assistant; Administrative Manager; Assistant Manager; Biochemist; Blue-Collar Worker Supervisor; Chemist; Clerical Supervisor; Controller; Customer Service Rep.; Desktop Publishing Specialist; Draftsperson; Electrical/Electronics Engineer; General Manager; Graphic Artist; Human Resources Manager; Industrial Engineer; Industrial Production Manager; Manufacturing Engineer; Mechanical Engineer; Operations Manager; Production Manager; Quality Control Supervisor; Sales Engineer; Sales Manager; Sales Rep.; Secretary; Systems Analyst; Systems Manager; Technical Writer/Editor; Typist/Word Processor; Webmaster. **Educational backgrounds include:** Accounting; Chemistry; Engineering; Liberal Arts; Marketing; Microsoft Word; Spreadsheets. **Benefits:** 401(k);

Casual Dress - Fridays; Dental Insurance; Disability Coverage; Financial Planning Assistance; Life Insurance; Medical Insurance; Profit Sharing; Sick Days (1 - 5); Tuition Assistance; Vacation Days (6 - 10). **Corporate headquarters location:** This Location. **Owner:** Robert W. Allington. **Number of employees at this location:** 420.

J&C STAINLESS FABRICATING COMPANY
860 Navajo Street, Denver CO 80204. 303/573-1700. **Toll-free phone:** 800/525-8966. **Fax:** 303/573-3776. **Contact:** Jeff Manion, President/ Owner. **Description:** Manufactures custom kitchen equipment for restaurants and school cafeterias. **Common positions include:** Accountant. **Educational backgrounds include:** Accounting. **Benefits:** 401(k); Casual Dress - Daily; Disability Coverage; Life Insurance; Medical Insurance; Profit Sharing; Sick Days (1 - 5); Tuition Assistance; Vacation Days (10 - 20). **Listed on:** Privately held. **Annual sales/revenues:** Less than $5 million. **Number of employees at this location:** 40.

JLG INDUSTRIES, INC.
One JLG Drive, McConnellsburg PA 17233. 717/485-5161. **Fax:** 717/485-6466. **Recorded jobline:** 717/485-6684. **Contact:** Gary M. Schweitzer, Corporate Employment Manager. **World Wide Web address:** http://www.jlg.com. **Description:** A leading manufacturer, distributor, and international marketer of mobile work platforms. Founded in 1969. **NOTE:** Entry-level positions are offered. **Common positions include:** Design Engineer; Electrical/Electronics Engineer; Industrial Engineer; Manufacturing Engineer; Mechanical Engineer. **Educational backgrounds include:** AS400 Certification; Business Administration; Engineering; Marketing; Microsoft Word. **Benefits:** 401(k); Casual Dress - Fridays; Dental Insurance; Disability Coverage; Employee Discounts; Life Insurance; Medical Insurance; Profit Sharing; Tuition Assistance. **Special programs:** Internships; Apprenticeships; Co-ops. **Office hours:** Monday - Friday, 8:00 a.m. - 4:45 p.m. **Corporate headquarters location:** This Location. **Other U.S. locations:** Bedford PA. **International locations:** Australia; Scotland. **Listed on:** New York Stock Exchange. **Stock exchange symbol:** JLG. **Number of employees at this location:** 1,840.

JAKEL, INCORPORATED
400 Broadway, Highland IL 62249. 618/654-2371. **Fax:** 618/654-5320. **Contact:** Jim Hartlieb, Director of Human Resources. **E-mail address:** jhartlieb@jakelinc.com. **World Wide Web address:** http://www.jakelinc.com. **Description:** Manufactures sub-fractional horsepower electric motors for the small appliance and HVAC industry. Founded in 1946. **NOTE:** Entry-level positions are offered. **Company slogan:** Quality starts here. **Common positions include:** Accountant; Administrative Assistant; Buyer; Chief Financial Officer; Customer Service Rep.; Design Engineer; Draftsperson; Human Resources Manager; Industrial Engineer; Manufacturing Engineer; Marketing Manager; MIS Specialist; Production Manager; Purchasing Agent/Manager; Quality Assurance Engineer; Quality Control Supervisor; Sales Manager; Sales Rep.; Secretary; Systems Manager. **Educational backgrounds include:** Accounting; Business Administration; Computer Science; Engineering; Microsoft Office. **Benefits:** Casual Dress - Daily; Life Insurance; Medical Insurance; Profit Sharing; Relocation Assistance; Tuition Assistance. **Special programs:** Internships; Co-ops. **Office hours:** Monday - Friday, 8:00 a.m. - 5:00 p.m. **Corporate headquarters location:** This Location. **Other U.S. locations:** Palestine IL; Clinton KY; Murray KY; East Prairie MO. **CEO:**

Robert K. Jakel. **Annual sales/revenues:** $51 - $100 million. **Number of employees at this location:** 300. **Number of employees nationwide:** 850.

JAMESBURY, INC.
NELES CONTROLS, INC.
P.O. Box 15004, Worcester MA 01615. 508/852-0200. **Physical address:** 640 Lincoln Street, Worcester MA. **Contact:** Marcia Siart, Employment Manager. **World Wide Web address:** http://www. jamesbury.com. **Description:** Manufactures valves and controls for the process control industry. **NOTE:** Entry-level positions and second and third shifts are offered. **Common positions include:** Accountant; Administrative Assistant; Applications Engineer; Buyer; Customer Service Rep.; Design Engineer; Draftsperson; Electrical/Electronics Engineer; Marketing Manager; MIS Specialist; Sales Rep. **Educational backgrounds include:** Accounting; Business Administration; Computer Science; Engineering; Finance; Marketing; Software Tech. Support. **Benefits:** 401(k); Dental Insurance; Disability Coverage; Job Sharing; Life Insurance; Medical Insurance; Pension Plan; Profit Sharing; Public Transit Available; Savings Plan; Tuition Assistance. **Special programs:** Summer Jobs. **Annual sales/revenues:** More than $100 million.

JEFFREY CHAIN CORPORATION
2307 Maden Drive, Morristown TN 37813. 423/586-1951. **Contact:** Human Resources. **Description:** Manufactures engineered chain products used in a variety of industrial equipment. **Common positions include:** Accountant; Buyer; Computer Programmer; Customer Service Rep.; Draftsperson; Human Resources Manager; Industrial Engineer; Mechanical Engineer; Metallurgical Engineer; Production Manager; Purchasing Agent/Manager. **Educational backgrounds include:** Accounting; Business Administration; Communications; Computer Science; Engineering; Finance. **Benefits:** 401(k); Dental Insurance; Disability Coverage; Life Insurance; Medical Insurance; Profit Sharing; Tuition Assistance. **Corporate headquarters location:** This Location. **Parent company:** Guardian Development (Fairway KS).

JOHNSON CONTROLS, INC.
BATTERY AUTOMOTIVE SYSTEMS GROUP
5757 North Green Bay Avenue, P.O. Box 591, Milwaukee WI 53201-0591. 414/228-1200. **Fax:** 414/228-0108. **Contact:** Human Resources. **E-mail address:** humanresources@jci.com. **World Wide Web address:** http://www.jci.com/bg. **Description:** Develops and manufactures lead acid storage batteries for automotive, communication, and industrial applications. **Common positions include:** Accountant; Chemical Engineer; Controller; Design Engineer; Financial Analyst; Manufacturing Engineer; Mechanical Engineer; MIS Specialist; Project Manager; Sales Engineer; Sales Rep.; Systems Analyst; Systems Manager. **Educational backgrounds include:** Accounting; Business Administration; Engineering; M.I.S. **Benefits:** 401(k); Daycare Assistance; Dental Insurance; Disability Coverage; Employee Discounts; Life Insurance; Medical Insurance; Pension Plan; Tuition Assistance. **Corporate headquarters location:** This Location. **Other U.S. locations:** Nationwide. **International locations:** Worldwide. **Listed on:** New York Stock Exchange. **Annual sales/revenues:** More than $100 million. **Number of employees at this location:** 300.

JORGENSEN CONVEYORS INC.
10303 North Baehr Road, Mequon WI 53092. 262/242-3089. **Fax:** 262/242-6942. **Contact:** James Sigl, Controller. **Description:** Manufactures metal conveyor belts for use in various industries. **Common positions include:** Buyer; Computer Operator; Controller; Draftsperson; Quality Control Supervisor; Sales Engineer. **Benefits:** Dental Insurance; Life Insurance; Medical Insurance; Profit Sharing. **Corporate headquarters location:** This Location. **Annual sales/revenues:** $5 - $10 million. **Number of employees at this location:** 110.

KBA-MOTTER CORPORATION
P.O. Box 1562, York PA 17405. 717/755-1071. **Contact:** Jack Cormack, Personnel Administrator. **Description:** Produces high-speed, web-fed rotogravure presses and related equipment. **Common positions include:** Accountant; Buyer; Computer Programmer; Draftsperson; Electrical/Electronics Engineer; Human Resources Manager; Machinist; Mechanical Engineer; Operations/Production Manager; Quality Control Supervisor. **Educational backgrounds include:** Accounting; Business Administration; Computer Science; Engineering; Mathematics. **Benefits:** Dental Insurance; Disability Coverage; Life Insurance; Medical Insurance; Pension Plan; Savings Plan; Tuition Assistance. **Corporate headquarters location:** This Location. **Parent company:** Koening & Bauer-Albert. **Number of employees at this location:** 135.

KENNAMETAL INC.
P.O. Box 231, 1600 Technology Way, Latrobe PA 15650-0231. 724/539-5000. **Fax:** 724/539-4711. **Contact:** Human Resources. **World Wide Web address:** http://www.kennametal.com. **Description:** As part of the Mining and Construction Division, this location manufactures wear-resistant parts through a metallurgical powder technology. Overall, Kennametal manufactures, purchases, and distributes a broad range of tools, tooling systems, supplies, and services for the metalworking, mining, and highway construction industries. The company's metal-cutting tools are made of cemented carbides, ceramics, and other hard materials. Kennametal manufactures a complete line of tool holders and tool holding systems by machining and fabricating steel bars and other metal alloys. The company's mining and construction cutting tools are tipped with cemented carbide and are used for underground coal mining and highway construction, repair, and maintenance. Metallurgical products consist of powders made from ore concentrates, compounds, and secondary materials. **Corporate headquarters location:** This Location. **Other U.S. locations:** Troy MI; Henderson NC; Roanoke Rapids NC; Fallon NV; Orwell OH; Solon OH; Bedford PA; Johnson City TN; New Market VA. **International locations:** Canada; China; England; Germany; the Netherlands. **Subsidiaries include:** Greenfield Industries, Inc.; JLK Direct Distribution Inc.; Kennametal Asia Pacific; Kennametal Hertel AG; Metalworking North America. **Listed on:** New York Stock Exchange. **Stock exchange symbol:** KMT. **President/CEO:** Robert McGeehan.

KEY TECHNOLOGY, INC.
150 Avery Street, Walla Walla WA 99362. 509/529-2161. **Fax:** 509/522-3378. **Contact:** Sherrie Mason, Human Resources Manager. **E-mail address:** smason@keyww.com. **World Wide Web address:** http://www.keyww.com. **Description:** A leading designer and manufacturer of process automation systems for the food processing industry. The company's automated systems convey, clean, grade, inspect, and process a wide variety of food products including vegetables, potatoes, snacks, cereals, nuts, and poultry. Key Technology is also a leader in the design and manufacture of high-speed machine vision systems. These systems inspect moving products for flaws in color, size, or other customer-

established criteria, and remove those items that do not meet the quality specifications. **Common positions include:** Mechanical Engineer. **Educational backgrounds include:** Engineering. **Benefits:** 401(k); Dental Insurance; Disability Coverage; Flexible Schedule; Life Insurance; Medical Insurance; Profit Sharing; Stock Purchase; Tuition Assistance. **Corporate headquarters location:** This Location. **Listed on:** NASDAQ. **Stock exchange symbol:** KTEC. **Number of employees at this location:** 440.

KIMBALL INTERNATIONAL, INC.

1600 Royal Street, Jasper IN 47549. 812/482-1600. **Contact:** Corporate Recruitment. **Description:** A leading supplier of high-quality wood furnishings for offices, hotels, resorts, and health care facilities. Products include office furniture and seating under the Kimball, National, and Harpers brand names; Kimball and Bosendorfer pianos; Kimball hospitality furniture; Kimball health care furniture; Harmony Woods home office furniture; and Kimball Victorian and French furniture reproductions. Kimball International operates as a contract/OEM manufacturer through its subsidiaries which produce electronic assemblies, cabinetry, molded plastics, carbide cutting tools, and metal stampings, and also produce a variety of brand name products marketed in such industries as home entertainment and furnishings, consumer electronics, marine, and automotive. **Common positions include:** Accountant/Auditor; Customer Service Representative; Electrical/Electronics Engineer; Financial Analyst; Industrial Engineer; Mechanical Engineer; Systems Analyst. **Educational backgrounds include:** Accounting; Computer Science; Engineering; Finance; Marketing. **Benefits:** 401(k); Dental Insurance; Disability Coverage; Life Insurance; Medical Insurance; Profit Sharing. **Special programs:** Internships. **Corporate headquarters location:** This Location. **Listed on:** NASDAQ. **Number of employees at this location:** 500.

KINGSBURY CORPORATION

80 Laurel Street, Keene NH 03431. 603/352-5212. **Fax:** 603/357-1955. **Contact:** Dianne Tisdale, Manager of Human Resources. **Description:** Designs and manufactures special purpose, high-production metal cutting assembly equipment and machining centers. **NOTE:** Entry-level positions and second and third shifts are offered. **Common positions include:** Applications Engineer; Electrical/Electronics Engineer; Electrician; Mechanical Engineer; Project Manager; Sales Engineer; Software Engineer. **Educational backgrounds include:** Engineering. **Benefits:** 401(k); Dental Insurance; Life Insurance; Medical Insurance; Pension Plan; Profit Sharing; Tuition Assistance. **Corporate headquarters location:** This Location. **Number of employees at this location:** 280.

KOHLER COMPANY

444 Highland Drive, Kohler WI 53044. 920/457-4441. **Contact:** Human Resources. **World Wide Web address:** http://www.kohlerco.com. **Description:** This location has a vitreous china pottery, a cast iron foundry, and enamel shop; manufactures faucets; and operates a plumbing distribution center. Overall, Kohler Company manufactures plumbing products, furniture, engines, and generators. Kohler's three plants in the United States specialize in the manufacture of plumbing products for homes, businesses, and institutions. Kohler's Power Systems Group manufactures generators, transfer switches, and accessories for power and recreational vehicles. The Engine Division manufactures air-cooled, 4-cycle engines.

The Interiors Group specializes in home furnishings and interior design. The Hospitality and Real Estate Group provides hospitality and land development to businesses nationwide. Kohler also has a design center which promotes new innovations for kitchens and baths. **Corporate headquarters location:** This Location. **International locations:** Mexico City, Mexico; Ontario, Canada. **Subsidiaries include:** Ann Sacks Tile & Stone, Inc. (Portland OR); Baker, Knapp & Tubbs, Inc. (Grand Rapids MI); Crosswinds Furniture Company (Los Angeles CA); Dapha, Ltd. (High Point NC); Kallista, Inc. (San Francisco CA); McGuire Furniture Company (San Francisco CA); Robern, Inc. (Bensalem PA); Sterling Plumbing Group (Rolling Meadows IL).

KOP-FLEX, INC.
EMERSON POWER TRANSMISSION

7565 Harmans Road, Hanover MD 21076. 410/787-8482. **Fax:** 410/787-8514. **Contact:** Colleen Rigatti, Employee Relations Representative. **Description:** A manufacturer of power transmission couplings and components for use in steel mills, paper mills, and navy ships. **NOTE:** Second and third shifts are offered. **Common positions include:** Accountant; Administrative Assistant; Blue-Collar Worker Supervisor; Buyer; Customer Service Rep.; Design Engineer; Draftsperson; Environmental Engineer; Manufacturing Engineer; Marketing Manager; Mechanical Engineer; MIS Specialist; Network/Systems Administrator; Production Manager; Project Manager; Sales Engineer; Sales Manager. **Educational backgrounds include:** Business Administration; Engineering. **Benefits:** 401(k); Dental Insurance; Disability Coverage; Life Insurance; Medical Insurance; Pension Plan; Profit Sharing; Savings Plan; Tuition Assistance. **Special programs:** Co-ops; Summer Jobs. **Corporate headquarters location:** This Location. **Listed on:** American Stock Exchange. **Annual sales/revenues:** $21 - $50 million.

KRAUSE CORPORATION

P.O. Box 2707, Hutchinson KS 67504. 316/663-6161. **Contact:** Personnel. **World Wide Web address:** http://www.krauseco.com. **Description:** Manufactures and markets farm and waste management equipment. The company is also engaged in captive-foundry forging and ductile iron forging. **Common positions include:** Accountant; Administrator; Agricultural Engineer; Blue-Collar Worker Supervisor; Buyer; Credit Manager; Customer Service Rep.; Department Manager; Draftsperson; Human Resources Manager; Industrial Engineer; Manufacturer's/Wholesaler's Sales Rep.; Manufacturing Manager; Marketing Specialist; Mechanical Engineer; Operations/Production Manager; Purchasing Agent/Manager; Quality Control Supervisor. **Educational backgrounds include:** Accounting; Business Administration; Engineering; Finance; Marketing. **Benefits:** Disability Coverage; Employee Discounts; Life Insurance; Medical Insurance; Profit Sharing; Savings Plan; Tuition Assistance; Vacation Days. **Corporate headquarters location:** This Location.

KURT MANUFACTURING COMPANY

5280 Main Street NE, Minneapolis MN 55421. 763/572-1500. **Contact:** Mr. Kern Walker, Vice President of Human Resources. **World Wide Web address:** http://www.kurt.com. **Description:** A manufacturer of a variety of industrial products including gauging and motion control systems, hydraulic products, precision gears, and workholding devices. Kurt Manufacturing Company also performs die casting, industrial precision machining, and screw machining. **Corporate headquarters location:** This Location.

KYOCERA MITA AMERICA, INC.
225 Sand Road, Fairfield NJ 07004. 973/808-8444. **Contact:** Human Resources. **World Wide Web address:** http://www.kyoceramita.com. **Description:** One of the world's largest manufacturers of copy machines. Kyocera MITA also offers computer peripherals such as fax machines, imaging systems, and laser printers. **Corporate headquarters location:** This Location.

KYSOR/WARREN
P.O. Box 8944, Columbus GA 31908. 706/568-1514. **Contact:** Beth Ferguson, Personnel Manager. **Description:** Designs and manufactures high-quality, energy-efficient commercial refrigeration equipment and display cases for food stores. **Corporate headquarters location:** This Location. **Parent company:** Kysor Industrial Corporation (Cadillac MI) produces commercial vehicle products, builders' hardware, and commercial refrigeration products.

LAMSON & SESSIONS COMPANY
25701 Science Park Drive, Cleveland OH 44122. 216/464-3400. **Toll-free phone:** 800/321-1970. **Fax:** 216/831-1876. **Contact:** Jim Erbacher, Manager of Salaried Employment. **World Wide Web address:** http://www.lamson-sessions.com. **Description:** Manufactures and markets thermoplastic enclosures, fittings, conduit and pipe, and wiring devices for the electrical, construction, consumer, power, communications, and wastewater markets. Founded in 1866. **NOTE:** Entry-level positions are offered. **Common positions include:** Accountant; Administrative Assistant; Chief Financial Officer; Computer Programmer; Controller; Credit Manager; Customer Service Rep.; Database Administrator; Database Manager; Design Engineer; Electrical/Electronics Engineer; Help-Desk Technician; Manufacturing Engineer; Marketing Manager; Mechanical Engineer; MIS Specialist; Network/Systems Administrator; Purchasing Agent/Manager; Sales Manager; Systems Analyst; Website Developer. **Educational backgrounds include:** Accounting; Business Administration; Computer Science; Engineering; Finance; Liberal Arts; Marketing; MBA; Microsoft Office; Microsoft Word; Spreadsheets. **Benefits:** 401(k); Casual Dress - Daily; Dental Insurance; Disability Coverage; Flexible Schedule; Life Insurance; Medical Insurance; Pension Plan; Profit Sharing; Tuition Assistance. **Special programs:** Co-ops. **Office hours:** Monday - Friday, 8:30 a.m. - 5:00 p.m. **Corporate headquarters location:** This Location. **Other U.S. locations:** Nationwide. **Listed on:** American Stock Exchange. **Stock exchange symbol:** LMS. **President/CEO:** John Schulze. **Annual sales/revenues:** More than $100 million. **Number of employees at this location:** 200. **Number of employees nationwide:** 1,000.

LANCER CORPORATION
6655 Lancer Boulevard, San Antonio TX 78219. 210/310-7000. **Contact:** Irene Prosperi, Human Resources Manager. **Description:** Manufactures soft drink and related food service equipment. **Corporate headquarters location:** This Location. **Listed on:** American Stock Exchange. **Number of employees at this location:** 200.

LANTECH INC.
11000 Bluegrass Parkway, Louisville KY 40299. 502/267-4200. **Contact:** Recruitment Specialist. **World Wide Web address:** http://www.lantech.com. **Description:** Researches, develops, and manufactures industrial packaging equipment, which uses stretch wrapping to palletize and/or wrap loads or individual products. **Common positions include:** Computer Programmer; Customer Service

Rep.; Draftsperson; Electrical/Electronics Engineer; Manufacturer's/Wholesaler's Sales Rep.; Marketing Specialist; Mechanical Engineer; Operations/Production Manager; Purchasing Agent/Manager; Quality Control Supervisor; Technical Writer/Editor. **Educational backgrounds include:** Accounting; Business Administration; Computer Science; Engineering; Marketing. **Benefits:** Dental Insurance; Disability Coverage; Life Insurance; Medical Insurance; Profit Sharing; Tuition Assistance. **Corporate headquarters location:** This Location. **President/CEO/Owner:** Jim Lancaster.

LEEDALL PRODUCTS INC.
351 West 35th Street, New York NY 10001. 212/563-5280. **Contact:** Ms. Leung, Personnel Department. **Description:** Produces perforating and duplicating machinery. **Corporate headquarters location:** This Location.

LETTS INDUSTRIES INC.
1111 Bellevue Avenue, Detroit MI 48207. 313/579-1100. **Contact:** Human Resources. **World Wide Web address:** http://www.letts.com. **Description:** Manufactures machining and forging equipment. Letts Industries also sells construction equipment parts. **Corporate headquarters location:** This Location.

LEYBOLD VACUUM PRODUCTS, INC.
5700 Mellon Road, Export PA 15632. 724/327-5700. **Toll-free phone:** 800/764-5369. **Contact:** Human Resources. **World Wide Web address:** http://www.leyboldvacuum.com. **Description:** A manufacturer of vacuum pumps and pumping equipment. **NOTE:** Entry-level positions and second and third shifts are offered. **Common positions include:** Electrical/Electronics Engineer; Marketing Specialist; Mechanical Engineer. **Educational backgrounds include:** C/C++; Internet Development; Microsoft Office; Microsoft Word; Novell; Software Development; Spreadsheets; Visual Basic. **Benefits:** 401(k); Casual Dress - Daily; Dental Insurance; Disability Coverage; Flexible Schedule; Life Insurance; Medical Insurance; Pension Plan; Profit Sharing; Relocation Assistance; Savings Plan; Sick Days (1 - 5); Telecommuting; Tuition Assistance; Vacation Days. **Special programs:** Internships; Training; Summer Jobs. **Office hours:** Monday - Friday, 8:00 a.m. - 4:45 p.m. **International locations:** Worldwide. **Listed on:** Privately held. **Annual sales/revenues:** $51 - $100 million. **Number of employees at this location:** 170. **Number of employees nationwide:** 230.

LIBERTY DIVERSIFIED INDUSTRIES (LDI)
5600 North Highway 169, New Hope MN 55428. 763/536-6600. **Fax:** 763/536-6813. **Contact:** Maureen Wheaton, Director of Human Resources. **E-mail address:** danpetrella@libertydiversified.com. **World Wide Web address:** http://www.libertydiversified.com. **Description:** A diversified organization comprised of seven companies located throughout the United States. Products include corrugated boxes; metal fabricated products; and plastic extruded products. Other subsidiaries include a paper mill and a manufacturer/wholesaler of office and industrial supplies. Founded in 1918. **NOTE:** Entry-level positions and part-time jobs are offered. **Common positions include:** Account Manager; Account Rep.; Accountant; Administrative Assistant; Advertising Executive; Applications Engineer; AS400 Programmer Analyst; Attorney; Blue-Collar Worker Supervisor; Clerical Supervisor; Computer Operator; Computer Programmer; Computer Scientist; Computer Support Technician; Computer

Technician; Controller; Cost Estimator; Credit Manager; Customer Service Rep.; Database Administrator; Database Manager; Design Engineer; Draftsperson; Electrical/Electronics Engineer; Electrician; General Manager; Human Resources Manager; Industrial Engineer; Industrial Production Manager; Internet Services Manager; Management Trainee; Manufacturing Engineer; Market Research Analyst; Marketing Manager; Marketing Specialist; Mechanical Engineer; MIS Specialist; Multimedia Designer; Network/Systems Administrator; Operations Manager; Production Manager; Project Manager; Public Relations Specialist; Purchasing Agent/Manager; Quality Assurance Engineer; Sales Engineer; Sales Executive; Sales Manager; Sales Representative; Secretary; Software Engineer; Systems Analyst; Systems Manager; Transportation/ Traffic Specialist; Typist/Word Processor; Webmaster. **Educational backgrounds include:** Accounting; AS400 Certification; Business Administration; Communications; Computer Science; Economics; Finance; Internet; Java; Marketing; Microsoft Word; Novell; QuarkXPress; Software Development; Software Tech. Support; Spreadsheets; Visual Basic. **Benefits:** 401(k); Casual Dress - Daily; Daycare Assistance; Dental Insurance; Disability Coverage; Employee Discounts; Financial Planning Assistance; Flexible Schedule; Life Insurance; Medical Insurance; Profit Sharing; Public Transit Available; Savings Plan; Sick Days (6 - 10); Tuition Assistance; Vacation Days (16+). **Special programs:** Internships; Apprenticeships; Training; Summer Jobs. **Corporate headquarters location:** This Location. **Other U.S. locations:** Baldwyn MS; Haltom City TX. **Operations at this facility include:** Divisional Headquarters. **President/CEO/Owner:** Mike Fiterman. **Number of employees at this location:** 350. **Number of employees nationwide:** 1,400.

LINK-BELT CONSTRUCTION EQUIPMENT CO.
2651 Palumbo Drive, Lexington KY 40509. 606/263-5200. **Fax:** 606/264-6214. **Contact:** Marsha Brock, Employee Relations Manager. **World Wide Web address:** http://www. linkbelt.com. **Description:** Produces construction machinery and equipment including cranes and excavators. **Common positions include:** Account Manager; Account Representative; Accountant; Administrative Assistant; Blue-Collar Worker Supervisor; Budget Analyst; Buyer; Chief Financial Officer; Computer Operator; Computer Programmer; Controller; Credit Manager; Design Engineer; Draftsperson; Human Resources Manager; Manufacturing Engineer; Marketing Manager; Marketing Specialist; Mechanical Engineer; Metallurgical Engineer; MIS Specialist; Public Relations Specialist; Purchasing Agent/ Manager; Quality Control Supervisor; Sales Executive; Sales Manager; Sales Rep.; Secretary; Software Engineer; Systems Analyst; Systems Manager; Technical Writer/Editor; Transportation/ Traffic Specialist; Typist/Word Processor. **Educational backgrounds include:** Accounting; Business Administration; Computer Science; Engineering; Finance; Marketing. **Benefits:** 401(k); Dental Insurance; Disability Coverage; Flexible Schedule; Life Insurance; Medical Insurance; Pension Plan; Tuition Assistance. **Corporate headquarters location:** This Location. **Parent company:** Sumitomo.

LONG AGRI-BUSINESS
P.O. Box 1139, Tarboro NC 27886. 252/823-4151. **Physical address:** 111 Fairview Street, Tarboro NC 27886. **Contact:** Human Resources Director. **Description:** Develops, manufactures, and markets a broad range of farm and industrial equipment including tractors, tillers, harrows, unloading equipment, elevators, backhoes, storage bins, furnaces, and wood-burning stoves. **Common positions include:** Administrator; Blue-Collar Worker Supervisor; Buyer; Computer Programmer; Department Manager; Draftsperson; Industrial Engineer; Manufacturer's/Wholesaler's Sales Rep.; Mechanical Engineer; Operations/Production Manager; Purchasing Agent/Manager; Quality Control Supervisor; Technical Writer/Editor. **Educational backgrounds include:** Business Administration; Computer Science; Engineering; Industrial Technology; Marketing. **Benefits:** Disability Coverage; Employee Discounts; Life Insurance; Medical Insurance; Profit Sharing. **Corporate headquarters location:** This Location. **Listed on:** Privately held. **Number of employees at this location:** 325.

LONG REACH MANUFACTURING CO.
P.O. Box 450069, Houston TX 77245-0069. 713/433-9861. **Physical address:** 12300 Amelia Drive, Houston TX 77045. **Contact:** Carol Gilder, Human Resources Manager. **Description:** Engaged in the manufacture of hydraulic forklift attachments. **Common positions include:** Accountant; Blue-Collar Worker Supervisor; Buyer; Customer Service Rep.; Draftsperson; Human Resources Manager; Manufacturer's/Wholesaler's Sales Rep.; Marketing Specialist; Mechanical Engineer; Plant Manager; Purchasing Agent/Manager; Systems Manager. **Educational backgrounds include:** Accounting; Business Administration; Computer Science; Engineering; Finance; Marketing. **Benefits:** 401(k); Credit Union; Dental Insurance; Disability Coverage; Life Insurance; Medical Insurance; Tuition Assistance. **Corporate headquarters location:** This Location. **Parent company:** Long Reach Holdings, Inc.

LOWELL MANUFACTURING COMPANY
100 Integram Drive, P.O. Box 385, Pacific MO 63069. 636/257-3400. **Contact:** John J. Lowell, President. **Description:** Manufactures baffles, enclosures, masking units, cabinets, racks, and accessories. **Common positions include:** Blue-Collar Worker Supervisor; Electrical/Electronics Engineer; Purchasing Agent/Manager. **Educational backgrounds include:** Engineering; Marketing. **Benefits:** Medical Insurance; Pension Plan. **Corporate headquarters location:** This Location. **Listed on:** Privately held. **Number of employees at this location:** 80.

LUFKIN INDUSTRIES, INC.
P.O. Box 849, Lufkin TX 75902. 936/634-2211. **Contact:** Human Resources. **World Wide Web address:** http://www.lufkin.com. **Description:** Designs and fabricates gears for power transmission products; iron castings; oil field pumps; and platforms and dump trailers for the over-the-road transportation industry. **Corporate headquarters location:** This Location. **Listed on:** NASDAQ. **Stock exchange symbol:** LUFK.

LYDALL, INC.
One Colonial Road, P.O. Box 151, Manchester CT 06045-0151. 860/646-1233. **Contact:** Mona Estey, Director of Human Resources. **World Wide Web address:** http://www.lydall.com. **Description:** Manufactures highly-modified, noncommodity products primarily in the areas of air and liquid filtration, thermal barriers and insulation, electrical insulation, and materials handling. Both wet-laid and needle-punched processes are utilized in fiber and fiber composite manufacturing. Lydall designs and produces specialty materials for critical, high-performance applications. The company's divisions include: Axohm Division; Composite Materials Divisions; Logistics Management Divisions); Lydall

& Foulds Division; Lydall International; Manning Non-wovens Division; Southern Products Divisions; Technical Papers Division; Westex Divisions. **Benefits:** 401(k); Incentive Plan; Pension Plan; Profit Sharing. **Corporate headquarters location:** This Location. **Listed on:** New York Stock Exchange.

MPB CORPORATION
P.O. Box 547, Optical Avenue Precision Park, Keene NH 03431-0547. 603/352-0310. **Contact:** Susan Metsack, Manager of Human Resources. **Description:** Manufactures ball and roller bearings. **Common positions include:** Accountant/Auditor; Aerospace Engineer; Blue-Collar Worker Supervisor; Buyer; Computer Programmer; Customer Service Rep.; Department Manager; Draftsperson; General Manager; Human Resources Manager; Industrial Engineer; Mechanical Engineer; Metallurgical Engineer; Operations/Production Manager; Purchasing Agent/Manager; Quality Control Supervisor; Systems Analyst. **Educational backgrounds include:** Business Administration; Engineering. **Benefits:** Dental Insurance; Disability Coverage; Employee Discounts; Life Insurance; Medical Insurance; Pension Plan; Profit Sharing; Savings Plan; Tuition Assistance. **Corporate headquarters location:** This Location.

MAKINO
7680 Innovation Way, Mason OH 45040. 513/573-4517. **Fax:** 513/573-7341. **Contact:** Mr. Ellery Joyeau, Human Resources Manager. **World Wide Web address:** http://www.makino.com. **Description:** A manufacturer of molds, gauges, small tools, lathes, single- and multiple-spindle drills, and milling machines. **Common positions include:** Design Engineer; Electrical/Electronics Engineer; Mechanical Engineer. **Educational backgrounds include:** Engineering. **Benefits:** 401(k); Dental Insurance; Disability Coverage; Life Insurance; Medical Insurance; Pension Plan; Profit Sharing; Tuition Assistance. **Corporate headquarters location:** This Location. **Other U.S. locations:** Los Angeles CA; Wichita KS; Detroit MI; Seattle WA. **International locations:** Germany; Japan; Mexico; Singapore.

MARCONI DATA SYSTEMS
P.O. Box 388, Belleville IL 62222. 618/234-1122. **Contact:** Trisha Bridges, Human Resources Manager. **Description:** Engaged in the manufacture of microprocessor-controlled and mechanical marking, coding, and packing equipment for industrial use. **Common positions include:** Buyer; Chemist; Computer Programmer; Customer Service Rep.; Draftsperson; Electrical/Electronics Engineer; Manufacturer's/Wholesaler's Sales Rep.; Mechanical Engineer. **Educational backgrounds include:** Chemistry; Computer Science; Engineering; Marketing. **Benefits:** Dental Insurance; Disability Coverage; Life Insurance; Medical Insurance; Savings Plan; Tuition Assistance. **Special programs:** Internships. **Corporate headquarters location:** This Location.
Other U.S. locations:
• 1500 North Mittel Boulevard, Wood Dale IL 60191-1073. 630/860-7300.

MARIETTA CORPORATION
P.O. Box 5250, Cortland NY 13045. 607/753-6746. **Physical address:** 37 Huntington Street, Cortland NY. **Contact:** Gail Sechrist, Manager of Human Resources. **World Wide Web address:** http://www.mariettacorp.com. **Description:** Marietta designs, manufactures, packages, markets, and distributes guest amenity programs to the travel and lodging industries. The company's guest amenity programs feature a wide variety of nationally branded toiletries, personal care products, and accessories which travel and lodging establishments provide for the comfort and convenience of their guests. Marietta is also a provider of customized sample-size and unit-of-use packaging products and services to companies in the toiletries, cosmetics, pharmaceuticals, and household products industries for purposes such as marketing promotions and retail sales. **Corporate headquarters location:** This Location.

THE MARLEY COOLING TOWER CO.
150 North Sinclair Avenue, Stockton CA 95215. 209/465-3451. **Contact:** Personnel. **Description:** Manufactures wooden cooling towers that are used in various industrial applications. **Corporate headquarters location:** This Location.

MAROTTA SCIENTIFIC CONTROLS INC.
P.O. Box 427, Montville NJ 07045. 973/334-7800. **Physical address:** 78 Boonton Avenue, Montville NJ. **Contact:** Robert Cooper, Personnel Manager. **Description:** Manufactures high-pressure valves for pneumatic and hydraulic equipment. The company is also a custom manufacturer of fluid control products. **Common positions include:** Mechanical Engineer. **Educational backgrounds include:** Engineering. **Corporate headquarters location:** This Location.

MARSHALL ENGINEERED PRODUCTS CO.
811 East Main Street, Marshalltown IA 50158. 515/752-4291. **Contact:** Dick White, Human Resources Manager. **World Wide Web address:** http://www.mepcollc.com. **Description:** A manufacturer of commercial steam and hot water heating system components and centrifugal pumps. Founded in 1903. **Common positions include:** Accountant; Advertising Clerk; Applications Engineer; Blue-Collar Worker Supervisor; Buyer; Controller; Credit Manager; Design Engineer; Draftsperson; Electrical/Electronics Engineer; General Manager; Human Resources Manager; Industrial Engineer; Manufacturing Engineer; Marketing Manager; Mechanical Engineer; MIS Specialist; Operations/Production Manager; Project Manager; Purchasing Agent/Manager; Quality Control Supervisor; Sales Manager. **Educational backgrounds include:** Accounting; Business Administration; Engineering; Finance; Marketing. **Benefits:** 401(k); Dental Insurance; Disability Coverage; Flexible Schedule; Life Insurance; Medical Insurance; Pension Plan; Tuition Assistance. **Corporate headquarters location:** This Location. **Other U.S. locations:** Nationwide. **International locations:** Worldwide.

MARTIN ELECTRONICS, INC.
10625 Puckett Road, Perry FL 32347. 850/584-2634. **Fax:** 850/584-2044. **Contact:** Director of Personnel. **Description:** Manufactures pyrotechnic and explosive devices for ordnance applications. **Common positions include:** Chemical Engineer; Manufacturing Engineer; Production Manager. **Educational backgrounds include:** Chemistry; Engineering. **Benefits:** 401(k); Disability Coverage; Life Insurance; Medical Insurance; Tuition Assistance. **Corporate headquarters location:** This Location. **Listed on:** Privately held. **Number of employees at this location:** 250.

MARTIN SPROCKET & GEAR INC.
P.O. Box 91588, Arlington TX 76015. 817/467-5181. **Contact:** Guy Young, Personnel Manager. **Description:** Manufactures chain sprockets and gears. **Corporate headquarters location:** This Location. **Other U.S. locations:** Nationwide. **Listed on:** Privately held. **Number of employees nationwide:** 1,200.

MATEC CORPORATION

75 South Street, Hopkinton MA 01748. 508/435-9039. **Fax:** 508/435-5289. **Contact:** Human Resources. **Description:** Designs, manufactures, imports, and sells quartz crystals and oscillators; designs and manufactures custom mechanical cable assemblies; develops and manufactures computer-controlled, ultrasonic test equipment to perform real-time measurements and analysis; and produces and sells instruments to evaluate the stability of colloidal dispersions. **Corporate headquarters location:** This Location. **Subsidiaries include:** Bergen Cable Technologies, Inc.'s product line includes mechanical cable control systems as well as a variety of special cable products; Matec Applied Sciences Inc. manufactures ultrasonic, scientific test equipment for analyzing the characteristics of colloids; Matec Instruments Inc. manufactures ultrasonic test instrumentation for non-destructive test material test applications and research purposes; ValpeyFisher Corporation manufactures and imports hybrid and surface-mount clock oscillators and quartz crystals for frequency control in computers, microprocessor-based instrumentation, and voice, data, and video communications equipment. **President/CEO:** Ted Valpey, Jr.

MATTHEWS INTERNATIONAL CORP.

2 Northshore Center, Pittsburgh PA 15212-5851. 412/442-8200. **Contact:** Human Resources. **World Wide Web address:** http://www.matthewsinternational.com. **Description:** Through its subsidiaries, Matthews International is a provider of creative surface graphics design, printing plates, cutting dies, and final press-side assistance in package printing operations. The company also designs and manufactures equipment and supplies used by industry to mark components, finished products, packaging, and packaging containers, and produces and distributes cast bronze memorial plaques, cremation urns, fabricated niche units, cemetery features, granite block and granite foundations for bronze memorials, and related products. **Corporate headquarters location:** This Location.

MAYFRAN INTERNATIONAL INC.

P.O. Box 43038, Cleveland OH 44143. 440/461-4100. **Physical address:** 6650 Beta Drive, Cleveland OH. **Contact:** Human Resources. **World Wide Web address:** http://www.mayfran.com. **Description:** Manufactures hinged steel belt and magnetic conveyors for the metalworking, resource recovery, municipal refuse, and automotive industries. **Common positions include:** Accountant; Administrator; Blue-Collar Worker Supervisor; Buyer; Customer Service Rep.; Department Manager; Draftsperson; Electrical/Electronics Engineer; Financial Analyst; Industrial Engineer; Operations/Production Manager; Sales Executive. **Educational backgrounds include:** Accounting; Business Administration; Engineering; Liberal Arts; Marketing. **Benefits:** Disability Coverage; Life Insurance; Medical Insurance; Pension Plan; Tuition Assistance. **Corporate headquarters location:** This Location.

A.Y. McDONALD MANUFACTURING CO.

P.O. Box 508, Dubuque IA 52004-0508. 319/583-7311. **Fax:** 319/588-0720. **Contact:** Human Resources. **World Wide Web address:** http://www.aymcdonaldmfg.com. **Description:** Manufactures water service valves and fittings, gas valves, pumps, water systems for domestic and commercial applications, plumbing and industrial valves, and petroleum equipment. Products are made of brass, cast iron, aluminum, stainless steel, and plastic. The company sells and distributes its five major product lines nationally and internationally. Founded in 1856. **Common positions include:** Accountant; Blue-Collar Worker Supervisor; Computer Programmer; Credit Manager; Customer Service Rep.; Electrician; Human Resources Manager; Manufacturer's/Wholesaler's Sales Rep.; Operations/Production Manager. **Educational backgrounds include:** Engineering; Liberal Arts; Marketing. **Benefits:** 401(k); Dental Insurance; Life Insurance; Medical Insurance; Pension Plan; Savings Plan; Tuition Assistance. **Corporate headquarters location:** This Location. **Listed on:** Privately held. **Number of employees at this location:** 270. **Number of employees nationwide:** 350.

MEISSNER TRACTORS, INC.

P.O. Box 1111, Havre MT 59501. 406/265-5457. **Contact:** Arnold Lalum, General Manager. **World Wide Web address:** http://www.meissners.com. **Description:** Manufactures scrapers for construction machinery and large farm tractors. **Common positions include:** Accountant/Auditor; Draftsperson; Industrial Designer; Industrial Engineer; Manufacturer's/Wholesaler's Sales Rep.; Mechanical Engineer; Quality Control Supervisor; Technical Writer/Editor. **Educational backgrounds include:** Accounting; Business Administration; Engineering; Finance; Marketing. **Benefits:** Dental Insurance; Employee Discounts; Life Insurance; Medical Insurance. **Corporate headquarters location:** This Location.

MEMRY CORPORATION

57 Commerce Drive, Brookfield CT 06804. 203/740-7311. **Contact:** Human Resources. **Description:** Operates through two segments: Research and Development produces and markets products and components that utilize a shape memory effect exhibited by certain alloys in response to changes in temperature; Manufacturing produces and markets screw machines, taper pins, and certain plumbing products. Memry Corporation is comprised of three operating divisions corresponding to its primary businesses: Memry Technologies covers the research and development segment; Memry Products is a sales and marketing division; and Memry Manufacturing is the production segment. **Corporate headquarters location:** This Location. **Number of employees at this location:** 60.

MEREEN-JOHNSON MACHINE CO.

4401 Lyndale Avenue North, Minneapolis MN 55412. 612/529-7791. **Contact:** Sharon Jurgens, Human Resources Manager. **Description:** Manufactures woodworking cutting machinery.

MERRITT EQUIPMENT COMPANY

9339 Highway 85, Henderson CO 80640. 303/287-7527. **Contact:** Personnel Department. **Description:** Manufactures livestock and commodity trailers and aluminum accessories for the trucking industry such as cab guards and tool boxes. **Common positions include:** Blue-Collar Worker Supervisor; Buyer; Industrial Engineer; Mechanical Engineer; Purchasing Agent/Manager; Structural Engineer. **Educational backgrounds include:** Computer Science; Engineering; Marketing. **Benefits:** Dental Insurance; Life Insurance; Medical Insurance; Profit Sharing. **Corporate headquarters location:** This Location. **Number of employees at this location:** 250.

MESTEK INC.

260 North Elm Street, Westfield MA 01085. 413/568-9571. **Contact:** Debra McCormick, Personnel Manager. **Description:** Manufactures industrial refrigeration and heating equipment. **Common positions include:** Accountant/Auditor;

Attorney; Blue-Collar Worker Supervisor; Customer Service Rep.; Financial Analyst; General Manager; Industrial Engineer. **Corporate headquarters location:** This Location.

METTLER TOLEDO INC.
1900 Polaris Parkway, Columbus OH 43240. 614/438-4510. **Fax:** 614/438-4534. **Contact:** Human Resources. **World Wide Web address:** http://www.mt.com. **Description:** This location manufactures precision instruments for global distribution. Overall, Mettler Toledo is a leading manufacturer and marketer of weighing instruments. The company also manufactures analytic, metal detection, laboratory, and dimensioning instruments. Founded in 1902. **NOTE:** Entry-level positions and part-time jobs are offered. **Common positions include:** Accountant; Administrative Assistant; Applications Engineer; AS400 Programmer Analyst; Attorney; Budget Analyst; Chemist; Chief Financial Officer; Computer Operator; Computer Programmer; Computer Support Technician; Computer Technician; Controller; Credit Manager; Customer Service Rep.; Database Administrator; Finance Director; Financial Analyst; Help-Desk Technician; Human Resources Manager; Internet Services Manager; Intranet Developer; Market Research Analyst; Marketing Manager; Network Engineer; Network/Systems Administrator; Operations Manager; Paralegal; Purchasing Agent/Manager; Quality Control Supervisor; Secretary; Software Engineer; SQL Programmer; Systems Analyst; Systems Manager; Technical Support Manager; Transportation/Traffic Specialist; Webmaster; Website Developer. **Educational backgrounds include:** Accounting; AS400 Certification; Business Administration; C/C++; Chemistry; Communications; Computer Science; Finance; HTML; Internet Development; Java; Marketing; MBA; MCSE; Microsoft Office; Microsoft Word; Software Development; Software Tech. Support; Spreadsheets; SQL; Visual Basic. **Benefits:** 401(k); Dental Insurance; Disability Coverage; Flexible Schedule; Life Insurance; Medical Insurance; Pension Plan; Profit Sharing; Relocation Assistance; Savings Plan; Sick Days (1 - 5); Telecommuting; Tuition Assistance; Vacation Days (10 - 20). **Special programs:** Internships; Co-ops. **Office hours:** Monday - Friday, 8:00 a.m. - 6:00 p.m. **Parent company:** AEA Investors Inc. (NY). **Listed on:** New York Stock Exchange. **Number of employees at this location:** 250.

MICRO MOTION, INC.
7070 Winchester Circle, Boulder CO 80301. 303/530-8400. **Fax:** 303/530-8007. **Recorded jobline:** 303/530-8000. **Contact:** Human Resources. **World Wide Web address:** http://www.micromotion.com. **Description:** Manufactures industrial flow meters. **Common positions include:** Blue-Collar Worker Supervisor; Customer Service Rep.; Electrical/Electronics Engineer; General Manager; Materials Engineer; Mechanical Engineer; Metallurgical Engineer. **Educational backgrounds include:** Business Administration; Engineering; Marketing. **Benefits:** 401(k); Dental Insurance; Disability Coverage; Life Insurance; Medical Insurance; Profit Sharing; Savings Plan; Tuition Assistance. **Corporate headquarters location:** This Location. **Parent company:** Emerson Electric Company. **Listed on:** New York Stock Exchange. **Number of employees at this location:** 650.

MICROFLUIDICS INTERNATIONAL CORP.
30 Ossipee Road, Newton MA 02464. 617/969-5452. **Contact:** Human Resources. **World Wide Web address:** http://www.microfluidics.com. **Description:** Manufactures and distributes high-performance mixing equipment primarily for the chemical, pharmaceutical, biotechnology, food, and personal care products industries. **Corporate headquarters location:** This Location.

MILACRON, INC.
2090 Florence Avenue, Cincinnati OH 45206. 513/487-5000. **Contact:** Human Resources. **World Wide Web address:** http://www.milacron.com. **Description:** A world leader in manufacturing technologies for the metalworking and plastic processing industries. Products include machine tools, numerical controls, plastic machinery, grinding wheels, coolants, coordinate measuring machines, composite processing systems, and Valenite metal-cutting tools. **Common positions include:** Accountant/Auditor; Ceramics Engineer; Chemical Engineer; Electrical/Electronics Engineer; Financial Analyst; Human Resources Manager; Industrial Engineer; Management Trainee; Materials Engineer; Mechanical Engineer; Metallurgical Engineer; Software Engineer; Structural Engineer. **Educational backgrounds include:** Accounting; Computer Science; Engineering; Finance. **Benefits:** 401(k); Dental Insurance; Disability Coverage; Life Insurance; Medical Insurance; Pension Plan; Profit Sharing; Savings Plan; Tuition Assistance. **Special programs:** Internships. **Corporate headquarters location:** This Location. **Other U.S. locations:** MI; PA; SC; TX; VA. **International locations:** Austria; France; Germany; Great Britain; Japan; Mexico; the Netherlands. **Listed on:** New York Stock Exchange. **Number of employees at this location:** 2,000.

MILLER DIAL CORPORATION
P.O. Box 5868, El Monte CA 91731. 626/444-4555. **Fax:** 626/443-3267. **Contact:** Human Resources. **Description:** One of the world's largest manufacturers of nameplates and other function identification products including panels, dials, membrane switches, and labels. **Corporate headquarters location:** This Location.

MILLER FLUID POWER CORPORATION
800 North York Road, Bensenville IL 60106. 630/766-3400. **Contact:** Tom Parker, Human Resources Director. **Description:** A manufacturer of pneumatic and hydraulic cylinders and components. **Common positions include:** Accountant; Branch Manager; Buyer; Computer Programmer; Credit Manager; Customer Service Rep.; Department Manager; Draftsperson; Human Resources Manager; Industrial Designer; Industrial Engineer; Manufacturer's/Wholesaler's Sales Rep.; Manufacturing Engineer; Marketing Specialist; Mechanical Engineer; Operations/Production Manager; Purchasing Agent/Manager; Quality Assurance Engineer; Systems Analyst. **Educational backgrounds include:** Accounting; Art/Design; Business Administration; Computer Science; Engineering; Finance; Liberal Arts; Marketing. **Benefits:** Disability Coverage; Life Insurance; Medical Insurance; Pension Plan; Profit Sharing; Savings Plan; Tuition Assistance. **Corporate headquarters location:** This Location.

HERMAN MILLER INC.
855 East Main Avenue, P.O. Box 302, Zeeland MI 49464. 616/654-3000. **Fax:** 616/654-5795. **Recorded jobline:** 616/654-3771. **Contact:** Staffing Department. **E-mail address:** jobs@hermanmiller.com. **World Wide Web address:** http://www.hermanmiller.com. **Description:** A manufacturer of interior systems, furnishings, and seating products for offices, public areas, and health care facilities. **Common positions include:** Accountant; Blue-Collar Worker Supervisor; Budget Analyst; Buyer; Computer Programmer; Customer Service Rep.; Designer; Draftsperson; Editor; Electrical/Electronics Engineer; Electrician;

Financial Analyst; Industrial Engineer; Industrial Production Manager; Mechanical Engineer; Operations/Production Manager; Purchasing Agent/ Manager; Quality Control Supervisor; Systems Analyst; Technical Writer/Editor. **Educational backgrounds include:** Accounting; Art/Design; Business Administration; Computer Science; Engineering; Finance. **Benefits:** 401(k); Bonus Award/Plan; Daycare Assistance; Dental Insurance; Disability Coverage; Employee Discounts; Life Insurance; Medical Insurance; Pension Plan; Profit Sharing; Savings Plan; Tuition Assistance. **Special programs:** Internships. **Corporate headquarters location:** This Location. **Other U.S. locations:** Rocklin CA; Roswell GA; Sanford NC. **Subsidiaries include:** Meridan; Milcare; Miltech; Phoenix Designs. **Listed on:** NASDAQ. **Number of employees at this location:** 3,000.

MILLER MULTIPLEX

1555 Larkin Williams Road, Fenton MO 63026. 636/343-5700. **Toll-free phone:** 800/325-5242. **Contact:** Alma L. Ruble, Human Resources Manager. **Description:** Manufactures store display fixtures. Founded in 1903. **NOTE:** Entry-level positions are offered. **Common positions include:** Accountant; Administrative Assistant; Controller; Credit Manager; Customer Service Manager; Design Engineer; Draftsperson; Human Resources Manager; Industrial Engineer; Marketing Manager; Operations Manager; Product Manager; Project Manager; Purchasing Agent/Manager; Sales Executive; Transportation/Traffic Specialist. **Educational backgrounds include:** Accounting; Art/Design; Engineering; Marketing; Microsoft Office; Microsoft Word; Spreadsheets. **Benefits:** 401(k); Casual Dress - Fridays; Dental Insurance; Disability Coverage; Life Insurance; Medical Insurance; Profit Sharing. **Office hours:** Monday - Friday, 8:00 a.m. - 4:30 p.m. **Corporate headquarters location:** Richmond VA. **President:** Frank G. Grelle. **Annual sales/revenues:** $11 - $20 million. **Number of employees at this location:** 135. **Number of employees nationwide:** 385.

MINCO PRODUCTS, INC.

7300 Commerce Lane NE, Minneapolis MN 55432. 763/571-3121. **Contact:** Jane Stoner, Human Resources Director. **World Wide Web address:** http://www.minco.com. **Description:** Manufactures temperature sensors, heaters, and flexible interconnecting devices. **Common positions include:** Draftsperson; Electrical/Electronics Engineer; Industrial Engineer; Mechanical Engineer. **Educational backgrounds include:** Engineering. **Benefits:** Dental Insurance; Disability Coverage; Life Insurance; Medical Insurance; Profit Sharing; Tuition Assistance. **Special programs:** Internships. **Corporate headquarters location:** This Location.

MINE SAFETY APPLIANCES CO. (MSA)

121 Gamma Drive, RIDC Industrial Park, O'Hara Township, Pittsburgh PA 15238. 412/967-3000. **Contact:** Mr. Benedict DeMaria, Human Resources Director. **World Wide Web address:** http://www.msanet.com. **Description:** Manufactures a variety of gas masks and respiratory protection products, protective headgear, and gas and vapor sensors. The company's products are generally supplied to the fire service, mining, construction, and industrial subcontracting industries. The company is divided into two major operating groups. MSA's Safety Products Division designs and manufactures full face pieces for self-contained breathing apparatuses, respirators, communication equipment for breathing apparatuses, cooling vests designed to combat heat stress, and a hand-held infrared heat detector. The company's Instrument Division makes a variety of monitors and sensors. MSA's international affiliates manufacture a wide array of equipment, ranging from thermal imaging cameras to air supply units. The company's products are sold worldwide. **Corporate headquarters location:** This Location.

MINOLTA CORPORATION

101 Williams Drive, Ramsey NJ 07446. 201/825-4000. **Fax:** 201/825-7605. **Contact:** Lisa Potenza, Human Resources Manager. **World Wide Web address:** http://www.minoltausa.com. **Description:** Markets, sells, and distributes photographic and business equipment, as well as document imaging systems. **Common positions include:** Accountant; Credit Manager; Customer Service Rep.; Software Engineer. **Educational backgrounds include:** Accounting; Business Administration; Computer Science; Marketing. **Benefits:** 401(k); Dental Insurance; Disability Coverage; Employee Discounts; Life Insurance; Medical Insurance; Pension Plan; Tuition Assistance. **Corporate headquarters location:** This Location. **Parent company:** Minolta Co., Ltd. (Osaka, Japan). **Number of employees at this location:** 500.

MOBILE TOOL INTERNATIONAL (MTI)

5600 West 88th Avenue, Westminster CO 80030. 303/427-3700. **Recorded jobline:** 303/657-2286. **Contact:** Director of Human Resources. **World Wide Web address:** http://www.mobiletool.com. **Description:** Manufactures products to serve the telecommunications, power utility, construction, and transportation industries. The five primary product groups are Puregas, Mopeco, Telsta, Holan, and PowerAll. Puregas is one of North America's leading brands of dry air pressurization systems. Puregas products are used in telecommunications, microwave, and industrial applications requiring moisture-free air to protect the quality of signal transmission or industrial processes. The Mopeco product line consists of a variety of heavy-duty ventilators and ventilator/heaters, which are used to ventilate and/or heat confined spaces. The Telsta line of non-insulated telescoping aerial lifts are sold by a nationwide direct sales force to telephone, CATV, and contracting companies. Holan is a leading manufacturer of insulated, articulated aerial lifts. These products are sold to power utilities through a nationwide network of independent distributors. The PowerAll Power Pak is a truck-mounted power source providing electric, pneumatic, and hydraulic power to support underground and road surface construction activities. Founded in 1954. **NOTE:** Entry-level positions and second and third shifts are offered. **Common positions include:** Account Manager; Account Rep.; Accountant/Auditor; Administrative Assistant; Administrative Manager; Assembler; Blue-Collar Worker Supervisor; Buyer; Controller; Customer Service Representative; Design Engineer; Draftsperson; Electrical/Electronics Engineer; Finance Director; Financial Analyst; Human Resources Manager; Industrial Engineer; Machinist; Manufacturing Engineer; Mechanical Engineer; Operations/Production Manager; Purchasing Agent/ Manager; Quality Control Supervisor; Sales Executive; Sales Manager; Sales Rep.; Secretary; Typist/Word Processor; Welder. **Educational backgrounds include:** Accounting; Business Administration; Engineering; Finance; Marketing. **Benefits:** 401(k); Dental Insurance; Life Insurance; Medical Insurance; Profit Sharing; Tuition Assistance. **Special programs:** Internships; Apprenticeships; Training. **Office hours:** Monday - Friday, 7:00 a.m. - 5:00 p.m. **Corporate headquarters location:** This Location. **Other U.S. locations:** Nationwide. **Parent company:** Penn Central Corporation.

MOCON
7500 Boone Avenue North, Suite 111, Minneapolis MN 55428. 763/493-6370. **Contact:** Human Resources. **World Wide Web address:** http://www. mocon.com. **Description:** Develops instruments that test packages and packaging materials for the pharmaceutical market. **Corporate headquarters location:** This Location. **Listed on:** NASDAQ. **Stock exchange symbol:** MOCO.

MODINE MANUFACTURING COMPANY
1500 DeKoven Avenue, Racine WI 53403. 262/636-1200. **Fax:** 262/636-1742. **Contact:** Cindy Noha, Employment/Recruiting Manager. **Description:** An independent, worldwide leader in heat transfer technology, serving vehicular (passenger car, van, truck, off-highway equipment, earth moving equipment, construction equipment, and agricultural equipment), industrial (a mixed category of OEM customers including the makers of engines, air compressors, refrigeration equipment, and hydraulic-pneumatic devices), commercial, and building/HVAC markets. The company's major products include radiators, oil coolers, vehicular air conditioning condensers and evaporators, building/HVAC products, charge-air coolers, and radiator cores. **Corporate headquarters location:** This Location. **Other U.S. locations:** Nationwide. **Subsidiaries include:** Langerer & Reich (L&R); Austria Warmetauscher GmbH (AWG).

MOORE PROCESS AUTOMATION SOLUTIONS
1201 Sumneytown Pike, Spring House PA 19477-0900. 215/646-7400. **Contact:** Personnel Manager. **Description:** Manufactures and sells process control systems and industrial instruments. **Common positions include:** Chemical Engineer; Computer Programmer; Electrical/Electronics Engineer; Industrial Engineer; Mechanical Engineer; Software Engineer. **Educational backgrounds include:** Computer Science; Engineering. **Benefits:** 401(k); Dental Insurance; Disability Coverage; Life Insurance; Medical Insurance; Pension Plan; Tuition Assistance. **Corporate headquarters location:** This Location. **Listed on:** NASDAQ.

MULTIGRAPHICS INC.
431 Lakeview Court, Mount Prospect IL 60056. 847/375-1700. **Contact:** Joyce Houston, Vice President of Human Resources. **World Wide Web address:** http://www.multigraphics.com. **Description:** Sells and services graphic arts products and machinery. **Corporate headquarters location:** This Location.

MURATA WIEDEMANN, INC.
10510 Twin Lakes Parkway, Charlotte NC 28269. 704/875-9280. **Fax:** 704/875-9898. **Contact:** Ms. C.A. Stahr, Director of Human Resources. **E-mail address:** astahr@muratawiedemann.com. **World Wide Web address:** http://www. muratawiedemann.com. **Description:** Develops, manufactures, and sells computer-controlled fabrication equipment, accessories, and systems, which provide flexibility and productivity for non-mass producers of parts made from flat materials (primarily sheet metal) in the world markets. Products include CNC Punch Press, Laser Contouring Equipment, Panel Bender, Plasma Arc, Right Angle Shears, and Twin Spindle Lathes. **NOTE:** Entry-level positions and part-time jobs are offered. **Common positions include:** Accountant; Administrative Assistant; AS400 Programmer Analyst; Buyer; Controller; Credit Manager; Customer Service Rep.; Electrical/Electronics Engineer; Industrial Engineer; Marketing Manager; Mechanical Engineer; Production Manager; Sales Executive; Sales Manager; Sales Rep.; Systems Manager; Transportation/Traffic Specialist; Vice President of Operations. **Educational backgrounds include:** Accounting; AS400 Certification; Business Administration; Computer Science; Engineering; Finance; Marketing; Novell. **Benefits:** 401(k); Casual Dress - Fridays; Credit Union; Dental Insurance; Disability Coverage; Life Insurance; Medical Insurance; Profit Sharing; Sick Days (1 - 5); Tuition Assistance; Vacation Days (10 - 20). **Special programs:** Internships; Co-ops; Summer Jobs. **Corporate headquarters location:** This Location. **Parent company:** Murata Machinery Ltd. **Listed on:** Privately held. **President:** D.R. Mitchell. **Annual sales/revenues:** $21 - $50 million. **Number of employees at this location:** 85. **Number of employees nationwide:** 115.

NCH CORPORATION
2727 Chemsearch Boulevard, Irving TX 75062. **Toll-free phone:** 800/527-9919. **Fax:** 972/438-0707. **Recorded jobline:** 972/721-6116. **Contact:** Human Resources. **World Wide Web address:** http://www.nch.com. **Description:** Manufactures and supplies specialty chemicals, water treatment products, fasteners, welding supplies, plumbing and electronic parts, and safety supplies to a worldwide customer base. Founded in 1919. **NOTE:** Entry-level positions and part-time jobs are offered. **Common positions include:** Account Rep.; Accountant; Administrative Assistant; Advertising Clerk; Applications Engineer; Assistant Manager; Attorney; Auditor; Biochemist; Blue-Collar Worker Supervisor; Chemist; Clerical Supervisor; Clinical Lab Technician; Computer Engineer; Computer Operator; Computer Programmer; Computer Support Technician; Cost Estimator; Credit Manager; Customer Service Rep.; Database Administrator; Desktop Publishing Specialist; Draftsperson; Editorial Assistant; Electrician; Environmental Engineer; General Manager; Graphic Artist; Graphic Designer; Human Resources Manager; Industrial Production Manager; Intellectual Property Lawyer; Internet Services Manager; Management Trainee; Market Research Analyst; Marketing Manager; Marketing Specialist; MIS Specialist; Multimedia Designer; Network/Systems Administrator; Operations Manager; Paralegal; Production Manager; Purchasing Agent/Manager; Quality Control Supervisor; Sales Manager; Sales Rep.; Secretary; Technical Writer/Editor; Telecommunications Manager; Typist/Word Processor; Webmaster. **Educational backgrounds include:** Accounting; Art/Design; Business Administration; Chemistry; Communications; Liberal Arts; Marketing. **Benefits:** 401(k); Adoption Assistance; Credit Union; Dental Insurance; Disability Coverage; Employee Discounts; Financial Planning Assistance; Flexible Schedule; Job Sharing; Life Insurance; Medical Insurance; Profit Sharing; Public Transit Available; Telecommuting; Tuition Assistance; Vacation Days (6 - 10). **Special programs:** Internships; Training. **Corporate headquarters location:** This Location. **Other U.S. locations:** El Segundo CA; Atlanta GA; Chicago IL; Paramus NJ; Seattle WA. **International locations:** Asia; Australia; Europe; South America. **Annual sales/revenues:** More than $100 million. **Number of employees at this location:** 600.

NSK CORPORATION
P.O. Box 1507, Ann Arbor MI 48106. 734/761-9500. **Fax:** 734/761-9509. **Contact:** Sherri L. Swanson, Employment Representative. **World Wide Web address:** http://www.nsk-corp.com. **Description:** Engaged in the manufacture of ball bearings. **Common positions include:** Accountant; Buyer; Computer Programmer; Customer Service Rep.; Electrical/Electronics Engineer; Financial Analyst; Marketing Specialist; Mechanical Engineer; Operations/Production Manager;

Purchasing Agent/Manager; Quality Control Supervisor. **Educational backgrounds include:** Accounting; Computer Science; Engineering; Marketing; Physics. **Benefits:** Dental Insurance; Disability Coverage; Life Insurance; Medical Insurance; Pension Plan; Savings Plan; Tuition Assistance. **Office hours:** Monday - Friday, 8:00 a.m. - 5:00 p.m. **Corporate headquarters location:** This Location. **Parent company:** NSK Tokyo. **Listed on:** Tokyo Stock Exchange. **President/CEO:** Larry McPherson.

NACCO INDUSTRIES, INC.
5875 Landerbrook Drive, Suite 300, Mayfield Heights OH 44124. 440/449-9600. **Contact:** Human Resources. **Description:** Produces and markets a variety of products for industrial and consumer markets. The company manufactures forklift trucks and produces coal from four surface mines in North Dakota, Texas, and Louisiana. NACCO also makes household appliances including blenders, food processors, electric knives, toasters, coffeemakers, and irons under the brand names Hamilton Beach and Proctor-Silex. The company operates more than 100 Kitchen Collection factory outlets nationwide that sell kitchenware and appliances. **Corporate headquarters location:** This Location. **Listed on:** New York Stock Exchange.

THE NASH ENGINEERING COMPANY
9 Trefoil Drive, Trumbull CT 06611. 203/459-3900. **Contact:** Mr. Lee Tsouris, Employment. **Description:** Manufactures, distributes, and services compressed air and vacuum systems for industrial use worldwide. **Common positions include:** Accountant; Blue-Collar Worker Supervisor; Budget Analyst; Buyer; Chemical Engineer; Computer Programmer; Credit Manager; Customer Service Rep.; Designer; Draftsperson; Financial Analyst; Human Resources Manager; Industrial Engineer; Materials Engineer; Mechanical Engineer; Quality Control Supervisor; Services Sales Rep.; Software Engineer; Systems Analyst. **Educational backgrounds include:** Accounting; Computer Science; Engineering; Finance. **Benefits:** Dental Insurance; Life Insurance; Medical Insurance; Pension Plan; Tuition Assistance. **Corporate headquarters location:** This Location. **Number of employees at this location:** 250.

NATIONAL ASSOCIATION OF MANUFACTURERS
1331 Pennsylvania Avenue NW, Suite 600, Washington DC 20004-1790. 202/637-3016. **Contact:** Human Resources. **World Wide Web address:** http://www.nam.org. **Description:** An association involved in lobbying for the interests of manufacturers. **Common positions include:** Attorney; Editor; Lobbyist; Reporter; Services Sales Representative. **Educational backgrounds include:** Communications; Liberal Arts; Political Science. **Benefits:** Dental Insurance; Disability Coverage; Life Insurance; Medical Insurance; Pension Plan; Savings Plan; Tuition Assistance. **Corporate headquarters location:** This Location.

NATIONAL SERVICE INDUSTRIES INC.
NATIONAL LINEN SERVICE
1420 Peachtree Street NE, Atlanta GA 30309. 404/853-1000. **Contact:** Human Resources. **Description:** A diversified manufacturing and service company with operations in five industries. The majority of revenue is made in lighting equipment, textile rental, and specialty chemicals, but the corporation also does business in insulation services and envelope manufacturing. National Linen Service (also at this location, 404/853-6000) is a linen rental supplier, serving the hospitality and health care industries. Products include napkins; table and bed linens; bath, bar, and shop towels;

uniforms; specialized garments; sterilized products; restroom products; mats; and mops. **Corporate headquarters location:** This Location. **Subsidiaries include:** Lithonia Lighting manufactures lighting fixtures for the commercial, industrial, institutional, and residential construction and renovation markets. Products include fluorescent lighting fixtures, indoor and outdoor high-intensity discharge fixtures, recessed down lighting fixtures, sports lighting fixtures, architectural outdoor fixtures, emergency lighting fixtures, controls, and wiring systems. Zep Manufacturing Company, Selig Chemical Industries, and National Chemical are manufacturers of specialty chemicals for the automotive, diversified manufacturing, food, hospitality, and institutional markets. Products include specialty chemicals and equipment used in cleaning, sanitizing, polishing, degreasing, and water treatment. North Brothers Company fabricates, distributes, and installs insulation and other building products and related services for the construction, renovation, cold storage, manufactured housing, process manufacturing, power generation, and services sectors. Products and services include insulation products, accessories, and contracting services. Atlantic Envelope Company manufactures custom and standard envelopes and related office products. **Listed on:** New York Stock Exchange.

NEOPOST
30955 Huntwood Avenue, Hayward CA 94544. 510/489-6800. **Contact:** Human Resources. **Description:** Engaged in the manufacture and sale of postage meters and related mailing equipment. **Common positions include:** Accountant/Auditor; Administrator; Buyer; Computer Programmer; Credit Manager; Customer Service Representative; Department Manager; Draftsperson; General Manager; Human Resources Manager; Management Trainee; Manufacturer's/Wholesaler's Sales Rep.; Marketing Specialist; Purchasing Agent/Manager; Quality Control Supervisor; Systems Analyst; Technical Writer/Editor; Transportation/Traffic Specialist. **Educational backgrounds include:** Accounting; Business Administration; Computer Science; Engineering; Finance; Liberal Arts; Marketing. **Benefits:** 401(k); Dental Insurance; Disability Coverage; Employee Discounts; Life Insurance; Medical Insurance; Tuition Assistance. **Corporate headquarters location:** This Location.

NESLAB INSTRUMENTS INC.
P.O. Box 1178, Portsmouth NH 03801. 603/436-9444. **Contact:** Bill Halley, Human Resources Director. **World Wide Web address:** http://www.neslabinc.com. **Description:** Manufactures temperature control equipment. **Common positions include:** Accountant/Auditor; Electrical/Electronics Engineer; Industrial Production Manager; Mechanical Engineer; Purchasing Agent/Manager; Services Sales Rep. **Educational backgrounds include:** Engineering; Marketing. **Benefits:** 401(k); Dental Insurance; Disability Coverage; Employee Discounts; Life Insurance; Meal Discounts; Pension Plan; Tuition Assistance. **Special programs:** Internships. **Corporate headquarters location:** This Location. **Parent company:** Life Sciences International. **Number of employees at this location:** 320.

NEW HAVEN MANUFACTURING CO.
446 Blake Street, New Haven CT 06515. 203/387-2572. **Fax:** 203/387-1922. **Contact:** Christian Dolan, Human Resources Manager. **Description:** Develops, manufactures, and markets time equipment, hydraulic control valves, and electronic hardware components. Founded in 1997. **NOTE:** Entry-level positions and second and third shifts are

offered. **Common positions include:** Accountant; Administrative Assistant; Blue-Collar Worker Supervisor; Buyer; Chief Financial Officer; Controller; Customer Service Rep.; Human Resources Manager; Manufacturing Engineer; Marketing Specialist; MIS Specialist; Operations Manager; Production Manager; Purchasing Agent/Manager; Quality Control Supervisor; Sales Executive; Sales Manager; Sales Rep.; Secretary; Typist/Word Processor. **Educational backgrounds include:** Accounting; Business Administration; Computer Science; Engineering; Liberal Arts; Software Tech. Support. **Benefits:** 401(k); Credit Union; Dental Insurance; Disability Coverage; Life Insurance; Medical Insurance; Pension Plan; Public Transit Available; Tuition Assistance. **Special programs:** Training; Summer Jobs. **Office hours:** Monday - Friday, 8:00 a.m. - 5:00 p.m. **Corporate headquarters location:** This Location. **Parent company:** Matthews Ventures. **CEO:** David McDonald. **Annual sales/revenues:** $11 - $20 million.

NEW HOLLAND, INC.
P.O. Box 1895, New Holland PA 17557-0903. 717/355-1121. **Fax:** 717/355-3650. **Contact:** Ted S. Lyon, Corporate Recruiting Manager. **World Wide Web address:** http://www.newholland.com. **Description:** Manufactures agricultural equipment including tractors and balers. **Common positions include:** Accountant; Agricultural Engineer; Budget Analyst; Buyer; Computer Programmer; Customer Service Rep.; Financial Analyst; Human Resources Manager; Industrial Engineer; Mechanical Engineer; Systems Analyst. **Educational backgrounds include:** Accounting; Business Administration; Computer Science; Engineering; Finance; Marketing. **Benefits:** 401(k); Dental Insurance; Disability Coverage; Employee Discounts; Life Insurance; Medical Insurance; Pension Plan; Profit Sharing; Savings Plan; Tuition Assistance. **Special programs:** Internships. **Corporate headquarters location:** London, England. **Parent company:** Fiat. **Number of employees at this location:** 2,000. **Number of employees nationwide:** 4,000.

NIBCO, INC.
1516 Middlebury Street, Elkhart IN 46515-1167. 219/295-3000. **Contact:** Human Resources. **World Wide Web address:** http://www.nibco.com. **Description:** Manufactures flow control solutions, fittings, and valves. **NOTE:** Entry-level positions are offered. **Common positions include:** Industrial Engineer; Mechanical Engineer; MIS Specialist; Operations/Production Manager; Systems Analyst. **Educational backgrounds include:** Engineering. **Benefits:** 401(k); Disability Coverage; Life Insurance; Medical Insurance; Pension Plan; Profit Sharing; Savings Plan; Tuition Assistance. **Special programs:** Internships. **Corporate headquarters location:** This Location. **Other U.S. locations:** Nationwide. **Listed on:** Privately held. **Number of employees nationwide:** 3,500.

NISSAN FORKLIFT CORPORATION, NORTH AMERICA
240 North Prospect Street, Marengo IL 60152-3298. 815/568-0061. **Toll-free phone:** 800/871-LIFT. **Fax:** 815/568-0181. **Contact:** Lee Van Syckle, Human Resources Manager. **World Wide Web address:** http://www.nissanforklift.com. **Description:** Manufactures forklifts including electrically powered and internal combustion engines. **NOTE:** Entry-level positions, part-time jobs, and second shifts are offered. **Common positions include:** Account Manager; Account Rep.; Accountant; Administrative Assistant; AS400 Programmer Analyst; Computer Support Technician; Computer Technician; Controller;

Customer Service Rep.; Desktop Publishing Specialist; Electrical/Electronics Engineer; Finance Director; Financial Analyst; Help-Desk Technician; Human Resources Manager; Industrial Engineer; Manufacturing Engineer; Marketing Manager; Marketing Specialist; Network Engineer; Network/ Systems Administrator; Operations Manager; Purchasing Agent/Manager; Quality Assurance Engineer; Sales Manager; Systems Analyst; Technical Writer/Editor; Vice President. **Educational backgrounds include:** Accounting; AS400 Certification; Business Administration; Computer Science; Engineering; Finance; Marketing; Microsoft Office; Microsoft Word; Novell; Publishing; Spreadsheets. **Benefits:** 401(k); Casual Dress - Fridays; Dental Insurance; Disability Coverage; Employee Discounts; Life Insurance; Medical Insurance; Relocation Assistance; Savings Plan; Vacation Days (10 - 20). **Special programs:** Internships; Summer Jobs. **Office hours:** Monday - Friday, 8:00 a.m. - 5:00 p.m. **Corporate headquarters location:** This Location. **International locations:** Japan; Spain. **Parent company:** Nissan Motor Company, Ltd. **Listed on:** Privately held. **President:** Mark Akabori. **Annual sales/revenues:** More than $100 million. **Number of employees at this location:** 500.

NORGREN
5400 South Delaware Street, Littleton CO 80120. 303/794-2611. **Fax:** 303/795-6200. **Contact:** Martha Parsley, Manager of Human Resources. **World Wide Web address:** http://www. usa.norgren.com. **Description:** Manufactures accessory and component parts for pneumatic systems. **Common positions include:** Accountant; Blue-Collar Worker Supervisor; Computer Programmer; Customer Service Rep.; Department Manager; Industrial Engineer; Operations/ Production Manager; Purchasing Agent/Manager; Quality Control Supervisor. **Benefits:** Dental Insurance; Disability Coverage; Life Insurance; Medical Insurance; Pension Plan; Savings Plan; Tuition Assistance. **Corporate headquarters location:** This Location.

NORTH AMERICAN PRODUCTS CORP.
1180 Wernsing Road, Jasper IN 47546. 812/482-2000. **Contact:** Dave Smith, Director of Human Resources. **World Wide Web address:** http://www. naptools.com. **Description:** Manufactures and services carbide-tipped cutting tools for the wood and metal industries. **Common positions include:** Accountant; Blue-Collar Worker Supervisor; Buyer; Credit Manager; Customer Service Rep.; Draftsperson; General Manager; Industrial Engineer; Industrial Production Manager; Mechanical Engineer; Services Sales Rep.; Systems Analyst. **Educational backgrounds include:** Accounting; Business Administration; Computer Science; Engineering; Finance; Marketing. **Benefits:** 401(k); Dental Insurance; Life Insurance; Medical Insurance; Profit Sharing; Savings Plan. **Corporate headquarters location:** This Location. **Other U.S. locations:** Nationwide. **Number of employees at this location:** 480.

NORTH HARTLAND TOOL CORP.
P.O. Box 38, 14 Evarts Street, North Hartland VT 05052. 802/295-3196. **Fax:** 802/295-2473. **Contact:** Human Resources. **Description:** Manufactures gages, fixtures, special tools, and precision parts. **NOTE:** Entry-level positions and part-time jobs are offered. **Common positions include:** Controller; Draftsperson; MIS Specialist; Production Manager; Purchasing Agent/Manager; Sales Rep.; Secretary. **Educational backgrounds include:** Art/Design; Engineering; Marketing; Microsoft Word; Spreadsheets. **Benefits:** 401(k);

Casual Dress - Daily; Dental Insurance; Disability Coverage; Life Insurance; Medical Insurance. **Special programs:** Apprenticeships; Co-ops; Summer Jobs. **Parent company:** Netam Corporation. **Listed on:** Privately held. **President:** John M. Mullen.

NUARC COMPANY INC.
6200 West Howard Street, Niles IL 60714. 847/967-4400. **Contact:** Personnel. **World Wide Web address:** http://www.nuarcco.com. **Description:** Manufactures graphic arts equipment such as exposure systems. **Corporate headquarters location:** This Location.

NUMATICS INC.
1450 North Milford Road, Highland MI 48357. 248/887-4111. **Contact:** Mr. L.A. Strauss, Director of Labor Relations. **World Wide Web address:** http://www.numatics.com. **Description:** Manufactures pneumatic air valves, controls, cylinders, dryers, and all types of ancillary equipment associated with the fluid power industry. **Common positions include:** Accountant; Budget Analyst; Buyer; Computer Programmer; Credit Manager; Customer Service Representative; Designer; Draftsperson; Electrical/Electronics Engineer; Financial Analyst; General Manager; Human Resources Manager; Industrial Engineer; Mechanical Engineer; Operations/Production Manager; Purchasing Agent/Manager; Quality Control Supervisor; Systems Analyst. **Educational backgrounds include:** Accounting; Art/Design; Computer Science; Engineering; Marketing. **Benefits:** 401(k); Dental Insurance; Disability Coverage; Life Insurance; Medical Insurance; Pension Plan. **Corporate headquarters location:** This Location. **Listed on:** Privately held. **Number of employees at this location:** 200.

OHIO ELECTRONIC ENGRAVERS, INC.
4105 Executive Drive, Dayton OH 45430-1081. 937/427-1022. **Fax:** 937/427-1375. **Contact:** Alene Loudermilk, Manager of Human Resources. **World Wide Web address:** http://www.ohioee.com. **Description:** A capital equipment manufacturer that designs and produces electronic engravers, scanners, and other prepress equipment; peripherals; and software for the gravure printing industry. Founded in 1978. **NOTE:** Entry-level positions and second and third shifts are offered. **Common positions include:** Account Manager; Administrative Assistant; Administrative Manager; Applications Engineer; Chief Financial Officer; Clerical Supervisor; Design Engineer; Draftsperson; Electrical/Electronics Engineer; General Manager; Human Resources Manager; Manufacturing Engineer; Mechanical Engineer; MIS Specialist; Project Manager; Purchasing Agent/Manager; Quality Control Supervisor; Sales Executive; Software Engineer; Systems Manager; Technical Writer/Editor; Telecommunications Manager. **Educational backgrounds include:** Engineering. **Benefits:** 401(k); Dental Insurance; Life Insurance; Medical Insurance; Profit Sharing; Tuition Assistance. **Special programs:** Internships. **Corporate headquarters location:** This Location. **Listed on:** Privately held. **Annual sales/revenues:** $21 - $50 million. **Number of employees at this location:** 250.

OLIVETTI OFFICE USA
765 U.S. Highway 202 North, P.O. Box 6945, Bridgewater NJ 08807. 908/526-8200. **Contact:** Personnel. **Description:** Manufactures and distributes a broad line of electronic office products including typewriters, calculators, word processors, cash registers, copiers, personal and small computers, business computers, complete data processing systems, teleprinters, video terminals, telephone-switching systems, minicomputers, automatic tellers, and associated equipment. **Corporate headquarters location:** This Location.

OMEGA ENGINEERING, INC.
One Omega Drive, P.O. Box 4047, Stamford CT 06907-0047. 203/359-1660. **Contact:** Human Resources. **World Wide Web address:** http://www.omega.com. **Description:** A manufacturer and worldwide distributor of process measurement and control instrumentation. Products include temperature, pressure, strain and flow devices, pH equipment, and a large selection of instrument and control tools. Omega Engineering also provides related consulting and engineering services. **Common positions include:** Accountant/Auditor; Advertising Clerk; Blue-Collar Worker Supervisor; Buyer; Computer Programmer; Credit Manager; Customer Service Rep.; Draftsperson; Electrical/Electronics Engineer; Human Resources Manager; Manufacturer's/Wholesaler's Sales Rep.; Marketing Specialist; Mechanical Engineer; Operations/Production Manager; Purchasing Agent/Manager; Technical Writer/Editor; Transportation/Traffic Specialist. **Educational backgrounds include:** Engineering; Marketing; Physics. **Benefits:** Dental Insurance; Medical Insurance; Tuition Assistance. **Corporate headquarters location:** This Location. **Other U.S. locations:** Bridgeport NJ.

OMNOVA
175 Ghent Road, Fairlawn OH 44333. 330/869-4200. **Contact:** Staffing. **World Wide Web address:** http://www.omnova.com. **Description:** A diversified holding company. **Corporate headquarters location:** This Location. **Subsidiaries include:** Aerojet specializes in aerospace and defense products; Decorative and Building Products include wallcoverings, films and laminates, and coated fabrics; Performance Chemicals produces emulsion polymers and chemicals; Vehicle Sealing Products produces a full-line of automotive sealing products.

ONAN CORPORATION
1400 73rd Avenue NE, Minneapolis MN 55432. 763/574-5000. **Contact:** Katie Pearson, Director of Human Resources. **World Wide Web address:** http://www.onan.com. **Description:** Manufactures generators. **Corporate headquarters location:** This Location.

OPTICAL COATING LABORATORY, INC.
2789 North Point Parkway, Santa Rosa CA 95407. 707/525-7555. **Contact:** Human Resources. **World Wide Web address:** http://www.ocli.com. **Description:** Manufactures thin-film coated components that are used in the manufacture of photographic products, office equipment, and computers. **Common positions include:** Electrical/Electronics Engineer; Industrial Engineer; Materials Engineer; Mechanical Engineer. **Educational backgrounds include:** Engineering. **Benefits:** 401(k); Dental Insurance; Disability Coverage; Life Insurance; Medical Insurance; Profit Sharing; Tuition Assistance. **Corporate headquarters location:** This Location. **Listed on:** NASDAQ. **Number of employees at this location:** 900.

OREGON CUTTING SYSTEMS
P.O. Box 22127, Portland OR 97269-2127. 503/653-8881. **Fax:** 503/653-4494. **Recorded jobline:** 503/653-4441. **Contact:** Employment Manager. **World Wide Web address:** http://www.oregonchain.com. **Description:** Manufactures saw chains and related power saw accessories. **Corporate headquarters location:** This Location. **Parent company:** Blount Inc.

ORSCHELN INDUSTRIES
P.O. Box 280, Moberly MO 65270. 660/263-4377. **Fax:** 660/269-4530. **Contact:** Employment Manager. **World Wide Web address:** http://www. orscheln.com. **Description:** A manufacturer of mechanical and electromechanical automotive and industrial equipment components; sealants; and adhesives for the automotive and construction industries. Orscheln also operates approximately 90 retail stores in eight midwestern states. Founded in 1946. **NOTE:** Entry-level positions and second and third shifts are offered. **Common positions include:** Accountant; Blue-Collar Worker Supervisor; Buyer; Chemical Engineer; Computer Programmer; Construction Contractor; Customer Service Rep.; Design Engineer; Draftsperson; Electrician; Financial Analyst; Human Resources Manager; Industrial Production Manager; Management Trainee; Mechanical Engineer; Operations/ Production Manager; Purchasing Agent/Manager; Quality Control Supervisor; Services Sales Rep.; Software Engineer; Systems Analyst; Transportation/Traffic Specialist. **Educational backgrounds include:** Accounting; Business Administration; Computer Science; Engineering; Finance; Marketing. **Benefits:** 401(k); Casual Dress - Daily; Dental Insurance; Disability Coverage; Employee Discounts; Flexible Schedule; Life Insurance; Medical Insurance; Relocation Assistance; Tuition Assistance. **Special programs:** Training. **Office hours:** Monday - Friday, 8:00 a.m. - 5:00 p.m. **Corporate headquarters location:** This Location. **International locations:** England. **Listed on:** Privately held. **Annual sales/revenues:** More than $100 million. **Number of employees at this location:** 750.

OSMONICS, INC.
5951 Clearwater Drive, Minnetonka MN 55343. 952/933-2277. **Fax:** 952/933-0141. **Contact:** Jeff Joyce, Human Resources Manager. **World Wide Web address:** http://www.osmonics.com. **Description:** Designs, manufactures, and markets fluid processing machines, systems, and components. **Common positions include:** Accountant; Agricultural Engineer; Biomedical Engineer; Blue-Collar Worker Supervisor; Buyer; Chemical Engineer; Chemist; Civil Engineer; Clerical Supervisor; Customer Service Rep.; Designer; Draftsperson; Electrical/Electronics Engineer; Human Resources Manager; Industrial Engineer; Industrial Production Manager; Mechanical Engineer; Metallurgical Engineer; Operations/Production Manager; Purchasing Agent/ Manager; Quality Control Supervisor; Systems Analyst; Technical Writer/Editor. **Benefits:** 401(k); Dental Insurance; Disability Coverage; Employee Discounts; Life Insurance; Medical Insurance; Profit Sharing; Tuition Assistance. **Corporate headquarters location:** This Location. **Other U.S. locations:** AZ; CA; MA; NY; WI. **Listed on:** New York Stock Exchange. **Number of employees at this location:** 505.

OTIS ELEVATOR COMPANY
One Farm Springs Road, Farmington CT 06032. 860/676-6000. **Contact:** Director of Recruitment. **World Wide Web address:** http://www. nao.otis.com. **Description:** Produces and distributes a line of elevators and escalators for commercial and industrial use. Founded in 1853. **Corporate headquarters location:** This Location. **Other U.S. locations:** Nationwide. **Parent company:** United Technologies Corporation.

PACCAR INC.
P.O. Box 1518, Bellevue WA 98009. 425/468-7400. **Fax:** 425/468-8206. **Recorded jobline:** 425/468-7011. **Contact:** Human Resources Department. **World Wide Web address:** http://www. paccar.com. **Description:** Manufactures, leases, and finances heavy duty on- and off-road trucks and industrial winches for industrial and commercial use. Brand names include Peterbilt, Foden, DAF, and Kenworth. **Common positions include:** Accountant/Auditor; Buyer; Computer Operator; Computer Programmer; Design Engineer; Industrial Engineer; Manufacturing Engineer; Mechanical Engineer; Purchasing Agent/Manager; Sales Rep. **Educational backgrounds include:** Accounting; Business Administration; Computer Science; Engineering; Finance. **Benefits:** 401(k); Dental Insurance; Disability Coverage; Life Insurance; Medical Insurance; Pension Plan; Savings Plan; Tuition Assistance. **Special programs:** Internships. **Corporate headquarters location:** This Location. **Other U.S. locations:** Nationwide. **International locations:** Australia; Canada; Mexico; the Netherlands; United Kingdom. **Annual sales/revenues:** More than $100 million. **Number of employees at this location:** 425.

PALL CORPORATION
2200 Northern Boulevard, East Hills NY 11548-1289. 516/484-5400. **Contact:** Patricia Lowy, Vice President. **World Wide Web address:** http://www. pall.com. **Description:** A leader in filtration technology, specializing in fluid clarification and high-end separation. The company's overall business is organized into three segments: Health Care, Aeropower, and Fluid Processing. **Common positions include:** Accountant; Biological Scientist; Biomedical Engineer; Chemist; Draftsperson; Operations/Production Manager; Public Relations Specialist. **Educational backgrounds include:** Accounting; Biology; Chemistry; Engineering; Physics. **Benefits:** Dental Insurance; Disability Coverage; Life Insurance; Medical Insurance; Pension Plan; Profit Sharing; Stock Option; Tuition Assistance. **Corporate headquarters location:** This Location. **Other U.S. locations:** Putnam CT; Fort Myers FL; New Port Richey FL; Pinellas Park FL; Cortland NY; Glen Cove NY; Hauppauge NY; Port Washington NY. **Subsidiaries include:** Pall Gelman Sciences Inc.

PALL GELMAN SCIENCES INC.
674 South Wagner Road, Ann Arbor MI 48103-9109. 734/665-0651. **Contact:** Human Resources. **Description:** Engaged in the manufacture of microfiltration devices. **Common positions include:** Biomedical Engineer; Chemical Engineer; Manufacturer's/Wholesaler's Sales Rep.; Quality Assurance Engineer. **Educational backgrounds include:** Biology; Chemistry; Engineering. **Benefits:** Dental Insurance; Disability Coverage; Life Insurance; Medical Insurance; Profit Sharing; Savings Plan; Tuition Assistance. **Corporate headquarters location:** This Location. **Parent company:** Pall Corporation. **Listed on:** American Stock Exchange. **Number of employees at this location:** 625.

PALL TRINITY MICRO
P.O. Box 2030, Cortland NY 13045. 607/753-6041. **Physical address:** 3643 Route 281, Cortland NY. **Fax:** 607/753-9653. **Contact:** Elizabeth Britt, Human Resources Specialist. **E-mail address:** Elizabeth_Britt@pall.com. **World Wide Web address:** http://www.pall.com. **Description:** Develops and manufactures filters and filtration devices and systems for global customers primarily in high-tech and industrial markets. **Company slogan:** Filtration. Separation. Solution. **Common positions include:** Accountant; Administrative Assistant; AS400 Programmer Analyst; Design Engineer; Draftsperson; Electrical/Electronics Engineer; Financial Analyst; Industrial Engineer;

Manufacturing Engineer; Mechanical Engineer; Metallurgical Engineer; MIS Specialist; Purchasing Agent/Manager. **Educational backgrounds include:** Accounting; Business Administration; Computer Science; Engineering; Finance; MBA; Microsoft Office; Microsoft Word; Spreadsheets. **Benefits:** 401(k); Casual Dress - Fridays; Dental Insurance; Disability Coverage; Holiday Bonus; Life Insurance; Medical Insurance; Pension Plan; Profit Sharing; Relocation Assistance; Stock Option; Tuition Assistance. **Corporate headquarters location:** East Hills NY. **Other U.S. locations:** CA; FL; MA; MI; TX. **International locations:** Germany; Ireland; Japan; United Kingdom. **Parent company:** Pall Corporation is a world leader in filtration technology, specializing in fluid clarification and high-end separation. The company's overall business is organized into three segments: Health Care, Aeropower, and Fluid Processing. **Listed on:** New York Stock Exchange. **Stock exchange symbol:** PLL. **Annual sales/revenues:** More than $100 million. **Number of employees at this location:** 680.

PAPER CONVERTING MACHINE CO.

P.O. Box 19005, Green Bay WI 54307-9005. 920/494-5601. **Contact:** Steve Herzog, Personnel Director. **World Wide Web address:** http://www.pcmc.com. **Description:** Designs and builds converting machinery for the paper, film, and foil industries. **Common positions include:** Electrical/Electronics Engineer; Mechanical Engineer. **Educational backgrounds include:** Engineering. **Benefits:** 401(k); Dental Insurance; Disability Coverage; Life Insurance; Medical Insurance; Profit Sharing; Tuition Assistance. **Corporate headquarters location:** This Location. **Number of employees at this location:** 860.

PARKER HANNIFIN CORPORATION

6035 Parkland Boulevard, Cleveland OH 44124. 216/896-3000. **Contact:** Dan Garey, Vice President of Employee Relations. **World Wide Web address:** http://www.parker.com. **Description:** This location manufactures hydraulic and pneumatic components and systems for the fluid industry. Overall, Parker Hannifin Corporation makes motion control products including fluid power systems, electromechanical controls, and related components. The Motion and Control Group makes hydraulic cylinders, actuators, and automation devices to remove contaminants from air, fuel, oil, water, and other fluids. The Fluid Connectors Group makes connectors, tube and hose fittings, hoses, and couplers which transmit fluid. The Seal Group makes sealing devices, gaskets, and packing which insure leak-proof connections. The Automotive and Refrigeration Groups make components for use in industrial and automotive air conditioning and refrigeration systems. The Aerospace Group makes hydraulic and pneumatic fuel systems and components. **Common positions include:** Accountant/Auditor; Aerospace Engineer; Computer Programmer; Financial Analyst; Mechanical Engineer. **Educational backgrounds include:** Accounting; Business Administration; Computer Science; Engineering. **Benefits:** Medical Insurance. **Corporate headquarters location:** This Location.

PAUL-SON GAMING CORPORATION

1700 Industrial Road, Las Vegas NV 89102. 702/384-2425. **Contact:** Human Resources Department. **World Wide Web address:** http://www.paulsongaming.com. **Description:** One of the leading manufacturers and suppliers of casino table game equipment in the United States. The company's products include casino chips, felt table layouts, playing cards, dice, gaming furniture, and miscellaneous table accessories such as chip trays, drop boxes, and dealing shoes. **Corporate headquarters location:** This Location. **Other U.S. locations:** Gulfport MS; Atlantic City NJ; Reno NV. **International locations:** San Luis, Mexico.

PAYMASTER TECHNOLOGIES, INC.

900 Pratt Boulevard, Elk Grove Village IL 60007. 773/878-9200. **Contact:** Personnel. **World Wide Web address:** http://www.paymastertech.com. **Description:** Manufactures and sells check-writing machines and check protectors. **Corporate headquarters location:** This Location.

PELLERIN MILNOR CORPORATION

P.O. Box 400, Kenner LA 70063. 504/467-9591. **Contact:** Mr. Sydney Lacoste, Human Resources Director. **Description:** An international manufacturer of industrial and commercial laundry machinery including washers, dryers, and presses. **Common positions include:** Accountant/Auditor; Blue-Collar Worker Supervisor; Buyer; Computer Programmer; Department Manager; Draftsperson; Electrical/Electronics Engineer; General Manager; Human Resources Manager; Industrial Engineer; Manufacturer's/Wholesaler's Sales Rep.; Mechanical Engineer; Operations/Production Manager; Product Manager; Purchasing Agent/Manager; Quality Control Supervisor; Systems Analyst; Technical Writer/Editor; Transportation/Traffic Specialist. **Educational backgrounds include:** Business Administration; Communications; Computer Science; Engineering; Finance; Liberal Arts; Marketing. **Benefits:** Credit Union; Dental Insurance; Disability Coverage; Life Insurance; Medical Insurance; Pension Plan; Profit Sharing. **Special programs:** Internships. **Corporate headquarters location:** This Location.

PENTAIR INDUSTRIES

Waters Edge Plaza, 1500 County Road B2 West, St. Paul MN 55113-3105. 651/636-7920. **Contact:** Human Resources. **World Wide Web address:** http://www.pentair.com. **Description:** A diverse firm with operations in the manufacturing of portable and stationary woodworking tools, pumps, lubrication systems, jacks, electrical enclosures, and sporting ammunition and accessories. **Common positions include:** Accountant; Blue-Collar Worker Supervisor; Branch Manager; Budget Analyst; Computer Operator; Computer Programmer; Customer Service Rep.; Department Manager; Designer; Dispatcher; Electrical/Electronics Engineer; Electrician; Employment Interviewer; Financial Manager; General Manager; Human Resources Manager; Industrial Engineer; Industrial Production Manager; Machinist; Management Analyst/Consultant; Management Trainee; Manufacturer's/Wholesaler's Sales Rep.; Marketing Manager; Mechanical Engineer; Metallurgical Engineer; Purchasing Agent/Manager; Quality Control Supervisor; Secretary; Systems Analyst. **Educational backgrounds include:** Accounting; Business Administration; Chemistry; Computer Science; Economics; Engineering; Finance; Liberal Arts; Marketing. **Corporate headquarters location:** This Location. **Listed on:** NASDAQ. **Number of employees at this location:** 40.

PERMACEL
A NITTO DENKO COMPANY

P.O. Box 671, New Brunswick NJ 08903. 732/418-2455. **Fax:** 732/418-2474. **Contact:** Human Resources. **Description:** Manufactures pressure-sensitive tape. **Common positions include:** Accountant; Administrator; Blue-Collar Worker Supervisor; Chemical Engineer; Chemist; Computer Programmer; Credit Manager; Customer Service Representative; Department Manager; Economist; Electrical/Electronics Engineer; Financial Analyst;

General Manager; Human Resources Manager; Industrial Engineer; Manufacturer's/Wholesaler's Sales Rep.; Marketing Specialist; Mechanical Engineer; Operations/Production Manager; Quality Control Supervisor; Systems Analyst; Transportation/Traffic Specialist. **Educational backgrounds include:** Accounting; Business Administration; Chemistry; Computer Science; Engineering; Finance; Liberal Arts; Marketing. **Benefits:** 401(k); Dental Insurance; Disability Coverage; Life Insurance; Medical Insurance; Pension Plan; Savings Plan; Tuition Assistance. **Corporate headquarters location:** This Location. **Listed on:** Privately held. **Number of employees at this location:** 500.

PERRY EQUIPMENT CORPORATION
P.O. Box 640, Mineral Wells TX 76068-0640. 940/325-2575. **Contact:** Doug Harcourt, Vice President of Human Resources. **Description:** Manufactures filtration separation cartridges, flow-measurement systems, and systems for the oil, gas, and chemical processing industries. **Common positions include:** Accountant/Auditor; Blue-Collar Worker Supervisor; Buyer; Chemical Engineer; Computer Programmer; Customer Service Rep.; Designer; Draftsperson; Electrical/Electronics Engineer; General Manager; Industrial Engineer; Industrial Production Manager; Manufacturer's/Wholesaler's Sales Rep.; Mechanical Engineer; Operations/Production Manager; Purchasing Agent/Manager; Quality Control Supervisor; Systems Analyst; Transportation/Traffic Specialist. **Educational backgrounds include:** Accounting; Business Administration; Computer Science; Engineering; Marketing. **Benefits:** Disability Coverage; Life Insurance; Medical Insurance; Pension Plan; Profit Sharing; Tuition Assistance. **Corporate headquarters location:** This Location. **Other area locations:** Amarillo TX; Houston TX. **Listed on:** Privately held. **Number of employees at this location:** 500.

PERSONA
700 21st Street SW, Watertown SD 57201. 605/882-2244. **Contact:** Cathy Duten-Hoffer, Human Resources Manager. **Description:** A multifaceted sign manufacturing operation with production facilities designed to handle the full range of sign and sign program needs, from standard to highly customized applications. PERSONA offers fabrication consultation during the design phase; interfacing with clients' design firms; complete materials evaluation; prototype fabrication; in-house design capability; and extensive, in-house computer support. The company's products and product features include aluminum frames and cabinets, steel frames and cabinets, flexible faces, rigid faces (both flat and formed plastic, and routed and non-routed aluminum), vinyl decoration, heat transfer decoration, awnings, channel letters, neon, and custom signs. The company's Corporate Identity Division, established for the sole purpose of project management on a national or regional basis, offers services such as image control sales coordinators, surveys and survey analysis, site analysis, obtaining permits and variances, elevation drawings, photo-scan and imaging services, sign installation and location coordination, detailed construction prints, complete customized location status reports, and indoor storage of inventory. **Corporate headquarters location:** This Location. **Other U.S. locations:** Madison SD. **Parent company:** ANZA, Inc.

PHILADELPHIA GEAR CORPORATION
181 South Gulph Road, King of Prussia PA 19406. 610/265-3000. **Fax:** 610/337-5651. **Contact:** Amy Elsea, Human Resources. **World Wide Web address:** http://www.philagear.com. **Description:** Produces a wide variety of gears and gear drives for various industrial uses. Founded in 1892. **Common positions include:** Account Manager; Accountant; Applications Engineer; Blue-Collar Worker Supervisor; Buyer; Chief Financial Officer; Computer Programmer; Credit Manager; Customer Service Rep.; Design Engineer; Electrician; Human Resources Manager; Industrial Engineer; Industrial Production Manager; Manufacturing Engineer; Mechanical Engineer; MIS Specialist; Quality Control Supervisor; Sales Engineer; Sales Executive; Vice President of Marketing and Sales. **Educational backgrounds include:** Accounting; Business Administration; Computer Science; Engineering; Finance. **Benefits:** 401(k); Dental Insurance; Life Insurance; Medical Insurance; Pension Plan; Tuition Assistance. **Corporate headquarters location:** This Location. **Other U.S. locations:** Lynwood CA; Houston TX. **Parent company:** American Manufacturing Group. **Listed on:** Privately held. **Annual sales/revenues:** $51 - $100 million. **Number of employees at this location:** 390.

PHOTO ELECTRONICS CORPORATION
17280 Wood Red Road NE, Suite 805, Woodinville WA 98072-9044. 425/806-9500. **Contact:** Human Resources. **Description:** A manufacturing company which specializes in photoanalyzing equipment utilized in professional color labs. **Common positions include:** Accountant/Auditor; Computer Programmer; Electrical/Electronics Engineer; Electronics Technician; Genetic Engineer; Human Resources Manager; Machinist; Manufacturer's/Wholesaler's Sales Rep.; Purchasing Agent/Manager. **Educational backgrounds include:** Accounting; Business Administration; Computer Science; Engineering. **Benefits:** 401(k); Dental Insurance; Disability Coverage; Employee Discounts; Life Insurance; Medical Insurance; Savings Plan; Tuition Assistance. **Corporate headquarters location:** This Location. **Listed on:** Privately held. **Number of employees at this location:** 15.

PITCO FRIALATOR, INC.
P.O. Box 501, Concord NH 03302. 603/225-6684. **Fax:** 603/228-5216. **Contact:** Leslie Campbell, Manager of Human Resources. **Description:** A manufacturer of commercial cooking equipment. **Common positions include:** Accountant; Administrative Assistant; Blue-Collar Worker Supervisor; Computer Programmer; Design Engineer; Designer; Quality Control Supervisor. **Educational backgrounds include:** Business Administration; Engineering; Spreadsheets. **Benefits:** 401(k); Casual Dress - Fridays; Dental Insurance; Disability Coverage; Employee Discounts; Life Insurance; Medical Insurance; Pension Plan; Sick Days (1 - 5); Tuition Assistance; Vacation Days (6 - 10). **Office hours:** Monday - Friday, 8:00 a.m. - 5:00 p.m. **Corporate headquarters location:** Burlington VT. **Parent company:** Maytag Corporation. **Listed on:** New York Stock Exchange.

PITNEY BOWES, INC.
One Elmcroft Road, Stamford CT 06926-0700. 203/356-5000. **Fax:** 203/351-6293. **Contact:** Staffing Department. **World Wide Web address:** http://www.pitneybowes.com. **Description:** Pitney Bowes operates within two industry segments: Business Equipment and Services and Financial Services. The Business Equipment and Services segment includes the manufacturing of postage meters; mailing, shipping, and facsimile systems; copiers and copier supplies; and mailroom reprographics. The Financial Services segment

includes the worldwide financing operations of the company. This segment provides lease financing for the company's products, as well as other financial services for the commercial and industrial markets. Founded in 1920. **Common positions include:** Accountant; Administrative Assistant; Attorney; Auditor; Buyer; Computer Programmer; Customer Service Rep.; Database Manager; Design Engineer; Electrical/Electronics Engineer; Environmental Engineer; Financial Analyst; Human Resources Manager; Intellectual Property Lawyer; Mechanical Engineer; MIS Specialist; Purchasing Agent/Manager; Software Engineer; Systems Analyst; Systems Manager. **Educational backgrounds include:** Computer Science; Engineering; Finance. **Corporate headquarters location:** This Location. **Listed on:** NASDAQ.

PLASTI-LINE, INC.
P.O. Box 59043, Knoxville TN 37950-9043. 865/938-1511. **Fax:** 865/947-8546. **Contact:** Julie A. Glibbery, Human Resources Manager. **Description:** Manufactures and distributes large illuminated plastic signs for corporations. **Common positions include:** Blue-Collar Worker Supervisor; Buyer; Customer Service Rep.; Designer; Draftsperson; Industrial Engineer; Industrial Production Manager; Mechanical Engineer; Purchasing Agent/Manager. **Benefits:** 401(k); Disability Coverage; Life Insurance; Medical Insurance; Profit Sharing; Savings Plan. **Corporate headquarters location:** This Location. **Other U.S. locations:** Fontana CA; Florence KY. **Listed on:** NASDAQ. **Number of employees at this location:** 600. **Number of employees nationwide:** 800.

PORTA-KAMP MANUFACTURING CO.
555 Gellhorn, Houston TX 77029. 713/674-3163. **Contact:** Personnel. **Description:** Manufactures offshore drilling equipment and metal portable buildings. **Corporate headquarters location:** This Location.

PRECISION OPTICS CORPORATION
22 East Broadway, Gardner MA 01440. 978/630-1800. **Fax:** 978/630-1487. **Contact:** Human Resources. **World Wide Web address:** http://www. poci.com. **Description:** Designs, develops, manufactures, and sells specialized optical systems and components and optical thin film coatings. The products and services are used in the medical and advanced optical systems industries. Medical products include endoscopes and image couplers, beamsplitters, and adapters which are used as accessories to endoscopes. Advanced optical design and developmental services provide advanced lens design, image analysis, optical system design, structural design and analysis, prototype production and evaluation, optics testing, and optical system assembly. **Corporate headquarters location:** This Location.

PRECISION TWIST DRILL COMPANY
One Precision Plaza, Box 9000, Crystal Lake IL 60039. 815/459-2040. **Contact:** Human Resources. **Description:** Manufactures drills and cutting tools for the aerospace, automotive, and construction industries. **Common positions include:** Accountant; Blue-Collar Worker Supervisor; Buyer; Computer Programmer; Cost Estimator; Credit Manager; Customer Service Rep.; Designer; Draftsperson; Electrical/Electronics Engineer; Electrician; Financial Analyst; General Manager; Human Resources Manager; Industrial Engineer; Mechanical Engineer; Metallurgical Engineer; Production Manager; Purchasing Agent/Manager; Quality Control Supervisor; Systems Analyst. **Educational backgrounds include:** Accounting; Business Administration; Engineering; Finance.

Benefits: 401(k); Dental Insurance; Disability Coverage; Employee Discounts; Life Insurance; Medical Insurance; Pension Plan; Profit Sharing; Savings Plan; Tuition Assistance. **Corporate headquarters location:** This Location. **Subsidiaries include:** Triumph Twist Drill Company. **Listed on:** Privately held. **Number of employees at this location:** 1,500.

PRECISION VALVE CORPORATION
700 Nepperhan Avenue, Yonkers NY 10703. 914/969-6500. **Fax:** 914/966-4637. **Contact:** Thomas F. Harrington, Industrial Relations Manager. **World Wide Web address:** http://www. precision-valve.com. **Description:** An international manufacturer of aerosol valves. **Common positions include:** Accountant/Auditor; Blue-Collar Worker Supervisor; Buyer; Computer Programmer; Customer Service Rep.; Designer; Draftsperson; General Manager; Human Resources Manager; Manufacturer's/Wholesaler's Sales Rep.; Operations/Production Manager; Purchasing Agent/Manager; Quality Control Supervisor; Services Sales Representative; Systems Analyst. **Educational backgrounds include:** Accounting; Business Administration. **Benefits:** 401(k); Disability Coverage; Employee Discounts; Life Insurance; Medical Insurance; Pension Plan; Tuition Assistance. **Corporate headquarters location:** This Location. **Other U.S. locations:** Greenville SC. **Number of employees at this location:** 390.

PREMIER-FARNELL
4500 Euclid Avenue, Cleveland OH 44101-4884. 216/391-8300. **Contact:** Corporate Recruiting. **Description:** A distributor of electronic components used in the production and maintenance of equipment; a supplier of maintenance products for industrial, commercial, and institutional applications; and a manufacturer of fire fighting equipment. **Corporate headquarters location:** This Location. **Listed on:** New York Stock Exchange.

PRESSTEK
55 Executive Drive, Hudson NH 03051. 603/595-7000. **Contact:** Cathleen Cavanna, Human Resources Manager. **World Wide Web address:** http://www.presstek.com. **Description:** PRESSTEK develops, manufactures, markets, and services products utilizing its proprietary, non-photographic, digital imaging technologies, system architectures, and consumables used primarily in the graphic arts and related imaging industries. Founded in 1987. **Benefits:** 401(k); Dental Insurance; Disability Coverage; Life Insurance; Medical Insurance; Tuition Assistance. **Corporate headquarters location:** This Location. **Operations at this facility include:** Administration; Divisional Headquarters; Manufacturing; Research and Development; Sales; Service. **Listed on:** NASDAQ. **Number of employees at this location:** 85.

PRIMESOURCE
355 Treck Drive, Seattle WA 98188. 206/575-9494. **Contact:** Bob Miller, Human Resources. **World Wide Web address:** http://www.primesource.com. **Description:** Manufactures and distributes electronic prepress equipment. **Corporate headquarters location:** This Location.

R&B MACHINE TOOL COMPANY
1705 East Woodland Drive, P.O. Box 100, Saline MI 48176. 734/429-9421. **Fax:** 734/429-4965. **Contact:** Sue Trachet, Human Resources Director. **Description:** A manufacturer of metal cutting machinery. **Common positions include:** Accountant/Auditor; CADD Operator; Computer Programmer; Electrical/Electronics Engineer; Electrician; Mechanical Engineer; Quality Control

Supervisor. **Educational backgrounds include:** Engineering. **Benefits:** 401(k); Dental Insurance; Disability Coverage; Life Insurance; Medical Insurance; Pension Plan; Profit Sharing; Savings Plan; Tuition Assistance. **Corporate headquarters location:** This Location. **Listed on:** Privately held. **Number of employees at this location:** 270.

RAGE, INC.
P.O. Box 1300, Plumsteadville PA 18949-1300. 215/766-7700. **Fax:** 215/766-0205. **Contact:** Human Resources. **Description:** Designs and engineers computerized turnkey bulk solid material handling systems for the industrial process industry. Typical systems transport dry powdered materials through closed pipes with air as the conveying medium. **Corporate headquarters location:** This Location.

RAYTECH CORPORATION
4 Corporate Drive, Suite 295, Shelton CT 06484. 203/925-8023. **Contact:** Human Resources. **World Wide Web address:** http://www.raytech.com. **Description:** Raytech Corporation is a multinational manufacturer and marketer of products for heat-resistant, inertia control, energy absorption, and transmission applications. Products are used in the automotive, aerospace, nucleonic, petrochemical, energy, metal working, construction, agricultural, utility, and electronics industries. **Benefits:** Incentive Plan; Stock Option. **Corporate headquarters location:** This Location. **International locations:** England; Germany. **Subsidiaries include:** Raybestos Products develops, manufactures, and markets friction materials for wet clutch and brake applications for vehicle and component manufacturers worldwide; Raybestos Aftermarket Products and Allomatic Products provide aftermarket products for domestic automobiles and trucks, which include automatic transmission filters, and friction and reaction plates.

REMMELE ENGINEERING
10 Old Highway 8, New Brighton MN 55112. 651/635-4100. **Contact:** Human Resources. **World Wide Web address:** http://www.remmele.com. **Description:** Operates a machine shop for large industrial equipment. **Corporate headquarters location:** This Location.

RESEARCH, INC.
6425 Flying Cloud Drive, Eden Prairie MN 55344. 952/941-3300. **Contact:** Karen O'Rourke, Vice President of Human Resources. **World Wide Web address:** http://www.researchinc.com. **Description:** Designs and manufactures product solutions based on the precise control and application of heat. Research, Inc. conducts business with companies worldwide in industries such as graphic arts, semiconductors and printed circuit boards, and plastic extrusion. **Common positions include:** Accountant; Buyer; Customer Service Rep.; Design Engineer; Draftsperson; Electrical/Electronics Engineer; Manufacturing Engineer; Mechanical Engineer; Sales Rep. **Educational backgrounds include:** Business Administration; Engineering. **Benefits:** 401(k); Casual Dress - Daily; Dental Insurance; Disability Coverage; Flexible Schedule; Life Insurance; Medical Insurance; Profit Sharing; Tuition Assistance. **Corporate headquarters location:** This Location. **Listed on:** NASDAQ. **Stock exchange symbol:** RESR. **Annual sales/revenues:** $21 - $50 million. **Number of employees at this location:** 160.

REULAND ELECTRIC
17969 East Railroad Street, City of Industry CA 91748. 626/964-6411. **Contact:** Employee Relations. **Description:** Manufactures custom-designed motors, brakes, and controls for industrial clients. **Common positions include:** Accountant; Administrator; Blue-Collar Worker Supervisor; Buyer; Claim Rep.; Computer Programmer; Credit Manager; Customer Service Rep.; Draftsperson; Economist; Electrical/Electronics Engineer; General Manager; Human Resources Manager; Industrial Designer; Industrial Engineer; Management Trainee; Manufacturer's/Wholesaler's Sales Rep.; Marketing Specialist; Mechanical Engineer; Operations/Production Manager; Public Relations Specialist; Quality Control Supervisor; Systems Analyst. **Educational backgrounds include:** Accounting; Communications; Engineering; Finance; Liberal Arts; Marketing. **Benefits:** Dental Insurance; Disability Coverage; Life Insurance; Medical Insurance; Profit Sharing; Tuition Assistance. **Corporate headquarters location:** This Location.

REVCOR, INC.
251 Edwards Avenue, Carpentersville IL 60110. 847/428-4411. **Fax:** 847/426-0589. **Contact:** Personnel. **World Wide Web address:** http://www.revcor.com. **Description:** Manufactures fans and blowers. **Common positions include:** Accountant; Blue-Collar Worker Supervisor; Customer Service Rep.; Designer; Human Resources Manager; Industrial Production Manager; Mechanical Engineer. **Educational backgrounds include:** Business Administration; Engineering; Finance; Marketing. **Benefits:** 401(k); Dental Insurance; Disability Coverage; Employee Discounts; Life Insurance; Medical Insurance; Profit Sharing; Savings Plan; Tuition Assistance. **Corporate headquarters location:** This Location. **Other U.S. locations:** Fort Worth TX. **Number of employees at this location:** 200.

REXAM CLOSURES
3245 Kansas Road, Evansville IN 47725. 812/867-6671x223. **Fax:** 812/867-6289. **Contact:** Scott Harrell, Manager of Employment. **Description:** Designs, develops, manufactures, and markets closure systems for the packaging industry. The company's products include child-resistant closures, dispensers, screw caps, and tamper-evident systems. Customers include pharmaceutical companies; over-the-counter drug companies; food and cosmetics companies; household, industrial, and agricultural chemical companies; swimming pool chemical companies; and packagers of household cleaners, automotive aftermarket products, and beverages. Founded in 1953. **Common positions include:** Accountant; Blue-Collar Worker Supervisor; Customer Service Rep.; Designer; Human Resources Manager; Mechanical Engineer; Operations/Production Manager; Plastics Engineer. **Educational backgrounds include:** Accounting; Business Administration; Communications; Engineering. **Benefits:** 401(k); Dental Insurance; Disability Coverage; Life Insurance; Medical Insurance; Savings Plan; Tuition Assistance. **Corporate headquarters location:** This Location. **Other U.S. locations:** Princeton IN. **Parent company:** Rexam. **Annual sales/revenues:** $51 - $100 million. **Number of employees at this location:** 325.

REXWORKS INC.
445 West Oklahoma Avenue, Milwaukee WI 53207. 414/747-7200. **Contact:** Human Resources. **Description:** Designs, manufactures, and sells truck-mounted concrete mixers, compaction equipment, and the Maxigrind materials reduction product. Compaction equipment includes sanitary landfill and soil compactors. The Maxigrind product grinds and reduces the volume of a variety of materials including asphalt, demolition debris, wood

products, and trash. The company's products are used to build and repair roads, bridges, airports, sewers, pipelines, and other infrastructure; to compact and cover sanitary landfill sites; and to reduce the volume of grindable material. **Corporate headquarters location:** This Location.

RICHARDS INDUSTRIES
dba JORDAN VALVE
3170 Wasson Road, Cincinnati OH 45209. 513/533-5600. **Toll-free phone:** 800/543-7311. **Fax:** 513/533-2583. **Contact:** Cheryl Koopman, Human Resources Administrator. **World Wide Web address:** http://www.jordanvalve.com. **Description:** A valve manufacturer. **Common positions include:** Accountant; Buyer; Computer Operator; Controller; Credit Manager; Customer Service Representative; Design Engineer; Human Resources Manager; Manufacturing Engineer; Marketing Manager; MIS Specialist; Purchasing Agent/Manager; Quality Control Supervisor; Sales Manager; Sales Representative; Secretary; Typist/Word Processor; Vice President of Sales. **Educational backgrounds include:** Accounting; Business Administration; Computer Science; Economics; Finance; Liberal Arts; Marketing. **Benefits:** 401(k); Dental Insurance; Disability Coverage; Life Insurance; Medical Insurance; Profit Sharing; Savings Plan; Tuition Assistance. **Corporate headquarters location:** This Location. **Other U.S. locations:** Frenchburg KY. **Subsidiaries include:** The Metalworking Group, Cincinnati OH.

RICHARDS-WILCOX, INC.
600 South Lake Street, Aurora IL 60506. 630/897-6951. **Fax:** 630/897-5014. **Contact:** Director of Human Resources. **World Wide Web address:** http://www.richardswilcox.com. **Description:** Engaged in the manufacture and distribution of materials handling equipment and office systems products. Products include overhead chain conveyors, horizontal and vertical carousels, general hardware, Aurora shelving, Timer 2, and mobile base. **Common positions include:** Accountant; Administrative Manager; Blue-Collar Worker Supervisor; Buyer; Clerical Supervisor; Computer Programmer; Credit Manager; Customer Service Representative; Design Engineer; Draftsperson; Electrical/Electronics Engineer; Electrician; Human Resources Manager; Industrial Engineer; Industrial Production Manager; Mechanical Engineer; MIS Specialist; Purchasing Agent/Manager; Quality Control Supervisor; Software Engineer; Systems Analyst; Typist/Word Processor. **Educational backgrounds include:** Accounting; Business Administration; Computer Science; Engineering. **Benefits:** 401(k); Dental Insurance; Disability Coverage; Life Insurance; Medical Insurance; Tuition Assistance. **Corporate headquarters location:** This Location.

ROCKWELL INTERNATIONAL CORP.
777 East Wisconsin Avenue, Suite 1500, Milwaukee WI 53202-5300. 414/212-5200. **Contact:** Human Resources. **World Wide Web address:** http://www.rockwell.com. **Description:** Manufactures products for the printing, military, automotive, and aerospace industries through its electronics, automotive, and graphics divisions. Products include military and commercial communication equipment, guidance systems, electronics, components for automobiles, and printing presses. Rockwell International provides the U.S. government with parts and services for bombers, as well as power systems for the space station. The company is also a contractor for the Space Shuttle Orbiter program. **Corporate headquarters location:** This Location. **Listed on:** New York Stock Exchange.

ROGERS CORPORATION
One Technology Drive, P.O. Box 188, Rogers CT 06263-0188. 860/774-9605. **Contact:** Jack Richie, Human Resources. **World Wide Web address:** http://www.rogers-corp.com. **Description:** Rogers Corporation develops and manufactures specialty polymer composite materials and components for the imaging, communications, computer and peripheral, consumer products, and transportation markets. Rogers Corporation is divided into segments according to the materials produced. The Poron Materials Unit (East Woodstock CT) manufactures urethane and silicone foam materials. The Elastomeric Components Unit (South Windham CT) manufactures foam and solid elastomeric components. The Microwave and Circuit Materials Divisions (Chandler AZ) manufacture high-frequency laminates used to make circuits for communications applications and flexible circuit materials used for interconnections in computers and peripherals. The Composite Materials Division (also at this location) manufactures dielectric material for most of these microwave laminates. The Molding Materials Division (Manchester CT) produces moldable composites using polymer engineering and filler technology. **Benefits:** 401(k); Incentive Plan; Investment Plan; Life Insurance; Medical Insurance; Pension Plan; Savings Plan; Stock Option. **Corporate headquarters location:** This Location. **Subsidiaries include:** Durel Corporation (Tempe and Chandler AZ) is a joint venture between Rogers and 3M, whose business focuses on electroluminescent lamps. **Listed on:** American Stock Exchange; Pacific Stock Exchange.

ROHM & HAAS COMPANY
100 North Riverside Plaza, Chicago IL 60606. 312/807-2000. **Contact:** Human Resources. **Description:** Manufactures industrial and consumer items including Morton brand salt. The company is also a large producer of inflatable air bags for the automotive industry, adhesives for the packaging industry, liquid plastic coatings for automobiles, electronic products used in printed circuit boards and semiconductor wafers, and dyes used by the printing industry. **Corporate headquarters location:** This Location. **International locations:** Bahamas; Canada; Europe; Mexico.

ROPER INDUSTRIES INC.
160 Ben Burton Road, Bogart GA 30622. 706/369-7170. **Fax:** 706/548-2262. **Contact:** Marilyn M. Messer, Director of Human Resources. **Description:** Manufactures industrial control systems, valves, pumps, and related equipment. **Common positions include:** Account Manager; Accountant; Administrative Assistant; Blue-Collar Worker Supervisor; Chief Financial Officer; Computer Operator; Computer Programmer; Controller; Customer Service Rep.; Electrical/Electronics Engineer; Electrician; Environmental Engineer; General Manager; Human Resources Manager; Industrial Engineer; Industrial Production Manager; Manufacturing Engineer; Marketing Manager; Marketing Specialist; Mechanical Engineer; Project Manager; Sales Manager; Sales Representative; Secretary; Software Engineer; Systems Analyst; Systems Manager; Vice President. **Educational backgrounds include:** Accounting; Biology; Engineering; Finance. **Benefits:** 401(k); Dental Insurance; Disability Coverage; Life Insurance; Medical Insurance. **Corporate headquarters location:** This Location. **Other U.S. locations:** Nationwide. **International locations:** France; United Kingdom. **CEO:** Derrick N. Key.

ROSS CONTROLS
P.O. Box 7015, Troy MI 48007-7015. 248/764-1800. **Fax:** 248/764-1850. **Contact:** Human

Resources. **World Wide Web address:** http://www. rosscontrols.com. **Description:** A manufacturer of directional air control devices and related pneumatic products. Founded in 1921. **Common positions include:** Accountant; Administrative Assistant; Administrative Manager; AS400 Programmer Analyst; Attorney; Buyer; Chief Financial Officer; Computer Support Technician; Controller; Desktop Publishing Specialist; Emergency Medical Technician; Human Resources Manager; Industrial Engineer; Manufacturing Engineer; Market Research Analyst; Marketing Manager; Mechanical Engineer; Network/Systems Administrator; Production Manager; Project Manager; Public Relations Specialist; Quality Assurance Engineer; Quality Control Supervisor; Sales Manager; Sales Representative; Secretary; Technical Writer/Editor; Telecommunications Manager; Transportation/ Traffic Specialist; Webmaster. **Educational backgrounds include:** Accounting; AS400 Certification; Business Administration; Communications; Computer Science; Engineering; Finance; Marketing; Microsoft Word; Public Relations. **Benefits:** 401(k); Casual Dress - Daily; Dental Insurance; Disability Coverage; Life Insurance; Medical Insurance; Pension Plan; Profit Sharing; Public Transit Available; Tuition Assistance. **Special programs:** Co-ops; Summer Jobs. **Corporate headquarters location:** This Location. **Other U.S. locations:** GA. **International locations:** Germany; Great Britain; Japan. **Subsidiaries include:** Ross Asia; Ross Europa; Ross Great Britain. **Number of employees at this location:** 45.

S-T INDUSTRIES, INC.
301 Armstrong Boulevard North, P.O. Box 517, St. James MN 56081. 507/375-3211. **Toll-free phone:** 800/326-2039. **Fax:** 507/375-4503. **Contact:** Personnel. **E-mail address:** rjf-st@prairie. lakes.com. **World Wide Web address:** http://www. stindustries.thomasregister.com. **Description:** Manufactures and sells precision measuring instruments, optical comparators, and video inspection systems. **NOTE:** Entry-level positions are offered. **Common positions include:** Accountant; Blue-Collar Worker Supervisor; Buyer; Computer Programmer; Design Engineer; Draftsperson; Electrical/Electronics Engineer; Industrial Engineer; Manufacturer's/Wholesaler's Sales Rep.; Mechanical Engineer; Purchasing Agent/Manager; Quality Control Supervisor. **Educational backgrounds include:** Accounting; Business Administration; Engineering; Liberal Arts. **Benefits:** Disability Coverage; Life Insurance; Medical Insurance; Pension Plan; Savings Plan. **Corporate headquarters location:** This Location. **Listed on:** Privately held. **President:** Michael J. Smith. **Annual sales/revenues:** $5 - $10 million. **Number of employees at this location:** 125.

SI TECHNOLOGIES
14192 Franklin Avenue, Tustin CA 92780. 714/505-6483. **Fax:** 714/505-6484. **Contact:** Human Resources. **World Wide Web address:** http://www. sitechnologies.com. **Description:** Designs, manufactures, and markets industrial sensors, and weighing and factory automation systems. **Corporate headquarters location:** This Location. **Other U.S. locations:** Chicago IL; Cumberland MD; Detroit MI; Mooresville NC; Eugene OR; Lynnwood WA; Seattle WA. **International locations:** Canada; France; Germany; the Netherlands; United Kingdom. **Listed on:** NASDAQ. **Stock exchange symbol:** SISI. **President/CEO:** Rick A. Beets. **Annual sales/revenues:** $21 - $50 million. **Number of employees worldwide:** 400.

SACO LOWELL, INC.
183 Rolling Hills Circle, Arial SC 29640. 864/859-3211. **Fax:** 864/850-4322. **Contact:** Brent O'Shields, Human Resources Director. **Description:** Saco Lowell, Inc. designs and manufactures textile machinery including parts, attachments, and accessories. The company's primary customers are textile mills. **Common positions include:** Accountant; Adjuster; Administrative Manager; Advertising Clerk; Blue-Collar Worker Supervisor; Buyer; CADD Operator; Claim Rep.; Computer Programmer; Cost Estimator; Customer Service Rep.; Designer; Draftsperson; Economist; Editor; Electrical/Electronics Engineer; Electrician; Emergency Medical Technician; Environmental Engineer; Financial Analyst; General Manager; Human Resources Manager; Industrial Engineer; Industrial Production Manager; Inspector/ Tester/Grader; Machinist; Management Trainee; Manufacturer's/Wholesaler's Sales Rep.; Marketing Manager; Mechanical Engineer; Metallurgical Engineer; Millwright; Payroll Clerk; Postal Clerk/ Mail Carrier; Purchasing Agent/Manager; Quality Control Supervisor; Receptionist; Sheet-Metal Worker; Systems Analyst; Technical Writer/Editor; Tool and Die Maker; Truck Driver; Typist/Word Processor; Water Transportation Specialist. **Educational backgrounds include:** Accounting; Business Administration; Computer Science; Engineering; Finance; Liberal Arts; Marketing; Mathematics; Physics. **Benefits:** Dental Insurance; Disability Coverage; Employee Discounts; Life Insurance; Medical Insurance; Pension Plan; Savings Plan; Tuition Assistance. **Corporate headquarters location:** This Location. **Number of employees at this location:** 500.

SAGEM MORPHO
1145 Broadway Plaza, Suite 200, Tacoma WA 98402-3253. 253/383-3617. **Fax:** 253/591-8856. **Contact:** Allyson Thomas, Human Resources Manager. **Description:** Manufactures and sells automated fingerprinting technologies to law enforcement and other civil service agencies. **NOTE:** Entry-level positions are offered. **Common positions include:** Account Manager; Accountant; Budget Analyst; Buyer; Computer Programmer; Design Engineer; Electrical/Electronics Engineer; Financial Analyst; Human Resources Manager; Multimedia Designer; Software Engineer; Systems Analyst; Technical Writer/Editor. **Educational backgrounds include:** Accounting; Business Administration; Computer Science; Engineering; Finance; Marketing; Mathematics; Physics. **Benefits:** 401(k); Dental Insurance; Disability Coverage; Job Sharing; Life Insurance; Medical Insurance; Parking; Profit Sharing; Tuition Assistance. **Special programs:** Internships. **Corporate headquarters location:** This Location. **Parent company:** Sagem Groupe. **Listed on:** Privately held. **Annual sales/revenues:** $21 - $50 million. **Number of employees at this location:** 150. **Number of employees nationwide:** 350.

SARGENT & GREENLEAF INC.
P.O. Box 930, Nicholasville KY 40340. 606/885-9411. **Contact:** Ms. Herron, Industrial Relations Manager. **Description:** Produces high-security locks and access controls and devices. **Common positions include:** Accountant/Auditor; Blue-Collar Worker Supervisor; Buyer; Computer Programmer; Credit Manager; Customer Service Rep.; Department Manager; Draftsperson; Financial Analyst; General Manager; Human Resources Manager; Industrial Designer; Industrial Engineer; Manufacturer's/ Wholesaler's Sales Rep.; Marketing Specialist; Mechanical Engineer; Operations/Production Manager; Purchasing Agent/Manager; Quality Control Supervisor; Systems Analyst. **Educational**

backgrounds include: Accounting; Business Administration; Engineering; Finance; Marketing. Benefits: Disability Coverage; Life Insurance; Medical Insurance; Pension Plan; Tuition Assistance. Corporate headquarters location: This Location.

SCHAFER GEAR WORKS
4701 Nimtz Parkway, South Bend IN 46628. 219/234-4116. Fax: 219/234-4115. Contact: Carol Senour, Human Resources Manager. World Wide Web address: http://www.schafergear.com. Description: A manufacturer of precision gears. Common positions include: Accountant/Auditor; Industrial Engineer; Mechanical Engineer. Educational backgrounds include: Accounting; Business Administration; Engineering. Benefits: 401(k); Life Insurance; Medical Insurance; Tuition Assistance. Corporate headquarters location: This Location. Other area locations: Elkhart IN; Fort Wayne IN. Number of employees at this location: 70.

SCHLUMBERGER MALCO, INC.
9800 Reisterstown Road, Owings Mills MD 21117. 410/363-1600. Fax: 410/363-4336. Contact: Gaye Saller, Employment Coordinator. World Wide Web address: http://www.slb.com. Description: Manufactures a variety of plastic products including credit cards and advertising specialties. Schlumberger Malco also provides screen process printing, lithography, and embossing services. Common positions include: Blue-Collar Worker Supervisor; Buyer; Chemist; Systems Analyst; Tailor. Benefits: Dental Insurance; Disability Coverage; Life Insurance; Medical Insurance; Pension Plan; Profit Sharing; Tuition Assistance. Corporate headquarters location: This Location. Parent company: Schlumberger. Listed on: New York Stock Exchange. Number of employees at this location: 300.

SCHUTTE & KOERTING, INC.
2233 State Road, Bensalem PA 19020. 215/639-0900. Fax: 215/245-4690. Contact: Ms. Sandy Flowers, Director of Human Resources. World Wide Web address: http://www.s-k.com. Description: Manufactures power and process vacuum equipment and turbine meter instrumentation. Founded in 1876. Common positions include: Electrical/Electronics Engineer; Sales Engineer. Educational backgrounds include: Engineering; Marketing. Benefits: 401(k); Dental Insurance; Disability Coverage; Life Insurance; Medical Insurance; Profit Sharing; Savings Plan; Tuition Assistance. Corporate headquarters location: This Location. Listed on: Privately held. Number of employees at this location: 100.

SCOTT TECHNOLOGIES
2000 Auburn Drive, Suite 400, Beechwood OH 44122. 216/464-6153. Contact: Human Resources. Description: A leading designer and manufacturer of high-performance respiratory systems including air packs and drop-down oxygen masks for aerospace, aviation, defense, fire fighting, government, and industrial markets. Corporate headquarters location: This Location. Listed on: NASDAQ.

SCULLY-JONES CORPORATION
1901 South Rockwell Street, Chicago IL 60608. 773/247-5900. Contact: Gerald Walton, Personnel Director. World Wide Web address: http://www.scullyjones.com. Description: A manufacturer of precision toolholders for machine tools. Common positions include: Accountant/Auditor; Computer Programmer; Customer Service Rep.; Industrial Engineer; Mechanical Engineer; Purchasing Agent/

Manager; Quality Control Supervisor; Systems Analyst. Educational backgrounds include: Business Administration; Computer Science; Engineering. Benefits: Dental Insurance; Disability Coverage; Life Insurance; Medical Insurance; Profit Sharing; Savings Plan; Tuition Assistance. Corporate headquarters location: This Location.

SEALED AIR CORPORATION
Park 80 East, Saddle Brook NJ 07663. 201/791-7600. Contact: Manager of Employee Benefits. World Wide Web address: http://www.sealedaircorp.com. Description: This location produces specialized protective packaging materials and systems that reduce or eliminate the damage to products that may occur during shipping. Overall, Sealed Air Corporation is a diversified worldwide enterprise consisting of specialty and agricultural chemicals, energy production and services, retailing, restaurants, and other businesses. The firm operates over 2,500 facilities worldwide. Benefits: 401(k); Dental Insurance; Disability Coverage; Life Insurance; Medical Insurance; Profit Sharing; Tuition Assistance. Corporate headquarters location: This Location. Other U.S. locations: Danbury CT; Holyoke MA; Scotia NY. Number of employees at this location: 35. Number of employees nationwide: 2,000.

SEAQUISTPERFECT DISPENSING
1160 North Silver Lake Road, Cary IL 60013. 847/639-2124. Contact: Rob Revak, Director of Human Resources. World Wide Web address: http://www.seaqperf.com. Description: Manufactures aerosol valves and spray pumps. Common positions include: Accountant/Auditor; Designer; Mechanical Engineer. Educational backgrounds include: Engineering. Benefits: 401(k); Bonus Award/Plan; Daycare Assistance; Dental Insurance; Disability Coverage; Life Insurance; Medical Insurance; Pension Plan; Savings Plan; Tuition Assistance. Special programs: Internships. Corporate headquarters location: This Location. Parent company: Aptar Group. Listed on: New York Stock Exchange. Number of employees at this location: 400.

SELAS CORPORATION OF AMERICA
2034 South Limekiln Pike, P.O. Box 200, Dresher PA 19025. 215/646-6600. Fax: 215/646-3536. Contact: Robert W. Mason, Director of Human Resources and Administration. World Wide Web address: http://www.selas.com. Description: A diversified firm that engages in the design, development, engineering, and manufacturing of a wide range of specialized industrial heat processing systems and equipment for steel, glass, and other manufacturers. Educational backgrounds include: Engineering. Benefits: 401(k); Dental Insurance; Disability Coverage; Life Insurance; Medical Insurance; Pension Plan; Tuition Assistance. Corporate headquarters location: This Location. Subsidiaries include: Deuer Manufacturing, Inc. manufactures spare tire holders, lifts, and related products, primarily based on cable winch designs, for use as original equipment by the pick-up truck and minivan segment of the automotive industry; Resistance Technology, Inc. designs and manufactures microminiature components and molded plastic parts primarily for the hearing instrument manufacturing industry worldwide. Listed on: American Stock Exchange. Stock exchange symbol: SLS. Annual sales/revenues: $51 - $100 million.

SEMICONDUCTOR PROCESS EQUIPMENT CORP.
25145 Anza Drive, Valencia CA 91355. 661/257-0934. Fax: 661/257-1083. Contact: Dede Long, Recruiter. Description: A leading manufacturer of

specialized processing equipment used by semiconductor manufacturers. Founded in 1986. **Common positions include:** Electrical/Electronics Engineer; Electrician; Mechanical Engineer; Project Manager; Sales Engineer; Software Engineer; Technical Writer/Editor. **Educational backgrounds include:** Engineering. **Benefits:** Dental Insurance; Disability Coverage; Employee Discounts; Life Insurance; Medical Insurance; Profit Sharing; Savings Plan. **Office hours:** Monday - Friday, 8:00 a.m. - 5:00 p.m. **Corporate headquarters location:** This Location. **Listed on:** Privately held. **Annual sales/revenues:** $11 - $20 million. **Number of employees at this location:** 125.

SHERWOOD

2200 North Main Street, Washington PA 15301. 724/225-8000. **Contact:** Douglas F. Patterson, Director of Human Resources. **World Wide Web address:** http://www.sherwoodvalve.com. **Description:** Produces a variety of flow control devices for the compressed gas, air conditioning, and refrigeration industry. **Common positions include:** Accountant; Economist; Human Resources Manager; Mechanical Engineer. **Educational backgrounds include:** Accounting; Business Administration; Engineering. **Benefits:** 401(k); Dental Insurance; Disability Coverage; Life Insurance; Medical Insurance; Pension Plan; Savings Plan; Tuition Assistance. **Corporate headquarters location:** Harrisburg PA. **Parent company:** Harsco Corporation. **Listed on:** New York Stock Exchange. **Number of employees at this location:** 285.

SIMMONS MANUFACTURING COMPANY

P.O. Box 509, McDonough GA 30253. 770/957-3976. **Contact:** Bob Engeman, Jr., Personnel Manager. **Description:** Produces a variety of flow control products including valves, seals, and hydrants. **Corporate headquarters location:** This Location.

SLOAN VALVE COMPANY

10500 Seymour Avenue, Franklin Park IL 60131. 847/671-4300. **Contact:** Personnel. **World Wide Web address:** http://www.sloanvalve.com. **Description:** An international manufacturer of valves for toilets, railroad cars, air brakes, and faucets. Brand names include Slimline, Flushmate, Act-O-Matic, and Optima. **Common positions include:** Accountant; Civil Engineer; Designer; Electrical/Electronics Engineer; Electrician; Industrial Engineer; Machinist; Mechanical Engineer. **Educational backgrounds include:** Business Administration; Engineering. **Benefits:** 401(k); Dental Insurance; Disability Coverage; Life Insurance; Medical Insurance; Pension Plan; Profit Sharing; Savings Plan; Tuition Assistance. **Corporate headquarters location:** This Location. **Other U.S. locations:** AR. **Listed on:** Privately held. **Number of employees at this location:** 750.

A.O. SMITH CORPORATION

P.O. Box 245010, Milwaukee WI 53223-0974. 414/359-4000. **Physical address:** 11270 West Park Place, Milwaukee WI 53224. **Contact:** Human Resources Department. **World Wide Web address:** http://www.aosmith.com. **Description:** A diverse manufacturer of products including chassis frames, electric motors, water heaters, and fiberglass piping systems for the construction, agricultural, financial, chemical, power generation, wastewater, and petroleum industries. **Corporate headquarters location:** This Location.

SONOCO PRODUCTS

North Second Street, Hartsville SC 29550. 843/383-7000. **Contact:** Human Resources. **World Wide Web address:** http://www.sonoco.com. **Description:** Manufactures paper and plastic cones, tubes, cores and spools; composite cans and containers; plastic bottles; plastic meter boxes and underground enclosures; specialties; partitions and pads; paperboard; aluminum and steel textile beams; machinery products; hardwood lumber; plastic grocery bags; metal, plastic, and wood reels; adhesives; fiber and plastic drums; and dual oven trays. **Corporate headquarters location:** This Location. **Other U.S. locations:** Orlando FL; Marietta GA.

SOUTHWORTH PRODUCTS

P.O. Box 1380, Portland ME 04104. 207/878-0700. **Contact:** John Lemire, Director of Human Resources. **World Wide Web address:** http://www.southworthproducts.com. **Description:** Manufactures hydraulic lift tables, packaging equipment, conveyors, and material handling systems. **Common positions include:** Accountant; Credit Manager; Customer Service Representative; Draftsperson; Electrical/Electronics Engineer; Industrial Designer; Manufacturer's/Wholesaler's Sales Rep.; Mechanical Engineer; Operations/Production Manager. **Educational backgrounds include:** Accounting; Business Administration; Engineering. **Benefits:** Dental Insurance; Disability Coverage; Life Insurance; Medical Insurance; Pension Plan; Savings Plan; Tuition Assistance. **Corporate headquarters location:** This Location.

SPACEMASTER

1400 North 25th Avenue, Melrose Park IL 60160. 708/345-2500. **Contact:** Linda Atkinson, Personnel Director. **World Wide Web address:** http://www. spacemaster.com. **Description:** Manufactures store fixtures, office furniture, and library equipment. **Corporate headquarters location:** This Location.

SPECIAL PRODUCTS COMPANY

15000 West 44th Avenue, Golden CO 80403. 303/279-5544. **Contact:** Larry Foot, Controller. **Description:** Engaged in custom steel fabrication, the fabrication of screw machine products, the manufacture of agricultural equipment attachments (blades, hitches, tractor accessories, specialized digging equipment), and the fabrication of other metal products. **Corporate headquarters location:** This Location.

SPIRAX SARCO INC.

1150 Northpoint Boulevard, Blythewood SC 29016. 803/714-2000. **Contact:** Human Resources. **Description:** A leading supplier of steam system solutions. The company manufactures regulators, controls, steam traps, strainers, pumps, and other steam specialty products. **Common positions include:** Advertising Clerk; Blue-Collar Worker Supervisor; Branch Manager; Buyer; Claim Representative; Clerical Supervisor; Computer Programmer; Credit Manager; Customer Service Representative; Designer; Draftsperson; Electrician; Environmental Engineer; General Manager; Human Resources Manager; Industrial Engineer; Industrial Production Manager; Management Trainee; Materials Engineer; Mechanical Engineer; Operations/Production Manager; Public Relations Specialist; Purchasing Agent/Manager; Quality Control Supervisor; Systems Analyst; Transportation/Traffic Specialist. **Educational backgrounds include:** Business Administration; Engineering; Marketing. **Benefits:** 401(k); Dental Insurance; Disability Coverage; Life Insurance; Medical Insurance; Pension Plan; Tuition Assistance. **Corporate headquarters location:** This Location. **Parent company:** Spirax Sarco Engineering plc. **Number of employees at this location:** 410.

SPRAYING SYSTEMS COMPANY
P.O. Box 7900, Wheaton IL 60189. 630/665-5000.
Contact: Jim Yehling, Director of Human
Resources. **World Wide Web address:** http://www.
spray.com. **Description:** Manufactures spraying
components for industrial use. Products include air
atomizing, tank wash, air control, spray/dry, and gas
conditioning nozzles; spray guns; and portable
spray systems. **Corporate headquarters location:**
This Location. **Number of employees at this
location:** 1,300.

STAINLESS INC.
One Stainless Plaza, Deerfield Beach FL 33441.
954/421-4290x224. **Fax:** 954/421-4464. **Contact:**
Elizabeth Mountcastle, Manager of Human
Resources. **Description:** Manufactures and
distributes commercial restaurant equipment.
Common positions include: Accountant/Auditor;
Administrator; Architectural Engineer; Blue-Collar
Worker Supervisor; Buyer; Computer Programmer;
Credit Manager; Customer Service Representative;
Department Manager; Draftsperson; Human
Resources Manager; Manufacturer's/Wholesaler's
Sales Rep.; Operations/Production Manager;
Quality Control Supervisor; Transportation/Traffic
Specialist. **Educational backgrounds include:**
Accounting; Business Administration; Liberal Arts.
Benefits: Dental Insurance; Disability Coverage;
Employee Discounts; Life Insurance; Medical
Insurance; Pension Plan; Profit Sharing; Tuition
Assistance. **Corporate headquarters location:**
This Location. **Number of employees at this
location:** 150.

STAR CUTTER COMPANY
P.O. Box 376, Farmington MI 48332. 248/474-
8200. **Contact:** Tim Zoia, Human Resources
Manager. **Description:** Manufactures machine tools.
Common positions include: Accountant/Auditor;
Blue-Collar Worker Supervisor; Buyer; Computer
Programmer; Customer Service Representative;
Design Engineer; Environmental Engineer;
Mechanical Engineer; Metallurgical Engineer;
Purchasing Agent/Manager; Quality Control
Supervisor; Services Sales Representative; Systems
Analyst. **Benefits:** 401(k); Dental Insurance;
Disability Coverage; Life Insurance; Medical
Insurance; Pension Plan; Profit Sharing; Tuition
Assistance. **Corporate headquarters location:**
This Location. **Listed on:** Privately held. **Number
of employees at this location:** 750.

STAR MANUFACTURING INTERNATIONAL
P.O. Box 430129, St. Louis MO 63143. 314/781-
2777. **Physical address:** 10 Sunnen Drive, St. Louis
MO. **Contact:** Human Resources. **World
Wide Web address:** http://www.star-mfg.com.
Description: Manufacturers of commercial food
service and concession equipment. **Common
positions include:** Accountant/Auditor; Buyer;
Computer Programmer; Credit Manager; Customer
Service Rep.; Draftsperson; Manufacturer's/
Wholesaler's Sales Rep.; Mechanical Engineer;
Purchasing Agent/Manager; Quality Control
Supervisor. **Educational backgrounds include:**
Accounting; Business Administration; Computer
Science; Engineering; Finance; Marketing.
Benefits: Dental Insurance; Disability Coverage;
Life Insurance; Medical Insurance; Pension Plan;
Profit Sharing; Tuition Assistance. **Corporate
headquarters location:** This Location. **Other U.S.
locations:** TN.

L.S. STARRETT COMPANY
121 Crescent Street, Athol MA 01331. 978/249-
3551. **Contact:** Personnel. **World Wide Web
address:** http://www.starrett.com. **Description:**
Manufactures industrial, professional, and consumer
products. Among the items produced are precision
tools, tape measures, levels, electronic gages, dial
indicators, gage blocks, digital-readout measuring
tools, granite surface plates, optical measuring
projectors, and coordinate measuring vises. Much of
the company's production is concentrated in hand
measuring tools and precision instruments. These
products are sold throughout the United States and
in over 100 foreign countries. **Corporate
headquarters location:** This Location. **Other U.S.
locations:** NC; OH; PA; SC. **International
locations:** Brazil; England; Puerto Rico; Scotland.

STEELCASE INC.
P.O. Box 1967, Grand Rapids MI 49501. 616/247-
2710. **Contact:** Tom Dryer, Employee Relations
Manager. **World Wide Web address:** http://www.
steelcase.com. **Description:** Manufactures office
furniture. **Corporate headquarters location:** This
Location.

STEVENS INDUSTRIES INC.
704 West Main Street, Teutopolis IL 62467.
217/857-6411. **Fax:** 217/857-3638. **Contact:**
Human Resources. **World Wide Web
address:** http://www.stevensind.com. **Description:**
A manufacturer of laminated case goods, integrated
component parts, and panels. **Common positions
include:** Blue-Collar Worker Supervisor; Computer
Programmer; Construction Contractor; Cost
Estimator; Customer Service Rep.; Draftsperson;
Industrial Engineer; Industrial Production Manager;
Mechanical Engineer; Operations/Production
Manager; Purchasing Agent/Manager; Quality
Control Supervisor; Systems Analyst;
Transportation/Traffic Specialist; Wholesale and
Retail Buyer. **Educational backgrounds include:**
Business Administration; Engineering; Industrial
Technology. **Benefits:** 401(k); Employee Discounts;
Life Insurance; Medical Insurance; Tuition
Assistance. **Corporate headquarters location:**
This Location.

STEWART & STEVENSON INC.
4516 Harrisburg Boulevard, Houston TX 77011.
713/923-2161. **Contact:** Ginnie Bordelone,
Personnel Director. **Description:** Manufactures a
broad line of products, primarily diesel or gas
turbine powered, serving a multitude of industries
and markets. Stewart & Stevenson Inc. has three
principal divisions. Engine Operations engineers
and builds power systems utilizing diesel or gas
turbine engines for such uses as irrigation systems,
oil well drilling rigs, and generators. Electric
Operations produces a line of switchgear and
control systems for numerous industries. Other
Operations include materials handling equipment
and refrigeration equipment for the transportation
industry. **Corporate headquarters location:** This
Location.

STILLMAN HEATING PRODUCTS
1011 Volunteer Drive, P.O. Box 789, Cookeville
TN 38501. 931/526-3351. **Contact:** Priscilla Cox,
Manager of Human Resources. **Description:**
Manufactures heating elements for domestic electric
ranges. **Parent company:** Zoppas Industries.

STORK GAMCO
P.O. Box 1258, Gainesville GA 30503. 770/532-
7041. **Contact:** Juanita Beasley, Personnel Director.
Description: Produces and markets a variety of
products and equipment used in the poultry
processing industry. **Corporate headquarters
location:** This Location.

STRATEGIC DIAGNOSTICS, INC.
111 Pencader Drive, Newark DE 19702. 302/456-
6789. **Toll-free phone:** 800/544-8881. **Fax:**

302/456-6770. **Contact:** Martha Reider, Vice President of Human Resources. **World Wide Web address:** http://www.sdix.com. **Description:** Develops, manufactures, and markets immunoassay-based test kits for rapid and cost-effective detection of a wide variety of substances in three primary market categories: agricultural, water quality, and industrial. Strategic Diagnostics is a leader in the field of immunoassay research, development, and manufacturing. The company develops products in markets where the attributes of immunoassay technology (speed, ease-of-use, low cost-per-test, quantitation, and flexibility) meet specific customer needs. The substances detected by the company's test kits include chemicals used to treat drinking water, proprietary chemicals used in industrial processes, environmental contaminants, pesticides, genetically engineered traits in plants, and diseases in commercial crops. Founded in 1990. **Common positions include:** Accountant; Administrative Assistant; Biochemist; Biological Scientist; Chief Financial Officer; Computer Technician; Controller; Customer Service Representative; Human Resources Manager; Marketing Manager; MIS Specialist; Production Manager; Project Manager; Quality Control Supervisor; Sales Executive; Sales Manager; Sales Representative; Systems Manager; Vice President of Operations. **Educational backgrounds include:** Biology; Marketing; Microsoft Office; Microsoft Word; Novell; Spreadsheets. **Benefits:** 401(k); Dental Insurance; Disability Coverage; Financial Planning Assistance; Flexible Schedule; Life Insurance; Medical Insurance; Sick Days (6 - 10); Tuition Assistance; Vacation Days (10 - 20). **Office hours:** Monday - Friday, 8:00 a.m. - 5:00 p.m. **Corporate headquarters location:** This Location. **Other U.S. locations:** Ramona CA; Windham ME. **International locations:** England. **Subsidiaries include:** Strategic BioSolutions. **Listed on:** NASDAQ. **Stock exchange symbol:** SDIX. **Vice President:** Martha Reider. **Annual sales/revenues:** $21 - $50 million. **Number of employees at this location:** 95.

SUNBRAND
3900 Green Industrial Way, Atlanta GA 30341. 770/455-0664. **Contact:** Personnel Director. **World Wide Web address:** http://www.sunbrand.com. **Description:** Engaged in the manufacture and distribution of sewing machine parts, a wide range of other related products including pressing and cutting equipment, and other supplies and equipment purchased by the apparel and related industries. **Corporate headquarters location:** This Location. **Parent company:** Willcox & Gibb (New York NY) manufactures and markets apparel and textile supplies and equipment.

SUNROC CORPORATION
P.O. Box 7054, Dover DE 19903-7054. 302/678-7800. **Fax:** 302/678-7810. **Contact:** Rhonda Davis, Personnel Manager. **World Wide Web address:** http://www.sunroc.com. **Description:** Manufactures a wide range of water coolers and drinking fountains. Founded in 1922. **NOTE:** Entry-level positions are offered. **Common positions include:** Accountant; Administrative Assistant; Buyer; Chief Financial Officer; Computer Operator; Computer Programmer; Controller; Credit Manager; Customer Service Rep.; Design Engineer; Draftsperson; Mechanical Engineer; Quality Control Supervisor; Sales Executive; Sales Representative; Secretary; Vice President of Operations; Vice President of Sales. **Educational backgrounds include:** Accounting; Business Administration; Engineering; Finance. **Benefits:** 401(k); Dental Insurance; Disability Coverage; Life Insurance; Medical Insurance; Profit Sharing; Tuition Assistance.

Special programs: Summer Jobs. **Corporate headquarters location:** This Location. **Listed on:** Privately held. **Number of employees at this location:** 300.

SYMONS CORPORATION
200 East Touhy Avenue, Des Plaines IL 60018. 847/298-3200. **Fax:** 847/635-9287. **Contact:** Richard M. Wolter, Corporate Personnel Manager. **E-mail address:** info@symons.com. **World Wide Web address:** http://www.symons.com. **Description:** An international manufacturer of standard, custom, and fiberglass concrete-forming equipment. The company also manufactures chemical systems including acrylic sealers, bonding agents, construction grouts, and curing compounds. **Common positions include:** Accountant/Auditor; Advertising Clerk; Buyer; Civil Engineer; Computer Programmer; Credit Manager; Customer Service Rep.; Draftsperson; Human Resources Manager; Industrial Engineer; Manufacturer's/Wholesaler's Sales Rep.; Purchasing Agent/Manager; Quality Control Supervisor. **Educational backgrounds include:** Business Administration; Computer Science; Engineering; Marketing. **Benefits:** Dental Insurance; Disability Coverage; Employee Discounts; Life Insurance; Medical Insurance; Pension Plan; Savings Plan; Tuition Assistance. **Corporate headquarters location:** This Location.

T&L AUTOMATICS INC.
770 Emerson Street, Rochester NY 14613. 716/647-3717. **Contact:** Human Resources. **Description:** A manufacturer of aluminum shop fittings. **Corporate headquarters location:** This Location. **Number of employees at this location:** 20.

TRW INC.
1900 Richmond Road, Cleveland OH 44124. 216/291-7000. **Contact:** Human Resources. **World Wide Web address:** http://www.trw.com. **Description:** Engaged in the research, development, and the engineering of materials, products, and processes; and offers metallurgical and chemical services. Other divisions of TRW produce electronics and space systems, car and truck equipment for both original equipment manufacturers and the replacement market, and a wide variety of industrial and energy components including aircraft parts, welding systems, and electromechanical assemblies. **Corporate headquarters location:** This Location. **Annual sales/revenues:** More than $100 million.

TAB PRODUCTS COMPANY
1400 Page Mill Road, Palo Alto CA 94304-1179. 650/852-2400. **Fax:** 650/852-2524. **Contact:** Human Resources. **World Wide Web address:** http://www.tab.com. **Description:** A document management company specializing in managing paper-based through electronic documents. Products and services include lateral color-coding filing supplies, storage and mobile systems, document management software, imaging services, and professional services. **Common positions include:** Accountant/Auditor; Adjuster; Budget Analyst; Buyer; Computer Programmer; Credit Manager; Customer Service Rep.; Economist; Financial Analyst; Services Sales Rep.; Software Engineer; Systems Analyst; Technical Writer/Editor. **Educational backgrounds include:** Accounting; Business Administration; Communications; Computer Science; Engineering; Finance; Marketing; Mathematics. **Benefits:** 401(k); Dental Insurance; Disability Coverage; Employee Discounts; Life Insurance; Medical Insurance; Pension Plan; Savings Plan; Tuition Assistance. **Corporate headquarters location:** This Location. **Other U.S. locations:** Nationwide. **Number of**

employees at this location: 120. Number of employees nationwide: 1,000.

TALLEY DEFENSE SYSTEMS
P.O. Box 34299, Mesa AZ 85277-4299. 480/898-2200. Contact: Ms. M. Franklin, Human Resources Manager. Description: An international development and manufacturing facility using forms of solid propellant material used in automotive airbag and defense systems and subsystems for the United States government. The company offers a broad product line built around innovative applications of propellant technology including automotive airbag inflators; gas generators; artillery range extension devices; rocket motors; ballistic devices; stores ejector racks; dispersion and inflation systems; and direct fire weapon systems. Common positions include: Aerospace Engineer; Chemist; Design Engineer; Mechanical Engineer. Educational backgrounds include: Chemistry; Engineering. Benefits: 401(k); Dental Insurance; Life Insurance; Medical Insurance; Pension Plan; Tuition Assistance. Listed on: New York Stock Exchange.

TEKTRONIX, INC.
P.O. Box 500, Mail Stop 55-545, Beaverton OR 97077-0001. 503/627-7111. Contact: Professional Staffing. World Wide Web address: http://www.tek.com. Description: This location manufactures oscilloscopes. Overall, Tektronix, Inc. produces electronic test and measurement, computer graphics, and communications equipment. Test and measurement products include oscilloscopes, logic analyzers, digitizers, and curve tracers. Computer graphics products include printers and terminals primarily for scientific and engineering uses. Communications equipment includes vectorscopes, waveform monitors, signal generators, cable and fiberoptic testers, demodulators, and television routing and switching items. Common positions include: Broadcast Technician; Ceramics Engineer; Chemical Engineer; Chemist; Computer Programmer; Credit Manager; Customer Service Rep.; Electrical/Electronics Engineer; General Manager; Human Resources Manager; Industrial Production Manager; Materials Engineer; Mechanical Engineer; Metallurgical Engineer; Operations/Production Manager; Public Relations Specialist; Purchasing Agent/Manager; Software Engineer; Systems Analyst; Technical Writer/Editor. Educational backgrounds include: Business Administration; Chemistry; Computer Science; Engineering; Finance. Benefits: 401(k); Dental Insurance; Disability Coverage; Employee Discounts; Life Insurance; Medical Insurance; Pension Plan; Profit Sharing; Sick Days; Tuition Assistance; Vacation Days. Special programs: Internships. Corporate headquarters location: This Location. Other area locations: Wilsonville OR. Other U.S. locations: Nationwide.

TELEDYNE TECHNOLOGIES INC.
2049 Century Park East, Los Angeles CA 90067. 310/277-3311. Contact: Human Resources Department. World Wide Web address: http://www.teledynetechnologies.com. Description: Manufactures avionics systems, broadband communications subsystems, and engines for the aerospace, defense, and manufacturing industries. The company also provides engineering and information technology services to corporate and government clients. Corporate headquarters location: This Location.

TELEFLEX INC.
SERMATECH
155 South Limerick Road, Limerick PA 19468. 610/948-5100. Contact: Human Resources. Description: This location houses administrative offices. Overall, Teleflex operates in two industry segments: The Technical Products and Services segment includes the manufacturing of precision mechanical and electromechanical control equipment and other products for the aerospace, chemical processing, and medical industries. The Commercial Products segment is engaged in the design and manufacture of commercial controls, control systems, hydraulics, instruments, and other products with applications in the automotive, marine, and other industries. NOTE: Please send all resumes to Ronald Boldt, Vice President of Human Resources, Teleflex Inc., 630 West Germantown Pike, Suite 450, Plymouth Meeting PA 19462. Corporate headquarters location: This Location.

TEMPLETON, KENLY & COMPANY, INC.
2525 Gardner Road, Broadview IL 60155. 708/865-1500. Contact: Manager of Personnel. Description: Manufactures hydraulic and mechanical jacks. Common positions include: Accountant/Auditor; Computer Programmer; Credit Manager; Customer Service Representative; Draftsperson; General Manager; Human Resources Manager; Industrial Engineer; Mechanical Engineer; Operations/Production Manager; Purchasing Agent/Manager; Quality Control Supervisor; Transportation/Traffic Specialist. Educational backgrounds include: Accounting; Computer Science; Engineering; Marketing. Benefits: Dental Insurance; Disability Coverage; EAP; Life Insurance; Medical Insurance; Profit Sharing; Savings Plan; Tuition Assistance. Corporate headquarters location: This Location.

TEMPTRONIC CORPORATION
55 Chapel Street, Newton MA 02458. 617/969-2501. Fax: 617/969-2475. Contact: Human Resources. World Wide Web address: http://www.temptronic.com. Description: Produces controlled temperature test equipment. NOTE: Entry-level positions are offered. Common positions include: Accountant; Blue-Collar Worker Supervisor; Customer Service Rep.; Design Engineer; Designer; Draftsperson; Human Resources Manager; Market Research Analyst; MIS Specialist; Quality Control Supervisor; Software Engineer; Systems Analyst; Technical Writer/Editor; Typist/Word Processor. Educational backgrounds include: Accounting; Art/Design; Business Administration; Chemistry; Computer Science; Engineering; Finance; Liberal Arts; Marketing. Benefits: 4-Day Work Week; 401(k); Dental Insurance; Disability Coverage; Life Insurance; Medical Insurance; Profit Sharing; Tuition Assistance. Special programs: Internships. Corporate headquarters location: This Location. Listed on: Privately held. Annual sales/revenues: $11 - $20 million. Number of employees at this location: 100.

TENNANT COMPANY
P.O. Box 1452, Minneapolis MN 55440. 612/540-1200. Physical address: 701 North Lilac Drive, Minneapolis MN. Fax: 612/513-1754. Contact: Human Resources. World Wide Web address: http://www.tennantco.com. Description: Manufactures floor maintenance equipment including industrial sweepers and scrubbers, floor coating machinery, and commercial equipment. Common positions include: Automotive Mechanic; Chemist; Customer Service Representative; Services Sales Representative; Systems Engineer. Educational backgrounds include: Business Administration; Chemistry; Computer Science; Engineering; Marketing. Benefits: 401(k); Dental Insurance; Disability Coverage; Life Insurance; Medical Insurance; Pension Plan; Profit Sharing; Tuition Assistance. Corporate headquarters location: This Location.

TERADYNE, INC.
321 Harrison Avenue, Boston MA 02118. 617/482-2700. **Contact:** Personnel. **World Wide Web address:** http://www.teradyne.com. **Description:** Designs and manufactures a variety of automatic test equipment. **NOTE:** Please refer to the company's Website for instructions about where resumes for each available position should be directed. If no applicable jobs are available, resumes may be directed to this location and will be entered into a searchable database. **Corporate headquarters location:** This Location.

TEREX CORPORATION
500 Post Road East, Suite 320, Westport CT 06880. 203/222-5905. **Contact:** Steven Hooper, Vice President. **Description:** Develops, manufactures, and markets a variety of vehicles and related components, primarily for the lifting and earth moving industries. Products include loaders, haulers, scrapers, cranes, trucks, tractors, and replacement parts. **Common positions include:** Accountant; Administrative Manager; Advertising Clerk; Attorney; Blue-Collar Worker Supervisor; Budget Analyst; Buyer; Clerical Supervisor; Computer Programmer; Economist; Financial Analyst; Human Resources Manager; Industrial Engineer; Industrial Production Manager; Management Analyst/Consultant; Management Trainee; Manufacturer's/Wholesaler's Sales Rep.; Materials Engineer; Mechanical Engineer; Metallurgical Engineer; Mining Engineer; Operations/Production Manager; Plant Manager; Purchasing Agent/Manager; Quality Control Supervisor; Services Sales Representative; Transportation/Traffic Specialist; Wholesale and Retail Buyer. **Educational backgrounds include:** Accounting; Business Administration; Computer Science; Economics; Finance; Marketing. **Benefits:** 401(k); Dental Insurance; Disability Coverage; Life Insurance; Medical Insurance; Tuition Assistance. **Corporate headquarters location:** This Location. **Other U.S. locations:** Waverly IA; Olathe KS; Baruga MI; Southaven MI; Wilmington NC; Tulsa OK; Conway SC; Huron SD; Watertown SD; Milwaukee WI. **Number of employees at this location:** 30.

TESA TAPE, INC.
5825 Carnegie Boulevard, Charlotte NC 28209. 704/554-0707. **Contact:** Charmaine Nephew, Human Resources. **Description:** Engaged in the production and sale of an extensive line of masking, cellophane, electrical, cloth, and other pressure-sensitive tape products for business, industrial, and household use. **Common positions include:** Accountant; Buyer; Chemical Engineer; Chemist; Claim Representative; Computer Programmer; Credit Manager; Department Manager; Financial Analyst; Human Resources Manager; Industrial Engineer; Manufacturer's/Wholesaler's Sales Rep.; Mechanical Engineer. **Educational backgrounds include:** Accounting; Business Administration; Chemistry; Engineering; Finance; Marketing. **Benefits:** Disability Coverage; Life Insurance; Medical Insurance. **Corporate headquarters location:** This Location. **Other U.S. locations:** Carbondale IL; Sparta MI; Middletown NY.

TEXTRON INC.
40 Westminster Street, Providence RI 02903. 401/421-2800. **Fax:** 401/457-3599. **Recorded jobline:** 877/4-TEXTRON. **Contact:** Lisa Whiting, Manager of Employment. **World Wide Web address:** http://www.textron.com. **Description:** A diversified conglomerate with over 30 separate companies in three primary areas: Aerospace and Defense Technology; Financial Services; and Communications. The company also manufactures automobile parts, outdoor equipment, and specialty fasteners. Founded in 1923. **NOTE:** Entry-level positions are offered. **Common positions include:** Accountant; Administrative Manager; Attorney; Auditor; Budget Analyst; Financial Analyst; Human Resources Manager; Marketing Manager; Marketing Specialist; Paralegal; Public Relations Specialist; Telecommunications Manager. **Educational backgrounds include:** Accounting; Business Administration; Communications; Economics; Finance; Liberal Arts; Marketing; Microsoft Word; Public Relations; Spreadsheets. **Benefits:** 401(k); Casual Dress - Fridays; Dental Insurance; Disability Coverage; Employee Discounts; Financial Planning Assistance; Flexible Schedule; Job Sharing; Life Insurance; Medical Insurance; Pension Plan; Profit Sharing; Public Transit Available; Savings Plan; Sick Days (6 - 10); Telecommuting; Tuition Assistance; Vacation Days (16+). **Special programs:** Internships; Training; Co-ops; Summer Jobs. **Office hours:** Monday - Friday, 8:30 a.m. - 5:00 p.m. **Corporate headquarters location:** This Location. **Other U.S. locations:** Nationwide. **International locations:** Worldwide. **Subsidiaries include:** Bell Helicopter; Cessna Aircraft Company. **Listed on:** NASDAQ. **Stock exchange symbol:** TXT. **President/CEO/Owner:** Lewis Campbell. **Number of employees at this location:** 400.

THERMADYNE HOLDINGS CORP.
101 South Hanley Road, St. Louis MO 63105. 314/721-5573. **Contact:** Employee Relations. **World Wide Web address:** http://www.thermadyne.com. **Description:** A diversified industrial holding company that engages in the manufacture of cutting and welding equipment and wear resistant alloys and specialty casting. **NOTE:** Managerial/administrative positions are based in St. Louis. Sales positions are offered nationwide. **Common positions include:** Accountant/Auditor; Financial Analyst; Manufacturer's/Wholesaler's Sales Rep. **Educational backgrounds include:** Accounting; Business Administration; Computer Science; Finance; Marketing. **Benefits:** 401(k); Dental Insurance; Disability Coverage; Life Insurance; Medical Insurance; Profit Sharing; Tuition Assistance. **Special programs:** Internships. **Corporate headquarters location:** This Location. **Subsidiaries include:** C&G Systems, Inc.; Stoody Company; Thermal Arc; Thermal Dynamics Corporation; Tweco Arcair; Tweco Products, Inc.; Victor Equipment Company; Victor Gas Systems.

THERMO ELECTRON CORPORATION
81 Wyman Street, Waltham MA 02454. 781/622-1166. **Contact:** Fred F. Florio, Director of Human Resources. **World Wide Web address:** http://www.thermo.com. **Description:** Provides a wide range of innovative products and services to the instruments; biomedical; recycling and resource energy; environmental energy; and advanced technology industries. Thermo Electron Corporation offers these services through its own operations as well as through the operations of its subsidiaries. **Common positions include:** Accountant; Administrator; Assistant Manager; Attorney; Department Manager; General Manager; Marketing Specialist; Paralegal; Systems Analyst; Technical Writer/Editor; Vice President. **Educational backgrounds include:** Accounting; Business Administration; Communications; Finance; Human Resources; Marketing; Mathematics. **Benefits:** Dental Insurance; Disability Coverage; Employee Discounts; Life Insurance; Medical Insurance; Pension Plan; Stock Option; Tuition Assistance. **Corporate headquarters location:** This Location. **Subsidiaries include:** Metrika Systems Corporation; ONIX Systems Inc.; Randers Killam Group; Thermedics Inc.; Thermo Bio Analysis

Corporation; Thermo Ecotek Corporation; Thermo Fibergen Inc.; Thermo Fibertek Inc.; Thermo Instrument Systems Inc.; Thermo Optek Corporation; Thermo Power Corporation; Thermo TerraTech Inc.; Thermo Vision Corporation; ThermoLase Corporation; ThermoQuest Company; ThermoRetec Corporation; ThermoSpectra Corporation; ThermoTrex Corporation; Trex Medical Corporation. **Listed on:** American Stock Exchange. **Number of employees at this location:** 400. **Number of employees worldwide:** 7,000.

THERMO INSTRUMENT SYSTEMS
P.O. Box 2108, Santa Fe NM 87504-2108. 505/438-3171. **Fax:** 505/473-9221. **Contact:** Human Resources. **Description:** Designs, manufactures, and markets advanced analytical and monitoring instruments used to detect and measure radioactivity, air pollution, toxic metals, chemical compounds, and other substances. The company also provides specialized environmental and radiochemical analysis and environmental science/engineering services. **Corporate headquarters location:** This Location. **Number of employees at this location:** 120. **Number of employees nationwide:** 3,700.

THOMAS & BETTS ELASTIMOLD
One Esna Park, Hackettstown NJ 07840. 908/852-1122. **Contact:** Kay Hedges, Manager of Human Resources. **Description:** A manufacturer of products and components for the industrial and consumer markets. Products are classified in the following three segments: Fluid Power and Metal Components; Electrical Components and Controls; and Consumer and Safety Products. Fluid Power and Metal Components include hose and tubing, flexible hose assemblies, metal fastener products, and high-precision metal molds used by automotive, industrial equipment, aerospace, and plastics manufacturers. Electrical Components and Controls includes a variety of molded rubber connectors and distribution systems components marketed under the Elastimold trademark. These products are used predominantly by electrical power distribution companies for the underground installation of power lines serving residential, commercial, and industrial customers. Elastimold also manufactures electromechanical and solid state time delay relays and switches, controls, and motors; battery separators; aviation lighting transformers; splice caps; terminal blocks; electronic packaging components; and crimping tools used in electronic installation, switch gear, and other industrial electrical and electronic equipment. Consumer and Safety Products include molded plastic key products for typewriters and telephones, and components for the automotive, appliance, computer, business machine, and hardware fields. **Corporate headquarters location:** This Location.

THOMAS INDUSTRIES
P.O. Box 35120, Louisville KY 40232-5120. 502/893-4600. **Contact:** Human Resources. **World Wide Web address:** http://www.thomasind.com. **Description:** Manufactures compressors and vacuum pumps for original equipment manufacturers. The primary product groups include piston, diaphragm, and rotary air compressors and vacuum pumps; vibrating diaphragm and linear air compressors and pumps; peristaltic liquid pumps; air motors; and air powered vacuum pumps. Products serve the medical, mobile, instrumentation, business, packaging, vapor recovery, and vending equipment markets. **Corporate headquarters location:** This Location. **Other U.S. locations:** Los Angeles CA; San Leandro CA; Tupelo MS; Sheboygan WI. **International locations:** Ontario, Canada; Quebec City, Canada.

3-D SYSTEMS INC.
26081 Avenue Hall, Valencia CA 91355. 661/295-5600. **Contact:** Human Resources. **World Wide Web address:** http://www.3dsystems.com. **Description:** Manufactures stereolithography equipment. Founded in 1986. **Corporate headquarters location:** This Location. **International locations:** China; France; Germany; Italy; United Kingdom. **Listed on:** NASDAQ. **Stock exchange symbol:** TDSC.

3M
3M Center, Building 224-1W-02, St. Paul MN 55144-1000. 651/733-0687. **Contact:** Staffing Resources. **World Wide Web address:** http://www.3m.com. **Description:** Manufactures products in three sectors: Industrial and Consumer; Information, Imaging, and Electronic; and Life Sciences. The Industrial and Consumer Sector includes a variety of products under brand names including 3M, Scotch, Post-it, Scotch-Brite, and Scotchgard. The Information, Imaging, and Electronic Sector is a leader in several high-growth global industries including telecommunications, electronics, electrical, imaging, and memory media. The Life Sciences Sector serves two broad market categories: health care, and traffic and personal safety. In the health care market, 3M produces medical and surgical supplies, drug delivery systems, and dental products; in traffic and personal safety, 3M is a leader in products for transportation safety, worker protection, vehicle and sign graphics, and out-of-home advertising. **Corporate headquarters location:** This Location. **International locations:** Worldwide.

TOMKINS INDUSTRIES INC.
P.O. Box 943, Dayton OH 45401-0943. 937/253-7171. **Physical address:** 4801 Springfield Street, Dayton OH 45431. **Contact:** Manager of Human Resources. **Description:** A manufacturer of a wide range of components for the manufactured housing and recreational vehicle markets, and of products for the commercial and industrial building industries. **Common positions include:** Accountant/Auditor; Administrator; Buyer; Computer Programmer; Electrical/Electronics Engineer; Financial Analyst; Human Resources Manager; Industrial Engineer; Marketing Specialist; Mechanical Engineer; Operations/Production Manager; Purchasing Agent/Manager; Quality Control Supervisor; Systems Analyst. **Educational backgrounds include:** Accounting; Business Administration; Engineering; Finance; Marketing. **Benefits:** Employee Discounts; Life Insurance; Medical Insurance; Profit Sharing; Tuition Assistance. **Corporate headquarters location:** This Location. **Listed on:** New York Stock Exchange.

THE TORRINGTON COMPANY
59 Field Street, Torrington CT 06790. 860/626-2000. **Fax:** 860/496-3603. **Contact:** Ken Keane, Manager, Professional Staffing & Recruiting. **World Wide Web address:** http://www.torrington.com. **Description:** The firm designs, develops, and manufactures antifriction needle, roller, and ball bearings. The Torrington Company also produces universal joints and precision metal components and assemblies. **NOTE:** Entry-level positions are offered. **Common positions include:** Accountant; Advertising Executive; Applications Engineer; Buyer; Chemical Engineer; Computer Programmer; Human Resources Manager; Internet Services Manager; IT Specialist; Manufacturing Engineer; Market Research Analyst; Marketing Specialist; Mechanical Engineer; MIS Specialist; Sales Engineer; Software Engineer; Systems Analyst; Systems Manager; Telecommunications Manager; Webmaster. **Educational backgrounds**

include: Accounting; Chemistry; Computer Science; Engineering. **Benefits:** 401(k); Dental Insurance; Disability Coverage; Financial Planning Assistance; Flexible Schedule; Life Insurance; Medical Insurance; Pension Plan; Savings Plan; Tuition Assistance. **Special programs:** Internships; Co-ops. **Internship information:** Summer internships and co-op opportunities are generally available for mechanical engineering assignments including design/test and special projects, information technology responsibilities, and chemical engineering projects. Applications for summer internships need to be received by April 15 and applications for co-ops by April 15 or October 15. **Corporate headquarters location:** This Location. **Other U.S. locations:** Nationwide. **International locations:** Australia; Brazil; Canada; England; Germany; Japan. **Parent company:** Ingersoll-Rand Company (Woodcliff Lake NJ). **Listed on:** American Stock Exchange. **Annual sales/revenues:** More than $100 million.

TRANSTECHNOLOGY CORPORATION
150 Allen Road, Liberty Corner NJ 07938. 908/903-1600. **Contact:** Human Resources. **World Wide Web address:** http://www.transtechnology.com. **Description:** Designs, manufactures, sells, and distributes specialty fasteners. **Corporate headquarters location:** This Location. **Subsidiaries include:** Breeze-Eastern (Union NJ) designs, develops, manufactures, and services sophisticated lifting and restraining products, principally helicopter rescue hoist and cargo hook systems, winches and hoists for aircraft and weapon systems, and aircraft cargo tie down systems. Breeze Industrial Products (PA) manufactures a complete line of standard and specialty gear-driven band fasteners in high-grade stainless steel for use in highly engineered applications. Industrial Retaining Ring (Irvington NJ) manufactures a variety of retaining rings made of carbon steel, stainless steel, and beryllium copper. The Palnut Company (Mountainside NJ) manufactures light- and heavy-duty single- and multithread specialty fasteners. The Seeger Group (Somerville NJ) manufactures retaining clips, circlips, spring pins, and similar components.

TRAULSEN & COMPANY INC.
4401 Blue Mound Road, Fort Worth TX 76106. 817/625-9671. **Contact:** Susan Pereira, Human Resources Manager. **World Wide Web address:** http://www.traulsen.com. **Description:** Manufactures an extensive line of commercial refrigerators and freezers. **Corporate headquarters location:** This Location.

TRENDWAY CORPORATION
P.O. Box 9016, Holland MI 49422. 616/399-3900. **Fax:** 616/399-8410. **Contact:** Ms. M. Serne, Human Resources Director. **World Wide Web address:** http://www.trendway.com. **Description:** A manufacturer of office systems furniture, floor-to-floor ceiling partitions, and seating. **Common positions include:** Buyer; Computer Programmer; Cost Estimator; Customer Service Rep.; Designer; Draftsperson; Human Resources Manager; Industrial Engineer; Mechanical Engineer; Public Relations Specialist; Purchasing Agent/Manager; Transportation/Traffic Specialist. **Educational backgrounds include:** Business Administration. **Benefits:** 401(k); Daycare Assistance; Disability Coverage; Employee Discounts; Life Insurance; Medical Insurance; Pension Plan; Profit Sharing; Tuition Assistance. **Special programs:** Internships. **Corporate headquarters location:** This Location. **Listed on:** Privately held. **Number of employees at this location:** 400.

TRICONEX CORPORATION
15091 Bake Parkway, Irvine CA 92618. 949/768-3709. **Contact:** Human Resources. **World Wide Web address:** http://www.triconex.com. **Description:** Manufactures fault-tolerant safety and control systems used in critical industrial process applications. **Corporate headquarters location:** This Location. **Other U.S. locations:** Lamarque TX. **Number of employees at this location:** 100.

TRINITY INDUSTRIES, INC.
P.O. Box 568887, Dallas TX 75356-8887. 214/631-4420. **Contact:** Human Resources Department. **World Wide Web address:** http://www.trin.net. **Description:** Manufactures an assortment of railroad and construction equipment and replacement parts. Trinity Industries also offers related services for the transportation, construction, aerospace, commercial, and industrial markets. Products include railcars, gas processing systems, petroleum transportation systems, guard rails, bridge girders and beams, airport boarding bridges, barges, tug boats, military marine vessels, and precision welding products. Trinity Industries also makes concrete and aggregates and produces metal components for the petrochemical, industrial, processing, and power markets. **Common positions include:** Accountant/Auditor; Data Entry Clerk. **Educational backgrounds include:** Accounting; Business Administration; Computer Science; Engineering. **Benefits:** Daycare Assistance; Disability Coverage; Employee Discounts; Life Insurance; Medical Insurance; Pension Plan; Profit Sharing; Savings Plan; Tuition Assistance. **Corporate headquarters location:** This Location. **Listed on:** New York Stock Exchange.

TUFCO INDUSTRIES
P.O. Box 23500, Green Bay WI 54305-3500. 920/336-0054. **Contact:** Mike Schilling, Vice President of Human Resources. **Description:** A leading specialty printer and converter of custom paper and nonwoven materials. The company provides custom converting services for industrial uses and converting of specialty and fine printing papers and paperboard, polyethylene film, and coated products. These converting services include thermal laminating, slitting and rewinding paper rolls, precision sheeting, folding, and packaging. Industrial products utilizing these custom converting services include reinforced towels, operating room towels, industrial wipes, medical drapes, and window insulation products. In addition, the company converts fine printing papers and paperboard for engineering, architectural, micrographic, geophysical, commercial, and other uses. Other services offered by the company include specialty printing services for paper tablecovers, food and gift wraps, feminine hygiene components, printed release liners, and novelty and holiday bathroom tissue. Tufco also manufactures a variety of disposable consumer products that include home improvement products such as CANVAX (a synthetic dropcloth developed by the company), polyethylene and canvas dropcloths, latex and vinyl gloves, paint strainers, and other allied products sold under the company's brand names or other private labels. **Corporate headquarters location:** This Location. **Other U.S. locations:** Manning SC; Dallas TX.

TUSCARORA INC.
800 Fifth Avenue, New Brighton PA 15066. 724/843-8200. **Contact:** Irene McAllister, Vice President of Corporate Services. **World Wide Web address:** http://www.tuscarora.com. **Description:** Designs and manufactures interior protective packaging and material handling solutions for a broad range of manufactured products. Tuscarora

also supplies customers with molded plastic thermoformed components for a number of industrial and consumer product applications. The company uses a variety of materials to develop customized internal protective packaging products, material handling solutions, and components, and integrates multiple materials such as corrugated paperboard, molded and/or die-cut foam plastics, thermoformed plastics, wood, and aluminum to meet customers' specific end use requirements. **Corporate headquarters location:** This Location. **Listed on:** NASDAQ.

TWIN CITY FAN COMPANIES
5959 Trenton Lane, Plymouth MN 55442. 763/551-7600. **Fax:** 763/551-7601. **Contact:** Leslie Barry, Director of Training. **World Wide address:** http://www.tcf.com. **Description:** Twin City Fan Companies is a leader in the design and manufacture of air-moving equipment. The company has a complete line of fans and blowers from 1/6 HP to over 1,000 HP for every commercial and industrial air-moving need. Products include airfoil design ventilating fans, packaged ventilating sets, material handling fans, high-pressure and induced draft fans, axial fans, propeller fans, and custom designs and accessories. Each fan and blower produced is manufactured to the customer's specifications. The company operates manufacturing facilities in Mitchell and Brookings SD and maintains a nationwide network of sales representatives. **Corporate headquarters location:** This Location. **Subsidiaries include:** TCF Aerovent, Inc.; Twin City Fan & Blower Company.

TYCO INTERNATIONAL
3 Tyco Park, Exeter NH 03833. 603/778-9200. **Contact:** John Helfrich, Vice President of Human Resources. **Description:** Manufactures fire protection equipment. **Corporate headquarters location:** This Location.

UFP TECHNOLOGIES, INC.
172 East Main Street, Georgetown MA 01833. 978/352-2200. **Fax:** 978/352-7169. **Contact:** Human Resources. **World Wide Web address:** http://www.ufpt.com. **Description:** Specializes in custom engineered packaging and specialty solutions that are produced by converting a wide range of foam, rigid plastic, fabric, fibre, and other composite materials. Packaging products and services include custom thermofoaming plastics and foams; designing and manufacturing precision, 100-percent recycled protective packaging and multimaterial solutions for durable, reusable inter- and intraplant product shipment; producing interior packaging; manufacturing complex product handling devices; and clean room manufacturing capabilities which enable particulate, temperature, and humidity controlled manufacturing. Specialty products include precision-molded foams, performance products, laminating and molding, custom footbeds, and medical components. **Corporate headquarters location:** This Location. **Listed on:** NASDAQ. **Stock exchange symbol:** UFPT.

U.S. NATURAL RESOURCES
P.O. Box 310, Woodland WA 98674. 360/225-8267. **Contact:** Human Resources. **Description:** Manufactures sawmill machinery. **Corporate headquarters location:** This Location.

USFILTER
40-004 Cook Street, Palm Desert CA 92211. 760/340-0098. **Contact:** Human Resources. **World Wide Web address:** http://www.usfilter.com. **Description:** Manufactures and services water purification and treatment equipment. Primary customers are the electronic, utility, and pharmaceutical industries. **Corporate headquarters location:** This Location. **Parent company:** Vivendi.

UNITED TECHNOLOGIES CORP.
One Financial Plaza, Hartford CT 06101. 860/728-7000. **Contact:** Human Resources. **World Wide Web address:** http://www.utc.com. **Description:** Provides high-tech products and support services to customers in the aerospace, building, military, and automotive industries worldwide. Products include large jet engines, temperature control systems, elevators and escalators, helicopters, and flight systems. The company markets its products under a variety of brand names including Carrier, Hamilton Standard, Otis, Pratt & Whitney, and Sikorsky. **Corporate headquarters location:** This Location. **International locations:** Asia; Australia; Canada; Europe; Latin America; Mexico.

UNIWELD PRODUCTS, INC.
2850 Ravenswood Road, Fort Lauderdale FL 33312. 954/584-2000. **Contact:** Erin Mumford, Personnel. **Description:** A manufacturer of gas welding and cutting equipment and pressure gauges. **Common positions include:** Accountant/Auditor; Buyer; Commercial Artist; Credit Manager; Customer Service Rep.; Draftsperson; Human Resources Manager; Industrial Engineer; Manufacturer's/Wholesaler's Sales Rep.; Mechanical Engineer; Purchasing Agent/Manager; Quality Control Supervisor. **Educational backgrounds include:** Accounting; Business Administration; Computer Science; Engineering. **Benefits:** Credit Union; Dental Insurance; Employee Discounts; Life Insurance; Medical Insurance; Tuition Assistance. **Corporate headquarters location:** This Location.

VALENITE, INC., DIE & WEAR WALMET DIVISION
510 Griffin Road, West Branch MI 48661. 517/345-2622. **Fax:** 517/345-7510. **Contact:** Brenda Klacking, Human Resources Administrator. **Description:** This location manufactures carbide die and wear parts. Overall, Valenite, Inc., Die & Wear is a manufacturer of pressed and extruded carbide products. **Common positions include:** Accountant; Blue-Collar Worker Supervisor; Customer Service Rep.; Data Entry Clerk; Draftsperson; General Manager; Industrial Production Manager; Manufacturer's/Wholesaler's Sales Rep.; Metallurgical Engineer. **Educational backgrounds include:** Business Administration; Material Sciences. **Benefits:** 401(k); Dental Insurance; Disability Coverage; Fitness Program; Life Insurance; Medical Insurance; Tuition Assistance. **Corporate headquarters location:** Madison Heights MI. **Other U.S. locations:** Nationwide. **Parent company:** Milacron, Inc. **Listed on:** New York Stock Exchange. **Number of employees at this location:** 200. **Number of employees nationwide:** 3,500.

VALLEN CORPORATION
13333 Northwest Freeway, Houston TX 77040. 713/462-8700. **Fax:** 713/462-7634. **Contact:** Human Resources. **World Wide Web address:** http://www.vallen.com. **Description:** Manufactures and distributes safety products. Founded in 1947. **Common positions include:** Accountant/Auditor; Assistant Manager; Branch Manager; Buyer; Computer Programmer; Customer Service Rep.; Department Manager; General Manager; Human Resources Manager; Industrial Engineer; Instructor/Trainer; Management Trainee; Manufacturer's/Wholesaler's Sales Rep.; Marketing Specialist; Operations/Production Manager; Purchasing Agent/Manager; Systems Analyst. **Educational backgrounds include:** Accounting; Business

Administration; Computer Science; Engineering; Liberal Arts; Marketing. **Benefits:** 401(k); Dental Insurance; Disability Coverage; Life Insurance; Long-Term Care; Medical Insurance; Profit Sharing; Savings Plan; Stock Option; Tuition Assistance. **Corporate headquarters location:** This Location. **Subsidiaries include:** Encon Safety Products, Inc.; Vallen Safety Supply Company. **Listed on:** NASDAQ. **Number of employees at this location:** 100. **Number of employees nationwide:** 1,000.

VARIAN ASSOCIATES
3100 Hansen Way, Mail Stop E-140, Palo Alto CA 94304. 650/493-4000. **Contact:** Human Resources. **World Wide Web address:** http://www.varian.com. **Description:** A diversified, international manufacturing company. Varian operates manufacturing facilities in seven countries and sales and service offices worldwide. The company is organized around the following core businesses: Health Care Systems; Instruments; Electronic Devices; and Semiconductor Equipment. People receive cancer treatments from over 2,300 Varian medical linear accelerators, treatment stimulators, and information management systems in service at hospitals and clinics worldwide. The company is also a leading supplier of X-ray tubes for imaging systems of all types. The company's instruments also aid physicians and researchers in treating diseases such as AIDS. Varian instruments regulate the quality of products such as petroleum, pharmaceuticals, ice cream, and champagne. Its vacuum pumps and leak detectors create a vacuum environment. Varian is a worldwide leader in the manufacture of devices that generate, amplify, and define signals for radio and television broadcasting and satellite communications. They are also used in air traffic control, navigation, radar, fusion energy, and other scientific research applications. **Common positions include:** Accountant/Auditor; Biomedical Engineer; Buyer; Ceramics Engineer; Chemical Engineer; Computer Programmer; Customer Service Rep.; Designer; Electrical/Electronics Engineer; Financial Analyst; Human Resources Manager; Materials Engineer; Mechanical Engineer; Metallurgical Engineer; Nuclear Engineer; Operations/Production Manager; Paralegal; Services Sales Rep.; Software Engineer; Systems Analyst; Technical Writer/Editor. **Educational backgrounds include:** Accounting; Business Administration; Chemistry; Computer Science; Engineering; Finance; Marketing; Physics. **Benefits:** 401(k); Daycare Assistance; Dental Insurance; EAP; Employee Discounts; Life Insurance; Medical Insurance; Profit Sharing; Tuition Assistance. **Special programs:** Internships. **Corporate headquarters location:** This Location. **Other U.S. locations:** AZ; MA; UT. **Listed on:** New York Stock Exchange. **Number of employees at this location:** 3,000. **Number of employees nationwide:** 6,500.

VARITRONIC SYSTEMS, INC.
6835 Winnetka Circle, Brooklyn Park MN 55428. 763/536-6400. **Fax:** 763/536-0769. **Contact:** Human Resources. **World Wide Web address:** http://www.varitronic.com. **Description:** Develops, produces, and sells business graphics products for communication materials. The products are made to satisfy presentation, labeling, and signage in a variety of markets including general office, manufacturing, and education. Varitronic sells lettering and labeling systems that generate print in a variety of styles, in sizes ranging from one-half inch to four inches, using thermal transfer technology. **Corporate headquarters location:** This Location. **Listed on:** NASDAQ. **Number of employees at this location:** 100. **Number of employees nationwide:** 290.

VEECO INSTRUMENTS INC.
Terminal Drive, Plainview NY 11803. 516/349-8300. **Contact:** Human Resources. **Description:** Designs, manufactures, markets, and services a broad line of precision ion beam etching and surface measurement systems used to manufacture microelectronic products. Veeco produces and sells its ion beam etching systems under the Microtech brand name. The company also sells leak detection/vacuum equipment, which is used for the precise identification of leaks in sealed components. Leak detectors are used in a broad range of electronics, aerospace, and transportation products, ranging from air conditioning components to fiberoptic cables. Veeco's surface measurement products include surface profilers, atomic force microscopy measurement systems, and X-ray fluorescence thickness measurement systems. **Corporate headquarters location:** This Location.

VICTORY ENGINEERING CORPORATION
Victory Road, P.O. Box 710, Springfield NJ 07081. 973/379-5900. **Contact:** Personnel. **World Wide Web address:** http://www.veco-net.com. **Description:** Manufactures and distributes thermistors, varistors, and specialty temperature sensing assemblies. **Common positions include:** Accountant; Administrator; Blue-Collar Worker Supervisor; Buyer; Chemist; Department Manager; Electrical/Electronics Engineer; General Manager; Human Resources Manager; Manufacturer's/Wholesaler's Sales Rep.; Operations/Production Manager; Purchasing Agent/Manager; Quality Control Supervisor. **Educational backgrounds include:** Accounting; Chemistry; Computer Science; Engineering; Finance; Marketing. **Benefits:** Disability Coverage; Life Insurance; Medical Insurance; Pension Plan; Tuition Assistance. **Corporate headquarters location:** This Location. **Parent company:** YSI Incorporated.

VISHAY INTERTECHNOLOGY INC.
VISHAY RESISTIVE SYSTEMS GROUP
63 Lincoln Highway, Malvern PA 19355-2120. 610/644-1300. **Fax:** 610/296-8775. **Contact:** William Spires, Vice President of Human Resources. **World Wide Web address:** http://www.vishay.com. **Description:** Operates in three business segments: Measurement Group develops, manufactures, and markets precision stress analysis products; Resistive Systems Group (also at this location) develops, manufactures, and markets high-precision resistive products; Medical Systems Group develops, manufactures, and markets dental products. **Corporate headquarters location:** This Location. **Listed on:** American Stock Exchange.

VISIONEERING, INC.
P.O. Box 127, Fraser MI 48026. 810/293-1000. **Contact:** Diane Hill, Human Resources Director. **Description:** Produces tooling for major automotive and aerospace manufacturers around the world. The company uses the latest CAD/CAM, machining, and material technologies in model and tooling techniques. **Common positions include:** Aerospace Engineer; Computer Programmer; Industrial Engineer; Mechanical Engineer. **Educational backgrounds include:** Engineering. **Benefits:** 401(k); Dental Insurance; Disability Coverage; Life Insurance; Medical Insurance; Tuition Assistance. **Corporate headquarters location:** This Location.

VOGEL PETERSON
347 North Lindbergh Road, St. Louis MO 63141. 314/993-8100. **Toll-free phone:** 800/942-4332. **Fax:** 314/993-0481. **Contact:** Human Resources. **Description:** Manufactures office furniture and hospitality industry products such as wardrobe hangers, lockers, cabinets, and accessories.

Common positions include: Accountant/Auditor; Advertising Clerk; Blue-Collar Worker Supervisor; Budget Analyst; Buyer; Clerical Supervisor; Computer Programmer; Credit Manager; Customer Service Rep.; Designer; Draftsperson; Electrical/Electronics Engineer; Electrician; Financial Analyst; General Manager; Human Resources Manager; Industrial Engineer; Industrial Production Manager; Manufacturer's/Wholesaler's Sales Rep.; Mechanical Engineer; Metallurgical Engineer; Operations/Production Manager; Purchasing Agent/Manager; Quality Control Supervisor; Systems Analyst. **Educational backgrounds include:** Accounting; Business Administration; Engineering; Finance; Marketing. **Benefits:** 401(k); Dental Insurance; Disability Coverage; Employee Discounts; Life Insurance; Medical Insurance; Pension Plan; Profit Sharing; Savings Plan; Tuition Assistance. **Corporate headquarters location:** This Location. **Other U.S. locations:** Nationwide. **Parent company:** Acco North America.

WALTER GRINDERS, INC.
5160 Lad Land Drive, Fredericksburg VA 22407. 540/898-3700. **Contact:** Human Resources. **World Wide Web address:** http://www.walter-ag.com. **Description:** Manufactures grinding machinery and related parts. **Corporate headquarters location:** This Location. **Parent company:** Walter AG (Germany).

WAREHOUSE EQUIPMENT, INC.
2500 York Road, Elk Grove Village IL 60007. 847/595-9400. **Contact:** General Manager. **World Wide Web address:** http://www.weinet.com. **Description:** Manufactures and distributes material handling products, provides engineering services for product handling systems, and designs storage and retrieval equipment. **Common positions include:** Civil Engineer; Design Engineer; Electrical/Electronics Engineer; Mechanical Engineer; Project Manager; Sales Engineer. **Educational backgrounds include:** Business Administration; Engineering. **Corporate headquarters location:** This Location. **Listed on:** Privately held. **Number of employees at this location:** 90.

WARNER ELECTRIC
23601 Hoover Road, Warren MI 48089. 810/758-5000. **Contact:** Kirby Smith, Human Resources Manager. **Description:** This location manufactures precision sprag-clutches for the machine tool and aerospace industries. Overall, Warner Electric is a global leader in the engineering, manufacturing, and marketing of products and systems for the worldwide vehicular, industrial, and mobile off-highway original equipment markets and is a major supplier to the related aftermarkets.

WATEROUS COMPANY
125 Hardman Avenue South, South St. Paul MN 55075. 651/450-5000. **Fax:** 651/450-5241. **Recorded jobline:** 651/450-5299. **Contact:** Human Resources. **World Wide Web address:** http://www.waterousco.com. **Description:** Manufactures and assembles parts for fire hydrants, underground valves for the waterworks industry, and pumps for fire services. **NOTE:** Entry-level positions, part-time jobs, and second and third shifts are offered. **Common positions include:** Accountant; AS400 Programmer Analyst; Buyer; Computer Operator; Computer Programmer; Controller; Credit Manager; Customer Service Rep.; Draftsperson; Human Resources Manager; Manufacturing Engineer; Network/Systems Administrator; Operations Manager; Production Manager; Quality Assurance Engineer; Sales Rep.; Secretary; Transportation/Traffic Specialist. **Educational backgrounds include:** AS400 Certification; Microsoft Word;

Spreadsheets. **Benefits:** 401(k); Casual Dress - Fridays; Dental Insurance; Disability Coverage; Life Insurance; Medical Insurance; Pension Plan; Profit Sharing; Sick Days (6 - 10); Tuition Assistance; Vacation Days (10 - 20). **Office hours:** Monday - Friday, 8:00 a.m. - 4:30 p.m. **Corporate headquarters location:** This Location. **Parent company:** American Cast Iron Pipe Company (ACIPCO). **Listed on:** Privately held.

WAUKESHA CHERRY-BURRELL
611 Sugar Creek Road, Delavan WI 53115. 262/728-1900. **Contact:** Human Resources. **World Wide Web address:** http://www.waukesha-cb.com. **Description:** Manufactures stainless steel valves, pumps, and fittings for the food and dairy industry. **Common positions include:** Accountant Blue-Collar Worker Supervisor; Buyer; Computer Programmer; Draftsperson; Industrial Designer; Industrial Engineer; Manufacturer's/Wholesaler's Sales Rep.; Operations/Production Manager; Purchasing Agent/Manager; Quality Control Supervisor. **Educational backgrounds include:** Accounting; Business Administration; Engineering; Finance; Liberal Arts; Marketing. **Benefits:** Dental Insurance; Disability Coverage; Life Insurance; Medical Insurance; Pension Plan; Savings Plan; Tuition Assistance. **Corporate headquarters location:** This Location.

WEB INDUSTRIES
1700 West Park Drive, Suite 110, Westborough MA 01581. 508/898-2988. **Contact:** Alan Harrington, Director of Human Resources. **Description:** A custom contractor that converts various foils (including aluminum), plastics, and woven and nonwoven materials into different forms for use by other companies. **Corporate headquarters location:** This Location.

WEB PRESS CORPORATION
22023 68th Avenue South, Kent WA 98032. 253/395-3343. **Fax:** 253/395-4492. **Contact:** Human Resources. **World Wide Web address:** http://www.webpress1.com. **Description:** Manufactures and sells rotary offset, web-fed printing presses. These products are designed for use in printing newspapers, advertising inserts, paperback books, and similar products. **Corporate headquarters location:** This Location.

WEBSTER INDUSTRIES, INC.
325 Hall Street, Tiffin OH 44883. 419/447-8232. **Contact:** Crystal Fry, Personnel Director. **World Wide Web address:** http://www.websterchain.com. **Description:** A producer of conveyors, materials handling components, and related items. **Common positions include:** Blue-Collar Worker Supervisor; Customer Service Rep.; Industrial Engineer; Industrial Production Manager; Mechanical Engineer; Operations/Production Manager; Transportation/Traffic Specialist. **Educational backgrounds include:** Business Administration; Communications; Engineering; Marketing. **Benefits:** 401(k); Disability Coverage; Life Insurance; Medical Insurance; Pension Plan; Tuition Assistance. **Corporate headquarters location:** This Location. **Other U.S. locations:** Meridian MS; Tualatan OR.

WEISS-AUG COMPANY INC.
P.O. Box 520, East Hanover NJ 07930. 973/887-7600. **Fax:** 973/887-6924. **Contact:** Mary Dante, Director of Human Resources. **World Wide Web address:** http://www.weiss-aug.com. **Description:** Manufactures stampings, moldings, insert moldings, and assemblies. Industries served include automotive, telecommunications, electronic and electrical connector, medical, and several specialty

markets. Services include design, tooling, production, and quality control. Founded in 1972. **NOTE:** Part-time jobs and second and third shifts are offered. **Common positions include:** Account Manager; Accountant; Administrative Assistant; Chief Financial Officer; Customer Service Rep.; Design Engineer; Environmental Engineer; Human Resources Manager; Industrial Engineer; Manufacturing Engineer; Marketing Specialist; Mechanical Engineer; Network/Systems Administrator; Production Manager; Purchasing Agent/Manager; Quality Assurance Engineer; Systems Manager. **Educational backgrounds include:** Accounting; Business Administration; Computer Science; Engineering; Microsoft Windows NT; Microsoft Word; Software Tech. Support; Spreadsheets. **Benefits:** 401(k); Casual Dress - Fridays; Dental Insurance; Disability Coverage; Fitness Program; Life Insurance; Medical Insurance; Tuition Assistance. **Corporate headquarters location:** This Location.

WESTERBEKE CORPORATION
41 Ledin Drive, Avon Industrial Park, Avon MA 02322. 508/588-7700. **Fax:** 508/559-9323. **Contact:** Iris Kennedy, Human Resources Manager. **World Wide Web address:** http://www.westerbeke.com. **Description:** Designs, manufactures, and markets marine engine and air conditioning products. The company's products consist of diesel and gasoline engine-driven electrical generator sets; inboard propulsion engines; self-contained, reverse cycle air-conditioners; and associated spare parts and accessories. Westerbeke's generator sets are installed in powerboats, houseboats, large sailboats, and other types of pleasure and commercial boats to provide electricity for operating, safety, and convenience needs. The company's propulsion engines are installed as auxiliary power systems for sailboats. In addition, the company manufactures and markets a limited number of electrical generator sets for use in nonmarine applications. Westerbeke's products are marketed through a nationwide and international network of 54 distributors and approximately 400 dealers, and through the company's direct sales personnel. Founded in 1930. **NOTE:** Entry-level positions are offered. **Common positions include:** Accountant; Blue-Collar Worker Supervisor; Chief Financial Officer; Controller; Electrical/Electronics Engineer; Human Resources Manager; Mechanical Engineer; Purchasing Agent/Manager; Quality Assurance Engineer; Quality Control Supervisor; Sales Manager; Sales Rep.; Secretary. **Educational backgrounds include:** Accounting; Business Administration; Engineering; Marketing; Microsoft Office; Microsoft Word. **Benefits:** 401(k); Bonus Award/Plan; Casual Dress - Fridays; Dental Insurance; Disability Coverage; Life Insurance; Medical Insurance; Public Transit Available; Tuition Assistance; Vacation Days (6 - 10). **Special programs:** Co-ops. **Office hours:** Monday - Friday, 8:15 a.m. - 5:00 p.m. **President:** Jack Westerbeke.

WESTERN LITHOTECH
3433 Tree Court Industrial Boulevard, St. Louis MO 63122. 636/225-5031. **Contact:** Personnel. **World Wide Web address:** http://www.westernlithotech.com. **Description:** Manufactures lithographic plates, chemicals, and high-speed exposure/processing systems. **Common positions include:** Accountant; Administrator; Advertising Clerk; Blue-Collar Worker Supervisor; Buyer; Chemical Engineer; Chemist; Civil Engineer; Computer Programmer; Credit Manager; Customer Service Rep.; Draftsperson; Electrical/Electronics Engineer; Financial Analyst; Human Resources Manager; Manufacturer's/Wholesaler's Sales Rep.;

Marketing Specialist; Mechanical Engineer; Operations/Production Manager; Purchasing Agent/Manager; Systems Analyst. **Educational backgrounds include:** Accounting; Business Administration; Chemistry; Computer Science; Engineering; Finance; Marketing. **Benefits:** Dental Insurance; Disability Coverage; Life Insurance; Medical Insurance; Pension Plan; Profit Sharing; Savings Plan; Tuition Assistance. **Corporate headquarters location:** This Location. **Other U.S. locations:** Springfield MO; Jacksonville TX. **Parent company:** Mitsubishi Chemical Co.

WHITING CORPORATION
15700 Lathrop Avenue, Harvey IL 60426. 708/331-4000. **Contact:** Human Resources. **World Wide Web address:** http://www.whitingcorp.com. **Description:** Manufactures heavy overhead gantry cranes, metallurgical process equipment, and transportation maintenance and repair equipment. **Common positions include:** Accountant; Credit Manager; Department Manager; Draftsperson; Electrical/Electronics Engineer; Human Resources Manager; Industrial Engineer; Manufacturer's/Wholesaler's Sales Rep.; Mechanical Engineer; Metallurgical Engineer; Operations/Production Manager; Purchasing Agent/Manager; Quality Control Supervisor; Services Sales Representative. **Educational backgrounds include:** Accounting; Business Administration; Engineering; Finance; Marketing; Mathematics. **Benefits:** 401(k); Disability Coverage; Life Insurance; Medical Insurance; Pension Plan; Profit Sharing; Tuition Assistance. **Corporate headquarters location:** This Location. **Number of employees at this location:** 200.

WICKS ORGAN COMPANY
P.O. Box 129, Highland IL 62249. 618/654-2191. **Fax:** 618/654-3770. **Contact:** Scott Wick, Vice President. **World Wide Web address:** http://www.wicks.com. **Description:** Manufactures church pipe organs. **Common positions include:** Electrical/Electronics Engineer. **Educational backgrounds include:** Marketing. **Benefits:** Medical Insurance. **Corporate headquarters location:** This Location. **Number of employees at this location:** 80.

A.R. WILFLEY & SONS
7350 East Progress Place, Suite 200, Englewood CO 80111. 303/779-1777. **Contact:** Bill Wilbur, Director of Communications and Human Resources. **World Wide Web address:** http://www.wilfley.com. **Description:** Manufactures centrifugal pumps.

WILKERSON CORPORATION
1201 West Mansfield Avenue, Englewood CO 80110. 303/761-7601. **Fax:** 303/783-2323. **Contact:** Human Resources Administrator. **Description:** Manufactures fluid power equipment including air dryers, filters, regulators, and lubricators. **NOTE:** Entry-level positions and second and third shifts are offered. **Common positions include:** Accountant; Administrative Assistant; Blue-Collar Worker Supervisor; Buyer; Computer Programmer; Customer Service Rep.; Design Engineer; Draftsperson; Electrical/Electronics Engineer; Graphic Designer; Human Resources Manager; Industrial Engineer; Mechanical Engineer; Operations/Production Manager; Quality Control Supervisor. **Educational backgrounds include:** Accounting; Business Administration; Engineering; Marketing. **Benefits:** 401(k); Dental Insurance; Disability Coverage; Flexible Schedule; Life Insurance; Medical Insurance; Tuition Assistance. **Corporate headquarters location:** This Location. **Number of employees at this location:** 330.

WILL-BURT COMPANY
P.O. Box 900, Orrville OH 44667. 330/682-7015. **Physical address:** 401 Collins Boulevard, Orrville OH 44667. **Fax:** 330/684-5261. **Contact:** Deborah Malta, Director of Human Resources. **Description:** Manufactures fabricated and machined original equipment including lights and antennae. **NOTE:** Second and third shifts are offered. **Common positions include:** Account Rep.; Blue-Collar Worker Supervisor; Buyer; Credit Manager; Customer Service Representative; Design Engineer; Purchasing Agent/Manager. **Educational backgrounds include:** Accounting; Business Administration; Engineering; Finance; Marketing. **Benefits:** Disability Coverage; Life Insurance; Medical Insurance; Pension Plan; Profit Sharing; Savings Plan; Tuition Assistance. **Special programs:** Internships; Summer Jobs. **Corporate headquarters location:** This Location. **Listed on:** Privately held. **CEO:** Dennis Donahue. **Number of employees at this location:** 370.

SHELBY WILLIAMS INDUSTRIES, INC.
150 Shelby Williams Drive, Morristown TN 37813. 423/586-7000. **Fax:** 423/586-2260. **Contact:** Human Resources. **World Wide Web address:** http://www.shelbywilliams.com. **Description:** Manufactures lounge, lobby, and casino seating; stacking chairs; folding tables; bar stools; service carts; booths; and related office furniture. **Corporate headquarters location:** This Location. **Other U.S. locations:** Los Angeles CA; Aurora CO; Plantation FL; Honolulu HI; Chicago IL; New York NY; Houston TX. **International locations:** San Juan, Puerto Rico.

WILLIAMS INTERNATIONAL CORP.
P.O. Box 200, Walled Lake MI 48390. 248/624-5200. **Fax:** 248/669-9172. **Contact:** Human Resources. **Description:** Engaged in the research, development, and manufacture of small gas turbine engines for military and commercial applications. Founded in 1955. **Common positions include:** Aerospace Engineer; Ceramics Engineer; Design Engineer; Electrical/Electronics Engineer; Materials Engineer; Mechanical Engineer; Metallurgical Engineer; Software Engineer. **Educational backgrounds include:** Engineering. **Benefits:** 401(k); Dental Insurance; Disability Coverage; Life Insurance; Medical Insurance; Pension Plan; Tuition Assistance. **Corporate headquarters location:** This Location. **Other U.S. locations:** Ogden UT. **Number of employees at this location:** 440.

THOMAS C. WILSON, INC.
21-11 44th Avenue, Long Island City NY 11101. 718/729-3360. **Fax:** 718/361-2872. **Contact:** Sharon Hanley, Marketing Director. **World Wide Web address:** http://www.tcwilson.com. **Description:** Manufactures tube cleaners and tube expanders for the boiler and condenser industry. **Educational backgrounds include:** Business Administration; Engineering. **Corporate headquarters location:** This Location.

WIS-CON TOTAL POWER CORP.
3409 Democrat Road, Memphis TN 38118. 901/365-3600. **Contact:** Ms. Pat McCaleb, Director of Human Resources. **World Wide Web address:** http://www.totalpower.com. **Description:** Manufactures, markets, and distributes industrial engines. Products range from three to 80 horse powered engines run by gasoline, natural gas, LPG, and diesel fuels. **Common positions include:** Accountant; Advertising Clerk; Branch Manager; Buyer; Clerical Supervisor; Computer Programmer; Credit Manager; Customer Service Representative; Draftsperson; Economist; Electrical/Electronics Engineer; Financial Analyst; General Manager;

Human Resources Manager; Industrial Engineer; Manufacturer's/Wholesaler's Sales Rep.; Mechanical Engineer; Purchasing Agent/Manager; Quality Control Supervisor; Systems Analyst. **Educational backgrounds include:** Accounting; Art/Design; Business Administration; Communications; Computer Science; Engineering; Finance; Marketing. **Benefits:** 401(k); Dental Insurance; Disability Coverage; Life Insurance; Medical Insurance; Tuition Assistance. **Special programs:** Internships. **Corporate headquarters location:** This Location. **Other U.S. locations:** Minneapolis MN; Dyer TN; Salt Lake City UT; Fredericksburg VA; Milwaukee WI. **Listed on:** Privately held. **Number of employees at this location:** 100.

WRIGHT INDUSTRIES INC.
P.O. Box 17914, Nashville TN 37217. 615/361-6600. **Contact:** Human Resources. **Description:** Designs and builds custom automated assembly equipment (non-metal-cutting) and large metal-working dies. The company is also engaged in precision-machine work. **Corporate headquarters location:** This Location. **Other U.S. locations:** Gilbert AZ.

XEROX CORPORATION
P.O. Box 1600, Stamford CT 06904. 203/968-3000. **Physical address:** 800 Long Ridge Road, Stamford CT 06904. **Contact:** Hector Motroni, Chief Staff Officer. **World Wide Web address:** http://www. xerox.com. **Description:** Develops, manufactures, markets, services, and finances information processing products including copiers, duplicators, scanners, electronic printing systems, word processing systems, personal computers, and computer peripherals. Xerox does business in over 120 countries. **Corporate headquarters location:** This Location.
Other U.S. locations:
* Xerox Square 27A, 100 Clinton Avenue South, Rochester NY 14644-1877.

XERXES CORPORATION
7901 Xerxes Avenue South, Suite 201, Minneapolis MN 55431. 952/887-1890. **Fax:** 952/887-1870. **Contact:** Barbara J. Meyer, Supervisor of Payroll and Accounting. **World Wide Web address:** http://www.xerxescorp.com. **Description:** Manufactures fiberglass structural products including multicompartment tanks, oil and water separators, and underground storage tanks. Other tank accessories include electronic gauging and leak detection products, hydrostatic monitoring systems, and secondary containment sumps. **Common positions include:** Accountant; Attorney; Chemical Engineer; Clerical Supervisor; Computer Programmer; Cost Estimator; Credit Manager; Designer; Draftsperson; Financial Analyst; Human Resources Manager; Industrial Engineer; Manufacturer's/Wholesaler's Sales Rep.; Mechanical Engineer; Purchasing Agent/Manager; Services Sales Representative; Structural Engineer; Systems Analyst. **Educational backgrounds include:** Accounting; Business Administration; Computer Science; Engineering; Finance; Marketing. **Benefits:** 401(k); Dental Insurance; Disability Coverage; Life Insurance; Medical Insurance; Tuition Assistance. **Corporate headquarters location:** This Location. **Other U.S. locations:** Anaheim CA; Lakeland FL; Tipton IA; Hagerstown MD; Avon OH; Seguin TX. **Listed on:** Privately held. **Number of employees at this location:** 35.

XTEK INC.
11451 Reading Road, Cincinnati OH 45241. 513/733-7800. **Contact:** Craig Fowler, Human Resources Manager. **World Wide Web address:** http://www.xtek.com. **Description:** A manufacturer

of engineered products for heavy industry including gearing, crane wheels, couplings, and cold rolling rolls. **Common positions include:** Manufacturer's/Wholesaler's Sales Rep.; Mechanical Engineer. **Educational backgrounds include:** Business Administration; Engineering; Marketing. **Benefits:** Life Insurance; Medical Insurance; Pension Plan; Profit Sharing; Savings Plan; Stock Option; Tuition Assistance. **Corporate headquarters location:** This Location.

YARWAY CORPORATION
480 Norristown Road, Blue Bell PA 19422. 610/825-2100. **Fax:** 610/832-2467. **Contact:** Personnel. **World Wide Web address:** http://www.yarway.com. **Description:** Manufactures gauges, valves, steam traps, and indicators. Yarway Corporation also provides steam services. **Corporate headquarters location:** This Location.

YORK INTERNATIONAL CORPORATION
P.O. Box 1592-36BH, York PA 17405-1592. 717/771-6578. **Contact:** Diane Yerkey, Corporate Employment Recruiter. **World Wide Web address:** http://www.york.com. **Description:** Manufactures a full line of residential, commercial, and industrial air conditioning and refrigeration equipment and systems, heating systems, and food refrigeration systems. The company markets its products in over 110 countries through exclusive distribution facilities, 10 co-owned centers, and over 200 other wholesalers. **Common positions include:** Accountant; Electrical/Electronics Engineer; Mechanical Engineer; MIS Specialist; Software Engineer. **Educational backgrounds include:** Accounting; Business Administration; Computer Science; Economics; Engineering; Finance; Marketing; Mathematics; Physics. **Benefits:** 401(k); Dental Insurance; Disability Coverage; Employee Discounts; Life Insurance; Medical Insurance; Pension Plan; Profit Sharing; Savings Plan. **Special programs:** Internships. **Corporate headquarters location:** This Location. **Subsidiaries include:** York Engineered Systems; York Refrigeration; York Unitary Products. **Listed on:** New York Stock Exchange. **Annual sales/revenues:** More than $100 million. **Number of employees worldwide:** 25,000.

ZENS MANUFACTURING
P.O. Box 12504, Milwaukee WI 53212-0504. 414/372-7060. **Contact:** Human Resources. **Description:** A knitting manufacturer that operates two divisions, both of which are housed at this location. One division knits medical hosiery and the other division makes industrial tubing, such as the tubes that are found in environmental cleanup equipment. **Corporate headquarters location:** This Location.

For more information on career opportunities in industrial manufacturing:

Associations

ASSOCIATION FOR MANUFACTURING EXCELLENCE
380 West Palatine Road, Wheeling IL 60090. 847/520-3282. World Wide Web address: http://www.ame.org.

ASSOCIATION FOR MANUFACTURING TECHNOLOGY
7901 Westpark Drive, McLean VA 22102. 703/893-2900. A trade association. World Wide Web address: http://www.mfgtech.org.

INSTITUTE OF INDUSTRIAL ENGINEERS
25 Technology Park, Norcross GA 30092. 770/449-0460. World Wide Web address: http://www.iienet.org. A nonprofit organization that conducts seminars and offers reduced rates on its books and publications.

NATIONAL ASSOCIATION OF MANUFACTURERS
1331 Pennsylvania Avenue NW, Suite 600, Washington DC 20004. 202/637-3000. World Wide Web address: http://www.nam.org.

NATIONAL TOOLING & MACHINING ASSOCIATION
9300 Livingston Road, Fort Washington MD 20744. Toll-free phone: 800/248-6862. World Wide Web address: http://www.ntma.org. Reports on wages and operating expenses, produces monthly newsletters, and offers legal advice.

PRECISION MACHINED PRODUCTS ASSOCIATION
6700 West Snowville Road, Brecksville OH 44141. 440/526-0300. Provides resource information.

SOCIETY OF MANUFACTURING ENGINEERS
P.O. Box 930, One SME Drive, Dearborn MI 48121. 313/271-1500. World Wide Web address: http://www.sme.org. Offers educational events and educational materials on manufacturing.

Directories

AMERICAN MANUFACTURER'S DIRECTORY
5711 South 86th Circle, P.O. Box 37347, Omaha NE 68127. Toll-free phone: 800/555-5211. World Wide Web address: http://www.infousa.com. Made by the same company that created *American Big Business Directory*, *American Manufacturer's Directory* lists over 531,000 manufacturing companies of all sizes and industries. The directory contains product and sales information, company size, and a key contact name for each company.

Online Services

CAREER PARK - MANUFACTURING JOBS
World Wide Web address: http://www.careerpark.com/jobs/manulist.html. This Website provides a list of current job openings in the manufacturing industry. The site is run by Parker Advertising Service, Inc.

Special Programs

BUREAU OF APPRENTICESHIP AND TRAINING
U.S. Department of Labor, 200 Constitution Avenue NW, Room N4649, Washington DC 20210. 202/219-5921.

Paper and Wood Products

You can expect to find the following types of companies in this chapter:

Forest and Wood Products and Services • Lumber and Wood Wholesale
Millwork, Plywood, and Structural Members • Paper and Wood Mills

Some helpful information: *The average salary range for a forester with a bachelor's degree is $19,000 - $25,000. Precision woodworkers generally earn approximately $20,000 per year (woodworkers that specialize in finished work and products such as decorative wood furniture may earn more).*

A.P.A. - THE ENGINEERED WOOD ASSN.
P.O. Box 11700, Tacoma WA 98411-0700. 253/565-6600. **Fax:** 253/565-7265. **Contact:** Human Resources. **World Wide Web address:** http://www.apawood.org. **Description:** A nonprofit trade association providing research, quality testing, and marketing services for its member mills. Members of the A.P.A. produce plywood, OSB, and I-joists. Founded in 1936. **NOTE:** Entry-level positions are offered. **Common positions include:** Accountant; Advertising Clerk; Advertising Executive; Architect; Civil Engineer; Construction Contractor; Editor; Editorial Assistant; Graphic Artist; Graphic Designer; Industrial Engineer; Market Research Analyst; Marketing Specialist; Mechanical Engineer; Sales Engineer; Sales Representative; Technical Writer/Editor. **Educational backgrounds include:** Art/Design; Communications; Engineering; Marketing; Wood Working. **Benefits:** 401(k); Dental Insurance; Disability Coverage; Flexible Schedule; Life Insurance; Medical Insurance; Pension Plan; Tuition Assistance. **Special programs:** Training. **Corporate headquarters location:** This Location. **Other U.S. locations:** Nationwide. **Number of employees at this location:** 170.

ATLANTIC VENEER CORPORATION
P.O. Box 660, Beaufort NC 28516. 252/728-3169. **Contact:** Human Resources. **Description:** Manufactures, produces, and sells veneer, hardwood lumber, and plywood. **Common positions include:** Accountant/Auditor; Administrator; Blue-Collar Worker Supervisor; Branch Manager; Buyer; Computer Programmer; Credit Manager; Department Manager; Financial Analyst; General Manager; Human Resources Manager; Industrial Engineer; Industrial Production Manager; Management Trainee; Manufacturer's/Wholesaler's Sales Rep.; Operations/Production Manager; Purchasing Agent/Manager. **Educational backgrounds include:** Accounting; Business Administration; Computer Science; Engineering; Finance. **Benefits:** Disability Coverage; Life Insurance; Medical Insurance. **Special programs:** Internships. **Corporate headquarters location:** This Location. **Number of employees at this location:** 700.

AUSTELL BOXBOARD CORPORATION
P.O. Box 157, Austell GA 30168. 770/948-3100. **Physical address:** 3300 Joe Jenkins Boulevard, Austell GA 30106-3227. **Contact:** Vice President of Human Resources. **Description:** A regional manufacturer and distributor of boxboard, paper box, and tubing products. **Corporate headquarters location:** This Location.

BALTEK CORPORATION
P.O. Box 195, Northvale NJ 07647. 201/767-1400. **Fax:** 201/387-6631. **Contact:** Human Resources. **Description:** Manufactures wood panels and other balsa wood products for marine and industrial use. **Corporate headquarters location:** This Location.

BEMISS-JASON CORPORATION
P.O. Box 699, Neenah WI 54957. 920/722-9000. **Contact:** Human Resources. **World Wide Web address:** http://www.bemiss-jason.com. **Description:** Produces a wide range of paper products for educational, arts and crafts, retail, display, and medical purposes. **Corporate headquarters location:** This Location.

BERLIN & JONES COMPANY, INC.
2 East Union Avenue, East Rutherford NJ 07073. 201/933-5900. **Contact:** Walt Lypowy, Controller. **Description:** Manufactures envelopes. **Corporate headquarters location:** This Location.

BLUE CIRCLE NORTH AMERICA
BLUE CIRCLE WILLIAMS
1800 Parkway Place, Suite 1100, Marietta GA 30067-8217. 770/499-2800. **Contact:** Personnel. **World Wide Web address:** http://www.bluecirclena.com. **Description:** Produces and supplies a wide range of construction products including ready-mixed concrete and rough and finished lumber. **Corporate headquarters location:** This Location.

BOISE CASCADE CORPORATION
P.O. Box 50, Boise ID 83728. 208/384-6161. **Contact:** Kathy Scott, Employment Manager. **World Wide Web address:** http://www.bc.com. **Description:** A producer and distributor of pulp and paper, a direct distributor of office products, and a manufacturer and distributor of building products. The company has more than 90 manufacturing and distribution locations in 27 states. Boise Cascade Corporation's paper is used for commercial printing and publishing, forms, envelopes, reprographics, tablets, and packaging. Overnight delivery and direct mail have made the company one of the largest distributors of its kind in the U.S. Boise Cascade Corporation provides customers with direct delivery of virtually any office product including office and computer supplies and xerographic paper. The company also produces engineered wood products such as laminated veneer lumber and wood I-joists. Founded in 1957. **Corporate headquarters location:** This Location. **Other U.S. locations:** Yakima WA.

BOWATER INC.
P.O. Box 1028, Greenville SC 29602. 864/271-7733. **Contact:** Human Resources. **World Wide Web address:** http://www.bowater.com. **Description:** Makes coated and uncoated groundwood papers, bleached kraft pulp, and lumber products. The company has 10 pulp and paper mills in the United States, Canada, and South

Korea. These operations are supported by 2.4 million acres of timberlands owned or leased in the United States and Canada and over 14 million acres of timber-cutting rights in Canada. The company is one of the world's largest users of recycled newspapers and magazines. **Common positions include:** Accountant/Auditor; Financial Analyst; Human Resources Manager; Marketing Specialist; Mechanical Engineer; Sales Representative. **Corporate headquarters location:** This Location. **Listed on:** London Stock Exchange; New York Stock Exchange. **Number of employees nationwide:** 8,000.
Other U.S. locations:
• P.O. Box 7, Catawba SC 29704. 803/981- 8000.

BRIGHT WOOD CORPORATION
P.O. Drawer 828, Madras OR 97741-0828. 541/475-2234. **Fax:** 541/475-7758. **Contact:** Personnel. **World Wide Web address:** http://www.brightwood.com. **Description:** Bright Wood is one of the largest millwork manufacturers in the world. Fourteen production plants work together to process over 150 million feet of board lumber annually. Bright Wood is a multiple species manufacturer using firs and pines from New Zealand, Chile, Canada, and other countries. **Corporate headquarters location:** This Location. **Number of employees at this location:** 1,150.

BUFFELEN WOODWORKING COMPANY
P.O. Box 1383, Tacoma WA 98401. 253/627-1191. **Contact:** Human Resources. **Description:** A large millwork manufacturing company. **Common positions include:** Accountant; Administrator; Blue-Collar Worker Supervisor; Buyer; Computer Programmer; Credit Manager; Customer Service Representative; Department Manager; Financial Analyst; General Manager; Human Resources Manager; Manufacturer's/Wholesaler's Sales Rep.; Operations/Production Manager; Purchasing Agent/Manager; Transportation/Traffic Specialist. **Educational backgrounds include:** Accounting; Business Administration; Computer Science; Finance. **Benefits:** Dental Insurance; Disability Coverage; Employee Discounts; Life Insurance; Medical Insurance; Savings Plan. **Corporate headquarters location:** This Location.

CALPINE CONTAINERS INC.
140 Gregory Lane, Suite 180, Pleasant Hill CA 94523. 925/798-3010. **Fax:** 925/686-0152. **Contact:** Jan Tibbetts, Personnel Director. **Description:** Produces wooden and corrugated paper boxes. **Common positions include:** Administrator; Branch Manager; Computer Programmer; Department Manager; Management Trainee; Manufacturer's/Wholesaler's Sales Rep. **Educational backgrounds include:** Accounting; Business Administration. **Benefits:** Dental Insurance; Disability Coverage; Life Insurance; Medical Insurance; Pension Plan; Profit Sharing; Vision Insurance. **Corporate headquarters location:** This Location. **Number of employees at this location:** 15. **Number of employees nationwide:** 300.

CARAUSTAR
P.O. Box 987, Hunt Valley MD 21031. 410/785-2233. **Contact:** Human Resources. **World Wide Web address:** http://www.caraustar.com. **Description:** Produces folding and corrugated boxes, recycled paperboard, custom packaging, plastics, and adhesives. **Common positions include:** Manufacturer's/Wholesaler's Sales Rep. **Educational backgrounds include:** Marketing. **Benefits:** Disability Coverage; Life Insurance; Medical Insurance; Pension Plan.

CHAMPION INTERNATIONAL CORPORATION
One Champion Plaza, Stamford CT 06921. 203/358-7000. **Contact:** Leslie Forrest, Staffing Manager. **World Wide Web address:** http://www.championpaper.com. **Description:** Manufactures paper, lumber, plywood, and forest products for the printing, construction, and home improvement markets. Champion International Corporation owns or controls over 5 million acres of timberland in the United States. The company has five major business units: Printing and Writing Papers; Publication Papers; Newsprint and Kraft; Forest Products; and Marketing, which includes two nationwide newspapers: Champion Export and Pulp Sales. The company's paper operations include the production of business papers, coated papers, bleached paperboard, and packaging materials. **Corporate headquarters location:** This Location. **Subsidiaries include:** Champion Papel e Celulose (Brazil); Weldwood of Canada. **Listed on:** New York Stock Exchange.

CHESAPEAKE CORPORATION
P.O. Box 2350, Richmond VA 23218-2350. 804/697-1000. **Contact:** Tom Smith, Vice President of Human Resources. **World Wide Web address:** http://www.cskcorp.com. **Description:** An integrated forest products company for the construction, institutional, health care, restaurant, hotel, and commercial industries. Products include paper, tissue, towels, placemats, pulp, paperboard, corrugated containers, and wood products. Chesapeake Corporation operates four saw mills in Virginia for kraft products and seven corrugated container plants. The company also provides graphic packaging services. **Corporate headquarters location:** This Location. **Listed on:** New York Stock Exchange. **Number of employees nationwide:** 5,200.

THE CINCINNATI CORDAGE & PAPER COMPANY
800 East Ross Avenue, P.O. Box 17125, Cincinnati OH 45217. 513/242-3600. **Fax:** 513/242-0836. **Contact:** Human Resources. **Description:** A wholesale distributor of printing paper. Founded in 1892. **NOTE:** Entry-level positions are offered. **Common positions include:** Accountant/Auditor; Branch Manager; Buyer; Computer Operator; Computer Programmer; Credit Manager; Customer Service Representative; Financial Manager; General Manager; Human Resources Manager; Manufacturer's/Wholesaler's Sales Rep.; Payroll Clerk; Sales Representative; Systems Analyst; Systems Manager. **Educational backgrounds include:** Accounting; Business Administration; Communications; Computer Science; Finance; Liberal Arts; Marketing. **Benefits:** 401(k); Dental Insurance; Disability Coverage; Life Insurance; Medical Insurance. **Special programs:** Training. **Corporate headquarters location:** This Location. **Other U.S. locations:** Indianapolis IN; Cleveland OH; Columbus OH; Dayton OH; Pittsburgh PA; Knoxville TN; Memphis TN; Nashville TN. **Listed on:** Privately held. **Annual sales/revenues:** More than $100 million. **Number of employees at this location:** 50. **Number of employees nationwide:** 210.

CLEAR PINE MOULDING
P.O. Box 309, Prineville OR 97754. 541/447-4195. **Fax:** 541/447-6479. **Contact:** Mr. Gene Schmidt, Human Resources Manager. **Description:** A sawmill and laminating company. **NOTE:** Second and third shifts are offered. **Common positions include:** Account Manager; Account Representative; Accountant; Administrative Assistant; Administrative Manager; Assistant Manager; Blue-Collar Worker Supervisor; Budget

Analyst; Buyer; Chief Financial Officer; Computer Engineer; Computer Operator; Computer Support Technician; Environmental Engineer; General Manager; Human Resources Manager; Industrial Production Manager; Internet Services Manager; MIS Specialist; Production Manager; Purchasing Agent/Manager; Quality Control Supervisor; Secretary; Typist/Word Processor; Vice President. **Educational backgrounds include:** Accounting; Business Administration; Microsoft Word. **Benefits:** 401(k); Casual Dress - Daily; Dental Insurance; Disability Coverage. **Special programs:** Summer Jobs. **Corporate headquarters location:** Portland OR. **Parent company:** Contact Lumber. **CEO:** Bob Donnelly. **Number of employees at this location:** 450.

CONSOLIDATED PAPERS, INC.
510 High Street, P.O. Box 8050, Wisconsin Rapids WI 54495. 715/422-3435. **Contact:** External Recruiter. **World Wide Web address:** http://www.consolidatedpapers.com. **Description:** Manufactures enamel papers, specialty papers, paperboard, and corrugated products for the print communication, food, and consumer product packaging industries. The company controls seven manufacturing facilities in Wisconsin. **Common positions include:** Chemical Engineer; Mechanical Engineer. **Listed on:** New York Stock Exchange.

COPELAND LUMBER YARDS INC.
901 NE Glisan Street, Portland OR 97232. 503/232-7181. **Fax:** 503/233-9759. **Contact:** Jennifer Goen, Employee Relations. **Description:** This location houses the executive offices. Overall, Copeland Lumber is a retail lumber yard with 68 locations. **Common positions include:** Account Manager; Accountant; Administrative Assistant; Advertising Clerk; Attorney; Buyer; Chief Financial Officer; Clerical Supervisor; Computer Programmer; Controller; Credit Manager; Human Resources Manager; Management Trainee; Marketing Manager; Marketing Specialist; Operations Manager; Project Manager; Real Estate Agent; Systems Analyst; Systems Manager; Vice President of Finance. **Educational backgrounds include:** Accounting; Business Administration; Communications; Computer Science; Finance; Marketing; Public Relations; Software Tech. Support. **Benefits:** 401(k); Dental Insurance; Disability Coverage; Employee Discounts; Flexible Schedule; Life Insurance; Medical Insurance; Pension Plan; Profit Sharing. **Corporate headquarters location:** This Location. **Other U.S. locations:** AZ; CA; NV; WA. **President/CEO:** Helen Jo Whitsell. **Facilities Manager:** Eric Taylor. **Number of employees at this location:** 140. **Number of employees nationwide:** 1,000.

COX INTERIOR, INC.
1751 Old Columbia Road, Campbellsville KY 42718. 270/465-2624. **Contact:** Human Resources. **Description:** Manufactures stair parts, doors, mantels, and other hardwood trim products. Primary materials are poplar, oak, and cherry woods. **Corporate headquarters location:** This Location. **Number of employees at this location:** 480.

DAISHOWA AMERICA COMPANY, LTD.
P.O. Box 271, Port Angeles WA 98362. 360/457-4474. **Fax:** 360/452-9004. **Contact:** David Flodstrom, Human Resources Manager. **Description:** Manufactures telephone directory paper. The company also operates pulp and de-ink facilities. **Common positions include:** Accountant; Blue-Collar Worker Supervisor; Chemical Engineer; Clerical Supervisor; Design Engineer; Electrical/Electronics Engineer; Electrician; Environmental Engineer; Financial Analyst; Human Resources Manager; Mechanical Engineer; Purchasing Agent/Manager; Systems Analyst; Typist/Word Processor. **Educational backgrounds include:** Accounting; Chemistry; Engineering. **Benefits:** 401(k); Dental Insurance; Disability Coverage; Life Insurance; Medical Insurance; Pension Plan; Tuition Assistance. **Corporate headquarters location:** This Location. **Listed on:** Privately held. **Annual sales/revenues:** More than $100 million. **Number of employees at this location:** 300.

DEXTER CORPORATION
One Elm Street, Windsor Locks CT 06096. 860/623-9801. **Contact:** Executive Recruiter. **World Wide Web address:** http://www.dexternonwovens.com. **Description:** This division manufactures specialty paper and nonwoven products. Overall, Dexter Corporation is a diverse manufacturing company whose primary products include chemical and medical products. The company is involved in molecular biology research items, as well as electronic, automotive, food packaging, and aerospace products. **NOTE:** Entry-level positions and second and third shifts are offered. **Common positions include:** Accountant; Chemical Engineer; Computer Programmer; Electrical/Electronics Engineer; Financial Analyst; Human Resources Manager; Marketing Manager; Mechanical Engineer; MIS Specialist; Purchasing Agent/Manager; Systems Analyst. **Educational backgrounds include:** Accounting; Business Administration; Computer Science; Engineering; Finance; Marketing; Mathematics. **Benefits:** 401(k); Dental Insurance; Disability Coverage; Employee Discounts; Financial Planning Assistance; Flexible Schedule; Life Insurance; Medical Insurance; Pension Plan; Profit Sharing; Savings Plan; Tuition Assistance. **Special programs:** Internships. **Corporate headquarters location:** This Location. **Listed on:** New York Stock Exchange.

DIXIELINE LUMBER COMPANY
P.O. Box 85307, San Diego CA 92186. 619/224-4120. **Contact:** Steve Solomon, Personnel Director. **World Wide Web address:** http://www.dixieline.com. **Description:** A lumber distributor. **Common positions include:** Accountant/Auditor; Branch Manager; Computer Programmer; Credit Manager; Customer Service Representative; Human Resources Manager; Systems Analyst. **Benefits:** 401(k); Dental Insurance; Disability Coverage; Employee Discounts; Life Insurance; Medical Insurance; Profit Sharing. **Corporate headquarters location:** This Location. **Listed on:** Privately held. **Number of employees at this location:** 100.

DIXON LUMBER COMPANY, INC.
P.O. Box 937, Galax VA 24333. 540/236-9963. **Fax:** 540/236-9490. **Contact:** Personnel. **Description:** A manufacturer of unfinished and finished hardwood flooring; and unfinished dimensions, stairs, and accessories. **Common positions include:** Accountant/Auditor; Blue-Collar Worker Supervisor; Buyer; Clerical Supervisor; Credit Manager; Customer Service Representative; Electrician; General Manager; Human Resources Manager; Manufacturer's/Wholesaler's Sales Rep.; Operations/Production Manager; Purchasing Agent/Manager; Quality Control Supervisor; Wholesale and Retail Buyer. **Benefits:** 401(k); Life Insurance; Medical Insurance. **Corporate headquarters location:** This Location. **Number of employees at this location:** 325.

DURO BAG MANUFACTURING COMPANY
Davies & Oak Street, Ludlow KY 41016. 606/581-8208. **Fax:** 606/371-5943. **Contact:** Michael Rick,

Employment and Training Coordinator. **E-mail address:** mrick@durobag.com. **World Wide Web address:** http://www.durobag.com. **Description:** A manufacturer of paper and plastic bags. Founded in 1953. **NOTE:** Entry-level positions and second and third shifts are offered. **Common positions include:** Accountant; Adjuster; Administrative Assistant; Buyer; Customer Service Representative; Graphic Artist; Human Resources Manager; Manufacturing Engineer; Marketing Manager; Marketing Specialist; Mechanical Engineer; Operations Manager; Production Manager; Purchasing Agent; Sales Manager; Sales Representative; Secretary. **Educational backgrounds include:** Business Administration; Marketing. **Benefits:** 401(k); Dental Insurance; Disability Coverage; Life Insurance; Medical Insurance; Pension Plan; Tuition Assistance. **Corporate headquarters location:** This Location. **Other area locations:** Covington KY; Walton KY. **Other U.S. locations:** Tampa FL; Brownsville TX; Richmond VA; Hudson WI. **International locations:** Rio Bravo, Mexico. **Listed on:** Privately held. **Annual sales/revenues:** More than $100 million. **Number of employees at this location:** 100. **Number of employees nationwide:** 1,400. **Number of employees worldwide:** 2,300.

ERB LUMBER, INC.

375 South Eton Road, Birmingham MI 48009. 248/644-5300. **Contact:** Human Resources. **Description:** A distributor of lumber and other building construction materials including tools, screws, windows, doors, and nails. **Common positions include:** Accountant/Auditor; Actuary; Administrative Manager; Advertising Clerk; Assistant Manager; Attorney; Budget Analyst; Buyer; Cashier; Clerical Supervisor; Computer Operator; Computer Programmer; Construction Contractor; Construction Trade Worker; Cost Estimator; Credit Clerk and Authorizer; Credit Manager; Editor; Employment Interviewer; Financial Manager; Health Services Manager; Management Trainee; Payroll Clerk; Receptionist; Sales Executive; Secretary; Systems Analyst; Teacher/Professor; Typist/Word Processor. **Benefits:** Dental Insurance; Disability Coverage; Employee Discounts; Life Insurance; Medical Insurance; Pension Plan; Profit Sharing; Savings Plan; Tuition Assistance. **Corporate headquarters location:** This Location. **Parent company:** Woslzy (Great Britain). **Number of employees at this location:** 300.

ELBERTA CRATE & BOX COMPANY

P.O. Box 795, Bainbridge GA 31718. 912/246-2266. **Contact:** D.R. Simmons Jr., President. **Description:** Produces a variety of wooden packaging and storage products including boxes, crates, and pallets. **Corporate headquarters location:** This Location.

FIBERMARK, INC.

P.O. Box 498, Brattleboro VT 05302-0498. 802/257-0365. **Fax:** 802/257-5973. **Contact:** Human Resources. **World Wide Web address:** http://www.fibermark.com. **Description:** Manufactures materials primarily for the office products market including types I, II, and III pressboards, pattern board, jacquard board, and electrical insulating paper and board; as well as guide stock; tube stock; trunk board; and cover stock. **NOTE:** Entry-level positions and second and third shifts are offered. **Common positions include:** Administrative Assistant; Administrative Manager; Chemical Engineer; Customer Service Representative; Electrical/Electronics Engineer; Industrial Production Manager; Mechanical Engineer; Operations Manager; Production Manager; Sales Representative; Secretary. **Educational**

Educational backgrounds include: Business Administration; Chemistry; Engineering. **Benefits:** 401(k); Dental Insurance; Disability Coverage; Employee Discounts; Financial Planning Assistance; Life Insurance; Medical Insurance. **Special programs:** Internships; Summer Jobs. **Corporate headquarters location:** This Location. **Other U.S. locations:** MA; MI; NJ; NY; PA; VA. **International locations:** Germany. **Listed on:** New York Stock Exchange. **Annual sales/revenues:** More than $100 million. **Number of employees at this location:** 240.

FOLD-PAK CORPORATION

P.O. Box 269, Newark NY 14513. 315/331-3200. **Contact:** John Holtz, Corporate Personnel Director. **Description:** Engaged in the manufacture of folding cartons. **Common positions include:** Accountantr; Administrator; Blue-Collar Worker Supervisor; Buyer; Commercial Artist; Computer Programmer; Credit Manager; Customer Service Representative; Department Manager; Draftsperson; Electrical Engineer; Financial Analyst; General Manager; Industrial Engineer; Management Trainee; Manufacturer's/Wholesaler's Sales Rep.; Marketing Specialist; Mechanical Engineer; Operations/Production Manager; Purchasing Agent/Manager; Quality Control Supervisor. **Educational backgrounds include:** Accounting; Art/Design; Business Administration; Computer Science; Engineering; Finance; Marketing. **Benefits:** Dental Insurance; Disability Coverage; Life Insurance; Medical Insurance; Profit Sharing; Savings Plan; Tuition Assistance. **Corporate headquarters location:** This Location. **Other U.S. locations:** Fresno CA; Columbus GA; Newark NJ; Nanuet NY.

FORT JAMES CORPORATION

1650 Lake Cook Drive, Deerfield IL 60015. 847/317-5000. **Contact:** Human Resources. **World Wide Web address:** http://www.fortjames.com. **Description:** A leading international consumer products company, serving consumers both at home and away from home with bathroom and facial tissue, paper towels, napkins, and cups and plates. The company's brands include Quilted Northern, Brawny, Dixie, Vanity Fair, Mardi Gras, Green Forest, Soft 'N Gentle, and So-Dri. Fort James also produces folding cartons for packaging food and pharmaceuticals, and communications papers such as printing, publishing, and office copy paper. The company has more than 60 manufacturing facilities in the U.S., Canada, and ten European countries. **Corporate headquarters location:** This Location. **Other U.S. locations:**
- 6802 Paragon Place, Richmond VA 23230. 804/662-8000.
- P.O. Box 19130, Green Bay WI 54307-9130. 920/435-8821.

FORTIFIBER CORPORATION

4489 Bandini Boulevard, Los Angeles CA 90023. 323/268-6783. **Contact:** Human Resources. **World Wide Web address:** http://www.fortifiber.com. **Description:** Manufactures and markets single-ply, saturated kraft paper for use in the construction industry. **Common positions include:** Accountant/Auditor; Administrator; Blue-Collar Worker Supervisor; Branch Manager; Buyer; Computer Programmer; Credit Manager; Customer Service Representative; Department Manager; Draftsperson; Electrical/Electronics Engineer; Financial Analyst; General Manager; Human Resources Manager; Industrial Engineer; Management Trainee; Manufacturer's/Wholesaler's Sales Rep.; Marketing Specialist; Mechanical Engineer; Operations/Production Manager; Production Manager; Purchasing Agent/Manager; Quality Control Supervisor. **Educational**

backgrounds include: Accounting; Business Administration; Computer Science; Economics; Engineering; Finance; Marketing. **Benefits:** 401(k); Dental Insurance; Disability Coverage; Life Insurance; Medical Insurance; Pension Plan; Tuition Assistance. **Corporate headquarters location:** This Location. **Other U.S. locations:** Portland CA; Tracy CA; Attleboro MA; Howard MI.

FRASER PAPERS INC.
51 South Elm Street, P.O. Box 66, West Carrollton OH 45449. 937/859-5101. **Contact:** Patti Dunham, Human Resources Advisor. **World Wide Web address:** http://www.fraserpapers.com. **Description:** Manufactures paper and related goods. **Common positions include:** Accountant/Auditor; Computer Programmer; Electrician; Environmental Engineer; General Manager; Human Resources Manager; Mechanical Engineer; Operations/ Production Manager; Purchasing Agent/Manager; Quality Control Supervisor; Stationary Engineer; Systems Analyst; Transportation/Traffic Specialist. **Educational backgrounds include:** Accounting; Business Administration; Computer Science; Engineering. **Benefits:** 401(k); Dental Insurance; Disability Coverage; Life Insurance; Medical Insurance; Pension Plan; Savings Plan; Tuition Assistance. **Corporate headquarters location:** Stamford CT. **Other U.S. locations:** Chicago IL; Madawaska ME; Dayton OH; Park Falls WI. **Parent company:** Nexfor, Inc. **Number of employees at this location:** 340. **Number of employees nationwide:** 1,200.

GAYLORD CONTAINER
500 Lake Cook Road, Suite 400, Deerfield IL 60015. 847/405-5500. **Contact:** Human Resources. **Description:** Manufactures and distributes corrugated containers, containerboard, unbleached kraft paper, specialty chemicals, multiwall bags, grocery bags, and sacks to manufacturing end users and converters. The company operates through two grocery bag and sack conversion plants, three paper mills, 19 corrugated container plants, two multiwall bag plants, and four other facilities. By-products of container production include dimethyl sulfide and dimethyl sulfoxide, which the company also markets. Gaylord Container also produces energy. **Corporate headquarters location:** This Location.

GENERAL VENEER MANUFACTURING
P.O. Box 1607, South Gate CA 90280. 323/564-2661. **Contact:** Doug E. DeWitt, Personnel Director. **Description:** Manufactures doors and plywood products for home, commercial, and industrial use. **Corporate headquarters location:** This Location. **Other U.S. locations:** Compton CA.

GEORGIA-PACIFIC CORPORATION
133 Peachtree Street NE, Atlanta GA 30303. 404/652-4000. **Contact:** Corporate Staffing. **World Wide Web address:** http://www.gp.com. **Description:** Manufactures, wholesales, and distributes building products, industrial wood products, pulp, paper, packaging materials, and related chemicals. The company is one of the world's largest manufacturers of forest products. **Common positions include:** Accountant/Auditor; Computer Programmer. **Educational backgrounds include:** Accounting; Business Administration; Computer Science. **Benefits:** Dental Insurance; Disability Coverage; Life Insurance; Medical Insurance; Pension Plan; Profit Sharing; Savings Plan; Tuition Assistance. **Corporate headquarters location:** This Location. **Other U.S. locations:**
- P.O. Box 1618, Eugene OR 97440. 541/689-1221.

P.H. GLATFELTER COMPANY
228 South Main Street, Spring Grove PA 17362. 717/225-4711. **Fax:** 717/225-6834. **Contact:** Mark A. Oberdick, Personnel and Training Administrator. **World Wide Web address:** http://www.glatfelter.com. **Description:** Manufactures fine quality papers for the printing, book publishing, business forms, and technical specialties markets. **NOTE:** Entry-level positions and second and third shifts are offered. **Common positions include:** Accountant/Auditor; Buyer; Chemical Engineer; Chemist; Computer Programmer; Customer Service Representative; Draftsperson; Electrical/Electronics Engineer; Electrician; Financial Analyst; Human Resources Manager; Mechanical Engineer; Systems Analyst. **Educational backgrounds include:** Accounting; Business Administration; Chemistry; Computer Science; Engineering; Liberal Arts; Marketing; Mathematics. **Benefits:** 401(k); Casual Dress - Fridays; Dental Insurance; Disability Coverage; Life Insurance; Medical Insurance; Pension Plan; Profit Sharing; Relocation Assistance; Tuition Assistance. **Special programs:** Internships; Apprenticeships; Training; Co-ops; Summer Jobs. **Corporate headquarters location:** York PA. **Listed on:** New York Stock Exchange. **Annual sales/revenues:** More than $100 million. **Number of employees at this location:** 1,100. **Number of employees nationwide:** 2,500. **Number of employees worldwide:** 3,700.

HANCOCK LUMBER COMPANY
P.O. Box 299, Casco ME 04015. 207/627-4201. **Physical address:** 4 Edes Falls Road, Casco ME. **Contact:** Personnel. **E-mail address:** info@hancocklumber.com. **World Wide Web address:** http://www.hancocklumber.com. **Description:** A lumber company. **Corporate headquarters location:** This Location.

HARTCO FLOORING COMPANY
P.O. Box 4009, Oneida TN 37841. 423/569-8526. **Physical address:** 418 South Main Street, Oneida TN. **Fax:** 423/569-9124. **Contact:** Human Resources. **Description:** Manufactures hardwood flooring. **Common positions include:** Accountant/Auditor; Blue-Collar Worker Supervisor; Chemical Engineer; Electrical/ Electronics Engineer; Electrician; General Manager; Industrial Engineer; Management Trainee; Mechanical Engineer. **Educational backgrounds include:** Accounting; Business Administration; Engineering. **Benefits:** 401(k); Cafeteria Plan; Dental Insurance; Disability Coverage; Employee Discounts; Life Insurance; Medical Insurance; Prescription Drugs; Profit Sharing; Tuition Assistance. **Corporate headquarters location:** This Location. **Other U.S. locations:** Somerset KY. **Listed on:** New York Stock Exchange. **Number of employees at this location:** 800.

HOBOKEN FLOORS
70 Demarest Drive, Wayne NJ 07470. 973/694-2888. **Contact:** Personnel. **Description:** Manufactures hardwood flooring. **Corporate headquarters location:** This Location.

HOLLINGSWORTH & VOSE COMPANY
112 Washington Street, East Walpole MA 02032. 508/668-0295. **Fax:** 508/668-3057. **Contact:** Human Resources. **World Wide Web address:** http://www.hollingsworth-vose.com. **Description:** Manufactures high-tech specialty filtration papers including nonwovens, battery separators, and engine filtration products. Founded in 1843. **NOTE:** Entry-level positions are offered. **Common positions include:** Account Manager; Accountant; Administrative Assistant; AS400 Programmer Analyst; Blue-Collar Worker Supervisor; Chemical

Engineer; Electrical/Electronics Engineer; Financial Analyst; Mechanical Engineer; Operations Manager; SQL Programmer. **Educational backgrounds include:** Accounting; Chemistry; Computer Science; Engineering; Finance. **Benefits:** 401(k); Casual Dress - Fridays; Dental Insurance; Disability Coverage; Financial Planning Assistance; Life Insurance; Medical Insurance; Pension Plan; Savings Plan; Tuition Assistance. **Special programs:** Co-ops. **Corporate headquarters location:** This Location. **Other area locations:** West Groton MA. **Other U.S. locations:** Hawkinsville GA; Greenwich NY; Floyd VA. **International locations:** Apizaco, Mexico; Winchombe, England. **Listed on:** Privately held. **Annual sales/revenues:** More than $100 million. **Number of employees at this location:** 200. **Number of employees nationwide:** 750. **Number of employees worldwide:** 900.

IMPERIAL PAPER BOX CORPORATION
252 Newport Street, Brooklyn NY 11212. 718/346-6100. **Contact:** Steven Sukoff, Personnel Director. **Description:** A manufacturer of paper containers including boxes and packaging materials. **Corporate headquarters location:** This Location.

INLAND CONTAINER CORPORATION
4030 Vincennes Road, Indianapolis IN 46268. 317/879-4222. **Contact:** Human Resources. **World Wide Web address:** http://www.inlandonline.com. **Description:** Manufactures corrugated shipping containers and boxes. **Corporate headquarters location:** This Location.

INTERNATIONAL PAPER COMPANY
2 Manhattanville Road, Purchase NY 10577. 914/397-1500. **Contact:** Human Resources. **World Wide Web address:** http://www.internationalpaper. com. **Description:** This location manufactures coated folding cartons and houses administrative offices. Overall, International Paper Company manufactures pulp and paper, packaging, wood products, and a range of specialty products. Millions of acres of timberland are controlled by International Paper, making it one of the largest private landowners in the United States. The company is organized into five business segments, Printing Papers, in which principal products include uncoated papers, coated papers, bristles, and pulp; Packaging, which includes industrial packaging, consumer packaging, and kraft and specialty papers; Distribution, which includes sales of printing papers, graphic arts equipment and supplies, packaging materials, industrial supplies, and office products; Specialty Products, which includes imaging products, specialty panels, nonwovens, chemicals, and minerals; and Forest Products which includes logs and wood products. **Corporate headquarters location:** This Location. **Listed on:** New York Stock Exchange. **Number of employees worldwide:** 72,500.

IVEX PACKAGING CORPORATION
100 Tri-State Drive, Suite 200, Lincolnshire IL 60069. 847/945-9100. **Contact:** Human Resources. **World Wide Web address:** http://www. ivexpackaging.com. **Description:** Manufactures paper and plastic packaging products including dessert trays, containers, and toilet tissue overwraps. **Corporate headquarters location:** This Location. **Operations at this facility include:** Administration.

THE A. JOHNSON CO.
995 South Route 116 Road, Bristol VT 05443. 802/453-4884. **Contact:** Human Resources. **Description:** Produces kiln-dried hardwood lumber. **Number of employees at this location:** 50.

JORDAN LUMBER & SUPPLY, INC.
P.O. Box 98, Mount Gilead NC 27306. 910/439-6121. **Contact:** Personnel Director. **Description:** A distributor of southern yellow pine lumber, wood chips, sawdust, bark, and related products. **Common positions include:** Accountant/Auditor; Blue-Collar Worker Supervisor; Department Manager; Forester/Conservation Scientist; Production Worker; Purchasing Agent/Manager; Quality Control Supervisor. **Educational backgrounds include:** High School Diploma/GED. **Benefits:** 401(k); Employee Discounts; Life Insurance; Medical Insurance; Profit Sharing; Savings Plan. **Corporate headquarters location:** This Location. **Number of employees at this location:** 150.

LETICA CORPORATION
P.O. Box 5005, Rochester MI 48308-5005. 248/652-0557. **Contact:** Director of Personnel. **Description:** Manufactures plastic and paper packaging materials. **Common positions include:** Accountant/Auditor; Buyer; Computer Programmer; Customer Service Representative; Draftsperson; Electrician; Environmental Engineer; Human Resources Manager; Industrial Production Manager; Maintenance Supervisor; Management Trainee; Mechanical Engineer; Plant Manager; Public Relations Specialist; Purchasing Agent/Manager; Quality Control Supervisor; Systems Analyst. **Educational backgrounds include:** Business Administration; Engineering; Marketing. **Benefits:** 401(k); Life Insurance; Medical Insurance; Profit Sharing. **Corporate headquarters location:** This Location. **Other U.S. locations:** Nationwide.

LYMAN LUMBER COMPANY
P.O. Box 40, Excelsior MN 55331. 952/474-0844. **Contact:** Human Resources. **Description:** A lumber and building materials company with several divisions in the Twin Cities metropolitan area, two in Wisconsin, and one in North Carolina. **Common positions include:** Accountant/Auditor; Architectural Engineer; Blue-Collar Worker Supervisor; Buyer; Credit Manager; Customer Service Representative; Draftsperson; Human Resources Manager; Management Trainee; Manufacturer's/Wholesaler's Sales Rep.; Operations/ Production Manager; Purchasing Agent/Manager; Truck Driver. **Educational backgrounds include:** Accounting; Engineering. **Benefits:** Dental Insurance; Disability Coverage; Employee Discounts; Life Insurance; Medical Insurance; Pension Plan; Profit Sharing; Tuition Assistance. **Corporate headquarters location:** This Location.

MACKAY ENVELOPE CORPORATION
2100 Elm Street SE, Minneapolis MN 55414-2597. 612/331-9311. **Contact:** Human Resources. **World Wide Web address:** http://www.mackayenvelope. com. **Description:** Manufactures envelopes. **Common positions include:** Accountant/Auditor; Customer Service Representative; Manufacturer's/ Wholesaler's Sales Rep. **Educational backgrounds include:** Accounting; Business Administration; Liberal Arts. **Benefits:** 401(k); Dental Insurance; Disability Coverage; Life Insurance; Medical Insurance; Profit Sharing; Tuition Assistance. **Corporate headquarters location:** This Location. **Listed on:** Privately held. **Number of employees at this location:** 250. **Number of employees nationwide:** 350.

MALNOVE INC.
P.O. Box 160128, Clearfield UT 84016-0128. 801/773-7400. **Contact:** Human Resources. **Description:** A packaging company that manufactures cardboard boxes.

MARCAL PAPER MILLS, INC.
One Market Street, Elmwood Park NJ 07407. 201/796-4000. **Contact:** James H. Nelson, Director of Human Resources. **World Wide Web address:** http://www.marcalpaper.com. **Description:** Manufactures and distributes a broad range of nationally advertised paper products including paper towels, toilet tissue, and napkins. **Common positions include:** Accountant/Auditor; Chemical Engineer; Computer Programmer; Customer Service Representative; Manufacturer's/Wholesaler's Sales Rep.; Mechanical Engineer; Operations/Production Manager. **Educational backgrounds include:** Accounting; Business Administration; Engineering. **Benefits:** 401(k); Dental Insurance; Disability Coverage; Employee Discounts; Life Insurance; Medical Insurance; Savings Plan; Tuition Assistance. **Corporate headquarters location:** This Location.

MEAD CORPORATION
Courthouse Plaza NE, Dayton OH 45463. 937/495-6323. **Contact:** Department of Human Resources. **World Wide Web address:** http://www.mead.com. **Description:** One of the world's largest manufacturers of paper. Mead produces more than 1.2 million tons annually for printing and business use and is a leader in the coated paperboard and multiple packaging markets. The company is also a distributor of paper, packaging, and business supplies made by manufacturers throughout the world. Mead is one of the largest makers of paper-based school and home-office supplies, as well as a developer of one of the world's leading electronic information retrieval services for law, patents, accounting, finance, news, and business information. **Corporate headquarters location:** This Location. **Listed on:** Chicago Stock Exchange; New York Stock Exchange; Pacific Stock Exchange. **Annual sales/revenues:** More than $100 million.

MENASHA CORPORATION
P.O. Box 367, Neenah WI 54957. 920/751-1000. **Contact:** Stevey S. Kromholz, Corporate Manager of Staffing. **World Wide Web address:** http://www.menasha.com. **Description:** A manufacturer of corrugated containers. **Common positions include:** Accountant; Attorney; Chemical Engineer; Computer Programmer; Customer Service Representative; Financial Analyst; General Manager; Health Services Manager; Human Resources Manager; Industrial Engineer; Industrial Production Manager; Management Trainee; Manufacturer's/Wholesaler's Sales Rep.; Mechanical Engineer; Operations/Production Manager; Paralegal; Purchasing Agent/Manager; Quality Control Supervisor; Systems Analyst. **Educational backgrounds include:** Accounting; Art/Design; Business Administration; Computer Science; Engineering; Liberal Arts; Marketing. **Benefits:** 401(k); Daycare Assistance; Dental Insurance; Disability Coverage; Life Insurance; Medical Insurance; Pension Plan; Profit Sharing; Tuition Assistance. **Corporate headquarters location:** This Location. **Other U.S. locations:** Nationwide. **Listed on:** Privately held. **Number of employees at this location:** 200. **Number of employees nationwide:** 4,800.

MOSINEE PAPER CORPORATION
1244 Kronenwetter Drive, Mosinee WI 54455-9099. 715/693-4470. **Contact:** Human Resources. **Description:** Manufactures specialty papers; towel and tissue papers; and laminated, saturated, and coated products. **Corporate headquarters location:** This Location. **Subsidiaries include:** Specialty papers are produced by the pulp and paper facility in Mosinee WI (715/693-2111), which manufactures a variety of products, primarily for industrial customers; and by Sorg Paper Company (Middletown OH) which produces specialty grades of paper and special-use tissue papers. Towel and tissue papers are produced by the Bay West Paper Corporation (Harrodsburg KY and Middletown OH), and marketed to industrial and commercial washroom supply distributors. Laminated, saturated, and coated products made of paper and other substrates are produced by Mosinee Converted Products (Columbus WI and Jackson MS). Mosinee Industrial Forest (Solon Springs WI) provides forest operations for Mosinee Paper Corporation, produces pulpwood, and sells sawlogs and landscape timber to area sawmills. **Listed on:** NASDAQ.

NVF COMPANY INC.
1166 Yorklyn Road, P.O. Box 68, Yorklyn DE 19736. 302/239-5281. **Contact:** Personnel Director. **World Wide Web address:** http://www.nvf.com. **Description:** Produces vulcanized fiber paper and industrial laminates. **Corporate headquarters location:** This Location. **Other U.S. locations:** Newark NJ.

NATIONAL SERVICE INDUSTRIES INC.
NATIONAL LINEN SERVICE
1420 Peachtree Street NE, Atlanta GA 30309. 404/853-1000. **Contact:** Vice President of Human Resources. **Description:** A diversified manufacturing and service company with operations in five industries. The majority of revenue is made in lighting equipment, textile rental, and specialty chemicals, but the corporation also does business in insulation services and envelope manufacturing. National Linen Service (also at this location, 404/853-6000) is a linen rental supplier, serving the hospitality and health care industries. Products include napkins; table and bed linens; bath, bar, and shop towels; uniforms; specialized garments; sterilized products; restroom products; mats; and mops. **Corporate headquarters location:** This Location. **Subsidiaries include:** Lithonia Lighting manufactures lighting fixtures for the commercial, industrial, institutional, and residential construction and renovation markets. Products include fluorescent lighting fixtures, indoor and outdoor high-intensity discharge fixtures, recessed down lighting fixtures, sports lighting fixtures, architectural outdoor fixtures, emergency lighting fixtures, controls, and wiring systems. Zep Manufacturing Company, Selig Chemical Industries, and National Chemical are manufacturers of specialty chemicals for the automotive, diversified manufacturing, food, hospitality, and institutional markets. Products include specialty chemicals and equipment used in cleaning, sanitizing, polishing, degreasing, and water treatment. North Brothers Company fabricates, distributes, and installs insulation and other building products and related services for the construction, renovation, cold storage, manufactured housing, process manufacturing, power generation, and services sectors. Products and services include insulation products, accessories, and contracting services. Atlantic Envelope Company manufactures custom and standard envelopes and related office products. **Listed on:** New York Stock Exchange.

THE NELSON COMPANY
2116 Sparrows Point Road, Baltimore MD 21219. 410/477-3000. **Fax:** 410/477-3577. **Contact:** Human Resources. **Description:** Produces wooden boxes, pallets, crates, angleboard, and corrugated boxes. The Nelson Company also recycles pallets. **Corporate headquarters location:** This Location.

NEW YORK ENVELOPE CORPORATION
29-10 Hunters Point Avenue, Long Island City NY 11101. 718/786-0300. **Contact:** Personnel

Department. **Description:** Manufactures a wide range of envelopes for distribution to wholesalers. **Corporate headquarters location:** This Location.

NORTH PACIFIC LUMBER COMPANY
P.O. Box 3915, Portland OR 97208-3915. 503/231-1166. **Contact:** Karen Austin, Personnel Manager. **World Wide Web address:** http://www.north-pacific.com. **Description:** A domestic and international wholesale distributor of forest products and other commodities. **Common positions include:** Accountant/Auditor; Buyer; Computer Programmer; Credit Manager; Sales Executive; Systems Analyst; Transportation/Traffic Specialist. **Educational backgrounds include:** Accounting; Business Administration; Finance; Liberal Arts; Marketing. **Benefits:** Dental Insurance; Disability Coverage; Life Insurance; Medical Insurance; Pension Plan; Profit Sharing; Savings Plan; Tuition Assistance. **Corporate headquarters location:** This Location.

NORTHWEST ARKANSAS PAPER COMPANY
755 Gray Drive, Springdale AR 72764. 501/751-7155. **Fax:** 501/756-6301. **Contact:** Human Resources Director. **Description:** A paper processing company. **Common positions include:** Accountant/Auditor; Administrative Manager; Automotive Mechanic; Buyer; Customer Service Representative; Human Resources Manager; Purchasing Agent/Manager; Services Sales Representative; Wholesale and Retail Buyer. **Educational backgrounds include:** Accounting; Business Administration; Communications; Computer Science; Marketing. **Benefits:** Dental Insurance; Employee Discounts; Life Insurance; Medical Insurance; Profit Sharing; Savings Plan. **Corporate headquarters location:** This Location. **Listed on:** Privately held. **Number of employees at this location:** 200.

PACIFIC LUMBER COMPANY
P.O. Box 37, Scotia CA 95565. 707/764-2222. **Contact:** Personnel Department. **World Wide Web address:** http://www.palco.com. **Description:** Manufactures redwood and douglas fir lumber. **Corporate headquarters location:** This Location. **Number of employees nationwide:** 1,400.

PACTIV CORPORATION
1900 West Field Court, Lake Forest IL 60045. 847/482-2000. **Contact:** Human Resources. **Description:** A worldwide manufacturer of paper, corrugated paper, paper board, aluminum, and plastic packaging material. Products are used in the packaging of food, paper and paper products, metal products, rubber and plastics, automotive products, point-of-purchase displays, soap, detergent, and food products, as well as residential construction. **Common positions include:** Accountant; Industrial Engineer; Manufacturer's/Wholesaler's Sales Rep.; Mechanical Engineer; Operations/Production Manager. **Educational backgrounds include:** Accounting; Engineering; Marketing. **Benefits:** Daycare Assistance; Dental Insurance; Disability Coverage; Employee Discounts; Life Insurance; Medical Insurance; Profit Sharing; Savings Plan; Tuition Assistance. **Special programs:** Internships. **Corporate headquarters location:** This Location. **Listed on:** New York Stock Exchange. **Number of employees worldwide:** 9,000.

PONDEROSA PRODUCTS INC.
P.O. Box 25506, Albuquerque NM 87125. 505/843-7400. **Contact:** Mary Fiedler, Office Manager. **Description:** Produces and distributes particleboard. **Corporate headquarters location:** This Location.

POTLATCH CORPORATION
P.O. Box 1388, Lewiston ID 83501. 208/799-0123. **Contact:** Darrell Daubert, Employee Relations Manager. **World Wide Web address:** http://www.potlatchcorp.com. **Description:** This location produces bleach kraft pulp, while the paperboard operation produces bleached paperboard. Overall, Potlatch Corporation is a diversified forest products company with approximately 1.5 million acres of timberland in Arkansas, Idaho, and Minnesota. Potlatch's manufacturing facilities convert wood fiber into two main product lines: bleached fiber products including bleached kraft pulp, paperboard, printing papers, and consumer tissue; and wood products including oriented strand board, plywood, particleboard, lumber, and wood specialties. **Corporate headquarters location:** This Location.

RAYONIER INC.
1177 Summer Street, Stamford CT 06905. 203/348-7000. **Contact:** Daniel Sassi, Human Resources. **Description:** A leading international forest products company primarily engaged in the trading, merchandising, and manufacturing of logs, timber, and wood products, and in the production and sale of specialty pulps. Rayonier owns, buys, and harvests timber stumpage and purchases delivered logs, primarily in North America and New Zealand, for subsequent sale into export markets (primarily to Japan, Korea, and China), as well as to domestic lumber and pulp mills. Rayonier also produces dimension and specialty products for residential construction and industrial uses. **Corporate headquarters location:** This Location. **Number of employees at this location:** 2,600.

RIVERWOOD INTERNATIONAL CORP.
3350 Riverwood Parkway SE, Suite 1400, Atlanta GA 30339. 770/644-3000. **Contact:** Robert Burg, Senior Vice President of Human Resources. **World Wide Web address:** http://www.riverwood.com. **Description:** Produces coated, unbleached kraft board and packaging products including beverage and folding cartons, packaging machinery, containerboard, corrugated boxes, lumber, and plywood. The company's primary machinery-based packaging system, which it produces and markets, is sold under the brand name Twin-Stack. **Corporate headquarters location:** This Location. **Parent company:** Manville Corporation. **Number of employees nationwide:** 8,500.

ROBBINS MANUFACTURING COMPANY
P.O. Box 17939, Tampa FL 33682. 813/971-3030. **Fax:** 813/972-3980. **Contact:** Human Resources. **Description:** A lumber mill. **Common positions include:** Blue-Collar Worker Supervisor; Branch Manager; Buyer; Clerical Supervisor; Computer Programmer; Credit Manager; Customer Service Representative; Draftsperson; Human Resources Manager; Manufacturer's/Wholesaler's Sales Rep.; Mechanical Engineer; Operations/Production Manager; Software Engineer; Systems Analyst; Wholesale and Retail Buyer. **Benefits:** 401(k); Medical Insurance; Profit Sharing. **Corporate headquarters location:** This Location. **Other U.S. locations:** CA; NC; TX; WA. **Listed on:** Privately held. **Number of employees at this location:** 250. **Number of employees nationwide:** 400.

ROCK-TENN COMPANY
P.O. Box 4098, Norcross GA 30091. 770/448-2193. **Contact:** Human Resources. **Description:** Manufactures 100 percent recycled paperboard and paperboard products. Over two-thirds of paperboard production is done by the company's own converting plants to produce folding cartons, book and notebook covers, components for the furniture

industry, and solid fiber partitions used in shipping glass and plastic containers. **Corporate headquarters location:** This Location. **Number of employees nationwide:** 5,900.

ROSEBURG FOREST PRODUCTS COMPANY
P.O. Box 1088, Roseburg OR 97470. 541/679-3311. **Contact:** John McAmis, Personnel Director. **World Wide Web address:** http://www.rfpco.com. **Description:** Manufactures softwood, plywood, and millwork. **Corporate headquarters location:** This Location.

SCHIFFENHAUS INDUSTRIES
2013 McCarter Highway, Newark NJ 07104. 973/484-5000. **Contact:** Human Resources. **Description:** Manufactures corrugated boxes and flexographic, preprinted liner board. **Common positions include:** Accountant/Auditor; Blue-Collar Worker Supervisor; Computer Programmer; Customer Service Representative; Manufacturer's/Wholesaler's Sales Rep.; Marketing Specialist; Operations/Production Manager; Purchasing Agent/Manager; Quality Control Supervisor. **Educational backgrounds include:** Accounting; Business Administration; Finance; Marketing. **Benefits:** Disability Coverage; Life Insurance; Medical Insurance; Pension Plan; Profit Sharing; Savings Plan; Tuition Assistance. **Corporate headquarters location:** This Location. **Listed on:** New York Stock Exchange. **Number of employees at this location:** 165.

SMEAD MANUFACTURING COMPANY
600 East Smead Boulevard, Hastings MN 55033. 651/437-4111. **Contact:** Dean Schwanke, Director of Human Resources. **World Wide Web address:** http://www.smead.com. **Description:** Manufactures die-cut paper. **Common positions include:** Accountant/Auditor; Administrator; Blue-Collar Worker Supervisor; Branch Manager; Buyer; Computer Programmer; Credit Manager; Customer Service Representative; Department Manager; Draftsperson; Financial Analyst; General Manager; Human Resources Manager; Industrial Engineer; Industrial Production Manager; Manufacturer's/Wholesaler's Sales Rep.; Marketing Specialist; Mechanical Engineer; Operations/Production Manager; Purchasing Agent/Manager; Quality Control Supervisor; Systems Analyst; Transportation/Traffic Specialist. **Educational backgrounds include:** Accounting; Business Administration; Computer Science; Engineering; Liberal Arts; Marketing. **Benefits:** Disability Coverage; Life Insurance; Medical Insurance; Pension Plan; Savings Plan; Tuition Assistance. **Corporate headquarters location:** This Location.

SMURFIT-STONE CONTAINER CORP.
150 North Michigan Avenue, Chicago IL 60601. 312/346-6600. **Contact:** Recruiting Specialist. **World Wide Web address:** http://www.smurfit-stone.com. **Description:** One of the world's leading paper-based packaging companies. Smurfit-Stone Container Corporation's main products include corrugated containers, folding cartons, and multiwall industrial bags. The company is also one of the world's largest collectors and processors of recycled products. Smurfit-Stone Container Corporation also operates several paper tube, market pulp, and newsprint production facilities. **Common positions include:** Accountant/Auditor; Computer Programmer; Credit Manager; Customer Service Representative; Financial Analyst; Human Resources Manager; Purchasing Agent/Manager; Systems Analyst. **Educational backgrounds include:** Accounting; Business Administration; Computer Science; Finance; Liberal Arts. **Benefits:** 401(k); Credit Union; Dental Insurance; Disability

Coverage; Life Insurance; Medical Insurance; Pension Plan; Profit Sharing; Savings Plan; Tuition Assistance. **Corporate headquarters location:** This Location. **Listed on:** NASDAQ. **Number of employees at this location:** 500.
Other U.S. locations:
• 5000 Flat Rock Road, Philadelphia PA 19127. 215/984-7000.

SORG PAPER COMPANY
901 Manchester Avenue, Middletown OH 45042. 513/420-5300. **Contact:** Human Resources. **Description:** A pulp and paper processor. **Common positions include:** Accountant/Auditor; Blue-Collar Worker Supervisor; Buyer; Chemist; Electrical/Electronics Engineer; Human Resources Manager; Industrial Engineer; Marketing Specialist; Mechanical Engineer; Operations/Production Manager. **Educational backgrounds include:** Accounting; Chemistry; Engineering. **Benefits:** Dental Insurance; Disability Coverage; Life Insurance; Medical Insurance; Pension Plan; Tuition Assistance. **Corporate headquarters location:** This Location. **Parent company:** Mosinee Paper Corporation.

SOUTH COAST LUMBER COMPANY
P.O. Box 670, Brookings OR 97415. 541/469-2136. **Contact:** Personnel. **Description:** A saw and planing mill which produces veneers and plywood. **NOTE:** This company hires through the Oregon State Employment Office. **Corporate headquarters location:** This Location. **Number of employees at this location:** 435.

STANDARD FOLDING CARTONS
85th Street & 24th Avenue, Jackson Heights NY 11370. 718/335-5500. **Contact:** Maureen Stokes, Personnel Department. **Description:** A manufacturer of folding boxes. **Corporate headquarters location:** This Location.

STATES INDUSTRIES INC.
P.O. Box 7037, Eugene OR 97401. 541/688-7871. **Contact:** Brenda Holloway, Human Resources Manager. **World Wide Web address:** http://www.statesind.com. **Description:** A lumbermill. **Corporate headquarters location:** This Location. **Number of employees at this location:** 300.

STERLING PAPER COMPANY
2155 East Castor Avenue, Philadelphia PA 19134. 215/744-5350. **Contact:** Human Resources. **Description:** Manufactures a wide variety of paper plates, cups, and related products. **Corporate headquarters location:** This Location.

THT INC.
33 Riverside Avenue, 5th Floor, Westport CT 06880. 203/226-6408. **Contact:** Human Resources Department. **Description:** A holding company. **Benefits:** Pension Plan. **Corporate headquarters location:** This Location. **Subsidiaries include:** Jackburn Manufacturing, Inc. manufactures fabricated steel parts; Setterstix Corporation manufactures rolled paper products for the confectionery and health care industries. **Number of employees nationwide:** 145.

TEMPLE-INLAND, INC.
P.O. Drawer N, Diboll TX 75941. 936/829-1313. **Contact:** Human Resources. **World Wide Web address:** http://www.templeinland.com. **Description:** A holding company offering corrugated packaging, bleached paperboard, building products, and financial services. **Corporate headquarters location:** This Location. **Annual sales/revenues:** More than $100 million.

TIMBER PRODUCTS COMPANY
P.O. Box 269, Springfield OR 97477-0055. 541/747-4577. **Physical address:** 305 South Fourth Street, Springfield OR 97477. **Contact:** Paul Haugen, Human Resources Manager. **Description:** Manufactures a wide variety of wood products. **Corporate headquarters location:** This Location. **Other area locations:** Grants Pass OR; Medford OR. **Subsidiaries include:** Selply Inc., White City OR.

TREESOURCE INDUSTRIES, INC.
P.O. Box 5805, Portland OR 97228-5805. 503/246-3440. **Fax:** 503/245-4229. **Contact:** Personnel Manager. **World Wide Web address:** http://www.treesource.com. **Description:** One of the 10 largest volume producers of lumber products in the United States. Its 12 mills in Oregon, Washington, and Vermont manufacture softwood stud and dimension lumber, as well as hardwood lumber. These products are marketed throughout the United States, Canada, and a number of other foreign markets under the TreeSource brand name. **Corporate headquarters location:** This Location.

TRUS JOIST MACMILLAN
200 East Mallard Drive, Boise ID 83706. 208/364-3300. **Contact:** Rob Adams, Director of Human Resources. **World Wide Web address:** http://www.trusjoist.com. **Description:** Markets industrial construction materials, concentrating on wood-and-steel composite truss. The company focuses on engineered wood, sized to fit custom needs. The engineered wood products are made from logs that are either peeled or stranded, and the resulting veneers or strands are coated with adhesives and pressed to permanently bond the wood fibers. The products resist warping, twisting, and changing shapes in most applications. Products include Microllam LVL; TimberStrand LSL; Parallam PSL, and Form-I Joists. **Corporate headquarters location:** This Location. **Parent company:** Weyerhaeuser Company. **Listed on:** NASDAQ. **Stock exchange symbol:** TJCO.

WAUSAU PAPER MILLS COMPANY
1244 Kronenwetter, Mosinee WI 54455. 715/675-3361. **Contact:** Human Resources. **Description:** Manufactures printing, writing, and technical papers, serving diverse markets throughout the United States and the world. The company consists of two operating divisions: the Printing and Writing Division and the Rhinelander Division. **Corporate headquarters location:** This Location. **Subsidiaries include:** The Printing and Writing Division (Brokaw WI), and Wausau Papers of New Hampshire, Inc. (Groveton NH) operate a paper mill. The division's product lines include recycled products made from 50 percent recycled fibers. These papers are sold to paper distributors and converters throughout the United States and Canada. The Rhinelander Division consists of Rhinelander Paper Company, Inc. (Rhinelander WI) which manufactures lightweight, dense, technical specialty papers which are sold directly to converters and end users. Small volumes of yeast and lignosulfonates are also manufactured and sold for use as food additives, pet food ingredients, and other end uses. **Listed on:** NASDAQ.

WERTHAN PACKAGING INC.
1400 Eighth Avenue North, Nashville TN 37208-1310. 615/259-9331. **Fax:** 615/242-2801. **Contact:** Human Resources. **World Wide Web address:** http://www.werthan.com. **Description:** Manufactures multiwall paper shipping sacks. **Common positions include:** Accountant; Administrative Assistant; AS400 Programmer Analyst; Chief Financial Officer; Computer Programmer; Controller; Customer Service Representative; Database Administrator; Marketing Manager; Purchasing Agent/Manager; Systems Manager; Transportation/Traffic Specialist. **Educational backgrounds include:** AS400 Certification; Microsoft Office. **Benefits:** 401(k); Casual Dress - Fridays; Dental Insurance; Disability Coverage; Life Insurance; Medical Insurance; Pension Plan; Relocation Assistance; Tuition Assistance. **Number of employees at this location:** 400.

WESTVACO CORPORATION
299 Park Avenue, New York NY 10171. 212/688-5000. **Contact:** Personnel Representative. **World Wide Web address:** http://www.westvaco.com. **Description:** A producer of paper packaging and specialty chemicals. Worldwide, Westvaco operates 50 facilities including paper and paperboard mills, converting plants, chemical plants, lumber mills, research and development laboratories, and real estate operations. **NOTE:** Resumes should be sent to Personnel, 1011 Boulder Springs Drive, Richmond VA 23225. **Common positions include:** Accountant; Financial Analyst; Manufacturer's/Wholesaler's Sales Rep. **Educational backgrounds include:** Business Administration; Engineering; Liberal Arts; Marketing. **Benefits:** Dental Insurance; Disability Coverage; Life Insurance; Medical Insurance; Savings Plan; Tuition Assistance. **Corporate headquarters location:** This Location. **Listed on:** New York Stock Exchange. **Number of employees nationwide:** 14,000.

WEYERHAEUSER COMPANY
P.O. Box 2999, CCB 507, Tacoma WA 98477. 253/924-2118. **Contact:** Recruiting and Staffing. **World Wide Web address:** http://www.weyerhauser.com. **Description:** A forest management and manufacturing company. Weyerhaeuser recycles pulp, paper, and packaging products; manufactures wood products; manages timberland; and develops real estate. **Company slogan:** Where the future is growing. **Common positions include:** Account Manager; Account Representative; Accountant; Adjuster; Administrative Assistant; Administrative Manager; Applications Engineer; AS400 Programmer Analyst; Assistant Manager; Attorney; Auditor; Biological Scientist; Blue-Collar Worker Supervisor; Budget Analyst; Buyer; Chemical Engineer; Chemist; Chief Financial Officer; Clerical Supervisor; Computer Animator; Computer Engineer; Computer Programmer; Computer Scientist; Computer Support Technician; Computer Technician; Consultant; Content Developer; Controller; Cost Estimator; Customer Service Representative; Database Administrator; Database Manager; Desktop Publishing Specialist; Draftsperson; Economist; Editor; Editorial Assistant; Electrician; Emergency Medical Technician; Environmental Engineer; Finance Director; Financial Analyst; General Manager; Geologist/Geophysicist; Graphic Artist; Graphic Designer; Human Resources Manager; Industrial Production Manager; Intellectual Property Lawyer; Internet Services Manager; Librarian; Licensed Practical Nurse; Management Analyst/Consultant; Management Trainee; Managing Editor; Manufacturing Engineer; Market Research Analyst; Marketing Manager; Marketing Specialist; Medical Assistant; MIS Specialist; Multimedia Designer; Network/Systems Administrator; Nurse Practitioner; Operations Manager; Paralegal; Production Manager; Project Manager; Public Relations Specialist; Purchasing Agent/Manager; Quality Assurance Engineer; Quality Control Supervisor; Real Estate Agent; Registered Nurse; Sales Engineer; Sales Executive; Sales Manager; Sales

Representative; Secretary; Software Engineer; SQL Programmer; Statistician; Systems Analyst; Systems Manager; Technical Writer/Editor; Transportation Specialist; Typist/Word Processor; Vice President; Video Production Coordinator; Webmaster. **Educational backgrounds include:** Accounting; AS400 Certification; ASP; Business Administration; C/C++; CGI; Chemistry; Cold Fusion; Computer Science; Engineering; Finance; HTML; Internet; Java; Marketing; Mathematics; MCSE; Microsoft Word; Novell; Public Relations; QuarkXPress; Software Development; Software Tech. Support; Spreadsheets; Visual Basic. **Benefits:** 401(k); Casual Dress - Fridays; Dental Insurance; Disability Coverage; Pension Plan; Profit Sharing; Public Transit Available. **Corporate headquarters location:** This Location. **Other U.S. locations:** Nationwide. **Listed on:** New York Stock Exchange. **Annual sales/revenues:** More than $100 million. **Number of employees nationwide:** 37,000.

WILLAMETTE INDUSTRIES INC.
1300 SW Fifth Avenue, Suite 3800, Portland OR 97201. 503/227-5581. **Contact:** Human Resources. **World Wide Web address:** http://www.wii.com. **Description:** A diversified, integrated forest products company with 90 plants and mills manufacturing containerboard, bag paper, fine paper, bleached hardwood market pulp, specialty printing papers, corrugated containers, business forms, cut sheet paper, paper bags, inks, lumber, plywood, particleboard, medium-density fiberboard, laminated beams, and value-added wood products. The company owns or controls over 1.2 million acres of forestland. Founded in 1906. **Common positions include:** Accountant/Auditor; Blue-Collar Worker Supervisor; Chemical Engineer; Computer Programmer; Credit Manager; Department Manager; Electrical/Electronics Engineer; Forester/ Conservation Scientist; General Manager; Human Resources Manager; Industrial Engineer; Management Trainee; Manufacturer's/Wholesaler's Sales Rep.; Marketing Specialist; Mechanical Engineer; Operations/Production Manager; Purchasing Agent/Manager; Quality Control Supervisor; Transportation/Traffic Specialist. **Educational backgrounds include:** Accounting; Business Administration; Communications; Engineering; Finance; Marketing. **Benefits:** Dental Insurance; Disability Coverage; Life Insurance; Medical Insurance; Pension Plan; Profit Sharing; Savings Plan; Tuition Assistance. **Corporate headquarters location:** This Location. **Listed on:** NASDAQ. **Number of employees at this location:** 180. **Number of employees nationwide:** 14,000.

ZUMBIEL PACKAGING
2339 Harris Avenue, Cincinnati OH 45212. 513/531-3600. **Contact:** Personnel Director. **Description:** A producer of paper and related packaging goods including Rewrite folding cartons, set-up boxes, and acetate beverage carriers including beer and soft drink 12- and 24-packs. **Common positions include:** Accountant/Auditor; Blue-Collar Worker Supervisor; Computer Programmer; Customer Service Representative; Manufacturer's/Wholesaler's Sales Rep. **Educational backgrounds include:** Accounting; Business Administration; Marketing. **Benefits:** Dental Insurance; Life Insurance; Medical Insurance; Profit Sharing; Savings Plan; Tuition Assistance. **Corporate headquarters location:** This Location.

For more information on career opportunities in the paper and wood products industries:

Associations

FOREST PRODUCTS SOCIETY
2801 Marshall Court, Madison WI 53705-2295. 608/231-1361. Fax: 608/231-2152. E-mail address: info@forestprod.org. World Wide Web address: http://www.forestprod.org. An international, nonprofit, educational association that provides an information network for all segments of the forest products industry, as well as an employment referral service.

NATIONAL PAPER TRADE ASSOCIATION
111 Great Neck Road, Great Neck NY 11021. 516/829-3070. World Wide Web address: http://www.papertrade.com. Offers management services to paper wholesalers, as well as books, seminars, and research services.

TECHNICAL ASSOCIATION OF THE PULP AND PAPER INDUSTRY
P.O. Box 105113, Atlanta GA 30348-5113. 770/446-1400. World Wide Web address: http://www.tappi.org. A nonprofit organization offering conferences and continuing education.

Directories

DIRECTORY OF THE WOOD PRODUCTS INDUSTRY
Miller Freeman, Inc., 600 Harrison Street, Suite 400, San Francisco CA 94107. 415/905-2200.

World Wide Web address: http://www. woodwideweb.com.

INTERNATIONAL PULP AND PAPER DIRECTORY
Miller Freeman, Inc., 600 Harrison Street, Suite 400, San Francisco CA 94107. 415/905-2200. World Wide Web address: http://www.pulp-paper.com.

LOCKWOOD-POST'S DIRECTORY OF THE PULP, PAPER AND ALLIED TRADES
Miller Freeman, Inc., 600 Harrison Street, Suite 400, San Francisco CA 94107. 415/905-2200. World Wide Web address: http://www.pulp-paper.com/lpdisk.htm.

Magazines

PAPERBOARD PACKAGING
Advanstar Communications, 131 West First Street, Duluth MN 55802. 218/723-9200. World Wide Web address: http://www.advanstar.com.

PULP & PAPER
Miller Freeman, Inc., 600 Harrison Street, Suite 400, San Francisco CA 94107. 415/905-2200. World Wide Web address: http://www.mfi.com.

WOOD TECHNOLOGY
Miller Freeman, Inc., 600 Harrison Street, San Francisco CA 94107. 415/905-2200. World Wide Web address: http://www.woodtechmag.com.

Printing and Publishing

You can expect to find the following types of companies in this chapter:
*Book, Newspaper, and Periodical Publishers • Commercial Photographers
Commercial Printing Services • Graphic Designers*

Some helpful information: *Printing press operators earn approximately $20,000 - $25,000 per year. The average salary range for an editorial assistant is $20,000 - $28,000, and associate editors earn around $30,000 annually. Managing editors and editorial directors generally earn $35,000 - $60,000 or more, depending on the size of the publishing house and years employed. Jobs in electronic publishing may pay considerably more.*

AARTISTIC GRAPHICS DIRECT
648-E Matthews-Mint Hill Road, Matthews NC 28105. 704/814-7160. **Fax:** 704/814-0514. **Contact:** Human Resources. **E-mail address:** info@aartistic.com. **World Wide Web address:** http://www.aartistic.com. **Description:** Engaged in the graphic design of brochures, catalogs, and packaging. The company also offers typesetting and animated Web design services. **Corporate headquarters location:** This Location.

THE ABERDEEN AMERICAN NEWS
P.O. Box 4430, Aberdeen SD 57402. 605/226-1600. **Fax:** 605/229-7532. **Contact:** Susan Rozell, Human Resources Director. **E-mail address:** srozell@aberdeennews.com. **World Wide Web address:** http://www.aberdeennews.com. **Description:** Publisher of one of the largest daily newspapers in South Dakota. **NOTE:** Part-time jobs are offered. **Common positions include:** Account Rep.; Administrative Assistant; Advertising Clerk; Advertising Executive; Chief Financial Officer; Computer Operator; Computer Programmer; Computer Support Technician; Controller; Customer Service Rep.; Editor; Financial Analyst; Graphic Artist; Graphic Designer; Human Resources Manager; Internet Services Manager; Managing Editor; Marketing Manager; Marketing Specialist; Reporter; Sales Rep.; Typist/Word Processor. **Educational backgrounds include:** Accounting; Art/Design; Business Administration; Communications; Finance; Internet; Management/ Planning; Marketing; Microsoft Word; Public Relations; QuarkXPress. **Benefits:** 401(k); Casual Dress - Fridays; Dental Insurance; Disability Coverage; Life Insurance; Medical Insurance; Pension Plan; Sick Days (6 - 10); Tuition Assistance; Vacation Days (6 - 10). **Corporate headquarters location:** San Jose CA. **Parent company:** Knight-Ridder, Inc. (San Jose CA). **Listed on:** New York Stock Exchange. **President/CEO/Owner:** Billie Smith. **Facilities Manager:** Everett Schnoor.

ACCESS: NETWORKING IN THE PUBLIC INTEREST
1001 Connecticut Avenue NW, Suite 838, Washington DC 20036. 202/785-4233. **Fax:** 202/785-4212. **Contact:** Executive Director. **Description:** Publishes a monthly newspaper for the nonprofit sector. **Corporate headquarters location:** This Location.

ADAMS MEDIA CORPORATION
260 Center Street, Holbrook MA 02343. 781/767-8100. **Toll-free phone:** 800/872-5627. **Fax:** 800/872-5628. **Contact:** Allan Tatel, Vice President of Finance and Administration. **E-mail address:** jobbank@adamsonline.com. **World Wide Web address:** http://www.adamsmedia.com. **Description:** A rapidly growing publisher of books and software products. Adams Media Corporation publishes books in a wide variety of nonfiction categories, including the *JobBank* series, which became available in electronic format in 1998 through the *JobBank* List Service. Major book series include the *Everything* series and the *Small Miracles* series. The company's line of business books includes the *Adams Small Business* series and the *Adams Streetwise* series. Travel titles include the bestselling *Mr. Cheap's* series of bargain shopping, eating, and travel books. Other nonfiction categories include self-help, weddings, humor, personal finance, parenting, and reference. The company also operates CareerCity.com (http://www.careercity.com) and BusinessTown.com LLC (http://www.businesstown.com). CareerCity.com is one of the largest and busiest job/career sites on the World Wide Web, offering thousands of current job openings from employers in a variety of industries. BusinessTown.com is a business assistance website geared toward helping small companies grow and manage their business. Adams Media Corporation's software and CD-ROM products focus on the career and small business categories. Founded in 1980. **Common positions include:** Accountant; Acquisitions Editor; Administrative Assistant; Advertising Clerk; Chief Financial Officer; Computer Programmer; Computer Support Technician; Controller; Credit Manager; Customer Service Representative; Database Manager; Editor; Editorial Assistant; General Manager; Graphic Artist; Graphic Designer; Internet Services Manager; Managing Editor; Marketing Manager; Marketing Specialist; Online Content Specialist; Operations Manager; Production Manager; Project Manager; Proofreader; Public Relations Manager; Public Relations Specialist; Publicist; Receptionist; Sales Executive; Sales Manager; Sales Rep.; Systems Manager; Technical Writer/Editor; Telemarketer; Webmaster. **Educational backgrounds include:** Accounting; Art/Design; Bachelor of Arts; Business Administration; Computer Science; English; Finance; Liberal Arts; Marketing; Microsoft Word; Public Relations; QuarkXPress. **Benefits:** 401(k); Bonus Award/Plan; Casual Dress - Daily; Direct Deposit; Disability Coverage; EAP; Employee Discounts; Free Parking; Insurance Discounts; Life Insurance; Medical Insurance; Non-Smoking Environment; Paid Holidays; Purchasing Plan; Section 125 Plan; Vacation Days. **Special programs:** Internships. **Internship information:** Adams Media Corporation's internship program runs throughout

the year. Positions are unpaid. For more information, contact Ms. Michelle Roy Kelly, Internship Coordinator, at the address, phone, or e-mail listed above. **Office hours:** Monday - Friday, 8:00 a.m. - 5:00 p.m. **Corporate headquarters location:** This Location. **Other area locations:** 270 Center Street, Holbrook MA 02343; Adams Media Warehouse, 301 Winter Street, West Hanover MA 02339. **Listed on:** Privately held. **President/Owner:** Bob Adams. **Facilities Manager:** Bill Arris. **Sales Manager:** Wayne Jackson.

ADDISON WESLEY LONGMAN
One Jacob Way, Reading MA 01867. 781/944-3700. **Contact:** Human Resources Manager. **World Wide Web address:** http://www.awl.com. **Description:** Publishes and distributes educational materials for use in elementary and high schools, universities, and certain businesses. Addison Wesley Longman publications cover all of the major disciplines. The company also publishes professional, reference, and nonfiction trade books. The company operates in three divisions: Higher Education; School; and General Books. **Corporate headquarters location:** This Location.

ADVANCE PUBLICATIONS INC.
950 Fingerboard Road, Staten Island NY 10305. 718/981-1234. **Contact:** Richard Diamond, Publisher. **Description:** Publishes the *Staten Island Advance*, a daily local newspaper. The paper has a weekday circulation of 80,000 and a Sunday circulation of 95,000. Founded in 1886. **Corporate headquarters location:** This Location. **Parent company:** Newhouse Newspapers Group. **Number of employees at this location:** 450.

ADVANCED MARKETING SERVICES (AMS)
5880 Oberlin Drive, Suite 400, San Diego CA 92121-9653. 858/457-2500. **Fax:** 858/452-2237. **Contact:** Molly Wood, Human Resources Representative. **World Wide Web address:** http://www.admsweb.com. **Description:** A leading distributor of general interest, computer, and business books to membership warehouse clubs and office product superstores. Advanced Marketing Services works with leading publishers and focuses on a limited number of titles. **NOTE:** Entry-level positions are offered. **Common positions include:** Account Manager; Accountant; Advertising Clerk; Buyer; Computer Programmer; Customer Service Representative; Financial Analyst; Graphic Artist; Marketing Specialist; Sales Executive. **Educational backgrounds include:** Accounting; Art/Design; Business Administration; Communications; Computer Science; Marketing; MBA; Microsoft Office; Publishing; QuarkXPress; Spreadsheets; Visual Basic. **Benefits:** 401(k); Casual Dress - Daily; Dental Insurance; Disability Coverage; Employee Discounts; Flexible Schedule; Life Insurance; Medical Insurance; Profit Sharing; Relocation Assistance; Telecommuting; Tuition Assistance. **Corporate headquarters location:** This Location. **Listed on:** NASDAQ. **Annual sales/revenues:** More than $100 million. **Number of employees at this location:** 400.

ADVANSTAR COMMUNICATIONS
7500 Old Oak Boulevard, Cleveland OH 44130. 440/243-8100. **Contact:** Human Resources. **World Wide Web address:** http://www.advanstar.com. **Description:** A U.S. business information company that publishes magazines and journals; coordinates expositions and conferences; and provides a wide range of marketing services. **Common positions include:** Administrative Worker/Clerk; Editor. **Educational backgrounds include:** Communications; Journalism; Marketing. **Benefits:**

401(k); Dental Insurance; Disability Coverage; Life Insurance; Medical Insurance; Tuition Assistance. **Corporate headquarters location:** This Location. **Other U.S. locations:** CA; IL; MN; NY; OR. **Listed on:** Privately held. **Number of employees at this location:** 250.

THE ADVOCATE
P.O. Box 588, Baton Rouge LA 70821. 225/388-1111. **Contact:** Human Resources. **World Wide Web address:** http://www.theadvocate.com. **Description:** Publishes *The Advocate*, a local newspaper. **Common positions include:** Accountant; Administrator; Advertising Clerk; Commercial Artist; Computer Programmer; Customer Service Rep.; Editor; Electrical/Electronics Engineer; Manufacturer's/Wholesaler's Sales Rep.; Marketing Specialist; Reporter; Systems Analyst; Technical Writer/Editor. **Educational backgrounds include:** Accounting; Art/Design; Business Administration; Communications; Journalism. **Benefits:** Dental Insurance; Disability Coverage; Employee Discounts; ESOP; Life Insurance; Medical Insurance; Profit Sharing; Stock Option; Vision Insurance. **Special programs:** Internships. **Corporate headquarters location:** This Location. **Number of employees at this location:** 560.

AFRO-AMERICAN NEWSPAPERS INC.
2519 North Charles Street, Baltimore MD 21218. 410/554-8221. **Fax:** 410/554-8218. **Contact:** Ms. Verdell Elliott, Director of Human Resources. **World Wide Web address:** http://www.afroam.org. **Description:** Publishes *The Baltimore Afro-American*, a newspaper marketed to the African-American community. Founded in 1892. **Common positions include:** Account Manager; Accountant; Administrative Assistant; Advertising Clerk; Computer Operator; Computer Programmer; Editor; Editorial Assistant; Graphic Artist; Graphic Designer; Human Resources Manager; Librarian; Production Manager; Reporter; Sales Executive; Secretary. **Educational backgrounds include:** Accounting; Communications; Computer Science. **Benefits:** Credit Union; Dental Insurance; Medical Insurance; Pension Plan; Tuition Assistance. **Special programs:** Internships. **Corporate headquarters location:** This Location. **Other U.S. locations:** Nationwide. **Listed on:** Privately held. **Number of employees at this location:** 55.

AGORA, INC.
14 West Mt. Vernon Place, Baltimore MD 21202. 410/783-8484. **Fax:** 410/783-8455. **Contact:** Nora Rogers, Personnel Manager. **Description:** A publisher of health, travel, financial, and entrepreneurial books and newsletters. Founded in 1979. **NOTE:** Entry-level positions and part-time jobs are offered. **Common positions include:** Advertising Executive; Computer Support Technician; Customer Service Rep.; Desktop Publishing Specialist; Editor; Editorial Assistant; Graphic Artist; Graphic Designer; Intranet Developer; Managing Editor; Marketing Manager; Marketing Specialist; Technical Writer/Editor; Web Advertising Specialist; Webmaster; Website Developer. **Educational backgrounds include:** Business Administration; HTML; Internet Development; Liberal Arts; Marketing; Microsoft Office; Microsoft Word; Publishing; QuarkXPress; Spreadsheets; Visual Basic. **Benefits:** 401(k); Casual Dress - Daily; Dental Insurance; Disability Coverage; Employee Discounts; Flexible Schedule; Life Insurance; Medical Insurance; Public Transit Available; Sick Days (1 - 5); Vacation Days (10 - 20). **Special programs:** Internships; Summer Jobs. **Office hours:** Monday - Friday, 8:30 a.m. - 5:30 p.m. **Corporate headquarters location:** This

Location. **Other U.S. locations:** Del Ray FL. **International locations:** Ireland. **Listed on:** Privately held. **Owner:** Bill Bonner. **Number of employees nationwide:** 200.

AIKEN STANDARD
P.O. Box 456, Aiken SC 29802. 803/648-2311. **Contact:** Judy Randall, Executive Secretary. **World Wide Web address:** http://www. aikenstandard.com. **Description:** Publishes *Aiken Standard*, a daily newspaper with a circulation of 15,000. **Corporate headquarters location:** This Location.

ALBANY DEMOCRAT-HERALD
P.O. Box 130, Albany OR 97321-0041. 541/926-2211. **Fax:** 541/926-7209. **Contact:** Personnel Officer. **E-mail address:** albanydh@proaxis.com. **Description:** A general interest information provider that publishes a daily newspaper (excluding Sundays), with a circulation of 22,000. The company also operates a commercial printing and distribution center. Founded in 1865. **Corporate headquarters location:** This Location. **Parent company:** ABC, Inc. **Number of employees at this location:** 110.

THE AMERICAN ASSOCIATION FOR THE ADVANCEMENT OF SCIENCE (AAAS)
1200 New York Avenue NW, Suite 100, Washington DC 20005. 202/326-6470. **Fax:** 202/682-1630. **Contact:** Dawn Graf, Human Resources Specialist. **World Wide Web address:** http://www.aaas.org. **Description:** Primary operations include the publication of *Science* magazine. Overall, the AAAS is one of the world's largest federations of scientific and engineering societies, with nearly 300 affiliate organizations. In addition, AAAS counts more than 142,000 scientists, engineers, science educators, policy makers, and interested citizens among its individual members, making it one of the largest general scientific organizations in the world. Founded in 1848. **Common positions include:** Accountant; Advertising Clerk; Art Director; Computer Graphics Specialist; Editor; Financial Analyst; Financial Manager; Librarian; Marketing Manager; Production Manager; Program Manager; Project Manager; Proofreader; Services Sales Rep.; Technical Illustrator; Writer. **Educational backgrounds include:** Accounting; Art/Design; Biology; Business Administration; Chemistry; Communications; Computer Science; Education; Engineering; English; Finance; International Relations; Liberal Arts; Marketing. **Benefits:** Dental Insurance; Disability Coverage; Employee Discounts; Life Insurance; Medical Insurance; Retirement Plan; Tuition Assistance. **Corporate headquarters location:** This Location. **Number of employees at this location:** 300.

AMERICAN BANK NOTE CORP.
410 Park Avenue, 12th Floor, New York NY 10022. 212/593-5700. **Contact:** Sheldon Cantor, Vice President of Corporate Services. **Description:** American Bank Note Corp. operates through three subsidiaries. American Bank Note Holographics, Inc. is one of the world's largest producers of the laser-generated, three-dimensional images that appear on credit cards and products requiring proof of authenticity. American Bank Note Company Brazil is one of Brazil's largest private security printers and a provider of personalized checks, financial transaction cards, and pre-paid telephone cards. American Bank Note Company is a printer of counterfeit-resistant documents and one of the largest security printers in the world. The company creates secure documents of value for governments and corporations worldwide. Products include currencies; passports; stock and bond certificates; and bank, corporate, government, and traveler's cheques; food coupons; gift vouchers and certificates; driver's licenses; product authentication labels; and vital documents. **Corporate headquarters location:** This Location. **Other U.S. locations:** Burbank CA; Long Beach CA; San Francisco CA; Washington DC; Atlanta GA; Bedford Park IL; Needham MA; St. Louis MO; Elmsford NY; Horsham PA; Huntington Valley PA; Philadelphia PA; Pittsburgh PA; Dallas TX. **Listed on:** New York Stock Exchange.

AMERICAN BIBLE SOCIETY
1865 Broadway, 6th Floor, New York NY 10023. 212/408-1269. **Contact:** Mr. S. King, Associate Director of Human Resources. **World Wide Web address:** http://www.americanbible.org. **Description:** Translates, publishes, and distributes *The Bible* and portions of the Scriptures, without doctrinal note or comment, in more than 180 nations. **Common positions include:** Accountant; Administrator; Customer Service Rep.; Department Manager; Editor; Financial Analyst; General Manager; Manufacturer's/Wholesaler's Sales Rep.; Operations/Production Manager; Public Relations Specialist; Purchasing Agent/Manager; Secretary; Systems Analyst. **Educational backgrounds include:** Accounting; Business Administration; Communications; Finance; Liberal Arts; Mathematics; Theology. **Benefits:** Dental Insurance; Disability Coverage; Employee Discounts; Life Insurance; Medical Insurance; Pension Plan; Savings Plan; Tuition Assistance. **Corporate headquarters location:** This Location. **Number of employees at this location:** 300.

AMERICAN BUSINESS PRODUCTS, INC.
CURTIS 1000, INC.
2100 Riveredge Parkway, Suite 1200, Atlanta GA 30328. 770/953-8300. **Contact:** Human Resources. **Description:** Manufactures and supplies business commodities including envelopes, forms, and labels. The company also engages in book printing, binding, and distribution; and specialty extrusion coating and laminating. **Common positions include:** Computer Programmer; Customer Service Rep.; Management Trainee; Manufacturer's/Wholesaler's Sales Rep.; Operations/Production Manager. **Educational backgrounds include:** Business Administration; Communications; Computer Graphics; Liberal Arts; Marketing. **Benefits:** Dental Insurance; Disability Coverage; Life Insurance; Medical Insurance; Profit Sharing. **Corporate headquarters location:** This Location. **Listed on:** New York Stock Exchange. **Number of employees nationwide:** 4,300.

AMERICAN GREETINGS CORPORATION
One American Road, Cleveland OH 44144. 216/252-7300. **Fax:** 216/252-6590. **Contact:** Human Resources. **World Wide Web address:** http://www.americangreetings.com. **Description:** One of the world's largest publicly-owned manufacturers and distributors of greeting cards and related novelty items. American Greetings Corporation's products are printed in 16 languages at more than 30 plants and facilities worldwide. Products are distributed through a global network of approximately 97,000 retail outlets in 68 countries. A creative staff of nearly 500 artists, designers, and writers works together to generate more than 20,000 new concepts each year. **Corporate headquarters location:** This Location. **Subsidiaries include:** Acme Frame Products manufactures picture frames under the brand names Acme and Royal Gallery of Frames; A.G. Industries designs and manufactures custom permanent display fixtures and merchandising systems for American Greetings, its

subsidiaries, consumer product companies, and retailers; CreataCard markets interactive, multimedia kiosks that allow consumers to write, personalize, and print greeting cards; Magnivision manufactures and distributes nonprescription, over-the-counter reading glasses produced primarily for mass retail distribution; Plus Mark manufactures and distributes promotional Christmas gift wrap, boxed cards, and accessories under the brand names Plus Mark and Greeneville Press; Those Charácters From Cleveland develops and markets licensed characters; Wilhold manufactures and distributes hair accessories. **Listed on:** NASDAQ.

AMERICAN LIBRARY ASSOCIATION
50 East Huron Street, Chicago IL 60611. 312/944-6780. **Contact:** Dorothy Ragsdale, Human Resources Director. **World Wide Web address:** http://www.ala.org. **Description:** A membership association focusing on library information science. The association works with legislators to obtain federal support for libraries; engages in public educational programs; maintains a library and research center; presents over 100 awards, scholarships, and grants including the Newbury and Caldecott Medals for children's literature; publishes journals, monographs, and reference works; and holds two conferences each year for its members. **Common positions include:** Accountant; Editor; Library Technician. **Educational backgrounds include:** Liberal Arts; Marketing. **Corporate headquarters location:** This Location. **Other U.S. locations:** Washington DC.

AMERICAN PRESS
4900 Highway 90 East, Lake Charles LA 70615. 337/433-3000. **Contact:** Anita Tinsley, Business Manager. **World Wide Web address:** http://www.americanpress.com. **Description:** A daily newspaper. **NOTE:** Part-time positions are offered. **Common positions include:** Account Rep.; Accountant; Advertising Clerk; Advertising Executive; Chief Financial Officer; Controller; Credit Manager; Database Manager; Desktop Publishing Specialist; Editor; Editorial Assistant; Graphic Artist; Graphic Designer; Managing Editor; Reporter; Systems Analyst; Technical Writer/Editor. **Educational backgrounds include:** Accounting; Art/Design; Business Administration; Communications; Computer Science; Economics; Finance; Liberal Arts; Marketing; MCSE; Microsoft Word; QuarkXPress; Software Tech. Support. **Benefits:** 401(k); Casual Dress - Daily; Disability Coverage; Life Insurance; Medical Insurance; Pension Plan; Sick Days (1 - 5); Vacation Days (1 - 5). **Special programs:** Internships. **Corporate headquarters location:** This Location. **Other U.S. locations:** CO; NM. **Annual sales/revenues:** $11 - $20 million.

AMERICAN SOCIETY OF COMPOSERS, AUTHORS & PUBLISHERS (ASCAP)
One Lincoln Plaza, New York NY 10023. 212/595-3050. **Contact:** Human Resources Department. **World Wide Web address:** http://www.ascap.com. **Description:** An international service organization serving the music, publishing, and other creative industries. The organization provides a wide range of services to members including the supervision and enforcement of copyrights. **Corporate headquarters location:** This Location.

AMOS PRESS INC.
P.O. Box 4129, Sidney OH 45365. 937/498-2111. **Fax:** 937/498-0888. **Contact:** Human Resources. **World Wide Web address:** http://www.amospress.com. **Description:** A printing and publishing company with operations in daily newspapers and a variety of periodicals including *Coin World* and *Linn's Stamp News.* **Common positions include:** Account Rep.; Computer Support Technician; Computer Technician; Customer Service Rep.; Desktop Publishing Specialist; Editor; Graphic Artist; Graphic Designer; Managing Editor; Network/Systems Administrator; Reporter; Sales Rep.; Systems Analyst; Webmaster. **Educational backgrounds include:** CGI; Computer Science; HTML; Internet; Journalism; MCSE; Novell; QuarkXPress; Spreadsheets. **Benefits:** 401(k); Casual Dress - Daily; Disability Coverage; Employee Discounts; Life Insurance; Medical Insurance; Tuition Assistance. **Corporate headquarters location:** This Location.

APPERSON BUSINESS FORMS, INC.
6855 East Gage Avenue, City of Commerce CA 90040. 562/927-4718. **Contact:** Human Resources. **Description:** Manufactures business forms. **Common positions include:** Manufacturer's/Wholesaler's Sales Rep. **Benefits:** 401(k); Dental Insurance; Disability Coverage; Employee Discounts; Life Insurance; Medical Insurance; Savings Plan. **Corporate headquarters location:** This Location. **Number of employees at this location:** 150.

APPLIED GRAPHICS TECHNOLOGIES (AGT)
450 West 33rd Street, 11th Floor, New York NY 10001. 212/716-6600. **Contact:** Jill Breheny, Human Resources Manager. **World Wide Web address:** http://www.agt.com. **Description:** One of the largest providers of integrated graphic communications services to advertising agencies, magazine and catalog publishers, and corporate clients in various industries worldwide. The company's services include commercial printing, color separation and retouching, facilities management, photo CD and digital image archiving, electronic imaging services, flexo/packaging services, publication and catalog services, satellite transmission services, creative design services, technical support and training services, and black and white ad production. **Corporate headquarters location:** This Location. **Other area locations:** Madison NY; Oceanside NY; Rochester NY. **Other U.S. locations:** Foster City CA; Glendale CA; Los Angeles CA; Boulder CO; Washington DC; Chicago IL; Detroit MI; Carlstadt NJ; Moonachie NJ.

ARKWRIGHT INC.
538 Main Street, P.O. Box 139, Fiskeville RI 02823-0139. 401/821-1000. **Fax:** 401/822-1559. **Contact:** David Patenaude, Director of Human Resources. **Description:** Manufactures imaging films for presentation graphics and design engineering applications. **Common positions include:** Chemical Engineer; Chemist; Mechanical Engineer. **Educational backgrounds include:** Chemistry; Engineering. **Benefits:** 401(k); Dental Insurance; Disability Coverage; Life Insurance; Medical Insurance; Pension Plan; Tuition Assistance. **Corporate headquarters location:** This Location. **Parent company:** Oce Van Der Grinten. **Listed on:** Privately held. **Number of employees at this location:** 240.

THE ASBURY PARK PRESS
3601 Highway 66, P.O. Box 1550, Neptune NJ 07754. 732/922-6000. **Contact:** Human Resources. **World Wide Web address:** http://www.injersey.com/app. **Description:** Publishes a daily local newspaper. **Common positions include:** Advertising Clerk; Blue-Collar Worker Supervisor; Branch Manager; Broadcast Technician; Computer Programmer; Credit Manager; Customer Service Representative; Electrician; General Manager; Human Resources Manager; Industrial Engineer; Management Analyst/Consultant; Management

Trainee; Manufacturer's/Wholesaler's Sales Rep.; Operations/Production Manager; Property and Real Estate Manager; Public Relations Specialist; Purchasing Agent/Manager; Radio/TV Announcer/ Broadcaster; Services Sales Rep.; Systems Analyst; Technical Writer/Editor; Transportation/Traffic Specialist; Travel Agent. **Educational backgrounds include:** Accounting; Art/Design; Business Administration; Communications; Computer Science; Economics; Finance; Liberal Arts; Marketing; Mathematics. **Benefits:** 401(k); Dental Insurance; Disability Coverage; Employee Discounts; Life Insurance; Medical Insurance; Pension Plan; Savings Plan; Tuition Assistance; Vision Insurance. **Special programs:** Internships. **Corporate headquarters location:** This Location. **Other U.S. locations:** Orlando FL.

THE ASSOCIATED PRESS
50 Rockefeller Plaza, 7th Floor, New York NY 10020. 212/621-1500. **Fax:** 212/621-5447. **Contact:** Staffing Department. **World Wide Web address:** http://www.ap.org. **Description:** One of the largest independent news-gathering organizations in the world. Founded in 1848. **Corporate headquarters location:** This Location. **Other U.S. locations:** Nationwide. **International locations:** Worldwide.

THE ATLANTA JOURNAL-CONSTITUTION
P.O. Box 4689, Atlanta GA 30302. 404/526-5151. **Contact:** Human Resources. **World Wide Web address:** http://www.accessatlanta.com/ajc. **Description:** Publishes a daily newspaper with a weekday circulation of 450,000. **Common positions include:** Accountant; Advertising Clerk; Computer Programmer; Customer Service Rep.; Editor; Reporter; Sales Executive; Systems Analyst; Technical Writer/Editor. **Educational backgrounds include:** Accounting; Business Administration; Communications; Computer Science; Marketing. **Benefits:** Disability Coverage; Employee Discounts; Life Insurance; Medical Insurance; Pension Plan; Savings Plan; Tuition Assistance. **Corporate headquarters location:** This Location.

AUGSBURG FORTRESS PUBLISHERS
P.O. Box 1209, Minneapolis MN 55440-1209. 612/330-3300. **Contact:** Jean Stanley, Human Resources Manager. **World Wide Web address:** http://www.augsburgfortress.org. **Description:** A publishing house for the Evangelical Lutheran Church of America. **Common positions include:** Administrative Manager; Advertising Clerk; Attorney; Blue-Collar Worker Supervisor; Branch Manager; Budget Analyst; Clerical Supervisor; Computer Programmer; Credit Manager; Customer Service Representative; Designer; Editor; Financial Analyst; General Manager; Human Resources Manager; Librarian; Operations/Production Manager; Quality Control Supervisor; Services Sales Rep.; Systems Analyst; Wholesale and Retail Buyer. **Educational backgrounds include:** Accounting; Art/Design; Business Administration; Communications; Computer Science; English; Finance; Journalism; Liberal Arts; Marketing. **Benefits:** Dental Insurance; Disability Coverage; Employee Discounts; Life Insurance; Medical Insurance; Pension Plan; Tuition Assistance. **Corporate headquarters location:** This Location. **Other U.S. locations:** Los Angeles CA; Omaha NE; Hicksville NY; Columbus OH; Harrisburg PA; Philadelphia PA; Columbia SC; Austin TX; Mountlake Terrace WA.

AUTOMATED GRAPHIC SYSTEMS, INC.
4590 Graphics Drive, White Plains MD 20695. 301/843-7185. **Contact:** Human Resources. **World Wide Web address:** http://www.ags.com.

Description: Provides printing and graphic communication services including design, desktop publishing, prepress services, on-demand printing, binding, fulfillment, mailing, and storage as well as CD-ROM production and disk replication. **Corporate headquarters location:** This Location.

BBF
10950 South Belcher Road, Largo FL 33777. 727/545-8703. **Fax:** 727/548-0711. **Recorded jobline:** 727/545-8703x208. **Contact:** Eric Kemerer, Human Resources Manager. **E-mail address:** hrmanager@bbfprinting.com. **World Wide Web address:** http://www.bbfprinting.com. **Description:** Supplies a full line of custom-printed forms, labels, envelopes, commercial printing, computer supplies, and promotional products. Founded in 1960. **NOTE:** Entry-level positions and second and third shifts are offered. **Common positions include:** Account Rep.; AS400 Programmer Analyst; Customer Service Rep.; Desktop Publishing Specialist; Press Operator. **Educational backgrounds include:** AS400 Certification; QuarkXPress. **Benefits:** 401(k); Casual Dress - Daily; Dental Insurance; Disability Coverage; Life Insurance; Medical Insurance; Profit Sharing; Savings Plan. **Special programs:** Training. **Office hours:** Monday - Friday, 8:00 a.m. - 5:00 p.m. **Corporate headquarters location:** This Location. **Listed on:** Privately held. **President/CEO:** Joseph P. Baker. **Annual sales/revenues:** $51 - $100 million. **Number of employees nationwide:** 400.

BET SERVICES
BLACK ENTERTAINMENT TELEVISION NETWORK
1900 W Place NE, Washington DC 20018. 202/608-2000. **Fax:** 202/608-2589. **Contact:** Curtis Scott, Vice President of Human Resources. **Description:** Operates the Black Entertainment Television Network (BET Network) which is an advertiser-supported basic cable television network. BET Services is also the publisher of *YSB* and *Emerge*, two magazines that are geared toward the African-American community. **Common positions include:** Accountant; Attorney; Broadcast Technician; Editor; Electrical/Electronics Engineer; Operations/ Production Manager; Systems Analyst. **Educational backgrounds include:** Communications; Computer Science; Liberal Arts. **Benefits:** 401(k); Dental Insurance; Disability Coverage; Life Insurance; Medical Insurance; Profit Sharing. **Special programs:** Internships. **Corporate headquarters location:** This Location. **Other U.S. locations:** Santa Monica CA; Chicago IL; New York NY. **Listed on:** New York Stock Exchange. **Number of employees nationwide:** 475.

BAILEY PUBLISHING & COMMUNICATIONS
P.O. Box 1769, Jacksonville FL 32201. 904/356-2466. **Contact:** James F. Bailey, Jr., Publisher. **World Wide Web address:** http://www. baileypub.com. **Description:** Publisher of the *Financial News and Daily Record*, a business and legal newspaper, and *Golf News*, a newspaper focusing on golf. **Common positions include:** Advertising Clerk; Editor; Reporter; Services Sales Rep. **Benefits:** Life Insurance; Medical Insurance. **Corporate headquarters location:** This Location.

BAKER & TAYLOR
44 Kirby Avenue, Somerville NJ 08876. 908/722-8000. **Contact:** Human Resources. **World Wide Web address:** http://www.btol.com. **Description:** A leading full-line distributor of books, videos, and music products. Customers include online and traditional retailers and institutional customers. Baker & Taylor also provides customers with value-

added proprietary data products and customized management and outsourcing services. Founded in 1828. **NOTE:** Entry-level positions and second and third shifts are offered. **Common positions include:** Administrative Assistant; Blue-Collar Worker Supervisor; Buyer; Computer Operator; Customer Service Representative; Industrial Engineer; Sales Representative; Secretary; Systems Analyst. **Educational backgrounds include:** C/C++; HTML; Library Science; Publishing; SQL; Visual Basic. **Benefits:** 401(k); Casual Dress - Fridays; Dental Insurance; Disability Coverage; Employee Discounts; Life Insurance; Medical Insurance; Tuition Assistance; Vacation Days (10 - 20). **Corporate headquarters location:** Charlotte NC.

THE BAKERSFIELD CALIFORNIAN INC.
P.O. Box 440, Bakersfield CA 93302. 661/395-7482. **Fax:** 661/395-7484. **Contact:** Human Resources. **World Wide Web address:** http://www.bakersfield.com. **Description:** *The Bakersfield Californian* is a mid-sized, family-owned newspaper with a daily circulation of 84,000 and a Sunday circulation of 93,000. **Common positions include:** Advertising Clerk; Management Trainee; Manufacturer's/Wholesaler's Sales Rep.; Reporter. **Educational backgrounds include:** Accounting; Communications; Marketing. **Benefits:** Dental Insurance; Life Insurance; Medical Insurance; Pension Plan; Savings Plan. **Special programs:** Internships. **Corporate headquarters location:** This Location. **Number of employees at this location:** 500.

BANK PRINTING COMPANY INC.
9102 Firestone Boulevard, Unit J, Downey CA 90741. 562/862-7001. **Contact:** Human Resources. **Description:** Prints bank checks and a variety of other banking papers. **Corporate headquarters location:** This Location. **Other area locations:** Cerritos CA.

BANTA CORPORATION
P.O. Box 8003, Menasha WI 54952-8003. 920/751-7777. **Physical address:** 225 Main Street, Menasha WI. **Contact:** Kristin Moore, Human Resources Specialist. **World Wide Web address:** http://www.banta.com. **Description:** Offers a wide variety of printing services including digital imaging. The corporation serves publishers of educational and general books, special-interest magazines, custom consumer and business catalogs, and direct marketing materials. Banta Corporation also offers multimedia and software packages, interactive media, point-of-purchase materials, and single-use products. The company's printing services include inkjet imaging, demographic binding, and digital printing. **Corporate headquarters location:** This Location. **Other U.S. locations:** CA; CO; CT; GA; IL; MA; MN; NC; UT; VA; WA. **International locations:** Apeldoorn, the Netherlands; Cork, Ireland; Dublin, Ireland; Limerick, Ireland. **Subsidiaries include:** Banta Book Group; Banta Catalog Group; Banta Digital Group; Banta Direct Marketing Group; Banta Global Turnkey Group; Banta Information Services Group; Banta Merchandising Products; Banta Publications Group; Banta Specialty Products. **Listed on:** NASDAQ.

BANTA DIGITAL GROUP
P.O. Box 390, Menasha WI 54952-0390. 920/751-7800. **Physical address:** 1457 Earl Street, Menasha WI. **Contact:** Human Resources. **Description:** Activities include data management for the creation of film and printing plates such as electronic and conventional prepress services; preparation and storage of customers' digital electronic files containing text and images; high-speed transmission of digitized text and graphics; digital photography; electronic layout and design; one- and four-color digital printing; television identity campaigns; corporate image videos; and interactive and alternative media programming. **Parent company:** Banta Corporation is a technology and market leader in printing and digital imaging. The corporation serves publishers of educational and general books, special-interest magazines, consumer and business catalogs, and direct marketing materials. In addition to printing and digital imaging, Banta offers multimedia and software packages, interactive media, point-of-purchase materials, and single-use products.

BAWDEN PRINTING, INC.
400 South 14th Avenue, Eldridge IA 52748. 319/285-4800. **Fax:** 319/285-8240. **Contact:** Human Resources. **World Wide Web address:** http://www.bawden.com. **Description:** A printing company offering a variety of services including complete test printing capabilities, typesetting, keylining, negatives, proofs, plates, printing, die-cutting, collating, stitching, trimming, consecutive numbering, sealing, wrapping, packaging, and distribution. Bawden Printing also has resources available for converting information from computer disks to camera-ready copy. Full distribution services are available including bulk mailing, first class, foreign mailing, UPS, and Federal Express. The four major operating areas of Bawden Printing are Finance; Manufacturing; Sales and Service; and Human Resources. Finance is responsible for the administrative management of the business. Manufacturing directs all production processes of the three daily shifts and includes the Prep, Litho, Electronic Imaging, Press, Bindery, and Distribution Departments. Manufacturing is also responsible for the staffing of all production departments, analysis of equipment needs, the efficient and timely scheduling of all Production Departments, plant and equipment maintenance, and effective operation of quality assurance systems. Sales and Customer Service is responsible for all sales and marketing efforts, beginning with the initiation and maintenance of customer relations, from job receipt through delivery and invoicing. The Service Department also includes the management of Bawden Printing's regional sales offices. Founded in 1908. **Educational backgrounds include:** Business Administration; Computer Science; Graphic Design; Liberal Arts. **Benefits:** 401(k); Dental Insurance; Disability Coverage; Life Insurance; Medical Insurance; Profit Sharing. **Corporate headquarters location:** This Location. **Other U.S. locations:** CA; IL; MA; NJ; TX. **Parent company:** Bawden Corporation also owns Bawden & Associates, a full-service advertising agency.

BAY TACT CORPORATION
440 Route 198, Woodstock Valley CT 06282. 860/974-2223. **Fax:** 860/974-2229. **Contact:** Human Resources. **Description:** Bay Tact is engaged in the dissemination of financial information for publicly traded companies. The information dissemination includes 10Ks, annual reports, press releases, and promotional material. Bay Tact's client base consists of over 2,800 companies. Annual reports are distributed through The Public Register's Annual Report Service. In addition, Bay Tact publishes the *Security Traders Handbook*, a national financial publication, and *Hornsmatch*, a buy-sell cattle publication; and provides investment screening services through the PaceSetters Database. **Corporate headquarters location:** This Location.

BEACON PRESS
25 Beacon Street, Boston MA 02108. 617/742-2110. **Fax:** 617/723-3097. **Contact:** Heather

Brown, Personnel Coordinator. **World Wide Web address:** http://www.beacon.org. **Description:** An independent publisher of nonfiction and fiction books. Founded in 1854. **Common positions include:** Advertising Clerk; Customer Service Rep.; Designer; Editor; Financial Manager; Order Clerk; Public Relations Specialist; Receptionist; Secretary. **Educational backgrounds include:** Fine Arts; Liberal Arts. **Benefits:** 403(b); Daycare Assistance; Dental Insurance; Disability Coverage; Employee Discounts; Life Insurance; Medical Insurance; Pension Plan; Savings Plan; Tuition Assistance. **Special programs:** Internships. **Corporate headquarters location:** This Location. **Parent company:** Unitarian Universalist Association.

BEAUTIFUL AMERICA PUBLISHING CO.
P.O. Box 244, Woodburn OR 97071. 503/982-4616. **Contact:** Beverly A. Paul, President. **Description:** A publisher of scenic photography books, calendars, and related products. **Benefits:** Dental Insurance; Employee Discounts; Medical Insurance. **Corporate headquarters location:** This Location.

MATTHEW BENDER & COMPANY, INC.
2 Park Avenue, New York NY 10016. 212/448-2000. **Contact:** Human Resources. **World Wide Web address:** http://www.bender.com. **Description:** A publisher of technical and reference books for law firms, real estate organizations, and industries. Publications include books about modern estate planning, banking law, deposition practice, advocacy, bankruptcy, state law, immigration law, international business, courtroom science, criminal law, natural resources, and taxes. The company also offers an online interactive legal practice data system, as well as other electronic publishing services. **NOTE:** Entry-level positions are offered. **Common positions include:** Administrative Assistant; Budget Analyst; Clerical Supervisor; Computer Operator; Computer Programmer; Controller; Credit Manager; Customer Service Rep.; Database Manager; Editor; Editorial Assistant; Finance Director; Financial Analyst; Graphic Artist; Graphic Designer; Human Resources Manager; Intellectual Property Lawyer; Internet Services Manager; Librarian; Managing Editor; Market Research Analyst; Marketing Manager; Marketing Specialist; MIS Specialist; Operations Manager; Paralegal; Secretary; Software Engineer; Systems Analyst; Systems Manager; Telecommunications Manager. **Educational backgrounds include:** Accounting; Art/Design; Business Administration; Communications; Computer Science; Economics; Finance; Liberal Arts; Marketing. **Benefits:** 401(k); Dental Insurance; Disability Coverage; Employee Discounts; Flexible Schedule; Job Sharing; Life Insurance; Medical Insurance; Pension Plan; Savings Plan; Telecommuting; Tuition Assistance. **Special programs:** Internships. **Corporate headquarters location:** This Location.

BERLITZ INTERNATIONAL, INC.
400 Alexander Park, Princeton NJ 08540. 609/514-9650. **Contact:** Donna Russomano, Director of Human Resources. **World Wide Web address:** http://www.berlitz.com. **Description:** A language services firm providing instruction and translation services through 298 language centers in 28 countries around the world. The company also publishes travel guides, foreign language phrase books, and home study materials. **Common positions include:** Accountant; Director; Instructor/Trainer; Services Sales Representative. **Educational backgrounds include:** Accounting; Business Administration; Finance; Foreign Languages; Liberal Arts. **Corporate headquarters location:** This Location. **Listed on:** New York Stock Exchange.

BERLYN INC.
9458 Lanham Severn Road, Seabrook MD 20706-2600. 301/306-9500. **Fax:** 301/306-0134. **Contact:** Human Resources. **World Wide Web address:** http://www.thesentinel.com. **Description:** Publishes two weekly newspapers, *The Prince George Sentinel* and *The Montgomery Sentinel*, with a combined circulation of more than 100,000. **NOTE:** Entry-level positions and part-time jobs are offered. **Common positions include:** Account Manager; Account Rep.; Accountant; Administrative Assistant; Advertising Clerk; Advertising Executive; Computer Operator; Credit Manager; Customer Service Rep.; Desktop Publishing Specialist; Editor; Editorial Assistant; Graphic Artist; Graphic Designer; Managing Editor; Marketing Manager; Marketing Specialist; Network/Systems Administrator; Operations Manager; Production Manager; Public Relations Specialist; Reporter; Sales Manager; Technical Writer/Editor; Typist/Word Processor. **Educational backgrounds include:** Accounting; Art/Design; Computer Science; HTML; Journalism; Liberal Arts; Mathematics; Microsoft Word; Public Relations; QuarkXPress; Spreadsheets. **Benefits:** Casual Dress - Daily; Dental Insurance; Flexible Schedule; Life Insurance; Medical Insurance; Public Transit Available; Sick Days (6 - 10); Telecommuting; Vacation Days (10 - 20). **Special programs:** Internships; Summer Jobs. **Office hours:** Monday - Friday, 8:30 a.m. - 5:00 p.m. **Corporate headquarters location:** This Location.

CHANNING L. BETE COMPANY INC.
200 State Road, South Deerfield MA 01373. 413/665-7611. **Fax:** 413/665-6397. **Contact:** Human Resources. **World Wide Web address:** http://www.channing-bete.com. **Description:** Publishers and printers of educational booklets, calendars, videos, coloring books, and posters. **Common positions include:** Accountant; Artist; Computer Programmer; Copywriter; Customer Service Rep.; Designer; Editor; Systems Analyst; Telemarketer; Writer. **Educational backgrounds include:** Accounting; Art/Design; Business Administration; Communications; Computer Science; Graphic Design; Liberal Arts; Marketing. **Benefits:** 401(k); Dental Insurance; Disability Coverage; Life Insurance; Medical Insurance; Pension Plan; Profit Sharing; Smoke-free; Tuition Assistance. **Corporate headquarters location:** This Location. **Listed on:** Privately held.

BLAIR PUBLISHING
1406 Plaza Drive, Winston-Salem NC 27103. **Toll-free phone:** 800/222-9796. **Fax:** 910/768-9194. **Contact:** Human Resources. **E-mail address:** blairpub@blairpub.com. **World Wide Web address:** http://www.blairpub.com. **Description:** A general trade publisher of specialty regional titles including history, travel, folklore, and biographies. The company publishes 15 - 20 books per year. **Corporate headquarters location:** This Location.

BOOK NEWS, INC.
5739 NE Sumner Street, Portland OR 97218. 503/281-9230. **Fax:** 503/287-4485. **Contact:** Human Resources. **E-mail address:** booknews@booknews.com. **World Wide Web address:** http://www.booknews.com. **Description:** Reviews newly published books. Book News reviews are carried by Barnes & Noble, Amazon.com, and BookScope, a library reference CD-ROM. **NOTE:** Book News uses Portland OR reviewers only. **Corporate headquarters location:** This Location.

BOOKAZINE COMPANY INC.
75 Hook Road, Bayonne NJ 07002. 201/339-7777. **Contact:** Richard Kallman, Vice President. **World**

Wide Web address: http://www.bookazine.com. **Description:** A general trade book wholesaler serving retail bookstores with an inventory of over 100,000 titles. **Corporate headquarters location:** This Location. **President/CEO:** Robert Kallman.

THE BOSTON GLOBE
P.O. Box 2378, Boston MA 02107-2378. 617/929-2000. **Fax:** 617/929-3376. **Contact:** Clare Larson, Assistant Manager, Human Resources. **World Wide Web address:** http://www.boston.com/globe. **Description:** One of New England's largest daily newspapers. Founded in 1872. **Special programs:** Internships; Co-ops. **Internship information:** The Boston Globe offers a Business Summer internship program to college sophomores and juniors. There are two internship positions available: one in advertising and one in accounting. The accounting intern is assigned to the Controller's Office and works on specific projects for the Credit, Accounting, and Payroll departments. The advertising intern is responsible for selling advertising space and servicing existing accounts. Summer interns work from June 1 through Labor Day and are paid approximately $550.00 per week. The deadline for applications (including resume and personal statement) is February 28. Questions about application procedures should be addressed to Clare Larson at 617/929-3483. **Parent company:** New York Times Company.

BOSTON MAGAZINE
300 Massachusetts Avenue, Boston MA 02115. 617/262-9700. **Contact:** Human Resources. **World Wide Web address:** http://www. bostonmagazine.com. **Description:** Publishes *Boston Magazine*, a monthly magazine focusing on local interest stories, politics, entertainment, theater, and dining. **Corporate headquarters location:** This Location. **Parent company:** MetroCorp (Philadelphia PA).

THE BOULDER COUNTY BUSINESS REPORT
3180 Sterling Circle, Suite 201, Boulder CO 80301-2338. 303/440-4950. **Contact:** Jerry Lewis, Editor/Vice President. **World Wide Web address:** http://www.bcbr.com. **Description:** Publishes a monthly business newspaper for the Boulder County area. **Common positions include:** Advertising Executive; Reporter; Secretary; Services Sales Rep. **Educational backgrounds include:** Advertising; Business Administration; Communications; Journalism; Liberal Arts. **Benefits:** Dental Insurance; Medical Insurance. **Corporate headquarters location:** This Location. **Number of employees at this location:** 5.

BOWNE OF NEW YORK CITY, INC.
345 Hudson Street, 10th Floor, New York NY 10014. 212/924-5500. **Fax:** 212/229-3400. **Contact:** Ellen McLynch, Human Resources Manager. **E-mail address:** jobs.bowne@ bowne.com. **World Wide Web address:** http://www.bowne.com. **Description:** Provides nationwide information management and compliance documentation services through principal business segments. Printing activities are divided into four segments: financial, corporate, commercial, and legal printing. Services in the legal printing segment include the typesetting and printing of compliance documentation relating to corporate and municipal financing, mergers, and acquisitions; the dissemination of information by companies through annual and interim reports and proxy material; and the printing of materials unrelated to compliance such as business forms and reports, newsletters, promotional aids, market letters, sales literature, and legal printing products. Founded in 1775. **NOTE:** Entry-level positions and second and third shifts are offered. **Company slogan:** Empowering your information. **Common positions include:** Accountant; Administrative Assistant; Administrative Manager; Advertising Clerk; Applications Engineer; AS400 Programmer Analyst; Computer Operator; Computer Programmer; Controller; Credit Manager; Customer Service Rep.; Database Manager; Electrician; Finance Director; Financial Analyst; Fund Manager; Human Resources Manager; Intranet Developer; Marketing Manager; Marketing Specialist; MIS Specialist; Network/Systems Administrator; Operations Manager; Production Manager; Project Manager; Public Relations Specialist; Purchasing Agent/Manager; Quality Control Supervisor; Sales Executive; Sales Manager; Sales Rep.; Secretary; Systems Analyst; Systems Manager; Transportation/Traffic Specialist; Typist/Word Processor; Vice President of Sales; Web Advertising Specialist; Website Developer. **Educational backgrounds include:** Accounting; AS400 Certification; Business Administration; Computer Science; Finance; HTML; Internet Development; Java; Marketing; MBA; MCSE; Microsoft Office; Microsoft Word; Novell; Printing; Software Tech. Support; Spreadsheets. **Benefits:** Adoption Assistance; Casual Dress - Fridays; Dental Insurance; Disability Coverage; Employee Discounts; Flexible Schedule; Life Insurance; Medical Insurance; Pension Plan; Profit Sharing; Relocation Assistance; Sick Days (1 - 5); Tuition Assistance; Vacation Days (10 - 20); Vision Plan. **Special programs:** Internships; Training; Co-ops; Summer Jobs. **Corporate headquarters location:** This Location. **Other U.S. locations:** Nationwide. **International locations:** Worldwide. **Parent company:** Bowne & Company. **Listed on:** New York Stock Exchange. **Stock exchange symbol:** BNE. **President:** Robert J. Baker. **Annual sales/revenues:** More than $100 million. **Number of employees at this location:** 900. **Number of employees nationwide:** 6,000. **Number of employees worldwide:** 7,800.

THE BRADENTON HERALD
P.O. Box 921, Bradenton FL 34206. 941/748-0411. **Contact:** Barbara Ferg, Human Resources Director. **E-mail address:** bferg@bradentonherald.com. **World Wide Web address:** http://www. bradentonherald.com. **Description:** Publisher of a daily newspaper. **Common positions include:** Account Rep.; Accountant/Auditor; Administrative Assistant; Advertising Clerk; Advertising Executive; Chief Financial Officer; Commercial Artist; Computer Operator; Computer Programmer; Computer Support Technician; Computer Technician; Credit Manager; Customer Service Rep.; Editor; Editorial Assistant; Graphic Artist; Graphic Designer; Help-Desk Technician; Human Resources Manager; Managing Editor; Market Research Analyst; Marketing Manager; MIS Manager; Network/Systems Administrator; Operations/Production Manager; Photographer/Camera Operator; Reporter; Sales Manager; Sales Representative; Services Sales Representative; Systems Manager. **Educational backgrounds include:** Accounting; Business Administration; COBOL; Communications; Computer Science; Finance; HTML; Internet Development; Liberal Arts; Marketing; MCSE; Microsoft Office; Microsoft Word; Publishing; QuarkXPress; Software Tech. Support; Spreadsheets; SQL; Visual Basic. **Benefits:** 401(k); Casual Dress - Daily; Dental Insurance; Disability Coverage; Employee Discounts; Life Insurance; Medical Insurance; Pension Plan; Savings Plan; Tuition Assistance. **Corporate headquarters location:** San Jose CA. **Parent company:** Knight-Ridder. **Listed on:** New York Stock Exchange. **Number of employees at this location:** 250.

BROWN COUNTY PUBLISHING CO.
P.O. Box 610, Denmark WI 54208. 920/863-2154.
Fax: 920/863-8653. **Contact:** Roger Wanek, Human Resources Director. **Description:** A publisher of a variety of newspapers, as well as newsletters and brochures for businesses. **NOTE:** Entry-level positions are offered. **Common positions include:** Accountant; Administrative Assistant; Administrative Manager; Advertising Clerk; Blue-Collar Worker Supervisor; Customer Service Representative; Editor; Editorial Assistant; General Manager; Graphic Artist; Human Resources Manager; Managing Editor; Production Manager; Reporter; Sales Manager; Sales Representative; Typist/Word Processor. **Educational backgrounds include:** Art/Design; Business Administration; Communications; Journalism. **Benefits:** 401(k); Dental Insurance; Disability Coverage; Life Insurance; Medical Insurance; Tuition Assistance. **Special programs:** Internships. **Corporate headquarters location:** This Location.

BROWNTROUT PUBLISHERS INC.
P.O. Box 280070, San Francisco CA 94128-0070. 310/316-4480. **Toll-free phone:** 800/777-7812. **Fax:** 310/316-1138. **Contact:** Human Resources. **World Wide Web address:** http://www. browntrout.com. **Description:** Publishers of 650 desk calendars and gift books on subjects including art, history, animals, sports, and travel. The company also customizes calendars for corporations and private businesses. **Corporate headquarters location:** This Location.

THE BULLETIN
P.O. Box 2060, Bend OR 97708. 541/382-1811. **Fax:** 541/385-5804. **Contact:** Kim Doran, City Editor. **World Wide Web address:** http://www. bendbulletin.com. **Description:** Publishes a daily newspaper with a circulation of approximately 28,000. **Common positions include:** Accountant; Advertising Clerk; Commercial Artist; Computer Programmer; Credit Manager; Customer Service Rep.; Designer; Editor; Reporter; Services Sales Representative; Systems Analyst. **Educational backgrounds include:** Accounting; Art/Design; Communications; Computer Science; English; Journalism; Liberal Arts; Marketing. **Benefits:** 401(k); Dental Insurance; Disability Coverage; Life Insurance; Medical Insurance; Profit Sharing; Tuition Assistance. **Internship information:** One reporting intern is hired each summer to work general assignment and vacation relief. The company requires a cover letter, resume, 10 to 12 clips, and three to four references with phone numbers by March 15. Pay is $1,500 per month. **Corporate headquarters location:** This Location. **Other area locations:** Baker OR; Brookings OR; Burns OR; Hermiston OR; La Grande OR; Redmond OR. **Other U.S. locations:** Crescent City CA. **Number of employees at this location:** 140. **Number of employees nationwide:** 275.

BULLETIN NEWSPAPERS
P.O. Box 99, Cottage Grove MN 55016. 651/459-3434. **Fax:** 651/459-9491. **Contact:** Jeff Patterson, General Manager. **Description:** Publishes two weekly newspapers, *The South Washington County Bulletin* and *The Woodbury Bulletin*. **Common positions include:** Editor; General Manager; Graphic Artist; Writer. **Educational backgrounds include:** Art/Design; Business Administration; Communications; Journalism. **Benefits:** 401(k); Life Insurance; Medical Insurance; Profit Sharing; Savings Plan. **Special programs:** Internships. **Corporate headquarters location:** Red Wing MN. **Parent company:** Red Wing Publishing. **Listed on:** Privately held. **Number of employees at this location:** 20.

THE BUREAU OF NATIONAL AFFAIRS
1250 23rd Street NW, 4th Floor, Washington DC 20037. 202/452-4335. **Fax:** 202/261-1583. **Contact:** Lois DeWeese, Recruitment Manager. **E-mail address:** bnajobs@bna.com. **World Wide Web address:** http://www.bna.com. **Description:** Prepares, publishes, and sells legal and economic periodicals and publications, books, and pamphlets. The Bureau of National Affairs also publishes labor, environmental, and safety services training and communications films. **Common positions include:** Accountant/Auditor; Attorney; Commercial Artist; Computer Programmer; Customer Service Rep.; Editor; Human Resources Manager; Marketing Specialist; Operations/Production Manager; Reporter; Systems Analyst; Technical Writer/Editor. **Educational backgrounds include:** Accounting; Art/Design; Business Administration; Communications; Computer Science; Finance; Journalism. **Benefits:** Daycare Assistance; Dental Insurance; Disability Coverage; Life Insurance; Medical Insurance; Pension Plan; Profit Sharing; Stock Option; Tuition Assistance. **Corporate headquarters location:** This Location.

BUTTERICK COMPANY, INC.
161 Avenue of the Americas, New York NY 10013. 212/620-2500. **Contact:** Roslyn Gardner, Personnel Manager. **Description:** Manufactures two lines of clothing patterns for the home sewing market and produces related fashion publications including *Weddings*, *Butterick Home Catalog*, *Vogue Patterns Magazine*, and *Vogue Knitting Magazine*. **Common positions include:** Apparel Worker; Editorial Assistant; Fashion Designer; Human Resources Manager; Public Relations Specialist; Technical Writer/Editor. **Educational backgrounds include:** Art/Design; Business Administration; Communications; Fashion; Liberal Arts; Marketing; Merchandising. **Benefits:** Dental Insurance; Disability Coverage; EAP; Employee Discounts; Life Insurance; Medical Insurance; Pension Plan; Savings Plan; Tuition Assistance. **Special programs:** Internships. **Corporate headquarters location:** This Location.

CMP MEDIA INC.
600 Community Drive, Manhasset NY 11030. 516/562-5281. **Fax:** 516/562-7243. **Contact:** Human Resources. **World Wide Web address:** http://www.cmp.com. **Description:** Publishes high-tech, computer-related magazines and trade publications. **Common positions include:** Advertising Clerk; Art Director; Artist; Customer Service Representative; Editor; Reporter; Sales Rep.; Systems Analyst. **Educational backgrounds include:** Art/Design; Communications; Marketing. **Benefits:** 401(k); Daycare Assistance; Dental Insurance; Disability Coverage; Life Insurance; Medical Insurance; On-Site Exercise Facility; Pension Plan; Profit Sharing; Savings Plan; Tuition Assistance. **Special programs:** Internships. **Corporate headquarters location:** This Location. **Listed on:** Privately held. **Number of employees at this location:** 1,000.

CPI CORPORATION
1706 Washington Avenue, St. Louis MO 63103. 314/231-1575. **Contact:** Director of Human Resources. **Description:** A holding company with subsidiaries operating professional portrait studios, photographic finishing laboratories, electronic publishing stores, and wall decor stores. **Common positions include:** Accountant/Auditor; Advertising Clerk; Computer Programmer; Marketing Specialist. **Educational backgrounds include:** Accounting; Business Administration; Computer Science; Marketing. **Benefits:** Dental Insurance; Disability Coverage; Employee Discounts; Life Insurance;

Medical Insurance; Pension Plan; Profit Sharing; Savings Plan; Tuition Assistance. **Corporate headquarters location:** This Location. **Listed on:** New York Stock Exchange. **Number of employees at this location:** 1,000.

CADMUS COMMUNICATIONS CORP.
6620 West Broad Street, Suite 240, Richmond VA 23230. 804/287-5680. **Fax:** 804/287-6267. **Contact:** Wayne Tennent, Director of Human Resources and Quality. **World Wide Web address:** http://www.cadmus.com. **Description:** A graphic communications company offering specialized products and services in three broad areas: printing, marketing, and publishing. Cadmus is one of the largest graphic communications companies in North America. Product lines include annual reports, catalogs, direct marketing financial printing, point-of-sale marketing, promotional printing, publishing, research journals, specialty magazines, and specialty packaging. **Corporate headquarters location:** This Location. **Other U.S. locations:** GA; MA; MD; NC. **Subsidiaries include:** Cadmus Consumer Publishing (Richmond VA); Cadmus Custom Publishing (Boston MA); Cadmus Direct Marketing, Inc. (Charlotte NC); Cadmus Interactive (Tucker GA); Cadmus Journal Services (Linthicum MD, Easton MD, and Richmond VA); Cadmus Marketing Services (Atlanta GA); Central Florida Press, L.C. (Orlando FL); Expert Brown (Sandston VA); Graftech Corporation (Charlotte NC); 3Score, Inc. (Tucker GA); Washburn Graphics, Inc. (Charlotte NC); The William Byrd Press (Richmond VA). **Listed on:** NASDAQ. **Number of employees nationwide:** 2,500.

CAHNERS BUSINESS INFORMATION
275 Washington Street, Newton MA 02458-1630. 617/964-3030. **Contact:** Human Resources. **World Wide Web address:** http://www.cahners.com. **Description:** One of the largest publishing companies in the U.S., providing over 50 magazines in the specialized business and consumer fields. Cahners also provides a variety of marketing and publishing services including direct mail, economic forecasting, and marketing research. **Corporate headquarters location:** This Location.

CAPITAL CITY PRESS
P.O. Box 546, Montpelier VT 05601. 802/223-5207. **Fax:** 802/223-7879. **Contact:** Dolores H. Cox, Human Resources Manager. **World Wide Web address:** http://www.capcitypress.com. **Description:** A printing press that provides a range of services including editorial, composition, and fulfillment. The company specializes in scientific, medical, and educational journals. Founded in 1908. **NOTE:** Second and third shifts are offered. **Common positions include:** Customer Service Representative; General Manager; Human Resources Manager; Internet Services Manager; MIS Specialist; Network/Systems Administrator; Operations Manager; Production Manager. **Educational backgrounds include:** Graphic Design; HTML; Internet; Printing; QuarkXPress. **Benefits:** 401(k); Dental Insurance; Disability Coverage; Flexible Schedule; Life Insurance; Medical Insurance. **Corporate headquarters location:** This Location. **Listed on:** Privately held. **President:** G. Paul Bozuwa. **Annual sales/revenues:** $21 - $50 million. **Number of employees at this location:** 310.

CAPITAL-GAZETTE COMMUNICATIONS
P.O. Box 911, Annapolis MD 21404. 410/268-5000. **Contact:** Tom Marquardt, Managing Editor. **World Wide Web address:** http://www. hometownannapolis.com. **Description:** Publishes the *Annapolis Evening Capital*, a newspaper with a daily circulation of 50,000. **Corporate headquarters location:** This Location. **Subsidiaries include:** Capital-Gazette Newspapers.

CENTRE DAILY TIMES
3400 East College Avenue, State College PA 16801. 814/238-5000. **Contact:** Human Resources. **World Wide Web address:** http://www.centredaily.com. **Description:** Publishes the *Centre Daily Times* newspaper.

CHARLESBRIDGE PUBLISHING
85 Main Street, Watertown MA 02472. 617/926-0329. **Toll-free phone:** 800/225-3214. **Fax:** 617/926-5720. **Contact:** Mary Ann Sabia, Vice President. **E-mail address:** books@ charlesbridge.com. **World Wide Web address:** http://www.charlesbridge.com. **Description:** Publisher of educational materials for the classroom and both fiction and nonfiction picture books for children. Picture books cover a wide range of topics including math, nature, multiculturalism, animals, history, geography, and nursery rhymes. Charlesbridge has two fiction imprints; *Talewinds* and *Whispering Coyote*, and a diversity imprint called *Shakti*. **Special programs:** Internships. **Corporate headquarters location:** This Location. **President:** Brent Farmer. **Number of employees at this location:** 25.

CHARRETTE CORPORATION
P.O. Box 4010, Woburn MA 01888-4010. 781/935-6000. **Physical address:** 31 Olympia Avenue, Woburn MA. **Fax:** 781/933-6104. **Contact:** Lawrence Mansfield, Director of Human Resources. **E-mail address:** charhr@aol.com. **World Wide Web address:** http://www.charrette.com. **Description:** Offers a variety of products and services to design professionals. Products include a wide range of art, design, and office products from mat boards and paints, to furniture and software. Services include digital imaging, offset printing, reprographics, and blueprinting. **NOTE:** Entry-level positions are offered. **Common positions include:** Accountant/Auditor; Buyer; Computer Programmer; Credit Manager; Customer Service Rep.; Financial Analyst; General Manager; Human Resources Manager; Management Trainee; Manufacturer's/Wholesaler's Sales Rep.; MIS Specialist; Systems Analyst. **Educational backgrounds include:** Accounting; Art/Design; Business Administration; Communications; Computer Science; Finance; Liberal Arts; Marketing. **Benefits:** 401(k); Daycare Assistance; Dental Insurance; Disability Coverage; Employee Discounts; Job Sharing; Life Insurance; Medical Insurance; Pension Plan; Tuition Assistance. **Special programs:** Internships. **Corporate headquarters location:** This Location. **Other U.S. locations:** New Haven CT; Chicago IL; Boston MA; Jessup MD; Detroit MI; Pennsauken NJ; Buffalo NY; New York NY; Rochester NY; Blue Bell PA; Philadelphia PA; Providence RI.

CHARTWELL INFORMATION PUBLISHERS
805 Cameron Street, Alexandria VA 22314. 703/519-3630. **Fax:** 703/519-7881. **Contact:** Human Resources. **World Wide Web address:** http://www.wasteinfo.com. **Description:** Publishes monthly newsletters about solid waste management. The company's publications include *Solid Waste Digest* and *Solid Waste Industry Statistics & Forecast*. **Corporate headquarters location:** This Location.

CHESAPEAKE PUBLISHING CORP.
P.O. Box 600, Easton MD 21601-0600. 410/822-1500. **Contact:** Human Resources. **World Wide Web address:** http://www.chespub.com. **Description:** This location publishes the *Star*

Democratic. Overall, Chesapeake Publishing publishes 50 newspapers including *Enterprise* (circulation: 14,000); *Maryland Independent* (circulation: 12,500); *South County Current* (circulation: 33,000); *Calvert County Recorder* (circulation: 5,500); and *Flightline* (circulation: 9,000). The company also provides commercial printing services. **Corporate headquarters location:** This Location. **Other U.S. locations:** Waldorf MD; Elkton MD.

CHICAGO SUN-TIMES INC.
401 North Wabash Avenue, Chicago IL 60611. 312/321-3000. **Contact:** Employment Manager. **World Wide Web address:** http://www. suntimes.com. **Description:** Publishes one of the largest daily newspapers in the United States. **Common positions include:** Accountant/Auditor; Computer Programmer; Customer Service Rep.; Financial Analyst; Systems Analyst. **Educational backgrounds include:** Business Administration; Communications; Computer Science; Finance; Liberal Arts; Marketing. **Benefits:** 401(k); Dental Insurance; Disability Coverage; Employee Discounts; Life Insurance; Medical Insurance; Pension Plan; Savings Plan; Tuition Assistance. **Special programs:** Internships. **Corporate headquarters location:** This Location. **Parent company:** American Publishing Company. **Listed on:** NASDAQ. **Number of employees at this location:** 1,700.

CHRISTIAN SCIENCE MONITOR
Christian Science Center, One Norway Street, Boston MA 02115-3195. 617/450-2000. **Contact:** Human Resources. **World Wide Web address:** http://www.csmonitor.com. **Description:** A daily newspaper focusing primarily on national and international news. Founded in 1908. **Corporate headquarters location:** This Location. **Operations at this facility include:** Publishing.

CHRISTIANITY TODAY, INC. (CTI)
465 Gundersen Drive, Carol Stream IL 60188. 630/260-6200. **Fax:** 630/260-0114. **Contact:** Kate Bryant, Employment Manager. **E-mail address:** ctihrdept@aol.com. **World Wide Web address:** http://www.christianitytoday.com. **Description:** A publisher of evangelical magazines. **Common positions include:** Accountant; Commercial Artist; Credit Manager; Editor; General Manager; Human Resources Manager; Manufacturer's/Wholesaler's Sales Rep.; Market Research Analyst; Marketing Specialist; Reporter. **Educational backgrounds include:** Accounting; Art/Design; Business Administration; Communications; Journalism; Liberal Arts; Marketing. **Benefits:** Dental Insurance; Disability Coverage; Employee Discounts; Life Insurance; Medical Insurance; Pension Plan; Tuition Assistance. **Special programs:** Internships. **Corporate headquarters location:** This Location.

THE CHRONICLE
P.O. Box 580, Centralia WA 98531. 360/736-3311. **Contact:** Human Resources. **World Wide Web address:** http://www.chronline.com. **Description:** Publishes a daily newspaper with a circulation of approximately 15,500. **Common positions include:** Administrator; Advertising Clerk; Editor; Reporter; Services Sales Representative. **Educational backgrounds include:** English; Liberal Arts. **Benefits:** Dental Insurance; Life Insurance; Medical Insurance; Profit Sharing; Savings Plan. **Corporate headquarters location:** This Location. **Number of employees at this location:** 100.

CITY PAGES, INC.
401 North Third Street, Suite 550, Minneapolis MN 55401. 612/375-1015. **Fax:** 612/372-3737.

Contact: Human Resources. **World Wide Web address:** http://www.citypages.com. **Description:** Publishes a weekly alternative newspaper. **Common positions include:** Account Manager; Advertising Executive; Controller; Credit Manager; Editor; Graphic Designer; Sales Manager; Systems Manager. **Educational backgrounds include:** Art/Design; Business Administration; Liberal Arts. **Benefits:** 401(k); Employee Discounts; Life Insurance; Medical Insurance. **Special programs:** Internships. **Corporate headquarters location:** This Location. **Listed on:** Privately held. **Publisher:** Mark Bartel. **Number of employees at this location:** 90.

THE CLARION-LEDGER
201 South Congress Street, Jackson MS 39201. 601/961-7000. **Toll-free phone:** 800/222-8015. **Fax:** 601/961-7329. **Contact:** Donna Wiggins, Recruitment/Retention Manager. **E-mail address:** dwiggins@jackson.gannett.com. **World Wide Web address:** http://www.clarionledger.com. **Description:** Publishes *The Clarion-Ledger*, a daily newspaper that is circulated statewide. **Common positions include:** Account Manager; Account Rep.; Accountant; Administrative Assistant; Advertising Clerk; Advertising Executive; Applications Engineer; AS400 Programmer Analyst; Budget Analyst; Controller; Credit Manager; Customer Service Representative; Desktop Publishing Specialist; Finance Director; Financial Analyst; Graphic Artist; Graphic Designer; Human Resources Manager; Managing Editor; Market Research Analyst; Marketing Manager; Marketing Specialist; Online Sales Manager; Public Relations Specialist; Reporter; Sales Executive; Sales Representative; Secretary; Systems Analyst; Systems Manager; Technical Writer/Editor. **Educational backgrounds include:** Accounting; Art/Design; Business Administration; Communications; Computer Science; Finance; Marketing. **Benefits:** Dental Insurance; Disability Coverage; Employee Discounts; Life Insurance; Medical Insurance; Pension Plan; Savings Plan. **Corporate headquarters location:** Arlington VA. **Parent company:** Gannett Corporation is a nationwide news and information company that publishes 81 newspapers including *USA Today*, and is the largest outdoor advertising company in North America. Gannett is also involved in marketing, television news and program production, research satellite information systems, and owns a national group of commercial printing facilities. Gannett has operations in 41 states, the District of Columbia, Guam, the Virgin Islands, Canada, Great Britain, Hong Kong, Singapore, and Switzerland.

CLARKE AMERICAN CHECKS, INC.
10931 Laureate Drive, San Antonio TX 78249. 210/697-8888. **Fax:** 210/558-5247. **Recorded jobline:** 210/690-6500. **Contact:** Personnel. **Description:** A leading printer of checks and share drafts for the financial industry. Founded in 1874. **Common positions include:** Accountant/Auditor; Administrative Assistant; Computer Programmer; Customer Service Rep.; Financial Analyst; Human Resources Manager; Industrial Engineer; Management Trainee; Marketing Specialist; Systems Analyst. **Educational backgrounds include:** Business Administration; Computer Science; Engineering; Finance; Marketing. **Benefits:** 401(k); Dental Insurance; Disability Coverage; Employee Discounts; Life Insurance; Medical Insurance; Tuition Assistance. **Special programs:** Internships. **Corporate headquarters location:** This Location. **Other U.S. locations:** Nationwide. **Parent company:** Caradon, Inc. **Number of employees at this location:** 300. **Number of employees nationwide:** 2,500.

COLOR-ART, INC.
10300 Watson Road, St. Louis MO 63127. 314/966-2000. **Fax:** 314/966-4725. **Contact:** Tim Murphy, Human Resources Manager. **Description:** A commercial printing company engaged in offset and letter press printing. **Common positions include:** Accountant; Blue-Collar Worker Supervisor; Computer Programmer; Customer Service Rep.; General Manager; Operations/Production Manager; Prepress Worker; Printing Press Operator; Purchasing Agent/Manager; Quality Control Supervisor; Services Sales Representative; Warehouse Manager; Warehouse/Distribution Worker. **Educational backgrounds include:** Marketing. **Benefits:** 401(k); Dental Insurance; Disability Coverage; Employee Discounts; Life Insurance; Medical Insurance; Profit Sharing; Section 125 Plan. **Other U.S. locations:** CA; FL; NY. **Subsidiaries include:** Lake Printing; Plus Communications. **Listed on:** Privately held. **Number of employees at this location:** 300.

COLOR-ART/BUXTON
2419 Glasgow Avenue, St. Louis MO 63106. 314/535-9700. **Contact:** Human Resources. **Description:** An offset, flexo, and letter press printer engaged in book manufacturing, labels, coasters, and general commercial printing. **Special programs:** Internships. **Number of employees at this location:** 95.

COLORADO SPRINGS BUSINESS JOURNAL
P.O. Box 1541, Colorado Springs CO 80901. 719/634-5905. **Fax:** 719/634-5157. **Contact:** Rob Wrubel, Publisher. **E-mail address:** publisher@aol.com. **World Wide Web address:** http://www.csbj.com. **Description:** Publishes a weekly business newspaper. Founded in 1989. **Common positions include:** Account Rep.; Administrative Assistant; Editor; Editorial Assistant; Graphic Artist; Market Research Analyst; Reporter; Sales Manager. **Educational backgrounds include:** Art/Design. **Benefits:** 401(k); Dental Insurance; Disability Coverage; Life Insurance; Medical Insurance. **Special programs:** Internships. **Corporate headquarters location:** This Location. **Annual sales/revenues:** Less than $5 million. **Number of employees at this location:** 20.

THE COLUMBIAN PUBLISHING COMPANY
P.O. Box 180, Vancouver WA 98666-0180. 360/694-3391. **Physical address:** 701 West Eighth Street, Vancouver WA. **Contact:** Human Resources. **World Wide Web address:** http://www.columbian.com. **Description:** Publishes *The Columbian*, a daily newspaper. **Common positions include:** Customer Service Rep.; Editor; Graphic Artist; Production Worker; Reporter; Services Sales Representative. **Educational backgrounds include:** Communications; Journalism; Liberal Arts; Marketing. **Benefits:** Dental Insurance; Disability Coverage; Employee Discounts; Life Insurance; Medical Insurance; Profit Sharing; Savings Plan; Tuition Assistance; Vision Insurance. **Corporate headquarters location:** This Location. **Number of employees at this location:** 350.

THE COLUMBUS DISPATCH
34 South Third Street, Columbus OH 43215. 614/461-5000. **Fax:** 614/461-5533. **Recorded jobline:** 614/461-8822. **Contact:** Human Resources. **World Wide Web address:** http://www.dispatch.com. **Description:** Publishes a morning newspaper with a daily circulation of over 250,000. **Common positions include:** Administrative Worker/Clerk; Customer Service Rep.; Editor; Human Resources Manager; Reporter; Sales Executive. **Benefits:** 401(k); Disability Coverage; Life Insurance; Medical Insurance; Pension Plan;

Tuition Assistance. **Special programs:** Internships. **Corporate headquarters location:** This Location.

COLWELL INDUSTRIES INC.
123 North Third Street, Minneapolis MN 55401. 612/340-0365. **Contact:** Human Resources. **World Wide Web address:** http://www.colwellind.com. **Description:** This location houses administrative offices. Overall, Colwell Industries is involved in the printing of brochures, albums, and color cards. **Corporate headquarters location:** This Location.

COMMTEK COMMUNICATIONS CORP.
9302 Lee Highway, Suite 600, Vienna VA 22182. 703/251-3000. **Contact:** Angela Anderson, Director of Operations/Human Resources. **World Wide Web address:** http://www.satelliteguide.com. **Description:** A magazine publisher of *satellite ORBIT* and *satellite DIRECT* television programming guides. **Common positions include:** Account Manager; Account Rep.; Accountant; Administrative Assistant; Administrative Manager; Advertising Clerk; Advertising Executive; Budget Analyst; Chief Financial Officer; Computer Programmer; Controller; Credit Manager; Customer Service Representative; Database Manager; Editor; Editorial Assistant; Finance Director; Financial Analyst; Graphic Artist; Graphic Designer; Human Resources Manager; Internet Services Manager; Managing Editor; Market Research Analyst; Marketing Manager; Marketing Specialist; MIS Specialist; Operations Manager; Production Manager; Public Relations Specialist; Reporter; Sales Executive; Sales Manager; Sales Representative; Secretary; Software Engineer; Systems Analyst; Systems Manager; Technical Writer/Editor. **Educational backgrounds include:** Accounting; Communications; Computer Science; Finance; Liberal Arts; Marketing; Public Relations. **Benefits:** 401(k); Dental Insurance; Disability Coverage; Employee Discounts; Life Insurance; Medical Insurance. **Corporate headquarters location:** This Location.

COMMUNITY PRESS
P.O. Box 265, Provo UT 84604. 801/225-2299. **Physical address:** 5600 North University Avenue, Provo UT. **Contact:** Richard Graves, Controller/Personnel. **Description:** A book printer and book binding firm with complete prepress facilities including typesetting, paste-up, camera, color/black & white presses, and multicolor presses. Community Press also offers a complete hardcover book binding line with cover making, embossing, stamping, and other services. **Corporate headquarters location:** This Location.

THE CONCORD MONITOR
One Monitor Drive, P.O. Box 1177, Concord NH 03302. 603/224-5301. **Contact:** Tracie Wager, Human Resources Manager. **World Wide Web address:** http://www.concordmonitor.com. **Description:** Publishes a daily newspaper with a circulation of 22,500. The Concord Monitor also does press runs for other area newspapers. **NOTE:** Entry-level positions and part-time jobs are offered. **Common positions include:** Customer Service Rep.; Editor; Reporter; Sales Rep. **Educational backgrounds include:** Microsoft Word; QuarkXPress. **Benefits:** 401(k); Dental Insurance; Disability Coverage; Life Insurance; Medical Insurance; Pension Plan. **Special programs:** Internships. **Corporate headquarters location:** This Location. **Listed on:** Privately held.

CONCORDIA PUBLISHING HOUSE
3558 South Jefferson Avenue, St. Louis MO 63118. 314/268-1252. **Contact:** Human Resources. **Description:** Publishers of religious curriculum,

periodicals, books, pamphlets, and Bibles. **Common positions include:** Accountant; Advertising Clerk; Blue-Collar Worker Supervisor; Buyer; Commercial Artist; Computer Programmer; Credit Manager; Customer Service Rep.; Department Manager; Financial Analyst; General Manager; Human Resources Manager; Industrial Production Manager; Management Trainee; Manufacturing Manager; Marketing Specialist; Operations/Production Manager; Purchasing Agent/Manager. **Educational backgrounds include:** Accounting; Art/Design; Business Administration; Communications; Finance; Marketing. **Benefits:** Dental Insurance; Disability Coverage; Employee Discounts; Life Insurance; Medical Insurance; Pension Plan; Tuition Assistance. **Corporate headquarters location:** This Location. **Number of employees at this location:** 335.

CONGRESSIONAL QUARTERLY
1414 22nd Street NW, Washington DC 20037. 202/887-8500. **Contact:** Linda Brashears, Human Resources Administrator. **World Wide Web address:** http://www.cq.com. **Description:** Publishes the *CQ Weekly* and the daily *Congressional Monitor*, as well as a wide range of government-related publications. **Common positions include:** Administrative Assistant; Editorial Assistant; Reporter.

THE CONNECTICUT POST
410 State Street, Bridgeport CT 06604. 203/333-0161. **Contact:** Human Resources. **World Wide Web address:** http://www.connpost.com. **Description:** A newspaper with a daily circulation of 77,000 and a Sunday circulation of 97,000. **Corporate headquarters location:** This Location.

CONSOLIDATED GRAPHICS, INC.
5858 Westheimer Road, Suite 200, Houston TX 77057. 713/787-0977. **Contact:** Human Resources. **World Wide Web address:** http://www. consolidatedgraphics.com. **Description:** Operates commercial printing companies nationwide. **Corporate headquarters location:** This Location. **Other U.S. locations:** Phoenix AZ; Denver CO; Dallas TX; San Antonio TX; Seattle WA. **Subsidiaries include:** Apple Graphics, Inc. (Los Angeles CA); Automated Graphics Systems (Washington DC and Cleveland OH); Bridgetown Printing Company (Portland OR); Byrum Lithographing Company (Columbus OH); CMI (Chicago IL); Emerald City Graphics (Seattle WA) produces technical and training manuals; Everett Graphics, Inc. (Oakland CA); Graphtec, Inc. (Washington DC); McKay Press, Inc. (Midland MI); Maryland Comp.com (Baltimore MD); Metropolitan Printing Service, Inc. (Bloomington IN); Mount Vernon Printing Company (Washington DC); Multiple Images Printing, Inc. (Chicago IL); Piccari Press, Inc. (Philadelphia PA); Precision Litho (Vista CA); Superior Colour Graphics (Kalamazoo MI); Wentworth Printing Corp. (Columbia SC). **Listed on:** New York Stock Exchange. **Stock exchange symbol:** CGX. **Chairman/CEO:** Joe R. Davis.

CONSTRUCTION DATA CORPORATION
11940 Jollyville Road, Suite 305 South, Austin TX 78759. 512/219-5150. **Toll-free phone:** 800/872-7878. **Fax:** 800/487-7878. **Contact:** Richard M. Griffin, Senior Editor. **World Wide Web address:** http://www.cdcnews.com. **Description:** A construction trade publication which provides planning news and bidding opportunities in Connecticut, Delaware, Massachusetts, New Jersey, New York, Pennsylvania, Rhode Island, and Texas. Founded in 1977. **NOTE:** Entry-level positions and part-time jobs are offered. **Common positions include:** Account Rep.; Desktop Publishing Specialist; Editor; Editorial Assistant; Reporter; Sales Rep. **Educational backgrounds include:** Business Administration; Communications; Internet; Liberal Arts; Microsoft Word; Novell; Software Tech. Support. **Benefits:** 401(k); Dental Insurance; Life Insurance; Medical Insurance; Profit Sharing; Tuition Assistance. **Special programs:** Internships. **Corporate headquarters location:** Vero Beach FL. **Other U.S. locations:** Denver CO; Cary NC; Hamilton NY. **Listed on:** Privately held. **Annual sales/revenues:** $11 - $20 million. **Number of employees at this location:** 20.

CONSTRUCTION DATA CORPORATION
3240 Cardinal Drive, Suite 200, Vero Beach FL 32963. 561/770-6003. **Toll-free phone:** 800/423-0500. **Fax:** 561/231-7247. **Contact:** Human Resources. **World Wide Web address:** http://www.cdcnews.com. **Description:** Publishes a construction trade publication which provides planning news and bidding opportunities in Connecticut, Delaware, Massachusetts, New Jersey, New York, Pennsylvania, Rhode Island, and Texas. **Common positions include:** Accountant; Clerk; Sales Rep.; Secretary; Typist/Word Processor. **Educational backgrounds include:** Accounting; Business Administration; Communications; Liberal Arts; Marketing. **Benefits:** 401(k); Dental Insurance; Life Insurance; Medical Insurance; Tuition Assistance. **Corporate headquarters location:** This Location. **Other U.S. locations:** Rockland MA; Lawrenceville NJ; Austin TX. **Listed on:** Privately held. **Annual sales/revenues:** $11 - $20 million. **Number of employees at this location:** 75.

CONTRA COSTA TIMES
P.O. Box 5088, Walnut Creek CA 94596. 925/935-2525. **Contact:** Laurie Fox, Human Resources Manager. **World Wide Web address:** http://www. contracostatimes.com. **Description:** Publishes a daily newspaper. **Common positions include:** Accountant; Advertising Clerk; Cashier; Clerical Supervisor; Computer Operator; Computer Programmer; Credit Clerk and Authorizer; Credit Manager; Customer Service Representative; Editor; Financial Manager; Human Resources Manager; Library Technician; Machinist; Market Research Analyst; Marketing Manager; Payroll Clerk; Printing Press Operator; Receptionist; Reporter; Secretary; Services Sales Representative; Truck Driver; Typist/Word Processor. **Educational backgrounds include:** Accounting; Art/Design; Business Administration; Communications; Computer Science; Finance; Liberal Arts; Marketing. **Benefits:** Dental Insurance; Disability Coverage; Life Insurance; Medical Insurance; Pension Plan; Savings Plan. **Corporate headquarters location:** This Location. **Parent company:** Contra Costa Newspapers also publishes *San Ramon Valley Times*, *Valley Times*, and *West County Times*. **Number of employees at this location:** 1,700.

COOK COMMUNICATIONS MINISTRIES
850 North Grove Avenue, Elgin IL 60120. 847/741-2400. **Contact:** Human Resources. **World Wide Web address:** http://www.cookministries.com. **Description:** Creates, designs, produces, prints, publishes, markets, and distributes evangelical material. **Common positions include:** Accountant; Blue-Collar Worker Supervisor; Buyer; Computer Programmer; Customer Service Representative; Department Manager; Human Resources Manager; Manufacturer's/Wholesaler's Sales Rep.; Marketing Specialist; Operations/Production Manager; Public Relations Specialist; Purchasing Agent/Manager; Statistician; Systems Analyst. **Educational backgrounds include:** Accounting; Art/Design;

Business Administration; Communications; Computer Science; Economics; Finance; Liberal Arts; Marketing; Mathematics; Religion. **Benefits:** 401(k); Daycare Assistance; Dental Insurance; Disability Coverage; Employee Discounts; Life Insurance; Medical Insurance; Tuition Assistance. **Corporate headquarters location:** This Location. **Number of employees at this location:** 450. **Number of employees nationwide:** 1,100.

CORPORATE REPORT WISCONSIN
P.O. Box 878, Menomonee Falls WI 53052-0878. 262/255-9077. **Contact:** Christine Schramek, Associate Publisher. **Description:** Publishes a monthly business magazine.

CORPTECH (CORPORATE TECHNOLOGY INFORMATION SERVICES)
12 Alfred Street, Suite 200, Woburn MA 01801. **Toll-free phone:** 800/333-8036. **Contact:** Human Resources. **World Wide Web address:** http://www. corptech.com. **Description:** Publishes company information in print and electronic formats. **Corporate headquarters location:** This Location. **Parent company:** OneSource.

COURIER EPIC, INC.
COURIER CORPORATION
15 Wellman Avenue, North Chelmsford MA 01863. 978/251-6000. **Contact:** Human Resources. **World Wide Web address:** http://www.courier.com. **Description:** As a division of Courier Corporation, Courier EPIC coordinates material for electronic publishers and software companies. Courier Corporation (also at this location) offers a full range of book production and distribution services. Publishing markets served include educational, religious, reference, medical, financial, trade, and software. Founded in 1824. **Corporate headquarters location:** This Location. **Other area locations:** Stoughton MA; Westford MA. **Other U.S. locations:** Kendallville IN; Philadelphia PA.

CURTIS MAGAZINE GROUP
INDIANA BUSINESS MAGAZINE
1000 Waterway Boulevard, Indianapolis IN 46202. 317/692-1200. **Contact:** Human Resources. **Description:** A monthly, statewide business publication. Curtis Magazine Group also issues a business directory of Indiana's top 2,500 firms. **Common positions include:** Administrator; Advertising Clerk; Editor; Sales Executive; Writer. **Educational backgrounds include:** Journalism; Liberal Arts. **Benefits:** Life Insurance; Medical Insurance. **Corporate headquarters location:** This Location.

DS GRAPHICS INC.
120 Stedman Street, Lowell MA 01851-2797. 978/970-1359. **Toll-free phone:** 800/536-8283. **Fax:** 978/970-1253. **Contact:** Human Resources. **World Wide Web address:** http://www. dsgraphics.com. **Description:** A commercial printer engaged in the printing of books, software documentation, and direct mail marketing materials. Founded in 1974. **Corporate headquarters location:** This Location.

DSI
11300 Lakefield Drive, Duluth GA 30097. 770/476-4455. **Contact:** Human Resources. **Description:** Provides customers with printing services and products including custom forms, notebooks, and memo pads. **Corporate headquarters location:** This Location.

THE DAILY ASTORIAN
P.O. Box 210, Astoria OR 97103. 503/325-3211. **Contact:** George Potter, Personnel Administrator.

E-mail address: astorian@dailyastorian.com. **World Wide Web address:** http://www. dailyastorian.com. **Description:** Publishes a local daily newspaper. **Common positions include:** Advertising Clerk; Customer Service Rep.; Graphic Artist; Reporter; Services Sales Rep. **Educational backgrounds include:** Art/Design; Business Administration; Journalism; Liberal Arts. **Benefits:** 401(k); Dental Insurance; Disability Coverage; Life Insurance; Medical Insurance; Profit Sharing. **Special programs:** Internships. **Corporate headquarters location:** Pendleton OR. **Other U.S. locations:** Salem OR; Long Beach WA. **Parent company:** East Oregonian Publishing Company.

DAILY CAMERA
P.O. Box 591, Boulder CO 80306. 303/442-1202. **Contact:** Human Resources. **World Wide Web address:** http://www.dailycamera.com. **Description:** Publishes a daily newspaper. **Special programs:** Internships. **Corporate headquarters location:** This Location. **Parent company:** E.W. Scripps Company (Cincinnati OH).

DAILY HERALD
PADDOCK PUBLICATIONS, INC.
P.O. Box 280, Arlington Heights IL 60006-0280. 847/427-4300. **Fax:** 847/427-1270. **Recorded jobline:** 847/427-4398. **Contact:** Diane Muchow, Employment Recruiter. **E-mail address:** hr@dailyherald.com. **World Wide Web address:** http://www.dailyherald.com. **Description:** Publishes a daily newspaper. Founded in 1872. **NOTE:** Entry-level positions, part-time jobs, and second and third shifts are offered. **Common positions include:** Account Manager; Account Representative; Accountant; Administrative Assistant; Administrative Manager; Advertising Clerk; Branch Manager; Computer Operator; Customer Service Representative; Desktop Publishing Specialist; Editor; Editorial Assistant; Graphic Artist; Graphic Designer; Internet Services Manager; Librarian; Managing Editor; Market Research Analyst; Marketing Manager; MIS Specialist; Multimedia Designer; Online Content Manager; Online Sales Manager; Reporter; Sales Representative; Secretary; Transportation/Traffic Specialist; Typist/Word Processor; Web Advertising Specialist; Webmaster. **Educational backgrounds include:** Accounting; Art/Design; Business Administration; Communications; Journalism; Microsoft Word; Publishing; QuarkXPress. **Benefits:** 401(k); Dental Insurance; Disability Coverage; Employee Discounts; Financial Planning Assistance; Flexible Schedule; Job Sharing; Life Insurance; Medical Insurance; Pension Plan; Profit Sharing; Tuition Assistance. **Special programs:** Internships; Training; Co-ops. **Corporate headquarters location:** This Location. **Listed on:** Privately held.

DAILY JOURNAL CORPORATION
P.O. Box 54026, Los Angeles CA 90054-0026. 213/229-5300. **Physical address:** 915 East First Street, Los Angeles CA 90012. **Contact:** Human Resources. **Description:** Publishes *The Los Angeles Daily Journal, Daily Commerce, California Real Estate Journal,* and *Nevada Journal,* each based in Los Angeles; *San Francisco Daily Journal* in San Francisco; *The Daily Recorder* in Sacramento; *The Inter-City Express* in Oakland; *Marin County Court Reporter* in San Rafael; *Orange County Reporter* in Santa Ana; *San Jose Post-Record* in San Jose; *Sonoma County Daily Herald-Recorder* in Santa Rosa; *San Diego Commerce* in San Diego; *Business Journal* in Riverside; and *Washington Journal* in Seattle. The company also serves as a newspaper representative specializing in public notice advertising. **Corporate headquarters location:** This Location.

THE DAILY RECORD INC.
800 Jefferson Road, Parsippany NJ 07054. 973/428-6200. **Contact:** Lori Aynat, Human Resources Director. **World Wide Web address:** http://www.dailyrecord.com. **Description:** Publishes a morning newspaper, *The Daily Record*. Circulation is approximately 63,000 on weekdays and 72,000 on Sundays. **Common positions include:** Account Representative; Accountant/Auditor; Administrative Manager; Advertising Clerk; Credit Manager; Customer Service Representative; Editor; General Manager; Graphic Artist; Reporter; Sales Representative. **Educational backgrounds include:** Accounting; Art/Design; Business Administration; Communications; Journalism; Microsoft Office; Microsoft Word; QuarkXPress; Spreadsheets. **Benefits:** 401(k); Casual Dress - Fridays; Dental Insurance; Disability Coverage; Employee Discounts; Life Insurance; Medical Insurance; Pension Plan; Sick Days (6 - 10); Vacation Days (10 - 20). **Corporate headquarters location:** Arlington VA. **Parent company:** Gannett Co. **Listed on:** New York Stock Exchange. **Number of employees at this location:** 300.

THE DAILY SOUTHTOWN
6901 West 159th Street, Tinley Park IL 60477. 708/633-6700. **Contact:** Human Resources. **World Wide Web address:** http://www.dailysouthtown.com. **Description:** A daily newspaper serving the Chicago metropolitan area. **Corporate headquarters location:** This Location.

DANNER PRESS CORPORATION
1411 Navarre Road SW, Canton OH 44706. 330/454-5692. **Fax:** 330/454-5693. **Contact:** Monica Howe, Personnel Director. **World Wide Web address:** http://www.dannerpress.com. **Description:** Provides a variety of printing services to area customers. Founded in 1923. **Common positions include:** Cost Estimator; Customer Service Rep.; Operations/Production Manager; Services Sales Rep. **Educational backgrounds include:** Graphic Design. **Benefits:** 401(k); Dental Insurance; Disability Coverage; Employee Discounts; Life Insurance; Medical Insurance; Tuition Assistance. **Corporate headquarters location:** This Location. **Listed on:** Privately held. **Number of employees at this location:** 360.

DARTMOUTH PRINTING COMPANY
69 Lyme Road, Hanover NH 03755. 603/643-2220. **Contact:** April Kurinskas, Director of Human Resources. **World Wide Web address:** http://www.dpc-nh.com. **Description:** A commercial printer. **Common positions include:** Accountant/Auditor; Customer Service Rep.; Department Manager; Prepress Worker; Printing Press Operator; Sales Executive. **Educational backgrounds include:** Accounting; Art/Design; Computer Science; Marketing; Printing. **Benefits:** 401(k); Dental Insurance; Disability Coverage; Employee Discounts; Life Insurance; Medical Insurance; Tuition Assistance; Vacation Days. **Corporate headquarters location:** This Location. **Annual sales/revenues:** $21 - $50 million.

DAY-TIMERS, INC.
One Day-Timer Plaza, Lehigh Valley PA 18195. **Toll-free phone:** 800/225-5005. **Contact:** Human Resources. **World Wide Web address:** http://www.daytimer.com. **Description:** Designs and manufactures personal and organizational calendars, accessories, and software. **Corporate headquarters location:** This Location.

DELORME MAPPING
2 DeLorme Drive, Yarmouth ME 04096. 207/846-7000. **Contact:** Human Resources. **E-mail address:** jobs@delorme.com. **World Wide Web address:** http://www.delorme.com. **Description:** Publishes atlases and gazetteers, CD-ROM phone directories, mapping software, and related computer hardware. **Common positions include:** Computer Programmer; Graphic Designer; Project Manager; Sales Manager. **Corporate headquarters location:** This Location.

DELUXE CORPORATION
3680 Victoria Street North, Shoreview MN 55126. 651/787-2759. **Contact:** Susan Pierre-Zilles, Employment Specialist. **World Wide Web address:** http://www.deluxe.com. **Description:** Provides check printing, electronic funds transfer processing services, and related services to the financial industry; check authorization and collection services to retailers; and electronic benefit transfer services to state governments. Deluxe also produces forms, specialty papers, and other products for small businesses, professional practices, and medical/dental offices; and provides tax forms and electronic tax filing services to tax preparers. Through the direct mail channel, Deluxe sells greeting cards, gift wrap, and related products to households. **Corporate headquarters location:** This Location. **International locations:** Canada; United Kingdom. **Listed on:** New York Stock Exchange. **Number of employees at this location:** 3,000. **Number of employees nationwide:** 18,000.
Other U.S. locations:
- 16505 West 113th Street, Lenexa KS 66219. 913/541-7952.

DESERET NEWS
P.O. Box 2220, Salt Lake City UT 84110. 801/237-2137. **Fax:** 801/237-2121. **Contact:** Sharon Thompson, Personnel Director. **World Wide Web address:** http://www.desnews.com. **Description:** Publishes a locally-owned, daily newspaper with a circulation of more than 70,000. Advertising, production, and circulation activities are carried out jointly with competitor *Salt Lake Tribune* through Newspaper Agency Corporation (Salt Lake City UT). **NOTE:** This location does not have an editorial division. **Common positions include:** Accountant; Administrative Assistant; Chief Financial Officer; Controller; Graphic Artist; Graphic Designer; Human Resources Manager; Internet Services Manager; Librarian; Marketing Manager; Reporter; Secretary. **Educational backgrounds include:** Art/Design; Communications; Computer Science; Public Relations. **Benefits:** 401(k); Dental Insurance; Disability Coverage; Life Insurance; Medical Insurance; Pension Plan; Tuition Assistance. **Special programs:** Internships. **Corporate headquarters location:** This Location.

DIRECT PRESS MODERN LITHO INC.
89 Cabot Court, Suite L, Hauppauge NY 11788. 631/952-0300. **Fax:** 631/952-2159. **Contact:** Human Resources. **World Wide Web address:** http://www.directpress.com. **Description:** Printers of brochures, catalogs, catalog sheets, inkjet posters, and postcards. Services include photography, design and typesetting, scanning, proofing, and off-set printing. **Educational backgrounds include:** Art/Design. **Benefits:** 401(k); Dental Insurance; Disability Coverage; Life Insurance; Medical Insurance. **Corporate headquarters location:** This Location. **Listed on:** Privately held. **Annual sales/revenues:** $11 - $20 million. **Number of employees nationwide:** 200.

DON TECH
200 East Randolph Drive, Chicago IL 60601. 312/240-6000. **Fax:** 312/240-2078. **Contact:** Sherry Evans, Human Resources. **Description:** Engaged in

publishing and selling the Yellow Pages. **Common positions include:** Graphic Artist; Sales Rep. **Educational backgrounds include:** Business Administration; Liberal Arts; Marketing. **Benefits:** 401(k); Medical Insurance; Tuition Assistance. **Corporate headquarters location:** This Location. **Number of employees at this location:** 600.

R.R. DONNELLEY & SONS COMPANY
77 West Wacker Drive, Chicago IL 60601-1696. 312/326-8000. **Fax:** 312/326-8169. **Contact:** Diana Gomez, Human Resources. **World Wide Web address:** http://www.rrdonnelley.com. **Description:** A world leader in managing, reproducing, and distributing print and digital information for publishing, merchandising, and information technology customers. The company is one of the largest commercial printers in the world, producing catalogs, inserts, magazines, books, directories, computer documentation, and financial printing. R.R. Donnelley has more than 180 sales offices and production facilities. Principal services offered by the company are conventional and digital prepress operations; computerized printing and binding; sophisticated pool shipping and distribution services for printed products; information repackaging into multiple formats including print, magnetic, and optical media; database management, list rental, list enhancement, and direct mail production services; turnkey computer documentation services including outsourcing, translation, printing, binding, diskette replication, kitting, licensing, republishing, and fulfillment; reprographics and facilities management; creative design and communication services; and digital and conventional map creation and related services. Founded in 1864. **Corporate headquarters location:** This Location. **Other U.S. locations:** Nationwide. **International locations:** Worldwide. **Listed on:** New York Stock Exchange. **Stock exchange symbol:** DNY.

DUKE COMMUNICATIONS INTERNATIONAL
P.O. Box 3438, Loveland CO 80539. 970/663-4700. **Fax:** 970/667-2321. **Recorded jobline:** 970/203-2909. **Contact:** Recruiter. **World Wide Web address:** http://www.duke.com. **Description:** Publishes technical information for IBM AS/400 and Windows NT users and financial analysts. The company produces numerous magazines, books, and textbooks. Founded in 1982. **Common positions include:** Account Manager; Accountant; Administrative Assistant; Advertising Executive; Chief Financial Officer; Computer Programmer; Computer Support Technician; Customer Service Representative; Database Administrator; Desktop Publishing Specialist; Editor; Editorial Assistant; Finance Director; Financial Analyst; Graphic Artist; Graphic Designer; Human Resources Manager; Internet Services Manager; Managing Editor; Market Research Analyst; Marketing Manager; Multimedia Designer; Network Administrator; Sales Manager; Sales Representative; Systems Manager; Technical Writer/Editor; Typist/Word Processor; Webmaster. **Educational backgrounds include:** Accounting; Art/Design; Cold Fusion; Computer Science; HTML; Internet; Java; Marketing; MCSE; Microsoft Word; Novell; QuarkXPress; Spreadsheets; Visual Basic. **Benefits:** 401(k); Casual Dress - Fridays; Dental Insurance; Disability Coverage; Flexible Schedule; Health Club Discount; Life Insurance; Medical Insurance; Telecommuting; Tuition Assistance. **Corporate headquarters location:** This Location. **Other area locations:** Lakewood CO. **Owner:** David Duke. **Annual sales/revenues:** $11 - $20 million.

EPX GROUP
P.O. Box 3878, Portland ME 04104. 207/774-6560. **Physical address:** 2273 Congress Street, Portland

ME. **Toll-free phone:** 800/866-6560. **Fax:** 207/775-4728. **Contact:** Kim Foglio, Human Resources Manager. **E-mail address:** hr@epx-group.com. **World Wide Web address:** http://www.epx-group.com. **Description:** A printing manufacturer providing business forms, commercial printing, digital printing, variable imaging, mailing, warehouse, and distribution services. **NOTE:** Entry-level positions, part-time jobs, and second and third shifts are offered. **Common positions include:** Account Manager; Administrative Assistant; Assistant Manager; Blue-Collar Worker Supervisor; Computer Programmer; Controller; Desktop Publishing Specialist; General Manager; Help-Desk Technician; Human Resources Manager; Network/Systems Administrator; Production Manager; Systems Manager. **Educational backgrounds include:** Accounting; Business Administration; Computer Science; Microsoft Office; Microsoft Word; Printing; Publishing; QuarkXPress; Spreadsheets. **Benefits:** 401(k); Casual Dress - Fridays; Dental Insurance; Disability Coverage; Employee Discounts; Life Insurance; Medical Insurance; Sick Days (1 - 5); Tuition Assistance; Vacation Days (6 - 10). **Office hours:** Monday - Friday, 8:00 a.m. - 5:00 p.m. **Corporate headquarters location:** This Location. **Other U.S. locations:** Woburn MA. **Subsidiaries include:** Maine Printing Company. **Listed on:** Privately held. **Annual sales/revenues:** $5 - $10 million. **Number of employees at this location:** 230. **Number of employees nationwide:** 245.

ECHO ROCK VENTURES
13620 Lincoln Way, Suite 380, Auburn CA 95603. 530/823-9600. **Fax:** 530/823-9650. **Contact:** Human Resources. **Description:** Operates through three business groups: the Quikset Organization designs, manufactures, and distributes underground, precast concrete structures. The group has developed a patented line of pre-cast concrete sectional boxes to house underground transformers, distribution systems, and splicing manholes; the Plastics Segment manufactures products using a fiber-reinforced plastic process and a structural foam process developed for injection molding; Surfer Publications publishes *SURFER Magazine*, *Powder*, *Snowboarder*, *Bike Magazine*, and *Skateboarder*. The group also produces cable television and home video programs. **Corporate headquarters location:** This Location.

EDITOR & PUBLISHER CO.
11 West 19th Street, 10th Floor, New York NY 10011-4234. 212/675-4380. **Contact:** Steve Yahn, Managing Editor. **World Wide Web address:** http://www.mediainfo.com. **Description:** Publishes a weekly trade periodical covering newspapers and an annual yearbook for the newspaper industry. **Common positions include:** Reporter. **Corporate headquarters location:** This Location.

EDITORS PRESS, INC.
6200 Editors Park Drive, Hyattsville MD 20782. 301/853-4900. **Contact:** Human Resources. **Description:** Provides a variety of commercial printing and direct mail services including the printing of advertising literature, brochures, folders, booklets, pamphlets, maps, catalogs, and periodicals. **Corporate headquarters location:** This Location. **Parent company:** Kiplinger Washington Editors Inc. (Washington DC).

ENCYCLOPAEDIA BRITANNICA
310 South Michigan Avenue, Chicago IL 60604. 312/347-7000. **Fax:** 312/294-2176. **Contact:** Human Resources. **Description:** An international publisher of reference books and other educational materials. **Common positions include:** Accountant;

Buyer; Computer Programmer; Customer Service Rep.; Editor; Indexer; Systems Analyst. **Benefits:** Disability Coverage; Education Assistance; Employee Discounts; Life Insurance; Medical Insurance; Pension Plan; Savings Plan. **Corporate headquarters location:** This Location.

ENERGY INTELLIGENCE GROUP, INC.
1401 New York Avenue NW, Suite 500, Washington DC 20005. 202/662-0700. **Fax:** 202/347-0851. **Contact:** Kathleen Smith, Coordinator of Human Resources. **Description:** Publishes oil and gas industry newsletters. **Common positions include:** Accountant/Auditor; Customer Service Rep.; Editor; Graphic Artist; Human Resources Manager; Marketing Manager; Receptionist; Reporter; Systems Analyst; Technical Writer/Editor. **Educational backgrounds include:** Accounting; Art/Design; Business Administration; Communications; Computer Science; Economics; Finance; Journalism; Marketing. **Benefits:** 401(k); Dental Insurance; Disability Coverage; Life Insurance; Medical Insurance. **Corporate headquarters location:** This Location. **Other U.S. locations:** New York NY; Houston TX. **Parent company:** EEOP. **President:** Edward Morse. **Number of employees at this location:** 35.

EUROPEAN JOURNALISM NETWORK (EJN)
270 Greenwich Avenue, Greenwich CT 06830. 203/661-1212. **Fax:** 203/661-0754. **Contact:** Human Resources. **E-mail address:** ejnwebsite@aol.com. **World Wide Web address:** http://www.ejn.org. **Description:** A nonprofit organization that trains and assists young journalists and publishers throughout the former Soviet Union. The main focus of the organization is to integrate democratic values into Soviet communist society. Founded in 1992. **Special programs:** Internships. **Corporate headquarters location:** This Location. **International locations:** Prague, Czech Republic.

EVA-TONE
P.O. Box 7020, Clearwater FL 33758. 727/572-7000. **Fax:** 727/571-3124. **Contact:** Human Resources. **World Wide Web address:** http://www.evatone.com. **Description:** Manufactures audio materials, CDs, CD-ROMs, cassettes, and soundsheets. The company also provides commercial printing, mailing, and packaging services. **Common positions include:** Factory Worker; Production Worker. **Educational backgrounds include:** Manufacturing Management. **Benefits:** 401(k); Dental Insurance; Disability Coverage; Life Insurance; Medical Insurance; Profit Sharing; Tuition Assistance. **Corporate headquarters location:** This Location. **Listed on:** Privately held. **Number of employees at this location:** 360.

F&W PUBLICATIONS INC.
1507 Dana Avenue, Cincinnati OH 45207. 513/531-2222. **Contact:** Human Resources. **World Wide Web address:** http://www.fwpublications.com. **Description:** Publishes how-to books covering a variety of topics including writing, genealogy, art, woodworking, graphic design, and other areas. Eight magazines and 125 new book titles are published annually. Founded in 1913. **NOTE:** Entry-level positions are offered. **Company slogan:** Helping our customers realize their dreams. **Common positions include:** Account Rep.; Accountant; Administrative Assistant; Advertising Clerk; Computer Support Technician; Customer Service Rep.; Editor; Editorial Assistant; Event Planner; Graphic Designer; Human Resources Manager; Managing Editor; Marketing Manager; Marketing Specialist; Network/Systems Administrator; Public Relations Specialist; Sales

Executive; Sales Manager; Sales Rep.; Website Developer. **Educational backgrounds include:** Accounting; Art/Design; English; HTML; Journalism; Liberal Arts; Marketing; Microsoft Office; Microsoft Word; Public Relations; Publishing; QuarkXPress; Spreadsheets. **Benefits:** 401(k); Casual Dress - Daily; Dental Insurance; Disability Coverage; Employee Discounts; Flexible Schedule; Life Insurance; Medical Insurance; On-Site Exercise Facility; Public Transit Available; Savings Plan; Sick Days (6 - 10); Tuition Assistance; Vacation Days (1 - 5). **Special programs:** Internships; Co-ops; Summer Jobs. **Office hours:** Monday - Friday, 8:00 a.m. - 5:30 p.m. **Corporate headquarters location:** This Location. **Listed on:** Privately held. **CEO:** Steve Kent. **Annual sales/revenues:** $21 - $50 million. **Number of employees at this location:** 310. **Number of employees nationwide:** 325.

FAIRCHILD PUBLICATIONS, INC.
7 West 34th Street, 6th Floor, New York NY 10001. 212/630-4300. **Fax:** 212/630-4295. **Contact:** Sharon Thorn, Director of Human Resources. **World Wide Web address:** http://www.fairchildpub.com. **Description:** A business and professional publisher. Fairchild Publications' primary focus is on the fashion industry. **Common positions include:** Accountant/Auditor; Advertising Clerk; Designer; Editor; Reporter. **Educational backgrounds include:** Accounting; Art/Design; Business Administration; Communications; Liberal Arts; Marketing. **Benefits:** 401(k); Dental Insurance; Disability Coverage; Employee Discounts; Life Insurance; Medical Insurance; Pension Plan; Tuition Assistance. **Special programs:** Internships. **Corporate headquarters location:** This Location. **Other U.S. locations:** Los Angeles CA; Washington DC; Chicago IL; Boston MA; Dallas TX. **Listed on:** New York Stock Exchange. **Number of employees at this location:** 550. **Number of employees nationwide:** 750.

FARRAR, STRAUS AND GIROUX
19 Union Square West, New York NY 10003. 212/741-6900. **Contact:** Peggy Miller, Human Resources Manager. **Description:** A general trade book publisher. Founded in 1946.

FAULKNER INFORMATION SERVICES
114 Cooper Center, 7905 Browning Road, Pennsauken NJ 08109-4319. 856/662-2070. **Toll-free phone:** 800/843-0460. **Fax:** 856/662-3380. **Contact:** Betsey Thomas, Operations/Personnel Administrator. **E-mail address:** faulkner@faulkner.com. **World Wide Web address:** http://www.faulkner.com. **Description:** An independent publishing and research company specializing in providing technical information to end users and communication and IT professionals. Faulkner Information Services publishes more than a dozen standard information services in both print and electronic formats. The company provides comprehensive intelligence on products, vendors, technological advancements, and management issues associated with a wide range of technologies from open systems and client/server to enterprise networking, workgroup computing, and telecommunications. Faulkner also offers custom research and publication capabilities in such areas as market studies, customer satisfaction surveys, competitive analysis reports, and custom databases. **Common positions include:** Accountant/Auditor; Customer Service Rep.; Human Resources Manager; Systems Analyst; Technical Writer/Editor. **Educational backgrounds include:** Communications; Computer Science; English. **Benefits:** 401(k); Dental Insurance; Disability Coverage; Life Insurance; Medical Insurance;

Tuition Assistance. **Corporate headquarters location:** This Location. **Number of employees at this location:** 45.

THE FLORIDA TIMES-UNION
FLORIDA PUBLISHING COMPANY
P.O. Box 1949, Jacksonville FL 32231. 904/359-4600. **Physical address:** One Riverside Avenue, Jacksonville FL 32202. **Fax:** 904/359-4695. **Recorded jobline:** 904/359-4588. **Contact:** Sherwin Pulmano, Human Resources Manager. **World Wide Web address:** http://www.jacksonville.com. **Description:** *The Florida Times-Union* is a daily newspaper that is published by the Florida Publishing Company. Florida Publishing Company provides other products and services in northeastern Florida and southeastern Georgia. **Common positions include:** Advertising Clerk; Blue-Collar Worker Supervisor; Branch Manager; Commercial Artist; Customer Service Rep.; Editor; Reporter; Services Sales Rep. **Educational backgrounds include:** Advertising; Art/Design; Communications; Journalism; Marketing. **Benefits:** Dental Insurance; Disability Coverage; Employee Discounts; Life Insurance; Medical Insurance; Profit Sharing; Savings Plan. **Special programs:** Internships. **Corporate headquarters location:** Augusta GA. **Parent company:** Morris Communications Corporation. **Listed on:** Privately held. **Number of employees at this location:** 1,200.

FORBES INC.
60 Fifth Avenue, New York NY 10011. 212/620-2200. **Contact:** Personnel. **World Wide Web address:** http://www.forbes.com. **Description:** One of the nation's leading book and magazine publishers. **Common positions include:** Accountant; Advertising Clerk; Editor. **Educational backgrounds include:** Accounting; Business Administration; Finance; Liberal Arts; Marketing. **Benefits:** 401(k); Dental Insurance; Disability Coverage; Employee Discounts; Life Insurance; Medical Insurance; Pension Plan; Tuition Assistance. **Special programs:** Internships. **Corporate headquarters location:** This Location.

FOUR CORNERS MAGAZINE
P.O. Box 1776, Sedona AZ 86339-1776. 520/282-7233. **Contact:** Human Resources. **World Wide Web address:** http://www.fourcornersmag.com. **Description:** Publishes a progressive magazine for residents in the four corners area of Arizona, Colorado, Utah, and New Mexico. **Corporate headquarters location:** This Location.

FREDERIC PRINTING
14701 East 38th Avenue, Aurora CO 80011. 303/371-7990. **Contact:** Personnel. **Description:** Provides a wide range of commercial printing services, from camera-ready art to binding. **Common positions include:** Accountant/Auditor; Blue-Collar Worker Supervisor; Buyer; Computer Programmer; Credit Manager; Customer Service Rep.; Department Manager; Electrical/Electronics Engineer; Management Trainee; Mechanical Engineer; Purchasing Agent/Manager; Services Sales Rep. **Benefits:** Dental Insurance; Disability Coverage; Life Insurance; Medical Insurance; Profit Sharing; Tuition Assistance. **Corporate headquarters location:** This Location.

FREY MEDIA
P.O. Box 5926, Hilton Head Island SC 29938. 843/842-7878. **Physical address:** 5 Office Park Road, Suite 205, Hilton Head Island SC. **Fax:** 843/842-5743. **Contact:** Human Resources. **Description:** Publishes regional magazines including *Golfer's Guide* and *Home Resource Book.* **Corporate headquarters location:** This Location.

FUJICOLOR PROCESSING INC.
27105 Industrial Boulevard, Hayward CA 94545. 510/783-7000. **Toll-free phone:** 800/999-4686. **Fax:** 510/783-0535. **Contact:** Tara Smith, Administrative Assistant. **Description:** Provides wholesale photofinishing services and related sales and service activities. **NOTE:** Entry-level positions, part-time jobs, and second and third shifts are offered. **Common positions include:** Account Rep.; Administrative Assistant; Administrative Manager; Advertising Clerk; Branch Manager; Customer Service Representative; Electrical/Electronics Engineer; Environmental Engineer; Operations Manager; Production Manager; Quality Assurance Engineer; Quality Control Supervisor; Sales Manager; Transportation/Traffic Specialist; Typist/Word Processor. **Educational backgrounds include:** Business Administration; Novell; Software Tech. Support. **Benefits:** 401(k); Casual Dress - Fridays; Dental Insurance; Disability Coverage; Employee Discounts; Life Insurance; Medical Insurance; Pension Plan; Profit Sharing. **Special programs:** Training; Summer Jobs. **Corporate headquarters location:** Elmsford NY. **Other U.S. locations:** Nationwide. **International locations:** Worldwide. **Parent company:** Fuji Film Ltd. **Listed on:** NASDAQ. **CEO:** Hank Hyyashi. **Annual sales/revenues:** More than $100 million. **Number of employees at this location:** 225. **Number of employees nationwide:** 8,000.

FUTURE MEDIA
207 South Elliott Street, Suite 215, Chapel Hill NC 27514. 919/933-2150. **Fax:** 919/942-0041. **Contact:** Human Resources. **E-mail address:** employment@futmedia.com. **World Wide Web address:** http://www.futmedia.com. **Description:** Offers graphic design services including corporate identity development, logos, letterhead, brochures, and annual reports. The company also provides Web and multimedia design. **Corporate headquarters location:** This Location.

GBF GRAPHICS INC.
7300 Niles Center Road, Skokie IL 60077. 847/677-1700. **Toll-free phone:** 800/423-8326. **Fax:** 847/677-5245. **Contact:** Keli Sullivan, Human Resources Representative. **E-mail address:** resumes@gbfgraphics.com. **World Wide Web address:** http://www.gbfgraphics.com. **Description:** A full-service commercial printer specializing in customized business forms and direct mail printing. **NOTE:** Entry-level positions and second and third shifts are offered. **Common positions include:** Account Manager; Administrative Assistant; AS400 Programmer Analyst; Buyer; Computer Operator; Computer Programmer; Controller; Graphic Artist; Graphic Designer; Human Resources Manager; Industrial Engineer; Manufacturing Engineer; Marketing Manager; MIS Specialist; Network/Systems Administrator; Production Manager; Purchasing Agent/Manager; Quality Control Supervisor; Sales Manager; Systems Analyst; Vice President. **Educational backgrounds include:** AS400 Certification; C/C++; Computer Science; Liberal Arts; Microsoft Office; Microsoft Word. **Benefits:** 401(k); Casual Dress - Fridays; Dental Insurance; Disability Coverage; Employee Discounts; Flexible Schedule; Life Insurance; Medical Insurance; Profit Sharing; Sick Days (1 - 5); Vacation Days (20+). **Special programs:** Internships; Apprenticeships. **Office hours:** Monday - Friday, 8:00 a.m. - 5:00 p.m. **Corporate headquarters location:** This Location. **Other U.S. locations:** Princeton IL. **Listed on:** Privately held. **President/CEO/Owner:** Richard Kuntz. **Annual sales/revenues:** $51 - $100 million. **Number of employees at this location:** 300. **Number of employees nationwide:** 350.

THE GALE GROUP
27500 Drake Road, Farmington Hills MI 48331. 248/699-4253. **Fax:** 248/699-8053. **Contact:** Corporate Recruiter. **World Wide Web address:** http://www.galegroup.com. **Description:** Offers complete business information solutions with various data delivery methods such as print, CD-ROM, database, and online services. The company's electronic information incorporates indexes, charts, photographs, glossaries, sound bites, video clips, and hypertext links to customize their business-related information. **Corporate headquarters location:** This Location. **Parent company:** International Thomson Organization.

GANNETT COMPANY, INC.
1100 Wilson Boulevard, Arlington VA 22234. 703/284-6224. **Fax:** 703/558-3506. **Recorded jobline:** 703/284-6054. **Contact:** Human Resources. **World Wide Web address:** http://www.gannett.com. **Description:** A nationwide news and information company that publishes 92 newspapers including *USA Today*, and is one of the largest outdoor advertising companies in North America. Gannett also is involved in marketing, television news and program production, and research satellite information systems, and owns a national group of commercial printing facilities. **Common positions include:** Accountant; Attorney; Buyer; Computer Programmer; Financial Analyst; Human Resources Manager; Operations/Production Manager; Paralegal; Purchasing Agent/Manager; Secretary. **Benefits:** 401(k); Adoption Assistance; Dental Insurance; Disability Coverage; Employee Discounts; Life Insurance; Medical Insurance; Pension Plan; Profit Sharing; Stock Option; Tuition Assistance. **Special programs:** Internships. **Corporate headquarters location:** This Location. **Other U.S. locations:** CA; CO; CT; MI; MO; NC; NJ; NY; TX. **International locations:** Canada; Great Britain; Guam; Hong Kong; Singapore; Switzerland. **Listed on:** New York Stock Exchange. **Annual sales/revenues:** More than $100 million.

THE GAZETTE
P.O. Box 511, Cedar Rapids IA 52406. 319/398-8211. **Contact:** Trish Thoms, Human Resources. **World Wide Web address:** http://www.gazetteonline.com. **Description:** Publishes a daily morning newspaper which serves eastern Iowa. *The Gazette* has a daily circulation of 70,500 and a Sunday circulation of 84,500. **Common positions include:** Accountant/Auditor; Advertising Clerk; Advertising Executive; Artist; Computer Programmer; Copywriter; Credit Manager; Customer Service Rep.; Department Manager; Editor; Graphic Artist; Human Resources Manager; Layout Specialist; Operations/Production Manager; Photographer/Camera Operator; Public Relations Specialist; Reporter; Systems Analyst. **Educational backgrounds include:** Accounting; Art/Design; Business Administration; Communications; Computer Science; Journalism; Marketing; Photojournalism; Public Relations. **Benefits:** 401(k); Dental Insurance; Disability Coverage; Employee Discounts; Fitness Program; Life Insurance; Medical Insurance; Tuition Assistance. **Special programs:** Internships. **Corporate headquarters location:** This Location. **Parent company:** The Gazette Company.

THE GLOBE PEQUOT PRESS
246 Goose Lane, Guilford CT 06437. 203/458-4500. **Toll-free phone:** 888/249-7586. **Contact:** Human Resources. **World Wide Web address:** http://www.globe-pequot.com. **Description:** Publishes travel books, maps, language books, and outdoor recreation books. Overall, the company produces 250 new titles annually. Founded in 1947.

Corporate headquarters location: This Location. **Parent company:** Morris Communications Corporation.

GOLFER MAGAZINES, INC.
10301 NW Freeway, Suite 418, Houston TX 77092. 713/680-1680. **Contact:** Sommy Littam, Publisher. **World Wide Web address:** http://www.golfermagazines.com. **Description:** Publishes two monthly tabloid format magazines geared toward serious golfers, with information on golfing techniques as well as news about the people, places, events, and results from the Texas golf scene. Founded in 1983. **Common positions include:** Advertising Manager; Editor; Reporter; Services Sales Rep. **Educational backgrounds include:** Business Administration; Communications; Journalism; Marketing. **Special programs:** Internships. **Office hours:** Monday - Friday, 8:30 a.m. - 5:30 p.m. **Corporate headquarters location:** This Location. **Listed on:** Privately held. **Number of employees at this location:** 10.

GRAPHLINE COMPANY
5701 NW 94th Avenue, Tamarac FL 33321. **Toll-free phone:** 800/998-3200. **Contact:** Director of Human Resources. **World Wide Web address:** http://www.graphline.com. **Description:** Distributes graphic arts and supplies equipment, and services traditional and prepress products. **Common positions include:** Accountant/Auditor; Advertising Clerk; Buyer; Computer Programmer; Credit Clerk and Authorizer; Customer Service Representative; Financial Manager; Management Trainee; Payroll Clerk; Receptionist; Secretary; Services Sales Rep.; Stock Clerk. **Educational backgrounds include:** Accounting; Business Administration; Marketing. **Benefits:** 401(k); Dental Insurance; Disability Coverage; Life Insurance; Medical Insurance; Profit Sharing. **Corporate headquarters location:** This Location. **Number of employees at this location:** 85. **Number of employees nationwide:** 125.

GREAT FALLS TRIBUNE COMPANY
P.O. Box 5468, Great Falls MT 59403. 406/791-1434. **Contact:** Personnel. **Description:** Publishes a daily newspaper. **Common positions include:** Accountant; Administrator; Advertising Clerk; Advertising Manager; Circulation Manager; Commercial Artist; Credit Manager; Customer Service Rep.; Editor; Marketing Specialist; Operations/Production Manager; Reporter; Technical Writer/Editor. **Benefits:** 401(k); Dental Insurance; Disability Coverage; Employee Discounts; Hearing Insurance; Life Insurance; Medical Insurance; Pension Plan; Savings Plan; Tuition Assistance; Vision Insurance. **Parent company:** Gannett Company.

GREAT WESTERN DIRECTORIES
2400 Lakeview Drive, Suite 109, Amarillo TX 79109. 806/353-5155. **Contact:** Human Resources. **Description:** A publisher of telephone directories. **Corporate headquarters location:** This Location.

WARREN H. GREEN, INC.
8356 Olive Boulevard, St. Louis MO 63132. 314/991-1335. **Fax:** 314/997-1788. **Contact:** Personnel. **World Wide Web address:** http://www.iwc.com/whgreen. **Description:** Publishes books in a broad range of categories including medical, law, art, history, and philosophy. **Common positions include:** Accountant; Credit Manager; Customer Service Rep.; Editor; Marketing Specialist; Purchasing Agent/Manager; Quality Control Supervisor; Reporter. **Educational backgrounds include:** Accounting; Communications; Computer Science; Marketing. **Benefits:** Disability Coverage; Life Insurance; Medical Insurance. **Special**

programs: Internships. **Corporate headquarters location:** This Location. **Number of employees at this location:** 10.

GROLIER, INC.
90 Sherman Turnpike, Danbury CT 06816. 203/797-3500. **Fax:** 203/797-3284. **Recorded jobline:** 203/797-3776. **Contact:** Laurie Scholl, Employment Coordinator. **E-mail address:** lscholl@grolier.com. **World Wide Web address:** http://www.grolier.com. **Description:** Publishes a variety of books ranging from encyclopedias to children's books. Founded in 1896. **NOTE:** Entry-level positions are offered. **Common positions include:** Accountant; Administrative Assistant; Computer Operator; Computer Programmer; Customer Service Rep.; Editor; Editorial Assistant; Financial Analyst; Graphic Artist; Multimedia Designer; Online Content Specialist; Production Manager; Project Manager; Sales Executive; Sales Manager; Sales Representative; Secretary; Software Engineer; Typist/Word Processor; Webmaster. **Educational backgrounds include:** Accounting; Art/Design; Business Administration; Computer Science; Finance; Marketing. **Benefits:** 401(k); Dental Insurance; Disability Coverage; Employee Discounts; Flexible Schedule; Life Insurance; Medical Insurance; Pension Plan; Public Transit Available; Savings Plan; Tuition Assistance. **Corporate headquarters location:** This Location. **Parent company:** Lagardere.

HARCOURT GENERAL, INC.
27 Boylston Street, Chestnut Hill MA 02467. 617/232-8200. **Contact:** Human Resources. **World Wide Web address:** http://www.harcourt-general.com. **Description:** A holding company with significant interests in the publishing and retail markets. **Common positions include:** Accountant; Attorney; Financial Analyst; Human Resources Manager; Paralegal. **Educational backgrounds include:** Accounting; Business Administration; Finance. **Benefits:** 401(k); Daycare Assistance; Dental Insurance; Disability Coverage; Employee Discounts; ESOP; Life Insurance; Medical Insurance; Pension Plan; Savings Plan; Tuition Assistance. **Corporate headquarters location:** This Location. **Subsidiaries include:** Academic Press is an international publisher of life, physical, and social science books and journals; Assessment Systems is a leading provider of computerized tests; Bergdorf Goodman is a high-end fashion retailer with two locations in New York City; Drake Beam Morin is a career counseling and outplacement firm; Harcourt Brace is one of the nation's largest publishers of textbooks and other educational materials, and fiction and nonfiction books for children and adults; Harcourt Brace Publishers International is the London-based division of Harcourt Brace; Harcourt Health Sciences is the world's largest medical publisher; Harcourt Professional Education Group provides legal, financial, and human resources professionals with educational materials; Holt, Rinehart and Winston publishes textbooks for junior and senior high school markets; ICS Learning Systems is the world's largest distance learning company; NETg is a leading provider of training materials for information technology professionals; NM Direct is the at-home catalog of Neiman Marcus; Neiman Marcus is a first-class, worldwide clothing retailer; The Psychological Corporation is the nation's largest publisher of psychological and other assessment tests; Steck-Vaughn publishes educational materials.

JOHN H. HARLAND COMPANY
2939 Miller Road, Decatur GA 30035. 770/981-9460. **Contact:** Arlene Bates, Director of Human Resources. **World Wide Web address:** http://www.harland.net. **Description:** A financial printing firm. Products include business and personal checks, as well as other forms and documents for the banking industry. **Corporate headquarters location:** This Location. **Listed on:** New York Stock Exchange. **Number of employees nationwide:** 7,300.

HARPERCOLLINS PUBLISHERS
10 East 53rd Street, New York NY 10022. 212/207-7224. **Contact:** Human Resources. **World Wide Web address:** http://www.harpercollins.com. **Description:** HarperCollins Publishers is one of the largest book publishers in the world. Titles include trade, fiction, nonfiction, and children's books. **Corporate headquarters location:** This Location. **Other U.S. locations:** San Francisco CA. **Number of employees at this location:** 600.

HARRIS INFOSOURCE
2057 East Aurora Road, Twinsburg OH 44087. 330/425-9000. **Contact:** Human Resources. **World Wide Web address:** http://www.harrisinfo.com. **Description:** Publishes magazine directories and software containing lists of manufacturers nationwide. Founded in 1972. **Common positions include:** Account Rep.; Administrative Assistant; Customer Service Rep.; Database Manager; Sales Representative; Secretary; Webmaster. **Educational backgrounds include:** Software Development; Software Tech. Support. **Benefits:** 401(k); Dental Insurance; Disability Coverage; EAP; Employee Discounts; Life Insurance; Medical Insurance. **Special programs:** Training. **Corporate headquarters location:** This Location. **Listed on:** Privately held.

HARVARD UNIVERSITY PRESS
79 Garden Street, Cambridge MA 02138. 617/495-2600. **Contact:** Human Resources. **World Wide Web address:** http://www.hup.harvard.edu. **Description:** A publisher of scholarly books and journals. **Corporate headquarters location:** This Location.

HEMMINGS PUBLISHING
P.O. Box 256, Bennington VT 05201. 802/442-3101. **Toll-free phone:** 800/227-4373. **Contact:** Lynne Latella, Manager of Human Resources. **World Wide Web address:** http://www.hemmings.com. **Description:** Publishes *Hemmings Motor News* magazine and *SIA*. Hemmings Publishing also hosts a large, interactive Website. **Common positions include:** Customer Service Representative; Data Entry Clerk; MIS Specialist; Sales Representative. **Benefits:** 401(k); Daycare Assistance; Dental Insurance; Disability Coverage; Employee Discounts; Life Insurance; Medical Insurance; Profit Sharing; Tuition Assistance. **Corporate headquarters location:** This Location. **Other U.S. locations:** Nationwide. **Parent company:** Watering, Inc. **Number of employees at this location:** 140.

THE HERALD
P.O. Box 930, Everett WA 98206. **Recorded jobline:** 425/339-3009. **Contact:** Human Resources. **World Wide Web address:** http://www.heraldnet.com. **Description:** Publishes one daily newspaper and five weekly newspapers. **NOTE:** Entry-level positions and part-time jobs are offered. This firm does not accept unsolicited resumes. Please call the jobline for a list of openings. **Common positions include:** Account Rep.; Accountant; Computer Support Technician; Credit Manager; Customer Service Rep.; Editor; Editorial Assistant; Graphic Artist; Librarian; MIS Specialist; Network/Systems Administrator; Reporter; Sales Executive; Sales Representative; Systems Analyst;

Webmaster. **Benefits:** 401(k); Casual Dress - Fridays; Daycare Assistance; Dental Insurance; Disability Coverage; Employee Discounts; Flexible Schedule; Job Sharing; Life Insurance; Medical Insurance; Tuition Assistance. **Special programs:** Internships. **Internship information:** Summer internships in news, photography, and advertising are sometimes offered. **Corporate headquarters location:** This Location. **Number of employees at this location:** 375.

THE HIBBERT GROUP
1601 Park Avenue West, Denver CO 80216-0525. 303/297-1601. **Contact:** Gordon Penley, Controller. **World Wide Web address:** http://www. hibbertco.com. **Description:** Provides commercial and offset printing services. **Corporate headquarters location:** This Location. **Parent company:** Hibbert Company (Trenton NJ).

HIGHLIGHTS FOR CHILDREN, INC.
2300 West Fifth Avenue, Columbus OH 43215. 614/486-0631. **Fax:** 614/487-2290. **Recorded jobline:** 614/487-2277. **Contact:** Human Resources. **Description:** Publishes a monthly, educational children's magazine. **Common positions include:** Accountant/Auditor; Computer Programmer; Customer Service Rep.; Editor; Operations/Production Manager; Public Relations Specialist; Services Sales Representative; Systems Analyst; Technical Writer/Editor. **Educational backgrounds include:** Accounting; Art/Design; Business Administration; Communications; Computer Science; Economics; Liberal Arts; Marketing. **Benefits:** Disability Coverage; Employee Discounts; Life Insurance; Medical Insurance; Profit Sharing; Savings Plan; Tuition Assistance. **Special programs:** Internships. **Corporate headquarters location:** This Location. **Listed on:** Privately held. **Number of employees at this location:** 670. **Number of employees nationwide:** 700.

HILLER INDUSTRIES
631 North 400 West, Salt Lake City UT 84103. 801/521-2411. **Contact:** Human Resources. **Description:** Offers bookbinding and other commercial printing services. Hiller Industries also manufactures custom loose-leaf binders, software packaging, and leather goods. **Common positions include:** Accountant/Auditor; Blue-Collar Worker Supervisor; Buyer; Commercial Artist; Computer Programmer; Credit Manager; Customer Service Representative; Human Resources Manager; Manufacturer's/Wholesaler's Sales Rep.; Operations/ Production Manager; Project Manager; Purchasing Agent/Manager; Quality Control Supervisor; Secretary; Systems Analyst. **Benefits:** Dental Insurance; Life Insurance; Medical Insurance; Savings Plan. **Corporate headquarters location:** This Location.

HINSHAW MUSIC, INC.
P.O. Box 470, Chapel Hill NC 27514. 919/933-1691. **Fax:** 919/967-3399. **Contact:** Manager. **Description:** A printer and publisher of choral music. Founded in 1975. **Corporate headquarters location:** This Location.

HOLDEN GRAPHIC SERVICES
607 Washington Avenue North, Minneapolis MN 55401. **Contact:** Human Resources. **Description:** Produces custom business forms. **Common positions include:** Customer Service Rep.; Department Manager; General Manager; Human Resources Manager; Manufacturer's/Wholesaler's Sales Rep.; Operations/Production Manager; Services Sales Representative. **Educational backgrounds include:** Business Administration;

Communications; Computer Science; Marketing; Printing. **Benefits:** 401(k); Daycare Assistance; Disability Coverage; Life Insurance; Medical Insurance; Savings Plan; Tuition Assistance. **Corporate headquarters location:** This Location. **Other U.S. locations:** Rockford IL; Arlington TX; Dallas TX. **Number of employees at this location:** 60. **Number of employees nationwide:** 280.

HOME NEWS TRIBUNE
35 Kennedy Boulevard, East Brunswick NJ 08816. 732/246-5500. **Contact:** Personnel Department. **World Wide Web address:** http://www. injersey.com/hnt. **Description:** Publishes an independently-owned daily newspaper with a weekday circulation of more than 51,000. **Corporate headquarters location:** This Location.

HONORIBUS PRESS
P.O. Box 4872, Spartanburg SC 29305. 864/597-4382. **Contact:** Human Resources. **World Wide Web address:** http://thehonoribuspress.com. **Description:** Engaged in the publication of nonfiction books in the areas of military history and memoirs. Founded in 1988. **Corporate headquarters location:** This Location.

HOUGHTON MIFFLIN COMPANY
222 Berkeley Street, Boston MA 02116. 617/351-5180. **Fax:** 617/351-1106. **Contact:** Human Resources. **World Wide Web address:** http://www. hmco.com. **Description:** A publisher of school textbooks; fiction, nonfiction, and reference works; educational software; and related multimedia products. **NOTE:** Entry-level positions are offered. **Common positions include:** Administrative Assistant; Attorney; Auditor; Customer Service Rep.; Designer; Editor; Editorial Assistant; Financial Analyst; Graphic Artist; Marketing Manager; Marketing Specialist; MIS Specialist; Multimedia Designer; Production Manager; Sales Representative; Software Engineer; Systems Manager; Webmaster. **Educational backgrounds include:** Accounting; Communications; Computer Science; English; Finance; Liberal Arts; Marketing. **Benefits:** 401(k); Dental Insurance; Disability Coverage; Life Insurance; Medical Insurance; Pension Plan; Public Transit Available; Tuition Assistance; Vision Insurance. **Special programs:** Internships. **Corporate headquarters location:** This Location. **Listed on:** New York Stock Exchange. **Stock exchange symbol:** HTN. **Annual sales/revenues:** More than $100 million. **Number of employees at this location:** 850.

THE HOUSTON BUSINESS JOURNAL
1001 West Loop South, Suite 650, Houston TX 77027. 713/688-8811. **Fax:** 713/963-0482. **Contact:** Personnel. **World Wide Web address:** http://www.bizjournals.com/houston. **Description:** A daily business journal. **Corporate headquarters location:** This Location. **Parent company:** American City Business Journal.

HOUSTON CHRONICLE
801 Texas Avenue, Houston TX 77002. 713/220-7171. **Contact:** Ann Turnbach, Personnel Director. **Description:** A daily newspaper. **Corporate headquarters location:** This Location.

HUNTER TEXTBOOKS, INC.
823 Reynolda Road, Winston-Salem NC 27104. 336/725-0608. **Fax:** 336/722-0530. **Contact:** Human Resources. **World Wide Web address:** http://www.huntertextbooks.com. **Description:** Specializes in the publication of college textbooks and laboratory manuals in the areas of physical education, biology, geology, and the humanities. **Corporate headquarters location:** This Location.

THE IMAGE BANK, INC.
2777 Stemmons Freeway, Suite 600, Dallas TX 75207. 214/863-4900. **Contact:** Human Resources. **World Wide Web address:** http://www. theimagebank.com. **Description:** Stocks and sells photographs obtained from various photographers. **Corporate headquarters location:** This Location.

IMAGING TECHNOLOGIES
655 Lambert Drive, Atlanta GA 30324. 404/873-5911. **Contact:** Human Resources. **Description:** Provides several printing and imaging services including blue printing, quick copying, laminating, mounting, and binding. **Corporate headquarters location:** This Location.

IMPERIAL LITHO & DRYOGRAPHY
210 South Fourth Avenue, Phoenix AZ 85003. 602/257-8500. **Fax:** 602/528-8401. **Contact:** Human Resources. **Description:** Provides a wide range of commercial printing and graphic services including lithography and offset reproduction. **NOTE:** Entry-level positions are offered. **Common positions include:** Account Manager; Accountant; Administrative Assistant; Blue-Collar Worker Supervisor; Computer Animator; Computer Operator; Controller; Cost Estimator; Customer Service Representative; Graphic Artist; Graphic Designer; Marketing Manager; MIS Specialist; Purchasing Agent/Manager; Sales Executive; Secretary; Technical Writer/Editor. **Educational backgrounds include:** Accounting; Art/Design; Computer Science; Marketing. **Benefits:** 401(k); Dental Insurance; Life Insurance; Medical Insurance; Public Transit Available; Tuition Assistance. **Corporate headquarters location:** This Location. **Other U.S. locations:** Austin TX.

IMTEK, INC.
P.O. Box 621, Bridgeport NJ 08014. 856/467-0047. **Physical address:** 110 High Hill Road, Bridgeport NJ. **Contact:** Personnel Director. **Description:** Provides complete lithography and bookbinding services. **Corporate headquarters location:** This Location.

INC. MAGAZINE
38 Commercial Wharf, Boston MA 02110. 617/248-8000. **Contact:** Personnel Department. **World Wide Web address:** http://www.inc.com. **Description:** Publishes a financial and business news magazine that is distributed worldwide. **Common positions include:** Accountant/Auditor; Credit Manager; Editor; Operations/Production Manager; Reporter; Sales Executive. **Benefits:** Daycare Assistance; Dental Insurance; Disability Coverage; Life Insurance; Medical Insurance; Profit Sharing; Savings Plan. **Special programs:** Internships. **Corporate headquarters location:** This Location.

INDIVIDUAL INVESTOR GROUP, INC.
125 Broad Street, 14th Floor, New York NY 10004. 212/742-2277. **Contact:** Deirdre Cavanagh, Human Resources Director. **World Wide Web address:** http://www.iionline.com. **Description:** A business information company that publishes and markets *Individual Investor* and *Individual Investor's Special Situations Report*. *Individual Investor* magazine is a monthly personal finance magazine which offers commentary and opinion on specific investment ideas in stocks and mutual funds. **Corporate headquarters location:** This Location. **Subsidiaries include:** I.I. Capital Management, Inc. is the general partner of a private investment fund.

INSTITUTE FOR SCIENTIFIC INFORMATION
3501 Market Street, Philadelphia PA 19104. 215/386-0100. **Fax:** 215/387-4231. **Contact:** Brian Richards, Employment/Employee Relations Manager. **World Wide Web address:** http://www. isinet.com. **Description:** Produces more than 50 products including indexes and databases that provide information from journals, books, and other significant materials published in the sciences, social sciences, and arts and humanities. Institute for Scientific Information supplies researchers and scientists with needed information in electronic formats. The company also offers online services and technical support. **Common positions include:** Accountant; Computer Programmer; Customer Service Representative; Database Manager; Editor; Financial Analyst; Indexer; Marketing Specialist; Operations/Production Manager; Proofreader; Quality Control Supervisor; Systems Analyst; Technical Writer/Editor; Translator. **Educational backgrounds include:** Accounting; Biology; Chemistry; Computer Science; Finance; Liberal Arts; Library Science; Marketing. **Benefits:** 401(k); Dental Insurance; Disability Coverage; Life Insurance; Medical Insurance; Tuition Assistance. **Corporate headquarters location:** This Location. **Other area locations:** Cherry Hill NJ; Mount Laurel NJ. **Parent company:** Thomson Company.

INTERNATIONAL EMPLOYMENT GAZETTE
423 Townes Street, Greenville SC 29601. 864/235-4444. **Toll-free phone:** 800/882-9188. **Fax:** 864/235-3369. **Contact:** Del McCaleb, General Manager. **E-mail address:** intljobs@aol.com. **World Wide Web address:** http://www. intemployment.com. **Description:** Publishes *International Employment Gazette*, a bi-monthly magazine with over 400 international job listings per issue. Job listings are primarily in the areas of science/technology, public/social services, computer science, construction and trades, and education. Founded in 1990. **Corporate headquarters location:** This Location.

INTERTEC PUBLISHING
9800 Metcalf Avenue, Overland Park KS 66212. 913/341-1300. **Fax:** 913/967-1846. **Contact:** Human Resources. **World Wide Web address:** http://www.intertec.com. **Description:** A publisher of business-to-business magazines and newsletters that allow manufacturers and suppliers to provide professionals with statistics, explanations, technical advice, and product introductions that ultimately make businesses more successful. Intertec Publishing also produces 450 technical books and valuation guides. **Corporate headquarters location:** This Location.
Other U.S. locations:
• 11 Riverbend Drive South, P.O. Box 4949, Stamford CT 06907. 203/358-9900.

IRONWOOD LITHOGRAPHERS, INC.
455 South 52nd Street, Tempe AZ 85281-7200. 480/829-7700. **Contact:** Human Resources. **Description:** Offers complete business communications services including electronic prepress, quality offset printing, Docutech on-demand printing, direct mail facilities, diskette duplication and packaging, and a full-service fulfillment department. **Corporate headquarters location:** This Location. **Number of employees at this location:** 100.

JAPS-OLSON COMPANY
7500 Excelsior Boulevard, St. Louis Park MN 55426. 952/932-9393. **Fax:** 952/912-1900. **Contact:** Mike Beddor, President. **World Wide Web address:** http://www.japsolson.com. **Description:** A commercial printer and direct mailer. Founded in 1907. **NOTE:** Second and third shifts are offered. **Common positions include:** Computer Operator; Computer Programmer;

Graphic Designer; Systems Analyst. **Educational backgrounds include:** Business Administration; Computer Science; Marketing; Microsoft Word; QuarkXPress; Visual Basic. **Benefits:** 401(k); Life Insurance; Medical Insurance. **Corporate headquarters location:** This Location. **Other U.S. locations:** Nationwide. **Listed on:** Privately held. **Number of employees at this location:** 700.

JEPPESEN SANDERSON
55 Inverness Drive East, Englewood CO 80112. 303/799-9090. **Fax:** 303/784-4121. **Recorded jobline:** 303/784-4444. **Contact:** Human Resources. **E-mail address:** jobs@jeppesen.com. **World Wide Web address:** http://www. jeppesen.com. **Description:** Publishes and distributes flight information manuals, flight training supplies, and informational products. **NOTE:** If you are faxing your resume, please specify the position that you are interested in and specify a desired salary. **Educational backgrounds include:** Aviation; Business Administration; Computer Science. **Benefits:** 401(k); Dental Insurance; Disability Coverage; Employee Discounts; Life Insurance; Medical Insurance; Pension Plan; Tuition Assistance. **Other U.S. locations:** Los Gatos CA. **Number of employees at this location:** 800. **Number of employees worldwide:** 1,100.

JOHNSON PUBLISHING COMPANY, INC.
820 South Michigan Avenue, Chicago IL 60605. 312/322-9200. **Contact:** LaDoris Foster, Personnel Director. **World Wide Web address:** http://www. ebony.com. **Description:** Publishes *Ebony* and *Jet* magazines. The company also markets the Fashion Fair cosmetics line. **Corporate headquarters location:** This Location. **Chairman/CEO:** John H. Johnson.

J.J. KELLER & ASSOCIATES, INC.
P.O. Box 368, Neenah WI 54957. 920/722-2848. **Fax:** 920/727-7522. **Contact:** Human Resources. **Description:** A provider of safety- and regulatory-based publications, training materials, printed forms, and services to various industries. Founded in 1953. **NOTE:** Entry-level positions are offered. **Common positions include:** Account Rep.; Computer Operator; Editor; Editorial Assistant; Market Research Analyst; Marketing Specialist; Sales Representative; Secretary; Systems Analyst; Technical Writer/Editor; Typist/Word Processor. **Educational backgrounds include:** Biology; Business Administration; Chemistry; Computer Science; Geology; Marketing. **Benefits:** 401(k); Dental Insurance; Disability Coverage; Life Insurance; Medical Insurance; Profit Sharing; Tuition Assistance. **Corporate headquarters location:** This Location. **Listed on:** Privately held. **Number of employees at this location:** 800.

KIPLINGER WASHINGTON EDITORS
1729 H Street NW, Washington DC 20006. 202/887-6400. **Contact:** Cindy Gentilcore, Director of Personnel. **World Wide Web address:** http://www.kiplinger.com. **Description:** Publishes business newsletters, a personal finance magazine, and books. **Corporate headquarters location:** This Location.

KNIGHT-RIDDER
50 West San Fernando Street, Suite 1500, San Jose CA 95113. 408/938-7700. **Fax:** 408/938-7755. **Contact:** Human Resources. **World Wide Web address:** http://www.kri.com. **Description:** A major newspaper publishing company that owns 28 dailies in 15 states and three non-dailies in suburban areas. The company also produces niche publications such as *Myrtle Beach's Golf*, *CubaNews* newsletter in Miami, and *Northland Outdoors* in Grand Forks. The larger papers include the *Miami Herald*, *Philadelphia Inquirer*, *Philadelphia Daily News*, *Detroit Free Press*, and *San Jose Mercury News*. **Corporate headquarters location:** This Location. **Subsidiaries include:** Knight-Ridder also has interests in the information distribution market through Knight-Ridder Information, Inc.; Knight-Ridder Financial; and Technimetrics. Knight-Ridder's online information retrieval serves the business, scientific, technology, medical, education communities in more than 100 countries. Knight-Ridder Financial provides real-time financial news and pricing information through primary products MoneyCenter, Digital Datafeed, ProfitCenter, and TradeCenter. Knight-Ridder also has interests in cable television and other businesses. TKR Cable, a 50-50 joint venture with Liberty Media Corporation, serves 344,000 basic subscribers in New Jersey and New York and manages Kentucky systems with 277,000 subscribers. Through TKR Cable Partners, Knight-Ridder owns a 15 percent share of TCI/TKR L.P. Cable Systems with 867,000 subscribers in five states. Other interests include partial ownership of the Seattle Times Company, two paper mills, a newspaper advertising sales company, and SCI Holdings. **Annual sales/revenues:** More than $100 million.

KUX MANUFACTURING
dba KUX GRAPHIC SYSTEMS
12675 Burt Road, Detroit MI 48223. 313/255-6460. **Contact:** Richard Johnson, Director of Human Resources. **Description:** A manufacturer of decals for automobiles, trucks, and industrial vehicles; building and window graphics; and corporate identification signage. **Common positions include:** Account Manager; Accountant; Architect; Blue-Collar Worker Supervisor; Buyer; Chief Financial Officer; Clerical Supervisor; Computer Operator; Controller; Cost Estimator; Credit Manager; Customer Service Rep.; Database Manager; Design Engineer; Draftsperson; General Manager; Graphic Artist; Graphic Designer; Human Resources Manager; Industrial Engineer; Manufacturing Engineer; Marketing Manager; MIS Specialist; Production Manager; Project Manager; Purchasing Agent/Manager; Sales Executive; Sales Manager; Secretary; Typist/Word Processor. **Educational backgrounds include:** Accounting; Art/Design; Business Administration; Communications; Computer Science; Marketing. **Benefits:** 401(k); Dental Insurance; Disability Coverage; Financial Planning Assistance; Flexible Schedule; Life Insurance; Medical Insurance; Profit Sharing; Tuition Assistance. **Corporate headquarters location:** This Location. **Annual sales/revenues:** $11 - $20 million.

LANCASTER NEWSPAPERS, INC.
P.O. Box 1328, Lancaster PA 17608. 717/291-8681. **Fax:** 717/293-4311. **Contact:** Susan Glouner, Personnel Coordinator. **E-mail address:** personnel@lnpnews.com. **World Wide Web address:** http://www.lancnews.com. **Description:** Publishes the morning *Intelligencer Journal*, the evening *Lancaster New Era*, and the *Sunday News*, with a combined daily circulation of over 100,000. Founded in 1794. **NOTE:** Entry-level positions and second and third shifts are offered. **Common positions include:** Account Representative; Accountant; Advertising Clerk; Blue-Collar Worker Supervisor; Buyer; Commercial Artist; Computer Programmer; Credit Manager; Customer Service Representative; Department Manager; Editor; Graphic Artist; Human Resources Manager; Librarian; Managing Editor; Marketing Manager; Marketing Specialist; MIS Specialist; Online Content Specialist; Purchasing Agent/Manager;

Quality Control Supervisor; Reporter; Sales Executive; Sales Manager; Sales Representative; Secretary; Systems Analyst; Systems Manager; Typist/Word Processor. **Educational backgrounds include:** Accounting; Business Administration; Communications; Computer Science; Finance; Journalism; Liberal Arts; Marketing. **Benefits:** 401(k); Dental Insurance; Disability Coverage; Employee Discounts; Life Insurance; Medical Insurance; Pension Plan; Tuition Assistance. **Special programs:** Internships. **Internship information:** Lancaster Newspapers offers internships in journalism and marketing/advertising. Please apply by March 1 for a 13-week summer internship. **Corporate headquarters location:** This Location. **Listed on:** Privately held. **Annual sales/revenues:** $51 - $100 million.

LAS VEGAS PRESS
3335 Winn Road, Las Vegas NV 89102. 702/871-6780. **Contact:** Human Resources. **World Wide Web address:** http://www.lvbusinesspress.com. **Description:** Publishes the *Las Vegas Business Press*, *CityLife*, and *Senior Press*.

LAS VEGAS REVIEW-JOURNAL
P.O. Box 70, Las Vegas NV 89125. 702/383-0224. **Fax:** 702/383-0435. **Contact:** Jim Hannah, Human Resources Director. **World Wide Web address:** http://www.lvrj.com. **Description:** Publishes a daily newspaper with a weekday circulation of approximately 170,400 and a Sunday circulation of more than 211,500. **Common positions include:** Advertising Clerk; Computer Programmer; Customer Service Rep.; Editor; Reporter; Sales Representative; Systems Analyst. **Educational backgrounds include:** Business Administration; Communications; Computer Science; Liberal Arts. **Benefits:** 401(k); Dental Insurance; Disability Coverage; Employee Discounts; Life Insurance; Medical Insurance; Profit Sharing; Tuition Assistance. **Corporate headquarters location:** Fort Smith AR. **Other U.S. locations:** Nationwide. **Parent company:** Donrey Media Group. **Number of employees at this location:** 720.

THE LEAHY PRESS INC.
P.O. Box 428, Montpelier VT 05601. 802/229-0818. **Contact:** Human Resources. **Description:** Offers full-service commercial offset printing, design, and typesetting. The company produces catalogs, magazines, and folders; and provides desktop publishing and graphic design services. **Common positions include:** Bindery Worker; Blue-Collar Worker Supervisor; Buyer; Commercial Artist; Computer Programmer; Cost Estimator; Credit Manager; Customer Service Rep.; General Manager; Graphic Artist; Management Analyst/Consultant; Quality Control Supervisor; Secretary. **Educational backgrounds include:** Accounting; Business Administration; Communications; Finance; Marketing; Mathematics. **Benefits:** Life Insurance; Medical Insurance; Pension Plan. **Corporate headquarters location:** This Location. **Number of employees at this location:** 25.

LEBHAR-FRIEDMAN INC.
425 Park Avenue, 6th Floor, New York NY 10022. 212/756-5000. **Contact:** Human Resources. **World Wide Web address:** http://www.lf.com. **Description:** A publisher of retail business publications including newspapers, magazines, and retail directories. **Common positions include:** Advertising Executive; Editor; Reporter; Secretary; Telemarketer. **Educational backgrounds include:** Journalism. **Benefits:** Dental Insurance; Life Insurance; Medical Insurance; Profit Sharing. **Corporate headquarters location:** This Location.

LEE ENTERPRISES
215 North Main Street, Suite 400, Davenport IA 52801. 319/383-2183. **Contact:** Human Resources. **World Wide Web address:** http://www.lee.net. **Description:** This location houses administrative offices. Overall, Lee Enterprises is a media company involved in newspapers, television, and graphic arts services. **NOTE:** Entry-level positions are offered. **Common positions include:** Editor; Human Resources Manager; Reporter. **Educational backgrounds include:** Business Administration; Communications; Liberal Arts; Marketing. **Benefits:** 401(k); Dental Insurance; Disability Coverage; Life Insurance; Medical Insurance; Profit Sharing; Tuition Assistance. **Special programs:** Internships; Training. **Corporate headquarters location:** This Location. **Other U.S. locations:** Nationwide. **Annual sales/revenues:** More than $100 million. **Number of employees at this location:** 85.

LEXIS LAW PUBLISHING
P.O. Box 7587, Charlottesville VA 22906. 804/972-7600. **Fax:** 804/972-7674. **Contact:** Human Resources. **World Wide Web address:** http://www.lexislawpublishing.com. **Description:** A publisher of legal materials. **NOTE:** Part-time jobs and second and third shifts are offered. **Common positions include:** Administrative Assistant; Computer Engineer; Computer Operator; Computer Programmer; Computer Support Technician; Customer Service Rep.; Database Administrator; Editor; Editorial Assistant; Network/Systems Administrator; Sales Executive; Sales Manager; Sales Rep.; Software Engineer; Systems Analyst. **Educational backgrounds include:** C/C++; HTML; Java; Microsoft Word; Novell; Software Development; Software Tech. Support. **Benefits:** 401(k); Casual Dress - Fridays; Dental Insurance; Disability Coverage; Employee Discounts; Flexible Schedule; Life Insurance; Medical Insurance; Pension Plan; Telecommuting; Tuition Assistance. **Special programs:** Internships. **Office hours:** Monday - Friday, 8:00 a.m. - 4:30 p.m. **Corporate headquarters location:** This Location. **Other U.S. locations:** CA; NY. **International locations:** Puerto Rico. **Parent company:** Lexis-Nexis. **Number of employees worldwide:** 840.

LIMRA INTERNATIONAL
300 Day Hill Road, Windsor CT 06095-4761. 860/298-3953. **Contact:** Brad M. Ragaglia, Managing Editor. **E-mail address:** bragaglia@limra.com. **World Wide Web address:** http://www.limra.com. **Description:** A publishing company. Publications include *Recruit* magazine, dedicated to recruiters and recruitees; *Managers Handbook*, dedicated to managers; *Market Facts*, dedicated to marketing effectiveness in the financial services industry; and *Vision Handbook*, dedicated to motivational issues in the work place.

LIPPINCOTT WILLIAMS & WILKINS
530 Walnut Street, Philadelphia PA 19106. 215/521-8300. **Contact:** Human Resources Assistant. **World Wide Web address:** http://www.lww.com. **Description:** A global publisher of medical, nursing, and allied health information resources in book, journal, newsletter, loose-leaf, and electronic media formats. **NOTE:** Entry-level positions and part-time jobs are offered. **Common positions include:** Account Manager; Accountant; Administrative Assistant; Computer Programmer; Computer Support Technician; Credit Manager; Database Administrator; Database Manager; Editor; Editorial Assistant; Financial Analyst; Graphic Artist; Graphic Designer; Managing Editor; Marketing Manager; Multimedia Designer; Network/Systems Administrator; Sales Rep.;

Software Engineer; Systems Analyst; Systems Manager. **Educational backgrounds include:** Accounting; Art/Design; AS400 Certification; Business Administration; C/C++; Communications; Computer Science; Finance; HTML; Internet; Java; Liberal Arts; Marketing; MCSE; Microsoft Word; Novell; Public Relations; QuarkXPress; Software Development; Software Tech. Support; Spreadsheets; Visual Basic. **Benefits:** 401(k); Casual Dress - Daily; Dental Insurance; Disability Coverage; Employee Discounts; Flexible Schedule; Life Insurance; Medical Insurance; Profit Sharing; Public Transit Available; Sick Days (6 - 10); Tuition Assistance; Vacation Days (6 - 10). **Special programs:** Internships; Co-ops; Summer Jobs. **Other U.S. locations:** Baltimore MD; Hagerstown MD; New York NY. **International locations:** Worldwide. **Parent company:** Wolters Kluwer.

LOS ANGELES MAGAZINE
11100 Santa Monica Boulevard, 7th Floor, Los Angeles CA 90025. 310/312-2200. **Contact:** Human Resources. **Description:** A city magazine that focuses on local issues, people, trends, events, and lifestyles. *Los Angeles Magazine* also includes options and opportunities available throughout the Southern California area. Founded in 1960. **NOTE:** Entry-level positions are offered. **Common positions include:** Advertising Clerk; Advertising Executive; Editor; Editorial Assistant; Graphic Artist; Graphic Designer. **Educational backgrounds include:** Art/Design; AS400 Certification; Business Administration; Marketing; Microsoft Word; QuarkXPress; Spreadsheets. **Benefits:** 401(k); Dental Insurance; Disability Coverage; Employee Discounts; Life Insurance; Medical Insurance; Savings Plan; Tuition Assistance; Vacation Days (6 - 10). **Special programs:** Internships. **Parent company:** Fairchild Publications, Inc. **Number of employees at this location:** 50.

LOS ANGELES TIMES
202 West First Street, Los Angeles CA 90012. 213/237-3700. **Contact:** Human Resources. **World Wide Web address:** http://www.latimes.com. **Description:** Publishes a daily newspaper with a circulation of over 1 million. **Parent company:** The Tribune Company (Chicago IL).

JOHN D. LUCAS PRINTING COMPANY
1820 Portal Street, Baltimore MD 21224. 410/633-4200. **Contact:** Personnel. **World Wide Web address:** http://www.johndlucas.com. **Description:** Involved in all aspects of printing and book-making including composition and binding services, typesetting, and lithography. **Common positions include:** Customer Service Rep.; Manufacturer's/Wholesaler's Sales Rep. **Educational backgrounds include:** Accounting; Business Administration; Liberal Arts. **Benefits:** Dental Insurance; Disability Coverage; Life Insurance; Medical Insurance; Profit Sharing; Tuition Assistance. **Corporate headquarters location:** This Location.

M&F CASE
717 School Street, Pawtucket RI 02860. 401/722-4830. **Contact:** Personnel Coordinator. **Description:** Manufactures custom loose-leaf binders and indexes. The company also provides screen process printing and decals. **Common positions include:** Accountant; Buyer; Commercial Artist; Computer Programmer; Credit Manager; Customer Service Rep.; Department Manager; Electrical/Electronics Engineer; General Manager; Human Resources Manager; Industrial Engineer; Management Trainee; Manufacturer's/Wholesaler's Sales Rep.; Marketing Specialist; Mechanical Engineer; Operations/Production Manager;

Purchasing Agent/Manager; Quality Control Supervisor. **Educational backgrounds include:** Accounting; Art/Design; Business Administration; Communications; Computer Science; Economics; Engineering; Finance; Marketing. **Benefits:** Dental Insurance; Disability Coverage; Employee Discounts; Life Insurance; Medical Insurance; Pension Plan; Profit Sharing; Savings Plan; Tuition Assistance. **Corporate headquarters location:** This Location.

M.I.T. PRESS
5 Cambridge Center, 4th Floor, Cambridge MA 02142. 617/253-5646. **Contact:** Human Resources. **World Wide Web address:** http://www-mitpress.mit.edu. **Description:** Publishes scholarly books. **Corporate headquarters location:** This Location.

MAGNUM DIGITAL SERVICES
6601 Lyons Road, Suite C-2, Coconut Creek FL 33073. **Fax:** 954/570-7808. **Contact:** Personnel. **World Wide Web address:** http://www.magnumds.com. **Description:** A printer of digital graphic images for banners, billboards, and bus displays. The company is also a Scotchprint manufacturer. **Corporate headquarters location:** This Location. **Number of employees at this location:** 10.

MAIL-WELL, INC.
23 Inverness Way East, Suite 160, Englewood CO 80112. 303/790-8023. **Fax:** 303/768-7380. **Contact:** Human Resources. **World Wide Web address:** http://www.mail-well.com. **Description:** Mail-Well is a leading consolidator in the envelope and specialty printing industries. The company specializes in customized envelopes, filing products, labels, and printed materials. Mail-Well operates approximately 70 printing plants and numerous sales offices throughout North America. **Common positions include:** Account Manager; Account Rep.; Accountant; Adjuster; Administrative Assistant; Administrative Manager; Advertising Clerk; Advertising Executive; Applications Engineer; Attorney; Auditor; Blue-Collar Worker Supervisor; Branch Manager; Chief Financial Officer; Computer Operator; Controller; Cost Estimator; Credit Manager; Customer Service Representative; Finance Director; Financial Analyst; General Manager; Graphic Artist; Graphic Designer; Human Resources Manager; Marketing Manager; MIS Specialist; Sales Executive; Sales Manager; Sales Representative; Secretary. **Educational backgrounds include:** Accounting; Business Administration; Finance; Marketing; Mathematics. **Benefits:** 401(k); Dental Insurance; Disability Coverage; Life Insurance; Medical Insurance; Pension Plan; Profit Sharing; Tuition Assistance. **Office hours:** Monday - Friday, 7:30 a.m. - 5:00 p.m. **Corporate headquarters location:** This Location. **Parent company:** Great Northern Nekoosa Corporation. **CEO:** Gerald Mahoney.

MALLOY LITHOGRAPHING, INC.
P.O. Box 1124, Ann Arbor MI 48106. 734/665-6113. **Contact:** Personnel Department. **World Wide Web address:** http://www.malloy.com. **Description:** A lithographing company which specializes in the printing of books. **Common positions include:** Blue-Collar Worker Supervisor; Computer Programmer; Customer Service Representative; Graphic Artist; Instructor/Trainer; Operations/Production Manager; Printing Press Operator. **Educational backgrounds include:** Art/Design; Computer Science; Engineering. **Benefits:** Dental Insurance; Disability Coverage; Life Insurance; Medical Insurance; Profit Sharing; Savings Plan; Tuition Assistance. **Corporate**

headquarters location: This Location. **Number of employees at this location:** 330.

MANUFACTURERS' NEWS, INC.
1633 Central Street, Evanston IL 60201. 847/864-7000. **Fax:** 847/332-1100. **Contact:** Human Resources. **World Wide Web address:** http://www.mninfo.com. **Description:** Compiles and publishes directories and databases of U.S. manufacturers. **NOTE:** Part-time jobs are offered. **Common positions include:** Customer Service Rep.; Researcher; Sales Executive. **Benefits:** 401(k); Casual Dress - Daily; Dental Insurance; Medical Insurance; Public Transit Available.

THE MAPLE-VAIL BOOK MANUFACTURING GROUP
THE MAPLE PRESS COMPANY
Willow Springs Lane, P.O. Box 2695, York PA 17405. 717/764-5911. **Contact:** Shirley Baker, Personnel Manager. **Description:** Provides book binding services including printing and photo composition. The Maple Press Company (also at this location) is a manufacturing facility. **Corporate headquarters location:** This Location.

MARATHON COMMUNICATIONS
P.O. Box 1908, Wausau WI 54402. 715/845-4231. **Physical address:** 2001 West Second Street, Wausau WI. **Fax:** 715/845-9267. **Contact:** Human Resources. **World Wide Web address:** http://www.marcomm.com. **Description:** A printing and communication services company. Marathon's technical publications division is engaged in the production of price books, manuals, and data sheets for corporations. **Common positions include:** Computer Programmer; Draftsperson; Sales Rep.; Technical Writer/Editor; Video Production Coordinator. **Educational backgrounds include:** Engineering. **Benefits:** 401(k); Dental Insurance; Disability Coverage; Life Insurance; Medical Insurance. **Corporate headquarters location:** This Location. **Other area locations:** Green Bay WI. **Number of employees at this location:** 170.

MARCEL DEKKER, INC.
270 Madison Avenue, New York NY 10016. 212/696-9000. **Fax:** 212/685-4540. **Contact:** Jennifer Foo, Human Resources Recruiter. **World Wide Web address:** http://www.dekker.com. **Description:** An international publisher of scientific, technological, and medical books, journals, and encyclopedias in the following fields: agriculture; biology; food science; chemistry; engineering; environmental science and pollution control; library information science and technology; material science and physics; mathematics; statistics; medicine; social science; business and economics; packaging and converting; and technology. Marcel Dekker distributes to libraries, societies, public institutions, hospitals, colleges, universities, and professionals. **Common positions include:** Accountant; Acquisitions Editor; Administrative Assistant; Designer; Editorial Assistant; Financial Analyst; Production Editor. **Educational backgrounds include:** Accounting; Art/Design; Business Administration; Communications; Computer Science; English; Finance; History; Journalism; Liberal Arts; Marketing; Psychology; Science. **Benefits:** 4-Day Work Week; 401(k); Dental Insurance; Flextime Plan; Life Insurance; Medical Insurance. **Corporate headquarters location:** This Location.

MAYFIELD PUBLISHING COMPANY
1280 Villa Street, Mountain View CA 94041. 650/960-3222. **Contact:** Personnel. **World Wide Web address:** http://www.mayfieldpub.com. **Description:** Publishes college textbooks. **Common**

positions include: Acquisitions Editor; Administrator; Art Director; Book Production Worker; Credit Manager; Customer Service Rep.; Editor; Human Resources Manager; Marketing Specialist; Operations/Production Manager; Order Clerk; Purchasing Agent/Manager. **Educational backgrounds include:** Communications; Liberal Arts. **Benefits:** Bonus Award/Plan; Dental Insurance; Disability Coverage; Employee Discounts; Life Insurance; Medical Insurance; Pension Plan; Tuition Assistance. **Corporate headquarters location:** This Location.

McARDLE PRINTING COMPANY, INC.
800 Commerce Drive, Upper Marlboro MD 20774. 301/390-8500. **Contact:** Human Resources. **World Wide Web address:** http://www.mcardleprinting.com. **Description:** A commercial printing firm. **Common positions include:** Accountant; Blue-Collar Worker Supervisor; Cost Estimator; Customer Service Rep.; Human Resources Manager; Manufacturer's/Wholesaler's Sales Rep.; Operations/Production Manager; Purchasing Agent/Manager. **Educational backgrounds include:** Accounting; Business Administration. **Benefits:** 401(k); Disability Coverage; Life Insurance; Medical Insurance; Profit Sharing. **Corporate headquarters location:** This Location. **Parent company:** Bureau of National Affairs. **Listed on:** Privately held. **Number of employees at this location:** 200.

McBEE SYSTEMS, INC.
299 Cherry Hill Road, Parsippany NJ 07054. 973/263-3225. **Fax:** 973/263-8165. **Contact:** Cynthia Burke, National Recruiting, T&D Manager. **World Wide Web address:** http://www.mcbeesystems.com. **Description:** Manufactures business forms designed specifically for small businesses and professional offices. **Common positions include:** Customer Service Rep.; Sales Representative. **Educational backgrounds include:** Accounting; Business Administration. **Benefits:** Dental Insurance; Disability Coverage; Life Insurance; Medical Insurance; Savings Plan; Tuition Assistance. **Corporate headquarters location:** This Location. **Parent company:** Romo Corporation.

THE McGRAW-HILL COMPANIES
1221 Avenue of the Americas, New York NY 10020. 212/512-2000. **Contact:** Human Resources. **World Wide Web address:** http://www.mcgraw-hill.com. **Description:** McGraw-Hill is a provider of information and services through books, magazines, newsletters, software, CD-ROMs, and online data, fax, and TV broadcasting services. The company operates four network-affiliated TV stations and also publishes *Business Week* magazine and books for the college, medical, international, legal, and professional markets. McGraw-Hill also offers financial services including *Standard & Poor's*, commodity items, and international and logistics management products and services. **Corporate headquarters location:** This Location. **Other U.S. locations:**
• 148 Princeton Hightstown Road, Hightstown NJ 08520. 609/426-5000.

MEDIA PROJECTS INC.
305 Second Avenue, Suite 342, New York NY 10003. 212/777-4510. **Contact:** Human Resources. **Description:** An independent book producer specializing in visual nonfiction. Media Projects handles all stages of book production in-house.

MEDICAL ECONOMICS COMPANY
5 Paragon Drive, Montvale NJ 07645. 201/358-7500. **Fax:** 201/722-2668. **Contact:** Human

Resources. **World Wide Web address:** http://www. medec.com. **Description:** Publishes medical books and journals. **Common positions include:** Accountant/Auditor; Advertising Clerk; Artist; Commercial Artist; Computer Operator; Computer Programmer; Customer Service Rep.; Designer; Editor; Financial Manager; Human Resources Manager; Librarian; Marketing Specialist; Receptionist; Services Sales Rep.; Systems Analyst; Technical Writer/Editor; Typist/Word Processor. **Educational backgrounds include:** Accounting; Art/Design; Business Administration; Communications; Finance; Marketing. **Benefits:** Dental Insurance; Disability Coverage; Life Insurance; Medical Insurance; Pension Plan; Savings Plan; Tuition Assistance; Vision Insurance. **Special programs:** Internships. **Corporate headquarters location:** This Location. **Other U.S. locations:** DC; IL; KS.

METRO CREATIVE GRAPHICS
33 West 34th Street, New York NY 10001. 212/947-5100. **Fax:** 212/967-4602. **Contact:** Human Resources. **Description:** Provides camera-ready graphics, editorial, and professional production services to the newspaper and graphic communication industries. **NOTE:** When submitting a resume, computer illustrators and artists should include nonreturnable samples of computer artwork. Some testing may be required. **Common positions include:** Computer Graphics Specialist; Copywriter; Customer Service Representative; Editor; Human Resources Manager; Sales Representative. **Educational backgrounds include:** Art/Design; Business Administration; Communications; Computer Science; Liberal Arts; Marketing. **Benefits:** 401(k); Credit Union; Dental Insurance; Direct Deposit; Disability Coverage; Life Insurance; Medical Insurance. **Corporate headquarters location:** This Location. **Number of employees at this location:** 60.

THE MIAMI HERALD PUBLISHING CO.
EL NUEVO HERALD
One Herald Plaza, Miami FL 33132. **Toll-free phone:** 800/437-2535. **Fax:** 305/995-8021. **Recorded jobline:** 305/376-2880. **Contact:** Human Resources. **Description:** Publishes a regional daily newspaper. **NOTE:** Entry-level positions and second and third shifts are offered. **Common positions include:** Account Manager; Account Rep.; Accountant; Administrative Assistant; Administrative Manager; Advertising Clerk; Advertising Executive; Assistant Manager; Budget Analyst; Customer Service Representative; Editor; Editorial Assistant; Financial Analyst; Graphic Artist; Graphic Designer; Human Resources Manager; Market Research Analyst; Marketing Manager; Marketing Specialist; Online Content Specialist; Operations Manager; Production Manager; Sales Executive; Sales Manager; Sales Representative; Systems Analyst; Systems Manager; Technical Writer/Editor; Typist/Word Processor; Webmaster. **Educational backgrounds include:** Accounting; Art/Design; Business Administration; Communications; Finance; Marketing. **Benefits:** 401(k); Daycare Assistance; Dental Insurance; Disability Coverage; Flexible Schedule; Job Sharing; Life Insurance; Medical Insurance; Pension Plan; Profit Sharing; Savings Plan; Tuition Assistance. **Special programs:** Internships. **Corporate headquarters location:** This Location. **Parent company:** Knight-Ridder. **Listed on:** New York Stock Exchange. **Number of employees at this location:** 2,200.

MIAMI METRO MAGAZINE
P.O. Box 019068, Miami FL 33132. 305/755-9920. **Physical address:** 1550 Biscayne Boulevard, Suite 300, Miami FL. **Fax:** 305/755-9921. **Contact:** Clara Cummings, Administrative Assistant. **E-mail address:** miametro@bellsouth.net. **World Wide Web address:** http://www.miamimetro.com. **Description:** Publishes a regional lifestyle magazine. **Common positions include:** Administrative Manager; Advertising Manager; Editor; Graphic Designer; Occupational Therapist. **Educational backgrounds include:** Art/Design; Business Administration; Communications; Marketing. **Benefits:** 401(k); Dental Insurance; Disability Coverage; Life Insurance; Medical Insurance. **Special programs:** Internships. **Corporate headquarters location:** Morristown NJ.

MIAMI TIMES
900 NW 54th Street, Miami FL 33127. 305/757-1147. **Contact:** Personnel. **Description:** Publishes a weekly newspaper. **Common positions include:** Advertising Clerk; Clerical Supervisor; Customer Service Representative; Editor; General Manager; Manufacturer's/Wholesaler's Sales Rep.; Reporter; Services Sales Representative. **Educational backgrounds include:** Business Administration; Communications; Liberal Arts; Marketing. **Benefits:** Dental Insurance; Life Insurance; Medical Insurance. **Special programs:** Internships. **Corporate headquarters location:** This Location. **Number of employees at this location:** 20.

MIAMI TODAY
P.O. Box 1368, Miami FL 33101. 305/358-2663. **Contact:** Michael Lewis, Publisher/Editor. **Description:** Publishes a weekly newspaper that focuses on the business community. Founded in 1983. **NOTE:** Entry-level positions are offered. **Common positions include:** Advertising Executive; Advertising Manager; Department Manager; Management Trainee; Marketing Specialist; Reporter. **Educational backgrounds include:** Business Administration; Communications; Liberal Arts; Marketing. **Benefits:** Life Insurance; Medical Insurance. **Special programs:** Internships. **Office hours:** Monday - Friday, 8:30 a.m. - 5:30 p.m. **Corporate headquarters location:** This Location. **Number of employees at this location:** 30.

MILWAUKEE JOURNAL SENTINEL, INC.
333 West State Street, Milwaukee WI 53203. 414/223-5171. **Fax:** 414/224-2897. **Contact:** Verona Morgan, Employment Manager. **World Wide Web address:** http://www.jsonline.com. **Description:** A newspaper with a daily circulation of 290,000 and 500,000 on Sundays. Founded in 1882. **NOTE:** Entry-level positions are offered. **Common positions include:** Account Rep.; Administrative Assistant; Computer Operator; Computer Programmer; Customer Service Rep.; Editor; General Manager; Graphic Designer; Management Trainee; MIS Specialist; Reporter; Sales Executive; Sales Representative; Systems Analyst. **Educational backgrounds include:** Accounting; Art/Design; Business Administration; Communications; Computer Science; Marketing. **Benefits:** 401(k); Dental Insurance; Disability Coverage; Employee Discounts; Life Insurance; Medical Insurance; Pension Plan; Profit Sharing; Tuition Assistance. **Special programs:** Internships; Apprenticeships; Summer Jobs. **Office hours:** Monday - Friday, 8:00 a.m. - 5:00 p.m. **Corporate headquarters location:** This Location. **Parent company:** Journal Communications (also at this location). **President:** Keith Spore. **Number of employees at this location:** 3,000.

MINNESOTA SUN PUBLICATIONS
10917 Valley View Road, Eden Prairie MN 55344. 952/829-0797. **Contact:** Human Resources. **World Wide Web address:** http://www.mnsun.

Description: Owns a group of suburban Minneapolis newspapers, including *Sun Current*, *Sun Post*, and *Sun Sailor*. **Common positions include:** Commercial Artist; Editor; Reporter; Sales Rep. **Educational backgrounds include:** Art/ Design; Business Administration; Journalism; Liberal Arts; Marketing. **Benefits:** 401(k); Dental Insurance; Disability Coverage; Life Insurance; Medical Insurance. **Corporate headquarters location:** This Location.

MINUTE MAN PRESS
9850 51st Avenue North, Suite 104, Plymouth MN 55442. 763/553-1561. **Contact:** General Manager. **World Wide Web address:** http://www.mmp-plymouth.com. **Description:** A national corporation that publishes magazines and is also engaged in commercial printing and mailing. **Common positions include:** Customer Service Rep.; Department Manager; General Manager; Manufacturer's/Wholesaler's Sales Rep.; Marketing Specialist; Operations/Production Manager. **Educational backgrounds include:** Art/Design; Business Administration; Communications; Marketing. **Benefits:** Dental Insurance; Medical Insurance; Tuition Assistance. **Special programs:** Internships. **Corporate headquarters location:** This Location. **Number of employees at this location:** 15.

THE MISSOULIAN
P.O. Box 8029, Missoula MT 59807. 406/721-5200. **Contact:** Personnel. **World Wide Web address:** http://www.missoulian.com. **Description:** Publishes a daily newspaper.

MONARCH SERVICES
GIRLS' LIFE
4517 Harford Road, Baltimore MD 21214. 410/254-9200. **Contact:** Human Resources. **Description:** Prints envelopes and publishes *Girls' Life* magazine. **Corporate headquarters location:** This Location.

MONTGOMERY NEWSPAPERS CO.
P.O. Box 1628, Fort Washington PA 19034. 215/542-0200. **Contact:** Diane Dumke, Human Resources. **World Wide Web address:** http://www.montgomerynews.com. **Description:** Publishes *Today's Spirit*, a daily newspaper for the Hatboro/ Warminster area and weekly newspapers in Ambler, Glenside, Huntingdon Valley, Jenkintown, King of Prussia, Springfield, and Willow Grove. **Common positions include:** Accountant/Auditor; Mail Distributor; Sales Representative. **Benefits:** 401(k); Dental Insurance; Disability Coverage; Life Insurance; Medical Insurance; Pension Plan; Profit Sharing. **Corporate headquarters location:** This Location. **Operations at this facility include:** Manufacturing. **Listed on:** Privately held. **Annual sales/revenues:** $5 - $10 million.

MOORE NORTH AMERICA
1200 South Lakeside Drive, Bannockburn IL 60015. 847/607-6000. **Contact:** Human Resources. **World Wide Web address:** http://www.moore.com. **Description:** A manufacturer of business systems, forms, and equipment. The company has more than 280 locations in 39 countries. **Common positions include:** Accountant; Computer Programmer; Customer Service Rep.; Department Manager; General Manager; Manufacturer's/Wholesaler's Sales Rep. **Educational backgrounds include:** Accounting; Business Administration; Communications; Computer Science; Engineering; Liberal Arts; Marketing. **Benefits:** 401(k); Dental Insurance; Disability Coverage; Life Insurance; Medical Insurance; Pension Plan; Savings Plan; Stock Option; Tuition Assistance. **Special programs:** Internships. **Corporate headquarters**

location: This Location. **Parent company:** Moore Corporation. **Listed on:** New York Stock Exchange. **Other U.S. locations:**
- 7801 Avenue 304, Visalia CA 93291. 559/651-2153.
- 2117 West River Road North, Minneapolis MN 55411. 612/588-7200.

MORRIS NEWSPAPER CORPORATION
P.O. Box 8167, Savannah GA 31412. 912/233-1281. **Contact:** Miriam Potter, Vice President of Human Resources. **World Wide Web address:** http://www.morrisnews.com. **Description:** A newspaper conglomerate that also operates broadcasting stations. **Corporate headquarters location:** This Location.

MOSBY
11830 Westline Industrial Drive, St. Louis MO 63146. 314/453-4248. **Toll-free phone:** 800/325-4177. **Fax:** 314/432-0719. **Contact:** Alicia K. Vernon, Human Resources Director. **World Wide Web address:** http://www.harcourt.com. **Description:** A publisher of books and periodicals in the field of health sciences. **Common positions include:** Accountant; Commercial Artist; Computer Programmer; Customer Service Rep.; Editor; Editorial Assistant; Manufacturer's/Wholesaler's Sales Rep.; Marketing Specialist; Systems Analyst. **Educational backgrounds include:** Art/Design; Biology; Communications; English; Journalism; Liberal Arts; Marketing. **Benefits:** 401(k); Daycare Assistance; Dental Insurance; Disability Coverage; Employee Discounts; Life Insurance; Medical Insurance; Pension Plan; Savings Plan; Telecommuting; Tuition Assistance. **Corporate headquarters location:** Philadelphia PA. **Parent company:** Harcourt General. **President:** Peter Hoenigsberg. **Annual sales/revenues:** More than $100 million.

MOTHERAL PRINTING COMPANY
P.O. Box 629, Fort Worth TX 76101. 817/335-1481. **Contact:** Personnel Department. **Description:** A commercial lithography and printing company. **Common positions include:** Bindery Worker; Blue-Collar Worker Supervisor; Customer Service Rep.; Department Manager; Printing Press Operator. **Educational backgrounds include:** Business Administration; Communications; Computer Science; Engineering. **Benefits:** Disability Coverage; Employee Discounts; Life Insurance; Medical Insurance; Pension Plan; Profit Sharing; Tuition Assistance. **Special programs:** Internships. **Corporate headquarters location:** This Location.

NCL GRAPHIC SPECIALTIES, INC.
North 29 West 22960 Marjean Lane, Waukesha WI 53186. 262/542-0711. **Fax:** 262/542-1475. **Contact:** Bill Menzel, Vice President. **World Wide Web address:** http://www.nclgraphicspecialties.com. **Description:** An offset web press, specializing in large-volume production of labels, on-pak, in-pak, and around-pak commercial printing. **Common positions include:** Account Manager; Account Rep.; Blue-Collar Worker Supervisor; Buyer; Cost Estimator; Credit Manager; Customer Service Rep.; Electrician; Environmental Engineer; General Manager; Graphic Artist; Operations/Production Manager; Production Manager; Purchasing Agent/Manager; Quality Control Supervisor; Systems Analyst; Typist/Word Processor. **Educational backgrounds include:** Accounting; Art/Design; Business Administration; Marketing. **Benefits:** 401(k); Dental Insurance; Financial Planning Assistance; Life Insurance; Medical Insurance; Pension Plan; Savings Plan. **Special programs:** Internships; Training. **Corporate headquarters location:** This Location.

Listed on: Privately held. **Annual sales/revenues:** $21 - $50 million. **Number of employees at this location:** 200.

NTC/CONTEMPORARY PUBLISHING GROUP
4255 West Touhy Avenue, Lincolnwood IL 60712. 847/679-5500. **Toll-free phone:** 800/323-4900. **Fax:** 847/679-2494. **Contact:** Human Resources Manager. **E-mail address:** ntchr@tribune.com. **World Wide Web address:** http://www.ntc-cb.com. **Description:** Publishes career, foreign language, travel, reference, business, and children's books. Divisions of the company include National Textbook Company, Passport Books, NTC Business Books, and VGM Career Horizons. This location also hires seasonally. **NOTE:** Entry-level positions and part-time jobs are offered. **Common positions include:** Account Manager; Account Rep.; Accountant; Administrative Assistant; Blue-Collar Worker Supervisor; Chief Financial Officer; Computer Programmer; Computer Support Technician; Computer Technician; Controller; Credit Manager; Customer Service Representative; Database Administrator; Database Manager; Desktop Publishing Specialist; Editor; Editorial Assistant; Finance Director; General Manager; Graphic Artist; Graphic Designer; Human Resources Manager; Industrial Engineer; Internet Services Manager; Intranet Developer; Managing Editor; Online Sales Manager; Operations Manager; Production Manager; Project Manager; Sales Manager; Sales Representative; Technical Writer/Editor; Typist/Word Processor; Webmaster. **Educational backgrounds include:** Accounting; Art/Design; Business Administration; Communications; Computer Science; Education; Finance; HTML; Internet Development; Java; Liberal Arts; Marketing; MBA; Microsoft Office; Microsoft Word; Public Relations; Publishing; QuarkXPress; Spreadsheets; SQL; Visual Basic. **Benefits:** 401(k); Casual Dress - Daily; Dental Insurance; Disability Coverage; Employee Discounts; Financial Planning Assistance; Flexible Schedule; Life Insurance; Medical Insurance; Profit Sharing; Public Transit Available; Savings Plan; Sick Days (1 - 5); Telecommuting; Tuition Assistance; Vacation Days. **Special programs:** Internships. **Corporate headquarters location:** This Location. **International locations:** Markham, Ontario. **Listed on:** New York Stock Exchange. **Stock exchange symbol:** TRB. **Annual sales/revenues:** More than $100 million. **Number of employees at this location:** 350. **Number of employees nationwide:** 425.

NACE INTERNATIONAL
1440 South Creek Drive, Houston TX 77084. 281/228-6256. **Fax:** 281/228-6356. **Contact:** Marcie Skinner, Human Resources Manager. **World Wide Web address:** http://www.nace.org. **Description:** NACE (National Association of Corrosion Engineers) International disseminates information about protection/performance in corrosive environments through its two monthly journals, one bimonthly magazine, and a variety of technical reports and journals. **Common positions include:** Advertising Clerk; Customer Service Representative; Editor; Public Relations Specialist; Technical Writer/Editor. **Educational backgrounds include:** Communications; Education; English; Journalism; Marketing. **Benefits:** 401(k); Dental Insurance; Disability Coverage; Life Insurance; Medical Insurance; Tuition Assistance. **Corporate headquarters location:** This Location. **Operations at this facility include:** Administration; Divisional Headquarters; Production; Service. **Executive Director:** Gerald Shankel. **Number of employees at this location:** 65.

NATIONAL ENQUIRER STAR GROUP, INC.
600 SE Coast Avenue, Lantana FL 33464. 561/586-1111. **Contact:** Personnel. **Description:** Publishes tabloid newspapers including *National Enquirer, Star, Weekly World News, Country Weekly*, and *Soap Opera Magazine*, with an aggregate weekly circulation of approximately 7 million copies. **Common positions include:** Computer Programmer; Editor; Layout Specialist; Reporter; Systems Analyst. **Educational backgrounds include:** Communications; Computer Science; Journalism; Liberal Arts. **Benefits:** Accident/Emergency Insurance; Dental Insurance; Disability Coverage; Employee Discounts; Fitness Program; Life Insurance; Medical Insurance; Profit Sharing; Savings Plan; Tuition Assistance. **Corporate headquarters location:** This Location. **Subsidiaries include:** Distribution Services, Inc. arranges for the placement of its periodicals in approximately 180,000 locations in North America. **Listed on:** New York Stock Exchange.

NATIONAL GEOGRAPHIC SOCIETY
1145 17th Street NW, Washington DC 20036. 202/857-7000. **Contact:** Eleanor Brown, Director of Employment. **World Wide Web address:** http://www.nationalgeographic.com. **Description:** This location houses the corporate offices as well as a museum. Overall, as one of the world's largest nonprofit organizations, the National Geographic Society offers various products and services. The National Geographic Education Program offers geography education programs to schools through films, computer software, videos, and other multimedia classroom materials. Since 1890, the society's Committee for Research and Exploration has supported more than 4,000 exploration and research projects in various locations. The society offers four major publications. *National Geographic* reaches over 9 million members and an estimated 40 million readers on a monthly basis. *National Geographic Traveler* provides travel information. *National Geographic World* is for children eight years old and over. *National Geographic Research and Exploration* is a scientific journal. *National Geographic* profiles geographic topics and locales from a very broad perspective. The society also offers maps and globes as well as books and games for young adults. *The National Geographic Explorer* is a two-hour cable television series with a magazine format. The society also offers various public services including an annual series of lectures and events, and the JASON Project, which provides students with access to interactive television links. **Special programs:** Apprenticeships. **Office hours:** Monday - Saturday, 9:00 a.m. - 5:00 p.m., and Sunday, 10:00 a.m. - 5:00 p.m. **Corporate headquarters location:** This Location. **Other U.S. locations:** Gaithersburg MD.

NATIONAL REVIEW INC.
215 Lexington Avenue, 4th Floor, New York NY 10016. 212/679-7330. **Contact:** Theresa Maloney, Circulation Director. **World Wide Web address:** http://www.nationalreview.com. **Description:** Publishes a nationally distributed conservative magazine focusing on current political issues. **Common positions include:** Editor; Reporter. **Educational backgrounds include:** Economics; Liberal Arts. **Benefits:** Disability Coverage; Life Insurance; Medical Insurance; Pension Plan; Savings Plan. **Corporate headquarters location:** This Location.

THE NEW AMERICAN THE DAILY CHALLENGE
1195 Atlantic Avenue, Brooklyn NY 11216. 718/636-9500. **Contact:** Thomas H. Watkins,

Publisher. **Description:** Publishes a nationally distributed, weekly newspaper (circulation of 130,000) primarily covering cultural, political, and social news of interest to African Americans. **Common positions include:** Accountant/Auditor; Administrator; Advertising Clerk; Computer Programmer; Editor; Human Resources Manager; Management Trainee; Marketing Specialist; Operations/Production Manager; Public Relations Specialist; Reporter; Sales Executive. **Educational backgrounds include:** Accounting; Art/Design; Business Administration; Communications. **Special programs:** Internships. **Corporate headquarters location:** This Location.

NEW ENGLAND BUSINESS SERVICE (NEBS)
500 Main Street, Groton MA 01471. 978/448-6111. **Contact:** Seth A. Canter, Corporate Employee Relations/Staffing Director. **World Wide Web address:** http://www.nebs.com. **Description:** A supplier of business forms and software for small businesses. The company's product line consists of over 1,000 standardized imprinted manual and computer business forms including billing forms, work orders, job proposals, and purchase orders; stationery including letterheads, envelopes, and business cards; checks and checkwriting systems; and marketing products including advertising labels, pricing tags and labels, signage, and greeting cards. The company offers a line of software that includes checkwriting, billing, and mailing applications, as well as a variety of simpler form-filling software; and One-Write Plus, a line of accounting software that integrates accounting and payroll functions with basic word processing, mail merge, a spreadsheet link, a backup utility, and a menu organizer. The computer forms are compatible with over 3,500 personal computer software packages developed by third parties and used by small businesses. **Common positions include:** Accountant/Auditor; Advertising Clerk; Buyer; Computer Programmer; Customer Service Representative; Department Manager; Editor; Financial Analyst; Human Resources Manager; Industrial Engineer; Management Trainee; Marketing Specialist; Operations/Production Manager; Purchasing Agent/Manager; Services Sales Representative; Systems Analyst; Technical Writer/Editor. **Educational backgrounds include:** Accounting; Art/Design; Business Administration; Communications; Computer Science; Engineering; Finance; Marketing. **Benefits:** 401(k); Dental Insurance; Disability Coverage; Employee Discounts; Life Insurance; Medical Insurance; Pension Plan; Profit Sharing; Tuition Assistance. **Special programs:** Internships. **Corporate headquarters location:** This Location. **Other area locations:** Townsend MA; Woburn MA. **Other U.S. locations:** Flagstaff AZ; Phoenix AZ; Maryville MO; Nashua NH; Peterborough NH. **Listed on:** Privately held.

NEW HAVEN REGISTER
40 Sargent Drive, New Haven CT 06511. 203/789-5200. **Contact:** Human Resources. **Description:** Publishes a newspaper with a weekday circulation of 110,000 and a Sunday circulation of 121,000. **Corporate headquarters location:** This Location.

NEW YORK TIMES COMPANY
229 West 43rd Street, New York NY 10036. 212/556-1234. **Contact:** Human Resources. **World Wide Web address:** http://www.nytco.com. **Description:** Publishes *The New York Times*, one of the largest newspapers in the world (daily circulation exceeds 887,000 weekdays and 1.4 million on Sundays). In addition to *The New York Times*, this diversified, publicly-owned communications firm publishes 30 dailies and weeklies in various cities; publishes three national magazines; and owns and operates three television stations, two radio stations, and a cable television system. The company also publishes syndicated news and features worldwide. The company also has interests in paper and newsprint manufacturing mills, and a partial interest in the *International Herald Tribune*. Newspaper subsidiaries are located throughout the country and have an average daily circulation of 272,000. **Corporate headquarters location:** This Location.

NEWPORT MEDIA
250 Miller Place, Hicksville NY 11801. 516/393-9300. **Fax:** 516/393-9242. **Contact:** Sue Annunziata, Manager of Human Resources. **Description:** A regional publisher involved in the publishing, printing, and distribution of weekly free-circulation newspapers, as well as circulars and other promotional and printed material. Newport Media's publications include *The Pennysaver*, *Shoppers Guide*, *Yankee Trader*, *Marketeer*, *Pocket Mailer*, and *Value Mailer*. **Common positions include:** Account Rep.; Accountant; Advertising Clerk; Blue-Collar Worker Supervisor; Commercial Artist; Computer Programmer; Customer Service Rep.; Department Manager; General Manager; Marketing Manager; Operations/Production Manager; Printing Press Operator; Promotion Manager; Telemarketer. **Educational backgrounds include:** Accounting; Advertising; Art/Design; Business Administration; Communications; Marketing. **Benefits:** 401(k); Dental Insurance; Disability Coverage; Life Insurance; Medical Insurance. **Corporate headquarters location:** This Location.

NEWS AMERICA PUBLICATIONS, INC.
TV GUIDE
4 Radnor Corporate Center, 100 Matsonford Road, Radnor PA 19088. 610/293-8500. **Contact:** Human Resources. **World Wide Web address:** http://www.tvguide.com. **Description:** Publishes *TV Guide* magazine. **Common positions include:** Accountant; Computer Programmer; Financial Analyst; Operations/Production Manager. **Educational backgrounds include:** Accounting; Business Administration; Communications; Computer Science. **Benefits:** Dental Insurance; Employee Discounts; Life Insurance; Medical Insurance; Pension Plan; Profit Sharing; Savings Plan; Tuition Assistance. **Special programs:** Internships. **Corporate headquarters location:** This Location. **Number of employees at this location:** 1,300.

THE NEWS SUN
1615 Lakeside Drive, Suite 100, Waukegan IL 60085. 847/336-7000. **Fax:** 847/249-7254. **Contact:** Richard Ribando, Human Resources Manager. **World Wide Web address:** http://www.copleynewspapers.com/newssun. **Description:** A daily newspaper that serves Waukegan and Lake counties. **Common positions include:** Advertising Clerk; Commercial Artist; Department Manager; Editor; Marketing Specialist; Reporter; Sales Executive. **Educational backgrounds include:** Art/Design; Journalism; Marketing. **Benefits:** Dental Insurance; Disability Coverage; Life Insurance; Medical Insurance; Pension Plan; Savings Plan; Tuition Assistance. **Other U.S. locations:** Lake Villa IL; Libertyville IL. **Parent company:** The Copley Press (La Jolla CA) publishes 45 newspapers nationwide.

NEWSDAY, INC.
235 Pinelawn Road, Melville NY 11747. 516/843-3561. **Fax:** 516/843-2550. **Recorded jobline:** 516/843-2120. **Contact:** Employment Services. **World Wide Web address:** http://www.

newsday.com. **Description:** One of the largest daily newspapers in the U.S. with a circulation of 750,000. **Common positions include:** Accountant; Advertising Clerk; Budget Analyst; Buyer; Clerical Supervisor; Computer Programmer; Customer Service Rep.; Editor; Human Resources Manager; Librarian; Operations/Production Manager; Public Relations Specialist; Reporter; Systems Analyst; Technical Writer/Editor; Transportation/Traffic Specialist. **Educational backgrounds include:** Accounting; Business Administration; Communications; Computer Science; Finance; Marketing. **Benefits:** 401(k); Daycare Assistance; Dental Insurance; Disability Coverage; Employee Discounts; Life Insurance; Medical Insurance; Pension Plan; Savings Plan; Tuition Assistance. **Special programs:** Internships. **Corporate headquarters location:** This Location. **Number of employees at this location:** 3,400.

NEWSEDGE CORPORATION

80 Blanchard Road, Burlington MA 01803. 781/229-3000. **Contact:** Human Resources. **World Wide Web address:** http://www.newsedge.com. **Description:** Provides customized, real-time news and information delivered to knowledge workers over their organizations' local area networks. The company's NewsEDGE service delivers up to 488 news and information sources, in real-time, to users' personal computers; automatically monitors and filters the news according to pre-established personal interest profiles; and alerts users to stories matching their profiles. The NewsEDGE service is used by executives, salespeople, marketers, lawyers, accountants, consultants, bankers, and financial professionals. News and information sources available on NewsEDGE include newswire from AFP/Extel News Limited; The Associated Press; Dow Jones; Knight-Ridder/Tribune Information Services; and the text of stories in *The Financial Post*, *Financial Times*, the New York Times News Service, *USA Today*, and *The Wall Street Journal*. Also available on NewsEDGE are the business sections of over 100 North American newspapers; periodicals such as *Forbes*, *Fortune*, *InfoWorld*, *MacWeek*, and *PC Week*; and newsletters such as those distributed by American Banker and Philips Business Information Services, Inc. **Corporate headquarters location:** This Location.

NEWSPAPER AGENCY CORPORATION

P.O. Box 45838, Salt Lake City UT 84145. 801/237-2800. **Contact:** Human Resources. **Description:** Provides business management, advertising, circulation, and production services for two editorially independent Salt Lake City newspapers published under the names *Salt Lake Tribune* and *Deseret News*. **Corporate headquarters location:** This Location.

NEWSWEEK MAGAZINE

251 West 57th Street, New York NY 10019. 212/445-4000. **Fax:** 212/445-4575. **Contact:** Director of Human Resources. **Description:** One of the most comprehensive weekly news magazines in the world. The company operates a global network of more than 60 correspondents and numerous stringers, reporting on important developments in politics, national and international affairs, business, technology, science, lifestyles, society, and the arts. In addition to its English language editions, the company also publishes two foreign language editions: *Newsweek Nihon Ban* in Japanese, and *Newsweek Hanuk Pan* in Korean and operates 23 bureaus throughout the United States and abroad. Weekly circulation is more than 4 million internationally, and more than 3 million in the United States. Founded in 1933. **Common positions include:** Art Director; Customer Service Rep.;

Editor; Marketing Specialist; Reporter; Sales Executive; Writer. **Educational backgrounds include:** Art/Design; Business Administration; Liberal Arts; Marketing. **Benefits:** 401(k); Adoption Assistance; Daycare Assistance; Dental Insurance; Disability Coverage; Employee Discounts; Life Insurance; Medical Insurance; Pension Plan; Tuition Assistance. **Corporate headquarters location:** This Location. **Parent company:** The Washington Post Company.

THE NEWTOWN BEE
BEE PUBLISHING COMPANY

5 Church Hill Road, Newtown CT 06470. 203/426-3141. **Contact:** Human Resources. **World Wide Web address:** http://www.thebee.com. **Description:** Publishes a daily community newspaper covering events and news in western Connecticut. **Corporate headquarters location:** This Location.

NORTH AMERICAN PUBLISHING CO.

401 North Broad Street, Philadelphia PA 19108. 215/238-5300. **Fax:** 215/238-5457. **Contact:** Human Resources. **World Wide Web address:** http://www.napco.com. **Description:** A publisher of trade and business magazines. **NOTE:** Entry-level positions are offered. **Common positions include:** Advertising Clerk; Customer Service Rep.; Editor; Sales Rep.; Telemarketer; Writer. **Educational backgrounds include:** Journalism; Liberal Arts; Marketing. **Benefits:** 401(k); Casual Dress - Daily; Dental Insurance; Disability Coverage; Life Insurance; Medical Insurance; Profit Sharing; Public Transit Available; Savings Plan; Tuition Assistance; Vacation Days (11 - 15). **Special programs:** Internships. **Office hours:** Monday - Friday 8:30 a.m. - 5:00 p.m. **Corporate headquarters location:** This Location. **President:** Ned S. Borowsky.

NORTHLAND PUBLISHING

2900 North Fort Valley Road, P.O. Box 1389, Flagstaff AZ 86001. 520/774-5251. **Toll-free phone:** 800/346-3257. **Fax:** 800/257-9082. **Contact:** Human Resources. **World Wide Web address:** http://www.northlandpub.com. **Description:** Publishes books on a wide range of topics including natural history, cooking, Western art and history, and Native American culture. Northland Publishing also publishes a number of children's books through Rising Moon (also at this location). Founded in 1958. **Corporate headquarters location:** This Location.

NOTICIAS DEL MUNDO

401 Fifth Avenue, 3rd Floor, New York NY 10016. 212/684-5656x8285. **Fax:** 212/576-0299. **Contact:** Maria Perez, Human Resources Director. **Description:** Publishes a daily Spanish newspaper. **NOTE:** Entry-level positions and part-time jobs are offered. **Common positions include:** Account Manager; Account Rep.; Administrative Assistant; Editor; Graphic Artist; Graphic Designer; Managing Editor; Reporter; Sales Executive; Sales Manager; Sales Rep.; Systems Manager. **Educational backgrounds include:** Accounting; Art/Design; Business Administration; Communications; Computer Science; Economics; Finance; Health Care; Liberal Arts; Marketing; QuarkXPress; Spreadsheets. **Benefits:** 401(k); Casual Dress - Fridays; Dental Insurance; Disability Coverage; Life Insurance; Medical Insurance; Pension Plan; Sick Days; Vacation Days (6 - 10). **Special programs:** Internships; Apprenticeships. **Corporate headquarters location:** This Location. **Parent company:** News World Communications Inc. **Listed on:** Privately held. **President:** Phillip V. Sanchez. **Annual sales/revenues:** Less than $5 million. **Number of employees at this location:** 60.

OMAHA WORLD-HERALD

1334 Dodge Street, Omaha NE 68102-1138. 402/444-1000. **Fax:** 402/444-1211. **Contact:** Mary Simmonds, Recruiter. **E-mail address:** msimmonds@owh.com. **Description:** Publishes a daily newspaper. The company is also engaged in advertising. **NOTE:** Entry-level positions, part-time jobs, and second and third shifts are offered. **Common positions include:** Account Manager; Account Rep.; Accountant; Administrative Assistant; Advertising Executive; Applications Engineer; Auditor; Blue-Collar Worker Supervisor; Budget Analyst; Chief Financial Officer; Clerical Supervisor; Computer Animator; Computer Engineer; Computer Operator; Computer Programmer; Computer Support Technician; Computer Technician; Controller; Credit Manager; Customer Service Representative; Database Administrator; Database Manager; Desktop Publishing Specialist; Editor; Editorial Assistant; Electrician; Finance Director; Financial Analyst; General Manager; Graphic Artist; Graphic Designer; Human Resources Manager; Industrial Production Manager; Internet Services Manager; Managing Editor; Market Research Analyst; Marketing Manager; Marketing Specialist; Multimedia Designer; Network/Systems Administrator; Production Manager; Public Relations Specialist; Purchasing Agent/Manager; Quality Assurance Engineer; Reporter; Sales Executive; Sales Manager; Sales Representative; Secretary; SQL Programmer; Systems Analyst; Technical Writer/Editor; Transportation/Traffic Specialist; Typist/Word Processor; Webmaster. **Educational backgrounds include:** Accounting; Art/Design; C/C++; Computer Science; English; Finance; HTML; Internet; Java; Journalism; Liberal Arts; Marketing; MCSE; Public Relations. **Benefits:** Dental Insurance; Disability Coverage; Employee Discounts; Life Insurance; Medical Insurance; Pension Plan; Savings Plan; Tuition Assistance; Vacation Pay. **Special programs:** Internships; Apprenticeships. **Corporate headquarters location:** This Location. **Listed on:** Privately held. **Number of employees at this location:** 900.

OPTIC GRAPHICS, INC.

101 Dover Road, Glen Burnie MD 21060. 410/768-3000. **Contact:** Human Resources Director. **World Wide Web address:** http://www.opticgraphics.com. **Description:** A book manufacturer utilizing both web and sheet-fed offset equipment. Optic Graphics provides a variety of finishing including saddle-stitch, perfect-binding, wire-o and plastic binding, loose-leaf binder manufacturing, index tabs printing, and foil stamping. **Corporate headquarters location:** This Location.

THE OREGONIAN

1320 SW Broadway Street, Portland OR 97201. 503/221-8327. **Contact:** Tom Whitehouse, Human Resources Director. **World Wide Web address:** http://www.oregonian.com. **Description:** A daily newspaper with a circulation of 350,000 weekly and 445,000 on Sundays. The newspaper maintains several bureaus in the Portland area and throughout Oregon, as well as a national bureau in Washington DC. **Corporate headquarters location:** This Location.

ORLANDO BUSINESS JOURNAL

315 East Robinson Street, Suite 250, Orlando FL 32801. 407/649-8470. **Fax:** 407/420-1625. **Contact:** Pat Beall, Editor. **World Wide Web address:** http://www.bizjournals.com/orlando. **Description:** A weekly business newspaper. **Common positions include:** Accountant/Auditor; Advertising Executive; Commercial Artist; Customer Service Rep.; Department Manager; Editor; Manufacturer's/Wholesaler's Sales Rep.; Operations/Production Manager; Reporter. **Educational backgrounds include:** Accounting; Art/Design; Communications; Economics; Finance; Journalism; Marketing. **Benefits:** 401(k); Disability Coverage; Life Insurance; Medical Insurance; Profit Sharing; Tuition Assistance. **Corporate headquarters location:** This Location. **Parent company:** American City Business Journals.

ORLANDO SENTINEL COMMUNICATIONS CO.

633 North Orange Avenue, Orlando FL 32801. 407/420-6253. **Fax:** 407/420-5766. **Recorded jobline:** 407/872-7200x9121. **Contact:** Employment Center. **E-mail address:** senthr@ aol.com. **World Wide Web address:** http://www.orlandosentinel.com. **Description:** Publishes the *Orlando Sentinel* newspaper and various niche publications. Other company divisions include interactive, direct mail, signage, and teleservices. The company is also involved in a joint venture with Time Warner Communications to produce a local 24-hour cable news channel. **NOTE:** Entry-level positions, part-time jobs, and second and third shifts are offered. **Common positions include:** Account Rep.; Accountant; Administrative Assistant; Advertising Executive; Applications Engineer; Broadcast Technician; Budget Analyst; Computer Engineer; Computer Operator; Computer Technician; Content Developer; Customer Service Representative; Database Administrator; Desktop Publishing Specialist; Editor; Editorial Assistant; Electrician; Financial Analyst; Graphic Artist; Graphic Designer; Market Research Analyst; Network/Systems Administrator; Purchasing Agent/Manager; Radio/TV Announcer/Broadcaster; Reporter; Sales Representative; Secretary; Systems Analyst; Webmaster. **Educational backgrounds include:** C/C++; CGI; HTML; Internet; Java; Microsoft Word; Novell; QuarkXPress; Spreadsheets; UNIX. **Benefits:** 401(k); Dental Insurance; Disability Coverage; Employee Discounts; Life Insurance; Medical Insurance; Tuition Assistance. **Special programs:** Internships; Co-ops. **Corporate headquarters location:** Chicago IL. **Other U.S. locations:** Nationwide. **Parent company:** Tribune Company.

OSHKOSH NORTHWESTERN

P.O. Box 2926, Oshkosh WI 54903-2926. 920/235-7700. **Contact:** Human Resources. **World Wide Web address:** http://www.thenorthwestern.com. **Description:** Publishes a daily newspaper. **Corporate headquarters location:** This Location.

PCA INTERNATIONAL, INC.

815 Matthews-Mint Hill Road, Matthews NC 28105. 704/847-8011. **Contact:** Personnel. **Description:** The exclusive operator of children's portrait photography services in over 1,400 Kmart stores. Adult and family portraits are marketed through the Institutional Division, which works primarily through church promotions. **Educational backgrounds include:** Accounting; Business Administration; Communications; Computer Science; Marketing; Phototechnology. **Benefits:** 401(k); Dental Insurance; Disability Coverage; Life Insurance; Medical Insurance; Profit Sharing. **Corporate headquarters location:** This Location. **Other U.S. locations:** Nationwide. **International locations:** Canada; Mexico; Puerto Rico; Virgin Islands. **Listed on:** NASDAQ. **Annual sales/revenues:** More than $100 million. **Number of employees nationwide:** 3,300.

PADGETT PRINTING CORPORATION

1313 North Industrial Boulevard, Dallas TX 75207. 214/742-4261. **Contact:** Personnel. **Description:** A printing company. **Common positions include:**

Accountant/Auditor; Bindery Worker; Customer Service Representative; Prepress Worker. **Benefits:** 401(k); Disability Coverage; Life Insurance; Medical Insurance; Profit Sharing; Savings Plan. **Corporate headquarters location:** This Location. **Number of employees at this location:** 110.

PANTONE
590 Commerce Boulevard, Carlstadt NJ 07072. 201/935-5500. **Contact:** Human Resources. **World Wide Web address:** http://www.pantone.com. **Description:** Produces color charts and color specification materials. **Common positions include:** Accountant; Assistant Manager; Blue-Collar Worker Supervisor; Chemist; Credit Manager; Customer Service Rep.; General Manager; Human Resources Manager; Manufacturer's/Wholesaler's Sales Rep.; Marketing Manager; Operations/Production Manager; Public Relations Specialist. **Educational backgrounds include:** Accounting; Chemistry; Computer Science; Finance; Marketing. **Benefits:** Dental Insurance; Life Insurance; Medical Insurance; Pension Plan; Savings Plan; Tuition Assistance. **Corporate headquarters location:** This Location.

PARADE PUBLICATIONS INC.
711 Third Avenue, New York NY 10017. 212/450-7000. **Fax:** 212/450-7200. **Contact:** Carol Unger, Employment Director. **Description:** Publishes weekly magazines, including *Parade* and *React.* **Common positions include:** Support Personnel. **Educational backgrounds include:** Liberal Arts. **Benefits:** 401(k); Dental Insurance; Disability Coverage; Employee Discounts; Life Insurance; Medical Insurance; Pension Plan; Tuition Assistance. **Corporate headquarters location:** This Location. **Listed on:** Privately held. **Number of employees at this location:** 200.

PARIS BUSINESS PRODUCTS, INC.
122 Kissel Road, Burlington NJ 08016. 609/387-7300. **Fax:** 609/387-0552. **Contact:** Vince Thompson, Personnel Manager. **World Wide Web address:** http://www.pariscorp.com. **Description:** Produces business forms. Founded in 1964. **Corporate headquarters location:** This Location.

THE PATRIOT LEDGER
P.O. Box 699159, Quincy MA 02269. 617/786-7246. **Physical address:** 400 Crown Colony Drive, Quincy MA. **Fax:** 617/786-7259. **Contact:** Cynthia Papil, Human Resources Manager. **Description:** Publishes a suburban daily newspaper, with a weekday circulation of more than 90,000. **NOTE:** Entry-level positions are offered. **Common positions include:** Customer Service Rep.; Editor; Editorial Assistant; Graphic Artist; Management Trainee; Reporter; Sales Rep.; Secretary; Typist/Word Processor. **Educational backgrounds include:** Accounting; Art/Design; Business Administration; Communications; Marketing; Public Relations. **Benefits:** 401(k); Dental Insurance; Disability Coverage; Employee Discounts; Life Insurance; Medical Insurance; Pension Plan; Profit Sharing; Public Transit Available; Tuition Assistance. **Special programs:** Internships; Apprenticeships. **Corporate headquarters location:** This Location. **Parent company:** Newspaper Media LLP. **Listed on:** Privately held. **Number of employees at this location:** 575.

PEARSON EDUCATION
1301 Sansome Street, San Francisco CA 94111. 415/402-2500. **Contact:** Human Resources. **World Wide Web address:** http://www.pearsoned.com. **Description:** This location primarily publishes higher education computer science and engineering materials. Overall, Pearson Education is one of the world's largest publishers and distributors of educational materials for use in elementary and high schools, universities, and businesses. **Common positions include:** Editor; Editorial Assistant; Graphic Designer; Managing Editor; Marketing Specialist; Software Engineer; Webmaster. **Educational backgrounds include:** Art/Design; Communications; Computer Science; Engineering; Liberal Arts. **Benefits:** 401(k); Dental Insurance; Disability Coverage; Employee Discounts; Life Insurance; Medical Insurance; Pension Plan; Public Transit Available; Savings Plan; Tuition Assistance. **Office hours:** Monday - Friday, 8:30 a.m. - 5:00 p.m. **Corporate headquarters location:** Reading MA. **Other U.S. locations:** Glenview IL; New York NY; White Plains NY. **Parent company:** Pearson plc.

PENGUIN PUTNAM INC.
375 Hudson Street, New York NY 10014. 212/366-2000. **Fax:** 212/366-2903. **Contact:** Human Resources. **E-mail address:** jobs@penguinputnam.com. **World Wide Web address:** http://www.penguinputnam.com. **Description:** One of the nation's largest publishers of trade fiction books. Penguin Putnam is a division of Penguin Group. **NOTE:** Entry-level positions are offered. **Common positions include:** Account Manager; Administrative Assistant; Budget Analyst; Computer Support Technician; Computer Technician; Desktop Publishing Specialist; Editor; Editorial Assistant; Financial Analyst; Graphic Artist; Graphic Designer; Help-Desk Technician; Human Resources Manager; Managing Editor; Marketing Manager; MIS Specialist; Operations Manager; Public Relations Specialist; Sales Manager; Sales Rep. **Educational backgrounds include:** Accounting; Art/Design; Business Administration; Communications; Economics; Liberal Arts; Marketing; Microsoft Office; Microsoft Word; Public Relations; Publishing; QuarkXPress; Spreadsheets. **Benefits:** 401(k); Casual Dress - Fridays; Dental Insurance; Employee Discounts; Life Insurance; Medical Insurance; Pension Plan; Tuition Assistance. **Special programs:** Internships. **Internship information:** Internship candidates should send resumes to the attention of Iris Milstein in Human Resources. **Corporate headquarters location:** This Location. **International locations:** Worldwide. **Parent company:** Pearson plc. is an international media group whose subsidiaries include Penguin Group.

PENTON MEDIA, INC.
1100 Superior Avenue, Cleveland OH 44114. 216/696-7000. **Contact:** Ms. Bobbi Navarra, Director of Human Resources. **World Wide Web address:** http://www.penton.com. **Description:** A diversified business media company. Products include 35 business publications, trade shows and conferences, Internet and electronic media, and direct marketing, research, and communications services. **Corporate headquarters location:** This Location. **Other U.S. locations:** Chatsworth CA.

PEORIA JOURNAL STAR, INC.
One News Plaza, Peoria IL 61643. 309/686-3000. **Contact:** Jamie Patton, Manager of Human Resources. **World Wide Web address:** http://www.pjstar.com. **Description:** Publishes a daily newspaper with a circulation of 72,000.

PERMANENT LABEL
801 Bloomfield Avenue, Clifton NJ 07012. 973/471-6617. **Contact:** Human Resources. **Description:** Engaged in decorating and printing labels for plastic products, primarily bottles. **Corporate headquarters location:** This Location.

PERRY JUDD'S INC.
P.O. Box 37, Waterloo WI 53594. 920/478-3551.
Fax: 920/478-1536. **Contact:** Human Resources.
Description: A printer of catalogs and magazines.
Common positions include: Accountant/Auditor;
Blue-Collar Worker Supervisor; Computer
Programmer; Cost Estimator; Customer Service
Representative; Designer; Draftsperson; Economist;
Electrical/Electronics Engineer; Human Resources
Manager; Industrial Engineer; Industrial Production
Manager; Manufacturer's/Wholesaler's Sales Rep.;
Operations Engineer; Quality Control Supervisor;
Registered Nurse; Services Sales Rep.; Systems
Analyst. **Educational backgrounds include:**
Business Administration; Communications;
Engineering; Finance; Marketing. **Benefits:** 401(k);
Dental Insurance; Disability Coverage; Employee
Discounts; Life Insurance; Medical Insurance;
Tuition Assistance. **Corporate headquarters
location:** This Location. **Other U.S. locations:**
Nationwide. **Number of employees at this
location:** 1,400.

PHILADELPHIA BUSINESS JOURNAL
400 Market Street, Suite 300, Philadelphia PA
19106. 215/238-1450. **Contact:** Personnel. **World
Wide Web address:** http://www.
bizjournals.com/philadelphia. **Description:** A
weekly business journal. **Common positions
include:** Accountant; Customer Service Manager;
Editorial Assistant; Event Planner; Marketing
Manager; Reporter; Sales Representative. **Number
of employees at this location:** 40.

PHONE DIRECTORIES COMPANY
P.O. Box 887, Provo UT 84603. 801/225-0801.
Contact: Human Resources. **World Wide Web
address:** http://www.phonedir.com. **Description:**
An independent publisher of telephone directories.
Corporate headquarters location: This Location.

PIPELINE PRESS, INC.
P.O. Box 9255, Chapel Hill NC 27515. 919/933-
6480. **Physical address:** 108 Main Street, Chapel
Hill NC. **Contact:** Human Resources. **E-mail
address:** info@pipelinepress.com. **World Wide
Web address:** http://www.pipelinepress.com.
Description: Publishes career guides and CD-
ROMS geared toward recent college graduates.
Corporate headquarters location: This Location.
Listed on: Privately held.

THE PLAIN DEALER
1801 Superior Avenue, Cleveland OH 44114.
216/999-5000. **Fax:** 216/999-6365. **Recorded
jobline:** 216/999-4366. **Contact:** Human
Resources. **World Wide Web address:** http://www.
pdnewmedia.com. **Description:** A newspaper
publisher. **NOTE:** Jobseekers interested in clerical
or secretarial positions may fill out an application
on Wednesday mornings between 9:00 a.m. and
11:00 a.m. Jobseekers interested in editorial
positions should call 216/999-4408 before applying.
Common positions include: Accountant/Auditor;
Commercial Artist; Computer Programmer;
Customer Service Rep.; Editor; Manufacturer's/
Wholesaler's Sales Rep.; Marketing Specialist;
Reporter; Systems Analyst. **Educational
backgrounds include:** Accounting; Art/Design;
Business Administration; Communications;
Computer Science; Journalism; Liberal Arts;
Marketing. **Benefits:** Dental Insurance; Disability
Coverage; Life Insurance; Pension Plan; Tuition
Assistance. **Special programs:** Internships.
Corporate headquarters location: This Location.

POLITICAL RESEARCH, INC.
16850 Dallas Parkway, Dallas TX 75248. 972/931-
8827. **Contact:** Personnel Director. **Description:**

Publishes reference services that offer information
on current state, federal, and international
governments. Primary customers include
educational institutions, libraries, government
offices, and businesses. **Common positions
include:** Accountant; Customer Service Rep.;
Marketing Specialist; Purchasing Agent/Manager;
Reporter; Researcher; Services Sales Rep.;
Technical Writer/Editor. **Educational backgrounds
include:** Accounting; Economics; Liberal Arts;
Marketing; Political Science. **Corporate
headquarters location:** This Location. **Number of
employees at this location:** 35.

THE POLK COMPANY
26955 Northwestern Highway, Southfield MI
48034. 248/728-7000. **Contact:** Human Resources.
World Wide Web address: http://www.polk.com.
Description: Publishers of city directories, book
directories, and statistical information. The Polk
Company also offers direct mail marketing and
specialty advertising services. **Common positions
include:** Payroll Clerk; Secretary; Stock Clerk;
Typist/Word Processor. **Benefits:** Dental Insurance;
Disability Coverage; Life Insurance; Medical
Insurance; Pension Plan; Tuition Assistance.
Corporate headquarters location: This Location.

PORTLAND MAGAZINE
578 Congress Street, Portland ME 04101. 207/775-
4339. **Fax:** 207/775-2334. **Contact:** Collin Sargent,
Publisher. **Description:** Publishes a monthly
periodical. **Common positions include:** Advertising
Clerk. **Educational backgrounds include:**
Art/Design. **Special programs:** Internships.
Corporate headquarters location: This Location.
Parent company: Sargent Publishing.

THE PROVIDENCE JOURNAL COMPANY
75 Fountain Street, Providence RI 02902-9985.
401/277-7000. **Contact:** Human Resources. **World
Wide Web address:** http://www.projo.com.
Description: Publishes *The Providence Journal*
with a daily circulation of 175,000 and *The Sunday
Providence Journal* with a circulation of 250,000.
Common positions include: Accountant/Auditor;
Customer Service Representative; Reporter.
Educational backgrounds include: Accounting;
Communications; Liberal Arts. **Benefits:** 401(k);
Dental Insurance; Disability Coverage; Life
Insurance; Medical Insurance; Pension Plan; Tuition
Assistance. **Special programs:** Internships.
Corporate headquarters location: This Location.
Other U.S. locations: Nationwide. **Subsidiaries
include:** Colony Communications; King
Broadcasting. **Listed on:** Privately held. **Number of
employees at this location:** 1,500.

THE PSYCHOLOGICAL CORPORATION
555 Academic Court, San Antonio TX 78204.
210/299-3616. **Fax:** 210/299-3662. **Recorded
jobline:** 210/299-2700. **Contact:** Lori Bowman,
Recruiter. **World Wide Web address:** http://www.
psychcorp.com. **Description:** One of the oldest and
largest commercial test publishers in the nation. The
company provides tests (e.g. the Stanford
Achievement Test Series, the Metropolitan
Achievement Tests, and Wechsler Intelligence
Scales for Children and Adults) and related services
to schools and colleges, clinicians and professional
organizations, businesses, and public entities. The
company's services include test research and
development, printing, marketing, distribution,
administration, and scoring. Psychological
Corporation has three divisions: an educational
measurement division; a psychological
measurement and communications division; and a
division that awards licenses and credentials.
NOTE: Entry-level positions and second and third

shifts are offered. **Common positions include:** Accountant; Administrative Assistant; Computer Operator; Computer Programmer; Customer Service Representative; Database Manager; Desktop Publishing Specialist; Editor; Financial Analyst; Graphic Designer; Human Resources Manager; Managing Editor; Market Research Analyst; Marketing Specialist; Occupational Therapist; Psychologist; Purchasing Agent/Manager; Research Assistant; Sales Rep.; Speech-Language Pathologist; Statistician; Systems Analyst; Teacher/Professor; Warehouse Manager. **Educational backgrounds include:** Business Administration; Computer Science; Psychology. **Benefits:** 401(k); Dental Insurance; Disability Coverage; Employee Discounts; Financial Planning Assistance; Flexible Schedule; Life Insurance; Medical Insurance; Pension Plan; Public Transit Available; Savings Plan; Tuition Assistance. **Corporate headquarters location:** This Location. **Annual sales/revenues:** More than $100 million.

PUBLISH PDQ
6700 France Avenue South, Suite 200, Edina MN 55435. 612/920-9928. **Contact:** Bob Larranaga, President. **Description:** Publishes financial and health articles for inclusion in newsletters. **Common positions include:** Accountant/Auditor; Advertising Clerk. **Educational backgrounds include:** Art/Design; Business Administration; Communications; Finance. **Benefits:** Disability Coverage; Life Insurance; Medical Insurance; Pension Plan; Profit Sharing; Tuition Assistance. **Corporate headquarters location:** This Location.

THE PUEBLO CHIEFTAIN
P.O. Box 4040, Pueblo CO 81003. 719/544-3520. **Contact:** Leonard Greggory, Executive Editor. **World Wide Web address:** http://www.chieftain.com. **Description:** Publishes *The Pueblo Chieftain*, a newspaper with a circulation of 51,000. **Corporate headquarters location:** This Location.

QUALEX, INC.
3404 North Duke Street, Durham NC 27704. 919/383-8535. **Contact:** Human Resources. **World Wide Web address:** http://www.onsitepictures.com. **Description:** Manufactures, markets, and services photofinishing equipment. Qualex also establishes one-hour photo labs. **Common positions include:** Accountant; Attorney; Credit Clerk and Authorizer; Graphic Artist; Industrial Engineer; Market Research Analyst; Paralegal; Payroll Clerk; Purchasing Agent/Manager; Secretary. **Benefits:** Dental Insurance; Disability Coverage; Employee Discounts; Life Insurance; Medical Insurance; Pension Plan; Profit Sharing; Savings Plan; Tuition Assistance. **Corporate headquarters location:** This Location. **Parent company:** Eastman Kodak. **Number of employees at this location:** 275. **Number of employees nationwide:** 7,500.

QUEBECOR PRINTING SAYERS INC.
9600 Manchester Road, St. Louis MO 63119. 314/968-5400. **Contact:** Personnel Director. **Description:** A commercial printing company. **Common positions include:** Accountant/Auditor; Customer Service Rep.; Department Manager; Manufacturer's/Wholesaler's Sales Rep.; Operations/Production Manager; Printing Press Operator; Purchasing Agent/Manager; Quality Control Supervisor. **Benefits:** 401(k); Dental Insurance; Disability Coverage; Life Insurance; Medical Insurance; Profit Sharing; Tuition Assistance. **Special programs:** Internships. **Other U.S. locations:** Nationwide. **Number of employees at this location:** 160.

QUEBECOR WORLD
BOOK SERVICES DIVISION
1133 County Street, Taunton MA 02780. 508/823-4581. **Fax:** 508/828-4356. **Contact:** Bruce Wynne, Director of Human Resources. **Description:** Prints books serving the education, technical, catalogue, and commercial markets. Quebecor World is one of the largest printers worldwide. **NOTE:** Entry-level positions and second and third shifts are offered. **Common positions include:** Accountant; Administrative Assistant; Blue-Collar Worker Supervisor; Controller; Customer Service Representative; Desktop Publishing Specialist; Electrician; General Manager; Human Resources Manager; Manufacturing Engineer; Mechanical Engineer; Operations Manager; Production Manager; Purchasing Agent/Manager; Quality Control Supervisor; Sales Representative; Secretary; Systems Manager. **Educational backgrounds include:** Accounting; Business Administration; Computer Science; Engineering; Finance; Graphic Design; MBA; Microsoft Office; Microsoft Word; Novell; Printing; Publishing; Spreadsheets. **Benefits:** 401(k); Casual Dress - Fridays; Dental Insurance; Disability Coverage; Financial Planning Assistance; Life Insurance; Medical Insurance; Pension Plan; Relocation Assistance; Tuition Assistance. **Special programs:** Co-ops. **Office hours:** Monday - Friday, 8:00 a.m. - 5:00 p.m. **Other U.S. locations:** Nationwide. **Listed on:** New York Stock Exchange. **Annual sales/revenues:** More than $100 million.

RAND McNALLY & COMPANY
8255 North Central Park Avenue, Skokie IL 60076. 847/329-8100. **Contact:** Human Resources. **World Wide Web address:** http://www.randmcnally.com. **Description:** A book, map, and road atlas publisher. **Corporate headquarters location:** This Location.

RANDOM HOUSE, INC.
1540 Broadway, New York NY 10036. 212/940-7894. **Fax:** 212/782-8450. **Contact:** Staffing Manager. **World Wide Web address:** http://www.randomhouse.com. **Description:** One of the largest trade publishers in the United States. Trade divisions include Villard Books, Vintage, Times Books, Pantheon/Schocken, and Knopf. Crown Publishing Group includes Crown Adult Books, Clarkson N. Potter, Fodor's Travel Guides, and Orion Books. Ballantine, Fawcett, Del Rey, and Ivy are mass-market imprints. **Common positions include:** Editor; Editorial Assistant; Financial Analyst; Graphic Artist; Graphic Designer; Managing Editor; Marketing Specialist; Public Relations Specialist; Sales Representative. **Educational backgrounds include:** Accounting; Art/Design; Business Administration; Communications; Economics; Finance; Liberal Arts; Marketing. **Benefits:** 401(k); Dental Insurance; Disability Coverage; Employee Discounts; Life Insurance; Medical Insurance; Pension Plan; Tuition Assistance. **Corporate headquarters location:** This Location. **Other U.S. locations:** Chicago IL; Westminster MD. **International locations:** Worldwide. **Parent company:** Bertelsmann, AG.

THE READER'S DIGEST ASSOCIATION
Reader's Digest Road, Pleasantville NY 10570. 914/238-1000. **Contact:** Human Resources. **World Wide Web address:** http://www.readersdigest.com. **Description:** A publisher of magazines, books, music, and video products. The flagship publication, *Reader's Digest*, is a monthly general interest magazine published in 17 languages with a circulation of approximately 100 million worldwide. Special interest magazines include *American Woodworker*, *The Family Handyman*, *New Choices*,

and *Walking*. **Common positions include:** Accountant; Budget Analyst; Computer Programmer; Customer Service Rep.; Designer; Economist; Editor; Financial Analyst; General Manager; Human Resources Manager; Management Analyst/Consultant; Public Relations Specialist; Purchasing Agent/Manager; Quality Control Supervisor; Statistician; Systems Analyst. **Educational backgrounds include:** Accounting; Art/Design; Business Administration; Communications; Computer Science; Economics; Finance; Liberal Arts; Marketing; Mathematics. **Benefits:** Dental Insurance; Disability Coverage; Employee Discounts; Life Insurance; Medical Insurance; Pension Plan; Profit Sharing; Tuition Assistance. **Special programs:** Internships. **Corporate headquarters location:** This Location. **Other U.S. locations:** New York NY. **Subsidiaries include:** Joshua Morris Publishing, Inc.; QSP, Inc. is a U.S. fundraising organization that work with schools and youth groups to raise money for educational enrichment programs. **Listed on:** New York Stock Exchange. **Number of employees at this location:** 1,500. **Number of employees nationwide:** 2,000.

REIMAN PUBLICATIONS
5400 South 60th Street, Greendale WI 53129. 414/423-0100. **Contact:** Human Resources. **World Wide Web address:** http://www.reimanpub.com. **Description:** Publishes 11 magazines focusing on country life, food, gardening, and nostalgia. Each magazine is supported solely by subscriptions.

RESEARCH INSTITUTE OF AMERICA GROUP
90 Fifth Avenue, New York NY 10011. 212/645-4800. **Contact:** Manager, Human Resources. **World Wide Web address:** http://www.riatax.com. **Description:** Publishers of tax and other professional services publications designed for attorneys, accountants, and the business community through print, electronic, and online media. **Common positions include:** Accountant; Administrator; Attorney; Computer Programmer; Credit Manager; Customer Service Representative; Department Manager; Editor; Editorial Assistant; Financial Analyst; Manufacturer's/Wholesaler's Sales Rep.; Marketing Specialist; MIS Specialist; Paralegal; Reporter; Software Engineer; Systems Analyst. **Educational backgrounds include:** Accounting; Computer Science; Finance; Law/Pre-Law; Liberal Arts. **Benefits:** Dental Insurance; Disability Coverage; EAP; Life Insurance; Medical Insurance; Pension Plan; Tuition Assistance; Vision Plan. **Corporate headquarters location:** This Location. **Other U.S. locations:** CA; DC; IL; NY; VA. **Parent company:** Thompson Corporation. **Number of employees at this location:** 300.

RICHMOND TIMES-DISPATCH
P.O. Box 85333, Richmond VA 23293. 804/649-6000. **Fax:** 804/649-6761. **Contact:** Human Resources. **World Wide Web address:** http://www.timesdispatch.com. **Description:** A newspaper publisher. **Corporate headquarters location:** This Location. **Parent company:** Media General. **Listed on:** American Stock Exchange. **Number of employees nationwide:** 7,300.

ROUTLEDGE INC.
29 West 35th Street, 10th Floor, New York NY 10001-2299. 212/216-7800. **Fax:** 212/564-7854. **Contact:** Mr. Andrey Harmaty, Human Resources. **World Wide Web address:** http://www.routledge-ny.com. **Description:** A progressive, international book and journal publisher focused on the humanities and social sciences. **Common positions include:** Editor; Editorial Assistant; Graphic Designer. **Educational backgrounds include:** Liberal Arts; Microsoft Word. **Special programs:** Internships. **Office hours:** Monday - Friday, 9:00 a.m. - 5:00 p.m. **President:** Colin Jones.

RUIDOSO NEWS
P.O. Box 128, Ruidoso NM 88355. 505/257-4001. **Physical address:** 104 Park Avenue, Ruidoso NM. **Contact:** Karen Payton, Office Manager. **Description:** A newspaper covering all of Lincoln County NM. *Ruidoso News* is printed twice a week.

WILLIAM H. SADLIER, INC.
9 Pine Street, New York NY 10005. 212/227-2120. **Contact:** Francis Marsh, Personnel Director. **World Wide Web address:** http://www.sadlier.com. **Description:** Publishes textbooks and related workbooks, teachers' guides, and other supplementary materials principally in the subject areas of religion, mathematics, language arts, and social studies. Founded in 1832. **Corporate headquarters location:** This Location.

SAGE PUBLICATIONS, INC.
2455 Teller Road, Thousand Oaks CA 91320. 805/499-0721. **Fax:** 805/375-1720. **Contact:** Stacy Entis, Director of Human Resources. **World Wide Web address:** http://www.sagepub.com. **Description:** Publishes academic journals and textbooks for graduate and upper-level college courses in various disciplines including political science and psychology. **NOTE:** Entry-level positions and second and third shifts are offered. **Common positions include:** Accountant; Administrative Assistant; Advertising Executive; Auditor; Claim Rep.; Clerical Supervisor; Computer Programmer; Computer Support Technician; Customer Service Rep.; Database Administrator; Database Manager; Desktop Publishing Specialist; Editor; Editorial Assistant; Graphic Artist; Graphic Designer; Marketing Manager; Network/Systems Administrator; Secretary. **Benefits:** 401(k); Casual Dress - Daily; Dental Insurance; Disability Coverage; Employee Discounts; Life Insurance; Medical Insurance; Profit Sharing; Tuition Assistance. **Special programs:** Internships; Training.

ST. MARTIN'S PRESS
HOLTZBRINCK PUBLISHERS
175 Fifth Avenue, New York NY 10010. 212/674-5151. **Contact:** Human Resources Manager. **World Wide Web address:** http://www.stmartins.com. **Description:** A national trade and scholarly book publisher. Founded in 1952. **NOTE:** Entry-level positions are offered. **Common positions include:** Accountant; Administrative Assistant; Advertising Clerk; Database Administrator; Editor; Editorial Assistant; Graphic Artist; Help-Desk Technician; Marketing Manager; Sales Manager; Technical Writer/Editor. **Benefits:** 401(k); Dental Insurance; Disability Coverage; Employee Discounts; Life Insurance; Medical Insurance; Tuition Assistance. **Corporate headquarters location:** This Location. **International locations:** Worldwide. **Subsidiaries include:** Farrar, Straus, & Giroux; Henry Holt and Company; St. Martin's Press; TOR Books. **Listed on:** Privately held. **CEO:** John Sargent. **Number of employees nationwide:** 930.

SALT LAKE TRIBUNE
143 South Main, Salt Lake City UT 84111. 801/237-2011. **Fax:** 801/521-9418. **Contact:** Personnel. **World Wide Web address:** http://www.sltrib.com. **Description:** Publishes an independent newspaper with a daily circulation of more than 126,000 and 162,000 on Sunday. Advertising, production, and circulation activities are carried out jointly with competitor *Deseret News* through

Newspaper Agency Corporation. **NOTE:** Part-time jobs are offered. **Common positions include:** Administrative Assistant; Computer Programmer; Editor; Editorial Assistant; Graphic Artist; Graphic Designer; Librarian; Managing Editor; Reporter; Typist/Word Processor. **Educational backgrounds include:** Microsoft Word; QuarkXPress. **Benefits:** 401(k); Dental Insurance; Disability Coverage; Life Insurance; Medical Insurance. **Special programs:** Internships; Summer Jobs. **Office hours:** Monday - Friday, 7:00 a.m. - 2:00 a.m. **Corporate headquarters location:** This Location. **Listed on:** Privately held.

HOWARD W. SAMS
2647 Waterfront Parkway East Drive, Indianapolis IN 46214-2041. 317/298-5611. **Toll-free phone:** 800/255-6989. **Fax:** 317/298-5604. **Contact:** Human Resources. **E-mail address:** hrhws@ hwsams.com. **World Wide Web address:** http://www.hwsams.com. **Description:** A technical publisher. **NOTE:** Second and third shifts are offered. **Common positions include:** Administrative Assistant; Graphic Artist; Human Resources Manager; Managing Editor; Marketing Specialist; Project Manager; Sales Engineer; Sales Manager; Sales Rep.; Systems Analyst; Technical Writer/Editor. **Educational backgrounds include:** Art/Design; Communications; Engineering; English; Liberal Arts; Marketing. **Benefits:** 401(k); Dental Insurance; Disability Coverage; Employee Discounts; Life Insurance; Medical Insurance; Tuition Assistance. **Corporate headquarters location:** This Location.

SANDHILLS PUBLISHING
P.O. Box 82545, Lincoln NE 68501-2545. 402/479-2181. **Fax:** 402/479-2195. **Contact:** Heather Thomas, Human Resources Consultant. **World Wide Web address:** http://www.sandhills.com. **Description:** An information processing company which publishes seven trade (advertising only) publications for buyers and sellers of heavy machinery, trucks, aircraft, and computer equipment. The company also produces two general interest computer magazines that cover personal computing fundamentals and computing options for small businesses. Sandhills Publishing also markets online services that offer instant access to nationwide dealers of personal computer parts and systems, as well as heavy equipment parts. Founded in 1978. **Common positions include:** Accountant; Advertising Manager; Computer Programmer; Customer Service Rep.; Designer; Editor; Electrical/ Electronics Engineer; Industrial Engineer; Manager of Information Systems; Manufacturer's/ Wholesaler's Sales Rep.; Mechanical Engineer; Sales and Marketing Manager; Software Engineer; Systems Analyst; Technical Writer/Editor. **Educational backgrounds include:** Accounting; Art/Design; Business Administration; Communications; Computer Science; Engineering; Marketing. **Benefits:** Dental Insurance; Disability Coverage; Employee Discounts; Medical Insurance; Savings Plan. **Special programs:** Internships. **Corporate headquarters location:** This Location. **Listed on:** Privately held. **Number of employees at this location:** 350.

W.B. SAUNDERS COMPANY
The Curtis Center, Independence Square West, Suite 300, Philadelphia PA 19106-3399. 215/238-7800. **Contact:** Human Resources. **Description:** The company publishes textbooks, clinical reference books, and periodicals for the medical, nursing, and health-related professions. Founded in 1888. **Common positions include:** Editor; Marketing Manager; Sales Representative. **Educational backgrounds include:** Art/Design; Business

Administration; English; Marketing; Science. **Benefits:** 401(k); Dental Insurance; Disability Coverage; Education Assistance; Employee Discounts; Life Insurance; Medical Insurance; Pension Plan; Savings Plan; Scholarship Program; Stock Option; Tuition Assistance. **Other U.S. locations:** St. Louis MO. **Parent company:** Harcourt General, Inc. (Chestnut Hill MA).

SCENIC ART
43176 Business Park Drive, Suite 103, Temecula CA 92590-3622. 909/587-6602. **Contact:** Mr. D.J. Sanders, Director of Operations. **Description:** Provides printing services. Founded in 1989. **Common positions include:** Account Rep.; Accountant; Graphic Artist; Graphic Designer; Operations Manager; Sales Executive. **Educational backgrounds include:** Art/Design. **Benefits:** Dental Insurance; Medical Insurance. **Corporate headquarters location:** This Location. **Annual sales/revenues:** Less than $5 million.

SCHAWK, INC.
1695 River Road, Des Plaines IL 60018. 847/827-9494. **Fax:** 847/827-8682. **Contact:** Personnel. **World Wide Web address:** http://www. schawk.com. **Description:** Provides prepress services for clients engaged in printing, publishing, advertising, and food and beverages packaging. **Common positions include:** Accountant/Auditor; Attorney; Computer Programmer; Credit Manager; Customer Service Representative; Systems Analyst. **Benefits:** 401(k); Dental Insurance; Disability Coverage; Life Insurance; Medical Insurance; Tuition Assistance. **Corporate headquarters location:** This Location. **Other U.S. locations:** GA; MI; MN; NJ; NY. **Listed on:** New York Stock Exchange. **Number of employees at this location:** 30. **Number of employees nationwide:** 830.

SCHLUMBERGER MALCO, INC.
9800 Reisterstown Road, Owings Mills MD 21117. 410/363-1600. **Fax:** 410/363-4336. **Contact:** Gaye Saller, Employment Coordinator. **World Wide Web address:** http://www.slb.com. **Description:** Manufactures a variety of plastic products including credit cards and advertising specialties. Schlumberger Malco also provides screen process printing, lithography, and embossing services. **Common positions include:** Blue-Collar Worker Supervisor; Buyer; Chemist; Systems Analyst; Tailor. **Benefits:** Dental Insurance; Disability Coverage; Life Insurance; Medical Insurance; Pension Plan; Profit Sharing; Tuition Assistance. **Corporate headquarters location:** This Location. **Parent company:** Schlumberger. **Listed on:** New York Stock Exchange. **Number of employees at this location:** 300.

SCHOLASTIC INC.
555 Broadway, New York NY 10012. 212/343-6912. **Fax:** 212/343-6934. **Contact:** Human Resources. **World Wide Web address:** http://www. scholastic.com. **Description:** Publishes and distributes children's books, classroom and professional magazines, software, CD-ROMs, and other educational materials. Products are generally distributed directly to both children and teachers in elementary and secondary schools. **Common positions include:** Accountant/Auditor; Editor; Software Engineer; Teacher/Professor; Technical Writer/Editor. **Educational backgrounds include:** Art/Design; Communications; English; Journalism; Marketing. **Benefits:** 401(k); Daycare Assistance; Dental Insurance; Disability Coverage; Employee Discounts; Life Insurance; Medical Insurance; Pension Plan; Profit Sharing; Savings Plan; Tuition Assistance. **Special programs:** Internships. **Corporate headquarters location:** This Location.

Other U.S. locations: Nationwide. **International locations:** Australia; Canada; France; Mexico; New Zealand; United Kingdom. **Listed on:** NASDAQ. **Number of employees at this location:** 1,400. **Number of employees nationwide:** 5,000.

SCHUMANN PRINTERS, INC.
701 South Main, Fall River WI 53932. 920/484-3348. **Fax:** 920/484-3661. **Contact:** Personnel. **Description:** Prints, binds, and mails publications and magazines. Founded in 1963. **NOTE:** Entry-level positions and second and third shifts are offered. **Common positions include:** Controller; Customer Service Rep.; Electrician; Graphic Artist; Internet Services Manager; Operations/Production Manager. **Benefits:** 401(k); Dental Insurance; Disability Coverage; Life Insurance; Medical Insurance; Pension Plan; Savings Plan. **Corporate headquarters location:** This Location. **Annual sales/revenues:** $21 - $50 million. **Number of employees at this location:** 170.

SCIENTIFIC AMERICAN, INC.
415 Madison Avenue, New York NY 10017. 212/754-0550. **Contact:** Personnel Department. **World Wide Web address:** http://www.sciam.com. **Description:** Publishes an international monthly magazine dealing with recent scientific research. **Corporate headquarters location:** This Location.

SCOTT FORESMAN
1900 East Lake Avenue, Glenview IL 60025. 847/729-3000. **Fax:** 847/486-3968. **Recorded jobline:** 847/657-3920. **Contact:** Angelina Bravo, Human Resources Generalist. **World Wide Web address:** http://www.scottforesman.com. **Description:** One of the largest educational publishers in the United States. The company publishes teaching materials including textbooks, computer software, video, and CD-ROM products for elementary and high school students in all major disciplines. **Common positions include:** Administrative Assistant; Administrative Manager; Advertising Clerk; Advertising Executive; Branch Manager; Budget Analyst; Cost Estimator; Database Manager; Editor; Editorial Assistant; Education Administrator; Financial Analyst; Graphic Artist; Graphic Designer; Human Resources Manager; Internet Services Manager; Librarian; Managing Editor; Market Research Analyst; Marketing Manager; Marketing Specialist; MIS Specialist; Multimedia Designer; Online Content Specialist; Operations/Production Manager; Project Manager; Purchasing Agent/Manager; Sales Manager; Sales Rep.; Secretary; Teacher/Professor; Typist/Word Processor; Webmaster. **Educational backgrounds include:** Accounting; Art/Design; Business Administration; Chemistry; Communications; Finance; Geology; Liberal Arts; Marketing; Mathematics; Physics. **Benefits:** 401(k); Dental Insurance; Disability Coverage; Employee Discounts; Financial Planning Assistance; Flexible Schedule; Life Insurance; Medical Insurance; Pension Plan; Profit Sharing; Public Transit Available; Reimbursement Accounts; Savings Plan; Tuition Assistance. **Special programs:** Internships. **Corporate headquarters location:** This Location. **Listed on:** Privately held. **Annual sales/revenues:** $21 - $50 million. **Number of employees at this location:** 500.

THE E.W. SCRIPPS COMPANY
312 Walnut Street, Suite 2800, Cincinnati OH 45202. 513/977-3000. **Contact:** Human Resources. **World Wide Web address:** http://www.scripps.com. **Description:** The E.W. Scripps Company operates 19 daily newspapers, nine large market television stations, cable systems, two television production companies, a 24-hour cable channel, the Home and Garden television network, and United Media, a licenser and syndicator of news features and comics. **Common positions include:** Accountant/Auditor; Human Resources Manager; Payroll Clerk; Secretary; Systems Analyst. **Benefits:** Dental Insurance; Disability Coverage; Life Insurance; Long-Term Care; Medical Insurance; Pension Plan; Savings Plan. **Corporate headquarters location:** This Location. **Other U.S. locations:** CA; IN; TN. **Listed on:** New York Stock Exchange. **Number of employees at this location:** 150. **Number of employees nationwide:** 8,200.

SEATTLE FILMWORKS
1260 16th Avenue West, Seattle WA 98119. 206/281-1390. **Fax:** 206/273-8373. **Contact:** Human Resources. **World Wide Web address:** http://www.filmworks.com. **Description:** Processes and sells 35mm film via mail-order. Seattle Filmworks has the capabilities to deliver customers' pictures over the Internet. **Common positions include:** Accountant/Auditor; Blue-Collar Worker Supervisor; Buyer; Chemist; Computer Programmer; Software Engineer; Systems Analyst. **Educational backgrounds include:** Marketing. **Benefits:** 401(k); Dental Insurance; Disability Coverage; Employee Discounts; Life Insurance; Medical Insurance; Profit Sharing; Tuition Assistance. **Corporate headquarters location:** This Location. **Operations at this facility include:** Administration; Manufacturing; Research and Development; Sales. **Number of employees at this location:** 400.

SEQUOIA PACIFIC SYSTEMS CORP.
1030 North Anderson Road, Exeter CA 93221. 559/592-2191. **Contact:** Director of Human Resources. **Description:** This location is the major manufacturing facility and corporate office. Overall, Sequoia Pacific Systems is engaged in the printing of labels, business forms, and election materials. **Corporate headquarters location:** This Location.

THE SHOPPING NEWS
4808 South Buckner Boulevard, Suite A, Dallas TX 75227. 214/388-3431. **Contact:** Personnel. **Description:** A weekly consumer publication with a circulation of 101,000. **Common positions include:** Advertising Clerk. **Educational backgrounds include:** Art/Design. **Benefits:** 401(k); Dental Insurance; Life Insurance; Medical Insurance. **Number of employees at this location:** 30.

SIERRA PUBLISHING GROUP, INC.
420 Central SW, Suite 104, Albuquerque NM 87102. 505/243-3444. **Contact:** Employment. **World Wide Web address:** http://www.nmbiz.com. **Description:** Publishes *The New Mexico Business Journal*, a monthly business journal with a circulation of 22,000 per month. Sierra Publishing Group is engaged in creating publications including visitor guides, directories, and magazines for a variety of organizations. Founded in 1976. **Corporate headquarters location:** This Location.

SIGNATURE PUBLISHING INC.
5000 Falls of Nuese Road, Suite 400, Raleigh NC 27609. 919/878-6151. **Fax:** 919/850-0873. **Contact:** Human Resources. **World Wide Web address:** http://www.sigpubs.com. **Description:** Publishes specialty magazines for the relocation, business, and health care industries. Publications include *City Facts* and *Newcomer Magazine*. **Corporate headquarters location:** This Location. **CEO:** Timothy Shaw.

SIMMONS-BOARDMAN PUBLISHING CORP.
345 Hudson Street, 12th Floor, New York NY 10014. 212/620-7200. **Contact:** Human Resources.

Description: Publishes trade magazines and books. **Common positions include:** Editor; Manufacturer's/Wholesaler's Sales Rep.; Operations/ Production Manager; Reporter; Technical Writer/ Editor. **Educational backgrounds include:** Art/ Design; Business Administration; Communications; Liberal Arts. **Benefits:** Life Insurance; Medical Insurance. **Special programs:** Internships. **Corporate headquarters location:** This Location.

SIMON & SCHUSTER, INC.
1230 Avenue of the Americas, New York NY 10020. 212/698-7000. **Fax:** 212/698-7640. **Contact:** Human Resources. **World Wide Web address:** http://www.simonandschuster.com. **Description:** Publishes consumer, educational, and professional books. **Common positions include:** Administrative Assistant; Designer; Editor; Marketing Specialist. **Educational backgrounds include:** Art/Design; Liberal Arts; Marketing. **Benefits:** 401(k); Dental Insurance; Disability Coverage; Employee Discounts; Life Insurance; Medical Insurance; Pension Plan; Savings Plan; Tuition Assistance. **Corporate headquarters location:** This Location. **Other U.S. locations:** CA; MA; NJ; OH. **Subsidiaries include:** Macmillan; Prentice-Hall. **Parent company:** Viacom. **Number of employees nationwide:** 4,000.

SOUTH COUNTY JOURNAL
P.O. Box 130, Kent WA 98035. 253/872-6600. **Contact:** Human Resources. **World Wide Web address:** http://www.southcountyjournal.com. **Description:** A newspaper. **Common positions include:** Advertising Clerk; Editor; Reporter. **Educational backgrounds include:** Art/Design; Liberal Arts. **Benefits:** 401(k); Dental Insurance; Life Insurance; Medical Insurance. **Special programs:** Internships. **Number of employees at this location:** 200.

THE SPORTING NEWS
10176 Corporate Square Drive, Suite 200, St. Louis MO 63132. 314/997-7111. **Contact:** Human Resources. **World Wide Web address:** http://www. sportingnews.com. **Description:** A national newspaper, covering a wide range of sports-related news. **NOTE:** For more information on professional hiring, please send resumes to 2 Park Avenue, New York NY 10016. **Corporate headquarters location:** This Location.

SPRINGER-VERLAG NEW YORK, INC.
175 Fifth Avenue, New York NY 10010. 212/460-1500. **Fax:** 212/614-3281. **Contact:** Human Resources. **World Wide Web address:** http://www. springer-ny.com. **Description:** An international publisher of scientific, technical, and medical books, journals, magazines, and electronic media. Founded in 1842. **NOTE:** Entry-level positions and part-time jobs are offered. **Common positions include:** Accountant; Administrative Assistant; Computer Programmer; Customer Service Representative; Editor; Editorial Assistant; Graphic Designer; Marketing Manager; Product Manager; Production Assistant; Production Editor; Sales Representative; Webmaster. **Educational backgrounds include:** Accounting; Art/Design; Biology; Business Administration; C/C++; Chemistry; Communications; Computer Science; Engineering; HTML; Liberal Arts; Marketing; Mathematics; Microsoft Office; Microsoft Word; Physics; Publishing; QuarkXPress; SQL; UNIX. **Benefits:** 401(k); Dental Insurance; Disability Coverage; Employee Discounts; Flexible Schedule; Life Insurance; Medical Insurance; Pension Plan; Tuition Assistance. **Special programs:** Internships; Co-ops. **Corporate headquarters location:** This Location. **Listed on:** Privately held.

STANDARD REGISTER COMPANY
P.O. Box 1167, Dayton OH 45401-1167. 937/443-1000. **Physical address:** 600 Albany Street, Dayton OH 45408. **Contact:** John Scarpelli, Vice President of Human Resources. **World Wide Web address:** http://www.stdreg.com. **Description:** Manufactures business forms, pressure sensitive products, and data systems forms for the business, health care, and other industries. The company also offers distribution, automation, management, and software products and services. **Common positions include:** Accountant/Auditor; Buyer; Chemical Engineer; Chemist; Computer Programmer; Draftsperson; Electrical/Electronics Engineer; Human Resources Manager; Industrial Engineer; Manufacturer's/ Wholesaler's Sales Rep.; Mechanical Engineer. **Educational backgrounds include:** Accounting; Business Administration; Chemistry; Computer Science; Engineering. **Benefits:** Disability Coverage; Life Insurance; Medical Insurance; Pension Plan; Savings Plan. **Corporate headquarters location:** This Location. **Other U.S. locations:** Nationwide. **Subsidiaries include:** Stanfast. **Listed on:** NASDAQ.

STANDARD-EXAMINER
P.O. Box 951, Ogden UT 84402. 801/625-4200. **Contact:** Jayne Dunn, Human Resources. **World Wide Web address:** http://www.standard.net. **Description:** Publishes an independent daily newspaper with a circulation of more than 60,000. **Corporate headquarters location:** This Location.

THE STATE NEWSPAPER
P.O. Box 1333, Columbia SC 29202. 803/771-8350. **Recorded jobline:** 803/771-8562. **Contact:** Holly Rogers, Human Resources Director. **World Wide Web address:** http://www.thestate.com. **Description:** Publishes *The State*, a daily newspaper with a weekday circulation exceeding 145,000. **Common positions include:** Advertising Clerk; Blue-Collar Worker Supervisor; Computer Programmer; Customer Service Representative; Editor; Manufacturer's/Wholesaler's Sales Rep.; Reporter. **Educational backgrounds include:** Communications. **Benefits:** Dental Insurance; Employee Discounts; Life Insurance; Medical Insurance; Pension Plan; Savings Plan; Tuition Assistance. **Corporate headquarters location:** This Location. **Parent company:** Knight-Ridder, Inc., a major newspaper publishing company, owns 28 dailies in 15 states, and three non-dailies. The company also publishes larger papers including the *Miami Herald, Philadelphia Inquirer, Philadelphia Daily News, Detroit Free Press,* and *San Jose Mercury News.* Knight-Ridder also has interests in the information distribution market through Business Information Services, with subsidiaries Knight-Ridder Information, Inc., Knight-Ridder Financial, and Technimetrics. Knight Ridder's online information retrieval serves the business, scientific, technology, medical and education communities in more than 100 countries. Knight-Ridder Financial provides real-time financial news and pricing information through primary products MoneyCenter, Digital Datafeed, ProfitCenter, and TradeCenter. Knight-Ridder also has interests in cable television and other businesses. Other interests include partial ownership of the Seattle Times Company, two paper mills, a newspaper advertising sales company, and SCI Holdings.

STEVENS GRAPHICS, INC.
713 R.D. Abernathy Boulevard SW, Atlanta GA 30310. 404/753-1121. **Contact:** Ricki Bryant, Staffing Supervisor. **Description:** A commercial printer of directories. **Common positions include:** Accountant; Blue-Collar Worker Supervisor; Computer Programmer; Customer Service Rep.;

Electrical/Electronics Engineer; Estimator; Financial Analyst; General Manager; Industrial Engineer; Management Trainee; Manufacturer's/Wholesaler's Sales Rep.; Marketing Specialist; Mechanical Engineer; Operations/Production Manager. **Educational backgrounds include:** Accounting; Business Administration; Computer Science; Engineering; Finance; Liberal Arts; Marketing. **Benefits:** 401(k); Dental Insurance; Disability Coverage; Employee Discounts; Life Insurance; Medical Insurance; Pension Plan; Savings Plan; Tuition Assistance. **Corporate headquarters location:** This Location. **Other U.S. locations:** Birmingham AL. **Parent company:** BellSouth.

STINEHOUR PRESS
853 Lancaster Road, Lunenburg VT 05906. 802/328-2507. **Contact:** Human Resources. **World Wide Web address:** http://www.stinehourpress.com. **Description:** A printing company whose products include art reproductions, museum catalogs, and posters. **Number of employees at this location:** 55.

SUN NEWS
256 West Las Cruces Avenue, Las Cruces NM 88005. 505/523-6464. **Contact:** Human Resources. **Description:** Publishes a daily newspaper with a circulation of more than 24,000. **Common positions include:** Accountant/Auditor; Administrative Worker/Clerk; Advertising Clerk; Credit Manager; Customer Service Representative; Editor; General Manager; Human Resources Manager; Librarian; Reporter; Services Sales Representative. **Educational backgrounds include:** Accounting; Art/Design; Communications. **Benefits:** 401(k); Dental Insurance; Disability Coverage; Life Insurance; Medical Insurance. **Special programs:** Internships. **Parent company:** Media News Group. **Operations at this facility include:** Sales. **Number of employees at this location:** 120.

SUTTLE PRESS, INC.
P.O. Box 370, Waunakee WI 53597. 608/849-1000. **Physical address:** 1000 Uniek Drive, Waunakee WI. **Fax:** 608/849-8264. **Contact:** John Berthelsen, President. **E-mail address:** john.berthelsen@suttlepress.com. **World Wide Web address:** http://www.suttlepress.com. **Description:** A commercial printing company providing flat-color and full-color printed products to a growing base of commercial customers. Founded in 1969. **NOTE:** Entry-level positions and second and third shifts are offered. **Common positions include:** Cost Estimator; Customer Service Rep.; Operations/Production Manager. **Educational backgrounds include:** Art/Design; Business Administration; Communications; Marketing. **Benefits:** 401(k); Dental Insurance; Disability Coverage; Life Insurance; Medical Insurance; Profit Sharing; Savings Plan; Tuition Assistance. **Corporate headquarters location:** This Location. **Parent company:** TDS (Telephone and Data Systems, Inc.). **Listed on:** American Stock Exchange. **Annual sales/revenues:** $5 - $10 million. **Number of employees at this location:** 75. **Number of employees nationwide:** 8,000.

TECHNICOMP, INC.
1111 Chester Avenue, Suite 750, Cleveland OH 44114. 216/687-1122. **Contact:** Human Resources. **World Wide Web address:** http://www.technicomp.com. **Description:** A publisher of training manuals, videotapes, and workbooks for use by industrial and commercial clients. **Common positions include:** Accountant/Auditor; Computer Programmer; Manufacturer's/Wholesaler's Sales Rep.; Systems Analyst; Technical Writer/Editor. **Educational backgrounds include:** Accounting;

Communications; Computer Science; Finance; Liberal Arts. **Benefits:** Dental Insurance; Disability Coverage; Life Insurance; Medical Insurance; Profit Sharing; Tuition Assistance. **Corporate headquarters location:** This Location.

TEXAS MONTHLY
P.O. Box 1569, Austin TX 78767. 512/320-6900. **Contact:** Gregory Curtis, Editor. **World Wide Web address:** http://www.texasmonthly.com. **Description:** *Texas Monthly* is a regional, general interest magazine. Articles range from health and travel to true crime. The magazine has a circulation of approximately 300,000. Founded in 1972. **Special programs:** Internships. **Corporate headquarters location:** This Location.

L.P. THEBAULT COMPANY
249 Pomeroy Road, P.O. Box 169, Parsippany NJ 07054. 973/884-1300. **Contact:** Human Resources. **Description:** One of the largest commercial printing companies in the United States. The company specializes in the print-buying market, with projects ranging from annual reports to promotional pieces. **Common positions include:** Management Trainee. **Educational backgrounds include:** Accounting; Business Administration; Finance. **Benefits:** 401(k); Dental Insurance; Disability Coverage; Employee Discounts; Life Insurance; Medical Insurance; Tuition Assistance. **Special programs:** Internships. **Corporate headquarters location:** This Location. **Other U.S. locations:** Detroit MI; New York NY. **Subsidiaries include:** LPT Express Graphics.

THIRD WORLD PRESS
P.O. Box 19730, Chicago IL 60619. 773/651-0700. **Contact:** Human Resources. **Description:** A publisher of fiction, nonfiction, and children's stories by African-American authors. Third World Press also publishes titles on audio and produces some videos. **Corporate headquarters location:** This Location.

THOMAS PUBLISHING COMPANY
5 Penn Plaza, New York NY 10017. 212/629-2100. **Contact:** Human Resources. **World Wide Web address:** http://www.thomaspublishing.com. **Description:** Publishes a directory of manufacturers, wholesalers, and distributors. **Common positions include:** Manufacturer's/Wholesaler's Sales Rep. **Educational backgrounds include:** Communications; Marketing. **Corporate headquarters location:** This Location.

TIME WARNER, INC.
75 Rockefeller Plaza, New York NY 10019. 212/484-8000. **Contact:** Human Resources. **World Wide Web address:** http://www.timewarner.com. **Description:** Publishes and distributes books and magazines including the weekly *Time* magazine. Time Warner also produces, distributes, licenses, and publishes recorded music; owns and administers music copyrights; produces, finances, and distributes motion pictures and television programming; distributes videocassettes; produces and distributes pay television and cable programming; and operates and manages cable television systems. **NOTE:** In January 2000, America Online, Inc. and Time Warner, Inc. announced plans to merge. The new company will be named AOL Time Warner Inc. Also in January 2000, EMI Group PLC and Time Warner, Inc. announced plans to merge their music businesses. Companies affected by this merger will be named Warner EMI Music. Please contact this location for more information. **Corporate headquarters location:** This Location. **Number of employees worldwide:** 38,100.

TIMES PUBLISHING COMPANY, INC.
P.O. Box 1121, St. Petersburg FL 33731. 727/893-8426. **Fax:** 727/893-8185. **Contact:** Human Resources. **World Wide Web address:** http://www.sptimes.com. **Description:** Publishes the *St. Petersburg Times* newspaper. **Common positions include:** Accountant/Auditor; Administrative Manager; Advertising Clerk; Blue-Collar Worker Supervisor; Budget Analyst; Buyer; Clerical Supervisor; Computer Programmer; Counselor; Credit Manager; Customer Service Manager; Editor; Electrical/Electronics Engineer; Electrician; Human Service Worker; Librarian; Library Technician; Management Analyst/Consultant; Management Trainee; Manufacturer's/Wholesaler's Sales Rep.; Operations/Production Manager; Quality Control Supervisor; Reporter; Securities Sales Representative; Services Sales Representative; Software Engineer; Systems Analyst; Technical Writer/Editor; Transportation/Traffic Specialist; Wholesale and Retail Buyer. **Educational backgrounds include:** Accounting; Business Administration; Communications; Computer Science; Finance; Liberal Arts; Marketing. **Benefits:** 401(k); Dental Insurance; Disability Coverage; Life Insurance; Medical Insurance; Pension Plan; Profit Sharing; Savings Plan; Tuition Assistance. **Corporate headquarters location:** This Location.

THE TIMES-HERALD RECORD
40 Mulberry Street, P.O. Box 2046, Middletown NY 10940. 914/346-3112. **Contact:** Patrick J. Clark, SPHR/Human Resources Director. **World Wide Web address:** http://www.th-record.com. **Description:** Publishes a daily newspaper, with a circulation of more than 80,000. **Common positions include:** Advertising Clerk; Customer Service Rep.; Editor; Human Resources Manager; Manufacturer's/Wholesaler's Sales Rep.; Operations/Production Manager; Reporter. **Educational backgrounds include:** Accounting; Art/Design; Communications; Computer Science; Journalism; Liberal Arts. **Benefits:** 401(k); Dental Insurance; Disability Coverage; Life Insurance; Medical Insurance; Pension Plan; Tuition Assistance. **Corporate headquarters location:** Campbell NY. **Other area locations:** New Paltz NY; Newburgh NY; Port Jervis NY. **Parent company:** Ottaway Newspapers

TOPFLIGHT CORPORATION
P.O. Box 2847, Glen Rock PA 17405. 717/227-5400. **Contact:** Human Resource Manager. **World Wide Web address:** http://www.topflight.com. **Description:** Manufactures pressure-sensitive labels. **Common positions include:** Customer Service Representative; Manufacturer's/Wholesaler's Sales Rep. **Benefits:** 401(k); Disability Coverage; Medical Insurance; Pension Plan; Profit Sharing; Tuition Assistance. **Corporate headquarters location:** This Location. **Subsidiaries include:** Adhesives Research. **Listed on:** Privately held. **Number of employees at this location:** 220. **Number of employees nationwide:** 420.

TOWER PUBLISHING COMPANY
588 Saco Road, Standish ME 04084. 207/642-5400. **Toll-free phone:** 800/969-8693. **Fax:** 207/642-5463. **Contact:** Michael Lyons, Publisher. **World Wide Web address:** http://www.towerpublishingcompany.com. **Description:** A publishing company specializing in business and legal directories for northern New England. Founded in 1820. **Common positions include:** Accountant/Auditor; Administrative Assistant; Managing Editor; Sales Representative. **Educational backgrounds include:** Business Administration; Marketing. **Benefits:** Medical Insurance; Profit Sharing. **Annual sales/revenues:** Less than $5 million.

THE TRIBUNE COMPANY
435 North Michigan Avenue, Chicago IL 60611. 312/222-9100. **Contact:** Human Resources. **World Wide Web address:** http://www.tribune.com. **Description:** Publishes daily newspapers including *The Baltimore Sun, The Chicago Tribune, The Fort Lauderdale Sun-Sentinel, The Los Angeles Times, The Hartford Courant, The Orlando Sentinel,* and *The Daily Press.* The company also owns eight independent TV stations in Illinois, New York, Colorado, Pennsylvania, California, Massachusetts, Georgia, and Louisiana; six radio stations in Illinois, New York, Colorado, and California; and a professional baseball team. **Corporate headquarters location:** This Location. **Subsidiaries include:** Contemporary Books; Independent Network News; The Wright Group; Tribune Entertainment Company. **Listed on:** New York Stock Exchange.

TUTTLE LAW PRINT, INC.
P.O. Drawer 110, Rutland VT 05702. 802/773-9171. **Physical address:** Quality Lane, Rutland VT 05701. **Contact:** Human Resources. **Description:** Provides printed stationery and related products for law and other professional offices. **Number of employees at this location:** 60.

TYNDALE HOUSE PUBLISHERS, INC.
P.O. Box 80, Wheaton IL 60189. 630/668-8300. **Contact:** Human Resources. **World Wide Web address:** http://www.tyndale.com. **Description:** Publishes *The Living Bible,* as well as other religious products including books, movies, calendars, audio books, and Bible reference products. Founded in 1962. **Common positions include:** Buyer; Commercial Artist; Customer Service Representative; Department Manager; Editor; Manufacturer's/Wholesaler's Sales Rep.; Marketing Specialist; Operations/Production Manager; Purchasing Agent/Manager. **Educational backgrounds include:** Art/Design; Business Administration; Communications; English; Liberal Arts; Marketing. **Benefits:** 401(k); Dental Insurance; Disability Coverage; Employee Discounts; Life Insurance; Medical Insurance; Profit Sharing; Tuition Assistance. **Office hours:** Monday - Friday, 8:00 a.m. - 4:30 p.m. **Corporate headquarters location:** This Location.

U.S. NEWS & WORLD REPORT
1050 Thomas Jefferson Street NW, Washington DC 20007. 202/955-2000. **Contact:** Human Resources. **Description:** A news magazine with more than 20 million readers. **NOTE:** Hiring is done out of the New York office. Please direct resumes to Ellen Weiss, Employment Manager, Human Resources, 450 West 33rd Street, New York NY 10001. 212/210-1864. **Common positions include:** Accountant/Auditor; Administrative Manager; Computer Operator; Computer Programmer; Market Research Analyst; Reporter; Services Sales Representative; Systems Analyst. **Educational backgrounds include:** Accounting; Business Administration; Computer Science; Finance; Liberal Arts; Marketing; Mathematics. **Benefits:** 401(k); Dental Insurance; Disability Coverage; Employee Discounts; Life Insurance; Medical Insurance; Savings Plan; Spending Account; Tuition Assistance. **Special programs:** Internships. **Corporate headquarters location:** This Location. **Other U.S. locations:** New York NY.

UNIMAC GRAPHICS
350 Michele Place, Carlstadt NJ 07072. 201/372-1000. **Contact:** Kathy Green, Payroll/Personnel. **Description:** Provides a full range of commercial printing services.

UNION LEADER

P.O. Box 9555, Manchester NH 03108. 603/668-4321. **Physical address:** 100 William Loeb Drive, Manchester NH. **Fax:** 603/668-8920. **Contact:** Sharon Ciechon, Director of Human Resources. **World Wide Web address:** http://www.theunionleader.com. **Description:** Publishes a daily newspaper with a weekday circulation of approximately 85,000 and 102,000 on Sundays. **Common positions include:** Account Rep.; Computer Programmer; Customer Service Rep.; Editor; Reporter. **Corporate headquarters location:** This Location. **Number of employees at this location:** 365.

UNISOURCE

P.O. Box 649, Exton PA 19341-0649. 610/280-5700. **Contact:** Human Resources. **Description:** Markets and distributes printing and imaging papers, packaging systems, and maintenance supplies. **Corporate headquarters location:** This Location. **Annual sales/revenues:** More than $100 million.

THE UNITED METHODIST PUBLISHING HOUSE

201 Eighth Avenue South, P.O. Box 801, Nashville TN 37202. 615/749-6535. **Fax:** 615/749-6366. **Contact:** Cindy Knight, Employment Manager. **World Wide Web address:** http://www.umph.org. **Description:** As The United Methodist Church's official publisher, the publishing house develops, produces, and distributes books for home, church, and official denominational church school curriculum. Overall, the company is one of the oldest and largest general agencies of The United Methodist Church. **Common positions include:** Accountant; Advertising Clerk; Cashier; Computer Operator; Computer Programmer; Customer Service Representative; Editor; Employment Interviewer; Management Trainee; Market Research Analyst; Receptionist; Secretary; Systems Analyst; Typist/Word Processor. **Benefits:** Dental Insurance; Disability Coverage; Employee Discounts; Life Insurance; Medical Insurance; Pension Plan; Savings Plan; Tuition Assistance. **Special programs:** Internships. **Corporate headquarters location:** This Location. **Number of employees at this location:** 850. **Number of employees nationwide:** 1,200.

UNITED PRESS INTERNATIONAL

1510 H Street NW, Washington DC 20005. 202/898-8200. **Contact:** Director of Personnel. **World Wide Web address:** http://www.upi.com. **Description:** One of the world's largest independent news gathering organizations with news bureaus located worldwide. **Common positions include:** Editor; Radio/TV Announcer/Broadcaster; Reporter. **Educational backgrounds include:** Journalism. **Benefits:** 401(k); Dental Insurance; Medical Insurance. **Special programs:** Internships. **Corporate headquarters location:** This Location. **Other U.S. locations:** Miami FL; Chicago IL; New York NY; Dallas TX.

UNIVERSITY FIELDING PRINTERS

2512 Paul W. Bryant Drive, Tuscaloosa AL 35401. 205/752-6184. **Contact:** Ray Woodbright, Owner. **Description:** A printing and publishing firm. **Common positions include:** Accountant/Auditor; Blue-Collar Worker Supervisor; Buyer; Commercial Artist; General Manager; Management Trainee; Purchasing Agent/Manager. **Educational backgrounds include:** Business Administration; Marketing; Mathematics. **Benefits:** Medical Insurance. **Corporate headquarters location:** This Location.

UNIVERSITY OF NORTH CAROLINA PRESS

P.O. Box 2288, Chapel Hill NC 27515. 919/966-3561. **Physical address:** 116 South Boundary Street, Chapel Hill NC. **Toll-free phone:** 800/848-6224. **Fax:** 919/966-3829. **Contact:** Human Resources. **E-mail address:** uncpress@unc.edu. **World Wide Web address:** http://uncpress.unc.edu. **Description:** Publishes nonfiction history, sociology, and related books as well as journals. **Corporate headquarters location:** This Location.

VALASSIS COMMUNICATIONS, INC.

19975 Victor Parkway, Livonia MI 48152. 734/591-3000. **Fax:** 734/591-4994. **Contact:** Corporate Human Resources. **World Wide Web address:** http://www.valassis.com. **Description:** A printer and publisher of four-color coupon newspaper inserts. The company also arranges the publication of promotions and offers design, printing, and distribution of promotional items including calendars, posters, and die-cuts. Founded in 1972. **Common positions include:** Account Manager; Account Representative; Administrative Assistant; Graphic Designer; MIS Specialist; Public Relations Specialist; Secretary; Video Production Coordinator; Webmaster. **Educational backgrounds include:** Business Administration; Computer Science; Liberal Arts; Marketing. **Benefits:** 401(k); Daycare Assistance; Dental Insurance; Disability Coverage; Life Insurance; Medical Insurance; Pension Plan; Profit Sharing; Tuition Assistance. **Special programs:** Internships. **Corporate headquarters location:** This Location. **Other U.S. locations:** Nationwide. **International locations:** Canada; France. **Listed on:** New York Stock Exchange.

VALENCIA COUNTY NEWS-BULLETIN

P.O. Box 25, Belen NM 87002. 505/864-4472. **Physical address:** 1837 Sosimo Padilla Boulevard, Belen NM. **Fax:** 505/864-3549. **Contact:** Chris Baker, Publisher. **E-mail address:** newsbltn@aol.com. **World Wide Web address:** http://www.news-bulletin.com. **Description:** A publisher of the twice-weekly newspaper *Valencia County News-Bulletin*, with a circulation of 23,000 on Wednesdays and Saturdays. This location also hires seasonally. Founded in 1911. **NOTE:** Entry-level positions, part-time jobs, and second and third shifts are offered. **Common positions include:** Account Manager; Account Representative; Accountant; Administrative Assistant; Advertising Clerk; Advertising Executive; Bank Officer/Manager; Controller; Editor; Editorial Assistant; Graphic Artist; Graphic Designer; Internet Services Manager; Managing Editor; Reporter; Sales Manager; Sales Representative; Secretary; Web Advertising Specialist; Webmaster; Website Developer. **Educational backgrounds include:** Bachelor of Arts; Marketing; Public Relations. **Benefits:** 401(k); Casual Dress - Fridays; Dental Insurance; Disability Coverage; Employee Discounts; Flexible Schedule; Life Insurance; Medical Insurance; Pension Plan; Profit Sharing; Relocation Assistance; Sick Days (6 - 10); Tuition Assistance; Vacation Days (6 - 10). **Special programs:** Internships; Apprenticeships; Training; Co-ops; Summer Jobs. **Office hours:** Monday - Friday, 8:00 a.m. - 5:00 p.m., Saturday 8:00 a.m. - 12:00 p.m. **Corporate headquarters location:** Lawrence KS. **Other area locations:** Ruidoso NM; Socorro NM. **Other U.S. locations:** Payson AZ; Craig CO; Steamboat Springs CO. **International locations:** Worldwide. **Parent company:** WorldWest. **Listed on:** Privately held. **Annual sales/revenues:** $5 - $10 million. **Number of employees at this location:** 40. **Number of employees nationwide:** 300.

WNC BUSINESS JOURNAL

P.O. Box 8204, Asheville NC 28814. 828/298-1322. **Fax:** 828/298-1312. **Contact:** Stephen Nason, Editor. **Description:** A monthly publication covering western North Carolina business news. The company also publishes *Today's Hospital Gift Shop*, the official newsletter of hospital gift shops. **Common positions include:** Accountant/Auditor; Advertising Manager; Editor; Operations/ Production Manager; Reporter. **Educational backgrounds include:** Accounting; Advertising; Art/Design; Communications; Economics; Finance; Liberal Arts; Marketing; Sales. **Corporate headquarters location:** This Location.

J. WESTON WALCH PUBLISHER

P.O. Box 658, Portland ME 04104-0658. 207/772-2846. **Physical address:** 321 Valley Street, Portland ME. **Contact:** Managing Editor. **World Wide Web address:** http://www.walch.com. **Description:** A book publishing company specializing in supplementary educational materials for middle schools, high schools, and adult learning schools.

WALLACE COMMERCIAL PRINTING

1718 Peachtree Street, Suite 1062, Atlanta GA 30309. 404/872-1202. **Contact:** Employment. **Description:** A graphic communications company offering services including corporate, commercial, and financial printing; and direct response, reprographic, and educational printing services. **Corporate headquarters location:** This Location. **Listed on:** NASDAQ. **Number of employees nationwide:** 2,800.

WARNER BROTHERS PUBLICATIONS

15800 NW 48th Avenue, Miami FL 33014. 305/620-1500. **Contact:** Marie Zaret, Director of Human Resources. **Description:** A printer and publisher of sheet music. **NOTE:** In January 2000, America Online, Inc. and Time Warner, Inc. announced plans to merge. The new company will be named AOL Time Warner Inc. Please contact this location for more information. **Common positions include:** Accountant/Auditor; Credit Manager; Customer Service Representative; Department Manager; Editor; Musician/Musical Arranger; Operations/Production Manager; Services Sales Representative. **Educational backgrounds include:** Accounting; Art/Design; Business Administration; Computer Science; Finance; Liberal Arts; Marketing; Music. **Benefits:** Dental Insurance; Disability Coverage; Employee Discounts; Life Insurance; Medical Insurance; Pension Plan; Savings Plan; Tuition Assistance. **Special programs:** Internships. **Corporate headquarters location:** This Location. **Parent company:** Time Warner.

THE WASHINGTON POST COMPANY

1150 15th Street NW, Washington DC 20071. 202/334-7174. **Contact:** Director of Human Resources. **World Wide Web address:** http://www. washpostco.com. **Description:** Publishes *The Washington Post*; *The Herald* (Everett WA); *Gazette* (MD); and *Newsweek*. The company also owns cable television stations as well as television broadcasting stations in Detroit, Hartford, Houston, Jacksonville, Miami, and San Antonio. **Benefits:** Adoption Assistance; Daycare Assistance; Dental Insurance; Disability Coverage; Employee Discounts; Legal Services; Life Insurance; Medical Insurance; Pension Plan; Savings Plan; Tuition Assistance. **Corporate headquarters location:** This Location. **Subsidiaries include:** Stanley H. Kaplan operates a regulatory computerized database. **Listed on:** New York Stock Exchange. **Number of employees nationwide:** 6,800.

THE WASHINGTON TIMES

3400 New York Avenue NE, Washington DC 20002. 202/636-3000. **Contact:** Human Resources Department. **World Wide Web address:** http://www.washtimes.com. **Description:** A daily metropolitan newspaper. **Common positions include:** Accountant; Administrative Manager; Advertising Clerk; Computer Programmer; Customer Service Rep.; Editor; Electrician; Employment Interviewer; Graphic Artist; Librarian; Library Technician; Mechanical Engineer; Paralegal; Payroll Clerk; Postal Clerk/Mail Carrier; Printing Press Operator; Receptionist; Reporter; Secretary; Services Sales Rep.; Typist/Word Processor. **Educational backgrounds include:** Accounting; Art/Design; Business Administration; Communications; Computer Science; Economics; Engineering; Finance; Liberal Arts; Marketing. **Benefits:** 401(k); Dental Insurance; Free Parking; Life Insurance; Medical Insurance; Vision Insurance. **Special programs:** Internships. **Corporate headquarters location:** This Location. **Other U.S. locations:** Lanham MD.

WAVERLY, INC.

351 West Camden Street, Baltimore MD 21201. 410/528-4065. **Contact:** Rosalind Grant, Human Resources. **Description:** Publishes and prints medical and scientific books, journals, and periodicals that are marketed and sold worldwide. Waverly's primary customers are medical and scientific practitioners, libraries, and universities. **Common positions include:** Accountant; Computer Programmer; Customer Service Rep.; Editor; Financial Analyst; Manufacturer's/Wholesaler's Sales Rep.; Marketing Specialist; Operations/ Production Manager; Purchasing Agent/Manager; Systems Analyst; Technical Writer/Editor. **Educational backgrounds include:** Accounting; Finance. **Benefits:** 401(k); Dental Insurance; Disability Coverage; Employee Discounts; Life Insurance; Medical Insurance; Pension Plan; Savings Plan; Tuition Assistance. **Corporate headquarters location:** This Location. **Other U.S. locations:** Easton MD; Malvern PA. **Number of employees at this location:** 400. **Number of employees nationwide:** 1,100.

WIDEN ENTERPRISES

2614 Industrial Drive, Madison WI 53713. 608/222-1296. **Toll-free phone:** 800/444-2828. **Fax:** 608/222-8346. **Contact:** Richard Junas, Human Resources Director. **World Wide Web address:** http://www.widen.com. **Description:** A graphic communications firm which provides prepress, digital printing, and information management services for the packaging, retail, catalog, and specialty markets. Founded in 1948. **Common positions include:** Graphic Artist; MIS Specialist; Sales Rep.; Software Engineer. **Educational backgrounds include:** Art/Design; Computer Science. **Benefits:** 401(k); Dental Insurance; Disability Coverage; Life Insurance; Medical Insurance. **Corporate headquarters location:** This Location.

JOHN WILEY & SONS, INC.

605 Third Avenue, New York NY 10158. 212/850-6000. **Fax:** 212/850-6088. **Contact:** Lynne Salisbury, Director of Staffing and Employee Relations. **World Wide Web address:** http://www. wiley.com. **Description:** An international publishing house. Wiley publishes in four categories: Educational, Professional, Trade, and Scientific, Technical, and Medical (STM). In Educational, Wiley publishes textbooks and instructional packages for undergraduate and graduate students worldwide. Publishing programs focus on the physical and life sciences,

mathematics, engineering, and accounting, with a growing business in economics, finance, business, MIS/CIS, and foreign languages. In Professional, Wiley publishes books and subscription products for lawyers, architects, accountants, engineers, and other professionals. In Trade, Wiley publishes nonfiction books in areas such as business, computers, science, and general interest. In STM, Wiley publishes approximately 260 scholarly and professional journals, as well as encyclopedias, other major reference works, and books for the research and academic communities. Major subject areas include chemistry, the life sciences, and technology. **NOTE:** Entry-level positions are offered. **Common positions include:** Account Rep.; Administrative Assistant; Applications Engineer; AS400 Programmer Analyst; Computer Programmer; Computer Support Technician; Customer Service Rep.; Database Administrator; Database Manager; Editor; Editorial Assistant; Graphic Artist; Internet Services Manager; Managing Editor; Market Research Analyst; Marketing Manager; MIS Specialist; Multimedia Designer; Network/Systems Administrator; Production Manager; Public Relations Specialist; Systems Analyst; Systems Manager; Technical Writer/Editor; Webmaster. **Educational backgrounds include:** Communications; HTML; Internet; Liberal Arts; Lotus; Marketing; Microsoft Word; Novell; Public Relations. **Benefits:** 401(k); Casual Dress - Fridays; Dental Insurance; Disability Coverage; Employee Discounts; Life Insurance; Medical Insurance; Pension Plan; Savings Plan; Sick Days (6 - 10); Tuition Assistance. **Special programs:** Internships. **Office hours:** Monday - Friday, 8:30 a.m. - 4:30 p.m. **Corporate headquarters location:** This Location. **Other U.S. locations:** Colorado Springs CO; Somerset NJ. **International locations:** Asia; Australia; Canada; Europe. **Listed on:** New York Stock Exchange. **Stock exchange symbol:** JWB. **Number of employees at this location:** 800.

WILLIAMSON PRINTING CORPORATION
6700 Denton Drive, Dallas TX 75235. 214/904-2670. **Toll-free phone:** 800/843-5423. **Fax:** 214/352-5698. **Recorded jobline:** 214/904-2603. **Contact:** Erica Sinch, Human Resources Administrator. **E-mail address:** jobs@twpc.com. **World Wide Web address:** http://www.twpc.com. **Description:** A commercial printing company. **NOTE:** Entry-level positions and second and third shifts are offered. **Common positions include:** Cost Estimator; Customer Service Rep.; Graphic Artist; Sales Rep. **Educational backgrounds include:** Art/Design. **Benefits:** 401(k); Dental Insurance; Life Insurance; Medical Insurance; Tuition Assistance. **Special programs:** Summer Jobs. **Corporate headquarters location:** This Location. **Subsidiaries include:** Classic Color Corporation; Image Express; The Fulfillment Center. **Listed on:** Privately held. **CEO:** Jerry Williamson.

WINSTON-SALEM JOURNAL
P.O. Box 3159, Winston-Salem NC 27102. 336/727-7211. **Physical address:** 418 North Marshall Street, Winston-Salem NC. **Toll-free phone:** 800/642-0925. **Fax:** 336/727-4096. **Recorded jobline:** 888/562-2864. **Contact:** Randy Noftle, Director of Human Resources. **E-mail address:** rnoftle@w-s-journal.com. **World Wide Web address:** http://www.journalnow.com. **Description:** A daily newspaper. **NOTE:** Entry-level positions, part-time jobs, and second and third shifts are offered. **Common positions include:** Account Rep.; Computer Operator; Computer Technician; Desktop Publishing Specialist; Editor; Editorial Assistant; Graphic Artist; Librarian; Managing Editor; MIS Specialist; Network/Systems

Administrator; Reporter; Typist/Word Processor. **Educational backgrounds include:** Accounting; Art/Design; Business Administration; Communications; Computer Science; HTML; Liberal Arts; Marketing; Microsoft Word; QuarkXPress; Spreadsheets. **Benefits:** 401(k); Casual Dress - Fridays; Dental Insurance; Disability Coverage; Employee Discounts; Financial Planning Assistance; Life Insurance; Medical Insurance; Pension Plan; Sick Days (1 - 5); Tuition Assistance; Vacation Days (10 - 20). **Special programs:** Internships. **Corporate headquarters location:** Richmond VA. **Other U.S. locations:** AL; FL; GA; KY; LA; MS; NJ; SC; TN; VA. **Parent company:** Media General, Inc. **Listed on:** American Stock Exchange. **Publisher:** Jon Witherspoon. **Annual sales/revenues:** $51 - $100 million. **Number of employees at this location:** 480. **Number of employees nationwide:** 9,000.

WISCONSIN COLOR PRESS INC.
5400 West Good Hope Road, Milwaukee WI 53223. 414/353-5400. **Fax:** 414/353-0829. **Contact:** Bruce Davie, Director of Personnel. **Description:** A commercial printer. Wisconsin Color Press uses four color web offset printing presses to print a wide variety of publications including upscale magazines, business-to-business catalogs, and newsstand publications. **Common positions include:** Customer Service Rep.; Industrial Engineer. **Educational backgrounds include:** Art/Design; Graphic Design; Industrial Technology. **Benefits:** 401(k); Dental Insurance; Disability Coverage; Employee Discounts; Life Insurance; Medical Insurance; Savings Plan; Tuition Assistance. **Corporate headquarters location:** This Location.

WOODWARD COMMUNICATIONS, INC.
P.O. Box 688, Dubuque IA 52004-0688. 319/588-5720. **Contact:** Betty Farrey, Human Resources. **World Wide Web address:** http://www.wcinet.com. **Description:** Operates a daily newspaper, radio stations, weekly publications, specialty publications, and offers Internet services. **Common positions include:** Accountant/Auditor; Advertising Clerk; Clerical Supervisor; Computer Programmer; Credit Manager; Customer Service Rep.; Editor; General Manager; Human Resources Manager; Librarian; Operations/Production Manager; Radio/TV Announcer/Broadcaster; Reporter; Systems Analyst. **Educational backgrounds include:** Accounting; Art/Design; Business Administration; Communications; Computer Science; Liberal Arts; Marketing. **Benefits:** 401(k); Dental Insurance; Disability Coverage; Employee Discounts; ESOP; Life Insurance; Medical Insurance; Pension Plan; Profit Sharing; Savings Plan; Tuition Assistance. **Special programs:** Internships. **Corporate headquarters location:** This Location. **Other U.S. locations:** IL; WI. **Listed on:** Privately held. **Number of employees at this location:** 300. **Number of employees nationwide:** 725.

WORCESTER TELEGRAM & GAZETTE
P.O. Box 15012, Worcester MA 01615-0012. 508/793-9260. **Physical address:** 20 Franklin Street, Worcester MA 01615. **Contact:** Peter H. Horstmann, Director of Human Resources. **World Wide Web address:** http://www.telegram.com. **Description:** Publishes the *Worcester Telegram & Gazette* with a daily circulation of over 107,000 and a Sunday circulation of over 133,000, and several weekly and semi-weekly newspapers. The company also provides the Telegram & Gazette online, an Internet access service and a wide range of online community information directories. **Parent company:** The New York Times Company.

WORLD TIMES INC.
210 World Trade Center, Boston MA 02210.
Contact: Human Resources. **World Wide Web address:** http://www.worldtimes.com. **Description:** Publishes the monthly *WorldPaper*, an international newspaper. Founded in 1978. **Corporate headquarters location:** This Location.

WORRALL COMMUNITY NEWSPAPERS INC.
P.O. Box 3109, Union NJ 07083-1919. 908/686-7700. **Contact:** Human Resources. **Description:** A publisher of 18 weekly newspapers in Union and Essex Counties with a total circulation of over 40,000.

YALE UNIVERSITY PRESS
P.O. Box 209040, New Haven CT 06520. 203/432-0960. **Physical address:** 302 Temple Street, New Haven CT. **Contact:** Human Resources. **World Wide Web address:** http://www.yale.edu/yup. **Description:** Publishes scholarly books. **Corporate headquarters location:** This Location. **Parent company:** Yale University.

YORK TAPE AND LABEL, INC.
P.O. Box 1309, York PA 17405. 717/266-9675. **Physical address:** 405 Willow Springs Lane, York PA 17402. **Contact:** Deidra A. Foore, Human Resources Manager. **World Wide Web address:** http://www.yorklabel.com. **Description:** Prints and converts pressure-sensitive labels used for product identification. **Common positions include:** Accountant; Blue-Collar Worker Supervisor; Buyer; Chemical Engineer; Commercial Artist; Credit Manager; Customer Service Rep.; Human Resources Manager; Industrial Engineer; Manufacturer's/Wholesaler's Sales Rep.; Mechanical Engineer; Printing Press Operator. **Educational backgrounds include:** Accounting; Business Administration; Engineering; Printing. **Benefits:** 401(k); Dental Insurance; Disability Coverage; Employee Discounts; Life Insurance; Medical Insurance; Pension Plan; Profit Sharing; Savings Plan; Spending Account; Tuition Assistance. **Corporate headquarters location:** This Location. **Other U.S. locations:** Columbia SC.

ZIFF-DAVIS PUBLISHING
28 East 28th Street, New York NY 10016. 212/503-3500. **Contact:** Personnel Department. **World Wide Web address:** http://www.ziffdavis.com. **Description:** A magazine publisher whose periodicals are primarily computer-related. Ziff-Davis also has minor broadcasting operations. **Corporate headquarters location:** This Location.

For more information on career opportunities in printing and publishing:

Associations

AMERICAN BOOKSELLERS ASSOCIATION
828 South Broadway, Tarrytown NY 10591. 914/591-2665. World Wide Web address: http://www.bookweb.org. Publishes *American Bookseller*, *Bookselling This Week*, and *Bookstore Source Guide*.

AMERICAN INSTITUTE OF GRAPHIC ARTS
164 Fifth Avenue, New York NY 10010. 212/807-1990. World Wide Web address: http://www.aiga.org. A nationwide organization sponsoring programs and events for graphic designers and related professionals.

AMERICAN SOCIETY OF NEWSPAPER EDITORS
11690-B Sunrise Valley Drive, Reston VA 20191. 703/453-1122. World Wide Web address: http://www.asne.org.

ASSOCIATION OF AMERICAN PUBLISHERS, INC.
71 Fifth Avenue, New York NY 10003. 212/255-0200. Fax: 212/255-7007. World Wide Web address: http://www.publishers.org. A national trade association for the book publishing industry that provides industry updates and news of upcoming events.

ASSOCIATION OF GRAPHIC COMMUNICATIONS
330 Seventh Avenue, 9th Floor, New York NY 10001-5010. 212/279-2100. World Wide Web address: http://www.agcomm.org. Offers educational classes and seminars.

THE AUTHORS GUILD
330 West 42nd Street, 29th Floor, New York NY 10036. 212/563-5904. Fax: 212/564-5363. World Wide Web address: http://www.authorsguild.org. A membership organization for published authors that promotes free speech, fair compensation, and copyright protection.

BINDING INDUSTRIES OF AMERICA
70 East Lake Street, Suite 300, Chicago IL 60601. 312/372-7606. Offers credit collection, government affairs, and educational services.

THE CHICAGO BOOK CLINIC
825 Green Bay Road, Suite 270, Wilmette IL 60091. 847/256-8448. Fax: 847/256-8954. World Wide Web address: http://www.chicagobookclinic.org. A membership organization for professionals involved in all aspects of book publishing. The organization offers educational programs, publications, and special events throughout the year.

THE DOW JONES NEWSPAPER FUND, INC.
P.O. Box 300, Princeton NJ 08543-0300. 609/452-2820. World Wide Web address: http://www.dj.com/newsfund.

ELECTRONIC PUBLISHING ASSOCIATION
One Rodney Square, 10th Floor, 10th & King Streets, Wilmington DE 19801. World Wide Web address: http://www.epaonline.com. An international association of companies that publish electronically using such formats as CD-ROM, DVD-ROM, and the Internet.

GRAPHIC ARTISTS GUILD
90 John Street, Suite 403, New York NY 10038. 212/791-3400. World Wide Web address: http://www.gag.org. A union for artists.

THE GRAPHIC ARTS TECHNICAL FOUNDATION
200 Deer Run Road, Sewickley PA 15143-2600. 412/741-6860. World Wide Web address: http://www.gatf.org. Provides information, services, and training to those in graphic arts professions.

MAGAZINE PUBLISHERS OF AMERICA
919 Third Avenue, 22nd Floor, New York NY 10022. 212/752-0055. World Wide Web address: http://www.magazine.org. A membership association.

NATIONAL ASSOCIATION OF PRINTERS AND LITHOGRAPHERS
75 West Century Road, Paramus NJ 07652. 201/634-9600. World Wide Web address:

http://www.napl.org. Membership required. Offers consulting services and a publication.

THE NATIONAL NEWSPAPER ASSOCIATION
1010 North Glebe Road, Suite 450, Arlington VA 22201. 703/907-7900. World Wide Web address: http://www.nna.org.

NATIONAL PRESS CLUB
529 14th Street NW, 13th Floor, Washington DC 20045. 202/662-7500. World Wide Web address: http://npc.press.org. Offers professional seminars, career services, and conference facilities, as well as members-only restaurants and a health club.

NEWSPAPER ASSOCIATION OF AMERICA
1921 Gallows Road, Suite 600, Vienna VA 22182. 703/902-1600. Fax: 703/902-1735. World Wide Web address: http://www.naa.org. Focuses on marketing, public policy, diversity, industry development, and newspaper operations.

PRINTING INDUSTRIES OF AMERICA
100 Dangerfield Road, Alexandria VA 22314. 703/519-8100. World Wide Web address: http://www.printing.org. Members are offered publications and insurance.

PUBLISHERS MARKETING ASSOCIATION
627 Aviation Way, Manhattan Beach CA 90266. Fax: 310/374-3342. A membership organization offering seminars and educational materials for professionals in the publishing industry.

TECHNICAL ASSOCIATION OF THE GRAPHIC ARTS
68 Lomb Memorial Drive, Rochester NY 14623. 716/475-7470. World Wide Web address: http://www.taga.org. Conducts an annual conference and offers newsletters.

WRITERS GUILD OF AMERICA WEST
7000 West Third Street, Los Angeles CA 90048. 310/550-1000. World Wide Web address: http://www.wga.org. A membership association which registers scripts.

Directories

GRAPHIC ARTS BLUE BOOK
A.F. Lewis & Company, Hudson Street, 4th Floor, New York NY 10014. 212/519-7398. $85.00. Lists manufacturers and dealers.

THE JOURNALISTS ROAD TO SUCCESS
The Dow Jones Newspaper Fund, P.O. Box 300, Princeton NJ 08543-0300. 609/452-2820. World Wide Web address: http://www.dj.com/newsfund.

Magazines

AIGA JOURNAL OF GRAPHIC DESIGN
American Institute of Graphic Arts, 164 Fifth Avenue, New York NY 10010. 212/807-1990. World Wide Web address: http://www.aiga.org. $22.00. A 56-page magazine, published three times per year, that deals with contemporary issues.

GRAPHIS
141 Lexington Avenue, New York NY 10016.

212/532-9387. $90.00. Magazine covers portfolios, articles, designers, advertising, and photos.

PRINT
RC Publications, 104 Fifth Avenue, 19th Floor, New York NY 10011. 212/463-0600. Offers a graphic design magazine. $57.00 for subscription.

PUBLISHERS WEEKLY
245 West 17th Street, New York NY 10011. 212/463-6758. Toll-free phone: 800/278-2991. World Wide Web address: http://www.publishersweekly.com. Weekly magazine for book publishers and booksellers. Each issue includes a listing of job openings.

Special Book and Magazine Programs

CENTER FOR BOOK ARTS
28 West 27th Street, 3rd Floor, New York NY 10001. 212/481-0295. Offers bookbinding, printing, and papermaking workshops.

EMERSON COLLEGE WRITING AND PUBLISHING PROGRAM
100 Beacon Street, Boston MA 02116. 617/824-8500. World Wide Web address: http://www.emerson.edu.

THE NEW YORK UNIVERSITY SUMMER PUBLISHING PROGRAM
11 West 42nd Street, Room 400, New York NY 10036. 212/790-3232.

THE RADCLIFFE PUBLISHING COURSE
6 Ash Street, Cambridge MA 02138. 617/495-8678. Fax: 617/496-2333. E-mail address: rpc@radcliffe.edu.

THE STANFORD PROFESSIONAL PUBLISHING COURSE
Stanford Alumni Association, Bowman Alumni House, Stanford CA 97305-4005. 650/723-2027. Fax: 650/723-8597. E-mail address: publishing.courses@stanford.edu. World Wide Web address: http://www.stanfordproed.org.

UNIVERSITY OF DENVER PUBLISHING INSTITUTE
2075 South University Boulevard, #D-114, Denver CO 80210. 303/871-2570.

Online Services

JOBS FOR JOURNALISTS
World Wide Web address: http://ajr.newslink.org/newjoblink.html. Offers links to newspapers and magazines, news articles, and an e-mail notification section for jobseekers.

JOURNALISM FORUM
Go: Jforum. A CompuServe discussion group for journalists in print, radio, or television.

PHOTO PROFESSIONALS
Go: Photopro. A CompuServe forum for imaging professionals.

PROPUBLISHING FORUM
Go: Propub. CompuServe charges a fee for this forum which caters to publishing and graphic design professionals.

Real Estate

You can expect to find the following types of companies in this chapter:
*Land Subdividers and Developers • Real Estate Agents, Managers,
and Operators • Real Estate Investment Trusts*

Some helpful information: *Real estate salespersons and brokers earn an average of approximately $50,000 annually (agents in their first year of sales, however, generally earn under $25,000). Experienced and successful agents that sell choice property (such as condominiums in large metropolitan areas) can earn over $200,000 annually.*

ACS DEVELOPMENT
80 Everett Avenue, Suite 319, Chelsea MA 02150.
617/889-6900. **Fax:** 617/889-6255. **Contact:**
Patricia Simboli, Vice President. **Description:** A
real estate corporation with assets in the
metropolitan Boston and Florida markets. Properties
include retail, office, and industrial locations.
Common positions include: Accountant/Auditor;
Administrator; Attorney; Construction Contractor;
General Manager; Marketing Specialist; Secretary.
Educational backgrounds include: Accounting;
Computer Science; Finance; Marketing;
Mathematics. **Corporate headquarters location:**
This Location. **Operations at this facility include:**
Administration; Sales.

ADLETA & POSTON, REALTORS
5956 Sherry Lane, Suite 100, Dallas TX 75225.
214/696-0900. **Fax:** 214/369-6996. **Contact:** Linda
Adleta, Partner. **World Wide Web address:**
http://www.adletaposton.com. **Description:** A
residential real estate brokerage specializing in the
luxury housing and corporate relocation markets.
Common positions include: Real Estate Agent;
Receptionist; Secretary. **Benefits:** Medical
Insurance; Profit Sharing. **Special programs:**
Internships. **Corporate headquarters location:**
This Location. **Number of employees at this
location:** 10.

ATLANTIC GULF COMMUNITIES CORP.
3030 Hartley Drive, Suite 270, Jacksonville FL
32257. 904/262-2112. **Contact:** Human Resources.
World Wide Web address: http://www.
atlanticgulf.com. **Description:** Engaged in real
estate and land development. Properties include The
Trails of West Frisco (Dallas TX), Saxon Woods
(Orlando FL), and Riverwalk Tower (Fort
Lauderdale FL). **Corporate headquarters location:**
This Location.

AVALONBAY COMMUNITIES, INC.
15 River Road, Wilton CT 06897. 203/761-6500.
Fax: 203/761-6555. **Contact:** Human Resources.
World Wide Web address: http://www.
avalonbay.com. **Description:** A self-administered
and self-managed equity real estate investment trust
that specializes in the development, construction,
acquisition, and management of apartment
communities in the mid-Atlantic and northeastern
U.S. AvalonBay Communities' real estate consists
of approximately 10,000 apartment homes in 33
communities located in six states and Washington
DC. **Corporate headquarters location:** This
Location. **Other U.S. locations:** Braintree MA;
Princeton NJ; Alexandria VA; Richmond VA.

BABBITT BROTHERS TRADING CO.
P.O. Box 1328, Flagstaff AZ 86002. 520/774-8711.
Contact: Human Resources. **Description:** A
holding company involved in a variety of activities
including commercial real estate rentals, the
operation of hotels and restaurants, and concession
services for the Grand Canyon. **Corporate
headquarters location:** This Location.

BAIRD & WARNER
1120 South LaSalle Street, Chicago IL 60603.
312/368-1855. **Fax:** 302/368-1490. **Contact:**
Christine Brown, Director of Human Resources.
World Wide Web address: http://www.
bairdwarner.com. **Description:** A full-service,
residential real estate broker operating 30 offices in
the Chicago area. **Corporate headquarters
location:** This Location.

BAY MEADOWS COMPANY
P.O. Box 5050, San Mateo CA 94402. 650/574-
7223. **Contact:** Human Resources. **Description:**
Operates Bay Meadows Race Track on the San
Francisco Peninsula, and California Jockey Club, an
equity real estate investment trust whose principal
asset is Bay Meadows Race Track. **Corporate
headquarters location:** This Location.

BEELER PROPERTIES, INC.
7500 San Felipe, Suite 750, Houston TX 77063.
713/785-8200. **Fax:** 713/785-4143. **Contact:**
Personnel. **Description:** Specializes in the
development, construction, and management of
apartment buildings. **Common positions include:**
Accountant/Auditor; Administrator; Blue-Collar
Worker Supervisor; Leasing Specialist/Consultant;
Property and Real Estate Manager. **Educational
backgrounds include:** Business Administration;
Marketing. **Benefits:** Dental Insurance; Flextime
Plan; Life Insurance; Medical Insurance; Tuition
Assistance. **Corporate headquarters location:**
This Location. **Parent company:** Beeler-Sanders,
Inc.

BINSWANGER
2 Logan Square, 4th Floor, Philadelphia PA 19103.
215/448-6000. **Contact:** Ellen Diorio, Director of
Human Resources. **Description:** Sells commercial
and industrial real estate. **Corporate headquarters
location:** This Location.

BLUEGREEN CORPORATION
4960 Blue Lake Drive, Suite 400, Boca Raton FL
33431. 561/912-8000. **Contact:** Human Resources.
World Wide Web address: http://www.bluegreen-
corp.com. **Description:** A national real estate
company specializing in rural land acquisitions and
sales. Bluegreen Corporation also serves as a
mortgage broker. **Common positions include:**
Accountant/Auditor; Advertising Clerk; Computer
Programmer; Human Resources Manager; Systems
Analyst. **Educational backgrounds include:**
Accounting; Business Administration; Computer
Science; Finance; Marketing. **Benefits:** 401(k);
Dental Insurance; Disability Coverage; Employee

Discounts; Life Insurance; Medical Insurance; Tuition Assistance. **Corporate headquarters location:** This Location. **Other U.S. locations:** Nationwide. **Operations at this facility include:** Administration. **Listed on:** New York Stock Exchange; Pacific Stock Exchange. **Number of employees at this location:** 70. **Number of employees nationwide:** 400.

BRESLER & REINER INC.
401 M Street SW, Waterside Mall, Washington DC 20024. 202/488-8800. **Contact:** Burton Reiner, President. **Description:** Engaged in two primary business segments: home and condominium construction, and rental property ownership and management. **Corporate headquarters location:** This Location.

BRUTGER EQUITIES, INC.
P.O. Box 399, St. Cloud MN 56302-0399. 320/529-2837. **Contact:** Thomas Etienne, Vice President of Human Resources. **Description:** Engaged in real estate development and management of properties including motels and apartments. **Common positions include:** Accountant/Auditor; Hotel Manager; Property and Real Estate Manager. **Educational backgrounds include:** Accounting; Business Administration; Hotel Administration; Marketing. **Benefits:** 401(k); Disability Coverage; Employee Discounts; Life Insurance; Medical Insurance; Tuition Assistance. **Special programs:** Internships. **Corporate headquarters location:** This Location. **Other U.S. locations:** AZ; CO; ID; MT; ND; SD; WY. **Listed on:** Privately held. **Number of employees at this location:** 25. **Number of employees nationwide:** 325.

JOHN BURNHAM & COMPANY
P.O. Box 122910, San Diego CA 92112. 619/236-1555. **Contact:** Personnel. **World Wide Web address:** http://www.johnburnham.com. **Description:** A real estate investor and syndicate. The firm serves as the general partner or investor in a number of real estate ventures including two public partnerships. **Corporate headquarters location:** This Location.

CAMDEN PROPERTY TRUST
3 Greenway Plaza, Suite 1300, Houston TX 77046. 713/354-2500. **Fax:** 713/354-2711. **Contact:** Amy Moers, Recruiting Manager. **World Wide Web address:** http://www.camdenprop.com. **Description:** A real estate investment trust that buys, sells, builds, and manages apartment communities throughout the Southwest. **NOTE:** Entry-level positions are offered. **Common positions include:** Administrative Assistant; AS400 Programmer Analyst; Attorney; Computer Support Technician; Construction Contractor; Controller; Financial Analyst; Human Resources Manager; Leasing Specialist/Consultant; Market Research Analyst; Property and Real Estate Manager; Secretary. **Educational backgrounds include:** Accounting; Business Administration; Microsoft Word; Spreadsheets. **Benefits:** 401(k); Casual Dress - Daily; Dental Insurance; Disability Coverage; Employee Discounts; Flexible Schedule; Life Insurance; Medical Insurance; Sick Days (6 - 10); Tuition Assistance; Vacation Days (6 - 10). **Corporate headquarters location:** This Location. **Other area locations:** Austin TX; Corpus Christi TX; Dallas TX; El Paso TX; Fort Worth TX; San Antonio TX. **Other U.S. locations:** AZ; CA; CO; FL; MO; NC; NV. **Number of employees at this location:** 140.

CARRAMERICA
1850 K Street NW, Suite 500, Washington DC 20006. 202/729-1700. **Contact:** Personnel Director.

World Wide Web address: http://www.carramerica.com. **Description:** A real estate, architectural, and construction management firm. The company specializes in the construction and/or renovation of mixed-use developments. CarrAmerica operates in four divisions: Acquisitions, which locates, evaluates, and purchases land and buildings; Development, which defines the market, creates the initial design concept, determines economic feasibility, and arranges financing; Construction, which supervises the final design and actualizes the plan; and Operations, which markets and manages the finished product. **Corporate headquarters location:** This Location.

CATELLUS DEVELOPMENT CORP.
201 Mission Street, 2nd Floor, San Francisco CA 94105. 415/974-4500. **Contact:** Human Resources. **World Wide Web address:** http://www.catellus.com. **Description:** Owns, develops, and manages industrial, retail, and office buildings. The company's properties, land holdings, and joint-venture interests are located in major markets in California and 11 other states. **Corporate headquarters location:** This Location.

CENDANT CORPORATION
9 West 57th Street, 37th Floor, New York NY 10019. 212/413-1800. **Contact:** Human Resources. **World Wide Web address:** http://www.cendant.com. **Description:** Provides a wide range of business services including dining services, hotel franchise management, mortgage programs, and timeshare exchanges. Cendant Corporation's Real Estate Division offers employee relocation and mortgage services through Century 21, Coldwell Banker, ERA, Cendant Mortgage, and Cendant Mobility. The Travel Division provides car rentals, vehicle management services, and vacation timeshares through brand names including Avia, Days Inn, Howard Johnson, Ramada, Travelodge, and Super 8. The Membership Division offers travel, shopping, auto, dining, and other financial services through Travelers Advantage, Shoppers Advantage, Auto Vantage, Welcome Wagon, Netmarket, North American Outdoor Group, and PrivacyGuard. Founded in 1997. **NOTE:** Resumes should be sent to Human Resources, Cendant Corporation, 6 Sylvan Way, Parsippany NJ 07054. **Corporate headquarters location:** This Location. **Listed on:** New York Stock Exchange. **Stock exchange symbol:** CD. **President/CEO:** Henry Silverman.
Other U.S. locations:
• 6 Sylvan Way, Parsippany NJ 07054. 973/428-9700.

CENTERTRUST RETAIL PROPERTIES
P.O. Box 10010, Manhattan Beach CA 90267. 310/546-4520. **Physical address:** 3500 Sepulveda Boulevard, Manhattan Beach CA 90266. **Fax:** 310/546-3396. **Contact:** Human Resources. **Description:** A real estate investment trust that develops, owns, and manages retail shopping centers throughout Southern California. Over 60 properties are owned or controlled by the company. **Corporate headquarters location:** This Location. **Listed on:** New York Stock Exchange. **Stock exchange symbol:** CTA. **President/CEO:** Edward Fox.

CENTRAL KINNEY PARKING SYSTEMS
360 West 31st Street, 12th Floor, New York NY 10001. 212/889-4444. **Contact:** Human Resources. **Description:** Operates parking garages and lots throughout New York. **Corporate headquarters location:** This Location. **Other U.S. locations:** FL; MA.

CENTURY 21 NEW MILLENNIUM
1700 Diagonal Road, Suite 700, Alexandria VA 22314. 703/549-0600. **Contact:** Manager. **E-mail address:** c21oldtown@aol.com. **Description:** A full-service real estate agency servicing the Washington DC metropolitan area's commercial and residential markets.

CHATEAU COMMUNITIES, INC.
6160 South Syracuse Way, Greenwood Village CO 80111. 303/741-3707. **Fax:** 303/741-3715. **Contact:** Human Resource Coordinator. **Description:** One of the largest real estate investment trusts in the nation. The company owns 128 manufactured home communities in 27 states and manages approximately 34 manufactured home communities owned by third parties. **Common positions include:** Accountant/Auditor. **Educational backgrounds include:** Accounting; Communications; Computer Science; Finance. **Benefits:** 401(k); Medical Insurance. **Corporate headquarters location:** This Location. **Listed on:** New York Stock Exchange. **Stock exchange symbol:** CPJ. **Number of employees at this location:** 350.

COLDWELL BANKER
BARBARA SUE SEAL PROPERTIES, INC.
4103 SW Mercantile Drive, Lake Oswego OR 97035. 503/241-5505. **Toll-free phone:** 800/342-7767. **Fax:** 503/635-4495. **Contact:** Vice President of Operations. **E-mail address:** seal@teleport.com. **World Wide Web address:** http://www.cbportland.com. **Description:** A residential real estate company with 13 sales offices. Founded in 1983. **Common positions include:** Administrative Assistant; Administrative Manager; Advertising Clerk; Advertising Executive; Branch Manager; Computer Operator; Controller; Human Resources Manager; Operations Manager; Purchasing Agent/Manager; Real Estate Agent; Systems Manager. **Benefits:** 401(k); Dental Insurance; Disability Coverage; Life Insurance; Medical Insurance; Vision Plan. **Listed on:** Privately held. **Annual sales/revenues:** More than $100 million. **Number of employees at this location:** 520.

COLDWELL BANKER HICKOK &
BOARDMAN REALTY
P.O. Box 1064, Burlington VT 05402-1064. 802/863-1500. **Fax:** 802/658-7616. **Contact:** Leslee MacKenzie, Broker/Manager. **World Wide Web address:** http://www.hbrealty.com. **Description:** An office of one of the largest residential real estate companies in the United States and Canada in total home sales transactions. Coldwell Banker Hickock & Boardman Realty provides residential and commercial real estate services. **Common positions include:** Administrative Assistant; Marketing Specialist; Real Estate Agent; Secretary; Typist/Word Processor.

COOPERATIVE HOUSING FOUNDATION
8300 Colesville Road, Suite 420, Silver Spring MD 20910. 301/587-4700. **Contact:** Human Resources. **World Wide Web address:** http://www.chfhq.org. **Description:** A foundation providing housing, economic, infrastructure, and health assistance. **Common positions include:** Accountant/Auditor; Architect; Economist; Real Estate Agent. **Educational backgrounds include:** Accounting; Business Administration; Communications; Economics; Engineering; Liberal Arts. **Benefits:** Credit Union; Dental Insurance; Disability Coverage; Life Insurance; Medical Insurance. **Corporate headquarters location:** This Location. **Operations at this facility include:** Regional Headquarters.

CROWN AMERICAN REALTY TRUST
P.O. Box 879, Johnstown PA 15907-0879. 814/536-4441. **Contact:** Andrew Herdman, Director of Human Resources. **World Wide Web address:** http://www.crownam.com. **Description:** Engaged primarily in the ownership, operation, management, leasing, acquisition, expansion, development, and financing of shopping malls. Crown American Realty Trust operates more than 20 malls in Pennsylvania and the surrounding areas. **Corporate headquarters location:** This Location.

CUSHMAN AND WAKEFIELD, INC.
51 West 52nd Street, 8th Floor, New York NY 10019. 212/841-7500. **Fax:** 212/841-5039. **Contact:** Melissa L. Madden, Employment Supervisor. **E-mail address:** mmadden@cushwake.com. **World Wide Web address:** http://www.cushwake.com. **Description:** This location provides assessment services, corporate services, brokerage services, financial and general administration, research, sales, and valuation advisory services. Overall, Cushman and Wakefield is an international commercial and industrial real estate services firm with 44 offices in 20 states. The company is engaged in appraisals, financial services, project development, research services and the management and leasing of commercial office space. **Common positions include:** Accountant/Auditor; Human Resources Manager; Market Research Analyst; Property and Real Estate Manager; Real Estate Broker. **Educational backgrounds include:** Accounting; Business Administration; Communications; Computer Science; Finance; Liberal Arts; Marketing. **Benefits:** 401(k); Dental Insurance; Employee Discounts; Life Insurance; Medical Insurance; Tuition Assistance. **Corporate headquarters location:** This Location. **Other U.S. locations:** Los Angeles CA; San Francisco CA; Chicago IL. **Parent company:** The Rockefeller Group Inc. **Listed on:** Privately held. **Annual sales/revenues:** More than $100 million. **Number of employees at this location:** 500. **Number of employees nationwide:** 5,000.

THE FRANK M. DARBY COMPANY
3384 Peachtree Road, Suite 400, Atlanta GA 30326. 404/812-5900. **Fax:** 404/812-5901. **Contact:** Gail Cleary, Senior Property Manager. **World Wide Web address:** http://www.fmdarby.com. **Description:** Specializes in the management and leasing of office, industrial, and investment properties in Atlanta. **Common positions include:** Administrative Assistant; Leasing Specialist/Consultant; Property and Real Estate Manager. **Educational backgrounds include:** Accounting; Business Administration; Computer Science; Liberal Arts; Marketing. **Benefits:** 401(k); Life Insurance; Medical Insurance. **Corporate headquarters location:** This Location. **Listed on:** Privately held. **President:** Frank M. Darby. **Number of employees at this location:** 30.

DeWOLFE NEW ENGLAND
80 Hayden Avenue, Lexington MA 02421. 781/863-5858. **Contact:** Human Resources. **World Wide Web address:** http://www.dewolfenewengland.com. **Description:** An integrated residential real estate service company which provides sales and marketing services to residential real estate consumers. In addition, the company originates, processes, and closes residential mortgage loans; provides corporate and employee relocation services; and provides asset management services to a variety of clients. In residential real estate and marketing, the company acts as a broker or agent in transactions through independent sales associates. **Corporate headquarters location:** This Location. **Other U.S. locations:** CT; NH. **Subsidiaries**

include: DeWolfe Relocation Services, Inc. offers employers a variety of specialized services primarily concerned with facilitating the resettlement of transferred employees. These services include sales and marketing of transferees' existing homes, assistance in finding new homes, educational and school placement counseling, customized videos, property marketing assistance, rental assistance, area tours, international relocation, group move services, career counseling, spouse/partner employment assistance, and financial services. **Number of employees nationwide:** 275.

DIAMOND PARKING SERVICES, INC.
3161 Elliott Avenue, Seattle WA 98121. 206/284-3100. **Contact:** Personnel Department. **Description:** Owns parking facilities and is involved in real estate. **Corporate headquarters location:** This Location. **Number of employees at this location:** 200.

DOGGETT ENTERPRISES, INC.
666 11th Street NW, Suite 300, Washington DC 20001. 202/638-2770. **Contact:** Human Resources. **Description:** Owns, manages, and operates parking facilities in the Washington DC area. **Common positions include:** Blue-Collar Worker Supervisor; Cashier; Management Trainee; Parking Attendant. **Benefits:** Bonus Award/Plan; Disability Coverage; Life Insurance; Medical Insurance. **Corporate headquarters location:** This Location.

THE DONOHOE COMPANIES, INC.
2101 Wisconsin Avenue NW, Washington DC 20007. 202/333-0880. **Contact:** Deirdre Robinson, Human Resources Manager. **World Wide Web address:** http://www.donohoe.com. **Description:** A real estate development company. **Common positions include:** Accountant/Auditor; Civil Engineer; Construction and Building Inspector; Construction Contractor; Construction Trade Worker; Cost Estimator; Heating/AC/Refrigeration Technician; Property and Real Estate Manager; Secretary. **Educational backgrounds include:** Accounting; Engineering. **Benefits:** Dental Insurance; Disability Coverage; Employee Discounts; Life Insurance; Medical Insurance; Profit Sharing; Savings Plan; Tuition Assistance. **Corporate headquarters location:** This Location. **Number of employees at this location:** 300.

DOUGLAS ELLIMAN GIBBONS & IVES
675 Third Avenue, Floor 6, New York NY 10017. 212/350-2800. **Contact:** Phyllis Dixon, Personnel. **Description:** A real estate firm engaged in apartment sales, rentals, and insurance. **Common positions include:** Accountant/Auditor; Administrative Worker/Clerk; Administrator; Computer Programmer; Customer Service Representative; Department Manager; Operations/Production Manager; Purchasing Agent/Manager; Secretary. **Benefits:** Disability Coverage; Life Insurance; Medical Insurance; Pension Plan. **Corporate headquarters location:** This Location.

DUKE-WEEKS REALTY CORPORATION
8888 Keystone Crossing, Suite 1200, Indianapolis IN 46240. 317/846-4700. **Contact:** Human Resources. **World Wide Web address:** http://www.dukereit.com. **Description:** Duke-Weeks Realty Corporation is a self-administered real estate investment trust which provides leasing, management, development, construction, and other tenant-related services for its properties and for about 12 million square feet of properties owned by third parties. The company provides leasing, property and asset management, development, construction, build-to-suit, and related services for more than 1,200 tenants at properties managed and

leased by Duke for third-party customers. **Common positions include:** Accountant/Auditor; Attorney; Construction Contractor; Financial Analyst; Paralegal; Property and Real Estate Manager; Real Estate Agent. **Educational backgrounds include:** Accounting; Business Administration; Finance; Real Estate. **Benefits:** 401(k); Dental Insurance; Disability Coverage; Life Insurance; Medical Insurance; Profit Sharing. **Corporate headquarters location:** This Location. **Annual sales/revenues:** More than $100 million. **Number of employees at this location:** 225. **Number of employees nationwide:** 455.

DUNES PROPERTIES OF CHARLESTON
P.O. Box 524, Isle of Palms SC 29451. 803/886-5600. **Toll-free phone:** 800/476-8444. **Fax:** 803/886-6537. **Contact:** John Taylor, Chief Operating Officer. **World Wide Web address:** http://www.dunesproperties.com. **Description:** A rental agent for resort and vacation properties. **Common positions include:** Accountant/Auditor; Administrator; Front Desk Sales Agent; Property and Real Estate Manager; Reservationist; Sales Executive. **Educational backgrounds include:** Accounting; Business Administration; Economics; Marketing. **Benefits:** Dental Insurance; Employee Discounts; IRA; Life Insurance; Medical Insurance. **Corporate headquarters location:** This Location. **Listed on:** Privately held. **Annual sales/revenues:** Less than $5 million. **Number of employees at this location:** 35.

FAIRFIELD COMMUNITIES, INC.
11001 Executive Center Drive, Little Rock AR 72211. 501/228-2700. **Contact:** Personnel Administrator. **World Wide Web address:** http://www.ffci.com. **Description:** A resort developer and one of the nation's largest vacation ownership companies. The company markets vacation products and manages resort properties in 11 states. **Common positions include:** Accountant/Auditor; Attorney; Clerical Supervisor; Computer Programmer; Credit Manager; Customer Service Representative; Property and Real Estate Manager; Restaurant/Food Service Manager; Services Sales Representative; Systems Analyst; Travel Agent; Typist/Word Processor. **Educational backgrounds include:** Accounting. **Benefits:** 401(k); Dental Insurance; Disability Coverage; Life Insurance; Medical Insurance; Profit Sharing. **Corporate headquarters location:** This Location. **Listed on:** New York Stock Exchange. **Number of employees at this location:** 200. **Number of employees nationwide:** 1,200.

FEDERAL REALTY INVESTMENT TRUST
1626 East Jefferson Street, Rockville MD 20852. 301/998-8100. **Contact:** Director of Personnel. **World Wide Web address:** http://www.federalrealty.com. **Description:** An equity real estate investment firm that acquires and develops prime retail properties. **Common positions include:** Accountant/Auditor; Attorney; Blue-Collar Worker Supervisor; Computer Programmer. **Benefits:** Dental Insurance; Flexible Benefits; Life Insurance; Medical Insurance; Pension Plan. **Corporate headquarters location:** This Location. **Listed on:** New York Stock Exchange.

FIRST WINTHROP CORPORATION
5 Cambridge Center, 9th Floor, Cambridge MA 02142. 617/234-3000. **Contact:** Human Resources. **Description:** A real estate agency specializing in commercial properties. Founded in 1978. **Common positions include:** Financial Analyst. **Educational backgrounds include:** Accounting; Finance. **Benefits:** 401(k); Dental Insurance; Disability Coverage; Life Insurance; Medical Insurance;

Tuition Assistance. **Corporate headquarters location:** This Location. **Listed on:** Privately held. **Number of employees at this location:** 30. **Number of employees nationwide:** 110.

FOLLMAN PROPERTIES
ONCOR INTERNATIONAL
165 North Meramec, Suite 500, St. Louis MO 63105-3798. 314/721-3444. **Contact:** Gary Follman, President. **Description:** A full-service, commercial real estate services firm. Follman Properties is part of Oncor International, serving office, industrial, retail, and investment brokerage requirements. The company is also involved in asset and property management, consulting, appraisal, and information services. **Common positions include:** Property and Real Estate Manager; Real Estate Agent. **Corporate headquarters location:** This Location. **Listed on:** Privately held. **Number of employees at this location:** 40.

GENERAL GROWTH MANAGEMENT
8251 Flying Cloud Drive, Suite 100, Eden Prairie MN 55344. 612/525-1200. **Contact:** Human Resources Manager. **Description:** Engaged in the third-party management of malls. **Common positions include:** Accountant/Auditor; Assistant Manager; Department Manager; General Manager; Marketing Specialist; Operations/Production Manager; Paralegal. **Educational backgrounds include:** Accounting; Business Administration; Communications; Economics; Liberal Arts; Marketing. **Benefits:** 401(k); Disability Coverage; Life Insurance; Medical Insurance; Savings Plan; Spending Account; Stock Option; Tuition Assistance. **Corporate headquarters location:** This Location. **Other U.S. locations:** Nationwide. **Listed on:** Privately held. **Number of employees at this location:** 250. **Number of employees nationwide:** 2,700.

GRUBB & ELLIS COMPANY
2215 Sanders Road, Suite 400, Northbrook IL 60062. 847/753-9010. **Contact:** Personnel Administrator. **World Wide Web address:** http://www.grubb-ellis.com. **Description:** A commercial and residential real estate brokerage firm. **Common positions include:** Accountant/Auditor; Administrator; Financial Analyst; Systems Analyst. **Educational backgrounds include:** Accounting; Business Administration; Computer Science; Finance; Liberal Arts. **Benefits:** 401(k); Dental Insurance; Life Insurance; Medical Insurance; Tuition Assistance. **Corporate headquarters location:** This Location.

THE HASSON COMPANY REALTORS
15400 SW Boones Ferry Road, Lake Oswego OR 97035. 503/635-9801. **Contact:** Human Resources. **World Wide Web address:** http://www.hasson.com. **Description:** Specializes in the buying and selling of residential property. **Corporate headquarters location:** This Location. **Number of employees at this location:** 50.

HAWTHORNE CORPORATION
P.O. Box 61000, Charleston SC 29419. 803/797-8484. **Contact:** Sue Johnson, Vice President. **World Wide Web address:** http://www.hawthornecorp.com. **Description:** A holding company whose companies are engaged in a variety of industries including aviation (operating airports); real estate operations; and financial services. **Corporate headquarters location:** This Location.

HEALTH AND RETIREMENT PROPERTIES TRUST
400 Centre Street, Newton MA 02458. 617/332-3990. **Fax:** 617/332-2261. **Contact:** Joyce Silver,

Human Resources. **Description:** A real estate investment trust which invests primarily in retirement communities, assisted living centers, nursing homes, and other long-term care facilities. **Corporate headquarters location:** This Location.

HELMSLEY-NOYES COMPANY INC.
230 Park Avenue, Suite 659, New York NY 10169. 212/679-3600. **Contact:** Personnel. **Description:** A commercial real estate agency engaged in the management of office buildings and a wide range of other institutional buildings including department stores and corporate offices. **Corporate headquarters location:** This Location.

HELMSLEY-SPEAR INC.
60 East 42nd Street, 53rd Floor, New York NY 10165. 212/880-0603. **Contact:** Human Resources. **Description:** One of the largest real estate service companies in the nation offering leasing (including industrial leasing, and retail and store leasing divisions); sales and brokerage; management; development; appraisals; and financing services. **Common positions include:** Accountant/Auditor; Actuary; Administrator; Assistant Manager; Attorney; Blue-Collar Worker Supervisor; Computer Programmer; Counselor; Electrical/Electronics Engineer; Financial Analyst; General Manager; Industrial Engineer; Industrial Production Manager; Instructor/Trainer; Management Trainee; Mechanical Engineer; Paralegal; Quality Control Supervisor; Real Estate Agent; Sales Executive; Systems Analyst. **Educational backgrounds include:** Accounting; Business Administration; Communications; Finance. **Benefits:** Disability Coverage; Life Insurance; Medical Insurance. **Corporate headquarters location:** This Location.

HIGH INDUSTRIES, INC.
P.O. Box 10008, Lancaster PA 17605-0008. 717/293-4486. **Contact:** Vincent F. Mizeras, Director of Human Resources. **World Wide Web address:** http://www.high.net. **Description:** Products and services include design and construction, food services, hotel management, prestress/precast concrete products, real estate development and management, and steel fabrication. **Common positions include:** Accountant/Auditor; Architect; Civil Engineer; Computer Programmer; Customer Service Representative; Draftsperson; Hotel Manager; Human Resources Manager; Services Sales Representative; Systems Analyst. **Educational backgrounds include:** Accounting; Business Administration; Computer Science; Engineering; Finance; Marketing. **Benefits:** Credit Union; Dental Insurance; Disability Coverage; Life Insurance; Medical Insurance; Pension Plan; Profit Sharing; Savings Plan; Tuition Assistance. **Corporate headquarters location:** This Location.

HINES PROPERTIES INC.
2800 Post Oak Boulevard, 48th Floor, Houston TX 77056. 713/966-2629. **Contact:** David LeVrier, Director of Human Resources. **Description:** Engaged in commercial real estate development and property management. The company has properties in 39 U.S. cities. **Common positions include:** Accountant/Auditor; Administrator; Property and Real Estate Manager; Stationary Engineer. **Educational backgrounds include:** Accounting; Business Administration. **Benefits:** 401(k); Dental Insurance; Disability Coverage; Employee Discounts; Life Insurance; Medical Insurance. **Corporate headquarters location:** This Location. **Number of employees at this location:** 120.

K. HOVNANIAN COMPANIES
10 Highway 35, Red Bank NJ 07701. 732/747-7800. **Contact:** Human Resources. **World Wide**

Web address: http://www.khov.com. **Description:** Designs, constructs, and sells condominium apartments, townhouses, and single-family residences in planned residential communities. The company is also engaged in mortgage banking. Founded in 1959. **NOTE:** Entry-level positions are offered. **Common positions include:** Accountant; Administrative Assistant; Architect; Attorney; Auditor; Civil Engineer; Computer Operator; Computer Programmer; Controller; Financial Analyst; Human Resources Manager; Market Research Analyst; Marketing Manager; Marketing Specialist; MIS Specialist; Online Content Specialist; Real Estate Agent; Sales Manager; Secretary; Systems Analyst; Systems Manager; Technical Writer; Webmaster. **Educational backgrounds include:** Accounting; Business Administration; Computer Science; Engineering; Marketing. **Benefits:** 401(k); Dental Insurance; Disability Coverage; Life Insurance; Medical Insurance; Profit Sharing; Tuition Assistance. **Corporate headquarters location:** This Location. **Other U.S. locations:** CA; FL; NC; NY; PA; VA. **Subsidiaries include:** New Fortis Homes. **Listed on:** American Stock Exchange. **Stock exchange symbol:** HOV. **Annual sales/revenues:** More than $100 million. **Number of employees at this location:** 90.

J&V URBAN RETAIL PROPERTIES CO.
900 North Michigan Avenue, Chicago IL 60611. 312/440-4800. **Fax:** 312/915-1768. **Contact:** Human Resources. **Description:** Owns and manages shopping malls and strip malls nationwide. **Common positions include:** Accountant/Auditor; Paralegal. **Educational backgrounds include:** Accounting; Business Administration; Marketing. **Benefits:** Dental Insurance; Disability Coverage; Life Insurance; Medical Insurance; Tuition Assistance. **Corporate headquarters location:** This Location. **Other U.S. locations:** Nationwide. **Listed on:** Privately held. **Number of employees at this location:** 500. **Number of employees nationwide:** 2,000.

KAUFMAN & BROAD HOME CORP.
10990 Wilshire Boulevard, 7th Floor, Los Angeles CA 90024. 310/231-4000. **Contact:** Gary Ray, Vice President/Human Resources. **World Wide Web address:** http://www.kaufmanandbroad.com. **Description:** Builds and markets single-family homes; provides mortgage banking services; develops commercial projects and high-density residential properties; and acquires and develops land. **Corporate headquarters location:** This Location.

J.I. KISLAK MORTGAGE CORPORATION
7900 Miami Lakes Drive West, Miami Lakes FL 33016. 305/364-4116. **Contact:** Director of Human Resources. **Description:** A mortgage banking and real estate firm. **Common positions include:** Accountant; Bank Officer; Branch Manager; Claim Representative; Computer Programmer; Customer Service Representative; Department Manager; Financial Analyst; Human Resources Manager; Industrial Agent/Broker; Loan Officer; Marketing Specialist; Systems Analyst; Underwriter/Assistant Underwriter. **Educational backgrounds include:** Accounting; Business Administration; Computer Science; Finance; Marketing. **Benefits:** Dental Insurance; Disability Coverage; Employee Discounts; Life Insurance; Medical Insurance; Pension Plan; Profit Sharing; Tuition Assistance. **Corporate headquarters location:** This Location.

LENNAR CORPORATION
700 NW 107th Avenue, Suite 400, Miami FL 33172. 305/559-4000. **Contact:** Carol Burgin,

Personnel Manager. **World Wide Web address:** http://www.lennar.com. **Description:** Builds and sells homes, develops and manages commercial and residential properties, and provides real estate-related financial services. The Homebuilding Division constructs and sells single-family attached and detached multifamily homes. These activities also include the purchase, development, and sale of residential land. The company is one of the nation's largest home builders with operations in Florida, Arizona, and Texas. The Investment Division is involved in the development, management, and leasing, as well as the acquisition and sale of commercial and residential properties. **Corporate headquarters location:** This Location. **Subsidiaries include:** Lennar Financial Services, Inc. invests in rated portions of commercial real estate mortgage-backed securities for which Lennar's investment division is the servicer, and an investor in the unrated portion of those securities. **Listed on:** New York Stock Exchange. **Number of employees nationwide:** 1,300.

LEXINGTON CORPORATE PROPERTIES TRUST
355 Lexington Avenue, 14th Floor, New York NY 10017. 212/692-7260. **Contact:** Human Resources. **Description:** A real estate investment trust that owns and manages office, industrial, and retail properties located in 25 states. Founded in 1993. **Corporate headquarters location:** This Location. **Number of employees at this location:** 25.

J.W. MAYS INC.
9 Bond Street, Brooklyn NY 11201. 718/624-7400. **Contact:** Frank Mollo, Personnel Director. **Description:** A real estate company operating commercial properties in Brooklyn, Jamaica, Levittown, Fishkill, and Dutchess County NY, as well as in Circleville OH. **Corporate headquarters location:** This Location.

McFARLAN REAL ESTATE
10100 North Central Expressway, Suite 200, Dallas TX 75231. 214/559-4599. **Contact:** Human Resources. **Description:** A commercial real estate agency. **Corporate headquarters location:** This Location.

MEDITRUST CORPORATION
197 First Avenue, Needham Heights MA 02494. 781/433-6000. **Contact:** Human Resources. **World Wide Web address:** http://www.reit.com. **Description:** A health care real estate investment trust. Meditrust invests primarily in health care facilities providing subacute and long-term care services. The company has investments in more than 400 health care facilities in 38 states. **Corporate headquarters location:** This Location. **Other U.S. locations:** Palm Beach FL. **Parent company:** The Meditrust Companies (also at this location) also consists of Meditrust Operating Company. **Listed on:** New York Stock Exchange. **Stock exchange symbol:** MT. **Number of employees at this location:** 50.

MERCHANDISE MART PROPERTIES
The Merchandise Mart, Suite 470, Chicago IL 60654. 312/527-7792. **Fax:** 312/527-7791. **Contact:** Tom Fitzpatrick, Director of Human Resources. **Description:** The management and leasing agent for prominent wholesale showroom facilities, which include the Merchandise Mart and Apparel Center (Chicago), the Decorators and Designers Building (New York), and the Washington Design Center (Washington DC). **Common positions include:** Accountant/Auditor; Advertising Clerk; Attorney; Construction Engineer; Credit Manager; Department Manager;

Draftsperson; Financial Analyst; Human Resources Manager; Marketing Specialist; Mechanical Engineer; Purchasing Agent/Manager; Sales Executive; Systems Analyst; Technical Writer/Editor. **Educational backgrounds include:** Accounting; Communications; Engineering. **Benefits:** 401(k); Dental Insurance; Life Insurance; Medical Insurance; Pension Plan; Savings Plan; Tuition Assistance. **Special programs:** Internships. **Corporate headquarters location:** This Location. **Other U.S. locations:** Washington DC; High Point NC. **Parent company:** Vornado Realty Trust. **Listed on:** Privately held. **Number of employees at this location:** 400. **Number of employees nationwide:** 430.

THE MICHELSON ORGANIZATION
7701 Forsyth Boulevard, Suite 900, St. Louis MO 63105. 314/862-7080. **Contact:** Human Resources. **World Wide Web address:** http://www.michelson-realty.com. **Description:** Develops, acquires, and manages real estate investments. **Common positions include:** Accountant/Auditor; Financial Analyst; Property and Real Estate Manager. **Benefits:** Dental Insurance; Life Insurance; Medical Insurance; Savings Plan. **Corporate headquarters location:** This Location. **Subsidiaries include:** Michelson Commercial Realty and Development Company assists corporate clients with a wide range of services.

NEW ENGLAND MANAGEMENT
214 Harvard Avenue, Allston MA 02134. 617/566-5571. **Contact:** Human Resources. **Description:** Acquires, develops, operates, and sells residential and commercial real estate. **Corporate headquarters location:** This Location.

NEW MEXICO AND ARIZONA LAND CO.
3033 North 44th Street, Suite 270, Phoenix AZ 85018. 602/952-8836. **Contact:** Hazel Guliford, Office Manager. **World Wide Web address:** http://www.nz-newmexariz.com. **Description:** Operates a land and natural resources management and development company. New Mexico and Arizona Land Company's principal source of income is through mineral sales and improved property rentals. Founded in 1908. **Corporate headquarters location:** This Location.

OASIS RESIDENTIAL, INC.
4041 East Sunset Road, Henderson NV 89014. 702/435-9800x2701. **Fax:** 702/547-1629. **Contact:** Kay Eatmon, Vice President of Human Resources. **Description:** A self-administered and self-managed real estate investment trust, engaged in the acquisition, development, and operation of multifamily properties in the greater Las Vegas NV area. The company owns and operates a portfolio of over 13,400 apartment units. Oasis Residential is one of the largest developers and owners of apartments in the greater Las Vegas area. Founded in 1993. **Common positions include:** Account Representative; Administrative Assistant; Computer Operator; Human Resources Manager; Management Trainee; Marketing Manager; MIS Specialist; Purchasing Agent/Manager; Sales Representative. **Educational backgrounds include:** Business Administration. **Benefits:** 401(k); Dental Insurance; Employee Discounts; Life Insurance; Medical Insurance; Tuition Assistance. **Corporate headquarters location:** This Location. **Listed on:** New York Stock Exchange. **Stock exchange symbol:** OAS. **Annual sales/revenues:** $51 - $100 million.

OMEGA HEALTHCARE INVESTORS, INC.
900 Victors Way, Suite 350, Ann Arbor MI 48108. 734/887-0200. **Contact:** Human Resources.

Description: Omega is a real estate investment trust, investing in and providing financing for the long-term care industry. The company's portfolio includes 193 health care facilities located in 20 states, operated by 23 independent health care companies. **Common positions include:** Accountant/Auditor; Financial Analyst; Typist/Word Processor. **Educational backgrounds include:** Accounting; Business Administration; Finance; Health Care. **Benefits:** 401(k); Dental Insurance; Disability Coverage; Life Insurance; Medical Insurance. **Corporate headquarters location:** This Location. **Annual sales/revenues:** $51 - $100 million. **Number of employees at this location:** 15.

OXFORD REALTY FINANCIAL GROUP
7200 Wisconsin Avenue, Suite 1100, Bethesda MD 20814. 301/654-3100. **Contact:** Human Resources. **Description:** Manages apartment complexes. **Common positions include:** Accountant/Auditor; Attorney; Financial Analyst; Human Resources Manager; MIS Specialist. **Educational backgrounds include:** Accounting; Business Administration; Finance. **Benefits:** 401(k); Dental Insurance; Disability Coverage; Employee Discounts; Life Insurance; Medical Insurance; Tuition Assistance. **Corporate headquarters location:** This Location. **Other U.S. locations:** Nationwide. **Number of employees at this location:** 40.

PM REALTY GROUP
1050 17th Street, Suite 1000, Denver CO 80265. 303/534-6611. **Contact:** Administrative Manager of Human Resources. **World Wide Web address:** http://www.pmrealtygroup.com. **Description:** Provides property management, leasing services, corporate services, construction management, asset management, engineering services, and related services. **Common positions include:** Accountant/Auditor; Building Engineer; Maintenance Technician; Paralegal; Property and Real Estate Manager; Receptionist; Secretary. **Educational backgrounds include:** Accounting; Business Administration; Finance; Real Estate. **Benefits:** 401(k); Dental Insurance; Disability Coverage; Life Insurance; Medical Insurance. **Corporate headquarters location:** Houston TX. **Operations at this facility include:** Administration. **Number of employees at this location:** 45. **Number of employees nationwide:** 80.

PORT ELIZABETH PARTNERS
220 Lenox Avenue, Westfield NJ 07090. 908/301-1344. **Contact:** Human Resources. **Description:** Engaged in real estate development. **Corporate headquarters location:** This Location.

PREFERRED EQUITIES CORPORATION
1500 East Tropicana, Suite 114, Las Vegas NV 89109. 702/891-6464. **Fax:** 702/736-5737. **Recorded jobline:** 702/225-9400. **Contact:** Human Resources. **Description:** One of the country's largest real estate and resort developers and marketing companies. The company develops and converts rental and condominium apartment buildings and hotels for sale as timeshare properties. **Common positions include:** Accountant/Auditor; Administrative Manager; Computer Programmer; Financial Analyst; MIS Specialist; Real Estate Agent; Services Sales Representative; Systems Analyst; Typist/Word Processor. **Educational backgrounds include:** Accounting; Business Administration; Computer Science; Economics; Finance; Marketing. **Benefits:** 401(k); Dental Insurance; Disability Coverage; Employee Discounts; Life Insurance; Medical Insurance; Tuition Assistance. **Corporate headquarters**

location: This Location. **Other U.S. locations:** CA; CO; FL; GA; KY; NC; NJ; OK; SC; TX; WA. **Parent company:** Mego Financial Corporation provides consumer financing to purchasers of its timeshare interests and land parcels; originates and purchases government-insured loans for home improvements; and sells and services receivables. **Listed on:** NASDAQ. **Stock exchange symbol:** MEGO. **Number of employees nationwide:** 1,700.

THE PRUDENTIAL NORTHWEST PROPERTIES
4970 SW Griffith Drive, Beaverton OR 97005. 503/646-7826. **Contact:** Personnel. **World Wide Web address:** http://www.pru-nw.com. **Description:** Provides a wide range of real estate services to corporate and residential clients. **Common positions include:** Accountant/Auditor; Administrative Manager; Advertising Clerk; General Manager; Property and Real Estate Manager; Real Estate Agent; Systems Analyst. **Educational backgrounds include:** Accounting; Business Administration; Computer Science; Marketing. **Benefits:** Dental Insurance; Disability Coverage; Life Insurance; Medical Insurance. **Corporate headquarters location:** This Location. **Listed on:** Privately held. **Number of employees at this location:** 80.

J.D. REECE REALTORS
7127 West 110th Street, Overland Park KS 66210. 913/491-1001. **Contact:** Sam Hartman, Director of Human Resources. **World Wide Web address:** http://www.jdreece.com. **Description:** Engaged in residential real estate, new home developments, resale, property management, and corporate relocation. **Common positions include:** Administrator; Branch Manager; Counselor; Financial Analyst; Instructor/Trainer; Management Trainee; Services Sales Representative. **Benefits:** Dental Insurance; Disability Coverage; Employee Discounts; Life Insurance; Medical Insurance; Tuition Assistance. **Corporate headquarters location:** This Location. **Number of employees nationwide:** 560.

FREDERICK ROSS COMPANY
717 17th Street, Suite 2000, Denver CO 80202. 303/892-1111. **Contact:** Personnel Director. **World Wide Web address:** http://www.frederickross.com. **Description:** A full-service commercial real estate firm. **Common positions include:** Accountant/Auditor; Administrative Manager; Brokerage Clerk; Financial Analyst; Human Resources Manager; Property and Real Estate Manager; Public Relations Specialist; Real Estate Agent; Systems Analyst. **Benefits:** 401(k); Dental Insurance; Disability Coverage; Life Insurance; Medical Insurance; Pension Plan; Tuition Assistance. **Corporate headquarters location:** This Location. **Parent company:** Oncor International. **Listed on:** Privately held. **Number of employees at this location:** 150.

THE ROUSE COMPANY
10275 Little Patuxent Parkway, Columbia MD 21044. 410/992-6000. **Contact:** Personnel. **World Wide Web address:** http://www.therousecompany.com. **Description:** Develops, acquires, owns, and manages commercial real estate projects, primarily large regional retail centers. The Rouse Company manages approximately 250 properties across the United States including Faneuil Hall Marketplace (Boston MA), South Street Seaport (New York NY), Harborplace (Baltimore MD), Bayside Marketplace (Miami FL), Arizona Center (Phoenix AZ), Pioneer Place (Portland OR), and Westlake Center (Seattle WA). **Corporate headquarters location:** This Location.

SCHULER HOMES, INC.
828 Fort Street Mall, 4th Floor, Honolulu HI 96813. 808/521-5661. **Fax:** 808/538-1476. **Contact:** Office Manager. **World Wide Web address:** http://www.schuler-hawaii.com. **Description:** Designs, builds, and sells single-family homes, townhouses, and condominiums. **Corporate headquarters location:** This Location. **Other U.S. locations:** CA; CO; OR; WA. **Listed on:** NASDAQ. **Stock exchange symbol:** SHLR. **President/CEO:** James K. Schuler.

SEA PINES ASSOCIATES, INC.
P.O. Box 7000, Hilton Head Island SC 29938. 843/785-3333. **Fax:** 843/842-1412. **Contact:** Monica Nash, Director of Human Resources. **World Wide Web address:** http://www.seapines.com. **Description:** A holding company. **Corporate headquarters location:** This Location. **Subsidiaries include:** Sea Pines Company, Inc. (also at this address) operates resort assets including three golf courses, a 28-court racquet club, a home and villa rental management business, retail sales outlets, food services operations, and other resort recreational facilities. Sea Pines Real Estate Company, Inc. is an independent real estate brokerage firm with 11 offices. Sea Pines Country Club, Inc. operates a full-service private country club providing golf, tennis, and clubhouse facilities for approximately 1,500 club members. **Number of employees at this location:** 250.

SERVICE CORPORATION INTERNATIONAL
1929 Allen Parkway, Houston TX 77019. 713/522-5141. **Contact:** Human Resources. **World Wide Web address:** http://www.sci-corp.com. **Description:** Engaged in the operation of cemeteries and also provides funeral services including cremation services and grief support counseling. **Number of employees nationwide:** 11,800.

STEWART ENTERPRISES, INC.
1333 South Clearview Parkway, Jefferson LA 70121. **Toll-free phone:** 800/553-8736. **Fax:** 504/729-1825. **Contact:** Ed Baucom, Director of Human Resources. **Description:** Stewart Enterprises, Inc. is one of the largest providers of funeral services in the U.S. Through its subsidiaries, the company operates 134 funeral homes and 95 cemeteries in 16 states, Puerto Rico, Mexico, and Australia. **Corporate headquarters location:** This Location.

TUCSON REALTY & TRUST COMPANY
1890 East River Road, Tucson AZ 85718. 520/577-7400. **Contact:** Human Resources. **World Wide Web address:** http://www.tucson-realty.com. **Description:** A real estate sales and management firm. **Common positions include:** Accountant/Auditor; Administrative Manager; Property and Real Estate Manager; Real Estate Agent. **Educational backgrounds include:** Accounting; Business Administration; Marketing. **Benefits:** 401(k); Dental Insurance; Life Insurance; Medical Insurance; Pension Plan. **Special programs:** Internships. **Corporate headquarters location:** This Location. **Number of employees at this location:** 250.

UNITED DOMINION REALTY TRUST
10 South Sixth Street, Richmond VA 23219. 804/780-2691. **Contact:** Human Resources. **World Wide Web address:** http://www.udrt.com. **Description:** One of the largest real estate investment trusts specializing in residential apartment communities in the Southeast. United Dominion is a fully-integrated real estate company handling acquisition, construction, and property management. The trust owns 138 properties

including over 29,000 apartments in 120 communities, 14 neighborhood shopping centers, and four other commercial properties. Founded in 1972. **Corporate headquarters location:** This Location.

UNITED PARKING, INC.
615 Peachtree Street, Suite 1150, Atlanta GA 30308. 404/658-9053. **Contact:** Alice Pittman, Payroll Manager. **Description:** Owns and manages a parking facility and offers consulting services in the design, construction, and operation of other such facilities. **Common positions include:** Branch Manager; Cashier. **Educational backgrounds include:** Business Administration. **Benefits:** Life Insurance; Medical Insurance; Pension Plan. **Corporate headquarters location:** This Location. **Other U.S. locations:** Tampa FL. **Number of employees at this location:** 250.

WATERMARK COMMUNITIES, INC.
P.O. Box 5698, Sun City Center FL 33571. 813/634-3311. **Contact:** Human Resources. **World Wide Web address:** http://www.wcicommunities.com. **Description:** Develops, builds, and manages resort communities in Florida. **Corporate headquarters location:** This Location.

WEICHERT REALTORS
1625 Route 10 East, Morris Plains NJ 07950. 973/267-7777. **Contact:** Human Resources. **World Wide Web address:** http://www.weichert.com. **Description:** A commercial real estate agency. **NOTE:** Jobseekers should specify a department of interest when applying. **Corporate headquarters location:** This Location.

WESTMINSTER HOMES
2706 North Church Street, Greensboro NC 27405. 336/375-6200. **Fax:** 336/375-6355. **Contact:** Human Resources. **World Wide Web address:** http://www.greensboro.com/westminster. **Description:** A real estate and construction company specializing in single-family home development and sales in North Carolina. **Common positions include:** Accountant; Computer Programmer; Customer Service Representative; Draftsperson; Human Resources Manager; Manufacturer's/Wholesaler's Sales Rep.; Marketing Specialist; Operations/Production Manager; Purchasing Agent/Manager; Quality Control Supervisor. **Educational backgrounds include:** Accounting; Business Administration; Computer Science; Marketing. **Benefits:** Dental Insurance; Disability Coverage; Employee Discounts; Life Insurance; Medical Insurance; Pension Plan; Profit Sharing; Savings Plan; Stock Option; Tuition Assistance. **Corporate headquarters location:** This Location. **Other U.S. locations:** Cary NC. **Parent company:** Weyerhaeuser Company. **Listed on:** New York Stock Exchange. **Number of employees at this location:** 60. **Number of employees nationwide:** 100.

WUKASCH COMPANY
2340 Guadalupe Street, Austin TX 78705-5218. **Contact:** Don C. Wukasch, President. **Description:** A diversified real estate and securities investment company providing real estate property management and securities portfolio management. **Common positions include:** Accountant/Auditor; Administrative Manager; Budget Analyst; Construction Contractor; Economist; Financial Analyst; General Manager; Real Estate Agent; Statistician; Systems Analyst; Typist/Word Processor. **Educational backgrounds include:** Accounting; Business Administration; Computer Science; Economics; Finance. **Benefits:** Medical Insurance. **Special programs:** Internships. **Corporate headquarters location:** This Location. **Listed on:** Privately held. **Annual sales/revenues:** Less than $5 million. **Number of employees at this location:** 5. **Number of employees nationwide:** 10.

WYNNE/JACKSON, INC.
600 North Pearl Street, Suite 650, Lock Box 149, Dallas TX 75201. 214/880-8600. **Contact:** Frank Murphy, Vice President. **Description:** A commercial real estate development and property management company. **Corporate headquarters location:** This Location.

For more information on career opportunities in real estate:

Associations

INSTITUTE OF REAL ESTATE MANAGEMENT
430 North Michigan Avenue, Chicago IL 60611. 312/661-1930. World Wide Web address: http://www.irem.org.

INTERNATIONAL REAL ESTATE INSTITUTE
1224 North Nokomis, Alexandria MN 56308. Offers seminars on issues relating to the real estate industry.

NACORE INTERNATIONAL
440 Columbia Drive, Suite 100, West Palm Beach FL 33409. 561/683-8111. World Wide Web address: http://www.nacore.com.

NATIONAL ASSOCIATION OF REAL ESTATE INVESTMENT TRUSTS
1875 Eye Street NW, Suite 600, Washington DC 20006. 202/739-9400. Toll-free phone: 800/3-NAREIT. World Wide Web address: http://www.nareit.com. Membership required.

NATIONAL ASSOCIATION OF REALTORS
430 North Michigan Avenue, Chicago IL 60611. 312/329-8200. World Wide Web address: http://www.realtor.com.

Magazines

JOURNAL OF PROPERTY MANAGEMENT
Institute of Real Estate Management, 430 North Michigan Avenue, Chicago IL 60610. 312/329-6000. World Wide Web address: http://www.irem.org.

NATIONAL REAL ESTATE INVESTOR
PRIMEDIA Intertec, 6151 Powers Ferry Road NW, Suite 200, Atlanta GA 30339. 770/955-2500. World Wide Web address: http://www.nreionline.com.

Online Services

REAL JOBS
World Wide Web address: http://www.real-jobs.com. This Website is designed to help real estate professionals who are looking for jobs.

Retail

You can expect to find the following types of companies in this chapter:
Catalog Retailers • Department Stores; Specialty Stores
Retail Bakeries • Supermarkets

Some helpful information: *The average salary of general sales staff is approximately $5.00 - $12.00 per hour (more if the salesperson earns a commission on successful sales). Store managers generally earn $24,000 - $45,000, district managers $40,000 - $70,000, and regional managers can earn as much as $100,000 and up.*

ACE HARDWARE CORPORATION
2200 Kensington Court, Oak Brook IL 60523. 630/990-6600. **Contact:** Director of Human Resources. **World Wide Web address:** http://www.acehardware.com. **Description:** A worldwide dealer-owned cooperative operating through 5,100 hardware retailers in 62 countries. Ace Hardware Corporation also produces a line of hand and power tools, plumbing products, lawn and garden products, cleaning supplies, and manufactures a line of paint. **Corporate headquarters location:** This Location. **Number of employees nationwide:** 3,000.

ACME MARKETS OF VIRGINIA, INC.
P.O. Box 246, North Tazewell VA 24630. 540/988-2561. **Contact:** Donny Meadows, Human Resources. **Description:** Operates a supermarket chain of 10 stores in Virginia and West Virginia. **Corporate headquarters location:** This Location.

ACO HARDWARE INC.
23333 Commerce Drive, Farmington Hills MI 48335-2764. 248/471-0100. **Contact:** Jayne Polisano, Director of Human Resources. **World Wide Web address:** http://www.acohardware.com. **Description:** Operates over 60 hardware stores throughout southeast Michigan. **NOTE:** Entry-level positions are offered. **Common positions include:** Management Trainee; Typist/Word Processor. **Educational backgrounds include:** Business Administration. **Benefits:** 401(k); Dental Insurance; Disability Coverage; Employee Discounts; Flexible Schedule; Life Insurance; Medical Insurance; Profit Sharing; Tuition Assistance. **Corporate headquarters location:** This Location. **Listed on:** Privately held. **Annual sales/revenues:** More than $100 million. **Number of employees at this location:** 200. **Number of employees worldwide:** 1,300.

ADVANCE STORES COMPANY, INC.
dba ADVANCE AUTO PARTS
5673 Airport Road, Roanoke VA 24012. 540/362-4911. **Contact:** Director of Human Resources. **Description:** Operates a chain of auto part stores. **Corporate headquarters location:** This Location.

ALAMO PLUMBING SUPPLY COMPANY
19 Burwood Lane, San Antonio TX 78216. 210/344-4950. **Fax:** 210/344-1253. **Contact:** Glenn Melton, Vice President. **Description:** A retail and wholesale distributor of plumbing supplies. **Corporate headquarters location:** This Location. **Number of employees at this location:** 30.

ALASKA COMMERCIAL COMPANY
550 West 64th Avenue, Suite 200, Anchorage AK 99518-1720. 907/273-4600. **Contact:** Henry Baldwin, Employment Manager. **Description:** Operates a retail chain of general merchandise stores. **Common positions include:** Accountant/Auditor; Advertising Clerk; Assistant Manager; Branch Manager; Buyer; Cashier; Computer Operator; Computer Programmer; Credit Clerk and Authorizer; Credit Manager; Department Manager; Food and Beverage Service Worker; General Manager; Graphic Artist; Management Trainee; Marketing Manager; Payroll Clerk; Receptionist; Retail Sales Worker; Secretary; Systems Analyst; Truck Driver; Typist/Word Processor; Wholesale and Retail Buyer. **Educational backgrounds include:** Accounting; Art/Design; Business Administration; Computer Science; Marketing; Retail Management. **Benefits:** Daycare Assistance; Dental Insurance; Disability Coverage; Employee Discounts; Life Insurance; Medical Insurance; Pension Plan; Profit Sharing; Savings Plan; Tuition Assistance. **Corporate headquarters location:** This Location. **Parent company:** The North West Company. **Annual sales/revenues:** $51 - $100 million. **Number of employees at this location:** 100. **Number of employees nationwide:** 750.

ALBERTSON'S INC.
3030 Cullerton Drive, Franklin Park IL 60131. **Toll-free phone:** 800/964-1434. **Fax:** 888/541-5793. **Contact:** Bobbie Riley, Director of Recruiting. **World Wide Web address:** http://www.albertsons.com. **Description:** One of the largest retail food-drug chains in the U.S. The company operates approximately 2,500 stores in 38 states. Founded in 1939. **NOTE:** Entry-level positions and part-time jobs are offered. **Common positions include:** AS400 Programmer Analyst; Computer Programmer; Management Trainee; Pharmacist; Systems Analyst. **Educational backgrounds include:** Accounting. **Benefits:** 401(k); Dental Insurance; Disability Coverage; Employee Discounts; Life Insurance; Medical Insurance; Profit Sharing; Relocation Assistance; Vacation Days. **Special programs:** Internships; Training. **Corporate headquarters location:** Boise ID. **President/CEO/Owner:** Gary Michael. **Number of employees nationwide:** 220,000.

ALBERTSON'S, INC.
P.O. Box 20, Boise ID 83726. 208/395-6200. **Fax:** 208/395-4880. **Contact:** Stacy Palsulich, Recruiting/Placement. **E-mail address:** employment@albertsons.com. **World Wide Web address:** http://www.albertsons.com. **Description:** One of the largest retail food-drug chains in the U.S. The company operates approximately 2,500 stores in 38 states. Founded in 1939. **NOTE:** Entry-level positions are offered. **Common positions include:** Accountant; Administrative Assistant; Architect; Attorney; Auditor; Computer Operator; Computer Programmer; Computer Support Technician; Computer Technician; Customer Service Representative; Draftsperson; Electrical/Electronics

Engineer; Help-Desk Technician; Intranet Developer; Mechanical Engineer; Network Engineer; Paralegal; Real Estate Lawyer; Secretary; SQL Programmer; Typist/Word Processor; Website Developer. **Educational backgrounds include:** Accounting; Business Administration; C/C++; Computer Science; HTML; Java; SQL; Visual Basic. **Benefits:** 401(k); Dental Insurance; Disability Coverage; Life Insurance; Medical Insurance; Profit Sharing; Relocation Assistance; Tuition Assistance; Vacation Days (6 - 10). **Office hours:** Monday - Friday, 8:00 a.m. - 5:00 p.m. **Corporate headquarters location:** This Location. **Other U.S. locations:** Nationwide. **Operations at this facility include:** Administration. **Listed on:** New York Stock Exchange. **Stock exchange symbol:** ABS. **Annual sales/revenues:** More than $100 million. **Number of employees at this location:** 1,600. **Number of employees nationwide:** 220,000.

ALDI INC.
1200 North Kirk Road, Batavia IL 60510. 630/879-8100. **Contact:** Personnel. **Description:** Operates a chain of discount grocery stores throughout the Midwest. **Corporate headquarters location:** This Location.

ALL STAR GAS CORPORATION
P.O. Box 303, Lebanon MO 65536. 417/532-3103. **Fax:** 417/532-8529. **Contact:** Debbie Neugebauer, Human Resources Manager. **Description:** Engaged in the retail sale of propane. **NOTE:** Entry-level positions are offered. **Common positions include:** Administrative Assistant; Auditor; Bank Officer/Manager; Blue-Collar Worker Supervisor; Branch Manager; Clerical Supervisor; Computer Operator; Computer Programmer; Customer Service Representative; Human Resources Manager; MIS Specialist; Operations Manager; Secretary; Systems Analyst; Typist/Word Processor. **Educational backgrounds include:** Accounting; Business Administration; Computer Science; Finance. **Benefits:** 401(k); Employee Discounts; Life Insurance; Medical Insurance; Tuition Assistance. **Special programs:** Training. **Corporate headquarters location:** This Location. **Other U.S. locations:** Nationwide. **President/CEO:** Paul Linsey. **Number of employees at this location:** 100. **Number of employees nationwide:** 630.

ROBERT ALLEN FABRICS
55 Cabot Boulevard, Mansfield MA 02048. 508/339-9151. **Contact:** Human Resources. **Description:** A fabrics retailer. **Office hours:** Monday - Friday, 8:30 a.m. - 5:00 p.m. **Corporate headquarters location:** This Location. **Other U.S. locations:** Nationwide.

ALLSUPS CONVENIENCE STORE
P.O. Box 1907, Clovis NM 88101. 505/769-2311. **Contact:** Personnel Department. **Description:** Operates a chain of convenience stores. **Corporate headquarters location:** This Location.

ALPINE LUMBER COMPANY
5800 North Pecos, Denver CO 80221. 303/458-8733. **Contact:** General Manager. **Description:** A retail lumber yard. **Corporate headquarters location:** This Location.

AMAZON.COM
P.O. Box 80185, Seattle WA 98108-0185. 206/622-2335. **Physical address:** 1516 Second Avenue, Seattle WA 98101. **Contact:** Strategic Growth. **E-mail address:** jobs@amazon.com. **World Wide Web address:** http://www.amazon.com. **Description:** An online store engaged in the sale of books, videos, music, toys, and electronics.

Amazon.com also offers online auctions and an online drugstore. Founded in 1995. **NOTE:** If sending a resume via e-mail, please be sure the information is in an ASCII-text format. **Corporate headquarters location:** This Location. **Other U.S. locations:** New Castle DE; McDonough GA; Coffeyville KS; Cambellsville KY; Lexington KY; Fernley NV. **International locations:** Europe. **Listed on:** NASDAQ. **Stock exchange symbol:** AMZN. **President/CEO:** Jeffrey Bezos.

AMERICAN EAGLE OUTFITTERS
150 Thorn Hill Drive, P.O. Box 788, Warrendale PA 15086. 724/779-5555. **Fax:** 724/779-5568. **Contact:** Mary B. Krentz, Human Resources Manager. **World Wide Web address:** http://www.ae.com. **Description:** A specialty retailer selling casual clothing and accessories for men and women. American Eagle Outfitters operates over 300 stores throughout the U.S. **Common positions include:** Management Trainee. **Educational backgrounds include:** Liberal Arts; Marketing. **Benefits:** 401(k); Dental Insurance; Disability Coverage; Employee Discounts; Life Insurance; Medical Insurance; Stock Option. **Corporate headquarters location:** This Location. **Operations at this facility include:** Sales; Service. **Listed on:** NASDAQ. **Number of employees nationwide:** 6,000.

AMERICAN FOODS, INC.
355 Benton Street, Stratford CT 06615. 203/378-7900. **Toll-free phone:** 800/233-5554. **Contact:** Bill Rappoport, Vice President of Sales. **World Wide Web address:** http://www.americanfoods.com. **Description:** Operates a customized shop-at-home food delivery service, delivering meats, vegetables, juices, desserts, and convenience items directly to the consumer. **Common positions include:** Branch Manager; Sales Manager; Sales Representative; Telemarketer. **Educational backgrounds include:** Business Administration; Liberal Arts. **Benefits:** Dental Insurance; Employee Discounts; Life Insurance; Medical Insurance; Pension Plan; Profit Sharing; Stock Option. **Other U.S. locations:** Nationwide. **Number of employees nationwide:** 1,200.

AMERICAN STORES COMPANY
299 South Main Street, Salt Lake City UT 84111. 801/539-0112. **Contact:** Curtis Rosentreter, Human Resources Director. **World Wide Web address:** http://www.americanstores.com. **Description:** Operates hundreds of retail food outlets and drug stores in 27 states. Chains include ACME Markets, Jewel-Osco, Lucky Stores, Jewel Food Stores, Osco Drug, and Sav-on Drugs. **Corporate headquarters location:** This Location. **Listed on:** New York Stock Exchange. **Annual sales/revenues:** More than $100 million.

AMES DEPARTMENT STORES, INC.
2418 Main Street, Mail Stop 0210, Rocky Hill CT 06067. 860/257-2167. **Contact:** Human Resources. **World Wide Web address:** http://www. amesstores.com. **Description:** Operates more than 300 discount department stores under the Ames name in 14 states in the Northeast, Mid-Atlantic, and Midwest, and in the District of Columbia. **Common positions include:** Accountant/Auditor; Administrative Manager; Advertising Clerk; Attorney; Budget Analyst; Buyer; Claim Representative; Clerical Supervisor; Computer Programmer; Construction Contractor; Credit Manager; Customer Service Representative; Financial Analyst; General Manager; Human Resources Manager; Management Trainee; Systems Analyst. **Educational backgrounds include:**

Business Administration; Computer Science; Finance; Liberal Arts. **Benefits:** 401(k); Dental Insurance; Disability Coverage; Employee Discounts; Life Insurance; Medical Insurance. **Corporate headquarters location:** This Location. **Listed on:** NASDAQ. **Number of employees at this location:** 1,000. **Number of employees nationwide:** 22,000.

ANCIRA ENTERPRISES INC.
6111 Bandera Road, San Antonio TX 78238-1643. 210/681-4900. **Contact:** Human Resources. **World Wide Web address:** http://www.ancira.com. **Description:** Sells new and used automobiles including Chevrolet, Subaru, and Volkswagen. This location also has a service, parts, and body shop. **Corporate headquarters location:** This Location.

ANDERSON LUMBER COMPANY
P.O. Box 9459, Ogden UT 84409. 801/479-3400. **Contact:** Personnel. **Description:** Operates a retail lumber yard. **Corporate headquarters location:** This Location. **Other U.S. locations:** ID; WY.

ANDRONICO'S MARKET
1109 Washington Avenue, Albany CA 94706. 510/649-6751. **Contact:** Ms. Paige Ellis, Human Resources Director. **E-mail address:** paige.ellis@andronicos.com. **World Wide Web address:** http://www.andronicos.com. **Description:** Operates a chain of retail grocery stores. Founded in 1929. **NOTE:** Entry-level positions and part-time jobs are offered. **Common positions include:** Administrative Assistant; Blue-Collar Worker Supervisor; Human Resources Manager; Vice President. **Benefits:** 401(k); Dental Insurance; Disability Coverage; Employee Discounts; Flexible Schedule; Life Insurance; Medical Insurance; Pension Plan; Sick Days. **Special programs:** Training. **Corporate headquarters location:** This Location. **Operations at this facility include:** Administration. **Listed on:** Privately held. **COO:** William J. Andronico. **Number of employees at this location:** 800.

ANGELICA CORPORATION
424 South Woods Mill Road, Suite 300, Chesterfield MO 63017-3406. 314/854-3800. **Contact:** Human Resources. **World Wide Web address:** http://www.angelica-corp.com. **Description:** This location houses the general offices for the Angelica Healthcare Services Group, Inc., a health care uniform rental store. Overall, Angelica Corporation provides textile rental and laundry services; manufactures and markets uniform and business career apparel; and operates specialty retail stores primarily for nurses and other health care professionals. Angelica's principal markets include health service networks and institutions (such as hospitals, nursing homes, outpatient service centers, health maintenance organizations, medical clinics, and laboratories) and health service personnel (such as doctors, dentists, and nurses); the hospitality market including lodging establishments (such as resorts, hotels and motels, and gaming establishments) and food service establishments (such as fast food, dinner and cafeteria chains, restaurants, food service management companies, amusement parks, clubs, and other eating and drinking places); other service industries including retailers (such as supermarkets and other food stores), drug and discount stores, financial institutions, transportation companies (such as car rental, cruise line, airline, bus, and other public transportation companies); manufacturers (such as food processors, drug and pharmaceutical, high-technology, and automotive companies); law enforcement and security companies; and educational and government institutions. **Common**

positions **include:** Accountant/Auditor; Credit Manager; Customer Service Representative; Industrial Designer; Manufacturer's/Wholesaler's Sales Rep.; Marketing Specialist; Operations/Production Manager; Quality Control Supervisor; Systems Analyst. **Educational backgrounds include:** Accounting; Art/Design; Business Administration; Computer Science; Liberal Arts; Marketing. **Benefits:** Dental Insurance; Disability Coverage; Employee Discounts; Life Insurance; Medical Insurance; Pension Plan; Savings Plan; Tuition Assistance. **Corporate headquarters location:** This Location. **Listed on:** New York Stock Exchange. **Number of employees nationwide:** 9,500.

ARDEN GROUP, INC.
P.O. Box 512256, Los Angeles CA 90051-2256. 310/638-2842. **Fax:** 310/604-4896. **Contact:** Human Resources. **Description:** A holding company for Gelson's Markets, which operates 13 Gelson's and two Mayfair supermarkets in the greater Los Angeles area. **Corporate headquarters location:** This Location. **Number of employees nationwide:** 1,900.

ARNOLDS ACQUISITIONS
7069 Consolidated Way, San Diego CA 92121. 858/549-6000. **Contact:** Personnel. **Description:** A furniture retailer operating stores under the name Arnolds Home Furnishings. **Common positions include:** Attorney; Buyer; Credit Manager; Customer Service Representative; Financial Analyst; Marketing Specialist; Services Sales Representative. **Educational backgrounds include:** Business Administration; Computer Science; Marketing. **Benefits:** Employee Discounts; Life Insurance; Medical Insurance. **Corporate headquarters location:** This Location.

ARVEY PAPER & OFFICE PRODUCTS
661 North LaSalle Drive, Chicago IL 60610. 312/951-5051. **Contact:** Manager of Human Resources. **Description:** A retailer of paper and office products. **Common positions include:** Accountant/Auditor; Administrator; Advertising Clerk; Assistant Manager; Branch Manager; Buyer; Customer Service Representative; Human Resources Manager; Management Trainee; Marketing Specialist. **Educational backgrounds include:** Accounting; Business Administration; Finance; Liberal Arts; Marketing. **Benefits:** Dental Insurance; Disability Coverage; Employee Sharing; Life Insurance; Medical Insurance; Pension Plan; Profit Sharing. **Corporate headquarters location:** This Location. **Parent company:** International Paper Company. **Listed on:** New York Stock Exchange.

AUSTAD'S
2801 East 10th Street, Sioux Falls SD 57103. 605/336-3135. **Contact:** Human Resources. **World Wide Web address:** http://www.mammothgolf.com. **Description:** A mail order company specializing in golf equipment. **Corporate headquarters location:** This Location.

AUTOZONE
123 South Front Street, Memphis TN 38103. 901/495-6500. **Contact:** Recruiting. **World Wide Web address:** http://www.autozone.com. **Description:** Operates a chain of do-it-yourself, retail auto parts stores. **Common positions include:** Retail Executive; Retail Manager; Retail Sales Worker. **Benefits:** Dental Insurance; Disability Coverage; Employee Discounts; Life Insurance; Medical Insurance; Pension Plan; Stock Option. **Corporate headquarters location:** This Location. **Listed on:** New York Stock Exchange. **Number of**

employees at this location: 850. **Number of employees nationwide:** 17,400.

AVEDA CORPORATION
4000 Pheasant Ridge Drive, Blaine MN 55449. 763/783-4000. **Fax:** 763/783-6850. **Recorded jobline:** 763/783-4282. **Contact:** Human Resources. **E-mail address:** jobs@aveda.com. **World Wide Web address:** http://www.aveda.com. **Description:** Manufactures perfume, makeup, and other beauty products. Aveda Corporation also operates salons and retail stores. **Special programs:** Internships. **Internship information:** Candidates should check the company's Website for application procedures. **Corporate headquarters location:** This Location. **Other U.S. locations:** New York NY. **International locations:** Worldwide.

AVON PRODUCTS INC.
1345 Avenue of the Americas, New York NY 10105. 212/282-5000. **Contact:** Human Resources Department. **World Wide Web address:** http://www.avoncareers.com. **Description:** A direct seller of beauty care products, fashion jewelry, gifts, fragrances, and decorative products. Avon, a *Fortune* 500 company, markets its products through a network of 2.8 million independent sales representatives in 135 countries worldwide. Founded in 1886. **NOTE:** Salespeople are considered independent contractors or dealers and most work part-time. If you are interested in becoming a sales representative, please call 800/FOR-AVON, or visit the company's Website for more information. **Corporate headquarters location:** This Location. **Listed on:** New York Stock Exchange. **President/CEO:** Andrea Jung. **Annual sales/revenues:** More than $100 million. **Other U.S. locations:**
• 6901 Golf Road, Morton Grove IL 60053. 847/966-0200.

B&B CORPORATE HOLDINGS, INC.
P.O. Box 1808, Tampa FL 33601. 813/621-6411. **Contact:** Linda Toledo, Director of Human Resources. **World Wide Web address:** http://www.usave.com. **Description:** Operates a chain of supermarkets and convenience stores under the USave name. **Common positions include:** Accountant/Auditor; Advertising Clerk; Blue-Collar Worker Supervisor; Human Resources Manager; Management Trainee. **Educational backgrounds include:** Food Services. **Benefits:** Dental Insurance; Disability Coverage; Life Insurance; Medical Insurance; Profit Sharing; Savings Plan. **Corporate headquarters location:** This Location. **Subsidiaries include:** USave Supermarkets.

BJ'S WHOLESALE CLUB
One Mercer Road, Natick MA 01760. 508/651-7400. **Contact:** Human Resources. **World Wide Web address:** http://www.bjs.com. **Description:** Sells food and general merchandise through more than 60 warehouses. **Corporate headquarters location:** This Location. **Parent company:** Waban Inc. (also at this location).

BMC WEST CORPORATION
P.O. Box 70006, Boise ID 83707. 208/331-4300. **Fax:** 208/331-4367. **Contact:** Neil Watterson, Director of Employment. **World Wide Web address:** http://www.bmcwest.com. **Description:** BMC West Corporation is a regional distributor and retailer of building materials in the western United States. Products are sold primarily to professional contractors and consumers. In addition to distributing products from other manufacturers, the company conducts value-added conversion activities that include pre-hanging doors, fabricating roof trusses, pre-assembling windows, and pre-

cutting lumber to meet customer specifications. **Common positions include:** Accountant/Auditor; Administrative Manager; Advertising Clerk; Clerical Supervisor; Computer Programmer; Credit Manager; Financial Analyst; General Manager; Human Resources Manager; Management Trainee; Operations/Production Manager; Systems Analyst; Transportation/Traffic Specialist; Wholesale and Retail Buyer. **Educational backgrounds include:** Accounting; Business Administration; Finance; Marketing. **Benefits:** 401(k); Dental Insurance; Disability Coverage; Employee Discounts; Life Insurance; Medical Insurance; Profit Sharing; Tuition Assistance. **Special programs:** Internships. **Corporate headquarters location:** This Location. **Operations at this facility include:** Administration. **Listed on:** NASDAQ. **Stock exchange symbol:** BMCW. **Number of employees at this location:** 100. **Number of employees nationwide:** 3,100.

BABBAGE'S ETC. LLC
2250 William D. Tate Avenue, Grapevine TX 76051. 817/424-2000. **Fax:** 817/424-2002. **Contact:** Human Resources. **World Wide Web address:** http://www.gamestop.com. **Description:** A national retailer of interactive games and accessories. Babbage's Etc. operates more than 475 stores in the U.S. and Puerto Rico under the Babbage's Etc., Software Etc., Gamestop, SuperSoftware, and Planet X names. **Corporate headquarters location:** This Location.

BABIES 'R US
605 Haywood Road, Greenville SC 29607. 864/297-9444. **Contact:** Human Resources. **World Wide Web address:** http://www.babiesrus.com. **Description:** A retailer of baby and young children's products. The company operates 46 stores in 13 states, primarily in the Southeast and Midwest. Founded in 1970. **Common positions include:** Cashier; Management; Sales Executive; Services Sales Representative; Stock Clerk. **Corporate headquarters location:** This Location. **Other area locations:** Augusta SC; Columbia SC; North Charleston SC. **Other U.S. locations:** Asheville NC; Charlotte NC; Greensboro NC; Raleigh NC. **Listed on:** NASDAQ. **Number of employees nationwide:** 2,470.

BACHMAN'S INC.
6010 Lyndale Avenue South, Minneapolis MN 55419. 612/861-7675. **Fax:** 612/861-7748. **Recorded jobline:** 612/861-9242. **Contact:** Julie Kingsley, Employment Manager. **E-mail address:** hr@bachmans.com. **Description:** A retail florist, landscaper, garden center, nursery, and greenhouse. **Common positions include:** Blue-Collar Worker Supervisor; Designer; Landscape Architect; Management Trainee. **Educational backgrounds include:** Horticulture. **Benefits:** 401(k); Dental Insurance; Disability Coverage; Employee Discounts; Life Insurance; Medical Insurance; Profit Sharing. **Special programs:** Internships. **Corporate headquarters location:** This Location. **Number of employees at this location:** 1,000.

W.S. BADCOCK CORPORATION
P.O. Box 497, Mulberry FL 33860. 941/425-4921. **Contact:** Jim Vernon, Director of Personnel. **World Wide Web address:** http://www.badcock.com. **Description:** Operates a chain of retail furniture stores. **Corporate headquarters location:** This Location.

J. BAKER, INC.
555 Turnpike Street, Canton MA 02021. 781/828-9300. **Contact:** Recruiter. **World Wide Web address:** http://www.workngear.com. **Description:** Engaged in the retail sale of footwear and apparel. J.

Baker sells footwear through self-service licensed shoe departments in mass merchandising department stores, through full- and semi-service licensed shoe departments in department and specialty stores, on a wholesale basis, and through its Fayva chain of self-selection family shoe stores, and its Parade of Shoes chain of women's shoe stores. The company is also involved in the retail sale of apparel through its chain of Casual Male Big & Tall men's stores and also through its chain of Work 'n Gear work clothing stores. **Common positions include:** Accountant/Auditor; Administrative Manager; Advertising Clerk; Blue-Collar Worker Supervisor; Buyer; Claim Representative; Computer Programmer; Designer; Draftsperson; Employment Interviewer; Financial Analyst; Receptionist; Retail Sales Worker; Stock Clerk; Transportation/Traffic Specialist; Typist/Word Processor; Wholesale and Retail Buyer. **Educational backgrounds include:** Accounting; Art/Design; Communications; Computer Science; Economics; Finance; Liberal Arts; Marketing. **Benefits:** Dental Insurance; Disability Coverage; Employee Discounts; Life Insurance; Medical Insurance; Pension Plan; Profit Sharing; Savings Plan; Tuition Assistance. **Special programs:** Internships. **Corporate headquarters location:** This Location. **Other U.S. locations:** Columbus OH. **Number of employees at this location:** 1,000. **Number of employees nationwide:** 13,260.

BARNES & NOBLE CORPORATION
122 Fifth Avenue, 2nd Floor, New York NY 10011. 212/633-3300. **Contact:** Melissa Church, Senior Employment Specialist. **World Wide Web address:** http://www.bn.com. **Description:** A nationwide bookstore chain. **Common positions include:** Accountant/Auditor; Administrative Worker/Clerk; Buyer; Customer Service Representative; Department Manager; Financial Analyst; Management Trainee; Store Manager. **Educational backgrounds include:** Accounting; Business Administration; Liberal Arts. **Benefits:** Dental Insurance; Disability Coverage; Employee Discounts; Life Insurance; Medical Insurance; Savings Plan. **Corporate headquarters location:** This Location. **Other U.S. locations:** Nationwide.

BARNEYS NEW YORK
660 Madison Avenue, New York NY 10021. 212/593-7800. **Contact:** Human Resources. **World Wide Web address:** http://www.barneys.com. **Description:** A national specialty retailer offering primarily men's and women's apparel collections from both American and international designers. **Common positions include:** Accountant; Administrator; Advertising Clerk; Assistant Buyer; Assistant Manager; Buyer; Customer Service Rep.; Department Manager; Human Resources Manager; Operations/Production Manager; Public Relations Specialist; Purchasing Agent/Manager; Sales Executive. **Benefits:** Dental Insurance; Disability Coverage; Employee Discounts; Life Insurance; Medical Insurance; Pension Plan; Savings Plan. **Corporate headquarters location:** This Location.

BARTELL DRUG COMPANY
4727 Denver Avenue South, Seattle WA 98134. 206/763-2626. **Contact:** Personnel Department. **World Wide Web address:** http://www.bartelldrug.com. **Description:** Operates a chain of drug stores in the Seattle area. **Corporate headquarters location:** This Location. **Number of employees nationwide:** 600.

E.C. BARTON & COMPANY
P.O. Box 4040, Jonesboro AR 72403. 870/932-6673. **Contact:** Chris Stevenson, Personnel

Manager. **Description:** Owners and operators of retail, wholesale, and discount building material stores. **Common positions include:** Accountant/Auditor; Advertising Clerk; Branch Manager; Brokerage Clerk; Buyer; Computer Programmer; Cost Estimator; General Manager; Human Resources Manager; Management Trainee; Manufacturer's/Wholesaler's Sales Rep.; Purchasing Agent/Manager; Systems Analyst; Wholesale and Retail Buyer. **Educational backgrounds include:** Accounting; Business Administration; Computer Science; Marketing. **Benefits:** Employee Discounts; Life Insurance; Medical Insurance; Profit Sharing. **Corporate headquarters location:** This Location. **Number of employees at this location:** 30. **Number of employees nationwide:** 450.

BASHAS'
P.O. Box 488, Chandler AZ 85244. 480/895-9350. **Contact:** Personnel Department. **World Wide Web address:** http://www.bashas.com. **Description:** Operates a chain of retail grocery stores. Founded in 1932. **Corporate headquarters location:** This Location. **Number of employees nationwide:** 3,400.

BASKIN-ROBBINS, INC.
31 Baskin-Robbins Place, Glendale CA 91201-2738. 818/956-0031. **Contact:** Suzanne Serguson, Director of Human Resources. **Description:** This location houses administrative offices. Overall, Baskin-Robbins is an ice cream manufacturer that also operates retail locations. **Corporate headquarters location:** This Location. **Number of employees nationwide:** 875.

BEALL'S DEPARTMENT STORES
P.O. Box 25207, Bradenton FL 34206. 941/747-2355. **Contact:** Human Resources. **World Wide Web address:** http://www.beallsflorida.com. **Description:** Operates department stores. **Corporate headquarters location:** This Location.

BEAR CREEK CORPORATION
HARRY & DAVID
P.O. Box 712, Medford OR 97501. 541/864-2121. **Physical address:** 2518 South Pacific Highway, Medford OR. **Recorded jobline:** 541/864-2232. **Contact:** Human Resources. **World Wide Web address:** http://www.bco.com. **Description:** Produces and markets fruit, gourmet food, and specialty gifts. Bear Creek Corporation is most famous for the Fruit of the Month Club, Royal Riviera Pears, Oregold Peaches, and roses. Mail order catalogs include Harry & David, Jackson & Perkins, and Northwest Express. **Common positions include:** Account Representative; Accountant/Auditor; Art Director; Buyer; Computer Programmer; Customer Service Representative; Distribution Manager; Financial Analyst; Human Resources Manager; Industrial Engineer; Logistics Manager; Market Research Analyst; Marketing Specialist; Merchandiser; Operations/Production Manager; Packaging Engineer; Plant Engineer; Product Engineer; Production Manager; Promotion Manager; Public Relations Specialist; Quality Control Supervisor; Retail Manager; Sales Representative; Systems Analyst; Transportation/Traffic Specialist. **Educational backgrounds include:** Accounting; Art/Design; Business Administration; Communications; Computer Science; Engineering; Finance; Liberal Arts; Marketing. **Benefits:** 401(k); Dental Insurance; Disability Coverage; Employee Discounts; Life Insurance; Medical Insurance; Pension Plan; Relocation Assistance; Scholarship Program; Tuition Assistance. **Corporate headquarters location:** This Location. **Listed on:** Privately held. **Annual sales/revenues:** More than $100 million.

Number of employees at this location: 1,500. **Number of employees nationwide:** 6,000.

BEE-GEE SHOES
3155 El-Bee Road, Dayton OH 45439. 937/643-7400. **Contact:** Human Resources. **Description:** A retailer of shoes. **Corporate headquarters location:** This Location.

BELK STORES SERVICES INC.
2801 West Tyvola Road, Charlotte NC 28217-4500. 704/357-1000. **Fax:** 704/357-1883. **Contact:** Human Resources. **Description:** Operates 260 department stores located in 14 southeastern states. **Common positions include:** Buyer; Management Trainee. **Educational backgrounds include:** Business Administration; Fashion; Home Economics; Merchandising. **Benefits:** Employee Discounts; Life Insurance; Medical Insurance; Pension Plan; Profit Sharing. **Special programs:** Internships. **Corporate headquarters location:** This Location.

JAN BELL MARKETING, INC.
14051 NW 14th Street, Sunrise FL 33323. 954/846-8000. **Toll-free phone:** 800/223-6964. **Fax:** 954/846-2787. **Recorded jobline:** 800/223-6964x5408. **Contact:** Human Resources. **Description:** A retailer, merchandiser, and distributor of jewelry, watches, sunglasses, fragrances, and collectibles. **Common positions include:** Accountant/Auditor; Blue-Collar Worker Supervisor; Buyer; Computer Programmer; Customer Service Representative; Department Manager; Financial Analyst; Graphic Artist; Human Resources Manager; Order Clerk; Payroll Clerk; Receptionist; Stock Clerk; Systems Analyst; Wholesale and Retail Buyer. **Educational backgrounds include:** Accounting; Art/Design; Business Administration; Communications; Computer Science; Economics; Finance; Liberal Arts; Marketing; Mathematics. **Benefits:** 401(k); Dental Insurance; Disability Coverage; Employee Discounts; Life Insurance; Medical Insurance; Stock Option. **Corporate headquarters location:** This Location. **Number of employees at this location:** 500. **Number of employees nationwide:** 2,500.

BENO'S FAMILY FASHIONS
1512 South Santee Street, Los Angeles CA 90015. 213/748-2222. **Contact:** Personnel. **Description:** Operates a chain of retail stores in California and Nevada selling a wide variety of merchandise, with emphasis on apparel for men, women, and children. More than 55 stores are operated under the name of Beno's. **Common positions include:** Accountant; Advertising Clerk; Branch Manager; Buyer; Retail Sales Worker. **Corporate headquarters location:** This Location. **Operations at this facility include:** Administration; Divisional Headquarters; Sales; Service. **Number of employees nationwide:** 550.

BEST BUY COMPANY, INC.
P.O. Box 9312, Minneapolis MN 55440-9312. 952/947-2000. **Physical address:** 7075 Flying Cloud Drive, Eden Prairie MN 55344. **Recorded jobline:** 952/947-2555. **Contact:** Jim Diesling and Helina Stefans, Region 1 Recruiters. **World Wide Web address:** http://www.bestbuy.com. **Description:** A national retailer of consumer electronics, appliances, and home office products. **Common positions include:** Accountant/Auditor; Advertising Clerk; Buyer; Computer Programmer; Customer Service Representative; General Manager; Human Resources Manager; Management Trainee; MIS Specialist; Systems Analyst. **Educational backgrounds include:** Accounting; Business Administration; Communications; Computer Science; Economics; Finance; Liberal Arts;

Marketing. **Benefits:** 401(k); Dental Insurance; Employee Discounts; Life Insurance; Medical Insurance; Pension Plan; Public Transit Available; Tuition Assistance. **Corporate headquarters location:** This Location. **Other U.S. locations:** Nationwide. **Listed on:** New York Stock Exchange. **Stock exchange symbol:** BBY. **Annual sales/revenues:** More than $100 million. **Number of employees at this location:** 1,500. **Number of employees nationwide:** 40,000.

BI-LO, INC.
P.O. Box 99, Mauldin SC 29662. 864/234-1600. **Contact:** Human Resources. **World Wide Web address:** http://www.bi-lo.com. **Description:** Operates a supermarket chain. The company has stores throughout the Southeast including South Carolina, North Carolina, Georgia, and Tennessee. **Corporate headquarters location:** This Location.

BIG V SUPERMARKETS INC.
176 North Main Street, Florida NY 10921-1098. 914/651-4411. **Contact:** Human Resources. **Description:** Operates and manages a chain of 30 supermarkets, primarily in the mid-Hudson Valley region of New York State. Big V Supermarkets offers both nationally-advertised brand names and a wide variety of ShopRite private label products. **Corporate headquarters location:** This Location.

BIG Y FOODS INC.
2145 Roosevelt Avenue, Springfield MA 01104. 413/784-0600. **Fax:** 413/732-7350. **Contact:** Jack Henry, Director of Human Resources. **World Wide Web address:** http://www.bigy.com. **Description:** Operates a chain of over 40 supermarkets. **Common positions include:** Accountant/Auditor; Administrative Manager; Advertising Clerk; Blue-Collar Worker Supervisor; Claim Representative; Computer Programmer; Construction Contractor; Customer Service Representative; Department Manager; Human Resources Manager; Investigator; Licensed Practical Nurse; Management Trainee; Property and Real Estate Manager; Public Relations Specialist; Purchasing Agent/Manager; Restaurant/Food Service Manager; Store Manager; Systems Analyst; Wholesale and Retail Buyer. **Educational backgrounds include:** Accounting; Business Administration; Computer Science; Finance; Marketing. **Benefits:** 401(k); Dental Insurance; Disability Coverage; Life Insurance; Medical Insurance; Profit Sharing; Tuition Assistance. **Special programs:** Internships. **Corporate headquarters location:** This Location. **Listed on:** Privately held. **Number of employees nationwide:** 7,200.

BLOCKBUSTER ENTERTAINMENT GROUP
1201 Elm Street, Suite 2100, Dallas TX 75270. 214/854-3259. **Fax:** 214/854-3241. **Contact:** Tom Grissom, Manager of Recruiting. **E-mail address:** career@blockbuster.com. **World Wide Web address:** http://www.blockbuster.com. **Description:** Operates a chain of video rental and music retail stores. There are approximately 7,100 Blockbuster locations worldwide. **NOTE:** Entry-level positions are offered. **Common positions include:** Accountant/Auditor; Buyer; Computer Operator; Financial Analyst; Market Research Analyst; MIS Specialist; Systems Analyst. **Educational backgrounds include:** Accounting; Business Administration; Computer Science; Finance. **Benefits:** 401(k); Dental Insurance; Disability Coverage; Employee Discounts; Financial Planning Assistance; Life Insurance; Medical Insurance; Tuition Assistance. **Corporate headquarters location:** This Location. **Other U.S. locations:** Nationwide. **International locations:** Worldwide. **Parent company:** Viacom. **Listed on:** New York

Stock Exchange. **CEO:** John Antioco. **Annual sales/revenues:** More than $100 million. **Number of employees at this location:** 1,600. **Number of employees nationwide:** 58,000.

BLOOMINGDALE'S
1000 Third Avenue, New York NY 10022. 212/705-2383. **Contact:** Human Resources. **Description:** Operates a chain of department stores. **Common positions include:** Administrator; Advertising Clerk; Blue-Collar Worker Supervisor; Branch Manager; Buyer; Commercial Artist; Customer Service Representative; Department Manager; General Manager; Management Trainee; Operations/Production Manager; Public Relations Specialist; Purchasing Agent/Manager; Quality Control Supervisor; Systems Analyst. **Educational backgrounds include:** Accounting; Business Administration; Communications; Economics; Finance; Liberal Arts; Marketing. **Benefits:** Dental Insurance; Disability Coverage; Employee Discounts; Life Insurance; Medical Insurance; Pension Plan. **Corporate headquarters location:** This Location. **Other U.S. locations:** Washington DC; Boca Raton FL; Miami FL; Palm Beach FL; Chicago IL; Boston MA; Minneapolis MN; Philadelphia PA. **Parent company:** Federated Department Stores Inc. **Listed on:** New York Stock Exchange.

BODY SHOP OF AMERICA, INC.
6225 Powers Avenue, Jacksonville FL 32217-2215. 904/737-0811. **Contact:** Judy Anderson, Assistant Controller. **Description:** A retail store offering apparel for juniors.

THE BOMBAY COMPANY, INC.
550 Bailey Avenue, Suite 700, Fort Worth TX 76107-2111. 817/870-1847. **Fax:** 817/348-7090. **Recorded jobline:** 817/339-3799. **Contact:** Human Resources. **World Wide Web address:** http://www.bombayco.com. **Description:** A specialty retailer of ready-to-assemble home furnishings, prints, and accessories. Products are sold through over 400 Bombay Company and Alex & Ivy Stores. **Common positions include:** Accountant/Auditor; Buyer; Customer Service Representative; Designer; Financial Analyst; Management Trainee; Retail Sales Worker; Secretary; Systems Analyst; Wholesale and Retail Buyer. **Educational backgrounds include:** Accounting; Art/Design; Business Administration; Finance; Liberal Arts; Marketing. **Benefits:** 401(k); Dental Insurance; Disability Coverage; Employee Discounts; Life Insurance; Medical Insurance; Profit Sharing; Stock Option; Tuition Assistance. **Special programs:** Internships. **Corporate headquarters location:** This Location. **Other U.S. locations:** Nationwide. **International locations:** Canada. **Listed on:** New York Stock Exchange. **Number of employees nationwide:** 8,000.

THE BON MARCHE
918 Idaho Street, Box 19, Boise ID 83707. 208/344-5521. **Contact:** Human Resources. **Description:** A retail department store chain with more than 35 locations. **Corporate headquarters location:** This Location. **Other U.S. locations:** ID; MT; OK; UT; WA. **Parent company:** Federated Department Stores.

THE BON-TON
2801 East Market Street, York PA 17402. 717/751-3185. **Fax:** 717/751-3083. **Contact:** Sue Hulme, Manager of Executive Employment. **E-mail address:** resumes@bonton.com. **World Wide Web address:** http://www.bonton.com. **Description:** One of the largest department stores in America with over 70 locations. The Bon-Ton offers brand-name

merchandise for men, women, children, and the home. **NOTE:** Entry-level positions are offered. **Common positions include:** Accountant; Administrative Assistant; Advertising Executive; Auditor; Branch Manager; Buyer; Chief Financial Officer; Computer Programmer; Computer Support Technician; Controller; Credit Manager; Customer Service Representative; Department Manager; Draftsperson; Financial Analyst; General Manager; Human Resources Manager; Industrial Engineer; Management Trainee; Network/Systems Administrator; Operations Manager; Planner; Project Manager; Purchasing Agent/Manager; Sales Manager; Secretary; Systems Analyst; Vice President; Wholesale and Retail Buyer. **Educational backgrounds include:** Microsoft Word; Spreadsheets. **Benefits:** 401(k); Casual Dress - Fridays; Daycare Assistance; Dental Insurance; Disability Coverage; Employee Discounts; Life Insurance; Medical Insurance; Profit Sharing; Sick Days; Vacation Pay. **Special programs:** Training; Summer Jobs. **Corporate headquarters location:** This Location. **Other U.S. locations:** MA; MD; NJ; NY; WV. **Operations at this facility include:** Administration. **Listed on:** NASDAQ. **President/CEO:** Heywood Wilansky. **Number of employees at this location:** 500. **Number of employees nationwide:** 12,000.

BOOKS-A-MILLION, INC.
402 Industrial Lane, Birmingham AL 35211. 205/942-3737. **Contact:** Personnel. **Description:** One of the country's largest book retailers with a network of 165 bookstores in 17 states. **Benefits:** 401(k); Stock Option. **Corporate headquarters location:** This Location. **Subsidiaries include:** American Wholesale Book Company, Inc. **Listed on:** NASDAQ. **Stock exchange symbol:** BAMM. **President/CEO:** Clyde B. Anderson. **Annual sales/revenues:** More than $100 million.

BORDERS GROUP, INC.
100 Phoenix Drive, Ann Arbor MI 48108. 734/477-1100. **Contact:** Human Resources. **World Wide Web address:** http://www.borders.com. **Description:** One of the nation's largest retail bookselling chains. Founded in 1933. **Corporate headquarters location:** This Location.

BRADLEES, INC.
One Bradlees Circle, Braintree MA 02184-5212. 781/380-3000. **Contact:** Human Resources. **Description:** A discount department store retailer in the Northeast, operating over 125 stores in eight states. Store offerings are mainly focused on apparel and home furnishings. **Benefits:** Deferred Compensation; Pension Plan; Retirement Plan; Stock Option. **Corporate headquarters location:** This Location. **Subsidiaries include:** Bradlees New England Holdings, Inc.; Bradlees New York Holdings, Inc.; Stop & Shop Holdings, Inc. **Listed on:** New York Stock Exchange.

BEN BRIDGE CORPORATION
P.O. Box 1908, Seattle WA 98111. 206/448-8800. **Contact:** Jonathan Bridge, Vice Chairman. **World Wide Web address:** http://www.benbridge.com. **Description:** A retailer of fine jewelry and related accessories. **Common positions include:** Accountant/Auditor; Buyer; Computer Programmer; Credit Clerk and Authorizer; Sales Executive; Services Sales Representative; Wholesale and Retail Buyer. **Benefits:** Dental Insurance; Disability Coverage; Employee Discounts; Life Insurance; Medical Insurance; Profit Sharing; Tuition Assistance. **Corporate headquarters location:** This Location. **Other U.S. locations:** AL; CA; HI; NV; OR. **Number of employees at this location:** 80. **Number of employees nationwide:** 475.

BRIDGESTONE/FIRESTONE, INC.
dba AMERICAN TIRE AND SERVICE CO.
2550 West Golf Road, Suite 400, Rolling Meadows IL 60008. 847/981-2200. **Fax:** 847/981-2350. **Contact:** Human Resources. **World Wide Web address:** http://www.bridgestone-firestone.com. **Description:** This location is the support center and headquarters for the Bridgestone/Firestone, Inc. retail stores. Founded in 1900. **NOTE:** Entry-level positions and part-time jobs are offered. **Common positions include:** Account Manager; Account Representative; Accountant; Administrative Assistant; Architect; Attorney; Buyer; Claim Representative; Computer Programmer; Computer Support Technician; Controller; Customer Service Representative; Database Administrator; Database Manager; Environmental Engineer; Financial Analyst; Graphic Artist; Human Resources Manager; Market Research Analyst; Marketing Manager; Media Planner; Multimedia Designer; Network/Systems Administrator; Paralegal; Public Relations Specialist; Purchasing Agent/Manager; Real Estate Lawyer; Secretary; Systems Analyst; Typist/Word Processor. **Educational backgrounds include:** Accounting; Art/Design; Business Administration; C/C++; Computer Science; Education; Engineering; Finance; HTML; Marketing; MBA; Microsoft Office; Microsoft Word; Software Tech. Support; Spreadsheets. **Benefits:** 401(k); Casual Dress - Daily; Dental Insurance; Disability Coverage; Employee Discounts; Life Insurance; Medical Insurance; Pension Plan; Savings Plan; Tuition Assistance. **Office hours:** Monday - Friday, 8:00 a.m. - 5:00 p.m. **Corporate headquarters location:** Nashville TN. **Other U.S. locations:** Nationwide. **International locations:** Worldwide. **Parent company:** Bridgestone. **Number of employees at this location:** 150. **Number of employees nationwide:** 15,000.

BROOKS BROTHERS
346 Madison Avenue, New York NY 10017. 212/682-8800. **Contact:** Personnel. **World Wide Web address:** http://www.brooksbrothers.com. **Description:** Operates over 150 retail stores and factory outlets in the United States. Founded in 1818. **Common positions include:** Advertising Clerk; Architect; Branch Manager; Buyer; Claim Representative; Computer Programmer; Customer Service Representative; Department Manager; Draftsperson; Editor; General Manager; Human Resources Manager; Management Trainee; Operations/Production Manager; Purchasing Agent/Manager; Receptionist; Reporter; Secretary; Stock Clerk; Systems Analyst. **Educational backgrounds include:** Accounting; Art/Design; Business Administration; Communications; Computer Science; Economics; Liberal Arts; Marketing; Mathematics. **Benefits:** Dental Insurance; Disability Coverage; Employee Discounts; Life Insurance; Medical Insurance; Pension Plan; Profit Sharing; Savings Plan; Tuition Assistance. **Corporate headquarters location:** This Location. **Parent company:** Marks & Spencer plc (London).

BROOKS CAMERA
125 Kearney Street, San Francisco CA 94108. 415/362-4708. **Contact:** Don Boyle, Manager. **Description:** A retailer of photography equipment. **Common positions include:** Accountant/Auditor; Buyer; Civil Engineer; Photographic Process Worker; Quality Control Supervisor; Retail Sales Worker. **Benefits:** Employee Discounts; Medical Insurance; Pension Plan. **Corporate headquarters location:** This Location. **Parent company:** Inventory Supply Company, Inc. **Number of employees at this location:** 10.

BROOKS/MAXI DRUG, INC.
50 Service Avenue, Warwick RI 02886. 401/825-3900. **Fax:** 401/825-3707. **Contact:** Roy Greene, Director of Human Resources. **Description:** Operates over 230 retail drugstores located throughout New England. **Common positions include:** Accountant; Administrative Assistant; Advertising Clerk; Advertising Executive; Assistant Manager; Auditor; Blue-Collar Worker Supervisor; Budget Analyst; Buyer; Chief Financial Officer; Computer Operator; Controller; Database Manager; Finance Director; Financial Analyst; Human Resources Manager; Management Trainee; Pharmacist; Quality Control Supervisor; Systems Analyst; Systems Manager. **Educational backgrounds include:** Accounting; Business Administration; Computer Science; Economics; Finance; Liberal Arts; Marketing; Pharmacology; Retail Management. **Benefits:** 401(k); Dental Insurance; Disability Coverage; Employee Discounts; Life Insurance; Medical Insurance. **Corporate headquarters location:** This Location. **Other U.S. locations:** CT; MA; ME; NH; VT. **Listed on:** Privately held. **President/CEO/Owner:** Michel Coutu.

BROOKSHIRE BROTHERS INC.
P.O. Box 1688, Lufkin TX 75902. 936/634-8155. **Contact:** Human Resources. **Description:** Operates a retail grocery chain. **Corporate headquarters location:** This Location.

BROOKSTONE COMPANY
17 Riverside Street, Nashua NH 03062. 603/880-9500. **Contact:** Laura Lundberg, Employment Coordinator. **World Wide Web address:** http://www.brookstone.com. **Description:** Operates a chain of over 200 specialty retail stores. **Corporate headquarters location:** This Location.

BRUNO'S SUPERMARKETS, INC.
P.O. Box 2486, Birmingham AL 35201. 205/940-9400. **Contact:** Human Resources. **E-mail address:** hrrecruiting@brunos.com. **World Wide Web address:** http://www.brunos.com. **Description:** Operates a chain of more than 150 supermarkets and smaller food and liquor stores. Stores include Food World; Bruno's; Food Fair; Food Max; and Food World Discount Liquors. **Corporate headquarters location:** This Location. **Listed on:** Privately held. **Annual sales/revenues:** More than $100 million. **Number of employees nationwide:** 13,000.

THE BUCKLE, INC.
2407 West 24th Street, Kearney NE 68845. 308/236-8491. **Fax:** 308/236-4493. **Contact:** Human Resources. **World Wide Web address:** http://www.buckle.com. **Description:** The Buckle, Inc. is a retailer of casual apparel for young men and women. The company operates over 260 retail stores in 35 states throughout the central United States. The company markets a wide selection of brand name casual apparel including denims, other casual bottoms, tops, sportswear, outerwear, accessories, shoes, and children's clothes. **Listed on:** New York Stock Exchange. **Stock exchange symbol:** BKLE.

BURDINE'S
22 East Flagler Street, 4th Floor, Miami FL 33131. 305/577-1998. **Contact:** Human Resources. **Description:** Operates a retail department store chain. **Corporate headquarters location:** This Location. **Parent company:** Federated Department Stores.

BURLINGTON COAT FACTORY
1830 Route 130 North, Burlington NJ 08016. 609/387-7800. **Contact:** Sarah R. Orleck, Recruiter.

World Wide Web address: http://www.coat.com. **Description:** An off-price apparel discounter. Product lines consist of brand name apparel including coats, sportswear, childrenswear, menswear, juvenile furniture, linens, shoes, and accessories. **Corporate headquarters location:** This Location. **Listed on:** New York Stock Exchange.

BUSY BEAVER BUILDING CENTERS INC.
3130 William Pitt Way, Building A6, Pittsburgh PA 15238. 412/828-2323. **Contact:** Personnel. **Description:** This location houses purchasing offices. Overall, Busy Beaver is a chain of building supply stores. **Corporate headquarters location:** This Location.

CVS
One CVS Drive, Woonsocket RI 02895. 401/765-1500. **Contact:** Human Resources. **World Wide Web address:** http://www.cvs.com. **Description:** A convenience and drug store chain operating more than 4,000 stores nationwide. **Corporate headquarters location:** This Location. **Parent company:** Mark Steven Service Merchandisers. **Listed on:** New York Stock Exchange. **Stock exchange symbol:** CVS. **President/CEO/Owner:** Tom Ryan. **Annual sales/revenues:** More than $100 million.

CAMELLIA FOODS
1157 Production Road, Norfolk VA 23502. 757/855-3371. **Contact:** Steve Rosa, Human Resources Manager. **Description:** Operates three chains of grocery stores: Meatland, Food City, and Fresh Pride. **Corporate headquarters location:** This Location.

CAMERA CORNER/CONNECTING POINT
529 North Monroe Street, Green Bay WI 54305. 920/435-2335. **Contact:** Human Resources Department. **World Wide Web address:** http://www.cccp.com. **Description:** Sells cameras and computer systems. Camera Corner/Connecting Point also provides service and technical support. **Corporate headquarters location:** This Location.

CARSON PIRIE SCOTT & COMPANY
331 West Wisconsin Avenue, Milwaukee WI 53203. 414/347-5109. **Fax:** 414/347-5337. **Contact:** Human Resources Department. **World Wide Web address:** http://www.saksincorporated. com. **Description:** A department store chain, with more than 50 stores located in the Midwest. The company operates 27 Carson Pirie Scott stores in greater Chicago, Indiana, and Minnesota; 12 Boston stores in Wisconsin; and 12 Bergner's stores in central Illinois. **Common positions include:** Buyer; Computer Programmer; Department Manager; Telecommunications Analyst. **Educational backgrounds include:** Accounting; Business Administration; Computer Science; Economics; Finance; Marketing. **Benefits:** Dental Insurance; Disability Coverage; Employee Discounts; Life Insurance; Medical Insurance; Pension Plan; Savings Plan; Tuition Assistance. **Corporate headquarters location:** This Location. **Parent company:** Saks Incorporated. **Listed on:** NASDAQ. **Number of employees at this location:** 700. **Number of employees nationwide:** 14,000.

CARVEL CORPORATION
20 Batterson Park Road, Farmington CT 06032. 860/677-6811. **Contact:** Ken Ward, Director of Human Resources. **Description:** Engaged in the manufacture of ice cream products and franchising operations for the chain of Carvel Ice Cream stores. **Corporate headquarters location:** This Location.

CATHERINE'S STORES CORPORATION
3742 Lamar Avenue, Memphis TN 38118. 901/363-3900. **Contact:** Human Resources. **World Wide Web address:** http://www.catherines.com. **Description:** A specialty retailer of women's plus-size clothing and accessories, operating 375 stores nationwide. **Common positions include:** Accountant; Advertising Clerk; Buyer; Clerical Supervisor; Credit Manager; Customer Service Rep.; Economist; Human Resources Manager; Property and Real Estate Manager; Public Relations Specialist; Technical Writer. **Educational backgrounds include:** Accounting; Communications; Computer Science; Finance; Marketing. **Benefits:** 401(k); Disability Coverage; Employee Discounts; Life Insurance; Medical Insurance; Profit Sharing. **Corporate headquarters location:** This Location. **Other U.S. locations:** Nationwide. **Subsidiaries include:** Added Dimensions; PS Plus Sizes; and The Answer. **Number of employees at this location:** 450. **Number of employees nationwide:** 3,800.

CHAMPS SPORTS
311 Manatee Avenue West, Bradenton FL 34205. 941/741-7158. **Fax:** 941/741-7170. **Contact:** Sue Campell, Vice President of Human Resources. **World Wide Web address:** http://www.champssports.com. **Description:** A specialty sporting goods retailer. Products include hardgoods, apparel, footwear, and accessories. **Common positions include:** Advertising Clerk; Buyer; Clerical Supervisor; Computer Programmer; Customer Service Representative; General Manager; Human Resources Manager; Management Trainee; Merchandiser; Operations Research Analyst; Purchasing Agent/Manager; Services Sales Representative; Systems Analyst. **Educational backgrounds include:** Business Administration; Communications; Liberal Arts; Marketing. **Benefits:** Dental Insurance; Disability Coverage; Employee Discounts; Life Insurance; Medical Insurance; Tuition Assistance. **Special programs:** Internships. **Corporate headquarters location:** This Location. **Other U.S. locations:** HI. **Parent company:** Woolworth Corporation. **Listed on:** New York Stock Exchange. **Number of employees at this location:** 115.

CHARMING SHOPPES, INC.
450 Winks Lane, Bensalem PA 19020. 215/245-9100. **Contact:** Phil Brunone, Director of Human Resources. **Description:** A retail holding company. **Common positions include:** Accountant/Auditor; Administrative Assistant; Assistant Buyer; Blue-Collar Worker Supervisor; Buyer; Clerk; Computer Programmer; Department Manager; Financial Analyst; Planner; Systems Analyst; Transportation/Traffic Specialist. **Educational backgrounds include:** Accounting; Business Administration; Communications; Computer Science; Finance; Liberal Arts; Marketing. **Benefits:** Medical Insurance. **Special programs:** Internships. **Corporate headquarters location:** This Location. **Subsidiaries include:** Fashion Bug and Fashion Bug Plus specialize in the sale of junior, miss, and plus size merchandise. There are more than 1,125 Fashion Bug and Fashion Bug Plus stores nationwide.

CHARRETTE CORPORATION
P.O. Box 4010, Woburn MA 01888-4010. 781/935-6000. **Physical address:** 31 Olympia Avenue, Woburn MA. **Fax:** 781/933-6104. **Contact:** Lawrence Mansfield, Director of Human Resources. **E-mail address:** charhr@aol.com. **World Wide Web address:** http://www.charrette.com. **Description:** Offers a variety of products and services to design professionals. Products include a

wide range of art, design, and office products from mat boards and paints, to furniture and software. Services include digital imaging, offset printing, reprographics, and blueprinting. **NOTE:** Entry-level positions are offered. **Common positions include:** Accountant/Auditor; Buyer; Computer Programmer; Credit Manager; Customer Service Representative; Financial Analyst; General Manager; Human Resources Manager; Management Trainee; Manufacturer's/Wholesaler's Sales Rep.; MIS Specialist; Systems Analyst. **Educational backgrounds include:** Accounting; Art/Design; Business Administration; Communications; Computer Science; Finance; Liberal Arts; Marketing. **Benefits:** 401(k); Daycare Assistance; Dental Insurance; Disability Coverage; Employee Discounts; Job Sharing; Life Insurance; Medical Insurance; Pension Plan; Tuition Assistance. **Special programs:** Internships. **Corporate headquarters location:** This Location. **Other U.S. locations:** New Haven CT; Chicago IL; Boston MA; Jessup MD; Detroit MI; Pennsauken NJ; Buffalo NY; New York NY; Rochester NY; Blue Bell PA; Philadelphia PA; Providence RI. **Listed on:** Privately held. **Annual sales/revenues:** $51 - $100 million. **Number of employees at this location:** 350. **Number of employees nationwide:** 750.

CHICO'S
11215 Metro Parkway, Fort Myers FL 33912. 941/277-6200. **Fax:** 941/277-5237. **Contact:** Human Resources. **Description:** A manufacturer and retailer of women's apparel. **Corporate headquarters location:** This Location. **Number of employees at this location:** 325.

CHRISTY SPORTS, LLC
875 Parfet Street, Lakewood CO 80215. 303/237-6321. **Fax:** 303/233-5946. **Contact:** Human Resources. **World Wide Web address:** http://www.christysports.com. **Description:** Operates Christy Sports, SportStalker, and Powder Tools sporting goods stores. The company specializes in retail skiing, snowboarding, and sport clothing. In addition, Christy Sports offers patio furniture and several golf retail stores. **NOTE:** Entry-level positions are offered. **Common positions include:** Administrative Assistant; Advertising Executive; Assistant Manager; Auditor; Buyer; Chief Financial Officer; Controller; General Manager; Human Resources Manager; Operations Manager; Sales Manager; Sales Representative; Systems Manager. **Benefits:** 401(k); Dental Insurance; Disability Coverage; Employee Discounts; Flexible Schedule; Life Insurance; Medical Insurance; Profit Sharing. **Special programs:** Training; Summer Jobs. **Corporate headquarters location:** This Location. **Other U.S. locations:** UT. **Number of employees at this location:** 75. **Number of employees nationwide:** 500.

CIRCUIT CITY STORES, INC.
9950 Mayland Drive, Richmond VA 23233-1464. 804/527-4000. **Toll-free phone:** 888/773-2489. **Fax:** 804/527-4086. **Recorded jobline:** 800/442-6177. **Contact:** Staffing & Planning. **E-mail address:** cc-jobs@ccnotes.ccity.com. **World Wide Web address:** http://www.circuitcity.com. **Description:** One of the largest U.S. retailers of brand-name consumer electronics and major appliances, as well as personal computers, music, and software. The company also sells used cars at CarMax Auto Superstores. Circuit City has over 600 Circuit City and Circuit City Express stores in operation nationwide. Founded in 1949. **NOTE:** Entry-level positions are offered. **Common positions include:** Accountant; Administrative Assistant; Advertising Clerk; AS400 Programmer

Analyst; Auditor; Budget Analyst; Buyer; Computer Operator; Computer Programmer; Computer Support Technician; Construction Contractor; Customer Service Representative; Database Administrator; Electrical/Electronics Engineer; Financial Analyst; General Manager; Graphic Artist; Graphic Designer; Human Resources Manager; Industrial Engineer; Market Research Analyst; Media Planner; Network/Systems Administrator; Operations Manager; Production Manager; Purchasing Agent/Manager; Software Engineer; Technical Writer/Editor; Website Developer. **Educational backgrounds include:** Accounting; Art/Design; AS400 Certification; Business Administration; C/C++; Communications; Computer Science; Economics; Engineering; Finance; Internet Development; Java; Liberal Arts; Marketing; Mathematics; MBA; PowerBuilder; Software Development; Software Tech. Support; UNIX; Visual Basic. **Benefits:** 401(k); Dental Insurance; Disability Coverage; Employee Discounts; Life Insurance; Medical Insurance; Pension Plan; Relocation Assistance; Savings Plan; Stock Purchase; Tuition Assistance. **Special programs:** Internships. **Office hours:** Monday - Friday, 8:30 a.m. - 5:00 p.m. **Corporate headquarters location:** This Location. **Other U.S. locations:** Nationwide. **Listed on:** New York Stock Exchange. **CEO:** Richard Sharp. **CIO:** Dennis Bowman. **Annual sales/revenues:** More than $100 million. **Number of employees at this location:** 3,000. **Number of employees nationwide:** 59,675.

CLOTHESTIME, INC.
5325 East Hunter Avenue, Anaheim CA 92807. 714/779-5881. **Fax:** 714/693-7402. **Contact:** Human Resources/Staffing. **World Wide Web address:** http://www.clothestime.com. **Description:** Operates a chain of women's apparel stores offering value-priced, fashionable sportswear, dresses, and accessories. **Benefits:** Dental Insurance; Disability Coverage; Employee Discounts; Life Insurance; Medical Insurance; Savings Plan. **Corporate headquarters location:** This Location. **Listed on:** NASDAQ. **Number of employees at this location:** 400. **Number of employees nationwide:** 4,200.

COMPUSA INC.
14951 North Dallas Parkway, Dallas TX 75240. 972/982-4000. **Contact:** Human Resources. **World Wide Web address:** http://www.compusa.com. **Description:** This location houses administrative offices. Overall, CompUSA Inc. operates over 75 high-volume computer superstores in 40 metropolitan areas throughout the U.S. Each computer superstore offers more than 5,000 computer products including hardware, software, accessories, and related products, at discount prices to retail, business, government, and institutional customers. The computer superstores also offers full-service technical departments and classroom facilities. **Common positions include:** Accountant/Auditor; Adjuster; Administrative Manager; Advertising Clerk; Attorney; Buyer; Clerical Supervisor; Collector; Computer Programmer; Credit Manager; Customer Service Representative; General Manager; Human Resources Manager; Investigator; Operations/ Production Manager; Property and Real Estate Manager; Public Relations Specialist; Purchasing Agent/Manager; Services Sales Representative; Systems Analyst; Technical Writer/Editor; Wholesale and Retail Buyer. **Educational backgrounds include:** Accounting; Advertising; Business Administration; Computer Science; Finance. **Benefits:** 401(k); Dental Insurance; Disability Coverage; Employee Discounts; Life Insurance; Medical Insurance. **Corporate headquarters location:** This Location. **Other U.S.**

locations: Nationwide. **Listed on:** New York Stock Exchange. **Number of employees at this location:** 620. **Number of employees nationwide:** 8,000. **Number of employees worldwide:** 17,300.

CONLEE OIL COMPANY
815 South Mill Street, Clio MI 48420. 810/686-5600. **Contact:** Jeff Conlee, Personnel Director. **Description:** This location houses administrative offices. Overall, Conlee Oil Company operates a chain of gasoline service stations and convenience stores. **Corporate headquarters location:** This Location. **Number of employees at this location:** 100.

CONSOLIDATED STORES CORP.
300 Phillipi Road, Columbus OH 43228. 614/278-6800. **Fax:** 614/278-6739. **Contact:** Human Resources. **World Wide Web address:** http://www.cnstores.com. **Description:** One of the nation's largest retailers of close-out merchandise. The company operates approximately 800 stores in 40 states under the names Odd Lots/Big Lots, All For One, Itzadeal, Toy Liquidators, Toys Unlimited, and It's Really One Dollar. The corporation has two wholesale divisions: Consolidated International and Wisconsin Toy. **Common positions include:** Accountant/Auditor; Adjuster; Advertising Clerk; Attorney; Budget Analyst; Buyer; Claim Representative; Collector; Computer Programmer; Credit Manager; Financial Analyst; Human Resources Manager; Investigator; Paralegal; Property and Real Estate Manager; Purchasing Agent/Manager; Systems Analyst; Transportation/Traffic Specialist; Wholesale and Retail Buyer. **Educational backgrounds include:** Accounting; Business Administration; Communications; Computer Science; Finance. **Benefits:** 401(k); Dental Insurance; Disability Coverage; Employee Discounts; Life Insurance; Tuition Assistance. **Corporate headquarters location:** This Location. **Listed on:** New York Stock Exchange. **Number of employees at this location:** 1,200. **Number of employees nationwide:** 20,000.

COOPER'S INC.
dba WESTERN WAREHOUSE
11205 Montgomery Boulevard NE, Albuquerque NM 87111-2648. 505/296-8344. **Toll-free phone:** 800/532-4888. **Fax:** 505/296-0278. **Contact:** Human Resources Administrator. **World Wide Web address:** http://www.westernwarehouse.com. **Description:** A retailer of western apparel. This location also hires seasonally. Founded in 1961. **NOTE:** Part-time jobs are offered. **Common positions include:** Administrative Worker/Clerk; Assistant Buyer; Assistant Manager; Cashier; Sales Representative; Store Manager. **Benefits:** 401(k); Dental Insurance; Disability Coverage; Employee Discounts; Flexible Schedule; Life Insurance; Medical Insurance. **Corporate headquarters location:** This Location. **Other U.S. locations:** AZ; CA; CO. **Annual sales/revenues:** $21 - $50 million. **Number of employees at this location:** 35. **Number of employees nationwide:** 500.

COSTCO WHOLESALE
999 Lake Drive, Issaquah WA 98027. 425/313-8100. **Contact:** Human Resources. **World Wide Web address:** http://www.costco.com. **Description:** A retailer of food, clothing, and numerous other products at wholesale prices. **Corporate headquarters location:** This Location. **Annual sales/revenues:** More than $100 million.

COURTESY CHEVROLET/GEO
1233 East Camelback Road, Phoenix AZ 85014. 602/279-3232. **Contact:** Human Resources. **World**

Wide Web address: http://www.courtesychev.com. **Description:** Provides automobile sales and service. **Common positions include:** Automotive Mechanic; Customer Service Representative; Services Sales Representative. **Benefits:** Dental Insurance; Employee Discounts; Life Insurance; Medical Insurance; Profit Sharing. **Corporate headquarters location:** This Location. **Listed on:** Privately held. **Number of employees at this location:** 260.

CRACKER BARREL OLD COUNTRY STORE
P.O. Box 787, Lebanon TN 37088-0787. 615/444-5533. **Fax:** 615/443-9476. **Recorded jobline:** 888/8-BARREL. **Contact:** Ms. Pat Williams, Employment Administrator. **E-mail address:** pwilliams@cbrl.com. **World Wide Web address:** http://www.crackerbarrelocs.com. **Description:** Operates a restaurant/retail chain with over 285 locations. **Common positions include:** Administrative Assistant; Computer Operator; Computer Programmer; Database Manager; Financial Analyst; Management Trainee; MIS Specialist; Restaurant/Food Service Manager; Retail Manager; Secretary; Systems Analyst; Systems Manager; Typist/Word Processor. **Educational backgrounds include:** Accounting; Business Administration; Computer Science. **Benefits:** 401(k); Dental Insurance; Disability Coverage; Employee Discounts; Flexible Schedule; Life Insurance; Medical Insurance; Savings Plan. **Corporate headquarters location:** This Location. **Listed on:** NASDAQ. **Stock exchange symbol:** CBRL. **Annual sales/revenues:** More than $100 million. **Number of employees at this location:** 700.

CREATIVE COMPUTERS INTEGRATED TECHNOLOGIES
2525 Busse Road, Oak Grove Village IL 60007. 847/860-4100. **Fax:** 847/616-0307. **Contact:** Human Resources. **Description:** Owns and operates a chain of retail stores that sell computers and related accessories. **NOTE:** Entry-level positions are offered. **Common positions include:** Accountant/Auditor; Administrative Assistant; Assistant Manager; Buyer; Computer Operator; Computer Programmer; General Manager; Graphic Artist; Marketing Specialist; Network Engineer; Sales Executive; Sales Representative. **Educational backgrounds include:** Accounting; Art/Design; Communications; Computer Science; Liberal Arts; Marketing; Mathematics. **Benefits:** 401(k); Dental Insurance; Disability Coverage; Employee Discounts; Life Insurance; Medical Insurance; Savings Plan; Tuition Assistance. **Corporate headquarters location:** This Location. **Other U.S. locations:** CO; IN; KS. **Annual sales/revenues:** More than $100 million. **Number of employees at this location:** 350. **Number of employees nationwide:** 750.

CROWLEYS
2301 West Lafayette Boulevard, Detroit MI 48216-1891. 313/962-2400. **Contact:** Manager of Human Resources. **Description:** Operates a chain of department stores. **Common positions include:** Advertising Clerk; Assistant Buyer; Buyer; Computer Programmer; Department Manager. **Educational backgrounds include:** Business Administration; Computer Science; Fashion; Liberal Arts; Marketing; Merchandising. **Benefits:** Disability Coverage; Employee Discounts; Life Insurance; Medical Insurance. **Corporate headquarters location:** This Location. **Number of employees at this location:** 1,200.

CROWN BOOKS CORPORATION
3300 75th Avenue, Landover MD 20785. 301/226-1200. **Contact:** Manager of Recruiting. **E-mail**

address: crownbooks@aol.com. **World Wide Web address:** http://www.crownbooks.com. **Description:** A bookstore chain. Crown Books operates over 100 Classic Crown Books and Super Crown Books. **Common positions include:** Assistant Manager; Retail Sales Worker; Store Manager. **Benefits:** 401(k); Dental Insurance; Disability Coverage; Employee Discounts; Life Insurance; Medical Insurance; Tuition Assistance. **Office hours:** Monday - Friday, 8:15 a.m. - 5:00 p.m. **Corporate headquarters location:** This Location. **Other U.S. locations:** Nationwide. **Parent company:** The Dart Group. **Listed on:** Over the Counter. **Stock exchange symbol:** CRWNQ. **President:** Anna Currence.

CUMBERLAND FARMS, INC.
777 Dedham Street, Canton MA 02021. 781/828-4900. **Fax:** 781/828-9012. **Contact:** Colleen Cesarini, Human Resources Manager. **Description:** Cumberland Farms operates a chain of retail convenience stores and gas stations. **Common positions include:** Accountant/Auditor; Advertising Clerk; Attorney; Automotive Mechanic; Blue-Collar Worker Supervisor; Budget Analyst; Buyer; Civil Engineer; Computer Programmer; Customer Service Representative; Draftsperson; Environmental Engineer; General Manager; Human Resources Manager; Manufacturer's/Wholesaler's Sales Rep.; Paralegal; Petroleum Engineer; Property and Real Estate Manager; Software Engineer; Systems Analyst; Wholesale and Retail Buyer. **Educational backgrounds include:** Accounting; Biology; Computer Science; Engineering; Marketing. **Benefits:** 401(k); Dental Insurance; Disability Coverage; Employee Discounts; Life Insurance; Medical Insurance; Savings Plan; Tuition Assistance. **Corporate headquarters location:** This Location. **Listed on:** Privately held. **Number of employees at this location:** 700. **Number of employees nationwide:** 8,000.

DM MANAGEMENT
25 Recreation Park Drive, Suite 200, Hingham MA 02043. 781/740-2718. **Fax:** 781/749-8523. **Contact:** Human Resources. **Description:** DM Management is a national direct marketer of a broad assortment of classic women's apparel and accessories. The company markets its products primarily through two catalog concepts, Nicole Summers and J. Jill. **Corporate headquarters location:** This Location. **Listed on:** NASDAQ. **Stock exchange symbol:** DMMC.

D'AGOSTINO SUPERMARKETS INC.
1385 Boston Post Road, Larchmont NY 10538. 914/833-4000. **Fax:** 914/833-4060. **Contact:** Human Resources. **Description:** A supermarket chain offering a full line of grocery, produce, and meats. The company operates more than 25 stores serving Westchester County, Brooklyn, Riverdale, and Manhattan. **Common positions include:** Accountant/Auditor; Cashier; Customer Service Representative; Department Manager; Management Trainee; Operations/Production Manager; Pharmacist; Retail Sales Worker. **Educational backgrounds include:** Accounting; Business Administration; Computer Science. **Benefits:** 401(k); Dental Insurance; Disability Coverage; Life Insurance; Medical Insurance; Tuition Assistance. **Special programs:** Internships. **Corporate headquarters location:** This Location. **Listed on:** Privately held. **Number of employees at this location:** 50.

DAIRY MART CONVENIENCE STORES
300 Executive Parkway West, Hudson OH 44236. 330/342-6600. **Fax:** 330/342-6752. **Contact:** Human Resources. **Description:** One of the nation's largest convenience store chains. Approximately 1,000 stores are operated or franchised in 11 states located in the Northeast, Midwest, and Southeast. The company also manufactures, processes, and distributes dairy products through its dairy plants and its distribution center. The company is also developing international operations through licensing and joint-venture agreements. **Benefits:** 401(k); Profit Sharing; Stock Option. **Corporate headquarters location:** This Location. **Other U.S. locations:** Louisville KY; Cuyahoga Falls OH; Toledo OH. **Listed on:** NASDAQ. **Number of employees nationwide:** 5,000.

DARLING'S INC.
P.O. Box 569, Bangor ME 04402. 207/941-1240. **Physical address:** 153 Perry Road, Bangor ME 04401. **Contact:** Personnel. **World Wide Web address:** http://www.darlings.com. **Description:** This location houses the corporate and accounting offices for the four Darling's automobile dealerships. **Corporate headquarters location:** This Location.

DAVID'S BRIDAL
27 West Athens Avenue, Ardmore PA 19003. 610/896-2111. **Contact:** Fred Postelle, Vice President of Human Resources. **World Wide Web address:** http://www.davidsbridal.com. **Description:** Sells a full line of bridal merchandise including apparel and accessories. **Common positions include:** Assistant Manager; Consultant; General Manager; Store Manager; Supervisor. **Educational backgrounds include:** Finance; Marketing; Merchandising; Personnel Relations. **Benefits:** Employee Discounts; Life Insurance; Medical Insurance. **Special programs:** Internships. **Corporate headquarters location:** This Location. **Number of employees at this location:** 215.

DAVIS FOOD CITY INC.
P.O. Box 8748, Houston TX 77249-8748. 713/695-2826. **Contact:** Personnel. **Description:** Operates a grocery store chain. **Corporate headquarters location:** This Location.

DAYTON HUDSON CORPORATION
700 On the Mall, Minneapolis MN 55402. **Fax:** 612/375-2795. **Contact:** Ms. Elix Colehour, Human Resources/Recruitment Manager. **World Wide Web address:** http://www.dhc.com. **Description:** Operates a chain of fashion department stores in eight midwestern states. **NOTE:** Interested jobseekers should fax a resume and cover letter to Human Resources. Part-time jobs are also offered. **Common positions include:** Auditor; Financial Analyst; Industrial Engineer; Management Trainee; Merchant Trainee; Sales Manager; Sales Representative. **Benefits:** 401(k); Casual Dress - Fridays; Daycare Assistance; Dental Insurance; Disability Coverage; Employee Discounts; Life Insurance; Medical Insurance; Pension Plan. **Special programs:** Training. **Corporate headquarters location:** This Location. **Other U.S. locations:** Chicago IL; Detroit MI. **Number of employees nationwide:** 34,000.

DEARDEN'S
700 South Main Street, Los Angeles CA 90014. 213/362-9600. **Contact:** Raquel Bensimon, President. **Description:** A retailer of furniture, appliances, televisions, and audio equipment. **Corporate headquarters location:** This Location.

DEB SHOPS, INC.
9401 Bluegrass Road, Philadelphia PA 19114. 215/676-6000. **Contact:** Ms. Pat Okun, Office Manager. **World Wide Web address:** http://www.debshops.com. **Description:** A chain of

specialty apparel stores offering moderately-priced, coordinated sportswear, dresses, coats, and accessories for juniors. The company operates 285 stores in 40 states. **Common positions include:** Buyer; District Manager; Regional Manager; Sales Executive; Store Manager. **Educational backgrounds include:** Art/Design; Business Administration; Communications; Fashion; Liberal Arts; Marketing; Merchandising. **Benefits:** 401(k); Employee Discounts; Life Insurance; Medical Insurance; Savings Plan. **Corporate headquarters location:** This Location. **Other U.S. locations:** Nationwide. **Listed on:** NASDAQ. **Stock exchange symbol:** DEBS. **Number of employees at this location:** 200. **Number of employees nationwide:** 2,500.

DEMOULAS SUPERMARKETS INC.
875 East Street, Tewksbury MA 01876. 978/851-8000. **Contact:** William Marsden, President of Operations. **Description:** Operates a grocery store chain with locations throughout northern and eastern Massachusetts. **Corporate headquarters location:** This Location.

DESIGNS, INC.
66 B Street, Needham MA 02494. 781/444-7222. **Fax:** 781/444-8999. **Contact:** Manager of Employment. **Description:** Operates a chain of more than 150 specialty retail stores that sell Levi Strauss & Company clothing and accessories. Forty of the locations are off-price outlet stores operating under the Levi's Outlet by Design name. Five of the locations are concept stores featuring a more focused selection of men's and women's apparel. Stores are located throughout the eastern United States. **NOTE:** Entry-level positions are offered. **Common positions include:** Management Trainee. **Educational backgrounds include:** Business Administration; Communications; Liberal Arts. **Benefits:** 401(k); Dental Insurance; Disability Coverage; Employee Discounts; Life Insurance; Medical Insurance; Tuition Assistance. **Special programs:** Training. **Corporate headquarters location:** This Location. **Listed on:** NASDAQ. **Annual sales/revenues:** More than $100 million. **Number of employees nationwide:** 1,940.

DILLARD'S DEPARTMENT STORES, INC.
1600 Cantrell Road, Little Rock AR 72201. 501/376-5200. **Contact:** Kim Kingsella, Director of Personnel. **World Wide Web address:** http://www.dillards.com. **Description:** Operates a retail chain. Dillard's offers a full line of fashion brand apparel and home furnishings. Dillard's stores are located primarily in the Southwest and Midwest including Texas, Florida, Louisiana, Oklahoma, Missouri, and Arizona. **Corporate headquarters location:** This Location. **International locations:** Mexico City, Mexico. **Annual sales/revenues:** More than $100 million.

DISCOUNT AUTO PARTS, INC.
P.O. Box 8080, Lakeland FL 33802. 941/687-9226. **Contact:** Director of Training. **Description:** A specialty retailer of automotive replacement parts, maintenance items, and accessories for do-it-yourself customers. The company operates a chain of over 300 stores located in Alabama, Florida, Georgia, and South Carolina. Founded in 1971. **Special programs:** Training. **Corporate headquarters location:** This Location. **Listed on:** New York Stock Exchange. **Number of employees nationwide:** 3,000.

DOLLAR GENERAL CORPORATION
100 Mission Ridge Road, Goodlettsville TN 37072. 615/855-4000. **Toll-free phone:** 888/877-9374. **Recorded jobline:** 800/909-5627. **Contact:** Recruiting Department. **World Wide Web address:** http://www.dollargeneral.com. **Description:** Operates general merchandise stores nationwide, primarily in the midwestern and southeastern states. Founded in 1939. **NOTE:** Entry-level positions and second and third shifts are offered. **Common positions include:** Accountant; Administrative Assistant; AS400 Programmer Analyst; Attorney; Blue-Collar Worker Supervisor; Claim Representative; Computer Operator; Computer Programmer; Computer Support Technician; Computer Technician; Customer Service Representative; Database Administrator; Help-Desk Technician; Human Resources Manager; Operations Manager; Paralegal; Real Estate Lawyer; Systems Analyst. **Educational backgrounds include:** AS400 Certification. **Benefits:** 401(k); Casual Dress - Daily; Daycare Assistance; Dental Insurance; Disability Coverage; Flexible Schedule; Life Insurance; Medical Insurance; On-Site Daycare; Relocation Assistance; Tuition Assistance. **Office hours:** Monday - Friday, 8:00 a.m. - 5:00 p.m. **Corporate headquarters location:** This Location. **Listed on:** New York Stock Exchange. **Stock exchange symbol:** DG. **Annual sales/revenues:** More than $100 million. **Number of employees at this location:** 1,000. **Number of employees nationwide:** 40,000.

DOLLAR TREE STORES, INC.
500 Volvo Parkway, Chesapeake VA 23320. 757/321-5000. **Contact:** David McDearman, Vice President of Human Resources. **Description:** A leading operator of discount variety stores offering merchandise for $1. The company's stores offer a wide assortment of everyday general merchandise in many traditional variety store categories including housewares, toys, seasonal goods, gifts, food, stationery, health and beauty aids, books, party goods, and hardware. The company operates more than 450 stores in 21 states. **Benefits:** 401(k); Incentive Plan; Profit Sharing; Stock Option. **Corporate headquarters location:** This Location. **Subsidiaries include:** Dollar Tree Distribution, Inc.; Dollar Tree Management, Inc. **Listed on:** NASDAQ. **Number of employees nationwide:** 4,500.

DOMINICK'S FINER FOODS
505 Railroad Avenue, Northlake IL 60164. 708/562-1000. **Fax:** 708/492-5210. **Contact:** Debbie Lange, Employment Specialist. **World Wide Web address:** http://www.dominick.com. **Description:** Operates a chain of retail grocery stores. **Common positions include:** Administrative Assistant; Buyer; MIS Specialist; Secretary; Systems Analyst. **Educational backgrounds include:** Business Administration; Marketing. **Benefits:** 401(k); Dental Insurance; Disability Coverage; Employee Discounts; Life Insurance; Medical Insurance; Tuition Assistance. **Corporate headquarters location:** This Location. **Listed on:** New York Stock Exchange. **Number of employees at this location:** 2,000. **Number of employees nationwide:** 18,000.

THE DRESS BARN, INC.
30 Dunnigan Drive, Suffern NY 10901. 914/369-4500. **Contact:** Human Resources. **World Wide Web address:** http://www.dressbarn.com. **Description:** Operates a chain of women's apparel stores. **Corporate headquarters location:** This Location.

DRUG EMPORIUM
155 Hidden Ravines Drive, Powell OH 43065. 740/548-7080. **Fax:** 740/548-8523. **Contact:** Human Resources. **Description:** Operates a chain of

retail drug stores. **Corporate headquarters location:** This Location.

DUCKWALL-ALCO STORES, INC.
401 Cottage Avenue, Abilene KS 67410. 785/263-3350. **Contact:** Dennis Alesio, Vice President of Personnel. **E-mail address:** duck-personnel@access-one.com. **Description:** Operates a chain of full-line discount stores and smaller variety stores. Founded in 1901. **Common positions include:** Assistant Manager. **Benefits:** Dental Insurance; Disability Coverage; Employee Discounts; Life Insurance; Medical Insurance; Profit Sharing. **Special programs:** Training. **Corporate headquarters location:** This Location. **Listed on:** NASDAQ. **Stock exchange symbol:** DUCK. **CEO:** Glen Shank. **Facilities Manager:** Tom Canfield. **Information Systems Manager:** Steve Spatz. **Purchasing Manager:** Mary Avery. **Number of employees at this location:** 200. **Number of employees nationwide:** 6,000.

DUNLAP COMPANY
200 Greenleaf Street, Fort Worth TX 76107. 817/336-4985. **Contact:** Human Resources. **Description:** Operates a chain of department stores with over 50 locations. The stores operate under the following names: Dunlaps, McClurkans, M.M. Cohn, Heironimus, Stripling & Cox, Porteus, and The White House. Founded in 1892. **Corporate headquarters location:** This Location. **Other U.S. locations:** Nationwide. **Listed on:** Privately held. **CEO:** Edward Martin. **Number of employees nationwide:** 2,100.

DURON PAINTS AND WALLCOVERINGS
711 First Avenue, King of Prussia PA 19406. 610/962-9907. **Contact:** Maria Rounds, Human Resources Manager. **World Wide Web address:** http://www.duron.com. **Description:** A retailer and wholesaler of paints, wallcoverings, window treatments, and related items. **Common positions include:** Branch Manager; Management Trainee. **Educational backgrounds include:** Business Administration; Marketing. **Benefits:** Disability Coverage; Employee Discounts; Life Insurance; Medical Insurance; Pension Plan. **Corporate headquarters location:** This Location.

EAGLE FOOD CENTERS INC.
P.O. Box 6700, Rock Island IL 61204-6700. 309/787-7730. **Fax:** 309/787-7895. **Contact:** Human Resources. **Description:** Owns and operates a supermarket chain offering a full line of groceries, meats, fresh produce, dairy products, delicatessen and bakery products, health and beauty aids, and other general merchandise. **Corporate headquarters location:** This Location.

EAGLE HARDWARE & GARDEN
981 Powell Avenue SW, Renton WA 98055. 425/227-5740. **Fax:** 425/204-5152. **Recorded jobline:** 425/204-5151. **Contact:** Human Resources. **Description:** Operates home improvement stores in the Pacific Northwest, Colorado, Utah, and Hawaii. **Common positions include:** Customer Service Representative; Retail Manager; Retail Sales Worker. **Benefits:** 401(k); Dental Insurance; Employee Discounts; Medical Insurance; Stock Purchase. **Corporate headquarters location:** This Location. **Listed on:** NASDAQ. **Number of employees at this location:** 160. **Number of employees nationwide:** 5,000.

ECKERD CORPORATION
P.O. Box 4689, Clearwater FL 33758. 727/395-6000. **Physical address:** 833 Bryan Dairy Road, Largo FL 33777. **Recorded jobline:** 727/395-6443. **Contact:** Human Resources. **Description:** One of the largest drug store chains in the United States, with over 1,715 stores in 13 states. The stores feature general merchandise, prescription and over-the-counter drugs, and photo development services. Eckerd operates more than 395 Eckerd Express photo centers offering overnight service. Non-pharmacy merchandise at Eckerd stores includes health and beauty aids, greeting cards, and other convenience products. The Eckerd Vision Group operates 47 optical superstores and 30 optical centers with one-hour service. Insta-Care Pharmacy Service centers provide prescription drugs and offer patient record and consulting services to health care institutions. **Common positions include:** Accountant/Auditor; Attorney; Buyer; Human Resources Manager; Operations/Production Manager; Paralegal; Pharmacist; Transportation/Traffic Specialist. **Educational backgrounds include:** Accounting; Business Administration; Communications; Finance; Marketing. **Benefits:** 401(k); Dental Insurance; Disability Coverage; Employee Discounts; Life Insurance; Medical Insurance; Pension Plan; Profit Sharing; Savings Plan. **Special programs:** Internships. **Corporate headquarters location:** This Location. **Listed on:** New York Stock Exchange. **Number of employees at this location:** 1,000. **Number of employees nationwide:** 40,000.

ECKERD DRUG
7245 Henry Clay Boulevard, Liverpool NY 13088-3571. 315/451-8000. **Contact:** Human Resources. **Description:** The company operates one of the largest chains of super drug stores in the Northeast under the name Eckerd Drugs. Eckerd Drug Store Division has over 250 drug stores located in New York, Pennsylvania, Vermont, and New Hampshire. **Corporate headquarters location:** This Location. **Parent company:** Eckerd Corporation.

EDDIE BAUER, INC.
P.O. Box 97000, Redmond WA 98073-9700. 425/882-6231. **Physical address:** 15010 NE 36th Street, Redmond WA. **Fax:** 425/869-4647. **Recorded jobline:** 425/861-4851. **Contact:** Human Resources. **World Wide Web address:** http://www.eddiebauer.com. **Description:** A multi-unit, private label retailer and catalog company for apparel and home accessories. **Common positions include:** Administrative Worker/Clerk; Computer Programmer; Customer Service Representative; Designer; Systems Analyst; Telecommunications Analyst. **Educational backgrounds include:** Accounting; Art/Design; Computer Science; Liberal Arts. **Benefits:** 401(k); Credit Union; Daycare Assistance; Dental Insurance; Disability Coverage; Employee Discounts; Life Insurance; Medical Insurance; Profit Sharing; Savings Plan; Tuition Assistance. **Corporate headquarters location:** This Location. **Other U.S. locations:** Nationwide. **Parent company:** Spiegel, Inc. **Number of employees at this location:** 1,000. **Number of employees nationwide:** 10,000.

EDISON BROTHERS STORES, INC.
P.O. Box 14020, St. Louis MO 63178. 314/331-6125. **Contact:** Personnel Administration. **Description:** A nationwide retailer of shoes and apparel. **Common positions include:** Accountant/Auditor; Administrator; Management Trainee; Marketing Manager; Merchandiser; Operations/Production Manager. **Benefits:** 401(k); Dental Insurance; Disability Coverage; Employee Discounts; Life Insurance; Medical Insurance; Pension Plan; Vacation Days. **Corporate headquarters location:** This Location. **Subsidiaries include:** 5-7-9; Bakers/Leeds; CODA; JW/Jeans West; Oaktree; Precis; Repp Ltd.; Sacha London Shoe Stores; Shifty's; The Wild Pair;

Velocity. **Listed on:** New York Stock Exchange. **Number of employees nationwide:** 24,200.

EDMUND SCIENTIFIC COMPANY
101 East Gloucester Pike, Barrington NJ 08007. 856/547-3488x6824. **Fax:** 856/546-9340. **Contact:** Lisa Verrecchia, Human Resources Representative. **E-mail address:** Lisa_Verrecchia@edsci.com. **World Wide Web address:** http://www.edsci.com. **Description:** This location is a retail store. Overall, Edmund Scientific Company is a retail supplier of industrial optics, lasers, telescopes, and precision optical instruments through two mail order catalogs. Founded in 1942. **NOTE:** Entry-level positions are offered. **Company slogan:** Bringing science into focus. **Common positions include:** Account Representative; Administrative Assistant; Computer Operator; Computer Programmer; Graphic Artist; Graphic Designer; Sales Representative; Statistician; Webmaster. **Educational backgrounds include:** Engineering; Graphic Design; Photoshop; Physics; QuarkXPress; Visual Basic. **Benefits:** 401(k); Casual Dress - Fridays; Disability Coverage; Employee Discounts; Life Insurance; Medical Insurance; Sick Days (1 - 5); Tuition Assistance; Vacation Days (6 - 10). **Special programs:** Internships. **Corporate headquarters location:** This Location. **Other U.S. locations:** Tucson AZ. **International locations:** Shanghai, China; Tokyo, Japan; United Kingdom. **Listed on:** Privately held. **CEO:** Robert Edmunc. **Facilities Manager:** Mike Reyes. **Annual sales/revenues:** $51 - $100 million. **Number of employees at this location:** 190. **Number of employees worldwide:** 210.

EMPIRE SOUTHWEST COMPANY
P.O. Box 2985, Mesa AZ 85062. 480/633-4300. **Contact:** Employment Manager. **World Wide Web address:** http://www.empiresouthwest.com. **Description:** A retailer and servicer of Caterpillar equipment. **Benefits:** 401(k); Dental Insurance; Disability Coverage; Employee Discounts; Life Insurance; Medical Insurance; Profit Sharing. **Corporate headquarters location:** This Location. **Other U.S. locations:** Phoenix AZ; Glendale AZ. **Subsidiaries include:** Empire Hydraulic Service; Empire Machinery; Empire Transport.

EMPORIUM DEPARTMENT STORES
P.O. Box 5467, Eugene OR 97405. 541/746-9611. **Contact:** Frank Murray, Personnel Director. **Description:** Operates a department store chain. Emporium Department Stores offers a wide variety of merchandise including apparel and home furnishings. **Common positions include:** Accountant/Auditor; Branch Manager; Buyer; Computer Programmer; Copywriter; Credit Manager; Department Manager; Designer; Purchasing Agent/Manager; Systems Analyst; Transportation/Traffic Specialist. **Educational backgrounds include:** Accounting; Business Administration; Communications; Computer Science; Finance; Marketing. **Benefits:** 401(k); Dental Insurance; Disability Coverage; Employee Discounts; Life Insurance; Medical Insurance. **Corporate headquarters location:** This Location. **Listed on:** Privately held.

ESPRIT DE CORP
900 Minnesota Street, San Francisco CA 94107. 415/648-6900. **Recorded jobline:** 415/550-3998. **Contact:** Human Resources. **World Wide Web address:** http://www.esprit.com. **Description:** A manufacturer and retailer of clothing, footwear, eyewear, bath and bed accessories, and watches. Founded in 1968. **NOTE:** Entry-level positions are offered. **Common positions include:** Account Manager; Account Representative; Accountant; Administrative Assistant; Assistant Manager; Budget Analyst; Buyer; Chief Financial Officer; Controller; Credit Manager; Customer Service Representative; Finance Director; Financial Analyst; Human Resources Manager; Marketing Manager; Operations Manager; Production Manager; Project Manager; Public Relations Specialist; Purchasing Agent/Manager; Quality Control Supervisor; Sales Executive; Sales Manager; Sales Representative; Systems Analyst; Systems Manager; Technical Writer/Editor; Transportation/Traffic Specialist; Webmaster. **Educational backgrounds include:** Accounting; Art/Design; Business Administration; Communications; Finance; Liberal Arts; Marketing; Mathematics; Public Relations; Software Development. **Benefits:** 401(k); Dental Insurance; Disability Coverage; Employee Discounts; Financial Planning Assistance; Life Insurance; Medical Insurance; Pension Plan; Profit Sharing; Public Transit Available; Savings Plan; Tuition Assistance. **Special programs:** Summer Jobs. **Office hours:** Monday - Friday, 8:00 a.m. - 6:00 p.m. **Corporate headquarters location:** This Location. **Other U.S. locations:** Nationwide. **Listed on:** Privately held. **CEO:** Jay Margolis. **Number of employees at this location:** 350. **Number of employees nationwide:** 1,400. **Number of employees worldwide:** 5,000.

ETHAN ALLEN INC.
Ethan Allen Drive, Danbury CT 06811. 203/743-8000. **Contact:** Charles Farfaglia, Human Resources. **World Wide Web address:** http://www.ethanallen.com. **Description:** An international retailer of home furnishings operating approximately 350 retail locations. **Corporate headquarters location:** This Location.

GENE EVANS FORD, INC.
4355 Jonesboro Road, Union City GA 30291. 770/964-9801. **Contact:** John Nessing, Hiring Coordinator. **World Wide Web address:** http://www.geneevansford.com. **Description:** An automobile dealer. **Common positions include:** Accountant/Auditor; Credit Manager; Customer Service Representative; Department Manager; Services Sales Representative. **Educational backgrounds include:** Accounting; Business Administration; Finance. **Benefits:** Dental Insurance; Employee Discounts; Life Insurance; Medical Insurance; Pension Plan. **Corporate headquarters location:** This Location.

EVANS SYSTEMS, INC. (ESI)
P.O. Box 2480, Bay City TX 77404-2480. 979/245-2424. **Fax:** 979/244-5070. **Contact:** Human Resources. **Description:** A holding company. **Corporate headquarters location:** This Location. **Subsidiaries include:** Way Energy distributes wholesale and retail refined petroleum products and lubricants and owns and operates convenience stores in southern Texas and Louisiana; Chem-Way Systems, Inc. produces, packages, and markets automotive aftermarket chemical products in 23 states; EDCO Environmental Systems, Inc. provides environmental remediation services and installations of underground storage tanks; Distributor Information Systems Corporation provides information systems and software for distributors and convenience store owners and operators. **Annual sales/revenues:** More than $100 million.

FACTORY 2-U STORES, INC.
4000 Ruffin Road, Suite B, San Diego CA 92123-1866. 858/627-1800. **Fax:** 858/637-4180. **Contact:** Human Resources. **E-mail address:** mailus@factory2-u.com. **World Wide Web address:** http://www.factory2-u.com. **Description:** Operates over 200 Factory 2-U and Family Bargain Center stores which primarily sell in-season family apparel and housewares at discounted prices. **NOTE:** Entry-

level positions are offered. **Common positions include:** Administrative Manager; Computer Programmer; Financial Analyst; Human Resources Manager; Market Research Analyst; Systems Analyst. **Educational backgrounds include:** Accounting; Economics; Finance; Liberal Arts; Marketing. **Benefits:** 401(k); Dental Insurance; Disability Coverage; Employee Discounts; Life Insurance; Medical Insurance. **Corporate headquarters location:** This Location. **Other U.S. locations:** AZ; NM; NV; OR; TX; WA. **Parent company:** Family Bargain Corporation. **Listed on:** NASDAQ. **Stock exchange symbol:** FTUS. **Chairman and CEO:** Mike Searles. **Annual sales/revenues:** More than $100 million. **Number of employees at this location:** 250. **Number of employees nationwide:** 3,700.

FAMILY DOLLAR STORES, INC.

P.O. Box 1017, Charlotte NC 28201. 704/847-6961. **Fax:** 704/845-0582. **Contact:** Mary D. Lauzon, Corporate Recruiter. **E-mail address:** mlauzon@familydollar.com. **World Wide Web address:** http://www.familydollar.com. **Description:** Owns and operates a chain of more than 3,300 discount stores. The company provides merchandise for family and home needs. Stores are located in a contiguous 39-state area ranging as far northwest as South Dakota, northeast to Maine, southeast to Florida, and southwest to New Mexico. Founded in 1959. **NOTE:** Entry-level positions and second and third shifts are offered. **Common positions include:** Accountant; Administrative Assistant; Advertising Clerk; Attorney; Blue-Collar Worker Supervisor; Buyer; Clerical Supervisor; Computer Engineer; Computer Operator; Computer Programmer; Computer Support Technician; Controller; Customer Service Representative; Database Administrator; District Manager; Draftsperson; Financial Analyst; Graphic Artist; Human Resources Manager; Industrial Engineer; Management Trainee; Market Research Analyst; Network/Systems Administrator; Operations Manager; Purchasing Agent/Manager; Registered Nurse; Secretary; SQL Programmer; Store Manager; Systems Analyst; Telecommunications Manager; Transportation/Traffic Specialist; Typist/Word Processor; Webmaster. **Educational backgrounds include:** Accounting; Business Administration; C/C++; Communications; Computer Science; Engineering; Finance; HTML; Internet; Microsoft Word; Oracle; QuarkXPress; Software Development; Software Tech. Support; Spreadsheets; Visual Basic. **Benefits:** 401(k); Casual Dress - Fridays; Dental Insurance; Disability Coverage; Life Insurance; Medical Insurance; Purchasing Plan. **Corporate headquarters location:** This Location. **Listed on:** New York Stock Exchange. **Stock exchange symbol:** FDO. **Annual sales/revenues:** More than $100 million. **Number of employees nationwide:** 26,000.

FAMOUS FOOTWEAR

7010 Mineral Point Road, Madison WI 53717-1701. 608/829-3668. **Contact:** Johnna Monkemeyer, Recruitment/Training Manager. **E-mail address:** jmonkeme@famousfootwear.com. **World Wide Web address:** http://www.famousfootwear.com. **Description:** A shoe retailer operating over 860 stores nationwide. **Common positions include:** Assistant Manager; Computer Programmer; Merchandiser; Retail Manager; Sales Executive. **Benefits:** 401(k); Dental Insurance; Disability Coverage; Employee Discounts; Life Insurance; Medical Insurance; Pension Plan; Savings Plan; Stock Option; Tuition Assistance. **Special programs:** Internships. **Corporate headquarters location:** This Location. **Other U.S. locations:** Nationwide. **Parent company:** Brown Group, Inc.

Listed on: New York Stock Exchange. **Number of employees nationwide:** 8,000.

FAMOUS-BARR COMPANY

601 Olive Street, St. Louis MO 63101. 314/444-3111. **Fax:** 314/444-3175. **Contact:** Executive Recruiting and Placement. **World Wide Web address:** http://www.mayco.com/fb. **Description:** Operates a retail department store chain with over 20 stores throughout Missouri, Illinois, and Indiana. **Common positions include:** Buyer; Department Manager; Financial Analyst; Human Resources Manager; Management Trainee; Sales Manager. **Educational backgrounds include:** Business Administration; Finance; Marketing. **Benefits:** 401(k); Dental Insurance; Disability Coverage; Employee Discounts; Life Insurance; Medical Insurance; Pension Plan; Profit Sharing. **Corporate headquarters location:** This Location. **Parent company:** The May Department Store Company.

FEDERATED DEPARTMENT STORES

7 West Seventh Street, Cincinnati OH 45202. 513/579-7000. **Contact:** David Clark, Human Resources Director. **World Wide Web address:** http://www.federated-fds.com. **Description:** Operates over 400 department stores nationwide. The retail segments include Bloomingdale's, The Bon Marche, Burdine's, Lazarus, Rich's, Goldsmith's, and Sterns. **Corporate headquarters location:** This Location. **Listed on:** New York Stock Exchange.

FIESTA MART INC.

5235 Katy Freeway, Houston TX 77007. 713/869-5060. **Contact:** Personnel. **Description:** Operates a Houston chain of grocery stores. **Corporate headquarters location:** This Location.

FIGI'S GIFTS INC.

2525 South Roddis Avenue, Marshfield WI 54449. 715/384-1425. **Toll-free phone:** 800/360-6542. **Fax:** 715/384-1177. **Contact:** Human Resources Recruiter. **World Wide Web address:** http://www.figis.com. **Description:** A leader in mail-order/catalog food gifts, with a full line of products including cheese, sausage, smokehouse specialties, candy, cookies, nuts, cakes, fruits, plants, and a variety of non-food gifts. This location also hires seasonally. Founded in 1944. **NOTE:** Part-time jobs are offered. **Common positions include:** Accountant; Administrative Assistant; Buyer; Computer Programmer; Marketing Specialist; Secretary; Systems Analyst. **Educational backgrounds include:** Business Administration; Marketing. **Benefits:** 401(k); Casual Dress - Daily; Dental Insurance; Disability Coverage; Employee Discounts; Life Insurance; Medical Insurance; Pension Plan; Profit Sharing; Relocation Assistance; Savings Plan. **Special programs:** Internships. **Corporate headquarters location:** This Location. **Other area locations:** Neillsville WI; Stevens Point WI. **Parent company:** Fingerhut. **Annual sales/revenues:** More than $100 million. **Number of employees at this location:** 2,250. **Number of employees nationwide:** 2,500.

FINE'S MEN'S SHOPS INC.

1164 Azalea Garden Road, Norfolk VA 23502-5612. 757/857-6013. **Contact:** Mitchell Fine, President. **Description:** Operates a chain of men's clothing stores. **Corporate headquarters location:** This Location.

FINISH LINE INC.

3308 North Mitthoeffer Road, Indianapolis IN 46235. 317/899-1022. **Contact:** Human Resources. **World Wide Web address:** http://www.thefinishline.com. **Description:** Finish Line Inc.

operates retail stores which offer a broad selection of current men's, women's, and children's brand name athletic and leisure footwear, activewear, and accessories. **Number of employees nationwide:** 5,000.

FINLAY ENTERPRISES, INC.
529 Fifth Avenue, New York NY 10017. 212/808-2079. **Contact:** Fran Galluccio, Human Resources Manager. **Description:** Operates through its subsidiary, Finlay Fine Jewelry Corporation, which sells jewelry through over 950 department store locations in the United States.

FIRST CASH, INC.
690 East Lamar Boulevard, Suite 400, Arlington TX 76011. 817/460-3947. **Contact:** Human Resources. **Description:** Acquires, establishes, and operates pawn stores that lend money on collateral of pledged personal property and retail previously owned merchandise acquired in forfeited transactions. First Cash also owns 26 check-cashing stores. **Common positions include:** Cashier; Computer Programmer; Inventory Control Specialist. **Benefits:** 401(k); Casual Dress - Daily; Dental Insurance; Medical Insurance. **Corporate headquarters location:** This Location. **Other U.S. locations:** CA; DC; IL; MD; MO; OK; SC. **Listed on:** NASDAQ. **Stock exchange symbol:** PAWN. **Number of employees at this location:** 800.

FOOD BASKET
P.O. Box 3766, San Angelo TX 76902. 915/658-5602. **Contact:** Personnel. **Description:** A grocery store chain with locations throughout Texas. **Corporate headquarters location:** This Location.

FOOD CITY MARKETS INC.
440 Sylvan Avenue, Suite 120, Englewood Cliffs NJ 07632. 201/569-4849. **Contact:** Barry Schwartz, Supervisor of Store Operations. **Description:** Operates a chain of supermarkets. **Corporate headquarters location:** This Location.

FOOD LION, INC.
P.O. Box 1330, Salisbury NC 28145-1330. 704/633-8250. **Contact:** Recruiting Manager. **Description:** Owns a chain of retail food stores in the southeastern United States. **Corporate headquarters location:** This Location.

FOODARAMA SUPERMARKETS
922 Highway 33, Building 6, Suite 1, Freehold NJ 07728. 732/462-4700. **Contact:** Bob Spires, Vice President of Personnel. **Description:** Operates supermarkets in New Jersey, New York, and Pennsylvania. **Common positions include:** Accountant/Auditor; Management Trainee. **Educational backgrounds include:** Accounting. **Benefits:** Dental Insurance; Disability Coverage; Life Insurance; Medical Insurance; Pension Plan. **Corporate headquarters location:** This Location. **Listed on:** American Stock Exchange.

FOODLAND
3536 Harding Avenue, Honolulu HI 96816. 808/732-0791. **Contact:** Personnel. **Description:** Operates 24 Foodland supermarkets. **Corporate headquarters location:** This Location.

FORTUNE BRANDS INC.
300 Tower Parkway, Lincolnshire IL 60069. 847/484-4400. **Contact:** Human Resources. **World Wide Web address:** http://www.fortunebrands.com. **Description:** A consumer products company offering home and office products, golf equipment, and spirits and wine. **Corporate headquarters location:** This Location. **Annual sales/revenues:** More than $100 million.

49ER SHOPS, INC.
6049 East Seventh Street, Long Beach CA 90840. 562/985-7854. **Contact:** Nancy Green, Personnel Director. **World Wide Web address:** http://www.csulb.edu/~bookstor. **Description:** Operates the bookstore, copy center, and food services on California State University's Long Beach campus. **Benefits:** Dental Insurance; Employee Discounts; Life Insurance; Medical Insurance; Pension Plan; Tuition Assistance. **Corporate headquarters location:** This Location. **Number of employees at this location:** 450.

THE FOSS COMPANY
1224 Washington Avenue, Golden CO 80401. 303/279-3373. **Contact:** Mike Minter, Personnel Manager. **World Wide Web address:** http://www.fossco.com. **Description:** A general store also offering a post office, pharmacy, and liquor store. This location is also headquarters for Ski Country Decanters, H.J. Foss Apparel, and The Golden Ram Restaurant. **Common positions include:** Accountant/Auditor; Buyer; Credit Manager; Department Manager; Management Trainee. **Benefits:** Dental Insurance; Employee Discounts; Life Insurance; Medical Insurance. **Corporate headquarters location:** This Location.

FRAME FACTORY LTD.
32 Worthington Access Drive, Maryland Heights MO 63043. 314/434-8882. **Contact:** Personnel Department. **Description:** This location houses the corporate office and warehouse. Overall, Frame Factory operates a chain of 11 area stores specializing in framing for various business needs. **Common positions include:** Customer Service Representative; Management Trainee; Manufacturer's/Wholesaler's Sales Rep. **Educational backgrounds include:** Art/Design. **Benefits:** Dental Insurance; Employee Discounts; Life Insurance; Medical Insurance; Savings Plan. **Corporate headquarters location:** This Location. **Number of employees at this location:** 100.

FRANK'S NURSERY & CRAFTS INC.
580 Kirts Boulevard, Troy MI 48084. 248/712-7000. **Fax:** 248/712-5007. **Contact:** Human Resources. **World Wide Web address:** http://www.franks.com. **Description:** A specialty retailer of nursery, craft, and Christmas items. Frank's operates over 260 stores in the Midwest, East, and in central Florida. This location also hires seasonally. Founded in 1949. **NOTE:** Entry-level positions are offered. **Common positions include:** Accountant; Administrative Assistant; Advertising Clerk; AS400 Programmer Analyst; Attorney; Computer Operator; Computer Programmer; Controller; Financial Analyst; Graphic Designer; Human Resources Manager; Marketing Manager; Media Planner; Real Estate Lawyer. **Educational backgrounds include:** Business Administration; Horticulture; Marketing; Microsoft Office; Spreadsheets. **Benefits:** 401(k); Dental Insurance; Disability Coverage; Employee Discounts; Life Insurance; Medical Insurance; Paid Holidays; Savings Plan; Vacation Days. **Office hours:** Monday - Friday, 8:30 a.m. - 5:30 p.m. **Corporate headquarters location:** This Location. **Parent company:** The Cypress Group LLC. **CEO:** Joseph Baczo. **Number of employees at this location:** 275. **Number of employees nationwide:** 5,500.

FRED MEYER, INC.
3800 SE 22nd Avenue, Portland OR 97202. 503/232-8844. **Contact:** Keith Lovett, Senior Vice President of Human Resources. **E-mail address:** fredmeyer@webhire.com. **World Wide Web address:** http://www.fredmeyer.com. **Description:** Operates a chain of approximately 400 retail stores

offering a wide range of food, products for the home, apparel, fine jewelry, and home improvement items. **Corporate headquarters location:** This Location. **Other U.S. locations:** AK; CA; ID; MT; UT; WA. **Parent company:** The Kroger Company. **Listed on:** New York Stock Exchange. **Annual sales/revenues:** More than $100 million.

FREE SERVICE TIRE COMPANY
P.O. Box 1637, Johnson City TN 37605. 423/928-6476. **Fax:** 423/461-1617. **Contact:** Lewis Wexler, Jr., Executive Vice President. **Description:** Engaged in the retail and wholesale of tires and related products. The company also offers some repair services. **Common positions include:** Automotive Mechanic; Clerk; Credit Clerk and Authorizer; Management Trainee; Manufacturer's/Wholesaler's Sales Rep.; Store Manager. **Educational backgrounds include:** Business Administration. **Benefits:** Disability Coverage; Employee Discounts; Life Insurance; Medical Insurance; Profit Sharing. **Corporate headquarters location:** This Location. **Listed on:** Privately held. **Number of employees at this location:** 205.

FURNITURE ROW COMPANY
13333 East 37th Avenue, Denver CO 80239. 303/371-8560. **Contact:** Personnel Department. **World Wide Web address:** http://www.furniturerow.com. **Description:** A retail furniture dealer. **Corporate headquarters location:** This Location.

GABBERTS INC.
3501 Galleria, Minneapolis MN 55435. 952/828-8500. **Contact:** Human Resources. **Description:** A retail furniture store. **Common positions include:** Accountant/Auditor; Computer Programmer; Credit Manager; Customer Service Representative; Department Manager; General Manager; Human Resources Manager; Operations/Production Manager; Retail Sales Worker. **Benefits:** Dental Insurance; Disability Coverage; Employee Discounts; Life Insurance; Medical Insurance; Profit Sharing; Savings Plan; Stock Option. **Corporate headquarters location:** This Location. **Other U.S. locations:** Dallas TX; Fort Worth TX. **Operations at this facility include:** Administration; Service. **Number of employees nationwide:** 700.

GALL'S INC.
2680 Palumbo Drive, Lexington KY 40509. 606/266-7227. **Contact:** Human Resources. **World Wide Web address:** http://www.gallsinc.com. **Description:** One of the largest catalog retailers of public safety equipment in the nation. Products include vehicle equipment (radar, lightbars, and security screens); bags and organizers; public safety accessories (scanners, cameras, surveillance systems); flashlights and spotlights; traffic safety products (lock picks, barrier tape, traffic warning supplies); law enforcement products (ear protection, weapon storage units, gun cleaning and lubrication systems, handcuffs, bullet proof vests, and breath tests); fire rescue products (helmets, hoods, and clothing); medical supplies; badges and identification; apparel and uniforms; and footwear. **Common positions include:** Customer Service Representative. **Benefits:** 401(k); Dental Insurance; Disability Coverage; Employee Discounts; Life Insurance; Medical Insurance; Tuition Assistance. **Corporate headquarters location:** This Location. **Listed on:** Privately held. **Number of employees at this location:** 275.

GAP INC.
900 Cherry Avenue, San Bruno CA 94066. 650/952-4400. **Contact:** Personnel. **World Wide Web address:** http://www.gap.com. **Description:** A nationwide retailer of moderately-priced, casual apparel for men, women, and children. The company operates over 1,800 stores in a number of metropolitan areas, under the names Gap, GapKids, BabyGap, Banana Republic, and Old Navy Clothing Company. **Corporate headquarters location:** This Location. **Other U.S. locations:** Nationwide. **International locations:** Canada; France; Germany; Japan; United Kingdom. **Listed on:** New York Stock Exchange.

KEN GARFF AUTOMOTIVE GROUP
531 State Street, Salt Lake City UT 84111. 801/521-6111. **Contact:** Human Resources. **World Wide Web address:** http://www.kengarff.com. **Description:** An automotive dealer group with six locations and 14 automotive product lines. **NOTE:** Entry-level positions are offered. **Common positions include:** Account Manager; Accountant/Auditor; Administrative Assistant; Administrative Manager; Assistant Manager; Blue-Collar Worker Supervisor; Buyer; Chief Financial Officer; Clerical Supervisor; Controller; Customer Service Representative; Electrical/Electronics Engineer; General Manager; Human Resources Manager; Sales Executive; Sales Manager; Sales Representative; Secretary; Systems Analyst. **Educational backgrounds include:** Accounting; Business Administration; Communications; Finance; Public Relations. **Benefits:** 401(k); Dental Insurance; Employee Discounts; Life Insurance; Medical Insurance. **Special programs:** Apprenticeships; Training. **Corporate headquarters location:** This Location. **Number of employees at this location:** 250. **Number of employees nationwide:** 850.

GART SPORTS
1000 Broadway, Denver CO 80203. 303/863-2297. **Fax:** 303/863-2240. **Contact:** Gigi Healy, Vice President of Human Resources. **World Wide Web address:** http://www.gartsports.com. **Description:** Operates a chain of retail sporting goods stores. **Common positions include:** Advertising Clerk; Apparel Worker; Buyer; Cashier; Management Trainee; Marketing Manager; Retail Sales Worker; Store Manager. **Educational backgrounds include:** Business Administration; Liberal Arts; Marketing. **Benefits:** 401(k); Dental Insurance; Employee Discounts; Life Insurance; Medical Insurance; Pension Plan. **Corporate headquarters location:** This Location. **Other U.S. locations:** ID; MT; NM; UT; WA; WY. **Parent company:** Leonard Green & Associates. **Number of employees nationwide:** 2,100.

GEERLINGS & WADE
960 Turnpike Street, Canton MA 02021. 781/821-4152. **Contact:** Human Resources. **Description:** Provides personal wine-buying services to consumers through direct marketing. The company purchases imported and domestic wines and delivers them directly to the customer's home or office. **Corporate headquarters location:** This Location.

GENERAL NUTRITION COMPANIES, INC.
GENERAL NUTRITION CENTERS (GNC)
300 Sixth Avenue, Pittsburgh PA 15222. 412/288-4600. **Fax:** 412/288-2074. **Contact:** Human Resources. **World Wide Web address:** http://www.gnc.com. **Description:** One of the largest specialty retailers of nutritional supplements and other health and self-care products in the United States. General Nutrition's products are sold through a network of more than 3,000 company and franchised locations in all 50 states and 16 foreign countries. The company also operates one of the largest vitamin supplement manufacturing facilities in the United States. Founded in 1935. **NOTE:**

Entry-level positions are offered. **Common positions include:** Account Manager; Accountant; Administrative Assistant; Assistant Manager; Attorney; Auditor; Buyer; Computer Operator; Computer Programmer; Customer Service Representative; Database Manager; Dietician/Nutritionist; Draftsperson; Financial Analyst; Graphic Artist; Human Resources Manager; Market Research Analyst; Marketing Manager; MIS Specialist; Paralegal; Project Manager; Secretary; Systems Analyst; Systems Manager; Telecommunications Manager. **Educational backgrounds include:** Accounting; Art/Design; Business Administration; Computer Science; Finance; Marketing; Nutrition; Software Development; Software Tech. Support. **Benefits:** 401(k); Dental Insurance; Disability Coverage; Employee Discounts; Life Insurance; Medical Insurance. **Special programs:** Summer Jobs. **Corporate headquarters location:** This Location. **Other U.S. locations:** Nationwide. **Annual sales/revenues:** More than $100 million. **Number of employees at this location:** 600. **Number of employees nationwide:** 10,000.

GENESCO, INC.
Genesco Administration Building, P.O. Box 731, Nashville TN 37202-0731. 615/367-7000. **Contact:** Human Resources. **Description:** Markets, distributes, and manufactures men's footwear. The company owns and licenses footwear brands, sold through both wholesale and retail channels, including Johnston & Murphy, Dockers, Nautica, and Jarman. Genesco products are sold at wholesale to a number of leading department, specialty, and discount stores. Products are also sold at retail through the company's own network of retail shoe stores including Johnston & Murphy, Jarman, and Journeys. **Corporate headquarters location:** This Location.

GEYERS' MARKET INC.
280 East Main Street, Lexington OH 44904-1194. 419/884-1373. **Contact:** Thomas S. Geyer, Vice President. **World Wide Web address:** http://www.geyers.com. **Description:** A grocery market. **Common positions include:** Retail Manager. **Educational backgrounds include:** Liberal Arts. **Benefits:** 401(k); Dental Insurance; Disability Coverage; Life Insurance; Medical Insurance; Profit Sharing. **Corporate headquarters location:** This Location. **Listed on:** Privately held. **Number of employees at this location:** 325.

GIANT FOOD, INC.
P.O. Box 1804, Washington DC 20013. 301/341-4100. **Contact:** Human Resources. **Description:** Operates a retail supermarket chain of approximately 115 stores. **Corporate headquarters location:** This Location.

GILLMAN COMPANIES
7611 Bellaire Boulevard, Houston TX 77036. 713/776-7162. **Contact:** Personnel Administration. **Description:** An automobile dealership group. Gillman operates dealerships selling Acura, Honda, Hyundai, Lincoln, Mazda, Mercury, Mitsubishi, Nissan, Subaru, and Suzuki automobiles. Founded in 1938. **Common positions include:** Accountant/Auditor; Advertising Clerk; Automotive Mechanic; Blue-Collar Worker Supervisor; Computer Operator; Computer Programmer; Credit Manager; Customer Service Representative; Department Manager; Dispatcher; Manufacturer's/Wholesaler's Sales Rep.; Payroll Clerk; Purchasing Agent/Manager. **Educational backgrounds include:** Accounting; Business Administration; Communications; Computer Science; Finance. **Benefits:** Credit Union; Dental Insurance; Disability Coverage; Employee Discounts; Life Insurance; Medical Insurance; Savings Plan. **Corporate headquarters location:** This Location. **Number of employees at this location:** 760.

GOLDEN BEAR GOLF INC.
11780 U.S. Highway One, North Palm Beach FL 33408. 561/626-3900. **Contact:** Sandy Zurnen, Personnel Administrator. **Description:** Franchises golf practice and instruction facilities, operates golf schools, constructs golf courses through Paragon Construction International (also at this location), and sells consumer golf products and apparel. **Common positions include:** Accountant/Auditor; Administrator; Architect; Civil Engineer; Marketing Specialist. **Educational backgrounds include:** Accounting; Art/Design; Business Administration; Finance; Marketing. **Benefits:** Dental Insurance; Disability Coverage; Life Insurance; Medical Insurance; Profit Sharing. **Corporate headquarters location:** This Location. **Listed on:** NASDAQ. **Stock exchange symbol:** JACK.

THE GOOD GUYS!
7000 Marina Boulevard, Brisbane CA 94005. 650/615-5000. **Contact:** Human Resources. **World Wide Web address:** http://www.thegoodguys.com. **Description:** Owns a chain of retail consumer electronic products stores specializing in televisions, videos, home audio systems, telephones, home office systems, car audio systems and cellular phones, photographic equipment, and other related electronic products. **Corporate headquarters location:** This Location.

GOODY'S FAMILY CLOTHING, INC.
400 Goody's Lane, Knoxville TN 37922. 865/966-2000. **Contact:** Human Resources. **Description:** An apparel retailer for women, men, and children. The company operates more than 250 stores in 16 states. **Corporate headquarters location:** This Location. **Other U.S. locations:** AL; AR; FL; GA; IL; IN; KY; MO; MS; NC; OH; SC; TN; VA; WV. **Listed on:** NASDAQ. **Stock exchange symbol:** GDYS. **Chairman and CEO:** Robert M. Goodfriend. **Number of employees nationwide:** 4,335.

GOTTSCHALKS
P.O. Box 28920, Fresno CA 93729-8920. 559/434-8000. **Fax:** 559/434-4806. **Contact:** Renee Jones, Director of Recruitment. **E-mail address:** hr@gottschalks.com. **World Wide Web address:** http://www.gottschalks.com. **Description:** A full-line fashion department store. This location also hires seasonally. Founded in 1904. **NOTE:** Entry-level positions and part-time jobs are offered. **Benefits:** 401(k); Casual Dress - Fridays; Dental Insurance; Employee Discounts; Medical Insurance; Stock Purchase; Vision Insurance. **Special programs:** Internships; Training. **Corporate headquarters location:** This Location. **Other U.S. locations:** NV; OR; WA. **Listed on:** New York Stock Exchange. **Stock exchange symbol:** GOT. **Annual sales/revenues:** More than $100 million. **Number of employees at this location:** 500. **Number of employees nationwide:** 5,000.

GREAT ATLANTIC & PACIFIC TEA CO. (A&P)
2 Paragon Drive, Montvale NJ 07645. 201/930-4416. **Contact:** Director of Personnel. **Description:** This location houses administrative offices for one of the nation's largest supermarket chains. Overall, The Great Atlantic & Pacific Tea Company maintains approximately 1,000 retail supermarkets throughout the East Coast, Mid-Atlantic, and Canada. **Common positions include:** Accountant/Auditor; Computer Programmer; Draftsperson; Financial Analyst; Systems Analyst.

Educational backgrounds include: Accounting; Business Administration; Computer Science. **Benefits:** 401(k); Dental Insurance; Disability Coverage; Life Insurance; Medical Insurance; Prescription Drugs; Retirement Plan; Vision Insurance. **Corporate headquarters location:** This Location. **Listed on:** New York Stock Exchange. **Number of employees at this location:** 650. **Number of employees nationwide:** 85,000.

GREEN MOUNTAIN COFFEE ROASTERS
33 Coffee Lane, Waterbury VT 05676. 802/244-5621. **Toll-free phone:** 800/545-2326. **Recorded jobline:** 802/244-6543. **Contact:** Human Resources. **World Wide Web address:** http://www.gmcr.com. **Description:** Roasts over 25 types of arabica beans to produce over 70 varieties of coffee which are sold through a multichannel distribution network consisting of wholesale, retail, and direct mail operations. **Common positions include:** Account Manager; Accountant; Administrative Assistant; Buyer; Chief Financial Officer; Computer Programmer; Controller; Customer Service Representative; Driver; Electrician; Finance Director; Graphic Artist; Human Resources Manager; Marketing Manager; MIS Specialist; Operations Manager; Production Manager; Project Manager; Public Relations Specialist; Purchasing Agent/Manager; Quality Control Supervisor; Sales Executive; Secretary; Systems Analyst; Systems Manager. **Educational backgrounds include:** Accounting; Art/Design; Business Administration; Computer Science; Finance; Marketing; Public Relations. **Benefits:** 401(k); Dental Insurance; Disability Coverage; Employee Discounts; Life Insurance; Medical Insurance. **Corporate headquarters location:** This Location. **Parent company:** Green Mountain Coffee, Inc. **Listed on:** NASDAQ. **Annual sales/revenues:** $21 - $50 million. **Number of employees at this location:** 200. **Number of employees nationwide:** 400.

GRIFFITH CONSUMERS COMPANY
2510 Schuster Drive, Cheverly MD 20781. 301/322-3111. **Contact:** Human Resources. **World Wide Web address:** http://www.griffithoil.com. **Description:** A full-service, independent, retail distributor of petroleum products, primarily heating oil and gasoline. Griffith Consumers Company also sells diesel fuel, heavy oils, kerosene, and products and services related to its energy business. Founded in 1898. **Common positions include:** Accountant/Auditor; Credit Manager; Customer Service Representative; Human Resources Manager; Sales Executive. **Educational backgrounds include:** Accounting; Finance; Marketing. **Benefits:** Dental Insurance; Employee Discounts; Life Insurance; Medical Insurance; Pension Plan. **Corporate headquarters location:** This Location. **Other U.S. locations:** DC; MD; NJ; PA; VA; WV.

GROW BIZ INTERNATIONAL
4200 Dahlberg Drive, Minneapolis MN 55422-4837. 612/520-8500. **Contact:** Human Resources. **World Wide Web address:** http://www.growbiz.com. **Description:** A retail franchiser which sells a variety of new and used merchandise. **Corporate headquarters location:** This Location. **Subsidiaries include:** It's About Games; Music Go Round; Once Upon A Child; Play It Again Sports; ReTool.

GYMBOREE
700 Airport Boulevard, Suite 200, Burlingame CA 94010. 650/579-0600. **Contact:** Human Resources. **World Wide Web address:** http://www.gymboree.com. **Description:** Operates a chain of retail stores that sell children's activewear and accessories. **Common positions include:** Accountant/Auditor; Designer; Operations/Production Manager; Paralegal; Systems Analyst; Transportation/Traffic Specialist. **Educational backgrounds include:** Accounting; Art/Design; Business Administration; Computer Science; Finance. **Benefits:** 401(k); Dental Insurance; Disability Coverage; Employee Discounts; Life Insurance; Medical Insurance; Tuition Assistance. **Corporate headquarters location:** This Location. **Listed on:** NASDAQ. **Number of employees at this location:** 100. **Number of employees nationwide:** 3,700.

HEB GROCERY COMPANY
646 South Main Street, San Antonio TX 78204. 210/938-8000. **Recorded jobline:** 210/938-5222. **Contact:** Dennis Galindo, Associate Recruiter. **E-mail address:** galindo.dennis@heb.com. **World Wide Web address:** http://www.heb.com. **Description:** Operates a chain of retail grocery stores. Founded in 1905. **NOTE:** Interested jobseekers should contact the jobline before sending a resume. **Common positions include:** Administrative Assistant; Construction Contractor; Customer Service Representative; Electrical/Electronics Engineer; Electrician; Environmental Engineer; Financial Analyst; Food Scientist/Technologist; Human Resources Manager; Industrial Engineer; Management Trainee; Manufacturing Engineer; Mechanical Engineer; Operations Manager; Production Manager; Quality Assurance Engineer; Sales Representative; Secretary; Transportation/Traffic Specialist. **Educational backgrounds include:** Biology; Chemistry; Engineering; Finance; Marketing; MBA. **Benefits:** 401(k); Casual Dress - Daily; Daycare Assistance; Dental Insurance; Life Insurance; Medical Insurance; Savings Plan; Sick Days (1 - 5); Tuition Assistance. **Office hours:** Monday - Friday, 8:00 a.m. - 5:00 p.m. **Corporate headquarters location:** This Location. **Listed on:** Privately held. **President:** Charles Butt. **Annual sales/revenues:** More than $100 million. **Number of employees at this location:** 5,000. **Number of employees nationwide:** 50,000.

HAGGEN, INC.
TOP FOOD & DRUG
P.O. Box 9704, Bellingham WA 98227. 360/733-8720. **Contact:** Human Resources Manager. **Description:** Operates over 25 grocery stores throughout the Pacific Northwest. . **Common positions include:** Accountant/Auditor; Chef/Cook/Kitchen Worker; Computer Programmer; Department Manager; Grocery Clerk; Meat Cutter; Pharmacist. **Educational backgrounds include:** Accounting; Business Administration; Communications; Computer Science; Liberal Arts; Marketing. **Benefits:** Dental Insurance; Disability Coverage; Life Insurance; Medical Insurance; Pension Plan; Profit Sharing; Savings Plan; Tuition Assistance. **Special programs:** Internships. **Corporate headquarters location:** This Location.

HAMILTON STORES, INC.
1709 West College Street, Bozeman MT 59715. 406/587-2208. **Fax:** 406/587-3105. **Contact:** Human Resources. **E-mail address:** jobs@hamiltonstores.com. **World Wide Web address:** http://www.hamiltonstores.com. **Description:** Operates 14 general stores in Yellowstone National Park. This location also hires seasonally. **Benefits:** Employee Discounts. **Special programs:** Internships. **Corporate headquarters location:** This Location. **Number of employees at this location:** 1,000.

J.L. HAMMETT COMPANY
P.O. Box 859057, Braintree MA 02185. 781/848-1000. **Physical address:** One Hammett Place, Braintree MA 02184. **Fax:** 781/843-4901. **Contact:** Lou Paress, Human Resources Supervisor. **World Wide Web address:** http://www.hammett.com. **Description:** Distributes educational supplies and equipment through catalog and retail stores. **Common positions include:** Accountant/Auditor; Administrator; Blue-Collar Worker Supervisor; Branch Manager; Buyer; Claim Representative; Computer Programmer; Credit Manager; Customer Service Representative; General Manager; Human Resources Manager; Marketing Specialist; Purchasing Agent/Manager; Sales Executive; Systems Analyst; Transportation/Traffic Specialist. **Educational backgrounds include:** Accounting; Business Administration; Computer Science; Finance; Marketing. **Benefits:** Dental Insurance; Disability Coverage; Employee Discounts; Life Insurance; Medical Insurance; Profit Sharing; Savings Plan; Tuition Assistance. **Corporate headquarters location:** This Location.

HAMRICK'S, INC.
742 Peachoid Road, Gaffney SC 29341. 864/489-6095. **Contact:** Maxine Elder, Director of Personnel. **Description:** Operates a chain of men's clothing stores. These stores are located in the southeastern United States at 23 different locations. **Corporate headquarters location:** This Location. **Other U.S. locations:** GA; NC.

HANNAFORD BROS. COMPANY
P.O. Box 1000, Portland ME 04104. 207/883-2911. **Physical address:** 145 Pleasant Hill Road, Scarborough ME. **Contact:** Human Resources. **World Wide Web address:** http://www.hannaford.com. **Description:** A multiregional food retailer located throughout Maine and in parts of New Hampshire, Vermont, upstate New York, Massachusetts, North Carolina, and South Carolina. Supermarkets operate primarily under the names Shop 'n Save, Wilson's, and Sun Foods. **Corporate headquarters location:** This Location.

HANOVER DIRECT, INC.
1500 Harbor Boulevard, Weehawken NJ 07087. 201/863-7300. **Fax:** 201/272-3465. **Contact:** Vice President of Human Resources. **Description:** A direct marketing company that sells products manufactured by other companies through its 12 core catalogs structured into operating groups. **NOTE:** Entry-level positions are offered. **Common positions include:** Accountant/Auditor; Buyer; Fashion Designer; Financial Analyst; Industrial Engineer; Market Research Analyst; Telemarketer. **Educational backgrounds include:** Accounting; Business Administration; Economics; Fashion; Finance; Liberal Arts; Marketing; Mathematics. **Benefits:** 401(k); Dental Insurance; Disability Coverage; Employee Discounts; Free Parking; Life Insurance; Medical Insurance; Public Transit Available; Tuition Assistance. **Corporate headquarters location:** This Location. **Other U.S. locations:** San Diego CA; San Francisco CA; Hanover PA; De Soto TX; Roanoke VA; La Crosse WI. **Annual sales/revenues:** More than $100 million. **Number of employees at this location:** 250. **Number of employees nationwide:** 3,000.

HARCOURT GENERAL COMPANY
27 Boylston Street, Chestnut Hill MA 02467. 617/232-8200. **Contact:** Human Resources. **World Wide Web address:** http://www.harcourt-general.com. **Description:** A holding company with significant interests in the publishing and retail markets. **Common positions include:** Accountant/Auditor; Attorney; Financial Analyst;

Human Resources Manager; Paralegal. **Educational backgrounds include:** Accounting; Business Administration; Finance. **Benefits:** 401(k); Daycare Assistance; Dental Insurance; Disability Coverage; Employee Discounts; ESOP; Life Insurance; Medical Insurance; Pension Plan; Savings Plan; Tuition Assistance. **Corporate headquarters location:** This Location. **Subsidiaries include:** Academic Press is an international publisher of life, physical, and social science books and journals. Assessment Systems is a leading provider of computerized tests. Bergdorf Goodman is a high-end fashion retailer with two locations in New York City. Drake Beam Morin is a career counseling and outplacement firm. Harcourt Brace is one of the nation's largest publishers of textbooks and other educational materials, and fiction and nonfiction books for children and adults. Harcourt Brace Publishers International is the London-based division of Harcourt Brace. Harcourt Health Sciences is the world's largest medical publisher. Harcourt Professional Education Group provides legal, financial, and human resources professionals with educational materials. Holt, Rinehart and Winston publishes textbooks for junior and senior high school markets. ICS Learning Systems is the world's largest distance learning company. NETg is a leading provider of training materials for information technology professionals. NM Direct is the at-home catalog of Neiman Marcus. Neiman Marcus is a first-class, worldwide clothing retailer. The Psychological Corporation is the nation's largest publisher of psychological and other assessment tests. Steck-Vaughn publishes educational materials. **Listed on:** New York Stock Exchange. **Number of employees at this location:** 120. **Number of employees nationwide:** 25,000.

HARRIS TEETER, INC.
P.O. Box 33129, Charlotte NC 28233. 704/845-3100. **Contact:** Director of Personnel. **World Wide Web address:** http://www.harristeeter.com. **Description:** Operates a regional supermarket chain with over 140 stores in five southeastern states. **NOTE:** All hiring for Harris Teeter is done at this location. **Corporate headquarters location:** This Location. **Parent company:** Ruddick Corporation (Charlotte NC) is a diversified holding company operating through wholly-owned subsidiaries American & Efird, Inc.; and Ruddick Investment Company. American & Efird (Mount Holly NC) manufactures and distributes sewing thread for worldwide industrial and consumer markets and handles its own hiring. **Listed on:** New York Stock Exchange.

THE HARVARD COOPERATIVE SOCIETY
1400 Massachusetts Avenue, Cambridge MA 02238. 617/499-2000. **Contact:** Personnel. **World Wide Web address:** http://www.thecoop.com. **Description:** A member-owned, collegiate department store selling a broad range of merchandise from clothing, books, and music, to housewares, electronics, and prints. **Common positions include:** Accountant/Auditor; Buyer; Customer Service Representative; Department Manager; Retail Sales Worker. **Educational backgrounds include:** Business Administration; Liberal Arts; Marketing. **Benefits:** Disability Coverage; Employee Discounts; Life Insurance; Medical Insurance; Profit Sharing; Savings Plan; Tuition Assistance. **Corporate headquarters location:** This Location.

HAVERTY FURNITURE COMPANIES
866 West Peachtree Street NW, Atlanta GA 30308. 404/881-1911. **Fax:** 404/877-9442. **Contact:** Human Resources. **E-mail address:** hr@havertys.com. **World Wide Web address:**

http://www.havertys.com. **Description:** A full-service home furnishings retailer with more than 100 showrooms in 14 states. The company distributes and sells furniture lines under the Thomasville, Drexel Heritage, and Broyhill names. Founded in 1885. **Company slogan:** Making it home. **Common positions include:** Accountant; Administrative Assistant; Advertising Clerk; Advertising Executive; Architect; AS400 Programmer Analyst; Budget Analyst; Chief Financial Officer; Computer Programmer; Computer Support Technician; Construction Contractor; Controller; Editor; Finance Director; Graphic Artist; Graphic Designer; Human Resources Manager; Marketing Manager; MIS Specialist; Network/Systems Administrator; Operations Manager; Secretary; Telecommunications Manager; Vice President of Operations; Web Advertising Specialist; Website Developer. **Educational backgrounds include:** Accounting; Art/Design; AS400 Certification; Business Administration; Communications; Economics; Finance; Marketing; Microsoft Office; QuarkXPress; Spreadsheets. **Benefits:** 401(k); Dental Insurance; Employee Discounts; Flexible Schedule; Life Insurance; Medical Insurance; Pension Plan; Tuition Assistance. **Special programs:** Training. **Corporate headquarters location:** This Location. **Other U.S. locations:** AL; AR; FL; KS; KY; LA; MO; MS; NC; SC; TN; TX; VA. **Listed on:** New York Stock Exchange. **President/CEO:** Jay Slater. **Annual sales/revenues:** More than $100 million. **Number of employees at this location:** 150. **Number of employees nationwide:** 3,400.

HECHINGER/HQ
1801 McCormick Drive, Largo MD 20774. 301/883-4500. **Contact:** Human Resources. **Description:** A specialty retailer operating over 100 home center stores in more than 20 states and the District of Columbia. **Common positions include:** Accountant/Auditor; Buyer; Computer Programmer; Economist; General Manager; Human Resources Manager; Management Trainee; Marketing Manager. **Corporate headquarters location:** This Location. **Subsidiaries include:** Hechinger Stores Company; Home Quarters Warehouse, Inc.

HECHT'S
685 North Glebe Road, Arlington VA 22203-2199. 703/558-1200. **Contact:** Bruce Kelso, Senior Vice President of Human Resources. **Description:** A general merchandise and apparel retailer. **Office hours:** Monday - Friday, 9:00 a.m. - 5:00 p.m. **Corporate headquarters location:** This Location.

HEILIG-MEYERS
8820 Park Central Drive, Richmond VA 23227. 804/553-1350. **Contact:** Human Resources. **Description:** Engaged in the retail sale of home furnishings including electronics, appliances, outdoor furniture, floor coverings, and bedding. The company operates approximately 650 stores in 24 states and Puerto Rico. **Corporate headquarters location:** This Location. **Subsidiaries include:** Berrios Enterprises of Caguas. **Listed on:** New York Stock Exchange; Pacific Stock Exchange. **Number of employees at this location:** 7,850. **Number of employees nationwide:** 12,510.

HELLO-DIRECT
5893 Rue Ferrari, San Jose CA 95138-1858. 408/972-1990. **Contact:** Human Resources. **World Wide Web address:** http://www.hello-direct.com. **Description:** A catalog retailer of telephone productivity items including headsets, cordless phones, line switches, digital adapters, and call recording devices. **Corporate headquarters location:** This Location.

HIT OR MISS, INC.
100 Campanelli Parkway, Stoughton MA 02072. 781/344-0800. **Fax:** 781/297-7268. **Contact:** Margaret Chapman, Staffing and Development Manager. **Description:** A women's discount fashion store. Hit or Miss operates over 330 stores in 35 states. **Common positions include:** Buyer; Computer Programmer; Management Trainee; Merchandiser; MIS Specialist; Retail Manager; Systems Analyst. **Benefits:** 401(k); Dental Insurance; Disability Coverage; Employee Discounts; Life Insurance; Medical Insurance. **Corporate headquarters location:** This Location. **Other U.S. locations:** Nationwide. **Listed on:** New York Stock Exchange. **Annual sales/revenues:** More than $100 million. **Number of employees at this location:** 180. **Number of employees nationwide:** 3,500.

HOLIDAY STATIONSTORES
4567 West 80th Street, Bloomington MN 55437. 952/832-8530. **Toll-free phone:** 800/745-7411. **Fax:** 952/832-8551. **Recorded jobline:** 952/832-8585. **Contact:** Wayne Nau, Recruiting Manager. **Description:** Operates retail convenience stores/gas stations with over 240 locations in 10 states. **NOTE:** Some post-secondary education in business management, accounting, or marketing is desired but not required. Entry-level positions are offered. **Common positions include:** Assistant Manager; Cashier; Management Trainee. **Benefits:** Bonus Award/Plan; Dental Insurance; Disability Coverage; Employee Discounts; Life Insurance; Medical Insurance; Profit Sharing; Tuition Assistance. **Special programs:** Internships; Training. **Corporate headquarters location:** This Location. **Other U.S. locations:** IA; ID; MI; MT; ND; NE; WA; WI; WY. **Parent company:** Holiday Companies. **Listed on:** Privately held. **Annual sales/revenues:** More than $100 million. **Number of employees at this location:** 500. **Number of employees nationwide:** 6,000.

HOLLYWOOD ENTERTAINMENT
9275 SW Peyton Lane, Wilsonville OR 97070. 503/570-1600. **Contact:** Human Resources. **World Wide Web address:** http://www.hollywoodvideo.com. **Description:** Owns and operates more than 1,600 video retail superstores. Each of the company's stores rents videocassettes, video games, and video game systems and sells videocassettes, accessories, and confectionery items. **Corporate headquarters location:** This Location. **Other U.S. locations:** Nationwide. **Number of employees nationwide:** 1,175.

THE HOME DEPOT
2455 Paces Ferry Road, Atlanta GA 30339-4024. 770/433-8211. **Contact:** Human Resources. **World Wide Web address:** http://www.homedepot.com. **Description:** Operates retail warehouse stores selling a wide assortment of building materials and home improvement products, primarily to the do-it-yourself and home remodeling markets. The company operates 900 full-service, warehouse-style stores. The stores stock over 40,000 different kinds of building materials, home improvement supplies, and lawn and garden products. Founded in 1978. **Common positions include:** Accountant; Administrative Assistant; Advertising Clerk; Advertising Executive; Applications Engineer; Assistant Manager; Attorney; Auditor; Broadcast Technician; Budget Analyst; Chief Financial Officer; Claim Representative; Clerical Supervisor; Computer Operator; Computer Programmer; Customer Service Representative; Design Engineer; Financial Analyst; Graphic Artist; Graphic Designer; Human Resources Manager; Marketing Manager; MIS Specialist; Paralegal; Purchasing

Agent/Manager; Quality Control Supervisor; Secretary; Software Engineer; Systems Analyst; Systems Manager; Technical Writer/Editor; Telecommunications Manager; Transportation/Traffic Specialist. **Benefits:** 401(k); Dental Insurance; Disability Coverage; Life Insurance; Medical Insurance; Profit Sharing; Tuition Assistance. **Corporate headquarters location:** This Location. **Other U.S. locations:** Nationwide. **International locations:** Canada; Chile; Puerto Rico. **Listed on:** New York Stock Exchange. **Annual sales/revenues:** More than $100 million. **Number of employees at this location:** 3,000. **Number of employees nationwide:** 211,000.

HOME SHOPPING NETWORK, INC.
One HSN Drive, St. Petersburg FL 33729. 727/872-1000. **Contact:** Human Resources. **Description:** A holding company that owns and operates Home Shopping Club, Inc. (HSC), which offers jewelry, hardgoods, softgoods, cosmetics, and other items via live television presentations; the Internet Shopping Network, which delivers online shopping; and HSN Direct division, which produces and airs infomercials and distributes infomercial products. **Corporate headquarters location:** This Location. **Listed on:** New York Stock Exchange. **Number of employees nationwide:** 5,000.

HOMESTEAD HOUSE
9410 Wadsworth Parkway, P.O. Box 499, Broomfield CO 80038-0499. 303/425-6544. **Toll-free phone:** 800/275-0345. **Fax:** 303/425-0541. **Contact:** Director of Human Resources. **Description:** Operates a chain of home furnishings stores. **Corporate headquarters location:** This Location. **President:** Richard L. Gill.

HUBCAP WORLD TOO
9425 SW Commerce Circle, Wilsonville OR 97070. 503/570-0663. **Contact:** Personnel. **Description:** Operates an Oregon retail chain that sells a variety of hubcaps. **Corporate headquarters location:** This Location.

INGLES MARKETS, INC.
P.O. Box 6676, Asheville NC 28816. 828/669-2941. **Contact:** Human Resources Director. **World Wide Web address:** http://www.ingles-markets.com. **Description:** Operates over 200 supermarkets in North Carolina, South Carolina, Georgia, Tennessee, Virginia, and Alabama. In conjunction with its supermarket activities, the company owns and operates neighborhood shopping centers. Ingles Markets also owns and operates a milk processing and packaging plant. **Corporate headquarters location:** This Location. **Listed on:** NASDAQ. **Number of employees nationwide:** 9,900.

INTERPACIFIC HAWAII RETAIL GROUP
P.O. Box 2480, Honolulu HI 96814. 808/971-4200. **Contact:** Human Resources. **Description:** Operates designer resort boutiques. **Common positions include:** Accountant/Auditor; Administrator; Buyer; Credit Manager; Customer Service Representative; Management Trainee; Sales Executive. **Educational backgrounds include:** Accounting; Business Administration; Communications; Liberal Arts; Marketing. **Benefits:** Dental Insurance; Disability Coverage; Employee Discounts; Life Insurance; Medical Insurance. **Special programs:** Internships. **Corporate headquarters location:** This Location.

JCPENNEY COMPANY, INC.
P.O. Box 10001, Dallas TX 75301. 972/431-1000. **Contact:** Human Resources. **World Wide Web address:** http://www.jcpenney.com. **Description:** This location houses administrative offices. Overall, JCPenney Company is a national retail merchandise

sales and service corporation with department stores nationwide. JCPenney sells apparel, home furnishings, and leisure lines in catalogs and 1,200 stores. **Corporate headquarters location:** This Location. **Subsidiaries include:** JCPenney Life Insurance Company, which sells life, health, and credit insurance; and JCPenney National Bank. **Listed on:** New York Stock Exchange. **Annual sales/revenues:** More than $100 million. **Other U.S. locations:**
- Oxford Valley Mall, 2300 East Lincoln Highway, Langhorne PA 19047. 215/752- 5300.

JEWEL OSCO
1955 West North Avenue, Melrose Park IL 60160. 708/531-6000. **Fax:** 708/531-6047. **Contact:** Employment Manager. **World Wide Web address:** http://www.jewelosco.com. **Description:** Operates a chain of retail food stores. **NOTE:** When sending a resume, please indicate department of interest. **Corporate headquarters location:** This Location.

JOAN FABRICS CORPORATION
100 Vesper Executive Park, Tyngsboro MA 01879-2710. 978/649-5626. **Contact:** Director of Human Resources. **Description:** Engaged in the manufacturing of woven and knitted fabrics for furniture and automotive manufacturers. The company also operates retail fabric stores nationwide. **Common positions include:** Accountant; Blue-Collar Worker Supervisor; Computer Programmer; Credit Manager; Customer Service Representative; Department Manager; Financial Analyst; Human Resources Manager; Industrial Engineer; Operations/Production Manager; Purchasing Agent/Manager; Quality Control Supervisor; Systems Analyst. **Educational backgrounds include:** Accounting; Business Administration; Computer Science; Engineering; Finance; Textiles. **Benefits:** 401(k); Disability Coverage; Life Insurance; Medical Insurance; Pension Plan; Tuition Assistance. **Corporate headquarters location:** This Location. **Other U.S. locations:** Fall River MA; Lowell MA; Hickory NC.

THE JONES COMPANY
P.O. Box 2149, Waycross GA 31502. 912/285-4011. **Contact:** Employment. **Description:** Owns and operates Flash Foods retail convenience stores. **Corporate headquarters location:** This Location.

JOS. A. BANK CLOTHIERS INC.
500 Hanover Pike, Hampstead MD 21074. 410/239-5728. **Toll-free phone:** 800/520-4473. **Fax:** 410/239-5868. **Contact:** Ami O'Meara, Employment Specialist. **World Wide Web address:** http://www.josbank.com. **Description:** A retailer of men's clothing. Founded in 1905. **NOTE:** Entry-level positions are offered. **Common positions include:** Accountant; Administrative Assistant; Buyer; Computer Operator; Computer Programmer; Financial Analyst; Marketing Specialist; Quality Control Supervisor; Sales Representative; Secretary. **Educational backgrounds include:** Merchandising; Retail. **Benefits:** 401(k); Dental Insurance; Disability Coverage; Employee Discounts; Flexible Schedule; Life Insurance; Medical Insurance; Tuition Assistance. **Corporate headquarters location:** This Location. **Other U.S. locations:** Nationwide. **Listed on:** NASDAQ. **President/CEO:** Tim Finley. **Annual sales/revenues:** More than $100 million. **Number of employees at this location:** 300. **Number of employees nationwide:** 1,400.

KANE FURNITURE
5700 70th Avenue North, Pinellas Park FL 33781. 727/545-9555. **Fax:** 727/548-0552. **Contact:** Human Resources Director. **Description:** A

furniture retailer. **Common positions include:** Accountant/Auditor; Administrative Manager; Clerical Supervisor; Customer Service Representative; Designer; Management Trainee; Services Sales Representative. **Educational backgrounds include:** Accounting; Business Administration; Communications; Marketing. **Benefits:** Dental Insurance; Disability Coverage; Employee Discounts; Life Insurance; Medical Insurance; Profit Sharing. **Corporate headquarters location:** This Location. **Listed on:** Privately held. **Number of employees at this location:** 250. **Number of employees nationwide:** 750.

KASH 'N KARRY FOOD STORES
6401A Harney Road, Tampa FL 33610. 813/620-1139. **Contact:** Director of Human Resources. **Description:** An operator of retail food and liquor stores. **Corporate headquarters location:** This Location. **Number of employees nationwide:** 8,400.

KEY FOOD STORES CO-OPERATIVE INC.
8925 Avenue D, Brooklyn NY 11236. 718/451-1000. **Contact:** Ronald Phillips, Controller. **Description:** Operates a chain of food stores. **Corporate headquarters location:** This Location.

KING KULLEN GROCERY COMPANY
1194 Prospect Avenue, Westbury NY 11590. 516/333-7100. **Contact:** Personnel Director. **Description:** Operates 55 supermarkets in Suffolk, Nassau, Queens, and Brooklyn, and maintains its own grocery, meat, and produce warehouses, as well as a fleet of delivery vehicles. **Corporate headquarters location:** This Location.

KITTERY TRADING POST
P.O. Box 904, Kittery ME 03904-0904. 207/439-2700. **Contact:** Manager. **World Wide Web address:** http://www.kitterytradingpost.com. **Description:** Sells a wide variety of sporting goods including clothing, footwear, camping gear, shooting and archery equipment, cross country skis, kayaks, and fishing gear.

KMART CORPORATION
3100 West Big Beaver Road, Troy MI 48084. 248/614-0906. **Contact:** Human Resources. **World Wide Web address:** http://www.bluelight.com. **Description:** One of the nation's largest owners and operators of general merchandise stores. The company operates 2,100 Kmart discount stores in 50 states and Puerto Rico, Guam, and Canada, and has formed joint ventures in Mexico and Singapore. These stores include 90 Super Kmart Centers, which offer foodstuffs in addition to general merchandise. **Common positions include:** Accountant/Auditor; Buyer; Computer Programmer; Designer; Financial Analyst; MIS Specialist; Software Engineer; Systems Analyst. **Educational backgrounds include:** Accounting; Business Administration; Finance; Marketing. **Benefits:** 401(k); Daycare Assistance; Dental Insurance; Disability Coverage; Life Insurance; Medical Insurance; Profit Sharing; Savings Plan; Tuition Assistance. **Corporate headquarters location:** This Location. **Other U.S. locations:** Nationwide. **Subsidiaries include:** Builders Square, a chain of retail home improvement centers. **Listed on:** New York Stock Exchange. **Annual sales/revenues:** More than $100 million. **Number of employees at this location:** 3,700. **Number of employees nationwide:** 300,000.

KNOWLAN'S SUPER MARKETS
111 East County Road F, Vadnais Heights MN 55127. 651/483-9242. **Contact:** Andrea Wellman, Human Resources Director. **Description:** Operates a chain of retail grocery stores. **Corporate headquarters location:** This Location.

KOHL'S DEPARTMENT STORES INC.
N56W 17000 Ridgewood Drive, Menomonee Falls WI 53051. 262/703-1600. **Contact:** Manager of College Relations. **World Wide Web address:** http://www.kohls.com. **Description:** A value-oriented, family-focused, specialty department store. The company's stores sell moderately priced apparel, shoes, accessories, soft home products, and housewares. **NOTE:** College graduates begin careers with Kohl's in a Store Management Trainee position. The first six weeks of the training program are spent in the corporate offices and in a structured, on-the-job training program. During this period, the trainees are exposed to merchandising, marketing, advertising, and distribution, as well as other support areas of the company. The following seven weeks are spent in the stores division, providing trainees with further exposure to customer service, merchandise presentation, and other non-selling areas. Upon successful completion of the trainee program, trainees are placed as assistant store managers-in-training. Kohl's will consider both business and liberal arts students for this program. **Common positions include:** Accountant/Auditor; Advertising Clerk; Assistant Manager; Buyer; Commercial Artist; Computer Programmer; Credit Manager; Draftsperson; Financial Analyst; General Manager; Human Resources Manager; Management Trainee; Systems Analyst. **Educational backgrounds include:** Accounting; Business Administration; Communications; Economics; Finance. **Benefits:** 401(k); Daycare Assistance; Dental Insurance; Disability Coverage; Employee Discounts; Life Insurance; Medical Insurance; Pension Plan; Profit Sharing; Savings Plan; Stock Option. **Corporate headquarters location:** This Location. **Other U.S. locations:** IA; IL; IN; MI; MN; OH; SD. **Listed on:** New York Stock Exchange. **Annual sales/revenues:** More than $100 million. **Number of employees at this location:** 650. **Number of employees nationwide:** 22,250.

THE KROGER COMPANY
1014 Vine Street, Cincinnati OH 45202-1100. 513/762-4000. **Contact:** Human Resources. **World Wide Web address:** http://www.kroger.com. **Description:** Operates more than 2,200 supermarkets and convenience stores. Kroger also has 37 food processing plants which supply over 4,000 private label products to its supermarkets. **Corporate headquarters location:** This Location. **Listed on:** New York Stock Exchange. **Number of employees worldwide:** 300,000.

K'S MERCHANDISE
3103 North Charles Street, Decatur IL 62526. 217/875-1440. **Contact:** Human Resources. **Description:** A retail catalog showroom chain. **Common positions include:** Accountant/Auditor; Advertising Clerk; Blue-Collar Worker Supervisor; Buyer; Commercial Artist; Computer Programmer; Department Manager; General Manager; Human Resources Manager; Management Trainee; Purchasing Agent/Manager; Transportation/Traffic Specialist. **Educational backgrounds include:** Accounting; Business Administration; Communications; Computer Science; Finance; Liberal Arts; Marketing. **Benefits:** Disability Coverage; Employee Discounts; Life Insurance; Medical Insurance; Pension Plan; Profit Sharing. **Corporate headquarters location:** This Location.

LAMONTS APPAREL, INC.
12413 Willows Road NE, Kirkland WA 98034. 425/814-5700. **Fax:** 425/814-5797. **Contact:** Human Resources. **E-mail address:** lamonts-

apparel@compuserve.com. **Description:** Owns and operates more than 35 retail clothing stores in the Northwest. This location also hires seasonally. Founded in 1967. **NOTE:** Part-time jobs are offered. **Common positions include:** Accountant; Administrative Assistant; Administrative Manager; Advertising Executive; Assistant Manager; Branch Manager; Broadcast Technician; Budget Analyst; Buyer; Computer Programmer; Financial Analyst; Graphic Designer; Help-Desk Technician; Management Trainee; Network/Systems Administrator; Systems Analyst; Technical Writer/Editor; Web Advertising Specialist. **Educational backgrounds include:** Accounting; Business Administration; Computer Science; HTML; Liberal Arts; Marketing; Microsoft Office; Microsoft Word; Software Tech. Support; Spreadsheets. **Benefits:** 401(k); Casual Dress - Daily; Daycare Assistance; Dental Insurance; Disability Coverage; Employee Discounts; Flexible Schedule; Life Insurance; Medical Insurance; Tuition Assistance; Vacation Days. **Special programs:** Internships; Training; Summer Jobs. **Office hours:** Monday - Friday, 8:30 a.m. - 5:00 p.m. **Corporate headquarters location:** This Location. **Other U.S. locations:** AK; ID; OR; UT. **Listed on:** NASDAQ. **Annual sales/revenues:** More than $100 million. **Number of employees nationwide:** 1,500.

LANDS' END, INC.
One Lands' End Lane, Dodgeville WI 53595. 608/935-9341. **Contact:** Human Resources. **World Wide Web address:** http://www.landsend.com. **Description:** An international direct merchant of a wide variety of casual clothing for men, women, and children; accessories; shoes; and soft luggage. The company's products are offered through its monthly catalogs. The company's specialty catalogs include the Kids Book catalog featuring casual clothing for children and infants; the Coming Home catalog, which features bed and bath items; the Beyond Buttondowns catalog, which offers classic tailored clothing for men; and Textures, a women's catalog featuring a selection of tailored clothing for the work setting. Lands' End also holds a majority interest in The Territory Ahead, a California-based, upscale casual clothing catalog for men and women. **Corporate headquarters location:** This Location. **International locations:** Rutland, England; Yokohama, Japan. **Number of employees worldwide:** 4,700.

LEATH FURNITURE
4370 Peachtree Road NE, 4th Floor, Atlanta GA 30319. 404/848-0880. **Contact:** Human Resources. **Description:** Owns and operates retail furniture stores across the state. **Corporate headquarters location:** This Location.

LECHTERS, INC.
One Cape May Street, Harrison NJ 07029. 973/481-1100. **Contact:** Employee Relations Manager. **World Wide Web address:** http://www.lechters.com. **Description:** A specialty retailer of primarily brand-name, non-electric basic housewares; tabletop items; and kitchen textiles. These products include cookware, bakeware, kitchen gadgets, kitchen utensils, microwave accessories, glassware, frames, household storage items, towels, place mats, napkins, and aprons. **Common positions include:** Accountant/Auditor; Buyer; Human Resources Manager; Management Trainee; Paralegal; Real Estate Agent. **Educational backgrounds include:** Accounting; Business Administration; Economics; Finance; Liberal Arts; Marketing. **Benefits:** 401(k); Dental Insurance; Disability Coverage; Employee Discounts; Life Insurance; Medical Insurance; Pension Plan. **Special**

programs: Internships. **Corporate headquarters location:** This Location. **Other U.S. locations:** Nationwide. **Listed on:** NASDAQ. **Number of employees at this location:** 400. **Number of employees nationwide:** 6,900.

LEVITZ FURNITURE CORPORATION
7887 North Federal Highway, Boca Raton FL 33487. 561/994-6006. **Contact:** Nicholas Masullo, Vice President of Human Resources. **World Wide Web address:** http://www.levitz.com. **Description:** Operates a national furniture store chain. **Corporate headquarters location:** This Location. **Other U.S. locations:** Nationwide.

LEWAN & ASSOCIATES, INC.
P.O. Box 22855, Denver CO 80222. 303/759-5440. **Physical address:** 1400 South Colorado Boulevard, Denver CO. **Contact:** Nancy Medley, Human Resources Manager. **World Wide Web address:** http://www.lewan.com. **Description:** A retail office products dealer. **Common positions include:** Administrator; Advertising Clerk; Buyer; Credit Manager; Customer Service Representative; Electrical/Electronics Engineer; Purchasing Agent/Manager; Services Sales Representative. **Educational backgrounds include:** Business Administration; Computer Science; Engineering; Marketing. **Benefits:** 401(k); Dental Insurance; Disability Coverage; Employee Discounts; Life Insurance; Medical Insurance; Pension Plan; Profit Sharing; Tuition Assistance. **Corporate headquarters location:** This Location.

LILLIAN VERNON CORPORATION
One Theall Road, Rye NY 10580. 914/925-1200. **Fax:** 914/925-1320. **Contact:** Human Resources. **E-mail address:** jobs@lillianvernon.com. **World Wide Web address:** http://www.lillianvernon.com. **Description:** Lillian Vernon markets gift, household, gardening, decorative, Christmas, and children's products through a variety of specialty catalogs. Catalog titles include: Lillian Vernon; Lillian Vernon Gardening; Neat Ideas; Personalized Gift; Christmas Memories; Lilly's Kids; Favorites; and Private Sale. Founded in 1951. **Common positions include:** Account Manager; Account Representative; Accountant; Administrative Assistant; AS400 Programmer Analyst; Auditor; Bank Officer/Manager; Budget Analyst; Buyer; Chief Financial Officer; Computer Programmer; Controller; Credit Manager; Database Manager; Desktop Publishing Specialist; Editor; Finance Director; Financial Analyst; Graphic Artist; Graphic Designer; Human Resources Manager; Internet Services Manager; Market Research Analyst; Marketing Manager; Marketing Specialist; Network/Systems Administrator; Public Relations Specialist; Purchasing Agent/Manager; Sales Representative; Secretary; Systems Analyst; Systems Manager. **Educational backgrounds include:** Accounting; Art/Design; AS400 Certification; Economics; Marketing; Merchandising; Microsoft Word; Novell; QuarkXPress; Spreadsheets. **Benefits:** 401(k); Casual Dress - Fridays; Dental Insurance; Disability Coverage; Employee Discounts; Flexible Schedule; Life Insurance; Medical Insurance; Profit Sharing; Tuition Assistance. **Office hours:** Monday - Friday, 8:30 a.m. - 5:00 p.m. **Corporate headquarters location:** This Location. **Other U.S. locations:** Virginia Beach VA. **Listed on:** American Stock Exchange. **Stock exchange symbol:** LVC. **Annual sales/revenues:** More than $100 million. **Number of employees at this location:** 175.

THE LIMITED STORES, INC.
3 Limited Parkway, Columbus OH 43230. 614/479-2000. **Contact:** Recruiting Office. **World Wide**

Web address: http://www.limited.com.
Description: Operates a nationwide chain of retail stores offering careerwear, sportswear, lingerie, and children's clothing. **Common positions include:** Accountant/Auditor; Computer Programmer; Management Trainee. **Educational backgrounds include:** Accounting; Computer Science. **Benefits:** Dental Insurance; Disability Coverage; Employee Discounts; Life Insurance; Medical Insurance; Pension Plan; Profit Sharing; Savings Plan. **Corporate headquarters location:** This Location. **Listed on:** New York Stock Exchange. **Annual sales/revenues:** More than $100 million.

LINENS 'N THINGS
6 Brighton Road, Clifton NJ 07015. 973/778-1300. **Fax:** 973/249-4604. **Contact:** Personnel. **E-mail address:** lntjobs@lnthings.com. **World Wide Web address:** http://www.lnthings.com. **Description:** A specialty retailer selling linens, home furnishings, and domestics. Linens 'n Things operates over 230 stores nationwide. **Common positions include:** Assistant Manager; Shipping and Receiving Clerk; Store Manager. **Educational backgrounds include:** Business Administration; Liberal Arts; Marketing; Retail Management. **Corporate headquarters location:** This Location.

LONDON FOG INDUSTRIES
1332 Londontown Boulevard, Eldersburg MD 21784. 410/795-5900. **Contact:** Human Resources. **Description:** London Fog is a manufacturer and retailer of traditional and contemporary men's and women's rainwear. The company is also manufacturer and retailer of men's, women's, and children's outerwear and sportswear. Founded in 1923. **NOTE:** Entry-level positions are offered. **Common positions include:** Accountant/Auditor; Adjuster; Administrative Manager; Attorney; Blue-Collar Worker Supervisor; Budget Analyst; Computer Programmer; Credit Manager; Customer Service Representative; Financial Analyst; Management Trainee; MIS Specialist; Systems Analyst; Transportation/Traffic Specialist. **Educational backgrounds include:** Accounting; Art/Design; Business Administration; Computer Science; Finance; Marketing. **Benefits:** 401(k); Dental Insurance; Disability Coverage; Employee Discounts; Life Insurance; Medical Insurance; Savings Plan; Tuition Assistance. **Other U.S. locations:** Nationwide. **Subsidiaries include:** Pacific Trail (also at this location). **Listed on:** Privately held.

LONGS DRUG STORES
P.O. Box 5222, Walnut Creek CA 94596. 925/937-1170. **Physical address:** 141 North Civic Drive, Walnut Creek CA 94596. **Fax:** 925/210-6335. **Contact:** Employment. **E-mail address:** employment@longs.com. **World Wide Web address:** http://www.longs.com. **Description:** Owns and operates a chain of more than 400 retail drug stores that offer a broad range of pharmaceuticals and personal care products. **Corporate headquarters location:** This Location.

LORD & TAYLOR
424 Fifth Avenue, New York NY 10018. 212/391-3344. **Contact:** Personnel Department. **World Wide Web address:** http://www.lordandtaylor.com. **Description:** A full-line department store offering clothing, accessories, home furnishings, and many other retail items. Founded in 1826. **Common positions include:** Branch Manager; Buyer; Credit Manager; Department Manager; Management Trainee. **Educational backgrounds include:** Business Administration; Communications; Economics; Finance; Liberal Arts; Marketing; Mathematics. **Benefits:** Dental Insurance; Employee

Discounts; Life Insurance; Medical Insurance; Pension Plan; Savings Plan. **Corporate headquarters location:** This Location. Nationwide. **Parent company:** The May Department Stores Company. **Annual sales/revenues:** More than $100 million.
Other U.S. locations:
- 450 Northpark Center, Dallas TX 75225. 214/691-6600.
- 5255 Western Avenue NW, Washington DC 20015. 202/362-9600.
- 7950 Tysons Corner Center, McLean VA 22102. 703/506-1156.

LOVE'S COUNTRY STORES
P.O. Box 26210, Oklahoma City OK 73126. 405/749-1744. **Fax:** 405/749-9145. **Contact:** Mr. Kerry Laws, Human Resources Director. **World Wide Web address:** http://www. lovescountrystores.com. **Description:** Operates retail convenience stores, travel stops, and restaurants. **Common positions include:** Management Trainee; Restaurant/Food Service Manager. **Educational backgrounds include:** Business Administration; Liberal Arts. **Benefits:** 401(k); Disability Coverage; Employee Discounts; Life Insurance; Medical Insurance; Savings Plan. **Special programs:** Internships. **Corporate headquarters location:** This Location. **Other U.S. locations:** AR; CO; KS; NM; TX. **Listed on:** Privately held. **Number of employees nationwide:** 2,000.

LOWE'S COMPANIES, INC.
P.O. Box 1111, North Wilkesboro NC 28656. 336/658-4000. **Contact:** Human Resources. **World Wide Web address:** http://www.lowes.com. **Description:** A discount retailer of consumer durables, building supplies, and home products for the do-it-yourself and home improvement markets. The company conducts operations through over 580 retail stores in 39 states, primarily in the south central and southeastern regions of the United States. Products sold include tools, lumber, building materials, heating, cooling, and water systems, and specialty goods. **CBenefits:** 401(k); Casual Dress - Daily; Daycare Assistance; Dental Insurance; Disability Coverage; Employee Discounts; ESOP; Life Insurance; Medical Insurance; Tuition Assistance. **Special programs:** Internships. **Corporate headquarters location:** This Location. **Listed on:** New York Stock Exchange. **Annual sales/revenues:** More than $100 million. **Number of employees nationwide:** 100,000.

LUND FOOD HOLDINGS BYERLY'S INC.
4100 West 50th Street, Suite 2100, Edina MN 55424. 612/927-3663. **Contact:** Personnel. **Description:** Lund Food Holdings owns and operates Byerly's, a retail grocery store chain with seven stores in the Minneapolis-St. Paul region. **Corporate headquarters location:** This Location.

MACY'S
151 West 34th Street, New York NY 10001. 212/695-4400. **Contact:** Human Resources. **Description:** This location houses administrative offices as well as a department store. **Corporate headquarters location:** This Location. **Parent company:** Federated Department Stores.

MAIL BOXES ETC.
6060 Cornerstone Court West, San Diego CA 92121. 858/455-8800. **Fax:** 858/625-3159. **Contact:** Human Resources. **World Wide Web address:** http://www.mbe.com. **Description:** Operates through two wholly-owned subsidiaries. Mail Boxes Etc. provides franchisees with a system

of business training, site location, marketing, advertising programs, and management support designed to assist the franchisee in opening and operating MBE Centers. **Corporate headquarters location:** This Location. **Subsidiaries include:** Mail Boxes Etc. USA grants territorial franchise rights for the operation or sale of service centers specializing in postal, packaging, business, and communications services. MBE Service Corp. offers electronic tax filing services.

MAILER'S SOFTWARE
22382 Avenida Empresa, Rancho Santa Margarita CA 92688-2112. **Toll-free phone:** 800/800-MAIL. **Contact:** Human Resources. **World Wide Web address:** http://www.800mail.com. **Description:** A catalog retailer of direct mail software. **Corporate headquarters location:** This Location.

MARSH SUPERMARKETS, INC.
9800 Crosspoint Boulevard, Indianapolis IN 46256. 317/594-2100. **Contact:** David Redden, Senior Vice President of Human Resources. **Description:** Through three divisions, the company operates Marsh Supermarkets, LoBill Foods, Village Pantry Convenience Stores in Indiana and Ohio, and CSDC, a convenience store distribution company. Founded in 1931. **Corporate headquarters location:** This Location.

MASS MARKETING, INC.
dba SUPER S FOODS
401 Isom Road, Building 100, San Antonio TX 78216. 210/344-1960. **Contact:** Human Resources Department. **Description:** A corporate division of the retail grocery store chain Super S Foods. **Corporate headquarters location:** This Location. **Number of employees at this location:** 50.

MAVERIK COUNTRY STORES, INC.
P.O. Box 8008, Afton WY 83110-8008. 307/885-3861. **Fax:** 307/886-3832. **Contact:** Val Dee Swenson, Payroll Supervisor. **World Wide Web address:** http://www.maverik.com. **Description:** Operates convenience stores. **Common positions include:** Accountant; Administrative Assistant; Administrative Manager; Auditor; Bank Officer/Manager; Chief Financial Officer; Claim Representative; Clerical Supervisor; Computer Operator; Computer Programmer; Credit Manager; Database Manager; Human Resources Manager; Internet Services Manager; Operations Manager; Secretary; Typist/Word Processor; Vice President of Operations. **Benefits:** 401(k); Dental Insurance; Life Insurance; Medical Insurance; Profit Sharing. **Corporate headquarters location:** This Location. **Listed on:** Privately held. **Number of employees at this location:** 20. **Number of employees worldwide:** 1,800.

THE MAY DEPARTMENT STORES CO.
611 Olive Street, St. Louis MO 63101. 314/342-6300. **Contact:** Richard Niemann, Manager of Human Resources. **World Wide Web address:** http://www.maycompany.com. **Description:** A retail organization with 13 department store companies and a discount shoe division. These department store companies operate under various names including Filene's, Lord & Taylor, and Kaufmann's. **Common positions include:** Accountant/Auditor; Architect; Attorney; Civil Engineer; Claim Representative; Computer Programmer; Draftsperson; Electrical/Electronics Engineer; Financial Analyst; Mechanical Engineer; Systems Analyst. **Educational backgrounds include:** Accounting; Computer Science; Engineering; Finance; Mathematics. **Benefits:** Disability Coverage; Employee Discounts; Life Insurance; Medical Insurance; Pension Plan; Profit Sharing; Tuition Assistance. **Corporate headquarters location:** This Location. **Listed on:** New York Stock Exchange. **Number of employees worldwide:** 127,000.

McCRORY STORES
12 West Market Street, York PA 17405. 717/757-8181. **Contact:** Larry Mynott, Personnel. **Description:** A national retail variety chain with operations in 38 states. **Corporate headquarters location:** This Location. **Number of employees nationwide:** 13,000.

McGLYNN BAKERIES, INC.
7350 Commerce Lane NE, Minneapolis MN 55432. 763/574-2222. **Toll-free phone:** 800/624-5966. **Fax:** 763/574-2210. **Contact:** Human Resources. **World Wide Web address:** http://www.mcglynn.com. **Description:** A producer of cookies and other baked goods that operates in three divisions: McGlynn's Retail Bakeries, which operates over 280 locations; Concept 2 Bakers, which produces and markets frozen bakery foods; and DecoPac, which markets cake decorating sets and supplies in the United States and Canada. **Corporate headquarters location:** This Location. **Parent company:** Pillsbury Company.

MEIER AND FRANK
621 SW Fifth Avenue, Portland OR 97204. 503/223-0512. **Contact:** Human Resources. **Description:** This location houses administrative offices and the downtown store. Overall, Meier and Frank operates a department store chain consisting of seven stores in Oregon. **Corporate headquarters location:** This Location. **Number of employees at this location:** 500.

MEIJER INC.
2929 Walker Avenue NW, Grand Rapids MI 49544. 616/453-6711. **Contact:** Employment Manager. **World Wide Web address:** http://www.meijer.com. **Description:** One of the largest privately-owned retail companies in the Midwest. The company operates 99 hypermarkets throughout Michigan, Ohio, Indiana, and Illinois. Hypermarkets are combination stores which allow customers to purchase general merchandise products as well as grocery items through one central checkout area. Founded in 1934. **Common positions include:** Food Service Manager; Hardgoods Manager; Management Trainee; Softgoods Manager; Supermarket Manager. **Educational backgrounds include:** Business Administration; Management/Planning; Marketing. **Benefits:** 401(k); Dental Insurance; Disability Coverage; Life Insurance; Medical Insurance; Pension Plan. **Corporate headquarters location:** This Location. **Number of employees nationwide:** 65,000.

METRO FOOD MARKET
5483 Baltimore National Pike, Baltimore MD 21229. 410/455-5400. **Contact:** Jane Mackie, Human Resources Manager. **World Wide Web address:** http://www.metrofoodmarket.com. **Description:** This location houses administrative offices. Overall, the company operates grocery stores under the names Basics and Metro Food. **Corporate headquarters location:** This Location.

MICHAEL'S STORES, INC.
P.O. Box 619566, Dallas TX 75261-9566. 972/409-1300. **Physical address:** 8000 Bent Branch Drive, Irving TX 75063. **Contact:** Human Resources. **World Wide Web address:** http://www.michaels.com. **Description:** A nationwide specialty retailer of art, crafts, and decorative items and supplies, offering over 30,000 items, from picture framing materials to seasonal and holiday

merchandise. Michael's Stores operates approximately 180 stores in 26 states. **Corporate headquarters location:** This Location.

MICRO WAREHOUSE, INC.
535 Connecticut Avenue, Norwalk CT 06854. 203/899-4000. **Fax:** 203/899-4242. **Contact:** Nancy Phillips, Human Resources Assistant. **World Wide Web address:** http://www.warehouse.com. **Description:** A specialty catalog and online retailer and direct marketer of brand name Macintosh and IBM-compatible personal computer software, accessories, and peripherals. Founded in 1987. **NOTE:** Entry-level positions are offered. **Common positions include:** Account Manager; Accountant; Administrative Assistant; Advertising Executive; Budget Analyst; Buyer; Computer Programmer; Credit Manager; Customer Service Representative; Database Manager; Financial Analyst; Graphic Artist; Graphic Designer; Market Research Analyst; Marketing Manager; Multimedia Designer; Online Content Specialist; Purchasing Agent/Manager; Sales Manager; Systems Analyst; Systems Manager; Webmaster. **Educational backgrounds include:** Accounting; Art/Design; Computer Science; Finance; Liberal Arts; Marketing; Software Tech. Support. **Benefits:** 401(k); Dental Insurance; Disability Coverage; Employee Discounts; Life Insurance; Medical Insurance; Public Transit Available; Tuition Assistance. **Special programs:** Internships. **Corporate headquarters location:** This Location. **Other U.S. locations:** Gibbsboro NJ; Lakewood NJ; Wilmington OH. **International locations:** Canada; England; France; Germany; Mexico; Sweden; the Netherlands. **Listed on:** NASDAQ. **Stock exchange symbol:** MWHS. **President/CEO:** Peter Godfrey. **Annual sales/revenues:** More than $100 million. **Number of employees at this location:** 600. **Number of employees nationwide:** 2,400. **Number of employees worldwide:** 3,500.

MIDWAY AUTO TEAM
2201 West Bell Road, Phoenix AZ 85023. 602/866-6611. **Fax:** 602/866-6648. **Contact:** Personnel. **Description:** An automotive dealership. **Common positions include:** Accountant/Auditor; Automotive Mechanic; Clerical Supervisor; Customer Service Representative; Financial Analyst; General Manager; Manufacturer's/Wholesaler's Sales Rep.; Marketing Manager; Operations/Production Manager; Public Relations Specialist; Quality Control Supervisor; Sales Manager; Sales Representative; Services Sales Representative. **Educational backgrounds include:** Accounting; Business Administration; Finance; Marketing. **Benefits:** 401(k); Dental Insurance; Disability Coverage; Employee Discounts; Life Insurance; Medical Insurance. **Special programs:** Internships. **Corporate headquarters location:** This Location. **Number of employees at this location:** 225.

MILLER INTERNATIONAL, INC.
8500 Zuni Street, Denver CO 80260-5007. 303/428-5696. **Contact:** Employment Manager. **Description:** A manufacturer, wholesaler, and catalog retailer of Western wear through its two divisions, Rocky Mountain Clothing Company and Miller Stockman. **Common positions include:** Accountant/Auditor; Administrative Manager; Advertising Clerk; Buyer; Credit Manager; Customer Service Representative; Human Resources Manager; Instructor/Trainer; Operations/Production Manager; Public Relations Specialist; Services Sales Representative; Systems Analyst; Warehouse/Distribution Worker. **Educational backgrounds include:** Art/Design; Business Administration; Computer Science; Marketing. **Benefits:** 401(k); Daycare Assistance; Disability Coverage; Employee Discounts; ESOP; Life Insurance; Medical Insurance; Tuition Assistance. **Special programs:** Internships. **Corporate headquarters location:** This Location. **Other U.S. locations:** GA. **Number of employees at this location:** 300. **Number of employees nationwide:** 800.

MINYARD FOOD STORES, INC.
P.O. Box 518, Coppell TX 75019. 972/393-8700. **Fax:** 972/304-3828. **Contact:** Personnel Department. **World Wide Web address:** http://www.minyards.com. **Description:** A retail grocery chain with over 85 stores. Stores include Minyard Food Stores, Sack n' Save, and Carnival Food Stores. **Common positions include:** Computer Programmer; Management Trainee; Pharmacist; Systems Analyst. **Educational backgrounds include:** Computer Science; Pharmacology. **Benefits:** 401(k); Dental Insurance; Disability Coverage; Life Insurance; Medical Insurance. **Corporate headquarters location:** This Location. **Listed on:** Privately held. **Number of employees at this location:** 350. **Number of employees nationwide:** 6,100.

MUSTANG TRACTOR & EQUIPMENT CO.
12800 Northwest Freeway, Houston TX 77040. 713/460-2000. **Fax:** 713/690-2287. **Recorded jobline:** 713/460-7267. **Contact:** Human Resources Manager. **Description:** Sells and services Caterpillar heavy equipment and engines. **Common positions include:** Blue-Collar Worker Supervisor; Management Trainee. **Educational backgrounds include:** Business Administration; Engineering; Marketing. **Benefits:** 401(k); Casual Dress - Daily; Dental Insurance; Disability Coverage; Life Insurance; Medical Insurance; Pension Plan; Profit Sharing; Savings Plan; Tuition Assistance. **Special programs:** Apprenticeships. **Corporate headquarters location:** This Location. Manufacturing; Sales; Service. **Number of employees at this location:** 360. **Number of employees nationwide:** 760.

NASH FINCH COMPANY
7600 France Avenue South, Minneapolis MN 55435. 952/832-0534. **Contact:** Ron Knkz, Personnel Administration. **World Wide Web address:** http://www.nashfinch.com. **Description:** Engaged in wholesale distribution, retail distribution, and produce marketing. The wholesale distribution segment supplies products to supermarkets, military bases, convenience stores, and other customers in 31 states. The retail distribution segment consists of approximately 128 company-owned retail stores in 16 states. Nash Finch's corporate stores operate under names such as Econofoods, Sun Mart, Family Thrift Center, Food Folks, and Easter's. Nash DeCamp markets fresh fruits and vegetables to wholesalers and retailers worldwide. **Corporate headquarters location:** This Location. **Listed on:** NASDAQ.

NATIONAL AUTOMOBILE DEALERS ASSN.
8400 Westpark Drive, McLean VA 22102. 703/821-7000. **Contact:** Human Resources. **World Wide Web address:** http://www.nada.org. **Description:** A trade organization representing nearly 20,000 new car and truck dealerships. The association publishes a used car guide for dealers that offers insurance information and retirement plans for dealerships. **Common positions include:** Accountant; Computer Programmer; Customer Service Representative; Economist; Education Administrator; Financial Analyst; Management Trainee; Market Research Analyst; Technical Writer/Editor. **Educational backgrounds include:** Accounting; Art/Design; Business Administration; Communications; Computer Science; Economics; Finance; Liberal

Arts; Marketing; Mathematics. **Benefits:** Dental Insurance; Disability Coverage; Employee Discounts; Life Insurance; Medical Insurance; Pension Plan; Tuition Assistance. **Corporate headquarters location:** This Location. **Number of employees at this location:** 400.

THE NEIMAN MARCUS GROUP, INC.
1618 Main Street, Dallas TX 75201. 214/573-5688. **Contact:** Crystal Curren, Manager of MDP Placement. **World Wide Web address:** http://www. neimanmarcus.com. **Description:** Operates two specialty retailing businesses: Neiman Marcus and Bergdorf Goodman. Combined, these two chains offer men's and women's apparel, fashion accessories, jewelry, fine china, and moderately-priced crystal and silver. **Corporate headquarters location:** This Location. **Subsidiaries include:** NM Direct is a direct marketing company, which advertises primarily through the use of such specialty catalogs as Neiman Marcus and Horchow.

NOODLE KIDOODLE
6801 Jericho Turnpike, Suite 100, Syosset NY 11791. 516/677-0500. **Contact:** Christine McDonough, Director of Human Resources. **World Wide Web address:** http://www.noodlekidoodle. com. **Description:** A location of the retail store chain offering a broad range of educationally-oriented children's toys and other products such as books, videotapes, audiotapes, computer software, and crafts. A product catalog is available. **Corporate headquarters location:** This Location. **Other U.S. locations:** Nationwide.

NORANDEX REYNOLDS INC.
8450 South Bedford Road, Macedonia OH 44056. 330/468-2200. **Contact:** Personnel Manager. **World Wide Web address:** http://www.norandex.com. **Description:** Operates a retail chain which sells windows and doors. Norandex Reynolds Inc. has over 100 locations nationwide. **Corporate headquarters location:** This Location. **Number of employees at this location:** 80.

NORDSTROM, INC.
1617 Sixth Avenue, Suite 500, Seattle WA 98101. 206/628-2111. **Contact:** Personnel. **World Wide Web address:** http://www.nordstrom.com. **Description:** This location is the flagship store of one of the largest independently-owned fashion retailers in the United States. The company operates more than 100 stores across the nation. Founded in 1901. **Common positions include:** Sales Representative. **Benefits:** 401(k); Dental Insurance; Employee Discounts; Medical Insurance; Profit Sharing. **Corporate headquarters location:** This Location. **Listed on:** NASDAQ. **Stock exchange symbol:** NOBE. **Annual sales/revenues:** More than $100 million.

OFFICE DEPOT
2200 Old Germantown Road, Delray Beach FL 33445. 561/278-4800. **Contact:** Human Resources. **World Wide Web address:** http://www. officedepot.com. **Description:** Operates a chain of large-volume, office products warehouse stores that sell brand name office merchandise primarily to small and medium-sized businesses. The retail locations also serve the growing home office market. Major merchandise categories include general office supplies, office furniture, computer hardware and software, copiers, telephones and fax machines, paper, writing instruments, briefcases, accounting supplies, and back-to-school supplies. **Corporate headquarters location:** This Location. **Other U.S. locations:** Nationwide. **International locations:** Canada. **Listed on:** New York Stock Exchange. **Number of employees nationwide:** 33,000.

OFFICEMAX
3605 Warrensville Center Road, Shaker Heights OH 44122-5203. 216/921-6900. **Contact:** Human Resources. **World Wide Web address:** http://www.officemax.com. **Description:** A retail store specializing in the sale of office supplies and equipment. **Corporate headquarters location:** This Location. **Annual sales/revenues:** More than $100 million.

ORCHARD SUPPLY HARDWARE
SEARS HARDWARE STORES
6450 Via Del Oro, San Jose CA 95119. 408/281-3500. **Fax:** 408/361-2884. **Recorded jobline:** 800/529-5229. **Contact:** Human Resources. **World Wide Web address:** http://www.osh.com. **Description:** Operates more than 250 retail stores nationwide. Products are primarily geared toward home repair and maintenance projects. Founded in 1931. **NOTE:** Entry-level positions and part-time jobs are offered. **Company slogan:** We are committed to providing our customers with legendary customer service. **Common positions include:** Account Manager; Account Representative; Accountant; Administrative Assistant; Administrative Manager; Advertising Clerk; Advertising Executive; AS400 Programmer Analyst; Assistant Manager; Attorney; Auditor; Bank Officer/Manager; Budget Analyst; Buyer; Chief Financial Officer; Claim Representative; Clerical Supervisor; Computer Programmer; Computer Support Technician; Computer Technician; Controller; Credit Manager; Customer Service Representative; Database Administrator; Database Manager; Desktop Publishing Specialist; Draftsperson; Finance Director; Financial Analyst; General Manager; Graphic Artist; Graphic Designer; Human Resources Manager; Internet Services Manager; Management Trainee; Market Research Analyst; Marketing Manager; Marketing Specialist; MIS Specialist; Operations Manager; Production Manager; Project Manager; Public Relations Specialist; Purchasing Agent/Manager; Quality Control Supervisor; Sales Executive; Sales Manager; Sales Representative; Secretary; Systems Analyst; Systems Manager; Typist/Word Processor; Vice President. **Educational backgrounds include:** Accounting; AS400 Certification; Business Administration; Communications; Computer Science; Economics; Finance; Internet; Liberal Arts; Marketing; Mathematics; Microsoft Word; QuarkXPress; Spreadsheets. **Benefits:** 401(k); Casual Dress - Fridays; Dental Insurance; Disability Coverage; Employee Discounts; Life Insurance; Medical Insurance; Pension Plan; Profit Sharing; Public Transit Available; Savings Plan; Sick Days (6 - 10); Tuition Assistance. **Special programs:** Internships; Training; Summer Jobs. **Corporate headquarters location:** This Location. **Other U.S. locations:** Nationwide. **Parent company:** Sears, Roebuck and Company. **Number of employees at this location:** 300. **Number of employees nationwide:** 13,000.

OSHMAN'S SPORTING GOODS INC.
2302 Maxwell Lane, Houston TX 77023. 713/928-3171. **Contact:** Human Resources. **World Wide Web address:** http://www.oshmans.com. **Description:** Offers a broad line of sporting goods and equipment as well as active sports apparel. Most stores operate under the name SuperSports USA. **Corporate headquarters location:** This Location.

PAMIDA, INC.
8800 F Street, Omaha NE 68127. 402/339-2400. **Fax:** 402/596-7708. **Recorded jobline:** 800/284-

7270. **Contact:** Human Resources. **World Wide Web address:** http://www.pamida.com. **Description:** A general merchandise retailer operating nearly 160 stores in 15 midwestern states. **NOTE:** Entry-level positions are offered. **Common positions include:** Buyer; General Manager; Management Trainee; MIS Specialist; Pharmacist. **Educational backgrounds include:** Business Administration; Marketing. **Benefits:** 401(k); Dental Insurance; Disability Coverage; Employee Discounts; Life Insurance; Medical Insurance; Tuition Assistance. **Special programs:** Training. **Corporate headquarters location:** This Location. **Parent company:** Shopko Stores, Inc. **Operations at this facility include:** Administration. **Listed on:** American Stock Exchange. **Stock exchange symbol:** PAM. **Annual sales/revenues:** More than $100 million. **Number of employees at this location:** 400. **Number of employees nationwide:** 5,000.

THE PANTRY, INC.
P.O. Box 23180, Jacksonville FL 32241. 904/464-7200. **Contact:** Office Manager. **World Wide Web address:** http://www.thepantry.com. **Description:** A chain of retail grocery and convenience stores. Stores operate under the names Depot, ETNA, Express Stop, Food Chief, Handy-Way, Kangaroo, Lil' Champ, Quick Stop, Smokers Express, Sprint, The Pantry, Wicker Mart, and Zip Mart. **Corporate headquarters location:** This Location.

PARISIAN
SAKS INCORPORATED
750 Lakeshore Parkway, Birmingham AL 35211. 205/940-4000. **Contact:** Human Resources. **World Wide Web address:** http://www.saksincorporated.com. **Description:** A specialty department store holding company. **Corporate headquarters location:** This Location.

PARK PLACE MOTORCARS
4023 Oak Lawn Avenue, Dallas TX 75219. 214/526-8701. **Toll-free phone:** 800/336-7073. **Fax:** 214/443-8270. **Contact:** Human Resources. **World Wide Web address:** http://www.parkplacetexas.com. **Description:** A new and preowned car dealership for Mercedes-Benz, Porsche, Lexus, and Audi automobiles. **NOTE:** Entry-level positions are offered. **Common positions include:** Administrative Assistant; Assistant Manager; Chief Financial Officer; Clerical Supervisor; Computer Operator; Computer Programmer; Controller; Finance Director; General Manager; Human Resources Manager; Management Analyst/Consultant; Management Trainee; Quality Control Supervisor; Sales Executive; Sales Manager; Sales Representative; Secretary; Typist/Word Processor. **Educational backgrounds include:** Accounting; Business Administration; Finance. **Benefits:** 401(k); Dental Insurance; Disability Coverage; Employee Discounts; Life Insurance; Medical Insurance; Savings Plan. **Corporate headquarters location:** This Location. **Other area locations:** Houston TX; Plano TX. **Number of employees at this location:** 230. **Number of employees nationwide:** 430.

PATHMARK STORES INC.
200 Milik Street, Carteret NJ 07008. 732/499-4019. **Contact:** Renee Perlman, Recruiter. **World Wide Web address:** http://www.pathmark.com. **Description:** Engaged primarily in the operation of large supermarket/drug stores. The company operates one of the largest supermarket chains in the country. Its Rickel Home Center division is among the largest do-it-yourself home center chains in the nation. The company's retail stores are located in the Mid-Atlantic and New England. **Corporate headquarters location:** This Location.

PAUL HARRIS STORES INC.
6003 Guion Road, Indianapolis IN 46254. 317/293-3900. **Fax:** 317/298-6940. **Contact:** Human Resources. **World Wide Web address:** http://www.paulharrisstores.com. **Description:** A specialty retailer of women's clothing, selling the Paul Harris Design private label brand. The company operates 300 stores nationwide. **Common positions include:** Accountant/Auditor; Wholesale and Retail Buyer. **Educational backgrounds include:** Accounting; Art/Design; Business Administration; Fashion; Merchandising. **Corporate headquarters location:** This Location. **Listed on:** NASDAQ. **Number of employees at this location:** 125. **Number of employees nationwide:** 2,500.

PAYLESS CASHWAYS, INC.
P.O. Box 648001, Lees Summit MO 64064. 816/347-6000. **Contact:** Staffing Department. **Description:** Payless Cashways, Inc. is a full-line building materials specialty retailer concentrating on tradespeople, remodelers, and do-it-yourselfers. The company's merchandise assortment includes lumber and building materials, millwork, tools, hardware, electrical and plumbing products, paint, lighting, home decor, kitchens, decorative plumbing, heating, ventilating and cooling, and seasonal items. **Common positions include:** Accountant/Auditor; Advertising Clerk; Attorney; Budget Analyst; Claim Representative; Clerical Supervisor; Computer Programmer; Cost Estimator; Credit Manager; Customer Service Representative; Design Engineer; Financial Analyst; Human Resources Manager; Human Service Worker; Management Trainee; Manufacturer's/Wholesaler's Sales Rep.; Market Research Analyst; MIS Specialist; Multimedia Designer; Paralegal; Public Relations Specialist; Software Engineer; Systems Analyst; Transportation/Traffic Specialist; Travel Agent; Typist/Word Processor. **Educational backgrounds include:** Accounting; Art/Design; Business Administration; Communications; Computer Science; Engineering; Finance; Marketing. **Benefits:** 401(k); Dental Insurance; Disability Coverage; Employee Discounts; Job Sharing; Life Insurance; Medical Insurance; Pension Plan; Profit Sharing; Savings Plan; Tuition Assistance. **Corporate headquarters location:** This Location. **Listed on:** NASDAQ. **Annual sales/revenues:** More than $100 million. **Number of employees at this location:** 700. **Number of employees nationwide:** 17,000.

PEARLE VISION, INC.
2534 Royal Lane, Dallas TX 75229. 972/277-5000. **Fax:** 972/277-5944. **Contact:** Human Resources. **Description:** Manufactures and retails prescription eyewear. **Common positions include:** Accountant/Auditor; Advertising Clerk; Attorney; Computer Programmer; Customer Service Representative; Department Manager; Financial Analyst; Human Resources Manager; Management Trainee; Manufacturer's/Wholesaler's Sales Rep.; Marketing Specialist; Purchasing Agent/Manager; Systems Analyst. **Educational backgrounds include:** Accounting; Business Administration; Computer Science; Finance; Marketing; Merchandising. **Benefits:** Dental Insurance; Disability Coverage; Employee Discounts; Life Insurance; Medical Insurance; Profit Sharing; Savings Plan; Tuition Assistance. **Corporate headquarters location:** This Location. **Parent company:** Grand Met USA. **Listed on:** London Stock Exchange.

PEEBLES DEPARTMENT STORES
One Peebles Street, South Hill VA 23970. 804/447-5297. **Contact:** Tim Moyer, Training and Recruitment Director. **World Wide Web address:** http://www.peebles-stores.com. **Description:** Operates a department store chain. **Common positions include:** Accountant; Advertising Clerk; Buyer; Credit Manager; Customer Service Representative; Department Manager; Human Resources Manager; Instructor; Management Trainee; Teacher/Professor; Transportation/Traffic Specialist. **Educational backgrounds include:** Accounting; Business Administration; Liberal Arts; Marketing. **Benefits:** Dental Insurance; Disability Coverage; Employee Discounts; Life Insurance; Medical Insurance; Pension Plan. **Special programs:** Internships. **Corporate headquarters location:** This Location. **Other U.S. locations:** DE; KY; MD; NC; SC; TN. **Number of employees at this location:** 2,200. **Number of employees nationwide:** 2,340.

THE PENN TRAFFIC COMPANY
P.O. Box 4737, Syracuse NY 13221. 315/457-9460. **Fax:** 315/453-8583. **Contact:** Training and Recruitment. **Description:** A food retailer and wholesaler. The company operates over 200 supermarkets in New York, Pennsylvania, Ohio, and West Virginia under the names Big Bear, Quality Markets, P&C Foods, and Bi-Lo Foods. Penn Traffic also operates wholesale food distribution businesses serving 106 licensed franchises and 90 independent operators, and the Penny Curtiss Bakery in Syracuse NY. Founded in 1942. **NOTE:** Entry-level positions and part-time jobs are offered. **Common positions include:** Accountant; Administrative Assistant; Administrative Manager; Advertising Clerk; AS400 Programmer Analyst; Auditor; Budget Analyst; Buyer; Claim Representative; Computer Programmer; Computer Support Technician; Computer Technician; Database Administrator; Draftsperson; Financial Analyst; Graphic Designer; Help-Desk Technician; Human Resources Manager; Management Trainee; Marketing Manager; MIS Specialist; Network/Systems Administrator; Paralegal; Secretary; Systems Analyst; Transportation/Traffic Specialist; Typist/Word Processor. **Educational backgrounds include:** AS400 Certification; Business Administration; Computer Science; Liberal Arts; Microsoft Office; Visual Basic. **Benefits:** 401(k); Casual Dress - Fridays; Dental Insurance; Disability Coverage; Employee Discounts; Life Insurance; Medical Insurance; Pension Plan; Profit Sharing; Relocation Assistance; Sick Days (6 - 10); Tuition Assistance; Vacation Days (6 - 10). **Special programs:** Internships; Training. **Corporate headquarters location:** This Location. **Other area locations:** Jamestown NY. **Other U.S. locations:** Columbus OH; DuBois PA. **Listed on:** NASDAQ. **Stock exchange symbol:** PNTE. **President/CEO:** Joe Fisher. **Annual sales/revenues:** More than $100 million. **Number of employees at this location:** 2,000. **Number of employees nationwide:** 16,000.

PEP BOYS
3111 West Allegheny Avenue, Philadelphia PA 19132. 215/227-9000. **Contact:** Human Resources. **World Wide Web address:** http://www.pepboys.com. **Description:** Primarily engaged in the retail sale of a wide range of automotive parts and accessories, and the installation of automobile components and merchandise. Pep Boys operates over 660 stores in 37 states. **Common positions include:** Accountant; Administrative Manager; Assistant Manager; Automotive Mechanic; Branch Manager; Buyer; Cashier; Claim Representative; Computer Operator; Computer Programmer;

Construction Contractor; Credit Manager; Customer Service Representative; Department Manager; Economist; Financial Manager; Graphic Artist; Human Resources Manager; Market Research Analyst; Payroll Clerk; Printing Press Operator; Receptionist; Retail Sales Worker; Secretary; Wholesale and Retail Buyer. **Educational backgrounds include:** Accounting; Art/Design; Business Administration; Communications; Computer Science; Finance; Liberal Arts; Marketing; Mathematics. **Benefits:** Dental Insurance; Disability Coverage; Employee Discounts; Life Insurance; Medical Insurance; Savings Plan; Tuition Assistance. **Corporate headquarters location:** This Location. **Listed on:** New York Stock Exchange. **Number of employees at this location:** 600. **Number of employees nationwide:** 15,000.

PETSMART, INC.
19601 North 27th Avenue, Phoenix AZ 85027. 623/580-6100. **Fax:** 623/580-6502. **Contact:** Human Resources. **World Wide Web address:** http://www.petsmart.com. **Description:** A national retail chain which sells pet supplies and animals. PETsMART also offers veterinary services, animal adoption centers, grooming services, and obedience classes. **Corporate headquarters location:** This Location. **Other U.S. locations:** Nationwide.

PICK QUICK FOODS INC.
83-10 Rockaway Boulevard, Ozone Park NY 11416. 718/296-9100. **Contact:** Krish Malik, Controller. **Description:** A grocery retailer. **Corporate headquarters location:** This Location.

PIER 1 IMPORTS
P.O. Box 961020, Fort Worth TX 76161-0020. 817/878-8000. **Contact:** Tawny McCarty, Staffing Manager. **World Wide Web address:** http://www.pier1.com. **Job page:** http://jobs.pier1.com. **Description:** This location houses administrative offices. Overall, Pier 1 Imports is engaged in the specialty retailing of handcrafted decorative home furnishings and accessories imported from approximately 50 countries around the world. **Common positions include:** Accountant/Auditor; Assistant Manager; Computer Programmer; Distribution Manager; Management Trainee; Real Estate Agent; Retail Merchandiser; Transportation/Traffic Specialist. **Educational backgrounds include:** Accounting; Business Administration; Communications; Finance; Liberal Arts; Merchandising. **Benefits:** Accident/Emergency Insurance; Dental Insurance; Disability Coverage; Employee Discounts; Life Insurance; Medical Insurance; Retirement Plan; Stock Option; Tuition Assistance; Vision Plan. **Corporate headquarters location:** This Location. **Other U.S. locations:** Nationwide. **Listed on:** New York Stock Exchange. **Number of employees at this location:** 520. **Number of employees nationwide:** 8,500.

THE PLEASANT COMPANY
8400 Fairway Place, Middleton WI 53562. 608/836-4848. **Fax:** 608/836-1999. **Contact:** Recruiting. **World Wide Web address:** http://www.americangirl.com. **Description:** Operates in four divisions: consumer catalogue and direct mail sales; book publishing, which markets *The American Girls Collection* and *American Girl Library*; the magazine division which publishes *American Girl* magazine; and customer programs, which provides programs and special events centered on an American Girl theme. Founded in 1986. **Common positions include:** Assistant Manager; Buyer; Chief Financial Officer; Computer Programmer; Controller; Database Manager; Editor; Editorial Assistant; Finance Director; Financial Analyst; General

Manager; Graphic Artist; Graphic Designer; Human Resources Manager; Industrial Engineer; Librarian; Managing Editor; Market Research Analyst; Marketing Manager; Multimedia Designer; Online Content Specialist; Production Manager; Project Manager; Public Relations Specialist; Purchasing Agent/Manager; Sales Manager; Sales Representative; Systems Analyst; Technical Writer/Editor; Telecommunications Manager; Webmaster. **Educational backgrounds include:** Accounting; Art/Design; Computer Science; Finance; Marketing; Public Relations; Software Development; Software Tech. Support. **Benefits:** 401(k); Casual Dress - Daily; Dental Insurance; Disability Coverage; Employee Discounts; Life Insurance; Medical Insurance; Public Transit Available; Tuition Assistance. **Office hours:** Monday - Thursday, 8:00 a.m. - 5:00 p.m.; Friday 8:00 a.m. - 1:00 p.m. **Corporate headquarters location:** This Location. **Other U.S. locations:** Chicago IL; DeForest WI; Eau Claire WI; Wilmot WI. **Parent company:** Mattel, Inc. **Listed on:** Privately held. **President/Owner:** Pleasant Rowland. **Number of employees at this location:** 750. **Number of employees nationwide:** 1,000.

PRESCOTT'S SUPERMARKETS, INC.
P.O. Box 818, West Bend WI 53095. 262/338-5620. **Fax:** 262/338-5630. **Contact:** Human Resources. **Description:** A retail grocer with six store locations throughout Wisconsin. **NOTE:** Entry-level positions are offered. **Common positions include:** Buyer; Chief Financial Officer; Clerical Supervisor; Computer Programmer; Database Manager; General Manager; Marketing Manager; MIS Specialist; Pharmacist. **Educational backgrounds include:** Accounting; Business Administration; Finance; Marketing. **Benefits:** 401(k); Dental Insurance; Disability Coverage; Life Insurance; Medical Insurance; Profit Sharing; Savings Plan; Tuition Assistance. **Corporate headquarters location:** This Location. **Listed on:** Privately held. **Annual sales/revenues:** More than $100 million.

PRICE CHOPPER SUPERMARKETS
501 Duanesburg Road, P.O. Box 1074, Schenectady NY 12301. 518/356-9556. **Fax:** 518/356-9348. **Recorded jobline:** 888/670-JOBS. **Contact:** Christine Tatko, Recruitment Specialist. **World Wide Web address:** http://www.pricechopper.com. **Description:** Operates a chain of grocery stores, gas stations, and convenience stores located in Connecticut, Massachusetts, New York, Pennsylvania, and Vermont. **NOTE:** Entry-level positions and part-time jobs are offered. **Special programs:** Internships; Apprenticeships; Training; Co-ops; Summer Jobs. **Office hours:** Monday - Friday, 8:00 a.m. - 5:00 p.m. **Corporate headquarters location:** This Location. **Parent company:** Golub Corporation (also at this location). **Listed on:** Privately held. **CEO:** Lewis Golub. **Number of employees at this location:** 18,000.

PRINCESS HOUSE, INC.
470 Myles Standish Boulevard, Taunton MA 02780. 508/823-0711. **Contact:** John McGuire, Vice President of Human Resources. **Description:** A national direct sales company specializing in crystal and china. **Common positions include:** Accountant/Auditor; Attorney; Buyer; Computer Programmer; Credit Manager; Customer Service Representative; Department Manager; General Manager; Human Resources Manager; Marketing Specialist; Operations/Production Manager; Purchasing Agent/Manager; Quality Control Supervisor; Systems Analyst. **Educational backgrounds include:** Accounting; Art/Design; Business Administration; Communications; Computer Science; Finance; Marketing. **Benefits:**

Dental Insurance; Disability Coverage; Employee Discounts; Life Insurance; Medical Insurance; Pension Plan; Savings Plan; Tuition Assistance. **Corporate headquarters location:** This Location. **Parent company:** Colgate-Palmolive Company.

PUBLIX SUPER MARKETS, INC.
P.O. Box 407, Lakeland FL 33802-0407. 863/688-1188. **Physical address:** 1936 George Jenkins Boulevard, Lakeland FL 33815. **Fax:** 863/680-5228. **Recorded jobline:** 863/680-5265. **Contact:** Employment Office. **World Wide Web address:** http://www.publix.com. **Description:** Operates a chain of retail supermarkets with 630 stores in Alabama, Florida, Georgia, and South Carolina. The company also produces dairy, delicatessen, and bakery items through four plants and conducts distribution operations through more than eight facilities in Florida and Georgia. Founded in 1930. **NOTE:** Jobseekers should address inquiries to the Employment Office, 1248A George Jenkins Boulevard, Lakeland FL 33815. Entry-level positions are offered. **Company slogan:** Where shopping is a pleasure. **Benefits:** 401(k); Casual Dress - Fridays; Dental Insurance; Disability Coverage; Life Insurance; Medical Insurance; Profit Sharing; Tuition Assistance. **Special programs:** Summer Jobs. **Corporate headquarters location:** This Location. **Listed on:** Privately held. **CEO:** Howard Jenkins. **Information Systems Manager:** Carla Morey. **Annual sales/revenues:** More than $100 million. **Number of employees at this location:** 5,000. **Number of employees nationwide:** 120,500.

QUALITY FOOD CENTERS
10116 NE Eighth Street, Bellevue WA 98004. 425/455-3761. **Contact:** Human Resources. **World Wide Web address:** http://www.qfci.com. **Description:** Operates a chain of retail supermarkets. **Corporate headquarters location:** This Location. **Number of employees nationwide:** 2,600.

RADIOSHACK
100 Throckmorton Street, Suite 500, Fort Worth TX 76102. 817/415-3700. **Fax:** 817/415-3243. **Contact:** Employment Opportunities. **World Wide Web address:** http://www.radioshack.com. **Description:** Sells a wide variety of consumer electronic parts and equipment through more than 7,000 stores nationwide. **Common positions include:** Accountant/Auditor; Advertising Clerk; Computer Programmer; Customer Service Representative; Services Sales Representative; Systems Analyst. **Educational backgrounds include:** Accounting; Computer Science. **Benefits:** Dental Insurance; Employee Discounts; Life Insurance; Medical Insurance; Pension Plan; Tuition Assistance. **Corporate headquarters location:** This Location. **Listed on:** New York Stock Exchange. **Annual sales/revenues:** More than $100 million.

RALEY'S & BEL AIR
P.O. Box 15618, Sacramento CA 95852. 916/373-6300. **Contact:** Ronnie Cobb, Corporate Recruiter. **Description:** A large supermarket chain with more than 145 locations in Northern California and Nevada. Raley's owns and operates Bel Air Markets (also at this location) a supermarket chain in San Francisco. **NOTE:** Entry-level positions are offered. **Common positions include:** Accountant; Administrative Assistant; Advertising Clerk; Advertising Executive; Applications Engineer; AS400 Programmer Analyst; Auditor; Benefit Analyst; Blue-Collar Worker Supervisor; Computer Engineer; Computer Operator; Computer Support Technician; Computer Technician; Construction

Contractor; Consultant; Controller; Customer Service Representative; Database Administrator; Database Manager; Design Engineer; Desktop Publishing Specialist; Editor; Finance Director; Financial Analyst; Graphic Artist; Graphic Designer; Human Resources Manager; Management Analyst/Consultant; Management Trainee; MIS Specialist; Network/Systems Administrator; Production Manager; Public Relations Specialist; Purchasing Agent/Manager; Secretary; Software Engineer; Systems Manager; Typist/Word Processor; Video Production Coordinator; Webmaster. **Educational backgrounds include:** Accounting; Art/Design; AS400 Certification; ASP; Biology; Business Administration; C/C++; CGI; Communications; Computer Science; Economics; Internet; Java; Microsoft Word; Novell; QuarkXPress; Software Development; Software Tech. Support; Spreadsheets; Visual Basic. **Benefits:** 401(k); Casual Dress - Daily; Dental Insurance; Employee Discounts; Flexible Schedule; Medical Insurance; Pension Plan; Tuition Assistance. **Special programs:** Internships. **Subsidiaries include:** Food Source; Nob Hill Foods.

RANDALLS FOOD MARKETS
P.O. Box 4506, Houston TX 77210-4506. 713/435-2400. **Fax:** 713/435-2499. **Recorded jobline:** 713/268-3404. **Contact:** Employment Manager. **World Wide Web address:** http://www.randalls.com. **Description:** Operates 1,650 retail grocery stores throughout the United States and Canada. **Corporate headquarters location:** This Location.

RECREATION USA
7851 Greenbriar Parkway, Orlando FL 32819. 407/363-9211. **Fax:** 407/363-2065. **Contact:** Paula Oulette, Personnel Director. **World Wide Web address:** http://www.recusa.com. **Description:** One of the largest retailers of recreational vehicles and boats in the United States. **Corporate headquarters location:** This Location. **Other U.S. locations:** CA; GA; SC. **Listed on:** NASDAQ.

RECREATIONAL EQUIPMENT INC. (REI)
P.O. Box 1938, Sumner WA 98390. 253/395-5965. **Physical address:** 6750 South 228th Street, Kent WA. **Recorded jobline:** 253/395-4694. **Contact:** Human Resources. **World Wide Web address:** http://www.rei.com/jobs. **Description:** A retailer of outdoor clothing and a wide variety of recreational equipment. **Common positions include:** Accountant/Auditor; Administrator; Computer Programmer; Customer Service Representative; Human Resources Manager; Instructor/Trainer; Operations/Production Manager; Public Relations Specialist; Purchasing Agent/Manager; Services Sales Representative; Systems Analyst; Technical Writer/Editor; Transportation/Traffic Specialist. **Educational backgrounds include:** Liberal Arts. **Benefits:** Dental Insurance; Disability Coverage; Employee Discounts; Life Insurance; Medical Insurance; Pension Plan; Profit Sharing; Savings Plan; Tuition Assistance. **Corporate headquarters location:** This Location. **Number of employees nationwide:** 3,000.

RENT-A-CENTER
5700 Tennyson Parkway, 3rd Floor, Plano TX 75024. 972/801-1100. **Toll-free phone:** 800/275-2696. **Fax:** 972/943-0112. **Contact:** Staffing. **World Wide Web address:** http://www.rentacenter.com. **Description:** Rents furniture, appliances, stereos, and other furnishings and equipment. **Special programs:** Internships. **Corporate headquarters location:** This Location. **Other U.S. locations:** Nationwide. **Annual**

sales/revenues: More than $100 million. **Number of employees at this location:** 500. **Number of employees nationwide:** 7,000.

RICE EPICURIAN MARKETS INC.
5333 Gulfston, Houston TX 77081. 713/662-7700. **Contact:** Personnel Director. **Description:** Operates and manages a chain of food stores. **Common positions include:** Accountant/Auditor; Blue-Collar Worker Supervisor; Management Trainee. **Educational backgrounds include:** Business Administration; Marketing. **Benefits:** Disability Coverage; Medical Insurance; Pension Plan; Profit Sharing; Savings Plan. **Corporate headquarters location:** This Location.

RICH'S
223 Perimeter Center Parkway, Atlanta GA 30346. 770/913-4123. **Contact:** Kathleen McManus, Senior Vice President of Human Resources. **World Wide Web address:** http://www.federated-fds.com. **Description:** Operates a chain of department stores. **Corporate headquarters location:** This Location. **Parent company:** Federated Department Stores, Inc.

RICHMAN GORDMAN 1/2 PRICE STORES
12100 West Center Road, Omaha NE 68144. 402/691-4000. **Fax:** 402/691-4269. **Contact:** Human Resources. **Description:** Operates a chain of off-price department stores. **Common positions include:** Accountant/Auditor; Advertising Clerk; Buyer; Computer Programmer; Customer Service Representative; Department Manager; Draftsperson; Financial Analyst; General Manager; Human Resources Manager; Management Trainee; Operations/Production Manager; Purchasing Agent/Manager; Wholesale and Retail Buyer. **Educational backgrounds include:** Accounting; Art/Design; Business Administration; Communications; Computer Science; Economics; Finance; Marketing. **Benefits:** 401(k); Dental Insurance; Disability Coverage; Employee Discounts; Life Insurance; Medical Insurance; Pension Plan. **Corporate headquarters location:** This Location. **Other U.S. locations:** CO; IA; IL; KS; MO; OK; SD. **Listed on:** NASDAQ. **Number of employees at this location:** 200. **Number of employees nationwide:** 2,500.

RITE AID CORPORATION
P.O. Box 3165, Harrisburg PA 17105. 717/761-2633. **Contact:** Human Resources. **World Wide Web address:** http://www.riteaid.com. **Description:** Operates 550 retail drug stores in 12 states. Founded in 1939. **Common positions include:** Pharmacist. **Educational backgrounds include:** Pharmacology. **Benefits:** Dental Insurance; Disability Coverage; Employee Discounts; Life Insurance; Medical Insurance; Pension Plan; Profit Sharing; Savings Plan. **Special programs:** Internships. **Corporate headquarters location:** This Location. **Other U.S. locations:** Nationwide. **Listed on:** New York Stock Exchange. **Annual sales/revenues:** More than $100 million. **Number of employees nationwide:** 83,000.

RIVERSIDE GROUP INC.
7800 Belfort Parkway, Suite 100, Jacksonville FL 32256. 904/281-2200. **Fax:** 904/281-0153. **Contact:** Personnel. **Description:** A holding company. **Corporate headquarters location:** This Location. **Subsidiaries include:** Wickes Lumber Company is a retail chain of building supply stores. **Number of employees at this location:** 35.

ROBINSONS-MAY COMPANY
6160 Laurel Canyon Boulevard, North Hollywood CA 91606. 818/508-5226. **Contact:** Central

Employment Office. **Description:** One of the nation's largest retailing organizations. Robinsons-May owns and operates a chain of department stores serving California, Arizona, and Nevada. **Corporate headquarters location:** This Location.

ROCKY MOUNTAIN CHOCOLATE FACTORY
265 Turner Drive, Durango CO 81301. 970/247-4943. **Fax:** 970/382-7371. **Contact:** Cathy Roberts, Human Resources Manager. **World Wide Web address:** http://www.rmcfusa.com. **Description:** A retail distributor of candy products including chocolate covered fruit, fudge, and caramel apples. The company operates over 200 retail stores worldwide. This location also hires seasonally. Founded in 1981. **NOTE:** Part-time jobs and second and third shifts are offered. **Common positions include:** Accountant; Administrative Assistant; Chief Financial Officer; Controller; Customer Service Representative; Human Resources Manager; Production Manager; Purchasing Agent/Manager; Quality Control Supervisor; Secretary. **Benefits:** 401(k); Casual Dress - Daily; Dental Insurance; Disability Coverage; Employee Discounts; Flexible Schedule; Life Insurance; Medical Insurance; Sick Days (6 - 10); Vacation Days (10 - 20). **Special programs:** Internships; Summer Jobs. **Corporate headquarters location:** This Location. **Other U.S. locations:** Nationwide. **International locations:** Canada; Taiwan; United Arab Emirates. **Listed on:** NASDAQ. **Stock exchange symbol:** RMCF. **CEO:** Franklin Crail. **Facilities Manager:** Bryan Merryman. **Information Systems Manager:** Key Jobson. **Purchasing Manager:** Sarah Mong. **Sales Manager:** Edward Dudley. **Annual sales/revenues:** $21 - $50 million. **Number of employees at this location:** 120. **Number of employees nationwide:** 400.

ROSES STORES INC.
P.O. Drawer 947, Henderson NC 27536. 252/430-2600. **Contact:** Recruitment Manager. **Description:** Operates a chain of retail variety stores. **Common positions include:** Management Trainee. **Corporate headquarters location:** This Location.

S&K FAMOUS BRANDS, INC.
11100 Broad Street, Glen Allen VA 23070. 804/342-2500. **Contact:** Human Resources. **World Wide Web address:** http://www.skmenswear.com. **Description:** Engaged in the retail sale of men's clothing, furnishings, sportswear, and accessories. S&K Famous Brands operates over 240 stores. **Corporate headquarters location:** This Location. **Listed on:** NASDAQ. **Number of employees nationwide:** 1,575.

SAFEWAY, INC.
5918 Stoneridge Mall Road, Pleasanton CA 94588-3229. 925/467-3383. **Contact:** Patty Carlson, Manager of Corporate Human Resources. **World Wide Web address:** http://www.safeway.com. **Description:** One of the world's largest food retailers. The company operates approximately 1,600 stores in the western, Rocky Mountain, southwestern, and mid-Atlantic regions of the United States and in western Canada. **Common positions include:** Computer Programmer; MIS Specialist; Systems Analyst. **Benefits:** 401(k); Dental Insurance; Disability Coverage; Employee Discounts; Flexible Schedule; Life Insurance; Medical Insurance; Pension Plan; Profit Sharing; Public Transit Available; Tuition Assistance. **Corporate headquarters location:** This Location. **Other U.S. locations:** Nationwide. **International locations:** Canada. **Subsidiaries include:** Casa Ley, S.A. de C.V. operates food/variety, clothing, and wholesale outlet stores in western Mexico; The Vons Companies, Inc. is one of the largest supermarket chains in southern California. **Listed on:** New York Stock Exchange. **Stock exchange symbol:** SWY. **President/CEO:** Steven A. Burd. **Annual sales/revenues:** More than $100 million. **Number of employees nationwide:** 111,000. **Number of employees worldwide:** 135,000.

ST. ANDREWS GOLF CORPORATION dba LAS VEGAS GOLF & TENNIS
2701 Crimson Canyon Drive, Las Vegas NV 89128. **Toll-free phone:** 800/873-5110. **Fax:** 702/798-6847. **Contact:** Barbara Allegrati, Human Resources Representative. **World Wide Web address:** http://www.lvgolf.com. **Description:** Saint Andrews Golf Corporation is the franchiser of the Las Vegas Discount Golf and Tennis retail stores, which sell a broad variety of golf and tennis equipment including apparel and accessories. The products sold by franchise stores include pro-line and private label merchandise. The company also operates the Saint Andrews Golf Center, which is designed to provide scaled-down franchises for driving ranges, golf course pro shops, and other small retail locations. Saint Andrews Golf Centers sell golf equipment, apparel, and accessories. The company owns and operates the All American Family Sports Park. The theme park includes a golf driving range and training center, a baseball batting stadium, a hotel-themed miniature golf course, a golf pro shop, go-cart tracks, a video arcade, a dry slide, restaurants, and other family-oriented facilities. **Corporate headquarters location:** This Location.

SCHNUCK MARKETS, INC.
11420 Lackland Road, St. Louis MO 63146-6928. 314/994-9900. **Fax:** 314/994-4465. **Contact:** Employment Manager. **World Wide Web address:** http://www.schnucks.com. **Description:** Operates a chain of supermarkets and restaurants. **Corporate headquarters location:** This Location. **Number of employees nationwide:** 2,530.

SEARS, ROEBUCK & CO.
3333 Beverly Road, Hoffman Estates IL 60179. 847/286-2500. **Contact:** Director of Personnel. **World Wide Web address:** http://www.sears.com. **Description:** Operates a chain of department stores. **Corporate headquarters location:** This Location. **Subsidiaries include:** Advantis, a partnership formed by Sears and IBM, is a networking technology company that provides businesses with data, voice, and multimedia services; Allstate Insurance Group is one of the nation's largest publicly-held property and casualty insurance companies, with more than 20 million customers and approximately 14,600 full-time agents in the U.S. and Canada. Allstate offers automobile insurance, homeowners insurance, life insurance, annuity and pension products, business insurance (insurance for small- and mid-size businesses, as well as reinsurance for other insurers), and mortgage guaranty insurance (through Allstate's wholly-owned subsidiary, PMI Mortgage Insurance Company); Homart is one of the country's leading developers, owners, and managers of regional shopping malls and community centers; Prodigy, a Sears/IBM partnership, is a home computer network providing a wide variety of personal Internet services including news, shopping, bulletin boards, travel ticketing, brokerage, banking, and e-mail services; and Sears Merchandise Group is a leading retailer of apparel, home, and automotive products and related services for families throughout North America. **Listed on:** New York Stock Exchange.

SERVICE MERCHANDISE COMPANY
P.O. Box 24600, Nashville TN 37202. 615/660-3195. **Fax:** 615/660-3319. **Contact:** Nancy Baker,

Director of Recruiting. **World Wide Web address:** http://www.servicemerchandise.com. **Description:** A general merchandise retailer and catalog store with over 200 locations nationwide. The company sells a variety of products including jewelry, cameras, toys, housewares, electronics, small appliances, and sporting goods. **Common positions include:** Accountant; Aircraft Mechanic/Engine Specialist; Architect; Attorney; Bindery Worker; Budget Analyst; Buyer; CADD Operator; Claim Representative; Computer Operator; Computer Programmer; Construction Contractor; Credit Manager; Employment Interviewer; Financial Manager; Graphic Artist; Human Resources Manager; Industrial Engineer; Market Research Analyst; Printing Press Operator; Receptionist; Retail Sales Worker; Secretary; Stock Clerk; Store Manager; Systems Analyst; Travel Agent; Wholesale and Retail Buyer. **Educational backgrounds include:** Accounting; Art/Design; Business Administration; Computer Science; Marketing. **Benefits:** Dental Insurance; Disability Coverage; Employee Discounts; Life Insurance; Medical Insurance; Pension Plan; Profit Sharing; Savings Plan; Tuition Assistance. **Special programs:** Internships. **Corporate headquarters location:** This Location. **Other U.S. locations:** Nationwide. **Number of employees at this location:** 1,400. **Number of employees nationwide:** 24,170.

SHARPER IMAGE CORPORATION
650 Davis Street, San Francisco CA 94111. 415/445-6000. **Contact:** Gary Frye, Human Resources Specialist. **World Wide Web address:** http://www.sharperimage.com. **Description:** A retailer of a wide variety of gifts in the following categories: automotive, outdoor and garden, travel and luggage, electronics, health and fitness, personal care, and home and safety. **Corporate headquarters location:** This Location.

SHAW'S SUPERMARKETS
P.O. Box 600, East Bridgewater MA 02333-0600. 508/378-7211. **Physical address:** 140 Laurel Street, East Bridgewater MA. **Contact:** Human Resources. **World Wide Web address:** http://www.shaws.com. **Description:** Administrative offices of the New England supermarket chain. **Corporate headquarters location:** This Location. **Subsidiaries include:** Star Markets; Wild Harvest. **Parent company:** J Sainsbury.

SHEPLER'S
6501 West Kellogg, Wichita KS 67209. 316/946-3600. **Contact:** David Faber, Vice President of Human Resources. **Description:** Engaged in retail and catalog sales of Western-style apparel. **Common positions include:** Accountant/Auditor; Clerical Supervisor; Customer Service Representative; Department Manager; Management Trainee. **Educational backgrounds include:** Accounting; Business Administration; Marketing. **Benefits:** 401(k); Disability Coverage; Employee Discounts; Life Insurance; Medical Insurance; Tuition Assistance. **Special programs:** Internships. **Corporate headquarters location:** This Location. **Listed on:** Privately held. **Number of employees at this location:** 350. **Number of employees nationwide:** 1,500.

THE SHERWIN-WILLIAMS COMPANY
2125 Oak Grove Road, Suite 324, Walnut Creek CA 94598. 925/932-3363. **Fax:** 925/930-7118. **Contact:** Jim Pfohl, Area Human Resources Manager. **E-mail address:** jim.m.pfohl@sherwin.com. **World Wide Web address:** http://www.sherwin-williams.com. **Description:** This location is a support office for area stores.

Overall, Sherwin-Williams operates in six business segments: Retail Stores, Coatings, Chemicals, Packaging Products, Specialty Products, and International. Products include Sherwin-Williams, Dutch Boy, Martin Senour, Baltimore, and Kem paints, as well as related packaging. Founded in 1866. **NOTE:** Entry-level positions are offered. **Common positions include:** Branch Manager; Human Resources Manager; Management Trainee; Manufacturer's/Wholesaler's Sales Rep.; Sales Manager; Sales Representative; Store Manager; Vice President of Sales. **Educational backgrounds include:** Business Administration; Management/Planning; Marketing. **Benefits:** 401(k); Dental Insurance; Disability Coverage; Employee Discounts; Life Insurance; Medical Insurance; Pension Plan; Profit Sharing; Savings Plan; Stock Purchase; Tuition Assistance. **Special programs:** Internships; Training; Summer Jobs. **Corporate headquarters location:** Cleveland OH. **Other U.S. locations:** Nationwide. **International locations:** Canada; Mexico. **Listed on:** New York Stock Exchange. **Stock exchange symbol:** SHW. **Annual sales/revenues:** More than $100 million. **Number of employees at this location:** 15. **Number of employees nationwide:** 23,000.

SHOPKO STORES, INC.
P.O. Box 19060, Green Bay WI 54307-9060. 920/497-2211. **Physical address:** 700 Pilgrim Way, Green Bay WI 54304. **Contact:** Human Resources. **Description:** A leading regional retailer operating Shopko Stores and Pamida Stores. The company's stores carry a wide selection of branded and private-label goods such as women's, men's, and children's apparel; shoes; jewelry; accessories; and home textiles; and hardline goods such as housewares; small appliances; furniture; music/videos; toys; sporting goods; cosmetics; and seasonal items. Most of ShopKo's stores also include pharmacy centers and optical centers. **Corporate headquarters location:** This Location. **Other U.S. locations:** CA; CO; IA; ID; IL; MI; MN; MT; NE; NV; OR; SD; UT; WA.

SMART & FINAL, INC.
P.O. Box 512377, Los Angeles CA 90051-0377. 323/869-7500. **Contact:** Human Resources. **World Wide Web address:** http://www.smartandfinal.com. **Description:** One of the largest nonmember warehouse grocery chains in the United States. Smart and Final operates 218 nonmembership stores and two food service distribution businesses located in southern Florida (Henry Lee Company) and Northern California (Port Stockton Food Distributors). Founded in 1871. **Common positions include:** Computer Programmer; Editor; Human Resources Manager; Internet Services Manager; MIS Specialist; Multimedia Designer; Purchasing Agent/Manager; Software Engineer; Systems Analyst; Technical Writer/Editor. **Educational backgrounds include:** Accounting; Business Administration; Communications; Computer Science; Economics; Finance; Liberal Arts; Marketing; Mathematics. **Benefits:** 401(k); Dental Insurance; Disability Coverage; Employee Discounts; Life Insurance; Medical Insurance; Pension Plan; Public Transit Available; Savings Plan. **Corporate headquarters location:** This Location. **Other U.S. locations:** AZ; CA; FL; NV. **International locations:** Mexico. **Listed on:** New York Stock Exchange. **Stock exchange symbol:** SMF. **Annual sales/revenues:** More than $100 million. **Number of employees at this location:** 600. **Number of employees nationwide:** 5,000.

SMITH'S FOOD & DRUG CENTERS
1550 South Redwood Road, Salt Lake City UT 84104. 801/974-1400. **Contact:** Human Resources.

World Wide Web address: http://www. smithsfoodanddrug.com. **Description:** Smith's Food & Drug Centers are designed for one-stop shopping and have specialty departments such as one-hour photo processing, hot prepared foods, delicatessen, seafood counter, frozen yogurt counter, bakery, florist, and pharmacy. **Corporate headquarters location:** This Location. **Listed on:** New York Stock Exchange. **Stock exchange symbol:** FMY.

SNYDER DRUG STORES
14525 Highway 7, Minnetonka MN 55345. 952/935-5441. **Fax:** 952/936-2512. **Contact:** Lisa Kraft, Manager of Human Resources Development. **E-mail address:** snyhr@fishnet.com. **World Wide Web address:** http://www.snyderdrug.com. **Description:** Operates a chain of retail drug stores. **Common positions include:** Computer Support Technician; Management Trainee; Pharmacist; Pharmacy Technician. **Educational backgrounds include:** Business Administration; Liberal Arts; Marketing. **Benefits:** 401(k); Dental Insurance; Disability Coverage; Employee Discounts; Flexible Schedule; Life Insurance; Medical Insurance; Sick Days (1 - 5); Vacation Days (10 - 20). **Special programs:** Internships; Training; Summer Jobs. **Corporate headquarters location:** This Location. **Listed on:** Privately held. **CEO:** Don Beeler. **Annual sales/revenues:** More than $100 million. **Number of employees at this location:** 125. **Number of employees nationwide:** 1,300.

SONIC AUTOMOTIVE INC.
5401 East Independence Boulevard, Charlotte NC 28212. 704/532-3320. **Contact:** Human Resources. **World Wide Web address:** http://www. sonicautomotive.com. **Description:** Operates a nationwide car dealership chain. Sonic Automotive also provides parts and services. **Corporate headquarters location:** This Location.

SOUND ADVICE, INC.
1901 Tigertail Boulevard, Dania FL 33004. 954/922-4434. **Contact:** Personnel. **Description:** Operates retail stores that sell and service audio and video equipment for the home and automobile markets. **Corporate headquarters location:** This Location. **Number of employees at this location:** 520.

SOUTHEAST FOODS
1001 North 11th Street, Monroe LA 71201. 318/388-1884. **Fax:** 318/322-0110. **Contact:** Manager of Human Resources. **Description:** This location houses the administrative offices for the grocery store chain located in Louisiana, Arkansas, and Mississippi. **Common positions include:** Accountant; Buyer; Clerical Supervisor; Computer Programmer; Construction and Building Inspector; Construction Contractor; Cost Estimator; Customer Service Representative; General Manager; Human Resources Manager; Management Trainee; Purchasing Agent/Manager; Systems Analyst; Wholesale and Retail Buyer. **Educational backgrounds include:** Accounting; Business Administration; Communications; Computer Science; Marketing. **Benefits:** 401(k); Daycare Assistance; Dental Insurance; Disability Coverage; Life Insurance; Medical Insurance; Pension Plan; Profit Sharing. **Corporate headquarters location:** This Location. **Number of employees at this location:** 30. **Number of employees nationwide:** 750.

SPARTAN STORES INC.
850 76th Street SW, P.O. Box 8700, Grand Rapids MI 49518. 616/878-2000. **Contact:** Human Resources. **World Wide Web address:** http://www.spartanstores.com. **Description:** Owns

and operates a chain of grocery stores. **Corporate headquarters location:** This Location.

SPECS LIQUOR WAREHOUSE
2410 Smith Street, Houston TX 77006. 713/526-8787. **Contact:** Personnel. **Description:** Operates a chain of liquor stores. **Corporate headquarters location:** This Location.

SPEEDWAY SUPERAMERICA LLC
1240 West 98th Street, Bloomington MN 55431. 612/887-6144. **Toll-free phone:** 800/328-2927. **Fax:** 612/887-6112. **Contact:** Pam Graupensperger, Recruiter. **E-mail address:** pgraupensperger@ ssallc.com. **World Wide Web address:** http://www.speedway.com. **Description:** Operates a chain of over 2,300 convenience store/gas stations in the Midwest and the Southeast. **NOTE:** Entry-level positions are offered. **Common positions include:** Assistant Manager; Customer Service Representative; General Manager; Management Trainee; Restaurant/Food Service Manager. **Educational backgrounds include:** Accounting; Business Administration; Finance; Liberal Arts; Marketing. **Benefits:** 401(k); Dental Insurance; Disability Coverage; Employee Discounts; Life Insurance; Medical Insurance; Pension Plan; Profit Sharing; Savings Plan; Tuition Assistance. **Special programs:** Internships. **Office hours:** Monday - Friday, 8:00 a.m. - 4:30 p.m. **Corporate headquarters location:** Enon OH. **Other U.S. locations:** IL; IN; MI; ND; OH; PA; SD; WI; WV. **Parent company:** Ashland, Inc. **Listed on:** New York Stock Exchange. **Number of employees at this location:** 100. **Number of employees nationwide:** 10,000.

SPIEGEL, INC.
3500 Lacey Road, Downers Grove IL 60515. 630/986-8800. **Fax:** 630/769-2012. **Contact:** Malcolm Harris, Director of Human Resources. **E-mail address:** careers@spgl.com. **World Wide Web address:** http://www.spiegel.com. **Description:** A retailer of goods and services for the home, as well as current fashions for women, men, and children. **Common positions include:** Accountant; Advertising Clerk; Architect; Attorney; Buyer; Computer Programmer; Copywriter; Customer Service Representative; Department Manager; Financial Analyst; General Manager; Industrial Engineer; Management Trainee; Marketing Specialist; Operations/Production Manager; Quality Control Supervisor; Systems Analyst. **Educational backgrounds include:** Accounting; Business Administration; Communications; Fashion; Marketing; Merchandising. **Benefits:** Dental Insurance; Disability Coverage; Employee Discounts; Life Insurance; Medical Insurance; Profit Sharing; Savings Plan; Tuition Assistance. **Corporate headquarters location:** This Location. **Subsidiaries include:** Eddie Bauer, Inc. **Listed on:** NASDAQ.

SPORTS SUPPLY GROUP, INC.
P.O. Box 7726, 1901 Diplomat Drive, Farmers Branch TX 75234. 972/484-9484. **Contact:** Human Resources. **World Wide Web address:** http://www. sportsgroup.com. **Description:** A catalog retailer of sporting goods and recreational products. **Corporate headquarters location:** This Location. **Listed on:** New York Stock Exchange. **Stock exchange symbol:** GYM.

STAMBAUGH HARDWARE COMPANY
4900 Market Street, Boardman OH 44512. 330/781-7100. **Contact:** Human Resources. **Description:** A retail home center providing home improvement and remodeling products. **Common positions include:**

Management Trainee. Educational backgrounds include: Business Administration; Marketing. **Benefits:** 401(k); Employee Discounts; Life Insurance; Medical Insurance; Pension Plan; Profit Sharing; Savings Plan. **Corporate headquarters location:** This Location.

STAPLES, INC.
500 Staples Drive, Framingham MA 01702. 508/253-5000. **Contact:** Human Resources. **World Wide Web address:** http://www.staples.com. **Description:** This location houses the corporate offices. Overall, Staples is a leading retailer of discount office products. The company operates over 350 high-volume office superstores in 18 states and the District of Columbia. **Common positions include:** Accountant/Auditor; Budget Analyst; Buyer; Computer Programmer; Management Trainee; Systems Analyst. **Educational backgrounds include:** Accounting; Business Administration; Computer Science; Finance; Marketing. **Benefits:** 401(k); Medical Insurance; Savings Plan; Tuition Assistance. **Corporate headquarters location:** This Location. **Listed on:** NASDAQ. **Number of employees at this location:** 850. **Number of employees nationwide:** 15,700.
Other U.S. locations:
* Staples Business Advantage, P.O. Box 1712, Atlanta GA 30303. 404/332-3000.

STAR FURNITURE COMPANY
P.O. Box 219169, Houston TX 77218-9169. 281/492-5445. **Fax:** 281/579-5909. **Contact:** Paige Olson, Director of Human Resources. **Description:** Engaged in the retail sale of home furnishings. **Common positions include:** Accountant/Auditor; Advertising Clerk; Blue-Collar Worker Supervisor; Buyer; Credit Manager; Customer Service Representative; Human Resources Manager; Management Trainee; Purchasing Agent/Manager; Retail Sales Worker. **Benefits:** Dental Insurance; Employee Discounts; Life Insurance; Medical Insurance; Savings Plan. **Corporate headquarters location:** This Location. **Other U.S. locations:** College Station TX. **Parent company:** Berkshire Hathaway Inc. **Listed on:** Privately held. **Number of employees at this location:** 200. **Number of employees nationwide:** 450.

STARBUCKS COFFEE CORPORATION
P.O. Box 34067, Seattle WA 98124. 206/447-1575. **Physical address:** 2401 Utah Avenue South, Seattle WA 98134. **Contact:** Human Resources. **Description:** Sells whole-bean coffees, along with hot coffees and Italian-style espresso beverages through more than 1,000 retail stores and licensed airport stores. The company purchases green coffee beans for its coffee varieties from coffee-producing regions throughout the world and custom roasts them. In addition to coffee beans and beverages, the company's stores offer a selection of coffee-making equipment, accessories, pastries, and confections. Also, the company sells whole-bean coffees through a specialty sales group and a national mail-order operation. **Corporate headquarters location:** This Location. **Other U.S. locations:** CA; CO; CT; DC; GA; IL; MA; MD; MN; NJ; NY; OR; VA. **International locations:** British Columbia, Canada; United Kingdom. **Subsidiaries include:** The Coffee Connection, Inc. **Number of employees worldwide:** 20,000.

THE STASH TEA COMPANY
P.O. Box 910, Portland OR 97224. 503/684-4482. **Contact:** Human Resources. **World Wide Web address:** http://www.stashtea.com. **Description:** A catalog retailer of specialty teas, cookies, breads, and related gift items. Founded in 1972. **Corporate headquarters location:** This Location.

THE STATIONERY HOUSE INC.
1000 Florida Avenue, Hagerstown MD 21741. 301/739-4487. **Contact:** Human Resources. **Description:** A catalog retailer of a wide range of holiday greeting cards for corporations. **Corporate headquarters location:** This Location.

PAUL STEKETEE & SONS
3615 28th Street SE, Grand Rapids MI 49512. 616/957-0188. **Contact:** Personnel. **Description:** Sells apparel for men, women, and children. **Corporate headquarters location:** This Location.

STERLING INC.
375 Ghent Road, Akron OH 44333. 330/668-5000. **Contact:** Recruitment Manager. **Description:** Operates over 900 jewelry stores nationwide. **Common positions include:** Accountant/Auditor; Computer Programmer; Customer Service Representative; Department Manager; Human Resources Manager; Management Trainee; Marketing Specialist; Operations/Production Manager; Retail Manager. **Educational backgrounds include:** Accounting; Business Administration; Communications; Marketing. **Benefits:** 401(k); Dental Insurance; Disability Coverage; Employee Discounts; Life Insurance; Medical Insurance; Pension Plan; Savings Plan; Tuition Assistance. **Corporate headquarters location:** This Location. **Subsidiaries include:** Belden Jewelers; Goodman Jewelers; J.B. Robinson Jewelers; Kay Jewelers; LeRoy's Jewelers; Osterman Jewelers; Rogers Jewelers; Shaws Jewelers; Weigfield Jewelers. **Parent company:** Signet Group plc. **Number of employees at this location:** 1,400. **Number of employees nationwide:** 12,000.

STERN'S DEPARTMENT STORES
Bergen Mall, Route 4, Paramus NJ 07652. 201/845-2426. **Fax:** 201/845-2383. **Contact:** Human Resources. **World Wide Web address:** http://www.federated-fds.com. **Description:** Operates a chain of full-line department stores. The company has 22 area branches. **Common positions include:** Management Trainee. **Educational backgrounds include:** Business Administration; Liberal Arts; Marketing. **Benefits:** 401(k); Dental Insurance; Employee Discounts; Medical Insurance; Pension Plan; Profit Sharing. **Corporate headquarters location:** This Location. **Other U.S. locations:** Woodbridge NJ; Flushing NY; Hicksville NY. **Parent company:** Federated Department Stores, Inc. **Listed on:** New York Stock Exchange.

STEW LEONARD'S DAIRY
100 Westport Avenue, Norwalk CT 06851. 203/847-7214. **Contact:** Christine Arnette, Recruiting Manager. **Description:** One of the world's largest retail dairy stores. Founded in 1969. **Common positions include:** Customer Service Representative; Management Trainee. **Educational backgrounds include:** Business Administration; Marketing. **Benefits:** 401(k); Dental Insurance; Disability Coverage; Life Insurance; Medical Insurance. **Special programs:** Internships. **Internship information:** Culinary and bakery internships are offered. **Corporate headquarters location:** This Location. **Other U.S. locations:** Danbury CT. **Annual sales/revenues:** $51 - $100 million. **Number of employees at this location:** 700. **Number of employees nationwide:** 1,400.

THE STOP & SHOP COMPANIES, INC.
1385 Hancock Street, Quincy MA 02169. 617/770-8700. **Contact:** Employment Manager. **Description:** A national supermarket retail chain. **Corporate headquarters location:** This Location.

STOP-N-GO OF MADISON, INC.
2934 Fish Hatchery Road, Madison WI 53713.
608/271-4433. **Fax:** 608/271-1222. **Contact:** Mark
Kiley, Director of Human Resources. **World Wide
Web address:** http://www.stop-n-go.com.
Description: Operates a chain of 45 convenience
stores and has developed partnerships with several
food service entities including Taco John's and
Blimpie Subs. Founded in 1963. **NOTE:** Entry-level
positions, part-time jobs, and second and third shifts
are offered. **Common positions include:** Assistant
Manager; Branch Manager; Management Trainee.
Special programs: Training; Summer Jobs.
Corporate headquarters location: This Location.
Annual sales/revenues: $51 - $100 million.
Number of employees nationwide: 320.

STORE 24, INC.
184 Riverview Avenue, Waltham MA 02453.
781/891-8880. **Fax:** 781/647-0320. **Contact:**
Human Resources. **Description:** A privately held
chain of 24-hour convenience stores. Stores are
located throughout New England and New York
City. **Benefits:** Dental Insurance; Disability
Coverage; Employee Discounts; Life Insurance;
Medical Insurance; Pension Plan; Profit Sharing;
Savings Plan; Tuition Assistance. **Corporate
headquarters location:** This Location.

WILLIAM A. STRAUB INC.
8282 Forsyth Boulevard, St. Louis MO 63105.
314/725-2121. **Contact:** Paul Poe, General
Manager. **Description:** Owners and operators of a
chain of retail grocery stores. **President:** Jack
Straub, Jr.

STRAUS-FRANK COMPANY
P.O. Box 600, San Antonio TX 78292-0600.
210/226-0101. **Contact:** Personnel Department.
Description: A wholesaler of automobile parts.
Straus-Frank Company owns the retail chain
automotive parts store Car Quest. **Corporate
headquarters location:** This Location.

STRAUSS DISCOUNT AUTO
9A Brick Plant Road, South River NJ 08882.
732/390-9000. **Contact:** Human Resources
Administrator. **Description:** Engaged in the retail
trade of automotive aftermarket products. **Common
positions include:** Accountant/Auditor; Advertising
Clerk; Automotive Mechanic; Budget Analyst;
Buyer; Computer Programmer; Construction
Contractor; Customer Service Representative;
Draftsperson; Human Resources Manager;
Management Trainee; Property and Real Estate
Manager; Systems Analyst. **Educational
backgrounds include:** Accounting; Business
Administration; Liberal Arts. **Benefits:** 401(k);
Dental Insurance; Disability Coverage; Employee
Discounts; Life Insurance; Medical Insurance;
Tuition Assistance. **Corporate headquarters
location:** This Location. **Listed on:** Privately held.
Number of employees at this location: 200.
Number of employees nationwide: 2,200.

STRAWBRIDGE'S
801 Market Street, Philadelphia PA 19107-3199.
215/629-6000. **Contact:** Personnel. **World Wide
Web address:** http://www.mayco.com.
Description: Operates a chain of more than 35
department and self-service stores in Pennsylvania,
Delaware, and New Jersey. **NOTE:** Strawbridge's
150-hour buyers training program begins in
September of each year. **Common positions
include:** Accountant/Auditor; Department Manager;
Management Trainee. **Educational backgrounds
include:** Business Administration; Economics;
Fashion; Liberal Arts; Marketing; Merchandising;
Retail Management. **Benefits:** 401(k); Dental

Insurance; Disability Coverage; Education
Assistance; Employee Discounts; Life Insurance;
Medical Insurance; Pension Plan; Prescription
Drugs; Savings Plan; Tuition Assistance. **Special
programs:** Internships. **Corporate headquarters
location:** This Location. **Parent company:** The
May Department Stores Company. **Number of
employees nationwide:** 12,000.
Other U.S. locations:
- 100 Christiana Mall, Newark DE 19702-3202.
  302/366-7399.
- 4747 Concord Pike, Wilmington DE 19803.
  302/478-1860.

J.D. STREETT & COMPANY INC.
144 Weldon Parkway, Maryland Heights MO
63043. 314/432-6600. **Contact:** Personnel. **E-mail
address:** info@jdstreett.com. **World Wide Web
address:** http://www.jdstreett.com. **Description:**
Retailers and wholesale marketers of petroleum
products. **Corporate headquarters location:** This
Location.

STRIDE-RITE CORPORATION
191 Spring Street, P.O. Box 9191, Lexington MA
02421. 617/824-6000. **Contact:** Mary Kuconis,
Human Resources Director. **World Wide Web
address:** http://www.striderite.com. **Description:**
Operated retail shoe stores. **Corporate
headquarters location:** This Location.

SUNSHINE FOOD MARKETS
1300 West Elkhorn Street, Sioux Falls SD 57104.
605/336-2505. **Contact:** Personnel Department.
Description: Operates a chain of grocery stores.
Corporate headquarters location: This Location.

SUPERMARKET INVESTORS
8109 Interstate 30, Little Rock AR 72209. 501/570-
0007. **Contact:** Human Resources. **Description:**
Operates a chain of supermarkets called Harvest
Foods. **Common positions include:** Accountant/
Auditor; Buyer; Computer Programmer; Human
Service Worker; Operations/Production Manager;
Structural Engineer; Systems Analyst. **Educational
backgrounds include:** Business Administration;
Marketing. **Benefits:** 401(k); Dental Insurance;
Disability Coverage; Life Insurance; Medical
Insurance. **Corporate headquarters location:** This
Location. **Listed on:** Privately held. **Number of
employees at this location:** 3,200.

SUPERVALU INC.
11840 Valley View Road, Eden Prairie MN 55344.
952/828-4000. **Fax:** 952/828-4803. **Contact:**
Michael Overline, General Director of Human
Resources. **World Wide Web address:**
http://www.supervalu.com. **Description:** One of the
nation's largest food retailers and distribution
companies, supplying grocery, health and beauty
aids, and general merchandise products. In the
corporate retail sector, SUPERVALU operates over
1,000 stores under the following names: bigg's, Cub
Foods, Shop 'n Save, Save-A-Lot, Scott's Foods,
Laneco, and Hornbachers. **Common positions
include:** Buyer; Computer Programmer; Human
Resources Manager; Management Trainee;
Pharmacist; Transportation Specialist; Wholesale
and Retail Buyer. **Corporate headquarters
location:** This Location. **Other U.S. locations:**
Nationwide. **Subsidiaries include:** Hazelwood
Farms Bakeries manufactures frozen bakery
products. **Listed on:** New York Stock Exchange.
Stock exchange symbol: SVU.

SYMS CORPORATION
One Syms Way, Secaucus NJ 07094. 201/902-9600.
Contact: John Tyzbir, Personnel Director. **E-mail
address:** symsih@aol.com. **World Wide**

Web address: http://www.symsclothing.com. **Description:** This location houses a retail location and a distribution center. Overall, Syms Corporation operates a chain of over off-price 45 apparel stores located throughout the Northeast, Midwest, Southeast, and Southwest. All stores offer men's tailored clothing; women's dresses, suits, and separates; and children's apparel. **Corporate headquarters location:** This Location.

THE TJX COMPANIES, INC.
770 Cochituate Road, Framingham MA 01701. 508/390-2000. **Fax:** 508/390-2650. **Recorded jobline:** 888/JOB-S597. **Contact:** Staffing Specialist. **E-mail address:** jobs@tjx.com. **World Wide Web address:** http://www.tjx.com. **Description:** The TJX Companies, Inc. is one of the world's largest off-price retailers. It comprises T.J. Maxx, Marshall's, Home Goods, A.J. Wright, Winners Apparel Ltd. in Canada, and T.K. Maxx in Europe. **NOTE:** Entry-level positions, part-time jobs, and second and third shifts are offered. **Common positions include:** Accountant; Administrative Assistant; AS400 Programmer Analyst; Auditor; Budget Analyst; Buyer; Claim Representative; Computer Programmer; Computer Support Technician; Customer Service Representative; Database Administrator; Database Manager; Graphic Artist; Graphic Designer; Help-Desk Technician; Human Resources Manager; Industrial Engineer; Marketing Specialist; Network/Systems Administrator; Project Manager; Public Relations Specialist; Purchasing Agent/Manager; Quality Assurance Engineer; Secretary; Software Engineer; SQL Programmer; Systems Analyst; Transportation/Traffic Specialist; Typist/Word Processor. **Educational backgrounds include:** Accounting; Business Administration; C/C++; Communications; Computer Science; Economics; Finance; Liberal Arts; Marketing; Microsoft Word; Novell; Software Development; Software Tech. Support; Spreadsheets; SQL; Visual Basic. **Benefits:** 401(k); Dental Insurance; Disability Coverage; Employee Discounts; Life Insurance; Medical Insurance; On-Site Daycare; Pension Plan; Profit Sharing; Tuition Assistance. **Special programs:** Internships; Training; Co-ops; Summer Jobs. **Corporate headquarters location:** This Location. **Other U.S. locations:** Nationwide. **International locations:** Canada; Europe. **Listed on:** New York Stock Exchange. **Annual sales/revenues:** More than $100 million. **Number of employees at this location:** 2,000. **Number of employees nationwide:** 60,000.

TRM COPY CENTERS CORPORATION
5208 NE 122nd Avenue, Portland OR 97230. 503/257-8766. **Contact:** Human Resources. **Description:** A leading provider of self-service photocopying centers. The company owns, maintains, and monitors over 33,000 TRM Centers located in independent retail establishments such as pharmacies, stationery stores, hardware stores, convenience stores, and gift shops. **Corporate headquarters location:** This Location. **International locations:** Belgium; Canada; France; United Kingdom.

TARGET STORES
P.O. Box 1392, Minneapolis MN 55440-1392. 612/304-6073. **Physical address:** 33 South Sixth Street, Minneapolis MN 55402. **Contact:** Human Resources. **World Wide Web address:** http://www.targetcorp.com. **Description:** Operates a retail chain of discount department stores. **Benefits:** Dental Insurance; Disability Coverage; Employee Discounts; Life Insurance; Medical Insurance; Pension Plan; Profit Sharing; Savings Plan; Tuition

Assistance. **Corporate headquarters location:** This Location.

THRIFTY WHITE STORES
55 West Office Center, Suite 300, 10700 Highway 55, Minneapolis MN 55441. 612/513-4300. **Contact:** David Rueter, Personnel Manager. **World Wide Web address:** http://www.thriftywhite.com. **Description:** Operates a retail drugstore chain with over 50 rural locations in Minnesota, the Dakotas, Iowa, and Montana. **Common positions include:** Accountant/Auditor; Advertising Clerk; Buyer; Clerical Supervisor; Credit Clerk and Authorizer; Department Manager; General Manager; Marketing Manager; Payroll Clerk; Pharmacist; Receptionist; Wholesale and Retail Buyer. **Educational backgrounds include:** Accounting; Business Administration; Liberal Arts. **Benefits:** 401(k); Dental Insurance; Employee Discounts; Life Insurance; Medical Insurance; Pension Plan; Profit Sharing. **Corporate headquarters location:** This Location. **Number of employees at this location:** 60. **Number of employees nationwide:** 1,150.

TODAY'S MAN, INC.
835 Lancer Drive, Moorestown NJ 08057. 856/235-0725. **Contact:** Human Resources. **World Wide Web address:** http://www.todaysman.com. **Description:** A leading menswear superstore specializing in tailored clothing, sportswear, and accessories. The company operates a chain of approximately 30 superstores. Today's Man carries a broad assortment of current-season brand name and private-label menswear at discount prices. **Common positions include:** Accountant/Auditor; Advertising Clerk; Buyer; Computer Programmer; Human Resources Manager; Management Trainee; Systems Analyst; Wholesale and Retail Buyer. **Educational backgrounds include:** Accounting; Art/Design; Business Administration; Computer Science; Liberal Arts; Marketing. **Benefits:** 401(k); Employee Discounts; Life Insurance; Medical Insurance; Profit Sharing. **Corporate headquarters location:** This Location. **Other U.S. locations:** CT; DC; FL; IL; MD; NY; PA; VA. **Number of employees at this location:** 200. **Number of employees nationwide:** 2,000.

TOM THUMB FOOD MARKETS, INC.
POLKA DOT DAIRY, INC.
110 East 17th Street, Hastings MN 55033. 651/437-9023. **Fax:** 651/438-2638. **Contact:** Todd Huffman, Director of Human Resources. **Description:** Tom Thumb Food Markets operates an area grocery and convenience store chain. Polka Dot Dairy (also at this location) is a distributor of bottled milk. **Common positions include:** Management Trainee. **Educational backgrounds include:** Accounting; Business Administration; Economics; Finance; Marketing. **Benefits:** Dental Insurance; Disability Coverage; Life Insurance; Medical Insurance; Profit Sharing. **Corporate headquarters location:** This Location.

TOYOTA OF DALLAS INC.
2610 Forest Lane, Dallas TX 75234. 972/241-6655. **Contact:** Paula Beaver, Controller. **Description:** Specializes in the retail sale of new and used Toyota cars. **Common positions include:** Accountant; Credit Manager; Customer Service Representative; Department Manager; General Manager; Management Trainee; Operations Manager; Retail Sales Worker; Technician. **Benefits:** Employee Discounts; Medical Insurance; Profit Sharing. **Corporate headquarters location:** This Location.

TOYS 'R US
461 From Road, Paramus NJ 07652. 201/262-7800. **Contact:** Director of Employment. **World Wide**

Web address: http://www.toysrus.com. **Description:** One of the largest children's specialty retailers in the world. The company operates over 1,450 stores worldwide. Founded in 1948. **NOTE:** Entry-level positions are offered. **Common positions include:** Accountant; Administrative Assistant; Assistant Manager; Computer Programmer; Financial Analyst; Management Trainee; MIS Specialist; Secretary; Systems Analyst. **Educational backgrounds include:** Accounting; Business Administration; Computer Science; Finance; Marketing. **Benefits:** 401(k); Daycare Assistance; Dental Insurance; Disability Coverage; Life Insurance; Medical Insurance; Profit Sharing; Savings Plan; Stock Option. **Special programs:** Training. **Corporate headquarters location:** This Location. **Other U.S. locations:** Nationwide. **Listed on:** New York Stock Exchange. **Stock exchange symbol:** TOY. **Annual sales/revenues:** More than $100 million. **Number of employees at this location:** 1,400. **Number of employees worldwide:** 94,000.

TRACTOR SUPPLY COMPANY (TSC)

320 Plus Park Boulevard, Nashville TN 37217. 615/366-4600. **Contact:** Human Resources. **World Wide Web address:** http://www.tractorsupplyco. com. **Description:** One of the largest operators of retail farm stores in the U.S., with over 220 stores in 26 states. The company supplies the daily farming and maintenance needs of hobby, part-time, and full-time farmers, as well as suburban customers, contractors, and tradesmen. The company sells farm maintenance products (fencing, tractor parts and accessories, agricultural spraying equipment, and tillage parts); animal products (specialty feeds, supplements, medicines, veterinary supplies, and livestock feeders); general maintenance products (air compressors, welders, generators, pumps, plumbing, and tools); lawn and garden products (riding mowers, tillers, and fertilizers); light truck equipment; and work clothing. **Corporate headquarters location:** This Location. **Listed on:** NASDAQ. **Stock exchange symbol:** TSCO. **Chairman and CEO:** Joe Scarlett. **Number of employees nationwide:** 2,200.

TRANS WORLD ENTERTAINMENT

38 Corporate Circle, Albany NY 12203. 518/452-1242. **Contact:** Human Resources. **Description:** A music and video retailer. Trans World owns 500 stores throughout the United States and Puerto Rico including Coconuts, Record Town, Music Express, and Saturday Matinee. **Corporate headquarters location:** This Location. **Number of employees at this location:** 800.

TREND-LINES, INC.

135 American Legion Highway, Revere MA 02151. 781/853-0900. **Contact:** Human Resources. **Description:** A distributor of woodworkers tools and accessories. Products are sold through Woodworkers Warehouse retail stores, with 100 Northeast locations, as well as its Trend-lines mail-order catalog, sent to customers in all 50 states. Founded in 1981. **Corporate headquarters location:** This Location.

TRI NORTH DEPARTMENT STORES

5700 Sixth Avenue South, Suite 214, Seattle WA 98108-2511. 206/767-7600. **Contact:** Human Resources. **Description:** Owns and operates a chain of retail clothing department stores located primarily throughout the Pacific Northwest. **Corporate headquarters location:** This Location.

TROY AIKMAN AUTO MALL

P.O. Box 121819, Fort Worth TX 76121-1819. 817/560-0500. **Fax:** 817/560-7982. **Contact:**

Personnel Office. **Description:** A new and used car dealership specializing in Chevrolet and Chrysler-Plymouth-Jeep lines. Founded in 1996. **NOTE:** Entry-level positions are offered. **Common positions include:** Administrative Assistant; Automotive Mechanic; Controller; Finance Director; General Manager; Human Resources Manager; Receptionist; Sales Executive; Sales Manager. **Educational backgrounds include:** Accounting; Business Administration; Finance. **Benefits:** 401(k); Dental Insurance; Disability Coverage; Employee Discounts; Life Insurance; Medical Insurance. **Special programs:** Apprenticeships; Training. **Corporate headquarters location:** This Location. **General Manager:** Jim Hardick. **Facilities Manager:** Jim Kappler. **Number of employees at this location:** 200.

TRUSERV CORPORATION

8600 West Bryn Mawr Avenue, Chicago IL 60631-3505. 773/695-5000. **Contact:** Human Resources. **World Wide Web address:** http://www.truserv. com. **Description:** A *Fortune* 500 company that operates the True Value, Home & Garden Showplace, and Taylor Rental national retail chains. **Corporate headquarters location:** This Location.

ULTIMATE ELECTRONICS, INC.

321-A West 84th Avenue, Thornton CO 80221. 303/412-2500. **Toll-free phone:** 800/260-2660. **Fax:** 303/412-2501. **Contact:** Personnel. **World Wide Web address:** http://www.ultimateelectronics com. **Description:** A specialty retailer of home entertainment and consumer electronics. The company operates stores under the SoundTrack, Audio King, and Ultimate Electronics names. Founded in 1968. **NOTE:** Entry-level positions and second and third shifts are offered. **Common positions include:** Accountant; Administrative Assistant; Advertising Clerk; Computer Operator; Computer Programmer; Customer Service Representative; Sales Representative. **Educational backgrounds include:** Accounting; Art/Design; Computer Science; Marketing. **Benefits:** 401(k); Dental Insurance; Employee Discounts; Life Insurance; Medical Insurance; Tuition Assistance. **Special programs:** Training. **Corporate headquarters location:** This Location. **Other area locations:** Arvada CO; Aurora CO; Boulder CO; Colorado Springs CO; Denver CO; Fort Collins CO; Littleton CO. **Other U.S. locations:** Albuquerque NM; Las Vegas NV; Murray UT; Orem UT; Salt Lake City UT. **Listed on:** NASDAQ. **Annual sales/revenues:** More than $100 million. **Number of employees at this location:** 700. **Number of employees nationwide:** 1,600.

ULTRAMAR DIAMOND SHAMROCK CORP.

P.O. Box 696000, San Antonio TX 78269. 210/592-2000. **Contact:** Human Resources. **World Wide Web address:** http://www.udscorp.com. **Description:** Owns and operates refineries which manufacture diesel, gasoline, and petroleum products. Ultramar Diamond Shamrock also owns and operates a large number of retail stores where its products are sold. **Common positions include:** Chemist; Computer Programmer; Draftsperson; Human Resources Manager; Mechanical Engineer; Petroleum Engineer; Purchasing Agent/Manager. **Educational backgrounds include:** Business Administration; Chemistry; Engineering; Mathematics. **Corporate headquarters location:** This Location. **Listed on:** American Stock Exchange.

UNI-MARTS, INC.

447 East Beaver Avenue, State College PA 16801-5690. 814/234-6000. **Contact:** Human Resources.

Description: An independent regional operator of over 400 convenience stores located in the mid-Atlantic region. **Corporate headquarters location:** This Location. **Other U.S. locations:** DE; MD; NJ; NY; OH; PA; VA; WV. **Listed on:** American Stock Exchange.

UNITED HARDWARE DISTRIBUTION CO.
P.O. Box 410, Minneapolis MN 55440. 763/559-1800. **Contact:** Renee Bourget, Human Resources. **Description:** This location houses the corporate offices. Overall, United Hardware Distribution Company operates the Hardware Hank and Trustworthy Hardware chains of hardware stores, and the Golden Rule Lumber chain of retail lumber stores. **Corporate headquarters location:** This Location.

UNITEDAUTO GROUP, INC.
One Harmon Plaza, 9th Floor, Secaucus NJ 07094. 201/325-3300. **Contact:** Human Resources. **World Wide Web address:** http://www.unitedauto.com. **Description:** Operates car dealerships. **Corporate headquarters location:** This Location. **Listed on:** New York Stock Exchange. **Stock exchange symbol:** UAG.

URBAN OUTFITTERS
1809 Walnut Street, Philadelphia PA 19103. 215/564-2313. **Contact:** Human Resources. **Description:** A clothing and housewares retail chain. **Corporate headquarters location:** This Location.

THE VERMONT TEDDY BEAR COMPANY
6655 Shelburne Road, Shelburne VT 05482. 802/985-3001. **Fax:** 802/985-1304. **Recorded jobline:** 802/985-1397x1718. **Contact:** Sue Schermerhorn, Human Resources Director. **E-mail address:** sues@vtbear.com. **World Wide Web address:** http://www.vermontteddybear.com. **Description:** Designs and manufactures hand-crafted teddy bears and markets them primarily as gifts called Bear-Grams, which are personalized teddy bears delivered directly to the recipient for special occasions such as birthdays, anniversaries, weddings, and holidays. This location also hires seasonally. Founded in 1983. **NOTE:** Entry-level positions and part-time jobs are offered. **Common positions include:** Administrative Assistant; Chief Financial Officer; Computer Operator; Computer Support Technician; Computer Technician; Controller; Cost Estimator; Customer Service Representative; Database Administrator; Help-Desk Technician; Human Resources Manager; Internet Services Manager; Market Research Analyst; MIS Specialist; Network/Systems Administrator; Operations Manager; Production Manager; Public Relations Specialist; Quality Control Supervisor; Sales Manager; Telecommunications Manager; Transportation/Traffic Specialist. **Educational backgrounds include:** Accounting; Art/Design; Business Administration; Communications; Computer Science; Finance; HTML; Internet Development; Marketing; MBA; Microsoft Office; Microsoft Word; Novell; QuarkXPress; Software Tech. Support. **Benefits:** 401(k); Casual Dress - Daily; Dental Insurance; Disability Coverage; Employee Discounts; Life Insurance; Medical Insurance; Public Transit Available; Sick Days (6 - 10); Vacation Days (16+). **Special programs:** Internships; Summer Jobs. **Corporate headquarters location:** This Location. **Other U.S. locations:** Newport VT. **Listed on:** NASDAQ. **Stock exchange symbol:** BEAR. **CEO:** Liz Roberts. **Facilities Manager:** Ann Lamb. **Information Systems Manager:** Bonnie West. **Sales Manager:** Katie Camardo. **Annual**

sales/revenues: $11 - $20 million. **Number of employees at this location:** 230.

VICTORY SUPERMARKETS
75 North Main Street, Leominster MA 01453. 978/840-2200. **Contact:** Dick Diotalevi, Director of Operations. **World Wide Web address:** http://www.victorysupermarkets.com. **Description:** An independent retail grocery store chain with 20 outlets located in Massachusetts and New Hampshire. **Corporate headquarters location:** This Location. **Other area locations:** Clinton MA; Fitchburg MA; Gardner MA; Marlborough MA; Uxbridge MA.

VILLAGE SUPERMARKET, INC.
733 Mountain Avenue, Springfield NJ 07081. 973/467-2200. **Contact:** Vic D'Anna, Personnel Director. **Description:** Operates 20 supermarkets, 17 of which are located in north central New Jersey and three of which are in eastern Pennsylvania. Village Supermarket offers traditional grocery, meat, produce, dairy, frozen food, bakery, and delicatessen departments, as well as health and beauty aids, housewares, stationery, and automotive and paint supplies. Six stores contain prescription pharmacy departments, and the company also owns and operates two retail package liquor stores and one variety store. **Corporate headquarters location:** This Location. **Other area locations:** Bernardsville NJ; Chester NJ; Florham Park NJ; Livingston NJ; Morristown NJ; The Orchards NJ; Union NJ. **Parent company:** Wakefern Food Corporation.

VISTA EYECARE
296 Grayson Highway, Lawrenceville GA 30045. 770/822-3600. **Contact:** Human Resources. **Description:** Operates over 300 retail vision centers. **Corporate headquarters location:** This Location.

VON MAUR, INC.
6565 Brady Street, Davenport IA 52806. 319/388-2200. **Contact:** Ms. Gayle Haun, Corporate Personnel Director. **World Wide Web address:** http://www.vonmaur.com. **Description:** A department store carrying a full line of clothing, shoes, and accessories for men, women, and children. **Common positions include:** Buyer; Computer Programmer; Department Manager; Management Trainee; Retail Manager. **Educational backgrounds include:** Business Administration; Computer Science; Marketing; Retail Management. **Benefits:** 401(k); Employee Discounts; Life Insurance; Medical Insurance. **Corporate headquarters location:** This Location. **Other U.S. locations:** Nationwide. **Number of employees at this location:** 300. **Number of employees nationwide:** 2,800.

THE VONS COMPANIES, INC.
P.O. Box 513338, Los Angeles CA 90051-1338. 626/821-7000. **Physical address:** 618 South Michillinda Avenue, Arcadia CA 91007. **Contact:** Human Resources. **Description:** One of the largest operators of supermarkets and drugstores in Southern California. **Corporate headquarters location:** This Location. **Parent company:** Safeway, Inc.

WAL-MART STORES, INC.
702 SW Eighth Street, Bentonville AR 72716. 501/273-4000. **Fax:** 501/273-1917. **Contact:** Corporate Recruiter, People Division. **World Wide Web address:** http://www.walmart.com. **Description:** One of the largest retail merchandise chains in the country, Wal-Mart Stores, Inc. operates a series of full-service discount department

stores. Wal-Mart Stores, Inc. has opened several stores in Mexico through a joint venture with Cifta, one of Mexico's largest retailers. **Common positions include:** Accountant/Auditor; Architect; Attorney; Biological Scientist; Broadcast Technician; Buyer; Chemical Engineer; Civil Engineer; Claim Representative; Clerical Supervisor; Computer Programmer; Construction and Building Inspector; Construction Contractor; Designer; Draftsperson; Editor; Electrical Engineer; Human Resources Manager; Industrial Engineer; Industrial Production Manager; Management Analyst; Management Trainee; Manufacturer's Sales Rep.; Mechanical Engineer; Operations Manager; Paralegal; Property and Real Estate Manager; Purchasing Agent; Quality Control Supervisor; Radio/TV Announcer; Securities Sales Representative; Services Sales Representative; Software Engineer; Systems Analyst; Technical Writer; Transportation Specialist; Wholesale and Retail Buyer. **Educational backgrounds include:** Accounting; Art/Design; Biology; Business Administration; Chemistry; Communications; Computer Science; Economics; Engineering; Finance; Liberal Arts; Marketing; Mathematics. **Special programs:** Internships. **Corporate headquarters location:** This Location. **Number of employees nationwide:** 910,000.

WALGREEN COMPANY
200 Wilmot Road, Deerfield IL 60015. 847/940-2500. **Contact:** Personnel Recruiting. **World Wide Web address:** http://www.walgreens.com. **Description:** Walgreen operates one of the largest retail drug store chains in the United States, which sells prescription and nonprescription drugs, cosmetics, toiletries, liquor and beverages, tobacco, and general merchandise. **Corporate headquarters location:** This Location. **Number of employees worldwide:** 75,000.

WAWA INC.
260 West Baltimore Pike, Wawa PA 19063-5699. 610/358-8000. **Contact:** Howard Anderson, Personnel Director. **Description:** This location houses administrative offices. Overall, Wawa is a convenience store chain with operations throughout Pennsylvania. **Corporate headquarters location:** This Location.

WEIS MARKETS, INC.
1000 South Second Street, Sunbury PA 17801. 570/286-4571. **Contact:** Allan Corcoran, Director/Human Resources. **World Wide Web address:** http://www.weis.com. **Description:** Operates over 165 supermarkets. **Common positions include:** Accountant; Buyer; Computer Programmer; Draftsperson; Management Trainee; Operations Manager; Quality Control Supervisor; Store Manager. **Educational backgrounds include:** Accounting; Business Administration; Computer Science; Marketing. **Special programs:** Internships. **Corporate headquarters location:** This Location. **Other U.S. locations:** MD; NJ; NY; VA; WV. **Number of employees nationwide:** 19,000.

WELCOME HOME, INC.
309 Raleigh Street, Wilmington NC 28412. 910/791-4312. **Contact:** Human Resources. **World Wide Web address:** http://www.welchome.com. **Description:** A retailer of giftware and home decor including fragrances, candles, framed art, furniture, and seasonal gifts. The company operates over 100 stores in 36 states. **Corporate headquarters location:** This Location. **Listed on:** Over the Counter. **Stock exchange symbol:** WELC. **Chairman and CEO:** Thomas H. Quinn. **Annual sales/revenues:** $51 - $100 million. **Number of employees nationwide:** 750.

WHEREHOUSE ENTERTAINMENT
19701 Hamilton Avenue, Suite 200, Torrance CA 90502. 310/538-2314. **Contact:** Rachel Centeno, Human Resources Manager. **Description:** A retailer of prerecorded music and videos. **Common positions include:** Accountant/Auditor; Administrative Manager; Advertising Clerk; Budget Analyst; Buyer; Claim Representative; Computer Programmer; Construction Contractor; Customer Service Representative; Designer; Financial Analyst; General Manager; Human Resources Manager; Management Trainee; Property and Real Estate Manager; Purchasing Agent/Manager; Software Engineer; Systems Analyst; Technical Writer/Editor; Wholesale and Retail Buyer. **Educational backgrounds include:** Accounting; Business Administration; Computer Science; Marketing. **Benefits:** 401(k); Dental Insurance; Disability Coverage; Employee Discounts; Life Insurance; Medical Insurance. **Special programs:** Internships. **Corporate headquarters location:** This Location. **Subsidiaries include:** Leopolos; Odyssey; Paradise Music; Record Shop; Rocky Mountain Records. **Parent company:** One Capitol Partners. **Listed on:** Privately held. **Number of employees at this location:** 230. **Number of employees nationwide:** 8,000.

WILD OATS MARKETS
3375 Mitchell Lane, Boulder CO 80301. 303/440-5220. **Contact:** Human Resources. **World Wide Web address:** http://www.wildoats.com. **Description:** Owns and operates health food supermarkets under the Wild Oats, Alfalfa's, and Caper's names. **Corporate headquarters location:** This Location. **Other U.S. locations:** Santa Fe NM.

WINN-DIXIE STORES, INC.
P.O. Box B, Jacksonville FL 32203-0297. 904/783-5000. **Physical address:** 5050 Edgewood Court, Jacksonville FL 32254. **Contact:** Human Resources. **World Wide Web address:** http://www.winn-dixie.com. **Description:** Winn-Dixie is one of the largest supermarket operators in the 14 Sunbelt states. Winn-Dixie stores operate under the names Winn-Dixie, Marketplace, and Buddies. Winn-Dixie also operates 16 warehousing and distribution centers and a host of manufacturing and processing facilities. A subsidiary of the company operates 14 stores in the Bahamas. **Corporate headquarters location:** This Location. **Number of employees nationwide:** 130,000.

WOLF CAMERA, INC.
4955 Marconi Drive, Alpharetta GA 30005. **Toll-free phone:** 800/955-WOLF. **Fax:** 770/754-4605. **Recorded jobline:** 888/WOLF-JOB. **Contact:** Tiffany Grayson, National Recruiting Manager. **World Wide Web address:** http://www.wolfcamera.com. **Description:** A retail distributor of photographic equipment and supplies. Wolf Camera is also a photofinisher. Founded in 1974. **Educational backgrounds include:** Accounting; AS400 Certification; Art/Design; Communications; Computer Science; Finance; HTML; Internet Development; Java; Marketing; Mathematics; Microsoft Certified Systems Engineer; Microsoft Office; Microsoft Word; Quark Xpress. **Benefits:** 401(k); Casual Dress - Fridays; Dental Insurance; Employee Discounts; Flexible Schedule; Life Insurance; Medical Insurance. **Corporate headquarters location:** This Location. **Listed on:** Privately held. **Number of employees at this location:** 450. **Number of employees nationwide:** 7,000.

YOUNKERS INC.
701 Walnut, Des Moines IA 50309. 515/362-8158. **Contact:** Mark Barkley, Vice President of Human

Resources. **World Wide Web address:** http://www.younkers.com. **Description:** Operates a chain of retail department stores. **Common positions include:** Accountant/Auditor; Administrator; Advertising Clerk; Branch Manager; Buyer; Commercial Artist; Computer Programmer; Credit Manager; Customer Service Representative; Department Manager; General Manager; Human Resources Manager; Management Trainee; Operations/Production Manager. **Educational backgrounds include:** Accounting; Business Administration; Communications; Computer Science; Finance; Marketing. **Benefits:** Dental Insurance; Disability Coverage; Life Insurance; Medical Insurance; Pension Plan; Profit Sharing; Savings Plan; Stock Option; Tuition Assistance. **Corporate headquarters location:** This Location. **Number of employees nationwide:** 7,000.

ZCMI
2200 South 900 West, Salt Lake City UT 84137. 801/579-6220. **Contact:** Ken Kraudy, Director of Human Resources. **World Wide Web address:** http://www.zcmi.com. **Description:** An Intermountain West department store offering over 3,000 brand names. There are 13 store locations covering every major city in Utah. ZCMI also offers full-service beauty salons; Tiffin Room Restaurants at the Salt Lake Downtown and Cottonwood stores; gift wrapping and shipping; a 24-hour, toll-free shopping service; and film and photographic supplies. CMI is the company's specialty store. An outdoor store is also located in Provo's East Bay complex. **Common positions include:** Accountant/Auditor; Advertising Clerk; Architect; Buyer; Commercial Artist; Computer Programmer; Credit Manager; Customer Service Representative; Draftsperson; Human Resources Manager; Purchasing Agent/Manager; Services Sales Representative; Systems Analyst. **Educational backgrounds include:** Accounting; Business Administration; Liberal Arts; Marketing. **Benefits:**

Dental Insurance; Disability Coverage; Employee Discounts; Life Insurance; Medical Insurance; Pension Plan; Savings Plan; Tuition Assistance. **Special programs:** Internships. **Corporate headquarters location:** This Location. **Number of employees nationwide:** 3,500.

ZALE CORPORATION
901 West Walnut Hill Lane, Mail Station 5B-12, Irving TX 75038. 972/580-4000. **Fax:** 972/580-5266. **Contact:** Manager of Corporate Staffing. **Description:** A specialty retail firm engaged in selling fine jewelry and related products. **NOTE:** Entry-level positions are offered. **Common positions include:** Accountant; Administrative Assistant; Architect; Attorney; Buyer; Computer Programmer; Customer Service Representative; Financial Analyst; Human Resources Manager; MIS Specialist; Property and Real Estate Manager; Systems Analyst; Typist/Word Processor. **Educational backgrounds include:** Accounting; Communications; Computer Science; Finance; Marketing. **Benefits:** 401(k); Daycare Assistance; Dental Insurance; Disability Coverage; Employee Discounts; Life Insurance; Medical Insurance; Profit Sharing; Savings Plan; Tuition Assistance. **Special programs:** Internships. **Corporate headquarters location:** This Location. **Other U.S. locations:** Nationwide. **Subsidiaries include:** Corrigan's; Gordon's; Linz. **Annual sales/revenues:** More than $100 million. **Number of employees nationwide:** 10,000.

ZALLIE SUPERMARKETS
1230 Blackwood-Clementon Road, Clementon NJ 08021. 856/627-6501. **Contact:** Laura Tabakin, Vice President of Human Resources. **Description:** This location houses administrative offices. Overall, Zallie Supermarkets operates a chain of six Shop-Rite supermarkets. **Corporate headquarters location:** This Location.

For more information on career opportunities in retail:

Associations

INTERNATIONAL COUNCIL OF SHOPPING CENTERS
665 Fifth Avenue, New York NY 10022. 212/421-8181. World Wide Web address: http://www.icsc.org. Offers conventions, research, education, a variety of publications, and awards programs.

NATIONAL ASSOCIATION OF RESALE & THRIFT SHOPS
P.O. Box 80707, St. Claire Shores MI 48080-0707. Toll-free phone: 800/544-0751. Fax: 810/294-6776. E-mail address: Webmaster@NARTS.org.

NATIONAL AUTOMOTIVE DEALERS ASSOCIATION
8400 Westpark Drive, McLean VA 22102. 703/821-7000. World Wide Web address: http://www.nada.com.

NATIONAL INDEPENDENT AUTOMOTIVE DEALERS ASSOCIATION
2521 Brown Boulevard, Arlington TX 76006. 817/640-3838. World Wide Web address: http://www.niada.com.

NATIONAL RETAIL FEDERATION
325 Seventh Street NW, Suite 1000, Washington DC 20004. 202/783-7971. World Wide Web address: http://www.nrf.com. Provides information services, industry outlooks, and a variety of educational opportunities and publications.

Directories

AUTOMOTIVE NEWS MARKET DATA BOOK
Crain Communications, 1400 Woodbridge Avenue, Detroit MI 48207-3187. 313/446-6000.

Online Services

THE INTERNET FASHION EXCHANGE
World Wide Web address: http://www.fashionexch.com. An excellent site for those industry professionals interested in apparel and retail. The extensive search engine allows you to search by job title, location, salary, product line, industry, and whether you want a permanent, temporary, or freelance position. The Internet Fashion Exchange also offers career services such as recruiting, and outplacement firms that place fashion and retail professionals.

RETAIL JOBNET
World Wide Web address: http://www.retailjobnet.com. This site is geared toward recruiting professionals and jobseekers in the retail industry.

Transportation/Travel

You can expect to find the following types of companies in this chapter:
Air, Railroad, and Water Transportation Services • Courier Services • Local and Interurban Passenger Transit • Ship Building and Repair • Transportation Equipment Travel Agencies • Trucking • Warehousing and Storage

Some helpful information: *Commercial truckers earn an average of $20,000 -$30,000 per year. Water transportation workers earn about $25,000 - $30,000. Travel agents with 10 or more years of experience earn around $30,000 - $35,000 annually.*

AAA
1000 AAA Drive, Heathrow FL 32746-5063. 407/444-7537. **Fax:** 407/444-7504. **Contact:** Human Resources. **World Wide Web address:** http://www.aaasouth.com. **Description:** A nonprofit organization that provides insurance, travel, and related services to its members. **Common positions include:** Accountant/Auditor; Administrative Assistant; Advertising Clerk; Architect; Attorney; Blue-Collar Worker Supervisor; Branch Manager; Budget Analyst; Buyer; Claim Representative; Clerical Supervisor; Computer Programmer; Counselor; Credit Manager; Customer Service Representative; Draftsperson; Economist; Editor; Education Administrator; Financial Analyst; General Manager; Human Resources Manager; Insurance Agent/Broker; Librarian; Library Technician; Management Trainee; Public Relations Specialist; Purchasing Agent/Manager; Restaurant/Food Service Manager; Services Sales Representative; Statistician; Systems Analyst; Technical Writer/Editor; Travel Agent; Underwriter/Assistant Underwriter. **Educational backgrounds include:** Accounting; Art/Design; Business Administration; Communications; Computer Science; Economics; Finance; Liberal Arts; Marketing. **Benefits:** Disability Coverage; Employee Discounts; Life Insurance; Medical Insurance; Pension Plan; Savings Plan; Tuition Assistance; Vacation Days. **Corporate headquarters location:** This Location. **Other U.S. locations:** AL; CA; DC; LA; MA; MD; MS; NH; NM; OK; TX; VA; WI; WY. **Number of employees at this location:** 1,100. **Number of employees nationwide:** 3,700.

AAR
One AAR Place, 1100 North Wood Dale Road, Wood Dale IL 60191. 630/227-2000. **Contact:** Human Resources Department. **Description:** Provides trading, overhaul, and manufacturing services, primarily to aviation-related customers including airlines, the government, original equipment manufacturers, and aviation service companies. In trading, AAR buys, sells, and leases aircraft, engines, and airframe components and distributes factory-new airframe and engine hardware. The company also customizes programs for airlines seeking inventory management. Overhaul includes the maintenance of aircraft and components including instruments; hydraulic, pneumatic, and electrical systems; landing gear; and engine parts. AAR also designs and manufactures many aviation products with an emphasis on air cargo transport systems and related materials. **Corporate headquarters location:** This Location.

ABC-NACO INC.
2001 Butterfield Road, Suite 502, Downers Grove IL 60515. 630/852-1300. **Contact:** Human Resources. **World Wide Web** address: http://www.abc-naco.com. **Description:** Manufactures and markets replacement and original equipment products for the railroad industry. Products include railroad tracks, wheels, brake shoes, and signals. **Corporate headquarters location:** This Location.

AEI LOGISTICS
120 Tokeneke Road, Darien CT 06820. 203/655-7900. **Contact:** Ms. Billie Raisides, Personnel Manager. **World Wide Web address:** http://www.aeilogistics.com. **Description:** An international freight forwarder serving customers in over 135 countries. **Corporate headquarters location:** This Location.

AMR CORPORATION
AMERICAN AIRLINES
P.O. Box 619616, Mail Drop 5106, Dallas Fort-Worth Airport TX 75261-9616. 817/963-1234. **Contact:** Human Resources Department. **World Wide Web address:** http://www.amrcorp.com. **Description:** An airline holding company. AMR Corporation's fleet consists of approximately 665 aircraft. **NOTE:** For positions other than flight attendants or pilots, request an application from American Airlines, Inc., P.O. Box 619040, Mail Drop 4146, Dallas Fort-Worth Airport TX 75261-9040. Send a self-addressed, 9-by-12 inch envelope with postage. **Common positions include:** Accountant; Customer Service Rep.; Electrical Engineer; Marketing Specialist; Sales Rep. **Educational backgrounds include:** Aviation. **Corporate headquarters location:** This Location. **Subsidiaries include:** American Airlines provides service to 106 domestic cities and 66 cities worldwide. Domestic hubs are located in Dallas-Fort Worth, Chicago, Nashville, San Juan, Raleigh-Durham, and Miami. SABRE Group conducts computer reservation operations and provides electronic data processing, information management, and computer services to clients in several industries. American Eagle Airlines is an airline that serves 170 cities in the U.S., Bahamas, and Caribbean. **Listed on:** New York Stock Exchange. **Number of employees at this location:** 27,000. **Number of employees nationwide:** 124,000.

ABILENE AERO INC.
2850 Airport Boulevard, Abilene TX 79602. 915/677-2601. **Fax:** 915/671-8018. **Contact:** Mr. Joe Crawford, General Manager. **World Wide Web address:** http://www.abileneaero.com. **Description:** Operates a small airport offering flight instruction, charter and pilot service, aircraft fueling, parts, and maintenance. Founded in 1968. **Common positions include:** Accountant; Aircraft Mechanic/Engine Specialist; Customer Service Representative; General Manager; Sales Manager; Secretary. **Benefits:** 401(k); Medical Insurance; Profit Sharing.

Corporate headquarters location: This Location. **Subsidiaries include:** Lubbock Aero, Lubbock TX. **Annual sales/revenues:** $5 - $10 million. **Number of employees at this location:** 35.

ACE DORAN HAULING & RIGGING CO.
1601 Blue Rock Street, Cincinnati OH 45223. 513/681-7900. **Fax:** 513/681-7908. **Contact:** Human Resources. **Description:** Provides truck transportation of heavy and specialized commodities such as steel, aluminum, self-propelled vehicles in excess of 15,000 pounds, and construction equipment. **Common positions include:** Accountant/Auditor; Administrator; Attorney; Claim Representative; Computer Programmer; Credit Manager; Customer Service Representative; Transportation/Traffic Specialist. **Educational backgrounds include:** Accounting; Business Administration; Communications; Computer Science; Economics; Finance; Marketing. **Benefits:** 401(k); Disability Coverage; Life Insurance; Medical Insurance.

AIR FRANCE
125 West 55th Street, New York NY 10019. 212/830-4000. **Contact:** Human Resources. **E-mail address:** mail.resume@airfrance.fr. **World Wide Web address:** http://www.airfrance.com. **Description:** An international airline. This location also hires seasonally. Founded in 1933. **NOTE:** Part-time jobs and second and third shifts are offered. **Common positions include:** Account Manager; Account Representative; Accountant; Administrative Assistant; Computer Programmer; Network/Systems Administrator; Sales Executive; Sales Manager; Sales Representative; Typist/Word Processor; Web Advertising Specialist. **Educational backgrounds include:** Accounting; Business Administration; Engineering; Finance; Liberal Arts; Marketing; Microsoft Office; Microsoft Word. **Benefits:** 401(k); Casual Dress - Fridays; Dental Insurance; Disability Coverage; Employee Discounts; Life Insurance; Medical Insurance; Public Transit Available; Relocation Assistance; Savings Plan; Sick Days (11+); Vacation Days (6 - 10). **Special programs:** Co-ops. **Corporate headquarters location:** Paris, France. **Number of employees at this location:** 830. **Number of employees worldwide:** 49,000.

AIR INDIA
570 Lexington Avenue, New York NY 10022. 212/407-1300. **Fax:** 212/838-9533. **Contact:** Personnel Manager. **World Wide Web address:** http://www.airindia.com. **Description:** An international airline with routes to major cities throughout the world. **Corporate headquarters location:** This Location.

AIR WISCONSIN AIRLINES CORP.
W6390 Challenger Drive, Suite 203, Appleton WI 54914-9120. 920/739-5123. **Contact:** Lisa Conover, Director of Human Resources. **Description:** Provides air transportation services. **Corporate headquarters location:** This Location.

AIRBORNE EXPRESS
3101 Western Avenue, Seattle WA 98121. 206/830-4600. **Contact:** Recruiting and Placement. **World Wide Web address:** http://www.airborne-express.com. **Description:** A domestic and international air express, air, and ocean freight services company. Operations include both domestic and international door-to-door, next-day delivery, and door-to-airport freight services. Airborne Express operates a fleet of more than 14,000 delivery vehicles. **Common positions include:** Aircraft Mechanic/Engine Specialist; Computer Programmer; Customer Service Representative; Driver; Industrial Engineer; Quality Control Supervisor; Services Sales Representative; Software Engineer; Supervisor; Systems Analyst; Telemarketer. **Educational backgrounds include:** Business Administration; Computer Science; Engineering; Liberal Arts; Marketing. **Benefits:** 401(k); Dental Insurance; Disability Coverage; Employee Discounts; Life Insurance; Medical Insurance; Pension Plan; Profit Sharing; Savings Plan; Tuition Assistance; Vision Insurance. **Corporate headquarters location:** This Location. **Listed on:** New York Stock Exchange. **Number of employees at this location:** 1,300. **Number of employees nationwide:** 16,500.

ALAMO RENT-A-CAR
P.O. Box 22776, Fort Lauderdale FL 33305. 954/522-0000. **Contact:** Recruitment. **Description:** One of the nation's leading car rental companies. **Common positions include:** Accountant/Auditor; Computer Programmer; Customer Service Representative; Financial Analyst; Secretary. **Educational backgrounds include:** Accounting; Business Administration; Computer Science; Finance; Marketing. **Benefits:** 401(k); Dental Insurance; Employee Discounts; Life Insurance; Medical Insurance; Tuition Assistance. **Corporate headquarters location:** This Location. **Listed on:** Privately held.

ALEXANDER & BALDWIN, INC.
P.O. Box 3440, Honolulu HI 96801-3440. 808/525-6611. **Contact:** John Gasher, Vice President of Human Resources. **World Wide Web address:** http://www.alexanderbaldwin.com. **Description:** Alexander & Baldwin, through its subsidiaries, is involved in ocean transportation, property development and management, trucking and storage, and sugar production and refinement. **Corporate headquarters location:** This Location. **Other U.S. locations:** Crokett CA; San Francisco CA; Kauai HI; Maui HI. **Subsidiaries include:** Matson Navigation offers a shuttle service across the Pacific serving ports in the continental U.S. and Canada, the Marshall Islands, and Johnston Island; Matson Terminals; Matson Services; Matson Leasing is one of the world's largest leasing companies involved in marine containers with 145,000 units; Matson Intermodal System; Hawaiian Commercial & Sugar; McBryde Sugar; A&B Hawaii; Kahului Trucking & Storage; East Maui Irrigation Company; Kauai Commercial Company; California & Hawaiian Sugar Company.

ALLIANCE SHIPPERS, INC.
15515 South 70th Court, Orland Park IL 60462. 708/802-7000. **Contact:** Manager. **World Wide Web address:** http://www.alliance.com. **Description:** Transports packages for businesses and consumers throughout the world. **Corporate headquarters location:** This Location.

ALLIED VAN LINES
215 West Diehl Road, Naperville IL 60563. 630/717-3150. **Fax:** 630/717-3164. **Contact:** Human Resources. **World Wide Web address:** http://www.alliedvan.com. **Description:** A moving company whose major markets are household goods moving and specialized transportation services. **Common positions include:** Transportation/Traffic Specialist. **Benefits:** Dental Insurance; Life Insurance; Medical Insurance; Pension Plan; Profit Sharing; Savings Plan; Tuition Assistance. **Corporate headquarters location:** This Location. **Parent company:** NFC (London, England).

AMERICAN BUS ASSOCIATION
1100 New York Avenue NW, Suite 1050, Washington DC 20005-3934. 202/842-1645.

Contact: Human Resources. **World Wide Web address:** http://www.buses.org. **Description:** An organization representing the inter-city busing industry. **Common positions include:** Administrative Worker/Clerk; Advertising Clerk; Public Relations Specialist. **Educational backgrounds include:** Business Administration; Communications; Liberal Arts. **Benefits:** Dental Insurance; Life Insurance; Medical Insurance; Pension Plan; Tuition Assistance. **Corporate headquarters location:** This Location.

AMERICAN CANADIAN CARIBBEAN LINE
P.O. Box 368, Warren RI 02885. 401/247-0955. **Fax:** 401/247-2350. **Contact:** Personnel Director. **World Wide Web address:** http://www.accl-smallships.com. **Description:** A small-ship cruise line sailing to domestic and foreign ports. **Common positions include:** Chef/Cook/Kitchen Worker; Cruise Director; Engineer; Ship's Captain; Ship's Deckhand; Ship's Mate; Stewardess. **Corporate headquarters location:** This Location. **Listed on:** Privately held.

AMERICAN CLASSIC VOYAGES CO.
Robin Street Wharf, 1380 Port of New Orleans Place, New Orleans LA 70130-1890. 504/586-0631. **Contact:** Vice President of Human Resources. **World Wide Web address:** http://www.amcv.com. **Description:** Owns and operates cruise lines. **Subsidiaries include:** The Delta Queen Steamboat Co.; Delta Queen Coastal Voyages; American Hawaii Cruises; United States Lines.

AMERICAN COMMERCIAL LINES HOLDINGS
P.O. Box 610, Jeffersonville IN 47130. 812/288-0100. **Fax:** 812/288-0413. **Contact:** Angie Sheckell, Human Resources Specialist. **World Wide Web address:** http://www.acbl.net. **Description:** A large, diversified transportation network operating in North and South America. American Commercial Lines Holdings also operates marine construction facilities and river terminals, and provides communications and repair services. **NOTE:** Entry-level positions, part-time jobs, and second and third shifts are offered. **Common positions include:** Accountant; Administrative Assistant; Attorney; Buyer; Computer Programmer; Computer Support Technician; Draftsperson; Financial Analyst; General Manager; Human Resources Manager; Industrial Engineer; Industrial Production Manager; Management Trainee; Operations Manager; Production Manager; Project Manager; Purchasing Agent/Manager; Quality Control Supervisor; Sales Manager; Secretary. **Educational backgrounds include:** Accounting; Business Administration; C/C++; Computer Science; Engineering; MCSE; Novell; Visual Basic. **Benefits:** 401(k); Casual Dress - Fridays; Dental Insurance; Disability Coverage; Life Insurance; Medical Insurance; Pension Plan; Savings Plan; Sick Days (6 - 10); Tuition Assistance. **Special programs:** Internships. **Corporate headquarters location:** This Location. **Other U.S. locations:** New Orleans LA; St. Louis MO. **International locations:** Argentina; Venezuela. **Subsidiaries include:** ACBL; ACT; Jeffboat; Louisiana Dock Company; Watercom. **Parent company:** CSX Corporation. **President/CEO:** Michael Hagan. **Facilities Manager:** Debbie Rice. **Number of employees at this location:** 300. **Number of employees nationwide:** 3,760. **Number of employees worldwide:** 4,030.

AMERICAN EXPRESS TRAVEL RELATED SERVICES
100 Cambridge Park Drive, Cambridge MA 02140. 617/868-9800. **Fax:** 617/349-1042. **Contact:** Recruiter. **World Wide Web address:** http://www.americanexpress.com. **Description:** A full-service travel agency. Founded in 1850. **Common positions include:** Accountant/Auditor; Computer Programmer; Travel Agent. **Benefits:** 401(k); Dental Insurance; Disability Coverage; Employee Discounts; Life Insurance; Medical Insurance; Tuition Assistance. **Corporate headquarters location:** This Location. **Parent company:** American Express is a diversified travel and financial services company operating in 160 countries. The company offers consumers Personal, Gold, and Platinum credit cards, as well as revolving credit products such as Optima Cards, which allow customers to extend payments. American Express Financial Advisors provides a variety of financial products and services to help individuals, businesses, and institutions establish and achieve financial goals. This company also employs more than 8,000 financial advisors in the United States and offers products and services that include: financial planning, annuities, mutual funds, insurance, investment certificates; and institutional investment advisory trust, tax preparation, and retail securities brokerage services. American Express Bank seeks to meet the financial services needs of wealthy entrepreneurs and local financial service institutions through a global network of offices in 37 countries. **Listed on:** Privately held. **Number of employees at this location:** 600. **Number of employees nationwide:** 3,700.

AMERICAN FREIGHTWAYS INC.
P.O. Box 840, Harrison AR 72601. 870/741-9000. **Fax:** 870/741-3003. **Contact:** Human Resources. **Description:** A trucking company providing scheduled, all-points, regional small shipment carrier service. The truckers ship a wide range of general commodities. The company uses its own drivers, equipment, and documentation process. **Common positions include:** Accountant/Auditor; Aircraft Mechanic/Engine Specialist; Automotive Mechanic; Budget Analyst; Claim Representative; Clerical Supervisor; Computer Operator; Computer Programmer; Customer Service Representative; Dispatcher; Management Trainee; Payroll Clerk; Printing Press Operator; Receptionist; Systems Analyst; Transportation/Traffic Specialist; Truck Driver. **Educational backgrounds include:** Accounting; Business Administration; Communications; Finance; Marketing; Transportation/Logistics. **Benefits:** 401(k); Dental Insurance; Disability Coverage; Employee Discounts; Life Insurance; Medical Insurance; Savings Plan; Tuition Assistance. **Corporate headquarters location:** This Location. **Other U.S. locations:** Nationwide. **Listed on:** NASDAQ. **Annual sales/revenues:** More than $100 million. **Number of employees nationwide:** 7,200.

AMERICAN TRUCKING ASSOCIATIONS
2200 Mill Road, Alexandria VA 22314. 703/838-1726. **Fax:** 703/836-5880. **Contact:** Kay Perkins, Director of Human Resources. **World Wide Web address:** http://www.trucking.org. **Description:** This national federation of the trucking industry represents all types of trucking companies. It is affiliated with 51 independent state trucking associations and 14 national conferences, which represent different segments of the trucking industry. American Trucking Associations consists of the Executive Office, the Foundation, and five divisions: Communications; Federation Relations; Law and Finance; Government Affairs; and Membership and Marketing. The association also publishes *Transport Topics*, a weekly trade newspaper. **Common positions include:** Customer Service Representative; Marketing Specialist; Transportation/Traffic Specialist; Writer. **Educational backgrounds include:** Accounting;

Business Administration; Communications; Economics; Finance; Marketing; Public Policy; Transportation/Logistics. **Benefits:** Dental Insurance; Disability Coverage; Employee Discounts; Life Insurance; Medical Insurance; Pension Plan; Tuition Assistance. **Corporate headquarters location:** This Location. **Number of employees nationwide:** 320.

ANCRA INTERNATIONAL LLC
4880 West Rosecrans Avenue, Hawthorne CA 90250. 310/973-5000. **Contact:** Tammy Carson, Human Resources Administrator. **World Wide Web address:** http://www.ancra-llc.com. **Description:** Manufactures cargo restraint equipment for the trucking and aircraft industries including aircraft fittings, winches, cam buckles, o/c buckles, shoring beams, cargo systems, and track. Ancra also maintains off-road and marine divisions. **Common positions include:** Accountant/Auditor; Customer Service Representative; Manufacturer's/Wholesaler's Sales Rep.; Manufacturing Engineer; Marketing Specialist; Operations/Production Manager; Purchasing Agent/Manager; Quality Control Supervisor. **Educational backgrounds include:** Accounting; Business Administration; Engineering; Finance; Liberal Arts; Marketing. **Benefits:** 401(k); Casual Dress - Fridays; Credit Union; Dental Insurance; Disability Coverage; Life Insurance; Medical Insurance; Tuition Assistance. **Corporate headquarters location:** This Location.

ARKANSAS BEST CORPORATION
P.O. Box 10048, Fort Smith AR 72917. 501/785-6000. **Contact:** Human Resources. **World Wide Web address:** http://www.arkbest.com. **Description:** Provides trucking and shipping services nationwide. **Common positions include:** Industrial Engineer; Management Trainee; Sales Representative. **Educational backgrounds include:** Business Administration; Transportation/Logistics. **Benefits:** 401(k); Dental Insurance; Disability Coverage; Life Insurance; Medical Insurance; Pension Plan; Tuition Assistance. **Corporate headquarters location:** This Location. **Other U.S. locations:** Nationwide. **Listed on:** NASDAQ. **Number of employees at this location:** 300. **Number of employees nationwide:** 10,500.

ATLANTIC COAST AIRLINES HOLDINGS
515A Shaw Road, Dulles VA 20166. 703/925-6000. **Contact:** Director of Human Resources. **World Wide Web address:** http://www.atlanticcoast.com. **Description:** One of the largest regional airlines operating in the United States, flying to 51 destinations in 24 states with approximately 560 scheduled departures each weekday. Atlantic Coast Airlines, operating as United Express, serves the eastern United States in the areas between Maine, Ohio, and South Carolina, from its hub at Dulles International Airport. **Corporate headquarters location:** This Location. **Listed on:** NASDAQ. **Number of employees nationwide:** 1,240.

ATLANTIC SOUTHEAST AIRLINES (ASA)
100 Hartsfield Center Parkway, Suite 800, Atlanta GA 30354-1356. 404/765-2000. **Contact:** Delta Employment Office. **World Wide Web address:** http://www.asa-air.com. **Description:** One of Atlanta's largest regional airlines and a Delta connection carrier. Founded in 1979. **NOTE:** Jobseekers can request an application by sending a self-addressed, stamped envelope to this location. **Corporate headquarters location:** This Location. **Parent company:** Delta Air Lines.

ATLAS VAN LINES, INC.
1212 St. George Road, Evansville IN 47711. 812/424-4326. **Fax:** 812/421-7125. **Contact:**

Patricia Walter, Assistant Vice President of Human Resources. **World Wide Web address:** http://www.atlasvanlines.com. **Description:** A worldwide common carrier, principally engaged in the transportation of used household goods, general commodities, special products, and freight forwarding. **Common positions include:** Accountant/Auditor; Adjuster; Budget Analyst; Claim Representative; Clerical Supervisor; Computer Operator; Computer Programmer; Customer Service Representative; Department Manager; Dispatcher; Financial Manager; Insurance Agent/Broker; Order Clerk; Payroll Clerk; Public Relations Specialist; Receptionist; Secretary; Systems Analyst; Transportation/Traffic Specialist; Travel Agent; Typist/Word Processor. **Educational backgrounds include:** Accounting; Business Administration; Communications; Computer Science; Finance; Liberal Arts; Marketing; Mathematics. **Benefits:** Dental Insurance; Disability Coverage; Life Insurance; Medical Insurance; Pension Plan; Tuition Assistance. **Corporate headquarters location:** This Location. **Number of employees at this location:** 430.

AVANT SERVICES CORPORATION
420 Lexington Avenue, New York NY 10170. 212/867-6845. **Fax:** 212/370-1452. **Contact:** Timothy Downs, Personnel Manager. **Description:** A delivery company. **NOTE:** Entry-level positions, part-time jobs, and second and third shifts are offered. **Common positions include:** Administrative Assistant; Assistant Manager; Driver; Human Resources Manager. **Special programs:** Summer Jobs.

AVIS GROUP HOLDINGS INC.
900 Old Country Road, Garden City NY 11530. 516/222-3000. **Toll-free phone:** 888/AVIS-270. **Contact:** Human Resources Department. **World Wide Web address:** http://www.avis.com. **Description:** A global leader in car rental services. Avis completes approximately 15 million rental transactions annually with a fleet of approximately 220,000 vehicles. Avis also provides leasing and management services. **Common positions include:** Architect; Auditor; Business Analyst; Customer Service Representative; Examiner; Executive Assistant; Financial Analyst; Human Resources Specialist; Marketing Specialist. **Educational backgrounds include:** Accounting; Business Administration; Communications; Computer Science; Finance; Hospitality; Liberal Arts; Marketing; Mathematics; Operations Research. **Benefits:** 401(k); Dental Insurance; Disability Coverage; EAP; Employee Discounts; Life Insurance; Medical Insurance; Pension Plan; Tuition Assistance. **Corporate headquarters location:** This Location. **International locations:** Argentina; Australia; Canada; New Zealand; Puerto Rico; U.S. Virgin Islands.

BEKINS VAN LINES
330 South Mannheim Road, Hillside IL 60162. 708/547-2000. **Fax:** 708/547-3478. **Contact:** Human Resources. **World Wide Web address:** http://www.bekins.com. **Description:** A moving and storage company. **Common positions include:** Account Representative; Accountant/Auditor; Adjuster; Administrative Assistant; Administrative Manager; Computer Programmer; Customer Service Representative; Database Manager; Financial Analyst; MIS Specialist; Project Manager; Sales Executive; Secretary; Systems Analyst. **Educational backgrounds include:** Accounting; Business Administration. **Benefits:** 401(k); Dental Insurance; Disability Coverage; Financial Planning Assistance; Life Insurance; Medical Insurance; Referral Bonus Plan; Tuition Assistance. **Corporate**

headquarters location: This Location. **Parent company:** The Bekins Company. **Listed on:** Privately held. **Annual sales/revenues:** More than $100 million. **Number of employees at this location:** 370.

BERTRAM YACHT, INC.
P.O. Box 520774 GMF, Miami FL 33152. 305/633-8011. **Contact:** Manager of Human Resources. **Description:** A manufacturer of yachts. **Common positions include:** Buyer; Computer Programmer; Draftsperson; Electrical/Electronics Engineer; Electrician; Financial Analyst; Human Resources Manager; Mechanical Engineer; Operations/Production Manager; Quality Control Supervisor; Structural Engineer; Systems Analyst. **Educational backgrounds include:** Accounting; Engineering; Finance; Marketing. **Benefits:** Dental Insurance; Disability Coverage; Life Insurance; Medical Insurance; Pension Plan; Savings Plan; Tuition Assistance. **Corporate headquarters location:** This Location. **Parent company:** Bertram, Inc. **Number of employees at this location:** 240.

BOATU.S.
880 South Pickett Street, Alexandria VA 22304. 703/823-9550. **Fax:** 703/461-4395. **Contact:** Evelyn Matey, Director of Human Resources. **World Wide Web address:** http://www.boatus.com. **Description:** One of the largest national associations of recreational boat owners. BoatU.S. provides marine insurance to its members, representation in Congress, water towing services, and discount boating equipment. Founded in 1966. **Common positions include:** Adjuster; Management Trainee; Technical Writer/Editor; Underwriter/Assistant Underwriter. **Educational backgrounds include:** Business Administration; Liberal Arts; Marketing. **Benefits:** 401(k); Dental Insurance; Employee Discounts; ESOP; Life Insurance; Medical Insurance; Tuition Assistance. **Corporate headquarters location:** This Location. **Number of employees at this location:** 500. **Number of employees nationwide:** 1,000.

BOWDEN TRAVEL SERVICE
CLEBURNE TRAVEL
410 West Chambers, Cleburne TX 76031. 817/641-3477. **Contact:** Human Resources. **Description:** A travel agency. **Common positions include:** Sales Executive; Transportation/Traffic Specialist. **Annual sales/revenues:** Less than $5 million. **Number of employees at this location:** 4.

BUDGET GROUP, INC.
125 Basin Street, Daytona Beach FL 32114. 904/238-7035. **Contact:** Human Resources. **World Wide Web address:** http://www.bgi.com. **Description:** A holding company. **Corporate headquarters location:** This Location. **Subsidiaries include:** Budget Airport Parking; Budget Rent A Car Corporation; Budget Car Sales, Inc.; Cruise America, Inc.; Premier Car Rental; Ryder TRS, Inc.; Van Pool Services, Inc.

BURLINGTON NORTHERN AND SANTA FE RAILWAY COMPANY
2650 Lou Menk Drive, Fort Worth TX 76131. 817/333-2000. **Contact:** Human Resources. **World Wide Web address:** http://www.bnsf.com. **Description:** A railroad transportation company operating on 24,500 miles of track in 25 western states and two Canadian provinces. The company is one of the largest haulers of low-sulfur coal and grain in North America. **Corporate headquarters location:** This Location. **Listed on:** New York Stock Exchange. **Annual sales/revenues:** More than $100 million.

BURRIS FOODS, INC.
P.O. Box 219, Milford DE 19963. 302/839-4531. **Fax:** 302/839-7588. **Contact:** Human Resources. **Description:** A frozen food distributor and warehouser. **Corporate headquarters location:** This Location. **Subsidiaries include:** Burris Retail Food Systems.

CCAIR, INC.
dba US AIRWAYS EXPRESS
P.O. Box 19929, Charlotte NC 28219-0929. **Toll-free phone:** 800/868-2515. **Fax:** 704/359-4575. **Contact:** Supervisor of Hiring. **Description:** An air carrier providing regularly scheduled passenger service to 25 cities in Alabama, Georgia, Kentucky, Maryland, Ohio, North Carolina, South Carolina, Virginia, and West Virginia, primarily from a hub at Charlotte/Douglas International Airport. The company operates a fleet of 26 turbo-prop, passenger aircraft with approximately 1,391 weekly departures over a 230,000 mile radius. The company provides services for business travelers from small and medium-sized communities in its market area to connecting flights of major carriers, principally US Airways, Inc. In addition, the company operates a small number of flights to US Airways Express's Baltimore hub and Raleigh NC location. **Common positions include:** Customer Service Representative. **Educational backgrounds include:** Communications; Public Relations. **Benefits:** 401(k); Dental Insurance; Employee Discounts; Life Insurance; Medical Insurance. **Corporate headquarters location:** This Location. **Parent company:** Mesa Air Group, Inc. **Listed on:** NASDAQ. **Number of employees nationwide:** 600.

CNF TRANSPORTATION CORPORATION
3240 Hillview Avenue, Palo Alto CA 94304. 650/494-2900. **Contact:** Personnel. **World Wide Web address:** http://www.cnf.com. **Description:** A motor freight carrier and air freight forwarder operating in all 50 states. Operations include import/export brokerage, overseas forwarding, and warehousing and distribution services. **Corporate headquarters location:** This Location. **Listed on:** New York Stock Exchange. **Number of employees nationwide:** 33,700.

CSX CORPORATION
P.O. Box 85629, Richmond VA 23285-5629. 804/782-1400. **Physical address:** 901 East Cary Street, Richmond VA. **Contact:** Linda Amato, Manager of Human Resources. **World Wide Web address:** http://www.csx.com. **Description:** An operator of container ship lines, railcars, and barges. CSX also provides intermodal and logistics services, operates two resorts, and conducts real estate activities. The company's rail system consists of 18,779 miles of track in 20 states and Ontario, Canada. **Corporate headquarters location:** This Location. **Subsidiaries include:** Sea-Land Service, which conducts operations in 100 ports in 70 countries with 83 vessels and over 160,000 containers; CSX Intermodal, Inc.; CTI; and American Commercial Lines which has a fleet of 3,353 barges and 123 tug boats. **Listed on:** New York Stock Exchange. **Annual sales/revenues:** More than $100 million.

CTI
10407 Centurion Parkway North, Suite 400, Jacksonville FL 32256. 904/928-1400. **Toll-free phone:** 888/LOGISTX. **Fax:** 904/928-1547. **Contact:** Recruiter. **World Wide Web address:** http://www.cti-logistics.com. **Description:** A third party logistics provider. Founded in 1980. **NOTE:** Entry-level positions and second and third shifts are offered. **Common positions include:** Accountant; Administrative Assistant; Applications Engineer;

AS400 Programmer Analyst; Attorney; Auditor; Clerical Supervisor; Computer Operator; Computer Programmer; Computer Technician; Cost Estimator; Credit Manager; Customer Service Manager; Database Administrator; Financial Analyst; Help-Desk Technician; Industrial Engineer; Internet Services Manager; Management Trainee; Network Engineer; Network/Systems Administrator; Operations Manager; Project Manager; Purchasing Agent/Manager; Quality Control Supervisor; Sales Executive; Secretary; Software Engineer; SQL Programmer; Systems Analyst; Systems Manager; Technical Support Manager; Transportation/Traffic Specialist; Website Developer. **Educational backgrounds include:** Accounting; AS400 Certification; Business Administration; C/C++; Computer Science; Engineering; Finance; Internet Development; MCSE; Microsoft Office; Microsoft Word; Software Development; Software Tech. Support; Spreadsheets; SQL; Visual Basic. **Benefits:** 401(k); Dental Insurance; Disability Coverage; Employee Discounts; Life Insurance; Medical Insurance; Pension Plan; Tuition Assistance. **Special programs:** Internships; Training. **Corporate headquarters location:** This Location. **International locations:** Argentina; Brazil; United Kingdom. **Parent company:** CSX Corporation. **Annual sales/revenues:** More than $100 million. **Number of employees at this location:** 200.

CAPITAL METRO
2910 East Fifth Street, Austin TX 78702. 512/389-7400. **Contact:** Personnel. **World Wide Web address:** http://www.capmetro.austin.tx.us. **Description:** Operates the public bus system for the metropolitan Austin area. **Corporate headquarters location:** This Location.

CAREY LIMOUSINE OF BOSTON
163 Adams Street, Braintree MA 02184. 617/623-8700. **Contact:** Kevin Muldenatto, General Manager. **Description:** A limousine service and executive travel specialist. Carey Limousine offers services for business meetings, airport transfers, dinner/theater events, weddings, and sightseeing activities. **Common positions include:** Accountant/Auditor; Automotive Mechanic; Chauffeur; Dispatcher; Reservationist; Services Sales Representative; Transportation/Traffic Specialist. **Benefits:** Medical Insurance; Profit Sharing. **Corporate headquarters location:** This Location. **Parent company:** Carey International. **Listed on:** Privately held. **Number of employees at this location:** 50.

CARLSON COMPANIES, INC.
CARLSON MARKETING GROUP
P.O. Box 59159, Minneapolis MN 55459-8246. 612/540-5000. **Contact:** Mr. Vern Lovstad, Human Resources. **World Wide Web address:** http://www.carlson.com. **Description:** A highly diversified corporation doing business through a variety of subsidiaries. Business areas include hotels, restaurant operations, and retail and wholesale travel. Carlson Marketing Group (also at this location) provides a variety of marketing services for sporting events and airlines; incentive programs for employees of other companies; and strategic consulting to help client companies create customer/brand loyalty. **Corporate headquarters location:** This Location. **Number of employees nationwide:** 50,000.

CATALINA YACHTS INC.
21200 Victory Boulevard, Woodland Hills CA 91367-2522. 818/884-7700. **Fax:** 818/884-3810. **Contact:** Human Resources. **World Wide Web address:** http://www.catalina.net. **Description:**

Manufactures yachts. **Corporate headquarters location:** This Location.

CELADON GROUP, INC.
9503 East 33rd Street, Indianapolis IN 46235. 317/972-7000. **Fax:** 317/897-8845. **Contact:** Rick Stewart, Human Resources Director. **World Wide Web address:** http://www.celadontrucking.com. **Description:** An international truckload carrier specializing in freight shipments between the U.S., Canada, and Mexico. **Common positions include:** Accountant; Administrative Assistant; AS400 Programmer Analyst; Claim Representative; Customer Service Representative; Human Resources Manager; Marketing Specialist; MIS Specialist; Network/Systems Administrator; Transportation/Traffic Specialist; Webmaster. **Corporate headquarters location:** This Location. **Other U.S. locations:** Laredo TX. **Subsidiaries include:** Cheetah Transportation (Mooresville NC); Gerth Transportation (Ontario, Canada); Jaguar Transportation (Mexico); and Zipp Express (Indianapolis IN). **President:** Stephen Russell. **Information Systems Manager:** Mike Gobbei. **Sales Manager:** Dave Gibbs. **Annual sales/revenues:** More than $100 million.

CELEBRITY CRUISES
1050 Caribbean Way, Miami FL 33132. 305/262-6677. **Contact:** Human Resources. **Description:** Operates an ocean cruise line. **Corporate headquarters location:** This Location.

CENDANT CORPORATION
9 West 57th Street, 37th Floor, New York NY 10019. 212/413-1800. **Contact:** Human Resources. **World Wide Web address:** http://www.cendant.com. **Description:** Provides a wide range of business services including dining services, hotel franchise management, mortgage programs, and timeshare exchanges. Cendant Corporation's Real Estate Division offers employee relocation and mortgage services through Century 21, Coldwell Banker, ERA, Cendant Mortgage, and Cendant Mobility. The Travel Division provides car rentals, vehicle management services, and vacation timeshares through brand names including Avis, Days Inn, Howard Johnson, Ramada, Travelodge, and Super 8. The Membership Division offers travel, shopping, auto, dining, and other financial services through Travelers Advantage, Shoppers Advantage, Auto Vantage, Welcome Wagon, Netmarket, North American Outdoor Group, and PrivacyGuard. Founded in 1997. **NOTE:** Resumes should be sent to Human Resources, Cendant Corporation, 6 Sylvan Way, Parsippany NJ 07054. **Corporate headquarters location:** This Location. **Number of employees worldwide:** 28,000. **Other U.S. locations:**
- 6 Sylvan Way, Parsippany NJ 07054. 973/428-9700.

CENTRAL PARKING CORPORATION
2401 21st Avenue South, Suite 200, Nashville TN 37212. 615/297-4255. **Contact:** Human Resources. **Description:** A leading provider of parking services in the United States. The company operates over 1,200 parking facilities in 34 states, and the District of Columbia. The company provides management services to multilevel parking facilities and surface lots. Central Parking Corporation also provides parking consulting services, shuttle services, valet services, parking meter enforcement services, and billing and collection services. **Corporate headquarters location:** This Location. **Other U.S. locations:** Nationwide. **International locations:** Chile; Germany; Ireland; Malaysia; Mexico; Puerto Rico; Spain; the Netherlands; United Kingdom. **Listed on:** New York Stock Exchange. **Stock**

exchange symbol: CPC. **Chairman and CEO:** Monroe J. Carell, Jr. **Annual sales/revenues:** More than $100 million.

CHIPMAN CORPORATION
1521 Buena Vista Avenue, Alameda CA 94501. 510/748-8700. **Contact:** Human Resources. **World Wide Web address:** http://www.chipmancorp.com. **Description:** Provides moving and storage services both domestically and internationally. **Corporate headquarters location:** This Location.

COLLINS INDUSTRIES, INC.
15 Compound Drive, Hutchinson KS 67502. 316/663-5551. **Fax:** 316/663-1630. **Contact:** Jack Cowden, Vice President of Human Resources. **Description:** Designs, manufactures, and sells specialty vehicles and accessories for various service niches of the transportation industry. Collins Industries is one of the world's largest manufacturers of ambulances and a leader in the production of small school buses, transit buses, terminal trucks, and wheelchair lifts. Founded in 1971. **Common positions include:** Accountant; Buyer; Controller; Customer Service Representative; Design Engineer; Draftsperson; Emergency Medical Technician; General Manager; Industrial Engineer; Industrial Production Manager; Marketing Manager; Production Manager; Sales Manager; Sales Representative. **Educational backgrounds include:** Accounting; Business Administration; Engineering; Finance; Marketing. **Benefits:** 401(k); Dental Insurance; Disability Coverage; Life Insurance; Medical Insurance; Profit Sharing; Tuition Assistance. **Corporate headquarters location:** This Location. **Subsidiaries include:** Capacity of Texas, Inc.; Collins Bus Corporation; Wheeled Coach Industries. **Listed on:** NASDAQ. **Annual sales/revenues:** More than $100 million. **Number of employees nationwide:** 950.

CON-WAY TRUCKLOAD SERVICES, INC.
2322 Gravel Drive, Fort Worth TX 76118. 817/284-7800. **Contact:** Jerry Casey, Director of Personnel. **Description:** Provides expanded services for over-the-road truckload transportation. As a full-service, multimodal truckload logistics company, its capabilities include expedited regional and transcontinental highway operations with drivers and company-owned trucks and trailers. CWT also retains the flexibility to offer its domestic intermodal operations. This service, marketed as the Con-Quest Premium Truckload Service, utilizes CWT's national long-haul alliances to provide time-definite, intermodal truckload transportation. In addition, the company continues to offer basic intermodal marketing services, local and interstate container drayage, and international LCL shipping with its GlobalRate program. **Common positions include:** Accountant/Auditor; Brokerage Clerk; Clerical Supervisor; Customer Service Representative; Operations/Production Manager; Services Sales Representative. **Educational backgrounds include:** Accounting; Business Administration; Marketing. **Benefits:** 401(k); Dental Insurance; Disability Coverage; Life Insurance; Medical Insurance; Pension Plan; Profit Sharing; Savings Plan; Tuition Assistance. **Corporate headquarters location:** This Location. **Parent company:** Con-Way Transportation Services. **Listed on:** New York Stock Exchange. **Number of employees at this location:** 140. **Number of employees nationwide:** 300.

CONNECTICUT LIMOUSINE SERVICE
230 Old Gate Lane, Milford CT 06460. 203/878-6867. **Contact:** Human Resources. **Description:** A shuttle bus service that provides transportation to and from John F. Kennedy International Airport (New York NY); LaGuardia International Airport (New York NY); Newark International Airport (Newark NJ); and Bradley International Airport (Windsor Locks CT). **Corporate headquarters location:** This Location.

CONSOLIDATED RAIL CORPORATION
2001 Market Street, Philadelphia PA 19101-1600. 215/209-5099. **Contact:** Human Resources. **World Wide Web address:** http://www.conrail.com. **Description:** A railroad company. **Corporate headquarters location:** This Location.

CONTINENTAL AIRLINES
1600 Smith Street, Houston TX 77002-4330. 713/324-4700. **Fax:** 713/324-5382. **Contact:** Human Resources. **World Wide Web address:** http://www.continental.com. **Description:** One of the largest airlines in the U.S., offering flights to 136 domestic and 86 international locations daily. Operating through its major hubs in Newark, Houston, and Cleveland, Continental offers extensive service to Latin America and Europe. Founded in 1934. **NOTE:** Entry-level positions and second and third shifts are offered. **Common positions include:** Accountant; Administrative Assistant; Computer Programmer; Computer Technician; Help-Desk Technician; Secretary. **Benefits:** 401(k); Daycare Assistance; Dental Insurance; Disability Coverage; Employee Discounts; Life Insurance; Medical Insurance; Pension Plan; Profit Sharing; Savings Plan. **Corporate headquarters location:** This Location. **Listed on:** New York Stock Exchange. **Annual sales/revenues:** More than $100 million. **Number of employees at this location:** 4,000. **Number of employees nationwide:** 50,000.

JOE CONWAY TRUCKING COMPANY
P.O. Box 1377, Glendale AZ 85311. 623/937-1684. **Contact:** Gene Cooper, President. **Description:** A trucking company. **Common positions include:** Truck Driver. **Benefits:** 401(k); Life Insurance; Medical Insurance. **Corporate headquarters location:** This Location. **Number of employees at this location:** 50.

COURTESY BUS COMPANY
107 Lawson Boulevard, Oceanside NY 11572. 516/766-6740. **Fax:** 516/678-0253. **Contact:** Personnel Office. **Description:** Provides bus service to local school districts, as well as a range of charter services through several area locations. **Common positions include:** Automotive Mechanic; Driver. **Corporate headquarters location:** This Location.

CUNARD LINE
6100 Blue Lagoon Drive, Suite 400, Miami FL 33126. 305/463-3000. **Toll-free phone:** 800/223-0764. **Fax:** 305/463-3035. **Contact:** Human Resources Department. **Description:** An ocean cruise line. **Corporate headquarters location:** This Location.

DAIMLERCHRYSLER RAIL SYSTEMS
1501 Lebanon Church Road, Pittsburgh PA 15236. 412/655-5700. **Contact:** Paul Overby, Executive Vice President of Shared Services. **Description:** A manufacturer of rapid transit systems including rail systems such as the Bay Area Rapid Transit (BART) in San Francisco CA, and conveyors found in airports and other public facilities. **Number of employees at this location:** 800.

DART TRANSIT COMPANY
P.O. Box 64110, St. Paul MN 55164-0110. **Toll-free phone:** 800/366-9000. **Fax:** 651/683-1650. **Contact:** Human Resources. **World Wide Web**

address: http://www.dartadvantage.com. **Description:** A trucking company with land-based transportation services throughout the U.S., Canada, and Mexico. **NOTE:** Entry-level positions, part-time jobs, and second and third shifts are offered. **Common positions include:** Account Manager; Account Representative; Accountant; Administrative Assistant; Blue-Collar Worker Supervisor; Clerical Supervisor; Customer Service Representative; Transportation/Traffic Specialist. **Educational backgrounds include:** Accounting; Business Administration; Marketing. **Benefits:** 401(k); Casual Dress - Fridays; Dental Insurance; Disability Coverage; Life Insurance; Medical Insurance; Profit Sharing; Sick Days (6 - 10); Vacation Days (6 - 10). **Special programs:** Internships; Summer Jobs. **Corporate headquarters location:** Eagan MN. **Other U.S. locations:** Sellersburg IN; Dallas TX. **Annual sales/revenues:** More than $100 million. **Number of employees at this location:** 225. **Number of employees nationwide:** 1,000.

DELAWARE OTSEGO CORPORATION
One Railroad Avenue, Cooperstown NY 13326-1110. 607/547-2555. **Fax:** 607/547-9834. **Contact:** Barbara Rogers, Human Resources. **Description:** Delaware Otsego Corporation is a non-rail holding company whose principal asset is the New York, Susquehanna, and Western Railway Corporation, which provides rail transportation service to customers in New York, New Jersey, and Pennsylvania. The company is also engaged in a real estate project to further develop the traffic base of the railroad. **Corporate headquarters location:** This Location.

DELTA AIR LINES
P.O. Box 20530, Atlanta GA 30320-2530. 404/715-2600. **Recorded jobline:** 800/659-2580. **Contact:** Employment Office. **World Wide Web address:** http://www.delta-air.com. **Description:** One of the largest airlines in the United States. The company provides scheduled air transportation for passengers, freight, and mail on an extensive route that covers most of the country and extends to 57 foreign nations. The route covers 153 domestic cities in 43 states, the District of Columbia, Puerto Rico, the U.S. Virgin Islands, and 57 cities abroad. Major domestic hubs include the Atlanta, Dallas/Fort Worth, Salt Lake City, and Cincinnati ports, with minor hubs located in Los Angeles and Orlando. Delta Airlines has 550 aircraft in its fleet with 125 planes on order and 233 on option. Founded in 1929. **NOTE:** Jobseekers must pick up an application at the Delta Airlines ticket counter in any airport and should then call the jobline to find out what positions are open, and in which cities jobs are available. Entry-level positions are offered. **Common positions include:** Accountant/Auditor; Aerospace Engineer; Aircraft Mechanic/Engine Specialist; Attorney; Buyer; Chemical Engineer; Computer Programmer; Customer Service Representative; Electrical/Electronics Engineer; Financial Analyst; Flight Attendant; Machinist; Mechanical Engineer; Operations Research Analyst; Pilot; Purchasing Agent/Manager; Reservationist; Secretary; Typist/Word Processor. **Educational backgrounds include:** Accounting; Business Administration; Computer Science; Economics; Engineering; Finance; Liberal Arts; Marketing; Mathematics. **Benefits:** Daycare Assistance; Dental Insurance; Disability Coverage; Employee Discounts; Flight Benefits; Life Insurance; Medical Insurance; Pension Plan; Savings Plan; Tuition Assistance. **Special programs:** Internships; Co-ops. **Corporate headquarters location:** This Location. **Listed on:** New York Stock Exchange. **Number of employees nationwide:** 73,000.

DiSALVO TRUCKING COMPANY
P.O. Box 193765, San Francisco CA 94119. 415/495-1800. **Contact:** Janet Mayer, Personnel Director. **World Wide Web address:** http://www.disalvo.com. **Description:** Operates an area trucking and trucking terminal services firm. **Corporate headquarters location:** This Location.

DORSEY TRAILERS INC.
2727 Paces Ferry Road, Building One, Suite 1700, Atlanta GA 30339. 770/438-9595. **Contact:** Human Resources. **Description:** A manufacturer of truck trailers. **NOTE:** Please send resumes to the Human Resources Department, 1409 Hickman Avenue, Elba AL 36323. **Corporate headquarters location:** This Location.

DYNAIR SERVICES INC.
Washington Dulles International Airport, 45025 Aviation Drive, Suite 350, Dulles VA 20166. 703/742-4300. **Contact:** Elaine Stott, Director of Human Resources. **Description:** Provides a wide range of ground-handling services for airlines and airports. **Common positions include:** Accountant. **Parent company:** Alpha Airports Group. **Annual sales/revenues:** More than $100 million. **Number of employees at this location:** 50. **Number of employees nationwide:** 6,000.

EZ LOADER BOAT TRAILERS INC.
P.O. Box 3263, Spokane WA 99220. 509/489-0181. **Contact:** Carol Mueller, Personnel Director. **World Wide Web address:** http://www.ezloader.com. **Description:** Manufactures boat trailers. **Common positions include:** Accountant/Auditor; Administrator; Blue-Collar Worker Supervisor; Buyer; Civil Engineer; Computer Programmer; Credit Manager; Department Manager; Financial Analyst; Industrial Engineer; Manufacturer's/Wholesaler's Sales Rep.; Mechanical Engineer; Operations/Production Manager; Purchasing Agent/Manager. **Educational backgrounds include:** Accounting; Business Administration; Computer Science; Engineering; Finance; Marketing. **Benefits:** Dental Insurance; Disability Coverage; Life Insurance; Medical Insurance; Pension Plan; Profit Sharing. **Corporate headquarters location:** This Location.

EL AL ISRAEL AIRLINES
120 West 45th Street, New York NY 10036-9998. 212/852-0625. **Contact:** Personnel Department. **Description:** An international air carrier operating a route system that includes major United States cities, and destinations in Israel, Europe, and Africa. **Corporate headquarters location:** This Location.

ENTERPRISE RENT-A-CAR
19500 Rockside Road, Bedford OH 44146. 440/786-8500. **Contact:** Human Resources. **World Wide Web address:** http://www.enterprise.com. **Description:** A car rental agency. **NOTE:** Jobseekers should send resumes to the Personnel Office at 6751 Engle Road, Suite B, Cleveland OH 44130. **Common positions include:** Account Representative; Accountant/Auditor; Adjuster; Customer Service Representative; Management Trainee. **Educational backgrounds include:** Accounting; Business Administration; Computer Science; Finance; Sales. **Benefits:** Dental Insurance; Life Insurance; Medical Insurance; Profit Sharing; Stock Option; Tuition Assistance. **Special programs:** Internships. **Corporate headquarters location:** This Location. **Listed on:** NASDAQ.

FARRELL LINES INCORPORATED
One Whitehall Street, New York NY 10004. 212/440-4402. **Contact:** Marge Nasco, Human Resources Manager. **World Wide Web address:**

http://www.farrell-lines.com. **Description:** Operates a steamship service with extensive shipping routes to the Mediterranean region, the Middle East, India, and Pakistan. **Common positions include:** Account Representative; Accountant; Buyer; Chief Financial Officer; Claim Representative; Computer Operator; Computer Support Technician; Computer Technician; Controller; Credit Manager; Customer Service Representative; Marketing Manager; MIS Specialist; Sales Executive; Sales Representative; Secretary; Transportation/Traffic Specialist. **Benefits:** 401(k); Disability Coverage; Life Insurance; Medical Insurance; Pension Plan. **Corporate headquarters location:** This Location. **Other U.S. locations:** GA; IL; MD; MI; NJ; OH; PA; SC; VA. **International locations:** Genoa, Italy; Tiblisi, Ukraine. **Listed on:** Privately held. **CEO:** George E. Lowman. **Facilities Manager:** Ulises J. Medina. **Information Systems Manager:** Spiros Zoulas. **Purchasing Manager:** Daniel Cappozalo. **Sales Manager:** Patrick Donovan. **Number of employees at this location:** 90. **Number of employees nationwide:** 140. **Number of employees worldwide:** 160.

FEDERAL EXPRESS CORP. (FEDEX)
P.O. Box 727, Memphis TN 38194-1095. 901/369-3600. **Contact:** Mark Bishop, Manager, Professional Recruiting/College Relations. **World Wide Web address:** http://www.fedex.com. **Description:** One of the world's largest express transportation companies serving 212 countries worldwide. FedEx ships approximately 3.2 million packages daily to 210 countries. FedEx operates more than 45,000 drop-off locations, and has a fleet that consists of more than 640 aircraft and 44,500 vehicles. Founded in 1973. **NOTE:** Entry-level positions, part-time jobs, and second and third shifts are offered. **Company slogan:** Be absolutely sure. **Common positions include:** Account Manager; Accountant; Administrative Assistant; Applications Engineer; AS400 Programmer Analyst; Budget Analyst; Cargo Handler; Computer Engineer; Computer Programmer; Computer Support Technician; Computer Technician; Content Developer; Courier; Customer Service Representative; Database Administrator; Database Manager; Electrical/Electronics Engineer; Financial Analyst; General Manager; Human Resources Manager; Industrial Engineer; Marketing Manager; Marketing Specialist; Mechanical Engineer; Multimedia Designer; Network/Systems Administrator; Operations Manager; Project Manager; Public Relations Specialist; Purchasing Agent/Manager; Quality Assurance Engineer; Sales Executive; Sales Manager; Secretary; Services Sales Representative; Software Engineer; SQL Programmer; Systems Analyst; Webmaster. **Educational backgrounds include:** Accounting; Business Administration; C/C++; CGI; Computer Science; Engineering; Finance; HTML; Internet; Java; Marketing; Novell; QuarkXPress; Software Development; Software Tech. Support. **Benefits:** Casual Dress - Fridays; Dental Insurance; Disability Coverage; Employee Discounts; Life Insurance; Medical Insurance; Pension Plan; Profit Sharing; Savings Plan; Tuition Assistance. **Special programs:** Internships; Summer Jobs. **Corporate headquarters location:** This Location. **International locations:** Worldwide. **Listed on:** New York Stock Exchange. **Stock exchange symbol:** FDX. **President:** Ted Weise. **Information Systems Manager:** Chris Hjelms. **Annual sales/revenues:** More than $100 million.. **Other U.S. locations:**

- 950 Tower Lane, Suite 1000, Foster City CA 94404. 650/578-5100.
- 1220 Riverbend, Dallas TX 75247. 214/634-3250.

FLORIDA EAST COAST RAILWAY CO.
P.O. Box 1048, St. Augustine FL 32085-1048. 904/826-2320. **Contact:** Gloria S. Taylor, Director of Human Resources. **Description:** A railway transportation company. **Common positions include:** Clerk; Engineer; Human Resources Manager; Maintenance Technician; Training Specialist; Transportation/Traffic Specialist. **Benefits:** Life Insurance; Medical Insurance. **Corporate headquarters location:** This Location. **Operations at this facility include:** Administration. **Number of employees at this location:** 200. **Number of employees nationwide:** 1,000.

FLORIDA ROCK INDUSTRIES
FLORIDA ROCK & TANK LINES/ SUNBELT TRANSPORT
P.O. Box 4667, Jacksonville FL 32201. 904/355-1781. **Contact:** Bob Banks, Director of Human Resources. **Description:** Manufactures concrete aggregates. Florida Rock & Tank Lines (also at this location) transports oil and gasoline. Sunbelt Transport (also at this location) is a flatbed transportation company. **Common positions include:** Accountant/Auditor; Administrator; Civil Engineer; Credit Manager; Department Manager; General Manager; Geologist/Geophysicist; Mining Engineer; Systems Analyst. **Educational backgrounds include:** Business Administration; Computer Science; Engineering; Geology. **Benefits:** Dental Insurance; Disability Coverage; Employee Discounts; Life Insurance; Medical Insurance; Profit Sharing; Savings Plan; Tuition Assistance. **Corporate headquarters location:** This Location. **Listed on:** American Stock Exchange.

FRITZ COMPANIES, INC.
706 Mission Street, San Francisco CA 94103. 415/904-8360. **Fax:** 415/904-8373. **Contact:** Human Resources. **World Wide Web address:** http://www.fritz.com. **Description:** A leader in global transportation and logistics, the company's services range from integrated logistics programs to traditional freight forwarding and customs brokerage. Fritz develops, implements, and delivers worldwide supply chain solutions for its clients. Founded in 1933. **NOTE:** Entry-level positions are offered. **Common positions include:** Transportation/Traffic Specialist. **Educational backgrounds include:** International Relations; Transportation/Logistics. **Special programs:** Internships. **Internship information:** Fritz Companies has an internship program with fall, winter, spring, and summer internships available in over 70 U.S. locations. All information concerning the internship program is available on the company's Website. **Corporate headquarters location:** This Location. **Other U.S. locations:** Nationwide. **International locations:** Worldwide. **Listed on:** NASDAQ. **Stock exchange symbol:** FRTZ. **Annual sales/revenues:** More than $100 million. **Number of employees at this location:** 4,500. **Number of employees nationwide:** 8,000.

GATX CORPORATION
500 West Monroe Street, Chicago IL 60661. 312/621-6200. **Fax:** 312/621-6665. **Contact:** Elysa Robin, Senior Human Resources Generalist. **World Wide Web address:** http://www.gatx.com. **Description:** A holding company engaged in the lease and sale of rail cars and storage tanks for petroleum transport; equipment and capital asset financing and related services; the operation of tank storage terminals, pipelines, and related facilities; the operation of warehouses; and distribution and logistics support. **NOTE:** Entry-level positions are offered. **Common positions include:** Account Manager; Account Representative; Accountant; Administrative Assistant; Assistant Manager;

Attorney; Auditor; Budget Analyst; Chemical Engineer; Chief Financial Officer; Computer Operator; Computer Programmer; Controller; Environmental Engineer; Finance Director; Financial Analyst; Graphic Designer; Human Resources Manager; Market Research Analyst; Marketing Manager; Mechanical Engineer; MIS Specialist; Operations Manager; Project Manager; Purchasing Agent/Manager; Sales Executive; Sales Manager; Sales Representative; Secretary; Systems Analyst; Systems Manager; Technical Writer/Editor; Telecommunications Manager; Transportation/Traffic Specialist; Vice President of Finance; Vice President of Sales. **Educational backgrounds include:** Accounting; Chemistry; Communications; Computer Science; Economics; Engineering; Finance; Marketing; Public Relations; Software Development; Software Tech. Support. **Benefits:** 401(k); Daycare Assistance; Dental Insurance; Disability Coverage; Employee Discounts; Life Insurance; Medical Insurance; Pension Plan; Public Transit Available; Savings Plan; Tuition Assistance. **Special programs:** Internships. **Corporate headquarters location:** This Location. **Other U.S. locations:** Nationwide. **International locations:** Worldwide. **Subsidiaries include:** American Steamship Company; GATX Capital Corporation; GATX Logistics; GATX Terminals Corporation; General American Trans. **Operations at this facility include:** Administration. **Listed on:** New York Stock Exchange. **Stock exchange symbol:** GMT. **Chairman and CEO:** Ronald H. Zech. **Annual sales/revenues:** More than $100 million. **Number of employees at this location:** 500. **Number of employees nationwide:** 6,500.

GENERAL DYNAMICS CORPORATION

3190 Fairview Park Drive, Falls Church VA 22042-4523. 703/876-3000. **Contact:** Human Resources. **World Wide Web address:** http://www.generaldynamics.com. **Description:** Designs and builds nuclear submarines including the Seawolf class attack submarine. The Land Systems Division designs and builds armored vehicles such as the M1 series of battle tanks for the U.S. Army, the U.S. Marine Corps, and a number of international customers. The company also has coal mining operations in central Illinois; provides ship management services for the U.S. government on prepositioning and ready reserve ships; and leases liquefied natural gas tankers. **Common positions include:** Accountant/Auditor; Secretary. **Educational backgrounds include:** Accounting; Business Administration; Finance. **Benefits:** Dental Insurance; Disability Coverage; Life Insurance; Medical Insurance; Pension Plan; Profit Sharing; Savings Plan. **Corporate headquarters location:** This Location. **Other U.S. locations:** CT; MI; NJ; OH; RI. **Listed on:** New York Stock Exchange. **Annual sales/revenues:** More than $100 million. **Number of employees at this location:** 60. **Number of employees nationwide:** 31,000.

GLOBAL VAN LINES

P.O. Box 14013, Orange CA 92863-1413. 714/921-1200. **Physical address:** 810 West Taft Street, Orange CA 92865. **Contact:** Manager/Administration. **World Wide Web address:** http://www.globalvanlines.com. **Description:** Provides shipping and storage services for the general public. **Corporate headquarters location:** This Location.

THE GREENBRIER COMPANIES, INC.

One Centerpointe Drive, Suite 200, Lake Oswego OR 97035. 503/684-7000. **Contact:** Jeanne Onchi, Human Resources. **Description:** Operates in two primary business segments: manufacturing and

refurbishing railcars and marine vessels; and leasing and managing surface transportation equipment and providing related services. **Corporate headquarters location:** This Location. **Subsidiaries include:** Gunderson Inc. manufactures and refurbishes railroad freight cars and marine barges.

GROUP VOYAGERS, INC.
dba GLOBUS & COSMOS

5301 South Federal Circle, Littleton CO 80123. 303/703-7000. **Toll-free phone:** 800/851-0728. **Fax:** 303/795-6615. **Contact:** Jackie Boyd, Recruiter. **World Wide Web address:** http://www.globusandcosmos.com. **Description:** A leader in escorted travel. The company provides travel packages to more than 70 countries on all seven continents. **NOTE:** Entry-level positions and part-time jobs are offered. **Common positions include:** Account Manager; Administrative Assistant; AS400 Programmer Analyst; Budget Analyst; Chief Financial Officer; Computer Operator; Computer Programmer; Computer Support Technician; Computer Technician; Controller; Credit Manager; Customer Service Representative; Database Administrator; Database Manager; Editor; Graphic Designer; Human Resources Manager; Market Research Analyst; Marketing Manager; Marketing Specialist; Network/Systems Administrator; Operations Manager; Public Relations Specialist; Sales Executive; Sales Manager; Sales Representative; Systems Analyst; Systems Manager; Technical Writer/Editor; Telecommunications Manager; Vice President; Webmaster. **Educational backgrounds include:** Accounting; Business Administration; C/C++; Communications; Computer Science; Finance; HTML; Java; Marketing; Microsoft Word; Novell; Software Tech. Support; Spreadsheets; Visual Basic. **Benefits:** 401(k); Casual Dress - Daily; Daycare Assistance; Dental Insurance; Disability Coverage; Employee Discounts; Life Insurance; Medical Insurance; Pension Plan; Sick Days; Telecommuting; Tuition Assistance; Vacation Days. **Special programs:** Training. **Corporate headquarters location:** This Location. **Other U.S. locations:** Pasadena CA. **International locations:** Worldwide. **Listed on:** Privately held. **President/CEO:** Paulo Mantegazza. **Sales Manager:** Jean Dorn. **Number of employees at this location:** 290.

GUNDERSON INC.

4350 NW Front Avenue, Portland OR 97210. 503/972-5700. **Toll-free phone:** 800/253-4350. **Recorded jobline:** 503/972-5901. **Contact:** Vanetta Shambry, Recruiting Coordinator. **World Wide Web address:** http://www.gundersoninc.com. **Description:** Manufactures and refurbishes railroad freight cars and marine barges. **NOTE:** Entry-level positions and second and third shifts are offered. **Common positions include:** Electrician; Welder. **Educational backgrounds include:** Accounting; Finance; Health Care; Welding. **Benefits:** 401(k); Casual Dress - Fridays; Dental Insurance; Disability Coverage; Life Insurance; Medical Insurance; Profit Sharing; Public Transit Available; Sick Days; Tuition Assistance; Vacation Days. **Special programs:** Training. **Corporate headquarters location:** Lake Oswego OR. **Other area locations:** Springfield OR. **Other U.S. locations:** Pine Bluff AR; Cleburne TX. **International locations:** Poland. **Parent company:** The Greenbrier Companies, Inc. **Number of employees at this location:** 1,200. **Number of employees nationwide:** 1,500.

HAWAIIAN AIRLINES, INC.

P.O. Box 30008, Honolulu HI 96820. 808/835-3700. **Fax:** 808/835-3692. **Recorded jobline:**

808/835-3950. **Contact:** Human Resources. **World Wide Web address:** http://www.hawaiianair.com. **Description:** A regional airline for passengers, cargo, and mail over a route consisting of six major Hawaiian islands, cities on the West Coast, and some cities in the South Pacific. **Common positions include:** Aircraft Mechanic/Engine Specialist; Airport Staff Worker; Customer Service Representative; Human Resources Manager; Mechanical Engineer; Reservationist; Structural Engineer; Systems Analyst. **Educational backgrounds include:** Accounting; Business Administration; Computer Science; Engineering; High School Diploma/GED; Liberal Arts; Marketing. **Benefits:** 401(k); Dental Insurance; Disability Coverage; Employee Discounts; Life Insurance; Medical Insurance; Pension Plan; Savings Plan. **Corporate headquarters location:** This Location. **Other U.S. locations:** Los Angeles CA; San Francisco CA; Las Vegas NV; Portland OR; Seattle WA. **Listed on:** American Stock Exchange; Pacific Stock Exchange. **Number of employees nationwide:** 2,500.

HAWTHORNE CORPORATION
P.O. Box 61000, Charleston SC 29419. 803/797-8484. **Contact:** Sue Johnson, Vice President. **World Wide Web address:** http://www.hawthornecorp. com. **Description:** A holding company whose subsidiaries are engaged in a wide variety of industries including aviation (operating airports); real estate operations that develop land for fixed base operations; and financial services (investor services). **Corporate headquarters location:** This Location.

HEARTLAND EXPRESS INC.
2777 Heartland Drive, Coralville IA 52241. 319/645-2728. **Contact:** Don McGlaughlin, Human Resources Director. **Description:** An irregular-route carrier that is authorized to transport general commodities in interstate commerce throughout the 48 contiguous states. **NOTE:** Entry-level positions are offered. **Common positions include:** Clerical Supervisor; Transportation/Traffic Specialist. **Educational backgrounds include:** Transportation/ Logistics. **Benefits:** 401(k); Medical Insurance; Profit Sharing. **Corporate headquarters location:** This Location. **Other U.S. locations:** Atlanta GA; Columbus OH. **Listed on:** NASDAQ. **Annual sales/revenues:** More than $100 million. **Number of employees nationwide:** 2,000.

THE HERTZ CORPORATION
225 Brae Boulevard, Park Ridge NJ 07656. 201/307-2000. **Fax:** 201/307-2644. **Contact:** Director of Personnel. **World Wide Web address:** http://www.hertz.com. **Description:** A large rental company which leases new and used cars, and industrial and construction equipment in 130 countries. The company also sells used cars in the U.S., Australia, New Zealand, and Europe. The fleet of cars consists of 283,000 automobiles which are leased through 5,300 offices. **Corporate headquarters location:** This Location.

HUDSON GENERAL CORPORATION
111 Great Neck Road, Great Neck NY 11022. 516/487-8610. **Fax:** 516/487-4855. **Contact:** Human Resources. **Description:** A nationwide aviation service company providing contracting services to airlines and airports including loading/unloading, cleaning planes, fueling planes, and cargo services. **Common positions include:** Accountant/Auditor; Administrative Manager; Automotive Mechanic; Customer Service Representative; General Manager. **Educational backgrounds include:** Business Administration. **Benefits:** 401(k); Dental Insurance; Disability

Coverage; Life Insurance; Medical Insurance; Profit Sharing; Tuition Assistance. **Special programs:** Internships. **Corporate headquarters location:** This Location. **Subsidiaries include:** Hudson Aviation Services, Inc. **Number of employees at this location:** 45. **Number of employees nationwide:** 3,400.

IFF INC.
452-A Plaza Drive, Cottage Park GA 30349. 404/305-9433. **Fax:** 404/209-6741. **Contact:** Yvonne May, Office Manager. **E-mail address:** admin@iffusa.com. **World Wide Web address:** http://www.iffusa.com. **Description:** A forwarder of international freight. Founded in 1983. **Common positions include:** Account Manager; Operations Manager. **Corporate headquarters location:** This Location. **Other U.S. locations:** Charlotte NC; Greenville SC; Richmond VA. **President:** Peter Halpaus. **Number of employees at this location:** 25.

ILLINOIS CENTRAL RAILROAD CO.
455 North Cityfront Plaza Drive, Chicago IL 60611-5317. 312/755-7500. **Contact:** Personnel. **Description:** Operates one of the largest rail networks in the U.S. The company's network includes 2,700 miles of main lines; 1,700 miles of passing, yard, and switching track; and 300 miles of secondary main lines. The company serves land shippers in Illinois, Louisiana, Michigan, Alabama, Kentucky, and Tennessee. Illinois Central's equipment consists of locomotives; freight cars; work equipment; and highway trailers and tractors. **Corporate headquarters location:** This Location. **Parent company:** Illinois Central.

INTERNATIONAL SHIPHOLDING CORP.
650 Poydras Street, Suite 1700, New Orleans LA 70130. 504/529-5461. **Contact:** Director of Human Resources. **Description:** Operates a diversified fleet of U.S. and foreign flag vessels which transport various shipments including forest products, automobiles, military cargo, petroleum products, and dry bulk cargo. **Common positions include:** Accountant/Auditor; Computer Programmer; Purchasing Agent/Manager; Systems Analyst. **Educational backgrounds include:** Accounting; Business Administration; Computer Science. **Benefits:** 401(k); Dental Insurance; Disability Coverage; Life Insurance; Medical Insurance; Pension Plan. **Corporate headquarters location:** This Location. **Other U.S. locations:** NY. **Subsidiaries include:** Central Gulf Lines; Lash Marine Services; Waterman Steamship Corporation. **Parent company:** I.S.C. **Listed on:** New York Stock Exchange. **Number of employees at this location:** 225. **Number of employees nationwide:** 800.

INTERNATIONAL TRAVEL ARRANGERS
1320 East Lake Street, Minneapolis MN 55407. 612/724-1484. **Contact:** Human Resources. **Description:** A tour wholesaler specializing in charter air travel packages to many destinations. **Common positions include:** Customer Service Representative; Transportation/Traffic Specialist; Travel Agent. **Benefits:** Employee Discounts; Life Insurance; Medical Insurance; Pension Plan; Profit Sharing. **Corporate headquarters location:** This Location.

INTRAV INC.
7711 Bonhomme Avenue, St. Louis MO 63105. 314/727-0500. **Contact:** Human Resources Director. **World Wide Web address:** http://www. intrav.com. **Description:** Intrav organizes, markets, and operates escorted, international travel programs. **Corporate headquarters location:** This Location.

IRON MOUNTAIN INC.
745 Atlantic Avenue, Boston MA 02111. 617/357-4455. **Contact:** Human Resources. **Description:** One of the nation's largest record management companies. Iron Mountain provides businesses with storage facilities for their records. **Corporate headquarters location:** This Location. **Other U.S. locations:** Nationwide.

JEFFERSON PARTNERS L.P.
2100 East 26th Street, Minneapolis MN 55404-4101. 612/332-8745. **Contact:** Human Resources Manager. **Description:** An intercity bus line and travel company. **Common positions include:** Accountant/Auditor; Customer Service Representative; Department Manager; Driver; Human Resources Manager; Operations/Production Manager; Payroll Clerk; Planner; Purchasing Agent/Manager; Services Sales Representative; Transportation/Traffic Specialist. **Educational backgrounds include:** Accounting; Business Administration; Communications; Finance; Liberal Arts; Marketing. **Benefits:** 401(k); Daycare Assistance; Dental Insurance; Disability Coverage; Employee Discounts; Flexible Benefits; Life Insurance; Medical Insurance; Savings Plan; Tuition Assistance. **Corporate headquarters location:** This Location. **Other U.S. locations:** Fort Smith AR; Des Moines IA; Kansas City MO; Oklahoma City OK; Tulsa OK. **Listed on:** Privately held. **Number of employees at this location:** 65. **Number of employees nationwide:** 250.

JEVIC TRANSPORTATION INC.
P.O. Box 5157, Delanco NJ 08075. 856/461-7111. **Contact:** Human Resources. **Description:** This location houses a dispatching center. Overall, Jevic Transportation is a trucking company providing freight services. **Corporate headquarters location:** This Location.

KELLAWAY TRANSPORTATION
One Kellaway Drive, P.O. Box 750, Randolph MA 02368. 781/961-8200. **Contact:** Human Resources. **World Wide Web address:** http://www.kellaway.com. **Description:** An intermodal distribution company. **Corporate headquarters location:** This Location.

KENAN TRANSPORT COMPANY
P.O. Box 2729, Chapel Hill NC 27515-2729. 919/967-8221. **Contact:** Human Resources. **Description:** A tank truck carrier serving the petroleum, propane gas, and chemical industries in the southeastern United States. The company conducts bulk trucking operations intrastate in Virginia, North Carolina, South Carolina, Georgia, and Florida; and interstate between these five states and points throughout the continental United States. The company transports a wide variety of products including gasoline to service stations; petroleum products to wholesalers and industrial plants; propane gas to agricultural, rural, and industrial consumers; and liquid and dry bulk chemicals to manufacturers. **Corporate headquarters location:** This Location. **Listed on:** NASDAQ. **Number of employees nationwide:** 740.

KIRBY CORPORATION
P.O. Box 1745, Houston TX 77251-1745. 713/629-9370. **Contact:** Jack M. Sims, Vice President of Human Resources. **World Wide Web address:** http://www.kmtc.com. **Description:** Provides marine transportation and diesel engine repair services. Kirby's marine transportation segment is conducted through Dixie Carriers, Inc., and its subsidiaries. The marine transportation segment is divided into three divisions. The Chemicals Division serves the inland industrial and agricultural chemical markets. The Refined Products Division serves the inland refined products market. The Offshore Division serves the offshore petroleum products and dry bulk cargo markets. The company's diesel repair business is conducted through the marine transportation segment. The company has diesel repair facilities in five locations nationwide that cater to specific markets. The company also writes property and casualty insurance in Puerto Rico. **Common positions include:** Accountant/Auditor; Administrator; Civil Engineer; Computer Programmer; Financial Analyst; Human Resources Manager; Manufacturer's/Wholesaler's Sales Rep.; Marketing Specialist; Quality Control Supervisor; Transportation/Traffic Specialist. **Educational backgrounds include:** Accounting; Business Administration; Computer Science; Engineering; Finance; Marketing. **Benefits:** Dental Insurance; Disability Coverage; Life Insurance; Medical Insurance; Profit Sharing; Savings Plan. **Corporate headquarters location:** This Location. **Listed on:** American Stock Exchange.

LAIDLAW EDUCATIONAL SERVICE INC.
2100 Highway 35, Sea Girt NJ 08750. 732/449-3530. **Contact:** Human Resources. **Description:** This location houses administrative offices. Overall, Laidlaw Educational Service provides school bus transportation services. **NOTE:** Entry-level positions and part-time jobs are offered. **Common positions include:** Accountant; Administrative Assistant; Administrative Manager; Blue-Collar Worker Supervisor; General Manager; Management Trainee; Secretary; Transportation/Traffic Specialist. **Benefits:** 401(k); Casual Dress - Daily; Dental Insurance; Disability Coverage; Job Sharing; Life Insurance; Medical Insurance; Savings Plan; Tuition Assistance; Vacation Days (11 - 15). **Special programs:** Apprenticeships; Training. **Corporate headquarters location:** Lawrenceville NJ. **Other U.S. locations:** Nationwide. **Listed on:** New York Stock Exchange. **Annual sales/revenues:** $21 - $50 million. **Number of employees nationwide:** 60,000.

LAND SPAN, INC.
P.O. Box 95007, Lakeland FL 33804. 941/688-1102. **Contact:** Human Resources. **Description:** Provides transportation of dry and refrigerated freight. **Common positions include:** Administrator; Computer Programmer; Credit Manager; Customer Service Representative; Department Manager; Human Resources Manager; Operations/Production Manager; Services Sales Representative; Transportation/Traffic Specialist. **Educational backgrounds include:** Business Administration; Communications; Computer Science; Finance; Marketing; Mathematics. **Benefits:** Dental Insurance; Disability Coverage; Employee Discounts; Life Insurance; Medical Insurance; Pension Plan; Profit Sharing; Savings Plan; Tuition Assistance. **Corporate headquarters location:** This Location. **Other U.S. locations:** Norcross GA; Chicago IL; Hagerstown MD; Charlotte NC; El Paso TX; Fort Worth TX. **Parent company:** Watkins Associated Industries, Inc. **Number of employees at this location:** 300.

LANDSTAR SYSTEM, INC.
13410 Sutton Park Drive, Jacksonville FL 32224. 904/398-9232. **Toll-free phone:** 800/862-9232. **Contact:** Human Resources. **Description:** Provides truckload transportation services through independent contractors and commissioned sales agents. **Corporate headquarters location:** This Location. **Subsidiaries include:** Landstar Expedited, Inc.; Landstar Express America, Inc.; Landstar Inway, Inc.; Landstar ITCO, Inc.; Landstar

Ligon, Inc.; Landstar Poole, Inc.; Landstar Ranger, Inc.; Landstar T.L.C., Inc.; and Landstar Transportation Service, Inc.

LIBERTY LINES
475 Saw Mill River Road, Yonkers NY 10703. 914/969-6900. **Fax:** 914/376-6440. **Contact:** Neil Erickson, Director of Human Resources. **Description:** One of the largest and most diversified bus services in the Yonkers/Westchester area. Services include commuter and transit bus operations. **Common positions include:** Bus Driver. **Benefits:** Dental Insurance; Disability Coverage; Life Insurance; Medical Insurance; Pension Plan. **Corporate headquarters location:** This Location. **President:** Jerry D'Amore.

LITTON INDUSTRIES
21240 Burbank Boulevard, Woodland Hills CA 91367. 818/598-5000. **Contact:** Human Resources. **World Wide Web address:** http://www.littoncorp. com. **Description:** A leader in defense and commercial electronics, shipbuilding, and information technology. Litton is involved in the electronic warfare and command, navigation, and guidance and control markets. Litton also designs, repairs, and modernizes ships. Founded in 1953. **Corporate headquarters location:** This Location. **International locations:** Canada; Germany; Italy. **Stock exchange symbol:** LIT. **Annual sales/revenues:** More than $100 million.

LONG ISLAND BUS
700 Commercial Avenue, Garden City NY 11530. 516/542-0100. **Contact:** Human Resources. **Description:** Provides public bus transportation services between various points in Nassau County and New York City. **Common positions include:** Administrative Assistant; Administrative Manager; Attorney; Auditor; Blue-Collar Worker Supervisor; Budget Analyst; Buyer; Claim Representative; Computer Programmer; Controller; Customer Service Representative; Electrical/Electronics Engineer; Financial Analyst; Graphic Artist; Human Resources Manager; Marketing Manager; Mechanical Engineer; MIS Specialist; Systems Analyst; Systems Manager; Transportation/Traffic Specialist; Typist/Word Processor. **Educational backgrounds include:** Accounting; Business Administration; Engineering; Finance; Liberal Arts. **Benefits:** 401(k); Dental Insurance; Disability Coverage; Life Insurance; Pension Plan; Public Transit Available; Savings Plan; Tuition Assistance; Vision Insurance. **Special programs:** Internships. **Internship information:** The company begins recruiting for interns in late April/early May. Interns are hired for the following departments: Accounting, Human Resources, MIS, Operations, Planning and Purchasing. **Corporate headquarters location:** This Location. **Other area locations:** Rockville Centre NY. **Parent company:** Metropolitan Transportation Authority.

THE LONG ISLAND RAILROAD CO.
Jamaica Station, Jamaica NY 11435. 718/558-7400. **Contact:** Human Resources. **World Wide Web address:** http://www.lirr.org. **Description:** Operates one of the oldest active railroads in the United States. The company has extensive commuter passenger and freight service railroad operations, primarily between New York City and numerous points on Long Island. The Long Island Railroad Company is one of the busiest passenger railroad operators in the United States. **Corporate headquarters location:** This Location.

LUFKIN INDUSTRIES, INC.
P.O. Box 849, Lufkin TX 75902. 936/634-2211. **Contact:** Human Resources. **World Wide Web** address: http://www.lufkin.com. **Description:** Designs and fabricates gears for power transmission products; iron castings; oil field pumps; and platforms and dump trailers for the over-the-road transportation industry. **Corporate headquarters location:** This Location. **Listed on:** NASDAQ. **Stock exchange symbol:** LUFK.

LUHRS CORPORATION
255 Diesel Road, St. Augustine FL 32086. 904/829-0500. **Fax:** 904/829-0683. **Contact:** Jane Wright, Personnel Manager. **World Wide Web address:** http://www.luhrs.com. **Description:** A manufacturer of fiberglass boats ranging from 25 to 47 feet long. **Common positions include:** Blue-Collar Worker Supervisor; Buyer; Carpenter; Customer Service Representative; Draftsperson; Electrician; Industrial Engineer; Mechanical Engineer. **Benefits:** 401(k); Dental Insurance; Life Insurance; Medical Insurance; Prescription Drugs; Vacation Days. **Corporate headquarters location:** This Location. **Number of employees at this location:** 375.

LUMINATOR
1200 East Plano Parkway, Plano TX 75074. 972/424-6511. **Contact:** Denise Boyd, Human Resources Manager. **World Wide Web address:** http://www.luminatorusa.com. **Description:** Manufactures aircraft parts, bus products, and rail products. Luminator aircraft products include batteries, lamps, search lights, interiors, and crew stations. Bus products include flip-out signs and voice systems. Rail products include various types of lighting, flip dot sign systems, electronic maps, voice systems, and air diffusers. **Corporate headquarters location:** This Location. **Parent company:** Mark IV Industries.

M.S. CARRIERS
P.O. Box 30788, Memphis TN 38130-0788. 901/332-2500. **Fax:** 901/344-6702. **Recorded jobline:** 901/344-4333. **Contact:** Employment Department. **World Wide Web address:** http://www.mscarriers.com. **Description:** An irregular-route truckload carrier transporting a wide range of commodities in the United States, Canada, and Mexico. The principal types of freight transported are packages, retail goods, nonperishable foodstuffs, paper and paper products, household appliances, furniture, and packaged petroleum products. **NOTE:** This company only accepts resumes for open positions. Please check the jobline before sending a resume. **Common positions include:** Accountant/Auditor; Automotive Mechanic; Buyer; Clerical Supervisor; Computer Programmer; Customer Service Representative; Financial Analyst; Human Resources Manager; Purchasing Agent/Manager; Sales Representative; Systems Analyst; Transportation/Traffic Specialist. **Educational backgrounds include:** Accounting; Business Administration; Computer Science; Finance; Marketing. **Benefits:** 401(k); Dental Insurance; Disability Coverage; Life Insurance; Medical Insurance; Profit Sharing; Tuition Assistance. **Corporate headquarters location:** This Location. **Other area locations:** Chestnut Hill TN. **Other U.S. locations:** Atlanta GA; Columbus OH; Port Clinton OH; Drums PA; Dallas TX; Martinsburg WV. **Listed on:** NASDAQ. **Number of employees at this location:** 450. **Number of employees nationwide:** 3,200.

MARITRANS INC.
1818 Market Street, Philadelphia PA 19103. 215/864-1200. **Contact:** Human Resources. **Description:** Maritrans provides marine transportation for the petroleum distribution process, delivers about 10.6 billion gallons a year, and owns oil storage terminals. Maritrans offers a

full line of distribution services including product exchanges, marine transportation, scheduling, terminal storage, and automated truck rack delivery systems. **Corporate headquarters location:** This Location. **Subsidiaries include:** Marispond Inc. serves the growing international need for oil spill contingency planning and spill management. This business capitalizes on Maritrans' spill response capabilities and also focuses on the related areas of safety training and dry cargo contingency planning; Maritank Philadelphia, Inc. operates storage terminals.

MARK VII, INC.
965 Ridge Lake Boulevard, Suite 103, Memphis TN 38120. 901/767-4455. **Contact:** Human Resources. **World Wide Web address:** http://www. markvii.com. **Description:** One of the country's leading providers of single-source transportation services to some of the largest shippers in the world. The company provides a full complement of logistics management services such as dedicated fleet, warehousing, and risk management, as well as the component services involved in these activities. The company's areas of operation include Intermodal Trucking Services; Carload, International, and Dimensional Traffic; Consolidation and Distribution Services; and Air Freight services. Services offered include double stack, trailers, and containers on rail cars; trucks; and ocean-going transportation. Commodities transported include paper, food, empty containers, retail products, and household goods. **Corporate headquarters location:** This Location. **Other U.S. locations:** Nationwide. **International locations:** Worldwide. **Subsidiaries include:** TemStar.

MASS BUYING POWER (MBP)
1076 Washington Street, Hanover MA 02339. 781/829-4900. **Contact:** Personnel. **E-mail address:** massbuy@massbuy.com. **World Wide Web address:** http://www.massbuy.com. **Description:** Provides discount purchasing benefits for employees of member companies. Mass Buying Power offers discounts on a wide variety of products and services including automobiles, major household appliances, furniture, consumer loans, and home improvements. Mass Buying Power also operates a full-service travel agency specializing in discount travel packages. **Corporate headquarters location:** This Location. **Listed on:** Privately held.

MAYFLOWER TRANSIT, INC.
P.O. Box 26150, Fenton MO 63026-1350. 636/305-4000. **Contact:** Human Resources. **World Wide Web address:** http://www.mayflower.com. **Description:** A diversified holding company whose subsidiaries provide a variety of transportation-related services including household moving services; services for goods that require special handling; and storage and distribution, freight forwarding, and flatbed hauling of containerized shipments. Mayflower Transit also owns and operates moving and storage agencies; provides school bus service to school districts; provides on-demand transportation services for local communities; operates a school bus dealership; sells tractor trailers; operates a road equipment maintenance facility; and sells moving supplies, equipment, and uniforms to agents and owner operators. Mayflower also provides a variety of insurance services including property and casualty coverage. **Corporate headquarters location:** This Location.

McALLISTER TOWING AND TRANSPORTATION COMPANY
17 Battery Place, Suite 1200, New York NY 10004. 212/269-3200. **Contact:** Ms. Jean Brown, Director of Personnel. **Description:** A marine services firm providing ship docking, deep-sea and coastal towing, oil transportation, bulk transportation, special projects such as positioning tunnel and bridge segments and other services for the transportation industry. McAllister also offers full-service, in-house capabilities through a complete packaged transportation service provided to shippers. The company operates one of the largest fleets of tugs and barges on the East Coast and in the Caribbean, with ship docking services in New York NY, Philadelphia PA, Norfolk VA, Charleston SC, Jacksonville FL, Baltimore MD, and Puerto Rico. Marine towing and transportation services are operated along the East Coast, in the Caribbean, through the New York State barge canal system, and in the Great Lakes and the St. Lawrence River. **Common positions include:** Accountant/Auditor; Administrator; Claim Representative; Computer Programmer; Department Manager; Financial Analyst; General Manager; Human Resources Manager; Management Trainee; Operations/Production Manager; Services Sales Representative. **Educational backgrounds include:** Accounting; Business Administration; Communications; Engineering; Finance; Marketing. **Benefits:** Dental Insurance; Disability Coverage; Life Insurance; Medical Insurance. **Corporate headquarters location:** This Location.

W.C. McQUAIDE, INC.
153 Mac Ridge Avenue, Johnstown PA 15904. 814/269-6000. **Fax:** 814/269-6189. **Contact:** Human Resources Department. **Description:** A freight carrier. **Common positions include:** Adjuster; Claim Representative; Customer Service Representative; Services Sales Representative; Transportation/Traffic Specialist; Truck Driver; Warehouse/Distribution Worker. **Benefits:** Employee Discounts; Life Insurance; Medical Insurance; Pension Plan. **Corporate headquarters location:** This Location. **Other U.S. locations:** NJ; NY; OH; WV. **Listed on:** Privately held. **Number of employees at this location:** 200. **Number of employees nationwide:** 415.

MESA AIRLINES, INC.
2700 Farmington Avenue, Building K, Suite 2, Farmington NM 87401. 505/327-0271. **Contact:** Personnel Assistant. **Description:** Provides regularly scheduled commuter and cargo airline services. **Common positions include:** Aircraft Mechanic/Engine Specialist; Flight Attendant; Pilot; Ticket Agent. **Corporate headquarters location:** This Location. **Number of employees at this location:** 300. **Number of employees nationwide:** 3,500.

MESABA AIRLINES
7501 26th Avenue South, Minneapolis MN 55450. 612/726-5151. **Contact:** Human Resources. **World Wide Web address:** http://www.mesaba.com. **Description:** A scheduled passenger airline carrier that provides services in over 40 U.S. cities and Canada. **Common positions include:** Accountant; Aircraft Mechanic/Engine Specialist; Buyer; Clerk; Computer Programmer; Customer Service Representative; Flight Attendant; Human Resources Manager; Pilot; Purchasing Agent/Manager. **Educational backgrounds include:** Accounting; Aviation. **Benefits:** 401(k); Dental Insurance; Disability Coverage; Employee Discounts; Life Insurance; Medical Insurance. **Corporate headquarters location:** This Location. **Other U.S. locations:** Detroit MI. **Listed on:** NASDAQ. **Number of employees at this location:** 300. **Number of employees nationwide:** 1,400.

METROPOLITAN ATLANTA RAPID TRANSIT AUTHORITY (MARTA)
2424 Piedmont Road, Atlanta GA 30324. 404/848-5000. **Fax:** 404/848-5687. **Recorded jobline:** 404/848-5627. **Contact:** Human Resources Manager. **Description:** Operates the bus and subway systems for the city of Atlanta. **Common positions include:** Accountant/Auditor; Automotive Mechanic; Budget Analyst; Buyer; Computer Programmer; Electrician; Human Resources Manager; Management Analyst/Consultant; Public Relations Specialist; Purchasing Agent/Manager; Systems Analyst; Technical Writer/Editor; Transportation/Traffic Specialist. **Educational backgrounds include:** Accounting; Business Administration; Finance; Liberal Arts; Marketing. **Benefits:** Dental Insurance; Disability Coverage; Life Insurance; Medical Insurance; Pension Plan; Tuition Assistance. **Special programs:** Internships. **Corporate headquarters location:** This Location. **Number of employees at this location:** 3,700.

METROPOLITAN TRANSPORTATION AUTHORITY
347 Madison Avenue, New York NY 10017. 212/878-7275. **Contact:** Human Resources. **World Wide Web address:** http://www.mta.nyc.ny.us. **Description:** A public benefit corporation primarily devoted to obtaining funding for mass transportation in the New York City area, as well as serving as the headquarters for the MTA's constituent agencies. **Common positions include:** Accountant/Auditor; Attorney; Computer Operator; Computer Programmer; Economist; Financial Analyst; Financial Manager; Market Research Analyst; Payroll Clerk; Purchasing Agent/Manager; Real Estate Agent; Secretary; Systems Analyst. **Educational backgrounds include:** Accounting; Business Administration; Communications; Computer Science; Economics; Engineering; Finance; Liberal Arts; Marketing. **Benefits:** Dental Insurance; Disability Coverage; Life Insurance; Medical Insurance; Pension Plan; Savings Plan; Tuition Assistance. **Corporate headquarters location:** This Location. **Number of employees at this location:** 400.

NATIONAL CAR RENTAL SYSTEM, INC.
7700 France Avenue South, Minneapolis MN 55435. 952/893-6060. **Contact:** Sandra Morrison, Director of Human Resources. **World Wide Web address:** http://www.nationalcar.com. **Description:** A car rental agency. **Common positions include:** Accountant/Auditor; Claim Representative; Reservationist; Sales Manager. **Educational backgrounds include:** Accounting; Business Administration; Finance; Marketing. **Benefits:** 401(k); Dental Insurance; Disability Coverage; Employee Discounts; Life Insurance; Medical Insurance; On-Site Exercise Facility; Tuition Assistance. **Corporate headquarters location:** This Location. **Other U.S. locations:** Nationwide. **Number of employees at this location:** 900.

NEW ORLEANS COLD STORAGE & WAREHOUSE COMPANY
3401 Alvar Street, New Orleans LA 70126. 504/944-4400. **Contact:** Human Resources. **Description:** Services include public refrigerated warehouses, custom house brokerage services, and USDA meat inspection facilities. **Common positions include:** Blue-Collar Worker Supervisor; Refrigeration Engineer. **Benefits:** Dental Insurance; Life Insurance; Medical Insurance; Pension Plan. **Corporate headquarters location:** This Location.

NEWPORT NEWS SHIPBUILDING
4101 Washington Avenue, Newport News VA 23607. 757/380-4878. **Fax:** 757/380-3114. Recorded jobline: 757/380-2142. **Contact:** Human Resources. **World Wide Web address:** http://www.nns.com. **Description:** Engaged in the design, construction, repair, overhaul, and refueling of conventional and nuclear-powered merchant and naval surface ships and submarines. **Common positions include:** Accountant/Auditor; Budget Analyst; Buyer; Civil Engineer; Computer Programmer; Cost Estimator; Designer; Draftsperson; Electrical/Electronics Engineer; Environmental Engineer; Financial Analyst; Human Resources Manager; Industrial Engineer; Materials Engineer; Mechanical Engineer; Medical Records Technician; Metallurgical Engineer; Naval Architect; Nuclear Engineer; Physician; Public Relations Specialist; Software Engineer; Structural Engineer; Systems Analyst; Technical Writer/Editor. **Educational backgrounds include:** Engineering. **Benefits:** 401(k); Daycare Assistance; Dental Insurance; Disability Coverage; Employee Discounts; Life Insurance; Medical Insurance; Pension Plan; Tuition Assistance. **Corporate headquarters location:** This Location. **Number of employees at this location:** 17,000.

NORFOLK SOUTHERN CORPORATION
3 Commercial Place, Norfolk VA 23510. 757/269-2600. **Recorded jobline:** 800/214-3609. **Contact:** Manager of Professional Recruiting. **World Wide Web address:** http://www.nscorp.com. **Description:** A railroad freight transportation and holding company controlling Norfolk Southern Railway, North American Van Lines, and Pocahontas Land Corporation. The company's rail lines extend through 20 states, primarily in the Midwest, Southeast, and Mid-Atlantic. **NOTE:** Entry-level positions are offered. **Common positions include:** Account Manager; Civil Engineer; Computer Programmer; Management Trainee; Marketing Manager; Mechanical Engineer; Operations/Production Manager. **Educational backgrounds include:** Accounting; Business Administration; Computer Science; Economics; Engineering; Finance; Marketing. **Benefits:** 401(k); Dental Insurance; Disability Coverage; Life Insurance; Medical Insurance; Pension Plan; Tuition Assistance. **Special programs:** Internships. **Corporate headquarters location:** This Location. **Other U.S. locations:** Nationwide. **Listed on:** New York Stock Exchange. **Annual sales/revenues:** More than $100 million. **Number of employees nationwide:** 24,300.

NORTHWEST AIRLINES
5101 Northwest Drive, Mail Stop A-1410, St. Paul MN 55111-3034. 612/726-3600. **Contact:** Personnel. **World Wide Web address:** http://www.nwa.com. **Description:** One of the world's largest airlines and one of America's oldest carriers. Northwest Airlines serves more than 240 cities in 22 countries. The U.S. system spans 45 states. Hub cities are located in Detroit, Minneapolis/St. Paul, Memphis, and Tokyo. Maintenance bases are in Atlanta and Minneapolis/St. Paul. Crew bases are in Anchorage, Chicago, Detroit, Memphis, San Francisco, Minneapolis/St. Paul, New York, Seattle/Tacoma, Boston, Los Angeles, Honolulu, and several international cities. Founded in 1926. **NOTE:** Jobseekers should call the jobline or view postings on the company's Website before sending a resume. Second and third shifts are offered. **Common positions include:** Account Manager; Accountant; Administrative Manager; Auditor; Budget Analyst; Computer Programmer; Computer Technician; Controller; Customer Service Representative; Database Administrator; Database Manager; Financial Analyst; Human Resources Manager; Market Research Analyst; Marketing Manager;

Mechanical Engineer; Operations Manager; Software Engineer; SQL Programmer; Systems Analyst; Systems Manager. **Educational backgrounds include:** Accounting; Business Administration; Computer Science; Engineering; Finance; SAS Programming; Spreadsheets. **Benefits:** 401(k); Casual Dress - Fridays; Dental Insurance; Employee Discounts; Medical Insurance; Pension Plan. **Special programs:** Co-ops. **Corporate headquarters location:** This Location. **Other U.S. locations:** Nationwide. **Listed on:** NASDAQ. **President:** John Dasburg. **Number of employees nationwide:** 50,000.

NORTON LILLY & CO. INTERNATIONAL
200 Plaza Drive, Secaucus NJ 07096. 201/392-3000. **Contact:** Human Resources. **Description:** This location handles collection, brokerage, and documentation. Overall, Norton Lilly & Company is a sea transportation firm specializing in cargohauling. **Corporate headquarters location:** This Location.

OMI CORPORATION
Metro Center, One Station Place, 7th Floor North, Stamford CT 06902. 203/602-6700. **Contact:** Human Resources. **Description:** A large bulk shipping company with interests in 46 ocean-going bulk carriers, tankers, and gas carriers. OMI also provides logistics, crewing, technical, and commercial operations for international clients. The company has interests in OMI Petrolink Corporation and in Chiles Offshore Corporation, which operates 14 drilling rigs. **Corporate headquarters location:** This Location. **Listed on:** New York Stock Exchange.

OHIO RIVER COMPANY
P.O. Box 1460, Cincinnati OH 45201. 513/721-4000. **Contact:** Human Resources. **Description:** Operates a fleet of barges and towboats, principally on the Ohio and Mississippi Rivers and their tributaries, the Gulf Intracoastal Waterway, and the Gulf of Mexico. The company also transports bulk commodities; performs repair work on marine equipment; operates two coal dumping terminals; runs a phosphate rock and phosphate chemical fertilizer terminal; and owns a marine fuel supply facility. **Corporate headquarters location:** This Location.

OLYMPIAN BEKINS MOVING & STORAGE
2225 South 43rd Avenue, Suite 2, Phoenix AZ 85009. 602/269-2225. **Contact:** Director of Human Resources. **World Wide Web address:** http://www.bekins.com. **Description:** Part of a nationwide company engaged in moving, storing, and distributing products. **Common positions include:** Accountant/Auditor; Adjuster; Branch Manager; Budget Analyst; Claim Representative; Customer Service Representative; Financial Analyst; General Manager; Management Trainee; Transportation/Traffic Specialist. **Educational backgrounds include:** Accounting; Business Administration; Finance; Liberal Arts; Marketing. **Benefits:** 401(k); Dental Insurance; Disability Coverage; Life Insurance; Medical Insurance; Tuition Assistance. **Special programs:** Internships. **Corporate headquarters location:** This Location. **Other U.S. locations:** Nationwide. **Parent company:** The Bekins Company. **Listed on:** Privately held. **Number of employees at this location:** 20. **Number of employees nationwide:** 900.

ORIENT OVERSEAS CONTAINER LINE
4141 Hacienda Drive, Pleasanton CA 94588. 925/460-4800. **Contact:** Human Resources. **E-mail address:** hrinfo@oocl.com. **World Wide Web address:** http://www.oocl.com. **Description:** Orient Overseas Container Line provides a containerized cargo distribution system to shippers worldwide. **NOTE:** Entry-level positions and part-time jobs are offered. **Company slogan:** We take it personally. **Common positions include:** Account Manager; Account Representative; Accountant; Administrative Assistant; Claim Representative; Computer Support Technician; Controller; Credit Manager; Customer Service Representative; Finance Director; General Manager; Human Resources Manager; Marketing Specialist; Operations Manager; Project Manager; Sales Executive; Sales Manager; Sales Representative; Transportation/Traffic Specialist. **Educational backgrounds include:** Business Administration; Finance; MBA; Microsoft Office; Spreadsheets. **Benefits:** 401(k); Casual Dress - Daily; Dental Insurance; Disability Coverage; Employee Discounts; Life Insurance; Medical Insurance; Pension Plan; Public Transit Available; Sick Days; Tuition Assistance; Vacation Days. **Special programs:** Internships. **Corporate headquarters location:** This Location. **Other U.S. locations:** Nationwide. **International locations:** Worldwide. **Listed on:** Hong Kong Stock Exchange.

OUTBOARD MARINE CORPORATION
100 Sea Horse Drive, Waukegan IL 60085. 847/689-5200. **Fax:** 847/689-5220. **Contact:** Judy Williams, Manager, Staffing. **World Wide Web address:** http://www.omc-online.com. **Description:** Produces marine products including outboard motors and engines under brand names including Johnson, Evinrude, and Cobra; and boats under brand names including Donzi, Four Winns, Grumman, Seaswirl, Javelin, Sunbird, Suncruiser, Ryds, Quest, Stacer, Roughneck, and Chris-Craft. The company also produces replacement parts and accessories, offers boat rentals, and provides related financial services. **NOTE:** Second and third shifts are offered. **Common positions include:** Account Manager; Accountant; Administrative Assistant; Applications Engineer; AS400 Programmer Analyst; Auditor; Budget Analyst; Buyer; Controller; Database Administrator; Design Engineer; Draftsperson; Electrical/Electronics Engineer; Financial Analyst; Industrial Designer; Industrial Engineer; Internet Services Manager; Intranet Developer; Manufacturing Engineer; Marketing Specialist; Network Engineer; Network/Systems Administrator; Purchasing Agent/Manager; Sales Manager; Sales Representative; Systems Manager; Technical Writer/Editor. **Educational backgrounds include:** Business Administration; Computer Science; Engineering; Finance; Marketing; MBA. **Benefits:** 401(k); Casual Dress - Daily; Dental Insurance; Disability Coverage; Employee Discounts; Life Insurance; Medical Insurance; Relocation Assistance; Tuition Assistance. **Special programs:** Internships; Co-ops. **Corporate headquarters location:** This Location. **Listed on:** Privately held. **Annual sales/revenues:** More than $100 million. **Number of employees at this location:** 980. **Number of employees nationwide:** 7,000.

PST VANS INC.
1901 West 2100 South, Salt Lake City UT 84119. 801/975-2513. **Contact:** Human Resources. **Description:** A nationwide truckload carrier. **Common positions include:** Accountant/Auditor; Adjuster; Budget Analyst; Claim Representative; Computer Programmer; Credit Manager; Customer Service Representative; Driver; Human Resources Manager; Human Service Worker; Systems Analyst. **Benefits:** 401(k); Dental Insurance; Life Insurance; Medical Insurance. **Corporate headquarters location:** This Location. **Listed on:** NASDAQ.

PILOT AIR FREIGHT CORPORATION
P.O. Box 97, Lima PA 19037. 610/891-8100.
Contact: Bill Morgan, Human Resources Director.
World Wide Web address:
http://www.pilotair.com. **Description:** A freight
forwarding company. **Common positions include:**
Accountant/Auditor; Adjuster; Claim
Representative; Collector; Computer Programmer;
Credit Manager; Customer Service Representative;
Human Resources Manager; Investigator; Public
Relations Specialist; Purchasing Agent/Manager;
Quality Control Supervisor; Systems Analyst;
Transportation/Traffic Specialist. **Educational
backgrounds include:** Accounting; Business
Administration; Computer Science; Finance;
Marketing. **Benefits:** 401(k); Dental Insurance;
Disability Coverage; Life Insurance; Medical
Insurance; Profit Sharing. **Corporate headquarters
location:** This Location. **Other area locations:**
Allentown PA; Folcroft PA. **Listed on:** Privately
held. **Number of employees at this location:** 85.

PORT OF OAKLAND
530 Water Street, Oakland CA 94607. 510/272-
1515. **Contact:** Manager of Personnel and
Employee Services. **Description:** Operates Oakland
International Airport, maritime facilities, and
commercial real estate properties. **Common
positions include:** Accountant/Auditor; Attorney;
Buyer; Civil Engineer; Claim Representative;
Clerical Supervisor; Computer Programmer;
Construction and Building Inspector; Construction
Trade Worker; Department Manager; Draftsperson;
Electrical/Electronics Engineer; Employment
Interviewer; Financial Manager; Heating/AC/
Refrigeration Technician; Human Resources
Manager; Human Service Worker; Payroll Clerk;
Property and Real Estate Manager; Public Relations
Specialist; Purchasing Agent/Manager;
Receptionist; Secretary; Systems Analyst;
Typist/Word Processor. **Educational backgrounds
include:** Accounting; Business Administration;
Computer Science; Finance; Marketing. **Benefits:**
Dental Insurance; Disability Coverage; Employee
Discounts; Life Insurance; Medical Insurance;
Pension Plan; Savings Plan; Tuition Assistance.
Special programs: Internships. **Corporate
headquarters location:** This Location. **Number of
employees at this location:** 600.

PORT OF STOCKTON
2201 West Washington Street, Stockton CA 95203.
209/946-0246. **Fax:** 209/941-0537. **Contact:**
Christeen Ferree, Human Resources Manager.
World Wide Web address: http://www.
portofstockton.com. **Description:** Provides berthing
and warehousing facilities for inbound and
outbound marine shipping. The port also provides
domestic offices and warehouse space, and has land
available for industrial development. **Common
positions include:** Accountant/Auditor; Blue-Collar
Worker Supervisor; Computer Programmer;
Department Manager; Environmental Engineer;
General Manager; Human Resources Manager;
Management Trainee; Marketing Manager; MIS
Specialist; Operations/Production Manager;
Police/Law Enforcement Officer; Property and Real
Estate Manager; Purchasing Agent/Manager;
Systems Analyst; Systems Manager;
Transportation/Traffic Specialist; Typist/Word
Processor. **Educational backgrounds include:**
Accounting; Business Administration; Computer
Science; Marketing; Transportation/Logistics.
Benefits: Dental Insurance; Disability Coverage;
Life Insurance; Medical Insurance; Pension Plan;
Tuition Assistance. **Corporate headquarters
location:** This Location. **Annual sales/revenues:**
$11 - $20 million. **Number of employees at this
location:** 80.

POTAMKIN AUTO CENTER
678 11th Avenue, New York NY 10019. 212/603-
7070. **Fax:** 212/603-7035. **Contact:** Jack Calamusa,
Vice President/General Manager. **Description:**
Operates a large automobile leasing company.
Benefits: Life Insurance; Medical Insurance.
Special programs: Internships. **Corporate
headquarters location:** This Location. **Other U.S.
locations:** Hollywood FL; Brooklyn NY; Westbury
NY. **Number of employees at this location:** 200.
Number of employees nationwide: 275.

PRESTIGE TRAVEL INC.
6175 Spring Mountain Road, Las Vegas NV 89146.
702/251-5552. **Contact:** Human Resources. **E-mail
address:** prestige@vegas.infi.net. **Description:** A
travel agency with 21 locations in the greater Las
Vegas area. **Corporate headquarters location:**
This Location.

PRINCESS TOURS
2815 Second Avenue, Suite 400, Seattle WA 98121.
206/728-4202. **Contact:** Human Resources.
Description: Operates rail and motorcoach tours in
Alaska and the Canadian Rockies for land-only
touring, or in conjunction with cruise ships. The
company also owns and operates seasonal and year-
round hotels in Alaska. **Common positions
include:** Accountant/Auditor; Customer Service
Representative; Public Relations Specialist;
Purchasing Agent/Manager; Reservationist.
Educational backgrounds include: Accounting;
Communications; Marketing. **Benefits:** 401(k);
Dental Insurance; Disability Coverage; Life
Insurance; Medical Insurance; Tuition Assistance.
Corporate headquarters location: This Location.
Other U.S. locations: AK. **Number of employees
at this location:** 150. **Number of employees
nationwide:** 300.

**PROVIDENCE AND WORCESTER
RAILROAD COMPANY**
75 Hammond Street, Worcester MA 01610.
508/755-4000. **Contact:** Human Resources.
Description: This location is the main freight
classification yard and the locomotive and car
maintenance facility. Overall, Providence and
Worcester Railroad Company is an interstate freight
carrier conducting railroad operations in
Massachusetts, Rhode Island, and Connecticut. The
railroad operates on approximately 470 miles of
track. Freight traffic is interchanged with
Consolidated Rail Corporation (ConRail) at
Worcester MA and New Haven CT; with
Springfield Terminal Railway Company at Gardner
MA; and with New England Central Railroad at
New London CT. Through its connections,
Providence and Worcester Railroad links
approximately 78 communities through its lines.
Founded in 1847. **Benefits:** Pension Plan; Profit
Sharing; Stock Option. **Corporate headquarters
location:** This Location. **Other U.S. locations:**
Plainfield CT; Cumberland RI. **Number of
employees nationwide:** 140.

PUGET SOUND FREIGHT LINES INC.
P.O. Box 24526, Seattle WA 98124. 206/623-1600.
Contact: Personnel Department. **Description:** A
regional common carrier, operating in Washington
and Oregon, using both company drivers and
owner/operators in truckload operations. **Benefits:**
Dental Insurance; Medical Insurance; Pension Plan;
Profit Sharing. **Corporate headquarters location:**
This Location.

QUEENS SURFACE CORPORATION
128-15 28th Avenue, Flushing NY 11354. 718/445-
3100. **Contact:** Kathleen O'Shea, Director of
Human Resources. **Description:** A public

transportation firm providing express and local service in Queens and Manhattan with more than 270 buses operating on nearly 20 routes. **Common positions include:** Accountant/Auditor; Automotive Mechanic; Blue-Collar Worker Supervisor; Buyer; Claim Representative; Clerical Supervisor; Computer Programmer; Cost Estimator; Electrician; Human Resources Manager; Purchasing Agent/Manager. **Educational backgrounds include:** Accounting; Liberal Arts; Marketing; Mathematics. **Benefits:** 401(k); Dental Insurance; Disability Coverage; Life Insurance; Medical Insurance; Pension Plan. **Special programs:** Internships. **Office hours:** Monday - Friday, 8:30 a.m. - 4:30 p.m. **Corporate headquarters location:** This Location. **Number of employees at this location:** 700.

REEVE ALEUTIAN AIRWAYS, INC.
4700 West International Airport Road, Anchorage AK 99502. 907/243-1112. **Contact:** Personnel. **Description:** An air transportation company that is also engaged in aircraft fueling. **Common positions include:** Accountant/Auditor; Blue-Collar Worker Supervisor; Flight Attendant. **Educational backgrounds include:** Accounting; Communications. **Benefits:** Dental Insurance; Employee Discounts; Life Insurance; Medical Insurance; Pension Plan. **Corporate headquarters location:** This Location.

ROADWAY EXPRESS INC.
P.O. Box 471, Akron OH 44309. 330/384-1717. **Physical address:** 1077 Gorge Boulevard, Akron OH 44310. **Contact:** Human Resources. **World Wide Web address:** http://www.roadway.com. **Description:** A leading less-than-truckload motor carrier. **Corporate headquarters location:** This Location. **Listed on:** NASDAQ. **Number of employees nationwide:** 26,000.

ROCKY MOUNTAIN HELICOPTERS
P.O. Box 1337, Provo UT 84603. 801/375-1124. **Contact:** Personnel Department. **World Wide Web address:** http://www.rmhllc.com. **Description:** A certified air carrier offering helicopter passenger services for goods and people. The company provides extensive maintenance and overhaul services for aircraft engines, components, and air frames. The company operates fixed base locations in 33 states and overseas. **Common positions include:** Accountant/Auditor; Aircraft Mechanic/ Engine Specialist; Computer Programmer; General Manager; Marketing Specialist; Pilot. **Educational backgrounds include:** Accounting; Business Administration; Finance. **Benefits:** Dental Insurance; Life Insurance; Medical Insurance; Pension Plan. **Corporate headquarters location:** This Location. **Number of employees nationwide:** 430.

ROYAL CARIBBEAN
1050 Caribbean Way, Miami FL 33132. 305/379-2601. **Contact:** Human Resources. **World Wide Web address:** http://www.rccl.com. **Description:** An ocean cruise line that operates 12 ships sailing to the Caribbean, the Bahamas, Bermuda, Mexico, Alaska, the Mediterranean, Europe, the Greek Isles, Panama Canal, Hawaii, Scandinavia/Russia, and the Far East. **Corporate headquarters location:** This Location. **Listed on:** New York Stock Exchange. **Number of employees nationwide:** 6,900.

RYDER SYSTEM, INC.
3600 NW 82nd Avenue, Miami FL 33166. 305/593-3726. **Contact:** Human Resources. **World Wide Web address:** http://www.ryder.com. **Description:** Leases trucks, hauls automobiles, provides contract carriage and logistics services, and provides school bus transportation. Truck leasing operations are conducted in the United States, Puerto Rico, United Kingdom, Germany, and Poland with over 78,000 vehicles. The company provides maintenance, leasing, and related supplies, and also maintains over 27,000 nonleased trucks. Ryder System's commercial truck fleet consists of 33,700 vehicles that operate through approximately 4,650 company locations and independent dealers. The company also operates 7,140 school buses in 19 states, and manages or operates 88 public transit systems. **Corporate headquarters location:** This Location. **Listed on:** New York Stock Exchange.

SCHNEIDER NATIONAL, INC.
P.O. Box 2545, Green Bay WI 54306-2545. **Toll-free phone:** 800/558-6767. **Fax:** 920/592-3252. **Contact:** Human Resources Department. **World Wide Web address:** http://www.schneider.com. **Description:** Offers a wide range of transportation and logistics services. Schneider National's transportation sector offers van, intermodal, flatbed, and bulk tank services. The company also offers solutions to supply chain management problems. Founded in 1935. **NOTE:** Entry-level positions, part-time jobs, and second and third shifts are offered. **Common positions include:** Accountant; Applications Engineer; Computer Support Technician; Customer Service Representative; Database Manager; Financial Analyst; MIS Specialist; Network Engineer; Network/Systems Administrator; Operations Manager; Sales Manager; Software Engineer; Transportation/Traffic Specialist. **Educational backgrounds include:** Accounting; Business Administration; C/C++; Computer Science; Economics; Engineering; Finance; HTML; Java; Liberal Arts; Marketing; Mathematics; MBA; Novell; Software Development; Software Tech. Support; Transportation/Logistics; Visual Basic. **Benefits:** 401(k); Casual Dress - Fridays; Dental Insurance; Disability Coverage; Financial Planning Assistance; Flexible Schedule; Job Sharing; Life Insurance; Medical Insurance; Pension Plan; Profit Sharing; Relocation Assistance; Telecommuting; Tuition Assistance. **Special programs:** Internships; Training; Co-ops; Summer Jobs. **Corporate headquarters location:** This Location. **Other U.S. locations:** Nationwide. **International locations:** Canada; Mexico. **Listed on:** Privately held. **Annual sales/revenues:** More than $100 million. **Number of employees nationwide:** 19,000.

SEABOARD CORPORATION
9000 West 67th Street, Shawnee Mission KS 66202. 913/676-8800. **Contact:** Doug Schult, Director of Human Resources. **World Wide Web address:** http://www.seaboardcorp.com. **Description:** Seaboard Corporation is a diversified international company with interests in food processing and transportation. Food operations include poultry and pork processing, primarily in the eastern U.S., with hog farrowing plants in Colorado and Oklahoma; flour milling and baked goods production in Puerto Rico; and fruit, vegetables, shrimp, flour, pen-raised salmon, and animal feed processing and production. Seaboard Corporation operates an oceanliner service for cargo, with routes running between Florida and Latin America; and operates bulk carriers in the Atlantic Basin. The company also trades bulk grain and oil seed commodities. **Corporate headquarters location:** This Location. **Listed on:** American Stock Exchange.

SECURITY MOVING & STORAGE
1701 Florida Avenue NW, Washington DC 20009-2697. 202/234-5600. **Contact:** Conrad S. Reid, Executive Vice President. **Description:** Provides general storage, cold storage, freight forwarding,

moving and packing, and international trading services. **Common positions include:** Accountant; Administrator; Blue-Collar Worker Supervisor; Branch Manager; Claim Representative; Computer Programmer; Customer Service Representative; Department Manager; Management Trainee; Operations/Production Manager; Quality Control Supervisor; Transportation/Traffic Specialist. **Educational backgrounds include:** Accounting; Business Administration; Computer Science; Finance; Marketing. **Benefits:** Dental Insurance; Disability Coverage; Employee Discounts; Life Insurance; Medical Insurance; Pension Plan; Stock Option; Tuition Assistance. **Corporate headquarters location:** This Location. **Number of employees at this location:** 160.

SHURGARD STORAGE CENTERS INC.
1155 Valley Street, Suite 400, Seattle WA 98109. 206/624-8100. **Contact:** Human Resources. **World Wide Web address:** http://www.shurgard.com. **Description:** Specializes in the self-storage industry. Shurgard Storage Centers Inc. is a self-administered, real estate investment trust. As one of the largest self-storage center operators in the U.S., the company operates over 280 storage centers nationally and abroad. Shurgard owns approximately 60 percent of these centers. **Corporate headquarters location:** This Location. **Listed on:** New York Stock Exchange.

SILVER EAGLE COMPANY
700 North Hayden Island Drive, Suite 170, Portland OR 97217. 503/285-9831. **Contact:** Linda Notestine, Human Resources Manager. **Description:** A warehouse and trucking company. **Corporate headquarters location:** This Location. **Number of employees at this location:** 550.

SKYWEST, INC.
444 South River Road, St. George UT 84790. 435/634-3000. **Fax:** 435/634-3306. **Contact:** Personnel Manager. **World Wide Web address:** http://www.skywest.com. **Description:** A holding company. **Common positions include:** Aircraft Mechanic/Engine Specialist; Customer Service Representative; Flight Attendant; Pilot. **Benefits:** 401(k); Dental Insurance; Disability Coverage; Employee Discounts; Life Insurance; Medical Insurance. **Corporate headquarters location:** This Location. **Subsidiaries include:** SkyWest Airlines is a large regional airline that operates as a Delta Connection carrier and offers scheduled passenger and cargo air services to 42 cities in 12 western states. Scenic Airlines provides air tours, general aviation, and scheduled airline services to Arizona, Nevada, and Utah. National Parks Transportation, Inc. rents AVIS vehicles in five of the airport locations served by SkyWest and Scenic Airlines. **Listed on:** NASDAQ. **Stock exchange symbol:** SKYW. **Number of employees at this location:** 150. **Number of employees nationwide:** 2,200.

SOUTHWEST AIRLINES COMPANY
P.O. Box 36644, Dallas TX 75235-1644. 214/792-4213. **Fax:** 214/792-7015. **Contact:** SWA People Department. **World Wide Web address:** http://www.southwest.com. **Description:** One of the U.S.'s only major short-haul, low-fare, high-frequency, point-to-point carriers. Southwest Airlines flies to 45 cities in 22 states and offers over 1,900 flights daily. **Common positions include:** Accountant; Administrator; Aircraft Mechanic/Engine Specialist; Computer Programmer; Customer Service Representative; Flight Attendant; Human Resources Manager; Marketing Manager; Public Relations Specialist; Receptionist; Sales Representative; Secretary; Systems Analyst. **Educational backgrounds include:** Accounting;

Computer Science; Liberal Arts; Marketing. **Benefits:** 401(k); Dental Insurance; Disability Coverage; Employee Discounts; Life Insurance; Medical Insurance; Profit Sharing; Savings Plan. **Special programs:** Internships. **Corporate headquarters location:** This Location. **Other U.S. locations:** Nationwide. **Listed on:** New York Stock Exchange. **Number of employees at this location:** 3,600. **Number of employees nationwide:** 17,000.

SPRINGFIELD AIRPORT AUTHORITY CAPITAL AIRPORT
1200 Capital Airport Drive, Springfield IL 62707-8419. 217/788-1060. **Contact:** Human Resources. **World Wide Web address:** http://www.flyspi.com. **Description:** Operates a community airport. **Corporate headquarters location:** This Location.

SWIFT TRANSPORTATION COMPANY
P.O. Box 29243, Phoenix AZ 85038-9243. 602/269-9700. **Physical address:** 2200 South 75th Avenue, Phoenix AZ 85043. **Contact:** Human Resources. **Description:** One of the largest truckload motor carriers in the United States. Swift Transportation Company offers a wide variety of trailers, with more than 5,600 on the road everyday. Swift Transportation has more than 2,400 power units to pull the widest variety of vans, flatbeds, and specialty trailers available to the industry. The company also provides full-service equipment leasing, dedicated fleet programs, and third-party logistics services for several major customers. **Corporate headquarters location:** This Location. **Listed on:** NASDAQ. **Stock exchange symbol:** SWFT. **President/CEO:** Jerry C. Moyes. **Annual sales/revenues:** More than $100 million.

THAI AIRWAYS INTERNATIONAL PUBLIC COMPANY LIMITED
222 North Sepulveda Boulevard, Suite 1950, El Segundo CA 90245. 310/640-0097x202. **Fax:** 310/640-7675. **Contact:** Ruth Campos, Personnel Coordinator. **Description:** An international passenger and freight air carrier. **NOTE:** Flight crews are only hired through the Bangkok, Thailand location. **Common positions include:** Services Sales Representative; Ticket Agent. **Benefits:** 401(k); Dental Insurance; Disability Coverage; Employee Discounts; Life Insurance; Medical Insurance; Profit Sharing; Vision Insurance. **Corporate headquarters location:** Bangkok, Thailand. **Other U.S. locations:** Nationwide. **Number of employees at this location:** 50. **Number of employees nationwide:** 100.

THERMO KING CORPORATION
314 West 90th Street, Bloomington MN 55420. 952/887-2200. **Fax:** 952/885-3404. **Contact:** Human Resources Manager. **Description:** Serves the refrigeration and air conditioning needs of buses and tractor-trailer centers. Thermo King is a world leader in temperature-controlled transport. **Common positions include:** Accountant/Auditor; Computer Programmer; Customer Service Representative; Designer; Draftsperson; Electrical/Electronics Engineer; Industrial Engineer; Materials Engineer; Mechanical Engineer; Purchasing Agent/Manager; Software Engineer; Systems Analyst; Test Engineer. **Educational backgrounds include:** Engineering. **Benefits:** 401(k); Dental Insurance; Disability Coverage; Employee Discounts; Life Insurance; Medical Insurance; Pension Plan; Savings Plan; Tuition Assistance. **Corporate headquarters location:** This Location. **Other U.S. locations:** Montgomery AL; Louisville GA; Hastings NE. **Subsidiaries include:** I.C.C. **Parent company:** Westinghouse. **Number of employees at this location:** 850. **Number of employees nationwide:** 2,000.

THRALL CAR MANUFACTURING CO.

2521 State Street, Chicago Heights IL 60411. 708/757-2285. **Fax:** 708/758-3290. **Contact:** Human Resources. **Description:** Manufactures railway freight cars. **Common positions include:** Accountant/Auditor; Buyer; Industrial Engineer; Industrial Production Manager; Mechanical Engineer; Registered Nurse; Stress Analyst. **Educational backgrounds include:** Accounting; Engineering; Finance; Marketing; Mathematics. **Benefits:** 401(k); Dental Insurance; Disability Coverage; Employee Discounts; Life Insurance; Medical Insurance; Profit Sharing; Tuition Assistance. **Corporate headquarters location:** This Location. **Number of employees at this location:** 900. **Number of employees nationwide:** 2,000.

THRIFTY RENT-A-CAR SYSTEM INC.

5310 East 31st Street, Tulsa OK 74135. 918/665-3930. **Contact:** Human Resources. **World Wide Web address:** http://www.thrifty.com. **Description:** A car rental company with a significant presence in both the airport and local car rental markets. In the airport market, Thrifty Rent-A-Car operates in every major airport in Canada and Australia and in nearly 40 cities in the U.S., the Caribbean, and Central and South America. In the U.S. local market, Thrifty maintains a relationship with Montgomery Ward and operates rental facilities in many of the retailer's Auto Express Centers. In Canada, Thrifty has a similar relationship with Canadian Tire. Thrifty is also one of the few car rental companies that features a self-contained, automated care rental center that operates in a manner similar to an automated teller machine. Thrifty Truck Rental is another local market the company pursues. **Corporate headquarters location:** This Location. **Parent company:** DaimlerChrysler.

TIGHE WAREHOUSING & DISTRIBUTION

45 Holton Street, Winchester MA 01890. 781/729-5440. **Fax:** 781/721-5862. **Contact:** Human Resources. **E-mail address:** personnel@tighe-co.com. **World Wide Web address:** http://www.tighe-co.com. **Description:** Provides warehousing, transportation, and related distribution services.

TITAN GLOBAL TECHNOLOGIES, LTD.

P.O. Box 617, Montvale NJ 07645. 201/930-0300. **Contact:** Human Resources. **World Wide Web address:** http://www.titan-global-tech.com. **Description:** Designs, manufactures, and installs monorail transportation systems. **Common positions include:** Accountant/Auditor; Administrative Manager; Advertising Clerk; Architect; Civil Engineer; Computer Operator; Computer Programmer; Cost Estimator; Electrical Engineer; Mechanical Engineer; Quality Control Supervisor; Systems Analyst; Transportation/Traffic Specialist. **Benefits:** Dental Insurance; Disability Coverage; Life Insurance; Medical Insurance. **Corporate headquarters location:** This Location.

TIX INTERNATIONAL GROUP

201 Main Street, Nyack NY 10960. 914/358-1007. **Toll-free phone:** 800/269-6849. **Fax:** 914/358-1266. **Contact:** Human Resources. **E-mail address:** travel@tixtravel.com. **World Wide Web address:** http://www.tixtravel.com. **Description:** A full-service travel agency and ticket broker for concerts, sports, and theater events. **Common positions include:** Travel Agent. **Corporate headquarters location:** This Location. **Listed on:** Privately held.

TRANS WORLD AIRLINES, INC. (TWA)

One City Center, 515 North Sixth Street, 18th Floor, St. Louis MO 63101. 314/589-3000. **Fax:** 314/589-3129. **Contact:** Employee Relations. **World Wide Web address:** http://www.twa.com. **Description:** Trans World Airlines provides scheduled air transportation of passengers, freight, and mail; and provides assistance and contractual services to other airlines. The company, with hubs in St. Louis and New York, provides service to cities in the U.S., Europe, and the Middle East. **Corporate headquarters location:** This Location.

TRANSPORT CORPORATION OF AMERICA

1769 Yankee Doodle Road, Eagan MN 55121. 651/686-2500. **Toll-free phone:** 800/345-0479. **Fax:** 651/686-2540. **Contact:** Karen Vesovich, Human Resources Manager. **World Wide Web address:** http://www.transportamerica.com. **Description:** An irregular route truckload motor carrier, covering 48 states. Founded in 1984. **NOTE:** Entry-level positions are offered. **Common positions include:** Account Manager; Accountant; AS400 Programmer Analyst; Chief Financial Officer; Claim Representative; Computer Operator; Computer Programmer; Computer Technician; Controller; Customer Service Representative; Database Administrator; Help-Desk Technician; Human Resources Manager; Marketing Manager; MIS Specialist; Network/Systems Administrator; Operations Manager; Sales Representative; Software Engineer; Systems Analyst; Systems Manager; Transportation/Traffic Specialist. **Educational backgrounds include:** Accounting; Business Administration; Software Development; Software Tech. Support. **Benefits:** 401(k); Casual Dress - Fridays; Dental Insurance; Disability Coverage; Life Insurance; Medical Insurance; Tuition Assistance; Vacation Days (6 - 10). **Corporate headquarters location:** This Location. **Listed on:** NASDAQ. **Stock exchange symbol:** TCAM. **President/CEO:** Robert Meyers. **Information Systems Manager:** Jon Seebach. **Vice President of Marketing:** Dan Van Alstine. **Annual sales/revenues:** Less than $5 million. **Number of employees at this location:** 275. **Number of employees nationwide:** 1,150.

THE TRAVEL COMPANY

1437 Old Square Road, Suite 204, Jackson MS 39211. 601/981-1133. **Fax:** 601/362-8966. **Contact:** Human Resources. **Description:** A travel agency. **Corporate headquarters location:** This Location. **Listed on:** Privately held. **Number of employees at this location:** 15. **Number of employees nationwide:** 35.

TRINITY INDUSTRIES, INC.

P.O. Box 568887, Dallas TX 75356-8887. 214/631-4420. **Contact:** Human Resources Department. **World Wide Web address:** http://www.trin.net. **Description:** Manufactures an assortment of railroad and construction equipment and replacement parts. Trinity Industries also offers related services for the transportation, construction, aerospace, commercial, and industrial markets. Products include railcars, gas processing systems, petroleum transportation systems, guard rails, bridge girders and beams, airport boarding bridges, barges, tug boats, military marine vessels, and precision welding products. Trinity Industries also makes concrete and aggregates and produces metal components for the petrochemical, industrial, processing, and power markets. **Common positions include:** Accountant/Auditor; Data Entry Clerk. **Educational backgrounds include:** Accounting; Business Administration; Computer Science; Engineering. **Benefits:** Daycare Assistance; Disability Coverage; Employee Discounts; Life Insurance; Medical Insurance; Pension Plan; Profit Sharing; Savings Plan; Tuition Assistance. **Corporate headquarters location:** This Location. **Listed on:** New York Stock Exchange.

U-HAUL INTERNATIONAL, INC.
2727 North Central Avenue, Phoenix AZ 85004.
602/263-6011. **Contact:** Henry Kelly, Human
Resources Director. **World Wide Web address:**
http://www.uhaul.com. **Description:** One of the
largest consumer truck rental operations in the
world, with a fleet of over 158,000 trucks and
trailers. The company operates in all 50 states and
all Canadian provinces, with over 12,000 dealers
and 1,100 U-Haul centers. The company is one of
the largest operators of self-storage units in the U.S.
with over 700 storage locations. U-Haul has a
computerized, nationwide storage reservation
system. U-Haul is one of the world's largest
installers of permanent trailer hitches, and is one of
the largest retailers of propane fuel. Founded in
1945. **Corporate headquarters location:** This
Location. **Number of employees nationwide:**
15,500.

US AIRWAYS, INC.
2345 Crystal Drive, Arlington VA 22227. 703/872-
7000. **Contact:** Senior Vice President of Human
Resources. **World Wide Web address:**
http://www.usairways.com. **Description:** Provides
air transportation of passengers, property, and mail;
reservations and ground support services to
commuter carriers; aircraft remarketing; aircraft
appraisal services; general aviation and spare parts
sales; fixed-based operations; fuel services; and
other aviation-related activities. **Corporate
headquarters location:** This Location. **Annual
sales/revenues:** More than $100 million.

USA TRUCK, INC.
P.O. Box 449, Van Buren AR 72957. 501/471-2510.
Fax: 501/471-3877. **Contact:** Jerry Seiter, Director
of Administration. **World Wide Web address:**
http://www.usa-truck.com. **Description:** A trucking
company that provides services for retail companies.
Common positions include: Transportation/Traffic
Specialist. **Educational backgrounds include:**
Business Administration. **Benefits:** 401(k); Dental
Insurance; Disability Coverage; Life Insurance;
Medical Insurance; Profit Sharing; Tuition
Assistance. **Corporate headquarters location:**
This Location. **Listed on:** NASDAQ.

USF RED STAR EXPRESS INC.
34 Wright Avenue, Auburn NY 13021. 315/253-
2721. **Contact:** Human Resources. **Description:** A
trucking company that serves as a national shipping
agent for other companies. **Corporate
headquarters location:** This Location. **Number of
employees at this location:** 150.

UNION PACIFIC CORPORATION
1416 Dodge Street, Omaha NE 68179. 402/271-
5777. **Contact:** Human Resources. **World Wide
Web address:** http://www.up.com. **Description:**
Provides transportation, computer technology, and
logistics services. Union Pacific Corporation
operates in three divisions: Union Pacific Railroad;
Overnite Transportation; and Union Pacific
Technologies. **Corporate headquarters location:**
This Location. **Listed on:** New York Stock
Exchange. **Stock exchange symbol:** UNP. **Number
of employees nationwide:** 65,000.

UNITED AIRLINES, INC. (UAL)
P.O. Box 66100, Chicago IL 60666. 847/700-4000.
Physical address: 1200 East Algonquin Road, Elk
Grove Township IL 60007. **Fax:** 847/700-5287.
Contact: Human Resources. **World Wide Web
address:** http://www.ual.com. **Description:** United
Airlines services 159 airports in the U.S. and 32
foreign countries in Europe, North and South
America, and Asia. Domestic hubs are located in
Chicago, Denver, San Francisco, and Washington
DC. International hubs are located in Japan and
England. **Common positions include:**
Accountant/Auditor; Aerospace Engineer; Aircraft
Mechanic/Engine Specialist; Budget Analyst;
Buyer; Computer Programmer; Customer Service
Representative; Financial Analyst; Industrial
Engineer; Meteorologist; Paralegal; Psychologist;
Software Engineer; Structural Engineer.
Educational backgrounds include: Accounting;
Business Administration; Computer Science;
Engineering; Finance. **Benefits:** 401(k); Dental
Insurance; Disability Coverage; Employee
Discounts; ESOP; Life Insurance; Medical
Insurance; Pension Plan; Savings Plan. **Special
programs:** Internships. **Corporate headquarters
location:** This Location. **Listed on:** New York
Stock Exchange.

UNITED PARCEL SERVICE (UPS)
55 Glenlake Parkway NE, Atlanta GA 30328.
404/828-6000. **Fax:** 404/828-6440. **Contact:**
Human Resources. **World Wide Web address:**
http://www.ups.com. **Description:** This location
houses the administrative offices. Overall, United
Parcel Service is a package pickup and delivery
service organization, providing service to all 50
states and to more than 185 countries and territories
worldwide. The company delivers approximately 12
million packages daily. **Common positions
include:** Accountant/Auditor; Administrative
Manager; Clerical Supervisor; Computer
Programmer; Draftsperson; Economist; Electrical/
Electronics Engineer; Financial Analyst; Industrial
Engineer; Mechanical Engineer; Paralegal; Public
Relations Specialist; Software Engineer; Systems
Analyst; Technical Writer/Editor; Transportation/
Traffic Specialist. **Educational backgrounds
include:** Accounting; Art/Design; Communications;
Computer Science; Economics; Engineering;
Finance; Marketing. **Benefits:** 401(k); Dental
Insurance; Disability Coverage; Life Insurance;
Medical Insurance; Pension Plan; Profit Sharing;
Tuition Assistance. **Special programs:** Internships.
Corporate headquarters location: This Location.
Listed on: Privately held. **Number of employees at
this location:** 2,000. **Number of employees
nationwide:** 300,000.
Other U.S. locations:
- 6800 South Sixth Street, Oak Creek WI 53154.
  Toll-free phone: 800/742-5877.

VAPOR CORPORATION
6420 West Howard Street, Niles IL 60714. 847/967-
8300. **Contact:** Anna Morales, Recruiting
Coordinator. **Description:** Manufactures railroad
passenger car heating and air conditioning
equipment, steam generators, electronic controls for
transit rails, and railroad speed indicating/
pacesetting controls. **Corporate headquarters
location:** This Location.

VIKING FREIGHT SYSTEM, INC.
6411 Guadalupe Mines Road, San Jose CA 95120.
408/268-9600. **Contact:** Human Resources.
Description: A trucking company. **Corporate
headquarters location:** This Location.

WE TRANSPORT INC.
303 Sunnyside Boulevard, Plainview NY 11803.
516/349-8200. **Contact:** Mary Prioli, Personnel
Manager. **Description:** An area school bus and van
transportation company. **Common positions
include:** Accountant; Accounting Clerk;
Administrative Assistant; Bus Driver; Claim
Representative; Computer Animator; Computer
Engineer; Computer Programmer; Customer Service
Representative; Department Manager; Dispatcher;
Draftsperson; Human Resources Manager;
Operations Manager; Payroll Clerk; Safety

Specialist; Transportation/Traffic Specialist; Vice President of Operations. **Educational backgrounds include:** Accounting; Business Administration; Communications; Computer Science; Liberal Arts. **Benefits:** 401(k); Casual Dress - Fridays; Dental Insurance; Disability Coverage; Life Insurance; Medical Insurance. **Special programs:** Internships. **Corporate headquarters location:** This Location. **Facilities Manager:** Pam DeRosse. **Number of employees at this location:** 70.

YELLOW FREIGHT SYSTEMS, INC.
P.O. Box 7270, Shawnee Mission KS 66207. 913/344-3000. **Physical address:** 10990 Roe Avenue, Overland Park KS 66211. **Contact:** Manager of Human Resource Services. **World Wide Web address:** http://www.yellowfreight.com. **Description:** A national, long-haul truckload carrier, with over 585 terminal locations in 50 states, Puerto Rico, and many Canadian provinces. **Corporate headquarters location:** This Location.

Parent company: Yellow Corporation. **Listed on:** American Stock Exchange. **Number of employees nationwide:** 28,000.

ZERO MOTOR FREIGHT INC.
P.O. Box 33940, San Antonio TX 78265. 210/661-4151. **Fax:** 210/666-0800. **Contact:** David Bishop, Vice President. **Description:** A freight trucking company that delivers goods to 48 states. Founded in 1949. **Common positions include:** Account Manager; Accountant/Auditor; Administrative Assistant; Assistant Manager; Blue-Collar Worker Supervisor; General Manager; Marketing Manager; Sales Executive; Secretary. **Benefits:** Dental Insurance; Life Insurance; Medical Insurance. **Special programs:** Training. **Corporate headquarters location:** This Location. **Annual sales/revenues:** $11 - $20 million. **Number of employees at this location:** 140.

For more information on career opportunities in transportation and travel industries:

Associations

AIR TRANSPORT ASSN. OF AMERICA
1301 Pennsylvania Avenue NW, Suite 1100, Washington DC 20004. 202/626-4000. World Wide Web address: http://www.air-transport.org. A trade association for the major U.S. airlines.

AIRLINE PILOTS ASSOCIATION INTERNATIONAL
535 Herndon Parkway, Herndon VA 20170. 703/481-4440.

AMERICAN BUREAU OF SHIPPING
2 World Trade Center, 106th Floor, New York NY 10048. 212/839-5000. World Wide Web address: http://www.abs-group.com.

AMERICAN SOCIETY OF TRAVEL AGENTS
1101 King Street, Suite 200, Alexandria VA 22314. 703/739-2782. World Wide Web address: http://www. astanet.com.

ASSOCIATION OF AMERICAN RAILROADS
50 F Street NW, Washington DC 20001. 202/639-2100. World Wide Web address: http://www.aar. com.

INSTITUTE OF TRANSPORTATION ENGINEERS
525 School Street SW, Suite 410, Washington DC 20024. 202/554-8050. World Wide Web address: http://www.ite.org. Scientific and educational association, providing for professional development of members and others.

MARINE TECHNOLOGY SOCIETY
1828 L Street NW, Suite 906, Washington DC 20036. 202/775-5966. World Wide Web address: http://www.mtsociety.org.

NATIONAL MOTOR FREIGHT TRAFFIC ASSOCIATION
2200 Mill Road, Alexandria VA 22314-4654. 703/838-1810. World Wide Web address: http://www.erols.com/nmfta/index.htm. Works towards the improvement and advancement of the interests and welfare of motor common carriers.

Books

FLIGHT PLAN TO THE FLIGHT DECK: STRATEGIES FOR A PILOT CAREER
Cage Consulting, Inc., 13275 East Fremont Place, Suite 315, Englewood CO 80112-3917. Toll-free phone: 888/899-CAGE. Fax: 303/799-1998. World Wide Web address: http://www.cageconsulting.com.

WELCOME ABOARD! YOUR CAREER AS A FLIGHT ATTENDANT
Cage Consulting, Inc., 13275 East Fremont Place, Suite 315, Englewood CO 80112-3917. Toll-free phone: 888/899-CAGE. Fax: 303/799-1998. World Wide Web address: http://www.cageconsulting.com.

Directories

MOODY'S TRANSPORTATION MANUAL
Financial Information Services, 60 Madison Avenue, 6th Floor, New York NY 10010. Toll-free phone: 800/342-5647.

NATIONAL TANK TRUCK CARRIER DIRECTORY
National Tank Truck Carriers, 2200 Mill Road, Alexandria VA 22314. 703/838-1700.

Magazines

AMERICAN SHIPPER
Howard Publications, P.O. Box 4728, Jacksonville FL 32201. 904/355-2601. Monthly.

FLEET OWNER
PRIMEDIA Intertec, 11 Riverbend Drive South, P.O. Box 4211, Stamford CT 06907-0211.

HEAVY DUTY TRUCKING
Newport Communications, P.O. Box W, Newport Beach CA 92658. 949/261-1636.

ITE JOURNAL
Institute of Transportation Engineers, 525 School Street SW, Suite 410, Washington DC 20024-2797. 202/554-8050. World Wide Web address: http://www.ite.org. One year subscription (12 issues): $60.00.

MARINE DIGEST AND TRANSPORTATION NEWS
Marine Publishing, Inc., 1710 South Norman Street, Seattle WA 98144. 206/709-1840.

SHIPPING DIGEST
51 Madison Avenue, New York NY 10010. 212/837-7029.

TRAFFIC WORLD MAGAZINE
1230 National Press Building, Washington DC
20045-2200. 202/783-1101.

Newsletters

AIR JOBS DIGEST
World Air Data, Department 700, P.O. Box 42360,
Washington DC 20015. This monthly resource
provides current job openings in aerospace, space,
and aviation industries. Subscription rates: $96.00
annually, $69.00 for six months, and $49.00 for
three months.

Online Services

**THE AIRLINE EMPLOYMENT ASSISTANCE
CORPS.**
World Wide Web address: http://www.avjobs.com.
Site for aviation jobseekers providing worldwide
classified ads, resume assistance, publications, and
over 350 links to aviation-related Websites and
news groups. Certain resources are members-only
access.

COOLWORKS
World Wide Web address: http://www.coolworks.
com. This Website provides links to 22,000 job
openings on cruise ships, at national parks, summer
camps, ski areas, river areas, ranches, fishing areas,
and resorts. This site also includes information on
volunteer openings.

INTERNATIONAL SEAFARERS EXCHANGE
World Wide Web address: http://www.jobxchange.
com. Over 300 listings on cruise ships or in other
maritime positions that can be searched by location,
title, skills, or salary.

JOBNET: HOSPITALITY INDUSTRY
World Wide Web address: http://www.westga.
edu/~coop/joblinks/subject/hospitality.html.
Provides links to job openings and information for
airlines and cruise ships.

TRAVEL PROFESSIONALS FORUM
Go: Travpro. To join this CompuServe forum, you
will need to send an e-mail to the sysop for
permission.

Alphabetical Index

EMCORE CORPORATION • 452
EMERSON COLLEGE • 412
EMERSON ELECTRIC CO. • 452
EMIGRANT SAVINGS BANK • 205
EMISPHERE TECHNOLOGIES • 235
EMMIS COMMUNICATIONS • 307
EMPI, INC. • 575
EMPIRE BLUE CROSS AND BLUE
    SHIELD • 664
EMPIRE SCIENTIFIC CORP. • 692
EMPIRE SOUTHWEST CO. • 860
EMPORIUM DEPT. STORES • 860
ENCAD, INC. • 349
ENCORE REAL TIME COMPUTING,
    INC. • 349
ENCYCLOPAEDIA BRITANNICA •
    806
ENDEVCO CORPORATION • 452
ENDOGEN, INC. • 235
ENDOSONICS CORP. • 575
ENERGETIC SOLUTIONS • 278
ENERGY INTELLIGENCE GROUP,
    INC. • 807
ENERQUIP INC. • 734
ENGINE COMPONENTS INC. • 86
ENGINEERED AIR SYSTEMS • 734
ENGINEERING SVC. • 86, 183
ENPLAS U.S.A., INC. • 278
ENSCICON CORPORATION • 350
ENSCO INC. • 452
ENTERPRISE RENT-A-CAR • 896
THE ENTERPRISE SYST GRP • 350
ENTERTAINMENT PUBLICATIONS,
    INC. • 72
ENTEX INFORMATION SVCS • 350
ENVIROMETRICS INC. • 489
ENVIRONMENTAL ELEMENTS
    CORP. • 734
ENVIRONMENTAL MATERIALS
    CORP. • 489
ENVIRONMENTAL MONITORING
    & TESTING CORP. • 127
ENVIRONMENTAL TECTONICS
    COMPANY • 735
ENVIROTEK PUMPSYSTEMS • 278,
    735
EPICOR SOFTWARE CORP. • 350
EPIMMUNE INC. • 235
EPISCOPAL MINISTRIES TO THE
    AGING • 575
EPITOPE, INC. • 235
EPIX MEDICAL INC. • 575
ePRESENCE, INC. • 350
EPSILON • 350
EPSON PORTLAND INC. • 350
EQUIFAX, INC. • 502
EQUITABLE LIFE & CASUALTY
    INSURANCE • 664
EQUITY ASSETS MGMT. • 508
MARSHALL ERDMAN AND
    ASSOCIATES • 128
ERICSSON INC. • 307
ERIM • 452
ERNEST ORLANDO LAWRENCE
    BERKELEY NTNL LAB • 242
ERNST & YOUNG • 53, 54
THE ERTL COMPANY INC. • 692
ESCO CORPORATION • 735
ESKIMO PIE CORPORATION • 528
ESPRIT DE CORP • 101, 860
ESSELTE CORPORATION • 692
ESSENTIAL COMMS. • 351
THE ESTEE LAUDER COS. • 693
ESTERLINE TECHNOLOGIES • 86,
    452
ETAK, INC. • 351
ETHAN ALLEN INC. • 860
ETHICON, INC. • 575
THE EUREKA COMPANY • 693

EURO RSCG TATHAM • 72
EUROPEAN JOURNALISM
    NETWORK (EJN) • 807
EUROPEAN LANGUAGE CENTER
    INC. • 160
EUTECTIC CORPORATION • 735
EVA-TONE • 735, 807
EVANS & SUTHERLAND
    COMPUTER CORP. • 351
J.C. EVANS CONSTRUCTION
    COMPANY • 128
GENE EVANS FORD, INC. • 860
EVANS INDUSTRIES • 279
EVANS SYSTEMS • 351, 489, 860
EVANSTON HOSPITAL
    CORPORATION • 575
EVEREST & JENNINGS • 575
EVEREST MEDICAL CORP. • 576
EVEREX SYSTEMS INC. • 351
EVERGREEN INTERNATIONAL
    AVIATION, INC. • 86
EX-CEL SOLUTIONS, INC. • 351
EX-CELL HOME FASHIONS • 693
EXAR CORPORATION • 452
EXCALIBUR TECHNOLOGIES
    CORP. • 351
EXCEL CORPORATION • 528
EXCHANGE NATIONAL
    BANCSHARES INC. • 205
EXCITE INC. • 351
EXECUSTAY, INC. • 638
EXECUTIVE SOFTWARE INTNL. • 351
EXECUTONE INFORMATION
    SYSTEMS, INC. • 307
EXEL INNS OF AMERICA • 638
EXEMPLAR LOGIC, INC. • 352
EXETER HOSPITAL • 576
EXIDE CORPORATION • 183, 735
EXIGENT INTERNATIONAL • 352
EXODUS COMMS. • 352
EXOTIC RUBBER & PLASTICS
    CORPORATION • 279
EXPERIAN • 72
EXPONENT FAILURE ANALYSIS
    ASSOCIATES • 128
EXPORT-IMPORT BANK OF THE
    U.S. • 205
EXTENDED SYSTEMS, INC. • 352
EYRING CORPORATION • 352

F

F&F FOODS, INC. • 529
F&W PUBLICATIONS INC. • 807
FAS TECHNOLOGIES • 453
FIC INSURANCE GROUP • 664
FKW INC. • 307
FM GLOBAL • 128
FMC CORPORATION • 279, 736
FSI INTERNATIONAL • 453
FWD/SEAGRAVE • 183
FACTORY 2-U STORES, INC. • 860
FAIR, ISAAC AND CO. • 55, 352
FAIRCHILD AEROSPACE
    CORPORATION • 86
THE FAIRCHILD CORP.• 307, 736
FAIRCHILD FASTENERS - U.S. • 86
FAIRCHILD PUBLICATIONS • 807
FAIRCOM • 353
FAIRFIELD COMMUNITIES • 840
FAIRFIELD UNIVERSITY • 412
FAIRMONT HOMES, INC. • 128
FAIRMONT HOTEL • 638
FAIRVIEW HEALTH SERVICES • 576
THE FALK CORPORATION • 736
FAMILY & CHILD SERVICES OF
    D.C. • 261
FAMILY DOLLAR STORES • 861
FAMILY GOLF CENTERS • 162

FAMILY INNS OF AMERICA • 638
FAMILY SERVICE & CONSUMER
    CREDIT COUNSELING
    SERVICE • 261
FAMOUS AMOS RESTAURANTS,
    INC. • 639
FAMOUS FOOTWEAR • 861
FAMOUS-BARR COMPANY • 861
FANUC ROBOTICS NORTH
    AMERICA, INC. • 453
FAR EAST NATIONAL BANK • 205
FARBERWARE HOME PRODUCTS,
    INC. • 693
FARBEST FOODS INC. • 529
FARGO ASSEMBLY CO. • 453
FARGO ELECTRONICS, INC. • 736
FARLEY INDUSTRIES • 101
FARM BUREAU FINANCIAL
    SERVICES • 664
LEON FARMER & CO. • 529
FARMER JOHN MEATS CO. • 529
FARMERS AND MERCHANTS
    BANK • 205
FARMERS INSURANCE GRP. • 664
FARMLAND INDUSTRIES • 529
FARMSTEAD TELEPHONE GROUP,
    INC. • 308
FARR COMPANY • 736
FARRAR, STRAUS & GIROUX • 807
FARREL CORPORATION • 279
FARRELL LINES INC. • 896
FARRELL'S ICE CREAM PARLOURS
    • 639
FAST • 453
FAULKNER INFORMATION
    SERVICES • 807
FAWN INDUSTRIES • 279, 453
FAY, SPOFFORD & THORNDIKE,
    INC. • 129, 489
FAYGO BEVERAGES, INC. • 529
FEDDERS CORPORATION • 693
FEDERAL BEEF PROCESSORS •
    529
FEDERAL DATA CORP. • 353
FEDERAL EXPRESS CORP. • 897
FEDERAL NATIONAL MORTGAGE
    ASSOC. • 503
FEDERAL PACKAGING
    CORPORATION • 279
FEDERAL REALTY INVESTMENT
    TRUST • 840
FEDERAL RESERVE BANK OF
    CHICAGO • 205
FEDERAL RESERVE BANK OF ST.
    LOUIS • 205
FEDERAL RESERVE BANK OF SAN
    FRANCISCO • 206
FEDERAL-MOGUL CORPORATION
    • 183
FEDERATED DEPARTMENT STORES,
    INC. • 861
FEDERATED DORCHESTER
    NEIGHBORHOOD HOUSES •
    261
FEDERATED INSURANCE • 664
FEDERATED-NATIONAL INC. • 639
FELD ENTERTAINMENT, INC. • 163
THE FEMALE HEALTH CO. • 236
FENDER MUSICAL INSTRUMENTS
    CORP. • 693
FENDERS & MORE, INC. • 183
FERRO CORPORATION • 279
FERRY CAP & SET SCREW
    COMPANY • 736
THE FERTILIZER INSTITUTE • 279
FIBERMARK, INC. • 783
FIBERVISIONS, INC. • 279
FIDELITY FEDERAL BANK &TRUST •
    206

FRU-CON CONSTRUCTION CORPORATION • 129
FUELLGRAF ELECTRIC COMPANY • 129, 454
FUGRO GEOSCIENCES • 129
FUJICOLOR PROCESSING • 808
FUJISAWA HEALTHCARE • 236
FUJITSU COMPUTER PRODUCTS OF AMERICA INC. • 354
FULLER COMPANY • 737
H.B. FULLER COMPANY • 280
FULTON FINANCIAL CORP. • 210
FULTON STATE HOSPITAL • 578
FUNK SOFTWARE, INC. • 354
FURNITURE ROW CO. • 863
FUTRON CORPORATION • 87
FUTURE MEDIA • 808
THE FUTURES GROUP INTERNATIONAL • 55

G

G&W ELECTRIC COMPANY • 454
GATX CAPITAL CORP. • 505
GATX CORPORATION • 897
GB TECH INC. • 87, 354
GBC/CCTV CORP. • 694
GBF GRAPHICS INC. • 808
GCC TECHNOLOGIES • 354
GCI GROUP • 73
GCI KAMER SINGER • 73
GE AIRCRAFT ENGINES • 87
GE AUTOMATION SERVICES • 454
GE CAPITAL CORP. • 505
GE CAPITAL IT SOLUTIONS • 354
GE FINANCIAL ASSURANCE PARTNERSHIP MARKETING • 73
GFI PREMIUM FOODS, INC. • 530
GKN AEROSPACE CHEM-TRONICS INC. • 87
GMAC INTEGON • 665
GMAC-RFC • 506
GN RESOUND CORP. • 579
GP STRATEGIES CORP. • 354
GPC BIOTECH • 236
GRC INTERNATIONAL, INC. • 355
GSI LUMONICS INC. • 454
GTE CORPORATION • 308
GZA GEOENVIRONMENTAL TECHNOLOGIES • 489
GAB ROBINS NORTH AMERICA INC. • 665
GABBERTS INC. • 863
GABLES ENGINEERING, INC. • 87
GABRIEL ENVIRONMENTAL SERVICES • 489
GAGE MARKETING GROUP • 73
GAI'S NORTHWEST BAKERIES • 530
GALACTIC TECHNOLOGIES • 355
GALE ASSOCIATES, INC. • 129
THE GALE GROUP • 809
GALENA-STRAUSS HOSPITAL & NURSING CARE FACILITY • 579
GALEY & LORD, INC. • 102
GALILEO INTERNATIONAL • 355
GALL'S INC. • 863
ARTHUR J. GALLAGHER & CO. • 666
GALLO SALAMI • 530
GALLO WINE COMPANY • 530
GALLUP-McKINLEY COUNTY PUBLIC SCHOOLS • 413
GANNETT COMPANY, INC. • 809
GANTON TECHNOLOGIES • 737
GAP INC. • 863
GARAN INC. • 102

GARDEN STATE TANNING • 184
GARDENBURGER, INC. • 531
GARDINER, KAMYA & ASSOCIATES PC • 55
THE GARDNER-ZEMKE CO. • 130
GARDUNO'S OF MEXICO/YESTERDAVE'S • 652
KEN GARFF AUTO. GRP • 863
GART SPORTS • 863
GARTNERGROUP, INC. • 73
GARY PLASTIC PACKAGING CORPORATION • 694
GAS-N-GO • 184
GASBOY INTERNATIONAL • 738
GASONICS INTNL. CORP. • 454
GATEFIELD CORPORATION • 355
GATES ARROW • 355
THE GATES RUBBER CO. • 280
GATEWAY • 261, 355
GAYLORD CONTAINER • 784
THE GAZETTE • 809
GEARY BREWING • 531
GECOM CORPORATION • 184
GEERLINGS & WADE • 863
GEHL COMPANY • 738
GEICO CORPORATION • 666
GEM ELECTRIC MFG CO. • 694
GEMINUS CORP. • 55, 261
GENAMERICA FINANCIAL • 506
GENENTECH, INC. • 237
GENERAL AUTOMATION • 355
GENERAL BEARING CORP. • 738
GENERAL CHEMICAL CORPORATION • 280
GENERAL COMMUNICATION, INC. (GCI) • 308
GENERAL DATACOMM • 355
GENERAL DISTRIBUTING CO • 531
GENERAL DYNAMICS ARMAMENT SYSTEMS • 738
GENERAL DYNAMICS CORPORATION • 898
GENERAL DYNAMICS ELECTRONIC SYSTEMS • 454
GENERAL ELECTRIC CO. • 738
GENERAL ELECTRIC INFORMATION SERVICES • 55
GENERAL ENGINEERING LABORATORIES, INC. • 489
GENERAL FIRE EXTINGUISHER CORPORATION • 694
GENERAL GROWTH MANAGEMENT, INC. • 841
GENERAL HOSE PRODS. • 184
GENERAL HOUSEWARES CORPORATION • 694
GENERAL KINETICS INC. • 454
GENERAL MILLS, INC. • 531, 639
GENERAL MOTORS CORP. • 184
GENERAL NUTRITION COS. • 863
GENERAL PHYSICS CORP. • 130
GENERAL REINSURANCE CORPORATION • 666
GENERAL RESOURCE CORPORATION • 130
GENERAL SCIENCES CORP. • 355
GENERAL VENEER MFG CO • 784
GENESCO, INC. • 102, 864
GENESEE CORPORATION • 531
GENESIS HEALTH VENTURES • 579
GENETIC THERAPY INC. • 237
GENETRACK SYSTEMS • 237
GENEVA PHARMACEUTICALS • 237
GENICOM CORPORATION • 356
GENOME THERAPEUTICS CORPORATION • 237
GENOVA PRODUCTS • 280
GENRAD INC. • 454

GENSLER • 130
GENTEX CORPORATION • 738
GENTEM COMMS CORP. • 308
GENUINE PARTS COMPANY • 185
GENUITY INC. • 356
GENUS, INC. • 455
GENZYME CORPORATION • 237
GEO QUEST • 356
GEO-MARINE, INC. • 490
GEOLABS, INC. • 490
THE GEON COMPANY • 280
GEORGIA DUCK & CORDAGE MILL • 281
GEORGIA GULF CORP. • 281
GEORGIA-PACIFIC CORP. • 784
GERBER PLUMBING FIXTURES CORPORATION • 130
GERBER SCIENTIFIC, INC. • 455
THE GESSERT GROUP • 73
GEUPEL DEMARS HAGERMAN • 130
GEYERS' MARKET INC. • 864
GIANT FOOD, INC. • 864
GIBSON USA • 694
GILBANE BUILDING CO. • 130
GILEAD SCIENCES • 238
THE GILLETTE COMPANY • 695
GILLMAN COMPANIES • 864
CHARLES E. GILMAN CO. • 455
GILMORE, GANNAWAY, ANDREWS, SMITH & CO. • 56
GILROY FOODS • 531
GIRL SCOUTS • 262
GISH BIOMEDICAL, INC. • 579
GIVEN ENTERPRISES • 640
GLACIER WATER SERVICES • 531
GLASGOW, INC. • 131
P.H. GLATFELTER COMPANY • 784
GLAXO WELLCOME • 238
THE GLEASON WORKS • 739
GLENAIR INC. • 455
GLENAYRE TECHNOLOGIES • 308
THE GLIDDEN COMPANY • 281
GLOBAL OUTDOORS INC. • 163
GLOBAL VAN LINES • 898
GLOBE MFG CO. • 102
THE GLOBE PEQUOT PRESS • 809
GLOBUS & COSMOS • 898
GNOSSOS SOFTWARE INC. • 356
GODDARD VALVE • 739
GOEDECKE COMPANY • 131
GOERLICH'S EXHAUST SYST. • 185
GOETTL AIR CONDITIONING INC. • 131
GOLD BUG INC. • 102
GOLD KIST, INC. • 531
GOLD PROSPECTOR'S ASSN. OF AMERICA • 163
S. GOLDBERG & CO. • 102
GOLDBERG MARCHESANO PARTNERS, INC. • 73
GOLDEN BEAR GOLF • 163, 864
GOLDEN CORRAL CORP. • 640
GOLDEN GEM GROWERS • 532
GOLDEN NUGGET HOTEL AND CASINO • 640
GOLDEN PEANUT CO. • 532
GOLDEN SOUTHWEST, INC. • 356
GOLDEN STATE BANCORP • 211
GOLDEN WEST & ASSOC. • 131
GOLDMAN SACHS & CO. • 506
SAMUEL GOLDWYN CO. • 163
GOLD'S GYM • 163
GOLFER MAGAZINES, INC. • 809
GOLFSMITH INTNL. • 695
GONNELLA BAKING CO. • 532
THE GOOD GUYS! • 864
GOODALL RUBBER CO. • 281

LOUISIANA TECH UNIVERSITY • 415
LOUISVILLE BEDDING CO. • 107
LOVE'S COUNTRY STORES • 871
LOVELACE RESPIRATORY RESEARCH INSTITUTE • 243
LOWE GROB HEALTH & SCIENCE • 75
LOWE'S COMPANIES, INC. • 871
LOWELL ENGINEERING • 187
LOWELL MFG. CO. • 750
LOWER WEST SIDE HOUSEHOLD SERVICES CORP. • 263
LOWRY COMPUTER PRODS. • 368
LOYOLA UNIVERSITY OF CHICAGO • 415
L3 COMMUNICATIONS • 311
LUBRICATION ENGINEERS • 285
LUBRIZOL CORPORATION • 285
LUBY'S CAFETERIAS • 644
LUCAS ARTS ENTERTAINMENT COMPANY • 369
LUCAS DIGITAL LTD. • 369
LUCAS DIGITAL LTD. LLC • 166
JOHN D. LUCAS PRINTING COMPANY • 815
LUCASFILM LTD. • 166
LUCENT TECHNOLOGIES • 311
LUDWIG BUILDING SYSTEMS • 138
LUFKIN INDUSTRIES • 750, 901
LUGARU SOFTWARE LTD. • 369
LUHRS CORPORATION • 901
LUMBER INSURANCE COS. • 671
LUMINANT WORLDWIDE CORPORATION • 369
LUMINATOR • 88, 901
LUND FOOD HOLDINGS • 871
LUSTINE GM PARTS DIST. • 188
LUTHERAN BROTHERHOOD COMPANY • 509, 671
LUXTEC CORPORATION • 587
LUZERNE OPTICAL LABS. • 587
LYCOS, INC. • 369
LYDALL, INC. • 750
LYMAN LUMBER COMPANY • 785
LYNNTECH INC. • 243
LYNTON AVIATION • 89
LYONDELL PETROCHEMICAL COMPANY • 285
LYONS LAVEY NICKEL SWIFT • 75
LYRIC OPERA OF CHICAGO • 166

M

M&F CASE • 815
M&G ELECTRONICS • 464
M&M/MARS INC. • 538
MAI SYSTEMS CORP. • 369
MBI, INC. • 75
MBIA INSURANCE CORP. • 671
MBNA AMERICA • 509
MCC PANASONIC • 311
MCT DAIRIES, INC. • 538
MDS HARRIS • 243
M.E. PRODUCTIONS • 166
MEMC ELECTRONIC MATERIALS, INC. • 464
MFA INCORPORATED • 538
MFS INVESTMENT MGMT. • 509
MGM GRAND HOTEL • 644
MGM INC. • 167
MGM/UNITED ARTISTS • 166
MHM SERVICES • 588
M.I.T. LINCOLN LAB. • 243
M.I.T. PRESS • 815
MMS (MEETING MGMT SVC) • 59
MPB CORPORATION • 751
MPCT SOLUTIONS CORP. • 375

MRC BEARINGS • 89
MRJ TECHNOLOGY SOLUTIONS • 369
M.S. CARRIERS • 901
MSE, INC. • 491
MTI TECHNOLOGIES CORP. • 369
MTS, INC. • 465
MZD (MONTGOMERY ZUKERMAN DAVIS, INC. • 76
MACALESTER COLLEGE • 415
MACAULAY-BROWN • 369, 465
MACDERMID INC. • 285
MACDONALD & PAGE • 60
MACE SECURITY INTNL. • 700
MACHEEZMO MOUSE RESTAURANTS INC. • 644
MACK MOLDING CO. • 285
MACK TRUCKS INC. • 188
MACKAY ENVELOPE CORP. • 785
MACOLA SOFTWARE • 370
MACROCHEM CORP. • 243
MACY'S • 871
MADISON AREA REHABILITATION CENTERS, INC. • 263
MADISON CIVIC CENTER • 166
MADISON OPERA & GUILD • 166
MADISON SQUARE GARDEN CORPORATION • 166
MAGAININ PHARMACEUTICALS INC. • 243
MAGLA PRODUCTS INC. • 700
MAGNET INTERACTIVE COMMUNICATIONS • 370
MAGNETEK, INC. • 465
MAGNUM DIGITAL SVCS • 815
MAGUIRE GROUP, INC. • 138
MAIL BOXES ETC. • 871
MAIL-WELL, INC. • 815
MAILER'S SOFTWARE • 872
MAINE STATE MUSIC THEATRE, INC • 167
MAINSTREAM, INC. • 263
MAJESTIC PRODUCTS CO. • 713
MAKINO • 751
MALIBU ENTERTAINMENT WORLDWIDE, INC. • 167
MALLINCKRODT, INC. • 243, 588
MALLORY AND CHURCH CORPORATION • 107
MALLOY LITHOGRAPHING • 815
MALNOVE INC. • 785
MANAGEMENT SCIENCE ASSOCIATES, INC. • 370
MANHATTAN TRANSFER • 167
MANN THEATRES • 167
MANOR CARE HEALTH SERVICES • 588
MANUFACTURED HOUSING ENTERPRISES, INC. • 139
MANUFACTURERS BANK • 212
MANUFACTURERS' NEWS • 816
MANUGISTICS, INC. • 370
THE MAPLE-VAIL BOOK MFG. GRP. • 816
MAR-JAC INC. • 538
MARATHON COMMS. • 816
MARATHON ENTERPRISES • 538
MARATHON POWER TECHNOLOGIES CO. • 89
MARCAL PAPER MILLS • 700, 786
MARCEL DEKKER, INC. • 816
MARCH OF DIMES • 264
MARCONI DATA SYSTEMS • 751
MARCONI MEDICAL SYST • 588
MARIETTA CORP. • 644, 751
MARIETTA MEMORIAL HOSPITAL • 588
MARIGOLD FOODS • 538

MARIN COMMUNITY COLLEGE • 416
MARINER POST-ACUTE NETWORK • 588
MARITRANS INC. • 901
MARK IV AUTOMOTIVE • 188
MARK IV INDUSTRIES, INC. • 188
MARK VII, INC. • 902
MARKEL CORPORATION • 671
MARKESAN RESIDENT HOME, INC. • 589
THE MARLEY COOLING TOWER COMPANY • 751
MAROTTA SCIENTIFIC CONTROLS INC. • 751
MARQUETTE BANK • 212
MARRIOTT INTERNATIONAL • 644
MARSH & McLENNAN COMPANIES, INC. • 671
MARSH SUPERMARKETS • 872
MARSH USA, INC. • 672
MARSHALL & ILSLEY TRUST CO. OF FLORIDA • 510
MARSHALL ENGINEERED PRODUCTS CO. • 751
MARSHALLTOWN MEDICAL & SURGICAL CTR. • 589
MARTEK BIOSCIENCES CORP. • 243
J.B. MARTIN COMPANY • 107
MARTIN ELECTRONICS • 751
MARTIN MEMORIAL HEALTH SYSTEMS, INC. • 589
MARTIN SPROCKET & GEAR • 751
MARTIN WILLIAMS ADVERTISING INC. • 76
MARTIN'S INC. • 645
THE MARTIN-BROWER CO. • 538
MARYKNOLL FATHERS AND BROTHERS • 264
MARYVALE HOSPITAL MEDICAL CENTER • 589
MARYVILLE ACADEMY • 264
MASCO CORPORATION • 700
MASS BUYING POWER) • 902
MASS MARKETING, INC. • 872
MASSACHUSETTS COLLEGE OF ART • 416
MASSACHUSETTS GENERAL HOSPITAL • 589
MASSACHUSETTS MUTUAL LIFE INSURANCE • 672
MASTECH SYSTEMS CORP. • 370
MASTER BUILDERS TECHNOLOGIES • 285
MATEC CORPORATION • 752
MATERIALS RESEARCH CORP. (MRC) • 465
MATEWAN BANK • 212
MATHSOFT, INC. • 371
MATICH CORPORATION • 139
MATRITECH, INC. • 243
MATRIX PHARMACEUTICAL • 244
MATSUSHITA KOTOBUKI ELECTRONICS INDUSTRIES OF AMERICA, INC. • 700
MATTEL INC. • 700
MATTEL INTERACTIVE • 371
MATTHEWS INTERNATIONAL CORPORATION • 752
MATTHEWS PAINT CO. • 285
MAVERIK COUNTRY STORES • 872
MAX & ERMA'S RESTAURANTS INC. • 645
MAXICARE HEALTH PLANS • 672
MAXTOR CORPORATION • 371
MAXVISION CORP. • 371
MAXWELL SHOE CO. • 107

MILLER MULTIPLEX • 754
THE MILLGARD CORP. • 140
MILLIKIN UNIVERSITY • 416
MILLIMAN & ROBERTSON • 60
MILLIPORE CORPORATION • 244
MILLWARD BROWN • 76
MILTOPE CORPORATION • 374
MILWAUKEE BALLET CO. • 167
MILWAUKEE ELECTRIC TOOL
    CORPORATION • 701
MILWAUKEE JOURNAL SENTINEL,
    INC. • 817
MILWAUKEE PUBLIC MUSEUM •
    168
MILWAUKEE PUBLIC SCHOOLS •
    417
MILWAUKEE SCHOOL OF ENG• 417
MIMBRES MEM. HOSPITAL &
    NURSING HOME • 595
MINCO PRODUCTS, INC. • 754
MINDSPRING ENTERPRISES • 375
MINE SAFETY APPLIANCES
    COMPANY (MSA) • 754
MINNESOTA RUBBER • 286
MINNESOTA SUN PUBLICATIONS
    • 817
MINNESOTA VIKINGS • 168
MINOLTA CORPORATION • 754
MINTZ & HOKE INC. • 76
MINUTE MAN PRESS • 818
MINYARD FOOD STORES • 873
MIPS TECHNOLOGIES, INC. • 375
MISENER MARINE
    CONSTRUCTION INC. • 140
MISSION ST. JOSEPH'S HOSPITAL •
    595
MISSISSIPPI CHEMICAL
    CORPORATION • 286
MISSISSIPPI STATE UNIVERSITY •
    417
THE MISSOULIAN • 818
MISSOURI ATHLETIC CLUB • 168
MISSOURI BOTANICAL GARDEN •
    168
MISSOURI SLOPE LUTHERAN CARE
    CENTER • 595
MITCHELLACE INC. • 108
MITEK PRODUCTS • 595
MITRE CORPORATION • 467
MITSUBISHI SILICON AMERICA •
    467
MITY-LITE, INC. • 701
MOBILE COUNTY PUBLIC
    SCHOOLS • 417
MOBILE TOOL INTNL. • 754
MOCON • 755
MODERN MEDICAL MODALITIES
    CORP. • 596
MODERN TECHNOLOGIES
    CORPORATION • 140
MODINE MFG CO. • 755
MODIS • 375
MOHAVE COMMUNITY COLLEGE
    (MCC) • 417
MOHAWK INDUSTRIES • 108
MOHAWK VALLEY COMMUNITY
    COLLEGE • 418
MOLDED FIBER GLASS CO. • 286
MOLEX INC. • 467
MOLTECH POWER SYSTEMS • 701
MONARCH LUGGAGE CO. • 702
MONARCH SERVICES • 818
THE MONROE CLINIC • 596
MONTANA STATE UNIVERSITY -
    NORTHERN • 418
MONTGOMERY COMMUNITY
    TELEVISION • 311
MONTGOMERY NEWSPAPERS
    COMPANY • 818

MONTGOMERY WATSON • 492
THE MONTICELLO CO. • 244
THE MONY GROUP • 510, 673
MOOG INC. • 89
MOORE MEDICAL CORP. • 244
MOORE NORTH AMERICA • 375,
    818
MOORE PROCESS AUTOMATION
    SOLUTIONS • 755
F.E. MORAN • 140
MOREHEAD STATE UNIVERSITY •
    418
MORETRENCH AMERICAN
    CORPORATION • 492
MORGAN BUILDING & SPAS, INC.
    • 140
MORGAN STANLEY DEAN WITTER
    & COMPANY • 511
MORGAN WIGHTMAN SUPPLY
    COMPANY • 140
MORONI FEED PROCESSING •
    540
JOHN MORRELL & CO. • 540
MORRIS NEWSPAPER CORP • 818
MORRISON KNUDSEN
    CORPORATION • 140, 492
JAMES D. MORRISSEY, INC. • 141
MORROW MEMORIAL HOME FOR
    THE AGED • 596
MORSE DIESEL INTNL • 141
M.A. MORTENSON CO. • 141
MORTGAGE GUARANTY
    INSURANCE CORP. • 673
MORTON PLANT MEASE HEALTH
    CARE • 596
MOSBY • 818
MOSES CONE HEALTH SYST. • 571
MOSINEE PAPER CORP. • 786
MOSS ADAMS LLP • 60
THE MOSSER GROUP • 141
MOTEL 6 • 645
MOTHERAL PRINTING CO. • 818
MOTOR CLUB OF AMERICA • 673
MOTORCAR PARTS &
    ACCESSORIES, INC. • 188
MOTORISTS INSURANCE
    COMPANIES • 673
MOTOROLA COMPUTER GROUP
    • 375
MOTOROLA, INC. • 311
MOTT ADULT HIGH SCHOOL •
    418
MOUNT ARBOR NURSERIES • 540
MOUNT MARY COLLEGE • 418
MOUNT VERNON MILLS • 108
MOUNTAIRE OF DELMARVA • 540
MOVIE STAR, INC. • 108
MRS. BAIRD'S BAKERIES • 540
MRS. FIELD'S ORIGINAL COOKIES,
    INC. • 540
MS DIVERSIFIED CORP. • 510, 671
MUHLENBERG COLLEGE • 418
MULTIGRAPHICS INC. • 755
MULTIMAX, INC. • 375
MULTIMEDIA TUTORIAL SVC • 168
MUNICIPAL THEATRE ASSN. OF ST.
    LOUIS • 168
MUNSON MEDICAL CENTER • 596
MURATA WIEDEMANN, INC. • 755
MURRY'S INC. • 540
JOS. L. MUSCARELLE, INC. • 141
MUSEUM OF CONTEMPORARY
    ART • 168
MUSEUM OF FINE ARTS - BOSTON
    • 168
THE MUSEUM OF FINE ARTS -
    HOUSTON • 169
MUSEUM OF MODERN ART • 169

MUSEUM OF SCIENCE &
    INDUSTRY • 169
MUSTANG ENGINEERING • 141
MUSTANG TRACTOR &
    EQUIPMENT COMPANY • 873
MUTUAL OF AMERICA • 673
MUTUAL OF OMAHA INSURANCE
    COMPANY • 674
MUZE INC. • 375
S.D. MYERS, INC. • 467
MYERS INDUSTRIES INC. • 188
MYLAN LABORATORIES • 244
MYLEX CORPORATION • 375
MYRON MFG CORP. • 702
MYSTIC AQUARIUM • 169

N

NBC • 311
NBC INTERNET • 311, 375
NCH CORPORATION • 286, 755
NCL GRAPHIC SPECIALTIES • 818
NCR CORPORATION • 375
NCUCOS INC. • 637
NDC HEALTH INFORMATION
    SERVICES • 376
NE RESTAURANT COMPANY • 645
NEC AMERICA • 311, 376, 467
NEC CORPORATION • 376
NFO WORLDWIDE, INC. • 77
NL INDUSTRIES, INC. • 287
NPC INTERNATIONAL • 645
THE NPD GROUP, INC. • 77
NSC CORPORATION • 492
NSK CORPORATION • 755
NTC/CONTEMPORARY
    PUBLISHING GROUP • 819
NVF COMPANY INC. • 786
NVR MORTGAGE FINANCE • 511
NVR, INC. • 141, 511
NYS THEATRE INSTITUTE • 169
NABISCO GRP HOLDINGS • 540
NABISCO INC. • 540
NAC RE CORPORATION • 674
NACCO INDUSTRIES • 702, 756
NACE INTERNATIONAL • 819
NACO INDUSTRIES, INC. • 287
NALCO CHEMICAL CO. • 287
NAN YA PLASTICS CORP.
    AMERICA • 287
NANIK GROUP • 702
NANTICOKE HOMES, INC. • 142
NAPCO SECURITY GROUP • 468
NAPLES MEDICAL CENTER • 596
NAPP TECHNOLOGIES • 244
THE NASH ENG. CO. • 756
NASH FINCH CO. • 541, 873
THE NASHVILLE NETWORK • 312
NASHVILLE SANCTION CENTER •
    264
NASHVILLE STATE TECHNICAL
    INSTITUTE • 418
NATIONAL ASSISTANCE LEAGUE •
    264
NATIONAL ASSN. OF BLACK
    ACCOUNTANTS • 60
NATIONAL ASSN. OF INSURANCE &
    FINANCIAL ADVISORS • 674
NATIONAL ASSN. OF
    MANUFACTURERS • 702, 756
NATIONAL ASSN. OF SECURITIES
    DEALERS, INC. • 511
NATIONAL AUTOMOBILE
    DEALERS ASSN. • 873
NATIONAL BENEFIT LIFE
    INSURANCE CO. • 674
NATIONALL CAR RENTAL
    SYSTEMS • 903

JobBank List Service
Custom-Designed For Your Job Search

Generated by the same editors who bring you the nationally renowned *JobBank* series, the electronic *JobBank List Service* is a compilation of company information that is important to you. Our huge database is updated year-round to ensure that our data is as accurate as possible. Our company information is available to you by e-mail or on disk in ASCII delimited text format.

Whether you're looking for a small company to work for, or a large corporation to do business with, *JobBank List Service* can help! *JobBank List Service* is not mass-produced for the general public; it is built for *you* through a personal consultation with a member of the *JobBank* staff.

While other services offer their company information on pre-generated disk or CD-ROM, we construct the data explicitly to match your criteria. Your *JobBank* consultant will work with you to find the company information that applies to your specific job search needs. Criteria for companies or employment agencies can be specified geographically, by industry, by occupation, or any variation or combination you can imagine... you decide.

With the most current information on companies in more than thirty industries, jobseekers, recruiters, and businesses alike will find the *JobBank List Service* the perfect solution to their personal and professional needs. Industries covered include:

- *Accounting and Management Consulting*
- *Advertising, Marketing, and Public Relations*
- *Aerospace*
- *Apparel, Fashion & Textiles*
- *Architecture, Construction, and Engineering*
- *Arts, Entertainment, Sports, & Recreation*
- *Automotive*
- *Banking/Savings and Loans*
- *Biotechnology, Pharmaceuticals & Scientific R&D*
- *Charities and Social Services*
- *Chemicals/Rubber & Plastics*

- *Communications: Telecommunications & Broadcasting*
- *Computer Hardware, Software, and Services*
- *Educational Services*
- *Electronic/Industrial Electrical Equipment*
- *Environmental & Waste Management Services*
- *Fabricated/Primary Metals & Products*
- *Financial Services*
- *Food & Beverages/ Agriculture*
- *Government*
- *Health Care: Services, Equipment & Products*
- *Hotels & Restaurants*

- *Insurance*
- *Manufacturing*
- *Mining/Gas/Petroleum/ Energy Related*
- *Paper & Wood Products*
- *Printing and Publishing*
- *Real Estate*
- *Retail*
- *Stone, Glass, Clay, and Concrete Products*
- *Transportation*
- *Utilities*
- *Miscellaneous Wholesaling and many others*

- NO MINIMUM ORDER — NO ORDER IS TOO SMALL!
- THOUSANDS OF PRIVATE & PUBLIC COMPANIES IN <u>ALL</u> 50 STATES & DC
- THOUSANDS OF EMPLOYMENT SERVICES
- EACH LISTING INCLUDES THE SAME TYPE OF DETAILED CONTACT & BUSINESS INFORMATION OFFERED IN THE *JOBBANK* BOOK SERIES
- STANDING ORDER DISCOUNTS ARE AVAILABLE

Contact a *JobBank* staff member now for your individual consultation and pricing information.
E-mail: jobbank@adamsonline.com
Phone: 800/872-5627 (in MA: 781/767-8100)
Fax: 781/767-2055

The JobBank Series

There are 30 *JobBank* books, each providing extensive, up-to-date employment information on hundreds of the largest employers in each job market. The #1 best-selling series of employment directories, the *JobBank* series has been recommended as an excellent place to begin your job search by the *New York Times*, the *Los Angeles Times*, the *Boston Globe*, and the *Chicago Tribune*. *JobBank* books have been used by millions of people to find jobs. Titles available:

The Atlanta JobBank ♦ *The Austin/San Antonio JobBank* ♦ *The Boston JobBank* ♦ *The Carolina JobBank* ♦ *The Chicago JobBank* ♦ *The Connecticut JobBank* ♦ *The Dallas-Fort Worth JobBank* ♦ *The Denver JobBank* ♦ *The Detroit JobBank* ♦ *The Florida JobBank* ♦ *The Houston JobBank* ♦ *The Indiana JobBank* ♦ *The Las Vegas JobBank* ♦ *The Los Angeles JobBank* ♦ *The Minneapolis-St. Paul JobBank* ♦ *The Missouri JobBank* ♦ *The New Jersey JobBank* ♦ *The Metropolitan New York JobBank* ♦ *The Ohio JobBank* ♦ *The Greater Philadelphia JobBank* ♦ *The Phoenix JobBank* ♦ *The Pittsburgh JobBank* ♦ *The Portland JobBank* ♦ *The San Francisco Bay Area JobBank* ♦ *The Seattle JobBank* ♦ *The Tennessee JobBank* ♦ *The Virginia JobBank* ♦ *The Metropolitan Washington DC JobBank* ♦ *The JobBank Guide to Computer & High-Tech Companies ($17.95)* ♦ *The JobBank Guide to Health Care Companies ($17.95)*

EACH JOBBANK BOOK IS 6" X 9¼", PAPERBACK, $16.95.
For ISBNs and ISSNs, please visit http://www.careercity.com/booksoftware/jobbank.asp

JobBank List Service: If you are interested in variations of this information in electronic format for sales or job search mailings, please call 800-872-5627, or e-mail us at jobbank@adamsonline.com.

Available wherever books are sold.

**For more information, or to order, call 800-872-5627
or visit www.adamsmedia.com**

Adams Media Corporation, 260 Center Street, Holbrook, MA 02343

Visit our exciting job and career site at www.careercity.com